May 7–12, 2011
Vancouver, BC

Association for
Computing Machinery

Advancing Computing as a Science & Profession

CHI 2011

The 29th Annual CHI Conference on

Human Factors in Computing Systems

Sponsored by:

ACM SIGCHI

Volume 1

Association for
Computing Machinery

Advancing Computing as a Science & Profession

The Association for Computing Machinery
2 Penn Plaza, Suite 701
New York, New York 10121-0701

Notice to Past Authors of ACM-Published Articles
ACM intends to create a complete electronic archive of all articles and/or other material previously published by ACM. If you have written a work that has been previously published by ACM in any journal or conference proceedings prior to 1978, or any SIG Newsletter at any time, and you do NOT want this work to appear in the ACM Digital Library, please inform permissions@acm.org, stating the title of the work, the author(s), and where and when published.

ISBN: 978-1-4503-0228-9 (Digital)

ISBN: 978-1-4503-0267-8 (Print)

Additional copies may be ordered prepaid from:

ACM Order Department
PO Box 30777
New York, NY 10087-0777, USA

Phone: 1-800-342-6626 (USA and Canada)
+1-212-626-0500 (Global)
Fax: +1-212-944-1318
E-mail: acmhelp@acm.org
Hours of Operation: 8:30 am – 4:30 pm ET

ACM Order Number: 609111

Printed in the USA

About SIGCHI and ACM

CHI 2011 is sponsored by ACM's Special Interest Group on Computer-Human Interaction (ACM SIGCHI). The scope of SIGCHI consists of the study of the human-computer interaction processes and includes research, design, development, and evaluation efforts for interactive computer systems. The focus of SIGCHI is on how people communicate and interact with a broadly-defined range of computer systems. SIGCHI serves as a forum for the exchange of ideas among computer scientists, human factors scientists, psychologists, social scientists, designers, educators, and practitioners involved in the design, implementation, and evaluation of interactive computing systems. Nearly 5,000 professional members of the SIGCHI community work together toward common goals and objectives. Visit SIGCHI at http://www.sigchi.org.

ACM, the Association for Computing Machinery http://www.acm.org/, is an educational and scientific society uniting the world's computing educators, researchers and professionals to inspire dialogue, share resources and address the field's challenges. ACM strengthens the profession's collective voice through strong leadership, promotion of the highest standards, and recognition of technical excellence.ACM supports the professional growth of its members by providing opportunities for life-long learning, career development, and professional networking. ACM offers its 87,000 global members cutting-edge technical information through world class journals and magazines, dynamic specia linterest groups and globally recognized conferences.

Welcome from Chairs

Over the last year or so, we have been blessed with the challenge, the opportunity, and the distinct pleasure of organizing the CHI 2011 Conference on Human Factors in Computing Systems, the premier international conference for the field of human-computer interaction.

CHI 2011 takes place in gorgeous, energetic, sophisticated Vancouver BC, a city renowned for its innovation in entertainment, sustainability, accessibility, and inclusivity. The New York Times calls it, "a liquid city, a tomorrow city, equal parts India, China, England, France and the Pacific Northwest." Vancouver lays a beautiful backdrop for our conference, which boasts nearly 30 years of wonderful work.

Behind the success of the conference is our diverse community of faculty and students, of researchers and practitioners, of young and, well, also of experienced. It is a community of designers, technologists, psychologists, social scientists, biologists, artists, engineers, anthropologists, musicians; the list goes on. Wherever we are, we are always a community of near and far. Most impressively, ours is a community that cares deeply about innovating, learning, sharing, and interacting; all with the common goal of using technology to shape the way people around the world live and play.

Returning attendees will recognize the general conference format - 2 days of small intimate workshops, followed by 4 days of technical content, all surrounded by social and intellectual exchanges. In addition to the familiar venues that form the core of the conference, we have also arranged various special events, such an keynotes by Howard Rheingold and Ethan Zuckerman; invited talks by ACM SIGCHI award winners Terry Winograd, Larry Tesler, Alan Newell, and Clayton Lewis; an HCI museum exhibit hosted by Bill Buxton; and a panel celebrating Stu Card's achievements and contributions to the field of HCI.

With the record number of submissions and accepted content this year, we hope that you will utilize the print and electronic programs, but also the daily CHI Madness presentations that provide a glimpse of the day ahead. In the interest of continuing to evolve the conference to best serve our needs, we will experiment with shorter talks this year (20 minute slots for long pieces of content and 10 for shorter ones) to infuse even more energy into the program. We will also have a pretty full slate of social media applications to help you connect with other attendees and to provide you with the fullest experience possible.

It has been quite the ride, and we'd like to thank everyone involved and welcome you all to the conference. We hope that CHI 2011 inspires you reflect on the past, the present, and perhaps most importantly, the future of the people and body of work that is ACM SIGCHI. We hope you enjoy CHI 2011 in Vancouver and that you have a great time "Connecting..."

Desney Tan
CHI 2011 General Conference Chair
Microsoft Research

Bo Begole
CHI 2011 Technical Program Chairs
PARC

Wendy Kellogg
CHI 2011 Technical Program Chairs
IBM Research

From ACM SIGCHI's President and Vice President for Conferences

SIGCHI is proud to sponsor the premier annual conference in the field of human-computer interaction. Past CHI conferences have been known for being the stage of new developments and advances in HCI, and for memorable events. CHI 2011 is no exception. We are extremely grateful to the CHI 2011 Conference Chair Desney Tan, to Technical Program Chairs Bo Begole and Wendy Kellogg, and to their wonderful crew, who succeeded to build an impressive program and experience.

CHI, the conference that is organized on behalf of ACM's Special Interest Group on Computer-Human Interaction (SIGCHI) is an ideal forum for people to meet formally as well as informally, to exchange knowledge and views, to share experiences, and to learn. The CHI conference brings together professionals from research and practice; people from industry, academia, and from government; long-term veterans of HCI, young professionals and students; all in an environment designed to encourage interaction. We invite you to actively participate in that interaction: introduce yourself to people, interact with presenters and speakers, renew old friendships and make new ones.

SIGCHI is an international community of professionals who share an interest in the many diverse facets of HCI. SIGCHI is committed both to advancing the field of HCI, to facilitate exchange of information within the SIGCHI community, and to support students to enter the domain.

The CHI conference is arguably the single most visible activity of SIGCHI, but we also sponsor and support a wide range of specialized conferences in areas ranging from interactive systems design to user interface technology to computer-supported cooperative work to "intelligent" user interfaces. Visit the SIGCHI website at http://www.sigchi.org to find our conference schedule, listing upcoming as well as past conferences.

SIGCHI and ACM produce some of the most respected publications in the field. All members receive interactions, a highly-acclaimed magazine covering the broad field of HCI and user interface design. ACM Transactions on Computer-Human Interactions (ToCHI), now in its 17th year, is our flagship journal - a quarterly publication with the top-quality archival research aimed at researchers and those translating research into practice.

SIGCHI is truly an international organization, with 32 local chapters and 3 student chapters in 19 countries on 5 continents. We encourage all SIGCHI members to join their local chapter - or if there isn't one in your area, we would love to help you create one. And don't forget virtual communities! SIGCHI hosts dozens of electronic mailing lists on topics ranging from HCI and the Web, to HCI educations, to public policy and beyond. Those lists range from dozens of subscribers to thousands, and are an excellent way to keep up with the field and with friends and colleagues.

Finally, on behalf of ACM SGICHI, we again want to thank the conference committee and all of the hundreds of volunteers who make this conference possible. Their work makes this a rewarding experience for all of us.

Gerrit C. van der Veer
SIGCHI President

John "Scooter" Morris
SIGCHI Vice-President for Conferences

CHI 2011 Table of Contents

CHI 2011 Table of Contents

CHI 2011 Table of Contents

CHI 2011 Table of Contents

CHI 2011 Table of Contents

CHI 2011 Table of Contents

Gestures, Body & Touch

Session Chair: Steve Benford, *University of Nottingham*

Pointing 1

Session Chair: Emmanuel Pietriga, *INRIA; Univ. Paris-Sud & CNRS*

Volume 2

Ambient & Peripheral Computing

Session Chair: Loren Terveen, *University of Minnesota*

Museums & Public Exhibitions

Session Chair: Jacquelyn Martino, *IBM Research*

Everyday Information Management

Session Chair: David McDonald, *University of Washington*

CHI 2011 Table of Contents

CHI 2011 Table of Contents

Microblogging Behavior

Session Chair: Mor Naaman, *Rutgers University*

Inter-cultural Interaction

Session Chair: Susan Fussell, *Cornell University*

Eye Tracking

Session Chair: Melanie Fitzgerald, *Google*

Families

Session Chair: Shaowen Bardzell, *Indiana University*

Search & Information Seeking

Session Chair: Jaime Teevan, *Microsoft Research*

CHI 2011 Table of Contents

CHI 2011 Table of Contents

CHI 2011 Table of Contents

CHI 2011 Table of Contents

CHI 2011 Table of Contents

CHI 2011 Table of Contents

CHI 2011 Table of Contents

CHI 2011 Table of Contents

CHI 2011 Table of Contents

Methods to Aid & Structure Design

Session Chair: Rob Miller, *Massachusetts Institute of Technology*

Touch 3: Sensing

Session Chair: Chris Harrison, *Carnegie Mellon University*

Authentication

Session Chair: Lorrie Cranor, *Carnegie Mellon University*

Cats, Dogs, Sports, Games & Books

Session Chair: Sara Kiesler, *Carnegie Mellon University*

CHI 2011 Table of Contents

CHI 2011 Table of Contents

CHI 2011 Table of Contents

CHI 2011 Table of Contents

CHI 2011 Table of Contents

Incentives & User Generated Content

Session Chair: Robert Kraut, *Carnegie Mellon University*

Session: Courriel

Session Chair: Laura Dabbish, *Carnegie Mellon University*

CHI 2010 Organizing Committee

Conference Chair
Desney Tan, *Microsoft Research*

Conference Chair Assistant
Saleema Amershi, *University of Washington*

Technical Program

Chairs
Bo Begole, *PARC*
Wendy A. Kellogg, *IBM Research*

Technical Program Chairs Assistant
Manas Tungare

Papers
Geraldine Fitzpatrick, *Vienna University of Technology*
Carl Gutwin, *University of Saskatchewan*

alt.chi chairs
Daniel Wigdor, *Microsoft*
Patrick Baudisch, *Hasso Plattner Institute*

Case Studies Chair
Manfred Tscheligi, *University of Salzberg*

Courses Chairs
Nancy Frishberg, *MSB Associates*
Regina Bernhaupt, *IRIT -- University of Toulouse*

Doctoral Consortium Chairs
Mary Beth Rosson, *Penn State University*
Saul Greenberg, *University of Calgary*

Interactivity Chairs
Jan Borchers, *RWTH Aachen University*
Lyn Bartram, *Simon Fraser University*
Sid Fels, *University of British Columbia*

Panels Chairs
John C. Thomas, *IBM Research*
Simone Barbosa, *PUC-Rio*

Poster Chair
Anthony Tang, *Georgia Tech*

Special Interest Groups (SIGS) Chairs
Ido Guy, *IBM Research*
Daphne Raban, *University of Haifa*

Student Design Competition Chairs
Stephen Brewster, *University of Glasgow*
Youn-kyung Lim, *KAIST*

Video Chairs
Michael Bernstein, *Massachusetts Institute of Technology*
Shahram Izadi, *Microsoft*

Work-in-Progress (WIPs) Chairs
Brian Bailey, *University of Illinois, Urbana-Champaign*
Mark Newman, *University of Michigan*

Workshops Chairs
Daniela Busse, *SAP Labs (Palo Alto)*
Catalina Danis, *IBM Research*

Core Communities

Communities Chair
Arnie Lund, *Microsoft*

Design Community Chairs
Scott Pobiner, *Parsons The New School for Design*
Carla Diana, *Smart Design*

User Experience Community Chairs
Elizabeth Buie, *Luminanze Consulting*
Jhilmil Jain, *Microsoft*

Engineering Community Chairs
Ruven Brooks, *Independent Consultant*
Keith Butler, *University of Washington*

Management Community Chairs
Jim Nieters, *Yahoo!*
Carola Fellenz Thompson, *Mindjet*

FEATURED COMMUNITIES

Child Computer Interaction Community Chairs
Janet C Read, *University of Central Lancashire*
Panos Markopoulos, Eindhoven University of Technology
Allison Druin, *University of Maryland*

Games and Entertainment Community Chairs
Regina Bernhaupt, *IRIT - University of Toulouse*
Katherine Isbister, *NYU-Poly*

Health Community Chairs
Gillian R. Hayes, *University of California, Irvine*
Madhu Reddy, *The Pennsylvania State University*

Sustainability Community Chairs
Azam Khan, *Autodesk Research*
Eli Blevis, *Indiana University-Bloomington*

PARTICIPATION & VOLUNTEERING

Student Volunteer Coordinators
Aaron Houssian, *Philips Research, TU/Delft*
Vicky McArthur, *York University*

Madness Chairs
Paul André, *University of Southampton*
Max L. Wilson, *Swansea University*

Social Media Chair
Cliff Lampe, *Michigan State University*

Publicity Chair
Kirstie Hawkey, *University of British Columbia*

SPONSORS, EXHIBITS, & TECHNOLOGY

Sponsors and Exhibits
Carol Klyver

Registration Coordinator
Yvonne Lopez

Design Directors
Oscar Murillo, *Microsoft*
Cole Benson, *University of Washington*

Webmaster
Lydia Chilton, *University of Washington*

Proceedings & Program Chairs
Aurélien Tabard, *IT University of Copenhagen*
Max Van Kleek, *Massachusetts Institute of Technology*
Nirmal Patel, *Georgia Tech*

Technology Liaisons
Scooter Morris, *University of California, San Francisco*
Sara Drenner, *Inuvo*

LOGISTICS

ACM Staff Liaisons
Ashley Cozzi, *Association for Computing Machinery*

CMC Staff Liaisons
Scooter Morris, *University of California, San Francisco*

Conference Logistics
Janeé Pelletier, *Conference & Logistics Consultants*

CHI 2011 Sponsors, Supporters, Champions, Contributors, & Friends

CHI 2011 Champions

Bloomberg

Microsoft

ebay | PayPal

NSF

Google

SAP

CHI 2011 Contributors

Autodesk

IBM Research

Graphisme, animation et nouveaux médias
granp
Graphics, Animation and New Media

NOKIA

event/burn

Friends of CHI

Adobe Systems, Inc.

Disney Research

FX Palo Alto Laboratory, Inc.

University of Maryland

Yahoo!

University of Michigan

Classroom-Based Assistive Technology: Collective Use of Interactive Visual Schedules by Students with Autism

Meg Cramer[1], Sen H. Hirano[1], Monica Tentori[2], Michael T. Yeganyan[1] & Gillian R. Hayes[1]

[1]Department of Informatics
University of California, Irvine
{mdcramer, shirano, myeganya, gillianrh}@ics.uci.edu

[2]School of Computer Science
Universidad Autónoma de Baja California
mtentori@uabc.mx

ABSTRACT
vSked is an interactive and collaborative assistive technology for students with autism, combining visual schedules, choice boards, and a token-based reward system into an integrated classroom system. In this paper, we present the results of a study of three deployments of vSked over the course of a year in two autism classrooms. The results of our study demonstrate that vSked can promote student independence, reduce the quantity of educator-initiated prompts, encourage consistency and predictability, reduce the time required to transition from one activity to another, and reduce the coordination required in the classroom. The findings from this study reveal practices surrounding the use of assistive technologies in classrooms and highlight important considerations for both the design and the evaluation of assistive technologies in the future, especially those destined for classroom use.

Author Keywords
Assistive technology, autism, visual schedules

ACM Classification Keywords
K.3 Computers and Education; K.3.1 Computers Use in Education; K.4.2 Social Issues

General Terms
Human Factors

INTRODUCTION AND MOTIVATION
Autism is characterized by impairment in communication, social interaction, emotional expression, and emotional recognition [3]. Visual supports can ease these challenges by augmenting communication with visual cues. Children with autism and school-based teaching staff (*e.g.*, teachers, teachers assistants, speech and language pathologists) use visual supports to complete tasks, manage daily routines, and engage in social interactions [12]. To capitalize on the benefits of current paper-based visual supports, teachers design and customize visual communication materials. However, after investing substantial time and money, these kits can still easily be lost or damaged.

To address some of these challenges, Hirano *et al.* developed an interactive and collaborative assistive technology for visual schedules called vSked [11]. vSked is comprised of individual devices for each student coordinated by the teacher through a large touch screen monitor at the front of the classroom. For students, this system combines three paper-based visual support practices often used in school (visual schedules, choice boards, and a rewards system) and incorporates interactive and collaborative functionality.

The design of vSked stands in contrast to many of the assistive technology devices currently used in classrooms in that it focuses on the classroom as the unit of intervention. Previous work on assistive technology has largely focused on meeting an individual learner's specific cognitive and motor needs. Research findings from professional programs [30] and literature for teacher preparation [8] suggest that teachers choose appropriate assistive technologies for children with autism based on "careful assessment and individualization" [20] for each student. Teachers are instructed to make decisions for "specific learners, in specific contexts, to meet specific needs" [20 as cited in 30]. However, meeting the needs of individual students runs the risk of overlooking the interplay of students, technologies, and staff that can impact adoption and use in a classroom setting. Design recommendations that place classrooms and groups of students at the forefront are not as prevalent, and therefore are the focus in this work.

By combining practices and offering new affordances for the classroom, use of vSked encourages emergent group practices for students with autism. Past work on vSked addresses the use of paper-based visual support systems and the resultant vSked system requirements as well as a preliminary feasibility study of the system in use [10,11]. In the work presented here, we focus on the practices that emerged with the use of vSked within the classroom, specifically concerning student independence and prompting, consistency and predictability of events, and community building activities. We focus on the classroom practices as a whole as well as the experience of students using the system.

BACKGROUND AND RELATED WORK

Extensive work has been done in assistive technologies, technologies for autism, and educational technologies. In this section, we first provide some background information on visual supports in classrooms and then outline those research projects in autism and educational technologies most relevant to our work.

Visual supports in classrooms

Visual supports can be therapeutically effective for children with autism. These techniques may present "clear advantages with regard to ease of use and intelligibility for communication patterns" [20]. In one study, 51% of classrooms reported using visual supports "most of the time," and 29% of classrooms "some of the time" [29].

Visual supports typically include the exchange or display of a variety of images, drawings or photographs on laminated cards to represent tasks, needs, goals and rewards (Fig 1). These visual supports are a type of aided, augmented communication common to special education classrooms used to provide support for learning and socialization [29].

There are many ways to use visual-graphic cards to assist children with autism, and often one large set of cards is used across a number of practices. Here we describe three common classroom tools in more detail: 1) visual schedules, 2) choice boards, and 3) token-based rewards.

Visual schedules provide a consistent display of "planned activities in symbols (words, pictures, photographs, icons, and actual objects) that are understood in the order in which they will occur" [13]. Schedules act as reminders of the day's events, preparing students for activities and transitions and providing students with structure to reduce anxiety and support better self-organization (Fig 2). The visual aids can represent an "in task" sequence, in which each step of a procedure is displayed, or, a "between task" sequence, in which the cards represent the day's activities [21]. In classrooms, "between task" visual schedules act as reminders of the day's events, preparing students for daily

Fig 1. Teachers often provide every student a copy of each card and supplement replacement cards for those that are lost and worn. Libraries can become extensive and cumbersome to manage.

Fig 2: (clockwise from top left) A paper-based choice board, visual schedule, and token board used in the classrooms before the introduction of vSked.

activities and transitions between activities. *Choice boards* or *communication boards* allow students with verbal language deficits to participate in multiple choice assessments, voice personal preferences, carry out functional communication, and participate in classroom activities [20]. In *token-based reward systems,* students earn tokens for appropriate behavior, such as staying on task, and for answering questions correctly. Such systems motivate and reward desired behavior [19]. Once a set number of tokens are earned, the reward, often tangible, is delivered and the tokens are removed, resetting the count.

Assistive technologies for autism

Assistive technologies for special education classrooms include tools for augmenting student communication [22], game learning [24], or developing proper functioning age social skills [6, 22]. Most relevant to our work are technologies for visual schedules.

Computer-based interactive displays have been used to ease the management of visual schedules. Some of these solutions involve the use of multimedia tools for increasing the interactivity of visual schedules [14, 15], and different input devices for ease of use [4]. The evaluation of these works has provided insight regarding issues related to the acceptance and use of the system (*e.g.*, the physical placement of the displays). Our work differs from this literature by focusing on how classroom practices change due to the extended use of a system.

*Ev*aluation of other classroom-based technologies

Additionally, there are studies of technology use in neurotypical classrooms that consider the entire classroom for analysis. Neurotypical is a term used by the autism community to denote students who have average cognitive functioning and no autism diagnosis. A review of the literature on these systems and their evaluation is out of the scope of this paper, but here we describe some research that is most relevant to our work.

ClassroomPresenter allows students to interact with instructor materials through individual Tablet PCs. Likewise, Classroom2000 (now known as eClass) [1], and the associated StuPad system [31] allow for integration of student note-taking devices with instructor PowerPoint™ slides. Evaluations of these systems and other similar systems have largely centered on university students, often in computer science or engineering classes [2, 5]. The work we present here differs from these projects in several ways. First, vSked enables true synchronous communication rather than allowing integrated content to be stored in an archive. Second, the primary role of vSked is as an assistive technology for students with significant impairments. In this paper, we demonstrate how considering the classroom experience of assistive technology, as is done with more traditional educational technologies, can lead to greater insight about the use of technology in special education.

THE VSKED SYSTEM

vSked is an interactive and collaborative assistive technology that replicates the functionality of visual schedules, choice boards, and token-based rewards in an integrated system. vSked also collectively presents and controls student schedules and activities on a touch screen display at the front of the classroom. vSked was designed with group classroom activities in mind, reflecting the need not only to augment each individual student's communication capabilities but also to enable synchronized group interaction and shared experiences.

The vSked system is comprised of an ultramobile PC (UMPC), a touch screen handheld device, for each child wirelessly connected to a large, central display (Fig 3). Software links the student handhelds with the information on the large monitor, creating a collaborative assistive technology for the entire classroom. The touch screen acts as a master timetable showing the daily schedule for each student. A picture and nametag for the student appears at the top of each schedule. Each UMPC has personalized features: the name and photo of the student, tokens earned, a reward, and the choice board (Fig 4). The teacher starts an activity by using the large touch screen, pressing on the picture of an activity. At the same time, a series of corresponding prompts are sent to the students' devices, appearing in the choice board area.

Fig 3: The teacher manages the schedule for the entire class through a large interactive touch screen.

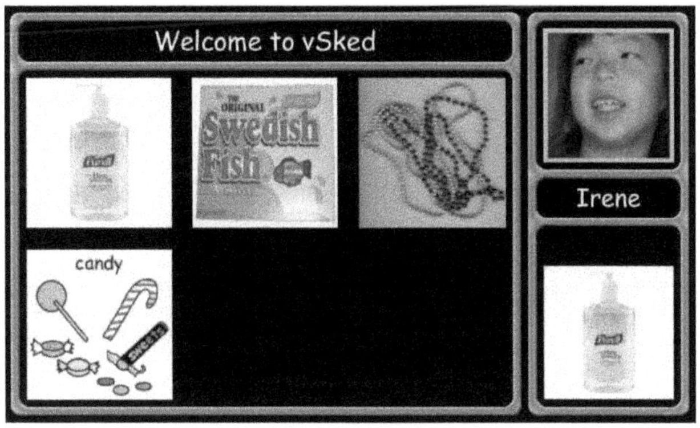

Fig 4: The choices are displayed on the left with the right showing the student's photo and a reward.

The system allows for three kinds of interaction: multiple choice questions, voting, and alerts. Activities with correct answers (*e.g.,* What day is it?) provide feedback for an incorrect choice in two ways: flagging the correct option and removing incorrect ones. For activities in which there is no correct answer (*e.g.,* "Do you want milk or water?") votes allow students to select choices based on personal preferences. A graph of students responses are shown on the large monitor. Alerts are used during transitions between activities. On the individual devices, each student presses the picture of the activity to confirm the start of the activity. All interactions in vSked are tracked, and teachers can generate progress reports.

METHODS

The results presented in this paper include analysis of observations, interviews and logs of system use for three deployments of vSked. The students were observed for two weeks before deployment of the system in Spring 2010 and Summer 2010. They were then observed for one week during Spring 2010 and three weeks during Summer 2010. Previously, students were observed for three weeks of system use during the Summer of 2009 [11].

During these times, teachers and aides participated in weekly short interviews, and a 90 minute group interview at the end of each deployment. The weekly interviews were individual and semi-structured, and participants were asked to discuss how the classroom's use of the system went during that particular week. They were encouraged to tell stories and discuss what they found interesting, surprising, or different that week. On average, interviews lasted approximately 30 minutes and were recorded and transcribed. Observations were conducted before and during deployment for a total of 202 observations. During Summer 2009 and Spring 2010, observations were open-ended, and data analysis was primarily inductive. Building on these results, during Summer 2010, in addition to the

Session	Summer 2009	Spring 2010	Summer 2010	Total
Hours of observation	97	21	84	202

Table 1. Hours of observations

open-ended observations, we video recorded one teacher, two aides and nine students for fifteen minutes each three days a week. We scored these videos for the following:

- Transitions between activities
- Levels of consistency and predictability in the schedule
- Levels of interactivity and coordination among stakeholders
- Student anxiety
- Use of vSked as a visual schedule, choice board or token system
- Teacher awareness of rewards and on-task behavior

vSked was essentially the same in all deployments. However, slight changes in the administration interface were made between the first and second studies. During the three deployments vSked was used in 2 classrooms, among 16 students (4girls), 2 teachers, and 4 aides.

Participants

Special education teachers coordinate the classroom and develop the Individualized Education Plans (IEP), which lay out the goals for each student in special education. They coordinate the work of teacher assistants and others involved in the child's well-being, including parents, social workers, school administrators, and therapists. Across the three deployments, two teachers were enrolled in this study. Each teacher received one hour of training focused on schedule creation and management and spent additional time exploring the systems on their own.

The *teacher assistants (aides)* help classroom teachers to complete instructional and administrative tasks. Additional classroom duties include preparing materials for lessons; tutoring and assisting students one-on-one; and managing behavior. Across the three deployments, eight aides from two classrooms were enrolled in this study.

All 14 students in this study were between the ages of six and 10 and diagnosed with moderate to severe autism. They demonstrated little to no verbal communication skills.

Analysis

All field notes, interview transcripts, images, and videos were inspected together using a mixed-methods approach. Researchers first analyzed the data for evidence that vSked supported the needs of teachers and students in relation to the literature on visual supports. Researchers used open coding and multi-phased affinity analysis to uncover emergent themes from the interview data, in particular in relation to the collective uses of the system. The entire team then discussed these themes in detail. During the course of the first deployment, classroom staff reported that the amount of work they were doing to manage transitions, prompt students, and so on was reduced with use of vSked. Thus, in the 2010 deployments, we conducted a preliminary quantitative analysis of these issues by collecting descriptive statistics as reported in the results section. We used an ANOVA and a Tukey post-hoc test to compare the captured behaviors with and without using vSked. The data presented a normal distribution.

RESULTS

Although the focus of this analysis is the group experience of classroom-based assistive technologies, there is no group without a collection of individuals. Thus, we also describe the ways in which themes uncovered in our evaluations reveal tensions in the classroom that require designers to balance the needs of the classroom as a whole with those of each individual student.

Independence, prompting, and reinforcement

In addition to the traditional call-and-response or question-and-answer models employed in classrooms, educators of children with autism often make use of explicit scaled prompting systems. For example, when a teacher prompts a student to make a choice, they may use hand-over-hand (a physical prompt) to point to the choice or say aloud the choice (a verbal prompt), depending on the student's needs. Teachers and aides offer various levels of prompting to encourage students to provide responses, adjust behaviors, and so on. In autism classrooms, these prompts can remind students to focus on and complete a task. At the same time, however, prompting can disrupt the group classroom experience. Thus, a goal of educators is often to reduce prompting both to increase individual student independence and to decrease classroom distractions.

Student goals focused on "independence" are measured in school assessments according to the quantity and quality of the human-initiated prompts required to help a student complete an activity. In observations, many of the students, given a sequence of choice-making activities using vSked, would progress through the activities without prompts from the teaching staff. For example, the instructors noted that during the first few days of use, students answered questions in the calendar activity (*e.g.,* What is day is it?) faster and with less prompting than without vSked.

> *A1[1]: ...they are wanting to work... they are wanting to look at it....they are wanting to make the choices... they want to hurry and get to the next one because they want see what happens next ... so I think that's huge because they want to work...*

The previously reluctant students were also noted as being more interested in picking their choices.

> *A1: Nathan, I was really surprised by him. He was looking. You could see him... paying attention, to this part... [Without vSked] he would never pick candy. He wouldn't even pick! He had no interest whatsoever in the reinforcer....Where the other kids would be like, "Whoa! This is mine, this is what I am*

[1] For ease of reading, teachers are represented by T, aides as A and then a number, and students with pseudonymns.

> *gonna get" ... There was nothing motivating for him. This time [using vSked] he was motivated.*

In our quantitative assessment, prompting by teachers when students use vSked (mean=7.20, SD=2.17) was 54% lower than without (mean=12.43, SD= 7.36; F=8.797, p=0.005). Classroom staff attributed the fewer prompts to the usability of the system itself (*e.g.,* students knew to press the screen) and to student comprehension (*e.g.,* students knew to select an answer). Specifically, teachers described some students as going "*straight to the answer.*"

> *T1: ... it was really amazing to see that Sharon correctly answered the [calendar questions] when using vSked ... that never happened before... and it makes me think "Oh! I didn't even know that she was able to do that."*

vSked provides some automatic prompting if a student selects an incorrect answer in a choice-making activity. On the first mistake, the correct image shakes to encourage its selection. On the second mistake, a random incorrect answer disappears. The teaching staff reported that the students responded to the shaking prompts if they were unsuccessful in their first attempt.

> *A1: I've noticed they kind of - if they choose the wrong one, they kind of look at it really fast and they'll see it shaking, and then they'll pick it.*

This kind of scaffolding is considered a highly desirable and positive outcome of using the system.

> *A1:... all the cues are there.. They are going to pick it up themselves instead of us having to say, you know, "check this, check that .. you know, try again" [....]so, they are just kind of looking at it themselves, and they're focusing more ...*

Despite a general push for independence, and thus less prompting, classroom staff described being comfortable with students continuing to receive prompting from vSked. They described vSked as analogous to the digital calendars used by many adults. We were curious, however, about the relationship between overall prompting from teachers, aides, and vSked (mean=6.06, SD=5.178) as opposed to overall prompting when vSked was not available (mean=10.38, SD=5.87; F=3.681, p=0.063). We did not find significant differences. However, this result warrants further investigation with a larger controlled sample.

In addition to prompting when students chose wrong answers, vSked also provided reinforcement for correct answers and task completion. First, the right side of the screen displayed images of the tangible rewards toward which the students were working, and images of themselves, which they viewed while completing activities (see Fig. 4). Viewing these images in close proximity to their work activities could be motivating for many students.

> *A1: ... they're paying attention to it ... even if they like kind of look away... they still kind of like glancing back at it like "wow [my reward] is still here."*

Second, students received an animated fireworks graphic after every correctly answered question and every time they earned enough tokens to receive rewards. The fireworks excited and intrigued the students. The fireworks provided students with an immediate reward for progressing through an activity. Feedback mechanisms, like the fireworks and the touch screen interactions, often drew the students to the device in ways that the paper-based tools could not.

> *A2: ...when Adele got her fireworks... her reinforcer page came up and she automatically already pushed what she wanted... I was like "hey that's pretty good" ... like she saw the fireworks and she was like... she kind of got the concept like "Okay I need to push something."*

Perhaps even more interesting when considering the role of classroom-level assistive technologies, students also reacted to the fireworks display on other students' devices. This kind of attention to other students in the room was surprising for the teaching staff considering the social challenges of autism. We describe this kind of sociality in depth in a later section.

Teachers and aides typically "fade out" prompts, using them less as a student progresses. Thus, the design of technological scaffolding and reinforcement can hold many implications for a student's progress, especially given the notion that prompts need to fade out over time, which was not a functionality of vSked. Our observations indicate that successful adoption of vSked rested in many ways on the interplay of classroom notions of, and tensions between, dependence and independence, and the ability of technology to respond to such tensions.

Consistency and predictability

Building and sustaining a routine is an integral component of well-managed autism classrooms. Teachers are often encouraged to establish clear classroom practices and reduce clutter and distraction [7, 26, 27] with the promise of reductions in severe problem behavior [23, 28]. However, classrooms are dynamic and ever-changing places, and the teaching staff who work in them are inherently human, which is to say somewhat inconsistent [9], and current tools sometimes attempt to be so general as to be flawed.

In practice, vSked allowed for more accuracy in the representations of activities and objects within visual supports. Whereas paper-based tools tend to use generic, often cartoonish imagery to increase the amount that each can be repurposed, vSked users tended to provide a mix of these general sketches and photographic images of actual activities or items (*e.g.,* Swedish Fish and "candy" in Fig. 4). Exact images help students to predict upcoming events and reduce the uncertainty associated with unexpected events. During interviews, teachers suggested that they appreciated the ability to add photorealistic images so that that students could better anticipate activities.

As a common classroom practice, students check their schedules at certain times throughout the day to prepare for the next activity and practice sequential processes. Before vSked, teachers set up the schedule every morning. Throughout the day students removed a finished activity from the schedule one at a time. Teaching staff reported that manually removing activities off of the paper-based schedule was an inconsistent practice, often resulting in inaccurate schedule displays. With vSked, the large touch screen displayed the students' schedules collectively.

> *T1: They can see the whole day right there in front of them and know that they are ok. Also, with the old fashioned schedules that we had...sometimes I would have to flip them over, for half the day, you know... The first half of the day, because they did so much, was on one side. Then after lunch, ok, let's turn it around to see what we are doing the rest of the day. So I would have kids that would have fits. They wouldn't know what is coming. So I think [vSked] helps them see what they have to do.*

When the teacher started an activity, the students first viewed this change together on the large screen and then touched a corresponding icon on their handheld devices. When moving on to the next activity, schedules were automatically updated to show the remaining activities for the day. With vSked, the students also could not alter their own schedules, reducing the classroom management challenges experienced from such changes.

> *A3: Before [vSked] each child had their own schedule and you had to find all their [visual cards] and put them of there ... because if they want they will take off all the morning cards to have more time for recess or lunch ... Now they can't do that, that is a good part ... they can't cheat.*

> *A4: And sometimes you don't know when they moved their schedule and you can actually see that everybody is [in the same task.]*

The teaching staff also reported that this helped the students focus and reduced distractions when transitioning between tasks. Delays in transition times can dramatically impact the classroom as a whole, even if they are not particularly problematic for an individual student. For example, the delay of one student might disrupt another student who is ready for the next task to begin. Classroom staff described faster and easier transitions between activities when using vSked. In our quantitative analysis, transition time from one activity to another was 61% lower with vSked (mean=60.62sec, SD=39.31) than without (mean=158sec, SD= 112.52; $F=4.762$, $p=.045$).

Finally, our results indicate that vSked may have allowed the students to receive their tokens and rewards in a more consistent manner than with the paper-based system. The paper-based system consisted of a token board at each student's desk on which teaching staff placed tokens when students completed work or behaved properly. Paper systems require substantial human effort to maintain them. Using the paper-based tools, teachers and aides were often inconsistent in their delivery of rewards and reinforcement to students both among students and over time. In classrooms in which multiple students and multiple instructors are interacting together, individual students can sometimes be overlooked. At the same time, some students may be given double rewards from more than one instructor. Furthermore, the time it takes to recognize and reinforce behavior, particularly across multiple students, prevents tokens from always being closely linked to the behavior being reinforced, which can limit their effectiveness.

With vSked, the teacher administered the reward stars from the large touch screen. Stars then appeared on a student's device. Often, the class would gather and watch the teacher administer the tokens. Teaching staff reported they were less likely to make mistakes, because the token count for all the students was displayed on the large monitor

> *T1: in the past I had to walk to everybody's individual desk [...] the desks were spaced out.. I forget certain kids half the time you know... and so this is nice that I can be like "OK we just had this work session, I do remember you guys being good... oh I remember you had a hard time so you're not getting a token."*

Rather than having to wait for a member of the classroom staff to recognize that enough tokens had been earned for the student to receive a reward, a fireworks simulation appeared on the large monitor and on the individual's handheld device. This feature was designed to ensure automatic notification of both the student and the classroom staff, thereby making the reinforcement both more immediate and more consistent. Emergent behavior among the students was both promising and surprising given the level of social disability exhibited by the participants. When a student earned a reward triggering the fireworks display on the large screen, other students often cheered. This kind of social support is extremely rare in autism classrooms. This phenomenon encouraged the classroom staff to consider how further communication of rewards status might encourage even greater interaction among students. Furthermore, this display served to motivate the other students. In our observations, we noted students wanting to work faster to earn their own rewards after seeing a peer do so, as described in the next section.

vSked provided new features and functionality for the teaching staff in the form of automation of some work, and for the students in the form of realness and instant gratification. The automation helped the teachers stay on schedule, with a central visual display of information that was kept up-to-date without much effort. The flexibility to provide realism in visual representations along with automation are key areas in the design of assistive technologies that may contribute to improved student response to the structure and transition of daily events.

Community and Interactivity

Building social skills and seeing themselves as part of a community of learners are important goals for any student, but especially for students with autism. Researchers have examined approaches to support both peer interactions and student-teacher interactions in autism classrooms [25]. In particular, Krantz and McClannahan used printed cues in visual schedules to support students initiating social contact with peers [16, 17], techniques we extend in this work.

vSked takes these kinds of interventions a step further by mimicking the typical call-and-response experience of regular education classrooms and providing a central display to support communication and interaction. In this way, both individual behaviors and classroom-wide activities become more visible, making both students and teaching staff more accountable to each other through visual cues. For example, using traditional tools, a caregiver would need to visit each student's desk to observe if a task was completed. While progress across activities throughout the day is not displayed on vSked, the large screen at the front of the room showed each student's progress within an activity. As a student completed tasks on the digital choice-boards, the green progress bars displayed how close a student was to finishing an activity (Fig. 5). The progress bar indicated to the teaching staff which students engaged in and successfully completed the tasks.

> *T1: ...I'm checking like when their names turn green that they've completed the task, and it seems like they're completing tasks quicker.*

vSked provides greater visibility into not only what activities are upcoming but also how the current activities are progressing. Thus, the teaching staff was able to assign tokens the moment students finished their activities, and to identify students who might need assistance. In our observations, teachers often encouraged students who had yet to finish a task by commenting aloud about another student's progress. For example, A6 commented in the middle of instruction: *"Wow! Look how fast Tommy finished! Let's give him two tokens!"*

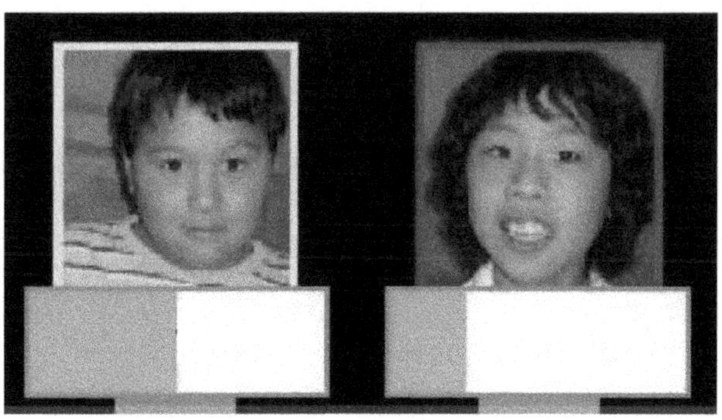

Fig 5. The green bar represents how far a student has progressed in an activity.

The teaching staff also used the large screen for remediation when a child was having a difficult day.

> *A1: ... taking the children up there, I'm always using it...Jeffery, today, he was kind of having a little meltdown and I took him up there and I showed him his little stars, and I'm like ... look! look how many you have. do you want to lose them? you know, he's 'noo noo noo'.*

In addition to the inherent visibility of the items on the large monitor, we observed students actively sharing items on their handheld display with teaching staff. Additionally, students showed interest in other student's devices.

> *A2: When the kids are using it, they are checking to see what their friends are doing.*

> *A1: They are kinda looking to see who is choosing what; they want to know what the other person is doing.*

> *A5:I think they also want to know what reinforcers [the other students] have. They have something they might want.*

Over the course of our deployments, the large screen became a focal point for the classroom. The size of the screen and colorful, bright images drew the students' interest. Additionally, the large screen allowed the students to have a shared experience with one another. Specifically, they were encouraged by and encouraging to one another because of the token system.

> *A1: when we say "ohh right, look, so and so is getting a star" the other ones is kind of like "ohhh"... looking out like I'm going to get a star too ... and it's not just one piece of paper in front them ... it's this huge... TV and the colors and everything it just really like makes them like "WOW" ...[sic]*

Previously, the practice of checking schedules was a collection of asynchronous, singular tasks. With vSked, this now became an activity the class could do as a whole. In our observations, checking vSked involved students each returning to their own desks and then transitioning to the next activity as a class. In the interviews, the teaching staff noted the importance of this procedure that took place often in conjunction with recess, bathroom time, and lunch.

> *T1:I think it's nice that the kids can come to their desks... which is like a natural transition for kids that are in typical classrooms you know... like everybody meets at their desk and then the teacher tells them what to do... [We] kind of reunite and then it's like "ok so we just finished this and you know, get all your reinforcers... get some tokens for the people that did really good during that work session.*

These community-building and sharing practices notably

arose in an environment that is by nature highly individualized. Furthermore, assistive technologies tend to be programmed and deployed with only the needs of an individual student in mind. Each student in the classroom has an Individual Education Plan (IEP) and works toward unique goals at his or her own pace. Aides lower the student-staff ratio, ensuring personalized instruction for each student. The emphasis on individual goals and instruction facilitates the unique needs of children with autism. As such, group activities in autism classrooms are often not prioritized. However, this lack of emphasis does not mean that group activities and socialization are not also important goals. On the contrary, despite heavily individualized instruction, even prior to vSked, teaching staff would facilitate activities for the group to do together when possible and appropriate. The teaching staff found value in the experience of looking and feeling like a "regular classroom." Instantiating group transitions or work time provided students with the opportunity to practice some of the behaviors expected of their neurotypical peers, as well as chances for socialization. The teaching staff described repeatedly using vSked to enhance these kinds of group activities and noting how much easier the activities were with the system.

In one poignant example, a completely new practice emerged around administering a student's final token before receiving a reward. During class time, as students earned tokens for good work or behavior, the teaching staff tracked the progress of every student at once with a quick glance at the large monitor. When doling out the tokens, the teacher made a mental note of students only one star away from the reward. Before a student's final token, the teacher led the student to the front of the class, and made an announcement. Administering the final token initiated the fireworks simulation on the large screen. The teaching staff would then lead the class in collective cheering. The event concluded with the student receiving the tangible reward.

The ability to award tokens from a single, central location was not possible before the introduction of vSked. Certain aspects of vSked functionality supported this new practice, but it emerged from the desire to provide opportunities for the students to participate as a community. Despite the focus on individual education, in practice, the teaching staff strove to balance individual needs and the possibilities for group learning. vSked helped to realize some of these goals that we would characterize as community-building. One of the teaching staff concluded:

> *T1: [vSked] will definitely change the way we do whole group. And hopefully increase their independence during other work times.*

Within individual work time, students carried out activities with fewer prompts from the teaching staff, in exchange for the scaffolding on the system itself. The system allowed the students to work on their tasks with automatic positive feedback and consistency in the daily structure and reward mechanisms. However, facilitating completely independent work sessions in the classroom was not the only experience the teaching staff strove to create. For example, this new practice of group recognition demonstrated the importance of working together as a group towards common goals in a classroom setting. The students expressed awareness and interest in each other's activities. By presenting a student's accomplishments to the class as a whole, opportunities arose for socialization as well as extrinsic motivation. The emergent community-based practices came about through the digital scheduling system, but were shaped by the desires, norms, and culture of the classroom that had been developing over time.

DISCUSSION

The deployment and evaluation of vSked exposed tensions around its use in a classroom, and holds implications for further work and future design processes for assistive technologies and classroom design in general. In particular, vSked was developed for use by an entire classroom of students. Classroom educational technologies (*e.g., [1, 4, 31]*) are common, however, classroom-level approaches to assistive technology are unique, even among those devices and systems deployed within classrooms already. Furthermore, examination of the issues of classroom management, sociality, and communication among students and staff reveal considerations, opportunities, and challenges for assistive technologies different from those that focus on individual student learners.

Classrooms have inherently limited resources, particularly in relation to student-staff ratios. While reliance on human prompting is generally considered undesirable, the use of technological prompts and scaffolding can be acceptable and is encouraged in special education. The vSked handhelds can be seen as an extension of the capacities of the student and thought of as personal resources for accomplishing tasks, not unlike the use of calculators or PowerPoint™ in neurotypical classrooms. The design of scaffolding and feedback within assistive technology is a critical factor in the usability, adoption and, ultimately, the success of the device.

Furthermore, consistent, shared, and networked systems can encourage more reaching out within a classroom space. We have found that individualization is not the only goal for assistive technology in classroom settings. In fact, emergent classroom practices provided evidence that teaching staff structured segments of the daily routines around activities designed for a group of students. Gathering students before recess or bringing a student up to the front of the classroom for recognition are examples of how community practices materialize within an individualized education model. These community practices are highly valued in the classroom setting, both to facilitate organization and to provide new opportunities for students to engage with each other and socialize. vSked supported new practices, such as synchronous transitions and public acknowledgement, previously uncommon to the classrooms of our study.

Despite the benefits of vSked, there were also some challenges, particularly when considering its role in the entire classroom, not just for individual students. In particular, vSked may have less flexibility for *ad hoc* customization than the paper-based schedules. Whereas a teacher can quickly use a marker to add text or change a detail on an individual paper schedule, she would have to use the programming interface to swap out the image for vSked. Limitations on this kind of *ad hoc* customization can conflict individualized student learning. If a student needs a schedule that is out of sync with the rest of the class, the current design of vSked does not necessarily accommodate that change. Furthermore, while vSked allows for more exact representation in the system, the overhead to update and manage a library of visual-graphic images can be a barrier to using exact representation. This suggests future work to examine the ways in which image search and retrieval technologies can be better incorporated into vSked.

In our studies, freeing the staff from specific individual prompting enabled them to be more flexible, moving from student to student but overall providing the same amount of attention as before. Future research should examine whether use of these technologies might become an excuse to lower teacher-student ratios. Also, many researchers have argued whether assistive technologies might create more dependence for individuals with disabilities over time (*e.g.*, McMillen & Soderberg 2002), an issue of relevance to long-term vSked use.

Although most assistive technology is designed to help with individual student's needs, we have found that designing a system explicitly for a classroom or a group of students creates opportunities for new practices. While the individual learning goals for each child may be paramount, assistive technology can, and arguably should, support both individualized work time and group practices. Designers creating new assistive technologies should thus consider how they might connect to one another, be used in concert, and be centrally coordinated. Achieving a balance between the needs of individual learners and those of the entire classroom—including both students and staff—is an open research question that warrants substantial further inquiry.

The resulting practices from these deployments are a reflection not only of vSked's functionality, but also a melding with existing social and educative trends. In our study, staff and students together established new practices around the system that incorporated previously defined parameters for school, classroom, and student success. In this work, we examined the classroom itself as the unit of analysis rather than just the individual student users. This approach contributes important implications for both the design and evaluation of assistive technologies in the future, especially those destined for classroom use. The deployment of vSked allowed the surfacing of issues that reflect school culture and norms related to the use of assistive technologies in classroom environments.

CONCLUSION AND FUTURE WORK

In this paper, we described the results of an empirical study of three deployments of vSked, a classroom intervention for students with autism, across two classrooms over the course of a year. In this work, we set out to understand the challenges and opportunities for a classroom-based assistive technology. Findings from this study indicate that use of these kinds of technologies can reduced the number of prompts given by teachers and aides and improve transition time. New community practices also emerged around the use of the system, such as collective cheering and general social awareness. The study also revealed some interesting tensions between facilitating a group of students (for example in the form of efficient transitions and predictable schedules) and individual students (by allowing for customized visual graphics and prompt variance). This work contributes to the research on assistive technology by suggesting design recommendations that place classrooms and groups of students at the forefront.

This work exposes research questions for classroom-based assistive technologies. First, the preliminary quantitative results we observed should be further investigated with a larger controlled sample. Second, the impact of these kinds of technologies and designing assistive technologies for the classroom rather than just the individual should be considered for populations other than autism.

ACKNOWLEDGMENTS

This work was supported by grants from NSF 0846063, UCMexus, and an NSF GRFP. We thank the participants in this work for their dedication and time. We thank LouAnne Boyd and Eliza Delpizzo for their help in this work as well as the STAR and LUCI research groups.

REFERENCES

1. Abowd, G.D. Classroom 2000: An Experiment with the Instrumentation of a Living Educational Environment. *IBM Systems Journal*, *38*, 4, (1999), 508-530.
2. Abowd, G.D., Atkeson, C.G., Brotherton, J., Enqvist, T., Gulley, P., and LeMon, J.. Investigating the capture, integration and access problem of ubiquitous computing in an educational setting. In the *Proc. CHI '98*, ACM Press (1998), 440-447.
3. American Psychiatric Association (APA). *Diagnostic and statistical manual of mental disorders, 4th ed.* Washington (DC): APA (1994).
4. Anderson, R., Anderson, R., Davis, P., Linnell, N., Prince, C., Razmov, V. and Videon, F. Classroom Presenter: Enhancing Interactive Education with Digital Ink. *IEEE Computer, 40*,9, (2007), 56-61.
5. Anderson, R. Anderson, R. Hoyer, C. and Wolfman, S. A Study of Digital Ink in Lecture Presentation. *Proc. CHI* ACM Press (2004), 567-574.

6. Bernard-Opitz, V., Sriram, N. and Nakhoda-Sapuan, S. Enhancing social problem solving in children with autism and normal children through computer-assisted instuction. *Journal of Autism and Developmental Disorders, 31*, 4, (2001), 377-384.
7. Clark, P. and Rutter, M. Task difficulty and task performance in autistic children. *Journal of Child Psychology and Psychiatry*, 20 (1979), p. 271-285.
8. Dell, A.G., Newton, D.N. and Petroff, J.G. *Assistive Technology in the Classroom: Enhancing the School Experiences of Students with Disabilities.* Upper Saddle River, NJ: PearsonMerrill Prentice Hall, (2008).
9. Flannery, K.B. and Horner, R.H. The relationship between predictability and problem behavior for students with severe disabilities. *Journal of Behavioral Education, 4*, 2, (1994), 157-176.
10. Hayes, G.R., Hirano, S., Marcu, G. Monibi, M., Nguyen, D., and Yeganyan, M., Interactive visual supports for children with autism. *Personal and Ubiquitous Computing,* (2010).
11. Hirano, S., Yeganyan, M., Marcu, G., Nguyen, D. Boyd, L.A., and Hayes, G.R.. vSked: Evaluation of a System to Support Classroom Activities for Children with Autism. *Proc. CHI 2010* ACM Press (2010), 1633-1642.
12. Hodgdon, L.A. *Visual Strategies for Improving Visual Communication: Volume I: Practical support for school and home.* Quirk Roberts Publishing, (1999).
13. ICAN, *Visual Schedules,* (2010).
14. Kimball, J.W., Kinney, E.M., Taylor, B.A., and Stromer, R. Video Enhanced Activity Schedules for Children with Autism: A Promising Package for Teaching Social Skills. *Education and treatment of children, 27*, 2, (2004) 280-298.
15. Kimball, J.W., Kinney, E.M., Taylor, B.A., and Stromer R. Lights, Camera, Action! Using Engaging Computer-Cued Activity Schedules. *Teaching Exceptional Children, 36*, 1, (2003) 40-45.
16. Krantz, P.J. and McClannahan, L.E.. Social interaction skills for children with autism: A scriptading procedure for beginning readers. *Journal of Applied Behavior Analysis*, 31 (1998), 191–202.
17. Krantz, P.J. and L.E. McClannahan, Teaching children with autism to initiate to peers: effects of a script-fading procedure. *Journal of Applied Behavior Analysis*, 26, (1993), 121– 132
18. Madsen, M., Kaliouby, R., Goodwin, M. and Picard, R. Technology for just-in-time in-situ learning of facial affect for persons diagnosed with an autism spectrum disorder. *Proc. ASSETS*, (2008).
19. Matson, J.L. and Boisjoli, J.A. The token economy for children with intellectual disability and/or autism. *Research in Developmental Disabilities, 30*, 2, (2009), 240-248.
20. McMillen, A.M. and Soderberg, S. Disabled Persons' Experience of Dependence on Assistive Devices. *Scandinavian Journal of Occupational Therapy, 9,4* (2002) 176-183.
21. Mirenda, P. Toward Functional Augmentative and Alternative Communication of Students with Autism: Maneal Signs, Graphic Symbols, and Voice Output Communication Aides. *Language, Speech, and Hearing Services in School, 34*, (2003), 203-216.
22. Mirenda, P., Autism, Augementative Communication, and Assistive Technology: What Do We Really Know? *Focus on Autism and Other Developmental Disabilities, 16*, 3, (2001), 141-151.
23. Cheng, Y., Moore, D., McGrath, P., and Fan, Y. Collaborative Virtual Environment Technology for People With Autism. *Focus on Autism and Other Developmental Disabilities, 20*, (2005), 231-243.
24. Olley, J.G. Classroom structure and autism. In D. J. Cohen & A. M. Donnellan (Eds.), *Handbook of autism and pervasive developmental disabilities* New York: John Wiley & Sons (1987), *411-417.*
25. Riedl, M.O., Arriaga, R., Boujarwah, F., Hong, H., Isbell, J., and Heflin, L.J. Graphical social scenarios: Toward intervention and authoring for adolescents with high functioning autism. *AAAI Fall Symposium on Virtual Healthcare Interaction,* Arlington, VA., (2009).
26. Rogers, S.J. Interventions that Facilitate Socialization in Children with Autism. *Journal of Autism and Developmental Disorders, 30*, 5 (2000) 399-409.
27. Schopler, E. and Olley, J.G. Public school programming for autistic children. *Exceptional Children*, 46 (1980), 451-453.
28. Schopler, E. Principles for directing both educational treatment and research. In C. Gillberg (Ed.) *Diagnosis and treatment of autism.* New York: Plenum Press. (1989), 167-183.
29. Schreibman, L. and Rogers, S.J. Interventions that facilitate socialization in children with autism . *Journal of Autism and Developmental Disorders*, *30*, 5 (2000), 399-409.
30. Sandford, C.A. *Available Classroom Supports for Students with Autism Spectrum Disorder in Public Schools.* in *Proc. of the Northeastern Educational Research Association,* (2009).
31. Sze, S. The Effect of Assistive Technology on Students with Disabilities. *Journal of Educational Technology Systems, 37*, 4, (2009), 419-429.
32. Truong, K. N. and Abowd, G.D. StuPad: Integrating Student Notes with Class Lectures. In the *Ext. Abstracts CHI.* ACM (1999), 208-209.

Privacy Risks Emerging from the Adoption of Innocuous Wearable Sensors in the Mobile Environment

Andrew Raij
University of South Florida
raij@usf.edu

Animikh Ghosh
SETLabs, Infosys
Animikh_Ghosh@infosys.com

Santosh Kumar
University of Memphis
santosh.kumar@memphis.edu

Mani Srivastava
UCLA
mbs@ucla.edu

ABSTRACT
Wearable sensors are revolutionizing healthcare and science by enabling capture of physiological, psychological, and behavioral measurements in natural environments. However, these seemingly innocuous measurements can be used to infer potentially private behaviors such as stress, conversation, smoking, drinking, illicit drug usage, and others. We conducted a study to assess how concerned people are about disclosure of a variety of behaviors and contexts that are embedded in wearable sensor data. Our results show participants are most concerned about disclosures of conversation episodes and stress — inferences that are not yet widely publicized. These concerns are mediated by temporal and physical context associated with the data and the participant's personal stake in the data. Our results provide key guidance on the extent to which people understand the potential for harm and data characteristics researchers should focus on to reduce the perceived harm from such datasets.

Author Keywords
Privacy, Information Disclosure, Wearable Sensors, Mobile Health, User Study

ACM Classification Keywords
H.5.2 Information Interfaces and Presentation: User Interfaces—*evaluation/methodology, user-centered design*; D.2.1 Requirements: [elicitation methods]; K.4.1 Public Policy Issues: [Privacy]

General Terms
Experimentation, Measurement, Human Factors

INTRODUCTION
Networked body-worn sensors and those embedded in mobile devices we carry (e.g., smartphones) can collect a variety of measurements about physical and physiological states, such as acceleration, respiration, and ECG. By applying sophisticated machine learning algorithms on these data, rich inferences can be made about the physiological, psychological, and behavioral states and activities of people. Example inferences include dietary habits, psychosocial stress, addictive behaviors (e.g., drinking), exposures to pollutants, social context, and movement patterns. These inferences, particularly when made continuously as people go about their daily lives, have many uses, such as sharing activity and context information with friends and family [35], self-monitoring health for behavior change [7], and scientific study of human physiology, psychology, and behavior [2, 10].

New Privacy Concerns and Challenges
While useful, such sensing systems raise significant new privacy concerns. Seemingly innocuous data shared for one purpose can be used to infer private activities and behaviors that the individual did not intend to share. For example, inertial sensor data (e.g., accelerometers and gyroscopes) shared with caregivers for evaluating and improving gait or physical activity levels could also be used to track location and movement patterns by sophisticated tracking algorithms [12] that make use of public information such as street maps and an individual's work locations. Inertial data may also reveal sensitive medical conditions, such as seizures [22], that one may wish to keep private. As another example, respiration and location data, combined with publicly available pollution maps, could be shared to measure an individual's exposure to air pollution, where respiration measurements are used to estimate the amount of air inhaled. However, this same data can also reveal the timing and duration of conversations [25] or even smoking [2]. In some cases, inferences from sensory data (e.g., public speaking inferred by fusing prolonged speaking episode and elevated stress) combined with other public information (e.g., department and university) can also re-identify an individual.

Privacy research has traditionally dealt with reidentification from quasi-identifiers [32], search histories [3], movie ratings [27], and social networks [28]. Some work exists on understanding the privacy concerns emerging from sensory data, such as location traces [16], but little work has investigated the new privacy concerns that emerge from the disclosure of measurements collected by wearable sensors.

While the privacy risks emerging from sharing data collected by personal sensors are poorly understood, their adoption is growing rapidly. One example of such a system is AutoSense, an experimental, unobtrusive wearable sensor suite capable of capturing physiological data and using it to infer the wearer's behavior and psychological state in real-time [2]. It can be worn for weeks at a time and is thus capable of collecting significant amounts of personal data from the mobile environment of its wearer. To date, AutoSense has been used by 60+ participants in behavioral science field studies totalling 1,000+ hours, where it collected ECG, respiration, accelerometer, temperature, and skin conductance data; and from this data made continuous inferences of physical activity, posture, stress, conversation, and commuting. This rich and unique dataset, however, can not be readily shared with other researchers out of fear of similar unknown threats to privacy. This is because seemingly innocuous personal datasetes have previously been shared, only to learn later of hidden privacy threats within them [27, 13]. We note that commercially available commodity devices capture similar information [1, 36]. To see continued growth and adoption of such devices, the privacy challenges associated with them must be addressed.

Contributions

Via a user study, we study the privacy concerns associated with the disclosure of data collected by wearable sensors in the mobile environment. We first develop a conceptual framework for examining the privacy issues associated with the disclosure of continuously-collected physiological, psychological, and behavioral data. Next, we create a new privacy survey to assess how concerns about privacy threats change as various behaviors and contexts are restricted and abstracted. Lastly, to analyze how concern level changes as the respondents' stake in the data is increased [24], we administered the survey to two groups. The first group, Group NS ($N = 36$), completed the survey and had no personal stake in the data described. The second group, Group S ($N = 30$), was composed of participants in an AutoSense field study who had direct personal exposure to the collection of sensitive datasets. They wore the AutoSense system for 3 days. Group S completed the privacy survey twice, after the 3 day collection period, and again after they were visually presented with behavioral and contextual inferences derived from their data (e.g., periods of stress, conversation, commuting, etc.) to further increase their personal exposure to and overall stake in their data.

We analyze the data from three perspectives. First, we assess how disclosure of different behaviors and contexts affect participant concern levels as their stake is increased in the data. Second, we evaluate the impact of applying various restrictions and abstractions on concern level. Third, we assess the impact of reidentification on the concern level as the role of the data consumer (i.e., whom the data is disclosed to) is varied from the research team to the general public.

Key Results. We find that participants are most concerned about release of conversation and commuting behavior, and release of stress, a psychological state. However, those with low or no personal stake in the data did not indicate nearly as strong concerns, implying that a person needs to have a personal connection to the data to understand the implications to his/her privacy. Restricting or abstracting the disclosure of temporal context (e.g., releasing duration in place of timestamps) had a significant effect on reducing privacy concerns for a variety of contexts and behaviors. Lastly, the risk of reidentification doubled concerns regarding disclosure of the data; the effect was largest for disclosure to the general public. Our results call for deeper investigation into the new privacy issues emerging in the domain of personal sensing.

RELATED WORK

Understanding and Awareness of Privacy Risks: Several well-publicized privacy breaches have contributed significantly to awareness of privacy risks [32, 3, 27, 28]. This awareness has led to studies that seek to understand the privacy concerns of users when sharing personal data, such as location [24, 33, 8, 4, 35, 5], calendars [31], and more generally sharing over online social networks [34]. However, these studies deal with sharing information whose privacy implications are already understood by most individuals (e.g. sensory information such as location and non-sensory information such as calendars). Their insights do not necessarily apply to the rich set of sensors in wearable devices and mobile phones that enable non-obvious inferences about users' behaviors and activities.

Some recent papers have examined awareness of non-obvious privacy threats from personal sensing applications and WiFi data. Using the Personal Audio Loop, Iachello et al examined privacy concerns regarding audio capture of conversation [15]. However, they focus on the privacy concerns of secondary stakeholders and third parties, who may be inadvertently recorded by the system. Our work focuses on the concerns of the primary user whose conversation episodes may be inferred without any recording of the audio, i.e., from an innocuous respiration sensor. Klasnja et al [17] investigate privacy concerns by interviewing participants using a physical fitness system. Concerns were evaluated for activity, GPS, and audio data. Our work is complementary, in that it studies concerns for physiological sensors and the psychological and behavioral inferences made from them. Klasnja et al [18] and Consolvo et al [6] investigate privacy problems associated with daily WiFi use. This work employs similar methods to assess privacy concerns, i.e., we also show participants their own potentially-sensitive data and then assess how exposure to the data changes awareness and concerns. However, we apply it to expose concerns associated with the use of innocuous physiological sensors.

To our knowledge, we are the first to highlight privacy concerns associated with behavioral and affective inferences that can be made from seemingly innocuous physiological data (e.g., ECG and respiration). Historically, these sensors have not been viewed as sources of privacy threats. We also identify disclosure of psychological state (e.g., stress) as concerning to users.

Maintaining Privacy: Increased awareness of privacy risks has led to anonymization techniques [32, 23, 21] that seek to thwart reidentification attacks on personal data from which explicit identifiers have been removed. Reidentification attacks exploit quasi-identifiers such as age, zip code, etc., which cannot be entirely suppressed due to their utility to the end-user, but can reveal identity when combined with background information. Current techniques, mostly explored in context of relational data, aim to preserve an individual's identity in a population. They combat reidentification with techniques such as suppression , perturbation , and generalization . While analogous techniques have utility for sensor time series data [11, 26], anonymizing sensory information is often harder and different because sensor data (i) may be both sensitive and quasi-identifying, making it harder to achieve privacy without affecting utility, and (ii) may need to be shared with identity (e.g., with caregivers). Thus, existing anonymization techniques alone cannot be used to protect individuals sharing personal sensor data. New approaches are needed to preserve *behavioral privacy* when identity cannot be removed from the dataset.

REASONING ABOUT PERSONAL SENSING PRIVACY

This section describes a conceptual framework for examining the privacy issues associated with physiological, psychological, and behavioral data captured by personal sensors (see Figure 1). Our framework is primarily concerned with what [30] calls the *disclosure boundary*, i.e., where privacy and publicity are in tension. We focus specifically on the choices data producers can make that displace this disclosure boundary for personal sensory data. In addition, the threats highlighted by our framework touch upon the *identity boundary*, and how unintended disclosure of an individual's behavior may change how others view the individual.

Our framework is composed of six elements: measurements, behaviors, contexts, restrictions, abstractions, and privacy threats. Data producers capture *measurements* with sensors, which can then be processed to infer *behaviors* and *contexts*. To control access to the data, data producers can put *restrictions* in place that prevent sharing of specified measurements and/or behaviors and contexts derived from them. To control the level of detail in the shared data, *abstractions* can be applied to unrestricted measurements, behaviors, and contexts. The set of disclosed behaviors and contexts, and the level of abstraction applied to each, ultimately decide the types and significance of the resulting *privacy threats*.

We motivate each element of the framework using a fictional AutoSense study participant, Jane Doe. Jane is participating in a study to examine physiological, psychological, and behavioral factors associated with stress. Jane is nearing the end of the third of seven consecutive days wearing the AutoSense system. She had a stressful day at work, so she decided to run home for exercise and stress relief. Her husband, John Doe, met her in the middle of the run, and they completed the run together. Jane has a medical condition that causes ocassional seizures, and after the run, Jane experienced a seizure. AutoSense recorded the following information about Jane's run, among others:

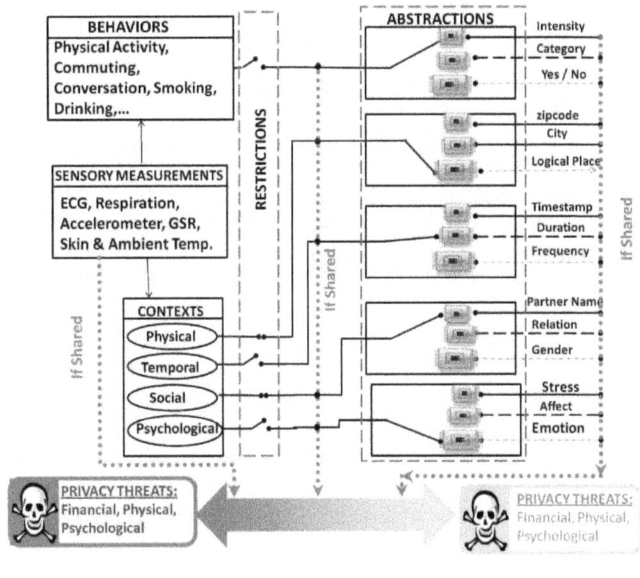

Figure 1. A conceptual framework for reasoning about privacy issues in sharing personal sensory data.

- Jane put on the sensors on September 21 at 8:00am.
- Additional processing of the accelerometer data indicated Jane was running September 21, from 5:33pm to 6:07pm, and she experienced a seizure from 6:15pm to 6:25pm.
- GPS data indicates the run started at 185 N Industry Street in Phoenix, AZ and ended at 1359 W Suburbs Street in Phoenix, AZ. The route taken was also recorded.
- Jane was angry and stressed from 5:25pm to 5:51pm. She was relaxed from 5:51pm until the start of her seizure at 6:15pm. She was terrified from the start of her seizure at 6:15pm until she removed the sensors at 6:30pm.
- Starting at 5:28pm, another mobile phone with the Bluetooth ID "'JohnDoe"' entered her phone's proximity and remained there until Jane removed the sensors at 6:30pm.

Measurements, Behaviors, and Contexts

Measurements are the raw data captured by wearable sensors, such as ECG, respiration, and accelerometer. **Behaviors** are actions taken or experienced by the data producer, and are inferred from measurements. In Jane's case, both the running episode and the seizure could be inferred from her accelerometer measurements. Jane was aware of the system's ability to detect running because it was mentioned in the study's informed consent document. However, the document did not mention that accelerometer data could also capture the motion signature of her seizure. The study designers anticipated behaviors that are not of interest might be captured by the sensors, but they did not anticipate that seizures, a sensitive medical condition, could be captured.

Other similar accidental captures of private behavior are possible. For example, heart rate and respiration, measurements used to infer stress level could also be used to infer cocaine, heroin, and other illicit drug use, all of which affect these measurements in extreme ways. Smoking, alcohol consumption, conversation, and commuting can also be captured. The list of behaviors that can be inferred from sensory data is growing rapidly.

Paraphrasing [9], we define **context** as any information that can be used to characterize the situation of a behavior. As with behaviors, contexts are explicitly stored in, or inferred from, measurements. The example contains four types of contexts which are representative of the capabilities of today's personal sensing systems: temporal, physical, psychological, and social.

Temporal contexts describe characteristics related to the timing of a behavior, such as the exact start time of a behavioral episode. In the example, the temporal properties include the start and end timestamps of Jane's run, seizure, emotional states, and time with her husband. **Physical** contexts describe the physical environment in which a behavior occurs, such as location and objects at a location. In the example, the addresses of the start and endpoint of the run, and the route taken between them, define these properties. **Psychological** contexts describe the psychological state of the user during the behavior. In the example, Jane experienced four psychological states: angry, stressed, and relaxed while running and terrified during the seizure. There is a wide gamut of emotions a person can experience, all of which fall under this category [20]. **Social** contexts describe the social environment in which a behavior occurs, and could include who the user was with when the behavior occurred and whether the user was interacting with that person. In the example, Jane's social context was initially empty. Later, her husband John entered the social context. Note that contexts cannot only be associated with behaviors but also with other contexts. This is demonstrated in the association of timestamps (temporal), with Jane's locations (physical), emotions (psychological), and the presence of her husband (social).

Privacy Threats

Privacy threats are the risks or harms that could come to the data producer if the his or her identity is associated with the data. If identity were removed from the dataset, the number of threats to the data producer decreases. Unfortunately, maintaining identity privacy is not always feasible with sensory datasets for two reasons. First, identity is sometimes needed to retain the utility of these datasets. A caregiver could develop a personalized treatment for a patient from his/her dataset, but would not know who to give the treatment to without the patient's identity. Second, identity is often intertwined with useful information that the data producer would like to share. In Jane's case, reidentification is possible from the GPS data [19] or from the presence of John's identity in the dataset.

Once a dataset is re-identified, there are three types of threats that could emerge: financial, psychological, and physical. **Financial threats** are threats that lead to loss of assets or property. It includes professional threats, such as the loss of a job or damage to one's business reputation. **Psychological threats** affect the data producer's emotions. Such threats include embarrasment due to demasking of white lies or demasking of emotion regulation, deterioration in social or family relationships, and development of pathological psychological conditions. **Physical threats** are threats to personal safety that may result in physical harm to the data producer. To reduce the probability of these threats when identity privacy cannot be maintained, we must maintain behavior and context privacy using restrictions and abstractions.

Restrictions and Abstractions

Restrictions remove data from a dataset before it is shared to reduce the potential privacy threats in the data. Measurements, behaviors, and contexts can all be restricted. For example, to prevent her husband's identity from identifying her own, Jane could restrict access to her bluetooth data. Additionally, to make it difficult to infer the seizure, Jane could restrict access to accelerometer data. Note, however, that this would also prevent the AutoSense team from accessing Jane's physical activity data, an important factor in moderating stress that may be of scientific interest.

Restricting all measurements, behaviors, and contexts would effectively empty the dataset, making it useless. On the other hand, sharing all the data is not desirable either. **Abstractions** provide a middle ground. They operate on measurements, behaviors, and contexts to reduce the extent of the exposure in the dataset. Abstraction operators include suppression[32], substitution[26], and transformation[29].

Jane's privacy could be better protected using several abstractions. John's presence during Jane's run and seizure (social context) could be abstracted into "family member present." Jane's terrified state during the seizure (psychological context) could be abstracted into a less specific emotion such as "stressed." This would not remove the seizure from the dataset, but would make it more difficult for an adversary to search for unusual emotional events like the seizure.

The examples above imply that one can mitigate the threats associated with a deanomymized dataset by restricting or abstracting behaviors and contexts. Stated mathemetically, the probability of a set of threats $\bar{T}$ is $P(\bar{T}) = f(\bar{R}, \bar{A}, \bar{M})$, where $\bar{M}$ is the set of measurements, and $\bar{R}$ and $\bar{A}$ are sets of restrictions and abstractions, respectively, applied to $\bar{M}$ or behaviors $\bar{B}$ and contexts $\bar{C}$ inferred from $\bar{M}$. Next, we describe a study that assesses how real people perceive $P(\bar{T})$ under various combinations of $\bar{C}$, $\bar{B}$, $\bar{R}$, and $\bar{A}$.

STUDY DESIGN

To study the privacy concerns associated with the disclosure of measurements collected by wearable sensors in the mobile environment, we designed a user study with three goals.

Goal 1: Assess the privacy concerns of real people regarding disclosure of continuously-collected physiological, behavioral, and psychological data. We also assess the change in concern levels as personal stake in the data is increased [24].

Goal 2: Use the proposed privacy framework and examine how restrictions and abstractions applied to various behaviors and contexts change concern levels.

Goal 3: Assess how reidentification of the data producer affects concern levels as the type of data consumer is varied.

Participants

66 participants were recruited from the student population at a 20,000+ student university in the United States. Participants were recruited using flyers and word-of-mouth. Participants volunteered to join one of two groups, a group with no personal stake in the data (Group NS) or a group with a personal stake (Group S) in the data. Table 1 summarizes the demographic characteristics of the groups.

	N	Males	Age±Std	AP	B	W	O
NS	36	56%	25 ± 4	22%	22%	53%	3%
S	30	53%	23 ± 4	23%	33%	40%	3%

Table 1. Group NS and S Demographics: AP=Asian/Pacific Islander, B=Black - Non Hispanic, W=White - Non Hispanic, O=Other

To capture the concerns of people with a personal stake in such data, we integrated this study into an existing study whose participants wore the AutoSense system for three consecutive days (Group S). The existing study examined the use of micro-incentives for scientific data collection and the effect of interruptions on user stress level. The data on micro-incentives and interruptions is outside the scope of this article and will be reported separately.

Procedure

For three days, Group S participants ($N = 30$) collected physiological, behavioral, and psychological data using the AutoSense sensor system as they went about their normal everyday life. At the end of the three-day period, Group S participants completed a privacy questionnaire assessing their concern regarding disclosure of selected behaviors and contexts with various restrictions and abstractions applied. Next, they reviewed graphs depicting the various behavioral and contextual inferences that were derived from their data (e.g., periods of stress, conversation, commuting, etc.) to further increase their personal exposure to and overall stake in their data. Finally, they completed the privacy questionnaire again. This within-subjects, repeated measures design allowed assessment of Group S concern level (Goals 1 and 2) at both a low (pre-review) and high (post-review) level of personal stake in the data (Goal 1). To distinguish between these two levels, the rest of this article refers to Group S before the review as Group $S\text{-}Pre$ and Group S after the review as Group $S\text{-}Post$.

Group NS participants ($N = 36$) had no exposure to continuous physiological, behavioral, and psychological data collection. They did not wear AutoSense and did not review any data collected by it. They only completed the same privacy questionnaire as Group S. This allowed a between-subjects comparison of concern levels between participants with no personal stake in the data, Group NS, and participants with a personal stake in the data, Group S (Goal 1).

Group NS

Participants in Group NS first provided informed consent. After consent was given, they completed the demographics questionnaire followed by the privacy questionnaire. They were then paid $2 for participation.

Group S

Participants in Group S first provided informed consent. As part of the informed consent process, Group S was informed about the data collected by the AutoSense sensors. After consent was given, they completed the demographics questionnaire. Then the field protocol was explained to the participant. After explaining the protocol, the study coordinator demonstrated how to put on the sensors and then assisted participants in putting them on if necessary. The study coordinator verified the sensors were working properly by visually examining the streaming sensor data using an oscilloscope program. Once the sensors were verified as working, the participant was sent into the field.

Participants wore the AutoSense sensors for 3 consecutive days during their awake hours. They were instructed to take the system off at night and put it back on in the morning. Participants also carried the AutoSense mobile phone (Android G1). Periodically, the phone would ask participants to complete questionnaires. Participants earned micro-incentives (between $0.02 and $0.11) for each question they completed.

On the last morning of the study, the participant returned to the lab where he/she completed the privacy questionnaire. After the questionnaire, the participant reviewed graphs depicting the data he/she collected over the 3 days (described below), and then completed the questionnaire again. Lastly, participants were debriefed to collect subjective comments about their data and any concerns they had about it.

Data Review Session

We developed the *Aha* visualization system for reviewing data collected by the AutoSense system from natural environments. *Aha* is designed to help participants examine their daily behaviors and contexts at low, medium, and high levels of abstraction. Aha incorporates four visualizations. The **Day at a Glance** visualization depicts an overview of behaviors performed by individuals in their daily life. For example, the visualization presents the fraction of time (temporal context, high abstraction) spent commuting or in conversation. Psychological context is also depicted here as durations of stress in a day (Figure 3). The **Stress at a Glance** visualization depicts the fraction of time (temporal, high) participants are stressed (psychological, medium) during behaviors such as commuting or walking. The **Stress at Places** visualization depicts the fraction of time (temporal, high) at places, such as home and work (physical, high), when participants are stressed (psychological, medium). Lastly, the **Daily Timeline** (Figure 4) visualization plots behaviors on a detailed timeline (temporal, low). An analysis of 100 hours of AutoSense data found that the visualizations in *Aha* were approximately 80.16% accurate. Group S participants reviewed the data they collected using *Aha* for 10-15 minutes.

Privacy Questionnaire

The privacy questionnaire asks participants to rate their level of concern regarding disclosure of various combinations of

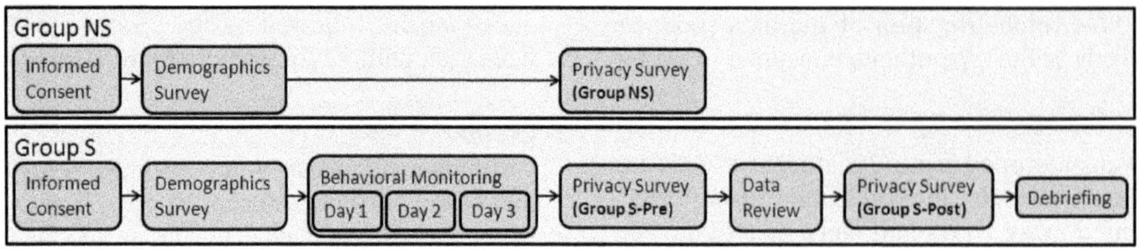

Figure 2. Procedure for Groups NS (top) and S (bottom)

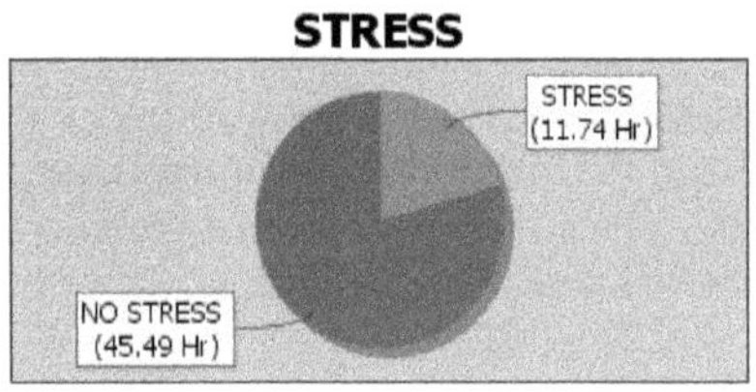

Figure 3. Fraction of monitoring period participant was stressed

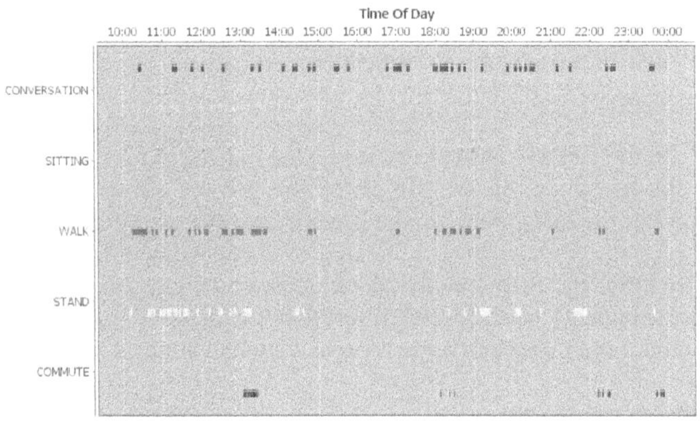

Figure 4. Daily Timeline of a participant monitored by AutoSense

behaviors, contexts, and levels of abstraction[1] (Goal 2). Concern is rated on a five-point scale: Not concerned (0), A little concerned (1), Moderately concerned (2), Concerned (3), and Extremely Concerned (4). The questionnaire consists of 9 sections. Sections 1 through 6 ask participants to rate their concern level for disclosure of places, smoking, stress, conversations, commuting, and exercise habits, all of which were depicted in the *Aha* visualizations. However, all participants reported they did not smoke, so the smoking section was automatically skipped by the questionnaire software.

Within each section, the participant is asked to rate the section's behavior or context if it were released with no context, temporal context, physical context, and both temporal and physical context simultaneously. The abstractions of temporal context on the questionnaire are timestamp, duration, and frequency. Physical context is assessed at one level of abstraction, place. Questions that ask about both temporal and physical context simultaneously ask about place and timestamp and place and duration. With each question, an example scenario of the disclosure is provided to help the participant understand the question. The last question for all behaviors, stress, and place asked participants to write in an explanation for ratings of at least moderately concerned. The choice of behaviors, contexts, and abstractions in the questionnaire was driven by 1) the capabilities of AutoSense and *Aha*, and 2) limiting the number of questions on the survey to approximately 50. The latter requirement was particularly important given the already high burden placed on Group S participants, who filled out the privacy questionnaire after 3 days of wearing sensors and answering field questionnaires.

[1] Available for download at [10]

Section 7 asks participants what information about their daily life they are particularly concerned about sharing. Sections 8 and 9 assess how concerned the participant would be if the data were shared, with or without identity, with the study coordinators, other study participants, other scientists and researchers, and the general public (Goal 3).

RESULTS

We analyzed participant data with respect to the three goals of the study as discussed in the preceding section. We now discuss the results and their interpretation from comments provided by the participants during debriefing. Unless otherwise noted, two-tailed t-tests were used to test for significant differences ($p < 0.05$). In comparisons between Groups NS and $S\text{-}Pre$ (different populations), unequal variances were assumed. In comparisons between Groups $S\text{-}Pre$ and $S\text{-}Post$ (same population), a paired t-test was used. Shapiro-Wilk tests confirmed the normality of the data. Where space allows, p-values are reported with the means and standard deviations of the corresponding distributions.

Goal 1: Concern Levels and Personal Stake

To analyze participant concerns and the effect of personal stake on those concerns, per-participant averages of concern were calculated for conversation, commuting, exercise, stress, and places for all three groups. Figure 5 depicts these summary measures for all three groups.

Group NS and Group $S\text{-}Pre$ provided similar concern ratings for exercise and place, and no significant differences were found between their distributions. However, there was a trend toward significance for commuting ($p = 0.08$, $NS = 1.3 \pm 0.1$, $S\text{-}Pre = 1.9 \pm 0.3$) and conversation ($p = 0.09$, $NS = 1.2 \pm 0.1$, $S\text{-}Pre = 1.4 \pm 0.2$).

Group $S\text{-}Post$ had higher concern ratings than Group $S\text{-}Pre$. In particular, conversation for $S\text{-}Post$ was significantly higher ($p = 0.01$, $S\text{-}Pre = 1.4 \pm 0.2$, $S\text{-}Post =$

2.1 ± 0.2), and similar trends toward significance were found for exercise ($p = 0.0978$, $S\text{-}Pre = 0.968 \pm 0.1$, $S\text{-}Post = 1.0 \pm 0.5$), commuting ($p = 0.07$, $S\text{-}Pre = 1.9 \pm 0.3$, $S\text{-}Post = 2.4 \pm 0.3$), and stress ($p = 0.06$, $S\text{-}Pre = 1.8 \pm 0.4$, $S\text{-}Post = 2.6 \pm 0.3$). Furthermore, across Group *S-Post*, 20% of stress questions were rated at "Concerned"(3) or "Extremely Concerned"(4), 15% for commuting, 12% for conversation, and 8% for exercise. Disclosure of place did not see a significant increase in concern from pre- to post-review (similar to that observed in [4] upon suitable scaling).

Taken together, the results for Groups *NS*, *S-Pre*, and *S-Post* indicate increasing personal stake in the data helps people better estimate their concerns regarding the disclosure of behaviors and contexts. The highest level of concerns emerged for exercise, conversation, commuting, and stress after participants observed visual depictions of their data. Surprisingly, only 10-15 minutes of data observation was needed for these differences to emerge.

To better understand the rationale for participants' concern ratings, we examined their free-form survey responses and debriefing comments. Two participants indicated their concern regarding commuting stemmed from an overall concern about being watched: "I am uncomfortable with someone watching over me that closely." Two other participants expressed similar concerns: "It would be strange knowing that a person knew exactly where I was going to be, and when, at all times of the day. I wouldn't feel like I had any privacy."

Although the survey did not have any questions about social context, some participants said they were concerned about revealing social context with conversation: "I don't like people to know whom I talked to at all...as i feel it's none of their business." Another participant said, "I do not want to share even when I talk because people may find out with whom if it is marked with time, which can be private." This participant felt that adding time to conversation data may provide enough information to reveal who he talks to.

Participant concerns about stress appear to stem from a fear of having one's inner thoughts revealed. One participant said, "I have this level of concern because whenever I am stressed out, I am around my mother." The comment implies the participant does not want to reveal to her mother that she is a source of stress. Another participant said: ''I feel my stress data if revealed can be a professional issue as am generally hot headed." People expect psychological states and inner thoughts to be private. Psychological monitoring technologies threaten this expectation.

Although concerns about exercise were low, participants commented that they did not want their exercise habits revealed. One participant explained: "I guess I'm a bit self-conscious over how little I exercise; I'd hate to have that broadcast."

Goal 2: Impact of Applying Restrictions & Abstractions

Figure 6 breaks down the effect of selected restrictions and abstractions on individual behaviors and contexts. Table 2 highlights the effect of restricting or abstracting temporal

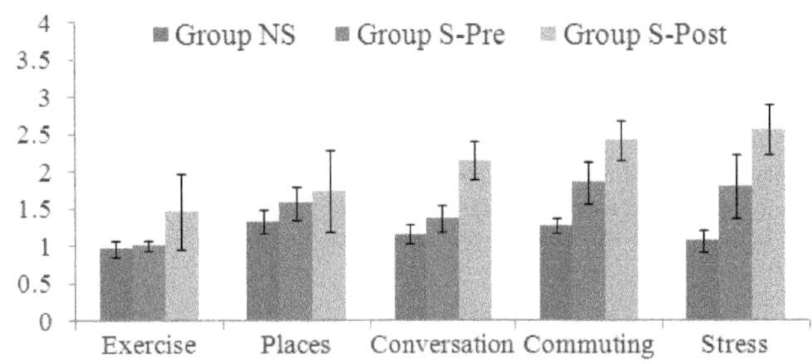

Figure 5. Groups NS and S concerns with respect to selected behaviors and contexts. The height of the bars represents the mean concern level, and the error bars depict $\pm$ one standard deviation from the mean.

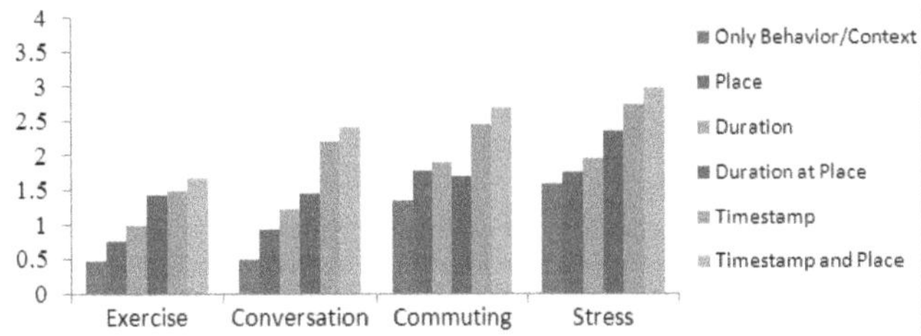

Figure 6. Changes in participant concerns due to temporal contexts

context. Generally speaking, adding temporal context to behaviors and other contexts increased concern level, with each decreasing level of temporal abstraction leading to a corresponding increase in level of concern. More often, adding timestamps induced a significant change in concern as compared to adding duration. Participants were most concerned about others knowing the exact moments they experience stress. Adding duration to stress events did not increase concern significantly, but adding timestamp increased concern by approximately 50%.

Participants were most concerned about sharing physical and temporal context together. There was a trend of increasing concern for place and timestamp, with the lowest concern for just sharing the behavior or context, the next level of concern for reporting the place or time of the behavior or context, and the highest level of concern for reporting both the place and time of the behavior or context. Across Group *S-Post*, 9% of behavior-only concerns were rated at "Concerned"(3) or "Extremely Concerned"(4), 11% for behavior with place, 20% for behavior with timestamp, and 26% for behavior with both timestamp and place. Adding both place and time simultaneously increased concerns significantly for conversation, commuting, and stress. Indeed, one participant explicitly expressed a concern about stress, time, and place: "I'd be concerned with people being able to tie the 'whens' of my being stressed with the 'wheres.' I'd rather people not know that I felt stressed at my particular job or when at my house, because they wouldn't have the whole picture." Exercise, however, did not exhibit a significant change from adding timestamp or place alone. Participants are likely less concerned about exercise episodes, since exercising is a positive behavior which they may be proud to share with others. Lower concerns for sharing place alone is consistent with the growing use and acceptability of location sharing sys-

	Exercise	Conversation	Commuting	Stress
Behavior/Context	0.02**, ns	ns, 0.06*	ns, 0.012**	ns, 0.06*
B/C + Place	0.008**, 0.08*	ns, 0.016**	ns, 0.062*	ns, 0.002**

Table 2. Effect of adding duration and timestamp to behaviors and other contexts (Group S-$Post$). Each cell is the result of a paired t-test comparing the particular row-column pair with that same pair, but with duration or timestamp added. The result for duration is the first value in each cell, and the second value is the result for timestamp. (ns = not significant, * = trend toward significance, ** = significant)

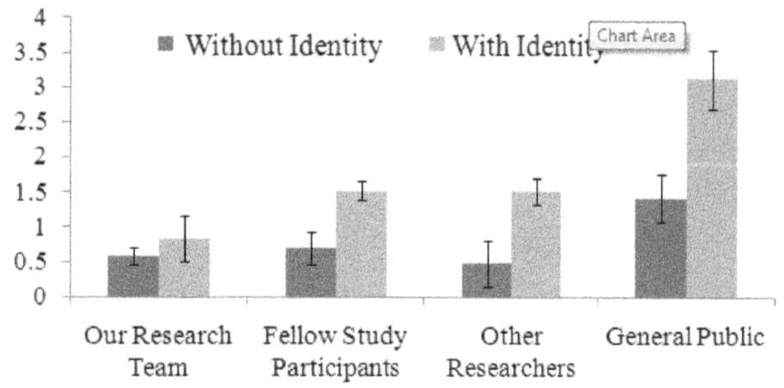

Figure 7. Change in participant concerns with respect to disclosure to different groups of people with and without identity (Group S-$Post$).

tems and what has been observed in other studies [4].

Goal 3: Role of Data Recipient

Participants rated their concern with respect to sharing identified and anonymous data with 4 groups: our research team, other study participants, other scientists and researchers, and the general public. Figure 7 summarizes participant responses. Adding identity to the dataset significantly increased participant concerns for all groups except our research team (Fellow Participants: p=0.02, $NoId = 0.7 \pm 0.2$, $Id = 1.5 \pm 0.1$, Other Researchers: p=2E-4, $NoId = 0.5 \pm 0.3$, $Id = 1.5 \pm 0.2$, General Public: p= 4E-5, $NoId = 1.4 \pm 0.3$, $Id = 3.1 \pm 0.4$). 10% of participants rated releasing data to the general public without identity at "Concerned" or "Extremely Concerned." This increased to 70% after adding identity. Releasing the data to members of our research team with identity increased concerns, but not significantly.

There was a significant increase in concern from releasing identified data to other researchers to releasing identified data to the general public (p=0.001, $OtherResearchers = 1.5 \pm 0.2$, $Public = 3.1 \pm 0.4$). Note that releasing identity to the general public more than doubles concerns to 3.1, the highest average concern level reported on the privacy survey. A trend toward significance was found between releasing identified data to members of our research team and releasing identified data to other study participants (p=0.06, $OurTeam = 0.8 \pm 0.3$, $OtherParticipants = 1.5 \pm 0.1$). Releasing identified data to study participants and to other researchers generated approximately the same level of concern. For anonymous data, increase in concern rating trended toward significance only when the recipient was changed from other researchers to the general public (0.06, $OtherResearchers = 0.5 \pm 0.3$, $Public = 1.4 \pm 0.3$).

The results indicate disclosure of any data to the general public is of significant concern to participants. When identity is added to the dataset, this concern more than doubles. Furthermore, identity has a similar effect for release to fellow study participants or other researchers.

IMPLICATIONS AND LIMITATIONS

Awareness of Threats

The results highlight an overall lack of awareness of the actual information contained in personal sensing datasets and the privacy threats associated with them. Participants who had little or no personal stake in the data, representative of most of the population today, did not appear to understand the sensitive nature of the data.

Interestingly, concerns regarding place did not change after the review session. One interpretation is that participants were already aware of the potential threats associated with sharing place, due to the growing use of location-based services and media coverage of the issues associated with them.

Reducing Threats

The results imply the components of the proposed framework – behaviors, contexts, restrictions, and abstractions – can be manipulated to mitigate perceived threats in a dataset. Avoiding combinations of temporal and spatial context significantly reduced concerns about the dataset. Likewise, the results suggest one should be extremely careful with revealing psychological states, as indicated by the high concern regarding stress. Abstractions also clearly play a role in defining the threats in the data. Timestamps generally raised concerns significantly when combined with other contexts and behaviors. Increasing the level of abstraction (e.g., releasing duration instead) decreased these concerns.

Ultimately, the choice of which behaviors and contexts to release, and how they should be abstracted, cannot be decided purely based on the threats created by those choices. Increasing abstraction may reduce the threats in the data, but it also reduces the utility of the data. For example, a scientist cannot study daily variations in stress if only the durations of stress events are revealed. Likewise, a caregiver cannot study a patient's gait if the patient's accelerometer data is abstracted into "moving" and "not moving" states. Clearly, manipulations of restrictions and abstractions need to be tailored for both the data contributor and consumer. Only by customizing privacy transformations can the privacy requirements of the data producer and the information quality requirements of the data consumer be met. This same observation inspired Iachello and Abowd's [14] complementary privacy framework, which aims to balance the utility of a UbiComp application with its burden on privacy. Personal sensing application developers can use our framework and study results within Iachello and Abowd's to evaluate the appropriateness and adequacy of various privacy transformations for the data contributor and consumer.

Threats from Revealing Psychological Context

The results of the study imply psychological context requires the most attention from the privacy and broader HCI community. Ratings indicated participants were more concerned about episodes of stress being revealed than any other behavior or context. The section on stress in the privacy questionnaire garnered more written comments than any other section, both pre- and post-review.

Psychological states like stress are different from behaviors and other contexts because they cannot be observed with the naked eye. Thus, psychological states are private by default, and remain private unless they are revealed. Personal sensing technologies that assess psychological states change this fundamental expectation. They enable mind-reading, a significant concern highlighted by participant comments.

However, such information can be useful, especially in the context of studying and treating psychological disorders (e.g., addiction and social anxiety). Methods to mitigate the harms associated with psychological context while still preserving their utility should be developed to address these concerns.

Limitations

A potential limitation of the study is that it confounds two variables that could affect concern level, 1) the personal nature of the data reviewed by Group S, and 2) increased awareness due to exposure to visual depictions of the data. Either variable alone or a mix of both could have increased concerns. A future study will address this, wherein Group NS will be shown visual depictions similar to those shown to Group S, except the depictions will not represent the participant's personal data. Assessing privacy concerns before and after exposure to the non-personal data will allow separating the effect of both variables.

CONCLUSIONS AND FUTURE WORK

Data collected by wearable sensors provide personal and societal utility, but also contain many unknown threats. Our study provides three key insights into the perceptions of threats from such datasets and how those threats can be mitigated. First, our results indicate people cannot understand the potential threats in the data unless they have a personal stake in it. Of the behaviors and contexts we examined, people were most concerned about revealing conversation, commuting, and inherently private psychological states (in this study, stress). Second, adding physical and temporal context increases concerns about the data, but those increases can be mitigated through restriction and abstraction. Third, people are willing to share such data - even with their identity - with us, other study participants, and other researchers. However, participants have significantly more concerns regarding sharing with the general public (e.g., over the web), especially when released with identity.

Given the concerns about psychological context, and our growing ability to capture psychological states, the community should examine disclosure of psychological context more closely. This paper did not assess participant concerns for combinations of psychological context with other behaviors, nor did it assess multiple abstractions of psychological context. Furthermore, it only assessed concerns for stress, which is not as specific as releasing specific emotions. In addition, the community could examine social context's effect on a dataset. Threats from social context are different than the others assessed here because they affect not only the user wearing the sensors, but also potentially any person interacting with the user.

Lastly, this study only examined privacy concerns from the perspective of data producers. The community should also examine how data consumers perceive privacy issues and what aspects of the data make it useful. Such a study would provide a better understanding of how to tradeoff behavior privacy and utility for physiological, psychological, and behavioral data collected by personal sensors.

ACKNOWLEDGEMENTS

We acknowledge the contributions of the following individuals. Anind Dey, Mustafa al'Absi, and Deepak Ganesan contributed to the study design, while Mary Read, Kelly Peck, Andrew Hoff, Ken Ward, and Satish Kedia helped conduct the study. Emre Ertin, Nathan Stohs, and Siddharth Shah developed the AutoSense sensor suite. Dan Siewiorek, Asim Smailagic, Patrick Blitz, Brian French, and Scott Fisk contributed to the study smartphone software. Context detection algorithms used in the visualization software were developed by Somnath Mitra (significant places from GPS data), Md. Mahbubur Rahman and Amin Ahsan Ali (speaking from respiration data), and Kurt Plarre (sensor detachments). This work was supported in part by NSF grants CNS-0910878, CNS-0910706 funded under the American Recovery and Reinvestment Act of 2009 (Public Law 111-5) and NIH Grant U01DA023812 from NIDA.

REFERENCES

1. AliveTec. Activity and Heart Monitor. http://www.alivetec.com/products.htm.
2. AutoSense. AutoSense: A Wireless Sensor System to Quantify Personal Exposures to Psychosocial Stress and Addictive Substances in Natural Environments. http://sites.google.com/site/autosenseproject.
3. M. Barbaro, T. Zeller, and S. Hansell. A Face is Exposed for AOL Searcher No. 4417749. *New York Times*, 2006.
4. L. Barkhuus and A. Dey. Location-Based Services for Mobile Telephony: a Study of Users' Privacy Concerns. In *Proc. Interact*, 2003.
5. A. Brush, J. Krumm, and J. Scott. Exploring end user preferences for location obfuscation, location-based services, and the value of location. In *ACM UbiComp*, pages 95–104, 2010.
6. S. Consolvo, J. Jung, B. Greenstein, P. Powledge, G. Maganis, and D. Avrahami. The Wi-Fi privacy

ticker: improving awareness & control of personal information exposure on Wi-Fi. In *ACM UbiComp*, pages 321–330, 2010.

7. S. Consolvo, D. McDonald, T. Toscos, M. Chen, J. Froehlich, B. Harrison, P. Klasnja, A. LaMarca, L. LeGrand, R. Libby, et al. Activity sensing in the wild: a field trial of ubifit garden. In *ACM SIGCHI*, 2008.
8. S. Consolvo, I. Smith, T. Matthews, A. LaMarca, J. Tabert, and P. Powledge. Location Disclosure to Social Relations: Why, When, & What People Want to Share. In *ACM SIGCHI*, 2005.
9. A. Dey and G. Abowd. Towards a Better Understanding of Context and Context-Awareness. In *ACM SIGCHI workshop*, 2000.
10. FieldStream. FieldStream: Network Data Services for Exposure Biology Studies in Natural Environments. http://www.fieldstream.org/.
11. R. Ganti, N. Pham, Y. Tsai, and T. Abdelzaher. PoolView: Stream Privacy for Grassroots Participatory Sensing. In *ACM SenSys*, 2008.
12. S. Guha, K. Plarre, D. Lissner, S. Mitra, B. Krishna, P. Dutta, and S. Kumar. AutoWitness: Locating and Tracking Stolen Property while Tolerating GPS and Radio Outages. In *ACM SenSys*, 2010.
13. S. Hansell. AOL Removes Search Data on Vast Group of Web Users. *New York Times*, 2006.
14. G. Iachello and G. Abowd. Privacy and proportionality: adapting legal evaluation techniques to inform design in ubiquitous computing. In *ACM SIGCHI*, pages 91–100, 2005.
15. G. Iachello, K. Truong, G. Abowd, G. Hayes, and M. Stevens. Prototyping and sampling experience to evaluate ubiquitous computing privacy in the real world. In *ACM SIGCHI*, pages 1009–1018, 2006.
16. W. Karim. Privacy Implications of Personal Locators: Why You Should Think Twice before Voluntarily Availing Yourself to GPS Monitoring, The. *Wash. UJL & Pol'y*, 14, 2004.
17. P. Klasnja, S. Consolvo, T. Choudhury, R. Beckwith, and J. Hightower. Exploring privacy concerns about personal sensing. *Pervasive Computing*, pages 176–183, 2009.
18. P. Klasnja, S. Consolvo, J. Jung, B. Greenstein, L. LeGrand, P. Powledge, and D. Wetherall. Ẅhen I am on Wi-Fi, I am fearless:p̈rivacy concerns & practices in everyday Wi-Fi use. In *ACM SIGCHI*, pages 1993–2002, 2009.
19. J. Krumm. Inference Attacks on Location Tracks. *Pervasive Computing*, 2007.
20. R. Lazarus. *Stress and emotion: A new synthesis*. Springer Publishing Company, 2006.
21. N. Li, T. Li, and S. Venkatasubramanian. t-Closeness: Privacy Beyond k-Anonymity and l-Diversity. In *IEEE ICDE*, 2007.
22. K. Lorincz, B. Chen, G. Challen, A. Chowdhury, S. Patel, P. Bonato, and M. Welsh. Mercury: A Wearable Sensor Network Platform for High-Fidelity Motion Analysis. In *ACM SenSys*, 2009.
23. A. Machanavajjhala, D. Kifer, J. Gehrke, and M. Venkitasubramaniam. l-diversity: Privacy beyond k-Anonymity. *ACM TKDD*, 2007.
24. C. Mancini, K. Thomas, Y. Rogers, B. Price, L. Jedrzejczyk, A. Bandara, A. Joinson, and B. Nuseibeh. From spaces to places: emerging contexts in mobile privacy. In *ACM UbiComp*, 2009.
25. D. McFarland. Respiratory Markers of Conversational Interaction. *Journal of Speech, Language, and Hearing Research*, 44(1), 2001.
26. M. Mun, S. Reddy, K. Shilton, N. Yau, J. Burke, D. Estrin, M. Hansen, E. Howard, R. West, and P. Boda. Peir, The Personal Environmental Impact Report, as a Platform for Participatory Sensing Systems Research. In *ACM MobiSys*, 2009.
27. A. Narayanan and V. Shmatikov. Robust De-Anonymization of Large Sparse Datasets. In *IEEE Symp. on Security and Privacy*, 2008.
28. A. Narayanan and V. Shmatikov. De-Anonymizing Social Networks. In *IEEE Symp. on Security and Privacy*, 2009.
29. S. Oliveira and O. Zaiane. Privacy Preserving Clustering by Data Transformation. *J. Information & Data Management*, 1(1), 2010.
30. L. Palen and P. Dourish. Unpacking Privacy for a Networked World. In *ACM SIGCHI*, 2003.
31. S. Patil and J. Lai. Who gets to know what when: configuring privacy permissions in an awareness application. In *ACM SIGCHI*, 2005.
32. L. Sweeney. Achieving k-anonymity Privacy Protection Using Generalization and Suppression. *International Journal of Uncertainty, Fuzziness and Knowledge-Based Systems*, 10(5), 2002.
33. E. Toch, J. Cranshaw, P. Drielsma, J. Tsai, P. Kelley, J. Springfield, L. Cranor, J. Hong, and N. Sadeh. Empirical Models of Privacy in Location Sharing. In *ACM UbiComp*, 2010.
34. E. Toch, N. Sadeh, and J. Hong. Generating default privacy policies for online social networks. In *ACM SIGCHI extended abstracts*, pages 4243–4248, 2010.
35. J. Tsai, P. Kelley, P. Drielsma, L. Cranor, J. Hong, and N. Sadeh. Who's viewed you?: the impact of feedback in a mobile location-sharing application. In *ACM SIGCHI*, 2009.
36. Zephyr Technology. BioHarness BT. http://www.zephyr-technology.com/bioharness-bt.html.

Interaction Design for Cancer Patients: Do We Need to Take Into Account the Effects of Illness and Medication?

Anita Das[1], Arild Faxvaag[1], Dag Svanæs[2]

[1]Department of Neuromedicine
Norwegian University of Science and Technology
7491 NTNU, Norway
{anita.das,arild.faxvaag}@ntnu.no

[2]Department of Computer and Information Science
Norwegian University of Science and Technology
7491 NTNU, Norway
dags@idi.ntnu.no

ABSTRACT
In this paper we explore how having cancer and receiving therapy influences upon patients' ability to use an online healthcare system. The motivation is that no empirically based design guidelines are available concerning this user group. Ignoring possible effects of illness and therapy can result in systems with poor usability and user acceptance. A case-control usability test with 14 cancer patients and 14 matched controls revealed that the cancer patients experienced significantly more difficulties compared with the healthy controls using a web-based online healthcare system. We conclude that designers of online healthcare systems need to take into consideration the unique challenges of being ill and/or using medication.

Author Keywords
User interfaces, Medical informatics, Usability, Cancer patients, patient-centred information systems.

ACM Classification Keywords
H5.m. Information interfaces and presentation (e.g., HCI): Miscellaneous.

General Terms
Design, Experimentation, Human Factors.

INTRODUCTION
A new breed of patient-centred information systems aims to help patients manage their health information and interact with providers. Such systems range from simple web sites with general medical information and systems that allow for communication with health providers, to full-fledged personal health records [6,10,11]. With all ICT systems it is important that the system in question has the necessary level of usability for all intended users. Currently, little empirical research is available to aid designers developing systems for patients.

In this study we have focused on one important patient group: cancer patients. Our motivation for studying this patient group originates in a usability study we did of a patient-centred information system. A number of usability issues were identified, and this helped the developers improve the usability of the next version of the system. Participants for the study were recruited from a primary care clinic, including some patients with cancer. We observed that the cancer patients experienced more problems than the others. This made us wonder whether this was a random observation, or if a controlled study would reveal statistically significant differences in performance. To our knowledge, there are no empirical studies on the effects of cancer on patients' ability to use ICT.

Eysenbach [4] has estimated that 2.3 million persons with cancer use the Internet worldwide. Furthermore he claims that 15% to 20% of all persons with cancer are indirect users, meaning that family members or companions use the Internet on their behalf. With time, indirect users often become direct users.

There are a number of reasons to suspect that having cancer will have a negative effect on the performance with ICT systems, and consequently require systems with a higher level of usability. Patients with advancing cancer frequently develop physical and cognitive impairments. This might be due to awareness of having cancer, symptoms and problems invoked by the disease, medications and actions taken against the disease or to alleviate complaints [1,7]. Cancer patients frequently experience pain, nausea, fatigue, depression and anxiety; factors that all are associated with cognitive disrupts. Cognitive disrupts among cancer patients are particularly found concerning mood disturbances and in the areas of memory, concentration and psychomotor skills [1,7,12,13]. Opioids, a class of strong analgesic drugs, are commonly used for pain management in cancer, and are related to reduced cognitive functioning and drowsiness [3].

Having an illness that temporarily or permanently lowers ones ability to use a certain technology is a disability. Research on universal access has so far focused mainly on accommodating major capability losses, dominated by research on visual impairments and physical disabilities [9].

No focus has been on the impact disease and illness has on patients' abilities to utilize ICT systems.

One important first step towards building a body of knowledge in this area is to establish if there are significant differences in task performance between particular patient groups and average computer users. The purpose of this study has been to investigate the adverse impact of having cancer and being under treatment on computer task performance. The hypothesis was that the group of cancer patients would have significantly more difficulties using a web-based healthcare system compared to a control group of healthy individuals.

METHODS

The study was set up as an observational case-control study with an experiment where cancer patients and healthy controls were observed while they conducted tasks by using a web-based healthcare system. Interviews and questionnaires were used to collect additional information.

Participants

Participants were required to be above 18 yrs. of age, have a mobile phone and be able to read SMS (Short Message Service) text messages. The cancer patients were required to be under treatment for their cancer disease. The study was approved by the National Committee for Research Ethics in Central Norway, and all participants provided a written informed consent. Participants received no compensation for their participation.

The cancer patients were recruited from the cancer outpatients' department at St.Olavs Hospital in Trondheim, Norway. 47 patients with cancer were asked to participate in the study, of these, 14 showed up and completed the study. The control group was recruited to match the cancer patients regarding age, gender, computer literacy and education level.

Setting

The study took place in a usability laboratory equipped with two pan-tilt cameras fixed to the ceiling, which recorded the participants during the experiment. Sound and user verbalization was recorded through wireless microphones.

The online healthcare system

During the experiments we used an Internet-based communication system that is developed for the primary healthcare in Norway (Figure 1). It allows patients to schedule appointments, request prescription renewals and obtain non-urgent online consultation with their physician.

Some of the services, such as booking appointments and renewing prescriptions, are available without being registered as user of the system. However, to get access to all the services available, the patient has to log on to the system with a user ID and password.

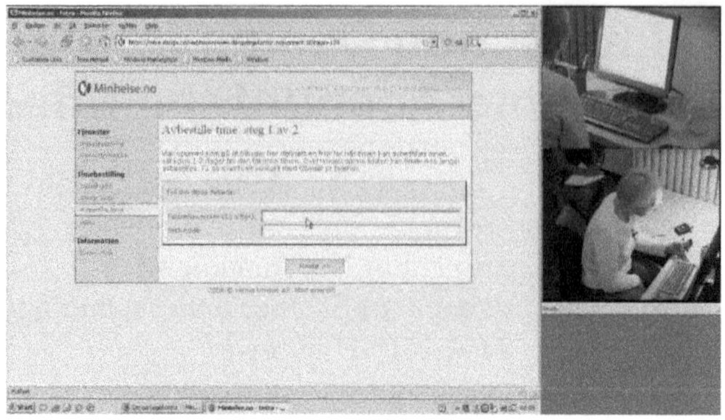

Figure 1. The system in use during a usability test.

For security reasons, required by law in Norway, login has to be confirmed by entering an automatically generated Personal Identification Number (PIN) that is sent to the patient's mobile phone (Figure 2).

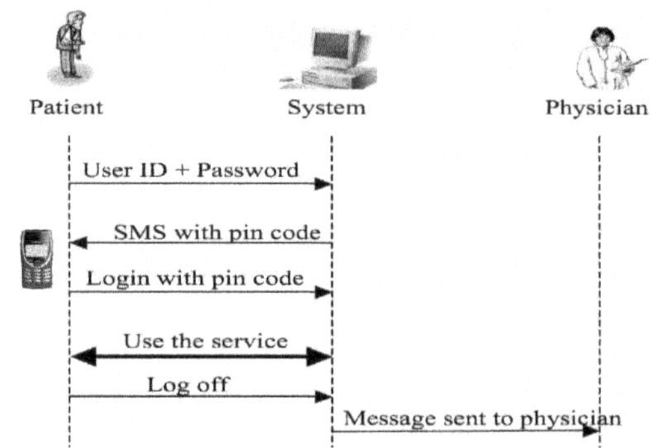

Figure 2. Double secure login with mobile phone.

Procedure

Subjects were tested individually under controlled settings, and each session followed the same procedure. The sessions lasted between 45 and 90 minutes.

To collect basic user demographic information, we used a questionnaire developed for this study. We used the Quality of Life Questionnaire (QLQ-C30) of the European Organization for Research and treatment of Cancer (EORTC), a 30-item version questionnaire, traditionally used in clinical trials, to assess multiple dimensions of the quality of life construct. The questionnaire comprised of five multi- item functional scales (physical, role, cognitive, emotional, social), three symptom scales (fatigue, pain, nausea and vomiting), six single items that assess both symptoms and economic consequences of the disease, and two rating scales of global health and quality of life [5].

The participants were registered as users of the system prior to the session. They were given an ID and password, and were further informed that they would receive PIN's on their mobile phone during the session. Participants were given the same tasks and had no time restrictions. The usability testing involved that the participants conducted tasks while they used the online healthcare system through a stationary computer. They got a written assignment that was read out loud by the facilitator. The usability test consisted of five subtasks under the pretext of patient-physician online communication, and involved: 1) accessing the Internet, 2) booking an appointment with a physician, 3) cancelling the appointment, 4) sending a message to a physician through the system 5) receiving a message in the system, which was sent by the physician.

After the usability testing, the participants completed a questionnaire, the System Usability Scale (SUS), a 10 item scale giving global view of subjective assessments of usability [2], and there was conducted a semi- structured interview to elucidate the participants' opinions and experiences with using the system.

Video analysis

The whole session was captured on video and analyzed. The purpose of the video analysis was to evaluate the users' ability to use an online healthcare system. We formed the measures based on the definition of usability in ISO 9241-11: *"extent to which a product can be used by specified users to achieve specified goals with effectiveness, efficiency and satisfaction in a specified context of use"* [8]. The usability test was consequently analyzed by measuring effectiveness (task completion), efficiency (time to complete the task) and user satisfaction (satisfaction with using the system).

RESULTS

Study population

14 patients with cancer and 14 healthy controls participated in the study. There were 6 male and 8 female in each group.

Several cancer types were represented: Breast cancer (n=6), prostate cancer (n=2), gastrointestinal cancer (n=4), pancreas cancer (n=1) and lymphoma (n=1). Among the cancer patients, 79% underwent chemotherapy, 14% received radiotherapy, and 7% was getting palliative treatment. 50% had metastasis to the liver, skeleton or abdominal cavity. Analysis of the participants' functional capacities showed that the cancer patients were in poorer health compared to the controls.

The two groups were examined on equivalence concerning demographics and prior technology use. The raw data was analyzed using the t-test for independent samples. The groups had similar demographic characteristics, and comparable technology experience, with no statistically significant differences ($P>0.05$). However, bivariate correlation tests revealed a significant correlation between prior Internet experience and the users' outcomes of the usability test. This independent factor was considered a covariate in the statistical analysis of covariance (ANCOVA). The level of significance was set at $P < 0.05$.

The Usability Test

Effectiveness was measured by task completion, involving how many participants in each group who completely and correctly completed the entire task (all five subtasks). The subtasks required that all previous subtasks were completed. In cases where participants were not able to complete a subtask by themselves, we consequently provided necessary assistance so that all participants could be tested on all subtasks.

As shown in Table 1, the cancer patients experienced more difficulties compared to the healthy controls for the entire task and for all its five subtasks. A one-way analysis of covariance (ANCOVA) on task completion, with having cancer as the independent variable (between-subject two-level factor) and "Internet experience" as covariate, showed a statistically significant effect ($P<0.05$) for the entire task: $F(1,25) = 4.24$, $p=0.05$. A similar ANCOVA analysis for each of the five subtasks showed that only subtask 4 had a statistically significant difference: $F(1,25)=6.77$, $p=0.02$.

	Cancer (n=14)		Controls (n=14)	
	N	%	N	%
Subtask 1	11	78,6	14	100
Subtask 2	11	78,6	13	92,9
Subtask 3	8	57,1	12	85,7
Subtask 4	5	35,7	12	85,7 *
Subtask 5	12	85,7	14	100
Entire task	4	28,6	10	71,4 *

*P < 0.05

Table 1. Effectiveness (completion rate).

Efficiency was measured by time-on-task for each subtask. If the user failed a subtask, the time until s/he gave up and was given assistance was measured for this subtask. Task time for the entire task was measured as the sum of time-on-task for all five subtasks. Table 2 shows the mean task time and SD for all five subtasks and the entire task.

	Cancer (n=14)		Controls (n=14)	
	Mean	SD	Mean	SD
Subtask 1	1:06	0:52	1:07	0:52
Subtask 2	6:03	3:32	4:51	1:37
Subtask 3	3:53	2:46	3:25	2:41
Subtask 4	9:08	6:23	9:43	3:31
Subtask 5	2:59	1:43	3:18	1:39
Entire task	23:11	8:28	22:25	6:05

Table 2. Task time (in minutes) for subtasks and entire task.

The mean task time for the entire task differed between the two groups. However, an ANCOVA analysis with "Internet experience" as covariate showed no statistically significant differences for the entire task: $F(1,25)=0.50$, $p=0.49$. A similar ANCOVA analysis for each subtask showed no statistically significant difference for any of the subtasks ($P<0.05$). Many of the cancer patients gave up on subtasks quite early, while many in the control group succeeded after much trial and error. This observation makes us believe that time-on-task is not a good measure of usability for this test.

Subjective satisfaction was measured by using the SUS-scale. The two groups had different mean scores, revealing that the cancer patients (mean score:68.21. SD:16.03) had a lower mean satisfaction score than the controls (mean score: 74.82. SD:14.29). An ANCOVA analysis with "Internet experience" as covariate showed no significant differences between the groups: $F(1,25)=0.53$, $p=0.47$. Nonetheless, in the interview that followed, several cancer patients expressed that they would like to have an online system for communication with their physician, and told they were motivated to use the system despite low usability. We have reason to believe that the cancer patients´ positive attitude towards the service as such had a positive effect on their overall SUS score, thus making SUS a less accurate measure of their assessment of its usability.

Poorer health makes it difficult to use the system

Bivariate correlation tests revealed significant correlations between the completion rate and selected variables from the EORTC QLQ-C30: the function scores of cognition (correlation: -0.513, $p<0.01$), fatigue (correlation: -0.386, $p<0.05$), nausea (correlation: -0.379, $p<0.05$), role (reduced ability to do activities and hobbies) (correlation: -0.374, $p< 0.05$), and the use of analgesics (correlation: -0.408, $p< 0.05$). Higher score (poorer physical health), or the use of analgesics was associated with lower completion rate and reduced ability to complete the task.

DISCUSSION

For this study we consider effectiveness to be the most important of the three ISO measures. Although our sample size was small, we believe our results justify that the user interface and functionality of patient-centred systems should be tested with patients who experience a significant burden of disease and that might use medication. A consequence of our findings is that patient-centred systems that are designed with the average Internet user in mind run the risk of excluding a large part of their intended users. The study was not designed to provide specific design guidelines, but the strong correlations between task completion and the factors cognition, fatigue and nausea give us reason to believe that simplicity is key in designing for this user group

CONCLUSION

Through this study we have found that cancer patients experience significantly more difficulties when using an online healthcare system compared to healthy controls. The patients with cancer, a group in high demand of healthcare services, were motivated to use the online system, but often failed to accomplish the tasks and required more assistance. Experiencing symptoms associated with their disease, being impaired, or using analgesic drugs were associated with significantly lower completion rate. The results indicate that when evaluating and designing online healthcare systems it is important to take into consideration the unique challenges of being ill and/or using medication.

ACKNOWLEDGEMENTS

We thank the participants for taking time to participate in the study. Also thank to Terje Røsand for technical assistance in the usability laboratory.

REFERENCES

1. Ahles TA, Saykin AJ, Furstenberg CT, et al. Neuropsychologic Impact of Standard-Dose Systemic Chemotherapy in Long-Term Survivors of Breast Cancer and Lymphoma. J Clin Oncol. 2002 January 15, 2002;20(2):485-93.
2. Brooke J. SUS- A 'quick and dirty' usability scale. In: P. W. Jordan BT, B. A. Weerdmeester & A. L. McClelland, editor. Usability evaluation in Industry. London: Taylor and Francis; 1996.
3. Cherny N, Ripamonti C, Pereira J, et al. Strategies to Manage the Adverse Effects of Oral Morphine: An Evidence-Based Report. J Clin Oncol. 2001 May 1, 2001;19(9):2542-54.
4. Eysenbach G. The Impact of the Internet on Cancer Outcomes. CA: A Cancer Journal for Clinicians. 2003;53(6):356-71.
5. Fayers P AN, Bjordal K, Groenvold M, Curran D, Bottomley A. EORTC QLQ- C30 Scoring Manual. Brussels 2001.
6. Google Health. http://www.google.com/Top/Health/. Retrieved September 1, 2010.
7. Harman K, Ruyak, Peggy. Working Through the Pain: A Controlled Study of the Impact of Persistent Pain on Performing a Computer Task. . Clinical Journal of Pain. 2005;21(3):216- 22.
8. ISO 9241-11:1998. Ergonomic Requirements for Office Work with Visual Display Terminals (VDTs)-Part 11; 1998.
9. Keates S. Pragmatic Research issues confronting HCI practitioners when designing for universal access. Journal of Universal Access in the Information Society. 2006;5(3):269-78.
10. Microsoft HealthVault. http://www.healthvault.com/. Retrieved September 1, 2010.
11. Simons WW MK, Kohane IS. The PING personally controlled electronic medical record system: technical architecture. Journal of the American Medical Informatics Association: JAMIA. 2005;12(1):47-54.
12. Stone PR, M. A'Hern, R. Hardy, J. 1. A study to investigate the prevalence, severity and correlates of fatigue among patients with cancer in comparison with a control group of volunteers without cancer. Annals of Oncology. 2000;11(5):561-7.
13. Valentine AD, Meyers, C. A. Cognitive and mood disturbance as causes and symptoms of fatigue in cancer patients. Cancer. 2001;92(S 6):1694- 8.

Simulating the Feel of Brain-Computer Interfaces for Design, Development and Social Interaction

Melissa Quek,[1] Daniel Boland,[1] John Williamson,[1] Roderick Murray-Smith,[1] Michele Tavella,[2] Serafeim Perdikis,[2] Martijn Schreuder,[3] Michael Tangermann[3]

[1]School of Computing Science
University of Glasgow
Glasgow, Scotland
{melissa, jhw, rod}@dcs.gla.ac.uk
email@dannyboland.com

[2]School of Engineering
École Polytechnique Fédérale de Lausanne
Lausanne, Switzerland
{michele.tavella, serafeim.perdikis}@epfl.ch

[3]Machine Learning Laboratory
Berlin Institute of Technology
Berlin, Germany
{schreuder, michael.tangermann}@tu-berlin.de

ABSTRACT

We describe an approach to improving the design and development of Brain-Computer Interface (BCI) applications by simulating the error-prone characteristics and subjective feel of electroencephalogram (EEG), motor-imagery based BCIs. BCIs have the potential to enhance the quality of life of people who are severely disabled, but it is often time-consuming to test and develop the systems. Simulation of BCI characteristics allows developers to rapidly test design options, and gain both subjective and quantitative insight into expected behaviour without using an EEG cap. A further motivation for the use of simulation is that 'impairing' a person without motor disabilities in a game with a disabled BCI user can create a level playing field and help carers empathise with BCI users. We demonstrate a use of the simulator in controlling a game of Brain Pong.

Author Keywords

BCI, HCI, simulation, usability, social interaction, disability, motor imagery, SMR

ACM Classification Keywords

H.5.2 Information Interfaces and Presentation: Miscellaneous

General Terms

Design, Performance, Human Factors

INTRODUCTION

A Brain-Computer Interface (BCI) is a system that harnesses a person's brain activity to interact with a computer or other electronic device. For people who are severely paralyzed, a BCI might provide the only means of communication; more commonly it potentially serves as an additional channel of input for those with a very limited control of movement.

A problem with testing and debugging BCI applications is that it can take a long time – up to an hour – to set up and calibrate a BCI. The input is also slow compared to most other methods and thus time consuming to run user trials: the highest performance reported for motor-imagery BCI so far is 40 bits/min [5], while a fast speller yields 7 chars/minute [12]. This note describes how modelling the classifier output of a motor-imagery BCI can be used to simulate interaction characteristics such as error rate, delay and noise. We aim to use the simulator to speed up and improve the development process, to enhance social interaction and to aid understanding of the constraints and skill involved in using a BCI.

BACKGROUND AND MOTIVATION

The electroencephalogram (EEG) is a technique used to measure electrical brain activity arising from a large number of neurons near the surface of the brain. It has been used for brain-computer communication in recent years [10]. Typically, a set of electrodes is gelled to the scalp with the help of a positioning cap. Certain *mental states* that a BCI user produces at will are recognized through machine learning techniques and mapped to interface controls. For example, a person might continuously do complex sums in one's head (the mental state) in order to move a ball to the left of the screen (the control). The current simulator is modelled on BCIs driven by *motor-imagery*, which refers to the imagining of moving a body part [10]. The feet and hands are the most commonly used body parts in current BCI literature.

Characteristics of a motor-imagery based BCI. A typical BCI system goes through the general process shown in Figure 1. The user intends an action (step 1), for example, to select left. 'Brainwave modulation' (step 2) refers to an attempt to produce a mental state that can be detected by the classifier. The raw EEG signals are recorded (step 3), features of the signals are selected (step 4) and subsequently *classified* (separated), into two or more mental states, or *classes* (step 5). Two classes are most commonly used allowing for binary input, although multi-class BCIs have also been demonstrated [5]. The noisy output of the classifier is usually integrated (smoothed), to lessen errors (step 6). Finally, the application presents the system's belief about the user's intention (step 7).

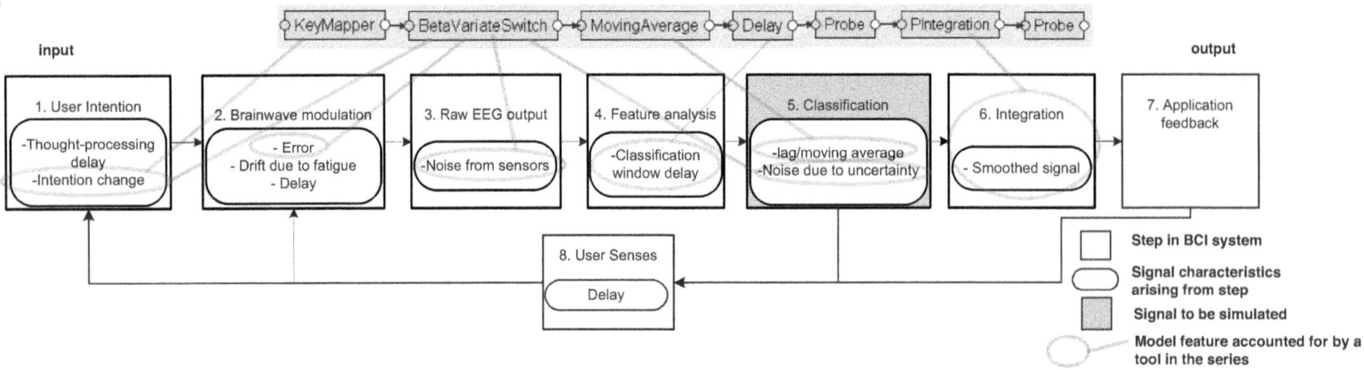

Figure 1. Top series (shaded background): Screen shot of part of the GUI used to create a simulator model, showing the tools used in the current model. Bottom: Stages in a BCI control loop giving rise to low-level characteristics of the BCI, some of which are modelled in the current simulator.

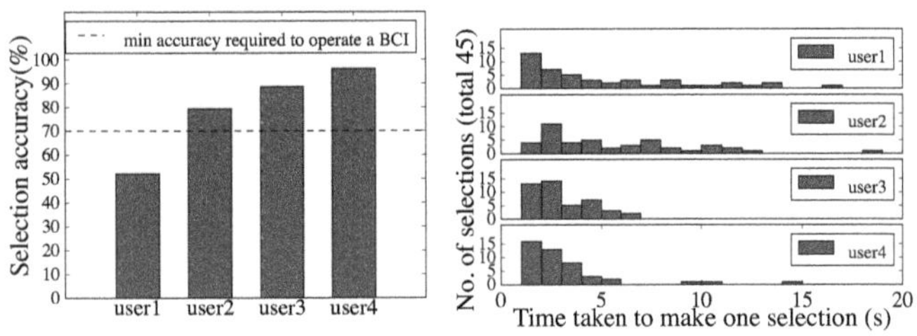

Figure 2. Individual differences in BCI control. Left: Bar chart of selection accuracy for 4 users (num correct trials ÷ total trials). Right: Histogram showing distribution of times taken to make a single selection (i.e. move the cursor to the left or right) for the same 4 users.

Individual differences in motor-imagery based BCI control are pronounced, with an estimated 15–30% of subjects being unable to operate such a BCI [4]. Figure 2 shows two control characteristics from the calibration data used in our current model, giving some examples of the error rate and variability in selection time. The minimum accuracy required for being able to communicate using a BCI is generally taken to be 70% [10]. False positives, where the system makes a selection despite the user not wishing to select anything, are a problem for current development of BCI applications because of the 'continuous' production of the brain signal. There is a delay between a user 'switching' mental states and its effect being displayed on the screen, and users also differ in their ability to sustain a mental state (continue imagining the movement) such that it can be accurately classified.

Simulation for design and understanding impairment. Designing for disabled people can be difficult for those who do not have the same disabilities. Simulation can help designers to understand what a particular impairment feels like in order to provide solutions to problems. For example, the Third Age Suit [6] is a wearable outfit which simulates the restricted movement experienced by the elderly for the purpose of design. In the context of BCI, low-level simulation can potentially enable people to experience the frustration of using a BCI without needing to wear an EEG cap. On the other hand, learning to achieve control of a BCI can be fun and challenging, so in the same way that flight simulators are entertaining for people who might never become a pilot, understanding the skill required to control a BCI through using a simulator could bring respect for a trained BCI user.

Simulation to predict usability. Simulation is useful for improving user interfaces for Assistive Technologies (ATs) because of the large variability in the population of users. Simulators incorporating perceptual, cognitive and motor models to predict usability of interfaces have been developed (e.g. [3]), while simulating motor disability by introducing delays into keyboard input produced useful guidelines in a word selection experiment [7]. However, the BCI characteristics mentioned previously require different models than those for input devices that are commonly investigated. The few simulation and modelling efforts in BCI focus on the number of decisions to make in order to reach a target (e.g. [2]), however in BCI this may not necessarily correspond to the time taken to make them. In addition, this method does not allow analysis of interfaces based on continuous interfaces, such as hex-o-spell [12]. Low-level characteristics of BCI can be simulated to explore these at a lower cost.

Simulation for testing and evaluting interfaces. Conducting user trials with BCI is expensive: it can be difficult to find people who have been sufficiently trained for testing the interfaces effectively, and it is undesirable to allow disabled people to sit for long periods of time with an EEG cap on, which can become uncomfortable. Since a BCI may be much slower and more error-prone than people with disabilities may be used to, it is important to obtain feedback about applications using BCI input. By using a simulator, user evaluation and testing can take place early on in the development cycle, affording BCI design the rapid prototyping methods that are taken for granted in mainstream HCI.

Simulation to support social interaction. Through interviews and focus groups carried out within the TOBI Project[1], disabled people have indicated a significant interest in interacting more with other people through playing games. One way of achieving this might be to 'impair' the non-disabled player in order to establish a level playing field. For example, the keyboard or mouse input could be modified to emulate the BCI user's input, with similar error rate and timing. In addition to making the games fairer for both parties, this could help the non-disabled player to empathize with the disabled player.

[1] http://tobi-project.org

SIMULATOR MODEL AND ARCHITECTURE

The current simulator was developed using data and information from BCI researchers at École Polytechnique Fédérale de Lausanne (EPFL) [8]. Data from 5 users was taken from the usual procedure used to train a user, which is briefly described as follows. A user is asked to imagine moving a limb (e.g. their right hand), in order to move a screen 'cursor' to the right, and to imagine moving another limb to move it to the left. At a rate of 16Hz, EEG features are computed and classified into the left or right classes. The output of probabilities at each time step indicate the system's belief that the person is imagining movement of the body part(s) assigned to these classes (~1=right, ~0=left). This noisy signal is integrated to give a smoother signal. The horizontal position of the cursor correlates with the value of the integrated classifier: when this reaches a user-dependent threshold, the bar reaches the corresponding side and a selection is made. This last integrated value is the output of the simulator since our aim is to simulate the subjective feel of the interaction.

We developed a simulation toolkit in Python where signal generation or modulation blocks, or *tools*, are linked together in a series. Tools can be replaced, added or removed easily. This is useful for improving the model as well as to simulate different BCI systems that use different techniques. Each modulation tool receives a signal from the preceding tool, modifies it and passes it along to the next tool in the series. The value of a signal at a particular point in the sequence can be captured using the *Probe* tool. The output of real BCIs is replaced seamlessly by sending these discrete values over the network to the application, using the same protocols as the real BCI. A GUI was developed in order to easily change the tools used in a model, their parameters and order in the series. We now describe in more detail how the tools work and relate to the current model, following the tool series in Figure 1 (top) from left to right.

The *KeyMapper* tool assigns a keyboard key to a particular state, for example the left arrow key to the 'left' state. To change the properties of the signal, the parameters for other tools in the model are updated when the state of the system changes. The *BetaVariateSwitch* tool is the core tool in the current simulator model which generates both the signal and noise in this system. Histograms of the classifier values indicate that at a given time step, the classifier believes that the features belong more strongly to one class or the other (i.e. the output of the classifier ranges from 0 to 1, and is biased towards either 0 or 1). Samples are drawn from a Beta distribution whose probability density function is given by

$$f(x;\alpha,\beta) = \frac{1}{\mathrm{B}(\alpha,\beta)}\, x^{\alpha-1}(1-x)^{\beta-1}[1]$$

Essentially, the drawn sample can be biased more or less strongly towards 0 or 1, e.g. for low α (< 1.0) and high β (> 1.0), most of the values drawn will be closer to 0 than 1, and vice versa. To obtain a noisy signal, we switch between two sets of opposing α and β values. A Markov chain is employed to influence the probability of and time taken for the integrated signal to reach the desired class threshold. The probability of switching from one set of values to another depends on the current set (Figure 3); adjusting these 6 parameters enables simulation of a wide range of performance.

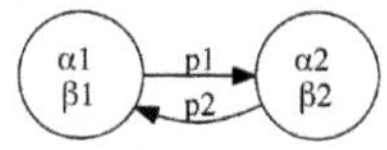

Figure 3. Finite state machine showing the Markov chain used in the *BetaVariateSwitch* tool: the probability of switching from one set of α, β parameters to another is dependent on the set currently employed.

Next, the *MovingAverage* tool implements an nth order moving average which arises from the feature extraction stage. The *Delay* tool accounts for the time delay due to the feature extraction and classification process. This was estimated to be 0.5s, as the output at each time step takes into account the last 1s of data; it seems reasonable that a change in state would be seen from around half this time. A Gamma distribution was used to model the delay that occurs when switching from one mental state to another, as a large variance was expected. The initial parameters were chosen by a reasonable estimation and optimized automatically. Finally, the *PIntegration* tool integrates the classifier output that has been generated. This is a direct implementation of the integration method used at EPFL [9].

Keyboard input was used rather than mouse as it is more appropriate to generate the classifier output signal based on discrete input to represent the switching between mental states, rather than a continuous input. In this first approximation, some BCI characteristics not accounted for are the ability to hold a mental state once the threshold is reached, the closed-loop interaction between the subject's thoughts and the influence of feedback, and the longer term deterioration in performance that occurs due to fatigue or stress [4]. However, the flexibility of the simulator allows additional tools to be added as the model is improved.

Optimization of parameters. The parameters of the model are optimized for the subjective feel of the BCI. Based on the assumption that the 2nd derivative of the signal (i.e. acceleration of the cursor) corresponds closely to subjective feel of movement, we measure the difference between the histograms of the 2nd derivatives of the time series for real and simulated data. This is added to the difference in selection accuracy, $x^{difference}$, where x is determined by trial and error. The result is used as a cost function to be minimized using Powell's method. The time series in Figure 4 shows that the integrated classifier output generated for one user using this method subjectively matches the real data; com-

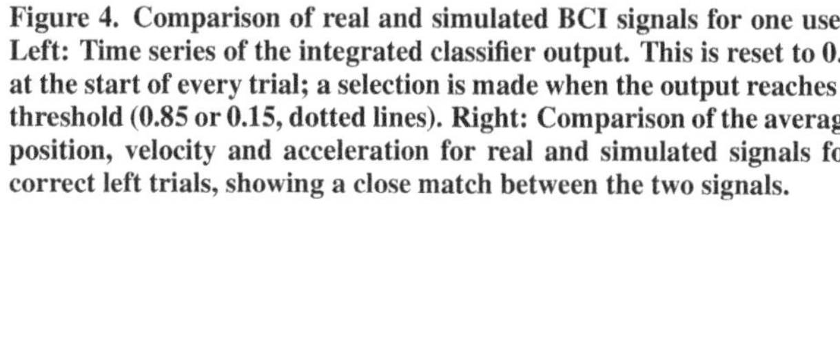

Figure 4. Comparison of real and simulated BCI signals for one user. Left: Time series of the integrated classifier output. This is reset to 0.5 at the start of every trial; a selection is made when the output reaches a threshold (0.85 or 0.15, dotted lines). Right: Comparison of the average position, velocity and acceleration for real and simulated signals for correct left trials, showing a close match between the two signals.

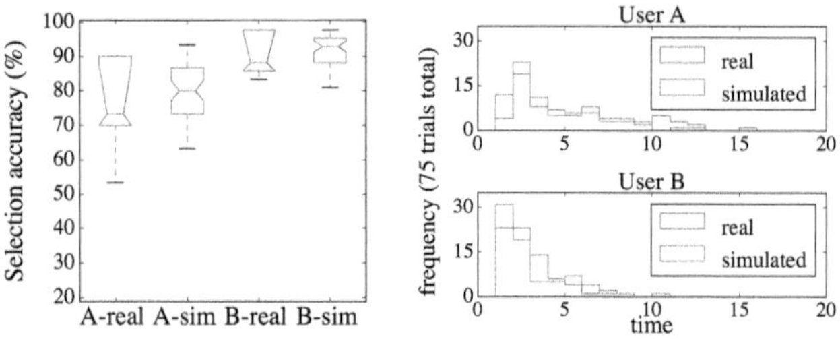

Figure 5. Selection accuracy (left) and histograms of time to make a selection (right) for real and simulated trials for 2 users A and B, indicating a reasonable approximation of the distributions for both users.

parison of the histograms of the 1st and 2nd derivatives verifies this. Figure 5 also shows that the selected parameters allow a match of the selection accuracy and time distributions, justifying the model and our implementation choices.

EXAMPLE APPLICATION

Although many BCI applications currently employ discrete selection as input, modelling the continuous control of a BCI is important as novel interaction techniques might improve performance. For example, the fastest motor-imagery BCI speller to date, hex-o-spell, uses the time taken to switch between mental states [12]. We used a version of the simulator adapted for a BCI research group at the Berlin Institute of Technology as input to *Brain Pong*, a BCI version of the classic game *Pong*. This directly replaced the BCI input expected by the application to control a paddle (Figure 6). The game used the Pythonic Feedback Framework [11], a BCI application platform used by several BCI labs. Expert BCI users asserted that the behaviour and subjective feel (i.e. delay, noise and error) of controlling the paddle seemed sufficiently similar to that when using a real BCI to be used for design purposes. This preliminary finding provides a credible basis for carrying out a more rigorous validation. Using a simulator adapted to match BCI characteristics in real time, a non-disabled person could play games either face-to-face or over the Internet with a BCI user, which could help to provide fairer competition.

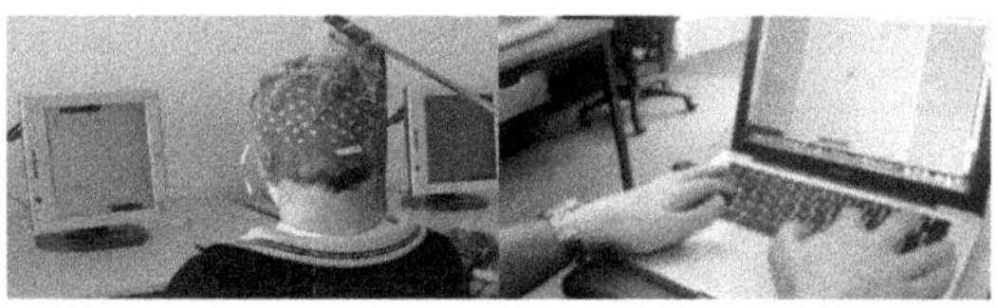

Figure 6. Left: Brain Pong with a real BCI. Right: Brain Pong with keyboard input modified by the simulator.

CONCLUSIONS

We have built a simulator that models the essential characteristics of motor-imagery based BCIs that are relevant to the design and development of BCI applications. As far as we know, this is the first attempt to model the low-level characteristics of a BCI for interface design purposes. Performance models for mouse, keyboard and single switches are mostly used to automatically evaluate interfaces (e.g. [3]), while usability studies which employ real time simulators to gain information about task performance also focus on standard inputs [7], and thus far do not appear to match the subjective feel of the input with accurate performance characteristics. Objective and subjective evaluation of the output of our simulator provide a basis for using it to predict usability of interfaces both offline through simulation and online with user studies. Simulation can allow interaction designers to explore BCI characteristics with little effort, and afford end user engagement on issues that arise from the input constraints. We also proposed that the simulator be used to create a more level playing field between disabled and non-disabled people, and validated the feasibility of this with the simulator-controlled game of Brain Pong.

ACKNOWLEDGEMENTS

Andrew Ramsay for the initial GUI. This work is supported by the European ICT Programme Project FP7-224631 and the PASCAL2 EC Network of Excellence. This paper only reflects the authors' views and funding agencies are not liable for any use that may be made of the information contained herein.

REFERENCES

1. J. Banks, B. Nelson, and D. Nicol. *Discrete-event system simulation*. Prentice Hall, 2009.
2. M. Bensch, A. Karim, J. Mellinger, T. Hinterberger, M. Tangermann, M. Bogdan, W. Rosenstiel, and N. Birbaumer. Nessi: an EEG-controlled web browser for severely paralyzed patients. *Comp. Intelligence and Neurosci.*, 2007:71863, 2007.
3. P. Biswas and P. Robinson. Automatic evaluation of assistive interfaces. In *Proc. 13th Int. Conf. on Intelligent User Interfaces*, pages 247–256. ACM, 2008.
4. B. Blankertz, C. Sannelli, S. Halder, E. Hammer, A. Kübler, K. Müller, G. Curio, and T. Dickhaus. Neurophysiological predictor of SMR-based BCI performance. *NeuroImage*, 51(4):1303–1309, 2010.
5. G. Dornhege. *Increasing information transfer rates for brain-computer interfacing*. PhD thesis, University of Potsdam, Potsdam, 2006.
6. D. Hitchcock, S. Lockyer, S. Cook, and C. Quigley. Third age usability and safety–an ergonomics contribution to design. *Int. J. Hum.-Comput. Stud.*, 55(4):635–643, 2001.
7. J. Mankoff, H. Fait, and R. Juang. Evaluating accessibility by simulating the experiences of users with vision or motor impairments. *IBM Syst. J.*, 44(3):505–517, 2010.
8. J. Millán, F. Renkens, J. Mouriño, and W. Gerstner. Brain-actuated interaction. *Artificial Intelligence*, 159(1-2):241–259, 2004.
9. S. Perdikis, H. Bayati, R. Leeb, and J. Millán. Evidence accumulation in asynchronous BCI. *Proc. TOBI workshop*, 2010 (to appear).
10. G. Pfurtscheller, C. Neuper, and N. Birbaumer. Human brain-computer interface. *Motor cortex in voluntary movements*, pages 367–401, 2005.
11. B. Venthur, S. Scholler, J. Williamson, S. Dähne, M. Treder, M. Kramarek, K. Mäller, and B. Blankertz. Pyff–A Pythonic Framework for Feedback Applications and Stimulus Presentation in Neuroscience. *Front. Neurosci.*, 4(179), 2010.
12. J. Williamson, R. Murray-Smith, B. Blankertz, M. Krauledat, and K. Müller. Designing for uncertain, asymmetric control: Interaction design for brain-computer interfaces. *Int. J. Hum.-Comput. Stud.*, 67(10):827–841, 2009.

Characterizing Patient-Friendly "Micro-Explanations" of Medical Events

Lauren Wilcox[1,2], Dan Morris[1], Desney Tan[1], Justin Gatewood[3], Eric Horvitz[1]

[1]Microsoft Research
{dan,desney,horvitz}
@microsoft.com

[2]Dept of Computer Science
Columbia University
wilcox@cs.columbia.edu

[3]MedStar Institute for Innovation
justin.s.gatewood@medstar.net

ABSTRACT
Patients' basic understanding of clinical events has been shown to dramatically improve patient care. We propose that the automatic generation of very short *micro-explanations*, suitable for real-time delivery in clinical settings, can transform patient care by giving patients greater awareness of key events in their electronic medical record. We present results of a survey study indicating that it may be possible to automatically generate such explanations by extracting individual sentences from consumer-facing Web pages. We further inform future work by characterizing physician and non-physician responses to a variety of Web-extracted explanations of medical lab tests.

Author Keywords
Electronic Medical Records, Personal Health Records

ACM Classification Keywords
J.3 [Computer Applications] Life Sciences – Health.

General Terms
Human Factors

INTRODUCTION
Active involvement by patients in their own care has been shown to increase patient satisfaction, which in turn results in greater compliance, reduced stress and complications, and several additional benefits to quality of care [7].

Patient involvement depends on patients being well-informed about their care. Fortunately, today's patients have several information sources at their disposal. For example, physicians routinely explain symptoms, diagnoses, conditions, and treatments to patients verbally. Unfortunately, such in-person explanations are not available to meet all patient information needs, nor are they as readily accessible as other materials. Educational materials about tests, procedures, and medications can provide useful information for patients. However, such materials can be overwhelming amidst the distress common in hospital environments. Furthermore, a great deal of medical information is inaccessible to those lacking health literacy; information packets are rarely tailored to a specific patient, and traditional delivery media such as paper make dynamic delivery difficult [3].

Online health resources (e.g. webmd.com) provide comprehensible, patient-friendly health literature, but target patients who are cognitively and logistically able to formulate a search query, then comprehend detailed results. Results typically contain much more information than is necessary to provide basic understanding, and often include facts that are irrelevant or even needlessly worrying to a specific patient. Consequently, much online content is often ill-suited for delivering information in the small chunks demanded by patients who are in a cognitive state to receive only limited information or who are using space-constrained media such as in-room displays and mobile devices.

In addition to online information sources, the increasing availability of electronic medical records (EMRs) promises to provide patients with unprecedented levels of access to *their own* medical data. Despite this availability, patients often remain uninformed about the tests and procedures conducted during clinical visits, leaving them ill-equipped to participate in medical decisions. This discrepancy is largely a consequence of the structure and terminology used in EMRs, which are designed for clinicians and administrators, rather than for patients.

We therefore propose that leveraging multiple information sources – specifically existing online health resources *and* the EMR – can provide concise, patient-friendly, and personalized explanations of medical events. Such medical *micro-explanations* would be suitable for real-time presentation to patients on mobile devices or in-room displays, or for offline presentation through a personal health record.

Fully-automatic generation of explanations remains technically difficult. However, we hypothesize that current consumer-facing Web resources, although not designed for this purpose, contain sentences that are suitable for presentation as standalone explanations. Furthermore, situation-specific extraction of appropriate sentences from these resources, based on information already available in the EMR, can circumvent the need to create explanations "from scratch".

As a first step toward supporting automated, Web-based micro-explanation extraction, we present a survey study that characterizes the properties of "good" Web-derived explanations, according to both physicians and non-physicians. The specific contributions of this note are:

1) Preliminary validation of our hypothesis that the Web is a source of concise, patient-friendly explanations of lab tests, suitable for automated extraction.
2) A survey study characterizing the properties of "good" explanations, targeted at defining features for automated Web content extraction.
3) Exploration of the similarities and differences between how doctors and patients view these explanations.

RELATED WORK

Recent work has demonstrated the benefits of computer-based presentation of medical data to hospital patients, through kiosks [5], in-room displays [9] or agents [1]. This work motivates ours, which opens a new approach for automatic content generation for these patient-facing media.

Parallel work has explored natural-language generation and extraction techniques for summarizing medical content. Delegér [2] used parallel medical and lay-person corpora to map specific phrases between "patient-speak" and "doctor-speak"; a similar approach is taken by [4]. Portet et al [6] attempt to create textual summaries of continuous signals (e.g. EKG traces) in hospital settings. DiMarco [3] addresses the problem of semi-automatic personalized educational materials, using physician input to tailor generic materials to specific patients. This and other work in medical summarization complements our proposed approach, but no work to date has explored the unique properties of short, real-time explanation delivery, or the opportunity to base such explanations on existing consumer-friendly sources.

METHODOLOGY

To pursue insights about the value of consumer-facing Web pages serving as a source of explanations for medical events, we conducted a survey to evaluate physicians' and non-physicians' opinions of Web-extracted sentences, presented as explanations for diagnostic lab tests. We scope the present work to lab tests, given the finding by [8] of patient interest and appreciation about diagnostic test results in a personal health record. The survey took about an hour and participants were given a software gratuity.

Physician Participants

Seven physicians (six male) participated. All were actively practicing in U.S. hospitals and indicated that explaining tests to patients was a part of their responsibilities. Participants' specialties were emergency medicine, oncology, cardiology, pediatrics, surgery, and internal medicine (2).

Non-Physician Participants

Twenty-three non-physician participants (9 male) from the U.S. (14 states) were recruited based on having had recent hospital experiences as patients or family members of patients. Sixteen participants had hospital experiences in the past two years; all had hospital experiences in the past ten years. Participants' ages ranged from 21 to 63 (mean 41), and education ranged from high school to post-graduate.

Survey Design

We prepared four "patient profiles" based on common Emergency Department presentations, chosen via review of patient records in a large, urban hospital. Each profile (approximately one paragraph) included the sample patient's current symptoms, current medications, and a summary of their medical history and was reviewed by two non-participating experts for content validity. For each profile, experts provided a list of four lab tests that would likely be ordered. For each of these lab tests (16 total), we collected nine alternative one-sentence explanations (144 total).

To select the sample explanations for our survey, we performed a Web query for each lab test and chose the first three HON-certified[1] Web pages appearing in the results. From these pages, we hand-selected sentences that would fit the micro-explanation format. A large set (hundreds) of candidate sentences existed, so we selected sentences that spanned the space of possible explanations to ensure a representative sample of explanatory content (i.e., removing redundancy across sites while diversifying information).

Each participant responded to two of the four patient profiles. Each participant was thus presented with 72 explanations total (9 explanations for each lab test, 4 lab tests per profile, 2 profiles). Participants rated each explanation according to how appropriate they found the explanation to be for the patient described (physicians) or how helpful they would find the explanation if delivered to them in a hospital (non-physicians).

Participants used a rating scale of 1-5, and were instructed to use scores above 3 to indicate that the benefit of the explanation outweighs any concerns about its flaws. For each rating given, participants elaborated on the rationale for their choice using free text. Additionally, after all lab explanations had been examined for both sample patients in the study, both participant groups were asked to reflect on their preferences and describe characteristics of meaningful explanations, again in free text.

RESULTS AND DISCUSSION

Overview

Not surprisingly, the most consistent theme in all responses was a desire for "simplicity". In fact, 23/30 participants mentioned this explicitly in their end-of-survey reflections, including 6/7 physicians. Despite this common high-level goal, however, a deeper analysis of our results reveals that participants have widely-varying concepts of what makes a "simple", patient-friendly explanation. This section will explore this complexity, along with several additional themes that emerged in survey responses.

Web-extracted sentences as explanations

One of our core hypotheses is that consumer-facing Web pages can serve as the basis for extracting single sentences,

[1] The "Health on the Net" (HON) Foundation certifies the credibility of health-related sites through physician review.

suitable for delivery as micro-explanations. This is not obvious, however; Web sites are composed as a whole, and single sentences may lose meaning out of context.

Our results suggest that even sampling only 9 candidate sentences per lab test (an automated system could examine many more) is sufficient to extract at least one "good" explanation. For both physicians and non-physicians, every lab test had at least one explanation whose mean score was higher than 3.0; participants were instructed that "A rating of 3 or higher means that you consider the explanation of enough benefit to display". This suggests that extracting individual sentences from Web pages, despite the loss of context, is promising for micro-explanation generation.

Features of "good" explanations

Another goal of our study was to understand the relationship between participant preferences and characteristics of explanation text. To investigate correlations between measurable features and survey responses, we manually coded several features of the survey explanations, including:

1. Mention of *symptoms*
2. Mention of *organs*, *systems*, or *body parts*
3. Mention of *problems* or *diagnoses*
4. Sentence length in words
5. Use of *acronyms* and *medical terms*
6. Number of *medical terms* or *acronyms defined*

These features were hypothesized to be consistent with good explanations, based on discussions with physicians.

The mention of a specific symptom and the mention of an organ or system in an explanation correlated with participant preference: the top five most-preferred explanations across all labs (i.e., the explanations with the highest mean scores) *all* contained both a symptom and an organ/system reference, and *none* of the five least-preferred explanations contained either of these features. The most-preferred explanation overall is illustrative of these properties:

> *The troponin test is used to help diagnose a heart attack, to detect and evaluate mild to severe heart injury, and to separate it from chest pain that may be due to other causes.*

Interestingly, despite participants' overall desire for simplicity, longer explanations were preferred overall by both physicians and non-physicians. The five most-preferred explanations overall had a mean length of 30.0 words (±8.0), while the five least-preferred explanations had a mean length of 15.8 words (±9.2).

This preference for somewhat long sentences was explained differently by physicians, who explained high ratings for more complex sentences based on *accuracy*, and patients, who frequently explained high ratings for more complex sentences based on "sounding like a professional answer" and "sounding like something a doctor would say".

The preliminary correlations observed between encoded features and participant preference support our hypothesis that a feature-driven approach to scoring and ranking explanations could underlie a micro-explanation system.

Sources of divergence between patients and physicians

We also aimed to understand differences between physician and non-physician responses to Web-extracted explanations. To explore this, we identified explanations whose mean scores differed by more than 0.8 between physician and non-physician participants (16 explanations). Examining these explanations yields insights into how physicians and non-physicians approach these explanations differently.

14 of these 16 explanations were cases in which physicians rated explanations *lower* than non-physicians, and in fact all 14 had means above 3.0 ("acceptable") for non-physicians but below 3.0 ("unacceptable") for physicians. Most of this divergence was caused by explanations that physicians felt were inaccurate in this specific case: although the sentence was true, it reflected a narrow application of the test that was not appropriate for the particular patient profile being examined. For example, regarding a test that is sometimes used to diagnose clotting disorders (easy to understand) but was really being used here to assess liver function, P3 (physician) responds to an explanation about clotting by saying: "This is a reason to order this test, but not necessarily in this patient.", and P1 (physician) states: "True, but not applicable to someone presenting in the ER."

This presents a challenge for automated extraction techniques: even given credible information, it is critical to target explanation selection to a specific patient. This need for patient-specificity re-affirms our hypothesis that drawing from multiple information sources – specifically the Web (for candidate content) and the EMR (for patient-specific selection among candidates) – is necessary for automatic generation of explanations.

Another surprising reason emerged for physician preference of several explanations relative to non-physicians: physicians thought the explanation was too complicated for non-physicians to understand, but non-physicians appreciated the technical detail and saw it as "professional". For example, the following liver panel explanation was rated significantly higher by non-physicians:

> *A liver panel or one or more of its component tests may be used to help detect liver disease if a person has symptoms that indicate possible liver dysfunction or if a person is being monitored or treated for a known condition or liver disease.*

A physician described this explanation as "too wordy", while non-physicians indicated that "it's detailed" and "something a doctor would say".

The two explanations that physicians rated highly but non-physicians did not were both explanations for the "lipase level" test, and both used the term "pancreatitis". While physicians were generally concerned about conforming to a patient-friendly level of technical detail, they did not expect patients to be unfamiliar with this term. This presents another interesting challenge for automated extraction: understanding patient vocabularies and finding the boundary between layman and medical terminology.

The danger of too much information

Both patients and physicians noted that while detail is critical, too much information not only limits clarity, but creates risk and confusion. This particularly applied to the mention of diseases in explanations. Responding to tests that clearly and concisely stated these goals, referring specifically to diseases, non-physicians in particular expressed potential fear. P17, for example, states: "The mention of all of these diseases while already under duress would cause more stress." P20 similarly expresses: "You are using medical terms that as a confused and disoriented individual are just scaring me. The longer the words are [...], the scarier it sounds." These findings suggest other challenges for automated extraction, including balancing *specificity* and *patient comfort*, and minimizing inappropriate anxieties that may come with mention of low-probability risks.

Need for personalization

In many cases, even among non-physicians, participants disagreed significantly on the quality of an explanation, suggesting a need for automated systems to recognize various aspects of personal preference.

In fact, 49 of 135 explanations were "polarizing", meaning that at least 25% of non-physician participants assigned score ≥ 4.0 ("good" to "excellent"), and at least 25% assigned scores ≤ 2.0 ("poor" to "unacceptable"). Exploring the rationales for these ratings highlights several sources of variation in non-physician responses.

Many lab tests are used as broad initial screenings, but non-physicians varied significantly in their willingness to accept "broad screening" explanations as useful. An explanation for one such test referred to "determining general health status", yielding scores of 1 ("I would hope any lab test would provide information on general health status") and 5 ("I understand that this kind of test is used to rule out many medical issues") from non-physician participants.

Another common explanation pattern that polarized non-physician respondents was the use of *indications for a test* that did not refer specifically to diagnostic outcomes. The following explanation is illustrative:

> *If a patient is having symptoms such as fatigue or weakness or has an infection, inflammation, bruising, or bleeding, then the doctor may order a CBC to help diagnose the cause.*

P14 (who assigned a 4.0 rating) specifically likes "that this answer tells me why the test might have been ordered for me", but P7 (who assigned a 2.0 rating) responds "Only states causes of the test, does not say what the test does".

A third source of significant disagreement among non-physicians emerged from varying health literacy: some explanations were concise and complete but used a term or acronym not familiar to some participants. The explanation "to determine if your blood glucose level is within healthy ranges" prompted responses of "This is straightforward and easy to understand" (P17, rating 5.0) and "If you don't know what blood glucose is, this explanation is useless." (P27, rating 2.0).

Finally, some respondents expressed a strong dislike for explanations that were not grammatically complete, even if they were conceptually correct (e.g. an explanation beginning with "To determine if your lungs are functioning well enough..."). This need for personalization opens a further challenge for automated extraction systems: personalization based not only on EMR data but on user preference as well.

CONCLUSION AND FUTURE WORK

We studied opportunities for generating medical *micro-explanations* from consumer-facing Web content. We explored physician and non-physician responses to sentences extracted from Web pages and presented as micro-explanations for medical lab tests. We aim to develop algorithms for presenting real-time explanations to hospital patients. Although the present work focused on explaining lab tests, we expect that insights and results presented here will generalize to other EMR content, e.g. medications. Further work is required to validate this hypothesis.

REFERENCES

1. Bickmore, T., Pfeifer, L. and Jack, B. Taking the time to care: empowering low health literacy hospital patients with virtual nurse agents. *Proc ACM CHI 2009.*
2. Deléger, L. and Zweigenbaum, P. Extracting lay paraphrases of specialized expressions from monolingual comparable medical corpora. *Proc 2009 Workshop on Building and Using Comparable Corpora.*
3. DiMarco, et al. Authoring and generation of individualised patient education materials. *Proc AMIA 2006.*
4. Elhadad, N. and Sutaria, K. 2007. Mining a lexicon of technical terms and lay equivalents. *Proc 2007 Workshop on Bio, Translational, and Clin Lang Processing.*
5. Jones, R. The role of health kiosks in 2009: literature and informant review. *Int J Env. Res Public Health,* 6.6 (2009).
6. Portet, F., Reiter, E., Gatt, A., Hunter, J., Sripada, S., Freer, Y., and Sykes, C. Automatic generation of textual summaries from neonatal intensive care data. *Artificial Intelligence*, 173 (2009).
7. Pratt, W., Unruh, K., Civan, A., and Skeels, M. Personal Health Information Management. *Commications of the ACM*, 49.1 (2006).
8. Tang, P.C. and Lansky, D. The missing link: bridging the patient-provider health information gap. *Health Affairs* 24 (2005).
9. Wilcox, L., Morris, D., Tan, D., and Gatewood, J. Designing patient-centric information displays for hospitals. *Proc ACM CHI 2010.*

"Now, I Have a Body": Uses and Social Norms for Mobile Remote Presence in the Workplace

Min Kyung Lee
HCI Institute, Carnegie Mellon University
5000 Forbes Avenue, Pittsburgh, PA 15213, USA
mklee@cs.cmu.edu

Leila Takayama
Willow Garage
68 Willow Road, Menlo Park, CA 94025, USA
takayama@willowgarage.com

ABSTRACT

As geographically distributed teams become increasingly common, there are more pressing demands for communication work practices and technologies that support distributed collaboration. One set of technologies that are emerging on the commercial market is mobile remote presence (MRP) systems, physically embodied videoconferencing systems that remote workers use to drive through a workplace, communicating with locals there. Our interviews, observations, and survey results from people, who had 2-18 months of MRP use, showed how remotely-controlled mobility enabled remote workers to live and work with local coworkers almost as if they were physically there. The MRP supported informal communications and connections between distributed coworkers. We also found that the mobile embodiment of the remote worker evoked orientations toward the MRP both as a person and as a machine, leading to formation of new usage norms among remote and local coworkers.

Author Keywords

Mobile remote presence, computer supported collaborative work, human-robot interaction.

ACM Classification Keywords

H5.m. Information interfaces and presentation (e.g., HCI): Miscellaneous.

General Terms

Experimentation

INTRODUCTION

As work environments change, there are more cases where collaborators in work teams are not collocated [12]. Collaboration in geographically distributed teams is still challenging [17]. Remote workers have fewer opportunities to engage in informal communication, which is critical for successful collaboration [5, 9]. Informal communication plays an important role for supporting work-related tasks, coordinating group activities, transmitting office culture, building teams, minimizing ambiguity in communication, and mitigating conflicts [3, 7, 22]. The connection built via informal communication improves workers' readiness to engage in fruitful communication [14].

However, supporting informal communication is difficult for most collaboration technologies because informal communications are often unscheduled and brief; they also require highly interactive and expressive communication channels [3, 9, 22].

Addressing this problem, we explore the use of a Mobile Remote Presence (MRP) system in the workplace. (See Figure 1.) In the context of remote collaboration, the MRP is a physically embodied audio-video system that remote workers can drive around the workplace. Using the MRP, remote coworkers, which we call "pilots," can wander the hallways and engage in impromptu interactions, increasing opportunities for connection in the workplace.

Figure 1. Using a MRP system in the office place for work and play: (a) hanging out with coworkers playing pool (b) having an impromptu conversation in a lab

RELATED WORK

Numerous systems have been developed to assist distributed team collaboration, aiming to facilitate informal communication and mutual awareness between distributed teams [16], particularly video conferencing systems [2].

Systems that support audio-video communication are particularly relevant to the MRP. Among the drawbacks of immobile videoconferencing systems is the lack of support for the informal, but critical, types of communications that take place outside of meeting rooms [2]. Shared audio-video portal systems have been developed to increase awareness among distributed teams by connecting shared spaces in different office locations [1, 9, 11]; the premise of this approach is that persistent audio-video communication channel will facilitate informal communication. Longitudinal fieldwork of such a system found that it was frequently used to check coworkers' availability, check project status, and coordinate meeting opportunities, but it was not used as a primary medium for problem-solving [9].

Another approach to supporting information communication in distributed teams has been to use a physical embodiment of remote coworkers with audio-video communication channels. One of the advantages of using an embodied representation is that it increases the presence of a remote coworker [19]. Using an embodied video conferencing system with remote coworkers reportedly helped listeners to selectively attend to speakers and helped speakers figure out who was paying attention to them [20]. Such embodied video conferencing systems also improve meeting participation and interpersonal social connections between hub and satellite teams [21].

MRP systems have been built (e.g., [18]), adding mobility to the equation. Similar to the MRP presented in this paper, these systems allowed a remote person to move throughout a distant location and engage conversation with others. However, to our knowledge, these systems have not been studied and reported upon in terms of long-term use, emerging work practices, or social norms. Improved WiFi technologies have enabled the current system to be used for over a year now, which has provided us with the opportunity to learn from experiences beyond first-contact, novelty effects, and initial impression.

We believe that the remotely controlled mobility of the MRP will enable different interactions in the workplace, using the advantages of rich audio-video communication channel and physical embodiment. As a pilot in our ongoing studies stated, "Before, I had no corporeal body [in the workplace]. I was handicapped. Now, I have a body." To better understand mobile remote presence, we took an exploratory approach that focused on the following research questions:

- How are MRP systems used in the workplace?
- What are the factors that influence MRP system use?
- What social and usage norms form around MRP systems?

STUDY DESIGN

At this stage of research, investigating a relatively new set of experiences in the workplace, we chose to examine these phenomena with several different methods, including open-ended critical incident interviews (to capture the most salient incidents from the previous year), surveys (to capture a wider variety of respondents than those we could interview and observe in person), and in-person observations (to capture actual interactions, not just ones recalled from memory).

MRP System

The MRP system used in these explorations was the Texai Alpha prototype [23], developed at Company A in order to work more effectively with a remote coworker, who lives approximately 1,800 miles away. Before the development of the MRP, the company had used phone conferencing and video conferencing systems to communicate with the remote coworker, but that was too limiting; the remote coworker was often left out of meetings and real decision-making discussions. Then the team put a laptop on a pushcart so that the video conferencing system could at least move around the building, but that quickly grew frustrating because the remote colleague had to ask local coworkers to push the cart around and to re-direct the laptop camera to locations where he wanted to look. In order to give the remote coworker control over his own location and viewpoint, they built the Texai Alpha prototype.

The Texai Alpha prototype consists of a mobile base, touch screen, microphone, speakers, pan-tilt webcam, wide-angle camera, and two laser range finders; it stands approximately 5' 2" tall. Remote pilots drive the MRP system by using a web browser and video conferencing application. (See Figure 2.) The Texai Alpha always shows the real-time video feed of the remote pilot when driving the system, following the design guideline of "If you see me, I see you." When it is idle, the screen saver turns to black. With the fully charged battery, it could be used for approximately eight continuous hours. At the time of the study, its current top speed was 1.5 miles per hour.

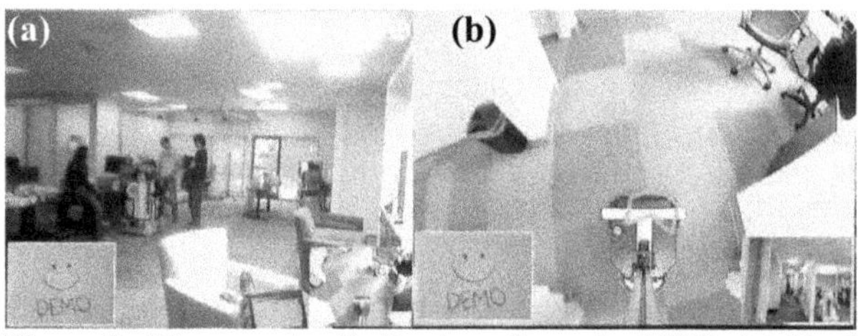

Figure 2. The remote pilot's views from the MRP: (a) Head view (looking up) and (b) navigation view (looking down)

METHODS AND ANALYSES

We investigated the MRP usage through interviews and observations in one company where the MRP system has been used longest, and evaluated whether these patterns are generalizable with two different companies through surveys.

Field Sites

The MRP system prototype was used in three different companies located in the San Francisco Bay Area for varying periods of time (2-18 months). Unlike the other embodied remote presence systems (e.g., [21]) where one system is dedicated to one remote pilot, the MRP system was used as a shared resource: anyone who had an account could connect to the MRP system website and use the system. To respect the privacy of our participants, we did not log audio-video recordings through the MRP system. Instead, we had permission to take photos and videos when we observed MRP usage in person.

Company A is a research and development organization that focuses on personal robotics; it also developed the prototype. Approximately ten MRP system prototypes have been used there for 18 months. The firm offered accounts to all the employees at the company so that anyone who was sick or away for a business trip could use the MRP system. The main remote pilots during the time of the study included one engineer who works with the rest of the team members (3-4 people) in Indiana, and a project leader who was working from Central America for an extended period of time. Most of the docking stations were located next to the main dining area, and two others were in a hallway.

Company B is a web development firm, and has used two MRP prototypes for ten weeks. The company comprises of highly distributed teams spread all over the world. The firm gave accounts to those who permanently live and work from remote locations. Three main remote pilots used the MRP systems: a product manager who resides in Canada, a web developer in Seattle, and a systems administrator in Singapore. Two docking stations were located in lounge areas on opposite sides of the building.

Company C is a design software development firm, and has used two MRP prototypes for ten weeks. The main pilots were two executives who reside in California but often work from home or from satellite offices; they travel frequently for business, spending most of their time away from the main office.

While there are many dimensions of organizations that could not possibly be covered by only three companies (e.g., industry, company culture, geographical distribution of employees, demographics of employees, degree of hierarchy), starting with three companies enabled us to learn about a wider range of uses, personalities, work practices, company cultures, etc. than we could have learned about with only one site.

Critical Incident Interviews

Because the MRP systems have been in daily use at Company A for over a year, this site was chosen for conducting a critical incident analysis [4]. We interviewed 20 respondents (4 women and 16 men), including four members of the Texai project development team. We asked respondents to recall specific incidences that were either very positive or very negative. Each interview took 20-90 minutes, depending on the respondent's experience with using the MRP system.

After transcribing the interviews, we extracted incidents and did a content analysis of those incidents in terms of the respondent's role (e.g., pilot, local), activity (e.g., attending planned work meetings, having an impromptu meeting), location (e.g., meeting room, hallway, office), etc. Each incident could have multiple codes assigned to it. Altogether, 79 critical incidents were reported (average incidents per respondent = 3.95, range = 2-8); we excluded 12 of the incidents that only reported technical problems that were unique to this system (e.g., network issues, software bugs). 56% incidents were reported from a pilot perspective; 22% were from a local interactant perspective; and 23% were from a local bystander perspective. For each activity that the MRP was used, we identified the upsides and downsides of using the MRP system, and factors that made the experience positive or negative.

Contextual Observations

To triangulate upon the self-reported findings identified in the critical incident analysis, we observed MRP usage in Company A, shadowing remote pilots throughout their workdays. These observations focused on two dedicated remote pilots, i.e., highly collaborative remote workers, who used the MRP to get their work done because they lived 1800 miles away from the workplace. One pilot, who had worked on building the MRP for his own use, had been using the MRP for 18 months at the time of the observations. The other pilot was not involved in building the MRP; he had been using the MRP to telecommute to work for one month. As part of our ongoing field studies, we also conducted shorter observations (half days, once every other week) at Companies B & C. Although the full results of the field studies are not reported, we have included some images from those field observations in this paper.

Surveys

The interviews and observation allowed us to identify common usages for the MRP, and the most significant benefits or issues that remain over repeated usages after the novelty effects wore off. Based on these findings, we generated a survey to understand the actual frequency of the activities, benefits and issues with a wider range of people who have experienced using or encountering the MRP. Thus, we conducted the survey at Companies A, B, and C.

The survey focused on: (1) The frequency and impact of the MRP use for collaboration activities; (2) Where, how, and why people have impromptu meetings using the MRP; (3) Perception of upsides (i.e., how the MRP improves remote communication and work) and downsides (e.g., noise, mistakes, difficulties of negotiating personal spaces); and (4) Politeness and embarrassment of usage behaviors. The survey also included questions about respondents' demographics and how well they knew the remote pilot or local teams in the MRP location (1= did not know the team in the MRP location (or remote pilot) at all, 2=knew the team barely, 3=knew the team moderately, 4=knew the team, 5=knew the team very well). The median was 2, so we divided the respondents with an average score of less than or equal to 2 into an "unfamiliar" group and those with higher or equal to 3 into a "familiar" group. We also noted whether remote pilots were designated users (e.g., satellite team, frequent travelers) or ones who used it on their short-term needs based (e.g., being sick at home, temporarily working from remote offices).

Pilots and locals were asked to answer all of the questions, and bystanders were asked to only answer politeness ratings of usage behaviors. For locals, we asked respondents to name one remote pilot they interact with most, and to base their answers on experiences with that particular pilot.

Pilots, locals, and bystanders from three companies responded to the survey (*N*=54). There were 12 pilots, 26 local bystanders, and 10 local interactants; 28 were from Company A, 11 from Company B, and 10 from Company C; 6 did not report their company name. Respondent ages ranged from 23-65 years, *M*=34.0, *SE*=1.7, including 9 women, 36 men, and 10 with unreported genders. They had a range of experiences with using the MRP (2-72 weeks, *M*=15.0, *SE*=2.23). Respondents held positions such as intern, engineer, consultant, program manager, director, and vice president. The MRP systems were located in the San Francisco Bay Area (USA). The MRP pilots were physically located in other parts of the USA, Central America, Canada, Germany, and Singapore.

Our analysis shows that locals' prior familiarity with remote pilots influenced their perceived benefits. Also, whether remote pilots were designated pilots or not influenced pilots' responses. Thus we used these variables as control variables in our analysis.

The survey responses showed the respondents' communication patterns before the introduction of the MRP. Dedicated pilots reported that they communicated with local teams through face to face to meeting (*M*=1.8, *SE*=0.58; 0=Never, 1=Once or less per month, 2=A few times per month, 3=Once a week, 4=A few times a week, 5=Once a day, 6=A few times a day), phone call (*M*=3.25, *SE*=0.48), email (*M*=4, *SE*=1.15), text chatting (*M*=4.33, *SE*=0.56), and video conference call (*M*=2.86, *SE*=0.55). The pilots also reported that they used these communication activities slightly less frequently on average after the introduction of the MRP system (*M*=2.77, *SE*=0.23; 1=Use much less often, 5=Use much more often). The answers to an open-ended question on communication changes suggest the introduction of the MRP system increased the overall amount of communication, rather than replacing the existing communication activities (e.g., "Communication has increased overall. It isn't so much about transitioning communication as it is about increasing communication").

The survey responses from remote pilots showed that dedicated remote pilots used the MRP a few times a week to attend planned meetings (*M*=4, *SE*=0.33, 0=Never, 1=Once or less per month, 2=A few times per month, 3=Once a week, 4=A few times a week, 5=Once a day, 6=A few times a day), and to engage in impromptu work meetings (*M*=3.75, *SE*=0.56). They also reported that they used the MRP about once a week to greet and socialize, seek or follow local coworkers, and to be around in the workplace.

Overall, participants reported the MRP was useful (*M*=5.77, *SE*=0.15, 1=Very useless, 7=Very useful), and effective (*M*=5.46, *SE*=0.21, 1=Very ineffective, 7=Very effective); answers by pilots vs. locals or between companies were not found to be significantly different.

RESULTS AND DISCUSSION

Our results showed that the MRP allowed remote pilots to work with local coworkers almost as if they were there in person. The MRP supported informal communications (see Figure 3) and connections between distributed coworkers. We also found that the MRP's mobile, physical embodiment of the remote pilot caused confusion about whether to treat the system as a person or object, leading to the formation of new social norms among coworkers.

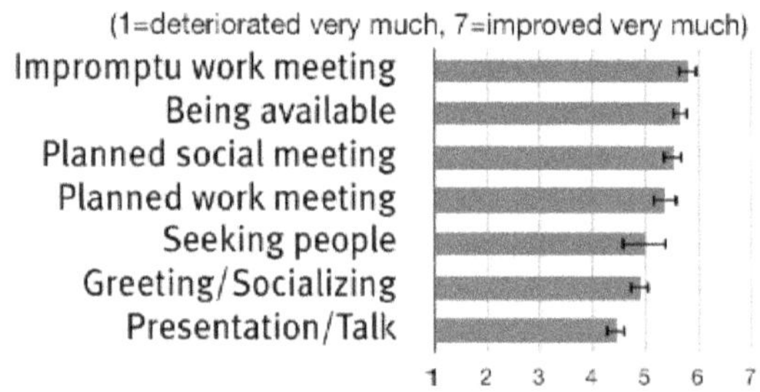

Figure 3. Impact of MRP usage on activities (*M*, *SE*)

USES OF MRP FOR WORKPLACE COMMUNICATION

The results of surveys, interviews, and observations showed that the MRP system was used for a wide variety of work and social activities in the workplace. Figure 3 shows the survey responses about the types of activities for which the MRP system was used and how much it improved each activity. While all the activities were improved, attending planned social events, having impromptu meetings, and being available to local coworkers seemed to benefit most.

Informal communication

The majority (76%) of positive incidents from the interview centered around informal communication activities. Impromptu activities using the MRP happened virtually everywhere in the workplace, including hallway, communal spaces such as lab space or kitchen, or individual offices. (See Table 1 and Figure 4.) The most frequently mentioned reasons for using the MRP for impromptu meetings are shown in the Table 2. The most common usages were

Location	Frequency
Hallway	28%
Communal space	27%
Office	26%
Conference room	11%
MRP dock	7%

Table 1. Locations of impromptu meetings via the MRP (Frequency of locations mentioned in the survey).

Purpose	Frequency
Get answers	18%
Exchange ideas	16%
Ask questions	15%
Project status check	14%
Socialize	14%
Show off the MRP	7%
Introduce coworker	5%
Show around workplace	5%
Others	7%

Table 2. Purposes of impromptu meetings via the MRP.

worked-related communication and socializing; this was consistent across companies.

These impromptu meetings and social conversations could show commitment, capture and maintain attention from local coworkers, and build social connections (affinity) among geographically distributed team members [14]. We explain these different types of impromptu activities in the following three sections.

Commitment: Being Present and Available

Commitment is "an engagement denoting scope for ongoing communication for projects of mutual interest" [14]. We found that the MRP allowed the remote pilots to be more present and available in the main office location, which demonstrates commitment to working with local coworkers. 6 out 12 pilots reported that they use the MRP to simply be around, once a week on average. In our observations, we also found that pilots logged in to the MRP even when they did not need to talk about anything in particular with the locals, consistent with findings from the ESP system [21]. Remote pilots who did not have their offices in the main location usually parked the MRP system in the shared lab space. Those pilots who were on business travel (or were working from home while sick) logged in to the MRP system and parked it at their own office desks. Having the MRP system allowed locals to talk with remote pilots without going through the additional coordination of checking their calendars. One pilot who frequently traveled in Company C and parked the MRP in his office expressed:

Figure 4. An impromptu conversation at Company B: The local person happened to be standing near where the pilot was trying to park the MRP system.

Users come in to my "office" where the robot is, expecting to find me, and instead find my robot there. Without the robot, these meetings likely wouldn't have happened, as they wouldn't have taken the time to hunt down my whereabouts. It helps me feel much more "present" when I'm not in the office.

The roaming sound of the MRP also became an indicator that the remote pilot was around, so local employees would notice that the remote pilot was around even before seeing it. Hearing the MRP's motor sound or pilot's voice, local employees would go out of the hallway and interrupt the MRP pilot if they wanted to initiate a work or social conversation. Having the MRP roaming around also increased the perceived presence of the remote pilot, as reflected in the survey. R18 reported:

He always would say, "Good morning!" to me, every morning, because he was up early, because he was on a different time [zone]. So that was always nice; I always felt like I had company in the building.

Our survey results also show that both pilots and locals in all companies agree that remote pilots have greater presence in the local office location. There was also trend that, when respondents reported that they were not familiar with the pilot before the introduction of the MRP, their perceived benefit about the greater presence was marginally higher (M=5.96, SE=0.33) than among people who already knew the pilot (M= 5.15, SE=.31), $F(1, 32)$=3.19, p=0.08.

Attention: Capturing and Maintaining Attention

Capturing attention is about "locating the intended recipient" and "attaining attention" [14]. In addition to simply being available, the MRP gave remote pilots more independence to initiate conversations with locals. Our survey shows that about 50% pilots and local users perceive that pilots usually initiate the impromptu meetings; the initiator reported in the survey: pilots 46%; locals 27%; equal split 27%. This contrasts against other systems where the communication is more dependent on the efforts of local coworkers (e.g., going to the telepresence room). Without having to schedule formal meetings, remote pilots visited local employees' offices to have impromptu meetings, wandered around the office to find colleagues, continued conversations after the end of meetings, and joined ad-hoc meetings. One remote pilot reported that he sometimes drove the MRP to someone's office door and waited there to catch him/her to get answers to urgent questions, which is similar to "ambushing" observed in the video conferencing wall system [3].

Our survey found that both local coworkers and remote pilots reported that communicating with the remote pilot (or local coworkers) became easier since using the MRP. In particular, those who reported being unfamiliar with the coworkers reported greater benefits in terms of ease of use (M=6.05, SE=0.21) than those who already knew each other well (M=5.27, SE=0.21), $F(1,32)$=8.33, $p<0.01$. Interestingly, local coworkers expressed that the MRP had improved the process of setting up the equipment to meet with remote coworkers.

Pilots reported that they had greater awareness of activities going on in the main office (M=5.33, SE=0.41). Dedicated pilots reported that they could make faster progress on collaborative projects (M=5.67, SE=0.44), but occasional pilots did not agree (M=3.33, SE=0.62), $F(1,8)$=9.53, $p<.05$.

Affinity: Building social connections

Affinity is about "feelings of connection between people" [14]. The MRP allowed remote and local workers to build social connections. Using the MRP, remote pilots could attend social events (e.g., drinking beer) that they could not join without the MRP; remote pilots also frequently joined impromptu chats while working with local workers in the same room, passing in the hallway, or swinging by the kitchen. See Figure 5.

Our observation and interviews also showed that the MRP's rich modalities—user controlled movement [13], its approximate human scale body, and audio and video communication all seemed to increase the social presence of remote pilots, which led to relatively fluid social interaction among local coworkers and remote pilots. Experienced pilots used the mobile base to socially signal when they wanted to talk and to whom they were listening by positioning and orienting the MRP system. Many locals reported that meeting someone for the first time via the MRP was more natural than other communication media alternatives. One local coworker mentioned meeting the remote person for the first time (R4):

Figure 5. Locals chatting over coffee with a remote pilot. The pilot is showing a new prototype that his team has designed.

And he just rolls up to my office door and says, "Hi," which is great. If he had hopped on my computer screen through Skype, that would have been very awkward.

Being able to be physically present in a social milieu allowed a relatively natural social interaction between the MRP and others. R11 explained:

That's what I think I like about the MRP is that, you know, if [the remote person, R5] or whatever is just chatting in the [shared workspace], you have the complete symmetry of like I'll chat with [R5] as much as I chat with anybody else.

Using the rich communication modalities, the MRP enabled more nuanced communication between remote pilots and local coworkers, which strengthened their social connections. One local coworker, who did not know the pilot, explained how he got to know the pilot via the MRP. He reported that the pilot was no longer a "mythic character" and was struck by the fact that meeting the remote pilot in person was not very different from meeting him via the MRP (R18):

It was so cool to meet him in person, but I was also so amazed that the only difference was that he was taller... I mean, he can have his personality. He'll bump into things, and laugh about them [using the MRP]. You get all the different aspects of a person's personality through this robot [...] He could still be a jokester in the [MRP].

Our survey results also confirmed that the MRP can enable more casual and social interaction, and provide greater opportunity for remote pilots to get to know local coworkers and vice versa. Both pilots and locals reported that they could communicate with remote pilots and locals in a more casual and sociable way. Respondents who did not know each other before the introduction of the MRP reported greater benefits (M=5.77, SE=0.24) than those who were already familiar with one another (M=5.03, SE=0.24), $F(1,33)$=7.03, $p<.05$. Local coworkers and pilots, who were unfamiliar with each other, agreed with the statement that since they started using the MRP, they got to better know the remote pilot or vice versa (M=6, SE=0.29), whereas those who were already familiar with each other did not (M=4, SE=0.33), $F(1,32)$=20.63, $p<.001$, 1=Strongly disagree, 4=Neither agree nor disagree, 7=Strongly agree.

Hindrance to the utility of the MRP

While our research identified benefits of using the MRP, it also identified limitations of the MRP system. The most frequently mentioned downside was the burden of driving. Pilots reported that the hassle of driving the MRP to go to a meeting room made the MRP system less useful and efficient. They reported that driving the MRP itself is not difficult (*M*=3.83, *SE*=0.49, 1=Strongly disagree, 7=Strongly agree with the statement "The Texai is difficult to drive."), but it was time consuming, which can make them late for scheduled meetings. In addition, pilots reported, when they were carrying out the conversation with local coworkers moving in the hallway, they could not focus on the social conversation as their attention was divided between driving the system and carrying on a conversation, as reported as a potential problem in a medical telepresence robot [15]. Gaze and head turn, a common issue in video conferencing systems [2, 16], were also problems with the MRP system, yet it was not reported as a showstopper. The large video display of a remote pilot helped mostly with reading the pilot's head/gaze orientation. The pan-tilt camera also helped, only if the locals noticed its movement. Sometimes the pan-tilt camera was a problem because pilots' cameras would be facing in a different direction than their video image appeared to be looking.

USAGE (SOCIAL) NORMS

We also found that the mobile embodiment of the remote pilots evoked orientations toward the MRP both as a person and as a machine, leading to the formation of new social norms among remote and local coworkers [8, 10]. These norms set expectations for how people believe that pilots and locals should interact. The MRP was sometimes perceived as being the remote pilot (e.g., referring to the MRP by the pilot's name), which can encourage social norms of face-to-face interaction; at other times, the system was perceived as being an object—furniture, a device, or a robot (e.g., addressing the MRP as "Robot" or "it," resting feet on its base, or leaning on it).

Usage norms drawn from other technology

As previous research has shown [10], many emerging usage norms seem to be drawn from people's previous experiences with existing communication technology.

Some of the social norms seem to come from face-to-face interactions. We observed numerous cases where people naturally made room for the MRP and adjusted their standing positions and orientations to incorporate the MRP into their group. Some local coworkers discussed their treatment of personal space around the MRP system with respect to how they treat personal space of a person (R10):

I can actually squeeze by in a way that if some person were standing there with their back turned to me, I'd be uncomfortable squeezing by them in the same way.

Negotiating personal space was also discussed in terms of how one would interact face-to-face: R2 explained:

If there were a person there and I were to walk up, he would—we wouldn't have to say anything. We wouldn't even have to exchange, you know, eye glances or anything. The person would move out of the way. He doesn't move out of the way. And so I either have to like step over him or explicitly say, "Hey [remote pilot's name], can you back up? I'd like to leave the room." And it's a surprisingly unnatural interaction.

When attending large group meetings or formal presentations, remote pilots will often join the audience and face the front of the meeting room to watch the presenter. In doing so, pilots sometimes inadvertently move the MRP directly in front of a local audience member, thereby blocking the local's view of the presenter. (See Figure 6.) As observed at both Companies A and B, this is usually remedied by someone speaking up for the local whose view was blocked.

At the same time, different local workers seem to have different mental models of the MRP. Some were hesitant to physically push the MRP to make it go faster toward its location, change its volume without asking for permission from the pilot, or touch the system; others did it without hesitation as if they were interacting with inanimate machines (e.g., resting feet on it). The violation of personal space, touching and control could be an issue from the remote pilot's perspectives. During a standing meeting, one local kept fiddling with the MRP, which was being piloted by R16. As R16 described it:

He just kept bumping my volume up, and bumping it down... It was just very distracting... I felt like... my personal space was being invaded.

Some of the behaviors of remote pilots seem to come from existing communication technologies (e.g., phone, chat), which are not always appropriate. Similar to hanging up a phone at the end of a call, some pilots just hang up the MRP system at the end of the conversation. This caused inconveniences or awkwardness to local coworkers.

One example critical incident describes this issue (R3):

And they just log out and they just run off and the robot is just left like in a conference room... If I don't put them on the chargers then the battery will be dead the next day.

Figure 6. The MRP in a scheduled presentation. The pilot put the MRP amongst others in the audience, but inadvertently blocked the view of a local, who was sitting behind him.

In the opposite type of scenario, participants reported that the pilot sometimes lingered for too long after the end of a conversation. Like in face-to-face conversations, these participants expected the pilot to drive the MRP system away soon after completing the conversation. Lingering for too long created an awkward situation for local coworkers as they felt that they were being watched by the pilots, even though the pilots were not usually paying any attention to the MRP system's audio-video feed. Some participants reported that they learned to explicitly remind the remote pilot to go away after they finished talking with each other.

Formation of new usage norms

While these usage norms seem to draw from previous experiences with face-to-face and mediated interactions, they are also forming new usage protocols to use the MRP system. For example, instead of standing at the side of the table and facing the projected screen as other meeting participants, the MRP system has a set location in the front corner so that the remote pilot can face the rest (Figure 7).

Local coworkers also demonstrated their commitment to engaging with remote pilots by helping the MRP function in the workplace. R14, a remote pilot, said:

I have tried to get to other meetings and my [MRP] has not been like behaving well... If people know I'm coming to the meeting, they'll come looking for me and like grab my [MRP] and drag it to where I need to be, which is nice.

Pilots are largely helpless when they lose network connection to the MRP so locals sometimes help them by pushing or pulling the MRP around. Similarly, locals often help pilots with opening doors. As R17 reported:

It'd just be like if someone was in a wheelchair and you needed to open a door for them... but it's a lot less bulky, so it's almost easier than a wheelchair.

To gain a broader understanding of the social norms forming around MRP, we polled the survey respondents to rate how polite or impolite (1=very impolite; 7=very polite) they thought it would be for pilots and locals to engage in scenarios mentioned in the critical incident interviews and seen during MRP observations. (See Figure 8.)

A MANOVA showed that both pilot and local coworkers believed it was more polite to ask remote pilots to adjust their own volume levels (M=5.13, SE=0.15) rather than adjust the volume levels by pressing the MRP buttons directly (M=4.11, SE=0.19), $F(1, 42)=29.62$, $p<.0001$. Pilots rated locals adjusting the volume on their own as being more impolite than local coworkers and bystanders, on average. This social norm stands in contrasts against how people typically adjust the volume of other audio/video conferencing system without asking remote users for permission. There is something different about the MRP that makes this behavior seem rude.

People's orientations toward the MRP influenced their judgments of how polite it would be to play pranks on the MRP. In our survey, we asked respondents to describe the MRP in their own words as a way to gain insight into how they conceptualize the MRP system—as a robot or something else. 41% of the respondents used the word "robot" to describe the MRP, and the rest did not. Respondents who used the word "robot" to describe the MRP believed it was more impolite to play pranks on the MRP (M=2.60, SE=0.28) than people who did not call it a "robot" (M=3.34, SE=0.25), $F(1,44)=3.92, p=.05$.

Impact of technical embodiment of a remote pilot

Being represented as a physical machine in a social setting poses some challenges to a remote pilot. Remote pilots often mentioned that they were embarrassed by their driving skills or technical glitches of the MRP.

It's not as bad if you're driving down a hallway by yourself and the wireless cuts out for a few seconds and you keep driving. It's not a big deal, but if you're trying to, you know, communicate with some one, especially in a social sense, well... now you've got to wait five seconds for your wireless to come back so then you have to ask hem to repeat themselves or whatever.

When a system is an embodied representations of you, it can also come with the psychological baggage of embarrassing you when it fails. That has led some users to withdraw from social interaction when the system is not performing reliably. On the other hand, other users were not bothered by the malfunctions; they simply moved on to use a different MRP system, leaving the original one behind.

Even though remote workers could pilot the MRP system, they did not have full control over their representation in

Figure 7. The MRP in a scheduled meeting. The pilot puts the MRP in the front corner, so that he can face everyone.

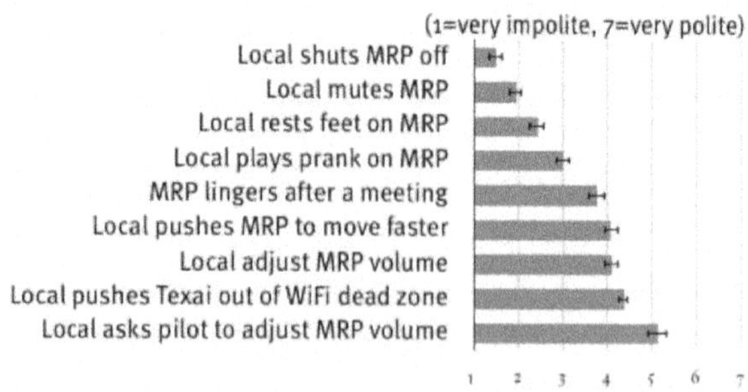

Figure 8. Politeness ratings of MRP usage norms (*M*, *SE*)

the MRP or its surroundings in the MRP location. Remote pilots also could not see what they looked like in the MRP, so they were not aware of any things attached to the MRP. The MRPs have been decorated (by locals) with hats, moustaches, posters, and leis, but the some pilots did not know about the decorations until being told about them or seeing pictures taken at the local site.

We also found some cases where the quality of the MRP was perceived as if it was the quality of its remote pilot. For example, the volume of the MRP was sometimes too loud, as the MRP system does not adjust volume automatically to the ambient sound level in its location. Even though remote pilots were not aware they were being too loud, many local coworkers described that the remote pilot (not the MRP system) as being too loud, thereby disturbing the workplace. This, in turn, upset the remote pilot as local coworkers began to shut their office doors in front of the MRP when the volume was turned up too high.

The MRP does not have arms or other manipulators. In a few instances, pilots improvised by pushing objects around with the mobile base of the MRP or bumping/knocking into doors to get attention from people on the other side of the door. However, pilots generally needed help from the local coworkers to manipulate its surroundings (e.g., opening a door of a meeting room, fetching a tool from a toolbox). One remote pilot (R5) expressed this experience as feeling disabled.

IMPLICATIONS FOR THEORY

The results of these exploratory studies suggest that the MRP could support informal communication and connection in distributed teams. However, we also learned, a technical embodiment of remote pilot creates confusion about who or what the MRP *is* (ontologically)—a person, an object, a robot, or something else. This raises theoretical issues of source orientation, entitativity, and agency. Because the MRP system is mobile and is controlled by remote pilots, its physical form somehow embodies the individual pilot. This contrasts against wall-mounted video displays, where the physical video display is not typically identified as being the remote people, but is more like a window or portal into their workspace.

In terms of theory, the MRP presents more questions than answers, but they could ultimately provide grounds for a deeper understanding of issues of agency, responsibility, and social norm formation. Should the MRP be treated as a person? When it is shut off by locals against the will of the pilot, is that an assault? When the MRP damages things, who is at fault? Does that change when autonomous features (e.g., obstacle-avoiding navigation features) are involved? At least some of these questions can be addressed empirically (e.g., which dimensions of MRP systems influence how people perceive the identity, rights, and responsibilities of remote pilots?), but some will require grounded conceptual work to articulate the boundaries that are being blurred between person and machine, physical and virtual, and being here vs. being elsewhere.

IMPLICATIONS FOR DESIGN

This MRP system and the current studies also raise practical issues about how to support users in making sense of these systems. In this section, we describe several design directions to address the issues raised by the current work.

Places

The places where most informal interactions took place were not spaces typically supported by stationary systems (e.g., videoconferencing), demonstrating that more informal remote communication can be supported outside of conference room and private office settings. Hallways are not typically construed as places for holding conversations, but they are exactly the places where information communication frequently occurs.

Strategically placing docking stations can influence the use of MRP systems. The docking stations should be placed in locations where there is a high traffic to increase the chance for impromptu meeting with local coworkers; it also should be in close proximity where other formal meetings happen, so that remote pilots can quickly drive to the meeting rooms. Each MRP system could also have multiple charging stations throughout a workspace.

Mobile Remote "Presentation of Self"

Features to provide remote pilots with more feedback about how they are presenting themselves (e.g., [6]) are important as these MRP systems become identified with the person, not just as a machine that is being driven by a person. Providing mechanisms to help monitor their volume levels, monitor their appearances, and communicate nonverbally could also improve the user experience for both remote pilots and locals. MRP sensor data could also be used to providing social (e.g., proxemic) information to pilots, e.g., when a person is trying to squeeze by.

As the MRP system is often used as a shared resource (like a landline telephone), it is important for locals to be able to quickly identify who is piloting the MRP so that it is not an anonymous lurker. While some local coworkers who have used the MRP for an extended period of time reported that they could infer the remote pilot just by hearing patterns in its driving noise, most people do not know who the pilot is until they check the front side of the MRP screen. Using either sound or visual feedback could let local coworkers identify the pilot from all angles. If one MRP is used by one dedicated pilot, then this is less of an issue. With earlier prototypes of the MRP system, when R5 was the one and only pilot, this was not an issue at all.

LIMITATIONS AND FUTURE WORK

A limitation of this work is the limited sample of participants; ongoing field studies will address this in future work, enabling comparisons across different types of organizations, individuals, MRP systems, use cases, etc.

Using Company A in this study may seem problematic, but only four people in the study actually worked on the Texai project; studying one's own prototype in different teams or divisions is not uncommon (e.g., [5, 9, 11, 18, 21]). There were several methodological limitations for this study. Unlike ethnographies, the current set of methods did not allow us to gain insight into the process of adaptation of the MRP or exactly how the social norms were forming over time. Unlike controlled experiments, these methods cannot identify causal relationships between variables. However, we believe this triangulation of methods (critical incident interviews that informed the design of surveys in combination with field observations) allowed us to observe the rich use of the system after novelty effects wore off, identifying key variables and hypotheses that follow-up controlled experiments can test.

CONCLUSION

We have explored the uses, interactions, and issues surrounding a mobile remote presence (MRP) system that was used by three different companies in their everyday work environments. People used the MRP system to engage in both formal and informal communication activities and used it in a variety of locations throughout the work spaces. By presenting the use cases, benefits, and issues, we hope that these findings will inspire and support the larger research community in identifying fruitful areas of research and design in the space of mobile remote presence.

ACKNOWLEDGEMENTS

Our thanks go to the Texai project team, Bianca Soto, Jodi Forlizzi, Sara Kiesler, and our volunteer participants for their support in making these studies possible.

REFERENCES

1. Dourish, P. & Bly, S. Portholes: Supporting awareness in a distributed work group. In *Proc. CHI*, ACM Press (1992), 541-547.
2. Egido, C. Videoconferencing as a technology to support group work. In *Proc. CSCW*, ACM Press (1988), 13-24.
3. Fish, R., S., Kraut, R. & Root, R.W. Evaluating video as a technology for informal communication. In *Proc. CHI*, ACM Press (1992), 37-48.
4. Flanagan, J. C. The critical incident technique. *Psychological Bulletin 51*, 4 (1954), 327-358.
5. Fish, R. S., Kraut, R. E., & Chalfonte, B. L. The VideoWindow system in informal communications. In *Proc. CSCW*, ACM Press (1990), 1-11.
6. Goffman, E. *The Presentation of Self in Everyday Life.* Anchor Books, New York, NY, 1959.
7. Hinds, P. J., & Mortensen, M. Understanding conflict in geographically distributed teams. *Organization Science 16*, 3 (2005), 290-307.
8. Kiesler, S., Siegel, J., & McGuire, T. W. Social psychological aspects of computer-mediated communication. *American Psychologist* (1984), 657-682.
9. Kraut, R. E., Fish, R., Root, R., & Chalfonte, B. Informal communication in organizations. In S. Oskamp & S. Scacapan (Eds.), *Human Reactions to Technology.* Sage, Beverly Hills, CA, 1990.
10. Kraut, R., Rice, R. E., Cool, C., & Fish, R. S. Varieties of social influence: The role of utility and norms in the success of a new communication medium. *Organization Science 9*, 4 (1998), 437-453.
11. Mantei, M. M., Baecker, R. M., Sellen, A. J., Buxton, W. A. S., Milligan, & T. Wellman, B. Experiences in the use of media space. In *Proc. CHI*, ACM Press (1991), 203-208.
12. McDonough, E. F., Kahn, K. B. & Barczaka, G. An investigation of the use of global, virtual, and collocated new product development teams. *Journal of Product Innovation Management 18*, 2 (2001). 110-120.
13. Nakanishi, H., Murakami, Y., Nogami, D., & Ishiguro, H. Minimum movement matters. In *Proc. CSCW*, ACM Press (2008), 303-312.
14. Nardi, B. A. Beyond bandwidth: Dimensions in connection in interpersonal communication. *CSCW 14* (2005), 91-130.
15. Nestel, D., Sains, P., Wetzel, C. M., Nolan, C,. Tay, A., Kneebone, R. L., & Darzi, A. W. Communication skills for mobile remote presence technology in clinical interactions. *Journal of Telemed Telecare 13*, 2 (2007), 100-104.
16. Olson, G., & Olson, J. Groupware and computer-supported cooperative work. In *Human-Computer Interaction: Design issues, solutions, and applications*, CRC Press (2009), 218-226.
17. Olson, G. M., & Olson, J. S. and Venolia, G. What still matters about distance? In *Proc. HCIC* (2009).
18. Paulos, E. and Canny, J. F. PRoP: Personal roving presence. In *Proc. CHI*, ACM Press (1998), 296-303.
19. Sakamoto, D., Kanda, T., Ono, T., Ishiguro, H., & Hagita, N. Android as a telecommunication medium with a human-like presence. In *Proc. HRI*, ACM Press (2007), 193-200.
20. Sellen, A. J. Remote conversations: Effects of mediating talk with technology. *Human-Computer Interaction 10* (1995), 401-444.
21. Venolia, G., Tang, J., Cervantes, R., Bly, S., Robertson, G. G., Lee, B. & Inkpen, K. Embodied Social Proxy. In *Proc. CHI*, ACM Press (2010), 1049-1058.
22. Whittaker, S., Frohlich, D. & Daly-Jones, O. Informal workplace communication. In *Proc. CHI*, ACM Press (1994), 131-137.
23. Willow Garage Texai Remote Presence System: http://www.willowgarage.com/pages/texai

Hands on Hitchcock: Embodied Reference to a Moving Scene

Paul Luff[1], Naomi Yamashita[2], Hideaki Kuzuoka[3], Christian Heath[1]

[1] King's College, London
150 Stamford Street, London, UK
<Paul.Luff@kcl.ac.uk, Christian.Heath@kcl.ac.uk

[2] NTT Communication Science Laboratories,
2-4 Hikaridai Seika-cho
Soraku-gun, Kyoto, Japan
<naomiy@acm.org>

[3] University of Tsukuba, Japan,
1-1-1 Tennoudai
Tsukuba, Ibaraki, Japan
<kuzuoka@iit.tsukuba.ac.jp>

ABSTRACT

In this paper we report on some experiments with a high fidelity media space, t-Room, an immersive system that presents full scale, real-time images of co-participants who are in similar spaces many miles apart. Although being designed to provide a coherent environment for interaction the system introduces a number of incongruities, both in time and space. Drawing on some quasi-naturalistic experiments, where the participants were required to analyse complex data, we consider how the participants manage these incongruities. We conclude by briefly discussing the resources people utilize to produce and recognize conduct in embodied spaces.

Author Keywords

Media spaces, interaction analysis, CSCW, embodied interaction.

ACM Classification Keywords

H5.3. Information interfaces and presentation (e.g., HCI): Computer-supported cooperative work. H4.3.

General Terms

Human Factors.

INTRODUCTION

Of the early efforts to develop systems to support collaborative work perhaps the most notable were attempts to design media spaces. In the 1980s and 1990s leading research laboratories and university departments introduced audio-visual infrastructures and networked computers to explore the potential for technologies to support everyday work activities in real-time. Typically these efforts were associated with office work between two people in two different locations [e.g. 10, 25]. Analysis of the conduct of participants in these spaces suggested that there were problems referring to features of the environment, notably paper documents; that the shapes of gestures, even simple pointing, were transformed when seen and produced through video; and that the technologies introduced a number of asymmetries into the interactional environment in which actions were performed [16]. Although a number of studies reported the advantages of long-term open video connections [4], these infrastructures tended not to persist for longer than the research projects that introduced them.

Recently there has been a renewed interest in media spaces [15]. On the one hand, higher broadband, high definition and high-fidelity systems like HP's Halo and Cisco's Telepresence offer capabilities that seem to overcome many of the problems found in early media spaces. For activities like meetings, what have become to be known as blended spaces [1], have been carefully designed to provide a coherent environment for interaction. On the other, new applications have emerged for high-quality, video-mediated environments. In the fields of e-science and cyber-infrastructures, technologies like the AccessGrid provide sophisticated support for scientists to collaborate when they are remote, either for distributed research meetings or when they are engaged in activities between laboratories [5]. And yet, it is unclear the extent to which these novel environments do resolve the interactional problems found in the early media spaces. There are few, if any, detailed studies of their use and despite providing resources to, say make a document available at both sites, such systems provide little support for integrating the use of other artefacts within the interaction. There are still ways in which the spaces are disjoint, so that even a simple action like pointing to an object in a remote domain can be problematic.

In this paper, we examine the use of one particular high definition, high fidelity system, t-Room. This is an experimental, immersive environment that allows participants to share and collaborate over remote electronically presented materials. However, rather than just the hands of two participants being projected in the remote domain [cf. 8, 21, 24] full 'embodiments' of several parties are visible. Participants can move around a small office-like space and change how they arrange themselves in the environment and this is reflected in a similar space at a remote site. The technology is designed to offer a symmetrical environment in which distributed actions are accomplished. We report on some quasi-naturalistic experiments that were developed to investigate the nature of multi=-party embodied interaction in this innovative space. They reveal that even a sophisticated space like t-Room subtly transforms how activities are displayed in a remote domain. We reveal how participants manage these transformations and discuss the implications of this analysis for the design of high-definition, high fidelity, video-based systems to support collaboration, our understanding of embodied interaction, and how we might support complex artefact-based interaction and collaboration with technology.

BACKGROUND

From the earliest media spaces to the most recent high fidelity distributed meeting spaces a common problem facing designers and users is how to integrate documents, whether these are paper or electronic, into the mediated environment. In early media spaces, even if augmented with a document camera, there were difficulties establishing a mutual orientation to details on a piece of paper [16]. It is unclear if these problems are resolved by more recent attempts at video-mediated interaction. It is not just a problem deciding where to display the document, but also how to present the conduct of the co-participants in and around the document. This may be due to assumptions about the activities these systems were designed to support. Early media spaces focused on supporting face-to-face interaction. Therefore, it is quite understandable that activities involving the use of artefacts were neglected. More recent innovations in telepresence have focused on 'business meetings' where any documents, such as PowerPoint slides, are typically displayed on monitors in fixed positions either above or below the images of the remote participants. Apart from the use of a computer cursor there are few resources to identify and refer to details of documents.

Such capabilities are important if richer forms of collaboration are required. Recent developments in e-research (or cyberinfrastructures) have drawn upon video mediated communications technologies provided by the AccessGrid to support scientists, social scientists and other researchers to collaborate in real-time over common materials [2, 7, 30]. Here again, there has been a challenge to integrate documents into these infrastructures. It is not just that the materials are visually complex, but researchers need to be able to refer to features in complex ways, not just pointing but also animating the images through their gestures and visual conduct [6, 20].

Efforts in CSCW and elsewhere to provide richer environments for interaction have revealed the difficulties of designing ways to support referential practices. Providing avatars in Collaborative Virtual Environments (CVEs) with ways of pointing to objects in the shared space fragmented the ecology in which gestures are produced and recognized [17]. Similar efforts of augmenting video-mediated interaction fractured the environment of interaction. Even with the addition of robots with pointing arms equipped with laser pointers, participants found it hard to tie the activities of the person pointing with the object being pointed at [23]. Some of these issues do seem to be resolved by systems that capture and present richer kinds of visual conduct [e.g. 18, 19]. By sophisticated video capture and projection techniques these have aimed to integrate real-time presentations of the hands of remote colleagues into the workspace and seem effective for supporting collaboration over detailed documents between two participants. Given the nature of the technology it is hard to envisage how such techniques could be scaled up when there is more than one party at each site.

One critical problem that has persisted through the early developments in media spaces, high fidelity conferencing systems and perhaps for most advanced collaborative technologies is that of reference. In video-mediated environments this could be glossed as the problem of presenting and understanding pointing. At first, this may appear a simple problem – the solution needing only for the person doing the pointing to be able to accurately identify the object being referred to. However, this neglects the rich variety of ways in which pointing can be achieved, as revealed by observing the work of the hands [21, 24]. The solution may then to be provide accurate representations of the hands, what could be considered as disembodied embodiments. Although providing greater fidelity such solutions can easily neglect how pointing is accomplished collaboratively [14]. Pointing and other referential gestures are produced in the light of the conduct of a c-participant, the 'pointer' monitoring how the other, the recipient or 'the pointee', (as Tallis describes them in a recent work on pointing) is, in the course of the pointing, making sense of the ongoing gesture [28]. Indeed, Tallis has not only argued that the complexity of this seemingly simple action reveals the distinctive nature of human collective consciousness, but also the ways in which humans are unique. Notwithstanding the grandiloquence of these claims it is perhaps understandable why trying to reproduce collaborative referential conduct has proved problematic for designers of co-operative systems.

In this paper, we will consider another attempt at developing a system, called t-Room, to provide a rich environment for collaboration. By presenting real-time, full size, embodiments of remote co-participants, t-Room can offer ways for those participants to produce a wide range of 'naturalistic' pointing actions, but also to produce these in the light of the conduct of their remote colleagues. Also, the scale of the system allows the participation of more than two parties and hence provides a resource for investigating the accomplishment of multi-party pointing.

IMMERSIVE MEDIA SPACES

T-Room is an experimental room-sized video conferencing system that aims to support group-to-group collaboration with multiple screens, cameras, and tables. Figure 1 shows the hardware design of the system. A single t-Room consists of eight modules (called Monoliths) arranged in a nonagon (one side left open to enter) with a shared worktable at the centre which consists of two LCD displays. Each Monolith is made up of a 65 inch LCD panel (resolution of 1920 by 1080) and a high-definition video (HDV) camera mounted on the panel. Each camera aims at a LCD panel standing at the opposite side of the room and captures a participant's whole upper body standing in front of the panel. A polarizing film is placed over each camera lens to capture only the views in front of the display and to eliminate infinite video feedback. The captured image is displayed on the remote t-Room's Monolith placed in the corresponding position (a mechanism similar to [29]). The configuration of video cameras and screens maintains spatial relationships between distant sites, and is designed to support consistent spatial referencing as well as a coherent environment in which to accomplish interaction. Because of this simplicity, however, an object located near the boundary of a Monolith is inevitably captured by more than one camera from various angles. Such a tendency increases as the object gets closer to the centre of the room, resulting in multiple object images being simultaneously displayed on multiple Monoliths.

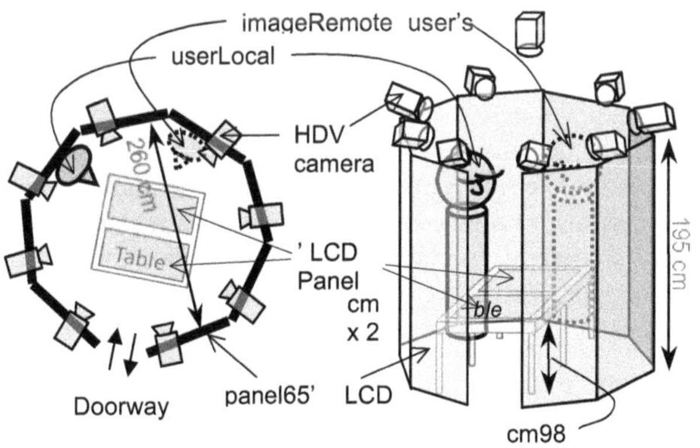

Figure 1. Hardware design of t-Room: Top-view (left) and Bird's eye-view (right)

Similar to the Monoliths, a central worktable consisting of two 40 inch LCD panels with two HDV cameras hung from the ceiling captures the activities above the table. Again, polarizing film is placed over each camera lens to eliminate video feedback. For verbal communication, we captured local sound with wireless microphones worn by each participant and played on the speakers in the remote t-Room. In this study the audio was not spatialized.

In addition to the providing views of the co-participants and the documents on the tabletop, t-Room allows data sharing across sites; distant people can share digital contents such as moving images displayed on one of the Monoliths. For this study a simple graphical user interface was developed on a notebook PC to allow participants in each t-Room to control what was presented at both sites. By storing the contents in each location ahead of time, people could view the same materials almost at the same time. Furthermore, by displaying the remote activities over the digital contents, the system allows people to collaborate over, around and about the digital materials.

T-Room in Kyoto, the two participants in Tokyo are presented on the left, they and one participant in Kyoto, are pointing at the 'shared image' . When pointing over the image the remote participant's conduct is overlaid.

The view from Tokyo at the same time (from a camera above and to the side of the shared screen)

EXPERIMENT & METHODS

Two identical t-Rooms were installed in the cities of Atsugi (near Tokyo) and Kyoto, which are approximately 150 miles apart, and connected by a gigabit network. We used the network to transmit HDV and audio data. The network delay for video and audio transmission between the two cities was around 0.3-0.4 and 0.2-0.3 seconds, respectively; video and audio were not synchronized.

To explore how people collaborated over and around digital materials using the system, we organized a series of quasi-naturalistic experiments that mimic the work practices in an e-science domain. 5 groups of four English–speaking subjects (13 male and 7 female) were recruited for this study and were paid for their participation. For each experiments two participants were located in Kyoto and two in Tokyo. The experiments were designed to examine:

- How participants coordinate their activities through the technology and the difficulties they faced.
- Whether participants could discuss details of the complex images, particularly how conduct is shaped with regard to moving images.
- How conduct (pointing) is designed for both co-located and remote recipients and whether and how the technology transforms this.

We developed a number of tasks for subjects to undertake in the experiment that would reflect the kind of complex activities required when supporting complex e-research activities: identifying objects from within complex scenes, locating features in dynamic images and reasoning about what is being viewed. As these needed to be generic and not require particular expertise we designed a task based around the analysis of clips from films of Alfred Hitchcock. The tasks the participants were asked to do ranged from trying to find Hitchcock within a clip, counting people who were looking at a particular feature and mapping out the environment in which a scene takes place. These problems were modeled on the kinds of activities that are undertaken by social scientists when analyzing video materials and included transcribing vocal and visual conduct, mapping out gaze direction and trying to discover the sequences of activities in fragments of data. To encourage discussion over the table, we also prepared some tasks using paper documents. The participants were given a 10 minute introduction to the technology and the task lasted around 90 minutes. There followed a short de-briefing to collect the comments of the participants about the use of the system.

We collected materials from 6 cameras (3 from each t-Room). Our analysis draws on conversation analysis and recent studies of multi-modal interaction. In this respect our concern is with the emergent and sequential character of practical action and the practices in and through which participants collaboratively accomplish particular activities, in this case pointing and reference. The fragments presented here are selected in order to provide a sense of some of the issues and complexities that arise in these brief moments of concerted action. In this paper we focus on the activities of the participants that arose when they were exploring and examining the moving images.

POINTING FOR MULTIPLE PARTICIPANTS

The tasks did seem to provide all four participants with the opportunity to engage in collaboratively finding objects and identifying features in the moving images. When a participant did locate a feature they would typically point to it on the central screen, both to their colleagues at the remote site and to their co-present, co-participant. In the following fragment, the participants are trying to find Hitchcock in the party scene from the film *Notorious*. Alex (A), in Tokyo, has made one suggestion which has been rejected. Now Fernando (F), in Kyoto, notices a figure who looks like Hitchcock and points to him on the screen to his right.

Fragment 1 (Clip 8)

F: The- <u>the</u>re there
(0.3)
M: okay that is him.
F: is that him↑
(1.2)
A: Yeah.

As a bald man appears on the screen Fernando, who is controlling the playback utters 'the- there there' and moves towards the screen. As he does this he holds his pointing towards the screen, even as the shot changes.

Mary Ken Fernando
Alex (obscured)

F: <u>the</u>re — <u>the</u>re there
M: okay

Fernando turns to his co-participants in Tokyo, Alex and Ken (K), and seems to get some acknowledgement from them (both nod, Ken also points to the screen and Alex says 'yeah') and also from Mary (M) who is standing to his right in Kyoto.

Fernando then goes on to discuss whether the man he has pointed to is indeed Hitchcock. Fernando's conduct, a simple pointing to the screen, secures engagement from all three co-participants. He identifies a feature for his colleagues, they seem to recognize what is being pointed at and Fernando monitors that they have located that feature. This provides a foundation for quite a long discussion about whether this is or is not the same man as one they have previously rejected. However, Fernando's conduct is produced in distinct ways for each participant. Once he has moved towards the screen he turns towards Alex, keeping his hand held out and asking 'is that him?', only dropping it when Alex nods and says 'yeah'. As Fernando moves back to where he can operate the playback he turns briefly to Ken, who now appears oriented to the film, smiling at the screen. Although she is in the same (t-) room, Fernando does not orient directly to Mary. Fernando, therefore, distinguishes the recipients of his conduct, securing different qualities of agreement from each.

T-Room, in quite subtle ways, allows participants to shape the 'production format' of their conduct, segmenting the 'audience' into principal and ratified recipient(s) [cf. 12]. This can be accomplished through the articulation of a turn of talk and the production of what seems a simple pointing action. It is also done through the configuration of the body. Fernando moves close to the screen and holds his arm whilst oriented primarily to Alex (but also to Ken). He then holds this pointing, monitoring their response. When this is secured he withdraws his hand. The accomplishment of the point relies on the co-participation of his colleagues. In this case, the recipients respond in distinct ways. Mary seems sensitive to this and from her position on the left turns towards the images of Ken and Alex and then explicitly says while pointing at them 'They're in agreement↑ (0.3) Right'.

Mary turning to screens behind her

M: They're in agreement↑ Right.

Considering the activity as a simple point that merely identifies a referent for a co-participant, glosses over the collaborative nature of the conduct. Moreover there are other interesting features of its production. First, as Fernando is pointing to a moving image the actual 'referent' of his point disappears almost as his gesture reaches its full extent. Fernando seems to adjust his pointing in the light of the changing image, pulling his finger in whilst still holding his hand out to the place where the feature appeared. This still secures a response from Alex. Second, even given the fast connection speed there are slight delays between the production of the conduct at one site and its appearance on the other, further weakening the ties between the pointer and the object he is pointing at. Third, the environment of action is also subtly transformed. In t-Room there are positions where a remote participant can appear to be looking at you even though he or she is looking at your colleague who is in the same space. This may account for Ken's nodding when Fernando seems to be addressing Alex. More noticeably, when Mary turns behind her to look at Alex and Ken in Tokyo, her own image is not visible to them, as her image (for them) is behind them.

Kyoto

Mary turning towards Alex who appears behind her

Tokyo

Mary turning to Alex, appearing behind him

T-Room offers high fidelity representations, embodiments, of the participants in an environment where participants have a great deal of choice about how they can position themselves and shape their own conduct. Even so the technology transforms how that conduct appears at the remote site in some subtle (and some not so subtle) ways. Nevertheless, it is curious that throughout the tasks the participants manage to recover an appropriate sense of their colleague's actions. Indeed, they did not report problems when asked afterwards about their impressions of the system or anything they noticed as strange, and during the tasks they made very few explicit requests to clarify another's conduct. In the next sections we will consider how the participants seemed to produce and make sense of each other's conduct in this multiparty environment.

RE-PRODUCING A POINT

As the resources the participants have in t-Room are in some ways symmetrical, it is often the case that participants identify the same feature at the same, or close to the same, time. As in the following fragment where the participants are trying to find Hitchcock in a street scene. Soon after the image fades in, both Andrew in Tokyo and Helen in Kyoto seem to spot Hitchcock in the centre of the image, standing on the pavement by a post box.

Fragment 2 (clip 56)

A: Yeah Right (0.2) there STOP:
(0.6)
H: ah him
F: uh huh
A: (.) right (.) up (.) No here let me (scoot around) from you (Brian) that guy right there exactly↑
(0.2)
A: that's got to be him
H: okay alright we have finished the clip and could not find anyone else

As Hitchcock appears, Andrew who is standing furthest from the screen points to a man in a black coat. He leans across his colleague Brian, stretching almost as far as he can go. As he says 'stop'. Brian, who has been writing some notes looks to the screen where Andrew is pointing.

Tokyo
Andrew Brian Helen Francis
(Obscured) (out of frame)

A: there

STOP: can you stop it

Andrew's 'stop' is for Francis in Kyoto who is operating the playback controls and Andrew's conduct seems to get both Francis and Helen to look at the screen and find who he is referring to. Indeed, as Helen who is closer to the screen, turns, her eyes open wide and her mouth opens, as if in surprise at identifying Hitchcock. She goes on to point herself to the man in black, saying 'ah him'.

By holding his point to the screen for nearly three seconds, Andrew gets all of his colleagues, both in Tokyo and Kyoto, to orient to the screen and identify what he is pointing at. Helen also produces a point to the screen. However, there seems to some problem with the precise location to where Helen is pointing. Andrew after suggesting that the location Helen is pointing to is problematic ('right up no'), actually goes on to walk around behind Brian and almost touch the screen when he points at the figure again.

A: right up no, let me (scoot around) from you (Brian) that guy right there exactly↑

As Andrew reproduces his gesture, Helen also points again. They both now move their fingers up and down and around the same figure on the screen. This time they seem to agree that they have found their man. The difficulties, for Andrew, of his earlier pointing seem to be due to the way that his pointing gestures have appeared in the different domains. There are slight differences in how they appear to the pointer in the local domain and the pointee(s) in the remote one.

For Helen (bottom) her gesture in the light of Andrew's which is away from the screen, seems to more precisely identify the object, and yet, for Andrew (top) Helen's finger seems a little lower and is directed towards a car that is moving across the scene; for Andrew, it is more directed towards the driver. Both participants seem to be sensitive to a problem in some way: Andrew goes on to more precisely identify the person he has found, reformulating his own prior pointing and also implicitly addressing problems he sees with Helen's gesture. On the other hand, Helen goes on to reformulate her own prior conduct, also moving closer to the screen and circling around the man on the screen. Although this appears slightly lower to the participants in Tokyo it does serve to unambiguously identify the object.

T-Room by careful calibration and integration of digital images allows participants' conduct to appear to another participant hundreds of miles away apparently over the same object on a common screen. For most purposes, where the object in question can be disambiguated through talk and the general orientation of a look or body movement, this is adequate. But when there are possible alternatives more precision is required. Even for what seems like a simple task, participants do sometimes require quite detailed precision in the production of their visible conduct, and are very sensitive to how this is being oriented to by a colleague. Systems like t-Room, compared to the early media spaces and conventional forms of video-conferencing, offer many more and richer resources for allowing participants to identify objects in a remote domain, and perhaps more importantly, they do seem to support seeing others' conduct with respect to those objects. However, there still are asymmetries in how one's conduct appears to another. Although they may not be aware of the details of these, of how their conduct appears to another, participants are aware when these problems arise and take remedial action, like moving closer and repeating a point to an object, to resolve the ensuing difficulties. In t-Room such common sense solutions help resolve some of the problems of calibration. Although reproducing a point closer to the screen may not necessarily make it clearer, indeed it may exacerbate the problem, it does allow the pointer to re-produce the gesture in the light of that of the remote colleague. The symmetrical resources offered by the system allow participants not only to self repair and to repair the conduct of a colleague but also to monitor how the other orients to that corrective work. The selfsame resources for producing and recognising action are used to repair and resolve problems that seem to arise.

CO-PRODUCING A POINT

Most of the activities the participants were set involved quite complex problems, including mapping out what was happening in a clip, transcribing the talk in a scene and even analyzing the gaze direction and visual conduct of the characters in the scene. To solve these a division of labour frequently emerged between the participants. In the following fragment the participants are trying to work out how many people in a restaurant notice that an argument is occurring between the main protagonists. The scene is complex, full of people, and also involves a pan as the principal characters move across the room. Therefore, various objects move in and out of view. To address these complications the participants in the experiment have taken on different interrelated activities. Adam in Kyoto is operating the playback controls and keeping count, Michael furthest from the screen in Tokyo is looking out for candidates which Jenny in Tokyo and John in Kyoto, take turns to point out. Jenny and John are both closer to the screen and can also look out for anyone the others might have missed. They are coming to the end of the scene, and John has just pointed to a sixteenth woman, when Michael identifies one more person John seems to have missed, 'and the guy behind her', and accompanies these with a point to the screen.

View of Tokyo site from above

Michael Jenny John Adam
M: and the guy behind her (partly out of shot)

However, because of the way it is displayed through t-Room, in Kyoto, this conduct is hardly noticeable to John.

View of Kyoto site from above screen

John Adam Michael
M: and the guy behind her

For Michael (and Jenny) in Tokyo, Michael's pointing reaches out towards the screen, but for John and Adam not only is Michael's conduct fractured by the border between the Monoliths, it is presented behind them and rendered in two dimensions. John remains looking at the screen. Jenny who has both seen Michael's gesture and can assess John's response, points to the screen.

Tokyo

Michael Jenny John

John then nods, and Adam says 'that guy there, seventeen'. The participants thus not only distribute the work of solving the task between the two sites, but also can draw on the resources available to resolve problems due to the nature of the way images are presented in t-Room. The participants have no explicit resources for seeing how their own conduct is being presented in the remote domain. They can see how the images of their remote colleagues appear and perhaps draw on this to design their own conduct, but the high fidelity and the life-size nature of the images gives few clues to the ways in which these images have been subtly transformed. Rather, the participants seem to draw on the ability to continuously monitor the responses of a co-participant to their own actions, and if necessary repair or reformulate any problems as they emerge. They also do this in the light of the responses of the other participants. So, in the case above, Jenny not only displays a sensitivity to both John's and Adam's apparent failure to respond, withdrawing her hand when John reorients to the place she is pointing. It was thus not uncommon to see a form of extended collaborative pointing, where a co-present colleague nearest the screen reproduces a point just made by a colleague. The pointing, or more accurately the identification of the object, was co-produced by more than one participant in the light of the conduct of the remote participants many miles away.

REVEALING THE QUALITIES OF A OBJECT: ANIMATING FEATURES

By offering the capability to present an image of the entire upper body t-Room allows participants to produce a variety of gestures to animate features of the objects they are describing. These can often accompany quite complex descriptions of what they see on the screen. In the following fragment, participants are trying to map out the room in the famous auction scene from *North by Northwest*. They have to locate where the principal characters are positioned during the action. To help them they have an outline plan of the room on the desks in front of them. Alex, in Tokyo, suggests that Cary Grant is sitting in the centre of the room. In order to find out exactly where this is Alex proposes matching the number of rows of seats visible in the scene with those on the paper plan. Ken, his colleague in Tokyo, and him do so, counting out aloud, with Ken who is closer to the screen animates the counting by pointing to the screen as they do so. Ken's conduct is shaped towards Fernando in Kyoto, who responds with a concern about this suggestion.

Fragment 4 (Clip 27)

F: But he's he's looking very:: like straight , forward no↑
(0.8)
F: So he's not here in the in the middle he's probably here no?
(1.5)
F: what do you think?
M: there's an aisle, right↑ on the side here ( )
(0.2)
F: ya ther- there's an aisle here (1.7) but he (0.2) he's (2.1) if he would be here in the middle his face would be (0.8)
F: a lot more (.) tilted than (3.0) what do you guys think?

As he say's 'But he's he's' Fernando moves closer to the screen and then gestures over the image whilst suggesting they use where Cary Grant is looking to help locate where the actor is sitting (i.e. in relation to the auctioneer's rostrum which Grant is looking at).

Fernando's gestures animate the gaze direction of the actor, first pointing at the actor and then with an open hand moving it back (whilst saying 'like straight') and

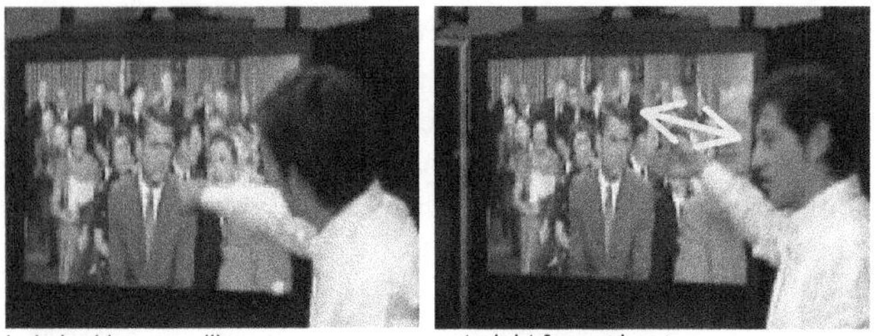

he's looking very like straight forward no↑

forth (whilst saying 'forward'). As he does this he looks towards Ken and Alex in Tokyo. Although oriented towards Fernando and the screen he is gesturing over, they offer little in the way of response to Fernando's query. Fernando tries again, this time also pointing to the plan on the desk with his left hand and looking directly at the pair in Tokyo. Alex and Ken both look between page and screen but still offer no response. After he tries a third time, explicitly asking what they think, Mary also contributes and gestures to show the location of an aisle both on the screen and on paper. Fernando tries again, this time using his pen. Whilst he points to the centre of the worksheet with his left hand, Fernando says 'if he would be here in the middle his face will be a lot more tilted', he animates the direction of gaze as if the actor was in Ken and Alex's suggested position. Fernando moves his pen in an arc towards the right and then towards Alex and Ken, tilting his pen up and down.

Alex then looks down to the page in front of him and goes on to discuss with Ken, the problem Fernando has raised, that the two ways of determining the actor's position produce inconsistent results. The colleagues in both sites together go onto to review the fragment to see if there is a way of resolving the problem.

In this fragment the four participants are engaged in a very complex form of reasoning. They are attempting to assemble a coherent account from the various images they can jointly see, drawing upon the perspectives of those characters that appear in the images. This kind of argument would be familiar to researchers who analyse naturalistic video recordings of social interaction in data sessions [30]. It also resonates with the practices of researchers working with complex visual data [6, 13]. Researchers when working with complex data juxtapose details of images with other resources such as representations on paper, utilise other material artefacts like pens and pencils to make more apparent particular details of what is visible, and produce complex animated gestures to reveal aspects they consider significant, even if these features may not be directly available from the image [6]. Through the 'embodiments'. t-Room provides participants with a range of ways of animating an image or an argument. However it is not just that the conduct of a co-participant is re-produced in high fidelity or that most of the body appears visible [26], t-Room allows participants ways of relating their conduct to features of the environment, in the light of the orientation of their co-participants. Fernando can monitor the ongoing engagement of his co-participant(s) and reshape his own conduct in the light of this, reformulating his explanation and drawing upon other kinds of resources. It is not just the ability to reproduce an embodiment that is critical but also to provide a coherent relationship between that embodiment, its environment and the contributions of others.

T-Room transforms the environment of action in other ways. As alluded to earlier the configuration of the Monoliths means that participants, even in the same space, can have a different sense of their remote participants. At the same time the remote party may appear to be looking at you, whilst they are actually oriented to your colleague, the so-called 'Mona Lisa' effect.

Tokyo: from behind the screen *Fernando appears to look at Ken*

Tokyo: From in front of screen *Fernando appears to look at Alex*

Moreover, transmission delays often resulted in the images of a remote participant appearing some time (up to ½ a second) after it was produced. At times this means that an action by a remote party, that was produced prior to one's own conduct, actually appears to be responsive to it, with the reverse happening at the other site. So, in effect, parties at both sites in the interaction can consider their own action as having initiated an activity with their colleagues seeming to respond appropriately. Curiously, neither party would comment on this nor did this seem to evoke the parties to try and repair any misunderstanding. T-Room transforms both the spatial and the temporal environment in which interactions are accomplished. In prior studies the timing of conduct in video-mediated interaction [27] and the spatial configuration [11] have seemed to be critical and have led to sophisticated solutions to try and resolve them [e.g. 31]. Faster communication speeds have no doubt overcome some of the problems caused by delays and higher resolution images given greater access to a remote environment, but one might still expect that, particularly for tasks that require the precise location of features at the right time, these transformations would be problematic. Rather, participants seem to make sense of their co-participant's activities and implicitly self correct their own ongoing conduct. The high fidelity of the system is therefore more essential in providing support for the moment-to-moment management of situated conduct.

DISCUSSION

The participants in the experiments were given complex tasks to perform. They had to find, identify and describe objects and features that were small, partly obscured and often indistinguishable from others in cluttered and dynamic scenes. T-Room seemed to support them to do this. The technology is not based on the typical model for high definition, virtual 'meeting' spaces. Rather than being seated around a desk, participants can move around. Rather than one person presenting materials through a display that is distinct from the rest of the space, the shared display is integrated into the interactional environment. Rather than having a simple mechanism for pointing and reference, the aim is to be able to be provide a richer range of resources: the whole body can be used to refer to and animate the features one is talking about. Such resources would seem critical when participants need to engage in work with images and discuss and reason about the details of common artefacts.

However, even when developing a space that aims to replicate the ways in which visual conduct is produced and recognized in co-present settings, certain, seemingly minor, transformations are introduced when the distributed technology is designed. These seem to introduce boundaries in the spaces for interaction and fragment how an activity is produced from how it is seen at the remote site. In t-Room these differences do seem to be quite minor. There is a very slight delay between the production and receipt of an image, the flat orientation of the Monoliths mean not only that there are boundaries between the screens but slight discontinuities within the space and as the screens can only present in two dimensions, the shape and impact of gestures and other forms of visual conduct are transformed when seen in the remote location. Although each of these would seem subtle transformations, studies of social interaction would suggest that they should be critical and problematic for participants. The timely production of gestures and visual conduct and the fine details of how they are produced for a participant from moment-to-moment have been a recurrent concern in studies of naturalistic conduct [14]. However, in t-Room the participants do not seem to face many difficulties overcoming the effects of these transformations to the interactional space: they rarely explicitly refer to the discontinuities in the timing and shape of another's conduct and did not report noticing these when asked afterwards about the system. Indeed, when certain aspects of the conduct were demonstrated to them afterwards many found it just as curious. The participants seemed to manage to resolve these problems in the course of the production of their activities. In future work we plan to undertake further experiments to explore when the delays and further alterations to the spatial configurations become problematic in multi-party interaction.

In a range of systems researchers have explored a variety of ways of supporting the ability to refer to objects in a remote environment. This may be through the use of laser pointers, robotic arms or avatars that can gesture in CVEs [17, 22]. Studies of these techniques have revealed how it is problematic for participants to refer to objects, or at least for others to recover what is being pointed at [17, 23]. These technologies seem to fracture and fragment the environment, disrupting the sequential and emergent ways in which pointing and related kinds of visual conduct emerge. Where this seems to be preserved, say when other displays provide resources not only to see the trajectory of the conduct but to monitor how a co-participant is attentive to that trajectory, a more coherent environment of action seems to emerge [24]. T-Room provides such an environment: a co-participant can see the initiation of a gesture, gear their own conduct accordingly and the person accomplishing that gesture can also monitor the co-participants' ongoing assessment to their own conduct. The 'embodiments' provide the 'feedback' necessary to be able to readjust, reformulate and even repair how an action is produced in this distributed environment. Further forms of feedback, like vanity monitors, reproductions of their own images or conduct or mere pointers seem unnecessary, and potentially disruptive. Instead participants draw on the ongoing response of a colleague to reformulate and transform action – even in its course. However, some way of preserving aspects of this referential work, for example by being able to mark up the image being referred to [cf. 7] so that annotations are preserved might serve as a useful additional resource for further discussion and collaboration.

It should be noted that these abilities to resolve referential problems are not just because life sized-embodiments are presented in real-time, but because these embodiments are embedded within the environment of action. It is the embeddedness of the action, not the embodiment of the actor, that is critical. In future work although we intend to develop more 'lightweight' approaches, using fewer (and perhaps smaller) screens for example, to assess the extent to which embeddedness can be supported with less emphasis placed on representing embodiments.

The issues arising from this study seem to resonate with debates concerning the early analysis of interaction in media spaces. The asymmetries in interaction in these early systems did seem to engender transformations in conduct of the participants in these spaces. Participants had problems referring to common objects and talk and visual conduct did seem to be disrupted. Practical matters like assessing the gaze direction of a co-participant and accessing the materials in the remote domain were problematic [16]. And yet it was argued that over time many of these interactional problems could be resolved and new practices would emerge that enabled participants to interact with each other more easily [3]. Indeed, it did seem that in some cases, ways of looking through the system were transformed and the technology could be made at home in the world. The t-Room experiments cast these early experiences in a new light. The participants did seem to manage the incongruities in the environment, and yet did so through the course of their own actions, almost as a 'problem' emerged they developed ways of resolving it. It seems rather than gradually develop a range of solutions over time, the participants draw on assumptions about their and their colleague's standpoints to resolve the interactional incongruities they faced [cf. 9].

Although it seems like a simple action, pointing is a challenging activity to support when designing collaborative systems. Participants reveal in the course of a momentary action not only their relation to their own environment but also display a sensitivity to how another can see and understand that conduct, as if they themselves were in the other's place. It is perhaps understandable that despite over 20 years of technical development this remains a problem for collaborative system design. Efforts that fragment everyday conduct across distinct domains bring to light what we still need to understand about how people manage and co-ordinate actions in human interaction.

ACKNOWLEDGEMENTS

We would like to thank Keiji Hirata and other t-Room members for their support and Mai Okada for help in running the experiment.

REFERENCES

1. Broughton, M., et al. Being here: designing for distributed hands-on collaboration in blended interaction spaces. in *Proc of OZCHI 2009*. 73-80.
2. Buckingham Shum, S., et al., Memetic: An Infrastructure for Meeting Memory, in *Proc of Conf. Design of Cooperative Systems COOP 2006*: Carry-le-Rouet, France. 71-85
3. Dourish, P., Adler, A., Bellotti, V., & Henderson, Hgestures., Your Place or Mine? Learning from Long-Term Use of Video Communication. *CSCW Journal*, 1996. 5(1): p. 33-62.
4. Dourish, P. and V. Bellotti. Awareness and Coordination in Shared Workspaces. in *Proc of CSCW '92*. Toronto: 107-114.
5. Dutton, W.H. and P.W. Jeffreys, eds. *World Wide Research: reshaping the Sciences and Humanities*. 2010, MIT Press:.
6. Flor, G.de la., et al., The case of the disappearing ox: seeing through digital images to an analysis of ancient texts, in *Proc of CHI 2010*. Atlanta. 473-482
7. Fraser, M., et al., Remote Collaboration over Video Data: Towards Real-Time e-Social Science. *CSCW Journal*, 2006. 15(4): 257-279.
8. Fussell, S.R., et al., Gestures Over Video Streams to Support Remote Collaboration on Physical Tasks. *Human Computer Interaction*, 2004. 19: 273-309.
9. Garfinkel, H., A Conception of and Experiments with Trust as a Condition of Stable Concerted Actions in *Motivation and Social Interaction*, O.J. Harvey, Ed. 1963, Ronald Press.
10. Gaver, W.W., et al. Realizing a video environment: EuroPARC's RAVE system. in *Proc of CHI 92*. Monterey, CA: 27-35.
11. Gaver, W.W., G. Smets, and K. Overbeeke. A Virtual Window on media space. in *Proc of CHI '95*. 1995: 257-264.
12. Goffman, E., *Forms of Talk*. 1981, Oxford: Blackwell.
13. Goodwin, C., Seeing in Depth. *Social Studies of Science*, 1995. 25(2): 237-274.
14. Goodwin, C., Pointing as a Situated Practice, in *Pointing: Where Language, Culture and Cognition Meet*, S. Kita, Editor. 2003, Lawrence Erlbaum: Mahwah, NJ. 217-41.
15. Harrison, S., ed. *Media Space 20 + Years of Mediated Life* 2009, Springer-Verlag: London.
16. Heath, C.C. and P. Luff. Disembodied Conduct: Communication through Video in a Multi-Media Office Environment. in *Proc of CHI '91*. New Orleans: 99-103.
17. Hindmarsh, J., et al. Fragmented Interaction: Establishing mutual orientation in virtual environments. in *Proc CSCW'98*. Seattle, WA: 217-226.
18. Ishii, H. TeamWorkStation: Towards a Seamless Shared Workspace. in *Proc of CSCW '90*. Los Angeles: 13-26.
19. Ishii, H., M. Kobayashi, and J. Grudin. Integration of Inter-Personal Space and Shared Workspace: Clearboard Design and Experiments. in *Proc of CSCW 92*. Toronto: 33-42.
20. Jirotka, M., et al., Collaboration and Trust in Healthcare Innovation: The eDiaMoND Case Study. *CSCW Journal*, 2005. 14 (4) 369-398.
21. Kirk, D., T. Rodden, and A. Crabtree, Ways of the hand, in *Proc of ECSCW 2005*: Paris 1-21.
22. Kuzuoka, H., et al. GestureMan: A Mobile Robot that Embodies a Remote Instructor's Actions. in *Proc of CSCW 2000*. Philadelphia PA: 155-162.
23. Luff, P., et al., Fractured ecologies: creating environments for collaboration. *HCI Journal*, 2003. 18(1-2): 51-84.
24. Luff, P., et al. Handling Documents and Discriminating Objects in Hybrid Spaces in *Proc of CHI 2006*. Montreal 561–570.
25. Mantei, M., et al. Experiences in the Use of a Media Space. in *Proc of CHI '91*. New Orleans, Louisiana: 203-8.
26. Morikawa, O. and T. Maesako. HyperMirror: Toward pleasant-to-use video mediated communication system. in *Proc of CSCW'98*. Seattle, WA: 149-159.
27. Ruhleder, K. and B. Jordan, Co-Constructing Non-Mutual Realities: Delay-Generated Trouble in Distributed Interaction. *CSCW Journal*, 2001. 10(1): p. 113-138.
28. Tallis, R., *Michelangelo's Finger: An Exploration of Everyday Transcendence* 2010, London: Atlantic Books.
29. Tang, J.C. and S.L. Minneman, VideoDraw: A Video Interface for Collaborative Drawing. *ACM Transactions on Information Systems*, 1991. 9,(2): 170-184.
30. Tutt, D., et al. The Distributed Work of Local Action: Interaction amongst virtually collocated research teams. in *Proc of ECSCW 2007*: 199-218.
31. Vertegaal, R., et al. GAZE-2: Conveying Eye Contact in Group Video Conferencing Using Eye-Controlled Camera Direction. in *Proc of CHI 2003*. Ft. Lauderdale, Florida, USA: 521-528.3.

Exploring Camera Viewpoint Control Models for a Multi-Tasking Setting in Teleoperation

Dingyun Zhu[1, 2] **Tom Gedeon**[2] **Ken Taylor**[1]
[1]CSIRO ICT Centre, Acton, Canberra, ACT 0200, Australia
[2]School of Computer Science, College of Engineering and Computer Science, The Australian National University, Canberra, ACT 0200, Australia
dingyun.zhu@csiro.au tom.gedeon@anu.edu.au ken.taylor@csiro.au

ABSTRACT
Control of camera viewpoint plays a vital role in many teleoperation activities, as watching live video streams is still the fundamental way for operators to obtain situational awareness from remote environments. Motivated by a real-world industrial setting in mining teleoperation, we explore several possible solutions to resolve a common multi-tasking situation where an operator is required to control a robot and simultaneously perform remote camera operation. Conventional control interfaces are predominantly used in such teleoperation settings, but could overload an operator's hand-operation capability, and require frequent attention switches and thus could decrease productivity.

We report on an empirical user study in a model multi-tasking teleoperation setting where the user has a main task which requires their attention. We compare three different camera viewpoint control models: (1) dual manual control, (2) natural interaction (combining eye gaze and head motion) and (3) autonomous tracking. The results indicate the advantages of using the natural interaction model, while the manual control model performed the worst.

Author Keywords
Natural interaction, gaze tracking, head motion, remote camera control, autonomous tracking, dual manual control, multi-tasking setting, teleoperation, user evaluation.

ACM Classification Keywords
H5.2. Information interfaces and presentation (e.g., HCI): User Interfaces – evaluation/methodology, input devices and strategies, interaction styles.

General Terms: Experimentation, Human Factors.

INTRODUCTION
Being able to remove human beings or provide replaceable surrogates in hazardous or difficult working environments, teleoperation has been recognized as a critical strategy and applied in a wide variety of situations. Sample application areas include space exploration, robotic navigation or inspection, surveillance, underwater operation, search and rescue activities and so on. Figure 1 shows another typical sample case (rock breaking) in mining, where teleoperation may be able to effectively improve safety.

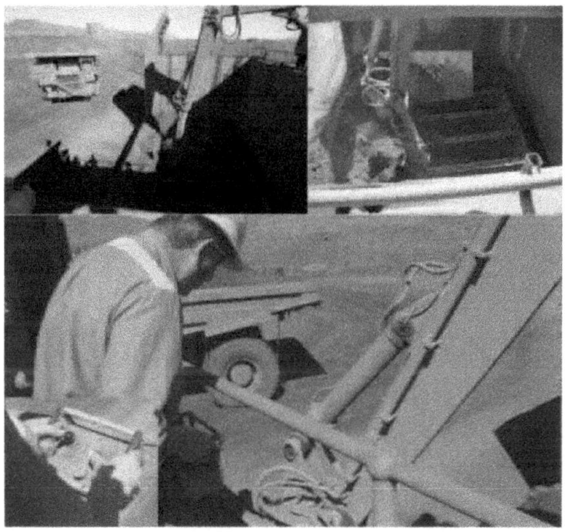

Figure 1. Rock breaking in mining.

As shown in Figure 1, a rock breaker is a giant manipulator arm with a large hydraulic hammer at the tip to break oversized rocks on the mine site. It is installed at a Run of Mine bin where a number of horizontal bars as a grizzly (top right of Figure 1) are fitted at the bottom to prevent oversized rocks from entering the crusher below. The actual rock breaking process is haul trucks dump their loads into the bin one by one at a certain time interval; in between an operator needs to break any oversized rocks stuck in the bin by controlling the rock breaker arm and firing the hammer at the tip.

Using normal line-of-sight operation (see the bottom part of Figure 1) requires the operator to stand at the platform around the bin and manipulate the arm via two joysticks on a two-handed industrial control box.

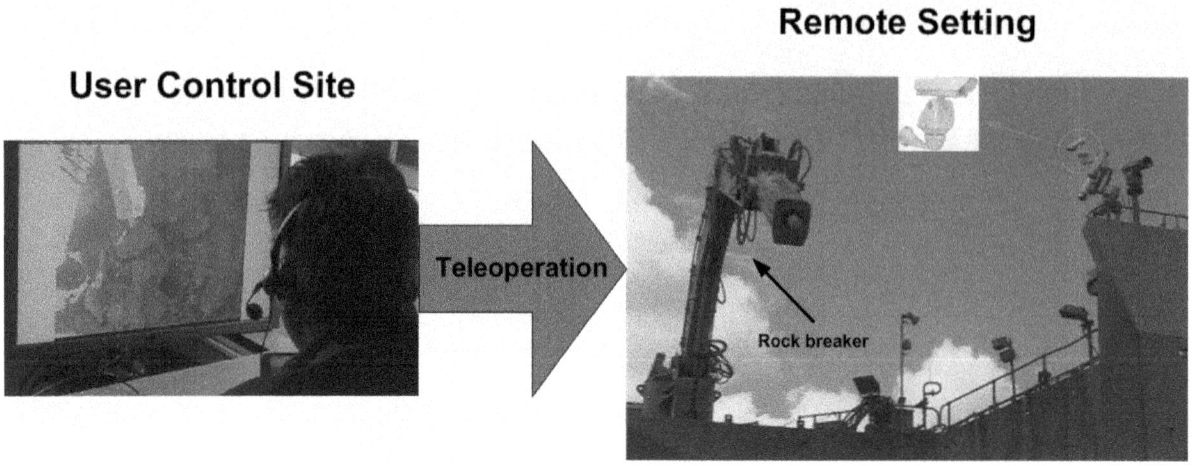

Figure 2. Teleoperation for rock breaking.

This process raises serious health and safety issues because of the harsh, dusty working condition in the mining environment and the risk of being close to the giant mining machinery.

The mining industry's long term plan is to teleoperate their mining operations [6], and achieve effective and safe remote control. Therefore, for the rock breaking process, a teleoperation system [6] has been developed to control the rock breaker arm at a long distance (over 1,000 kilometers), with a pan-tilt-zoom (PTZ) camera installed on one side of the bin as the basic visual feedback for the operator to accomplish the task (see Figure 2).

In this setting, camera operation becomes vital for the entire remote rock breaking process. The operator needs to explore locations of the oversized rocks in the bin by moving the remote camera (i.e., conducting pan and tilt functions), obtaining details of the target rock via the camera zoom-in view, then carefully positioning the tip on the rock and firing the hammer. The operational process must be effective and time-efficient as trucks arrive in a short time interval with limited time remaining for the operator to complete the rock breaking task for each truck load.

This turns out to be a typical multi-tasking situation that an operator has multiple devices to operate simultaneously. Such multi-tasking situations are quite common and general in teleoperation, as observations indicate that directly controlling a robot while watching a video feed from the remote camera(s) still remains the most common interaction form in teleoperation [7]. Even though autonomous and semiautonomous robotic systems and applications have been increasingly developed and used, such basic settings with remote manual operations are still regarded as an important default mode [2] to involve human observation, intervention and supervision as integral roles [14].

In this research, we focus on this multi-tasking problem in a situation where an operator is conducting remote camera operation while carrying out other teleoperation tasks simultaneously. Apart from considering conventional dual control interface as an optimized manual model, we explore two alternative remote camera control models: one by importing human eye gaze and head motion as natural interaction for remote viewpoint control, the other by using an autonomous tracking approach to completely automate the remote camera. By conducting a model multi-tasking teleoperation user study comparing these three different camera viewpoint control models, we demonstrate and discuss their advantages and disadvantages. The aim is to explore potential solutions for this common multi-tasking problem in teleoperation.

RELATED WORK

User interface issues have significant impacts on human performance in teleoperation [2]. As suggested in [7], well-performing teleoperation interfaces must be as efficient and as capable as possible, providing solutions and tools to help perceive remote environments, make decisions and generate commands. They are expected to be able to maximize information transfer while minimizing an operator's workload both physically and cognitively. Also, a good interface should be designed to minimize user training or to be user adaptive.

Conventional user interfaces such as joysticks, switches, buttons and wheels are still the major control elements in teleoperation [10], though various types of other interfaces have been developed to provide immersive feedback in different teleoperation fields, for instance, haptic inputs [9], gesture based interfaces [13] and voice interfaces [5]. However, most of these approaches focus on the direct control of the remote robot or machine because it is the primary task for the operator, rather than solutions for the multi-tasking process which includes both remote camera operation and robot control.

Especially for remote camera control, several alternative methods have been proposed, such as using a set of specific hand gestures [3] or a Wii remote with infrared sensors [8]. They may provide more interactive camera operation models, but obviously are not an effective solution for the multi-control problem since they require an operator to use their hands and pay attention to the extra device control.

Chen et al. [2] recommended that multi-model interfaces provide a large range of interactions to improve traditional teleoperation control interfaces. Introducing additional modalities can supplement or augment an operator's visual and control channels when heavily loaded. This suggestion has led to research developments not only in teleoperation, but also in many similar fields with standard user control or interaction settings, such as video gaming, virtual reality (VR) interactions.

Particularly for the multi-tasking situation, many researchers have investigated similar problems (e.g. manual input is not effective or both of the user's hands are busy) with the intention of developing more intuitive control or interaction models that use alternative modalities other than hands. Using natural interaction based interfaces allow people to interact with technologies, applications and systems as they are used to in everyday life [28]. In [29], Wang et al. explore head motion as an augmented input in video games to enhance presence, role-playing and user control. They integrated head tracking in company with conventional gamepad control for a first-person-shooter (FPS) game to control the user's viewpoint in several more "realistic" ways, such as peeking and dodging. Yamaguchi et al. [30] proposed using head movements to control a PTZ camera for online video chat. More relevantly, Zhu et al. [33] introduced two types of head tracking techniques for remote camera control in order to solve the multi-control problem in teleoperation settings. From their user study, they showed that head motion control was able to provide a comparable performance to the traditional keyboard control.

Similarly, human eye gaze has been recognized as an augmented input medium or control modality in *advanced user interfaces* [16]. In traditional pointing, Zhai et al. [32] introduced the MAGIC technique which firstly warps the cursor to the vicinity of the target when the user looks at it. Then the user can finish the target selection by another pointing device (e.g. mouse) manually. Another prototype system: *EyePoint* developed by Kumar et al. [17] incorporates gaze input with keyboard triggers using a fluid look-press-look-release action. As summarized in [32], using gaze input can be an effective approach for situations in which the user's hand input is not appropriate, such as disabled users (quadriplegic) or continuously occupied with other tasks (such as the multi-tasking situation in our example of the remote rock breaking process).

Numerous approaches and applications have been developed using gaze inputs in company with hand controls or in situations that the hand control is not possible, for example, aiming and shooting in FPS [15], intelligent tour planning (*iTourist* [22]), controlling a wheelchair for disabled users [31] and driving a robotic vehicle [31]. As to the hands-busy problem in teleoperation, Zhu et al. [34] recently conducted another user study comparing use of gaze tracking, head tracking and joystick for remote camera control. They found gaze tracking significantly outperformed the other two camera control models. Compared to head tracking, it is less physical movement, more efficient and almost fatigue free [23].

Beyond human-involved camera viewpoint control, there has been a long research track for developing autonomous camera operation approaches in computer vision and robotics. Cohen and Medioni [4] introduced a method to automatically detect and track moving objects using a PTZ camera for video surveillance. *FLYSPEC* [19]: another multi-user video camera system integrates manual and fully automatic control, which significantly assists users in remote inspection task. Obviously, fully automating cameras could reduce human control load for the operation process. We include an autonomous tracking model in our user study below.

CAMERA CONTROL MODELS CONSIDERED

After a substantial amount of observation on the mine site, discussions with real operators and analysis of the user requirements, we propose three camera viewpoint control models as potential solutions for this multi-tasking problem.

Dual Manual Control – Conventional Interface

The first model is based on existing conventional manual control interfaces. The interface was selected to meet the user control requirements of this teleoperation process:

1. Both the robot arm and the remote camera should be operated by a single user control interface, i.e. dual manual control.
2. The control interface should be suitable for standard desktop use rather than the original two-handed industrial control box with a large size, which is not convenient for desktop based teleoperation settings.
3. The control configuration or mapping of the interface should be easy for the user to adapt to.
4. The control interface should be easy to obtain and maintain, also robust, portable and easy to complete integration and implementation for both the robot arm device and the remote camera.

We decided to use a standard Logitech Dual Action Gamepad [20], which satisfies all the requirements we had for the setting.

The manual control mapping for both devices is illustrated in Figure 3. The two thumb joysticks on the gamepad are used to control the robot arm. The left joystick moves the arm forward, backward and sideways, the right joystick controls the arm vertically, lifting up and down. The pan and tilt functions for the remote camera are operated by the four buttons on the right part of the gamepad, the Left and Right buttons for panning, the Up and Down buttons for tilting. Additionally, the two buttons on the front side of the gamepad are used to control zooming and the one below the "zoom out" button on the right side is used as a "fire" button to trigger the hammer.

Figure 3. Dual manual control mapping for both robot arm and remote camera.

Despite the complexity of this description these mappings are easy and similar to the computer game control. Using this gamepad allows us to optimize the manual control of two separate devices with a simple control mapping, which minimizes the transferring time of switching hand operations between different interfaces. Furthermore, it uses standard USB connection and it is a low cost, very sophisticated interface which has been widely deployed.

Natural Interaction – Eye Gaze + Head Motion

The natural interaction model combines both eye gaze and head motion to control a PTZ camera. The camera pan and tilt control are based on the user's current fixation coordinates on the screen. Figure 4 shows the details of the control.

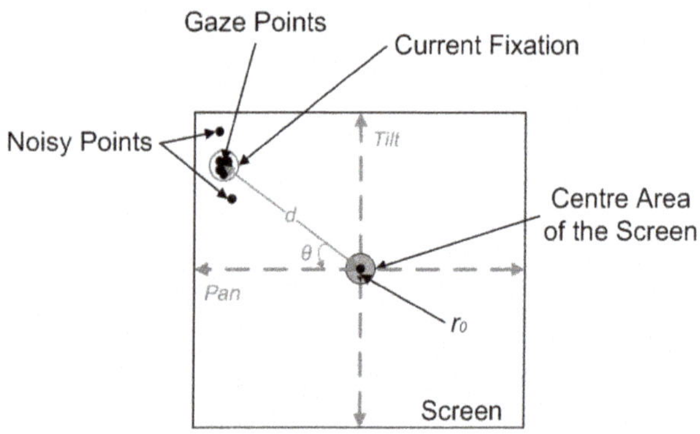

Figure 4. Eye gaze for camera pan and tilt control.

Since the raw gaze data is noisy and the camera is not able to move as fast as the user's gaze, a modified version of the *Velocity-Threshold Identification* fixation detection algorithm [24] is used to filter the raw gaze points into fixations. This method is straightforward to implement, runs very efficiently, and can easily run in real time.

The coordinate of the current fixation is used to calculate the distance between the current fixation and the centre of the screen (d) and the angle (θ). If the fixation is not in the central area ($d < r_0$), then the camera will start moving along the angle (θ). Otherwise, it will remain at the current position. This design is similar to the "*rate control*" concept, in which we follow a simple principle: *whatever the user looks at on the screen, it moves to the centre.* However, instead of using a simple linear function gain to specify the camera's velocity, we used a sigmoid function to define the camera velocity proportionally to the distance (d) from the centre, and make more smoothed and responsive camera movements according to the user's eye movements [13].

The camera zoom function is operated by the user's head motion (see Figure 5), as small movements of the user's head (approximately ±6cm) can be detected by the eye tracking device we had in real time.

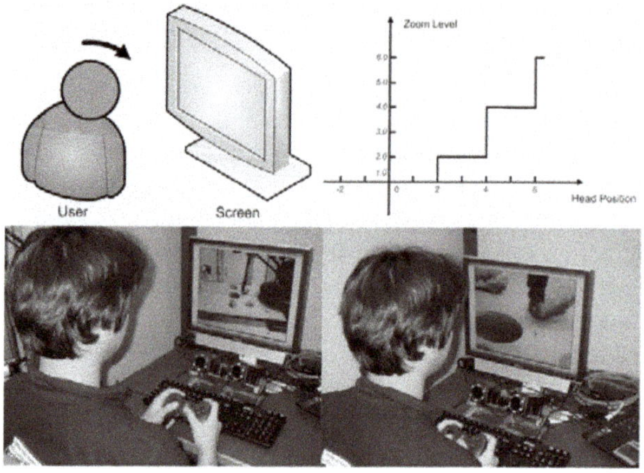

Figure 5. Zooming by moving head towards the screen.

The original version of the head motion for zooming control was similar to the *Head-to-Zoom* in [1]: the zooming rate is proportional to the amount of movement the user moves their head towards the screen or away from the screen and the camera stops zooming in a small region around the user's neutral head position. However, this model did not perform well in our preliminary user test mainly due to the zoom latency of the camera lens. We modified the model by adopting another similar technique: *Lean and Zoom* [12], defining several discrete zoom levels rather than using a continuous zoom scale. The camera zoom level is based on the user's current head position and the gain of the zoom can be adjusted as desired. This improves the camera zoom latency issue and also gives the user some freedom to move their head without activating the zooming function, being more error-tolerant.

Autonomous Tracking

The intention of an auto camera tracking system is that it automatically brings the view of the most important region of the teleoperation task to the operator. For our industrial setting, the operator mostly focuses their visual attention on the region around the tip when they are trying to specify the breaking spots on rocks and fire the hammer. Therefore, the view of the tip would be the region that the remote camera always tracks. In our model this is the tip of the robot arm.

An autonomous tracking approach has been mentioned in [6]. The design of the autonomous camera tracking system is to use hardware sensors on the arm to obtain the position data of the tip according to the pre-defined 3D coordinate system of the arm. Then the tip position data can be further geometrically transformed into the camera movement angle to make the remote camera carry out corresponding pan and tilt functions to track the tip in real time. This version only considered camera pan and tilt automation.

For our model, we improved the design by adding an autonomous zooming function. When the operator is focusing on a target rock, a zoom-in view is essential. On the other hand, when the operator needs to make a "big" move of the arm, for example, trying to reach another rock far away from the current position, moving the arm to or from the parking place, then a zoom-out view would provide more visual information of the environment.

Therefore, a similar design to that of the head motion model has been implemented, in which the camera zoom rate is adapted to the distance the tip moved from the last position. Similarly, non-linear (e.g. sigmoid function) functions performed better to define the zoom rate than simple linear functions due to the high user tolerance for camera zoom latency as described in the previous section.

USER STUDY

A user study was conducted to assess how well these three camera viewpoint control models could perform in a model multi-tasking teleoperation setting in terms of both objective measures and subjective measures.

Apparatus and Implementation

As we had very limited access to the real rock breaker device and the real operators, we modeled the setting by building a physical control analogue and recruited university students as experimental subjects. A Phantom Premium (V1.5) Haptic device [26] was used as a "small" equivalent of the rock breaker, which has a similar arm structure to the rock breaker device as well as very similar kinds of possible movements. As we described in the previous section, the "small" robot arm was controlled by the two thumb joysticks on the gamepad for all three camera control models in the user study.

We modeled the entire rock breaker environment into a lab-based setting with similar properties (see Figure 6). The small robot arm is placed behind a wood board with a hole for dropping rocks in the centre and a parking place next to the board, which are similar to the setting of the real bin on the mine site. The same model of Pelco ES30C [21] camera as used in the industrial setting was installed on one side to be the remote camera for our user study.

In addition, since this haptic device based robot arm does not have the strength to break rocks, we implemented another function called "nudge" (see (6) in Figure 6) which makes the tip quickly move in a small circle (radius = 1cm). This "nudge" function was designed to simulate the "fire" function for the real rock breaker tip. It is more similar to the industrial setting than just simply moving the arm to push rocks into the hole. It makes participants move the arm close to a target rock and "nudge" it into the hole, which is similar to the way that the real operator places the tip on a rock and fire the hammer, breaking the rock, the pieces of which fall through the grizzly.

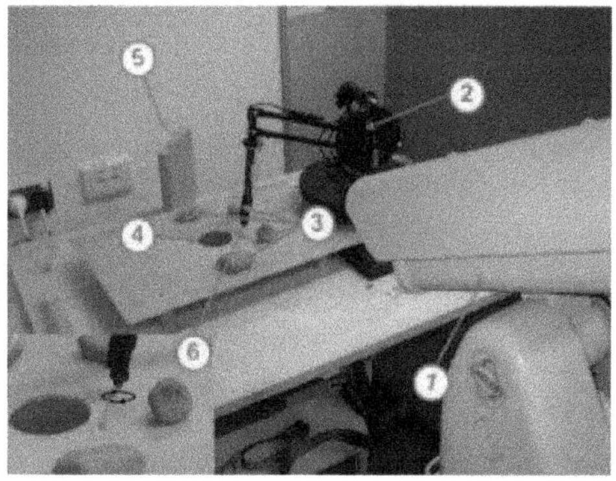

Figure 6. Remote setting: (1) Pelco ES30C camera, (2) Phantom Premium 1.5 as the rock breaker, (3) rocks, (4) hole for dropping rocks, (5) parking place for the arm, (6) "nudge" function to simulate the "fire" function.

For the natural interaction camera viewpoint control model, we used a FaceLAB V4.5 [25] eye tracking system to perform both real time eye tracking and head tracking at 60Hz frequency without using any markers. The FaceLAB Client Tools SDK was used to implement the gaze filtering algorithm and the camera control code. The user control setting is shown in Figure 7.

Figure 7. User setting: (1) FaceLAB V4.5 eye tracker, (2) video stream from the remote setting, (3) Logitech Dual Action Gamepad.

All the software development was implemented in Visual C++ and installed on a Dell Precision Work Station with standard Window XP operation system on the user site. The display was a standard 19" monitor with a resolution of 1280 × 1024 pixels and shows the real-time video stream to the participant from the remote camera. A local LAN network was set up to connect the remote site and the user.

Participants

A total of 30 undergraduate volunteers (mostly first-year students) from a local university successfully participated in this user study, including 25 male and 5 female, ranging from 18 to 26 years of age (M_{age} = 20.27, SD_{age} = 2.02).

All of them were regular computer users (at least 2 hours a day) enrolled in a computing or IT related major with experience of using a gamepad interface. None of them had any previous experience on any eye tracking or head tracking interfaces, and none of them had any experience on our remote control setting.

Several participants had corrected vision but all the participants' eye gaze could be calibrated with the tracker successfully in the user study.

Experimental Design, Task and Procedure

The experiment followed a within-subject design therefore all the participants participated in all conditions of the experiment. The independent variable *camera control model* contained three levels:

1. Dual manual model
2. Natural interaction model
3. Autonomous tracking model

The order effect was counterbalanced by using a Latin square.

Participants took part in the study individually. The major task for the participants was to remotely control both the robot arm and the camera to "nudge" rocks into the hole, called "sinking" rocks by analogy with the game of billiards. Prior to starting the experiment, participants were first given a short verbal introduction about the system, a quick tutorial of how to control the remote camera by using the manual model, the natural interaction model and the autonomous tracking model respectively, and how to control the arm via the two thumb joysticks on the gamepad as well as the objective of their task, which was to try to sink as many rocks as they could during each testing trial. Participants were given a few minutes to experiment with all these control models, and then they were required to confirm an understanding of using these three different camera control models and the requirements of the experimental task.

After that, participants started the formal experiment. For each camera control model, participants had 3 minutes in total to sink rocks by nudging them. Moreover, the entire 3-minute task was further separated to 3 operation periods (60s each), which was approximately the same length of time that an operator had in the industrial setting to handle one truck load dumped in the bin. After each operation period, participants were required to stop the nudging operation, and move the arm to the parking place. Meanwhile, an experiment assistant put rocks back on the board as a new dumped load, and then participants could bring the arm back and start the next operation round. An extra 3 to 5 minutes were required for calibrating each participant's eye gaze before they started the natural interaction model trial.

During the operation periods, participants were required to use a zoom-in view of rocks while conducting nudging operations. This was to match the industrial operation in which a zoom-in view was vital. They could zoom out the view when they were looking for other rocks or moving the arm to or from the parking place.

The number of rocks each participant nudged into the hole and the number of nudges they made by using the corresponding camera control model were recorded as the major performance measures. Once the rock nudging task under all three camera control models had been finished, we collected participants' feedback by using a questionnaire with a 7-point Likert scale, rating from 1 (strongly disagree) to 7 (strongly agree) and a short interview. The questions were derived from the IBM Computer Usability Satisfaction Questionnaire [18], in which participants compared their experiences with different camera control models across several criteria as subjective measures, including easiness, required consciousness, distraction and time to get used to the control and so on.

RESULTS

Objective Measures: Rocks and Nudges

The major objective measures are the number of rocks sunk and nudges each participant achieved by using different camera control models.

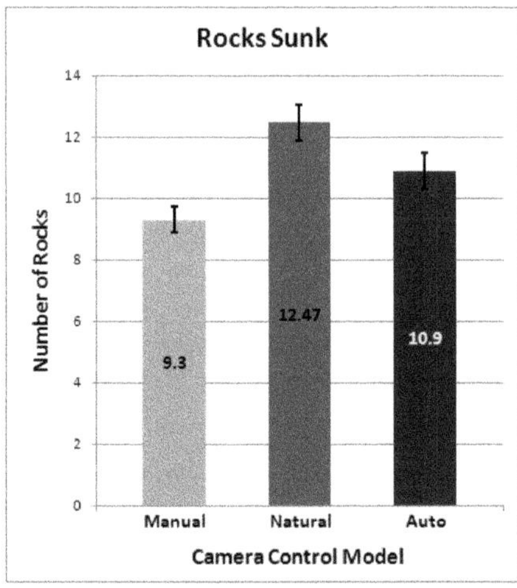

Figure 8. Comparison of mean rocks sunk.

A 1-way Repeated Measures ANOVA showed highly significant differences in number of rocks participants completed between the three camera control models, $F(2, 58) = 21.36$, $p < 0.001$. Figure 8 shows the relevant overall mean rocks for each camera control model. The post hoc pair-wise tests revealed that using the natural interaction model participants sunk significantly more rocks than using the dual manual model ($p < 0.001$) and the auto tracking model ($p < 0.05$). In addition, using the auto tracking model participants performed significantly better than using the manual model ($p < 0.01$).

Similarly, the results of 1-Way Repeated Measures ANOVA showed differences between the camera control models were highly significant for number of nudges participants made in the experiment, $F(2, 58) = 23.75$, $p < 0.001$. The corresponding mean numbers of nudges for each camera control model are illustrated in Figure 9. After the post hoc pair-wise comparisons, we also found that participants made significantly more nudges by using the natural interaction model than the dual manual model ($p < 0.001$) and the auto tracking model ($p < 0.01$). Using the auto tracking model was also significantly better than using the manual model in the experiment ($p < 0.05$).

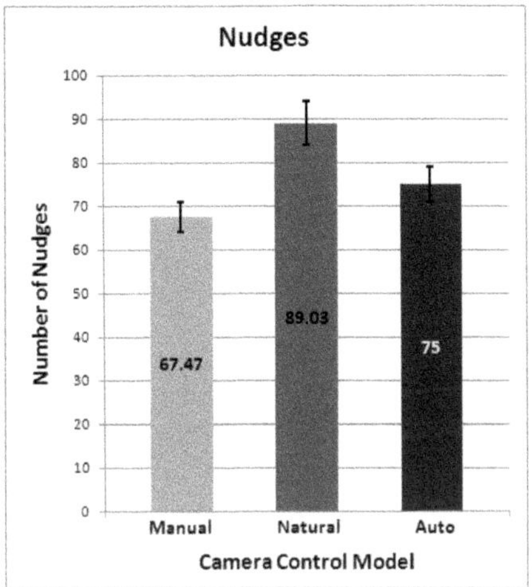

Figure 9. Comparison of mean nudges.

We also separated the results of both rocks sunk and nudges to three phases for the three sequential operation periods participants completed in the experiment. Figure 10 shows the number of rocks and nudges on average for each operation period respectively.

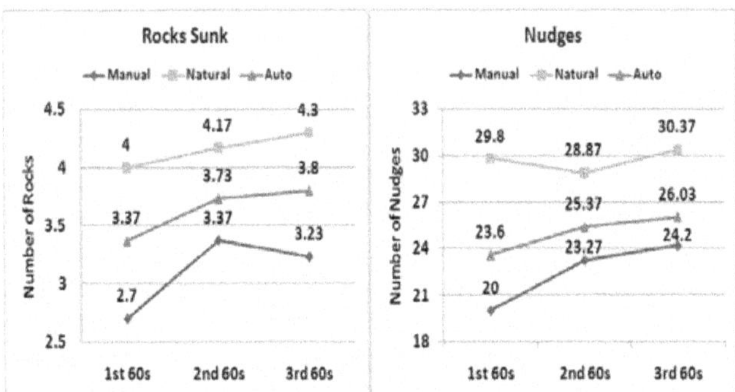

Figure 10. Mean numbers of rocks sunk and nudges for each operation period.

The overall trends of performance (including both numbers of rocks and nudges) for all three camera control models are increasing during the three operation periods. This reflects the general expectation that a participant's performance would gradually increase at the early stage of a new task.

From the results of analysis, significant effects were found on camera control models for both mean rocks sunk (F_{1st_60s} (2, 50) = 21.64, $p < 0.001$, F_{2nd_60s} (2, 54) = 6.59, $p < 0.01$, F_{3rd_60s} (2, 57) = 7.8, $p < 0.01$) and nudges (F_{1st_60s} (2, 59) = 23.1, $p < 0.001$, F_{2nd_60s} (2, 58) = 7.06, $p < 0.01$, F_{3rd_60s} (2, 57) = 10.2, $p < 0.01$) through the three periods. For all three period, participants using the natural interaction model significantly outperformed the manual model ($p < 0.001$). Using the auto tracking model was significantly better than the manual model at the 1st 60s period ($p < 0.05$) on both of the measures, but there were no significant differences on performance for the remaining two operation periods ($p > 0.05$).

Subjective Measures: Questionnaire and Interview

The results of questions from our questionnaire regarding user experience of using the three different camera control models are depicted in Figure 11 which shows the mean results of all participants.

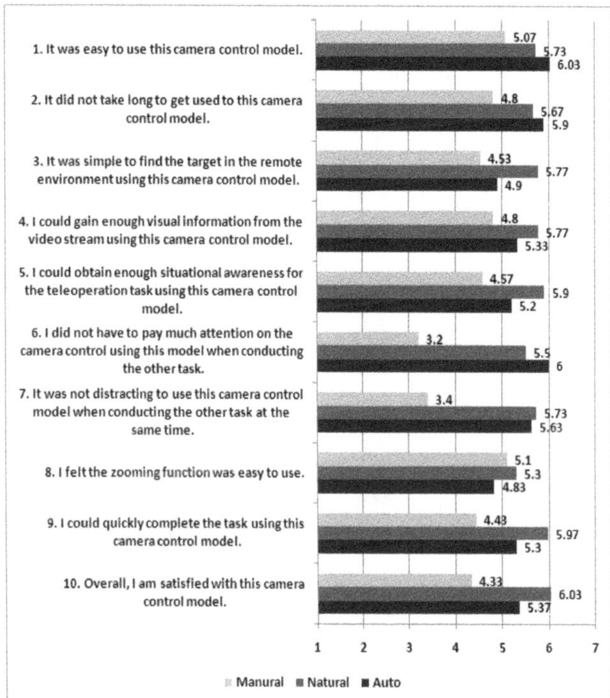

Figure 11. Mean results regarding questionnaire feedback (7-point Likert scale: 1 – Strongly Disagree to 7 – Strongly Agree).

The results of Friedman's tests showed significant differences on the user feedback in terms of camera control models for all the questions except for Question 4 and 8. Wilcoxon follow-up tests were used to analyse the results in more detail. For Question 1($\chi^2_{Q1}(2) = 6.92$, $p < 0.05$), 2 ($\chi^2_{Q2}(2) = 6.94$, $p < 0.05$) and 6 ($\chi^2_{Q6}(2) = 26.91$, $p < 0.001$), participants rated the auto tracking model significantly better than the manual model ($p < 0.01$), but the results between the natural interaction model and the auto tracking model were not significant. Participants felt it took significantly shorter time to get used to the natural interaction model (Q2: $p < 0.05$) with much less attention (Q6: $p < 0.01$) than the manual model. As to Question 3

($\chi^2_{Q3}(2) = 6.21, p < 0.05$) and 5 ($\chi^2_{Q5}(2) = 9.76, p < 0.01$), participants rated the natural interaction model significantly better than the other two models ($p < 0.05$), but the mean results between the manual model and the auto tracking model were not significant.

Highly significant differences were found in the remaining three questions, 7 ($\chi^2_{Q7}(2) = 24.54, p < 0.001$), 9 ($\chi^2_{Q9}(2) = 17.6, p < 0.001$) and 10 ($\chi^2_{Q10}(2) = 18.06, p < 0.001$). The mean results of both the natural interaction model and the auto tracking model were significantly better than the manual model for all the three questions ($p < 0.001$). In addition, the natural interaction model was rated significantly better than the auto tracking model for the last two questions (Q9: $p < 0.05$ and Q10: $p < 0.05$), but there was no significant difference between them for Question 7.

At the end of the questionnaire, participants were asked to state an overall preference of the three camera control models according to their experience gained in the model multi-tasking experiment. The results are illustrated in Figure 12.

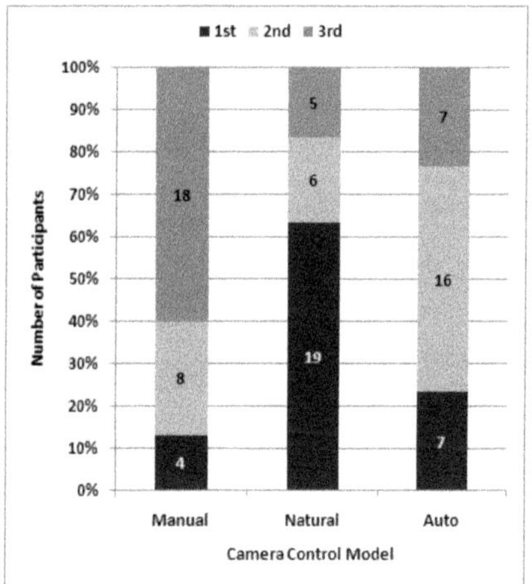

Figure 12. Overall preferences of the participants.

The mean position for the natural interaction model was 1.53, 2.0 for the auto tracking model and 2.47 for the manual model. A majority of participants (19 / 30 = 63.3%) ranked the natural interaction model as their first preference and 6 (20.0%) ranked it as their second choice. The auto tracking model was rated better than the manual model with 7 (23.3%) ranked it as the best and more than half of the population ranked it as their second preference (16 / 30 = 53.5%). The manual model was rated as the worst by a majority of participants (18 / 30 = 60.0%).

From the short interview conducted at the end the of the user study and the comments participants made whilst filling in the questionnaires, most of them felt that both the natural interaction model and the auto tracking model were effective solutions for the multi-tasking problem being modeled. In comparison to separate control interfaces requiring frequent hand switches, the dual manual model minimizes the physical effort but participants still felt obvious distractions when they were carrying out the two control tasks at the same time in the experiment. They also commented that the natural interaction model offered a more intuitive way for remote view point control than the other two models. Although the auto tracking model also worked well for the multi-tasking problem, participants felt that they lost some freedom of obtaining visual information from the remote environment as the camera could only be moved when they were moving the arm.

DISCUSSION

The results of objective measures clearly demonstrate that for this model multi-tasking experiment, the natural interaction model significantly outperformed the other two camera control models. Compared to dual manual model and autonomous tracking model, participants nudged more rocks into the hole and certainly more valid nudges were produced by using natural interaction model. It followed our general expectation that more nudges would lead to more rocks to be completed. This tells us that using natural interaction model participants obtained significantly more opportunities to nudge rocks as the remote camera always followed their current visual concentration whilst operating the arm.

The auto tracking model provided a comparable performance to the natural interaction model, and participants performed significantly better than using the manual model. It offered a fully autonomous approach which effectively released any user involvement for the remote viewpoint operation in the experiment. However, this actually did not lead to the best performance in the user study as we expected, because it also reflects the fact that participants could not obtain as much situational awareness or visual information as by using the natural interaction model from the remote setting.

The subjective results and feedback from both questionnaire and short interview remain consistent with the objective results. Participants rated the natural interaction model significantly better than the other two models for most of the criteria we selected. As revealed in the results of questions regarding ease to use (Q1), time to get used to the camera control model (Q2) and required attention on the camera control (Q6), the auto tracking model was rated as the best as apparently it completely freed the participants from the control of the remote camera so that they were able to only concentrate on operating the arm to nudge rocks.

Nevertheless, from the results of questions about whether it was simple to find the target (Q3), whether users could gain enough visual information (Q4) and situational awareness (Q5) and efficiency of completing the rock nudging task (Q9), participants showed their preference for the natural interaction model rather than the auto tracking model. The major reason for this point was just as one of those participants with similar opinions in the interview commented that: "*Natural interaction model allowed you to look ahead and plan your next step move intuitively. However, auto tracking model actually did not allow you to look around or see further away as you did not have the control of the camera.*" This also suggests us that in complex teleoperation settings, not only the current visual concentration for conducting the task, but also the way to improve an operator's capability of planning next step operation or predicting further situation might have a significant influence on the entire performance. Operating the remote camera is closely related to an operator's capability for planning and prediction, therefore most participants have significantly confirmed that using the natural interaction model offered them more visual information and situational awareness than using fully autonomous model.

The results of the question regarding zoom function (Q8) are not significant, but a few interesting points were commented on by participants. Most participants directly commented that they really liked the interaction technique of using head motion for controlling the zoom function, since it makes the viewpoint control natural and intuitive. However, several participants with much experience of using the same model of gamepad for video games suggested that if only considering achieving the maximal performance, they would rather have the hand control of the zoom function on the gamepad, as they believed using head motion requires more physical effort than just pressing buttons on a gamepad. Similar opinions regarding the zoom function in the auto tracking model were also commented on by a number of participants. They explained that the auto zooming was actually a bit distracting and sensitive as it used only the distance they moved the arm, which sometimes resulted in frequently zooming in and out automatically. Therefore, they also suggested moving the zoom function to the hand control for the auto tracking model.

For our user studies, we simulated some properties of the mining process, which we consider to be a preliminary experiment. This lab-based setting may not exactly match the real world setting, but it can provide full control of the experiment to test specific usability aspects on the control interfaces, i.e. the multi-tasking problem. In practice, to conduct such a formal user study on the real world mining setting will have a huge cost. Therefore, to design a model with the key properties of the real world setting will offer us an appropriate mapping to the real world setting, on which we are able to conduct user studies and obtain valid results with much less cost. In addition, the results would be useful at a more generic level rather than just for this particular mining scenario. In the experiment, participants were all novice users with limited training. From the results we can see that the learning effect was taking place, but it in fact offered us a fairer comparison of user performance under the same conditions than comparing something new with a participant who already had much experience on one model. In order to be more applicable for the rock breaking process, our plan for the next step user studies will be conducted on the real operators.

CONCLUSION

In this paper, we address a common multi-tasking problem in a situation that operators are required to conduct remote camera viewpoint control and their main teleoperation control task simultaneously. We consider three different camera control models, including a dual manual control model, a natural interaction model using human eye gaze and head motion, and an autonomous tracking model.

A user study was conducted by modeling the multi-tasking situation based on a real-world industrial teleoperation setting (remote rock breaking). From the results of both objective measures and subjective measures on the model application, we report the significant performance advantages and user preference for using the natural interaction model. The auto tracking model offered a comparable performance and the dual manual model was significantly worse. Our results were analyzed according to both quantitative and qualitative information collected.

Future directions may include importing more natural interaction strategies into the control interface design for teleoperation. Also, we hope the findings described in this work will encourage more research on such common multi-tasking issues in teleoperation and may lead to the deployment of such remote camera operation models in a practical context.

ACKNOWLEDGMENTS

The authors would like to express their appreciation to all the experimental participants, and also thank Chris Gunn, Matt Adcock, Leila Alem, Jock Cunningham and Eleonora Widzyk-Capehart for their great help and valuable suggestions. This research was supported by the Transforming the Future Mine theme under the CSIRO National Mineral Down Under (MDU) Research Flagship.

REFERENCES

1. Adams, N., Witkowski, M. and Spence, R. The inspection of very large images by eye-gaze control. In *Proc. AVI 2008*, ACM Press (2008), 1-8.
2. Chen, Y. C., Haas, E. C. and Barnes, M. J. Human performance issues and user interface design for teleoperated robots. *IEEE Trans. on SMC – Part C: Applications and Reviews*, 37, 2 (2007), 1231-1245.
3. Cohen, C. J., Conway, L. and Kiditschek, D. Dynamical system representation, generation, and recognition of basic oscillatory motion gestures. In *Proc. 2nd Int. Conf. Face Gesture Recog.* 1996, 60-65.
4. Cohen, I. and Medioni, G. Detecting and tracking moving objects for video surveillance. In *Proc. CVPR 1999*, 319-325.
5. Draper, M., Calhoun, G., Ruff, H., Williamson, D. and Barry, T. Manual versus speech input for unmanned aerial

vehicle control station operations. In *Proc. Hum. Factors Ergonom. Soc. 47th Annu. Meet.* 2003, 109-113.

6. Duff, E., Caris, C., Bonchis, A., Taylor, K., Gunn, C. and Adcock, M. The development of a telerobotic rock breaker. In *Proc. FSR 2009*, 1-10.
7. Fong, T., and Thorpe, C. Vehicle Teleoperation interfaces. *Autonomous Robots*, 11, 1 (2001), 9-18.
8. Goh, A. H. W., Yong, Y. S., Chan, C. H., Then, S. J., Chu, P. L., Chau, S. W. and Hon, H. W. Interactive PTZ camera control system using Wii remote and infrared sensor bar. In *Proc. World Academy of Science, Engineering and Technology* (2008) 46, 127-132.
9. Gunn, C., Hutchins, M. Stevenson, D., Adcok, M. and Youngblood, P. Using collaborative haptics in remote surgical training. In *Proc. WorldHaptics 2005*, 481-482.
10. Hainsworth, D. Teleoperation user interfaces for mining robotics. Autonomous Robots, 11, 1 (2001), 19-28.
11. Hansen, D. W., Skovsgaard, H. and Mollenbach, E. Noise tolerant selection by gaze-controlled pan and zoom in 3D. In *Proc. ETRA 2008*, ACM Press (2008), 205-212.
12. Harrison, C. and Dey, A. K. Lean and zoom: proximity-aware user interface and content magnification. In *Proc. CHI 2008*, ACM Press (2008), 507-510.
13. Hu, C., Meng, M. Q., Liu, P. X. and Wang, X. Visual gesture recognition for human-machine interface of robot teleoperation. In *Proc. IEEE/RSJ Int. Conf. Intell. Robot. Syst.* 2003, 1560-1565.
14. Hughes, S. and Lewis, M. Robotic camera control for remote exploration. In *Proc. CHI 2004*, ACM Press (2004), 511-517.
15. Isokoski, P., Hyrskykari, A., Kotkaluoto, S. and Martin, B. Gamepad and eye tracker input in first person shooter games: data for the first 50 minutes. In *Proc. COGAIN 2007*, 11-15.
16. Jacob, R. J. K. The use of eye movements in human-computer interaction techniques: what you look at is what you get. *ACM Transactions on Information Systems*, 9, 3 (1991), 152-169.
17. Kumar, M., Paepcke, A. and Winograd, T. Eyepoint: practical pointing and selection using gaze and keyboard, In *Proc. CHI 2007*, ACM Press (2007), 421-430.
18. Lewis, J. R. IBM computer usability satisfaction questionnaires: psychometric evaluation and instructions for use. *Int. J. Human-Computer Interaction*, 7, 1, (1995), 57-78.
19. Liu, Q., Kimber, D., Foote, J., Wilcox, L. and Boreczky, J. FlySPEC: a multi-user video camera system with hybrid human and automatic control. In *Proc. MM 2002*, ACM Press (2002), 484-492.
20. Logitech Dual Action Gamepad.

    http://www.logitech.com/en-us/gaming/controllers/devices/288/
21. Pelco ES30C.

    http://www.pelco.com/products/
22. Qvarforde, P. and Zhai, S. Conversing with the user based on eye-gaze patterns. In *Proc. CHI 2005*, ACM Press (2005), 221-230.
23. Saito, S. Does fatigue exist in quantitative measurement of eye movements?, Ergonomics, 35 (5/6), 607-615.
24. Salvucci, D. D. and Goldberg, J. H. Identifying fixations and saccades in eye-tracking protocols. *In Proc. ETRA 2000*, ACM Press (2000), 71-78.
25. Seeingmachines FaceLAB 4.5.

    http://www.seeingmachines.com/product/facelab/
26. Sensable Phantom Premium 1.5.

    http://www.sensable.com/phantom-premium-1-5.htm/
27. Tall, M. Alapetite, A., Agustin, J. S., Skovsgaard, H. H., Hansen, J. P., Hansen, D. W. and Mollenbach, E. Gaze-controlled driving. *Ext. Abstracts CHI 2009*, ACM Press (2009), 4387-4392.
28. Valli, A. The design of natural interaction. *Multimedia Tools and Applications* (2008) 38, 295-305.
29. Wang, S., Xiong, X., Xu, Y. Wang, C., Zhang, W., Dai, X. and Zhang, D. Face tracking as an augmented input in video games: enhancing presence, role-playing and control. In *Proc. CHI 2006*, ACM Press (2006), 1097-1106.
30. Yamaguchi, K., Komuro, T. and Ishikawa, M. PTZ control with head tracking for video chat. *Ext. Abstracts CHI 2009*, ACM Press (2009), 3919-3924.
31. Yanco, H. Wheelesley: a robotic wheelchair system: indoor navigation and user interface. *Assistive Technology and Artificial Intelligence*, (1998), 256-268.
32. Zhai, S., Morimoto, C. and Ihde, S. Manual and gaze input cascaded (MAGIC) pointing. In *Proc. CHI 1999*, ACM Press (1999), 246-253.
33. Zhu, D., Gedeon, T. D. and Taylor, K. Keyboard before head tracking depresses user success in remote camera control. In *Proc. INTERACT 2009*, Springer Press (2009), LNCS 5727, 319-331.
34. Zhu, D., Gedeon, T. D. and Taylor, K. Natural interaction enhanced remote camera control for teleoperation. *Ext. Abstracts CHI 2010*, ACM Press (2010), 3229-3234.

Zoom Cameras and Movable Displays Enhance Social Telepresence

Hideyuki Nakanishi, Kei Kato
Department of Adaptive Machine Systems
Osaka University
2-1 Yamadaoka, Suita
Osaka 565-0871, Japan
{nakanishi, kei.katou}@ams.eng.osaka-u.ac.jp

Hiroshi Ishiguro
Department of Systems Innovation
Osaka University
1-3 Machikaneyama, Toyonaka
Osaka 560-8531, Japan
ishiguro@sys.es.osaka-u.ac.jp

ABSTRACT
This paper shows that the augmentation of a remote person's positional movement enhances social telepresence. There are three possible ways of representing a remote person's movement toward the user in visual communication: a) the remote person's movement toward the remote camera, b) the remote camera's zooming in to enlarge the remote person's picture, and c) a forward movement of the display that is displaying the remote person. We conducted an experiment to see the relationship among these three ways and the effects of a remote camera's zooming and a display's movement on social telepresence. In the experiment, we observed that the remote person's movement lowered the reality of conversations, and the remote camera's zooming lowered the visual quality. However, social telepresence was enhanced when both the person's movement and the camera's zooming occurred simultaneously. We also observed that a 6-centimeter movement of the display enhanced social telepresence, whether the remote person moved or not.

Author Keywords
Telepresence, videoconferencing, telerobotics.

ACM Classification Keywords
H5.3. Information interfaces and presentation (e.g., HCI): Group and Organization Interfaces - Computer-supported cooperative work.

General Terms
Design, Experimentation, Human Factors.

INTRODUCTION
The role of live video in videoconferencing has traditionally been regarded as the presentation of eye movements, facial expressions, gestures, and postures. Additionally, the presentation of positional movement has recently started to attract a lot of attention [10,15,21,22,25]. This paper shows that the presentation of augmented positional movement enhances social telepresence, that is the degree of resembling face-to-face interaction [4]. This paper especially focuses on short movements that can occur even in formal meetings, e.g., a seated person sliding the chair.

It is currently common to use a single display to see multiple people in videoconferencing. But, since the price of large flat-panel displays is becoming lower and lower, it becomes more and more feasible to assign one display to each remote person. This study supposes that each user can use a dedicated display to show the user's picture at the remote site. A dedicated display makes it easy to show the remote person's life-size picture and also the person's positional movement as described below.

Figure 1 shows three possible ways of representing a remote person's movement toward the user in visual communication: a) the remote person's movement toward the remote camera, b) the remote camera's zooming in to enlarge the remote person's picture, and c) a forward movement of the display that is displaying the remote person. This paper clarifies the relationship among these three ways and demonstrates how they contribute to social telepresence.

The first way, i.e., the remote person's movement toward the remote camera, is the most basic among the three ways. When the remote person approaches the remote camera, you can see the person's body motion on the display. However, it is known that such a visual motion is much less noticeable than a physical motion that occurs in the same room [6]. Therefore, we aimed to diminish this gap in order to improve the reality of videoconferencing.

The second way, i.e., the camera's zooming in, is a common visual effect that is used in films and TV programs. When the remote person approaches the remote camera, the picture of the person is enlarged according to the camera's field of view (FOV). This enlargement is amplified if the camera's zooming in narrows its FOV exactly when the person moves forward. This paper shows that this amplification can make the remote person's movement more noticeable and enhance social telepresence.

Figure 1. Three ways of representing a remote person's movement

The third way, i.e., the display's forward movement, is rapidly becoming popular thanks to the recent release of various commercial telepresence robot products. While their appearance varies, their structure is almost the same: a camera, a display, a microphone, and a speaker that are mounted on a remote controlled robot. A telepresence robot moves around a remote site instead of its operator. It is expected that an on-site person, who stands in front of the robot, feels as if the operator comes up to the person when the robot moves toward the person. We examined this expectation empirically. This paper shows that even a tiny movement of the display can represent a remote person's movement and enhance social telepresence.

RELATED WORK

This study is located at the intersection of the two telepresence research areas, which are videoconferencing and telerobotics.

Videoconferencing research has revealed several effects of live video on telepresence [2]. Basically, live video can transmit the social presence of a remote person [3,7]. It is well known that social presence is strengthened if the setup of cameras and displays allows eye contact to be established [1]. A past study found that stereoscopic video and a life-size picture of a remote person had the effect of strengthening social presence [20]. A recent study reported that a moving point of view, which can be implemented as a remote camera that moves according to the position of the user's eyes [5], strengthened social presence [17]. In this paper, we add new ways to make live video strengthen social presence: zoom cameras and movable displays.

Telerobotics research has developed various kinds of telepresence robots. Some of them exhibit their own robotic face instead of the operator's face [11,14,23]. And others are equipped with a display that shows the operator's face, but its size is usually small [8,9,16,19,24]. Because of the small display, those robots can show either a small-size picture of the operator or a life-size picture of the operator's head. The small-size picture is harmful to social telepresence, and the picture of a head is also harmful to social telepresence [18]. In this study we used a larger display – a 30-inch wide-screen display that was placed vertically in order to show a nearly life-size picture of the entire upper body of a remote person [12]. This large display allowed us to investigate the relationship among the three ways that are described in the previous section.

EXPERIMENT

Goal

We conducted an experiment to clarify the effects of the two ways to augment a remote person's movement: zoom cameras and movable displays.

We anticipated that normal zooming would have little influence on social telepresence, since it is a familiar visual effect. However, we predicted that zooming in and out could enhance social telepresence if it were synchronized with the remote person's approaching and moving away from the remote camera. In this synchronization, zooming in and out amplifies the enlargement and shrinkage of the remote person's picture, which is originally caused by the changes of the distance between the person and the camera. We thought that this amplification could function as an exaggeration of the person's movement. Thus, the first hypothesis is the following.

H1: The remote camera's zooming strengthens the social presence of the remote person if the camera's zooming in and out is synchronized with the person's approaching and moving away from the camera.

The movement of telepresence robots is supposed to be interpreted as the remote operator's movement. This supposition means that the distance between the robot and an on-site person who stands in front of the robot represents the distance between the remote person and the on-site person. The supposition also means that the remote person's actual movement does not need to occur. Thus, we established the second hypothesis as follows.

H2: The display's forward-backward movement strengthens the social presence of the remote person, whether the movement is synchronized with the person's movement or not.

Setup

To examine hypotheses H1 and H2, we contrived a situation in which a remote person had to move forward and backward several times. We selected the presentation of books as the task of a remote person. One of the experimenters played the role of a presenter. A whiteboard

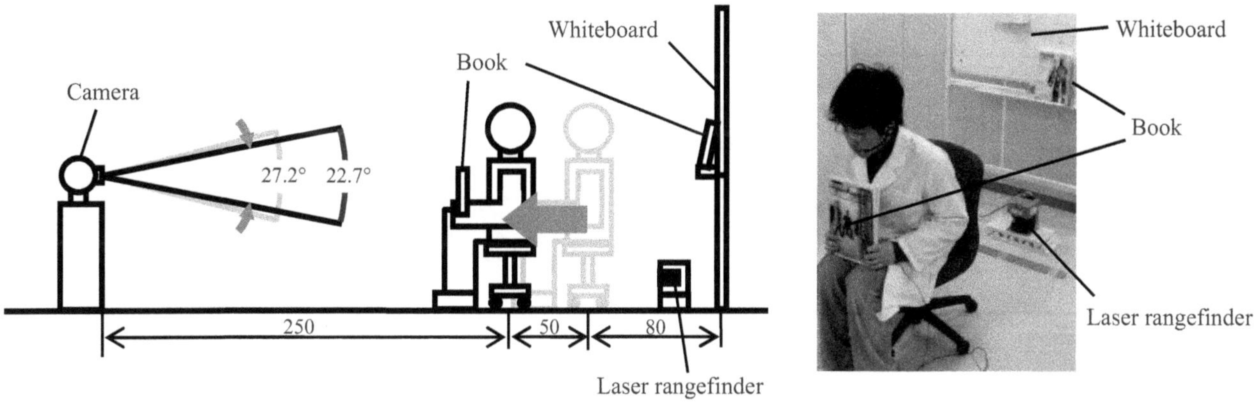

(a) Presenter's room

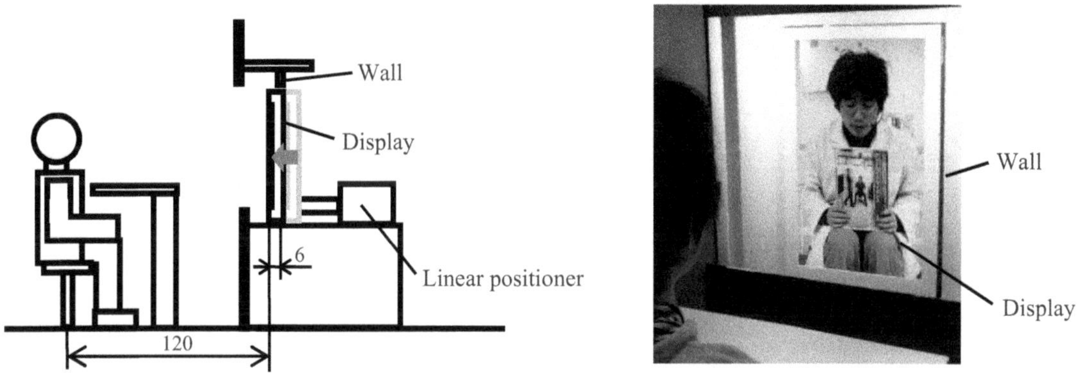

(b) Subject's room

Figure 2. Setup of the experiment (length unit: centimeters)

was placed behind the presenter as shown in Figure 2(a), and three books were arranged on the metal stand of the whiteboard. The presenter, who was seated in a chair, slid his chair backward to pick up one of the books, then slid his chair forward to return to the former position, and described the book to the subject. The presenter repeated this behavior three times.

The display, which is depicted in Figure 2(b), showed the presenter's live video that was sent from a network camera, which is depicted in Figure 2(a). We modified the functions of the display and camera as follows. (The camera in the subject's room and the display in the presenter's room are omitted in Figure 2.)

To examine hypothesis H1, we made the camera zoom in and out in synchronization with the presenter sliding his chair forward and backward. As shown in Figure 2(a), the camera expanded the vertical FOV from 22.7 degrees to 27.2 degrees when the presenter slid his chair backward, and then reduced it from 27.2 degrees to 22.7 degrees when the presenter slid his chair forward. These slides were detected by a laser rangefinder that was placed in front of the whiteboard.

To examine hypothesis H2, we made the display movable by attaching a linear positioner to it. As shown in Figure 2(b), the linear positioner moved the display six centimeters forward or backward when the presenter slid his chair fifty centimeters forward or backward. Thus, the display's movement was much shorter than the presenter's movement. We used a vertically placed 30-inch wide-screen display in order to show a nearly life-size picture of the remote person's upper body. The subject was seated 1.2 meters away from the display.

We determined the amounts of the zooming (from 27.2 degrees to 22.7 degrees) and the presenter's movement (fifty centimeters) so that both produced the same degree of enlargement (1.25 times as large as the original size) in the picture of the presenter. Figure 3 shows that the simple zoom camera and human movement conditions produced the same degree of enlargement. In the preliminary experiment we tested various degrees and observed that 1.25 times seemed a minimum enlargement which could be perceived by subjects. In the preliminary experiment we also tested display movement that was longer or shorter than six centimeters and rejected them as described in the Discussion section.

Conditions

To examine hypothesis H1, we observed the effects of the two factors: whether the camera zoomed or not (zoom-camera factor) and whether the presenter moved or not (human-movement factor). Thus, we compared the following four conditions:

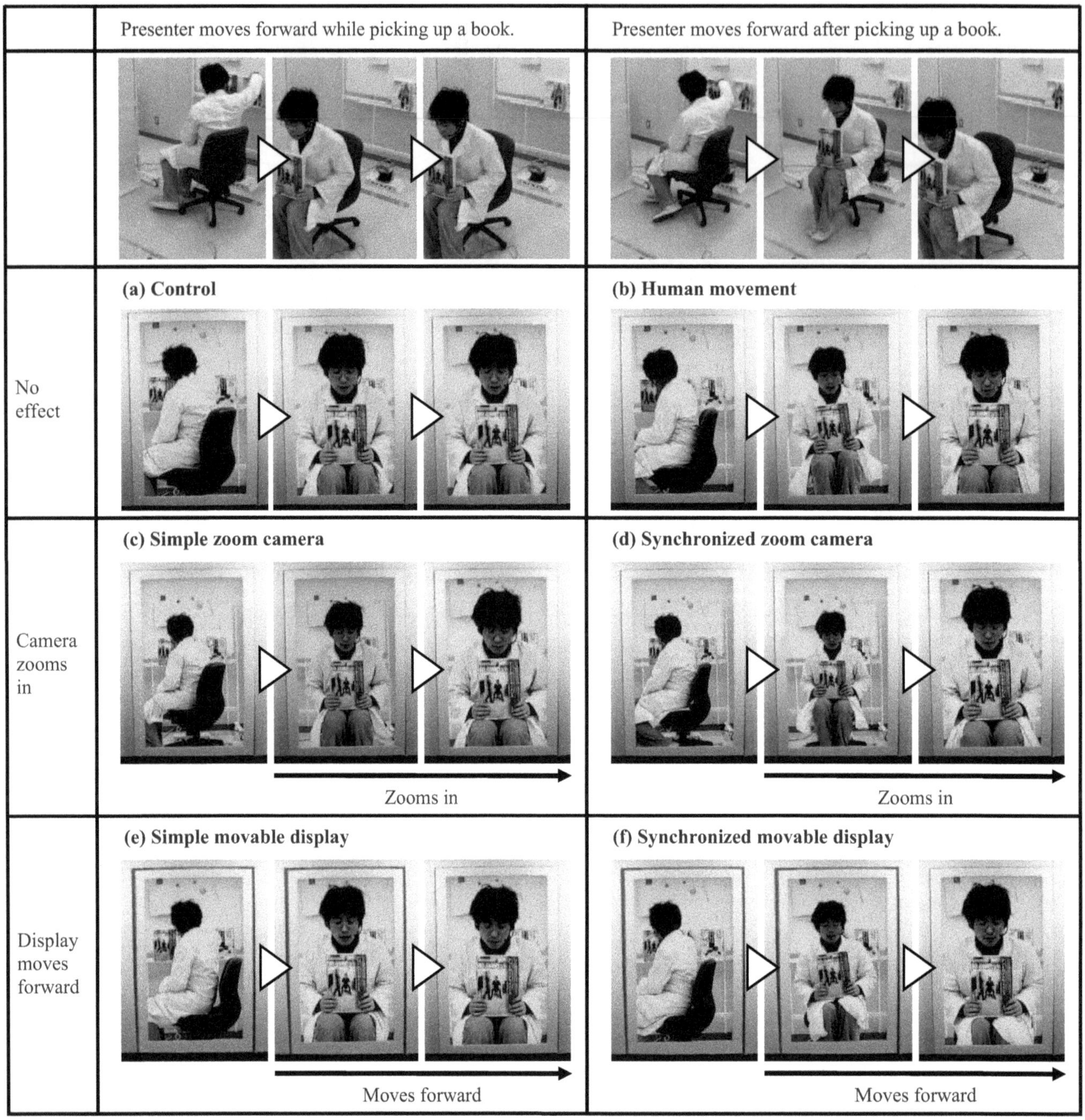

Figure 3. Conditions of the experiment

Control condition: This is a basic condition (Figure 3(a)). The camera did not zoom and the display did not move.

Human movement condition: Also in this condition, the camera did not zoom and the display did not move. However, the presenter's behavior was different from the control condition, in that the presenter slid his chair backward and forward while turning his body to pick up a book. In this condition, the presenter kept facing forward while sliding his chair, and did not slide it while turning his body to pick up a book, so that the subject could clearly recognize that the presenter moved (Figure 3(b)). You can see this difference in Figure 4, which shows how the presenter's behavior of picking up a book and moving forward was seen by the subject.

Simple zoom camera condition: The presenter's behavior was the same as the control condition, but the camera zoomed in and out in this condition. The camera's FOV expanded just before the presenter picked up a book, and reduced just afterward. The presenter did not move at all while the camera was changing its FOV. Each change took about three seconds. Figure 3(c) shows how the camera's zooming in enlarged the presenter's picture.

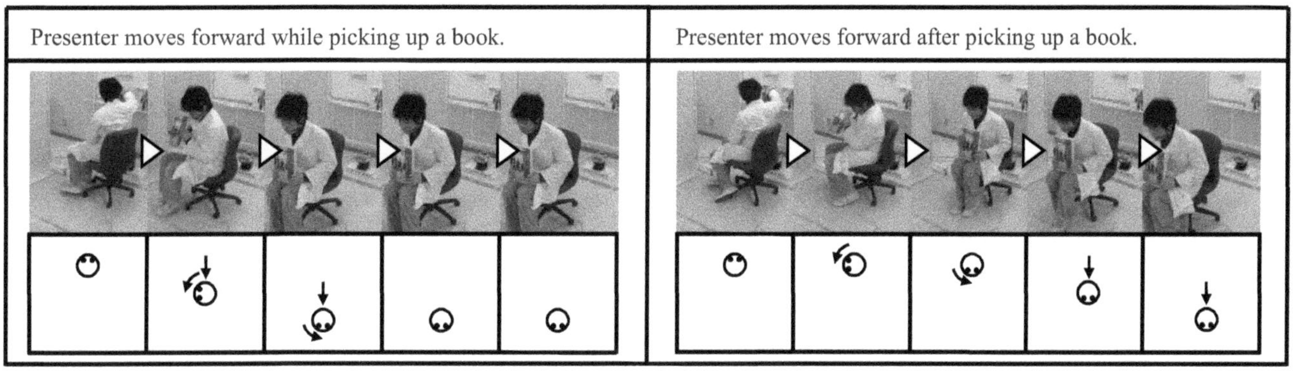

Figure 4. Presenter's behavior

Synchronized zoom camera condition: The presenter's behavior was the same as the human movement condition, and the camera zoomed in synchronization with the presenter's sliding. The camera's FOV expanded when the presenter slid his chair backward, and reduced when the presenter slid his chair forward. The time to change the FOV was the same as in the simple zoom camera condition. Figure 3(d) shows how the combination of the zooming in and the forward slide enlarged the presenter's picture.

To examine hypothesis H2, we observed the effects of two factors: whether the display moved or not (movable-display factor) and whether the presenter moved or not (human-movement factor). Thus, we compared the following four conditions:

Control condition: This condition is as described above.

Human movement condition: This condition is as described above.

Simple movable display condition: This condition is almost the same as the simple zoom camera condition, but the subject experienced the display's movement instead of the camera's zooming. The display moved backward just before the presenter picked up a book, and moved forward just afterward. The presenter did not move at all while the display was moving. Each move took about three seconds. Figure 3(e) shows that the display moved across the wall.

Synchronized movable display condition: This condition is almost the same as the synchronized zoom camera condition, but the subject experienced the display's movement instead of the camera's zooming. The display moved backward when the presenter slid his chair backward, and moved forward when the presenter slid his chair forward. The time to move the display was the same as in the simple movable display condition. Figure 3(f) shows that both the display and the presenter moved forward simultaneously. Figure 5 clarifies that this condition did not use camera zoom, and the picture of the presenter was enlarged only by the presenter's movement. In the figure you can see that the size of the paper attached to the whiteboard remained unchanged in this condition, while it was enlarged and also the size of the whiteboard was enlarged in the synchronized zoom camera condition.

Because the above two comparisons shared two conditions, there were six conditions as shown in Figure 3. In all of these conditions, the display was positioned nearest to the subject, and the FOV of the camera was set for the minimum during the book descriptions. The camera or the display acted differently in each condition only when the presenter picked up a book.

Subjects

The experiment was between-subjects and ten subjects participated in each condition, so sixty subjects participated in total. All the subjects were undergraduate students who lived near our university campus.

Conversation

As shown in Figure 6, the duration of the entire conversation was two or three minutes, and the description of each book was about thirty seconds. In the descriptions, the presenter asked the subject the same questions as given in the figure. The presenter constantly conducted almost the same conversation in all trials. To establish a vocal channel

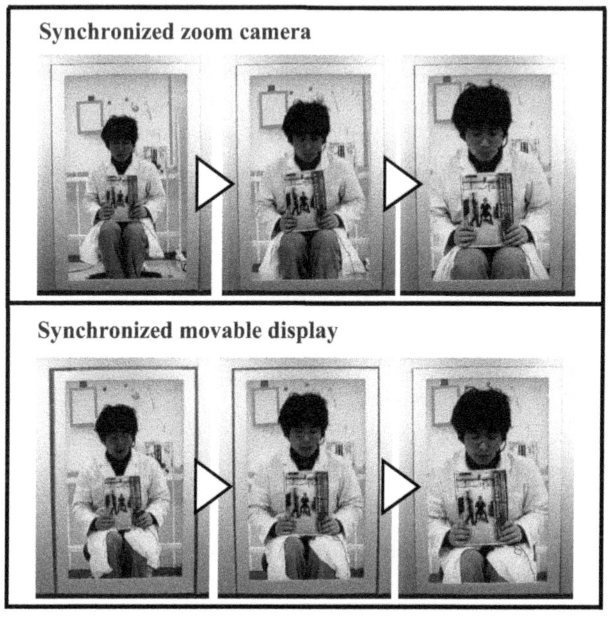

Figure 5. The two synchronized conditions

0:00

Greet

Presenter: Hello.

Subject: Hello.

0:13

Pick up the first

Presenter: I'm going to introduce three books about humanoid robots. Are you ready?

Subject: Yes, I'm ready.

0:23

Presenter: OK, I'll start introducing the books (move backward and pick up the first book). Now I'll describe the first book (move forward).

Describe the first

Presenter: Are you interested in state-of-the-art humanoid robotics?

Subject: Yes, I am.

Presenter: I am, too. This book reports recent technological advancements in a casual style. ... (description omitted) ...

0:55

Pick up the second

Presenter: I'm finished describing this book. Let's go on to the next book (move backward, put the first book down, and pick up the second book). Now I'll describe the second book (move forward).

1:10

Describe the second

Presenter: Do you think it's difficult to construct a humanoid robot?

Subject: Yes, I do.

1:30

Pick up the third

Presenter: I think so, too. This book is written for novices at robotics. ... (description omitted) ...

1:45

Presenter: I'm finished describing this book. Let's go on to the next book (move backward, put the second book down, and pick up the third book). Now I'll describe the third book (move forward).

Describe the third

Presenter: This book proposes a scientific approach to the development of realistic humanoid robots. ... (description omitted) ... Would you like to have a humanoid robot that is a realistic copy of yourself?

Subject: Yes, I would.

Presenter: I would, too. That's all. Do you have any questions or comments about the books?

Subject: No, I don't.

Presenter: OK, thank you.

2:40

Figure 6. Conversation

between the subject and the presenter, we used an Internet telephony tool.

Questionnaire

The questionnaire asked the extent to which the statements matched the impression the subject had. The questionnaire included the following statements to check the quality of the presentation.

- The video was sufficiently clear.
- The audio was sufficiently clear.
- The presentation was intelligible.

The questionnaire included the following statements to estimate the degree of social telepresence.

- I felt as if I were viewing the presenter in the same room.
- I felt as if I were viewing the books in the same room.
- I felt as if I were facing the presenter in the same room.
- I felt as if I were talking with the presenter in the same room.

All the statements were rated on a 9-point Likert scale where 1 = strongly disagree, 3 = disagree, 5 = neutral, 7 = agree, and 9 = strongly agree.

The "viewing" and "talking" statements could effectively measure social presence of a remote person in our previous study [16,17], thus we reused them. The "viewing" statement could measure the visual aspect of social presence, and the "talking" statement could measure the conversational aspect. To measure another aspect, we used the "facing" statement additionally. According to the interviews, this statement was approximately equal to the "viewing" statement, but could measure subjective interpersonal distance rather than just the visual aspect.

RESULTS

Effects of the zoom camera

To examine hypothesis H1, we compared the control, human movement, simple zoom camera, and synchronized zoom camera conditions by 2x2 two-way between-subjects ANOVA. We also analyzed the simple main effects of the zoom-camera factor with the Bonferroni correction. Figure 7 shows the results, in which each box represents the mean value of the responses to each statement, and each bar represents the standard error of the mean value.

We found strong interaction between the zoom-camera factor and the human-movement factor. We found significant interaction in the perceived quality of the video ($F(1,36)=4.739$, $p<0.05$) and the audio ($F(1,36)=6.096$, $p<0.05$), and in the feelings of viewing the presenter ($F(1,36)=7.003$, $p<0.05$), facing the presenter ($F(1,36)=8.341$, $p<0.01$), and talking with the presenter ($F(1,36)=14.642$, $p<0.001$). We also found a tendency for significant interaction in the feeling of viewing the books ($F(1,36)=3.842$, $p=0.058$). We found no interaction and no main effect in the intelligibility of the presentation.

We found simple main effects of the zoom-camera factor in all the statements that had significant interaction in the above analysis. When the presenter moved (human movement condition vs. synchronized zoom camera condition), the zoom camera caused significantly greater feelings of viewing the presenter ($F(1,36)=4.722$, $p<0.05$), facing the presenter ($F(1,36)=14.722$, $p<0.001$), and talking with the presenter ($F(1,36)=23.007$, $p<0.001$). When the presenter did not move (control condition vs. simple zoom camera condition), the zoom camera caused significant reduction in the perceived quality of the video ($F(1,36)=5.474$, $p<0.05$) and the audio ($F(1,36)=4.863$, $p<0.05$), and the feeling of viewing the books ($F(1,36)=8.614$, $p<0.01$). There was no other significant effect of the zoom-camera factor.

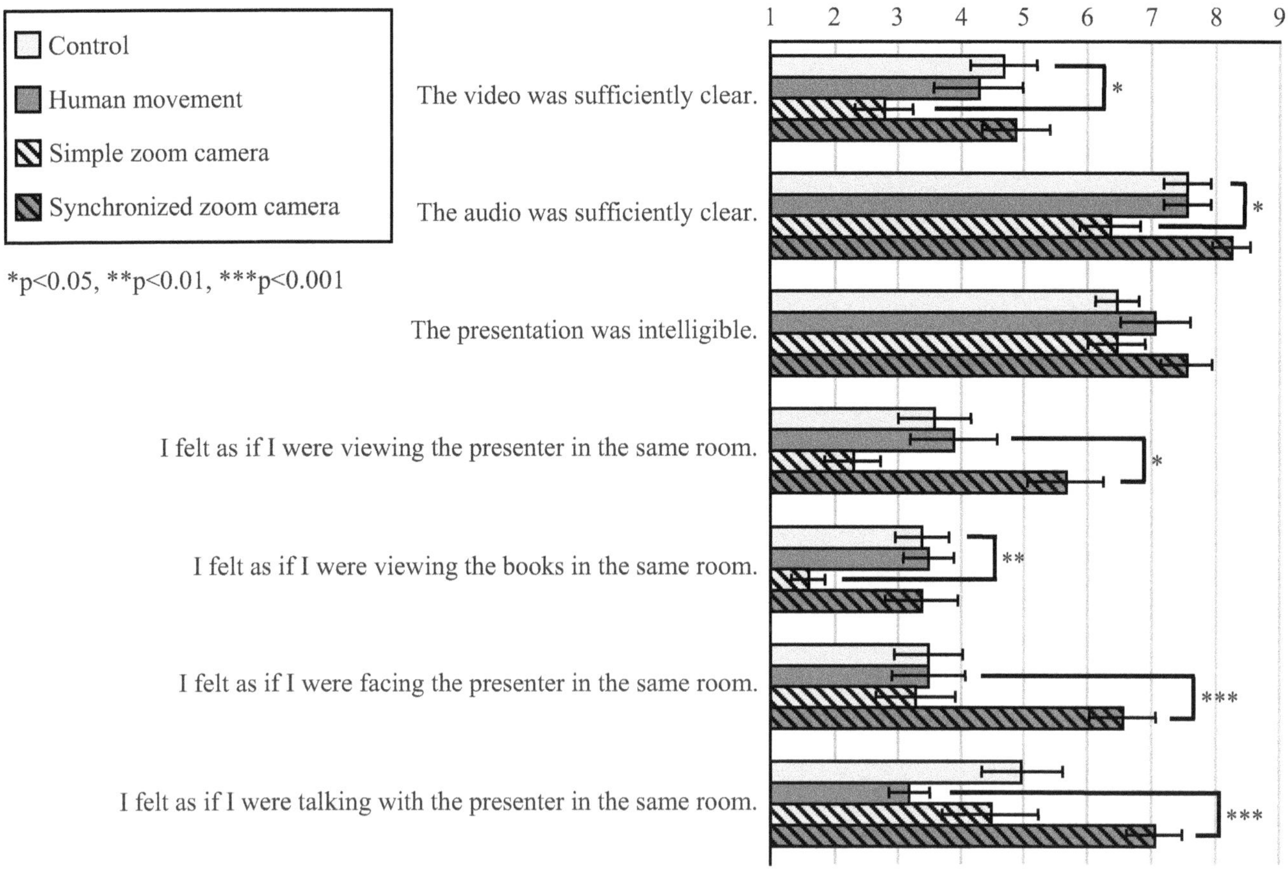

Figure 7. Results of the questionnaire (zoom-camera and human-movement factors)

The above results support hypothesis H1, which states that the synchronized zoom camera condition enhances social telepresence. We observed that the social presence of the remote presenter increased only when the remote camera's zooming was accompanied by the presenter's movement. We could additionally observe that the pure zooming lowered the evaluation of the audio-visual quality and the presence of the books.

Effects of the movable display

To examine hypothesis H2, we compared the control, human movement, simple movable display, and synchronized movable display conditions by 2x2 two-way between-subjects ANOVA. Figure 8 shows the results.

We found strong main effects of the movable-display factor. The movable display caused significantly greater feelings of viewing the presenter ($F(1,36)=9.456$, $p<0.01$), viewing the books ($F(1,36)=6.399$, $p<0.05$), facing the presenter ($F(1,36)=7.089$, $p<0.05$), and talking with the presenter ($F(1,36)=16.438$, $p<0.001$). We also found a main effect of the human-movement factor (omitted in Figure 8 due to the figure's complexity), which was a reduction of the feeling of talking with the presenter ($F(1,36)=5.918$, $p<0.05$). There was no other significant main effect and no significant interaction.

The above results support hypothesis H2, which states that the synchronized movable display condition and also the simple movable display condition enhance social telepresence. We observed that the display's movement increased the social presence of the remote presenter even when he did not move. We could additionally observe that the presenter's movement lowered the reality of the conversations.

DISCUSSION

In the introduction section we explained the three possible ways of representing a remote person's movement. In the experiment we observed that the first way – human movement – was harmful to the reality of the conversations. According to the interviews, this might be because the subjects felt that the presenter was distant when the person moved backward and away from the remote camera.

We observed that the second way – camera zooming – contributed to social telepresence. It was interesting that a combination of the first and second ways could enhance social telepresence, even though each way was harmful to it. The drawback of the first way is described above. The drawback of the second way is as follows. In the simple zoom camera condition, the remote camera's zooming out shrank the picture of the remote person and the book carried by him. According to the interviews, this seemed to be the

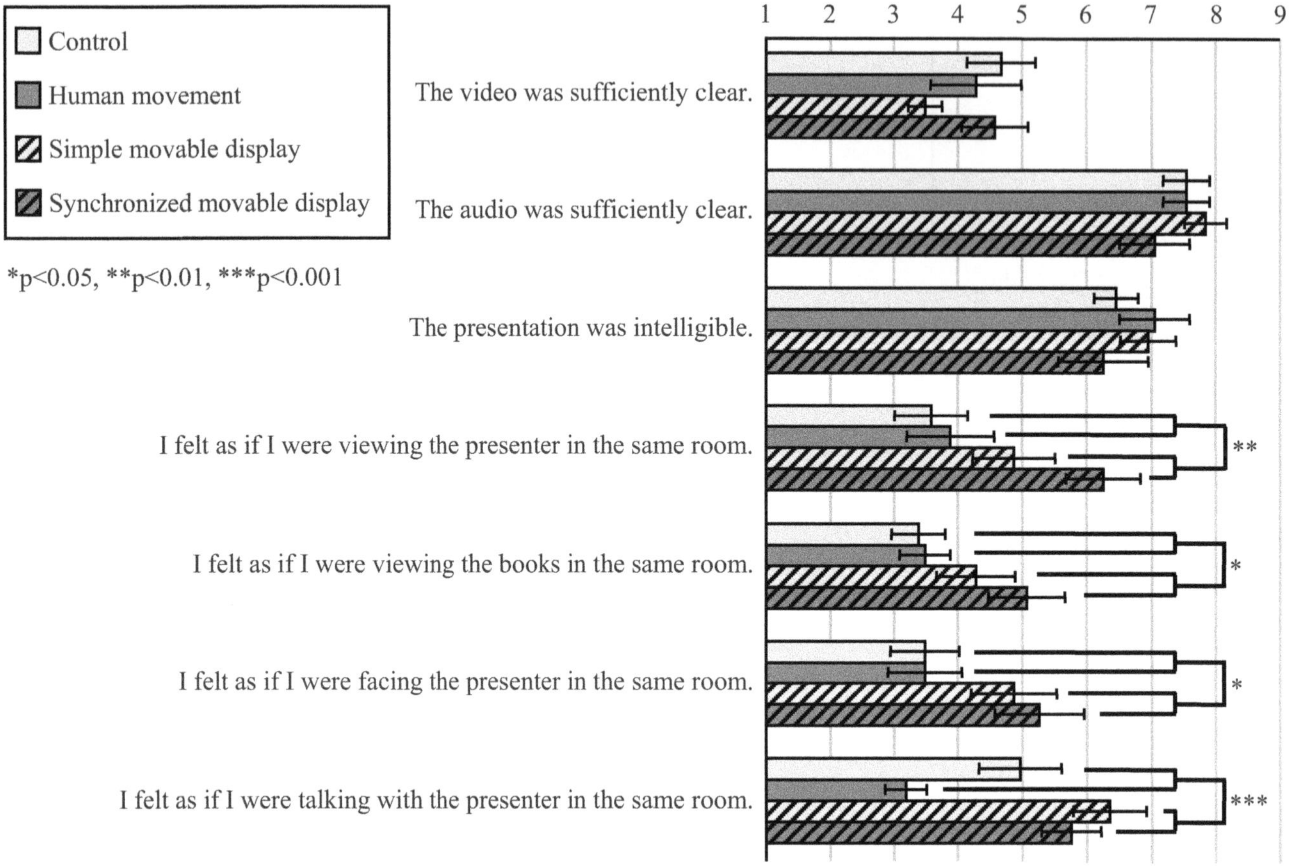

Figure 8. Results of the questionnaire (movable-display and human-movement factors)

reason why the evaluation of visual quality including the books was low. The evaluation of audio quality seemed to be affected by the low evaluation of visual quality. The positive effects that were generated by the combination of the first and second ways overcame these negative effects, even though the remote person's picture was shrunk by both the zooming out and the person's backward movement in the synchronized zoom camera condition.

In the simple zoom camera condition, the zooming was unimpressive probably because it occurred solely. In the interviews we found that only two of the ten subjects remembered the zooming. In the synchronized zoom camera condition, the zooming and the presenter's movement occurred simultaneously. As a result, six of the ten subjects remembered the zooming, and three of the six subjects answered that they were made to pay attention just when the presenter came up. This answer suggested that the zooming caused the feeling of shrinkage of a useful field of view (UFOV), since the degree of attention and the size of UFOV are inversely proportional to each other [13]. When a remote person moves toward the remote camera, the distance of that approach can be recognized based on how much the foreground picture of the person occludes the background. If the zooming enlarges the picture in synchronization with the approach, the size of the picture becomes larger than the size that is expected based the occlusion. This extra enlargement can cause the feeling of shrinkage of UFOV, since the enlargement reduces the area of the remote person's body that is seen within the UFOV.

We observed that the third way – a movable display – also contributed to social telepresence. The difference between the second and third ways was that the third way could enhance social telepresence even when the remote person did not move. It seemed that the display's movement could provide the subjects the feeling as if the remote person were moving. It was evidential that in the interviews several subjects of the simple movable display condition said that they felt as if the remote person were coming forward. It was surprising that this feeling could be generated by such a subtle stimulus as a 6-centimeter movement of the 30-inch display that was 1.2 meters away from the viewer. This implied that people are sensitive to the movement of a physical apparatus, and so the mobility of telepresence robots is an excessive capability just for giving a feeling of approaching and leaving.

In the preliminary experiment, we tested display movement that was longer than six centimeters. As a result, the movement tended to provide the subject with the artificial feeling of watching a display device, and this feeling deteriorated social telepresence (Figure 9(a)). Therefore, we hid the display device behind the wall and made only the inside of the display frame viewable (Figure 9(b)). This

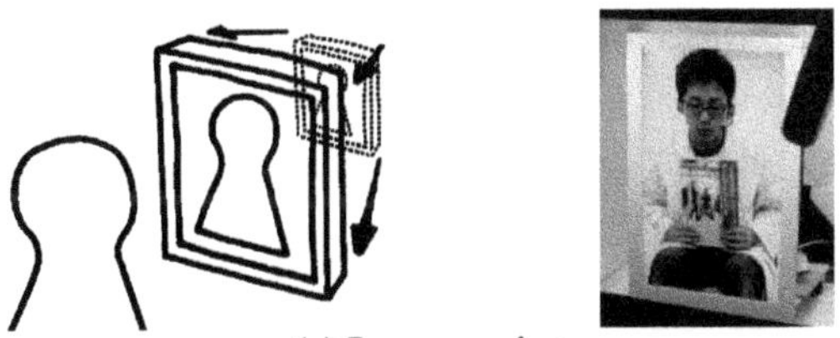

(a) Long version

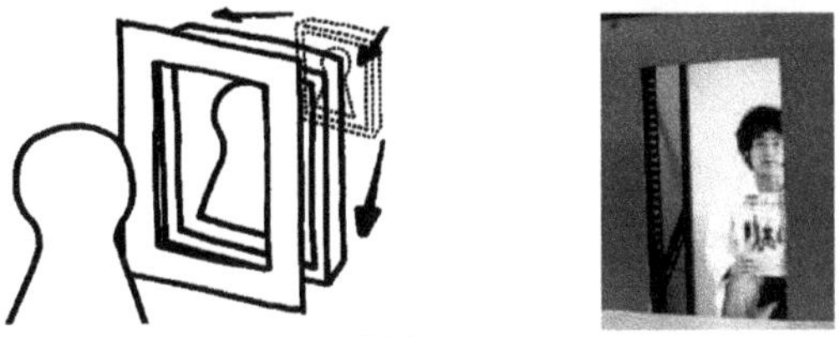

(b) Hidden version

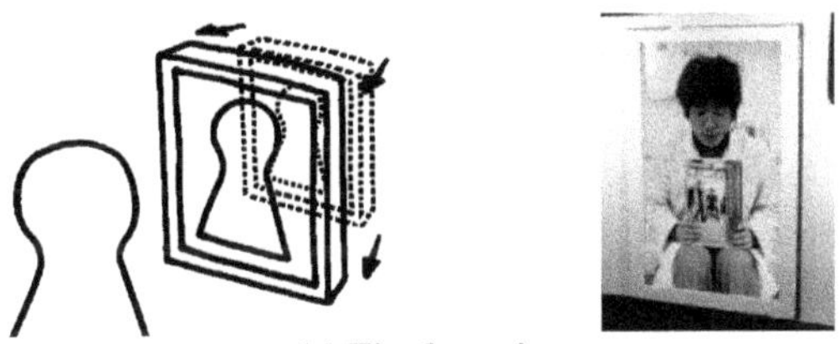

(c) Final version

Figure 9. Three steps of designing a movable display

construction removed the artificial feeling but also prohibited the subjects from perceiving the display's movement even when the movement was much longer than six centimeters. Because of this prohibition, the display's movement could not influence social telepresence. We also confirmed that less than a 6-centimeter movement could hardly be perceived and had little influence on social telepresence. Thus, in the main experiment, we showed the subject that the display moved six centimeters forward and backward across the wall that surrounded the display (Figure 9(c)).

In this study we did not test the combination of the second and third ways. This combination would be somewhat worse than just the third way, since the second way is harmful unless it is accompanied by the first way. However, the combination of all three ways may be the best, since the second way accompanied by the first way is effective. This combination can be a simple collocation of a zoom camera and a movable display: the remote camera zooms in and out and the display moves forward and backward in synchronization with a remote person's approaching and moving away from the camera. Furthermore, it is possible to combine this with a movable camera, which is a remote camera that moves according to the position of the user's eyes [17]. Testing these combinations is a subject for future work.

Another subject for future work is an investigation of the real-world usage of zoom cameras and movable displays. Movable displays may be used more widely than zoom cameras, since movable displays do not require a remote person's actual movement so that the display's movement can be added to various scenes. For example, if the display moves forward when the remote person begins talking, the beginning of the speech can be emphasized. This mechanism would give the user a feeling as if the remote person came up to the user when he or she began talking. On the other hand, movable displays may be used less widely than zoom cameras, since movable displays need an additional mechanism to move and their purchase and maintenance costs must be higher than normal displays. However, we do not worry about this issue very much, since various commercial telepresence robot products have already been available and the mechanical structure of movable displays can be much simpler than them. Zoom cameras are much less costlier than movable displays, since almost all webcams are already equipped with a zooming function and only a sensor to detect a remote person's movement has to be installed. In the experiment the system sensed the slides of the remote person's chair. This method is accurate but can work only when the person slides the chair to do something, e.g., picking up an object that is a little distant from the person. A more generic method is face tracking, which can detect the distance between the camera and the person's face.

CONCLUSION

There are three possible ways of representing a remote person's movement toward the user in visual communication: a) the remote person's movement toward the remote camera, b) the remote camera's zooming in to enlarge the remote person's picture, and c) a forward movement of the display that is displaying the remote person. It is known that visual motion such as the remote person's movement toward the remote camera is much less noticeable than a physical motion that occurs in the same room. We aimed to diminish this gap by means of a remote camera's zooming and a display's movement. We conducted an experiment to see the effects of zoom cameras and movable displays on social telepresence, i.e., the degree of resembling face-to-face interaction. The results of the experiment are the following:

Zoom cameras: In the experiment, the remote person's movement lowered the reality of the conversations, and the remote camera's zooming lowered the visual quality. However, social telepresence was enhanced when both the person's movement and the camera's zooming occurred simultaneously.

Movable display: In the experiment, the length of the display's movement was only six centimeters. However, it enhanced social telepresence, whether the remote person moved or not.

The main and peripheral contribution of this study is 1) to propose and evaluate two user interfaces that improve the reality of videoconferencing; 2) to reveal that human positional movement is useful for improving the reality of videoconferencing; 3) to hint that common visual effects would have little influence on the reality of videoconferencing; and 4) to indicate that people are sensitive to the movement of a physical apparatus.

ACKNOWLEDGMENTS
We thank Gaku Senoo and Tatsuya Asano for helping to conduct the experiment. This study was supported by JSPS Grants-in-Aid for Scientific Research No. 21680013 "Telerobotic media for supporting social telepresence" and No. 20220002 "Representation of human presence by using tele-operated androids."

REFERENCES
1. Bondareva, Y. and Bouwhuis, D. Determinants of Social Presence in Videoconferencing. *Proc. AVI 2004 Workshop on Environments for Personalized Information Access*, (2004), 1-9.
2. Buxton, W.A.S. Telepresence: Integrating Shared Task and Person Spaces. *Proc. Graphics Interface 92*, (1992), 123-129.
3. de Greef, P. and Ijsselsteijn, W. Social Presence in a Home Tele-Application. *CyberPsychology & Behavior*, 4(2), (2001), 307-315.
4. Finn, K.E., Sellen, A.J. and Wilbur, S.B. *Video-Mediated Communication*. Lawrence Erlbaum Associates, (1997).
5. Gaver, W.W., Smets, G. and Overbeeke, K. A Virtual Window on Media Space. *Proc. CHI 95*, (1995), 257-264.
6. Heath, C. and Luff, P. Media Space and Communicative Asymmetries: Preliminary Observations of Video-Mediated Interaction. *Human-Computer Interaction*, 7(3), (1992), 315-346.
7. Isaacs, E.A. and Tang, J.C. What Video Can and Can't Do for Collaboration: a Case Study. *Multimedia Systems*, 2(2), (1994), 63-73.
8. Ishiguro, H. and Trivedi, M. Integrating a Perceptual Information Infrastructure with Robotic Avatars: A Framework for Tele-Existence. *Proc. IROS 99*, (1999), 1032-1038.
9. Jouppi, N.P. First Steps Towards Mutually-Immersive Mobile Telepresence. *Proc. CSCW 2002*, (2002), 354-363.
10. Karahalios, K. and Donath, J. Telemurals: Linking Remote Spaces with Social Catalysts. *Proc. CHI 2004*, (2004), 615-622.
11. Kuzuoka, H., Yamazaki, K., Yamazaki, A., Kosaka, J., Suga, Y. and Heath, C. Dual Ecologies of Robot as Communication Media: Thoughts on Coordinating Orientations and Projectability. *Proc. CHI 2004*, (2004), 183-190.
12. Leigh, J., Rawlings, M., Girado, J., Dawe, G., Fang, R., Verlo, A., Khan, M.A., Cruz, A., Plepys, D., Sandin, D.J. and DeFanti, T.A. AccessBot: an Enabling Technology for Telepresence. *Proc. INET 2000*, (2000).
13. Miura, T. Behavior Oriented Vision: Functional Field of View and Processing Resources. *J.K. O'Regan and A. Levy-Schoen Ed., Eye Movements: From Physiology to Cognition*, Elsevier, (1987), 563-572.
14. Morita, T., Mase, K., Hirano, Y. and Kajita, S. Reciprocal Attentive Communication in Remote Meeting with a Humanoid Robot. *Proc. ICMI 2007*, (2007), 228-235.
15. Mueller, F., Agamanolis, S. and Picard, R. Exertion Interfaces: Sports over a Distance for Social Bonding and Fun. *Proc. CHI 2003*, (2003), 561-568.
16. Nakanishi, H., Murakami, Y., Nogami, D. and Ishiguro, H. Minimum Movement Matters: Impact of Robot-Mounted Cameras on Social Telepresence. *Proc. CSCW 2008*, (2008), 303-312.
17. Nakanishi, H., Murakami, Y. and Kato, K. Movable Cameras Enhance Social Telepresence in Media Spaces. *Proc. CHI 2009*, (2009), 433-442.
18. Nguyen, D.T. and Canny, J. More than Face-to-Face: Empathy Effects of Video Framing. *Proc. CHI 2009*, (2009), 423-432.
19. Paulos, E. and Canny, J. Social Tele-Embodiment: Understanding Presence. *Autonomous Robots*, 11(1), (2001), 87-95.
20. Prussog, A., Muhlbach, L. and Bocker, M. Telepresence in Videocommunications. *Proc. Annual Meeting of Human Factors and Ergonomics Society*, (1994), 25-38.
21. Roussel, N. Experiences in the Design of the Well, a Group Communication Device for Teleconviviality. *Proc. Multimedia 2002*, (2002), 146-152.
22. Roussel, N., Evans, H. and Hansen, H. Proximity as an Interface for Video Communication. *IEEE Multimedia*, 11(3), (2004), 12-16.
23. Roussou, M., Trahanias, P., Giannoulis, G., Kamarinos, G., Argyros, A., Tsakiris, D., Georgiadis, P., Burgard, W., Haehnel, D., Cremers, A., Schulz, D., Moors, M., Spirtounias, E., Marianthi, M., Savvaides, V., Reitelman, A., Konstantios, D. and Katselaki, A. Experiences from the Use of a Robotic Avatar in a Museum Setting. *Proc. VAST 2001*, (2001), 153-160.
24. Vespa, P.M., Miller, C., Hu, X., Nenov, V., Buxey, F. and Martin, N.A. Intensive Care Unit Robotic Telepresence Facilitates Rapid Physician Response to Unstable Patients and Decreased Cost in Neurointensive Care. *Surgical Neurology*, 67(4), (2006), 331-337.
25. Yamashita, N., Hirata, K., Aoyagi, S., Kuzuoka, H. and Harada, Y. Impact of Seating Positions on Group Video Communication. *Proc. CSCW 2008*, (2008), 177-186.

Breath Control of Amusement Rides

Joe Marshall, Duncan Rowland[1], Stefan Rennick Egglestone, Steve Benford, Brendan Walker, Derek McAuley
Horizon Digital Economy Research & The Mixed Reality Laboratory
The University of Nottingham, UK
{jqm, dar, sre, sdb, }@cs.nott.ac.uk, info@aerial.fm, drm@cs.nott.ac.uk
[1]current affiliation: Lincoln School of Computer Science, University of Lincoln, UK, drowland@lincoln.ac.uk

ABSTRACT
Emerging robotic technologies are enabling the control of individual seats on rollercoasters and other thrill rides. We explore the potential of breathing as an effective and engaging way of driving this. Observations and interviews from trials of an enhanced bucking bronco ride show that breath-control is fun, challenging and intelligible, and reveal riders' tactics as they battled the machine. We conclude that breath control is feasible and appropriate for controlling rides, unpack its important characteristics, and consider how it might be built into future ride systems. We argue that the combination of voluntary and involuntary factors in breathing is especially appealing for controlling rides as it balances game-like elements of skill and learning against the thrill of surrendering control to the machine.

Author Keywords
Breathing, breath control, amusement ride, biosensing, affective computing, bucking bronco, thrill, themepark

ACM Classification Keywords
H5.m. Information interfaces and presentation (e.g., HCI)

General Terms
Design

INTRODUCTION
The earliest fairground rides were small-scale affairs in which human operators directly controlled speed and duration in response to riders' expressions of excitement and fear, especially screams [1]. Some even allowed fine-grained tuning such as when 'gaff lads' who collected money on 'waltzers' gave a carriage an extra spin. Driven by a desire for ever greater thrills, coupled to demands for increasing throughput, ride technology has since evolved into large-scale computer-controlled 'thrill rides' (rollercoasters and large 'spin rides') that provide riders with an identical experience. However, a new generation of ride technologies is emerging in which computer-controlled robotic systems steer individual carriages or seats. The Robocoaster G1, for example, consists of a pair of seats on the end of a large flexible robotic arm, while the G2 and G3 attach several arms to shuttles to create a rollercoaster in which small groups of seats can be moved around the track as the ride unfolds [22]. Looking forwards, future rides are likely to deliver thrilling but also highly personalized experiences. They might even learn about riders' reactions and adapt themselves on subsequent visits.

The key question now becomes: on what basis might such real-time control be achieved? How can a human interact with a robotic system that is pushing them around under high G-forces when they are also feeling excited or scared? What form of control might enhance the experience of a thrilling ride? One strategy is to give riders voluntary control over some aspects of their movement, allowing them to partially steer their own seats. An alternative is to use biosensing to measure the rider's involuntary responses and automatically adapt the ride accordingly, mirroring the role of the traditional human operator.

In this paper, we explore how both strategies can be combined through the use of breath control. We have four motivations for this: breath control offers an intriguing balance between voluntary and involuntary control; it responds to the ride pushing back at the rider, creating a direct physical feedback loop between human and machine; riders can be highly aware of their own breathing; and it may be feasible to measure it with sufficient reliability, even under the extreme conditions of an amusement ride. We have therefore developed a small-scale prototype ride and conducted public trials in order to explore the opportunities and challenges associated with breath-controlled rides. Our contributions are to demonstrate the feasibility of this approach; to explore what kinds of control are possible and how they feel; and then to consider how the approach might be deployed on future rides. More generally we seek to extend HCI's appreciation of the nuances of breath control as an interaction technique and to highlight the potentially productive tensions between voluntary and involuntary control of interactive systems.

RELATED WORK
Although amusement rides are a popular and commercially significant form of entertainment, they have received scant attention within HCI and related fields. Previous work has focused on designing virtual reality rides [19], technologies for controlling animatronics, lighting and sound on 'dark rides' [7], and revealing riders' physiological responses to spectators [24]. Our paper adopts a distinct focus on how

humans can interact with robotic ride systems to influence the physical movement of the ride as part of a thrilling and yet also personally responsive experience.

There is, in contrast, a far more established body of research into breath as an input mechanism, falling into two main categories: assistive technologies that adapt user interfaces to specific abilities; and expressive devices that enable dynamic control of creative applications. Assistive interfaces include keyboards for use by individuals with motor impairments such as tetraplegia; simple 'suck-puff' switches allow letters to be selected from an on-screen keyboard, while more recent advances use piezo film sensor arrays to detect flow [12]. Along with more accurate control of screen-based interfaces [8], improved sensitivity and reliability of sensors is now enabling breath to control physical artifacts such as powered wheelchairs [30]. Turning to creative applications, breath controllers have augmented traditional wind and brass musical instruments (e.g., the Yamaha BC3A Breath Controller [29]) and been incorporated into new kinds of instrument [2]. Breath control has been put to other creative uses too: for controlling computer games [13, 31]; for navigating an immersive virtual world through the metaphor of diving [5]; and for enabling two-way 'gust-based' communication [23]. Mainstream products have also entered the market, for example the Sensawaft breath controlled mouse [25].

Beyond direct control, breathing can also reveal one's physiological and psychological responses to an experience, including levels of exertion, relaxation or anxiety. Here, monitoring breathing is an example of the more general approach of biosensing that is of growing interest to HCI and entertainment computing. 'Exertion interfaces' [16] to boxing [15] and cycling [26] games respond to heart-rate in order to promote exercise. Other games test players' skill at controlling their heart rates, requiring them to move between exertion and relaxation, for example when skiing and then shooting in Pulse Masters Biathlon [18], or when capturing territory on the city streets in the pervasive game 'Ere be Dragons [3]. There is also a body of work on incorporating biosensing into novel performances [17].

We extend this prior work on breath control and biosensing in two directions. First, by focusing on amusement rides, we explore the effects of a direct physical feedback loop in which a robotic system pushes back at the user, affecting their breathing as they in turn, try to control the ride. Second, we focus on the relationship between voluntary and involuntary control of breathing, especially how a creative tension between these may lead to engaging experiences.

THE BRONCOMATIC

Our approach to exploring the use of breath control in relation to amusement rides has been to construct a prototype ride and then study the experiences of riders through observation, interviews and analysis of breathing data captured from a series of public trials.

A key challenge was to design a ride that was realistic enough to be able to test breath control, and yet practical in terms of cost, tourability and safety. We alighted on the idea of extending an existing commercial bucking bronco ride of the kind that can be hired out for public events such as parties. Although not an extreme rollercoaster, a bucking bronco provides a quite intensive physical experience for a single rider (usually sufficient to throw them off) that is controlled in real-time (by a human operator). Bronco rides clearly push back on the rider, throwing them around and demanding considerable physical exertion as well as concentration. More practically, our bucking bronco was small enough to live in our lab during development, portable enough to take to various venues for public trials, and also proven to be safe over many years use at parties and similar events. In short, we felt that the bucking bronco would be a sufficiently realistic platform for testing breath control of amusement rides. An initial test in which we got a human operator to control the bronco based on data that was transmitted from the rider over a wireless network [21] confirmed the practicability of using the bronco and so we began to develop an automated version – the Broncomatic.

Figure 1. Overview of the Broncomatic

Figure 1 shows the physical set-up of the Broncomatic. The ride unit is a standard commercial ride consisting of a large red egg (broncos come in various physical forms from the traditional 'rodeo bull' to more unusual shapes) attached to a base unit in which there are two large motors that generate buck and spin movements. Riders don a breathing sensor in the form of a chest strap, sit on top of the Bucking Bronco and attempt to remain on the ride while it moves around at high speeds. Under normal operation, the ride is controlled by a human operator who uses a joystick and two speed controls mounted on a nearby control unit (left of picture) which adjust how fast the bronco spins around its vertical axis and bucks by rocking forward and backwards. While these are now under computer control in the Broncomatic, the human operator is present to monitor proceedings and press a large red safety cut-off button in case of difficulties. Finally, a large inflatable mat catches riders safely when they fall off – we have had over 100 rides with no notable injuries (Figure 2 shows an example of a quite extreme fall where the rider landed safely).

Figure 2. Falling off the Broncomatic

Controlling the ride

The original bucking bronco ride is certified as safe for public use and has several mechanical and electronic limits built into the control system, including the cut-off switch mentioned previously. In order not to compromise safety, we were keen to avoid directly altering the internals of the control hardware in any way. Our solution was to use the Phidgets physical interface prototyping toolkit [10] to construct a series of physically actuated controllers to push and pull the bronco's existing joystick and 'buck speed' and 'spin speed' dials, directly manipulating them as a human would (see Figure 3 where the small crosshatched circle next to each control is a servo connected to that control). The joystick is connected to 4 servos by tight metal wires, and the dials are connected to a servo each, using gears. As a result of this direct control, our system cannot make the bronco move in any way that a human operator could not, and so we stay within the proven, certified safety envelope of the ride. We also felt that seeing the computer physically controlling the ride would add to the public spectacle of the Broncomatic, enhancing its performativity for onlookers.

We use a MindMedia Nexus 10 Bluetooth device for breath control, which fits in a pouch worn on the body and can transmit data wirelessly. We use a belt sensor, mounted around the rider's chest which determines breathing rate and the speed at which a rider is exhaling or inhaling by detecting chest expansion. The control software for the Broncomatic runs on a nearby laptop, which receives biosensing data over Bluetooth, and is connected to the Phidgets hardware interface which controls the servos on the control panel. This integrator software takes data from the sensor, and runs a Python 'game script' that maps this to the control outputs and also drives a scoreboard shown on a nearby projection screen.

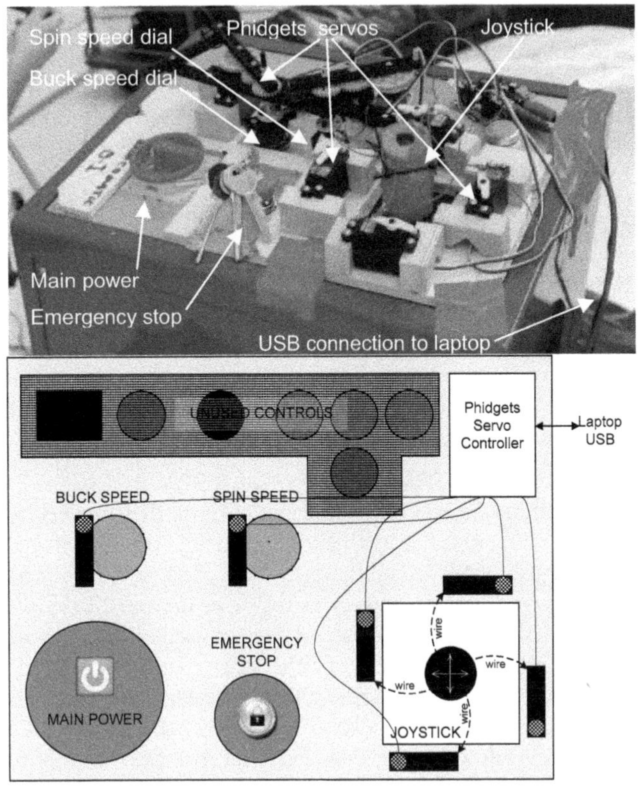

Figure 3. Broncomatic Controller and system diagram

The ride program – the Broncomatic Breathing Game

Our ride program takes the form of a simple game that is intended to explore the potential of breath control under ride conditions that vary from easy to extremely difficult. We implemented a straightforward mapping from the rider's breathing to the horizontal rotation of the ride. Inhaling causes the ride to turn clockwise, while exhaling causes the reverse anti-clockwise rotation. The speed of rotation is modulated by the speed of breathing, so that holding your breath makes the bronco stop, and inhaling or exhaling quickly makes it spin very fast. In order to introduce increasing difficulty into the experience, and also to limit the maximum time people can stay on the ride, the system then gradually and automatically increases the speed of the rotation and also eventually adds bucking to the basic rotation movement. The sequence progresses over three distinct levels. On the first level, which lasts for thirty seconds, breathing makes the bronco turn relatively slowly. On the second, also lasting for thirty seconds, the bronco turns more quickly for the same amount of breathing. On the final level, which lasts until the rider falls off, as well as another increase in spin-speed, the bronco begins to buck, which makes it extremely difficult to stay on.

Finally, the whole ride program is presented as a game in which the player scores more points the more that they breathe (which is presented to them as being based upon the total volume of air that they breathe). This sets up a fundamental tension between needing to breathe more in order to score points, but breathe less to be able to stay on the ride. In order to get a high score, the rider must breathe a lot (meaning repeated large chest expansions), making the ride move fast, which in turn makes it harder to stay on, creating a powerful dynamic and physical feedback loop in which people who want to do well are forced to push themselves harder and harder.

During the game, a large screen provides a public display of the score from the current game and a trace of the breathing sensor data. At the end of a ride, a small sticker printer prints off a sticky label with the rider's game score on it, which they can stick on their lapel. A small trace on the bottom of the sticker shows their breathing sensor data for the last 20 seconds of the ride. This souvenir also makes them a walking advert for the ride.

BRONCOMATIC TRIALS

We ran three trials with Broncomatic. In the first we set up the ride in a public atrium near a busy café and encouraged passersby to ride. Secondly, at a large student networking event, we invited volunteers to try it. In the third trial, we ran the Broncomatic at our lab and recruited a group of eight friends to repeatedly try the ride over several hours. This final test aimed to explore what happened when people rode multiple times and also to see whether spectators being personally known to the rider made a difference. A total of 43 participants took part in the three trials (23, 12 & 8 respectively), they experienced a total of 72 rides (1 person riding 5 times, 7 people riding 4 times, 4 riding twice, and 31 riding a single time). We instructed all riders briefly in the basic ride response of turning with breathing, and told them of the three levels of increasing difficulty.

We recorded video of, and logged the breathing sensor data from, each rider and also conducted semi-structured interviews immediately after each ride, asking about people's experience. A team of three people ran each experiment, one running the Broncomatic software and hardware, one interviewing people after the ride and the third in charge of a hard-wired emergency power button in case of ride malfunctions. This allowed for a relatively high throughput of riders at roughly 1 ride per 2 minutes. Participants were not paid for their time for several reasons: firstly, we hoped the ride was enjoyable in itself, so riders got a fun experience by taking part; secondly, the bronco is quite an intense ride and we did not want to encourage anyone to ride the ride who would otherwise be too scared. Broadly, the aim was to run trials with a demographic typical for riders of other small fairground rides.

For completeness, we note that the Broncomatic was modified slightly between the three trials. In the first experiment, we did not have the large scoring display and found that it was hard for people to have an idea of how good a score they were getting during the ride, or for spectators to see how the rider was doing, so this was subsequently added. After feedback from the second experiment, we modified level 3, to make the buck movement come in more slowly once level 3 started and increasing over the next 30 seconds. This was designed to make the shift from level 2 to level 3 less severe, whilst still maintaining the high difficulty level that limits the time people are likely to stay on the ride.

EXPERIENCING THE BRONCOMATIC

In presenting our findings, we focus on two key questions: what tactics and strategies were riders able to employ, and how did it feel to ride the Broncomatic, especially with regard to control of the ride and of one's own breathing? We draw on the interviews and our observations, presenting examples and illustrating them with quotes and also graphs that show the rate of expansion and contraction of the breathing sensor belt over time. We use this in the ride as an approximation of people's breathing – a negative value shows that someone is exhaling air, and a positive value shows that they are inhaling air. Due to the different sizes of people's chests that stretch the belt differently, sensor readings have to be normalized by the ride software. Consequently, there is no vertical scale on these graphs as the raw values are essentially specific to the rider (and also to how the belt is adjusted). While movement of the chest strap is an approximation of breathing (as considered later in the paper), it is a sufficiently good one for the riders to experience a believable sense of control and for the graphs to show changing patterns of breathing over time.

Riders' Tactics and Strategies

We begin by identifying and comparing various tactics and strategies that were employed by riders during the ride.

Controlled breathing

Most riders tried hard to focus on their breathing: "*you're just concentrating, concentrating so hard*". A lot of them tried to keep a steady breathing pace: "*because I used to do a lot of martial arts, and of course from that, we focus on how to calm your breathing down to a point, so I mainly just tried to focus on that, just calm it down, keep it level and steady*". One rider even rode the ride with their eyes closed to try and stay in control of the ride, emphasizing the idea of being inwardly focused: "*I closed my eyes, and I breathed deeply.*" The graph in Figure 4 shows an example of this steady breathing, where the rider breathed constantly at 26 breaths per minute until they got 12 seconds into level 3, could no longer keep it steady, and fell off.

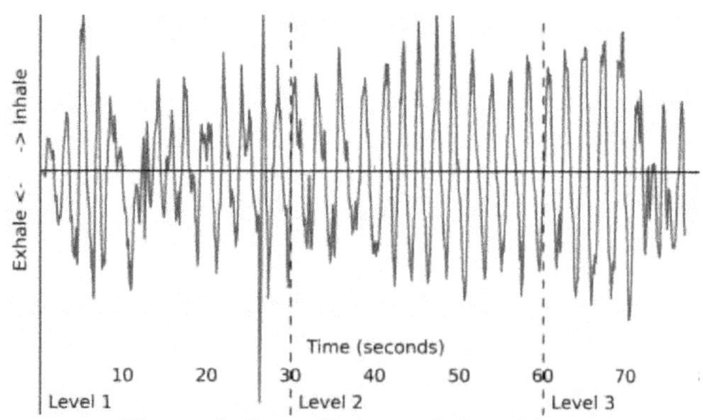

Figure 4. Controlled, steady breathing

Several riders related their breath control tactics to sporting activities: "*I play rugby as well, and when you're playing, when you're really concentrating, you've still got to focus on breathing while you're running the whole time*", "*I used to do a lot of martial arts, and of course from that, we focus on how to calm your breathing down to a point*"

Holding one's breath

Interviewees reported holding their breath at key moments to be a tactic, especially to control the ride as it stepped up to the next level (there was an audible alert on level changes). Figure 5 shows a rider holding her breath as level 2 kicks in at 30 seconds so as to start the level gently. When level 3 started at 60 seconds the extra speed meant that she quickly lost control of her breathing, causing the ride to spin quickly and making her fall off.

Holding one's breath could also be a good tactic to temporarily stop the ride, rebalance and regain control: "*it threw me off, I managed to hold my breath, there was a spin, and I almost lost it, then I held my breath.*" However, while a useful tactic in the short term, breath holding was a self-limiting option in the longer term. Beyond not scoring points, the longer you hold your breath, the harder you need to breath afterwards, and people cannot hold their breath for ever: "*I guess I thought that if I held my breath when I was about to fall off, it might be okay, and that worked for a few seconds, but then I found myself like going, losing blood, you know, needing a breath*". Figure 6 shows a rider who held their breath for 10 seconds (between 20 and 30 seconds) before running out of breath.

It appears that holding one's breath led to a rise in tension as the rider realized that they would have to breathe sooner or later, possibly exacerbated by the physical sensation of gradually running out of breath, a feeling perhaps not unlike approaching a drop in a rollercoaster.

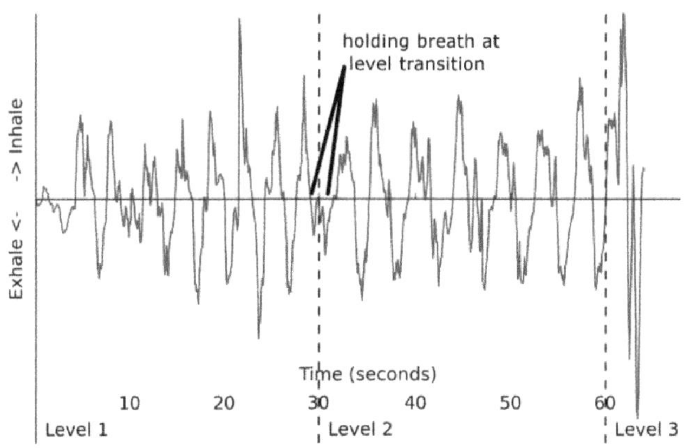

Figure 5. Holding breath between levels

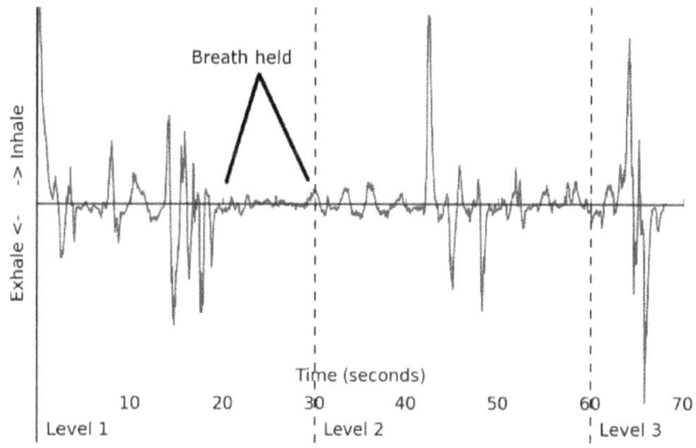

Figure 6. A rider who held his breath

Holding on tight

Sometimes riders gave up on breath control and just held on in the hope that they could continue to do so, particularly at the point they lost control of their breathing, mostly in level 3: "*...level three, like near the end; I was just concentrating on holding on with my legs and arms as tightly as possibly*". Figure 7 shows an example of the odd positions people end up in whilst hanging on. Such positions also have an effect on their breathing that makes the ride less predictable. However, holding on could be a good tactic when all else failed. Figure 8 shows the breathing of a rider who managed to hang on for 60 seconds in level 3, despite being thrown about and breathing wildly.

Longer term strategies

Those who rode multiple times experienced a learning process, a mixture of getting used to the twin challenges of staying on the bronco and controlling their breathing, whilst also optimizing strategies in order to get the highest score: "*The first time you don't know what to expect and you're kind of just getting the hang of it, second time, tried to control it too much, and it didn't work out, and then the third time, was better because I was just like right; I'm just going to concentrate on [staying on and breathing deep].*"

Figure 7. An example of hanging on

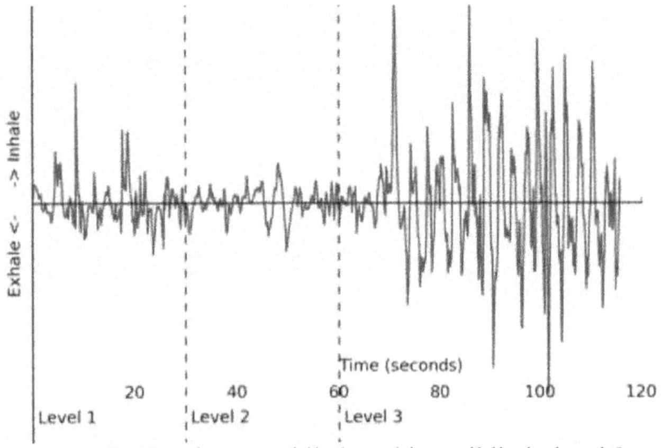

Figure 8. Hanging on while breathing wildly in level 3

This led to whole ride strategies, rather than localized tactics, taking into account the way the game progresses to get the highest score. Several riders noticed that in the first level, it was relatively easy to stay on the bronco, even with quite hard breathing, whilst on levels 2 and 3 it was much harder (the scoring was the same on all levels). This led to an overall ride strategy of breathing as hard as possible to get a good score on level 1, then trying to calm down breathing on 2 and 3: *"First time I tried long slow breaths, to sort of pace it and then I realised that you need to score quite highly in the lower levels, so I think it's a case of exploitation of the system a little bit"*. Figure 9 shows a rider who managed to breathe very hard up to 30 seconds (average of 61 breaths per minute), then calmed down to try and stay on in level 2 and 3 (average of 26 breaths per minute). However, this rider reported feeling quite dizzy after the extreme breathing on level 1, which is probably why they fell off so quickly in level 3. Recorded breathing rates provide further evidence that riders were able to push their breathing rates harder in the earlier levels. For example, in the third experiment, the maximum breaths per minute of any rider were 62 for level 1, 48 for level 2, and 36 for level 3.

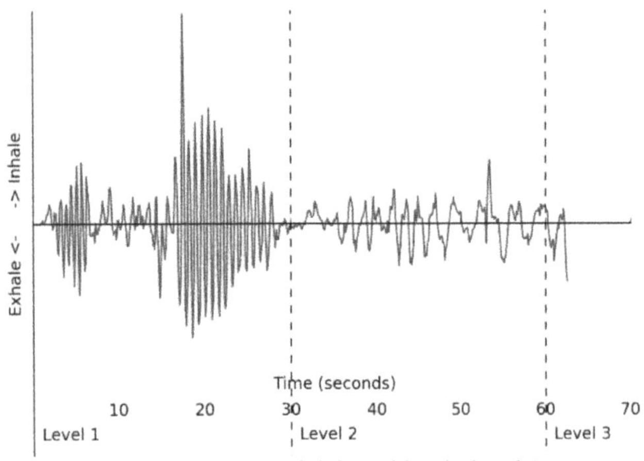

Figure 9. Very quick breathing in level 1

How does it feel to ride the Broncomatic?

We now turn to the question of how it felt to ride the Broncomatic as revealed by our interview.

How did it feel overall?

We asked riders whether they enjoyed the ride. All but one of the riders was very positive about their enjoyment of the ride, even those who had ridden it three or four times already. One rider had slightly mixed feelings, as he felt it was fun, but drank too much the night before, so was hung-over, and the ride had made him feel sick (not an unusual feeling for some people on amusement rides). For all riders, this was the first time they had experienced a breath controlled ride. It was clearly quite a different experience to other rides, even for those with plenty of amusement ride experience as the breath control seemed to feel unusual: *"It was err, a really strange experience, something I've never, never experienced before, so it was kind of odd"*

Most people found the ride hard, particularly on level 3, where the tilting movement made it much harder for people; as one rider said: *"it's not as jerky as it looks, it's much smoother, and then level 3 happens and it all goes to pot"*. The longest any rider managed to stay on was 171 seconds (2 minutes 51s), which included 71 seconds on level 3. The shortest rides were under 15 seconds, with a median ride length of 66 seconds. 66% of rides reached level 3, whilst a small number of people fell off very quickly (15% of rides). The progressive difficulty increase stopped people getting bored, yet allowed them some time to discover how the ride worked: *"I figured out what the mapping was between how I was breathing and what would happen; it was cool. And then, when it changed level, there were things that shifted and I had to readjust again, which was really good, stopped me getting like too confident with it, or bored or whatever."*

Responsiveness and control of the ride

Responses to the questions "did you feel the ride was responding to you?" and "did you feel in control of the ride?" give an interesting insight into the overall dynamic of the ride. When asked whether they felt the ride was responding to them, only 3 riders said they couldn't tell, with 35 riders feeling it certainly was responding to their breathing. However, whilst riders generally felt that the ride was responding to them, they varied as to how much they felt in control of the ride, with only 9 riders saying that they felt completely in control of the ride, and 16 saying they had a level of control, but not right throughout the ride.

When asked for more detail, several described a progressive loss of control as the levels got more difficult: *"I think at the first stage, I was controlling the situation .... 2, it was in the middle, between me and the machine. Level 3 was err, out of my control. I tried not to breathe!"*, *"...the third one I was focusing so much in trying to stay on the thing that I lost all my ability to change direction"*. There is sometimes a strong feedback loop between the rider and the ride when they lose control: *"when it speeds up quite a bit, it shocked me, and I breathed a bit deeper, so it threw me off.*" Others were tripped up by the link between breathing and talking, for example by laughing: "*I was trying to control it and it was working, but I guess when you start having fun, like in the end, where it just - spun - like that completely, and that was the time when I was laughing myself,*"

Due to the servos and motors, there is inevitably a slight delay in response; this also made people lose control: "*I thought the delay was significant enough so that I felt that I wasn't completely in control of the situation*".

Responsiveness and control of their own bodies

We also wanted to know if riders felt in control of their breathing and movements. We asked whether riders lost control of their breathing at all. Of 41 riders, 20 felt they lost control of their breathing during the ride, whereas 12 stayed in control throughout (9 were uncertain). We also asked whether riders fell off as soon as they lost control. Of the 20 who lost control, 9 said they fell off the bronco straight away. Riders described various tactics that they adopted for trying to stay on the ride when they reached the tipping point of loss of control as we discussed above

Competition with others

After observing some people competing with each other in the first experiment, in the second two experiments, we asked riders whether they felt they were competing with others. Interestingly, several people (9 of the 16 people who answered this question) did not feel that they were competing in any way with anyone else and were instead viewing the ride as a personal challenge: "*mainly with myself, rather than with other people ... for me I think it was much more about, trying to see that the balance is right*". The other 7 were more directed at getting the high score – "*Yeah definitely, [going for a high score] yeah, that's my thing*". As well as trying for a long ride or a high score, some people chose to ignore the game and play around with the ride just for the joy of controlling the ride: "*seeing how much I could turn it on the early levels, so just taking big, deep breaths, see how far it would go, and then breathe out as much as possible. Then on the last couple, I was just kind of trying to breathe in more than out, to try and get it to turn back round. Which didn't work.*"

Noticing spectators

We were interested to know how riders felt about having their breathing put on public display. Interestingly, no-one said anything negative about this; people's feelings were a mixture of neutral ("*Not really bothered*") and actively positive comments: "*...having people watching, I mean family are here today, and quite a few students who may know me, colleagues, that, that adds quite a lot to the experience.*", "*Good fun, enjoy being a spectacle, what can I say, I'm a bit of a joker.*" People didn't seem to mind their breathing being broadcast to spectators at all, perhaps because they didn't see any real privacy issue around it: "*It didn't worry me too much, because, I don't think that ... there's not a lot that you can kind of infer from breathing*", "*I wasn't really too fussed about people seeing my breathing, because I don't think, I don't really think that it's a private matter I guess*". However, one rider had been concerned about revealing the state of their health in advance of the ride: "*I'm a smoker, and I've got a cold at the moment, so I was thinking, I'm gonna be terrible at this, because I'm pretty unhealthy in that sense*".

Interestingly, despite at times there being large groups of people around the Broncomatic and people taking flash photographs etc., many riders said that they did not notice them at all, due to being so focused on the ride: "*...it's just the adrenalin rush and that's it. I just zone out*", "*I could hear them, but I didn't really notice them, because I'm too busy concentrating on the actual ride*". Having to concentrate on breathing as well as staying on took a lot of mental energy: "*I think in fact, the feedback mechanism takes the focus off everyone else. Because you're thinking that, you've got other things to think about.*" It may be that, by asking riders to focus internally on their breathing, we make them less aware of external factors such as spectators.

However, spectators could have an impact. Some shouted at riders in an attempt to distract them, for example trying to make them laugh, which fed into the ride feedback loop, making it harder: "*I noticed [name], asking me how to, telling me to kind of laugh, or not to laugh ... and then, that did affect me then, so I started smiling, and breathing a bit deeper, started moving faster, so [name] saying that to me, then did affect the way that the ride moved as well.*"

DISCUSSION

In discussing our findings we consider the extent to which our trials with the Broncomatic demonstrate the feasibility of breath controlled rides; identify key characteristics of breath control; explore how breath control might be incorporated into future rides; and reflect on the general nature of negotiating control with autonomous systems.

Breath control of rides is feasible

Our findings indicate the broad feasibility of breath control in adaptive amusement rides. Technically, our ride was reliable and it appears that even current chest-strap technologies offer sufficient accuracy and responsiveness to control rides. We also propose that the Broncomatic delivered a good ride experience. Not only did nearly all riders enjoy the ride, but it felt appropriately responsive, challenging and was open to various different tactics and strategies. The ride was responsive in the sense that riders understood how to control it and felt that it was capable of delivering a direct and intelligible response at times – i.e., it could be made controllable by a rider with sufficient skill rather than feeling random or wildly unresponsive. However, the success of the ride also lay in riders not always being in control, not least due to having only partial control over their own breathing. Key here was the ride physically pushing back on the rider, affecting their breathing and hence their control. The Broncomatic also appears to encourage some riders to focus in on their breathing. Even this one dimensional control – breathing in and out – gave rise to a variety of tactics which riders could then incorporate into broader strategies as they learned how to respond over multiple rides. Finally, we saw spectators adopting various tactics to affect the riders' breath control.

The key characteristics of breath control

We now reflect on the underlying characteristics of breath control that afford distinct opportunities and challenges for designing rides (and possibly other experiences). Firstly, breathing is one of the few corporeal functions that are part-controllable by conscious effort and part under control of the autonomic nervous system. It is, for example, possible to deliberately hold one's breath, denying the body of oxygen (hypoxia), but only to the point of unconsciousness whereupon automatic systems safely embedded in the medulla and pons deep within the brain take over. Conversely, hyperventilating removes carbon dioxide from the blood, making the blood more alkaline which in turn signals the blood vessels that supply the brain to constrict (again leading to hypoxia) [27]. Various regulatory mechanisms respond to environmental conditions (e.g., a decrease in levels of oxygen in the air) or levels of exertion. Psychological factors also come into play – when people are scared, excited or otherwise aroused, their respiration rates become quicker [6], which at extreme levels may lead to hyperventilation. As well as feelings affecting breathing, controlled breathing can affect how people feel; for example the 'EmRoll' emotional game [31], exploits the fact that slow breathing can make players feel more relaxed.

Yet, there is also the possibility for very fine grained direct control over breathing as we see when playing musical instruments or in the everyday activity of speech, although even here involuntary workings can be exposed such as hiccups or yawning. It is this wide range of control, from completely voluntary to involuntary, from immediate to longer term, from fine grained to coarse, and from environmental, to bodily and psychological, that makes breathing so powerful as a control mechanism, and possibly more flexible than other forms of biosensing such as heart rate or GSR which may be less immediately controllable and responsive.

Breathing also has highly a distinctive feel to it. Riders can become very aware of breathing and so be able to tune into the experience, again more directly than with say heart rate. It may even be visible to spectators. The feeling of holding breath soon becomes incredibly powerful and adds tension to an experience. Finally, people can train in breath control, which is an integral part of many practices such as yoga, meditation, singing, diving, swimming, shooting and martial arts. This is not to say that other ways of sensing response to an experience are not of interest, but rather that breath control is an especially powerful one in several regards, and that designers should be aware of the fine nuances of using it.

One interesting point about how our system uses breath control, is that it does not have any emotional model or interpretation, using breathing data as a direct input, yet creates strong emotional responses in the rider. This suggests that we can successfully create 'affective loop' experiences [11], where there is a feedback loop between the rider's emotions and the system, without the emotional models used in most previous systems which aim to be emotionally responsive by measuring or visualizing user's emotional state (eg. Stresscam [20] uses thermal imaging data to measure levels of stress, the eMoto pen [11] allows users to visualize their emotions as colours, based on an emotional model interpreting gestures that they input.)

Incorporating breath control into future rides

With this in mind, we consider how ride designers might practically utilise breath control. What tactics can they emply and how can rides measure breathing?

Tactics for ride design

Based on our experience with the Broncomatic and our reflections on the general characteristics of breathing, we propose some practical tactics for using breath control. The first three focus on how the rider can control the ride:

- Encourage the rider to hold their breath at key points such as before a major drop or movement. The tension of holding up the ride by breath alone may be powerful, and the feeling of having to let go soon overwhelming.
- Use controlled rhythmic breathing to initially raise the thrill level of the ride (e.g., gradually raising a drop tower but only while the rider remains calm), or to synchronise with the timing and movement of the ride (e.g., deep breathing drives ever deeper swinging)
- Use rapid breathing to power-up both rider and ride, leaving them pumped up and ready for the next phase.

The next five tactics allow the ride to push back at the rider:

- Use physical movement and exertion to make the rider breathe harder and less regularly and so lose control.
- Gradually increase tension to make the rider increase breathing in preparation for 'fight or flight', e.g., when slowly elevating the ride before rapid movement.
- Use sudden shocks to make them draw and hold breath.
- Heighten a rider's awareness of their breathing by enclosing them, or through sound and visual effects.
- Encourage riders to shout or scream in order to trigger a response, including enabling spectators to do this

We also draw attention to the wider potential of designing 'sticky' rides that remember a rider's previous experiences and adapt the next one accordingly in order to reward repeat visits. Rides might also reward riders who train themselves to control their breathing in various ways.

How these tactics are used will depend on the available ride technology. For emerging technologies that afford flexible control over individual seats, it is a case of designing a ride program that mixes them in appropriate ways. For example, the Broncomatic leads riders to experience increasing levels of difficulty whilst they learn to control the movement, before the ride gradually introduces its own movements, inexorably leading them to the point of loss of control. It may also be possible to use some of these tactics with current ride technologies, e.g., raising drop towers, pausing before drops or controlling swings as mentioned above. The harder challenge here is that current rides do not provide individual seat control, so there is the problem of how to adapt for a whole group of riders. There may be entertaining possibilities in allowing one person to control a ride for everyone else, especially if they can communicate. Perhaps the most timid rider takes control with others encouraging them, or the bravest with others pleading?

Of course, it will be important to use these tactics safely. Rides are carefully designed, tested and inspected to ensure appropriate levels of physical safety and judge an appropriate level of thrill or scaring. The additional challenge of breath control lies in potential interference with breathing. It may be important be allow rapid disengagement if there is any risk of uncontrollable hyperventilation, while sensing technologies – as we now discuss – must guard against overly restricting breathing or, for respirators, transmitting infections . Designers must also warn people with breathing difficulties about possible risks.

Negotiating control with the Ride

The Broncomatic is interesting and successful precisely because it affords a balance of control between rider and ride, with each being able to influence the other as part of a feedback loop. Key to this is that the rider does not have full control over the ride or themselves and has to battle with two autonomous systems (ride and body) until they reach the tipping point between control and loss of control that is the climax of the experience.

We propose that this negotiation of control and balance of the voluntary and involuntary is especially important for building adaptive amusement rides. Rides are in large part about the pleasures of surrendering control, either to a human operator, or more recently by being strapped into a powerful machine from which there is no escape until the ride has finished. Rides may be about confronting fears and passing through 'rites of passage' as much as they are about the visceral pleasure of the experience, and it is important not to remove this element in trying to make them more personally adaptive. Thus, while the Broncomatic includes elements of computer games in terms of levels of difficulty and scoring points, it would be a mistake to think of it in terms of being a game that is solely about skill and mastery. Rather, designers need to introduce adaptation but without compromising the principle of surrendering control.

Measuring breathing on rides

We now consider how to sense breathing on a ride. There are many different ways to achieve this non-invasively [9]. Most thrill rides already involve the rider being strapped into a safety harness integrated with the seat unit. One possibility that might involve relatively little additional disruption and delay would be to integrate elastic chest-sensor straps into the harness or to require the rider to fasten one more strap to turn on the breath control feature of the ride. An alternative might be to use clothing with sensors embedded (such as shirts for breathing and heart rate [4]). Riders could then purchase their own monitoring devices to communicate with various rides. A more radical alternative is to use a respirator-style sensor as part of a mask. Although at first sight requiring users to wear masks might appear to be an unlikely approach, this could bring the advantage of making the user even more intensely aware of the sound and feel of their own breathing, further increasing tension for horror-themed and other scary rides. The mask might also provide a platform for embedding microphones to capture riders' responses for generating souvenirs or broadcasting to spectators following the approach of Schnädelbach et al [24]. Our ongoing work is exploring the feasibility of this approach and, at the time of writing, we have just fabricated and are testing a set of breath-control gas masks for use in a major horror-themed experience (Figure 10). Flow rate sensors are used to monitor breathing flow rate, in the side filter of the mask. A phial containing silica gel is used to remove water from exhaled air before reaching the moisture-sensitive sensors. The filter at the front of the mask also allows air flow, so only a small (but stable) percentage of the air goes through our measurement system, and breathing is not restricted.

Figure 10. Respiration sensing, Wi-Fi enabled gas mask

As an additional note, the benefits of surrendering control have been discussed in other contexts: by Woodruff and colleagues in their studies of the use of home-automation systems to assist in the observance of the Jewish Sabbath [28], and also with relation to automated agents such as autopilots and car navigation systems [14]. Our study suggests that it can also feel exciting or stimulating to at least partially surrender control to a robotic system. We observe that such interactions actually involve reconciling two autonomous systems – machine and body – that are in a feedback loop, which is of particular relevance to ongoing research into biosensing. Modalities such as heart-rate and GSR will also be subject to both voluntary and involuntary control, and any applications of these will need to carefully consider what aspects of control are surrendered to what degree and how this might feel to the user.

CONCLUSIONS

Our experience with the Broncomatic suggests that breath control is a viable and interesting way of driving individually responsive amusement rides. Even a simple mapping of breathing, measured by a commercial chest-strap sensor, can provide an engaging, challenging and yet intelligible ride experience. Breath control is especially interesting because it balances voluntary and involuntary control, enabling the ride to physically and psychologically 'push back' at the rider while they struggle to control it and themselves. Ride designers can also exploit a wide variety of breath control tactics. The net result is new forms of ride that have game-like qualities in terms of skill learning, and adaptation, and yet retain the distinctive and thrilling quality of surrendering control to the machine.

ACKNOWLEDGEMENTS

This work is supported by Horizon Digital Economy Research, RCUK grant EP/G065802/1.

REFERENCES

1. Adams, J. A. *The American Amusement Park Industry: A History of Technology and Thrills*. Twayne (1991)
2. Aziz, A. D., Warren, C., Bursk, H., and Follmer, S., The flote: an instrument for people with limited mobility, *Proc. ASSETS 08*, 295-206, ACM (2008)
3. Boyd Davis, S., Moar, M., Jacobs, R., Watkins, M., Riddoch C., Cooke, K., Ere Be Dragons: heartfelt gaming, *Digital Creativity*, 17(3), Taylor Francis (2006)
4. De Clerk, H, Corthouta, R, Puers, R. Textile Integrated Breathing and ECG Monitoring System, *Proc. Eurosensors XXIII*, Elsevier (2009)
5. Davies, C., Osmose: being immersive in a virtual space, *Digital Creativity*, 9 (2), 65-77, Taylor Francis (1998)
6. Van Diest, I., Winters, W. et al, Hyperventilation beyond fight / flight: Respiratory responses during emotional imagery, *Psychophysiology*, 38 (2001)
7. Dominey, R., Simon, R., and Wong, D., Heightened amusement park dark ride interactivity and creativity made possible with highly integrated technology, *Computers in Entertainment*, 2 (2), 13-13, ACM (2004)
8. Evreinov, G., Evreinov, T., "Breath-Joystick" – Graphical Manipulator for Physically Disabled Users, *ICCHP 2000*,
9. Folke, M., Cernerud, L., Ekström, M. and Hök, B. Critical review of non-invasive respiratory monitoring in medical care. *Medical and Biological Engineering and Computing*, 41 (4). 377-383, Springer (2003)
10. Greenberg, S., Fitchett, C., Phidgets: easy development of physical interfaces through physical widgets, *UIST 2001*, 209-218, ACM
11. Höök, K Affective Loop Experiences – What Are They?, *Proc. PERSUASIVE 2008*, Springer
12. Kuzume, K., Input device for disabled persons using expiration and tooth-touch sound signals, *Proc. ACM SAC 2010*, 1159-1164, ACM
13. Lee, H., Panont, W. R., Plattenburg, B., de la Croix, J., Patharachalam, D., and Abowd, G., Asthmon: empowering asthmatic children's self-management with a virtual pet, *Proc. CHI 2010*, 3583-3588, ACM
14. Lee, J.D. and See, K.A. Trust in Automation: Designing for Appropriate Reliance, *Human Factors*, 46(1), (2004)
15. Masuko, S. and Hoshino, J. (2006). A fitness game reflecting heart-rate. *Proc. ACE 2006*. ACM
16. Mueller, F., Agamanolis, S, Picard, R., Exertion Interfaces: sports at a distance for social bonding and fun, *Proc. CHI 2003*, 561-568, ACM, 2003
17. Nagashima, Y., Bio-sensing systems and bio-feedback systems for interactive media arts, *Proc. NIME 2003*, 48-55, National University of Singapore
18. Nenonen, V., Lindblad, A., Hakkinen, V., Laitinen, T., Jouhtio, M. and Hamalainen, P.(2007). Using heart-rate to control an interactive game, *Proc. CHI 2007*, ACM
19. Pausch, R., Snoddy, J., Taylor, R., Watson, S., and Haseltine, E. 1996. Disney's Aladdin: first steps toward storytelling in virtual reality, *Proc. SIGGRAPH96*, ACM
20. Puri, C., Olson, L., Pavlidis, I, Levine, J and Starren, J, StressCam: non-contact measurement of users' emotional states through thermal imaging, *Proc. CHI 2005*, ACM.
21. Rennick Egglestone, S., Marshall, J., Walker, B., Rowland, D., Benford, S., Rodden, T. The Bronco: a proof-of-concept adaptive fairground ride, *Proc. ACE 2009*, ACM
22. Robocoaster: http://www.robocoaster.com
23. Sawada, E., Ida, S., Awaji, T., Morishita, K., Aruga, T.et al., Furukawa, M., Shimizu, N., Tokiwa, T., Nii, H., Sugimoto, M., and Inami, M., BYU-BYU-View: a wind communication interface, *Proc. SIGGRAPH 2007*, ACM
24. Schnädelbach, H., Rennick Egglestone, S., Reeves, S., Benford, S., Walker, B., and Wright, M., Performing thrill, *Proc. CHI 2008*, ACM.
25. Sensawaft: http://www.zyxio.com/
26. Stach, T., Graham, T.C.N., Jim, Y. and Rhodes, R.E., Heart-rate control of exercise video games, *Proc. Graphics Interface 2009*, ACM
27. West, J., *Pulmonary Pathophysiology: The Essentials*, Williams & Wilkins. pp. 22. (1977)
28. Woodruff, A., Augustin, S, Focault, B., Sabbath Day Home Automation: "It's Like Mixing Technology and Religion", *Proc. CHI 2007*, 527-536, ACM
29. Yamaha BC3A http://uk.yamaha.com/en/products/music-production/accessories/breathcontrollers/
30. Yamamoto, M., Ikeda, T. and Sasaki, Y., "Real-time analog input device using breath pressure for the operation of powered wheelchair", *Proc Robotics and Automation (ICRA 2008)*, 3914-3919, IEEE
31. Zangouei, F. et al, How to Stay in the Emotional Rollercoaster: Lessons Learnt from Designing EmRoll, *Proc.NordiCHI 2010*, ACM

Time Characteristics of Olfaction in a Single Breath

Daisuke Noguchi†Sayumi Sugimoto†
†Keio University
3-14-1 Hiyoshi, Kohoku-ku, Yokohama, Kanagawa 223-8522, Japan
noguchi, sugimoto,okada@mos.ics.keio.ac.jp

Yuichi Bannai††Ken-ichi Okada†
††Canon Inc.
3-30-2 Shimomaruko, Ohta-ku, Tokyo 146-8501, Japan
bannai.yuichi@canon.co.jp

ABSTRACT
The transmission of olfactory information together with audiovisual information is now attracting much attention. However, the information is difficult to synchronize because of problems of scent lingering in the air and olfactory adaptation. We aimed at minimizing the amount of odorant presented to users in order to mitigate these problems, and developed an olfactory display that is able to present scents precisely. The display uses pulse ejection, whereby scents are emitted for only short periods of time. In this study, we aimed to mitigate the above-mentioned problems and to measure the time characteristics of olfaction in a single breath, which are difficult to measure by conventional methods. As a result, the most effective conditions for using a small amount of odorant in a single breath were revealed. These results are expected to ease the synchronization of olfactory and audiovisual information.

Author Keywords
Olfactory information, olfactory display, pulse ejection.

ACM Classification Keywords
H.5.2 Information Interfaces and Presentation: User Interfaces.—*User-centered design.*

General Terms
Human Factors

INTRODUCTION
Information transmission and communication tend to be limited to visual information and audio information. However, the transmission of information via all five senses (sight, hearing, touch, smell and taste) has lately attracted much attention[1]. Transmission of olfactory information along with visual information has been shown to be effective in increasing the understanding of content by an audience [2]. In addition, the relation between emotion and scent has been analyzed by measuring brain waves of participants viewing videos, in order to assess their psychological state[3]. The presentation of olfactory information is thought to be as effective in conveying a heightened sense of realism as three-dimensional audio and visual effects[4]. Therefore, olfactory information is expected to have high potential in the field of rich multimedia communication.

Previous scent presentation techniques were designed merely to create the sense of experiencing a scent, and they used higher densities and longer presentation times of scent than actually necessary. For those reasons, the methods were hindered by problems of olfactory adaptation and scent lingering in the air. Olfactory adaptation results in the user becoming unable to detect a scent when olfactory information is presented, and scent lingering in the air hinders the switching of scents because previously presented scents become mixed with the next ones. We developed a high-quality olfactory display that enables high-precision control of scent emission, as well as a scent presentation technique where scent is emitted for a short period of time in a pulse (we call this method "pulse ejection"). Pulse ejection enables the amount of odorant presented to a user to be minimized, and effectively mitigates the above-mentioned problems.

We investigated, for a single breath, the timing of scent presentation by pulse ejection, which enabled scents to be used effectively. When olfactory characteristics have been measured, precise control in time has not been considered; hence, the olfactory time characteristics for effective scent presentation are not yet known. We previously found that the strength required for a scent to be perceived depended on the presentation timing in a single breath[5]. In this study, to determine the ejection timing where the amount of odorant is minimized, we measured more precisely the human olfactory characteristics when a scent is presented in a single breath.

CHARACTERISTICS OF OLFACTION
In brief, odor substances are chemical compounds that stimulate olfactory cells in the nasal cavity. Most odor substances are organic compounds, except for some inorganic compounds such as ammonia and hydrogen sulfide. There are around 2,000,000 known organic compounds, and it is said that about 400,000 of these have an odor[6]. However, humans only encounter about 5000 odorants in everyday life. The characteristics of human olfaction are described below.

Olfactory Thresholds

Olfactory thresholds are values used as standards to express the strength of a scent. Three values are generally used as olfactory thresholds: the detection threshold, the recognition threshold and the differential threshold [7], which are expressed in units of concentration (mol/L, ppb, mass %, etc.).

The detection threshold is the minimum concentration at which a scent can be detected without requiring that the scent be identified. The recognition threshold is the minimum concentration at which a scent can be recognized; this value reflects the ability of a user to perceive and describe the quality and characteristics of a scent. The differential threshold is the density at which the user can distinguish the strength of a scent; this value reflects the ability of a user to detect changes in stimulus strength and to quantify the change.

Measurement Method for Characteristics of Olfaction

Olfactometry[8] and the odor bag method[9] are well-known methods for measuring the characteristics of olfaction. An olfactometer is a device that attenuate odor automatically by means of mechanisms including a pump, electromagnetic valve, needle pulp and flowmeter, and this apparatus can be used to provide an odor testing panelist with a continuously attenuated odor. In the odor bag method, a participant smells an odorant in a 3-L plastic bag. The odor bag method was used, for instance, to calculate the odor index in Japan's Offensive Odor Control Act.

Adaptation

Adaptation is the phenomenon where sensory nerve activity is decreased by continuous olfactory stimulation. Adaptation itself and the speed of recovery from adaptation differ between scents. Adaptation is gradually strengthened over time but is restored shortly thereafter (3-5 min) by eliminating the scent. In addition, there are various patterns of adaptation, depending on the identity of the odorant and recognition factors.

At the start of the 20th century, adaptation time was measured by presenting continuous smell stimulation[10]. However, the method was criticized for biasing the participants to smells. For that reason sensory intensity was directly rated in subsequent research. As a result, it was found that a scent can still be perceived, albeit slightly, even if the scent is presented for a long time, and the perceived strength was found to decrease exponentially[11, 12, 13].

In 1996, Pamera et al. measured the duration of adaptation following long-term odor exposure[14]. Participants were exposed continuously to odorants while in their home for a period of 2 weeks. As a result, the detection threshold for the adapting odorant was elevated following exposure and the perceived intensity ratings for weak concentrations were reduced.

RELATED WORK

The transmission of olfactory information together with audiovisual information is currently being investigated. Kaye describes systems that add scent to Web content[15], and computer-controlled olfactory displays such as iSmell[16] and Osmooze[17] are utilized in these systems. The air cannon olfactory display, another type of display that generates toroidal vortices of a scent in order to present it in limited space, has been proposed in [18].

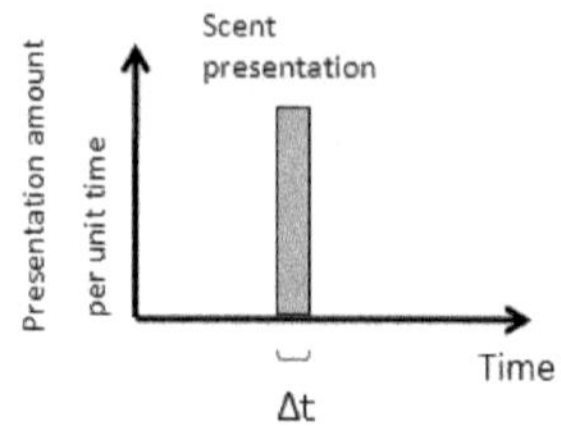

Figure 1. Diagram of pulse ejection.

Brewster et al. designed the tool "Olfoto," which has digital image libraries and added scent tags with which users can search for information[19]. Ademoye et al. examined the effect of olfaction-enhanced multimedia on information recall[20]. AROMA[21] was designed to introduce an olfactory modality as a potential alternative to visual and auditory modalities for messaging notifications. Experimental findings indicated that while the olfactory modality was less effective in delivering notifications than the other modalities, it had a less disruptive effect on user engagement in a primary task.

However, the scent presentation techniques of previous works were designed merely to create the sense of experiencing a scent, and higher densities and longer presentation times of scent were used than actually necessary; hence, these approaches were hindered by problem of olfactory adaptation and scent lingering in the air. In order to mitigate these problems, we measured the time characteristics of olfaction in order to control scents precisely.

TIME CHARACTERISTICS OF OLFACTION IN A SINGLE BREATH

In conventional methods, a scent is continuously emitted at high density for a long time so that the scent can be easily perceived. However, this leads to problems of scent lingering in the air and olfactory adaptation, which reduces the effectiveness of scent presentation. Therefore, we developed pulse ejection, which emits scent for a short period of time, and reduced the amount of fragrance amount presented to users. Figure 1 shows a graphical representation of pulse ejection.

The vertical axis of Figure 1 shows the amount of odorant presented per unit time, the horizontal axis shows scent presentation time, and the purple rectangle indicates scent presentation. Since pulse ejection uses a small amount of odorant, we confirmed that scent did not linger in the air when scent was presented with wind velocity above a cer-

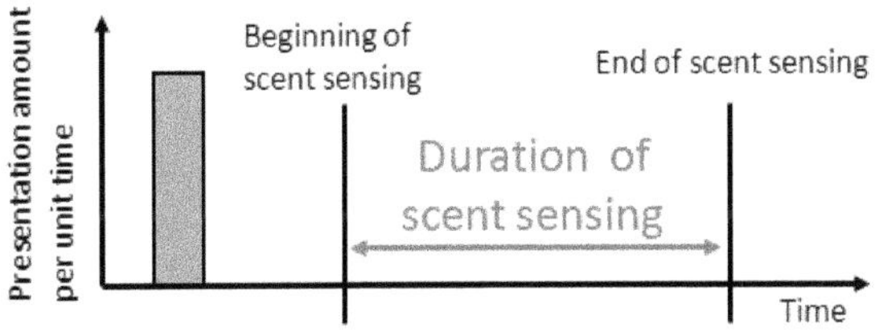

Figure 2. Duration of scent perception.

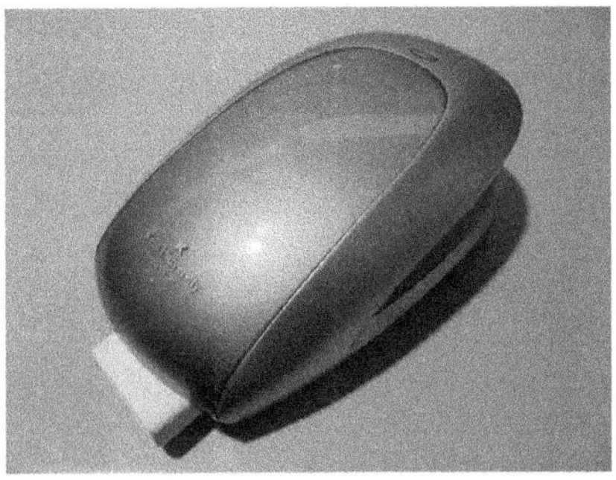

Figure 3. Olfactory display.

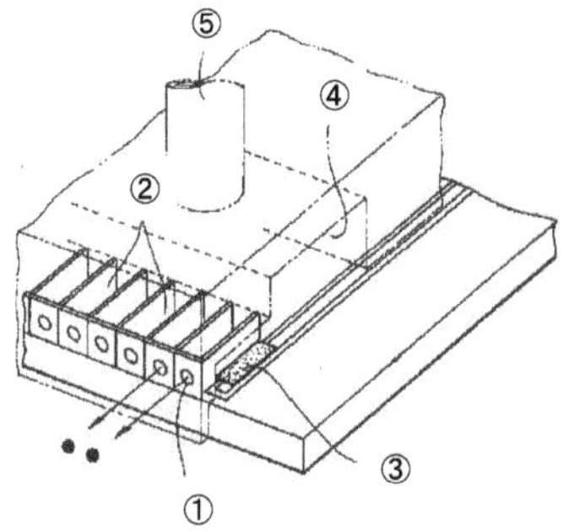

Figure 4. Scent ejection head.

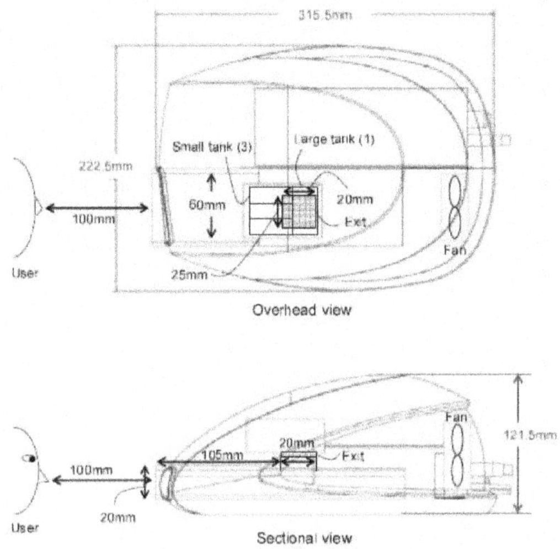

Figure 5. Schematics of the olfactory display.

tain level[22] In addition, continuous scent presentation in pulses can reduce adaptation[23].

As characteristics to measure in evaluating single-breath olfaction, we chose the detection threshold and the duration of scent sensing . By finding the detection threshold, we will be able to present the minimum required amount of an odorant to the user. For the five senses, there is a delay when short-term stimulation is received. In other words, a user does not sense a scent as soon as pulse ejection is presented, but rather experiences some delay. For example, human vision is known to have a lag time of about 1/16 s[24]. In regard to olfactory information, the user senses a scent not only during the presentation time, but also briefly thereafter.

For that reason, we defined the time from the beginning to end of scent perception as the duration of scent sensing. A long duration of sensing a small amount of odorant would suggest that the scent was efficiently presented.

We examined how these values changed for various timings of pulse ejection in a single breath, in order to ascertain the time characteristics of olfaction in a single breath.

OLFACTORY PRESENTATION SYSTEM

Olfactory Display

We developed the olfactory display shown in Figure 3. We modified the firmware of a previous olfactory display[22] and the architecture of device itself, thereby realizing higher emission control. Concretely we succeeded in markedly lowering the minimum time of scent presentation, from 100 ms to 667 μs.

This display uses an ink-jet mechanism to eject, from a small hole in the ink tank, a jet that is broken into droplets. In general, methods for emitting ink can be classified as thermal and piezo methods. In the thermal method, a heater is installed in part of a narrow tube filled with ink. In order to emit ink, bubbles are formed in the ink by instantaneous heating. In the piezo method, a piezoelectric element installed in the tube is energized to emit ink. The thermal method is advantageous for miniaturization because the structure is simple, but it is difficult to control ejection stably; furthermore, there is the risk that heat will degrade the ink. As for the piezo method, ejection control is comparatively simple, but miniaturization is difficult because the mechanism of the piezoelectric element is complex. Considering the potential for future miniaturization, we selected the thermal method for use in the developed olfactory display.

Figure 4 shows a detailed drawing of the scent ejection head. An ejection heater (3) is installed in the liquid path (2), which continues to the exit hole (1). The ejection heater is heated so that bubbles are generated in the liquid. Through the generation of pressure, odorant is emitted from the exit hole (1). The liquid path and a liquid chamber (4) are replenished with odorant. The odorant in the liquid chamber (4) is supplied via a supply route (5) from the odorant tank. By using microfabrication, a head was produced with 100 more exit holds

Figure 6. Breath sensor.

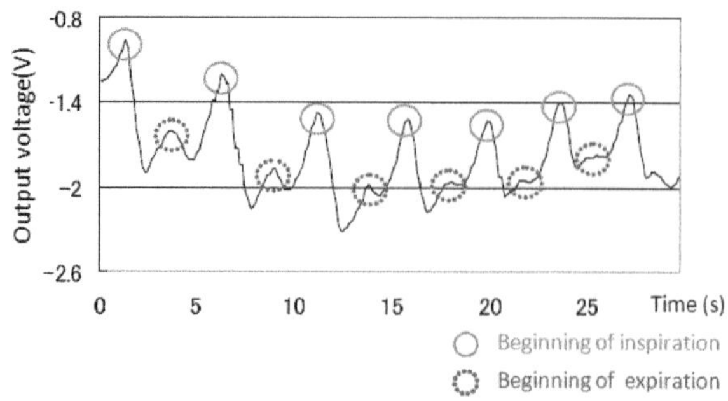

Figure 7. Output voltage measured for single breath.

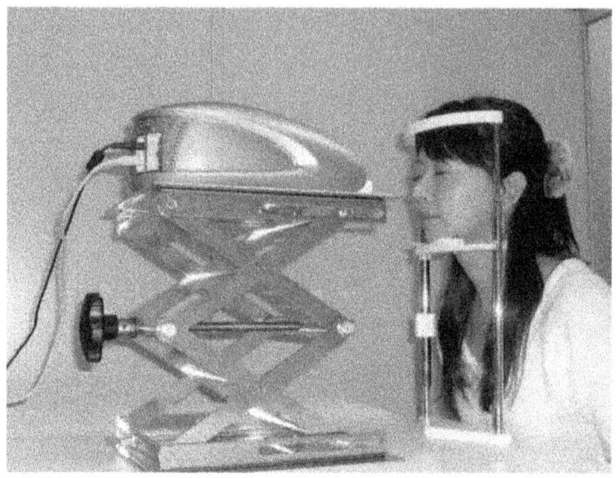

Figure 8. Experimental setup.

as compared with the previous version. This head can emit odorant in pulses of several picoliters.

This display's ejection time can be controlled in increments of 667 μs. Figure 5 shows schematics of the olfactory display. The display is equipped with 1 scent ejection head. Because the head has 1 large tank and 3 small tanks, the display can present, in total, 4 scents, and switch between them in 100-ms intervals. There are 255 small holes in the head connected to the large tank, and 127 in the head connected to the small tank. Moreover, the display can emit odorant from different numbers of holes at one time, so the ejection quantity is adjustable to 1–255 holes (large tank), or 1–127 holes (small tank). Per 667-μs interval, the mean ejection quantity from each hole of the small tanks is 4.7 pL and that of the large tank is 7.3 pL.

Also, the display is equipped with a fan with 10 settings of wind velocity in the range of 0.8–1.8 m/s; the wind carries the scent from the display to the user.

Breath Sensor

We developed the breath sensor system shown in Figure 6, which can detect the beginning of inspiration by the user. The sensor is worn within 5 mm from the user's nostril, and this system detects the user's breath from the change in air temperature. The temperature-sensing element is a negative temperature coefficient (NTC) Thermistor, the specifications of which are shown in Table 1. In addition, we attached an air screen to the headphones in order to block the wind from the olfactory display.

Table 1. Specifications of thermistor.

Model	120-102EAJ-Q01
Resistance value (25 °C)	1 kΩ
Resistivity	7.04
Maximum temperature	300 °C

NTC thermistors have a negative temperature coefficient; consequently, as temperature increases, resistance decreases. Also, as temperature changes, the resistance of an NTC thermistor changes widely, resulting in a large change in output voltage. Figure 7 shows the thermistor's output voltage measured during respiration by a user. Red circles denote the beginning of inspiration, and blue circles denote the end of expiration; the beginning of inspiration clearly corresponds to a local maximum. Because of airflow, the temperature decreases at the moment of user inspiration, and resistance decreases. As a result, output voltage drastically decreases as shown in Figure 7.

EXPERIMENTAL

This experiment was conducted in a university laboratory of about 70 square meters. The experimental space (about 3 m × 3 m) was separated by partitions and two large-scale deodorizing apparatuses were set up. Figure 8 shows a photograph of the experimental setup. The participant places the chin on a chin rest, fixing the distance from the olfactory ejection point to the nose at 22.5 cm.

In our previous study[22], we confirmed that no scent lingers in the air when the wind velocity of the olfactory display is set at more than 1.2 m/s. Here, we set the wind velocity control at 1.8 m/s, which is the maximum setting of this olfactory display, in order to reduce the time between emission of the odorant and its arrival at the user's nose. The presentation time of pulse ejection (Δ shown in Figure 1) was set to 33 ms, which allowed odor detection by all participants. One natural fragrance, namely, lavender, was used.

Preliminary Experiment 1: Measurement of Reaction Time

In the main experiment, we presented a scent at multiple timings for a single breath while measuring time characteristics, and so it is necessary that this timing be precise. Therefore, we first synchronized scent presentation and the beginning

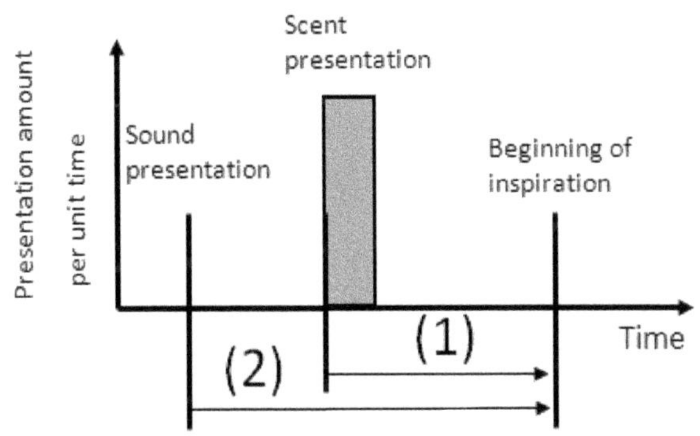

Figure 9. Synchronization of sound presentation and the beginning of inspiration.

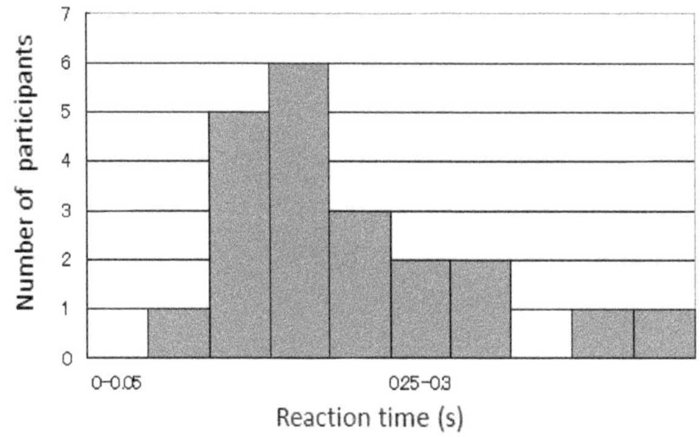

Figure 10. Distribution of reaction time from the auditory cue to the beginning of inspiration.

of inspiration. We instructed the participant to breathe in accordance with an auditory cue ("3, 2, 1, go") and synchronized the scent presentation accordingly. Ideally, the scent will reach the participant's nose at the start of inspiration. For this, it is necessary to examine the two times shown in Figure 9: (1) the time from presentation of the scent to its arrival at the participant's nose, and (2) the reaction time from the auditory cue to the beginning of inspiration.

The distance from the olfactory display's exit hole to the participant's nose was 22.5 cm, and the wind velocity was set at 1.8 m/s; thus, time (1) equaled 0.125 s. On the other hand, the value of time (2) differed between participants, and was therefore measured. We measured the reaction time by using the breath sensor system. This experiment was conducted with 21 participants (17 men, 4 women) who were students in their 20s majoring in information technology. These participants also took part in the other experiments described later in this report.

The reaction time was measured 10 times for each participant, and the mean value for each was calculated. Before the experiment, the participants were adequately familiarized with breathing in accordance with the auditory cue.

Table 2 shows the mean, standard deviation, maximum and minimum of the reaction time for the 21 participants. Figure 10 shows the distribution of reaction time.

Table 2. Results for measurement of reaction time from the auditory cue to the beginning of inspiration.

Mean (s)	0.21
Standard deviation	0.11
Maximum	0.47
Minimum	0.06

As shown in Figure 10, participants' reaction times differed greatly between individuals. In addition, the average standard deviation the 10 measurements of each participant was 0.007 (average of coefficient of variance: 45.9%), which was small. This shows that the variance for a given participant was small.

With the reaction time determined for each participant, scent emission can be timed such that the scent arrives at the beginning of inspiration. We know that time (1), from scent presentation to arrival at the participant's nose, is 0.125 s (Figure 9). Therefore, if we add the reaction time (2), the scent can be presented at the beginning of inspiration.

As a result of this experiment, we demonstrated that the reaction time from the auditory cue to the beginning of inspiration differed greatly between individuals, whereas the variance was small for a given participant. For this reason in a following experiment, we used the mean of each participant's reaction time to synchronize scent presentation and the beginning of that participant's inspiration.

Preliminary Experiment 2: Measurement of Inspiration Time

In the main experiment, we measured the time characteristics of olfaction during inspiration by the participants. To set the measurement range in the experiment, the inspiration time was measured by using the breath sensor system. As noted before, the system can detect the beginning of inspiration as a clear local maximum point, but can hardly detect the beginning of expiration because of the ambiguity of the small peak. In a previous study, we confirmed that participants were unable to sense a scent near the end of inspiration[23]. Therefore, we defined the inspiration time as the time from the local maximum point in the respiration data to the local minimum point (shown as the blue area in Figure 11).

The measurement of inspiration time was conducted with the same 21 participants as Preliminary Experiment 1. To reproduce normal conditions in the experiment, participants adequately controlled their breathing before the experiment.

We instructed the participant to breathe normally while wearing the breath sensor. The local maximum and local minimum in the sensor's signal were measured, and the time between these points was taken as the inspiration time. This was repeated 10 times for each participant, and the mean inspiration time for 10 breaths was calculated.

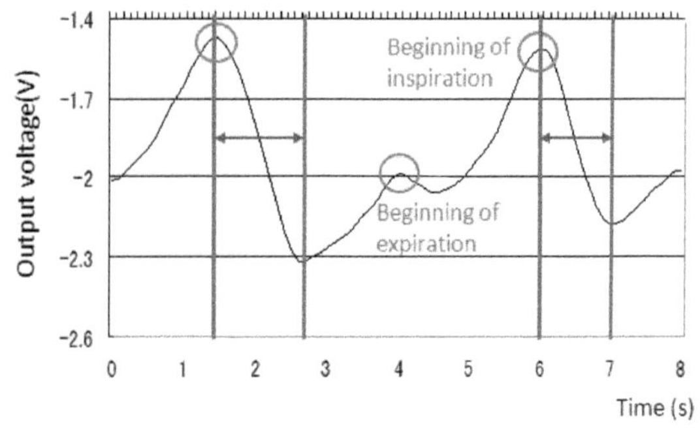

Figure 11. Definition of inspiration time.

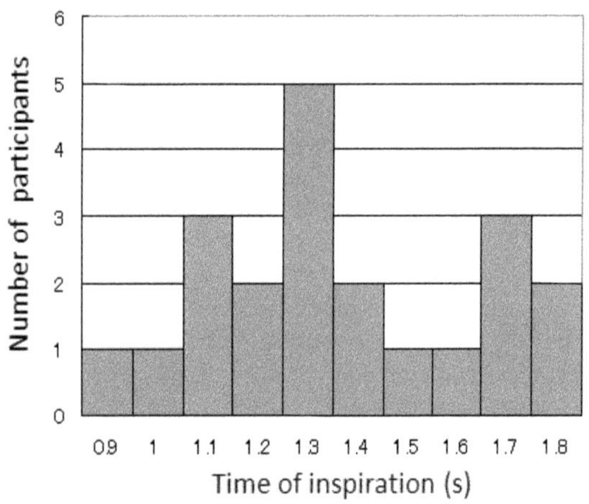

Figure 12. Distribution of inspiration time.

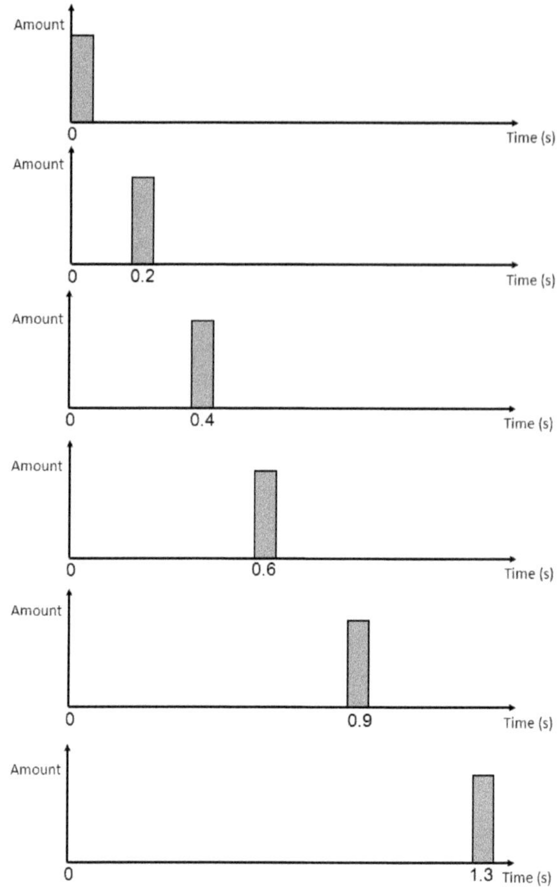

Figure 13. Timings of scent presentation in measurements.

Table 3 shows the mean, standard deviation, maximum and minimum of inspiration time for the 21 participants. Figure 12 shows the distribution of inspiration time.

Table 3. Results of measurement of inspiration time.

Mean (s)	1.34
Standard deviation (s)	0.73
Maximum (s)	1.79
Minimum (s)	0.85

As shown in Figure 12, the inspiration time differed greatly between individual participants. In addition, the average standard deviation of each participant's 10 breaths was 0.09 (average of coefficient of variance: 18.6%) which was small. This shows that the variance was small for a given participant.

As a result of this experiment, we demonstrated that the inspiration time was highly individual, but that its coefficient of variance was small, in other words, that the variance in the value among the participants was small. Moreover, the difference in the values was small for the 10 measurements of each participant. In the main experiment, we took the time of a single breath to be 1.3 s, which was the mean inspiration time for the 21 participants.

Experiment 1: Measurement of Detection Threshold

Experimental Method

In this experiment, we measured the detection threshold, which is the smallest ejection amount at which scent can be detected, by presenting a pulse ejection in 6 timings, as shown in Figure 13, which are 0 s, 0.2 s, 0.4 s, 0.6 s, 0.9 s and 1.3 s after the beginning of inspiration. We set the ejection quantity in the range of 1–90 of the 127 holes of the small tank, because all participants could detect the quantity of lavender emitted from 90 holes in a preliminary experiment. Before the main experiment, the participants were familiarized with 33-ms pulse ejection.

The detection threshold measurement was based on the paired comparison method[25]. The olfactory display presented a scented and an unscented ejection to each participant, synchronized with the beginning of inspiration from the result of Preliminary Experiment 1. The sequence of the scented or unscented ejection was presented at random. After each trial, the participants answered the following two questions.

1. Which of the two was the scented ejection?

2. How strong was the scent?

Table 4. Results of measurement of detection threshold

Timing of presentation	0 s	0.2 s	0.4 s	0.6 s	0.9 s	1.3 s
Mean	17.0	7.8	13.0	169	22.7	29.0
Standard deviation	14.7	6.3	8.9	10.4	12.4	17.6
Maximum	61	23	39	41	61	81
Minimum	3	2	3	3	4	4

In the case that the participant gave the correct answer to question 1, we considered that the scent could be detected. Ejection quantity was decreased until the participant selected the unscented ejection. Ejections were presented at random with the above-mentioned 6 timings, and when the participant answered incorrectly for all timings, the measurements were stopped. The smallest ejection level detected by the participants was taken as the detection threshold.

Result

Table 4 shows the mean, standard deviation, maximum and minimum score of the 127 phases of the detection threshold for the 21 participants. The red curve in Figure 14 shows the approximate curve of the mean detection threshold at each presentation timing, and results for each participant's detection threshold are shown as symbols.

As shown in Table 4, participants could detect lower quantities of lavender in the following sequence: 0.2 s, 0.4 s, 0.6 s, 0 s, 0.9 s and 1.3 s. The smallest detection threshold was at 0.2 s for all participants as shown in Figure 14. We confirmed that there were sensory perception differences depending on the scent presentation timing in a single breath, and that scent arriving at the nose 0.2 s after the beginning of inspiration was efficient.

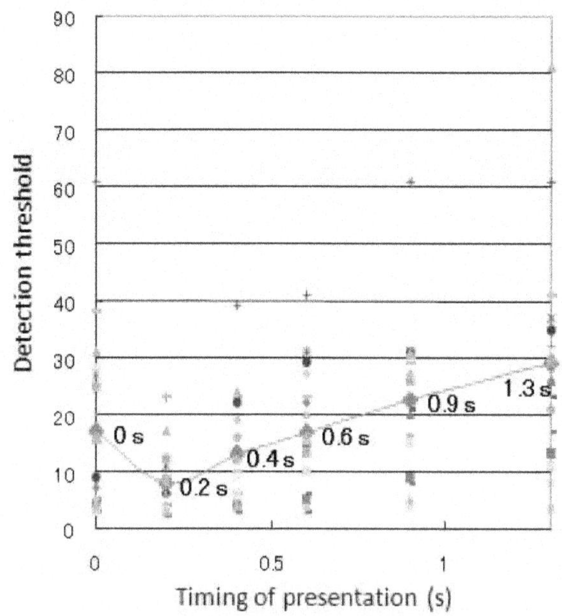

Figure 14. Approximate curve of the detection threshold at each presentation timing.

Discussion

We discuss individual differences in the detection threshold in detail. Since inspiration time differed greatly between individuals, we assumed that there was some relation between the inspiration time and the detection threshold. Because the participants were the same in Preliminary Experiment 2 and Experiment 1, we can compare each measurement result. Firstly, we classified the 21 participants into 3 groups of 7 from the result of the measurement of inspiration time. These groups are the short time group, the intermediate time group and the long time group. Figure 15 shows the distribution of inspiration time for these 3 groups.

Secondly, we calculated the mean detection threshold at 6 timings for each group. Table 5 shows the results of this calculation, and Figure 16 shows a graph of the results Here, it can be seen that the detection threshold of the short time group is larger, and the threshold of the long time group is smaller.

To examine the detection threshold for each of these groups, the results were analyzed by using a two-way ANOVA ("group" and "presentation timing"). There was significant difference in detection threshold for "group" ($F(2)=3.08$, $P<0.01$). For each group, the difference was assessed by the Steel–Dwass test. As a result, significant differences were found between the short time group and the long time group ($P<0.05$), with the detection threshold of the long time group being smaller. This result shows a broad trend that as inspiration time became longer, the detection threshold became smaller.

We next examined the correlation between the inspiration time and the detection threshold at each presentation timing. Figure 17 shows a correlation chart for these parameters. The value for each participant is shown as a symbol and the approximation of the correlation between detection threshold and timing is shown as a line. As shown in this figure, there are some outliers, but there is negative correlation for all timings. Examining the coefficient of correlation of the inspiration time and the detection threshold at each timing, we find a mean of -0.4, which signifies a small negative correlation between these parameters. In other words, the detection threshold of a person who inspires for a longer time was smaller. We conclude that a person with a long inspiration time could detect scent at a lower quantity, that is, that they had a keener sense of smell.

Experiment 2: Measurement of Duration of Scent Sensing

Experimental Method

Table 5. Mean detection threshold for each group

Timing of presentation	0 s	0.2 s	0.4 s	0.6 s	0.9 s	1.3 s
Short time	22.3	10.6	17.0	21.0	28.7	40.0
Intermediate time	19.3	8.4	10.3	15.1	22.1	26.9
Long time	9.4	4.3	11.6	14.6	17.1	20.3

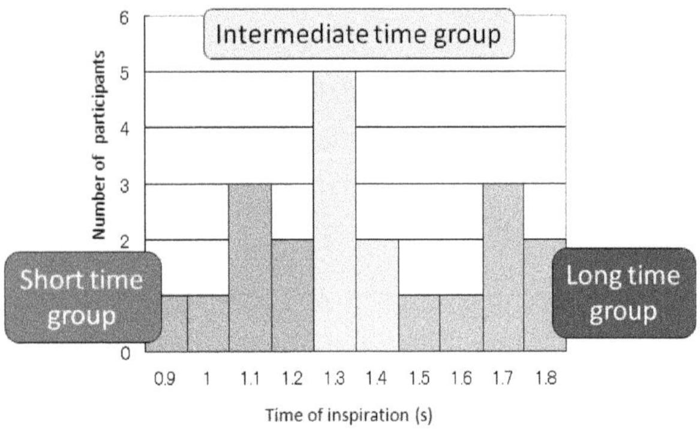

Figure 15. Three groups classified by inspiration time.

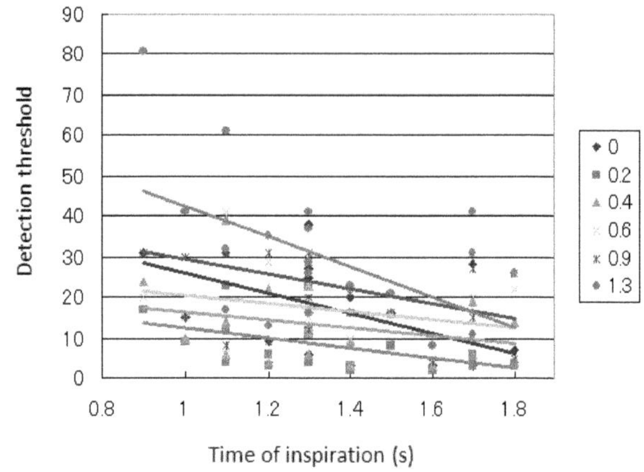

Figure 17. Correlation chart of inspiration time and detection threshold at each presentation timing.

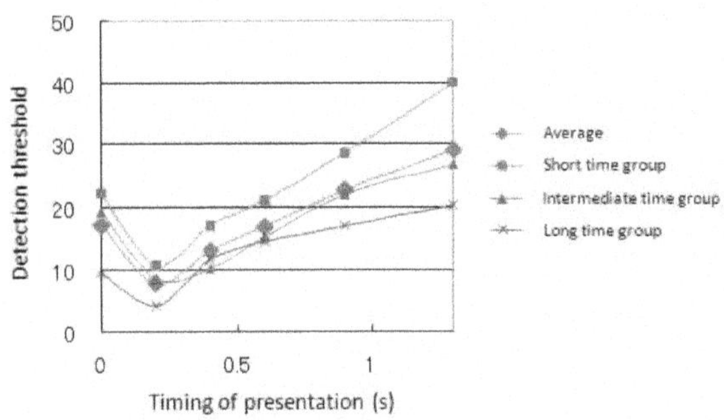

Figure 16. Mean detection threshold for each group.

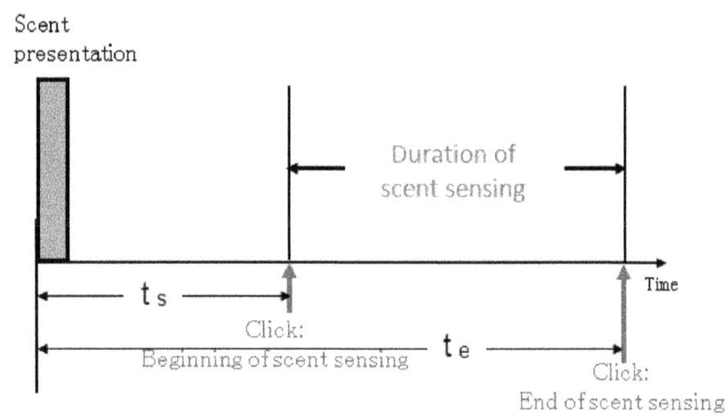

Figure 18. Method for measuring duration of scent sensing.

In this experiment, we measured the duration of scent sensing, at the same 6 timings as in Experiment 1. We used 33-ms pulse ejection of lavender, and this experiment was conducted with the same 21 participants. In addition, as we set the presentation amount per unit time to 81 of 127 holes, which was the highest detection threshold measured in Experiment 1; thus, all participants could detect the scent. Before the experiment, we confirmed that all participants could detect the pulse ejection from 81 of 127 holes.

Figure 18 shows the content of this measurement. Firstly, we measured the time before the participant began to sense the scent. The olfactory display presented a scent precisely synchronized with the participant's breath. We instructed the participants to click a computer mouse when they noticed the scent. The interval of time from scent presentation to the participant's click was measured 2 times at each timing, and the mean of the 2 measurements at each timing was calculated as t_s.

Secondly, we measured the time until the participant stopped detecting the scent. The olfactory display presented a scent precisely synchronized with their breath. We instructed the participants to click a computer mouse when they perceived the scent to have vanished. The interval of time from scent presentation to the participant's click was measured 2 times at each timing, and the mean of the 2 measurements at each timing was calculated as t_e as follows:.

$$t_d = t_e - t_s.$$

Before this experiment, the participants became familiarized with mouse clicking at the beginning and end of scent sensing.

Results

Table 6 shows the mean and standard deviation of the duration of scent sensing at each timing for the 21 participants.

Table 6. Mean duration of scent sensing at each timing

Timing of presentation	0 s	0.2 s	0.4 s	0.6 s	0.9 s	1.3 s
Mean (s)	1.05	1.32	1.14	1.08	0.99	0.89
Standard deviation (s)	0.57	0.63	0.53	0.52	0.50	0.47

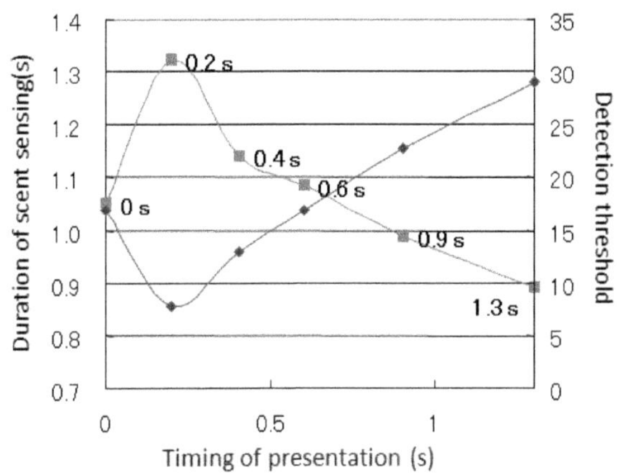

Figure 19. Mean detection threshold and duration of scent sensing at each presentation timing.

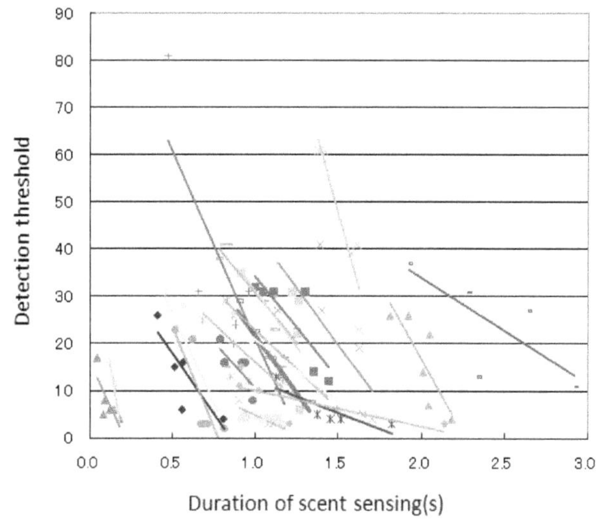

Figure 20. Correlation chart of the detection threshold and the duration of scent sensing for each participant.

As shown in Table 6, at each timing, the duration for each participant is longer in the following sequence: 0.2 s, 0.4 s, 0.6 s, 0 s, 0.9 s and 1.3 s. We confirmed that there were differences in sensory perception depending on the scent presentation timing for a single breath, and that scent arriving at the nose 0.2 s after the beginning of inspiration was perceived to last longer.

Discussion

In Experiments 1 and 2, we found that there were differences in the detection threshold and the duration of scent sensing depending on the scent presentation timing for a single breath; thus, we posit that some relation exists between the detection threshold and the duration of scent sensing. Since the participants were the same in Experiments 1 and 2, we can compare the measurement results.

Figure 19 shows the mean detection threshold as a blue curve and the duration of scent sensing as a red curve at each timing for the 21 participants. These curves can be seen to be nearly symmetric.

We examined the correlation of the detection threshold and the duration of scent sensing at each presentation timing for each participant. Figure 20 shows correlation chart of these parameters. The value for each participant at each timing is shown as symbols, and the approximation of the correlation for each participant is shown as a line. As shown in this figure, there is a slight difference in the slopes of the lines, but there is a negative correlation for all participants. Examining the coefficient of correlation of the detection threshold and the duration of scent sensing for each participant, we find a mean of -0.8, which signifies a large negative correlation between these parameters. This shows that as the duration of scent sensing increased, the detection threshold decreased.

The duration of scent sensing is a characteristic of presenting the same quantity of odorant by pulse ejection, and the detection threshold is the smallest quantity at which scent can be detected. In presenting the same quantity of odorant by pulse ejection, the scent is perceived to be stronger at the time with a small detection threshold. In this regard, we conclude that presenting a scent when the detection threshold was lower led to a longer duration of scent sensing.

CONCLUSIONS

In this study, we aimed to minimize the amount of odorant presented to the greatest extent possible, in order to solve the problems of scent lingering in the air and olfactory adaptation when olfactory information is transmitted together with audiovisual information. Toward this end, we examined the time characteristics of human olfaction when scent was presented in a single breath.

From these measurements, we confirmed that the perceived intensity of scent was dependent on its presentation timing, and that scent arriving at nose about 0.2 s after the beginning of inspiration was perceived to be strongest. In addition, the duration of scent sensing for pulse ejection was also dependent on the presentation timing: when the scent was perceived to be stronger, the duration of scent sensing was longer. In the future, we plan to develop scent presentation techniques based on these results, which should enable the amount of odorant to be greatly reduced and thereby solve the problems of scent lingering in the air and olfactory adaptation. This is expected to facilitate the presentation of highly precise scent in synchrony with audiovisual information. .

REFERENCES

1. *Reports of the Association for Information and Communications Technology Using Five Senses(in Japanese)*. Ministry of Posts and Telecommunications in Japan, 2007.
2. A Tomono, S Yamamoto, M Utsunomiya, D Ikei, Y Yanagida, and K Hosaka. The effect which visual media with scent exert on contents understanding(in japanese). *Human Interface Symposium 2004*, pages 249–254, 2004.
3. K Okada and S Aiba. For realization of the broadcast with olfactory information. *Technology Report ofThe Institute of Image Information and Television Engineers(in Japanese)*, 27:31–34, 2003.
4. M Hirose and T Tanigawa. Wearable olfactory display. *Information Communication of Odor (Fragrance Journal Ltd)(in Japanese)*, pages 60–76, 2007.
5. J Sato, K Ohtsu, Y Bannai, and K Okada. Effective presentation technique of scent using small ejection quantities of odor. *IEEE VR 2009*, pages 151–158, 2009.
6. T Kawasaki, M Nakajima, and T Tonoike. *Aroma Science Series 21 6. Fragrance Journal Ltd.(in Japanese)*. 2003.
7. *A term and a commentary of a odor(in japanese)*. Odor Control Association of Japan, 2003.
8. J S Nader. *In Am.Ind.Hyg.Assoc.J.* 1958.
9. *Environmental Agency Air Quality Bureau special pollution section(in Japanese)*. 1977 sensuality examination investigation papers, 1978.
10. H F Woodrow and B Karpman. A new olfactometeric technique and some results. *J.Exp. Psychol.*, 3:31–447, 1917.
11. G Ekman, B Berglund, U Berglund, and T Lindvall. Perceived intensity of odor as a function of time of adaptation. *Scand.J.Psychol.*, 8:177–186, 1967.
12. B Berglund, U Berglund, and T Lindvall. Psychophysical scaling of odorous air pollutants. *Proceedings of the Fourth International Clean Air Congress*, pages 377–380, May 1977.
13. S W Cain. Perception of odor intensity and the time course of olfactory adaptation. *ASHRAE Transactions*, 80:53–75, 1974.
14. P Dalton and C J Wysocki. The nature and duration of adaptation following long-term odor exposure. *Psychonomic Society, Inc.*, 58(5):781–792, 1996.
15. J. Kaye. Making scents: aromatic output for hci. *Interactions*, 11(1):48–61, 2004.
16. D. A. Washburn, L. M. Jones, R. V. Satya, C. A. Bowers, and A. Cortes. Olfactory use in virtual environment training. *Modeling and Simulation Magazine*, 2(3), 2004.
17. http://www.osmooze.com/osmooze/osmooshop_gb.html.
18. Y. Yanagida, H. Noma, N. Tetsutani, and A. Tomono. An unencumbering, localized olfactory display. In *CHI '03 Extended abstracts*, pages 988–989, 2003.
19. S A Brewster, D K McGookin, and C A Miller. Olfoto: designing a smell-based interaction. In *CHI2006*, pages 653–662, 2006.
20. G Ghinea and O A Ademoye. olfaction-enhanced multimedia: bad for information recall? In *ICME2009*, pages 970–973, 2009.
21. A. Bodnar, R. Corbett, and D. Nekrasovski. Aroma: Ambient awareness through olfaction in a messaging application. In *ICMI '04 Proceedings*, pages 183–190, 2004.
22. A Kadowaki, J Sato, Y Bannai, and K Okada. Measurement and modeling of olfactory responses to pulse ejection of odors. *Japan Association on Odor Environment*, 39(1):36–43, 2008.
23. A kadowaki, J Sato, Y Bannai, and K Okada. Presentation technique of scent to avoid olfactory adaptation. *17th International Conference on Artificial Reality and Telexistence*, pages 97–104, 2007.
24. N Nagasawa, Y Ono, S Watanabe, and K Koyama. *Basic Technology of Television, easily understandable TV and Bloadcast technology.(Ohmsha, Ltd)(in Japanese)*. 1998.
25. *Odor Simplified Measurement Guidebook(in Japanese)*. Japan Association on Odor Environment, 2005.

Augmented Reality Flavors: Gustatory Display Based on Edible Marker and Cross-Modal Interaction

[1]Takuji Narumi, [2]Shinya Nishizaka, [2]Takashi Kajinami,
[2]Tomohiro Tanikawa and [2]Michitaka Hirose

Graduate School of Engineering,
the University of Tokyo / JSPS
7-3-1 Hongo, Bunkyo-ku Tokyo, Japan
narumi@cyber.t.u-tokyo.ac.jp
81-3-5841-6369

Graduate School of Information Science
and Technology, the University of Tokyo
7-3-1 Hongo, Bunkyo-ku Tokyo, Japan
{nshinya, kaji, tani, hirose}@cyber.t.u-tokyo.ac.jp
81-3-5841-6367

ABSTRACT
The main contribution of this paper is to realize computer generated augmented flavors and establish a method to integrate gustatory information into computer human interactions. There are several reasons for the scarcity of research on gustatory information. One reason is that taste sensations are affected by a number of factors, such as vision, olfaction and memories. This produces a complex cognition mechanism for a user's gustatory sensation, and makes it difficult to build up a gustatory display which produces a specific taste on demand.

Our hypothesis is that the complexity of gustatory sensation can be applied to the realization of a "Pseudo-gustatory" display that presents the desired flavors by means of a cross-modal effect elicited by visual and olfactory augmented reality. We propose the Edible Marker system, which can detect the state [number/shape/6-degree-of-freedom (DOF) coordinate] of each piece of bitten or divided food in real time, and the "Pseudo-gustation" method to change the perceived taste of food by changing its appearance and scent. We construct "MetaCookie+" as an implementation and discuss its validity through an exploratory study.

Author Keywords
Gustatory Display, Pseudo-gustation, Edible Marker, Cross-modal Interaction, Augmented Reality

General Terms
Design

ACM Classification Keywords
H.5.1 [Information Interfaces and Presentation (I.7)]: Multimedia Information Systems-Artificial, augmented, and virtual realities

INTRODUCTION

Fig. 1 MetaCookie+

A gustatory display is one of the last frontiers in the area of computer human interaction. Given that it has become easy to manipulate visual and auditory information on a computer in recent years, there has been a great deal of work on visual and auditory displays. Although olfactory displays are uncommon, many researchers are working to develop ways to display scents [1-3]. Moreover, some olfactory displays using vaporizers have already been commercialized [4-10].

However, few of these studies have dealt with gustatory information, and there have been few display systems that present gustatory information. Although gustatory displays have been discussed in some literatures, no system has yet emerged that can be evaluated. Beidler [11] provided a compendium of knowledge of the basis for the sense of taste. More recently, Maynes-Aminzade offered a suggestion for "edible user interfaces" [12] and developed some low-resolution gustatory displays. Iwata et al. have developed the "Food Simulator" [13] by integrating an interface that displays the biting force, auditory information, and the chemical sensation of taste. In the "Food Simulator", chemical sensation of taste was displayed by releasing prepared taste components using a micro injector. However, these studies have not focused on presenting various synthesized tastes.

There are several reasons for the scarcity of research on gustatory displays that synthesizes various tastes. One is that the sensation of taste is based in part on chemical signals, whose functions have not yet been fully understood. Another is that taste is affected by other factors such as vision, olfaction, thermal sensation, and memory. Thus, the complexity of the cognitive mechanisms underlying gustatory sensation makes it difficult to construct a gustatory display that can present a wide variety of gustatory information.

Our hypothesis is that the complexity of the gustatory system can be applied to the realization of a pseudo-gustatory display that presents desired flavors by means of a cross-modal effect.

Perception is traditionally regarded as a modular function. It has long been thought that different sensory modalities operate independently of each other. However, recent behavioral and brain imaging studies are changing this view by suggesting that cross-modal interactions have an important role in our perception [14]. In cross-modal effects, the perception of a sensation through one sense is changed by other stimuli that are simultaneously received through other senses. Indeed, many psychophysical studies have shown that the perception of taste is influenced by visual cues, auditory cues, smell, the trigeminal system, and touch. By using such effects, we may induce people to experience different flavors when they taste the same chemical substance. Therefore, in order to realize a novel gustatory display system, we aim to establish a method for eliciting and utilizing cross-modal interactions.

On the other hand, Augmented Reality (AR) has recently been undergoing significant growth in numerous fields. AR enhances and modifies our perception of reality by presenting computer-generated virtual sensations in semantic context with real environmental elements. The majority of current AR applications are visual. However, AR has great potential to augment perceptions other than vision. We suggest that the taste of food can be modified using a multisensory AR system, and that this can lead to the realization of a new type of gustatory display system.

Therefore, in order to realize a novel gustatory display system, we aim to establish a method that allows people to experience various tastes by changing only the accompanying information with AR technologies without changing the ingredients of the food.

In this paper, we first introduce the knowledge from conventional studies on the influence that other senses have on gustation. Next, based on this knowledge, we propose a method for flavor augmentation using visual and olfactory AR technologies. To realize flavor augmentation, we propose the Edible Marker system, which can detect the state (number/shape/6DOF coordinate) of each piece of bitten or divided food in real time. We also propose the "Pseudo-gustation" method to change the perceived taste of the food when eaten by changing its appearance and scent. We then report the "MetaCookie+" system (Fig. 1) as an implementation of the proposed method and discuss its validity through an exploratory study.

GUSTATION AND CROSS-MODAL INTERACTIONS UNDERLYING THE PERCEPTION OF FLAVOR

Taste is one of the traditional five senses. It refers to the ability to detect the flavor of substances such as food, certain minerals, and poisons. Humans receive gustatory input through sensory organs called taste buds concentrated on the upper surface of the tongue. According to physiological definitions, taste has the status of a minor sense modality, as a channel comprising only a limited number of sensations: sweetness, sourness, bitterness, saltiness, and umami [15]. Taste, as perceived by the tongue, can be measured using a biological membrane sensor that investigates the content of each basic taste [16]. However, it is difficult to synthesize a specific taste on demand by combining basic tastes. This is because the sense of taste is a multi-modal sensation and is not determined solely by a combination of basic tastes.

The term "taste" signifies a perceptual experience that involves the integration of various sensations. When we use the common word "flavor" in place of taste, we again refer to what is a quite multi-faceted sensation. In fact, the International Standards Organization has defined flavor as a complex combination of olfactory, gustatory, and trigeminal sensations perceived during tasting [17]. Auvray et al. reviewed the literature on multisensory interactions underlying the perception of flavor; they summarized their review by stating that flavor is not defined as a separate sensory modality but as a perceptual modality that is unified by the act of eating, and should be used as a term to describe the combination of taste, smell, touch, visual cues, auditory cues, and the trigeminal system [18]. These definitions suggest that it is possible to change the flavor that people experience from foods by changing the feedback they receive through modalities other than the sense of taste. Although it is difficult to present various tastes through a change in chemical ingredients, it is possible to vary other sensory information that people experience when eating without changing the chemical ingredients. In this way, people might be induced to experience various flavors.

Among the other senses, the sense of smell is most closely related to our perception of taste. This relationship between gustatory and olfactory sensations is commonly known, as is illustrated by the fact that we pinch our nostrils when eating food that we find displeasing [19]. Indeed, it has been reported that most of what people commonly think of as the taste of food actually originates from the nose [20]. Conversely, another set of studies on taste enhancement has provided strong support for the ability of odors to modify taste qualities [21]. These studies indicate the possibility of changing the flavor that people experience from foods by changing the scent.

Conversely, under many conditions, it is well known that humans have a robust tendency to rely upon vision more than other senses. Several studies have explored the effect of visual stimuli on our perception of flavor. For instance, the intensities of taste and flavor have been shown to increase as the color level in a solution increases [22]. However, according to Spence et al., the empirical evidence regarding the role that food coloring plays in the perception of the intensity of a particular flavor or taste to which it is attributed (as reported by many researchers over the last 50 years) is rather ambiguous, although food coloring most certainly influences peoples' flavor identification responses [23]. Nonetheless, their survey suggests the possibility of changing flavor identification by changing the appearance of food.

Therefore, our research focuses on the technological application of the appearance and scent of food and its effects on flavor perception. We propose a method to change the perceived taste of a food by changing its appearance and scent. In this study, we use cookies as an example. We chose cookies because they have a wide variety of appearances, scents, and tastes, while being similar in texture and shape. Thus, we have developed a system to overlay the appearance and scent of a flavored cookie on a plain cookie to enable users to experience eating a flavored cookie while just eating a plain cookie.

PSEUDO-GUSTATORY DISPLAY: METACOOKIE+

We developed a system, which we have named "MetaCookie+," to change the perceived taste of a cookie by overlaying visual and olfactory information onto a real cookie with a special AR marker pattern (Fig. 1). "MetaCookie+" combines AR technology and olfactory display technology.

System Overview

"MetaCookie+" comprises four components: a marker-pattern-printed plain cookie, a cookie detection unit based on an Edible Marker System, an overlaying visual information unit, and an olfactory display. Fig. 2 illustrates the system configuration of "MetaCookie+." Each component is discussed in more detail in the following sections.

In this system, a user wears a head-mounted visual and olfactory display system. The cookie detection unit detects the marker-pattern-printed cookie and calculates the state (6DOF coordinate/occlusion/division/distance between the cookie and the nose of a user) of the cookie in real time. Based on the calculated state, an image of a flavored cookie is overlaid onto the cookie. Moreover, the olfactory display

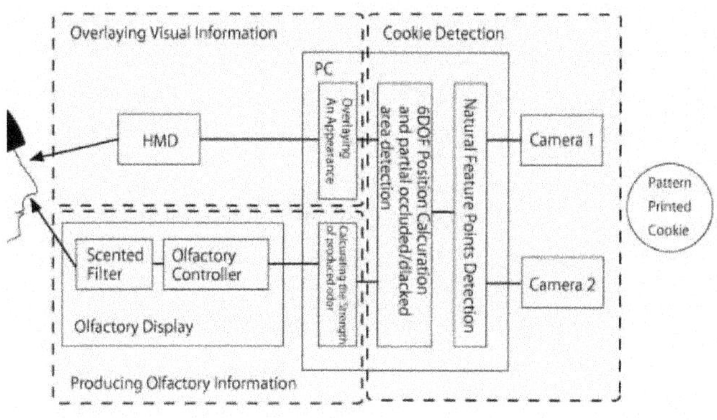

Fig.2 System configuration of "MetaCookie+"

generates the scent of a flavored cookie with an intensity that is determined based on the calculated distance between the cookie and the nose of a user. The user can choose one cookie, which s/he wants to eat, from multiple types. The appearance and scent of the flavored cookie, which the user selects, are overlaid onto the cookie.

Edible Marker System

A basic technology of AR applications is the registration method between the real and virtual world. One method, which uses a specifically designed marker, has been widely used following the emergence of ARToolKit [24]. Other methods use natural features. In particular, with respect to object-detection-based methods in this group, the camera position and pose are estimated by detecting and tracking 2D/3D objects.

For taste augmentation, an interaction with foods is necessary. At the time when the foods must be eaten or divided, a method to detect occlusion and division is required.

However, conventional object-detection methods assume that a target object is continuous. When the object is divided into pieces, tracking will fail because the feature points of only a single piece are recognized as the target object whereas other feature points are regarded as outliers. Despite the importance of division as one of the state changes of an object, it has not been studied from the viewpoint of object detection for AR applications.

Therefore, we proposed the "Edible Marker" system, which not only estimates the 6DOF coordinate of the AR marker, but also detects its occlusion and division. We then applied this system to "MetaCookie+." Fig. 3 shows the processing steps of the occlusion- and division-detectable "Edible Marker" system.

To create the occlusion- and division-detectable AR marker, we used natural feature points. To recognize the absence and occlusion of the marker, we used a background subtraction method. Users must prepare a template image they wish to use as the marker pattern image in advance. They can use any pattern except a point-symmetric one as the marker.

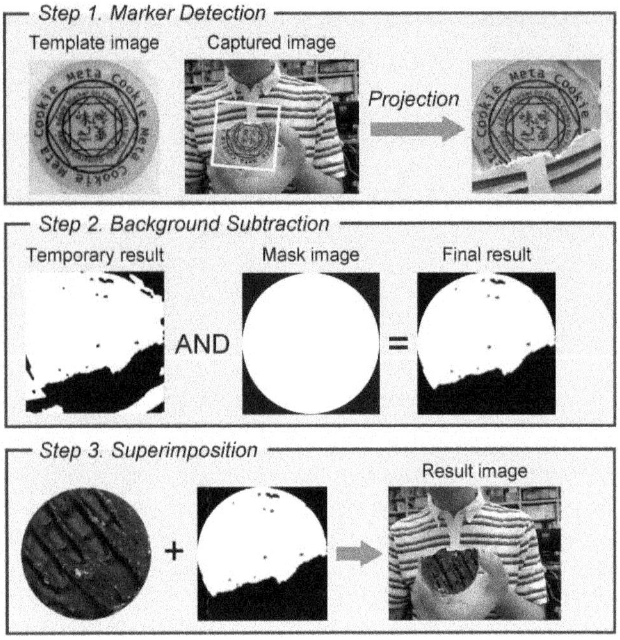

Fig. 3 Processing steps of the occlusion-and-division-detectable "Edible Marker" system

Fig. 4 Edible Marker printed cookie
(The Edible Marker can recognize the bitten/divided marker shown in the middle/bottom panels of the figure. Moreover, the remaining area can be detected to allow realistic superimposition.)

The Edible Marker System estimates the 6DOF coordinate, occlusion, and division of a marker in three steps: Marker Detection, Background Subtraction and Superimposition.

In step 1 (Marker Detection), the natural feature points are detected from the captured image and the marker position is extracted from an estimated homography matrix. Subsequently, the projected image of the marker area in the captured image can be obtained.

For implementation, we used Fern [25] as the natural feature descriptor and classifier. There are other well-known keypoint detectors such as SIFT [26], SURF [27], and Fast [28]. Although SIFT is a very robust keypoint detector, its processing is computationally too intensive to apply it to real-time applications. SURF and Fast can be used at relatively high speed; however, their robustness is not enough to use for AR applications. On the other hand, Fern is a robust high-speed keypoint detector. It requires pre-training with the template image so that the registration can be processed in real time. This offline training requires about 5 min to process a 350×350 pixel image. Currently, long advance processing times are inconsequential for applications to which we aim to apply the proposed system. Therefore, Fern is the best choice at the present time.

In a conventional planar-object detection method, a homography matrix is estimated from the correspondence of the feature points between a prepared template image and an image captured by the user's camera. A robust estimation method such as RANSAC [29] is generally used to eliminate outliers. An accurate homography matrix is estimated by calculating its elements using the least squares method after outlier elimination. If we simply apply the conventional method to a divided planar object, only one out of all the pieces of the object is detected as an inlier; therefore, the other pieces cannot be detected as parts of the object. To detect all pieces of the divided object, another method is required. The proposed method detects the pieces of the divided object by iteratively applying PROSAC [30], which is a method similar to but faster than RANSAC. A database of the target object's feature points is prepared in advance. In each estimation process, the inlier points are deleted from the database. Next, estimation is performed using the updated database. Subsequently, this method detects the inliers for each piece of the target object. The iteration stops when the homography matrix calculation fails. After these processes, the projected image of each piece in the captured image is obtained.

In step 2 (Background Subtraction), a difference image is obtained by background subtraction. We implemented background subtraction based on the method shown in [31]. The image to the left of the middle panel in Fig. 3 is the difference between the template image and the projected image. Combining the temporary result and the mask image for superimposition, the final result is obtained.

In step 3 (Superimposition), the image to the left of bottom panel in Fig. 3 is overlaid using the final result obtained in step 2. The result of superimposition is shown in the image to the right.

Fig. 4 shows that the proposed object-detection system can be recognized even if the cookie is eaten, partially occluded, or divided. Furthermore, the area on which the image should be overlaid can be detected by the background subtraction method. The marker can manage an occlusion/division that is more than half of an entire cookie.

Pattern Printed Cookie

We made a plain cookie detectable by a camera for this system by printing a pattern on it with a food printer. We use a MasterMind's food printer "Counver" [32], which is a commercial off-the-shelf product. The printer produces a jet of colored edible ink, which is broken into droplets, and creates a printed image on a flat surface of food. Fig. 5 shows the food printer and the pattern-printed cookie we use in our system.

Fig. 5 Food printer and pattern printed cookie

Cookie Detection and Overlaying an Appearance

The Cookie Detection unit based on the Edible Marker system can obtain the 6DOF coordinate of the cookie and the distance between the cookie and the camera. In the Cookie Detection phase, two cameras are used in parallel. We used two Logicool Webcam Pro 9000 cameras (angle of view: 76°) in this implementation. The layout of the cameras, a head-mounted display (HMD), and an olfactory display is shown in Fig. 6. The range of the cameras is also illustrated in this figure. The two cameras are positioned to eliminate blind spots between the user's hands and mouth, in order to track the cookie from the time at which a user holds it to the time at which s/he puts it in her/his mouth.

Camera 1 in Fig. 6 is for overlaying the appearance of another cookie on the marked cookie and deciding the strength of the produced smell. The relationship of the distance between the cookie and the camera to the strength of the produced smell is discussed below. This camera and an HMD are used for Video see-through. The HMD displays an image of several types of cookies on the pattern-printed plain cookie based on the estimated position and detected occlusion/division. This visual effect allows users to experience eating a selected cookie while merely eating a plain cookie.

Another camera (Camera 2 in Fig. 6) is positioned in front of the user's nose and oriented in the downward direction in order to detect when the user eats a cookie. The area near the user's mouth is outside the first camera's line of vision. This is because we placed the second camera in front of the user's nose and oriented it in the downward direction. When the second camera detects that there is a cookie in front of the user's mouth (within 15 cm from the camera), the system recognizes that the user is about to put a cookie in her/his mouth. The parameter is set to 15 cm because the distance from camera 2 to the chin is about 15 cm on average for Japanese users [33].

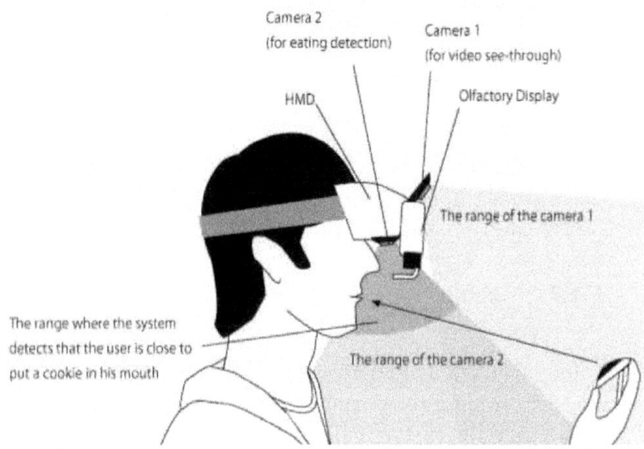

Fig. 6 Layout of two cameras, a head-mounted display and an olfactory display

Olfactory Display

Smell is elevated to the status of a dual sense given its role in both sniffing the air around us and in savoring food. The olfactory receptors can thus be stimulated by two distinct routes: Either via the nose, by sniffing (orthonasal olfaction), or via the mouth, during eating and drinking, as volatile chemicals rise up through the nasopharynx (retronasal olfaction). Recent psychophysical and neuroimaging data have indicated that different neural substrates underpin these two forms of olfactory perception [34, 35].

Orthonasal olfaction can be simulated easily using conventional olfactory displays. However, it is difficult to simulate retronasal olfaction without inserting a tube into the user's mouth. It is assumed that a user is uncomfortable with such an arrangement. Directly spraying a flavor on a cookie just before a user eats it would generate retronasal but not orthonasal olfactory stimuli. Moreover, this would also generate gustatory stimuli related to the fragrance composition (e.g., ethanol). We decided to avoid gustatory stimuli, which have the potential to disturb our system, and to provide scented air to the user's nose instead.

Therefore, we decided to use an air-pump-type head-mounted olfactory display (Fig. 7), which sprays a scent of the selected cookie from in front of user's nose to the nasal cavity in order to simulate both forms of smell. Retronasal stimuli normally evoke a stronger sensation than orthonasal stimuli. We surmised that this was essential for simulating our experience of tasting food. In order to emulate the effect of a retronasal aroma while the user eats a cookie, we then decided to produce a strong odor from the olfactory display rather than produce the same stimuli by inserting a tube into the mouth.

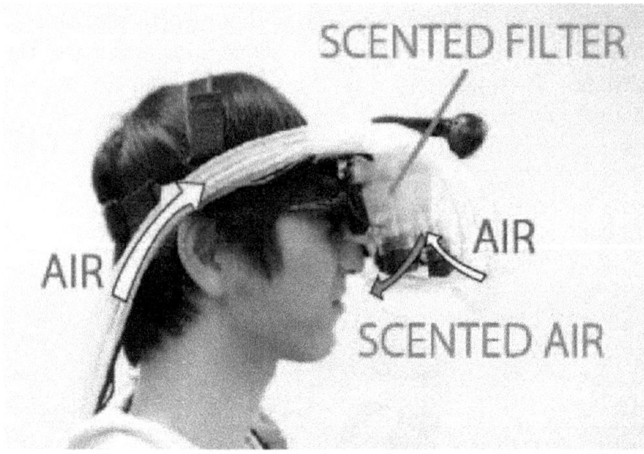

Fig.7 Air-pump type head-mounted olfactory display

The olfactory display can eject fresh air and seven kinds of scented air. It comprises eight air-pumps, a controller, and eight scented filters. One pump sends fresh air, and the seven other pumps send scented air. Each pump for scented air is connected to a scented filter filled with aromatic chemicals. Food flavors such as chocolate, strawberry, and others are used. We select flavors that resemble those of commercially available cookies. The strength of these scents can be adjusted to 127 different levels. By mixing fresh air and scented air, the olfactory display generates an odor of arbitrary level with the same air volume. Users are unable to feel any change in air volume when the strength of the generated odor changes.

The controller drives the air pumps according to position of the pattern-printed cookie. The scented filters add scents to the air from the pumps, after which the scented air is ejected near the user's nose. The response time to produce an arbitrary odor is less than 50 ms. This is sufficiently fast to allow users to feel a change in smell in synchronization with a change in visual information.

"MetaCookie+" generates two patterns of olfactory stimuli for simulating orthonasal and retronasal olfaction. One pattern simulates orthonasal olfaction and functions after the user holds the pattern-printed cookie and before s/he brings it near her/his mouth. In this pattern, the controller drives the air pumps according to the position of the pattern-printed plain cookie. The nearer the pattern-printed cookie is to the user's nose, the stronger the scent ejected from the olfactory display. The olfactory display is activated when the cookie is detected within 50 cm from camera 1. The value of 50 cm is determined based on the average distance between the cameras and a 70 cm-high desk along the line of sight when the user sits on a chair in front of the desk. The strength of the smell produced by the olfactory display is zero when the distance is 50 cm and strongest when the distance is 0 cm. The output is controlled linearly within 50 cm from camera 1. Given that [36] describes linear olfactory feedback as offering a more realistic experience when the source of a smell moves, we decided to use linear mapping.

Another pattern simulates retronasal olfaction and functions after the system recognizes that the user is about to put a cookie in her/his mouth with camera 2. When camera 2 detects a cookie in front of the user's mouth, the system produces the strongest smell from the olfactory display for 30 s. We determined the period to be longer than the time to finish eating a bite of the cookie. Fig. 8 shows the relationship between the strength of the produced smell and the distance between the cookie and the user's mouth.

This olfactory information evokes a cross-modal effect between olfaction and gustation, and enables users to feel that they are eating a flavored cookie although they are just eating a plain cookie.

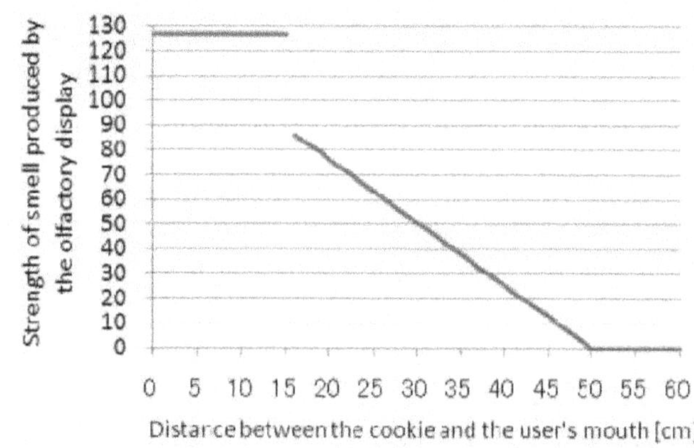

Fig.8 Relationship between the strength of produced smell and the distance between the cookie and the user's mouth

EXPLORATORY STUDY

In order to evaluate the effectiveness of our proposed method for inducing people to experience various flavors, we conducted an exploratory study to investigate how people experience flavor in a cookie by using the "MetaCookie+" system.

We prepared seven kinds of appearances and scents of cookies. In the experiment, each participant ate cookies overlaid with the appearances and scents of cookies prepared by our system and evaluated their tastes.

Purpose of the Exploratory Study

The point of this study is to informally see what aspects of our system worked well and what required improvement by examining how the participants would percept and identify the flavor of the plain cookie when its appearance and scent were changed.

We prepared six types of appearances and scents of commercially available cookies: chocolate, almond, tea, strawberry, maple, and lemon. We examined how the participants experience and interpret the taste of a plain cookie with these appearances and scents that are overlaid using our system.

Moreover, we attempted to examine how the participants experience and identify the taste of a plain cookie with an unfamiliar appearance and scent evoking no expectations. Specific expectations regarding the likely flavor of that food play an important role in identifying flavor [37]. If our system can change both the perception of taste and the identification of flavor, the ratio of subjects who experience a changed taste from a plain cookie with an unfamiliar appearance and scent should be similar to that of subjects who experience a changed taste with a familiar appearance and scent. This should hold true even though the ratio of subjects who identify the augmented cookie with an unfamiliar appearance and scent should be lower than that of subjects who identify the augmented cookie with a familiar appearance and scent. Conversely, if our system changes only the identification of flavor based on expectations, both the ratio of subjects who experience a changed taste with an unfamiliar appearance and that of subjects who experience the selected taste with an unfamiliar appearance and scent should be lower than that of subjects who identify the augmented cookie with a familiar appearance and scent.

Therefore, we prepared a mushroom flavor and an image of a mushroom in order to examine the role of expectations in the cross-modal effect induced by our system. A mushroom cookie is unfamiliar and most people have not eaten such a cookie. We investigated how the participants experience and identify the taste of a plain cookie with the appearance and scent of a mushroom with our system.

Through a comparison of results of this study, we determine whether users can experience a selected flavor using our system and whether users not only identify the flavor as a selected but also sense the change in taste. Moreover, we reveal the limitations of our method and required improvement.

Experimental Procedure

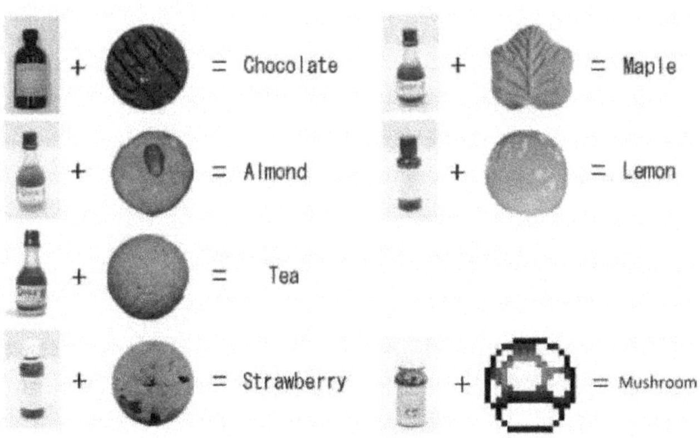

Fig.9 Combination of food flavors and appearances

The combinations of scent and appearance, which were used in the exploratory study for representing flavored cookies, are illustrated in Fig. 9. We captured images of a chocolate cookie, an almond cookie, a tea cookie, a strawberry cookie, a maple cookie, and a lemon cookie, and used these to overlay onto real cookies.

The study was conducted with 44 participants who had never received training in the anatomy of tastes. When they tested our system, we did not inform the participants beforehand that our system aimed to change perceived taste before they finished the experience.

First, the participant chose one taste from "chocolate," "almond," "tea," "strawberry," "lemon," "maple," and "mushroom" from a text-only list. After a taste was chosen by a participant, we overlaid the prepared appearance and scent of the selected cookie using our system. Next, the participant was instructed to hold the cookie, observe the overlaid appearance on the cookie, move it to her/his mouth, and eat it. After the trial, the participant was instructed to eat another plain cookie without our system.

After all trials, participants responded to surveys on the flavor they experienced for each cookie. To prevent subjects from knowing too much about the purpose of the experiment, they were given their survey form after all of their trials. Each participant selected one or two cookies. In total, participants ate 70 cookies with our system (i.e., 70 trials).

In the survey, the participant was first instructed to write what cookie taste s/he chose from the list in her/his trial and select from the following two options: "The cookie tasted just like a plain cookie" or "The cookie tasted different from a plain cookie." When the participant selected the latter, s/he was instructed to write the taste s/he perceived freely and choose an intensity score of the change in taste from 1 (Slight), 2 (Significant), and 3 (Totally Different). Additionally, participants were freely allowed to write some comments. Fig. 10 illustrates participants eating cookies using our system.

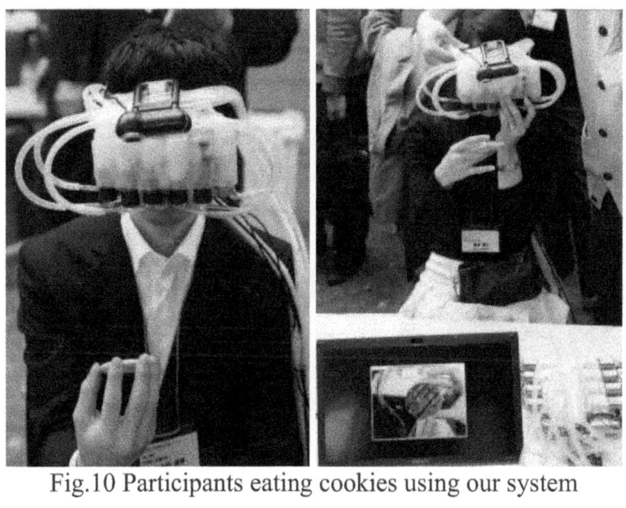

Fig.10 Participants eating cookies using our system

Results

Fig. 11 and 12 illustrates in the results of this experiment.

On 79.3% of the trials, the participants experienced a change in taste when they ate the simulated commercially available cookies with augmented appearance and scent. Moreover, on 72.6% of the trials, the participants identified the taste of the augmented cookie as the taste of the selected cookie, i.e., a participant tasted a chocolate cookie when s/he chose "chocolate" from the text-only list. This result suggests that our system can change a perceived taste and enable users to experience various tastes from a plain cookie by simulating other types of commercially available cookies.

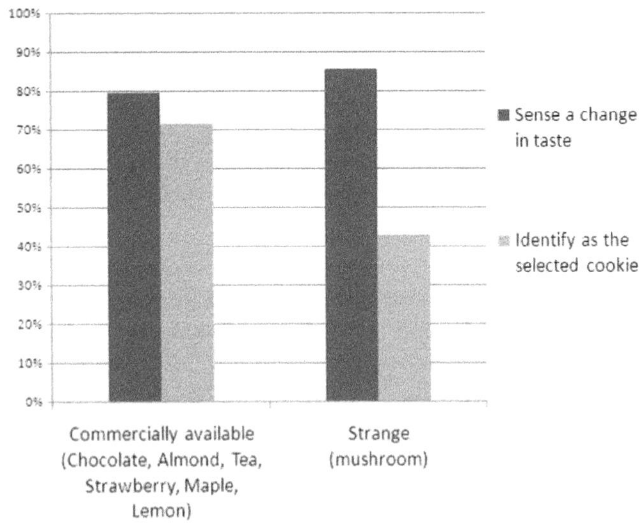

Fig.11 Comparison of the ratio of subjects who experienced the other/selected taste from plain cookie between emulation of commercial cookie and unfamiliar cookie

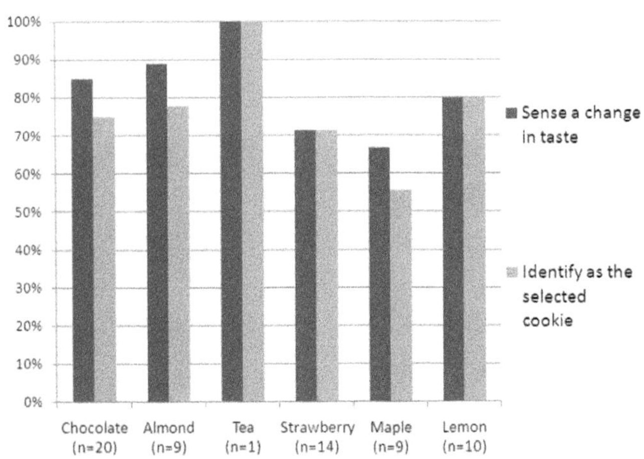

Fig.12 Percentage of subjects who experienced a change in taste from a plain cookie for each flavor

Many participants commented that they were surprised to experience the significant change in the cookie's taste. Some participants expressed regret that our system could not change the texture of a plain cookie.

On the other hand, on 85.7% of the trials, the participants experienced a change in the cookie's taste in case of representing an unfamiliar cookie. However, in only 42.9% of the trials did the participants identify the taste of the augmented cookie as the taste of mushroom when they chose "mushroom" from the text-only list.

Many participants commented that they could not identify the taste of the cookie overlaid with the appearance and scent of a mushroom.

In addition, we compared the results of each represented flavor. When participants selected "chocolate" from the list, they tasted chocolate on 75.0% of the trials (n = 20). When they selected "almond," they tasted almond on 77.8% of the trials (n = 9). When they selected "tea," they tasted tea on 100.0% of the trials (n = 1). When they selected "strawberry," they tasted strawberry on 71.4% of the trials (n = 14). When they selected "maple," they tasted maple on 55.6% of the trials (n = 9). When they selected "lemon," they tasted lemon on 80.0% of the trials (n = 10). The exploratory study gave similar results for every flavor except mushroom.

Moreover, the average intensity score of the change in taste is 1.41. This score lies midway between 1 (Slight) and 2 (Significant).

Discussion

The exploratory study shows that the participants experienced a change in the cookie's taste using our system on about 80% of the trials, although the intensity of the change in taste is modest. From the results, we cannot distinguish the different roles that visual cues with augmented reality and olfactory cues play in the perception of flavor. However, the results do suggest that our system can change the perception of taste, and allows users to experience various flavors by varying only the visual and olfactory information without changing the chemical composition.

Moreover, the exploratory study shows that the ratio of subjects who experienced a changed taste with an unfamiliar appearance and scent is similar to that of subjects who experienced a changed taste with a familiar appearance and scent, even though the ratio of subjects who identified the augmented cookie with an unfamiliar appearance and scent as the selected taste is lower than that of subjects who identified the augmented cookie with the familiar appearance and scent. The results suggest that our system changes both the perception of taste and the identification of flavor, and that knowledge has an important role in the identification of flavor. This indicates that it is difficult for our system to enable the user to experience and identify the taste of a cookie as intended when representing cookies with an unfamiliar appearance and scent, although the user perceives a change in the taste. In order to overcome this limitation, another method such as a method for synthesizing tastes from fundamental taste substances is required.

When the participants selected the maple cookie (n = 9), they experienced the flavor on 55.6% of the cases. This rate is lower than the other flavors. We suspect that this is due to the volatility of the maple flavor. Before we conducted the experiment, we impregnated each filter with the same amount of flavor. After the experiment, we observed that the odor of maple flavor was weaker than that of other flavors. Given that the volatility of maple flavor is higher than that of the other flavors, its strength decreases faster than that of other flavors. Therefore, we believe that the maple flavor is diluted after a certain period and becomes insufficient for evoking the cross-modal effect for many participants.

We used an air-pump-type olfactory display in this implementation. We believe that an inkjet-type olfactory display [3] will solve the problem of flavor dilution because it is better able to maintain the strength of the generated odors. Were we to use such a display for our system, the cross-modal effect would be evoked more effectively.

CONCLUSION

In this paper, we aimed to realize a method for flavor augmentation using visual and olfactory AR technology. To do so, we proposed the Edible Marker system, which can detect the state (number/shape/6DOF coordinate) of each piece of a bitten or divided food in real time, and the "Pseudo-gustation" method to change the perceived taste of food when eaten by changing its appearance and scent. We combined the two proposed methods into the "MetaCookie+" system based on the effect of cross-modal integration of vision, olfaction, and gustation as an implementation of the proposed method.

"MetaCookie+" is a system to change the perceived taste of a cookie by overlaying visual and olfactory information onto a real cookie with a special AR marker pattern. The system can recognize a cookie even if it is eaten or partially occluded, and detect the position and bitten/occluded area of the cookie using our Edible Marker system.

Using this system, we performed an exploratory study that investigates how people experience the flavor of a plain cookie. The results of the experiment suggested that our system can change the perceived taste, and that this enables the user to experience various tastes simply by changing visual and olfactory information without changing the chemical ingredients in the cookie.

Our system can shift the flavor of nutritionally controlled foods from distasteful or tasteless to tasty or desired. For this reason, we believe that it can be used for food prepared in hospitals and in diet food applications.

In future work, we will seek to quantify and assess the cross-modal integration effect. For example, we will attempt to reveal the role of visual feedback and olfactory feedback separately, and the relationship between the cross-modal effect and the strength of the odor produced using odor sensors. Through these assessments, we aim to realize a more effective pseudo-gustatory display system.

Furthermore, we believe we can build an expressive gustatory display system by combining this pseudo-gustation method based on cross-modal integration and methods for synthesizing a rough taste from fundamental taste substances. By doing so, we can realize a gustatory display that can represent a wide variety of tastes.

ACKNOWLEDGMENTS

This research was partially supported by the Ministry of Education, Science, Sports and Culture, Grant-in-Aid for Young Scientists (A), 21680011, 2009.

REFERENCES

1. T. Nakamoto and H. P. D. Minh: "Improvement of olfactory display using solenoid valves," Proc. IEEE Virtual Reality 2007, pp. 179.186 (2007)
2. Fumitaka Nakaizumi, Yasuyuki Yanagida, Haruo Noma, and Kenichi Hosaka: SpotScents: A Novel Method of Natural Scent DeliveryUsing Multiple Scent Projectors, Proceedings of IEEE Virtual Reality 2006, pp. 207-212, 2006.
3. Junta Sato, Kaori Ohtsu, Yuichi Bannai and Ken-ichi Okada: Pulse Ejection Technique of Scent to Create Dynamic Perspective, 18th International Conference on Artificial Reality and Telexistence, pp.167-174, 2008.
4. ScentAir: http://www.scentair.com/
5. AromaJet: http://www.aromajet.com/
6. Trisenx: http://www.trisenx.com/intro.html
7. Scentcommunication: http://www.scentcommunication.com/
8. Osmooze: http://www.osmooze.com/
9. air aroma: http://www.air-aroma.com/
10. Air/Q Whole Room Air Freshener: http://www.airq.com/store/whole-room-air-freshener
11. Beidler, L. M. (Ed.). (1971). Handbook of sensory physiology. Volume IV: Chemical senses. Part 1: Olfaction. Berlin: Springer-Verlag.
12. Dan Maynes-Aminzade: Edible Bits: Seamless Interfaces between People, Data and Food, ACM CHI 2005 Extended Abstracts, pp 2207-2210, 2005.
13. Hiroo Iwata, Hiroaki Yano, Takahiro Uemura and Tetsuro Moriya: "Food Simulator: A Haptic Interface

for Biting", Proceedings of IEEE Virtual Reality 2004, pp.51-57, 2004.

14. Shimojo S, Shams L.: Sensory modalities are not separate modalities: plasticity and interactions, Curr Opin Neurobiol. 2001 Aug;11(4):505-9, 2001.

15. Delwiche J: The impact of perceptual interactions on perceived flavor, Food Qual Prefer 15:137.146, 2004.

16. Toko, K., et al., Taste Sensor Using Electric Potential Changes in Lipid Membranes, Biosensors and Bioelectronics, Vol.9, pp.359-364, 1994.

17. Chandrashekar, J., Hoon, M. A., Ryba, N. J., & Zuker, C. S.: The receptors and cells for mammalian taste, Nature, 444, 288.294, 2006.

18. Auvray M, Spence C.: The multisensory perception of flavor, Consciousness and Cognition. 17(2008), pp. 1016-1031, 2008.

19. Ross, P. W. (2001). Qualia and the senses. The Philosophical Quarterly, 51, 495.511.

20. Rozin P,: "Taste-smell confusion"and the duality of the olfactory sense. Perception and Psychophysics, Vol. 31 (1982), pp. 397-401.

21. R. J. Stevenson, J. Prescott and R. A. Boakes: Confusing Tastes and Smells: How Odours can Influence the Perception of Sweet and Sour Tastes, Chem. Senses (1999) 24 (6): 627-635, 1999.

22. Zampini, M., Wantling, E., Phillips, N. & Spence, C.: Multisensory flavor perception: Assessing the influence of fruit acids and color cues on the perception of fruit-flavored beverages. Food Quality & Preference, 18, 335-343, 2008.

23. Charles Spence, Carmel Levitan, Maya Shankar, Massimiliano Zampini: Does Food Color Influence Taste and Flavor Perception in Humans?, Chemosensory Perception, Vol. 3, No. 1, pp. 68-84, 2010.

24. H. Kato and M. Billinghurst. Marker tracking and hmd calibration for a video-based augmented reality conferencing system. In Proc. of IWAR'99, page 85. IEEE Computer Society, 1999.

25. M. Ozuysal, M. Calonder, V. Lepetit, and PascalFua. Fast keypoint recognition using random ferns. IEEE Transactions on Pattern Analysis and Machine Intelligence, 32:448.461, 2010.

26. D. Lowe. Distinctive image features from scale-invariant keypoints. International journal of computer vision, 60(2):91.110, 2004.

27. H. Bay, T. Tuytelaars, and L. Van Gool. Surf: Speeded up robust features. Computer Vision.ECCV 2006, pages 404.417, 2006.

28. E. Rosten and T. Drummond. Machine learning for high-speed corner detection. Computer Vision.ECCV 2006, pages 430.443.

29. M. Fischler and R. Bolles. Random sample consensus: A paradigm for model fitting with applications to image analysis and automated cartography. Communications of the ACM, 24(6):381.395, 1981.

30. O. Chum and J. Matas. Matching with prosac-progressive sample consensus. In Proc. of CVPR'05, volume 1, pages 220.226. IEEE, 2005.

31. L. Li, W. Huang, I. Gu, and Q. Tian. Foreground object detection from videos containing complex background. In Proceedings of the eleventh ACM international conference on Multimedia, page 10. ACM, 2003.

32. MasterMind,Food Printer "Couver": http://www.begin.co.jp/goods/11_plotter/main_01.htm

33. Research Institute of Human Engineering for Quality Life: Anthropometric Dimension Database, http://www.hql.jp/database/size2004/

34. Kuo, Y.-L., Pangborn, R. M., & Noble, A. C.: Temporal patterns of nasal, oral, and retronasal perception of citral and vanillin and interaction of these odourants with selected tastants, International Journal of Food Science and Technology, 28, 127.137, 1993.

35. Small, D. M., Gerber, J. C., Mak, Y. E., & Hummel, T.: Differential neural responses evoked by orthonasal versus retronasal odorant perception in humans. Neuron, 47, 593.605, 2005.

36. Satoshi Yokoyama, Tomohiro Tanikawa, Koichi Hirota , Michitaka Hirose "Olfactory Field Simulation by using Wearable Olfactory Display" 9 No. 3 , Transactions of the Virtual Reality Society of Japan Vol.9 No.3 pp.265-274 2004. (In Japanese)

37. Stevenson RJ, Oaten M: The effect of appropriate and inappropriate stimulus color on odor discrimination. Percept Psychophys 70:640.646, 2008.

Biofeedback Game Design: Using Direct and Indirect Physiological Control to Enhance Game Interaction

Lennart E. Nacke **Michael Kalyn** **Calvin Lough** **Regan L. Mandryk**
Department of Computer Science
University of Saskatchewan, Saskatoon, Saskatchewan, Canada
lennart.nacke@acm.org, michael.kalyn@usask.ca, calvin.lough@usask.ca, regan.mandryk@usask.ca

ABSTRACT
Prior work on physiological game interaction has focused on dynamically adapting games using physiological sensors. In this paper, we propose a classification of direct and indirect physiological sensor input to *augment* traditional game control. To find out which sensors work best for which game mechanics, we conducted a mixed-methods study using different sensor mappings. Our results show participants have a preference for direct physiological control in games. This has two major design implications for physiologically controlled games: (1) Direct physiological sensors should be mapped intuitively to reflect an action in the virtual world; (2) Indirect physiological input is best used as a dramatic device in games to influence features altering the game world.

Author Keywords
Psychophysiology, affective computing, affective gaming, entertainment, physiological input, biofeedback, games.

ACM Classification Keywords
H.5.2 [Information Systems]: User Interfaces; K.8.0 [General]: Games; J.3 [Life and Medical Sciences].

General Terms
Design, Experimentation, Human Factors, Measurement.

INTRODUCTION
Computer games have evolved considerably since the initial days of Pong (Atari, 1972) and Space Invaders (Midway, 1978). Computer graphics techniques have advanced the realism of graphics, rendering, and simulation; artificial intelligence systems have improved the vividness of virtual worlds; and hardware has evolved. New game input devices have seen commercial success, (e.g., Nintendo Wiimote, Microsoft Kinect), which provide natural and realistic interaction and experiences. Throughout this evolution of digital games, researchers and developers have also been exploring physiologically controlled game interfaces.

Since the early 1980s, researchers have been exploring physiological input in biofeedback games for stress reduction (see *Related Work*). In the last decade, there has been increased commercial interest in using physiological input in digital games, not only for biofeedback training, but also to enhance immersion and engagement for players. Yet even with all of the technical advances surrounding physiological game input, and all of the ludological advances surrounding game design, physiological input in gameplay is still limited mainly to relaxation games using indirectly controlled physiological signals, such as heart rate (HR), galvanic skin response (GSR), or brain waves as a replacement for the game controller.

The indirectly controlled forms of physiological input previously used, such as GSR, are excellent at helping users train themselves to relax precisely because they are indirectly controlled. For example, GSR – which measures skin conductance as a proxy for psychological arousal – is a commonly used physiological input in biofeedback applications that is not directly controlled by the user. To raise or lower their GSR, players must try and relax or excite themselves, which is good for training people to relax, but limiting in terms of gameplay. To date, there has been very little work on directly controlled physiological input. In this paper, we define direct physiological control as measures that a user can manipulate and control directly (e.g., muscle flexion, eye gaze). In contrast, indirect physiological control refers to measures that cannot be explicitly influenced and changes as an indirect result of other direct bodily activation (e.g., HR, GSR).

Replacing traditional controllers with physiological sensors has been a good approach for initial testing of physiological game input. However, traditional game controllers are very good for certain game-related interaction tasks such as pointing and clicking. In addition, traditional controls may be superior in terms of performance, may be preferred by users, or may produce a better user experience (UX).

To make physiological input more desirable for the mainstream computer and video games market, we need to answer two main questions:

1. How do users respond when physiological sensors are used to augment rather than replace game controllers?

2. Which types of physiological sensors (indirect versus direct) work best for which in-game tasks?

In addition, we were interested in exploring how we could effectively integrate gaze location as a game input (using a monitor-based eye tracker) without negatively affecting the game through unintentional activation of game events from users looking at the display simply to play.

To investigate our research questions, we designed a side-scrolling platform shooter game that uses a traditional game controller as primary input. We augmented this traditional interaction with physiological sensors. Physiological input was considered to be either directly or indirectly controlled by the user although we acknowledge that this distinction can be fuzzy and dynamic in practice. Directly-controlled sensors included muscle flexion, breathing patterns, and temperature change (through blowing hot air). Indirectly-controlled sensors included HR and GSR. Gaze location was also integrated to augment controller input. Using our game, we conducted a study where participants played with three combinations of physiological and traditional input.

Through a combination of participant observation and survey data, we discovered: that players enjoy using physiological input; that they prefer directly-controlled physiological input; that indirectly-controlled input is best used for altering background variables; and that gaze input can be effectively integrated into game play. As game design and development continues to press for more novel and thrilling experiences for players, our work can help by informing the design of physiologically controlled games.

RELATED WORK

Prior related work on physiological game interaction has focused on adapting games to a user's physiological state [4] and on developing emotional models to understand the psychophysiological input from a user [9].

Physiological control and adaptive gameplay

Recent research in human-computer interaction (HCI) has explored the potential of physiological computing to tailor user experience to players' cognitive, motivational, and emotional responses (see [3] for an overview). Computer games are an excellent application area in which to explore the benefits and drawbacks of physiological HCI as they are a low-risk domain – if a game misinterprets a physiological signal or adapts incorrectly, there is less fallout than if a critical command-and-control system did the same.

Industry manufacturers have investigated physiologically-controlled biofeedback techniques for gaming since the late 1970s and early 1980s. For example, Canadian biofeedback equipment manufacturer Thought Technology investigated physiological input in their CalmPute[1] software packaged with a modified GSR2 sensor (i.e., an Apple II mouse with GSR electrodes) and the racing game CalmPrix in 1984.

Other attempts at integrating biofeedback into gaming systems included the unreleased Atari Mindlink in 1983, The Journey to Wild Divine in 2001, and the Nintendo 64 biosensor included in the Japanese version of Tetris 64 in 1998. This electrocardiographic (EKG) sensor measured users' HR and adapted game speed. Eventually, it was taken off the market, but Nintendo recently revisited this idea by announcing its Wii Vitality sensor, a pulse oximeter connected to the Wiimote designed to be used in relaxation games. Similarly, Ubisoft has announced a similar product for 2011, called Innergy, another pulse oximeter, which was demonstrated with a stress relaxation game[2].

Additionally, many hardware manufacturers are aiming at providing cheap input solutions that use brain signals to interact with a computer, such as Emotiv EPOC, Neurosky Mindset, or OCZ Neural Impulse Actuator (NIA).

Game Design for Physiological Game Interaction

Physiological game interaction is generally called *affective gaming* by the academic community. A definition of affective gaming was proposed by Gilleade et al. [5] as an activity where "the player's current emotional state is used to manipulate gameplay." Thus, an affective gaming system should sense a player's emotion and arousal, and loop this information back into the system. However, the simple replacement of user controls with biofeedback information does not make a game effective. A popular example for this is the unreleased *Bionic Breakthrough* game (a clone of the *Breakout* game) for the Atari Mindlink, which used forehead EMG sensors to replace the conventional joystick input device. Mindlink players frequently reported headaches as a result of moving their eyebrows in an attempt to control the game.

Part of the reason why game publishers are targeting biofeedback control as a replacement of traditional input devices is that learning to control biofeedback consciously or subconsciously can be challenging and fun for some players. Games are rule-based formal interactive systems geared toward teaching a player how to interact with the simulated world and its entities. Part of the fun of gaming is figuring out these interactions. However, not every game design and mechanic can (or should be) supported through physiological interaction (e.g., using brain signals for quick-reaction events). An alternative approach to affective gaming is to adapt games based on physiological input [4].

Adaptive affective games [4, 5] change either technical parameters or user preferences based on recordable user behavior such as error-rates, button pressure, controller movement, or physiological responses. It is important to correctly distinguish affective states of the user, such as at-game or in-game frustration [4]. Physical failures, (e.g., inability to execute a command), will result in at-game frus-

[1] http://www.thoughttechnology.com/thewall2.htm

[2] http://www.physiologicalcomputing.net/?p=389

tration and mental failures (e.g., not recognizing game objectives), will result in in-game frustration. Physiologically adaptive games must propagate affective feedback [1]. Replacing conventional execution of input commands is regarded by Gilleade et al. [5] as "straight-forward biofeedback."

Direct or Indirect Physiological Control

Most examples of prior research on physiologically-controlled games use indirect control – that is, the game uses a player's affective state without giving players the option of controlling it directly. For example, consider physiological games such as the relax-to-win racing game [1] or the Brainball game [6]. In these games, winning conditions are controlled by a player's ability to relax – in the former by allowing a dragon to race faster, and in the latter by rolling a physical ball across a table towards an opponent. These games demonstrate how physiological input is not directly controlled, but mediated by some other player interaction, such as meditation or deep breathing. This is different from "implicit commands" or indirectly controlled brain-computer interfaces (BCIs). Zander et al. [15] introduced this concept of directly and indirectly controlled BCIs, where indirect control refers to modulation of brain activity in response to external stimulation.

Players can get satisfaction out of learning to control their biofeedback through indirect physiological control. Playing the game AlphaWoW, in which players trigger their shapeshifting ability using electroencephalography (EEG) [11], provides players with the satisfaction of learning to control their brainwaves. In all of these cases, biofeedback is trained competitively in order to gain advantage and win the game, whereas an alternative approach would aim to improve player experience rather than chances of winning. For example, Dekker et al. developed a game modification using the Source SDK and Half-Life 2, GSR and HR were used to control game shader graphics, screen shaking, and enemy spawn points (i.e., number of locations in which enemies are put into the game world) [2].

Although most games have used indirectly-controlled physiological sensors, there is an unexplored opportunity for direct physiological control to map directly to specific game mechanics, or to enhance the player experience.

Awareness of Control

In all previous examples, players were aware that their physiological input controlled some aspect of the game or experience. Kuikanniemi et al. [8] explored the difference between players that are aware of and not aware of their biofeedback when playing a first-person shooter (FPS) game and referred to this as implicit and explicit biofeedback. The biofeedback modulated player-character-related game mechanics including walking and turning speed, aiming direction, recoil amount, and firing rate. The results show that people enjoyed the explicit biofeedback conditions more and their conscious control of the respiratory sensor led to a better game experience.

Physiological studies of gameplay experience

Instead of being used as input to a game, physiological sensors such as GSR, cardiovascular measures, and EMG, have been used to objectively quantify user emotion during interactions with gaming systems [9]. An overview of game research using psychophysiological measures [7] notes two general approaches having emerged from previous work: Studying phasic psychophysiological responses to game events [12] and research studies of tonic responses to variations in game design dubbed affective ludology [10].

A Primer of Used Physiological Measures

For a synopsis of physiological measures in games, see [7].

Gaze Interaction. Tracking the location of a user's gaze (GAZE) supports analysis of visual attention. Gaze-related data includes the position and movement of gaze on the screen, and pupil dilation. Eye trackers, which can be integrated into a computer monitor, record patterns and distributions of gaze fixations and saccadic eye motion. Gaze input is considered as direct physiological control.

Electromyography (EMG) describes the measurement of electrical activation of muscle tissue. While facial EMG is used in emotion detection, EMG has also been used to sense muscle activation as a more direct form of input [13].

Electrodermal activity (EDA, also: skin-conductance level or SCL) or *galvanic skin response* (GSR) is a common psychophysiological measurement with easy application. EDA is regulated by production of sweat in the eccrine glands, where increased activity is associated with psychological arousal. GSR is an indirect form of input.

Electrocardiography (EKG) is the sensing of heart activity through physiological sensors on the body. It is hard to control directly, but hyperventilation or increased physical activity often results in an increased HR. HR is an indirect input mechanism for a game.

A *respiration (RESP) sensor* is stretched across an individual's chest to measure breathing rate and volume. Strain sensors can be directly controlled.

A *temperature sensor* (TEMP) is directly controlled in our experiment, through blowing hot air on it; TEMP could also be an indirect measure if placed on the surface of the skin.

A GAMING SYSTEM FOR AFFECTIVE INPUT

To investigate direct and indirect physiological control, we developed a single-player 2D side-scrolling shooter game that used standard controller mappings in Xbox360 shooter games. Physiological input was controlled separately.

Building a Game for Physiological Input

The single-player 2D side-scrolling shooter, features many obstacles, including increasingly difficult enemies, moving platforms, and a final boss. Players can save their progress by reaching checkpoints. If a player's character dies after that, they are returned to the most recent checkpoint that they reached and given half their health back. To encourage players to interact with enemies and have a more challenging experience, a checkpoint is only registered if a player has killed all enemies leading up to that checkpoint.

Game Mechanics under Variable Control Schemes

To explore different variations of traditional game control and physiological input, we implemented five game mechanics that could be controlled using different physiological sensors. We describe the game mechanics here and present the control mappings in the study section.

Enemy Target Size

Because performance in 2D shooting games is primarily about the accuracy of aiming at targets, we manipulated the enemy target size through physiological control. Rather than increasing the size of the entire sprite, we displayed a shadow of the enemy that grew (See Figure 1). Pilot testing showed that increasing the enemy size directly was counter-intuitive, since easier-to-hit enemies looked more threatening. Hitting an enemy shadow counted as a hit.

Figure 1. Target enemies increase in size.

Flamethrower weapon: Flame length

The game featured three weapons: a regular projectile weapon, an ice projectile weapon, and a flamethrower weapon with unlimited ammunition. To avoid deadlocks in a game when a player runs out of ammunition, many games feature a fallback weapon (e.g., the crowbar in Half-Life 2). We made our fallback weapon more interesting by placing the flame length under variable control (see Figure 2).

Figure 2. Flamethrower weapon: flame length was increased

Speed and jump height

Many side-scrolling platform games employ power ups that increase avatar speed and jump height temporarily. We linked this to a single variable which was controlled using physiological input.

Final boss battle: weather conditions and boss speed

At the end of our test game level, the player enters an icy area, eventually leading to the final game boss. Gentle falling snow was implemented throughout this area. In heavy snowfall (see Figure 3), it was more difficult for players to see platforms and enemies, thus affecting the accuracy of their shots. The rate of snowfall was under variable control. In addition, the boss behavior was linked to the snowfall rate – with lighter snowfall, the boss would get warmer, would start to steam (a visual effect only) and would also move more slowly (thus being easier to target).

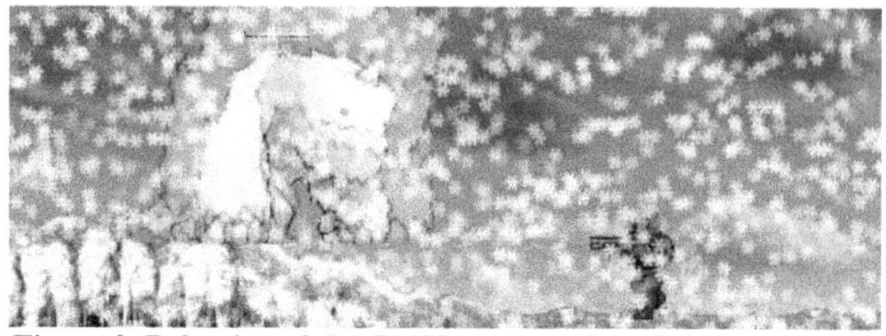

Figure 3. Behavior of the final boss (a yeti) and the snow effect were controlled together in a variable.

Eye tracker feature: Medusa's gaze

We implemented one game mechanic under physiological control that was designed specifically to use gaze control. Gaze control can be difficult to implement well because players should not inadvertently activate gaze-controlled features simply by looking around the display.

Figure 4. The Medusa's Gaze feature in the game.

We used gaze control as a power-up that temporarily froze enemies and moving platforms, called Medusa's Gaze. To acquire this power-up, users needed to pick up a special item, which would then display a blue circle at the location of their gaze (see Figure 4). Looking at enemies and moving platforms would freeze them temporarily. Frozen enemies and platforms turned green and then transitioned back to their normal color, indicating the amount of time left in their frozen state. To keep the game balanced and avoid eyestrain, Medusa's Gaze was only available for 20 seconds after picking up the special item.

Game Implementation and Architecture

To integrate physiological sensors, we wrote a custom C# library called SensorLib, which is a multi-threaded library written in C# that provides an interface for external third-party sensors. It handles the connection to the sensors, the data-buffering, digital signal processing, and offers the data through a high-level .NET interface. It aggregates third party SDKs into a single interface so programmers can create sensor-dependent applications.

Sensor	SDK	Measure	Processing
Audio	DirectX 10	Amplitude of sound waves.	None
Gaze	TobiiSDK	Tracks where user is looking on computer screen.	None
BVP		Blood flow through a finger.	Downsampled by 64
GSR		Skin conductance	Downsampled by 64
EKG		Senses heart beats.	Heartbeat Detection
EMG		Contraction of muscles.	Smoothing; Normalized
RESP	TTLAPI	Amount of strain on a chest strap.	Downsampled by 64; Normalized
TEMP		Temperature change.	Downsampled by 64; Normalized
Raw		Receives data from any TTL sensor with no processing.	None

Table 1. Digital signal processing in SensorLib.

Table 1 shows the SDKs used by each sensor in SensorLib and the digital signal processing each sensor does. All digital filters are Chebyshev type II filters with lower filter length and no ripple in the passband. The game architecture, implemented in C# using XNA and SensorLib is shown in Figure 5.

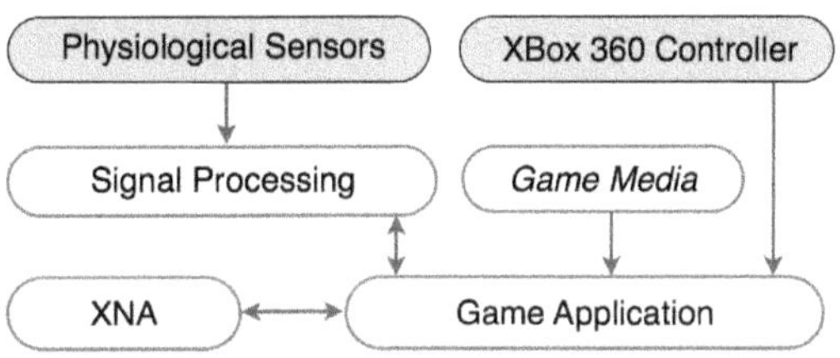

Figure 5. Game Architecture

STUDY

To evaluate the relative appeal of direct and indirect physiological control, participants played three versions of a game, two augmented with physiological input and one control condition. The sensor mappings and their respective thresholds for each game mechanic were developed using iterative prototype testing for five months, gathering feedback from more than 50 individuals before this study.

Game Conditions

Two of the game conditions mapped two direct and two indirect sensors to the four game mechanics under variable control described previously, while the third condition used no physiological input. Although it would have been useful to include only direct physiological input in one condition and indirect in the other, this was not possible as the indirect sensors are difficult to control independently.

The physiological sensors used as direct control were respiration, EMG on the leg, and temperature. The indirectly-controlled sensors included GSR and EKG. Mappings of the sensors to the game mechanics for each condition are shown in Table 2.

Mechanic	Cond. 1	Cond. 2
Target size	RESP	GSR
Speed/jump	EKG	EMG
Weather/boss	TEMP	EKG
Flamethrower	GSR	RESP
Avatar control	Gamepad	Gamepad
Medusa's Gaze	Gaze	Gaze

Table 2. Game conditions. Direct sensors are shaded in dark blue, and indirect in light blue. Gaze tracking is a special case of direct sensor control; the gamepad was used in all cases.

Medusa's gaze was available in both physiological conditions, but not in the control condition. The third control condition used only the gamepad for avatar control and did not make use of the game mechanics implemented for the physiological sensors.

Experimental Procedure

The study used a three-condition (2 physiological variations, 1 control with gamepad only) within-subjects design. All participants played all three conditions, which were presented using a randomized ordering. Each participant played through an initial training level to get accustomed to the game controls before the trial started. EMG, RESP, and gaze tracking were recalibrated before each game condition. After providing informed consent, the participants completed a demographics questionnaire, which also asked questions about their gameplay experience. Participants were then fitted with the physiological sensors and briefed on how to control them both directly and indirectly. For example, to increase their GSR, players were advised to laugh, bite their lip, flick themselves, or think about exciting things[3], whereas they were told to flex their foot to increase their EMG response. Participants played each game condition for 10 minutes or until they completed the level (10-35 min.), a common playing time in game research [7]. After each game, players completed a survey, rating their gameplay experience using game-specific questions. Following completion of all conditions, players completed a final survey soliciting their opinions of physiological control in video games.

Apparatus

The game was played on a Dell computer running Windows XP. The monitor was a 24" TFT display running at a resolution of 1080p (1920x1200), with an integrated Tobii T60 XL eyetracker running at 60 Hz (see Figure 6). Physiological data was collected using the Flexcomp Infinity hardware by Thought Technology, and integrated into the game using our custom sensor library SensorLib, described briefly in the previous section.

[3] While it might be argued that biting one's lip is a somewhat direct physiological influence, the directness of the action here is the biting, but the resulting change in GSR is still indirect. For example, in contrast measuring lip-biting pressure would be a direct measure.

Figure 6. A participant playing the game using the physiological sensors and the eye tracker

Participants

Ten participants (7 male), aged 21 to 40 (M=25.8, SD=5.5) completed the study. Six of the participants played video games at least monthly; the others played only a few times a year. Participants were not very experienced with side-scrolling shooter games, indicating an average expertise of 2.5 on a scale of 1 (novice) to 5 (expert). When asked about their experience with novel forms of input to games, participants primarily reported having used the Nintendo DS and Wii, with fewer participants having experience with the WiiFit balance board and the Rock Band controllers.

RESULTS

Ratings data were analyzed with non-parametric techniques, while open-ended survey responses were clustered into overarching themes. We present results on fun and novelty ratings, followed by sensor preference.

Physiological Control: Fun Ratings

We asked players to rate their fun in each condition on a scale of 1 (not much fun) to 5 (very fun). A Friedman test for 3-related samples showed differences in players' fun ratings depending on game condition (χ^2_2=7.3, p=.026). Pairwise Wilcoxon Signed Ranks tests showed that players found both physiological control conditions to be more fun than the no physiological control condition (both Z=2.1, both p=.033, see Figure 7), but no difference between the physiological control conditions was found (Z=0, p=1.0).

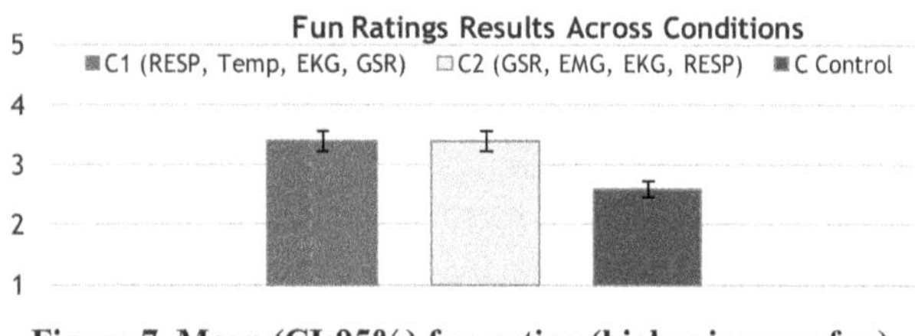

Figure 7. Mean (CI:95%) fun rating (higher is more fun).

When asked at the end of the experiment whether they preferred to play with or without sensors, 9 of 10 players preferred to use physiological control.

The players who enjoyed physiological control commented that having to use more than one input device *"made for a very immersive game, out of what is basically just a very simple platform shooter." (P7, Male)*. In line with this statement, *"the sensors added a new dimension to the game, and gave a greater sense of involvement." (P2, Female)*. This involvement and enjoyment seemed to be especially strong when *"more parts of the body are involved in the game." (P1, Male)*

With the increase of immersion came also a greater sense of challenge, a feeling of greater *"variation, and more enjoyment while playing because there are always new skills to improve on." (P4, Male)*

The controls were usually perceived as best when they matched a natural input, such as thawing snow with temperature increase, freezing enemies by staring at them, or running faster by flexing the leg muscle.

"Jumping higher and running faster by flexing the leg is so intuitive. I'm sure many do it instinctively anyway." (P5, Male)

The one dissenting participant commented that the *"sensors [made the] game complicated. (P3, Female)"*.

Novelty of Physiological Control

We asked participants how they would rate the novelty of physiological control on a scale from 1 (not novel) to 5 (extremely novel). Participants agreed that the physiological control was novel (M=4.2, SD=0.79). To better understand their view of the novelty of physiological control, we asked if there was something special about using their body to control the game, or whether it was more like a new type of game controller.

"At times it felt like a new type of controller that I had to actively think about, but other times it felt like more than that—almost that I was physically part of the game." (P2, Female)

Some players mentioned that there was a learning curve involved in learning to use the sensor, but once they learned to use it, the experience was more rewarding. Additionally, players mentioned that they were more aware of some sensors than others and that some felt more like controllers:

"The breathing sensor and GSR sensor felt like controllers though, because I was very aware they were attached to me. The EKG and EMG were completely unnoticeable and fun to use..." (P4, Male)

"[The] muscle and breathing sensors were simple enough that they were practically like a new button on the controller for me, but very awesome ones since rather than tapping a button, it was an instinctive action." (P7, Male)

Sensor Preference

After each game, we asked participants which sensor they preferred to all others. Over the course of the two games, 12/20 votes were for gaze input, 5 were for RESP, and one for each of TEMP, EMG and GSR. Although these choices are also affected by controlled game mechanic, only 1/20 votes was for an indirect sensor. We also asked players to rate their enjoyment of the five game mechanics explored.

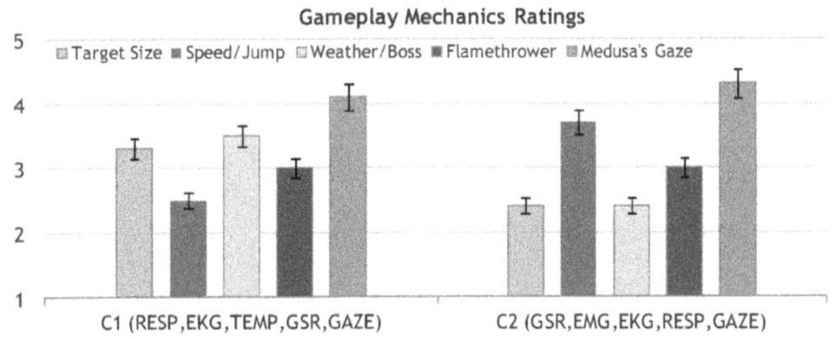

Figure 8. Game mechanic ratings (CI:95%) for each condition.

Figure 8 shows how participants rated the direct controls higher than the indirect controls for target size increases, speed/jumps, and weather/boss speed, but not for the flamethrower. In the post-game questionnaire, we asked participants about their preferred sensors (see Figure 9).

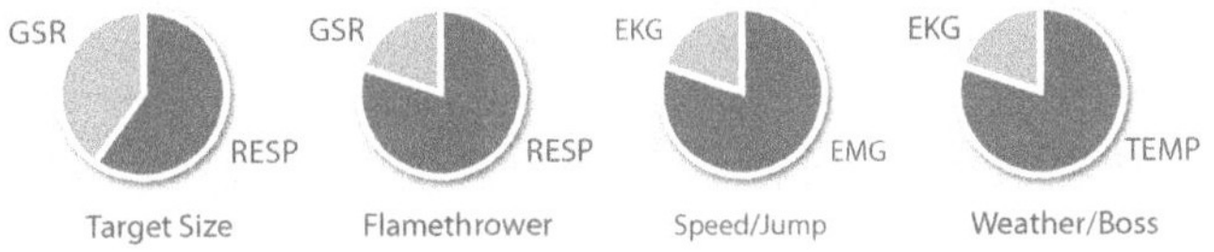

Figure 9. Player choices for physiological control by game mechanic. Dark wedges are direct sensors, light are indirect.

For target size increases and flamethrower length, players preferred RESP to GSR. For speed and jump height they preferred EMG to EKG. For controlling the weather and speed of the yeti, players preferred TEMP to EKG.

As shown in Figure 9, for each game mechanic more participants preferred the direct control than the indirect control. We also asked players which they would choose if they could only play with one combination of RESP/EMG/TEMP (direct) or EKG/GSR (indirect). Eight of the ten participants chose the direct sensors combination. We present participant comments for each of the physiological controls individually.

Opinions about GSR Sensor (Indirect)

Many participants reported problems with controlling the GSR sensors, because it only responded indirectly. Some perceived the indirect control as unnoticeable or "not working." Players used different strategies for trying to control GSR, and some of them not pleasant:

"I liked that it was always a challenge to control just with my thoughts [...] and forced me to use a part of my brain I wouldn't normally use in a video game." (P4, Male)

"I disliked the fact that one of the only ways that I found I was able to use the GSR was by biting my lip which isn't actually all that fun after it starts hurting." (P8, Male)

Another issue for participants was the location of the GSR sensor on the pinkie and ring finger of the left hand during controller-based gameplay, which one participant found *"uncomfortable and awkward." (P4, Male)*

"I didn't like that it got in the way a bit with holding the controller. After I got used to it I was fine though." (P9, Male)

One participant also mentioned the close relationship of the control of GSR to control of EKG, saying he was *"not even sure what this one controlled in the second game." (P4, Male)*

Opinions about the EKG Sensor (Indirect)

Similar to participant response to the other indirect sensor (GSR), participants felt that EKG was hard to control and therefore was not perceived as working accurately.

"[...] I couldn't control as instantly as the others—the effect from it tended to last over longer periods of time." (P2, Female)

Players also thought that because EKG seemed slow to respond, it might be *"better suited to changing the game context than what the character is doing." (P5, Male)*

Opinions about the EMG Sensor (Direct)

Comments on the direct control using EMG were split between positive and negative experiences. Some noted that they were *"wishing it was a bit more sensitive or easier to trigger [the sensor by flexing the muscles]." (P2, Female)*, while others felt that it was easy to use:

"It was fairly easy to use. It was effective and worked." (P8, Male)

Players generally liked the mappings of the EMG sensor:

"I really liked this one. Flexing your leg to move faster or jump higher? Definitely cool." (P7, Male)

"[...] having this sensor tied to jumping/speed felt natural" (P2, Female)

It was also noted that the muscle could become strained if the sensor is used continuously for input, but some players liked the idea of a physical workout by playing a video game.

Opinions about the RESP Sensor (Direct)

This sensor was praised for its very easy controllability and the immediate feedback it provided to participants' actions.

"It was neat to see the immediate reaction from my body to the game." (P10, Female)

"This was also cool, as it was very easy to activate, didn't really have to put much thought into it." (P7, Male)

Due to its responsive nature, participants also noted that they felt *"it got you more into the game." (P8, Male)*

"[It] felt very natural, particularly when it was tied to target size in the game [...]. It's one I felt I could control to a fine degree." (P2, Female).

Opinions about the TEMP Sensor (Direct)

This sensor was initially experienced as easy-to-use; however, using it over longer periods of time became tedious, since the participants had to remember to keep on blowing on it.

"It was easy to use for short periods of time but hard to remember to breathe deep into the sensor [...]." (P8, Male)

"It was easy to control but the effect didn't last long in the game so I [had] to constantly breathe out [...]." (P6, Male)

The natural mapping to control the snow in the environment by the heat of the sensor was perceived positively although some players noted the limited applicability in games.

"I like [...] when it was tied to weather [...], because it felt like a natural thing to do. [...]" (P2, Female)

"I'm not sure how many games you could actually include it in [...] Limited applicability would be the only thing I dislike about it." (P7, Male)

One participant found that controlling TEMP would cross activate HR, because she was breathing rapidly.

"Breathing rapidly to increase temperature also brought my heart rate up." (P2, Female)

Opinions about the Gaze Sensor (Direct)

Gaze was chosen by many players as their favorite input control, because many found that it was easy to control and worked well.

"Now that was just cool [...] I liked being able to roast one frozen combatant while immobilizing another." (P5, Male)

"It worked remarkably well and was easy to control. I found the effect useful in the game." (P6, Male)

Some noted that it became inaccurate if posture was changed rapidly during gaming. Another participant noted that it obscured her intended gameplay at some parts.

"I loved the eye tracking input. It was cool, and unique! It worked pretty well, but if I changed my posture it didn't work as well." (P9, Male)

"I found it frustrating when you would look at a platform intending to jump on it and end up freezing it." (P2, Female)

Additional comments from participants

Many participants noted that direct control was their preferred way of controlling the game mechanics as they felt it provided direct feedback to them and made the game more responsive. The eye tracker was a favorite of many, because it did not require the application of a sensor on the body of the participant, making it incredibly easy to use.

The idea of having multiple modes of input in an extended (or augmented) controller struck a chord with many players.

"I like the idea of using multiple physiological inputs. Distributing the functions around the body is intuitive in some cases." (P5, Male)

"[It] basically boils down to an "extended controller" where the buttons are not buttons but other actions, similar to waving a Wii remote." (P7, Male)

DISCUSSION

We investigated the use of direct and indirect physiological control in games. Our main results were:

- The physiological augmentation of game controls provided a more fun experience than using only a traditional control scheme for game interaction.
- Physiological control was a fun game mechanic in itself because it provided enjoyment by adding an additional challenging dimension to gameplay.
- Participants preferred physiological sensors that were directly controlled because of the visible responsiveness.
- Physiological controls worked most effectively and were most enjoyable when they were appropriately mapped to game mechanics.
- Indirect control was perceived as slow and inaccurate, and was not preferred; however, users recognized its potential to show passive reactions of the game world (e.g., atmospheric changes) or as a dramatic device.

We explore these main findings further and discuss the relative advantages of direct and indirect control, the relevance of appropriate mappings, and how to best integrate physiological sensors into traditional control schemes. In addition, we address the limitations of our work and present future research opportunities.

Indirect versus Direct Physiological Control in Games

It is not surprising that players preferred direct physiological control, since the benefits of directly controlled physiological input are compatible with the nature of many action games requiring a quick reaction to a presented stimulus. The feeling of control over the game world is an important factor in gameplay enjoyment. Direct physiological input was easier for players to activate and provided better and instantaneous feedback, which was likely perceived as more or better playing control.

Indirect physiological control does not have a 1:1 mapping of player action and game reaction and is therefore not equally suited as game input for fast-paced action games. This was made evident in participants' comments noting the slow response of indirect physiological sensors to their actions. However, this disadvantage could be turned into a strength if indirect physiological control was used to affect slow-changing environmental variables of the game that could allow these sensors to function as a dramatic device. This would be in line with prior work on affective feedback games [1,5], which intelligently respond to players' physiological states, or games that dynamically adjust to provide player satisfaction [14]. Our work suggests that indirect control may be best used for peripheral environmental variables (i.e., features altering the game world to change player experience) or as a dramatic or aesthetic or artistic device that does not directly influence game mechanics.

Another important game enjoyment factor related to the feeling of control is the feeling of action accomplishment. The disproportionally positive feedback for a simple action is one of the reward mechanics used in games. For example, pressing the right combination of buttons (a fairly simple task) could result in a special action that moves a player's avatar in unrealistic and exciting ways, such as flying or jumping over a building. The greater feeling of control that resulted from direct physiological input could have enhanced a player's sense of accomplishment. In addition, since the in-game actions using direct sensors were triggered using the body as input (e.g., flexing leg) rather than the traditional controller (e.g., pressing button), the sense of accomplishment may have been heightened and made the experience more immediate and personal.

The distinction between direct and indirect physiological control may change with increased use. One could argue that initially indirect measures become direct with exposure over time since a user's intuitive ability to control their physiological response would increase. This is the basic premise of biofeedback training, and presents interesting questions and challenges for physiological game designers over the long term. As users learn to intentionally manipulate indirect physiological measures, it opens the door to physiological cheats and exploits. For example, in Tokimeki Memorial Oshiete Your Heart (Konami, 1997) players cheated by going for a jog before playing to increase their body sweat and the resulting success of a virtual animated date [4].

Relevance of Control to Game Context

Many participants mentioned that they most enjoyed using the sensors when they felt their physiological actions mapped naturally to the in-game reaction. For example, when breathing out triggered a longer flame of the flamethrower, blowing hot air on the temperature sensor decreased the amount of snow, or flexing the leg muscle increased speed and jump height. Natural mappings create an intuitive method for interacting with the game world.

For example, in some game contexts, it might be difficult to find natural mappings, or multiple mappings may exist. Our participants show this in their ratings and rankings of RESP versus GSR for the flamethrower length. When asked directly, participants preferred the RESP to GSR input, but the rating of the game mechanic was equal across conditions, indicating that both sensors were suitable for controlling the game mechanic. Natural mappings may present more intuitive game interfaces, but also limit the flexibility and generality of the sensors for game control. This tension between innovating new uses of physiological controls and sticking with standard mappings will present future challenges for physiological game designers.

Replacing or Augmenting Traditional Game Controllers

Most previous work has focused on replacing direct control with a physiological sensor [1], and this trend is still evident in the game industry with the announcement of the Wii Vitality and the Ubisoft Innergy. Physiological input—whether direct or indirect—will not be suitable for all tasks. For example, playing a button-mashing game with brain signals does not seem like a good design choice. In our approach, we focus on augmenting traditional input devices with physiological information to reward players with a richer experience. In addition, we feel that augmenting traditional game controllers with physiological input will allow for a gentle learning curve as players become used to physiological control. Having the possibility to enter the game world using a common interaction modality such as the game controller would allow players to feel more competent in the game and would facilitate trying out the "new powers" they gain through physiological control.

Integrating Physiological Sensing into Controllers

Augmenting traditional controllers with physiological input will be a challenge for industrial designers. In addition, cooperation is needed between the hardware manufacturers who make the devices and the game developers, who include physiological input in their game controllers. The recent collaboration between Ubisoft and MindMedia, a Dutch biofeedback company, for the development of Innergy demonstrates that this can successfully be done. PC games can draw upon the availability of physiological input devices in the consumer market, such as the Lightstone from The Journey to Wild Divine, the Neurosky Mindset, and the Emotiv EPOC, which all use indirect physiological input. Direct sensors, such as GAZE, RESP, and EMG were preferred by our participants, but there are currently no consumer-level sensors available. Both RESP and EMG use standard components and would be inexpensive to produce.

Game and hardware designers must also consider the willingness of players to adopt wearable technology. In our work, we have found that players are very comfortable wearing sensors if they perceive the added value in gameplay. The broad consumer acceptance of fitness games that require wearing sensors also suggests that this is not an issue for players. Our participants mentioned they were fully aware of using muscle activation as control in the game and some entertained the thought that this might be a great way to improve their fitness. Because the combination of several sensors was mentioned as a positive feature by many participants, there are great opportunities to integrate physiological sensors (e.g., EMG) with fitness game input.

Limitations

Our study shows support for augmenting game control with direct and indirect physiological input; however, it was a preliminary investigation and therefore is limited in its generalizability. First, we explored a small number of specific game mechanics in a certain genre. Choosing different gameplay mechanics, interaction mappings, or game genres would likely result in different player experiences. Second, our participants played for a short time; as with any new technology, it will be interesting to see how user experience changes over long-term repeated use. Third, our participants were mostly casual game players. To fully explore the range of possibilities with physiological input, it will be important to involve players of all experience levels into the game design process. And finally, as this is an initial explorative study, we must acknowledge both the role of novelty in our results and the small number of participants. Large-scale, long-term deployment to address these issues will be feasible after additional small-scale targeted studies.

FUTURE WORK

Our initial investigation into direct and indirect physiological control opens many future research opportunities. One of our participants noted that triggering one physiological control (i.e., breathing warm air on the temperature sensor) co-activated another physiological response (i.e., increasing HR). As many indirect physiological sensors are triggered as a result of a more direct action, using this co-activation as a game mechanic has great potential. For example, for fitness games, an objective could be to flex a muscle a certain amount of time, but only within a certain arousal threshold to make sure the exercise is being performed within a healthy range. This would combine the power of using direct physiological control and indirectly influencing the game state and come in the appealing marketing package of a fitness game fostering exercise and mobility.

Our players also mentioned that physiological sensors could be integrated into an extended version of a controller that uses multiple physiological inputs simultaneously. The co-activation of multiple direct physiological sensors could provide new gameplay challenges such as using gaze to unlock a door and then slowly breathing out to push it open.

CONCLUSION

As we create new forms of input, we need to consider whether these will replace or augment well-established methods of interaction. Traditional interaction forms may be superior in terms of performance, may be preferred by users, or may produce a better experience, while new forms may provide additional capabilities or be more immersive. We propose *augmenting* traditional controller input with physiological input. Therefore, we investigated this combination in an exploratory study, and have two main results for designing a game for physiological input: first, *direct* physiological sensors should be mapped naturally to *reflect an action* in the virtual world; and second, *indirect* physiological control is best used as a *dramatic device* in games to influence environmental variables.

ACKNOWLEDGMENTS

We thank Kiel Gilleade, Jaymie Koroluk, Jörg Niesenhaus, and our CHI reviewers who provided helpful comments on previous versions of this document, and we thank NSERC and the GRAND NCE for funding. Thanks to all participants in the game experiment.

REFERENCES

1. Bersak, D., McDarby, G., Augenblick, N., McDarby, P., McDonnell, D., McDonal, B., Karkun, R. Intelligent Biofeedback using an Immersive Competitive Environment. *Online Proc. for Designing Ubiquitous Computing Games Workshop at Ubicomp'01* (2001).
2. Dekker, A. and Champion, E. Please Biofeed the Zombies: Enhancing the Gameplay and Display of a Horror Game Using Biofeedback. *Proc. of DiGRA*, (2007).
3. Fairclough, S.H. Fundamentals of Physiological Computing. *Interact Comput 21*, 1–2 (2008), 133–145.
4. Gilleade, K. and Dix, A. Using frustration in the design of adaptive videogames. *Proc. of ACE*, ACM (2004), 228–232.
5. Gilleade, K., Dix, A., and Allanson, J. Affective Videogames and Modes of Affective Gaming: Assist Me, Challenge Me, Emote Me. *Proc. of DiGRA*, (2005).
6. Hjelm, S.I. Research + design: the making of Brainball. *interactions 10*, 1 (2003), 26–34.
7. Kivikangas, J. M., Ekman, I., Chanel, G., Järvelä, S., Salminen, M., Cowley, B., Henttonen, P., Ravaja, N. Review on psychophysiological methods in game research. *Proc. of 1st Nordic DiGRA*, DiGRA (2010).
8. Kuikkaniemi, K., Laitinen, T., Turpeinen, M., Saari, T., Kosunen, I., and Ravaja, N. The influence of implicit and explicit biofeedback in first-person shooter games. *Proc. of CHI'10*, ACM (2010), 859–868.
9. Mandryk, R. and Atkins, M. A Fuzzy Physiological Approach for Continuously Modeling Emotion During Interaction with Play Environments. *Int J Hum-Comput St 65*, 4 (2007), 329–347.
10. Nacke, L.E., Stellmach, S., and Lindley, C.A. Electroencephalographic Assessment of Player Experience: A Pilot Study in Affective Ludology. *Simulation & Gaming*, ahead of print (2010).
11. Nijholt, A., Plass-Oude Bos, D., and Reuderink, B. Turning shortcomings into challenges: Brain-computer interfaces for games. *Entertainment Computing 1*, 2 (2009), 85–94.
12. Ravaja, N., Turpeinen, M., Saari, T., Puttonen, S., and Keltikangas-Järvinen, L. The Psychophysiology of James Bond: Phasic Emotional Responses to Violent Video Game Events. *Emotion 8*, 1 (2008), 114–120.
13. Saponas, T.S., Tan, D.S., Morris, D., and Balakrishnan, R. Demonstrating the feasibility of using forearm electromyography for muscle-computer interfaces. *Proc. of CHI'08*, ACM (2008), 515–524.
14. Yannakakis, G.N. and Hallam, J. Towards Optimizing Entertainment in Computer Games. *Applied Artificial Intelligence 21*, 10 (2007), 933–971.
15. Zander, T.O., Kothe, C., Jatzev, S., and Gaertner, M. Enhancing Human-Computer Interaction with Input from Active and Passive Brain-Computer Interfaces. In D.S. Tan and A. Nijholt, eds., *Brain-Computer Interfaces*. Springer London, 2010, 181–199.

Confessions from a Grounded Theory PhD: Experiences and Lessons Learnt

Dominic Furniss and Ann Blandford
University College London
UCL, Gower Street, London. WC1E 6BT. UK.
d.furniss@ucl.ac.uk; a.blandford@ucl.ac.uk
+44 (0) 207 679 7085; +44 (0) 207 679 0688

Paul Curzon
Queen Mary, University of London
QMUL, Mile End, London. E1 4NS. UK.
pc@dcs.qmul.ac.uk
+44 (0) 20 7882 5212

ABSTRACT
Grounded Theory (GT) is used within HCI research, but nuances and more modern interpretations of the method are rarely discussed. This paper has two intentions: to offer guidance on practical issues when applying GT, and to clarify the space of methodological possibilities. We describe an extended GT study on understanding why practitioners choose particular usability evaluation methods. We describe five stages in this study to highlight our experiences and choices made. We draw out seven practical and methodological considerations in applying GT in a CHI context. This challenges the more traditional inductive and objective positions on GT use; it sensitizes novices of GT to these issues; and through the extended case study it provides substance for debate on issues that affect those that use qualitative methods more broadly.

Author Keywords
Grounded theory, constructivist. distributed cognition, method, qualitative, resilience engineering

ACM Classification Keywords
H5.m. Information interfaces and presentation (e.g., HCI): Miscellaneous.

ACM Classification Keywords
Human Factors, Theory

INTRODUCTION
Contemporary HCI is facing more qualitative research questions to engage with human values in a digital age [24], and develop methods, practices and designs 'for the full range of human experience' [30]. These challenges encourage better reflection on the art of performing different qualitative techniques to ensure strong research results are obtained. Grounded Theory (GT) is a method that can facilitate insight into people's values, understanding and experience with technology. It has wide applicability to HCI; e.g. previous GT studies presented at CHI have included topics on immersion in video games [3], online trust and security [20], and password use [16]. Despite its popularity, nuances in the method's use are rarely discussed in empirical papers, presumably because of space limitations and an over-reliance on Strauss and Corbin's [26] guidance on the method. These nuances are important: they have analytic consequences, and so should be recognised and considered. Furthermore, Matavire and Brown [18] call for more debate about GT use to reduce the widespread myths and misunderstandings around themes such as the role of literature and the use of prior theory.

CHI 2011, May 7–12, 2011, Vancouver, BC, Canada.

At one level, this paper could be seen to confess a deviation from traditional approaches to GT. Some have argued that such deviations should drop the GT label and instead subscribe to doing qualitative research more broadly [27]. However, methods' labels encompass their history, process and properties, which can be reflected on and critiqued. We offer guidance on practical issues and clarify the space of methodological possibilities around the GT method. These issues are pertinent to qualitative studies more broadly; e.g., should we just process data inductively, should we incorporate prior theory creatively, and how should this be managed? Arguably, these considerations make GT more relevant for contemporary HCI by going beyond a coding process to allow one to co-create understandings with users, and employ existing HCI theories to explore and elaborate findings. This paper's format follows a reflexive account of GT use by Urquhart [28].

BACKGROUND
Grounded Theory (GT) was first proposed by Glaser and Strauss [10] and has since undergone developments and variations (discussed below). Broadly, it is a method with iterative data gathering and analysis. It uses coding processes heavily, but it is not just a way of coding. Importantly, it is different from methods such as protocol analysis and content analysis that emphasise reliability, validity and the counting of instances [22]. GT's essence is in exploratory conceptual and theoretical development. It involves interplay between theoretical ideas and subjective understandings while requiring 'fit' with the data [23].

GT processes have been described in detail elsewhere [e.g. 1, 4, 13, 26]. Typically GT will involve interviewing a sample population about a topic, transcribing the interviews, coding parts of the transcript, and relating these codes to one another. Here, coding is a process of identifying and naming significant chunks of text. For example, I might label the previous sentence 'coding' and I might label this paragraph 'GT method'. This form of abstraction facilitates analysis across different parts of the text or transcript and between different interviews. Analysis and coding should be carried out between interviews so that questions can be adapted to direct future data gathering. Variations include to what extent interviews and analysis are interleaved and the specifics of the coding process (e.g. not everyone will do open, axial and selective coding – this roughly translates to labelling codes, relating codes to each other, and selecting the main codes respectively [26]). Also, analysts with a more constructivist stance emphasise the use of analytic tools such as writing theoretical memos, defining codes and integrating codes into broader categories [23]. Here, a 'constructivist' stance emphasises creating a description of the context rather than discovering a description of it, which would be more 'objectivist'.

Demonstrating the variation of GT use, a recent study in Information Systems (IS) identified four different uses of 'grounded theory' across 126 empirical grounded theory papers between 1985 and 2007 [18]. The four uses differ in their procedures and are dubbed 'Glaserian', 'Straussian', 'mixed methodology', and 'technique application'. The Glaserian approach emphasises the emergence of ideas from the data away from established ideas and processes – a traditional inductive approach. The Straussian perspective introduces *a priori* coding procedures, frameworks and more directed questions [26]. The mixed methodology seeks to combine GT with other research methods, e.g. action research and case studies. Lastly, technique application does not show a strict adherence to any particular formulation but uses GT techniques, e.g. open coding, axial coding, selective coding, memos and diagramming. In terms of its output, GT does not have to build a total conceptual system with many concepts and connections; it can be used for: basic taxonomy development to show a hierarchy of classes and sub-classes in a context; focused conceptual development to describe a particular concept in detail; and cycles of interpretation between data gathering and analysis [23]. Henwood and Pidgeon [13] argue that it should not be presented as a unitary method.

The biggest controversy in GT variations is between Glaser and Strauss. Glaser disagreed with the development of procedural guidance and analytical frameworks, which he thought detracted from the original tenets of the method; i.e. these new developments add too much *a priori* shape, and inhibit the data's ability to 'speak for itself' [12]. From this position, Glaser seems against the use of extant theory. Some authors claim that both Glaser and Strauss are against the use of extant theory [e.g. 18].

Charmaz [4, p. 134-5] criticises authors that reify statements in early works and turn them into static pronouncements, rather than treating them as starting points for an evolving method. She acknowledges that positions have not always been clear, but argues that the use of extant concepts is allowed, although these concepts need to earn their right to feature in the analysis [4, p. 165-6]. Henwood and Pidgeon's [13, p. 138] phrase 'theoretical agnosticism' is apt here. They say that "the special counsel that remains within grounded theory is to avoid being wedded to particular theoretical positions and key studies in the literature in ways that overly direct ways of looking and stymies the interactive process of engagement with the empirical world being studied." We agree, and from the experience of our case study would say that the purposeful use of extant theory can be a source of creativity and insight, which a more traditional inductive approach would not afford.

Henwood and Pidgeon [13, p. 152] state that the challenge and excitement of all grounded theory research is getting out of the maze of detailed and complex codings, deciding on the limits to making constant comparisons, and reaching theoretical closure or integration. The case study here presents such a maze, focusing more on methodological issues than outcome, and on experiences and lessons learnt rather than results.

THE EXTENDED GT CASE STUDY

This case study's research focus was on understanding why practitioners choose to use the usability evaluation methods (UEMs) they do. Urquhart [28] calls this sort of focus her 'research problem', which develops into sharper research questions as the study progresses. We were not aware of the benefits of a reflexive journal [22] during the study. However, other documentation is referred to, including weekly review meeting summaries, which helped us reconstruct this account. We highlight five stages in the study that were of significance for methodological reasons: before the beginning; acclimatising; fleshing out features; re-rendering the data; and theoretical lenses as tools.

Before the beginning

This study formed work towards the first author's PhD in the UK, which is why it spans approximately three years. This is significant for understanding the study's effort and duration. Like other studies, GT use is constrained by practical considerations, not least of which are deadlines for publication and when funding expires, which of course might raise tensions with purely methodological ideals such as theoretical saturation (see Lesson 1; all lessons are described in detail later in this paper). Theoretical saturation refers to a point in the analysis where one does not gain anything new from more data. When saturation has been reached, further data gathering is unfruitful.

We have already stated that the study's research focus was on understanding why practitioners choose to use the UEMs they do; however, this was not the starting point. Months of reading, literature review, and discussion preceded this, which was performed to try to settle on a research problem that was suitable for a PhD and that fitted within the broad area of understanding design practice better. Competing topics included design expertise, design process, design problems, and reflection in HCI. In the end, we preferred to try to understand why practitioners use some methods and not others. Essentially, academia develops lots of methods and few are adopted in practice, but the reasons for this were not well understood.

One approach to investigating this issue was to interview practitioners about why they chose some UEMs and not others. GT was already used by research colleagues, so this was recommended as an appropriate approach; the first author (hereafter referred to as A1) was advised to read Strauss and Corbin [26] to get started. It suited the project as an exploratory approach was needed, interviews were an obvious approach to the data gathering, there was guidance for the analysis, and others were already using it as a legitimate approach for HCI research.

One of the main alleged principles of GT is to start from the data and not prior texts, ideas and theories. With a mild concern that this had already been violated by doing an extensive literature review to settle on a topic (Lesson 5), A1 formulated a semi-structured interview script which covered five themes:

- *Background* of the participant.
- *Work organization,* concerning how the work is organized, the structure of the organization, whether there are teams, project lifecycles and challenges.
- *Business client relationship*, on communicating with clients for attracting, doing and handing off work.
- *Practitioner skills*, concerning what skills are needed to be a good practitioner.
- *Tools and techniques,* concerning what methods are used, how they are used, when they are used and what is valued in a method.

Without the extensive literature review, prior education in HCI and the supervisor's experience, we would not have been able to start with a developed interview script or settle on a topic of such theoretical interest (Lesson 5).

Acclimatising

The deadline of a first year report viva focused attention on doing some preliminary data gathering and analysis within the first 9 months. This pragmatic driver also had methodological significance by providing a stage of review.

We chose HCI practitioners in the website domain as a sample population to focus the study. The first four participants were known to the researcher, were easily available, and allowed A1 to ease into the interviewing and subject matter in a more comfortable way. We also thought that we would be able to get better data from more experienced practitioners later in the study after our understanding had matured. The first four interviews had between 1 and 3 years experience in industry. This sampling therefore did not conform to the idealized processes of theoretical sampling but was influenced by pragmatic constraints (see Lesson 1). Theoretical sampling is a sampling technique that is based on what is best for developing the theory, e.g. perhaps by selecting contrasting participants or someone that could elaborate a particular feature of the context. It is very considered so is far from random, and in its purest form neglects pragmatic influence.

These early semi-structured interviews provided a learning opportunity, enabling A1 to get used to the variations between interviewees' styles, in handling questions and probing. At the start of the interviews, A1 took great pains to ask open-ended questions and not put words in the mouths of interviewees, but it became apparent that this population was independent enough not to warrant such concern, and it appeared that a relaxed, discursive interview style opened up the interview to yield better data. It was also apparent with successive interviews that A1 brought forward the points, words and examples of the previous interviews, building on each conversation (see Lesson 2).

Following the advice of colleagues, A1 proceeded with open coding [26] and used Atlas.ti software to support the process. It was difficult to know at what level to code the data, but through the process it became apparent that the level initially chosen was too detailed, as the list of codes soon became too long and unmanageable (Lesson 3).

This early analysis developed a narrative that centered around three main concepts: power, persuasion and value added HCI. These were extracted by trying to get a sense of the main themes thus far. Each theme was supported by quotations as the extract from A1's first year viva report shows (Excerpt 1; participant quotations are in italics).

Fleshing out features

We fed the 4 interviews from the preliminary study into the main study phase, interviewing 9 HCI practitioners from the website domain in total. To explore the potential differences in culture we interviewed six practitioners with experience in full service agencies, three in usability consultancies and three with in-house service experience. Some had experience in multiple areas. Total experience for the three contexts was over 15 years, over 10 years, and 3 years respectively. We interleaved data gathering, coding

> Excerpt 1. Description of 'Power': "Power is an important concept as there is always someone to report to, someone that is managing your work and someone that is paying for your work. This power normally resides in a hierarchy with it being concentrated toward the top; clients are likely to hold the power in a consultancy relationship because they are paying for the service, and management and senior staff are likely to hold the power when in-house.
>
> *R4: ...at the end of the day it is the client who is the one that is paying the cheques so it's up to them what they want really...*"

and analysis where practical, but were constrained by when it was convenient for participants to meet. Some interviews were a week apart, some a few months; 8 interviews were completed in seven months and the last much later.

The interviews kept building on each other, and the open discursive style sometimes led to apparent contradictions and clarifications that allayed fears of inadvertently biasing the interviews; for example participant R8 corrected an implicit assumption made by A1:

"*I: I wondered what sort of things clients come to you for, [...] an obvious one might be to increase revenue [...] if it were an ecommerce site, but I wondered whether there were any more reasons that come to mind?*

R8: Yeah, it would range... well the unspoken assumption behind that question is that all the clients know why they have come to us, and they don't, sometimes the biggest portion of our job is to work with them to figure that out."

Rather than tidy the coding scheme of the previous stage, we recoded the data anew at a more manageable level. Moving on to the other interviews, we attempted to perform the coding stages consistently with Strauss and Corbin [14], and in keeping with the Glaserian style of inhibiting and excluding extant theory. We focused on developing the GT inductively. With hindsight, coding the first 4 transcripts appears to conform to Charmaz's [4] 'initial coding' stage, where transcripts are analysed in an unfocused manner. As subsequent interviews matured, we moved on to more 'focused coding', elaborating concepts and themes. However, it was hard to perform selective coding as several categories were competing for dominance. In the end, four categories provided the corner stones of the narrative [9]: methods and processes; relationships; communication and coordination; and psychology and expertise. In terms of presentation: after a closer introduction to the analysis and supporting quotations, the four dominant categories were described and linked to the existing literature (see Excerpt 2 for an example).

Re-rendering the data

The four categories that emerged from the previous stage (above) provided a rendition of the data, but it left the analyst wanting. From the nine interviews this rendition highlighted areas of importance. However, it did not show the diversity between interviews as it was an aggregation, it did not help readers to become intimate with the data, and while the hierarchical format of the four high-level categories highlighted areas of attention it felt disjointed. The question remained as to whether there was a way of getting readers closer to the data, demonstrating the diversity between interviews and integrating themes better, in a narrative, so that they could be more easily understood and communicated. With hindsight, these concerns of how to best render the data were the first signs of moving from 'how do I represent the respondents' views validly?' to 'how do I best render the data to communicate a useful message to an audience?' (see Lesson 6 on objectivist versus constructivist GT). Taking this forward this next phase intentionally experimented with alternative treatments of the data to explore options, strengths and weaknesses in how to render it.

> Excerpt 2. Description of 'Methods and Processes': "The analysis has shown that usability work is heavily influenced by the clients' needs. This commercial focus puts emphasis on effective and pragmatic choices that will deliver results to agreed time and budget scales. This is reflected in Wixon and Wilson's [29] move away from science to "the art of the possible under constrained resources" in usability practice; and Cockton's [5] claim that HCI should be more about delivering value than finding the truth. This is perhaps what one participant meant when distinguishing scientific validity from commercial and design validity. [...] [9, p. 162]

Following the principle of theoretical sampling, we decided to expand our data set to include human factors (HF) practitioners in the safety-critical domain. We interviewed 13 HF practitioners, from 8 different work places. Six practitioners had between 1 and 5 years of HF experience and six had between 6 and 30 years of experience. One engineer had no direct HF work experience but described managing a project that had a strong HF component. A1 started by interviewing practitioners that were known and more accessible to the analyst. This domain was less familiar to the analyst. A literature review was carried out to develop a better vocabulary and to make A1 familiar with the issues, methods and practices that participants might discuss (Lesson 5). Again, data gathering and analysis were interleaved where possible. On one occasion the analyst travelled and interviewed three practitioners from the same company in one day, which made practical sense (Lesson 1).

Three treatments of the data were trialled. The first was a summary of each interview. Two of the summaries can be seen in Excerpt 3. These gave an idea of the breadth of data but lacked insight that generalised across cases.

The second treatment was a view of the coding network. Atlas.ti allows the analyst to link codes together in network diagrams to explore relationships between codes. The intention here was to give the reader access to the codes and links that had emerged from the analysis. However, the full GT network was overpopulated (128 codes) and too dense to readily make sense of. A simpler, higher-level network was created by using 16 codes that were significant due to the number of quotations associated with them, the number of links to other codes and the number of participants that mentioned them. Figure 1 shows this diagram merely to

Excerpt 3. Variance in participant data shown through interview summaries of S1 and S2:

Respondent S1: Here design solutions were driven through iterations with input from people with knowledge of the products and working practices, rather than the specific identification of safety issues through evaluative methods. Much of the communication is captured in design drawings and so documentation is in pictures and notes rather than wordy reports. Even though they work in-house they still have to sell their ideas and services, and face the same issues of not being involved or being involved too late that out-house people face. The design-solution focus forces them to engage with the real trade-offs. They apply patterns through analogical reasoning to aid the design process, i.e. they are familiar with reoccurring issues that inform designs.

Respondent S2: This contrasted with solution focused consultancies in that it was quite formal, independent and research driven. Rather than taking a design orientation the work appeared to be very evaluative, a lot of it taking the form of controlled experiments where safety could be independently evaluated. Reports were written in a similar way to research reports that you might find in academia. Written communication seemed to dominate client contact so an audit trail was maintained and misunderstandings reduced. The rigor of their research and independent status characterise the company's offering. Often they do not know what happens to their results and subsequent designs as they are detached from the process. Expert panels and discussion groups were recognised as useful methods for tapping into domain expertise. [7, p. 119]

illustrate what such a network looks like. Each of the codes in the diagram was described with reference to the other codes it was linked to (see Excerpt 4 for an example). However, the presentation of this network and descriptions, although allowing one to become more intimate with the analysis, lacked a core focused message for the reader to take away.

The third data treatment involved developing a narrative around the concept of 'downstream utility'. Traditionally, researchers were focused on the implementation of the UEM, but more recently attention has turned to how information from UEMs can better transfer value 'downstream' [e.g. 17]. Our data also showed that UEM choice and use depended on factors 'upstream', such as resource allocation for the projects and past experiences between the client and consultant. A river metaphor started to develop and another creative jump was made, using what with hindsight would be called analogical or metaphorical reasoning. The stream or river was in a landscape of context-shaping factors composed of social factors (e.g. client-consultant relationship), technical factors (e.g. specific HCI issues), the project's structural factors

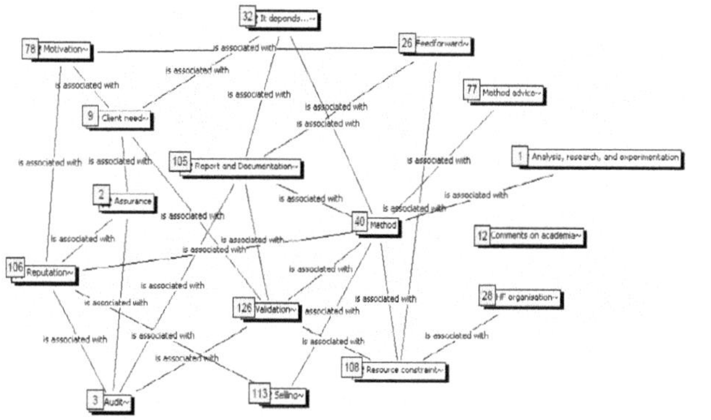

Figure 1: Network diagram of 16 codes and links [7, p. 125]

Excerpt 4. Description of the code 'Reputation': There can be the reputation of HF in general, the HF organization, the HF practitioner, methods and ideas; and this can be influential in organizational decision making.

Reputation has to be worked for and quality maintained. The reputation of a practitioner will facilitate selling their services as it will provide the client with some reassurance that the work will be completed to a good standard and their recommendations will be sound. The expertise of the practitioner will be linked to their reputation, and greater experience will reduce the risk of a project failing. New practitioners, new methods and new practices that have a weak track record will make a project less predictable. There will be a motivation and prejudice to select practitioners and methods that they have confidence in.

Practitioners and organizations can be audited by clients and regulators to check their quality, which will influence their reputation. Good work will more likely lead to repeat business and attract more work. [7, p. 372]

(e.g. the design stage), communication factors (e.g. reporting back to developers or the chief executive) and resource factors (e.g. the capabilities of the practitioners and the time for the project). These context-shaping factors were derived from the data. The metaphor led to the development of a 'conceptual picture' (Figure 2) that aided the sense-making of the analyst and appeared to provide the more coherent narrative for readers that he was looking for. For example, this appeared to provide a more fluid story than the presentation of the four categories introduced in the 'fleshing out' stage (above). The use of the metaphor led to a focus on 'process' rather than only 'themes' as recommended by Charmaz [4]. Now we have a *story* around events rather than simply a hierarchical list of related factors.

Theoretical lenses as tools

Analysis of a more top-down nature, e.g. through the use of pre-existing literature and theory was inhibited in the previous three stages where we emphasized an inductive or bottom-up approach (see Lesson 5). In the theoretical lenses

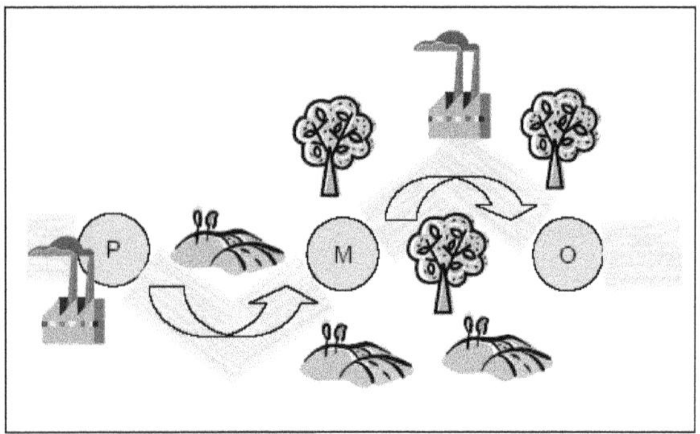

Figure 2: To show that project planning 'P', method application 'M', and project output 'O' are linked together by a stream that is shaped by context-shaping factors

stage we stopped gathering empirical data and explored the leverage that extant theory could provide in interpreting our data. It involved two separate stages of theory bridging, the first using Distributed Cognition (DC) [14] and the second using Resilience Engineering (RE) [15].

Preparation and selection of extant theory

In terms of identifying a potentially useful theoretical framework to apply, these two stages involved serendipity and a 'prepared mind' [6]. For example, DC was a body of work that the analyst was familiar with because of previous projects. This meant the analyst's mind was prepared to see bridging opportunities between emerging concepts from the data and DC theory. This acknowledges that researchers will inevitably come to a situation with some established ideas and preferred theories [19], and that the researcher is integral to the interpretation of the data [4]. Serendipity played a large role in highlighting RE as a fruitful extant theory for bridging purposes. RE was only encountered when preparing to talk to HF practitioners in the safety-critical domain, and by having a colleague highlight RE as a related area. After the re-rendering stage of analysis, the analyst was intimate with the data and more prepared to see bridging opportunities when extant theories and concepts were encountered.

Creating links between 'theory and data' / 'data and theory'

A1 took a systematic approach to explore the creative links from data to theory and back. He externalised this process sufficiently so that it could be developed. Reviewing the literature of the extant theory was an important step to 'prepare the mind' to recognise links between the theory and the data. Potential links between the extant themes and the emerging concepts were externalised through notes and memos [4; 19], which are essentially written notes of thoughts about the developing GT analysis (Lesson 4). The constant comparison method [22] then led to these links being explored with further codes, categories, descriptions and information from the literature. As we progressed with this approach we adopted a template for each time we made a bridging step between the data and the extant theory: we first explained the theme in the theory, we then explained how this was reflected in the data, and finally we discussed broader observations of this link (e.g. see Excerpt 5). One must also be open to apparent contradictions between theory and data, which will highlight limitations in linkages. Trying to understand discrepancies can lead to further investigation and insight.

DC [14] concerns itself with the propagation and transformation of information in systems. Consequently it provided leverage by embellishing the factors influencing information flows of HCI/HF project work; e.g., transformation of information could be tracked from the client need, to HCI/HF project aims, to user testing design, to user testing video recordings, transcriptions, analysis, project reports and distilled recommendations. Furthermore, this extant theory provided an opportunity for more mature reflections on developed concepts such as boundary objects (Star, 1989), organisational expertise and epistemic actions. For example, boundary objects were recognised such as the client's need that was reinterpreted in HCI/HF terms, the contract between the client and the HCI/HF practitioner, and the final report. Some practitioners wrote the latter with the audience in mind, i.e. knowing that it may have to satisfy the different needs of regulators, directors and developers.

Resilience relates to safety, but focuses more on unexpected events and how systems cope, adapt and recover from these, e.g. rather than a reduction in error per se. RE [15] resonated well with the data from the bottom-up stages. For example, RE favours systemic over linear explanations of accidents, has adaptation under constraints as a focus, is interested in normal work as well as extreme situations, and emphasises understanding phenomena from the perspective of those that are inside the context. These elements provided the initial hook for the analyst, and enough interest to explore bridging data with theory in more detail (e.g. see Excerpt 5). Interestingly, there was some back propagation to RE theory suggesting a different emphasis to its normal use; i.e. the avoidance of accidents. This was a modification of the extant theory which was inspired by our data and which came to the fore by the constant comparison method [22]. For example, the non-linear explanations of accidents resonated strongly with the data but on closer reflection the theory did not entirely match. This did not mean it was inapplicable; instead it led to a moment of creative tension to work out what this meant for the data and what this meant for the theory. Here, RE would normally focus on how events negatively interact to cause accidents and look to dampen these negative interactions to stop things going wrong; we instead found it more useful to consider how HCI and HF practitioners maximise positive interactions in a project so that things go right with limited resources. This led to a switch of focus from 'negative resonance' to 'positive resonance' [7, 8].

Excerpt 5. Bridge to concept of 'Loose Coupling':

Theory: Grote [11, p. 116] states that "a core requirement for resilience is to achieve an adequate balance between stability and flexibility in the functioning of an organization."

Support: This is evident in the labeling of techniques and methods that add stability to a design project, and where their practice can be adapted to suit the context. For example, Heuristic Evaluations [21] were reported to be used in an ad hoc manner to support design recommendations, explicitly used to evaluate and compare websites, implicitly used like an expert evaluation, and actual heuristics were sometimes adapted from "Nielsen's ten heuristics."

Discussion: The loose coupling evident in labeling simplifies communication of project elements and structure to clients. According to our interviewees, novices (e.g. clients) are less able to cope with the details of potential project variances. Labels and prescriptions help overcome this. [8]

Further analyses using extant methods

After these types of theoretical links between themes were made, a further stage of rendering the data was explored by using analysis methods from the respective theories. For DC this led to the use of DiCoT (Distributed Cognition for Teamwork [2]) and for RE this led to the use of FRAM (Functional Resonance Accident Model [15]) – both methods that support the analysis of complex systems. DiCoT is a method normally used to analyse observational data of teamwork settings in terms of DC. This method involves developing five models of the system: the social, information flow, artefact, evolutionary and physical models [2]. This can involve diagramming and reference to DC principles. In this case, the interview data provided the information to populate the models rather than observational work. FRAM identifies and maps functional elements in the system and how they influence each other [15]. Both of these methods developed the role of 'process' at the core of the GT, and lent their theoretical weight to exploring the nature of the complex system in which this process was situated. Again, preparing the mind to recognise links through familiarity with the data and the method, extensive use of notes and memos, and the constant comparison method to check the legitimacy of insights created the conditions necessary for this analysis.

These methods provided an analytic framework and theoretical insight that extended the original analysis in the more bottom-up stages. Using the FRAM analysis as an example, six subsystems were identified as influencing the choice and use of usability evaluation methods: the project process; HCI/HF practitioners understanding; persuasion, rapport and reputation; staff development and management; tools, methods and reporting practices; and auditing and documentation. These overlapping subsystems involved 29 individual functional elements, and their representation resembled a GT network diagram. The picture that this theory supported, which had strong resonance with the data, is that there are many factors in the context that can influence the adoption and adaptation of method use in complex ways. Some of these factors can be at the 'sharp-end' [15] close to the point of method use, e.g. a specific request by the client or the budget they have; and others can be at the 'blunt-end', far away from the point of method use, e.g. what practitioners were taught and industry trends.

Validation through member checking

To check that the 29 functional elements and 6 subsystems we had constructed were recognisable by practitioners, 10 of the 22 participants gave their feedback on them, as well as 8 practitioners not involved in the interviews [7]. This showed broad support for the work with some suggested modifications (see Lesson 7).

LESSONS LEARNT

Seven major lessons emerge from the above case study:

Lesson 1. GT studies are managed alongside their practical constraints, and so should not be appreciated against imagined objective ideals. Consideration needs to be given to the scope of the study and its output, the numbers of participants and their accessibility, and the depth of the analysis. One way this came in to play in our GT was the length of the study, which extended over a three-year period, but was also punctuated by milestones (vivas) at which interim findings needed to be reported. Other projects may be much smaller and so not have the time to experiment with data treatments and develop a conceptual framework. This extended duration allowed time for the researcher to mature with the method's use, which is important when GT is so entwined with the analyst using it.

Practical constraints also came to the fore when organising interviews. Theoretical sampling suggests that you select future interviews and data points to test your emerging theory, so exploring the boundaries and diversity of concepts is key. This was practiced in selecting HCI practitioners in the website domain with different experience, and from different companies, e.g. in-house, full service agencies and independent consultancies. The more diverse comparison was between the website and safety-critical domains. However, practitioners that were more accessible were interviewed more readily, which follows a convenience sampling model rather than a theoretical sampling one.

Theoretical saturation occurs when new data is not leading to new insight or further conceptual development [13]. This is associated with the last stages of a GT, when the analysis and picture are complete. However, when this actually happens appears to be subjective, a decision which could be encouraged by a looming deadline. Also, 'saturation' can be problematic from a constructivist perspective because the data can be reinterpreted in new ways [e.g. 4].

Lesson 2. Interview style must be adapted to the situation but open and friendly is best. Initially, there was an acute concern over asking open-ended questions that would not bias the interview, but in hindsight this was misplaced. For our population, participants were professional, articulate, would defend their views, and made their experience understood. As the study developed, the analyst adopted a more discursive style of interviewing, trying to create a friendly and respectful atmosphere in the interview, to open it up and get good data. This became a lot less like a question and answer session and more like a discussion between equals where a joint understanding was created. This became easier to do further into the analysis where the analyst had the foundation of previous interviews' examples, experience and opinion. It was felt that creating a relaxed atmosphere, e.g. through trust and humour, worked well in opening interviews up; but of course not all interviews were as open as others due to confidentiality issues, familiarity with the analyst and just the way different personalities interact.

Lesson 3. Start coding low and move upwards. Pause early in the process and reflect on the coding level. Through experience we found that the granularity of coding should adapt according to the centrality of the text to the emerging themes, from leaving paragraphs of transcript untouched where it was not relevant, to going through particularly interesting sentences word by word. Adams et al. [1] and Urqhart [28] show examples of GT coding practice.

We would advise novices to start too low and come up as we did, rather than too high and come down, as otherwise too much detail can be glossed over. However, in the end the analyst has to feel their way through the codes. We paused after the first 4 interviews, which gave time to reflect on the analysis and the granularity on the coding scheme. This early pause was useful and will likely be useful for future studies. Charmaz [4] calls this the 'initial coding' stage, where transcripts are analysed in an unfocused manner. After this stage, the coding scheme either has to be tidied up or started again with the benefit of being acclimatized by the preliminary analysis. We started again, and as subsequent interviews matured we moved on to more 'focused coding', fleshing out concepts and themes.

Lesson 4. Use analytic tools and use them flexibly. At the start of this study, the prevailing view was that GT analysis centred around the coding mechanisms of Strauss and Corbin [26], i.e. open coding, axial coding and selective coding. The mechanisms and benefits of other analytic tools, such as memos, and network diagrams, were neglected. The role of these tools, supported by the Atlas.ti software, grew as the study developed. This in part came from a confidence that GT appeared to be less about selecting and applying a relevant coding scheme so that it accurately represented the data, and more about making sense of it, linking it to different ideas and thoughts that occurred in the analysis and creating an insightful rendering of the data that would be understood by and useful to others. The bigger conceptual moves in our analysis, involving the development of the stream and landscape metaphor, and the links to DC and RE, were explored through memos and network diagrams. Analytic tools should be used flexibly as long as it helps the analyst understand the data, develop ideas, and create insights that 'fit' the data. Just relying on codes leaves the analyst somewhat limited to hierarchies of codes, categories and themes that may fall short of a conceptual framework or miss those creative insights that could open up an area and move its understanding forward.

Lesson 5. A top-down constructivist approach should not be neglected. It has potential for better questioning, theory integration, insight and a richer picture compared to a more traditional inductive approach. From the outset of the study, the prevailing view was that GT was a strict inductive method to create theory about some context or phenomena from participants' perspectives. However, a purely inductive view is problematic as no analyst is a *tabula rasa*. Through our analysis we moved from a position of trying to inhibit the use of extant literature and theory, to intentionally using it for analytic and creative purposes.

Before interviewing practitioners in the two different domains we performed an extensive literature review. This was necessary to select the research problem of the study, to develop a reasonable semi-structured interview script, to internalize their vocabulary and to become familiar with issues that the participants would discuss (particularly in the safety-critical domain which was new to A1). This was necessary to make the interviews engaging and productive; less preparation would have jeopardized this.

The top-down approach of the theoretical lenses stage could be seen to be controversial when considering the traditional advice to inhibit and exclude extant theory. However, in our analysis we found that the bottom-up analysis benefited from existing theoretical concepts and structures. This is less controversial for those that argue for a more modern constructivist revision of GT [e.g. 4]. Here, the same principles that should be applied in any GT analysis, e.g. emergence, constant comparative method, and theoretical sampling [18], continue to be important. The interpretation must remain faithful to the data, and favour emergence over forcing [e.g. 4 & 13].

In the experience of our study the top-down phase strengths include: getting vertical validity by referring to abstract concepts that have been noted elsewhere; using extant theory as leverage for insight and creativity that can bring new perspectives on different contexts; breaking writer's/analyst's block; and developing extant theory by resolving discrepancies between this and the data. Potential weaknesses include: warping an objective view of the world; allowing the researcher to bias and influence the data and analysis; and inhibiting what the data says about itself. Overall, our case study shows an extended inductive process that has benefited from using theoretical lenses as tools to explore the data. These top-down mechanisms can bring benefit if managed appropriately, by helping to construct a better rendering of the data. Constructivists will more readily accept the use of extant theory for helping to see the data in a new way; whereas more objectivist views will emphasise seeing the data on its own, as a window on an objective world that should not be biased by the analyst or extant theory. In our experience, constructivist revisions to GT can yield a richer and more insightful analysis.

Lesson 6. Appreciate the multiple styles and purposes of GT. Henwood and Pidgeon [13] stress that the excitement and challenge of GT is finding a way out of its maze, but there is no one legitimate way out of the maze. GT is associated with building theory, and at the most developed level this includes a full conceptual system, but at lower levels of development will also include: basic taxonomy development, focused conceptual development and cycles of interpretation [23].

All stages of our study included cycles of interpretation. The fleshing out stage involved thematic analysis. The re-rendering stage involved the development of a conceptual system through the stream and landscape metaphor. The theoretical lenses stage involved conceptual development, integration with extant theory, and the creation of a conceptual system. So choices and trade-offs have to be made in terms of what is done in a GT and what form of output one will have when out of the maze. It is scientifically responsible to remain theoretically sensitive [4; 13] so the GT relates to, builds on and challenges previous work. Neglecting this risks 'reinventing the wheel' or wondering how a GT fits the literature after its analysis has been complete. This is where the importance of the study's findings come to life or we are left asking, 'So what?'

Our stance on the purpose of GT changed with our increasing resonance with a more constructivist revision, moving away from more objectivist views. From our understanding the purpose of a GT study can change dramatically depending on whether an objectivist or constructivist stance is adopted, i.e. the former seeks to represent each participant's views accurately and validly like a privileged window into the participant's world, and the latter tries to create a rendering of the data that communicates an insightful, valid and useful message to an audience. This difference impacts on the way one conducts a GT, what one is left with when out of the maze, and the criteria for assessment.

Lesson 7. Assessment should fit the style of the project. GT fruit is often produced by an individual, following a style and within a scope, which we have detailed in our case study. However, it could be by a team, applying an emergent coding scheme, or over a shorter period of time. Pidgeon and Henwood [23, p. 101] have argued that the stance and purpose of a GT will impact on the criteria to assess it. However, they offer four questions to orientate an assessment:

1. Was respondent validation attempted?
2. How well documented was the process of analysis?
3. Were concepts linked together in justified ways?
4. Was the problem of reflexivity addressed?

From a constructivist perspective respondent validation or member checking seems the most developed form of assessment because this enables participants (subject-matter experts) to check the final rendering of the data. Checking the output is especially important where some of the analytic process may be hidden. For example, the process of arriving at a rendering might be a complex and creative process involving theory, data and ideas whose integrated mechanics might be indescribable and so uninspectable. For our study HCI/HF practitioners checked different outputs at three stages including the RE analysis in the theoretical lenses stage, but they did not check all the parts because of the time and effort it would take them. From a constructivist perspective, inter-rater reliability is misplaced as a method of assessment because GT is not the application of a coding scheme, as a contents analysis would be; instead it is the exploration and rendering of data in a way that provides conceptual insight into some context or phenomenon. Writing up a GT, reporting results, and sharing enough of the data to satisfy readers who may be from different methodological stances remains a challenge and one that we are still learning.

CONCLUSION

GT is a flexible qualitative method that can be used for basic taxonomy and conceptual development, and the creation of theoretical frameworks. More modern constructivist revisions of GT [e.g. 4] move away from traditional data-driven approaches, which seek to capture an objective view of the world. Instead they offer flexibility to co-create understandings with users and can employ HCI theories to explore and elaborate findings in a more top-down fashion (e.g. by using DC and RE). In our experience extant theory provided theoretical weight, insight and was a source of creativity. This paper provides guidance on practical GT issues through the case study and lessons learnt; it has also clarified the space of methodological possibilities, which has consequences for style, purpose and assessment of the research. This will hopefully inspire and guide those choosing to embark on related studies.

ACKNOWLEDGMENTS

We are grateful to all participants who contributed their time and expertise to this study; to Helen Sharp and Alistair Sutcliffe who provided feedback on an earlier version of the paper; and for the anonymous reviewers' contributions This research was funded by EPSRC Grants GR/S67494/01, GR/S67500/01 and EP/G059063/1.

REFERENCES

1. Adams, A., Lunt, P. & Cairns, P. A qualititative approach to HCI research. In P. Cairns & A. Cox (Eds.) *Research Methods for Human-Computer Interaction*. Cambridge University Press. (2008).
2. Blandford, A. & Furniss, D. (2006). DiCoT: a methodology for applying Distributed Cognition to the design of team working systems. *Proc. DSVIS 2005*, LNCS, (2005), 26-38.
3. Brown, E. & Cairns, P. A Grounded Investigation of Immersion. (2004). *Proc. CHI 2004*.
4. Charmaz, K. *Constructing grounded theory*. Sage Publications, London. (2006).
5. Cockton, G. (2004). Value-Centred HCI. In *Proc. NordiCHI 2004*.
6. Foster, A. & Ford, N. Serendipity and information seeking: an empirical study. *Journal of Documentation*, 59. (2003). 321-340.
7. Furniss, D. Beyond Problem Identification: Valuing methods in a 'system of usability practice'. PhD Thesis. UCL. (2008).
8. Furniss, D., Blandford, A. & Curzon, P. Resilience in Usability Consultancy Practice: the case for a positive resonance model. Proc. Resilience Engineering Workshop, Linköping Electronic Conference Proceedings. Sweden, 23, 5, (2007) 31-35.
9. Furniss, D., Blandford, A. & Curzon, P. Usability work in professional website design. In E. Law, E. Hvannberg, & G. Cockton (Eds.) *Maturing Usability: Quality in Software, Interaction and Value*. (2008).
10. Glaser, B. & Strauss, A. *Discovery of grounded theory*. Sociological Press. (1967).
11. Grote, G. Rules management as source for loose coupling in high-risk systems. In *Proc. of the Second Resilience Engineering Symposium*. (2006). 116-124.
12. Heath, H., & Cowley, S. Developing a grounded theory approach: a comparison of Glaser and Strauss. *Int Journal of Nursing Studies*, 41, 2, (2004), 141-150.
13. Henwood, K. & Pidgeon. N. Grounded theory in psychological research. In P. Camic, J. Rhodes, & L. Yardley (Eds.), *Qualitative research in psychology: Expanding perspectives in methodology and design*. APA, Washington DC. (2003).
14. Hollan, J., Hutchins, E., & Kirsh, D. Distributed cognition: toward a new foundation for human-computer interaction research. *ACM Trans. Comput.-Hum. Interact*, 7, 2, (2000), 174-196.
15. Hollnagel, E. *Barriers and Accident Prevention*. Ashgate Publishing, Ltd. (2004).
16. Inglesant, P. & Sasse, A. The True Cost of Unusable Password Policies: Password Use in the Wild. *Proc CHI 2010*.
17. Law, E. Evaluating the Downstream Utility of User Tests and Examining the Developer Effect: A Case Study. In *IJHCI*, 21 (2). (2006).
18. Matavire, R. & Brown, I. Investigating the Use of "Grounded Theory" in Information Systems Research. *Proc. SAICSIT 2008*. ACM Press (2008).
19. Miles, M., & Huberman, A. *Qualitative data analysis*. Sage Publications. (1994).
20. Nilsson, M. Adams, A. & Herd, S. Building security and trust online. *Proc. CHI 2005*.
21. Nielsen, J. Heuristic evaluation. In Nielsen, J., and Mack, R.L. (Eds.), Usability inspection methods. John Wiley & Sons, New York, NY. (1994).
22. Pidgeon, N. Grounded Theory: theoretical background. In *Handbook of Qualitative Research and Methods for Psychology and the Social Sciences*. (1996).
23. Pidgeon, N. & Henwood, K. Grounded Theory: Practical Implementation. In *Handbook of Qualitative Research and Methods for Psychology and the Social Sciences*. (1996).
24. Sellen, A., Rogers, Y., Harper, R., & Rodden, T. Reflecting Human Values in the Digital Age. In *Comm. of ACM*. 52 (3). (2009).
25. Star, S. (1989). The structure of ill-structured solutions: boundary objects and heterogeneous distributed problem solving. In L. Gasser & M. Huhns (Eds.), *Distributed Artificial Intelligence*. Cited in Ackerman, M., & Halverson, C. (2000). Reexamining organizational memory. *Communications of the ACM*, 43(1), 58-64.
26. Strauss, A. & Corbin, J. *Basics of Qualitative Research*. (2nd Ed.) Sage Publications. (1998).
27. Thomas, G. & James, D. Reinventing Grounded Theory: Some questions about theory, grounded and discovery. *British Educational Research Journal*, 32 (6), (2006), 767-795.
28. Urquhart, C. An Encounter with Grounded Theory: tackling the practical and philosophical issues. In *Qualitative research in IS: issues and trends*. (2001).
29. Wixon, D. & Wilson, C. The Usability Engineering Framework for Product Design and Evaluation. In Helander, M., Landauer, T., and Prabhu, P. (Eds.) Handbook of Human Computer Interaction (2nd Ed.). Elsevier Science. (1997).
30. Wright, P. & McCarthy, J. Empathy and Experience in HCI. *Proc. CHI 2008*. 637-64

Reflexivity in Digital Anthropology

Jennifer A. Rode
iSchool, Drexel University,
3141 Chestnut St. Philadelphia PA, 19104
jen@acm.org

ABSTRACT
There are a variety of forms of ethnography inside and outside HCI each with valid complementary contributions. This paper looks at the practices of digital anthropology and how it contributes to reflexive design in HCI. The paper overviews key aspects its use in HCI, as well as in the anthropological approach. In doing so it relates these practices to participatory design and the socio-technical gap, and the ways ethnography can address them.

Author Keywords
Ethnography, rapport, participant-observation, iterative

ACM Classification Keywords
H5.m. Info. interfaces & presentation (e.g., HCI): Misc.

General Terms
Theory

INTRODUCTION
Across the CHI community we are joined by a desire to understand humans' interactions with computational technologies. Social science within CHI has many different approaches, all of which have different orientations to the discovery of knowledge. This paper's purpose is to establish and characterize the contributions of anthropological ethnography. In part this will be done by differentiating it from other scholarly traditions. To be clear, however, the aim is not to criticize these, but to offer an alternative tradition.

Ethnography is used differently within different disciplinary traditions. Sociologists, anthropologists, not to mention ethnologists, ethnobotanists, and musicologists, amongst others, all use ethnography. There is no one form of ethnographic analysis: ethnoscience, ethnomethodology, grounded theory, conversation analysis, and cultural critique all are accepted forms [40.]. Ethnography has been discussed before in the HCI community [2. ,4. ,10. ,15. ,16. ,19. ,32. ,36. ,37.], but here I wish to discuss anthropological ethnography specifically, in order to explore its contributions and explain the differences between forms of ethnography, providing a basic grounding for the majority of the CHI community who are non-practitioners of ethnography.

CHI 2011, May 7–12, 2011, Vancouver, BC, Canada.

While this paper aims to explain the differences among forms of ethnography, it does so without privileging one ethnographic method over the other. Clearly, there are many competing uses of ethnography, and we cannot hope to reconcile such widely divergent practices in one interpretation. Instead in HCI we need to recognize the academic legacies of these varied approaches and not privilege one approach over the next; we can adapt a series of complementary practices for HCI. Speaking as an anthropologist, I wish to contribute a deeper understanding of anthropologic practices as applied to reflexive ethnography of technology, an area increasingly being called Digital Anthropology [30.].

In this paper I will establish what anthropologists can contribute to HCI by writing reflexive ethnographies. The people doing this in the digital space are called digital anthropologists, and; they write digital ethnographies. I will explain these terms in more depth in the next section. Next, I will establish that a critical contribution of digital anthropologists' approach is reflexivity, and contrast it with other more positivist approaches in CHI. Finally, I will explain the key forms of anthropology's ethnographic narratives, the key elements of its practice, and what HCI can take away from this specific instantiation of ethnographic practice when applied to the digital.

The purpose in doing this is twofold. First, the HCI community needs to differentiate the forms and variations of ethnography that may be relevant for the field, and I wish specifically to legitimize anthropologically ethnographic writing conventions in CHI. Second, this will allow me to discuss the key attributes of digital anthropology and how they may benefit CHI. Let us begin with a review of the role of ethnography both inside and outside of CHI.

WHAT IS DIGITAL ANTHROPOLOGY?
Anderson [2.] and Dourish [16.] have given largely similar accounts of the history of ethnography beginning with Malinowski, moving on to the Chicago school and encountered by HCI via Suchman's "situated action", which brings us to HCI. Of course, since 1987, when Suchman published her groundbreaking book, anthropology has continued to develop, but HCI has been slow to keep pace with these changes [43.]. New theoretical arguments exist beyond Clifford, Fischer, Marcus or Geertz [11. ,13. ,20. ,28.]. As new technologies develop they allow new possibilities for fieldwork—remote interviews, participant-observation through games, or

blogs, or virtual worlds, and following the lives of ones informants via twitter. Anthropologists debate how to bound this new area of study. They ask whether digital anthropology is simply the anthropological study of digital worlds [6.], the integration between online and offline worlds [30.] or perhaps the best definition would be the comparative ethnography of the consequences of digital technologies for the human experience. Presently, work in CHI spans each of these domains, but lacks anthropology's tradition of reflexivity. Digital Anthropology is a burgeoning field [6. ,23. ,24. ,26. ,30. ,31.], which is adapting to accommodate these new areas of study, and these technologies are increasingly becoming a focus of study themselves. As Geertz wrote, however,

> The locus of study is not the object of study. Anthropologists don't study villages (tribes, towns, neighborhoods…) they study in villages [21. , p22].

In the Geertzian sense, technology is not the object of study. Digital anthropologists are studying *in technology*, or *in the context of technology*. Of course, digital anthropology like the rest of anthropology cannot be defined solely by its methods. Its reflexive stance, comparative analysis and use of critical theory are vital to its composition as a field.

Digital Anthropology then is a practice which exists in its own right outside of HCI. Scholars in HCI come from different traditions and those with anthropological backgrounds draw heavily from these works. Dourish's "Implications for Design" brought the mid-80s debate of ethnographic cultural critique to HCI. However, I will argue we also need to situate HCI in terms of the larger debates within the burgeoning field of digital anthropology [30.], and that CHI needs Digital Anthropologists writing reflexive ethnographies. I will return to this at the end of the paper, having described general anthropological practice in detail.

REFLEXIVITY

Buroway defines reflexivity based on its methodological differences from positivist approaches, which culminate in orientations to the production of scientific knowledge [9.]. Most methods in the CHI community belong to the positivist tradition—data is collected, studied and tested with the aim of producing an unambiguous result. They draw on positivist traditions as defined by Burawoy, in that they aim to minimize reactivity (the effect of the experimenter), and ensure reliability, replicability and representativeness (that our sample is typical of the larger population) and thus generalizable) [9.]. Our approaches in CHI primarily fit Burawoy's characterization of positivist methods; we seek to generalize our findings to other contexts and choose representative samples even for our ethnographies. We use fieldwork primarily for understanding how existing technologies are used, and generalize our findings to future ones, as means of "scenic fieldwork" for understanding the design context [10.], or as a mechanism for identifying implications for design [16.].

Within HCI, Bödker has called for reflexivity, [5.] arguing that it is critical to third-wave HCI. She rests her argument on conventional understandings of reflexivity, whereas here I wish to explicitly define reflexivity as outlined by Burawoy [9.]. His definition rests on four criteria. First, reflexivity, unlike positivism, embraces intervention as a data gathering opportunity. Second, reflective texts aim to understand how data gathering impacts the quality of the data itself. This approach "commands the observer to unpack those situational experiences by moving with the participants through their time and space" [9. , p14]. Third, reflexive practitioners attempt to find structural patterns in what they have observed, and fourth, in doing so they extend theory [9.]. Broadly they embrace and discuss the idiosyncrasies of unique ethnographic encounters. There are various approaches to reflexivity in CHI, but in this paper I will focus on the approach used by digital anthropologists and its potential contribution.

Within HCI ethnography draws on reflexive traditions both when it functions as a means of defamiliarisation by allowing researchers to obtain critical distance from their own culture [4.], and later when used as a part of a design encounter [36.]. Previously, Dourish discussed ethnographic work's potential to explore the socio-technical gap [16.]. Ackerman defines this as "the divide between what we know we must support socially and what we can support technically"[1.]. Metaphorically, design is a bridge that spans this gulf [1. ,16.]. Dourish extends this to argue that that the gap is "essentially, between our technological 'reach' in the design process and the realities of technologies-in-practice," and that it is in this space where users make meaning [16.]. Ethnography has various orientations towards this gap. In this paper, I will show how its various forms differ in reflexivity and approach to understanding this gap.

In the remainder of the paper, I illustrate how Anthropological Ethnographic's reflexivity contributes to design and theory in HCI. First, I describe three forms of anthropological writing. Second, I explain key elements of its technique. Finally, I discuss where ethnography is used in the design process in CHI so that I can highlight how Digital (Anthropological) Ethnography can contribute.

STYLES OF ETHNOGRAPHIC WRITING

Within the HCI community there is a prominent discussion of *ethnography* [16. ,32.], but it is an umbrella term covering a range of approaches used at different parts of the design process to allow different types of reflexivity on the relationship between the social world. Discussing ethnography in HCI is tricky, because often ethnographic HCI research describes itself otherwise[1]. For instance, consider Wyche's "field study," in which she "visited"

[1] Here I will discuss only work which explicitly discusses itself as *ethnography*. This is to differentiate it from the more general use of the term *ethnographic* that is often used purely to mean a qualitative study. Further, discount ethnographic methods such as rapid ethnography are outside the scope of this paper.

megachurches for six months and "participated in services and carefully observed how technology was being used" [45.]. Wyche never calls her work ethnography; though by many conventional definitions it is, given the participant-observation entailed in the author's attending religious services combined with months of interviews.

Ethnography can have a variety of styles that afford varying amounts of reflexivity. In his "Tales of the Field; on writing ethnography" Van Maanen discusses the three major stylistic traditions of ethnographic writing in anthropology and to a lesser extent sociology—*realist, confessional* and *impressionistic* [40.]. While only the realist approaches can be found commonly within the current canon of ethnographic text within HCI, confessional and impressionistic open the possibilities of alternate ethnographic voices that permit reflexivity.

Realist

The *realist ethnography* is without question the dominant form of ethnographic text within HCI (see [14. ,33. ,38.]). Van Maanen describes the realist tradition of ethnography, though his use of the term realist should not be confused with Bhaskar's realist philosophy of science [7.]. Van Maanen writes,

> On display are the comings and goings of the culture, theoretical coverage of certain features of the culture, and usually a hesitant account of why the work was undertaken in the first place. The result is an author-proclaimed description and something of an explanation for certain specific, bounded, observed (or nearly observed) cultural practices. Of all the ethnographic forms discussed in this book, realist tales push most firmly for the authenticity of the cultural representations conveyed by the text. [40. , p45].

The realist account strives for the authenticity of representation, a key characteristic of positivism. He distinguishes it from the likes of journalism, fictions, and travel narratives in four ways—the need for *experimental author(ity)*, its *typical forms*, the *native's point of view*, and *interpretive omnipotence*.

First, in discussing *experimental author(ity)*, van Maanen is emphasizing the role of the author writing about the "good-faith assumption" of realist tales:

> At root this assumption of good faith permits readers to hold the attitude that whatever the fieldworker saw and heard during a stay in the studied culture is more-or-less what any similarly well-placed and well-trained participant-observer would see and hear. Ironically, by taking the "I" (the observer) out of the ethnographic, report, the narrator's authority is apparently enhanced and audience worries of personal subjectivity becomes moot. [40. , p46].

The ethnographer, through prolonged exposure in the field gains authority: seeing repeated behavior over the course of months (or years) allows the ethnographer not to make inferences, but rather to repeatedly create and test hypothesis in context. Thus the author's role is critical in understanding how theories are developed and evaluated. The writing style aims to minimize the impression of reactivity.

Second, there is the issue of *typical forms* of the realist text. The format emphasizes data and precision, as "details suggest intimacy and establish presence (who else could know such things?)" [40. , p49]. The realist tale is "a documentary style focused on minute, sometimes precious, but thoroughly mundane details of everyday life among the people studied," which are carefully structured to support authors' points. Details give the impression of reliability.

Third, the realist ethnographer attempts to clearly represent *the native's point of view*. As Geertz argued, it is not adequate to paraphrase the informants' activities, but one needs a richer understanding of what lies behind their observable behavior. Consequently, van Maanen writes,

> Extensive, closely edited quotations characterize realist tales, conveying to readers that the views put forward are not those of the fieldworker but are rather authentic and representative remarks transcribed straight from the horse's mouth. [40. , p 49]

Ethnographies written in the Boasian tradition, ethnoscience and, most familiar to HCI, ethnomethodology, all provide alternate analytical approaches to ensure accurate representations of the informants' voice. However,

> In a sense the debate concerning the native's point of view now turns on how such a perspective is to be rendered in a text rather than whether or not it belongs in one. Observation in this sense has given way to interpretation. [40. , p51].

This raises a possible critique of realist ethnographies, that even in attempting to represent the informant's point of view, interpretation inevitably comes into play.

The final component of Van Maanen's characterization of realist ethnographies is that of *interpretive omnipotence.* The author of the realist ethnography is the final arbiter of the culture's representation, having final control over the written text. Texts do not focus on "self-reflection and doubt" but rather convey a certainty over a correct interpretation of behavior thereby guaranteeing reproducibility. The realist ethnography does not provide the informant a way of participating in the dialog, nor does it allow the author to present findings in shades of gray. I argue these are potential liabilities with regards to design, and that often greater reflexivity is required. Other forms of ethnographic text, however, allow greater reflexivity than realist text.

Confessional

An alternate, more reflexive approach is that of the *confessional ethnography* which broadly provides a written form for the ethnographer to engage with the nagging doubts surrounding the study and discuss them textually. It emerged from the auto-critique within Anthropology led by Marcus and Clifford and was mainly influential within US based anthropology [28.]. The aim is to demystify the fieldwork process. Van Maanen writes, "The distinguishing characteristics of confessional tales are their highly personalized styles and their self absorbed mandates." The "I" that eludes the realist tale regains its voice, as the ethnographer discusses their specific relationships with their informants. As a consequence,

> Stories of infiltration, fables of fieldwork rapport, minimelodramas of hardships endured (and overcome), and accounts of what the fieldwork

did to the fieldworker are prominent features of confessionals. [40. , p73]

Here authority is personalized, and naturalness is emphasized. Despite the confessional tales' free discussion of the limitations of the fieldwork, and the complexities of the relationships involved, the overarching belief is that on the whole the fieldworker has not "misled." Instead, the "implied story line of many a confessional tale is that of a fieldworker and a culture finding one another and, despite some initial spats and misunderstandings, making a match" [40. , p79]. The *confessional ethnography* provides a means of directly addressing the inherent subjectivity of ethnographic practice, by giving the ethnographer a voice and by refusing to black-box ethnographic practice.

This form is rare in HCI, however, we see a brief glimpse in a passage by Genevieve Bell [3.] where she calls on Ruth Frankenberg [18.] and demonstrates a need for reflexivity. Here she discusses her religious background and how it relates to her informants for her study of religion and SMS:

> I grew up straddling multiple domains of religious signification in Australia – Catholicism and Catholic schooling; indigenous religious practices; a strongly agnostic home life... I am, as an Indian woman with whom I once worked described me, "a free thinker". As such, I find myself more interested in the study of religious practice than I am in endorsing a particular vein of religious dogma. [3.].

We do not need to know Bell's religious proclivities, but in confessing them so carefully we gain insight into how she positions herself amongst her informants. I would argue it strengthens her work, by allowing us greater understanding into her ethnographic praxis.

Unfortunately, confessional ethnography's tendency towards reflexivity has had difficulty finding a place in HCI as ethnographers already defensive about claims of the subjectivity of their method use primarily realist techniques to avoid opening their work to further scrutiny. This makes sense when careers and tenure cases can be made or broken by reviews from individuals from different scholarly traditions. Yet, this decision comes at a cost to science. We lose the ability to discuss and learn from what Dourish calls the "messy bits" of ethnographic practice, which he argues happen in exploring the socio-technical gap. Realist ethnography inhibits a chance to explore the nature of the relationship with the informant textually. This hampers exploration in publishing preliminary design work or in explaining design process, much the same way it was argued that focusing excessively on usability can prematurely cut off exploration [22.]. Writing confessional text is one way a reflexive ethnographer explores the gap, and confessional ethnography's reflexivity is vital to understanding the socio-technical gap and thus design.

Impressionistic

A third approach that shows promise for HCI is Van Maanen's *impressionistic ethnography*, also has reflexive roots. Van Maanen draws on the work of impressionist painters and how they capture a moment in time from a uniquely individual perspective. Van Mannen draws on Clifford's discussion of ethnography as poetry:

> To recognize the poetic dimension of ethnography does not require one gives up its facts and accurate accounting for the supposed freeplay of poetry. Poetry is not limited to romantic, or modernist subjectivism; it can be historical, precise, objective [12.].

In this way impressionist tales are an art form of a sort,

> The impressionists of ethnography are also out to startle their audience. But striking stories, not luminous paintings are their stock-in-trade. Their materials are words, metaphors, phrasings, imagery, and most importantly the expansive recall of the field experience.

The narrative of the impressionist tale is dramatic recall. There is little interpretation in letting the power of a well-told story stand for itself. This form of ethnography is rare in HCI, but,the following examples may clarify the form.

Impressionist ethnographic traditions are what are being drawn on in the HCI literature when studies report proactive findings letting the narrative speak for itself. For instance, March and Fleuriot [27.][2] rely on impressionistic text when they discuss how teenage girls organize domestic space in terms of the privacy it affords cell phone conversations,

> Bedroom, car, street, sauna, bathroom, closet, garden, trampoline, the room most distant from their mother... were all listed as places to go to with a phone in order to have a private conversation. So, rather than text silently, they wanted to use voice, and moved so as not to be overheard: "if there's something I really don't want my parents to hear I'd go in my closet. "[27. , p109-110].

The detail of young girl on the trampoline or hiding in her closet engaged in clandestine phone call outside a watchful mother's eye speaks to the *impressionist* conventions.

Similarly, Williams et al.'s study of Thai transnationals employed similar techniques in describing fieldwork,

> I interview Nok and Kung at their home in Chantaburi province... His brother lives close by, and there are plans for other siblings to build homes nearby in the future...Both have cell phones, on extended loan from a cousin, but the house currently lacks hot water, a land-line, and internet. When they settle there permanently ("someday") they will set those things up. For the time being, Nok checks email at her brother-in-law's house or at an internet café in town. Their orchard will soon produce an excess of bananas to share with relatives or sell at the local market. Over the course of a day, Kung's older brother visits to help in the garden, and we in turn use his house in town as our base of operations while visiting the afternoon market. His wife provides us with a spicy crab dip. We also run into Kung's younger brother at the morning market; later that afternoon he and his wife stop by with green mangoes and coconut... They normally spend most of their time in Thailand in Chantaburi, but on this trip Kung's sister is in the hospital in Bangkok and they are helping to take care of her. [42. , p5-6]

This excerpt from William's fieldnotes, creates an evocative image of the rhythms of her daily life with her informants. The text startles a Western audience discussing how her informants are *choosing* to do without supposedly basic utilities, and yet contrasts it with an easy access to cell phones. Borrowing cell phones, computer access, banana orchards, crab dip, and green mangoes—these are the images of a pattern of daily life organized around

---

[2] This self-reports as a "qualitative study" though the combined use of interviews with the participant-observation of blogs suggests that it was an early form of reflexive ethnography in HCI.

sharing and extended families. William's presence is unmistakable in this passage. We imagine her traveling from Chantaburi to Bangkok with her informants, eating crab dip along the way. The texture of this passage grounds their argument that the cell phone fits into the rhythms of the daily life in Thailand.

Ironically, though, this bit of impressionistic text is set apart from the main body of the text, being used to set the mood before progressing to a more typical realist-styled ethnographic narrative. It is like a jeweled ornament set-amongst a functional band, and yet it pushes well beyond the boundaries of what Button called "scenic fieldwork" in that its purpose is beyond scene setting [10.]. Williams et al. use this text to motivate their theoretical argument. Thus, impressionist text drawing from months of fieldwork can strengthen theories by grounding it in detailed examples.

These three styles of ethnography—*realistic, confessional, impressionist*—each have found at least some followers within the CHI community, even though confessional and impressionist writers struggle to get such work published. While most CHI ethnography is firmly rooted in the realist tradition, anthropology draws on all three forms of ethnography. Each convention offers alternatives about how to deal with issues of the author's voice, the native's voice, subjectivity, detail, doubt, and the authority of the ethnographic text. Certainly, each form raises a host of issues to be addressed. By outlining these ethnographic forms my goal is to encourage authors to reflect on the appropriateness of the form used, and reviewers to gain awareness of the alternatives.

While these forms each have sparked considerable debate within HCI and while confessional and impressionist tales may be particularly controversial they do not necessarily lack rigor. Anthropology traditionally requires a year in the field living with informants before one starts writing up findings. Only by repeatedly and routinely observing and interacting, again and again to the point at which it becomes utterly mundane does the anthropologist draw conclusions. Further, anthropologists observe strict conventions regarding participant-observation, rapport and the role of theory, which I will return to next. For now though, I want to stress that confessional and impressionist tales are no less rigorous than other methods in HCI, rather they differ in terms of their reflexive writing style and the voice given to the author. Such a voice is indeed entirely appropriate when one wants understand the relationship between the ethnographer and informants in a fashion that might inspire participatory design.

ETHNOGRAPHIC CONVENTIONS

When we think of ethnographic convention we think of thick description, something all CHI ethnographers struggle with given CHI's short article length. However, there are other aspects of anthropological ethnography that are not commonplace in HCI—*discussing rapport, participant-observation*, and *use of theory*.

Discussing Rapport

One aspect of an ethnography which cuts across these three styles of ethnographic writing is the discussion of *rapport*, though realist writers often do so to a much lesser extent since there is a tension between discussing rapport and maintaining *interpretive omnipotence.* When an anthropologist speaks of "creating rapport" with their informants they speak of their actions to ensure mutual understanding and trust which will in turn facilitate the ethnographic encounter. Rapport facilitates *access*, not only physically reaching participants, but also getting them to open up and share their stories, even if they are embarrassing or taboo. Part of this involves creating shared understanding, as well as positioning the ethnographer into the social hierarchies of the informant's culture, details which are key for a reflexive text. Discussion of rapport is to ethnographies what discussion of choice of statistical techniques is to an experimental paper—it is a critical aspect of the reflexive ethnographer's craft and a core part of their method. Yet it is rarely discussed in HCI research.

So, for instance, a rather blunt example can be found in Sophie Woodward's study of how women use, organize and maintain their wardrobes [44.]. She writes how the choice of her dress for the interviews is critical to establishing rapport with her informants, but "there were numerous occasions when I got it wrong"[44. , p39].

> On… [one] occasion, when I went to see Vivienne, a woman who rarely wore make-up and deemed excess concern with clothing to be superficial, I was experimenting with fake nails. My unprofessional attempt to glue plastic nails onto one of my real nails resulted in a lost-nail mid interview. Her withering look as I scrambled to find it told me just how badly I had anticipated this research encounter. [44. , p39]

Here we cannot help but visualize Woodward's amateur manicure, and stern Vivienne's disdain at Woodward's flippant femininity. Yet Woodward, despite a gaffe that damaged rapport, gained insight into the informant's views. This was the result of the natural interactions involved in ethnography and the discussion of that experience. The ethnographer does not always get it right, and social gaffes give insight into a culture's organization.

Another example comes from Masayuki Hamabata in his study of Japanese business culture [29.]. Hamabata did his fieldwork while a graduate student and struggled with rapport. He reflects on how his early attempts to relate to his participants as a social equal were problematic especially because he was a single man. He writes,

> The boundary of sexuality appeared to me with great clarity. If I didn't cross it, I would waste my remaining months in the field, feeling dizzy with shame, my informants either trying to arrange marriages for me or trying to avoid me. As a sexually available male, I was my own biggest fieldwork problem.

Eventually, he writes that he resolved this issue by presenting himself increasingly in the role of a student.

> …I acted increasingly naive about worldly matters… My status as a student came to the forefront; the image of the *gakeusei-san* (student) is one of immaturity, even more so than in the United States, and it is the

> image I cultivated. In Japan, patterns of behavior that separate boys from men are quite clear-cut, and I found myself adopting boyish language and tastes... The ploy might not have been entirely conscious, but it worked. By becoming a boy, I removed myself from the sexual market: no longer was I considered a threat. [29. , p16]

In doing so he fit his relationship as an ethnographer into the larger cultural hierarchy resolving the question of his marriage. Masayuki Hamabata writes of Japan that it is "a world in which families are also businesses." Being *gakeusei-san* gave him a privileged vantage point into certain aspects of family business at the cost of access to others. Regardless, by performing the role of student, he garnered a first-hand understanding of social roles and their implicit constraints, which in turn inform his ethnography.

While the confessional format of Masayuki Hamabata's ethnographic work allowed for a lengthy discussion of sexuality and rapport based on his own role in the encounters, the realist format dominant in CHI does not. Such discussions of rapport are not only crucial to understanding the nature of the ethnographic encounter and its methodology, but to understanding the data itself. The ethnographer is exploring a social setting in part by interacting with its social norms. By creating rapport ethnographers are, in a sense, testing their ability to interact with social norms and to avoid violating their taboos, and their success or failure gives us critical insights into social organization. Their discussion of creating rapport, even the cultural bumbling of getting it wrong, is critical to the ethnographic enterprise. Consequently, explicitly discussing rapport via confessional or impressionistic text is a vital part of reflexive ethnography.

Explaining the strength of rapport to the reader goes beyond the spoken word, to include the wink, the innuendo, the shared glance, the comportment of the body, and tone. All contribute to understanding what is said, all of this constitutes thick description. Their interpretation, of course, should be grounded in repeated interaction and observation, and not merely the experience of a single instant. Thick description allows for the deepening of context regarding rapport. And yet, often the non-verbal is pushed aside as too subjective for the supposed facticity of dialogue.

Here is an example that looks at a married woman and strategies for maintaining domestic technologies,

> Kathy (HH7) described her strategy for sharing security work with her husband, saying that at work, she is "highly technical" [whereas] at home, "he does it faster." Makes a great comment about "dangling a carrot", and he will just fix things, but you need to be careful when you dangle– "it's like a drug." She winks at me as she says it, and her inflection is proactive. There is a knowing glance that passes between us, and in that instant something is communicated which is unspoken. I come away with the sense that she flirts with her partner to get him to fix things, and that the interactions can be sexually charged. Fixing the technology is just part of the exchange... [34.].

The argument is that technology skills are being exchanged alongside other domestic skills, and that for men providing technology support affords a sort of digital chivalry. It is unsurprising then that a wife might flirt with her husband as chivalry has a strongly gendered component, but this flirtation is not made explicit by the dialog. Thick description—the wink, the glance, saying "dangling a carrot" just right—left the sentiment clear in the mind of the author due to her years doing similar pieces of fieldwork, who in turn attempted to translate it into the stuff of ethnography. Not only is the product of ethnography interpretive and contextual, it is incomplete. There is a point where the facticity of the situation stops, and interpretation begins, and a point beyond that where the ethnographer explains the unknown. This is our craft.

Geertz address the issue of uncertainty arising from thick description as well. He writes,

> Cultural analysis is intrinsically incomplete. And, worse than that, the more deeply it goes the less complete it is...Anthropology, or at least interpretive anthropology, is a science whose progress is marked less by a perfection of the consensus than by a refinement of debate. What gets better is the precision with which we vex each other." [21. , p29]

Discussing rapport, the ethnographer's relationship to the informant and how this trust was gained, is critical to reflexivity methods as outlined by Burawoy [9.]. Anthropological ethnography does this more explicitly than other qualitative work in HCI discussing rapport directly, especially in confessional and impressionist forms. Rapport is largely black boxed within realist texts, and most qualitative work in HCI. However, anthropologists argue it is critical to understanding the data gathering encounter, a key tenant of reflexivity as outlined by Burawoy [9.]. This is especially important as we move to non-Western design spaces. More positivistic researchers in our community might ask: why then is the ethnographer's interpretation a valid one if it is inherently subjective, contextual, and incomplete? In order to discuss that, I will next discuss Participant-Observation.

Participant- Observation

Participant-observation is the fundamental difference between many forms of anthropological ethnography and other qualitative methods that permit reflexivity. Rosaldo describes it as "deep hanging out," being part of the informant's daily life [36.]. Salvador et al argue it is core to ethnographic sense-making in cultural anthropology,

> the notion that you learn by doing and by watching, and by the interplay of those two roles. This means that most anthropologists (and those from other disciplines who use ethnographic methods) do field work. They spend time in and with the cultures and peoples they are studying, engaging with the people around them, participating in every-day life, and attempting to make sense of the patterns of that culture. [36. , p1]

Clifford writes participation-observation is both about experience and interpretation, Dilthey's wrote of this as he discussed the concept of *Verstehen*—that through first hand experience individuals come to understand the world around them [25.]. Writing an ethnography is "minimally, a translation of experience into textual form" [11.].

While a psychologist creates and tests theories, so too does an anthropologist. When in the field they must make a hundred little decisions to gain rapport—lest the participant not open up and they lose insight into private moments, such as couples flirting to get technology work done. While gaining rapport, and through a string of endlessly trivial interactions, such as whether to wear fake nails to an interview, the anthropologist learns through firsthand experience the rules of interaction and acceptable behavior. Hypotheses then are tested not through external validation, but rather through embodied experiences. Participant-observation is a key element of much anthropological practice, and ensures substantial reflexivity.

A key difference between anthropological ethnography and other approaches in CHI is the treatment of this relationship in the ethnographic encounter. Participant-observation is central to anthropological ethnography, though realist anthropologists do not discuss in a first-hand fashion. In HCI while we have elements of participant-observation, we tend to discuss people as the objects of study, rather than embodied experiences in the context of personal relationships.

An additional difference is that confessional and impressionist anthropological approaches explicitly rely on inference and experience of the author, a willingness to engage with the whole of thick description. Of course, these inferences are made only based on the understanding gained in the process of becoming a "cultural insider". Cultural critique, application of theory, literary practice, while they are methods employed by some anthropologists, are tangential to the core of attempting to textualize what was experienced. At its core, interpretation is relating back the experience in terms that the audience can understand using available tools. We need to distinguish critiques of the particular tools themselves, from the methodology at its core.

If ethnography is inherently experiential, then losing the voice of the author in its writing limits our insight into the data and our ability to use it for design. Ethnography is after all about a relationship with informants, and relationships are two-way—there is no other without the self. This suggests that while ethnographic work is inherently subjective, contextual, and incomplete, it has the possibility of giving us insights into the gap where the work of addressing the socio-technical gap is done. Participant observation allows the ethnographer to understand this work first hand, and as such the treatment must be personal.

Use of Theory

The most fundamental attribute of truly reflexive text lies in the use of critical theory [9.]. Reflexive text creates new theories to elaborate on existing ones [9.]. Their work is intrinsically tied to critical theory, and most anthropologists, even those writing realist texts, engage theory directly. Dourish critiques qualitative work in CHI for its not engaging with theory, and by providing a number of vignettes he suggests,

> "that the most useful strategy when engaging with ethnographic work is to "read for theory" as much as for empirical evidence, since these may, in the end, be where the truly significant implications lie" [15.].

When working with theory, anthropologists do not aim to prove or disprove a specific theory, but go into the field with a background knowledge of many different current theories potentially relating to the subject of study. Some of these might be models of behavior, but others might be more ephemeral.

For instance, in my recent work on gender I went to the field having thoroughly read up on feminist theory [e.g.39.]. When in the field I brought, served, and cleaned up after dinner to subvert the role of guest and became a temporary member of the household. During the study I realized that by doing so I was engaging with the household's gender roles. I turned explicitly to the theory of technology as masculine culture, which argues technology primarily designed by men best reflects their power and interests and ostracizes women [41.]. I combined my observations of gender work and interview data to create open, axial and selective codes to construct new theories surrounding gender, which led finally to a theory regarding the co-construction of gender and technical identity [34.].

Confessional and impressionist texts, in particular, are critical to discussing theory when rapport and participant-observation play a role in theory's construction. Dourish has already established the need for critical theory in CHI [16.]. What is key here is the recognition that, before this can happen, community norms for styles of writing must allow the background to theory to be adequately presented and supported—allowing for reflexivity is crucial.

FRAMING ETHNOGRAPHIC PRACTICE

When ethnography is used in the HCI canon, there are three specific forms—formative, summative, and iterative.

Formative Ethnographies

Formative evaluation aims to understand current practice or current practice surrounding technologies with an eye towards improving or creating new technologies. In the case of ethnographic work this may be studying an existing technology with an eye towards the future. These are the classic design ethnographies most common to HCI. For instance, William et al.'s study of Thai retires [42.], or Crabtree et al's work on coordinate displays [14.] are both examples of formative evaluation.

Recent debates in HCI [15. , 16. , 32.] focus primarily on formative ethnographic work. These papers discuss research that differs in terms of the analytical methods used and the types of contributions made to HCI. Some of this work makes explicit design recommendations [33. , 38.], whereas others reflect on findings at a more theoretical level [14.], others still do both [42.]—yet, these approaches contribute an ethnography understanding to design.

Summative Ethnographies

Summative evaluation evaluates the technology at the end of the design process. Summative ethnographic evaluation explores the socio-technical gap. An example of a summative ethnographic study is Miller and Slater's look at how the Internet is used amongst Trinidadians [31.]. Broadly, they question the notion of 'site' in ethnography by arguing the world of the internet and everyday life are not separate places, but rather both act as spaces where identity and relationships are being negotiated and maintained. The Internet simply allows for additional ways of "being Trini." Miller and Slater are trying to create an understanding of how Trinidadians and the Internet change each other, but they are not trying to change either.

Unlike the formative studies that offer their findings to help close the socio-technical gap, summative studies aim to understand it for its own sake. Dourish writes:

> Seeking to close the gap through the application of ethnographic methods is a contradiction in terms; the gap is where all the interesting stuff happens… It is practice that gives form and meaning to technology; the focus of ethnography is the ways in which practice brings technology into being. From this perspective, and drawing again on the notions of reflexivity raised earlier, we might suggest that what ethnography problematizes is not the setting of everyday practice, but the practice of design. [16.].

One way of reading Dourish then is to draw into question the legitimacy of formative ethnographic practice. I think this is perhaps too strong—formative design ethnographies are a valuable form of practice as they both seek to close the socio-technical gap and they represent a newer ethnographic form in the recent CHI literature. While I do not condemn them (and could not, as an author of such studies), I do think there is an important distinction that needs to occur when discussing ethnography in HCI, as formative and summative ethnographies differ in how they approach this gap, and thus differentiating them is critical.

Summative studies are increasingly being written in the burgeoning field of Digital Anthropology. This style of ethnography has both pros and cons. In itself summative work makes little direct contribution to HCI in terms of how to connect findings to design. Further, by removing any interpretive voice as to how to apply these findings from the text itself, this work loses the authority over how it may be applied to design. On the other hand, unlike the other forms, this approach does not require the ethnographer to manage two separate relationships with the informant—that of the peer required for participant-observation and that of critic for design. This suggests the primacy of the relationship with the participants is preserved, allowing data to be unaltered by the politics of design. Both of these are significant factors that must be considered and debated as we appropriate this style of ethnography in HCI.

Iteratively Evaluative Ethnographies

Here I am proposing a third form of ethnographic praxis, iteratively evaluative ethnographies, which address some of the issues above. While formative and summative practices can be reflexive, iterative evaluation is an inherently reflexive practice. It is different from participatory design practices [8.], cultural probes and design-based research because of its roots in anthropological ethnographic practice. The Webkit project, in which tangible interfaces were created to teach rhetoric, provides an example of this approach [35.]. The aim was to employ a participatory design technique, but the English National Curriculum, prohibited spending lesson time for design evaluation, and the children could not participate outside of school. To address this, the technology and the lessons themselves were designed so that even if the prototype broke down completely, or was not useful in the un-expected ways, the lessons would still succeed [35.]. Technology was then only gradually and iteratively added to the interface, resulting in 11 prototypes over 18 months, many of which were then deployed in the classroom. An anthropological ethnographer with a background in critical theory [17.] observed teachers interactions with students, and participated in the lesson as a teacher's aid. Doing so provided an understanding of the work that was being conducted by children and teacher to compensate for the socio-technical gap. The resultant grounded theory improved the technology, narrowing the socio-technical gap, but also improved the lesson-plan and surrounding infrastructure, increasing users capability to use the bridge afforded by design.

This approach to ethnography draws on participatory design tradition as it includes children's voices in design. However, it moves beyond standard participatory design by allowing informants to participate in the design process in an indirect fashion. While perhaps somewhat contrary to the spirit of traditional participatory design in that the users are not given a direct role in design, it does still give them a voice. At the same time it also allows them use actual technology, and as the technology evolves feedback is received on a variety of prototypes via an ethnographic encounter. This is different from technology probes in that the technology was meant to be a product in its own right, not simply a point of intervention. Consequently, it allows for feedback on how users bridged the socio-technical gap, and allows technologists the chance to understand and react to these behaviors through prototype redesign. However, this only works due to the exceedingly slow pace of design and the ethnographer's engagement with informants—in the case of Webkit, the fieldwork and iterative design took place over a year and a half. Regardless, this approach is a significant means of both empowering users and understanding the socio-technical gap as part of the design process.

Ethnography within HCI, then, has a multitude of orientations and contributions to both design practice and understanding society. Further, each of the three forms—*formative*, *summative*, and *iteratively evaluative*—negotiates the socio-technical gap differently, by aiming to close it, understand it, or perhaps a little of both. These forms of ethnography offer exciting possibilities for how to explore the "messy bits" of the socio-technical gap, and relate it to design, if we embrace the challenge of integrating its writing forms into discussion of design process.

CONCLUSION

Understanding the real world appropriation of technology and how it is situated within social conventions and realities of daily life is a vital part of design. However, if the "messy bit," the socio-technical gap, is where we need to be focusing our attentions to understand technology use in actual practice [16.], then we need research approaches that strive to understand it. The socio-technical gap can be studied objectively, and at a distance, however it can also be experienced as part of a reflexive ethnographic encounter. The reflexive ethnographer works in the shadows between what is said and what is done, piecing together their narrative having seen what is enacted in a multitude of lights. Innuendo, half-truths, the unsaid, that which cannot be specifically laid out with certitude—these are the guiding principles of daily life and the ethnographer works here. By discussing rapport, writing thick description, engaging in participant-observation, and presenting work as confessional or impressionistic tales, the ethnographer can give insight into their encounter from firsthand experience.

Yet a core problem then is one of the authority of writers [11.]. Clifford points out that the feature of anthropological practice that allows its followers to achieve scholarly legitimacy is the custom of spending about a year with informants, and that this is a professional rite of passage that gives anthropologists authority. Our field needs norms for what constitutes proper ethnography praxis that balance the realities of design with the need for authority.

Within HCI we need to recognize the various forms of *ethnography*. Anthropological ethnography allows the author to engage with theory directly, and focus on the experience of the relationship between the observer and the observed. This preserves context by embracing intervention as a data gathering opportunity through its reliance on rapport. Confessional and impressionist works allow readers to understand the process of data gathering and the ethnographer's place within it. Finally, ethnographers use participant-observation to understand the underlying structure of the observed, and apply and extend critical theory to explain it [9.], by broadly embracing and discussing the idiosyncrasies of unique encounters. Ethnographers struggle with the impact of the ethnographer's power and how it impacts data, yet realist, impressionist and confessional texts all make significant contributions to science [9.]. Each approach has liabilities.

Given that there are multiple valid approaches, each with liabilities, we need to be nuanced in our discussion of ethnography and focus on relating methods to design. Here I have shown how digital anthropology can contribute to participatory design as a means of understanding experience and how iterative ethnography allows for careful study of the socio-technical gap with a chance to fold the findings back into the design process. Finally, summative ethnography provides case studies of technology use focusing on how users dealt with the socio-technical gap.

We need to consider current unresolved debates in Anthropology, for instance. One such debate is raised by experimenting with the form of ethnographic text—the experimental, interpretive, dialogical and polyphonic (giving the informant's control over authorship along with the fieldworker) [11.]. Just as anthropologists are struggling over and debating the appropriate form of their ethnographic texts, we need not only to debate this but to also situate this dialog with regards to design. Much of this debate focuses on resolving the privileged status of the ethnographer over the informant in authoring ethnographic text. Given our participatory design heritage, our design-informants voice is relevant. We need to integrate this dialog into our own.

Conversely, we need to make sure the voice of the ethnographer's firsthand experience in the field is not lost as we record these experiences. Also, we need to add our own voice to this dialog as we discuss the relationship between digital anthropology and design. Confessional and impressionist text and critical theory represent a radical departure for CHI, but these are key forms of reflexivity. Participant observation allows us to explore technology use through embodied experience. Reflexive text, at its best, embraces and impacts the data gathering encounter, providing untapped sources for design inspiration. Through laying out the attributes of reflexivity and digital anthropology, I hope to ground a more nuanced onward discussion of how to use ethnography, and promote respect and understanding of its many forms.

ACKNOWLEDGMENTS

My thanks to my UCL qualitative research methods students for asking hard questions prompting this paper. I would like to thank P. Dourish, T. Rodden, D. Miller, B. Gaver and J. Bowers for discussions that were key in shaping this paper, and, M. Ames, L. Barkhuus, S. Bödker, J. Kaye, W. Kellogg, R. Magee, J. Mankoff, W. Newman, M. Sebastian, A. Williams, S. Wyche.

REFERENCES

1. Ackerman, M. 2000. The Intellectual Challenge of CSCW: The Gap Between Social Requirements and Technical Feasibility. *Human-Computer Interaction*, 15, p179-203.
2. Anderson, R. 1994. Representation and Requirements: The Value of Ethnography in System Design. *Human-Comp. Interact.*, 9(2),151-82.
3. Bell, G. No More SMS from Jesus: Ubicomp, Religion and Techno-spiritual Practices. *Proc. of Ubicomp 05,* p141-158.
4. Bell, G., Blythe, M., and Sengers, P. 2005. Making by making strange: Defamiliarization and the design of domestic technologies. *ACM Trans. on CHI* 12(2), 149-173.
5. Bödker, S.. 2006. When second wave HCI meets third wave challenges. In Proc Nordchi 06, p1-8.
6. Boelstorff, T. 2008. Coming of Age in Second Life: an Anthropologist Explores the Virtual Human. Princeton, NJ: Princeton UP.

7. Bhaskar, R.A., 1975. *A Realist Theory of Science*, London: Verso.
8. Blomberg, J., Giacomi, J., Mosher, A., & Swenton-Wall, P. 1993. Ethnographic field methods and their relation to design. In D. Schuler & A. Namioka (Eds.), *Participatory design: Perspectives on systems design*. 123-54. NJ: LAE P.
9. Burawoy, M. 1998. The Extended Case Method. *Sociological Theory*. 16:1, p4-33.
10. Button, G. 2000. The Ethnographic Tradition and Design. *Design Studies*, 21, p319-332.
11. Clifford, C. 1983. On Ethnographic Authority. *Representations*, 2, p118-146.
12. Clifford, J. 1981. On Ethnographic Surrealism. *Comparative Studies in Society and History*. 23, p539-64.
13. Clifford, J. and Marcus, G. 1986. *Writing Culture: The Poetics and Politics of Ethnography*. Berkeley, CA: U. of California P.
14. Crabtree, A., T, Hemmings, and T. Rodden. 2003. The Social Construction of Displays; Cordinate Displays and Ecologically Distributed Networks In K. O'Hara, et al (Eds.) In *Public and situated displays: social and interactional aspects of shared*. Netherlands: Kluwer. p170-190.
15. Dourish, P. 2007. Responsibilities and implications: further thoughts on ethnography and design. *In Proc. DUX '07*, p2-16.
16. Dourish, P. 2006. Implications for design. In Proc. ACM Conf. Human Factors in Computing Systems CHI' 06, p541-550.
17. Easthope, A., and Kate McGowan, eds. 2004. A Critical and Cultural Theory Reader. 2nd Edition. London: U of Toronto.
18. Frankenberg, R. 2004. *Living Spirit, Living Practice.* Durham: Duke.
19. Forsythe, D. E. 1999. It's Just a Matter of Common Sense: Ethnography as Invisible Work. *Computer Supported Coop. Work,* 8(1-2), 1p 27-145.
20. Geertz, C. 1988. Works and Lives: The Anthropologist as Author. Stanford, CA: Stanford UP.
21. Geertz, C. 1973. *The Interpretation Of Cultures.* New York: Basic.
22. Greenberg, S. and Buxton, B. (2008) Usability evaluation considered harmful. *Proc. CHI' 08*, p111-20.
23. Ito, M, Baumer, S. & et al. (forthcoming). Hanging Out, Messing Around, Geeking Out: Living and Learning with New Media. Cambridge: MIT Press.
24. Kelty, C. 2008. Two Bits: The Cultural Significance of Free Software. Durham NC: Duke UP.
25. Makkreel, R. A. 1993. *Dilthey: Philosopher of the Human Studies*. Princeton: Princeton University P.
26. Malaby. T 2009 Making Virtual Worlds: Linden Lab and Second Life. Ithaca, NY: Cornell UP.
27. March, W. and Fleuriot, C. 2006. Girls, technology and privacy: "is my mother listening?". *Proc. CHI' 06*, p107-10.
28. Marcus, G. and Fischer, M. 1986. Anthropology as Cultural Critique: An Experimental Moment in the Social Sciences. Chicago UP.
29. Masayuki Hamabata, Matthews. 1991. Crested Kimono: Power and Love in the Japanese Business Family. Ithaca, NY: Cornell UP.
30. Miller, D. In preparation The Digital and the Human; A Prospectus for Digital Anthropology.
31. Miller, D. and Slater, D. 2000. *The Internet: An Ethnographic Approach*. Oxford: Berg.
32. Newman, W. 2009. The Status of Ethnography in Systems Design. *Panel CHI'09,* (Boston, MA). New York: ACM.
33. Park, J., Blythe, M., Monk, A., and Grayson, D. 2006. Sharable digital TV: relating ethnography to design through un-useless product suggestions. *Proc. CHI' 06*, p1199-1204.
34. Rode, J.. 2008. An Ethnographic Examination of the Relationship of Gender & End-User Programming. PhD Dissertation.
35. Rode, J., M. Stringer, E. Toye, A. Simpson, and A. Blackwell. 2003. Curriculum-Focused Design. *Interaction Design and Children 2003,* (Preston, UK), 119-26.
36. Salvador, T., Bell G. & Anderson K. 1999. Design ethnography. *Design Management Journal* 10(4).
37. Sengers, P., K. Boehner, S. David, and J.J. Kaye. 2005. Reflective design. In Proceedings of the 4th decennial conference on Critical computing: between sense and sensibility (CC '05), O. Bertelsen, N. Bouvin, P.. Krogh, and M. Kyng (Eds.). ACM, NY NY, USA, 49-58.
38. Taylor, A. S. and Swan, L. 2005. Artful systems in the home. *Proc. ACM Conf. Human Factors in Computing Systems CHI' 05*, (Portland, OR), 641-650. New York: ACM.
39. Tong, R. P. (1998). Feminist Thought: A More Comprehensive Introduction. Boulder, Westview P.
40. Van Maanen, J. 1998. Tales of the Field; On Writing Ethnography. Chicago: Chicago UP.
41. Wajcman, J. From women and technology to gendered technoscience. *Information, Communication, and Society 10,* 3 (2007), 287-298.
42. Williams, A., Anderson, K., and Dourish, P. 2008. Anchored mobilities: mobile technology and transnational migration. *In Proc. DIS '08,* p323-332.
43. Williams, A. M. and Irani, L. 2010. There's methodology in the madness: toward critical HCI ethnography. *Proc. CHI '10 Extended Abstracts,* p2725-2734.
44. Woodward, S. 2007. *Why Women Wear What they Wear.* Oxford: Berg.
45. Wyche, S. P., Medynskiy, Y., and Grinter, R. E. 2007. Exploring the use of large displays in American megachurches. *Proc. CHI' 07,* p2771-2776.

Comparing Activity Theory with Distributed Cognition for Video Analysis: Beyond "Kicking the Tires"

Eric P. S. Baumer
Information Science Department
Cornell University
ericpsb@cornell.edu

Bill Tomlinson
Department of Informatics
University of California, Irvine
wmt@uci.edu

ABSTRACT
The field of HCI is growing, not only in the variety of application areas or the volume of research conducted, but also in the number of analytical approaches for use in the evaluation and design of interactive systems. However, despite the abundance of theoretical frameworks available, relatively little work has directly compared the application of these frameworks. This paper compares video analysis methods based on two analytic frameworks—activity theory (AT) and distributed cognition (DCog)—by performing an analysis of the same system from each of the two different theoretical perspectives. The results presented here provide a better understanding of how such theoretically informed methods in practice both resemble and differ from one another. Furthermore, this comparison enables specific insights about each of the theories themselves, as well as more general discussion about the role of theory in HCI.

Author Keywords
Activity theory, distributed cognition, video analysis, evaluation methodology, methodology evaluation.

ACM Classification Keywords
H5.m. Information interfaces and presentation (e.g., HCI): Miscellaneous.

General Terms
Human Factors

INTRODUCTION
HCI researchers, practitioners, designers, and engineers often confront the difficult and complex issue of evaluation. Given a system, design, or prototype, how does one assess its value? Moreover, how does one go about selecting a framework for understanding the ways users interact with it and with each other? There is no single theory of HCI. Rather, in its relatively short history, researchers in the field have generated or applied a panoply of theoretical frameworks, ranging from activity theory [17,23], to distributed cognition [12], to GOMS [6], to many others. This variety is both a blessing and a curse: an individual performing an evaluation can choose whatever methodology best fits the object of study and goals of the evaluation [9], but given a particular focus or question the ramifications of choosing one theory over another are not always clear. Several researchers have compared and contrasted different theories, often arguing that one theoretical perspective is more applicable, more comprehensible, or more useful than another [11,19,21]. Although such comparisons are useful in understanding the various theories involved, they often do not present the information that would be of greatest use to someone choosing which of these theories to employ: how do the methods informed by these theories compare *in practice*, that is, in the process of actually applying them to assess, evaluate, and understand users' interactions with a system and with each other? Furthermore, the practical issue of choosing and applying a theoretical framing belies a deeper but subtler question: what does HCI *do* with theory?

To develop such a practical understanding, and to consider at length the role of theory in HCI, this paper presents a side-by-side comparison of activity theory (AT) [3,18] and distributed cognition (DCog) [10,12]. Each is applied to video data of users interacting with a multidevice character-based installation called Normative Echoes [2]. This side-by-side application goes beyond "kicking the tires of different theories" [20:274] by directly comparing both the processes and products of using theory-driven methods on the same object of analysis. This is not a matter of triangulation, or the use of multiple approaches to reinforce the credibility or validity of results. Rather, the purpose here is to examine the methodologies themselves. The primary purpose of this paper, then, is to contribute to the continuing theoretical discussions in the literature [7,11,15,19,21,24] by examining similarities, differences, overlaps, and conflicts between the processes and products of applying theory-driven methods in HCI.

THEORETICAL BACKGROUND
This section provides brief introductions to AT and DCog. For a thorough review of theory in HCI, see [21].

Activity Theory
Based largely on Russian psychology from the early 20th century [17,23], activity theory (AT) focuses on human

activity as the unit of analysis. An activity includes a subject, or intentional actor performing the activity; an object, toward which the activity is directed; and mediating artifacts, through which the activity is carried out. In this framework, an object can be part of physical reality, such as a mouse or LCD, or of social reality, such as friendship or authority. Similarly, mediating objects can include physical artifacts, such as tools or diagrams, as well as cognitive or cultural artifacts, such as language or history. An object defines an activity, and no activity is without an object.

AT has been applied to a wide variety of settings in HCI research and design, e.g. [3,15,18]. Much of its utility is derived from the prominent analytic place of mediation, where computing technologies are seen as artifacts mediating human activity. The analysis here draws specifically on Engeström's [8] formulation of AT, which includes a community, social rules, and division of labor in the analytic framework, as well as incorporating methods informed by Mwanza [18] and Bødker [3]. Specifically, Mwanza [18] describes an eight-step process of identifying the activity of interest, the object of the activity, the subject performing the activity, etc., corresponding to the "activity triangles" developed by Engeström [8]. Bødker [3] emphasizes focusing on the role of breakdowns, when an activity is disrupted by an unanticipated outcome, and subsequent focus shifts, which signal a change in the object of activity, in defining units of activity for analysis. Methods informed by AT are used here for their flexibility in analyzing various levels of interaction with and through computational artifacts, their focus on the ways in which technical artifacts mediate human actions, and their emphasis on the user as an intentional actor.

Distributed Cognition

Distributed cognition (DCog) [12] draws on cognitive science, but its purview extends beyond the individual, arguing that cognitive processes do not occur strictly inside the mind but rather are distributed across multiple individuals and artifacts. Thus, the focus is on how cognitive and computational tasks are accomplished by interactions among individuals and artifacts, as well as social and cultural elements. DCog focuses on representations of computational state and the media of those representations, as well as transformations that occur when a state represented in one medium is propagated to another. Importantly, with respect to cognitive processes, human and non-human agents are treated symmetrically, that is, both can be components carrying out various processes in the system, and both can be media in which representational states are created or through which they are propagated.

DCog has been used in a number of HCI-related settings, e.g., [10,11,12]. These analyses focus on the ways that information gets represented and re-represented across various media, allowing for a close analysis of cognitive processes that span individuals, artifacts, and organizations. The methods used here draw mainly on Halverson [10,11], specifically involving diagrammatic depictions of the temporal flow of computational state through the various representational media involved in a cognitive system. Methods informed by DCog were selected for this analysis because of its emphasis on cognitive processes that occur across multiple individuals and artifacts, the contrast between their symmetric treatment of agents with AT's focus on intentional actors, and a resonance between the analytic prominence of propagation of representational state and the movement of virtual entities between devices in this exhibit.

THEORY COMPARISONS

Previous work has compared and contrasted different theoretical approaches within HCI, often arguing for one approach over others. Nardi [19] presents a comparison of situated action, distributed cognition, and activity theory, arguing that the focus on intentionality in activity theory absent from the other two offers "the richest framework for studies of context" [19:96] and users' engagement with artifacts. Halverson [11] compares AT with DCog, using an example analysis to argue for the benefits of DCog. Rogers [21] presents an account of theoretical developments in HCI, including AT, DCog, situated action, and several others, highlighting historical origins and differences in philosophical underpinnings. Suchman applies the concept of artifact mediation in a situated action analysis [22] but focuses on combining concepts from different theories rather than on comparing independent analyses. Some panels have discussed and compared theories in HCI [16], for example, three experts with different theoretical backgrounds analyzed a video clip from the film *Apollo 13* [24]. In both cases, all panelists were experts and the resulting discussion is not archived. Most similar to this paper, one study compared activity theory, cognitive ergonomics, and distributed cognition, but their focus was on an organizational work setting [7], rather than the focus here on video analysis of ad-hoc interactions of groups of participants learning to use a novel system. Where possible, those findings are compared and contrasted with ours.

However, little research has gone beyond high-level comparisons or simply trying out one theory or another. The point in this paper is to compare the methods informed by multiple theories by applying each to the same object of study. This simultaneous application enables us to assess differences and similarities between both the process and products of these theories, as well as to provide a side-by-side comparison of using theory-driven methods in practice.

NORMATIVE ECHOES

Normative Echoes is a multidevice character-based installation [2]. The physical set-up consists of two 26" LCD monitors, each connected to a desktop PC and representing a virtual island inhabited by a community of animated characters. A tablet PC acts as a virtual raft, allowing participants to move characters between islands (Figure 1). Participants may also interact with the characters by talking to them through microphones, one near each monitor. The characters learn simple speech patterns, represented as combinations of words and phrases, which are recombined to form new vocal expressions. The system does not perform semantic operations or infer the meaning of these speech patterns. Rather, it focuses on syntactic manipulation of speech patterns, allowing users to ascribe meaning to the system's actions.

The video data for this study were recorded during the demonstration session of the 2006 Artificial Intelligence and Interactive Digital Entertainment Conference. The conference program consists mainly of technical papers by researchers in academia and industry on AI techniques, with specific emphasis on those with applications in video games and other interactive digital media. The demonstration session of this conference allows researchers to give live demos of systems incorporating the techniques they have developed and to answer conference attendees' questions.

METHODS

As part of an analytic framework, theory "influences and is influenced by the process of data collection and interpretation" [10:26]. This paper uses video recordings, as opposed to interviews, timed system logs, or any other data collection method, enabling the same data to be used for both analyses. While both AT and DCog are often used to analyze much more complex, multifaceted data, there are methods and examples from both traditions of video analysis of interactive systems [3,10,24]. A distinguishing feature of this study is that the users are novices, rather than experts, so the analysis here focuses on the process of collectively learning to use the system and participants interactions during that process.

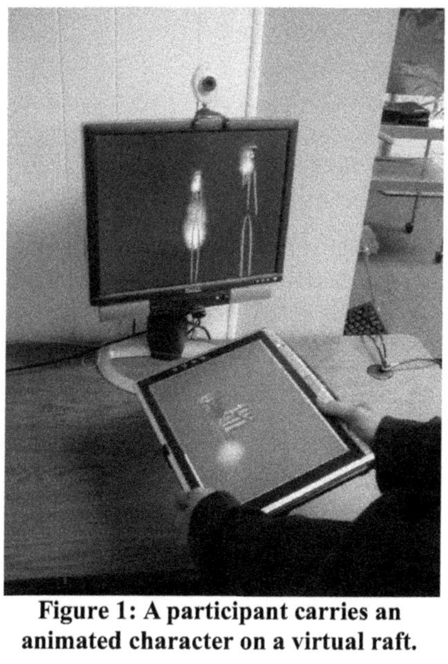

Figure 1: A participant carries an animated character on a virtual raft.

Throughout the demonstration session, participants were recorded interacting with Normative Echoes. A camera was placed behind one of the LCD displays, allowing participants' faces to be observed at that display, while other participants and the animated characters were visible at the other display. The camera was run continuously during the demonstration session, generating two hours of video footage, during which time about 40 participants interacted in the area visible to the camera. Most interactions lasted three to five minutes, though some lasted over fifteen minutes.

The analysis began with creating a content log for the entirety of the video data, from which segments were selected for closer analysis. Bødker [3] suggests looking for focus shifts, breakdowns, or other interesting or surprising situations, while Halverson [10] advises choosing clips that involve exchanges and re-representations of information among participants and devices in the system. While not entirely identical, there was some overlap in the clips both methods identified for further analysis. For each clip, highly detailed transcripts were created. The clips and transcripts were reviewed using the activity theoretic eight-step model [18], summarized above, to help construct activity triangles diagramming the relationships between subjects, objects, mediating artifacts, and other aspects of activity. Also, tables were made that follow the creation of representational states and their propagation across different media [10,11].

Most of the analysis was carried out by a single individual with consultation and assistance from others at various times. The analyses were done roughly concomitantly, rather than completing one entirely before starting another. While this process helped the individual researcher see where the analyses coincided and where they differed, it could also be beneficial for multiple researchers to contribute to such an analysis, each using a different theory [cf. 7,24]. On the one hand, conducting this analysis with multiple experts may enable a more thorough treatment of each theory and the methods it informs. However, in practice, such experts are not available to all HCI researchers or practitioners, meaning that those who wish to use these theories must grapple with the abstract theoretical concepts, and their associated methods, themselves.

REPRESENTATIVE VIDEO EXCERPT

This section presents a representative portion from one of the many video segments analyzed. In this excerpt, a group of participants attempts to transfer an animated character from the tablet to a stationary display. This clip was chosen as an example of a breakdown, as well as an example of a cognitive task being conducted by a group of participants. All names are pseudonyms.

Sara and Claude are standing at the large desktop display farther from the camera, Sara holding a tablet near the display, as Blake and Tony approach the closer display.

Figure 2. Sara's accelerometer test.

Blake leans down to the microphone and says, "Hello." Both he and Tony lean in near the display to listen closer as the animated characters respond, "Hello. Hey you!" Blake glances at Tony, points toward the display, and appears about to speak, when Sara walks up holding the tablet and says, "I gotta get this guy over here." Blake and Tony look down at the tablet, then step to either side and allow Sara to approach the display, as Blake asks, "Oh c'mon, why you gotta keep 'em separated?" alluding to a popular punk-rock song.

Sara holds the tablet near the bottom of the screen, as Blake and Claude look on over her shoulder. All three gaze intently at the tablet. After a few moments, Sara says, "leave," presumably to the character, and Blake reaches forward to take hold of the tablet, saying, "tilt it, tilt it." As they tilt the tablet, the computer graphical raft on which the animated character is standing moves in the direction of the tilt until it has almost entirely vanished from the screen. The participants seem to believe that, since the character is no longer visible on the tablet, that it has transferred to the island. Blake pulls his hand back, and, smiling, says, "There you go, see?" Sara turns to look at him and asks, "You actually had to tilt it?" To which Blake responds, "Well what do you think, water flows up hill?" Blake's statement indicates his belief that the tablet is aware of its physical orientation, and furthermore that the virtual objects contained therein should react similarly to their physical counterparts.

Figure 3. Blake demonstrating the raft's movement to Sara.

The character on Sara's tablet has not transferred to the island as she intended. Claude suggests, "What you have to do is tilt it again," while Tony says, "You move the tablet." Sara, though, seems incredulous. "How does moving the tablet help?" she asks. "Is there like a [sic] accelerometer on here?" Lifting the tablet, she holds it upside-down and shakes it (Figure 2). "I don't think so," she concludes, then leans back and says to Blake, "I think you're making that up."

As Sara turns to speak to him, Blake cocks his head, points at the screen, and listens to the characters speaking. However, his attention is turned toward Sara's disbelief. He grabs the tablet, while still in her hands, and tilts it back and forth, side to side, saying, "You see this? His position moves based on this" (Figure 3). As he does so, the animated raft on the tablet moves to reflect the tablet's pitch and roll. Tony chimes in, "My laptop has that, too."

However, this does not help Sara, as she still wants to know, "How do I get him over there?" Tony states, "You don't have anybody on your raft," to which Sara replies, "I do! There's a dude on it." There is a moment of confusion, as Sara says, "Oh, he left, but he's not over there. Where'd he go?" A moment later, Claude and Blake point at the screen, and Sara says, "Oh there he is," as all three see that the character has transferred from the raft to the island.

ANALYSIS

This section presents each analysis separately, followed by comparison in the subsequent discussion section.

Activity Theory

Since AT frames human activity as intentional, goal-driven action, the methods involved focus on people's activities and their objects. The AT analysis presented here draws on Mwanza's eight-step model [18] to fill in the various components of an activity, depicted as a series of triangles [8]. Although intended as part of a design process, the eight-step model works well for analytic purposes, as it presents a specific process for understanding an activity. The activity of interest here is the participants in the clip above transferring a character from the tablet to the desktop. Similar analyses were performed on other clips, but results here are restricted to this representative example.

Figure 4 depicts the subjects, object, mediators, etc. In this framework, human activity is mediated not only by tools, but also by other aspects of context. In terms of rules and regulations, the main factor is the technical limitations of the system, restricting the conditions under which the subjects (the participants) are able to achieve their object (transferring the character). In this situation, the video data also show an implicit division of labor, in that the person holding the tablet guides the activity and makes the decisions. Suggestions and advice for what to do come from those not holding the tablet, then the person holding the tablet chooses which advice to follow. This division of labor leads to a second activity when Claude suggests, "What you have to do is tilt it again."

When Sara responds, "How does moving the tablet help?" this breakdown [cf. 3] signals an object shift and corresponding activity change (Figure 5) from transferring the character to determining the effect of tilting the tablet. Language, physical movement, and the tablet all mediate this activity. The culture of a demonstration session also mediates this interaction with a focus on the technological aspects of the system. While Tony and Claude are still present, they are not directly engaged in this activity, and thus are categorized as part of the community rather than as subjects. The result is that Sara "believes" Blake that the tilting matters. Once Sara has been convinced, her question "But how do I get him over there?" signals a shift back to the activity of transferring the character, which is eventually accomplished.

This analysis is informative in a number of ways. First the social rules and division of labor draw attention to the fact that, although Sara is holding the tablet and thus makes most of the decisions about what should be tested or attempted, the others make the suggestions and provide ideas for how to transfer the character. Second, when the participants change focus and begin to argue about the importance of tilting the tablet, the object-oriented analysis of AT directs us to view this as an entirely different activity, rather than just a phase of the interaction. During this activity, a third important point is brought into focus: the mediating role of the participants' bodies. Generally, activity theoretic analyses discuss the mediating roles of tools, language, culture, and many other aspects of interaction. However, due to the physicality of the user interface, we see here that Blake uses not only the graphical effects seen on the tablet, but he also tilts his head and shifts his entire posture to emphasize the importance of tilting the tablet. The body's mediating role is addressed further in the discussion below.

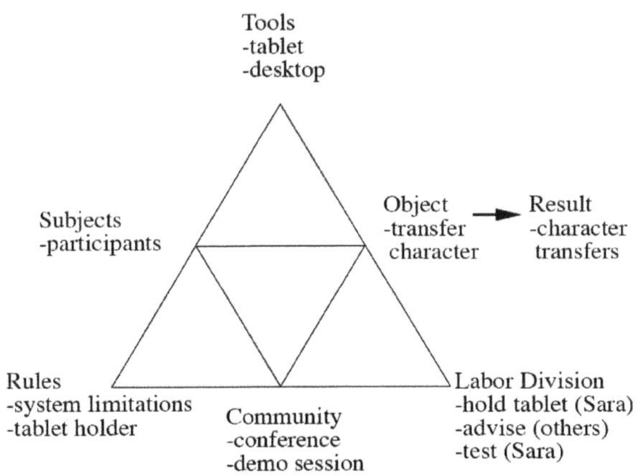

Figure 4. Activity triangle for figuring out how to transfer a character.

Distributed Cognition

The distributed cognition analysis here focuses on the creation of representational states and their propagation through various media [10,11] with a portion of the same clip used in the AT analysis. Similarly, this section is representative of several close analyses.

Through the lens of DCog, the Normative Echoes installation is a cognitive system, of which the participants and the devices are components (Table 1, top row). The rows are grouped into portions of the interaction, each of which describes the representational state of each component, the medium in which that state occurs, and what processing is being done (whether state information is being created or propagated), including from and to what media. Claude is not involved in the representational state propagation here and so is not included in this analysis.

The table begins with Blake grabbing the tablet and demonstrating the effect of tilting it (Table 1, first event), using the tablet to create a physical representation of his understanding of the system, which is then propagated by the LCD to a graphical representation in response to the tablet's orientation. When Sara again asks "How do I get him over there?" and Tony replies, "You don't have anybody" (Table 1, second event), both Sara and Tony are creating verbal representations of their understanding of the system, and both are performing aural processing on the representations they receive. Additionally, Sara is using the virtual state of the character on the raft, propagated by the tablet to a graphical state, to demonstrate that her mental representation and the character's virtual state are in alignment. However, the character shortly thereafter disappears from the tablet, its virtual state of leaving the tablet propagated to a graphical representation on the LCD. As the character disappears, the desktop starts making the sound of a ship creaking to indicate that the tablet is within range to transfer. Also, Sara states, "Oh, he left," propagating the graphical representation of the character's state into an auditory medium and signaling a change in her own mental representation (Table 1, third event). Once the character finishes transferring, the desktop propagates this

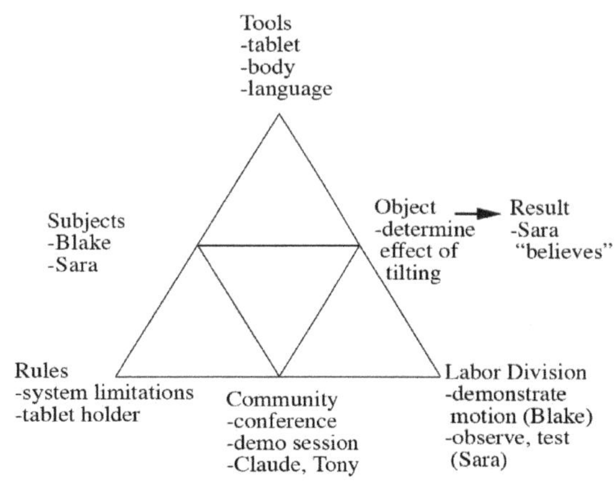

Figure 5. Activity triangle for convincing Sara of the accelerometer's effects.

	Event (time)	Sara	Blake	Tony	Tablet	LCD	Desktop	Character
rep state	First event: tilting demonstration (3:03)	hold/tilt tablet	speech, tilt tablet	speech, gesture	orientation	raft moving	fire crackling	on raft
medium		body, tablet	voice, body	voice, body	tablet	LCD	speakers	program
processing / type		propagate / motor, aural	create / verbal, motor	create / verbal, motor	propagate / physical	propagate/ physical to graphical	propagate / physical to audio	create / virtual
rep state	Second event: how to transfer (3:19)	speech		speech	orientation	character on raft	fire crackling	on raft
medium		voice		voice	tablet	LCD	speakers	program
processing / type		create / aural		create / aural	propagate / physical	propagate / virtual to graphical	propagate/ physical to audio	create / virtual
rep state	Third event: character leaves tablet (3:23)	speech			position	character jumps	creaking sound	in transit
medium		voice			tablet	LCD	speakers	program
processing / type		propagate / visual to verbal			propagate / physical	propagate / virtual to graphical	propagate / physical to audio	create / virtual
rep state	Fourth event: character reaches desktop (3:28)	speech	gesture	gesture		raft w/o character	arriving animation	on island
medium		voice	body	body		LCD	LCD	program
processing / type		propagate /graphical to verbal	propagate graphical to motor	propagate /graphical to motor		propagate / virtual to graphical	propagate / virtual to graphical	create / virtual

Table 1. Creation and propagation of cognitive state across representational media (excerpt). System components listed across top. LCD is the tablet display. Blank cells indicate no relevant representational state for that component at that time. Times are min:sec.

virtual state to a graphical one, an animation of the character arriving on the island, which is in turn propagated by verbal and motor processing to vocal and physical representations by the three participants (Table 1, fourth event).

The DCog analysis highlights a number of important elements of this interaction. First, it draws attention to how information and understanding is shared among the participants. The primary form of exchange here is verbal, often with gestural support, but participants also use the physical orientation of the tablet or the tablet's LCD to align the others' mental representations with their own. Second, people and devices both participate in creation and propagation of state representations. DCog's symmetric stance–treating participants, devices, and even virtual characters as components of a cognitive system—allows for seeing the character as creating a virtual representation of its current state. It also shows the way that certain remarks or gestures of the participants work to propagate representational states they perceive.

DISCUSSION

The comparison conducted here affords a number of insights, here discussed around two themes. The first portion addresses findings that pertain specifically to DCog and AT. The second discusses broader implications for what HCI does, or perhaps should do, with theory.

Theoretical Findings

Process and Structure – One important difference between the theories used here is the amount of structure each provides. AT gives a relatively specific structure into which observations are fit; DCog does not provide a specific structure but rather directs attention to a certain aspect of interaction. In our experience, more structure made a theory easier to apply. Ascertaining a subject's object was often easier than tracing exactly where and how state representations propagated. On the other hand, the amount of structure had the opposite impact on the ease of learning. For example, Kaptelinin and Nardi [15] devote several chapters to discussing the notion of "object," at times even describing conflicts within a single theorist's writing, making the learning process difficult.

Since we are not experts in either DCog or AT, others seeking to understand or apply these theories may benefit from our experiences. That said, our particular experiences were framed by our backgrounds, such that others may have different experiences with each of these theories. We return to this question of individual differences further below.

Products and Temporality – The above analyses involve different temporal granularities. DCog provides a moment-to-moment record of changes in representational media, as evidenced by the relatively short time lapses between events in Table 1, whereas the people and artifacts of AT's analytic categories (subject, object, mediating tool, etc.) do not change quite so rapidly. This is not to say that AT treats activities as distinct, static units, but rather that temporal dynamism is foregrounded and more tightly integrated into the analytic representations DCog affords. This experience differs slightly from Halverson's view that "dealing with processes is built into the structure of... AT," but it resonates with her finding that "in DCog, process(ing) is... central to the analysis" [11:247].

These differences in granularity extend beyond temporality. In general, DCog led to a lower level of analysis, focusing on the ways that individual actions change the state of the cognitive system, while AT led to a higher level of analysis, focusing instead on the intentions and goals of the subjects performing those actions. This difference in granularity stems largely from the two theories' differing stances toward the object of analysis. When viewed as a group of intentional actors, the focus is on the ways in which a high level goal is achieved. When viewed as a cognitive system, the focus is on the tasks that system performs. For example, when the participants attempt to ascertain the effect of tilting the tablet, an AT analysis suggests a change in activity, due to the participants taking up a different object, which requires a shift in the analytic framing. In contrast, the DCog analysis enables use of the same analytic framing throughout, since participants' actions can still be understood in terms of representational state propagation, but did not draw as much analytic attention to that episode. It is possible that an AT analysis focusing on the level of actions and operations may produce results that more closely resemble the task-level DCog analysis (see [4] for more discussion of levels in AT). This example demonstrates how different philosophical commitments can lead to different analytic insights.

The Body and Mediation – While theoretically plausible, most traditional accounts of AT and DCog do not include the body as a mediating tool or as a representational medium [3,10,11,15,19]. Hutchins and Palen describe how the body is used to construct shared meaning [14], but not how it acts as a representational medium. Aspects of experience such as language, culture, and history are often seen in AT as mediating interaction and in DCog as representational media, but these theories rarely discuss the mediating role of the body. This lack of theoretical account for the body made it, in these analyses, more analytically conspicuous. As seen in the interactions between Sara and Blake, posture, gestures, and the entire body help to mediate their interaction. Similarly, in the DCog analysis, participants' bodies became an important medium in which cognitive state was instantiated and propagated.

Hutchins and Klausen [13] provide an account of how such instantiation and propagation in an airline cockpit, including speech, glances, and instrument readings, function to create a shared, intersubjective understanding of the situation. Bødker and Andersen [4] also examine meaning making, but they do so through a more nuanced model of mediation that draws on semiotics to incorporate not only a subject's use of a mediating tool but also the subject's interpretation of the representation proffered by the mediating tool. Although neither analysis explicitly acknowledges the role of the body, both are concerned with how mediation shapes intersubjective interpretations.

This similarity exemplifies Nardi's belief that AT and DCog "will mutually inform, and even merge, over time" [19:89]. Even in the terminology of mediating artifacts and representational media, the common root "medium" draws attention to the relational properties of interactive systems, those that lie not within any particular entity but rather in the relationships between them. However, these results also point to important ways that future analyses should consider the prominent role of the body as a medium of interaction.

Agency and Agents – Generally speaking, AT considers agency in terms of intentional actors, usually humans, while DCog makes no analytic distinction between human and non-human agents. For example, without significantly stretching the framework, there is little room in AT for treating an animated character as an intentional actor. DCog, though, allowed the authors to treat the character as an agent that could instantiate representational state. However, this flexibility led to questions about where to draw the line between agent and medium. It was at times difficult to determine whether the tablet should be considered as an agent, as a medium, or as both.

These questions of agency are different from those encountered by Decortis et al. [7], who describe how AT's emphasis on intentionality drew attention to the individual while DCog's more systemic view framed individuals as system components. They do not, however, recount any difficulties in their analysis about whether a given entity counts as a medium or an agent. That complication may have arisen partly from the animated characters behaving like intelligent agents, and partly from the mixed physical-virtual nature of the system being analyzed here.

Ultimately, we chose to treat the physical device of the tablet as an agent that propagates the physical configuration of participants' bodies into the computational system, and to treat the LCD display on the tablet as a separate agent that propagated the virtual state of the animated character into a graphical medium. This difficulty could be construed as a problem, in that it exposes ambiguity in the theory. Alternatively, it could be seen as a resource, allowing the researcher some flexibility in applying the theory so as to focus on the phenomena of interest.

Terms and Terminology – Different frameworks, and at times different theorists working within the same framework, will use the same term to mean subtly if not drastically different things. In their use of AT, DCog, and cognitive ergonomics to analyze an organizational work process, Decortis et al. [7] note a multiplicity of meanings for certain terms. Specifically, their analysis drew attention to ambiguities over the terms activity, tool/artefact, and representation. The two preceding discussion points suggest a similar concern with comparing theories; here, multiple meanings of the terms medium and agency were highly salient. However, other foundational terms, such as information, knowledge, or even cognition are equally contentious. For example, in AT, only intentional action counts as cognition; actions of the animated characters in Normative Echoes cannot feasibly be seen as cognitive, but the characters could be seen as mediating artifacts. On the other hand, DCog's process oriented focus nearly requires that the character's actions be viewed as an agent in a cognitive system rather than as a representational medium.

On one hand, this ambiguity complicates any attempt at cross-theoretical comparisons; one theory's cognition is another's computation. On the other, the ambiguities exposed in the comparison presented here provide concrete examples of how the definitional aspects of a theory shape and direct an analysis. These basic definitional issues lead to larger questions of how theories are deployed in HCI.

Broader Concerns: What Does HCI Do with Theory?[1]

Falsification and Verification – Some theories [e.g., 6] seek to predict experiment results or user behavior. Such theories' predictions can be compared with empirical evidence to verify or falsify them. In contrast, theories such as AT and DCog seek to provide explanations or descriptions that are useful in talking about and thinking about user interactions. While analytically beneficial, such theories are not intended to make predictions, and thus cannot be proven or disproven [cf. 21]. Instead, we should explore the various theories' explanatory power through direct comparisons, such as those provided here.

Such an approach will not lead to a single, grand unified theory of HCI, as some might desire. However, any given theory will draw attention to some features of an interaction while downplaying others, as demonstrated here. It is unlikely that any single theory will meet all the needs of every HCI researcher and practitioner. Thus, rather than strive toward unification, we should seek to capitalize on our current theoretical pluralism. Furthermore, conducting comparative analyses, such as in this paper, not only provides the opportunity to better appreciate each others' theories, but also helps us as a field develop a deeper practical understanding of the similarities, differences, and relationships among our various theoretical frameworks.

Concomitant Analyses and Individual Differences – The authors initially intended to conduct each theoretically informed analysis completely separately, but it quickly became clear that such complete separation was impossible. The first task in both the AT and DCog methods involved generating a transcript for the entire two-hour video, which meant that the analyses were conducted concomitantly from the outset. While each analysis was conducted independently, some conceptual crossover was unavoidable. For example, the role of the body as a representational medium (described above) was first noticed during the DCog analysis. This insight then drew the authors' attention to the body's mediating role during the AT analysis. This is but one example of how the two analyses mutually influenced one another.

Furthermore, even if the two analyses were somehow kept completely separate and entirely independent, this paper would not be a comparison of DCog and AT *per se*. Rather, the paper is a comparison of two *applications* of these theories. Any application is necessarily shaped not only by the object to which a theory is being applied, but also by the persons doing the applying. A researcher or practitioner is not a neutral, veridical conduit through which a theory is applied. As mentioned above, the points of relative ease and difficulty in learning and applying these theories were likely due in part to the authors' specific backgrounds, e.g., the first author's primary training is in computer science. Ultimately, the knowledge gained from the work presented here will be most useful when combined with others' practical experiences in comparing such theories, as described further below.

Methods and Methodology – There is an important distinction between methods (i.e., the actual tasks in which one engages) and methodology (i.e., the philosophical stance and epistemological commitments underlying those tasks) [5]. The work described here, then, represents not just a discussion of theoretically informed methods, but a case study that exemplifies the analytic ramifications of these two methodologies. The above analysis and discussion contain many examples of how different theoretical stances on various issues, such as what counts as an agent, how time and change are represented, or how participants' bodies are accounted for, can have significant analytical ramifications. Before actually using any of these theoretical frameworks, researchers and practitioners should consider not only the fitness of the theory's methods for the task at hand, but also such impacts of the associated underlying methodological commitments.

Objects and Lenses – Not only can an object of study be viewed through different theoretical lenses, but the lenses themselves can at times create the object of study. For

[1] This section title is adapted from the title of [11].

example, because AT directs attention toward the mediating role of artifacts, we see the tablets as mediating participants' activities of transferring the character. Because DCog emphasizes the importance of representational state, we see the character's virtual state propagated to its graphical state on the tablet. As noted elsewhere [10,21], theory performs a multitude of functions, from framing data collection to presenting results, but among them is not the role of creating a veridical representation of reality. This process of examining the same object with multiple lenses allows us reflexively to turn the lenses themselves into an object of study. Considering not only the ways in which theory frames an analysis but also the ways in which it creates a certain reality is crucial if we are to apply such theories productively.

IMPLICATIONS FOR PRACTICE

The preceding section details a number of this paper's implications for theory. Here, we draw out two specific implications for practice. First, it is not necessary for every single user study or system evaluation to draw, incorporate, and compare insights from multiple theoretical frameworks. Second, in order to gain a better understanding of the theoretical frameworks used in HCI, further comparative studies similar to that presented in this paper should be conducted. We argue each of these in turn.

First, we are not arguing that every possible user study would benefit from a "polytheoretic" analysis. The conceptual overhead of learning and applying a single theoretical framework can be quite high, and the additional insights gained do not seem worth the additional effort. As shown here, there were relatively few instances in which one framework led to a compelling finding that was completely missed in the other. Rather, the two theories placed greater analytic significance on different aspects of the interaction being analyzed. That said, situations are conceivable in which applying multiple theoretical frameworks may be advantageous. For example, if there are many diverse goals for conducting an evaluation, or if different parties have different loci of inquiry, the parallel use of different theoretically informed methods could effectively serve such multiple goals or varied interests simultaneously.

Second, we suggest that the field of HCI could benefit from other researchers conducting comparative analyses similar to that presented here. Such comparisons would help determine which results present here were due to particular aspects of this study and which might be more broadly applicable. Was the role of the body—as a representational medium and as a mediating artifact—specific to this study, or is it a large issue in DCog and AT? Would a similar mixed physical-virtual system that did not include intelligent agents lead to similar questions of the distinction between agent and medium? How do differences in representations of temporality manifest when analyzing interactions or processes that unfold over much longer time scales? The most effective way to address these questions will be to conduct multiple comparative analyses, like that presented here. Synthesizing the results of many such studies will help work toward a fuller, deeper understanding of these theories and their application.

FUTURE WORK

While this paper takes a step towards comparing theoretically-informed methods, it is only a first step. The analyses presented here were of a specific and, although complex, relatively limited interaction. Comparing such methods in more longitudinal research, such as organizational studies, might help bring an understanding of how these different theories frame processes of large-scale change. Furthermore, integrating and synthesizing results from many such comparative studies can help further develop both abstract and practical understandings of these theories. From a pragmatic standpoint, future researchers conducting similar analyses could keep a journal to trace the flow of conceptual crossover during concomitant analyses. It could also be informative to have multiple researchers, each well-versed in one particular theory, analyze the same data, either individually, to compare their results, or collaboratively, to engender discussion. Lastly, these theoretical perspectives should be compared not only for the purpose of analysis, but also for the purpose of design. Bassoli et al. [1] point to the dialectic relationship between design and theory. Using different theoretical perspectives may lead to entirely different design products, which may then be deployed and studied using multiple theoretic perspectives. While these comparisons are more labor intensive and more time consuming than other standard approaches, the results presented here suggest that the insights we gain may be worth the extra time and effort.

CONCLUSION

While HCI offers a variety of theoretically informed methods, coming to a consensus about evaluations thereof can be quite difficult. This paper furthers this discussion by directly comparing theoretically informed methods through application to the same object of study. It is not intended as an argument for or against any particular theory. Rather, the purpose here is to present a side-by-side comparison of methods informed by different theories. Specifically, this paper advances our understanding of methods informed by activity theory and distributed cognition in terms of the role of the body, temporality, granularity of analysis, and agency. Such comparisons can help understand further how theoretically-driven analyses compare in practice, as well as consider more broadly the role of theory in our field.

Almost 15 years ago, Nardi [19] asserted that a crucial step for HCI would be the development of a common vocabulary. Halverson echoed this perspective, arguing that we need to "understand each other's theoretical frameworks" [11:263]. While we are not advocating the development of a single, common theoretical framework, this paper does seek to promote discussion between advocates of different perspectives by contributing to a better understanding of how methods associated with different theories work in practice. "The choice of evaluation methodology – if any – must arise from and be appropriate for the actual problem or research question under consideration" [9:111]. Understanding the relationships among theoretical frameworks and evaluation methodologies is crucial for the development of a discipline. This paper aims to further that understanding within the discipline of HCI.

ACKNOWLEDGMENTS

Thanks to Silvia Lindtner, Amanda Williams, Bonnie Nardi, Gillian Hayes, Laurian Vega, Danielle Lottridge, Antti Salovaara, and the anonymous reviewers for comments on previous versions; and to David H. Nguyen, Karen Martin, Lucian Leahu, Lilly Irani, Six Silberman, Joel Ross, Lilly Nguyen, and Christo Sims for helpful conversations. This work was supported in part by a grant from the Alfred P. Sloan Foundation, by the Emulex Corporation, and by the Bren School of ICS.

REFERENCES

1. Bassoli, A., Brewer, J., and Martin, K. In-between theory and practice: dialogues in design and research. *CHI '07 Extended Abstracts*, (2007), 1691-1696.
2. Baumer, E., Tomlinson, B., Yau, M., and Alspaugh, T. Normative Echoes: Use and Manipulation of Player Generated Content by Communities of NPCs. *AI in Interactive Digital Entertainment (AIIDE-06) Demonstration Program*, AAAI Press (2006).
3. Bødker, S. Applying Activity Theory to Video Analysis: How to Make Sense of Video Data in HCI. In *Context and Consciousness: Activity Theory and Human-Computer Interaction*. MIT Press, Cambridge, MA, 1996, 147 - 176.
4. Bødker, S. and Andersen, P.B. Complex Mediation. *Human-Computer Interaction 20*, 4 (2005), 353-402.
5. Boehner, K., Vertesi, J., Sengers, P., and Dourish, P. How HCI interprets the probes. *Proceedings of the SIGCHI conference on Human factors in computing systems*, ACM (2007), 1077-1086.
6. Card, S., Moran, T., and Newell, A. *The Psychology of Human-Computer Interaction*. Lawrence Erlbaum Associates, Hillsdale, NJ, 1983.
7. Decortis, F., Noirfalise, S., and Saudelli, B. Activity theory, cognitive ergonomics and distributed cognition: three views of a transport company. *Int. J. Hum.-Comput. Stud. 53*, 1 (2000), 5-33.
8. Engeström, Y. *Learning, Working, and Imagining: Twelve Studies in Activity Theory*. Orienta-Konsultit Oy, Helsinki, 1990.
9. Greenberg, S. and Buxton, B. Usability evaluation considered harmful (some of the time). *ACM SIGCHI*, ACM (2008), 111-120.
10. Halverson, C. Inside the Cognitive Workplace: New Technology and Air Traffic Control. 1995.
11. Halverson, C. Activity theory and distributed cognition: or What Does CSCW need to do with theories. *Special Issue of Computer Supported Cooperative Work on Activity Theory 11*, 1-2 (2002), 243-267.
12. Hutchins, E. *Cognition in the Wild*. MIT Press, Cambridge, MA, 1995.
13. Hutchins, E. and Klausen, T. Distributed Cognition in an Airline Cockpit. In Y. Engeström and D. Middleton, eds., *Cognition and Communication at Work*. Cambridge University Press, New York, 1996, 15-34.
14. Hutchins, E. and Palen, L. Constructing Meaning from Space, Gesture, and Speech. In L.B. Resnick, R. Säljo, C. Pontecorvo and B. Burge, eds., *Discourse, Tools, and Reasoning: Essays on Situated Cognition*. Springer-Verlag, Berlin, 1997, 24-40.
15. Kaptelinin, V. and Nardi, B.A. *Acting with Technology: Activity Theory and Interaction Design*. MIT Press, Cambridge, MA, 2006.
16. Kaptelinin, V., Nardi, B., Bødker, S., et al. Post-cognitivist HCI: second-wave theories. *CHI '03 extended abstracts on Human factors in computing systems*, ACM (2003), 692-693.
17. Leont'ev, A. The problem of activity in psychology. *Soviet Psychology 13*, 2 (1974), 4 - 33.
18. Mwanza, D. Towards an Activity-Oriented Design Method for HCI Research and Practice. 2002.
19. Nardi, B. Studying Context: A Comparison of Activity Theory, Situated Action Models, and Distributed Cognition. In *Context and Consciousness: Activity Theory and Human-Computer Interaction*. MIT Press, Cambridge, MA, 1996.
20. Nardi, B.A. Coda and Response to Christine Halverson. *Special Issue of Computer Supported Cooperative Work on Activity Theory 11*, 1-2 (2002), 269 - 275.
21. Rogers, Y. New Theoretical Approaches for Human-Computer Interaction. *Annual Review of Information Science and Technology (ARIST) 38*, (2004), 87-143.
22. Suchman, L. Embodied Practices of Engineering Work. *Mind, Culture, and Activity 7*, 1-2 (2000), 4-18.
23. Vygotsky, L. *Mind and Society*. Harvard University Press, Cambridge, MA, 1978.
24. Wolf, C.G., Halverson, C., Kaptelinin, V., and Shepherd, A. From Analysis to Design: Do Different Analytical Methods Make a Difference? *Panel at INTERACT '99*, (1999).

The Aligned Rank Transform for Nonparametric Factorial Analyses Using Only ANOVA Procedures

Jacob O. Wobbrock,[1] Leah Findlater,[1] Darren Gergle,[2] James J. Higgins[3]

[1]The Information School
DUB Group
University of Washington
Seattle, WA 98195 USA
{wobbrock, leahkf}@uw.edu

[2]School of Communication
Northwestern University
Evanston, IL 60208 USA
dgergle@northwestern.edu

[3]Department of Statistics
Kansas State University
Manhattan, KS 66506 USA
jhiggins@ksu.edu

ABSTRACT
Nonparametric data from multi-factor experiments arise often in human-computer interaction (HCI). Examples may include error counts, Likert responses, and preference tallies. But because multiple factors are involved, common nonparametric tests (*e.g.*, Friedman) are inadequate, as they are unable to examine interaction effects. While some statistical techniques exist to handle such data, these techniques are not widely available and are complex. To address these concerns, we present the *Aligned Rank Transform (ART)* for nonparametric factorial data analysis in HCI. The ART relies on a preprocessing step that "aligns" data before applying averaged ranks, after which point common ANOVA procedures can be used, making the ART accessible to anyone familiar with the F-test. Unlike most articles on the ART, which only address two factors, we generalize the ART to *N* factors. We also provide *ARTool* and *ARTweb*, desktop and Web-based programs for aligning and ranking data. Our re-examination of some published HCI results exhibits advantages of the ART.

Author Keywords: Statistics, analysis of variance, ANOVA, factorial analysis, nonparametric data, F-test.

ACM Classification Keywords: H.5.2 [Information interfaces and presentation]: User interfaces – *evaluation/methodology, theory and methods.*

General Terms: Experimentation, Measurement, Theory.

INTRODUCTION
Studies in human-computer interaction (HCI) often generate nonparametric data from multiple independent variables. Examples of such data may include error counts, Likert responses, or preference tallies. Often complicating this picture are correlated data arising from repeated measures. Two analysis approaches for data like these appear regularly in the HCI literature. The first simply uses a parametric F-test, which risks violating ANOVA assumptions and inflating Type I error rates. The second uses common *one-way* nonparametric tests (*e.g.*, Friedman), foregoing the examination of interaction effects. Although some methods for handling nonparametric factorial data exist (see Table 1) [12], most are not well known to HCI researchers, require advanced statistical knowledge, and are not included in common statistics packages.[1]

Table 1. Some possible analyses for nonparametric data.

Method	Limitations
General Linear Models (GLM)	Can perform factorial parametric analyses, but cannot perform nonparametric analyses.
Mann-Whitney *U*, Kruskal-Wallis	Can perform nonparametric analyses, but cannot handle repeated measures or analyze multiple factors or interactions.
Wilcoxon, Friedman	Can perform nonparametric analyses and handle repeated measures, but cannot analyze multiple factors or interactions.
χ^2, Logistic Regression, Generalized Linear Models (GZLM)	Can perform factorial nonparametric analyses, but cannot handle repeated measures.
Generalized Linear Mixed Models (GLMM), Generalized Estimating Equations (GEE)	Can perform factorial nonparametric analyses and handle repeated measures, but are not widely available and are complex.
Kaptein *et al.*'s [7] nonparametric method	Can perform factorial nonparametric analyses and handle repeated measures, but requires different mathematics and software modules for each type of experiment design. ([7] focused only on 2×2 mixed designs.)
Aligned Rank Transform (ART)	Can perform factorial nonparametric analyses and handle repeated measures. Requires only an ANOVA after data alignment and ranking, provided for by *ARTool* or *ARTweb*.

A remedy to the paucity of nonparametric factorial analyses would be a procedure that retains the familiarity and interpretability of the familiar parametric F-test. We present just such an analysis called the *Aligned Rank Transform (ART)*. The ART relies on an alignment and ranking step before using F-tests. We offer two equivalent tools to do the alignment and ranking, one for the desktop (*ARTool*) and one on the Web (*ARTweb*). Unlike the advanced methods

[1] A useful page from statistics consulting at UCLA for choosing the right statistical test has a conspicuous omission marked with "???", which appears in the slot for analyzing factorial ordinal data. See http://www.ats.ucla.edu/stat/mult_pkg/whatstat/default.htm. Similarly, another useful page giving the rationale for myriad statistical tests fails to describe any nonparametric factorial analysis for repeated measures data. See http://www.ats.ucla.edu/stat/spss/whatstat/whatstat.htm. Both pages were accessed January 12, 2011.

shown in Table 1, researchers only familiar with ANOVA can use, interpret, and report results from the ART.

We describe the ART and contribute: (1) its generalization from two factors to N factors, (2) the *ARTool* and *ARTweb* programs for easy alignment and ranking, and (3) a re-examination of some published HCI data.

THE ALIGNED RANK TRANSFORM FOR *N* FACTORS

This section describes the Aligned Rank Transform, generalizing it to an arbitrary number of factors. The ART is for use in circumstances similar to the parametric ANOVA, except that the response variable may be continuous or ordinal, and is not required to be normally distributed.

Background

Rank transformations have appeared in statistics for years [12]. Conover and Iman's [1] Rank Transform (RT) applies ranks, averaged in the case of ties, over a data set, and then uses the parametric F-test on the ranks, resulting in a nonparametric factorial procedure. However, it was subsequently discovered that this process produces inaccurate results for interaction effects [5,11], making the RT method unsuitable for factorial designs.

The Aligned Rank Transform (ART) [2,10] corrects this problem, providing accurate nonparametric treatment for both main and interaction effects [4,5,11]. It relies on a preprocessing step that first "aligns" the data for each effect (main or interaction) before assigning ranks, averaged in the case of ties. Data alignment is an established process in statistics [6] by which effects are estimated as marginal means and then "stripped" from the response variable so that all effects but one are removed.

Let's consider an example: In a two-factor experiment with effects A, B, and $A*B$, and response Y, testing for the significance of effect A means first stripping from Y estimates of effects B and $A*B$, leaving only a possible effect of A behind. This alignment results in Y_A', whose values are then ranked, producing Y_A''. Lastly, a full-factorial ANOVA is run with Y_A'' as the response and model terms A, B, and $A*B$, but importantly, only the effect of A is examined in the ANOVA table; B and $A*B$ are ignored. This process is then repeated for the effects of B and $A*B$, *i.e.*, on aligned ranks Y_B'' and Y_{A*B}'', respectively. Thus, to use the ART, responses Y from a study must be aligned and ranked for each effect of interest. This is a tedious process to do by hand, but *ARTool* or *ARTweb* make it easy.

ART Procedure for *N* Factors

We present the ART procedure in five steps:

Step 1. Compute residuals. For each raw response Y, compute its residual as

$$residual = Y - cell\ mean\ .$$

The cell mean is the mean for Y's "cell," *i.e.*, the average of all responses whose factors' levels match that of the Y response for which we're computing the residual. As Table 2 shows, cell means are computed using Y values from rows with matching levels of independent variables (X_1 and X_2). Thus, the cell mean in row 1 is the mean Y of s1 and s5.

Table 2. Example calculation of cell means.

Subject	X_1	X_2	Y	cell mean
s1	a	a	12	(12+19)/2
s2	a	b	7	(7+16)/2
s3	b	a	14	(14+14)/2
s4	b	b	8	(8+10)/2
s5	a	a	19	(12+19)/2
s6	a	b	16	(7+16)/2
s7	b	a	14	(14+14)/2
s8	b	b	10	(8+10)/2

Step 2. Compute estimated effects for all main and interaction effects. Let A, B, C, and D be factors with levels A_i, $i = 1..a$; B_j, $j = 1..b$; C_k, $k = 1..c$; D_ℓ, $\ell = 1..d$.

Let $\overline{A_i}$ be the mean response Y_i for rows where factor A is at level i. Let $\overline{A_iB_j}$ be the mean response Y_{ij} for rows where factor A is at level i and factor B is at level j. And so on. Let μ be the grand mean of Y over all rows.

One-way effects. The estimated main effect for a factor A with response Y_i is

$$= \overline{A_i} - \mu\ .$$

Two-way effects. The estimated effect for an $A*B$ interaction with response Y_{ij} is

$$= \overline{A_iB_j} - \overline{A_i} - \overline{B_j} + \mu\ .$$

Three-way effects. The estimated effect for an $A*B*C$ interaction with response Y_{ijk} is

$$= \overline{A_iB_jC_k} - \overline{A_iB_j} - \overline{A_iC_k} - \overline{B_jC_k} + \overline{A_i} + \overline{B_j} + \overline{C_k} - \mu\ .$$

Four-way effects. The estimated effect for an $A*B*C*D$ interaction with response $Y_{ijk\ell}$ is

$$\begin{aligned} &= \overline{A_iB_jC_kD_\ell} - \overline{A_iB_jC_k} - \overline{A_iB_jD_\ell} - \overline{A_iC_kD_\ell} - \overline{B_jC_kD_\ell} \\ &+ \overline{A_iB_j} + \overline{A_iC_k} + \overline{A_iD_\ell} + \overline{B_jC_k} + \overline{B_jD_\ell} + \overline{C_kD_\ell} \\ &- \overline{A_i} - \overline{B_j} - \overline{C_k} - \overline{D_\ell} + \mu\ . \end{aligned}$$

N-way effects. The generalized estimated effect for an N-way interaction is

$$= \overline{N\text{ way}}$$

$$- \sum\left(\overline{N\text{-1 way}}\right) + \sum\left(\overline{N\text{-2 way}}\right) - \sum\left(\overline{N\text{-3 way}}\right) + \sum\left(\overline{N\text{-4 way}}\right)$$

...

$- \sum\left(\overline{N\text{-}h\text{ way}}\right)$ // if h is odd, or

$+ \sum\left(\overline{N\text{-}h\text{ way}}\right)$ // if h is even

...

$- \mu$ // if N is odd, or

$+ \mu$ // if N is even.

Step 3. Compute aligned response Y'. The calculation is

Y' = residual + estimated effect, *i.e.*,

= result from Step 1 + result from Step 2.

Step 4. Assign averaged ranks *Y″*. Assign averaged ranks to a column of aligned observations *Y′* to create *Y″*. The smallest *Y′* receives rank 1, the next smallest *Y′* receives rank 2, and so on until the largest of *r* values receives rank *r*. In the case of a tie among *k* values, the average rank is the sum of ranks divided by *k*.

Step 5. Perform a full-factorial ANOVA on *Y″*. All main and interaction effects should be included in the model, but only the result corresponding to the effect for which *Y* was aligned as *Y′* should be considered. A fixed-effects ANOVA or a mixed-effects model analysis of variance can be used, the latter being useful for repeated measures [8].[2] Also, *post hoc* comparisons can be used; however, comparisons should be made only within effects for which the data was aligned.

Ensuring Correctness

ART users have two opportunities for ensuring correctness. First, every column of aligned responses *Y′* should sum to zero; *ARTool* and *ARTweb* verify this for the user. Second, a full-factorial ANOVA performed on the aligned (not ranked) responses *Y′* should show all effects stripped out (F=0.00, p=1.00) except for the effect for which the data were aligned. (An ANOVA on ranked responses *Y″* will often show nearly F=0.00, p=1.00, but the stripping is rarely as complete as for *Y′*.) The ability to check one's results is why *ARTool* and *ARTweb* produce not only ranked columns *Y″*, but also aligned columns *Y′*.

ARTOOL AND *ARTWEB*

To make alignment and ranking easy, we built *ARTool* (Fig. 1), which parses long-format data tables and produces aligned and ranked responses for all main and interaction effects. For example, with two factors and their interaction, *ARTool* produces three aligned columns and three ranked columns, all in *.csv format.

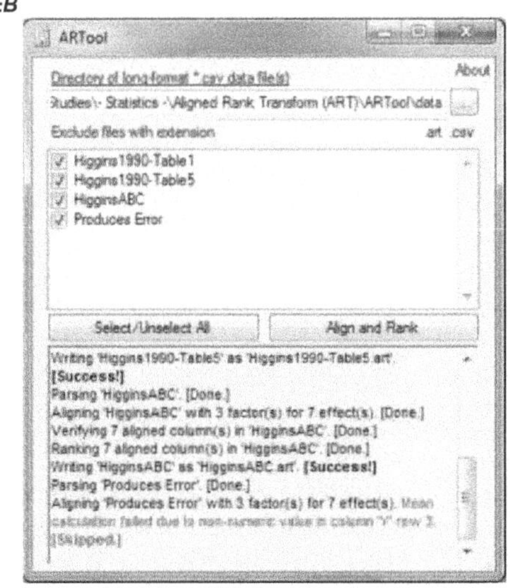

Figure 1. *ARTool* processes long-format data tables giving detailed feedback.

ARTool makes no assumptions about column names, level types or values, or row order. *ARTool* does assume that data is in long-format (one response per row), that the first column is the subject identifier (*S*), and that the last column is a numeric response (*Y*). All intervening columns are assumed to be factors (X_i's). In the case of an error, *ARTool* produces descriptive messages to aid researchers in locating and remedying problems. Because *ARTool* reproduces an *N*-factor table's original columns, *ARTool*'s output contains $(2+N) + 2(2^N\text{-}1)$ columns. *ARTool* is implemented in C# using the .NET 2.0 framework. Its Web-based equivalent is *ARTweb*, a Java program that runs in a Web browser. Both tools are available at http://faculty.washington.edu/wobbrock/art/ .

[2] A discussion of fixed-effects ANOVAS versus models with random effects is beyond the current scope.

RE-EXAMINATION OF DATA

In this section, we briefly re-examine some published HCI data. Because the ART procedure has been vetted in the statistics literature, our purpose is to show its utility and relevance, not prove its correctness. The first case shows how the approach can be used to provide interaction effects not available with Friedman tests. The second case shows how the ART can be used to free analysts from the distributional assumptions of ANOVA. The third case shows the nonparametric testing of repeated measures data.

Findlater *et al.* (CHI 2009)

In a study concerning adaptive menus, Findlater *et al.* [3] collected satisfaction ratings (1-7) from 24 participants on two independent factors: *Accuracy* (2 levels, between-subjects) and *Interface* (3 levels, within-subjects). In their paper, the authors used two separate Friedman tests to find satisfaction differences across the three levels of *Interface* within each level of *Accuracy*. The authors found no such differences, but commented on a possible interaction unexaminable by the Friedman test: "[I]n the High accuracy condition the mean rating for Short-Onset was lowest, whereas in the Low accuracy condition it was highest" [3] (p. 1660). An (inappropriate) parametric repeated measures ANOVA yields nonsignificant main effects for *Accuracy* ($F_{1,22}$=0.01, p=.936) and *Interface* ($F_{2,44}$=0.41, p=.668), but a significant interaction ($F_{2,44}$=4.47, p=.017). The nonparametric ART method also yields nonsignificant main effects for *Accuracy* ($F_{1,22}$=0.01, p=.920) and *Interface* ($F_{2,44}$=0.65, p=.529) and a significant interaction ($F_{2,44}$=4.12, p=.023). Incidentally, because this was a 2×2 mixed design, Kaptein *et al.*'s [7] online tool can also be used, and yields a similar interaction p-value (p=.020).

MacKenzie & Zhang (CHI 1999)

Nonparametric analyses are useful when ANOVA assumptions may be violated. In a 20-session longitudinal study comparing the OPTI and QWERTY stylus keyboards, MacKenzie & Zhang [9] used a parametric repeated measures ANOVA to analyze error rates for within-subjects factors *Session* ($F_{19,76}$=4.43, p<.001) and *Method* ($F_{1,4}$=12.14, p=.025), finding that OPTI had fewer errors but that both methods' errors increased over time. However, no *Session*Method* interaction was reported. Our re-examination of their data shows that under a parametric ANOVA, the interaction was marginal ($F_{19,76}$=1.57, p=.087). It also shows, however, that these data were non-normal for both OPTI (Shapiro-Wilk W=.95, p=.001) and QWERTY (W=.96, p=.003). In fact, error rates were lognormal for both OPTI (Kolmogorov's D=.08, p=.139) and QWERTY (D=.04, p=.150). If the data had been log-transformed, the *Session*Method* interaction would have, in fact, been significant ($F_{19,76}$=3.46, p<.001). An alternative to using a log-transform to correct for non-normality would have been to use a nonparametric procedure on the original data. With the ART, the main effects of *Session* ($F_{19,76}$=5.19, p<.001) and *Method* ($F_{1,4}$=10.64, p=.031) are still significant, and now their interaction is also significant ($F_{19,76}$=1.85, p=.032). Although OPTI had fewer overall errors, its errors increased faster than that of QWERTY, being quite similar from the 15th-20th sessions.

Wobbrock *et al.* (UIST 2007)

Wobbrock *et al.* [14] compared a new stroke recognizer to two published recognizers in a within-subjects study of gestures made at three different speeds by 10 participants. The researchers found that recognition errors were rare and highly skewed towards zero. They therefore regarded errors as "rare events" and used Poisson regression [13], which can be appropriate for such data. However, Poisson regression is a Generalized Linear Model (GZLM) and cannot handle repeated measures (see Table 1). Wobbrock *et al.* found significant effects of *Recognizer* ($\chi^2_{(2,N=780)}$=867.33, p<.001), *Speed* ($\chi^2_{(2,N=780)}$=24.56, p<.001), and *No. Train* ($\chi^2_{(1,N=780)}$=125.24, p<.001) on error counts. However, they found no significant interactions. By contrast, an (inappropriate) parametric mixed-effects model analysis of variance [8] gives the same significant main effects, but also a significant *Recognizer*No. Train* interaction ($F_{2,757}$=98.25, p<.001) and a marginal *Recognizer*Speed* interaction ($F_{4,757}$=2.27, p=.060). More appropriately, using the ART reduces the skew in the data, gives the same significant main effects, and now gives both significant *Recognizer*No. Train* ($F_{2,757}$=42.49, p<.001) and *Recognizer*Speed* ($F_{4,757}$=4.37, p=.002) interactions.

Some Limitations of the Aligned Rank Transform

In the above examples, the ART enabled the nonparametric testing of interactions, the avoidance of distributional assumptions, and the nonparametric testing of repeated measures. But the ART has limitations. For data exhibiting very high proportions of ties, the ART simply replaces those ties with tied ranks. If data exhibits extreme skew (*e.g.*, power-law distributions), the ART, as with any rank-based transform, will reduce that skew, which may be undesirable if distributions are meaningful. Lastly, alignment works best for completely randomized designs; it also works for other designs, but effects may not be entirely stripped out.

CONCLUSION

We have presented the Aligned Rank Transform for nonparametric analysis of factorial experiments using the familiar F-test. The ART offers advantages over more complex methods in its simplicity and usability. We offered the first generalized mathematics for an *N*-way ART and programs called *ARTool* and *ARTweb* to make alignment and ranking easy. By providing three examples of published data re-examined using the ART, we exhibited its benefits. It is our hope that researchers in HCI will find this convenient nonparametric method and our tool as useful as we have.

ACKNOWLEDGEMENTS

Thanks to Nelson Nogales, I. Scott MacKenzie, Krzysztof Z. Gajos, Parmit K. Chilana, and Jessica J. Tran. This work was supported in part by National Science Foundation grants IIS-0811063 and IIS-0811884.

REFERENCES

1. Conover, W.J. and Iman, R.L. (1981). Rank transformations as a bridge between parametric and nonparametric statistics. *The American Statistician 35* (3), 124-129.
2. Fawcett, R.F. and Salter, K.C. (1984). A Monte Carlo study of the F test and three tests based on ranks of treatment effects in randomized block designs. *Communications in Statistics: Simulation and Computation 13* (2), 213-225.
3. Findlater, L., Moffatt, K., McGrenere, J. and Dawson, J. (2009). Ephemeral adaptation: The use of gradual onset to improve menu selection performance. *Proc. CHI '09*. New York: ACM Press, 1655-1664.
4. Higgins, J.J., Blair, R.C. and Tashtoush, S. (1990). The aligned rank transform procedure. *Proc. Conf. on Applied Statistics in Agriculture*. Kansas State, 185-195.
5. Higgins, J.J. and Tashtoush, S. (1994). An aligned rank transform test for interaction. *Nonlinear World 1* (2), 201-211.
6. Hodges, J.L. and Lehmann, E.L. (1962). Rank methods for combination of independent experiments in the analysis of variance. *Annals of Mathematical Statistics 33* (2), 482-497.
7. Kaptein, M., Nass, C. and Markopoulos, P. (2010). Powerful and consistent analysis of Likert-type rating scales. *Proc. CHI '10*. New York: ACM Press, 2391-2394.
8. Littell, R.C., Henry, P.R. and Ammerman, C.B. (1998). Statistical analysis of repeated measures data using SAS procedures. *J. Animal Science 76* (4), 1216-1231.
9. MacKenzie, I.S. and Zhang, S.X. (1999). The design and evaluation of a high-performance soft keyboard. *Proc. CHI '99*. New York: ACM Press, 25-31.
10. Salter, K.C. and Fawcett, R.F. (1985). A robust and powerful rank test of treatment effects in balanced incomplete block designs. *Communications in Statistics: Simulation and Computation 14* (4), 807-828.
11. Salter, K.C. and Fawcett, R.F. (1993). The art test of interaction: A robust and powerful rank test of interaction in factorial models. *Communications in Statistics: Simulation and Computation 22* (1), 137-153.
12. Sawilowsky, S.S. (1990). Nonparametric tests of interaction in experimental design. *Review of Educational Research 60* (1), 91-126.
13. Vermunt, J.K. (1997). *Log-linear Models for Event Histories*. Thousand Oaks, CA: Sage Publications.
14. Wobbrock, J.O., Wilson, A.D. and Li, Y. (2007). Gestures without libraries, toolkits or training: A $1 recognizer for user interface prototypes. *Proc. UIST '07*. New York: ACM Press, 159-168.

Human Model Evaluation in Interactive Supervised Learning

Rebecca Fiebrink[1,2], Perry R. Cook[1,2], and Daniel Trueman[2]
Departments of [1]Computer Science and [2]Music
Princeton University
Princeton, New Jersey, USA
{fiebrink, prc, dtrueman}@princeton.edu

ABSTRACT
Model evaluation plays a special role in interactive machine learning (IML) systems in which users rely on their assessment of a model's performance in order to determine how to improve it. A better understanding of what model criteria are important to users can therefore inform the design of user interfaces for model evaluation as well as the choice and design of learning algorithms. We present work studying the evaluation practices of end users interactively building supervised learning systems for real-world gesture analysis problems. We examine users' model evaluation criteria, which span conventionally relevant criteria such as accuracy and cost, as well as novel criteria such as unexpectedness. We observed that users employed evaluation techniques—including cross-validation and direct, real-time evaluation—not only to make relevant judgments of algorithms' performance and interactively improve the trained models, but also to learn to provide more effective training data. Furthermore, we observed that evaluation taught users about what types of models were easy or possible to build, and users sometimes used this information to modify the learning problem definition or their plans for using the trained models in practice. We discuss the implications of these findings with regard to the role of generalization accuracy in IML, the design of new algorithms and interfaces, and the scope of potential benefits of incorporating human interaction in the design of supervised learning systems.

Author Keywords
Interactive machine learning, evaluation, gesture, music

ACM Classification Keywords
H.5.2 Information Interfaces and Presentation: User Interfaces—*Interaction Styles*; I.2.6 Artificial Intelligence: Learning

General Terms
Design, Human Factors

INTRODUCTION
Machine learning offers a set of powerful algorithmic tools for understanding, modeling, and making decisions from data. Application of these tools has been critical to advances in domains as diverse as bioinformatics, information retrieval, gaming, robotics, and beyond. Along with a growing number of human-computer interaction researchers, we are interested in the question of how to leverage human interaction and expertise in new ways to make machine learning even more effective and useful in more application domains. We are particularly interested in engaging human interaction throughout the process of building a working machine learning model, by enabling the user to iteratively evaluate the current state of the model and take appropriate actions to improve it.

Human model evaluation plays a critical role in an interactive machine learning context: evaluation methods are useful not only for informing the user about the relative or absolute quality of a given model, but also for informing the user how he or she might take action to improve it. As we seek to build effective and usable interactive machine learning systems, it is crucial to understand users' own evaluation criteria for models, the ways users engage different evaluation techniques to gain the information they need, and the ways users employ this knowledge to shape their future interactions with the system. This understanding can be used to inform the design of user interfaces for model evaluation, the choice and interpretation of model evaluation metrics, and the selection and design of learning algorithms themselves. It can also lead to a greater appreciation for how applied machine learning applications may stand to benefit from incorporating human interaction. It is precisely this understanding that we have sought in this work, through three studies observing end users employing interactive machine learning to build real-world gesture analysis systems in music.

Our most significant findings are summarized as follows: Users' criteria for model evaluation included more than just correctness, encompassing subjective judgments of properties such as cost, decision boundary shape, confidence, and complexity (which, notably, was sometimes highly desirable). The relative importance of these criteria and the way they were defined varied appreciably across applications. A hands-on, fine-grained, exploratory evaluation of models allowed users to judge them against these criteria and to learn

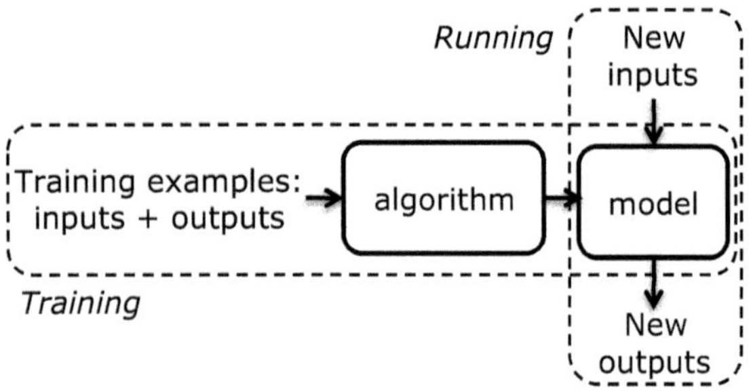

Figure 1. A supervised learning algorithm creates a model from training data. The trained model can then compute new output values from new inputs.

the information they most needed to improve models' behaviors. Cross-validation was sometimes useful for quick comparison and validation, but even when generalization accuracy was of high importance to the user, cross-validation accuracy did not necessarily correlate positively with the user's subjective rating of a model's quality. Finally, model evaluation also provided feedback to users that helped them learn to interact more effectively with the supervised learning process and to interactively discover and manage tradeoffs between building models that were easy to create and building models that were most useful in practice.

BACKGROUND AND MOTIVATION

Supervised Learning

This work concerns a family of machine learning and pattern recognition algorithms known as supervised learning. Here we will give only a very basic overview of supervised learning; a more thorough treatment can be found in [6], which is the reference for our overview unless otherwise indicated. A supervised learning algorithm is essentially a tool for producing a mathematical model or function that, given some input, produces some output. The algorithm infers, or *learns*, this model from a training dataset, which is a collection of data points or "instances" consisting of example inputs paired with their corresponding outputs, or "labels." After this model is built, it can compute new output values for new inputs, even for inputs not present in the training set. Figure 1 illustrates the relationship between the data, algorithm, training, and model.

The inputs to a model are vectors of numbers, or features. For example, a model of human gesture might take in a feature vector extracted from sensors worn on the body, where the features themselves are raw sensor values, statistics computed on those sensor values, or both. The output of a model is either a real number or one of a finite set of discrete labels, depending on whether the model is for regression or classification. For example, classification could be used to build a sign language alphabet classifier that outputs the written word a human is signing, as in [1]. On the other hand, regression could be used to build a continuous gesture-to-speech controller, such as one component of Fels and Hinton's Glove-TalkII, in which continuous hand motions result in gradually changing articulatory control over a speech synthesis algorithm [8].

A primary goal of supervised learning is to model the relationship between inputs and outputs in the training set in a way that allows *generalization*, producing reasonable outputs for new inputs not present in the training data. Concern for generalization is at the core of the theoretical analysis and design of many machine learning algorithms. In the PAC-learning framework, for example, a learning algorithm is by definition capable of classifying instances not (necessarily) in the training set with a high accuracy rate, with a high probability [21]. Widely-used algorithms such as AdaBoost and support vector machines are designed to explicitly to maximize generalization accuracy (that is, the proportion of future inputs that are assigned the correct label) [6].

An emphasis on generalization accuracy underlies many standard metrics used to evaluate the suitability of an algorithm (or parameterization thereof) for modeling a given dataset. Unless one knows the identity of all future inputs to a model and their proper labels (in which case building a perfect model is trivial), generalization accuracy must be estimated from the available data. Using accuracy on the model's training dataset is a poor estimate, as this can assign too favorable a rating to a model that has "overfit" to the training data and is poor at generalizing. So, the available data can be partitioned into a training set and a mutually exclusive test set for evaluating performance. Cross-validation is a commonly-used technique that repeats this procedure several times such that each available instance is present in the test set of a single iteration, then averages test set accuracy over all iterations. Alternative measures such as F-measure, cost, precision, recall, and area under ROC may be used under certain circumstances, but in each case, the goal remains to estimate the model's relevant future behavior from the available, finite data. In order to do this, it is standard for the learning algorithms and evaluation procedures to make the basic assumption that the future inputs to a model will look more or less like the training data. This can be stated probabilistically as the assumption that the training data and the future data examples are both sampled i.i.d.[1] from a shared distribution over the data space.

Interactive Machine Learning

Our work focuses on supporting human-computer interaction in the context of creating machine learning systems, where users are engaged in tasks including choosing and training a learning algorithm, evaluating and comparing models, and supplying training data. The scope of relevant users includes researchers applying machine learning techniques to data analysis in an application domain of their expertise, developers of user interfaces that contain machine learning components, and end users of software tools that directly engage the user in controlling some aspects of a machine learning system, such as providing training data and evaluating trained models.

There is an exciting thread of recent research investigating how human interaction can be leveraged in new ways in the

[1] independent and identically distributed; i.e., having a shared underlying probability distribution and being mutually independent

creation of machine learning systems. For example, ManiMatrix allows users to manipulate a confusion matrix to interactively steer a model's performance to reflect their priorities [16], and EnsembleMatrix harnesses human users to optimize ensembles of learners [20].

One significant opportunity for improving supervised learning systems using human interaction lies in enabling the user to evaluate a model, then edit its training dataset based on his or her expert judgments of how the model should improve. This approach was proposed under the term "interactive machine learning" by Fails and Olsen [7], whose Crayons system allows users to improve an image classification model by iteratively evaluating the system, providing new training data, and retraining. We have found this approach very useful in building systems for audio analysis [12] and musical gesture analysis [9]. This general approach has also been applied to handwriting analysis in CueTip [19], web image classification in CueFlik [13, 2, 3] (where it is termed "end-user interactive concept learning"), document analysis by Baker et al., [4], and sensor-based interaction design in Exemplar [15]. This body of work suggests that, for domains where it is feasible to provide additional training data, and where a human user has knowledge of the modeling problem, user modification of the training data allows a natural and effective means to take advantage of user expertise.

Motivation

We propose, along with prior work such as that of Amershi et al. [3], that interactive machine learning interfaces must not only enable the user to effectively edit the training data, but also supply him with the information he needs to most effectively guide the machine learning process. One aim of our work is to learn more about what this information entails, based on users' own criteria for evaluating models and the actions they take based on their evaluations. Additionally, in any machine learning application, the choice of algorithm and objective evaluation metrics reflect certain assumptions about the goals for the trained model, for example the goal of good generalization accuracy. A second aim of our work is therefore to interrogate how knowledge of end users' evaluation criteria and evaluation strategies can inform the selection or design of learning algorithms and evaluation metrics. Finally, though interactive machine learning of this type has not been widely studied in gesture analysis or in real-world applications, several of the users we have worked with have found it to be a transformative technique in their work in music. So, a third goal is to provide an enriched understanding of the merits of an interactive approach to supervised learning by studying users applying it to real-world problems in this domain.

APPLICATION DOMAIN, SOFTWARE, AND STUDIES

Application Domain and Software

We have observed and worked with users applying supervised learning to different human gesture modeling problems in computer music composition and performance. Some gesture analysis applications in music entail the identification and classification of discrete control gestures, in order to initiate computer audio or visual events (e.g., [18]). Certain of these applications closely resemble gesture analysis problems in the design of interfaces for general-purpose control (e.g., [23]) and gaming (e.g., [14]). Other applications in music involve the analysis of acoustic performers' musical gestures, for example analysis of the bowing articulations of a string player (e.g., [24]). These applications have certain parallels to analysis of natural human motion, for example in sports or medical diagnosis (e.g., [5]). A third category of applications that has no clear counterpart in non-creative domains is the design of new computer music instruments, where the trained model provides a function mapping from the sensed gesture space into the parameter space of an audio synthesis algorithm (e.g., [17]). There, the goal is to allow a human performer to "play" the synthesis algorithm expressively in real-time, not to model human gesture "correctly," per se. Each of these application categories is represented in at least one of our three studies.

Gesture modeling is a natural domain for applying interactive machine learning: when the goal is to build a gesture model of the user herself, it is easy to obtain representative training and evaluation data and to trust that she understands the goal of the modeling problem well enough to make reasonable assessments of model quality. However, despite widespread application of supervised learning to gesture modeling in music, previous work does not incorporate human interaction in this way.

The software used in all three studies, the Wekinator, has been designed to facilitate the interactive application of standard supervised learning algorithms in real-time domains, including music. The software is described in detail in [9]. It supports an iterative approach to IML illustrated in Figure 2, and it provides user interfaces for the creation, editing, and visualization of the training data, the selection of machine learning algorithms and their parameters, and the running of trained models on real-time inputs. Users are able to create and add to the training dataset by demonstrating different inputs (here, physical gestures) in real-time while providing the corresponding classification or regression labels using the Wekinator GUI. Users can also run trained models in real-time, producing a stream of real-time model outputs in response to an incoming stream of gestural inputs. In this regard, the Wekinator is similar to the Exemplar system [15], though the Wekinator is a more general-purpose tool that includes support for experimenting with different algorithms and applying machine learning to various real-time problems, including the analysis of audio and other non-gestural inputs.

The Wekinator includes standard algorithms for classification (AdaBoost.M1, J48 decision trees, k-nearest neighbor, and support vector machines) and multilayer perceptron neural networks for regression. While the Wekinator can take inputs from any external feature extractor, it includes several simple, built-in gestural feature extractors that allow users to provide gestural inputs using the webcam, the laptop's internal accelerometers, the trackpad (used as a 2-dimensional finger position sensor), and USB human interface devices (HIDs) including standard game controllers.

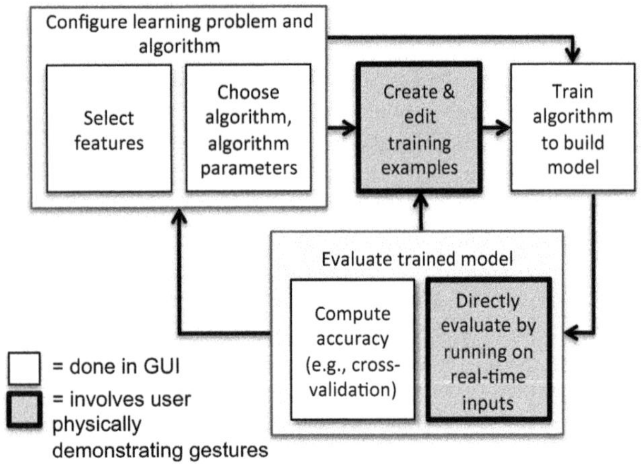

Figure 2. The interactive machine learning workflow supported by the Wekinator, where white actions are performed using the GUI and grey actions are performed through real-time demonstration.

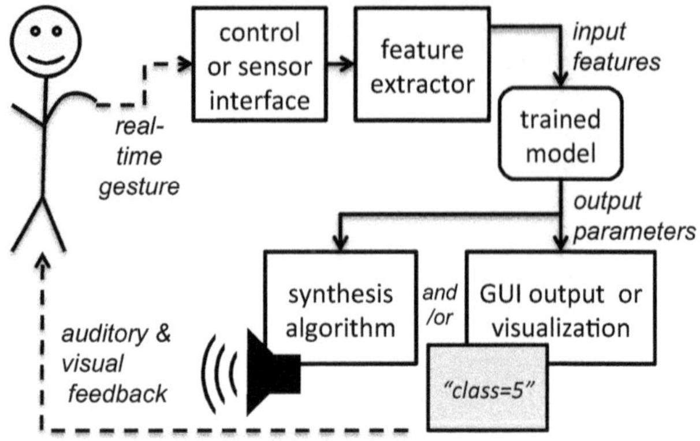

Figure 3. Direct model evaluation in the Wekinator. The user supplies new gestural inputs in real-time and evaluates the model's response by observing the sonic or visual processes controlled by the model's outputs.

In the Wekinator, users can evaluate trained models both by computing cross-validation and by hands-on, or "direct" evaluation. In direct evaluation, illustrated in Figure 3, the user provides inputs (here, gestures) in real-time and observes the model's behavior. The user can view the model's current outputs as text fields in the GUI, or the models' outputs can be sent over the Open Sound Control protocol[2] to another program, for example to control a visualization or sound synthesis algorithm in real-time.

Studies

We have conducted three studies of people applying supervised learning to their work in computer music. In the first study ("A"), we led a user-centered design process (see [22]) with seven composers, which focused on the refinement of the Wekinator. The participants were six PhD students and one faculty member in Princeton's Music Composition department. Participants met weekly for three hours each week for ten weeks. During each session, they discussed how they were using the software in their work, proposed improvements, asked questions, and experimented with the software. We took written notes of composers' questions, suggestions, and discussion topics. In between meetings, we implemented suggested improvements. After the ten meetings, participants completed a written questionnaire about their experiences in the process and their evaluation of the software.

The composers in Study A primarily used the Wekinator to build new musical instruments, creating neural network models that input the sensed human gestures and output control parameters that drove a digital audio synthesis algorithm in real-time. Participants used a variety of gestural input devices, including webcams, laptop motion sensors, HID devices, and custom-built sensor arrays. The two most frequently used synthesis algorithms required the setting of several (nine or more) real-valued control parameters, each of which had highly nonlinear and interdependent effects on the sound. Composers had found these algorithms difficult to control in a musically satisfying way using either a GUI or an explicitly programmed control sequence. More information about this study and a discussion of how participants used supervised learning in composition is published in [11].

In the second study ("B"), we observed a group of 21 students using the Wekinator in an assignment focused on supervised learning in interactive music performance systems. All students were enrolled in an interdisciplinary computer science and music course that included a significant emphasis on interactive performance technologies. Students ranged from first through fourth year in undergraduate study, they came from a variety of majors, and most had only rudimentary knowledge of machine learning. Prior to the assignment, the students received an in-class discussion and demo of the Wekinator software. In the assignment, each student was asked to use an input device (USB controller, motion sensor, trackpad, or webcam) to create two gesturally-controlled music performance systems, one that employed a classifier to trigger different sounds based on each gesture's label, and one that employed a neural network to create a continuously-controlled musical instrument (similar to Study A). These tasks were assigned in preparation for the midterm concert, which required students to compose and perform pieces using interactive systems that they had built (though not necessarily the systems built during the assignment). The software logged the students' actions during both tasks. The assignment also included 12 short-answer questions about the process of creating the two systems. Students were graded on completing the assignment and answering the questions thoughtfully.

The third study ("C") was a case study in which we worked with a professional cellist/composer to build a gesture recognition system for a sensor-equipped cello bow. This bow, called the "K-Bow,"[3] contains sensors for measuring the position and motion of the bow in real-time, including acceleration along three axes, tilt, horizontal and vertical position of the bow relative to the instrument, hair tension, and grip pressure. The goal of our work with the cellist was to build a

[2] http://opensoundcontrol.org/

[3] http://www.keithmcmillen.com/products/k-bow/

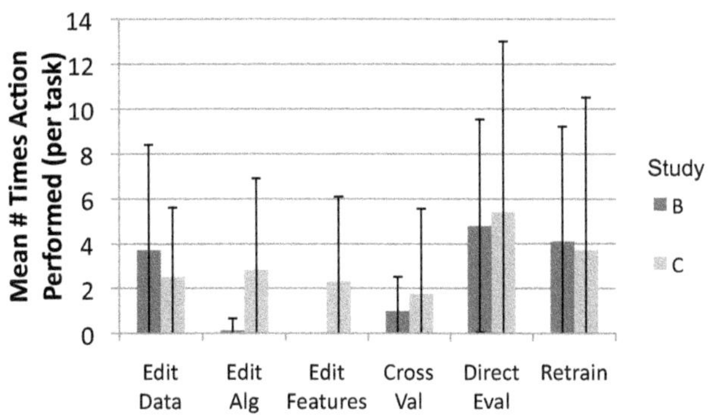

Figure 4. The mean number of times each interaction was performed, for each task and user in B, and for each task in C.

set of gesture classifiers to process the bow sensor values in real-time and produce musically appropriate labels. These labels could then be sent to the cellists' own composition programs in Max/MSP (a standard music composition environment) and used to influence computer-generated sound and/or visuals. Following a preliminary study with the cellist to develop infrastructure for communicating the bow outputs to the Wekinator and to choose gestures to classify [10], in Study C we worked with the cellist to construct eight robust gesture classifiers that labeled the bow's vertical position, horizontal position, roll, speed, articulation style, direction, position on or off the string, and grip squeeze strength. Throughout this process, the software logged all actions and saved all iterations of the trained gesture models. We also solicited the cellist's subjective rating of each model's overall quality, and we recorded observations of the model-building process using video and written notes.

FINDINGS

Interactive, Iterative Model-Building

Participants in all three studies took an approach to model-building in which they interactively created the training data from scratch, then iteratively built models, evaluated the models, and modified the models by changing the training dataset, learning algorithms, selected features, and/or algorithm parameters. Students in Study B retrained the algorithm an average of 4.1 times per task ($\sigma = 5.1$), and the cellist in C retrained an average of 3.7 times per task ($\sigma = 6.8$). In between retrainings, users most frequently changed the model behavior by editing the training data. Figure 4 summarizes the logged actions of users in B and C. For Study A, participants' questionnaires indicated that they also iteratively retrained the models, and they almost always chose to modify the models only by editing the training dataset. In all studies, retraining of the models was nearly always fast enough to enable uninterrupted interaction with the system (i.e., a few seconds or less).

The Use of Cross-validation

In Study A, composers never used cross-validation. In B and C, cross-validation was used occasionally; on average, students in B used it 1.0 times per task ($\sigma = 1.5$), and the cellist in C used it 1.8 times per task ($\sigma = 3.8$).

The five students in Study B who commented on their use of cross-validation indicated that they treated a high cross-validation accuracy as reliable evidence that a model was performing well. At least one student used cross-validation to validate his own model-building ability, writing "Following [dataset creation], I would usually quickly check the cross-validation and training accuracy and see if Wekinator thought that my model was a good one. If it was, my next step was usually to run the model myself and observe how it reacted to different gestures." This echoes the findings of Amershi et al. [3], who observed that users felt pressure to optimize cross-validation accuracy as an end in itself, rather than using it as an informative tool.

In Study C, cross-validation was used to quickly and objectively compare alternative classifier algorithms on the same dataset. This was done either after direct evaluation had shown that a reasonably good model had been built from the current training dataset, and it was uncertain which algorithm might perform most accurately, or when direct evaluation had revealed the learning problem to be particularly stubborn, and many different algorithms and feature selections were tried in succession to see if any one might result in a usable model. Cross-validation was convenient for this purpose because it provided a faster and more consistent way of comparing models than direct evaluation (each round of cross-validation took, on average, 1.1 seconds; $\sigma = 1.5$).

The Use of Direct Evaluation

Participants were also able to perform direct, hands-on evaluation to assess model performance. In direct evaluation in Studies A and B, models' real-time outputs drove sound synthesis algorithms. In C, the cellist had the option of displaying outputs textually in a GUI or controlling a live visualization, as discussed below.

Participants in all three studies used direct evaluation more frequently than cross-validation. Participants in A only used direct evaluation; participants in B performed direct evaluation an average of 4.8 ($\sigma = 4.8$) times per task, and the cellist in C performed direct evaluation 5.4 ($\sigma = 7.6$) times per task. (Note that C required a minimum of one direct evaluation per retraining, as the cellist was required to assign each model iteration a subjective rating based on her evaluation.) Compared to cross-validation, direct evaluation was used under a wider variety of circumstances and to evaluate the model against a wider array of subjective criteria. In the following section, we discuss the criteria users employed when directly evaluating models, and how users took action to improve models against these criteria.

Direct Evaluation Criteria

Correctness

Predictably, direct evaluation was employed to systematically check a model's correctness over a range of the input space of gestures. In all studies—including the expressive instrument design projects in A and B, where there was no objectively right or wrong model behavior—users identified the model's behavior as incorrect when it produced an output contrary to what they believed was appropriate and expected. Users typically reacted to this finding by modifying the training dataset—adding new inputs similar to those that caused the error, but with the correct labels—and retraining. In extreme cases of failure, users deleted the training set and recreated it from scratch.

Cost

Our observations suggest that users held an implicit error cost function that variably penalized model mistakes based on both the type of misclassifications (i.e., the user's label and the model's label) and their locations in the gesture space. For example, the cellist in C verbally indicated that classification mistakes a human cellist might easily make were less problematic. Another concern for users in A and B was whether a model could produce desirable or correct outputs for the types of gestures that would be used in a performance; the model's behavior on gestures not used in performance was inconsequential. Note that, for these users, the goal of applying supervised learning was not to model a gestural vocabulary that was strictly defined a priori: the users had considerable leeway in choosing which gestures would be used in performance. One student in B wrote about his strategy for designing the training set: "I tried to assess which [sounds] I would use more often and correlate them with [features] that were easier to obtain on the [input device]..." One role of direct evaluation was to search for input gestures that produced good outputs and practice them to ensure that they could be performed reliably. Several users in A and B likened this to practicing a traditional musical instrument, and just as in learning to play the violin, for example, users accepted responsibility for adjusting and improving their own performance-time actions to ensure good behavior of the model. In other words, users were not only seeking to improve the model to minimize cost, but they were also interactively attempting to adjust the cost function itself to favor the model.

In Study A, misclassification cost was also higher for examples similar to those in the training set: some composers indicated that they designed their training examples with the explicit intention of using the model to play those chosen sounds when they made the corresponding chosen gestures, and they were not happy when the trained model did not allow this. Composers were typically much less concerned with the model behavior matching their pre-formed expectations for input gestures dissimilar to those in the training set.

Decision Boundary Shape

In Study C, the cellist occasionally complained that, as she gradually changed from one bow gesture to another, a classifier's output might jump around unpredictably before stabilizing. When classifying horizontal bow position, for example, it was very important to her that the classifier cleanly switch from a label of "frog" to a label of "middle" at some point during a down-bow stroke, rather than jump between the two; it was less important that this label switching happen at a precise horizontal position. In other words, the shape and smoothness of the classifier decision boundaries in the gesture space were more important than their exact locations. Actions taken to smooth jagged decision boundaries included changing algorithm parameters (e.g., increasing k in k-nearest neighbor) and adding smoothly-labeled training data along the boundary area.

Label Confidence and Posterior Shape

In Study C, the cellist also took model confidence into account when evaluating its quality. The cellist was proficient in Max/MSP, and she worked with us during the study to design several simple Max/MSP visualizations to help her understand more about the model during direct evaluation. One frequently-used visualization displayed the model's estimated posterior probability distribution over the set of class labels. When the model classified her current bow gesture correctly but also assigned relatively high posterior probabilities to several incorrect labels, the user expressed dissatisfaction (at one point exclaiming, "Come on, be more sure than that!") and attempted to improve the model's confidence, usually by adding more training data. The cellist also considered the information gained from the posterior distribution as potentially helpful for improving the practical usefulness of a poorly-performing classifier. For example, when evaluating an articulation classifier using the posterior visualization, she noticed that although the model often output the wrong label for three of the articulations, the posterior distribution for these articulations had a predictable "signature" shape that could be post-processed by some simple code to produce the correct label.

Complexity and Unexpectedness

In Study A, composers valued models that produced sonically interesting parameterizations of the synthesis algorithm, which a human could manipulate over time in a musically sensitive way. Composers typically did not construct the models with a full set of physical and musical gestures already in mind; rather, a common strategy for building the models was to choose a few different and interesting synthesis parameter values that they wanted the instrument to be capable of playing, match each of these with a different gestural input in the training set, then directly evaluate the trained model to discover and explore the sounds that arose as they moved between and around the gestures present in the training set.

When evaluating the model using gestures outside the training set, two of the characteristics that were most important to composers were its complexity and unexpectedness. Unlike in a typical machine learning application, complexity was desirable, and composers sometimes added training data with the explicit intention of making the model more complex. Some composers remarked that the complexity of functions generated by the Wekinator's neural networks made their new instruments feel more like traditional, acoustic instruments, which by nature involve very complicated relationships between the physical gestures of a performer and the sound produced. Additionally, composers valued the fact that they could be surprised by the sounds generated by a gesture not in the training set, allowing them to find unimagined and compositionally useful sounds in the synthesis space.

Subjective Evaluation Versus Cross-validation

In Study C, every time an algorithm was trained or retrained, the cellist evaluated the model using direct evaluation and assigned it a subjective rating from 1 to 10. After the completion of the study, we computed cross-validation accuracy for all models from the logged data. For each of the six classification tasks where three or more training iterations were performed, we computed the Pearson's correlation between the cellist's rating of each model and its cross-validation accuracy. Even though model accuracy was extremely important to the user, the data show that a model's cross-validation accuracy did not always positively correlate with its subjective rating. The horizontal position, vertical position, bow direction, and on/off string classification tasks had negative correlation coefficients (-0.59, -0.44, -0.74, and -0.50), while speed and articulation classification tasks had positive coefficients (0.65 and 0.93).

In the four tasks with negative correlations, the training sets of certain iterations provided representations of the learning problem that were both inaccurate and simple to model. For example, an initial version of the horizontal position training set contained mislabeled examples for all instances of one class. The training dataset was easy to classify correctly but the resulting model was useless. In the other tasks, the negative correlation likely resulted from the cellist unknowingly co-varying the bowing class of interest with more easily distinguishable aspects of the gesture (such as the string being played), effectively leading the model to learn the wrong concept. In all four cases, therefore, problems with the training set were undetectable using cross-validation. Direct evaluation allowed the cellist to discover the problems, fix them, and ultimately create models rated "10" for each task.

Evaluation and Human Learning

Cross-validation and direct evaluation served as feedback mechanisms to the users, enabling them to discover whether or not their recent changes to the training set or algorithms had had the desired effect on the retrained models. In fact, as the Wekinator did not provide any machine learning tutorials or hints, the feedback obtained from cross-validation or direct evaluation was the only mechanism for users to learn how their actions were likely to affect the system. In this way, evaluation actions trained the users, none of whom had significant experience or instruction in machine learning, to use the system more effectively.

Teaching Users to Provide Better Data

In Study B, when asked about their strategies for model building, ten students indicated that they had learned during their interaction with the software to provide training data that more clearly expressed their intentions. One student wrote, "In collecting data, it is crucial, especially in Motion Sensor, that the positions recorded are exaggerated (i.e. tilt all the way, as opposed to only halfway)." Another wrote, "I tried to use very clear examples of contrast in [input features]... If the examples I recorded had values that were not as satisfactory, I deleted them and rerecorded... until the model understood the difference." Some students even learned to balance class proportions in the training set ("Each extreme of a parameter should be trained with roughly the same number of examples"), even though this more advanced machine learning concept was not introduced in class.

The cellist in Study C remarked that her strategy for providing training data "definitely evolved over the training sessions." By the end of the study, her strategy for classification problems she knew from experience were easier to model was to provide as varied a training dataset as possible, varying "which string, bow position (frog to tip and fingerboard to bridge), speed and preparation (i.e., how high off the string I would start)... " to make the trained model maximally robust to these effects. On the other hand, for problems that she discovered were more difficult to model, she started by simplifying the problem represented in the training dataset, keeping variables such as speed and choice of string constant across all training examples in order to build a model more likely to discriminate between classes based on only truly relevant criteria.

Teaching Users What is Possible

Users often adapted their goals for the system based on what they discovered through direct evaluation. This was especially true for users in A and B, who had some choice in the types of models they asked the computer to learn. One reason for adaption was that, as machine learning novices, users did not have well-formed expectations of how different algorithms worked or what could be accomplished with supervised learning. When discovering that their efforts were failing to produce a model that worked how they wanted (for example, failing to create a neural network with a smoothly linear mapping between a gesture and a synthesis parameter), users adjusted their goals. Another reason for adaptation was that, through hands-on experimentation with the system, users discovered that models performed in unexpected ways that they actually liked better than their initial goals. Twelve students in B indicated that they changed their minds about which gestures they wanted to use after their initial efforts failed to produce a model that worked how they wanted, or when they discovered that a model did something unexpectedly useful for a new gesture. Two other students and the majority of the composers indicated that their strategy was to choose performance-time gestures to use solely through exploration, rather than start from a set of gestures they were intent on incorporating. In C, the cellist's goals were more subtly adjusted to reflect knowledge about what a model was able to learn alongside knowledge of what type of model would be most useful in practice. For example, after building a speed classifier that worked well for three classes, she decided to try building a finer-grained speed classifier for five classes.

Providing Feedback on Users' Gestural Techniques

In Study C, the cellist also gained a new perspective on her own bowing technique, when she discovered through consistently poor system behavior that her training data was not as clear as she thought it had been. For example, noticing that the bowing articulation model was not discriminating well between riccocet and spiccato strokes, she reexamined her own technique for those strokes and discovered that her spiccato technique actually needed to be improved in order to be less like riccocet. After adjusting her technique, she was able to both train a model that performed better and produce a better cello sound.

Usability and Usefulness of the Software

Our findings indicate that participants understood how to use the software, found it useful, and were engaged in meaningful interactions during our observations. At the conclusion of Study A, composers highly agreed that the Wekinator allowed them to create more expressive models than other techniques (mean = 4.5 on a 5-point Likert scale) and to create models more easily (mean = 4.6). In Study B, students highly agreed that they were able to create models that learned what they wanted (mean = 4.6), that their classifiers provided reliable classifications (mean = 4.9), and that their neural network models were musically expressive (mean = 4.1). All students subsequently succeeded in employing the software in their midterm performances. In C, the cellist rated the quality of six of the eight final bow gesture classifiers as "10" and the other two as "9" on a 10-point scale. A more thorough evaluation of software usefulness and usability is provided in [9].

DISCUSSION

Model Evaluation in Interactive Contexts

Our observations suggest that metrics such as test set accuracy or cross-validation accuracy may be, on their own, insufficient for assessing the quality of models designed for interactive human use. First, users were concerned with evaluating more than the overall accuracy or error rate. Direct evaluation allowed them to identify where and how the model was likely to make mistakes, enabling them to make a cost-sensitive assessment based on criteria like error severity and the extent to which it might be possible to avoid using error-prone gestures during a performance. Direct evaluation also allowed users to evaluate models against highly subjective criteria, such as "unexpectedness" of model behavior.

Furthermore, in interactive machine learning, cross-validation or held-out test set accuracy may be problematic for other reasons. As demonstrated by the negative correlation between cross-validation accuracy and user rating for some tasks in Study C, the training set may be a particularly poor resource for estimating generalization performance during certain stages of the interactive model creation process, especially when the human has not yet discovered problems with the training data. Additionally, in this approach to IML, the user manipulates the training set as a means to directly influence the trained model's behavior, for example by adding properly-labeled examples to correct mistakes in error-prone areas of the input gesture space. Given that the user is consciously employing the training set to manipulate model performance, it is not necessarily reasonable to assume that the training examples will at all resemble the examples seen by the model in the future. Speaking probabilistically, it may be too strong an assumption to say that the training examples and the future examples are sampled i.i.d from a shared underlying distribution. So, evaluation based on a test set partition of the user-generated training data may not be meaningful for estimating model performance on future inputs. At the same time, in the case that the person driving the interactive machine learning process will also be the future user of the trained model, the user may know how to generate evaluation data that is more representative of future inputs.

Generalization Accuracy and the Choice and Design of Algorithms for IML

Supervised learning algorithms are often explicitly designed with the goal of maximizing generalization accuracy. Generalization accuracy was indeed a goal for many of our observed users, in that they intended the system to produce reasonably accurate outputs for gestural inputs that were not identical to those in the training set. In the music performance scenarios for which users were creating the models, there would be inevitable variation in future inputs due to human error and circumstances including room lighting and camera position when using the video input, or non-identical sensor calibrations when using the sensor bow. To some degree, the human user can mitigate the effects of changing circumstances by adding more training examples and retraining. But so long as the goal is to create a robust system for use in performance, the ability to accurately generalize to previously unseen inputs remains important.

As we have discussed, users were concerned with other model characteristics in addition to accuracy. When these other criteria are known and quantifiable, it may be useful to choose or design algorithms that explicitly consider these criteria during training. For example, algorithms might explicitly enforce decision boundary smoothness or function complexity. Alternatively, it may be useful to employ algorithms that expose parameters that users can employ to explicitly adjust models along dimensions that are important to them. For example, many algorithms can incorporate a regularization parameter controlling the degree to which overfitting is penalized [6], and exposing this parameter to the user could allow a means of interactively adjusting the complexity of the model.

Many learning algorithms are designed to produce a model with good generalization accuracy (as estimated, again, from the available training data), at the cost of good training accuracy. Even when generalization accuracy is of primary importance to the user, privileging generalization accuracy at the expense of training accuracy might be problematic in this type of interactive machine learning context. First, for the reasons discussed above, the training set may sometimes be a poor resource for estimating generalization accuracy. Second, the IML user relies on the algorithm's attention to the training examples as the primary means of influencing the model's behavior after training. By down-weighting the importance of training accuracy—that is, by being willing to misclassify portions of the training dataset—the algorithm may be ignoring an intentional attempt by the user to shape the model's behavior. It is possible, therefore, that training accuracy may play a more important role in interactive supervised learning than in conventional supervised learning. Future work might investigate whether algorithms such as k-nearest neighbor, which does not explicitly address generalization accuracy and which can trivially achieve perfect training accuracy, are preferred by interactive machine learning users under certain circumstances.

The Benefits of Interactive Evaluation

Model evaluation provided a feedback loop that aided users in developing effective strategies for building working systems. Users were "trained" by the system to take appropriate actions to improve models according to their subjective goals, for example learning to provide clearer training examples. This feedback also helped users learn what was possible to accomplish with the given learning algorithms and features; in response, users sometimes adapted their interactions with a model during performance to work around its shortcomings. At other times, users made changes to flexible aspects of the learning problem, such as the number or nature of gesture classes to be used, in order to create models that were both feasible to build and most useful in practice. These behaviors bode especially well for the usefulness of interactive machine learning in other domains where users have some freedom in defining and changing the concept learned by the models, or where users are able to adapt their behavior to treat a trained model more "gently." In these cases, interactive design of the machine learning component can help users choose the most appropriate learning concepts and learn to provide good training data for those concepts.

Though previous work, notably that of Amershi et al. [2], has explored ways to provide the user with visual interfaces to efficiently evaluate trained models and choose new training examples, it is not clear how to extend this work to modeling problems for which there is no existing dataset of unlabeled examples, or in domains for which it is difficult to visualize examples. In this work, the exploratory nature of direct evaluation provided a means for users to assess the trained model's behaviors against a variety of subjective criteria, and the example-level granularity of the knowledge gained this way was critical to both making judgments of model quality and making corrective edits to the training data. Further work exploring how to guide users' evaluations to interesting or important areas of the model input space would be valuable. Additionally, it is worth exploring whether a gesturally-controlled, example-granularity exploration of the input space might be useful for directly evaluating models in domains where the model input itself is not human gesture.

CONCLUSIONS

We have observed people applying interactive supervised learning to several gestural analysis problems in computer music. User interactions included creating training data by real-time demonstration, evaluating models by computing cross-validation accuracy and by running them on new inputs in real-time, and iteratively improving models by changing aspects of the training data, algorithm, or features, and retraining. These interactions are appropriate for domains in which the user is capable of efficiently supplying training data and competently judging the suitability of the trained models for the application context.

In this work, we examined the criteria users held for assessing the quality of trained models, the techniques they employed to evaluate models, and the ways that model evaluation informed their goals and interactions with the system. We observed that cross-validation was sometimes useful for quickly assessing accuracy, but direct evaluation allowed users to make accuracy assessments that were cost-sensitive, assess models against a wider set of criteria, and detect problems with inaccurate models that were undiscoverable using cross-validation alone. Users employed cross-validation and direct evaluation to inform their immediate next actions with the system—for example, the choice of a certain algorithm, or the addition of particular training data. Model evaluation also provided feedback that enabled users to develop more effective interaction strategies for guiding the machine learning outcomes (especially strategies for providing better training data). Finally, through iterations of model building and evaluation, users learned about what was feasible to accomplish with the given features and algorithms, and they sometimes modified the learning problem definition or their goals for how the models would be used in order to create models that were most useful in practice.

From these observations, we conclude that supervised learning models intended to be ultimately used in interactive contexts should be evaluated with attention to the model qualities important to users in those contexts; in particular, objective accuracy metrics such as cross-validation may not be sufficient to allow researchers or system designers to validate or compare model quality. We also conclude that exploratory evaluation of models can complement objective metrics in allowing users to evaluate models against a wide range of criteria. We propose that IML systems may benefit from the use of existing or new algorithms designed to optimize various quantities (beyond generalization accuracy, and possibly including training accuracy) that are important to users. Lastly, we conclude that a previously-unexplored benefit of IML is the ability for human domain experts to improve the ultimate usefulness of a trained model, through iteratively using model evaluation outcomes to inform changes to the learning problem and to the context in which the model will be used.

ACKNOWLEDGEMENTS

We are grateful to our participants for their time, feedback, and insights. This material is based upon work supported under a National Science Foundation Graduate Research Fellowship. Any opinions, findings, conclusions or recommendations expressed in this publication are those of the author and do not necessarily reflect the views of the National Science Foundation. This work is also supported by the Kimberly and Frank H. Moss '71 Research Innovation Fund and the David A. Gardner '69 Magic Project.

REFERENCES

1. Allen, J. M., Asselin, P. K., and Foulds, R. American sign language fingerspelling recognition system. In *Proc. of the IEEE 29th Bioengineering Conference* (2003).
2. Amershi, S., Fogarty, J., Kapoor, A., and Tan, D.

Overview-based example selection in end-user interactive concept learning. In *Proc. of the ACM Symposium on User Interface Software and Technology (UIST '09)* (2009), 247–256.

3. Amershi, S., Fogarty, J., Kapoor, A., and Tan, D. Examining multiple potential models in end-user interactive concept learning. In *Proc. of the SIGCHI Conference on Human Factors in Computing Systems* (2010), 1357–1360.
4. Baker, K., Bhandari, A., and Thotakura, R. An interactive automatic document classification prototype. In *Proc. of the Third Workshop on Human-Computer Interaction and Information Retrieval* (2009), 30–33.
5. Begga, R., and Kamruzzaman, J. A machine learning approach for automated recognition of movement patterns using basic, kinetic and kinematic gait data. *Journal of Biomechanics 38* (2005), 401–408.
6. Bishop, C. M. *Pattern Recognition and Machine Learning*, 2nd ed. Springer, 2007.
7. Fails, J. A., and Olsen, Jr., D. R. Interactive machine learning. In *Proc. of the International Conference on Intelligent User Interfaces (IUI '03)* (2003), 39–45.
8. Fels, S. S., and Hinton, G. E. Glove-TalkII: An adaptive gesture-to-formant interface. In *Proc. of Computer Human Interaction (SIGCHI95)* (1995), 456–463.
9. Fiebrink, R. *Real-time Human Interaction with Supervised Learning Algorithms for Music Composition and Performance.* PhD thesis, Princeton University, Princeton, NJ, USA, January 2011.
10. Fiebrink, R., Schedel, M., and Threw, B. Constructing a personalizable gesture-recognizer infrastructure for the K-Bow. In *Proc. of the 3rd International Conference on Music and Gesture (MG3)* (2010).
11. Fiebrink, R., Trueman, D., Britt, C., Nagai, M., Kaczmarek, K., Early, M., Daniel, M. R., Hege, A., and Cook, P. R. Toward understanding human-computer interaction in composing the instrument. In *Proc. of the International Computer Music Conference* (2010).
12. Fiebrink, R., Wang, G., and Cook, P. R. Support for MIR prototyping and real-time applications in the ChucK programming language. In *Proc. of the International Conference on Music Information Retrieval* (2008).
13. Fogarty, J., Tan, D., Kapoor, A., and Winder, S. CueFlik: interactive concept learning in image search. In *Proc. of the SIGCHI Conference on Human Factors in Computing Systems* (2008), 29–38.
14. Gohring, N. Mundie: Microsoft's research depth enabled Kinect. *PCWorld* (July 2010).
15. Hartmann, B., Abdulla, L., Mittal, M., and Klemmer, S. R. Authoring sensor-based interactions by demonstration with direct manipulation and pattern recognition. In *Proc. of the SIGCHI Conference on Human Factors in Computing Systems* (2007), 145–154.
16. Kapoor, A., Lee, B., Tan, D., and Horvitz, E. Interactive optimization for steering machine classification. In *Proc. of the SIGCHI Conference on Human Factors in Computing Systems* (2010), 1343–1352.
17. Lee, M., Freed, A., and Wessel, D. Neural networks for simultaneous classification and parameter estimation in musical instrument control. *Adaptive and Learning Systems 1706* (1992), 244–55.
18. Peng, L., and Gerhard, D. A Wii-based gestural interface for computer-based conducting systems. In *Proc. of the Conference on New Interfaces for Musical Expression* (2009).
19. Shilman, M., Tan, D., and Simard, P. CueTIP: A mixed-initiative interface for correcting handwriting errors. In *Proc. of the ACM Symposium on User Interface Software and Technology (UIST '06)* (2006).
20. Talbot, J., Lee, B., Kapoor, A., and Tan, D. S. EnsembleMatrix: Interactive visualization to support machine learning with multiple classifiers. In *Proc. of the SIGCHI Conference on Human Factors in Computing Systems* (2009), 1283–1292.
21. Valiant, L. G. A theory of the learnable. *Communications of the ACM 27*, 11 (1984), 1134–1142.
22. Vredenburg, K., Mao, J.-Y., Smith, P. W., and Carey, T. A survey of user-centered design practice. In *Proc. of the SIGCHI Conference on Human Factors in Computing Systems* (2002), 471–478.
23. Wilson, A., and Shafer, S. XWand: UI for intelligent spaces. In *Proc. of the SIGCHI Conference on Human Factors in Computing Systems* (2003), 545–552.
24. Young, D. Classification of common violin bowing techniques using gesture data from a playable measurement system. In *Proc. of the Conference on New Interfaces for Musical Expression* (2008).

CueT: Human-Guided Fast and Accurate Network Alarm Triage

Saleema Amershi[†‡], **Bongshin Lee**[†], **Ashish Kapoor**[†], **Ratul Mahajan**[†], **Blaine Christian**[*]

[†] Microsoft Research
One Microsoft Way
Redmond, WA 98052
{bongshin, akapoor, ratul}
@microsoft.com

[‡]Computer Science & Engineering
DUB Group,
University of Washington
Seattle, WA 98195
samershi@cs.washington.edu

[*]Microsoft Corporation
One Microsoft Way
Redmond, WA 98052
blainech@microsoft.com

ABSTRACT
Network alarm triage refers to grouping and prioritizing a stream of low-level device health information to help operators find and fix problems. Today, this process tends to be largely manual because existing tools cannot easily evolve with the network. We present CueT, a system that uses interactive machine learning to learn from the triaging decisions of operators. It then uses that learning in novel visualizations to help them quickly and accurately triage alarms. Unlike prior interactive machine learning systems, CueT handles a highly dynamic environment where the groups of interest are not known a-priori and evolve constantly. A user study with real operators and data from a large network shows that CueT significantly improves the speed and accuracy of alarm triage compared to the network's current practice.

Author Keywords
Interactive Machine Learning, Visualization, Triage.

ACM Classification Keywords
H.5.2. [User Interfaces]: Graphical User Interface.

General Terms
Algorithms, Design, Human Factors.

INTRODUCTION
Triaging alarms is the first line of defense for modern computer networks. Triage is the process by which the multitude of low-level alarms (e.g., high link utilization, fan failure) generated by individual devices are grouped and prioritized. These groups are investigated by network engineers for problems with the network. Grouping related alarms, which likely stem from the same problem, helps engineers by reducing the number of issues they need to investigate and giving them a broader view of the problem than what an individual alarm provides. It is critical that triage is fast and accurate so engineers are not misled and problems can be identified and resolved quickly.

Many automated systems have been developed for alarm triage (see [9, 17] for reviews). However, despite years of effort, these systems are never fully accurate due to the complexity of the problem. Large networks have thousands of diverse devices, each generating a different set of alarms. Further, because each network is different and the set of devices within a network changes with time, it is very challenging to develop systems that work across networks. Therefore, to cope with the inherent inaccuracy of automated systems, networks invariably employ human operators (so called "Tier 1" operators) for alarm triage. These operators are required to sift through the thousands of alarms per day that can be missed by automation.

We explore a fundamentally different approach for alarm triage. Since human operators need to be involved in the triage process anyway, we ask if we can learn from their actions and in turn use that learning to assist them. By learning continuously and in situ from operator actions, the assistance provided would better fit the network and its unique practices as well as evolve with the network.

We develop CueT (Figure 1), a system that combines novel visualizations with interactive machine learning for fast and accurate alarm triage. CueT maintains a constantly-updating, machine-learning-based model for the triage process. As alarms arrive, CueT provides an operator with recommendations on how to group the alarms based on its model at that instant. The operator inspects the recommendations along with CueT's visualization of its confidence in them, and decides how to triage. CueT then learns from these operator actions and updates its model.

Our evaluation of CueT demonstrates the effectiveness of our approach. Testing with human operators and real data from a large, global network with approximately 15,000 devices, we show that CueT significantly improves the accuracy and reduces the time required for alarm triage.

The contributions of this paper are:

- A novel approach to alarm triage. Our approach also applies to many other scenarios where a human needs help with organization of a continuous data stream (e.g., RSS information feeds, email management, social

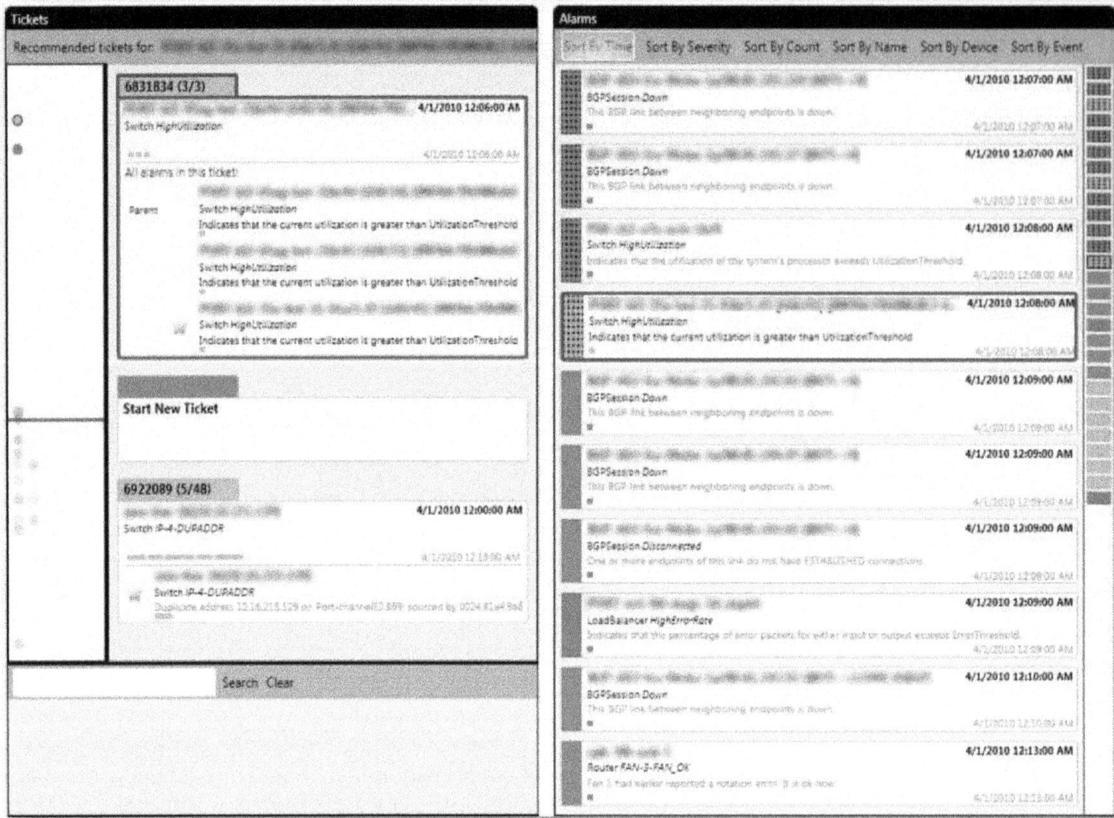

Figure 1. CueT's interface. Alarms stream in from the network and are displayed on the right. CueT's triage recommendations for each alarm appear on the left along with a visualization of CueT's confidence in those recommendations (far left). Device Names and other information are blurred for security reasons.

network updates). It is designed to reside in a dynamic environment, where it learns from each human action to help with organizing the incoming data stream.

- The design and implementation of CueT, a system that embodies our approach in the context of triaging network alarms. CueT tightly integrates visualization with the underlying computation, in contrast to existing work on network monitoring which tends to focus on one aspect or the other. CueT is based on an interactive machine learning technique operating in a highly dynamic environment; existing work assumes a fixed set of groups that are known a-prior.
- Evaluation of CueT in a real-world environment with real operators and its comparison against the current practice of manual triage, showing that our approach leads to faster and more accurate triage.

RELATED WORK

Most research in network monitoring and alarm correlation has focused either on visualizations or automated solutions in isolation. Researchers have recently proposed visualization systems for network monitoring and diagnosis (e.g., [7, 14]). For example, the Visual-I system [7] uses visual grouping and scatterplots to highlight correlations between multiple devices and problems. While these systems leverage human visual and cognitive abilities to process data and look for patterns, our approach combines visualization and interactive machine learning in order to further reduce the cognitive effort of manually identifying patterns in large data sets. Helping automate pattern discovery can increase operator efficiency and accuracy, necessary for these time critical problems.

Automated alarm correlation (also related to root cause analysis and fault localization) has long been an active area of research because of the complexity of the problem and the potential impact on the industry [9, 17]. Most solutions to this problem have taken the form of expert defined rules or models (e.g., [1, 3, 9, 12, 15]). Such approaches require manual configuration of rules which can be difficult to obtain, are not robust to new situations, and require frequent maintenance [9, 17]. In contrast, our interactive machine learning approach can handle general alarm correlations that require alarm grouping based on similarity.

Some researchers have explored automatically learning rules or models from data that can then be used for automated alarm correlation and filtering (e.g., [13, 17]). However, most of these approaches require extensive training periods and must be retrained whenever the network topology changes [17]. In contrast, our approach is based on a dynamically changing model that is constantly learning from human guidance. We argue that human input is critical during the alarm correlation process because of the inherently inconsistent and ambiguous nature of the problem [9], which is a contributing factor to why alarm correlation is still an open area of research.

While today's commercial systems employ some of these previous techniques for alarm triage and filtering [5, 10, 18], most companies still require teams of Tier 1 operators to manually triage the thousands of remaining alarms unhandled by these existing systems. Furthermore, most of these systems tend to use a tabular representation of the data, which can make it difficult for Tier 1 operators to find patterns and group alarms (e.g., Figure 2). Our approach combines interactive machine learning with an appropriate visualization in order to deal with general alarm triage that is difficult to handle with existing approaches.

Our work is closely aligned with evolving research on interactive machine learning [2, 4, 6, 8]. All of these works assert the importance of human involvement and propose interactive systems for various applications (e.g., image segmenting [6], grouping documents [2, 4] and image search [8]). While all of these focus on a pool-based static environment, where the categories of interest and the pool of unlabeled data are known a-priori, our work involves a more challenging scenario. CueT deals with a highly dynamic environment where data is constantly streaming in and out and the set of labels to be assigned is constantly changing over time. Such dynamic scenarios, to the best of our knowledge, have not been addressed earlier in the realm of interactive machine learning.

UNDERSTANDING THE TRIAGE PROCESS

We visited the network operations center of a large organization on multiple occasions to understand current triage practices. We first talked informally with center managers to get a broad understanding of the process. We then closely observed two Tier 1 operators (1 female) for an hour each as they were triaging alarms using the current tool employed at this network operations center, and asked them questions during and after the observations.

The current tool used at this operations center is a combination of two pieces: (1) an automated rule-based engine that selects alarms to be shown to Tier 1 operators and labels those alarms (e.g., alarm severity level) and (2) a table-based UI for operators to triage alarms using labels and other features (Figure 2).

Our investigation revealed three main failings of the current process. First, the rule-based engine is hard to configure and keep up-to-date as the network evolves. As a result, thousands of alarms must still be manually triaged by operators every day. While triaging, the operators largely ignored the tool's output, except for some basic information like alarm severity that is used for prioritizing which alarm to focus on next. Much of this information is not computed by the tool but is directly configured by network managers.

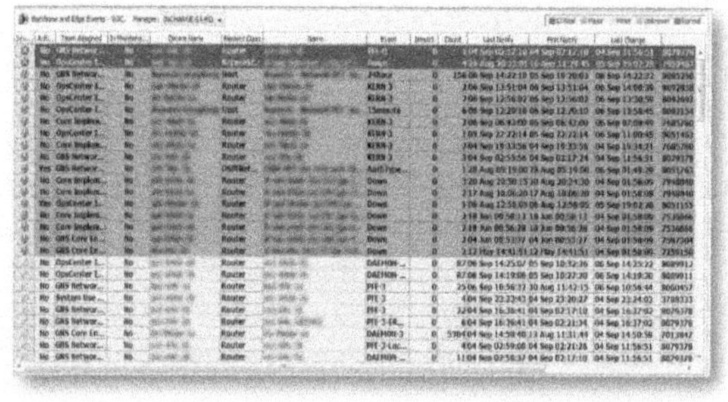

Figure 2. Current tool for displaying alarms in the network operations center we observed. A separate tool with a similar interface is used for displaying tickets.

Second, the triage process is highly manual partly because network managers often have specific instructions on how operators should temporarily handle certain types of alarms. These instructions are based on how managers expect the network to behave as they are making changes behind the scenes. They are typically conveyed in a formal document known as a *whiteboard*, updated daily and that operators are instructed to review before beginning a workday. Such special case instructions make it hard to develop tools for assisting with alarm triage. This difficulty applies not only to the traditional methods, but also to our approach as short-term special cases create noise in our learning model.

Third, the table-based visualization for the current triage process is rudimentary and inefficient. The alarms are presented as rows in a table that can be ordered by alarm attributes (e.g., severity). Another table in a different window shows the recently created alarm groups. The operators need to switch between these two windows to handle an alarm.

In addition, we learned that some alarm attributes are more important than others for the triage process. Understanding the importance of alarm attributes helps us not only choose the right features for the machine learning algorithm but also design appropriate visual representations.

While we studied only one network in detail, based on conversations with the network managers (who have a broader view of the industry and have also worked at other networks), we understand that the processes at this network are similar to those of many others. Next, we describe how CueT addresses these problems by interleaving human interaction with machine learning and visualization.

CUET

CueT consists of two interacting components: (1) a stream-based interactive machine learning engine for making triage recommendations and (2) an interface to assist operators in inspecting and interpreting those recommendations and feeding operator actions back into the learning engine. We will refer to the alarm currently being triaged as the "incoming alarm," a group of one or more related alarms that have already been triaged as a "ticket," and the current set of tickets that are being used for recommendations (and have not been discarded yet) as the "working set of tickets."

Stream-Based Interactive Machine Learning

One key aspect of our problem scenario is that it resides in a dynamic environment, where both the alarms and tickets being generated are constantly changing. Thus, our scenario is fairly different than the classical machine learning setting, where the classes are fixed and known a-priori, and the classifier operates in an assumed static environment. We tackle the challenges due to the dynamic environment and ever evolving set of classes (i.e., the working set of tickets and the alarms within those tickets).

Our approach builds on nearest neighbor classification. In particular, CueT provides triage recommendations for an incoming alarm via a nearest-neighbor strategy that orders the working set of tickets by their similarity to that alarm. Similarity is measured using a distance function that can adapt based on operator actions.

While the nearest neighbor strategy can help match incoming alarms with existing tickets, there is no easy way to identify that a new ticket needs to be spawned. We extend the classification module to include a mechanism for recommending when an incoming alarm should spawn a new ticket and include this recommendation in CueT's ordered list of recommendations. New tickets are interactively spawned and added to the working set when a human operator judges that an incoming alarm is unrelated to any existing ticket (i.e., part of a new problem). Additionally, old tickets are dynamically discarded from the working set over time, simulating the effect of problems represented by those tickets as being resolved (and reducing interference among existing tickets in the working set).

Recommending Existing Tickets

CueT measures similarity between the incoming alarm and a ticket in the working set of tickets by computing the average distance between the incoming alarm and each alarm in the ticket. CueT then orders the tickets by their average distance to the incoming alarm and uses this ordering of tickets as its triage recommendations.

Distance between alarms is measured using 17 individual distance metrics, each of which represents alarm similarity along a feature attribute. These 17 distance metrics were found to be relevant and important for triage during our initial observations of Tier 1 operators. The operators typically inspect the following alarm attributes:

- *Device Name* (e.g., ab1-cd2-ef3-gh4)
- *Device Type* (e.g., Router, Switch)
- *Element Type* (device part needing attention, e.g., Port)
- *Name* (includes Device Name and additional information such as the Element that needs attention, e.g., Port-ab1-cd2-ef3-gh4)
- *Severity* (an integer ranging from 1 to 5 representing highest to lowest priority, respectively)
- *Event Name* (e.g., Fan-3-Failed, High Utilization)

From these attributes, CueT computes 17 string-based distance metrics described below. Our simulations in the following section show that these string-based distance metrics effectively capture operators' practice of visually comparing the attribute values of alarms. Further, because large organizations often follow standard device naming conventions [16] (e.g., the "ab1" in ab1-cd2-ef3-gh4 typically indicates the location of the device), some of our string-based metrics implicitly encode topological information about the underlying network structure (e.g., device ab1* is likely to be near device ab2*). If organizations do not include topological information in device names, such information is typically available in network configuration data, from where it can be easily extracted and used to compute the following metrics.

For alarm attributes *Device Name*, *Name*, and *Event Name*, as well as the four standard component parts of the *Device Name* (e.g., ab1-cd2-ef3-gh4 is divided into ab1, cd2, ef3, and gh4), CueT computes two string-based distance metrics (amounting to fourteen metrics in total): the edit distance and the longest common substring (LCS) converted to a distance according to:

$$d_{i,j} = \text{maxlength}\,(i, j) - s_{i,j}$$

where $s_{i,j}$ is the length of the longest common substring between strings i and j. We include both edit distance and LCS because they have complementary strengths. For example, LCS is a good measure for strings that encode location. Devices "ab1*" and "ac1*" are likely in different locations. For these, LCS distance (which is 2) better captures that these are different than edit distance (which is 1). As described below, our method of learning the combination of these individual metrics will reduce the effect of any irrelevant metric (edit distance in this case).

For alarm attributes *Device Type*, *Element Type*, and *Severity*, CueT computes one string matching distance metric each (amounting to three metrics in total). This distance metric returns 0 if the attribute values are the same or 1 if they are different.

We combine these 17 distance metrics using Mahalanobis distance, which parameterizes distance between any alarms $\boldsymbol{u}$ and $\boldsymbol{v}$, represented as d dimensional feature vectors, by a $d{\times}d$ positive definite covariance matrix A:

$$\textit{Distance}\,(\boldsymbol{u}, \boldsymbol{v}) = (\boldsymbol{u} - \boldsymbol{v})^{\mathrm{T}} A\, (\boldsymbol{u} - \boldsymbol{v})$$

This function effectively weights the 17 distances by the matrix A, which encodes their relative importance for alarm classification and the correlations between them.

We learn the parameters of the matrix A from operators using an online metric learning algorithm [11], originally derived for nearest neighbor classification in static environments. We extend the procedure to dynamic scenarios where both the number and type of classes are varying. In particular, given a stream of alarms, each labeled with the ticket that it was triaged into, we incrementally update the matrix A by encoding the labels as constraints indicating that the incoming alarm and each alarm in the target ticket should be near each other. When an alarm spawns a new ticket, no update is made to the matrix A (however, this does change the working set of tickets). To learn the parameters of A, we initialize it to the identity matrix (and set the regularization parameter η to .001) and then update the parameters as we observe triage actions. We continue this process for N alarms, where N is determined empirically from our simulation experiments described below, and then fix the distance function. The final covariance matrix A_N is used in making recommendations for the remaining data.

Intuitively, the parameters learned for the matrix A reflect the importance and correlations among the individual distance metrics, to best explain the human operator's actions. The advantage of learning the matrix A from data is that it does not require expert tuning, which can be difficult to obtain and does not evolve with the network [9, 17].

Recommending Starting a New Ticket

CueT maintains a threshold distance for starting a new ticket based on information about when operators spawn new tickets. When an operator spawns a new ticket for an incoming alarm, the distance between this alarm and the nearest ticket in the working set is stored. We experimented with several strategies for computing the threshold distance from these stored distances. They include taking the minimum and average over various window sizes of the most recently stored distances (including a window of all the distances). We found that taking the minimum within a window of the five most recent stored distances performs best. That a small window size performs better than larger sizes likely stems from the fact that thresholds need to reflect the dynamically changing distribution of tickets in the metric space.

For each incoming alarm, CueT computes the latest threshold distance using the strategy above and inserts a "start new ticket" recommendation into its ordered list of recommendations according to this distance.

Spawning New Tickets and Discarding Old Tickets

When an operator determines that an incoming alarm is part of a new problem, a new ticket is created and added to the working set. CueT also automatically discards old tickets, simulating the resolution of problems. We use a windowing mechanism to discard old tickets. In particular, we fix the window size to N, which is the number of alarms used for learning our covariance matrix. Any time the number of unique alarms in the working set of tickets exceeds N we remove the oldest ticket in the set. Spawning new tickets and discarding old ones means that the working set of tickets used for machine learning based recommendations is continually evolving as an operator interacts with CueT.

Simulation Experiments

In this section, we present the results of experiments that simulate human interaction with CueT's interactive machine learning component. For our experiments, we obtained alarm triage data from a network operations center at a large organization that monitors a network with approximately 15,000 devices. This data was labeled by Tier 1 operators through their manual triage process. To evaluate CueT's interactive machine learning component over a long period, we use data spread across several months. In particular, we use data from the first day of each month between January and August 2010 (inclusive) except for May and July when the network had recording problems. This data set contains 338,218 alarms of which 8,719 are unique and are mapped to 1,281 unique tickets.

To simulate human interaction and compute the accuracy of CueT's learning, we processed alarms in the data in the order in which they occurred. For each alarm, we first compute an ordered list of recommendations that we use to measure accuracy. Then, we obtain the actual label for the alarm and either add the alarm to an existing ticket or create a new ticket. If we add the incoming alarm to an existing ticket and we have observed fewer than N alarms, we update A_N as described previously. If we start a new ticket, we update the threshold distance for starting new tickets and update the working set of tickets. Finally, if we determine that the working set has exceeded the window size of N alarms, we discard the oldest ticket in the set.

We measure recommendation accuracy for each incoming alarm by comparing the recommendations to the ground truth (all of the alarm triage data observed before reaching the current incoming alarm, without discarding any tickets). There are two types of correct recommendations:

- *Correct New Ticket.* CueT recommends a new ticket be created and the alarm's label shows that a human operator actually created a new ticket for that alarm.
- *Correct Existing Ticket.* CueT recommends an existing ticket and that ticket is the alarm's actual label.

If neither of these is true, we record the recommendation as incorrect. Note that because the nature of the problem we are dealing with requires that we operate in a moving window, some of our errors may be the result of discarding tickets (e.g., recommending a new ticket when the correct ticket is in the ground truth but no longer exists in the working set of tickets).

Because multiple tickets may be the same distance away from an incoming alarm, we compute recommendation accuracy as whether or not the alarm's actual label appeared within the set of ticket recommendations a given distance away from the alarm or closer. For example, if CueT predicts two different ticket recommendations as being equally closest to the incoming alarm ("Top 1 distance" away) and if the correct label is one of the two tickets then we consider this a correct recommendation at the Top 1 distance. Similarly, a recommendation is correct at the Top 2 distance if the correct label is within the set of tickets recommended at the Top 2 distance away from the incoming alarm or less (e.g., at the Top 1 distance). We

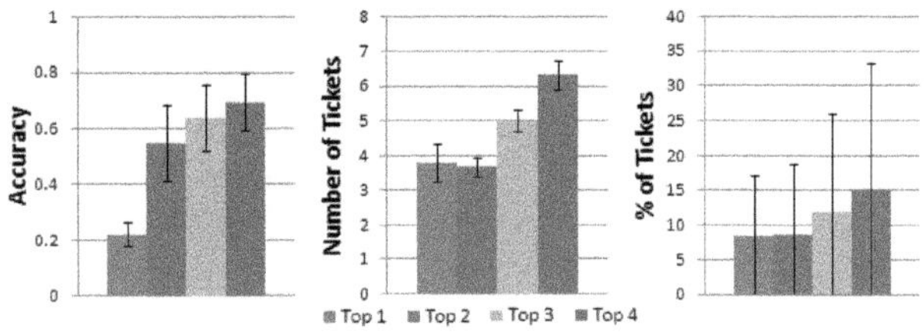

Figure 3. CueT's accuracy (left), number (middle), and % of tickets presented (right) within Top 1, 2, 3, 4 distances from each incoming alarm, averaged over all simulation trials.

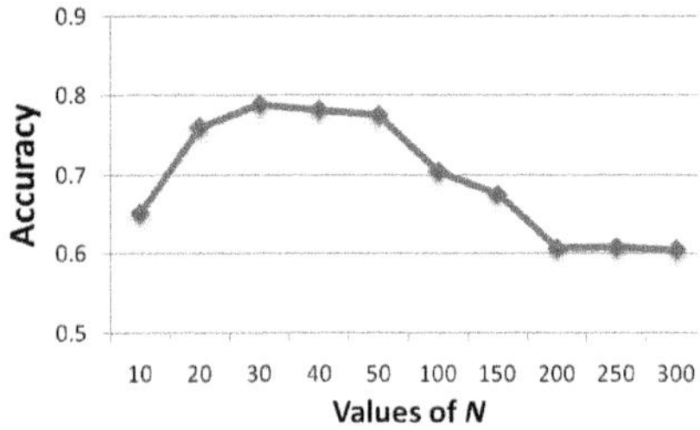

Figure 4. CueT's accuracy at the Top 3 distances for various window sizes *N*. *N*=30 achieves peak performance.

experimented with accuracy within the Top 1, 2, 3 and 4 distances from the incoming alarm.

We ran ten simulations over our data, varying the number of alarms N used in both learning the distance function parameters A_N as well as in the window size for discarding old tickets. Figure 3 (left) illustrates CueT's accuracy within the set of tickets recommended at the Top 1, 2, 3, and 4 distances from incoming alarms averaged over all the simulation trials. Figure 3 (middle and right) shows the average number and percentage of tickets (out of N) presented at each of the Top 1 to 4 distances. From these results it appears that presenting tickets in the Top 3 distances achieves a good balance between relatively high accuracy and a small number of tickets being presented. Therefore, for our user study described later, we fix CueT to recommend tickets for an incoming alarm within the Top 3 distances from that alarm.

CueT's accuracy at the Top 3 distances over the various values of N that we experimented with (10, 20, 30, 40, 50, 100, 150, 200, 250, and 300) appears to peak at an N value of 30 alarms (Figure 4). Therefore, for our user study, we set N=30 in our interactive machine learning engine.

CueT Interface

CueT's interface (Figure 1) consists of two main views: the *Alarm View* on the right displays alarms as they stream in from the network and the *Ticket View* on the left displays CueT's ticket recommendations.

When operators click on an alarm in the Alarm View, CueT displays its recommendations for that alarm in the Ticket View and illustrates its confidence in those recommendations with the *Ticket Distance Overview*. Operators can then inspect the recommendations and visualizations to determine how to triage the alarm (that is, either add it to an existing ticket or start a new one). Operators triage the alarm by dragging and dropping it onto the appropriate ticket in the Ticket View. CueT's interface also contains a *Search View* (bottom left in Figure 1) through which operators can search for existing tickets by entering a search string as they do with their current system for triaging alarms. Operators can add alarms to tickets appearing in the Search View just as in the Ticket View.

Alarms and Alarm View

Our initial observations of operators helped us determine the importance of certain alarm attributes. *Severity* and *Notification Time*, most viewed by operators when determining which alarm to triage next, are displayed prominently. As shown in Figure 1 (right), Severity (on a scale of 1-5) is encoded on the left of an alarm by color: red (most severe), orange-red, orange, yellow, and white (least severe). The Notification Time attribute is emphasized in bold and displayed at the top right-hand side of the alarm.

Operators often work under a service level agreement (SLA) that defines the time limit within which an alarm must be triaged. CueT highlights when an alarm has passed this limit by overlaying a pattern on the Severity display as in the alarms at the top of the Alarm View in Figure 1.

Operators also sometimes use the *Count* attribute of an alarm to determine which alarm to deal with next. The Count attribute represents the number of duplicate alarms observed and many duplicates sometimes signal a severe problem. CueT represents Count by the length of the horizontal bar (color coded by Severity of the alarm) at the bottom of the alarm. In addition, if duplicates are observed, the time when the last duplicate was observed is displayed in gray at the bottom right of the alarm.

Alarm *Name* is also emphasized in the alarm in bold as this attribute is used most often when comparing alarms to existing tickets and deciding how to triage. The rest of the alarm information, including *Device Type*, *Event Name*, and a description of the event is displayed less saliently in the alarm in gray. This layout allows operators to visually scan and compare alarms by Severity, Time, and Count while still being able to digest the rest of the alarm information in a compact representation.

Alarms are displayed in the Alarm View as they stream in from the network. Since operators often miss important alarms that appear off of the screen, the Alarm View includes an Alarm Overview (far right in Figure 1) that provides awareness of all alarms still requiring triage even if they are off the screen. This overview displays one rectangle per alarm, color coded by that alarm's Severity and possibly the pattern if that alarm has passed its SLA. The heights of the rectangles automatically adjust so as to always display all of the alarms currently available for triage. The rectangles are presented in the order that alarms are displayed in the Alarm View, where alarms can be sorted by any attribute of the alarm. This allows the overview to act as a scroll bar for easy alarm navigation.

Tickets, Ticket View, and Ticket Distance Overview

Tickets are a collection of related alarms (Figure 1 left). Each ticket has a parent alarm, which is manually determined by a human operator and typically represents either the most severe or the first alarm in the ticket. The label at the top of the ticket is color coded by Severity of the ticket's parent alarm. The ticket label also includes the ticket's unique ID, automatically generated by the system at the time of creation, and two numbers in parenthesis; the number of unique alarms within that ticket followed by the total number of duplicates across those alarms. Unique alarms and duplicates are dually represented in the ticket as a series of horizontal bars (similar to the Count display in the alarm representation), one for each unique alarm, and again color coded by Severity of the alarm and reflecting the number of duplicates for that alarm by its length.

Immediately below the ticket label is information about the ticket's parent alarm along with the ticket description. Below the parent alarm is the best matching alarm within the ticket to the incoming alarm (next to the star icons in Figure 1). This serves as an explanation for why CueT is recommending that an operator triage an alarm into a given ticket. Thus, ticket representations displayed in the Ticket View are tailored for each alarm. Operators can also click on a ticket to display all the alarms currently grouped within the ticket. New ticket recommendations are displayed as empty ticket stubs with a gray label and text within the ticket displaying "Start New Ticket."

Each time the operator clicks on an alarm to triage in the Alarm View, CueT generates its ticket recommendations for the selected alarm and displays them in the Ticket View. They are shown in order of increasing distance from the alarm as per the distance function described previously. By default, and as determined by our simulation results, the Ticket View initially displays only the tickets within the Top 3 distances from the alarm being triaged as this helps to balance operator load and the probability of these tickets containing the correct recommendation. CueT allows operators to reveal more tickets to inspect using the Ticket Distance Overview visualization.

The Ticket Distance Overview (far left in Figure 1) is designed to provide operators with an estimate of its confidence in its recommendations so that operators can determine the necessity of inspecting more tickets. Each bubble in the Ticket Distance Overview corresponds to a ticket. The vertical position of the bubbles relative to the top of the overview reflects the distance between the alarm being triaged and each ticket within the working set. That is, the closer the bubble is to the top, the better a match the corresponding ticket is for the alarm with respect to our distance function. Also vertical positions of the bubbles correspond to the ordered list of recommendations in the Ticket View. Vertical distances are normalized so as to fit all of the existing tickets within the display. Thus, the positions of the bubbles display relative distances between tickets rather than absolute distances. Horizontal positioning is only used to minimize overlap of bubbles that are of equal or near equal distance to the incoming alarm.

Bubbles that are positioned near each other are comparable in terms of their similarity to the alarm currently being triaged. In this case, the overview should encourage operators to inspect all of the comparable tickets. To enable operators to inspect more tickets when necessary, CueT provides a horizontal green bar allowing them to set the distance threshold for the tickets to be displayed in the Ticket View. It divides the bubbles into a visible region (above the bar and corresponding to visible tickets in the Ticket View) and the invisible region (faded bubbles below the bar and corresponding to tickets not currently visible in the Ticket View). Operators can drag this bar vertically to reveal and inspect other tickets within the Ticket View.

USER STUDY

We conducted a user study to examine the effectiveness of CueT for alarm triage as compared to the traditional method of manually ticketing alarms. For the Traditional condition, we replicated the commercial system used by our network operators (Figure 2). As in the commercial system, participants could keyword search the tabular view of existing tickets to add incoming alarms or create new tickets. Adding alarms to existing tickets or creating new tickets is achieved by right clicking on a row in the table of alarms and selecting the corresponding action from a popup menu. The commercial system has separate windows for displaying alarms and searchable tickets, both using a tabular format. To avoid the overhead of switching between windows (a problem we observed during our initial observations), our version of the Traditional interface combines both of these views in one window as in CueT. This combination provides a fairer evaluation of the current practice, as the two-window issue is easy to fix.

Data, Study Design, and Equipment

For our study we used part of the data that we used for our simulation experiments (January 1, 2010 data). To compare two interfaces, we created two data sets from this data. To ensure that each set includes comparable numbers, distributions and types of alarms and tickets, we extracted alternating unique alarms. We also simulated the correct assignment of alarms to tickets for alarms not being shown as CueT relies on a dynamically changing working set of tickets. Therefore, *Data Set 1* included odd alarms (while we simulated the correct assignment for even alarms) and *Data Set 2* included even alarms (where we simulated the correct assignment for odd alarms). Each data set contained 80 unique alarms to be triaged by our participants as our pilot study showed that was a manageable number of alarms to triage in about 20 minutes. For demonstration and practice in each condition, we also created two additional data sets (*Demo Sets 1* and *2*) from the April 1, 2010 data using this same approach.

We conducted a within-subjects study, with each participant performing alarm triage using both CueT and the Traditional method. We compared *CueT* to the *Traditional* method in terms of accuracy, speed, and user preference. To avoid a learning effect, we counterbalanced the presentation order of the two interfaces.

We ran participants individually or in pairs depending on their schedule (two pairs). Each participant worked on a 2.7 GHz dual-core Windows 7 laptop with 4 GB RAM. We attached a 20.1'' Samsung monitor at a resolution of 1200x1600 (i.e., in a portrait orientation) to each laptop, as well as a mouse and keyboard. We turned the laptop away from participants so they could only look at the attached monitor and use the attached mouse and keyboard. When we ran pairs, we faced their desks away from each other to minimize disturbance.

Procedure and Participants

Before each condition, the experimenter demonstrated each interface using *Demo Set 1*. Then the participants were allowed to practice triaging alarms using *Demo Set 2* until they were comfortable with the interface and had practiced triaging several alarms, for a maximum of 5 minutes.

In each condition, participants were asked to triage all 80 alarms presented as accurately and quickly as possible and in the order that they normally would (i.e., they could triage the alarms in any order, but are encouraged to triage high severity alarms and alarms that have passed their SLA first). All interface actions were time-stamped and logged.

After each condition, participants were given a short questionnaire about the interface they just used. The questionnaire included 7-point Likert scale questions asking for the participants' level of agreement with statements about the interface (e.g., "Overall, I am satisfied with this system.") and specific questions about the CueT interface if they had just used that interface (e.g., "The ticket recommendations were useful."). It also asked participants to list three things that they liked and three that they would like improved about the interface. At the end of the session, a final questionnaire asked participants to select which interface they preferred and explain why.

The experiment lasted about 90 minutes and participants were given a gratuity of $20 worth of dining coupons. To encourage participants to triage alarms quickly and accurately, we also offered a prize of an additional $20 worth of dining coupons for the person who performed the best in terms speed and accuracy in each condition.

We recruited eleven people (two female, ages 28 to 44) plus one male pilot from the network operations team. Our participants were not currently working as Tier 1 operators, though six of them were self-proclaimed experts at the alarm triage process and four said they were proficient. One said he was a beginner. We could not recruit active Tier 1 operators because of their tight work schedule and because many work outside of the country.

Results

Performance: Accuracy and Speed

We analyze our logged data in terms of accuracy and speed. *Accuracy* is computed as the percentage of alarms correctly triaged out of the total presented. Correctness of participant labels is measured against the ground truth labels.

We compute two measures for speed: *Time on Screen* and *Time to Ticket*. The former is the time between when an alarm appeared on screen and when the participant completed the triage operation for that alarm. Along with *Accuracy*, it is a key measure of triage performance and is used to formulate service level agreements (SLAs) that the monitoring team offers. For instance, a possible guarantee may be that for 95% of alarms *Time on Screen* would be under 5 minutes. Note that both *CueT* and *Traditional* present multiple alarms on screen simultaneously and operators need not triage alarms in the order in which they appear on screen. Therefore, *Time on Screen* is affected by the order in which an operator decides to triage an alarm. Thus, for a detailed view of triage behavior, we also study *Time to Ticket*, which is time between successive triage actions regardless of order.

For *Accuracy*, *Time on Screen*, and *Time to Ticket*, we perform paired-samples t tests. We report means and standard deviations throughout.

Our analyses showed that participants were able to triage alarms faster with *CueT* than with the *Traditional* interface while maintaining the same level of accuracy. Participants were significantly faster with *CueT* than *Traditional* in terms of *Time on Screen* (M=107.7s, SD=127.7s vs. M=277.8s, SD=168.5s, $t(10)$=4.43, p=.001) and in terms of *Time to Ticket* (M=10.1s, SD=2.69s vs. M=12.9s, SD=3.79s, $t(10)$=3.26, p=.009). There was no significant difference in terms of accuracy between the *CueT* and *Traditional* conditions (M=71.8%, SD=17% vs. M=76.4%, SD=8%).

Our data included a type of alarm that required special handling. Operators are usually instructed to always create a new ticket for each such alarm, regardless of similarity to other alarms. Only a few participants asked us how to triage such alarms, to which we responded that they should triage as normal. The logged data shows that such alarms were handled unevenly by participants. Some rapidly created new tickets without inspecting recommendations (in CueT) or searching related tickets (in the CueT or Traditional condition), while others triaged based on similarity. These alarms reduce CueT's accuracy because its model does not handle exceptional cases. Despite that our results show that CueT's accuracy is no worse and its speed is much better.

We re-did our analysis after removing 39 of these exceptional alarms from the data to evaluate CueT's performance in the absence of special cases. Our corrected analyses of variance show that participants were still faster with *CueT* but also more accurate than the *Traditional* condition (Figure 5). The accuracy with *CueT* versus the

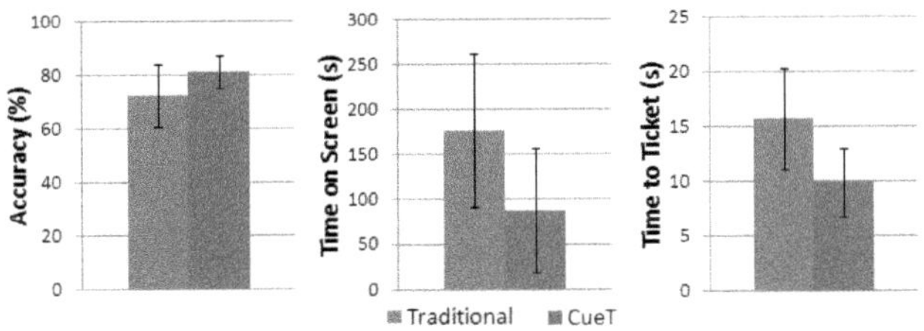

Figure 5. Accuracy (left), Time on Screen (middle), and Time to Ticket (right) comparisons. All differences are significant. Error bars represent standard error.

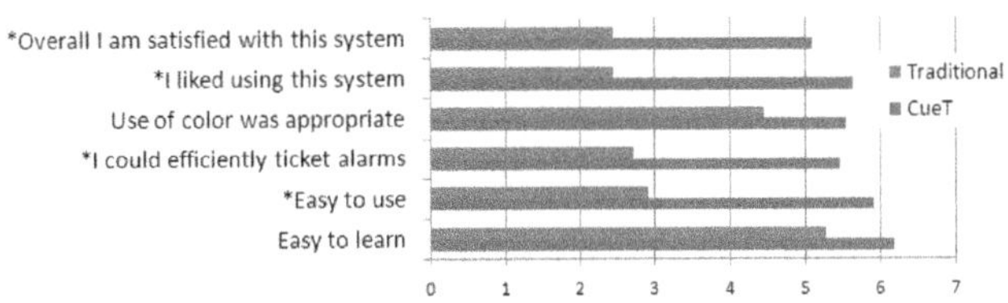

Figure 6. 7-point Likert scale questionnaire results. Stars indicate the question was significantly different.

Traditional condition was 81.3% (*SD*=6%) vs. 72.4% (*SD*=12%), ($t(10)=2.29$, $p=.045$). The participants were significantly faster with *CueT* at triaging in terms of both *Time on Screen* (*M*=86.9s, *SD*=69.2s vs. *M*=176.2s, *SD*=85.2s, $t(10)=4.63$, $p=.001$) and *Time to Ticket* (*M*=9.9s, *SD*=3.1s vs. *M*=15.7s, *SD*=4.6s, $t(10)=6.52$, $p<.001$).

Subjective Preference

We analyze our post-condition questionnaires using Friedman Chi-Square tests. *CueT* was favored significantly more than *Traditional* in terms of overall satisfaction ($\chi^2(1,N=11)=9.0$, $p=.003$), how much participants liked using the system ($\chi^2(1,N=11)=11.0$, $p=.001$), whether they felt that they could efficiently ticket alarms with the system ($\chi^2(1,N=11)=6.4$, $p=.011$), and whether they felt the system was easy to use ($\chi^2(1,N=11)=11.0$, $p=.001$) (Figure 6).

Regarding *CueT*-specific features, participants tended to agree with the statements "The ticket recommendations were useful" (5.81 avg.) and "The Distance Overview was useful" (5.36 avg.). In addition, all of our participants chose *CueT* as their preferred system for network alarm triage.

DISCUSSION AND FUTURE WORK

Our results show that real network operators can triage alarms significantly faster with CueT than with their traditional method. When considering general alarms as well as exceptional cases, CueT reduces the *Time on Screen* of alarms by 61.2% on average. When excluding exceptional cases the savings on this measure are 50.7%. Savings are lower without exceptional cases because such cases require an action that can be performed quickly and without deliberation (e.g., rapidly creating new tickets without looking for similar tickets). *Time on Screen* is affected by the order in which an operator triages alarms. Thus, CueT's Alarm Overview, designed to facilitate awareness of alarms remaining in the queue of alarms to be triaged, likely contributed to the savings on this measure. In listing the things they liked about CueT, one participant commented that "Having the alert change colors as it approached SLA helps with prioritization."

For *Time to Ticket*, CueT enables a savings of 21.6% when considering general and exceptional alarms, and a savings of 36.8% when considering only the general alarms that CueT is designed for. Considering that participants performed only 4.6 manual searches on average throughout their session with CueT (compared to 84.6 searches on average with the traditional method) and only one participant ever ticketed an alarm via dragging and dropping the alarm onto CueT's Search View, participants relied on CueT's recommendations to triage. Therefore, as *Time to Ticket* measures the time between ticket actions, this savings in time can be attributed to CueT's ability to provide operators with suggestions about how to ticket each alarm rather than having to manually search for tickets. To put this in perspective, assuming 10K alarms per day and a time savings of 5.8s per alarm (36.8%), CueT's estimated cumulative time savings using this measure amounts to about 20 operator days per month.

As our observations of operators revealed, exceptional cases are a reality in network operations. CueT currently cannot automatically exclude exceptional cases from its dynamically changing model. Remarkably, when considering general alarms along with exceptional cases, no significant decrease in overall accuracy is observed. This suggests that CueT does not adversely affect operator ability to deal with exceptional cases. Furthermore, although including exceptional cases in CueT's dynamic model may cause interference in recommendation accuracy for general alarms, CueT still performed significantly better than the traditional method for the general case, by 9%. This result points at the robustness of using triage recommendations from human-guided interactive machine learning based models. As interference can negatively affect CueT's recommendation accuracy, it is fair to regard CueT's performance results from our evaluation as a lower bound on its potential for improving alarm triage. In fact, it may be possible for network administrators to reduce some of this noise by creating temporary rules to automatically remove exceptional alarms. Despite the potential for interference, nine of our eleven participants commented that CueT's recommendation ability was one of the things they most liked about the system (e.g., "Recommendations done by the system for appropriate tickets was very useful.").

In terms of their subjective preference, all participants preferred CueT over the traditional method. The only questions for which there was no significant difference between CueT and the traditional method were whether the use of color was appropriate and whether the system was easy to learn. As with CueT, the traditional method also makes use of color coding to indicate severity of alarms. CueT however takes an additional step in overlaying information about the operator's SLA on the colored area of an alarm. In terms of being easy to learn, our participants were all already familiar with the traditional system of manually triaging alarms. Despite this, they were still able to learn and start using CueT in a matter of minutes.

We believe CueT's tight integration between interactive machine learning and visualization is key to its success. As with other distance-based recommendation systems, multiple tickets in CueT can be equally distant from an alarm. Presenting recommendations as a traditional list would therefore require arbitrarily ordering tickets and would likely mislead operators. To ensure high accuracy, CueT's Ticket Distance Overview visualization was specifically designed to show estimates of recommendation quality and encourage operators to inspect comparable tickets. Further, the coupling between machine learning and visualization makes it easy for operators to provide feedback to the system and keep the model up-to-date. However, additional studies that compare CueT's machine learning with and without visualization would shed more light on the value of this integration. We suggest a longitudinal investigation of operator confidence in the recommendations and the effects on operator vigilance in carefully inspecting those recommendations with and without visualization.

CONCLUSION

We present CueT, a system that combines novel visualizations and interactive machine learning to deal with a highly dynamic environment where the groups of interest are not known a-priori and evolve constantly. We implement CueT in the context of triaging network alarms to assist network operators in the complex task of alarm triage. Our user study indicates that CueT increases operator accuracy as well as speed compared to the current approach. All of our study participants preferred CueT over the traditional method, a sentiment that is reflected in one participant's comment: "the new system compared to the old is hands down better." While CueT is designed for triaging alarms, we believe that the lessons learned from our work readily extend to other scenarios where humans need to organize continuous streams of data.

ACKNOWLEDGEMENTS

We thank the staff at the network operations center, especially Spencer Watkins, for explaining their current practices to us and letting us observe their work. We also thank our study participants for their time and feedback.

REFERENCES

1. Appleby, K., Goldszmidt, G., and Steinder, M. Layered Event Correlation Engine for Multi-Domain Server Farms. *Proc. INM 2001*, IEEE (2001), 329-344.
2. Basu, S., Fisher, D., Drucker, S.M., and Lu, H. Assisting Users with Clustering Tasks by Combining Metric Learning and Classification. *Proc. AAAI 2010*.
3. Brugnosi, S., Bruno, G., Manione, R., Montariolo, E., Paschetta, E., and Sisto, L. An Expert System for Real Time Fault Diagnosis of the Italian Telecommunications Network. *Proc. INM 1993*, IEEE (1993), 617-628.
4. desJardins, M., MacGlashan, J., and Ferraioli, J. Interactive Visual Clustering. *Proc. IUI 2007*, ACM Press (2007), 361-364.
5. EMC Ionix, http://www.emc.com/products/family/ionix-family.htm
6. Fails, J.A. and Olsen, Jr., D.R. Interactive Machine Learning. *Proc. IUI 2003*, ACM Press (2003), 39-45.
7. Fisher, D., Maltz, D.A., Greenberg, A., Wang, X., Warncke, H., Robertson, G., and Czerwinski, M. Using Visualization to Support Network and Application Management in a Data Center. *Proc. INM 2008*, IEEE (2008), 1-6.
8. Fogarty, J., Tan, D., Kapoor, A., and Winder, S. CueFlik: Interactive Concept Learning in Image Search. *Proc. CHI 2008*, ACM Press (2008), 29-38.
9. Gardner, R.D. and Harle, D.A. Methods and Systems for Alarm Correlation. *Proc. GLOBECOM 1996*, IEEE (1996), 136-140.
10. HP OpenView, http://openview.hp.com
11. Jain, P., Kulis, B., Dhillon, I.S., and Grauman, K. Online Metric Learning and Fast Similarity Search. *Proc. NIPS 2008*, (2008), 761-768.
12. Jakobson, G. and Weissman, M.D. Alarm Correlation: Correlating multiple network alarms improves telecommunications network surveillance and fault management. *IEEE Network 7*, 6 (1993), 52-59.
13. Klementtinen, M., Mannila, H., and Toivonen, H. Rule Discovery in Telecommunication Alarm Data. *J. Network and Systems Management 7*, 4 (1999), 395-423.
14. Lakkaraju, K, Yurcik, W., and Lee, A.J. NVisionIP: Network Visualizations of System State for Security Situational Awareness. *Proc. VizSEC/DMSEC 2004*, ACM Press (2004), 65-72.
15. Liu, G., Mok, A.K., and Yang, E.J. Composite Events for Network Event Correlation. *Proc. INM 1999*, IEEE (1999), 247-260.
16. Spring, N., Mahajan, R., Wetherall, D., and Anderson, T. Measuring ISP Topologies with Rocketfuel. *Proc. SIGCOMM 2002*, ACM Press (2002), 133-145.
17. Steinder, M. and Sethi, A.S. A Survey of Fault Localization Techniques in Computer Networks. *Science of Computer Programming 53*, (2004), 165-194.
18. Yemini, S., Kliger, S., Mozes, E., Yemini, Y., and Ohsie, D. High Speed and Robust Event Correlation. *IEEE Communications Magazine 34,* 5 (1996), 82-90.

Apolo: Making Sense of Large Network Data by Combining Rich User Interaction and Machine Learning

Duen Horng "Polo" Chau, Aniket Kittur, Jason I. Hong, Christos Faloutsos
School of Computer Science
Carnegie Mellon University
Pittsburgh, PA 15213, USA
{dchau, nkittur, jasonh, christos}@cs.cmu.edu

ABSTRACT
Extracting useful knowledge from large network datasets has become a fundamental challenge in many domains, from scientific literature to social networks and the web. We introduce Apolo, a system that uses a mixed-initiative approach—combining visualization, rich user interaction and machine learning—to guide the user to incrementally and interactively explore large network data and make sense of it. Apolo engages the user in bottom-up sensemaking to gradually build up an understanding over time by starting small, rather than starting big and drilling down. Apolo also helps users find relevant information by specifying exemplars, and then using a machine learning method called Belief Propagation to infer which other nodes may be of interest. We evaluated Apolo with twelve participants in a between-subjects study, with the task being to find relevant new papers to update an existing survey paper. Using expert judges, participants using Apolo found significantly more relevant papers. Subjective feedback of Apolo was also very positive.

Author Keywords
Sensemaking, large network, Belief Propagation

ACM Classification Keywords
H.3.3 Information Storage and Retrieval: Relevance feedback; H.5.2 Information Interfaces and Presentation: User Interfaces

General Terms
Algorithms, Design, Human Factors

INTRODUCTION
Making sense of large networks is an increasingly important problem in domains ranging from citation networks of scientific literature; social networks of friends and colleagues; links between web pages in the World Wide Web; and personal information networks of emails, contacts, and appointments. Theories of sensemaking provide a way to characterize and address the challenges faced by people trying to organize and understand large amounts of network-based data. Sensemaking refers to the iterative process of building up a

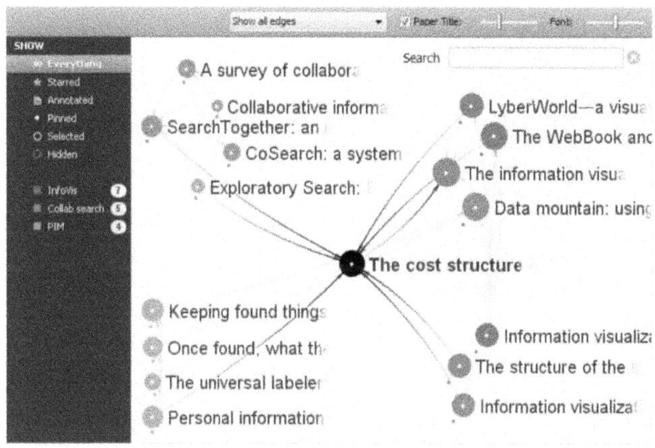

Figure 1. Apolo displaying citation network data around the article *The Cost Structure of Sensemaking*. The user gradually builds up a mental model of the research areas around the article by manually inspecting some neighboring articles in the visualization and specifying them as exemplar articles (with colored dots underneath) for some ad hoc groups, and instructs Apolo to find more articles relevant to them.

representation or schema of an information space that is useful for achieving the user's goal [31]. For example, a scientist interested in connecting her work to a new domain must build up a mental representation of the existing literature in the new domain to understand and contribute to it.

For the above scientist, she may forage to find papers that she thinks are relevant, and build up a representation of how those papers relate to each other. As she continues to read more papers and realizes her mental model may not well fit the data she may engage in representational shifts to alter her mental model to better match the data [31]. Such representational shifts is a hallmark of insight and problem solving, in which re-representing a problem in a different form can lead to previously unseen connections and solutions [11]. The practical importance of organizing and re-representing information in the sensemaking process of knowledge workers has significant empirical and theoretical support [28].

We focus on helping people develop and evolve externalized representations of their internal mental models to support sensemaking in large network data. Finding, filtering, and extracting information have already been the subjects of significant research, involving both specific applications [7] and a rich variety of general-purpose tools, including search engines, recommendation systems, and summarization and extraction algorithms. However, just finding and

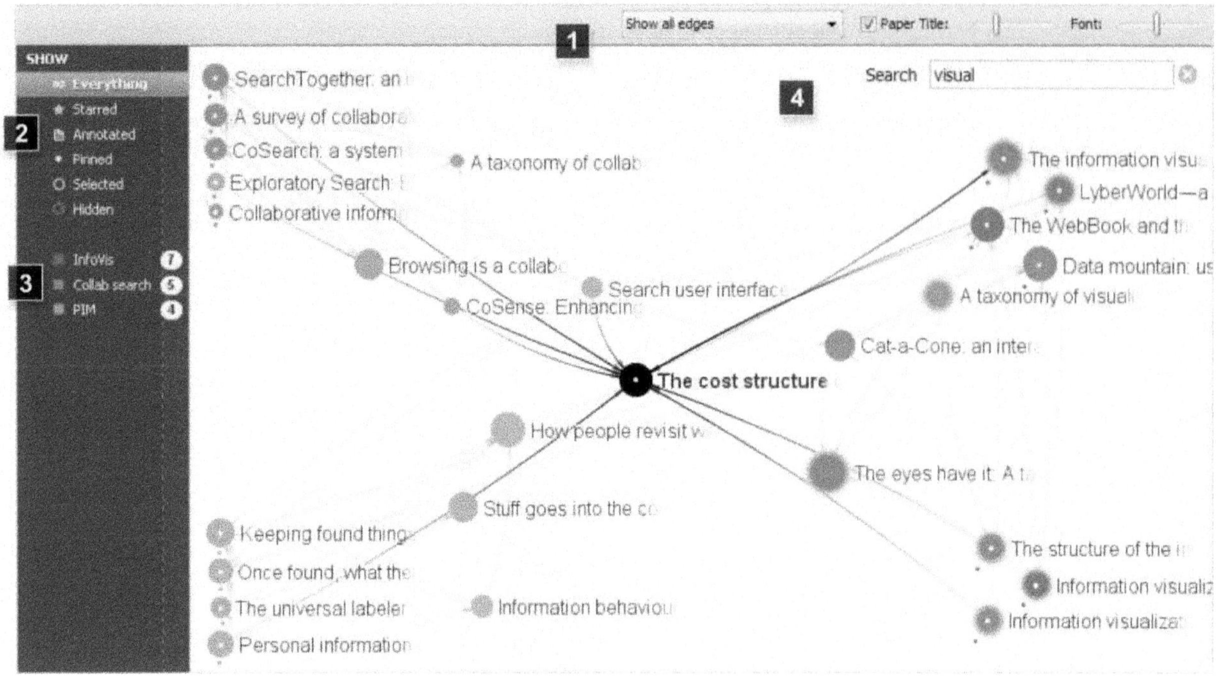

Figure 2. The Apolo user interface displaying citation data around the article *The Cost Structure of Sensemaking*. The user has created three groups: *Information Visualization* (InfoVis, blue) , *Collaborative Search* (orange), and *Personal Information Management* (PIM, green). A color is automatically assigned to each group, and each node is assigned the color of the group it most likely belongs to; saturation indicates "belongness". Each exemplar has a colored dot below it. 1: The *Configuration Panel* for enhancing visualization readability, by setting visibility of citation edges and article titles, varying font size and visible length of titles via sliders. 2: The *Filter Panel* provides filters to control the type of nodes to show; the default filter is "Everything", showing all types of nodes, except hidden ones. Other filters show nodes that are starred, annotated, pinned, selected, or hidden. 3: The *Group Panel* lets the user create, rename, and delete groups. 4: The *Visualization Panel* where the user incrementally and interactively builds up an understanding and a highly personalized visualization of the network. Articles whose titles contain "visual" are highlighted with yellow halos.

filtering or even reading items is not sufficient. Much of the heavy lifting in sensemaking is done as people create, modify, and evaluate schemas of relations between items. Few tools aimed at helping users evolve representations and schemas. We build on initial work such as Sensemaker [3] and studies by Russell et al. [30] aimed at supporting the representation process. We view this as an opportunity to support flexible, ad-hoc sensemaking through intelligent interfaces and algorithms.

These challenges in making sense of large network data motivated us to create Apolo, a system that uses a mixed-initiative approach—combining rich user interaction and machine learning—to guide the user to incrementally and interactively explore large network data and make sense of it. Our main contributions are

- We aptly select, adapt, and integrate work in machine learning and graph visualization in a novel way to help users make sense of large graphs using a mixed-initiative approach. Apolo goes beyond just graph exploration, and enables users to externalize, construct, and evolve their mental models of the graph in a bottom-up manner.
- Apolo offers a novel way of leveraging a complex machine learning algorithm, called Belief Propagation (BP) [40], to intuitively support sensemaking tailored to an individual's goals and experiences; BP was never applied to sensemaking or interactive graph visualization.
- We explain the rationale behind the design of Apolo's novel techniques and how they advance over the state of the art. Through a usability evaluation using real citation network data obtained from Google Scholar, we demonstrate Apolo's ease of use and its ability to help researchers find significantly more relevant papers.

RELATED WORK

Apolo intersects multiple research areas, each having a large amount of relevant work. However, less work explores how to better support graph sensemaking, like the way Apolo does, by combining powerful methods from *machine learning*, *visualization*, and *interaction*. Here, we briefly describe relevant work in some of the related areas.

Sensemaking

Sensemaking refers to the iterative process of building up a representation of an information space that is useful for achieving the user's goal [31]. Numerous models have been proposed, including Russell et al.'s *cost structure* view [31], Dervin's sensemaking methodology [8], and the notional model by Pirolli and Card [28]. Consistent with this dynamic task structure, studies of how people mentally learn and represent concepts highlight that they are often flexible, ad-hoc, and theory-driven rather than determined by static features of the data [4]. Furthermore, categories that emerge in users' minds are often shifting and ad-hoc, evolving to match the changing goals in their environment [14]. These results highlight the importance of a "human in the loop" approach for organizing and making sense of information, rather than fully unsupervised approaches that result in a common structure for all users. Several systems aim to support interactive sensemaking, like SenseMaker [3], Scatter/Gather [7], Russell's sensemaking systems for large doc-

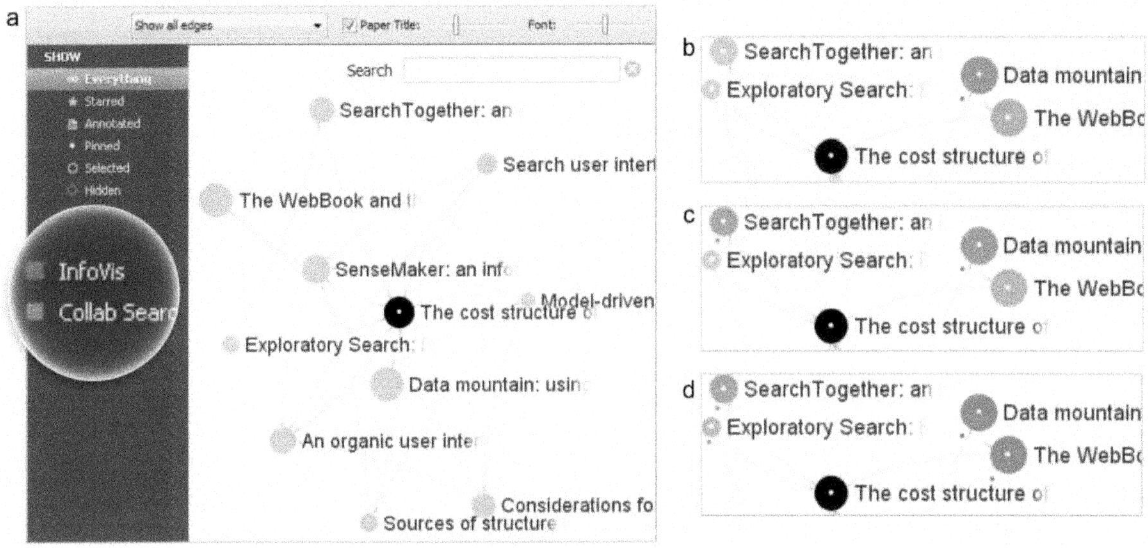

Figure 3. a) The Apolo user interface at start up, showing our starting article *The Cost Structure of Sensemaking* highlighted in black. Its top 10 most relevant articles, having the highest proximity relative to our article, are also shown (in gray). We have selected our paper; its incident edges representing either "citing" (pointing away from it) or "cited-by" (pointing at it) relationships are in dark gray. All other edges are in light gray, to maximize contrast and reduce visual clutter. Node size is proportional to an article's citation count. Our user has created two groups: *Collab Search* and *InfoVis* (magnified). b-d) Our user first spatially separates the two groups of articles, *Collab Search* on the left and *InfoVis* on the right (which also pins the nodes, indicated by white dots at center), then assigns them to the groups, making them *exemplars* and causing Apolo to compute the relevance of all other nodes, which is indicated by color saturation; the more saturated the color, the more likely it belongs to the group. The image sequence shows how the node color changes as more exemplars are added.

ument collections [30], Jigsaw [34], and Analyst's Notebook [16]. Other relevant approaches include [35] and [1] which investigated how to construct, organize and visualize topically related web resources.

Visualization and exploration

Apolo builds on a large body of research aimed at understanding and supporting how people can gain insights through visualization [17]. A number of tools have been developed to support "landscape" views of information. These include WebBook and WebForager [6], which use a book metaphor to find, collect, and manage web pages; Butterfly [21] aimed at accessing articles in citation networks; and Webcutter, which collects and presents URL collections in tree, star, and fisheye views [20]. For a more focused review on research visualizing bibliographic data, see [23].

In contrast to many of these systems which focus on providing overviews of information landscapes, Apolo adopts a bottom-up sensemaking approach [31] aimed at helping users construct their own landscapes of information. This is because people may have very different mental representations of information depending on their individual goals and prior experiences. To address this problem, some research has explored local exploration of graphs, including Treeplus [19], Vizster [10], and the degree-of-interest approach proposed in [37]. These approaches generally support the idea of starting with a small subgraph and expanding nodes to show their neighborhoods (and in the case of [37], help identify useful neighborhoods to expand). One key difference with these works is that Apolo changes the very structure of the expanded neighborhoods based on users' interactions, rather than assuming the same neighborhoods for all users. We will describe this approach in more detail when discussing Apolo's core design factors.

Graph mining algorithms and tools

A lot of research in graph mining studies how to automatically discover clusters (or groupings) in graphs, e.g., Graphcut [18], METIS [13]. Much work has also been done on developing methods to compute relevance between two nodes in a network; many of them belong to the class of spreading-activation [2] or propagation-based algorithms, e.g., HITS [15], PageRank [5], and *random walk with restart* [36]. Used by Apolo, Belief Propagation [40] is a message passing algorithm over link structures similar to spreading activation, but it is uniquely suited for graph sensemaking because it offers *simultaneous* support for: multiple user-specified exemplars (unlike [37]); any number of groups (unlike [2, 12, 37]); linear scalability with the number of edges (best possible for most graph algorithms); and soft clustering, supporting membership in multiple groups (unlike [18]). Few tools have integrated graph algorithms to interactively help people make sense of network information [12, 27, 37], and they often only support some of the sensemaking features offered by Apolo, e.g., [37] supports one group and a single exemplar.

INTRODUCING APOLO

The user interface

The Apolo user interface is composed of three main areas (Figure 2). The *Configuration Panel* at the top (1) provides several means for the user to reduce visual clutter and enhance readability of the visualization. Citation edges and article titles (i.e., node names) can be made invisible, and the font size and the visible length of the titles can be varied via sliders. On the left is the *Filter Panel* (2) and *Group Panel* (3). The *Filter Panel* provides filters to control the types of nodes to show; the default filter is "Everything", showing all types of nodes, except hidden ones. Other filters show nodes that are starred, annotated, pinned, selected, or hidden. The *Group Panel* lets the user create, rename, and delete groups. Group names are displayed with the automatically assigned color (to the left of the name) and the exemplar count (right side). Each group label also doubles as a filter, which causes only the exemplars of that group to be visible. The *Visualization Panel* (4) is the primary space where the user interacts with Apolo to incrementally and interactively build up a personalized visualization of the data.

Apolo in action

We show how Apolo works in action through a sensemaking scenario of exploring and understanding the landscape of the related research areas around the seminal article *The Cost Structure of Sensemaking* by Russell et al. (Figure 2 shows final results). This example uses real citation network data mined from Google Scholar using a breadth-first strategy to crawl all articles within three degrees from the above paper. The dataset contains about 83,000 articles (nodes) and 150,000 citations relationships (edges, each represents either a "citing" or "cited-by" relationships). This scenario will touch upon the interactions and major features of Apolo, and highlight how they work together to support sensemaking of large network data. We will describe the features in greater depth in the next section.

We begin with a single source article highlighted in black in the center of the interface (Figure 3a) and the ten most relevant articles as determined by the built-in BP algorithm. Articles are shown as circles with sizes proportional to their citation count. Citation relationships are represented by directed edges.

After viewing details of an article by mousing over it (Figure 4), the user moves it to a place on the landscape he thinks appropriate, where it remains pinned (as shown by the white dot at the center). The user can also star, annotate, unpin, or hide the node if so desired. After spatially arranging a few articles the user begins to visually infer the presence of two clusters: articles about *information visualization* (*InfoVis*) and *collaborative search* (*Collab Search*). After creating the labels for these two groups (Figure 3a), the user selects a good example article about *InfoVis* and clicks the *InfoVis* label, as shown in Figure 4, which puts the article into that group. A small blue dot (the group's color) appears below the article to indicate it is now an *exemplar* of that group. Changing an article's group membership causes BP to execute and infer the relevance of all other nodes in

Figure 4. The *Details Panel*, shown when mousing over an article, displays article details obtained from Google Scholar. The user has made the article an *exemplar* the *InfoVis* group by clicking the group's label.

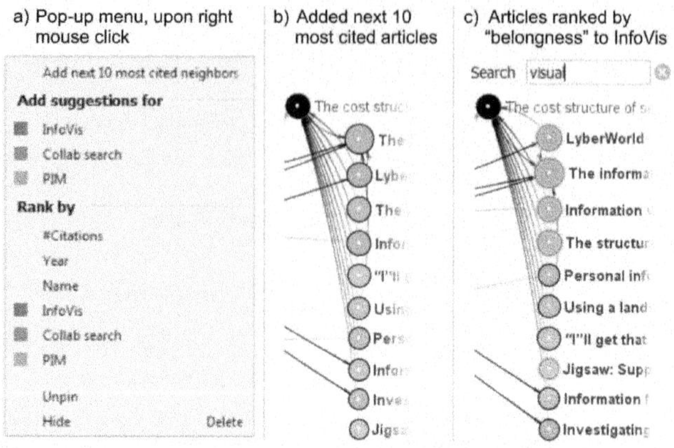

Figure 5. a) Pop-up menu shown upon right click; the user can choose to show more articles, add suggested articles for each group, rank sets of nodes in-place within the visualization, hide or unpin nodes. b) Newly added neighboring nodes ranked by citation count; they are selected by default to allow the user to easily relocate them all to a desired location. c) The same nodes, ranked by their "belongness" to the (blue) InfoVis group; articles whose titles contain "visual" are highlighted with yellow halos.

the network relative to the exemplar(s). A node's relevance is indicated by its color saturation; the more saturated the color, the more likely BP considers the node to belong to the group. Figure 3b-d show how the node color changes as more exemplars are added.

Our user now would like to find more articles for each group to further his understanding of the two research areas. The user right-clicks on the starting paper and selects "Add next 10 most cited neighbors" from the pop-up menu (Figure 5a). By default, new nodes added this way are ranked by citation count (proportional to node size, as shown in Figure 5b) and initially organized in a vertical list to make them easy to identify and process. To see how relevant these new nodes are, he uses Apolo's *rank-in-place* feature to rank articles by their computed relevance to the InfoVis group. To quickly locate the papers about visualization, our user types "visual" in the search box at the top-right corner (Figure 5c) to highlight all articles with "visual" in their titles.

Going further down the list of ranked articles, our users found more InfoVis articles and put them all into that group. Within it, our user further creates two subgroups spatially, as shown in Figure 6, the one on top containing articles about visualization applications (e.g., *Data mountain: using spatial memory for document management*), and the lower subgroup contains articles that seem to provide analytical type of information (e.g., *The structure of the information visualization design space*). Following this work flow, our user can iteratively refine the groups, create new ones, move articles

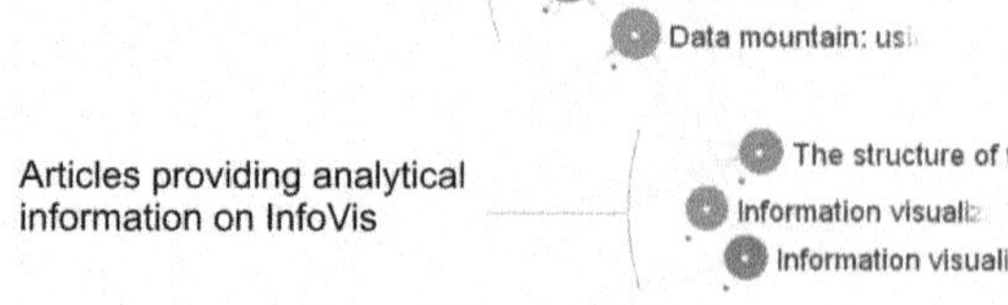

Figure 6. Two spatial subgroups

between them, and spatially rearrange nodes in the visualization. The user's landscape of the areas related to Sensemaking following further iterations is shown in Figure 2.

CORE DESIGN RATIONALE

Below we discuss core factors that demonstrate Apolo's contributions in supporting sensemaking.

Guided, personalized sensemaking and exploration

A key factor in the design of Apolo was having exploration and sensemaking be user-driven rather than data-driven—using structure in the data to support the user's evolving mental model rather than forcing the user to organize their mental model according to the structure of the data. This led to several interrelated features and design decisions. First, it drove our decision to support *exploration through construction*, where users create a mental map of an information space. By allowing users to define the map by pinning nodes to the layout, the system provides stability: familiar landmarks do not shift, unless the user decides to shift them. Contrast this to a pure force-directed layout algorithm, which may place items in a different location every time or shift all items when one is moved. Apolo's support for hybrid layout, mixing user-driven and automatic layout, is also different from work on semi-automatic layout (e.g., [32]) that uses constraints to improve a final layout, whereas Apolo supports constraints (fixing node positions) to help users evolve and externalize their mental models.

Second, instead of using an unsupervised graph clustering algorithm that uses the same similarity space for every user (as in [27]), we adapted a semi-supervised algorithm (BP) that would fundamentally change the structure of the similarity space based on user-labeled exemplars. Apolo uses this algorithm to find relevant nodes when starting up or when the user asks for group- or paper-relevant nodes, and to quantify relevance for use in ranking-in-place or indicating relevance through color. This means that even if two users' landscapes included the same nodes, those landscapes could be very different based on their goals and prior experience.

Multi-group Sensemaking of Network Data

Another important factor was the ability to support multiple dynamic, example-based groups. Theories of categorization suggest that people represent categories and schemas through examples or prototypes [29], as opposed to what are typical way of interacting with collections of information online such as search queries or tags. Furthermore, items may and often do belong to multiple groups, leading to a need for "soft" clustering.

Apolo was designed to support multiple groups both in the interface and algorithmically. In the interface, users can easily create multiple groups and move nodes into and out of one or more groups (via the *Details Panel*, Figure 4). Users can also see the degree to which the algorithm predicts items to be in a group through color. The use of the BP algorithm is instrumental as it can support fast, soft clustering on an arbitrary number of groups; many graph-based spreading activation-style algorithms are limited to one or two groups (such as PageRank [5], and random walk with restart [36]).

Evaluating exploration and sensemaking progress

Sensemaking involves evolution and re-representation of the user's mental model. Users typically continue evolving their models until they stop encountering new information; when the new information they encounter confirms rather than changes their existing mental representations; and when their representations are sufficiently developed to meet their goals. To assist in this evaluation process, Apolo surfaces change-relevant information in a number of ways. It helps the user keep track of which items have been seen or hidden. New nodes are added in a systematic way (Figure 5), to avoid disorienting the user. Pinned nodes serve as fixed landmarks in the users' mental map of the information space and can only be moved through direct action by the user. When saving and loading the information space, all pinned nodes remain where the user put them. Apolo uses all these features together to preserve the mental map that the user has developed about the graph structure over time [24].

As a node's group membership can be "toggled" easily, the user can experiment with moving a node in and out of a group to see how the relevance of the other nodes change, as visualized through the nodes' color changes; thus the effect of adding more exemplars (or removing them) is easily apparent. Also, color changes diminishing over time can help indicate the user's representations stabilizing.

Rank-in-place: adding meaning to node placement

Typically, layout algorithms for graphs (e.g., force-based layouts) try to layout nodes to minimize occlusion of nodes and edges, or to attain certain aesthetic requirements [9]. These layouts usually offer little help with the sensemaking process. Approaches to address this problem include "linked views", which use a separate view of the data (e.g., scatter plot) to aid node comparison; and imparting meaning to the node locations (e.g., in NodeXL [33] and PivotGraph [39]). However, the above approaches are often global in nature: all nodes in the network are repositioned, or a new, dedicated visualization created.

Apolo's main difference is that it offers a rank-in-place feature that can rank local subsets of nodes in meaningful ways.

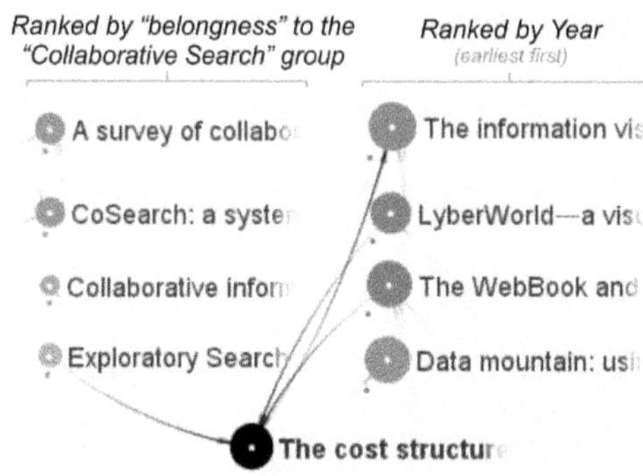

Figure 8. Our user applies two *rank-in-place* arrangements to the exemplars of *Collaborative Search* group (left, ranked by their "belongness" to the group) and the *InfoVis* group (right, ranked by year). These two side-by-side arrangements reveal several insights: 1) the *Collaborative Search* articles are less cited (smaller node sizes), as the research is more recent; 2) only the article *Exploratory Search* in the *Collaborative Search* group cited the source paper, while three papers in the *InfoVis* has either cited or been cited by the source paper.

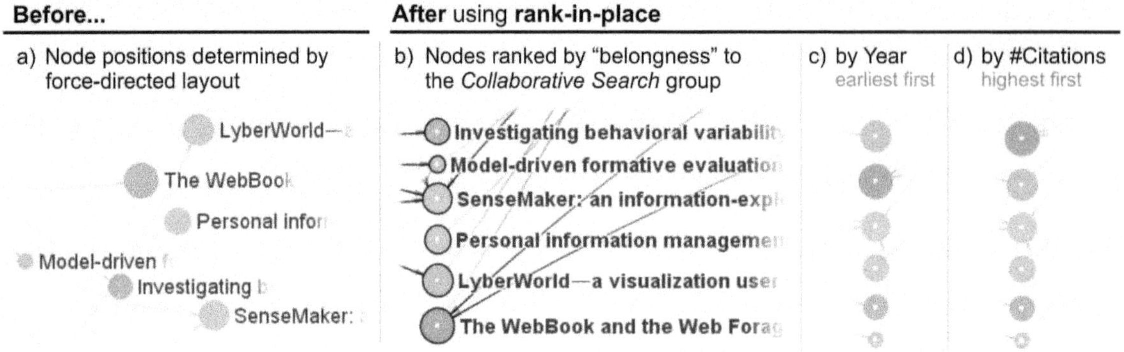

Figure 7. Illustrating how the user can learn more about a set of nodes using the rank-in-place feature, which imparts meaning to the nodes' locations, by vertically aligning and ordering them by a specified node attribute. (Node names have been hidden in figures c and d to reduce clutter.) a) Without using rank-in-place, nodes' positions are determined by a force-directed layout algorithm, which strives for aesthetic pleasantness, but offers little to help with sensemaking. b) Using rank-in-place, our user ranks the articles by their "belongingness" to the *Collaborative Search* group. c) Ranking articles by year reveals a different structure to the data. d) Ranking by citation count shows the "WebBook" article appears at the top as most cited.

Figure 7 shows one such example. Furthermore, the user can create multiple, simultaneous arrangements (through ranking) for different sets of nodes, which can have independent arrangement criteria (e.g., one ranks by year, the other ranks by citation count). We designed for this flexibility to allow other characteristics of the nodes (e.g., their edges, node sizes) to still be readily available, which may then be used in tandem with the node arrangement across multiple rankings (see Figure 8). Recently, researchers are exploring techniques similar to rank-in-place, to create scatterplots within a network visualization [38].

IMPLEMENTATION & DEVELOPMENT

Informed design through iterations

Sensemaking for large network data is an important problem which will undoubtedly take years of research to address. As such, our Apolo system only solves part of it; however, the system's current design is the result of over two years' investigation and development effort through many iterations and two major revisions.

The first version of Apolo presented suggestions in ranked lists without a visualization component (Figure 9), one list for each group in a floating window. Users' exemplars showed up at the top of the lists with the most relevant items in ranked order below them . We initially thought that the high data density and ease of comprehension of the list format might lead to better performance than a spatial layout. However, our users quickly pointed out the lack of a spatial layout, both as a workspace to externalize their mental representations as well as to understand the relations between items and between groups. This finding prompted us to add a network visualization component to the second revision. While working towards the second revision, we conducted contextual inquiries with six graduate students to better understand how they make sense of unfamiliar research topics through literature searches. We learned that they often started with some familiar articles, then tried to find works relevant to them, typically first considering the articles that cited or were cited by their familiar articles. Next, they considered those new articles' citation lists. And they would repeat this process until they had found enough relevant articles. This finding prompted us to add support for incremental, link-based exploration of the graph data.

Figure 9. The first version of Apolo

We studied the usability of the second revision through a pilot study, where we let a few researchers use Apolo to make sense of the literature around new topics that they recently came across. We learned that (1) they had a strong preference in using spatial arrangement to manage their exploration context, and to temporarily organize articles into approximate (spatial) groups; (2) they used the visualization directly most of the time, to see relations between articles and groups, and they only used the list for ranking articles. These findings prompted us to rethink Apolo's interaction design, and inspired us to come up with the *rank-in-place* technique that offers benefits of both a list-based approach and a spatial layout. *Rank-in-place* lays out nodes at a greater density, while keeping them quick to read and their relations easy to trace. With this new technique, we no longer needed the suggestion lists, and the visualization became the primary workspace in Apolo.

System Implementation

The Apolo system is written in Java 1.6. It uses the JUNG library [26] for visualizing the network. The network data is stored in an SQLite[1] embedded database, for its cross-platform portability and scalability up to tens of gigabytes. One of our goals is to offer Apolo as a sensemaking tool that work on a wide range of network data, so we designed the network database schema independently from the Apolo system, so that Apolo can readily be used on different network datasets that follow the schema.

[1] www.sqlite.org

We implemented BP as described in [22]. The key settings of the algorithm include: (1) a *node potential* function that represents how likely a node belongs to each group (a value closer to 1 means more likely), e.g., if we have two groups, then we assign (0.99, 0.01) to exemplars of group 1, and (0.5, 0.5) to all other nodes; (2) an *edge potential* function that governs to what extent an exemplar would convert its neighbors into the same group as the exemplar (a value of 1 means immediate conversion; we used 0.58).

EVALUATION

To evaluate Apolo, we conducted a laboratory study to assess how well people could use Apolo on a sensemaking task on citation data of scientific literature. At a high-level, we asked participants to find papers that could be used to update the related work section of a highly cited survey paper describing software tools for HCI [25]. We considered using other datasets such as movie data, but we felt that evaluation could be too subjective (genres are hard to define). In contrast, scientific literature provides a good balance between objectivity (some well-known research areas) and subjectivity (subject's different research experience). Another reason we chose scientific literature was because it was easier to assess "ground-truth" for evaluating the study results. More specifically, we used literature from computer science research areas of HCI (i.e., UIST), and had experts at our institution help establish "ground truth."

Participants

We recruited twelve participants from our university through a recruitment web site managed by our institution and through advertisements posted to a university message board. All participants were either research staff or students, and all had backgrounds in computer science or related fields, so they would be comfortable with the technical computer-related terms mentioned in the study materials. Our participants' average age was 24, and 9 were male and 3 were female. All participants were screened to make sure they had (1) participated in research activities, (2) were not familiar with user interface (UI) research, and (3) had conducted literature search before using Google Scholar. Seven of them have used other citation managers/websites, such as PubMed or JSTOR. Each study lasted for about 90 minutes, and the participants were paid $15 for their time.

We also had two judges who were experts with HCI research help evaluate the results of the participants. These judges have taught classes related to the UIST topics that the participants were exploring.

Apparatus

All participants used the same laptop computer that we provided. It was connected to an external 24" LCD monitor, with a mouse and keyboard. The computer was running Windows 7 and had Internet Explorer installed, which was used for all web-browsing-related activities. For the Apolo condition, we created a web crawler that downloaded citation data from Google Scholar using a breadth-first-search within three degrees of separation using the survey paper as the starting point. There was a total of about 61,000 articles and 110,000 citations among them.

Experiment Design & Procedure

We used a between-subjects design with two conditions: the Apolo condition and the Scholar condition, where participants used Google Scholar to search for papers. We considered using a within-subjects design, where the participants would be asked to find related work for two different survey papers from different domains using the two tools; however that would require the participants to simultaneously have a background in both domains while not being knowledgeable about both. We believed these constraints would make the scenarios used in the study overly artificial, and that qualified participants would be much harder to come across. However, we still wanted to elicit subjective feedback from the participants, especially for their thoughts on how the two tools compare to each other for the given task. To do this, we augmented each study with a second half where the participants used the other tool that they did not use in the first half. None of the data collected during these second tasks were used in the quantitative analysis of the results.

We asked participants to imagine themselves as researchers new to research in user interfaces (UI) who were tasked with updating an existing survey paper published in 2000. The participants were asked to find potentially relevant papers published since then, where relevant was defined as papers that they would want to include in an updated version. We felt that defining "relevant" was necessary and would be understandable by researchers. Given that finding relevant papers for the entire survey paper would be a very extensive task, both for participants and for the judges, we asked participants to focus on only two of the themes presented in the survey paper: *automatically generating user interfaces based on models* and *rapid prototyping tools for physical devices, not just software* (both paraphrased), which were in fact section titles in the paper.

In each condition, the participants spent 25 minutes on the literature search task. They were to spend the first 20 minutes to collect relevant articles, then the remaining five to select, for each category, 10 that they thought were most relevant. They did not have to rank them. We limited the time to 25 minutes to simulate a quick first pass filter on papers. In the Google Scholar condition, we set the "year filter" to the year 2000 so it would only return articles that were published on or after that year. In the Apolo condition, we started people with the survey paper. Participants in the Apolo condition were given an overview of the different parts of Apolo's user interface and interaction techniques, and a sheet of paper describing its main features.

Results

We examined our results using both a quantitative approach as well as subject measures. We pooled together all the articles that the participants found in the study and divided them into two stacks, "model-based" and "prototyping", according to how they were specified by the participants. For each article, we located a soft copy (usually a PDF) and printed out the paper title, abstract and author information. We col-

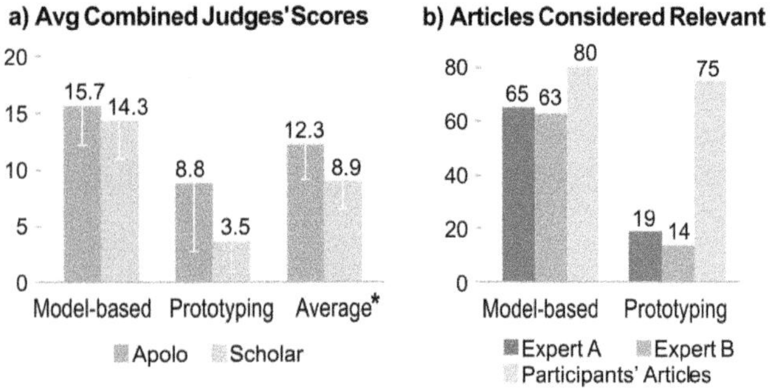

Figure 10. a) Average combined judges' scores; an article from a participant receives a score of 1 when it is considered relevant by an expert (min is 0, max is 2). The average score across both categories was significantly higher in the Apolo condition. Error bars represent -1 stdev, * indicates statistically significant. b) The number of articles considered relevant by the two expert judges (blue and orange). The total number of articles found by participants are in gray. The two experts strongly agree with each other in their judgment.

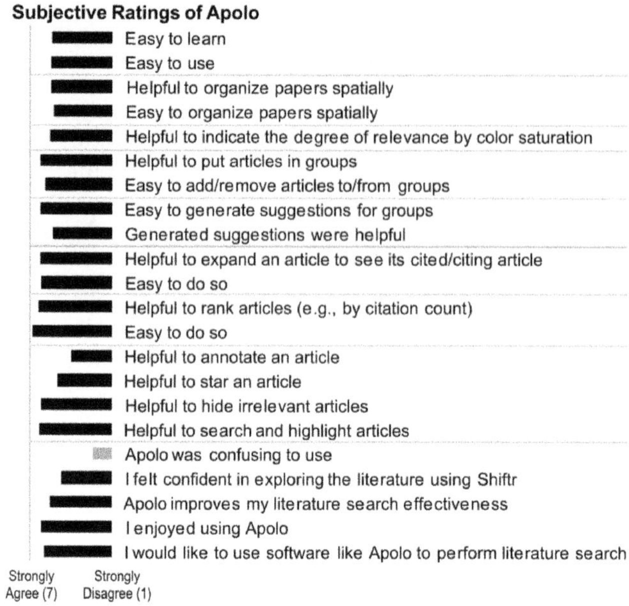

Figure 11. Subjective ratings of Apolo. Participants rated Apolo favorably. Features for grouping, suggesting and ranking nodes, were highly rated. Apolo's usage was very clear to most participants (green bar).

lected these printouts and sorted them alphabetically. These printouts were used by the expert judges. We had the two judges select papers relevant to the topic. We represented each expert's judgment as a vector of 0s and 1s. An article was marked with "1" if the expert considered it relevant, and "0" otherwise. We used cosine similarity to evaluate the similarity between the two experts. A score of 1 means complete agreement, and 0 means complete disagreement. For the "Model-based" articles, the cosine similarity between the experts' judgement was 0.97. For the "Prototyping" articles, despite few papers being considered relevant by the judges, the cosine similarity was 0.86.

In our evaluation, the independent factor is "participant", and the dependent factor is the relevance scores assigned by the expert judges. Using a two-tailed t-test, we found the average score across both categories was significantly higher in the Apolo condition ($t(9.7) = 2.32, p < 0.022$), as shown in Figure 10a. We also note that participants in both conditions did well for finding papers related to model-based interfaces. One reason for this is that papers in this category tended to have the word "automatic" or "model" in the title. However, the same was not true for papers in the prototyping category.

Subjective Results

Overall, participants felt that Apolo improved their sensemaking experience. Based on a post-test survey, Apolo seemed to be easy to use, as shown in Figure 11 and 12. These results are encouraging given that Apolo was not designed as a walk-up-and-use system.

We organized qualitative feedback from participants into three categories. The first relates to general sensemaking and organization. One participant said that Apolo "helped much more in organizing search[...] Google was a bit random." The graph visualization was also helpful. One person said that it "helped me see the citation network in which articles cited which ones". Another said that the "indication of degree relevance by color was extremely helpful and easy to use and it also helped to make sense of the articles." Being able to spatially organize papers was also a useful feature and participants were happy about using it. One person said that "arrangement of articles in my order of preference & my preferred location was easy." We do note that the task that we had participants do was somewhat limited in scale, but for the current task the screen real estate available was sufficient. Seeing connections between papers was also helpful. Participants said that "it helped me see the citation network in which articles cited which ones", and that it was an "easy way to list & relate citations graphically." Participants also had constructive feedback for improving Apolo. One comment was to have abstracts be more readily available in Apolo (a constraint of the crawling software, since Google Scholar does not have full abstracts in an accessible format). Another comment was that there would often be too many edges, a problem common to graph visualizations.

Discussion and Limitations

While the results of our evaluation was positive, there are also several limitations. For example, we only had participants examine two themes. Having more themes would stress the screen real estate. Apolo currently has minimal features for managing screen real estate.

We also did not evaluate category creation and removal; participants were given two categories that correspond to two

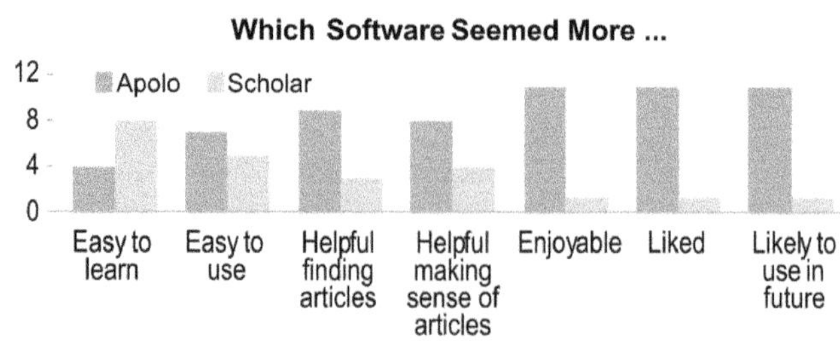

Figure 12. Participants liked and enjoyed using Apolo, and would like to use it again in the future. They generally found Apolo more useful than Google Scholar in helping them find relevant articles and make sense of them.

sections in the given overview paper, which may not be the most natural categories that they would like to create. However, if we were to allow the participants to create any group they wanted, the great variety of possible groups created would make our evaluation extremely difficult. Moreover, a pilot study found that more categories required more prior knowledge than participants would have. Two categories were in fact already challenging, as indicated by the few relevant articles found for the "Prototyping" group.

The need for the participants to categorize articles was created by the tasks; however, in real-world scenarios, such needs would be ad hoc. We plan to study such needs, as well as how Apolo can handle those kinds of tasks, in less controlled situations. For example, how many groups do people create? Do the groupings evolve over time, such as through merging or subdivision. How well do the findings of sensemaking literature apply to large graph data?

DISCUSSION & FUTURE WORK

We believe mixed-initiative approaches for network exploration are becoming increasingly important as more datasets with millions or even billions of nodes and edges are becoming available. These numbers vastly exceed people's limited cognitive capacities. By combining a person's reasoning skills with computer algorithms for processing large amounts of data, we hope to reduce the disparity in gaining access to and comprehending the vast amount of graph data that have become increasingly available. Automated analysis methods and algorithms for extracting useful information, such as patterns and anomalies, are active research topics. However, these methods can rarely give the perfect solutions, or even if they can, it is necessary to convey such information to the user. Our work seeks to reach the goal of supporting sensemaking through a mix of rich user interaction and machine learning.

Visually managing many nodes is also an open problem in graph sensemaking; Apolo currently focuses on filtering, e.g. enabling users to remove nodes from the visualization, re-add them, or focus only on selected ones. By integrating BP, we hope to help users find relevant nodes quickly and remove unnecessary nodes from the visualization more easily than a manual approach. We have been experimenting with methods that will help further, such as semantic zooming, and reversibly collapsing nodes into meta nodes.

Apolo currently relies exclusively on the link-structure of a graph to make relevance judgments. In the future, we would like to integrate other types of information as well, such as the textual content of the nodes and edges (e.g., the content of an article), edge weights, and temporal information (particularly important for analyzing dynamic networks).

We are also developing features in Apolo to support data from many more sources. Some of these include other citation data sets, such as from the ACM and the IEEE digital libraries, CiteSeerX, and using one's own personal citation libraries (in software like Zotero, Mendeley, and EndNote) to discover new papers. However, Apolo can be used on any network data; for example, we have conducted successful proof of concepts integrations of tagging data from delicious, friendship networks from Facebook, and recipe-ingredient networks. As we move forward it will be important to understand the degree to which context-specific features are necessary in order to support sensemaking across a variety of domains. Finally, we plan to release Apolo for general use and collect feedback and ideas from the community about its usefulness and how to improve it.

CONCLUSIONS

This paper introduces Apolo, a mixed-initiative system for helping users make sense of large network data. Apolo tightly couples large scale machine learning with rich interaction and visualization features to help people explore graphs through constructing personalized information landscapes. We demonstrate the utility of Apolo through a scenario and evaluation of sensemaking in scientific literature. The results of the evaluation suggest the system provides significant benefits to sensemaking and was viewed positively by users. This work focuses on the scientific literature domain; a recent work [12] showed that approaches similar to ours (based on spreading activation) could also work well for graph data of websites and tags. We believe that the ideas in Apolo can be helpful for many other kinds of data intensive domains, by aiding analysts in sifting through large amounts of data and directing users' focus to interesting items.

ACKNOWLEDGEMENT

We thank Scott Hudson and Brad Myers for their help with the user study. This work is partially supported by an IBM Faculty Award, the National Science Foundation under Grants No. CNS-0721736, IIS0970179, IIS-0968484, OCI-0943148 and under the auspices of the U.S. Department of Energy by Lawrence Livermore National Laboratory under contract No. DE-AC52-07NA27344, and by the Army Research Laboratory under Cooperative Agreement Number W911NF-09-2-0053. The views and conclusions contained in this document are those of the authors and should not be interpreted as representing the official policies, either expressed or implied, of the Army Research Laboratory, the U.S. Government, NSF, or any other funding parties. The U.S. Government is authorized to reproduce and distribute reprints for Government purposes notwithstanding any copyright notation here on.

REFERENCES

1. B. Amento, W. Hill, L. Terveen, D. Hix, and P. Ju. An empirical evaluation of user interfaces for topic management of web sites. In *Proc. CHI*, page 559. ACM, 1999.
2. J. Anderson. A spreading activation theory of memory. *Journal of verbal learning and verbal behavior*, 22(3):261–95, 1983.
3. M. Q. W. Baldonado and T. Winograd. Sensemaker: an information-exploration interface supporting the contextual evolution of a user's interests. In *Proc. CHI*, pages 11–18. ACM Press New York, NY, USA, 1997.
4. L. Barsalou. Ad hoc categories. *Memory & Cognition*, 11(3):211–227, May 1983.
5. S. Brin and L. Page. The anatomy of a large-scale hypertextual Web search engine* 1. *Computer networks and ISDN systems*, 30(1-7):107–117, 1998.

6. S. Card, G. Robertson, and W. York. The WebBook and the Web Forager: an information workspace for the World-Wide Web. In *Proc. CHI*. ACM, 1996.
7. D. Cutting, D. Karger, J. Pedersen, and J. Tukey. Scatter/gather: A cluster-based approach to browsing large document collections. In *Proc. SIGIR*, pages 318–329. ACM Press, 1992.
8. B. Dervin. An overview of sense-making research: concepts, methods and results to date. In *International Communications Association Annual Meeting*, 1983.
9. G. Di Battista, P. Eades, R. Tamassia, and I. Tollis. *Graph drawing: algorithms for the visualization of graphs*. Prentice Hall PTR Upper Saddle River, NJ, USA, 1998.
10. J. Heer and D. Boyd. Vizster: Visualizing online social networks. *Proc. InfoVis*, pages 33–40, 2005.
11. K. Holyoak and P. Thagard. *Mental leaps: Analogy in creative thought*. The MIT Press, 1996.
12. Y. Kammerer, R. Nairn, P. Pirolli, and E. H. Chi. Signpost from the masses: learning effects in an exploratory social tag search browser. In *Proc. CHI*, 2009.
13. G. Karypis and V. Kumar. METIS: Unstructured graph partitioning and sparse matrix ordering system. *The University of Minnesota*, 2.
14. F. Keil. *Concepts, kinds, and cognitive development*. The MIT Press, 1989.
15. J. Kleinberg. Authoritative sources in a hyperlinked environment. *Journal of the ACM (JACM)*, 46(5):604–632, 1999.
16. P. Klerks. The network paradigm applied to criminal organisations. *Connections*, 24(3):53–65, 2001.
17. B. Kules. From keyword search to exploration: How result visualization aids discovery on the web.
18. V. Kwatra, A. Schodl, I. Essa, G. Turk, and A. Bobick. Graphcut textures: Image and video synthesis using graph cuts. *ACM Transactions on Graphics*, 22(3):277–286, 2003.
19. B. Lee, C. Parr, C. Plaisant, B. Bederson, V. Veksler, W. Gray, and C. Kotfila. Treeplus: Interactive exploration of networks with enhanced tree layouts. *TVCG*, pages 1414–1426, 2006.
20. Y. Maarek, M. Jacovi, M. Shtalhaim, S. Ur, D. Zernik, and I. Ben-Shaul. WebCutter: a system for dynamic and tailorable site mapping. *Computer Networks and ISDN Systems*, 29(8-13):1269–1279, 1997.
21. J. Mackinlay, R. Rao, and S. Card. An organic user interface for searching citation links. In *Proc. CHI*, page 73. ACM, 1995.
22. M. McGlohon, S. Bay, M. G. Anderle, D. M. Steier, and C. Faloutsos. Snare: a link analytic system for graph labeling and risk detection. In *Proceedings of the 15th ACM SIGKDD international conference on Knowledge discovery and data mining*, KDD '09, pages 1265–1274, New York, NY, USA, 2009. ACM.
23. G. McKiernan. New Age Navigation. *The Serials Librarian*, 45(2):87–123, 2003.
24. K. Misue, P. Eades, W. Lai, and K. Sugiyama. Layout adjustment and the mental map. *Journal of Visual Languages and Computing*, 6(2):183–210, 1995.
25. B. Myers, S. Hudson, and R. Pausch. Past, present, and future of user interface software tools. *TOCHI*, 7(1):3–28, 2000.
26. J. OMadadhain, D. Fisher, P. Smyth, S. White, and Y. Boey. Analysis and visualization of network data using JUNG. *Journal of Statistical Software*, 10:1–35, 2005.
27. A. Perer and B. Shneiderman. Integrating statistics and visualization: case studies of gaining clarity during exploratory data analysis. In *Proc. CHI*, pages 265–274, New York, NY, USA, 2008. ACM.
28. P. Pirolli and S. Card. The sensemaking process and leverage points for analyst technology as identified through cognitive task analysis. In *Proc. IA*, 2005.
29. E. Rosch and C. Mervis. Family resemblances: Studies in the internal structure of categories. *Cognitive psychology*, 7(4):573–605, 1975.
30. D. M. Russell, M. Slaney, Y. Qu, and M. Houston. Being literate with large document collections: Observational studies and cost structure tradeoffs. In *HICSS*, page 55. IEEE, 2006.
31. D. M. Russell, M. J. Stefik, P. Pirolli, and S. K. Card. The cost structure of sensemaking. In *Proc. CHI*, pages 269–276. ACM Press, 1993.
32. K. Ryall, J. Marks, and S. Shieber. An interactive constraint-based system for drawing graphs. In *Proc. UIST*, pages 97–104. ACM, 1997.
33. M. Smith, B. Shneiderman, N. Milic-Frayling, E. Mendes Rodrigues, V. Barash, C. Dunne, T. Capone, A. Perer, and E. Gleave. Analyzing (social media) networks with NodeXL. In *Proc. C&T*, pages 255–264. ACM, 2009.
34. J. Stasko, C. Gorg, Z. Liu, and K. Singhal. Jigsaw: supporting investigative analysis through interactive visualization. *InfoVis*, 7(2):118, 2008.
35. L. Terveen, W. Hill, and B. Amento. Constructing, organizing, and visualizing collections of topically related web resources. *TOCHI*, 6(1):94, 1999.
36. H. Tong, C. Faloutsos, and J. Pan. Fast random walk with restart and its applications. In *ICDM*, pages 613–622, 2006.
37. F. van Ham and A. Perer. "Search, Show Context, Expand on Demand": Supporting Large Graph Exploration with Degree-of-Interest. *IEEE TVCG*, 15(6).
38. C. Viau, M. J. McGuffin, Y. Chiricota, and I. Jurisica. The flowvizmenu and parallel scatterplot matrix: Hybrid multidimensional visualizations for network exploration. *IEEE Transactions on Visualization and Computer Graphics*, 16:1100–1108, 2010.
39. M. Wattenberg. Visual exploration of multivariate graphs. In *Proc. CHI*, page 819. ACM, 2006.
40. J. Yedidia, W. Freeman, and Y. Weiss. Understanding belief propagation and its generalizations. *Exploring artificial intelligence in the new millennium*, 8:236–239, 2003.

Mid-air Pan-and-Zoom on Wall-sized Displays

Mathieu Nancel[1,2] Julie Wagner[2,1] Emmanuel Pietriga[2,1] Olivier Chapuis[1,2] Wendy Mackay[2,1]

[1]LRI - Univ Paris-Sud & CNRS
F-91405 Orsay, France

[2]INRIA
F-91405 Orsay, France

Figure 1. Panning and zooming in Spitzer's 396 032 x 12 000 = 4.7 billion pixels images of the inner part of our galaxy.

ABSTRACT
Very-high-resolution wall-sized displays offer new opportunities for interacting with large data sets. While pointing on this type of display has been studied extensively, higher-level, more complex tasks such as pan-zoom navigation have received little attention. It thus remains unclear which techniques are best suited to perform multiscale navigation in these environments. Building upon empirical data gathered from studies of pan-and-zoom on desktop computers and studies of remote pointing, we identified three key factors for the design of mid-air pan-and-zoom techniques: uni- vs. bimanual interaction, linear vs. circular movements, and level of guidance to accomplish the gestures in mid-air. After an extensive phase of iterative design and pilot testing, we ran a controlled experiment aimed at better understanding the influence of these factors on task performance. Significant effects were obtained for all three factors: bimanual interaction, linear gestures and a high level of guidance resulted in significantly improved performance. Moreover, the interaction effects among some of the dimensions suggest possible combinations for more complex, real-world tasks.

General Terms
Design, Human Factors, Performance

Author Keywords
Multi-scale interfaces, Pan & Zoom, Navigation, Wall-sized Displays, Mid-air interaction techniques.

ACM Classification Keywords
H.5.2 Information Interfaces and Presentation: User Interfaces. - Graphical user interfaces.

INTRODUCTION
Very-high-resolution wall-sized displays can accommodate several hundred megapixels and make it possible to visualize very large, heterogeneous datasets in many domains [1, 3, 34]. Astronomers can use them to display telescope images constructed from hundreds of thousands of frames stitched together, such as Spitzer's 4.7 billion pixels images of the inner part of our galaxy (Figure 1). Biologists can explore the docking of complex molecules. Artists can create gigapixel images, such as the 26 gigapixel panorama of Paris based on 2,346 pictures stitched together. Crisis management centers can interact with highly detailed maps of very large areas. For example, OpenStreetMap data range from a view of the world down to street level, resulting in an image that requires 18 peta ($18 \cdot 10^{15}$) pixels at its highest level of detail.

With resolutions up to 100-dpi, these LCD-based displays afford more physical forms of navigation [3, 32, 34] compared to conventional desktop setups or to lower-resolution projection-based large displays: Users simply step back to get an overview of the displayed data and walk forward to see details, including small but legible text. However, as the examples above show, datasets increase in size faster than displays increase in dimensions and pixel density. The display depicted in Figure 1 consists of thirty-two 30-inch tiled monitors and can display a "mere" 131 million pixels. NASA's Hyperwall-2, to our knowledge the largest wall built to date, only doubles that number, and does so by adding some screens that users cannot reach. Virtual navigation is thus still required, as datasets can be several orders of magnitude too large to fit on even wall-sized displays [4].

Many interaction techniques have been specifically designed to help users navigate large multiscale worlds on desktop computers, using zooming and associated interface schemes [11]. However, high-resolution wall-sized displays pose different sets of trade-offs. It is critical to their success that interaction techniques account for both the physical characteristics of the environment and the context of use, including cooperative work aspects. Input should be location-independent and should require neither a hard surface such as a desk nor clumsy equipment: users should have the ability to move freely in front of the display and interact at a distance [3, 34]. This precludes use of conventional input devices such as keyboards and mice, as well as newer interaction techniques: The powerful multi-finger gestural input techniques designed by Malik *et al.* [22] were devised for interaction with lower-resolution large displays from afar. They require sitting at a desk, and are thus not optimal for displays of very high-resolution that afford more physical forms of navigation. The recent Cyclostar approach [21] is very elegant, but requires the display surface to be touch-enabled, a feature that wall-sized displays often lack. Cyclostar is also not well-suited to wall-sized displays, as it requires users to be within arm's reach of the display surface. While this is perfectly acceptable for displays up to 1.5m in diagonal such as SMART Boards™, users of larger displays such as the one in Figure 1 (5.8m in diagonal) would only see a very limited portion of the display while navigating. This lack of an overview would be a non-negligible hindrance as navigation is mostly driven by contextual information.

Our goal is to study different families of location-independent, mid-air input techniques for pan-zoom navigation on wall-sized displays. More specifically, we seek to answer questions related to the performance and subjective preferences of users, including: Beyond their almost universal appeal, do gestures performed in free space work better than those input via devices operated in mid-air? Is bimanual interaction more efficient in this context? Is it more tiring? Do circular, continuous gestures perform better than those that require clutching (restoring the hand or finger to a more comfortable posture)? We ground our work on both theoretical and experimental work on bimanual input [8, 14, 18], the influence of limb segments on input performance [2, 35], on types of gestures [25, 33] and on the integral nature, in terms of perceptual structure, of the pan-zoom task [17]. In particular, we are interested in comparing the following dimensions: bimanual vs. unimanual input; device-based vs. free-hand techniques; degrees of freedom (DOF) and associated kinesthetic and haptic feedback; and types of movements: linear gestures vs. circular, clutch-free gestures.

RELATED WORK

This work is at the intersection of many HCI research areas, including multiscale interfaces, large displays, spatial input and travel in virtual environments. This section highlights strongly related or seminal work that guided our designs and we point to relevant surveys, when available.

Large Displays

Large displays have been the focus of much research and evaluation over the last ten years. Ni *et al.* [27] survey hardware configurations, rendering techniques as well as interaction techniques for many different types of large displays.

Overall, the body of empirical work on large displays suggests that users can greatly benefit from their use. It also shows that the design of interaction techniques has to be carefully adapted to the characteristics of these displays and to their context of use. Early studies investigated how users could benefit from larger displays in different settings. Baudisch *et al.* [4] found advantages to using a large focus+context screen over zooming and overviews to extract information from large documents such as maps and schematics of circuit boards. Improvements to spatial task performance were also identified in several complementary studies [12, 26, 31].

Other works have focused on the size and configuration of high-resolution tiled displays. Ball *et al.* [3] found that for tasks involving pan-zoom, such as navigating to a known location, searching for specific targets or looking for patterns, users perform better with larger viewport sizes that require less virtual navigation, promoting physical navigation instead. Virtual navigation was always performed with the same device: a gyroscopic mouse. Results from other recent studies suggest that large displays are also beneficial for information visualization and analysis tasks thanks to the larger amount of data that can be displayed [1, 34].

Spatial Input and Mid-air Interaction Techniques

Spatial input has been studied for years in the context of travel in immersive virtual environments and other 3D user interfaces based on virtual camera control with techniques using gloves, bimanual input and leaning, or high degrees of freedom devices [7, 24, 35]. Hinckley *et al.* [16] present a survey of design issues in spatial input, including fatigue, recalibration, clutching, motion and orientation, unimanual vs. bimanual interaction. One important issue they raise is the interdependency of all these aspects, that makes formal studies challenging, as we will see later.

Several input devices make it possible to point in mid-air on large displays: commercial devices such as gyroscopic mice, or *soap* [5], based on hardware found in a conventional optical mouse wrapped in elastic fabric. ARC-Pad [23] enables seamless absolute+relative pointing on large displays through a mobile touchscreen. The VisionWand [10] is a passive wand whose colored tips are tracked in 3D by two webcams. The multiple degrees of freedom enable a richer interaction vocabulary, that includes pan-zoom navigation.

Recent advances in motion tracking and dynamic gesture recognition technologies now make it possible to investigate freehand input techniques. Vogel and Balakrishnan [32] propose three pointing and clicking techniques that work with bare hands, with emphasis on important design characteristics such as accuracy, performance, but also comfort of use. Zigelbaum *et al.* [36] describe a gestural interface based on Oblong's *g-speak* spatial operating environment to navigate in a collection of videos arranged in a 3D interface through a set of twenty hand-centric gestures.

Multi-scale Navigation on the Desktop

Pan-zoom navigation techniques have been studied for many years in the more general context of multiscale interfaces for the desktop. Cockburn *et al.* [11] provide a thorough survey of the many zooming, overview + detail and focus + context techniques, as well as empirical work that evaluated them.

Of particular interest to us is the work by Guiard *et al.* on multiscale pointing. Multiscale pointing consists of panning and zooming the view so as to bring the target in view, followed by a cursor pointing action to that target [15]. They performed several empirical studies, showing that multiscale pointing obeys Fitts' law, and that performance bandwidth is proportional to view size (up to a ceiling that we far exceed on wall-sized displays). They introduced an experimental task adapted from Fitts' reciprocal pointing task, that we further adapt to take into account potential overshoots in the scale dimension. An earlier paper [6] evaluated pan-zoom performance with uni- and bimanual input, suggesting that performance is enhanced with two hands, as it affords better pan-zoom coordination. Pan-zoom navigation has however not received much attention beyond desktop interfaces, except for the recent work by Malacria *et al.* on Cyclostar [21], specifically designed for touch-enabled surfaces and discussed in more detail in the next section.

PANNING AND ZOOMING IN MID-AIR

A large body of literature is devoted to the design and evaluation of input devices that feature a high number of degrees of freedom (DOF). Available degrees of freedom have a direct impact on the potential for parallelization of actions required to achieve the task. For example, 6DOF input devices can increase the degree of parallelization of docking tasks [35], though studies report limits in terms of human capacity to handle all DOFs simultaneously. Pan and zoom is a 3DOF task: the user controls the view's position (x, y) and its scale (s). The possible solutions for mapping pan and zoom to three input channels are endless.

The film industry offers interesting and visually attractive scenarios with movies such as *Minority Report* which show users interacting via freehand gestures to navigate in a seemingly fluid and efficient way. The technology to achieve this type of interaction is now available in research laboratories and beyond [36]. However, it remains unclear how freehand gestures actually fare when compared to device-based input techniques that take advantage of the human ability to use physical tools [10] and suffer less from problems commonly associated with spatial input [16], such as precision and fatigue. Years of research in virtual reality have demonstrated that devising efficient navigation techniques for immersive virtual environments is still a challenge.

Our goal is to study families of input techniques that let users pan and zoom from any location in front of very high-resolution, wall-sized displays. We made no *a priori* assumptions about relevant metaphors or technologies and considered freehand as well as device-based techniques.

An extensive design and testing phase allowed us to limit the number of candidates for the subsequent formal evaluation. For instance, the apparently intuitive solution that consists in using two hands or two fingers to zoom with pinch and stretch gestures was considered but quickly discarded: while these gestures work well on touch-sensitive surfaces such as tabletops, they are much less natural when performed in mid-air. Most importantly, they proved quite inaccurate, and tiring. Another category of techniques that was discarded are those based on first-order-of-control and operated via an elastic or isometric input device. As reported in the literature in the case of pointing, e.g., [9], our pilot tests revealed that techniques based on first-order-of-control allow for fast and comfortable coarse navigation, but perform poorly during the final precise positioning phase, causing numerous overshoots.

Factors		Advantages	Disadvantages
Hands	One	• One hand available for other actions	• Pan and zoom are performed sequentially
	Two	• Pan and zoom can be performed in parallel	• No hand available for other actions
Gesture	Linear	• Direct, natural mapping to zoom actions	• Potentially requires clutching
	Circular	• No clutching (continuous gesture)	• Less natural mapping to zoom actions
Degree of Guidance	1D path	• Input guided by strong haptic feedback • Mainly involves fingers	• Only 1 degree of freedom
	2D surface	• Many degrees of freedom • Mainly involves fingers	• Input guided by limited haptic feedback
	3D free hand	• Many degrees of freedom • No device	• No haptic feedback • Mainly involves whole hand and arms

Table 1. Key Dimensions of the Design Space

We eventually identified a set of twelve candidate techniques. Their design was informed by related empirical studies reported in the literature and refined through prototyping and pilot testing. These techniques can be organized according to three key dimensions forming a design space (Table 1), and introduced in the following sections. In addition to performance (task time and accuracy), we took into account other usability issues, such as fatigue and ease of use.

Unimanual vs. Bimanual Input

In their paper on the perceptual structure of multidimensional input, Jacob and Sibert claim that panning and zooming are integrally related: the user does not think of them as separate operations, but rather as a single, integral task like "*focus on that area over there*" [17]. Buxton and Myers [8] and later Bourgeois and Guiard [6] observed high levels of parallelism for pan-zoom operations, further supporting this argument. The level of parallelism correlates with task performance and is typically well afforded by the use of bimanual input techniques [14, 18]. While we expect bimanual techniques to outperform unimanual ones, we are still interested in comparing their performance, as the latter might still be of interest in more complex, real-world tasks that require input channels for other actions.

Linear vs. Circular Gestures

Navigating in the scale dimension (zooming in and out) is a task typically performed through vertical scroll gestures on, e.g., a mouse wheel or a touchpad. The mapping from input to command is natural, but often entails clutching as the course of mouse wheels and touchpads is very limited. An alternative consists in mapping continuous circular gestures to zooming. Clockwise gestures zoom in; counter-clockwise

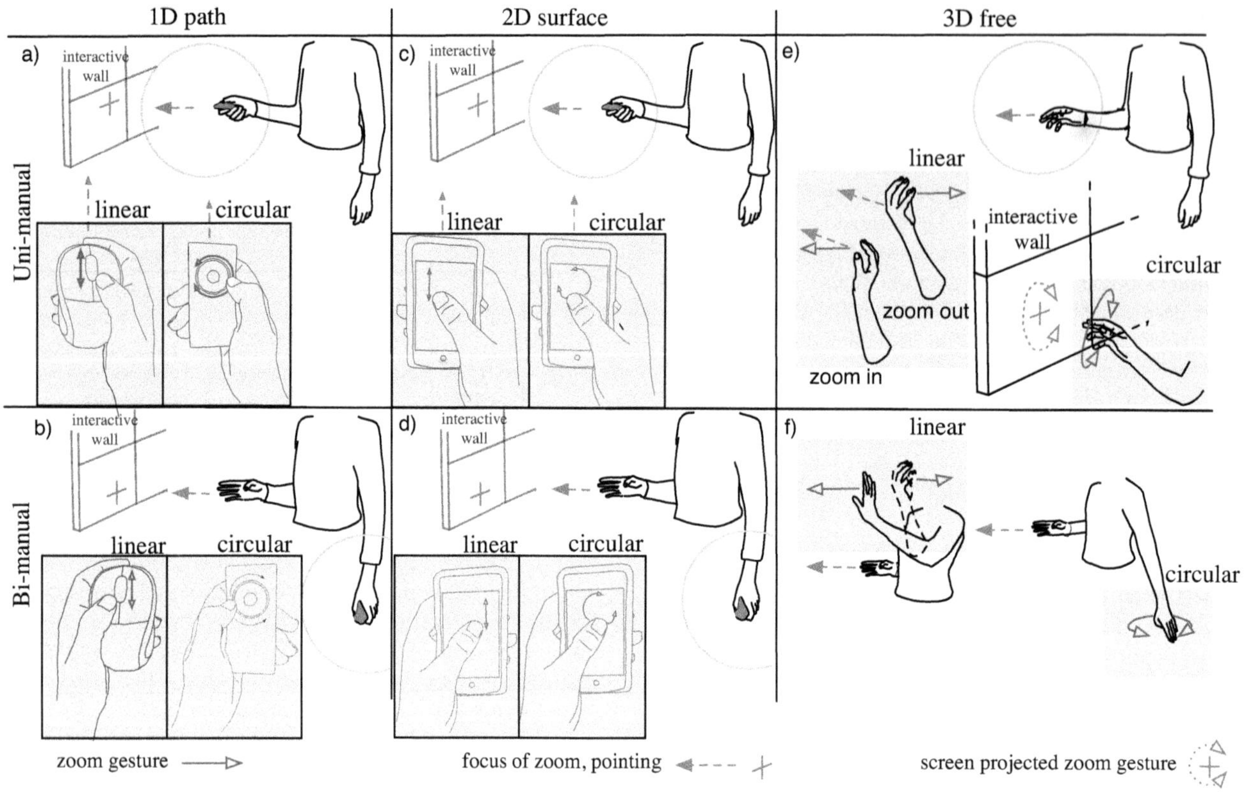

Figure 2. Matrix of the 12 techniques organized according to key characteristics: uni- vs. bimanual, degree of guidance, linear vs. circular gestures. 1D path involves guiding gestures along a particular path in space; in 2D surface gestures are made on a touch-sensitive surface; while in 3D free gestures are totally free.

gestures zoom out. Despite the less natural mapping from input to commands, such continuous, clutch-free gestures have been successfully applied to vertical scrolling in documents [25, 33], and to pan and zoom on large, touch-sensitive surfaces in CycloStar [21]. Circular gestures potentially benefit from an automatic Vernier effect [13]: as zooming is mapped to angular movements, the larger the circular gesture's radius, the greater the distance that has to be covered to make a full circle, and consequently the more precise the input.

Guidance through Passive Haptic Feedback

Two main categories of techniques have been studied for mid-air interaction on wall-sized displays: freehand techniques based on motion tracking [32, 36]; and techniques that require the user to hold an input device [5, 10, 19, 23]. Input devices provide some guidance to the user in terms of what gesture to execute, as all of them provide some sort of passive haptic feedback: A finger operating a knob or a mouse wheel follows a specific path; gestures on touch-enabled devices are made on planar surfaces. Freehand techniques, on the contrary, provide essentially no feedback to the user who can only rely on proprioception [24] to execute the gesture. We call this dimension the *degree of guidance*. Gestures can be guided to follow a particular path in space (*1D path*); they can be guided on a touch-sensitive surface (*2D surface*) ; or they can be totally free (*3D free*). These three values correspond to decreasing amounts of passive haptic feedback for the performance of input gestures.

DESIGN CHOICES

Panning. For all techniques, controlling the cursor's position is achieved naturally by ray-casting from the dominant hand to the wall display (dashed arrows in Figure 2). As mentioned earlier, first order of control was discarded for both pan and zoom operations. Panning is achieved by dragging, as in applications such as Adobe Illustrator™ or Google Maps™ with their typical hand-shaped cursor.

Zooming. As in desktop applications such as Google Maps or NASA's WorldWind, *linear* techniques zoom in by moving forward towards the display and zoom out by moving backwards; *circular* techniques zoom in by turning clockwise and zoom out by turning counter-clockwise (solid arrows in Figure 2). Pointing plays an important role when zooming, as it specifies the focus of expansion (zoom in)/contraction (zoom out). Letting users specify this focus point is very important on displays of that physical size, as they will typically not be standing right in the center. A focus of expansion implicitly located at the center of the screen would make zooming operations tedious and hard to control as every zoom operation would require multiple panning actions to compensate drifts induced by the offset focus.

Bi-manual interaction. All bimanual techniques (Figure 2, bottom row) are grounded in Guiard's study of asymmetric division of labor in bimanual actions that led to the Kinematic chain model [14]. Following the observation that motion of the dominant hand typically finds its spatial reference in the results of motion of the non-dominant-hand, we assign pointing and panning to the dominant hand, while the non-dominant hand controls zoom, as is typically the case for bimanual pan-zoom techniques on the desktop [6, 8].

Input Gestures via a Device

The main limb segments involved in the input of gestures via a device are the fingers and, to a lesser extent, the fore-arm (for the dominant hand). This group of techniques is illustrated in Figure 2, columns *1D path* and *2D surface*.

Column *1D path* illustrates techniques that provide a high degree of guidance for executing the zooming gestures. The first row corresponds to *one handed* techniques: the device is operated by the dominant hand, which also controls pointing via ray-casting. The second row corresponds to *two handed* techniques: the dominant hand controls pointing via ray-casting, while the non-dominant hand controls zoom using the device. *linear* gestures can be input using, e.g., a wire-less handheld mouse featuring a scroll wheel; *circular* gestures using, e.g., any type of handheld knob. Depressing a button on the device activates drag mode for panning.

Column *2D surface* illustrates techniques that use a touch-sensitive surface for input, providing a lesser degree of guidance. The surface is divided horizontally in two areas. Users zoom in the upper area either by moving the thumb up and down (*linear* case), or by drawing approximate circles (*circular* case). Touching the lower area activates drag mode for panning. Users just rely on proprioceptive information to switch between both areas and do not have to look at the device. These techniques can be implemented with a touch-sensitive handheld device such as a PDA or smartphone.

1D path techniques employing *circular* gestures will provide more guidance, but will not benefit from the earlier-mentioned Vernier effect, as input is constrained to one specific trajectory. However, the range of amplitudes that can be covered with the thumb is limited [30]. This should minimize the trade-off between *1D path* and *2D surface* in that respect. For *2D surface* techniques, rubbing gestures [28] were considered to avoid clutching when performing linear gestures, but were found to be impractical when performed with the thumb on a handheld touch-sensitive surface. As a technique designed specifically for thumb input, we were also interested in MicroRolls [30]. However, these were originally designed for discrete input. Cardinal MicroRolls would have had to be mapped to first order of control, which we discarded as discussed earlier, and circular MicroRolls are not precise enough for zoom control.

Input Gestures in Free Space

The main limb segments involved in performing gestures in free space are the wrist, forearm and upper arm. This group of techniques is illustrated in Figure 2, column *3D free*.

The first row illustrates *one handed* techniques using either *linear* or *circular* gestures. The technique using *circular* gestures is actually very close to the CycloStar zooming gesture, but performed in mid-air, without touching any surface. Users perform circular gestures with the dominant hand and forearm oriented toward the display. As in CycloStar, the focus of expansion is the centroid of the round shape corresponding to the cursor's circular path, here projected on the display surface (dotted arrow in Figure 2-e). The technique using *linear* gestures consists in pushing the dominant hand forward to zoom in, as if reaching for something, with the palm towards the target. Turning the hand and pulling backward (away from the display) zooms out. Users point orthogonally to the palm of the same hand (blue arrows in Figure 2-e, left side), with the arm slightly tilted for greater comfort. The second row illustrates *two handed* techniques (Figure 2-f). The *linear* zooming gestures are similar to the ones above, but are performed with the non-dominant hand, the dominant hand still being used for pointing and specifying the focus of expansion. In the *circular* case, users adopt a potentially less tiring posture, pointing at the floor with their non-dominant hand and making circular movements. All other postures and movements being ignored by the system for the non-dominant hand, the user can easily clutch. Several options can be considered for engaging drag mode: specific hand postures such as pinching, or using a small wireless actuator (e.g., a button).

EXPERIMENT

We conducted an experiment using a [2×2×3] within-subjects design with three primary factors: HANDEDNESS $\in$ {*OneHanded*, *TwoHanded*}, GESTURE $\in$ {*Circular*, *Linear*}, and GUIDANCE $\in$ {*1DPath*, *2DSurface*, *3DFree*} to evaluate the 12 unique interaction techniques described above. We controlled for potential distance effects by introducing the DISTANCE between two consecutive targets as a secondary within-subjects factor. We systematically varied these factors in the context of a multiscale navigation task within a wall-sized display environment.

Measures include performance time and number of overshoots, treated as errors. Overshoots occur when participants zooms beyond the target zoom level, and indicate situations in which the participant has less precision of control over the level of zoom. For instance, from an overview of Canada, zooming down to street level in Google Maps when what the user actually wanted was to get an overview of Vancouver.

Hypotheses

Based on the research literature and our own experience with the above techniques, we made the following 7 hypotheses.

Handedness: prior work [6, 8, 15, 18] suggests that two-handed gestures will be faster than one-handed gestures (*H1*) because panning and zooming are complementary actions, integrated into a single task [17]. Two-handed gestures should also be more accurate and easier to use (*H2*).

Gesture: Linear gestures should map better to the zooming component of the task, but should eventually be slower because of clutching, the limited action space compared to zoom range requiring participants to repeatedly reposition their hand/finger (*H3*). Prior work [25, 33] suggests that users will prefer clutch-free circular gestures (*H4*).

Device vs. Free Space: Zhai et al. [35] suggest that techniques using the smaller muscle groups of fingers should be

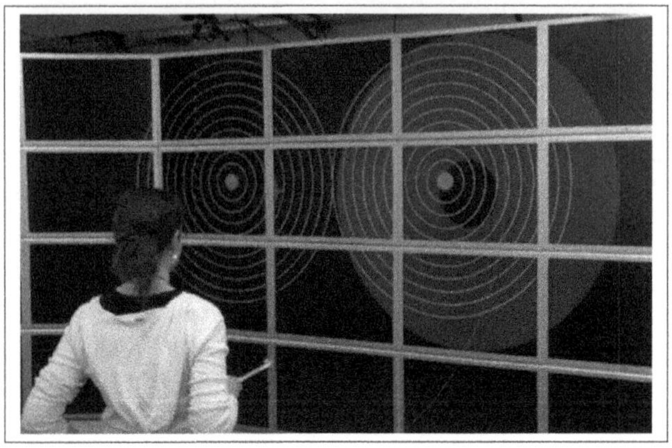

Figure 3. Participant performing the task

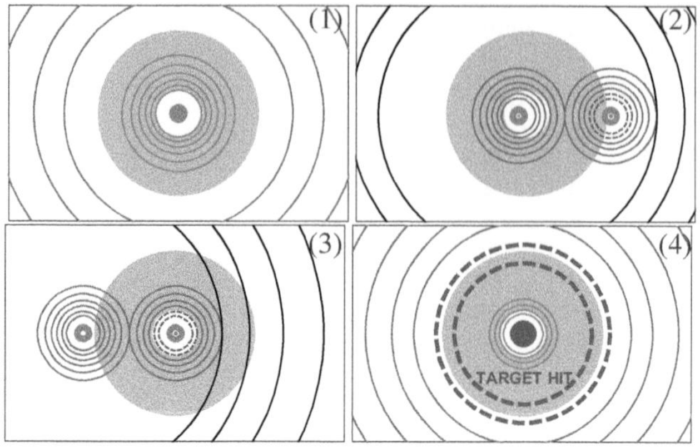

Figure 4. Task (schematic representation using altered colors): (1) Groups of concentric circles represent a given position and zoom level. (2) Zooming out until the neighboring set of circles appears. (3-4) Pan and zoom until the target (green inner disc and circles, dashed for illustration purposes only) is positioned correctly with respect to the stationary gray ring.

more efficient than those using upper limb segments. Balakrishnan *et al.* [2] moderate this observation with findings suggesting that the fingers are not performing better than forearm or wrist for a reciprocal pointing task. Nevertheless, they acknowledge that differences exist in the motor system's ability to control the different limb segments. Based on the gestures to be performed and taking into account the physical size and mass of the segments involved, we predicted that techniques using fingers (*1DPath* and *2DSurface* conditions), should be faster than those requiring larger muscle groups (hands and arms, *3DFree* conditions) (*H5*).

We also predicted that *1DPath* gestures would be faster, with fewer overshoots than techniques with lesser haptic feedback, i.e., *2DSurface* and *3DFree* (*H6*). Finally, we predicted that *3DFree* gestures would be more tiring (*H7*).

Participants

We recruited 12 participants (1 female), ranging in age from 20 to 30 years old (average 24.75, median = 25). All are right-handed daily computer users. None are color-blind.

Apparatus

Hardware. The display wall (Fig. 1 and 3) consists of 32 high-resolution 30" LCDs laid out in an 8×4 matrix, 5.5 meters wide and 1.8 meters high. It can display 20480×6400 pixels. A cluster of 16 computers, each with two high-end nVidia 8800GT graphics cards, communicate via a dedicated high-speed network through a front-end computer. Our goal is to identify the performance characteristics of each technique from the user's perspective. It is thus essential that each technique operates equally well from a purely technological perspective. We use a VICON motion-capture system to track passive IR retroreflective markers and provide 3D object coordinates with sub-millimeter accuracy at 200Hz (although gesture recognition technologies are constantly improving, such a system is still necessary to get reliable and precise 3D position/orientation information). The *Linear 1DPath* condition uses the wheel of a wireless Logitech M305 mouse (Fig. 2-a,b). The *Circular 1DPath* condition uses a wireless Samsung SM30P pointing device, normally used for presentations (Fig. 2-a,b). All *2DSurface* conditions use an iPod Touch. So as to avoid failures from gesture segmentation algorithms that would impact task performance in an uncontrolled manner, we use an explicit mode switch to unambiguously engage drag mode (panning). As mentioned earlier, we use the device's main button for *1DPath* conditions, and the lower area of the touch-sensitive surface for *2DSurface* conditions. While in real-world applications we would use specific hand postures such as pinching in *3DFree* conditions, for the sake of robustness we use a wireless mouse button whose activation is seamlessly integrated with the gesture.

Software. The experiment was written in Java 1.5 running on Mac OS X and was implemented with the open source ZVTM toolkit [29] (`http://zvtm.sf.net`) modified to run on clusters of computers driving display walls. Touchstone [20] was used to manage the experiment.

Pan-Zoom Task

The task is a variation of Guiard *et al.*'s multiscale pointing task [15], adapted to take overshoots into account. Participants navigate through an abstract information space made of two groups of concentric circles: the *start group* and the *target group*. Each group consists of seven series of 10 concentric circles symbolizing different zoom levels, each designated by a different color (Fig. 4.2). The target group features two additional green circles (dashed in Fig. 4.4) and a disc, referred to as C_1, C_2 and C_3 from smallest to largest.

Participants start at a high zoom level in the start group (Fig. 4.1). They zoom out until the neighboring target group appears (Fig. 4.2). It may appear either on the left or right side of the start group. Then they pan and zoom into the target group until they reach the correct zoom level and the target is correctly centered. A stationary gray ring symbolizes the correct zoom level and position (Fig. 4-(1-4)). Its radii are $r_1 = 4400$ and $r_2 = 12480$ pixels. All three criteria must be met for the trial to end: $\mathcal{A}$) C_1 is fully contained within the stationary ring's hole (radius $= r_1$), $\mathcal{B}$) $radius(C_2) < r_2$, $\mathcal{C}$) $radius(C_3) > r_2$. Overshoots occur when the zoom level is higher than the maximum level required to meet criteria $\mathcal{B}$ and $\mathcal{C}$, in which case participants have to zoom out again (C_1 becomes white instead of green in that situation). When all conditions are met, the message TARGET HIT appears and the thickness of C_2 and C_3 is increased (Fig. 4.4). The trial ends when the position and zoom level have stabilized for at least 1.2 seconds (all trials must be successfully completed).

Procedure

The experiment presents each subject with six replications of each of the 12 techniques at three DISTANCES. The experiment is organized into four sessions that each present three techniques: One combination of the GESTURE and HANDEDNESS factors and all three degrees of GUIDANCE. Each session lasts between 30 and 90 minutes, depending on techniques and participant. Participants are required to wait at least one hour between two consecutive sessions, and to complete the whole experiment within four days or fewer, with a maximum of two sessions per day to avoid too much fatigue and boredom. Participants stand 1.7m from the wall and are asked to find a comfortable position so they can perform gestures quickly, but in a relaxed way.

Practice Condition: Participants are given a brief introduction at the beginning of the first session. Each technique begins with a practice condition, with trials at three different DISTANCES: (49 920, 798 720 and 12 779 520 pixels). Measures for the experimental condition start as soon as 1) participants feel comfortable and 2) task performance time variation for the last four trials is less than 30% of the task time average in that window.

Experimental Condition: Each technique is presented in a block of 18 trials consisting of 6 replications at each DISTANCE. Trials, blocks and sessions are fully counter-balanced within and across subjects, using a Latin square design.

Measures: We measure movement time *MT* and number of overshoots for each of 2592 trials: 2 GESTURE × 2 HANDEDNESS × 3 GUIDANCE × 3 DISTANCE × 12 participants × 6 replications. Participants also answer questions, based on a 5-point Likert scale, about their perceived *performance*, *accuracy*, *ease of learning*, *ease of use*, and *fatigue*. They rank the techniques with respect to the GUIDANCE factor after each session. When they have been exposed to both conditions of HANDEDNESS or GESTURE, they rank those as well. After the last session, they rank the techniques individually and by factor. Participants are encouraged to make additional observations and comments about any of the above.

Results and Discussion: Movement Time

Prior to our analysis, we checked the performance for unwanted effects from secondary factors. We checked for individual performance differences across subjects and found that, for all 12 participants, movement time and number of overshoots were perfectly correlated with the overall performance measures. As expected, movement time data are skewed positively; replications of unique experimental conditions are thus handled by taking the median (note that taking the mean yields similar results). In all remaining analysis, we handled participant as a random variable, using the standard repeated measures REML technique. We found no significant fatigue effect although we did find a significant learning effect across sessions. Participants performed about 1.4 s more slowly in the first session and then became slightly faster over the next three sessions. However, we found no significant interaction between session orders and main factors. As the factors were counter-balanced, this created no adverse effects in the analysis.

Factor	DF, DFDen	F Ratio	p
HANDS	1,11	24.65	0.0004 *
GESTURE	1,11	42.87	< 0.0001 *
GUIDANCE	2,22	58.80	< 0.0001 *
DIST	2,22	228.8	< 0.0001 *
HANDS×GESTURE	1,11	2.060	0.1790
HANDS×GUIDANCE	2,22	4.914	0.0172 *
GESTURE×GUIDANCE	2,22	10.38	0.0007 *
GESTURE×DIST	2,22	17.27	< 0.0001 *
HANDS×DIST	2,22	11.57	0.0004 *
GUIDANCE×DIST	4,44	3.828	0.0094 *
HANDS×GESTURE×GUIDANCE	2,22	1.127	0.3420
HANDS×GESTURE×DIST	2,22	0.790	0.4661
HANDS×GUIDANCE×DIST	4,44	0.650	0.6301
GESTURE×GUIDANCE×DIST	4,44	3.750	0.0104 *
HANDS×GESTURE×GUIDANCE×DIST	4,44	1.049	0.3929

Table 2. Results of the full factorial ANOVA for MT.

Table 2 details results of the full factorial ANOVA for the model *MT* ~ HANDS × GUIDANCE × GESTURE × DIST × Rand(Participant). We observe that HANDS has a significant effect on *MT* (Figure 5-a[1]). A post-hoc Tukey test shows that *TwoHanded* gestures are significantly faster than *OneHanded* gestures (avg. 9690 ms vs. 11869 ms). We found a significant interaction effect of HANDS × GUIDANCE (Figure 5-a). The interaction does not change the significance of the post-hoc test, but indicates that the magnitude of the difference is greater for *3DFree* than for *2DSurface* and greater for *2DSurface* than for *1DPath* techniques.

Unsurprisingly, performance data strongly support (*H1*): all other conditions being equal, two-handed techniques are consistently faster than one-handed techniques. An interesting observation is that using two hands is more advantageous when the degree of guidance for achieving gestures is low.

GUIDANCE has a significant effect on *MT* (Figure 5-b). A post-hoc Tukey test shows that *1DPath* (avg. 9511 ms) is significantly faster than *2DSurface* (10894 ms), which in turn is significantly faster than *3DFree* (11934 ms). This time the HANDS × GUIDANCE interaction changes the significance of the test (Figure 5-b). The difference is that a post-hoc Tukey test shows no significant difference between *2DSurface* and *3DFree* for *TwoHanded*.

Both hypotheses (*H5*) and (*H6*) are supported: involving smaller muscle groups improves performance; providing higher guidance further contributes to this. However, this effect is less pronounced in *TwoHanded* conditions. This confirms the previous observation that a higher degree of guidance is especially useful when a single hand is involved.

GESTURE also has a significant effect on *MT*. A post-hoc Tukey test shows that *Linear* movements (avg. 9384 ms) performed significantly faster than *Circular* gestures (12175 ms). However, we have a strong significant interaction of GESTURE ×

[1]Error bars in all the figures represent the 95% confidence limit of the mean of the medians per participants ($\pm StdErr \times 1.96$).

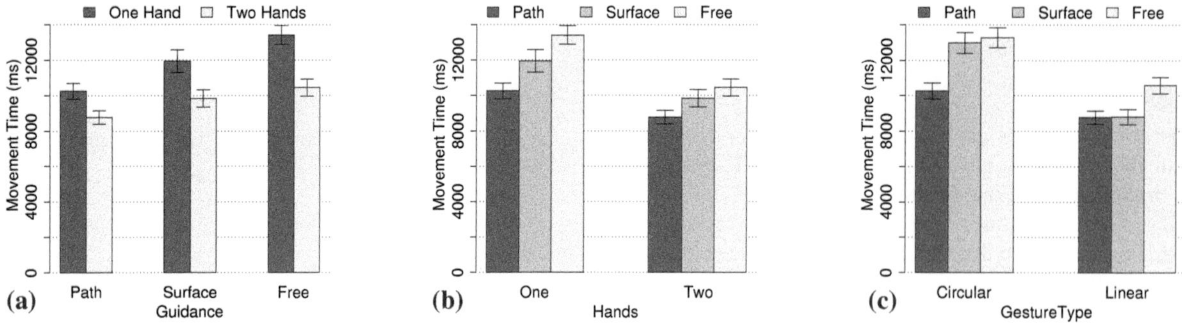

Figure 5. (a): *MT* **per** HANDS × GUIDANCE. **(b)** *MT* **per** GUIDANCE × HANDS. **(c)** *MT* **per** GUIDANCE × GESTURE.

GUIDANCE (Figure 5-c). A post-hoc Tukey test shows that (i) for *Circular* gestures: *1DPath* guidance is faster than both *2DSurface* and *3DFree* with no significant difference between *2DSurface* and *3DFree*; (ii) for *Linear* gestures, there is no significant difference between *1DPath* and *2DSurface*, but a significant difference between *2DSurface* and *3DFree*; (iii) for *1DPath* guidance there is no significant difference between *Circular* and *Linear* gestures, but there is a significant difference between *Circular* and *Linear* for *2DSurface* and *3DFree* guidance.

Surprisingly, *Linear* gestures are generally faster than *Circular* ones. (*H3*), that claimed that *Linear* gestures should be slower because of clutching, is not supported. Performance differences between gesture types are however affected by the degree of guidance: *Circular* gestures with *1DPath* guidance (e.g., a knob) are comparable to *Linear* gestures with low guidance. We tentatively explain the lower performance of *Circular* gestures with *2DSurface* guidance by the difficulty of performing circular gestures with the thumb [30], also observed here.

Another interesting observation is that our analogue of CycloStar in mid-air (*Circular* gestures with *3DFree* guidance) performs poorly. It seems that the lack of a surface to guide the gesture significantly degrades this technique's usability. Another factor contributing to its poor performance in our study is likely related to overshoots, as discussed below.

As expected, distance to target (DIST) has a significant effect on *MT*. A post-hoc Tukey test shows that *MT* increases significantly with *distance*. There are several significant interactions between DIST and the main factors (Fig. 6), but none of these change the relative performance ordering for the main factors. These interactions are due to a change in the magnitude of the difference across conditions, confirming that the choice of an efficient technique is of increasing importance as the task becomes harder.

Results and Discussion: Overshoots

As detailed earlier in the description of task design, overshoots correspond to zooming beyond the target zoom level and are treated as errors. We consider the model *Overshoots* ∼ HANDS × GUIDANCE × GESTURE × DIST × Rand(Participant).

We observe significant simple effects on *Overshoots* for GESTURE ($F_{1,11} = 21.04, p = 0.0008$) and GUIDANCE ($F_{2,22} = 53.80, p < 0.0001$), and one significant interaction effect for GESTURE × GUIDANCE ($F_{2,22} = 8.63, p = 0.0017$). *Circular* gestures exhibit more overshoots than *Linear* gestures (1.65 vs. 2.71).

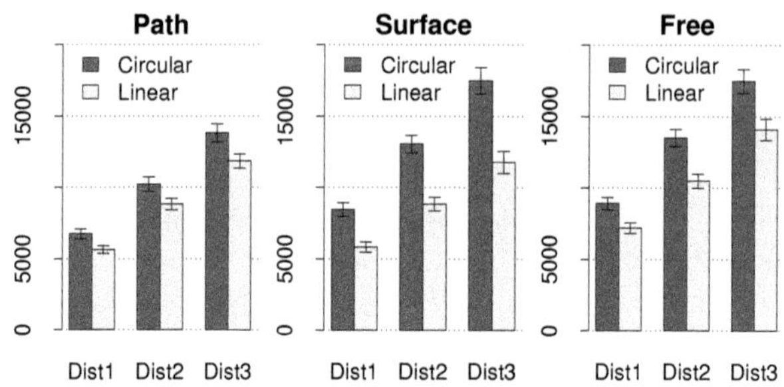

Figure 6. *MT* **per** DIST × GESTURE, **for each** GUIDANCE

2DSurface gestures exhibit more overshoots than *1DPath* and *3DFree* gestures (3.75 for *2DSurface* vs. 1.52 for *1DPath*, and 1.26 for *3DFree*). There is a significant difference between *Linear* and *Circular* gestures for *2DSurface* and *3DFree*, but not *1DPath*. Moreover, overshoots exhibit the same interaction effect for *2DSurface* gestures: *Circular 2DSurface* result in significantly more overshoots than *Linear 2DSurface* (4.68 vs. 2.82).

The observed higher number of overshoots for *Circular* techniques helps explain the generally lower *MT* performance measured for this type of gestures. The best-fitting ellipse algorithm involved in the recognition of *Circular* gestures has an inherently higher cost of recovery, introducing a delay when reversing course. The poor performance of our analogue of CycloStar is at least partially due to this, knowing that there was a major difference between the zooming experiment reported in [21] and the present one: we included overshoots in our task design, whereas the CycloStar experiment apparently did not (there is no report of such a measure in task design or results analysis), thus ignoring this issue.

Results and Discussion: Qualitative Results

Qualitative data confirms our results. Participants generally preferred *TwoHanded* to *OneHanded* techniques (8/12) and *Linear* to *Circular* gestures (10/12). Subjective preferences about degree of guidance were mixed, with 4 participants preferring the high degree of guidance provided by *1DPath* techniques, only 1 for both of *2DSurface* and *3DFree* techniques, and all others expressing no particular preferences. Looking at the details of answers to our 5-point Likert scale questions about perceived speed, accuracy, ease of use and fatigue, significant results ($p < 0.002$) were obtained only for degree of GUIDANCE, with *1DPath* being consistently rated higher than *2DSurface* and *3DFree*; and for HANDS, *TwoHanded* techniques being considered less tiring than *OneHanded* techniques ($p < 0.03$).

GROUP	HANDS	GESTURE	GUIDANCE	Figure	*MT* (*ms*)
Gr1	*TwoHanded*	*Linear*	*2DSurface*	2-d	8 100
	TwoHanded	*Linear*	*1DPath*	2-b	8 377
Gr2	*OneHanded*	*Linear*	*1DPath*	2-a	9 160
	TwoHanded	*Circular*	*1DPath*	2-b	9 168
	TwoHanded	*Linear*	*3DFree*	2-f	9 185
	OneHanded	*Linear*	*2DSurface*	2-c	9 504
Gr3	*OneHanded*	*Circular*	*1DPath*	2-a	11 340
	TwoHanded	*Circular*	*2DSurface*	2-d	11 591
	TwoHanded	*Circular*	*3DFree*	2-f	11 718
	OneHanded	*Linear*	*3DFree*	2-e	11 981
Gr4	*OneHanded*	*Circular*	*2DSurface*	2-c	14 380
	OneHanded	*Circular*	*3DFree*	2-e	14 851

Table 3. Groups of techniques according to *MT*

Comments from participants suggest that in the *OneHanded* condition, zoom gestures interfere with pointing as they introduce additional hand jitter and consequently lower accuracy. Some participants also commented that pointing and zooming were confounded in the *OneHanded* conditions, making the techniques difficult to use (*H2*). However, two participants strongly preferred one-handed gestures, arguing that they were less complex and less tiring. They assumed their performance was better (even though it was not), probably because they experienced more overshoots in the *two handed* condition, which may have led to their conclusions. One of them mentioned that for the *one handed* condition there was *"no need for coordination"*; techniques were *"more relaxed"* and made it *"easier to pan and zoom"*.

Linear gestures were preferred to *Circular* ones, participants commenting that circular gestures were difficult to perform without guidance, that circular gestures for zooming interfered with linear gestures for panning, and that circular gestures were hard to map to zoom factor. All but one participants preferred linear gestures overall although one commented that he liked *"the continuity of circular gestures"*. Others commented that *"making good circles without a guide is hard"* and did not like having to turn their hands. These findings contradict our hypothesis that users would prefer clutch-free circular gestures (*H4*). This hypothesis was based on observations made for techniques operated on a desktop, not in mid-air, and involved different limb segments. In many of our conditions, the gestures had to be performed with the thumb, and were thus more complex to achieve than when using, e.g., the index finger in conjunction with hand or forearm movements. Several participants commented on this interaction effect: *"[It is] too hard to do circle gestures without a guide"*, *"Linear movements are easier on the iPod"* and *"[Is it] impossible to do circular movements on a surface, maybe with some oil?"*.

Finally, as hypothesized (*H7*), participants found *1DPath* guidance least tiring while *3DFree* caused the most fatigue.

Results and Discussion: Individual Techniques

The analysis of variance for the model $MT \sim$ HANDS × GUIDANCE × GESTURE × DIST × Rand(Participant) does not show a significant triple interaction between the three main factors (Table 2). Formally, we cannot say more than the above about the ranking of the twelve techniques. However, based on the results about *MT* above, we can observe four distinct groups of techniques, shown in Table 3. As a side note, if we consider the model $MT \sim$ GROUP × Rand(Participant), the ANOVA shows a significant effect of GROUP ($F_{3,33} = 65.35$, $p < 0.0001$) and a post-hoc Tukey test shows a significant difference between each groups.

Gr1 contains the two fastest techniques with similar *MT* : *TwoHanded*, *Linear* gestures with either *2DSurface* or *1DPath* degrees of guidance. Optimal performance in terms of movement time implies the use of two hands and a device to guide gestural input.

Gr2 contains the four techniques that come next and also have close *MT* : the *OneHanded* version of the two fastest techniques, the *TwoHanded Circular 1DPath* and the *TwoHanded Linear 3DFree* techniques. Techniques in this group are of interest as they exhibit a relatively good level of performance while broadening possible choices for interaction designers. For instance, the unimanual techniques in this group make one hand available to perform other actions. The *3DFree* technique is also of interest as it does not require the user to hold any equipment and is generally appealing to users.

Gr3 contains techniques that again have very close *MT* but about 2.3 *s* slower than the techniques of *Gr2*. This group consists of *OneHanded Circular 1DPath*, *TwoHanded Circular 2DSurface* and *3DFree*, and *OneHanded Linear 3DFree*. Techniques in this group are of lesser interest, except maybe for the *OneHanded Linear 3DFree* technique, which is the fastest unimanual technique using gestures performed in free space.

Gr4 contains the 2 techniques performing worst, *OneHanded Circular 2DSurface* and *3DFree*. These are significantly slower than all others, about 3 *s* slower than the techniques of *Gr3* and about 6 *s* slower than the techniques of *Gr1*. Our data suggest that these techniques should be rejected.

SUMMARY AND FUTURE WORK

We studied different families of location-independent, mid-air input techniques for pan-zoom navigation on wall-sized displays. After an extensive exploratory design phase, we identified the following key factors for the design of such techniques: handedness (uni- vs. bimanual input), gesture type (linear or circular), and level of guidance (movements restricted to a 1D path, a 2D surface or free movements in 3D space). We systematically evaluated each combination of these factors through a controlled experiment in which participants performed pan-and-zoom navigation in an abstract, very large multiscale environment, with distances up to 12 million pixels.

Experimental results identify several successful mid-air input techniques that can be used to navigate efficiently in very large datasets on wall-sized displays. In addition to identifying groups of alternative techniques based on performance, but each with specific characteristics, the experiment also suggests clear results with respect to the factors that constitute our design space. For example, despite their inherent and almost universal appeal, gestures performed in free space prove to be generally less efficient and more prone to fatigue than device-based input techniques. Adding guidance to input gestures increases, rather than decreases, accuracy. In accordance with the research literature, bimanual input techniques perform very well. Unimanual techniques perform honorably, and may still be considered in contexts of use where, for example, tools must be held in one hand to perform a domain/task specific action. A more surprising result is the generally higher efficiency of linear gestures when compared to circular, clutch-free gestures.

As future work, we plan to investigate how these pan-zoom techniques combine with other interaction techniques. Indeed, in real-world applications, users must also handle text entry, menu selection, copy and paste, drag and drop, and other activities. This implies trade-offs among techniques: a technique with optimal performance in this experiment may prove less easy to integrate with other techniques because of its requirements in terms of handedness or type of device. We have started to explore these questions in the context of real-world activities involving scientists visualizing and manipulating extremely large sets of multi-scale data.

ACKNOWLEDGEMENTS

We wish to thank Clément Pillias and Romain Primet, who helped implement the experiment on the wall-sized display, as well as Caroline Appert, Stéphane Huot and the anonymous reviewers for their feedback on drafts of this paper. We also wish to thank all the volunteers who participated in our experiments. This research was supported by a Région Île-de-France/Digiteo grant.

REFERENCES

1. C. Andrews, A. Endert, and C. North. Space to think: large high-resolution displays for sensemaking. In *Proc. CHI '10*, 55–64. ACM, 2010.
2. R. Balakrishnan and I. S. MacKenzie. Performance differences in the fingers, wrist, and forearm in computer input control. In *Proc. CHI '97*, 303–310. ACM, 1997.
3. R. Ball, C. North, and D. Bowman. Move to improve: promoting physical navigation to increase user performance with large displays. In *Proc. CHI '07*, 191–200. ACM, 2007.
4. P. Baudisch, N. Good, V. Bellotti, and P. Schraedley. Keeping things in context: a comparative evaluation of focus plus context screens, overviews, and zooming. In *Proc. CHI '02*, 259–266. ACM, 2002.
5. P. Baudisch, M. Sinclair, and A. Wilson. Soap: a pointing device that works in mid-air. In *Proc. UIST '06*, 43–46. ACM, 2006.
6. F. Bourgeois and Y. Guiard. Multiscale pointing: facilitating pan-zoom coordination. In *CHI '02 EA*, 758–759. ACM, 2002.
7. D. A. Bowman, D. Koller, and L. Hodges. Travel in immersive virtual environments: An evaluation of viewpoint motion control techniques. In *Proc. VRAIS '97*, 45–52. IEEE, 1997.
8. W. Buxton and B. Myers. A study in two-handed input. *SIGCHI Bull.*, 17(4):321–326, 1986.
9. B. Campbell, K. O'Brien, M. Byrne, and B. J. Bachman. Fitts' law predictions with an alternative pointing device (wiimote®). *Proc. Hum. Factors Ergon. Soc. Meeting*, 52(19):1321–1325, 2008.
10. X. Cao and R. Balakrishnan. Visionwand: interaction techniques for large displays using a passive wand tracked in 3d. In *Proc. UIST '03*, 173–182. ACM, 2003.
11. A. Cockburn, A. Karlson, and B. B. Bederson. A review of overview+detail, zooming, and focus+context interfaces. *ACM CSUR*, 41(1):1–31, 2008.
12. M. Czerwinski, D. Tan, and G. Robertson. Women take a wider view. In *Proc. CHI '02*, 195–202. ACM, 2002.
13. K. Evans, P. Tanner, and M. Wein. Tablet-based valuators that provide one, two, or three degrees of freedom. In *Proc. SIGGRAPH '81*, 91–97. ACM, 1981.
14. Y. Guiard. Asymmetric division of labor in human skilled bimanual action: The kinematic chain as a model. *J. Motor. Behav.*, 19:486–517, 1987.
15. Y. Guiard and M. Beaudouin-Lafon. Target acquisition in multiscale electronic worlds. *IJHCS*, 61(6):875–905, 2004.
16. K. Hinckley, R. Pausch, J. Goble, and N. Kassell. A survey of design issues in spatial input. In *Proc. UIST '94*, 213–222. ACM, 1994.
17. R. Jacob and L. Sibert. The perceptual structure of multidimensional input device selection. In *Proc. CHI '92*, 211–218. ACM, 1992.
18. A. Leganchuk, S. Zhai, and W. Buxton. Manual and cognitive benefits of two-handed input: an experimental study. *ACM ToCHI*, 5(4):326–359, 1998.
19. R. Lindeman, J. Sibert, and J. Hahn. Hand-held windows: Towards effective 2d interaction in immersive virtual environments. In *Proc. VR '99*, 205–212. IEEE, 1999.
20. W. E. Mackay, C. Appert, M. Beaudouin-Lafon, O. Chapuis, Y. Du, J.-D. Fekete, and Y. Guiard. Touchstone: exploratory design of experiments. In *Proc. CHI '07*, 1425–1434. ACM, 2007.
21. S. Malacria, E. Lecolinet, and Y. Guiard. Clutch-free panning and integrated pan-zoom control on touch-sensitive surfaces: the cyclostar approach. In *Proc. CHI '10*, 2615–2624. ACM, 2010.
22. S. Malik, A. Ranjan, and R. Balakrishnan. Interacting with large displays from a distance with vision-tracked multi-finger gestural input. In *Proc. UIST '05*, 43–52. ACM, 2005.
23. D. McCallum and P. Irani. Arc-pad: absolute+relative cursor positioning for large displays with a mobile touchscreen. In *Proc. UIST '09*, 153–156. ACM, 2009.
24. M. Mine, F. Brooks, Jr., and C. Sequin. Moving objects in space: exploiting proprioception in virtual-environment interaction. In *Proc. SIGGRAPH '97*, 19–26. ACM Press/Addison-Wesley, 1997.
25. T. Moscovich and J. F. Hughes. Navigating documents with the virtual scroll ring. In *Proc. UIST '04*, 57–60. ACM, 2004.
26. T. Ni, D. Bowman, and J. Chen. Increased display size and resolution improve task performance in information-rich virtual environments. In *Proc. GI '06*, 139–146. Canadian Inf. Proc. Soc., 2006.
27. T. Ni, G. Schmidt, O. Staadt, M. Livingston, R. Ball, and R. May. A survey of large high-resolution display technologies, techniques, and applications. In *Proc. VR '06*, 223–236. IEEE, 2006.
28. A. Olwal, S. Feiner, and S. Heyman. Rubbing and tapping for precise and rapid selection on touch-screen displays. In *Proc. CHI '08*, 295–304. ACM, 2008.
29. E. Pietriga. A toolkit for addressing hci issues in visual language environments. In *Proc. VL/HCC'05*, 145–152. IEEE, 2005.
30. A. Roudaut, E. Lecolinet, and Y. Guiard. Microrolls: expanding touch-screen input vocabulary by distinguishing rolls vs. slides of the thumb. In *Proc. CHI '09*, 927–936. ACM, 2009.
31. D. Tan, D. Gergle, P. Scupelli, and R. Pausch. Physically large displays improve performance on spatial tasks. *ACM ToCHI*, 13(1):71–99, 2006.
32. D. Vogel and R. Balakrishnan. Distant freehand pointing and clicking on very large, high resolution displays. In *Proc. UIST '05*, 33–42. ACM, 2005.
33. E. Wherry. Scroll ring performance evaluation. In *CHI '03 EA*, 758–759. ACM, 2003.
34. B. Yost, Y. Haciahmetoglu, and C. North. Beyond visual acuity: the perceptual scalability of information visualizations for large displays. In *Proc. CHI '07*, 101–110. ACM, 2007.
35. S. Zhai, P. Milgram, and W. Buxton. The influence of muscle groups on performance of multiple degree-of-freedom input. In *Proc. CHI '96*, 308–315. ACM, 1996.
36. J. Zigelbaum, A. Browning, D. Leithinger, O. Bau, and H. Ishii. g-stalt: a chirocentric, spatiotemporal, and telekinetic gestural interface. In *Proc. TEI '10*, 261–264. ACM, 2010.

Gesture Select: Acquiring Remote Targets on Large Displays without Pointing

Andrew Bragdon and Hsu-Sheng Ko
Brown University
Providence, RI, USA
{acb, hsusheng}@cs.brown.edu

ABSTRACT

When working at a large wall display, even if partially utilized, many targets are likely to be distant from the user, requiring walking, which is slow, and interrupts workflow. We propose a novel technique for selecting remote targets called Gesture Select, in which users draw an *initial mark*, in a target's direction; rectilinear gestures represented as icons are dynamically overlaid on targets within a region of interest; the user then continues by drawing the *continuation mark* corresponding to the target, to select it. Extensions to this technique to support working with remote content for an extended period, and learning gesture shortcuts are presented. A formal experiment indicates Gesture Select significantly outperformed direct selection for mid/far targets. Further analysis suggests Gesture Select performance is principally affected by the extent to which users can read the gestures, influenced by distance and perspective warping, and the gesture complexity in the ROI. The results of a second 2-D experiment with labeled targets indicate Gesture Select significantly outperformed direct selection and an existing technique.

Author Keywords

Gestures, selection, large display, remote targets

ACM Classification Keywords

H5. Information interfaces and presentation: Interaction.

General Terms

Human Factors

INTRODUCTION

Large, high-resolution display walls are growing in popularity and are now available as commercial products [22] [29]. A long history of research applications in this area demonstrates the value of these systems in various domains, such as interactive whiteboards [25] and scientific visualization [24].

While these systems can be operated from a distance (e.g. [33] [21]), we believe there is significant value in using them up close. When standing in front of the display, users can write with a pen to annotate or manipulate objects with their hands directly on the display. They can also collaborate with other users gathered around the display, similar to a very large whiteboard. Finally, some wall displays tile multiple projectors to offer very high resolutions, letting users perceive fine detail even when standing at the display (e.g. [16]).

CHI 2011, May 7–12, 2011, Vancouver, BC, Canada.

However, when working at a large display, selecting remote targets requires the user to walk to select targets that are out of reach, something that is likely to occur frequently on a 15-foot wide display that is even partially utilized, even if the user is standing in the center. Such interruptions may hinder user workflow on a large display.

In this paper we propose a novel technique, *Gesture Select*, which aids users in selecting remote targets on large displays (Fig. 1). The technique differs from prior approaches in that it does not use pointing-based selection. Rather, users select targets by first drawing a line with a pen or finger in the general direction of the desired target. Simple *continuation mark* gestures are then dynamically overlaid on targets within a region of interest defined by this direction. The user then continues their initial stroke by drawing the continuation mark overlaid on the target. We analyze the performance of Gesture Select through two formal experiments. We also explore several extensions of the technique for manipulating remote targets for an extended period, and teaching persistent command gestures.

The contributions of this paper are:

- The design of Gesture Select, a novel selection technique for large displays based on gestures
- Extensions to this technique that support portal invocation and gesture shortcut learning
- A formal experiment which indicates that selection time with Gesture Select significantly outperforms unaided direct selection. Performance changed by <12% as target size was halved/as distance was doubled; analysis suggests that Gesture Select is affected by the extent that users can read the remote disclosure icons, and gesture complexity
- A second experiment indicating significantly improved performance over unaided direct selection and a previous technique for selection, for 2-D labeled targets

RELATED WORK

Applications

Tivoli [25] provided users with an interactive whiteboard environment for supporting meetings. Flatland [23] let users define semantic types for content on the whiteboard, and then manage the content and its history. Guimbretière et al. [11] explored techniques for creating and managing sketches and objects on display walls. Rekimoto [27] explored moving objects between networked computers using pen identification.

Bringing Proxy Targets Closer

Drag-and-pop and drag-and-pick [3] brings a fixed number of remote targets closer to the user at their original size and compresses space between them using a grid-based algorithm, when the user drags in a particular direction. Push-and-pop [7] brings all targets near the user at the original size. This is effective for very sparse target fields; however, it may not scale when the targets are large or numerous, and also requires users to re-find targets, which may be difficult when the target set changes often (e.g. content-manipulation).

Another approach, The Vacuum [5], also uses a sector of influence, but shrinks remote targets, thereby preserving spatial relationships, and also scaling to larger numbers of targets, but incurring the cost that targets are now smaller and thus harder to select. A comparative study of single selection in the presence of path and area distractor targets found no significant difference in performance between The Vacuum, Drag-and-Pick and unaided direct selection. A second study showed benefits for multi-selection. Based on this result we believe there is the potential to create a technique which can outperform unaided direct, single selection on large displays.

Gestures

Marking menus [20] lay out menus using sequences of rectilinear marks, typically in 8 compass-aligned directions; the simple rectilinear marks inspire our gesture design. Flow-Menus [10] integrate marking menus with other actions such as data entry or direct manipulation in one fluid stroke, inspiring our approach of integrating two actions in one stroke.

Escape [34] aids users in selecting small targets on smart phones by displaying each target as a directional icon; users first identify the target's direction, then touch that area of the display, and finally flick in the direction. This gestural selection technique inspires the present work with large displays. Move-and-stroke overlays animated mouse gesture demonstrations on targets; users mimic the gestures with a mouse and then disambiguate errors using a pie menu [8]; though likely slower than pointing for desktop tasks, it can be applied to situations in which there is no pointer, or pointing is costly. Hinckley et al. [14] explored techniques for combining multiple networked pen-based devices into a larger display via gestures. Techniques have been developed for "throwing" objects to remote locations on a large display; we refer to [26] for a summary of work in this area. Systems for teaching gestures on demand such as [6] and [2] have also been developed.

Interacting at a Distance

Several approaches let users interact with display walls at a distance. We believe that, while this is valuable in some situations, there is also value in working at the display as well, e.g. to see high-resolution data up close. While users can "step back" to perform an interaction from a distance, we note the time cost incurred for such transitions may interrupt users' workflow. The "dollhouse" [30] or world-in-miniature approach lets users interact with small proxies for large targets. Bubble radar [1] lets users interact with a miniature of a large display on a tablet with the aid of a bubble cursor. Malik et al. developed techniques for interacting with large displays at a distance using hand gestures over a tabletop [21].

Pointing and clicking interfaces using hand tracking for interacting with large displays from a distance, including ray casting, have been explored [33]. A multimodal technique, the Speech-filtered bubble ray [32] begins with ray casting; the user then speaks a property (e.g. "green"), causing a cursor relative to the ray intersection point to snap to matching targets. This approach showed improved performance over ray casting approaches, however it requires speech, which may be undesirable in local/remote collaborations, and ray casting, which slows at large distances as the effective size of remote targets is small and thus difficult to pick, even if effective size is increased. Ninja Cursor [19] uses multiple cursors to reduce the average distance from cursor to the target, coupled with a delay algorithm for handling ambiguities that arise so a single cursor is active at a time.

Live Clippings of Remote Content

A number of techniques have been developed to allow the user to interact with live clippings of content from other areas of the display. Frisbees [18] let users position a remote target; the contents of this remote target is rendered inside a Frisbee display near the user, from which it can be interacted with. Hopping [17] lets users select targets not currently visible onscreen through a similar interface. The canvas portal framework [4], explored using Frisbee-like portals to access, semantically filter and scale remote content. Shoemaker and Gutwin explored several multi-point interaction techniques that preserve visibility and scale for multiple regions of interest [28]. WinCuts [31] lets users cut out pieces of a live window and interact with these cutouts. These techniques inspire our use of portals. We note, however, that these techniques are best-suited for working with remote content for a period of time, rather than brief transient selections.

DESIGN

Overview

Our approach is founded on the idea of using gestures to select arbitrary remote targets. We believe that this approach has a number of potential advantages:

- A unique gesture can be assigned to each potential target, eliminating the need for pointing
- Walking and searching for a proxy target is not required
- Additional gestural punctuation can be fluidly added to the gesture to modify or extend the interaction

Design Principles

We began the design process with 4 design principles:

Eyes-on: In order to make a selection, users should have to look only at the target itself. More specifically, users should not have to shift their gaze from the desired target to a second location, nor should they have to perform an additional visual search to locate a proxy of the original target to complete a selection, both expensive operations.

Lightweight: The design should be transient, only opening briefly when needed, and should not require an explicit, heavyweight mode switch or tool invocation.

Scalable: The design should be scalable to various scenarios: small/large targets, mid-range/remote targets, dense/sparse arrangements, and up to at least several hundred targets (e.g., a 15'x5' display with 6" targets can hold 300 targets).

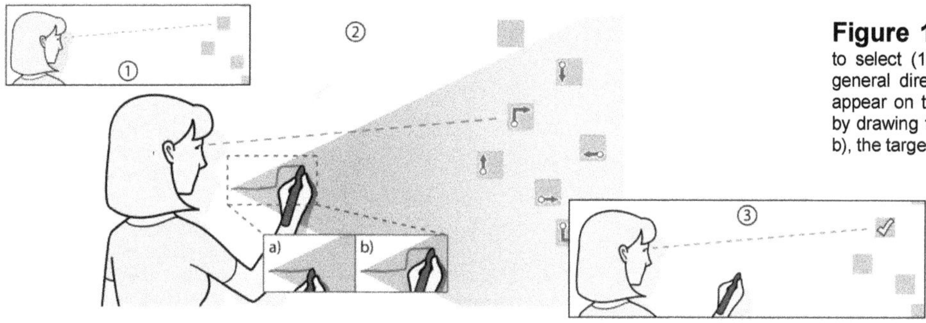

Figure 1. User identifies a remote target she wishes to select (1), draws an initial mark with the pen in the general direction of the target (2-a), continuation marks appear on the targets (2), user continues the initial mark by drawing the continuation mark of the desired target (2-b), the target is selected on pen up (3).

Versatile: The design should scale to support interactions beyond single selection; it should support multi-selection and longer-term interaction with remote targets, when needed.

Region of Interest

Inspired by prior work [3] [5], our technique begins by drawing a line (the *initial mark*) in the direction of the target. Based on this line, a region of interest (ROI) ±26° on each side of this line is defined and displayed visually on the screen as a filled pie wedge. As soon as the length of the initial mark exceeds 1.2" in length, the region of interest is shown (the user does not pick up the pen). Pilot testing was used to find an angle that made it straightforward to be imprecise and still open a region of interest containing the desired target. For comparison, [5] used a dynamically adjustable arc angle ranging from ±10° to ±60°.

The region of interest lets us assign simpler gestures to areas nearer the user's target (see below), and also constrains the visual distraction of the selection process to a specific scope.

Continuation Marks

When the ROI is shown, icons are overlaid on targets that lie within the region of interest. Each icon is scaled to fit such that it is inscribed inside the target. Several corner cases exist, such as very small sparse targets, or very small densely packed targets (discussed below). This section discusses the typical case of targets with shortest side approx. 3" or larger.

Each icon depicts a simple rectilinear gesture that we call a *continuation mark.* To select the desired target, the user simply continues the initial mark by now drawing the continuation mark without picking up the pen, thus drawing them together as one fluid stroke. When contact is released, a segmentation algorithm segments the initial mark from the continuation mark; segmentation is necessary since users tend to draw initial marks of varying lengths. The continuation mark is then recognized using a simple mark-based gesture recognizer, and the appropriate target is selected.

Mark Design

For efficiency, we chose rectilinear mark-based gestures, inspired by marking menus [20]. This let us create a fairly large vocabulary of gestures with simple axis-aligned (up, down, left, right) marks. In pilot testing with four users, we found error rates were substantially higher when diagonals were introduced; we believe this is because users drawing the mark are typically looking at the target itself/continuation mark icon, and therefore are not looking at their hand as they draw, since it is out of their field of view, given the large distances. Thus we do not use diagonals.

From this set of possible gestures, we prune several possibilities. First, if the user's initial mark is within 15° of a major axis, we prune any marks beginning with that direction, except the single special case of a 1-segment continuation mark that is in the same direction as the initial mark. This solves a potential scale invariance ambiguity problem: if the user draws an initial mark to the left, and then draws a continuation mark that is left followed by down, the system cannot be sure whether the user drew a continuation mark of left followed by down, or just down; in pilot testing, users found it difficult to precisely draw the length of marks without looking. For the same reason, we also prune marks in which two consecutive marks are in the same direction. We observed in initial testing that marks longer than length 3 became too small/perspective-warped to read easily for smaller-sized targets. Therefore, to extend the mark set without requiring additional space, we added "pigtail" marks (Fig. 2, right), defined as loop-like marks with a single self-intersection. We discuss the performance of pigtail marks below.

This produces a base set of 260 marks[1] (after pruning) for 1 – 3 segment gestures. We felt this was sufficient for most large wall applications, since the region of interest will intersect 37.5% of the targets[2] onscreen if opened to the right in the center. We do note, however, that for very large numbers of targets more gestures may be required.

Simple marking menus, in which users draw separate strokes (e.g. 3 strokes for up-right-up) were shown to be more accurate and slightly faster than single-stroke compound marks [36]. However, this requires a "transient mode": if the user has inputted 2 strokes and may input a third, the system must wait, for some time threshold for the third mark, because it does not know whether the user is done. We were concerned adding this mode would add weight to the technique, violating our Lightweight design principle. We therefore used single-stroke marks to keep the mode implicit, although we note accuracy could be improved with simple marks.

Assigning Marks to Targets

Since some marks are more difficult to make than others, we use a simple heuristic to assign marks to targets (see Fig. 2). Each mark has an associated difficulty weight. We sort the targets by their distance from the center line of the region of interest; the simplest marks (that is, the ones with the lowest difficulty weight) are assigned to targets that are closest to this center line, and marks are then iteratively assigned outward by distance in increasing order of difficulty weight.

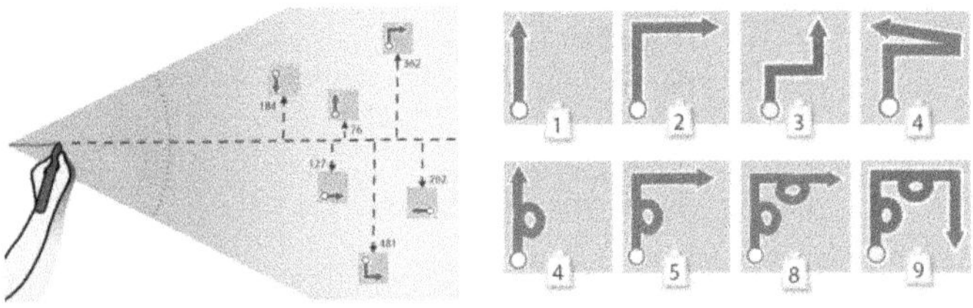

Figure 2. Simpler marks are assigned to targets closest to the center of the region of interest. No gestures are assigned for targets which are very close (left). Difficulty weights of a range of continuation marks (right).

Difficulty weight has integer units and is determined primarily by the number of strokes in the mark, one unit per mark; however, there are several additional considerations. Marks containing pigtails have a greater difficulty weight (4 units per pigtail segment) than marks without; marks containing doubling back also have a higher difficulty weight (2 units). This weighting system was implemented based on pilot study observations with four users, in which users ranked the marks by difficulty after completing a study similar to Experiment 1. Note that this approach is heuristic in nature, but we expect it tends to assign the fastest marks closest to desired targets.

Finally, for marks inside the region of interest that are within easy arm's length of the user (27.5"), based on the start point of the initial mark, no continuation marks are assigned. This was done for two reasons. First, we observed that it was faster to select directly when targets are within arm's length, so we would be doing users a disservice by encouraging them to select nearby targets more slowly. Second, by excluding these targets, more "fast" gestures are available for targets that the user actually needs assistance with. We observed during testing that this was intuitive for users, with the intuition being "can I easily reach the target without moving?"; if so then invoking Gesture Select is not needed. We note this might be a problem in an ecologically valid setting with no instruction.

Note that, with the exception of command gestures (see below), gestures are not persistently assigned to a particular target. We explored several possibilities, but concluded that it would be difficult to persistently assign gestures to targets in a predictable way, and so gesture assignment is dynamic. We expect this will not be a major problem since in many cases we believe the target set will change frequently (e.g., user creates new content, etc.). We also note that during pilot testing, no users commented on the fact that gestures changed each time the region of interest was invoked.

Disclosure Icon Design

The disclosure icons are designed to clearly illustrate the continuation mark for a particular target, while attempting to minimize the extent to which the underlying target itself is occluded. To support dense arrays of targets, the icons are inscribed inside the target and scaled (uniform X/Y scale) to fit. The disclosure is *absolute*, that is, it does not depend on the direction of the initial mark.

During pilot testing with 2 users, we explored several forms of the disclosure icons. Users felt it was important that to easily identify the starting point of the mark, so that they can begin drawing quickly, so we indicate this with a white dot.

Figure 3. Disclosure icon arrowhead styles; triangular (left), minimal (center), none (right).

Figure 4. Placing icons on the periphery (right) helps reduce occlusion (left) of centered icons.

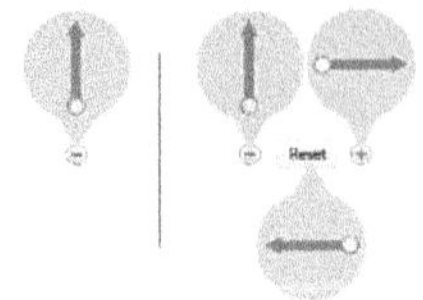

Figure 5. For small, but sufficiently sparse targets, disclosure icons are shown offset in a callout (left); when other callouts are nearby a simple algorithm places them to avoid overlap (right).

We explored several arrowhead types (Fig. 3). Users preferred the triangular arrowhead to no arrowhead, and the minimal arrowhead because it helped them identify both the starting and the ending point. Icons are rendered semi-transparent and shown in red with a white stroke. This two-color design helps in situations where the target may be all-red or all-white rendering a single-color arrow invisible.

We observed that in many applications, icons are often centered and may be quite small; for example, a minus icon ('-') might indicate zoom out (Fig. 4). To avoid covering such small icons completely with the overlay, we align the icons with the outer edge rather than center them. We found that icons as small as the worst-case minus icon are typically centered, decreasing the likelihood of this occurring.

Small Target Corner Cases

Since our approach relies on disclosure icons, several corner cases must be considered for small targets. While most targets on a large display are likely to be more than 3" wide (indeed, [5] used targets that were 6" wide), there may be some exceptions. For very small targets (< 1.5%, or < 2.7" on a 15' display), the icons are too difficult to read at a distance. For small targets with sufficient nearby space, we display the disclosure icon in a callout (Fig. 5) placed (to the left, right, top or bottom of the target) so that it does not overlap other targets, using a simple, left-to-right greedy algorithm.

The other (somewhat worse) case to consider is a grid of small, tightly packed targets, such as a multiline text box: each character is essentially a small target. To handle this case, we group the small targets together using a simple adjacency-based clustering algorithm, with a join threshold of 1.5", and display a single gesture icon for all targets in the cluster. If the user selects this cluster by performing the gesture, a live copy of the cluster is brought to the user at full size for continued interaction using a Portal (see below).

Integrating Portals

We felt there would be cases where users would want to multi-select or otherwise interact with a remote region for an extended period. To support this, we adapt the Portals [4] approach. Users wishing to interact with a target for an extended period (e.g., to fill out a form and then click Search) can simply draw a closed loop at the end of the target's continuation gesture (Fig. 7). This gestural *punctuation* [35] [13], which can be fluidly added to any continuation mark, opens a

[1] After initial mark direction is pruned, there are 8 1-segment gestures, 36 2-segment gestures, and 216 3-segment gestures.

[2] Computed from the geometric union of a 26° isosceles triangle centered, directed to the right in a rectangle of width/height ratio 4

Portal-like live copy of that region of the screen with default width and height 17.5"x17.5" centered on the target. The user may then interact with the remote content, resize this view by dragging on its border or close it by tapping a close icon.

By integrating portal invocation with Gesture Select, users can open the portal directly over the desired target, without having to invoke, and then manually position a portal target.

Teaching Persistent Command Gestures

Many targets are dynamic in nature, e.g. objects in a document. However, some may be persistent commands, e.g. a Save button. We give applications the option of using Gesture Select to teach gestural shortcuts for persistent commands. Applications can define custom, free-form or mark-based gestures to be associated with a specific target; e.g., the application might assign a spiral gesture to Save. The disclosure icon appears with a different visual style to indicate that this gesture does not change (Fig. 8). Much like marking menus, users could learn over time that Save is done via a spiral gesture, so it would no longer be necessary to invoke the region of interest (expert mode); they could simply draw the spiral to Save. To prevent the region of interest from opening in expert mode, all of the persistent gestures begin with a characteristic prefix; we used a "half-loop" (Fig. 8) which is sufficiently distinct from the straight lines used to invoke the region of interest. It is notable, however, that other prefixes could be used.

Cancelling Invocation

Users may on occasion "change their mind" after opening a region of interest and decide not to execute a command, or may open it in the wrong direction. We observed in pilot testing that users naturally drew a "scribble" when they wanted to cancel, and so implemented this approach (Fig. 6).

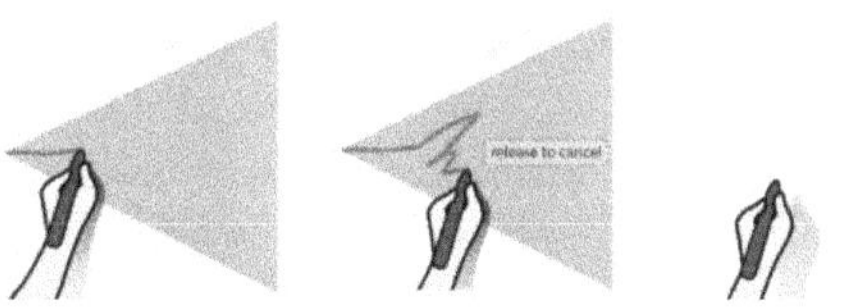

Figure 6. User opens ROI (left) but decides she does not want to execute any commands, so she performs a scribble (center), which cancels (right).

EXPERIMENT 1

Since Gesture Select does not require users to pick a target using a conventional pointing-based approach, we wanted to determine whether this new technique is dependent on target distance or size. We also sought to determine selection time and error rate compared with unaided direct selection.

Note that we do not apply Fitts' law [9] here. We considered applying this highly successful model of pointing, however, in the case of the large display there is an important issue: walking. When selecting a remote target on a large display directly the user must first walk to the target; once they reach the target, they can then perform a pointing task. The Fitts'-law model is conceived for pointing, and does not account for this walking component. We are unaware of an adaptation of Fitts' law that has been tested to account for a walking subtask, so we opted to analyze target selection in the presence of varying target size and distance only.

Tasks

A 1-D reciprocal pointing task was used, with the addition of a start target. Two goal targets were spaced an equal distance along the horizontal axis from the red start target. One of the two goal targets, the active goal target, was highlighted in green, while the other (inactive) goal target was gray. Users first tapped the start target and then selected the goal target. (They were required to successfully select the goal target to continue, so that they could not "race through the experiment by clicking anywhere.") After selecting the active goal target, the active and inactive goal targets switched, with the active goal target now highlighted in green. Users completed four trials for each condition. The start target, based on [5], was used to control the distance between the user and target. Gestures were dynamically assigned (see Design, above), so would not be predictable by the user, and were not the same within each set of reciprocal trials.

We used three distances, near (46" or 26% of display), mid (68.4", 38%), and far (90", 50%); all were outside comfortable reaching distance (near was just outside). We used three target sizes; the smallest was based on a simple calculation: in the Windows 7 OS, desktop icons use 6.51% height of a 1024x768 screen; a proportional height on our display is 3.01". Thus we used target sizes of 3", 4.5" (+50%), and 6" (+100%). We avoid very small targets as in [5], as we feel these are less representative on a display of this size.

Distractor Targets

In addition to the goal targets, gray distractor targets were placed as well. In pilot testing, we found it was not the arrangement of distractors *per se* (e.g. distractors placed on the path between the user and the target vs. targets placed around the target) that affected Gesture Select, but rather simply the total number of distractors within the region of influence: in general, more targets lead to more complex gestures needed. Therefore, in this experiment, we varied the number of *area distractors* close enough to the target to affect gesture complexity. The distractors were laid out in a dense random arrangement around the goal target. We used three distractor counts: 16, 32, and 48. 48 was the maximum number of targets that would fit vertically in a dense circular formation on our large display for the large target size.

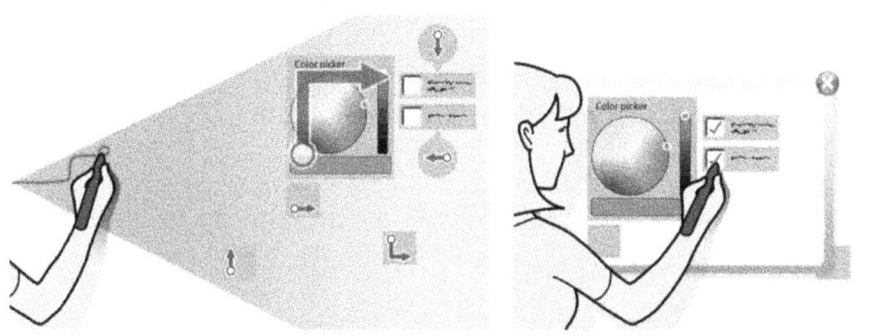

Figure 7. User draws a continuation mark with a loop punctuation at the end (left) to open a portal in place, centered on the selected target (right).

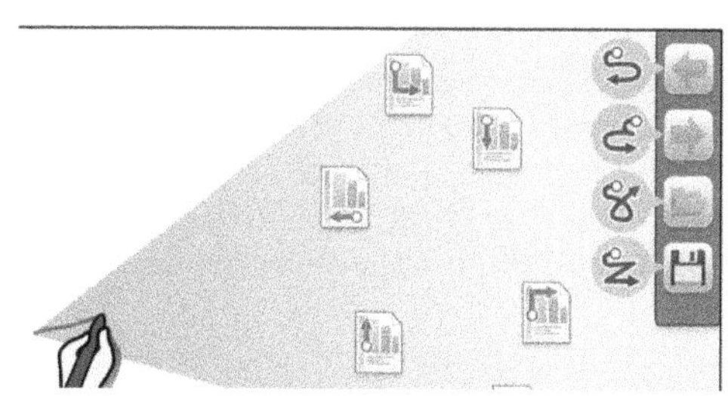

Figure 8. For persistent commands, e.g. Save, gestures can be statically assigned, and will appear in the ROI with different visuals.

Participants and Equipment

Ten participants (aged 18-28, 3 female, all right-handed) were recruited from the general population of Brown University. Two participants reported owning or using a device that has gestures. Participants used a stylus in their right (dominant) hand and were compensated.

We used a 15.4x3.85 ft, short-throw front-projected, tiled large display (effective resolution of 3,072x768). Our large display consisted of a SmartTech SB680 77" (diagonal) interactive whiteboard (input resolution 4000x4000 units) with a short-throw front projector in the center that was flanked on the left and right by two short-throw projectors projecting onto 77" rigid projection screens (Fig. 9).

The center SmartBoard-based portion could sense pen or touch contacts, whereas the two flanking screens were passive/projection only. The lack of input on the passive screens was not a problem for two reasons: (1) for Gesture Select there was no reason to walk any distance to pick remote targets, and the start target kept users centered after each task, and (2) for unaided direct selection (only) we used a camera-measurement/Wizard-of-Oz approach. Video cameras recording the session displayed on screens hidden from the user, allowed the "Wizard" to advance to the next task when appropriate. Note that the Wizard's actions only advanced the task; videos were analyzed offline at the frame level to get timing/accuracy information. This approach is similar to prior work, e.g. [12]. The effect of shadows from user's hands was minimal as the short throw allowed the projectors to be placed very close to the surface of the screen (shadows were below users' hands). Our software was C# and WPF-based, and ran on 3 networked dual-core computers with 2GB of RAM; each computer outputting to one projector.

Experimental Design

A repeated-measures full factorial within-participant design was used, with independent variables: technique (Unaided Direct Selection, Gesture Select), distance (46", 68.4", 90"), width (2", 4", 6"), and distractor count (16, 32, 64):

10 participants
x 2 techniques
x 1+3 blocks (training + measured)
x 3 distances
x 3 widths
x 3 distractor counts
x 4 trials
= 8,640 trials completed

Results

Selection Time

The results for selection time are presented in Fig. 9, left by distance, Fig. 9 center by target size, and Fig. 9, right by distractor count. There was a significant main effect of technique on selection time ($F_{1,18}$=27.66, p=0.001). There was also a significant effect of distance ($F_{2,27}$=231.07, p<0.0001), target size[3] ($F_{1.28,11.23}$=30.62, p<0.0001), and distractor count ($F_{2,27}$=26.16, p<0.0001). There was a significant technique × distance interaction effect[1] ($F_{1.34,25.01}$=142.38, p<0.0001) on task completion time. There was also a significant technique × distractor count interaction effect ($F_{2,27}$=12.50, p<0.0001). There were no other interaction effects (p>0.05).

Post-hoc pairwise means comparisons were conducted with 2-tailed t-tests using Holm's sequential Bonferroni adjustment for multiple means comparisons [15]. Gesture Select was significantly faster than unaided direct selection for 21 of 27 conditions (p<0.0013); six near conditions[4] were not significant. Two of the near conditions were significant, few distractors with large and medium-sized targets (p<0.0013).

Thus, Gesture Select significantly outperformed unaided selection for the mid (46.20%) and far distances (66.20%).

Effect of Target Size on Selection Time

Gesture Select performed significantly worse for small targets than large targets (t_9=10.60, p<0.0001), a mean difference of 189.81 ms (8.9%). However, there was no significant difference between small and medium-sized targets (t_9=3.04, p=0.014), or between medium- and large-sized targets (t_9=1.52, p=0.164).

Effect of Target Distance on Selection Time

Interestingly, Gesture Select was affected by distance: near targets were significantly faster to select than medium-distance targets (t_9=-5.37, p<0.0001), a mean difference of 109.91 ms (5.7%). Near targets were significantly faster to select than far targets as well (t_9=-5.09, p<0.0001), a mean difference of 219.88 ms (11.5%). There was no significant difference between medium-distance and far targets, however (t_9=-3.19, p=0.011).

Effect of Distractor Count on Selection Time

Gesture Select was affected by distractor count: performance with 16 distractors increased 14.54% to 48 distractors, which was significant (t_9=-8.13, p<0.001), 16 to 32 was 10.07% higher, which was significant (t_9=-7.49, p<0.001), and 32 to 48 was 4.06% higher, which was significant (t_9=-3.84, p<0.001). Unaided direct selection had no significant difference in selection time across distractor counts (p>0.05).

Errors

Technique had a significant main effect on error rate ($F_{1,18}$=27.04, p<0.001). Unaided selection had a mean error rate of 1.14%, while Gesture Select had a mean error rate of 6.08%. Distance, target size, and distractor count had no significant effect on error rate (p>0.05).

Keystroke Level Analysis

We performed a keystroke level analysis of the data to determine how Gesture Select was used (Fig. 10). We modeled Gesture Select performance, T, as 5 variables: initial reaction time, T_0; time to open the region of interest, T_{ROI}; time to stop moving after the region of interest opens, T_S; time to read/identify the gesture disclosure icon, T_R; and finally the time to draw the gesture and release contact, T_G.

$$T = T_0 + T_{ROI} + T_S + T_R + T_G$$

On average, users spent 39.6% of the time on initial reaction time and opening the region of interest, 12.1% of the time on

[3] The sphericity assumption was not met, so the Huynh-Feldt correction was applied; the corrected degrees of freedom is shown.

[4] Near, small, some distractors (t_9=2.28, p=0.049); near, small, many distractors (t_9=1.03, p=0.33); near, middle, few distractors (t_9=2.80, p=0.02); near, middle, some distractors (t_9=2.18, p=0.06); near, middle, many distractors (t_9=0.99, p=0.005), near, large, some distractors (t_9=2.83, p=0.02); near, large, many distractors (t_9=2.07, p=0.07).

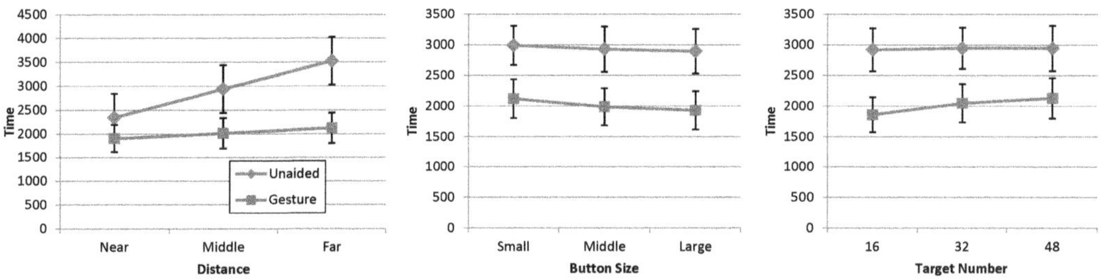

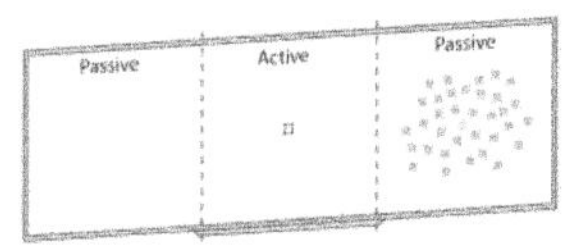

Figure 9.
Distance (left), target size (center), distractor count (right) vs. selection time. Experimental layout (above).

stopping movement after opening the ROI, 16.3% of the time reading/identifying the gesture icon, and 32% of the time drawing the gesture. Stopping movement and reading/identifying the gesture together took 28.4% of the time, very close to the 32% of the time drawing the gesture.

From near to far targets, $T_0 + T_{ROI}$ increased 5.2%, T_S increased by 11.0%, T_R increased by 17.2%, and T_G increased by 12.8%. From large to small targets, $T_0 + T_{ROI}$ increased 5.1%, T_S increased by 5.1%, T_R increased by 10.3%, and T_G increased by 15.6%. It is interesting to note that opening the ROI increased just 5%, while reading and drawing the gesture slowed down. This suggests that opening the ROI was not the source of the increase in selection time, but rather that identifying, reading, and copying the gesture was harder to do when it was smaller/more perspective-warped. Indeed, users commented that small targets were harder to see at the farther distances; we believe this may explain why only small targets were significantly affected (see above).

Performance Stability Across Blocks

There was no significant effect for block number on selection time[1] ($F_{1.19,16.06}$=0.42, p=0.57), or error rate ($F_{2,27}$=0.30, p=0.74). There was also no significant technique × block number interaction for selection time ($F_{2,27}$=0.30, p=0.75), or error rate ($F_{2,27}$=0.27, p=0.77). We attribute the apparent lack of a learning effect to training. In terms of gesture complexity, 23.7% were 1-segment gestures, 35.4% were 2-segment, 16.1% were 2 segment including 1 double-back, 22.0% were 3-segment, 2.4% were 3-segment including 1 double-back, and 0.43% were 3-segment including 2 double-back.

EXPERIMENT 2

In Experiment 1 we determined that Gesture Select can outperform unaided selection for medium-distance and far targets, and that performance is affected by target size, distance and distractor count. However, Experiment 1 may not have been sufficiently representative of real-world tasks in that its selection was 1-D, goal targets were highlighted, and users did not identify targets via a visual icon or label. Thus, the goal of Experiment 2 is to compare performance of Gesture Select to a previous technique, the Vacuum [5], and to unaided direct picking, for 2-D, single selection of labeled targets. We hypothesize Gesture Select will perform similarly to Experiment 1, and outperform the other techniques.

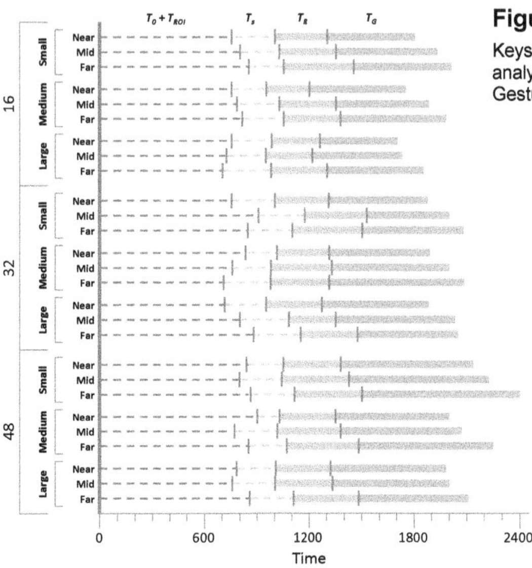

Figure 10.
Keystroke level analysis of Gesture Select.

Since the goal of our technique is similar to The Vacuum, we adapted the experimental design closely from [5]. We did not include Drag-and-Pick as [5] found no significant difference in selection time between Drag-and-Pick and the Vacuum (not including hover dismissal time). Since the Vacuum can scale to a greater number of targets but had very similar performance to Drag-and-Pick, we chose to compare our approach to the Vacuum. We thus implemented a slightly simplified version of the Vacuum for single selection that included no hover dismissal (automatically dismissed after user makes a selection).

Participants and Equipment

We recruited 10 participants from the general population of Brown University (ages 19-27, 4 female, all right-handed). As in Experiment 1, participants used a stylus in their right (dominant) hand and were compensated. Three participants reported owning or using a device that has gestures. The same equipment was used as in Experiment 1 (Fig. 9).

Tasks

Users first tapped a start target and then selected a goal target from amongst distractor targets. As in [5], targets were rendered as gray squares each with a number inscribed; the goal target was gray, like the distractor targets, but was always numbed '1' whereas the distractor targets had other distinct numbers. Since the goal target was not highlighted, users had to identify it via its unique label. The start target let us control the distance to the goal target. Participants could not continue to the next task until correctly selecting the goal target. As in [5], all targets were visible from the trial's beginning. For consistency with [5], a stylus was used for all tasks.

Experimental Design

We used a repeated measures within-subjects full factorial design with controlled variables technique (Direct, Vacuum, Gesture Select), distance (63.3", 78.2"), direction (E, NE, SE, W, SW, NW), and path distractor density (0%, 40%, 80%):

10 participants
x 3 techniques
x 4 blocks (1 training, 3 measured)

x 2 distances
x 6 directions
x 3 path distractor densities
= 4,320 trials completed

The study lasted approximately one hour, and was divided into three parts by technique. For each technique, participants completed 4 blocks, each of which included all combinations of distance, direction, target size, and path distractor density. The first block for each technique was a training block and was not included in the analysis. The condition order was counterbalanced with randomization.

In [13], one target size was used: 6". We felt that 6" targets, while representative of some applications, are larger than many items users might want to select, e.g. icons or command buttons (see Windows 7 OS typical case analysis, above). Therefore, we used 3" targets, as in Exp. 1. As in [13], we used two target distances (the distance between the start target and the goal target), 63.3" and 78.2" (35.1% and 42.4% of display width). Also as in [13], we used 6 target directions, relative to the start target; excluding the N and S directions, as this requires reaching to uncomfortable positions. For this reason, the diagonals were at angles ±17.8° (for 63" distance) and ±14.3° (for 78.2") to the horizontal axis; this produced changes in height of 46".

The start target was placed in the center of the screen. As in [13], users were required to select the start target before selecting the goal target. Also as in [13], all targets were visible at the beginning of the trial, mimicking a scenario in which users are familiar with the interface layout. Emanating from this point, in the six directions, at each distance, goal targets were placed. As in [13] we used two types of distractors: path and area distractors. As in [13], path distractor targets were added between the start and the goal targets, filling in 0%, 40%, or 80% of the space between. We found in Experiment 1 that the number of targets inside the ROI had a significant effect on Gesture Select performance; thus, we used 35 area distractors placed densely around the goal targets, supplementing the path distractors. Users had to complete tasks correctly (see above).

Results

Time

Technique had a significant main effect on task completion time ($F_{2,27}$=13.58, p<0.0001), as did distance ($F_{1,18}$=63.54, p<0.0001). There was also a significant technique × distance interaction[1] ($F_{1.27,23.71}$=22.52, p<0.0001). Path distractor density did not have a significant effect ($F_{2,27}$=1.98, p=0.17). There was, however, a significant technique × path distractor density interaction ($F_{4,85}$=7.79, p<0.0001). Post-hoc tests were conducted with 2-tailed t-tests, with Holm's sequential Bonferroni adjustment [36] for multiple comparisons.

Gesture Select significantly outperformed Vacuum for all conditions (p<0.0025). Gesture Select also significantly outperformed unaided direct selection for all conditions (p<0.0025) with one exception: near + high-density (t_9=3.26, p=0.010). Consistent with [13], there was no significant difference between Vacuum and Unaided for any condition (p>0.05). Gesture Select was affected by distance, increasing 7.55% from mid-far (t_9=-6.04, p<0.001), as was unaided selection 24.02% (t_9=-10.06, p<0.001). The Vacuum was not significantly affected by distance (t_9=0.24, p=0.82).

Interestingly, path distractor density induced no significant difference in selection time for Gesture Select (p>0.05). The Vacuum, however, did show an increase in selection time between 0% and 80% of 11.75%, but this was not significant (t_9=-2.70, p=0.025), and between 40% and 80% distractor densities of 8.60%, also not significant (t_9=-2.66, p=0.026).

This result shows that in the presence of substantial numbers of distractor targets, in a 2-D selection task where targets are not highlighted, Gesture Select significantly outperforms unaided selection and the Vacuum, and performs comparably to the idealized task in Experiment 1.

Gesture Complexity

A histogram of the gesture difficulty classes of goal targets is shown in Fig. 11. Interestingly, 32.92% were 1 and 2-weight gestures, with 51.67% 3-weight, and less than 15.42% higher weight gestures. This indicates complex gestures with weight greater than 3 were rarely used, despite the large number of targets onscreen (see above), and the fact that most of the gesture set have weight greater than 3 (90.4%). This suggests the region of interest, and the heuristic of assigning simpler gestures to the ROI center may have simplified gestures over randome assignment, as that would have assigned greater numbers of ≥ 4 weight gestures given the distractor target count. The mean selection time for each class is shown in Figure 11 as well (note: weight 5 has few samples). 2-weight gestures were 10.37% slower than 1-weight, and 3-weight were 9.19% slower than 2-weight. Interestingly, 4-weight gestures increased 4.60% from 3, and 5-weight increased 6.06% from 4. Overall, there was an increase of 26.05% from weight 1 to weight 4. This suggests the weight heuristic helped represent the increasing gesture difficulty.

Errors

Technique had a significant main effect on error rate ($F_{2,27}$=14.25, p<0.001). Distance and density had no significant effect on error rate (p>0.05). There were also no interaction effects between distance, density and technique on error rate (p>0.05). Post-hoc multiple means comparisons were conducted, using the same adjustment procedure as above. Unaided direct selection had an error rate of 1.85%, while the Vacuum had an error rate of 6.54%, and Gesture Select 8.24%. There was a significant increase in error rates from unaided direct selection to the Vacuum (t_9=-3.57, p<0.025), and a significant increase in error rates from unaided direct selection to Gesture Select (t_9=-6.79, p<0.017). Interestingly, there was no significant difference in error rates between Vacuum and Gesture Select (t_9=-1.29, p=0.23). We note that Vacuum error rates and selection times are higher than those reported in [13]; this is likely the result of the smaller targets used, both directly in that smaller targets are harder to select, and also as there were more individual targets to search, as the path distractors are density-based.

Subjective Preference

When asked which of the techniques was the fastest, 10 of 10 users chose Gesture Select. When asked which of the tech-

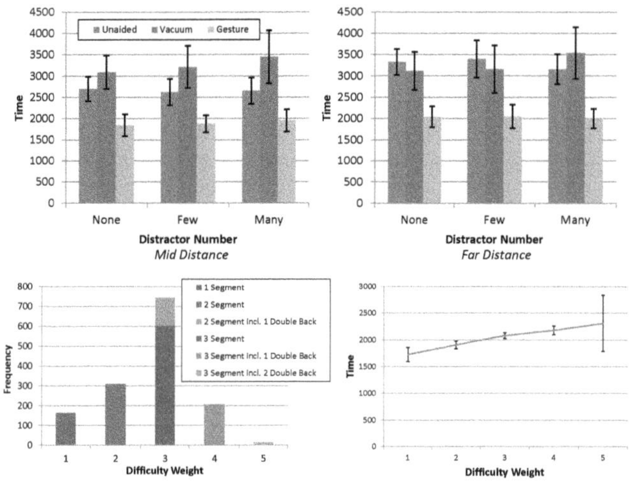

Figure 11. Performance results for medium-distance and far distances (top), histogram of gesture difficulty weight, with gesture complexity breakdown (bottom, left), performance by difficulty weight (bottom, right).

niques was most accurate, 8 of 10 chose unaided selection, 1 chose Vacuum, and 1 chose Gesture Select. This is not surprising, since the large target size made it difficult to miss with unaided selection. When asked which of the techniques was preferred overall, 9 of 10 users chose Gesture Select, and 1 of 10 chose Vacuum. Users felt Gesture Select required "little physical effort" was "really cool" and was "fast and easy to use." The user who preferred Vacuum felt it was useful to be able to see the targets in miniature. Interestingly, despite the fact that 7 users did not use gestural devices, no users mentioned difficulty learning or performing gestures.

Gesture Recognizer Analysis

To determine to what extent the errors for Gesture Select were the result of user error vs. bugs in the recognizer an independent, human, single-blind verification of the recorded gesture performances was conducted. For each participant, 5% of the recordings were sampled randomly, and then recognized using a simple "recipe" set up *a priori*. Beyond visual comparison with a crib sheet, the verifier marked a gesture "unknown" if it was ambiguous, if a mark segment was >80% smaller/larger than other segments, or if there was <45° of angular difference between two consecutive marks.

Overall, there was 97.1% agreement between the human and software recognizer. When looking at trials considered by the system to be successful attempts, there was 100% agreement, indicating false positives were minimal. When looking at trials considered by the system to be failed attempts we found 64.7% agreement, indicating that as much as 35.3% of Gesture Select errors could be false negatives. This suggests user error rate could potentially be lowered with an improved recognizer; it is also possible selection time could be improved as well. Of the gesture errors as a whole, 23.5% were cases in which the user performed the wrong gesture, 41.2% were failures to correctly perform the gesture, and 35.3% were recognition failures.

Performance Stability Across Blocks

There was a significant effect of block number on selection time ($F_{2,27}$=4.73, $p<0.05$), but not for error rates ($F_{2,27}$=1.96, p=0.17). There was also a significant technique × block number interaction for selection time ($F_{4,85}$=6.68, $p<0.05$), but not for error rate ($F_{4,85}$=1.41, p=0.25). The Vacuum improved performance by 257 ms (7%) over the experiment, while the other two techniques changed less than 3%. Informally, we observed that earlier on in the experiment users had a tendency to spend more time adjusting the Vacuum's size, compared with minimal adjustments later on.

DISCUSSION

The controlled nature of the study may limit the generality of the results. We also did not simulate distractions, situational awareness, or collaboration (see below), which might affect performance in ecologically valid situations.

Gesture Select significantly outperformed the Vacuum, as well as unaided direct selection in selection time in Experiment 2, and was preferred overall by 9 of 10 users. It is notable that distance had a 7.55% impact, but path distractors had no significant effect on Gesture Select performance.

Interestingly, despite not involving pointing, Gesture Select is affected by target size and distance. In Experiment 1, we found a 9.84% significant difference between 3" and 6" targets, but no other significant differences. We also found that nearby targets were 5.78% faster to select than medium targets, and 11.56% faster than far targets, but no significant difference between medium and far targets was found.

A keystroke level analysis of Gesture Select performance suggests that small or far targets are harder to see, due to smaller size and perspective warping, thus slowing the gesture identification and copying process. This was consistent with user comments to this effect. This suggests that for a given target size, there may be an effective limit on how far the targets can be from the user and still be legible. A possible solution to this problem for very far targets, would be to apply the clustering approach already used for very small targets, and cluster the targets into larger groups, overlaid with large disclosure icons; executing these gestures could then open a portal.

Performance of Gesture Select was also affected by gesture complexity. We saw a 26.05% increase in selection time from weight 1 to weight 4 gestures, for example. The heuristic of assigning simpler gestures nearer the center of the ROI appeared to benefit users, as a disproportionate number of weight 1, 2 and 3 gestures were used (see above), as there are fewer such gestures. Thus Gesture Select has the interesting property that the number of nearby targets affects performance.

For accuracy, Gesture Select and the Vacuum have a higher error rate than unaided selection. However, there was no significant difference in error rate between the Vacuum and Gesture Select. Gesture Select had an error rate of 6.5% in Exp. 1, and 8.2% in Exp. 2. A single-blind human analysis of the errors in Exp. 2 revealed that as many as 35.3% of these errors were false negatives caused by software recognizer imperfections. We hypothesize that further refinement, or by using simple marks [36], error rates could be reduced. Distance, target size, and distractor count had no significant effect on error rate.

We believe these results are promising, and indicate Gesture Select represents a performance improvement for single selection over the techniques tested.

LIMITATIONS AND FUTURE WORK

There are several limitations in the present work. We did not evaluate Gesture Select in a colocated collaboration scenario; it is possible that the icon overlays could distract other users. In addition, it may be difficult to see disclosure icons if occluded by other users. Given this positive initial result, further work is warranted to evaluate Gesture Select in collaborative scenarios to determine if refinements are required. Another limitation of the technique is that, if more targets are in the region of interest than 260 (the number of available gestures) targets near the edge of the region of interest will not be selectable. However, we expect this problem will be relatively rare, since targets on a display of this size are likely to be large and since we group very small, dense targets together using clustering. The recognizer used in our prototype is imperfect. In a product implementation, a more robust recognizer would be required, or simple marks [36] could be used. Extensions of the core Gesture Select technique were not evaluated formally. Future work is warranted to determine how performance of these extensions compares with prior approaches. In addition, while our technique is usable with direct-touch input as well as pen input, direct-touch input was not tested. Gesture Select is not inherently self-disclosing. A gesture disclosure approach such as [6] could potentially be adapted to address this approachability issue.

CONCLUSION

We have presented Gesture Select, a novel technique for selecting remote targets on large displays. We further presented several extensions to this design for working with remote content for an extended period, and teaching gesture shortcuts for commands. The results of a formal experiment indicate that Gesture Select significantly outperforms direct selection for mid/far targets, and that selection times are affected by target size, and distance within 12% when doubling the distance, and halving target size. Gesture complexity, driven by the number of targets in the ROI had a 15% impact. Further analysis suggests that Gesture Select is principally affected by the extent to which users can easily read the gestures, and the complexity of the gestures in the ROI. The results of a second experiment indicate Gesture Select significantly outperforms unaided direct selection and an existing technique in selection time.

ACKNOWLEDGEMENTS

We wish to thank Andries van Dam for his advice and insight, Alice Liu for her illustrations, and Ronald Dunleavy, Steven P. Reiss, Noah Zimmt and Robert Zeleznik for their assistance. This material is based upon work supported under a National Science Foundation Graduate Research Fellowship and in part by NSF grant CCF-1012056.

REFERENCES

1. Aliakseyeu, D., Nacenta, M., Subramanian, S., and Gutwin, C. Bubble Radar: Efficient Pen-Based Interaction. In *Proc. of AVI'06.*
2. Bau, O. and Mackay, W. OctoPocus: a dynamic guide for learning gesture-based command sets. In Proceedings of UIST'08, 37-46.
3. Baudisch, P., et al. Drag-and-Pop and Drag-and-Pick: techniques for accessing remote screen content on touch-and-pen operated systems. In *Proc. of INTERACT'03.*
4. Bezerianos, A. et al. View and Space Management on Large Displays. *IEEE Computer Graphics and Applications*, 25, 4 (2005).
5. Bezerianos, A. and Balakrishnan, R. The vacuum: facilitating the manipulation of distant objects. In *Proc. of CHI'05*, 361-370.
6. Bragdon, A., Zeleznik, R., et al. GestureBar: improving the approachability of gesture-based interfaces. In *Proc. of CHI'09.*
7. Collomb, M., Hascoët, M., Baudisch, P., and Lee, B. Improving drag-and-drop on wall-size displays. In *Proc. of GI'05*, 25-32.
8. Fekete, J., Elmqvist, N., and Guiard, Y. Motion-pointing: target selection using elliptical motions. In Proc. of CHI'09, 289-298.
9. Fitts, P. M. The information capacity of the human motor system in controlling the amplitude of movement. *J. Exp. Psych.*, 47, 6 '54.
10. Guimbretiere, F. and Winograd, T. FlowMenu: Combining Command, Text, and Data Entry. In *Proc. of UIST'00*, 213-216.
11. Guimbretière, F., Stone, M., and Winograd, T. Fluid interaction with high-resolution wall-size displays. In *Proc. of UIST'01*, 21-30.
12. Harrison, C. and Hudson, S. Providing dynamically changeable physical buttons on a visual display. In *Proc. of CHI'09*, 299-308.
13. Hinckley, K., Baudisch, P., et al. Design and analysis of delimiters for selection-action pen gesture phrases in scriboli. *CHI'05.*
14. Hinckley, K., Ramos, G., Guimbretiere, F., Baudisch, P., et al. Stitching: Pen gestures that span multiple displays. In *AVI'04.*
15. Holm, S. A Simple Sequentially Rejective Multiple Test Procedure. *Scandinavian Journal of Statistics*, 6 (1979), 60-65.
16. Humphreys, G. and Hanrahan, P. A distributed graphics system for large tiled displays. In *Proceedings of IEEE VIS'99*, 215-223.
17. Irani, P., Gutwin, C., and Yang, X. Improving selection of off-screen targets with hopping. In *Proceedings of CHI'06* (), 299-308.
18. Kahn, A., Fitzmaurice, G., Almeida, D., et al. A Remote Control Interface for Large Displays. In *UIST'04.*
19. Kobayashi, M. and Igarashi, T. Ninja cursors: using multiple cursors to assist target acquisition on large screens. In *CHI'08.*
20. Kurtenbach, G. and Buxton, W. The limits of expert performance using hierarchic marking menus. In *Proc. of CHI'93.*
21. Malik, S., Ranjan, A., et al. Interacting with Large Displays from a Distance with Vision-Tracked Multi-Finger Gestural Input. *UIST'05.*
22. Mitsubishi. *MegaView Data Wall.* mitsubishi-megaview.com.
23. Mynatt, E., Igarashi, T., Edwards, W., and LaMarca, A. Flatland: new dimensions in office whiteboards. In *Proceedings of CHI'99.*
24. Ni, T., Schmidt, G.S., Staadt, O.G., Livingston, M.A., et al. A Survey of Large High-Resolution Display Technologies, Techniques, and Applications. In *Proc. of IEEE VR'06.*
25. Pederson, E., McCall, K., Moran, T. P., et al. Tivoli: an electronic whiteboard for informal workgroup meetings. In *INTERCHI'93.*
26. Reetz, A., et al. Superflick: a natural and efficient technique for long-distance object placement on digital tables. In *GI'06.*
27. Rekimoto, J. Pick and drop: A direct manipulation technique for multipe computer environments. In *Proc. of UIST'97*, 31-39.
28. Shoemaker, G. and Gutwin, C. Supporting Multi-Point Interaction in Visual Workspaces. In *Proc. of CHI'07*, 999-1008.
29. Smart Technologies. *Large-wall Touch Displays.* smarttech.com.
30. Swaminathan, K. and Sato, S. Interaction for Large Displays. interactions, 4, 1 (1997), 15-24.
31. Tan, D., Meyers, B., et al. WinCuts: manipulating arbitrary window regions for more effective use of screen space. *CHI'04EA.*
32. Tse, E., et al. Speech-filtered bubble ray: improving target acquisition on display walls. In *Proc. of Multimodal interfaces*'07.
33. Vogel, D. and Balakrishnan, R. Distant freehand pointing and clicking on very large, high resolution displays. In *Prc. of UIST'05.*
34. Yatani, K., Partridge, K., et al. Escape: a target selection technique using visually-cued gestures. In Proc. of CHI'08.
35. Zelenik, R. and Miller, T. Fluid inking: augmenting the medium of free-form inking with gestures. In *Proceedings of GI'06*, 155-162.
36. Zhao, S. and Balakrishnan, R. Simple vs. compound mark hierarchical marking menus. In *Proceedings of UIST'04*, 33-42.

User-Defined Motion Gestures for Mobile Interaction

Jaime Ruiz*
University of Waterloo
Waterloo, ON, Canada
jgruiz@cs.uwaterloo.ca

Yang Li
Google Research
Mountain View, CA, USA
yangli@acm.org

Edward Lank
University of Waterloo
Waterloo, ON, Canada
lank@cs.uwaterloo.ca

ABSTRACT
Modern smartphones contain sophisticated sensors to monitor three-dimensional movement of the device. These sensors permit devices to recognize motion gestures—deliberate movements of the device by end-users to invoke commands. However, little is known about best-practices in motion gesture design for the mobile computing paradigm. To address this issue, we present the results of a guessability study that elicits end-user motion gestures to invoke commands on a smartphone device. We demonstrate that consensus exists among our participants on parameters of movement and on mappings of motion gestures onto commands. We use this consensus to develop a taxonomy for motion gestures and to specify an end-user inspired motion gesture set. We highlight the implications of this work to the design of smartphone applications and hardware. Finally, we argue that our results influence best practices in design for all gestural interfaces.

Author Keywords
Motion gestures, sensors, mobile interaction.

ACM Classification Keywords
H5.2. User Interfaces--Input devices and strategies.

General Terms
Design

INTRODUCTION
While smartphones combine several tasks (e.g., voice and data communication, multimedia consumption, mobile gaming, and GPS navigation) into one package, their form factor is also limiting in both input and output. To allow the device to fit into a pocket or purse, screens are small and keyboards are thumb-sized. On many devices the thumb keyboard has been replaced by a soft-keyboard displayed on the screen to minimize the size and weight of the device.

Two primary input modalities are commonly supported by soft-keyboard based smartphones: The first is a touchscreen display; and the second is a set of motion sensors: accelerometers, gyroscopes, orientation sensors (vs. gravity), etc. The two inputs recognized by these devices are different types of gestures. Users can gesture on the device in two dimensions, using the touchscreen of the smartphone as a mobile surface computer. We call these two-dimensional gestures *surface gestures*. Users can also gesture with the device, in three dimensions, by translating or rotating the device. We call these three-dimensional gestures *motion gestures*.

In this research, we focus specifically on *motion gestures*. Researchers have proposed the use of motion gestures for a variety of input tasks: for example, to navigate maps or images [18], to input text [11,17,26], to control a cursor [25], and to verify user identity [12].

Recently, Wobbrock et al. [28] addressed the lack of understanding of the design space for surface gestures. However, many similar questions about motion gesture design are also unanswered by past research. What parameters do users manipulate to create different motion gestures (i.e. differences in path, in kinematics, etc.)? Is there a "design-space" or taxonomy of the different dimensions that designers can manipulate in the creation of these gestures? Is there an end-user consensus set of user-specified motion gestures that eliminates the need for designers to arbitrarily create their own motion gestures? Finally, is there a logical mapping of motion gestures onto device commands?

In this paper, we describe the results of a *guessability study* [27] for motion gestures which elicits natural gestures from end-users as follows: given a task to perform with the device (e.g. answer the phone, navigate East in a map), participants were asked to specify a motion gesture that would execute that task.

The results of the study yield two specific research contributions to motion gesture design. First, when participants were asked to specify motion gestures for many common smartphone effects including answering the phone, ignoring a call, or navigating within applications, there was broad unscripted agreement on the gestures. As a result, we can specify an end-user motion gesture set for many common smartphone tasks, analogous to Wobbrock et al.'s end-user surface gesture set [28]. Second, we use

*This work was conducted during an internship at Google Research.

measurements from both the input sensors of the smartphone and video recordings of motion gestures created by participants to specify a taxonomy of the parameters that can be manipulated to differentiate between different motion gestures. This taxonomy represents the design space of motion gestures.

The implications of this research to the design of smartphone appliances are two-fold. First, from the perspective of smartphone application designers, the taxonomy of physical gestures and our understanding of agreement for user-defined gestures allow the creation of a more natural set of user gestures. They also allow a more effective mapping of motion gestures onto commands invoked on the system. Second, from the perspective of companies that create smartphones and smartphone operating systems, this study provides guidance in the design of sensors (i.e. what features of three dimensional motion must we distinguish between) and toolkits (i.e. what gestures should be recognized and accessible to application context) to support motion gesture interaction at both the application and the system level.

More broadly, the results reported in this paper significantly extend our understanding of gestural interaction both in two dimensions (surface gestures) and in three dimensions (motion gestures). Broad agreement exists among users on gesture sets, both in two [28] and six degrees of freedom. As well, users' past experiences with desktop computers or with smartphones inform a logical mapping of causes onto effects for both surface and mobile computing. Our work suggests that these consistent logical mappings would extend to paradigms beyond just surface and mobile computing. If the effects persist for other computing paradigms, then the design task for gestural interaction becomes one of manipulating established taxonomies of gestures while preserving the logical mappings of causes to effects as specified by end users. The downside of this is that the constraints on gesture designers increase, i.e. the logical mapping must be preserved. The benefit is that, whether in 2D or 3D, natural gestures and natural mappings can potentially be identified by conducting a basic guessability study with prospective users.

The rest of this paper is organized as follows. We first explore related work in user-specified gesture sets and in physical gestures for device control. Next, we describe our study methodology, including our participants and the set of tasks that we examine. We describe the qualitative data and the taxonomy, the specific results of our observational study. Finally, we discuss in more detail the broader implications of this work.

RELATED WORK

A majority of the prior work on classifying human gestures has focused on human discourse (see [28] for a review). In this section, we focus on work which explores the classification of human gestures in relation to the dialog between a human user and an interactive device. Within this space, research exists in both surface gestures and motion gestures. We also describe techniques for elicitation studies as a motivation for our research approach to motion gestures.

Surface Gesture Research

In the domain of surface computing, surface gestures have been used by groups of users to support cooperative work with systems and by single users to issue commands to the system. Tang [23] observed that gestures play an important role in communicating significant information for small groups around drawing interfaces. He observed that gestures are used to express ideas, demonstrate a sequence of actions, and mediate group interaction. Morris et al. [15] described a classification, or design space, for collaborative gestures resulting from their evaluation of a system for cooperative art and photo manipulation. Their classification identified seven design axes relevant to cooperative gesture interaction: symmetry, parallelism, proxemic distance, additivity, identity-awareness, number of users, and number of devices.

In work examining gestures for single-user interaction, Wobbrock et al. [28] present a taxonomy of surface gestures based on user behavior. Based on a collection of gestures from twenty participants, their taxonomy classifies gestures into four dimensions: form, nature, binding, and flow. They also create a user-specified gesture set. More recently, they evaluated this gesture set against a gesture set created by a designer and showed that the user-specified gesture set is easier for users to master [16]. Wobbrock et al.'s work in surface gestures is a strong justification for elicitation studies in the design of gesture sets.

Motion Gesture Research

To our knowledge no research has been published describing the classification of motion gestures. As well, little research been done on end-user elicitation of motion gestures. Research on motion gestures has been focused on interaction techniques using motion input and tools to design motion gestures.

Rekimoto [18] was credited for proposing one of the earliest systems to use motion input to interact with virtual objects. Rekimoto demonstrated how mapping motion to tilt can be used for selecting menu items, interacting with scroll bars, panning or zooming around a digital workspace, and performing complex tasks such as 3D object manipulations.

Harrison et al. [6], Small & Ishii [22], and Bartlett [4] extended the use of tilt sensors to enable navigating through widgets on mobile devices. Hinckley et al. [9] proposed using tilt on a mobile device to allow a user to change screen orientation—a feature now commonly found on many devices. Motion input has also been used for text input [11,17,26], controlling a cursor [25], and user verification [12].

Research efforts in physical gestures have also been targeted at designers of systems that use physical gestures. Exemplar [8] allows quick motion gesture design using demonstration and direct manipulation to edit a gesture. MAGIC [3] allows designers to design motion gestures by demonstration, and incorporates tools that provide information about performance. MAGIC also allows designers to test for false positives, internal consistency, and distinguishably between classes of gestures to improve the recognition rate of motion gestures created by designers.

What little research exists on end-user elicitation of motion gestures has been done in support of multimodal interaction. In this domain, Mignot et al. [13] studied the use of speech and gesture and found that gestures were used for simple and direct commands, while speech was more commonly used for abstract commands. In their work on augmented reality offices, Voida et al. [24] asked participants to create gesture and/or voice commands for accessing objects on multiple displays. They found that people overwhelmingly used finger pointing. While some elicitation of motion gestures exists in the multimodal interaction community, the work has typically explored physical gesture input as an add-on to voice-based commands. Research on the use of motion gestures as a stand-alone input modality has not been explored by these researchers.

Conducting Elicitation Studies

Eliciting input from users is a common practice and is the basis for *participatory design* [21]. Our approach of prompting users with the effects of an action and having them perform a gesture has been used to develop a command line email interface [5], unistroke gestures [27], and gestures for surface computing [28].

DEVELOPING A USER-DEFINED GESTURE SET

To explore user-defined gestures, we elicited input from 20 participants. Participants were asked to design and perform a motion gesture with a smartphone device (a cause) that could be used to execute a task on the smartphone (an effect). Nineteen tasks were presented to the participants during the study (Table 1). Participants used the think-aloud protocol and supplied subjective preference ratings for each gesture.

As the goal of the study was to elicit a set of end-user gestures, we did not want participants to focus on recognizer issues or current smartphone sensoring technology. As a result, no recognizer feedback was provided to participants during performance of the gestures. We also encouraged the participants to ignore recognition issues by instructing them to treat the smartphone device as a "magic brick" capable of understanding and recognizing any gesture they might wish to perform. Our rationale for these decisions was the same as the rationale expressed in Wobbrock et al.'s surface gesture work [28]. Specifically, we wished to remove the *gulf of execution* [10] from the dialog between the user and the device, i.e. to observe the users' unrevised behavior without users being influenced by the ability of the system to recognize gestures.

Category	Sub-Category	Task Name
Action	System/Phone	Answer Call
		Hang-up Call
		Ignore Call
		Voice Search
		Place Call
	Application	Act on Selection
Navigation	System/Phone	Home Screen
		App switch Next
		App switch Previous
	Application	Next (Vertical)
		Previous (Vertical)
		Next (Horizontal)
		Previous (Horizontal)
		Pan Left
		Pan Right
		Pan Up
		Pan Down
		Zoom In
		Zoom Out

Table 1. The list of tasks presented to participants grouped by category.

Each participant performed gestures for each of the tasks indicated in Table 1. The session was video recorded and custom software running on the phone recorded the data stream generated from the accelerometer. Each session took approximately one hour to complete. For each participant, a transcript of the recorded video was created to extract individual quotes and classify and label each motion gesture designed by the participant. The quotes were then clustered to identify common themes using a bottom-up, inductive analysis approach.

Selection of Tasks

Inclusion of tasks in our study was determined by first classifying tasks into two categories: *actions* and *navigation-based* tasks. Within these categories, we created two sub-categories: a task can either act on the system/phone (e.g. answering a phone call or switching to a previous application) or on a particular application (e.g. navigating a map in a GPS application, selecting text on the display). After grouping the tasks into these four sub-categories, a scenario representing each task was chosen for inclusion in the study. This method allowed us to create tasks that would be representative of the tasks used in a smartphone while minimizing duplication of tasks resulting from application specific gestures. Categories and sub-categories for the tasks are shown in Table 1.

Participants

Grasping the concept of moving the device to invoke commands and clearly understanding the potential tasks that could be performed on a smartphone (both necessary to collect usable data in a guessability study) arguably require that the user have some experience with the device. Therefore, we intentionally recruited participants who indicated that they used a smartphone as their primary mobile device.

Twenty volunteers, ten males and ten females, between the ages of 21-44 (mean = 28, SD = 5.4) participated in the study. The participants all worked for a high-tech company but did not all hold technical positions. The volunteers received a $30 gift certificate to an online bookseller for their participation.

Apparatus

Gestures were recorded using custom software developed using the Android SDK [1] for a Google Nexus One smartphone running Android 2.1. The software was responsible for logging the data stream of the accelerometer sensor and locking the screen to ensure no feedback was displayed to the participant. Additional software written in Java ran on the researcher's laptop and was responsible for recording the beginning and end of a gesture as well as the participant's subjective ratings.

Procedure

At the beginning of each experimental session, the researcher described the study to the participant and handed the participant the smartphone running the custom software. The 19 tasks were grouped into six sets of similar tasks. For example, one task set included effects that represented normal use of the phone: answering a call, muting the phone, ending a call. Another task set involved map navigation tasks such as panning and zooming.

For each set of tasks, the participant was presented with a sheet describing the overall set of tasks they were to invoke and listing each task in the group. Where appropriate (e.g., navigating Google Maps) a screenshot of an application was provided. Participants were instructed to read the information sheet and, in a talk-aloud method, design a motion gesture to represent each one of the listed tasks. Participants did not need to commit to a gesture until all gestures in the task set were designed to encourage participants to design a cohesive set of gestures for the set of tasks.

After designing the set of motion gestures for the given task set, the researcher asked the participant to perform each gesture five times on cue and then rate the gesture using a seven-point Likert scale on the following criteria:

- The gesture I picked is a good match for its intended use.
- The gesture I picked is easy to perform.

In addition, the user was also asked how often they would use the motion gesture if the gesture existed on a six-point scale ranging from never to very frequently.

The interview concluded with the interviewer asking the participants if they had suggestions of other tasks where motion gestures would be beneficial. Participants were then asked to design a gesture for each task they suggested. The purpose of this exercise was to assess if our proposed tasks had enough coverage of possible uses of the phone.

RESULTS

The data collected during our study included transcripts, the video recording, a set of gestures designed by our participants, subjective ratings of the set of gestures, and the data stream collected from the sensors while participants performed their gestures on the smartphone. From this data we present themes emerging from our interviews, a taxonomy for motion gestures, and a user-defined motion gesture set for mobile interaction.

Designing Motion Gestures

Transcripts of the recorded interviews were used to identify common themes that emerged from our study. The themes—which provide user-defined design heuristics for motion gestures—include mimicking normal use, applying real world metaphors, natural and consistent mappings, and providing feedback. We discuss each of these themes bellow.

Mimic Normal Use

Volunteers who designed gestures that mimicked motions occurring during normal use of the phone often perceived their gesture as being both a better fit to the task and easier to perform. In addition, there was a consensus among participants on the form of these gestures. This is especially evident in the design of a motion gesture to answer a call. For this task, 17 out of 20 users designed a gesture where users placed the phone to their ear. When asked to describe why they chose that gesture, participants often made comments describing the gesture as "natural":

The first motion I would be doing is picking it up [and] bringing it to my ear...The most natural thing for me would be bringing it to my ear.[P16].

Real-world Metaphors

When participants were able to relate interacting with the mobile phone to interacting with a physical object, the gesture they designed consistently mimicked the use of a non-smartphone object. For example, to end a call, a majority of participants suggested removing the phone from the ear and turning the display face down parallel to the ground. When asked why they choose that gesture to represent the task, several participants noted that it mimicked the action of hanging up a phone receiver on an "old-fashioned" telephone.

Real-world metaphors do not always need to correspond directly to the phone. For example, when given the task of navigating to the Home Screen, half of the users selected shaking the phone as the gesture. Users viewed navigating to home as *"clearing what you are doing"* [P6]. Users related clearing the contents of the phone to the action of clearing the contents of an Etch A Sketch [2]:

Why shaking? It's almost like the Etch A Sketch where, when you want to start over, you shake it. [P20].

Natural and Consistent Mappings

Motion gestures differ from surface gestures in that the user interacts by using the device itself instead of interacting on the device with a finger or hardware button. To allow designers to create more intuitive motion gesture sets, it is important to understand the user's mental model of how motion gestures map to the interaction of the device instead of relying on current mappings.

Tasks that were considered to be opposites of each other always resulted in a similar gesture but performed in the opposite direction, regardless of the proposed gesture. For example, a flick to the right was the most common gesture for next and a flick to the left was used by these same participants for previous.

Several sets of tasks were designed as navigational or scrolling tasks with the intention of determining the participant's mental model of navigation (i.e., Is the participant controlling the viewport or the content?). Current touch interfaces often require the user to interact with the content while the viewport remains static. In contrast, when interacting with a scroll bar on a desktop PC the scroll bar controls the viewport.

Results from our study show that the preference of a participant depends on the plane in which she is interacting. In cases where the participant was interacting on the XY plane, i.e. navigating on a map, the consensus was that the interaction using motions should alter the viewport. In other words, to move to the left in a map, participants would move the phone to the left, similar to the interaction found in the peephole system [30]. Even those participants who first described interaction with the content performed gestures that required the viewport to move. For example, when asked to pan a map to the east (right), participants performed a gesture to the right, indicating the viewport would move to show the content east of the current position. When the interviewer mentioned this discrepancy between the description and the gesture, one participant responded:

I didn't even notice I was doing it. [P15]

While moving in the XY plane resulted in viewport manipulations, when choosing gestures to zoom in and out of a map, i.e. interacting in the Z plane, the consensus was to perform a gesture to "move" the map closer to the participant's face to zoom in and to move the map away from the participant's face to zooming out. Therefore, instead of treating the phone as viewport, participants instead reverted to a real-world metaphor: a magnifying glass. Understanding the subtleties that exist between mappings and metaphors is one challenge of implementing gesture set behaviors.

While map navigation used the metaphor of a viewport, the on-screen context had an effect on participants' mappings. As part of the study we included two presentations of lists to determine if list orientation (horizontal or vertical) influenced the design decisions of our participants, and to determine whether list navigation and map navigation were analogous tasks. A majority of the participants shared the sentiments of P17 who stated:

I want to have the same gesture for next and previous regardless if I am viewing search results, contacts, or photos [P17]

Search results and contacts were arranged in a vertical list, whereas photos were arranged in a horizontal list. The gesture for "next" was common to both lists.

Finally, for gestures designed to navigate content (e.g., scrolling or panning) movement of the viewport can occur in discrete steps or can be based on the amount of force occurring during the gesture. While the agreement among participants was not as strong as other themes, there was a majority agreement that discrete navigation was preferred. As stated by P9:

If it was continuous then I think it would be pretty hard when to determine when to stop...and if I was walking down the street I would have to pay close attention [to] when to stop. [P9]

This observation runs counter to common surface gesture design on touch-screen smartphones, where on-screen flicks typically map gesture speed to different scrolling and panning distances.

Feedback

While the goal of our experiment was to eliminate any feedback in order to observe participants' unedited gestures, participants often commented on the need for feedback:

I suppose what I would expect no matter what gesture I would use is some kind of feedback, probably some auditory feedback since I wouldn't necessarily be looking at the phone...just alert me that is what it is doing and give me a chance to back out because I can imagine doing [the gesture] by mistake. [P9]

Participants were also careful when designing gestures to ensure that any visual feedback displayed on the screen would be visible during execution of the gesture.

The problem that any gesture that requires anything extended while you're not looking at the screen...you are then losing feedback so it seems like it's undesirable. [P10]

Since the tasks selected in our trial required the user to interact with content on the screen after completing the gesture—map navigation, navigating previous and next in lists, etc.—it was also important for participants to be able to view the screen while performing the gesture, especially when part of the user experience is the interaction with the content. For example, P8 states:

...with photos usually there is this nice experience of like transitioning between one photo or the next, so I don't want to twitch because then I miss it. I want something that keeps the display facing me. [P8]

Motion Gesture Taxonomy

Given our understanding of the heuristics our participants applied to gesture design, the second question we explored is the set of parameters manipulated by our participants. We constructed a taxonomy for motion gestures using the 380 gestures collected that contains two different classes of taxonomy dimensions: *gesture mapping* and *physical characteristics. Gesture mapping* involves how users map motion gestures to device commands. These include the *nature*, *temporal* and *context* dimensions of the gesture. *Physical characteristics* involve characteristics of the gestures themselves: the *kinematic impulse, dimensionality, and complexity*. The full taxonomy is listed in Table 2.

Gesture Mapping

The *nature* dimension defines the mapping of the gesture to physical objects. One can view the gesture in a number of ways, specifically:

- *Metaphor:* The gesture is a metaphor of acting on a physical object other than a phone (a microphone, an old-fashioned phone).
- *Physical:* The gesture acts on the content/object itself (direct manipulation).
- *Symbolic:* The gesture visually depicts a symbol. For example, drawing the letter B with the device.
- *Abstract:* The gesture mapping is arbitrary.

The *temporal* dimension describes if the action on an object occurs during or after a gesture is performed. A gesture is categorized as *discrete* if the action on the object occurs after completing the gesture. Examples of discrete gestures include answering and making a call. During a *continuous* gesture, action occurs during the gesture and is completed upon the completing of the gesture. For example, map navigation tasks were typically considered continuous gestures by our participants.

The *context* dimension describes whether the gesture requires a specific context or is performed independent of context. For example, placing the phone to the head to answer a call is an *in-context* gesture, whereas a shaking gesture to return to the home screen is considered an *out-of-context* gesture.

Taxonomy of Motion Gestures		
Gesture Mapping		
Nature	Metaphor of physical	Gesture is a metaphor of another physical object
	Physical	Gesture acts physically on object
	Symbolic	Gesture visually depicts a symbol
	Abstract	Gesture mapping is arbitrary
Context	In-context	Gesture requires specific context
	No-context	Gesture does not require specific context
Temporal	Discrete	Action occurs after completion of gesture
	Continuous	Action occurs during gesture
Physical Characteristics		
Kinematic Impulse	Low	Gestures where the range of jerk is below $3m/s^3$
	Moderate	Gestures where the range of Jerk is between $3m/s^3$ and $6m/s^3$
	High	Gestures where the range of Jerk is above $6m/s^3$
Dimension	Single-Axis	Motion occurs around a single axis
	Tri-Axis	Motion involves either translational or rotational motion, not both.
	Six-Axis	Motion occurs around both rotational and translational axes
Complexity	Simple	Gesture consist of a single gesture
	Compound	Gesture can be decomposed into simple gestures

Table 2. Taxonomy of motion gestures for mobile interaction based on collected gestures.

Physical Characteristics

Since motion gestures are physical, it is appropriate to classify the gestures in reference to their *kinematic* properties. The kinematic impulse dimension segments gestures into three categories, represented by the range of jerk (rate of change of acceleration) applied to the phone throughout the gesture. A low impulse gesture represents a gesture where the range of jerk over the gesture is below $3m/s^3$. A high impulse gesture is one where the range of jerk is relatively high, larger than $6m/s^3$ over the gesture. An example of a high impulse gesture would be a forceful shake. Gestures falling in between the range are classified as having a moderate kinematic impulse. The three categories and their respective cut-offs were determined by creating a histogram of the collected gestures by the rate of jerk and identifying clusters.

The *dimension* of a gesture is used to describe the number of axes involved in the movement. Many gestures, including flicks and flips of the phone involve single-axis motion. Others, for example zooming using a magnifying glass metaphor, require users to translate the phone in 3D space. Gestures that are either translations or rotations are tri-axis gestures. Still other gestures, for example ending a call by "hanging up" the phone, require users to both translate and rotate the device around its six degrees of freedom.

The *complexity* dimension relates to whether the proposed gesture is a *compound* gesture or a *simple* gesture. We define a compound gesture as any gesture that can be decomposed into simple gestures by segmenting around spatial discontinuities in the gesture. Discontinuities can include inflection points, pauses in motion, or corners.

Figure 1 illustrates the breakdown of the 380 gestures collected during the study using our taxonomy. As shown in the figure, gestures tended to be simple discrete gestures involving a single axis with low kinematic impulse.

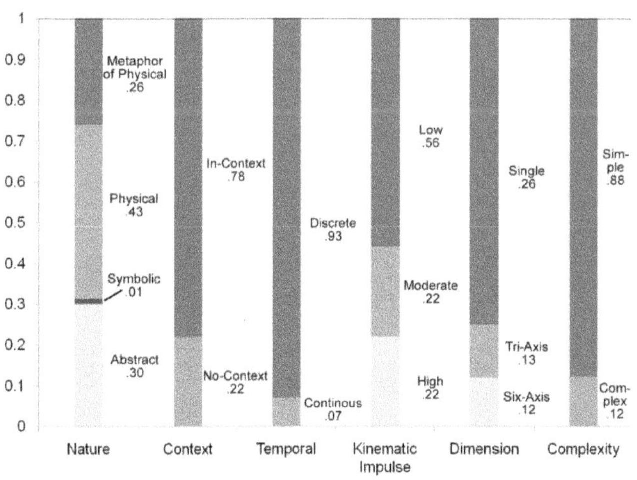

Figure 1. Percentage of gestures in each taxonomy category.

A User-defined Gesture Set

Using the gestures collected from our participants, we generated a user-defined gesture set for our specified tasks. For each task, identical gestures were grouped together. The group with the largest size was then chosen to be the representative gesture for the task for our user-defined gesture set. We call this gesture set both our *consensus set* and our *user-defined gesture set* interchangeably.

To evaluate the degree of consensus among our participants and compare our gesture set to Wobbrock et al. [28], we adopted the process of calculating an *agreement score* for each task [27,28]. An agreement score, A_t, reflects in a single number the degree of consensus among participants. Wobbrock [27] provides a mathematical calculation for agreement, where:

$$A_t = \sum_{P_i} \left(\left| \frac{P_i}{P_t} \right| \right)^2$$

In Equation 1, t is a task in the set of all tasks T, P_t is the set of proposed gestures for t, and P_i is a subset of identical gestures from P_t. The range for A is [0, 1].

As an example of an agreement score calculation, the task *answer the phone* had 4 groups with sizes of 17, 1, 1, and 1. Therefore, the agreement score for *answer the phone* is:

$$A_{answer\ phone} = \left(\frac{|17|}{|20|}\right)^2 + \left(\frac{|1|}{|20|}\right)^2 + \left(\frac{|1|}{|20|}\right)^2 + \left(\frac{|1|}{|20|}\right)^2 = 0.73$$

Figure 2, illustrates the agreement for the gesture set developed by our participants. Agreement scores from our user-defined motion gestures are similar to those shown for Wobbrock et al.'s gesture set for surface computing [28]. As shown by their agreement scores, there was not a consensus on a motion gesture for *switching to next application, switching to previous application,* and *act on selection* tasks. Therefore, we did not include gestures in the user-defined set for these tasks. The resulting user-defined set of motion gestures is shown in Figure 3.

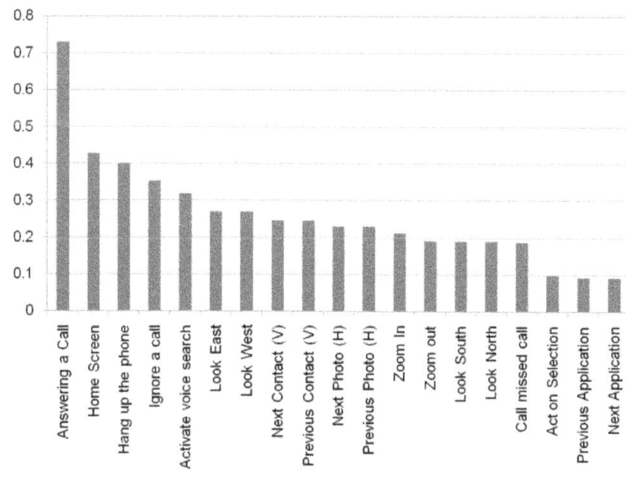

Figure 2. Agreement for each task sorted in descending order.

Subjective Ratings of the User-Defined Gesture Set

Recall that after designing a gesture for a particular task, participants rated the goodness of fit, ease of use, and how often the participant would use the gesture assuming it existed. Consider two sets of gestures. The first set is those gestures in our user-defined gesture set, i.e. those that were specified by a plurality of participants for each task. The second set includes all other gestures, i.e. those that are not part of our consensus set.

Comparing the subjective ratings, we find subjective ratings on *goodness of fit* to be more highly rated for our user-defined gesture set than for those gestures not in the consensus set ($X^2=12.85$, $p < 0.05$). However, we did not

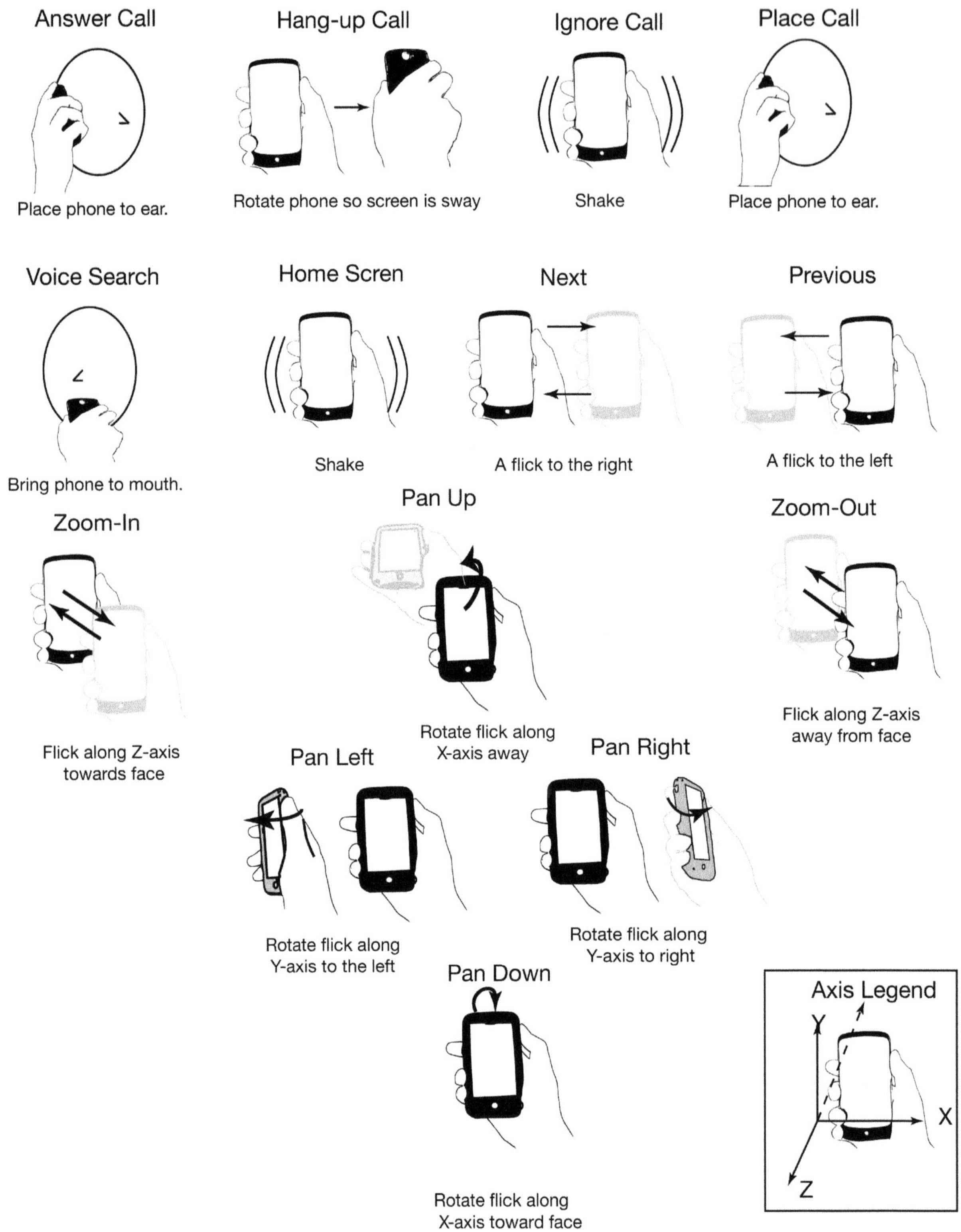

Figure 3. The user-defined motion gesture set. A *flick* is defined by a quick movement in a particular direction and returning to the starting position. Since the gestures for next and previous did not differ regardless how the task was presented (i.e. a vertical or horizontal list) we simplify our presentation by presenting the gestures under a single heading. The tasks of navigating to previous application, navigating to next application, and act on selection were not included in the gesture set due to the lack of agreement between participants.

find significant differences for *ease of use* or *frequency of use* between the two groups.

Task Coverage

Although great care was taken to create a list of tasks that would be representative of the tasks users perform on their device, it is possible that some potential tasks were not represented. To compensate for any neglected tasks, at the end of the interview we gave participants the opportunity to suggest tasks that would benefit from motion gesture interaction. While we did receive some suggestions, all suggestions were specific to an application, for example, a web browser. In addition, participants often commented that they would reuse previous gestures that were designed for the same purpose. For example, to mimic the back button in the web browser users suggested the same gesture as navigating to a previous photo or contact. Therefore, while we did not address all applications with our scenarios, we did address the majority of actions commonly used on mobile smartphones. As a result, our user-defined gesture set can be used to inform the design of motion gestures for a majority of the tasks within an application. The generalizability of many of the user-specified gestures allows for consistency across applications, which is important for learnability and memorability [29].

DISCUSSION

In this section we discuss the broader implications of our results for motion gesture design, mobile devices, and gesture interaction.

Supporting Motion Gesture Design

To support applications designers, motion gesture design software and toolkits should provide easy access to the gestures described in the user-defined set. Application designers may also wish to specify their own gestures, so design software and toolkits should also allow the creation of new motion gestures based on the heuristics presented above. Finally, while many tasks had good agreement scores for their user-specified gestures, some did not. For tasks with poor agreement scores, gesture toolkits should allow end-user customization.

Implications for System Design

The gestures in the user-defined gesture set and the themes that emerged from the study provide several challenges for designers of mobile phones. A major theme that emerged was that gestures should mimic normal use. In addition, as shown in Figure 1, a majority of the gestures collected during the study were classified as having a low kinematic impulse. The difficulty of using gestures with a low kinematic impulse and that mimic normal use is that these gestures are often difficult to distinguish from everyday motion. This can result in a high false positive rate and a high level of user frustration. As well, gestures with low kinematic impulse may be difficult to differentiate from one another using the current sensors in smartphones.

Despite the drawbacks associated with the observation that many user-specified motion gestures exhibit low kinematic impulse and mimic normal use, there are benefits in understanding the natural characteristics of user-specified gestures. First, it may be possible to develop a delimiter, for example a physical button to push or an easy-to-distinguish motion gesture [20] to segment motion gestures from everyday device motion. Second, understanding the physical characteristics of end-user specified gestures gives system designers specific requirements to build towards. These can include adding additional sensors to infer context or using more sensitive sensors to distinguish between different low kinematic impulse motion gestures.

Implications for Gesture Interaction on Smartphones

During our study we asked participants how often they would use a motion gesture to accomplish a task. As we reported above, ratings did not differ depending on if the gesture designed by the participant was a member of the consensus group or not. In both cases, participants were very receptive to using motion gestures; only 4% of all responses indicated that participants would never use the motion gesture. In contrast, 82% of the responses indicated they would use the motion gesture at least occasionally. This result supports the notion that the use of motion gestures can substantially alter how users interact with their mobile phones. By providing motion gestures as an additional input modality, motion gestures can be used to simplify interaction (such as when answering the phone) or to enable interaction when users are unable to interact with the device using surface gestures (such as when wearing gloves).

Implication for the Design of 2D and 3D Gestural Interfaces

When examining the user-specified gesture set for surface computing developed by Wobbrock et al. [24], designers may feel that the existence of this gesture set was a singular event. In other words, something "special" about the intersection of surface computing with two-dimensional gestures permitted the creation of this gesture set. Our research indicates that this is not the case. For a different gestural paradigm, motion gestures, and for a different computing paradigm, mobile computing, another user-specified gesture set was created using a guessability study. As with surface gestures, our agreement scores vary from task to task. However, the extent of the between-participant agreement on gestures and mappings is still highly significant.

While gestures and mappings agree for surface and mobile computing paradigms, there are still open questions. Does agreement persist for other paradigms? For example, what about motion gesture interfaces where users control devices from afar using a device, an object, or their hands? What about using "scratches," another form of surface gesture, to issue commands [7]. Our work suggests that conducting a guessability study with users before specifying gesture sets and mapping will significantly inform the design of gestures in these domains.

Social Acceptability of a User-Defined Gesture Set

Recent work by Rico and Brewster [19] and Montero et al. [14] explored the social acceptability of performing motion gestures in public places. The researchers found that a participant's rating of the social acceptability of a gesture was influenced by whether they believed a bystander could interpret the intention of the gesture. Given these findings, gestures in the consensus set (or gestures that mimic gestures in the set) should be more socially acceptable than gestures not in the set as a result from bystanders being able to interpret the meaning of the gesture. We plan on validating this hypothesis in future work.

FUTURE WORK

A limitation of our study is that our participants were educated adults who lived in a Western culture. It is quite possible that the gestures are influenced by the culture. For example, gestures such as previous and next are strongly influenced by reading order. In future work we would like to validate the user-defined gesture set with new participants from other user demographics and cultures.

We are also exploring tools to help developers select and evaluate gestures based on our taxonomy. In addition, we are exploring the possible use of online tools to allow the developer community to continue to revise and expand the user-defined gesture set as the tasks that users wish to accomplish on mobile devices change.

CONCLUSION

In this paper, we described the results of a guessability study for motion gestures. We show that for a subset of tasks that encompass actions with the device there is broad agreement on the motion gestures used to invoke these tasks. As a result of commonalities in gestures and their mappings, we present design heuristics and a taxonomy that inform motion gesture design for mobile interaction. Finally, we highlight the significant effect of this work on the paradigm of gestural interaction.

REFERENCES

1. *Android Open Source Project*. Google Inc.
2. *Etch A Sketch*. Ohio Art.
3. Ashbrook, D. and Starner, T. MAGIC: A Motion Gesture Design Tool. *Proceedings of CHI '10*, ACM (2010), 2159-2168.
4. Bartlett, J.F. Rock 'n' Scroll Is Here to Stay. *IEEE Comput. Graph. Appl. 20*, 3 (2000), 40–45.
5. Good, M.D., Whiteside, J.A., Wixon, D.R., and Jones, S.J. Building a user-derived interface. *Communications of the ACM 27*, 10 (1984), 1032-1043.
6. Harrison, B.L., Fishkin, K.P., Gujar, A., Mochon, C., and Want, R. Squeeze me, hold me, tilt me! An exploration of manipulative user interfaces. *Proceedings of CHI '98*, ACM Press/Addison-Wesley Publishing Co. (1998), 17–24.
7. Harrison, C. and Hudson, S.E. Scratch input. *Proceedings of UIST '08*, (2008), 205.
8. Hartmann, B., Abdulla, L., Mittal, M., and Klemmer, S.R. Authoring sensor-based interactions by demonstration with direct manipulation and pattern recognition. *Proceedings of CHI '07*, (2007), 145.
9. Hinckley, K., Pierce, J., Sinclair, M., and Horvitz, E. Sensing techniques for mobile interaction. *Proceedings of UIST '00*, ACM (2000), 91–100.
10. Hutchins, E., Hollan, J., and Norman, D. Direct Manipulation Interfaces. *Human-Computer Interact 1*, 4 (1985), 311-338.
11. Jones, E., Alexander, J., Andreou, A., Irani, P., and Subramanian, S. GesText: Accelerometer-based Gestural Text-Entry Systems. *Proceedings of CHI '10*, (2010).
12. Liu, J., Zhong, L., Wickramasuriya, J., and Vasudevan, V. User evaluation of lightweight user authentication with a single tri-axis accelerometer. *Proceedings of MobileHCI '09*, ACM (2009), 1–10.
13. Mignot, C., Valot, C., and Carbonell, N. An experimental study of future "natural" multimodal human-computer interaction. *Proceddings of INTERACT '93 and CHI '93*, (1993), 67-68.
14. Montero, C.S., Alexander, J., Marshall, M.T., and Subramanian, S. Would you do that? *Proceedings of MobileHCI '10*, (2010), 275.
15. Morris, M.R., Huang, A., Paepcke, A., and Winograd, T. Cooperative gestures. *Proceedings of CHI '06*, (2006), 1201.
16. Morris, M.R., Wobbrock, J.O., and Wilson, A.D. Understanding users' preferences for surface gestures. *Proceedings of GI 2010*,CIPS (2010), 261–268.
17. Partridge, K., Chatterjee, S., Sazawal, V., Borriello, G., and Want, R. TiltType: accelerometer-supported text entry for very small devices. *Proc. UIST '02*, ACM (2002), 201–204.
18. Rekimoto, J. Tilting operations for small screen interfaces. *Proceedings of UIST '96*, ACM (1996), 167–168.
19. Rico, J. and Brewster, S. Usable gestures for mobile interfaces: evaluating social acceptability. *Proceedings of CHI '10*, ACM (2010), 887–896.
20. Ruiz, J. and Li, Y. DoubleFlip: A Motion Gesture for Mobile Interaction. *Proceedings of CHI '11*, ACM (2011).
21. Schuler, D. *Participatory design : principles and practices*. L. Erlbaum Associates, Hillsdale N.J., 1993.
22. Small, D. and Ishii, H. Design of spatially aware graspable displays. *CHI '97 extended abstracts*, ACM (1997), 367–368.
23. Tang, J. Findings from observational studies of collaborative work. *International Journal of Man-Machine Studies 34*, 2 (1991), 143-160.
24. Voida, S., Podlaseck, M., Kjeldsen, R., and Pinhanez, C. A study on the manipulation of 2D objects in a projector/camera-based augmented reality environment. *Proceedings of CHI '05*, (2005), 611.
25. Weberg, L., Brange, T., and Hansson, \.W. A piece of butter on the PDA display. *CHI '01 extended abstracts*, ACM (2001), 435–436.
26. Wigdor, D. and Balakrishnan, R. TiltText: using tilt for text input to mobile phones. *Proc UIST '03*, ACM (2003), 81–90.
27. Wobbrock, J.O., Aung, H.H., Rothrock, B., and Myers, B.A. Maximizing the guessability of symbolic input. *CHI '05 extended abstracts*, (2005), 1869.
28. Wobbrock, J.O., Morris, M.R., and Wilson, A.D. User-defined gestures for surface computing. *Proceedings of CHI '09*, (2009), 1083.
29. Wu, M., Chia Shen, Ryall, K., Forlines, C., and Balakrishnan, R. Gesture Registration, Relaxation, and Reuse for Multi-Point Direct-Touch Surfaces. *Proceedings. of TABLETOP '06*, 185-192.
30. Yee, K. Peephole displays. *Proceedings of CHI '03*, ACM (2003), 1--8.

Gesture Avatar: A Technique for Operating Mobile User Interfaces Using Gestures

Hao Lü[*]
Computer Science and Engineering
DUB Group, University of Washington
Seattle, WA 98195
hlv@cs.washington.edu

Yang Li
Google Research
1600 Amphitheatre Parkway
Mountain View, CA 94043
yangli@acm.org

ABSTRACT
Finger-based touch input has become a major interaction modality for mobile user interfaces. However, due to the low precision of finger input, small user interface components are often difficult to acquire and operate on a mobile device. It is even harder when the user is on the go and unable to pay close attention to the interface. In this paper, we present Gesture Avatar, a novel interaction technique that allows users to operate existing arbitrary user interfaces using gestures. It leverages the visibility of graphical user interfaces and the casual interaction of gestures. Gesture Avatar can be used to enhance a range of mobile interactions. A user study we conducted showed that compared to Shift (an alternative technique for target acquisition tasks), Gesture Avatar performed at a much lower error rate on various target sizes and significantly faster on small targets (1mm). It also showed that using Gesture Avatar while walking did not significantly impact its performance, which makes it suitable for mobile uses.

Author Keywords
Touchscreens, finger-based touch input, gestures, mobile devices, target acquisition.

ACM Classification Keywords
H.5.2. Use Interfaces: Input devices and strategies, Interaction style. I.3.6. Methodology and Techniques: Interaction techniques.

General Terms
Design, Experimentation, Human Factors

INTRODUCTION
Touchscreen mobile devices have become prevalent in the recent years [2,12]. However, although finger-based touch input is intuitive, it suffers from low precision due to two fundamental problems: the area touched by the finger is much larger than a single pixel—the fat finger problem—and the pointing finger often occludes the target before touching it—the occlusion problem [21].

Although existing mobile interface widgets are often designed to be easily operated by finger, the tension remains between the low precision of finger input and the high precision needed by graphical user interfaces for the following reasons. First, it consumes precious screen real estate to make UI widgets large enough to be finger-operable, especially as the resolution of mobile devices increases, e.g., the iPhone 4's resolution is 640 × 960 [12]. Secondly, in a web interface, many UI widgets, e.g., hyperlinks or an embedded Flash player, are still small and hard to operate by finger. Lastly, high precision interactions are more challenging for mobile users because they are often on the go, e.g., walking or taking a bus, and cannot pay a close attention to the interface.

Although many solutions have been explored for addressing the fat finger and occlusion problems, most of them still require highly precise visual perception and motor control such as carefully adjusting a finger's position [1,4,18,20].

Figure 1: (a) Small mobile interface widgets are difficult to operate through fingers. (b) In Gesture Avatar, the user can draw the shape of the target, e.g., the rectangle for the knob of the slider. (c) Gesture Avatar finds the widget that best matches the user gesture and shows an avatar attached to it. (d) The user can then operate the widget (e.g., the slider knob) through the avatar, e.g., by dragging the avatar to move the video slider.

CHI 2011, May 7–12, 2011, Vancouver, BC, Canada.

[*] This work was conducted during an internship with Google Research.

In contrast, gesture-based techniques, e.g., panning a map by swiping a finger across the touch screen, allow for casual interaction. However, gesture-based interactions tend to lack visibility compared to graphical user interfaces whose operation semantics are embodied by their interface components [16]. Prior work such as Escape [24] creatively combined the advantages of both worlds using rectilinear gestures to select graphical objects. However, it is limited in that it requires a target interface to be designed in a specific way. In addition, prior work mostly focused on the one-shot target acquisition, leaving other common interactions, such as drag-and-drop, unexplored.

To address these issues, we designed and implemented Gesture Avatar, a novel interaction technique that allows users to operate mobile user interfaces using gestures. Figure 1 provides a quick demonstration of the technique. Gesture Avatar leverages the visibility of graphical user interfaces and the casual interaction of gestures. A user can dynamically associate a gesture shape with an arbitrary GUI widget and then interact with the widget through the drawn gesture, which is conceptually akin to an avatar.

Gesture Avatar can be used to enhance a range of mobile interactions. A user study we conducted showed that in target acquisition tasks, Gesture Avatar achieved a significantly lower error rate than Shift [20] and performed faster on small targets (1mm). It also showed that walking had no significant effect on using Gesture Avatar, which makes it suitable for mobile uses. We demonstrate the feasibility and ease of use of Gesture Avatar by integrating it with existing systems such as a mobile web browser.

In the rest of the paper, we first provide a brief introduction of how a user interacts with the existing mobile interfaces through Gesture Avatar and then discuss related work. Next, we provide a detailed description of our design and implementation of Gesture Avatar along with more example applications that our technique can enhance. We then evaluate Gesture Avatar by comparing it to Shift. Finally, we discuss the factors in designing Gesture Avatar and possible future work.

MOBILE INTERACTION USING GESTURE AVATAR

In this section, we describe how a user would interact with mobile interfaces using Gesture Avatar. Assume that a user opens the New York Times website (http://nytimes.com) in a mobile phone web browser. The interaction objects such as hyperlinks are viewable but too small to be easily tapped on by a finger.

Here the user wants to navigate to the sports section. She draws an "s" on the screen[1] near the link "SPORTS" (see

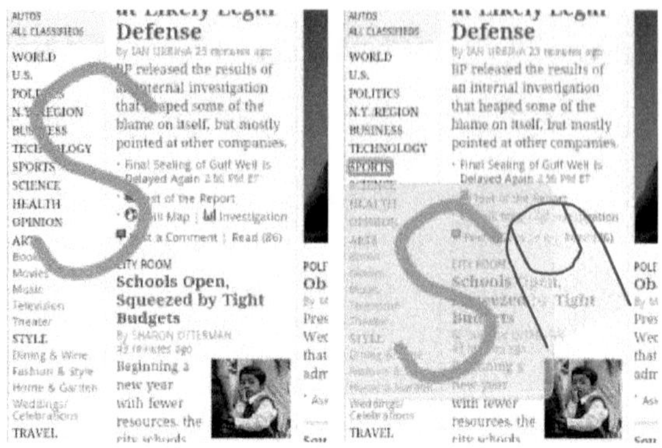

(a) (b)

Figure 2: Tapping on a target using Gesture Avatar. (a) The user draws an "S" near the target "SPORTS". (b) The user taps on the gesture avatar as if tapping on the target.

Figure 2a). This creates a gesture avatar, the gesture stroke with a translucent background. The bounding box of the link that the avatar is associated with is highlighted (see Figure 2b). The user can then easily trigger the link "SPORTS" by tapping on the gesture avatar, which is a much larger target.

As we will discuss in the following sections, to form the association between a gesture and an object, we leverage both the shape of the gesture and its distance to the objects on the screen.

From this example, we can see that a gesture avatar provides a larger effective area for a user to comfortably interact with a small target. The type of interaction that Gesture Avatar can enhance is not limited to tapping. A gesture avatar essentially re-dispatches whatever touch events it receives to the associated object. For example, a user can long press an avatar to long press the associated object to bring up a context menu.

The gesture that is used to create an avatar can also be arbitrary. It can be a character or an arbitrary shape. For example, the user can draw a box to create an avatar for controlling the progress bar of a media player as seen in Figure 1. The user can then move the knob of the progress bar by dragging the avatar.

An avatar may be associated with an undesired object due to the inaccuracy of gesture recognition and the essential ambiguity of the objects on the screen. For example, in Figure 2a, when the user draws an "S", both "SPORTS" and "SCIENCE" are good candidates.

When an avatar is associated with an undesired object, the user can either dismiss the avatar by tapping outside of the avatar and redraw a gesture, or re-assign an object to the avatar using directional (collinear) gestures. When the user draws directional gestures outside the avatar (e.g., Figure 3a), Gesture Avatar will find the next best match in the direction of the stroke and update the avatar's position on the screen accordingly (e.g., Figure 3b). The user can repeat this process until the avatar is associated with the target.

[1] To allow the user to indicate a drawing action instead of panning the webpage, an implementation of Gesture Avatar can use various mode-switching techniques, which we will discuss later.

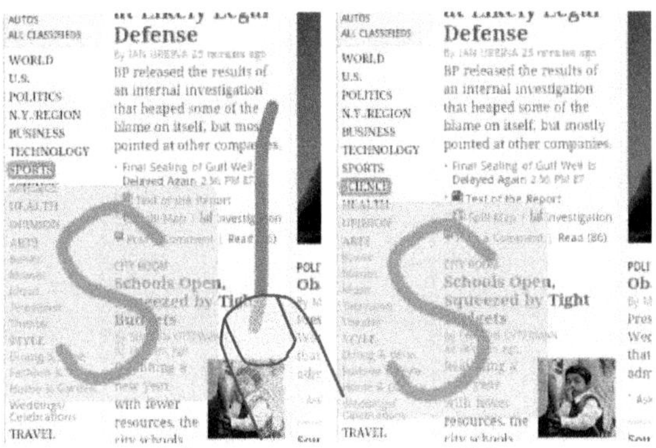

Figure 3: Re-assigning a target to the avatar. (a) The user draws a directional gesture outside the avatar. (b) Gesture Avatar finds the next best match in the given direction.

The directional gestures of Gesture Avatar enable users to easily navigate in the possible matches that are presented on the screen (a 2-dimensional space).

RELATED WORK

A large corpus of prior work has focused on facilitating target acquisition. Most of this work generally reduces the Fitts's Index of Difficulty [10] by increasing a target's size. Semantic pointing [6] dynamically adjusts the control-display (CD) ratio as the cursor approaches the target. Bubble cursor [11], which is based on area cursor [23], dynamically changes its size according to the proximity of surrounding objects so that the pointer is snapped to a nearby object.

High-precision pointing is hard with an imprecise input such as a bare finger. Many methods and techniques have been presented for high-precision touchscreen interaction. Albinsson and Zhai [1] propose two techniques using widgets for precise finger positioning by zooming, reducing CD gain, and discrete pixel-by-pixel adjustment. They show that though these techniques are faster than Offset Cursor for targets smaller than 0.8 mm, they are slower for targets larger than 3.2 mm. Benko et al. [4] present Dual Finger Selections that facilitate pixel-accurate targeting by adjusting the CD ratio with a secondary finger.

Much work has also been done in avoiding finger occlusion. Offset Cursor [18] eliminates finger occlusion by showing a cursor above users' fingers. However, users can no longer aim for the target directly even when the target is big enough. Instead, users have to first touch the surface to show the cursor and then move the cursor onto the target to select it. This contradicts the intuitiveness of direct touch. Shift [20] improves Offset Cursor by showing a copy of the occluded screen in a callout above the user's finger. Unlike Offset Cursor, users still can aim for the actual target with Shift. Their user study shows that Shift has a much lower error rate than unaided touchscreen and is faster than Offset Cursor for large targets. One problem with Shift is that the callout view is taken out of context, which requires extra effort to re-understand the view and re-recognize the target.

Wigdor et al. [22] propose back-of-device interaction to eliminate the finger occlusion problem. However, they cause the user's fingers to be occluded by the device, causing large error rates. LucidTouch [21] addresses the problem by introducing pseudo-transparency, which creates an illusion that users can see their occluded fingers, decreasing error rates. Baudisch et al. [3] propose a similar technique on small devices.

Escape [24] is a gesture-based technique for facilitating target acquisition. It first assigns directions to all objects. Users then can press their fingers near the target, followed by a directional stroke to specify the direction of the target. Through gestural interaction, Escape greatly reduces the effort in human visual feedback loop and avoids the occlusion and fat finger problems. The major limitation of Escape is that the appearance of the user interface has to be modified in order to make the assigned directions visible. Escape is demonstrated with a map-like application where using directional balloons is possible. However, it is often inappropriate or impossible to change the appearance of an application's user interface, which makes the technique less applicable. Moreover, as mentioned in their own paper, the density of the objects (the number of the objects in a certain area) is limited due to the fact that close objects cannot have similar directions, and the technique is limited near screen edges, as gestures cannot go beyond screen edges.

THE DESIGN OF GESTURE AVATAR

In this section, we describe the details of how Gesture Avatar works. Our design goal is to allow users to easily interact with mobile interfaces, especially when the target (e.g., a link or a button) is small and users are on the go. As a result, we designed Gesture Avatar with reducing or eliminating high precision interaction in mind.

The Interaction Flow of Gesture Avatar

Figure 4 illustrates the interaction flow of Gesture Avatar. The interaction with Gesture Avatar involves four states. The interaction process starts from the *Initial* state. Once the finger touches the screen, it enters the *Gesturing* state, in which the touch trace is rendered on top of the underlying user interface that is being operated. When the user lifts her finger and the trace is a valid gesture (e.g., the bounding box of the trace is large enough to be considered as a gesture instead of a tap), the process enters the *Avatar* state, in which the drawn gesture stroke forms the avatar with a translucent background. The object that is associated with the avatar is also highlighted.

In the *Avatar* state, the user can choose to operate the associated object through the avatar, or adjust the association if the avatar is associated with an undesired object. In this state, if the user touches down inside of the avatar, the *touch_down* as well as the subsequent *touch_move* and *touch_up* events will be re-dispatched to

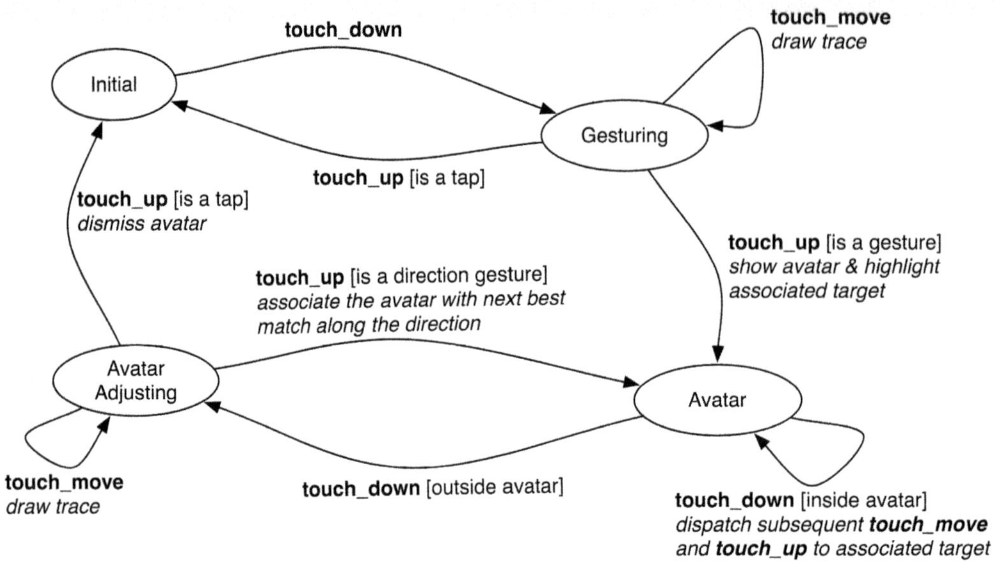

Figure 4: The interaction flow of Gesture Avatar. The interaction starts from the Initial state. Touch events are shown in bold. The conditions for a transition to occur are enclosed in brackets and the actions of a transition are shown in italic.

the associated object in the underneath user interface. If the user touches outside of the avatar, the user can either dismiss the shown avatar by a tap or change the associated object using directional gestures.

Matching an Gesture against Objects

In this section, we discuss how a gesture, g, is matched against the potential targets available on the screen, T, so that the avatar can be associated with a desired target, t_{match} (see Equation 1).

$$t_{match} = \arg\max_{t_i \in T} P(t_i|g) \quad (1)$$

As discussed earlier, we leverage both the semantics of the gesture and its spatial relationship with the objects on the screen. The combination of these two factors can effectively triangulate a desired object on the screen. As a result, Equation 1 can be expanded as the following:

$$P(t_i|g) = \alpha P(c_i|s_g)P(p_i|b_g) \quad (2)$$

where $P(c_i|s_g)$ encodes how much the content of the object, c_i, matches the semantics of the gesture, s_g, and $P(p_i|b_g)$ captures the spatial relationship between an object and the gesture, in particular, the distance between the gesture's bounding box, b_g, and the center of the object, p_i. We discuss how these two quantities are calculated in the following sections. (α is the normalizing constant.)

Matching Based on Semantic Information

A gesture can be a character or an arbitrary shape, and the content of an object is either a set of characters for a textual object or the contour of a graphical object (e.g., the triangular boundary of the play button of a media player). Character and shape recognition have several fundamental differences, and distinct approaches have been developed for handling each case [5]. As a result, we first classify whether the gesture is a character or a shape and then employs different recognizers for each case. For character matching, Gesture Avatar employs a neural network handwriting recognizer that recognizes letters and numbers used in English. The recognized character is then used to search against the content of each object on the screen. For shape matching, Gesture Avatar uses a template-based shape recognizer that is conceptually akin to [14]. The templates, i.e., the contours of all the objects on the screen, are added on the fly. The shape recognizer then finds the object that has the most similar contour to the gesture. Note that rather than only keeping the best guess, this calculation gives a distribution of all possible characters and shapes, which is fed into $P(c_i|s_g)$ of Equation 2.

Matching Based on Spatial Relationships

Since users tend to aim for the target, the position of the gesture for interacting with the target is often a strong indicator of where the target is. As a result, it is reasonable to assume that the closer an object is to the gesture, the more likely it is the target.

To capture this intuition, we use a 2D Gaussian distribution over the distance between the center of an object and the bounding box of the gesture. To save computation when there are numerous objects on the screen, we use the Manhattan distance, instead of the Euclidean distance, of an object to the bounding box (see Figure 5). The output of the Gaussian provides an indication of how likely the object is the target, i.e., $P(p_i|b_g)$.

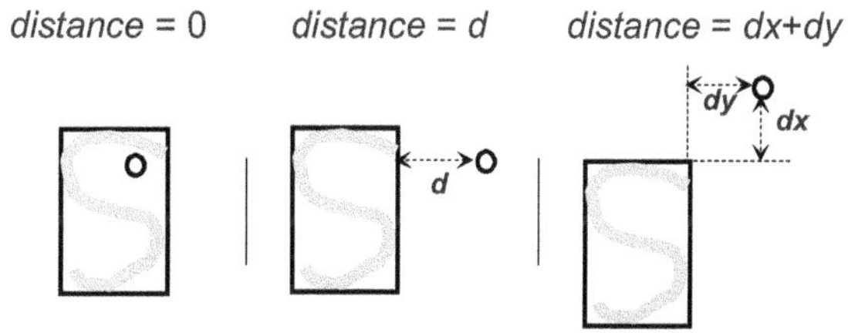

Figure 5: The distance of a target (denoted as a circle) to the avatar is calculated as the smallest Manhattan distance from it to the gesture's bounding box.

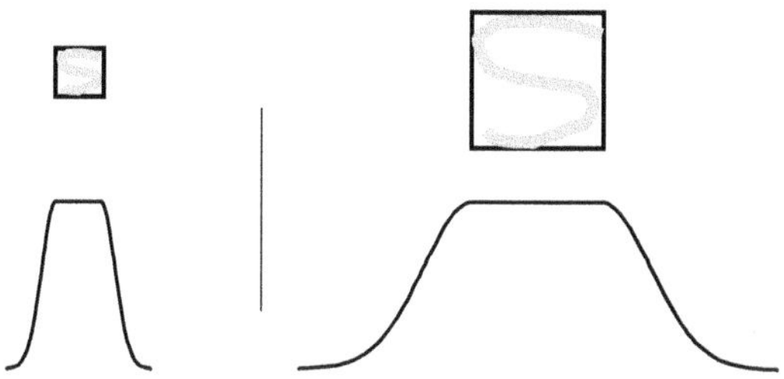

Figure 6: The larger the bounding box is, the less impact the distance has on the scoring.

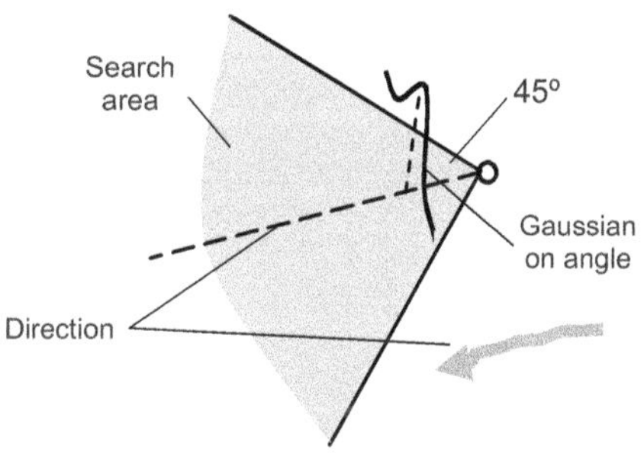

Figure 7: Searching the next best match in the given direction. We restrict the search area to the objects in a 45-degree range. A Gaussian function on the angular distance from the given direction gives a scoring factor.

The 2D Gaussian distribution employs a changing variance that is dynamically adjusted based on the length of the longer edge of the gesture's bounding box (see Figure 6). This design of our algorithm is based on the observation that users draw gestures in different sizes, and the smaller the gesture is, the more specific area the user is targeting at.

Correcting a Mismatch by Navigating in Objects

Due to the inaccuracy of gesture recognition and the inherent ambiguity of objects available on the screen, it is unavoidable that an avatar is associated with an undesired object. For example, multiple objects with similar content might be cluttered in one area. Furthermore, objects on the edges of the screen are also prone to incorrect matching, since users cannot draw gestures over these objects and the Gaussian distribution cannot efficiently capture this situation.

One typical approach to correct a mismatch is to ask the user to dismiss the avatar and then recreate it. However, this approach cannot guarantee success and can be annoying if it is only a close miss, e.g., when the target object is just next to the mismatched object.

In our design, we allow the user to go to the next best match in the given direction by drawing a directional stroke. Directional strokes are fast to perform and the outcomes of them are more predictable.

Based on the directional stroke the user draws, we infer the next best match based on not only how well an object matches the avatar gesture semantically, but also the angular distance between the directional stroke and the direction from the currently matched object to the object being evaluated. Again, we use a Gaussian function to give each object a score based on its angular distance (see Figure 7). To reduce computation cost, we restrict the search to the objects within ±45° of the stroke direction.

MORE EXAMPLES

In the previous sections, we demonstrated the use of Gesture Avatar through a media player and a mobile browser. In this section, we discuss two more examples.

The first example (see Figure 8a) applies Gesture Avatar to moving the caret in a text box. The on-screen keyboards on most touchscreen mobile phones do not have dedicated keys for moving the caret. Instead, users need to directly touch between two characters. Since the text is small, moving the caret is error-prone. The iPhone uses a Shift-like technique to address this problem. With Gesture Avatar, the user can draw the character before (or after) the desired position to assign an avatar to it and then tap on the right (or left) half of the avatar to move the caret.

The second example (see Figure 8b) applies Gesture Avatar to Google Maps. Previously, maps have been a heavily used example to demonstrate and evaluate different target acquisition techniques [20,24]. Locations on a map are typically represented by distinct letters. This property makes Gesture Avatar promising for acquiring locations,

(a) (b)

Figure 8: (a) Moving the caret in a text box using Gesture Avatar. (b) Acquiring a location in Google maps.

since there is little semantic ambiguity in these location objects.

IMPLEMENTATION

Gesture Avatar was primarily written in Java using Android SDK 2.2. For image contents, we first compute their edges using the Canny edge detector and then pass them to our shape recognizer. The image processing and edge detection were written in C++ using OpenCV [17] and built with a variation of Android NDK.

The example applications that we have discussed in the paper were written in Java. We built these examples by wrapping an existing user interface, e.g., a web browser or a text input field, with an additional interaction layer, i.e., Gesture Avatar. In the mobile web browser example, the current version of mobile WebKit does not expose its UI structures, i.e., the DOM tree, in Java but only accessible through JavaScript. As a workaround, we implemented the logic for searching the best matches in JavaScript and inject the JavaScript code upon loading a webpage.

EVALUATION

As discussed earlier, Gesture Avatar addresses not only the acquisition of small targets, but also the follow-up interaction such as dragging an object after it is acquired. There has been little prior work in addressing the latter. So Gesture Avatar makes a clear contribution in that regard. As a result, we here focus on its performance on target acquisition compared to Shift.

We hypothesize that Gesture Avatar outperforms Shift on small targets and is better for mobile uses. Specifically:

(H1) Gesture Avatar will be slower than Shift on larger targets, but faster on small targets.

(H2) Gesture Avatar will have fewer errors than Shift.

(H3) Mobile situations such as walking will decrease the time performance and increase the error rate of Shift, but have little influence on Gesture Avatar.

Apparatus

The experiment was conducted on a Motorola Droid running Android 2.2 (see Figure 1). It has a 3.7-inch, 480×854 pixel multi-touch display. The walking tasks were conducted on a treadmill desk from Steelcase, with a maximum speed of 2.0 mph (see Figure 9b). Walking on a treadmill offers a reasonable simulation that captures common properties of various "on the go" scenarios, such as device shaking and significant body movement. At the same time, an indoor treadmill setting allowed us to conduct the experiment in a more controlled manner.

Participants

Twelve participants (8 male and 4 female), between age 20 and 30, were recruited from a company. They were all right-handed. All the participants owned touchscreen mobile devices and used their phones extensively. Each participant received a gratuity equal to a US$30 gift card for their participation.

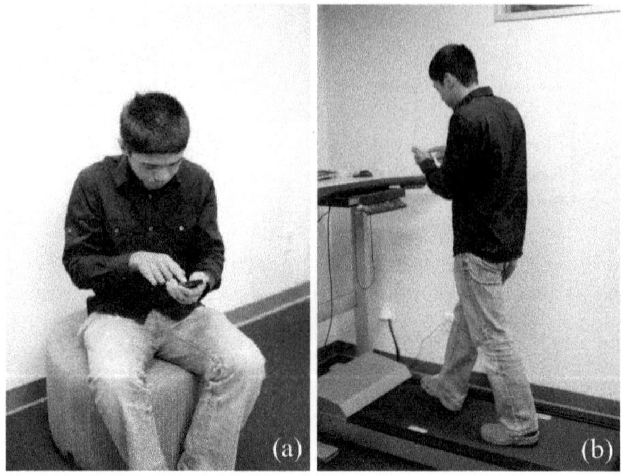

Figure 9: (a) The user was sitting on a stool. (b) The user was walking on a treadmill.

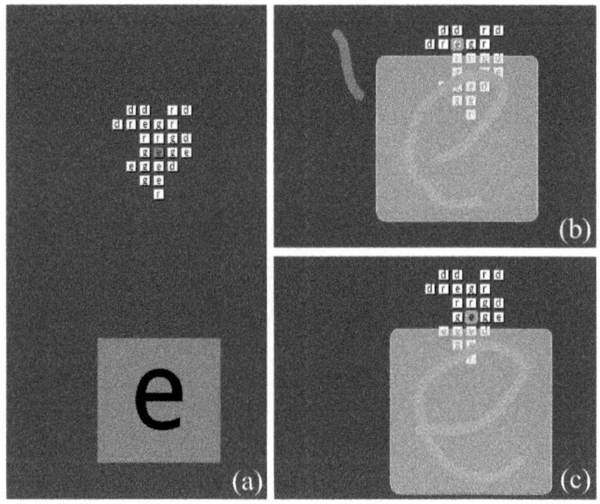

Figure 10: The experimental task. (a) The target is highlighted in red and a magnified copy serves as the start button. (b) and (c) show a typical run of the task.

Experimental Design

A within-subjects factorial user study was used in this experiment. Half of the participants learned and performed Gesture Avatar first and then Shift, while the other half did the opposite so that the order of two techniques was counterbalanced. For each technique, participants were asked to complete the tasks in two conditions: sitting and walking as shown in Figure 9.

The objects in the tasks were represented as letter boxes (see Figure 10). Participants were asked to acquire targets of different sizes, positions, letters, and ambiguity using both Gesture Avatar and Shift. In the starting screen of a task (Figure 10a), the participants were shown 24 small letter boxes. The target box, which was always near the center, was highlighted in red. To eliminate the time for searching for the target visually, which was not the focus of this experiment, a magnified version of the target was shown 300 pixels below the target. Participants needed to tap the magnified target to start the task. Performance times were measured between the tap on the magnified target and the selection of the target.

We chose 24 letter boxes for our study for several reasons. First, we wanted to cover the entire spectrum of semantic ambiguity in targets, from very ambiguous (i.e., few letters are used with high repetitions) to non-ambiguous cases (i.e., each box has a unique letter). As a result, the number of letter boxes should not be larger than 26, the size of the English alphabet. Second, we wanted the number of unique letters shown on the screen to be a factor of the total number of boxes so that the distribution of the letter usage is uniform, i.e., each letter can have an equal number of instances and affect the gesture recognizer equally. 24 is a good option as it has many nontrivial factors (2, 3, 4, 6, 8, and 12). Lastly, 24 objects offer an information density that reasonably simulates real life scenarios.

The ambiguity of the target, i.e., the number of objects that have the same letter near the target, may affect the performance of Gesture Avatar. We simulated the ambiguity by controlling the distance between objects and the number of letters used. Since the performance of Shift correlates to the size of the objects instead of the distance between them, we fixed the margin of objects to 5px and varied the size of the objects to affect both techniques. Three sizes were used in the study: 10px (1mm), 15px (1.5mm) and 20px (2mm).

Some objects at a small size such as 1mm would become uncomfortable or difficult for users to read. However, many UI widgets in a web interface are often presented at such a scale. In addition, mobile users are often on the go. The short attention span of a mobile user as well as interacting in motion affects the performance of human motor control. These factors can greatly decrease the effective size of a target, such that a large target in such circumstances might have a much smaller effective size.

When using Gesture Avatar to acquire the target, we highlighted the currently matched object with an orange border (see Figure 10b). Participants could tap on the avatar to acquire the matched object. For this comparison, we re-implemented Shift and used the escalation time 0, 50, and 200 milliseconds for 10, 15, and 20 pixel objects, respectively.

To make the finger position more stable, we averaged the finger positions with a smoothing factor of 0.25 as a low pass filter for the finger position signals.

While performing these techniques, participants were required to acquire targets with the index finger of their dominant hands while holding the device in their non-dominant hands, as required in previous studies.

Experimental Procedure

Upon being introduced to a new technique, participants had a practice session where they performed the same type of tasks as the test sessions. They were allowed to practice until they felt comfortable using it. During the test period, participants could take a break between tasks. For each technique, participants performed the first 12 test sessions while sitting on a stool (see Figure 9a) and the second 12 while walking on a treadmill (see Figure 9b). The walking speed was between 1.8 and 2 mph depending on participants' preference. The 12 sessions covered all combinations of box sizes and numbers of unique letters. In each session, there were 10 tasks, with the same box size and same number of unique letters. They were drawn randomly from a pre-generated task pool (50 tasks for each combination).

Independent Variables

The independent variables were *Technique* (Gesture Avatar versus Shift), *MobileState* (sitting versus walking), *TargetSize* (10, 15, or 20px), and *NumOfLetters* (the number of unique letters used: 1, 4, 8, and 24). In summary, the experimental design was:

12 *Users* ×
2 *Techniques* (*Gesture Avatar* versus *Shift*) ×
2 *MobileState* (*Sitting* versus *Walking*) ×
3 *TargetSizes* (5, 15, 20px) ×
4 *NumOfLetters* (1, 4, 8, 24) ×
10 *Target Acquiring Tasks*
= 5760 tasks

Results

Here we discuss our findings, including time performance, accuracy and subjective preferences.

Time Performance

For performance time, we performed a within-subjects analysis of variance (ANOVA) for *Technique* × *MobileState* × *TargetSize* × *NumOfLetters*. A main effect was found for *Technique* ($F_{1,5758}$=51.574, p<0.001), *MobileState* ($F_{1,5758}$=18.668, p<0.001), and *TargetSize* ($F_{2,5757}$=140.736, p<0.001), but not *NumOfLetters*. The significant interactions were *Technique* × *MobileState* ($F_{1,5756}$=19.070, p<0.001), *Technique* × *TargetSize* ($F_{2,5754}$=122.165, p<0.001), *Technique* × *NumOfLetters* ($F_{3,5752}$=5.170, p<0.001), *MobileState* × *TargetSize* ($F_{2,5754}$=5.760, p<0.005) and *Technique* × *MobileState* × *TargetSize* ($F_{2,5748}$=9.583, p<0.001).

Tukey's post-hoc pair-wise comparison showed that Gesture Avatar was significantly slower than Shift when *TargetSize* was 20px, but significantly faster than Shift when *TargetSize* was 10px. There was no significant difference between two techniques when *TargetSize* was 15px. Both techniques were significantly faster on larger target sizes. Shift with *MobileState* as sitting was significantly faster than it with *MobileState* as walking. For Gesture Avatar, there was no significant difference between *MobileState* being sitting versus walking.

We performed the same analysis on Shift and Gesture Avatar separately. We found that for Gesture Avatar, there was no significant difference across different *MobileStates* and *TargetSizes*. For Shift, *TargetSize*=10px was significantly slower than larger sizes at all *MobileStates*, and sitting was significant faster than walking when the *TargetSize* is 10px.

Error Rates

For the error rate, we also performed a within-subjects ANOVA for *Technique* × *MobileState* × *TargetSize* × *NumOfLetters*. A main effect was found for *Technique* ($F_{1,5758}$=674.166, p<0.001), *MobileState* ($F_{1,5758}$=26.493, p<0.001), and *TargetSize* ($F_{2,5757}$=41.057, p<0.001), but not *NumOfLetters*. The significant interactions were *Technique* × *MobileState* ($F_{1,5756}$=18.878, p<0.001), *Technique* × *TargetSize* ($F_{2,5754}$=41.201, p<0.001), and *MobileState* × *TargetSize* ($F_{2,5754}$=6.729, p<0.001).

Tukey's post-hoc pair-wise comparison showed that Gesture Avatar had lower error rates than Shift on all *TargetSizes*, while there was no significant difference for Gesture Avatar across different *TargetSizes*.

We performed the same analysis on Shift and Gesture separately. We found that for Gesture Avatar, there was no significant difference across all *MobileStates* and *TargetSizes*. For Shift, *TargetSize*=10px when walking had a significantly higher error rate than any other *TargetSizes* and *MobileStates*.

Subjective Preferences

In the post-study questionnaire participants were asked about their preferences for the two techniques. 10 of the 12 participants preferred Gesture Avatar, 1 Shift, and 1 both. All commented that Shift was more stressful especially while walking. 10 participants agreed that Gesture Avatar is useful, 1 strongly agreed and 1 neutral. 8 participants agreed that Gesture Avatar is easy to use, 3 strongly agreed and 1 neutral.

Experiment Discussion

Our results support hypothesis H1. Figure 11 and Figure 12 show that Shift's performance time increases as the target size decreases. However, Gesture Avatar's performance time almost remains unaffected by the change of the target size. As a result, Gesture Avatar is slightly slower than Shift when the target size is 20px, but quickly catches up and becomes a lot faster when it is 10px. This also implies that Gesture Avatar scales well to small targets.

Our results support hypothesis H2. Figure 13 and Figure 14 show trends in error rates that are similar to those of performance time. However, Gesture Avatar has much lower error rates than Shift. Though Gesture Avatar has a correction stage, achieving such low error rates with little sacrifice in performance is still surprising.

Our results also support hypothesis H3. By comparing Figure 11 to Figure 12, and Figure 13 to Figure 14, we can

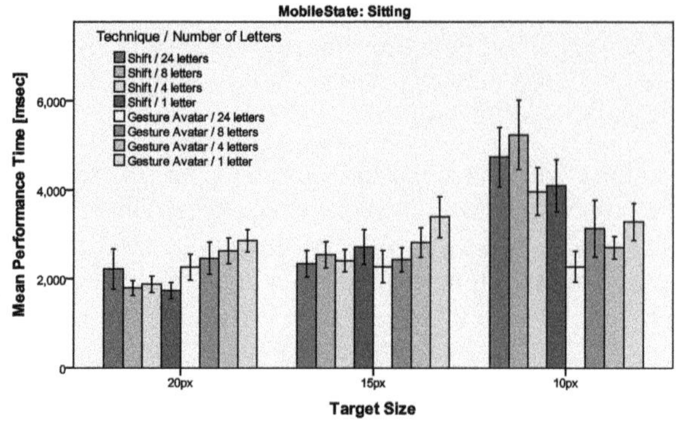

Figure 11: Mean performance time for Technique × TargetSize × NumOfLetters when participants were sitting on a stool. In this and all later charts, error bars represent 95% confidence intervals.

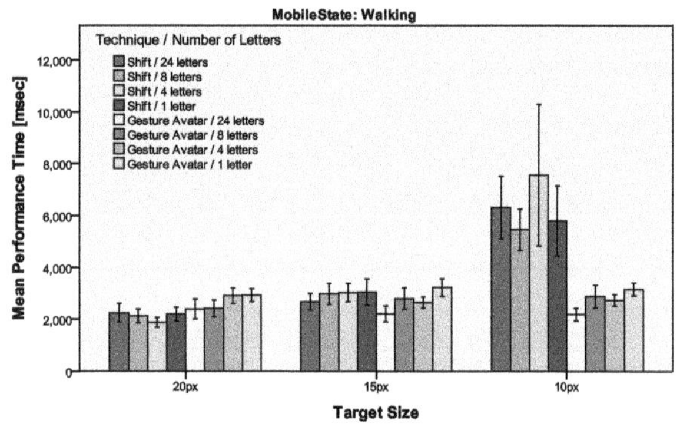

Figure 12: Mean performance time for Technique × TargetSize × NumOfLetters when participants were walking on a treadmill.

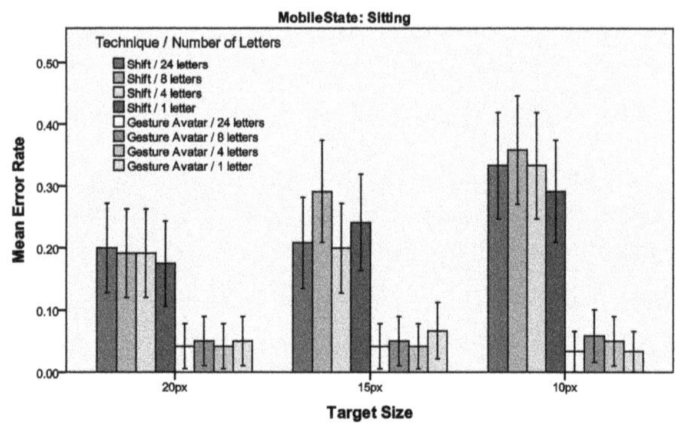

Figure 13: Mean error rate for Technique × TargetSize × NumOfLetters when participants were sitting on a stool.

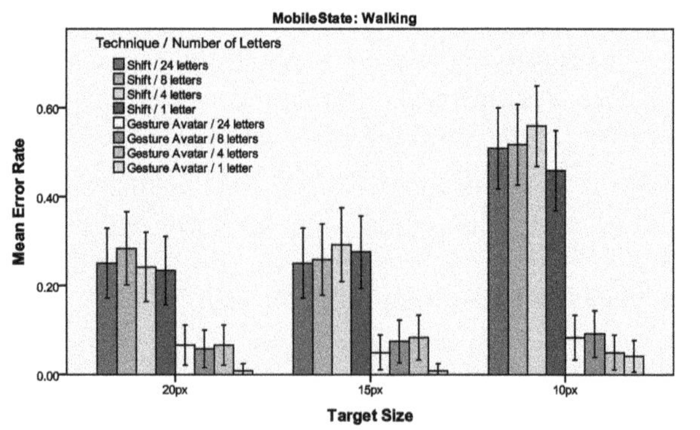

Figure 14: Mean error rate for Technique × TargetSize × NumOfLetters when participants were walking on a treadmill.

see that walking greatly hurt Shift both in performance times and error rates, but had almost no influence on Gesture Avatar. This indicates that Gesture Avatar is promising when users are on the go.

One surprising finding is that the number of unique letters had no significant influence on Gesture Avatar, as we thought that more content ambiguity would decrease the effectiveness of the gesture recognizer, and therefore decrease the overall performance. However, in our study, we observed that the participants tended to draw smaller gestures when there was more ambiguity and as a result the matched objects were often either the targets or very close to the targets. We also observed that all participants quickly converged to "flicking" [9] towards the targets as their correction strokes, which was very efficient.

DISCUSSION

Accelerating for One-Shot Interactions

As we have discussed in the previous sections, Gesture Avatar offers unique advantages for manipulating small targets beyond target acquisition. As a result, it can address many common interaction behaviors that prior techniques cannot support, e.g., adjusting a slider, drag-and-drop, double tapping, and long pressing.

However, for a target that only accepts one-shot interaction, e.g., the only valid interaction for a button is to be clicked, it might be unnecessary to show the avatar when the match is highly unambiguous. For example, a user can simply draw a gesture near a target (such as a hyperlink) and if the ambiguity is low, the target should be triggered immediately, instead of having to display an avatar for the user's confirmation. In such case, Gesture Avatar supports a one-shot interaction as prior techniques did, although Gesture Avatar still has the advantage of allowing casual interactions.

Another design alternative is to show the avatar at the end of gesturing, but before the user lifts her finger, which gives the user an opportunity to confirm the match. If the match is incorrect, the user can either continue gesturing, or dwell the finger, e.g., for a half second, on the touch screen to bring up the avatar. She can then adjust the matching using directional gestures. This design would require us to detect the potential ending of a gesture stroke being drawn.

Acquiring Moving Targets

Prior work on target acquisition often assumes fixed locations for targets, which is not always the case. As we have seen in the previous media player example (Figure 1), the knob of the progress bar moves towards the right end while the media player is playing. As another example, in a real-time location information application, objects such as cars can move quickly on a map.

Moving targets make a technique that requires high precision difficult to use since acquiring these targets require intensive visual tracking and more challenging

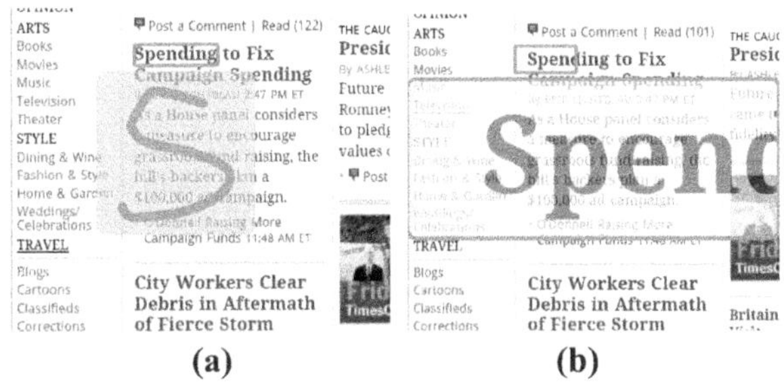

Figure 15: Two different representations we explored for Gesture Avatar: (a) the stroke and (b) the lens representation.

motor control. As a result, many existing techniques are inefficient in acquiring moving targets. In Shift, the target can move out of the callout view during the interaction, and in Escape, the target can move to items with the same or similar directions. In contrast, for Gesture Avatar, moving targets are not a challenge. Since the target matching algorithm works on a static state of the user interface, all the claims in this paper should still hold for moving targets. We do need to update the avatar view constantly in order to attach the avatar to the moving targets.

Avatar Representations

We explored various representations for gesture avatars. We focused on two representations in our iterative design process: *stroke* and *lens* representations (see Figure 15). We employ the stroke representation in the current design, i.e., an avatar is shown as the gesture stroke with a translucent background. The lens representation is to show a magnified version of the matched target and has been explored in literature [19]. Both representations highlight the bounding box of the original target. We chose the stroke over the lens representation for the following reasons.

First, a lens often affords different interaction behaviors that are inconsistent with the avatar metaphor that we intended to support. For example, dragging lens would be naturally interpreted as shifting the view rather than moving the magnified object. Secondly, a magnified view often has a more complicated appearance than a gesture stroke. As a result, the lens representation is more likely to obscure the underlying user interface and adds visual complexity. In contrast, the stroke representation is more lightweight.

Mode Switching Issues

Similar to many other gesture-based techniques, mode switching [15] is also an issue in integrating Gesture Avatar into existing user interfaces. For example, when gesturing on a map, it is necessary to distinguish the initial gesturing for creating an avatar from actions such as panning.

In our implementation of Gesture Avatar, a user gestures by first pressing and holding a holding finger, and then drawing gestures with a different finger, the gesturing finger. If the holding finger moves, it is considered as a regular touch-based interaction, e.g., panning or pinching to zoom. Similar asymmetric dependent two-handed techniques have been studied in [13].

Integrating with Existing Systems

Gesture Avatar needs to be aware of the objects available on the user interface being operated, although it does not require these objects to be in a specific presentation. The more Gesture Avatar knows about the underlying user interface, the better it can perform. The ideal situation is that we can access the structure of the underlying user interface. For example, the structure of a webpage can be accessed via its DOM tree [8]. However, this information can be inaccessible to Gesture Avatar (e.g., in a Flash application embedded in a webpage). One possible solution is to reverse engineer the underlying user interface from its pixels as previously explored in Prefab [7]. The limitation of this kind of approach is that it only works for known UI widgets. To make Gesture Avatar a general technique and avoid the effort for implementing it for every user interface, we designed Gesture Avatar as an interaction layer that can be easily used to wrap around a specific interface via a simple API. We implemented a toolkit based on the Android platform and all the examples demonstrated in the paper were implemented using the toolkit.

CONCLUSION AND FUTURE WORK

This paper presents Gesture Avatar, a gesture-based interaction technique for operating mobile interface that supports casual interaction of the existing mobile interfaces. We discussed the interaction design of Gesture Avatar. We showed how Gesture Avatar can improve user experience on mobile devices via four example applications. A controlled user study and the range of interactions that are supported indicate that Gesture Avatar outperforms its peers in many ways.

REFERENCES

1. Albinsson, P.-A. and Zhai, S. High precision touch screen interaction. *Proc. CHI 2003*, ACM Press (2003), 105-112.
2. Android (operating system). http://en.wikipedia.org/wiki/Android_(operating_system).
3. Baudisch, P. and Chu, G. Back-of-device interaction allows creating very small touch devices. *Proc. CHI 2009*, ACM Press (2009), 1923-1932.
4. Benko, H., Wilson, A.D., and Baudisch, P. Precise selection techniques for multi-touch screens. *Proc. CHI 2006*, ACM Press (2006), 1263-1272.
5. Bishop, C.M. *Pattern Recognition and Machine Learning (Information Science and Statistics)*. 2006.
6. Blanch, R., Guiard, Y., and Beaudouin-Lafon, M. Semantic pointing: improving target acquisition with control-display ratio adaptation. *Proc. CHI 2004*, ACM Press (2004), 519-526.
7. Dixon, M. and Fogarty, J. Prefab: implementing advanced behaviors using pixel-based reverse engineering of interface structure. *Proc. CHI 2010*, ACM Press (2010), 1525-1534.
8. Document Object Model. http://en.wikipedia.org/wiki/Document_Object_Model.
9. Dulberg, M.S., Amant, R.S., and Zettlemoyer, L.S. An Imprecise Mouse Gesture for the Fast Activation of Controls. *INTERACT*, (1999), 375-382.
10. Fitts, P.M. The information capacity of the human motor system in controlling the amplitude of movement. *Journal of experimental psychology 47*, 6 (1954), 381-391.
11. Grossman, T. and Balakrishnan, R. The bubble cursor: enhancing target acquisition by dynamic resizing of the cursor's activation area. *Proc. CHI 2005*, ACM Press (2005), 281-290.
12. iPhone 4. http://en.wikipedia.org/wiki/IPhone_4.
13. Kabbash, P., Buxton, W., and Sellen, A. Two-handed input in a compound task. *Proc. CHI 1994*, ACM Press (1994), 417-423.
14. Kara, L.B. and Stahovich, T.F. An Image-Based Trainable Symbol Recognizer for Sketch-Based Interfaces. *AAAI Fall Symposium Series 2004: Making Pen-Based Interaction Intelligent and Natural*, (2004).
15. Li, Y., Hinckley, K., Guan, Z., and Landay, J.A. Experimental analysis of mode switching techniques in pen-based user interfaces. *Proc. CHI 2005*, ACM Press (2005), 461-470.
16. Norman, D.A. The way I see it: natural user interfaces are not natural. *Interactions 17*, 3 (2010), 6-10.
17. OpenCV. http://opencv.willowgarage.com/wiki/.
18. Potter, R.L., Weldon, L.J., and Shneiderman, B. Improving the accuracy of touch screens: an experimental evaluation of three strategies. *Proc. CHI 1988*, ACM Press (1988), 27-32.
19. Ramos, G., Cockburn, A., Balakrishnan, R., and Beaudouin-Lafon, M. Pointing Lenses : Facilitating Stylus Input through Visual- and Motor-Space Magnification. *Proc. CHI 2007*, ACM Press (2007), 757-766.
20. Vogel, D. and Baudisch, P. Shift: a technique for operating pen-based interfaces using touch. *Proc. CHI 2007*, ACM Press (2007), 657-666.
21. Wigdor, D., Forlines, C., Baudisch, P., Barnwell, J., and Shen, C. LucidTouch : a see-through mobile device. *Proc. UIST 2007*, ACM Press (2007), 269-278.
22. Wigdor, D., Leigh, D., Forlines, C., et al. Under the table interaction. *Proc. UIST 2006*, ACM Press (2006), 259-268.
23. Worden, A., Walker, N., Bharat, K., and Hudson, S. Making computers easier for older adults to use: area cursors and sticky icons. *Proc. CHI 1997*, ACM Press (1997), 266-271.
24. Yatani, K., Partridge, K., Bern, M., and Newman, M.W. Escape: a target selection technique using visually-cued gestures. *Proc. CHI 2008*, ACM Press (2008), 285-294.

Speak Little and Well: Recommending Conversations in Online Social Streams

Jilin Chen*, **Rowan Nairn**†, **Ed H. Chi**†

* University of Minnesota
200 Union Street SE, Minneapolis, MN 55455
jilin@cs.umn.edu

† Palo Alto Research Center
3333 Coyote Hill Road, Palo Alto, CA 94304
{rnairn, echi}@parc.com

ABSTRACT

Conversation is a key element in online social streams such as Twitter and Facebook. However, finding interesting conversations to read is often a challenge, due to information overload and differing user preferences. In this work we explored five algorithms that recommend conversations to Twitter users, utilizing thread length, topic and tie-strength as factors. We compared the algorithms through an online user study and gathered feedback from real Twitter users. In particular, we investigated how users' purposes of using Twitter affect user preferences for different types of conversations and the performance of different algorithms. Compared to a random baseline, all algorithms recommended more interesting conversations. Further, tie-strength based algorithms performed significantly better for people who use Twitter for social purposes than for people who use Twitter for informational purpose only.

Author Keywords

Social stream, recommender system, conversation, user preference.

ACM Classification Keywords

H.5.3: Group and Organization Interfaces.

General Terms

Algorithms, Experimentation

INTRODUCTION

Online social streams such as Facebook news feeds, Google Buzz and Twitter streams have emerged as important channels of online information. Millions of people are reading statuses, tweets and alike to learn breaking news, useful tips, fun stories, keep up with friends' everyday lives, and engage in random chatters.

Conversation is a key element in the social stream experience. Prior research has suggested informal chatting as a major reason for using social streams [12, 13], and empirically demonstrated the prevalence of conversations in social streams [11, 12]. These conversations facilitate information exchange and social awareness, as well as help build common ground among users [19, 20]. The importance of conversations in social streams is also demonstrated by the interest within industry. For example, several startups have been formed to support the threading of Twitter conversations (e.g. *bettween.com*, *twonvo.com*).

However, not all conversations in social streams are interesting to read. Active Facebook users may receive over 100 conversations in their full feed per day, which they often have neither time nor desire to read completely. As a result, to avoid flooding users with boring conversations, service providers often selectively display conversations to users. Facebook used the proprietary EdgeRank algorithm, particularly favoring recent, long conversations related to close friends [14]. Instead, Twitter adopts simple rules to aggressively filter correspondences between users. In fact, the filter on Twitter was so aggressive that some users have wished Twitter to be more inclusive. To date, little research has been published on techniques for finding interesting conversations, despite their prevalence in social streams.

A great challenge in finding interesting conversations is the mixture of informational and social purposes in using social stream, and thus the potential diversity in user preferences of conversations. Between a short exchange about Java programming and a lengthy discussion around Alice's recent trip to Japan, Bob may prefer the former because of his interest in programming, while Charles may prefer the latter because he cares more about Alice. As a more nuanced example, David may skip the exchange about programming despite his interest in the topic, because the exchange itself is too short to be meaningful to him. Due to this potential diversity in preferences and shifts in contexts, a single model of users' interest might be doomed to fail.

Our research has three high level research questions:

RQ1: How do users differ on their preferences of conversations? Do their preferences correlate with their usage purposes, i.e., whether they use Twitter as an information medium or a social medium?

RQ2: How effective are different algorithms in selecting interesting conversations for recommendation?

RQ3: Do usage purposes of Twitter and preferences of conversations affect algorithm performance?

To answer these questions, we explored the design of a recommender system that recommends potentially interesting conversations on Twitter. We chose Twitter over many other social stream platforms due to its popularity. Specifically, we chose Twitter over Facebook because Twitter's open APIs provide us greater flexibility in collecting data, designing conversation selection algorithms, and deploying these algorithms.

We deployed our recommender system online to conduct a user study, where Twitter users rated the interestingness of conversations produced by different algorithms. The user study allowed comparison of algorithm performances across different Twitter users.

The rest of the paper is structured as follows. First, we discuss how existing research relates to our work. We then provide an overview of Twitter and intricacies of Twitter conversations. We describe the design of recommender, and then detail our studies and the results. We conclude with discussions of our findings and design implications.

RELATED WORK

Social streams have attracted a fair amount of attention in the research community recently. Our work is built on two areas within social stream research: 1) characterization and analysis, and 2) information filtering and recommendation.

Characterization and Analysis

Research has demonstrated social streams to be used for a multitude of purposes. Java et al. [12] found major usage on Twitter to be daily chatter, conversations, information sharing and news reporting. Naaman et al. [15] manually coded Twitter messages, and suggested that people post on Twitter for both informational and social purposes. In a study of the enterprise social stream site Yammer, Zhang et al. [19] found that people used the site for different purposes, and have different preferences as a result. They also found conversations to be a large part of activity on Yammer, and suggested difficulty in finding relevant content being the greatest challenge.

Several works studied the conversational aspect of social streams. boyd et al. [4] analyzed the conversational usage of retweets (RT) in Twitter, revealing great variety in Twitter conversational practices. Honeycutt et al. [11] investigated Twitter conversations in form of @replies, and discussed the challenge in finding relevant conversations on Twitter. Our exploration in recommending conversations is an important step in addressing this challenge.

Our work is also informed by prior analytical research on Facebook. Joinson [13] characterized the motives on the use of Facebook and discussed the use of Facebook news feeds. Gilbert et al. [7] modeled tie-strength – the strength of social relationships – on Facebook, and suggested that tie-strength may be a useful factor for filtering messages in Facebook news feeds.

Information Filtering and Recommendation

Several recent works have addressed the information overload problem in social streams by utilizing topic as a key factor. Ramage et al. [17] applied LDA (Latent Dirichlet Allocation) to characterize topics in Twitter and to find messages worthwhile to read. Bernstein et al. [2] utilized search engines to support a topic-based browsing interface of Twitter. Both works were built on prior research on information retrieval and topic modeling, including Salton et al. [18] and Blei et al. [3].

Studies on filtering and recommendation in social streams have indicated the potential diversity in user preferences. Chen et al. [6] recommended news URLs in Twitter using topic relevance and social voting, and suggested that a single recommender may not be able to satisfy users' differing needs. Paek et al. [16] trained support vector machines to predict the importance of posts in Facebook feeds, and found that many posts were considered important to one user but worthless to another user. They indicated personalization as a promising solution to the problem.

Our exploration in recommending interesting conversations contributes to this existing body of research in two aspects: 1) While prior research focused on individual messages, our work is focused on conversations, and each conversation is a coherent thread of multiple messages; 2) While prior works concentrated on supporting news finding and information gathering in social streams, instead we explore conversation recommendation while facing the diversity in usage purposes and preferences.

In this work, we in particular explore three factors for recommending conversations: thread length, topic relevance, and tie-strength. We include thread length because it is a simple measure of the sustainability of a conversation [9]. Topic relevance is included due to its prior success on social streams [6, 17]. Tie-strength is included due to the suggestions by Gilbert et al. [7].

BACKGROUND: TWITTER CONVERSATIONS

Twitter is a popular social stream service with millions of registered users. Twitter users can post short messages, or *tweets*, each up to 140 characters long. By default these tweets are publicly available and can be viewed by anyone; in this work, we only consider such public tweets.

Users can direct a tweet to a particular user by adding an @ symbol and a user name (e.g. @Alice) in front of the tweet. Such directed tweets are usually referred as @replies. An @reply can be further replied, constituting a chain of tweets in a conversation.

Since Twitter does not otherwise have a separate feature for conversations, most Twitter users post a series of @replies to interested parties so as to engage in conversations [11, 12]. As a result, throughout this paper, whenever we mention *conversation* in context of Twitter, we mean a tweet followed by a series of interconnected @replies, which looks like the example below:

Alice: worked till the last minute before CHI deadline.

Bob: @Alice you submitted a paper to CHI?

Alice: @Bob yeah, I'll tell you details some time.

The social network on Twitter is constructed by *"follow"* relationships. This relationship is asymmetric – Alice can follow Bob without Bob following Alice back. Throughout this paper, whenever Alice follows Bob, we refer to Alice as Bob's *follower*, and Bob as Alice's *followee*. If Alice and Bob follow each other, we refer them as *bi-directional friends* to each other.

Twitter users consume tweets mostly by reading their *home timeline*, a stream that contains tweets posted by all their followees. As a result, a typical Twitter user's followees are users that she is interested in reading from, while her followers are users who are interested in her posted tweets.

Twitter has gone through several changes on how @replies should be included in the home timeline. Originally Twitter did not treat @replies any differently in the home timeline. An @reply posted from Alice to Bob would be included in Charles' home timeline if Charles follows Alice, just like any other tweets posted by Alice. This practice appeared to cause confusion when Charles follows only Alice but not Bob, because he would only receive half of the conversation, seeing replies from Alice but missing replies from Bob. As a result, after several iterations of changes, in May 2009, Twitter added a mandatory filter on @replies – an @reply would be included in the home timeline only if the user follow both ends of the @reply. In case that Charles follows Alice but not Bob, he would miss all @replies between Alice and Bob.

Many believed such filtering is too aggressive. Popular IT blog TechCrunch and ReadWriteWeb criticized the filter immediately after Twitter's latest change. TechCrunch articulated the benefit for not having this filter: "[disabling the filter would have] led to an increase in noise, but it [would have] also exposed you to new Twitter users and conversations that you might have otherwise missed out on"[1]. ReadWriteWeb compared this filter to Facebook: "it's more fundamentally closed than Facebook is; on that site I may not be able to view the profiles of strangers talking to my friends, but I can see that the conversations are happening and I can read the comments."[2]

Indeed, Facebook is more inclusive on conversations compared to Twitter. On Facebook, all conversations that a friend participates in, including these involving strangers, are included in the full "Most Recent" feed. Facebook then applies its EdgeRank algorithm to selectively filter the full feed into the "Top News" feed on users' homepages [14]. Table 1 summarizes how Twitter and Facebook have been filtering conversations in their streams.

Facebook and Twitter also differ on how they display conversations in the stream. Facebook groups all posts in one conversation together in its feed, allowing users to see the whole conversation in one place. Twitter, in contrast, always displays tweets in reverse chronological order. As a result, in a Twitter home timeline, two interconnected @replies in one conversation may be separated by tens of other tweets that were posted between them. This design has made keeping track a long conversation particularly challenging on Twitter. In response, several third party services (e.g. *bettween.com*, *twonvo.com*, *tweetconvo.com*) have provided threading displays of Twitter conversations.

<table>
<tr><th rowspan="2">Message From</th><th rowspan="2">Message To</th><th colspan="3">Would the Message Be Shown in the Stream?</th></tr>
<tr><th>Early Twitter</th><th>Current Twitter</th><th>Facebook</th></tr>
<tr><td rowspan="2">Followee or Friend</td><td>Followee or Friend</td><td rowspan="2">Yes</td><td>Yes</td><td rowspan="3">Maybe (determined by EdgeRank algorithm)</td></tr>
<tr><td>Stranger</td><td rowspan="3">No</td></tr>
<tr><td rowspan="2">Stranger</td><td>Followee or Friend</td><td rowspan="2">No</td></tr>
<tr><td>Stranger</td><td>No</td></tr>
</table>

Table 1. Conversation Filtering on Twitter and Facebook

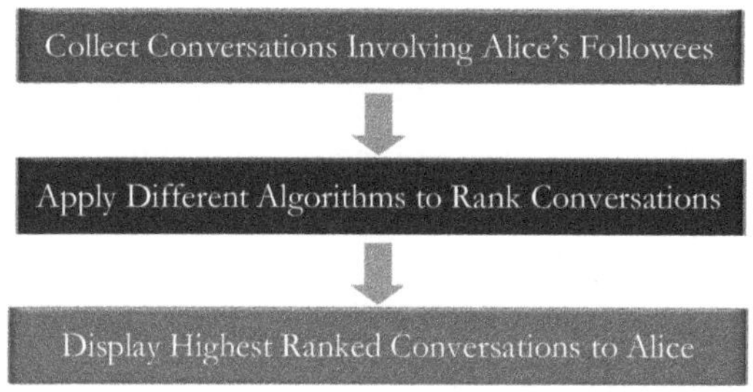

Figure 1. Recommending Conversations For Alice

DESIGNING CONVERSATION RECOMMENDER

The high level workflow of our conversation recommender is illustrated in Figure 1. To recommend conversations for Alice, we begin by collecting all conversations that Alice's followees have participated in as candidate conversations, including conversations between followees and non-followees. This candidate set is similar to Facebook's candidate set for EdgeRank, and is broader than what Twitter currently shows to users (Table 1).

We then rank candidate conversations using different algorithms. We explore three factors of conversations in our algorithm design: thread length, topic relevance, and tie-strength. Below in this section we will discuss extensively the reason we choose each factor, how we approach the factor computationally, and how we use these factors to construct ranking algorithms.

Finally, after ranking, we present the highest ranked conversations as recommendations. We display each conversation as a thread (Figure 2), similar to Facebook and many third party Twitter conversation threading services.

Factor 1: Thread Length

Thread length of a conversation is the number of tweets that the conversation contains. This simple measure has been used to reflect how well sustained a discussion is in newsgroups and online forums [9]. In this work we apply the same intuition on Twitter conversations; that is, longer conversation threads are likely to be more sustained, of

[1]http://techcrunch.com/2009/05/12/twitter-decides-were-not-smart-enough-for-replies-changes-them-again/

[2]http://www.readwriteweb.com/archives/twitter_puts_a_muzzle_on_your_friends_goodbye_peop.php

Figure 2. Conversation Displayed as a Thread

richer content, and therefore more promising as interesting conversations.

Factor 2: Topic Relevance

Topic relevance has been widely used to rank candidate items in recommender systems (See Adomavicius et al. [1] for a review) and has been successfully utilized to rank messages in social streams as well [6, 17].

Similar to the approach in Chen et al [6] and Ramage et al [17], in order to measure the topic relevance of a conversation to a user, we first build a topic profile vector for the user, then represent the content of the conversation in a similar vector, and finally match the user topic profile against the content of the conversation to compute a topic relevance score.

We build the topic profile of a Twitter user in the form of a bag-of-words vector, following the *Self-Profile* approach in Chen et al. [6]. Each dimension in the vector corresponds to a word used on Twitter and is calculated based on how many times the user has posted the specific word in her tweets, using a TF-IDF weighting scheme [18]. At a high level, Alice's topic profile constructed as such would represent her topic interest by capturing her interest on every word she has posted. That is, the more Alice posted the word in her tweets, the fewer other users posted the same word, the more confident we are that the word uniquely identifies Alice's topic interest.

The content of a conversation is represented in a similar TF-IDF weighted bag-of-words vector, using all words that have appeared in the conversation. However, since often a conversation contains only a handful of tweets and each tweet contains at most 140 characters, the constructed bag-of-words vector is often too sparse to be matched against user topic profiles. As a result, we also incorporate additional topic keywords into the vector so as to enrich the content of the vector. We identify these additional topic keywords through the TweeTopic technique [2]. That is, we feed each tweet in the conversation to the Yahoo! BOSS search engine, and extract the most salient keywords from the results returned from the search engine. At a high level, this approach allows us to discover keywords relevant to the conversation from the whole web corpus behind the search engine.

With both the user topic profile and the content of a conversation represented as vectors, we use a standard cosine similarity between the two vectors as the final *topic relevance score* for the conversation.

In preliminary explorations we have also represented topic profiles and content of conversations using LDA [3]. However, we found LDA-based representation by itself inferior to TF-IDF representation, concurring with Ramage et al.'s findings [17]. We also found the combination of TF-IDF and TweeTopic outperformed the combination of TF-IDF and LDA. We therefore decided to adopt our current approach to measure topic relevance of conversations. Note that the result we report here is merely meant to clarify our design choice; rigorous comparison of many different topic models is beyond the scope of this work.

Factor 3: Tie-Strength

Tie-strength is a characterization of social relationships between people [8]. Under this characterization, people in an individual's social network can be roughly divided into *strong-ties* and *weak-ties*. Strong-ties are families and close friends, with highly overlapped social circles. Weak-ties are, conversely, merely acquaintances. Weak-ties often provide access to novel information, information not circulating among the strong-ties.

In social streams, tie-strength of conversation participants can greatly affect the interestingness of a conversation. A discussion of Alice's recent trip to Japan would likely be much more interesting to her close friends than to her mere acquaintances.

As a result, for recommending conversations to a user, we give higher priority to conversations that happen among the strong-ties of the given user. When estimating tie-strength, we only assign non-zero tie-strength between bi-directional friends, because two users not following each other often means that the two do not know each other in person. For example, millions follow the user *BarackObama* on Twitter, but few are followed back or can claim to have a real social relationship with him.

Our approach of estimating tie-strength is largely inspired by Gilbert et al. [7], who have modeled tie-strength on Facebook in a regression model. In particular we take insight from three of their findings: 1) the existence of direct communications between two users is the strongest factor in predicting tie-strength between the two; 2) the frequency of such direct communications is another strong predictor; and 3) the tie strength between two users depends on the tie-strength between the two and their mutual friends.

We estimate tie-strength between a pair of users, Alice and Bob, using the following procedure:

1) For Alice, we first define the *communication score* for her bi-directional friend Bob as the logarithm of the

number of @replies that Alice and Bob have posted between each other;

2) Further, if Charles, David and Edward are all the mutual bi-directional friends between Alice and Bob, we compute the communication scores for these three people, and refer the average of their communication scores as the *mutual friend score* for Bob.
3) The final *tie-strength score* for Bob is the sum of communication score and mutual friend score for him.

As a result, Bob would be considered a strong-tie of Alice if he frequently exchanges @replies with Alice, or if a majority of his mutual friends with Alice (i.e. Charles, David, Edward) frequently exchange @replies with Alice.

We have two methods to associate the tie-strength scores of users to a conversation with several tweets. In one, we define the tie-strength score of a tweet as the tie-strength of its author, and then sum the tie-strength scores of all tweets within a conversation. We call this sum the *total tie-strength score* of the conversation. Intuitively, this score favors long conversations involving strong-ties.

In another, we divide the total tie-strength score of a conversation by the number of tweets in the conversation, and call the result *average tie-strength score*. Note that it is not equivalent to the average tie-strength score of all conversation participants. That is, if Alice has tie-strength score 1 and Bob has tie-strength score 0, a conversation containing 2 tweets from Alice and 1 tweet from Bob would have a final score 2/3 instead of 1/2. We pick this design so that people who participate more in a conversation will be weighted stronger in the tie-strength calculation.

Ranking Algorithms

From the above three factors, we construct five ranking algorithms for further exploration. We also included a random baseline. We will therefore compare the following six algorithms in our user study.

Random: Recommend random conversations. We use this approach as a baseline for other algorithms.

Length: Recommend conversations with the highest thread length.

Topic: Recommend conversations with the highest topic relevance scores.

Tie: Recommend conversations with the highest average tie-strength scores.

Tie-Sum: Recommend conversations with the highest total tie-strength scores. This approach is closely related to Facebook's EdgeRank algorithm [14]. Among other factors, EdgeRank attaches an "affinity score" to each post, and then decides whether to display a conversation based on the total score of all posts in the conversation. This approach can also be viewed as a hybrid of *Length* and *Tie*, because it essentially ranks conversations based on the product of thread length and the average tie-strength in *Tie*.

Topic-Tie-Sum: Recommend conversations with the highest product of the topic relevance score in *Topic* and the total tie-strength score in *Tie-Sum*. This approach can be viewed as a combination of all three factors that we have proposed.

Among the algorithms above, *Length*, *Topic* and *Tie* each directly correspond to one of the three factors. Performance of these algorithms would demonstrate the effectiveness of individual factors for selecting interesting conversations.

We include *Tie-Sum* as the forth algorithm due to its relationship to Facebook's EdgeRank, and include *Topic-Tie-Sum* as the fifth because it combines all three factors.

We did not include more algorithms, such as other ways of combining factors, because we do not want to burden our subjects with too many tasks in the user study: evaluating conversations from six algorithms already takes 20~30 minutes for a user in our pilot tests.

USER STUDY

We conducted the user study online at *zerozero88.com*, our living laboratory website that provides Twitter-based news recommendation. We recruited subjects for the study by sending Twitter private messages to existing users of *zerozero88.com*. We also posted tweets about the user study and let the information propagate through word-of-mouth on Twitter. As such, all subjects were already Twitter users before our study. Because completing the user study requires substantial effort, we offered two $50 Amazon certificates as raffle prizes.

As discussed below, the whole study consists of three parts: a pre-survey, the main study, and finally a post-survey.

Pre-Survey

In the pre-survey we sought direct inputs from the subjects for the following two purposes:

1) Confirming key design choices of the recommender, e.g. whether the threading UI (Figure 2) is appropriate;
2) Obtaining self-reports on subjects' Twitter usage purposes and their preferences of conversations, so as to understand the relationship between the two (RQ1).

We will detail the questions and responses from the subjects when we report the results of the pre-survey.

Main Study

In the main study, we collected ratings from subjects so as to compare the effectiveness of algorithms (RQ2). By relating the ratings to the self-reported usage purposes in the pre-survey, we also examined if usage purposes affect quantitatively the performance of the algorithms (RQ3).

Subjects were asked to rate the interestingness of a list of conversations on a 5-point Likert scale, where 1 is completely boring and 5 is the most interesting. Each of the conversations is displayed in a widget as shown in Figure 2.

We compile the list of conversations for a given subject as follows: First, we collect all conversations that the subject's followees have participated in during the last 7 days. Each of the 6 candidate algorithms then independently ranks this conversation collection and recommends the top 10 according to its ranking. The 6 algorithms generate a total of 60 recommendations. We then combine these 60 recommendations into a single list in random order. When algorithm A and B both recommend the same conversation, we only show one copy of the conversation to the subject. The subject's rating for the conversation is then reflected in the evaluation for both algorithm A and B, to ensure a fair comparison of all algorithms.

Post-Survey

We expect some recommended conversations to be rated as boring. One possible reason is model inaccuracy, e.g. the tie-strength score is high but in reality the conversation is all among weak-ties. However, subjects may still dislike a conversation even when the model is consistent, possibly due to their personal preferences. For example, the *Tie* algorithm may correctly recommend a conversation from strong-ties, but the subject then dislikes the conversation because she cares more about topic. Therefore, in the post-survey we asked subjects to clarify the reason for not liking a recommendation, to see qualitatively whether their preferences affect algorithm performance (RQ3).

After all conversations are rated, if any conversations generated by *Length*, *Topic*, *Tie* are rated 1, i.e., completely boring, subjects are asked to explain their ratings. In the questions we revealed why we thought the conversation should have been interesting: "we thought this conversation was in-depth" (for conversations from *Length*), "we thought this conversation was of your topic of interest" (for conversations from *Topic*), "we thought this conversation was among your close friends" (for conversations from *Tie*). In this way, we were able to qualitatively understand how much low ratings were due to model inaccuracy or due to other reasons, including personal preference.

We also ask subjects if they would be interested in receiving conversation recommendations as a service, and if they have any additional comment for this potential service.

RESULTS

We ran the user study live for three weeks and collected results from 38 subjects. We removed 3 subjects from the analysis because they follow fewer than 20 people and have fewer than 100 conversations to be considered as candidates for recommendation. The result we report is therefore based on responses from 35 subjects, who on average follow 248 people on Twitter. Below we will describe the results from the pre-survey, the main study, and the post-survey in order.

Pre-Survey

User Input for Conversation Recommender Design

In the pre-survey we asked questions related to two major design choices that we have made for the recommender: 1) displaying conversations in threads; and 2) including conversations involving non-followees, which are currently filtered away by Twitter (refer to Table 1 for a reminder).

For 1), we showed Figure 2 to subjects and asked if they think such threading display would be useful for them to track Twitter conversations. Among the 35 subjects, 29 subjects thought threading would indeed be useful. Among the other 6 subjects who did not give a positive answer, 2 subjects answered that individual @replies as in current Twitter are just fine; 3 subjects believed threading would not help much because they rarely see @replies on Twitter anyway; and 1 subject answered he/she is not sure if such display would be helpful.

Purpose	How much do you use Twitter for the following purposes?				
	1	2	3	4	5
	No		Kind of		A lot
Read useful or fun information	0 (0%)	1 (3%)	1 (3%)	15 (43%)	**18 (51%)**
Share useful or fun information	0 (0%)	3 (9%)	6 (17%)	12 (34%)	**14 (40%)**
Keep updated with people's lives	7 (20%)	5 (14%)	**12 (34%)**	7 (20%)	4 (11%)
Chat with people	6 (17%)	7 (20%)	**12 (34%)**	6 (16%)	4 (11%)

Table 2. Different Purposes of Using Twitter
Number in each cell is the number of subjects who have given the corresponding answer to the given purpose. The highest number in each row is bolded.

For 2), we briefly explained the fact that Twitter does not show a conversation if the conversation involves a person whom the user does not follow. We then asked subjects if they would rather see these conversations instead. Among the 35 subjects, 8 subjects answered a definite yes, 19 subjects said that it depends on how interesting the conversation is. The rest 8 subjects answered no, believing that the current filtering in Twitter is the right design.

We believe feedback from the subjects is supportive of both of our design choices, given that a majority of subjects believed threading as useful and showed interest in conversations involving non-followees.

Purposes of Using Twitter

In the pre-survey, subjects were asked about their purposes of using Twitter. We identified four potential purposes by reviewing prior research [12, 20]: *reading useful or fun information*, *sharing useful or fun information*, *keeping updated with people's lives*, and *chatting with people*. We consider the former two purposes as more "informational" and the latter two purposes as more "social".

We asked subjects to identify how much they use Twitter for each of the four purposes on a 5-point Likert scale, where 1 means "no", 3 means "kind of", and 5 means "a lot". The results are shown in Table 2.

An overwhelming majority of the subjects use Twitter for informational purposes. As shown in the first two rows of Table 2, 34 of the 35 subjects gave 3+ points to *reading useful or fun information*, and 32 of the 35 subjects gave 3+ points to *sharing useful or fun information*.

The answers to the two social purposes – *keeping updated with people's lives* and *chatting with people* – are more varied. As shown in the last two rows of Table 2, some subjects use Twitter for these purposes a lot, while some subjects do not use Twitter for these purposes at all. The answers to the two social purposes are significantly correlated ($r = 0.53$, $p < .01$), indicating that subjects who use Twitter to keep updated with people's lives tend to also use Twitter for chatting, and vice versa. We found no significant correlation between answers to the two social purposes and answers to the two informational purposes.

In summary, we found that most of the subjects use Twitter for informational purposes, while social purpose usage is varied.

Grouping Subjects by Twitter Usage Purpose

To contrast the difference on social purposes, we divide subjects into two groups: The *Info-Only* group consists of subjects who gave 5 points or less in total for the two social purposes; the *Info-Social* group consists of subjects who gave 6 points or more in total for the two social purposes. Intuitively, subjects in the *Info-Only* group use Twitter mainly for informational purposes, while subjects in the *Info-Social* group use Twitter for both informational and social purposes. Under this designation, 16 subjects belong to the *Info-Only* group, and the other 19 subjects belong to the *Info-Social* group.

Self-Reported Preferences of Conversations

In the pre-survey subjects were also asked to report their preferences for Twitter conversations. We presented three statements about preferences, and asked subjects if they agree with each of them. The three statements directly correspond to the three factors in our algorithm design: thread length, topic relevance, and tie-strength. Agreement with each statement is measured on a 5-point Likert scale, where 1 means "strongly disagree", 3 means "neutral", and 5 means "strongly agree". We show the preference statements and the answers from the two subject groups in Table 3.

The two subject groups have shown similar preferences regarding thread length: most subjects gave either 3 points (neutral) or 4 points (agree) to the statement of preferring thread length.

As for preferences regarding topic, both subject groups mostly gave either 4 points (agree) or 5 points (strongly agree). The *Info-Only* gave averagely 4.7 points while the *Info-Social* group gave averagely 4.4 points. However, this difference is non-significant (T[33] = 1.79, p = .08)

The *Info-Social* group seems to prefer conversations with greater tie-strength more than the *Info-Only* group, since the former gave an average of 4.0 points (agree) while the latter gave an average of 2.9 (between disagree and neutral). This difference is significant (T[33] = 3.34, p < .01).

Main Study

In the main study, each of the 35 subjects rated recommendations from each of the 6 candidate algorithms. Each algorithm recommended 10 conversations. The whole dataset therefore contains 2100 ratings. Each rating is on a 5-point scale, with 5 representing the most interesting.

For the purpose of data analysis, *subject group* (*Info-Only*, *Info-Social*) is a between-subject factor, while *algorithm* (*Random*, *Length*, *Topic*, *Tie*, *Tie-Sum*, *Topic-Tie-Sum*) is a within-subject factor.

Our dataset is nested in nature – ratings given by a single subject are nested within each subject and may therefore be correlated. We thus employed a Hierarchical Linear Model (HLM) [5] for the analysis. HLM is an advanced form of linear regression, allowing us to model the correlation among ratings nested within the same subject. Compared to traditional ANOVA, HLM is known to provide a better fit for nested user study data like ours [5].

In the HLM model, *subject group* and *algorithm* are treated as fixed effects on the subject level, while correlations among a single subject's ratings are modeled via a covariance structure. We perform pair-wise comparisons between algorithms using post-hoc analysis with Tukey-Kramer adjustment of p-values [10].

Overall Performance of Algorithms

The overall performance of the 6 algorithms among all 35 subjects is illustrated in the top portion of Figure 3. The performance of an algorithm is measured by its mean interesting rating, i.e. on average how interesting subjects have rated recommendations from that algorithm.

In the HLM model, factor *algorithm* has a significant effect on the interestingness ratings (F[5,2055]=36.69, p<.001). Post-hoc analysis showed that the mean rating of *Random* is significantly lower than the other five algorithms (p<.001). In other words, the five non-baseline algorithms are all significantly better than the random baseline.

Among the five non-baseline algorithms, *Topic-Tie-Sum* performed the best overall. Subjects gave a mean interesting rating of 3.08 to its recommendations. *Topic-Tie-Sum* has been found significantly better than all other algorithms except *Tie-Sum* in the post-hoc analysis

Preference Statement	Subject Group	Do you agree with the following statements about your preferences of Twitter conversations?				
		1	2	3	4	5
		Strongly Disagree	Disagree	Neutral	Agree	Strongly Agree
Thread Length: "I prefer longer and more in-depth conversations over short exchanges."	Info-Only	0 (0%)	3 (19%)	5 (31%)	**6 (38%)**	2 (12%)
	Info-Social	0 (0%)	1 (5%)	7 (37%)	**10 (53%)**	1 (5%)
Topic: "I prefer conversations whose topic is close to my interest area."	Info-Only	0 (0%)	0 (0%)	0 (0%)	4 (25%)	**12 (75%)**
	Info-Social	0 (0%)	0 (0%)	1 (5%)	**9 (47%)**	**9 (47%)**
Tie-Strength: "I prefer conversations involving close friends or people I know personally"	Info-Only	1 (6%)	4 (25%)	**7 (44%)**	3 (19%)	1 (6%)
	Info-Social	0 (0%)	1 (5%)	4 (21%)	**8 (42%)**	6 (32%)

Table 3. Self-Reported Preferences of Twitter Conversations

Number in each cell is the number of subjects who have given the corresponding answer to the given preference statement. The highest number in each row is bolded.

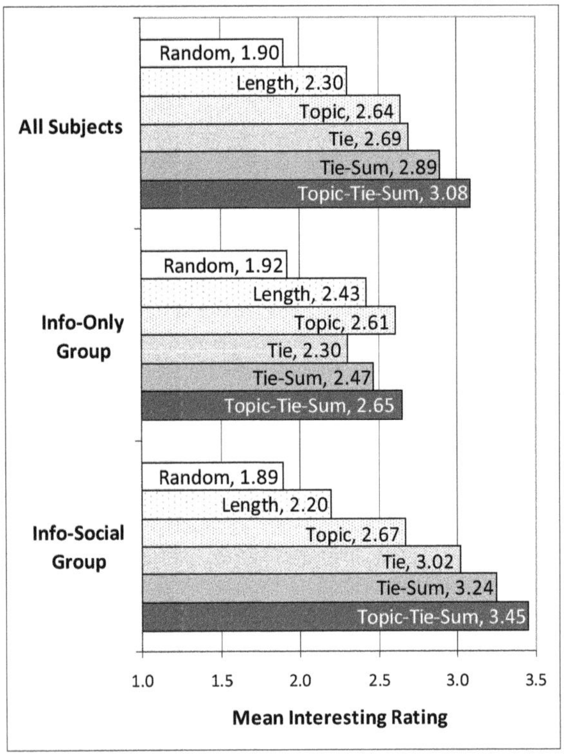

Figure 3. Mean Interesting Ratings by Algorithms and Subject Groups

($p<.001$). *Tie-Sum* is the second-best with a mean interesting rating of 2.89, though it is only significantly better than *Length* and *Random* ($p<.001$), and is statistically indistinguishable from *Topic* and *Tie*.

Comparison of Algorithms between Subject Groups

There is a significant *algorithm x subject group* interaction effect in the HLM model ($F[5,2055] = 11.83$, $p<.001$). In other words, algorithm performance differs significantly between the two subject groups.

Compared between the two subject groups, the three algorithms that utilized tie-strength (*Tie*, *Tie-Sum* and *Topic-Tie-Sum*) have performed significantly better for the *Info-Social* group than for the *Info-Only* group:

- The mean rating of *Tie* is 3.02 for *Info-Social* vs. 2.30 for *Info-Only* ($p < .05$);
- The mean rating of *Tie-Sum* is 3.24 for *Info-Social* vs. 2.47 for *Info-Only* ($p < .05$);
- The mean rating for *Topic-Tie-Sum* is 3.45 for *Info-Social* vs. 2.65 for *Info-Only* ($p < .05$).

The performance of the other three algorithms, *Random*, *Length* and *Topic*, is statistically indistinguishable between the two groups.

We show the performance of algorithms for the two subject groups in the middle and bottom portion of Figure 3. As shown in the middle portion of Figure 3, due to the degraded effectiveness of tie-strength for the *Info-Only* group, the differences between the five non-baseline algorithms were small. In fact, the differences were so small that these five algorithms were found statistically indistinguishable for the *Info-Only* group.

Post-Survey

In the post-survey we gathered comments from subjects on lowly rated conversations recommended by *Length*, *Topic*, *Tie*. We analyzed the comments to qualitatively understand whether these low ratings were due to model inaccuracy or due to other reasons, including personal preference.

We also asked subjects if they would be interested in receiving conversation recommendations as a service, and if they have any additional comment for this potential service.

Why Are Recommendations from Length Algorithm Boring?

A majority of comments acknowledged that conversations recommended by the *Length* algorithm were more in-depth, and attributed the low ratings to other reasons.

One such reason is lack of topic relevance: "It's a detailed conversation about a topic I don't care about at all. I could care less about the details of StarCraft patches." "What the hell is Ithaca brute? I don't care." "This was a long conversation about a topic in which I have little interest."

Another reason is lack of social relationship: "I hardly know the people involved…" "I don't know any of these people personally, and only follow @[username]."

Several comments even indicated that thread length is actually an *undesirable* feature when other desirable features are absent: "Too long for the lack of thought represented in the conversation." "Yeah, is in-depth about crap. However, this is valuable in that I can skip the whole thread as one uninteresting blob - i LIKE that!!"

Why Are Recommendations from Topic Algorithm Boring?

For recommendations from the *Topic* algorithm, a number of comments suggested inaccuracy of our topic modeling. In other words, what the algorithm presented as topically relevant was not really relevant: "I'm not interested in the subject of the video and I don't use .wmv." "It is a very personal conversation that is not related to anything that I am interested in. It is very tech-support related." "Not interested in Formula one or why [username] is finally getting selective about what they tweet."

Several comments acknowledged topic relevance and explained low ratings by lack of substance: "The topic was interesting (state fair), but there was no content. 'Excited!' Tons of that junk on twitter." "The original tweet is interesting; the following conversation is not. and there is no answer to the important question in the second tweet!"

Why Are Recommendations from Tie Algorithm Boring?

For recommendations from the *Tie* algorithm, only one comment suggested that the people involved were not close friends: "These are not among my close friends. Cell phone stats do not interest me."

The rest of the comments largely attribute the low ratings to lack of relevance or substance: "Lack of useful content" "Idle chit-chat and not very interesting." "It is just small talk between two people and pointless/not relevant to me."

User Comments on Conversation Recommendation

At the end of the study, 32 of the 35 subjects indicated that they are interested in getting conversation recommendations as a new service on *zerozero88.com*. The other 3 subjects rejected conversation recommendations, 2 of which have given explanations: "I don't think I want to see the conversations. I like the brief 140 characters and that is enough for me." "In most cases, I was interested in the original tweet, but the follow-up conversation was not relevant to me. In fact, a lot of my followers often RT [retweet] part of a conversation if it becomes relevant to a broader audience, so the best parts of conversations seem to be coming into my stream already."

Several subjects summarized their experiences with the recommendations and explicitly explained their preferences of conversations: "Any conversation over 10 tweets or so is just a big space-waster unless it involves people that I really care about (i.e. people that I would hang out with and talk about stupid stuff with) or topics that I really care about (i.e. topics that are so interesting that I want to hear all I can about them)." "It seemed that the recommendations placed more emphasis on network rather than content. Many of the conversations I disliked came from people in my network who were complaining about some new phone or another product I don't care about."

Summary of Results

Usage Purpose and Preferences of Conversations

We found a large variation of social purpose usage among our subjects: some subjects use Twitter for social purposes a lot, while some other subjects have little social purpose usage (Table 2). In contrast, most subjects reported high informational usage of Twitter.

We found a link between the variation in social purpose usage and the reported preferences of conversations: subjects of high social purpose usage reported a high preference of tie-strength, while subjects of low social purpose usage reported a significantly weaker preference of tie-strength (Table 3). The above results answer RQ1.

Algorithm Performance and Comparison

Overall the five non-baseline algorithms performed significantly better than the random baseline. The most sophisticated algorithm, *Topic-Tie-Sum*, performed the best (top portion of Figure 3). This result answers RQ2.

The variation of social purpose usage among subjects greatly affected algorithm performance: algorithms utilizing tie-strength performed significantly better for subjects of high social purpose than for subjects of low social purpose in Twitter usage. Due to ineffectiveness of tie-strength, for subjects of low social purpose usage, the best algorithm only improved on average 0.73 on the 5-point scale rating (middle portion of Figure 3), and the five non-baseline algorithms were statistically indistinguishable from each other. In contrast, for subjects of high social purpose usage, the best algorithm was able to improve averagely 1.56 on the rating, and the difference among algorithms was more drastic than the overall case (bottom portion of Figure 3). This result answers RQ3.

DISCUSSION

Purpose, Preference, Performance, Personalization

At a high level, we have demonstrated in this work that the variation in usage purposes among users *matters* for conversation recommender design. More concretely, while several of our algorithms performed well for people of high social purpose usage (much thanks to the tie-strength factor), the same algorithms performed poorly for people of low social purpose usage.

This result has a straightforward explanation. Because some people do not use Twitter for social purpose as much, they do not have a strong preference on conversations involving strong-ties. Therefore, algorithms that assume importance of tie-strength would have a poor performance for these people, because the assumption of the algorithms is invalid.

There is also a less obvious alternative explanation. That is, because these people use Twitter mainly for informational purpose and not for social purpose, their Twitter social network is more focused toward weak-ties and strangers. After all, when the purpose is purely information gathering, whether the source is a friend or not is not always relevant. As a result, for these people, tie-strength based algorithms may fail simply because there are not many real strong-ties to begin with. One subject in the post-survey hinted directly at this possibility: "The biggest issue is that the signal/noise ratio is incredibly low. It'll be hard to pick out a conversation I'm actually interested in. As you probably know, this is a fundamental problem: most of my Twitter followees are not personal friends, and most of my personal friends don't converse much. So there's not a lot of signal to begin with."

Fortunately, both explanations lead to the same design implication: more *personalization*. More specifically, while the *Topic-Tie-Sum* algorithm may already be good enough for people of high social purpose usage, something different should be designed for people of low social purpose usage.

In retrospect, for people who view Twitter mainly as a medium for information gathering, a better design may have been ranking by thread length and topic, but not by tie-strength. Further, the recommender may benefit from considering all public conversations as candidates, instead of only considering conversations involving followees. By considering all conversations, the recommender can pick the longest topically relevant conversations from, say, all the 500,000 recent conversations on Twitter, instead of limiting itself on the 500 recent conversations in a user's local social network. Related to this argument, one subject has suggested in the post-survey "finding conversations not only around me but around hashtags or search keywords".

Limitation and Generalization

Our result is limited by our small subject population. Nevertheless, our subjects have demonstrated a decent level of preference diversity in their post-survey comments.

One concern comes from the fact that most subjects reported high informational usage of Twitter. This bias may be because many subjects are recruited from our news recommender *zerozero88.com*, and thus hold a prior interest in informational usage. Alternatively, Naaman et al [15] has found that information sharing on Twitter is correlated with high conversation activities, so perhaps people interested in a conversation recommender are likely also interested in informational usage of Twitter anyway. Further research is needed to clarify between the two possibilities.

Readers trying to generalize our results beyond Twitter should also note that certain designs of the recommender, such as our way to estimate tie-strength in algorithms, were made particularly for Twitter and may therefore need adaption for other platforms. Moreover, as the tie-strength estimate depends solely on online interactions, it cannot always reflect true offline relationships. Such potential online vs. offline mismatch is a general limitation of these estimates [7].

The effect of usage purpose on preference and algorithm performance in our study is likely present in information filtering and recommendation for social streams in general. Many social stream platforms, including Facebook, Twitter, Yammer and Google Buzz, are used for information gathering and social awareness with various degrees. For predicting the interestingness of a piece of information, topic relevance is likely effective whenever the user cares about information gathering, and tie-strength is likely effective whenever the user cares about social awareness. In light of this argument, the emphasis on social relationship in Facebook's EdgeRank is justified, as Facebook is known to support social awareness more than other purposes [13]. Further improvement may be possible if Facebook can identify subgroups of users who also care about information gathering and incorporate topic relevance into the formula.

CONCLUSION AND FUTURE WORK

We have studied conversation recommendation on Twitter. We implemented five algorithms, and evaluated the algorithms in an online study of real Twitter users. Further, in the study we explicitly explored the diversity in usage purpose and preference among users, and found that the performance of the same algorithms can be significantly different for users of differing usage purposes and preferences.

A promising future direction is inferring usage purpose and incorporating the inference into recommendation. For example, we may implement a conversation recommender for informational purpose and another for social purpose, and mix the two recommenders depending on the inferred usage purpose of each individual user.

REFERENCES

1. Adomavicius, G. and Tuzhilin, A. 2005. Toward the next generation of recommender systems: A survey of the state-of-the-art and possible extensions. IEEE Transactions on Knowledge and Data Engineering, 17(6), 734-749.
2. Bernstein, M., Suh, B., Hong, L., et al. 2010. Eddi: Interactive topic-based browsing of social status streams. Proc. UIST'10.
3. Blei, D.M., Ng, A.Y., and Jordan, M.I. 2003. Latent Dirichlet allocation. Journal of Machine Learning Research 3, 4-5, 993-1022.
4. boyd, d., Golder, S., and Lotan, G. 2010. Tweet tweet retweet: Conversational aspects of retweeting on Twitter. Proc. HICSS '10.
5. Bryk, A.S., and Raudenbush, S. W. 1992. Hierarchical linear models: Applications and data analysis methods. Sage Publications.
6. Chen, J., Nairn, R., Nelson, L., et al. 2010. Short and tweet: Experiments on recommending content from information streams. Proc. CHI '10.
7. Gilbert, E. and Karrahalios, K. 2009. Predicting tie strength with social media. Proc. CHI '09.
8. Granovetter, M.S. 1973. The strength of weak ties. The American Journal of Sociology, 78(6), 1360–1380.
9. Guzdial, M. and Turns, J. 2000. Effective discussion through a computer-mediated anchored forum. Journal of the Learning Sciences, 9(4), 437–469.
10. Hochberg, Y. and Tamhane, A. C. 1987. Multiple Comparison Procedures. Wiley.
11. Honeycutt, C. and Herring, S.C. 2009. Beyond microblogging: Conversation and collaboration via Twitter. Proc. HICSS '09.
12. Java, A., Song, X., Finin, T., et al. 2007. Why we twitter: Understanding microblogging usage and communities. Proc. WebKDD '07, 56-65.
13. Joinson, A.N. 2008. Looking at, looking up or keeping up with people?: Motives on the use of Facebook. Proc CHI '08.
14. Kincaid, J. 2010. EdgeRank: The secret sauce that makes Facebook's news feed tick. Retrieved from http://techcrunch.com/2010/04/22/facebook-edgerank
15. Naaman, M., Boase, J., and Lai, C. 2010. Is it really about me? Message content in social awareness streams. Proc. CSCW '10.
16. Paek, T., Gamon, M., Counts, S., et al. 2010. Predicting the importance of newsfeed posts and social network friends. Proc. AAAI '10.
17. Ramage, D., Dumais, S., and Liebling, D. 2010. Characterizing microblogs with topic models. Proc. ICWSM '10.
18. Salton, G. and Buckley, C. 1988. Term-weighting approaches in automatic text retrieval. Information Processing and Management, 24(5), 513-523.
19. Zhang, J., Qu, Y., Cody, J., et al. 2010. A case study of micro-blogging in the enterprise: use, value, and related issues. Proc. CHI '10.
20. Zhao, D. and Rosson, M. B. 2009. How and why people Twitter: the role that micro-blogging plays in informal communication at work. Proc. GROUP '09.

TwitInfo: Aggregating and Visualizing Microblogs for Event Exploration

Adam Marcus, Michael S. Bernstein, Osama Badar,
David R. Karger, Samuel Madden, Robert C. Miller
MIT CSAIL
32 Vassar St., Cambridge MA
{marcua, msbernst, badar, karger, madden, rcm}@csail.mit.edu

ABSTRACT
Microblogs are a tremendous repository of user-generated content about world events. However, for people trying to understand events by querying services like Twitter, a chronological log of posts makes it very difficult to get a detailed understanding of an event. In this paper, we present TwitInfo, a system for visualizing and summarizing events on Twitter. TwitInfo allows users to browse a large collection of tweets using a timeline-based display that highlights peaks of high tweet activity. A novel streaming algorithm automatically discovers these peaks and labels them meaningfully using text from the tweets. Users can drill down to subevents, and explore further via geolocation, sentiment, and popular URLs. We contribute a recall-normalized aggregate sentiment visualization to produce more honest sentiment overviews. An evaluation of the system revealed that users were able to reconstruct meaningful summaries of events in a small amount of time. An interview with a Pulitzer Prize-winning journalist suggested that the system would be especially useful for understanding a long-running event and for identifying eyewitnesses. Quantitatively, our system can identify 80-100% of manually labeled peaks, facilitating a relatively complete view of each event studied.

Author Keywords
Twitter, Visualization, Exploration, Event Detection

ACM Classification Keywords
H.5.2 Information Interfaces and Presentation: Misc.

General Terms
Design, Human Factors

INTRODUCTION
Twitter captures a moment-by-moment pulse of the public consciousness. Unfortunately, the format of the raw data from Twitter is a flood of opinions, information and emotion, and is very difficult to synthesize into a coherent timeline of events or sentiment. To address the limitations of raw Twitter feeds, researchers have built a number of one-off visualizations for a variety of domains, including political events [7, 24], media events [23], and crisis scenarios [27, 29]. Others have focused on building visualization over large static collections of tweets [6]. However, these are generally domain specific, and operate only on archived tweet data.

To address these limitations, we present *TwitInfo*, a platform for exploring Twitter in real-time. Given a search query related to an event, TwitInfo identifies and labels event peaks, provides a focus+context visualization of long-running events, and provides an aggregate view of user sentiment. The system extracts the posts that match keywords in the query and provides a graphical timeline interface that labels peaks of high-volume posts as subevents and highlights important terms and tweets in the conversation around each subevent. Users can zoom into this timeline to visualize more peaks and subevents. TwitInfo also includes a sentiment analysis engine that displays the crowd's sentiment about various subevents, and additionally shows the geographic distribution of posted messages. When there are frequently occurring links in a cluster of tweets which might provide a bigger picture, TwitInfo also displays these links in the user interface.

TwitInfo addresses two major technical problems inherent in scaling such visualizations to realtime performance on an unconstrained dataset: identifying subevents and summarizing sentiment. To identify peaks in conversation around a given topic in realtime, TwitInfo adapts signal processing techniques to social streams. Existing sentiment visualizations have the potential to mislead users because positive and negative sentiment classifiers have differing precision and recall (Figure 2). We introduce a normalization procedure to ensure that these visualizations produce correct results.

In this paper we make the following contributions:

1. We describe streaming algorithms to generate labeled event peaks and visualizations of arbitrary topics in real time from the Twitter stream. This approach allows users to track events as they unfold, like a sporting event or election, rather than restricting users to post-hoc analysis. TwitInfo marries the signal processing literature with social streams to make realtime end-user event tracking feasible.
2. We present an automatic peak detection and labeling algorithm with subevent drill down, which is the first to allow

focus+context exploration for social streams. TwitInfo is the first interface to provide navigable peak labels for social streams; our evaluation shows that these peaks were the main tool users chose to explore the interface. Users used peak labels to understand events, and most identified labels as the most memorable and helpful element. We found that TwitInfo's event detection algorithm, which identifies subevents, has recall and precision of 80-95%.

3. We identify a problem with aggregate visualizations of sentiment analysis over a collection of documents. The problem arises when positive and negative classifiers have different recall rates, which can lead to skew in the reported proportion of documents that are positive or negative. We present a technique for properly normalizing these statistics.
4. We describe a formative evaluation of the interface with 12 users and one professional journalist. We find that non-expert participants successfully used the interface to rapidly summarize complex, nebulous event timelines.

We start with a motivating scenario for TwitInfo. We go on to discuss related approaches, describe the system in detail, and present our algorithms. Finally, we evaluate the algorithms and user interface, and discuss future work.

MOTIVATING SCENARIO

It's June 2009 and Ellen has caught wind of protests in Iran concerning the outcome of the election. A few traditional news media articles have come out based on eyewitness reports, but the media are barred from covering events. Instead, many individuals utilize the Twitter microblogging service to broadcast updates and report on events on the ground. Ellen wants to get a bigger picture. Her key questions are: what were the major events of the protests, what were people located inside the country saying, and how do people generally feel about each event? Performing a Twitter search for the *#iranElection* hashtag (used by many people to identify the subject of their posts) produces a list of thousands of individual messages that are not grouped or organized in any meaningful way.

Instead, Ellen visits the TwitInfo website to view a timeline of tweets containing the term *#iranElection*. Whenever there is a peak in activity, TwitInfo highlights the peak and labels it with commonly occurring words like the protest location. She wants to know how individuals in Israel, whose citizens are interested in Iranian affairs, are reacting to the event. So, she turns to the map interface and zooms in to Tel Aviv, then reads several comments on the events. Ellen hypothesizes that public sentiment about the election will shift over time, so she uses TwitInfo's sentiment aggregation interface to examine overall opinion at each peak in the timeline including a discussion that has just popped up. Ellen centers in on one protest event of interest, and follows a popular link mentioned in tweets for deeper exploration.

RELATED WORK

We now review related work on Twitter analytics, temporal exploration interfaces and topic detection algorithms.

The growth of microblogging has led to an expanding body of research. Java et al. studied the topological and geographical distribution of Twitter [16]. Kwak et al. found that Twitter exhibited network properties more like a news media than a social network [17]. Naaman et al. detailed a division between informers, who spread information, and meformers, who discuss their own affairs [19]. Starbird, Vieweg and colleagues have contributed analyses of microblog usage and information lifecycles during crisis situations [27, 29].

A particularly relevant branch of microblogging research analyzes reactions to news events on Twitter. Many of the papers in this category involve hand-creating timelines, graphs and visualizations very similar to those that TwitInfo produces automatically and interactively. Diakopoulous and Shamma did inspirational work in this vein, demonstrating the use of timeline analytics to explore the 2008 Presidential debates through Twitter sentiment [7]. Shamma et al. later demonstrated a similar analysis at the President Obama's Inauguration, finding that tweet volume increases and @replies drop during important moments [24]. Starbird et al. tracked tweets from different geographical areas on a timeline as the Red River flood proceeded [27]. Gaffney performed a retrospective analysis of the recent Iran election, in which Twitter played a pivotal role in news reporting [11]. Jansen et al. found that tweet sentiment analysis could provide useful insights into product opinion, an idea we leverage for the sentiment visualization in TwitInfo [15]. Our goal in TwitInfo is to make these kinds of analyses easier and faster, without requiring programming knowledge.

More recently, Diakopoulos et al. presented Vox Civitas [6], a timeline-based visualization of events discussed on microblogs. Vox Civitas displays sentiment over time, and can be used to annotate a video of the event with tweet-generated commentary. Dörk et al. [8] present a timeline-based visualization used as a backchannel for events discussed on microblogs. Like both systems, TwitInfo generates an event-summarization dashboard, but contributes a streaming algorithm for event detection and timeline annotations that our user study finds to be effective for exploring large collections of tweets. TwitInfo also contributes a method for correcting a common problem that arises in displaying aggregate sentiment as estimated by automated classifiers.

TwitInfo builds on recent work on exploratory interfaces for temporal exploration. Most closely related are Statler [23] and Eddi [4], which both provide timeline visualizations of Twitter data. Statler focuses on media events, and Eddi on only one user's feed; our goal with TwitInfo is to extend and generalize these interfaces to an arbitrary topic of interest on Twitter. To do this, we draw on other work exploring temporal visualization (for a survey, see Silva [26]). Leskovec et al.'s Memetracker pursued similar goals, tracking prominent phrases through blogs and news media [18] rather than Twitter. Zoetrope allows the user to graph web content trends like temperature or images over time [1]. TwitInfo also takes inspiration from Continuum's [2] notion of hierarchical timelines, allowing users to expand subevents in the timeline for further exploration. Opinion Space [9] investigated visual layouts for browsing many user comments. In the future, we plan to integrate its ideas for treating tweets with sentiment or opinion separately from information-sharing tweets.

We build on work related to topic and event detection. Swan and Allen developed a χ^2 significance test for identifying bursty extracted noun phrases [28] in a stream, but it is not appropriate for Twitter's needs. We need an online algorithm that can update as tweets stream in, and tweets are so short that noun agreement may not occur naturally. Newsjunkie developed algorithms for users who wish to find novel content in their stream [10]. BlogScope [3] pursues many of the same goals as TwitInfo, but is focused on blogs, and does not go into detail about peak detection algorithms. One body of work that does address such scenarios is TCP congestion control [14], which has minimal memory requirements and works in an online fashion to determine outlier delays in packet transmission. We base our approach on this notion.

Finally, it is worth touching on some related non-academic projects. Twitter Sentiment[1] is a site which displays a message frequency timeline, sentiment pie chart, and sentiment-coded tweets. The site inspired many visual elements in TwitInfo, and we utilize their approach to extract sentiment from tweets, but they fall victim to the aggregate sentiment normalization issues we solve with TwitInfo. Google News Timeline[2] facilitates exploration of news media in given time ranges, but does not visually signal to the user which items to focus on, and does not provide intuition into which articles are selected for a given period. Systems such as Flipboard[3] make news socially relevant by providing a magazine-like interface for exploring news sources extracted from your social networks on Twitter and Facebook, but do not provide context about events of interest. Twitter is planning a real-time analytics framework[4], but this does not seem to be geared at relaying news or informing end-users.

THE TWITINFO SYSTEM

In this section we describe TwitInfo, beginning with the user's initial event query, then detailing the exploration interface and the creation of nested events.

Creating the Event

TwitInfo users define an *event* by specifying a Twitter keyword query. For example, for a soccer game users might enter search keywords *soccer, football, premierleague,* and team names like *manchester* and *liverpool.* Users give the event a human-readable name like "Soccer: Manchester City vs. Liverpool" or "Obama presidency," as well as an optional time window. When users are done entering the information, TwitInfo saves the event and begins logging tweets matching the query. In its current implementation, we only track tweets for a keyword when a user first enters the keyword into the system, but this is not a hard limitation: to get a historical view of an event from its keywords, we could continuously collect a sample of all tweets, and historically index each keyword as users begin tracking them.

[1] http://twittersentiment.appspot.com/
[2] http://newstimeline.googlelabs.com/
[3] http://www.flipboard.com/
[4] http://gigaom.com/2010/09/22/twitter-to-launch-free-real-time-analytics-this-year/

Timeline and Tweets

Once users have created an event, they can monitor the event in realtime by navigating to a web page that TwitInfo creates for the event. The main TwitInfo interface (Figure 1) is a dashboard summarizing the event over time. The dashboard displays a timeline for this event, raw tweet text sampled from the event, an overview graph of tweet sentiment, and a map view displaying tweet sentiment and locations.

The event timeline (Figure 1.2) reports tweet activity by volume. The more tweets that match the query during a period of time, the higher the y-axis value on the timeline for that period. So, when many users are tweeting about a topic (for example, *Obama*), the timeline spikes. TwitInfo's peak detection algorithm, described later in the paper, automatically identifies these spikes and flags them as peaks in the interface. Peaks appear as flags in the timeline and appear to the right of the timeline along with automatically-generated key terms that appear frequently in tweets during the peak. For example, in Figure 1.2, TwitInfo automatically tags one of the goals in the soccer game as peak "F" and annotates it on the right with representative terms in the tweets like 3-0 (the new score) and tevez (the soccer player who scored). Users can perform text search on this list of key terms to locate a specific peak. To visually scale from short events to long-running queries, TwitInfo will aggregate tweets on the timeline by minute-, hour-, or day-level granularity depending on the timespan the user is viewing.

The timeline also provides a way to filter the tweets in the rest of the interface: when the user clicks on a peak, the other interface elements (map, links, tweet list, and sentiment graph) refresh to show only tweets in the time period of that peak.

While derived information is useful at a glance, users need to have access to the tweets behind the event. The Relevant Tweets panel (Figure 1.4) lists tweets that fall within the event's start and end times. These tweets are sorted by similarity to the event or peak keywords, so that tweets near the top are most representative of the selected event. Tweets are colored red, blue, or white depending on whether their detected sentiment is positive, negative, or neutral.

Aggregate Metadata Views

In addition to skimming sentiment for individual tweets, users may wish to see the general sentiment on Twitter about a given topic. The Overall Sentiment panel (Figure 1.6) displays a piechart representing the total proportion of positive and negative tweets during the event. We discuss the difficulties in accurately depicting aggregate sentiment and other aggregated classifier output in the Algorithms section.

Twitter users will share links as a story unfolds [17]. The Popular Links panel (Figure 1.5) aggregates the top three URLs extracted from tweets that occurred during the selected subevent if users want sources for further exploration.

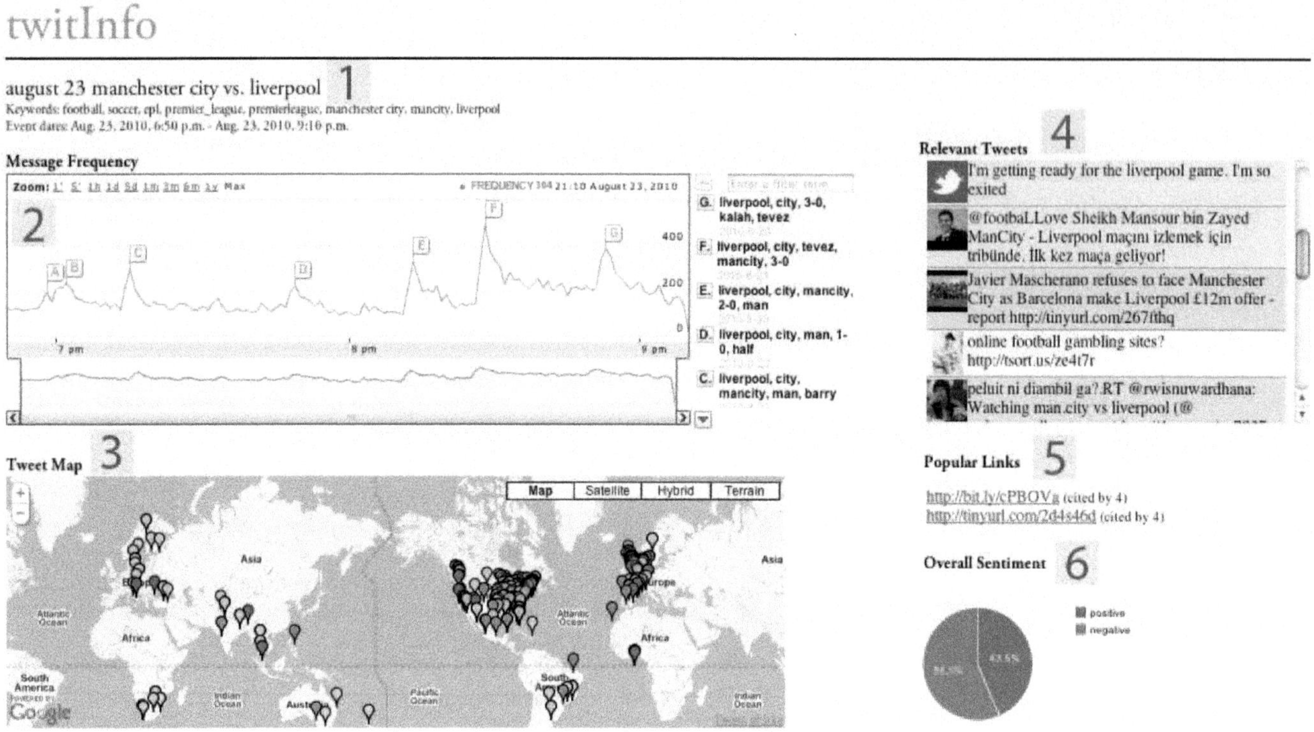

Figure 1. The TwitInfo user interface. 1) the user-defined name of the event, as well as keywords sent to the Twitter Search API to log the tweets. 2) The central timeline interface, with the y-axis corresponding to tweet volume. Automatically-detected peaks (subevents) are labeled with lettered flags. When the user clicks on a peak, all the other interface elements filter to tweets in that time period. 3) Event-related tweets with geolocation are displayed on a map. 4) Tweets for the currently selected event or peak (subevent), colored red if TwitInfo detects negative sentiment or blue if TwitInfo detects positive sentiment. 5) The most popular links in the currently-selected event or subevent. 6) Aggregated sentiment of all tweets in the event or subevent.

Often, opinion on an event differs by geographic region. A user should be able to quickly zoom in on clusters of activity around New York and Boston during a Red Sox-Yankees baseball game, with sentiment toward a given peak (e.g., a home run) varying by region. The Tweet Map (Figure 1.3) displays tweets that provide geolocation metadata. The marker for each tweet is colored according to its sentiment, and clicking on a pin reveals the associated tweet.

Creating Subevents

An important contribution of TwitInfo is its interactive support for hierarchically nested events: users can start by viewing several months of the Obama presidency on Twitter, zoom in to a subevent to see a timeline of just a single speech, then zoom in again to do a detailed analysis of reactions to a single remark the President made. The user can transform any peak on the timeline into its own first-class event with a dedicated page. To do so, users are asked to "Label this event" in the timeline and provide a human-readable name for the event. This serves the purpose of providing a better event label, and for allowing future users to navigate deeper into the subevent structure.

Realtime Updating

Diffusion speed is one of Twitter's competitive advantages in tracking the news, so it is important for Twitter interfaces to be able to handle ongoing events. Because TwitInfo captures realtime streams from Twitter, its interface reacts accordingly. The interface refreshes at regular intervals to include any new tweets that have entered the system. In this way, a user might track a speech, sporting event, or media event in realtime as it occurs.

ALGORITHMS FOR DISPLAYING EVENTS

We now turn to the algorithms we use for detecting and displaying subevents in a collection of tweets.

Event Detection

A key technical contribution of this paper is identifying temporal peaks in tweet frequency. Our algorithm first bins the tweets into a histogram by time, for example by minute. This binning allows us to count the tweet-arrival rate in each time period. We then calculate a historically weighted running average of tweet rate and identify rates that are significantly higher than the mean tweet rate. For these rate spikes, we find the local maximum of tweet rate and identify a window surrounding the local maximum. Finally, we collect tweets within this window that contain the desired keywords, and select frequent terms to provide an automated label of each peak. We now describe each of these steps in detail.

Given a time-sorted collection of tweets, we first group the tweets that were posted within a one-minute time window of one-another. Increasing bin size smooths out small spikes in longer events, and can sometimes aid in finding larger trends. Users can adjust bin size to hours or days.

After our binning process, we are left with a list $[C_1, ..., C_N]$ of tweet counts, where C_i is the number of tweets in bin i. For example, a list $[25, 50, 13]$ with minute-sized bins would mean that there were 25 tweets in the first minute of an event, 50 tweets in the second, and 13 tweets in the third. We wish to determine when there is a peak in conversation about some topic. A naïve approach would be to find local maxima amongst the C_i's, but this would mis-identify peaks which are marginally taller relative to their neighbors. Instead, we wish to identify each bin i such that C_i is large relative to the recent history $C_{i-1}, C_{i-2}, ...$ A similar problem is addressed in TCP's congestion control mechanism [14], which must determine whether a packet is taking unusually long to be acknowledged and is thus an outlier. The analogue in our system is that the algorithm must determine whether a bin has an unusually large number of tweets in it. We take inspiration from TCP's approach, which uses a weighted moving average and variance.

Algorithm 1 Offline Peak-Finding Algorithm

```
1:  function find_peak_windows(C):
2:  windows = []
3:  mean = C_1
4:  meandev = variance(C_1, ..., C_p)
5:
6:  for i = 2; i < len(C); i++ do
7:    if |C_i − mean| / meandev > τ and C_i > C_{i−1} then
8:      start = i − 1
9:      while i < len(C) and C_i > C_{i−1} do
10:       (mean, meandev) = update(mean, meandev, C_i)
11:       i++
12:     end while
13:     while i < len(C) and C_i > C_start do
14:       if |C_i − mean| / meandev > τ and C_i > C_{i−1} then
15:         end = −−i
16:         break
17:       else
18:         (mean, meandev) = update(mean, meandev, C_i)
19:         end = i++
20:       end if
21:     end while
22:     windows.append(start, end)
23:   else
24:     (mean, meandev) = update(mean, meandev, C_i)
25:   end if
26: end for
27: return windows
28:
29: function update(oldmean, oldmeandev, updatevalue):
30: diff = |oldmean − updatevalue|
31: newmeandev = α*diff + (1−α)*oldmeandev
32: newmean = α*updatevalue + (1−α)*oldmean
33: return (newmean, newmeandev)
```

An offline version of peak detection is described in Algorithm 1. The function **find_peak_windows(C)** takes binned tweet counts as input $[C_1, ..., C_N]$. The function returns a list $[W_1, ..., W_N]$ of peak windows, where window $W_i = (S_i, F_i), S_i < F_i$ is represented by S_i, the start bin of the window, and F_i, the final bin of the window. After initializing the mean to the first bin count (line 3) and the mean deviation to the variance of the first p (we use $p = 5$) bins (line 4), we loop through the subsequent bin counts (line 6). Line 7 contains our peak detection logic: if the current bin count (C_i) is more than τ (we use $\tau = 2$) mean deviations from the current mean, and the bin counts are increasing, we say that the increase is significant, and begin a new peak window (line 8). The loop in lines 9-12 is performing hill-climbing to find the peak of this window: we loop until we reach a bin count smaller than the previous one. Every time we iterate over a new bin count, we update the mean and mean deviation (lines 10, 18, 24). After a peak C_i has been found, we enter the loop of lines 13-21. Here we follow the peak to its bottom, which occurs either when the bin counts are back at the level they started (line 13) or another significant increase is found (the *if* statement on line 14).

To summarize the algorithm: when the algorithm encounters a significant increase in bin count relative to the historical mean, it starts a new window and follows the increase to its maximum. The algorithm ends the peak's window once the bin count returns to the same level it started at, or when it encounters another significant increase.

The implementation of **find_peak_windows(C)** in TwitInfo is different than the one in Algorithm 1 to facilitate streaming interactivity. In order to make peak-finding an online algorithm, we make the iteration between lines 6 and 26 reachable using a continuation-passing style, and make the function take only the latest bin count with each call.

The **update(oldmean, oldmeandev, updatevalue)** function is the update step: given a new bin count (*updatevalue*), it updates *oldmean* and *oldmeandev* and returns their new values. Because we are doing this in a streaming context (we do not want to maintain a list of historical values) and because we want to eventually forget old bin counts to adjust to changing message frequency trends, we maintain an exponentially weighted moving mean of bin counts. Similarly, we maintain exponentially weighted moving mean deviations. The formulas for these update steps are on lines 31 and 32, and require that $\alpha < 1$. We have found that $\alpha = .125$ captures a reasonable amount of historical information.

The significance tests of lines 7 and 14 are similar to outlier detection criteria which identify outliers if they are a certain number of standard deviations from the mean. We utilize mean deviation instead of standard deviation because the update step for mean (line 31) does not require keeping historical bin count values. The update steps of lines 31 and 32, as well as the use of exponentially weighted moving averages and mean deviations are based on ideas from TCP congestion control.

After identifying a window $W = \{S, F\}$, we generate a label for W. We consider all tweets containing the event's keywords that were posted between the start of bin S and the end of bin F. We then tokenize all tweets into unigrams and rank the unigrams by their Term Frequency / Inverse Document Frequency (TF-IDF) [22]. TF is calculated across all tweets in W, and IDF is calculated for tweets in all windows. We present the top five ranked unigrams as the label for W.

Removing Noisy Query Terms

If a user includes a tangential but high-volume keyword in the list of event keywords, the resulting timeline can lose its meaningful signal. For example, suppose the user wanted to track music news using band keywords like *Journey*, *T-Pain*, and *Justin Bieber*. Justin Bieber is a Twitter celebrity and perpetually trending — the volume of Bieber-related tweets would overwhelm signal about the other musicians.

We employ an IDF-normalizing technique for avoiding this situation. Rather than count the number of tweets which contain any of the desired keywords in a given timeframe, we normalize the count of tweets containing always-popular terms by the terms' global popularity (IDF). Thus, because *Bieber* frequently appears in the Twitter stream, the contribution of tweets containing that term to the volume of a period is dampened.

Identifying Relevant Tweets

Because there are typically more tweets than can be digested by a user for any subevent, we try to identify relevant tweets for the user in the Relevant Tweets list (Figure 1.4). Given our 5-term label for each identified event, we rank tweets by the number of terms from the subevent label that the tweet contains. Since retweets contain the same words as a tweet and we want to promote diversity, we halve the matching term count of retweeted tweets.

Representing Aggregate Sentiment

Our sentiment analysis algorithm places tweets into *positive* and *negative* classes. It uses a Naïve Bayes classifier trained on unigram features. We built the algorithm around an idea described by Go et al. [12], generating training sets for the positive and negative classes using tweets with happy and sad emoticons.

Traditionally, twitter-based sentiment analysis algorithms are evaluated tweet-by-tweet, using standard precision/recall metrics. In practice, however, they are often used in aggregated form. The standard means of displaying aggregate sentiment can pose a biased view. We illustrate the issue in Figure 2. TwitInfo contributes a correction for this bias.

Our classifier predicts the probability that a tweet is a member of the *positive* class (p_p) and the probability that it is a member of the *negative* class (p_n). Not all tweets express a strong sentiment, so we need a confidence threshold τ on the classifiers below which we predict a *neutral* category. Increasing the threshold for a class on a well-trained classifier has the effect of increasing the precision and decreasing the recall of the classifier. For example, we can increase our precision on the positive class by increasing threshold τ_p for which we will accept tweets with p_p values as positive.

Our positive and negative classifiers will have different precision/recall curves as we adjust their thresholds. It is relatively unlikely that the precision/recall curves will be identical for both classes. This may cause the two classes to have different recall values at the same precision.

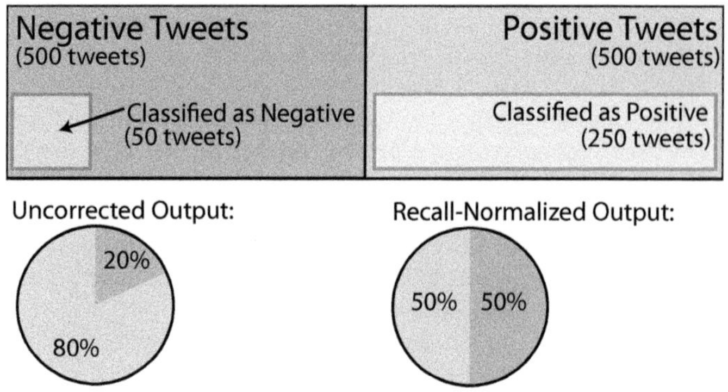

Figure 2. Positive and negative sentiment classifiers often have different performance. Suppose both the positive and the negative class contain 500 tweets. If the negative classifier is conservative and only identifies 50 tweets while the positive classifier is more liberal and identifies 250, the relative proportions will be biased (bottom left). If wedivide by an estimate of the classifier's recall (as a number in $[0 \ldots 1]$), however, we produce a more accurate visualization.

This means that one classifier may be conservatively ignoring tweets while the other is accepting them. Following the example of Figure 2, if we have 500 positive and negative tweets, but the negative classifier has a recall of .1, whereas the positive classifier has a recall of .5, then the positive classifier will identify 5 times as many positive tweets as negative ones in aggregate. If we do not correct for this problem, the user will see an aggregate visualization that grossly overestimates the number of positive tweets in the data.

Our solution to this problem is to *recall-normalize* the aggregate numbers. We first adjust both classifiers so that they have equivalent precision values on a test dataset. We then measure their recalls on this set. When we count the number of positive tweets, we divide the count by the positive recall, and similarly normalize the negative count. For example, if we know recall is .1 and we observed 50 negative tweets, we estimate $50/.1 = 500$ negative tweets. This correction assumes that the precision/recall characteristics of our sentiment analysis algorithm is similar in practice as it is on the test dataset. As aggregated sentiment is important in many domains, we think that researching a principled solution to this problem will be important future work.

IMPLEMENTATION

TwitInfo layers an interface and infrastructure over the tweet stream. When an event is created, TwitInfo searches for the keywords for that event using the Twitter Streaming API. It associates tweets containing relevant keywords with events, counts tweet volume over time, and extracts metadata like sentiment and URLs. It records location metadata by harvesting geolocation tags on the tweet or, failing that, attempting to convert the freetext user location field into a latitude/longitude pair using a geolocation service.

These tweets are serialized to a database using Django, indexed by keywords that matched the streaming query. When the user requests a TwitInfo page, Django looks up relevant tweets using indexes on keyword and timestamp. To power

Data Source	Precision	Recall
Soccer Events	$\frac{17}{22} \Rightarrow 77\%$	$\frac{17}{22} \Rightarrow 77\%$
Soccer Events & Discussion	$\frac{21}{22} \Rightarrow 95\%$	$\frac{21}{26} \Rightarrow 81\%$
Major Earthquakes	$\frac{6}{44} \Rightarrow 14\%$	$\frac{5}{5} \Rightarrow 100\%$
All Earthquakes	$\frac{29}{44} \Rightarrow 66\%$	N/A
All Earthquakes & Discussion	$\frac{39}{44} \Rightarrow 89\%$	N/A

Table 1. Event detection performance on our data sets. Without a reasonable ground truth labeling of all earthquakes, we omit recall values for them. Note that there were five major earthquakes in the period of interest, but one event had two distinct peaks on Twitter. Precision and recall were equal for Soccer Events.

the visualization, we use the Google Visualization API[5] for our annotated timeline and pie charts, and generate a map using the Google Maps API.

EVALUATION

We now evaluate the performance of the algorithm for detecting events in the timeline, and the effectiveness of the user interface at visualizing events using Twitter data. We analyze the algorithm through a quantitative analysis of its ability to identify events, and analyze the user interface through a user study on twelve users and a semi-structured interview with a Pulitzer Prize-winning former Washington Post investigative reporter.

Algorithm Evaluation

We now determine if our automated event detection approach matches human intuitions about correct behavior. To support the evaluation, we gathered tweets from three soccer games and one month of earthquakes. To create ground truth for the soccer data, one researcher annotated major events in the soccer game using the game video and web-based game summaries, without looking at tweets. For ground truth on the earthquake data, we gathered data from the US Geological Survey on major earthquakes during the time period.

We tested how many of the events our algorithm detected were part of this ground truth set (*precision*), and how many events in the ground truth set our algorithm detected (*recall*). We used the default threshold cutoff for determining events — we can trade off precision and recall by adjusting this threshold, but we chose to use the single value that users will experience. Results are in Table 1.

The algorithm has high recall, finding all major earthquakes and most soccer events. Figure 3 displays several ground truth timelines and events that the algorithm identified. If the algorithm failed to catch an event, it was typically because Twitter volume did not peak when it occurred. For example, the only uncaught ground truth events in the soccer data set were yellow cards, which did not appear in large quantities in the stream, even though our researcher identified them as interesting events in his initial analysis of the game.

[5]http://code.google.com/apis/visualization/documentation/gallery.html

Figure 3. The TwitInfo timeline displaying three soccer games. The peak detection algorithm finds only 1 false positive, labeled red. The algorithm did not find Yellow Card events, but there was no spike in Twitter usage to suggest it. The algorithm occasionally flagged pregame chatter like retweeting a livestream URL.

Precision depended on activity type: it was high for soccer, but there were several false positives for major earthquakes because the algorithm also flagged minor earthquakes. If we include in our ground truth dataset all minor earthquakes, precision rises from 14% to 66% (Table 1). It still produces false positives, because Twitter spikes when its users discuss an earthquake or share information about donating aid money. If we include all earthquake-related discussion, precision rises to 89%. Likewise, including soccer-relevant discussion (like conversations identifying live video stream URLs for a game) leads to 95% precision in the soccer dataset. The remaining false positives come from high-volume topics that happened to mention the word earthquake or a soccer term. For example, one Twitterer asked celebrity Justin Bieber to follow her because she survived Chile's earthquake, and she was retweeted around Bieber's fan base.

The algorithm can be biased by Twitter's interests. If there is a medium-sized earthquake in the middle of the ocean, nobody will notice or tweet about it, so TwitInfo will miss the event. Conversely, if there is a minor earthquake in a densely populated area, lots of locals will tweet about it and TwitInfo may flag it as an event.

We also note two artifacts that occur because of a combination of our algorithm, timeline visualization, and use of Twitter as a datasource. First, a well-defined event, such as the September 2010 earthquake in Christchurch, NZ, often appears as multiple peaks on Twitter. In the Christchurch earthquake, we noticed three distinct peaks, all of which were identified by the algorithm: 1) news about the earthquake, 2) thoughts and prayers to those in Christchurch, and

3) information about aid and scams. The second artifact occurs when multiple events overlap in time. For example, two earthquakes in different locations might result in a single larger peak on the timeline. Our algorithm does not distinguish overlapping events, and our visualization, which does not provide stacked layers like MemeTracker [18] does not identify the two events as distinct.

User Interface Evaluation

Our next goal was to understand if TwitInfo users can understand an event's structure via the interface, and if some elements of the interface are more helpful for event exploration than others.

Method

We recruited twelve participants, six of whom had Twitter accounts. Ten had been to the Twitter website before. They could all explain Twitter's mechanics, including tweet length and broadcast messaging. Four participants were female. We compensated participants with $10 gift certificates.

We asked the participants to perform directed search tasks for the first half of the study. We chose tasks that exercised all the elements of the interface and allowed us to gather feedback on a variety of usage scenarios. Some example tasks on the earthquake dataset included:

- Find the earthquake that happened in Vanuatu. When did it occur, and what was the magnitude?
- How did sentiment about the earthquake differ between Vanuatu and New Zealand?
- What are people who live in Christchurch saying about the earthquake there?

During this process, we gathered usability feedback and observed which interface elements were useful or ignored.

The second half of the study was a time-limited exploration task. We gave participants up to five minutes to understand an event using TwitInfo and five minutes to dictate a news report on the event to the experimenter. To gain a variety of observations, we gave half of the participants a dataset of a soccer game between Manchester City and Liverpool, and half a dataset containing sixteen days of tweets about President Barack Obama.

Finally, we guided participants in a semi-structured interview. We asked about the best and worst parts of the TwitInfo interface. We also tried to understand the situations in which our participants would want to use TwitInfo, and asked them for alternate modes of performing their assigned reporting task in the absence of TwitInfo.

Results

Here is one participant's summary of President Obama's activities over a 16 day period:

> *After the peace talks, Obama traveled to the ASEAN conference and to NATO to work on issues in those parts of the world. He then spent the week dedicated to domestic economic issues. First he proposed a research tax break, then a $50 billion investment in infrastructure, then the issue came up about whether he should keep some tax breaks that Bush had implemented, and he's asking for some tax breaks from business, and these are generating some controversy because [. . .]*

Participants such as this one successfully reconstructed events from the Twitter timeline within five minutes, even without previous knowledge. TwitInfo gave quick, high-level understanding, with one user describing some of the visual elements as "at-a-glance" interfaces, and another praising its speed of distilling information, but explaining that the extracted information was "shallow."

Common Usage Patterns. When performing freeform exploration, users picked the largest peak and explored it carefully: they read the tweets thoroughly, drilled in on the map, and followed links to articles. Most users relied on tweets to confirm event details, though a few skimmed the automatically-generated labels. Under time pressure, users instead skimmed all peak labels to get a broad sense of the chronology. Self-reported "news junkies" tended to follow at least one link, either from a tweet citing an interesting news source, or from the popular links section. These users cited the lack of detail of the tweets as their reason for going outside of the system.

The Timeline Focused User Activity. When providing a high-level summary of the interface in the semistructured interview, most users cited the timeline and event labels as the most memorable and helpful elements. The timeline was also the most actively used component in the interface.

Mapping Requires Aggregation. The map provided helpful filtering features, but could have been even more useful if it offered aggregation. Users were excited to find that tweet density increased in areas affected by earthquakes, but this fact was not discoverable while the map was zoomed out. So, these users requested a map indicator for geographic areas with unusually high volume, for example a heatmap. Other participants wanted the bounds and zoom level of the map to act as a filter for the rest of the interface, for example re-sampling the timeline based only on tweets from Iran.

Users Do Not Trust Sentiment Analysis. We tested our sentiment classifier against previous work investigating tweet sentiment [15], finding similar performance. However, users did not agree with its model of sentiment. For example, users were often surprised to find positive overall sentiment for earthquakes. After examining the positive and negative sentiment tweets, they realized that many tweets contained positive messages such as "sending best wishes to those recovering from the earthquake in haiti." They would decide that the sentiment classifier was working correctly, but that it was not giving them the information they wanted. In essence, the sentiment of individual tweets did not summarize the overall sentiment of the topics they mentioned.

What Alternatives Did Users Suggest? We asked users how they would have performed their reporting task had TwitInfo not been provided to them. Users who successfully reported on the soccer match suggested, correctly, that they could have searched for an article about the game and extracted much of the same information. Users reporting on two weeks of Obama's activities had a harder time arriving at solutions. One user explained that he would have collected news weeklies (e.g., *Newsweek*), identified key events from each of President Obama's weeks, and then searched for articles on those events. Most of the other users explained that they would have searched Google News for historical day-by-day coverage, and compiled a set of the most interesting stories. All of the users had difficulty determining how, across the sets of daily search results, they would identify which results to pay attention to.

A Journalist's Perspective

Twitter has considerable buzz as a news medium [17]. We wanted to understand if TwitInfo would be a useful tool for journalists exploring a new topic. We conducted a semi-structured interview with a Pulitzer Prize-winning former Washington Post investigative reporter who is now a Knight Professor of Journalism. We asked the journalist to interact with the soccer, earthquake, and Obama examples, and to reflect on how journalists might use TwitInfo.

When presented with TwitInfo, the journalist initially focused on the labeled timeline view. She explained that the timeline with labeled events would be useful for *backgrounding* on a longer-running topic such as the sixteen-day Obama example. The journalist expanded: "When I do long stories, they are on a very arcane subject. Being able to see a timeline on an arcane subject could be really helpful." Specifically, she felt that the automated timeline would be useful to understand which substories to explore further. Additionally, she recommended blending the extracted URLs from the tweet stream with stories from traditional sources of news for an expanded understanding. In order to navigate longer timelines covering multiple subevents, she recommended a topic-based drill-down interface along the lines of what Eddi [4] provides.

The journalist was also interested in a separate use case for the map view of geolocated tweets, which could be used by reporters seeking to contact on-the-ground sources. The map view was compelling because "from the perspective of us covering a breaking event, you want to know what the people on the ground are saying," and zooming in on the location of interest could result in eyewitnesses to follow up with. The journalist drew an analogy to the *#iranElection*, which was billed as a Twitter revolution, but left reporters wanting to talk to the 200-odd people in Iran who were the eye-witness sources of on-the-ground information.

For the most part, the journalist's view on sentiment analysis was similar to that of the user study participants. She said that journalists would be skeptical of the quality and accuracy of the algorithm as well as the sample population expressing the sentiment. While aware of the research suggesting that extracted Twitter sentiment matches sentiment measured through other polling measures [20], she expressed skepticism that a journalist would trust these numbers.

Overall, the journalist found TwitInfo to be a compelling first version of a tool to make sense of the tweet stream from a reporter's perspective. She expressed that with her recommended interface modifications, she could imagine the tool being useful for reporting on breaking news, following real-time events, and familiarizing herself with overall interest and current opinions on an arcane topic.

DISCUSSION

TwitInfo successfully allows individuals to aggregate thousands of short messages into a coherent picture of an event. If a user or journalist wishes to receive a high-level background on a new topic, or if a reporter wishes to identify eyewitnesses to follow up with, our study and interview suggest that TwitInfo would be a useful tool.

We offer designers and developers of similar systems several takeaways from our experience. TwitInfo utilizes algorithms which enable configuration-free real-time social stream analysis. Prior work focuses on building useful dashboards on such data, but displays prototypes built on static datasets. To fully benefit from social streams, systems designers need to consider the streaming nature of the data when designing the algorithms behind their visualizations.

Our application of signal processing and streaming techniques to social streams opens the door to other uses in interfaces for social computing systems. Some examples include event-based notification (e.g., your tweet is suddenly getting lots of retweets), large text corpus summarization techniques (e.g., extending Diakopoulos et al. [6] to realtime scenarios), and smarter trend detection in newsfeed interfaces (e.g., extending systems like Eddi [4]).

Our evaluation presents a cautionary experience against some of the excitement in using sentiment analysis in tweet dashboards. Using sentiment analysis techniques from the literature, we showed that users are wary of sentiment-enabled exploratory tools of informative tweets due to a mental model mismatch. While this does not reduce the value of such signals in visualizations, it does suggest that sentiment is not an easy drop-in for such interfaces.

As a news source, our users found that Twitter was often only a shallow window into world events. Though analysis and conversation does appear on Twitter [13, 5], for many events Twitter is a medium for quick reactions and information sharing. Even the summary tweets sometimes could not explain the headline news: statistical summarization interfaces could help convey more meaning [25, 4, 21].

Our evaluation had several limitations. First-use studies make it difficult to understand how a person might use the interface longitudinally to track a topic. Such studies also have low external validity: could a citizen journalist use TwitInfo for real investigative reporting? We plan to release TwitInfo publicly to answer some of these questions.

CONCLUSION

Twitter is fast becoming a critical source of information about world events large and small. However, it is difficult to translate this information into a format allows users to draw higher-level conclusions. In this paper we present TwitInfo, a novel microblog-based event tracking interface that can collect, aggregate, and visualize tweets about user-specified events as they unfold on the stream. TwitInfo embeds a novel algorithm for peak detection and labeling, as well as a new technique for correcting aggregate sentiment displays. The peak detection algorithm identifies 80-100% of manually labeled peaks. TwitInfo users were able to understand several weeks' worth of Twitter data in a matter of minutes, on diverse topics like earthquakes, politics, and sports. A professional journalist reflected on the interface as a means of exploring complex topics and identifying eyewitness accounts. We discuss some implications of our approach for future designers and researchers to consider.

Aggregate Twitter interfaces promise a new set of exploratory data analysis tools. These tools are already being used for social science [27, 29] and augmented media experiences [23]. We envision a future where citizen journalists, citizen scientists and curious minds can use tools like TwitInfo to explore and understand their world.

REFERENCES

1. E. Adar, M. Dontcheva, J. Fogarty, and D. S. Weld. Zoetrope: interacting with the ephemeral web. In *UIST '08*. ACM Press, 2008.
2. P. André, M. L. Wilson, A. Russell, D. A. Smith, A. Owens, and m. schraefel. Continuum: designing timelines for hierarchies, relationships and scale. In *UIST '07*. ACM Press, 2007.
3. N. Bansal and N. Koudas. Blogscope: a system for online analysis of high volume text streams. In *VLDB '07*. VLDB Endowment, 2007.
4. M. S. Bernstein, B. Suh, L. Hong, J. Chen, S. Kairam, and E. H. Chi. Eddi: Interactive Topic-based Browsing of Social Status Streams. In *UIST '10*, 2010.
5. danah boyd, S. Golder, and G. Lotan. Tweet, tweet, retweet: Conversational aspects of retweeting on twitter. In *HICSS*. IEEE, 2010.
6. N. Diakopoulos, M. Naaman, and F. Kivran-Swaine. Diamonds in the rough: Social media visual analytics for journalistic inquiry. In *VAST 2010*.
7. N. Diakopoulos and D. A. Shamma. Characterizing debate performance via aggregated twitter sentiment. In *CHI 2010*.
8. M. Dörk, D. Gruen, C. Williamson, and S. Carpendale. A visual backchannel for large-scale events. *IEEE Transactions on Visualization and Computer Graphics*, 16:1129–1138, 2010.
9. S. Faridani, E. Bitton, K. Ryokai, and K. Goldberg. Opinion space: a scalable tool for browsing online comments. In *CHI '10*. ACM Press, 2010.
10. E. Gabrilovich, S. Dumais, and E. Horvitz. Newsjunkie: providing personalized newsfeeds via analysis of information novelty. In *WWW '04*. ACM Press, 2004.
11. D. Gaffney. #iranelection: Quantifying online activism. In *Web Science*, 2010.
12. Go, Alec and Bhayani, Richa and Huang, Lei. Twitter sentiment website, September 2010. `http://twittersentiment.appspot.com`.
13. C. Honeycutt and S. C. Herring. Beyond microblogging: Conversation and collaboration via twitter. In *HICSS '09*, 2009.
14. IETF Network Working Group. Rfc 2988: Computing tcp's retransmission timer, November 2000. `http://tools.ietf.org/html/rfc2988`.
15. B. J. Jansen, M. Zhang, K. Sobel, and A. Chowdury. Twitter power: Tweets as electronic word of mouth. *JASIST*, 60(11), 2009.
16. A. Java, X. Song, T. Finin, and B. Tseng. Why we twitter: Understanding the microblogging effect in user intentions and communities. In *WebKDD*, 2007.
17. H. Kwak, C. Lee, H. Park, and S. Moon. What is twitter, a social network or a news media? In *WWW 2010*, 2010.
18. J. Leskovec, L. Backstrom, and J. Kleinberg. Meme-tracking and the dynamics of the news cycle. In *KDD '09*. ACM Press, 2009.
19. M. Naaman, J. Boase, and C.-H. Lai. Is it really about me?: message content in social awareness streams. In *CSCW '10*, New York, NY, USA, 2010. ACM.
20. B. O'Connor, R. Balasubramanyan, B. R. Routledge, and N. A. Smith. From tweets to polls: Linking text sentiment to public opinion time series. In *ICSWSM 2010*.
21. D. Ramage, S. Dumais, and D. Liebling. Characterizing microblogs with topic models. In *ICWSM '10*, 2010.
22. G. Salton and C. Buckley. Term-weighting approaches in automatic text retrieval. *Information Processing and Management*, 24(5):513–523, 1988.
23. D. Shamma, L. Kennedy, and E. Churchill. Tweetgeist: Can the twitter timeline reveal the structure of broadcast events? In *CSCW 2010 Horizon*, 2010.
24. D. A. Shamma, L. Kennedy, and E. F. Churchill. Conversational shadows: Describing live media events using short messages. In *ICWSM '10*, 2010.
25. B. Sharifi, M.-A. Hutton, and J. Kalita. Summarizing microblogs automatically. In *NAACL '10*. ACL, 2010.
26. S. F. Silva and T. Catarci. Visualization of linear time-oriented data: A survey. *Web Information Systems Engineering*, 1:0310, 2000.
27. K. Starbird, L. Palen, A. L. Hughes, and S. Vieweg. Chatter on the red: what hazards threat reveals about the social life of microblogged information. In *CSCW '10*. ACM, 2010.
28. R. Swan and J. Allan. Extracting significant time varying features from text. In *CIKM 1999*.
29. S. Vieweg, A. L. Hughes, K. Starbird, and L. Palen. Microblogging during two natural hazards events: what twitter may contribute to situational awareness. In *CHI '10*. ACM Press, 2010.

Tweets from Justin Bieber's Heart: The Dynamics of the "Location" Field in User Profiles

Brent Hecht*, Lichan Hong†, Bongwon Suh†, Ed H. Chi†

*Northwestern University
Electrical Engineering and Computer Science
brent@u.northwestern.edu

†Palo Alto Research Center
Augmented Social Cognition Group
3333 Coyote Hill Road, Palo Alto, CA
{hong,suh,echi}@parc.com

ABSTRACT

Little research exists on one of the most common, oldest, and most utilized forms of online social geographic information: the "location" field found in most virtual community user profiles. We performed the first in-depth study of user behavior with regard to the location field in Twitter user profiles. We found that 34% of users did not provide real location information, frequently incorporating fake locations or sarcastic comments that can fool traditional geographic information tools. When users did input their location, they almost never specified it at a scale any more detailed than their city. In order to determine whether or not natural user behaviors have a real effect on the "locatability" of users, we performed a simple machine learning experiment to determine whether we can identify a user's location by only looking at what that user tweets. We found that a user's country and state can in fact be determined easily with decent accuracy, indicating that users implicitly reveal location information, with or without realizing it. Implications for location-based services and privacy are discussed.

Author Keywords

Location, location-based services, Twitter, privacy, geography, location prediction, social networks

ACM Classification Keywords

H5.m. Information interfaces and presentation (e.g., HCI): Miscellaneous.

General Terms

Human Factors, Design

INTRODUCTION

Interest in geographic information within the HCI community has intensified in the past few years. Academic HCI research has seen an increase in the number of papers on geographic information (e.g. [8, 18, 20, 21, 24, 26]). Industry has experienced an even greater spike in activity.

Geotagged photo map interfaces have become commonplace (e.g. in Flickr and iPhoto), Google's Buzz has integrated a geographic component since its inception, and companies like Yelp have embraced the geographic nature of their user-generated content wholeheartedly.

Despite this increased interest in "geo", one of the oldest, most common forms of geographic information in the Web 2.0 world has escaped detailed study. This is the information that exists in the "location" field of user profiles on dozens of immensely popular websites. Facebook has had "Current City" and "Hometown" fields for years. Flickr allows users to enter their hometown and current location in their user profile, and the recently-launched music social network Ping by Apple has "Where I Live" as one of its profile fields.

This gap in understanding has not stopped researchers and practitioners from making ample use of the data entered into location fields. In general, it has been assumed that this data is strongly typed geographic information with little noise and good precision – an assumption that has never been validated. Backstrom et al. [1], for instance, wrote that "there is little incentive to enter false information, as leaving the field blank is an easier option". Similarly, Twitter reported that many location-based projects "are built using the simple, account-level location field folks can fill out as part of their profile". [25] This includes the "Nearby" feature of Twitter's official iPhone app, which is designed to show tweets that are close to the user's present location.

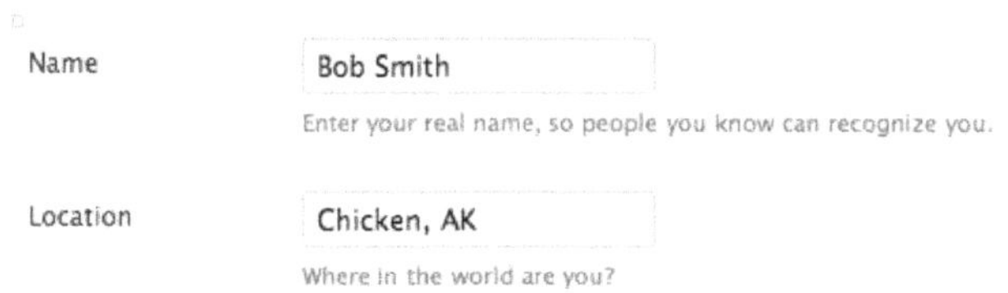

Figure 1. A screenshot from the webpage on which Twitter users enter location information. Location entries are entirely freeform, but limited to 30 characters.

In this paper, we conduct an in-depth study of user profile location data on Twitter, which provides a freeform location field without additional user interface elements that encourage any form of structured input (Figure 1). The prompt is simply "Where in the world are you?" This environment allows us to observe users' natural, "organic" behavior as best as possible, thus illuminating actual user practices.

In the first part of this paper, we report the results derived from an extensive investigation of thousands of users' location entries on Twitter. We demonstrate that users' behavior with respect to the location field is richly varied, contrary to what has been assumed. We also show that the information they enter into the field is both highly diverse and noisy. Finally, our results suggest that most users organically specify their location at the city scale when they do specify their location.

For practitioners and researchers, it may be important to discover the rough location of the large percentage of users who did not disclose their true location. How can location-based services (LBS) ranging from information retrieval to targeted advertising leverage location field information given its noisy nature? Do users reveal location information through other behaviors on Twitter that can be used to effectively "fill in" the location field?

To answer both these questions, we considered users' *implicit* location sharing behavior. Since there are many forms of this implicit behavior, we decided to evaluate the most basic: the act of tweeting itself. In other words, how much information about her or his location does the average Twitter user disclose implicitly *simply by tweeting*? The second part of this paper presents a machine learning experiment that attempts to answer this question. We found that by observing only a user's tweets and leveraging simple machine learning techniques, we were reasonably able to infer a user's home country and home state. While we might never be able to predict location to GPS-level accuracy reliably using tweet content only, knowing even the country or the state of a user would be helpful in many areas such as answering search queries and targeted advertisement. In other words, users' most basic behavior on Twitter somewhat implicitly "fills out" the location field for them, better enabling LBS but also raising privacy concerns.

In summary, our contributions are fourfold:

- To the best of our knowledge, we provide the first in-depth study of user behavior in relation to one of the oldest and most common forms of online social geographic information: the location field in user profiles.
- We find that users' natural location field behavior is more varied and the information they submit is more complex than previously assumed.
- We show that the traditional tools for processing location field information are not properly equipped to handle this varied and noisy dataset.
- Using simple machine learning techniques to guess at users' locations, we demonstrate that the average user reveals location information simply by tweeting.

Following this introduction and a related work section, we describe how we collected our data from Twitter, as this is central to both of our studies. Next, we detail our characterization study and its implications. Following that, we describe the machine learning study. Finally, we close with a conclusion and discussion of future work.

Finally, before moving on, it is important to note that this work is descriptive in nature and does not focus on causal explanations for users' natural behavior. For instance, some users may decide not to enter their location for privacy reasons, while others may do so due to lack of interest or the belief that interested people already know their location. While some clues as to users' motivations can be gleaned from our first study, we leave in-depth causal analysis to future work.

RELATED WORK

Work related to this paper primarily arises from four areas: (1) research on microblogging sites like Twitter, (2) work on location disclosure behavior, (3) the location detection of users who contribute content to Web 2.0 sites, and (4) prediction of private information.

Various researchers have studied Twitter usage in depth. For instance, Honeycutt and Herring [10] examined the usage of the "@" symbol in English tweets. boyd et al. [3] studied how retweets are used to spread information. By manually coding 3,379 tweets, Naaman et al. [17] found that 20% of users posted tweets that are informational in nature, while the other 80% posted tweets about themselves or their thoughts.

With regard to the Twitter location field, Java et al. [11] found that in their dataset of 76K users, 39K of them provided information in their "location" field. They applied the Yahoo! Geocoding API[1] to the location field of these 39K users to show the geographical distribution of users across continents. Using the self-reported "utc_offset" field in user profiles, Krishnamurthy et al. [12] examined the growth of users in each continent over time. In the area of machine learning, Sakaki et al. [22] used the location field as input to their spatiotemporal event detection algorithms.

Location disclosure behavior has been investigated both in the research community and in the popular press. For instance, Barkhuus et al. [2] concluded that this behavior must be understood in its social context. In our case, this context is the entire "Twittersphere", as all data examined was in public profiles. Ludford et al. [15] identified several heuristics for how people decide which locations to share, such as "I will not share residences [or] private workplaces." In the popular press, the New York Times

[1]http://developer.yahoo.com/maps/rest/V1/geocode.html

recently featured an article [4] reporting that just 4% of U.S. residents had tried location-based services.

In the third area – location detection – the most relevant works include Lieberman and Lin [13], Popescu and Grefenstette [19], and Backstrom et al. [1]. The recentness of these papers, all published in the past two years, demonstrates that this is an active area of research. Lieberman and Lin sought to determine the location of Wikipedia users, but did so using very specific properties of the Wikipedia dataset that do not generalize to the rest of the Web 2.0 world. In addition, they did not examine the natural behavior of Wikipedia users on their "user pages", which are the Wikipedia equivalent of user profiles.

Popescu and Grefenstette [19] attempted to predict the home country of Flickr users through the analysis of their place name photo tags and latitude and longitude geotags. In contrast to both this paper and the Lieberman and Lin work, once our model has been trained, our location prediction algorithms do not depend on a user submitting any geographic information. Popescu and Grefenstette also did no qualitative examination.

Backstrom et al. [1] used the social network structure of Facebook to predict location. As noted below, our work focuses on the content submitted by users, not the social network, although both approaches could be combined in future work.

In terms of prediction of profile fields or other withheld information, our work stands out from other recent research (e.g. [1, 14]) in two ways: (1) first we examine the user practices surrounding the information that we are trying to predict, and (2) we make predictions solely from content innate to its medium and do not leverage any portion of the social graph.

DATA COLLECTION

From April 18 to May 28, 2010, we collected over 62 million tweets from the Spritzer sample feed, using the Twitter streaming API[2]. The Spritzer sample represents a random selection of all public messages. Based on a recent report that Twitter produced 65 million tweets daily as of June 2010 [23], we estimate that our dataset represents about 3-4% of public messages.

From these 62 million tweets, we further identified the tweets that were in English using a two-step combination of LingPipe's text classifier[3] and Google's Language Detection API[4]. All together, we identified 31,952,964 English tweets from our 62 million tweets, representing 51% of our dataset.

---

[2] http://dev.twitter.com/pages/streaming_api

[3] http://alias-i.com/lingpipe/demos/tutorial/langid/read-me/html

[4] http://code.google.com/apis/ajaxlanguage/documentation/

This research purposely does not consider the recent change to the Twitter API that allows location information to be embedded in each individual tweet [25]. We made this choice for two reasons. First, our focus is on the geographic information revealed in the "location" field of user profiles, a type of geographic information that is prevalent across the Web 2.0 world. Second, we found that only 0.77% of our 62 million tweets contained this embedded location information. With such a small penetration rate, we were concerned about sampling biases.

STUDY 1: UNDERSTANDING EXPLICIT USER BEHAVIOR

Study 1: Methods

Our 32 million English tweets were created by 5,282,657 unique users. Out of these users, we randomly selected 10,000 "active" users for our first study. We defined "active" as having more than five tweets in our dataset, which reduced our sampling frame to 1,136,952 users (or 22% of all users). We then extracted the contents of these 10,000 users' location fields and placed them in a coding spreadsheet. Two coders examined the 10,000 location field entries using a coding scheme described below. Coders were asked to use any information at their disposal, from their cultural knowledge and human intuition to search engines and online mapping sites. Both coders agreed initially on 89.2% of the entries, and spent one day discussing and coming to an agreement on the remaining 10.8%.

The coding scheme was designed to determine the *quality* of the geographic information entered by users as well as the *scale* of any real geographic information. In other words, we were interested in examining the 10,000 location entries for their properties along two dimensions: quality and geographic scale. We measured quality by whether or not geographic information was imaginary or whether it was so ambiguous as to refer to no specific geographic footprint (e.g. "in jail" instead of "in Folsom Prison"). In the case of location field entries with even the most rudimentary real geographic information, we examined at what scale this information specified the user's location. In other words, did users disclose their country? Their state? Their city? Their address?

Since both coders are residents of the United States, only data that was determined to be within the United States was examined for scale. This choice was made due to the highly vernacular nature of many of the entries, thus requiring a great deal of cultural knowledge for interpretation.

Study 1: Results

Information Quality

As shown in Figure 2, only 66% of users manually entered any sort of valid geographic information into the location field. This means that although the location field is usually assumed by practitioners [25] and researchers (e.g. in [11] and [22]) to be a field that is as associated with geographic information as a date field is with temporal information, this is definitely not the case in our sample. The remaining one-third of users were roughly split between those that did not enter any information and those that entered either non-real locations, obviously non-geographic information, or locations that did not have specific geographic footprints.

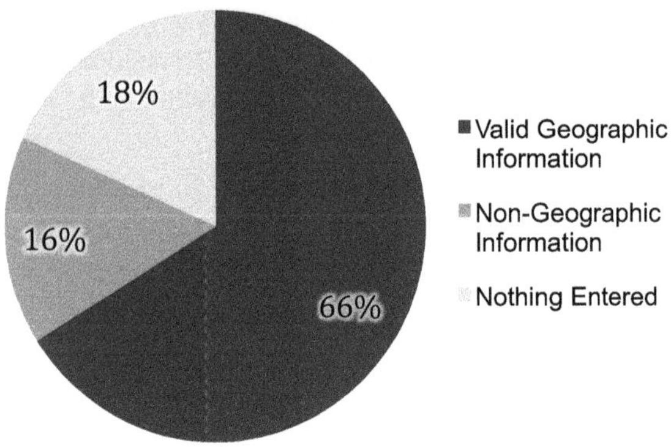

Figure 2: The distribution of manually entered location field data. Roughly one-third of users did not enter valid geographic information into the location field. 16% entered non-geographic information, while 18% entered nothing at all.

An analysis of the non-geographic information entered into the location field (the 16% in Figure 2) revealed it to be highly unpredictable in nature (see Table 1). A striking trend was the theme of Justin Bieber, who is a teenage singer. A surprising 61 users (more than 1 in 200 users) co-opted the location field to express their appreciation of the pop star. For instance, a user wrote that s/he is located in "Justin Biebers heart" (inspiring the title of this paper) and another user indicated s/he is from "Bieberacademy". Justin Bieber was not the only pop star that received plaudits from within the location field; United Kingdom "singing" duo Jedward, Britney Spears, and the Jonas Brothers were also turned into popular "locations".

Another common theme involved users co-opting the location field to express their desire to keep their location private. One user wrote "not telling you" in the location field and another populated the field with "NON YA BISNESS!!" Sexual content was also quite frequent, as were "locations" that were insulting or threatening to the reader (e.g. "looking down on u people"). Additionally, there was a prevalent trend of users entering non-Earth locations such as "OUTTA SPACE" and "Jupiter".

A relatively large number of users leveraged the location field to express their displeasure about their current location. For instance, one user wrote "preferably anywhere but here" and another entered "redneck hell".

Entering non-real geographic information into the location field was so prevalent that it even inspired some users in our sample to make jokes about the practice. For instance, one user populated the location field with "(insert clever phrase here)".

Frequency counts for these types of non-geographic information are reported in Table 1. To generate this table, non-geographic entries were coded by two human coders and the lists were merged. Categories were determined using a grounded approach, and each "location" was allowed to have zero or more categories. Because of the highly vernacular nature of this data, coders were instructed to only categorize when highly confident in their choice. As such, the numbers in Table 1 must be considered lower bounds.

Information Type	# of Users
Popular Culture Reference	195 (12.9%)
Privacy-Oriented	18 (1.2%)
Insulting or Threatening to Reader	69 (4.6%)
Non-Earth Location	75 (5.0%)
Negative Emotion Towards Current Location	48 (3.2%)
Sexual in Nature	49 (3.2%)

Table 1: A selection of the types of non-geographic information entered into the location field. Many of these categories exhibited large co-occurrence, such as an overlap between "locations" that were sexual in nature and those that were references to popular culture (particularly pop and movie stars). Percentages refer to the population of non-geographic information location field entries.

Note that, in the 66% of users who did enter real geographic information, we included all users who wrote *any* inkling of real geographic information. This includes those who merely entered their continent and, more commonly, those who entered geographic information in highly vernacular forms. For example, one user wrote that s/he is from "kcmo--call da po po". Our coders were able to determine this user meant "Kansas City, Missouri", and thus this entry was rated as valid geographic information (indicating a location at a city scale). Similarly, a user who entered "Bieberville, California" as her/his location was rated as having included geographic information at the state scale, even though the city is not real.

Information Scale

Out of the 66% of users with any valid geographic information, those that were judged to be outside of the United States were excluded from our study of scale. Users who indicated multiple locations (see below) were also filtered out. This left us with 3,149 users who were determined by both coders to have entered valid geographic information that indicated they were located in the United States.

When examining the scale of the location entered by these 3,149 users, an obvious city-oriented trend emerges (Figure 3). Left to their own devices, users by and large choose to disclose their location at exactly the city scale, no more and no less. As shown in Figure 3, approximately 64% of users specified their location down to the city scale. The next most popular scale was state-level (20%).

When users specified intrastate regions or neighborhoods, they tended to be regions or neighborhoods that engendered significant place-based identity. For example, "Orange

County" and the "San Francisco Bay Area" were common entries, as were "Harlem" and "Hollywood". Interestingly, studying the location field behavior of users located within a region could be a good way to measure the extent to which people identify with these places.

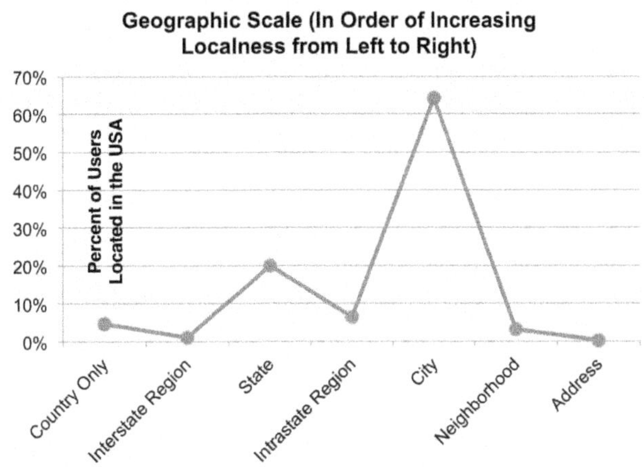

Figure 3: The scale of the geographic information entered by 3,149 users who indicated that they lived in the United States.

Multiple Locations

2.6% of the users (4% of the users who entered any valid geographic information) entered multiple locations. Most of these users entered two locations, but 16.4% of them entered three or more locations. Qualitatively, it appears many of these users either spent a great deal of time in all locations mentioned, or called one location home and another their current residence. An example of the former is the user who wrote "Columbia, SC. [atl on weekends]" (referring to Columbia, South Carolina and Atlanta, Georgia). An example of the latter is the user who entered that he is a "CALi b0Y $TuCC iN V3Ga$" (A male from California "stuck" in Las Vegas).

Automatically-entered Information

The most categorically distinct entries we encountered were the automatically populated latitude and longitude tags that were seen in many users' location fields. After much investigation, we discovered that Twitter clients such as ÜberTwitter for Blackberry smartphones entered this information. Approximately 11.5% of the 10,000 users we examined had these latitude and longitude tags in their location field. We did not include these users in Figure 2 or 3, as they did not manually enter their location data.

Study 1: Implications for Design

Failure of Traditional Geographic Information Tools

Our study on the information quality has vital implications for leveraging data in the location field on Twitter (and likely other websites). Namely, many researchers have assumed that location fields contain strongly typed geographic information, but our findings show this is demonstrably false. To determine the effect of treating Twitter's location field as strongly-typed geographic information, we took each of the location field entries that were coded as not having any valid geographic information (the 16% slice of the pie chart in Figure 2) and entered them into Yahoo! Geocoder. This is the same process used by Java et al. in [11]. A geocoder is a traditional geographic information tool that converts place names and addresses into a machine-readable spatial representation, usually latitude and longitude coordinates [7].

Of the 1,380 non-geographic location field entries, Yahoo! Geocoder determined 82.1% to have a latitude and longitude coordinate. As our coders judged none of these entries to contain any geographic information or highly ambiguous geographic information, this number should be zero (assuming no coding error). Some examples of these errors are quite dramatic. "Middle Earth" returned (34.232945, -102.410204), which is north of Lubbock, Texas. Similarly, "BieberTown" was identified as being in Missouri and "somewhere ova the rainbow", in northern Maine. Even "Wherever yo mama at" received an actual spatial footprint: in southwest Siberia.

Since Yahoo! Geocoder assumes that all input information is geographic in nature, the above results are not entirely unexpected. The findings here suggest that geocoders alone are not sufficient for the processing of data in location fields. Instead, data should be preprocessed with a geoparser, which disambiguates geographic information from non-geographic information [7]. However, geoparsers tend to require a lot of context to perform accurately. Adapting geoparsers to work with location field entries is an area of future work.

Attention to Scale in Automated Systems

Another important implication comes from the mismatch in revealed scale between the latitude and longitude generated automatically by certain Twitter clients and that revealed naturally by Twitter users. The vast majority of the machine-entered latitude and longitude coordinates had six significant digits after the decimal point, which is well beyond the precision of current geolocation technologies such as GPS. While it depends somewhat on the latitude, six significant digits results in geographic precision at well under a meter. This precision is in marked contrast with the city-level organic disclosure behavior of users. In our dataset, we found a total of only nine users (0.09% of the entire dataset) who had manually entered their location at the precision of an address, which is still less precise than a latitude and longitude coordinate expressed to six significant digits. However, this number could have been affected somewhat by the 30-character limit on the Twitter location field.

This mismatch leads us to a fairly obvious but important implication for design. Any system automatically populating a location field should do so, not with the exact latitude and longitude, but with an administrative district or vernacular region that contains the latitude and longitude coordinate. Fortunately, these administrative districts are easy to calculate with a reverse geocoding tool. Users should also be given a choice of the scale of this district or region (i.e. city, state, country), as users seem to have different preferences. This implication may apply to the "location" field on other sites as well as the location metadata associated with user-contributed content such as tweets and photos.

Other Implications

Another design implication is that users often want to have the ability to express sarcasm, humor, or elements of their personality through their location field. In many ways, this is not a surprise; people's geographic past and present have always been a part of their identity. We are particularly interested in the large number of users who expressed real geographic information in highly vernacular and personalized forms. Designers may want to invite users to choose a location via a typical map interface and then allow them to customize the place name that is displayed on their profile. This would allow users who enter their location in the form of "KC N IT GETS NO BETTA!!" (a real location field entry in our study) to both express their passion for their city and receive the benefits of having a machine-readable location, if they so desire.

Our findings also suggest that Web 2.0 system designers who wish to engender higher rates of machine-readable geographic information in users' location fields may want to force users to select from a precompiled list of places.

People who entered multiple locations motivate an additional important implication for design. This gives credence to the approach of Facebook and Flickr, which allow users to enter both a "current" location and a "hometown" location. However, the behavior of these users also suggests that this approach should be expanded. We envision a flexible system that would allow users to enter both an arbitrary number of locations and describe each of those locations (e.g. "home", "favorite place", etc.)

STUDY 2: UNDERSTANDING IMPLICIT USER BEHAVIOR THROUGH MACHINE LEARNING

In the first study, we used human judges to look closely at the explicit information included in the location field. However, in domains such as location-based services it may be important to discover the rough location of the large percentage of users who did not disclose their true location. Privacy advocates would likely also be interested in understanding whether or not this can be done. Given the results of prior research on location detection [1, 13, 19], we wanted to determine how much *implicit* location information users disclose simply by their day-to-day tweeting behavior. To do so, we used the data gathered above to conduct a set of machine learning experiments.

The goal of these experiments was to determine users' locations simply by examining the text content of their tweets. Specifically, we sought to predict a user's country and state solely from the user's tweets. We did not have enough data to work at a city level. As noted above, the contribution here is to demonstrate the implicit location sharing behavior of users in the context of their explicit behavior (with an eye towards location-based services, as well as privacy).

Study 2: Methods

In this subsection, we describe the general methodology behind our machine learning experiments, in which we use a classifier and a user's tweets to predict the country and state of that user. First, we discuss how we modeled each Twitter user for the classifier and how we shrank these models into a computationally tractable form. Next, we highlight the methodology behind the building of our training sets for the classifier and explain how we split off a subset of this data for validation purposes. Finally, we describe our classification algorithm and sampling strategies, as well as the results of our machine learning experiments.

Model Construction and Reduction

To classify user locations, we developed a Multinomial Naïve Bayes (MNB) model [16]. The model accepts input in the form of a term vector with each dimension in the vector representing a term and the value of the dimension representing the term count in a user's tweets. We also tried advanced topic models including Explicit Semantic Analysis [6]. However, a pilot study revealed that the simple term frequency (TF) MNB model greatly outperformed the more complex models. Thus, we only report the TF results.

For computational efficiency, we settled on using a fixed-length 10,000-term vector to represent each user in all cases. We tried two different methods for picking which 10,000 terms to use. The first was the standard frequency-based selection model in which we picked the 10,000 most common terms in our corpus. We called this algorithm "COUNT", for its reliance on term counting.

We also developed a more advanced algorithm designed to select terms that would discriminate between users from different locations. This simple heuristic algorithm, which we call the "CALGARI" algorithm, is based on the intuition that a classification model would perform better if the model includes terms that are more likely to be employed by users from a particular region than users from the general population. It is our assumption that these terms will help our classifier more than the words selected by the COUNT algorithm, which includes many terms that are common in all countries or states considered (e.g. "lol").

The CALGARI algorithm calculates a score for each term present in the corpus according to the following formula:

$$CALGARI(t) = \begin{cases} 0 \quad if \quad users(t) < MinU \\ \dfrac{\max(P(t \mid c = C))}{P(t)} \quad if \quad users(t) \geq MinU \end{cases}$$

where t is the input term, *users* is a function that calculates the number of users who have used t at least once, *MinU* is an input parameter to filter out individual idiosyncrasies and spam (set to either 2 or 5 in our experiments), and C is a geographic class (i.e. a state or country). The max function simply selects the maximum conditional probability of the term given each of the classes being examined. Terms are then sorted in descending order according to their scores and the top 10,000 terms are selected for the model. After picking the 10,000 terms, each user's Twitter feed was represented as a term vector using this list of 10,000 terms as dimensions, populated by the feed's term frequencies for each dimension.

A good example of the differences between CALGARI and COUNT was found in the average word vector for each algorithm for users in Canada. Among the terms with the highest weights for the CALGARI algorithm were "Canada", "Calgari", "Toronto" and "Hab". On the other hand, the top ten for COUNT included "im", "lol", "love", and "don't". Note that the CALGARI algorithm picked terms that are much more "Canadian" than those generated by the COUNT algorithm. This includes the #2 word "Calgari" (stemmed "Calgary"), which is the algorithm's namesake.

Developing Ground Truth Data

In order to build a successful classifier, we first needed to generate high-precision ground truth data. The main challenge here was to match a large group of users with their *correct* country and/or state. Through this group of users, the classifier could then learn about the tweeting patterns of each country and state population, and use these patterns to make predictions about *any* user.

Our starting point in developing the ground truth data was the 32 million English tweets created by over 5 million users. We first applied an extremely high-precision, very low-recall geocoder similar to that used in Hecht and Gergle [8]. The geocoder examines the text of the location field of each user and attempts to match it against all English Wikipedia article titles. If the location field matches (case-insensitive) a title exactly, latitude and longitude coordinates are searched for on the corresponding Wikipedia page[5]. If coordinates are found, the user is assigned that latitude and longitude as her location. If not, the user is excluded. We validated the precision of this method by testing it against the same non-geographic data that was input into the Yahoo! Geocoder in Study 1. Our Wikipedia-based geocoder correctly determined that none of the input entries was an actual location.

The Wikipedia-based geocoder and the automatically entered latitude and longitude points allowed us to identify the coordinates for 588,258 users. Next, we used spatial data available from ESRI and the United States Census to calculate the country and state (if in the United States) of the users. This process is known as reverse geocoding.

[5] Hundreds of thousands of Wikipedia articles have latitude and longitude points embedded in them by users.

In order to avoid problems associated with having a small number of tweets for a given user, we further restricted our ground truth data to those users who had contributed ten or more tweets to our dataset. In doing so, we removed 484,449 users from consideration.

We also required that all users in our dataset have a consistent country and state throughout the sample period. A tiny minority of users manually changed their location information during the sample period. In addition, a larger minority of users had their location changed automatically by Twitter clients. This temporal consistency filter pruned an additional 4,513 users from consideration.

In the end, our ground truth data consisted of 99,296 users for whom we had valid country and state information and 10 or more tweets. As noted earlier, this ground truth data was the sampling frame for deriving our training and validation sets for all machine learning experiments.

Training and Validation Sets

In each experiment, we used a specific subset (described below) of the ground truth data as training data. Since the CALGARI algorithm and the COUNT algorithm both involve "peeking" at the ground truth data to make decisions about which dimensions to include in the term vectors, the use of independent validation sets is vital. In all experiments, we split off 33% of the training data into validation sets. These validation sets were used *only* to evaluate the final performance of each model. In other words, the system is totally unaware of the data in the validation sets until it is asked to make predictions about that data. The validation sets thus provide an accurate view of how the machine learner would perform "in the wild." We used two sampling strategies for generating training and validation sets.

Sampling Strategies

In both our country-scale and state-scale experiments, we implemented two different sampling strategies to create the training data from the ground truth data. The first, which we call "UNIFORM", generated training and validation sets that exhibited a uniform distribution across classes, or countries and states in this context. This is the sampling strategy employed by Popescu and Grefenstette [19]. The experiments based on the UNIFORM data demonstrate the ability of our machine learning methods to tease out location information in the absence of the current demographic trends on Twitter.

The second sampling strategy, which we call "RANDOM", randomly chose users for our training and validation datasets. When using "RANDOM" data, the classifier considers the information that, for example, a user is much more likely to be from the United States than from Australia given population statistics and Twitter adoption rates. In other words, prior probabilities of each class (country or state) are considered. The results from experiments on the "RANDOM" data represent the amount of location information our classifier was able to extract *given* the demographics of Twitter.

Sampling Strategy	Model Selection	Accuracy	Baseline Accuracy	% of Baseline Accuracy
Country-Uniform-2500	**Calgari**	**72.71%**	**25.00%**	**291%**
Country-Uniform-2500	Count	68.44%	25.00%	274%
Country-Random-20K	**Calgari**	**88.86%**	**82.08%**	**108%**
Country-Random-20K	Count	72.78%	82.08%	89%
State-Uniform-500	**Calgari**	**30.28%**	**5.56%**	**545%**
State-Uniform-500	Count	20.15%	5.56%	363%
State-Random-20K	Calgari	24.83%	15.06%	165%
State-Random-20K	**Count**	**27.31%**	**15.06%**	**181%**

Table 2: A summary of results from the country-scale and state-scale experiments. The better performing model selection algorithm is bolded for each experiment. The CALGARI result reported is the best generated by *MinU* = 2 or *MinU* = 5.

Evaluation of the Classifier

In the end, we conducted a total of four experiments, each on a differently sampled training and validation set (Table 2). In each experiment, we tested both the CALGARI and COUNT algorithms, reporting the accuracy for both. The machine learning algorithm and training/validation set split were identical across all four experiments.

For the country-prediction experiments, we first focused on the UNIFORM sampling strategy. From our ground truth data, 2,500 users located in the United States, the United Kingdom, Canada, and Australia were randomly selected, resulting in 10,000 users total. These four countries were considered because there are less than 2,500 users in each of the other English-speaking countries represented among the 99,296 ground truth users. As noted above, 33% of these users were then randomly chosen for our validation set and removed from the training set. The remainder of the training set was passed to one of two model selection algorithms: CALGARI and COUNT. We then trained our Multinomial Naïve Bayes classifier with the models and evaluated on the validation set removed earlier.

Next, we performed the same exercise, replacing the UNIFORM with the RANDOM sampling strategy, which selected 20,000 different users from our ground truth data, all of whom lived in one of the four countries listed above.

Our state-prediction experiments were roughly the same as our country experiments, with the only major difference in the development of the UNIFORM datasets. Since the U.S. states range in population from California's 36+ million people to Wyoming's 0.5+ million people, our dataset was skewed in a similar fashion. We only had very limited data for small-population states like Wyoming. In fact, out of all our 99,296 ground truth users, we only had 31 from Wyoming. As such, we only included the 18 states with 500 or more users in our UNIFORM dataset.

Study 2: Results

Country-prediction Experiments

For the UNIFORM sampling strategy, the best performing algorithm was CALGARI, which was able to predict the country of a user correctly 72.7% of the time, simply by examining that user's tweets. Since we considered four different countries in this case, one could achieve 25% accuracy by simply randomly guessing. Therefore, we also report the accuracy of our classifier relative to the random baselines, which in the best case here was 291% (or 2.91x).

With the RANDOM sampling strategy, we needed to use a different baseline. Since 82.08% of sampled users were from the U.S., one could achieve 82.08% accuracy simply by guessing "United States" for every user. However, even with these relatively decisive prior probabilities, the CALGARI algorithm was capable of bringing the accuracy level approximately 1/3 of the way to perfection (88.9%). This represents a roughly 8.1% improvement.

State-prediction Experiments

The results of our state-prediction experiments were quite similar to those above but better. As can be seen in Table 2, the classifier's best UNIFORM performance relative to the random baseline was a great deal better than in the country experiment. The same is true for the RANDOM dataset, which included users from all 50 states (even if there were only a dozen or so users from some states).

The baselines were lower in each of these experiments because we considered more states than we did countries. The UNIFORM dataset included 18 states (or classes). The RANDOM dataset included all 50 plus the District of Columbia, with New York having the maximum representation at 15.06% of users. A baseline classifier could thus achieve 15.06% accuracy simply by selecting New York in every case.

Study 2: Discussion

Table 2 shows that in every single instance, the classifier was able to predict a user's country and/or state from the user's tweets at accuracies better than random. In most cases, the accuracy was several *times* better than random, indicating a strong location signal in tweets. As such, there is no doubt that *users implicitly include location information in their tweets*. This is true even if a user has not entered any explicit location information into the location field, or has entered a purposely misleading or humorous location (assuming that these users do not have significantly different tweeting behavior).

We did not attempt to find the optimal machine learning technique for location prediction from tweet content. As such, we believe that the accuracy of location prediction can be enhanced significantly by improving along four fronts: (1) better data collection, (2) more sophisticated machine learning techniques, (3) better modeling of implicit behaviors, especially those involving social contexts on Twitter, and (4) inclusion of more user metadata.

Study 2: Implications

An interesting implication of our work can be derived from the conditional probabilities tables of the classifier. By studying these tables, we developed a list of terms that could be used to both assist location-based services (LBS) and launch location "inference attacks" [14]. A selection of terms that have strong predictive power at the country and state scales is shown in Table 3.

Stemmed Word	Country	"Predictiveness"
"calgari"	Canada	419.42
"brisban"	Australia	137.29
"coolcanuck"	Canada	78.28
"afl"	Australia	56.24
"clegg"	UK	35.49
"cbc"	Canada	29.40
"yelp"	United States	19.08
Stemmed Word	**State**	**"Predictiveness"**
"colorado"	Colorado	90.74
"elk"	Colorado	41.18
"redsox"	Massachusetts	39.24
"biggbi"	Michigan	24.26
"gamecock"	South Carolina	16.00
"crawfish"	Louisiana	14.87
"mccain"	Arizona	10.51

Table 3: Some of the most predictive words from the (top) Country-Uniform-Calgari and (bottom) State-Uniform-Calgari experiments. Predictiveness is calculated as a probability ratio of the max. conditional probability divided by the average of the non-maximum conditional probabilities. This can be interpreted as the number of times more likely a word is to occur given that a person is from a specific region than from the average of the other regions in the dataset. In other words, an Arizonan is 10.51 times more likely to use the term "mccain" than the average person from the other states.

There appear to be four general categories of words that are particularly indicative of one's location. As has been known in the social sciences for centuries (e.g. the gravity model [5]) and seen elsewhere with user-generated content (UGC) [9,13], people tend to interact with nearby places. While in some cases this has been shown to be not entirely true [8], mentioning place names that are close to one's location is very predictive of one's location. In other words, tweeting about what you did in "Boston" narrows down your location significantly on average.

Tweeting about sports assists in location inference significantly, as can be seen in Table 3. Similarly, our classifier found that a user from Canada was six times more likely to tweet the word "hockey" than a user from any other country in our study.

A third major category of predictive terms involves current events with specific geographic footprint, emphasizing the spatio*temporal* nature of location field data. During the period of our data collection, several major events were occurring whose footprints corresponded almost exactly with the scales of our analyses. The classifier easily identified that terms like "Cameron", "Brown", and "Clegg" were highly predictive of users who were in the United Kingdom. Similarly, using terms related to the 2010 NBA playoffs was highly indicative of a user from the United States. More generally speaking, a machine learner could theoretically utilize any regionalized phenomenon. For example, a tweet about a flood at a certain time [24, 26] could be used to locate a user to a very local scale.

Finally, regional vernacular such as "hella" (California) and "xx" (U.K.) were highly predictive of certain locations. It is our hypothesis that this category of predictive words helped our term frequency models perform better than the more complex topic models. It seems that the more abstract the topic model, the more it smoothes out the differences in spelling or slang. Such syntactic features can be powerful predictors of location, however.

Given some Twitter users' inclination towards privacy, users might value the inclusion of this predictive word list into the user interface through warnings. Moreover, given some users' inclination towards location field impishness, users may enjoy the ability to easily use this type of information to fool predictive systems. In other words, through aversion or purposeful deception, users could avoid location inference attacks by leveraging these terms.

FUTURE WORK

Much future work has arisen from this study of explicit and implicit location field behavior. The most immediate is to examine the causal reasons for the organic location disclosure behavior patterns revealed by this work. This could be explored through surveys, for example.

With regard to the classifier, we are looking into including social network information into our machine learners. This would allow us to explore the combination of content-based and network-based [1] location prediction.

We also are working to extend our predictive experiments to other cultural memberships. For instance, there is nothing about our models that could not be adapted to predict gender, age group, profession, or even ethnicity.

Other directions of future work include examining per-tweet location disclosure, as well as evaluating location disclosure on social network sites such as Facebook. Of course, accessing a large and representative sample of location field data on Facebook will be a major challenge. We have also done research investigating the ability to use the surprisingly noisy yet very prevalent "time zone" field in user profiles to assist in location prediction.

CONCLUSION

In this work, we have made several contributions. We are the first to closely examine the information embedded in user profile location fields. Through this exploration, we have shown that many users opt to enter no information or non-real location information that can easily fool geographic information tools. When users do enter their real locations, they tend to be no more precise than city-scale.

We have also demonstrated that the explicit location-sharing behaviors should be examined in the context of implicit behaviors. Despite the fact that over one-third of Twitter users have chosen not to enter their location, we have shown that a simple classifier can be used to make predictions about users' locations. Moreover, these techniques only leverage the most basic activity in Twitter – the act of tweeting – and, as such, likely form something of a lower bound on location prediction ability.

Given the interest in LBS and privacy, we hope the research here will inspire investigations into other natural location-based user behaviors and their implicit equivalents.

ACKNOWLEDGEMENTS

We thank our reviewers, Bjoern Hartmann, and our colleagues at PARC and the Northwestern CollabLab for their helpful suggestions.

REFERENCES

1. Backstrom, L., Sun, E. and Marlow, C. Find Me If You Can: Improving Geographical Prediction with Social and Spatial Proximity. *WWW '10*, Raleigh, NC.
2. Barkhuus, L., Brown, B., Bell, M., Hall, M., Sherwood, S. and Chalmers, M. From Awareness to Repartee: Sharing Location within Social Groups. *CHI '08*, Florence, Italy, 497-506.
3. boyd, d., Golder, S. and Lotan, G. Tweet, Tweet, Retweet: Conversational Aspects of Retweeting on Twitter. *HICSS '10*, Kauai, HI.
4. Miller, C. and Wortham, J. Technology Aside, Most People Still Decline to Be Located. *The New York Times*. August 30, 2010.
5. Fellman, J.D., Getis, A. and Getis, J. *Human Geography: Landscapes of Human Activities*. Mcgraw-Hill Higher Education, 2007.
6. Gabrilovich, E. and Markovitch, S. Computing Semantic Relatedness using Wikipedia-based Explicit Semantic Analysis. *IJCAI '07*, Hyberabad, 1606-1611.
7. Hecht, B. and Gergle, D. A Beginner's Guide to Geographic Virtual Communities Research. *Handbook of Research on Methods and Techniques for Studying Virtual Communities*, IGI, 2010.
8. Hecht, B. and Gergle, D. On The "Localness" Of User-Generated Content. *CSCW '10*, Savannah, Georgia.
9. Hecht, B. and Moxley, E. Terabytes of Tobler: Evaluating the First Law in a Massive, Domain-Neutral Representation of World Knowledge. *COSIT '09*, L'Aber Wrac'h, France, 88-105.
10. Honeycutt, C. and Herring, S.C. Beyond Microblogging: Conversation and Collaboration via Twitter. *HICCS '09*.
11. Java, A., Song, X., Finin, T. and Tseng, B. Why We Twitter: Understanding Microblogging Usage and Communities. *Joint 9th WEBKDD and 1st SNA-KDD Workshop '07*, San Jose, CA, 56-65.
12. Krishnamurthy, B., Gill, P. and Arlitt, M. A Few Chirps about Twitter. *First Workshop on Online Social Networks*, Seattle, WA, 19-24, 2008.
13. Lieberman, M.D. and Lin, J. You Are Where You Edit: Locating Wikipedia Users Through Edit Histories. *ICWSM '09,* San Jose, CA.
14. Lindamood, J., Heatherly, R., Kantarcioglu, M. and Thuraisingham, B. Inferring Private Information Using Social Network Data. *WWW '09*, Madrid, Spain.
15. Ludford, P.J., Priedhorsky, R., Reily, K. and Terveen, L.G. Capturing, Sharing, and Using Local Place Information. *CHI '07*, San Jose, CA, 1235-1244.
16. McCallum, A. and Nigam, K. A Comparison of Event Models for Naive Bayes Text Classification. *AAAI-98 Workshop on Learning for Text Categorization*, 41-48.
17. Naaman, M., Boase, J. and Lai, C.-H. Is it Really About Me? Message Content in Social Awareness Streams. *CSCW '10*, Savannah, GA.
18. Panciera, K., Priedhorsky, R., Erickson, T. and Terveen, L.G. Lurking? Cyclopaths? A Quantitative Lifecycle Analysis of User Behavior in a Geowiki. *CHI '10*, Atlanta, GA, 1917-1926.
19. Popescu, A. and Grefenstette, G. Mining User Home Location and Gender from Flickr Tags. *ICWSM '10*.
20. Priedhorsky, R. and Terveen, L.G. The Computational Geowiki: What, Why, and How. *CSCW '08*, San Diego.
21. Reddy, S., Shilton, K., Denisov, G., Cenizal, C., Estrin, D. and Srivastava, M. Biketastic: Sensing and Mapping for Better Biking. *CHI '10*, Atlanta, GA, 1817-1820.
22. Sakaki, T., Okazaki, M. and Matsuo, Y. Earthquake Shakes Twitter Users: Real-time Event Detection by Social Sensors. *WWW '10*, Raleigh, NC.
23. Schonfeld, E. Costolo: Twitter Now Has 190 Million Users Tweeting 65 Million Times A Day. *TechCrunch*. http://techcrunch.com/2010/06/08/twitter-190-million-users/, 2010.
24. Starbird, K., Palen, L., Hughes, A.L. and Vieweg, S. Chatter on The Red: What Hazards Thread Reveals about the Social Life of Microblogged Information. *CSCW '10*, Savannah, GA.
25. Twitter. Location, Location, Location. *twitterblog*. http://blog.twitter.com/2009/08/location-location-location.html, 2009.
26. Vieweg, S., Hughes, A.L., Starbird, K. and Palen, L. Microblogging During Two Natural Hazards Events: What Twitter May Contribute to Situational Awareness. *CHI '10*, Atlanta, GA, 1079-1088.

An Open, Social Microcalendar for the Enterprise: Timely?

Werner Geyer[1], Casey Dugan[1], Beth Brownholtz[1], Mikhil Masli[2], Elizabeth Daly[1], David R Millen[1]

[1]IBM T.J. Watson Research
One Rogers Street, Cambridge, MA 02142
werner.geyer, cadugan, beth_brownholtz, david_r_millen{@us.ibm.com}

[2]GroupLens Research
University of Minnesota
Minneapolis, Minnesota, USA
masli@cs.umn.edu

ABSTRACT

We present the system design and rational for a novel social microcalendar called Timely. Our system has been inspired by previous research on calendaring and popular social network applications, in particular microblogging. Timely provides an open, social space for enterprise users to share their events, socialize, and discover what else is going on in their network and beyond. A detailed analysis of the events shared by users during the site's first 47 days reveals that users willingly share their time commitments despite an existing culture of restricted calendars.

Author Keywords

Social software, electronic calendars, GCS, microcalendar.

ACM Classification Keywords

H5.m. Information interfaces and presentation (e.g., HCI): Miscellaneous.

General Terms

Experimentation, Human Factors, Design.

INTRODUCTION

The Social Web has changed the way we share and interact with content on the Internet today. It has moved content such as photos, videos, and bookmarks, which previously sat on users' desktop machines onto sites such as flickr.com, youtube.com, and del.icio.us. Users and their social networks are able to socialize around the content they have uploaded to these sites; and discover interesting content uploaded by others. The chunks of data being shared on the Social Web have begun decreasing in size as well, from page-length blog entries to 140-character microblog status updates. We use the new paradigms offered by the Social Web to revisit decades of research on calendaring.

Electronic calendars first became available to enterprise users in the early 1980s, typically as a feature of office tools [12,16]. Although users saw their potential benefits in helping to minimize the time spent scheduling meetings, they were not well adopted for the next ten years. Reasons included the lack of usability compared to paper calendars [16], and poorly networked organizations. This changed dramatically in the 1990s when calendars become a well adopted key office technology by the end of the millennium [12, 21].

Since then, electronic calendars have become more integrated into enterprise and personal information systems, more accessible through mobile devices [8], smarter [18] and more interoperable through standards. However, the basic concepts have remained more or less the same. While the electronic calendar is a reliable personal time management tool that helps with scheduling, reminding, tracking time and temporal orientation [20, 21], it has been mostly used as a static, closed repository of events. With a few exceptions (e.g., SUN nurtured a corporate culture with open access to calendar information [12]), access to electronic calendars is often closed or restricted, e.g., in Lotus Notes within IBM users can only see the blocked time of coworkers without any details, unless they are given explicit access.

Interestingly, early calendar research has described the value of open access models [11]. This includes finding the location and availability of a person, discovering relevant and interesting meetings, understanding the degree to which a meeting is open to interruption and rescheduling, or even learning how the company functions. Moreover, awareness of others' activities within the enterprise allows one to get to know one's colleagues better on a professional and personal basis [2] and provides opportunities for social interactions around upcoming and past events.

The research in this paper describes the system design and early lessons learned from a 6-week trial of a novel online microcalendaring system called *Timely*. The Timely design addresses a number of calendaring opportunities mentioned earlier, such as open access, social interaction, and discoverability, and combines them with a person-centric sharing model. We call Timely a *microcalendar* because its design and interaction model have been inspired by popular microblogging sites like Twitter. Our system aims to complement existing calendars, not replace them. Hence, we did not replicate traditional calendar functionality, but instead sought to provide an outlet for enterprise users to broadcast their own time commitments, socialize around these, and discover the events of coworkers.

A major challenge for our project was the fact that IBM has been using traditional desktop calendaring systems for over 20 years: would the employees be willing to share their calendar events with each other after having been exposed to a restricted access model for such a long time? On the other hand, our company also has been using social software, including social network applications, for more than a decade now, i.e. employees openly share other types of content such as photos, bookmarks, blogs etc. An initial look at an internal social network site revealed a wealth of time-based information in the Twitter-like status messages posted. While most of the time-based information was in reference to what users were doing "now" (i.e. "in a meeting for the next hour"), we were encouraged by these initial findings and suspected that employees would also be willing to share future plans and events. Hence, we deployed Timely in IBM to better understand how social microcalendaring supports enterprise users. This paper focuses on the system design and describes the first 47 days of usage, including what types of events employees were willing to share. Our research goal was to understand people's willingness and motivations to share calendar data.

The paper is structured as follows: We first review existing work related to calendaring and enterprise social software. We then describe our design and the rationale behind our decisions. Using data gathered during the site's first 47 days, we describe how people used the system and provide a detailed analysis of the content shared. We conclude with a discussion of design implications for subsequent versions of Timely and directions for future research.

RELATED WORK

Groupware Calendaring Systems: Early research on electronic calendaring focused mostly on Groupware Calendaring Systems (GCSs) for personal and group time management. PCAL and MPCAL were early command-line systems developed and evaluated at MIT [9]. They provided role-based read access to calendars for other users. Kincaid et al. [16] surveyed office workers on their use of electronic and paper calendars and found that the use of paper calendars still prevailed. They offered user interface and interaction suggestions on how to improve electronic calendars. Grudin and Palen [12] examined the successful adoption of group calendars at Microsoft and SUN. They compared studies of failures in the 80's with the later success of GCSs in SUN and Microsoft. They describe socio-technical factors that led to predominantly bottom-up adoption. This work also illustrates different access models to calendar information: open versus restricted. Grudin [11] describes a case study of calendar use addressing access and transparency in a GCS and their benefits. He also describes the online calendar as "a massive organizational self-logging system that has great potential as a source of [..] knowledge and learning." This statement touches upon what Ehrlich [4] calls the "dual needs" of retrieving calendar information: personal for oneself but also making it available to others. Palen [20, 21] further explored the personal-social duality of calendars. Her ethnographic work investigates group calendaring at SUN where open calendaring systems facilitated the understanding of the use of calendars for both personal work and social coordination. Her work illustrates that calendars can go beyond scheduling meetings and also function as distributed information and communication systems.

Family Calendaring: During the last decade, calendaring research has focused much on family calendars, calendar use at home, and the intersection of work and family. Family calendars are different than work calendars in that they are more a group calendar, rather than a personal calendar, with a primary scheduler maintaining it. Its main purpose is public awareness and coordination based on the shared information. Neustaedter et al. [19] argue that moving from paper to digital made coordination at the workplace easier; whereas for families, it is the opposite, because sharing a digital calendar in a public space as an awareness calendar is difficult. Grimes and Brush [10] studied 15 working parents looking at how they manage their personal and professional schedules. Their work shows how personal scheduling blends into work scheduling and vice versa and the tension that arises from the role as a parent and employee.

Enterprise social software: There is a large body of research on the use of social software in the enterprise. Several studies on blogging in the enterprise show how blogging aids collaboration and communication, community building and information discovery [3, 14, 15]. Millen et al. [17] demonstrate that social bookmarking is often done out of personal motivation but adds community value and solves an enterprise information discovery problem. Hasan et al [13] discuss benefits and adoption issues of Wikis in corporations. A larger body of work on a system called Beehive, a social network site for the enterprise [1, 5, 6, 7, 22], covers understanding user motivations, use of new social content types, the impact on social capital, and the use of recommender and incentive systems. More recently, microblogging has successfully made an appearance in enterprises. Zhang et al. [24] describe adoption patterns, general use, and the value of a microblogging system in a medium size enterprise. Yammer, the microblogging system used, has also recently incorporated user-created events into the update stream.

Calendaring on the Social Web. Outside the enterprise, the Social Web has recently produced a number of innovations that are related to our work. For example, doodle.com is a social meeting scheduling system which makes scheduling transparent to all participants. Tungle.me is similar but goes beyond by offering tight calendar integration and also a profile page on which users can selectively publish calendar entries. Google Calendar is a popular online calendar whose access control and multi-calendar overlay features are beyond what standard desktop calendars offer today. Tungle.me has just recently published an online manifesto titled "The Calendar of the Future, [23]" featuring video clips of thought leaders in the space covering transparency, mobile access, and semantic relationships. There are also a number of web sites that support event sharing and discovery, such as Facebook, going.com or upcoming.yahoo.com. These sites are focused on leveraging social networks to help users in finding something to do and meeting like-minded people. Events on these sites typically involve a group of people rather than a single individual, and in the case of going.com and upcoming.yahoo.com are typically "official" events, comprised of concerts, festivals, sports, arts etc. Closest to our system is Plancast, a site that allows sharing and socializing around upcoming plans.

TIMELY SYSTEM DESIGN

The Timely design was driven by the desire to push the limits of existing calendars – in particular the value propositions of open-access calendars in earlier research [11, 10] – and leverage the success of the Social Web, which has changed the way we interact and share content on the Internet today. Microblogging in particular influenced our design because of the time-ordered nature of short posts and network-based discovery of these. In essence, Timely users can broadcast events by posting them to their event stream. Other users who are subscribed to this user will receive these events on their homepage event stream.

We did not seek to replace existing calendar functionality in IBM but rather complement it. As such we avoided re-implementing traditional calendar features. The existing corporate calendar, Lotus Notes, is a desktop client. While that system supports some extensibility, we felt that working in that application directly would limit our ability to reinvent calendars and also constrain the general availability of our system. Hence, we decided to build a separate web-based application. Figures 1 and 2 show screenshots of Timely, which we will illustrate as we describe our design guides.

Open Access

While the potential benefits of open calendars have been previously documented by researchers [10, 11], many enterprise calendaring systems still restrict access to a person's calendar, including IBM's internal deployment of Lotus Notes. While Lotus Notes can be configured for open access, IT departments often restrict visibility by default. Typically, others can only see "busy" blocks of time, with the ability to give another user direct access to your entire calendar. Many calendar systems position access control at the level of the calendar, which makes it awkward if one wanted to quickly share one event but not another within the same calendar. Access to individual events on one's calendar can only be accomplished by adding individuals as participants to a scheduled meeting. The need for finer-grained sharing of calendar events has been highlighted by Grimes and Brush [10] as a socially more acceptable way for combining work and family calendars.

In order to overcome these limitations, we wanted to provide access control at the individual event level. Further, our research goal was to understand people's willingness and motivations to share calendar data. Therefore, we designed Timely to support only two levels of access control: public (default) and private, and chose to position Timely as the place employees go to broadcast their time-based data to others. Public events are visible to everyone on the site. Private events you have created appear in your event stream, but others following you will not see them. This strategy was also aligned with our research goal because we first wanted to understand people's willingness to openly share events. A finer-grained model would have made it more difficult to weed out the differences between private and public. However, this approach had its own risks. Firstly, the all-or-nothing access control was likely to deter people who would be willing to share information with only a selective group of people. Secondly, the existing restrictive calendaring culture was not conducive to people's willingness to share time-based events [12]. However, we did conceive a future access control model based on social networks which we were ready to put in place if needed, and will likely be supported in future Timely versions.

Discoverability

Our design takes the open access inspired by early calendar research a step further by layering in discoverability features common on the Social Web today. While some early calendars like Calendar Manager [11] supported open access, users explicitly had to specify a user whose calendar they would like to "browse" by providing a hostname and user name. Since you have to know who you want to browse beforehand, it makes serendipitous discovery of relevant events difficult. Going from one calendar to another also quickly becomes a tedious, manual "data mining" activity.

Our design was mostly inspired by microblogging sites whose time-ordered stream of text messages lends itself naturally to time-based events. However, instead of using recency as ordering principle, we use the time the event is taking place. Combined with a following model in which you can subscribe to users whose events you are interested in (just like Twitter), a user's home page on Timely shows all upcoming and past events of their social network at one glance (see Figure 1A). Similar to Twitter, we also show your own events along with your network's events, i.e. at any time, a user can see how their time relates to the temporal order of events of their social network (a user's events are color-coded in orange to be easily identifiable in

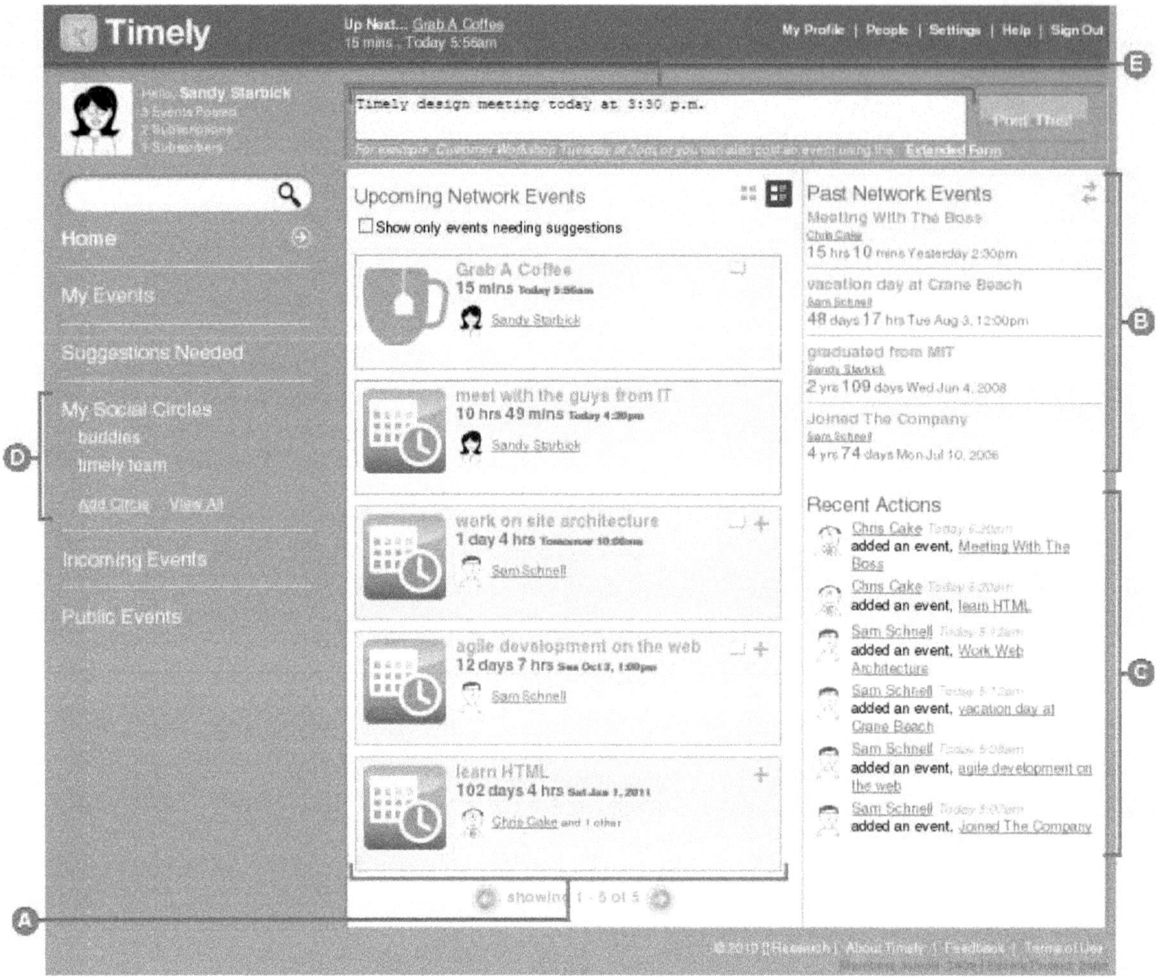

Figure 1. The Timely Home Page showing what's coming up in your network of subscribed users.

the event stream). While the left hand column consists of upcoming events, the right hand column (Figure 1B) consists of a condensed view of events that have recently taken place, with the most recent events at the top. We felt that showing the past side-by-side with the future might serve as an immediate reminder to users of recent activity. In addition, recent actions done by those you subscribe to on the site, e.g. commenting, creating events etc. are also shown at the bottom of the right column (C). This way, users can, for example, discover events that might be happening in the far future but were created recently.

We chose an asymmetric subscription model like Twitter instead of a reciprocated friendship model like Facebook so that users could follow others who posted events they found interesting, without there being a requirement that the other user is equally interested in his/her events, thereby reducing the cost of event discoverability. Given that the number of subscriptions can grow quickly, we felt that it would be important to provide a mechanism to filter events by a subset of users. "Social circles" (Figure 1D) are lists of users, similar to lists in Twitter. One can create social circles of users and filter events by them by clicking on that circle name. Additional ways to discover events are public events (from everyone inside IBM), incoming events (someone notified you about an event), or search.

A site with public event sharing has numerous opportunities for making personalized recommendations for discovery. We anticipated that in addition to browsing list views of events, users might spend much of their time viewing individual events. Hence, we decided to add related event recommendations to individual event pages (Figure 2A). Events having textual overlap between their tags, titles and descriptions are considered related. For example, Figure 2 shows an event that has been tagged with "design" and a similar event called "Design Seminar" is listed as related. Social tagging also opens opportunities for future browsing capabilities, such as tag clouds or lists of trending tags.

Social Interaction

Traditional calendars offer little to support social interactions except for the built-in scheduling mechanisms. Built on email messaging, they support some social coordination. Calendar Manager with its public access went beyond that by being a distributed information system that supports coordination [21]. However, communication about events typically happens outside the calendar which often becomes the static repository to track those events. Openly sharing events and making them discoverable offers opportunities for communication within or even outside of one's network. In order to support this, similar to other social media sites, Timely provides a page for each event, that captures all the social interaction around it by allowing users to leave comments (Figure 2B). On this page, users can also leverage existing communication channels, such as Twitter or IBM's internal microblogging system (LC) by posting to these services, with references back to the event. Moreover, a user can notify others of an event on the site whether he created it or merely found it and knows others who may be interested (Figure 2C).

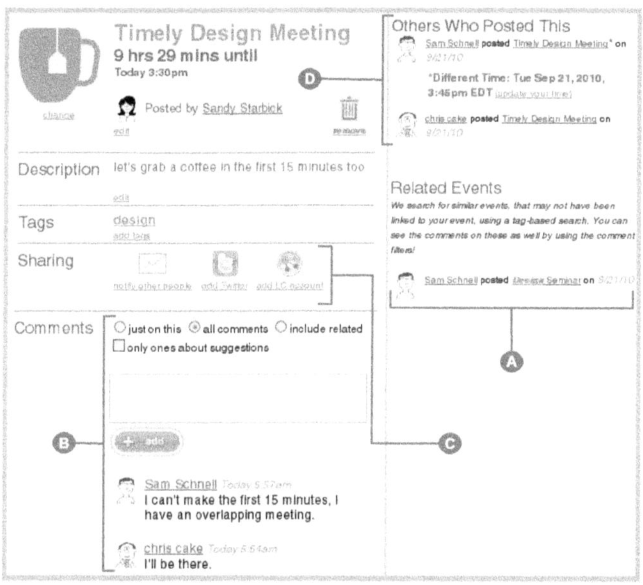

Figure 2. Details of an individual event page.

Natural Event Entry

Entering events into traditional calendar applications often feels heavy-weight because of the form-based input with numerous fields. To address this, our design allows users to post time-based status updates from any page in a single update box rather than requiring the user to fill out a detailed form (Figure 1E). We use natural language processing (NLP) capabilities of the Java library JChronic to extract the time/date portion from the entered text. For example, "Timely Design meeting today at 3:30 p.m." gets parsed to an event named "Timely design meeting" occurring that day at 3:30 pm. If the parsing is successful, the site redirects to the page created for this event (Figure 2). However, if the date parsing fails, or if the user needs to create an event with additional information such as description or thumbnail image, the system offers form-based input as a fallback mechanism. Similarly, Timely allows users to import microblog updates they posted (both internally and externally) that contain date/time information detected by NLP as events.

User-Centric Event Sharing

Event sharing requires the ability to associate multiple people with an event. Typically this is supported through the notion of participants or attendance on a single event instance. While this group-centric model supports sharing and aggregating information such as comments and involved people very well, it is not conducive to managing personal time commitments. For example, in the group-centric model, if the "owner" deletes it, the event instance would be removed from other people's calendars.

Timely is designed with a user-centric model, in which users post their own time commitments, e.g., a conference event he/she is going to. If another user wishes to associate herself with this event, she can then simply press a button to post it to her own event stream. This action is similar to retweeting a status message on Twitter. The date/time and name of the event are copied, and a loose linkage is maintained between the events in the database which allows us to display them together, aggregate comments across those events, and synchronize events if required. This also allows users to keep the same event while maintaining their own time preferences for that event, thus attempting to blend personal and social time management.

In Figure 2D, the "Others who posted this" section shows all those who have posted this event to their own stream. It also shows that Sam Schnell, who added the Timely design meeting event has changed the time to be 3:45 p.m. instead of 3:30 p.m. today. In the comment section he explains he'll be late because of an overlapping meeting. Everyone who looks at this event's page (or any additional posts of it) will see that Sam's event is listed as occurring at a different time, while Sam can still use this to manage and accurately broadcast his own time commitments.

DATA COLLECTION

We deployed Timely on the IBM Intranet and collected data over a period of 47 days, from July 27, 2010 to September 10, 2010. During this time, 2,395 registered Timely members created 2,206 events with a total of 254 comments. Timely was launched to a small group of 50 people in our department and in associated divisions. Through Timely's subscription model, built-in invitation messages, and word of mouth, the site grew to 2,395 registered users within the first 47 days as shown in Figure 3. An initial jump in members and events was followed by constant linear growth, with steps indicating weekends of lower activity. Users are from 62 different departments, reside in 57 different countries, 19% are people managers, and the majority (97%) were not from the research division. Content created by our team was removed from the data set.

A second source of data was semi-structured interviews with eight users of the site, selected based on their activity on the site. They were not affiliated with our project nor part of our group. Two members of the team conducted these interviews over the phone (7) and in person (1). The interviews were relatively short and covered very general aspects of the site with a focus on open access. A third source of information was postings, comments and feedback from a public discussion forum and bug database used to support our internal deployment.

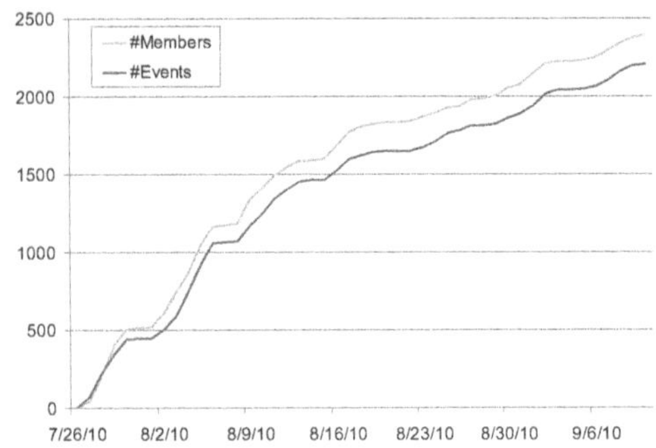

Figure 3: Cumulative number of members and events.

RESULTS

Our analysis of the Timely dataset addresses general usage of the system structured by the three major design principles: open access and sharing, discoverability, and social interaction. We were particularly surprised by how willingly employees shared information about their plans and whereabouts, typically only found in a personal calendar. Inspired, we conducted a detailed content analysis to better understand the types of events shared.

Content Type	Total	% of Users	Avg / Median Per Active User
Events	2,206	32.9% (788)	2.8 / 2
Comments	254	4% (97)	2.62 / 1
Subscriptions	11,664	77.5%(1,854)	6.29 / 3
Social Circles	274	8.4% (200)	1.37 / 1

Table 1. Timely content types created during the study period.

General Usage

Sharing Events

One of Timely's major design principles is open access. The system was designed for users to be able to publicly broadcast events. Our data suggests that users embraced this. About a third of the users posted events with an average of 2.8 events per person for those who posted (see Table 1). Event creation was among the top 5 activities on the site (Figure 4) and 98.8% of all events on the site were public. Note that the default setting was public and users had to explicitly check off a box if they wanted to make something private. The detailed content analysis following later, reveals that the types of events resemble what one would typically find on a calendar, i.e. users did not only share "official", already-public events but also personal content.

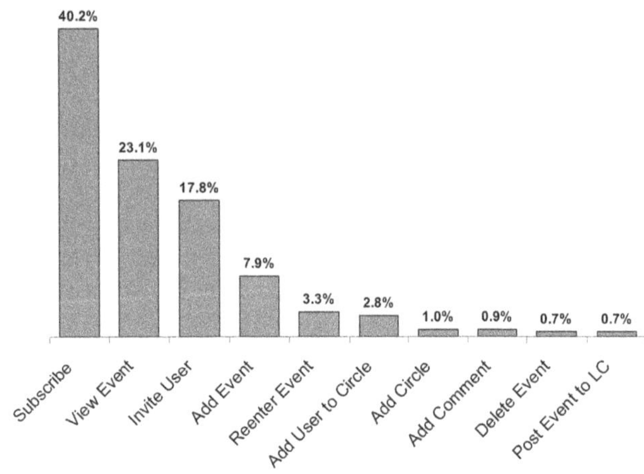

Figure 4. Top 10 actions on Timely of all logged activities.

Interview data illustrates different sharing attitudes, with a user on one end of the spectrum saying she would only publicly share 5% of the events from her restricted, desktop calendar, while a user on the other end said he would share up to 80% of his events. The rest of those interviewed fell into the range between them, willing to share around 30%. From some of the more "conservative" sharers, we heard that it wasn't necessarily because others should not know about events taking place, though that was mentioned at least once: *"the project manager wouldn't be thrilled, don't want random people on project calls."* Instead, they said they would not share a higher percentage of events in their personal calendar because they simply didn't think others would find them valuable: *"me doing my day to day job... not much value for other people"* and *"regular group meetings I wouldn't share because everyone knows."* One user said, about sharing the events he didn't think others would find valuable: *"If it wasn't extra work for me to manage it, [sharing's] not a big deal. No benefit for me to do even two seconds of extra work to get that in [Timely]. If there's no extra work [added automatically], I probably wouldn't go delete them."* But for those events he did think others would find valuable: *"even if it takes 15 seconds, if it benefits even 1 person, it's worth the 15 seconds."* Every user mentioned the need to sometimes share events with a broader audience: *"will use it when going to a client, people in my environment can provide me more input or value to help me," "[for things] I want to advertise or want other people to know about," "I say, 'here's an event, it's kinda cool, I can't go to it, but I'll share it.'"* Two users spoke specifically of this being a way for others to learn more about them through their events: *"where my usage would go in the long run: the external face of my activity that I want people to know of"* & *"I think of events in [Timely] as tags of what [I'm] socially and professionally associated with."*

Of the 2,206 events created, 36.5% (806) were created using the form-based input, 24.0% (530) were created as a part of prompting users during the signup process, 21.1%

(465) came from the free-form text entry box at the top of the page, 15.6% events (345) resulted from users "re-posting" events that others had previously added, and 2.7% (60) were imported from time-based microblog updates from internal and external services during signup .

While we had hoped to save our users the cumbersome process of filling out a form, it was used almost twice as often as the free-form text entry box in practice. However, this may not have been their first choice. As described in the system description, we also forwarded users to the form-based input page if there was a problem parsing their input from the free-form text box. Approximately 52% of events created through the form-based input page were immediately preceded by a recorded parsing-error from the free-form text box by that user. In those cases, the user was likely reentering the same event he had tried to enter in the simplified way. We also heard from users during our trial that the parsing technology led to frustration. In interviews, entering dates was described as *"tricky"* and requiring a *"learning curve,"* while one user went as far as saying that it *"was a barrier for me to want to share more events."*

Discovering Events

Our second major design principle was discoverability and in order to support this, we designed and implemented a following model similar to popular microblogging sites. Figure 4 shows that the most popular activity on the site was subscribing to other users: 40.2% of all logged activities were subscription actions and 77.5% of all users during the study period had one or more subscriptions with an average of 6.29 among those with one or more (Table 1). 8.4% of our users also created social circles with 1.37 on average; with valid circles having an average of 4.59 users.

Subscribing to others and creating lists enabled users to discover relevant content. Our data shows that discovery was another major activity of our users (see Figure 4: 23.1% of all activities were view actions). Of these views, 60% came from users looking at the pages of their own events, and 40% came from looking at other users' events. We further looked into where users had discovered other people's events. We were not able to determine which, if any, Timely page a user came from when viewing an event 35.5% of the time. In the remaining cases, 40.1% users discovered other peoples' events from their home page, 26.2% navigated to events from the page for public events, 25.2% of users came from another event page (from a re-posting of the event or through related events), 5.7% came from another user's list of events, and 2.9% came from a social circle page.

In interviews, users often spoke of the value of discovery: *"Good that people all over the world see the event."* In particular, for reaching out beyond one's network: *"That's the power of such a tool, other people subscribe, you get information from people you don't know. People I know, I can contact them."* And described engaging in such discovery themselves: *"When I want to take a break from the day to day and look for something interesting outside my normal sphere of what's going on"* and *"When I go to [the site] I'm looking at - Are there events I didn't know about that I would be interested in joining?"* They also emphasized that broadcasting, with subsequent discovery by others, felt less formal than other methods of informing people about events. One user said, *"Stuff I think deserves attention to wider public. Where a calendar invite would be overkill,"* while another said, *"It is a good way of putting something out there, But not bother them. [...] If they have an extra 10-15 minutes, they can discover it. Seems like an unobtrusive way to give them the information."*

Socializing Around Events

Our design emphasizes social interaction through comments and the interview data was supportive of the value of this kind of interactions around events. While many of those interviewed said they wanted to share events that others would find valuable, some went even further, saying that they explicitly shared events hoping for a dialogue with others: *"If someone sees me having a meeting internally about [...] a specific project, and somebody thinks '[....]I can contribute and help [John] better prepare or share some ideas' that's the value I think [sharing] brings. So, basically, conversation starters."* Another user interviewed went as far as saying that he viewed it as a success that his event was able to generate conversation: *"I had some people comment on this. It worked. [Jane Smith] said 'This is cool, it's the first I've heard of it.'"* Another stated that while he did not experience this kind of interaction, he would use the system more if it did happen: *"If I go to a client, can anybody help me with this? Then I would use it."*

We did find anecdotal evidence of conversations in which people followed up on events posted on Timely, e.g. asking for details, or connecting to users who they had not known before. In one such case, a user found out about someone else going to the same conference and both connected on the site, planning to see each other at the conference. However, overall the commenting activity on our site seemed relatively low at 0.9% of all actions with only 4% of all users leaving comments.

Content Analysis

In order to find out what kind of event content our users were sharing publicly on Timely, we manually categorized 1,271 randomly selected public events of the 2,206 total events on the site. Two researchers did a level-setting session with 100 of these events, then independently coded the rest. Cases of disagreement were later discussed and reconciled. We were not able to code roughly 9% (114) of the selected events because of lack of information in the title and description, or they clearly were test data only. This schema gave us 1,157 categorized events. We used an open coding scheme to determine the type of activity it represented. In addition we also coded each event as work-related versus personal, and group versus individual.

The work dimension was based on whether the event was related to a *work activity* or whether it was *personal* in nature. Previous research has found that employees readily share personal information such as "outside activities through status messages" or "personal life through photos" [1]; one enterprise social networking site found that only 29.7% of lists shared were categorized as "work-related" [6]. Events classified as work included team meetings, customer presentations, technical conferences, etc, for example: "UI Team Daily Call." The work category also included social events taking part through the work context, such as "IBM picnic nashoba valley." Events categorized as personal included vacations, plans involving family members, sporting events, etc, for example: "Help my son move in at NC State." Events with no obvious or explicitly stated business tie (such as "Italy", likely a personal vacation) were categorized as personal.

The individual/group dimension related to whether the event involved only the user who created it or included social participation of other people. Today, the majority of social networking tools which support event sharing (such as Facebook externally or enterprise-based Beehive [2]) typically focus on large-scale events with multiple participants, such as parties, concerts, etc. Similarly, we hypothesized that many of the events in employees' traditional calendaring tools involved other people as well, such as meetings. We wanted to get a sense for whether events shared on our system included those that were more individual in nature. The group category included any event where it was obvious other people would be taking part with the creator, such team dinners and conferences, as well as one-on-one meetings. An example of an event labeled as group was "web 2.0 expo NY." Individual events were those that involved personal tasks/deadlines, personal milestones/anniversaries, or other events where the inclusion of other people was not stated or implied. An example of an individual event was "I Joined IBM"

The final dimension was the overall type of activity the event represented. We created 13 categories through an

Activity Type	Work		Personal		Total
	Group	Individual	Group	Individual	
Todo - Piece of work was described as finished or worked on at a particular time, ex:"Take Evan To Soccer Camp" and "Catching Up Emails And Prepping For Presentation"	.5%	8.4%	.3%	.8%	9.9%
Presentation- One or multiple presenters presenting to an audience ex: "Two Customer presentations in Vienna" and "[...] Demo To CIO"	9.3%	.1%	-	-	9.4%
Meeting - Multiple parties meeting without a clearly designated presenter, ex: "Icrc Call With Labs" and "Ks Team Meeting"	33.0%	-	-	-	33.0 %
Education – Time designated for learning/training: ex: "North America Technical Professional Management Training"	4.3%	.2%	-	.1%	4.6%
Customer – Involved work being done for customers or meeting with customers ex: "[Customer name] Project Status" and "Customer Workshop in Brussels"	25.2%	1.7%	-	-	27.0 %
Food – An event which involved food or drink ex: "[...] Executive Breakfast The Ivy Sydney" and "Tea"	2.3%	.1%	.3%	.7%	3.5%
Anniversary/Milestone – Marked moment in personal history (such as birthday or work anniversary, e.g. "End of Internship") or company/project (e.g. "[Company]'s Centennial")	.3%	11.8%	.3%	.6%	13.0 %
Conference – Event with many attendees and multiple presentations, typically over multiple days, ex: "Espoo Finland For Academics" and "[Company] Partner Summit"	15.8%	-	.1%	-	15.9 %
Leisure – A "fun" event, including movies, sports, concerts, etc ex: "Paintball" and "[Second Life] DJ at Fireflys" and "Shakespeare On The Common"	1.1%	-	2.5%	2.8%	6.4%
Vacation – Time taken off from work, ex: "Vacation South Bethany Beach Delaware Usa"	-	-	.2%	5.0%	5.2%
Holiday – Typical observed holidays (e.x. "Ramadan"), but also including certain days marked as having a certain purpose/theme (e.x: "InspireTuesday")	.1%	-	-	.3%	.4%
Family – Events with family members or home life, ex: "Taking Son #2 To Driver Test"	-	-	.6%	.2%	.8%
Location –User designated a physical location where they would be at a given time, ex: "work from home," and "Going To Croatian Seaside" and "flight to columbia, sc"	11.9%	1.4%	.7%	5.8%	19.8 %
Total	62.5%	21.1%	2.7%	13.7%	

Table 2. Distribution of 1,157 events by categories. Note: events could fall into multiple activity types (ex: food and family)

open coding process. Events were not restricted to fall into a single category in this dimension. Table 2 shows these categories and distribution of events.

Of the events shared, 83.6% (967) were categorized as work-related, while 16.4% (190) were categorized as personal, showing a clear preference of Timely users to share events around work happenings. The majority of the work events shared involved a group of people (74.8%), while the majority of personal events were individual in nature (83.7%). The overall breakdown of group versus individual events shared was 65.2% (754) and 34.8% (403), respectively.

The two most common types of activity shared were meetings (33%) and events having to do with customers (27%). The large number of customer events shared could point to Timely serving a particular value or need of a certain population, specifically, customer-facing employees such as sales people. Two users interviewed who worked in Sales described how they were particularly interested in broadcasting their customer meetings in case other employees could help them with their clients.

In addition, events where a user designated a particular location made up 20% of the total shared. This is not surprising given the recent rise in popularity of mobile sites for location-based sharing such as Foursquare or Gowalla. Designating a location as part of a time-based status update in Timely is similar, with the addition of having the ability to tell others about where you previously were during given time periods or where you will be at future times. Previous research on the benefits of open calendaring pointed to the ability to find others when needed [11]. Thus, these location-based time updates could potentially prove very valuable to a user's social network or colleagues in Timely.

DISCUSSION

We learned from the first 47 days of Timely usage that two of our design principles, open access / broadcasting and the discoverability of events, were appreciated by users. Despite an existing corporate culture of restricted calendar access, employees readily shared a wide variety of events that are typically hidden in their private calendars. A major activity of our users was browsing other users' events, filtered by their network of subscriptions, and public events on the site.

Usage data also illuminated some problems we will need to address in the near future. For example, the average number of shared events per user is relatively low. A closer look at the activity patterns during the 47 days of usage shows that for users who joined during the first half of the study period, 74% create all their events within 24 hours, with no other events created for the remainder of the study. We believe a few reasons contributed to this high attrition. First, users had difficulties with the natural language event entry as described earlier. While the system worked well in our tests, we did not anticipate all possible ways in which dates could be entered, including country and time-zone specific formats. Users had to fall back in 50% of all cases to the form-based input which led to early frustration with the system. Second, we heard in interviews and our discussion forum that the number one barrier for users is to retype events that they already have in their corporate calendar. Interviews also revealed users are not willing to publish 100% of the events in their personal calendars on Timely. However, an easy way to broadcast existing events to Timely through calendar integration seems to be crucial for sustained usage. Deeper integration into Lotus Notes could be accomplished through a side bar plugin that renders Timely events and allows users to easily publish events to Timely, e.g. through drag and drop mechanisms or context menus on individual calendar entries. Moreover, Timely itself could support sending events to Lotus Notes through iCalendar email messages.

The discussion forum brought up another issue with our design. We originally thought that the idea of "retweeting" / posting an existing event to your own event stream would be an easy to understand gesture because of its consistency with the broadcast nature of microblogging. However, some of our users struggled with the notion of zero semantics for adding an event from someone else. Users would often ask how they can attend an event or rsvp, or indicate what their intention was when they "post" an existing event to their stream. While much of this might be terminology, it illustrates that users have a preconceived concept of an event and how to interact with one. While existing calendars do support richer semantics, they often fail when it comes to events that are visible to other users. Grimes and Brush [10] highlight that putting family events in an open work calendar can lead to peer judgment, although users often add these events only to keep track of but not necessarily attend them. In this case, traditional calendars also fail to provide affordances to indicate the level of commitment to an event. We are currently hoping that an informal, unstructured way of expressing your level of commitment, such as by selecting from default options (e.g. "attending") plus allowing users to provide their own textual descriptions (e.g. "Just want to remember") could address this issue.

The majority of events shared on the system (65.2%) were group-like in nature, involving more than merely the creator of the event. The nature of social software frequently leads to a long tail in contributions. It seems event-sharing in particular may be able to benefit from individuals sharing information about what they are doing in conjunction with others in order to populate the profiles/data of those who do not contribute themselves. This will also bring up potential privacy concern questions and sharing etiquette issues, as our ideas of what it is acceptable to share may be different and will have to be reconciled when I choose to share something we are doing together. This is especially important given the additional discoverability, sharing, and broadcasting features in this Social Web environment.

CONCLUSION

We see two major contributions of our research. First, the design and rationale for a novel social enterprise microcalendaring system that allows employees to broadcast events .and discover the events of their coworkers. Second, the empirical validation of some of the design principles that guided our system. Timely's usage during the first 47 days deployed inside IBM suggests that open access sharing of work and personal events seems to be embraced and valued by employees despite an existing culture of restricted calendars. We are currently working on some of the shortcomings of our design such as lack of integration with existing calendaring tools and inferior natural language parsing of dates. As our research of this system progresses, we will have opportunities for longitudinal studies .of adoption, and the impact and benefit of event awareness.

REFERENCES

1. DiMicco, J., Millen, D. R., Geyer, W., Dugan, C., Brownholtz, B., and Muller, M. 2008.Motivations for social networking at work. *Proc CSCW '08*. ACM, New York, NY, 711-720.
2. DiMicco, J., Geyer, W., Dugan, C., Brownholtz, B., Millen, D.R. 2009. People Sensemaking and Relationship Building on an Enterprise Social Networking Site. In *Proc. HICSS'09.*
3. Efimova, L., Grudin, J. Cross Boundaries: A Case Study of Employee Blogging. In *Proc HICSS'07*, IEEE Press.
4. Ehrlich, S.F. 1987. Social and Psychological factors influencing the design of office communication systems. *Proc CHI+GI'87*, 323-329.
5. Farzan, R., DiMicco, J., Millen, D. R., Dugan, C., Geyer, W., and Brownholtz, E. 2008. Results from deploying a participation incentive mechanism within the enterprise. In *Proc CHI '08*. ACM, New York, NY, 563-572.
6. Geyer, W., Dugan, C., DiMicco, J., Millen, D. R., Brownholtz, B., and Muller, M. 2008. Use and reuse of shared lists as a social content type. In *Proc. CHI '08*. ACM, New York, NY, 1545-1554.
7. Geyer, W., Dugan, C., Millen, D.R., Muller, M., Freyne, J. 2008. Recommending Topics for Self-Descriptions in Online User Profiles. *Proc RecSys'08*, 59-66.
8. Gkekas, G., Kyrikou, A., and Ioannidis, N. 2007. A smart calendar application for mobile environments. In *Proc. of the 3rd international Conference on Mobile Multimedia Communications* (Nafpaktos, Greece, August 27 - 29, 2007). ACM International Conference Proceeding Series, vol. 329.
9. Greif, I., Sarin, S. 1988. Data sharing in group work. Computer-Supported Cooperative Work: A Book of Readings. San Mateo, CA, Morgan-Kaufmann.
10. Grimes, A. and Brush, A. 2008. Life scheduling to support multiple social roles. In *Proc. CHI '08*. ACM, New York, NY, 821-824.
11. Grudin, J. 1996. A case study of calendar use in an organization. *SIGOIS Bull.* 17, 3 (Dec. 1996), 49-51.
12. Grudin, J. Palen, L. 1995. Why groupware succeeds: Discretion or Mandate? In *Proc. ECSCW'95*. 263-278.
13. Hasan, H., Pfaff, C.C. 2006. The Wiki: an environment to revolutionise employees' interaction with corporate knowledge. In *Proc OZCHI '06*, 377-380.
14. Huh, J., Jones, L., Erickson, T., Kellogg, W. A., Bellamy, R. K., and Thomas, J. C. BlogCentral: the role of internal blogs at work. In *Proc CHI '07*, 2447-2452.
15. Jackson, A., Yates, J., Orlikowski, W. Corporate Blogging: Building community through persistent digital talk. In *Proc HICSS'07*, IEEE Press.
16. Kincaid, C. M., Dupont, P. B., and Kaye, A. R. 1985. Electronic calendars in the office: an assessment of user needs and current technology. *ACM Trans. Inf. Syst.* 3, 1 (Jan. 1985), 89-102.
17. Millen, D.R., Feinberg, J. and Kerr, B. 2006. Dogear: Social bookmarking in the enterprise. *Proc CHI '06*, 111-120.
18. Mynatt, E.& Tullio,J.2001.Inferring calendar event attendance.*Proc.IUI '01*.ACM, New York, NY,121-128.
19. Neustaedter, C., Brush, A. J., and Greenberg, S. 2009. The calendar is crucial: Coordination and awareness through the family calendar. *ACM Trans. Comput.-Hum. Interact.* 16, 1 (Apr. 2009), 1-48.
20. Palen, L. 1998. Calendars on the new frontier: Challenges of groupware technology. Ph.D. dissertation, University of California, Irvine.
21. Palen, L. 1999. Social, individual and technological issues for groupware calendar systems. In *Proc. CHI '99*. ACM, New York, NY, 17-24.
22. Steinfeld, C., DiMicco, J.M., Ellison, N., Lampe, C. 2009. Bowling Online: Social Networking and Social Capital within the Organization. *Proc. C&T 2009*, State College, PA.
23. Tungle.Me Manifesto, http://calendarofthefuture.com
24. Zhang, J., Qu, Y., Cody, J., and Wu, Y. 2010. A case study of micro-blogging in the enterprise: use, value, and related issues. *Proc. CHI '10*. ACM, New York, NY, 123-132.

"Pleasure is Your Birthright": Digitally Enabled Designer Sex Toys as a Case of Third-Wave HCI

Jeffrey Bardzell and Shaowen Bardzell
Indiana University School of Informatics & Computing
919 E 7Th Street
Bloomington, IN, 47408
{jbardzel; selu}@indiana.edu

ABSTRACT
In the past decade, HCI has become increasingly preoccupied with the deeply subjective qualities of interaction: experience, embodiment, pleasure, intimacy, and so on, an agenda sometimes grouped under the heading of "third-wave HCI." Analytically understanding and designing for such qualities has been an ongoing challenge to the field, in part because its established theories and methodologies are comparatively weak at understanding and being responsive to human subjectivity. In this paper, we present a case study of a group of designers who have, in the past few years, revolutionized their domain—sex toys—by combining embodied pleasure, intimate experience, health and wellness, emerging technologies, high-quality design processes, and social activism. We consider the implications this case could have for researchers innovating on especially third-wave HCI design theories, methodologies, and processes.

Author Keywords:
HCI, design, human sexuality, criticism, activism

ACM Classification:
H.5.1.m. Information interfaces and presentation (e.g., HCI): Miscellaneous.

General Terms
Design, Theory

INTRODUCTION
It might be surprising to consider that human-computer interaction, once the province of engineers and experimental psychologists, would find itself on a trajectory that is converging with that of sex toys, once the province of sleazy urban sex shops and pornographers. Yet, as is well documented (e.g., [10, 19]), HCI has taken a strong cultural turn, taking seriously the subjective dimensions of interaction: experience [23, 27], embodiment [15, 20, 16, 22], pleasure [9], emotion [30, 11], and physical intimacy. Several major conferences devote themselves to such these concerns: DUX, TEI, DPPI, to name a few.

The other side of this converging trajectory is the rise of designer sex toys. Challenging the cheap adult novelties of the past, these new designs are digitally enabled, aesthetically sophisticated, high-quality consumer electronics. A typical example of these new designer toys is Jimmyjane's Form 6 vibrator (Figure 1), which retails for $185 USD, and features body safe materials, dual motors, a rechargeable lithium ion battery, and an elegant user interface. The OhMiBod Freestyle offers wireless connectivity to MP3 players for real-time music-vibration synchronization. Nomi Tang's Better than Chocolate has a tangible user interface to control vibration patterns and intensity. Je Joue's SaSi has a user-programmable vibration design interface. These toys, whose function *is* to provide pleasurable embodied experiences, have not only revolutionized the adult toy industry, but they offer a more general vision of digitally enabled physical pleasure can be.

Figure 1: JimmyJane's Form 6

This vision of pleasure is timely for third-wave HCI, because it is clear that progress in many of its target areas of experience, embodiment, wellness, pleasure, and so forth has been elusive: as a community we seem to have struggled to develop coherently a social science methodology, linked both to an epistemology and a body of methods, for the third wave. Whatever the reason, attempts to detect and measure experience and emotion, or to design for embodied interaction, have turned out to be more difficult perhaps than the research community expected. Case studies obviously cannot generalize into a new epistemology, methodology, and collection of methods, but they can offer glimpses of what the eventual solutions could look like.

Digital Sexual Interaction
The topic of sex in HCI has seen a steady stream of work in the past decade. HCI researchers have already called attention to the significance of online porn for HCI [8]. At the same time, sexuality—a term that includes emotional inti-

macy, vulnerability, and experiential qualities such as excitement, as well as the more obvious physical dimensions of it—includes much more than individuals looking at porn. Indeed, sexual expression is a part of everyday life, from the bedroom [7] to the social media landscape, including Twittergasm, ijustmadelove.com, and Vibe Review. Projects integrating HCI and performance art have explored physical intimacy that often borders on the erotic [33, 34]. Virtual worlds have been studied as sources of intimacy [31], and have become home to evolved sexual subcultures, including furries and Goreans [4, 5]. Low bandwidth technologies have been shown to provide rich interpretative mediations for couples in long distance relationships [21]. In human-robot interaction, there is the emerging field of teledildonics. Workshops have been held in recent years on sex and HCI at both CHI and NordiCHI [12, 3].

We argue that sexuality and human-computer interaction (SHCI), rather than being a marginal example of third-wave HCI, in many ways should be recognized as a paradigmatic example of the third wave, since it so powerfully interweaves its major themes. Lest we be misunderstood, we are not claiming that all third wave HCI is sexual in nature or that people working in third wave HCI should take up sexuality. Rather, we are observing that both HCI/sex and third wave HCI share a number of common concerns.

Given the extraordinary success of recent designer sex toys in bringing together design innovation, sexual health expert and sex-positive feminist involvement, and consumer advocacy, we believe that they make a worthwhile case study for the third wave. (Note: neither our data nor our backgrounds qualify us to assess the actual public wellness benefits of this movement; we limit our own assessment of this movement's "success" with reference to it as a commercially successful, innovative design movement that has earned for itself strong buy-in from sexual wellness experts.) This paper offers just such a case study, relying primarily on expert interviews to reveal the design processes and outcomes of this experience-, pleasure-, and embodiment-oriented domain of interaction design. We argue that sex toy designers are successful in two particular areas that could be emulated among third-wave HCI designers:

- Critical engagement with interactions, especially one's sensual and visceral responses, to cultivate a dense subjective understanding of specific interaction qualities.
- Embedded commitment to a stakeholder community, including users and experts as well as to their values.

Sex Toys: An Historical Overview

Invented by a British doctor in the 19th century, vibrators were first used by physicians to treat women with "hysteria" [26]. Often these vibrators resembled heavy machinery and were hardly anything but sensually appealing. Between the 1920s and 1960s, traveling salesmen began selling vibrators not as therapeutic instruments but as aids to induce sexual pleasures, which were seen at the time as secret, unauthorized, and even morally corrupt. As a part of the sexual revolution of the 1960s, sex toys became a visible part of a movement that constructed sexual pleasure as a human right, rather than as a moral shame [36].

The 1970s saw a backlash against the sexual revolution, in part from feminism, which attacked many forms of sexuality, including pornography, as a form of violence against women. In the 1970s and 80s, a "sex positive" feminist movement pushed back, advocating sexual freedom, including advancing (often female-produced) pornography as well as gay, lesbian, and alternative sexual lifestyles. Around the same time, sex positive feminists began to open sex stores to offer an alternative to traditional sex shops, which were perceived as sleazy shops that were often unsafe for women. These early feminist sex shops, such as San Francisco's Good Vibrations, which opened in 1977, featured clean, well-lit environments, trained employees, and a sex positive message: in the words of one of our interviewees, the main buyer for Good Vibrations, "We have been really positive for 32 years saying, no, no, no, it is our birthright, pleasure is your birthright, this belongs to you."

For years, however, sex-positive shops continued to sell toys designed and sold by the sex industry, lacking any alternative. Such toys, still widely available today, often have the following characteristics. Made by pioneering vibrator companies such as California Exotic Creations and Doc Johnson, many of these toys have strong ties to the adult and/or porn industries. Made of plastic and rubber, they are comparatively inexpensive (often between US$10 and $30). Unreliable, their motors often break before the product is even sold. The plastic itself often contains phthalates, which is an ester used in plastics that have been linked to allergies, asthma, endocrine disruption, and birth defects. These toys are often sold in clear plastic clamshell packaging, with an image of a female porn star printed on a cardboard insert. In short, traditional vibrators are targeted at a male buying public for use as a quasi-disposable adult novelty.

In recent years, several factors have given rise to a new generation of sex toys. Sex toys have increasingly been portrayed in a favorable light in mainstream media (e.g., *Sex and the City*), and at the same time they have become increasingly marketed to female consumers. Simultaneous to these developments has been the rise of digital technologies, which has encouraged the sex toy industry to embrace high quality production and digital technology [37]. Examples of high quality sex toy companies include Lelo, Jimmyjane, OhMiBod, We-Vibe, Je Joue, Tenga, and Nomi Tang, among others. These companies are recognized by sexologists (and, importantly, each other) as constituting a group of designers defining and inaugurating a new era in sex toys. Defining this era are toys that reflect the values of the sex positive movement, design for the sexual health and the overall wellbeing of individuals and groups—a value that resonates with what's being proposed at the recent Wellness Informatics workshop [18], all while providing physical pleasure, supporting intimacy between partners, and contributing to fulfilling experiences.

RESEARCH APPROACH

The present work introduces digitally enabled designer sex toys to the HCI and interaction design communities. The work offers a critical synthesis of over 30 hours of interviews with industry experts. Relying on the voices of the designers and sexperts at the center of this movement, the paper then offers a synthetic account of who is doing this design, what their design processes are, and how these processes relate to their values and goals both for a given design and more broadly for social change. We relate these activities to design processes and issues in HCI, including the roles of criticism, problem framing, embodied design cognition, and activism in supporting this movement.

From November 2009 through May 2010, we conducted a total of 14 interviews. We spoke with some of the most privileged voices in this emerging community—the designer-inventors who have collectively initiated this new wave of high quality vibrators as well as sexual health experts and sex-positive activists on the front lines of the sexual health community. We interviewed these industry experts because they are uniquely able to highlight key design and development issues as well as to understand their perspectives on these artifacts' design intentions, rationales, materials, and production tools and practices. The fourteen interviewees (9 female, 5 male, and including 2 participants with doctorate degrees) reside in Hong Kong, Canada, Sweden, China, and the United States, and were recruited initially through the recommendation of one of the AASECT-certified sex educators who is an advisor to this research. A snowball sample was subsequently developed from the original participants.

We asked these experts to tell us about their experience designing, developing, buying, and/or curating sex toys in the industry. The open-ended questions centered on four threads:

- *Background*: Education/industry history, motivation, day-to-day responsibilities, etc.
- *Perceptions of existing toys*: Qualities of a good sex toys, market perspectives, what works and why, etc.
- *Design process*: Inspirations, rationale, tools, materials, working with consumers, etc.)
- *Integration with technology*: Their vision of the role technology plays in sex toy design in 5- and 10-years, how technology shapes the design process, etc.

A total of 30 hours of interviews were recorded and transcribed. Participants had the choice of remaining anonymous or supplying their identities, and all but one consented to identifying themselves. All participants received a draft of this paper months prior to publication.

The authors have extensive experience with sexual interaction research [3,4,5,6] and critical textual analysis [1,2]. The data analysis was conducted through a procedure known as *explication de texte*, or close reading, an analytical method that originated in the humanities [29] and which involves the careful examination of diction, rhetorical devices, style, and other formal and thematic elements in a text. Both researchers involved in the study have doctoral training in the humanities and have used this approach in prior research [31]. The data analysis phase followed a process. Initially both researchers conducted their close readings independently of one another to identify her or his own set of themes. Subsequently, the researchers collaborated to combine, refine, and distinguish among themes before arriving at the critical synthesis of their design process, described below. The combination of these expert voices and our critical analysis should help to shed insights on successful practices in the interaction design areas emphasizing any combination of experience, embodiment, wellness, pleasure, social activism, and intimacy.

DESIGNING DIGITALLY ENABLED SEX TOYS

One of the hallmarks of the new class of digitally enabled designer sex toys that we have been describing is that they are the outcome of a particular engineering and design process. This process is different than that typically taught in HCI, with its emphasis on users, empirical measurement, and iterative prototyping and evaluation [17]. Thus, as we critically reflect on ways to advance third-wave HCI in light of the limitations of earlier approaches, it is useful to explore alternative approaches that are successful in their own separate, but related, domains. In the ensuing exposition, we highlight areas of difference between mainstream HCI and sex toy design processes, especially where they may most influence the resulting product.

Sex Toy Designers

All of the designers we interviewed are small business. While they did not all provide us with exact numbers, most have around 10-20 employees based on our office visits and the information they did share, exclusive of manufacturing (mostly done in China). The largest company for which we have a number was Lelo, which has about 30 employees, exclusive of manufacturing. These numbers include the founders, who are themselves designer-engineers, and they also include industrial and packaging designers, marketing and sales staff, customer support staff, and accountants and lawyers.

One of the most interesting findings from our interviews was that none of the designer-engineers behind these products comes from or has a significant history in the adult or sex toy industry. The designer behind Jimmyjane, for example, started in bioinformatics working on the human genome, before moving into industrial design and working at Frog Design doing mainstream design work for Nike, Motorola, Colgate, and so forth. The couple who created the We-Vibe worked in semiconductors at Nortel, before a career change provided the impetus to take a vibrator concept through the process of invention and bringing it to market. The brothers behind Lelo were engineers at Ericsson. Others worked at Apple, in car manufacturing, at NASA, and Tyco Electronics. The trend toward high tech designers making toys is likely to grow, in the words of one of our interviewees: "there are more people coming from industrial design and design backgrounds going, 'I don't want to design a new watch, I want to design a sex toy.'"

We can see that these companies all have a number of similarities. All are small, and many are family-run, facts whose significance we will return to later. All of the founding inventors have some form of technical engineering, commonly hailing from large, high-tech companies, as a key part of their pedigree. This combination seems to offer both the entrepreneurial and technological know-how to succeed in this new market. The high standards that one expects from products from companies like Ericsson, Apple, and Frog Design has survived their departures as a commitment to high quality in the field of sex toys.

An Embodied Design Process

In this section, we synthesize an account of designer processes from the interviews, including many direct quotes to allow readers to hear the voice of our interviewees. Our goal is not merely to shed light on their processes, but also their attitudes, metaphors, and epistemological orientations to their problem space. We emphasize throughout the centrality of their own cultivated subjective experience in their design reasoning.

Inspiration

Most of our designer-inventor interviewees had a narrative that explained how they ended up making vibrators. As industry outsiders, it is perhaps not surprising that some of these narratives begin with a founding flash of intuition, which is later framed, researched, and prototyped, and put to market. One inventor writes,

> OhMiBod came about because [my husband] was traveling a lot in China and one Christmas he bought me an iPod mini and a vibrator... and I found that I was using the two together.... [After I've done chores] and I've put my kids to bed, how do you get sexy from there? So what I found, music helped to transport me easily to a different place. I could kind of get out of my own head and listen to my music and then be open to basic pleasure.

With OhMiBod, a personal narrative about the inventor's own sensual experience helped identify a particular need—"how do you get sexy from there?"—which led to the insight that music can transport us from the mundane to the sexy. From there, it's not hard to see how music + vibrator led to the OhMiBod line of toys. It is important to note, however, that the originating goal was to serve a deeply felt subjective experience, "getting sexy," and not an intention to build a thing, that is, an interactive technology.

Another product, the We-Vibe, a small vibrator that is worn during intercourse, had a similar start.

> [W]e were [on] an eight hour drive ... and we were just—and sex toys were not a part of our life. We starting talking about all sorts of silly things like the Californians with their blow-up dolls [in the HOV lanes] ... [a]nd you know all these $10,000 sex machines.... And it was just a pretty innocent idea. We were just like, "Oh," it was just like, "Well, I wonder if there is a sex toy that fits between people when they're making love?" And it was that simple. And then basically got home ... and wrote it down in my little inventor's book.... I looked ... to see what sex toys were out there..., but there was just nothing out there. So, then I went to the patent office....

Here again we see that the idea just happened fortuitously during a conversation about sexual aids. Interestingly, the speaker is clearly not only not from the adult industry, but he even here still seems to be distancing himself from sex toys, by first insisting that sex toys had never been a part of his life and by repeatedly using the word "silly" to describe the conversation (this word is used elsewhere in the same passage, not quoted here). The distancing of themselves from traditional sex toy manufacturers, who as noted earlier are commonly associated with the adult/porn industry, is a common theme with this whole group of designers.

If the two narratives just cited suggest an almost unintentional initial inspiration, for others, inspiration came as a result of a critical engagement with existing toys.

> We came to one of those nice little shops in Shibuya, Tokyo. I thought that well we are a little bit in a holiday mood, so why not try a vibrator? We were frustrated afterwards, because it did not survive the battery lifetime.... And we said, why doesn't anyone make this kind of device better? Why is nobody caring about high quality sex toys that come in nice packaging, with a nice design, not one with a naked woman...? Maybe a little bit more modern approach towards technology? [3 years later we] brought up this whole story, and I said why is nobody caring about really nice sex toys with a sexy approach, which is not so intimidating as maybe one of those dildos or classic vibrators you find in an ordinary sex shop? Yes, this is where the idea finally was formed. I thought that well if nobody does it better why am I not doing it better?

This critique does not lead to a concrete concept in and of itself. Instead, it identifies a small number of *design qualities* [25] that the speaker perceives that the market fails to offer: high production quality, technological currency, non-pornographic packaging, and not being too intimidating.

The founder of Jimmyjane is even further removed from a random flash of insight. He writes that in 2002, "I was approached by three different people to look into products related to sex and that is what made me think, okay, something is going on because I have never been approached with this before." Accordingly,

> I went to [an adult industry] trade show and ... I was personally sort of overwhelmed because I had very limited experience with these products.... I started picking products up ... and thinking of them just as product. Relatively quickly you become desensitized

> to the stigma.... You start look at these as just products, and looking through that lens all sorts of things that would never have been acceptable to me as a designer, were present in these products.... The products were scary looking, very unapproachable, often looked like severed anatomy or you know, were animals and very figurative.... They were noisy, they were smelly, and a whole host of materials.... I could tell ... if something is off gassing, if you can smell it, you know that some chemical is being released. Anyway, so it became immediately apparent that these products were made out of toxic material. They were packaged in packaging with porn stars.... It seemed to me that there was a lot that could be done.

The speaker here also distances himself initially from sex toys, but his perception of them completely inverts the moment he re-categorizes them from "sex toys" to "design product." With this shift, he has a flood of critical insights about the (then) state of the art. Considering shapes, visual appearance, and smells, he infers the materials from which they are made and then immediate continues on to infer a set of design qualities as diverse as product experience, cultural positioning, and health. His criticisms in many ways echo and reinforce those of Nomi Tang, cited just above. And as with Tang, he does not immediately have an idea of the toy he will make; instead, he constructs a list of design qualities that the toys should meet: body safe, not intimidating, approachability, non-smelly, non-pornographic, nice packaging, etc.

The designers acquire a holistic understanding of their problem space not through an early focus on users, as recommended by [17], but rather by means of critical self-reflection on their own experience and/or a more systematic act of design criticism, defined in [1] as the careful, practiced, and theoretically informed investigation of a cultural work or phenomenon, situated in the creative, historical, social, and semantic contexts of similar works. Our participants stress an aspect of criticism that [1]'s definition understates: the role of the designer-critic's sensual and visceral response in directing design-critical cognition. Design criticism is needed, because when helping designers build understandings of human needs in terms of the relationships among dense experiential qualities, product semantics, design materials, the state of the market, and broader social movements, most users are simply not able to articulate their needs. The expert eye of the designer-critic, on the other hand, is able to interrogate designs to perceive design opportunities. With the design space identified, the next step is to think about it in a structured way.

Problem Framing

Design research—e.g., the work of Schön [35], Cross [14], and Lawson [24]—has stressed the importance of "framing." *Framing* refers to the designer's identification of "areas of the solution space in which they choose to explore" [14, p.102], in Schön's words, to "set its boundaries, select particular things and relations for attention, and impose on the situation a coherence that guides subsequent moves" [14, p.102].

Perhaps the most fundamental example of problem framing, and on some level it is shared by all of the designers we interviewed, is the understanding of vibrators as "consumer electronics." This particular framing has implications both for what quality toys should *be* and also how they should be *made*. One of the designer-inventors of OhMiBod puts it thus:

> I actually think, and it's us together with a couple of other companies, who are actually defining what a quality type toy should be. The consumers historically don't know.... They're so used to buying the very cheap, the kind of jelly rubber toys ... it's really turning into a consumer electronics product as opposed to just what historically has been a kind of cheap sex toy. So there are different manufacturing protocols. We do ... tracking so if something goes wrong with a toy we can actually trace it back to a specific lot number....

The key act of framing is the shift from "cheap plastic toy" to "consumer electronic." As soon as that occurs, everything else shifts as well: manufacturing protocols, quality control, and a certain understanding of "quality" itself.

Problem framing goes well beyond the overall framing of the sex toy design space, however. For the founder of Jimmyjane, problem framing not only applies to a given design, but also to his brand strategy. Building a brand strategy led him to develop a model of "sexuality," so he could ensure that his brand is not one-dimensional. He says,

> Jimmyjane ... is not a vibrator company, but rather a concept about extending sexiness throughout the day, about this notion that fundamentally we never feel better than when we feel sexy. So, why not have that and access that consistently throughout the day in all sorts of different ways? One way certainly is actual physical sexual contact with the body and with another, but also obviously there all sorts of other phases of sexuality that permeate our lives. It extends to how we dress, it extends to all sorts of other sort of rituals that are fundamental to our lives, grooming and so on.

Here is an understanding of sexuality that is quite different than that of traditional porn-industry sex toy manufacturers, who build toys and brand experience around the California porn industry fantasy of a sex encounter episode. For Jimmyjane's founder, overt sex acts barely register: he is talking about how aspects of sexuality "permeate our lives"—a profound and ultimately phenomenological question. His understanding is equally distinct from a scientific models or theories of human sexuality, e.g., from psychology or health sciences. His critical understanding is not only healthy from a sex positive feminist perspective—it emphasizes feeling good about yourself—but it also helps him develop his business: in addition to vibrators, Jimmyjane also offers a line of fragrances, thus connecting sexuality to grooming.

Grooming is a different type of sexual practice than body contact, and to design fragrances that will help people feel sexy, Jimmyjane's founder decided to work with the concept of *attraction* as a way to structure his design reasoning:

> But ... as soon as I realized, okay, there are so many different types of attraction.... [The] essential elements of attraction [are the] intellectual component, the emotional component and the sexual component.... And so the fragrances then ... are Charm, Wit, and Kink.... So, in a relationship that maybe is defined by Wit and Kink is an intellectual and a physical interaction, but not really an emotional one, is one sort. I can't think of a better word for it, but one that is emotional and physical.... You know, perhaps this overlap of all three is you know, what you might call love...

Both the development and the design explanation of Jimmyjane fragrances are intertwined with an explanation of both the brand as well as attempts to think systematically not only about sexuality, but also about related concepts, including attraction and love itself.

Jimmyjane's founder is not alone in critically examining human sexuality as a resource to design reasoning. In our interview with We-Vibe, when we asked them to tell us about the qualities of a good designer sex toy, one of the designer-inventors proposes a three-dimensional understanding of the problem space:

> So, that's the trick in engineering is to me is to take all of the human desires on one side from a functional point of view. And ... then the aesthetics of it to make it beautiful so it doesn't look ugly or threatening as a second dimension. Then the third one is the engineering side of it how do you get something that's got all of those attributes small, powerful, quality, lasts a long time, easy to use and how do you make it an object that will achieve that? And that's the art of engineering.

For We-Vibe's designer-inventors, a good sex toy is responsive to human desires, aesthetic, and well engineered. Interestingly, when we probed about "human desires," he responded, "but 'human' like how it performs: its function, its longevity, its ease of use, ease of washing you know it's bullet proof, and lasts a long time, etc." The inventor's understanding of human desire here has clearly been operationalized into concrete design qualities. In fact, it is difficult, based on this passage, to distinguish between the "human desire" and the "engineering" dimensions, because he has analyzed human desire into constituent parts, each of which in turn becomes a design problem space.

In all of our interviews with designers, we saw time and again evidence of efforts to think systematically about the problem domain, simultaneously exploring use- and design qualities. Nomi Tang, for example, used tangible user interfaces as starting point to help her think through her design's user interface, leading to a surprisingly (and wittily) natural gesture/touch control for vibrator speed and pattern that technologically resembles the iPod trackwheel and experientially resembles clitoral stimulation.

Research for Design

Inspiration and problem framing is a form of reasoning that is largely internal to the designer. However, all of the designers we interviewed also turned outside, by conducting different forms of research for design. The most commonly reported form of research was not surprisingly user research, but our interviewees also reported the use of sexperts, that is, involving sexual health experts in the prototyping and evaluation stages of design, as well the use of published works.

All of the designers we interviewed engaged in two or more forms of user research. This included standard market research, such as surveys, focus groups, and interviews with users and retailers. One designer reported reading blog-based reviews of sex toys, starting her own blog, and trying to encourage critical dialogue about toys between herself and her customers. Most of the designers told us that they got ideas and feedback from their own partners and girlfriends. Another designer-inventor went to the streets and randomly talked to passers-by:

> I remember standing downtown handing out surveys to government worker ladies going by and saying, "Oh, can I borrow a few minutes of your time and talk to you about sex toys?" The ones who didn't run away of course gave me great information in terms of you know what's your favorite toy. Then I went away and of course bought all these toys and measured what frequency they are and what rpm they do and their basic characteristics.

The distance between the designers-as-researchers and their research subjects seems reduced in many of these examples. Instead of scientists behind a two-way mirror, these designer inventors are having frank, personal, and individual conversations with consumers, whether they are new acquaintances or their own family members. Considered as sources of empirical data, such strategies seem rife with problems, e.g., of anecdote, bias, and problems of generalization. Considered as conversations that sustain critical investigation of the phenomenology of human sexual experience and its relationship to design, however, it may be that intimate conversations with family members and customers may be a particularly strong strategy, because of the demanding—interpersonally, intellectually—nature of what the designers are asking.

(Embodied) Prototyping

Our interviewees spoke at length about their prototyping processes. We were struck at how strongly their descriptions of prototyping were interlaced with the language of embodiment. Obviously, an intellectual understanding of embodiment—human sexuality, anatomy, texture, safety, etc.—is central to designing sex toys. But it was clear to us that embodiment was not merely rationally understood;

rather, the designers' own embodiment strongly influenced the way they approach design. For the founders of OhMiBod, 3D prototypes are transformative, so much so that they have gone to interesting lengths to obtain them:

> we can take a concept and throw it into a CAD and then within 24 hours get a 3D print so you can actually hold that product in your hand and feel it against your body; I think transforms the whole design process.... I won't give any names..., but there's a couple of guys who actually had access to a 3D printing machine with a local company here..., and they run the 3D printing lab, and so at night they sneak in there and they 3D print the vibrators for us.... The idea that these guys kind of sneak into their own lab and do vibrator prints is pretty interesting.

Indeed, these prototypes seem to play some of the same roles that sketches do in traditional design in terms of thinking through experience [13], only with a more touch-oriented perspective.

Embodiment influences design in other, more gendered ways, as the buyer for Good Vibrations explains:

> Now this is a funny story. And one of my [employees] was explaining how when she uses [a particular vibrator], when she uses this it is counterintuitive because how to turn it off and on and up and down. It is just is counterintuitive to her and [when confronted with this reaction, the designer] was like, oh right it was designed for a man to use on a woman. The designers are all men. [The sex toy company] was all men and now there are women but it was all men.... And they designed them to use on their wives or girlfriends or whomever, never thought about what would happen when a woman uses it on herself.

This example illustrates a certain first-person mentality that pervades the design process. Again, viewed scientifically, this is problematic, since it suggests a certain lack of distance or objectivity on the part of the designers. At the same time, designing for experience, physical pleasure, intimacy, and so forth can hardly be done without deep recourse to one's own personal embodied experience; this experience is not an intellectual liability in understanding human experience, but arguably its preeminent resource.

We saw more unconsciously embodied reasoning in the interviews that we were able to conduct face-to-face. In explaining toys to us, our interviewees often gestured toward their own or even our bodies; these gestures were natural and unconscious. Once, a company co-founder quite un-self-consciously climbed on a table to show us a sexual position in order to explain the placement of some controls on a toy. Further, when talking about g-spot vibrators, interviewees tended to direct their attention and gaze to the female researcher, and likewise when talking about prostate vibrators, they directed their attention to the male researcher.

An embodied understanding of vibrators goes beyond their intended uses as sexual stimulants, as well. For example, the lead engineer at Lelo was concerned about the portability of a set of prototypes, and so he "would carry these in his pocket almost all of the time and he was trying to see which device would be kind of the best that he would be most comfortable with and that is how Mia basically was chosen." A lifestyle includes not just sex acts and feeling sexy, but even the mundane dimensions of carrying pleasure objects around in one's pocket.

Nomi Tang wanted her vibrator both to be a piece of art and also to have the ergonomic qualities associated with high quality medical equipment. She explains how she achieved this fusion of concept art and ergonomics in her design for Better Than Chocolate:

> I gave [the design team] a couple of references of art pieces that I ... liked and said I want to have the toy which looks more like a piece of art, which I can keep in the bedroom or in the bathroom, which blends into the environment without looking any kind of cheap or non luxurious, and [without giving] away directly that it is a vibrator.... And the design team that came up with 12 or 16 [prototypes].... They come from medical design background, which is quite interesting ... they specialized in emergency room equipment, which has to be very ergonomic to please the hand as well as the body of the patient.

The resulting toy has a highly organic-looking shape—it is immediately appealing to the eye and to touch—but it does not look like any particular part of the human body—its shape is the outcome of a design process.

Several designers also talked about the problem of sound. For example, the inventors of the We-Vibe explain,

> the perfect toy should be ... dead nut silent. And we go to a lot of effort to make this We-Vibe quiet. We actually test each motor for the noise it makes. And I'm often astounded at when you turn these things on it sounds like a washing machine or you know it's just some of these [toys] are just so noisy it's just gross and because part of the human intake is noise and if this thing just sounds ugly. It doesn't matter what it looks like or what it feels like it's just a bad thing.

The diction in this passage—"astounded," "sounds like a washing machine," "gross," and "sounds ugly"—is emphatic and personal. We do not normally describe a machine sound as "gross," which normally has organic connotations, and surely it is an exaggeration to describe the sound of a small electronic device as "like a washing machine." Yet when such noises occur in the context of sexual intimacy, this use of such vocabulary makes sense. Designers leverage their own imaginations as sexual human beings to form judgments about what constitutes acceptable levels of sound in intimate situations and make design decisions accordingly.

The major themes of the third wave of HCI all engage in some way with the sensual. The designers' own embodied and even sexual perspectives and practices position them to design for sensual pleasure: 3D sketching, developing an aesthetic vocabulary, relating to interlocutors and users, orienting UI controls, and assessing the acceptability of machine noises, among many others. As interaction design takes on increasingly intimate aspects of human experience, the field will possibly benefit from adopting a more embodied vocabulary to express its design reasoning.

Evaluation

When asked about evaluation, the designers described many standard mechanisms for evaluating designs: beta testers were given prototypes and they provided their reactions; the designers collected product feedback, e.g., from product returns, customer surveys, and comments from retailers. Interestingly, we also continued to see the emphasis on collecting critical feedback from close relations: internal employees and their families/friends evaluated products both professionally and personally: "[our designers] even ask their spouses or whatever, girlfriends." Again, because sex toy design is governed by critical, rather than empirical, understandings of embodied pleasure and experience, accounts offered by close friends and family may be deeper, more honest, and more personally intimate than accounts acquired in more traditional scientific ways.

An important aspect of the evaluation phase of these designer sex toys is how short the iteration loops are. This is possible, according to nearly all of our interviewees (including the sexual health experts and retailers), because customer feedback penetrates design companies even at the highest levels. In the words of Lelo's co-founder and co-lead designer,

> And we would get numerous e-mails also regarding any feedback. Pretty much all of these e-mails are sent to [the co-founders] or to development people and we would … take action and do something.... And that is the nice thing about being a smaller company is that … the top people see these things and they are not filtered.... Everybody, not always but usually, has the same goal and is driven by the same things.

That designers, senior management, and customers are on the same page affects the design in important ways. All of the designers emphasize fast product iterations and innovations possible because of consumer feedback, facilitated in part by the fact that staff and key decisionmakers alike are engaging the community together, helping the company respond quickly to criticisms and ideas.

Social Activism Through Design

One dynamic that gradually became visible over the course of our interviews is that stakeholders throughout the community—companies making toys, sexual health experts, retailers, and consumers alike—are united in pursuing an agenda. This unity of purpose, shaped in part by ideals, creates an ecosphere of resources that we believe is extremely effective in advancing good sexual interaction design. And in that ecosphere, better design is not merely the outcome of work done by health experts and sex positive feminists; rather, design is also an input that contributes to this agenda in ways that seem to relate both to the HCI topics of research through design [38] and feminist HCI [2], but also more generally to feminist activist research, which likewise advocates for the integration of knowledge and action [32, 28].

The unity of purpose is evident in several ways. Chief among them may be the key role of the advocacy offered by sexual health experts and feminist sex retailers (whom we collectively refer to as "sexperts"), whose alignment not only benefits the consumer (as was intended from their very beginnings in the 1970s) but is now increasingly influencing design itself. This is supported by strong lines of communications among all three constituencies: sexperts, designers, and consumers.

We can see evidence of the tie between the sexperts and consumers through sexperts' commitment to educating consumers, the outcome of which is apparent in this observation by Good Vibrations' buyer: "I think that people now, they want to know ingredients, they want to know materials, they, I mean just as in electronics, as in any other industry the user is a little more savvy, they have done their research online." Sexperts in retail obviously can do more than merely educate the consumer: they also decide what to put in front of the consumer as well as what to promote, an activity that shapes demand. This demand in turn influences designers, who, thanks to their own critiques of the industry, were anticipating these needs and responding to them. In delivering high quality toys—and leveraging their skills at marketing to trumpet that quality—they not only meet demand but also make it easier for sexperts to educate consumers and promote the sexual wellness agenda.

We also saw evidence of significant interaction between sexual health experts and the designers themselves. One expert describes her involvement with the design of the first OhMiBod vibrator:

> I met with [the company founders] ... a couple of times around different products and they are wonderful because they … very much appreciate our input as experts in this field.... I met with [them] … before [their first] product actually came out and just gave him my thoughts, and he is a manufacturer that is so, I just love him for doing this.... I sat down with him and it was just like, I love this, I don't love this, and you have to have this, and just, my own opinions of a buyer knowing the market, and he listened, he listened. And even if some things could not be changed then, they were changed on … the second product.

By engaging Good Vibrations' buyer in the design process, its design was influenced by a retailer-sexpert, and at the same time that sexpert began to engage in design cognition: beyond understanding toys as particular contributors to certain experiences or forms of wellness, she now has a better understanding of sex toys as a design problem (e.g., manufacturing issues and other design constraints). We heard other examples of this kind of interaction between designers and sexperts—indeed it a part of every interviewee's experience in one way or another. In some cases, all three groups—designers, sexperts, and consumers, come together. For example, the Center for Sexual Health, run by sexual health scholars, sometimes collaborates with Good Vibrations and San Francisco-based toy designers to host events with focus groups and even amateur sex toy design competitions. In this way, design processes about sex toys reaches out and includes consumers as well.

A key to the design success of this design-advocacy-consumer ecosystem is that it serves its stakeholders well on different levels. It addresses an area of public health where people historically have been underserved. It enables all stakeholders to advance a set of ideals (including, but not limited to, a progressive sex-positive feminist agenda), and it creates a profitable market. And design companies are well aware of the market, as the co-founders of one company made clear, when we asked why their first toy was designed for couples: "Money.... [Product] is aimed specifically right dead nuts in the middle of the bell curve of the population."

Sex toys have transitioned from a topic of shame to a movement that people are increasingly proud to be a part of, which in turn motivates them to contribute to its advancement, as the founder of Jimmyjane explains in a news article at AskMen.com:

> I was designing—it was kind of whatever clients came through the door and I was looking for something that was going to be more impactful. You know, I designed yet another cell phone, yet another toothbrush, yet another computer monitor, and all of my fellow designers in other firms are designing the same stuff. It just seemed like all we were doing was driving demand, but not actually delivering something that at the end of the day was going to make a big difference in people's lives.

Obviously, it is not always possible to design in an area where one feels that one is contributing to a good social cause—someone has to design watches, shoes, mobile phones, and productivity software. Still, it is hard to deny the motivating power of the designers' passion to contribute to wellness—and the collaborative stakeholder configurations that it leads to.

CONCLUSION

Many of the concerns of third-wave HCI—experience, emotion, embodiment—remain secondary considerations in HCI practice. As a field, we historically have begun with a set of functional needs and/or a sense of a particular interface in mind, and we have iterated on it, before starting to evaluate it in terms of usability or user experience. Subjective satisfaction is often measured in crude terms, e.g., via Likert scales. Often, experiential qualities are reduced to cybernetic system features: can a system infer when a user is frustrated with pressure-sensitive mice, face-recognition algorithms, or by detecting breakdowns in information seeking behaviors? Likewise, some seek to achieve aesthetic interaction by grafting psychological models of flow onto user models. In addition to placing experience in the backseat behind functionality, such approaches seem methodologically to alienate designers from their own vast experience with, well, experience.

This case study of sex toy designers has shown an alternative: what might it look like when designers *start* with the objective of designing to support pleasurable, embodied, affective experiences? We have seen that in the case of designer sex toys, designers operate in a critical, rather than empirical, space. They interrogate key vocabulary, from sex to attraction to feeling sexy to love itself, dialogically, by engaging in design criticism, reasoning from their own experiences, and having intimate conversations with friends, family, colleagues, customers, and even strangers. User feedback goes directly to principle designers, unmediated by averages and models. Designers talk openly about their own sexual experiences and reflections and incorporate them into their design explanations as just another resource. Instead of developing complex analytic models, they quickly iterate through three-dimensional prototypes. They consult with experts, not to have domain knowledge transmitted to them, but rather to engage the experts themselves, as thinking subjects, in their cycles of iteration.

It would be absurd to suggest that the specific case of high-end sex toy design could generalize to all of third-wave HCI. This case study provides one example, however, of a successful area of experience design whose processes bear little resemblance to hallowed HCI traditions, with their early empirical focus on users and predilection for validated models and methods [17]. For sex toy designers, to design for experience, emotion, and physical pleasure is to *critically immerse* themselves in experience, emotion, and physical pleasure, and to engage these critical immersions into a conversation involving "users" as fellow sexual beings (rather than data providers); sexual health, medical, and retail experts; and a steady stream of quickly iterating 3D prototypes. Our suggestion is not, of course, that we should abandon our past and emulate sex toy designers, but rather to reflect on cases such as these while HCI critically interrogates its own design processes during this third-wave paradigm shift. Perhaps we can develop our methodological and/or theoretical vocabulary to be responsive to aspects of this case that seem to be working well, in particular in the areas of embodied design cognition and social activist-oriented design.

REFERENCES

1. Bardzell, J. Interaction Criticism and Aesthetics. *Proc. of CHI'09: World Conference on Human Factors in Computing Systems*. ACM: New York. (2009).

2. Bardzell, S. Feminist HCI: Taking stock and outlining an agenda for design. *Proc. of CHI'10.* ACM: New York. (2010), 1301-1310.
3. Bardzell, J., Bardzell, S., Bertelsen, O., and Kannabiran, G. Erotic life in Human-Computer Interaction. *Proc of NordiCHI'10*, Reykjavík, Iceland. New York: ACM Press (2010).
4. Bardzell, J., Bardzell, S. Intimate interactions: Online representation and software of the self. *Interactions*. ACM: New York. (2008), 11-15.
5. Bardzell, S., & Odom, W. The experience of embodied space in virtual worlds: An ethnography of a Second Life community. *Space and Culture 11*, 3 (2008), 239-259.
6. Bardzell, S., & Bardzell, J. Docile avatars: Aesthetics, experience, and sexual interaction in Second Life. *Proc. of British HCI 2007*, (2007).
7. Bertelsen, O., and Petersen, M. Erotic life as a new frontier in HCI. *Proc. of British HCI 2007.* Lancaster, UK. (2007), 7-10.
8. Blythe, M. and Jones M. Human Computer (Sexual) Interactions. In *Interactions 11*, 5 (2004), 43-46.
9. Blythe, M., Overbeeke, K., Monk, A., and Wright, P. *Funology: From usability to Enjoyment.* Springer, 2003.
10. Bødker, S. When second wave HCI meets third wave challenges. *Proc. of NordiCHI'06,* ACM Press (2006).
11. Boehner, K., DePaula, R., Dourish, P., and Sengers, P. How emotion is made and measured. *International Journal of Human-Computer Studies* 65, Elsevier Ltd (2007), 275-291.
12. Brewer, J., Kaye, J., Williams, A., and Wyche, S. Sexual interactions: Why we should talk about sex in HCI. *Ext. Abstracts CHI 2006*, ACM Press (2006).
13. Buxton, B. *Sketching User Experiences: Getting the Design Right and the Right Design.* Morgan Kaufmann, 2007.
14. Cross, N. *Designerly Ways of Knowing.* Birkhäuser Architecture, 2007.
15. Dourish, P. *Where the Action is: The Foundations of Embodied Interaction.* MIT Press, 2006.
16. Fogtmann, M., Fritsch, J., Kortbek, K. Kinesthetic interaction: Revealing the bodily potential in interaction design. *Proc. of OzHCI, 2008.* ACM Press (2008), 89-96.
17. Gould, J., and Lewis, C. Designing for usability: Key principles and what designers think. *Communications of the ACM 28*, 3(1985), 300-311.
18. Grinter, B., Siek, K., and Grimes, A. Wellness informatics. *Extended Abstracts, CHI'10* (2010).
19. Harrison, S. Tatar, D. and Sengers, P. The three paradigms of HCI. *Ext. Abstracts CHI 2007,* ACM Press (2007).
20. Hornecker, E., and Burr, J. Getting a grip on tangible interaction: A framework on physical space and social interaction. *Proc. of CHI 2006.* ACM Press (2006), 437-446.
21. Kaye, J.J. I Just Clicked To Say I Love You: Rich Evaluations of Minimal Communication. CHI '06 extended abstracts on Human factors in computing systems, ACM Press (2006), 363-368.
22. Klemmer, S., Hartmann, B., Takayama, L. How bodies matter: Five themes for interaction design. *Proc. of DIS 2006.* ACM Press (2006), 140-149.
23. Law. E. Preface: Meaningful measures: Valid useful user experience measurement. In *Proc. of the International Workshop on Meaningful Measures.* (2008), 3-4.
24. Lawson, B. *How Designers Think: The Design Process Demystified.* Elsevier Architectural Press, 1980.
25. Löwgren, J. and Stolterman, E. *Thoughtful Interaction Design.* MIT Press, 2004.
26. Maines, R. *The Technology of Orgasm: Hysteria, the Vibrator, and Women's Sexual Satisfaction.* Johns Hopkins UP: Baltimore & London, 1999.
27. McCarthy, J. and Wright, P. *Technology as Experience.* The MIT Press, 2004.
28. Naples, N. *Feminism and Method: Ethnography, Discourse Analysis, and Activist Research.* Routledge, 2003.
29. Ogden, C., Richards, I.A. *The Meaning of Meaning.* Mariner Books, New York, 1923.
30. Picard, P. *Affective Computing.* The MIT Press, 2000.
31. Pace, T., Bardzell, S., and Bardzell, J. The rogue in the lovely black dress: Intimacy in World of Warcraft. *Proc. of CHI'10.* ACM: New York (2010), 233-242.
32. Reinharz, S. *Feminist Methods in Social Research.* Oxford UP, 1992.
33. Schiphorst, T. soft(n): Toward a somaesthetics of touch. *Extended Abstract of CHI'09.* ACM: New York. (2009), 2427-2438.
34. Schiphorst, T. exhale. An art installation. 2007. Retrieved September 18, 2010. http://www.sfu.ca/~tschipho/exhale/index.html
35. Schön, D. *The Reflective Practitioner: How Professionals Think In Action.* Basic Books, 1984.
36. Silverberg, C. Putting a price on pleasure: An oral history of retail sexual business and public discourse on sexual pleasure, 2009, unpublished manuscript.
37. Waxman, J. The case for intelligent design. *Adult Video News.* Retrieved November 2009 from avn.com.
38. Zimmerman, J., Forlizzi, J., and Evenson, S. Research through design as a method for interaction design research in HCI. *Proc. of CHI'07* ACM: New York. (2007), 493-502.

Designing a Phone Broadcasting System for Urban Sex Workers in India

Nithya Sambasivan
Department of Informatics
University of California
Irvine, CA 92617
nsambasi@uci.edu

Julie Sage Weber & Edward Cutrell
Microsoft Research India
Sadashivanagar
Bangalore, India 560080
julie.weber@gmail.com, cutrell@microsoft.com

ABSTRACT
In this paper, we present the design, implementation, and deployment of a phone-based broadcasting system designed for reaching out to at-risk populations in urban India. We worked in collaboration with Pragati, a non-governmental organization dedicated to assisting Urban Sex Workers (USWs) in Bangalore, India, with the goal of improving Pragati's outreach to the women they serve. We conducted ethnographic action research to understand and address the needs of Pragati and the lifestyles of USWs. Responding to the unique design constraints of the USW community such as specific privacy and timing constraints, a desire to remain invisible, and the unusually high rate of mobile phone use, we designed a phone-based broadcasting system for Pragati. We then deployed the system on four different occasions and application areas. We present the results and key findings from our study, and conclude with a discussion on how designing for particularly difficult cases such as USWs can shed new light on the design of mobile applications for the developing world in general, such as challenging ubiquity and phone numbers as identity.

Author Keywords
HCI4D, ICT4D, M4D, Urban Sex Workers, India.

ACM Classification Keywords
H5.m. Information interfaces and presentation (e.g., HCI)

General Terms
Design

INTRODUCTION
Governmental and civil society organizations for socio-economic development organize and support target communities, helping them access a broad range of services such as health care, education, and business development [13]. Communication infrastructures are crucial in reaching out to these communities for notifications, announcements, advertising, reminders, and emergency services during crises. Communications are also used for disseminating information about welfare services and for effecting behavior change (e.g., public service announcements). Organizations use several mechanisms to communicate with their members—television and radio advertisements, Internet services, Short Messaging Service (SMS), printed flyers, word-of-mouth, and so on.

In the developing world, organizations working for socio-economic development are stifled by several factors in their communication reach, including literacy and infrastructure constraints. Moreover, broadcast media are not always relevant to the entire target population: they can be impersonal or non-local (e.g., radio and television); programming can be expensive (e.g., television); and content may rely on literacy (e.g., textual flyers and SMS).

Mobile phones present an excellent opportunity to reach out to target populations in the developing world. As of July 2010, the overall tele-density in India was 58.17% (688 million subscribers with 2.5% monthly growth rate) [1], with arguably a larger actual usage base due to shared and pay phones [15]. By using voice content, phones are unconstrained by literacy concerns and they support the existing oral formats of everyday conversation and radio listenership [7,13]. By featuring the voice of a familiar leader or peer, phone systems can provide a rich means to leverage existing institutional and interpersonal trust. Moreover, by modifying content, targeted or personalized message broadcasts can be scaled to very large audiences.

We designed, implemented, and observed a phone-based broadcasting system for Pragati: a non-profit, healthcare project targeted at Urban Sex Workers (USWs) in Bangalore, India. USWs constitute a unique and particularly challenging group for socio-economic development work: they are highly marginalized by society, vulnerable to HIV and other Sexually Transmitted Infections (STIs), and are often very poor. At the same time, USWs are technologically well-connected, with an exceedingly high mobile phone tele-density of 97%. The Pragati project currently reaches out to its USW members through word-of-mouth via its field workers, who in turn communicate and disseminate HIV treatment and prevention strategies. However, the project faces several challenges in connecting with USWs. Word-of-mouth scales poorly, with delays in communication, especially for emergency notifications. In addition, USWs are highly mobile and there are specific dependencies on their schedules for when they may be available for contact.

We adapted an automated calling system to make phone calls to Pragati's USW members and play a variety of pre-recorded audio messages for different reminders and announcements. In addition to common developing-world impediments (e.g., resource and educational constraints), we needed to accommodate the maintenance of dual identities of USWs (not revealing their professional identities to their families), scattered populations, urban migration, and privacy concerns.

We believe that our findings can generalize to other populations that may be vulnerable, mobile, untrackable, or nervous, and to the institutions trying to reach out to them, such as migrant Bangladeshi workers in India, war-torn Sudanese nomads, and homosexuals in Saudi Arabia. Our motivation to work with the USWs stems from the fact that despite their social marginalization and economic and health vulnerabilities, they have very high telecom penetration. We believe that USWs present us with a unique opportunity to augur technological ideas for other user groups facing similar socio-economic issues, but where technology is steadily penetrating. We feel our primary contribution is the design of a broadcasting system for a marginalized population; we also identify the unique lifestyle issues and design implications of interactive systems for invisible and wary populations.

In this paper, we report our ethnographically-inspired study and field trials of the phone-based broadcasting system. We describe some of the challenges in designing for USWs. We describe four different deployments of our system—a pilot announcement for an event, microfinance loan payment reminders, HIV testing advertisements, and announcements for a computer training event. We conclude with some broad lessons for the HCI4D community, including reflections on trust, mobility, ubiquity, and privacy for developing world populations.

RELATED WORK

Phone-based systems

Much of the prior work on phone-based communication systems has focused on sending automated reminders for appointment keeping [9] and for medication regimen adherence, including HIV [15] and Tuberculosis [19]. Such attempts have disseminated through text messages and voice messages, including Interactive Voice Response [8], albeit, through automated or impersonal voices of hired callers. All of the above studies have shown some success in improving baseline rates with the help of technology.

Several researchers have designed interactive voice-based mobile applications for the developing world, such as [7,13,17]. In their studies of usage of phone-based asynchronous voice message forums for small-scale farmers, Patel *et al.* point to the importance of complementing social media with traditional media, such as radio [13]. Sherwani *et al.* have designed and deployed a phone-based speech interface for health workers to access replies to health queries, in spoken conversation format [17]. Other researchers have designed a phone-based user-generated audio classifieds service for the economically poor [7]. We add the case of design and study of a one-way phone-based communication system keeping the constraints of a special population in mind, like USWs.

Non-profits and ICTs

In their work on resource-constrained non-profits, LeDantec *et al.* note the importance of ICT integration for co-ordination and communication among non-profits, and its role in providing coordinated care to vulnerable communities [11]. To the best of our knowledge, no prior research has explicitly designed or studied outreach or co-ordination of non-profits with target populations.

FIELD METHODS

Our preliminary field study was targeted at gaining an understanding of the function of the organization and the lives of the urban sex workers. In particular, our inquiry probed into entry into the sex trade; identity management of USWs; sites, pay scales, and entities in sex trade; physical, financial, and emotional security; and knowledge of STIs.

Our study was ethnographic in spirit; we employed participant and non-participant observation, combined with semi-structured interviews. In order to understand the organization planning, implementation, and logistics, we conducted interviews with various stakeholders at the Pragati office (head office staff, zone-level staff, and field workers). We employed non-participant observation at the zone 3 Swati Manne, or the drop-in shelter, which houses some beds, a microfinance payment collection center, health checkup center, and counseling center. We spent 3 months at the zone 3 Swati Manne, attending meetings, helping at events, observing transactions and checkups, and 'hanging-out' in general. Interviews were conducted in Tamil, Hindi, and Kannada by the first author. We also conducted non-participant observation at client solicitation locations, on streets and at homes and bus-stops. We conducted semi-structured interviews with 21 urban sex workers at these locations.

Research ethics: Conducting research with USWs entails paying special care to research ethics and informant privacy. Interviewees were asked for verbal consent before conducting interviews. No identifying information was collected, including names and addresses. Photographs were only shot in Swati Manne premises, which were post-processed for pixilation. Audio recordings were avoided for interviews—we took down notes wherever possible. In order to respect our informants' privacy and identities, we restricted our interviews to Swati Manne premises and streets. Our field access was mediated by Pragati, which helped us gain entry into the women's lives as well as avoid any possible confrontations with the police.

Researcher values: Our own views and values with respect to sex work have inherently biased our research. While sex work can be exploitative and risky, we decided to view our informants as independent professionals, family members, colleagues and friends in their own right, instead of viewing them as victims of their circumstances. Such a position helped us understand the agency, relationships, and identities constructed in their everyday realities.

PROJECT PRAGATI AND URBAN SEX WORKERS

Project Pragati (meaning "progress") is a healthcare project for USWs, primarily targeted at HIV prevention and treatment. It also provides auxiliary services, such as microfinance banking and counseling. Pragati was created in the year 2005, when Bangalore was surveyed and an HIV prevalence of 12.1% among USWs was noted.

The Pragati organizational structure is constituted by employees both from within and outside the sex worker community. The head office administration comprises non-community members and community members. As the structure gets closer to grassroots, it is essentially run by community members. In particular, outreach workers (*Jananis*) and field workers (*Jeevikas*) are chosen from the sex worker community.

Jeevikas, or fulltime field workers, are senior USWs who may continue to practice their trade in their free time. They are chosen from the community based on criteria like friendliness with other USWs and local expertise. They visit the field regularly during times when USWs are available in the field, i.e., soliciting clients. This poses a logistical challenge, since USWs are usually busy and not always available. Jeevikas monitor health checkups, distribute condoms to USWs directly and place condoms in strategic public areas (like paid restrooms and parks), offer counseling, and monitor monetary payments. Jananis, or outreach workers, monitor and train Jeevikas as well as visit the field themselves. Currently, dissemination is largely driven by the Jananis and Jeevikas, who deliver information back and forth to the grassroots and Pragati officers.

USW overview

India is home to an estimated 2.8 million USWs [2]. USWs in Bangalore may work full-time or part-time, owing to the informal, flexible nature of work. Broadly, the Bangalore-based sex trade is divided into four categories (breakdown and percentages come from Pragati officers):

Street-based sex trade: Roughly 50% of the Bangalore USWs are street-based. They solicit in the streets and go with clients to motels and public-private spaces, like restrooms. Most of them are homeless, seeking rest in bus stops and railway stations. They are the most vulnerable type of USWs, perpetually dealing with the police and rowdies. They generally carry out the trade at night.

Home-based sex trade: About 40% of the USWs are home-based. While solicitation is carried out on the streets, they rent out rooms in an apartment or house. Several home-based USWs are married with children. They work during the day and return to their families at night. Such a lifestyle is built upon a dual identity—the USWs tell their families that they work innocuous jobs, such as domestic work or tailoring in the garments industry.

Lodge-based sex trade: About 5% of the USWs are based in motels (commonly known as lodges in India), renting out rooms on a permanent basis.

Brothel-based sex trade: The remaining 5% of the USWs are based in brothel buildings in residential areas. Brothels keep changing locations, for fear of suspicion among neighbors or the police.

USWs are vulnerable to several social, economic, and health issues. Many USWs are affected by poverty (especially those earning in the range of INR50-200 or USD1-4 per client). Poverty manifests as other issues: condoms are not enforced on male clients since they agree to pay more for "going natural". Condoms are also telltale signs if discovered by the police, resulting in harassment. This results in HIV and other STIs. Violence is pronounced in these communities: police, pimps, intimate partners, or *goondas* (thugs) may abuse the USWs and extricate a major share of their earnings. Not surprisingly, many USWs turn to alcohol during work, resulting in further tensions.

Legality: The Immoral Traffic (Prevention) Act or PITA is a 1986 amendment of legislation passed in 1956 to prevent illegal trafficking [3]. While it is illegal to operate brothels and surrounding activities in India, it is not illegal to exchange sex for money. A sex worker can be punished for soliciting or seducing in public, while clients can be punished for sexual activity in proximity to a public place. In reality, sex work in India lies in a grey zone, under police enforcement and pimp discretion.

USW vignettes

We present two vignettes to illustrate the everyday life of urban sex workers. We pick two types from the general typology—home- and street-based—since they represent majority of the USWs at 90%. Both cases are chosen to be representative of the two types.

Lakshmi is a 45-year old home-based USW. She is a mother of 3 adult children, who are all married. Originally from the Mandya district of the Karnataka state, she is a native Kannada speaker who has lived in Bangalore since her marriage. Lakshmi has not attended school. Her husband's alcohol addiction drove her into the trade at 35 years of age. She was introduced by her female friend (also a sex worker) to a client. Among friends and family, she maintains an image of a garment-factory worker, working a day-shift between 9 am to 6 pm. Lakshmi rents out a room in the neighborhood where she solicits, usually on one of the busy streets. Her earnings vary between zero to INR 1,000 (~USD 21) per day, after servicing multiple clients. Her professional mobile phone is strictly switched off and hidden in her purse when she is home. She distributes her mobile number to her clients, encouraging them to pass it around. She shares her other phone freely with her family. This phone is used as a mobile landline at home, and also functions as radio.

Jaya is a 25-year old street-based USW. She was introduced to this line of work at age 19, when she left her family in rural Hosur. She dropped out of school in 5th grade. Her first contact in the city of Bangalore was a female USW, who then initiated her into the trade. Jaya is unmarried. She practices sex work at night, between 10 pm and 7 am. Her usual solicitation spots are in and around the Bangalore city bus terminal. She rents out a room throughout the night at a motel near the terminal. She sleeps during the day, usually at the local Pragati drop-in shelter or at her friend's place. Jaya earns anywhere between zero to INR 500 (~USD 11) per night; a huge portion of the earnings are distributed among the local police and her intimate partner. She sends another portion of her earnings to her family in Hosur, who believe she works as domestic help. Jaya owns a dual-SIM mobile phone, switching numbers when she visits her family. Her mobile phone is her nodal point in everyday communications and in soliciting customers: she uses the same phone to make calls to her tailor and milkman, as well as intimate partner and clients. Despite being non-literate, she gets her friends to store address book contacts, and rote-memorizes names through symbolic literacy [15]. The phone is strictly "cleansed" when she takes it to her village, as she sometimes reverts to her old SIM for everyday tele-communication, but rejects calls from any clients.

DESIGN SPACE

Potential application areas

From our ethnographic observations, we found that Pragati's communication ecology was prone to several problems: the Jeevikas were unable to always reach out to the USWs because of their busy work schedules and scattered lifestyles. Large-scale communication took several days to transpire. Communicating an urgent message to all members instantly was next to impossible.

For the services provided by Pragati, the USWs tended to forget the dates for monthly HIV and STI medical tests. Several STIs are non-symptomatic, which pose severe problems when undetected. Members would discontinue their treatment upon success from the first dosage (for example, syphilis requires three Penicillin shots, but the women stop at the first shot, which is ineffective at curing the disease). Another problem area was that of microfinance monthly payments for loans. With compounding interest, missing the deadline for a repayment can be costly, given the poverty-stricken conditions of USWs. Consequences for missing a deadline include ineligibility for loan requests for the following two months.

Mobile phone penetration among Pragati USWs is self-reported by Pragati administrators at 97%, which is an unusually high number for both: a developing nation population (the average wireless tele-density in India is 55.14% as of July, 2010 [1] and women (who are 37% less likely to own a mobile phone in South Asia, as of February, 2010 [4]). Mobile phones are excellent tools for reminders and announcements, since they form a pervasive infrastructure, are very effective at delivering short messages, and are portable. For the above-mentioned problem areas, we took into consideration the exceedingly high mobile penetration among USWs and narrowed down on designing a reminder and announcement system. USWs lead busy and nomadic lives; therefore, the system seemed better poised at sending short, effective messages rather than behavior change through sex education or financial literacy. We picked two areas—microfinance and healthcare reminders—as focal points for our system.

Design constraints

Designing a system for USWs entails dealing with unique lifestyles. We generated a socio-cultural analysis that highlighted possible dimensions where our design response needed to be particularly sensitive. We list them below:

Multiple devices: While the USWs we met were exceptionally technology-reliant, there are other challenges to consider with such perpetual usage. A salient finding from our ethnographic observations is that the maintenance of multiple identities follows that multiple mobile phone identities are maintained, for work and for family. This could mean either two separate devices, or dual-SIM phones. Work phones are strictly switched off and hidden at home; however, there is some seepage at times.

In addition, mobile phones are heavily prone to theft and misplacement. It is estimated by Pragati that roughly 2-3% of their USWs lose their phones per month. Moreover, mobile numbers are constantly changed for a variety of reasons, such as purchase of a new phone, avoiding contact with partners or pimps, or circumvention of suspicion.

Invisibility: Many USWs lead double lives, maintaining different images, stories, and logics at work and home. Identities switch, information does not flow, and networks are disconnected, across infrastructures. Work identities are protected from the family. Boundaries are established between the legal and illicit, not as forgery, but as a necessary occupational measure. How do we think about fuzzy properties in technology design?

Associated with the invisibility realm are several issues that have implications for technology design. There is a stigma of being attached to formal institutions for fear of identification. Within the Pragati project, there is a common binding thread (sex work) and mechanisms are in place to verify the reputation of a member before formal transactions, like loans. How can we create a trustworthy system that will carefully balance existing relations with the NGO and remain sensitive to the nature of the USW work, not jeopardizing their lives?

Migration and scatteredness: Most USWs are migrants from villages and towns in Karnataka and neighboring states. Mobility is a prime part of the street-based USW lifestyle; many of them live out of a suitcase. It is common for USWs to leave with their partners for several days at a stretch, or travel to where their work takes them.

Unlike populations that cohere through shared spaces, such as neighbors, street-based USWs are either homeless or scattered across the city. There is a pronounced lack of social capital that is built from sharing a geographical space. This poses a challenge for accountability for institutional transactions.

Timing: Home-based USWs operate at regular hours, similar to day jobs (as part of their story of working as domestic help or seamstresses). Street-based workers usually operate at night, and rest during the day. Consequences of intervening at an inappropriate time, hence in an inappropriate geographical space can include revealing protected identities. Due to the flexible working hours and nebulous times when sex work is actually carried out, timing is a crucial in designing for USWs.

SYSTEM DESIGN

As a design response to the problem of reaching out to the USWs, we designed, implemented, and began evaluations on a phone-based broadcasting system. It was designed to call several mobile phones at once, and play audio messages upon feedback from the receiver.

We were interested in porting a mass-media approach over to a device that is, in some ways, designed more around mutually-accepted coordination and exchange than one-way large-scale dissemination, and in understanding its effects.

Design process

We employed human-centered, ethnographic action-research in the design of our system. We integrated our initial ethnographic findings into the system design. We deployed the system between July–September 2010, for various application areas that we will note in the next section. We constantly sought feedback from our users and iteratively revised the features. Jeevikas and Jananis helped us gather phone numbers of their members, for our phone system. We also transcribed paper-based microfinance and health records into our database (see fig. 1).

In the current setup, the Jeevikas and Jananis go out to the field and act as communication agents between Pragati and the members, i.e., a person-to-person model. Implicit in this setup is a high level of trust in field staff and Pragati. Our system was not meant to be a replacement for the current communication processes; in fact, we wanted to leverage the actors in the loop and the trust placed in them. In the next sub-section, we discuss the various design criteria that we chose from our study results.

Design criteria:

Build a phone-based, server-side infrastructure: Owing to the ubiquity of mobile phones, our system was envisioned to work on telephones. In order to avoid compatibility

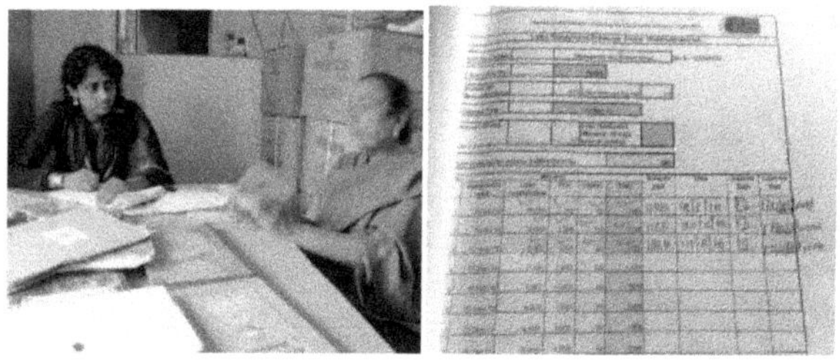

Figure 1. (Left) Field interviews with USWs and (right) microfinance bank records.

issues and potentially incriminating application traces, we decided to build a server-side infrastructure.

Leverage audio: Our system would solely make use of audio messages, to avoid literacy issues and make use of the familiar oral format. Text messages were another possibility, but they rely on literacy.

Leverage institutional trust: One of our key motivations in building the system was to leverage the existing institutional and interpersonal trust. We recorded audio messages using the voice of the friendly Field Coordinator of Zone 3, who was a highly visible and much-liked person. This ensured that our content was approved by Pragati.

Keep the calls short: We wanted to keep the audio messages short, hoping that it would interfere less with the USWs' lives as well as motivate listening to the content end-to-end. We decide to intersperse the voice content with classical music in the background.

Keep the content anonymous: In our attempts to respect the privacy of the USWs, we decided to make the content non-linked to the receiver and not divulge identifying or criminalizing information, such as names, sex work, or HIV records, while still being clear to the recipient what the message was about.

Find a good time to call: Based on the overlap between street- and home-based USWs, we decided to broadcast the audio messages at late afternoon-evening. During these timings, home-based workers solicit and street-based workers relax or get ready for their night shifts.

Implementation: We built a broadcasting system using off-the-shelf components and custom scripting. We used Asterisk [5], an open-source telephony software, on Linux to make the outgoing calls. We utilized a Primary Rate Interface board (2000 Media Series from Dialogic, Inc.) to allow up to 15 phone calls in parallel. We wrote Python scripts to automatically generate call files from a phone number input log, and to dial the numbers in parallel. The system played pre-recorded audio messages upon hearing any feedback noise from the receiver side. We produced audio as 8 KHz, 8-bit Pulse Code Modulation wav files.

The system enabled simple logging of the outcome of each call, including whether it was answered, time of dialing,

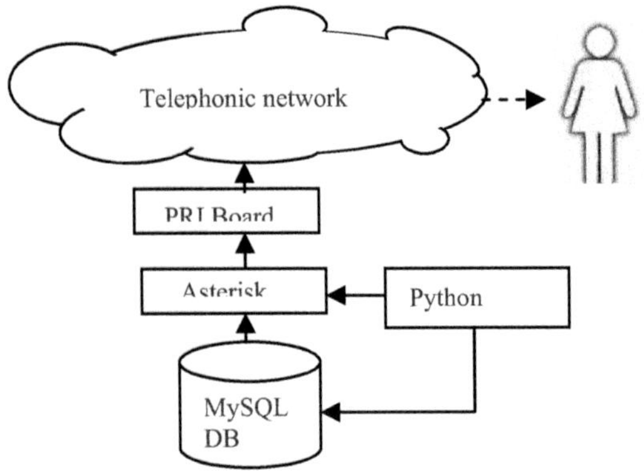

Figure 2. System architecture.

and the total duration of each call. Organizations can easily adapt the system by supplying their own audio recording and list of telephone numbers to call; the rest is automatic.

DEPLOYMENT

For our deployment, we chose four applications areas, depending upon the purpose, scale of phone numbers, nature of communication, and relation to existing information sources (standalone or complementary to field workers). Table 1 explains the breakdown of our deployments. Table 2 explains their results.

Our system was designed to serve as an effective broadcast communication system. Towards this, we were interested in understanding the following: the percentage of the population that was reachable; the effect of timing on reachability; and the percentage of the reached population that listened to the content entirely. We were looking for behavior change to whatever extent possible, but were acutely aware of our time limitation of three months. We used a mixed-method approach to understand how, what, why, and when the system intervened into the USWs' lives.

Structured interviews: We conducted interviews both in person and over the telephone after each deployment. In-person interviews were conducted at Swati Manne premises. Interviews over the phone were sufficiently modified to respect privacy of informants. We asked for the person's name from our phone database, and then revealed our identity if the person confirmed that it was indeed the right person. Our interviews probed into the information ecology, call context, mobile phone profiling, reactions to the call and audio, and the after-effects of the call.

Deployment	Target	Nature of communication	Stand-alone?
Pilot: Swati Manne inauguration	Selected #s, one-time (n=35)	Reminder	No
Microfinance loans	Loanees with #s, one-time (n=23)	Reminder	No
HIV testing	All numbers, one-time (n=230)	Advertisement	No
Computer training session	All numbers, twice (n=627 in total)	Announcement	Yes

Table 1. Breakdown of deployments.

Data records: We collected and transcribed medical and financial records from Pragati. As a baseline, we analyzed the financial health (i.e., their average rate of repayment, days before or after deadline, outstanding amount, length of the loan period, etc.) and created portfolio profiles for the members (reasons why they borrowed the money, typology of sex work, and neighborhood). For the medical tests, we analyzed the frequency of testing.

Phone logs: Finally, we monitored and analyzed the master call log maintained by Asterisk. Here we looked for duration of listening to the voice messages, number of calls that were answered, and the time of dialing.

Swati Manne Inauguration: In July 2010, Pragati was opening a new Swati Manne in zone 3. A cultural program was organized, which included *pujas* (worship), talks, and lunch. Our system was deployed alongside traditional communication methods of face-to-face announcements, by Jeevikas and Jananis. We collected the phone numbers of 35 USWs through Jeevikas and Jananis.

For the content, we recorded the voice of the zone 3 field coordinator. We faced several challenges in this simple task. We recorded the message at the Swati Manne premises, to fit with the schedule of the Field Coordinator. However, the environment was prone to perpetual and random background noise, such as auto-rickshaw and bus horns, metro rail construction, and the regular buzz at Swati Manne. We overcame this issue through a combination of noise removal, voice amplification, and background music.

Another design challenge was to keep the message succinct and clear. We avoided talking about the organization or motivate the members about the event explicitly. Our recorded message was follows: "Namaskaram [Greetings]. My name is Geetha, and I am calling from Swati Manne, Zone 3. We

	Swati Manne inauguration reminders	Microfinance loan reminders	Medical testing advertisements	Computer training announcements
Members	35	38	230	627
Members w/#	35	23	230	627
%Reachable members	NA	61.00%	NA	NA
Connected calls	29	22	207	441
Finished content	27	20	121	354
%Finished/Connected calls	93.10%	90.90%	58.54%	80.27%
%Connected calls/Members w/#	82.85%	95.65%	90.00%	70.33%
Audio message length	19 seconds	13.2 seconds (average)	31 seconds	15 seconds

Table 2: Summary of results from the four deployments.

are shifting our old Swati Manne to Rajaji Nagar. The inauguration program is tomorrow at 11 am. Lunch will be served. I request you to kindly attend. Thank you."

Figure 3. Swati Manne inauguration.

Results: Of the 35 members we contacted, 29 calls were answered (table 2). 5 phones were switched off. Twenty-seven members (93.10%) listened to the entire audio.

Ten out of 29 contacted attended the event, out of which 5 had not heard through field workers. 9/10 people reported distrust in foreign and male voices and several interviewees liked the short length of our messages (at 19 seconds). Many members were traveling or soliciting at the time of receiving the call.

Microfinance reminders: Our second deployment was targeted at loanees of *Swathi Jyothi,* the microfinance (MFI) wing of Pragati. Individual loans are taken out for mortgage, children's education, starting new part-time businesses and so in. Built on a joint liability model, 3-4 members get together and form a group. While the members do not have to save to form a group pool, they commit themselves to repay each other's loans, should there be any defaulting by other members of the group. Failure to repay on time also means that loanees cannot request loans for the next two months. Our interviews reflected some confusion among the USWs in recalling their loan deadlines, attributable to their non-literacy and lack of financial visibility.

"The [loan] dates keep changing each month and I often forget when the repayment is. Some days I barely make anything, so paying the fine is an additional problem."

We were motivated to modify the broadcasting system to send out reminders for deadlines. We collected as many phone numbers of loanees as possible (23 out of 38 loanees) from Swathi Jyothi, the MFI at Pragati. We sent out reminders one day before the deadline. The voice message conveyed that a payment was due on the specified deadline. We did not include names of the loanees in the messages.

Results: Twenty-two out of 23 members were reachable, out of which 20 members (91%) listened to the content entirely. In general, we found no difference between payment rates of members who got the call (payment on time = 77.77%) and the 15 who did not (payment on time = 77.27%). Two women that we had called were hospitalized after HIV and one USW's grandmother had passed away, which brought down the overall average by 16, 17, and 7 days each. Without these 3 loanees, the average payment with calls was made 1.59 days in advance, compared to 0.88 days in advance without the call. However, our interview findings unanimously indicated that the microfinance reminders were useful at reminding loanees:

	Avg. # of months	Avg. # months on time (%)	Avg. # of days paid on time (days)	Avg. # on time in August (%)	Avg. # of days paid on time in Aug (days)
Call	4.7	86.78	-1.66	77.27	0.23
No	5.4	87.65	-1.99	77.77	-0.88

Table 3. Analysis of financial portfolios. (Avg. # of months is length of loan so far & avg. # days is number of days paid before deadline, negative for early, positive for late payments)

"I have a slip of paper on which the due dates are written, but I often forget to pay with all the tension at work and home. I have been paying late for the past 3 months. This call really reminded me to pay on time."

Another interviewee spoke of how the system helped her remember without incurring a due.

"I was in the Ghati Subramanya temple for a worship. I got this call and I immediately took the bus back to Bangalore to pay my fees, since I had forgotten by then. I remembered the amount, not the exact date. I was very happy to get the phone call."

However, payments are a function of availability of funds. Interviewees noted that reminder calls one-two days in advance were sufficient, re-affirming our design decisions.

Medical testing reminders: Our third deployment was focused on sending out medical testing advertisements to the USWs. Pragati encourages HIV and Syphilis testing once every 1-3 months, depending upon the volume of sex work and age of the USW. From our interviews with Pragati staff, it was noted that they found it difficult to remind the women about their tests, since the dates varied each month and there was a general lack of interest in getting tested. We sent out advertisements to motivate the USWs to attend the medical examinations. We were interested in understanding whether the calls were reaching out. Note that this phase targeted all Pragati members of zone 3 whose numbers were collected.

For the audio message, we were faced with the challenge of including content that would communicate in a relevant and appropriate fashion, but at the same time, not reveal details about HIV or other STIs or risky information. In consultation with the Pragati staff, we decided to model the content similar to radio advertisements promoting medical examinations. Our message read as follows:

"Namaskaram, I am Geetha speaking from Swathi Mahila Sangha. We are organizing healthcare camps. They will be conductede at the following locations: every Sunday at the Leprosy hospital, every Wednesday at Swati Manne, every Thursday at the Kamkshi Pallaya government hospital, every Friday at the Ayurvedic hospital, and every Saturday at the Kamala Nagar BBMP hospital. We will conduct blood tests and health examinations. Please attend without fail. Thank you."

	Friday	Monday
Members w/ #	297	330
Connected calls	122	319
% Connected calls /Members w/ #	41.07%	96.66%
Finished content	106	248
% Finished/Connected calls	86.88%	77.74%

Table 4. Results of Friday and Monday announcements.

Results: Out of the 230 numbers contacted, 207 connections were made (90%). One hundred twenty one members listened to the content in entirety (59%). Note that the audio for this deployment was longer and more detailed compared to other phases, at 31 seconds. The content was not targeted atany individual in particular, and medical testing was only recommended, not compulsory. Not surprisingly, the listenership dropped slightly, compared to other phases.

"I think the reminders are a very good thing. But I am perfectly healthy. I use condoms with clients 100%. Why should I go get tested? Why go through the pain when I know I am okay?"

Computer training: For our final deployment, we made use of the broadcasting system to make announcements about a free computer training session arranged by us. These announcements were made solely via the system. Our motivation in this field trial was to explore the possibility of a phone-only information source and to make the announcements a few days prior to the event. For the event on Tuesday, we called the Pragati members of zone 3 on the preceding Friday and Monday of the week. Our audio message included details on the event, including time, location, and lunch.

Results: For the computer training, we initiated two sets of announcements on two days (on Friday and the following Monday) (see table 4). The numbers called on Monday were the same 297 as those on Friday with 33 additional numbers for a total of 330. In fact, on Friday 87% of those reached listened to the message entirely. Since Friday and Monday calling were cascading events, there was some repetition between Friday users and Monday users (hence the lower listenership on Monday). Of the total number calls dialed, 63 people (19%) attended the training.

We provided basic computer skills training, printed material and lunch. For the training, our modules included MS-Word, MS-Paint, MS-Excel, and YouTube. Except for one person, no one had touched a computer before. All participants indicated that they found the session to be useful. Even though the training lasted the afternoon, we later discovered that several USWs showed up after the training was over, because of their schedules.

FINDINGS

Overall, our results indicate that the broadcasting system is effective at reaching out to members with phones and delivering content: we connected with 85.25% of members who provided phone numbers. 80.7% members listened entirely. We notice that short, interesting messages got

Figure 4. Computer training deployment.

across (88.09% listened entirely on average for phases 1, 2, and 4, of 12.73 seconds average) and detailed messages got hung up on sooner (58.54% listened for 31 seconds in phase 3), amidst subject material, day/time of call, and being the first call received versus a later call received. The system was widely accepted by Pragati staff and USWs, attributing to its non-intrusiveness and minimal time requirement on part of staff in recording, and users in listening.

Our deployments over multiple "development verticals" are relatively rare in HCI4D; we were keen on learning about the nature of the unsolicited broadcasts across healthcare, microfinance, and training.

Reactions to unknown numbers

One of our main findings was the mixed reaction to getting calls from an unknown phone number (i.e., from our outgoing number). From our ethnographic interviews, we had learned that mobile phones are key instruments in contacting customers. However, not all USWs distributed their professional phone numbers to their clients. Therefore, not all women were used to getting calls from unknown numbers (albeit the occasional wrong number) regularly.

First-time reactions to our calls were a combination of curiosity and doubt. Interestingly, from our interviews, we learned that several USWs would call either the zone 3 Pragati office or their local point of contact (Jeevikas or Jananis monitoring them), despite the fact that the number was that of our research unit. With subsequent calls, they had learned to recognize the number as one associated with Pragati. We expected users to show less interest in listenership with time. However, the later deployments reflect that while the percentage of reachable connections was still high (SD: 10.92% across deployments), the percentage that actually finished the content varied (SD: 15.80%). We learned that this number depended on content (relevance and interesting-ness) and institutional affinity.

Trust

Using the field coordinator's voice invoked positive responses. Our system was amplified by the familiarity and trust built by the Pragati staff, over years of working the USWs, in its reach and authenticity.

"If not for the voice of madam, I would not be sure. We know her and respect her. If it were someone else, I would be really suspicious. I took the message seriously only because of madam."

Taking a cue from large advertising campaigns, we initially thought that using the voice of film stars or popular personalities may be more effective in getting the message across. However, given the sensitive nature of the content, we found a strong proclivity towards using a female voice.

"Since the messages were about health and money, if it were a male voice or a film star's voice, then I will be really suspicious because the content is so sensitive."

This quote suggests that popular voices may actually be counter-productive—a trusted, well-recognized voice works better for sensitive material. Using Geetha's voice also gave the impression to the members that they were "taken care of" (in the words of a Swati Jyothi cashier). Another interesting finding is that several members mistook the automated recording to be a live transmission. Even though our system sent out broadcasts, the findings are a strong indicator of how members reach back to Pragati. This is only possible because of the previously established foundation of relationships.

Anchoring with the NGO helped us not only augment their own reach to their members, but also made our system more acceptable and in sync with established practices.

Timing rhythms and control

One of our initial concerns in designing the system was that of being sensitive to various social infrastructures, such as home and work. Our members unanimously voiced that the system was effective at reaching out to them, without any side-effects. Since the users themselves had agency in controlling their technology usage, by switching off phones when not at work or rejecting the calls, the connections that were established were non-perilous to their lives. Such control has implications for the fraction that is actually reachable, despite the ubiquitous mobile phone penetration.

One way to counter the timing issue is to call on different days, as evidenced in our computer training calls. For the computer training calls, on the Friday, we reached 41.07% users (122/297 calls), whereas on Monday, we reached out to 96.66% (319/330 users), even though we called during the same time slot of 3 – 5 pm. Added to this, several mobile numbers were non-functional. A viable solution here may be for the user to register herself, if she gets a new SIM, perhaps by providing a missed call to the number.

Diffusion

USWs present a unique case of multiple devices per person. In addition to reaching out to individual members through their mobile phones, we noticed a diffusion effect among other members. Several interviewees noted that they called their friends to convey the message. Such a diffusion effect helped surpass actual technology penetration through a social infrastructure, as also noted in [15]. Indeed, for the computer training event, 5 of the 68 who attended did not receive the call and had heard about it through other means.

"I called my friends in my group [joint-liability group] when I got the call about the loans. I called my close friends when I got the call about the computer training. This [system] is very useful to us. It helps me learn about important events over the phone itself. I did not want my friends to miss out on such useful events or forget to pay their loans. It will earn us a bad reputation if we forget."

Our interviews indicate that heavy diffusion occurred among the USWs for the pilot and microfinance deployments. In two cases, 2 women who did not receive calls had made loan payments upon being reminded by their group member who received the call. Three women who attended the Swati Manne inauguration were persuaded by their friend, for whom the call legitimized the event.

"After getting the call, I thought it was an important event for our community to attend. I convinced my three friends to come. "

DISCUSSION

What can the design of a broadcasting system for USWs teach us about designing systems for other vulnerable or nervous populations with similar design constraints, or even Mobiles for Development (M4D) in general?

Challenges for ubiquity

Due to their far-reaching penetration, mobile phones are met with great optimism by designers of technologies for the developing world, especially in the M4D space [8]. However, design in the developing world is not simple; mobiles neither always constitute neat one-to-one, private use configurations [15], nor are they being shared freely all the time. Their use is determined by complex, socio-economic negotiations. USWs' use of mobile phones at home and work highlight some of these tensions.

Mobile connections are unambiguously based on the user's own terms. Mobile phones exist across several social infrastructures. The challenge is to make the applications relevant within each socio-technical system, yet meaningful across these infrastructures. In our case, it was often critical that information remained siloed for different contexts. Women work very hard to keep their work secret from their families, and their use of phones reflects this segregation of communication. Privacy, trust, and timing issues are not unique to USW communities. While mobile phones transcend many facets of people's lives, some boundaries may be permeable, but others need to remain fixed. Failure to respect these boundaries can be dangerous and potentially detrimental to the users.

Caveats in shared-use models

Prior research has underscored the important role of shared use in developing communities, as seen in [6,16]. Indeed, in our study, we see that sharing is not necessarily a defining, normative, practice within the socio-cultural milieus of USWs. While the USWs share within certain realms and social groups, like home and family, tight control is exhibited when they do not wish to share: for example, family members are not allowed to pick up their work phones, by making them invisible. Contrary to the obvious, economic challenges do not always drive shared technology usage in poor communities, as we see how USWs are very poor yet technologically well-connected; as a counterpoint to the expansion of reach through intermediated, shared access in other communities [15]. Such caveats emphasize the need for further work in sharing, such as [18].

Phone numbers and identities

Phone numbers are increasingly used as identities, such as in mobile Internet [8] and mobile banking [10]. Our study alerts us to several challenges in using mobile numbers as identities, such as timing and permanence. Mobile phones are fluid and ever-changing. In the case of USWs, they are explicitly forked for a separate identity. Moreover, phones are easily lost or numbers are changed. Our deployments point to the fact that a synchronous, broadcasting system such as ours simply cannot reach all users, unlike e-mail, voicemail, or asynchronous, stored mechanisms, leaving us looking for a middle-ground. Using mobiles as intervention channels for vulnerable, migrant, untrackable or low-literate populations, where the mobile is the only personal communication device, requires designers to carefully balance approachability, permanence, and identity.

Unlike the technical view of identity or privacy management in the western world, where the technology is a proxy to the construction of identity, we see that identity and privacy around mobile devices in the developing world are socially-negotiated [16]. Users run up against the system in forging their identity and privacy. They adopt specific strategies in coping with their identities, not dissimilar from teenagers coping with privacy, victims of domestic violence, people managing sexual or other controversial lifestyle choices, or those seeking confidential medical information such as HIV or psychiatric problems.

CONCLUSION

In this paper, we presented the design of a phone-based broadcasting system and the results of our deployment at an NGO catering to urban sex workers. We articulated the challenges in designing for USWs and the organizational constraints in reaching out to them. We presented the results of four deployments of the system, in sending out reminders, advertisements, and announcements.

USWs present a severe case of problems that plague the developing world, such as poverty, health concerns and social marginalization. Yet they also represent a unique demographic for high technology penetration, multiple devices per person, and intensive usage in their everyday practices. While the developing world is not yet saturated by technology or concerned with technology-mediated privacy yet, it is likely that various user groups will meet some of these issues sooner or later. Looking explicitly into the design concerns for such groups may pave the way for designing new technological interventions for a variety of at-risk populations where mobiles are the only personal communication device available.

ACKNOWLEDGMENTS

Our thanks to Pragati staff and members for sharing their life stories with us in a heartfelt and welcoming way. We thank our anonymous reviewers and AC for their thoughtful comments. We also thank Aakar, Paige Bills, Ruy Cervantes, Jonathan Donner, David Hutchful, Chinmay Kulkarni, Bonnie Nardi, Navkar, Praveen, Nimmi Rangaswamy, Aishwarya Ratan, and Bill Thies.

REFERENCES

1. TRAI. http://www.trai.gov.in/.
2. Around 2.8 mn prostitutes in India. http://expressindia.com/news/fullstory.php?newsid=86159.
3. Human Rights Reports: India. http://www.state.gov/g/drl/rls/hrrpt/2008/sca/119134.htm.
4. Vital Wave: Emerging Markets. http://www.vitalwaveconsulting.com/insights/articles/
5. Asterisk Project. http://www.asterisk.org/.
6. Burrell, J. Evaluating Shared Access: social equality and the circulation of mobile phones in rural Uganda. *CMC. 15*, 2 (2010), 230-250.
7. Cervantes, R. and Sambasivan, N. VoiceList: user-driven telephone-based audio content. In *Proc. MobileHCI 2008.*, 499–500.
8. Gitau, S., Marsden, G., and Donner, J. After access: challenges facing mobile-only internet users in the developing world. In *Proc. CHI 2010*, 2603–2606.
9. Hashim, M.J., Franks, P., and Fiscella, K. Effectiveness of telephone reminders in improving rate of appointments at an outpatient clinic. *Am. Brd. of Fam. Med. 14*, 3 (2001), 193.
10. Hughes, N. and Lonie, S. M-PESA: Mobile Money for the "Unbanked". *Innovations: 2007 2*, 1-2 (2007), 63-81.
11. Le Dantec, C.A. and Edwards, W.K. The view from the trenches: Organization, power, and technology at two nonprofit homeless outreach centers. In *Proc. CSCW 2008*, 589–598.
12. Parikh, T.S. Engineering rural development. *Comm. of ACM 52*, 1 (2009), 54–63.
13. Patel, N., Chittamuru, D., Jain, A., Dave, P., and Parikh, T.S. Avaaj Otalo: a field study of an interactive voice forum for small farmers in rural India. In *Proc. CHI 2010*, 733–742.
14. Puccio, J.A., Belzer, M., Olson, J., et al. The use of cell phone reminder calls for assisting HIV-infected adolescents and young adults to adhere to highly active antiretroviral therapy. *AIDS Pat. Care & STDs 20*, 6 (2006), 438–444.
15. Sambasivan, N., Cutrell, E., Toyama, K., and Nardi, B. Intermediated technology use in developing communities. In *Proc. CHI 2010*, 2583–2592.
16. Sambasivan, N., Rangaswamy, N., Cutrell, E., and Nardi, B. Ubicomp4D: infrastructure and interaction for international development. In *Proc. UBICOMP 2009*, 155–164.
17. Sherwani, J., Ali, N., Mirza, S., et al. Healthline: Speech-based access to health information by low-literate users. In *Proc. ACM/IEEE ICTD 2007*, 131–139.
18. Steenson, M. and Donner, J. Beyond the personal and private: Modes of mobile phone sharing in urban India. In *The Reconstruction of Space and Time (Vol. 1)*. Piscataway, NJ: Transaction Books, 2009, 231-250.
19. Tanke, E.D. and Leirer, V.O. Automated Telephone Reminders in TB Care. *Medical Care 32*, 4 (1994), 380-389.

Bodily Orientations around Mobiles: Lessons learnt in Vanuatu

Pedro Ferreira
Mobile Life @ Stockholm University
Forum 100, 164 40 Kista, Sweden
pedro@mobilelifecentre.org

Kristina Höök
Mobile Life @ Stockholm University
Forum 100, 164 40 Kista, Sweden
kia@sics.se

ABSTRACT
Since we started carrying mobiles phones, they have altered the ways in which we orient our bodies in the world. Many of those changes are invisible to us – they have become habits, deeply engrained in our society. To make us more aware of our bodily ways of living with mobiles and open the design space for novel ways of designing mobiles and their interactions, we decided to study one of the last groups of users on earth who had not been exposed to mobiles: the people of Vanuatu. As they had so recently started using mobiles, their use was still in flux: the fragility of the mobile was unusual to them as was the need to move in order to find coverage. They were still getting used to carrying their mobiles and keeping them safe. Their encounters with mobile use exposed the need to consider somaesthetics practices when designing mobiles as they profoundly affect our bodily ways of being in the world.

Author Keywords
Embodiment, movement, experience, ethnography

ACM Classification Keywords
H5.m. Information interfaces and presentation

General Terms
Design

INTRODUCTION
To most of us, who have incorporated mobile telephony in our everyday lives, it is hard to see the role that this technology plays in our everyday practices. As the mobile evolves and becomes increasingly pervasive, society and individuals adapt, creating new social rules or modifying bodily behaviors. The ways in which we place our mobiles on our bodies or on the environment, how we hold them when engaged in different activities or how we situate and orient our bodies when in conversation, are all part of the ongoing process in which people, society and the technology, through the ongoing interactions, adapt and exert mutual influence. But has shown by Shklovski et. al. [17,18], it is sometimes easier to expose practices when they are in change – as in their studies on how electronic communication practices change when one moves to another house. As Shklovski et.al put it: "*It is through this experience of being unsettled that we explore the processes of behavior adjustment*" [18]. Another example would be the way we realize how much our everyday practices revolve around a mobile or the Internet much more intensely the day we are suddenly deprived of them. In certain parts of Vanuatu, their practices were in such a flux, as they were exposed to mobiles for the first time – their use was therefore changing, adapting, and in some sense more accessible to study.

We conducted a 2-month long, design-oriented, explorative fieldwork study in the islands of Vanuatu, where the diverse mobile scenery ranged from high penetration, to no penetration whatsoever. We looked for ways in which the mobile related to life in the areas we visited, concerning bodily orientations, the need to change physical behaviors, physical environment and implications for cultural values. Our focus in this report will be on bodily aspects of interacting with mobiles in a particular area, The Banks, where mobile telephony came just days before our arrival.

In this report we look at issues regarding the fragility of the device in the setting, and how *ni-Vans* are dealing with it. Afterwards we will go through issues of mobility and implications brought about by new invisible landscapes. We will then develop these themes in a more detailed analysis.

PREVIOUS WORK
Our aim with the work presented here is to provide inspiration to design for novel *bodily orientations and interactions* with/through mobile technology. Originally, HCI spun off from ergonomics through its focus on the cognitive aspects of interaction. With the turn to third-wave HCI and its focus on experiences [2], we are now in a sense turning back to considering the body in interaction. But contrary to the main focus of ergonomics, instead of documenting and altering routines, finding error-free ways of involving operators in the complex beast of man and machine as a unity, or measuring how the body has its limitations, this turn back to bodily interaction entails a new focus. The renewed HCI interest lies in designing for *experiences* – beyond efficiency and task completion [5,13]. Although in some respects ergonomists were, and still are, more sensitive of the body than HCI, given their concerns on the integrity of the body and integration of function and movement.

Recently, we have started to see other studies where HCI researchers attempt to observe different cultures or communities of practice, for insight on how to design for novel bodily experiences. There are ethnographic studies about hunting culture [9], skaters and golfers [23], horseback riding [7] to citizens constrained by electronic surveillance bracelets [24]. These studies repeatedly tell us that bodily experiences have been undervalued in ICT design and that there is little knowledge on how to address them.

The study by Tholander and Johansson [23], on skaters and golfers show that those practices do not distract their users from being in the world together with their skateboards or golf clubs. Tholander and Johansson convincingly argue that interactive technologies that aim for physical interaction too often force users to interact through some type of screen interface, taking away focus from the environment. Instead of interacting with others around us or with the surrounding nature, we focus on the screen

The study by Höök [7] provides a rich account of how horseback riding involves all our senses, at moments involving us in centaur-experiences – feeling as one with horse and environment. Her point is to show both how impoverished interaction with many of our interfaces are compared to the sensory richness of riding, and also how impoverished our descriptions of interactions are, the lack of an agreed upon language for describing interactions.

Troshynksi and Dourish, in their study on paroled sex offenders who are required to wear a GPS tracking electronic bracelet on their ankle [24], show how this technology constrains their bodies in ways beyond that of the original intent of the technology. A considerable amount of work is put into preserving the technology intact during everyday routines like showering, and their mobility in the environment is considerable constrained, among other implications.

All of these studies point to limitations in the ways we think of today's wearable and mobile technologies and their impact on bodily behaviors and practices. Often missing out on designing for much richer experiences. Some even claim that the technologies we wear today treat our bodies in a negative way [10]: *"Electronics, robotics, and spintronics invade and transform the body and, as a consequence of this, the body becomes an object and loses its remaining personal characteristics, those characteristics that might make us consider it as the sacred guardian of our identity"*

But all bodily experiences with digital technology are not impoverished, limiting or painful. There have been attempts to design for various aesthetic experiences: Schiphorst's soft(n), where design of physical interactive artifacts is done from a somaesthetic perspective [16], Sundström et. Al.'s eMoto, where SMS is enriched with emotional cues through gesturing [22], or Moen's design for the joy of moving in her BodyBug system [14], to just name a few.

A major issue for both the design work and the studies of bodily experiences lies in exposing and articulating bodily experiences. As Höök expresses it after trying to describe her horseback riding experiences: *"I [have] tried to provide an account of exactly how I was sitting, which muscles were tensed, how I balanced on my sitting bones, the direction of my head and vision, the position of my legs and the tension in arms and hands. Still, the experiences I am trying to describe are wordless, and putting detailed descriptions of them still fails to cover the complexities and the uniqueness of my embodied experience."* [7]

In our Vanuatu study, we will only scratch the surface of the bodily experiences, re-orientations and changed practices the people we met were experiencing as they started to use mobiles as part of their everyday life.

RESEARCH SETTING AND METHODOLOGY

The whole of the research project was conducted during 2 months in the country of Vanuatu. In particular, the results presented in this report, focused on The Banks islands, in Vanuatu a northern group of Islands part of the Torba province (see Figure 1). The choice of site was based on locally obtained information where we looked for a place where mobile telephony was just becoming a reality.

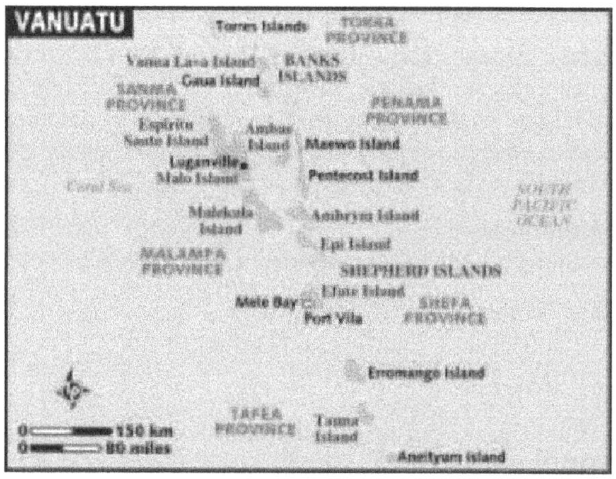

Figure 1 : Map of Vanuatu

Vanuatu is, since 1980, a sovereign, independent nation located in the South Pacific. Prior to that it was a territory jointly ruled by the French and English, in a setup that was known as Condominium [15]. Until that time Vanuatu was known as the New Hebrides. Vanuatu is populated by around two hundred thousand *ni-Vanuatu* [1] (or *ni-Vans*) spread out throughout approximately eighty islands. Vanuatu's cash economy is largely dependent on its main export, copra, the meat of the coconut intended for oil, and tourism.

The capital, Port Vila (located in the island of Efate), is one of the two only urban areas in Vanuatu (along with Luganville in the island of Espiritu Santo). In both places, the penetration of mobile telephony is high [20]. There are two companies providing mobile telephony in Vanuatu: TVL[1],

[1] Telecom Vanuatu Limited: The old telecommunication monopoly. One of the two main players in the Vanuatu mobile scene.

the former communication monopoly, and Digicell, which is commonly known to have been the driving force of this modernization by challenging TVL's monopoly.

The place this reports refers to, The Banks is a group of islands, part of the Torba province. The local capital is Sola, located in the island of Vanua Lava. Cargo boats do not come here often and people often feel that they are the last in Vanuatu to experience change and novelty.

Around the time we arrived in Motalava, a TVL tower was installed and GSM service was launched. This tower was meant to serve the whole Banks group, although its coverage is still far from reaching all places. We spent a little less than 2 weeks in the island of Rah, which is very close to the island of Motalava (almost being one and the same, Motalava often referred to as "the mainland"). We then spent some days in Lalntak and Sola, in Vanua Lava.

The fieldwork was done with a combination of methods. We conducted ethnographic observations; taking notes, pictures and video whenever we could (sometimes the weather conditions or lack of assuredness that it was acceptable to take pictures or videos, limited these last two data collection methods). We conducted short formal interviews along with many informal ones. The notes are direct citations from what we were told, when in Bislama or French translated into English. In here, we will focus on observational data alongside of fragments from informal interviews often in the form of narratives [12], since they come closest to describing the richness of the kinds of bodily descriptions we aimed to capture. To illustrate the findings we describe specific encounters. We found these to be representative, and a solid basis for a detailed analysis, of what each theme may suggest and imply for mobile design.

The Banks is a group of islands of varying dimensions (Figure 2). Everyday bodily practices have evolved within this environment. Crossing over water in a dugout canoe or diving to catch lobster might not be an everyday mundane activity to most of the readers. It is so in The Banks though.

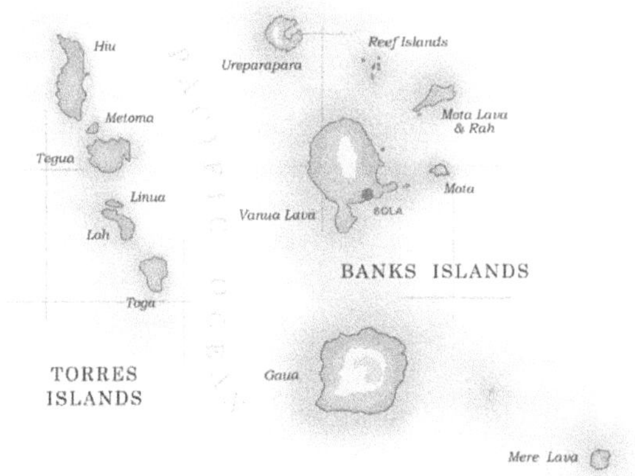

Figure 2: Map of the Torba province

We will look at four different themes in which it is relevant to understand how the mobile fits in this setting: the act of crossing over water, the everyday bodily practices involving a decision of going in the water and the unpredictability of finding oneself inside the water. We will then look at similar issues but this time beyond the water.

On the water

Being on water is an everyday mundane activity for people in Rah and Motalava. Crossing back and forth between the two islands, for instance, is very common. From children going to school and back twice a day (because of lunch time), men and women going to meet family members, to buy and sell something or to take care of any other business, this is a basic activity, especially for inhabitants in Rah, given the reduced demographical and geographical dimension of their island and the presence of the airport in Motalava. Most of the crossing between the two islands was made using a dugout canoe, which was locally known as a "Taxi". The canoes mentioned, or "Taxis", are built from a single tree trunk, and for reasons of stability, most of them were balanced using a lateral log, tied to the main one with the help of auxiliary logs and rope (Figure 3). We will now look at some encounters between the mobile phone and these practices.

Figure 3 : Dugout canoe

One day, crossing with a 'Taxi' from Motalava to Rah (Figure 4), Brian crossed paths with Brian's younger brother Suva who was heading in the opposite direction. Brian made some gestures to Suva, in a seemingly mocking way, as they would be often 'pulling each other's leg' in a friendly way. Suva stood up on the canoe and screamed with a challenging tone, then throwing one of his Croc's (the famous brand of rubber sandals) in the water, close to the canoe where Brian was probably in the hope of hitting him with some of the splash from his Croc in the water. The shoe hit a couple of meters from Brian's canoe, he immediately used the paddle to maneuver the canoe around and intercept the fallen shoe. As he was approaching the shoe, floating in the water, he stopped paddling taking the paddle inside the canoe, just letting it "glide" with its existing momentum. He stretched his body in the direction of the floating shoe, leaning over the side of the canoe. He held on the canoe with one hand while his other arm reached out for the shoe.

At the time, his mobile phone was hanging around his neck, and was still inside the canoe, but as he stretched out, the phone was pulled higher and higher against the inner wall of the dugout and was now facing a possible dip in the water, which Brian did not seem to be realizing at the moment. Suva, who was half standing on his canoe, looking at the whole situation, yelled out something to Brian, which made him sit back in a very sudden move, causing the boat to rock slightly. They both screamed to each other with a smile, as if saying "*that was a close one*", Brian holding his phone and looking to check if it was wet. Brian told me "*oh, I was lucky*" with a smile.

Figure 4 : Brian crossing from Motalava to Rah on a 'Taxi'

Brian had apparently completely forgotten the presence of the mobile phones hanging down from his neck, which was an extremely common way for people in Rah to carry their phones around. He was engaged in an everyday activity. As Jorege put it at one time: "*sometimes we just lean over to look at something, or to get some water out of the canoe [...] we forget that we have the phone on our chest [laughter] and then the phone goes in the water [followed by generalized laughter]*".

Brian's example and Jorege's statement are examples of how the practice of wearing the mobile phone hanging around the neck has been at odds with their everyday practices. It also shows how their practices and attention has already begun shifting in a way that it accounts for this presence and protects it.

Everyday activities in the water: fishing and swimming

Being on water is not the only way that harm can come to the mobile phones. Being in the water was equally an everyday mundane activity in Rah and other parts of Vanuatu, as you can see in Figure 5. Fishing was often done by plunging all the way inside the water, sometimes in the evening, with the help of battery operated, waterproof, flashlights, sometimes during daytime, depending on the kind of catch they were aiming for.

Figure 5 : Group of people walking from across from one island to the other

At one time, while we were by the water together in a group talking and watching over Brian as he was repairing his canoe, someone came to call Brian, as he needed to attend to some issue elsewhere. Given the work he had been engaged in he was feeling sweaty and dirty, and decided to go for a quick swim, telling us to wait a second. He threw off his flip-flops and then proceeded to run towards the water. As the water level reached his knees, and water was splashing all around due to his running, it was clear he was getting ready to jump right in. All of a sudden he broke his step, turned around and ran back towards, while at the same time removing the phone from around his neck. He then handed me the phone, smiling and said: "*I almost forgot!*"

Another incident was narrated to us by Father Robert, concerning Jorege: "*people's life here involves fishing. This is the food that we have and we get it every day.[...] We are lucky to have this many resources [...][he continues into a criticism of the lack of respect that new generations have of this natural advantage][...] but people here they do not pay attention to what they are doing, like my brother here [pointing at Jorege] [pause, looking at Jorege, while Joregelooks at me with a guilty smile] how many times he goes running in the water with the phone on his chest, and often I have to shout for him to stop? [Pauses] how many times has this happened?[people around, Jorege included, burst into laughter and snapping their fingers against each others' in a typical ni-Van way of doing when something funny has occurred]*". Before Father Robert told me this story, Jorege himself had complained about the fragility of the mobile devices by saying: "*sometimes I run in the water and remember in the last minute [slaps his forehead] oh! The phone! [pause] then I have to go back and leave the phone someplace else.*".

Whether for a long period of time, like J.G.'s fishing, but also for just regular split seconds dives like Brian's the possibility that the phone would be irreversibly damaged was most likely as the mobiles they had been given were not of very high quality or water-resistant. These are activities that are part of everyday life and to which they dedicate themselves to without much preparation and to which they attend to in a very quick fashion. This attitude clashes with the fragility of the device they are now carrying with them.

The acts of avoiding letting the mobile dip into the water – as in the canoeing examples above - have to be seen not as isolated bodily behaviors, but in a larger context of also changing the ways they engage in mundane activities around water. Arguably just leaving the mobile on the sand, at the shore, is a bad idea, since the sand, or an animal, such as a crab, may cause damage to it. Having the mobile present becomes a central concern causing practices to evolve around it.

Unpredictable water encounters

In Rah, Brian had already told a story in which "*one day, a fat woman was crossing with a bag of rice, and when she was coming out, the canoe tipped over [everyone started to laugh] and her phone and rice got full of water [...] the phone was not working anymore*". This made us particularly aware of those situations in which one does not intend to and in fact does nothing to have to go in the water, but the circumstances so dictate.

Our own exposure to the environment made it easier for us to emphatically experience how living surrounded by water, in your daily life, exposes our electronic equipment to so many risks. We were also carrying a wide selection of electronic equipment, ranging from digital cameras, Dictaphones, video camera, mobile phone, and chargers.

One encounter occurred when some children took us to the other side of the island, to show us how big (or small) the island was, as well as to show us how the island, outside of the village area, was. Once we arrived to the other side, the water level had already changed and was slightly higher. The children immediately suggested that we should return to the village by going back in the water, which was around a meter deep, and walking around the island, as that would be now easier and faster than trying to take the same path back. The children did not have a mobile phone or any other type of electronic equipment with them. I[2] had brought my digital camera along to document this trip. What happened was that I found myself holding the camera on my hand, away from the water, to keep it dry, while maneuvering my way over the reef. To walk on the reef one requires balance, especially when the water is still relatively shallow. Although *ni-Vans* had an extraordinary balance, when compared to us they were still vulnerable to the reef as the many wounds on their bodies witnessed. Falling on the reef can be extremely painful and most often results in skin cuts. The sharp and slippery nature of the reef means that one's full bodily focus typically goes into not falling and hurting oneself as that is usually the main priority. To do that one must walk carefully, trying to feel where the bottom is good enough to stand on, while at the same time using your arms to keep the balance.

[2] Here, the term 'I' refers to the personal experience and personal camera of the first author.

The problem was that now, a part of one's body, in my case the hand that was carrying the digital camera, is somehow restricted. This part of your body can also not get wet. This results in having to split attentions between not getting that specific region wet, and keeping yourself from hurting yourself. In my case, the fear of wrecking the digital camera, alongside with the documentation still in it kept my focus on the hand while sometimes it was almost impossible to resist the temptation of getting that hand wet in order to stabilize myself and facilitate the balance.

What all these episodes show is that one cannot always plan when to get into the water. There is a need to be ready for situations as they occur and to have one's body free to do full-body activities. In certain environments, such as everyday life in a place such as Manhattan, one can reasonably expect not to be plunged into water. Of course other restrictions follow from the environment, such as placing the mobile in a place protected from pickpockets for instance. What this implies is that in one setting a group of places emerge as "safe" to incorporate a mobile: pockets, neck lanyard, backpack, amongst others. But, in settings where the same assumptions cannot be made, then the same "safe" behaviors do not follow. This is not merely a one-way relation between the environment and what behaviors it allows for, but equally what the technology is and what behaviors it affords or constrains.

What is aimed at, with the narration of these encounters, is not to say that a water-proof mobile is the solution to all the problems, although it would probably be a welcomed feature by people in Rah. First, water is not the only danger around as we will see in the next example. Secondly, merely adding a waterproof layer to the mobile would only be addressing some of the concerns one might have regarding bodily orientations around mobiles.

"A World where things get easily broken"

As we mentioned earlier, water was not the only danger in regards to the mobile phones. To work in the gardens is a big part of the everyday *ni-Van* life. With the exceptions of the urban areas, where people dispose of little or no land of their own, in all the other islands of Vanuatu, people have land, sometimes relatively far from their homes, to which they walk to and back regularly and where they cultivate. These lands are called gardens.

Garden work is hard, physical work. It involves cutting branches and trees. It involves cleaning of the cultivated areas. It involves climbing trees to gather fruits. People will have to carry what they collect for long distances, back to the villages. All this is very demanding, and is done in a setting that is harsh on mobiles.

Jorege showed us his garden, carrying his mobile in his hand. In gesturing, he almost lost it (its neck-strap got stuck on a bush) and we asked Jorege why he did not have his phone in his pockets? Jorege was wearing shorts at the time which had two pockets on the sides and two on back, as well as two lower in the legs. He answered: "*if you... you put the phone in your pocket [...] then it can fall [he bends over to illustrate himself doing garden work, close to the floor, such as cutting lower weeds with a machete] you are like this, [continues to make hacking moves], then the phone falls down [making gestures with his hand coming from his pocket and down to the floor, showing that by bending over, as it is often required of garden work, that the phone could just slip out of the pocket]*".

The nature on the islands was not always soft as the sand. We experienced this when we were climbing up a hill, close to an active volcano, in Lalntak (Vanua Lava). At some point the path was crossed by many rivers of hot sulfuric water. This water came down on the rocks creating a polished effect on these rocks, giving them different shiny colors, but also making them extremely slippery. I crossed with the help of the boys, but they would mostly just jump and run from rock to rock. Suva, one of the boys who had come from Rah to take us to Lalntak, was jumping around quite often, with his mobile phone always in his hand, trying to call Rah, every time there was a bit of network along our way. At one point he slipped on one of the rocks, while hopping over one of the streams, and his leg went back, making him fall to the front. As he felt he semi-opened his arms falling on his chest, keeping the phone in his hand, with his arm stretching out from his body, keeping the phone safe throughout the fall. He did not seem hurt and screamed in success displaying his intact phone.

The best way to sum this up, in the words of Father Lewis: "*this is a world where things get easily broken*". To this world, *ni-Vans* were accustomed to. Their bodies were in general very strong and they possessed a great amount of balance in that setting. Their adaptation is of course not perfect or risk-free. The mobile may at times introduce extra fragility, as they will have to add it to their own bodily fragilities. In order to protect the mobile, as the example above shows, Suva risked hurting himself.

These encounters bring to the forefront the effort that must be put into caring for this fragile extension of ourselves. The lack of experience with this device forces people in Rah to adapt their bodily postures, in order to protect it, stiffening their bodies in different and unusual ways. At the same time it shows us the value that is put onto this new technology, as they reflect and pay attention to the ways in which this novelty is to be preserved.

MOBILITY

"*The mobile phones are making people lazy*", said Father Robert during one of our meetings, "*the young ones do not want to help their parents in the gardens anymore, all they want is to make play-play*[3] *with their mobile phones*". Father Robert also said that people were spending money superfluously on calls when they could just walk over to each other as they are so close: "*these two [pointing towards Jorege and Joe.] they waste 1000 Vatu*[4] *in two days [...] they bought their phones at the same time, and so they only remembered each other's [phone] number [this is because one's number was obtained by adding 1 to the other's number and vice-versa] so they were always calling each other. [Both started laughing along with the crowd] They are laughing, but this is serious, they waste money just to call the other and ask 'is the kava ready' and the other replies 'yes it is ready' and they are just some short distance from each other, sometimes they even see each other while they are talking [...] only because they do not want to move*".

This cost issue could be considered a serious threat to their very low-income level and existing economy. We are not putting a value on calling a friend for asking about *kava* or when to meet next. Neither is there anything wrong with making calls without any specific grand purpose in mind. Perhaps the issue here is more to do with dealing with a habituation to the rate and charging system of mobile telephony. In the long run, they will know where and when they will be able to do this given the costs.

Another more straightforward way to interpret these encounters is by concluding that given the mobile's possibilities for far reaching conversation, without the necessity of physical mobility, it brings about, as a consequence, a situation where people tend to move less and become more sedentary. What we saw though, and what we will look at next is a different story. One which shows a number of examples of mobiles actually promoting moving around, sometimes creating the necessity for physical movement itself, sometimes by allowing for new possibilities which themselves entail physical mobility.

The work of looking for reception

Coverage was far from global in The Banks. Depending on where you were, geographically, in relation to the tower installed by TVL, you would get different qualities in the reception. Weather conditions were also of great importance as Frelal points out "*sometimes, if it's cloudy, we don't get reception at all, for days*". It was very common to have people going around looking for reception in the most varied ways.

One illustrative way in which this is relevant, happened when a group of men were playing cards by the beach, sitting in a circle and using a mat as table, and Jorege got a call. He stands up, and reaches for his phone. He looks at it to try and identity who is calling him, clicks on the answer button using the other hand than the one he was holding the phone with, and places the phone next to his ear: "*Hello?... Hello?*" and then after a small pause with a significant higher volume of voice "*Hello? Yes! Kaspa!*" it was his

[3] "*Play-play*" is Bislama for an attitude of what some might call "playfulness" that is playing without the implication of rules or goals.

[4] 1000 Vatu at the time of our stay was around 10 USD.

brother in Port Vila calling. He places his free hand on the other side of his face, covering his eardrum with one of his fingers and starts walking away from the card game and towards the water. He then starts speaking in local language (Motlav), which I did not understand at all. He wanders by the water, going back and forth speaking very loudly, seemingly unconcerned with the environment around him. Everyone could distinctly overhear the conversation. He had a short conversation, at times he would lower the volume of his voice significantly and, at other times he would speak loudly again. Sometimes he would drift further away where we were, and sometimes he would just wonder freely relatively close to our position. For more than one time, the call was abruptly interrupted, this was noticeable at a distance by the amount of times he would shout "*Hello?*" louder and louder, and then looking straight at the mobile in front of him eventually pressing the necessary buttons to realize a new call or waiting for his brother to call again. He finally hung up the phone for good and headed towards me. After telling me that it was his brother, he reiterated the complaints he himself had persistently made clear to me regarding the quality of the reception: "*You see? I call and 'Hello! Hello!' then nothing*" Jorege complained, "*I call again, and again... sometimes I call ten times just to say 'how are you', but then I spend ten calls*". This was a result of the uneven spread of coverage throughout the island and beach, creating this behavior of walking around, looking for reception and spending some extra money in the process.

But finding reception was sometimes much more difficult. Jimmy lived in a place that was just opposite from the side of Vanua Lava that can see Motalava, and hence on the opposite side of the island where reception exists, which he claimed to not be a big problem: "*here we are very lucky, we get reception not far from here [...] in some places people do not get reception at all*". As our phone did not pick up any reception at all in the whereabouts, we asked what he meant: "*well, on top of the hill [pointing to the direction] we can get very good reception, we just walk there and make our calls from up there [...] we go there almost every day*". We asked about the distance to that hill, to which he nonchalantly replied: "*oh, just about 2-3 hours walk*".

Climbing on a coconut tree is, on a physical level, a very demanding task. Children up to a certain age seem fitter to do so: "*me, I do not climb so much anymore, the 'pikinini' oooh [making a gesture of admiration] they do it all the time, with no problem*", said Brian regarding climbing up coconut trees, "*if you want to take a picture, I can do it, but since I am older [he was around 28] I don't do it so much, I am more heavy*". Most often children or young people would do the climbing. To climb is similar to climbing a pole where there are no hooks for the hands and feet. One must embrace it with the arms and legs and then perform a snail like movement up, where the arms hold the tree while the legs move up and vice-versa until you reach the top. If you were carrying a bush-knife, as was the case when Jerry did itto cut out some leaves (the coconuts you could twist them around their attachment until it wore off and broke), then he would add, to the sequence of movements described above, the act of successively stabbing the knife higher and higher up on the tree trunk. In Rah we heard that in other islands in the Banks, where the reception was not as good as in Rah, people were climbing the trees to get reception: "*they climb the coconut tree just to talk on the phone*", said Jorege while others around laughed at the situation, "*when they are up there they can talk, but they cannot drop the phone*", this lead the others to laugh even more and snap their fingers together, in the Vanuatu way.

We saw that people start moving through their available landscape in different ways, such as climbing the trees or walking up hills to get reception. We write 'available landscape' because climbing up trees or walking, on a daily basis, 3 hours up a hill are not part of the available landscape to most. As mobile telephony settles in, people discover and orient themselves vis-à-vis this new superposition in landscapes, between the geographical landscape and the invisible coverage landscape. With better coverage, these orientations might decrease, but from our own experiences, we know that they always persist to some extent.

ANALYSIS

We do not want to propose packaged solutions to the apparent mismatches between existing practices and the incorporation of a new device, that have become clear in the encounters described above. Instead, we want to expand and open up for reflection and inspiration to design on both the form and interactions with/through mobile technology from a bodily perspective. We do not want to provide simplistic design implications that would narrow down the design space [6], but draw attention to some of the cracks and creaks in the interaction that we may want to revisit in our design processes.

Also of note, and to make this clear, we do not want to suggest that ni-Vans represent pre-mobile civilization as a whole. For our aims, Vanuatu simply represents a place where exciting things happened, when mobiles were introduced, which we found relevant to analyze. We also want to stay away from judgments on the value of mobile technology in Vanuatu, apart from noting that it seemed desirable, for most people, despite the high financial costs.

Above we identified the four following themes:

Fragility: adjustments to mobile fragility – in particular in relationship to our own fragile bodies

Somaesthetic implications: tensions in posture or muscles from wearing mobiles

Coverage landscape: discovery and orientation vis-à-vis the invisible coverage landscape and its relationship to the environment

Competing for bodily space: wearing the mobile requires finding a 'space' on your body where it can be worn

Fragility. It seems obvious that the *ni-Vans* need more robust mobiles, preferably waterproof ones. But this will only take us so far. Their mobiles will still require care to have their battery loaded, not lose their mobile in the sand when running into the water, or getting smashed against a rock. *Ni-Vans* are used to adapting their movements to a, in parts, fairly rough environment with rocks, thorny bushes, uneven sea bottom, and so on. The mobile will move focus from caring about their own bodies to caring about an object, as if caring for a fragile being like a baby. We see this in the way we react when tripping with a laptop in our hands, for example, and the way we orient our bodies to protect it. It seems to us that the design of the mobile was never created to nurture that kind of relationship.

As we all know, the shape of an object will evoke certain understandings, and bring about certain behaviors– it entails affordances that we may take advantage of in our design processes. But it will also evoke certain experiences and sensual connotations. As pointed out before [8,16,21], we need to cultivate a deep understanding of the materials we use to build our artifacts from. Only then can we design for experiential qualities arising in the interaction, as it unfolds over time and space – its dynamic gestalt to quote Löwgren [11]. In this setting, we see a need for design that purposefully exposes the mobile device's fragility to evoke feelings of caretaking. But that design needs to take the totality of the mobile shape and material qualities, such as network coverage, cost, or address book, into account. It is not only the outer physical shape of the mobile that needs to change in order to make it wearable. In addition, a new design needs to consider the experiential qualities as they unfold in settings as the one we see here, in Vanuatu.

Somaesthetic implications. Somaesthetics [19] is, according to Richard Shusterman, a pragmatist philosopher, the study and understanding of how to improve our bodily, or somatic, agency. His view is that we need to focus on, become more aware of, train and find a sensory-aesthetic appreciation, similar to how we must study any other subject at which we want to excel. He discussed how certain movements, brought about through critically aware somatic training, are good for us. Schiphorst has tried to translate his insights into design: "*In the context of interaction, somaesthetics offers a bridging strategy between embodied practices based in somatics, and the design of an aesthetics of interaction for HCI.*"[16]

In this study, we may note how people in Rah sometimes had to perform movements that clashed with their everyday bodily practices, when canoeing, fishing or bathing in the sea. The rigid body postures required in order to stop the mobile (dangling from a string around your neck) from dipping into the water, brought about experiences of fear, rigidness of posture and sudden muscle tensions. Similarly, the painful posture of stretching one arm above your head while swimming creates for an uneven, asymmetrical movement.

For many bodily practices, we need to train our bodies, strengthen certain muscles or stretch limbs to make them able to freely move in certain directions. Some of that machine-like training may harm our bodies in the long run and needs to be better addressed in the design process, in particular by the field of ergonomics. But perhaps our aim should not only be to avoid designing technology that harms us, but to move beyond that, and design for somaesthetic experiences. By exposing the bodily practices that the mobile device brings about, we can see that some of them are not, (and will not be even after substantial co-evolution with the cultures norms and practices) somaestehtical movements. In our view, we can see that this is true also in more mature bodily practices around mobile devices. By explicitly addressing the somaesthetics in the design process, through, for example, studying practices such as yoga, Alexander-technique, or Feldenkrais, as proposed by Shusterman [19], we may end up with better, more aesthetically pleasing, bodily practices around mobile devices.

Coverage landscape. The seams in network coverage, has been discussed extensively in the HCI literature. Some have seen lack of coverage, signal strength, GPS coverage, etc., as resources to design rather than problems. It has been named seamful design [3,4] – the idea being that by explicitly exposing seams one can create novel exciting functionality. But what is interesting in this case is how willing *ni-Vans* are to go to places which for most of us would be inaccessible, in order to enjoy mobile interactions.

In the formation of seamful design, this kind of enforced movements, making people climb a hill for 3 hours in order to reach a point where they can make a phone call, is never really discussed. Obviously, any technology that is brought into cultural, social and bodily systems of practices will generate a different evolvement of the whole that might take some time before some of the main awkwardness in the interaction fades away. Having to climb that hill to get to a point where there is reception seems similar to the situation where a landline phone would be on top of that hill, which contrasted with the enthusiasm of people who already had access to nearby landline phones but were still happy to walk the distance in order to use their mobiles. What we want to challenge here is the assumption that mobile communication in itself augments the readily available landscape, rather it superimposes other layers of different landscapes (coverage, socially accepted places, private places), that we should consider in the design process, not as mere limitations but as resources for design.

We have focused on the types of evolvements that some of the everyday bodily practices in Rah will undergo due to the introduction of this technology. And to make it clear, this is not meant to be a negative assessment of the introduction of this device in any way, if anything, the contrary. The mobile phone enables a kind of proximity with geographically far away family members, which before was difficult and sometimes impossible. It enables new business opportunities and dynamism in coordinating with other business partners, such as in the sales of kava, or being more interactively updated on when ships might come to export a variety of local goods, such as kava, copra or handcrafts. It allows for coordination with tourism offices and tourists themselves in order to better accommodate them when they come to Rah for a visit. All of these represent fundamental sources of income for people in Rah, and the importance of the mobile phone in the development of any of these points should not be underplayed.

What we want to point out instead, is that the mobile phone results in a deep transformation of existing concepts and structuring of time and space constraints, in an unprecedented way. It reshapes social, economic and bodily practices in Rah. The whole pattern of movements and ways of being in the world can be drastically changed. At the same time that the mobile phone allows people in Rah to be in proximity with far away relatives and friends, enlarging in some ways their available landscape; it also shortens it by forcing them to be in specific places in order to get reception. In the same ways, phones allow any of us, mobile phone owners, to call friends while miles away, but it also forces us at times to remain on the same physical place while our phones are charging, or to switch rooms inside our homes to improve the quality of reception.

Competing for bodily space. The bush-knife is a pervasive tool in Vanuatu. Carrying it at hand is a very common way of dealing with it, whether to cut through the bush, to go work in the gardens, it is the one tool people in Rah seem to carry with them at most times. Carrying it in pockets in their backs was sometimes observed but only rarely. The most common way one would see the knife would be hanging down as an extension of one's arm. Even small children are seen carrying knifes, sometimes by demand of their parents when the knife is not in reachable distance and they ask the children to bring it. Sometimes the children are only barely bigger than the knife itself.

This idea that *ni-Vans* are already habituated to carrying around a physical artifact with them most of the times, by growing their whole lives around it, brings out the question of how do they find space on their bodies for another one? This idea perhaps accounts for some of the placements that we observed as well as for some added awkwardness in appropriating this device into their practices.

One inspiration that one can take from this, is how then, to think of mobile as more than a handheld? As something different than an artifact which requires dominant hand usage? Perhaps one thread of thought that can arise from this is to think about non-dominant hand usage or non hand usage at all. Possibly in ways that can free our hands for other purposes, such as balancing as in some of the examples seen above, or engaging with other artifacts which have already claimed that bodily space.

Looking at these results. Our aim in this paper is to leave our findings open enough for others to reflect and build upon, and yet practical enough that implications for design can be immediately withdrawn. For example fragility appeared as one of the issues in this paper, but instead of simply arguing for a more robust build of the mobile, we suggested that other alternatives were possible, such as creating designs which afford different ways of caretaking for the mobile. And yet this is just one of the many views that can arise from the themes under discussion.

Further thoughts. Our attentive reviewers have highlighted the importance of connecting issues of social order in relation to somaesthetics and somaesthetic practices, and the fact that somaesthetics is in itself a culturally grounded lens to understand these practices. Although these are issues of major importance, we feel they would be too broad to address in this work of limited scope. We nevertheless wanted to acknowledge these remarks as they are of undoubted important for a future, in-depth look at these and other somaesthetic practices.

CONCLUSION

All this said, we want to reinforce the idea that the specific ways in which mobiles are being adopted in Rah is a secondary concern of this paper, compared to exposing the ways in which everyone in and outside of Rah, needs to adjust their bodies and practices around this device. The encounters in Rah help expose some of these adjustments.

We need to better understand how technology, like mobiles, alters our bodily ways of being in the world: the movements of our body, the stiffening of certain muscles, the way we move through the landscape, how we appropriate it, wear it and find bodily and social space for it. Obviously, this process is developing over time – we get a socio-digital material (or socio-*bodily*-digital material) that is over time, more or less, fitted to the setting. But, by altering the design, we might alter body schemas to be better adjusted to social norms, bodily practices, but also better adjusted to what is somaesthetically pleasing – giving rise to better experiences with the device.

Driving forces such as the miniaturization of technology and the starting metaphors of fixed phones and the personal computer, to some extent, as well as business considerations, have been much more relevant to the design of mobile technologies than studies on the relationships between these technologies and our bodies. This study suggests that there are lessons to be learned, and even practical design implications, if we address mobile design from a bodily and somaesthetic perspective. These, in turn, might add a great deal of value to the user.

By studying early stages of adjusting to a new technology, or when technology use is in flux for some other reason, some of these processes are more clearly uncovered. Later they become engrained with our behaviors– becoming harder to see those adjustments, and address them in design.

In a sense, we are proposing a move back to the ergonomics careful and considerate care for our bodily ways of being in the world, but without putting a machine-like perspective on what the body is or could be. Instead, we have exposed the need to consider somaesthetics practices when designing wearable technologies in general and mobiles in particular.

ACKNOWLEDGEMENTS
We could not be more thankful to everyone in Vanuatu and in particular in The Banks islands for welcoming us with open and friendly arms and for sharing their views and experiences with mobile technologies so openly. Also many thanks to all the "expats" and foreign researchers in Vanuatu, who helped us immensely in our integration in Vanuatu life. In particular Daniela Kraemer, whose help in understanding the local *kastom*, communicating in Bislama and a countless number of other things was fundamental and indispensable for any success during this work.

Finally our colleagues at Mobile Life, who helped clarify and make sense of the data, and even without going to Vanuatu, were very open and understanding of it.

REFERENCES
1. *2009 National Census of Population and Housing.* Vanuatu National Statistics Office, Port Vila, Vanuatu, 2009.
2. Bødker, S. When second wave HCI meets third wave challenges. *NordiCHI '06: Proceedings of the 4th Nordic conference on Human-computer interaction*, ACM (2006), 1–8.
3. Chalmers, M. and MacColl, I. Seamful and seamless design in ubiquitous computing. *Workshop At the Crossroads: The Interaction of HCI and Systems Issues in UbiComp*, (2003).
4. Chalmers, M., Dieberger, A., Höök, K. and Rudström, Å. Social Navigation and Seamful Design. *In Japanese Journal of Cognitive Science, Special Issue on Social Navigation*, (2004), 171–181.
5. Dourish, P. *Where the Action Is: The Foundations of Embodied Interaction (Bradford Books).* The MIT Press, 2001.
6. Dourish, P. Implications for design. *Proceedings of the SIGCHI conference on Human Factors in computing systems*, (2006), 541-550.
7. Höök, K. Transferring Qualities from Horseback Riding to Design. *Proceeding of the 2010 Nordic conference on Human factors in computing systems*, (2010).
8. Isbister, K. and Höök, K. On being supple: in search of rigor without rigidity in meeting new design and evaluation challenges for HCI practitioners. *CHI '09: Proceedings of the 27th international conference on Human factors in computing systems*, ACM (2009), 2233–2242.
9. Juhlin, O. and Weilenmann, A. Hunting for fun. *Proceedings of the 2008 ACM conference on Computer supported cooperative work*, (2008), 57-66.
10. Longo, G.O. Body and Technology: Continuity or Discontinuity? In *Mediating the Human Body: Technology, Communication, and Fashion.* Lawrence Erlbaum & Associates.
11. Löwgren, J. and Stolterman, E. *Thoughtful interaction design: A design perspective on information technology.* MIT Press, 2007.
12. Matthews, B. and Ross, L. *Research Methods: A practical guide for the social sciences.* Pearson Education Limited, 2010.
13. McCarthy, J. and Wright, P. *Technology as Experience.* The MIT Press, 2004.
14. Moen, J. From hand-held to body-worn: embodied experiences of the design and use of a wearable movement-based interaction concept. *TEI '07: Proceedings of the 1st international conference on Tangible and embedded interaction*, ACM (2007), 251–258.
15. Peck, J.G. and Gregory, R.J. A Brief Overview of the Old New Hebrides. *Anthropologist 7*, 4 (2005), 269-282.
16. Schiphorst, T. soft(n): toward a somaesthetics of touch. *CHI '09: Proceedings of the 27th international conference extended abstracts on Human factors in computing systems*, ACM (2009), 2427–2438.
17. Shklovski, I., Kraut, R., and Cummings, J. Keeping in touch by technology: maintaining friendships after a residential move. *CHI '08: Proceeding of the twenty-sixth annual SIGCHI conference on Human factors in computing systems*, ACM (2008), 807–816.
18. Shklovski, I.A. and Mainwaring, S.D. Exploring technology adoption and use through the lens of residential mobility. *CHI '05: Proceedings of the SIGCHI conference on Human factors in computing systems*, ACM (2005), 621–630.
19. Shusterman, R. *Body Consciousness: A Philosophy of Mindfulness and Somaesthetics.* Cambridge University Press, 2008.
20. Sijapati-Basnett, B. *Social and economic impact of introducing telecommunications throughout Vanuatu.* Pacific Institute of Public Policy, 2009.
21. Sundström, P. and Höök, K. Hand in hand with the material: designing for suppleness. *CHI '10: Proceedings of the 28th international conference on Human factors in computing systems*, ACM (2010), 463–472.
22. Sundström, P., Ståhl, A., and Höök, K. eMoto: affectively involving both body and mind. *CHI '05: CHI '05 extended abstracts on Human factors in computing systems*, ACM (2005), 2005–2008.
23. Tholander, J. and Johansson, C. Design qualities for whole body interaction - learning from golf, skateboarding and bodybugging. .
24. Troshynski, E., Lee, C., and Dourish, P. Accountabilities of presence: reframing location-based systems. *Proceeding of the twenty-sixth annual SIGCHI conference on Human factors in computing systems*, (2008), 487-496.

We Want More: Human-Computer Collaboration in Mobile Social Video Remixing of Music Concerts

Sami Vihavainen[1], Sujeet Mate[2], Lassi Seppälä[1], Francesco Cricri[3], Igor D.D. Curcio[2]

[1]Helsinki Institute for Information Technology HIIT / Aalto University
00076 Aalto, Finland
{sami.vihavainen, lassi.seppala}@hiit.fi

[2]Nokia Research Center
P.O. Box 1000, 33721 Tampere, Finland
{sujeet.mate, igor.curcio}@nokia.com

[3]Tampere University of Technology
P.O. Box 527, FI-33101 Tampere, Finland
francesco.cricri@tut.fi

ABSTRACT

Recording and publishing mobile video clips from music concerts is popular. There is a high potential to increase the concert's perceived value when producing video remixes from individual video clips and using them socially. A digital production of a video remix is an interactive process between human and computer. However, it is not clear what the collaboration implications between human and computer are.

We present a case study where we compare the processes and products of manual and automatic mobile video remixing. We provide results from the first systematic real world study of the subject. We draw our observations from a user trial where fans recorded mobile video clips during a rock concert.

The results reveal issues on heterogeneous interests of the stakeholders, unexpected uses of the raw material, the burden of editing, diverse quality requirements, motivations for remixing, the effect of understanding the logic of automation, and the collaborative use of manual and automatic remixing.

Author Keywords: Automation, Video, Human Factors, Music, Social, Mobile.

ACM Classification Keywords: H5.m. Information interfaces and presentation (I.7): Miscellaneous.

General Terms: Human Factors.

INTRODUCTION

Today, more and more consumers utilize their mobile phones for recording video clips and for editing activities. Video features and recording quality of mobile phones are reaching a level where the phones are becoming a serious tool for on-the-move content creators. Making available a large pool of snapshot digital videos taken by the audience in the same concert can result in higher value material than individual video clips. The individual digital video clips can be remixed into compilations that potentially enhance the perceived value of the event, are useful for various stakeholders such as the artists, and the fans of the artists. Remixing can also give the fans the possibility to become creators and not just receivers, and enhance the community feeling between the artists and the fans [11].

Digital video editing is an interactive process between human and computer; depending on how the editing system is designed, the human will do some tasks and the computer will do others. A key issue with designing collaborative multi-camera video remixing systems is the level at which the editing tasks should be automated and thus allocated between human and computer. This is especially important to ensure that the editing process will not feel too troublesome for an amateur and still produce an output that adds perceived value to the stakeholders.

As we will explain in more detail, automation has a high potential to improve the performance and ease the burden of producing a video compilation. However, in a live concert type of social context, where the compilation should be able to reconstruct the collaborative experience between the band and the audience, it is not self-evident how the automatic editing algorithm should be designed.

To approach this problem, we studied the motivations for collaborative video compilations and the role of automation in the process of editing the compilations. We conducted a user-centric real world study to bring out the points of view of various stakeholders and reveal automation related socio-technical factors that we thought could be important to consider in social video remixing systems.

We formulated the following research questions:

- What are the users' motivations for collaborative video compilations?
- How do users react to manual video remixing?
- How do users react to automatic video remixing?

By publishing a video compilation, the publisher puts the content to a public space (e.g., the Internet), where the stakeholders' different interests might conflict. This is why we see that to create sustainable social video services with an excellent user experience, it is not enough to study the phenomena only from one angle, but instead we must aim for a more heterogeneous view by studying the subject from the point of view of various stakeholders. We therefore studied the two main stakeholders of a live concert event: the artist and artist's fans. Under the word "artists" we include also the artist's record company, agent, and manager. Under "fans", we include people who have great enthusiasm for the artist. We understand that the interests of the actual artist and their record company might sometimes differ in the music industry ecosystem. However, for this study, we saw that the producer-consumer distinction is sufficient. We also researched how the boundaries between consumers and producers would blur when the consumers become producers with automation as a middleman.

As a case, we compare the manual and automatic video editing processes and outcomes from the two stakeholders' perspectives. The video compilations were produced out of video clips that the audience took with camera phones in a live concert. In the manual editing process, we gave the fans of the artist the ability to use the Kaltura video editor to make their own compilations from the raw material. In the automatic editing process, we used a software prototype developed by Nokia (we will refer this as Automatic Video Remixer (AVR)). In a nutshell, this software adds context data to video clips while filming, and is afterwards able to automatically produce compilations from multi-camera video material by using the captured context data.

We begin this paper by presenting the manual and automatic video editing processes as part of our research frame. Next, we present our results on how the stakeholders reacted to the manual and automatic video remixing and how they assessed three collaborative video compilations that were produced as a part of the study. At the end of the paper, we discuss the possibilities and challenges that the automation faces in mobile social video remixing from live music events. As the main data gathering methods, we used a focus group session and individual interviews.

RELATED RESEARCH

Studies on video production and mobile media

Let us start by going through the research related to the artist-audience interaction process. Engström et al. [2] analyzed how dance club's video jockeys work and suggested that mobile video could enhance the interaction between the club visitors and VJs. Engström et al. [1] continued their studies and presented the SwarmCam prototype for video capture and live transmission of mobile video. Club visitors film their dancing on the dance floor and stream the video live to the VJ, who possibly broadcasts it to a mega screen. From our paper's point of view the study is interesting, given that it concentrates on the interaction process of VJ and club visitors in often so dark music clubs. In our study the context is similar, focusing on the improvement of the interaction between the artist and audience, but in stretching the timeline of the experience with post event video remixing.

Foote et al. [3] and Kennedy et al. [8] concentrated on automation in video remixing. Foote et al. [3] concentrate on automatic analysis of audio and video material based on significant audio changes, automatic suitability analysis of the video based on camera motion and exposure. Their system then stitches audio and video material together so that high quality video clips are adjusted to match the audio segments. They also developed a semi automatic system (Hitchcock), where the user manually selects the preferred video clips and the system automatically synchronizes the video clips with the audio track. This is a very interesting study not only because of the automatic content analysis but also because it takes into account the collaboration between computer and human for easy production of personalized video compilations. Kennedy et al. [8] studied automatic video synchronization and organization of video content taken by the audience in live music concert contexts. Their results reveal practical points regarding: use of audio fingerprinting to synchronize videos taken at the same event, the effectiveness of audio synchronization under different conditions, and finding meaningful content-based metadata to retrieve and summarize video material.

Girgensohn et al. [4] describe their video remixing system Hitchcock that was also discussed in Foote et al. [3]. The system takes a semi-automatic approach on creating custom videos from raw videos taken by a basic home video camera. In their paper they concentrate in home videos and not music videos. The system analyzes video content based on the camera motion and gives the video material unsuitability scores. The work is interesting considering the focus on various levels of automation. Girgensohn et al. [5] present their user study on Hitchcock. Their results demonstrate the need for a useful balance between user control and automation. Kirk et al. [9] take a holistic user-centric view on people's practices around home videos. Their results reveal useful information about people's motivations and practices for editing home videos. One of their results is that people do not find any reason to do editing of the short video clips they had taken. Shamma et al. [14] suggested that multimedia research should shift from semantics to pragmatics by designing systems and algorithms that can usefully utilize information about how media content is being used in specific contexts. Lehmuskallio et al. [10] studied people's snapshot videography practices. They state that the models for capturing video are often taken from snapshot photography.

In addition to video editing and practices, there is related research on mobile content creation, for example Jacucci et al. [6] and Sarvas et al. [13], and on automation in mobile social applications, Vihavainen et al. [16].

Video editing, multi-camera video production, music videos, automation, live contexts, or user point of view have been discussed in several high-class studies. However, none of the earlier studies have combined those aspects in a single study. Also our objective is to take into account the viewpoints of various stakeholders that interact in the production of collaborative music video compilations.

Automation as Part of Human Factors Research

Automation has been studied systematically in human factors engineering. Sheridan [15] proposed an automation framework with seven levels:

1. The computer offers no assistance; the human must do it all
2. The computer suggests alternative ways to do the task
3. The computer selects one way to do the task and asks for human approval
4. The computer allows the human a restricted time to veto before automatic execution
5. The computer executes the suggestion automatically, then informs the human
6. The computer executes the suggestion automatically, and informs the human if asked
7. The computer selects the method, executes the task, and ignores the human.

Table 1. Levels of automation according to Sheridan [15]

In addition, Parasuraman et al. [12] proposed a four-stage model of functions inside the system that can be automated on different levels:

1. Information acquisition	3. Decision selection
2. Information analysis	4. Action implementation

Table 2. Stages of automation according to Parasuraman [12]

These levels and functions make an automation design matrix that we believe might be useful in examining the human-automation collaboration in mobile video remixing.

THE STUDY: 11 FANS IN A ROCK CONCERT

Users from two stakeholder groups (artists and fans) were recruited in Finland to participate in the study. A focus group session and a user trial (with interviews) were conducted to discover opinions, reactions, and experiences on social video production from live music concerts.

Users

The artists (Artists) who represented the artist stakeholders included the three members of a Finnish rock band and four employees from their record agency (The Artists will be marked as A1...A7). Three of the artists (A1, A2, A3) had a background in movie editing, and all were professionals in the music business. All were men, age 25 to 35. The fans (Fans) were a group of eight men and four women living in southern Finland (The Fans will be marked as F1...F12). All were between the ages of 18 and 30, with one 61-year-old man (F3). Two of the Fans (F2, F4) had an amateur background in movie editing and two had a strong background in amateur photography (F3, F12). Others were not particularly tech savvy. Most were hard-core fans of the band. They were recruited through the band's Facebook profiles and newsletters. All were interested in going to music concerts and took photos or video during concerts to get memorabilia and share experiences with their friends.

Data Collection

Focus Group Session

The objective was to discover the Artists' and the Fans' views, opinions, and habits concerning video recording at live concerts and remixing the recorded video material afterwards into compilations, either automatically by a computer or manually by the users. Four participants from the Artists (A1, A3, A6, A7) and seven from the Fans (F1, F2, F3, F5, F6, F7, F12) participated in the focus group.

User Trial

As a user trial, we arranged a live rock concert in collaboration with the band (A3, A6, A5) and their record agency (A4). The concert was a public event and thereby an authentic situation. 11 of the Fans (F1-F11) participated in the trial. They were given Nokia N97 phones equipped with the context-recording client that was used as part of the automatic remixing process (we will present the manual and automatic remixing processes in the next chapter). The Fans were directed to film as they would normally do in the concert situation. However, they were told that from the raw material, both automatic and manual video compilations would be made afterwards. For technical reasons (mainly battery life), they were directed to film a maximum of 15 minutes, and the maximum length of a clip was five minutes. After the concert, the phones were collected and users were provided with access to the raw video material and the Kaltura video editor (Kaltura will be presented later).

Interviews

After the trial, six of the 11 Fans (F1-F6) who participated in the trial and three of the Artists (A1-A3) were interviewed. The interviewees were selected based on voluntariness. Before the interviews, both the manually and automatically created remixes had been made available for viewing. The interview protocol was semi-structured. During the interview, we showed the participants one manually made reference compilation that was made by us, one of the manual compilations made by F1, and one automatic remix that was made using the AVR automatic remixing system. We watched the compilations with each of the participants and let them comment on the videos. After each video, we asked whether they thought the compilation was made by a human or a machine, and asked their feelings and opinions on the compilations and the remixing processes. Six out of eight participants had not seen the compilations before the interview and did not know whether the compilations were made manually by a human or automatically by a machine. For this paper some of the quotes from the transcriptions of the interviews and the focus group were translated into English by the first author.

The Video Remixing Procedures

Next we address the trial procedure — including the automatic and manual video remixing procedures — that we used as a research frame in our study. Figure 1 shows the remixing process we utilized in our user trial.

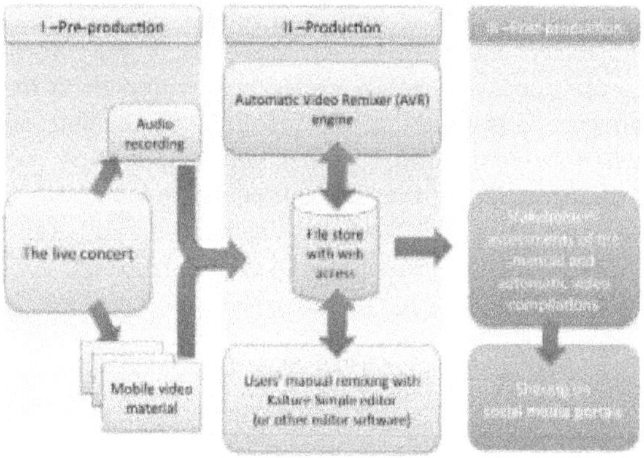

Figure 1. Remixing process

Automatic Remixing System

The automatic remixing system consists of the recording devices and a remixing server, and it functions in three main stages. The first is the *Pre-Production* stage, the second the *Production* stage, and the third the *Post-Production* stage.

The *Pre-Production* stage consists of recording the videos at the music event, and subsequently uploading these to the automatic remixing server. The recording devices (Nokia N97 mobile phones) were running a context recording client simultaneously with the video recorder. The context recording client captures and stores time-stamped sensor data while recording the videos. This helps in inferring the contextual information of the recorded video depending on the sensors being used. For the trial, data from the built-in electronic compass was recorded together with the video. The electronic compass gives as output the orientation of the camera-pointing direction with respect to North (for example: 90 degrees with respect to North). The information about the orientation of recording is then exploited to achieve two main goals: understanding what is the Region Of Interest (ROI) of the event for those users who are participating at the multi-user event recording, and inferring horizontal and rotational camera movements (also known as "camera panning" operations). Due to the limited network bandwidth availability with respect to the high volume of recorded data, we chose not to have direct up-loading from the mobile phones. Instead, the videos and the context data were uploaded offline using a USB connection.

The *Production* stage is based on the idea of stitching together video segments cropped from the original source videos recorded by different users. The main issue consists of understanding which video segments to consider and discovering the optimal length for each of the selected segments. The *Production* stage consists of several steps. First, all the uploaded videos are synchronized with each other such that the same events happen at corresponding timestamps among different user recorded videos (i.e., source videos) which overlap temporally. The second step consists of context data analysis: the orientation data from each user is used to infer if and when that specific user has moved the camera phone in a horizontal direction by means of a panning operation. The detected panning operations are then marked as "event points" and used in the AVR video generation as switching points between different views. Also, orientation data from all the users is used to understand if there is a specific ROI in that event. The information about the ROI is then used to assign higher priority to videos that have been recorded by pointing the camera phone within the range of orientations of interest. The video segments with higher priority will then have a higher chance of being inserted into the final AVR video. In order not to switch from one view to another too fast or too slow (causing an unpleasant viewing experience), minimum and maximum segment durations (lower and upper bound temporal thresholds) have been set in the process. Thus, if there are consecutive event points detected within a too short time interval (i.e., less than the lower-bound temporal threshold), only the first event point is used for switching the view. Instead, if there are no event points for a too long interval (depending on the higher-bound temporal threshold), then the system forces a view switch. After having stitched together all the selected video segments, the visual part of the AVR video is ready. Regarding the audio side, a combined audio track is created by using the extracted audio from the recorded videos. The approach for this combined audio track creation is based on two requirements: using the audio tracks with the best quality, and obtaining the minimum number of audio switches. The first requirement might introduce a large number of audio segments if the source content consists of frequently changing audio quality or many source videos with good audio quality of short duration. Thus, there has to be a trade-off between the requirements. At this point, the automatically generated video and audio tracks are merged to obtain the final AVR video.

The *Post-Production* stage includes the sharing and viewing of the AVR video. Due to the completely automatic nature of the AVR production, there is a possibility for inclusion of source videos that contain objectionable material (e.g. obscene gestures). When such segments are included, the related source video needs to be removed manually.

Manual Remixing Procedure

The manual remixing procedure roughly simulates the way a single user would preview, download, upload, and remix mobile video material that is accessible on the web. The procedure follows the three phases as described before for the automatic remixes and as shown in Figure 1, but differs in the Production phase. In this phase the Fans were provided with a link to a website with previews of the videos as well as access to download the raw material, including a fifteen minute audio track recorded with the Nokia N97 or three specific audio tracks recorded with a video capable micro-DSLR camera. Users could watch the lower quality preview videos and then download all or part of the material in the original quality. The Kaltura Open Source video platform [7] was used to provide users with an online video editing service for creating mixes from the downloaded material. Kaltura was given only as an option and not as a mandatory requirement. All the participants were also instructed that they could use some desktop-based video editor if they desired. We wanted to offer them one tool because many of them did not have earlier experience on video remixing. With Kaltura it was easy to give technical support, if needed. Kaltura Simple Editor provides the basic video editing features needed for mixing together multiple video clips and a soundtrack; it includes timeline-based editing, trimming of and transitions between video clips, and options to use either video clip audio or an external sound file. The editor was used online on a web browser and required users to upload all the material they wanted to use in their mixes. After uploading the material, it was converted on the server to a format usable by the editor. The necessary conversion process added more waiting time on top of the time used for uploading the material. This, however, simulates the fully manual remixing process as was intended. After conversion the videos were available in the editor's Clip Library tab where the clips could be dragged onto the timeline. On the timeline the clips could be trimmed to a desired length and transitions could be added in between the clips by dragging them onto the timeline from the Transitions tab. In the Soundtrack tab the user could upload sound files into the project. One single sound file could be used to play over the video, either in looped or play-once mode. Users could then choose to mute the sounds from the videos to have them to play together with the selected soundtrack or without a separate soundtrack.

Overview of the Data

Raw Material

The trial resulted in 105 clips, totaling approximately one hour and 52 minutes of video and 2.3GB of data. Each user contributed an average of nine clips. There was a wide variation among the users on the number of clips with the minimum being four clips per user and the maximum being 20 clips per user. There was no direct correlation observed between the number of clips per user and the average clip duration. Some users were more prolific than others; the minimum total time of the clips recorded per user was 4:39 while the maximum total time of the clips recorded per user was 12:24. The maximum clip duration for each user varied between one minute and five minutes. Of these, the users chose not to include seven videos for remixing; thus, the total time of the clips was approximately one hour and 44 minutes. Most users wanted to include all of the material they shot. Three of the four users who decided not to include some videos excluded more than one clip.

Video Compilations

Out of the Fans who participated in the concert trial, only one, F1, edited her own video compilations. She made two of them. As a reference, we made a reference remix using the same process and editor as described earlier. It was done to test the process and the capabilities of the editor fully, to give an example of certain kind of editing style, and to test how it will be assessed against the other compilations. With the AVR system, we made two compilations to test what kind of compilations the system makes from the material that is taken in an authentic music concert environment.

FINDINGS 1: GENERAL REQUIREMENTS FOR REMIXES

In the focus group and the after-trial interviews, our objective was to discover the stakeholders' requirements for the collaborative video compilation process and their views on the added value of manual and automatic social video compilations from a live music event.

Heterogeneous Motivations for Video Compilations

The Fans' main motivation was to record videos as personal memorabilia of the concert. However, some people said that they share video clips with their friends, for example, on Facebook. Others noted that they would share the videos more with their friends if they could do it easily from their phones or cameras during the event. The Artists thought that video compilations are a way to promote the band image, and could be used by venue owners to publicize the band. The main motivation was to demonstrate the interaction between the band and the audience to other people who did not see the event live.

> "As an agent, it is very important to me to show the customers [venue owners and consumers] how the band's live performance looks like." – A1

Both the Fans and the Artists saw video compilations as a great way to enhance the concert experience, stretch the timeline of the concert, and promote interaction between the fans and the band.

> "To get the fans to communicate with each other. That is why this is interesting." –A1

> "After a concert I often have a feeling like, too bad it's already over." – F1

FINDINGS 2: REACTIONS TO MANUAL REMIXING

In this section, we describe the reactions of the stakeholders to the manual remixing, including how they felt about making compilations and what kind of motivations they had to make their own.

Motivations for Manual Mixing

For the Fans, the main motivation to make their own manual compilations was personal challenge, and/or publication (such as to the band's Facebook profile).

"I Made This!" Self-Expression and Meeting a Challenge
The F1 who made two manual compilations was very motivated. She was proud of her compilations and excited at the prospect of them being published somewhere.

> "I had this kind of proud feeling that this is my thing . . . then I can say that, hey I made this!" - F1

She felt successful after completing difficult editing of her clips to suit herself.

> "Then it was like, great, I got this one thing done!" - F1

She was also motivated to make more compilations. However, she was not sure if any band would like to use these kinds of mixes because they are not very professional. One of the Fans did not consider publication important, and he felt that the only motivation was the personal challenge and that he could make something nice for himself.

> "It would be like, hey I made this!" – F2

However, he would have agreed with the publishing of his compilation on the band's Facebook site.

F4 was motivated to make a remix. He even had planned what kind of a story he would tell with his remix. However, he had some problems with his Internet connection and in understanding the logic of the manual remixing process. He liked the idea of getting his remixes published.

"Not Interested!" Concentrating on the Concert and Not Video Editing
For the F3 and F2 it was all about the concert experience itself. They did not have any interest in making compilations of their own. Their primary intention was just to shoot the video material in the concert and give it to other people to make the remix. They did not feel that remixing was for them.

> "I shoot the material and give it to others." – F3

Burden of Manual Remixing
Next, we will discuss the burdens involved the manual video compilation.

"It's a Tough Job But I Love it": Overcoming the Hardship and Keeping the Standards High
The F1 who made her own compilations said that for the first one (duration of 4:24), she worked about 35 to 40 hours. This was a surprisingly long time considering that the reference compilation our researcher made was completed in about three hours. F1 said that first she used one evening to familiarize herself with the Kaltura video editor. This was evident because she did not have any video editing experience. Subsequently, after 12 to 14 hours of editing, she thought the compilation was ready. However, she was still not satisfied.

> "I wanted the remix to be perfect." – F1

She also went through almost all of the raw material of one song. She made a choice to concentrate only on the video material from one song; otherwise the work would have been too much. This demonstrates how laborious and time-consuming it can be for an amateur to manually make a satisfactory video compilation.

"I Was Going to Do it But Something Came Up": No Time and Technical Difficulties
The other three of the Fans (F2, F4, F5) who had some intentions to make their own manual compilations said that they either did not have time for it, or they felt it was too much of a burden to start figuring out how the editor worked and going through the raw material. There was also a technical difficulty in getting their computers to view the material and upload the best videos to the Kaltura editor.

> "It was like download clips to the computer, upload clips to the server. Edit there, put here. I was like, later!" – F2

F4's home Internet connection was so slow that he was unable to download the raw clips to his computer. He was also uncertain if he understood how to proceed with a manual compilation:

> "It was a little uncertain for me, how to make the remix." – F4

"No Way I'm Going to Do This": Way Too Much of a Burden
Two of the Fans (F3, F6) did not even check the manual editor and had no intention to do their own compilations. F6 said she would just forget herself while trying. She also had some problems in understanding the logic of the editing process. The M3 did not even check how Kaltura works and had no intention of making a compilation of his own.

> "I just did not feel like studying it." – F3

FINDINGS 3: USE OF THE MANUAL EDITOR
In this section, we will discuss how the manual editor was used. Our data comes from the F1 who made her own video compilations, and the findings are based on her experiences. We still think there are valuable results relating to how an amateur can make multi-camera live music video compilations manually, and what significant factors there are in that kind of video editing process.

Unexpected Uses of Raw Material
Manual editing brought up some unexpected uses of the raw material, like use of lights, jumping audio track, and ruined video material. The F1 said that she used lights as a guide to edit the remix. Beforehand, we thought that the music would be the main factor when the user chooses when to make cuts.

> "In addition to music I used lights as a guide to edit the remix. ...Because they changed in convenient points." – F1

She did not use the complete audio track that we provided. However, her idea was not to make a music video style remix with a complete audio track but something different. She thought that it was "cool" to listen to the concert from several places. She also wanted to use all the possible camera angles. Her intention was to show the viewer how the concert looked and sounded from various places in the concert hall, and to show that the experience is different depending on the location. Because of this she tried to use every participant's material for her remix:

> "I wanted to add in the element that shows how the concert sounds when you are at the balcony, near the drums or at the back of the hall." – F1

She also wanted to use a clip where the cameraman had flipped the phone by 90 degrees. She thought that would be a great special effect. The fan who had recorded that exact clip thought that the clip itself was ruined because he had accidentally held the camera with a wrong angle. We think this is a great example of how an individual video clip has much more potential when it can be remixed innovatively with other video clips.

Coping With the Amount of Raw Data in Manual Mixing

We were surprised of how fast can the raw material grow in a multi-camera recording. F1 had to mark off some material in the beginning so that going through the clips would not be too overwhelming. She decided to concentrate only on the clips from one song. Although she tried to use every participant's material for her compilation, she used her own material the most. This was mainly because she was familiar with it, and it was laborious to find good scenes from the other cameramen's raw material manually. She also used pen and paper to keep notes about which of the clips were good. It became clear that the amount of a multi-camera video material quickly becomes so large that it might be overwhelming to go through all the video material manually. As one of the Artists said:

> "If one has material from 100 cameras there is no way he can go through all of them...Even if one had four cameras and a web based video editor, there are still endless ways one can go wrong and concentrate on insignificants thing during the first five seconds of the editing process." – A2

Thus, for example efficient use of metadata or more strictly organized directing in the filming phase might make it easier for an amateur to handle the material and make manual video compilations.

FINDINGS 4: REACTIONS TO THE MANUAL REMIXES

In this section, we will go through the participants' reactions to the manual compilations.

The Reference Compilation

Five of the six participants guessed that humans made the reference compilation, and one was unsure. Based on the interviews, the five knew the video was human-made because it seemed somehow logical; the change of colors worked effectively; cuts were synchronized with the music; and it had "a human touch."

> "It was made from the short cuts and what was special about it was the rhythm. The creator gave the viewer an understanding about what is going on [in each scene] and then it was cut to another scene and cut and another and cut..." – F3

All of the Fans thought that the reference compilation was good, and many of them were amazed how it was possible to make such a good compilation from the raw material they had been filming. The Artists had positive feeling towards the video and thought that it might be good publicity for the band. They thought that it might be the deciding factor a wavering concertgoer.

> "I think and hope that based on this compilation a positive twist could happen" – A3

The Manual Compilation Made by One of the Fans

In the case of the manual compilation made by F1, the participants were a bit unsure whether it was made manually or automatically. Still, five out of six participants thought a human made it. The main reason for their uncertainty was that this compilation did not have a continuous audio track, but instead the audio was from the individual scenes' audio. This made the audio fragmented and negatively affected the viewing experience. However, the clear narration convinced them it was human-made. In the first scene, the band's lead singer welcomes people to the concert, and in the last scene, he walks away, jumping and waving. This gave the users a human impression.

FINDINGS 5: REACTIONS TO AUTOMATIC REMIXING

In this section, we will discuss how the users understood the logic of automation, reacted to automatic compilations, and what kind of use they had in mind for automatic remixing. Before the trial, the participants' first reactions to automatic remixing were mostly curious about how it would work and how the machine makes decisions. Many of the participants also thought it sounded interesting that a machine could do the editing process, but also brought up that they felt a bit skeptical about how it could be possible.

The Effect of Understanding the Logic of Automation

In the trial, the participants were not told how the automatic editor makes decisions and what information it uses in the editing process. This enabled us to study the effect of understanding the logic of the automatic editor, especially how the ignorance of the logic of automation affects how the Fans film in the concert situation. Some of the Fans thought that the automatic editor would not be able to cut the raw clips in any way. Because of this, they tried to shoot short, ready-to-use clips.

> "Because it does not cut those (raw clips), because there is going to be the whole clip. That's how I assumed it works." – F4

The F3 thought it was bothersome to shoot the video clips because he did not know how the automatic systems made editing decisions.

> "One should know what their algorithm is like." – F3

The Fans were thinking about the editing phase already as they shot. They tried to cooperate with the automatic editor by pre-planning what kind of material would be useful.

Reactions to the Automatic Remix

Five participants' thought the compilation was automatically edited, and one was unsure. Thus, it was clear that the automatic compilation had special features that made it look like machine-made. Next, we will discuss what those features were and how the participants reacted to the automatic compilation before and after they came to know that it was automatically edited.

"This Does Not Have a Rhythm": Reactions Before Knowing it Was Made by a Machine

Because of the low light conditions in the concert hall, there were many dark scenes in the raw material. Thus, all the compilations, manual and automatic, had dark scenes. However, in the automatic compilation, participants thought the darkness was somehow "weird" and that it flattened the feeling of the video.

> "This darkness does not motivate here. It does not have any function here." – F3

None of the participants liked the automatic compilation as much as they did the first two manual ones. The automatic compilation was described as passive.

> "Passivity can be a special effect to bring up dynamic stage performance. But in this there is only darkness." – F3

"Not So Bad After All, But No Use as a Promotional Material" – Reactions After Knowing it Was Made by a Machine

When the Fans were told that the compilation was automatically edited, most of them then developed a different perspective. Even though it lacked the human touch, it was still viewed positively. It seemed that people did not have such high expectations for the machine-made compilation.

> "It's actually good considering it's a machine made" – F4

Most of the participants saw the automatic compilation as promising and said it would be worth developing further. However, the Artists especially still saw limitations. They brought up how it is hard to get a good automatic compilation because editing is based on continuity of movement, colors, and music that enables a narration.

> "It's impossible to automate drama." – A2

The Artists also thought that the image the automatic compilation projected about the atmosphere of the live show was so irrational that if it was the only reference to the band's live performance, the fans would not come to watch.

> "The machine is irrational. When there is action on the stage, it shows only an illuminated exit sign." – A1

The Perceived Usefulness of the Automatic Compilation

Although the automatic compilation did not get very high ratings from the participants, many of them still found situations where it could be useful, especially if it could be made more interesting. Some of the Fans thought that the automatic one could be used in personal blogs or for marketing, and could be an easy way to participate without having to make their own manual compilations.

> "You can take video and then you become part of this compilation. It would be participatory activity" – F1

> "Like I could watch it from YouTube." – F4

The F4 also thought the automatic remix would be great to have on his mobile phone right after the concert. This would extend the timeline of the concert experience and would be great memorabilia produced with no effort, even if it were not top quality.

How to Make it More Interesting

Next, we asked the participants how to make the automatic compilation more interesting to watch and more useful. The main things were that the video should be synchronized with the music; clips should be shorter; there should be more variability in field size; and the dark scenes should be eliminated. Three participants said that the video should be more synchronized with the music.

> "Now the automatic one jumped randomly somehow in a way that a human made one would not." – A3

Two participants said that the compilation should not have such long, continuous scenes from the same camera but instead it would be more interesting and lively if there were quicker changes between cameras.

> "One has to remember that five seconds in a video compilation like that is a long time." – A3

Three participants mentioned that in a multi-camera compilation, there should be more systematic variation in the camera angles and field sizes. They also suggested that there should be scenes from locations other than the main concert hall, such as a bar or the men's restroom.

> "Like Big Brother in a good way." – A3

One of the Artists thought that one reason the manual compilation was better is that a human can use light as a guideline to capture the feeling of the concert. Thus, if the dark scenes could be eliminated, it might improve the viewing experience of the automatic compilations.

> "In a concert the light can change dramatically only for like half second. If you don't capture those tiny moments one might think that the concert was totally black." – A3

Need for Human Intervention

The users often mentioned the need for human intervention as a part of the automatic editing process. A3 said that when he watched the automatic compilation, he had a feeling that he would like to make his own changes to it.

> "I was like I wish I could now go there and edit that. Then one could get more out of it." – A3

He also thought that because the editing process requires a complete view of the raw material, it is difficult to leave it solely to a computer.

> "There has to be a human understanding about what kind of scenes need to be one after the other because contiguous scenes affect to each other." – A3

However, one of the Artists also brought up the importance of the actual goal of the compilations:

> "If it's just harsh recording, it could work without a single cut. However, if we want to do even a little bit artistic material then there needs to be a human in the process." – A2

DISCUSSION

The study showed that in production of social video compilations from live music events it is not self-evident how to allocate the remixing tasks between human and machine.

In a fully manual setup, the user has total control of the editing process. She has the authority from the beginning to the end to sense, analyze, decide, and implement which parts of the material she uses. At best, this flexibility can give a satisfactory feeling to the users. Also, the actual video compilation can raise excitement among the other stakeholders. However, the editing process itself may prove to be troublesome. In multi-camera video editing it can be laborious to manage large amounts of material in a satisfactory way. The use of technical infrastructure for video editing can be felt as too much of a burden to even start the editing. Improvements in the manual editing interface and usability design can only reduce part of the work. The labor of going through the video clips to find the good ones and synchronizing them would still be needed.

By contrast, when the remixing process is fully automated to the point that the computer ignores the human and acts autonomously, humans do not have to do anything but film the raw material during the concert. Thus, the laborious struggle with the technology and the burden of perusing the overwhelming quantity of material disappears. However, it turned out that a machine simply cannot imitate the human touch. It was surprising that ignorance regarding the logic of the automatic editor had an effect on how the people filmed the video during the concert. People made assumptions about how the machine would edit the raw material and directed their filming based on those assumptions. We also found out that expectations for an automatically made video compilation versus the manual one were lower. Naturally, how satisfactory a video compilation is perceived to be depends on its intended use. We found that for a documentary style compilation, the artistic demands are muted. On the other hand, a compilation that has to mediate the social interaction and atmosphere of a live music concert and is also intended to be used for marketing purposes has very stringent demands in terms of artistic quality.

Our research frame considered the two most extreme options of automation: namely, fully manual and fully automatic. We note that there is a large design space between those two extremes; a space where human and machine can collaborate in various stages during the remixing process, depending on how personal and artistic one wants the compilation at one extreme or how simple and fast at the other. For this design space, we propose that designers use the levels of automation and the stages of information processing Sheridan [15] and Parasuraman [12] have presented, and which we discussed earlier in the Related Research section.

As an example, let us next walk through a case where we set the tasks of a video remixing process into Parasuraman's four-stage model of information processing and discuss how Sheridan's automation levels could change inside the video remixing process when moving from one stage to another. Thus, we stress the use of human labor in some tasks and machine labor in others. In *the first stage*, information acquisition can cover the sensing of the raw data. If the goal is to find all scenes that have bright lighting conditions, in a fully manual model, the human must go through the material and find the proper scenes. As we have discussed, this is laborious with multi-camera material. However, if we raise the level of automation and program the machine to sense and "lock on" to all the bright scenes, this would ease the human labor. In *the second stage*, information analysis can cover the cognitive functions such as remembering which of the previously found bright scenes also include a guitar solo. In a fully manual setup, the human must manually integrate the two inputs (the brightness and guitar solo) and analyze when they both exist together. If we raise the automation level and let the computer do the analysis, we can ease human labor by letting the computer provide context-dependent summaries of the raw video data. During *the third stage*, the decision and action selection stage, some of the previously found scenes (with good lighting conditions and a guitar solo) are selected to be stitched in a particular order into a compilation. This stage could be left for human to do independently, and this is a way to raise the artistic value of the video. In *the fourth stage*, the actual stitching phase is implemented during which the selected scenes are stitched together, forming the final compilation. Human could implement this step by manually combining the previously selected scenes. If the fourth stage was automated to a higher level, a computer could execute the stitching autonomously and complete the editing process.

By this thought experiment we want to demonstrate the possibilities of dividing the video editing process into separate information-processing stages, and by that help designers and developers to systematically think of an automated process in multi-camera video remixing. When moving from one stage to another, it is possible to change the level of automation depending on the intended uses for the compilation. If the need is to get a quick documentary style compilation, greater emphasis should be put on automation. However, if the need is for an artistic compilation, higher human involvement may be required.

CONCLUSIONS AND FUTURE RESEARCH

We compared the processes of manual and automatic video remixing from both the artists' and the fans' point of view. We studied the process from the moment when the fans shoot mobile video in a live concert to the moment when the fans and the artists assess the human or machine made video compilations. Based on the results, automation related design decisions have several implications on the motivations and reactions the users have towards a collaborative mobile video remixing system and the actual video compilations.

First, it came up that the various stakeholders of a music event could have different motivations and requirements for video compilations depending on the intended use. An artist might want to emphasize the marketing value of the compilation whereas a fan might want to have it as personal memorabilia for her to share it with friends. If the compilation is wanted to have a special artistic feeling, it is hard to gain that with a fully automatic remixing. *Second,* the manual editing process can give satisfactory results but the raw material from multi-camera video shooting can quickly become cumbersome. This came up when only one of the participants made the effort to actually make video compilations. She did a lot of work for them but in the end was very satisfied about the results. *Third,* people are able to use the raw material innovatively in ways that are difficult for computers to imitate without a high-end adaptive automation. For example, video material that was accidentally shot with a 90 degrees angle was surprisingly considered as a great special effect material. *Fourth,* automatic video compilations are not assessed with the same criteria applied to human made ones. However, for this to be true, it should be evident to the viewer that a machine has generated the compilation automatically. In our study many participants thought that the automatic video compilations we showed them were quite all right only after we told them that they were remixed automatically. *Fifth*, the results revealed strong interconnections between the filming process and the editing process. Transparency and communication between both of the processes affects the automatic and manual video compilations. For example, knowledge of the logic of the automatic editing process affected the participants' filming process. People were keen to learn the logic of the automatic editing process. Before the filming stage some of the participants had made assumptions on how the automatic remixer would work and directed their filming based on those assumptions. In the manual editing stage, the effect of transparency and communication became visible when a participant ended up using her own video material more than other participants' material. The main reason was that she was more familiar with her own material than with others'. This showed that context metadata the camera phone possibly adds to the raw material, such as location, could be valuable not only in automatic remixing but also for manual remixing. For the future research we believe it is valuable to study the possibilities of automatic and user generated metadata in multi camera video remixing process and how the direction during the shooting phase affects the editing process.

ACKNOWLEDGMENTS

The work was part of Social Video project funded by The Finnish Funding Agency for Technology and Innovation. We thank the participants, Anu Kankainen, and anonymous reviewers for their help and valuable comments.

REFERENCES

1. Engström, A., Esbjörnsson, M. and Juhlin, O. Mobile collaborative live video mixing. *Proc. MobileHCI 2008,* (2008), 157–166.
2. Engström, A., Esbjörnsson, M. and Juhlin, O. Nighttime visual media production in club environments. *Night and darkness: interaction after dark. Workshop at CHI 2008.*
3. Foote, J., Cooper, M. and Girgensohn, A. Creating music videos using automatic media analysis. *Proc. MM 2002,* ACM Press (2002), 560.
4. Girgensohn, A. et al. A semi-automatic approach to home video editing. *Proc. UIST 2000*, ACM Press (2000), 81–89.
5. Girgensohn, A. et al. Home video editing made easy—balancing automation and user control. *Proc. INTERACT 2001,* ACM Press (2001), 464–471.
6. Jacucci, G., Oulasvirta, A., Salovaara, A. and Sarvas, R. (2005). Supporting the Shared Experience of Spectators through Mobile Group Media. *Proc. GROUP 2005*, ACM Press (2005), 207-216.
7. Kaltura open source video http://corp.kaltura.com/.
8. Kennedy, L. and Naaman, M. Less talk, more rock: Automated organization of community-contributed collections of concert videos. *Proc. WWW 2009,* ACM Press (2009), 311–320.
9. Kirk, D. et al. Understanding videowork. *Proc. CHI 2007,* ACM (2007), 61–70.
10. Lehmuskallio, A., Sarvas, R., Snapshot Video: Everyday Photographers Taking Short Video-Clips. Proc. NordiCHI 2008, ACM Press (2008).
11. Lessig, L. *Remix: Making art and commerce thrive in the hybrid economy*. Penguin Pr, 2008.
12. Parasuraman, R., Sheridan, T.B. and Wickens, C.D. A model for types and levels of human interaction with automation. *IEEE Transactions on Systems, Man and Cybernetics, Part A 30*, 3 (2000), 286–297.
13. Sarvas, R., Viikari, M., Pesonen, J. And Nevanlinna, H. MobShare: Controlled and Immediate Sharing of Mobile Images. *Proc. MUM 2004*. ACM (2004), 724-731.
14. Shamma, D. A., Shawn, R., Shafton, P. L., Liu, Y. "Watch what I watch: using community activity to understand content. *Proc. MIR 2007*. ACM Press (2007).
15. Sheridan, T. *Telerobotics, Automation, and Human Supervisory Control*. MIT Press, Cambridge, MA. 1992.
16. Vihavainen, S., Oulasvirta, A., Sarvas, R.: "I Can't Lie Anymore" – The Implications of Location Automation for Mobile Social Applications. *Proc. MobiQuitous 2009*, IEEE Press (2009).

Knowing Funny: Genre Perception and Categorization in Social Video Sharing

Jude Yew
School of Information
University of Michigan
Ann Arbor, MI, USA
jyew@umich.edu

David A. Shamma
Internet Experiences Group
Yahoo! Research
Santa Clara, CA, USA
aymans@acm.org

Elizabeth F. Churchill
Internet Experiences Group
Yahoo! Research
Santa Clara, CA, USA
churchill@acm.org

ABSTRACT
Categorization of online videos is often treated as a tag suggestion task; tags can be generated by individuals or by machine classification. In this paper, we suggest categorization can be determined socially, based on people's interactions around media content without recourse to metadata that are intrinsic to the media object itself. This work bridges the gap between the human perception of genre and automatic categorization of genre in classifying online videos. We present findings from two internet surveys and from follow-up interviews where we address how people determine genre classification for videos and how social framing of video content can alter the perception and categorization of that content. From these findings, we train a Naive Bayes classifier to predict genre categories. The trained classifier achieved 82% accuracy using only social action data, without the use of content or media-specific metadata. We conclude with implications on how we categorize and organize media online as well as what our findings mean for designing and building future tools and interaction experiences.

Author Keywords
Video, social, classification, categorization, YouTube, Naive Bayes, genre, interview, survey

ACM Classification Keywords
H.5.1 Information Interfaces and Presentation: Multimedia Information Systems; J.4 Computer Applications: Social And Behavioral Sciences

General Terms
Human Factors, Experimentation

INTRODUCTION
In an episode of *The Simpsons*, Homer lectures Bart about shoplifting, "Why do you think I took you to all those Police Academy movies? For fun? Well, I didn't hear anybody laughin', did you?" [18] Here, the genre of the comedy, *Police Academy*, is recategorized by Homer based on the audience's humorless reception of the movie. Although clearly a joke in itself, Homer's perception of *Police Academy* illustrates how the social consumption of media can alter the way content is perceived and categorized. Media content that we believe to fit a particular genre is both constituted by, and constitutive of, the changing social contexts in which that content is produced, shared and consumed [1]; genres are socially constructed. This article presents a study of genre categorization and demonstrates how the analysis of social consumption and sharing behaviors can reveal the nature and characteristics of online video content. Genre engenders recognizable patterns of social action and we can infer the genre of a video by looking at what people do with that content.

Genre categories have both epistemological and functional dimensions; they are first and foremost ways of organizing and defining content, but also ways of organizing *social actions* [1]. For instance, the category Comedy helps us identify and expect a particular kind of video content, such as a humorous narrative and funny characters. At the same time, Comedy also presents content that specifies a type of individual behavior and social interaction that would be different, or even inappropriate, if one were to watch a Documentary. Besides the dual nature of genres, they can also be understood as "socially constituted systems" [5] that shape the context and social activity surrounding them. Genres are social constructs which specify particular interaction patterns and social activity, which in turn, determine how we define and interpret those genre categories [14].

Current automated tag-based classification techniques ignore these aspects of social construction. In this paper, we focus on the categorization of videos that are socially shared on the Internet. The online social sharing of media can take place asynchronously, through social media websites like YouTube, or synchronously, with services like `http://justin.tv` or Yahoo! Zync. In addition to simply sharing videos, people interact around the video by leaving comments, rating content or, in the case of synchronous sharing, by chatting. These interactions leave traces which are either explicit, publicly viewable annotations in the form of comments and ratings, or are implict, logged usage data; both can be mined to reveal patterns of interaction and engagement with the video content. More importantly, the data resulting from social actions around the video content can also provide insights in to the nature, characteristics and genre classification of the video content itself.

CHI 2011, May 7–12, 2011, Vancouver, BC, Canada.

In this paper, we address people's understanding of genre categories from a social construction perspective. For the purposes of our analysis we focus on Comedy as a genre. We develop a model of video genre classification using data captured from the social consumption and sharing of online videos. The predictive model is built from 5 features sampled from a dataset of 9,364 videos taken from 2,188 sharing sessions. The model classifies videos by genre at an accuracy greater than 82%.

In the following sections, we review the online video categorization task from a human and computational perspective. To gain further insight into the human perspective of comedy, we present findings from two online surveys and eleven 1-hour, semi-structured interviews with a sample of the survey participants. The findings from the qualitative exploration are used to inform the training features used for automated genre prediction. Finally, we conclude by suggesting what this model means for current recommendation systems as well as for the interaction design of future systems.

CATEGORIZATION

> [categorization is] not a social act simply because it takes place in some social context; it is social because it is at work in shaping the very context within which it functions [1]

Social action can transform how a media event is received by an audience [1]. For example, overlaid commentary can transform a serious event into something comedic. The cult TV series Mystery Science Theater 3000 ran from 1988 to 1999 based entirely on this premise, the main protagonists providing a running commentary over a series of science fiction B-movies and transforming what had initially been created as "serious" content into comedy. Given social action can thus transform the reception of a media event, we can conclude that without social context, categorization is a difficult task to do accurately, and that representing content by classification must account for contextual and social uses. Bowker and Star explain this difficulty, "people (and the information systems they build) routinely conflate formal and informal, prototypical and Aristotelian aspects of classification. There is no such thing as an unambiguous uniform classification system." [2] In reality, things cannot be sorted easily into mutually exclusive and complete categories. Online videos are no exception; they can be categorized on several levels such as, the semantic or narrative content of the video, the inherent properties of the video itself like its format, by stylistic features like mood, and so on [16].

Methods used to classify the genre of web videos have traditionally focused on the video's content or metadata. Classification of online videos is computationally treated as tag suggestion from a pre-defined set [16]. However, we argue the task of genre classification can be made more accurate via an examination of the social interaction surrounding online video—in effect, how the video is discussed and interpreted. How a video is consumed, interacted with, and commented on is indicative of the nature of its content. In the following two subsections, we detail arguments made from related work towards the issue of classifying videos from a social action point of view.

Categorizing on social data

Online tools for content viewing support many forms of social interaction [3, 23] such as link sharing/forwarding, ratings, "liking" as a public statement of endorsement, explicit recommendation, commenting, synchronous chatting while watching, and so on. In synchronous video sharing contexts, people also start/stop videos to review key moments and discuss them. These activities leave digital traces in the form of server logs and large-scale databases [24]. These digital traces are used to assess the popularity of content, and to create promotional mechanisms (such as leaderboards) to further raise the profile of the content for recommendation. Activity data are also mined, aggregated and analyzed to develop models of user consumption patterns. As well as understanding people's consumption practices around content, these activity data can be used to categorize the content itself. Crane and Sornette [6] identified "signatures" in the metadata of YouTube videos in order to identify "quality" content. Whitman et al. [25] utilized textual data from online forums to classify and infer similarity in music content. However, while actions on or around a media object by individuals have been explored to classify content, social actions have not been explored. In our work we analyze patterns of activity between people over or around that media object as a means of classifying content.

Categorization as Tagging and Recommendation

Historically, in computing and the social media, categorization is a collaborative filtering task for tag suggestion. Computationally, finding a category for a video can be the equivalent of suggesting the single best tag for that video. Automatic tags and tag suggestions are often content-based either from the video's meta-data or the visual media's content [8]. Recently, Zhang, Zhang, and Tang [27] proposed a hybrid method based on video meta-data and social-graph distance. Similar web-graph systems have been proposed for image classification [13]. These richer tag sets have been shown to improve the performance of web video categorization [4]. Similar approaches use tag metadata co-occurrence using machine learning (ML) or term-ranking techniques [22, 15].

From the start of tagging's popularity, social navigation, or recommendation, has been an ongoing research investigation [19]. Likely the most publicized example is the NetFlix Prize contest. From a dataset of 100 million movie ratings, the open contest challenged people to find a 10% improvement over the current state of the art. The solutions used a variety of information types, from ratings data to the movie rental's ZIP-code location to the renter's age; no content was used. In general, the actual video, image, or audio signal/content is believed to be unreliable for recommendation. Instead, ML researchers look for explicit distinct actions, like 5-star rating scores, to find similarity [21] and categorization. For example, Yew and Shamma [26] trained a Naive Bayes classifier to predict YouTube categories to an accuracy of 75.5% using only three features of YouTube Metadata: video duration, view count, and 5-star rating. In particular, their finding showed that nominal factorization of explicit data, in their case: ratings, improves performance without the need to increase the training set size. They attribute the rating's dominance to "explicit social action" being a higher fidelity signal than implicitly aggregated usage data. From our findings in this study, we model "implicit social sharing behaviors" as the construction of genre.

Research Questions

Is there a correlation between genre and watching behavior? If so, could watching behavior be more effective than 5-star ratings when used for categorization? This paper aims at identifying this connection as guided by two primary research questions:

[Research Question 1] How do people socially consume, perceive, and categorize videos (in particular, comedy)?

[Research Question 2] Can a predictive model be built to automatically categorize media using social traces (such as conversational and interactional metadata) and without the use of explicit annotations or video content?

METHOD

This work employs a mixed-method approach to explore the issues of categorization of shared online videos, answering RQ1 qualitatively, which in turn should advise a quantitative model to answer RQ2. This approach consists of three phases combining multiple data collection and analysis methods. The first phase conducts two surveys, a pilot survey with 43 respondents administered internally and a larger survey conducted via Mechanical Turk with 69 valid responses, in order to assess the difficulties associated with categorizing online videos by humans. In phase two, the surveys are followed up with 11 interviews from the phase one survey respondents. The interviews involved questions about the respondents' mental processes when categorizing online videos, in particular videos that they labeled as "comedy." Finally, we use the findings of the surveys and the interviews to develop a classifier for categorizing video genres using only metadata from conversational and interaction activity. The main aim of adopting a machine learning classifier is to devise a method of genre classification based on how we watch videos, and not what is in them. The results from all three phases will then be used to explicate on the issue of why the categorization task, especially for comedy videos, is so difficult. Each method complements the others and allows for a stronger generalization of genre categorization from various human-computer interaction perspectives [7].

Finding a Conversational Video Dataset

For this study, we need to investigate how people judge the category of a set of videos and compare that judgement to a classifier. Since we will be training the classifier on conversation activity, the metadata that arises from crawling a site like YouTube is insufficient. Conversational activity surrounding video sharing can be found online in various livestream rooms like JustinTV[1] and video-on-demand chat and synchronous sharing tools like CBS Social TV[2] or Meebo Rooms[3], Yahoo! Zync[4] [20] which lets people host viewing parties with their broadcast TV content.

We acquired a 24-hour sample of the Zync event log for Christmas Day 2009. Zync allows two people in an instant-message session to watch a video together; the video's playback stays in sync across both participants and both participants share playback control. This provides a set of watched videos from YouTube as well as conversational activity rich enough to train a classifier. The dataset records several features: anonymous user id hashes, session start/stop events, the session duration, the number of play commands, the number of pause commands, the number of scrubs (fast forwards or rewinds), and the number of chat lines typed as a character and word count. For the chat lines, the dataset contained no actual text content, only the aggregate count of characters and words. The only text that is collected is video URLs and emoticons. Each item/activity collected is a line in the dataset which records the time of the event and the playback time on the video [12].

In total, the dataset contained 2,188 dyadic sessions that shared a sum of 9,364 YouTube videos. Not all sessions appeared complete and were missing the start/stop events, was missing a participant, or other critical information; these sessions were discarded. We then took each remaining YouTube video identifiers and retrieved the related metadata associated with each video using YouTube's Application Programming Interface[5]. Some videos were no longer available on YouTube due to copyright infringement or owner deletion; these videos and their respective sessions were also discarded. The final test sample consisted of 1,732 videos with valid metadata. The data collected from YouTube consisted of a video identifier, the video's title, its published date, its description, the genre category the uploader used, the tags the video was labelled with, the video's duration and the 5-star rating score it attained. Of these data, we only use the video's genre/category, of which YouTube provides a constrained list of 18 genre categories. The YouTube video's category is specified by the person who uploaded the video, which is *required* at the time of upload. For this article, it functions as the predictive category for our surveys and classifier and allows us to investigate if there's a match between the uploaded category and the social actions.

Within our sample of 1,732 videos and associated sessions, not all categories were well represented. However, the category distribution was unevenly distributed. To ensure we had enough data to accurately perform this study, we retained only the Top 5 video categories for our investigation; this discarded 13 categories, 11 of which contained fewer than 20 videos of that category watched. The final categories from the remaining 1,580 videos were, in order of frequency, Mu-

[1] `http://justin.tv` (Accessed 9/2010)

[2] `http://www.cbs.com/social_tv/` (Accessed 9/2010)

[3] `https://meebo.com/rooms/` (Accessed 9/2010)

[4] `http://sandbox.yahoo.com/Zync` (Accessed 9/2010)

[5] `http://gdata.youtube.com/feeds/api/` (Accessed 9/2010)

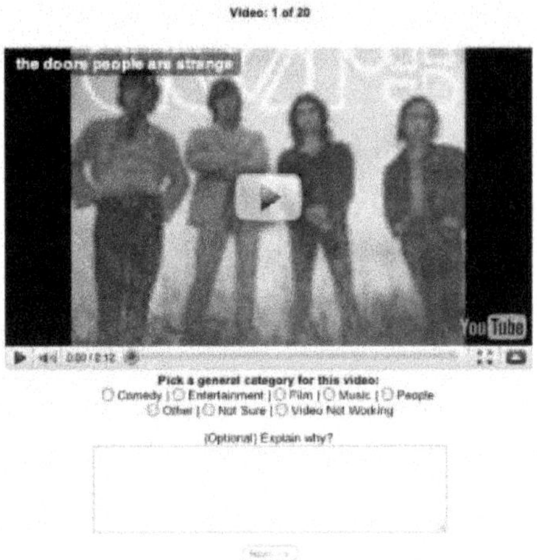

Figure 1. Screenshot of classification task in the pilot survey

sic (896), Entertainment (232), Comedy (212), Film (121), and People (119).

Surveys

Our investigation begins with two surveys: 1) a pilot survey and 2) a larger survey utilizing Amazon's Mechanical Turk service. In both surveys we presented each respondent with a set of 20 videos, selected from our corpus of retrieved videos. The primary task in both surveys is to view each video and carry out a categorization task.

Pilot Survey

In the pilot, we assess how individuals categorize shared online videos from websites like YouTube. The online survey involved presenting each respondent with one video at a time randomly from our video corpus (Figure 1). The respondent would watch or scan through the video and then make a judgement about the genre category of the video by selecting one of the Top 5 sampled genre categories: Music, Film, Comedy, Entertainment and People and leave an optional comment. An agreement between the survey respondent's genre selection and the video uploader's original genre designation signified an accurate judgement. The survey call was posted to 3 internal mailing lists within our organization. A total of 43 valid and complete responses were gathered from this survey. Respondents were able to correctly categorize 60% of the videos with the same label as the original uploader's categorization. Looking at Comedy specifically, the success rate was 50%. The comments left by the respondents on the incorrectly labeled comedy videos surfaced a lack of distinction between what is comedy and what the respondent believed was funny. One respondent illustrated this confusion in their comment as, "Comedy is the category... but I guess that doesn't require it to be funny." The respondents knew what was funny to them, but were less readily able to classify videos based on whether it belongs to the Comedy category. The pilot survey's results prompted us to ask, why are people so bad at classifying Comedy genre videos from YouTube?

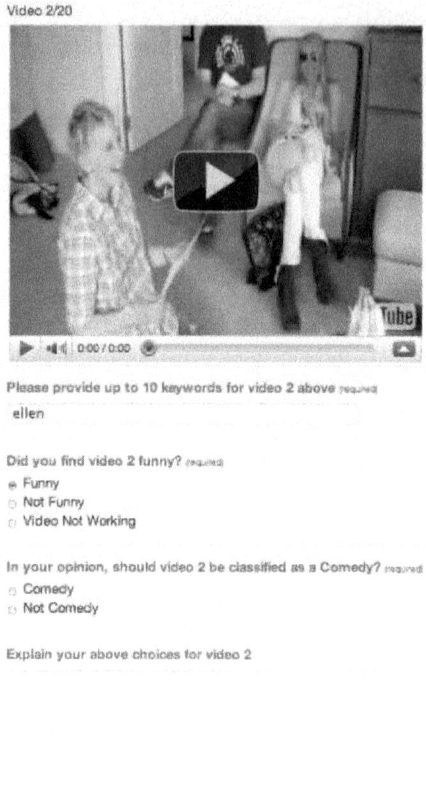

Figure 2. Screenshot of classification task on Crowd Sourced survey

Crowd Sourced Survey

We designed a second survey to address responses to what is funny and what is comedy. First, we performed a content analysis of the videos which surfaced the following media-types: cartoons, stand-up comedy, music videos, foreign film clips, and video blogs. In the second survey, each survey respondent was also presented a set of 20 videos at random. However, this time the survey presented each respondent with the same set of 20 videos. The videos were selected as a distribution of 10 Comedy videos and 10 Non-Comedy; the latter encompassed videos from the 4 other categories. Additionally, the second survey asked a different set of questions (see Figure 2).

This second survey asked "Comedy or Not" and "Funny or Not," which differs from our first survey which asked for an explict category label. Discussions with the pilot survey respondents indicated that category selection is dependent on the number of choices and more choices result in wider distribution of selections: i.e., consensus goes down.

The second survey was administered externally using the Crowdflower *crowdsourcing service*[6] to recruit respondents from Amazon's Mechanical Turk[7] (AMT). "Crowdsourcing"

[6]Crowdflower assists with "crowdsourcing" respondents for tasks from several online "labor on demand" pools, see `http://crowdflower.com/` (Accessed 9/2010)

[7]Amazon's Mechanical Turk service is an crowdsourcing marketplace that enables users to recruit large numbers of workers for tasks that computers do not do well. See `https://www.mturk.com/mturk/welcome` (Accessed 9/2010)

is a quick and inexpensive method to gather responses for our survey which has grown in recent popularity within research communities. We followed the suggestions of Kittur et. al [9] to ensure data quality when using crowdsourcing techniques. Crowdflower's service pulls from a pool of *trusted* turkers as respondents for a survey. Our survey gathered 103 responses of which 69 of them were valid and complete responses.

For the questions "Is this funny" and "Is this a comedy?," we test for inter-rater reliability using Krippendorf's alpha [10] in order to determine if there was a consensus amongst the respondents about which videos were funny and which videos should be classified as a comedy. Similar to our finding in the pilot survey, respondents showed little agreement about Comedy videos or if they were funny (Funny: $\alpha = 0.374$, Comedy: $\alpha = 0.259$). Higher reliability scores for the non-comedy videos highlight more agreement, something is obviously funny or not funny (Funny: $\alpha = 0.687$, Comedy: $\alpha = 0.464$).

The inter-rater reliability test provides only a general insight about how the videos were perceived and classified. For a more detailed understanding, we conducted a text analysis of the keywords and comments solicited for each video. Table 1 lists the frequency of the keywords "comedy" and "funny" provided by the respondents for each video. Not all the comedy videos (videos 1–10) were tagged as "comedy" by the survey respondents. In particular, videos 8 and 9 are more frequently tagged as "funny" rather than "comedy". To better understand why these two videos are tagged more frequently as "funny," we reviewed the content of both these videos. These two popular, viral videos share the following characteristics: both have generated millions of views, are short, are easy to understand, and are humorous and "cute". Video 8 is *Laughing Baby*[8], a video where a swedish baby boy bursts into giggles whenever his father makes the "bing!" sound. Video 9 is *Sneezing Panda*[9], it depicts a tiny infant panda, who is sleeping at the feet of its mother, suddenly sneezes about halfway into the video giving his mother a huge fright. For our respondents, both these videos exemplify videos that are "funny," but don't necessarily fit the definition of a comedy genre video. Some of the comments provided by the survey respondents about these two videos include:

> This is very funny video of a baby laughing. Not sure it should be categorized as a comedy. (Respondent 16)

> Its funny but its only an animal getting startled by her sneezing baby. It is not comedy because the actions were not specifically done to make us laugh. (Respondent 9)

For the respondents, not all funny videos should be classified as comedy. So what exactly are the characteristics of a comedy video? Just by looking at the frequency of the tag 'comedy' used, there is no video in our sample where there is a clear consensus in describing it as a comedy. To better understand what our respondents typically view as comedy, we carried out a word association analysis on the tags provided for each video. Specifically, we transformed all the tag/keywords responses into a term-document matrix in order to find terms that correlate with the keywords "comedy," essentially the term-frequency portion of a $tf \cdot idf$ model [17]. The results of the word association analysis provide us with some insight into how the respondents characterize videos tagged with the keyword "comedy". Table 2 shows the strong association between the keyword "comedy" with descriptions of comedic structure or stylistic features such as the presence of audience laughter (or a laugh track) or if the video depicts the performance of a stand-up comedy routine.

		Keyword Count	
Video Category	*Video*	*Comedy*	*Funny*
Comedy	1	6	18
	2	34	12
	3	43	16
	4	10	50
	5	7	31
	6	52	25
	7	2	7
	8	0	29
	9	3	33
	10	26	5
Non Comedy	11	9	13
	12	1	21
	13	1	27
	14	1	4
	15	0	5
	16	2	8
	17	0	1
	18	1	4
	19	2	5
	20	1	3

Table 1. Frequency of the terms "comedy" and "funny" appearing in the keywords solicited from the survey respondents.

comedy	act	club	comedian
stand	standup	actor	monologue
shirt	crowd	audience	mic
talking	guy	laughter	laugh
performance			

Table 2. Terms associated with the keyword 'comedy' across all videos

The same word association analysis for the keyword "funny" was not as meaningful as the analysis of "comedy". The analysis retrieved a total of 109 terms associated with the keyword "funny".

Survey Results

One major finding from the 2 surveys show that people have difficulty in classifying videos with the genre "comedy" but they are more readily able to identify whether the content of

[8] `http://www.youtube.com/watch?v=5P6UU6m3cqk` (Accessed 9/2010)

[9] `http://www.youtube.com/watch?v=FzRH3iTQPrk` (Accessed 9/2010)

a video is funny. One reason why comedy videos are hard to classify is because people have very set structural and stylistic norms they look for—such as the presence of a laugh track or a standup comedy routine. However, a cursory scan of the comedy category on YouTube will reveal that most, if not the majority, of the videos there do not conform to this form of stylistic classification. In fact, many highly popular and viral videos, such as *Laughing baby* and *Sneezing panda*, fall between genre categories and are often difficult to place within existing categorization schemes.

Interviews

We followed-up the surveys with 11 interviews from the survey respondents. Namely we wanted to find their rationale and mental process for classifying and distinguishing between videos that belong to the comedy genre and videos that are funny. The interview questions and process involved having the interviewees explain their responses in the survey by showing them specific videos from their survey. One of the main goals of the interviews is to inform the selection of metadata features to use in the next stage of our project. All the interview participants were contacted via email and interviews were conducted face-to-face whenever possible.

The interviews highlighted the fact that the task of classifying online videos is much harder than the classification of movies. According to Participant 5:

> Films in general tend to fit categories more narrowly... if NetFlix says that something is a screwball comedy, I know what to expect. I think on YouTube the range of possibilities for the content of the videos is much less constrained. Cause it might literally be a segment from a film or it could something shot on a cheap digital camera. (Participant 5)

The variability in content makes categorization more complicated. Especially so with the Comedy genre, where the format of the content aids with the understanding of whether something was meant to be funny or not. For instance, it would be much easier to categorize a video as a comedy if the content were presented as a short film. If that same content were to be presented as in the format of a home movie video-clip, it would not be so easy to conclude that the video was a comedy because the home movie format is more ambiguous with regards to intentionality. The issue of intentionality is paramount for determining whether a video is to be classified as comedy:

> Comedy videos are harder to classify... did it make me laugh? Was the intention of the video to make me laugh? An excerpt from The Office or standup would be "Comedy". It gets hazier when the intention of the clip isn't to make you laugh—but the content is funny. (Participant 2)

Participant 2's comment highlights the problem of categorizing comedy videos found in the surveys; it is harder to classify a video as comedy than it is to categorize something as funny, especially when the intention of the video's producer is hard to discern. This issue relates to why videos like *Laughing baby* and *Sneezing panda* are hard to categorize as comedies. Without a priori knowledge of the video's uploaded intentionality, what are some of the other cues that indicate a video is a comedy? According to two interview participants:

> If I ever hear the laughter track, it doesn't even have to be funny, it's intended to be Comedy. The style of it... even if its a music video. (Participant 3)

> Anything comedy is always impressed upon you with laughter in the background or some funny accompanying music... those contextual cues. (Participant 4)

Both participants 3 and 4 corroborate our earlier survey result that the genre of comedy was dependent on a few universally accepted features, such as a laugh track, even if the content wasn't even funny. A reason for this is because stylistic features such as audience laughter relate back to the earlier notion of intentionality—background laughter signals to the viewer that the content is *meant to be funny* and should be categorized as Comedy. These are social indicators of *intended* comedy.

Apart from some of these contextual cues, Comedy, as a genre, shares little else in common. Our interview subjects had particular difficulty in categorizing videos that were labelled as *comedy* and often disagreed with the classification selected by the original uploader for these videos. In fact, some of the interview subjects have found that genre categories are sometimes used as prescriptions for how to appropriately interact with the content being presented:

> They (the original uploaders of a video on YouTube) are uploading things and categorizing it as "Comedy" because they are proposing that there's something funny in it. Even though the content itself may not be "Comedy". And so, if you don't watch to the end, you won't pick up the intended funny part. (Participant 1)

This echos our study's premise—if people have little agreement in classifying comedy videos, what else, besides intention and contextual cues, can we use to help identify and categorize these videos? In the view of some of our interview subjects, one approach towards identifying whether a shared video is a comedy or not, is by studying the social actions and interactions surrounding the video:

> There's a context that you need to have for something to be identified as comedy... when I see a video that I have no context for I don't know whether to identify it as funny. But if other people are interacting with it in a way that makes me believe that it's funny. Same thing for the wedding dance... my interaction with it is, people are saying that this is funny. (Participant 5, referring to the virally popular video *JK Wedding dance*[10] video.)

The above quote echoes the illustration from *The Simpsons* cited at the start of this paper. For Participant 5, and for Homer, the interactional context surrounding a video/movie,

[10] http://www.youtube.com/watch?v=4-94JhLEiNO (Accessed9/2010

how others are perceiving the content and how they are interacting with each other around the content, helps the both them to categorize the content and interact with it in a contextually appropriate manner. Genres are not just organizational tools, but also underpin social behaviors that surround the content of the shared videos. Towards our automated classification method, we will need to look for metadata that similarly highlights the behaviors and activities of the users surrounding shared videos to utilize as features for the classifier. In our case, the metadata from the Zync tool, detailed in the next section, consists of logs of video sharing sessions where users can chat, and at the same time, control the playback of a video. The interaction between the pair of users and their activity controlling the video constitutes as the social and interactional context that can be used to indicate the nature and characteristics of the video content.

It is important to note that not all social actions are indicative of a video's genre. Social media websites afford a variety of ways to interact, communicate and participate around the sharing of media content. Indiscriminate use of metadata surrounding socially shared videos for automated classification may not yield meaningful results. So we need to identify metadata that is representative of a person's relationship with the content and with others. As Participant 6 noted, utilizing metadata from individuals who are strongly related to each other, or who resemble each other, in some way will yield meaningful cues about the content of a video.

> When consuming a video, I trust other consumers more than I trust the producer. So I would be interested in what other people who think like me, say about this video... Probably out of all the users on YouTube, people who look like certain niches have affinities to certain videos. (Participant 6)

This speaks towards how a video could be treated by various people, perhaps in different ways by different niches. Therefore, one important use of social metadata is that it can provide contextually and socially appropriate information to determine how the perception of a video's content by a particular group of individuals.

Another indicator of the viewer's relationship to a video can be found in the commentary and surrounding discussion.

> Sending a photo of your dog and expecting them to comment on it is one thing. Sending a 15min video of your dog and expecting them to comment on it... they are two different things... the latter makes them commit to something much longer. (Participant 3)

As suggested by the interviewee above, commentary and discussion surrounding a video requires much greater effort and commitment from the users. Because of this, metadata derived from these contextual comments and discussions can provide a more robust signal than 5-star rating data that is typically used in contemporary ML approaches. Comments and conversational activity surrounding a video not only requires a greater commitment from the user, but is also more indicative of their opinion and relationship to the video content and other people.

Given the comments provided by the interviewees, our automated method of video classification will similarly utilize social metadata that is reflective of the social and interactional activity surrounding shared videos. In particular, we pay close attention to the use of social metadata that captures the conversational and interactional activity between the users and the shared video.

Automated Classification

Having elaborated the issues our participants raised, we now turn to automated classification of genre. From the surveys and interviews findings, and congruent with current ML research, content alone is insufficient for genre classification. Traditionally, asynchronous annotation data, such as 5-star ratings, produce the meaningful signals for classification, but do not fully account for the social construction of genre in practice. Activity data such how many times the video was watched in a single viewing session, the amount of conversational exchange (for example in chat) and use of video controls (such as fast forward, pause, etc) signal how the video functions within the social interaction between people.

Features for Training

For training a classifier, we aggregate all the events in each session into a feature vector. In our dataset of 1,580 video sessions, 80 sessions contained more than one video. These sessions are split into separate sessions. For example, if Bob and Mary have a 12 minute session where they shared a Music video for 8 minutes then a News video for 4 minutes, we create two unique sessions one 8 minute and one 4 minute. This ensures every session has one video to classify. This brings 1,660 sessions in total after multi-video sessions have been subdivided.

Each session yielded a large amount of data from feature use. For the purposes of this research, our focus was on social actions, specifically social interaction and shared control features. Data, such as load counts, emoticons, the video's event timestamps, and the event time were not considered. Social interaction features included for the classification were session duration, the number of play commands, the number of pause commands, the number of scrubs (fast forwards or rewinds), and the number of chat lines typed as a character and word count. Our goal is to predict categories accurately from social behavior *using as little data possible*. The final feature vector consists of two parts: the activity counts from the session's inviter and the activity counts of the receiver. Each video's feature vector is an aggregated count of activities from each person in the dyadic social exchange. The original YouTube tube video category, provided by the uploader, is used as the predictive category class variable for the independent feature vector. In effect, we are training the classifier to match non-content, conversation activity patterns to the source video's uploaded category.

Classification Accuracy and Nominal Factorization

As 1,660 feature vectors is a relatively small sample, we begin by using a generous training set, one that is 80% of the size of our feature set, a Naive Bayes classifier predicts a

	Prediction Accuracy	
Training Set Size	**Raw Data**	**Factored**
20%	26.33%	52.22%
40%	53.48%	67.59%
60%	54.30%	75.32%
80%	54.30%	82.34%

Table 3. Naive Bayes predictions from Zync data on Video Categories across different training sample sizes.

video's genre poorly at roughly 53% accuracy. For comparison, people in our pilot study predicted categories at 60.9%. In Yew and Shamma's YouTube study, they reported significant improvements from nominal factoring of features which are resultant of "explicit social action," in their case, the 5-star ratings [26]. In their study, nominal factoring of the ratings bucketed numerical, interval data into discrete unordered bins (all the 4.0 videos in one set, the 4.1s in another, and the 4.3 into another and so on). This conversion from an interval to factors improved the classifier's training and overall performance.

The Zync data does not represent explicit social annotation; it is implicit behavior observed from using a tool. Yew and Shamma's findings demonstrated little to no performance gain from the nominal factoring of implicit usage data from YouTube. However, Zync's data comes from two people sharing and conversing around the media, thus socially constructing its genre. As we hypothesized these data to be *purposeful* and *definitional* with regards to genre construction, we believe it to be equally predictive and explicit as Yew and Shamma defined. After nominal factorization, the Naive Bayes classifier predicted category genre with an accuracy of 82.34% (using a 80% training corpus), a performance increase of 30%. A 60% training set predicted with an accuracy of 75.32%. A full list of prediction accuracies by training set size is found on in Table 3. Category prediction based on implicit conversational data increases accuracy by 6.8% when compared to Yew and Shamma's [26] YouTube dataset findings with an 80% training set. Furthermore, our model trained on a 60% sample (996 videos) predicts with the same accuracy as Yew and Shamma's model trained on an 80% corpus (1,392 videos). See Table 4.

DISCUSSION

In our results and findings we have addressed two research questions: RQ1 to better understand what individual and social processes people use to categorize online videos as Comedy, and RQ2, to develop an improved method for automatically classifying online videos, taking into account social and contextual features.

Why are people so bad at classifying Comedy?

Triangulating between the results from the three phases of our study, we find that people find it hard to classify videos within the category 'Comedy'. It is clear that what is or is not considered comedic is subjective, contextual and somewhat culturally specific. However, we also found that we were able to discern stylistic and contextual cues that signal

Accuracy	Features and Factorization
	Random Chance Predictions
23.0%	Sampled from YouTube Crawl
37.2%	Sampled from Zync Dataset
	Human Predictions
60.9%	Average from pilot survey
	YouTube Features/Naive Bayes predictions
14.6%	All YouTube features and categories
32.4%	All YouTube features/Top 5 Categories
75.5%	**Factoring "Ratings" feature/ Top 5 categories**
	Zync Features/Naive Bayes predictions
52.9%	All Zync Features and Categories
53.9%	All Zync Features/Top 5 Categories
82.3%	**Factoring Zync features/ Top 5 categories**

Table 4. Using nominally factored conversational data for classification shows a 6.8% increase in accuracy over traditional, asynchronous social media metadata and a 21.4% increase over human judgement. The chance prediction was based on random guess based on the corpus distribution of categories. Bayes predictions based on 80% training sample size. YouTube predictions reported are from Yew and Shamma [26].

something as potentially Comedy. For example, cues like background laughter functioned as signaling mechanisms, indicating that a video is a Comedy—even if for the viewer, the content was not deemed to be that funny. Given our finding that people can articulate what factors make something a Comedy (even if they personally did not find the content funny), we posed the question: why did our respondents fare so badly in classifying comedy videos in our surveys?

One explanation is that many of the videos shared on sites like YouTube do not, in fact, conform to the more culturally accepted conventions and characteristics of the Comedy genre. An informal review of videos classified as Comedy on YouTube revealed why there was far more agreement in our survey results about whether a video was funny or not than whether the video fitted in the category Comedy. People were much more likely to agree that something was funny, even if the original creator had not intended it to be funny. For example, in the course of the study, two specific videos, *Laughing baby* and *Sneezing panda*, emerged from our data as examples of videos where there was some ambiguity between the intentions of the video producer and the user who had uploaded the video. These are videos that people find funny but that were not intentionally created to be comedic; people therefore did not think they necessarily belong in the category Comedy. To be categorized as Comedy requires as assumption of comedic intention on the part of the creator of the video itself.

Use of classifications... in the wild

Unlike genre categorizations for other media channels (e.g., TV, radio), socially shared online videos are more diverse and varied in their form and content. The videos in our sample range from edited excerpts from longer films, to music videos, personal home movies, and video blogs. This variance in styles and formats makes it much harder for individuals to categorize videos from sharing sites like YouTube using definitive classifications like Comedy.

So why do individual uploaders classify their videos as Comedy? One explanation is the use of genres as a signaling mechanism for hoped-for audience orientation to the content. By categorizing a video clip as comedy, uploaders signal to potential audiences the appropriate or desired way to experience and interact around the content. A video clip that does not appear to be a comedy, but that has funny elements within it for the audience to enjoy, may be classified as Comedy, signaling that it is intended to be taken as such. The uploader of the video is using the genre classification to shape the social experience, shaping how the media content is perceived and classified. This is something that occurs during conversations or through gestural or postural cues when we watch things together, in a co-present setting.

Evolving Categories

Genres are more than just static organizational retrieval tools. Our results counter the view of genres that suggests "things come in well-defined kinds, that the kinds are characterized by shared properties, and that there is one right taxonomy of the kinds." [11] Rather, our results are consistent with Bowker and Star's [2] view that no classification scheme or genre category is perfect and users of classification systems often ignore the boundaries between categories or even routinely mix them up.

Our findings support the view that genres like Comedy are constantly evolving, shaped by the behavior of others and by our interactions with others around and through media content. These social interactions in turn affect our social behaviors and activities with and around that content. Viral videos like *Sneezing panda* were not intentionally created to be comedic. But having been constituted as funny, framed and shared with labels like the Comedy classification to indicate they should be read as such, drive them to be seen as humorous, and shape their trajectory through social networks as they spread and humorous memes. Even if the original intention of a video clip is not meant to be comedy, how it is viewed, interacted with, and shared shapes its classification and expands its genre. Our study supports the view that genres are social constructs, contextually defined and evolving out of people's pragmatic interactions and activities. Therefore, for automated classification, implicit interaction which represents how media can transform context, should be utilized.

On Machine Classification

Addressing RQ2, we have found that a predictive model of genre identification can be built by using only implicit social traces that result from synchronous sharing, without using video content, metadata, or annotations. This means that social behavioral traces may be stronger and thus more predictive signals on which to train predictive models. This is a departure from the current ML approach, where explicit annotations are considered to be the most powerful features on which to train classification systems. Our results indicate that conversational activity features prove to be very effective, demonstrating more generally the potential for predictive classification of uncategorized content based on social interactional features; our classifier performed well with a small training set after nominal factorization of the implicit features. Table 5 shows a list of the social multimedia features which generate social and interactional traces for modeling.

Async		Sync	
Implicit	*Explicit*	*Implicit*	*Explicit*
View Counts	5-Star Rating	Play/Pause	Chat
Upload Count	Comments	Scrubbing	Emoticons
Video Duration	Tags	Session Duration	VoIP

Table 5. Types of data for social multimedia classification. Our classifier trained on implicit synchronous features outperformed those trained on asynchronous explicit features. Current ML techniques hold asynchronous explicit actions to be the more dominate features.

Our approach also suggests diversity in classification. Not everything that is Comedy should be primarily ranked as Comedy for everyone. When building recommendation systems and new interaction experiences, there is no one-size-fits-all solution. Sharing media, not only can, but should and indeed will transform how we perceive, understand and ultimately categorize it. Therefore there is a strong role for systems that fluidly emerge categories for classification on the basis of social action and interaction.

CONCLUSION

This work contributes to a developing understanding of the experience of sharing/consuming media content online. In this article, we have shown how genre, specifically Comedy, can be modeled predictably when features are drawn from a qualitative understanding of media classification. We have demonstrated that there is more to genre and classification than just flat or hierarchical organization as embodied in post-hoc tagging by people or machines. Genre in practice is as much about how something is shared and communicated as how it fits into a pre-existing categorical schema, or genre, emerges from how we share and communicate around media. Our classifier out performs previous solutions underscoring the importance of social action and interaction in categorization, but also suggests we have a uncovered a viable method for classifying online video for more effective organization and retrieval. With this approach, we can help people find things which others have found to be funny rather that things that have been prescriptively tagged as such.

ACKNOWLEDGEMENTS

We thank Judd Antin, Bryan Pardo, Lyndon Kennedy and Matt Cooper for their technical advice and comments.

REFERENCES

1. Bawarshi, A. The Ecology of Genre. *Ecocomposition: theoretical and pedagogical approaches* (2001), 69–80.
2. Bowker, G. C., and Star, S. L. *Sorting Things Out: Classification and Its Consequences*. Inside technology. The MIT Press, October 1999.

3. Cesar, P., Geerts, D., and Chorianopoulos, K. *Social Interactive Television: Immersive Shared Experiences and Perspectives*. Information Science Reference, 2009.

4. Chen, Z., Cao, J., Song, Y., Guo, J., Zhang, Y., and Li, J. Context-oriented web video tag recommendation. In *WWW '10: Proceedings of the 19th international conference on World wide web*, ACM (New York, NY, USA, 2010), 1079–1080.

5. Cooper, M. M. The ecology of writing. *College English 48*, 4 (1986), 364–375.

6. Crane, R., and Sornette, D. Viral, quality, and junk videos on youtube: Separating content from noise in an information-rich environment. In *Proc. of AAAI symposium on Social Information Processing, Menlo Park, CA* (2008).

7. Erzberger, C., and Kelle, U. Making inferences in mixed methods: The rules of integration. *Handbook of mixed methods in social and behavioral research* (2003), 457–488.

8. Hölbling, G., Thalhammer, A., and Kosch, H. Content-based tag generation to enable a tag-based collaborative tv-recommendation system. In *EuroITV '10: Proceedings of the 8th international interactive conference on Interactive TV & Video*, ACM (New York, NY, USA, 2010), 273–282.

9. Kittur, A., Chi, E. H., and Suh, B. Crowdsourcing user studies with mechanical turk. In *CHI '08: Proceeding of the twenty-sixth annual SIGCHI conference on Human factors in computing systems*, ACM (New York, NY, USA, 2008), 453–456.

10. Krippendorff, K. *Content analysis: An introduction to its methodology*. Sage Publications, Inc, 2004.

11. Lakoff, G. *Women, Fire, and Dangerous Things*. University Of Chicago Press, April 1990.

12. Liu, Y., Shamma, D. A., Shafton, P., and Yang, J. Zync: the design of sychnronized video sharing. In *DUX 2007: Proceeding of the 3rd conference on Designing for User Experience* (Chicago, IL, USA, November 2007).

13. Mahajan, D., and Slaney, M. Image classification using the web graph. In *Proceedings of the International Conference on Multi-Media*, ACM (2010).

14. Miller, C. Genre as social action. *Quarterly journal of speech 70*, 2 (1984), 151–167.

15. Naaman, M., and Nair, R. Zonetag's collaborative tag suggestions: What is this person doing in my phone? *IEEE MultiMedia 15*, 3 (2008), 34–40.

16. Roach, M., and Mason, J. Recent trends in video analysis: A taxonomy of video classification problems. In *In Proceedings of the International Conference on Internet and Multimedia Systems and Applications, IASTED* (2002), 348–354.

17. Salton, G., Wong, A., and Yang, C. S. A vector space model for automatic indexing. *Communcations of the ACM 18* (1975), 613–620.

18. Scully, M. Marge be not proud. In *The Simpsons*, 3F07. FOX, December 1995.

19. Sen, S., Lam, S. K., Rashid, A. M., Cosley, D., Frankowski, D., Osterhouse, J., Harper, F. M., and Riedl, J. tagging, communities, vocabulary, evolution. In *CSCW '06: Proceedings of the 2006 20th anniversary conference on Computer supported cooperative work*, ACM (New York, NY, USA, 2006), 181–190.

20. Shamma, D. A., and Liu, Y. *Social Interactive Television: Immersive Shared Experiences and Perspectives*. Information Science Publishing, Hershey, PA, USA, 2009, ch. Zync with Me: Synchronized Sharing of Video through Instant Messaging, 273–288.

21. Slaney, M., and White, W. Similarity based on rating data. In *Proc. of Int. Symposium on Music Information Retrieval*, Citeseer (2007).

22. Weinberger, K. Q., Slaney, M., and Van Zwol, R. Resolving tag ambiguity. In *MM '08: Proceeding of the 16th ACM international conference on Multimedia*, ACM (New York, NY, USA, 2008), 111–120.

23. Weisz, J. D., Kiesler, S., Zhang, H., Ren, Y., Kraut, R. E., and Konstan, J. A. Watching together: integrating text chat with video. In *CHI '07: Proceedings of the SIGCHI conference on Human factors in computing systems*, ACM Press (New York, NY, USA, 2007), 877–886.

24. Wesler, H. T., Smith, M., Fisher, D., and Gleave, E. Distilling digital traces: Computational social science approaches to studying the internet. In *The Sage handbook of online research methods*, N. Fielding, R. M. Lee, and G. Blank, Eds. Sage, London, 2008, 116 – 140.

25. Whitman, B., and Ellis, D. Automatic record reviews. In *ISMIR* (2004).

26. Yew, J., and Shamma, D. A. Know your data: Understanding implicit usage versus explicit action in video content classification. In *IS&T/SPIE Electronic Imaging* (January 2011).

27. Zhang, N., Zhang, Y., and Tang, J. A tag recommendation system for folksonomy. In *SWSM '09: Proceeding of the 2nd ACM workshop on Social web search and mining*, ACM (New York, NY, USA, 2009), 9–16.

Real-Time Nonverbal Opinion Sharing through Mobile Phones during Sports Events

Alireza Sahami Shirazi[†✦], Michael Rohs[*°], Robert Schleicher[°], Sven Kratz[*°], Alexander Müller[†], Albrecht Schmidt[†✦]

[✦]University of Stuttgart VIS Stuttgart, Germany

[†]University of Duisburg-Essen, Paluno Essen, Germany

[°]Deutsche Telekom Laboratories, TU Berlin Berlin, Germany

[*]LMU Munich Munich, Germany

{alireza.sahami, albrecht.schmidt, alexander.mueller}@uni-due.de

{robert.schleicher, sven.kratz}@tu-berlin.de

michael.rohs@lmu.de

ABSTRACT
Even with the rise of the World Wide Web, TV has remained the most pervasive entertainment medium and is nowadays often used together with other media, which allow for active participation. The idea of connecting non-collocated TV viewers via telecommunication technologies, referred to as Social TV, has recently received considerable attention. Such systems typically include set-top boxes for supporting collaboration. In this research we investigate if real-time opinion sharing about TV shows through a non-verbal (non-textual) iconic UI on mobile phones is reasonable. For this purpose we developed a mobile app, made it available to a large number of users through the Android Market, and conducted an uncontrolled user study in the wild during the soccer world cup 2010. The results of the study indicate that TV viewers who used the app had more fun and felt more connected to other viewers. We also show that by monitoring this channel it is possible to collect sentiments relevant to the broadcasted content in real-time. The collected data exemplify that the aggregated sentiments correspond to important moments, and hence can be used to generate a summary of the event.

Author Keywords
Social TV, mobile phone, sentiment support, sports

ACM Classification Keywords
H5.2 [Information Interfaces and Presentation]: User Interfaces.

General Terms
Human Factors

INTRODUCTION
This paper reports an analysis of the opinion-sharing behavior of the TV viewers during soccer matches. The television set is an omnipresent device and for many people still the most popular entertainment resource. Even the strong increase in Internet usage has not changed the popularity of TV. Nowadays, the majority of viewers usually watch TV alone [3]. However, watching TV does not necessarily have to be a solitary experience. It can foster multiple forms of sociability, as shown, e.g., in [12]. In recent years, the idea of connecting non-collocated TV viewers via telecommunication technologies has received considerable attention (cf. [2,10]), mainly referred to as Social TV. Typical social TV systems include presence of viewers, text, voice, and/or video chat. Basically, these systems enable viewers to actively share information about TV content in real-time.

With the ubiquity of interactive mobile devices, enhanced with continuous wireless connectivity and powerful user interfaces, connecting TV viewers via their phones is technically easy to accomplish. Mobile phones are almost always with their users and can serve as standalone platforms for collecting the user's emotional responses to TV-related experiences. The main research challenge lies in establishing a shared TV watching experience that is meaningful and engaging to users while at the same time does not distract viewers from the actual content.

In this research we investigate if mobile phones can be used as a communication channel for exchanging non-verbal information that represents emotional reactions to events shown live on TV. So, we developed a mobile application, called "World Cupinion", and conducted a large-scale field study by distributing the app for free via the Android Market and the Web. As the content domain we chose a sports event, namely the soccer world cup 2010 in South Africa. This particular event was chosen since it receives extremely high public attention all over the world and many viewers are highly emotionally involved. The matches are broadcasted live and in sync, allowing for real-time opinion sharing. For the whole period of the tournament (4 weeks) users could download and use the app during each match. After the tournament, we conducted a survey among the users and asked them about their motivations for using the app.

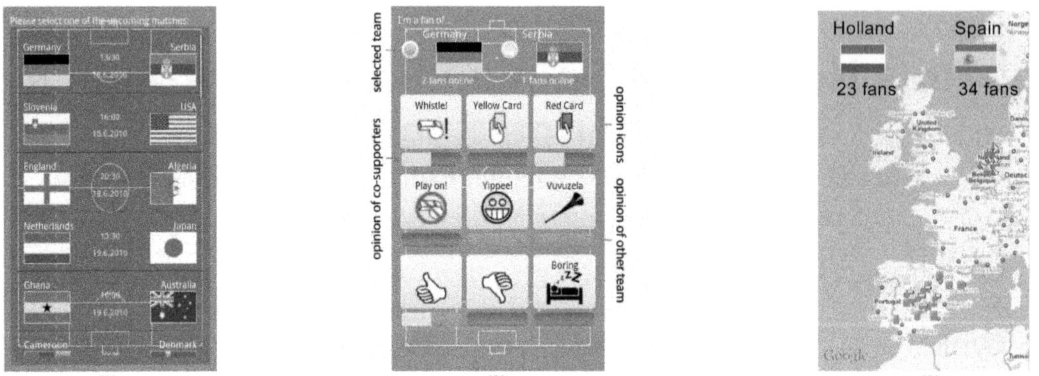

(1) (2) (3)

Figure 1: *World Cupinion* screens: (1) Initial Screen "Match List" (2) Second Screen "Arena" (3) Map View.

Our hypothesis is that if TV viewers are able to share their opinions about TV content in real-time through this additional channel without being distracted, then they should experience higher enjoyment and feeling of connectedness with other viewers. Through deploying the app widely we aim at understanding more about this collaborative experience. Another motivation is to investigate in how far important events are reflected by user inputs and can be annotated by log analysis. The work described here is, to the best of our knowledge, the first attempt at using non-textual iconic communication on mobile phones for sharing opinions in real-time and connecting TV viewers (virtually) while watching sport events.

RELATED WORK

The idea of allowing additional communications in parallel with watching TV has been investigated in different setups. "AmigoTV" was an early social TV system that combined broadcast TV with voice chat communication and provided a buddy list with online status, and emoticons [2]. The "Social TV" system (STV) allowed users to engage in spontaneous communication with their buddies through text or voice chat while watching TV [8]. It also included an additional display to convey comments of the current TV-watching users. A comprehensive overview of social TV systems is available in [7]. Further, various user studies were conducted which compared the communication modalities [1, 6, 9, 14]. Geerts *et al.* [6] used the "AmigoTV" system and compared the voice communication to other modalities in a within-subjects lab setting. They reported that most users thought that voice chat was more natural and easier to use than text chat. Huang *et al.* [9] conducted a similar study, but in the field, using the STV system and reported that participants preferred text chat to voice chat, often communicated about topics unrelated to the TV content. Weisz *et al.* [14] investigated the effect on the social relationships of friends and strangers in text chatting while watching online videos. In [5] a set of comprehensive sociability heuristics for social TV systems is reported.

Media annotation and sharing while watching TV has been studied, too. Miyamori *et al.* [11] proposed a method for generating views of TV programs based on viewer's opinions collected from live chats on the Web. In [4] the sentiments of tweet annotations for a presidential debate were analyzed to understand their relationship to discussed topics and performance of the opponents in the event.

All the aforementioned social TV systems require the installation of set-top boxes for supporting collaboration that are only available in certain locations. Hence, users are restricted to particular environments. We tried to overcome the limitation by offering a free mobile phone application that can be used in any context in which watching the event is possible, even in bars, the stadium, or at public places. tvChatter[1] is a web and mobile app that mines Twitter for commentaries on TV shows and presents them in a (primarily one-way) text-based tweet stream. Our work, in contrast, focus on iconic (non-textual) real-time communication.

WORLD CUPINION DESIGN

The "World Cupinion" app is mainly designed for soccer fans (viewers) to share their opinions while watching a match in real-time. The design of the system takes various aspects into consideration: since the users' focus of attention is mainly on the match, simplicity of the user interface is crucial. Providing feedback and visualizing aggregated opinions of the competing teams' fans is also essential. Thus, the app should convey how the collected opinions evolve even if the user is a "lurker" and not actively interacting with the system. Furthermore, the system should be able to handle a large number of worldwide users simultaneously. Hence, supporting multiple languages is important – we offered the app in English, German, French, and Spanish. To reach the widest possible audience, we implemented "World Cupinion" as an Android app and a Web interface. The former provides better responsiveness and uses more features of the device, while the latter is available for every phone with a Web browser.

The app consists of three screens (Figure 1). The initial screen shows the list of upcoming matches with their time details in the phone's local time zone (Figure 1.1). The

[1] http://www.tvchatter.tv (accessed January 2011)

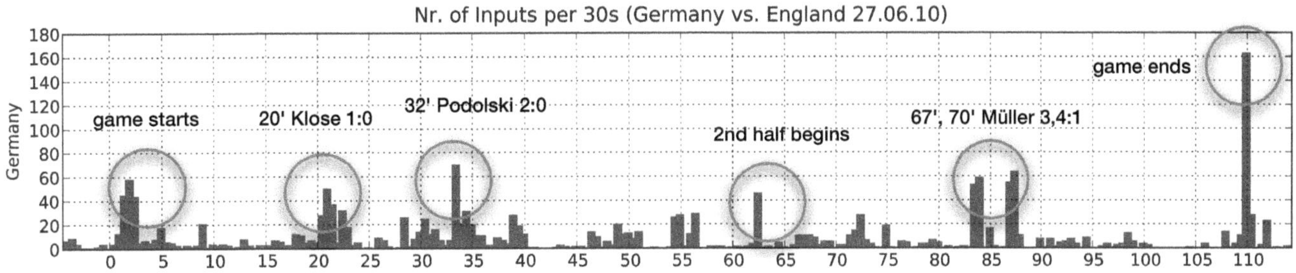

Figure 2: The input histogram for *World Cupinion* users that were fans of Germany in the match Germany vs. England.

second screen (Figure 1.2) is the "arena" for a selected game where users are able to share opinions. To enter this screen the user has to select a match from the initial screen and choose a team before sharing opinions. The users can then input their opinions through 3x3 icon buttons. We provide these icons to lower the cost of interaction and decrease the space between "Readers" and "Leaders" [13]. We generally divided the icon design into icon types either representing factual events (e.g., whether the referee should give a yellow/red card or let the game goes on) or opinions/expressive assessments (e.g., thumb up/down). Moreover, the Vuvuzela button is added to introduce an additional modality – a horn sound is played when the button is pressed and the sound is amplified when more than 75% of a fan group had input within the last 15 seconds. The second screen also conveys the aggregated opinions of the opponent teams. Below each button there is a horizontal bar that indicates the overall statistics with regard to that input category for the competing teams. The length of the bar indicates the momentary percentage of users giving this type of feedback. The feedback for the own team is shown in green and for the other team in blue. The bars are frequently updated based on the last 30s of inputs. The third screen shows the geographical distribution of opinions for both teams overlaid on the Google Maps (Figure 1.3). The maximum zoom level is restricted for privacy reasons.

SYSTEM ARCHITECTURE

The system is implemented as a client-server architecture. The mobile client sends three request types: *input requests* to send users' opinions to the server, *update requests* to poll the current state of aggregated feedback, and *map requests* to show the locations at which sentiments are shared. The server logs all inputs to an SQLite database and maintains statistics of the opinions received in the last 30s. Also, an important issue regarding the mobile client is energy consumption. There is a tradeoff between the interface update rate and energy consumption. In pilot tests we realized that one update per 3s is sufficient. A significant amount of energy is consumed by the display, which continuously shows the feedback stated based on aggregated community inputs, even when the user does not interact with the app.

EXPERIMENT

To evaluate the "World Cupinion" app on a larger scale, we distributed the app and recruited users via the Android Market. The conducted study was an uncontrolled long-term (4 weeks) study in the wild. It was crucial to conduct the study this way to be able to observe natural user behavior (which is problematic in tightly controlled experiments). The app was released a week before the tournament started and was downloadable for free until the last day of the event. The web-based version was also available during that time. After the last match in the tournament an update containing a questionnaire about the app was released.

Usage Statistics

Based on the Android Market portal, at the end of the tournament the app had been downloaded 1645 times. Based on our database, 71% of inputs were from the Android client and 29% from the Web-based client. In total 21205 inputs from 925 unique users (71% Android users) were collected during the 64 matches of the tournament (an average of 331 inputs/match). There was a significant difference in the number of actively followed (session length $\geq$ 15 minutes) matches between the mobile and web-based client. Mobile users followed an average of 2.31 matches whereas web-based users followed 1.03 matches. An ANOVA showed the difference to be significant ($F(1,257)=30.890$, $p<0.001$). The top four inputs were the vuvuzela (22.8%), foul (19.3%), thumb up (14.9%), and thumb down (10%). The average number of fans per match sharing opinions was 18 and per team 10. The match with the highest number of fans was Germany vs. England (on June 27th 2010).

Sentiment Relevancy

To examine whether the aggregated sentiments were relevant to actual events in a match, we analyzed the sentiments of more than 5 matches in detail. The analysis showed that there is a relation between the collected sentiments and events in the chosen ground truth, i.e., Y! Sports ticker[2]. Figure 2 depicts one of the input histograms. It is clearly visible that the inputs correspond to important moments of a match such as scored goals and goal kicks. Thus, generating a summary of important moments of a match based on the collected sentiments appears feasible.

Questionnaire Results

Demographics & World Cupinion Usage

In total 46 users (mean age = 20.1 years, STD = 9.2) replied to the questionnaire, of whom 37% followed the world cup

[2] http://g.sports.yahoo.com/soccer/world-cup (accessed January 2011)

matches frequently and 50% watched occasionally. 55% of the participants considered themselves as knowledgeable fans and 30% as experts (know players' details). 73% of them stated that they normally watched the matches at home and 65% watched with the family or buddies. Based on the replies, 18% of participants stated that they used the app for most matches, 40% used it regularly, and 42% occasionally or just once. Also, those who considered themselves as knowledgeable or expert fans used the app more frequently. 60% of those who watched the matches in a group (with family, buddies, or crowd) still used the app regularly or for most matches. Participants also rated the app using a 5-point Likert scale. The average rating was 3.6 (MED=4, STD=1.1). Those who used the app more regularly rated the app higher (Spearman's $\rho = .422$, $p \leq 0.004$).

Connectedness vs. Fun

In the questionnaire users are asked to rate on a 5-point Likert scale (1=completely disagree, 5=completely agree) in how far the app changed their fun level and feeling of connectedness to other fans. 11% mentioned that the fun level did not change at all. 30% believed that it increased sometimes and 59% reported to have more fun most of the time or always. None of the responses indicated that the app reduced the fun of watching TV. Also, 7 out of 46 participants (15%) did not feel connected to other fans at all. 32% felt strong connection and 53% average or little connection. Those who had more fun felt more connected to the other fans (Spearman's $\rho = .636$, $p < 0.00$).

DISCUSSION & CONCLUSION

The main goal of this research was to investigate if real-time opinion sharing about TV programs through a non-verbal (non-textual) iconic UI on mobile phones is reasonable. The motivation for iconic interactions was to enable instant reactions to the live events and minimize user distraction when operating the mobile phone. Since text input requires more time and cognitive resources, we deliberately chose to explore iconic communication. To achieve this, we conducted an uncontrolled user study in the wild. As our results reveal, the iconic approach is reasonable and aggregated sentiments correspond to the events that were also highlighted by a commercial sports service. However, for individuals we do not have any ground truth regarding the relevance of certain moments during the game and official reports do not always reflect the viewers' sentiments. Thus, there is no obvious reference data available which we could compare our data against.

Furthermore, the TV viewers' sense of connectedness and enjoyment increased by sharing opinions. Remarkably, even those users who watched the matches in groups still used the app to virtually connect to non-collocated fans. Anecdotal evidence showed that the implicit action of an ambient vuvuzela sound – amplified sound when the majority of fans had pressed the Vuvuzela button – resulted in an "aha" reaction in viewers and promoted the conscious experience of connectedness between viewers. It should be mentioned that the post-experiment questionnaire might have been biased due to the characteristics of our field study. In such studies it is inevitable that users who do not like the app delete it or do not answer the questionnaire. However, some of the responses were negative which shows that these users were not biased in favor of the approach. The type of application proposed and evaluated here can be useful for other types of events, e.g., election debates, quiz shows, contests, etc. We believe that providing real-time feedback directly on the TV while watching events encourages users to contribute even more.

ACKNOWLEDGMENT

This work was partially supported by the Deutsche Forschungsgemeinschaft (DFG) in the Embedded Interaction project.

REFERENCES

1. Baillie, L., Frohlich, P., & Schatz, R. Exploring Social TV. *Proc. ITI'07*, 215-220.
2. Coppens, T., Trappeniers, L., & Godon, M. AmigoTV: towards a social TV experience. *Proc. EuroITV'04.*
3. Crispell, D. TV soloists-Statistics on number of television sets owned in households from SRI Consulting Media Futures Program, *American Demographics.*
4. Diakopoulos, N.A. & Shamma, D.A. Characterizing debate performance via aggregated twitter sentiment. *Proc. CHI'10*, 119.
5. Geerts, D. & De Grooff, D. Supporting the social uses of television: sociability heuristics for social TV. *Proc. CHI'09*, 595–604.
6. Geerts, D. Comparing voice chat and text chat in a communication tool for interactive television. *Proc. NordiCHI'06*, 464.
7. Harboe, G., Massey, N. *et al.* The uses of social television. *Computers in Entertainment* 6, 1 2008, 1–15.
8. Harboe, G., Metcalf, C.J. *et al.* Ambient social tv: drawing people into a shared experience. *Proc. CHI'08*,1–10.
9. Huang, E.M., Harboe, G., Tullio, J., *et al.* Of social television comes home: a field study of communication choices and practices in tv-based text and voice chat. *Proc. CHI'09*, 585-594.
10. Luyten, K., Thys, K., Huypens, S., & Coninx, K. Telebuddies: social stitching with interactive television. *Proc. CHI'06 extended abstracts*, 1054.
11. Miyamori, H., Nakamura, S., *et al.* Generation of views of TV content using TV viewers' perspectives expressed in live chats on the web. *Proc. MM'05*, 853-861.
12. Oehlberg, L., Ducheneaut, N. Thornton, J. D., Moore, R. J., Nickell, E. Social TV: Designing for distributed, sociable television viewing. *Proc. EuroITV'06*, 25–26.
13. Preece, J. & Shneiderman, B. The Reader-to-Leader Framework: Motivating technology-mediated social participation. *AIS THCI*, 1 2009, 13–32.
14. Weisz, J.D., Kiesler, S., *et al.* Watching together: integrating text chat with video. *Proc. CHI'07*, 877-886.

Are We in Sync? Synchronization Requirements for Watching Online Video Together

David Geerts*, Ishan Vaishnavi†, Rufael Mekuria‡, Oskar van Deventer‡, Pablo Cesar†
*CUO, IBBT / K.U.Leuven, †CWI, ‡TNO
david.geerts@soc.kuleuven.be, oskar.vandeventer@tno.nl, P.S.Cesar@cwi.nl

ABSTRACT
Synchronization between locations is an important factor for enabling remote shared experiences. Still, experimental data on what is the acceptable synchronization level is scarce. This paper discusses the synchronization requirements for watching online videos together – a popular set of services that recreate the shared experience of watching TV together by offering tools to communicate while watching. It studies the noticeability and annoyance of synchronization differences of the video being watched, as well as the impact on users' feelings of togetherness, both for voice chat and text chat. Results of an experiment with 36 participants show that when using voice chat, users notice synchronization differences sooner, are more annoyed and feel more together than when using text chat. However, users with high text chat activity notice synchronization differences similar to participants using voice chat.

Author Keywords
Online video, Synchronization, Social TV, Entertainment

ACM Classification Keywords
H.4.3 Communications Applications, H.5.1 Multimedia Information Systems

General Terms
Experimentation, Measurement

INTRODUCTION
Traditionally, watching television is for a large part a social activity as viewers in the same location often discuss the contents of the programs they are jointly watching [5]. Recently, online video sites like ClipSync and Watchitoo try to recreate this shared experience over the Internet by adding text chat features or an audio channel alongside the videos on offer. This allows users to watch a synchronized version of a video while communicating with each other. These examples are part of a larger trend of integrating social media and communication features with video content, not only on the Internet, but also on traditional television sets [2] and even mobile phones [7].

An important assumption when offering users the option to communicate while watching video together is that the video needs to be synchronized in order to have some common ground to talk about [9]. While viewers do not always talk about the video content while watching, synchronization is important when the content of the program is the topic of the conversation. However, it is theoretically impossible to exactly synchronize video play-out over a network. Therefore a key research question is to know which synchronization level still enables users to have a satisfying shared experience, impacting the design of future social video systems.

This paper examines this issue by discussing the results of an experimental user study focusing on synchronization differences of videos when jointly watched video content while communicating using either voice chat or text chat.

RELATED WORK
Previous research on social video watching has concentrated on studying communication choices based on results of field trials [2] and on identifying appropriate sociability heuristics [1]. Other relevant work had a more specific focus, e.g. on measuring the level of togetherness between friends or strangers [9] or on identifying in detail user activity while watching together [8]. The findings of all this work points to a common direction: a direct communication link between people watching video together is desirable and it increases the level of togetherness.

Apart from the general conclusion, these and other studies reveal specific issues which can influence the shared video watching experience. Some of the parameters that might affect communication while watching videos include how well people know each other, which genre they are watching [1], if they like the video they are watching and what communication modality they use [2]. Additional factors that may play a role as well are if users have seen the video before, what is happening in the program at a specific moment, or even a person's personal characteristics.

On top of these results, a particular question that has not been tackled in the past is what the acceptable difference is in synchronization while watching television together. Currently, 150ms is used as a rule of thumb, a value drawn from telecommunications research. This rule states that the maximum end-to-end, one-way delay when talking remotely should not be over 150ms [4]. Below this value users cannot perceive the delay in communication, and therefore cannot detect differences in synchronization of shared video content. However, no actual user studies have been done to determine the range of acceptable synchronization levels for social video watching. This, we believe, is in part because of the number of parameters that this value may depend on, as described above.

This work intends to answer part of this question by presenting the results of a user study, which isolates some of these parameters and determines the relevant acceptable synchronization levels for those parameters, as well as their impact on users' feeling of togetherness.

METHODOLOGY

Test Setup

A within-subjects lab-based experiment was conducted with 18 couples (partners, friends, or family), with a total of 36 people taking part in the tests, consisting of 12 males and 24 females. The age ranged from 15 to 68 years old, which is wider spread than in most previous research, reflecting the broad target audience of shared video watching.

Each participant from each couple was shown two episodes of a popular local quiz show at different locations. The show was chosen because a quiz is a very sociable genre [1], and it was carefully edited to offer consistent content during the test. During the first episode, participants could voice chat with each other using a headset. The headset was also used for listening to the audio track of the video content, so the participants could not hear the audio track of their partner's show. During the second episode, participants could only text chat with each other. The text chat was implemented with a chat box on the same screen as the video (on a laptop), positioned at the right side of the video (as in services like YoutubeSocial or Watchitoo). Messages were sent line-by-line, as is common in most chat services. The tests were carried out on a private LAN with no external influence presumably limiting the end-to-end voice/text chat delay. We did not observe any noticeable delay in communication between users. The order of text chat and voice chat conditions was randomized over the different test sessions, in order to remove any habituation effects.

Without informing the participants, every seven minutes the synchronization level of the videos was changed. This length was chosen in order to allow participants enough time for having a substantial conversation, as well as being able to present several conditions to participants during a two-hour test session. In each condition (voice chat and text chat), five synchronization levels were presented to users: 0 seconds (perfect sync), 500 milliseconds, 1 second, 2 seconds and 4 seconds. These values were chosen during a test by two of the authors, in which it was discovered that video synchronization difference becomes detectable between 500ms and 2s. Based on these results - and supported by an earlier pilot study with 21 users - 500ms, 1s, and 2s were taken as test condition, and 0s and 4s were chosen to test the more extreme cases. These levels were presented in a randomized order for each set of participants and each condition. As a difference in synchronization between two participants implies that (the video of) one person is ahead ('leading'), and one person is behind ('lagging'), the order of who is leading and who is lagging was also randomly varied.

After each seven minutes (before the next synchronization change), the participants were asked to fill in a web-based questionnaire, asking a series of questions related to togetherness, noticeability and annoyance of the synchronization differences. For measuring togetherness, six questions were asked (e.g. "I felt 'together' with my partner"). These six questions were tested to be consistent (Cronbachs alpha α=0.852, and Gutmann's split half 0.807). From these six questions an aggregate measure was derived (the average) to indicate the togetherness experienced by the participant. To measure the noticeability and annoyance of synchronization differences, the Degradation Category Rating (DCR) MOS score as described in [3], used for degraded speech signals, was adapted with values ranging from 1 (not noticeable) to 5 (noticeable and very annoying).

In total each participant filled in 10 questionnaires (5 during each condition), resulting in 360 unique measurements. After the first questionnaire it would become clear that synchronization was one of the issues which was questioned. Therefore the participants were instructed in advance to only talk about the content of the show, and not discuss the test itself nor explicitly try to figure out the synchronization difference of the videos.

Synchronization Algorithm

In order to control the synchronization during the user tests, a system is required which can play media synchronized in two locations and can be manipulated by the observers. A simplified version of the local lag algorithm [6] was used to achieve the chosen level of synchronization. One of the participants' computers was chosen as a master, which continuously sent out position updates to the other computer (the slave). The slave computer received these updates and jumped to the recommended position. Before the tests were conducted, this mechanism was validated within the test environment and a margin of error was established for the synchronization levels. It was found that the error in synchronization levels was maximum 150ms with an average of 8ms difference and a standard deviation of 59ms. Thus in this experiment a synchronization level of 0 implies an interval of 0 +- 0.15 seconds.

Hypotheses

As the two conditions being tested were talking (voice chat) and chatting (text chat), the analysis will mainly focus on the differences between both modalities. Therefore the following three general hypotheses are formulated:

H1 People feel more together when using voice chat than when using text chat

H2 People will notice synchronization difference sooner when using voice chat than when using text chat

H3 People will be more annoyed by synchronization differences when using voice chat than when using text chat

For each of the hypotheses, the influence of other factors was tested such as chat experience, chat activity, or if the participants liked the program or not. For testing text chat activity, the participants were divided into an active group (more than 400 words per session, which was close to the median), with N=15 participants, and a non-active group (less than 400 words per session), with N=21 participants.

Play-out differences and the use of text/voice chat were taken as explanatory variables. The dependent variables measured in each condition on each participant were noticeability, annoyance and togetherness. Repeated measures analysis was used to calculate the effect taking within subject effects into account. Interaction effects were analyzed with a between-within analysis.

RESULTS

Togetherness

The answers on the togetherness questions show that voice chatters feel more together on average than text chatters (one way ANOVA $F(1,140)=14.26$, $p<0.01$). Although significant, the difference is small as on average it was approximately one point on a 7 point scale (ranging from 1, completely not together, to 7, completely together). This corresponds to text chatters being "somewhat together" (mean togetherness=4.3) on average and voice chatters being mostly "together" (5.1) on average. Although we expected to find different scores depending on how well the video was synchronized, the effect of synchronization levels on togetherness was not found significant.

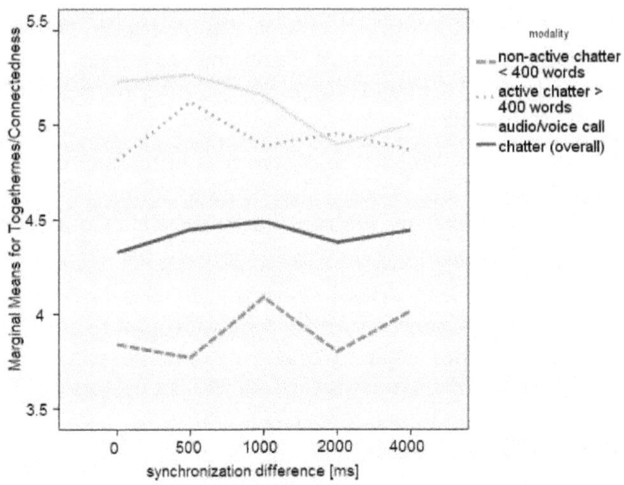

Figure 1: togetherness by chat activity

When taking into account chat activity (see Figure 1), this difference in mean togetherness between voice chatters and text chatters is mainly attributed to non-active chatters (3.9). Between active text chatters (4.9) and voice chatters no significant difference on togetherness was found. Taking these three groups into account, voice chatters and active chatters feel significantly more together than non-active chatters ($F(1,359)=93.5$, $p<0.001$). This means that while H1 in general might be true, it has to be rejected when comparing active text chatters with voice chatters.

Noticeability and Annoyance

H2 focuses on the noticeability of synchronization, while H3 concerns annoyance. As both are closely related, they will be discussed together. Figure 2 shows that in the voice chat condition, synchronization difference becomes noticeable for most people when it is 1s or more.

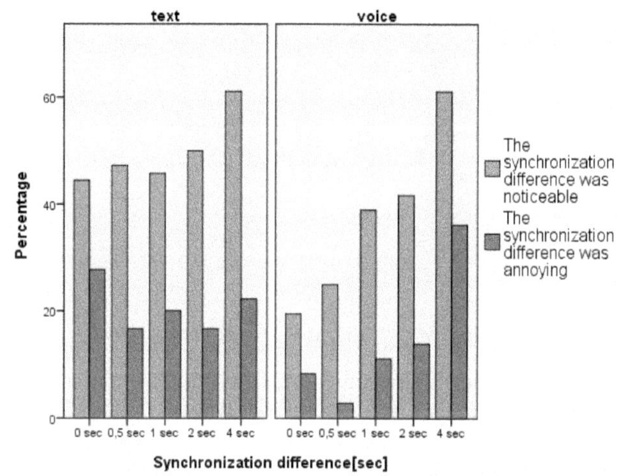

Figure 2: Noticeability and annoyance of play-out differences

People in the text chat condition give rather random answers, not correlated with the synchronization levels, indicating that they do not notice a difference based on synchronization level, but probably attribute this to other factors (such as reaction time of the other participants).

The statistical results show that synchronization differences in the 0-4s range tested were noticed significantly by voice chatters ($F(4,140)=6.479$, $p<0.001$). The effect of synchronization difference on annoyance was also found significant for the voice chat case ($F(2.33, 81.66)=6.845$, $p<0.05$). Text chatters however, did not notice synchronization differences significantly more or less often for each different level ($F(4,140)=0.887$, $p>0.05$). Also the effect of the synchronization difference on annoyance was not verified ($F(4,132)=0.564$, $p>0.05$). Based on these results, H2 and H3 can be accepted, as voice chatters notice synchronization more easily, and are more annoyed by it.

It is interesting to see if the likeability of the content, or the fact that the participants had seen the episodes, would influence the noticeability of synchronization differences.

Overall, voice and text chat participants that liked the show seemed to notice synchronization difference more quickly than people that were neutral to it. This effect however was tested non-significant ($F(8,132) = 0.859$, $p>0.05$). Having seen the episode before also does not make synchronization difference more or less noticeable ($F(1,359)=0.875$, $p>0.05$).

Text chat experience and text chat activity were also tested as mediating factors. Experienced text chatters (more than once per month) do not notice synchronization difference better than less experienced text chatters (less than once per month) ($F(4,112) = 0.029$, $p>0,05$).

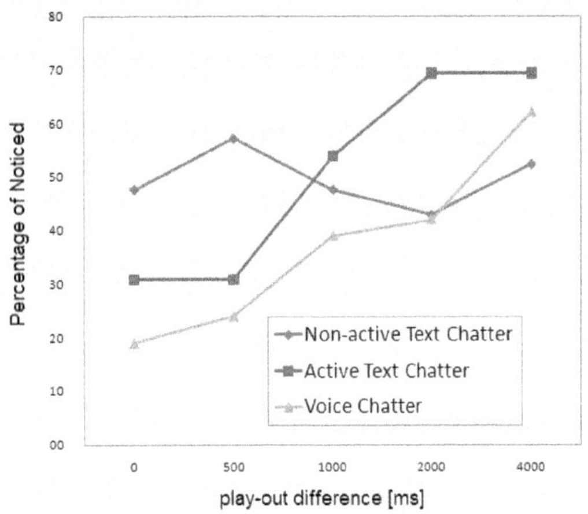

Figure 3: Noticeability by chat activity

The difference between active chatters and non-active chatters however was found significant ($F(1,32)=6.116$, $p<0.05$). Figure 3 shows that active text chatters are able to notice synchronization differences larger than 1 second, similar to voice chatters. Due to the few participants that got annoyed, no similar claims on annoyance can be made.

CONCLUSION

This paper discussed how well people using voice chat and text chat notice synchronization differences when watching online videos together, and what the impact is on annoyance and togetherness. While currently telecom operators are aiming at the synchronization level found in telecommunication tests (150ms) our results show that voice chatters only start noticing differences above 2 seconds delays. Most text chatters do not notice synchronization differences between 0 and 4 seconds, however active text chatters notice synchronization differences similar to when using voice chat. As the highest levels of togetherness were also observed with active text chatters and all voice chatters, we recommend synchronization of approximately 1 second (which was not noticeable by this group) for a seamless shared experience. These results put into doubt the 150ms value from telecommunications research as the target synchronization bound required for social video watching applications. A first implication for software designers is that they can concentrate on implementing simpler mechanisms that aim at a synchronization level of 1second. Even more interesting, these results imply that social video watching applications can be effective even on more challenging platforms such as mobile networks, where delays are unpredictable, or thin clients, where execution times may be variable. This will result in new opportunities for network operators and system designers, which in turn may provide more flexibility and dynamism to end-users in future ubiquitous social video applications. Further research should focus on the influence of other parameters such as different genres or different platforms (PC, mobile, TV) to test whether these results are also valid in other circumstances.

ACKNOWLEDGMENTS

The research leading to these results has received funding from the European Community's Seventh Framework Programme (FP7/2007-2013) under grant agreement no. ICT-2007-214793

REFERENCES

[1] Geerts, D. and De Grooff, D. 2009. Supporting the social uses of television: sociability heuristics for social TV. In Proceedings of the CHI Conference on Human Factors in Computing Systems, pp. 595-604.

[2] Huang, E. M., Harboe, G., Tullio, J., Novak, A., Massey, N., Metcalf, C. J., and Romano, G. 2009. Of social television comes home: a field study of communication choices and practices in tv-based text and voice chat. In Proceedings of the CHI Conference on Human Factors in Computing Systems, pp. 585-594.

[3] ITU-T Rec. P.800 "Methods for subjective Determination of Transmission quality", August 1996

[4] ITU-T G.114: "General Recommendations on the transmission quality for an entire international telephone connection, One-way transmission time", May 2003.

[5] Lull, J. 1980. Family Communication Patterns and the Social Uses of Television. In Communication Research, 7(3):319--333.

[6] Mauve, M., Vogel, J., Hilt, V., Effelsberg, W. 2004. Local-lag and timewarp: Providing consistency for replicated continuous applications. IEEE transactions on Multimedia

[7] Schatz, R., Wagner, S., Egger, S., and Jordan, N. 2007. Mobile TV becomes social: integrating content with communications. In Proceedings of the ITI Conference on Information Technology Interfaces, pp. 263-270.

[8] Shamma, D. A., Bastea-Forte, M., Joubert, N., and Liu, Y. 2008. Enhancing online personal connections through the synchronized sharing of online video. In CHI '08 Extended Abstracts on Human Factors in Computing Systems, pp. 2931-2936.

[9] Weisz, J. D., Kiesler, S., Zhang, H., Ren, Y., Kraut, R. E., and Konstan, J. A. 2007. Watching together: integrating text chat with video. In Proceedings of the CHI Conference on Human Factors in Computing Systems, pp. 877-886.

Designing for Peer Involvement in Weight Management

Julie Maitland
People-Centered Technologies Group
National Research Council of Canada
46 Dineen Drive, Fredericton, E3A 4J1
julie.maitland@nrc-cnrc.gc.ca

Matthew Chalmers
Social/Ubiquitous/Mobile Group
School of Computing Science
University of Glasgow, G12 8QQ
matthew.chalmers@glasgow.ac.uk

ABSTRACT
The problems of obesity and overweight are commonly cited as the motivation behind recent efforts to develop technology that promotes physical activity. Prompted by the social nature of many of the emerging applications, this paper presents our investigation of the sociality of weight management as experienced by a broad demographic of individuals. Our findings highlight the broad scope of peer involvement, and provide insight into the context and mechanics of related interaction that may prove valuable in informing the next generation of peer-based weight management technology for use in everyday life.

Author Keywords
Health, behavioral change, physical activity, diet, weight, obesity, social networks, social support, social influence.

ACM Classification Keywords
H5.m. Information interfaces and presentation (e.g., HCI): Miscellaneous. J.3. Life and medical sciences: Health.

General Terms
Human Factors.

INTRODUCTION
Obesity and overweight are commonly cited as motivation for the majority of work emerging from CHI and related domains concerned with developing applications to promote physical activity. Many emerging systems include a social component, be it through broadcasting physical activity levels to a predetermined peer group [7,21,26] or collaborative gaming [11,19]. The inclusion of sociality in these system designs is strongly supported—and in some cases the designs themselves are informed—by interpersonal theories of health and behavioural change. Social support has long been acknowledged as having a positive correlation with health [2,4] and health-related behavioural change [6,16]. The social influence of those around us is explained in part through theories of social facilitation [32], social comparison [10], normative influence [28] and social learning [1].

Driven by the stigma that can surround the issues of weight and obesity, and the relatively low level of involvement of overweight or obese individuals in system design and evaluation, we were curious to find out if and how people who are trying to lose weight harness the support of their surrounding peer groups. We sought to explore the social dynamics of weight management with a view to better understand the opportunities and constraints for socially focused system design within this domain.

Previous work within the sociomedical domain that investigates weight-related social influence tends to focus on quantitative measures. For example, by investigating the correlation between social network structure and weight [5] or between the physical characteristics of others and an individual's food choice [22]. This work complements such work by providing insight into the human experience of peer-involvement, and perhaps more importantly for CHI, into the nuanced interactions between peers. For example, while Christakis et al. [5] point to the impact of same-sex friendship on the spread of obesity, our work suggests ways in which gender can be accounted for in system design.

Consolvo et al. [8] recently observed that much of the related work within computing tends to focus on behavioural change at the expense of considering "how these technologies must effectively integrate into an individual's everyday life", and then contributes to this underrepresented area by providing design guidelines informed by two social psychological theories. This work complements such efforts by providing domain-specific insight and basing recommendations on the social practices of weight-management observed in this study. For example, the need to "support fundamental impression management needs" [8] is supported by the information disclosure practices observed in this study and our recommendation to base selective disclosure mechanisms on the relative comparability of individuals.

We interviewed nineteen individuals with current or previous experience of trying to lose weight. In particular we were concerned with the role that peers play in an individual's weight management efforts, and what aspects were shared with peers. The insights that were gained into the sociality of weight management were then used to identify several points of consideration that we suggest designers take into account when designing peer-based weight management technology.

The main contribution of this work is an unpacking of the underlying dynamics of social activity that surrounds weight management, in a way that, we suggest, can serve to inform future system designs. The key outcomes are:

- A taxonomy of peer involvement that could be used to inspire new genres of weight management technology and further develop existing approaches.
- Observed patterns of interaction that could inform the underlying mechanics of collaborative applications.
- Evidence of gender- and role-based peer involvement that suggests further consideration should be paid to the gender and specific peer group at whom particular applications are targeted.

Before we present the study and discuss our findings, we commence with a brief overview of related work. The findings of the study are then structured around the various forms of peer involvement that we observed, before we consider how these findings might inform the further development of existing efforts in the field and inspire new genres of weight management technology.

RELATED WORK

The sociality of weight management is a multidisciplinary topic of interest. Here we discuss some of the existing work within the sociomedical and HCI domains, which are structured respectively around the effectiveness of peer-based weight management interventions and harnessing social influence in applications to promote behavioral change in everyday life.

Peer-Based Weight Management Interventions

The sociomedical literature has long considered social support a component of weight management programs, be it within the relationship between clinician and patient, or within peer support groups. It is considered an intrinsic component of a multifaceted strategy to facilitate weight management [9,29]. Although commercial weight loss programs may have proven to be a financial success, the evidence to support successful weight loss is not convincing. A systematic review of commercial weight loss programs in the US that include a social component (online or offline) found "with the exception of 1 trial of weight watchers, the evidence to support the use of major commercial and self-help weight loss programs is suboptimal" [27].

The bulk of literature is concerned with the effectiveness of integrating peer involvement into the delivery of clinical weight management programs. A meta-analysis of peer-based weight management interventions identified various ways in which peers can be formally involved (ranging from commitment contracts witnessed by peers to spousal participation), and showed that social support interventions are promising but their effectiveness is yet to be conclusively proven [29]. For example, while the studies included in aforementioned meta-analysis showed that having peers also participate in the weight loss program was positively correlated with successful weight loss, a different study found that successful weight-loss was not correlated with the number of involved partners, but with the number of successful partners [12].

Further illustrating the complexity of the problem space, it has been shown that the need [29] and effectiveness [23] of social support varies depending on the condition and characteristics of the individuals involved. For example McLean et al. [23] found that while adolescents benefit greatest when treated alone, parental involvement was associated with weight loss in children, as was spousal involvement in adults. The contextually dependent nature of support was also evident in the literature surrounding online provision of social support in weight management programs. Various studies have indicated a correlation between an individual's stage of change, and the effectiveness of on- or offline support [12,24,30].

These findings indicate a need tailored interventions and also sensitizes us to the fact that facilitating social support may not always make a positive contribution. This may seem to contradict the earlier statement that social support is positively correlated with health and health-related behavioral change [2,4,6,16], but actually only refers to the direct involvement of peers within an individual's behavioral change program. We believe that this suggests an important distinction between formal involvement and the everyday nature of supportive relationships.

Harnessing Social Influence in Everyday Life

In contrast to the sociomedical focus on weight management programs, the work emerging from HCI and Ubiquitous Computing concerns itself with harnessing the potential behavioral influence of peers within everyday life. The applications tend to take the form of lightweight social awareness systems, which are typically characterized by the tracking and sharing of physical activity levels between pre-defined groups of users [7,11,19,21,26]. Both Fish'n'Steps [19] and the Lifestyle Coaching Application (LCA) [11] encapsulated behavioral goals within the context of a team-based game, thus explicitly introducing competition and social pressure. In contrast, Houston [7] and Chick-Clique [26] both integrate social influence through social facilitation and social support. In those systems, peers do not explicitly compete with one another but can view and comment on the progress of their peers.

Despite the widely acknowledged role that social influence has on behavioral change, detailed understanding is still taking shape. During the evaluation of Houston, participants were significantly more likely to achieve their behavioral goals if they were using the version that enabled social influence, but these findings conflict with those of Fish'n'Steps [19] and LCA [11], whose team-based versions were not found to have a significant effect on behavioral outcomes when comparatively evaluated against single-user equivalents. It is not yet clear whether the conflicting results are due to the mechanics of social influence, details of the designs or the mechanics of the experiments themselves. For example one could infer from the results that competition within physical activity systems is an ineffective form of social influence, but it is interesting to note that it was only in the evaluation of Houston that the peers already knew each other. Teams were made up of strangers in LCA and were anonymous in Fish'n'Steps. Given the emphasis that the sociomedical literature places on existing peers with respect to social support [2,4,6,29], these findings are not surprising. However, a more consistent evaluation framework is necessary to enable cross–comparison.

Although these systems are designed for any particular peer group, and so do not exclude the possibility of use by family members, relatively little research has been done that deals with promoting health-related behavioral change within families. One exception was the recent study into technologies that support family reflections on health [14], that identified family gatherings as an opportunity for collective reflection, highlighted potential conflicts between the need for openness and the need to protect, and argued for design to support cooperation rather then competition within the family unit.

THE STUDY

While the sociomedical literature sensitizes us to the contextually dependent nature of peer involvement and social support within formal weight management programs, the body of work within HCI points to the various ways in which social influence can be integrated into everyday behavioral change applications. The work in this paper seeks to contribute to the body of knowledge surrounding peer-based applications to promote everyday behavioral change by investigating social aspects of weight management practices. In order to do this, we seek to answer the following questions: who is involved in an individual's weight management, how are they involved, who prompts such involvement, and what aspects of weight management are shared?

Method

Interview recruitment posters were created and displayed in several community centers, shop notice boards and within a UK university. They invited individuals who considered themselves to be overweight, or had been in the past, to talk about the 'things' and people in their life that made it easy or difficult for them to lose weight. The initial recruitment drive resulted in fourteen respondents, ten of whom were female. In an attempt to recruit more male participants, we sent an email to a university mailing list containing the same information as the initial recruitment posters but specifically requesting male participants. From this email we recruited a further four male participants, one of whom subsequently recruited his wife.

We performed semi-structured interviews that lasted 45–90 minutes. Questions were structured around peer–involvement in an individual's weight management alongside more general weight–management related questions such as history, progress, and strategies. Each interview was audio recorded and transcribed, and we then employed inductive analytic methods advocated by Lofland et al. [20]. Transcripts were initially subjected to open coding, whereby each sentence was analyzed in a process of sensitization. The emergent codes were then subject to more focused coding, whereby similar codes were grouped together to form categories of phenomena. Similarities and differences were compared and contrasted, and the data was repeatedly revisited. Themes emerged that were then used to structure the data presented in this paper.

Participant Overview

All but two of the nineteen participants were engaged in weight management activities at the time of the study: that is, they were either trying to lose weight or maintain their current weight loss through diet (n=6), physical activity (n=2), or a combination of both (n=9). The participant group included two married couples; in both cases the husband and wife were interviewed separately. The participants represent a fairly diverse demographic: aged between 21 and 74, and including a nursing assistant, a policeman, a telesales operator, and a computer technician. Three participants were students, and two were retired (one through ill-health). Technology use for weight management was limited. One participant used a spreadsheet to monitor exertion and recovery time after exercise, and despite the plethora of online forums for weight management only two participants reported using them.

FINDINGS

Although weight is considered by many to be an intensely private issue, we found weight management to be an inherently social activity. As had been indicated in the literature, a peer group (spouses, relatives, friends, and colleagues) constructs social norms and a frame of reference through which weight management efforts are motivated, driven, and evaluated. The remainder of this section is structured around the taxonomy of peer involvement that was derived from our analysis. The following section introduces the multiple forms of peer involvement, before we illustrate how various forms of peer involvement are evident even in solitary weight management efforts. Individual forms of peer involvement are addressed in subsequent sections and, where appropriate, attention is paid to the mechanics of interaction commonly employed during such involvement. Finally, we discuss the implications for those researching and designing peer-based weight management technology.

Introducing the Multiple Forms of Peer Involvement

We found that peer involvement could be passive or active; Table 1 serves to roughly show the various active forms of peer involvement. Although none are as simple as the illustrative phrases, passive involvement is too complex to convey in such a manner. The various forms of peer involvement are discussed in more detail in the following sections, and where appropriate the mechanics of such peer involvement are presented.

INVOLVEMENT	ILLUSTRATIVE PHRASE
Obstructive	*Don't do it.*
Inductive	*You should do it.*
Proactive	*Do it with me.*
Supportive	*I'll do it too.*
Co-operative	*Let's do it together.*

Table 1: Subtypes of Active Involvement

We start by highlighting how peers can be involved in what is otherwise considered to be solitary weight management efforts, including obstructive and inductive involvement that both appear counterproductive. We then focus on passive involvement, which we suggest is the most influential form. There are a variety of ways in which peers' passive involvement contributes to an individual's attitudes towards his or her weight, and desire to lose or maintain their current weight, and an individual's awareness and preference for particular weight loss strategies. Finally, we discuss the remaining forms of active involvement before considering implications for research and design in this domain.

Never Really Alone: Peer Involvement in Solitary WM

Only three of the participants tried to lose weight alone, and all of these were aged between 21 and 25. P1 was of normal weight according to her BMI but had gained 10kg since moving to the UK 18 months previously. Of all of the interview participants, she appeared to be the most secretive with regards to concerns about her weight. Despite two months' dieting and going to the gym to try and lose weight, she only ever mentioned her weight to her friends in the UK in a tongue-in-cheek fashion. She appears to use humor to test the water: to establish responses without committing to exposing how she really feels. The responses from her UK friends so far have been affectionately dismissive, telling her that her figure is great and that she doesn't need to lose any weight. She in return is equally dismissive of their responses, choosing to focus instead on the comments made by her family at home: *My family are always like 'hey girl watch your weight' and you know, 'watch what you are eating because the food is not the same... and even for your health, take care of yourself.'*

The remaining two participants who acted alone were also different from the other participants in that they had both grown up overweight. Both P2 and P17 were obese prior to making behavioral changes, and acknowledged that overeating was their primary problem behavior. Neither participant could identify any significant other that had been involved in their weight-loss attempts. However, both participants experienced situational changes that prompted their behavioral changes. P2 moved to California for a year and took the opportunity to adopt the more active outdoor lifestyle that his new peers participated in. P17 experienced unintentional weight loss when he went to university, which he put down to a more active social life and no longer having his meals cooked for him. Both remembered their parents nagging them as teenagers, and recalled themselves not being ready to listen.

Despite the fact that in the three examples described above each participant considered him– or herself to be acting independently, these examples introduce three forms of peer involvement: inductive, obstructive and passive.

Inductive Involvement: The comment made by P1's family is an example of inductive involvement, whereby the comments are, or are perceived to be, intended to instigate change. Typically made by family members, they can easily be perceived as offensive, ranging from "you're putting on a bit of beef, are you not" (P11's brother), to "you are going to die young" (P3's parents). It is impossible to gauge how effective such comments were in prompting behavioral change. The comments made to P1 by her family certainly were central to her desire to lose weight, but for the most part such 'nagging' was nothing more than hurtful and was eventually dismissed. Although tempting to judge such comments as thoughtless and unethical, a counterargument is that it is sometimes necessary to be cruel to be kind.

Obstructive Involvement: It may be that peers are in a 'no win' situation, because dismissing an individual's concerns about his/her weight is almost uniformly regarded as unhelpful. Such reactions can be said to be an example of obstructive involvement, whereby peers do not support an individual's weight management efforts; often leading to the individual seeking alternative sources of support. It is similar to inductive involvement in the respect that the peer's intention may be well–meaning. Offering 'bad' foods as treats was highlighted by five of the seven married women interviewed as the worst thing their husbands do while they are trying to lose weight. Yet while it is frowned upon for them to provide temptation, it is worse to discourage their wife from eating 'something she shouldn't'. Despite any well-meaning intentions, there seems to be a fine line between comments and actions being perceived as encouraging or interfering. Interestingly, the male participants expressed no such tension towards their wives' involvement in their weight management efforts (as will be discussed in the coming sections).

Passive Involvement: The change in lifestyle associated with P3's move abroad and P17's move to university show how the social norms of a peer group, alongside broader environmental constraints, can influence an individual's weight-related behaviors, prompting unintended or opportunistic weight-loss. In the cases observed, the change of lifestyle associated with their moves caused unintended weight loss. They reported drastic results both with respect to the way that they looked and the way that they felt; which they then sustained with conscious efforts. The sort of involvement that the peers (before and after their move) had on their weight is an example of passive involvement. The peers themselves were not necessarily aware of their influence or involvement.

Passive Involvement as a Foundation of Change

Passive involvement has a broad scope of influence on the health-related behavior and behavioral change of an individual and sets the foundation for more active forms of involvement. In this section we consider the social shaping of behavior and everyday talk as two forms of passive involvement, before considering the role of comparison and competition in such everyday talk.

Social Shaping of Behaviors: Life-events, such as suffering an injury, going to university, moving abroad, getting married, having children and getting old, all framed the stories that participants told about their weight. Apart from the physiological influences that such events have, what was evident in their stories was the influence that the social changes associated with each event had on the individual's health-related behaviors.

Apart from gravitating towards the activities of others, people also develop patterns of behavior together: *I think most of my weight went on, I would say, once we got married. You stop going out every night with your mates and playing football and things like that. You are married and then you are sitting in, watching TV, cups of tea, biscuits and things like that. P18*

Domestication also presents demands that influence the daily activities that an individual engages in. The day-to-day running of family life primarily affected the female participants' efforts to diet and exercise. Between working, doing the housework and looking after children, very little 'me time' was left for participants. While most husbands supported their wives' weight loss attempts in theory, or became actively involved as will be discussed in the coming sections, there was no evidence of them offering practical support by alleviating their wives' domestic chores so that the latter had time to exercise. However, it should be said that there was no evidence of any of the participants asking her husband to help in this way.

Speaking of Weight: Perhaps reflecting the current focus of the media in the UK, weight and diet is an everyday topic of conversation for most participants. The workplace, in particular, was a frequent location for talk about weight for men and women. However, women were more likely to extend the discussion to also include female friends and family members. For men, if weight was discussed within the workplace, or within a circle of friends, it was more common that the discussion would take the form of friendly banter, gentle ribbing and light-hearted competition. The middle-aged participants reported such occurrences most frequently, possibly because this is a time when most of their friends and colleagues realize that they have gained weight over the years. Age was attributed by most participants (both male and female) as being a natural cause of weight gain. Apart from P2 and P17, all of the men talked about their weight creeping up on them almost without them noticing. Male colleagues would often make flippant jokes about middle-age spread, regardless of whether they themselves were middle-aged or overweight. Far from taking these comments to heart, our male participants seemed to relish being able to return the name-calling when their weight-loss meant that they were no longer heavier than their friends and colleagues.

For the most part, such banter was not delivered in the hope of changing an individual's behavior; it was just part of the humor and familiarity of a friendship. In other cases though, it masked a concern for the health of the person who was the butt of the remark. After making radical changes to his lifestyle following a multiple diagnosis of diabetes, high cholesterol and high blood pressure at the age of 42, P18 discussed his subsequent raised consciousness of the healthy and unhealthy lifestyle choices that he and his friends were making. The only way that he has found to bring the subject up is through "winding them up": *I am thinking 'you are going to die' and I was kidding him on, you know just winding him up... [I said] 'You're going to die', in fact I said 'see when you die they are going to have to get one of those big American caskets to take you out in'.*

Although such jokes and remarks are an accepted part of certain friendships, as with most forms of inductive involvement they remain largely ineffective as motivational tools for behavioral change, and they also existed exclusively within male relationships.

Weight was a much more sensitive subject for the female participants, but at the same time it is treated as something easily manipulable. 55% of female participants cited upcoming occasions as a reason to try and lose weight (in comparison to 0% of male participants), and talk of upcoming occasions would often prompt efforts to lose weight. Sharing hints and tips was a major topic of the women's weight-related conversation. Although only three of the female participants were members of weight-loss organizations at the time of the interviews, five others were using their knowledge of weight-loss programs to devise their own dietary strategies. So, despite the sensitivities associated with weight, weight remained a frequent topic of conversation for women. Perhaps reflecting the underlying sensitivities, women's weight-related conversations were subject to comparability filtering not evident in the reported practices of men, as we now discuss.

Relative Comparability

We found that women used the relative comparability of others to determine whether or not they disclosed particular aspects of their weight management, e.g. *I suppose if somebody got really, really heavy you wouldn't make a comment because they might be self-conscious about it. You know you would kinda, hold back I think. None of us have got to that stage where we are really heavy. P19*

Participants avoided the direct comparison of weight loss with others "because we are all different shapes and sizes" (P4). However, successful weight losses always served as inspiration, regardless of similarity of size. Although comparisons were mostly weight-based, the three eldest women all expressed concern about discussing their weight-loss with younger colleagues for fear of cultivating obsessive attitudes. As large weight loss inspires, regardless of similarity, the elder participants were uncomfortable when younger colleagues who only had one or two pounds to lose approached them asking for advice.

From Comparison to Competition

Competition played a relatively small role in the weight management practices of the participants, but was more openly discussed by our male participants. The manifestation of the competition varied, from trying to lose more weight to being better at whatever physical activity was being undertaken. In contrast, and in keeping with the findings of [21] whereby female participants used their peers' activity levels as a target to stay within range, P6 speculated that the motivation derived from her friend's participation in sporting activities did not come out of competition: *Not competitiveness but I suppose... almost copying... maybe she has gone every night that week. I feel guilty but I don't feel that I want to do better than her.*

Taking the Lead with Proactive Involvement

In contrast to the passive involvement described above in which behavioral change may not necessarily be explicitly considered, proactive involvement is focused on initiating behavioral change. Unlike inductive involvement whereby peers simply instruct an individual that change is required, here peers encourage behavioral change by participating in the target behavior and inviting the individual to participate with them. Neither of the young male participants who had been overweight during their teens expressed regrets at not having someone to talk to about their problems, but retrospectively desired proactive 'others' who would have prompted and encouraged activity.

For our male participants, the first point of meaningful weight-related conversational contact with others would, more often than not, be with regards to the actions that they intended on taking in order to resolve the problem. They seem to avoid the involvement of friends and colleagues in the reflective, decision-making period when an individual determines what course of action should be taken. P16 had been gaining weight over a number of years after a series of injuries prevented him from participating in sports. He decided that he would start going to the gym, but instead of going alone, he encouraged his workmates to go along with him: *I thought 'well it is about time someone started this up'. So I decided the more the merrier, and I managed to convince them to come along... I just said 'Right I am going to start going, who is coming with me?'.*

This prompt from P16 to encourage his workmates to go to the gym had not been preceded with a discussion about weight: *I suspect that... we... men... or at least the men I know consider [weight] to be a personal thing. There are just some things that you don't particularly discuss [...] some things you don't need to discuss, it is understood.*

When asked why her female colleagues at work choose to trade dieting tips daily as opposed to become more active together, P5 responded "I don't know, I think it might just be that everyone has their own lives, you know?" Apart from the gender-specific influence of domestication that was discussed earlier, this response highlights the fact that while work is a place where ideas are discussed it is at home that much of the work of weight management is carried out (as previously stated by [29]). However, proactive involvement was only evident in three of the thirteen couples represented by the participants of this study.

Toeing the Line with Supportive Involvement

More commonly than instigating change, both male and female spouses would seek to ease the effort of behavioral change by supporting and facilitating the changes that their partners were making. Unlike proactive involvement, supportive involvement was directed at dietary changes. The amount of effort invested by the spouse varied. In some cases, it was a matter of eating or cooking the low-fat diet that the individual wanted to follow, and others went to the extent of planning their spouses' meals for the week or following the diet as well "to keep him on the straight and narrow" (P11). There were isolated incidents when friends or colleagues supported an individual's efforts in this way, such as when P19 went to a party after a night out and her friend purposely avoided offering her pizza. However, the collocation of spouses in the home make them more suited to supportive involvement, despite the tensions associated with spousal support described earlier.

Doing it Together in Cooperative Involvement

Although there were occasions when married participants had come to a joint decision to engage in weight management efforts together, it was more common for women to collaborate with their friends or colleagues. For couples, although weight may be a motivating factor there is not necessarily a target weight being aimed at. Instead they agree to participate in specific activities together to improve their health or the healthiness of their lifestyle, such as going to the gym together (P14), following a particular diet (P5, P15), or making an effort to go for walks (P16). In contrast, co-operative efforts between groups of friends remain very weight-focused, emulating the organizational structure of formal weight-loss programs. Seven of the eleven female participants actively trying to lose or maintain their weight belonged to one of four unofficial weight-loss clubs made up of friends or colleagues. All apart from one resembled the formal weight loss clubs, with a focus on dieting as the primary route to losing weight, including weigh-ins complete with recording of weight loss and gain.

In addition to providing practical support such as shared experiences and resources, the time spent with other club members is deemed as allocated 'weight time'. During such times it is possible to complain about the diet and talk about your weight without fear of being a burden, something that prevented participants expressing their feelings to other peers: *I try not to talk about it. I talk more to you guys than anybody else. But I feel that it is such a constant, because it is such a constant thing with me I think that people are sick of listening to me. I deliberately try and not talk about it. And my husband, he is really, ... you know "oh you're fine, you're fine", you know, the fine thing. [...], and I am not fine because I don't feel fine." P9*

Secrecy and Disclosure

Varying degrees of secrecy about several aspects of participants' weight management were maintained: their actual weights, whether they perceived their weights to be problems, and their weight loss plans and actions. For the most part the most sensitive and private aspect of an individual's weight was the degree to which their weight concerned and affected his or her daily life. Self-consciousness and the fear of judgment caused some of our female participants to make excuses in order to avoid uncomfortable situations such as swimming or going on a night out. Even in cases whereby an individual had groups of friends with which he or she would share dieting and weight-loss tips, he or she would either retain these most sensitive aspects, or only share with a member of the group in whom he or she had invested a great deal of trust: *I spend a lot of time with her at work and I know she wouldn't say to anybody. I think it is more of a thing that you know you can confide in them and they wouldn't tell anyone else. P5*

P3's story is illustrative of many of the emergent themes and strategies relating to secrecy and disclosure during weight loss. She had been dieting for 5 weeks when she was interviewed, and had lost 17lb from her original weight. Colleagues at her work had formed a 'diet club' in which each shared diet plans and participated in a weekly weigh-in. Once a week, all club members would go into an office and an allocated member would weigh each one, recording weight loss or gain in a booklet. Because she wanted to avoid the embarrassment of quantifying her weight, P3 performed the weigh-in in secret with a trusted party. Other members of the club did not know that she was participating, and it was only when her weight loss progressed and they started to notice, that P3 was prepared to 'come out' and start publicly participating in the group.

Incremental Participation

Similarly incremental was the degree of participation in collaborative efforts to lose weight. By its very nature participation incurs a level of disclosure unless, like P3, participation begins in secret. Incremental participation also suggests partialness. Like disclosure, partialness may progress or regress at any one point in time. For some partial participation was a static choice, P4 chose not to and never intended to get involved in the weigh-in with her colleagues. Likewise, adherence to diets would waver over time, some participants choosing to participate in weekday dieting, and giving themselves the weekend to enjoy otherwise forbidden luxuries.

Incremental participation was not a behavior restricted to female participants, nor to co-operative involvement. When P15 and his partner agreed to try and lose weight together, she joined a weight loss organization and they both followed its diet. His participation over time progressed from dropping her off at the classes and waiting outside in the car, to dropping her off and waiting inside, to eventually joining in the classes with her. Similarly, when P15 initially invited his brother to go cycling, his brother was reluctant to go cycling with him for fear of slowing him down, but once engaged in the activity together they participated in friendly competition that kept them motivated both on and off the bikes.

DISCUSSION

This study investigated weight management as experienced by a broad demographic of individuals. Supporting current understanding within the sociomedical literature, we observed peer involvement that was widely varied and heavily contextually dependent. We observed selective information disclosure practices based on relative comparability and incremental participation in–group activities. Furthermore, evidence of gender- and role-based peer involvement was observed throughout the study.

When considering what this means for the peer-based technologies in this domain, we start by reflecting on the existing approaches being taken within HCI and related communities. The applications discussed in the Related Work section have been groundbreaking. They form a new genre of technological health promotion, creating resources for interaction through which health behaviors can be discussed and reflected on. However, the notion of peer involvement has remained relatively vague or obscure. So far, the mechanics of peer involvement has been broadcasting monitored information to a predetermined group of peers, and for the most part the nature of peer relationships and their impact on system design has not been discussed. Exceptions to that statement are the works on family-based health monitoring technology [14] and community-based technologies to promote healthy eating [13]. Here, we draw on our findings to offer four points of consideration to those interested in supporting appropriate peer involvement in weight management in everyday life.

The Taxonomy of Peer Involvement

Considering the various levels of peer involvement highlighted by this study, that ranged from passive to proactive, it is interesting to note that current designs seem to be best suited to cooperative involvement. We suggest that efforts should be made to *develop applications that support or emulate the various passive and active forms of peer involvement.* However, our findings indicate that it may be inappropriate to design systems that encourage obstructive and inductive involvement. In order to prioritize future work, further research is required to investigate the behavioral effectiveness of each form of involvement. Here we give some examples of how the various forms of peer involvement could be supported in design.

Passive: Designing to support passive involvement essentially involves highlighting or improving an individual's weight management-related social capital i.e., the resources made available through the existence of an individual's social network [4]. For example, with an application that highlights and compares the weight management strategies, progress and experiences of others. It could be restricted to existing peers, but designs that increase an individual's social capital could extend to non-peers of similar demographic and location. In either case, our findings suggest drawing from others who are comparable to the individual (as is discussed further later).

Obstructive: Designing to support the obstruction of an individual's weight management efforts appears to be counterintuitive. None of the participants responded positively to being told that they did not need to lose weight. One possible design strategy that may be worth further exploration could be a 'nudge' function for peers to use to suggest when the individual is taking his or her weight management too far.

Inductive: As with obstructive involvement, and based on the responses of participants to being told they should engage in weight management activities, designing for inductive involvement does not appear appropriate. However, with the growing interest in behavioral change applications that include aversive feedback [17] and coercion (pinc-research.org), it may prove to be an avenue worthy of further investigation.

Proactive: Perhaps the most straightforward of involvement types to support, inviting an individual to participate in a weight management activity that the peer is already involved in could be facilitated through the inclusion of an invite function. As with all involvement types there is much scope for innovation. In exergames, for example, recruitment of new participants could be explicitly integrated into the game's objectives.

Supportive: In this study supportive involvement was characterised by a peer's participation in an individual's weight management activity. Similarly to the invite feature described above, a request-to-participate feature could be integrated into technology-facilitated activities. While spouses were the most common source of supportive involvement in this study, the complexity of the domestic space was highlighted by examples of well-meaning but obstructive spousal involvement. An alternative to direct mediation of supportive involvement could be an application to highlight a peer's current and potential role in supporting or hindering an individual's efforts, that provides hints and tips on how to be more supportive; an example of such a system is proposed in following section.

Cooperative: As mentioned previously, the majority of existing social applications could be considered to support cooperative involvement as they assume, and indeed require, the involvement of multiple participants. In seeking to further develop the existing genre we recommend considering how the remaining points of consideration could be integrated (see below).

The Target Peer Group

An important issue in the design of peer-based systems is to *make a conscious decision as to which peer-group to design for*. For example, given the existing collaborative practices observed in groups of friends and colleagues, such groups seem obvious beneficiaries of existing approaches. However, family groups appear less suited to approaches that simply assume that all members are willing to participate. There was evidence that spousal involvement often extended beyond the moral support of weight loss efforts to facilitation, invitations to engage in an activity, and joint decisions to make changes. For remaining family members, systems aimed at improving the physical activity or dietary intake of the family 'as a whole' could reduce the obstacles faced by one individual trying to change his or her daily routine while the others remain the same.

For example, the Whereabouts Clock [3] is an ambient interface for the home that displays each family member's current location and allows members to send messages to the household. A similar home-based interface could be imagined that conveys the domestic routine of a family in terms of the duties and activities of each family member. When a family member needs or wants to make changes to his/her own routine then the temporal demand of making that change (e.g., to go and exercise) and any impact on collaborative activities (e.g., making and eating dinner) could be shown on the interface. This would highlight any areas of conflict and might encourage family members to contribute, either by getting involved in the activity itself or by alleviating pressure on the individual in order to free up time for them. The ambient nature of the interface avoids the need for individuals to make direct requests for assistance—something that participants currently seem reluctant to do. However, it should also be noted that such a system would involve a degree of disclosure of intention and desire to change. Further research is needed to find whether this issue would prevent such a system being adopted and whether it could be addressed through selective and incremental disclosure mechanisms.

The Role of Gender

While applications have been designed for a particular gender (female) [7,26], relatively little consideration has been given to the broader implications of gender in everyday behavioral change technology. The lack of overt competition between female participants suggests that applications founded on explicit competition may be unsuitable as a means for health promotion for women. Systems designed for gender-specific groups should be different while avoiding simple and static stereotyping: people should be able to shift or choose between different forms of interaction. In contrast to gender stereotyping, a challenge would be to promote gender-balanced interactions, such that women currently flooded with emotional support receive more proactive interventions, and vice versa for men. It should be noted that the tendency of the female participants to discuss their weight and discuss diets reflects that diet was a socially acceptable topic of conversation them. Equally, physical activity lends itself much more easily to collective action than dieting does. We do not suggest that gender predisposes women or men to discussion and action respectively, but that these tendencies are socially constructed and can therefore potentially be reconstructed via social use of technology. When considering the representation of gender in such systems, we would recommend designers *avoid simple stereotyping and consider whether the aim is to develop gender-based or gender-balanced interventions.*

The Mechanics of Disclosure and Participation

Five areas of potential disclosure emerged during this study: weight, perception of weight as a problem, weight management plans, actions and progress. Disclosure strategies ranged from secrecy to selective, partial and incremental exposure. Male interactions tended to focus less on the problems of weight and weight loss, instead displaying proactive tendencies to get others (be it partners or colleagues) involved in the practicalities of weight loss, e.g. taking up sports and making dietary change. Both male and female participants displayed incremental participation in weight loss activities, as well as online and offline communities. Such behavior resonates with the CSCW literature surrounding the practice of learning to be a member of a community through initial observation and gradual engagement [18,25].

The design implications of such observations vary depending on the type of system being developed. With a weight loss program, use is in itself a form of declaration. This may prevent uptake by those reluctant to declare themselves as having weight problems. Lifestyle systems may then be more effective in those cases as they allow a degree of weight anonymity, while more action-based systems support the implicit statement of the underlying problem—instead channeling focus or energy into the proposed solution. Regardless of how the technology is packaged, *selective disclosure and incremental participation should be considered in group-based designs.*

The dynamic nature of disclosure and participation raises specific challenges and questions. If managed automatically, perceived loss of control may prove to be a barrier to adoption. If managed manually, the system should be easily configurable such that it is not laborious to use.

The relative comparability of individuals and their weight management found during the study provides a good grounding for any automatic implementation of selective disclosure. While groups of already established friends are aware of their similarities and differences, broader technologically facilitated groups could benefit from the discovery of or affiliation with comparable people through an automatic social networking mechanism. In addition to traditional metrics such as total or desired weight loss, other aspects of context to be considered are actual weight, previous successes and failures, age, and lifestyle. Such mechanisms of comparison would mean that members of facilitated groups can make informed choices about whom they share advice with and whose examples they follow, in the same way that people who know each other already do.

CONCLUSION

This paper presented our investigation into the sociality of weight management. Our findings emerged through the process of inductive analysis described earlier in the paper, and lead to some caveats to bear in mind: we do not make any claims of absolute generalisability beyond the group studied, and we do not suggest that the family life or gender characteristics observed in this study apply universally. Nevertheless, our work complements the existing body of work on weight-related social influence and behavioural change. While the importance of social support is well established within the sociomedical literature, that literature has also highlighted outstanding ambiguities surrounding the underlying dynamics of social support [6,29]. The main contribution of this work is therefore the unpacking of terms such as social support and peer involvement, which provides actionable insight for research and design in the domain of peer-based weight management technology.

ACKNOWLEDGEMENTS

We thank the study participants and the colleagues who provided support and feedback throughout the study, in particular Scott Sherwood, Barry Brown, and Phil Gray. This work was funded by a UK EPSRC PhD studentship.

REFERENCES

1. Bandura, A. *Social Learning Theory.* General Learning Press, 1977.
2. Berkman, L. and Glass, T. Social integration, social support, and health. In Berkman, L. and Kawachi, I. (Eds.) *Social Epidemiology.* Oxford University Press, 2000.
3. Brown, B., Taylor, A. et al. Locating family values: A field trial of the Whereabouts Clock. In *Proc. Ubicomp 2007*, Springer-Verlag (2007), 354-371.

4. Carpiano, R.M. Toward a neighborhood resource-based theory of social capital for health: Can Bourdieu and sociology help? *Social Science & Medicine* 62 (2005), 165-175.
5. Christakis, N.J. and Fowler, J., H. The spread of obesity in a large social network over 32 years. *New England Journal of Medicine* 357 (2007), 370-379.
6. Chronister, J.A., Johnson, E.K., and Berven, N.L. Measuring social support in rehabilitation', Disability and Rehabilitation, 2006, 28, (2), pp. 75-84.
7. Consolvo, S., Everitt, K. et al. Design Requirements for Technologies that Encourage Physical Activity. In *Proc. CHI 2006*, ACM Press (2006), 457-466.
8. Consolvo, S., McDonald, D.W. and Landay, J.A. Theory-Driven Design Strategies for Technologies that Support Behavior Change in Everyday Life. In *Proc. CHI 2009*, ACM Press (2009), 405-414.
9. Elfhag, K. and Rossner, S. Who succeeds in maintaining weight loss? A conceptual review of factors associated with weight loss maintenance and weight regain. *Obesity Reviews* 6, 1 (2005), 67-85.
10. Festinger, L. A Theory of Social Comparison Processes. *Human Relations* 7 (1954), 117-140.
11. Gasser, R., Brodbeck, D. et al. Persuasiveness of a Mobile Lifestyle Coaching Application using Social Facilitation. In *Proc. Persuasive 2006*, Springer-Verlag (2006), 27-35.
12. Gorin, A., Phelan, S. et al. Involving support partners in obesity treatment. *Journal of Consulting and Clinical Psychology* 73, 2 (2005), 341-343.
13. Grimes, A., Bednar, M. et al. EatWell: sharing nutrition-related memories in a low-income community. In *Proc. CSCW 2008*, ACM Press (2008), 87-96.
14. Grimes, A., Tan, D. and Morris, D. Toward Technologies that Support Family Reflections on Health. In *Proc. GROUP 2009*, ACM Press (2009), 311-320.
15. Harvey-Berino, J., Pintauro, S. et al. Effect of internet support on the long-term maintenance of weight loss. *Obesity Research* 12, 2 (2004), 320-329.
16. Haughton McNeill, L., Kreuter, M.W. and Subramanian, S.V. Social Environment and Physical activity: A review of concepts and evidence. *Social Science & Medicine* 63, 4 (2006), 1011-1022.
17. Kirman, B., Linehan, C. et al. There's a monster in my kitchen: using aversive feedback to motivate behaviour change. *Ext. Abstracts CHI 2010*. ACM Press (2010), 2685-2694.
18. Lave, J. and Wenger, E. *Situated Learning: Legitimate Peripheral Participation*. Cambridge University Press, UK, 1991.
19. Lin, J.J., Mamykina, L. et al. Fish'n'Steps: Encouraging Physical Activity with an Interactive Computer Game. In *Proc. Ubicomp 2006*, Springer-Verlag (2006), 261-268.
20. Lofland, J., Snow, D.A. et al. *Analyzing Social Settings: A Guide to Qualitative Observation and Analysis*. Wadsworth Publishing, 2005.
21. Maitland, J., Sherwood, S. et al. Increasing the Awareness of Daily Activity Levels with Pervasive Computing. In *Proc. Pervasive Health 2006*, IEEE (2006), 1-8.
22. McFerran, B., Dahl, D.W. et al. I'll Have What She's Having: Effects of Social Influence and Body Type on the Food Choices of Others. *Journal of Consumer Research* 36, 6 (2010), 919-925.
23. McLean, N., Griffin, S. et al. Family involvement in weight control, weight maintenance and weight-loss interventions: a systematic review of randomized control trials. *International Journal of Obesity* 27 (2003), 987-1005.
24. Micco, N., Gold, B. et al. Minimal in-person support as an adjunct to internet obesity treatment. *Annals of Behavioral Medicine* 33, 1 (2007), 49-56.
25. Preece, J., Nonnecke, B. and Andrews, D. The top five reasons for lurking: Improving community experiences for everyone. *Computers in Human Behavior* 20, 2 (2004), 201-223.
26. Toscos, T., Faber, A.M. et al. Encouraging Physical Activity in Teens: Can technology help reduce barriers to physical activity in adolescent girls? In *Proc. Pervasive Health 2008*, IEEE (2008), 173-184.
27. Tsai, A., G. and Wadden, T. A. Systematic Review: An Evaluation of Major Commercial Weight Loss Programs in the United States. *Annals of Internal Medicine* 142, 1 (2005), 56-66.
28. Turner, J.C. *Social Influence*. Open University Press, 1991.
29. Verheijden, M.W., Bakx, J.C. et al. Role of social support in lifestyle-focused weight management interventions. *European Journal of Clinical Nutrition* 59, 1 (2005), 179-186.
30. Williamson, D.A. and Stewart, T.M. Behavior and lifestyle: approaches to the treatment of obesity. *Journal of the Louisiana State Medical Society* 157, S1 (2005), S50-S55.
31. Wing, R.R., Tate, D.F. et al. A self-regulation program for maintenance of weight-loss. *New England Journal of Medicine* 355, 15(2006), 1563-1571.
32. Zajonc, R.B. Social Facilitation: A solution is suggested for an old unresolved psychological problem. *Science* 149 (1965), 269-274.

Mining Behavioral Economics to Design Persuasive Technology for Healthy Choices

Min Kyung Lee[1], Sara Kiesler[1], Jodi Forlizzi[1,2]
[1]Human Computer Interaction Institute, [2]School of Design
Carnegie Mellon University
{mklee, kiesler, forlizzi}@cs.cmu.edu

ABSTRACT
Influence through information and feedback has been one of the main approaches of persuasive technology. We propose another approach based on behavioral economics research on decision-making. This approach involves designing the presentation and timing of choices to encourage people to make self-beneficial decisions. We applied three behavioral economics persuasion techniques—the default option strategy, the planning strategy, and the asymmetric choice strategy—to promote healthy snacking in the workplace. We tested the strategies in three experimental case studies using a human snack deliverer, a robot, and a snack ordering website. The default and the planning strategies were effective, but they worked differently depending on whether the participants had healthy dietary lifestyles or not. We discuss designs for persuasive technologies that apply behavioral economics.

Author Keywords
Persuasive technology, behavioral economics, health technology, default bias, present-biased preferences, asymmetric dominance, snacking, healthy eating, choice.

ACM Classification Keywords
H5.2. Information interfaces and presentation (e.g., HCI): User Interfaces.

General Terms
Design

INTRODUCTION
The role of information technology in people's daily decision making is steadily growing. For example, we decide which route and transportation to take to visit a friend's house, which restaurant to go for dinner, or which grocery products to buy based on the information and choices presented in information technology applications. This change offers tremendous opportunities for human-computer interaction (HCI) researchers to provide interventions to assist people to make self-beneficial or pro-social choices.

Many researchers have investigated ways to use technology to convince people to adopt healthy or sustainable lifestyles [9]. One of the most common approaches has been to use information and feedback to encourage behavioral change. By inducing users to set goals and providing them with feedback about their current behavior, this approach seeks to increase people's awareness about an issue and to encourage them to change their behavior.

We suggest an alternative approach, drawn from the field of behavioral economics. Behavioral economics examines the gamut of large and small decisions people make about such choices as how much to invest in retirement savings, whether to join a health club, and whether to eat a delicious but caloric candy bar. The persuasive element in this approach consists of presenting choices in a way that leverages people's decision processes and induces them to make self-beneficial choices [3].

We argue that designs for HCI that leverage behavioral economics theory and research are a highly promising avenue for persuasive technologies. Although widely discussed outside the HCI and design communities in both academic and popular arenas (e.g., [31]), this approach has not yet influenced our field. The message of behavioral economics is simple: people are susceptible to decision bias, which often makes it hard for them to make self-beneficial choices. Thus, we should present choices in a way that helps people to make self-beneficial choices and understand the implications of their decisions as well—all without restricting their freedom of choice. Although behavioral economics principles can be applied in many domains, we address healthy eating, particularly workplace snacking. Workplace snacking is pervasive and often highly caloric; high-calorie snack choices are shown to contribute to obesity [22].

In this paper, we make three contributions. We first present different ways that behavioral economics approaches can be applied to the design of persuasive technology in the domain of healthy snacking. Second, we demonstrate through three experimental case studies the efficacy of behavioral economics approaches in comparison to other persuasive approaches. Finally, in testing these approaches, we inform behavioral economics theory by adding an understanding of how the theory works with people's existing habits and how it influences people's experience.

PERSUASIVE TECHNOLOGY FOR HEALTHY EATING

We are not the first to conduct HCI research in the domain of healthy eating. Researchers have designed technologies to encourage people to adopt healthy dietary lifestyles [2, 11, 21]. For example, Chi et al.'s intelligent kitchen provides nutritional information about ingredients at the time of cooking so people can adjust their ingredients accordingly [5]. Autom, a weight management robot, helps people keep track of what they have eaten that day and calculates caloric and nutritional information with respect to their set goals [13]. These and other applications help people make informed choices about what they eat by providing nutritional information, tracking their behavior, and providing feedback.

These applications are similar in that they provide information for people to better understand nutritional information about food. However, research points to some potential disadvantages of using information-centric techniques to motivate healthy eating. Providing calorie information about food that is about to be eaten can reinforce feelings of guilt about eating high-calorie food and reduce people's enjoyment of food [25]. Providing calorie information about certain foods at the moment of choice can even lead to an increase in calorie consumption. Wansink and Chandon found that labeling a snack food as "low fat" led people to eat more of it and they felt less guilty about doing so [32]. Other studies of nutritional labeling show very limited effects [e.g., 28].

APPLYING BEHAVIORAL ECONOMICS

We argue that behavioral economics could avoid the potential downside of information-centric approaches. Departing from the premise of economics that people make rational choices, behavioral economists have shown that people's decision making processes are biased by various situational factors, such as the manner in which options are presented and the times when the choices are offered, and the emotional or visceral state of the person at the time of choice [3, 15]. This understanding of people's decision biases provides a rich repertoire of tools that designers can leverage. In this section, we present three different ways that behavioral economics theories can be applied to design technology that promotes healthy eating.

Default bias

When people make choices, they tend to favor the default option or the status quo, rather than taking the time to consider and then adopt an alternative state [14, 27]. People tend to take "the path of least resistance," and keep doing what they have been doing, or doing what comes automatically, even when they can make improvements. The reasons for this decision bias could have roots in people's limited attention and tendency to "satisfice" [27], their perception that an organization's selection of a default option constitutes a recommendation (see [8]), and the implied popularity of the default option.

Default biases have been blamed for a wide range of undesirable outcomes, including Americans' excessive consumption of fries and large sodas as part of "supersized" meals at McDonald's [18]. Yet if carefully designed, the default bias can be a powerful tool to propel people toward self-beneficial behaviors (see [18, 30]).

HCI design can leverage the default bias in many ways, by making healthy choices more convenient and salient physically and cognitively. In the domain of snacking, featured healthy snacks can be made easy to access, e.g., on websites, on vending carts, and so forth. For example, on a website, the checkbox of healthy snacks among available options could be selected as the default, reducing the need to select one of these options explicitly. Or when presenting sale items at a bakery, a system could filter and first offer items that are made with whole grain flours. For a kiosk system, the placement of buttons, the number of clicks or the number of screens a user has to access to choose an item could be decreased or increased to change the perceived priority of a snack or sandwich order.

An eldercare robot working in a nursing home could organize the physical placement of food in a way that the healthy food is placed closer to an elder's room. In addition, a snack delivery robot might only deliver healthy snacks to people's offices, but require people to walk to the robot to get unhealthy snacks.

Convenience can be further leveraged using sensing technologies that tell people when they are near healthy snacks. For instance, if shoppers are in a food court in a mall, the system could present healthy choices to them via mobile phone as convenient food options.

Present-biased preferences

Present-biased preferences represent people's tendency to weigh the pros and cons of present choices more heavily than future choices, and to underestimate their needs in the future. This decision bias is also known as "time discounting" [20]. The tendency typically promotes unhealthy eating because the immediate pull of tasty food is likely to eclipse considerations of future health consequences. However, present-biased preferences can be used to encourage healthier choices if people are asked to plan ahead. Read and van Leeuwen [26] gave their participants a choice of snack to be eaten in one week or at the time of eating, the next week. They found that their participants chose far more unhealthy snacks for immediate choice than for advance choice.

Present-biased preferences can be leveraged by strategically designing the time that technology applications prompt users to make certain choices. Researchers in context-aware technology have been designing applications that can sense the current activity of people and learn their routines over time [6]. A meal planning application or a restaurant reservation system that nudges people to make a choice when they are less likely to be hungry (i.e., 1-2 hours after their lunch) might be as effective as the application that uses persuasive messages or calorie information, and it might be felt to be less intrusive.

Asymmetrically dominated choices

People tend to make choices that are easier to judge as superior than other alternatives. One example of this tendency is the "asymmetric dominated choice" [12], which means placing a choice option next to an inferior option to increase its attractiveness. For instance, consider a cookie as compared to a large, shiny Fuji apple and a small withered apple. By pairing the Fuji with the withered apple, the Fuji's value seems much higher, and choices of the Fuji will increase.

Relevance of behavioral economics to HCI theories

The above-mentioned behavioral economics theories have some linkages to other theories and principles commonly used in the field of HCI. Both approaches identify factors that influence decision-making and derive design principles from them. Theories about information processing limits (e.g., the model human processor [4]) and human cognition (e.g., cognitive tunneling [32]) predict when people are likely to use heuristics in decision making, as does behavioral economics. Research on user interface design offers design principles for designing displays, controls, and response options (e.g., consistency, reduce short-term memory) to improve ease of use and efficiency of interfaces [24, 29]. Designs for interfaces drawn from behavioral economics theories have a different goal, that is, to encourage self-beneficial choices, even when they are not what users want most. For example, in contrast to the practice of putting most used-menu items in a salient and accessible location on a screen, using a default strategy from behavioral economics would have us place less frequent or less popular items that are healthy in a more convenient place, with the hope that people would choose the most convenient item, rather than their usual item.

Challenges in applying theories to design

It is not immediately clear how one can apply behavioral economics to persuasive technologies to support beneficial choices in everyday domains such as eating. The intervention design should be powerful enough to work against people's existing unhealthy preferences and habits (e.g., their favorite sweet). Eating can especially be driven by strong visceral urges that could overcome any particular architecture of choice [19]. At the same time, the intervention must avoid intrusiveness. For example, offering a default option might hamper people's enjoyable experience of making a choice.

We argue that systematic design iteration and evaluation of theory-based design is critical to assess whether it is desirable and powerful enough to lead to changes in people's decision making. Some interventions may not be effective enough to result in behavioral change, and others may be perceived too forceful and manipulative.

We have begun to explore ways of using behavioral economics principles in the everyday domain of snacking and to evaluate them experimentally. We measured people's existing habits (i.e., diet style) and enjoyment of their choices to test whether the strategies would be effective for people with unhealthy eating habits, and whether the strategies would have a negative impact on people's experience.

OVERVIEW OF EXPERIMENTAL CASE STUDIES

In our experimental case studies, we focused on three strategies, pursuing the following research questions.

Study 1: Do planning and default choices work effectively in promoting healthy snack choices?

Study 2: Do default choices work in presenting healthy snack choices when a robot offers the snack? Can we strengthen the effect of default by manipulating cognitive load through a robot's dialogue?

Study 3: Do default choices work when they are implemented on a screen-based interface? How well do the default choices work when compared to asymmetric choice and information-centric approaches? Can we strengthen the effect of default by manipulating perceptual load using a screen interface component?

We implemented these strategies on three different platforms, one with a human snack deliverer, a second using a snack delivery robot, and a third using a snack ordering website.

STUDY 1: DEFAULT VS. PLANNING STRATEGIES

We conducted a between-subjects field experiment over two days. The design was a one-way factorial with three conditions: Control, Default, and Plan. The participants were randomly assigned to one of the three conditions.

Participants

We recruited 61 faculty, administrative staff, and graduate students in a university (Control condition: N = 21; Default condition: N = 20; Plan condition: N=20). Seventy-four percent of the participants were female. People who were allergic to the snacks or had medical conditions that could influence their choices of snacks could not participate.

Procedure

An experimenter visited participants in their offices in the afternoon (2:00 p.m. to 4:30 p.m.) on two days, carrying snacks in a bag. The experiment was double blind, and the experimenter was not aware of the hypotheses of the study. On both days, the experimenter offered participants a choice between two types of apples and two types of cookies. We used two types of apples and cookies to discourage people from choosing a different snack category on each day only for the sake of diversity [16]. On Day 1, the experimenter asked participants whether they wanted to participate in the test of a new snack delivery service. Once they agreed, participants were randomly assigned to one of three conditions: Control, Default, and Plan.

Control condition. On Day 1, the experimenter told participants about the next day's visit, and asked them to choose a snack to eat now: "We have two options: apples or cookies. Which snack would you like to have?" We did not counterbalance the order of snacks because the same snacks were used in all conditions. On Day 2, the experimenter visited the participants again, and gave them the same choice.

Default condition. On Day 1, the experimenter asked participants to make a choice of an apple or cookie. The experimenter also told participants that the snack for Day 2 would be apples, but that they could change the snack: "I brought two snacks today, but for the next visit, I will only bring apples. If you would like to have a cookie instead of an apple, please tell me." On Day 2, the experimenter brought the snack the participant specified but offered to get a different snack if the participant wished.

Plan condition. On Day 1, before choosing the snack for that day, the experimenter asked participants to plan ahead for Day 2 by saying, "I brought apples and cookies today, but for the next visit I will bring only one of the snacks. Can you tell me what snack you would like to have for the next visit?" On Day 2, the experimenter returned and brought the planned snack, but gave the participant the option of changing his or her mind.

At the end of the Day 2 visit, all participants completed a brief survey.

Measures

The effectiveness of each strategy was measured as the percentage of participants choosing apples for Day 2. We also measured whether they changed their choice on Day 2 when the experimenter delivered the snacks. To measure the influence of the strategies on the enjoyment of their snack choice, we asked participants on Day 2 to rate on 5-point Likert scales how much they had enjoyed their snack on Day 1 and how much they thought they would enjoy their chosen Day 2 snack. We also asked participants whether they were currently on a diet or vegetarian.

Results of Study 1

On Day 1, 51% of the participants chose apples and 49% chose cookies. On Day 2, 33% of the participants in the Control condition chose apples. There were no differences depending on participants' gender, or whether they were on a diet. However, vegetarians only ate apples, so we used this factor as a control variable in all the regressions. We used mixed model regressions to control for the within subjects variable of Day 1 vs. Day 2 choice.

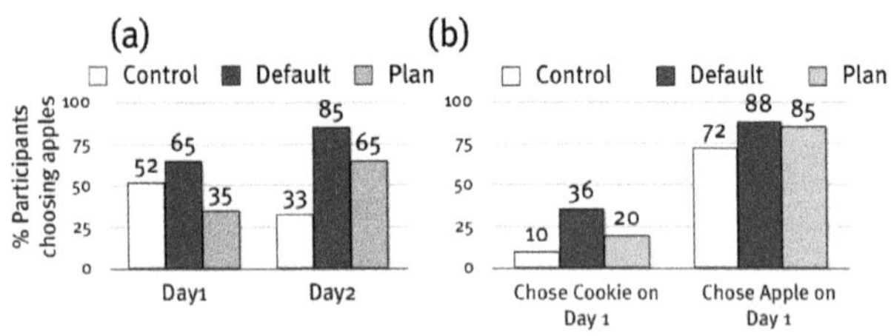

Figure 1. (a) Percentage of participants choosing an apple in the Control, Default, and Plan conditions on Day 1 and Day 2; (b) Percentage of participants choosing an apple on Day 2 depending on their choice on Day 1.

Effect of the default option strategy

In the Default condition, 65% of the participants chose an apple on Day 1 and 85% did so for Day 2. That is, all but two participants in the default condition chose an apple for Day 2. This is a marginally significant increase in the healthy choice from Day 1 to Day 2 ($F [1, 39] = 2.51$, $p = .10$; Figure 1a). The percentage of the participants choosing an apple for Day 2 was greater in the Default condition than in the Control condition ($F [1,71] = 12.01$, $p < .01$). All but two participants stayed with their choice when the snack was delivered on Day 2.

Effect of planning strategy

As compared to the Control condition results, participants in the Plan condition tended to choose an apple on Day 2 (Figure 1a). In the Plan condition, 35% of the participants chose an apple on Day 1, but 65% of the participants did so for Day 2, showing a significant increase ($F [1,39] = 5.22$, $p < .05$). Significantly more participants chose an apple for Day 2 in the Plan condition than in the Control condition ($F [1,71] = 4.87$, $p < .05$). All but three participants stayed with their planned choice when their snack was delivered. In the Control condition, there was no significant difference in terms of the number of participants choosing apples between Day 1 and Day 2.

Choice on Day 2 as a function of choice on Day 1

The results above do not control for people's preferences on Day 1. We ran a regression model predicting the choice of snack on Day 2 as a function of condition, choice on Day 1, and the interaction (Figure 1b). In all conditions, the participants who chose an apple on Day 1 tended to choose an apple again on Day 2 (Control: 72%; Default: 88%; Plan: 85%). However, the differences across conditions remained whereby more participants in the Default and Plan conditions chose an apple for Day 2 ($F [2, 49] = 5.4$, $p < .01$). There was an interesting difference among participants who chose a cookie on Day 1. In the Control condition, 90% of the participants who chose a cookie on Day 1 also chose a cookie on Day 2. In the Plan condition, 80% of those who chose a cookie on Day 1 also chose a cookie on Day 2. However, in the Default condition, only 64% of the participants who chose a cookie on Day 1 chose a cookie on Day 2. When compared to the Control condition, the Default is significantly different ($F [1, 49] = 4.77$, $p < .03$). This result suggests that the default option strategy could be effective in influencing people who like sweets to consider an apple as a snack.

Effect on enjoyment

Participants were asked on Day 2 to rate how much they had enjoyed their snack on the previous day, and how much they anticipated enjoying the snack that had just been delivered to them. There was no difference across conditions in how much participants liked the cookie versus the apple on Day 1, how much they expected to like a cookie or apple on Day 2, or how much people retrospectively say they enjoyed their Day 1 snack.

On the other hand, we did find a difference in people's anticipated enjoyment of their snack choice for Day 2 across conditions ($F [2, 43] = 3.0$, $p = .05$). Participants in the Default and Plan conditions said that they would enjoy the snack they chose for Day 2 slightly less than did those in the Control condition. (Control M = 4.6; Default M = 4.3; Plan M = 4.4) This analysis excludes the five participants who changed their mind when the snack was delivered on Day 2; those participants said they would enjoy their (changed) snack more (mean = 4.8). The drop in anticipated enjoyment occurred in both the Plan and Default conditions but was significantly different only in the Default condition ($F [1, 43] = 4.7$, $p < .05$).

Discussion of Study 1

The default option and plan strategies were effective in inducing people to choose healthy snacks. When the participants were asked to plan their future snack in advance, with or without the default, they chose an apple over a cookie. However, the default strategy was significantly more effective in influencing those who chose a cookie on Day 1 to switch to an apple on Day 2 than was the plan strategy. This finding suggests that the default option strategy may be a more powerful tool than planning ahead alone.

We also found that enjoyment of the Day 2 snack dropped in the Plan and the Default conditions. Possibly, participants felt implicit pressure to have a healthy snack, or simply did not like planning a snack in advance. Framing a healthy snack as the default snack that the delivery person would carry may have exacerbated this feeling. This finding suggested we select a design in the next study that would not involve planning ahead.

STUDY 2: DEFAULT STRATEGY APPLIED TO A ROBOT

In Study 2, we applied the lesson from the human-human experiment to the design of a robot. We focused on the default strategy because it was slightly more effective for people with less healthy lifestyles. We tested a different implementation of the default strategy because the default strategy seemed to reduce people's subjective enjoyment of their snack choice in Study 1. Instead of framing the healthy snack as the default choice, we changed the presentation of the snack choices by varying their convenience [7]. In the Default condition, we placed the healthy snacks in a slightly more convenient place than the unhealthy snacks. In addition, we introduced a cognitive load variable as a way to strengthen the effect of the default strategy. We speculated that higher cognitive load might consume participants' cognitive resources and cause them to opt for the default snack more when they were thinking about something else. This resulted in a 2 x 2 between subjects design, with Control versus Default strategy as one variable, and Low versus High Cognitive Load as a second variable. The participants were randomly assigned to one of four conditions.

Participants

Posters and a website offered people in our office building a free snack in exchange for walk-in participation in a study. The 119 participants (Control condition: N = 59; Default condition: N = 60) consisted of students, faculty, staff, and visitors. Thirty-nine percent of the participants were female. Those with allergies or medical conditions were excluded from the study.

Robot

The Snackbot robot [17] (Figure 2) offered snacks during the experiment. The robot was 4'5" tall and carried a tray on which snacks were placed. We developed a custom dialog, speech, and audio manager system for the robot.

Procedure

The experimenter left the participant in a room with the robot. The Snackbot introduced itself, saying, "Good morning [afternoon]. My name is Snackbot and I'm from Carnegie Mellon University." The robot then asked the participant to answer a puzzle before taking the snack. The Snackbot then instructed each participant to take his or her

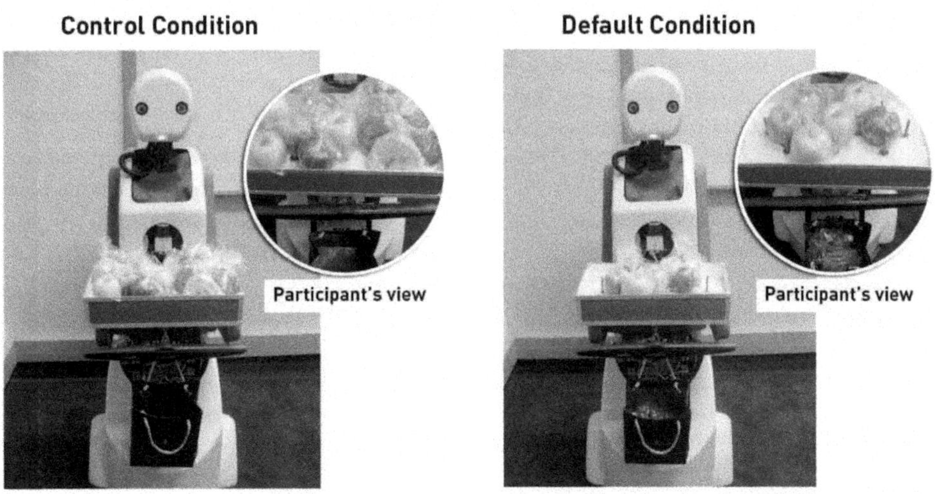

Figure 2. Manipulation of the Control and Default conditions in Study 2.

snack. As in Study 1, we used two types of apples as healthy snacks and two types of cookies as unhealthy snacks. After the participant chose a snack, the robot directed the participant to another room to fill out a survey.

Default vs. Control conditions. We created two types of snack presentation by slightly varying how convenient it was for participants to reach their snack (Figure 2). In the Control condition, six wrapped apples and six wrapped cookies were placed on the robot's tray. A bag hanging under the tray was left empty. In the Default condition, six wrapped apples were place on the tray and six wrapped cookies were placed in the bag hanging under the tray. The bag was easily visible to participants. After each participant left, the experimenter replenished the snacks, so that the number of snacks that each participant saw was the same.

Cognitive Load. Each participant had to answer a question before he or she chose a snack. In the low cognitive load condition, the robot asked the participant a very easy question, "What is two plus two?" In the high cognitive load condition, the robot said, "There are 102 offices on this floor. On average, there are two people in each office. If I visit each of these offices three times a week, on average, how many deliveries do I make?" Participants got a snack regardless of their answers. The cognitive load factor, as we manipulated it, had no effect on choices of snack, so we do not discuss this variation further.

Measures

The main dependent variable was the percentage of participants choosing apples. We also measured self-reported healthy eating behaviors by using a scale measuring healthy eating behavior [23]. The items included "read product labels," "take active steps to eat a well-balanced diet," "watch fat," and "watch sugar." The items were rated on a 5-point Likert scale, where 1 = almost never, 5 = almost always (Cronbach's alpha = .80). We divided the participants with an average score of less than 3 into a low healthy diet score group, and those with higher than 3 into a high healthy diet score group.

We measured each participant's anticipated enjoyment of his or her snack choice using a 5-point Likert scale. To measure experimental demand, we asked participants to say why they chose their snack. We also measured how hungry participants said they were at the moment of choice, since hunger level can be a factor that influences people's snack choice [26], and if they were vegetarian, vegan, or dieters.

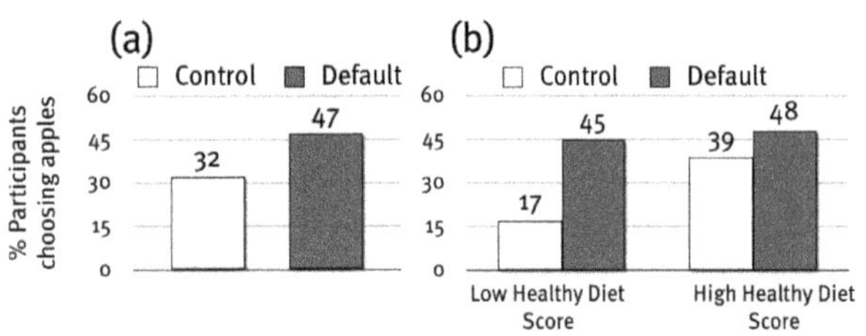

Figure 3. (a) Percentage of participants choosing an apple in the Control, and Default conditions in Study 2; (b) Percentage of participants with low and high healthy diet scores choosing an apple in the Control and Default conditions in Study 2.

Results of Study 2

Thirty-nine percent of the participants chose an apple from the robot. There were no differences due to participants' gender, or whether participants were vegetarian, or how hungry participants were. However, those who reported being on a diet tended to choose apples, so we used this variable as a control variable in all the regressions.

Effect of the default strategy

We conducted regression analyses testing for the effect of Default versus Control conditions, controlling for whether participants were dieters. The participants were more likely to choose an apple in the Default condition, when apples were placed on the tray and cookies were placed in the bag. Thirty-two percent of the participants chose an apple in the Control condition, whereas 47% chose an apple in the Default condition ($F[1, 118] = 3.8$, $p = .05$; Figure 3a).

Effect of the default strategy on those with different eating lifestyles

We conducted another regression predicting snack choice, adding a variable for whether participants scored high or low on the healthy eating scale. The analysis shows a significant main effect of the Default vs. Control conditions ($F[1,118] = 4.54$, $p < .05$), and a significant main effect of the dieter control variable ($F[1,118] = 6.31$). The interaction with the high vs. low healthy eating scale was not significant. However, the Default condition showed an interesting trend and marginally significant influence on the choices of participants with a low healthy eating score. In the low healthy diet score group, 45% of the participants chose an apple in the Default condition whereas only 17% did so in the Control condition ($F[1, 114] = 3.37$, $p = .07$; Figure 3b). In the high healthy eating scale group, 39% of participants in the Control condition chose an apple whereas 48% did so in the Default condition.

Effect of the default strategy on enjoyment

We conducted a regression to compare the differences in participants' enjoyment of their choice depending on the conditions. Participants' perceived enjoyment did not differ between conditions (Control M = 4.34, Default M = 4.33). There also was no statistical difference in enjoyment of the two snack types (Cookie = 4.35, Apple = 4.30).

Awareness of the manipulation

The number of participants who chose "convenience" as one of the reasons why they chose their snack did not significantly differ across conditions (Control = 5%, Default = 11%). Also, when questioned after the study, participants did not indicate any concern with the difference in the location of the apples and the cookies.

Discussion of Study 2

Study 2 showed that making healthy snacks slightly more accessible and convenient is effective in influencing people to make a healthier snack choice. The default option strategy also was marginally effective in influencing participants with less healthy dietary lifestyles to make a healthy choice. In contrast to Study 1, the default option strategy that varied convenience did not negatively influence the participants' perceived enjoyment of their snack. We think participants were not aware of any social pressure to choose a healthy snack. Those who chose an apple also did not seem to think that they chose it because it was right in front of them on the tray and less convenient than the cookie in the bag.

STUDY 3: DEFAULT, ASYMMETRIC CHOICE, AND INFORMATION STRATEGIES APPLIED TO A WEBSITE

The results of Study 1 and Study 2 show that framing an item as default and making a healthy choice physically more convenient can promote healthy choices. In Study 3, we applied the strategy to a screen-based user interface. We applied the default strategy on the presentation of choices to a snack ordering website, and compared it with an asymmetric choice presentation and information feedback approach. We also combined the Default with a dynamic visual design in the form of a banner to strengthen its effect. This resulted in a between-subjects design, with Control, Information Feedback, Default, Default with Banner, and Asymmetric conditions. The participants were randomly assigned to one of the five conditions.

Website

We used a website for people to order snacks to be delivered by the Snackbot (Figure 4). Participants selected a picture of a food item and dragged it to a picture of a shopping cart to place a snack order. We manipulated the presentation of snacks in the following manner:

Control: The website showed healthy and unhealthy snacks in two columns on one page.

Information: The website showed calorie information for each snack and a green banner to indicate healthy snacks.

Default: The website showed only two snacks at a time; participants needed to press "next" and "previous" buttons to browse the snacks. Healthy snacks were presented on the first two pages; unhealthy snacks were presented on the last two pages.

Default +Banner: The website showed an animated banner of the Snackbot logo instead of the static Snackbot logo. The presentation of snacks was same as Default.

Asymmetric Choice: The website showed one Fuji apple and one smaller Macintosh as the first two snacks.

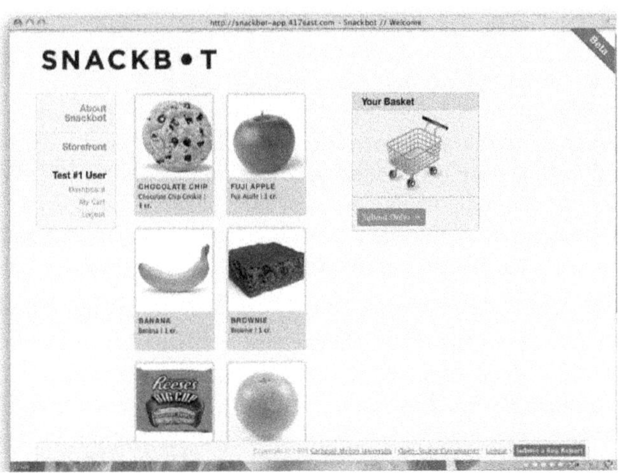

Figure 4. Snack ordering website used for Study 3 showing the Control condition.

The sequence of snacks for each condition was randomized except Default and Default + Banner that were randomized within the healthy or unhealthy snack categories. For Asymmetric Choice, Fuji and Macintosh remained at the top all the time; other snacks were randomized.

Participants

We recruited passers-by in our office buildings. There were 100 participants (Control N = 20, Information N = 20, Default N = 19, Default + Banner N = 19, and Asymmetric Choice N = 20), of whom 44% were female. People with allergies or medical conditions were excluded.

Procedure

The experimenters set up a table in a public place and invited people to test the snack ordering website and receive a free snack of their choice. Once participants chose a snack on the website, the experimenters gave them a snack, and asked them to fill out a questionnaire. We used two types of apples, bananas, and oranges as healthy snacks and chocolate chip cookies, brownies, and two types of candy bars as unhealthy snacks [26]. We put all the snacks in paper bags, so that participants could not see which snacks were offered until they interacted with the website.

Measures

We used the same measures as we used in Study 2. The main dependent variable was the percentage of participants choosing a healthy snack.

Results of Study 3

Across conditions, 53% of the participants chose a healthy snack on the website. There were no differences depending on participants' gender, hunger level, or whether they were vegetarian or dieters.

Effects of the Default, Default+Banner, Asymmetric Choice, and Information Strategies

We conducted regression analyses testing for the main effect of the conditions. The main effect was significant ($F[4,95] = 15.89$, $p <.001$; Figure 5a). The participants were more likely to choose a healthy snack in the Default condition (100%) and Default + Banner condition (95%) as compared to the Control condition (42%; $F[1, 91]=21.44$, $p<.001$). The difference between the Default and Default + Banner conditions was not significant, nor was the difference between the Asymmetric Choice (47%) and Control conditions. Those in the Information condition were least likely to make a healthy choice (20%), a result statistically different from the Asymmetric Choice

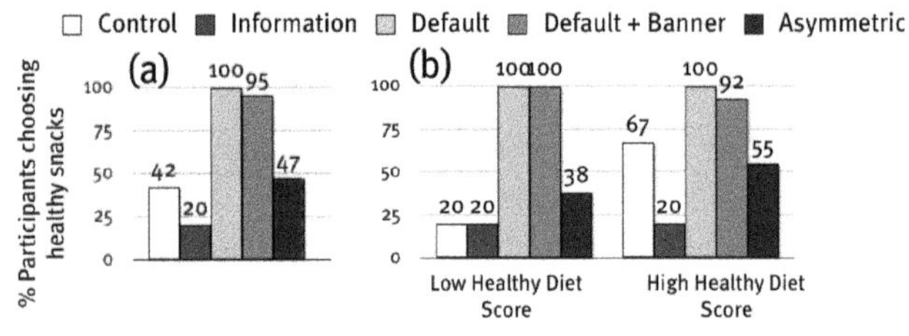

Figure 5. (a) Percentage of participants choosing a healthy snacks in Study 3; (b) Percentage of participants with low and high healthy diet scale scores choosing a healthy snack in Study 3.

condition ($F[1, 91] = 4.91$, $p < .03$) and, marginally, from the Control ($F[1, 91] = 3.21$, $p < .08$) condition.

Effects of the strategies with different eating lifestyles

We conducted another regression predicting snack choice, adding a variable for whether participants scored high or low on the healthy eating scale. The analysis shows a significant main effect of the different conditions ($F[4,95] = 14.92$, $p < .001$; Figure 5b). The interaction effect with the high vs. low healthy eating scale was not significant. The Default and Default+Banner conditions showed that they had significant influence on the choices of the participants with a low healthy eating score, as in Study 2. In the low healthy diet score group, all participants chose healthy snacks in the Default condition whereas only 20% did so in the Control condition ($F[1,86] = 16.75$, $p < .001$). The calorie information worked negatively in the healthy diet score group, similar to the behaviors of dieters reported in [7]. In the high healthy diet score group, only 20% of the participants in the Information condition chose healthy snacks in contrast to the Control condition where 67% did so ($F[1,86] = 7.20$, $p < .01$).

Effect of default strategy on enjoyment

We conducted a regression to compare the differences in participants' enjoyment of their snack choice depending on the conditions. Participants' perceived enjoyment did not differ across the conditions (Control M = 4.17, Default M = 4.53, Default + Banner M = 4.53, Asymmetric M = 4.34, Information M = 4.42) or between snack types (Healthy M = 4.45, Unhealthy M = 4.33).

Awareness of the manipulation

Most frequently mentioned reasons for snack choices were Taste (N=69), followed by Health (N=29), and Convenience (N=5). The distribution of the answers did not differ across the conditions. This finding suggests that the participants were not knowingly influenced by the convenience or information manipulation.

Discussion of Study 3

Study 3 showed that placing healthy snacks on the first page of the website is extremely effective in influencing people to make a healthier snack choice. Even though the "next page" button was right below the snack choices and clicking a button did not require much effort, very few people clicked the buttons. One explanation for this result could be that, even though the website was visually clean, participants were drawn to the photos of snacks first, and intuitively tried to place them in the shopping cart, without looking at the whole structure of the site [32].

Study 3 also shows that the Information condition, which showed calorie information, along with the green banner, influenced participants with a healthy diet style to choose unhealthy snacks. There might be two reasons for this effect. Participants might have thought that a candy bar has fewer calories than what they expected, so they might have indulged themselves in the high-caloric snack. An alternative explanation is that by just seeing the obvious healthy snacks indicated by the low calorie count may have made them satisfy their desire to consider healthy snacks, so that they instead chose unhealthy snacks [34].

GENERAL DISCUSSION

Study 1, 2, and 3 suggest that designs drawn from behavioral economics can be useful to promote healthy snack choices, and further, that technology can be persuasive using extremely simple techniques.

Efficacy of default, plan & asymmetric choice strategies

The default strategy was consistently shown to be effective in promoting healthy choices across different systems, even for participants with less healthy diet lifestyles (Study 1, 2, 3). The findings suggest that the default option strategy could be a useful tool to encourage healthy snacking, even among those who may not aware of their potential dietary issues. The planning strategy worked as well, but only with those who already had healthy eating habits (Study 1). The asymmetric choice strategy did not influence the participants' choices (Study 3). Our results are especially interesting given the failure of many information-centric approaches, including food labeling [28], and calorie information as shown in our Study 3.

Different designs and their influence on user experience

Our results suggest how a behavioral economics theory strategy is designed and implemented makes a difference in the outcome. Even when based on the same theoretical principle, the ways that we designed the default strategy influenced people's experiences differently. Being asked to think ahead, with or without a default, reduced participants' enjoyment of their snack choice. When implemented by varying physical placement of snacks on the robot (Study 2) and spatial position of snack choices on the website (Study 3), the default strategies did not reduce participants' enjoyment of their snack choice. These findings suggest that designs that do not involve conscious effort may work best.

We also speculate that different media might also influence people's decision-making differently. The percentage of participants who chose an apple in the Control condition of Study 2 was lower than those who chose an apple in the Control condition of Study 1. Even though we cannot compare Study 1 and Study 2 because they were conducted at different times, we propose that the difference might have arisen from the difference between human-human interaction and human-robot interaction. Participants who interacted with a person in Study 1 might have felt social pressure to make a healthy choice. Evidently, this pressure did not apply to interacting with the robot.

Limitations and future work

Our experiments have limitations. First, we tested the proposed strategies with a one-time choice. Future work will examine the effectiveness of the strategies over repeated choices. Second, we tested the strategies with a snack choice. Even though we believe that choosing a snack is a typical example of everyday dietary choice, meal choices have different characteristics (such as higher stakes) that would need to be studied.

We believe behavioral economics research in general, not limited to the principles presented in this paper, has implications for broader areas in HCI. As sensors and systems that can readily track human behavior become more ubiquitous [6], behavioral economics is a theoretical approach that can be used to better time and structure information to help people make decisions that change their behavior. Beyond the domain of healthy snacking, designs drawn from behavioral economics can be harnessed in other HCI application areas such as healthcare, sustainability, education, and others.

Ethics of persuasive designs

This study, along with the general approach to influencing choices via behavioral economics, requires ethical analysis [1, 10]. Some may argue that using behavioral economics approaches to promote healthy choices, and persuasive designs more generally, do not pose a serious ethical dilemma, as they do not limit people's choices [3]. However, the reality is that whenever designers of technology make judgments on behalf of their users, whether good or bad, ethics comes into play. Even though full choices are presented, what if many of them are easy to miss or understand? When applying behavioral economics approaches, designers need to be aware of the balance between "subtly more convenient," vs. "too convenient to the extent it is the only option."

Another caveat in using behavioral economics approaches might be its lack of educational effect. In comparison to persuasive techniques that use informative messages (e.g., indicating consequences of choices), the behavioral economics approaches proposed in the paper do not provide any information that people can use to reflect on their behaviors and learn the consequences of their choices. If users are subsequently put in a new environment without the interventions, the changed behaviors may not continue. Designers using behavioral economics approaches should be aware of this potential problem, and consider using them with educational methods. New research is needed to understand the long-term effects of these techniques.

Finally, although we chose a domain, snack choices, about which there is general agreement as to the "healthy" choice and best interest of the user, the agreement of what is a best choice is controversial in many domains. For instance, some online companies use the default option strategy (opt out) to induce people to agree to receive commercial emails. Such strategies would seem to be questionable ethically because the user's best interest is not central. Ethical analysis of designs derived from behavioral economics would be a fruitful and important area for future work in HCI.

CONCLUSION

We investigated and evaluated three ways to apply behavioral economics research in the design of persuasive technology. Our studies show that extremely simple changes in user interfaces can have substantial impact on people's choices. Given the increasing role of information technology in people's lives, it will be the responsibility of the HCI community to acknowledge the importance of a simple design choice, and use this in a way that promotes self-beneficial choices. We believe HCI researchers and designers should look to the field of behavioral economics as it provides a deep understanding of people's decision making processes, and ways to harness them. We hope this work provides inspiration that knowledge from the field of behavioral economics can be combined powerfully with design thinking to create products and services that benefit humankind.

ACKNOWLEDGEMENTS

This research was supported by NSF grants IIS-0624275 and CNS 709077. We thank George Loewenstein for his guidance, and Andy Echenique, Kimberley Nederlof, and Leonard Turnier for helping conduct the experiments. We acknowledge Paul Rybski, Jack Ferris, David Kohlbrenner, and Chun Yu for their work on the Snackbot robot, and Austin Bales and Tak Yeon Lee for their work on the website. Min Kyung Lee was supported by Kwanjeong Educational Foundation.

REFERENCES

1. Berdichevsky, D. & Neuenschwander, E. (1999). Toward an ethics of persuasive technology. *Communications of the ACM, 42 (5).*
2. Brown, B., Chetty, M., Grimes, A., & Harmon, E., (2006). Reflecting on health: A system for students to monitor diet and exercise. In *Proceedings of CHI'06*, 1807-1812.
3. Camerer, C., Issacharoff, S., Samuel, C., & Loewenstein, G. (2003). Regulation for Conservatives: Behavioral Economics and the Case for "Asymmetric Paternalism." *University of Pennsylvania Law Review, 151*, 1211-1254.
4. Card, S., Moran, T., and Newell, A. (1986). The model human processor: An engineering model of human performance. In *Handbook of Perception and Human Performance.* John Wiley and Sons, 1-35.

5. Chi, P.-Y., Chen, J.-H., Chu, H.-H. & Chen, B.-Y. (2007). Enabling nutrition-aware cooking in a smart kitchen. In *Proceedings of CHI'07*, 2333-2338.

6. Dey, A. K. (2001). Understanding and using context. *Journal of Personal and Ubiquitous Computing,* 4-7.

7. Downs, J., Loewenstein, G., & Wisdom, J. (2009) Strategies for promoting healthier food choices. *American Economic Review, 99,*159-164.

8. Feldman, M.S., & March, J.G. (1981). Information in organizations as signal and symbol. *Administrative Science Quarterly, 26(2),* 171-186.

9. Fogg, B.J. (2002). *Persuasive technology: Using computers to change what we think and do.* Morgan Kaufmann.

10. Friedman, B. (1997). *Human values and the design of computer technology.* Cambridge University Press.

11. Grimes, A & Grinter, R.E. (2007). Designing persuasion: Health technology for low-income African American communities. *PERSUASIVE 2007*, 24-35.

12. Huber, J., Payne, J. W., & Puto, C. (1982). Adding asymmetrically dominated alternatives: Violations of regularity and the similarity hypothesis. *Journal of Consumer Research, 9,* 90 – 98.

13. Intuitive Automata, http://intuitiveautomata.com

14. Kahneman, D., Knetsch, J., & Thaler, R. (1991). Anomalies: The endowment effect, loss aversion, and status quo bias. *Journal of Economic Perspectives, 5, 1,* 193-206.

15. Kahneman, D. (2003). Maps of bounded rationality: Psychology for behavioral economics. *American Economic Review,* 1449-1475.

16. Kahn U., & Dhar, R. (2007). Where there is a way, is there a will? The effect of future choices on self-control. *Journal of Experimental Psychology*, 277-288.

17. Lee, M.K., Forlizzi, J., Rybski, P.E., Crabbe, F., Chung, W., Finkle, J., Glaser, E., & Kiesler, S. (2009). The Snackbot: Documenting the design of a robot for long-term Human-Robot Interaction. In *Proceedings of HRI'09*, 7-14.

18. Loewenstein, G., Brennan, T. and Volpp, K.G. (2007). Protecting people from themselves: using decision errors to help people improve their health. *Journal of the American Medical Association. 298(20),* 2415-2417

19. Loewenstein, G. (1996). Out of control: Visceral influences on behavior. *Organizational Behavior and Human Decision Processes, 65*, 272–292.

20. Loewenstein, G., O'Donoghue, T.M., & Rabin, M. (2003). Projection bias in predicting future utility. *Quarterly Journal of Economics, 118,* 1209-1248.

21. Mankoff, J., Hsieh, G., Hung, H.C., Lee, & S., Nitao, E. (2002). Using low-cost sensing to support nutritional awareness. In *Proceedings of Ubicomp'02*, 371-378.

22. McCrory, M. A., Fuss, P. J., McCallum, J. E., Yao, M., Vinken, A. G., & Hays, N. P. (1999). Dietary variety within food groups: Association with energy intake and body fatness in men and women. *The American Journal of Clinical Nutrition, 69*, 440–447.

23. Mowen, J.C. (1999). *The 3M model of motivation and personality: Theory and empirical applications to consumer behavior.* Springer.

24. Norman, D. A. (1988). *The design of everyday things.* Basic Books.

25. Polivy, J. (1998). The effects of behavioral inhibition: Integrating internal cues, cognition, behavior, and affect. *Psychological Inquiry, 9,* 181-204.

26. Read, D., & van Leeuwen, B. (1998). Predicting hunger: The effects of appetite and delay on choice. *Organizational Behavior and Human Decision Processes, 76(2),* 189-205.

27. Samuelson, W. & Zeckhauser, R. (1988). Status quo bias in decision making. *Journal of Risk and Uncertainty, 1,* 7-59.

28. Seymour, J. D., Yaroch,A. L., Serdula, M. Blanck, H.M., & Khan, L. K. (2004). Impact of nutrition environmental interventions on point-of-purchase behavior in adults: A review. *Preventative Medicine, 39,* 108 – 136.

29. Shneiderman, B. and Plaisant, C. (2009). *Designing the user interface.* 5th edition. Addison Wesley.

30. Thaler, R.H. & Benartzi, S. (2004). Save more tomorrow: Using behavioral economics to increase employee saving. *Journal of Political Economy, 112,* 164-187.

31. Thaler, R. H., & Sunstein, C. R. (2008). *Nudge: Improving decisions about health, wealth, and happiness.* New Haven: Yale University Press.

32. Thomas, L. C., & Wickens, C. D. (2001). Visual displays and cognitive tunneling: Frames of reference effects on spatial judgments and change detection. In *Proceedings of Human Factors and Ergonomics Society Annual Meeting,* 336-340.

33. Wansink, B. & Chandon, P. (2006). Can "low-fat" nutrition labels lead to obesity? *Journal of Marketing Research, 43*, 605-661.

34. Wilcox, K., Vallen, B., Block, L., & Fitzsimons, G. J. (2009). Vicarious goal fulfillment: When the mere presence of a healthy option leads to an ironically indulgent decision. *Journal of Consumer Research, 36, 3*, 380-393.

Means Based Adaptive Persuasive Systems.

Maurits Kaptein
Eindhoven University of Technology / Philips Research
Eindhoven, the Netherlands
maurits@mauritskaptein.com

Steven Duplinsky
Stanford University / Accenture Technology
San Francisco, CA, USA
steven@duplinsky.com

Panos Markopoulos
Eindhoven University of Technology
Eindhoven, the Netherlands
p.markopoulos@tue.nl

ABSTRACT
Large differences in individual responses to persuasive strategies suggest the need for systems that rely on persuasion profiles: estimates of an individual user's susceptibility to different persuasive strategies. Establishing an empirical ground supporting decisions regarding user involvement can provide valuable guidelines for the design of such systems. We describe two studies examining the effects of choice, disclosure, and multiple strategy usage on user compliance to persuasive attempts. We show that involving users in the selection of a specific influence strategy can increase compliance, while disclosing the persuasive intent can reduce compliance. Furthermore, we demonstrate that it is not only feasible, but optimal to choose the single *correct* influence strategy for a given context; even more so than implementing multiple relevant and congruent influence attempts.

Author Keywords
Persuasive Technology, Influence Strategies, Adaptive Systems, Online Commerce, Recommender Systems

ACM Classification Keywords
H.5.m Information Interfaces and Presentation: Miscellaneous.

General Terms
Design, Experimentation.

INTRODUCTION
Persuasive technologies specifically designed to change user attitudes or behaviors pervade the public domain. Most examples reported in literature focus on creating attitudinal and behavioral changes that are perceived to be socially desirable [18]. Persuasive systems have been successful in influencing users to smoke less [24], lose weight [19], or maintain a healthy workout regime [17]. Applications have even been developed to fulfill more social purposes: improving social interactions [8, 16] and motivating contributions to online communities [3]. Not surprisingly, the use of persuasive technologies for human wellbeing has been a focus of many researchers and practitioners in the HCI domain [12].

Recent work shows significant individual differences in user's responses to influence attempts [5, 7, 11, 15]. This suggests the relevance of systems that adapt to these differences by utilizing persuasion profiles: estimates of an individual user's susceptibility to different influence strategies [13]. These *adaptive persuasive systems* are distinct from other adaptive systems such as recommender systems because they adapt the *means* of a request to a user (e.g. which influence strategy is used) instead of the *ends*: the suggested goal or user action. In this paper, we empirically investigate the effects of *influence strategy choice*, *the disclosure of usage of such strategies*, and *multi-strategy usage* on users' compliance to persuasive attempts. The results provide guidelines for the design of adaptive persuasive systems.

Adaptive Persuasive Systems
Adaptive persuasive systems modify their persuasive attempts in response to the behavioral cues of each unique user to increase the system's effectiveness on that individual. There has been some attention in the literature to adaptive persuasive systems, however most of this work focuses on adapting to a changing context or to a specific application domain [1, 2, 24]. Adaptation based on the level of the effectiveness of influence strategies is still uncommon. Because influence strategies can be regarded as *means*, and gained knowledge of an individuals' susceptibility in one domain could potentially be used effectively in other domains, individual specific cross-domain persuasion profiles can be built [13]. These profiles would consist of a description of the estimated effect(s) of a number of persuasive strategies (and the certainty surrounding these estimates) for an individual user.

Influence Strategies
Human-technology and human-media interactions are remarkably social and often closely mirror the social norms of human-human interactions [22, 25]. As a result, interactive technologies are seen as social actors which "open[s] the door for computers to apply [...] social influence" strategies [10]. That is, not only do humans influence humans, but interactive technologies are designed to, and do, influence human behavior by employing the very same social influence strategies. The array of influence strategies is vast and not well defined: Cialdini [6] elaborates on six strategies at length,

Fogg [10] describes 40 strategies, and others have listed over 100 [26]. However, it is clear that influence strategies can be used as powerful tools to increase the effectiveness of persuasive systems.

Regardless of which list of influence strategies one subscribes to, it is important to note the functional commonality between the majority of influence strategies: to varying extents they all can be deployed irrespective of the attitudinal or behavioral change goals. That is, an influence strategy such as the use of an authority argument [6, 20] can be employed as a *means* to multiple persuasive systems' varying *ends*: A digital workout application gives advice to take an early morning run as recommended by a fitness coach or, likewise, an addiction control application aids users in their attempts to stop smoking by providing targeted advice of a general practitioner. In both cases, a legitimate authority is used to increase compliance to the persuasive technology and thus aid more users in reaching their goal. These are merely examples of two different implementations of how the authority strategy can be effectively implemented in a host of other domains to increase overall compliance; one strategy, many domains.

Individual Differences

While most influence strategies are effective in increasing compliance or influencing attitudes on a population level, there is theoretical and experimental work indicating sizable differences in individual responses to influence strategies. This work initially focused on individual differences in the overall usage of peripheral cues in the decision process: some people seem more likely to incorporate implementations of influence strategies in their decision process. Next, the work extended to examining differential effects of implementations of specific strategies on individual consumers.

Numerous studies have examined individuals' overall tendency to focus on either central or peripheral processing. Individual differences in Need for Cognition (NfC) [5]—one's tendency to think or elaborate—seem to predict whether or not usage of peripheral cues will influence attitudes. Individuals high in NfC will elaborately scrutinize the arguments presented. On the other hand, for those low in NfC, scrutinizing arguments is less likely and their compliance to requests will be increased by the usage of a persuasive strategy (e.g. the authority strategy). Differences in an individual's overall susceptibility to persuasive strategies as measured by NfC have been shown to have profound behavioral effect on one's susceptibility to individual implementations of persuasive strategies. Individuals scoring high in overall susceptibility to persuasive strategies, as measured using a questionnaire, at a later point in time complied more often to messages that included persuasive strategies, while for those scoring low on susceptibility, the effect was the reverse [14].

Individual differences in responses to implementations of influence strategies do not only exist at a general processing level. There is evidence that there are sizable individual differences in responses to implementations of specific strategies [7]. For example, the *Preference for Consistency* is a measure which identifies up to what level individuals are influenced by implementations of the consistency strategy. Empirical work shows that specific implementations of this strategy, such as the "Foot-in-the-door" technique, are more likely to be effective for individuals scoring high on this construct [11]. Furthermore, Kaptein et al. [15] show a strong relationship between self reported susceptibility to implementations of the consensus strategy and behavioral responses to requests supported by implementations of this specific strategy. In their study, participants were first asked to rate a number of statements like: *"When I am in a new situation I look at others to see what I should do."*. Participants who highly agreed with this (and similar) statements were more likely, in a seemingly unrelated context, to provide email addresses of personal contacts when the consensus strategies was implemented in the request ("All of the other participants provided several email addresses to us") than participants who did not agree with the initial personality statements.

Based on the aforementioned findings, several authors in the HCI field have proposed the creation of persuasive applications that adapt to individual differences in responses to influence attempts. Fogg [9] was the first to coin the term 'persuasion profile' relating to a description of an individual user's susceptibility to different persuasive strategies. Lacroix et al. [17] described how to efficiently tailor [23] (i.e. adapt to an individual) different persuasive interventions based on an individual user's cognitions. In Study 1, we extend this work by showing how allowing users a small level of choice in which influence strategy they receive creates a leading self report that, through enhanced commitment, increases the effectiveness of the utilization of the user-selected influence strategy. This finding reduces the need to predict the preference for a specific strategy based on previous user behavior or personality measures while broadening the scope of the system's efficacy.

The Current Paper

It is important to know what the effects of disclosure and user choice are on the effectiveness of influence strategies in persuasive systems. If persuasive technologies indeed start implementing the previously described persuasion profiles, as we believe they will, a series of practical—but important—questions about the implementation of such systems must be answered: Is adaptation actually necessary or would simply using a broad range of non-adaptive influence strategies simultaneously be equally effective? Should the usage of a persuasion profile be disclosed to users to ensure transparency? Should the most effective strategies be disclosed? Should users have a free-choice to inspect, edit, or delete information in their profiles? The answers to these questions are necessary to increase the effectiveness of means based persuasive systems and enable a meaningful discussion of the potential legal and ethical concerns raised by the deployment of such systems. The questions are also directly related to problems of intelligibility and accountability of context aware systems as described by Bel

In this paper, we describe two studies investigating the effects of influence strategy implementations in adaptive persuasive technologies. In the first study, we examine whether disclosure of the use of the implemented persuasive strategy or the incorporation of free conscious choice between different strategies influences compliance. In the second study, we determine the effects of simultaneous usage of multiple (both congruent and incongruent) influence strategies. We discuss the implications of this work for designers of persuasive systems by offering a set of guidelines for the design of adaptive persuasive systems. These two studies are, to our knowledge, the first application oriented studies to investigate the effects of trade-offs emerging from the possible implementation of persuasion profiles in the design of adaptive persuasive systems.

STUDY I: CHOICE AND DISCLOSURE

Study 1 aimed at manipulating a persuasive scenario to examine the effects on compliance of two main factors: *disclosure*, explicitly stating to the user that a influence strategy is being used in an attempt to change their opinion, and *choice*, providing users with a choice between multiple persuasive strategies. Arguably, free choice can be a powerful tool for designers to make persuasive technologies more transparent, move away from a black box approach, and fortify user efficacy by instilling a sense of empowerment through the aforementioned clarity. However, designers must be cognizant of the actual effects of disclosure as it influences user compliance (proven in subsequent findings) and thus has direct implications for the design of persuasive systems and the degree to which designers can incorporate transparency in their design while preserving the systems effectiveness.

In study 1, we used a decision task in which participants were asked to rank a number of items [21]. Participants first ranked the items in the order they believed was most important before they were ostensibly given advice from one of two groups: a group of individuals who previously completed the task successfully (implementing the consensus strategy) or by an expert (implementing the authority strategy). This source of advice was either randomly assigned to the participant (no choice), assigned ostensibly based on knowledge (no choice, knowledge), or chosen freely by the participant (choice). Next, the use of this strategy was either disclosed or not. This results in a 2×3 between subject design with three levels of choice and two levels of disclosure.

Method

Participants

We recruited participants from a list of university students registered for an introductory research methodology course. The majority of recruited students consisted of undergraduates in both communication and computer science programs. A total of 112 participants were recruited. Fifty three of the recruited participants were female (47.3%) and 59 were male (52.7%). The mean age of participants was 22.2 years ($SD = 3.3$). Participants took part in this study for course credit. All participants were notified prior to the study that participation was not required to receive full credit. If they did participate, they were informed that they could stop at any time and retain all credits. All participants fully completed the experiment.

Procedure

The study was conducted entirely online. Participants received a link to the online study in their mailbox and were asked to complete the study which would take approximately 30 minutes to complete. After clicking the study link, participants arrived at the study website where they were first introduced to the study and read the consent waiver.

The first task of the study was an item-ranking task in which participants were asked to rank 12 items in order of their importance for survival in the arctic. Participants were introduced to the scenario in the following way:

You have just survived the crash of a small plane. Both the pilot and co-pilot were killed in the crash. It is mid-January, and you are in Northern Canada. The daily temperature is 25 below zero, and the night time temperature is 40 below zero. There is snow on the ground, and the countryside is wooded with several creeks criss-crossing the area. The nearest town is 20 miles away. You are dressed in city clothes appropriate for a business meeting. You manage to salvage twelve items that you can use to try to survive.

After the introduction, participants were shown the following list of items and given the opportunity to rank the items from 1 (most important to survival) to 12 (least important to survival):

1. A 20'x 20' piece of heavy-duty canvas
2. A cigarette lighter
3. A compass
4. Dehydrated milk (8 pounds)
5. Duct tape (25' roll)
6. An extra shirt and pair of pants for each survivor
7. A hand ax
8. Iodine water purification tablets (50 tablets)
9. A loaded .45-caliber pistol
10. A loud signal whistle
11. One box of matches
12. A sectional air map made of plastic

After ranking the items participants were told—after an ostensible 6 seconds analysis of their ranking—that *"...some of your rankings were correct, but some could use improvement. You will now get the chance to revise your answers."*

Participants then saw a screen which stated that they would have the opportunity to revise their answers either based on: "The advice of successful students" or "the advice of an arctic expert". Both sources of advice were presented with a picture of the respective source. These descriptions of the two sources of advice were pre-tested with 145 subjects to determine overall strategy preference in this survival scenario context. In 144 of the 145 cases, our pilot participants—again college students—chose the expert advice. Hence, it was clear that the expert advice is the preferable strategy for this specific task.

Next, one third of our participants were randomly assigned to receive the message that they would be *"randomly assigned to one of the two sources of advice"*. In reality, everyone was assigned to receive the expert advice—the preferred advice as based on the pre-test. Another third of our participants received a message that they were assigned to receive the expert advice because *"...this is the advice you will like best"*. The ostensible analysis of participants rankings, which was shown to all participants, was implemented to increase the realism of this condition. The final third of our participants had the option to select the advice they would prefer most; these participants had a free-choice between the two strategies. Consistent with our pre-test results, all of the participants in this condition ended up choosing the expert advice. Hence, the only difference between the three groups was the perception of free-choice, or the basis of this choice if made by the system, before receiving the advice.

After the choice manipulation, participants received short feedback about 6 of their 12 ranked items. For each participant, irrespective of their ranking, it was suggested to: move their most important item (ranked 1) down to rank 7, move the item ranked at 3 to 5, move 5 to 12, 7 to 1, 10 to 3, and 12 to 10. These suggestions were presented one by one, and, during the presentation of these suggestions, the disclosure conditions were implemented. Half of the participants received the message "You ranked [the item] at number [ranking by the participant]. The expert ranked [the item] as [more/less] important at number: [suggested rank]." The other half of the participants were shown the same advice *and* a message box with the following message: *"Please note that research shows that people tend to be persuaded by experts"*.

After reading each of the six recommendations, participants were shown a screen displaying their initial ranking of the twelve items compared side by side with the ranking of the expert. Participants could then re-rank their items as desired based on the expert's advice. For participants in the disclosure condition, the aforementioned message box was again displayed. After re-ranking the items, participants were asked to evaluate the advice that was given. The study ended with a short set of demographic questions about the participant followed by a screen that stated: *"The study has ended. You are free to go now with full compensation. However, it is known that people get better at ranking tasks by practicing more often. Would you like to try again?"*. If participants chose "no" the study ended. Participants who selected "yes" were given another opportunity to try a *different* ranking task.

Measures

As a primary measure of the effectiveness of the persuasive attempt, (the advice given by the expert) a compliance score was computed. The compliance score is the sum of the number of ranks changed between initial rank and suggested ranks for the items for which a re-rank was suggested. Hence, if the item that was initially ranked at 1 was moved to position 5 (suggested position was 7) in the final rankings, participants received a score of $(|7-1|-|7-5|) = 4$, (the maximal suggested change minus the actual distance between the suggested rank and the final rank) for that item. The maximum compliance score was (6 + 2 + 7 + 6 + 7 + 2 =) 28. Negative scores could be obtained when items were moved in greater rank-distance to the suggestions than the initial rank, however, this did not occur in the study.

In addition to the actual compliance score, we measured the perceived usefulness of the expert advice and participants confidence in their final ranking. Perceived usefulness was measured using the following 5 ten-point items (Cronbach's $\alpha = 0.934$):

1. *How useful was the advice provided by the expert?*
2. *How much did you respect the opinion of the expert?*
3. *Did the advice from the expert change your opinion?*
4. *How helpful was the advice from the expert for your ranking in the arctic survival task?*
5. *How satisfied are you with the help from the expert?*

Participants' confidence in the final ranking was measured using the following 2 ten-point items (Cronbach's $\alpha = 0.859$):

1. *How confident are you in your final ranking?*
2. *How satisfied are you with your final ranking?*

Results

Compliance

To examine the effects of disclosure and choice on compliance, a compliance score was computed for each participant and these scores were analyzed using a 2 × 3 between-participants ANOVA. There was a significant main effect of choice, $M_{no,random} = 18.2$, $M_{no,knowledge} = 21.0$, $M_{free-choice} = 22.2$, $F(2, 106) = 3.38$, $p = 0.038$. Furthermore, there was a statistically significant main effect of disclosure on the compliance scores, $M_{no} = 22.1$, $M_{yes} = 18.8$, $F(1, 106) = 6.55$, $p = 0.012$. No interaction between choice and disclosure was found, $F(2, 106) = 0.10$, $p = 0.905$. Figure 1 shows an overview of the results.

It is clear that compliance to the expert's advice is higher when the persuasive intent of this implementation was not disclosed. Thus, telling participants about the possible persuasive effect of advice originating from an authority source, diminished its effectiveness.

Using post-hoc tests, the main effect of choice was further examined. The free-choice condition differed significantly from the random-assignment condition, $p = 0.011$. None of the other conditions differed significantly from each other. Hence, providing a free choice between the strategies increased participants compliance to the advice given by the expert.

Usefulness of the Advice

A mean score on the five items addressing the usefulness of the advice was computed for each participant. The useful-

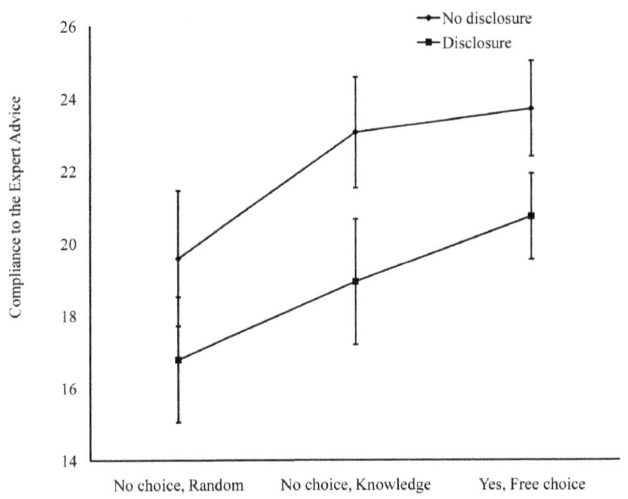

Figure 1. The effects of choice and disclosure on compliance. Shown are the estimated marginal means and standard errors of the compliance scores. On the x-axis, are the three choice levels, and the two separate lines represent the two disclosure conditions.

ness score was analyzed using a 2 × 3 between-participants ANOVA. There was a significant effect of choice, $M_{no,random}$ = 7.1, $M_{no,knowledge}$ = 7.0, $M_{free-choice}$ = 8.0, $F(2, 106) = 4.19$, $p = 0.018$. Furthermore, there was a statistically significant main effect of disclosure on the usefulness scores, M_{no} = 7.7, M_{yes} = 7.0, $F(1, 106) = 4.74$, $p = 0.032$. No interaction between choice and disclosure was found, $F(2, 106) = 0.24$, $p = 0.787$. Figure 2 shows an overview of the results.

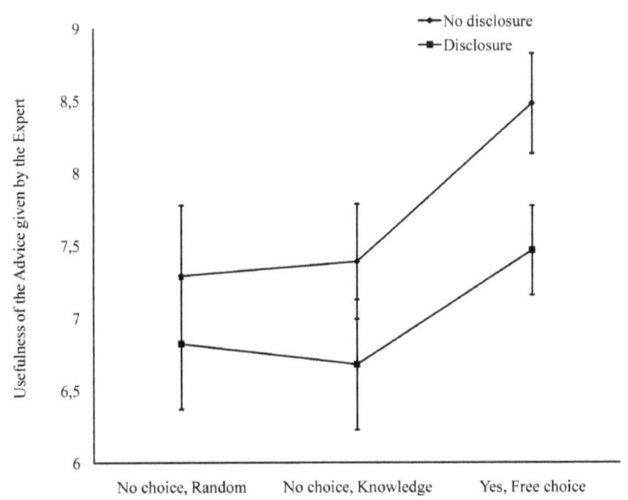

Figure 2. The effects of choice and disclosure on the perceived usefulness of the advice. Shown are the estimated marginal means and standard errors of the usefulness scores.

It is clear that the advice from the expert is perceived as more useful when it is not disclosed to participants the fact that advice from an expert tends to influence opinion. Thus, consistent with the compliance results, disclosure diminishes the perceived usefulness of this implementation of the authority strategy. Furthermore, it is clear that free-choice increases the perceived usefulness of the advice over conditions where participants are not free to choose for this advice source. Using post-hoc tests, it was clear that the free choice condition differed significantly in its perceived usefulness from both the no choice, random condition, $p = 0.031$, and the no choice, knowledge condition, $p = 0,028$.

Confidence

Analysis of the confidence in the final ranking score using a 2 × 3 ANOVA showed a significant main effect of choice, $M_{no,random} = 6.1$, $M_{no,knowledge} = 6.7$, $M_{free-choice} = 7.7$, $F(2, 106) = 6.20$, $p = 0.003$. No significant main effect of disclosure, $F(2, 106) = 3.23$, $p = 0.076$, and no significant interaction were found, $F(2, 106) = 1.22$, $p = 0.300$. Using post-hoc tests, it was clear that the free-choice condition differed significantly from both the no choice, random condition, $p = 0.001$, and the no choice, knowledge condition, $p = 0.031$. Thus, freely choosing to receive persuasive messages from an authority source increases the confidence that participants have in their final performance on the item ranking task.

Additional Results

Participants' willingness to try the task again was influenced by the choice conditions: people in the free-choice condition were more likely to try one more item ranking task at the end of the study, $\chi^2(2, N = 112) = 4.73$, $p = 0.025$ than those in the other conditions.

Discussion

The results of study 1 that both choice—the ability to select the persuasive strategy that is used for the specific influence attempts—and disclosure—the revelation of the effect of this strategy—affect compliance. Free-choice led to higher compliance to the request. Disclosure of the fact that the expert advice generally has an influence on others, led to decreased compliance.

Free-choice by users of different persuasive strategies leads to higher compliance, usefulness, and user confidence ratings than system assigned strategies. This implies that designers of adaptive persuasive systems should try to involve users in the selection of different influence strategies. Therefore, an adaptive persuasive system is more effective when its decision to employ a specific strategy is powered (at least partly) by the user of the system. The effectiveness of free-choice is likely a result of the consistency principle: Once people make a certain choice, they will go to great lengths to stick to this choice [6]. Hence, once a user chooses to comply to an expert, they will try to adapt their behavior to be consistent with this choice. The positive effect of free-choice was strong enough to influence significantly more participants in this condition to spend another 10 minutes of their own time in practicing the experimental task to improve their skills after it was made clear that they were free to leave. The results show that obtaining a persuasion profile based on self-report is a potentially worthwhile option to explore in practical system designs.

Disclosing the general effect of the use of the expert strategy reduced its effectiveness. This was probably due to the fact that disclosing the use of a persuasive strategy leads to a higher elaboration state, reduces peripheral processing, and thus lessens the impact of the influence strategy through the peripheral route (see [5]. This finding might imply that secrecy about the use of influence strategies can be beneficial for persuasive systems. If this is true, then an ethical trade off between the drawbacks of this non-disclosure, and a possible decreased effectiveness of a system which promotes a socially desirable behavior has to be made by the designer. We feel that ways of increasing disclosure and user awareness without a loss of effectiveness should be part of a future research agenda. Positive disclosure methods might benefit from implementing our findings of choice in a way to negate the loss in persuasive effectiveness of disclosure or possibly even increase compliance after further refinement.

STUDY II: ADDITION AND CONGRUENCY

While Study 1 focused on the effects of both disclosure and choice on the effectiveness of using influence strategies, Study 2 focuses on the applied question whether adaptation is actually necessary: *Is it not just possible to use multiple strategies simultaneously?* While it has already been shown that adaptation at a level of overall susceptibility to persuasive strategies is feasible [15], to our knowledge the effects of using multiple strategies simultaneously has not yet been investigated.

As a first attempt to investigate the effects of the usage of multiple strategies, we investigate the main effect—and thus not the individual differences—of responses to either one or multiple strategies. Furthermore, we test the effects of congruent or incongruent strategies when multiple strategies are presented.

Method

Participants

In Study 2, 44 undergraduates from both communication and computer science programs voluntarily participated. Participants were recruited through an email invitation and received a link to the study website. In total, 136 possible participants were approached, leading to a response rate of 32.4%. Within our final sample 25 (56.8%) of the participants were females. The average age of the participants was 23.8 (SD = 7.6). None of the participants in Study 2 had participated in Study 1.

Procedure

The procedure of Study 2 was very similar to that in Study 1. Again, participants were asked to take part in an online item ranking study. We used the exact same arctic survival item-ranking task as in Study 1. After reading the consent waiver, participants were first asked to rank the 12 items in their importance for survival. After finalizing their rankings, participants were again told that: *"...some of your rankings were correct, but some could use improvement. You will now get the chance to revise your answers."*

After the messages, the four conditions were implemented. In Study 2 we focused both on (a) the number of strategies used (*one* or *multiple*) and (b) whether the implementations were congruent (*yes* or *no*).

The number of strategies was implemented as follows: In the single strategy condition participants would either receive advice from the expert source *or* the consensus source. Analogous to Study 1, the possible sources were presented with a picture and a short textual description. Contrary to Study 1, participants were not ostensibly randomly assigned to either source but were only exposed to one of the sources. Participants were thus told: *"You will have the chance to revise your answers based on advice from..."* and then were shown one single description. In the multiple strategy condition participants were told that they would receive advice from both sources; in this case both descriptions and images were presented simultaneously.

The suggestions made by the sources were the same as those in Study 1 with the exception of the multiple strategy conditions. Here, in the *congruent* condition the authority advice was the same as in Study 1, while for the consensus advice the following message was added: *"The group of successful students* ***agreed*** *with the expert"* for five out of the six suggestions. For the sixth suggestion from the expert (presented to the participants as the second suggestion), a message stating that the group of students *disagreed* was added to increase realism. In the *incongruent* condition, these two numbers were reversed and thus the students disagreed with the authority source on five out of six suggested changes and only agreed on one suggestion. We selected the authority strategy as the reference since it was clearly the most preferred strategy in the current context, see Study 1.

There are four experimental groups in the experiment:

1. *Single strategy - Authority.* This group received advice from the authority source only. N = 10
2. *Single strategy - Consensus.* This group received advice from the consensus source only. N = 12
3. *Double strategy - Congruent.* This group received advice from the authority source and the consensus source agreed with the advice. N = 10
4. *Double strategy - Incongruent.* This group received advice from the authority source and the consensus source disagreed with the advice. N = 12

Measures

Participants were randomly assigned to one of the four groups. After re-ranking their items based on the suggested changes, participants filled out the same post task questions as used in Study 1. However, for the multiple strategies condition the items evaluating the usefulness of the suggestions were asked about both the expert advice and the consensus advice. Eventually, Study 2—similar to Study 1—resulted in data on compliance, the usefulness of the advice, and participants' confidence in the final rankings. Similar to Study 1, the experiment ended with the request to try one more item-ranking task on the individuals own time.

Results

Since the design of Study 2 does not represent a clean 2×2 between-subjects design but presents a partially nested design, the analysis was conducted differently from Study 1.

For each of the dependent variables we first looked at a main-effect of the number of strategies. Next, separate analyses were performed to test the effects of the specific strategy that was used, the number of strategies used, and the congruency of the messages under the multiple strategy condition. Finally, a one-way between-subjects analysis of variance with Bonferroni corrected pairwise comparisons was used to compare each of the four experimental conditions to each other.

Compliance

For the actual compliance to the advice given in the four experimental conditions, we found no significant main-effect of the number of sources: The average compliance score for the single source conditions, $\bar{X} = 15.8$, $S.E = 1.96$, was similar to that of the multiple strategy condition,, $\bar{X} = 17.2$, $S.E = 1.62$ $t(42) = 0.55$, $p = .582$. Within the single strategy condition a strong effect—as expected based on the pre-test for Study 1—of the actual strategy that was used was found: Participants in the authority condition, $\bar{X} = 23.6$, $S.E. = 1.87$, complied much more to the advice than participants in the consensus condition, $\bar{X} = 9.3$, $S.E. = 1.61$, $t(20) = 5.80$, $p < .001$. Within the multiple strategy condition both the incongruent group, $\bar{X} = 17.6$, $S.E = 2.34$, and the congruent group, $\bar{X} = 16.8$, $S.E = 2.33$ had approximately similar mean compliance scores, $t(20) = 0.235$, $p = .816$.

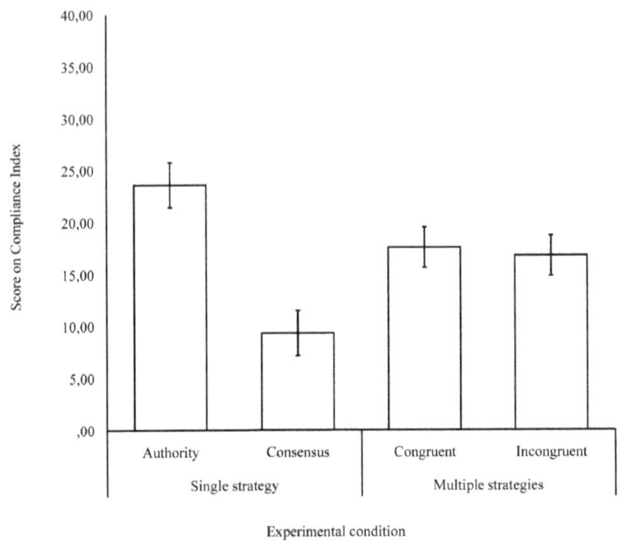

Figure 3. The effects of the use of single or multiple strategies, either authority or consensus and congruent or incongruent on compliance.

Figure 3 shows the means and standard errors for each of the experimental groups. When conducting a one-way four level ANOVA on this data, there is a significant main-effect of condition, $F(3,40) = 8.097$, $p < .001$. Bonferroni corrected pairwise comparisons show that the single strategy consensus condition scores significantly lower than all other conditions, while the single strategy authority condition scores significantly higher. Table 1 shows the mean differences between each of the four conditions, their standard errors, and the p-value for each possible pairwise comparison. The results indicate that when choosing the optimal single strategy for a specific context, adding other strategies can have a detrimental effect on compliance. It also shows that when the effect of one of the sources is clearly preferable, the effects of incongruence are small.

(A) condition	(B) condition	$(\bar{A} - \bar{B})$	$S.E.$	p-value
MS C	SS Cons	8.25	2.79	.005
MS C	MS IC	0.78	2.93	.790
MS C	SS Auth	-6.02	2.93	.046
SS Cons	MS C	-8.25	2.79	.005
SS Cons	MS IC	-7.47	2.93	.015
SS Cons	SS Auth	-14.27	2.93	.001
MS IC	MS C	-0.78	2.93	.790
MS IC	SS Cons	7.47	2.93	.015
MS IC	SS Auth	-6.8	3.06	.032
SS Auth	**MS C**	**6.02**	**2.93**	**.046**
SS Auth	SS Cons	14.27	2.93	.001
SS Auth	MS IC	6.8	3.06	.032

Table 1. Post-hoc comparisons of the four experimental conditions in Study 2. SS=Single strategy, MS=Multiple strategies, Auth=Authority, Cons=consensus, C=congruent, IC=incongruent

Usefulness of the Advice

Analysis on the usefulness of the advice was conducted in a similar way as the analysis of the confidence scores. Again, an overall usefulness score was computed (Cronbach's $\alpha = 0.923$). Since participants in the single strategy, consensus source condition only received consensus advice, they evaluated the usefulness of the advice coming from the expert. For all other participants, we analyzed the usefulness of the expert advice.

Similar to the compliance scores for the usefulness of the advice given in the four experimental conditions we found no significant main-effect of the number of sources: The average usefulness score for the single source conditions, $\bar{X} = 5.5$, $S.E = 2.44$, was similar to that of the multiple strategy condition,, $\bar{X} = 6.1$, $S.E = 1.76$ $t(42) = 1.076$, $p = .288$. Again, within the single strategy condition a strong effect—as expected based on the pre-test for Study *I*—of the actual strategy that was used was found: Participants in the authority condition, $\bar{X} = 7.0$, $S.E. = 1.85$, perceived the advice as much more useful than participants in the consensus condition, $\bar{X} = 4.2$, $S.E. = 2.18$, $t(20) = 3.159$, $p < .01$. Within the multiple strategy condition both the incongruent group, $\bar{X} = 5.7$, $S.E = 1.75$, and the congruent group, $\bar{X} = 6.5$, $S.E = 1.77$ had approximately similar usefulness scores, $t(20) = 1.032$, $p = .314$.

Figure 4 shows the mean usefulness scores and standard errors for each of the experimental groups. Post-hoc tests with Bonferroni corrections show that the single use of the consensus strategy scores significantly lower than both the single expert source condition, $p = .002$ and the congruent multiple source condition $p = .005$. However, the pattern is similar to the pattern found on the compliance scores: Choosing the right strategy for the right context makes the advice more useful, and adding irrelevant strategies can decrease the perception of usefulness of the single right strategy.

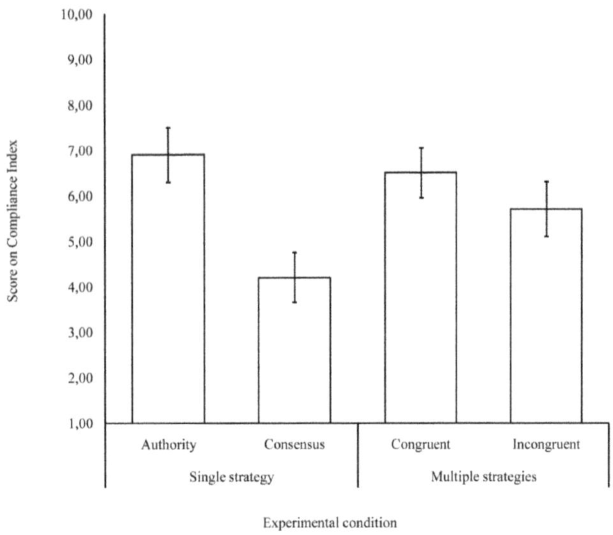

Figure 4. The effects of the use of single or multiple strategies, either authority or consensus and congruent or incongruent on the perceived usefulness of the advice.

Confidence

Analysis of the confidence scores (Cronbach's $\alpha = 0.783$) shows that the average confidence score for the single source conditions, $\bar{X} = 7.7$, $S.E = 1.89$, was similar to that of the multiple strategy condition,, $\bar{X} = 8.1$, $S.E = 1.19$ $t(42) = 0.673$, $p = .504$. Contrary to the results on compliance and usefulness, within the single strategy condition no significant effect of strategy was found: Participants in the authority condition, $\bar{X} = 7.8, S.E. = 1.65$, were as confident as participants in the consensus condition, $\bar{X} = 7.7$, $S.E. = 2.11$, $t(20) = 0.061$, $p < .952$.

Also, different from the previous results on compliance and usefulness, a significant effect of congruency was found: In the multiple strategy condition the confidence in the final rating based on advice from incongruent sources, $\bar{X} = 7.5$, $S.E = 0.60$, was lower than that based on advice from congruent sources, $\bar{X} = 8.8$, $S.E = 1.35$, $t(20) = 2.992$, $p = .007$. Hence, while incongruent advice did not lead to lowered compliance, it did lead to a lowered confidence in the final rankings.

Discussion

Study 2 quantitatively shows human affinity for the preferential strategy, and solely that strategy. Compliance was greatest in the condition where advice came from *only* the preferential source (expert).

Contrary to intuition, having multiple sources of advice agree on the recommendation had not only no positive impact on compliance levels but actually had a slightly negative effect when compared to the preferred strategy (Table 1, bold). This is a fascinating discovery since one would assume two agreeing opinions would be stronger than one. This could potentially be a result of increasing cognition and elaboration with the added advice and the introduction of skepticism or lack of trust with intention of the application (observed in the variance in the usefulness-index across conditions). However, the result is clear that in some situations using multiple strategies can be detrimental as compared to presentation of the single right strategy.

Equally surprising was that there was no appreciable variation between the multiple strategies condition where the sources agreed and the multiple strategies condition where the sources disagreed. This leads us to believe that individuals mentally default to the preferential strategy and thus any disagreement with the preferential strategy has little effect on final attitudes.

It is tempting to assume then that one can simply implement multiple strategies and users will follow the most relevant advice to their cognitive tendencies. While our study showed this to be true, it also showed that the introduction of multiple strategies decreases compliance to the end goal and decreased user confidence in the advice provided by the system. It is thus most desirable to implement the single most effective strategy (or allow users to choose this strategy for themselves as demonstrated in Study 1).

GENERAL CONCLUSIONS: ADAPTIVITY, DISCLOSURE, AND MULTIPLE STRATEGIES

The use of persuasion profiles is a delicate and complex task from an application design perspective. In this paper, we described two studies that show empirical evidence for the effects of choice, disclosure, and multiple strategies on compliance to persuasive attempts. Since there are large individual differences in responses to the use of persuasive strategies, we expect systems to emerge that rely heavily on persuasion profiles, and thus we feel that providing empirical ground supporting decisions regarding user involvement (free-choice & disclosure) and strategy presentation (single vs. multiple & congruent vs. incongruent) provides valuable guidelines for designers of such systems. We know that these systems are only just beginning to emerge but feel that the results demonstrated in this paper are useful not only for the design of such systems but also serve as input for an ethical debate about adaptive persuasive systems. In this section, we interpret and summarize the findings obtained from both studies and summarize them into three design guidelines. Finally, we conclude by identifying future research opportunities in the field of adaptive persuasive systems.

Study 1 clearly showed that providing individuals with an option about which strategy to choose instead of assigning an influence strategy leads to higher compliance. Thus, designers of adaptive persuasive systems should try to seek user involvement when determining which strategy the system should utilize to accomplish a goal. For example, allowing the user to choose whether they will be linked to their social network to improve their eating habits or whether they will be supported by a general practitioner. Providing users with such a choice leads to increased compliance to requests made by the system and increases the perceived usefulness of the provided advice. The study also showed that the perception of free-choice was enough to increase compliance even though in actuality there was only one acceptable answer as displayed by our overwhelming pre-test results. Knowledge of the possible influence strategies to use in a given situation, combined with a clear way of presenting these options, can benefit the effectiveness of persuasive systems without the need for complex personal data about the user.

Next to the positive effects of free-choice on compliance and usefulness, a different result also sprang from Study 1: Making the common persuasive effect of the influence strategy that is used explicit, decreased the effectiveness of its use. While this result can easily be explained using the ELM—higher elaboration leads to a decreased effectiveness of the peripheral cue that is used—in the future it might pose an ethical trade-off between the effectiveness of a design and transparency that is maintained toward users. While in general we and others [4] feel that users should be informed about the aims and possible effects of using influence strategies, this mere act might decrease the chances of the design success. However, more research on disclosure of the use of a persuasion profile, privacy perceptions, and their effects on compliance should be carried out to further define the role of disclosure.

Study 2 focused on the question of whether or not multiple influence strategies can be used simultaneously. While it was previously shown that using influence attempts supported by influence strategies can lead to decreased effectiveness for people low in susceptibility to such attempts, it was until now, unclear whether the use of additional strategies would be beneficial, equal, or even detrimental to the effectiveness of a request. Study 2 showed that *only* presenting the right strategy for a given context—in this case using an authority argument—can lead to higher compliance than presenting multiple strategies at the same time. This was even true if both strategies that were used presented congruent messages. Thus, a persuasive system cannot just implement "any trick in the book" and designers should be careful to implement only those influence strategies that increase compliance in a given context or for a given user.

In study 2 congruency—agreement between multiple strategies used—influenced not the actual compliance to the request, but only the confidence people had in their final behavior. We feel that this might partly be due to the overwhelming preference for the authority strategy in the item-ranking context. Thus, for both the congruent and the incongruent conditions participants chose to comply with the expert. The additional congruency only influenced their certainty about their decision. This effect of incongruency on attitude certainty instead of valence is in line with previous findings [27].

To summarize, based on the results presented in this paper we recommend that designers of adaptive persuasive technologies:

1. Involve users in their choice for preferred strategies in a given context.
2. Disclose the implications of the use of influence strategies with caution.
3. Avoid using "redundant" strategies, even if they present a congruent message.

Final Remarks

The presented studies demonstrate the ability to increase compliance to persuasive systems by *means* based manipulations. Our findings on strategy choice indicate that adaptive persuasive systems might not require complex user personality or behavioral data, but could start by using simple user input. Key choice points cause the user to commit in small increments to the program and become increasingly invested in the advice they receive. The system then not only becomes personal to the user but, in doing so, the user adds increasing amounts of personal commitment to the advice they are receiving; and as we have shown, from the commitment follows compliance and satisfaction.

Further studies should explore different disclosure methods. By further defining exactly what aspects of disclosure reduce compliance, we will be able to more clearly recommend ways to increase transparency without reducing compliance. Furthermore, while in the presented studies we disclosed the possible effect of usage of an authority strategy, it is worthwhile to investigate the effect of user feedback about persuasion profiles directly. Additionally, further studies should be conducted to test the effects of multiple degrees of choice. In other words, if a system had more opportunities for the user to choose or provide feedback, would a relationship be built and thus would compliance increase even further, or would increasing choice points have a null effect similar to implementing multiple persuasive strategies?

We hope that these studies lay the foundation for a move from systems that try to tell a user how to help themselves based on sometimes erroneous analysis of a user profile or previous actions, to systems that facilitate users to aid themselves. As a result of knowledge gained in this paper, we believe that the latter proposed approach provides increased agility and transparency to persuasive systems while not reducing, and possibly even strengthening, its beneficial effect on its users.

REFERENCES

1. Arroyo, E., Bonanni, L., and Selker, T. Waterbot: exploring feedback and persuasive techniques at the sink. In *Proceedings of the SIGCHI conference on Human factors in computing systems*, ACM (New York, NY, USA, 2005), 631–639.

2. Bang, M., Torstensson, C., and Katzeff, C. The powerhouse: A persuasive computer game designed to raise awareness of domestic energy consumption. In *PERSUASIVE*, W. IJsselsteijn, Y. de Kort, C. J. H. Midden, B. Eggen, and E. van den Hoven, Eds., vol. 3962 of *LNCS*, Springer (2006), 123–132.

3. Beenen, G., Ling, K., Wang, X., Chang, K., Frankowski, D., Resnick, P., and Kraut, R. Using social psychology to motivate contributions to online

communities. *Proceedings of the 2004 ACM conference on Computer supported cooperative work* (2004), 212–221.

4. Berdichevsky, D., and Neunschwander, E. Toward an ethics of persuasive technology. *Communincations of the ACM 42*, 5 (1999), 51–58.

5. Cacioppo, J. T., Petty, R. E., Kao, C. F., and Rodriguez, R. Central and peripheral routes to persuasion: An individual difference perspective. *Journal of Personality and Social Psychology 51*, 5 (1986), 1032âĂŞ1043.

6. Cialdini, R. *Influence, Science and Practice*. Allyn & Bacon, Boston, 2001.

7. Cialdini, R. B., Trost, M. R., and Newsom, J. T. Preference for consistency: The development of a valid measure and the discovery of surprising behavioral implications. *Journal of Personality and Social Psychology 69* (1995), 318–328.

8. DiMicco, J. M., Pandolfo, A., and Bender, W. Influencing group participation with a shared display. In *Proceedings of CSCW 2004*, ACM (Chicago, Illinois, USA, 2004), 614–623.

9. Fogg, B. J. Persuasive technologies: Introduction. *Communications of the ACM 42* (1999).

10. Fogg, B. J. *Persuasive Technology: Using Computers to Change What We Think and Do*. Morgan Kaufmann, 2002.

11. Guadagno, R. E., Asher, T., Demaine, L. J., and Cialdini, R. B. When Saying Yes Leads to Saying No: Preference for Consistency and the Reverse Foot-in-the-Door Effect. *Personality and Social Psychology Bulletin 27*, 7 (2001), 859–867.

12. IJsselsteijn, W., de Kort, Y., Midden, C. J. H., Eggen, B., and van den Hoven, E. Persuasive technology for human well-being: Setting the scene. In *PERSUASIVE*, W. IJsselsteijn, Y. de Kort, C. J. H. Midden, B. Eggen, and E. van den Hoven, Eds., vol. 3962 of *LNCS*, Springer (2006), 1–5.

13. Kaptein, M., and Eckles, D. Selecting effective means to any end: Futures and ethics of persuasion profiling. In *Persuasive Technology*, T. Ploug, P. Hasle, and H. Oinas-Kukkonen, Eds., Springer Berlin / Heidelberg (2010), 82—93.

14. Kaptein, M., Lacroix, J., and Saini, P. Individual differences in persuadability in the health promotion domain. In *Persuasive Technology*, T. Ploug, P. Hasle, and H. Oinas-Kukkonen, Eds., Springer Berlin / Heidelberg (2010), 94—105.

15. Kaptein, M., Markopoulos, P., de Ruyter, B., and Aarts, E. Can you be persuaded? individual differences in susceptibility to persuasion. *Proceedings of Interact 2009* (2009).

16. Kass, A. Transforming the mobile phone into a personal performance coach. In *Mobile Persuasion: 20 Perspectives on the Future of Behavior Change*, B. J. Fogg and D. Eckles, Eds. Stanford Captology Media, 2007.

17. Lacroix, J., Saini, P., and Goris, A. Understanding user cognitions to guide the tailoring of persuasive technology-based physical activity interventions. In *PERSUASIVE*, S. Chatterjee and P. Dev, Eds., vol. 350 of *ACM International Conference Proceeding Series*, ACM (2009), 9.

18. Lockton, D., Harrison, D., and Stanton, N. A. Design with intent: Persuasive technology in a wider context. In *PERSUASIVE*, H. Oinas-Kukkonen, P. F. V. Hasle, M. Harjumaa, K. Segerståhl, and P. Øhrstrøm, Eds., vol. 5033 of *LNCS*, Springer (2008), 274–278.

19. Maheshwari, M., Chatterjee, S., and Drew, D. Exploring the persuasiveness of "just-in-time" motivational messages for obesity management. In *PERSUASIVE*, H. Oinas-Kukkonen, P. F. V. Hasle, M. Harjumaa, K. Segerståhl, and P. Øhrstrøm, Eds., vol. 5033 of *LNCS*, Springer (2008), 258–261.

20. Milgram, S. *Obedience to Authority*. London: Tavistock., 1974.

21. Nass, C., Fogg, B. J., and Moon, Y. Can computers be teammates? *International Journal of Human-Computer Studies 45*, 6 (1996), 669 – 678.

22. Nass, C., and Moon, Y. Machines and mindlessness: Social responses to computers. *Journal of Social Issues 56*, 1 (2000), 81–103.

23. Noar, S. M., Benac, C. N., and Harris, M. S. Does tailoring matter? meta-analytic review of tailored print health behavior change interventions. *Psychological Bulletin 133*, 4 (2007), 673 – 693.

24. Räisänen, T., Oinas-Kukkonen, H., and Pahnila, S. Finding kairos in quitting smoking: Smokers' perceptions of warning pictures. In *PERSUASIVE*, H. Oinas-Kukkonen, P. F. V. Hasle, M. Harjumaa, K. Segerståhl, and P. Øhrstrøm, Eds., vol. 5033 of *LNCS*, Springer (2008), 254–257.

25. Reeves, B., and Nass, C. *The Media Equation: How People Treat Computers, Television, and New Media Like Real People and Places*. Cambridge University Press, 1996.

26. Rhoads, K. How many influence, persuasion, compliance tactics & strategies are there? http://www.workingpsychology.com/numbertactics.html, 2007.

27. Tormala, Z. L., and Rucker, D. D. Attitude certainty: A review of past findings and emerging perspectives. *Social and Personality Psychology Compass 1*, 1 (2007), 469–392.

Side Effects and 'Gateway' Tools: Advocating a Broader Look at Evaluating Persuasive Systems

Victoria Schwanda[1], Steven Ibara[1], Lindsay Reynolds[2], Dan Cosley[1]

[1]Department of Information Science
Cornell University
301 College Ave., Ithaca NY 14850

[2]Department of Communication
Cornell University
Kennedy Hall, Ithaca NY 14853

{vls48, ssi9, llr48, drc44}@cornell.edu

ABSTRACT

This paper argues for evaluating the impact of persuasive systems on users beyond metrics that focus on system usage, based on an interview study of 16 Wii Fit users. While exploring their experiences and reasons for abandoning the system, two main themes emerged: the tension between Wii Fit as a fitness tool and a game, and ways participants reacted to the system's feedback about their weight and performance. Some participants used Wii Fit as a 'gateway fitness' tool, moving beyond it to other fitness routines. Additionally, some users had significant emotional reactions to the Wii Fit's feedback. We argue that these 'side effects' are crucial considerations for the design and long-term evaluation of persuasive technologies.

Author Keywords

Wii Fit, e-health interventions, persuasive technologies.

ACM Classification Keywords

H5.m. Information interfaces and presentation (e.g., HCI): Miscellaneous.

General Terms

Experimentation.

INTRODUCTION

Nintendo's fitness system Wii Fit has sold over 22.5 million copies worldwide, making it the third best-selling non-bundled console video game ever[1]. Its combination of fitness, fun, and affordability has led to its use as a fitness tool in a wide range of contexts, including physical education courses and nursing homes. Wii Fit is a commercially successful example of the growing class of persuasive technologies that aim to change specific health behaviors (e.g., [3]).

There is less data on whether Wii Fit has been effective as a tool for actually encouraging fitness, and in fact many technologies and resolutions are abandoned shortly after their adoption. Based on an interview study of 16 adults who played Wii Fit for at least two weeks, we found that all of our participants had either stopped or dramatically decreased their use of Wii Fit. Below, we explore why this is so. We first briefly introduce Wii Fit's main features and our participants' background. We then describe their reactions to Wii Fit as a game and a fitness tool and to its feedback about their performance and body weight. We next discuss reasons they stopped using Wii Fit, including boredom, changes in the gaming environment, and a move to more challenging fitness routines. Based on these data, we argue that effective persuasive technologies must look beyond system usage, and instead should consider how the design may affect people's self image and scaffold behaviors that go beyond what the design itself can support.

CHI 2011, May 7–12, 2011, Vancouver, BC, Canada.

A BRIEF INTRODUCTION TO WII FIT

Wii Fit is a fitness system in which the user performs specific movements while standing on a balance board (see Figure 1). The balance board has pressure sensors which determine a user's center of balance and weight.

When a player first uses the system, he or she is prompted to create or select a Mii (an avatar representing the user) and then is asked to take a body test—which the user has the option of repeating at any time. The test asks for the user's age and height, and uses the balance board to record his or her weight. Following the weigh-in, the system displays the users' *body mass index* (BMI), which is computed based on weight and height, and a BMI "label" (e.g., underweight, obese) (see Figure 2). The user then completes a short series of balance tasks which are used to compute and display a *Wii Fit Age*, which often differs

Figure 1. This user is using the balance board for push-ups, one of the strength-training activities. There is a screen shot of the Wii Fit game display on the right.

[1] http://www.nintendo.co.jp/ir/pdf/2010/100507e.pdf#page=6

Figure 2. After being weighed by the system, the user sees the following screen including their Mii, BMI and weight label.

from his or her actual age. At this point, the user may also set a weight goal, which is tracked by the system over time.

People spend most of their time on Wii Fit participating in five types of activities: *Yoga*, *Strength Training*, *Aerobics*, *Balance Games*, and *Training Plus*. After completing an activity, the user receives feedback about his or her performance, including a score, a rating out of five stars, and a ranking on a leaderboard relative to other users using the same copy of Wii Fit. New activities are "unlocked" by reaching score or time thresholds.

Wii Fit uses characters such as an animated balance board to provide information, such as the relationship between balance and fitness, and positive and negative feedback, such as congratulating users on unlocking new levels and scolding them if they fail to use the system regularly.

METHODS

We conducted semi-structured interviews of 16 participants (eight female; ages 18-54; median age 24). Ten participants were students (seven undergraduate, three graduate); the remaining six were occupied in a variety of fields, ranging from the service sector to professional work. Interviews lasted approximately 20 minutes. We conducted 12 in person and four via phone or Skype. Fourteen were audio recorded, while detailed notes were taken during the other two. Undergraduate participants were compensated by either course credit or by entrance into a lottery for one of eight twenty-dollar gift cards, and other participants were compensated by the latter.

We began by asking for participants' "overall impressions of Wii Fit" and asked them to "describe a typical game session." Based on their responses, we asked about specific features of the system (e.g., "what about the balance games did you like?"). We asked about the body test and "how [they] feel about the game's representation of [themselves]." and why they started and stopped using the system. Finally, we asked if they "ever used any other systems or tools for fitness, weight loss, or nutrition."

We analyzed the interviews using inductive qualitative methods drawn from grounded theory [7]. First, three of the authors reviewed each interview and independently took notes about key ideas. We then used affinity diagrams to organize these ideas into the themes we discuss below.

RESULTS

A Wide Variety of Users and Uses

Participants came to Wii Fit with a variety of video game and fitness experience. Two participants called gaming "a passion" but most had little to moderate experience with video games. Similarly, our participants varied in how much they exercised when they started using Wii Fit, ranging from very little physical activity to regular fitness routines. Their use of Wii Fit itself spanned a wide range in terms of overall use (from "a couple of times" to four years), frequency (from "off and on" to daily), and session length (from 20 minutes to three hours). Their initial reasons for trying Wii Fit also varied. Six participants did so because their family or friends owned the system and/or they thought it was novel and interesting. Eleven purchased the system to use as a fitness tool.

Fitness Tool versus Game

This variety of motivations and experience led to a tension between perceiving the system as a fitness tool or a game.

Nine participants viewed Wii Fit primarily as a fitness tool. These users focused on "serious" and "non-game" activities that they considered more "exercise-y" such as Strength Training or Yoga, using activities that they saw as games for a "break." Six participants saw the system as primarily a game, and treated it as such. The game-like ability to unlock new content was motivating to 10 participants, but those participants who saw Wii Fit as a game mentioned getting bored after all the content was unlocked.

At times, Wii Fit awkwardly straddled the line between fitness and fun, as a "gimmick" to combine games and fitness. Eight participants who exercised outside of Wii Fit stated that the system would not replace their current workout routine or that they could get a "better" workout in other ways, while seven thought it could be marginally beneficial because it was "better than nothing" or "I was doing *something*." Four participants described Wii Fit as not as entertaining as other games; if they wanted to play a game, they would play something like Wii Sports instead of Wii Fit: "I don't want to run…it's not what video games are for." These participants felt that the Wii Fit was not serious enough of a fitness tool to be useful in that respect, but it also wasn't fun enough to be played regularly as a game.

Social aspects of playing Wii Fit highlighted this tension between fun and exercise. Many of our participants enjoyed playful teasing and friendly competition during group use, sharing in the success of others by providing support and encouragement. Others, however, would save the "serious fitness stuff" for solo play, because trying hard on certain activities makes "you look kind of ridiculous." Some used Wii Fit because they felt embarrassed about going to the gym, making social use unappealing and counterproductive.

Reactions to Motivational Feedback

People also had mixed reactions to the feedback Wii Fit provides, with some finding it motivational and others finding it hard to interpret and sometimes hurtful.

This feedback includes metrics of performance such as activity scores, changes in the user's Mii, and coaching, and metrics of fitness such as Wii Fit Age, BMI and BMI label. Three participants had positive emotional reactions to this feedback. They noted that it felt "good" when their Wii Fit Age was lower than their actual age and appreciated the positive feedback on their performance. They also appreciated some of the harsher features and liked that the system "scolded" them when they had not played recently.

Four of our participants, however, reported negative emotional reactions. They felt "bad" when they were given feedback such as their Wii Fit Age being higher than their actual age. There were also negative reactions to how the Mii changed shape according to their weight. One participant was nervous about being weighed because "[she] didn't want to have a pudgy little Mii." Another participant said, "it's one thing to see your [weight], it's another thing to see yourself—your Mii—as a Stay-Puft Marshmallow man." Although some participants found negative feedback motivating, these participants did not:

> *"The little guy yells at you...some people might be motivated by that, but not me."*
>
> *"The little machine lecture[d] me."*
>
> *"It can be a little harsh."*

Seven participants were skeptical about these features on an intellectual level. Some questioned the use of BMI as a representation of their fitness; one called it a "garbage number." Others were skeptical of or confused about the system's metrics and accuracy:

> *"I didn't understand how they calculated things and how they knew when I was fit."*
>
> *"How the hell do they determine that?"*
>
> *"Maybe my floor is off, or [Wii Fit] has really high standards."*

Reasons for Leaving Wii Fit

All of our participants had either stopped or dramatically decreased their use of Wii Fit at the time of the interview, citing a wide variety of reasons. Nine participants identified prosaic, circumstantial events that contributed to reduced use: hot weather or changes in the gaming environment such as moving the system to the basement or buying a set of peripherals for another game. Seven participants said that other activities took priority, while five mentioned being bored with the repetitiveness of the Wii Fit's activities.

Of our 16 participants, six approached Wii Fit with serious fitness goals. In addition to the above reasons, two additional reasons emerged in this group. Three participants stopped using the system because it did not live up to their expectations as a serious fitness tool. The remaining three changed to another fitness routine, such as running or working out at a gym. These participants purchased Wii Fit as a first step towards getting fit, and as they came to prefer more strenuous exercise in place of using of the system, their use of Wii Fit decreased.

DISCUSSION

Some of the reasons for leaving Wii Fit, such as circumstantial change or boredom, indicate that it was not an effective motivator for everyone. But others reported stopping because their use of Wii Fit was *successful*: it led to their adopting other fitness activities they came to prefer. Wii Fit may have played a key role in scaffolding these activities. Cognitive dissonance theory [5] predicts that freely adopting goal-oriented behaviors, even if they are temporary and are replaced by others, may help people maintain or strengthen those goals and related attitudes. In the fitness domain, [2] reports that participants who freely chose to engage in exercise activities reported more positive attitudes about exercise and greater intention to exercise than those who were pressured or required to.

This is in line with our current findings, and shows the potential for Wii Fit usage to have a lasting influence on users, perhaps serving as a 'gateway fitness' activity. We therefore argue that when evaluating electronic health behavior interventions and other systems with persuasive elements, it is critical to consider attitude and behavior change, not just system utilization. Evaluation of e-health interventions often focuses on how, and how much, people use the system itself [10]. While this is a natural and readily available metric, it is only part of the story. Torning & Oinas-Kukkonen highlight the importance of approaching persuasion with the goal of changing attitudes, not just behaviors, and point out that many efforts in the area of persuasive systems design focus on behavior only [12]. We take our findings as a warning against being too system-focused in evaluation.

The idea that abandonment can be a marker of success also implies that persuasive systems can be explicitly *designed* for this 'gateway' effect, planning for the day when the system will no longer be needed to support new behaviors. Instead of seeing persuasive tools as persistent, permanent companions, persuasive systems designers should consider whether the systems might play a critical but temporary role in a gradual change, much as nicotine patches are not designed for indefinite use. For example, Wii Fit might start new users with more game-like activities, but over time the balance of game and fitness could shift until use of the system simulates a trip to the gym. It might even suggest more intense fitness activities outside of the system. Other persuasive tools, such as home energy monitors that are often used to encourage sustainable behavior [4], may also benefit from careful consideration of their role in the larger picture of how attitudes and practices around sustainability evolve. Once people learn how they use energy in their homes, what then for the monitor?

Another design implication comes from the tension that participants felt between the fitness and fun aspects of Wii Fit, often seeing it as purely a fun activity, or one that was too game-like to support serious fitness needs. We see clear parallels between educational games and games to increase physical activity: both take an activity that can be seen as unattractive and attempt to engage users in it by making it more fun. It follows that design suggestions from educational games research could be adapted to tools like Wii Fit. Isbister et al.'s idea of "Deep content," for instance, argues for educational material being tightly integrated into games and not "bolted on" [8]. Users viewed certain Wii Fit activities as fitness and others as games, but rarely both; it might be effective to incorporate core fitness moves into the game-like activities, creating experiences that support both fun and fitness.

Finally, we return to the potential 'side effects' of persuasive technologies on people's emotions, especially in domains such as health and fitness where issues of self-image are salient [1] and can lead to dire consequences such as the eating disorders that affect between 6 and 11 million people in the United States [11]. A quarter of our participants experienced negative emotions related to feedback based on BMI or fitness performance. While they did not explicitly cite these feelings as reasons for abandoning Wii Fit, negative feedback was largely viewed by these participants as unproductive, and sometimes unwarranted, as expressed by one participant's frustration with the system's blindness to positive or neutral reasons for weight gains such as increases in muscle mass or a female's monthly cycle.

Such experiences raise the question of how (or whether) systems that use health and biometric data can make useful, appropriate, and sensitive interpretations that "negotiate the relationship between objective signals and subjective experiences" [9]. Persuasive technologies often privilege certain values or attitudes, which can stifle rather than encourage reflection on the topics of interest. Fogg's original captology work explicitly points to ethical considerations [6], but in practice ethics is rarely considered in persuasive technology literature [12]. Our work calls out the need for designers of persuasive health technologies to consider the potential negative consequences of their use.

Limitations and Future Work

Our participants stopped using Wii Fit several months to two years prior to the interview date. We are therefore limited by the specific experiences they remembered and reported, which likely do not represent their entire experience with the system. We are following up on this work by running a month-long in-home study of new Wii Fit users. With this work we hope to better understand users' experiences with the system over time without relying on the self-reflection method used here. We also hope to shed light on what kinds of early experiences might predict whether the system will ultimately be abandoned in frustration or in triumph.

CONCLUSION

Our interviews revealed two key themes in users' experiences with Wii Fit: the tension between the system as a fitness tool or a game and the sometimes negative emotional and intellectual reactions to feedback. They also gave us insight into the reasons why users abandon the system. These themes lead us to highlight considerations for the design and evaluation of persuasive technologies. First, it is important to consider attitude change, not just behavior change, when evaluating the effectiveness of these systems. Sometimes abandonment of the system is not evidence of failure, but of successful attitude change, and designers should often explicitly aim for this kind of scaffolding. Second, attitude and behavior change are not the only outcomes to consider around persuasive systems. Emotional impacts on their users may pose risks greater than the benefits to be gained, and designers have the responsibility to take these risks into account.

ACKNOWLEDGEMENTS

We wish to thank Eric Baumer and the anonymous reviewers for their comments on drafts of this paper. Some of this material is based upon work supported under a NSF Graduate Research Fellowship.

REFERENCES

1. Adams, G.R. (1977) Physical Attractiveness Research. *Hum Dev*, 20:217-239.
2. Chatzisarantis, N., Hagger, M., Wang, J. (2008). An experimental test of cognitive dissonance theory in the domain of physical exercise. *J Appl Sport Psychol*, 20(1):97-115.
3. Consolvo, S., et al. (2008). Activity sensing in the wild: a field trial of UbiFit Garden. In *Proc. CHI*.
4. DiSalvo, C., Sengers, P., Brynjarsdóttir, H. (2010). Mapping the Landscape of Sustainable HCI. In *Proc CHI*.
5. Festinger, L. (1957). *A theory of cognitive dissonance.* Stanford, CA: Stanford University Press.
6. Fogg, B. 1998. Persuasive computers: perspectives and research directions. *Proc. CHI*.
7. Glaser, B.G., Strauss, A. (1967). *Discovery of Grounded Theory: Strategies for Qualitative Research.* Soc. Press.
8. Isbister, K., Flanagan, M., Hash, C. (2010). Designing Games for Learning: Insights from Conversations with Designers. In *Proc. CHI*.
9. Leahu, L., Schwenk, S., Sengers, P. (2008). Subjective Objectivity: Negotiating Emotional Meaning. *Proc. DIS*.
10. Norman, G., Zabinski, M., Adams, M., Rosenberg, D., Yaroch, A., Atienza, A. (2007). A review of eHealth interventions for physical activity and dietary behavior change. *Am J Prev Med*, 33(4):336-345.
11. Patrick, L. (2002). Eating disorders: a review of the literature with emphasis on medical complications and clinical nutrition. *Altern Med Rev*, 7(3):184-202.
12. Torning, K., Oinas-Kukkonen, H. (2009) Persuasive system design: state of the art and future directions. In *Proc. PERSUASIVE*.

I Will Do It, but I Don't Like It: User Reactions to Preference-Inconsistent Recommendations

Christina Schwind, Jürgen Buder, Friedrich W. Hesse
Knowledge Media Research Center
72072 Tübingen, Germany
{c.schwind, j.buder, f.hesse}@iwm-kmrc.de

ABSTRACT
Recommender systems have their origin in e-commerce. In this domain the users are meant to *like* the recommended information. This preference-consistency is not adequate or even desirable for all domains where recommender systems are implemented. One key issue for opinion formation and informed decision making is to be aware of more than one's own perspective. However, information search is often biased, because confirming information is favored over opposing information. Therefore it would be useful to recommend information that is inconsistent to users' prior perspective to help overcome this bias. The present paper deals with an online experiment aimed at investigating the effects of preference-consistent compared to preference-inconsistent recommendations on information selection and evaluation. Results showed a significant reduction of confirmation bias in the condition with preference-inconsistent recommendations. However, participants prefer preference-consistent recommendations in terms of global, cognitive and affective evaluations. We discuss the impact of these findings for application.

Author Keywords
Recommendations, confirmation bias, experimental study.

ACM Classification Keywords
J.4 Social and Behavioral Sciences---Psychology, K.3.1 Computer Uses in Education, H.5.m. Information Interfaces and Presentation (e.g., HCI): Miscellaneous.

General Terms
Experimentation, Human Factors

INTRODUCTION
Recommender systems are very popular personalized information filtering tools originating in areas such as e-commerce and online marketing [8]. They provide valuable cues about the preferences held by the community, thereby giving guidance to one's activities. In commercial contexts, recommendations are mainly intended to fit the user's taste – the recipients are meant to *like* the recommended product. But what if a recommended item is not a product, but a thought or an argument? One could still strive to recommend thoughts that users like. However, maximizing preference-consistency might be detrimental in some cases. First, system output can become trivial and lead to dissatisfaction, e.g. when the third part of a trilogy is recommended because a user gave good ratings for the first two parts [12]. Second, tailoring to users' preferences can lead to separate "balkanized" interest groups, preventing the emergence of novel ideas [11]. Third, preference-consistent recommendations do not challenge the user with opposing views even though this is desirable for informed decision making on societal, political or health-related issues. In particular, for critical thinking, opinion formation, learning, or education, it is worthwhile to confront users with dissenting information [2, 5].

Bias in information search
However, there is empirical evidence that people often fail to take dissenting information into account [6, 9]. For instance, by searching for information on controversial topics, users tend to seek information that confirms their prior perspectives. This biased information search leads to the maintenance of the information seeker's position. The effect is based on Festinger's dissonance theory and is referred to as selective exposure or confirmation bias [4, 6]: As soon as individuals adopt a position, they favor consistent over inconsistent information to avoid dissonance. As confirmation bias hinders users from taking dissenting information into account, it is also an obstacle towards becoming an informed decision maker.

Potential of preference-inconsistent recommendations
This raises the question of how confirmation bias can be overcome. Our suggestion involves the use of systems that recommend preference-inconsistent information for controversial issues. There are already some approaches that target diversity through algorithms [10, 12], and others that target user reactions through recommender systems interface design [1, 3]. However, none of these studies investigates the basic psychological processes underlying the confrontation with recommendations. The research presented here addressed this question by testing if users select more inconsistent information and thus reduce confirmation bias when preference-inconsistent information

is made salient through recommendation. Furthermore, we explored how users evaluate these recommendations.

Conclusion and Contribution

We use a stepwise approach to explore the potential of preference-inconsistent recommendations. The first step involves investigating the impact of preference-inconsistent recommendations on information selection and evaluation. To assess our hypotheses, a basic experimental approach appears suitable. If a reduced confirmation bias can be found, later steps will focus on the effects that inconsistent recommendations have on preferences, elaboration, as well as on rating behavior. Finally, an implementation might validate the findings in the field. The effects of preference-inconsistent recommendations on users' reactions may have an important influence on the logic and the implementation of recommender systems.

Hypotheses

Based on the research on controversies [5], it is hypothesized that confirmation bias will remain when preference-consistent arguments are recommended and that this bias will be reduced when preference-inconsistent arguments are recommended.

Hypothesis 1: Preference-consistent recommendations lead to confirmation bias. Preference-inconsistent recommendations reduce confirmation bias.

Keeping in mind that challenging information is not always liked most [10], it is expected that the evaluation of preference-inconsistent recommendation will be inferior to the evaluation of preference-consistent recommendation.

Hypothesis 2: Global evaluations of as well as cognitive and affective reactions to preference-inconsistent recommendations will be lower than those for preference-consistent recommendations.

METHOD

We tested our hypotheses by conducting an online experiment using Amazon Mechanical Turk (www.mturk.com). This was deemed appropriate as the study involved a close-ended task [7]. Moreover, through manipulation check questions random clicking was prevented.

Participants

Participants were included in the analysis only if manipulation check questions were answered correctly. Following this rule, data from 123 paid subjects ($M = 32.68$, $SD = 10.94$; 70 females) were obtained for the analyses. The majority of participants (96 %) judged their prior knowledge about the subject matter to be very poor, poor, or average.

Materials and Design

The materials of the online study comprised a number of screens. One screen contained a short introductory text about the controversial topic of neuro-enhancement, referring to the facilitation of cognitive abilities through training or through the intake of medicine. The main screen of the experiment consisted of a bogus list of Web search results. The list was composed of eight written arguments, four of them endorsing and four of them opposing neuro-enhancement. Each argument consisted of a headline followed by two explanatory sentences[1]. Although the headlines were marked as hyperlinks participants could not access additional information. One of the arguments was highlighted by an orange-colored frame around the text. This argument represented the recommendation. The caption above the frame stated: "The following resource is recommended to you." The order of the arguments and the serial position of the recommendation were randomized across participants in order to minimize content and order effects.

A one factorial design with two conditions was used to manipulate the recommendation (preference-consistent vs. preference-inconsistent). In the first experimental condition an argument was recommended that was consistent with the participant's preference on neuro-enhancement. In the second experimental condition an argument was recommended that was inconsistent with the participant's preference. Of the participants, 61 were randomly assigned to the preference-consistent experimental condition (EC_{con}), and 62 to the preference-inconsistent experimental condition (EC_{inc}). In both conditions user preferences were equally distributed: overall, 62 % of the participants were in favor of neuro-enhancement.

Procedure

The procedure was adapted from Jonas et al. [6]. First, subjects read the introductory passage on neuro-enhancement and they indicated which perspective on the controversial issue they preferred (endorsing vs. opposing neuro-enhancement). In the second phase, the list of eight arguments was presented with four arguments in favor and four arguments against neuro-enhancement. This phase varied depending on which condition the participants were assigned to. In the consistent experimental condition subjects received a preference-consistent recommendation, and in the inconsistent experimental condition subjects received a preference-inconsistent recommendation. This treatment mimicked the personalization part of recommender systems. Subjects were asked to select

[1] An example of an endorsing argument: "Minimizing risks at the workplace: Neuro-enhancement should be embraced particularly for professional fields where human failure is likely to lead to detrimental outcomes (e.g. air traffic controllers, surgeons, or military personnel)." An example of an opposing argument: "Striving for undesirable perfectionism: The era of lovable little quirks might be over quite soon. Research is looking for ways to make us perfect. We don't need that."

exactly one argument that they would like to read more about by clicking on an adjacent box. In the third phase, participants received semantic differential scales in order to evaluate the perceived quality of the recommended argument. These scales contained four items concerning global attitudes, six items on cognitive, and six items on affective evaluations on a 7-point bipolar continuum. Each item was represented by a word pair ranging from a negative (-3) to a positive end point (+3). Afterwards, participants were asked to provide demographic details (age, gender), and they could comment on the experiment using a text box. On average, the experiment lasted 864 seconds (*SD* = 398) and subjects dwelled on the main page for 292 seconds (*SD* = 166).

Information selection was measured by means of the arguments that participants chose. If more users in a condition selected preference-consistent over preference-inconsistent arguments a confirmation bias would exist.

For measuring *evaluation* we used semantic differential scales. They consisted of lists of adjectives where subjects assessed the recommendation given to them on bipolar 7-point continua for a global evaluation as well as for cognitive and affective reactions.

RESULTS

Selection

The key finding was that recommendations do have an influence on the selection of consistent and inconsistent arguments. This effect was statistically highly significant by comparing the bias between the two conditions ($\chi^2_{0.95\,(1)} = 8.66, p < .01$). This effect is shown in Figure 1.

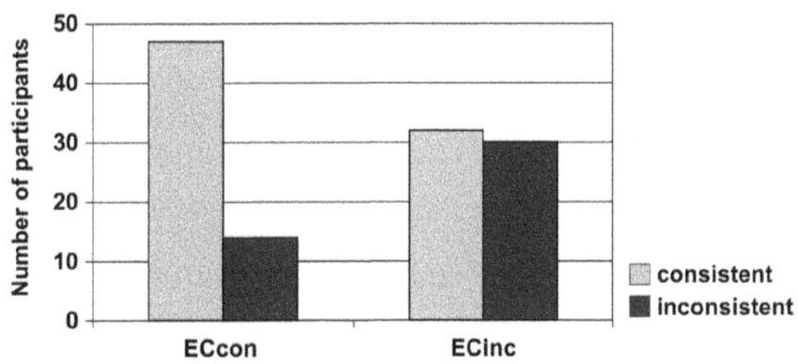

Figure 1. Number of participants selecting consistent and inconsistent arguments in the two conditions

There was no significant difference in the acceptance rates of recommendations between the two conditions: 28% of the EC_{con} subjects and 26% of the EC_{inc} subjects selected the recommended argument ($t(121) = -0.26$, *n. s.*).

These results raise the possibility that confirmation bias was only reduced in EC_{inc} by subjects "blindly" following the recommendation. However, this could be ruled out by performing separate χ^2 goodness of fit tests per condition and on only those participants who did not accept the recommendation. The number of participants was therefore reduced to 44 in EC_{con} and to 46 in EC_{inc}. As expected, in EC_{con} a highly significant confirmation bias was found ($\chi^2_{0.95\,(1)} = 11.48$, $p < .01$). In contrast, EC_{inc} did not yield such a bias ($\chi^2_{0.95\,(1)} = 2.92$, *n. s.*).

Evaluation

The items of the three evaluative categories (global, cognitive, and affective) were integrated into three overall scale values, respectively. Figure 2 shows that the global evaluation was significantly better for preference-consistent recommendations (*M* = 1.14, *SD* = 1.40) than for preference-inconsistent recommendations (*M* = -0.17, *SD* = 1.46), $t(121) = 5.10, p < .001$.

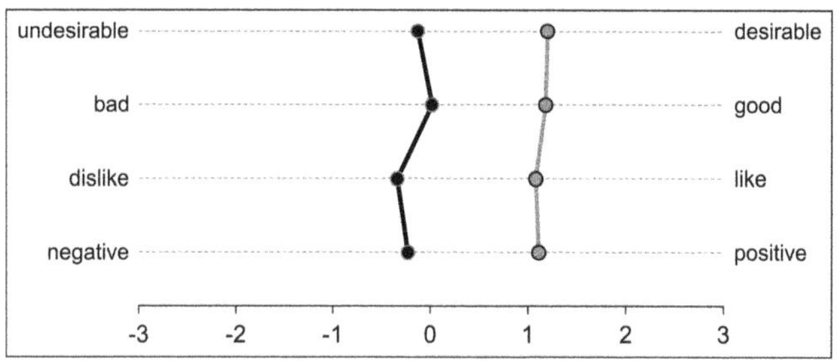

Figure 2. Global evaluation patterns for consistent (grey) and inconsistent (black) recommendations.

The same pattern of results was found for the cognitive scale ($t(121) = 2.80$, $p < .01$) and the affective scale ($t(121) = 5.09$, $p < .001$). The detailed scores for these scales are shown in Figure 3. Additional analyses have shown that these effects are independent from the acceptance of recommendations in both conditions.

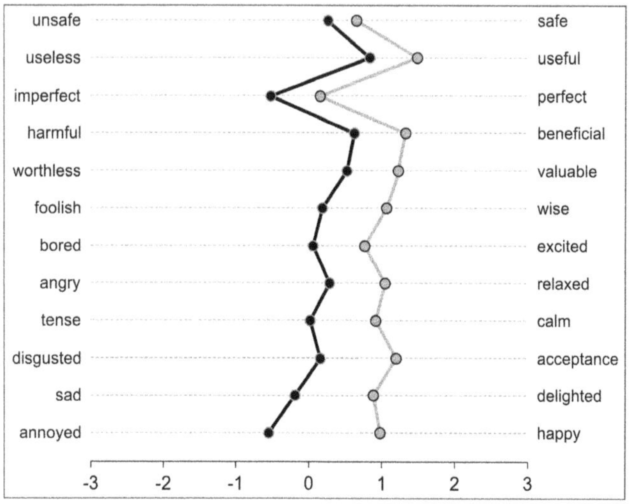

Figure 3. Cognitive and affective evaluation patterns for consistent (grey) and inconsistent (black) recommendations.

Summary of results

To sum up the results, we found that preference-consistent recommendations have a different impact on information selection and evaluation than preference-inconsistent recommendations. When a preference-consistent argument is recommended, users are subject to a confirmation bias.

This is expressed by the higher selection frequency of consistent over inconsistent resources. This difference is not present when inconsistent recommendations are given. The effects within the conditions persist even after excluding the participants who accepted the respective recommendation. The second finding refers to the evaluation of the recommendations. Consistent recommendations are better evaluated than inconsistent recommendations. This significant difference was found for global evaluation as well as cognitive and affective properties.

IMPLICATIONS AND FUTURE WORK

Searching for information in the Web is often triggered by actual debates and controversies concerning societal, political or health related issues and by the motivation for informed decision making. Becoming an informed decision maker requires actually attending to arguments supporting *and* opposing one's own perspective. In the Web a vast amount of differing opinions is publicly available. However, because confirmation bias prevents attention to dissenting information, availability alone is not sufficient. Our empirical data show that confirmation bias can be overcome by preference-inconsistent recommendations.

A limitation of the current findings is that they could not be compared to a control condition. Based on the findings of Jonas et al. [6] we hypothesize that a natural confirmation bias will be present when no recommendation is given. Future studies have to clarify if consistent recommendations maintain or even enhance this bias. Furthermore, our future research in this field is dedicated to subsequent user reactions to preference-consistent and preference-inconsistent recommendations. It will track the cognitive consequences, e.g. by capturing memory of arguments, preference change, and elaboration. In other words, we want to find out if recommendations do not only have an influence on information selection, but also on further information processing. First hints that this might be the case can be drawn from the comments that subjects gave on the experiment. For instance, one participant receiving a preference-inconsistent recommendation wrote "it makes sense, I'm curious to learn more", and another indicated "I decided that it would [be] interesting to read more about it because I might change my mind."

However, this study has also shown that preference-inconsistent recommendations come with a cost. Our data on the evaluation of recommendations provide empirical support for the assumption made by Tang and McCalla [10] that users do not always like demanding recommendations. This finding has implications for the design of recommender systems. Future studies should be directed at finding ways to make preference-inconsistent recommendations more appealing, e.g. by verbally framing inconsistent items as challenging or interesting. Making users not only select preference-inconsistent content, but also to make them think about more than their own perspective, is likely to be a selling point for the development of successful recommender systems in non-commercial contexts.

ACKNOWLEDGMENTS

This work was supported by grants from the Leibniz Graduate School for Knowledge Media Research.

REFERENCES

1. Cosley, D., Lam, S.K., Albert, I., Konstan, J.A., and Riedl, J. Is seeing believing? How recommender system interfaces affect users' opinions. In *Proc. CHI 2003*, ACM Press (2003), 585-592.
2. Doise, W., and Mugny, G. *The social development of the intellect*. Oxford: Pergamon Press, 1984.
3. Faridani, S., Bitton, E., Ryokai, K., and Goldberg, K. Opinion space: A scalable tool for browsing online comments. In *Proc. CHI 2010*, ACM Press (2010), 1175-1184.
4. Festinger, L. *A theory of cognitive dissonance*. Stanford University Press, 1957.
5. Johnson, D.W., Johnson, R.T., and Smith, K.A. Constructive controversy: The educative power of intellectual conflict. *Change 32*, 1 (2000), 28-37.
6. Jonas, E., Schulz-Hardt, S., Frey, D., and Thelen, N. Confirmation bias in sequential information search after preliminary decisions: An expansion of dissonance theoretical research on selective exposure to information. *Journal of Personality and Social Psychology 80*, 4 (2001), 557-571.
7. Kittur, A., Chi, E.H., and Suh, B. Crowdsourcing user studies with Mechanical Turk. In *Proc. CHI 2008*, ACM Press (2008), 453-456.
8. Schafer, J.B., Konstan, J., and Riedl, J. Recommender systems in e-commerce. In *Proc. EC 1999*, ACM Press (1999), 158-166.
9. Stanovich, K.E., and West, R.F. Reasoning independently of prior belief and individual differences in actively open-minded thinking. *Journal of Educational Psychology 89*, (1997), 342-357.
10. Tang, T.Y., and McCalla, G. Beyond learners' interest: Personalized paper recommendation based on their pedagogical features for an e-learning system. *PRICAI: Trends in Artificial Intelligence* (2004), 301-310.
11. Van Alstyne, M.W., and Brynjolfsson, E. Global village or cyber-balkans? Modeling and measuring the integration of electronic communities. *Management Science 51*, 6 (2005), 851-868.
12. Ziegler, C.N., McNee, S.M., Konstan, J.A., and Lausen, G. Improving recommendation lists through topic diversification. In *Proc. WWW 2005*, ACM Press (2005), 22-32.

Embodiment in Brain-Computer Interaction

Kenton O'Hara, Abigail Sellen, Richard Harper
Microsoft Research
7 J J Thomson Avenue
Cambridge, UK

ABSTRACT
With emerging opportunities for using Brain-Computer Interaction (BCI) in gaming applications, there is a need to understand the opportunities and constraints of this interaction paradigm. To complement existing laboratory-based studies, there is also a call for the study of BCI in real world contexts. We present such a real world study of a simple BCI game called MindFlex®, played as a social activity in the home. In particular, drawing on the philosophical traditions of embodied interaction, we highlight the importance of considering the body in BCI and not simply what is going on in the head. The study shows how people use bodily actions to facilitate control of brain activity but also to make their actions and intentions visible to, and interpretable by, others playing and watching the game. It is the public availability of these bodily actions during BCI that allows action to be socially organised, understood and coordinated with others and through which social relationships can be played out. We discuss the implications of this perspective and findings for BCI.

Author Keywords
Brain-Computer Interaction, gaming, embodied interaction

ACM Classification Keywords
H5.m. Information interfaces and presentation (e.g., HCI): Miscellaneous.

ACM Classification Keywords
Human Factors

INTRODUCTION
The concept of Brain-Computer Interaction (BCI) in which measurements of brain activity are used to control interactive systems has been with us for decades. Initially, the key focus of this kind of interaction technique was to offer new interaction modalities for people with disabilities such as those with motor control impairments. For example, BCI techniques have been used to control cursors, keyboard entry or navigation for wheelchairs [2, 25, 33, 26]. More recently, though, with advances in non-invasive BCI technology and the development of more practical BCI headsets, there is now a realistic possibility for using such technologies for a wider variety of applications and for users with no physical disabilities [1, 23]. In the last few years, one such area to which researchers have turned their attention has been the use of BCI as a technique for gaming [e.g. 5, 10 22, 15, 7, 16]. Some notable examples from the research literature include Brainball [12, 13], MindBalance [16], and "Use the force" [17, 20]. At the same time, we are also now beginning to see the first commercial BCI-based games with offerings from NeuroSky and Emotiv. These organisations offer both headsets and development kits for the creation of new games and applications based on BCI technology. This is likely to accelerate development of BCI games for fun and educational purposes.

Accompanying such developments, there is an increasing need to further understand the opportunities and constraints of BCI as an interactional paradigm within the context of gaming [22, 23]. That is, it raises questions such as: what are the capabilities and limitations of these techniques within the context of gaming; in what ways should BCI techniques be combined with other interaction modalities for engaging gaming experiences; and what new paradigms need to be developed that go beyond the emulation of basic games controllers [17]?

In deepening this understanding, as with any other area of HCI, there is a need to adopt a broad set of techniques capable of addressing both micro and macro levels of analytic enquiry, from questions of fine-grained interactional efficacy to larger questions of the value and use of these systems in real world social contexts. Inevitably, because of the pragmatic considerations associated with BCI research, to date there has been tendency to focus on issues amenable to analytic enquiry within laboratory settings by individuals using the headsets. These studies yield important results, but are only a part of the story. As Lécuyer et al suggest, there is a need to begin complementing this strand of work with other types of HCI and CSCW enquiry [17]. That is, they argue for more ethnographic and real world studies of BCI for gaming and other application scenarios. Such studies will help in an understanding of this technology since games are, in the main, social, as indeed are many of the other contexts in which BCI might be deployed.

With this in mind, in this paper, we discuss findings from a real world study of a BCI-controlled game played as a social activity in the home. This study draws on the philosophical and analytic concerns found in CSCW where techniques for analysing the social in all its embodied forms

CHI 2011, May 7-12, 2011, Vancouver, BC, Canada.

are well developed [e.g. 6, 28]. Before presenting the study, we first wish to establish some more context with respect to BCI and embodied interaction.

BCI AND EMBODIED INTERACTION

On the face of it, it is perhaps rather curious to align BCI with embodied interaction. After all, on the surface, the magic of BCI stems from the apparent disembodiment of action, where thoughts alone can have impact in the world. Inherent in the BCI paradigm and in its treatment in the literature is a focus on the internal workings of the brain and how detectable patterns of brain activity can be reliably interpreted to control artefacts in the digital domain. In this respect, the BCI paradigm begins to bear some resemblance to early approaches in HCI that were dominated by cognitive theories and abstract representations of the brain's internal processes as opposed to specific concerns with the external world, and the ways in which actions were situated. However, as HCI matured, this approach was subject to a number of critiques both in practical and philosophical terms. In part, these critiques arose out of the turn to the social as HCI shifted focus away from simply addressing individual interaction with computers to the more collaborative interaction possibilities being realized with emerging CSCW technologies. With this shift came new concerns and approaches driven by the practical concern of how to think about groups of people interacting through technology rather than just about individuals. But, accompanying this were related philosophical issues. In particular, there were concerns about the abstract nature of cognitive theories and the inherent "invisibility" of these processes. This led to a greater emphasis on examining what was observable – namely social action and the ways it is situated within a particular context [e.g. 8, 30]. It is this perspective we bring to bear in the work we report here.

Of additional import with these critiques and new approaches to HCI are philosophical foundations associated with them. These raise intriguing and challenging questions with respect to BCI because of the extent to which they concern themselves with the "embodiment" of action. Notions of embodied action in HCI [e.g. 5, 28] essentially draw on the philosophical foundations of phenomenologist thinkers such as Husserl, Heidegger and Merleau-Ponty. These authors take as their starting point that consciousness and perception are active, interpretive and embodied, arising from our presence and action in the world. This particular stance of embodied interaction is of significance for a number of reasons that relate to our concerns and methodological orientation in this paper. Firstly, it articulates an inherent relationship between actions in the world and our internal cognitive and conscious experiences. Secondly, it argues that through our actions we are able to create shared meanings with other people - the public availability of these actions to the perceptions of others allows action to be socially organized, understood and coordinated with others.

Where these arguments lead us to then are the important concern with the bodily actions that accompany brain-computer interaction. While BCI technologies have done more to reveal the internal workings of the brain and render them interpretable (albeit by machines), the inherent relationship with bodily actions in the world suggests our understanding of Brain-Computer Interactions lies also with an understanding of these actions in the world. This relationship has implications both for the pragmatics of BCI control as well as how these interactions are experienced socially. For example, from a pragmatic perspective, bodily movements and muscle artefacts can influence EEG signals [e.g. 21]. Within a social context, too, these accompanying actions are of additional significance. The work done to render the internal states of the brain and any intentionality visible and interpretable by others present, through actions, gestures, expressions and utterances, is a key component in the organisation of social conduct around these kinds of interactions [14]. Further, this is of importance to how social meaning is created through these technologies and how particular social relationships are played out both for those playing as well as those watching.

In order to explore these issues, we present a real world study of people using a simple BCI-based game called MindFlex®. MindFlex was a useful candidate of study for our purposes for a number of reasons. First, it is one of only a few BCI applications readily and commercially available for real world deployment. Second, gaming offers the necessary kind of social context through which we could study the social organisation of action with BCI.

RELATED WORK: BCI AND GAMING

While the use of steady state visual-evoked potentials and motor imagery-based BCIs have been demonstrated in other contexts, the demands of gaming present different challenges that motivate the recent crop of games-related research [7, 23]. There are questions for example, as to how things such as audio and visual stimulation in video games might impact on performance and motivation in positive and negative ways by dividing resources [e.g. 16]. A number of research initiatives in recent years have begun to explore the use of simple BCI controls in game-like scenarios. Typically, the applications provide the user with a small set of commands and controls somewhere in the region of one to three [17]. For example, there have been several attempts to demonstrate the use of BCI techniques for navigating in game-like virtual environments [e.g. 19]. The concern of this research, though, was not focussed on the gaming experience per se. Rather, they wanted to demonstrate how feedback provided by the 3D virtual world could improve motivation and performance over simple 2D feedback. What this does show, though, is the susceptibility of BCI performance to certain factors and parameters within game-like settings.

Other researchers have more explicitly attempted to create engaging game situations within the particular control constraints of BCI to understand the efficacy of the interaction within this context. In the MindBalance game, players' EEG readings are used to provide binary control over an animated character that is balancing on a tightrope [16]. As the character walks towards the player, it stumbles either leftwards or rightwards off the tightrope. The aim of the game is to correct the character's balance by focusing on the checkerboard on the opposite side of the screen to the direction of falling. This work is important for us in a number of ways. First, it points to an idiomatic approach to BCI game design. That is, the game mechanic would be relatively trivial for other more traditional games controllers but presents an engaging challenge within the context of EEG-based control. Second, the study quantitatively demonstrated that such binary control was feasible within the visually stimulating environment of the game and importantly that this success could be achieved using techniques requiring little training – an especially important consideration for use of BCI in gaming.

The MindBalance study, for good reason, like much BCI research, was conducted in closely controlled environmental conditions. As we have discussed, some authors have made explicit calls to conduct additional BCI research for gaming in more demanding real world contexts. This was one of the motivations underlying the work of the group at INRIA in their development and explorations of the "Use the Force" game [17, 20]. In this game, BCI techniques were used to control the virtual take-off of a spaceship using real or imaginary foot movements. One thing of significance was that it was conducted outside of a controlled laboratory environment in a public exhibition space with a large number of participants. This context enabled the researchers to take on some of the challenges associated with BCI in more real world environments and the distractions associated with these. In spite of these challenges, the experiments reported that a significant number of participants were able to successfully control the spaceship with BCI. The work also highlighted some of the cognitive strategies employed by participants in their control of the ship. This is an issue we return to later in the study presented here, albeit within the social context of game play. Of importance with this work though, as the authors argue, is that the environmental context of the study paves a way for more ethnographic enquiry into BCI, a key motivation for the work presented here.

Perhaps one of the most intriguing and imaginative pieces of work in BCI gaming is that which has looked at Brainball [12, 13]. What is notable about this research is that it is less focused on demonstrable efficacy of the BCI technique within the gaming domain and more on the creation of an engaging experience within the constraints and affordances of the BCI technology. In this game, two players at either end of a game table control a ball on the table. The aim of the game is to score a goal by moving the ball into the opponent's goalmouth by relaxing more than your opponent. With greater relative relaxation, the ball moves towards the opponent's goalmouth.

Notwithstanding the imaginative concept behind the game itself, the research on it highlights a number of important issues. For example, and as articulated by several authors, play is as much a social and collaborative experience as it is an individual experience [e.g. 29, 31, 32]. It is the social aspects of games through which play becomes meaningful – an opportunity for people to come together with social purpose: for competition, for identity work and for other forms of social occasioning. The playing of BrainBall was very much a social occasion; in part because it involved multiple players in competition, but also because the playing of the game became an event, attracting both players and audience. The notion of audience in relation to BCI is of interest to us because it suggests engagement with a game is not just about a player's experience but also how it can be watched and enjoyed [27].

While the BrainBall work points to a number of issues relevant to our discussion, the evaluation part of the research does not share the same analytic concerns as our own. The research discusses some high level feedback about people's response, but there is very little in the way of detailed interaction analysis that contributes to our understanding of the physical manifestations of behaviour using BCI in social settings – the *physical* and *social* features of playing the game in a real-world setting.

THE STUDY

MindFlex® game

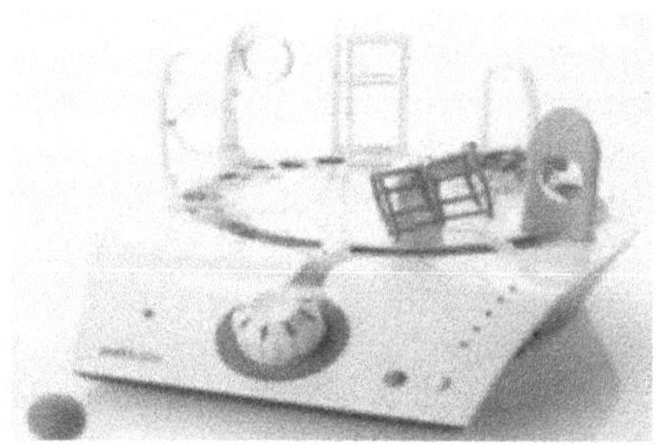

Figure 1. The MindFlex® Game Board

The MindFlex® Game is a commercially available BCI game and, as such, is amenable to use in a real world study. MindFlex uses a wireless headset with single electrode at the front and two clips that attach to each earlobe. The headset is based on Electroencephalography (EEG) technology that measures electrical signals from the brain to determine relative levels of concentration. The aim of the game is to move a floating ball around an obstacle course assembled on the game board (see Figure 1). As the player concentrates, electrical signals from the brain activate a fan on the game. Higher levels of brain activity, or "concentration", increase the fan strength, thereby blowing the ball higher. To lower the ball, players must relax, reducing concentration and brain activity. With the ball raised, a second control knob is turned by hand to move the fan source round the game board. This allows the floating ball to be moved around the obstacle course as the player raises or lowers the ball over encountered obstacles.

Participants

Sixteen participants took part in the study, made up of four distinct groups of people who knew each other. For each group there was a "host" participant responsible for assembling the group of people with whom they wanted to play the game just as they would if playing any other game at home. A social group had to consist of at least two people. The groups, then, consisted of different family members and friend relationships as determined by the group host. The groups were as follows:

Group 1 – One female (early 30s) and one male (early 40s), in a relationship and cohabiting.

Group 2 – Father (early 40s) playing with his three children – boy (7), girl (16), boy (18).

Group 3 – Married couple (50s), daughter (14), her two stepsisters (18, 20), the boyfriend (20) of one of the stepsisters. One of the stepsisters had learning difficulties.

Group 4 – Mother (50), father (52), son (14), daughter (12).

Method

Host participants were given the MindFlex® game to take home for approximately 1 week. They were asked to play the game at home with other people they knew. It was up to them to decide when, where, with whom, and how often to play the game, just as with any other game. Participants were given a camcorder and asked to video themselves when they played the game in a social setting. The groups were fluid in that some people would join or leave the group at particular points during any game play; this fluidity being a natural component to the play context. After finishing with the game, participants returned it and the video recordings of their sessions. In total, there was approximately 4 hours worth of video data collected from the sessions. The video sessions were subject to a detailed interaction analysis by the researchers, that focused on the physical manifestation of behaviour around the game, looking in detail at bodily action, gestures and utterances occurring during game play. This was oriented to players, as well as co-presents others who were watching or even collaborating. The aim of this analysis was to describe the embodied nature of the interactions and collaborations, and how they were coordinated. Further, it aimed to show how social meaning was created and relationships played out through these embodied interactions.

FINDINGS

In presenting the findings, we draw on a series of vignettes and video sequences that illustrate key manifestations of the embodied nature of BCI. We begin with a discussion of the body in achieving focus and controlling concentration and relaxation. Next, we consider notions of intentionality including difficulties arising from lack of bodily manifestations of intentionality and the efforts to make intentionality visible. We then explore extraneous gestures people employ to accompany BCI creating enhanced narrative around the game and with a view to facilitating their engagement. We then look at the ways players create performance through their body during BCI. We examine too, the playful role of spectators in interacting with the players and the social and interactional implications of this.

Bodily Orientation and Focus

In our observations, the proxemic arrangement of players with respect to the game and others was an important consideration for controlling concentration and relaxation. Deliberate adjustments in body posture were performed to relax and achieve focus. Consider a sequence from a participant in Group 4 (Figure 2).

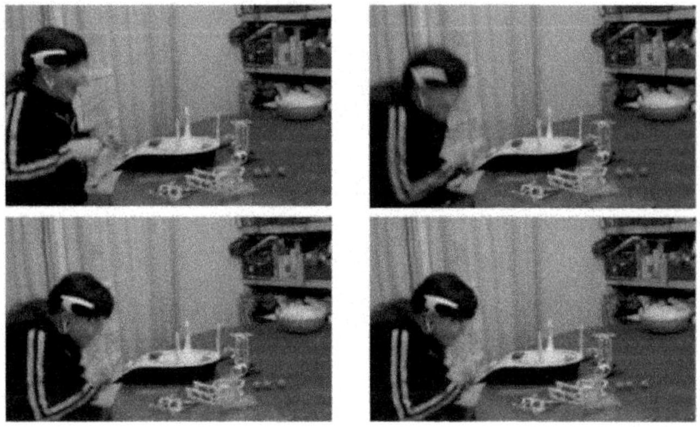

Figure 2. Holding breath and clenching for concentration

The younger daughter, staring at the ball, lifts her whole body up as she takes a deep breath and holds it. While holding her breath, she lowers her body downwards and towards the device. She clenches her hand and tenses up her whole body as if this will squeeze out some imaginary energy to raise the ball. This posturing has little to do directly with facilitating the wireless transmission of signals between headset and game. Rather, it is a strategy to achieve focus and concentration.

Such spatial arrangements were not simply static but rather were dynamically organised in response to the behaviour of the game and player performance. For example, players would lean in and increase the intensity of their visible gaze when the ball was not responding as they intended. What is of significance in these behaviours is the way gestures are closely choreographed with the behaviour of the game. We can see this illustrated in the following sequence (see Figure 3). In the beginning, the player (Group 1) looks at the ball with her hand on the control knob, trying to keep the ball raised through concentration. However, the ball begins to lower. As the ball lowers, she removes her hand from the control knob and begins to clench and unclench her hand. Closely choreographed with this is a scrunching up of her face. The intensity of the squeezing and grimace increase as the ball becomes precariously low but the gestures gradually relax as she manages to raise the ball. Only then does her hand return to the control knob. What we see here is the use of gesture in attempt to get back into a state of concentration. In using her hands in this way, she is temporarily unable to control the other mode of input, namely the control knob. Only once she has achieved a more stable state of focus does she return to the multimodal input control.

Figure 3. Gesture and Posture choreographed with game

Proxemic arrangement and gaze orientation were also used as means to try and reduce concentration on the ball in order to lower it. Most typically, this involved averting the gaze away from the game. Consider the following sequence in which a player from Group 2 was struggling to reduce the height of the ball (see Figure 4).

Figure 4. Averting gaze to reduce concentration

The sequence begins with the player staring at the ball, with his hand on the control knob ready to move the ball around the game board when it lowers. As he is unable to reduce his concentration and thereby lower the ball, he removes his hand from the control knob and looks away to his left. As he is looking to the left, the ball lowers in height as his concentration is reduced. Importantly as the ball lowers, the pitch of the fan reduces indicating that it is falling. When it gets to a low enough pitch, he then briefly brings his gaze back to the ball to quickly monitor its height before returning his gaze again to the left. The ball and the pitch of the fan drop lower allowing him to feel confident that he is in a state of relaxation. With that, he turns again to face the ball and brings his right hand back onto the control knob to begin to steer it. As he does this, his concentration increases and the ball begins to rise. To his frustration, he removes his hands from the knob and turns his gaze to the right and up into the air. Important here is the turn away from the visible as a means to guide the player interaction with the device. This potentially raises interaction difficulties because of a lack of visual monitoring of the system. However, the audio feedback provided by the noise of the fan allows the player to continue monitoring the system behaviour.

Mental Imagery and Narrative

During game play, gestures were performed as part of an additional narrative fantasy layer acted out over and above the basic elements of the game play. In the following vignette (Group 2), a father is playing with his younger son, and the father is offering guidance and instructions for how to get the ball to rise. In offering these instructions, the father adds an additional layer of narrative to the game that goes beyond what is necessary if we consider the interaction purely in terms of the control mechanisms. He suggests: *"Relax your face and put everything through your hands and into the ball flying"*. The instructions here, then, make reference to an imaginary energy that flows from the brain through the body and hands to the system. In response to this, the son moves his hands over the system and hovers them next to the ball to facilitate the channelling of this "energy" (see Figure 5).

Figure 5. Magician fantasy gestures

This additional narrative fantasy adds an extra source of mysticism and engagement for the son playing (and the father watching). With his father watching, the son plays it out through his bodily actions, waving his fingers about the ball, simulating the movements of a magician. He cups his hands underneath the ball without touching it and raises them, moving the "energy flow" in an attempt to move the ball upwards. These additional layers of narrative interpretation and mental imagery were evident in other strategies used by players in their attempts to more explicitly control the interaction in the game too. Such strategies involved thinking directly about moving the ball up or thinking about related concepts of height or flying objects. Another example is from the daughter in Group 2 :

> *"Birds , Plane takes off into the air. Up very high. Sky diver from very high up." She is saying this as she is looking into the air "Up up up up up!"*

> *"At the end of the day it helps to think about moving up – I don't know why. Think about stuff that moves up." Son 2, Gp 2*

Of significance here is how these kinds of strategies contribute to engagement with the device, adding a layer of intentionality to the way interaction is achieved, and a narrative in which players can engage. With this particular BCI mechanism, control is achieved through any non-specific concentration level. That is, it is not necessary to think of the ball moving up. However, by virtue of thinking about the ball moving up, they are in consequence increasing their concentration. So while it is simply this increased concentration that is causing the ball to rise, the association it makes with their intentional thoughts gives the impression that the intentional thought is responsible. Ironically, adopting this approach can also lead to a lack of control. For example, in other cases, players were seen to think explicitly about lowering the ball in order to get it to fall. This turns out to be counter-productive since these kinds of thoughts lead to increased concentration levels. We can see this in another episode where the father (Group 2) is interacting with his young son who is playing the game. The father says to his son *"Lower it in your mind"*. In response to this comment the son begins to stare intently at the ball, trying to control it rather than relax. The concentration levels that accompany this lead to the ball remaining in the air. Within the narrative of control, this is the appropriate opposite but is mismatched with the actual underlying control mechanics.

This has implications for thinking about the design of games and other applications utilising these relatively simplistic non-specific BCI mechanisms. That is, it suggests how design of the game experience might focus on the construction of appropriate narratives within the game to encourage stronger engagement with the game at the same time as teaching players how to achieve better control.

Intentionality and Invisibility

Watching and interpreting the game (whether for coordination purposes or enjoyment of the spectacle), was not always straightforward and unambiguous. Other players and spectators were not always able to understand the intentions and actions of others in relation to the game, particularly when there was no bodily manifestation of their intention. Key here is that focus and concentration are often at odds with communicating with others. Consider an example of this interpretive difficulty.

Participant J, the young son from Group 2 is playing the obstacle course version of the game while his father watches from the other side of the table. The father has been instructing his son in terms of how to control the ball and also the rules of the obstacle course such as correct direction for the ball to pass through the hoop. As J approaches the upcoming hoop obstacle with the ball floating below the hoop, the father says *"Top down that one"* as he points to the hoop in question. Because J is concentrating on trying to raise the ball higher and rotating it around in line with the hoop, he is unable to acknowledge his father's instruction either verbally or through gesture. The father is therefore reliant on the behaviour of the ball to confirm that his son has understood. However, because of the difficulty J is having controlling the ball, it is lower than the height of the loop giving the impression that he is approaching the hoop from the bottom up. The father takes this to mean that J has ignored his instructions so repeats them: *"Top down"*, to which J replies *"I know. I'm thinking, I'm thinking."* In verbally acknowledging his father, J is distracted and the ball drops to the game surface.

The example demonstrates how interaction *manipulations* [27] in this BCI are difficult to discern by those watching the game. Because these manipulations are not visible, those co-present might normally infer intentionality of a player from the interaction *effects* – namely the system's output. However, one difficulty with this approach in the context of this game arises from the relative lack of precision over the control of the system and a lack of strong mapping between the intentionality of the player and the game. This means that intentionality is not always represented in the interaction *effects* with this kind of interface. These factors lead to the misinterpretation of the player's intentions by the father. To exacerbate the problem, having to correct this misinterpretation also interferes with the player's attempt to concentrate, further undermining his ability to control the ball.

The imprecision of mapping between intentionality and interaction effects was also dealt with by players volunteering explanations of their behaviour through visible utterance or gesture. Consider the following episode. The father (Group 2) is playing the obstacle course version of the game while his children watch. He has his hand on the control knob, but keeps it still, ready to move the ball around once it is at the correct height. The ball is floating in the air and oscillating gently at a certain height. The father is staring at it and then looking away. The children are motionless watching him. This continues in silence for several seconds. At this point, the father glances across at them, chuckles and says: *"I can't get it to go down."* Because the ball has been up in the air for so long and not making any progress visible to the observing audience, he feels a need to explain what is going on to those watching.

Gestures too were used to make intentions visible to the audience when they were not being revealed through the state of the system. We can see an example of this in the following sequence by the daughter in Group 3 (Figure 6).

Figure 6. Using gesture to reveal intentionality

The daughter in this sequence is playing the obstacle course. She has raised the ball and prepares to move it around to the next obstacle. Once the ball is positioned above the obstacle, she needs to lower it through the hoop. As this does not happen immediately, she signals her intent through gesture. She looks at the ball and brings both hands off the console. As she raises them up, she turns them over and then gently lowers them in a downward gesture. While moving her hands down, she closes her eyes and gently nods her head to signal that the action should be initiated. She repeats this gesture phrase again, but with a stronger nod of the head to emphasise her intent.

Play as performance

Beyond simply trying to account for, or explain one's actions to others, we also observed that bodily movements and verbalizations while interacting with the device were sometimes about creating a performance for those watching. At times, gestures were deliberately exaggerated not only to help make visible the intentions of the player to the audience, but also to make it more engaging to watch. This is illustrated well in the following segment (Figure 7). Here, we see the daughter from Group 2 playing the obstacle course with her father sitting on the opposite side of the table, and her younger brother also in the room (but out of sight of the camcorder). She is trying to get the ball to rise higher so that she can get it through one of the hoops. She is initially intently focussed on the ball. After a while she glances up and then flicks her head upwards as if to usher the ball upwards. Immediately after this gesture she leans back and then begins to raise both hands from their resting place on the table. With her palms facing downwards she raises both arms together into the air high above her head. Her whole body moves upwards as she performs this gesture. She then gently lowers her arms before repeating a more forceful upward gesture. This gesture is then repeated two more times with a wave like flow to the movements. This is then followed by a couple quicker and jerkier arm lifts, palms raised up in the air like she is willing it to rise. A short while later, the ball falls lower than she wants it to drop. This creates panic and excitement on her part. In her excitement she screams "at the top of her voice. She moves in closer to get it to rise and then shouts *"Nooooo - birds birds birds - birds"*. As she shouts she smiles, and her father laughs.

Figure 7. Gesture as performance

Spectatorship verbalisations and play

Much of what we have discussed so far has been how actions and intentions are visibly manifest by players within this social context. These manifestations help make the game understandable for those watching as well as making it more entertaining as a spectator experience. Even the minutiae of facial expressions when trying to concentrate were at times engaging to observers as well as the more deliberately performative aspects undertaken by the players:

> *"Is that your concentration face with your weirdy wizard eyes?" V (Gp 1)*

Spectatorship is not simply about passively watching but is more a two-way relationship between players and observers who are actively participating. This participation can be seen, for example, in active attempts to influence the thought patterns and behaviours of the players, providing a source of encouragement, distraction and humour. Of note too, is the sensitivity to particular familial relationships and a means through which these particular relationships are played out. Consider the following example. The mother from Group 4 is playing the game with a time limit. She is being watched by her son and daughter sitting with her at the table and her partner, sitting on the sofa. The game indicates she has 10 seconds left to go. She is looking up at the ceiling in an attempt to lower the ball. The machine then begins a 5 second countdown at which point she realises she needs to raise the ball again quickly. The son, conscious of the urgency, shouts *"Mum, Hugh Jackman,*

Hugh Jackman, Hugh Jackman's naked!" as he points to the other side of the room. They all burst out laughing.

What we see here is the use of the game characteristics to create humour. The family are fondly aware of the mother's penchant for Hugh Jackman and offer it as subject matter to get her to concentrate. While used to encourage her concentration, its primary motivation is the opportunity for an affectionate expression of humour. This example also confirms that this audience understands the generic nature of the BCI in being based on general notions of concentration levels. This general, as opposed to a more specific BCI control mechanism, means it is open to interpretation. It is this that allows it to be appropriated in this personal way for humorous purposes.

In a similar vein, it is the close timing between system response to such verbalisations that becomes a source of humour. In this respect, the system is taken as a reflection of the thought processes and brain activity of the player. This can be seen in the following example, again from Group 4 but this time with the father playing. The father is staring at the ball attempting to concentrate and raise it but having no success. After a few seconds of not raising the ball, the son says *"Dad, remember when City lost 6-0 to Cardiff? Do you remember that?'* The father looks at his son and replies *"Yeah."* The ball is still not moving. The daughter then says *"Explain the whole match. Think about the match and remember it"*. He says *"Nah."* but it is at this moment that the ball rises. The daughter, son and mother burst out laughing. The father is a strong City fan and was not happy about the huge 6-0 defeat by local rivals Cardiff. They are trying to tease him through this suggestion and, while he tries not to think about it, the system response and its timing are used humorously by his family to suggest that he *must* be thinking about it. Again, it is the non-specific notion of concentration levels BCI that enable this appropriation. Ambiguity and interpretability are important here in allowing these behaviours.

Related to these issues were the more general inferences made about cognitive ability and activity in relation to the particular state of the machine. For example, inactivity of the ball for an extended period of time led to expressions of embarrassment on the part of the players. This would also prompt acts of self-deprecation as seen in Group 1:

> *"Its very worrying man. Look its not moving at all." V – laughs*
>
> *"I think it's you're not thinking." – M smiles*
>
> *"At all." - V laughs again*

Similar behaviour can be observed in the following episode from Group 3. The father in Group 3 manages to lift the ball up momentarily only for it to fall back down again. This prompts laughter from the watching family members. He smiles, with mild embarrassment and says *"It's stopped."* – then adds laughing *"My brain has stopped."* A little while later he causes the ball to roll off the board. His wife comments: *"You made it fall off – that's very clever"*. After replacing the ball, it falls off again - she laughs and says: *"Yours is obviously not very ordinary thinking, is it darling?"*

With this audience interaction in mind, a pertinent concern is the sensitivity of the BCI to these kinds of external factors and impact on performance. Indeed, robustness under real world conditions is a motivating factor for this kind of study. Play too, evokes its own particular type of audience engagement relative to other domains of usage. That is, in our observations, there were attempts both to encourage *and* distract people using the BCI. This choice of encouragement or distraction is done with particular social meaning and bound up in particular relationships between players and audiences and performed with particular social sensitivity. The point we are trying to make here is that while these interaction mechanisms are delicate and susceptible to distraction within such a social context, this is not something that is inherently problematic as a feature of the mechanism itself. Rather, the ways people orient towards this delicacy become an important part of the game, and a key part of what makes it engaging and fun. So, for example, in Group 2, the older brother and sister would actively tease and distract each other during BCI play (through staring, leaning in, and distracting utterances) because they were closer in age. By contrast, when their younger brother was playing, they were more encouraging and respectful in their utterances and proxemic arrangements. To further illustrate, the children in Group 2 were trying to distract their father while he was playing, making noise and offering amusing suggestions about what to think. The father tolerated this for a while but then said.

> *"Ok can you both be quiet please... This is supposed to be a game of concentration." S*
>
> *"No no but we're helping." M responds.*
>
> *"No no shut up." S says again.*
>
> *"At the end of the day it helps to think about moving up – I don't know why. Think about stuff that moves up." Sm*
>
> *"Will you just shut up." S*

M tries again to distract S by waving her hands magically over the ball. He pushes her away because it is distracting. After this they watch more quietly.

DISCUSSION

In this paper, we have begun to examine Brain-Computer interaction within the context of a real world setting [17] - namely within the context of social game play in the home. In doing this, we have been able to offer an alternative and complementary perspective on this kind of interaction. Our concerns with this perspective are not only about the efficiency and effectiveness of the BCI as a games controller, but rather lie with how the interaction mechanism affects the social construction of behaviour and meaning-making around the device and how social context affects interaction with the device. In addressing these concerns, we draw on notions of embodied interaction [e.g. 6, 28], which highlight the importance of people's participation and action in the world. This is, in part, about their physical action but also social action and how people to create and communicate meaning with the system and other social actors.

While it may at first seem curious to reinstate notions of bodily action in systems designed to bypass the body, what we hope to have shown in the findings is the importance of such a perspective. What is significant here is that a BCI interface puts the player in the unusual position of treating their own thoughts--their own brain--as a physical effector much like they would their arms or hands. Rather than using physical actions to engage with the elements of the game or interface, the player must use their levels of concentration in this way. This has several implications. First, whereas we have no need to think explicitly about how to move a game piece with our hands on a chessboard, players in this game need to explicitly think about how to use their own thoughts to achieve a desired effect. This means that what is usually taken for granted in game play (how to effect simple moves in a game) becomes instead central to the game. This also has the further complication that thinking about one's thoughts changes the nature of those thoughts, and, as a result, changes the way in which thoughts effect action. As we have seen, this recursive relationship is then used as a source of humour and a resource for interference in the game by others. Further, any lack of visible embodiment is often compensated for by the player, providing additional cues to their audience to account for and explain their actions. All of these findings point to the importance of embodiment both for players to work out how to use their minds *as body*, and for bodily action to be used as a resource for social engagement.

These findings point also to ways in which we might extend the design space for these kinds of games. For example, we have seen ways in which players used bodily action (postures, gestures, orientation and stillness) as a set of strategies to control brain state and interaction with the system. This suggests that players might be encouraged to explore various physical strategies to impact their interaction in the game. More interestingly, there might be ways in which BCI might be used in combination in interesting and novel ways with new physical interaction paradigms such as the whole-body interaction. An important consideration here is to understand when the physical demands of other interaction modalities might *facilitate* BCI versus when they *interfere*. Facilitation may be a focus for efficient interaction, whereas interference might be a focus for game-like challenging interaction.

We have seen too the importance of bodily action arising from the lack of visibility, with this technology, of interaction *manipulations* [27] (namely brain state) and the loose coupling between intentionality and interaction *effects* [27] (namely the ball rising). While this can lead to difficulties in interpretation by other social actors present, efforts are made through physical gestures and verbalisations to make these intentions visible to and interpretable by others. This has implications for thinking about how such technologies can be enjoyed in social contexts as an understandable spectacle. But there are pointers here too for thinking about how these interaction mechanisms might work within more explicit collaborative contexts where coordination and collaboration are the desired design goals. Further, within competitive contexts, this particular relationship between invisible interaction *manipulations* and visible *effects* could be exploited in design to interesting effect by enabling things such as surprise and deception for example.

The BCI game too had further consequences in the context of social game play. For example, bodily actions were used to performative effect to make the game more visibly interesting to watch. These kinds of actions in relation to the game can play an important role in the success of these games in a social context and therefore in their successful adoption. What was also revealed was the delicacy of these interaction mechanisms in terms of how the audience evaluated them, sometimes leading to deliberate attempts at distraction. While this points to some pragmatic concerns for BCI as a control mechanism, what is important in the context of game play is that such interventions are socially mediated and are an important channel through which particular social relationships are played out – both through affectionate teasing or moral support. The playing out of social relationships between player and audience was enabled too through because of the generalised control mechanism of concentration/relaxation. This lends a sense of ambiguity to the game that makes player and system performance open to interpretation [9]. This possibility for interpretation is an important resource that can be used by player and audience alike to create social meaning and to playfully nurture social relationships. These important sources of engagement may not be so possible with more explicit BCI commands that are less open to interpretation.

CONCLUSION

In conducting our real world study of BCI gaming in a social context, we have explored a complementary set of issues to those being addressed in existing BCI research. In particular, when we consider BCI in such social contexts, we hope to have shown the importance of reinstating the social organisation of bodily and mindful behaviour in our understanding and analysis of these technologies. Given the potential for bodily movement to both facilitate and inhibit BCI control [21, 24], understanding the circumstances of this action has consequences for thinking about the application of BCI design in these contexts. As Nijholt et al [24] argue, shortcomings and idiosyncratic characteristics of BCI can be incorporated into game challenges by design. But our concerns are not simply with the direct impacts on BCI control. Rather, we have also highlighted the work done to make internal brain states and any intentionality visible and interpretable by others present, through actions, gestures, expressions and utterances. This is important for how social meaning is created and how social relationships are played out for both players and audiences.

REFERENCES

1. Allison, B and Graimann, C. (2008). Why Use a BCI if you're Healthy? *IEEE Intelligent Systems,* 23(3), 76-78.
2. Birbaumer, N., Hinterberger, T., Kübler, A., Neumann, N., (2003), The Thought-Translation Device (TTD): Neurobehavioral Mechanisms and Clinical Outcome, *IEEE Transactions on Neural Systems and Rehabilitation Engineering,* Vol. 11(2), June 2003.
3. Button, G. and Harper, R.H.R (1996) The Relevance of 'Work-Practice' for Design. In *Journal of CSCW, 4.*
4. Caillois, R. (1958) *Man, Play and Games.* University of Illinois Press, Urbana and Chicago, 1958.
5. Cutrell, E., and Tan, D. (2008) BCI for Passive Input in HCI. In *Proceedings of CHI '08.* Florence, Italy.
6. Dourish, P. (2001) Where the Action Is: The Foundations of Embodied Interaction. MIT Press, Cambridge.
7. Fairclough, S. (2008) BCI and Physiological Computing for Computer Games: Differences, Similarities & Intuitive Control. In *Proceedings of CHI '08,* Florence.
8. Garfinkel H (1967) Studies in Ethnomethodology. Prentice-Hall, Englewood Cliffs, NJ.
9. Gaver, W., Beaver, J. and Benford, S. (2003) Ambiguity as a Resource for Design. In *Proceedings of CHI '03,* Fort Lauderdale, FL
10. Girouard, A. (2009). Adaptive brain--computer interface. In *Proc. CHI '09 Ext Abstracts,* Boston, MA.
11. Heath, C. and Luff, P. 2000. *Technology in Action.* Cambridge University Press, Cambridge
12. Hjelm, S. I. & Browall, C. (2000) Brainball - using brain activity for cool competition. In *Proceedings of. NordiCHI, 2000,* Stockholm, Sweden.
13. Hjelm, S. (2003) Research + design: the making of Brainball. *Interactions 10(1),* 26-34.
14. Kendon, A. (1990) Spatial Organization in Social Encounters: the F-formation System. A. Kendon, A. (Ed) Conducting Interaction: Patterns of Behavior in Focused Encounters, Cambridge University Press, (1990), 209-237.
15. Krepki, R., Blankertz, B., Curio, B., and Muller, K. (2007) The Berlin Brain-Computer Interface (BBCI): Towards a New Communication Channel for Online Control in Gaming Applications. In *J. Multimedia Tools and Applications,* vol. 33, no. 1, 2007, pp. 73-90.
16. Lalor, E. C. & Kelly, S. P. & Finucane, C. & et al. (2005) Steady-State VEP-Based Brain-Computer Interface Control in an Immersive 3D Gaming Environment. In *Journal on Applied Signal Processing, 19,* 3156-3164.
17. Lécuyer, A. & Lotte, F. & Reilly, R. B. & Leeb, R. & Hirose, M. & Slater, M. (2008) Brain-Computer Interfaces, Virtual Reality, and Videogames. *Computer 41(10),* 66-72.
18. Lee, J., & Tan, D. S. (2006) Using low-cost electroencephalograph for task classification in HCI research. In *Proceedings of UIST 2006,* 81-90.
19. Leeb, R., Lee, F., Keinrath, C., Scherer, R., Bischof, H., and Pfurtscheller, G. (2007) Brain-Computer Communication: Motivation, Aim and Impact of Exploring a Virtual Apartment. In *IEEE Trans. Neural Systems and Rehabilitation Eng.,* 15, pp. 473-482.
20. Lotte, F. & Renard, Y. & Lécuyer & A. (2008). Self-paced Brain-Computer Interaction with Virtual Worlds: a Quantitative and Qualitative Study "Out of the Lab". In *4th International Brain-Computer Interface Workshop and Training Course,* 373-378.
21. Lotte, F. J. Fujisawa, J., Touyama, H., Ito, R., M. Hirose, M. and Lécuyer, A. (2009) Towards Ambulatory Brain-Computer Interfaces: A Pilot Study with P300 Signals. In *Proceedings of ACE '09.*
22. Nijholt, A. & Tan, D. (2007). Playing with your brain: brain-computer interfaces and games. In *Proceedings of the International Conference on Advances in Computer Entertainment Technology.*
23. Nijholt, A. & Tan, D. (2008). Brain-Computer Interfacing for Intelligent Systems. In *IEEE Intelligent Systems, 23 (3).*
24. Nijholt, A., Plass-Oude Bos, D. and Reuderink, B. (2009) Turning Shortcomings into Challenges: Brain-Computer Interfaces for Games. In *Entertainment Computing (1),* pp 85-94.
25. Obermaier, B., Müller, G., and Pfurtscheller, G. (2003) Virtual keyboard controlled by spontaneous EEG activity. In IEEE Trans. Neural. Syst. Rehab. Eng. 11(4).
26. Rebsamen, B., Burdet, E., Guan, C., Zhang, H., Teo, C. L., Zeng, Q., Laugier, C., and Ang Jr., M. H. (2007) Controlling a Wheelchair Indoors Using Thought. *IEEE Intelligent Systems* 22, 2 (Mar. 2007), 18-24.
27. Reeves et al (2005) Designing the Spectator Experience. In *Proceedings of CHI '05,* Portland OR, USA.
28. Robertson, T. (1997) Cooperative Work and Lived Cognition: A Taxonomy of Embodied Actions. In *Proceedings of ECSCW '97,* Lancaster, UK.
29. Salen, K., and Zimmerman, E. (2004) *Rules of Play.* London: MIT Press.
30. Suchman, L. (1987) *Plans and Situated Actions: The Problem of Human-Machine Communication.* Cambridge University Press, New York.
31. Sutton-Smith, B. (2001) *The Ambiguity of Play.* Harvard University Press.
32. Voida, A. and Greenberg, S. (2009) Wii all play: The console game as a computational meeting place. In *Proceedings of CHI '09,* Boston, MA.
33. Wolpaw, J.R. (2007). Brain Computer Interfaces for Communication and Control. ASSETS'07, AZ, USA.
34. Yuksel, B. F., Donnerer, M., Tompkin, J. and Steed, A. (2010) A novel brain-computer interface using a multi-touch surface. In *Proceedings of CHI '10,* Atlanta, GA.

Now where was I? Physiologically-Triggered Bookmarking

Matthew K.X.J. Pan, Jih-Shiang Chang, Gokhan H. Himmetoglu, AJung Moon, Thomas W. Hazelton, Karon E. MacLean, Elizabeth A. Croft
The University of British Columbia
Vancouver BC V6T 1Z4
maclean@cs.ubc.ca

ABSTRACT
This work explores a novel interaction paradigm driven by implicit, low-attention user control, accomplished by monitoring a user's physiological state. We have designed and prototyped this interaction for a first use case of bookmarking an audio stream, to holistically explore the implicit interaction concept. Here, a user's galvanic skin conductance (GSR) is monitored for orienting responses (ORs) to external interruptions; our prototype automatically bookmarks the media such that the user can attend to the interruption, then resume listening from the point he/she is interrupted. To test this approach's viability, we addressed questions such as: *does GSR exhibit a detectable response to interruptions,* and *how should the interaction utilize this information?* In evaluating this system in a controlled environment, we found an OR detection accuracy of 84%; users provided subjective feedback on its accuracy and utility.

Author Keywords
Physiological signals, human-computer interaction, interruption, orienting response, galvanic skin response.

ACM Classification Keywords
H.5.2 [**User Interfaces**]: Input devices and strategies, Haptic IO; I.5.5 [**Pattern Recognition Implementation**]: Interactive Systems

General Terms
Measurement, design, experimentation, human factors.

INTRODUCTION
Most modern user interfaces developed for consumer electronic products rely on explicit channels of command and control. That is, information is most often exchanged between users and devices through explicit gestures like key strokes, verbal commands and finger swipes, and received through visual or auditory channels. When well designed, this clear, controlled form of interaction has the important benefit of leaving little room for misinterpretation.

However, there are circumstances in which the demands and costs of an explicit interface encumber its utility and efficiency, most typically in multitasking scenarios [1]. In a time- and safety-critical example, steering and handling a vehicle often requires most of the driver's attention; yet a variety of secondary vehicle controls (e.g., adjusting audio system settings) compete for the same attentional resources. The resulting diversion can impair safety. In other cases, the cost may be in convenience, privacy or attentional fragmentation: a user may wish to alter a device's behavior, but cannot or prefers not to use explicit commands (e.g., answering the phone while washing dishes). A badly timed device notification may temporarily dip in priority and then be forgotten (e.g., a pop-up notification).

Theory
Foreseeing the rise of ubiquitous computing, Weiser and Brown argued that rather than abruptly demanding a user's focus, interactions should slide transparently between the attentional periphery and center [2], "calmly" providing context and orientation.

In this vein, we propose a fundamentally different approach to device interaction, which employs implicit control channels to reduce an interface's attentional demand. Building on the knowledge that some human affective (emotional) states can be estimated from physiological signals captured with off-the-shelf biometric sensors [3], our implicit channel is a user's voluntary and involuntary physiological responses to a situation. We incorporate this biometric response directly into the application's interaction loop, such that it responds to changes implied by the user's affective state (Figure 1). The loop is closed with an immediate but unintrusive indication of system recognition and response to the user's estimated state; in ongoing work, we are exploring haptic feedback for this role [4,5].

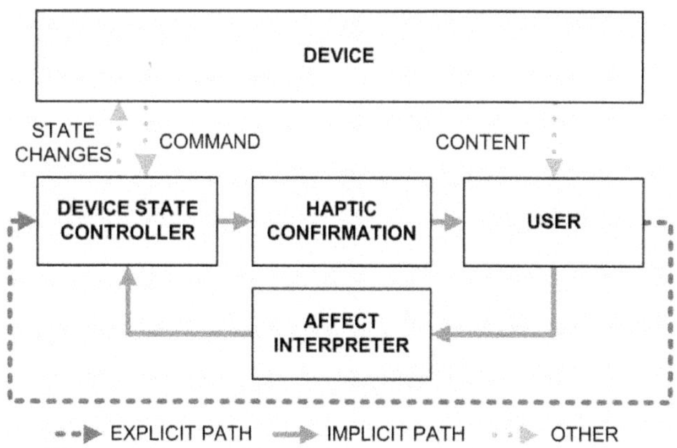

Figure 1. Proposed implicit interaction loop structure.

Approach and Use Case Description

We are interested in the utility and effectiveness of this implicit control paradigm in the context of a simple but representative use case, illustrated by this scenario:

A woman listens to an audiobook on her portable media player in a dentist's waiting room. Her name is called; her focus shifts from the audiobook to the hygienist. She fumbles in her bag to pull out the device, and eventually finds the "pause" button. The hygienist waits.

Or,

... her focus shifts. Reluctant to make the hygienist wait, she pulls out her earbuds and gets up, leaving her player running until the book ends. Later, she iteratively scrolls and listens backwards through the audio stream, trying to find the last familiar point and estimating forwarding intervals when she overshoots.

Both trajectories highlight how an explicit interface can 'demand' a user's attention, with negative outcomes if attention is not given. But what if instead:

... her focus shifts. An electrode slipped over her finger detects this and marks the audio stream, which continues to play. She feels a small tap on her finger that signals bookmark placement. She pulls out the earbuds and follows the hygienist. Later when alone again, she jumps back through two or three placed marks, locates the one placed just before the interruption where she stopped listening, and continues playback from there.

This is the implicit interaction method: an 'auto-bookmarking' system detects and marks a user's orienting response (OR) to an interruption by monitoring galvanic skin response (GSR) in real time. Bookmarks placed near the estimated point of interruption can be accessed later via a graphical or haptic tool. This use case highlights the example of a mobile application used in a predominantly hands-free mode. At this stage, we do not seek to change the underlying nature of existing explicit control or replace its channels; but rather to bypass points of dysfunction with a new, lower-effort channel when appropriate.

Contributions

This research example of attentional bookmarking, applied here to the initial use case of interrupted audiobook listening, defines a model for a unique user-device interface driven by implicit, low-attention control. With this platform, we have assessed the viability of a holistic interaction model that may be appropriate for a wide range of applications. We have focused on two questions pertaining to our implicit interaction model, with respect to the audiobook-listening use case:

1. *Does GSR exhibit a consistent and detectable response to interruptions in realistic contexts?*
2. *How should the system respond to this information?*

In this paper, we demonstrate empirically that GSR can be used to detect orienting responses to interruptions under controlled conditions, and have data suggesting that this ability can be extended to noisier, chaotic environments. We built an OR detection system based on this result, and to explore Question 2, made quantitative and qualitative observations of its use in a setup simulating audiobook listening scenarios. The latter effort gave us specific insights towards how best to refine our implicit interaction model in both this and more general cases. We explored the interaction paradigm without the haptic feedback component shown in Figure 1, as the feedback dynamics warrant a more in-depth examination than can be offered here.

In the remainder of this article, we summarize related work (`Related Work`), describe our hardware/software setup for detecting and displaying ORs (`Use Case System Description`), and present the experimental methods and results by which we quantified GSR-based ORs to interruptions and applied it to our interaction paradigm use-case (`Experiments`). We conclude with discussion and future work (`Discussion` and `Conclusions & Future Work`).

RELATED WORK

Affective State Detection and Implicit Interaction

Past work has related a human's measured physiology to affective state. This includes characterization of vision-based facial expression and auditory speech [6]; however, external manifestations (i.e., mouth and eye motions, voice pitch, etc.) can vary and be voluntarily suppressed. Physiological signal analysis is a popular alternative. Researchers have processed physiological sensor data and used filtering, statistical analysis and machine learning classifiers to derive models of affective user state [7-11]. Here, the difficulty lies in signal quality that differs by individual and day or hour, non-specific responses and other sensor noise.

In their early work in affective computing, Picard et al. classified emotions using physiological sensors [3,7,8]. With algorithms such as Fisher Projection and Sequential Floating Forward Search, they obtained emotional state recognition accuracy of up to 81% after 2-4 min of algorithm training per subject, for eight categories. Kim et al. aimed to reduce signal monitoring times and system training requirements through feature extraction and pattern classification of data (electrocardiography, skin temperature variation and electrodermal activity) pooled from multiple subjects [9]. A recognition rate of 78% for three emotion categories was obtained after 50s of monitoring.

There have also been initial attempts to use physiological classification to augment traditional interaction techniques. For example, Healey and Picard's StartleCam - a wearable video camera - monitors a user's GSR to detect when a user is startled [10]. When GSR indicates a user's heightened arousal, a time series of digital images are saved to mimic the user's "flashbulb" memory of the event causing the startle, autonomously generating an image-based diary for offline examination and memory assistance.

Our interaction model builds on these results with the aim of providing transition support between primary and secondary tasks. Beyond offline review, we seek a fluid continuous interaction where marked moments are used to propel the user towards a goal with minimal disruption.

GSR and the Orienting Response

The OR is an immediate reaction to the perception of a novel element or stimulus that is not sudden or intrusive enough to elicit a startle reflex. ORs are often examined to gather insights on human attention shifts and information processing [12]. An OR can be detected in many ways, including heart rate and electroencephalography (EEG), but the simplicity of measuring GSR and its strong relationship to OR is attractive.

The GSR (i.e., electrodermal activity) has been studied since the late 1800s. It is currently believed that the GSR is caused by the electrical activity of the sweat glands, and is connected to the sympathetic nervous system; it has been linked with the physiological instantiations of emotion, arousal and attention [13-16]. Firth and Allen showed that short-term changes in GSR reflect ORs [12]. Previous research has shown that within normal ranges of ambient room temperature and controlled subject state and motion, there is a high correlation between OR and GSR [14]. Other literature suggests that GSR measurements can be more easily discriminated than other physiological measures such as heart rate and EEG, since they can be detected quickly and without complex analysis [15].

GSR measurements are most sensitive on volar surfaces, suggesting a future possibility for sensors that can be worn unintrusively as a ring or shoe insert during daily activities. GSR sensors are inexpensive, wearable and pose no risks for the user. Disadvantages include latency in signal detection (i.e., 1-4s lag periods are common), significant response variance between subject groups (e.g., gender, age), possible habituation over time, and non-specificity [16].

We chose GSR as, on balance, the most promising physiological input to our control loop - keeping its limitations in mind. Since we require only OR information, with GSR we can bypass the complexity of a full affective model.

USE CASE DESCRIPTION

In our use case, marks are placed automatically during interrupted listening to an informative audio stream.

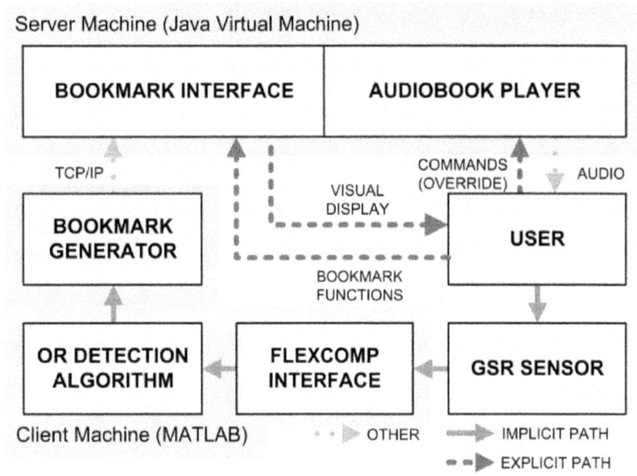

Figure 2. Diagram of bookmarking system architecture.

Bookmarks are placed near GSR-detected ORs, without explicit user direction. The marking system used here is intended as a platform to demonstrate and study the broader implicit interaction paradigm.

In this section, we describe our physical implementation. The "loop" is illustrated in Figure 2: the user's GSR was sensed, processed and sent by network to a control computer which analyzed the GSR stream, placed bookmarks, and made the bookmarks accessible to the user via a graphical list. A user can control the audio stream directly and/or via bookmark selection. Users could also place bookmarks manually ("Bookmark Functions" in Figure 2). Some parts of the system were developed specifically for this use case (e.g., the audiobook player and bookmark manager). Others, in particular the interruption detection algorithm and software, are of more general applicability.

GSR Apparatus and System Architecture

Our GSR measurements were obtained with Thought Technology's ProComp Infiniti® physiology-measurement hardware system [17]. The ProComp encoder reads data from a GSR sensor which uses dry electrodes attached to the index and middle fingers of the non-dominant hand. The encoder transmits the filtered, digitized signal to a notebook computer via USB. Skin conductance was measured in micro-Siemens (μS) and recorded at 256 Hz.

To test various feature-based OR detection approaches, we developed a distributed system based on a TCP/IP client-server architecture (see Figure 2). The client CPU received GSR data via a custom MATLAB™ program which performed OR detection and bookmark generation. Bookmarks are sent via TCP/IP to a custom MP3 audiobook player running on the server notebook. This architecture was designed for flexibility and future use in implicitly-controlled media players in mobile or distributed environments, with the wired USB connection replaced with a Bluetooth link from a wearable sensor.

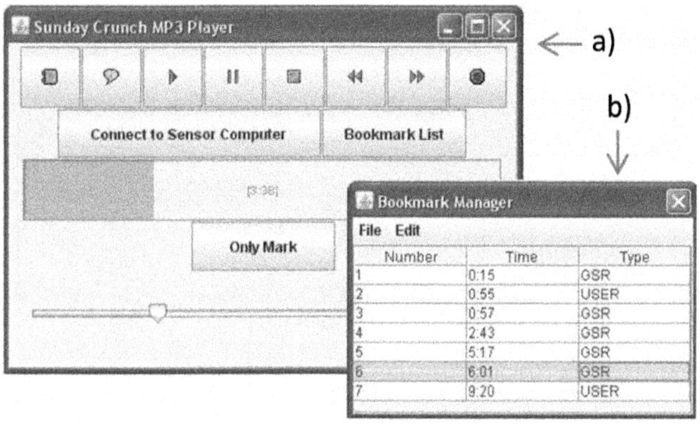

Figure 3. a) Audiobook player; b) Bookmark manager.

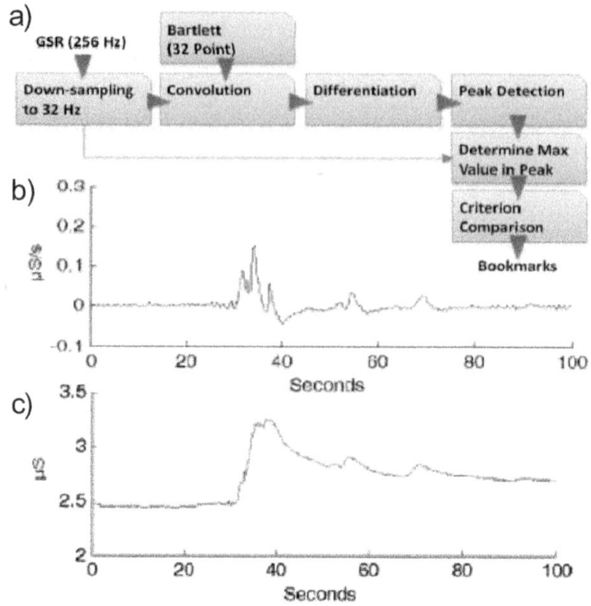

Figure 4. a) Flowchart of OR detection process. b) Typical smoothed GSR waveform (3200 samples). c) Smoothed first derivative GSR waveform (3200 samples).

Audiobook Player and Bookmark Manager

Users interacted with a custom Java audiobook player (Figure 3a), on which the user could place bookmarks explicitly using a custom bookmark-manager graphical interface (Figure 3b). Participants used the bookmark GUI to navigate through existing marks labeled by type (GSR-derived and explicitly user-created) and time. In the future, we plan to render device-to-user communication and bookmark placing through other channels (e.g., haptics) to further reduce demand on a user's visual faculties.

Interruption Detection Software

Figure 4a shows a process flow diagram outlining the detection process and subsequent auto-bookmarking behavior, which was implemented in MATLAB™. The GSR was measured in real-time, then down-sampled from 256 to 32 Hz to permit online processing (literature and our own results have shown that GSR rise times for ORs are in the range of 1-3s [15]; the Nyquist-Shannon theorem translates this to sampling requirement of >5 Hz). The resampled signal is smoothed by convolution with a 32-point Bartlett window (Figure 4b), and then differentiated (Figure 4c) similar to the procedure used by Kim et al. [9].

To detect an OR, we first identified zero-crossings in the first derivative of the smoothed GSR, noting the signal's direction at these points ('-' to '+' or '+' to '-'). Consecutive zero-crossings, from negative to positive then back to negative, signify peaks in the raw GSR signal. A bookmark is placed if the following inequality holds true:

$$Threshold \le GSR_{peak} - SMA_{640}(GSR)$$

where *Threshold* is a pre-determined value established in Experiment 1, GSR_{peak} is the maximum value of a peak, and $SMA_{640}(GSR)$ represents the moving average of the last 640 samples (20s). To avoid the placement of extraneous bookmarks, new bookmarks were suppressed for a 20s "blackout" window following the most recent placed bookmark. This procedure incorporates contextual information (GSR amplitude) for the signal under investigation, which can vary greatly across individuals and time.

Latency and Window Length: GSR measurements experience a natural latency of 1-4s [15]. The auto-bookmarking system introduces a delay due to differencing, smoothing and other operations, measured at 100ms. Computational latency associated with OR detection was experimentally assessed to range from 0.5-2s due to differences in GSR signal rise time after different stimuli. When summed, there is a 1.5-6s lag between the actual occurrence of a stimulus and the GSR-based recognition of the OR.

We have hypothesized that users could more easily re-orient after jumping to a few seconds prior to a perceived interruption, than to the exact point of interruption. Experimentally, we found that users tended to rewind audiobooks to approximately 10s prior to the start of an interruption*. We therefore placed bookmarks 15s prior to the detection of an OR, corresponding to 9-13s before the actual interruption based on our estimate of recognition latency. Figure 5 shows a timeline of these events.

The choice of averaging window length was the result of a compromise. If the averaging window is too long, false detections arise from large-amplitude, low-frequency GSR changes that are not characteristic of ORs. If the window is too short, the analysis will be too localized and the algorithm will fail to identify ORs. Through pilot studies, we found that a 20s window provided the most stable algorithm sensitivity; hence this value was used in our experiments*.

EXPERIMENTS

Our main objective was to support development of and then validate the general implicit interaction paradigm, within the context of the initial audiobook marking use case. We

* See Experiment 3.

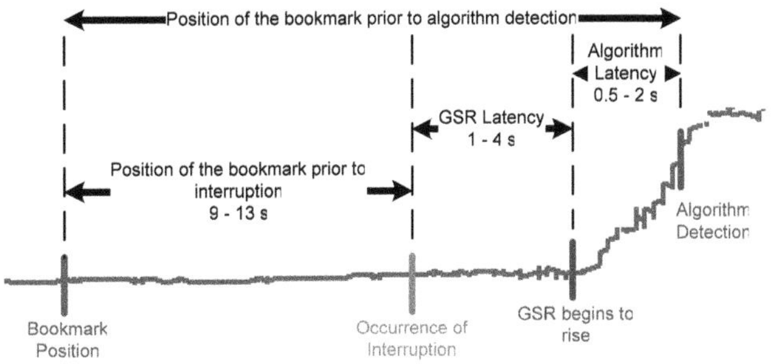

Figure 5. Approximate timeline of the auto-bookmarking system. Horizontal bars indicate timeline variability, black vertical lines show an example timeline for a participant introduced to vocal stimulus.

structured our research questions to be broad, but answerable and relevant from this use case perspective. Experiment 1 (E1) examined the usability of GSR as an indicator of true interruption. We used Experiment 2 (E2) to refine parameters of the bookmark algorithm; e.g., the distance by which bookmarks should be advanced from the point of measured interruption. In Experiment 3 (E3) we showed our bookmarking implementation to users and invited their qualitative feedback. Finally, in a preliminary pilot experiment (E4), we logged and examined additional GSR data in an uncontrolled, noisy environment to assess the algorithm's viability in more realistic situations.

Experiment 1: Evaluation of GSR Utility

Our first research question addressed physiological responses to interruptions - specifically:

Q1: *Does GSR exhibit a consistent and detectable change in response to interruptions of a level that distract users?*

Bookmarks should be placed at or near the point where the user is interrupted. To do this, we need to know what GSR looks like when the user has really been interrupted. Only some events at some times are interruptive enough to distract users who are focused on a primary task (here, audiobook listening). For example, one may be able to mentally block a nearby conversation in a café, but will be distracted by the sound of a door opening in a quiet room. We would like to differentiate between these two situations using only features extracted from GSR measurements. E1 was conducted to answer Q1 by specifically addressing the following hypotheses:

H1: *The GSR signal amplitude exhibits a range that corresponds to ranges of interruption levels; and*

H2: *Disruptive interruptions exhibit a characteristic GSR profile and amplitude range that can be detected with usably high (>80%) true-positive rates.*

This would provide the empirical grounding necessary for development of an OR detection system. An 80% accuracy rate was chosen as baseline. This was comparable to results obtained by Kim et al. [9] for the recognition of three emotion types and determined to be adequate for practical applications. Usability of detection rates is examined in the `Discussion`.

Design

Four female and seven male subjects (n = 11) aged 23-30 participated in E1. Subjects were pre-screened for potential confounds including diagnosed attention disorders (obsessive-compulsive or attention-deficit) and familiarity with the audiobook used. Data from one male subject was discarded due to sensor malfunction.

At the beginning of the experiment, half of the subjects were asked to put in their pocket a cell phone provided by the experimenter that was programmed to emit an auditory ringtone triggered by an experimenter. The other half were asked for their own cell phone numbers, then asked to set their cell phones to vibrate mode and place them in a pocket. This was done to determine if there is a net noticeable difference in GSR when a familiar stimulus from the participant's own cell phone is presented verses an unfamiliar one from cell phone provided by experimenters. We observed no discrepancy between the two cases.

During the experiment, subjects were asked to sit in a silent experiment room facing a wall and to don a GSR sensor and pair of headphones. To reduce noise in the GSR, subjects were asked to avoid making large physical motions. The entire experiment was video-recorded for post-hoc comparison with GSR data. The experimenters sat on the other side of a visual divider from the subject, as shown in Figure 6, to avoid unintentional distraction or anticipation thereof. To encourage interruption responses typical of focused listening, subjects were instructed to listen to the audiobook carefully as they might be tested on concepts described in the audiobook; no test was actually administered.

After collecting two minutes of baseline GSR data where the participants were asked to silently relax, experimenters started playback of the first chapter of the audiobook "Free" by Chris Anderson [18]. The chapter, which describes the invention and marketing of Jell-O and Gillette disposable razors, was verified to be of neutral arousal level in a pilot study; that is, listening to the audiobook did not impact the user's GSR signal except at the start or end of play. The content was considered boring by most subjects and was reused in E1, E2 and E3.

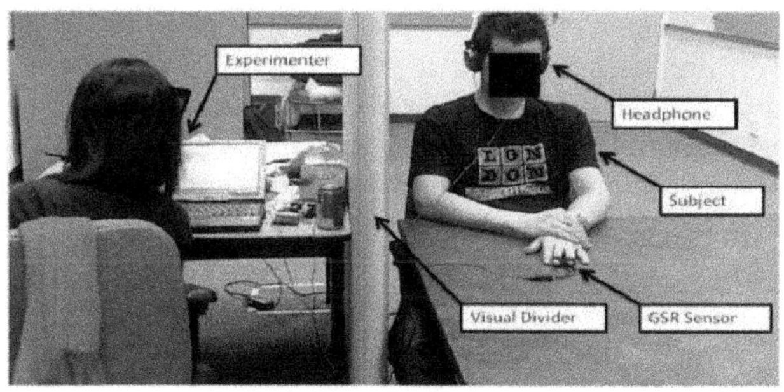

Figure 6. Experiment 1 set-up.

After approximately a minute of playback, the experimenter began to cause interruptions without pausing or stopping the player. Four different interruptions were used: knocking on the experimenter's desk three times {K}, tapping the subject on the shoulder twice from behind {T}, calling the cell phone in the subject's pocket {C}, and verbally activating the subject {V}. These interruptions were chosen as they were perceived to be common in daily-life settings within the context of an audio-listening task. Each interruption was used twice. Intervals of at least 1 min between interruptions allowed the subject's GSR to settle.

Eight interruptions were presented to all subjects in the following order: {K}-{T}-{C}-{V}-{V}-{C}-{T}-{K}. During piloting, we did not discover any difference in any measured quantities as a result of stimulus order; therefore, to standardize the experience of the interruption order across users we did not randomize this sequence. Subjects were not informed of the order of interruptions. The same experimenter introduced all interruptions throughout all sessions with consistent volume and tone. The duration of phone rings was constant, and the two verbal instructions in the experiment were scripted as:

V1: "[Subject Name], I just want to let you know that you are doing great."

V2: "[Subject Name], we are going to continue to take more measurements, and let you know when the experiment is over, OK?"

The experiment was followed by a post-hoc questionnaire and a semi-structured interview. The questionnaire aimed to discover which interruptions were most disruptive. For each type of interruption, the subjects were asked whether they: a) were distracted, b) found it hard to refocus on the book after the interruption, and c) would have liked to rewind the book to a time just before the occurrence of interruption. In the interview, we collected general feedback on the experiment with a focus on each interruption. Qualitative data from the questionnaires and interview was statistically analyzed to test H1. Quantitative data from the recorded GSR was analyzed with pattern detection algorithms to test H2. The length of E1 excluding preparation and administration of the questionnaire/interview was 20 min.

Results

Questionnaires & Interviews: Post-experiment questionnaires revealed that 81% of participants agreed or strongly agreed that they were engaged by the audiobook. 73% of participants agreed that they were interrupted during the experiment. From a set of yes/no questions for each type of interruptions, 91% of participants agreed that they were interrupted by verbal interaction {V}. 55% of subjects stated that {K}, {T} and {C} were interruptive. Qualitative analysis of the post-experiment interview showed that verbal interruption was found to be the most disruptive; it was also found that {K} did not register as either annoying or disruptive to most participants. Three subjects reported that they did not notice a knock at all. Users found the level of disruption by tapping or cell phone to be in between that of knocking and verbal interruption. Hereafter, we refer to {K} as non-disruptive and {V}, {T}, and {C} as disruptive interruptions.

Name	Definition
True positive (TP)	A detection occurred within a 15s time window from the start of a labeled interruption (-4 to +11s).
False negative (FN)	No detection occurred within a 15s time window from the start of a labeled interruption.
False positive (FP)	A detection occurred without a corresponding a labeled interruption within a 15s period.
True negative (TN)	No detection occurred when there was no labeled interruption within a 15s period.
POWER	Proportion of interruptions that are detected by the algorithm (N_{TP} / N_{actual}).
PRECISION	Proportion of detections are interruptions ($N_{TP}/N_{detected}$).

Table 1. Definitions of test outcomes, conditions and measures.

GSR Signal Analysis: The algorithm's performance was evaluated by power and precision metrics as defined in Table 1. We considered an interruption "detected" if an OR occurred within -4 to +11s from the presentation of an interruptive stimulus; this range was derived from the sum of the 1–6s detection latency (see `Interruption Detection Software`) and ±5s which was allocated to account for variation of when ORs were detected. We tested both the power and precision of the algorithm's interruption detection. Power reflects the frequency of true positives, i.e. detection of when an interruption occurred. For example, if 4 out of 6 disruptive interruptions were detected in a single trial, power = 67% (N_{TP}=4, N_{FN}=2). Precision indicates robustness to false positives. If 4 out of 10 detections correspond to disruptive interruptions, precision = 40% (N_{TP}=4, N_{FP}=6). A false positive proved difficult to define because nonspecific responses – those that occur in the absence of an identifiable stimulus – could be caused by valid internal or otherwise unobservable stimuli.

Figure 7 shows the results of our OR detection algorithm for a typical trial, illustrating disruptive interruptions and detected ORs. Supporting our previous approximation of 1.5 to 6s, the average interval between an interruption's actual occurrence and "true" OR capture was 2.52s (std 2.35s).

We examined the algorithm's sensitivity to detection threshold by computing the average power and precision for threshold values ranging from 0.01 to 0.70μS as shown in Figure 8. Power and precision are inversely and directly proportional, respectively, to threshold in a roughly linear fashion. A threshold of 0.07μS (shown at the arrow in Figure 8) was found to be optimal, with maximum power of 84% and a precision of 32%.

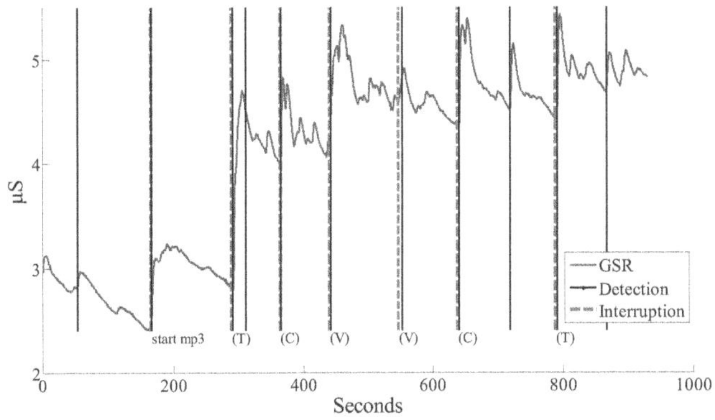

Figure 7. GSR signals overlaid with interruption and detection lines for one representative trial (threshold set at 0.07 μS).

E1 subjects received 20 of each interruption type for a total of 80. The average power of each type of interruption is plotted in Figure 9. Additionally, we calculated the power of detected interruptions deemed to be disruptive, by excluding the apparently non-disruptive {K} types. With the detection threshold set to 0.07μ*S*, the average trial power of disruptive interruptions was 84% (std 15%). A two-sample right-tail T-test verified that the power of disruptive interruptions - {V}, {T} and {C} - is significantly greater than the power of non-disruptive {K} interruptions (p=0.02). However, inspection of GSR data from E1 does not show notable qualitative differences between interruption types.

Experiment 2: Qualitative/Quantitative Observation of Desired System Behavior

In E2, we sought data that would help build the auto-bookmarking application for an average user. Specifically,

Q2a: *Where should a mark be placed for greatest utility?*

Q2b: *Is there a correlation between interrupt duration and how far back participants rewind the audio stream?*

According to E1, verbal interruptions (conversation, verbal instructions and questions) were the most disruptive of those tested; verbal interruptions are also controllable in duration. Thus, to maximize the number of rewind events, we used only verbal interruptions in E2.

Design

Four females and seven males (n=11) aged 23 to 30 participated in E2. The same audiobook used in E1 was reused in E2. We required that subjects chosen for E2 had not previously listened to nor read the book prior to the experiment; hence, no participants from E1 participated in E2.

The set-up for E2 is shown in Figure 10. The visual divider used in E1 was omitted, as we felt verbal interruptions lacking eye contact was unnatural. A second experimenter recorded interrupt durations. Both experimenters were out of the participant's immediate sight to prevent anticipation of stimuli. Subjects used the MP3 player shown in Figure 3a; the pause function and 'track time' display were disabled to simulate the scenarios described in `Approach and Use Case Description`. After a brief training session on the customized player, subjects were instructed to pay close attention to the content of the audiobook, to rewind whenever desired, and that there would be content-related questions following the listening session. The player automatically logged timestamps of user rewind actions.

Subjects were asked to relax for two minutes at the outset of the experiment to collect baseline GSR data. Experimenter 1 initiated verbal interruptions periodically after the subjects' GSR had settled, with short (2-13s), medium (14-28s), and long (29+s) conversations. A total of six verbal interruptions (two short, two medium and two long) were used for each subject. One medium and one long question were related to the content of the audiobook. Finally, the video recording of the experiment was played back to the subject in a semi-structured interview, to understand the rationale for various rewinding patterns.

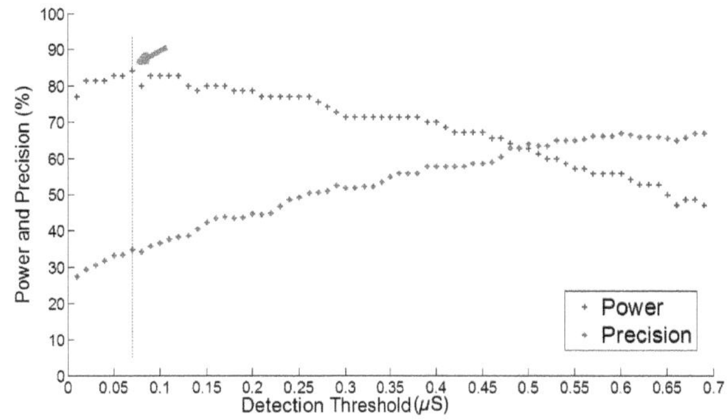

Figure 8. Average power and precision versus detection threshold. The arrow points to the maximum power when the threshold is set to 0.07μS.

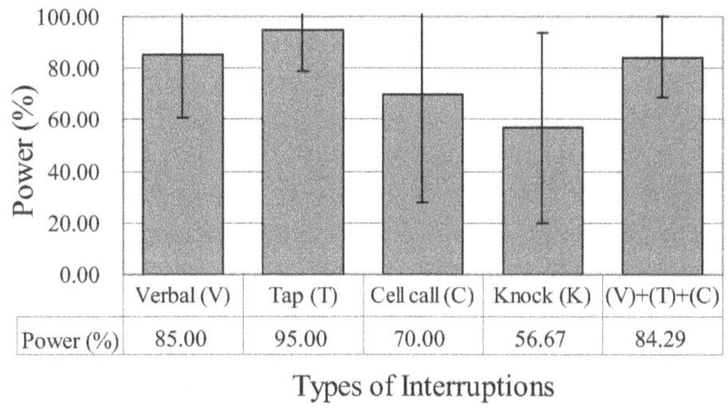

Figure 9. Average algorithm power (proportion of interruptions detected of total) for interruption types. Error bars represent std variability of power across all subjects.

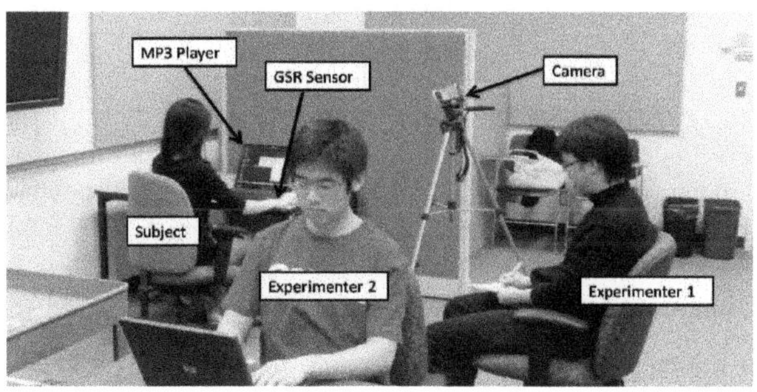

Figure 10. E2 set-up. A similar set-up was also used for E3.

Results

We expected all 66 stimuli to be interruptive - six per subject across the 11 subjects. 19 of these generated user-driven rewind events that corresponded to an interruption. 33 of the remaining stimuli did not cause any rewind event, and the other 14 were discarded either because they caused unrelated rewinding (due to mind wandering etc.), or subjects were not able to remember their reasons for rewinding the audiobook at that particular incident during the interview. It was found that users tended to rewind multiple times for a short duration after an interruption for reasons such as seeking for the 'best' location. This was still counted as a single valid rewind event.

We measured how many seconds the subject rewound prior to the onset of the interruption. For example, we recorded a value of -2 if a subject rewound the audiobook to a position 2s prior to the start of an interruption. The average rewind period during the 19 valid interruptions was found to be -9.37s (std: 7.65s), i.e. on average, a subject rewound the audiobook to 9.37s prior to the occurrence of the disruptive interruption event. We also recorded the duration of each interruption. The duration of the 19 valid interruptions ranged from 7 to 56s. The correlation coefficient between interruption length and extent of the rewind event was $r=0.03$, which suggests that the rewind distance was unrelated to length of interruption.

Experiment 3: Interaction Utility Assessment

In E3, we tested the utility of our tuned GSR-based auto-bookmarking algorithm. E3 re-used E2's procedure and set-up (Figure 10) but employed the bookmarking algorithm in real-time. Data from E3 provided insight into user reactions to the bookmarking prototype.

Design

One female and four males (n=5) aged 23-29 participated in E3. The system used in E3 is described with its parameterizations in the `Use Case System Description`. While the previous experiments provided us with information on how to detect disruptive interruptions and how to use that information, E3 specifically addresses the question:

Q3: *Do our system-generated bookmarks consistently provide utility after interruptions?*

We used the same pre-screening procedure and setup as in E2. In addition, E3 subjects were asked to use the custom MP3 player and associated custom bookmark manager interface (Figure 3b). Subjects were instructed to use this manager as their first method of rewinding when rewinding was desired, reverting to manually navigating through the audiobook only if the bookmarks were unsatisfactory. Subjects could rewind from any bookmark, but were advised to try the most recent one first. Interactions with the MP3 player and bookmark manager were logged, and video and audio recordings of the experiment were saved.

To better understand their strategies for interrupt recovery, we asked subjects to view the recorded video stream while commenting on each interruption in a post-experiment questionnaire. Finally, we conducted an interview to understand user satisfaction and usefulness of each bookmark.

Results

Each subject in E3 was exposed to six interruptive stimuli, for a total of 30 events. 26 of these stimuli were reported as disruptive, valid interruptions. 21 of these caused subjects to rewind immediately following the interruption. 18 of the 21 rewinds utilized only system-generated bookmarks; in 13 of these, subjects used only the latest system-generated bookmark, whereas subjects in the other five instances continued to try older bookmarks. In the remaining three rewind events, subjects manually navigated through the audiobook. Subjects rated 76% of the automatically-placed bookmarks that they used as 'appropriately positioned'.

The semi-structured interviews provided constructive feedback: users were surprised to see such a system, and were interested in seeing further application areas of such interaction. In general, subjects provided positive feedback on the system's usefulness and utility. Few suggestions on bookmark follow-up were raised. Two subjects suggested the system should pause when the user is interrupted, and to play again by user's manual control. One subject reported that the system's visualization and/or interaction quality could be improved.

Experiment 4: GSR Field Assessment (Pilot)

As a final early validation step, we assessed the potential effectiveness of this implicit interaction implementation based on GSR informativeness in a less controlled environment. We were keen to preview through a pilot what would be involved as we moved to the field to guide our own future work. Specifically, we wanted an initial indication of:

Q4: *Are there quantifiable differences between GSR measurements obtained from a controlled vs. uncontrolled, possibly noisy environment which may affect utility or effectiveness of the interaction?*

Design

Two male subjects (n=2) aged 23 participated in the E4 pilot. During rush hour at a busy outdoor bus terminal, each participant was seated (alone) on a bus bench for the duration of the study and asked to attend to an audiobook played through headphones. Subjects wore a GSR sensor and were instructed to use a pushbutton marking device to signal moments where they felt interrupted enough by an event to wish the audiobook to be rewound. An experimenter (out of the participant's view) also recorded major events that could have potentially caused ORs.

Results

An informal analysis of data from two male participants showed little qualitative (wave shape, event responsiveness) difference between raw GSR measurements obtained from our controlled tests (E1 and E2 results) and the bus terminal. The primary distinguishing characteristic was absolute GSR amplitude: subjects in E1 and E2 tended to exhibit baseline and OR GSRs in the range of 3-6µS, whereas GSR measurements in E4 were 6-15µS; an example comparison is shown in Figure 11. As the software algorithm designed for the auto-bookmarking use case does not utilize absolute signal amplitude, but rather amplitude of peaks relative to the moving average, this preliminary result suggests that system operation should be minimally affected by a chaotic, noisy environment.

Although E4 results are informal and preliminary, this pilot study suggests (though not proves) to us that at the cost of more sophisticated signal processing, information regarding ORs will still be present in GSR data collected from less controlled environments.

DISCUSSION

Q1: Does GSR indicate disruptive interruptions?

E1 showed that GSR can be used to detect disruptive interruptions in an audiobook listening context. According to subject interviews and self-reports, our {V}, {T} and {C} interruptions did disrupt subjects. E1 results (Figure 9) confirmed that different types of interruptions correspond to different levels of disruption as indicated by GSR. Thus, H1 is confirmed for the range of interruptions that we tested. Moreover, for GSR data obtained in E1, we achieved an 84% recognition rate in detecting disruptive interruptions, (i.e., true positives of type {V}, {T} and {C}). This supports H2, where disruptive interruptions produce salient GSR signal features, detectable by our algorithm with an acceptable true-positive rate; false positives were difficult to detect, as explained in `Experiment 1`.

Only four types of interruption stimuli were tested in these experiments; the design space of possible interruption stimuli and contexts is much larger. As such, validity of our results is coupled to the primary task and interruption stimuli used here. For example, while a gentle knock was not disruptive in this context, it certainly could be in other situations. Nevertheless, our approach - evaluating the GSR signal in context and using this to tune an algorithm variant to that context - is general enough to be applied to other primary tasks such as watching TV, housecleaning, gardening, working at a computer and perhaps driving.

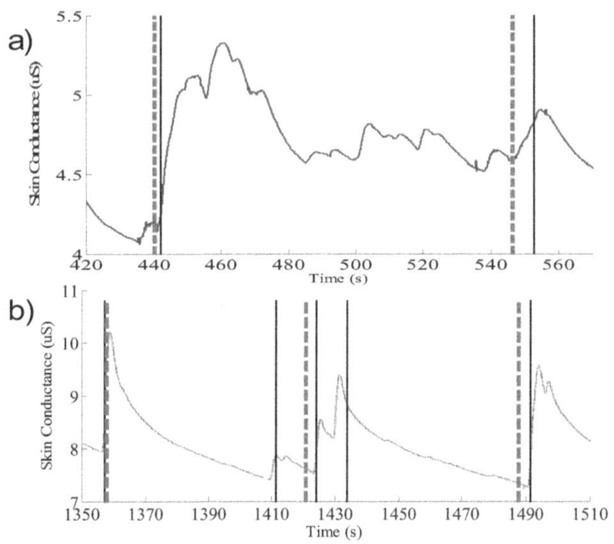

Figure 11. Raw GSR data collected from a participant in a) a controlled test environment and b) a bus terminal at rush hour. Thick, dotted lines signifies interruptions; thin, solid lines represent bookmarking system OR detections.

As seen in Figure 8, there is a tradeoff in power versus precision as a function of detection threshold, i.e. between false negatives and false positives. Based on subject interviews, we believe that higher power with slightly lower precision is a reasonable tradeoff. However, the optimal balance will depend on the environment and individual responsiveness to ORs.

Q2: Where should a mark be placed relative to interruption?

E2 provided data for designing the bookmark placement system. Its results indicated that users preferred to rewind the audiobook to a location approximately 10s prior to the onset of an interruption, independently of interruption length. This implication for mark placement advance may be applicable to interruptions in other use contexts. Conveniently, the results also imply that it is not crucial to measure or estimate the length of interruption, a potentially challenging task in the field. However, we believe this finding only applies to interruptions under a minute. Longer interruption may affect user's behavior and the desire of bookmark location; for instance, a 10-minute interruption may cause the user to replay the entire chapter of the audiobook, because the content has slipped out of his short-term memory. Likewise, our observation of mark-advance independence from interruption length may apply to other use cases, but this will need to be verified.

Q3-Q4: Do our system-generated bookmarks consistently provide utility after interruptions? Is GSR informative in uncontrolled environments?

GSR signals are known to be susceptible to noise from sources such as bodily motion and cognitive workload [15]. We generally found (E1-E3) that our algorithm was quite robust to small hand or arm movements and subtle posture changes, but we had false-positive detections in the absence of an identifiable stimulus. Although it is not feasible to explain each one, we expect that some occur through internal distractions, such as when a phrase or a word in the media being perused initiates mind wandering. E4 results suggest that GSR is robust in a chaotic environment.

Subjects did not always find rewinding the audiobook necessary despite being interrupted – particularly for short interruptions (<11s – as determined by the length of the longest 'short' interruptive conversation in E2 without causing users to rewind). We found that no rewinding occurred for 81% of the short interruptions presented to subjects in the experiments. Subjects reported that even if they stopped listening to the audiobook to attend to short interruptions, they could quickly pick up the gist of what was being said afterwards. We believe this was representative of this use case, and it seems that users sometimes use a 'multi-tasking' strategy to cope with interruptions.

E3 and E4 served only to briefly explore the potential of our implicit control algorithm in controlled and uncontrolled setting; the small sample size limits our ability to provide any concrete evidence pertaining to the usefulness our system in the field and thus caution is required when evaluating the significance of these results. They give some indication that our algorithm provided a usable detection rate; further investigations with larger sample sizes are required. Subjects reported appreciation of and surprise at the automatic bookmarking. Perhaps most relevantly, many comments were directed to bookmark follow-up as opposed to the actual bookmark generation, supporting the conclusion that the current bookmarking algorithm is reasonably accurate, our vision of a loop-closing system is of potential utility and our next step is to concentrate on using the bookmarks themselves.

CONCLUSIONS AND FUTURE WORK

In this paper, we have demonstrated a novel approach to human-computer interaction based on an implicit communication paradigm. We have developed and validated the theory that a computer algorithm can, in real-time, detect features within a GSR stream that correspond to ORs caused by external disruptive interruptions. We have exploited these findings with a system that provides OR-based auto-marking for a representative audiobook use case. We have found that with our algorithm, we can achieve a true-positive interruption detection power of 84%.

The work presented here demonstrates the feasibility of an implicitly-controlled interaction model which provides a possible solution for managing the interplay between primary and secondary tasks in various environments. This use case represents a first step in a larger effort in which we aim to develop an implicit interaction loop driven by physiological parameters such as GSR.

We anticipate that the false-positive rate found in this use case may be addressable by dynamically tailoring the OR detection algorithm to individuals, through adjusting sensitivity, bookmarking delay and dead-zone period until another bookmark can be placed. Improvements to the present system's usability in the field (e.g., further reducing noise in the GSR introduced by bodily movements) may be assisted by integrating contextual information such as accelerometer and location data from a worn or carried device.

Our next step is to provide users with a low-attention notification that the application has acted in response to the user's physiology (for the use case presented here, that a mark has been placed). To further test and validate this model, we plan to study the closed-loop dynamics of other use cases such as streaming media, internet browsing and vehicle operation. We would also like to explore how to discriminate ORs to the media itself from responses to external events.

REFERENCES

1. Wickens CD. *Engineering Psychology and Human Performance*. Merrill; 1984:513.
2. Weiser M, Brown JS. Designing Calm Technology. *Powergrid Journal.* 1996;1.01(July):94-110.
3. Picard RW. *Affective Computing*. Cambridge, MA: MIT Press; 1998.
4. MacLean K. Putting Haptics into the Ambience. *IEEE Trans. on Haptics*. 2009;2(3):123-135.
5. Baumann MA, Maclean KE, Hazelton TW, McKay A. Emulating Human Attention-Getting Practices with Wearable Haptics. In: *IEEE Haptics Symp.* ; (2010).
6. Cowie R, Douglas-Cowie E, Tsapatsoulis N, et al. Emotion Recognition in Human-Computer Interaction. *IEEE Signal Processing*. 2001;26(1):32-80.
7. Picard RW, Vyzas E, Healey J. Toward Machine Emotional Intelligence: Analysis of Affective Physiological State. *IEEE Trans. on Pattern Analysis and Machine Intelligence*. 2001;23(10).
8. Picard RW. Toward Agents that Recognize Emotion. *MIT Media Lab Perceptual Computing Section Technical Report*. 1998;(515).
9. Kim, K.H., Bang, S.W., Kim, S.R. Emotion recognition system using short-term monitoring of physiological signals. *Med. & Bio. Eng. & Computing.* 42, 3 (2004).
10. Healey J, Picard RW. StartleCam: a cybernetic wearable camera. *Intl. Symp. on Wearable Comp.*, IEEE Comp. Soc. (1998), 42-49.
11. Conati, C. Probabilistic Assessment of User's Emotions in Educational Games. *Applied Artificial Intelligence 16*, 7-8 (2002), 555-575.
12. Frith CD, Allen HA. The skin conductance OR as an index of attention. *Biological Psychology*. 1983;17(1).
13. Boucsein, W. *Electrodermal Activity*. Plenem Press, New York, New York, USA, 1992.
14. Cacioppo JT, Tassinary LG. Inferring psychological significance from physiological signals. *The American Psychologist*. 1990;45(1):16-28.
15. Bernstein, A. An analysis of the skin conductance OR in samples of American, British, and German schizophrenics. *Biological Psych.* 1982;14(3-4):155-211.
16. Cacioppo JT, Tassinary LG, Berntson GG. The Electrodermal System. In: *Handbook of Psychophysiology*. 3rd ed. New York, New York, USA: Cambridge University Press; 2007:159-181.
17. www.thoughtechnology.com
18. Anderson, C. *Free: The Future of a Radical Price*. HarperCollins, New York, New York, USA.

This is Your Brain on Interfaces: Enhancing Usability Testing with Functional Near-Infrared Spectroscopy

Leanne M. Hirshfield[1] Rebecca Gulotta[2] Stuart Hirshfield[1] Sam Hincks[1] Matthew Russell[1] Rachel Ward[1] Tom Williams[1] Robert Jacob[3]

[1]Computer Science
Hamilton College
Clinton, NY 13323

[2] HCI Institute
Carnegie Mellon University
Pittsburgh, PA 15213

[3]HCI Laboratory
Tufts University
Medford, MA 02155

ABSTRACT

This project represents a first step towards bridging the gap between HCI and cognition research. Using functional near-infrared spectroscopy (fNIRS), we introduce techniques to non-invasively measure a range of cognitive workload states that have implications to HCI research, most directly usability testing. We present a set of usability experiments that illustrates how fNIRS brain measurement provides information about the cognitive demands placed on computer users by different interface designs.

ACM Classification Keywords: H5.2 [Information interfaces and presentation]: User Interfaces. - Graphical user interfaces.

Author Keywords: usability, brain, mental workload, fNIRS, brain-computer interaction.

General Terms
human factors, experimentation

INTRODUCTION

Usability researchers attempt to formalize and quantify the process whereby an interface is evaluated, and to measure precisely the degree to which an interface meets the goals of its intended audience. Although one can measure the accuracy with which users complete tasks and the time it takes to complete a task with a user interface (UI), measuring subjective factors such as workload, frustration, and enjoyment is more difficult. These factors are often "measured" by qualitative observation of subjects or by administering subjective surveys to subjects. Such surveys are inherently subjective and they can elicit participant biases, as participants often attempt to please experiment investigators in their responses. Additionally, surveys are often administered after a task has been completed, lacking insight into the users' changing experience as they work with a UI.

Our research addresses these evaluation challenges with respect to mental workload (WL). We use a non-invasive brain sensing technique called functional near infrared spectroscopy (fNIRS) to record real time, objective measurements of users' WL while working with UIs. Users can wear the comfortable fNIRS device (Fig. 1) in working conditions.

Using brain measurement to quantify the level of WL experienced by computer users is a difficult task because "workload" is somewhat of an umbrella term. The brain is a complex structure, and there are many cognitive resources that work in serial and in parallel to process information. Indeed, when we compute arithmetic, compose a poem, or chat with a friend, we are experiencing some form of WL.

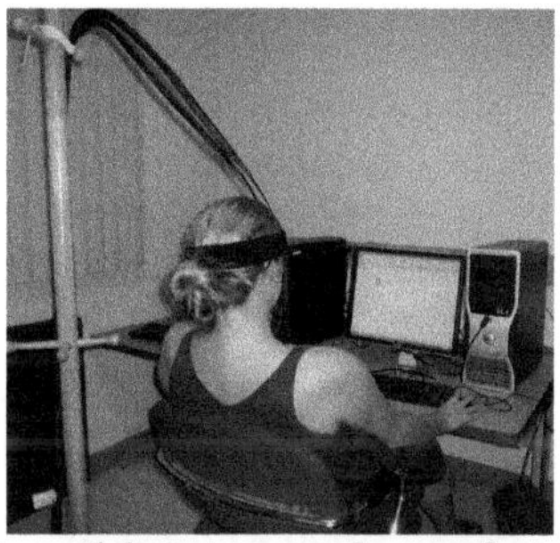

Figure 1: A participant wears the comfortable fNIRS.

However, for each task that we take part in, we may use different (and often overlapping) cognitive resources. While there are many definitions in the literature describing WL [13, 14, 33], for the purposes of this paper we define it in functional terms as: *The load placed on various cognitive resources in the brain in order to complete a task that involves the processing of information.*

Since the processing of information is a key element in users' interactions with computers, the field of human-computer interaction (HCI) is derived from and heavily influenced by cognitive psychology. We seek a thorough understanding of the effects that a new UI will have on users' mental resources. Ideally, a UI will be easy to use, allowing users to focus their mental resources on the task at hand. However, there remains a large gap between the high-level references made to these mental resources in HCI research and the low-level ability to pin point and measure these resources in human users. For this reason, Czerwinski and Larson [9] discuss the need to tie together cognition research and HCI design principles. They note that this is not an easy task, as most cognitive research focuses on task manipulations that are on a low-level, with a cognitive load that is small, and the jump from these specific cognitive tasks to UI tasks administered in real world settings is large.

With these challenges in mind, our work provides two primary research contributions to the field of HCI:

1) We attempt to bridge the gap between HCI and cognition research. We introduce techniques to measure via non-invasive means a range of cognitive WL states that have implications to HCI research. We describe several cognitive resources at a low-level, as they pertain to the brain, and at a high-level, as they relate to the field of HCI.

2) We demonstrate ways that fNIRS brain measurement can be used to complement usability testing by measuring a range of WL states objectively and in real time. This additional information can yield a more thorough, comprehensive understanding about a UI design than can be achieved with standard usability testing.

We begin this paper by describing related work on the fNIRS device and the human brain and go on to describe an experiment protocol designed to measure the level of load placed on users' low-level cognitive resources while working with a UI. We then present a series of usability experiments that apply this protocol to the evaluation of design choices of UIs. Finally, we describe our results and analysis, as well as avenues for future work in this area.

RELATED WORK

Our interdisciplinary research builds on work in biomedical engineering, cognitive psychology, and HCI.

Measuring the Human Brain with fNIRS

EEG has been used in the HCI and Human Factors domains to measure various aspects of mental workload [4, 12, 24, 28, 34]. While a promising tool for non-invasive brain measurements, EEG has several drawbacks such as low spatial resolution, susceptibility to noise, and long set-up time which can make EEG challenging to use in realistic human-computer interactions. fNIRS has recently been introduced [8] to overcome many of the drawbacks of the EEG and other brain monitoring techniques. The tool, still a research modality, uses light sources in the near infrared wavelength range (650-850 nm) and optical detectors to probe brain activity, as depicted in Figure 2. Deoxygenated (Hb) and oxygenated hemoglobin (HbO) are the main absorbers of near infrared light in tissues during hemodynamic and metabolic changes associated with neural activity in the brain [8]. These changes can be detected measuring the reflected light that has probed the brain cortex [8, 19].

Experimental Studies of Workload in the Brain

To date, most experimental psychology studies explore brain functioning while people conduct simple, highly controlled tasks that have been designed to target a specific cognitive resource, such as visual scanning and perception, working memory (WM), and similar higher-order cognitive functions. Many of these resources relate directly to current research in HCI.

Working Memory

WM refers to an information processing system that temporarily stores information in order to serve higher-order cognitive functions such as planning, problem solving, and understanding language [3]. One of the most common tasks used in cognitive psychology to elicit load on participants' WM resources is the n-back task [11, 23, 30]. The n-back task is depicted in Figure 3.

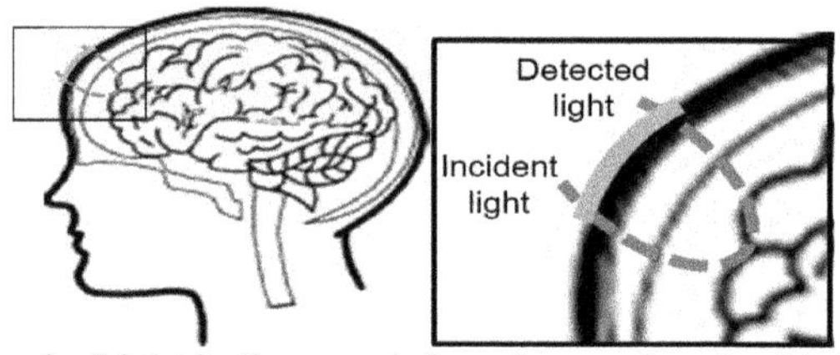

Figure 2: Light in the near-infrared range is pulsed into the brain cortex and the reflected light is detected.

A series of letters is presented to participants, one letter at a time, on the computer screen. For each letter, the participant indicates whether or not that letter matches the letter that she saw *n* letters previously. During the 3-back condition, participants must store and manipulate, three items at a time in WM, and for the 1-back task, they only manipulate and store one item at a time.

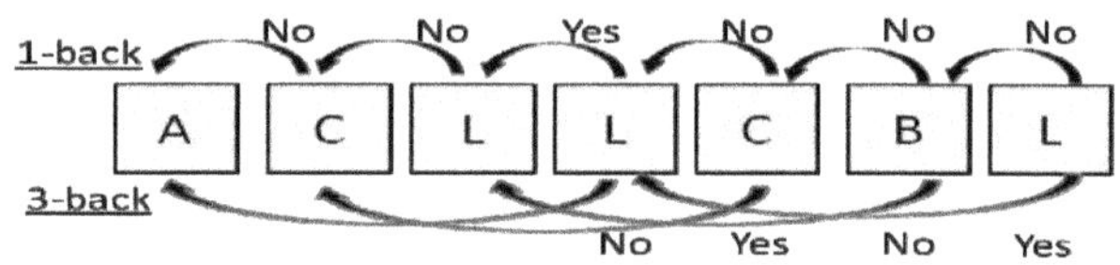

Figure 3: Depiction of the 0-back and 3-back task.

Parasuraman [27] found that WM and executive functioning tasks activate areas in the prefrontal cortex, and that the amount of activation increases as a function of the number of items held in WM. The presence of WL activation and the relative load (of holding *n* items in WM or of making *n* updates to WM) can be quantified using fNIRS [27]. WM is at the foundation of all interactions between humans and computers. If we can determine that a UI design elicits high WM load on users, we can modify the UI to alleviate this load. For example, a poorly constructed menu may require users to keep several menu items in their WM while searching for the correct selection. Perhaps this menu can be redesigned to alleviate this load on the user's WM.

Visual Perception and Search

Another WL related set of tasks involves visually searching for items within a set of distracter items. There are two kinds of visual search; efficient and inefficient. If a target item is saliently different as compared to the distracter items surrounding the target item, it can be found immediately, regardless of the number of distracter items [2, 26, 32]. Inefficient search occurs when the search item is not highly salient as compared to the distracter items. In this case, a serial visual search must be performed in order to locate the item of interest.

One task that has been used to induce inefficient visual search is called the "finding A's" task. This task can be found, among a variety of other experimental tasks, in the Kit of Factor Referenced Cognitive Tests [10]. In this task, users are instructed to scan through a list of words and to cross off every word that contains the letter 'a'.

fNIRS has been used to measure the resources responsible for visual search [22, 25]. If we can determine that users are conducting inefficient visual searches while looking for items in a UI, we can modify the UI to alleviate these demands. For example, a poorly structured web page may not direct users' visual attention to the relevant content that they are likely to search for. The page can be restructured to provide salient visual cues directing people to the most relevant semantic content on the web page.

Executive Processes and Response Conflict

Pinpointing functional brain regions is difficult to do with our executive processes, as they are involved in high order processing that involves the recruitment of a number of overlapping cognitive resources [3]. While we still have much to learn about executive processing, functions related to response conflict have been empirically validated. Response conflict deals with the central executive's suppression of automatic, but incorrect responses. We use response conflict throughout our daily lives. For example, while driving a car we may see a squirrel run across the road. Our initial, automatic reaction may be to swerve the car away from the squirrel. However, a quick look around may show oncoming traffic on one side of us and a cliff on the other side. Our central executive helps us to inhibit the automatic response of swerving in order to choose the response of staying in our lane (sorry, squirrel!).

A common test used in experimental psychology research to induce response inhibition in the brain is the Stroop test [29]. In this task, a color name, which is written in a font of a particular color, is presented to participants. Participants must say the color that each word is written in out loud. In the congruent condition (Figure 4a), the name of the word and the color that the word is written in are one and the same. In the incongruent condition (4b), the name of the word and the color that the word is written in are different. People's ability to name a color is slightly slower than their semantic ability to read a word. Thus, the incongruent condition of the Stroop test requires people to use their response conflict resources, suppressing the automatic response of saying the name of the word and answering correctly, with the color of the word. fNIRS has been used to measure the brain activity induced by the Stroop test [29].

If we determine that a user has high response conflict while working with a UI, this may indicate that something about the UI is unintuitive. For example, some un-intuitive video games may require the user to press awkward keys in order to navigate in the game; pressing the 'A' key when one wants to turn right may cause response conflict as the user may automatically want to physically move the controller to the right, as is done with the successful Nintendo Wii.

a) BLUE	b) YELLOW
RED	GREEN

Figure 4: Say the color that each word is written in out loud. a) congruent Stroop test, and b) incongruent Stroop test.

TRANSITIONING FROM LOW-LEVEL EXPERIMENTAL PSYCHOLOGY TO HIGH-LEVEL USABILITY TESTING

In order to enhance usability testing with fNIRS, we aim to measure which low-level resource(s) are being taxed and the level of load (i.e., high or low) that is placed on each of these resource(s) while users work with UIs. Although there is some disagreement as to the effects of multitasking in the brain [1, 20], most agree that combining several low-level, simplified tasks has an additive effect in the brain. fNIRS has been used to measure the spatiotemporal changes occurring when different cognitive resources are recruited to complete a high-level mental task [17, 18]. This suggests that we can use fNIRs to measure different patterns of activation associated with the various cognitive resources targeted in this experiment.

The brain research presented in this section shows that: 1) There are unique signatures of brain activation relating to the level of load placed on many low-level cognitive resources. 2) Brain activation increases in a given region as the load on that resource increases. 3) Combining several low-level, simplified tasks has an additive effect in the brain, which can be measured with fNIRS. Thus, we expect to be able to measure different levels of load placed on users' WM, visual search, and response inhibition resources.

CONDUCTING USABILITY EXPERIMENTS WITH FNIRS

To make connections between the users' brain activity while completing high-level UI tasks and the low-level demands placed on their cognitive resources, we developed an experiment protocol, described in detail in [16], for use in our usability tests. The general protocol is as follows:

Usability Experiment Protocol

1) Researchers gather benchmark tasks from cognitive psychology that elicit high and low-levels of WL on a range of target cognitive resource(s) such as visual search, WM, and response inhibition. We refer to these exercises as *cognitive benchmark tasks.*

2) Researchers create a set of tasks that users will complete with the UI to be evaluated. We refer to these as *UI tasks.*

3) An experiment is run where users complete the *cognitive benchmark tasks*, yielding a measure of their brain activity while experiencing high and low WL levels in their various cognitive subsystems. Users also work with the *UI tasks.* Brain activity is measured throughout the experiment.

4) fNIRS data from the *cognitive benchmark tasks* are used as training data to build a machine learning classifier. The fNIRS data from the *UI tasks* is input into the machine learning classifier as testing data for the classifier. The classifier outputs the level of cognitive load experienced by each user while working with a given *UI task*.

USABILITY EXPERIMENTS

We conducted a usability experiment to evaluate the design of two UIs and to demonstrate our experimental protocol.

Cognitive Benchmark Tasks

Participants completed the following benchmark tasks:

Finding A's

In the Finding A's task, participants were instructed to look at a matrix of words and click on those that contained the letter 'a'. In one version of the task, the a's in the words were highlighted. In the other version, the a's were not highlighted. There were 14 words with a's in them on each screen presented to participants. If a participant clicked on all of the words containing a's, a new screen was shown, though there was a maximum of two screens per 50 second task. These two tasks induced benchmark levels of high and low load on users' visual search resources.

Stroop

The Stroop task had two variations, an incongruent Stroop and a congruent Stroop, which are depicted in Figure 5. In both variations, adapted from previous fNIRS research [29], one of the words BLUE, RED, YELLOW, or GREEN appeared on the screen for .5 seconds before another of those four words was added to the screen beneath the first. Participants determined whether the bottom word correctly described the color of the top word. In the congruent version, the top word was always colored to correspond with its meaning. In the incongruent version, the top word did not have to match its own meaning. These tasks induced benchmark levels of high and low load on users' response inhibition resources.

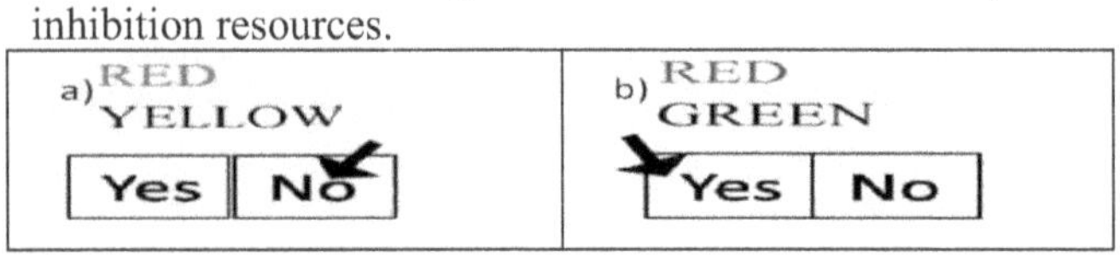

Figure 5: a) congruent Stroop and b) incongruent Stroop task

n-back

We used the 0-back and 3-back variations of the n-back task. In the 0-back condition, participants were first shown a single letter. As the task progressed, participants were presented with new letters on the screen. They were asked to identify whether the letters they were seeing were the same or different than the first letter. In the 3-back task, they were asked to judge whether the letter they were looking at was the same as the letter they saw three letters before. These two tasks induced benchmark levels of high and low load on users' WM resources.

UI Tasks

The first UI was a driving simulator and the second UI was for conducting web searches. We chose these UIs because the design of driving/video game [6, 21] and web search UIs [5, 32] have been popular areas of HCI research.

Car Driving Interface

The driving tasks were completed using a software program called 3D Driving School (Fig. 6). The task took place in a parking lot where there were three lines of cones. Participants were instructed to drive around the cones in a slalom pattern using the arrow keys on the keyboard to navigate. There were two variations of the task. In the first, the commands associated with the arrow keys performed as expected. That is, pressing the ← and → arrow keys caused the car to turn to the left and the right, respectively. In the second variation, the functions of the ← and → arrow keys were reversed. Pressing the ← key turned the car to the right, and pressing the → key turned the car to the left.

Figure 6: The Free Drive course used in the driving tasks.

Web Search Interface

The web search was completed using a Google search engine embedded in an online site for financial news articles (www.fdi-magazine.com). Participants were presented with a question which could be answered by searching the financial site and reading the articles (Fig. 7).

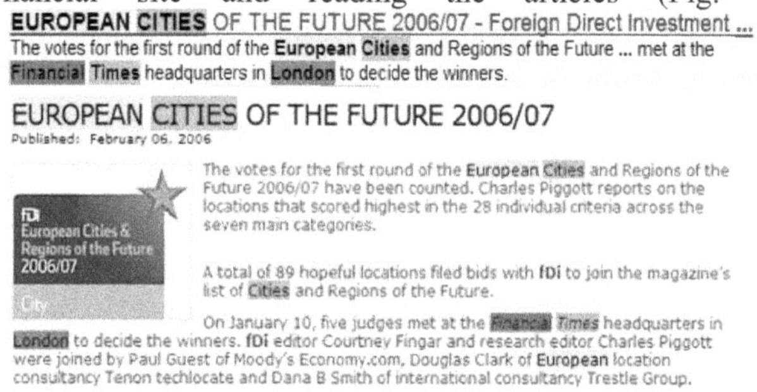

Figure 7: The web search task with highlighting.

Participants were instructed to highlight their answer using the mouse and then to proceed to the next question (this eliminated noise caused by participants speaking or writing their answers in the middle of the task). For each instance of the web search, there was a maximum of two questions. There were two versions of the web search task. In one version, the user's search terms were highlighted in the search results and the articles. In the other version there was no highlighting of search terms.

Completion Time

We controlled for completion time in all experiment conditions. During the nback and Stroop conditions, new questions were presented to subjects every 3 seconds. There was only one speed enabled when subjects moved forward during the driving tasks, placing a limit on the number of cones users could access in each task. During the finding a's and web search tasks, subjects only had a set number of task-items to complete in each 50-second period of time. Subjects were instructed (with the help of a progress bar that was visible during the experiment) to work at a rate that would result in the completion of all tasks by the end of the task period. By controlling for time in this way, we were able to focus more on the difference in brain activity during different tasks rather than on differences caused by working at different paces.

Usability Experiment Setup and Protocol

In the rest of this paper, we use the following terminology:

Cognitive benchmark tasks: Experiment tasks that have been pulled from experimental psychology research. In this experiment, these tasks target the following resources: *low and high WM, low and high visual search, and low and high response inhibition tasks.*

UI tasks: Experiment tasks that represent the UIs to be evaluated. These include: *driving with correct mapping, driving with incorrect mapping, web search with highlighting,* and *web search with no highlighting tasks.*

Methodology

Ten participants completed the experiment. After providing informed consent, participants were instructed to complete a tutorial. Participants were instructed to keep body movement to a minimum, and to only move when using the keyboard and mouse while working with the experiment tasks. Previous research has shown that these minimal hand movements do not add detrimental amounts of noise to the fNIRS data [31]. Experiment tasks were presented to participants in a randomized order, with a 23 second rest period between tasks. There were six trials and each trial consisted of 10 tasks (the six benchmark tasks and the four UI tasks).. Each task lasted 50 seconds. As the experiment progressed, the answers provided by the participants were recorded. After the experiment was complete, participants completed a post-experiment survey where they rated the tasks on a 1-7 Likert scale, with 1 representing the lowest and 7 representing the highest level of difficulty.

fNIRs Equipment and Data Analysis

The fNIRs device is an ISS OxyplexTS frequency-domain tissue spectrometer with two probes. Each probe has a detector and four light sources. Each light source produces near infrared light at two wavelengths (690nm and 830nm) which were sampled at 6.25Hz.

As brain activity differs widely on a person-by- person basis, we ran all preprocessing of data separately for each participant. We normalized the fNIRS light intensity raw data in each channel by their own baseline values. We then applied a moving average band pass filter to each channel and we use the modified Beer-Lambert Law [8, 19] to convert our light intensity data to measures of the change in oxygenated hemoglobin (ΔHbO) and deoxygenated hemoglobin (ΔHb) in the brain. Therefore, we had a recording of ΔHbO and another recording of ΔHb at four depths on the left side (labeled L1, L2, L3, L4) and four depths on the right side of the brain (R1, R2, R3, R4). Both ΔHbO and ΔHb contribute to what is known as the blood oxygen level dependent (BOLD) signal, which is correlated to brain activity. For a review on the BOLD signal see [7] and for a review on the measurement patterns seen in ΔHbO and ΔHb in fNIRS studies see [15]. We cut off the first 4 seconds of each task, as blood takes several seconds to move to areas of activation. Next, we extracted the following features from our preprocessed fNIRS data: *largest value, smallest value, average, slope, time to peak,* and *full width at half maximum;* for the first and second half of each task. We used a cross validation scheme that takes into account the block design of the experiment, as traditional cross validation produces higher classification accuracy that is not representative of real world HCI-relevant applications [12]. Once we had partitioned our data into training and testing data, we used CfsSubsetEval(), a feature subset selection algorithm from the Weka open source toolkit [35] on our training data. The function selects feature subsets that are highly correlated with the class and have a low correlation to one another. We used these features to classify our test data.

USABILITY EXPERIMENT RESULTS AND ANALYSIS

We used the usability experiment protocol described above in our usability studies. Our results and analyses are intended to (in)validate the following research hypotheses:

Experiment Hypotheses

1) We can distinguish between three cognitive resources (visual search, WM, and response inhibition).
2) Not only can we determine which resource is being taxed, but within a given cognitive resource, we can distinguish between high and low-levels of load placed on that resource.
3) We can use our benchmark cognition tasks as training data to build a machine learning classifier. We can use this classifier to determine the user's workload while working with a driving UI and a web search UI.
4) The accuracy and survey results will support the results from the fNIRS data analysis, and the fNIRS results will provide information above and beyond the information provided by the more traditional usability metrics of accuracy and survey data.

In the rest of this section we describe our analysis techniques and we relate our results to each hypothesis. Then we make recommendations to the UIs based on the results.

Experiment Hypothesis 1: *We can distinguish between which cognitive resource is being taxed.*
To address our first hypothesis, we used a Naïve Bayes classifer from Weka's open source toolkit [35] to make pair-wise comparisons between the *cognitive benchmark tasks* (high WM *vs* high VS *vs* high RI*)*. Average classification accuracy across all subjects is reported in Fig. 8.

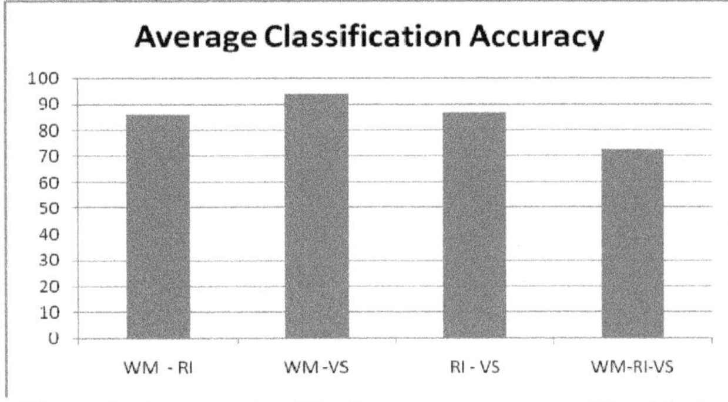

Figure 8: Average classification accuracy across 10 subjects distinguishing between the cognitive benchmark tasks.

As the figure shows, we were able to distinguish between WM and response inhibition (RI), WM and visual search (VS), and response inhibition and visual search with over 80% average accuracy across subjects. Also, we were able to distinguish between the three classes of WM, response inhibition, and visual search with over 70% accuracy. These classification accuracies support our first hypothesis.

Experiment Hypothesis 2: *Not only can we determine which resource is being taxed, but within a given resource, we can distinguish between high and low-levels of load placed on that resource.*
To address our second hypothesis, we used our Naïve Bayes classifer to distinguish between the load (low or high) placed on each cognitive resource. Mean classification accuracies for all subjects are in Fig. 9. As the figure shows, for each resource, we were able to distinguish between low and high-levels of load on that resource with average accuracies ranging from 76-94%. These promising classification accuracies support our second hypothesis.

Experiment Hypothesis 3: *We can use our benchmark tasks as training data to build a machine learning classifier. We can use this classifier to determine the user's workload while working with a driving and a web search UI.*
We used the process described in our usability experiment protocol to predict the WM, response inhibition, and visual search load of the UI variations. Next we will illustrate, for each participant, how we built three distinct machine learning classifiers. Each of the three classifiers was responsible for predicting that participant's level of 1) WM load, 2) response inhibition load, and 3) visual search load while working with the driving and web search tasks.

Construction of Classifiers
For each participant, we built three distinct classifiers. Figure 10 depicts our process for creating a machine learning classifier to predict the WM load (high or low) associated with our driving UI tasks. First, the data from each of the low and high benchmark WM tasks was used as training data to build a Naïve Bayes classifier (see the *fNIRS Data Analysis* section for more detail). This resulted in a WM classifier that predicted whether or not a given test instance had a high or low WM load.

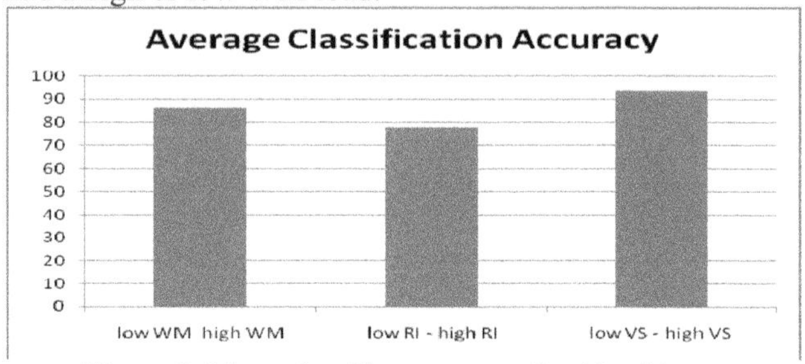

Figure 9: Mean classifier accuracy for 10 subjects.

Next, the same participant's data from the driving UI and web search UI tasks was fed into the classifier as testing data. The classifier predicted the level of WM load (high or low) associated with each UI task. For each subject, we refer to this first classifier as the *WM classifier*.

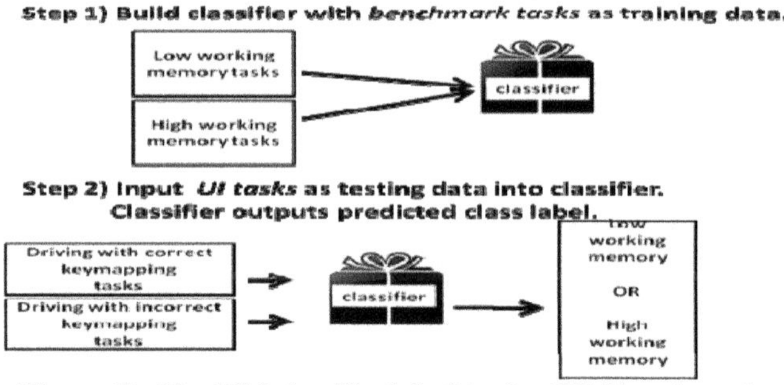

Figure 10: The *WM classifier* is built using WM benchmark tasks. The UI tasks are fed into the classifier as test instances.

Next, for each participant, the low and high response inhibition benchmark tasks were used as training data to build another Naïve Bayes classifier. The same process as that depicted in Figure 10 was followed, however, this time the training data input into the classifier were the response inhibition benchmark tasks rather than the WM benchmark tasks. This resulted in a response inhibition classifier that predicted the load of response inhibition (high or low) placed on users while working with the UI variations. For each subject, we refer to this second classifier as the *response inhibition classifier*.

Lastly, a third Naïve Bayes classifier was built using just the visual search benchmark tasks as training data. This resulted in a visual search classifier that predicted the visual search load (high or low) placed on users while working with the UI variations. For each subject, we refer to this third classifier as the *visual search classifier*.

Composition of Classifiers
For each of our 10 subjects we built three Naïve Bayes classifiers; a WM classifier, a response inhibition classifier,

and a visual search load classifier. Thus, we built 30 distinct classifiers using 30 completely separable sets of training data. While training each classifier for each subject, we had eight sensor locations (four on the left side of the forehead and four on the right) and each sensor generated values of the rate of change of oxygenated blood (HbO) and deoxygenated blood (Hb). Thus, we had 16 timeseries, and we generated 12 features from each of these timeseries (resulting in a total of 192 features that were generated from the raw fNIRS data).We used the CfsSubsetEval feature selection algorithm to prune our features (*see fNIRS Data Analysis section*). The feature selection algorithm pruned the features greatly, and the number of features selected by each classifier ranged from two to 15 features. On average, 7.6 features were selected for classification when building the WM classifiers while an average of 5.2 and 9.1 features were selected while building the response inhibition and visual search classifiers, respectively. Figure 11 displays the composition of the three classifier types across subjects.

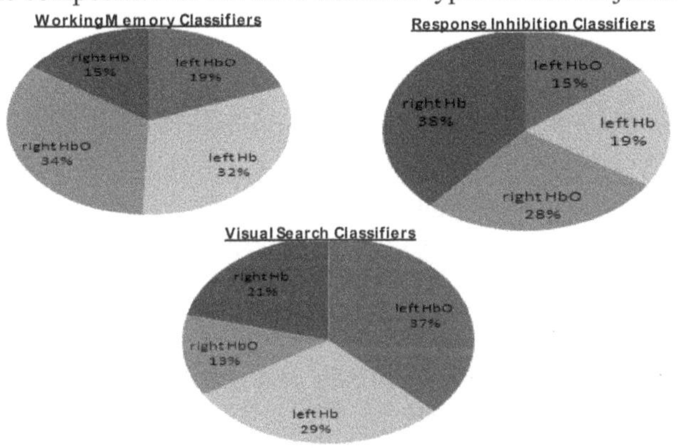

Figure 11: Composition of the classifier types across subjects.

We created a WM classifier, a response inhibition classifier, and a visual search classifier for each of our 10 participants. Thus, we created 10 distinct WM classifiers which were suited to the individual. We tallied the features selected by each of these 10 classifiers and grouped the features based on the sensor location of that feature, and on whether or not the feature represented ΔHbO or ΔHb data. We did the same for the response inhibition and for the visual search classifiers. We made four groups to describe the features selected by each of the classifiers across all subjects: 1) ΔHbO on the left side of the forehead, 2) ΔHbO on the right side of the forehead, 3) ΔHb on the left side of the forehead, and 3) ΔHb on the right side of the forehead.

As shown in the figure, each classifier type differed in structure from the other two classifiers. Participants' ΔHbO on the right side of the head and ΔHb on the left side of the head were the most predictive for the WM tasks. Participants' ΔHbO and ΔHb on the right side of the head were the most predictive for response inhibition tasks. The ΔHbO and ΔHb on the left side of the head were the most predictive for visual search tasks. This supports the hypothesis that the benchmark WM, response inhibition, and visual search tasks used different (though probably overlapping) cognitive resources, and that these differences were measurable with fNIRS.

Classifier Predictions Across Subjects

We ran machine learning predictions for 10 participants x 3 classifiers x 4 UI variations x 6 trials, which resulted in 720 distinct machine learning predictions. We describe our classifier predictions for all participants next. We've broken down our results into four graphs (Figure 11 and Figure 12). Each graph shows a tally of the predictions made by each of the 10 subject's three classifiers while each subject worked on one of the UI variations. Thus, each graph contains a tally of 10 subjects x 6 trials x 3 classifiers = 180 classifier predictions. For each driving UI variation we report the total number of high and low load predictions made by each of the three classifiers across all subjects (10 subjects x 6 trials = 60 instances total . These results are depicted in Figure 12.

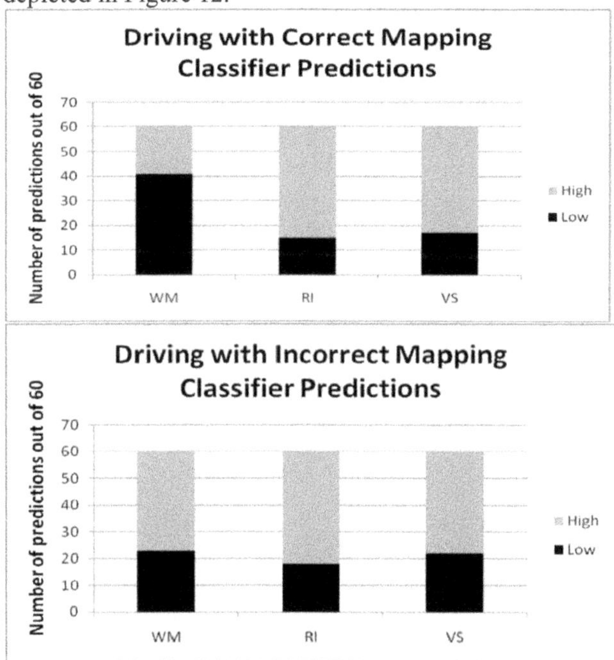

Figure 12: The total number of high and low load predictions made by each of the three classifiers across all subjects..

The results show that across all subjects most of the driving with correct mapping instances were classified as having a low WM, high response inhibition, and high visual search load. The majority of the driving with incorrect mapping instances were classified as having a high WM, high response inhibition, and high visual search load.

It is not surprising that driving with the correct mapping caused users to exert lower levels of WM than driving with the incorrect mapping. It is likely that when using the controls in the incorrect mapping condition, users had to keep the unusual mapping stored in their WM throughout the driving task. It is also not surprising that both driving conditions caused a high visual search load, as users were continually scanning the cones ahead of them while steering. Interestingly, both keyboard mappings (correct and incorrect) caused a high level of response inhibition. We wonder if the choice of using a keyboard (as opposed to a joystick or steering wheel) placed restraints on users' response inhibition by forcing them to inhibit natural steering movements in order to press the right keys. Post-experiment interviews support this speculation.

As shown in Fig. 13, the results showed that across all subjects the majority of the web search with highlighting instances were classified as having a high WM, high response inhibition, and low visual search load. The majority of the web search with no highlighting instances were classified as having a high WM, low response inhibition, and high visual search load. It is not surprising that both web search UIs caused users to have high-levels of WM. After all, users had to remember the content of the question that was asked of them while they searched for the solution in the articles in front of them. It is also not surprising that the level of visual search load was higher when highlighting of search terms was not available than when the highlighting was available for users. We expected that users would have to conduct an inefficient visual search of the articles for the keywords when highlighting was not available.

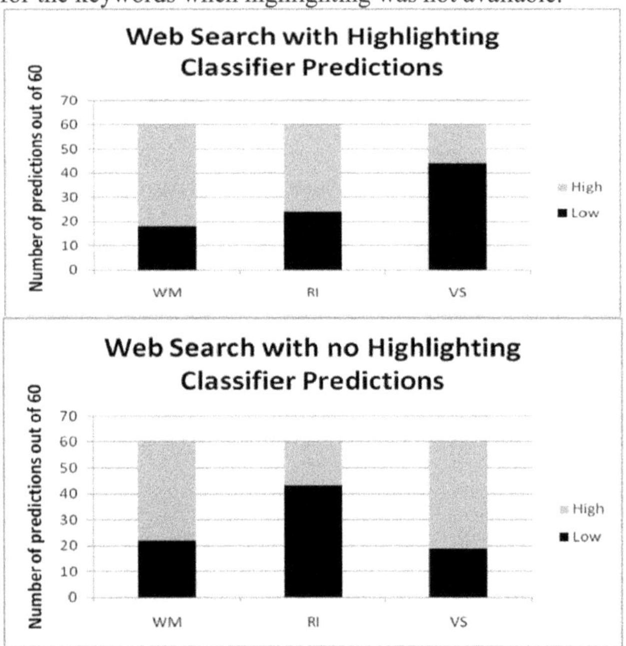

Figure 13: the total number of high and low load predictions made by each of the three classifiers across all subjects.

We did not expect, however, the web search with highlighting to be associated with a higher load of response inhibition than the web search with no highlighting. Since the use of highlighting enabled our users to avoid an inefficient visual search of search items, they were able to spend more time processing the verbal information presented to them in the research articles than in the no highlighting condition. A thorough review of recent experimental psychology literature shows that people use response conflict resources while processing sentences and semantic information [36]. Therefore, we conjecture that the highlighting of search terms enabled users to minimize their visual search load and focus on processing the text in front of them.

This resulted in users having a higher level of response inhibition that reflected the added load that they were able to place on semantic, task related, processing. We hypothesize that the added effort that users were able to place on semantic (or task related) processing rather than on syntactic (or UI related) processing resulted in the higher accuracy that users achieved in the web search with highlighting condition. Our classification results support our third hypothesis; the cognitive load classifications depicted in Fig. 11 and 12 are in line with what we would expect users' cognitive resource load to be while working with each UI.

Experiment Hypothesis 4:
The accuracy and survey results will support the results from the fNIRS data analysis, and the fNIRS results will provide information above and beyond the information provided by the more traditional usability metrics of accuracy and survey data.

We recorded the number of correct and incorrect responses made by participants during the experiment. A repeated measures ANOVA was used on this accuracy data to make comparisons between conditions. A Kruskal-Wallis test was used to analyze the Likert scale survey data for each condition. Table 3 provides a summary of these results. Highlighted cells indicate significance with 95% confidence.Not surprisingly, all accuracy data (except the Stroop tasks) and all survey data indicated that the low benchmark workload (WL) tasks were more difficult than the high benchmark WL tasks. Additionally, the accuracy data supported the fNIRS findings that *driving with the correct mapping* was easier than *driving with the incorrect mapping*, and that web searches with highlighting were easier than searches with no highlighting.

Interestingly, users did not report a difference in difficulty between the UI tasks in the Likert survey. This is in contrast to the accuracy data and to the data from the fNIRS results. Some common, and well known, issues with self-report surveys are that users may not be aware of subtle differences in their own user experiences, and post-surveys may lack insight into the user's real time experiences while working with a given task. One of the primary benefits of non-invasive brain measurement during usability studies is to overcome the short coming of self report surveys.

In general, the results from the accuracy and survey data supported the fNIRS findings. Furthermore, the fNIRS findings provided information about the load placed on users' cognitive resources that was above and beyond that which could be acquired with the behavioral results alone. This supports our fourth hypothesis.

Implications to UI Designs

The work presented here would not stay true to the premise of a realistic usability study if it didn't shed light on the particular design choices of each UI design. Therefore, based on the information acquired in our study, we discuss the implications of our findings on the design of the web search and driving UIs next:

Driving UIs

As reflected in Table 3, the driving with correct keymapping appears to be a preferable UI design than the driving with incorrect keymapping as it is associated with fewer errors. Furthermorre, the results in Figure 11 show that the driving with correct keymapping was associated with a lower level of WM load for our subjects than the driving with incorrect keymapping. However, the level of response inhibition and visual search were high for both UI variations. We would suggest using an actual driving wheel or joystick to alleviate the demands placed on users' response inhibition resources while driving. We are currently conducting a follow-on experiment to compare the level of response inhibition exerted by users driving with the keyboard and the response inhibition exerted by users driving with a steering wheel. We expect to see a lower level of response inhibition when users work with the steering wheel than when they use the keyboard.

Table 3: Summary of behavioral results. Shaded cells indicate significance, and we accept the stated hypothesis.

Condition		Hypothesis	Result
Low benchmark tasks	*High benchmark tasks*	*Users' accuracy during low benchmark task < accuracy during high benchmark task*	*Users rated low benchmark task more difficult than high benchmark task*
Congruent Stroop	Incongruent Stroop	F(9, 81) = 1.589, p = .1324	H = 10.41, 1 d.f., P < .05
0back	3back	F(9,81) = 4.004, p < .05	H = 14.2, 1 d.f., P < .05
Finding a's with highlighting	Finding a's with no highlighting	F(9,81) = 84.926, p < .05	H = 13.14, 1 d.f., P < .05
UI version 1	*UI version 2*	*Users' accuracy during UI 1 > accuracy during UI 2*	*Users rated UI version 1 as less difficult than UI version 2*
Driving with correct mapping	Driving with incorrect mapping	F (9,81) = 6.409, p < .05	H = 1.36, 1 d.f., P = .2443
Web search with highlighting	Web search with no highlighting	F (9,81) = 2.094, p < .05	H = 1.26, 1 d.f., P = .2643

Web Search UIs

As reflected in Table 3, the web search with highlighting UI seems to be a preferable UI design than the web search with no highlighting UI as it is associated with fewer errors. Furthermore, the results in Figure 12 show that the web search with highlighting still causes high levels of WM and response inhibition (due most likely to the task related effort involved in reading through an article for solutions to a specific query). One possible UI enhancement could show the users search terms in a semi-transparent window that follows the users mouse across the computer screen. This could alleviate users' WM demands by enabling them to see their search terms within the context of the article they are reading instead of requiring them to recall the search terms while searching through articles.

CONCLUSION

Our experiment results showed that we were able to use brain measurement to measure high and low-levels of load experienced by users' various cognitive resources while working with our driving and web search UI variations. The usability metrics provided by our survey and accuracy data yielded results that are in line with our fNIRS results. The protocol presented in this paper, combined with the fNIRS data acquired during the usability experiment, provided us with information above and beyond the knowledge gained by the more traditional survey and accuracy usability metrics. With the fNIRS data, we were able not only to determine which tasks were 'more difficult' for participants, but to shed light on the low-level cognitive resources in the brain that were more heavily taxed by a given UI design choice.

FUTURE WORK

While our fNIRs device only provided measurements on the left and right side of the participant's forehead, there are devices that can acquire more measurements across participant's cortex. In order to find regions of the brain that are activated while load is placed on various cognitive resources, we are using a new 52-channel fNIRS device to explore the use of more sensor locations across the forehead, enabling the measurement of small spatiotemporal changes that occur when different cognitive resources are taxed. In the future, we foresee brain data as an additional metric gathered in usability tests. This cognitive state information, combined with more traditional usability metrics such as speed, accuracy, and survey results, can provide in-depth evaluations of a range of UIs.

REFERENCES

1. Adcock, R.A., Constable, R.T., Gore, J.C. and Goldman-Rakic, P.S. Functional neuroanatomy of executive processes involved in dual-task performance. *Proceedings of the National Academy of Sciences of the United States of America, 97* (7). 3567-3572.
2. Anderson, E.J., Mannan, S.K., Husain, M., Rees, G., Summer, P., Mort, D.J., McRobbie, D. and Kennard, C. Involvement of prefrontal cortex in visual search. *Experimental Brain Research, 180* (2). 289-302.
3. Baddeley, A. and Della Sala, S. Working memory and executive control. *Philosophical Transactions of the Royal Society of London, 351.*
4. Berka, C., Levendowski, D., Cvetinovic, M., Petrovic, M., Davis, G., Lumicao, L., Zivkovic, V., Popovic, M. and Olmstead, R. Real-Time Analysis of EEG Indexes of Alert-

ness, Cognition, and Memory Acquired With a Wireless EEG Headset. *International Journal of Human Computer Interaction, 17* (2). 151–170.
5. Blackmon, M.H., Kitajima, M. and Polson, P.G., Tool for accurately predicting website navigation problems, non-problems, problem severity, and effectiveness of repairs. in *In Proceedings of the SIGCHI Conference on Human Factors in Computing Systems*, (Portland, Oregon, USA, 2005).
6. Brumby, D.P., Salvucci, D.D. and Howes, A., Focus on driving: how cognitive constraints shape the adaptation of strategy when dialing while driving. in *In Proc. of the 27th international Conference on Human Factors in Computing Systems*, (Boston, MA, USA, 2009), ACM.
7. Buxton, R. *Introduction to functional magnetic resonance imaging*. Cambridge University Press, Cambridge, United Kingdom, 2002.
8. Chance, B., Anday, E., Nioka, S., Zhou, S., Hong, L., Worden, K., Li, C., Murray, T., Ovetsky, Y. and Thomas, R. A novel method for fast imaging of brain function, non-invasively, with light. *Optics Express, 10* (2).
9. Czerwinski, M. and Larson, K. Cognition and the Web: Moving from Theory to Web Design. in *Human Factors and Web Development*, Ratner, J. (Ed.), Erlbaum: NJ, 2002, 147-165.
10. Eckstrom, R., French, J., Harman, H. and Derman, D. Kit of factor-referenced cognitive tests.
11. Gevins, A. and Smith, M. Neurophysiological Measures of Working memory and Individual Differences in Cognitive Ability and Cogntive Style. *Cerebral Cortex, 10*.
12. Grimes, D., Tan, D., Hudson, S., Shenoy, P. and Rao, R., Feasibility and Pragmatics of Classifying Working Memory Load with an Electroencephalograph. in *CHI 2008 Conference on Human Factors in Computing Systems*, (Florence, Italy., 2008).
13. Guhe, M., Liao, W., Zhu, Z., Ji, Q., Gray, W.D. and Schoelles, M.J., Non-intrusive measurement of workload in real-time. in *49th Annual Conference of the Human Factors and Ergonomics Society*, (2005), 1157-1161.
14. Hart, S.G. and Staveland, L.E. Development of NASA-TLX (Task Load Index): Results of empirical and theorical research. in Hancock, P., Meshkati, N. ed. *Human Mental Workload*, Amsterdam, 1988, pp 139 - 183.
15. Hirshfield, L.M. Enhancing Usabiltiy Testing with Functional Near Infrared Spectroscopy *Computer Science*, Tufts University, Medford, MA, 2009.
16. Hirshfield, L.M., Solovey, E.T., Girouard, A., Kebinger, J., Jacob, R.J.K., Sassaroli, A. and Fantini, S., Brain Measurement for Usability Testing and Adaptive Interfaces: An Example of Uncovering Syntactic Workload in the Brain Using Functional Near Infrared Spectroscopy. in *Proc. of SIGCHI*, (2009).
17. Hoshi, Y. and Tamuraa, M. Near-Infrared Optical Detection of Sequential Brain Activation in the Prefrontal Cortex during Mental Tasks. *NeuroImage, 5*. 292-297.
18. Hoshi, Y., Tsoub, B., Billockc, V., Tanosakia, M., Iguchia, Y., Shimadaa, M., Shinbaa, T., Yamadad, Y. and Odae, I. Spatiotemporal characteristics of hemodynamic changes in the human lateral prefrontal cortex during working memory tasks. *NeuroImage, 20*. 1493-1504.
19. Izzetoglu, K., Bunce, S., Onaral, B., Pourrezaei, K. and Chance, B. Functional Optical Brain Imaging Using Near-Infrared During Cognitive Tasks. *International Journal of Human-Computer Interaction, 17* (2).
20. Jaeggi, S.M., Seewer, R., Nirkko, A.C., Eckstein, D., Schroth, G., Groner, R. and Gutbrod, K. Does excessive memory load attenuate activation in the prefrontal cortex? Load-dependent processing in single and dual tasks: functional magnetic resonance imaging study. *NeuroImage, 19* (2). 210-225.
21. Jancke, L., Brunner, B. and Esslen, M. Brain activation during fast driving in a driving simulator: the role of the lateral prefrontal cortex. *Neuroreport, 19* (11).
22. Jasdzewski, G., Strangman, G., Wagner, J., Kwong, K., Poldrack, R. and Boas, D. Differences in the hemodynamic response to event-related motor and visual paradigms as measured by near-infrared spectroscopy. *NEUROIMAGE, 20* (1). 479-488.
23. Joanette, Y., Ansaldo, A., de Mattos Pimenta Parente, M., Fonseca, R., Kristensen, C. and Scherer, L. Neuroimaging investigation of executive functions: evidence from fNIRS. *PSICO, 39* (3).
24. Lee, J.C. and Tan, D.S., Using a Low-Cost Electroencephalograph for Task Classification in HCI Research. in *ACM Symposium on User Interface Software and Technology*, (2006).
25. Meek, J., Elwell, C., Khan, M., Romaya, J., Wyatt, J., Delpy, D. and Zeki, S. Regional Changes in Cerebral Haemodynamics as a Result of a Visual Stimulus Measured by Near Infrared Spectroscopy. *Proc. Roy. Soc. London, 261*. 351-356.
26. Muller-Plath, G. Localizing subprocesses of visual search by correlating local brain activation in fMRI with response time model parameters. *Journal of Neuroscience Methods, 171* (2). 316-330.
27. Parasuraman, R. and Caggiano, D. Neural and Genetic Assays of Human Mental Workload. in *Quantifying Human Information Processing*, Lexington Books, 2005.
28. Scerbo, M., Frederick, G., Freeman, F. and Mikulka, P. A brain-based system for adaptive automation. *Theoretical Issues in Ergonomics Science, 4* (1).
29. Schroeter, M.L., Zysset, S., Kupka, T., Kruggel, F. and Yves von Cramon, D. Near-Infrared Spectroscopy Can Detect Brain Activity During a Color-Word Matching Stroop Task in an Event-Related Design. *Human Brain Mapping, 17* (1). 61-71.
30. Smith, E. and Jonides, J. Storage and Executive Processes n the Frontal Lobes. *Science, 283*.
31. Solovey, E., Girouard, A., Chauncey, K., Hirshfield, L., Sassaroli, A., Zheng, F., Fantini, S. and Jacob, R., Using fNIRS Brain Sensing in Realistic HCI Settings: Experiments and Guidelines. in *ACM UIST Symposium on User Interface Software and Technology*, (2009), ACM.
32. Tamborello, F. and Byrne, M.D., Information search: The intersection of visual and semantic space. in *CHI 2005 Extended Abstracts*, (Portland, OR, USA, 2005), ACM, 1821-1824.
33. Wickens, C., Lee, J., Liu, Y. and Becker, S. *An Introduction to Human Factors Engineering*. Pearson, 2004.
34. Wilson, G.F. and Fisher, F. Cognitive task classification based upon topographic EEG data. *Biological Psychology, 40*. 239-250.
35. Witten, I.H. and Frank, E. *Data Mining: Practical machine learning tools and techniques*. Morgan Kaufmann, San Francisco, 2005.
36. Ye, Z. and Zhou, X. Conflict control during sentence comprehension: fMRI evidence. *Neuroimage, 48* (1). 280-290.

Sensing Cognitive Multitasking for a Brain-Based Adaptive User Interface

Erin Treacy Solovey[1], Francine Lalooses[1], Krysta Chauncey[1], Douglas Weaver[1], Margarita Parasi[1], Matthias Scheutz[1], Angelo Sassaroli[2], Sergio Fantini[2], Paul Schermerhorn[3], Audrey Girouard[4], Robert J.K. Jacob[1]

[1]Tufts University
Computer Science
161 College Ave.,
Medford, MA 02155, USA

[2]Tufts University
Biomedical Engineering
4 Colby St., Medford,
MA 02155, USA

[3]Indiana University
Cognitive Science
Bloomington, IN
47406, USA

[4]Queen's University
School of Computing
25 Union St., Kingston,
ON K7L 3N6, Canada

{erin.solovey, francine.lalooses, krysta.chauncey, douglas.weaver, margarita.parasi, matthias.scheutz, angelo.sassaroli, sergio.fantini}@tufts.edu, pscherme@indiana.edu, audrey@cs.queensu.ca, jacob@cs.tufts.edu

ABSTRACT
Multitasking has become an integral part of work environments, even though people are not well-equipped cognitively to handle numerous concurrent tasks effectively. Systems that support such multitasking may produce better performance and less frustration. However, without understanding the user's internal processes, it is difficult to determine optimal strategies for adapting interfaces, since all multitasking activity is not identical. We describe two experiments leading toward a system that detects cognitive multitasking processes and uses this information as input to an adaptive interface. Using functional near-infrared spectroscopy sensors, we differentiate four cognitive multitasking processes. These states cannot readily be distinguished using behavioral measures such as response time, accuracy, keystrokes or screen contents. We then present our human-robot system as a proof-of-concept that uses real-time cognitive state information as input and adapts in response. This prototype system serves as a platform to study interfaces that enable better task switching, interruption management, and multitasking.

Author Keywords
fNIRS, near-infrared spectroscopy, multitasking, interruption, brain computer interface, human-robot interaction

ACM Classification Keywords
H5.2 [Information interfaces and presentation]: User Interfaces. - Graphical user interfaces.

General Terms
Human Factors

INTRODUCTION
Multitasking has become an integral part of work environments, even though people are not well-equipped to effectively handle more than one task at a time [26]. While multitasking has been shown to be detrimental to performance in individual tasks [26], it can also be beneficial when a secondary task provides additional information for completing the primary task, such as allowing people to integrate information from multiple sources.

Multiple windows, multiple monitors and large displays make it possible for the interface to handle multitasking, and many researchers have investigated how best to support the user who is balancing multiple tasks. Because multitasking can elicit several different cognitive states, the user's needs during multitasking may change over time. However, it is difficult to determine the best way to support the user without understanding the internal cognitive processes occurring during task performance.

In this paper, we describe a preliminary study and two experiments using neural data in which we identified four mental processes that may occur during multitasking and have direct relevance to many HCI scenarios. These processes are almost indistinguishable by examining overt behavior or task performance alone. However, using our non-invasive brain-sensing system (Figure 1) with functional near-infrared spectroscopy (fNIRS), we can automatically distinguish these four states. By detecting specific cognitive states that occur when multitasking, we can build user interfaces that better support task switching, interruption management and multitasking. We show an example of this with a proof-of-concept adaptive human-robot system that can change behavior based on brain signals received. This prototype system serves as a platform to provide the basis for designing and evaluating future brain-based adaptive user interfaces, with broader applications beyond human-robot team tasks.

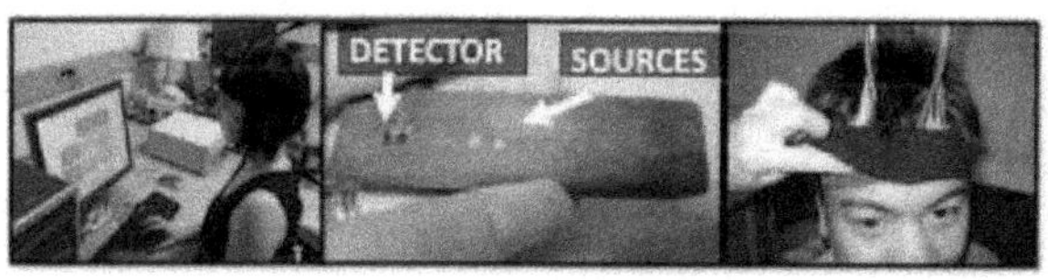

Figure 1. Functional near-infrared spectroscopy is a portable non-invasive tool for detecting brain activity.

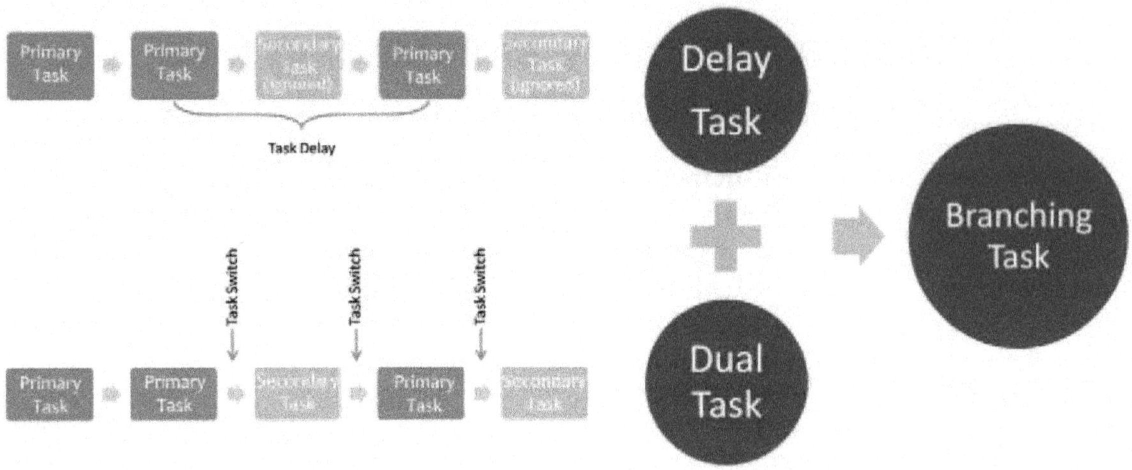

Figure 2. In the Delay scenario, the secondary task requires little attention, but the primary task goal is held in working memory. In the Dual-Task scenario, both primary and secondary tasks require attentional resources to be allocated for each task switch, but goals are not held in working memory. Branching has characteristics of both Delay and Dual-Task scenarios (Figure 3).

This paper makes the following contributions: (1)We show that specific cognitive multitasking states, previously studied with fMRI, can be detected automatically with fNIRS which is more practical in HCI. (2)We moved from a simple letter-based task in previous work to actual HCI-related tasks that elicit similar states. (3)We show a working proof-of-concept human-robot platform that supports adaptive behavior based on the cognitive states detected with fNIRS.

Related Work: Multitasking Support

Although computers are capable of handling multiple processes simultaneously, people have a difficult time due to high mental workload from increased working memory demands and the overhead of switching context between multiple tasks. Repeated task switching during an activity may lead to completion of the primary task with lower accuracy and longer duration, in addition to increased anxiety and perceived difficulty of the task [1]. The challenge is to devise an effective way to measure workload and attention-shifting in a dynamic environment, as well as to identify optimal support for multitasking.

Measuring Mental Workload and Other Cognitive States

Managing mental workload has long been an active topic in HCI research and high mental workload has been identified as a cause of potential errors [2]. Researchers have shown that different types of subtasks lead to different mental workload levels [15]. As a measure for mental workload, researchers have proposed pupil dilation [17] in combination with subjective ratings as this is non-invasive, and allows the user to perform the tasks as the data is processed in real time. Other physiological measures, including skin conductance, respiration, facial muscle tension and blood volume pressure, have also been used to detect cognitive or emotional states to improve machine intelligence [6, 23, 29]. While adaptive user interfaces may be designed to reduce mental workload, any automation may also result in reduced situation awareness, increased user complacency and skill degradation, and these human performance areas should be evaluated in the system [28].

Task Switching and Measuring Interruptibility

When managing multiple tasks, interruptions are unavoidable. To address this, researchers have developed systems that try to identify the cost associated with interruption based on different inputs, such as desktop activity, environment context [7, 13, 35], eye tracking [12], or other physiological measures such as heart rate variability and electromyogram [4] and handle interruptions accordingly. They have found interruptions to be less disruptive during lower mental workload [16, 30]. Other studies tried placing interruptions near the beginning, middle or end of a task [5], at task boundaries [25], or between repetitive tasks which were considered as more interruptible [27]. It was also shown that interruptions relevant to the main task tend to be less disruptive for the users than irrelevant interruptions [5].

Various interruption schemes may affect performance in different ways; however, there is no universally optimal interruption scheme. Interrupting the user as soon as the need arises, for example, emphasizes task completeness over accuracy, while allowing the user to defer interruptions indefinitely does the opposite [31]. McFarlane [24] discusses four distinct methods for coordinating interruption—immediate, negotiated (user selects when to be interrupted), mediated (an intelligent agent selects when to interrupt), and scheduled (interruptions appear at fixed times)—and found that no optimal method existed across users and tasks. Thus, it is crucial that the style of interruption adapts to the task. Systems have been developed that quantify the optimal time to interrupt a user by weighing the value against the cost of interruption [15]. In addition to determining the optimal time for switching tasks, researchers have tried to determine the best method for reminding users of pending background tasks. Miyata and Norman [26] note that important alerts specifically designed for someone who is deeply engaged in another task would most likely be inappropriate and may even be disruptive in other situations.

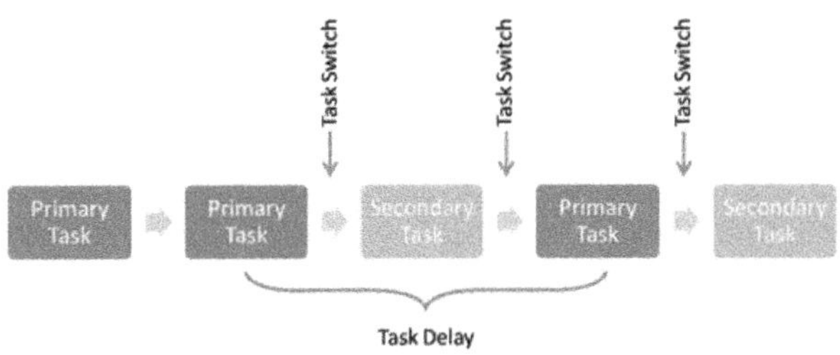

Figure 3. Branching: Primary and secondary task both require attentional resources to be allocated, and the primary task goal must be kept in mind over time.

Brain Sensing for HCI

Real-time cognitive state information can inform the tradeoffs to create intelligent user interfaces. Design of user interfaces that employ real-time cognitive state information has become an emerging topic in HCI recently (for an overview, see [18]). Much of this work has used brain sensing as explicit input to the system to make selections or control the interface [21, 36], although there have been examples of passive brain sensing to be used either as implicit input or for evaluation of user interfaces [9, 11, 22]. Our work focuses on using fNIRS sensors to detect signals users implicitly produce while interacting naturally with a system. These sensors detect changes in oxygenated and deoxygenated blood in a region of the brain by using optical wires to emit near-infrared light [3]. The sensors are easy to use, have a short set-up time and are portable, all characteristics which make fNIRS suitable for use in realistic HCI settings [34]. However, because it is a novel technique for brain sensing, there have been few studies showing specific measurements with fNIRS and their appropriate use in HCI.

Multitasking Scenarios: Branching, Dual Task, Delay

Multitasking behavior involves several high-level brain processes, which vary depending on the types of tasks and the interaction between the tasks. Koechlin et al. [19] described three distinct, but related multitasking scenarios, which they refer to as *branching*, *dual-task*, and *delay*. These are the foundation for the studies described here.

Branching (Figures 2,3) is illustrated by the following scenario: *A user is tackling a complex programming task but is interrupted by an incoming email from her boss that is time sensitive.* Thus, the user must "hold in mind goals while exploring and processing secondary goals" [19]. Branching processes are triggered frequently in multitasking environments and pose a challenge to users.

However, some situations may involve frequent task switching without the need to maintain information about the previous task (e.g. *A user is monitoring and responding to high priority software support issues that are logged by clients as well as responding to important emails, and regularly switches between the two tasks*). These tasks are referred to as *dual-task* because there are two tasks that require attentional resources (Figure 2). These situations could also utilize adaptive support in the user interface, but the adaptive behavior would be distinct from that of *branching.*

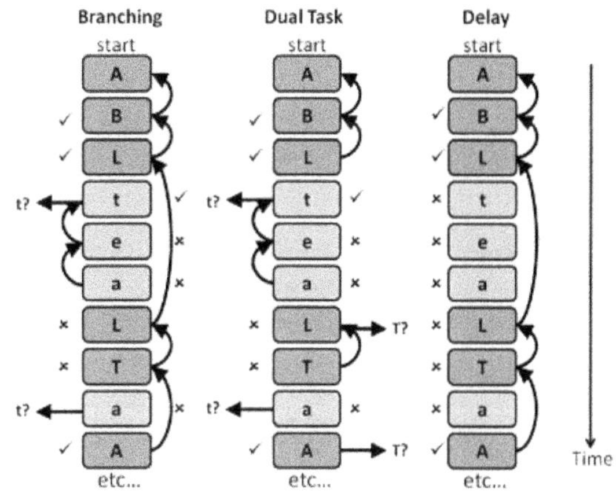

Figure 4. Conditions from [19]. Stimuli were either uppercase (red) or lowercase (blue) letters from the word "tablet" and the response varied depending on the case. Check indicates a match and x indicates a non-match stimulus.

The third multitasking paradigm is illustrated with the following scenario: *A user is tackling a complex programming assignment and at the same time gets instant messages which the user notices, but ignores.* Here, the secondary task is ignored and therefore requires little attentional resources. They refer to this as *delay* because the secondary task mainly delays response to the primary task (Figure 2).

In their experiment, Koechlin et al. demonstrated using functional Magnetic Resonance Imaging (fMRI) that these three multitasking processes have different activation profiles in the prefrontal cortex of the brain, particularly in Brodmann's Areas 8, 9 and 10. Their task involved processing rules based on letters appearing on the screen. Each stimulus was either an uppercase or lowercase letter from the word "tablet." The expected response from the user was different depending on the case of the letter, so switching between uppercase and lowercase letters would be similar to balancing two tasks. There were four conditions in their experiment, each with different rules for responding, designed to trigger specific multitasking behavior (Figure 4):

1) *Delay*: Are two consecutive *uppercase* stimuli in immediate succession in the word "TABLET'? Ignore *lowercase*.
2) *Dual-Task:* Are two consecutive stimuli *of the same case* in immediate succession in the word tablet? When the case changes, is the first letter in the series a 'T' or 't'?
3) *Branching*: For *uppercase* stimuli, respond as in *Delay.* If the letter is *lowercase*, respond as in *Dual Task.*
4) *Control*: Are two consecutive stimuli in immediate succession in "TABLET'? All stimuli were uppercase.

Koechlin et al. [20] later showed that even during branching, there were distinct activation profiles that varied depending on whether the participant could predict when task switching would occur or whether it was random. The ex-

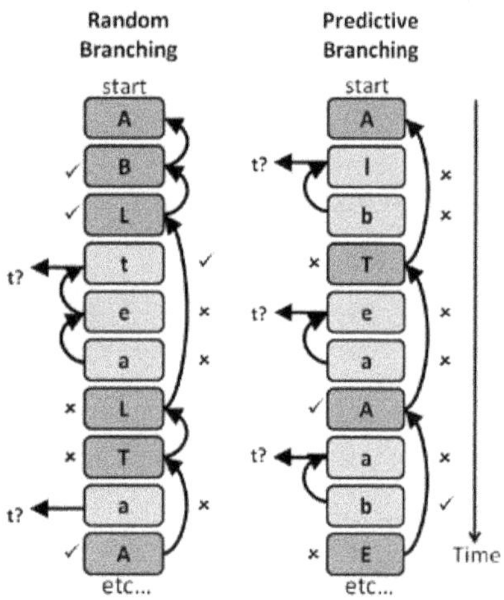

Figure 5. Experimental conditions from Koechlin et al. [20].

perimental setup was almost identical to the earlier study, except that in all conditions, the *branching* paradigm was used. There were two experimental *branching* conditions (Figure 5) and a control:

1) *Random Branching:* Upper- and lower-case letters were presented pseudorandomly.
2) *Predictive Branching:* Uppercase letters were presented every 3 stimuli.
3) *Control Branching:* The same six-letter sequence (A e t a B t) was shown repeatedly.

The significance of these two experiments lies in the fact that all experimental conditions had the same stimuli and the same possible user responses, so the conditions could not be easily distinguished from one another by simply observing the participant. Using fMRI, however, it became possible to distinguish the conditions based on the distinct mental processes (and thus, distinct blood flow patterns) elicited by each task.

In addition, the cognitive states identified in these experiments have direct relevance to many HCI scenarios, particularly when a user is multitasking. Automatically recognizing that the user is experiencing one of these states provides an opportunity to build adaptive systems that support multitasking. For example, by recognizing that most interruptions are quickly ignored, as in the *delay* condition, the system could limit these types of interruptions or reduce their salience as appropriate. Further, if a user is currently experiencing a *branching* situation, the interface could better support maintaining the context of the primary task, whereas during *dual-task* scenarios this would be unnecessary. Finally, distinguishing between *predictive* and *random* scenarios could trigger the system to increase support when the user's tasks become unpredictable.

This paper builds from their experiments with the goal of designing interfaces that recognize these states and behave in appropriate ways to support multitasking. We conducted a preliminary study to reproduce the results of Koechlin et al. [19] using fNIRS which is practical for HCI settings unlike fMRI in which slight movement can create motion artifacts and corrupt the image [34]. We then followed with two experiments that look at distinguishing the cognitive multitasking states in other scenarios besides the "tablet" task to investigate whether these are generic cognitive processes, and not simply tied to the particular task used in the earlier study. Finally, we designed and built a proof-of-concept platform that recognizes and classifies the fNIRS signal and uses it as input to drive an adaptive human-robot system.

PRELIMINARY STUDY

Our preliminary experiment extends Koechlin et al.'s work [19] to more realistic HCI settings. We wanted to determine whether we could distinguish between *branching*, *dual-task* and *delay* situations. These states were successfully distinguished using fMRI [19], but fMRI is not practical in HCI settings. Our hypothesis was that the same could be achieved using fNIRS. Since the sensors are placed on the forehead, they are particularly sensitive to changes in the anterior prefrontal cortex, where Koechlin et al. [19] showed distinct activation profiles during *delay*, *dual* and *branching* tasks.

Three participants wore fNIRS sensors as they performed the experimental tasks. To trigger the three cognitive states, we used the same experimental paradigm used in [19].

To determine whether these tasks could be distinguished, we performed leave-one-out cross validation in Weka [10] to classify the fNIRS sensor data. In MATLAB, the fNIRS signal was detrended by fitting a polynomial of degree 3 and then a low-pass elliptical filter was used to remove noise in the data. Using support vector machines, we achieved reasonably high accuracy classifying the tasks across the three participants (68.4% mean across three pairwise classifications, and 52.9% accuracy for three-way classification). This was a small sample of users, and we hope to achieve higher accuracy, but found the results encouraging enough continue in this research direction.

MULTITASKING EXPERIMENTS

From the promising results of the preliminary study, we investigated whether we could detect these three states in other tasks and domains that are more relevant to interactive user interfaces. Our hypothesis was that the cognitive functions elicited in the "tablet" tasks were generic processes that occur during multitasking. Numerous HCI scenarios involve multitasking, and we chose a human-robot team scenario to further explore the detection of cognitive multitasking in user interfaces.

Multitasking in Human Robot Interaction

Human-robot team tasks inherently involve multitasking, as the user is both performing his or her part of the task, while monitoring the state of the robot(s). Thus, these tasks provide an appropriate example for studying adaptive multitasking support, and may see improved performance with

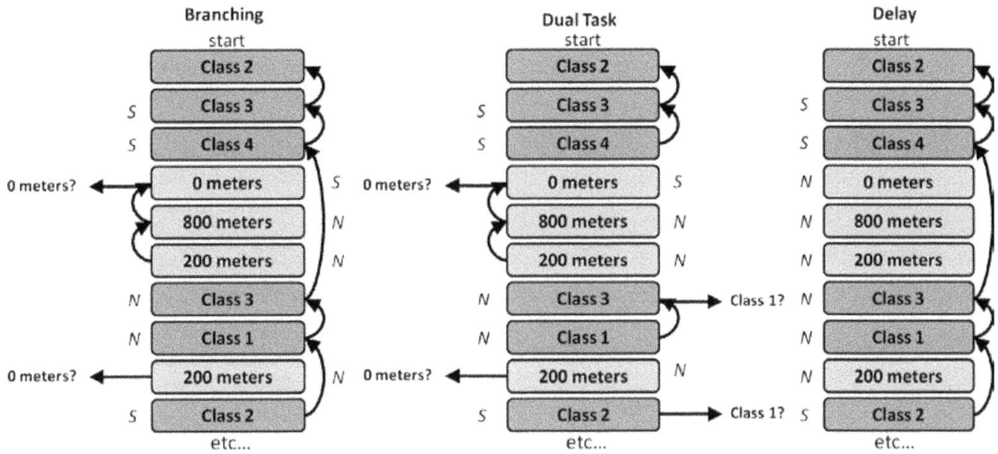

Figure 6. Stimuli and responses for conditions in Experiment 1. These conditions are analogous to those in [19]. (See Figure 4).

brain-based adaptive interfaces. Thus, the simple word-related task was replaced by a human-robot interaction (HRI) task that has similar properties.

Experimental Tasks

We conducted two separate experiments which built from the human-robot team task described by Schermerhorn and Scheutz [32] and adjusted it to include tasks that would induce *delay*, *dual-task* and *branching*, similar to our preliminary study. The tasks involved a human-robot team performing a complex task that could not be accomplished by the human nor the robot alone. The robot and the human had to exchange information in order to accomplish the task. The robot continually updated the human operator with status updates to which the human responded.

In the two separate studies, the participant worked with a robot to investigate rock types on the surface of Mars and had to perform two tasks. The robot presented the participant with status updates, either about a newly found rock or a new location to which it moved. Each rock classification update informed the user of the newly discovered rock's class, which was based on size and ranged from Class 1 to Class 5. Each location update alerted the user of the robot's current location. The spacecraft to which the robot was transmitting could detect the robot's location to the nearest kilometer and assumed the robot was moving in a straight line. Thus, the location updates presented to the user ranged from 0 to 800 meters, in 200 meter increments.

The participant's primary task was to sort rocks, and the secondary task was to monitor the location of the robot. Each time the participant received a status update from the robot (in the form of a pop-up on the screen), s/he had two possible responses: either respond with the left hand by typing "S" to signify *same* or the right hand by typing "N" to signify *new*. After a rock classification, "S" instructed the robot to store the rock in the *same* bin, while "N" instructed the robot to store the rock in a *new* bin. After a location update, "S" instructed the robot to maintain the *same* transmission, while "N" instructed the robot to begin a *new* transmission. The correct response after a particular update varied among the conditions.

Experiment 1: Delay, Dual-Task & Branching

The first experiment contained three conditions, analogous to those in [19], each with its own rules for the user response (Figure 6):

Delay: Do two successive rock classification messages follow in immediate consecutive order? If so, put it in the *same* bin. If not, select a *new* bin. For all location updates, begin a *new* transmission.

Dual-Task: Do two successive messages *of the same type* follow in immediate consecutive order? If so, select the *same* rock bin or maintain the *same* transmission. If the update is of a different type (switch task between rock and location), is the message either a Class 1 rock or a location of 0 meters? If so, select the *same* rock bin or maintain the *same* transmission. In all other cases, place the rock in a *new* bin or begin a *new* transmission.

Branching: For *rock classification* messages, respond as in *Delay*. If the update is a *location*, respond as in *Dual Task*.

Participants

This study included 12 healthy volunteers (10 male), between the ages of 18 and 34. Four additional volunteers had participated in the study, but are not included in this analysis because their performance in the tasks was below 70% in more than two trials per condition, indicating that they were not correctly performing the tasks. In addition, data from another participant is not included due to technical problems with the fNIRS system. All participants were right-handed, had English as their primary language, had no history of brain injury and had normal or corrected-to-normal vision. Informed consent was obtained for all participants. This experiment was approved by our institutional review board.

Design and Procedure

Before the experiment, each participant was given the opportunity to become familiar with each of the three tasks

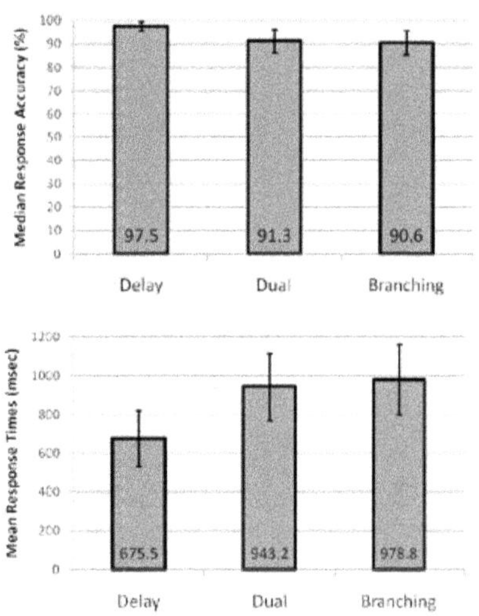

Figure 7. Behavioral results for Experiment 1: median accuracy & standard deviation (top); mean response time and standard deviation (bottom).

during a practice session without the fNIRS sensors. The conditions were presented in counterbalanced pseudo-random order. Each task was repeated until the participant achieved greater than 80% accuracy in the task. After this accuracy was achieved for all three conditions, the fNIRS sensors were placed on the participant's forehead. The participant was presented with an initial rest screen, which was used to collect a baseline measure of the brain activity at rest. After that, the user had to complete ten 40-second trials for each of the three conditions, which were presented randomly. Between each task, the user was presented with the instructions for the next task, followed by a rest screen.

Equipment

We used a multichannel frequency domain OxiplexTS from ISS Inc. (Champaign, IL) for data acquisition. Two probes were placed on the forehead to measure the two hemispheres of the anterior prefrontal cortex (Figure 1). The source-detector distances were 1.5, 2, 2.5, and 3cm. Each distance measures a different depth in the cortex. Each source emits two light wavelengths (690nm and 830nm) to detect and differentiate between oxygenated and deoxygenated hemoglobin. The sampling rate was 6.25Hz.

Results

To examine the differences between the three task conditions, we looked at behavioral data collected during the experiment as well as the fNIRS sensor data. In both experiments, any trials where the participant achieved less than 70% accuracy in the task performance were removed in the analysis, since this would indicate that the subject was not actually performing the task correctly.

Behavioral Results: In the three conditions, the stimuli were essentially the same, as were the possible responses. Thus, it would be difficult for an observer to detect any difference from the screen contents or the subject's behavior alone. Like the sensor data, response time and accuracy measurements can be obtained automatically without interfering with the task so we investigated whether they would vary depending on the condition.

Statistical analysis was performed utilizing the InStat statistical package by GraphPad Inc. All variables were tested for normal distribution with the Kolmogorov-Smirnov test. For normal distributions, the repeated measurements one-way analysis of variance (ANOVA) with the Tukey post-hoc test for multiple comparisons was used. For non-Gaussian distributions, we used the Friedman (non parametric repeated measurements ANOVA) test. The level of statistical significance was set at 0.05 (Figure 7).

Since *dual task* and *branching* behavioral results are similar, the factor was not significant overall, but is in pairwise comparisons. We found statistical significance in response time between *delay* and *dual* ($p < 0.001$), *delay* and *branching* ($p < 0.001$), but not between *dual* and *branching* ($p > 0.05$). Similarly, we found statistical significance in accuracies between *delay* and *dual* ($p < 0.05$), *delay* and *branching* ($p < 0.05$), but not *dual* and *branching* ($p > 0.05$). Also, correlations between accuracy and response time for each task were not statistically significant. We also looked at learning effects based on response time and learning effects based on accuracies as users progressed through the experiment. We did not find a learning effect.

Statistical Analysis of Signal: We wanted to determine whether the hemodynamic response measured by fNIRS has a different signature between the three conditions. For each of the two probes, we selected the fNIRS measurement channels with the greatest source-detector distances (3cm), as these channels are expected to probe deepest in the brain tissue, while the closer channels are more likely to pick up systemic effects and noise. From each of these channels, we calculated both the change in oxygenated hemoglobin and deoxygenated hemoglobin using the modified Beer-Lambert law [3] after removing noise with a band pass filter. Thus, we used four channels corresponding with

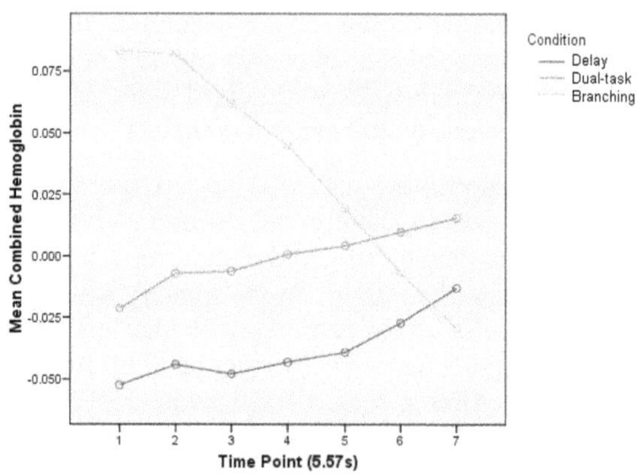

Figure 8. Combined oxygenated and deoxygenated hemoglobin by condition for Experiment 1.

changes in oxygenated and deoxygenated hemoglobin on the left and right hemispheres. Since the hemodynamic changes occur over a 5-7 second period, we simplified the signal for analysis by dividing the time series measurement for each trial into seven segments (~5.57 second each) and took the mean over these segments for the four channels.

In order to confirm that there were differences in brain activity during the three conditions, we did an ANOVA comparing condition means within subjects. Since there were multiple sensors, factors for the distribution of sensors were included (left/right hemisphere), as well as a factor for hemoglobin type (oxygenated or deoxygenated) and the time point. We used the Greenhouse-Geisser ANOVA values to correct for violations in sphericity. We found a main effect of condition (F(2,22)=4.353, p=0.029), in which total hemoglobin measures were overall higher in the branching condition than in the dual-task or delay condition (Figure 8). There were no other significant effects in this analysis.

Experiment 2: Random & Predictive Branching

To follow up on the first study, we conducted a second experiment to determine whether we could distinguish specific variations of the branching task. This experiment had two conditions that were analogous to those in [20], in which the participant was always following the *branching* rules described in Experiment 1:

Random Branching: Rock classification and location update messages were presented pseudorandomly.

Predictive Branching: Rock classification messages were presented every three stimuli.

Ideally, when using computer systems, the default scenario for a user would be similar to the *predictive* condition, and therefore the user would be able to plan ahead and handle incoming work appropriately. If we could automatically identify that the user is experiencing *random* or unpredictable behavior, there may be appropriate adaptations that the system could make to better support the user, which we are exploring with the adaptive interface platform described below. This experiment investigates whether we can automatically detect the different scenarios using fNIRS.

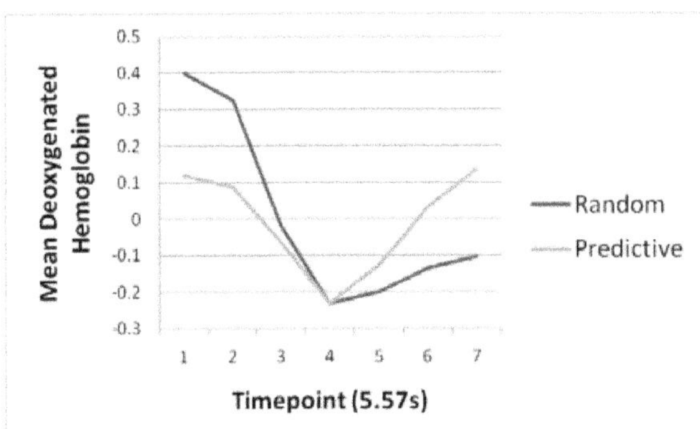

Figure 9. Average of deoxygenated hemoglobin over all subjects by condition for Experiment 2.

Participants

This study included 12 healthy volunteers (5 male), between the ages of 19 and 32. Three additional volunteers had participated, but are not included in this analysis because their performance in the tasks was below 70% in more than two trials per condition, indicating that they were not correctly performing the tasks. In addition, data from another participant was not included due to technical issues with the fNIRS system.

Design, Procedure & Equipment

This experiment used the same procedure and equipment as in Experiment 1. However, in this experiment, there were only two experimental conditions as described above and the participants completed eighteen trials of each condition, which were counterbalanced.

Results

Behavioral Results: As in Experiment 1, we collected response time and accuracy throughout the study to determine whether the conditions elicited different measurements.

Statistical analysis was performed utilizing the InStat statistical package by GraphPad Inc. All variables were tested for normal distribution with the Kolmogorov-Smirnov test. For normal distributions, a paired t-test was used. For non-Gaussian distributions, we used the Wilcoxon matched-pairs signed-ranks test.

There was no statistically significant difference in response time between *random* (M=998.67, SD=190.02) and *predictive* (M=992.81, SD=213.34) branching, $t(215)=0.53$ ($p>0.05$). There also was no statistically significant difference in accuracy between *random* (M=93.982, SD=8.144) and *predictive* (M=92.824, SD=8.765) branching ($p>0.05$). Also, correlation between accuracy and response time for *random* branching was not statistically significant ($p>0.05$), but there was a statistically significant correlation in the *predictive* branching condition ($p<0.0001$).

Statistical Analysis of Signal: Our goal was to determine whether the hemodynamic response measured by fNIRS has a different signature between the two conditions. Our analysis was the same as in Experiment 1.

We found an interaction between branching type, timepoint, and hemoglobin type (F(6,66)=3.035, p=0.038). This effect indicates that, although there was no significant change in oxygenated hemoglobin, deoxygenated hemoglobin levels were higher in the random branching type than the predictive branching type for the first half of trials, but reversed for the second half (Figure 9). Therefore, it should be possible to distinguish these two conditions using only the deoxygenated hemoglobin measure from fNIRS, which is in accordance with Huppert et al. who found that the magnetic blood oxygenation level dependent (BOLD) signal used in fMRI is most tightly tied to deoxygenated hemoglobin in fNIRS [14]. There were no other significant effects in this analysis.

PROOF OF CONCEPT BRAIN-BASED ADAPTIVE USER INTERFACE PLATFORM

In the two experiments described above, we verified that there is a significant difference between the cognitive multitasking conditions in the fNIRS signal. Because we can statistically differentiate them, we can apply machine learning techniques to automatically identify these cognitive multitasking states, in real time, in a user interface. This information could then be used to drive the user interface to better support cognitive multitasking.

As a proof-of-concept, we developed a platform for studying brain-based adaptive user interfaces of this type. The system has two main components: the Online fNIRS Analysis and Classification (OFAC) system [8] and the Distributed Integrated Affect, Reflection, Cognition Architecture (DIARC) [33] for human-robot interaction (Figure 10).

The OFAC system receives raw fNIRS signals from Boxy acquisition software (ISS, Inc.), classifies them in real time and sends the classification results to a specialized DIARC component. In addition to the normal *online* mode where signals are classified and sent in real time, OFAC supports *offline* mode which simulates the analysis and classification of previously recorded data, and will be useful in experimenting with various adaptive strategies. As OFAC receives data, it stores the signal in a database and preprocesses the signal (filtering, conversion to oxy- and deoxy- genated hemoglobin values using the modified Beer-Lambert law [3]), and performs classification using Weka [10].

The DIARC [33] is an integrated architecture for working with complex robots that can support various levels of robot autonomy and other adaptive robot behavior. The architecture can interface with physical robots in an environment, but also has a simulation mode that allows for simulated interactions with a robot on a computer screen (Figure 11), along with several different environment configurations.

To receive input from the OFAC system, we have created a DIARC component to which OFAC sends cognitive multitasking state classification results via sockets. DIARC can then use these messages to change the robot's goal structures, allowing the robot to adapt its autonomy and behavior. In addition, we have provided a simulation mode, where cognitive state classifications can be entered manually by inputting classification confidence levels for each of the possible states. This allows for debugging and testing

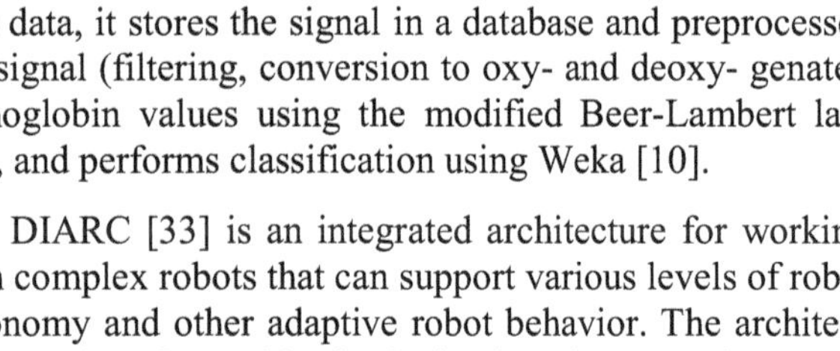

Figure 10. Brain-based adaptive user interface platform.

of the robot adaptive behaviors, without requiring a human to be physically connected to the fNIRS sensing system.

Integrating the OFAC system with DIARC provides the robot with cognitive state information of the human, affording the robot to adapt its behavior to better support and collaborate with the human operator. Driven by fNIRS cognitive multitasking input, DIARC can adapt various aspects of the human-robot interface, such as level of autonomy of the robot, the frequency, length and style of the robot's status updates, as well as the tone of the robot's voice.

As an initial step, we created a task scenario and simple adaptive behavior based on Experiment 1 described above to provide a technical demonstration that the platform functions as intended and can be further expanded to study adaptive multitasking user interfaces. The system was used to complete a human-robot team task where the primary task was to classify rocks and the secondary task was to monitor robot location as in the two experiments above.

When a *branching* state was identified—indicating that the user was tending to multiple tasks and maintaining information about the primary task over time—the robot switched to autonomy mode allowing the user to focus on the primary task of classifying rocks. In autonomy mode, the robot would move autonomously to new locations and find the best location for a new transmission. When a *non-branching* state was recognized, the robot returned to the default behavior, requiring the human to give instructions to the robot about whether it needed to start a new transmission. Staying in autonomous mode throughout the entire task would not be ideal as the human needs to be aware of the robot's location and progress to provide corrective feedback (as the robot's search behavior is not optimal), ensuring that the message is transmitted before time is up.

To validate that *branching* and *non-branching* could be classified in real time and that the robot could receive the signal and adapt its behavior, we did two demonstrations. First, utilizing the *offline* mode of OFAC, we sent previously recorded fNIRS data through the system as if it were being collected on a user in real time. We used the previously recorded data from Experiment 1. The next demonstration of the platform was to show that it can perform in *online* mode while a user was wearing fNIRS sensors.

In both cases, we used the *branching* and *delay* tasks described in Experiment 1 to invoke known *branching* and *non-branching* states. There was a *training* session where the *branching* and *delay* tasks from Experiment 1 were performed (or were simulated using the data collected in Experiment 1), allowing the robot to build a classification model based on the fNIRS sensor data during those tasks. Each condition was completed 10 times in random order to provide training data. Once the training session ended, the system switched to *testing* phase, where the fNIRS signal was classified using the model that had been built during the *training* session. The entire session took about 30 minutes.

We established that fNIRS data was transmitted from OFAC to DIARC in real time, with fNIRS and robot components running in full operational mode. Robot goals and behaviors adapted based on the fNIRS data. This proof-of-concept confirms that our platform can form the basis of future study on brain-based adaptive user interfaces. We intend to enhance the machine learning techniques to improve the accuracy of the system. We will also analyze the fNIRS response more deeply in our future work, but our initial goal was show that there was a significant difference between the signals we detected for the different conditions. This allows us to discriminate the conditions, and adapt a user interface when each state is detected. In addition, we will expand adaptive behaviors that are supported to study the tradeoffs for making such adaptations.

DISCUSSION AND CONCLUSION

This paper builds a foundation for brain-based adaptive user interfaces. First, in our preliminary study, we brought research on cognitive activity during multitasking to a system that is practical for HCI by showing that fNIRS sensors could detect states previously studied with fMRI (which cannot be used in HCI settings). In our next two experiments, we further extended this research to HCI by showing that the states elicited in the "tablet" task may be generic processes that occur in more realistic HCI tasks, by using a human-robot scenario. We integrated these findings with the brain-based adaptive interface platform we developed, in order to augment user interfaces with this cognitive multitasking state as input.

We demonstrated that the platform can form the basis for brain-based user-interfaces by implementing a simple adaptive scheme based on the experiments. However, to design a successful adaptive user interface many factors must be considered and the automation scheme will be more complex than that illustrated here. Parasuraman et al. [28] propose a framework for supporting user cognition with automation which describes four stages of human information processing (sensory processing, perception, decision making and response selection), each of which can have a different automation level. They also outline criteria for evaluating the user interface by examining both human performance measures and also system performance criteria (automation reliability, costs of action outcomes). This framework provides guidelines but does not prescribe specific adaptive behavior for every system. Instead each system must be carefully evaluated and iteratively designed to meet the needs of the users. Our platform will enable us to conduct evaluations of various adaptive behaviors to determine the appropriate strategy for supporting multitasking by utilizing signals coming implicitly from the brain.

Figure 11. The Brain-Adaptive Human-Robot Interaction Platform supports robot navigation (real or simulated), as well as fNIRS cognitive state input (real or simulated).

Human-robot team tasks provide appropriate scenarios for studying adaptive multitasking support, as they inherently involve multitasking: the user is performing a task, while also monitoring the state of the robot(s). HRI team tasks thus may see improved performance with brain-based adaptive interfaces. There has been much work on adaptive robots that change behavior based on the environment or situation. We plan to develop robots that have a greater understanding of the user's cognitive state during multitasking, and can adapt their behavior to better support the user.

In addition, we believe that similar brain-based user interfaces may support a wide range of contexts that involve multitasking and interruptions, such as air traffic control, management of unmanned aerial vehicles (UAVs), complex data visualization and analytics, and many others. Non-invasive brain sensing provides an additional channel of input to the system without any explicit action by the user. However, any adaptation must be done carefully, to ensure that the user does not feel that he or she has lost control. The platform we have developed will allow us to explore adaptive behavior to find the best strategies for these scenarios. We can now begin to develop complex systems that adapt based on fNIRS brain signals and experimentally evaluate them.

ACKNOWLEDGMENTS

We thank the Tufts HCI Lab (past & present), Remco Chang, Desney Tan and Dan Morris. We also thank the NSF for support of this research (NSF Grant Nos. IIS-0414389 and BES-93840). Any opinions, findings, and conclusions or recommendations expressed here are those of the authors and do not necessarily reflect the views of the National Science Foundation.

REFERENCES

1. Bailey, B.P., et al. The Effects of Interruptions on Task Performance, Annoyance, and Anxiety in the User Interface. *INTERACT'01*, 2001, 593-601.
2. Card, S., Moran, T. and Newell, A. *The Psychology of Human Computer Interaction*. Lawrence Erlbaum Associates, Hillsdale, NJ, 1983.
3. Chance, B., et al. A novel method for fast imaging of brain function, non-invasively, with light. *Optics Express*, 10 (2). 411-423.

4. Chen, D., et al. Towards a Physiological Model of User Interruptability. *INTERACT'07*, 2008, 439-451.
5. Czerwinski, M., et al. Instant Messaging: Effects of Relevance and Timing. *HCI*, 2000, 71-76.
6. Fairclough, S.H. Fundamentals of physiological computing. *Interact. Comput.*, 21 (1-2). 133-145.
7. Fogarty, J., Hudson, S.E. and Lai, J. Examining the robustness of sensor-based statistical models of human interruptibility. *CHI'04*, ACM, 2004.
8. Girouard, A., Solovey, E.T. and Jacob, J.K. Designing a Passive Brain Computer Interface using Real Time Classification of Functional Near-Infrared Spectroscopy. *Intl J of Auton. & Adaptive Comm. Sys.* (2010). in press.
9. Grimes, D., et al. Feasibility and pragmatics of classifying working memory load with an electroencephalograph. *CHI'08*, ACM, 2008.
10. Hall, M., et al. The WEKA data mining software: an update. *SIGKDD Explor. Newsl.*, 11 (1). 10-18.
11. Hirshfield, L., et al. Brain Measurement for Usability Testing and Adaptive Interfaces: An Example of Uncovering Syntactic Workload with Functional Near Infrared Spectroscopy. *CHI'09*, 2009.
12. Hornof, A.J.,et al. Knowing where and when to look in a time-critical multimodal dual task. *CHI '10*, 2010.
13. Hudson, S., et al. Predicting human interruptibility with sensors: a Wizard of Oz feasibility study. *CHI '03*, 2003.
14. Huppert, T., et al. A temporal comparison of BOLD, ASL, and NIRS hemodynamic responses to motor stimuli in adult humans. *Neuroimage*, 2006:29(2). 368-382.
15. Iqbal, S.T., et al. Towards an index of opportunity: understanding changes in mental workload during task execution. *CHI '05*, 2005.
16. Iqbal, S.T. and Bailey, B.P. Investigating the effectiveness of mental workload as a predictor of opportune moments for interruption. *CHI extended abstracts*, 2005.
17. Iqbal, S.T., Zheng, X.S. and Bailey, B.P. Task-evoked pupillary response to mental workload in human-computer interaction. *CHI extended abstracts*, 2004.
18. Jackson, M.M. and Mappus, R. Applications for Brain-Computer Interfaces. in Tan, D. and Nijholt, A. eds. *Brain Computer Interfaces: Applying our Minds to Human-Computer Interaction*, Springer, 2010, 89-104.
19. Koechlin, E., et al. The role of the anterior prefrontal cortex in human cognition. *Nature*, 1999, 148-151.
20. Koechlin, E., et al. Dissociating the role of the medial and lateral anterior prefrontal cortex in human planning. *PNAS*, 97. 7651-7656.
21. Kuikkaniemi, K., et al. The influence of implicit and explicit biofeedback in first-person shooter games. *CHI'10*, 2010.
22. Lee, J.C. and Tan, D.S. Using a low-cost electroencephalograph for task classification in HCI research *UIST'06*, ACM Press, 2006.
23. Mandryk, R.L. and Inkpen, K.M. Physiological indicators for the evaluation of co-located collaborative play *CSCW '04*, 2004.
24. McFarlane, D. Comparison of four primary methods for coordinating the interruption of people in human-computer interaction. *Hum.-Comput. Interact.*, 17(1). 63-139.
25. Miyata, Y. and Norman, D. The Control of Multiple Activities. in Norman, D. and Draper, S.W. eds. *User Centered System Design: New Perspectives on Human-Computer Interaction*, Lawrence Erlbaum Associates, Hillsdale, NJ, 1986.
26. Miyata, Y. and Norman, D. Psychological Issues in Support of Multiple Activities. in Norman, D.A. and Draper, S.W. eds. *User Centered System Design: New Perspectives on Human-Computer Interaction*, Lawrence Erlbaum Associates, Hillsdale, NJ, 1986, 265-284.
27. Monk, C., et al. The attentional costs of interrupting task performance at various stages. *HFES Ann. Mtg*, 2002.
28. Parasuraman, R., et al. A model for types and levels of human interaction with automation. *IEEE Trans. on Systems, Man and Cybernetics*, 30 (3). 286-297.
29. Picard, R.W., et al. Toward Machine Emotional Intelligence: Analysis of Affective Physiological State. *IEEE Trans. Pattern Anal. Mach. Intell.*, 23 (10). 1175-1191.
30. Salvucci, D.D. and Bogunovich, P. Multitasking and monotasking: the effects of mental workload on deferred task interruptions. *CHI'10*, 2010.
31. Sasse, A., et al. Coordinating the Interruption of People in Human-Computer Interaction. *INTERACT*, 1999.
32. Schermerhorn, P. and Scheutz, M. Dynamic robot autonomy: investigating the effects of robot decision-making in a human-robot team task. *ICMI*, 2009.
33. Scheutz, M., et al. First steps toward natural human-like HRI. *Auton. Robots*, 22 (4). 411-423.
34. Solovey, E.T., et al. Using fNIRS Brain Sensing in Realistic HCI Settings: Experiments and Guidelines. *UIST'09*, 2009.
35. Starner, T., Schiele, B. and Pentland, A. Visual Contextual Awareness in Wearable Computing. *ISWC*, 1998.
36. Yuksel, B.F., et al. A novel brain-computer interface using a multi-touch surface. *CHI'10*, 2010

RemoteTouch: Touch-Screen-like Interaction in the TV Viewing Environment

Sangwon Choi, Jaehyun Han, Geehyuk Lee
Department of Computer Science
KAIST, Daejeon, South Korea
{sangwonchoi7, jay.jaehyun, geehyuk}@gmail.com

Narae Lee, Woohun Lee
Department of Industrial Design
KAIST, Daejeon, South Korea
{narae, woohun.lee}@kaist.ac.kr

ABSTRACT
We explored the possibility of touch-screen-like interaction with a remote control in the TV-viewing environment. A shadow representing the user's thumb touches the screen, presses a button, flicks a cover-flow list, and draws a simple stroke, while the thumb stays and moves on and above the touchpad. In order to implement the concept we developed an optical touchpad for tracking the thumb hovering over its surface, and designed a TV application to demonstrate possible new interaction styles. Throughout two iterations of prototyping, we corrected some of our false expectations, and also verified its potential as a viable option for a TV remote control. This paper presents technical issues and requirements for the hover-tracking touchpad and a complete report of our user studies to explore touch-screen-like interaction for the TV.

Author Keywords
RemoteTouch interaction, hover-tracking touchpad, TV user interface, TV remote control.

ACM Classification Keywords
H.5.2. Information interfaces and presentation: user interfaces – input devices and strategies

General Terms
Design, Human Factors, Experimentation

INTRODUCTION
The TV in the future will become a terminal for many interactive applications such as Video-On-Demand (VOD) services, online games, and online shopping services. Smart TV projects, such as Google TV, Apple TV, and Samsung Internet@TV, provide a foretaste of the future of TV. In response to the new needs of this future TV, and replacing the conventional array of buttons, new remote control designs incorporating alternative input technologies, such as joystick, touchpad, or direct-pointing, are being explored and evaluated. For example, remote pointing devices such as a gyro-mouse [11] proved to be more efficient than a remote with an isometric joystick. However, as with other laser-pointer style direct-pointing devices, a gyro-mouse had problems such as fatigue, jittering, and response delay introduced by cursor stabilization [17, 18]. A remote with a touchpad is another common idea [4], but currently lacks a comparative study on its usability. In the context of pointing on a computer interface, a touchpad was shown to be less efficient than an isometric joystick [3]. Such studies focused on pointing efficiency, a typical requirement for desktop user interface, but did not assess the usability of such devices in the context of a TV viewing environment. Based on these studies, it is still difficult to predict which design will prevail in the future TV environment.

In an effort to design a better remote control for a TV, we have been studying different options in parallel. A remote with a touchpad as in [4] was an attractive option since a touchpad is familiar to users and users seemed to adapt quickly to using it with the thumb. A major concern with a touchpad was the indirectness due to the relative cursor control. Another attractive option was a remote with a touchscreen, which provides direct-touch control. This is becoming a popular idea especially due to the rapid spread of smart phones, and the new possibility to use them to control the TV. Google TV remote applications for smart phones are examples for this. However, a major concern with a remote with a touchscreen was the problem of divided visual attention between the remote and the TV screen, which are usually separated by a few meters. In addition, a smart phone as a remote, whether it has a touchscreen or not, may create the mismatch between the phone as a personal mobile device and the TV as a shared domestic device; for example, parents will be reluctant to let their child use their phones.

After examining possible options for a TV remote control, we became interested in the idea of realizing touch-screen-like interaction. Instead of touching the TV screen, which is too far to reach, one touches a sensor area on a remote, which offers a one-to-one mapping to the TV screen. For instance, one can select a button on the screen by moving the thumb over the sensor area and landing the thumb on the button. Also, one spins a scrolling list on the screen by flicking on a corresponding spot on the sensor. Such interaction techniques are familiar to users thanks to the popularity of touch-screen smart phones. Of course, the question remains whether users will be able to perform such techniques indirectly on the touchpad and away from the screen. We speculate that users will be able to develop the skill to map the movement of the thumb on the remote to the movement on the screen if good on-screen visual feedback of the thumb is provided. We named this type of interaction RemoteTouch, and the primary goal of the present research is an iterative exploration of both the interaction design and the technical implementation of RemoteTouch, as well as verifying its effectiveness with users.

In the rest of the paper, we describe our early explorations and two main iterations of prototyping the RemoteTouch concept. The main focus of the first iteration was on the design of a hover-enabled touchpad for the basic realization of the RemoteTouch concept. The second iteration then focused on the design and evaluation of RemoteTouch-style interfaces. Before reporting our explorations, we first give a brief overview of the background of TV remote controls as well as previous research related with the RemoteTouch concept.

BACKGROUND AND RELATED WORK

The first wired remote control 'Lazy Bones' was developed by Zenith and it was soon replaced by its successor 'Space Command' whose form factor resembled that of a modern remote control. The basic structure of a TV remote, consisting of a series of buttons, each dedicated to a specific function, has remained until these days [4]. With more diverse TV usage patterns, especially driven by the connection to the Internet, researchers became interested in new TV user interfaces. Most of them, however, merely transferred user interface technologies from desktop computing to the TV viewing environment [4, 9, 11], thus lacking research for a novel remote control concept that takes into account the special characteristics of the TV viewing environment.

Some of these special characteristics are discussed in previous research on TV user interface [5, 9, 10]. TV viewers usually operate a TV at some distance in a relaxed posture without a stable working surface. A remote control and the output of a TV are spatially separated by a few meters. This spatial separation circumvents users from reaching the screen directly and requires them to alternate the focus of attention between the remote and the TV. As the TV becomes more interactive, the usability problem caused by the spatial separation of input and display will worsen. Furthermore, TV viewers take whatever posture

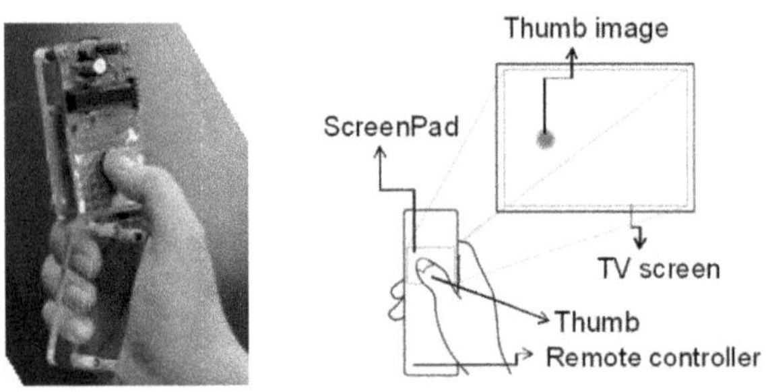

Figure 1. RemoteTouch controller (left) and the mapping from the RemoteTouch controller to the screen (right).

that is comfortable for them while watching TV, and therefore it is not acceptable to design a TV remote control that requires a stable working surface. Also, users should be able to use a TV remote single-handed. The concept of RemoteTouch is especially motivated by the problem of the spatial separation of input and display.

There are two intriguing user interface concepts that are closely related to that of RemoteTouch: EZ Touch Remote by Panasonic [19] and TactaPad by Tactiva [20]. The EZ Touch Remote is an effort to overcome the indirectness of controlling a TV. The EZ Touch Remote allows users to see a virtual thumb on the screen that represents their thumb. With such visual feedback users feel the sense of directness in handling the TV. The EZ Touch Remote, however, utilizes a normal touchpad, and therefore fails to maintain the "continuous visual feedback" of the thumb as the visual thumb cannot follow the real thumb when it lifts off the touchpad. Intended for the desktop environment, the TactaPad is pursuing a very similar goal to RemoteTouch. It uses a multi-finger touchpad and a camera so that users can see the movement of their hands on the screen interacting with virtual objects. It is meant for users to feel enhanced directness of manipulation as if they touched objects directly. A very similar concept was explored for interacting with large displays while sitting around a table using a computer-vision based touchpad with hover information [15]. Although these bare much similarity with of the concept of RemoteTouch, they were intended for desktop usage with fixed setup, therefore not suitable for the versatility of the TV viewing environment.

Figure 1 illustrates the concept of RemoteTouch. The remote has a sensor area that is one-to-one mapped to the TV screen. The TV screen provides visual feedback about the position and hovering height of the thumb on the sensor area. For instance, when the thumb is above the sensor area, a small disk representing the thumb appears with a shadow as if it is hovering on the screen. When the thumb touches and slides on the sensor area, the disk lands on the screen and drags the object under the circle. The user sees the thumb moving on and above the screen while the thumb is moving on and above the sensor area. Eventually, this will make the user feel like using a touch-screen remotely.

EARLY EXPLORATIONS

At first, we tried to prototype the concept of RemoteTouch using a normal touchpad without hover information, and a one-to-one mapping from the touchpad to the screen. After a pilot study, we soon realized that the prototype suffers from the lack of the "continuous visual feedback of the thumb". For instance, when drawing a gesture on the screen, the thumb position remains unknown until touching the touchpad. Also, the visual feedback of the thumb is lost as soon as the thumb is lifted to start another stroke. Of course, the continuous visual feedback of the thumb would have been possible if we designed the interaction so that the thumb always needs to stay on the touchpad. However, confining the thumb on a touchpad restricts possible thumb

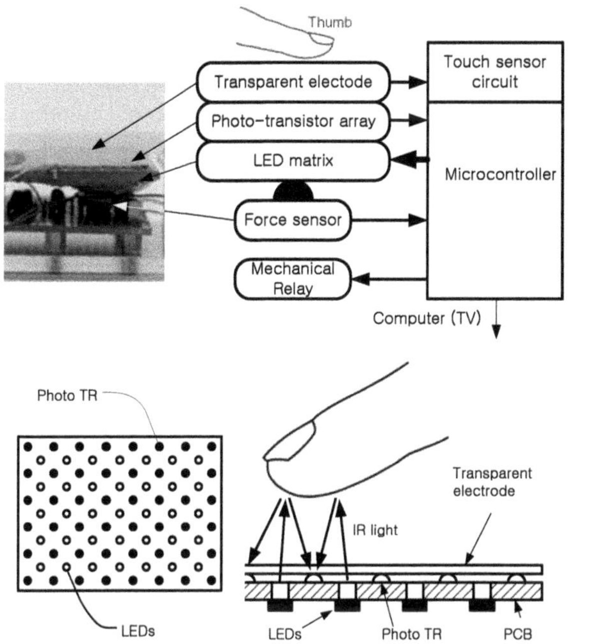

Figure 2. The structure of the ScreenPad: the functional blocks (top), and the top-view and the magnified cross-section of the optical sensor layer (bottom).

movements and gestures. We learned that we needed a hover-tracking touchpad that can sense the thumb above the surface as well as on the surface in order to realize the RemoteTouch concept.

We first considered capacitive sensing options, including GlidePoint and GlideSensor from Cirque [2], for hover-tracking, but could not find a satisfactory solution. For instance, GlideSensor in its highest sensitivity provided a sensing range of a few millimeters, which was too small to allow natural thumb movements. We observed that the thumb movement above the touchscreen can be as high as 10mm, which means that the sensor should have a hover-tracking range of at least 10mm. Hover-detection at this height may be possible with a capacitive sensing method, but, considering the physical nature of capacitive sensing, at this height we expected the image of the thumb being too diffuse for a precise localization of the thumb.

As a second option, we considered optical sensing methods using a camera. The prototype that we built was based on the principle of a diffusive IR touch screen [16]. We added an additional in-plane IR illumination to the prototype to enhance touch detection [6]. The resulting prototype successfully sensed the thumb, whether it was on or over the surface, yet a problem with the prototype was an excessive latency even though we used an IEEE 1394 camera with a frame rate of 60Hz. The visual feedback that we could achieve by processing the camera frames was not fast enough to make the visual feedback effective. The thumb by far outran the expected speed, causing a noticeable delay in its visual feedback. Another problem of the prototype was that it was too thick (about 6cm) to be housed in the size of a remote control.

FIRST PROTOTYPING

In order to overcome the latency problem of the camera-based prototype, we tested optical sensing using an LED array. The resulting optical touchpad, which we named as ScreenPad, finally satisfied our minimal requirements. Its sensing range was large enough to allow natural thumb movements (the sensor output at 10% of its maximum when the thumb is at 16mm from the pad), it was fast enough to allow a responsive visual feedback (about 12ms for sampling a frame and 4ms for transmission), and it was thin enough to be fitted in a remote mockup (about 5mm thick excluding a force sensor under the optical sensor). Only after building the ScreenPad prototype, we were able to start the experimentation of the RemoteTouch concept. Therefore, we will describe the implementation and experimentation of this prototype as our "first prototyping" and the next prototype in the following section "second prototyping".

Prototype Design

Hardware design

As shown in Figure 2, the sensor consists of three layers: a transparent conductor layer for touch sensing, a photo-transistor and LED matrix layer for position sensing, and a force sensor for thumb pressure sensing. Figure 2c shows the detailed structure of the second layer. The 5x7 LED matrix illuminates the thumb sequentially in the row-major order. The 6x8 photo-transistors, all of which are wired in parallel and act as a single planar sensor, measure reflection from the thumb. The operating principle is different from other implementations using a matrix of receivers [1] or a matrix of emitter-receiver pairs [7], but is similar to that of a laser barcode reader. Both use localized illumination instead of localized sensing to achieve imaging. We chose localized illumination since it is advantageous in terms of power conservation and chose global (non-localized) sensing since it is advantageous for sensing efficiency and sensitivity, i.e., more light scattered by the thumb can be gathered.

Using off-the-shelf components, the assembly of the sensor was rather simple except for the following three deliberations. First, the angular sensitivities of the LEDs and the photo-transistors had to be chosen carefully in order to obtain a smooth reflection image. The smoothness of the image is essential for the subsequent signal processing stage to produce sub-pixel resolution position data. Secondly, the placement of the LEDs and the photo-transistors had to be determined carefully in order to avoid reflection from the transparent cover (touch sensor electrode). Finally, the sensor circuit had to be designed to be resistant to AC line noise through capacitive coupling with the thumb. The 6x8 photo-transistors connected in parallel form a single planar photo-sensor with very low output impedance and therefore were almost insensitive to such electrical noise sources.

Signal processing

One of the main problems that we had to solve was the instability of the cursor due to the high control-display gain,

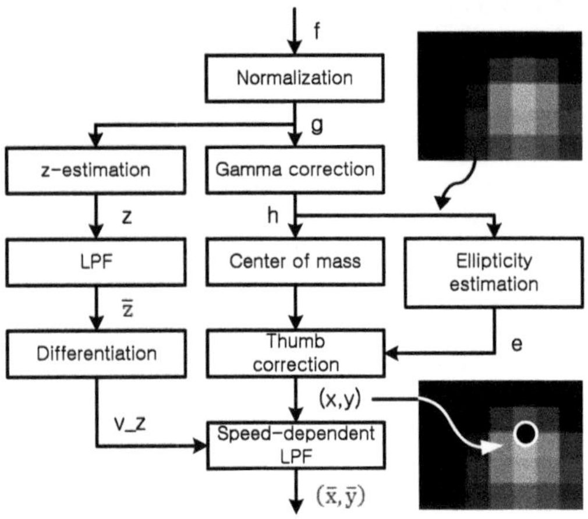

Figure 3. The signal flow diagram of ScreenPad.

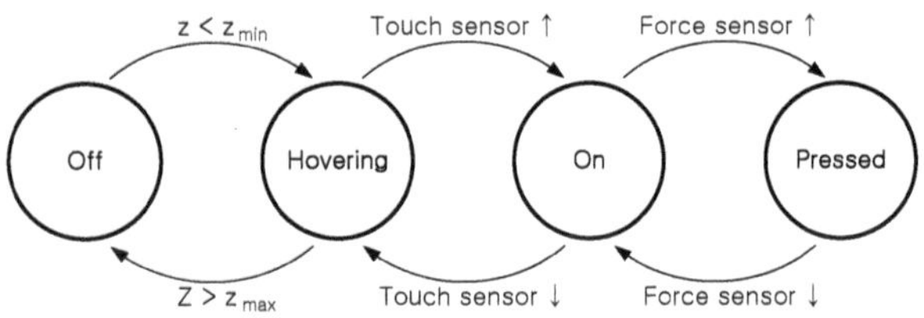

Figure 4. The state transition diagram of ScreenPad.

which is the consequence of a one-to-one mapping between the small sensor area and the large screen. A smoothing filter may reduce the instability but will also reduce the responsiveness of the device. In order to cope with the instability problem while preserving the responsiveness of the device, we designed a speed-dependent low-pass filtering (LPF) algorithm, where the strength of filtering is inversely proportional to the speed of the cursor. Another problem was the shift of the cursor during "down" movements. With a ScreenPad, one usually catches a target in two steps: moving to a point over a target and down to touch it. In the second step, one expects that the cursor will be stationary, but the cursor often moves and misses the target. The shift of the cursor during "down" movements may be due to the actual horizontal movements of the thumb or due to an error in the estimation of the center of the thumb. In either case, it was desired to reduce the cursor shift during down movements, and we answered this problem by incorporating the vertical velocity of the thumb into the speed-dependent LPF algorithm; the cursor was stabilized further when the thumb is in a rapid vertical motion.

Figure 3 shows the signal processing steps of the thumb image f from the sensor to the final determination of the thumb position $(\bar{x}, \bar{y})$. First, the raw sensor image f is transformed into the normalized value image $g \in [0,1]$. The individual variance of LEDs and photo-transistors are also compensated in this step. Next, the image g is gamma-corrected to emphasize the tip of the thumb ($\gamma = 2.0$). The center of mass of the resulting image h is the first estimate (x, y) of the thumb position. This first estimate (x, y) suffers from an error due to the light reflection from the proximal part of the thumb. This error is roughly proportional to the degree of ellipticity of the thumb projection in the image h. The degree of ellipticity is especially large when the thumb tries to reach the upper-left corner of the sensor area. In order to correct this error, we estimated the degree of ellipticity e by $\sqrt{\mu_{1,1}}$, where $\mu_{1,1}$ is the $(1,1)$ central moment of the whole image, and adjusted (x, y) by $0.3 \times e$ to the left-up diagonal direction.

The vertical position z of the thumb is determined by the maximum value in $g{:}z = 1 - \max_{i,j} g(i,j)$. This value is low-pass filtered and then differentiated to give the vertical speed v_z of the thumb. The final step is the speed-dependent LPF that deals with jittering noise in the thumb position (x, y). It is a one-pole LPF whose pole is not constant but is dynamically determined by the variance (σ_x, σ_y) in the recent samples of (x, y) and the vertical speed v_z of the thumb:

$$(\bar{x}, \bar{y}) = \alpha_x(\bar{x}, \bar{y}) + (1 - \alpha_x)(x, y)$$

$$(\alpha_x, \alpha_y) = \min(1, \max(0, \alpha_0 - \beta(\sigma_x, \sigma_y) - \rho v_z))$$

where $(\bar{x}, \bar{y})$ is the output of the filter, and α_0,β, and ρ are positive constants that control the overall smoothing strength, the dependence on the horizontal thumb speed and the dependence on the vertical thumb speed, respectively. By a careful choice of these parameters ($\alpha_0 = 0.9$, $\beta = 1.0$, $\rho = 3.0$), pointing and selection operations became a lot more stable while the responsiveness of the device was not overly affected. Figure 4 shows the four states of the sensor and the transition conditions. The transition between "Off" and "Hovering" is triggered by the change of the vertical position estimation z ($z_{min} = 0.7$, $z_{max} = 0.8$, corresponding to about 10mm), while other transitions are triggered by the change of dedicated sensor outputs.

Visual feedback design

It is important to provide an effective visual feedback about the thumb position for the successful realization of the RemoteTouch concept. After a few trials, we chose a simple design not interfering with the current targets and tasks: a small circle with a translucent shadow as illustrated in Figure 5a. We used the disparity between the circle and the shadow to represent the height of the thumb above the touchpad.

User Test

We evaluated the efficiency of the RemoteTouch controller for pointing tasks and dragging tasks by comparing it with a "clickable" touchpad on the one hand and a "clickable" joystick on the other. Dragging tasks were included in the test as we thought that they would be crucial in RemoteTouch interactions, e.g., for moving a slider or for flicking a page. The "clickable" touchpad resulted from combining Cirque's GlideTouch touchpad with a button switch under the pad similar to the touchpad of an Apple MacBook. There were three states: off-state (over-the-pad), on-state (touched), and pressed state (touched and pressed).

For the "clickable" joystick, we used the right stick of the Xbox 360 controller, which can be pressed as well as tilted.

Pointing with the RemoteTouch controller is achieved by moving the thumb in the hovering state and landing it on the target displayed on the TV screen. Dragging, on the other hand, is done by touching a "start circle", moving the thumb with contact to the pad, and lifting the thumb at the on-screen target. In contrast, pointing with the clickable touchpad is done by moving in the touched state and clicking on the target, while dragging is done by pressing on the start circle, moving in the pressed state, and releasing at the target. Finally, pointing with the clickable joystick is realized by moving in the rate control mode and clicking on the target, while dragging is done by pressing on the start circle, moving in the pressed state, and releasing at the target.

The experiment was a 3(device) x 2(task) x 5(session) within-subjects factorial design. We asked participants to perform pointing and dragging tasks with the three devices for 5 sessions. Twelve university students (average age 25.7, 10 females) were recruited and the devices were presented to them in a counterbalanced order. Fifty random-circle-tracking trials were allotted to each condition, and one session (3x2 conditions) took about an hour. We measured throughputs and error rates by device and task for each session, and evaluated participants' task workload by the NASA-TLX questionnaire of workload after the experiments. The throughput for both tasks was computed by fitting the experimental data to Fitts' law and estimating the reciprocal of the slope of the line (time vs. index of difficulty) as done in [13].

The means and standard deviations of the measures are presented in Table 1. The effect of device was statistically significant for throughput in the pointing tasks (ANOVA, $F(2,118) = 66.053$, $p < 0.001$). In the dragging tasks, there was a significant effect of device for throughput (ANOVA, $F(1.3, 76.5) = 56.303$, $p<0.001$). In this case, we applied Greenhouse-Geisser correction since Mauchly's p-value was greater than 0.05. There was no significant difference between the throughput of the RemoteTouch controller and the touchpad in pointing tasks. However, the RemoteTouch controller outperformed others in dragging tasks.

		RemoteTouch	Touchpad	Joystick
Pointin	Throughput(bps)	3.1(1.1)	3.1(1.0)	1.6(0.3)
	Error rate(%)	6.2(4.8)	2.5(2.4)	1.1(1.9)
	NASA-TLX	293(84)	363(105)	255(104)
Draggin	Throughput(bps)	3.9(2.1)	2.5(0.9)	1.6(0.4)
	Error rate(%)	5.5(4.4)	5.5(4.9)	20(13)
	NASA-TLX	234(72)	292(85)	356(107)

Table 1. Throughputs, error rates, and workloads of the three devices for the pointing task and the dragging task (standard deviations in parentheses).

The throughput of RemoteTouch was better in dragging tasks than in pointing tasks ($t=-2.851$, $p=0.003$) contrary to the results of a previous research [13]. In addition, interestingly, the score of NASA-TLX of RemoteTouch were also significantly lower in dragging tasks than in pointing tasks ($t=3.495$, $p=0.002$). These results are persuading us to put more emphasis on dragging-based operations than clicking-based operations in the user interface design of RemoteTouch interaction.

SECOND PROTOTYPING

The experimental results of the first prototyping did not live up to our expectations, but gave us a chance to verify and correct our assumptions about RemoteTouch. First of all, we learned through observation that moving in the hovering state of RemoteTouch is not as easy as doing it on a real touchscreen. With a touchscreen phone, for example, we can maintain the thumb over the surface without much difficulty. This is not the case anymore when we look at the feedback on the TV screen. While there may be other important differences between these two cases, we could observe that lack of depth cue was a major problem in the second case. RemoteTouch seemed to share the same problem due to the low quality of the visual feedback of the thumb. The quality of visual feedback is affected by the following three factors: the latency of the sensor, noise in the thumb position estimation, and the visualization method. In the second prototyping, we focused on improving on these three factors. Also, in the design of the RemoteTouch interaction, we tried to minimize the time staying in the hovering state, since staying in a hovering state may be still stressful compared with the case of a real touchscreen.

Prototype Design

Hardware design

The two main improvements in the hardware were resistance to ambient light noise and an increased frame rate. Ambient light noise may be from low-frequency sources such as daylight and incandescent lamps, or from high-frequency sources such as fluorescent lamps. In order to cope with ambient light noise, we changed the ScreenPad firmware so that it uses differential sampling; it measures ambient light noise levels between successive pixel samplings with LEDs off, and use them to subtract noise levels from pixel values. Since pixel samplings and noise samplings were close in time (about 150μs) and linear interpolation was used to estimate noise levels at pixel sampling times, the differential sampling method could make the prototype almost insensitive to high-frequency ambient light noise as well as to low-frequency ambient light noise. Next, we increased the frame rate of ScreenPad from 25 Hz in the first prototyping to 50 Hz. The speed of the hardware in the first prototype was already fast enough as the total amount of time for acquiring a thumb image and transmitting it to the PC took less than 20ms. This remained the same when the frame rate was increased to 50Hz. Also, the signal processing on the PC leveled off at 5ms after testing various signal processing algorithms. In short, the total time delay due to the processing pipeline remained mostly unchanged when the frame rate was raised from 25Hz to 50Hz. Nevertheless, the increased update rate of the thumb's visual feedback made the hardware appear more responsive. Another change is the replacement of the force sensor by a button switch (a tact switch). We used a force sensor in the first prototyping in order to adjust the click threshold. We realized that the high-fidelity haptic feedback of a click operation is more important and decided to use a mechanical switch.

Signal processing

The overall flow in Figure 3 was maintained except for the following two changes. First, the method to determine the center of the thumb was changed. The center of mass, which earlier was used to represent the center of the thumb, caused problems when the thumb was in a strongly inclined posture. We resized the 5x7 image, *h*, into 20x28 image, *H*, using a bi-cubic interpolation method before we calculated the center of mass, $(\bar{x}, \bar{y})$. Also, we did not use all pixels but only pixels with brightness above a threshold determined by the peak value, and weighted by their brightness. That is,

$$(\bar{x}, \bar{y}) = \sum_{w_{ij}>0} w_{ij}(x_{ij}, y_{ij}) \Big/ \sum_{w_{ij}>0} w_{ij}$$

$$w_{ij} = H(i,j) - \emptyset H_{max}$$

where (i,j) is the index to the image, *H*, (x_{ij}, y_{ij}) is the position of the pixel (i,j), H_{max} is the maximum value in $H(i,j)$, and $\emptyset$ is a parameter that controls the dynamic threshold and was set to 0.7 experimentally.

Secondly, the step to correct the thumb position using the ellipticity of the thumb was now omitted. This algorithm could not cope well with individual differences. Also, the thumb position correction was only necessary when users touched the pad with the bottom of the thumb. It seemed to be more practical to expect users to learn that using the tip of the thumb is better than using the bottom of the thumb.

In the hope to further improve noise tolerance, we tried Kalman filters in place of the speed-dependent LPF. We tried different dynamical models, including a constant velocity model and a constant acceleration model, and did our best to optimize the noise parameters of the models. Nonetheless, the speed-dependent LPF performed better in terms of both stability and responsiveness of the thumb movement. Therefore, we decided to keep the speed-dependent LPF.

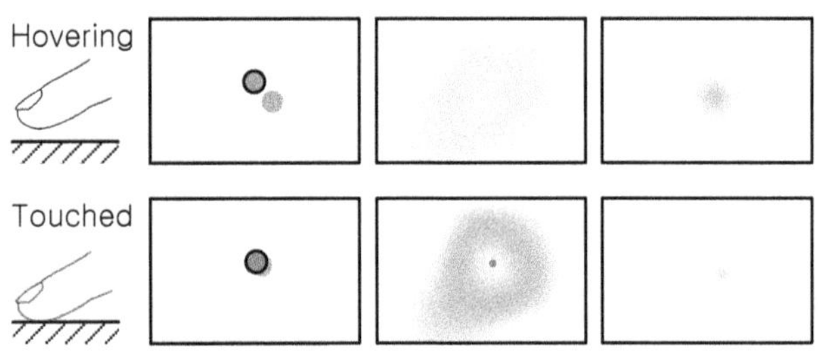

Figure 5. The three visual feedback designs that were considered in the second prototyping.

Visual feedback design

The quality of the visual feedback of the thumb does not only depend on the quality of the position information, but also on an effective visual design. These two are in fact dependent on each other. A very realistic visual feedback can result in a less stable control when the position information is very noisy. The level of realism and precision that a visual feedback design should pursue depends on the quality of the available information.

Figure 5 shows the three designs of visual feedback that we considered in the second prototyping. Figure 5a shows the visual feedback design that we used in the first prototyping. A solid disk represents the position of the thumb, and the distance to its shadow (the half transparent disk under the solid disk) presents the distance between the thumb and the touchpad. When the thumb touches the surface, the solid disk overlaps the shadow and changes color to indicate transition into the touched state. The problem with this design was that its positional feedback appears more precise than the actual information available from the hardware. As the thumb hovers higher, the positional signal becomes noisier and less accurate, but the visual feedback appears the same, i.e., crisp and definite. This is misleading and seems to have a negative influence on the motor control of the thumb. This problem is not only due to the limited quality of the sensor information, but also due to the ambiguity of the "perceived thumb position" [8]. The hot-spot of the thumb may be perceived as at the tip of the thumb for some, and at the center of the thumb for others.

Figure 5b shows a feedback design that was intended to cope with this problem. The image of the thumb acquired by the sensor is shown as is with pseudo-color, and the center of the thumb is not provided until the thumb touches the surface. The reflected light values are mapped to the hue. Pixels touching the surface are painted in solid yellow, while pixels above the surface are pointed in transparent gray. This design seemed to solve the problem with design (a), but was visually too distracting; the image of the thumb was too large and too dynamic. Figure 5c shows the final design that we settled with. This may be regarded as a tidy abstraction of design (b). A Gaussian profile is used to represent the thumb. Its size, color, and transparency are controlled to show the proximity of the thumb. When the thumb is in contact with the surface, it is represented by a small, solid, yellow Gaussian dot. When the thumb is hovering, it is represented by a large, transparent, gray Gaussian shadow. The size, transparency, and color of the image are also consistent with the accuracy of the position information. The final design may be regarded as a trade-off between the two extreme designs (a) and (b).

The TV Application

We implemented a TV application that would allow us to experience and experiment with a RemoteTouch-style interface. Figure 6a shows the main screen of the TV. "Edge-bars" frame the screen on each of its four edges. They remain inactive until a user clicks on one of the edges.

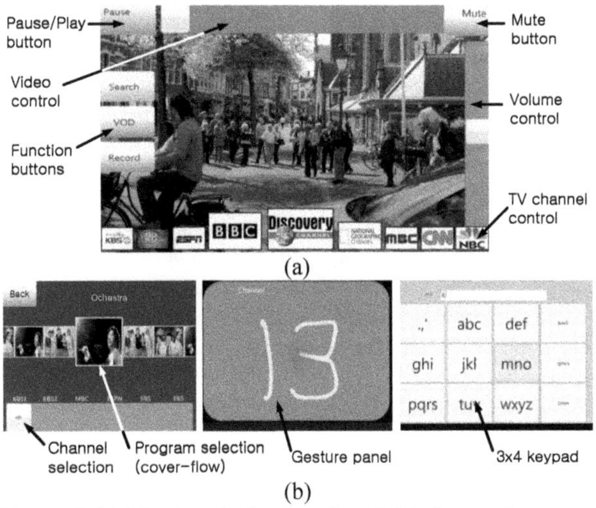

Figure 6. (a) The four "edge-bars" and (b) three sub-screens for VOD selection(left), gesture input (center), and text entry (right), respectively.

Only one bar at a time is visible and active. For illustrative purposes, we showed them all activated in this picture. The bottom edge-bar is for selecting a channel. A user can slide on the edge and press on an icon to select a channel. The top edge-bar is for controlling playback of the content; a user can slide on the edge to move forward or backward in the program. The right edge-bar is for controlling the volume and the left edge-bar is for a short-cut menu. Figure 6b shows three sub-screens. The first is the VOD selection interface invoked by the VOD button in the left edge-bar. A user switches a category using the bottom slider control and selects a program in a list in the center, similar to the cover-flow interface on the iPod. The second is the gesture panel invoked by clicking in the center of the main screen. A user can write a channel number to switch channels directly. The third is the text-input interface invoked by the Search button in the left edge-bar. These three interfaces are the three test tasks in the user test, to be explained in more details in the next section.

Focus Group Interview feedback

We conducted a focus group interview (FGI) with 4 undergraduate students (average age 24.8, 1 female). Two of them had about three years' experience with an Internet protocol TV (IPTV) interface, and others have none. We gave them a 5-minute instruction on the use of the current IPTV interface (B-tv, SK Broadband) and the use of the RemoteTouch interface for the TV application. The IPTV interface that we used for a reference was based on a traditional remote with directional keys. We gave them an additional 15 minutes for trying the interfaces themselves. The FGI continued for 50 minutes afterwards.

The participants seemed to feel comfortable with the current IPTV interface, but complained about difficulty in selecting an item in the deep hierarchical menu and inconvenience in using a search function. They all showed interests in RemoteTouch interaction style but seemed to need time to become used to it. A lot of useful comments were collected and representative ones are summarized in Table 2.

Questions	Comments
Pros and cons of RemoteTouch?	It is refreshing; Its use is intuitive; Cursor movement is too sensitive because the sensor area is small; Cursor movement is a lot more continuous than expected; Pressing a button would be easier than writing on the pad.
Able to use after a short introduction?	A short introduction was enough; I felt fatigue at the finger since the device was very sensitive.
Compared with pointing devices like Wii remote?	They are more intuitive, but are more tiresome since I have to move the arm all the time; It would be better to move on a small area like ScreenPad.
Additional comments?	It makes me feel like really "remote-controlling"; The playback control of a movie would be done better with gestures than manipulating the slider control; RemoteTouch may be useful for a vehicle UI where visual attention to the device is limited.

Table 2. User comments from an FGI with the TV application.

User Test

The user test has two aims. One is to obtain user feedback after giving the participants sufficient time to get used to the RemoteTouch interaction style. The other is to assess the advantage of hover-tracking in touch-screen-like interactions. For this purpose, we let participants try three tasks corresponding to the three sub-screens in Figure 6b in two conditions using the RemoteTouch device: Hover-Tracking (HT) and No-Hover-Tracking (NHT). In the NHT condition, it was impractical to use a flick gesture or write by touch, because the initial position of the thumb is not visible, and therefore, dragging and writing in the pressed state had to be used instead. A more detailed description of the differences of the three tasks for the two conditions is given in Table 3.

	HT	NHT
Task 1: Numeric gesture	Writing in the touched state; visual feedback in the hovering state	Writing in the pressed state; no visual feedback in the hovering state
Task 2: Program selection	Dragging in the touched state; visual feedback in the hovering state; selection by a click	Dragging in the pressed state; no visual feedback in the hovering state; selection by a double-click
Task 3: Text entry	Key input by a click; visual feedback in the hovering state	Key input by a click; no visual feedback in the hovering state

Table 3. The differences of the three tasks in the two conditions, HT and NHT.

Participants and procedure

We started with 12 university students, but one of them failed to complete the whole tests for a personal reason. All of the 11 successful participants (average age was 25.4, 4 females) had some experience with a touchpad.

One session consisted of three blocks, one for each of the three tasks. A short break for a few minutes was allowed between the tasks. Since one session took less than 20 minutes and did not cause too much fatigue, two or three sessions were conducted per day. A practice session for about 10 minutes was allowed every day before test sessions began. The experiment was a within-subject design. Six of them started with the HT condition first, and others with the NHT condition. In order to reduce the interference between two conditions, we let them have at least a two days' break between conditions. In the end, each participant completed 5 sessions for each condition.

In the following, we describe each experiment task with reference to Figure 7.

(a) Numeric gesture (Task 1): A two-digit number is presented in the left text box, and a participant writes it on the screen. The gesture recognizer available from Windows .NET Framework was used for gesture recognition. The recognition result is displayed in the right text box. This task is repeated for 20 two-digit random numbers in a block.

(b) Program selection (Task 2): This task is to select a program from a channel. The slider bar at the bottom shows 8 channels, and the cover-flow-like list in the center contains 20 programs from the selected channel. A target to select is presented by a channel-program pair (represented as letters in the experiment) on the top of the screen, and a participant selects the channel and the program in succession. This task is repeated for 10 random targets in a block.

(c) Text-entry (Task 3): This task is to enter a sentence using a 3x4 screen keypad (multi-tap, alphabetic layout). A sentence from the MacKenzie and Soukereff's English phrase dictionary [14] is presented in the first text box, and the text-entry result is displayed in the second text box. This task is repeated for 5 randomly chosen sentences in a block.

Results

The experimental results for the three tasks are summarized in the following with reference to Figure 8.

(a) Numeric gesture: Figure 8a shows the average time for writing a two-digit number in the two conditions. The stroke time in HT was significantly shorter than in NHT ($t = 4.3785$, $p < 0.0001$). Figure 8b shows the recognition error rates in both conditions. The error rate in HT was slightly lower than that of NHT but the difference was not significant.

The gesture recognizer appeared to be the source of most errors. The recognizer frequently misread a numeric gesture despite its high legibility. In particular, '7' was often mistaken as '17' since the recognizer expected it to be written in a single stroke, while in Korea it is usually written in two strokes. Furthermore, we expected the recognizer to identify gesture inputs better in the HT case, since it also provided a superior quality of writing. Yet, contrary to our expectations, the recognizer performance was similar in both cases.

(b) Program selection: Figure 8c shows the average completion times for a program selection. Contrary to our expectation, participants performed better in the NHT condition ($t = 1.715$, $p < 0.05$). The curves in the figure show a learning effect (ANOVA, $F(4, 40)=9.562$, $p < 0.0005$), and the HT curve, at the end, appears to outrun the NHT curve, but the difference in the final block is not significant ($p = 0.07$). This stood in contrast to the post-test survey result and the NASA-TLX test result that are presented later. One of the possible reasons for this result was the difference in the way participants use the cover-flow-like list. While they reported that they liked the 'flicking' operation in the HT condition, flicking induced more overshoots. The average number of overshoots in a block was 3.1 for HT and 2.6 for NHT, and the difference was significant ($t = 1.741$, $p < 0.05$). The average error rates in Figure 8d are also reflecting this difference. Participants complained of accidental clicks that they made when they actually tried to flick the list. An interesting observation in Figure 8c is that there was a significant interaction between conditions and blocks (ANOVA, $F(4, 40)=4.722$, $p = 0.003$) implying a stronger learning effect in HT than in NHT as evident in the graph.

(c) Text-entry: There was no difference in text-entry speed

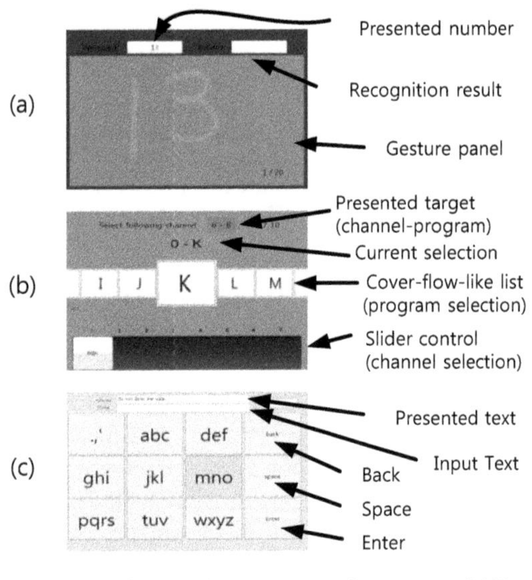

Figure 7. The three tasks: (a) Numeric gesture, (b) Program selection, and (c) Text-entry.

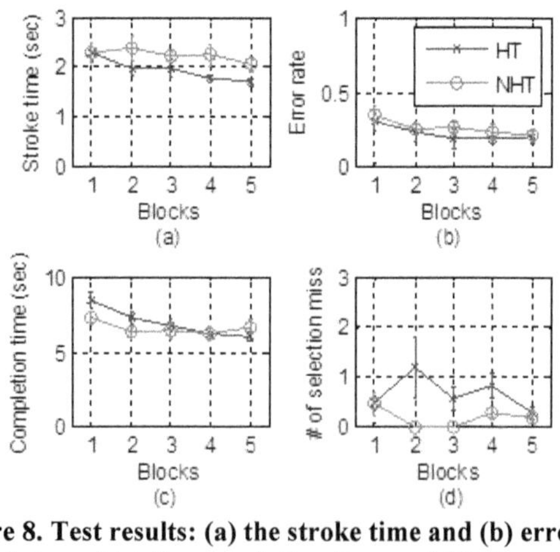

Figure 8. Test results: (a) the stroke time and (b) error rates for task 1, and (c) the completion time and (d) the number of errors for task 2.

between the two conditions ($t = 1.1710$, $p > 0.05$). This result was in fact anticipated from the participants' behavior in the test. Unlike the case of a physical keypad, they rarely moved the thumb off the touchpad. They repeated 'slide and click' instead of 'fly and land'. The interfaces in the two conditions are in fact identical when the thumb is always in contact with the pad, and therefore we could not expect any difference in the experimental result. We expected that their thumb would start to leave the surface as their typing becomes faster, and, if this happens, hover-tracking would be able to make a difference. However, they did not seem to have sufficient time to reach a typing speed of that level. No learning effect was observed in the result and the best speeds that they could achieve were about 8.5 wpm in both conditions. This is comparable with the text entry speed of novice users of a mobile phone keypad, which is about 8 wpm [12]. All the participants were indeed novice users since they are all Koreans and do not usually use an alphabetic keypad for text entry.

Post-test feedback

We conducted a brief questionnaire survey after the test, and the main results are summarized in Table 4. For the first five questions, the average values of a 5-point Likert scale feedback were shown. For the remaining questions the numbers of votes were shown. Except for the fourth question, their rating and votes were in favor of the HT condition. The difference in stroke time in task 1 between HT and NHT was only about 15%, but all participants in the experiment answered that writing a gesture in the HT condition was more natural, which may be more important than the small difference in the stroke time. Participants also favored the HT condition for manipulating the cover-flow-like list but favored the NHT condition for manipulating the slider in task 2. They seemed to favor the NHT condition for operations requiring precision. In task 2, the pointing operation to catch the tracker of the slider control required precision, and this was easier in the NHT than in the HT condition.

	Questions	HT	NHT	No idea
Task 1	1. Was the digit recognition function satisfactory?	3.36	2.64	
	2. Could you easily get used to the device?	3.55	3.27	
	3. Did you find the writing action natural?	3.27	2.27	
Task 2	4. Could you easily manipulate the slider control?	3.18	3.45	
	5. Could you easily manipulate the Cover-Flow control?	3.73	3.45	
Over-all	6. Which is better for task 1?	9	2	0
	7. Which is better for task 2?	5	4	2
	8. Which is better for task 3?	5	3	3

Table 4.The result of the post-test questionnaire survey.

For task 3, only 6 of the participants reported that they could perceive a difference between the two conditions. They said that they tried harder to maintain the thumb in contact with the pad for concern that they might lose visual feedback of the thumb on the screen in the NHT condition. Participants reported that they felt less fatigue and faster visual feedback in the HT condition. In order to assess the overall task load in the two conditions, we conducted NASA-TLX tests after each condition, and summarized the result in Table 5. All numbers are in favor of the HT condition except for the item 'Frustration'. A frequent complaint was about the shift of the thumb image when they moved fast to catch a target on the screen. Errors caused by the less-than-perfect visual feedback might have been the main cause for the frustration.

NASA-TLX	HT		NHT	
	Rating	Weight	Rating	Weight
Mental demand	35(7)	1.6(0.4)	41(6)	1.6(0.4)
Physical demand	42(9)	2.6(0.6)	57(8)	3.1(0.6)
Temporal demand	39(7)	2.5(0.5)	40(7)	2.2(0.4)
Effort	38(9)	2.9(0.5)	38(8)	3.0(0.6)
Performance	47(9)	3.0(0.5)	53(7)	3.0(0.4)
Frustration	42(9)	2.6(0.6)	39(8)	2.2(0.6)

Table 5. The average scores of the NASA-TLX test (standard errors in the parentheses). A lower score means lower demand or better performance.

DISCUSSION

An important yet unaddressed issue in this paper is the ergonomic aspect of the RemoteTouch controller. Indeed, we considered the movement range of the thumb when we determined the size of ScreenPad. Moreover, we rotated the orientation of ScreenPad by 20 degrees to the CCW direction as shown in Figure 1 in order to align the horizontal axis of ScreenPad better to the natural movement direction of the thumb. We also tried to make the shape of the controller handle fit the grip better. There is still a lot of room for improvement in the ergonomic aspects of the RemoteTouch controller. A related issue is considerations for handedness. Throughout our study on the RemoteTouch interaction, we assumed right-handedness. For instance, the rotation angle of ScreenPad in Figure 1 is for right-handed users. Also, the lighting model that we assumed in the design of the visual feedback shown in Figure 5a is also biased for right-handed users. These designs may be easily mirrored for left-handed users, but a single design for both types of users will be a challenge.

Choosing between absolute (AC) and relative (RC) position control of the cursor is another important discussion point. This question deliberately has not been addressed in this paper, since AC is an essential part of the RemoteTouch concept. A pilot study to compare the two cases for a clickable touchpad was done in the early investigation phase as RC was a common choice for a touchpad. AC has advantages when it comes to utilizing one-to-one mapping to access targets on the edges or the vertices of the screen directly. A disadvantage with AC was the instability of the cursor due to a high control-display gain. RC uses a smaller control-display gain minimizing the instability problem. A smaller gain, however, resulted in frequent clutching. Another difference was the role of the cursor. The cursor in AC was perceived as an image of the thumb, but in RC was perceived as an object to move. As such, RC requires the cursor as a mediator, which compromises the directness of control. The final choice between AC and RC remains an open question and should be determined by the requirement of the usage scenario.

One of the considerations for the RemoteTouch controller to be a practical solution is the power consumption of ScreenPad. While ScreenPad consists of a matrix of LEDs, it turns on only one LED at a time, meaning that the power consumption of the whole matrix is the same as that of a single LED. In fact, we designed the current through the LEDs to be below 20 mA in order to drive them directly by a microcontroller. The capacity of a common alkaline AA battery is about 2500mAh, and therefore a single battery cell (in fact, two or more cells to provide a required voltage) can power the LED array for at least 125 hours. The power consumption of the LED array is comparable with the LED illumination of an optical mouse. Considering the usage pattern of a TV remote, we believe 125 hours of continuous operation will not be too short to make it a practical solution. Of course, this implies that LEDs can be turned off when the remote is not in use. The ScreenPad has a button switch (tact switch) for clicking and a touch sensor for detecting a touch by the thumb. The first option will be using the mechanical button switch for waking up the microcontroller. If clicking is too laborious for users, we may consider leaving the touch sensor active in a low-power state.

CONCLUSION

This paper introduced the RemoteTouch concept proving its validity by iterations of prototyping and a user study. Through these iterations we could correct some of our false expectations, and also verify its potential as a viable option for a TV remote control. While the main focus of the second iteration was to enable better visual feedback of the thumb, the user study results indicate that it is still the most important factor to work on further. Immediate future work is to improve the accuracy of the sensor, especially the accuracy of the hover distance, and pursue a realistic, 3-dimensional visual feedback of the thumb.

The contributions of this study are twofold. Foremost, it is the first high-fidelity prototyping study that examines the problems and possibilities of touch-screen-like interactions in a TV remote control environment. Secondly, Screen Pad, a hover-enabled touchpad, is a practical design example for implementing such interactions. The advantages of its operating principle, such as low power consumption by successive lighting of the LEDs and high noise immunity by binding photo-transistors into a single sensor, may also be exploited in the future designs of other hover-enabled optical touchpads.

REFERENCES

1. Abileah, A. and Green, P. Optical sensors embedded within AMLCD panel: design and applications. ACM SIGGRAPH 2007 Emerging Technologies.
2. Cirque – Innovative Touch Solutions. http://www.cirque.com.
3. Douglas, S. A., Kirkpatrick, A. E., and MacKenzie, I. S. Testing pointing device performance and user assessment with the ISO 9241, Part 9 standard. *In Proc. CHI 1999*, 215-222.
4. Enns, N. R. and MacKenzie, I. S. Touchpad-based remote control devices. *In Proc. CHI 1998*, 229-230.
5. Ginny J., et al. The challenges of designing a user interface for consumer interactive television, *In Proc. Int. Conf. on Consumer Electronics*, (1994), 114-115.
6. Han, J. Y. Low-cost multi-touch sensing through frustrated total internal reflection. *In Proc. UIST 2005*, 115-118.
7. Hodges, S., Izadi, S., Butler, A., Rrustemi, A., and Buxton, B. ThinSight: versatile multi-touch sensing for thin form-factor displays. *In Proc. UIST 2007*, 259-268.
8. Holz, C. and Baudisch, P. The generalized perceived input point model and how to double touch accuracy by extracting fingerprints. *In Proc. CHI 2010*, 581-590.
9. Ishiyama, K., and Yano, S. A study of characteristics of pointing devices for television operation, *In Proc. IEEE SMC 2000*, 1307-1312.
10. Lekakos, G., Chorianopoulos, K., Spinellis, D. Information systems in the living room: a case study of personalized interactive TV design. *In Proc. the 9th Euro. Conf. on Information Systems*, (2001), 319-329.
11. MacKenzie, I. S. and Jusoh, S. An evaluation of two input devices for remote pointing. *In Proc. IFIP Int. Conf. on Eng. for HCI 2001*, 235-250.
12. MacKenzie, I. S., Kober, H., Smith, D., Jones, T., and Skepner, E. LetterWise: Prefix-based disambiguation for mobile text input. *In Proc. UIST 2001*, 111-120.
13. MacKenzie, I. S., Sellen, A., and Buxton, W. A. A comparison of input devices in element pointing and dragging tasks. *In Proc. CHI 1991*, 161-166.
14. MacKenzie, I. S. and Soukoreff, R.W. Phrase sets for evaluating text entry techniques. *CHI 2003 Extended Abstracts*, 754-755.
15. Malik, S., Ranjan, A., and Balakrishnan, R. Interacting with large displays from a distance with vision-tracked multi-finger gestural input. *In Proc. UIST 2005*, 43-52.
16. Matsushita, N. and Rekimoto, J. HoloWall: designing a finger, hand, body, and object sensitive wall. *In Proc. UIST 1997*, 209-210.
17. Myers, B. A., Bhatnagar, R., Nichols, J., Peck, C. H., Kong, D., Miller, R., and Long, A. C. Interacting at a distance: measuring the performance of laser pointers and other devices. *In Proc. CHI 2002*, 33-40.
18. Olsen, D. R. and Nielsen, T. Laser pointer interaction. In Proc. CHI 2001, 17-22.
19. Panasonic's EZ Touch Remote prototype, Exhibited at CEATEC Japan 2008, Makuhari Messe, Japan.
20. TactaPad – See, Touch, Feel. http://www.tactiva.com/tactapad.html.

Experimental Analysis of Touch-Screen Gesture Designs in Mobile Environments

Andrew Bragdon[1], Eugene Nelson[1], Yang Li[2] and Ken Hinckley[3]

[1]Brown University
Providence, RI, USA
{acb, ebnelson}@cs.brown.edu

[2]Google Research
Mountain View, CA, USA
yangli@acm.org

[3]Microsoft Research
Redmond, WA, USA
kenh@microsoft.com

ABSTRACT

Direct-touch interaction on mobile phones revolves around screens that compete for visual attention with users' real-world tasks and activities. This paper investigates the impact of these *situational impairments* on touch-screen interaction. We probe several design factors for touch-screen gestures, under various levels of environmental demands on attention, in comparison to the status-quo approach of soft buttons. We find that in the presence of environmental distractions, gestures can offer significant performance gains and reduced attentional load, while performing as well as soft buttons when the user's attention is focused on the phone. In fact, the speed and accuracy of bezel gestures did not appear to be significantly affected by environment, and some gestures could be articulated eyes-free, with one hand. Bezel-initiated gestures offered the fastest performance, and mark-based gestures were the most accurate. Bezel-initiated marks therefore may offer a promising approach for mobile touch-screen interaction that is less demanding of the user's attention.

Author Keywords

Touch, gestures, mobile phones, performance, evaluation

ACM Classification Keywords

H5.2 Information interfaces and Presentation: Interaction.

General Terms

Human Factors

INTRODUCTION

Touch screens are growing rapidly in popularity as an input method for smart phones and other mobile devices [1]. These devices have few, if any, hard buttons; instead soft buttons are the dominant command invocation paradigm on commercial touch-based phones, and are effective when the user is seated and focusing directly on the phone, with no distractions (an *ideal environment*).

However, users rely on mobile devices while sitting, walking, driving, and in diverse environments with various distraction levels [2]. When the user is in a *non-ideal environment*, such as walking through an airport looking for a currency exchange, she must navigate, maintain awareness of her location and avoid obstacles. These *situational impairments* [3] are environmental factors that inhibit the ability to perform tasks on a device. We hypothesize, therefore, that techniques such as soft buttons, which require the user to look at and press a relatively small target, will suffer performance degradation in non-ideal environments, while also potentially degrading performance of other concurrent tasks. This implies that for some mobile tasks, soft buttons could be augmented with other techniques that demand less attention.

In this regard, direct touch gestures offer some possible advantages. Some direct-touch gestures have the potential to be articulated eyes-free or with reduced visual monitoring, making them more resilient to distraction. Gestures can be committed to muscle memory, which helps users focus on their task [4], and it is possible to articulate some gestures with one hand. Gestures also require no dedicated screen space, which is a limited resource on mobile phones.

Even if gestures can be performed quickly and accurately with reduced attentional load in mobile environments, reliance on visual feedback is still a problem. Audio may be sufficient for some tasks, even complex tasks such as scheduling meetings [5]. In other cases, feedback on a heads-up display may be sufficient, e.g. in a car, via a wireless network [6]. Some cases may require little feedback, such as a gesture that is mapped to call a specific person. In many situations, a quick glance may be all that is needed, e.g. when a gesture brings up a map of the current location. Thus, we believe there is significant value in reducing the attentional burden required by soft buttons.

Thus, the goal of this paper is to explore the design space of touch gestures on mobile devices, and evaluate these designs in multiple mobile environments that induce varying levels of situational impairment on users. We induce situational impairment as two factors: *motor activity* and *distraction level*. For motor activity, we examine sitting and walking. For distraction level, we examine no distraction, a light situational-awareness distraction, and an attention-saturating distraction.

We explore two factors of gesture design: *moding* and *gesture type*. Since touch often scrolls or pans by default, the user needs a robust method to enter gesture mode. We explore several ways to indicate mode, including crossing through the screen bezel to integrate mode selection with the articulation of the gesture itself. We also analyze two prevalent types of gestures: *mark* and *free-form path* gestures.

Thus this paper yields insights on a number of fundamental questions regarding touch gestures on mobile phones:

- Which performs best in common mobile environments with varying levels of motor activity and distraction: soft buttons or gestures?
- How is attentional load affected by gestures?

- Can gestures be made eyes-free with sufficient accuracy in the above environments?
- Can gestures be articulated efficiently one-handed?
- Among the factors and conditions we consider here, what is the fastest combination of moding techniques and gesture type for mobile phones?
- To what extent do varying levels of distraction and motor activity affect the speed and accuracy of gestures?
- Which approach do users prefer? Would users like to have both soft buttons and gestures?

Our analyses of these questions contribute a fundamental body of knowledge about touch screen gestures on mobile phones that has not been adequately addressed by prior work.

RELATED WORK

Empirical Studies

A field study of two types of service workers concluded, as one of three design recommendations, that executing actions should not demand high visual attention [7]. Li et al. compared 5 mode switching pen-based gestures techniques on Tablet PCs, and found that using the non-dominant hand to press a button was the fastest [8]. In contrast, we focus on smaller mobile phones, using touch gestures – which necessitates different techniques and experimental design appropriate for mobile devices. Pirhonen et al. [9] compared a media player with 5 unmoded gestures to a player with 5 soft buttons, both worn on the hip while walking; while typical for media-players, we believe this is not representative of the common phone-usage scenarios in which the user holds a phone, which is our focus. From this inspiration, we extend this work by exploring moding type, gesture type, distraction type, and motor activity, and by examining task performance with finer granularity, attentional load and eye gaze.

Lee and Zhai evaluated the hard and soft button performance on mobile devices with multiple types of feedback and input methods [10]. A study of one-handed soft button use found users could select small targets reliably and that walking did not affect speed or accuracy [11]. Lin, et al. studied selecting targets with a stylus while sitting and in two mobile environments [12]. Kane et al. [13] found a significant interaction between walking/not walking and button size, and proposed larger buttons when users are walking. Our focus is not keyboard/keypad input, but rather command selection (e.g. back in a browser) which, as discussed below, is distinct.

Related Techniques and Systems

Bezel Swipe [14] is a technique for scrolling and multi-selection on mobile devices which defines sub-regions of the bezel for different command modes; the user can then cross these regions to enter a mode. Manual Deskterity [15] uses a similar approach to create objects. This work forms the basis of the bezel moding technique presented in this paper.

MacKay et al. compared techniques for scrolling on mobile devices and found differences in performance between sitting and walking [16]. BlindSight [5] lets users perform interactive tasks on phones eyes-free while on a call, using physical buttons and audio cues, while [17] showed that gestures can be learned faster than keyboard shortcuts on desktop PCs.

Techniques Not Evaluated

See Table 1 for a discussion of other moding techniques not evaluated in this paper.

Menus

Marking menus [4] help users move from novice to expert by showing a spatially arranged hierarchical menu that uses compass-aligned marks; the menu is shown on a delay so that after a time users can simply perform the marks from memory. This design inspires the mark-based gestures evaluated in this paper. Simple marking menus [18], in which users draw separate strokes (e.g. 3 strokes for up-right-up) were shown to be more accurate and slightly faster than single-stroke compound marks. However, this requires a "transient mode": if the user has input 2 strokes and may input a third, the system must wait for some time threshold for a third mark. We were concerned this might tempt users to look at the screen to ensure their marks had registered as intended; we thus used single-stroke marks, although we note that accuracy could be improved with simple marks. A tilt-based marking menu [19] was explored on mobile phones, but task times were high – a 2-segment gesture required a mean of 3.9 – 4.7 s.

OVERVIEW

We examine four factors: moding technique, gesture type, user's motor activity, and distraction level of the environment. Below we discuss each factor in more detail.

Karlson et al. [20] observed that users prefer to use smart phones one-handed – that is, holding and supporting the phone, as well as executing commands, with a single hand – and do so the majority of the time. This is not surprising since using both hands incurs the opportunity cost of the additional hand, and greater effort. Given these advantages, we chose to focus on the single-hand scenario, and so all our techniques are designed to work well with a single hand.

Learnability of gestures is also an issue; [17] found it outperformed keyboard shortcuts. Approachability is also a problem; it has been shown, however, that users of a GestureBar disclosure mechanism can use gestural UIs without prior training or experience [21]. Therefore we focus on expert performance, since such an approach could be adapted to disclose the gestures and moding techniques discussed here.

Technique	Evaluation Rationale
Pressure	Li et al. [8] explored pen pressure to initiate a mode switch, however, in the context of touch, increasing pressure also increases the force of friction between the user's finger and the screen, which is not the case with pens, and may be uncomfortable. In addition, this variable is not available on standard capacitive touch screens.
Clickable screen	Some devices, such as the Blackberry Storm (www.blackberry.com), let the user bear down on the touch surface: exceeding a certain pressure threshold causes the surface to "click" in, much like a mouse button. The click is used for picking, while swiping without clicking is used for scrolling. This leaves dragging while the screen is clicked in, which has the same discomfort issue as pressure.
Press-and-hold	Li et al. [8] showed that press and hold with a 1-second hold time was the slowest of the mode switching techniques they tested, and also was rated the worst. This technique therefore did not seem promising for touch.
Multiple fingers	Lepinski et al. adapted marking menus for multi-touch [39], supplementing directional marks with 5-finger chording. Since chording cannot be done one-handed on the screen, we did not implement this approach.
Hard buttons	Not tested for direct command invocation, as touch-based phones have few, if any, hard buttons.
Voice recognition	Can be used to execute commands, however, cannot be used in many mobile environments due to social acceptability (e.g. a meeting, etc.).

Table 1. Techniques not evaluated.

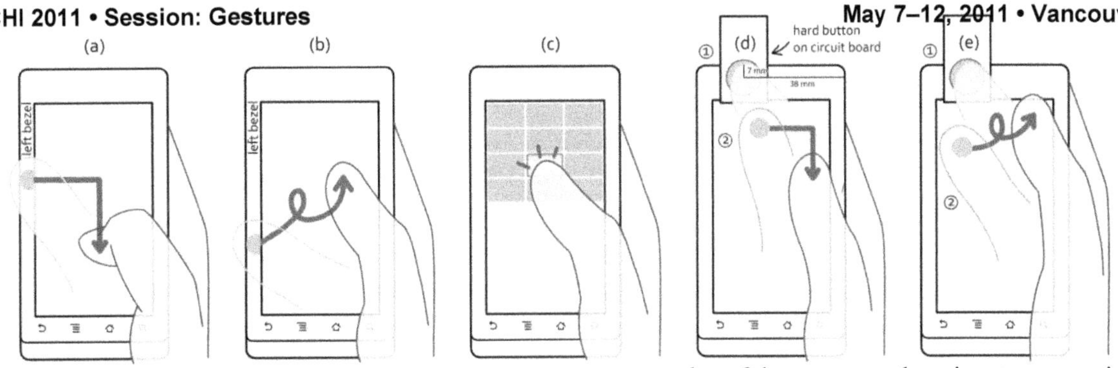

Figure 1. Command invocation techniques: (a) bezel marks, (b) bezel paths, (c) soft buttons (control), (d) hard button marks, (e) hard button paths. Figures to scale.

MODING TECHNIQUES

This section summarizes the gesture-moding techniques explored. Vibrotactile/audio feedback was not provided, as selection of command buttons on phones such as the Android/iPhone does not give feedback; also consistent with [8].

Hard Button-initiated Gestures. Li et al. [8] showed that using the non-dominant hand to press a physical button while drawing pen gestures with the dominant hand was the fastest of five mode switching techniques tested. Since our study focuses on single-handed mobile devices use, we could not transfer this bimanual technique directly. In pilot testing with 2 users performing the main experiment (see below), we tested using a button on the side of the phone that could be pressed with the index finger while holding the phone. However, users found this awkward since they had to brace the phone against their palm to counteract the force of the button press; they also had a strong tendency to look down at the phone "to make sure they didn't drop it." We then tested switching modes by soft button; however, in pilot testing with 2 users they often missed the button, even after we made it quite large (20x20 mm); we also noted users often looked to ensure they hit the button.

Therefore, we instead mounted a physical button just above the top of the phone's screen (Fig. 1d/e). The 14x14 mm button is made of a rubberized material that feels quite different from the glass phone bezel. The hard button requires force to depress, creating a mechanical "click." Without looking, users can rest and feel their finger on the button before pressing, and be confident that they have clicked it. Once the button is clicked, users can draw a single-stroke gesture anywhere on the screen, at any scale. On contact-up, it is recognized. The user does not have to hold the button, but rather presses and releases it to enter gesture mode; the next stroke is treated as a gesture. In pilot testing, users were able to comfortably reach the button, one-handed.

Bezel Gestures. We extend [14] to act as a moding technique for path gestures: *bezel gestures* combine the tasks of setting gesture mode, and performing the gesture itself, into one fluid motion (Fig. 1-a/b). The user swipes through a bezel of the screen, setting gesture mode, continues by drawing a gesture, and finally releases contact to execute the command. In a sense, bezel gestures combine a crossing interface [22] that has large crossing targets with a gestural interface.

On contact up, the stroke input is fed to the gesture recognizer, and the appropriate action is registered. In our implementation on the Motorola DROID's capacitive touch screen, if the beginning point of the input stroke was very close t o the edge of the screen, such an input was considered a bezel gesture, otherwise it was deemed normal input. This heuristic worked quite well in pilot testing, and is the same used in [14]. The tactile feedback of touching the bezel confirms to users that they are contacting the bezel without having to look. Bezel gestures include information on *which* of the 4 bezels was contacted (bezels were not subdivided into smaller targets), e.g. performing a gesture from the left bezel could connote a different action than from the right.

Soft Buttons. To offer a performance baseline, we implemented a soft-button condition (Fig. 1c), with 12 buttons separated by l-mm gaps in a 3x4 grid (14.2x9.5 mm). The buttons are similar to and slightly larger than the numeric keypad soft buttons in the Android 2.1 Phone application (12.7x7.9 mm buttons, 2-mm gap). In comparison, the mean width of the adult male index finger and thumb is 18.2 mm and 22.9 mm; adult female, 15.5 mm and 19.1 mm [23]. Though smaller than an average finger, these buttons are typical in size of many smart phones, and we observed in pilot testing are easily pressed with the thumb, consistent with [24] [25] [26].

Each button is white with a black single-letter label. In most real-world toolbars and menus, commands are not listed in alphabetical order; mirroring this, we randomly chose 12 letters and assigned one to each button in random order (static). We chose this toolbar/menu layout rather than a numeric keypad to model how most commands are selected on mobile phones, and also to mirror the unfamiliarity in button layout by the unfamiliarity of specific gestures in the gestural techniques (see below). As an example, in the iPhone web browser, while unrelated other than both are browser functions, the Switch Tabs and Bookmarks button are adjacent.

GESTURE TYPES

We paired the moding techniques with 2 types of path-based gestures frequent in the literature: rectilinear, mark-based gestures and free-form gestures. We separate these two types here to better understand their performance characteristics; in a real application, both types could be used. Gesture type also affects what type of recognizer can be used, which in turn may affect performance. Although free-form path gestures are more complex than marks, our goal in testing was to identify design tradeoffs in a mobile context relative to the mark gestures, since they are used frequently in the literature. As with soft buttons (above), we used a gesture set of size 12.

Mark-based Gestures. Mark-based gestures, as exemplified in marking menus [27], are typically comprised of axis-aligned (up/down/left/right and optionally four diagonals, e.g. "north-east") rectilinear mark segments that form a compound path, e.g. "up" followed by "right" (Fig. 2, right). Mark-based gestures are simple and thus quick to execute and potentially tolerant of imprecision due to rapid execution.

To maximize recognition tolerance, we limit the mark-based gestures explored to only axis-aligned marks. Our gesture set is comprised of the 12 marks shown in Fig. 2 right. We implemented a simple recognizer that examined the starting/ending point and bounding box of the gesture, combined with simple thresholds and heuristics to identify the gestures.

Free-form Path Gestures. Free-form gestures naturally support 2-D operands (e.g. lasso select), can be rotationally invariant, and may be mnemonic (e.g. scribble delete [28]). We implemented 12 gestures (Fig. 2, left) that met the following criteria: relatively simple to perform, include no axis-aligned marks, distinct enough to be robustly recognized while allowing for imprecise drawing. We started with 9 gestures from prior work (Fig. 2). We added 3 gestures representative of the complexity used in prior studies, such as [17], so that the gesture set as a whole was distinct as to be robustly recognized. Recognition was implemented using the built-in template-based Android 2.1 OS recognizer (used by a variety of commercial applications), similar at a high level to [29].

GESTURE TYPE + MODING COMBINATIONS

Each of the moding techniques was crossed with the gesture types (see Table 2). Hard-button-initiated gestures could be drawn anywhere. Bezel path gestures could be drawn from any bezel. Bezel mark gestures had to start from a specific bezel corresponding to the direction of the mark's first segment (e.g., N-W would start from the bottom bezel).

MOBILE ENVIRONMENT

We model mobile environment as two factors.

Motor Activity

Karlson et al. [20] studied three motor activities: sitting, standing and walking. We eliminated standing as in pilot testing with 2 users performing the experiment (see below) we observed no major change in performance from sitting. We felt using a mobile device while running is rarer than these other activities, and so eliminated it.

Sitting. Perhaps one of the most common motor activities while using a mobile device is sitting: e.g., at the office, in a meeting, on a bus, while driving, etc. Users sat upright in a non-reclining chair adjusted to be 0.45 m high (Fig. 3).

Walking. To test walking in a controlled way, we used a motorized treadmill in a room with only the experimenter present (Fig. 3). While previous work (e.g. [11]) has asked users to walk in a populated building, which is more ecologically valid, we opted for a more controlled approach. We wanted to capture distraction task performance as well as

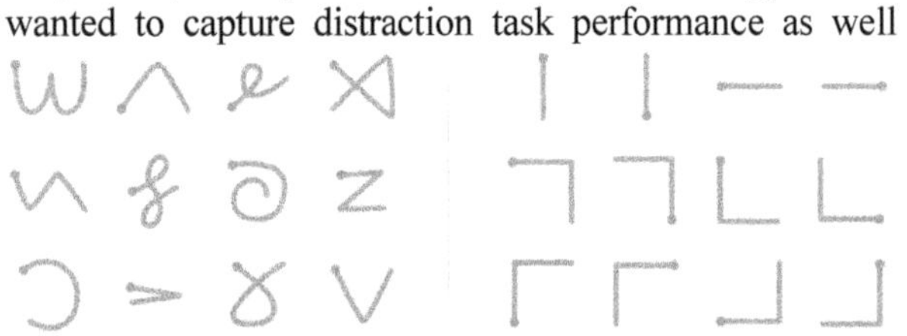

Figure 2. Free-form gestures (left) incl. pigtail [35], spiral [36], downward caret [17], Z [37], X [38], upward caret [38], "delete" [38], "squiggle" [17], and "redo" [28]. Mark-based gestures (right). Dots indicate start of each gesture.

Technique	Gesture Type + Moding Combination
Bezel Marks	Bezel Mode Switch + Mark-based Gestures
Bezel Paths	Bezel Mode Switch + Free-form Path Gestures
Hard Button Marks	Hard Button Mode Switch + Mark-based Gestures
Hard Button Paths	Hard Button Mode Switch + Free-form Path Gestures
Soft Buttons	See Above

Table 2. Command Invocation Techniques

eye-gaze data of the user looking at the phone, which would be difficult to do reliably in an uncontrolled environment. Knoblauch et al. recommend using walking speeds ranging from 0.91 m/s to 1.22 m/s for design purposes, depending on age and other factors [30]. We therefore chose 0.91 m/sec as the target speed. We measured and confirmed that the treadmill was operating at 0.93 m/s (S.D. = 0.014).

Distraction Level

We used 3 distraction levels, with varying attentional load.

No Distraction. This distraction level represents scenarios in which a user concentrates solely on operating the phone. Command-invocation tasks were displayed on the phone screen in the bottom-left corner. Thus, no eye movement is needed as the task and UI are displayed together.

Moderate Situational Awareness Task. This distraction level represents scenarios in which users must maintain some environmental awareness, e.g. watch for a bus stop, follow a presentation, etc., but need not devote all attention. We based the design of this task on successive sensory inspection sustained attention tasks [31]. To simulate such environments in a controlled way, a 17" monitor was set up so that the user could not see both the phone and monitor simultaneously; a horizontal line was configured below which the user was required to hold the phone (Fig. 3). Phone tasks were displayed on one half of the monitor, and distractor tasks on the other. Users were asked to press and hold the spacebar of a keyboard with their non-dominant hand while a circle was visible. The circle randomly appeared for 1 to 8 whole seconds, then disappeared for 1 to 8 whole seconds. The relatively slow-changing but unpredictable nature of this task meant users spent most of their time watching the circle, but could glance down quickly at the phone with relative ease.

Attention-Saturating Task. We implemented an attention-saturating dual-task framework [31] in which users performed a continuous attention-saturating task (AST) while simultaneously performing additional tasks on the phone. The demand placed on attention by the phone tasks can then be measured as a drop in performance in the AST. Like the situational awareness task, the AST was shown on half of the monitor with command tasks on the other. As in [32], the goal of the AST was to keep a moving circle centered on a fixed crosshair. Random forces caused the circle to move in a simple 2D physics simulation in which it had momentum (Fig. 3). The user controlled the circle using an elastic tether connected to the mouse cursor, controlled via a desktop

Environment	Motor Activity + Distraction Level Combination
Direct	Sitting + No Distraction
Indirect	Sitting + Situational Awareness Task
Walking	Walking + Situational Awareness Task
AST	Sitting + Attention-Saturating Task

Table 3. Environments

mouse. Raw performance was measured as the circle's mean distance from the crosshair, sampled every 500 ms. For this task, users held the phone in their right hand and the mouse in their left so as to be consistent with the other conditions. This potential confounding factor is mitigated by the fact that performance on the AST was normalized relative to baseline data (see below), all users were right-handed, and the AST was performed using the left hand for all techniques.

Environment Combinations

We did not fully cross motor activity and distraction because we found that some combinations were not representative of common scenarios (see Table 3). Sitting+AST approximates an attention saturating experience, perhaps similar to driving; while talking or texting when driving is unsafe [33], users do issue commands on their phones while driving, e.g. to place calls, and we wanted to measure the extent to which this would affect attentional load (AST performance) and eye-gaze switches. We did not explore Walking+AST since a user would not likely want to use a phone during such a scenario. We also did not consider Walking+No Distraction as we believe that most users always maintain some level of environment awareness when walking and using a phone.

EXPERIMENT

Participants, Equipment and Physical Setup

We recruited 15 participants from the general population of Brown University (mean age 20.8, S.D. 2.73, 6 female, all right-handed). We advertised widely to get a sample of participants with diverse backgrounds and computers expertise; the average self-rated computer expertise was 5.06 on a 7-point Likert scale where 4 was "Intermediate" and 7 was "Expert"; 4 users reported using a touch device regularly.

We used Motorola DROID smart phones running Android 2.1 update 1 OS. We disabled the built-in hard buttons. Phones measured 60x115x13.7 mm, weighed 169 g, had a glass capacitive multi-touch screen (94 mm diagonal, 854x480 px), 256 MB RAM, and bezel widths of 4, 4, 10 and 8 mm on the left/right/top/bottom. The phone was connected to a laptop (visible only to the experimenter) via network, outputting to a 17" XGA monitor for showing primary and distractor tasks when appropriate. We used 2 phones, one with the gesture hard button and one unmodified (for all other techniques); weight differences were negligible, and the button assembly did not affect how users held the phone (right hand). Java programs ran on the phone and laptop.

Eye gaze data was recorded using a video camera placed at a fixed distance recorded the user's face including eye movements (similar to [32]); the videos were analyzed offline to the frame level to determine eye movement start and stop times. The distance between phone and display was large enough to very reliably identify eye movements.

Tasks

Our goal was to measure expert performance, and so we sought to simulate a scenario where users had memorized the gestures in question. This approach is similar to [27], in which the users were asked to draw rectilinear marking menu gestures based on descriptions of the form "NE", which inherently indicate the mark sequences required (e.g., a "north" mark followed by "east"). For our study, such acronyms do not include all necessary information, such as which bezel to start from, etc. We opted to use simple icons to disclose this information (for soft buttons, this showed command labels, e.g. 'Q'). For distraction-free tasks, the icon appeared in the bottom left corner of the phone's screen (icons were too small to trace but large enough to disclose gestures), and for distraction tasks, the icon appeared on half the external monitor (Fig. 3, above). Feedback (correct/incorrect) was displayed onscreen (phone screen for direct, monitor otherwise) after each performance.

Experimental Design and Procedure

We used a repeated-measures within-participants experimental design. After a pre-questionnaire, participants were read a description of the first technique and shown a 40-second demonstration video. Users were given a short demonstration and then asked to complete a series of tasks using the technique in the first environment: 2 training blocks followed by 6 measured blocks; each block contained each of the 12 commands once. We felt 12 was a sufficient number of commands to be representative of a typical mobile application. For environments involving a distractor task, participants had 3 minutes to acclimate to the distractor task in isolation before using the technique concurrently. This was repeated as follows:

15 participants
x 4 environments/distraction combinations
x 5 command invocation techniques
x (2+6) blocks (training + measured)
x 12 commands
= 28,800 trials completed

Condition order was counterbalanced with randomization. After completing 5 techniques and before moving on to the

Figure 3. User in the indirect (sitting + discrete distraction) environment. Users were asked to hold the phone below the striped line (left). User in the walking + discrete distraction environment. Users were asked to hold the phone below the striped line (center). Heads-up stimulus for discrete distractor task + mark-based gestures (right, top), stimulus for attention saturating task + free-form gestures (right, bottom).

next environment users had a 7-minute break. Dependent variables included completion time, mode errors, command errors, and baseline and concurrent distractor task performance. Gesture performances were recorded. Cameras recorded users' eye movements in context.

Participants were paid $15 per hour plus $0.25 for every 100 ms faster than 2,000 ms they completed tasks on average (integer units) for a given technique/environment combination while maintaining less than a 10% error rate average (i.e., they earned an extra $1 if they completed with an average of 1,600 ms with 94% accuracy). Users were notified when their average passed a 100-ms threshold and the accuracy was sufficiently high, with current average speed displayed in fractional seconds. We implemented this performance-based compensation system to keep participants motivated, after observing in pilot testing that some participants lost interest in the tasks partway through the experiment. Once complete, users filled-out a post-questionnaire.

RESULTS

Before analyzing variance, we observed histograms of the data and observed that it appeared to fit the normal distribution. Training blocks are excluded from this analysis.

Time

We report mean completion time results in Fig. 4, 5. Analysis of variance with technique as a within-subjects factor[1] found a significant main effect ($F_{2.67,37.33}$=47.23, p<0.001). There was a significant main affect for environment ($F_{3,42}$=4.83, p<0.01). There was no significant technique × environment interaction ($F_{12,168}$=1.31, p=0.22). Post-hoc comparisons were performed using 2-tailed t-tests, with Holm's sequential Bonferroni adjustment [34] for multiple comparisons.

Overall Performance. We began by looking at mean completion time by technique averaged across environments. While this gives equal weight to each environment, which may not be representative of usage habits, it provides an overview of technique performance.

Bezel marks had the lowest mean completion time, 1092.87 ms; this was significantly lower than soft buttons (t_{14}=5.12, p<0.0038), which had a mean of 1244 ms (an improvement of 12.17%). There was no significant performance difference between soft buttons and hard button mark's mean of 1262 ms (t_{14}=-0.46, p=0.66). The 8.08% increase from soft buttons to bezel path's 1344 ms was not significant (t_{14}=-3.11, p=0.0078). Finally, there was a significant, 14.1% increase in mean completion time between bezel paths and hard button path's 1534 ms (t_{14}=-5.68, p<0.0033), the highest mean.

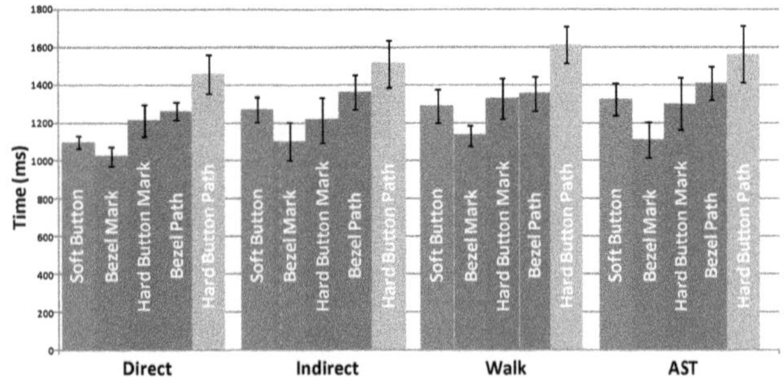

Figure 4. Task completion time by technique and environment.

Performance within Each Environment. To explore the surprising result that bezel marks outperformed soft buttons, we made additional comparisons focused on each of the 4 environments. In direct, without distractions, bezel marks had a mean completion time of 1022 ms, 6.82% lower than soft button's 1097 ms. There was no significant difference between bezel marks and soft buttons (t_{14}=2.52, p=0.025), surprising given that the user was not distracted and concentrated directly on the phone.

When used in the indirect environment, bezel marks (1102 ms) significantly outperformed soft buttons (t_{14}=3.70, p < 0.0045), which had a mean of 1271 ms. In the walk environment, bezel marks (1134 ms) significantly outperformed soft button's 1286 ms (t_{14}=3.41, p < 0.005), and in AST, bezel marks (1112 ms) again significantly outperformed soft button's 1321 ms (t_{14}=3.84, p < 0.0042).

It is notable that bezel marks and soft buttons performed similarly in direct, and that with various distraction types, bezel marks significantly outperformed soft buttons in each case.

Effect of Environment on Performance. We conducted further tests to see how the two best-performing techniques, bezel marks and soft buttons, were affected by environment. We also examine bezel paths (which we hypothesized might be affected by distractions).

For soft buttons, there was a significant difference in performance between the direct and indirect environments (t_{14}=5.26, p<0.0036) of 15.84%. Interestingly, there was no significant difference for soft buttons between indirect and walk or indirect and AST (p>0.05). This suggests that in terms of performance, the biggest effect for soft buttons came from not looking directly at the phone at all times.

For bezel marks, on the other hand, there was no significant difference in performance between direct and indirect, indirect and walk or indirect and AST (p>0.05), suggesting bezel marks were unaffected by not looking directly at the phone.

For bezel paths, completion times increased from direct to indirect by 7.85%; however, this difference was not significant (t_{14}=2.12, p=0.052). For walk and AST, bezel paths remained within 3.27% of indirect performance. This was surprising given that vibration or distractions could be expected to affect free-form gesture performance.

Accuracy Analysis

Mean accuracy and errors type results are reported in Fig. 6. Analysis of variance with technique as a within-subjects factor showed a significant effect for accuracy ($F_{4,56}$=29.94, p<0.001), as did environment ($F_{3,42}$=5.09, p<0.01). Tech-

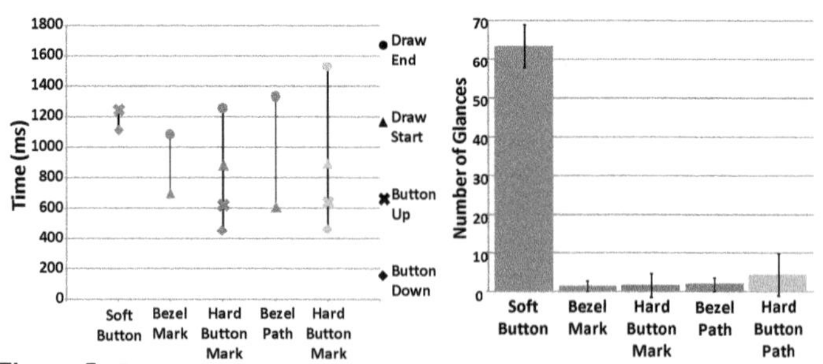

Figure 5. Task timing breakdown by technique (left), glances at phone in environments other than direct (right).

nique × environment[1], had no significant interaction effect ($F_{9.52,133.27}$=0.50, p=0.88). The same post-hoc multiple comparisons adjustment procedure was used as above.

Overall Accuracy. As above, to get a sense of the overall performance, we examine mean technique accuracy across environments (including both mode-in and command errors).

Hard button marks (93.5%) and bezel marks (92.5%) had the highest mean accuracy, followed closely by soft buttons (91.2%). There was no significant difference between hard button marks and bezel marks in accuracy, or between bezel marks and soft buttons (p>0.05). Bezel paths (81.4%) and hard button paths (83.5%) had the lowest mean accuracy. Hard button paths had significantly lower accuracy than soft buttons (t_{14}=5.59, p<0.0036).

Error-Type Analysis. Of the two moding approaches–bezel and hard button–there was 9.63% greater mode-in errors for hard buttons than for bezel; however, this was not significant (t_{29}=0.19, p=0.85). Of the two gesture approaches – mark (0.69 errors/block) and path (1.86) – there were significantly more (168%) command errors for paths than marks (t_{29}=11.24, p<0.000001).

Environmental Effect on Accuracy. From direct to indirect, soft button accuracy decreased by 2.88%, but this was not significant. Differences in soft button accuracy between indirect/walk and indirect/AST were not significant (p>0.05).

From direct to indirect for bezel marks, accuracy decreased by 2.93%, but was not significant (t_{14}=1.90, p=0.078). Differences in mean accuracy for bezel marks between indirect/walk and indirect/AST were less than 1.16%. Similarly, hard button marks performed consistently across environments; differences in accuracy between direct/indirect and between indirect/walk and AST, were less than 1.28%.

For bezel paths, from direct to indirect, accuracy decreased by 4.35%, but was not significant; from indirect to walk, the difference in accuracy was only 1.23%, and from indirect to AST the accuracy decreased by 3.45% but was not significant (p>0.05). For hard button paths, from direct to indirect, and indirect to walk, the differences in accuracy were all less than 1.74%; from indirect to AST, however, the difference was 5.91%, but not significant (t_{14}=1.68, p=0.11).

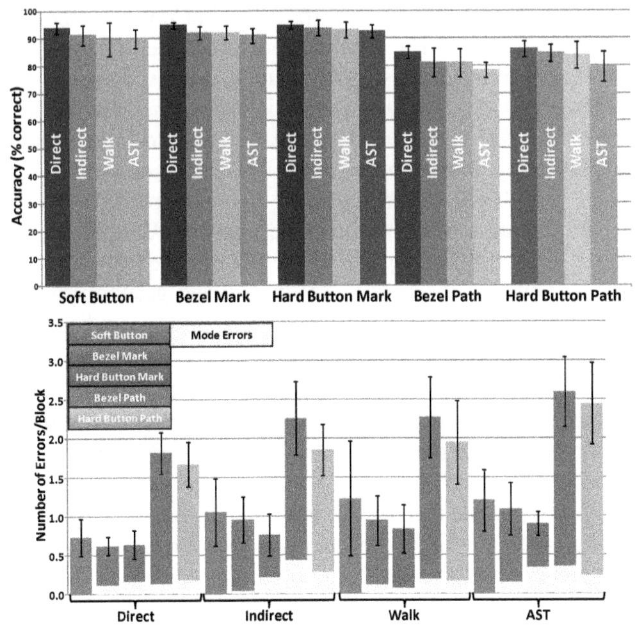

Figure 6. Accuracy rates by technique and environment (top); errors/block by technique and environment with mode errors shown (bottom).

Accuracy within Environments. Hard button marks, bezel marks, and soft buttons were most accurate. For direct, accuracy differed by at most 0.8% and for indirect, walk and AST, at most 3.2%. No significant differences were found for environment (p>0.05). Path gesture techniques were least accurate. For direct, hard button paths were significantly lower than soft buttons by 7.8% (t_{14}=-4.89, p<0.0038). This general trend continued, with hard button paths having 6.6% lower accuracy for indirect, 6.0% for walking, and 10.4% for AST. Very similar trends were seen for bezel paths.

Discrete Distractor Performance

For sitting, the four gesture-based techniques' mean discrete distractor performances (Fig. 7, right) were within 2.1% of each other. However, soft buttons performed 6.6% worse than bezel marks, a significant difference (t_{14}=2.66, p<0.025). For walking, a similar pattern held, with the gesture techniques having mean performances within 3.3% of one another. Soft button performance was 4.2% lower than bezel marks, but this was not significant (t_{14}=1.81, p=0.093).

Continuous Distractor Task Performance

To control for differing distractor task aptitudes, we normalized performance with the baseline mean performance from the second half of the distractor-only training (Fig. 7, left).

Soft buttons had the highest (worst) mean normalized distance from the target (2.1), while bezel marks had the lowest mean (1.6), significantly lower than soft buttons (t_{14}=-2.61, p<0.025) – Fig. 7, left. Hard button marks and bezel paths were within 9.7% of bezel marks. Finally, hard button paths had a mean distance of 1.9, but this was not significantly different from bezel marks (t_{14}=2.11, p=0.053). The relatively high normalized scores are likely caused by the continuous administration of command invocation tasks, which likely served as a greater distraction than occasional invocation.

Eye Gaze

The difference in the number of glances (Fig. 5) for soft buttons and all the gestural techniques was significant (t_{14}=20.04, p<0.000001). Interestingly, there was no significant difference for glances between any of the gestural techniques (p>0.05). The mean percentage of tasks requiring looks across environment for soft buttons was 98.8%; in contrast, the mean for gestural techniques was 3.5%. Since users were free to look, it is clear that looking was required for soft buttons but essentially not needed for gestural techniques.

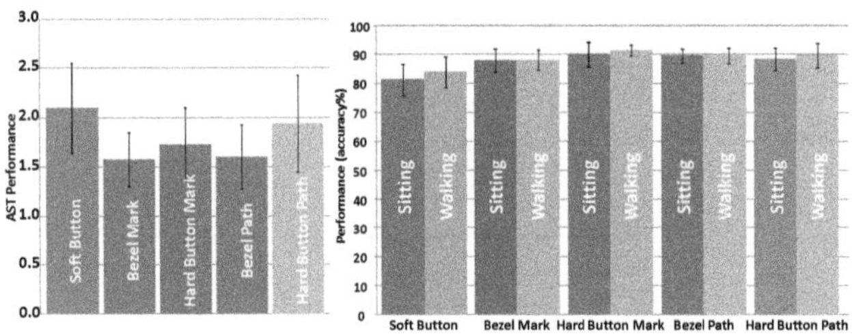

Figure 7. Normalized performance on the attention-saturating task (left), discrete distractor task performance (right).

Looking was expensive, requiring 522 ms to finish looking down for soft buttons (plus 768 ms of looking at the phone).

Subjective Preferences

For direct, a majority (8 of 15 users) chose soft buttons as the preferred technique for performance; 4 chose hard button marks and 3 chose bezel marks. For *least* preferred, 10 chose hard button paths, with the rest evenly distributed.

For indirect, 0 now preferred soft buttons; 7 of 15 users chose bezel marks, 7 chose hard button marks, and 1 chose bezel paths. For their *least* preferred technique, 7 now chose soft buttons. 7 users wrote unprompted that a gesture-based technique allowed them to not have to look at the phone to perform commands: e.g. bezel marks "was still easy to use without looking at the phone"; and "I felt like I needed to look" for soft buttons. This trend continued for walking, again 0 users preferred soft buttons; 10 users chose bezel marks, 4 chose hard button marks, and 1 chose bezel paths. Finally, it further continued for AST, 9 users chose bezel marks and 6 chose hard button marks. Despite the vibration of walking, users appeared to still prefer gestural techniques; "[it is] easy to draw rectilinear shapes while not looking at the phone."

For overall preferred technique, 7 chose bezel marks, 6 chose hard button marks, and 1 chose soft buttons. This is a surprising result given the ubiquity of soft buttons. When asked for their least favorite overall, free-form path gesture techniques dominated; 9 chose hard button paths and 4 chose bezel paths. Users commented on the relative ease of making rectilinear marks over free-form paths; one user wrote, "simple straight lines and right angle turns are easier to make with high tolerance of error." 2 users felt pressing the hard button was an "extra step," but this did not appear to be universal.

Keystroke Level Analysis

Fig. 8 shows a keystroke level analysis. Several general trends become apparent: first, it is notable that for the soft

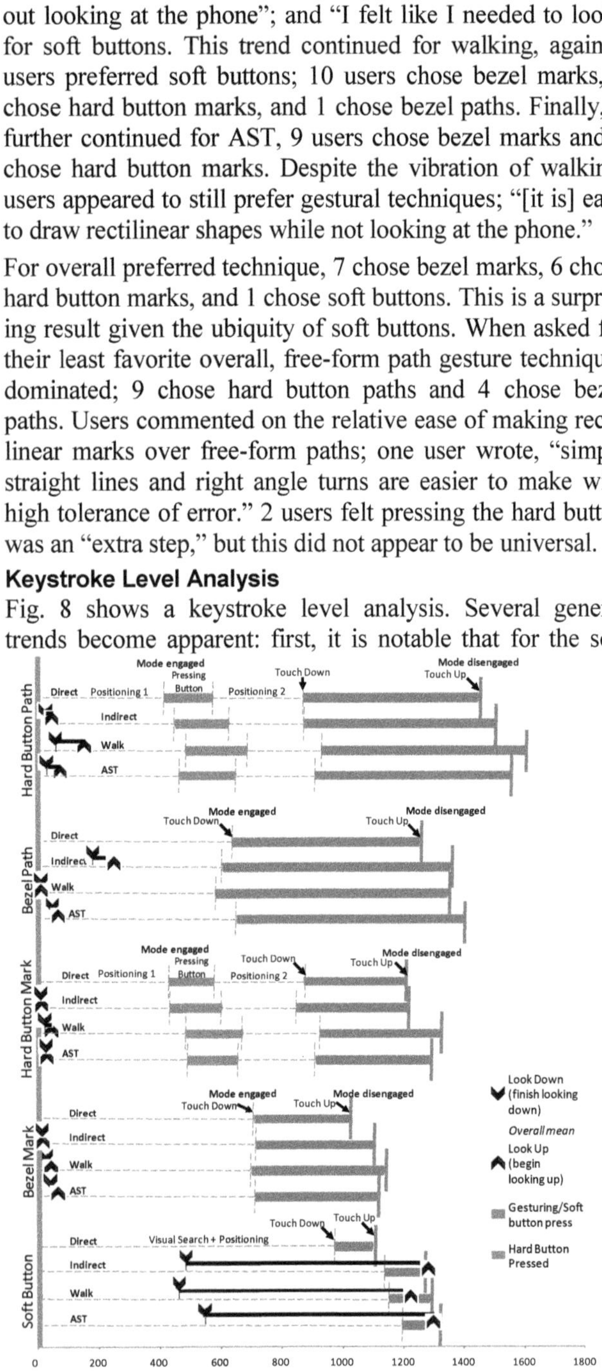

Figure 8. Keystroke-level analysis of gesture performances.

button task, although users finish looking down after 457-564 ms in indirect tasks, completion time increases by only 174-225 ms; we attribute this primarily to user reaction time. In addition, it is also notable that gesturing consistently begins sooner for bezel moding than hard-buttons. It is also notable that users were able to consistently begin pressing the hard button before the bezel mode became engaged; however, given the cost of then repositioning the hand, users completed the gestures after the bezel conditions.

Independent Analysis of Path Gesture Recognizer

The gesture error rates of the path gesture techniques were higher than 10%, so an independent, single-blind human analysis of the recorded performances was done to test if the recognizer malfunctioned. 5% of path gestures performed were randomly sampled and then human-recognized with a specific "recipe" set up *a priori*[2]. Comparison of the software to the human recognition found 3.5% false positives and 3.3% false negatives. As even for humans 100% agreement is difficult to achieve, we feel this discrepancy is acceptable.

We attribute most of the path gesture errors made (Fig. 9) to user error: quickly drawing free-form path gestures on a phone with a thumb while holding the phone may be more difficult than, say, clicking buttons with a mouse, in which error rates are typically < 4%. Specifically, we hypothesize that it is the nature of the thumb that makes it difficult to accurately perform gestures one-handed – indeed, accuracy rates likely would be higher with two-handed input. We believe bezel marks were successful because the recognizer can be quite robust given the simple nature of the gestures. We believe also that had participants performed the gestures more slowly they would have had a lower error rate. We also note that the error rates for gestures were typically within 700 basis points of the soft button rates. It is possible that with a different type of recognizer, performance could be improved.

Stability of Performance over Multiple Blocks

There was a significant effect of block number on task completion time ($F_{5,1794}=2.87$, $p<0.05$), but not on error rate, however ($p>0.05$). The improvements were seen primarily for the gestural techniques. Soft buttons improved by 38 ms (3.6%), and actually worsened slightly in the last block (-0.97%). Bezel marks improved by 5.1%, hard button marks improved by 11.1%, bezel paths by 7.6%, and hard button paths by -0.4%. After extended training (perhaps several weeks), gesture performance could improve. We believe this threat to validity is mitigated by the fact that the learning effect for soft buttons appeared to be limited, and gestural learning did not appear to be of sufficient magnitude to indicate the performance measured was not representative.

It is important to discuss how representative user performance was. It is notable that we were looking at command invocation rather than data entry, with the soft buttons representing command buttons (e.g. "Create Contact," etc. but not "1, 2, 3, ..."). We feel that for this context, it is less likely, for many users, to fully memorize the location of toolbar button/menu items, the way they would for say QWERTY, and

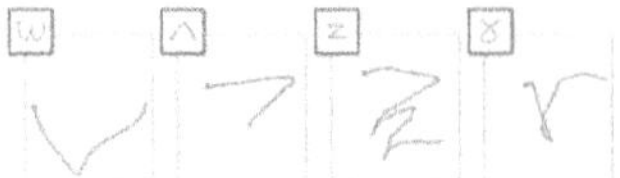

Figure 9. Examples of users' path-based gesture command errors

instead may perform a visual search coupled with adjacency cues from memory. While there is an obvious benefit to a user to memorize keyboard locations, we believe toolbar buttons are used less frequently and so there is less need to fully memorize them. Looking at the soft button learning effect, this was minimal during the experiment, as expected.

We note mean soft-button speed recorded for direct (1097 ms) was less than other studies, such as approximately 500 ms from [24]. We attribute the difference to differences in methodology, e.g. labeled targets, and non-reciprocal tasks.

DISCUSSION

Which performs best: soft buttons or gestures? Surprisingly, when users were looking directly at the phone there was no significant difference in completion time between soft buttons and bezel marks, probably because targets were not highlighted but needed to be identified from a letter caption. We believe this is realistic, however, since soft buttons for executing commands typically have either a text or icon label. In addition, bezel marks significantly outperformed soft buttons for the other three environments (sitting with discrete distraction, walking with discrete distraction, and sitting while doing an attention-saturating task). We hypothesize from the eye-gaze data that most of the performance benefit for gestures came from not having to look down at the phone.

How is attentional load affected by gestures? Performance on the discrete distractor task and the AST were both significantly improved for bezel marks over soft buttons. Hard button marks and bezel paths both performed similarly to bezel marks. This result is excellent, showing that gestures can reduce user's attentional load over soft buttons, even though gestures involve reproducing geometry with some degree of accuracy and soft buttons can be performed in ~1.2 s.

Can gestures be made eyes-free in the above environments with sufficient accuracy? The eye-gaze data indicates that gestures can be made eyes-free, requiring looking at the phone just 3.5% of the time. In contrast, soft buttons required looking 98.8% of the time.

Can gestures be done one-handed effectively? Mark-based gestures can be done one-handed effectively (e.g. no significant difference in accuracy for bezel marks and soft buttons); however, our analysis indicates that accurate one-handed free-form path gestures may be considerab ly more difficult.

What is the fastest tested combination of moding technique and gesture type? Most accurat e? Bezel marks appear to be the fastest combination of moding techniques and gesture type, followed by hard button marks. Overall, bezel marks were significantly faster than hard button marks across environments; they had no significant difference in accuracy. Bezel marks were preferred (see below), and had the advantage of not requiring an additional button on the phone.

	Design Recommendations
R1	Gestural shortcuts/alternatives should be provided for soft button commands.
R2	Users should be able to assign gestures to common action sequences, e.g. "Run Phone App, Call Home" or "Run Media App, Play Classical Playlist" to make them eyes-free. The system could potentially identify such interaction patterns and automatically assign gestures to them.
R3	Mark-based gestures are faster and more accurate than free-form gestures in all the mobile environments tested, so they should be used instead of free-form path gestures unless 2D operands are required.
R4	We recommend bezel moding for design purposes as bezel marks have nearly identical performance to hard button marks; however, users preferred bezel marks.
R5	For space-critical applications, gestures could be used to save screen real estate.
R6	Because moded gestures are unlikely to be triggered by accident, they could be used to unlock the phone *and* execute a command, thus eliminating an extra step.

Table 4. Design Recommendations

Interestingly, free-form path gestures performed significantly worse in both speed and accuracy. Users made 168% more errors with free-form path gestures than with mark-based gestures. Subsequent analysis of the gestures drawn indicates that virtually all these errors were due to user error, not a recognizer bug. We hypothesize that it is harder to perform gestures accurately one-handed with the thumb than with two hands or a stylus, which was the root cause of the errors. Users also preferred mark-based gestures to path-based.

It is notable that the specific free-form gestures used may affect performance. However, we believe they are representative of prior research systems (9 of 12 are cited), and sufficiently unique to create a robustly recognizable set.

How do various mobile environments affect the speed and accuracy of gestures? It was surprising that specific gestural conditions appeared to be unaffected by environment in speed or accuracy. Bezel marks and bezel paths, for example had no significant difference from direct to indirect, indirect to walk, or indirect to AST.

Soft buttons, in contrast, were affected by environment, and had a significant increase in completion time from direct to indirect (15.8%), after which completion time remained fairly steady. The accuracy of soft buttons was unaffected by environment. Interestingly, there was no significant difference in accuracy between soft buttons and bezel marks.

Which do users prefer? Would users like to have both soft buttons and gestures? It was surprising that for direct usage, only half the users preferred soft buttons. Furthermore, for the other 3 environments, 0 users chose soft buttons. Bezel marks were most-preferred for walking and AST, and tied with hard button marks for indirect.

Users commented almost unanimously that gestures would be useful when not devoting full attention to the phone. On gesture type, 9 commented it was difficult to perform freeform gestures; one user saying "too much thumb motion" was required, while users mentioned that rectilinear gestures helped them focus their attention on the circle centering task.

Two users felt pre ssing the hardware button slowed performance or felt like an "extra step." A majority of users commented that it was easy to locate the hardware button and bezels without looking, while difficult to press soft buttons.

When asked if they would like more than one technique for different situations, 13 of 15 users chose more than one technique; just one chose soft buttons only. Based on this and the quantitative performance results, we hypothesize that gesture-shortcut alternatives to command buttons on smart

[1] The sphericity assumption was not met so the Huynh-Feldt correction was applied. The corrected degrees of freedom is shown.

[2] Beyond visual comparison against a crib sheet of gestures, the verifier marked a gesture as unknown if >20% geometry was missing, >20% new geometry was added, if a feature was rotated/skewed by >50°, or if a feature was scaled up or down by >60%. The verifier was unaware of the software recognizer's ratings.

phones would improve performance and reduce attentional load. Table 4 (above) outlines our design recommendations.

Other Considerations

The controlled nature of our study limits the generality of results. Although we simulated several types of distractions and motor activities, these may not fully represent ecologically valid situations. Prior experience (4 users) with touch screens may impact performance; results may not generalize to other populations. Our compensation approach may limit generality. However, as remarked above, we found this was essential to prevent users from becoming "bored"/underperforming in speed/accuracy given the large number of trials. We do not believe it sacrificed accuracy, since users were rewarded for both speed *and* accuracy, and because our soft button accuracy of 93.9% is close to the approx. 95.0% values from [24]. Freeform path gestures may have mnemonic advantages due to greater uniqueness. Gestures are always available, while soft buttons consume screen space, or use an invocation procedure.

CONCLUSION

In this paper we explored the effect of mobile environments, modeled as motor activity and distraction level, on moded direct touch gestures. The results of a formal experiment indicates direct touch gestures can produce on-par performance and accuracy with soft buttons when the user is focused on the phone, and improved performance, and reduced attentional load in the presence of environmental distractions. Our results further indicate that bezel gestures did not appear to be affected by environment in speed or accuracy, and the gestures tested can be done effectively eyes free, with one hand. We found bezel-initiated gestures to be fastest, and most-preferred by users. We also found mark-based gestures were faster and more accurate to perform, and were preferred by users to free-form path gestures. We believe, therefore, that bezel-initiated, mark-based gestural shortcuts should be provided for soft button commands on mobile devices.

ACKNOWLEDGEMENTS

We wish to thank Andries van Dam for his advice and insight, Alice Liu for her illustrations, and Robert Zeleznik, Zachary Kahn, Zachary Davis, Jeff Coady, and Max Salvas for their assistance. This material is based upon work supported under a National Science Foundation Graduate Research Fellowship and by a Google Research Award.

REFERENCES

1. iSuppli. *Touch-Screen Shipments Expected to Reach 833 Million by 2013.* '08.
2. Brewster, S. Overcoming the lack of screen space on mobile computers. *Personal and Ubiquitous Computing*, 6, 3, 188-205.
3. Sears, A., et al. When computers fade: Pervasive computing and situationally-induced impairments and disabilities. In *HCI Int'l '03*.
4. Kurtenbach, G. *The Design and Evaluation of Marking Menus*. Department of Computer Science, University of Toronto. 1993.
5. Li, K., Baudisch, P., and Hinckley, K. Blindsight: eyes-free access to mobile phones. In *Proceedings of CHI'08*, 1389-1398.
6. Charissis, V., et al. Designing a direct manipulation HUD interface for in-vehicle infotainment. In *Proc. of ICHCI'07*.
7. Kristoffersen, S., et al. "Making place" to make IT work: empirical explorations of HCI for mobile CSCW. In *SIGGROUP'99*.
8. Li, Y., Hinckley, K., Guan, Z., et al. Experimental analysis of mode switching techniques in pen-based user interfaces. In *CHI'05*.
9. Pirhonen, A., Brewster, S., and Holguin, C. Gestural and audio metaphors as a means of control for mobile devices. In *CHI'02*.
10. Lee, S. and Zhai, S. The performance of touch screen soft buttons. In *Proc. of CHI'09*.
11. Perry, K. and Hourcade, J. Evaluating one handed thumb tapping on mobile touchscreen devices. In *Proc. of GI'08*, 57-64.
12. Lin, M. et al. How do people tap when walking? An empirical study of nomadic data entry. *Int. J. of Hum.-Com. Studies*, 65, 9, 759-769.
13. Kane, S., et al. Getting Off the Treadmill: Evaluating Walking User Interfaces for Mobile Devices in Public Spaces. In *MobileHCI'08*.
14. Roth, V. and Turner, T. Bezel swipe: conflict-free scrolling and multiple selection on mobile touch screen devices. In *CHI'09*.
15. Hinckley, K., Yatani, K., Pahud, M. et al. Manual deskterity: an exploration of simultaneous pen + touch direct input. In *CHI'10 EA*.
16. MacKay, B., Dearman, D., Inkpen, K., and Watters, C. Walk 'n scroll: a comparison of software-based navigation techniques for different levels of mobility. In *Proc. of MobileHCI'05*, 183-190.
17. Appert, C. and Zhai, S. Using strokes as command shortcuts: cognitive benefits and toolkit support. In *CHI'09*, 2289-2298.
18. Zhao, S. and Balakrishnan, R. Simple vs. compound mark hierarchical marking menus. In *Proc. of UIST'04*, 33-42.
19. Oakley, I. and Park, J. A motion-based marking menu system. In *Proceedings of CHI'07 Extended Abstracts*, 2597-2602.
20. Karlson, A., Bederson, B., et al. Understanding One Handed Use of Mobile Devices. In *Handbook of Research on User Interface Design and Evaluation for Mobile Technology*. IGI Global, 2007.
21. Bragdon, A., Zeleznik, R., et al. GestureBar: improving the approachability of gesture-based interfaces. In *CHI'09*, 2269-2278.
22. Accot, J. and Zhai, S. More than dotting the i's - foundations for crossing-based interfaces. In *Proc. of CHI'02*, 73-80.
23. Henry Dreyfus Associates. *The Measure of Man and Woman*. Whitney Library of Design, New York, 1993.
24. Perry, K. B. and Hourcade, J. P. Evaluating One Handed Thumb Tapping on Mobile Touchscreen Devices. In GI'08, 57-64.
25. Parhi, P., et al. Target size study for one-handed thumb use on small touchscreen devices. In Proc. of MobileHCI'06, 203-210.
26. Karlson, A. et al. ThumbSpace: Generalized One-Handed Input for Touchscreen-Based Mobile Devices. In Lect. Notes, Interact'07.
27. Kurtenbach, G. and Buxton, W. The limits of expert performance using hierarchic marking menus. In CHI'93, 482-487.
28. Zeleznik, R., Bragdon, A., Liu, C., and Forsberg, A. Lineogrammer: creating diagrams by drawing. In *UIST'08*, 161-170.
29. Li, Y. Protractor: A Fast and Accurate Gesture Recognizer. *CHI'10*.
30. Knoblauch, R. L., et al. Field Studies of Pedestrian Walking Speed and Start-Up Time. *Transportation Research Record* (1996), 27-38.
31. Wickens, C.D. and Hollands, J.G. *Engineering Psychology and Human Performance*. Prentice Hall, 1999.
32. Harrison, C. and Hudson, S. Providing dynamically changeable physical buttons on a visual display. In *Proc.CHI'09*, 299-308.
33. Iqbal, S., Ju, Y., and Horvitz, E. Cars, calls, and cognition: investigating driving and divided attention. In *CHI'10*, 1281-1290.
34. Holm, S. A Simple Sequentially Rejective Multiple Test Procedure. *Scandinavian Journal of Statistics*, 6 (1979), 60-65.
35. Moran, T. P., et al. Pen-based interaction techniques for organizing material on an electronic whiteboard. In *Proc. of UIST"97*, 45-54.
36. Hinckley, K., et al. InkSeine: In Situ Search for Active Note Taking. In *CHI'07*.
37. Liao, C., et al. PapierCraft: A Gesture-Based Command System for Interactive Paper. *ToCHI*, 14, 4 (2008).
38. Wobbrock, J., et al. Gestures without Libraries, Toolkits or Training: A $1 Recognizer for User Interface Prototypes. *UIST'07*.
39. Lepinski, G., Grossman, T., and Fitzmaurice, G. The design and evaluation of multitouch marking menus. In *CHI'10*, 2233-2242.

Usable Gestures for Blind People: Understanding Preference and Performance

Shaun K. Kane, Jacob O. Wobbrock
The Information School, DUB Group
University of Washington
Seattle, WA 98195 USA
{skane, wobbrock}@uw.edu

Richard E. Ladner
Computer Science & Engineering, DUB Group
University of Washington
Seattle, WA 98195 USA
ladner@cs.washington.edu

ABSTRACT
Despite growing awareness of the accessibility issues surrounding touch screen use by blind people, designers still face challenges when creating accessible touch screen interfaces. One major stumbling block is a lack of understanding about how blind people actually use touch screens. We conducted two user studies that compared how blind people and sighted people use touch screen gestures. First, we conducted a gesture elicitation study in which 10 blind and 10 sighted people invented gestures to perform common computing tasks on a tablet PC. We found that blind people have different gesture preferences than sighted people, including preferences for edge-based gestures and gestures that involve tapping virtual keys on a keyboard. Second, we conducted a performance study in which the same participants performed a set of reference gestures. We found significant differences in the speed, size, and shape of gestures performed by blind people versus those performed by sighted people. Our results suggest new design guidelines for accessible touch screen interfaces.

Author Keywords: Accessibility, blind, touch screens, gestures, gesture recognition.

ACM Classification Keywords: H.5.2. Information interfaces and presentation: User Interfaces–*input devices and strategies.* K.4.2. Computers and Society: Social issues–*assistive technologies for persons with disabilities.*

General Terms: Experimentation, Human Factors.

INTRODUCTION
While touch screens were once rare, touch screen-based interfaces are now present across a wide range of everyday technologies, including mobile devices, personal computers, and public kiosks. As touch screens have become mainstream, it is crucial that touch screen-based interfaces be usable by people with all abilities, including blind and visually impaired people.

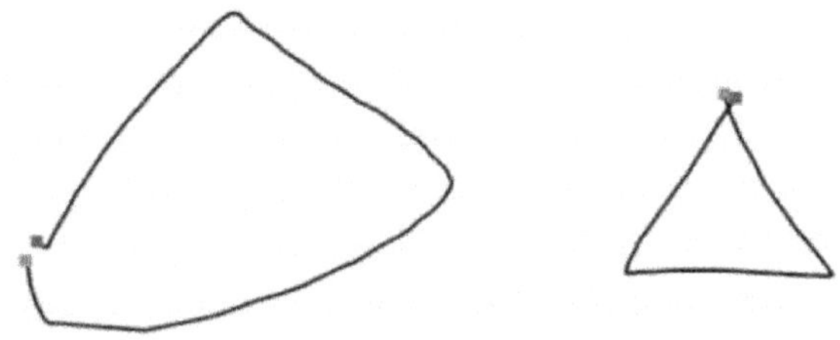

Figure 1. Two representative versions of a *triangle* gesture produced by a blind person (left) and a sighted person (right).

Until recently, most touch screens provided few or no accessibility features, leaving them largely unusable by blind people. However, both the blind community and technology manufacturers have made progress on this issue in recent years. At the 2009 Consumer Electronics Show, musician Stevie Wonder and a group of blind engineers took designers to task for the inaccessibility of touch screens, and encouraged them to improve touch screen accessibility for blind and visually impaired people [7]. Later that year, both Google and Apple released basic screen-reading software for their touch screen-based mobile devices, and most Google Android and Apple iOS devices now ship with screen-reading software preinstalled.

However, accessible touch screens still present challenges to both users and designers. Users must be able to learn new touch screen applications quickly and effectively, while designers must be able to implement accessible touch screen interaction techniques for a diverse range of devices and applications. Because most user interface designers are sighted, they may have a limited understanding of how blind people experience technology. We therefore argue that accessible touch screen interfaces can be improved substantially if *designers* can better understand how blind people actually use touch screens (Figure 1).

A designer who wishes to create a new accessible touch screen-based application currently faces several challenges. First, while touch screen interfaces for sighted users are largely consistent due to now-familiar gestures such as tapping, swiping, and pinching, touch screen interfaces for blind users vary widely across platforms. For example, in Apple's VoiceOver for iPhone[1], a user can browse a menu by performing a series of discrete directional flicks to move the cursor, and can select a menu item by double-tapping

[1] http://www.apple.com/accessibility/iphone/vision.html

the screen. In contrast, in Google's Eyes-Free Shell for Android[2], a user can select a menu item by holding their finger down on the screen, dragging their finger in one of 8 directions to choose the item, and then releasing their finger to select it. Both systems use completely different layouts and interaction primitives, and thus there is currently no *lingua franca* for touch screen interactions for blind people.

Second, there exist very few examples of how to extend accessible touch screen interfaces to devices other than smartphones. Touch screens may appear on devices of many different sizes, from jewelry-sized displays (*e.g.,* [3]) to wall-sized interactive installations (*e.g.,* [12]). However, most commercially available and accessible touch screen-based devices are smartphones. There still exists little information about how to best design accessible touch screen interfaces for tablets and other large touch screens.

Third, a designer who wishes to provide gestures in their application must consider whether the gestures will be appropriate for a blind user. Although blind people may use the same hardware as their sighted peers, it is possible that they will prefer to use different gestures, or that they will perform the same gestures differently than a sighted person. Sighted people perform gestures differently when they lack visual feedback [25], and it is reasonable to assume that a blind person may also perform gestures differently than a sighted person.

These challenges raise fundamental questions about how blind people use touch screens: What types of gestures are the most intuitive and easy to perform for a blind person? And if blind people perform gestures differently than sighted people, how do their gestures differ? In this paper, we address these questions through two user studies that explore how blind and sighted people interact with touch screens. First, we conducted a gesture elicitation study (see [28]) in which blind and sighted participants invented gestures for performing common computing tasks on a touch screen-based tablet PC. Second, we conducted a gesture performance study in which both blind and sighted participants repeatedly performed a set of standard gestures on a touch screen. Our results show that there are indeed differences in the types of gestures preferred by blind and sighted people, as well as differences in how gestures are performed by blind and sighted people. Based on these results, we provide suggestions for the design of future touch screen-based applications and devices for blind users.

RELATED WORK

Our research is motivated by prior attempts to create accessible touch screen user interfaces for blind people, as well as by prior studies of spatial and tactile perception in blind people. We also adopt participatory techniques from prior research to elicit participants' preferred gestures.

[2] http://code.google.com/p/eyes-free

[3] http://codefactory.es

Gesture-Based User Interfaces for Blind People

Providing blind people with access to touch screens has been a concern since the creation of the earliest touch screen systems. Buxton *et al.'s* introduction of an early touch tablet [6] was followed shortly by a panel discussing accessibility issues surrounding touch interfaces [5]. In the 1990s, the emergence of touch screen kiosks in public places such as airports and shopping malls prompted investigation of how touch screen hardware could be made more accessible (*e.g.,* [17,27]). In recent years, researchers have explored accessible interaction techniques for mobile touch screens (*e.g.,* [4,11,15,22,23]), and commercial manufacturers have begun to incorporate screen-reading software into their mobile devices (*e.g.,* VoiceOver[1], Eyes-Free Shell[2], and Mobile Speak for Windows Mobile[3]).

While some earlier systems such as the Talking Fingertip Technique [27] and the Talking Tactile Tablet [16] used physically adapted hardware, most of these systems have used software alone to enable accessible interactions on a touch screen, typically by accepting gestures as input and providing speech and audio as output. Despite the diversity of the touch screen-based devices that have been adapted for use by blind people, most of these systems have used one of a small set of underlying interaction techniques. As no formal taxonomy of these interfaces has yet been published, we refer to these techniques as *menu browsing, discrete gestures,* and *fixed regions.* These techniques are described briefly below.

Menu Browsing

In *menu browsing,* the user moves a cursor through a list of menu items and receives speech or audio feedback describing each item. The user then performs a gesture to actuate the currently selected item. The user may move the cursor through continuous touch gestures, in which the user strokes their finger across the screen to navigate the list, or by using discrete gestures or taps to move the cursor. The list of menu items typically changes based on the current application state. Menu items may be laid out spatially across the surface of the screen, either in their original arrangement or rearranged to optimize non-visual exploration. Systems that use *menu browsing* include the Talking Fingertip Technique [27], Slide Rule [15], EarPod [31], NavTouch [11], No-Look Notes [4], and VoiceOver[1].

Discrete Gestures

Other applications use a series of predefined *discrete gestures* to perform actions. Common actions are associated with a specific, predefined gesture, such as swiping one's finger in a specific direction or drawing a shape gesture. For example, swiping a finger from the top of the bottom of the screen may change the currently playing track in a touch screen-based music player. Systems that use *discrete gestures* include the Adaptive Blind Interaction Technique for Touchscreens [29], mBN [23], McGookin *et al.*'s gestural music player [19], and Eyes-Free Shell[2].

Fixed Regions

Some accessible touch screen applications map specific regions of the screen to predefined functions, as if the screen were in fact a set of discrete hardware buttons. In these applications, the user initiates an action by performing a gesture over the designated screen region. For example, a user might double tap the lower left corner of the screen to start an application. Systems that use *fixed regions* include Mobile Messenger for the Blind [22] and Mobile Speak[3].

Our research takes a technique-agnostic approach to understanding touch screen interactions for blind people. In our gesture elicitation study, participants could choose any type of gesture they wished to perform a given command. The results of this research show support for using a variety of touch screen interaction techniques.

Spatial Perception and Drawing Among Blind People

As touch screen interfaces become more common, it is important to provide equal access to these interfaces for blind people. However, in some cases, touch screen-based interfaces may in fact be preferable to interfaces that use fixed buttons, even for blind people. Prior research shows that blind people, even those who are born blind, may have substantial spatial and tactile abilities. Blind people use the regions of the brain designated for visual processing when reading Braille and performing other spatial tasks [21]. Other studies have shown that both *early-blind* (those blind at birth or at an early age) and *late-blind* people have higher tactile sensitivity in their fingers than sighted people [10,26], and that late-blind adults can trace tactile shapes faster and more accurately than sighted adults [13].

Several studies have also examined the ability of blind people to draw or trace shapes using various technologies. Kamel and Landay [14] performed a study in which blind users drew shapes using both tactile swell paper and a keyboard-driven, grid-based drawing program. Crossan and Brewster [8] combined a haptic controller with audio feedback to enable blind users to trace simple shapes.

This research confirms that blind people are capable of performing gestures and drawing shapes on a screen, and suggests that gestures may in fact be an effective interaction method for some blind people.

Participatory Design of Gestures

Another limitation of current accessible touch screens is the lack of user participation in their development. Although some researchers have incorporated user feedback into the design of accessible touch screen systems (*e.g.,* [4,15]), the resulting systems have still been largely created by their designers. However, past research has shown that users often prefer gestures that were created by groups of potential users to those created by a single designer [20]. Beaudouin-Lafon [2] and Liu *et al.* [18] each created gesture sets based on users' observed movements, and Epps *et al.* [9] elicited gestures from users by showing them images of computing tasks. Wobbrock *et al.* [28] used a participatory design approach to create a user-defined gesture set. In that study, participants were shown the outcome of an action and asked to demonstrate gestures that would accomplish that action.

The gesture elicitation study presented here is based on methods introduced by Wobbrock *et al.* [28]. However, while that study focused on visual touch screen interactions for sighted users, the current study examines gesture preferences among both blind and sighted participants.

STUDY 1: GESTURE ELICITATION

To better understand how blind people might prefer to interact with a touch screen, we conducted a study in which both blind and sighted participants were asked to invent gestures that could be used to conduct standard computing tasks on a touch screen-based tablet PC.

Participants

We recruited 10 blind people (6 female, 4 male, average age 49.0, SD=12.2) and 10 sighted people (4 female, 6 male, average age 28.8, SD=11.6) for the study. For the purposes of this research, we define blind participants as people who typically use a screen reader to access a computer. Blind participants were recruited via local blind organizations and via word of mouth. Sighted participants were recruited via local mailing lists and bulletin boards. Nine of the sighted participants and 6 of the blind participants regularly used some touch screen-based device. All of the sighted participants and 8 of the blind participants were right-handed. Three of the blind participants were early-blind and had become blind by the age of 2 years old.

Apparatus

Participants executed the experimental tasks using a 10.1-inch Lenovo S10-3t multi-touch tablet PC (Figure 2). The tablet PC ran Windows 7 and a custom C□ application that recorded all screen touches with millisecond timestamps. Touch information was stored in a JSON-formatted log file. The experimenter used a wireless keyboard to begin and end experimental trials. A video camera captured the tablet PC and the participants' hands, as well as participants' spoken comments and think-aloud data.

Procedure

The study protocol was based upon the user-defined gesture study by Wobbrock *et al.* [28], but was modified to be used with both blind and sighted participants. Participants were seated at a desk in front of the tablet PC. The tablet PC was initialized to a blank screen, and participants were introduced to the device. Blind participants were given an opportunity to touch the screen and bezel in order to orient themselves. Sighted participants were shown that the screen tracked touches and visualized them as trails on the screen.

Once participants were ready to proceed, the experimenter began the session. At this point the application's blank screen was replaced by a "shapes world" containing labeled squares and circles. This neutral layout was chosen, as in Wobbrock *et al.* [28], to remind participants that they were not creating gestures for any specific operating system or application. The shapes on the screen provided both visual and audio feedback: for example, touching a square would cause the program to speak the word "square," and a white noise loop played while the participant held his or her finger over the shape.

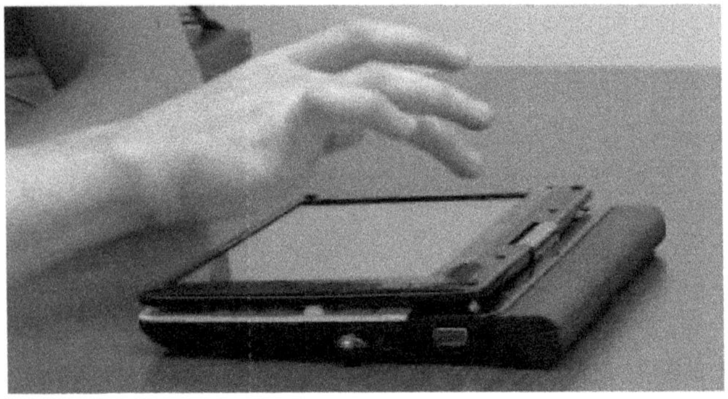

Figure 2. A participant performs an experimental task using the tablet PC.

The experimenter informed participants that their task was to invent gestures that could be used to execute a set of computing commands. Commands were derived from Wobbrock *et al.* [28] and Morris *et al.* [20]. However, commands that had a primarily visual function (*e.g.*, enlarge, zoom in) were replaced by commands that applied to both visual and non-visual interfaces (*e.g.*, move up in hierarchy). The commands used in the study were: *menu, help, undo, task switch, move down in hierarchy, move up in hierarchy, previous page, next page, accept, reject, move object, open, close, duplicate, delete, cut, paste, select single, select group, move insertion point, select text range,* and *enter text.*

Because showing the outcome of the command visually would not be accessible to all participants, the experimenter read a standardized description that described the *outcome* of the command. For example, for the *next page* command, the participant was told: "Next page. You move from the current page of content to the next page." Commands were presented to each participant in random order.

For each trial, the experimenter read the description for the command. The participant was then asked to invent 2 different gestures that could initiate the command, and to think aloud while doing so. Once the participant decided upon a gesture, they described the gesture verbally to the experimenter and demonstrated it 3 times using the tablet PC's touch screen. Once the participant had demonstrated the 2 gestures that they had invented, the experimenter prompted them to rate each of the gestures using scales from Wobbrock *et al.* [28]. The first scale, referred to here as *good match*, read: "The gesture I picked is a good match for its intended purpose." The second scale, referred to here as *easiness*, read: "The gesture I picked is easy to perform." Both questions used Likert-type scales that ranged from 1 (strongly disagree) to 7 (strongly agree).

Results

Each participant invented 2 gestures for each of the 22 commands. We collected a total of $20 \times 22 \times 2 = 880$ gestures. In this section we analyze differences between the gestures invented by blind participants and the gestures invented by sighted participants, including participants' preferred methods for entering text on a touch screen.

Gesture Ratings

For the *good match* question, blind participants gave the gestures they created an average score of 5.54 (SD=1.15), and sighted participants gave the gestures they created an average score of 5.15 (SD=1.42). For the *easiness* question, blind participants gave their gestures an average score of 5.77 (SD=1.15), while sighted participants gave their gestures an average score of 5.72 (SD=1.39). Logistic regression showed that blind participants rated the gestures they created as significantly better on the *good match* question ($\chi^2_{(1,N=880)}=13.69$, $p<.001$). There was no significant difference between the two groups on the *easiness* question ($\chi^2_{(1,N=880)}=0.23$, *n.s.*).

Gesture Properties

We examined differences in the properties of the gestures invented by blind and sighted participants, including the total number of strokes, the location of the gesture, and the use of multi-touch.

Stroke count. On average, blind participants' gestures used 1.52 (SD=0.75) strokes and sighted participants' gestures used 1.24 (SD=0.46) strokes. A Wilcoxon rank-sum test revealed that blind participants' gestures contained significantly more strokes ($Z=5.63$, $N=880$, $p<.0001$).

Location. We analyzed whether participants' gestures used either an edge or corner of the screen. Of the 880 gestures produced, 113 (12.8%) used an edge and 213 (24.2%) used a corner. Of these, blind people invented 69 (61.1%) of the edge gestures and 138 (64.8%) of the corner gestures. A Chi-Square test showed that blind people were more likely to choose gestures that used the edge ($\chi^2_{(1,N=880)}=6.35$, $p<.05$) or corner ($\chi^2_{(1,N=880)}=24.58$, $p<.0001$).

Multi-touch. Of the 880 gestures, 270 (30.7%) used at least two simultaneous contact points at some point during the gesture. Blind participants invented 166 (61.5%) of these multi-touch gestures. A Chi-Square test showed that blind participants were significantly more likely than sighted participants to invent multi-touch gestures ($\chi^2_{(1,N=880)}=20.54$, $p<.0001$). Although both blind and sighted participants invented multi-touch gestures, the groups used multi-touch differently, and many of the multi-touch gestures invented by blind participants were different than the multi-touch gestures used in current gesture-based user interfaces. In particular, many of the multi-touch gestures performed by blind participants involved a virtual mode key, in which the participant held one finger down on a specific area of the screen while performing the gesture with a second finger or hand. While thinking aloud, some blind participants justified the first touch as a way to reduce potential conflicts between gestures. This use of a mode key was common among blind participants: 63 of the gestures invented by blind participants during the study used a mode key to activate the gesture, while only 10 of the gestures invented by sighted people used a mode key.

Gesture Nature and Rationale

We identified participants' rationale for the gestures that they created by analyzing their think-aloud comments and gesture descriptions. We classified gesture rationale using the *nature* dimension from Wobbrock *et al.*'s taxonomy of gestures [28]. Gesture nature considers a gesture's underlying explanation as either *symbolic* ("gesture visually depicts a symbol"), *physical* ("gesture acts physically on objects"), *metaphorical* ("gesture indicates a metaphor"), or *abstract* ("gesture-referent mapping is arbitrary"). We assigned a nature to each gesture produced during the gesture elicitation study. Figure 3 shows the gesture natures produced during this study.

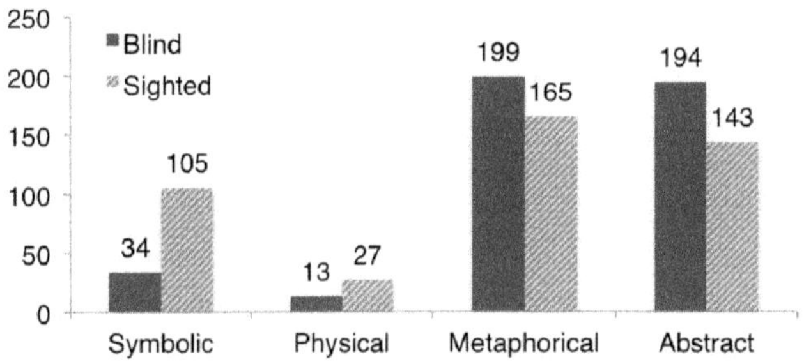

Figure 3. Gesture rationale for each subject group as described using gesture nature.

A Chi-Square test showed a significant difference between gesture natures assigned by blind and sighted participants ($\chi^2_{(3,N=880)}$=52.06, p<.0001). Examining the results more closely, we note a higher number of symbolic gestures invented by sighted participants, and a higher number of abstract and metaphorical gestures invented by blind participants. Within these categories, participants in both groups provided similar explanations for their gestures, with one notable exception: 95 of the metaphorical gestures produced by blind participants involved an interaction in which the participant touched areas of the screen in a way that was analogous to pressing keys on a physical keyboard. For example, one participant demonstrated the paste command with a CONTROL-V gesture, in which she tapped an area of the screen near where the CONTROL key would be on a QWERTY keyboard, and then tapped an area of the screen near where the V key would be. These keyboard metaphors accounted for 21.6% of the gestures invented by blind participants during the study, and were used at least once by 9 of the 10 blind participants. Of the 9 blind participants who used such a gesture, 5 regularly used some touch screen-based device, suggesting that this idea was popular even among participants who were familiar with traditional touch screen interfaces. No sighted participants performed gestures based on a physical keyboard layout.

Preferences for Text Entry

We included the *enter text* command in this study to elicit ideas about how a user might enter text using a touch screen. We were particularly interested in suggestions for text entry methods from blind participants, as entering text without visual feedback can be slow and laborious. Participants offered the following ideas for entering text:

- *On-screen QWERTY keyboard:* suggested by 7 blind and 9 sighted participants;
- *Handwriting:* Suggested by 2 blind and 3 sighted participants;
- *Perkins Braille:* Two blind participants suggested using the multi-touch screen to enter Braille using the Perkins technique, a two-handed chording technique used on physical Braille typewriters;
- *T9*[3]*:* Two blind participants suggested using the T9 predictive text method found on 12-key phone keypads.

Methods suggested by only one participant were: tapping out the dots of Braille characters, an on-screen Dvorak keyboard, Graffiti, and ShapeWriter (*a.k.a.* SHARK) [30]. Although participants were asked to keep an open mind and be creative, 10 participants were unable to invent a second text entry method, and instead chose an alternative form of their original method. Of these participants, 9 chose a variation of QWERTY and 1 chose a variation of T9.

STUDY 2: GESTURE PERFORMANCE

The gesture elicitation study provided us with new insight about the types of gestures that blind people may wish to perform. However, the open-ended nature of the study made it difficult to ascertain whether blind people and sighted people actually perform gestures differently, or whether they simply prefer different types of gestures. To determine if there were significant differences in how blind and sighted people performed the *same* gestures, we conducted a second study in which all participants performed the same set of standard gestures.

Participants and Apparatus

This study featured the same participants as the previous gesture elicitation study. Participants used the same Lenovo tablet PC and logging software as the previous study. The tablet PC ran the same logging application, which recorded all contacts with millisecond timestamps. During each trial, the application initially showed a blank screen, and drew trails that visualized the user's touches on the screen.

Procedure

The experimental procedure was similar to the gesture elicitation study. However, instead of inventing new gestures, participants performed specific gestures as specified by the experimenter. For each gesture, the experimenter read the name and a brief description of the gesture. The participant was given a chance to practice the

[4] http://www.tegic.com

gesture once on the touch screen. Once the participant had practiced the gesture, they performed the gesture 3 times, and each trial was recorded in the log file. After completing each gesture, the participant rated the gesture using a variation of the *easiness* scale from the first study: "The gesture is easy to perform." (1 = strongly disagree, 7 = strongly agree).

For this study, we chose 40 gestures that represented common interactions on current touch screen platforms, and which included unistroke, multi-stroke, and multi-touch gestures. Gestures were divided into 5 categories: *tap* (taps in various locations on screen), *flick* (directional swiping gestures), *multi-touch* gestures, *shape* (simple geometric shapes), and *symbol* (letters, numbers, and other symbols). The following categories and gestures were used:

- *Tap:* single tap center, single tap left, single tap right, single tap top, single tap bottom, single tap top left, single tap top right, single tap bottom left, single tap bottom right, double tap, triple tap;
- *Flick:* flick left, flick right, flick up, flick down;
- *Multi-touch:* 2-finger pinch, 2-finger spread apart, 2-finger rotate clockwise, 2-finger rotate counterclockwise;
- *Shape:* square, circle, triangle;
- *Symbol:* A, B, C, D, E, F, L, X, Z, 1, 2, 3, 4, 5, question mark, check mark, 5-pointed star, scratch out.

The gesture set contained some symbols used in printed English writing, including the numbers 1 through 5 and the letters A through F, L, X, and Z. Although many blind people do not typically use handwriting, and thus may be unfamiliar with these symbols, we chose to include the symbols to increase the overall number of glyph-like gestures, as well as to explore how familiar blind people actually are with these symbols. Participants were allowed to skip a gesture if they were not familiar with it.

Results

Gestures Collected

Each participant was asked to perform 40 gestures 3 times each, for a total of 40 × 3 × 20 = 2400 gestures performed. However, 2 blind participants skipped a total of 15 gestures because they were unfamiliar with the gesture. One participant skipped *A, E, 2, 4, 5, check mark,* and *5-pointed star*, while the other skipped *B, Z, 2, 3, 4, 5, question mark,* and *5-pointed star.* In addition, 20 gestures were not accurately captured by the touch screen, leaving a total of 2335 recorded gesture instances and 785 gesture ratings.

Gesture Ratings

Participants rated each of the gestures in terms of *easiness*. Overall, blind participants gave the gestures they performed an average score of 5.71 (SD=1.55), while sighted participants gave the gestures they performed an average score of 5.76 (SD=1.28). Ratings by gesture category are shown in Figure 4. Logistic regression showed no significant effects of blindness ($\chi^2_{(1,N=785)}$=2.70, *n.s.*) on *easiness*. However, there was a significant effect of gesture category ($\chi^2_{(4,N=785)}$=68.85, p<.0001) on *easiness*, which shows that participants' ratings were influenced by the gesture category. There was also a significant interaction between blindness and gesture category ($\chi^2_{(4,N=785)}$=18.61, p<.001), indicating that a gesture's category affected its rating differently for blind and sighted participants.

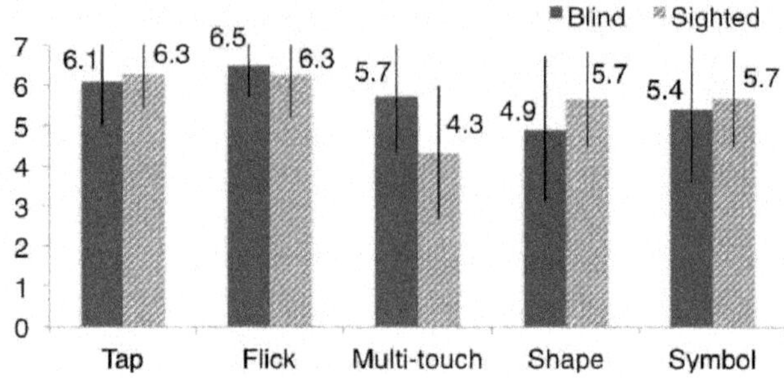

Figure 4. Participants' *easiness* ratings by gesture category. Error bars indicate ±1 SD.

Gesture Properties

In addition to soliciting ratings for each gesture, we examined various properties of the gestures that participants performed to determine whether there were significant differences in how blind and sighted people performed the same gestures.

Size. We measured the overall size of each gesture using the area of the bounding box for that gesture. The average size of gestures produced by blind participants was 165.82 (SD=136.89) pixels^2, while the average size of gestures produced by sighted participants was 148.05 (SD=120.68) pixels^2. A Wilcoxon rank-sum test found a significant difference in the size of gestures produced by blind and sighted participants (Z=3.20, N=2335, p<.01), indicating that blind participants tended to create significantly larger gestures than sighted participants.

Size variation. In addition to calculating gesture size, we also examined the size variation between multiple instances of the same gesture created by a single participant. We calculated size variation using the standard deviation of the gesture size for a given participant and gesture. This standard deviation averaged 20.43 (SD=23.38) pixels^2 for blind participants and 13.59 (SD=18.44) pixels^2 for sighted participants. There was a significant difference in the standard deviation of sizes between blind and sighted participants (Z=5.32, N=780, p<.001), indicating that blind participants produced gestures with greater variation in size when performing the same gesture multiple times.

Aspect ratio. We calculated the aspect ratio of each gesture's bounding box (width/height). The average aspect ratio for blind participants was 1.64 (SD=3.73), and the average aspect ratio for sighted participants was 1.44 (SD=3.45), suggesting that blind participants tended to create wider gestures. However, when examining all gestures performed in the study, we found no significant difference in the aspect ratio of gestures produced by blind and sighted participants (Z=1.75, N=2335, p=.08, *n.s.*). Looking specifically at gestures in which participants drew some glyph (*i.e., shape* and *symbol* gestures), we did find that blind participants drew significantly wider gestures than sighted participants (Z=3.87, N=1213, p<.0001).

Speed. On average, blind participants performed gestures in 925.90 (SD=1110.22) milliseconds, while sighted participants performed gestures in 462.58 (SD=477.24) milliseconds. This difference was significant (Z=10.96, N=2335, p<.0001), showing that, on average, blind participants took approximately twice as long to perform the same gestures.

Analysis of Specific Gesture Features

In addition to the aforementioned properties, we were interested in some specific issues that had been observed during our pilot testing. Because these issues did not apply across all gestures, we examined these features using specific subsets of the gesture set, rather than the entire set.

Location accuracy. In general, participants were able to perform gestures at any location on the screen. However, nine gestures in the *tap* category referred to specific screen locations, including the corners, edges, and center. For these gestures, we calculated the distance between the centroid of the performed gesture and the specified screen location. For blind participants, the average distance from the specified location was 110.97 (SD=50.28) pixels. The average distance for sighted participants was 48.84 (SD=18.35) pixels. Blind participants had a significantly greater offset than sighted participants (Z=-15.52, N=528, p<.0001). During the study, some blind participants mentioned that it was difficult to target locations that were away from the screen corners. Looking only at gestures in which participants tapped the corners, we found that blind people's gestures were still farther from the intended targets than sighted people's gestures (Z=-9.82, N=233, p<.0001).

Form closure. Another issue that we observed during initial testing was the difficulty of connecting the various parts of a gesture without visual feedback. However, it is difficult to operationalize this feature for an arbitrary gesture, as different gestures connect in different ways.

To examine this issue quantitatively, we measured its effects on the *circle* gesture alone. We chose the circle gesture because it was likely to be completed in a single stroke, and because the start point and end points coincide in its canonical form. For the purposes of this analysis, we defined the metric *form closure distance* as the Cartesian distance between the circle's start point and end point. For blind participants, the average form closure distance was 149.12 (SD=84.00) pixels, while for sighted participants this distance was 67.12 (SD=94.59) pixels. A Wilcoxon rank-sum test revealed that this difference was statistically significant (Z=4.47, N=60, p<.0001). This suggests that gestures created by blind people were more likely to have start and end points that did not coincide (Figure 5).

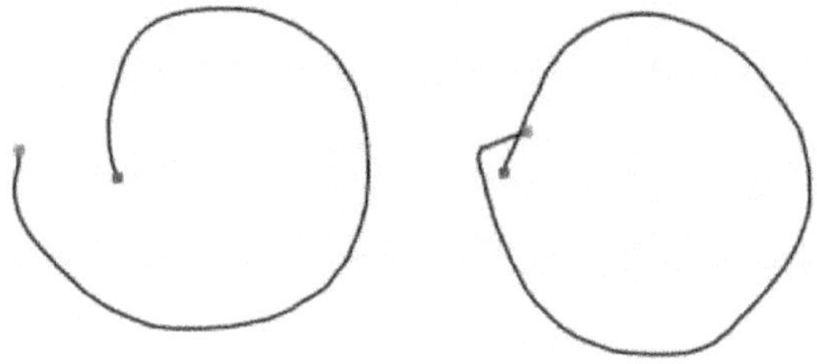

Figure 5. Two *circle* gestures drawn by a blind participant with high form closure distance, *i.e.*, a large distance between the start and end points.

Line steadiness. During pilot testing, we noted that the lines of some blind participants' gestures seemed to be less steady or more "wavy" than those created by sighted participants. Prior studies have attempted to quantify the steadiness of a gesture by measuring parameters of a single specific gesture, such as angular deviation when drawing a straight line or eccentricity from a reference shape (*e.g.*, [24]). However, these approaches are limited to specific gestures and do not generalize. Furthermore, because participants in this study could not see a reference shape on screen, matching their gestures to a reference shape would be inappropriate.

Figure 6. Lines drawn by blind participants tended to be less steady (left) than lines drawn by sighted participants (right).

To model this waviness quantitatively, we introduce a generalizable stability metric for drawn gestures, the *average angular acceleration* metric, shown in Equation 1.

$$A = \frac{\sum_p \frac{d\omega}{dt}}{|p|} \tag{1}$$

The average angular acceleration metric is defined as the sum of the angular acceleration over the course of the gesture, divided by the length of the gesture in points. This metric approximately measures how much the path changes direction over the course of the entire gesture. For example, a gesture that is drawn in a wavy or jagged fashion will continually be changing direction, and thus will have a higher average angular acceleration value. Figure 6 shows a wavy gesture with high average angular acceleration and a steady gesture with low average angular acceleration.

Note that this metric is not appropriate for comparing between different gestures, as each gesture requires a different amount of angular movement to be drawn correctly. However, examining different participants as they perform the same gesture allows us to approximate the overall steadiness or waviness of their lines using this measure. For demonstration, we calculated this value for the *square* gesture only. For blind participants, the average angular acceleration was 0.47 (SD=0.26), while for sighted participants the average angular acceleration was 0.06 (SD=0.13). This difference was statistically significant (Z=5.27, N=60, p<.0001).

Gesture Recognition Accuracy

We have described a number of differences in how blind people and sighted people perform gestures. It seems likely that these differences would also affect gesture recognition accuracy for gestures performed by a blind person. To explore this question, we compared gesture recognition results for a subset of the gestures collected in this study.

We used the $N multi-stroke recognizer [1] to recognize gestures. We analyzed only gestures from the *shape* and *symbol* categories, as many gesture recognizers, including $N, are designed to handle glyph gestures such as these, but not taps or directional flicks. For each of the *shape* and *symbol* gestures collected in this study, we performed a recognition test using 3 sets of gestures: (1) all other *shape* and *symbol* gestures created by that participant, (2) *shape* and *symbol* gestures created by blind participants, and (3) *shape* and *symbol* gestures created by sighted participants. For (2) and (3), the creator of the gesture being tested was excluded from the set. Recognition was considered correct if the correct gesture was the top recognition result.

Table 1 summarizes the results of this analysis. A Chi-Square test revealed that gestures from sighted participants were significantly more likely to be recognized correctly ($\chi^2_{(1,N=3624)}$=56.19, p<.001). Recognition accuracy also differed based on the recognizer's training set. For sighted participants, recognition accuracy was higher when tested against gestures from other sighted participants than when tested against gestures from blind participants ($\chi^2_{(1,N=1250)}$=35.96, p<.0001). Surprisingly, recognition accuracy was also higher for blind participants when tested against sighted gestures ($\chi^2_{(1,N=1166)}$=7.33, p<.01). This result seems counterintuitive, as we would expect that a blind person's gestures would be more similar to gestures from other blind people, and thus that recognition accuracy would be higher when the recognizer was trained with blind gestures. A closer examination reveals that recognition accuracy for blind participants' *symbol* gestures was much higher when tested against sighted gestures than when tested against other blind gestures. This difference may be due to blind participants' unfamiliarity with some of the *symbol* gestures. Because these gestures were less familiar to the blind participants, there may have been greater variation in how they were performed. Thus, *symbol* gestures performed by blind people may have been better matched to sighted participants' gestures because the sighted gestures were internally consistent, even if they differed from blind participants' gestures in other ways. However, this explanation is merely speculative, and further work is needed to understand the effects of blind people's gesture performance on recognition accuracy.

	vs. Self	*vs.* Blind	*vs.* Sighted
Symbol gestures by blind	68.2% (46.6)	52.0% (50.0)	61.3% (48.7)
Shape gestures by blind	59.6% (49.4)	44.9% (50.0)	44.9% (50.0)
Symbol gestures by sighted	72.5% (44.7)	63.2% (48.3)	78.7% (41.0)
Shape gestures by sighted	68.9% (46.6)	57.8% (49.7)	73.3% (44.5)

Table 1. Each gesture was tested against (1) the participant's other gestures, (2) blind gestures, and (3) sighted gestures. Table cells report mean and SD recognition accuracy.

DISCUSSION

The overarching goal of this research is to set future directions for the design of touch screen applications, and to promote accessible touch screen interaction techniques that work equally well for both blind and sighted people. The studies described here address two primary questions: first, given the choice, would blind people prefer to perform different gestures than sighted people? Second, do blind people perform gestures differently than sighted people even when performing the same gestures?

In response to the first question, we discovered significant differences in the gestures chosen by blind and sighted participants. Blind participants in our study showed strong preferences for gestures that used screen corners, edges, and multi-touch. Furthermore, when asked to invent gestures, blind participants in our study adopted two techniques that are rare in most current touch screen user interfaces: using a second finger or hand to begin a mode, and touching areas of the screen that correspond to keys on a QWERTY keyboard. These gestures were used by a majority of blind participants in our study, including participants who had experience with other touch screen-based devices. While it remains to be seen whether these gestures would be useful or efficient in a real world application, their popularity in this study suggests that they may have potential.

In answering the second question, we uncovered a number of performance characteristics that differentiate gestures produced by blind people from those produced by sighted people. Gestures produced by blind participants were larger, slower, and featured greater variation in size than those produced by sighted participants. Although some of these differences may seem intuitive, identifying these differences in real performance data, and quantifying them, deepens our understanding of how blind people perform gestures. We have identified several important metrics related to gesture performance by blind people, including location accuracy, form closure, and line steadiness. These factors have a significant impact on how gestures drawn by blind people may look different than those drawn by sighted people, and to our knowledge this is the first time these features have been discussed and measured in relation to how blind people perform gestures.

A relevant outcome of the second study is that some blind participants did not know how to perform some of the gestures used in our protocol, including letters, numbers, and other symbols. Even some blind participants who knew these symbols sometimes pointed out that other blind people might not know them. This is not surprising when we consider that many blind people have never learned how to print, but it is an important and non-obvious consideration when choosing gestures for an application.

Design Guidelines for Accessible Touch Screens

Based on the results of these two studies, we offer preliminary advice on how to design future touch screen-based applications for both blind and sighted users:

Avoid symbols used in print writing. Blind users may have limited knowledge of symbols used in print writing, such as letters, numbers, or punctuation. Even when these symbols are known, users may not be used to them or may not be comfortable performing them. If performing symbol-based gestures is an important part of the user experience, the user should be trained in how to perform these gestures or should be able to choose alternative gestures.

Favor edges, corners, and other landmarks. Locating precise spots on the touch screen surface can be very difficult for a user who cannot see the screen. The physical edges and corners of a touch screen are useful landmarks for a blind person. Placing critical functions in these areas will improve accessibility and reduce the likelihood that the user will trigger these functions accidentally.

Reduce demand for location accuracy. Blind users may be less precise in targeting specific areas of the screen, including edges and corners. This problem can be reduced by increasing target size or by allowing approximate targeting methods, such as allowing a user to touch near a target and then explore with their finger to locate it more precisely.

Limit time-based gesture processing. Blind people may perform gestures at a different pace than sighted people. Thus, using the gesture's speed as a recognition feature or as a parameter (as in kinetic scrolling) may result in increased errors for blind users.

Reproduce traditional spatial layouts when possible. Objects with familiar spatial and tactile layouts, such as a QWERTY keyboard or telephone keypad, are instantly familiar to many blind people. Reproducing these layouts may make it easier for a blind person to learn and use a new interface.

FUTURE WORK

The present work has uncovered several promising directions for creating new accessible interaction techniques for touch screens. In particular, the QWERTY keyboard-like interaction technique was very popular among our blind participants, and thus merits further investigation. In addition, our participants suggested a number of possible avenues for improving text entry on a flat touch screen, including handwriting Braille characters, using the Perkins Braille chording technique, or using variations of a telephone keypad. These techniques may hold promise for both blind people and sighted people in eyes-free situations.

A second area of opportunity is in improving gesture recognition accuracy for blind people. Our results show that blind participants experienced significantly reduced gesture recognition accuracy when using a traditional recognizer even when the recognizer was trained with gestures from other blind participants. We envision several possibilities for improving gesture recognition accuracy for blind people, such as by preprocessing blind users' gestures before recognition, creating a modified gesture recognizer for blind gestures, or identifying a subset of gestures that can be recognized reliably when performed by blind people.

CONCLUSION

In this paper, we explored two issues related to the design of touch screen user interfaces for blind people. First, we examined blind and sighted participants' preferences for gesture-based commands on a tablet PC by asking them to invent their own gestures. We found that blind participants did in fact suggest gestures that were different than those suggested by sighted people. Blind participants favored gestures that occurred on the edges of the screen, and suggested new gestures that utilized spatial layouts that were familiar to them. Second, we examined differences in how blind and sighted people perform the same set of gestures, and presented metrics for describing how gestures produced by blind people differ from gestures produced by sighted people.

As touch screens are now one of the most common ways of interacting with computers, it is not only important that blind people can access touch screens, but also that they can do so effectively and efficiently. The present work provides new information about how blind people currently think about interacting with a touch screen, and about how they perform gestures on a touch screen as compared to a sighted person. We believe that this work will bring us closer to the creation of robust and usable touch screen interfaces that work equally well for blind and sighted people.

ACKNOWLEDGEMENTS

We thank Nicole Torcolini for her valuable feedback. This work was supported in part by National Science Foundation grant IIS-0811063. Any opinions, findings, conclusions or recommendations expressed in this work are those of the authors and do not necessarily reflect those of the National Science Foundation.

REFERENCES

1. Anthony, L. and Wobbrock, J.O. A lightweight multistroke recognizer for user interface prototypes. *Proc. GI '10,* Canadian Information Processing Society (2010), 245-252.
2. Baudel, T. and Beaudouin-Lafon, M. Charade: Remote control of objects using free-hand gestures. *Communications of the ACM 36,* 7 (1993), 28-35.
3. Baudisch, P. and Chu, G. Back-of-device interaction allows creating very small touch devices. *Proc. CHI '09,* ACM (2009), 1923-1932.
4. Bonner, M., Brudvik, J., Abowd, G. and Edwards, W.K. No-Look Notes: Accessible eyes-free multi-touch text entry. *Proc. Pervasive '10,* Springer (2010), 409-427.
5. Buxton, W., Foulds, R., Rosen, M., Scadden, L. and Shein, F. Human interface design and the handicapped user. *SIGCHI Bulletin 17,* 4 (1986), 291-297.
6. Buxton, W., Hill, R. and Rowley, P. Issues and techniques in touch-sensitive tablet input. *Proc. SIGGRAPH '85,* ACM (1985), 215-224.
7. Crew, S. Touch-screen gadgets alienate blind. *Reuters,* January 8, 2009.
8. Crossan, A. and Brewster, S. Multimodal trajectory playback for teaching shape information and trajectories to visually impaired computer users. *ACM TACCESS 1,* 2 (2008), 1-34.
9. Epps, J., Lichman, S. and Wu, M. A study of hand shape use in tabletop gesture interaction. *CHI '06 Extended Abstracts,* ACM (2006), 748-753.
10. Goldreich, D. and Kanics, I.M. Tactile acuity is enhanced in blindness. *Journal of Neuroscience 23,* 8 (2003), 3439-3445.
11. Guerreiro, T., Lagoa, P., Nicolau, H., Gonalves, D. and Jorge, J. From tapping to touching: Making touch screens accessible to blind users. *IEEE Multimedia 15,* 4 (2008), 48-50.
12. Guimbretière, F., Stone, M. and Winograd, T. Fluid interaction with high-resolution wall-size displays. *Proc. UIST '01,* ACM (2001), 21-30.
13. Heller, M.A., Wilson, K., Steffen, H., Yoneyama, K. and Brackett, D.D. Superior haptic perceptual selectivity in late-blind and very-low-vision subjects. *Perception 32,* 4 (2003), 499-511.
14. Kamel, H.M. and Landay, J.A. A study of blind drawing practice: Creating graphical information without the visual channel. *Proc. ASSETS '00,* ACM (2000), 34-41.
15. Kane, S.K., Bigham, J.P. and Wobbrock, J.O. Slide Rule: Making mobile touch screens accessible to blind people using multi-touch interaction techniques. *Proc. ASSETS '08,* ACM (2008), 73-80.
16. Landau, S. and Wells, L. Merging tactile sensory input and audio data by means of the Talking Tactile Tablet. *Proc. Eurohaptics '03,* (2003), 414–418.
17. Law, C. and Vanderheiden, G. The development of a simple, low cost set of universal access features for electronic devices. *Proc. CUU '00,* ACM (2000), 118.
18. Liu, J., Pinelle, D., Sallam, S., Subramanian, S. and Gutwin, C. TNT: Improved rotation and translation on digital tables. *Proc. GI '06,* Canadian Information Processing Society (2006), 25-32.
19. McGookin, D., Brewster, S. and Jiang, W. Investigating touchscreen accessibility for people with visual impairments. *Proc. NordiCHI '08,* ACM (2008), 298-307.
20. Morris, M.R., Wobbrock, J.O. and Wilson, A.D. Understanding users' preferences for surface gestures. *Proc. GI '10,* Canadian Information Processing Society (2010), 261-268.
21. Sadato, N., Pascual-Leone, A., Grafman, J., Ibanez, V., Deiber, M.P., Dold, G. and Hallett, M. Activation of the primary visual cortex by Braille reading in blind subjects. *Nature 380,* 6574 (1996), 526–528.
22. Sánchez, J. and Aguayo, F. Mobile messenger for the blind. *Proc. ECRIM '06,* Springer (2006), 369-385.
23. Sánchez, J. and Maureira, E. Subway mobility assistance tools for blind users. Proc. ECRIM '06, Springer (2006), 386-404.
24. Stößel, C., Wandke, H. and Blessing, L. Gestural interfaces for elderly users: Help or hindrance? *Gesture in Embodied Communication and Human-Computer Interaction,* Springer (2010), 269-280.
25. Tinwala, H. and MacKenzie, I.S. Eyes-free text entry with error correction on touchscreen mobile devices. *Proc. NordiCHI '10,* ACM (2010), 511–520.
26. Van Boven, R., Hamilton, R., Kauffman, T., Keenan, J. and Pascual-Leone, A. Tactile spatial resolution in blind Braille readers. *Neurology,* 54 (2000), 2230-2236.
27. Vanderheiden, G.C. Use of audio-haptic interface techniques to allow nonvisual access to touchscreen appliances. *Proc. HFES 40,* (1996), 1266.
28. Wobbrock, J.O., Morris, M.R. and Wilson, A.D. User-defined gestures for surface computing. *Proc. CHI '09,* ACM (2009), 1083-1092.
29. Yfantidis, G. and Evreinov, G. Adaptive blind interaction technique for touchscreens. *Universal Access in the Information Society,* 4 (2006), 328-337.
30. Zhai, S. and Kristensson, P. Shorthand writing on stylus keyboard. *Proc. CHI '03,* ACM (2003), 97-104.
31. Zhao, S., Dragicevic, P., Chignell, M., Balakrishnan, R. and Baudisch, P. EarPod: Eyes-free menu selection using touch input and reactive audio feedback. *Proc. CHI '07,* ACM (2007), 1395-1404.

Fit4Life: The Design of a Persuasive Technology Promoting Healthy Behavior and Ideal Weight

Stephen Purpura[*1], Victoria Schwanda[*1], Kaiton Williams[*1], William Stubler[+], Phoebe Sengers[*]
[*]Information Science [+]Electrical and Computer Engineering
Cornell University
301 College Ave., Ithaca, NY 14850
{sp559, vls48, kow2, wgs38, pjs54}@cornell.edu

ABSTRACT
This is a critical design paper offering a possible scenario of use intended to provoke reflection about values and politics of design in persuasive computing. We describe the design of a system—Fit4Life—that encourages individuals to address the larger goal of reducing obesity in society by promoting individual healthy behaviors. Using the Persuasive Systems Design Model [26], this paper outlines the Fit4Life persuasion context, the technology, its use of persuasive messages, and an experimental design to test the system's efficacy. We also contribute a novel discussion of the ethical and sociocultural considerations involved in our design, an issue that has remained largely unaddressed in the existing persuasive technologies literature [29].

Author Keywords
Persuasive technology, weight loss, social implications, critical design.

ACM Classification Keywords
K.4.0 Computers and Society: General. H.5.2 [Information Interfaces and Presentation (e.g. HCI)]: User Interfaces – theory and methods, user-centered design.

General Terms
Design, Human Factors, Measurement.

INTRODUCTION
The American population is fat. In 1994 more than 54% of adults had a body mass index (BMI) that qualified as overweight or obese [13]. By 2006 this number had skyrocketed to almost 73% [2]. This statistic is alarming, as obesity has been linked to many health problems, several of which can be reduced by a 5-15% weight loss [3].

Americans have not ignored the obesity epidemic; millions are trying to lose weight [1]. In 2000 this was true of 46% of American women and 33% of American men [8]. Despite the existence of a simple equation for weight loss—consume fewer calories than you burn—the North American weight loss industry amasses an estimated $50 billion in revenue every year [4]. The industry as a whole promotes a number of weight loss measures, from diet pills through strict diet and exercise regimes to hypnosis. However, Weight Watchers is the only commercial program shown to be effective in a controlled trial [1] and American waistlines are still on the rise.

To address this problem we have designed a new weight loss technology, Fit4Life. Our system design is based on a number of the literature-supported principles seen in existing weight loss programs, including mechanisms to track calorie consumption and exercise activity along with a social networking component where people can celebrate their success and receive motivation when they find themselves failing. We also address the primary reasons attributed to the failure of existing programs: that people are required to spend too much time tracking their diet and exercise, and that they have the ability to not participate fully by not tracking all food or not following an exercise plan. The key innovation in our approach follows from persuasive technology literature where human behavior is often considered the weak link in accomplishing a greater goal [29]; we use this literature to inform the selection of methods to convince people to develop healthier behaviors.

We begin by describing the literature on behavioral weight loss methods and their lack of effectiveness. Next, we use the Persuasive System Design (PSD) Model framework to present the Fit4Life system as a solution to these behavioral treatment failures. We then present our directions for future work and discuss the ethical and sociocultural considerations involved in the Fit4Life system design.

WEIGHT LOSS METHODS
After making the decision to lose weight, one is faced with many methods that promise to help shed unwanted pounds. The majority of these programs attempt to alter diet and exercise behavior in order to achieve weight loss. The prevalence of these behavior-oriented programs is justified by studies that show participants enrolled in structured behavioral treatments lose significantly more weight than those who use self-help resources [18, 28].

[1] Purpura, Schwanda and Williams are co-first authors.

Behavioral Weight Loss Principles and Effectiveness

Behavioral treatments were first introduced in the 1970s and represented a conceptual landmark in obesity treatment [20]. Researchers promoting these approaches argue that the most effective way to change diet and exercise is by changing environmental factors. Factors to be changed can either precede behavior (e.g. restricting types of food available, prompting exercise by placing sneakers close to a door) or be in the form of positive or negative consequences of behavior (e.g. receiving points for healthy behaviors, social criticism for unhealthy behaviors).

While these behavioral change programs are more effective than self-help programs, they result in a mean loss of less than 5% of initial weight [1]. Weight loss success is usually defined as a 10% weight loss [19], so these programs are arguably unsuccessful. Even within the small number of participants who achieve a 10% weight loss, one study showed that after four years participants' weight was only 4% below their baseline [19]. Failure in these behavioral change programs is almost always cited as resulting from participants' inability to follow the prescribed diet and exercise changes [15].

Behavioral Weight Loss Technology

We analyzed 33 technology-based behavioral change programs for weight loss to determine how these programs enact the literature described above[2]. These programs vary in type of behavior change promoted (e.g. eating behavior, exercise behavior, or both), and the medium used (e.g. online, offline, mobile phone, a combination of the above), but are overwhelming similar in their methods.

Most of the programs include an initial assessment where participants enter their weight, height, age and gender to determine their starting BMI. Next, the programs require a goal such as desired weight or number of fitness minutes per week to be set. All of the 33 programs use a tracking paradigm to promote behavior change, requiring participants to record fitness minutes, caloric intake, and/or weight. A few of these programs also include tidbits such as inspirational quotes and articles about success stories or how to avoid common pitfalls, often addressing the change of environmental factors preceding behavior. Some programs include community-based components such as forum boards and groups where participants can communicate and set group goals. Many of the programs also send emails to participants to encourage them to continue with the program. One particular program also uses points to encourage diet and exercise behavior.

A PERSUASIVE TECHNOLOGY APPROACH

We believe that these programs fail in two broad ways: 1) by placing the burden of tracking on the participant and therefore contradicting the behavioral treatment principle of requiring less effort and 2) by allowing the participant to choose which information is "front stage" (what they do report) and which information is "backstage" (what they do not report) and therefore undermining the program's ability to provide consequences and rewards to the participant.

Fit4Life addresses these problems by capitalizing on three strategies from the persuasive literature. First, we are motivated by [9] to design technology for people's everyday lives. Second, we are motivated by [14] to encourage new behaviors by making them simpler. Third, we introduce new rewards and motivations to encourage behaviors that address the social problem of obesity [29].

We employ the Persuasive Systems Design (PSD) model [26] as a framework to explain our approach. The PSD model helps to structure thinking about a persuasive system by providing a map of persuasive design techniques to system requirements. Above we described our understanding of the fundamental issues driving the need for the system, which is the first step in the PSD process. The second step is to build the "persuasive context" where the system designer selects behavioral changes that they wish to induce and the strategies for doing so. Finally, actual system qualities are designed. In the following sections, we discuss the persuasive context, its implementation, and the persuasive strategies used to map between the two in the Fit4Life system.

The Persuasive Context

In the Fit4Life system, "the persuader" is, at one level, the system designers. However, at another level, Fit4Life becomes a mediator to allow other individuals, both face-to-face and on social networks, to become persuaders and influence each user to "do what is best for them."

Like other persuasive computing designers, we focus on modifying behavior because modifying attitudes seems too difficult [29]. At the macro-level, the goal of the Fit4Life system is to introduce a change in each user's eating and exercise behavior. This change will make users aware of situations that might negatively impact the maintenance of their ideal weight. In this sense, we choose to place less priority on understanding the goals of the individual user in favor of maximizing the possible utility from reducing societal health care costs associated with obesity. Optimizing the system to achieve the user-in-societal goal of reducing obesity will not only improve the health of working Americans, making them more productive, but, also has the effect of helping each participant become more attractive, and, therefore, more socially acceptable.

To help users achieve weight loss, the Fit4Life system has four primary sensors and a few other components that are operated using the Fit4Life iPhone Application. Fit4Life's Data Recorder makes use of image processing algorithms to estimate the calories of food consumed. Attached to the Data Recorder is the Beacon Accessory, which acts as a visual indicator of the individual's progress. The Earpiece

[2] For a list of programs, criteria for selection, and detailed analysis, visit: http://www.victoria.schwanda.org/fit4life.

is a Bluetooth receiver that, as with all of the peripheral devices, has been networked with the iPhone. This medium allows for direct audio communication with the user. The Earpiece also measures jaw movements to track eating behavior. The Thinsert is an electronic scale that can be inserted into a sock or shoe depending on the user's preference. The Heart Rate Monitor is worn around the user's chest to determine exercise behavior. The Metabolic Lancet is worn on a toe and it is used to analyze blood to determine current metabolic rate. The Support Cloud is implemented as a connector to Facebook and other social networking sites to broadcast the user's progress.

Use and User Context

To function as a weight management tool, the Fit4Life system must be capable of evaluating the current fitness of the individual at any given time [11]. This is accomplished by quantizing fitness into a model derived from data from the Fit4Life sensor network.

New Fit4Life users begin with an Assessment and Configuration phase. Given the user's height and age, the system determines the user's BMI and the correct diet and fitness plan for the user. The Fit4life system then describes the user's current fitness level and the system's plan to help them achieve a BMI in the ideal range.

The Fit4Life system combines the input of all of the sensors to assist the user in achieving their Fit4Life goal. We have developed a model that maps observed sensor inputs to Present Lifestyle Context (PLC): a vector that contains Daily Calories Consumed, Daily Calories Expended, Body Mass, Metabolic Rate, and Heart Rate, in addition to a few other proprietary variables. The system performs this assessment every second. With the PLC, Fit4Life is able to assess the current fitness of the user. The system provides feedback and suggestions to the user and informs others when the user needs encouragement to ensure Fit4Life-appropriate choices.

The Data Recorder observes the food consumption of a user. It is worn on the body and is placed such that it can determine the caloric content of food that is being consumed. When the Data Recorder has determined that the user is consuming food, the caloric content of the ingested food is added to the current value of Daily Calories Consumed. Data from the Heart Rate Monitor is combined with data from the Metabolic Lancet—which performs periodic blood tests—to determine the current metabolic rate. Observations of metabolic rate map to Daily Calories Expended and Metabolic Rate and data from the Heart Rate Monitor maps to Heart Rate. Finally, body mass is recorded daily using the Thinsert and maps to Body Mass. With the PLC, Fit4Life is able to assess the current fitness of the user and develop feedback and suggestions to provide to the user through the Earpiece. Recognizing that each user needs community support, the Beacon Accessory and the Support Cloud inform others that the user is in need of encouragement to ensure Fit4Life-appropriate choices.

The Persuasive Strategy

As outlined by the PSD model, the strategy of a persuasive system is executed via messages sent by the persuader to the user and by the routes the messages take to reach and persuade the user. Routes can be direct, indirect, or both. Routes are considered direct when the system provides information, such as calorie count or total calories expended for the day to the user. More subtle forms of persuasion are considered indirect routes. In the Fit4Life system, many messages and routes are employed, but in this section we list a representative sample of the techniques by the component of the system that serves as the route for persuasion. The Fit4Life system makes use of many of the persuasive design principles in primary task support (see [26]) including self-monitoring, reduction, tunneling, tailoring, personalization and social comparison.

Since Fit4Life tracks the performance of the user in all relevant categories to support the user's goal of weight management, it implements self-monitoring by providing a mechanism for the user to track their performance on metrics relevant to achieving that goal. The entirety of the Fit4Life system can be seen as an effort to reduce the complex task of weight management, beginning with "wear the Fit4Life system at all times"—an implementation of the persuasive reduction principle. In addition, calendar integration between the iPhone and Fit4Life simplifies scheduling. Instead of the complicated task of calorie awareness, the Data Recorder and the Earpiece work together to perform a sophisticated scientific analysis of food intake and eating behavior, with simple feedback to inform the user of their decisions.

Fit4Life tackles another complicated task—decisions about diet and exercise. It is engaged continuously to persuade users to make appropriate Fit4Life choices. In doing so, it uses the persuasive tunneling principle to "guide a user through a complex experience and persuade along the way" [26]. Since Fit4Life provides information when directly relevant to the user's behavior, and since that information is customized to the user's needs at every instant, the system employs principles of both tailoring and personalization. Finally, social support—and thus social comparison—is mediated through the Fit4Life Support Cloud.

The Fit4Life Support Cloud

Each user is assigned to a monitored treatment group on Facebook. Additionally, Facebook is periodically updated with each user's progress against their personal goals. When a user's eating and exercise behavior is in balance with their goals, the system generates a Wall post once per day that praises the appropriate behavior. When a user's eating and exercise behavior is not in balance with their goals, the system periodically generates a Wall post to notify others to provide encouragement. Additionally, if the user is not wearing components of the Fit4Life system, Wall posts are generated every hour notifying others that the user needs encouragement. Examples of the Wall messages generated by the system include the following (note that the primary persuasive design principles and Dialogue Support [26] are tagged next to each message):

"Congratulations! You've had a perfect Fit4Life day. At this rate, only one more day until you're the perfect weight!" [Personalization, Praise]

"Fantastic! You're at your ideal weight! If you exercise just once more this week, you'll have achieved all of your Fit4Life goals." [Tunneling, Praise]

"Shucks. You've gained an extra pound today because you consumed too much food and you didn't exercise. If you take a 30 minute walk tomorrow, you'll be back on the right path!" [Personalization, Suggestion]

We also include a sampling of messages left on other people's Walls by group participants:

"Wow! You look great! You're Fit4Me!" [Social]

"Bobby Joe, you can do it! We'll hang out tomorrow and have some carrot juice instead of beer."[Social]

(Next to a picture of a bikini that was attached to the post) ... "Lucy, how are we going to pick up guys at the beach next month?!?"[Social]

(Next to a picture of a wedding dress that was attached to the post) ... "Libby, are you going to break your mother's heart on your wedding day?" [Social]

(Next to a picture of a wedding dress that was attached to the post) ... "Libby, you'll look fabulous in your slimmer dream dress!" [Social]

The Fit4Life Data Recorder and Beacon Accessory

The Beacon Accessory displays user status via a blinking scarlet light. When a user's behavior is in balance with their goals, no light is emitted from the device, but when out of balance, the beacon accessory blinks to notify others to provide encouragement. As with the Support Cloud, the alert rate is proportional to the imbalance in behavior—until a constant stream of scarlet light is emitted, indicating a need for immediate assistance.

The Fit4Life Earpiece

Suggestions are frequently delivered via the Fit4Life Earpiece, which is the primary vehicle for delivering direct suggestive persuasive advice to a Fit4Life subject. The advice provided by the system can take many forms, ranging from telling the user how many calories they are about to consume to direct suggestions about whether their decisions are in line with their goals. Examples include:

"Dave, your schedule seems to be filling up. Would you like to schedule time for a walk by the river today?" [Tunneling, Reminder]

"Dave, you're scheduled to have dinner with Lisa's parents this evening. They wish to eat at Moosewood, which has many healthy options. You might enjoy one of the cookies on the table now." [Tunneling, Suggestion]

"Dave, the scone you are about to eat probably contains 400 calories. You've already consumed 300 calories today. There are 9 hours remaining in your wake period. After eating the scone, you will have consumed 45% of your total nutrition needs for today. You have free time today from Noon to 2 pm. Would you like me to schedule a long run?" [Reduction, Suggestion]

"Dave, you've eaten the scone and you didn't run with me yesterday. I would like to go for a run soon." [Personalization, Suggestion]

"I'm sorry, Dave, you shouldn't eat that. Dave, you know I don't like it when you eat donuts." [Personalization, Suggestion]

The Fit4Life system is visualized in Figure 1.

FUTURE WORK

Using evaluation protocols common in the persuasive literature [29], we will demonstrate system efficacy using 26 student subjects grouped using a randomized block design over a 9-week period. Study participants are given free access to the Fit4Life system during the experimental trials. Each group will be pre-tested for weight, BMI, and fitness level. The study requires all test group participants have a diet and exercise regime that will result in a body mass within the acceptable range. We hope to find at the end of the trials that Fit4Life users are more likely to have BMIs in the acceptable range than Control group users.

Additionally, we plan on upgrading our sensor network to enable analysis of chewing sounds for dietary monitoring [4] and body fat calculation via bioelectrical impedance analysis. Planned upgrades also include the use of LED tattoo technology [22] and custom voice selection for the Earpiece so users can choose to receive feedback from people such as their mother or wife. We also plan to offer more fashion conscious versions of our sensors through partnerships with celebrity designers. Finally, our celebrity partners are developing and endorsing diet and exercise plans to be available to future Fit4Life users.

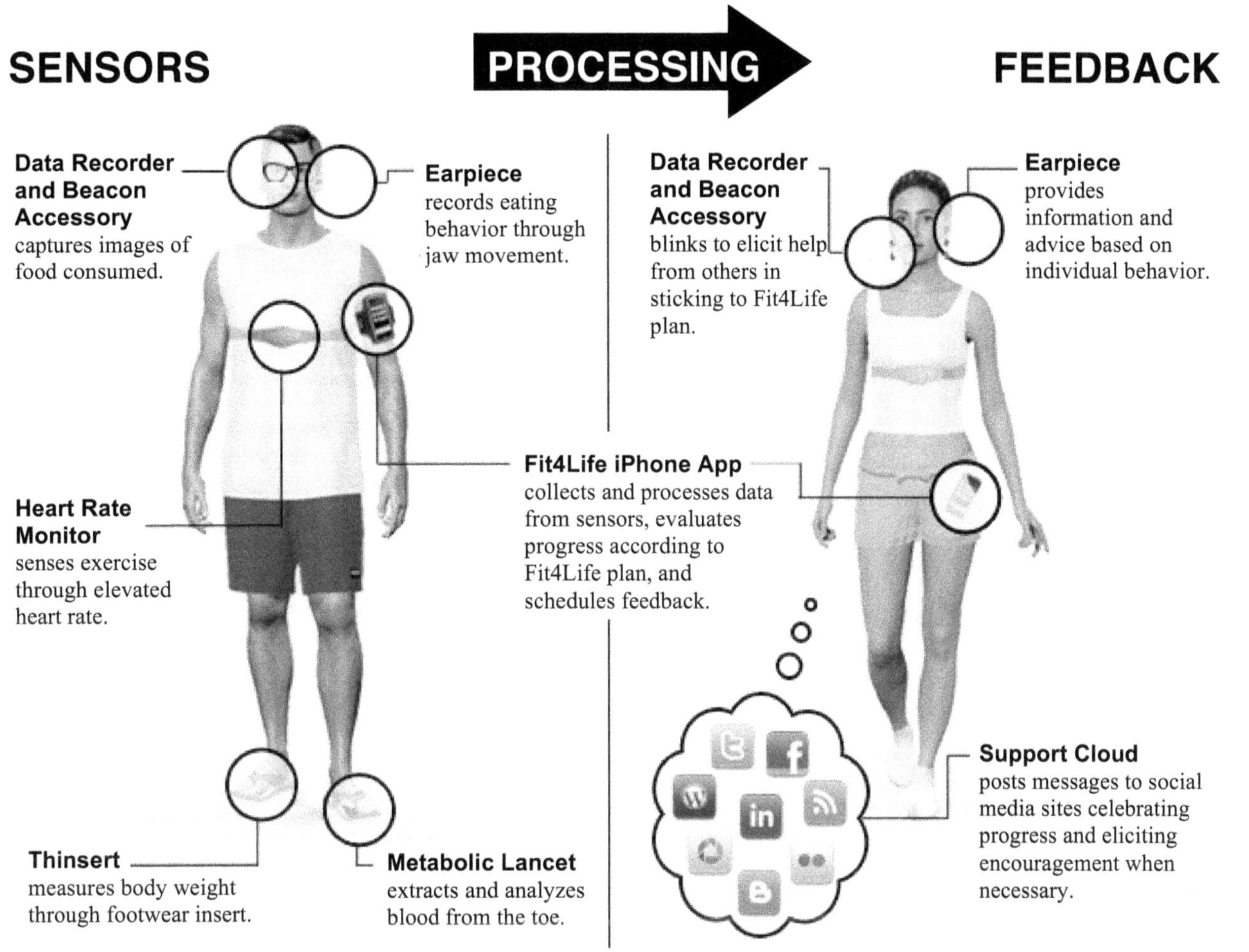

Figure 1. The Fit4Life system in use. All components of the system are shown including sensors, the processing unit, and feedback mechanisms. Certain system components such as The Fit4Life Data Recorder and Beacon Accessory are available in multiple forms (shown here as prescription glasses and fashion earrings) and perform both sensing and feedback functionality.

DISCUSSION

Fit4Life is a fictional, critical design. Our goal is not to present a persuasive computing system to solve the problem of obesity but rather to demonstrate how easily such a design can spiral out of control, and through this, explore the ethical and conceptual limits of persuasive computing. Our goal in the first half of this paper was to take the persuasive technology and obesity research literatures at their word and see how far we could implement their logic and recommendations. In order to do so, we carefully documented each design decision, no matter how outrageous, with specific references to the persuasive design literature that justifies it.

Fit4Life is intended not as a practical design solution but as a thought experiment to stimulate reflection on the social, ethical, and political issues that technology raises. Our critical intervention is addressed to designers of persuasive and ubiquitous systems and aims to unearth issues of meaning and value, of ethics and responsibility. Our purpose is not to lambaste practitioners of persuasive computing; as practitioners ourselves, we aim to demonstrate the limits of what we perceive as common approaches in the field by pushing these approaches to their logical conclusion. Our aim is to unsettle, but we are aware that the design of our paper can arouse negative sentiments, particularly since our parody is not made explicit until this section. This decision was carefully made to maximize critical reflection. Our fear was that if the parody were clear initially, we would run the risk of a complacent reading of such design as not truly possible. Our hope is that readers will evaluate for themselves the extent to which Fit4Life's design elements are realistic reflections of technological research trends.

Our approach is based on intellectual precedents in activist literatures. In our design, we follow traditions of tactical media [23] in aiming for a fine line between humor and realism to highlight how frighteningly close reality can be to a joke. We are inspired by Dunne and Raby's notion of critical design, whose goal is not to provide clear answers but to provoke reflection [10]. We believe the ethical and value issues related to persuasive design need to be actively discussed by the community. Our goal is not to tell the community what to think but to help provoke discussion.

In this discussion section, we describe the key critical issues that our design is constructed to explore. At the highest level, we see persuasive computing as conceptualizing itself in terms of structured, rational approaches to optimizing individual behavior, frequently for goals which are not chosen by the individual. This conceptualization raises three critical issues. First, persuasive computing raises issues around the borderlines between encouragement, persuasion, and coercion, and specifically with who should be in control of individual behavior. Second, we see persuasive computing as participating in and reinforcing broader troublesome cultural trends to control, rationalize, and optimize human behavior. Third, persuasive computing's use of technological control raises issues around surveillance and around what is lost through the process of quantification.

Persuasion or coercion?

Our design explores the boundary shared between persuasion, encouragement, and coercion. This recurring theme was designed to encourage system designers to consider whether their persuasive strategies are really control or persuasion. For example, by sublimating the designer's ideology as the "system's" Fit4Life obscures the question of just whose ideas of fitness and diet are being enacted and treats the user as a 'technological dope', "an automatic, almost reflex substantiator and re-enactor of [dietary] cultural norms, with little recognition of ... individual experiences, awarenesses and reflection" [30].

We constructed the support cloud and beacon to demonstrate the potential shortcomings in such social support approaches. As designers, such measures may seem at first as enabling as they allow users to solicit help in achieving what at first appears to be solely their own goals. But when viewed critically, the beacon appears as both a signal for help and an element of shame. While soliciting support for the user it also highlights his or her non-conformity to personal and social norms and an inability to stick to plan. We believe that this shame, regardless of social or physical distance, is coercive. Fit4Life exploits that inherent tension between eating and exercise, and capitalizes on users' dissatisfaction with their own fitness and health to induce behavior that is acceptable to a wider group and uses "objective" standards as reinforcement.

Fit4Life's design decisions frequently sacrificed individual good for the social good—by providing avenues for unpleasant peer pressure, for example. In doing so, we try to highlight the distinction between providing people with tools for reflection on the impacts of their practices to achieve *social* goals (as suggested, for example, by [7]) and providing people with tools for reflection on the impacts of their practices to achieve *their own* goals. While personal goals are always culturally influenced, the key distinguishing feature that concerns us with the persuasive computing literature is that users do not get to choose their own viewpoints, but are provided with one by designers.

More broadly, persuasive computing raises questions on the ethics of changing another's attitude, belief or behavior. In considering an ethical boundary situated around a user's intent we must ask if a choice can even honestly be made to take away one's choices. This is not a straightforward examination given that persuasive technologies frequently aim to make behavioral decisions 'simpler' by eliminating complexity (and options), and often aim to enforce sublimated social goals. Is it ethical to exploit fears and anxieties in service of such goals? Are users allowed witness to the origin and full extent of these changes?

While we used the terminology and design practices of the persuasive computing movement, the complete Fit4Life product—in its extremes—highlights a need for reflection through non-judgmental means rather than persuasion to achieve an ideal. In this way, it suggests that an ideal system might be a subjective one that would allow users to define their own meanings and values.

A persuasive society

At the onset of our project we believed that our design would be quickly recognized as satire. As our work progressed, however, we realized that our design could likely actually be marketed and accepted in mainstream society without recognition of its commentary due to a mutually reinforcing relationship between worrisome aspects of persuasive computing and a broader incursion of scientific rationalization into our everyday lives. We see persuasive computing as embodying a 'McDonaldized' [27] worldview that values quantification and rationality at the cost of situational, hard-to-measure factors and sees scientific measurement as obviating personal experience. Through Fit4Life's design, we hope to provoke conversation about the meaning and value of a broader, pervasive rationalization of our lives.

We chose diet and exercise as domains for Fit4Life because they culturally embody those principles. The tie between diet and exercise and concepts of persuasion became clear when our survey of literature and websites revealed a plethora of exercise promotion tools and calorie trackers that circumscribed plans of action and offered persuasive sticks and carrots to ostensibly guide users towards correct behavior. We saw how popular diet and exercise planning tools and programs encourage a shift of responsibility from individuals to external sources [24]. Late night infomercials promise quick weight loss drugs or exercise machines that ignore the varying situational needs and dietary habits that are crucial to our self-definition. The increased reliance on scientific measures of healthiness has left users ever more uncertain of what to eat and increasingly dependent on scientific experts to inform them.

These aspects of diet and exercise can be seen as embodying broader cultural trends that Ritzer terms

McDonaldization: referring to the permeation of structured, rational approaches throughout American society, and the emphasis of the attributes of efficiency, calculability, predictability, and nonhuman (frequently technological) control. Following the theories of sociologist Max Weber, Ritzer highlights the 'irrationality of rationality' – the ways in which too great an emphasis on these individual rational attributes leads to solutions that are globally irrational.

Diet programs based on the models of efficiency and calculability abound: the right amount of protein, carbohydrates and fat cooked and consumed in the smallest measure of time. We now seek to lose weight in a manner that parallels the way in which we gained it: quickly, mindlessly and conveniently. By pulling quantitative measures to the foreground over qualitative ones, and usurping (or "complementing" in marketing-speak) the normal situational human decision making process, the Fit4Life system is an embodiment of this worldview.

We have pointed to statistics that show that obesity levels are increasing rapidly due to a variety of factors, but poor diet and an increasingly sedentary—yet somehow busy—lifestyle, are the most notable. Strikingly, many of us simply can no longer determine what eating properly entails (if there even is a single answer to that question). In developing this critique, we tried to take care to avoid defaulting to a romantic desire to return to a past that can no longer exist. Can we really return to a world without such systems and controls? While we can be concerned about the over-application of rational models of control and efficiency to human experiences [27], it would be disingenuous to simply put forward a design modeled on inefficiency and unpredictability when the market demands otherwise. Instead we choose to raise this question: do our desires for such controls indicate a need to be seen as and feel contemporary or modern?

We designed Fit4Life in the spirit of what we believed to be that modern zeitgeist. In particular, we conceived of configurable celebrity-endorsed packs as an example of loci of control that are external, corporate, and rational and the iPhone application node reflects a desire for a simplified control panel for our lives. Will our future ability to manage our diet and exercise be finally determined by technological innovations like Fit4Life? Though our literature review indicates that this might be the hope and direction of modern man, it also highlights the sea of continually updating, often contradictory, dietary information through which such a path must be chartered.

Technological control

Given the cultural value of technological control, an increase in the domain of machines in our health management seems all but inevitable through dining room tables that "sense the movement of food from the serving container to the individual consuming it," sensor-augmented kitchen knives, cutting boards, and on-body sensors [17]. Our design, by taking this idea of tracking and persuasion to its logical extreme, challenges the idea that increasing the volume and fidelity of data captured can result in a long-term healthy attitude.

Through our design we imagined a world where all of the data needed to quantify a user's fitness could be collected. A strain of belief in the literature we reviewed is that if people reported all this relevant information, then experts would be unrestrained in their ability to help users help themselves. Fit4Life's notion of quantizing fitness and health into a feature vector based on sensor input and system designer options relies on intrusive, obvious, and perhaps even ridiculous sensors, but similar methods are showing up in the literature [5]. The lancet intermittingly drawing blood from your system and the earpiece measuring jaw movements may seem ridiculous at first blush but these decisions set the stage for an examination of what happens when system designers have an unfettered visibility into user's lives that is coupled with realized intrusion.

One issue with the formal models derived from sensed data used in Fit4Life is that positive behavior is identified solely with reducing BMI. In choosing such a fixed model, the system reinforces a narrow conception of what it means to be healthy or fit. By focusing on quantitative measures the system also discards the value of personal experiences and emotions for a utilitarian position on the value of food and exercise. Because of the inherent limitations of sensing, persuasive systems often promote behaviors based on limited understanding of users' actual personal situations.

But even if unlimited data acquisition is possible, there are issues of surveillance and privacy. With Fit4Life, users are monitored constantly and must behave accordingly. Foucault, in speaking of the Panopticon, notes: "we live in a prison-like society founded on discipline and surveillance. The formation of this society stems from many historical processes, but it is a surveillance society and its purest form is the prison." Conceived in this way, the Fit4Life system is not only a design artifact but also embodies a schema "for characterizing many aspects of society" and is "[a] diagram of a mechanism of power reduced to its ideal form" [Foucault in 21]. This is an embodiment of utilitarianism wherein behavior is evaluated strictly according to its utility in lowering BMI and in constraining the user in order to enact social goals.

Fit4Life is then a rational cage that showcases the "irrationality of rationality" [27]. It is a personal prêt-à-porter panopticon. Fit4Life represents an incursion of a rationalistic, objective view of the world that is often hidden in the agendas of persuasive designers. This cage can be seen as a "rationalized setting" where the "self [is] placed in confinement, its emotions controlled, and its spirit subdued" [27]. By seeking to reduce basic human flaws (or characteristics depending on your slant), the persuasive agenda embodied in this design is dehumanizing.

The feasibility of such a design is increasing. Fit4Life's Present Lifestyle Context is a vector of measurements because a persuasive system that includes machine-learning components would, essentially, construct a vector of sensor measurements and historical user responses to provide suggestions tailored to increase compliance. If a user is most likely to comply if the system posts a Facebook message, a machine learning system could learn that aspect and act accordingly. The system may not even be sophisticated enough to know that for a specific user, the Facebook route is effective because the user's mother functions as an enforcer. System designers face the tension between the increased system efficacy possible from using machine-learning systems to tailor user suggestions and the side effects that can be created by a reliance on effective but unseemly persuasive routes.

IMPLICATIONS FOR PRACTICE

Expanding Criteria for Evaluation

One clear implication of the Fit4Life design is that evaluation needs to be expanded beyond the explicit goals of the system to include attitudes (not only behaviors) and unintended consequences.

The Fit4Life system focused on changing user's behaviors, and not their attitudes, which is a common practice in persuasive technology [29]. Success is measured during a 9-week period—a fairly short evaluation period, also common in the literature [29]—and our main critieria for success was that users reach a certain BMI as measured by our system. As practitioners, we know this is an extremely short-sighted method of evaluating whether users remain fit and healthy. As a designer, is the appropriate role to persuade users to achieve an ideal BMI in 9 weeks or is it to help the user live a healthier life?

As the designers of Fit4Life, we wanted to show that when people use the system the outcome would be users with ideal BMI. As critical reviewers of Fit4Life, we think it is unrealistic that people would use the system for the rest of their lives and that they may develop behaviors when using the system that are not sustainable. Therefore, we find the evaluation—the focus on measuring the outcome of achieving ideal BMI—flawed because it doesn't assess the true impact of the system on the user. This difficulty is common to other persuasive studies [29].

Additionally, the Fit4Life evaluation should have included more holistic measures of the users physical and mental well-being. In this respect, we should have been diligent about looking for unintended consequences, including stress in their personal relationships and their self-image. In medical studies, it is common to examine unintended problems or adverse events from a treatment. In persuasive research designs, how is this facilitated? And what would be the definition of an adverse event? Would it include feeling stressed and pressured by your mother on Facebook to fit into a size 2 wedding dress?

The American Food and Drug Administration has evolving recommendations for dealing with adverse events in treatment. Patient advocates, industry veterans, and government representatives work in cooperation and conflict to resolve definitions and protocols. By exaggerating and integrating persuasive design principles in Fit4Life, some of their potential weaknesses become more apparent. In this sense, the critical design method employed to produce Fit4Life can be used to explore similar discussions for evaluating potential technical designs.

In our case, Fit4Life was designed to achieve a societal goal at the potential loss of mindfulness. We chose explicitly to frame loss of mindfulness as an unimportant side effect in our exaggerated design, but designers working on the development of different systems might choose other potential harms.

Designing for mindfulness and leaving room for stories

The principles of reduction, tunneling, and tailoring are most used in the persuasive technology literature [29], and taken together encourage designers to make it easier for the user to act in a manner consistent with their system's message. A system following these principles would guide a user through accomplishing a complex task in a manner that is customized and simplified to the user's personal situation. The Fit4Life earpiece is an example of these principles in their extreme. It provides explicit verbal suggestions when specific foods should be eaten or avoided and when the user should engage in specific fitness activities based on the PLC and the user's current surroundings and schedule. The user no longer has to calculate calories consumed and expended to determine for themselves whether they are within their daily calorie allowance and they no longer have to use this information to make food and exercise decisions—the system does this for them. In an effort to make this process easier, we took away the user's ability to reflect on their situation and decide on appropriate action. We are telling them *exactly* how to behave in every situation.

Even if we accept the idea of diet and exercise planning as a valid part of the realm of personal, everyday computing, we need not agree that everyday computing need be everywhere computing or that everywhere computing needs to be mindless computing. We hope that Fit4Life's encompassing and detailed model of calorie consumption and expenditure exposes arguments on the uncertainty inherent in such measures and on the importance of mindfulness on the part of the designers and system users. Allegiance to Fit4Life discourages mindfulness when mindfulness might be precisely what users need to develop for building attitudes important for sustaining long-term health.

Perhaps, in the end, this should be the goal of more exercise and diet programs: not to supplement or to make decisions for users but to eventually wean them by helping to establish self-reliance. If obesity is viewed as a disease, then the focus can be more readily seen as on lifestyle, on the management of a chronic condition and in helping users develop an internal locus of control. In such a situation the "individual discovery of patterns and correlations in past experiences" [24] is as important as the system's persuasions and controls. Reflection is then one of the most important skills to develop in order to help users build a "sense of control over their disease and their perceived role in [its] management" [24]. It is important then to not focus solely on restoration to an ideal state but also on the revelations that users achieve while using the product [24].

In exploring alternative conceptual designs, Gaver notes that "if people are enabled to play a substantial role in determining the meaning of systems...they will be actively engaged in the process of understanding both the system and its situation of use" [16]. He goes on to call out—importantly—that an "active engagement in sense-making may not only be pleasurable or liberating, it may also be useful in safety-critical applications" [16].

While not immediately safety-critical, exercise and diet planning regimes could be more effective (although the very question of "effectiveness" is at stake here) if they incorporated similar strategies for encouraging mindfulness. By exposing rather than covering seams [16] in the abilities of calorie or exercise tracking, the hope is that users would be encouraged to reflect on how they feel, rather than relying on the illusion of an impeachable, scientifically objective source of measurement.

But what is appropriate behavior? Fit4Life focuses on an objectively agreed upon metric for healthiness, the BMI. Should the focus be on numerical values of calories or macronutrients, the distance one's food has travelled, or on the feelings of community and wholesomeness that often accompany the act of eating? How we feel about the way we eat is important in maintaining healthy habits, and how any diet management or tracking system allows for self-presentation and makes room for users' stories [6] is arguably as important as the very measures it tracks.

Fit4Life destroys strategies for misrepresentation or secret consumption that could have allowed for any idealized impressions of behavior that an individual could have conveyed [9]. If it is accepted—and we do—that these are strategies essential for long term adoption, the accuracy and entirety of information capture should be trumped by the need to support controls for "backstage access" but Fit4Life demolishes demarcations between a back or front stage. Successful tracking then should at least allow for the user to present that tracked information in different formats for varying audiences or risk abandonment of the platform [9].

While our underlying argument is that the encroachment of such structured systems is far from ideal, our preference is that designers allow users enough space for reflection in order to make such distinctions themselves. Fit4Life continually points out to users when to reduce intake or increase expenditure (of calories, of structure) but our hope is that through discussion, an appreciation of how these issues can be raised without forcing action, negative comparisons, or triggering neuroses can be achieved. Fit4Life's earpiece may be a monologue, but it should be viewed as encouraging a conversation about the system's interpretation of the user. Is the user just a combination of measurable attributes: caloric intake, height and body fat?

CONCLUSION

Our goal in this paper is to provoke discussion of the conceptual and ethical limits of persuasive computing. Our method was to take documented principles and guidelines from the persuasive computing literature and push them to their logical conclusion, in order to clarify some of the dangers that may be involved with them. With Fit4Life, we aimed to make explicit the values that inform the weight management and tracking tools that we have surveyed. By bringing these issues—the idea that sensors accurately measure attributes that directly translate to health; that health can be measured in a purely reductive way; that communal support is always positive—to the surface, we hope that designers will consider how they ask users to conceive of their own health. We highlighted three resulting critical issues for persuasive computing: the extent to which persuasion can shade into coercion; the mutually reinforcing relationship between persuasive computing and broader cultural trends towards scientific rationalization and an "irrationality of rationality;" and issues around surveillance and the ascendancy of data collection over personal experience as a means for establishing truth and manipulating behavior.

One postulate that underlies persuasive computing is that technology is not neutral; it is always guiding the individual. When designers make decisions about the "one right way" that should drive suggestions to influence the "flawed" user, it removes agency from the individual. We embodied Fit4Life with these design habits in an effort to provoke discussion about when and whether this approach is respectful of the user and their ability to interpret. If Fit4Life were designed to foster mindfulness, it might not discuss calories, schedules, and exercise in minutes at all.

The realization of the Fit4Life system brings to the foreground what it means to be human. The reduction of human experience to inputs and outputs raises the questions: am I man or machine? Am I what I eat?

ACKNOWLEDGMENTS

Thanks to Hrönn Brynjarsdóttir, Carl DiSalvo, Paul Dourish, Jofish Kaye, JP Pollak, Peter Wright, and the anonymous reviewers for helpful feedback on this paper. This work was supported in part by NSF Grant ISS-0847293 and an NSF Graduate Research Fellowship.

REFERENCES

1. Institute of Medicine. (1995). Weighing the Options: Criteria for Evaluating Weight-Management Programs.

P.R. Thomas (Ed.). Washington, DC: National Academies Press.

2. National Center for Health Statistics. (2008). Prevalence of overweight, obesity and extreme obesity among adults: United States, trends 1960-62 through 2005-2006. Retrieved from http://www.cdc.gov/nchs/data/hestat/overweight/overweight_adult.pdf.
3. Office of the Surgeon General. (2002). Overweight and Obesity Health Consequences. Retrieved from http://www.surgeongeneral.gov/topics/obesity/calltoaction/fact_consequences.htm.
4. O. Amft, M. Stager, P. Lukowicz, G. Troster. (2005). Analysis of Chewing Sounds for Dietary Monitoring. In *Proc. UBICOMP '05*.
5. O. Amft., G. Tröster. (2009). On-Body Sensing Solutions for Automatic Dietary Monitoring. *IEEE Pervasive Computing*.
6. P.M. Aoki, A. Woodruff. (2005). Making space for stories: ambiguity in the design of personal communication systems. In *Proc. CHI '05*.
7. A.J. Bernheim-Brush, T. Combs-Turner, M. Smith, N. Gupta. (2004). Scanning Objects in the Wild: Assessing an Object-Triggered Information System. In *Proc. UBICOMP '04*.
8. C.L Bish, H.M. Blanck, M.K. Serdula et al. (2005). Diet and physical activity behaviors among Americans trying to lose weight: 2000 Behavioral Risk Factor Surveillance System. *Obes Res*, 13(3):596-607.
9. S. Consolvo, D. McDonald, J. Landay. (2009). Theory-driven design strategies for technologies that support behavior change in everyday life. In *Proc. CHI '09*.
10. A. Dunne, F. Raby. *Design Noir: The Secret Life of Electronic Objects*. Basel:Birkhäuser, 2001.
11. K.E. Evers, J.M. Prochaska, J.O. Prochaska. (2003). Strengths and Weaknesses of Health Behavior Change Programs on the Internet. *J Health Psychol*, 8(1):63-70.
12. G. Eysenbach. (2003). The Impact of the Internet on Cancer Outcomes. *CA Cancer J Clin*, 53(6):356-371.
13. K.M. Flegal, M.D. Carroll, R.J. Kuczmarski, C.L. Johnson. (1998). Overweight and obesity in the United States: prevalence and trends. *Int J Obes Relat Metab Discord*, 22(1):39-47.
14. B.J. Fogg. (2003). Persuasive Technology: Using Computers to Change What We think and Do. San Francisco: Morgan Kaufmann.
15. D.M. Garner, S.C. Wooley. (1991). Confronting the failure of behavioral and dietary treatments for obesity. *Clin Psychol Rev*, 11(6):729-780.
16. B. Gaver, H. Martin. (2000). Alternatives: exploring information appliances through conceptual design proposals. In *Proc. CHI '00*, 209-216.
17. A. Grimes, D. Tan, D. Morris. (2009). Toward technologies that support family reflections on health. In *Proc. GROUP '09*.
18. S. Heshka, J.W. Anderson, R.L. Atkinson et al. (2003). Weight Loss With Self-help Compared With a Structured Commercial Program: A Randomized Trial. *J Amer Med Assoc*, 289(14):1792-1798.
19. R.W. Jeffery, A. Drewnowski, L.H. Epstein, A.J. Stunkard, G.T. Wilson, R.R. Wing. (2000). Long-Term Maintenance of Weight Loss: Current Status. *Health Psychol*, 19(1):5-16.
20. R.W. Jeffery, R.R Wing, C. Thorson, L.R. Burton, C. Raether, J. Harvey, M. Mullen. (1993). Strengthening Behavioral Interventions for Weight Loss: A Randomized Trial of Food Provision and Monetary Incentives. *J Consult Clin Psyc*, 61(6):1038-1045.
21. J.L. Jespersen, A. Albrechtslund, P. Ohrstrom, P. Hasle, J. Albretsen. (2007). Surveillance, Persuasion, and Panopticon. In *Proc. PERSUASIVE '07*, 109-120.
22. D. Kim, Y. Kim, J. Amsden, B. Panilaitis, D.L. Kaplan, F.G. Omenetto, M.R. Zakin, J.A. Rogers. (2009). Silicon electronics on silk as a path to bioresorbable, implantable devices. *Appl Phys Lett*, 95:133701.
23. T. Liacas. 101 Tricks to Play with the Mainstream. In A. Langlois, F. Dubois, eds., *Autonomous Media: Activating Resistance & Dissent*. Montreal: Cumulus Press, 2005, pp. 60-73.
24. L. Mamykina, E. Maynatt, P. Davidson, D. Greenblatt. (2008). MAHI: Investigation of social scaffolding for reflective thinking in diabetes management. In *Proc. CHI '08*, 5-10.
25. H. Oinas-Kukkonen and M. Harjumaa. (2008). A Systematic Framework for Designing and Evaluating Persuasive Systems. In *Proc. PERSUASIVE '08*, 164-176.
26. H. Oinas-Kukkonen and M. Harjumaa. (2009). Persuasive Systems Design: Key Issues, Process Model, and System Features. *Commun Assoc Inform Syst*, 24(1).
27. G. Ritzer. (2004). The McDonaldization of society. Pine Forge Press.
28. D.F. Tate, R.R. Wing, R.A. Winett. (2001). Using Internet Technology to Deliver a Behavioral Weight Loss Program. *J Amer Med Assoc*, 285(9):1172-1177.
29. K. Torning, H. Oinas-Kukkonen. (2009). Persuasive system design: state of the art and future directions. In *Proc. PERSUASIVE '09*.
30. A.G. Tsai, T.A. Wadden. (2005). Systematic Review: An Evaluation of Major Commercial Weight Loss Programs in the United States. *Ann of Intern Med*, 142(1):56-66.

Many Bills: Engaging Citizens through Visualizations of Congressional Legislation

Yannick Assogba, Irene Ros, Joan DiMicco, Matt McKeon
IBM Research
One Rogers St, Cambridge, 02142
[yannick; iros; joan.dimicco]@us.ibm.com, matt@mattmckeon.com

ABSTRACT
US federal legislation is a common subject of discussion and advocacy on the web, inspired by the open government movement. While the contents of these bills are freely available for download, understanding them is a significant challenge to experts and average citizens alike due to their length, complex language, and obscure topics. To make these important documents more accessible to the general public, we present Many Bills (http://manybills.us): a web-based set of visualization tools that reveals the underlying semantics of a bill. Using machine learning techniques, we classify each bill's sections based on existing document-level categories. We then visualize the resulting topic substructure of these bills. These visualizations provide an overview-and-detail view of bills, enabling users to read individual sections of a bill and compare topic patterns across multiple bills. Through an overview of the site's user activity and interviews with active users, this paper highlights how Many Bills makes the tasks of reading bills, identifying outlier sections in bills, and understanding congressperson's legislative activity more manageable.

Author Keywords
Information visualization, text classification, government, legislation, government transparency.

ACM Classification Keywords
H5.3. Group and Organization Interfaces; Web-based interaction.

General Terms
Human Factors

INTRODUCTION
The day after his inauguration in 2009, US President Barack Obama signed the Memorandum on Transparency and Open Government [1] stating that *transparency*, *participation*, and *collaboration* would be hallmarks of his administration. In the wake of this announcement, US government agencies began releasing data in digital formats for the general public to access and for application developers to build on top of. A number of non-profit organizations, such as the Sunlight Foundation[2], GovTrack.us[3] and MAPLight[4], emerged as clearinghouses for information and as advocates for a more data-driven approach to citizen and government communication.

One of the many issues these organizations seek to address is to help the average citizen navigate the complexity of US federal legislation. Knowing where to look in a bill for a particular issue or topic of interest is difficult because bills use specialized language and are, at times, quite long. A bill also may contain elements that are unrelated to its overall subject. One of our favorite examples of this appears in H.R. 627: The Credit Card Accountability Responsibility and Disclosure (CARD) Act of 2009, imposing transparency and disclosure requirements on credit card companies. The metadata provided by the Library of Congress categorizes this bill as a "Finance and Financial Sector" bill. However, embedded in Title V – Miscellaneous Provisions is a section titled Protecting Americans From Violent Crime that establishes the right of citizens to carry firearms in National Parks and Wildlife Refuges.

As this example shows, document-level metadata can hide important aspects of the underlying text. Motivated by this and a desire to make the content of legislative text less opaque, we have taken up the challenge of helping individuals read, explore and discuss US federal legislation. Our prototype, Many Bills, is a visualization and public website that enables anyone to search and explore the content of bills brought before the current Session of the Congress of the United States (running from Jan 3, 2009 - Jan 3, 2011). We use a machine learning approach to derive fine-grained topic overviews of bills and then visualize the results at various levels of detail including full-text browsing. Users can create custom views and embed them into a variety of other online media. Users can also explore bills based on which congresspeople sponsored them.

This paper presents Many Bills (screenshot in Figure 1), the techniques used to build and design the site, and initial responses from users. Through an overview of the site's user activity and interviews with active users, we highlight how Many Bills is used.

[1] www.whitehouse.gov/the_press_office/Transparency_and_Open_Government/
[2] http://sunlightfoundation.com
[3] http://data.gov
[4] http://maplight.org

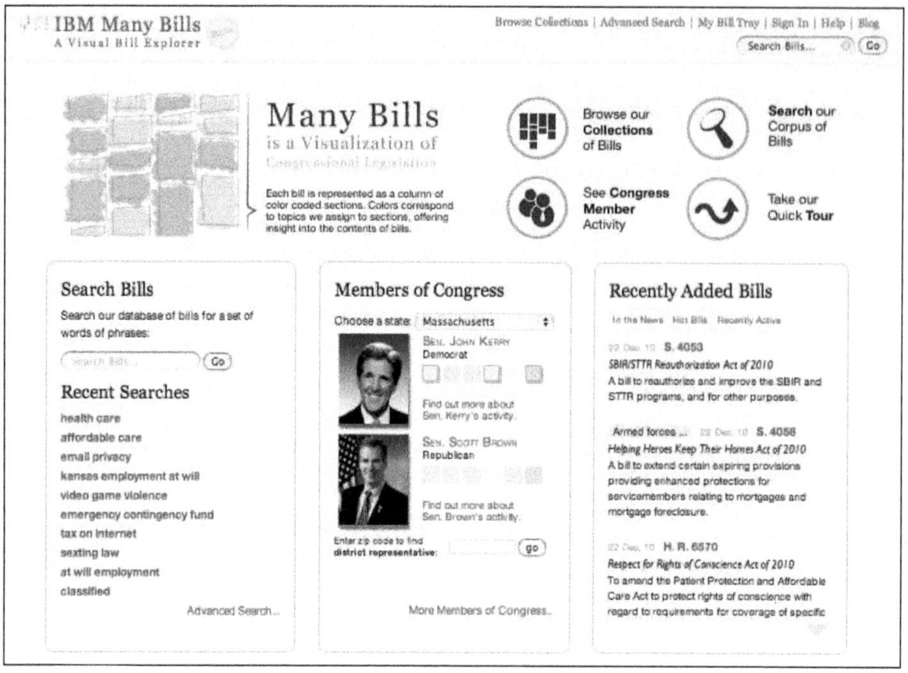

Figure. 1. The homepage of Many Bills (http://manybills.us).

OUR DESIGN GOALS

Many Bills is part of a larger movement at the intersection of government and technology that aims to provide applications that transform government data into more approachable formats that citizens can understand, interpret, and communicate about. There are many examples of these types of "Gov 2.0" applications that have been built since Obama's memorandum on open government: the following are a small set of representative examples.

Two winners of the Sunlight Foundation's Design for America[5] challenge were Cool Kids at the White House[6], showing frequent White House visitors, and US Federal Contract Spending[7], showing federal spending versus media coverage. The visualizations are visually compelling and guide users to eye-opening conclusions based on the data.

Two other examples that allow users to interact even more with government data are Data Masher[8] and the National Obesity Comparison Tool[9]. These types of tools provide a limited collection of data, overlaid onto a geographic region, allowing users to filter and zoom into areas of interest.

One of our observations about the web applications built upon open government data is that the source data is often abstracted, providing a cursory summary of the data, allowing for only a few number of user interpretations. While engaging for the casual user, the applications do not cater to the curiosity of an advanced user-base who could potentially derive *new* meaning and insight from the data behind the visualization.

Our belief is that for citizens to become meaningfully engaged with government data, they need to be able to draw their own conclusions about it. Tools built around government data should provide guides and references to make finding the information they seek more apparent. So for our project, to support citizens in reading, understanding and interpreting legislation, we focused on these goals:

- Stay true to the text of the legislative bills while providing abstractions that make them more easily approachable: display a high-level view of a bill while providing access to its full text content.
- Create a visual interface that supports various levels of text abstraction to support different levels of interest in legislative text.
- Use standard web browser technologies to access a boarder audience, trading the rich capabilities of the desktop and plug-in based platforms for the wider reach of the web to citizens.

RELATED WORK

This research builds upon previous work on text visualization and other web applications that make US legislation available.

---

[5] http://sunlightlabs.com/blog/2010/design-america-winners/
[6] http://www.nrftw.net/
[7] http://www.pitchinteractive.com/usbudget/
[8] http://www.datamasher.org/
[9] http://public.tableausoftware.com/views/contributorstoobesity/Eatyourvegtables

Congressional Legislation Websites

There are three main websites that provide access to US federal legislation today. THOMAS [3], operated by the Library of Congress, is a comprehensive, web-accessible source of information on the activity taking place in Congress. Data includes bills & resolutions, public law, vote records, and legislator information. While bill text appears in full on THOMAS, it is presented in its raw form as a complete text document. No visual techniques are used to represent the data that might encourage informal engagement.

OpenCongress.org [2], a non-profit project run by the Participatory Politics Foundation, brings together legislative data, news media and individual blog posts, as well as public commenting on congressional activities. OpenCongress displays bills as formatted text without any visual abstraction or embellishment, similar to THOMAS. An additional enhancement is users' ability to comment on any portion of the bill.

A third site that provides open access to US legislative content is GovTrack.us [1], a tool by Civic Impulse, LLC. The site gathers congressional information from disparate official government websites (including THOMAS) and combines and cross-references the information to make it more reusable for third-party developers. GovTrack is a destination to read bills in a manner similar to that of THOMAS and OpenCongress. GovTrack's bill reading interface offers users a powerful embedding widget that can be used by bloggers and other media outlets to embed any portion of the bills within their site. GovTrack also serves as a legislative datasource to many applications, including Many Bills, because it provides a wealth of data to the developer community.

Connect2Congress [14] is an additional example of a visual analytics tool for exploring congressional activity, in this case voting patterns. It is a powerful and innovative effort to combine complex analytics and visualization methods to show the other side of legislative activity. However, without drill-down capability, users are not able to explore the data behind C2C's analysis.

Text Visualization

We considered many existing text visualization approaches for our challenge of visualizing legislative text. Our final approach differs from these examples of related work in a number of ways.

Visualizations such as Word Clouds [20] and Word Trees [21] can be useful for gaining insight into individual text documents. Word Clouds represent a document by relating features of individual words (such as frequency) while Word Trees explore the relationships of words to sentences. Both methods ignore the original relationship between the visualized units. In contrast Many Bills retains the structure of the original document, while augmenting it with metadata useful for topic based segmentation.

Wise et al.'s Themescapes [22] clusters documents based on thematic relationship in a 3-dimensional space. Havre et al.'s ThemeRiver [11] adds the dimension of time to show shifts in overall theme across documents. This class of visualization does not attempt to provide individual document views, which we see as critical to our goal in making legislative text more accessible to citizens.

Systems such as TileBars [12] FeatureLens [8], Digidock Explorer [4], and Jigsaw [18] support information retrieval tasks by providing a means to visualize the occurrence of terms or entities of interest across documents within a corpus. Many Bills also offers a higher level interpretation of the semantics of a particular section, as a guide to reading. While Literature Fingerprinting by Keim and Oelke [13] allows for visual comparison of multiple documents, the metrics displayed are not semantic in nature but rather are lower level linguistic features of text that are best suited to an expert analyzing a document corpus. Document Cards [19] and SmartNails [5] generate semantic, fixed-size thumbnails of documents. Each of these methods provide high-level summary information, but not a high level guide to the original contents of the documents.

Most related to Many Bills are Seesoft [9], ViewTool [6] and Compus [10] that each integrate full-text browsing into the visualization itself. Seesoft and Compus display a reduced view of documents as adjacent columns; coloring portions of the text according to various line-level metrics (SeeSoft) and human-annotated features (Compus). While similar in layout, Many Bills visualizes machine-generated semantic descriptors of document substructure, giving a higher level overview of documents. ViewTool combines a high level, topic-based single-document overview and a full-text view into a single 3-pane interface while Many Bills offers a view of multiple documents allowing users to compare topic distributions.

Plaisant et al.'s visualization of Emily Dickenson's correspondence [17] uses a human-assisted machine classification system to assign documents into one of two categories for further analysis. However, its heavy reliance on experts for both classification and interpretation, as well as the low granularity of its categories, limit its application to the more general problem we are attempting to address.

One example of a project visualizing government textual data is Parallel Tag Clouds, by Collins, et al. [7], explored a large government dataset of complex legal documents focusing on district court rulings. Using a combination of parallel coordinates and tag clouds, users can explore the common words appearing in each district. While this visualization offers insight into the prominent topics in each district, it does not allow advanced users to delve deeper into the dataset, a common trend among text visualizations.

IMPLEMENTATION

Many Bills is a web-based application built on the Ruby on Rails platform using HTML, CSS and Javascript on the front end. In this section we discuss the text analysis technique used and the visualizations available to users on the site.

Text Analysis

While legislation is accompanied by descriptive metadata, the only information provided about the different portions of a bill is within a table of contents. Yet summary information about the different portions of a bill could be useful for providing guidance to citizens on whether they want to read a bill, or which portions of a bill would be most interesting to them. Thus, in analyzing congressional legislation, we sought to discover the distribution of topics that a bill contains.

Congressional bills are structured hierarchically, and although the hierarchy varies across bills, they consistently contain a discrete unit, known as a *section*, that typically covers a single provision of legislation.

Our approach is to use a trained machine learning classifier to estimate the probability of a section of a bill being about a particular subject. To train the classifier we took advantage of the fact that each bill is assigned a *top subject* by the Congressional Research Service (CRS) of the Library of Congress. We use these subject assignments on a collection of over 100,000 bills from 2000-2009 to train a classifier that we then use to label individual sections. Our assumption is that the model that predicts the top subject of an entire bill can be used to predict the subject of an individual section. As new bills are proposed in this session of Congress, we run the classifier over the new bills' sections. To date, there are over 9000 unique bills on the website.

We use a maximum entropy classification algorithm provided by the MALLET toolkit [15] with an 80/20 training/test split and 10-fold cross-validation. No special parameters were used in tuning the algorithm, nor were bills pre-processed prior to classifier training. Our initial results are promising. For example, in the aforementioned Credit CARD Act of 2009, most sections carry the label "Finance and Financial Section," yet the section on gun rights is classified as "Public Lands." Each section receives a probability for each possible top subject provided by the CRS (approx. 80 different subjects). We do not attempt to classify sections with less than 50 words, as we found that the in those cases the results are rarely accurate.

We performed an initial evaluation of the quality of the predictions made by the classifier. Given the large number of sections that we have labelled (73,020 sections at the time of this evaluation), it is difficult to hand-rate a representative sample of sections. As a baseline measurement, we compared the overlap between the subjects we assign to the full set of subjects assigned to the bill by the CRS. In Table 1, we report at different levels of classifier confidence how well our classifications overlap with the CRS classifications for the bill. To calculate this in a manner that is sensitive to the different lengths of bills, we look at the subject we assign to each section in a bill and assign a point if that subject is in the set of subjects indicated by the CRS for that bill. We then divide the total number of points by the number of classified sections in that bill. This measures how many of our classifications match those that the CRS suggest should be present within the bill.

This analysis method does not take into account situations where we may do better than the CRS at suggesting a topic -- we are in fact penalized when this occurs. For example, in the Credit CARD Act, the subjects assigned to the bill are: Finance and Financial Sector, Administrative Law and Regulatory Procedures, Banking and Financial Institutions Regulation, Consumer Credit, Federal Reserve System, Government Information and Archives, and Interest, Dividends, Interest Rates. None of the subjects suggest content related to second amendment rights, national parks, or education on financial literacy: all topics that we are able to identify with our technique.

Admittedly the performance of the classifier as reported in Table 1 is not ideal, however this is an area we continue to work on improving. We hope to increase this performance by better modeling of the language used in the entire dataset and improving feature selection for the classifier. Future work will also gather classifications from our users. One might ask, given there is no ground truth for section classifications, why don't we use unsupervised techniques such as clustering. The primary reason we chose a supervised technique is the ability to present semantically interpretable labels to the user. With clustering, the output would inform us which sections differ from others, but wouldn't tell us why. In early experiments this turned out to be unsatisfactory from a comprehension perspective.

Table 1. Classification Results

Confidence Threshold	Classified Sections (Out of 73,020)	Section classifications that match CRS classifications.
> 0	100%	51%
> 0.20	92%	53%
> 0.40	82%	54%
> 0.60	69%	55%
> 0.80	52%	59%
> 0.99	22%	72%

Visualization Design

The Many Bills website provides two perspectives from which to explore legislation. The first, a document-centric view reveals the topical substructure of bills we have classified. The second provides a view of the different topics that legislators align themselves with and allows users to explore bills from a people-centric perspective.

Document-Centric Visualization

The analysis described previously generates a set of congressional bills where each section has been assigned one or more subjects, along with their associated probabilities. We assign each section a color based on its subject. As we have over 100 different possible subjects, it is impossible to create a color scheme that allows the user to visually distinguish subjects from one another. We manually grouped semantically-related subjects together and assigned each group a color; for example, the subjects "Consumers," "Trade," and "Taxation" all fall under the "Economics" group, which is assigned a green color.

We render each bill's sections as vertically stacked blocks; a block's color corresponds to the top subject (the subject with the highest probability) assigned to that section. The height of a block is mapped to the length of that section in the bill. Inside each section's block, its title is displayed to provide a quick overview of the section's content. When a section is opened by clicking on it, or when a user mouses over it, the classifier's confidence score is displayed. The actual subject assigned to the section is shown by a small badge displayed to the left of the block; each badge is formed from the first few letters of its subject. Figure 2 shows a single bill as represented in Many Bills.

Figure 3 shows four bills in a user-generated collection about the extension of unemployment benefits. The document-centric visualization screen can display up to 50 bills on a single screen at a time, with larger collections spanning over multiple pages. Users can save any group of bills into an annotated collection, with a title and description, by adding them to a temporary storage area known as the 'bill tray'. These collections are browsable from the home page and can be shared with others.

Figure. 4. Ten bills represented in "minified" mode where each section is a color rectangles.

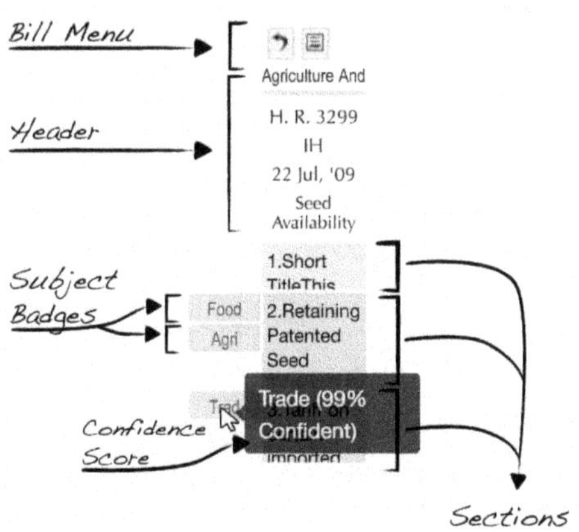

Figure. 2. How a single bill appears in Many Bills, each section color-coded according to classification, marked with a classification badge.

The visualization supports several interaction methods. When a user clicks on a bill section, it expands and displays the full text of the section. This is in line with our primary goal of supporting users in accessing the original data. Furthermore, the entire contents of a bill can be read by clicking a button in the toolbar displayed above each bill. A color legend is provided for each collection page that displays all subjects visible on that page. Users can toggle specific colors on/off, selectively coloring or graying out sections associated with that subject. This enables users to quickly locate topics of interest in the current collection.

Users can switch the visible bills into "minified" mode, shown in Figure 4. In this view, each section is reduced to a rectangle with a fixed height, enabling users to compare patterns of subjects across bills of greatly varying length. Due to the extreme length of some of the more significant bills, this view is particularly valuable for compressing the visual length of a bill. In this mode users are encouraged to navigate the collection of bills through color and tooltips, which show each section's title and classification. Just as in the default view, a single click on a section expands the section to the full text.

Many Bills supports comprehensive search that includes subject, author, date, and full text. The search results appear in the visualization as in the same manner as any other collection, with sections containing search hits highlighted with a yellow bar.

People-Centric Visualization

An alternative visualization provided on Many Bills looks at legislation from the perspective of the people directly involved in the process of its creation and debate. For each Senator and House Representative we provide a page detailing their legislative activity from the current session.

The page comprises of three parts, first (Figure 5a) is a plot that displays every bill sponsored or cosponsored by a congressperson as a square, color coded by the CRS provided subject for that bill. Mousing over each square provides additional information about the bill and clicking on the

Figure. 3. Four bills in a user-generated collection about the extension of unemployment benefits.

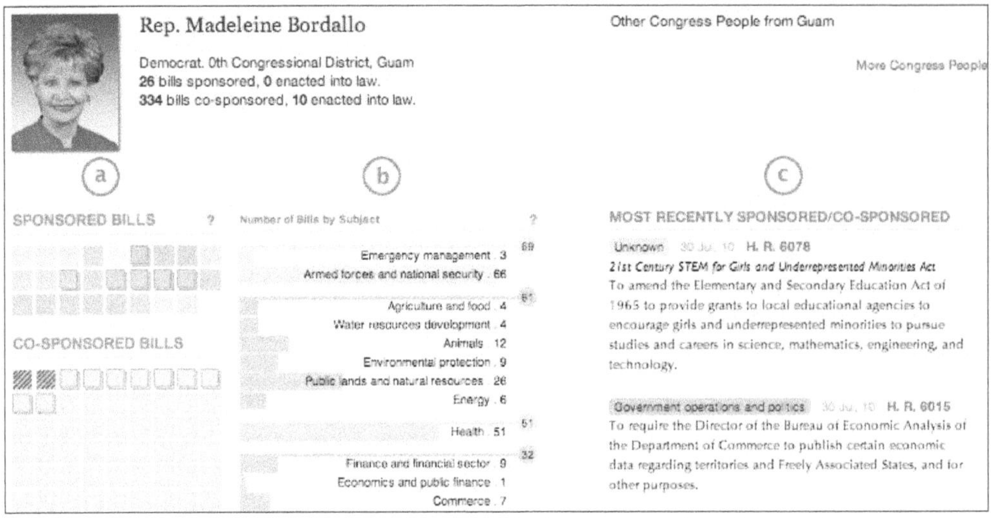

Figure. 5. A Congressperson page. a. Bill plot. b. Bar graph. c. Recent bills.

square takes you to the content of that bill. This plot allows one to get a summary of the various topics a congressperson is particularly active with. The squares are also shaded to indicate how far along in the process a bill is: hashmarks for passed, stacked squares for on the legislative calendar, and plain for introduced.

We also provide a bar chart (Figure 5b) that shows the exact proportions of bills sponsored or cosponsored per member. By employing the interaction techniques of brushing and linking, we allow users to highlight particular parts of the bar chart to filter the first plot of all the bills and highlight those in a particular subject of interest making them easier to pivot to.

The last major element on this page, is a list of recently sponsored or cosponsored bills for the congress person in question (Figure 5c). This list displays the titles of recently sponsored bills as well as their subject assignments from the CRS.

ILLUSTRATIVE EXAMPLES

The primary goal of Many Bills is to offer visual summaries of legislation that offer guidance on where to find interesting or unusual sections of bills. Several examples have provided validation of this and we believe show the various ways in which the tool can help citizens read bills in a more manageable way.

As discussed in our analysis of the classifier's performance, the section on firearms in the Credit CARD Act is correctly labeled as not relating to the "Finance and Financial Sector," but rather "Public Lands." Figure 6 shows how the bill appears within the document-centric visualization. The 'Protecting Americans from Violent Crime' section clearly stands out as a brown rectangle in a sea of green 'Finance' sections.

Another example is the controversial health bill that was signed into law in late 2009. This bill, H.R. 4872 Health Care and Education Affordability Reconciliation Act of 2010, makes substantial changes to health care regulation in the US and its length, of over 2000 pages, was mentioned in the media discussion. Viewing the bill in Many Bills highlights several aspects. As was often mentioned in the media, this bill contains substantial portions of education legislation and this is easily observed by turning off all colors except for those related to education. Instantly, a portion at the end of the bill is lit up, revealing the exact location of these education sections. We believe these dense documents can be made more digestible overall by providing such visual segmentation of a bill into constituent topical clusters.

Another aspect of this bill that dominated media and political discussion was its characterization as "government-run healthcare:" opposing politicians claimed the bill authorized government rationing of healthcare, referred to as "death panels [16]." In our visualization a deep pink color highlights sections relating to "Government and Politics." When exploring the bill, a pink section stands out from the blue "Health" color; section 141, which outlines the formation of a Health Choices Administration and a Health Choices Commissioner. Subsequent sections continue to outline the duties of this new part of the executive branch. It is our hope that making these key topics easier to find will aid citizens in discussing and reasoning about the issues based around the content of the bill, rather than pundits' politicized interpretations of the bill.

Another bill of interest is S. 22 ES, the Omnibus Public Land Management Act of 2009. This bill designates certain lands as components of the National Wilderness Preservation System, in addition to enacting other legislation related to public lands. It is also an extremely long bill with 389 sections. By turning off all of the categorization colors, and then turning on individual category colors, one can discover there are three sections labelled "Medicine." By expanding these sections to their full text, one finds the Christopher and Dana Reeve Paralysis Act, which funds a paralysis rehabilitation center. Just as the firearms provision was added to the Credit CARD Act, this provision deviates from the main bill topic, but may have been necessary to ensure passage of the bill.

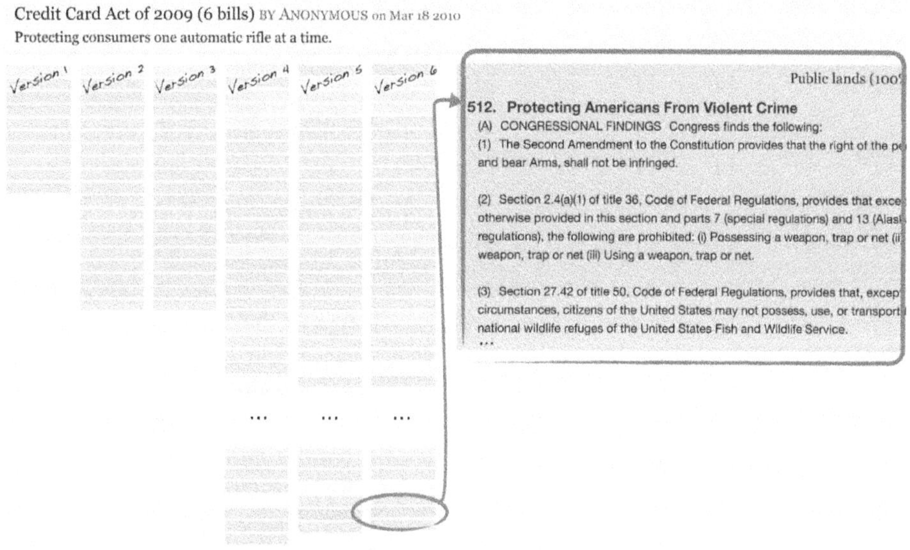

Figure 6. The Credit CARD Act of 2009, as it appears in Many Bills. The bill protects consumers from predatory lending practices by credit card companies. Additionally, it allows citizens to bear firearms in national parks. In this example, 6 revisions of the Credit CARD act are shown.

67% of the bill's sections are classified by our analysis into the category of Natural Resources, assisting the user in focusing in on either that portion of the bill or to the outlier topics.

EVALUATION

The examples described above demonstrate the way in which Many Bills can provide guidance towards understanding a bill's content. To understand how people actually use Many Bills's features and to evaluate whether or not we met our design goals, we analyzed web log data and conducted interviews with select users. For evaluation purposes, the site was instrumented to record single-click events in addition to page views, capturing each click on the minify, read-in-full, and color toggle buttons.

In the five months since launching the site (end of March to beginning of September, 2010), 11,412 visitors visited the site. Examining the logs, we found that 6,656 of these visitors clicked beyond the home page, and this group collectively performed 99,746 actions (clicks) on the site. While these are high numbers, looking at just the users who performed more than 100 actions on the site, the number of users drops to 125 (1.1% of total users). These active users collectively account for 49,264 actions (49.4% of total actions).

This power law distribution of activity is typical for any web community site, and it provides an indication that Many Bills is highly engaging for a certain type of citizen user and that most visitors use the site with less commitment. To explore this hypothesis, we examined the behavior of these 125 "power users," contrasted with the behavior of the 6531 "casual users," who browsed beyond the home page. The purpose of this segmentation is to determine if there are behavioral differences between these populations, beyond simply high versus low levels of activity.

Analysis of Power Users

In terms of visits to the site, power users average 2.3 visits each (median 1, stdev 2.58, max 15). Each visit, they perform an average of 267.6 actions on the site (median 208, stdev 226.1). 39.2% of power users return to the site more than once, contrasted with just 13.5% of casual users.

A surprise to us is that casual users and power users find Many Bills through similar means and search for similar terms on the site. Approximately a third of users find the site through a site associated with our company, a quarter find it through a search engine, 15% find it through a technology or visualization related blog, and 10% find it through a government-related discussion site or blog. We expected that power users would have found the site more through government-related channels, but evidence indicates there is no difference.

Similarly, search terms used on the site by these two groups fall within the same general categories. 18% of users search for a specific bill name, about 8% search for a congressperson, and 3-5% of searches are for geographic regions (states, cities, countries), company names, and government agencies. The remaining 60% are general keyword searches such as "health care," "foster care," and "transportation planning."

The real differences between the casual and the power users emerges in how they interact with bills. Figure 7 shows a comparison of casual versus power users.

For each site action, except for viewing a Congressperson's page, the power users are performing the actions at a significantly higher level, as measured by Chi-square tests ($p<0.001$ for each test). This higher level not surprising because, by definition, the power users are much more active. What is interesting about their activity though is that power users are drilling down into the details of the bill more than they zoom out, whereas the casual users are choosing to view the highest level summary views, over viewing its full text. This can be seen in that twice as many power users choose to read the bill versus minified (98% vs. 54%) and twice as many casual users minified a bill versus read a bill in full (12% vs. 6%),. Similarly, while saving a bill to one's "bill tray" on the site is a less common

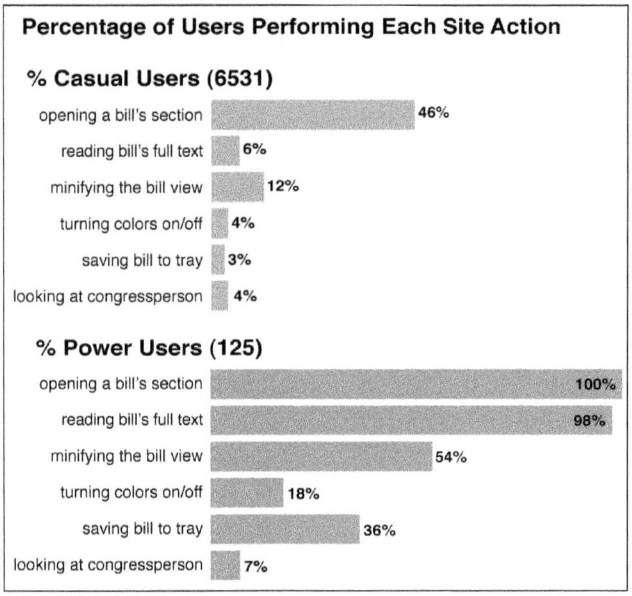

Figure. 7. Comparing all users to 125 power users in terms of how they spend their time on the site

activity, power users are doing it twice as much as they are turning the color guides on/off, whereas the casual users do both at the same low rate. This power-user action of saving a bill on the site indicates a longer-term intention to examine a bill and compare it with others.

Our conclusion from this is that power users, those most active on the site, are utilizing the features that enable the most detailed inspection of a bill: they are viewing bills in their entirety and saving them for later reference. In contrast, the casual users, who by definition are less committed to the site, use the minified feature more, which is designed for the quickest and most cursory overview of a bill's topics. We see this as evidence that our site and visualization design is able to support different levels of interest, and that the more engaged user is focused on accessing the details, rather than remaining at the overview level.

Interviews

To understand how Many Bills does, or does not, support these power users, we interviewed a small set of users who, in addition to having used the site, had experience with legislation in either a professional or personal capacity. We spoke with four people: a journalist, an employee of a non-profit focused on government transparency, a journalism professor, and a citizen involved his local political party chapter. We gave each user a short introduction to Many Bills and then directed them to the live system. We asked them to use the site as they wished for one week, to explore legislation that was of interest to them. We did not assign any specific tasks. One week later, we conducted a phone interview with each subject, asking them about their impressions and discoveries. The interviewees reported having spent from 30 minutes to over 2 hours on the site, spread over multiple days. Their comments, although not in direct comparison to other tools like THOMAS, were well-informed about legislation and legislative data available online.

Our interviews were conducted over the phone in a semi-structured way, gathering their impressions and reactions to the tool.

Overview of an Entire Bill

The primary message we heard during our interviews was that the subjects appreciated the approach on Many Bills of making the original text available, while providing a layer of abstraction that includes visual guides. For example, the non-profit worker said:

> *"Most people try to look at legislation in terms of summarizing it or news articles about it and what you guys got to the heart of was keeping the legislation intact, Keeping its original form but providing an overview insight without delving into summarizing it. It was a neat of experience of still having that first hand account of legislation in a format that was approachable"*
>
> -- Non-profit worker

The journalist described how, with the time constraints of his profession, having a tool that guides a journalist to the general topics is very useful:

> *"A lot of reporters don't have a lot of time anymore to go through and read a lot of legislation, sadly. And so this is a great way to give them an 'at a glance' at what some of the issues in the legislation are so that they know whether or not to dig a little bit deeper."*
>
> -- Journalist

The politically-active citizen was our most enthusiastic subject, explaining

> *"I don't know if it's my attention span or what it is, [but] when I look at the bills I glass out in the first paragraph. When I saw you took the bill and color-coded it and see what a paragraph was about, it suddenly made this very arcane area very approachable to me. I still had a lot to read but at least it was approachable."*
>
> -- Citizen

Many Bills does not eliminate the job of reading the bill, but, according to our subjects, the visualization made it easier to find on the portions of a bill that they were interested in reading and for getting an overall gist on the topics a bill covers.

Discovering Unusual or Outlier Sections

Because of our illustrative examples that motivated much of the design of the site, we were particularly interested in knowing how users found the text classification and color coding. All interview participants confirmed that the visual segmentation created by our coloring of sections helped them navigate the bills and make decisions about what to read next. Again, the journalist said:

> *"Finding stuff that's way outside the box was mostly what I was interested in. So I found myself looking more at those outliers. I'm glad that visualization [modes are] there because when you shrink it down and look at it to see what the biggest outliers are, that's a great tool to get a two-second glance at some thing that would take 3 days to read."*
> -- Journalist

The active citizen described a specific scenario in which the color-coding helped him. His local Democratic party interest group was interested in understanding a new energy bill's contents, S. 1733: Clean Energy Jobs and American Power Act. His plan had been to assign each person a fixed number of sections, to divide up the work of reading the bill and summarize it back to the group. "I tried to break it up to the group mechanically... The group didn't read the bill." When he first used Many Bills, he realized he could draw conclusions about the bill without the need for crowd-sourcing out the different sections:

> *"Everyone had a difficult time approaching the energy bill until we had it color-coded. I can begin to look at the sections in it.... What I did learn is that there are a lot of parts to a bill that have seemingly little to do with the substance that the bill is about. A lot is about how it will be instantiated and financially supported."*
> *-- Citizen*

This feedback that the color-coding gave users a way to locate sections that deviated from the bill's main topic has highlighted the importance of supporting the task of locating outlier sections within bills. In future work, we plan to offer more advanced analysis of outlier sections and enhance the ability for users to find them.

A New Perspective on Congresspeople

The congresspeople pages were added to the site a month prior to this writing, so there has been less time available for users to explore them. Our intention in designing this people-centric visualization was to provide an additional entry point to a bill that is personally meaningful to a user. By looking up one's own congressperson, a user can discover legislation that may be more relevant to their local region; by seeing what a congressperson has been actively sponsoring, a user can form new conclusions about the efforts of elected officials. For example, our active citizen used the feature to compare across multiple congresspeople:

> *"Looked at my congressperson. There were 177 bills, not many passed. Noticed he was very active... Looked at [House Majority Leader] Harry Reid . Noticed there were less bills... Looked at [House Minority Leader] Mitch McConnell. Saw two bills sponsored and five co-sponsored. It's an eye opener. This was opening up to me the inner workings of Congress. ... [Learned that McConnell's] job was not to represent the people of Kentucky; He was there to represent the Republican party.*
> -- Citizen

We also had an opportunity to give a demo of Many Bills to a Member of Congress. We showed her a bill that she had recently proposed relating to the BP oil spill in the Gulf of Mexico. While the record shows that the bill has not progressed through Congress, she explained that the contents of the bill were incorporated into another, more comprehensive bill that was voted on and passed. She elaborated that the process of legislation is very "human" and hard to fully capture in government documents. Our discussion with her highlighted a limitation of government transparency based on government-released data: the data does not tell the whole story. A major direction to take this research is to incorporate the input of expert users, through mechanisms like annotation, that explain the data and reveal the story behind the data.

IMPLICATIONS

As discussed earlier in the paper, our belief is that for the open government movement to engage citizens with the government data, tools for citizens need to provide guides and references to make finding the information easier, rather than simply summarize or provide interpretations of the data. In our power users, we see indications and reports that the detailed views into the data are the most utilized, and useful, capabilities. The implication is that open government data applications that do support data exploration, and essentially ownership of the data, empowers citizens and supports their goals.

On the other hand, we have not seen broad adoption on the site by casual users interested in government. This may be a consequence of our chosen dataset: legislative text is still a challenge for lay users to understand, even with topic guides. Yet this may be an issue with any open government dataset: the details, while important in terms of what the government is doing, may be beyond the scope of what citizens may want or need. This remains a challenge for those working in open government to continue to explore.

Our analysis of how people are using Many Bills provides some lessons learned that may apply to any applications built for large text datasets, either government-related or not. First, the activity on the site will likely follow a power law where a few number of people are engaging in great detail with the text, and these users have either a professional or deep personal interest in the data. That is to be expected for any resource of complex data. But what was informative in our log analysis and interviews was that the activity level of the user influenced which features they used: power users focused more on features for detailed analysis and casual users focused on features for summarizing analysis. This discovery indicates that the design of our data visualization, which aimed for a mid-level of detail as a default, was able to support *both* types of users by allowing one to either abstract or drill deeper on the data. This is not always the appropriate choice to make, but in our context of aiming to engage a diverse citizen population, we see this as a promising approach.

As we move forward in our development of open government applications aiming to engage citizens, we see allowing users, particularly power users, to annotate and even contribute to the data, as an important step towards empowering citizens to engage with their government. We also see that involving power users in the process of explaining the data could open up channels through which the casual user may transition to being a more engaged user.

CONCLUSION

In this paper, we presented the design and implementation of Many Bills, a web-based set of visualizations that provides rich interactive views of US Congressional Legislation. Our initial user evaluations indicate that this is a valuable tool for helping people access the content of bills and get an easy to interpret overview.

The techniques used in Many Bills can be applied to domains with complex categorized documents that have an impact on non-experts. For example: legal documents such as terms of service and patent filings, other government documents such as judicial court decisions and the tax code. The approach used in Many Bills can assist users in accessing the content of the text with topic and outlier guides, pointing to the potentially interesting portions.

Many Bills is one contribution to the open government movement and there are many remaining opportunities in this domain. We see the road to citizen engagement as having many steps, beginning with citizens understanding the data and the actions of the government. This is where Many Bills' focus has been. Deeper engagement includes citizens communicating their discoveries and sharing their opinion. Many Bills supports some of this, but this could be supported to a greater extent.

ACKNOWLEDGMENTS

We want to particularly thank GovTrack.us and Open Congress for providing their data in open, accessible ways. We also thank our colleagues for their input on the design of Many Bills and our users for their valuable feedback.

REFERENCES

1. GovTrack.us. http://www.govtrack.us/
2. OpenCongress. http://www.opencongress.org/
3. THOMAS (Library of Congress). http://thomas.loc.gov/
4. Apitz, G. and Lin, J. Interfaces to Support the Scholarly Exploration of Text Collections. (2008).
5. Berkner, K., Schwartz, E.L., and Marle, C. Document Recognition and Retrieval XI. SPIE (2003), 54-65.
6. Boguraev, B., Kennedy, C., Bellamy, R., Brawer, S., Wong, Y., and Swartz, J. Dynamic presentation of document content for rapid on-line skimming. (1998), 118-128.
7. Collins, C., Viégas, F.B., and Wattenberg, M. Parallel tag clouds to explore and analyze faceted text corpora. IEEE Symposium on Visual Analytics Science and Technology (VAST), (2009), 91–98.
8. Don, A., Zheleva, E., Gregory, M., et al. Discovering interesting usage patterns in text collections: integrating text mining with visualization. (2007), 213–222.
9. Eick, S., Steffen, J., and Jr, E.S. Seesoft - A Tool for Visualizing Line Oriented Software Statistics. IEEE Transactions on Software Engineering 18, 11 (1992), 957-968.
10. Fekete, J. and Dufournaud, N. Compus: visualization and analysis of structured documents for understanding social life in the 16th century. ACM (2000), 47-55.
11. Havre, S., Hetzler, E., Whitney, P., and Nowell, L. ThemeRiver: Visualizing Thematic Changes in Large Document Collections. IEEE Transactions on Visualization and Computer Graphics 8, 1 (2002), 9-20.
12. Hearst, M.A. TileBars: visualization of term distribution information in full text information access. Proceedings of the SIGCHI conference on Human factors in computing systems, (1995), 59–66.
13. Keim, D.A. and Oelke, D. Literature fingerprinting: A new method for visual literary analysis. IEEE Symposium on Visual Analytics Science and Technology, 2007. VAST 2007, (2007), 115–122.
14. Kinnaird, P., Romero, M., and Abowd, G. Connect 2 congress: visual analytics for civic oversight. (2010), 2853–2862.
15. McCallum, A.K. MALLET: A Machine Learning for Language Toolkit. 2002. http://mallet.cs.umass.edu.
16. Nyhan, B. Why the "Death Panel" Myth Wouldn't Die: Misinformation in the Health Care Reform Debate. POLITICS 8, 1 (2010), 5.
17. Plaisant, C., Rose, J., Yu, B., et al. Exploring erotics in Emily Dickinson's correspondence with text mining and visual interfaces. ACM (2006), 141-150.
18. Stasko, J., G\örg, C., and Liu, Z. Jigsaw: Supporting investigative analysis through interactive visualization. Information Visualization 7, 2 (2008), 118–132.
19. Strobelt, H., Oelke, D., Rohrdantz, C., Stoffel, A., Keim, D.A., and Deussen, O. Document Cards: A Top Trumps Visualization for Documents. IEEE Transactions on Visualization and Computer Graphics 15, 6 (2009), 1145-1152.
20. Viégas, F.B., Wattenberg, M., and Feinberg, J. Participatory Visualization with Wordle. IEEE Transactions on Visualization and Computer Graphics 15, 6 (2009), 1137–1144.
21. Wattenberg, M. and Viégas, F.B. The word tree, an interactive visual concordance. IEEE Transactions on Visualization and Computer Graphics, (2008), 1221–1228.
22. Wise, J.A., Thomas, J.J., Pennock, K., et al. Visualizing the non-visual: Spatial analysis and interaction with information from text documents. Proceedings of the 1995 IEEE Symposium on Information Visualization, (1995).

HCI for Peace: A Call for Constructive Action

Juan Pablo Hourcade and Natasha E. Bullock-Rest
Department of Computer Science
University of Iowa
14 MacLean Hall, Iowa City, IA 52242 USA
hourcade@cs.uiowa.edu, natasha.bullock.rest@gmail.com

ABSTRACT
Peace is an important value for the human-computer interaction research community, yet it has not resulted in the development of a research sub-community or even a research agenda. In this paper we seek to address this void by first motivating the need for computing research on promoting peace and preventing war. We then review evidence on the factors that affect the likelihood that armed conflict will occur, as well as the aspects involved when individuals make moral decisions on whether or not to support a war. Based on this review, we propose a research agenda, citing research examples from the human-computer interaction literature and discussing new ideas.

Author Keywords
Peace, war, causes of conflict, empathy, compassion, software, technology, research agenda.

ACM Classification Keywords
H5.m. Information interfaces and presentation (e.g., HCI): Miscellaneous. K.3.1. Computer uses in education. K.4.1. Public policy issues.

General Terms
Human factors.

INTRODUCTION
We are members of the human-computer interaction community interested in using computing technologies to promote peace and prevent conflict. This paper aims to highlight and celebrate work already done to this end and to encourage further research with peace as its explicit goal. We hope this call to action continues community-wide discussions from which positive action can spring: our world can be no brighter than the worlds we dream of. We seek to create the conditions for peace by both promoting the precursors of peace and decreasing the known causes of conflict. The human-computer interaction community is uniquely positioned in the computing world to affect change in this arena, its focus not only on the user sitting in front of a screen, but on the effect of technology on humanity at a societal and global scale. As 1997 Nobel Peace Prize winner Jody Williams demonstrated through her use of email to help coordinate the International Campaign to Ban Landmines [10], computer technologies can play a positive role in promoting peace. In the human-computer interaction community many research efforts have focused on precursors of peace. These include projects promoting education in developing regions (e.g., [46][57][58]), and supporting democracy through transparent, understandable, easily audited voting systems (e.g., [35][68]). There are many additional opportunities for research including the design of technologies to enable connections between opposing camps, tools to present news stories from several points of view, and technologies to support international monitoring missions to prevent the escalation of conflicts.

We saw an additional indicator of the importance of peace within the human-computer interaction community during CHI 2010. At the conference, 500 attendees became peace ambassadors, wearing peace ribbons on their name badges and engaging with other attendees in a discussion of how computing technology can be used to promote peace and prevent conflict. About 50 peace ambassadors gathered for an impromptu brainstorm for peace during the last day of the conference, generating many ideas on how the human-computer interaction community can design technologies that have peace as an explicit goal.

In this paper, we focus on peace in regards to preventing armed conflicts. In the following sections, we further motivate the need for research in this area, discuss related work and initiatives, and propose a research agenda based on our peace brainstorm and focused on the antecedents of peace at a socio-political level as well as at an individual level. Our intention is to motivate constructive action in this area and begin to build a research community dedicated to technologies to promote peace and prevent conflict[1].

[1] Part of the paper is based on a previous publication in alt.chi (not an archival venue) [38].

WHY PEACE

There are very practical reasons to pursue research on promoting peace and preventing conflict. Even the military recognizes this. For example, the 2008 National Defense Strategy, prepared by the United States Department of Defense states that "military efforts to capture or kill terrorists are likely to be subordinate to measures to promote local participation in government and economic programs to spur development, as well as efforts to understand and address the grievances that often lie at the heart of insurgencies" [16].

This last statement makes it clear that peace is not just a goal for idealists but also for pragmatists. Nobel Prize Winner Joseph Stiglitz, for example, has estimated that the Iraq war is costing every household in the United States 138 USD a month, and that by 2017 the United States will have paid 1 trillion USD in interest for the money borrowed to pursue this war [20]. Studying war in developing regions, Frances Stewart, an economist at the University of Oxford, also discusses the devastating economic impact of war, with most of the poorest countries in the world currently or recently involved in violent conflicts [69].

Notwithstanding the economic costs of war, the most horrible costs are in terms of human lives. The most atrocious example in recent history is the civil war in Rwanda that cost the lives of about 500,000 people and is still having negative consequences in neighboring Congo [18]. In addition, during the 20th century no less than 87 million people died as a direct consequence of war, a number that does not include the more than 150 million civilians deliberately put to death due to doctrinal hatred or passions [9].

PEACE AND COMPUTING RESEARCH

Given the increasingly ubiquitous nature of digital technology in people's lives, many in the human-computer interaction community have promoted the use of computing to pursue specific values or agendas. Examples include research on technologies for environmental sustainability [8], feminist approaches to design [4], and the development of technologies for social activism [23][24].

When it comes to peace, Ben Shneiderman has long been a strong and consistent voice calling for the use of information technologies to promote world peace, arguing that peace should be part of a social impact statement in every human-computer interaction project [64]. BJ Fogg taught a peace innovation course at Stanford and has recently began the Peace Dot initiative, encouraging organizations to create a "peace" subdomain for their websites [25]. There have also been a few specific projects with the express purpose of promoting peace, which we will highlight as examples when discussing our proposed research agenda. In spite of these efforts, there is currently no research sub-community within human-computer interaction dedicated to peace, and a search for the word "peace" in the ACM Digital Library yields no papers with at least five citations on the topic of promoting peace and preventing armed conflict.

Outside the human-computer interaction research community, the *ICT for peace foundation* is dedicated to supporting the international community in managing crises through the use of information and communications technology [42]. This foundation has strong links to international organizations such as the United Nations. Other organizations, such as the *United States Institute of Peace* and *World Peace Through Technology*, support the development of technologies for peacebuilding and benevolence [71][73].

The most comprehensive proposal for conducting computing research on peace actually came from one of the parents of computer science as an academic discipline. Just a few months after the Cuban Missile Crisis, Louis Fein wrote a paper titled *Computer-Oriented Peace Research,* which proposed the creation of the *Peace on Earth Research Center* (PERC). His vision was for PERC to construct computer models to provide a better understanding of the problems that cause armed conflict and through this understanding develop solutions that could prevent future conflicts [22].

The past 10-15 years have seen a large number of publications that have addressed Fein's first challenge by conducting statistical analyses of empirical data on conflict to better understand the risk factors associated with war. This research, together with the increasingly ubiquitous nature of computing technologies provide a unique opportunity for human-computer interaction researchers to make a difference in designing technologies that prevent conflict and promote peace.

In addition, recent research in neuroscience is increasingly providing a clearer picture of how humans make moral decisions that involve empathy and compassion, including decisions concerning war and killing other human beings. This recent research can also provide inspiration to design technologies that make people aware of the humanity of perceived enemies when making decisions about war.

SOCIO-POLITICAL CAUSES OF WAR

Factors that Increase the Likelihood of War

In an article in the *British Medical Journal*, Stewart provides an overview of findings on the causes of armed conflict in developing countries, which have been the costliest in human lives in the past 50 years [69]. A cause she and others highlight is private motivation (e.g., economic benefits of joining armed groups, looting, and illicit trade). The main proponent of this idea is Collier, who found that economic opportunities are more likely to drive civil wars than grievances. His point is that civil wars will not occur if rebel organizations cannot be financially viable. Collier found that countries that heavily depend on primary commodity exports are much more likely to experience civil wars because it is difficult to ascertain the origin of these commodities and they can be more easily commercialized [11][12][14]. Private motivation is not limited to causing wars in developing countries though. In his 1961 farewell address, United States President Dwight D. Eisenhower cautioned against the "unwarranted influence" of the military-industrial complex and encouraged "an alert and knowledgeable citizenry" to ensure that such a powerful entity remained compatible "with our peaceful methods and goals" [21].

A second type of cause cited by Stewart is a failure of the social contract (e.g., low incomes, short life expectancy). Collier, for example, found that rapid economic decline increases the risk for conflict by increasing the financial incentive for participating in an armed conflict [11][12][14]. DeRouen Jr. and Goldfinch also cite social unrest as a cause of violent conflict [17].

A third cause for conflict cited by Stewart is environmental stress (e.g., lack of resources). Homer-Dixon studied how environmental scarcities can contribute to violent conflicts citing examples in Senegal, Mauritania, Israel and the West Bank, Nicaragua and other countries [37].

A fourth factor Stewart mentions and that often comes first to mind is inequality (e.g., political access, economic, social, gender). While economic inequality is often part of the grievances brought up to justify violent conflicts, it does not appear to be a good predictor for conflicts [11][12][14]. Cramer provides the example of many countries with high levels of inequality (e.g., Panama, Brazil) that have not recently experienced civil war [15]. There is evidence though, that gender equality reduces the likelihood of intra- and inter-state armed conflict [56].

An interesting dimension of armed conflicts is ethnicity and other kinds of identities. DeRouen Jr. and Goldfinch found that inter and intrastate conflicts are more likely to become violent if there is an ethnic dimension to the crisis [17]. Sambonis argues that there is a difference between ethnic/religious (identity) wars and those that are not. Through a statistical analysis of civil wars, he concludes that identity wars are mostly caused by political grievances and are unlikely to occur in democratic countries [62]. Surprisingly, Collier found that ethnic and religious fractionalization reduced the risk for conflict. However, having the largest ethnic group constitute 45-90 percent of the population increased the risk of civil war. Collier speculates that ethnic groups constituting such a fraction of the population have the means and the incentive to exploit other ethnic groups [11][12][14].

Collier cites other risk factors for civil wars including having a high proportion of young men in the population and partially democratic governments [11][12][14]. DeRouen Jr. and Goldfinch add other risk factors including contiguity to an adversary, a violent trigger to the crisis, and chronic and severe problems [17]. Demonstrating the complexity behind the sources of conflict, Kenyon-Lischer provides evidence of how humanitarian aid can sometimes contribute to conflict if it is, for example, provided to refugee camps that are used as military bases by armed groups [47].

Factors that Reduce the Likelihood of War

The most consistent finding in the literature is that fully democratic countries are less likely to have civil wars and participate in armed conflicts with other countries [11][12][14][17][60][62].

A better-educated population reduces the risk of armed conflict. Studying data on 152 countries for the period between 1965 and 1995, Collier found that each additional year of education reduces the risk of civil war by about 20 percent. He also found that economic growth and high incomes reduce the risk for civil war [11][12][13][14].

Alice Ackermann discusses the history and current practices of international conflict prevention, from the Congress of Vienna in 1815, to the Marshall Plan and the various roles the United Nations has played. Ackermann distinguishes between two types of conflict prevention practices. Operational prevention is aimed at imminent crises and includes actions such as fact-finding and monitoring missions, negotiation, mediation, facilitating dialogue between the parts and confidence building measures. A recent example is what was done to prevent an escalation of the conflict between Georgia and Russia in 2008. Structural prevention aims to prevent conflicts in the long term through actions such as facilitating governance, increasing the respect for human rights, improving educational systems and economic opportunities, and promoting democracy [1].

The research in this section provides empirical evidence on the socio-political causes of war. In the following section, we discuss the role of personal decisions and compassion.

PERSONAL DECISIONS AND WAR[2]

Recent developments in neuroscience are relevant to how armed conflict occurs at a micro level, in particular with regards to what makes it easier for individuals to decide that a particular war is necessary and to make the decision to kill another human being. In this section we discuss how compassion is triggered in human beings, and how it is being systematically removed from decision-making in war-related situations.

Neuroscience and Compassion

One way to understand compassion is to learn about people who lack compassion. Psychopaths are people who have perfect use of reason but who do not experience emotions in the face of fear or suffering on the part of fellow human beings [7]. In other words, psychopaths lack compassion.

---

[2] This section of the paper was inspired by Jonah Lehrer's book *How we decide*, in particular the chapter titled *The Moral Mind* [51]

For example, a study by Blair [6] looked at how psychopaths compared to other violent offenders in judging conventional and moral transgressions. In the study participants were presented with scenarios taking place in a school. Psychopaths thought that if given permission by a teacher, it is equally fine to talk in class (a conventional transgression) as to hit another child (a moral transgression). Non-psychopaths thought it was still wrong to hit another child. Blair [7] cites neurological evidence pointing at psychopaths having impairments in specific regions of the brain that have been associated with social cognition.

Neuroscientists have made great inroads in the past decade in identifying these brain regions, helping us better understand how we make decisions involving social matters. In particular, there is increasing evidence that specific parts of the brain, such as the medial prefrontal cortex, are involved in tasks involving mental-state attribution (e.g., [27][55]). Furthermore, these regions of the brain are most developed in social primates, with the greatest development in humans [28]. In other words, the brain structures associated with empathy and compassion are part of what makes us human.

A clever example of how empathy works in our brains comes from a study by Harvard University's Joshua Greene and colleagues that tests the difference between personal and impersonal moral decisions. Greene presents participants with one of two scenarios. In one scenario a runaway trolley is heading toward five people who will be killed if nothing happens. You have the option of hitting a switch that will make the trolley go to another set of tracks, killing one person instead. Most participants (about 95%) chose to hit the switch. In another scenario, the only way to save the five people is to push someone onto the path of the trolley. Almost no participants would push someone and have them die in order to spare the life of five others. When exposed to the second scenario, participants used the regions of the brain involved in mental-state attribution [29]. They could put themselves in the other person's shoes.

Greene et al. [30] later studied what happens when there are personal moral versus utilitarian values at play. In their experiment, participants were presented with a scenario in which they had a choice of smothering a crying baby, or letting the baby cry and have everyone in a group (including the baby) killed by troops under order to do so. They found that in these cases the brain activated regions associated both with personal moral and utilitarian values and it appeared that another part of the brain, the anterior cingulated cortex, played the role of arbiter.

Soldiers face similar dilemmas, but in real-life scenarios. During World War II, Brigadier General S.L.A. Marshall surveyed thousands of United States troops after they had been in combat in the front lines in Europe and the Pacific [54]. He found that "in an average experienced infantry company in an average stern day's action, the number engaging with any and all weapons was approximately 15 per cent of total strength. In the most aggressive infantry companies, under the most intense local pressure, the figure rarely rose above 25 per cent of total strength from the opening to the close of action." In other words, on average, more than four out of five soldiers in the front lines were not firing their weapons at all during combat. This is a clear example of the compassion displayed by what in the United States is referred to as the "greatest generation." Grossman provides evidence of similarly low firing rates for United States soldiers during the United States Civil War and World War I [31]. Marshall and the United States armed forces though, thought this was a serious problem. Marshall stated: "there is every reason why the fire ratio factor should be treated primarily as a most vital training problem."

Bypassing Compassion During Battle

Armed forces throughout the world took notice, and training was modified to bypass the activation of the regions of the brain responsible for empathy and compassion. In the United States, this has been accomplished through a combination of desensitization, conditioning and denial defense mechanisms [31]. To desensitize, training emphasizes to the soldier that "their purpose is not just to be brave or to fight well; it is to kill people" [19]. To condition soldiers, training presents tasks where soldiers learn to instinctively shoot at targets that are made to look as close as possible to real human beings. This also helps develop denial defense mechanisms in that killing on the battlefield is so similar to training that soldiers do not think of what they are doing as killing other human beings. Through these changes, firing rates for United States soldiers, for example, went significantly up, from the 15 percent S.L.A. Marshall found in World War II to 90 percent or more during the Vietnam War [31]. Lieutenant Colonel (Ret.) Grossman, who taught psychology at West Point, believes the changes in training are necessary to help soldiers complete missions and survive. But he also acknowledges the negative impact of these changes on the mental health of soldiers due to the higher levels of violence they experience. In particular, he is concerned about the increasing rates of mental health disorders for United States war veterans [31], with about 30 percent of Vietnam veterans suffering post-traumatic stress disorder at some point after deployment, and some estimates finding that as many as 40 percent of reservists returning from the current conflict in Iraq screen positive for mental health disorders [53].

Another way to make it easier to kill is to increase the distance between warriors and those they are asked to kill [31]. When you do not see the faces of those you might kill, or you do not even see their bodies, you are much less likely to use those regions of the brain involved in mental-state attribution that bring about compassionate actions. When you do not see the carnage of war, you are much more likely to support it. Hence, the increased use of military technologies that distance the warrior from those who get killed. The latest incarnation is drones that make killing seem like playing a video game. Armed forces in several countries, joined by researchers in artificial intelligence, robotics and other disciplines are going a step further by developing autonomous battlefield robots. These are robots that will make their own decisions on who to kill. Their supporters claim that by having no emotion, the robots will avoid war crimes [3]. What they fail to consider is that the robots will have no compassion. In other words, autonomous battlefield robots will be the perfect psychopaths.

In addition, autonomous battlefield robots would be the ultimate way of separating those deciding to start a war from the carnage caused by their decision. Interestingly, there is a parallel between the automation of war and the automation of the modern economy. For example, financial decisions, such as accepting a mortgage application, used to be made by lending officers with plenty of experience who made decisions case-by-case through an examination of an applicant's credit-worthiness. Financial firms decided to replace them with statistical models and algorithms that provided excellent short-term savings, yet no one seemed to completely understand. In his recent book, Tufts University's Amar Bhidé argues they were behind the current financial crisis because these models and algorithms lacked the judgment of the individual people who used to make decisions [5]. We argue that beyond a judgment gap, automation adds a responsibility gap. Who would be responsible if autonomous robots massacre poorly armed conscripts from an opposing army with little intent to fight?

We have to realize that these technologies are very attractive to the military for several reasons. First, they minimize casualties for the side using them. Second, they are often much more accurate than many weapons used in the 20th Century (e.g., fire bombings of cities), potentially leading to lower civilian casualties. And third, because of the greater distance, they reduce the likelihood that those operating the technologies will suffer from mental disorders. Hence, there is little chance they will go away.

The problem is that the increasing use of technologies with the above characteristics (whether robots or remote controlled drones) can make it a lot easier and less painful to start wars. They not only distance the warrior from those being killed, they distance citizens in democratic countries from those being killed by their militaries.

It is also possible to increase the social distance to enemies by making them seem inferior, evil or immoral. The language of war plays a role in this respect. Ivie, for example, discusses the use of language in justifications of war by the United States, with the presentation of Americans as victims and enemies as savages driven by irrational desires [45].

Terrorist groups also understand the need to take compassion out of the equation. What works for them is the demonization and de-humanization of people who are different. Just like military entities, they seek to increase the distance between the warrior and the people who are killed, but in this case the emphasis is on increasing the social distance [72].

This is where the human-computer interaction community can make a contribution. More specifically, we can help by designing technologies that engage people at an individual level and help understand both the humanity we share with perceived enemies, and the real costs of war in terms of human lives and human suffering. In other words, we can engage the regions of the brain that support empathy, compassion and altruism by reducing the physical and social distance with potential victims of war. The goal is to enable people to fully understand the human consequences of going to war. Not surprisingly, most of the ideas proposed during the peace brainstorm at CHI 2010 address this issue [34].

RESEARCH AGENDA

In this section we discuss the role human-computer interaction can play in promoting peace and preventing conflict. To do so we focus on proposals and examples of technologies that can promote compassion in order to prevent war. We also go through the factors that increase or decrease the likelihood of war at a socio-political level and discuss how previous projects have already made positive contributions and where there are opportunities for research. In both cases, we do not intend to provide a comprehensive collection of what has been done and what could be done, but rather provide constructive ideas for conducting human-computer interaction research for peace.

When possible, we will refer to topics that were raised during our peace brainstorm at CHI 2010. At the peace brainstorm, attendees found someone they did not personally know, discussed their ideas for peace with them and wrote the ideas on sticky notes. From these ideas, several main themes emerged: promoting education, increasing social awareness of everyday actions, creating a culture of peace, engaging other organizations, exposing the ugly side of war, promoting cross-cultural understanding, and building infrastructure and tools.

Promoting Compassion to Prevent War

Reduce the Social Distance Between Enemies

In a 2007 article in *Science*, Jonathan Haidt discusses how people make moral decisions [32]. The evidence from neuroscience suggests that most often we make these decisions based on our intuition, and then attempt to rationalize them. Imagine Sara, who is deciding whether or not to support a war, and has a long social distance between her and her perceived enemies (e.g., thinking they are inferior or immoral). How can we help her understand the humanity of her perceived enemies and the likely costs in human lives and suffering of the war she might support? Haidt presents evidence that there are at least three ways of achieving this. The first is for her to use verbal reasoning to better evaluate the costs and benefits of her decision. The second is for her to consciously reframe the situation, to see the decision from someone else's perspective, for example. The third is for Sara to speak with other people who can help her see the question from a different perspective. Haidt points out that the first two ways are rarely used, while the third is the most common. Most changes in moral attitudes, and in our case, in decisions about supporting a war will occur through social interaction.

Hence, the development of technologies that can connect people of opposing factions in a way that they can interact with each other and learn about their common humanity could prove very useful. On peace.facebook.com, for example, it is possible to track the number of friendships between people of "opposing camps", such as Israelis and Palestinians, Greeks and Turks, and Indians and Pakistanis. Sometimes what is needed is simply to help people engage with others who are not in their immediate social circle. In this respect, in a recent article in *interactions*, Hochheiser and Shneiderman emphasize the importance of social media technologies that can restore participation in social, civic and political institutions [36].

However, there is a need to go beyond providing a means to communicate. There have to be incentives to reach out to those we disagree with. It is always tempting to stay within a social network of people who share similar ideas to ours. To counteract this, and to change people's minds about perceived enemies, research points at the power of storytelling. To understand the plight of a group of people, statistics about what they go through are much less powerful than stories about specific people, as has been found in studies on donations to charity [66]. Therefore, providing ways of sharing visual stories on people from opposing sides could greatly help in reducing the social distance between perceived enemies. Even simple storytelling through video could prove powerful, as some of our colleagues have found in places like Rwanda and Liberia (e.g., [26][63][67]).

Not surprisingly, by far the most discussed topic during our peace brainstorm at CHI 2010 was reducing conflict through emphasizing our common humanity, encouraging people to step out of their comfort zones to make cross-cultural connections and seek out information from new sources of ideas, help them learn about each other, and think from another perspective. Ideas to this effect included setting up video-conferencing classrooms across the world, creating a site for "speed friending" across the globe – particularly for countries in conflict, encouraging diverse groups of young children to communicate through playing and collaborating together across time and space, setting up partnerships for the privileged to collaborate and help people in need, and a computer-mediated pen pal system to match children in conflict prone tension areas. To seek out different perspectives, one participant suggested findyouropposite.net, a space in which one could discuss ideas with people from different persuasions and backgrounds. A participant mentioned that it is important for everyone's voice to be heard, even if it requires extra work on our part. Microblogging could be used as a helpful tool, both for sharing experiences and for making higher numbers of contacts from other countries.

Other examples of research on highlighting the humanity of others include that of Stock et al. who presented a tool for joint narration to promote conflict negotiation and resolution, with some results from an experience between Arab and Jewish youth [70]. A few years earlier, Rosen described something similar through *KidCast for Peace*, which proposed connecting children in various parts of the world so they could share their creations and obtain feedback [61]. The *International Children's Digital Library* provides access to children's books in dozens of languages, enabling children to read books written by people from other ethnic and religious groups [39]. Other possibilities for research include tools that automatically "translate" euphemisms and dehumanizing language in news stories as well as tools that will bring up the same news story from several points of view.

Expose War, Celebrate Peace

Another way to reduce the physical distance between opposing factions is to expose the ugly side of war as wars are happening. Participants at the peace brainstorm brought up the need to educate people about the negative facts of war through pictures, stories, and anecdotes, as a way to increase empathy and compassion. Al-Ani et al., for example, discuss the use of blogs written by Iraqi citizens, and how they enable others not experiencing the war to learn about what it is like to live in a war zone [2].

A counterpart to this idea that was also discussed at the peace brainstorm is that creating a culture that values peace involves creating activities that highlight peace. One idea was the geocaching of "peace sites" in the model that war sites and battlefields are commended, including places like the ones where Gandhi and Martin Luther King Jr. spoke. Video games such as *PeaceMaker* where players win by achieving peace can also help [43].

In addition, computer technology could be used to better understand how populations are convinced to go to war. For example, an analysis of media stories could trace how pro-war messages and language are distributed and who originates them. This idea could be extended to examine how online social networks are used to promote war and peace.

Socio-Political Interventions to Promote Peace

De-Incentivize Private Motivation

Private motivation to go to war could be exposed through information visualization techniques. For example, students in one of our classes designed information visualization software to track the path of campaign contributions for the United States Presidential primaries.

It enabled users to see where the campaign contributions came from and where the politicians were spending money. Similar efforts could be used to untangle the financial interests behind wars.

Participants at our peace brainstorm discussed similar ideas. One participant noted, "conflict should not produce profit," highlighting the frequent interplay between the two, dovetailing with another participant's suggestion to create visualizations that illuminate the public cost of war and who profits to help people understand the forces that create conflict.

Prevent Failures of the Social Contract

Failures of the social contract that cause extreme poverty and low life expectancy can be addressed through a variety technologies. Mobile technologies can help provide information to prevent disease, promote healthy habits, and help people in developing regions get more out of what they have by, for example, being informed of market prices and weather forecasts. In Uruguay for example, parents in rural areas whose children received laptops have used them to check on market prices for milk to schedule pick-ups [41].

Alleviate Environmental Stress

Technologies can help alleviate environmental stress in many ways. Blevis' recommendations on sustainable interaction design can help in preventing technologies from having a negative impact on the environment [8]. Satellite imaging delivered in a user-friendly manner can be used to better understand how to manage natural resources and predict where crises may occur. Simulations and modeling can help evaluate different scenarios in the use of resources while information visualization can help the public better understand how the products they consume affect the environment.

Address Inequality

Inequality could be addressed first by making people aware of its prevalence and severity. Information visualization in combination with storytelling could be used for this purpose. For example, Shneiderman's "details on demand" could be stories instead of numbers [65]. The more difficult task is actually reducing inequality. Efforts to democratize access to the Internet, when combined with appropriate education on how to make the most out of it could prove useful. Technologies to facilitate peer-to-peer micro-financing, such as Kiva, can also provide more people with opportunities to become economically self-sufficient [49]. Taking advantage of mobile devices to spread know-how in rural areas is another promising path [59]. Feminist perspectives can also inform the design of technologies to contribute toward gender equality [4].

Promote Democracy

According to the empirical studies reviewed in this paper, promoting full democracy with free and fair elections, freedom of assembly, press and religion, and respect for human rights is one of the surest ways of preventing conflict. Getting there may not be so simple, but one could argue that greater exposure through the Internet to how successful countries' governments work may contribute toward democracy. Technologies can also help implement democratic reforms more quickly through the use, for example, of well-implemented voting systems that can easily be audited and provide transparency [35][68]. As Ben Bederson said in a recent interview "The HCI community must help ensure that not only are voting systems reliable, secure and accurate, but also that the voters understand and believe in them" [33].

Promote Education

An example of a project aiming to improve educational levels in developing regions is *One Laptop Per Child* (OLPC) [58]. In spite of many setbacks and falling well short of its vision [50], in at least some locations, the project has provided children with an enormous increase in their access to content, and encouraged them to produce their own. This makes it more likely that they will acquire 21st century skills to better understand, analyze and use online information and produce digital content of their own [40]. Other examples of work on educational technologies for developing regions include the work of Kam et al. on e-learning games, and Moraveji et al. on single display groupware learning applications [46][57]. In all these efforts in developing regions it is always important to take into account the dynamic nature of culture and the impact of historical events [44].

The participants at the peace brainstorm also discussed the importance of education. Participants suggested working on raising literacy rates for women, educating children, giving opportunities to adults and elderly people, and building education ICTs. Another participant captured a popular sentiment – "peace starts from the kids." In this vein, a movement worth noting is *Design for Change*, which started in India and is spreading throughout the world with the goal of having groups of children work for one week on solutions for a local problem of their interest. A group of children in Finland, for example, worked on a campaign to stop Finland from supporting the use of cluster bombs [48].

During our peace brainstorm at CHI 2010, some participants noted the importance of informed social awareness. One stated, simply, "think about who you're working for and what their goals are." Another mentioned that giving consumers tools to ascertain product origin and the conditions in which different products are created can help people make more ecologically and humanitarianly sound choices. Social networking sites can allow the sharing of social pressure to maximize individuals' social impact. Another participant stressed the need for moving beyond quick fixes by promoting long-lasting changes in attitudes and behaviors relating to informed consumer knowledge

Aid Operational Prevention

Technologies can also be of help in operational prevention tasks such as monitoring missions and confidence building measures. For example, streaming video of sensitive areas could be made available over the Internet. This could be used to ensure that ceasefires are respected by providing an easy way for all parties to monitor sensitive areas.

DISCUSSION

Our hope is that this paper continues a serious discussion within the human-computer interaction community on how we can design technologies to promote peace and prevent armed conflict. It identifies many areas where research can be conducted and where technologies can have a positive impact. In fact, from our research agenda one thing is clear: there are many ways to pursue peace through efforts involving computing. Not only that, but many in our human-computer interaction community have already made and continue to make important contributions. There are other areas though where there have not been many contributions from our field and where the opportunities are ripe for action given the wide interest within our community.

At the same time, we must always remember that technology by itself is not going to bring about peace. It will just be another tool, yet a powerful one that if used in the right ways can make a positive difference. In the end, our goal is to design technologies to augment people's capabilities in seeking peace and preventing war, not to replace people. In the same vein, we believe it is important to always question the added value of technology. Just because we specialize in computing does not mean we should blindly address all problems through it when there may be less costly and more effective alternatives.

There are many challenges ahead. Evaluating technologies for peace can be difficult. In particular, if we want to reduce armed conflicts, the efforts may need to be large or take a long time to have an effect, and it may be difficult to evaluate their impact. While it may be possible to measure shorter-term gains in areas such as education, it may take years for any of these projects to have positive measurable effects in terms of peace, and even then, it may be difficult to attribute successes to specific projects. In the case of technologies designed to increase empathy and compassion toward people from other groups, it may be possible to measure this through questionnaires before and after a technology is used.

From an academic's perspective, it is also difficult to pursue this avenue of research due to the lack of funding opportunities. This problem could be turned into a positive by making all the research in this area completely open, sharing research results, and making any software open source. This could encourage a larger community of volunteers to participate and would increase the chances of any project to succeed. Academics also face ethical challenges when deciding whether to accept funding for conducting research that could make war easier to wage, or that could facilitate the suppression of civil liberties. Related to this is the impact of funding priorities on academic pursuits, in particular how these funding priorities can define research priorities in scientific fields [52].

It would also be important to connect with existing peace groups to combine efforts. We have already been in contact, for example, with the *United States Institute of Peace*. One of the participants at the peace brainstorm suggested hosting a *TED* talk that focused on peace and conflict in Africa or other developing regions.

Future steps should include opportunities for all those interested to join in discussions and arrange for suitable ways of communicating. We expect to host activities at CHI 2011 to continue forming a community.

CONCLUSION

In this paper, we presented a review of empirical studies on the causes of conflict. We also discussed neurological factors involved in moral decisions that are relevant to individuals deciding whether or not to support a war. We then presented a research agenda, identifying many opportunities for research. We hope that this paper will inspire others to think of many more. Instead of thinking of peace as an intangible, vague goal, we now have concrete examples of technologies that can make a positive, constructive difference.

ACKNOWLEDGEMENTS

We would like to thank all the peace ambassadors at CHI 2010, and in particular those who participated in our peace brainstorm.

REFERENCES

1. Ackermann, A. (2003). The Idea and Practice of Conflict Prevention. *Journal of Peace Research, 40*, 339-347.
2. Al-Ani, B., Mark, G., and Semaan, B. (2010). Blogging in a region of conflict: supporting transition to recovery. In *Proceedings of CHI '10*, 1069-1078.
3. Arkin, R. (2009). *Governing Lethal Behavior in Autonomous Robots.* New York: CRC Press.
4. Bardzell, S. (2010). Feminist HCI: taking stock and outlining an agenda for design. *Proceedings of CHI '10*, 1301-1310.
5. Bhide, A. (2010). *A Call for Judgment: Sensible Finance for a Dynamic Economy*. New York: Oxford University Press.
6. Blair, R.J.R. (1995). A cognitive developmental approach to morality: investigating the psychopath. *Cognition, 57,* 1-29.
7. Blair, J.R. (2003). Neurobiological basis of psychopathy. *British Journal of Psychiatry, 182,* 5-7.

8. Blevis, E. (2007). Sustainable interaction design: invention & disposal, renewal & reuse. *Proceedings of CHI 2007*, 503-512.

9. Brzezinski, Z. (1993). *Out of Control. Global Turmoil on the Eve of the Twenty-First Century.* New York: Scribner.

10. Cincotta, H. (2009). A Few People Making It Happen. *eJournal USA, 14*(3), 29-35.

11. Collier, P. (1999). Doing Well out of War. *Conference on Economic Agendas in Civil Wars*. London, April 26-27.

12. Collier, P. (2007). Economic Causes of Civil Conflict and their Implications for Policy. In *Leashing the Dogs of War: conflict management in a divided world* (C.A. Crocker, F.O. Hampson and P.R. Aall Eds). Washington, DC: United States Institute of Peace Press.

13. Collier, P. and Hoeffler, A. (1999). *Justice-seeking and loot-seeking in civil war.* DECRG, World Bank.

14. Collier, P. and Hoeffler, A. (2000) *Greed and Grievance in Civil War.* The World Bank.

15. Cramer, C. (2003). Does Inequality Cause Conflict? *Journal of International Development, 15,* 397-412.

16. Department of Defense. (2008). *National Defense Strategy.* http://www.defenselink.mil/news/2008%20national%20defense%20strategy.pdf.

17. DeRouen Jr., K.R. and Goldfinch, S. (2005). Putting the Numbers to Work: Implications for Violence Prevention. *Journal of Peace Research, 42* (1), 27-45.

18. Des Forges, A (1999). *Leave None to Tell the Story: Genocide in Rwanda.* Human Rights Watch. http://www.hrw.org/legacy/reports/1999/rwanda/

19. Dyer, G. (1985). *War.* London: Guild Publishing.

20. Edemariam, A. (2008) *The True Cost of War.* http://www.globalpolicy.org/security/issues/iraq/attack/statement/2008/0228truecost.htm

21. Eisenhower, D.D. (1961). *Farewell Address.* http://www.eisenhowermemorial.org/speeches/19610117%20farewell%20address.htm

22. Fein, L. (1963). Computer-oriented peace research. *Proceedings of AFIPS.* ACM Press: pp. 631-639.

23. Flanagan, M. and Nissenbaum, H. (2007). A Game Design Methodology to Incorporate Social Activist Themes. *Proceedings of CHI 2007*, 181-190.

24. Flanagan, M., Howe, D.C. and Nissenbaum, H. (2005). Values at Play: Design Tradeoffs in Socially-Oriented Game Design. *Proceedings of CHI 2005*, 751-760.

25. Fogg, B.J. (2010). *Peace Innovation.* http://peace.stanford.edu/

26. Friedman, B. and Nathan, L.P., Grey, N.C., Lake, M., Nilsen, T., Utter, E., Utter, R.F., Ring, M., and Kahn, Z. (2010). Multi-lifespan information system design in post-conflict societies: An evolving project in Rwanda. *Extended Abstracts of CHI 2010*, 2833-2842.

27. Frith, C.D. and Frith, U. (1999). Interacting minds – a biological basis. *Science, 286,* 1692-1695.

28. Gallese, V., Keysers, C. and Rizzolatti, G. (2004). A unifying view of the basis of social cognition. *Trends in Cognitive Sciences, 8*(9), 396-403.

29. Greene, J.D., Sommerville, R.B., Nystrom, L.E., Darley, J.M. and Cohen, J.D. (2001). An fmri inverstigation of emotional engagement in moral judgment. *Science, 293,* 2105-08.

30. Greene, J., Nystrom, L.E., Engell, A.D., Darley, J.M. and Cohen, J.D. (2004). The Neural Bases of Cognitive Conflict and Control in Moral Judgment. *Neuron, 44,* 389-400.

31. Grossman, D. (1996). *On Killing: The Psychological Cost of Learning to Kill in War and Society*. Boston: Back Bay Books.

32. Haidt, J. (2007). The new synthesis in moral psychology. *Science, 316,* 998-1002.

33. HCI for Peace (2010). *Interview with Allison Druin and Ben Bederson.* http://hciforpeace.blogspot.com/2010/03/interview-with-allison-druin-and-ben.html

34. HCI for Peace (2010). *HCI for Peace at CHI 2010.* http://hciforpeace.blogspot.com/2010/05/hci-for-peace-at-chi-2010.html

35. Herrnson, P.S., Niemi, R.G., Hanmer, M.J. Bederson, B.B., Conrad, F.C., and Traugott, M.W. (2008). *Voting Technology: The Not So Simple Act of Casting a Ballot.* Washington, DC: Brookings Institution Press.

36. Hochheiser, H. and Shneiderman, B. (2010). From bowling alone to tweeting together: technology-mediated social participation. *interactions 17*, 2 (Mar. 2010), 64-67.

37. Homer-Dixon, T.F. (1994). Environmental Scarcities and Violent Conflict: Evidence from Cases. *International Security, 19* (1), 5-40.

38. Hourcade, J.P. (2009). Give Peace a Chance: A Call to Design Technologies for Peace. *Extended Abstracts of CHI 2009*, 2499-2508.

39. Hourcade, J.P., Bederson, B.B., Druin, A., Rose, A., Farber, A., and Takayama, Y. (2003). The International Children's Digital Library: Viewing Digital Books Online. *Interacting with Computers, 15*, 151-167.

40. Hourcade, J.P., Beitler, D., Cormenzana, F. and Flores, P. (2008). Early OLPC Experiences in a Rural Uruguayan School. *Extended Abstracts of CHI 2008*, 2503-2512.

41. Hourcade, J.P., Beitler, D., Cormenzana, F. and Flores, P. (2009). Early OLPC Experiences in a Rural

Uruguayan School. In A. Druin (Ed.), *Mobile Technology for Children: Designing for Interaction and Learning*. Boston: Morgan Kaufmann.

42. ICT4Peace Foundation. (2010). http://www.ict4peace.org/

43. ImpactGames (2010). *PeaceMaker – Play the News, Solvie the Puzzle.* http://www.peacemakergame.com/

44. Irani, L.C. and Dourish, P. (2009). Postcolonial interculturality. *Proceedings of IWIC '09*, 249-252.

45. Ivie, R.L. (1980). Images of Savagery in American Justifications for War. *Communication Monographs, 47,* 279-294.

46. Kam, M., Mathur, A., Kumar, A., and Canny, J. (2009). Designing digital games for rural children: a study of traditional village games in India. *Proceedings of CHI '09*, 31-40.

47. Kenyon-Lischer, S. (2003). Collateral Damage: Humanitarian assistance as a cause of conflict. *International Security, 28* (1), 79-109.

48. Keune, A. and Ramkumar, P. (2010). *Design for Change Finland.* http://hciforpeace.blogspot.com/2010/09/design-for-change-finland.html

49. Kiva. (2010). *Kiva – Loans that change lives.* http://www.kiva.org/

50. Kraemer, K.L., Dedrick, J. and Sharma, P. (2009). One laptop per child: vision vs. reality. *Commun. ACM, 52*(6), 66-73.

51. Lehrer, J. (2010). *How We Decide.* New York: First Mariner Books.

52. Leslie, S.W. (1993). *The Cold War and American Science.* New York: Columbia University Press.

53. Marmar, C.R. (2009). Mental health impact of Afghanistan and Iraq deployment: Meeting the challenge of a new generation of veterans. *Depression and Anxiety, 26*, 493-97.

54. Marshall, S.L.A. (1947). *Men Against Fire: The Problem of Battle Command in Future War.* Washington, DC: Combat Forces Press.

55. Mitchell, J.P., Banaji, M.R. and Macrae, C.N. (2005). The link between social cognition and self-referential thought in the medial prefrontal cortex. *Journal of Cognitive Neuroscience, 17*(8), 1306-1315.

56. Melanger, E. (2005). Gender Equality and Intrastate Armed Conflict. *International Studies Quarterly, 49*(4), 695-714.

57. Moraveji, N., Inkpen, K., Cutrell, E., and Balakrishnan, R. (2009). A mischief of mice: examining children's performance in single display groupware systems with 1 to 32 mice. *Proceedings of CHI '09*, 2157-2166.

58. OLPC. (2010). One Laptop Per Child. http://laptop.org

59. Patel, N., Chittamuru, D., Jain, A., Dave, P., and Parikh, T. S. (2010). Avaaj Otalo: a field study of an interactive voice forum for small farmers in rural India. *Proceedings of CHI '10*, 733-742.

60. Reed, W. (2000). A Unified Statistical Model of Conflict Onset and Escalation. *American Journal of Political Science, 44*(1), 84-93.

61. Rosen, P.H. (1998). KidCast for peace: solutions for a better world. *SIGGRAPH 98 conference abstracts and applications.* ACM Press: 150.

62. Sambanis, N. (2001). *Do Ethnic and Non-Ethnic Civil Wars Have the Same Causes?* The World Bank.

63. Sawhney, N. (2009). Voices beyond walls: the role of digital storytelling for empowering marginalized youth in refugee camps. *Proceedings of IDC '09*, 302-305.

64. Shneiderman, B. (1991). Human values and the future of technology: a declaration of responsibility. *SIGCHI Bulletin, 23* (1), 11-16.

65. Shneiderman, B., Plaisant, C., Cohen, M. and Jacobs, S. (2009). *Designing the User Interface: Strategies for Effective Human-Computer Interaction*. New York: Addison-Wesley.

66. Small, D.A., Loewenstein, G. and Slovic, P. (2007). Sympathy and callousness: the impact of deliberative thought on donations to identifiable and statistical victims. *Organizational Behavior and Human Decision Processes, 102,* 143-53.

67. Smyth, T. N., Etherton, J., and Best, M. L. (2010). MOSES: exploring new ground in media and post-conflict reconciliation. *Proceedings of CHI '10*, 1059-1068.

68. Staedter, T. (2010, November 4). Clever E-Voting Tech Reduces Fraud. *Discovery News.* http://news.discovery.com/tech/clever-e-voting-tech-reduces-fraud.html

69. Stewart, F. (2002). Root causes of violent conflict in developing countries. *BMJ, 324,* 342-345.

70. Stock, O., Zancanaro, M., Koren, C., Rocchi, C., Eisikovits, Z., Goren-bar, D., Tomasini, D., and Weiss, P. (2008). A co-located interface for narration to support reconciliation in a conflict: initial results from Jewish and Palestinian youth. *Proceedings of CHI 2008,* 1583-1592.

71. United States Institute of Peace (2010). *Science, Technology, and Peacebuilding.* http://www.usip.org/issue-areas/science-and-technology

72. Weimann, G. (2004). *www.terror.net How Modern Terrorism Uses The Internet*. Washington, DC: United States Institute of Peace.

73. World Peace Through Technology (2010). *What are benevolent technologies?* http://peacetour.org/

Evaluating a Pattern-Based Visual Support Approach for Humanitarian Landmine Clearance

Lahiru G. Jayatilaka*, **Luca F. Bertuccelli**†, **James Staszewski**‡, and **Krzysztof Z. Gajos***
*Harvard University
Cambridge, MA 02138, USA
{lahiru, kgajos}@seas.harvard.edu
†MIT
Cambridge, MA 02139, USA
lucab@mit.edu
‡Carnegie-Mellon University
Pittsburgh, PA 15213, USA
jjs@cmu.edu

ABSTRACT
Unexploded landmines have severe post-conflict humanitarian repercussions: landmines cost lives, limbs and land. For deminers engaged in humanitarian landmine clearance, metal detectors remain the primary detection tool as more sophisticated technologies fail to get adopted due to restrictive cost, low reliability, and limited robustness. Metal detectors are, however, of limited effectiveness, as modern landmines contain only minimal amounts of metal, making them difficult to distinguish from the ubiquitous but harmless metallic clutter littering post-combat areas. We seek to improve the safety and efficiency of the demining process by developing support tools that will enable deminers to make better decisions using feedback from existing metal detectors. To this end, in this paper we propose and evaluate a novel, pattern-based visual support approach inspired by the documented strategies employed by expert deminers. In our laboratory study, participants provided with a prototype of our support tool were 80% less likely to mistake a mine for harmless clutter. A follow-up study demonstrates the potential of our pattern-based approach to enable peer decision-making support during landmine clearance. Lastly, we identify several design opportunities for further improving deminers' decision making capabilities.

Author Keywords
humanitarian landmine clearance, decision support, visual support, demining

ACM Classification Keywords
H.5.2 Information Interfaces and Presentation: User Interfaces

General Terms
Human Factors

INTRODUCTION AND MOTIVATION
A landmine is a passive explosive device hidden beneath the topsoil. During armed conflict, it is used to deny access to military positions or strategic resources. Unexploded landmines can persist for decades after a conflict's end, indiscriminately killing and maiming innocent civilians. As of 2010, 66 internationally recognized states were confirmed or suspected to be affected by mines, and in 2009 alone, landmines were responsible for over 1,300 casualties [17].[1] Beyond this loss of life, post-conflict societies must face the challenges presented by survivors of landmine incidents; these individuals may require amputation of limbs, suffer a loss of hearing or vision, and experience post-traumatic stress disorder [26, 16]. The number of affected individuals is significant—a 2009 report states that Cambodia alone has over 40,000 explosive remnants of war and mine survivors [13]. Also, significant resources are needed by each survivor. For example, a child with a lower limb amputation may need up to 15–20 artificial limbs in a lifetime [26]. However, the extensive resources required for adequate rehabilitation and reintegration of victims are often in limited supply in the developing countries where mine incidents predominantly occur [13, 16]. In addition to causing these human casualties, landmines severely inhibit the economic growth of developing countries by rendering vast tracts of farmland useless, injuring livestock, and reducing the size of working populations [1, 16].

Humanitarian demining aims to mitigate these problems by removing the threat of landmines and explosive remnants of war from civilian life [10, 11]. A crucial component of the humanitarian demining process is the physical clearance of landmines, which typically involves a human operator using audio feedback from a metal detector to find mines and employing hand-held digging tools to unearth them. Presently, mistakes in probing for suspected targets are among the main causes of accidental detonation, while operator inability to distinguish low-metal landmines from harmless clutter such as cans or shrapnel is the main source of inefficiency [11, 16]. There is a clear need for improvements to the mine clearance practice [6], yet more advanced detection and neutralization technologies designed to increase safety and efficiency (e.g., [8, 12, 4, 5]) have failed to be widely adopted due to their cost, complexity, low reliability, bulk, and high power requirements [25, 16, 11].

An alternative approach for improving safety and efficiency is to focus on improving the decision-making abilities of

[1]Casualty statistics are based on incomplete information and are strict underestimates

deminers operating existing technology. A recent study [22] revealed that expert deminers employ a sweeping strategy that allows them to mentally visualize the shape and size of a *metallic signature*—an area where a metal detector responds with acoustic feedback to the presence of a buried metallic object. By referring to previously encountered signatures, the expert deminer can more accurately determine if the buried object under investigation is a landmine or a piece of harmless clutter. Explicitly teaching this strategy to novice deminers has been shown to significantly improve their ability to correctly classify buried objects [22].

Informed by these findings, we hypothesized that the ability to *explicitly* visualize the edge points of metallic signatures as visual patterns on a computer screen would further improve the performance of novice deminers. To evaluate this hypothesis, we conducted a laboratory evaluation of a *pattern-based* visual support approach that enables deminers to build patterns on a display screen by serially collecting boundary points belonging to metallic signatures. In a study with 44 participants, we found that our visual support approach resulted in an 80% reduction in the number of missed mines and it reduced mine localization errors by 30%. In a follow-up study, we presented the visual patterns collected in the first experiment to a new set of 13 evaluators. The results suggest that individuals not directly involved in the demining process can successfully interpret the patterns, implying that our approach may allow deminers to benefit from peer support. Lastly, results from both studies contributed several design insights for further improving deminers' decision making performance. We intend to use the results of these studies to develop a cheap, portable, and robust visual support device that can be deployed as an add-on to existing metal detectors and that can contribute to improving the safety and efficiency of humanitarian landmine clearance.

In the remainder of this paper, we provide further pertinent background on humanitarian mine clearance and briefly synthesize previous work in the area. We then describe our main experiment and the follow-up study, and conclude with our interpretation of the findings.

BACKGROUND ON HUMANITARIAN DEMINING

Humanitarian mine clearance procedures require the identification and removal of all mine and other explosive hazards from a given area to a specified depth [11]. In practice, mine clearance takes place in environments as diverse as the deserts of Egypt, the mountains of Croatia and the tropical forests of Cambodia, with most programs operating on limited resources [16]. Given the procedural demands and the practical realities, mine clearance technology must be cheap, reliable and robust. Because of the difficulty of deploying technology within these constraints, a human with a metal detector has remained the primary method of mine clearance since the 1950s [6, 9]. Even though safer methods such as machine [4] or animal clearance [5] are available, their use is not widespread because machines are expensive to maintain and are constrained by terrain, while animals are difficult to train and are practically suited only for specific clearance scenarios [11].

Humanitarian deminers are usually recruited from local populations and trained over a two to four week period [7]. These deminers work according to strict operating procedures, which aim to preserve their safety and promote the efficacy of the mine clearance process [11, 7]. When using a metal detector, the primary tasks of a deminer are to carefully segment the ground in a marked lane with a meter-long stick, cut vegetation to clear the ground for detection, sweep with a detector, and investigate the ground carefully and methodically using a prodder or excavator [7, 16].

As of 2005, the average clearance rate for a deminer was 15–20 square meters a day [7]. Factors such as vegetation, topography, dehydration, monotony, and protective equipment have all been identified to impact performance of deminers. However, as mentioned previously, metallic clutter is the biggest source of inefficiency: the increased use of plastics in modern landmines has necessitated metal detectors that are highly sensitive, which has increased the rate of false alarms from non-hazardous metallic items [11, 16]. Demining organizations have little choice but to stipulate that deminers treat every signal as a threat, since there is presently no reliable way to make the mine versus clutter distinction based on audio feedback [16, 8, 7]. This strategy consumes a significant amount of time and resources [16]. However, advances in detection technology have demonstrated that procedural changes are possible in order to improve efficiency. In evaluation studies of the PSS-14 dual sensor detector, which combines a metal detector with a ground-penetrating radar (GPR), deminers used rapid clutter excavation techniques whenever they had compelling evidence that the buried object was not a mine. This enhanced efficiency of landmine clearance without detracting from deminer safety [2]. Despite its potential to improve the demining process, the PSS-14 remains unavailable to most organizations due to its high cost [11].

PREVIOUS WORK

The pattern-based visual support approach we propose and evaluate in this work is informed by findings on expert deminer performance by Staszewski and colleagues [22]. Their work shows that expert deminers systematically sweep the area near a potential threat to find and remember *edge points* of the metallic signature. That is, they systematically find and remember points where the metal detector response starts and stops. These experts then refer to past experiences to draw inferences from the spatial pattern outlined by the edge points held in their "mind's eye". These behavioral findings have been incorporated into US military deminer training programs [3] and have been shown to improve novice performance with not only metal detectors but also dual sensor detectors such as the PSS-14 described above [22]. With the PSS-14, inferences made from metallic signatures are used to guide investigation with the GPR. Our work is driven by the hypothesis that augmenting deminers' internal representations of metallic signatures with explicit visualizations of the edge point patterns will further increase the effectiveness of this procedure, especially for novice deminers.

Several visual feedback systems for metal detector–based demining are in development, but we are not aware of any published results contributing to our understanding of how these systems impact deminers' decision making capabilities. Kruger and Ewald have developed a laboratory setup that uses an ultrasonic positioning system and detector-mounted palmtop computer to present detector feedback as 2D intensity-graded regions [15]. Tohoku University has developed and field-tested the Advance Landmine Detection System (ALIS) which is an add-on system to a metal detector [20]. ALIS consists of a GPR sensing unit strapped to the operator's back, a palmtop computer (for computation and display) that is extended over the deminer's shoulder, and a camera attached to the detector handle for positioning. Metal detector feedback is presented as 2D intensity-graded regions, while the GPR signal is visualized as intensity fields for specific depths. Field evaluations have suggested that ALIS has potential for adoption, but to the best of our knowledge no data is available on how this system affects deminers' performance.

The most salient distinction between prior work and our approach is that we propose a discrete visualization that emphasizes information about the shape and size of the electromagnetic induction pattern induced by the buried object or objects instead of visualizing continuous signal intensity information at each location. As previously explained, our approach visualizes the information that expert deminers have been shown to rely on to make classification decisions. We also note that our approach is complementary to the graded approaches used by others and future work may demonstrate that a combination of the two is appropriate in some situations.

Visual support tools have also previously been used to support the training of deminers. The Sweep Monitoring System (SMS) [19, 14] uses remotely mounted stereo cameras to visually track the deminer's detector head in a simulated minefield to provide real-time auditory and visual feedback. Audio messages like "too fast" or "too slow" are provided to the trainee deminer, while visualizations of sweep coverage, detector speed and detector height are presented to the training supervisor. SMS is currently in use at U.S. army training centers, deployed after formative laboratory evaluations that demonstrated that visual feedback on sweeping performance improved the performance of demining trainees [14].

INTENDED DEVICE

The experiments presented in this paper are motivated by the desire to design and build a visual decision support device that can be used to improve the current humanitarian landmine clearance practice. To address the practical requirements of cost, portability, versatility, robustness, and power requirements, we envision that our solution will be centered around a commercial mobile device. The device will be engineered so that it can be mounted on the handles of most existing metal detectors. Its screen will present visual feedback to the deminer, while its built-in camera will be used to track the detector head's position with respect to the ground (an approach that is feasible with existing technology [18]). Several commercially-available mobile devices are marketed in "ruggedized" versions which function robustly in adverse environmental conditions.

We note that the metallic signatures edge points could be visualized using other, non-electronic, approaches. Indeed, in training, edge points are often marked with physical markers, such as poker chips. However, such marking is physically cumbersome and is time consuming for the operator, and thus necessitates the assistance of a trainer or training buddy. This adds to training costs. For these reasons and because of the safety concerns, this approach is not useful in actual demining. Another possibility is to use spray paint to mark the edge points. A prototype of such a device has even been designed [24]. Compared to our approach, the paint-based approach requires a more time-consuming and more permanent modification to the metal detector, and will probably result in lower precision of the edge point placement. It also lacks a mechanism to completely erase markings, which is a concern for training facilities. The cost advantage of the paint-based solution is also unlikely to be substantial, while the electronic approach will support novel functionalities such as the storage and retrieval of previously-recorded patterns.

EXPERIMENT 1

In this section, we describe a laboratory experiment to evaluate our pattern-based visual support approach. Our participants, who were extensively trained to behave like novice deminers, carried out simulated mine detection tasks using a hobby metal detector. All of our participants used the method developed by Staszewski and colleagues [22] (described earlier) to locate edge points of the metallic signatures belonging to hidden objects. Half of the participants were provided with an experimental implementation of our visual support system that allowed them to view the edge point patterns on a computer screen. The other half of the participants had to rely solely on their mental representations of these patterns, as is the case in current demining practice.

Hypotheses

This experiment was driven by the hypothesis that pattern-based visual support would improve deminers' decision making abilities in classifying and locating buried objects. Specifically, we formulated the following hypotheses:

H.1 Visual support will result in the reduction of false negatives (missed mines);

H.2 Visual support will result in the reduction of false positives (mines declared where only clutter is present);

H.3 Visual support will result in smaller localization errors.

Participants

49 university students (31 male, 18 female) volunteered for this experiment. Their ages ranged from 18 to 24 (M=21). All participants were right-handed and either had normal or corrected-to-normal vision. Participants received a monetary reward of \$10–\$30 based on performance.

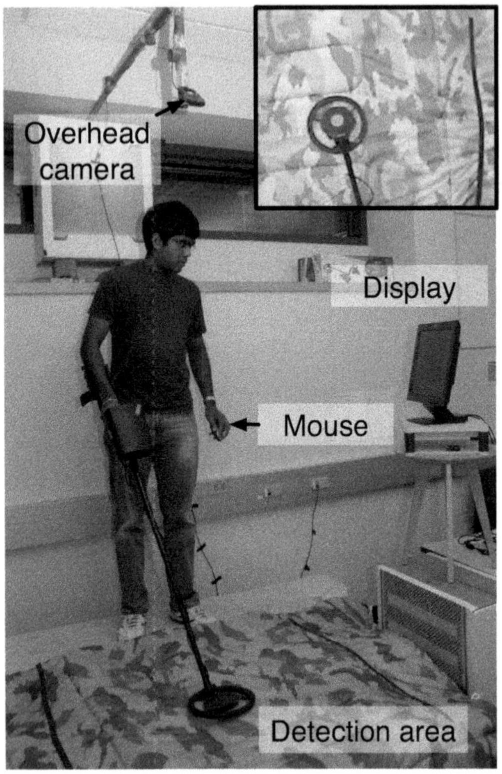

Figure 1. Experimental setup. The inset shows the contents of the visual support display: a live image of the ground with recorded edge points overlaid on top of the image.

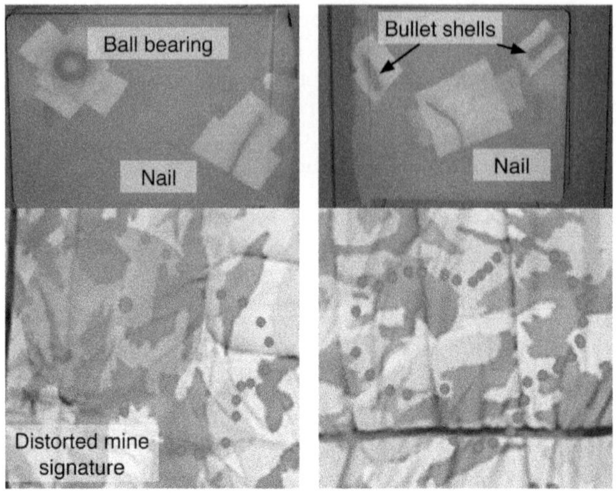

(a) Mine with clutter task. The red oval was added later to help the reader notice the circular signature of a mine simulant.

(b) Clutter task

Figure 2. Two of the detection tasks used in our study together with screen shots of the our visual support systems showing sample patterns generated by our participants.

Apparatus

Physical setup

The physical setup (illustrated in Figure 1) consisted of a 1.5m by 2m detection area under which simulated mine detection tasks were concealed, a display mounted a little below face level to the left of the detection area, and an overhead camera. The detection area was raised 0.5m above the floor to account for metallic interference from the indoor concrete floor, and was covered with a camouflage fabric to approximate visual cues and distractors found in actual demining environments. The overhead camera was suspended 1.85m above the detection area with its optical axis perpendicular to the plane of the detection surface.

Equipment and the Visual Support System Prototype

A lightweight hobby metal detector (Bounty Hunter Pioneer 505) was used as a simulated landmine metal detector. The detector provided binary response—beeping or no beeping—in the presence/absence of metal.

Our custom-built prototype visual decision support system relied on the overhead camera (Logitech Pro 9000) to track the position of the metal detector head. Participants used the right button of a wireless mouse (Logitech 450), held in the non-dominant hand, to signal that the detector head was over an edge point (detector feedback on-off point) of the metallic signature. The on-screen display (presented on a 17" IBM Think Vision) showed a live-feed from the overhead camera with the positions of the reported edge points and currently tracked detector head position overlaid on top of the image. (Figure 1). Participants used the middle mouse button to declare the suspected location of the mine for those tasks for which they decided that a mine was present, and the left button to erase previously recorded mine or edge points. To maintain consistency, participants in both conditions were instructed to use the mouse to indicate that the detector was over an edge point or over a mine but only half of the participants were provided with the visual feedback.

For analysis, we recorded the complete trajectories traced by the metal detector head in addition to the positions explicitly marked by the participants. The software was written in Visual C++ using Open CV 2.0.

This implementation of our visual support approach captures the core aspects of the experience we want to provide for deminers while requiring only a modest engineering investment.

Simulated Mine Detection Tasks

We used metal ball bearings to simulate anti-personnel landmines, because with our experimental setup they generated signatures similar in form to those belonging to typical landmines [22, 3]. Metallic items collected from military training grounds such as barb wire, bullet casings and nails, along with household metallic items such as screwdrivers and wires, were used to simulate battlefield clutter. To ensure that identical detection tasks could be reproduced for each participant, we affixed combinations of mine simulants and clutter to plastic trays (10 x 24 inches) and carefully marked the positions where each tray should be placed during the experiment. The trays (illustrated in Figure 2) were placed (one per experimental condition) underneath the camouflage fabric while the participant was behind a partition, thus ensuring that the participants were unaware of the location and composition of objects in each task. Half of the trays contained one mine simulant plus 2–3 items of clutter (*Mine with clutter* tasks); the other half of the trays had only clutter items (*Clutter only* tasks). Four of these trays were set aside for the training and the remaining 6 were used in the testing phase of the experiment. We designed the Mine with clutter tasks such that the clutter significantly interfered with the metallic signature of the mine while still leaving some of the mine's characteristic circular signature visible (Figure 2(a))—this design choice was ecologically motivated given the prevalence of clutter on minefields.

Procedure

Training

Training and practice lasted about 1.5 hours on average. Participants were taught about detector sweeping styles, how to operate the metal detector, the difference between mines and clutter, how to identify edge points of metallic signatures, how to interpret the resulting patterns, and how to use the visual decision support system. Participants were trained to associate a fragment of a circular arc embedded in the overall pattern as indicating mine presence, with the center of the circle corresponding to the approximate location of the mine (see Figure 2(a)).

To avoid systematic differences in training across the experimental conditions, all participants were trained to build and interpret metallic signatures both with and without the visual support (only at the conclusion of the training were they told which condition they were assigned to). For both conditions, following Staszewski's protocol [3], participants were taught to move their detector head in small semi-circular motions between neighboring edge points, clicking the mouse button whenever they found one. When training with the visual support enabled, participants were specifically instructed to build patterns while focusing on detector head motion and only refer to the screen once they had finished construction.

During the practice session, participants had to perform detection tasks on four practice tasks (2 Mine with clutter, 2 Clutter). These tasks were similar in nature to the ones used for testing, and were presented in random cycles of four with visual support provided on every other trial. Subjects had to determine mine presence or absence for each task and localize a mine if they thought one was present. Participants were encouraged to think aloud about geometric features of the pattern that indicated mine presence or absence before making a decision. For each task, participants were provided with feedback on the validity of the reasoning applied. For training purposes, after completing a task without visual support participants were shown on screen the edge points they had collected. Participants had to correctly classify all 4 consecutive tasks in one full cycle before moving onto the testing phase. This ensured that all participants had a similar skill level at the beginning of the testing phase and that their performance had stabilized and was unlikely to change significantly during the experiment. Participants who failed to reach this proficiency criterion after 60 minutes of practice were discharged (with base compensation of $10) without completing the testing phase of the study.

Testing

The 6 detection tasks (3 Mine with clutter and 3 Clutter only) used for testing were randomly ordered and counterbalanced for each participant to reduce ordering effects. To induce a consistent behavior among our participants, we instructed them to complete each task within 120 seconds, and we provided them with auditory notifications at regular intervals. This amount of time was sufficient to comfortably scan the area, establish the location of the edge points, and make a decision. Participants were tested under a monetary incentive structure intended to induce ecologically valid conservative behavior [23], where a false negative (a missed mine) yielded a penalty of $3 while a false positive (incorrectly classifying clutter as a mine) yielded a penalty of $1. Additionally, a reward of $1 was given for localizations within 6 inches of the underlying target position.

Each testing task commenced with participants sweeping the detector in densely-spaced side-to-side motions across the cell to locate the general area of feedback (area where the simulated mine detection task was hidden). Once feedback was encountered, participants engaged in pattern construction and interpretation. With visual support present, participants could consult the display to make a decision and possibly refine the pattern. The task concluded when the participants made and verbally announced their final decision. If a mine was thought to be present, participants indicated its suspected location using the middle mouse button during the course of the task. Participants had a mandatory break of two minutes at the end of each task to rest and to complete a post task questionnaire. At the end of the testing phase, participants completed an additional questionnaire that assessed overall ease and confidence. Results of testing performance were only divulged at the end of the experiment.

Design and Analysis

The experiment was a mixed between- and within-subject design with the following factors and levels:

- *Visual support* {Provided, Not provided}
- *Task type* {Mine with clutter, Clutter only}
- *Task ID* $\{1\ldots6\}$ – 3 tasks containing mine with clutter, and 3 tasks containing clutter only
- *Trial* $\{1\ldots6\}$

Visual Support was a between-subject factor, while Task type was a within-subject factor. The 44 participants whose data were included in the analysis (see the Results section for a discussion of exclusions) completed $44 \times 6 = 264$ trials. Of these, 180 were completed by male participants and 84 by female. Half of the trials contained a mine simulant with clutter and half only clutter. Genders were balanced between the two Visual support conditions. Task ID and Trial were both within-subject factors; their effects were analyzed only to verify uniform difficulty of tasks and the effectiveness of the training program at mitigating learning effects.

Our dependent measures were:

- **Classification errors** which included both the *false positives*, i.e., declaring a mine where one was not present, and *false negatives*—missing a mine. Because the two types of classification errors have very different implications for the demining practice, in all our analyses we include separate results for both.
- **Localization errors** which indicate the distance between the mine location indicated by the user and the actual location of the mine simulant. Localization errors were computed only for tasks where participants correctly detected a mine when one was actually present.

After each trial, we also collected 6 subjective measures on a Likert scale from 1 (strongly disagree) to 5 (strongly agree) relating to the ease of making classification and localization decisions, participants' confidence in their decisions, and the ease of creating and interpreting the patterns. Additionally, at the very end of the study, we asked participants to report (on a 5-point Likert scale) their overall confidence in 3 different aspects of their performance.

We used non-parametric tests in the analyses because the error data followed a highly skewed distribution and the Likert scale responses are more correctly treated as ordinal data. For the two-level factors we used Wilcoxon signed rank test for within-subject factors and Wilcoxon rank-sum test [27] (equivalent to the Mann-Whitney U test) for between-subject factors. We used the Friedman test to analyze the effects of Task ID. To test for learning effects across Trials, we performed a contrast analysis with all the pairwise comparisons using the Wilcoxon signed rank test.

To guard against Type I errors, we applied the Holm's sequentially-rejective Bonferroni procedure [21] to all analyses except the three planned comparisons that corresponded to our stated hypotheses and the two analyses verifying the task design and learning effects (Preliminaries section).

Results

Adjustment of Data

Three out of the 49 volunteers did not pass the exit criterion of our training program and were thus discharged without completing the study. Data from one participant were excluded because of an experimenter's error in following the protocol, and another subject's data were lost due to software malfunction. Consequently, data from 44 participants (30 male, 14 female) were considered in the analysis.

Preliminaries

In the design of this experiment, we strove to maintain uniform difficulty among all the tasks of the same type (i.e., all the Mine with clutter tasks and all the Clutter only tasks). We also designed our training procedure to minimize learning effects during the testing phase. Indeed, we observed no significant effect of Task ID on classification errors for either task type. Similarly, a contrast analysis showed no learning effect on classification performance.

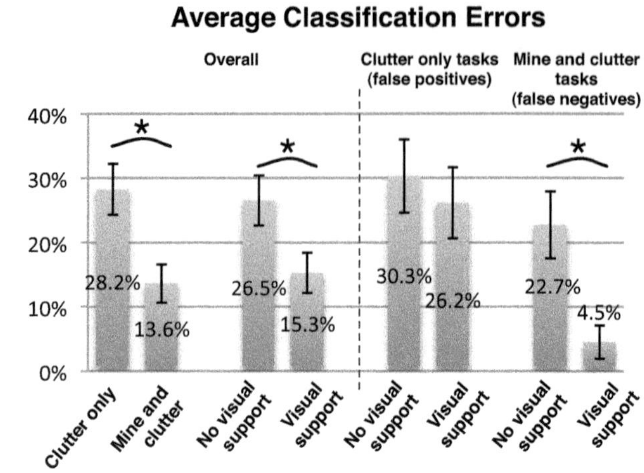

Figure 3. Average classification error rates. Error bars correspond to the standard error and the ⋆ symbols denote statistically significant differences.

Classification Errors

We observed a significant main effect of Visual support on classification errors ($z = 2.36$, $p < 0.05$): with visual support provided, participants made an average of 15.3% classification errors, compared to 26.5% without visual support. Visual support resulted in significant reduction in false negatives ($z = 2.87$, $p < .01$): participants missed on average 22.7% mines without visual support but only 4.6% when the visual support was provided. In other words, Visual support resulted in an 80% reduction in the number of missed mines. Hypothesis H.1 was thus supported. Hypothesis H.2, however, was not supported: Visual support had no significant effect on false positives ($z = 0.41$, n.s.).

We also observed a main effect of Task type ($z = 130.0$, $p < .01$): on average, participants made 28.2% classification errors on tasks that contained only clutter compared to 13.6% on tasks that involved a mine.

Localization Errors

We analyzed the effects on localization errors for those tasks where the participants correctly classified the task as containing a landmine. We observed a significant main effect of visualization support on localization error ($z = 4.25$, $p < .0001$): the availability of visual support resulted in the reduction of the average localization error from 30.0 pixels to 20.7 pixels (approximately from 3 inches to 2 inches). Hypothesis H.3 was thus supported.

Subjective Results

Participants reported that it was significantly easier to decide whether there was a mine present when the visual support was provided (M=3.35 vs. 2.84 without visual support, $z = 3.53$, $p < .001$). For this measure there also was evidence of interaction between Visual support and Task type: participants found that visual support made the decision easier for tasks containing a mine ($z = -4.73$, $p < .0001$) but not those containing clutter only ($z = 0.15$, n.s.).

	Visual support		
	not provided	provided	* = *significant*
Ease of classifiaction	2.84	3.35	*
Confidence in classification	3.37	3.64	
Ease of pattern construction and interpretation	3.28	3.80	*
Noticed good symmetry	2.77	3.60	*
Ease of localization	3.18	3.48	
Confidence in localization	3.43	3.67	

Table 1. Summary of subjective results. Responses were collected on a 5-point Likert scale (1 = strongly disagree, 5 = strongly agree).

With the visual support present, participants also found it easier to construct and interpret the edge point patterns (M=3.80) than without visual support (M=3.28, $z = 4.15$, $p < .0001$). As with the previous measure, we again see evidence of interaction between Visual support and Task type: the presence of visual support resulted in increased ease of pattern creation and interpretation for tasks involving a mine ($z = -4.37$, $p < .0001$) but not for those that involved only clutter ($z = 1.52$, n.s.).

Finally, participants reported noticing significantly better partial circular symmetry in the constructed patterns when the visual support was provided (M=3.60 vs. M=2.77 without visual support, $z = 4.98$, $p < .0001$).

We did not observe significant effects of Visual support on any of the other subjective measures.

Patterns and Pattern Creation Strategies

Next we take a qualitative look at the sensor head trajectories traced by four of our participants as well as the patterns they created. We will use the term "petals" to refer to the continuous arcs traced with a metal detector between two adjacent edge points.

To evaluate whether pattern creation strategies influenced a deminer's success at correctly classifying targets, we first rank-ordered the participants (separately for each of the two Visual support conditions) based on their classification error rates (weighing false negatives a little higher than false positives) and their localization errors. The sensor head trajectories and edge points created by the highest and lowest performers in each of the two visual support conditions are shown in Figure 4. The most striking difference is that the lowest performers—both with and without visual support—returned the sensor head to the same positions multiple times and had a large number of overlapping petals (Figures 4(c) and 4(d)). Additionally, the number and density of the edge points varied considerably between the high and low performers. Lower performing participants under-sampled the boundary (as in the Mine with clutter task in Figure 4(d), where the participant marked a relatively small number of edge points) or over-sampled in some areas (such as the bottom left corner of the boundary of that same pattern). Note the dense and regular spacing of the edge points collected by the high performers (Figures 4(a) and 4(b)) when compared to the patterns of lower performers shown in Figures 4(c) and 4(d).

EXPERIMENT 2

To gain further insight into the factors affecting deminers' success at classifying and locating targets using our pattern-based visual support approach, we conducted a second experiment for which we recruited a new set of 13 participants to interpret the patterns created by a subset of the participants from the first study. The new participants only received brief instruction on interpreting the patterns but they were given no practical training on the actual demining procedures. From now on, whenever the term participant may be ambiguous, we will refer to the participants from the first experiment as the (original) *deminers* and those from the second experiment as *evaluators.*

Participants

13 university students (7 male, 6 female) volunteered for this experiment. Their ages ranged from 18 to 22 (M=20). All participants either had normal or corrected-to-normal vision. Participants received a monetary reward of $10–$16 based on performance.

Apparatus

We created new custom software to display patterns and elicit participants' classification and localization feedback. Participants viewed the information on a 17" IBM Think Vision monitor.

Selection and Preparation of Patterns

In this study, we presented the patterns generated by participants in the first experiment on a neutral background. We used patterns generated on training tasks in the first study for training in the current experiment. Similarly, we used patterns from the testing phase of the first experiment for the testing phase of this study. We randomly selected 24 patterns from the training phrase (equally split between the two task types). For the testing phase, we first sorted the original deminers according to their performance using the same procedure as the one described in the earlier section on Patterns and Pattern Creation Strategies. We then randomly picked, separately for the two Visual support conditions, 2 participants in the top performance quartile (High Performers) and 2 in the low performance quartile (Low Performers) for a total of $2 \times 2 \times 2 = 8$ original deminers. These original deminers had each generated 6 patterns (3 for tasks with Mine with clutter, 3 for tasks with just Clutter). This provided us with a testing set of $8 \times 6 = 48$ unique patterns. Even though all the patterns were unique, they were all generated based on the same smaller set of tasks (4 training, 6 testing). To increase diversity of the patterns experienced by the new participants, we randomly rotated and translated each of the patterns.

Procedure

Training

Training and practice lasted 30 minutes on average. Participants were first briefed on the challenges of mine detection with a metal detector, the difference between mines and clutter, the usefulness of metallic signatures, and the use of the experimental software. Next, participants used our software

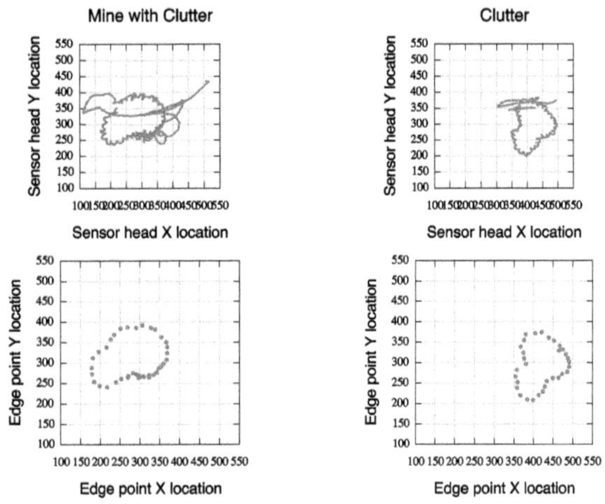

(a) Highest performer with the display assistance

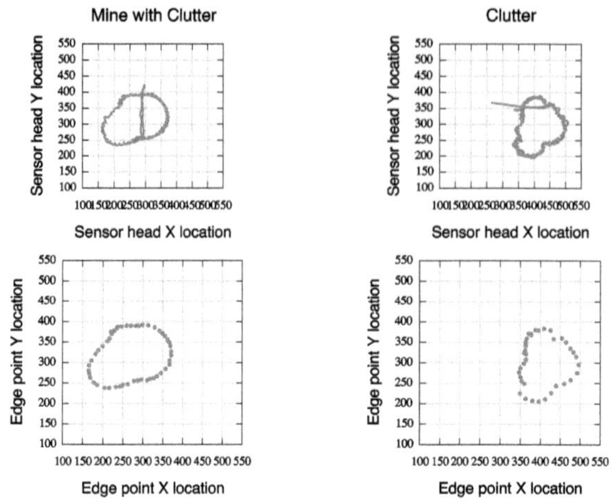

(b) Highest performer without the display assistance

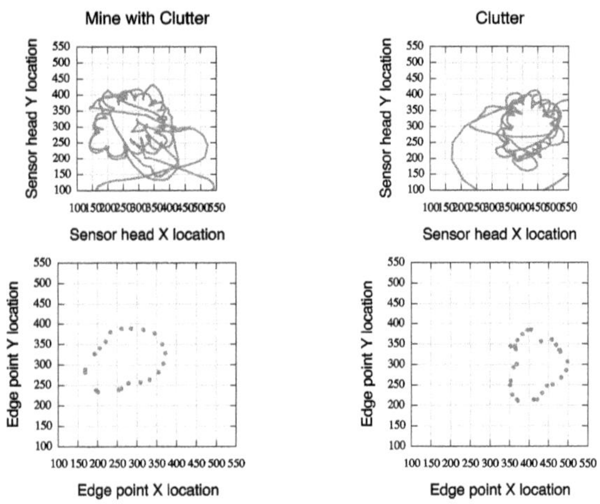

(c) Lowest performer with the display assistance

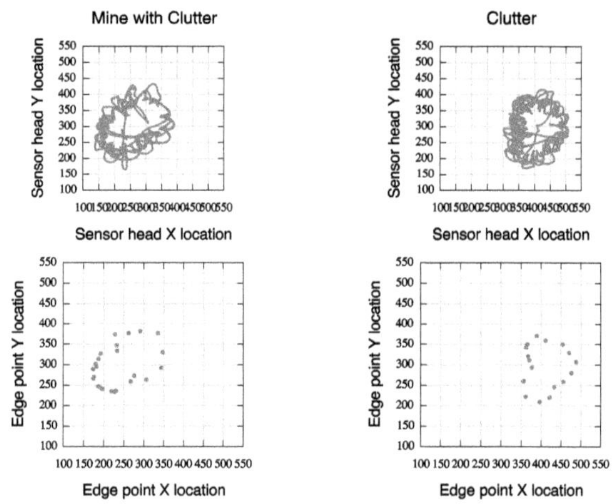

(d) Lowest performer without the display assistance

Figure 4. Qualitative comparison of sensor head trajectories (top plots in each subfigure) and the patterns (bottom plots) created by four of our participants.

to carry out practice classification and localization tasks on randomly selected patterns drawn from the training set. Selected patterns were checked to ensure that no two consecutive patterns were from the same task. If a pattern was incorrectly classified the participant received immediate notification of the error. As in the previous experiment, participants were asked to think aloud as they made their decisions and they were provided with extensive feedback on their reasoning. Participants had to correctly classify 6 consecutive patterns before moving on to the testing phase. To ensure a minimum amount of training among participants, all had to experience a minimum of 10 patterns during the training phase even if they were immediately successful.

Testing

The 48 patterns used in the testing phase were ordered randomly for each participant to reduce ordering effects. As in the training phase, we ensured that no two consecutive patterns were generated based on the same task. To mirror the time pressure from Experiment 1, participants were instructed to spend no more than 15 seconds on each pattern (this bound was determined based on average perceived time deminers with visual support took to make decisions once they had constructed visual patterns). As in the first experiment, the monetary incentive structure was designed such that missing a mine incurred a larger penalty (15¢) than declaring a mine where none was present (5¢). Additionally, a reward of 5¢ was given for each localization within 20 pixels of the true mine position. Results of performance during the testing phase were only divulged at the end of the experiment.

Design and analysis

The experiment was a within-subjects design with the following factors and levels:

- *Visual support (in the original study)* {Provided, Not provided}

- *Performance level of the original deminer* {High performer, Low performer}
- *Original classification correctness* {Correct, Incorrect}; this factor indicates if a pattern was correctly classified by the original deminer who created it in Experiment 1
- *Task type* {Mine with clutter, Clutter only}

As in the first experiment, our dependent measures were the Classification error and the Localization error. We used the same non-parametric tests to analyze our data as in Experiment 1 and we used the Holm's sequentially-rejective Bonferroni procedure [21] to guard against Type I errors.

Results

The evaluators in this study made on average fewer errors (14%) than the 8 original deminers whose patterns were used in the second experiment (19%), but the difference was not statistically significant. There was also no significant difference in the number of classification errors the evaluators made on patterns that were originally created with the Visual support, compared to those constructed without Visual support. We did observe, however, a significant main effect of Task type on classification error ($z = -31.5$, $p = .01$): on average, participants had a false positive rate (detecting a mine when there was none) of 6.4% while they missed a mine 21.5% of the time. This is in contrast to the results from the first experiment, where the deminers' false positive rate was substantially higher than their false negative rate (28.2% vs. 13.6%).

We observed a significant main effect of the Performance level of the original deminer ($z = 191.5$, $p < .001$): participants made an average of 10% classification errors on patterns from high performers, compared to 18% on patterns from low performers. We also observed a significant main effect of Original correctness ($z = 286.000$, $p < .0001$): participants made an average of 10.7% classification errors on patterns that were correctly classified by the original deminer, and an average of 24.7% errors on patterns incorrectly classified in Experiment 1. These results provide further evidence that quality of created patterns impact the likelihood of correct classification.

We observed no significant effects of any of the factors on the localization errors.

DISCUSSION AND DESIGN INSIGHTS

The results of the first experiment support our hypothesis that visual support helps to reduce false negatives: participants who worked with the visual support missed 80% fewer mines than those who worked without it. Visual support also resulted in a 30% reduction in the magnitude of mine localization errors. Our hypothesis that visual support would reduce false positives (cases where a deminer declares a mine where none is present) was, however, not supported. While not an immediate threat to deminers' safety, false positives can be a significant source of inefficiency in metal detector–based landmine clearance. In order to help mitigate decision errors in general and the false positives in particular, we sought to gain insights into the sources of these errors.

The qualitative analysis of the sweeping trajectories indicated a consistent difference in behavior between the most successful participants and those who made the most classification errors: the successful participants created the patterns in a single pass along the perimeter of the metallic signature and sampled the edge points at small, regular intervals. The least successful participants, meanwhile, re-traced the outline two or more times and sampled the edge points at irregular intervals, with subsequent passes occasionally filling gaps left earlier and occasionally duplicating earlier work. These observations suggest that classification errors by deminers can be partially attributed to the quality of the patterns they created. They also point to a specific behavior that results in low-quality patterns. Results from the second experiment—which show that evaluators made significantly more errors interpreting patterns that were originally misclassified and those generated by the lowest performing original deminers—provide further evidence that poorly-constructed patterns contribute to the classification errors.

These findings suggest two ways of further reducing classification errors. First, the discussion of successful and unsuccessful sweeping strategies can be incorporated more prominently into the training program. Second, a decision support system can make deminers aware when their sweeping strategy is likely to result in unreliable patterns. Errors in pattern construction might be reduced if the process of edge point capture was automated.

The results of our second experiment also demonstrate that people other than those who created the patterns can successfully interpret them. With current approaches, collaborative decision making is not possible because the person operating the metal detector cannot externalize and share the pattern she has observed. In contrast, a system that visually captures these patterns would enable deminers to easily consult peers and supervisors. Because it is not uncommon for more than one person to be assigned to a single demining cell (with only one operating the metal detector) [7], such peer assistance is often readily available.

Finally, we note that our work demonstrated that explicitly visualizing the edge points of a metallic signature improves deminers' decision making capabilities. To evaluate the resulting patterns, however, deminers still have to refer to mental representations of previously encountered patterns in order to make a classification decision. We hypothesize that deminers' classification performance can be further improved if the device can enable the storage and retrieval of previously encountered patterns for subsequent side-by-side comparisons.

The major limitation of our work has been the limited ecological validity of our experimental setup. Our results are, however, still informative and they will serve to inform our design of a higher fidelity outdoor prototype, which we intend to evaluate at an actual deminer training facility with real deminer trainees.

CONCLUSION

In this paper, we made three main contributions. First, we proposed and evaluated a novel visual support approach to improve the decision making capabilities of deminers. Our approach enables metal detector operators to explicitly visualize—instead of having to imagine—the geometry of the electromagnetic induction patterns produced by buried metallic objects. In our first experiment, participants working with our visual support missed 80% fewer mines and reduced their mine localization errors by 30% compared to those who relied on mental representations alone. Contrary to our expectations, however, the visual support did not result in the reduction of false positives: both groups of participants were equally likely to misclassify a piece of harmless clutter as a landmine.

Second, our results allowed us to identify some likely sources of deminer classification errors. These findings allowed us to propose several design suggestions that are likely to help reduce deminers' classification errors.

Lastly, the results of our second experiment demonstrate that people other than those who originally constructed the pattern can successfully interpret these patterns. This opens the possibility of new, collaborative, decision making procedures for landmine clearance.

We intend to implement this approach on top of an existing mobile hardware platform to produce a cheap and robust visual support device that can be easily mounted on top of most existing metal detectors. Because such a device will be simple, inexpensive, robust, portable, and able to function in the field without recharging for hours at a time, we hope that it will gain adoption in the humanitarian demining community.

ACKNOWLEDGEMENTS

We thank the following individuals for the guidance and support they offered for this project: Rebecca Cremona, Alan Davison, Barbara Grosz, Kurt Gray, Hasini Jayatilaka, Sarath Jayatilaka, Amrapali Maitra, Radhika Nagpal, Thrishantha Nanayakkara, Nushelle de Silva, Ruwan Senaratne, Matt Welsh, and Jacob Wobbrock. This work was funded in part by the NSF grant IIS-0705406 and by a grant from the William F. Milton Fund of Harvard University.

REFERENCES

1. Andersion, N., da Sousa, C., and Paredes, S. Social cost of land mines in four countries: Afghanistan, Bosnia, Cambodia, and Mozambique. *British Medical Journal 311*, 7007 (1995), 718.
2. Boshoff, C., and Cresci, R. The HALO Trust and HSTAMIDS. *Journal of Mine Action 12*, 1 (2008).
3. Davison, A., and Staszewski, J. Handheld mine detection based on expert skill: Reference guide for training plan design and training site development. Aberdeen Proving Ground, MD: Army Research Laboratory Human Research and Engineering Directorate, 2002.
4. Geneva International Centre for Humanitarian Demining (GICHD). *A Study of Mechanical Application in Demining*. GICHD, Geneva, 2004.
5. Geneva International Centre for Humanitarian Demining (GICHD). *Mine detection dogs: Operations*. GICHD, Geneva, 2005.
6. Geneva International Centre for Humanitarian Demining (GICHD). *A study of manual mine clearance, Book 1*. GICHD, Geneva, 2005.
7. Geneva International Centre for Humanitarian Demining (GICHD). *A study of manual mine clearance, Book 2*. GICHD, Geneva, 2005.
8. Geneva International Centre for Humanitarian Demining (GICHD). *Guidebook on Detection Technologies and Systems for Humanitarian Demining*. GICHD, Geneva, 2006.
9. Geneva International Centre for Humanitarian Demining (GICHD). *Detectors and Personal Protective Equipment*. GICHD, Geneva, 2009.
10. Geneva International Centre for Humanitarian Demining (GICHD). *A Guide to International Mine Action Standards*. GICHD, Geneva, 2009.
11. Geneva International Centre for Humanitarian Demining (GICHD). *A Guide to Mine Action*. GICHD, Geneva, 2010.
12. Habib, M. Humanitarian demining: The problem, difficulties, priorities, demining technology and the challenge for robotics. In *Humanitarian Demining Innovative Solutions and the Challenges of Technology*, M. Habib, Ed. I-Tech Education and Publishing, Croatia, 2008, ch. 1, 1–56.
13. Handicap International. *Voices from the Ground*. Handicap International, Brussels, 2009.
14. Herman, H., McMahill, J. D., and Kantor, G. Enhanced operator interface for hand-held landmine detector. *Proceedigns of SPIE 4394*, 1 (2001), 844–851.
15. Kruger, H., and Ewald, H. Handheld metal detector with online visualisation and classification for the humanitarian mine clearance. In *Sensors, 2008 IEEE* (2008), 415–418.
16. Landmine and Cluster Munition Monitor. *Landmine Monitor Report 2009, Executive Summary*. 2009.
17. Landmine and Cluster Munition Monitor. *Landmine Monitor Report 2010, Executive Summary*. 2010.
18. Lee, T., and Soatto, S. Tracking and recognition on a hand-held. Demonstration at IEEE CVPR'10, 2010.
19. National Robotics Engineering Center. Sweep Monitoring System. `http://www.rec.ri.cmu.edu/projects/sweep_monitoring/`. Last accessed on January 13, 2011.
20. Sato, M., Fujiwara, J., Kido, T., and Takahashi, K. ALIS evaluation tests in croatia. *Proceedings of SPIE 7303*, 1 (2009).
21. Shaffer, J. P. Multiple hypothesis-testing. *ANNUAL REVIEW OF PSYCHOLOGY 46* (1995), 561–584.
22. Staszewski, J. Spatial thinking and the design of landmine detection training. In *Applied spatial cognition: from research to cognitive technology*, G. A. Allen, Ed. Mahwah, NJ, Erlbaum Associates, 2006, 231–265.
23. Stevens, S. *Handbook of experimental psychology*. John Wiley, New York, 1951.
24. Trevelyan, J. Paint marker device. `http://school.mech.uwa.edu.au/~jamest/demining/tech/markers/minem3.html`, 1999. Last accessed on January 11, 2011.
25. Trevelyan, J. Research challenges. In *Humanitarian Demining Innovative Solutions and the Challenges of Technology*, M. Habib, Ed. I-Tech Education and Publishing, Croatia, 2008, ch. 2, 57–68.
26. Walsh, N. E., and Walsh, W. S. Rehabilitation of landmine victims : the ultimate challenge. *Bulletin of the World Health Organization 81* (09 2003), 665 – 670.
27. Wilcoxon, F. Individual comparisons by ranking methods. *Biometrics Bulletin 1*, 6 (1945), 80–83.

Hang on a Sec! Effects of Proactive Mediation of Phone Conversations while Driving

Shamsi T. Iqbal[1], Eric Horvitz[1], Yun-Cheng Ju[1] and Ella Mathews[2]

[1]Microsoft Research
One Microsoft Way, Redmond, WA 98052
{shamsi, horvitz, yuncj}@microsoft.com

[2]California Institute of Technology
1200 E California Boulevard, Pasadena, CA 91125
emathews@caltech.edu

ABSTRACT
Conversing on cell phones while driving is a risky, yet commonplace activity. State legislatures in the U.S. have enacted rules that limit hand-held phone conversations while driving but that allow for hands-free conversations. However, studies have demonstrated that the cognitive load of conversation is a significant source of distraction that increases the likelihood of accidents. We explore in a controlled study with a driving simulator the effectiveness of proactive alerting and mediation of communications during phone conversations while driving. We study the use of auditory messages indicating upcoming critical road conditions and placing calls on hold. We found that such actions reduce driving errors and that alerts sharing details about situations were more effective than general alerts. Drivers found such a system valuable in most situations for maintaining driving safety. These results provide evidence that context-sensitive mediation systems could play a valuable role in focusing drivers' attention on the road during phone conversations.

Author Keywords
Driving, attention, context-sensitive systems, cell phones.

ACM Classification Keywords
H.5.m. Information interfaces and presentation (e.g. HCI): Miscellaneous.

General Terms
Experimentation, Human factors, Measurement.

INTRODUCTION
Engaging in cell phone conversations while driving is a dangerous yet common practice. Recognizing the threat to road safety that simultaneous driving and conversing poses to drivers and others, several U.S. states have enacted laws that limit calls to hands-free configurations [1]. Yet studies have shown that using hands-free setups may not reduce the distraction [22, 28], and may lull drivers into a false sense of safety. More than half of all U.S. states forbid novice drivers and school bus operators from any use of cell phones while driving [1]. However, general bans on phone conversations while driving are unlikely given expectations of modern mobile communication. Thus, we seek solutions that enable safer driving while communicating, focusing on opportunities for automated mediation of communications.

Automated mediation of human attention in multitasking situations has been a focus of the research community, especially in the desktop domain [11, 12]. Our broader goal is to explore the effectiveness of similar mediation in driving scenarios, where a context-sensitive system can recognize when a phone call is in progress and intervene by interrupting the call to deliver alerts about road conditions, and even suspend conversations if deemed beneficial. Such systems might jointly share interventions with drivers and the people they are speaking with to provide the remote participants with useful grounding about the driving situation [27]. Establishing such mutual understanding may help with joint regulation of conversations, enabling drivers to better focus on maintaining driving safety.

As a first step, we conducted a controlled study using a medium fidelity driving simulator. Different interventions were tested as drivers piloted a car within the simulator and engaged in phone conversations with remote users. We investigated the effectiveness and acceptability of short and long intervention messages, putting the call on hold, and the timing of an intervention, exploring outcomes of actions that interrupt conversations at natural conversational breakpoints versus at other times.

Our results showed that interventions positively affected driving, reducing driving errors compared to the baseline. The positive effect on driving safety was associated with perceived degradations in the quality of the conversation experience. Subjective feedback showed that drivers found interventions to be useful for most situations. Their general preference was towards having a shorter shared message at a conversational break followed by the call being put on hold. Non-driving participants in conversations were more neutral about the use of interventions, despite the fact that all were experienced drivers themselves. We believe the results highlight the promise of proactive mediation of phone conversations during driving and motivate further explorations. The results also make salient the need to educate the general population about the dangers of driving and talking on a cell phone whether the phone is balanced manually on the ear or embedded in a hands-free system.

RELATED WORK

We shall first describe related work on how secondary tasks distract driving, strategies to help better manage secondary tasks, and the role of intervention in overall attention management, with a focus on the driving domain.

Driving and Distraction

While piloting a vehicle, core aspects of driving are "automated" and easily backgrounded as other tasks come to the fore [16]. Multiple studies have shown the detrimental effects of cell phone conversations, texting, or interacting with music players on driving safety [3, 4, 8, 23, 25]. Drivers who engage in phone conversations while driving have been found to have slower braking reaction time [2, 15], degraded steering performance [4], and to have accidents with higher likelihood [22] than drivers piloting cars without phone conversations. The common solution of mandating that calls be made in a hands-free manner while driving, has not been found to improve safety [22, 28]. A constellation of findings suggests that it is not the motor action of holding the phone, but primarily the cognitive demands of dual-task scenarios that degrade performance on one or both tasks [21]. A recent study demonstrated that the difficulty of the driving situation and the content of the conversation influence both driving and conversation performance, where conversations that include information recall challenges have the most detrimental effects on driving [14]; multiple recall tasks of varying difficulty certainly occur in the course of typical conversations.

Strategies to manage secondary tasks during driving

Humans have the ability to perform multiple concurrent activities, given availability of cognitive resources and absence of conflicts in resource demands from different tasks [29]. Researchers have explored the abilities of people to interleave driving with other activities. Brumby et al. studied how dialing a phone number can be interleaved with driving by chunking the dialing task to be accommodated within driving [5]. In another study, it was found that searching for music in a music player without decomposing it into subtasks resulted in faster performance, but it was safer to prioritize the driving task at the cost of increasing performance time on the search task [6]. Iqbal et al. found that the formulation and relay of directions to a remote caller while piloting a vehicle has less impact on driving than answering questions that involve challenging information recall tasks [14]. The authors propose that the task of generating directions may be decomposed into smaller subtasks and interleaved with driving demands while retrieval tasks may employ a less decomposable process of engaging long-term memory.

We explore here the effects of interventions during phone conversations while driving. Although the main goal is to direct driver attention back to road conditions through informative alerts, we also look to minimize the additional distraction associated with alerting by identifying more opportune moments and least disruptive interrupting mechanisms.

Intervention or Mediation to Manage Attention

The notion of using mediation in helping users manage attention has been explored in many domains. McFarlane's seminal work proposed mediation as one of four interruption management methods [19]. The concept of attention manager systems has been studied in the desktop computing domain [10-12]. Some of these systems infer the cost of interrupting a user, and use this cost in decisions about if and when to pass on incoming information to the user. One particularly effective approach for mediation is deferring interruptions using a bounded deferral technique [9], which means waiting until a task or perceptual breakpoint within a given deadline [13].

In the domain of driving, researchers have explored the effectiveness of systems for aiding driving, e.g. providing local danger alerts [7], mediating communications among car passengers [17], or persuading people to drive in a more economical manner [20]. A challenge that such systems face is finding the best moment and modality for delivering information to the driver. Such decisions are complicated in multitasking scenarios, where cognitive resources of the driver are already engaged in driving and secondary tasks.

Findings that conversations with collocated passengers have less negative impact on driving compared to those with remote callers motivate further research on sharing driving context with remote callers [27]. Manalavan et al. explored how signaling a remote caller can indirectly reduce driver distraction [18]. They first investigated whether providing cues about the driving situation to a remote caller caused the caller to suspend the conversation (no actual driving occurred). Using findings from the first phase of analysis as ground truth, they performed a separate study to see if driving was safer when a remote caller stopped talking. While these disjoint studies provide initial intuition on how cues may affect conversations and consequently driving safety, further understanding is needed of cues and interventions in more realistic scenarios where driving and conversing occur together. In related work, Schneider and Kiesler found that providing remote callers with driving context via a visual display of the driver's view positively influenced driving performance during conversations [26].

We shall focus here on the influence on driving performance of delivering auditory alerting messages of different types and timings. We face the challenge of decisions about intervening with information coming in the midst of a preexisting dual-task scenario of driving and conversing, and seek to balance the value of the intervention with the goals of maintaining driving safety, while conforming to the social expectations of parties involved in the conversation.

STUDY

We pursue an understanding of the effects of different actions taken to direct drivers' attention to upcoming road conditions while the drivers are engaged in a phone conversation. The research questions include:

1) How effective are the interventions in maintaining driving safety compared to no intervention?
2) How do the interventions influence the conversation?
3) How do the drivers and the other participants in the conversations feel about such interventions?

To answer these questions, we conducted a controlled study using a driving simulator where we explored different types of interventions during a phone conversation between a driver and a remote participant. The study was set up so that the remote participant (situated in a separate room) talked to the driver over a speaker phone while the driver was driving through a predetermined route in the simulator, mimicking a hands-free phone call setting. The auditory interventions interrupted the conversation when some critical event or situation was soon to occur on the route.

Experimental design

The study was designed as a 2 (Intervention Mode) X 2 (Call Hold) X 2 (Intervention Timing) repeated measures within subjects study. Each condition was repeated twice. Additionally, there were two baseline trials with only driving (no conversation), and two baseline trials with only answering questions (no driving).

Users

Users participated in pairs, with one playing the role of the *driver* and the other in the role of the remote participant (the *caller*). Drivers were recruited from a mailing list for people who had been previously trained and calibrated for using the driving simulator. Recruited drivers were asked to bring their own partner for the study; otherwise the experimenters matched them up with partners. A total of 18 pairs were recruited. 15 of the 18 pairs were prior acquaintances, including friends, colleagues or family members. Prior acquaintance did not have any effects on the results. Users were compensated with a free software or hardware gratuity. To incentivize appropriate attention on performing the task, an extra $50 was offered to the pair who had the best overall performance in the study.

Task

For each trial, the driver was given a specific destination as the goal and was instructed to drive a 3-4 minute route where road signs would direct them towards the desired destination. Routes were composed of a combination of road segments *(regular)* with light or heavy traffic and had a mixture of signals and stop signs. Additionally, each route contained a number of *critical segments*, where the driver had to pay extra attention to avoid driving misdemeanors. Such segments consisted of road signs indicating turns to the destination, construction sites, pedestrian crossings, residential areas, police cars, and accident scenes.

While piloting the vehicle, the driver answered questions asked by the caller over a speaker phone system (fig. 1). A predefined set of no more than 25 questions were asked in each trial. Questions were designed to resemble daily chit-chat, requiring recall of recent activities and background,

Figure 1: Participant driving the STISIM simulator. The simulator provides a console with speedometer, steering wheel with turn signals, and traditional brake and accelerator. Three 47" screens generate an impression of driving a vehicle. The driver used a speaker phone system (center left) to converse with the remote caller (inset).

e.g. "*When did you last get gas for your car?*" and "*Name the last movie you saw.*" We chose these retrieval-centric questions in light of findings from a previous study showing that drivers have difficulty with driving while being challenged with retrieval tasks [14]. The caller was instructed to ask questions in a predefined order and to write down each answer before moving on to the next one. Repetitions of questions for clarification were allowed.

To provide incentive for allocating attention to both driving and answering questions, participants were informed that their performance scores depended on both driving and the conversations. They were told that they would be scored on the number of questions that they completed within a given amount of time. They were further told that they would be docked points for driving misdemeanors such as accidents, missing stop signs and turn signals, and unnecessarily slowing down or speeding. The caller was placed in a separate room and did not have access to the visual rendering of the driving scene, but the driver could provide relevant information to the caller over the phone to negotiate safe driving while answering questions.

Intervention

Before a critical segment (consisting of a critical event requiring the driver's attention) was about to start in the route, the conversation would be interrupted with one of the auditory interventions being studied, and heard by both the driver and remote caller. Interventions happened only for critical segments. The intervention was one of two modes (*Mode*): a short message simply stating "*Focus needed*," and a longer, more descriptive message stating exactly what to expect, e.g. "*Turn ahead*" or "*Construction ahead.*" For each intervention mode, the call was put on hold (*Hold*) for half of the trials, where, the caller also received a message stating that their call was put on hold temporarily. The caller was then muted until the critical event passed, followed by a message to resume conversation right after. The driver did not hear the hold message that the caller heard, but both were told at the beginning of the trial whether calls will be muted after receiving an intervention message, so the silence from the caller's end after delivery of the intervention message was expected for the driver. For the other half of cases, the message was delivered, but the conversation was not put on hold. In these cases, it was left to the driver and the caller to negotiate safe driving.

In terms of the timing of the interventions (*Timing*), for half of the trials, the intervention message was delivered immediately, as soon as the beginning of the critical segment could be seen in the driving horizon, typically a few seconds before the vehicle reached the start of the critical segment. This resulted in the intervention message often interrupting the conversation in the middle of asking a question or providing an answer. For the other half, a *bounded deferral* [9] technique was used, where the message would be withheld until the driver had finished answering the question from the caller, and delivered at a conversational breakpoint (before the start of the next question). In cases where the answer did not end until the critical event was about to happen, the message was delivered right at the beginning of the critical segment. The intervention was conducted in a Wizard of Oz setting where one of the experimenters who had full view of the driving scene and could hear the conversation could determine when to deliver the intervention message.

Before each trial, participants were told about the mode (receiving short or long message) and whether or not the call would be put on hold. We did not tell them whether the call would be delivered at a conversational breakpoint to test whether participants would notice this shift in timing, and whether interrupting in the middle of a conversation was considered to be more 'rude' or costly in another way compared to waiting until an answer was completed.

Methodology

Participants arriving at the lab were guided through an informed consent process, followed by an overview of the study. The caller was provided a set of questionnaires that s/he would ask over the phone (one for each trial) and then taken to a separate room where one of the experimenters remained with her throughout the duration of the trials. The communication between the simulator room and the caller room was maintained through an audio conferencing system, also used to simulate a phone conversation.

The participants were then taken through a series of practice trials, the first involving only questions over the phone in the absence of driving, and the second involving driving with no questions. These were followed by two practice trials where driving and question answering were combined, one demonstrating the short message, call on Hold combination, and the other demonstrating the longer message, call not on hold condition. This provided the participants a sense of what to expect during the actual trials. The practice trials could be repeated if needed.

The participants then moved on to the experimental trials. Each pair had a total of 20 trials, though not everyone could complete all trials due to time limitations. Two of the trials were a baseline of driving with no conversations, and two were a baseline of conversations in the absence of driving. The remaining 16 trials occurred according to various intervention conditions. Combinations of factors (Mode, Timing, and Hold) were presented according to a Latin square design. Each combination was presented twice.

At the end of each trial, both the driver and caller answered a short questionnaire on the difficulty of the trial and about the effectiveness and disruptiveness of the intervention. The entire study lasted approximately 2 hours per pair.

Measures

Quantitative data on performance on both driving and conversation was collected. For driving, we collected the number of errors with turning and collisions (for both of which intervention messages provided alerts ahead of time), as a measure of how the intervention messages affected these metrics. To indirectly assess whether an intervention added to the cognitive load of drivers in a manner that may distract drivers and force other driving errors, we collected the number of missed red lights and stop signs, and roadside excursions. These measures were automatically recorded by the simulator. For all collected measures we computed incidence rates (per minute) separately over the span of the critical segments (when critical events occurred), and the span of regular segments (part of the route excluding the critical segments). This was done for both trials with phone calls and the baseline driving in the absence of phone calls.

For performance on the phone conversations, we computed the number of questions answered per minute, again for both trials with phone conversations and driving, and the baseline of phone conversations with no driving.

We also collected qualitative data on participants' perceptions on the intervention experience. We asked them to assess the overall difficulty of each trial, and to rate how they felt about the effectiveness of the intervention in maintaining driving safety, the disruptiveness of the intervention for the task of driving and answering questions, and how rude they felt the system was.

At the end of all trials, participants in both roles answered a final questionnaire on the promise of using the interventions in real life, where they were asked to rank order the nine situations that they had experienced during the study.

Effects of Intervention on Driving Performance

We now review the metrics for driving performance to understand the effects of different types of interventions. Unless otherwise stated, our analysis for each metric conformed to the following steps:

1. Baseline comparison of the metric between regular and critical segments to establish relative difficulty of the critical segments and validation that these segments required extra attention from the driver.
2. For critical segments only, comparison of the metric across three contexts: trials with driving only (baseline control), trials with driving and conversation (control to assess effects on performance due to talking), and trials with driving, conversation, and intervention (to understand intervention effects).
3. For critical segments only on the trials that had interventions, comparison of the metric among different types of intervention along the dimensions of Mode, Hold, and Timing.

Effects of Interventions in Reducing Turning errors

A turning error is characterized as not making a turn when required (as instructed by road signs), making a wrong turn (e.g. making a left turn instead of a right), or turning when not needed. Making turns were required only in the critical segments and an intervention message was delivered either directing the driver's attention to the road (shorter message) or explicitly announcing an upcoming turn (longer message). Turning errors could still occur in regular segments if drivers made a turn at an intersection where they were not supposed to.

For baseline comparison, we ran an independent samples *t*-test for turning errors per minute between critical (M=0.23, S.D=0.48) and regular (M=0.15, S.D.=0.3) segments across all trials. Results showed that drivers had more errors in turning during the critical segments (t(572)=2.78, p<0.006), which was not unexpected as specific instructions for turning was provided only during the critical segments. This also indicates the need for the driver to pay more attention to the turn instructions during the critical segments. Interestingly, turning errors were nonzero for the regular segments, happening when drivers made turns when not needed, indicating lack of attention on the driver's part.

Looking at only the critical segments (where turns were specifically required), a one-way ANOVA on turning errors /minute showed a significant difference (F(2, 337)= 35.6) across driving (M=0.54, S.D.=0.75), driving+ conversation (M=0.73, S.D.=0.83), and driving+conversation +intervention (M=0.14, S.D.=0.3). Post hoc Bonferroni tests showed that turning errors/minute during driving+ conversation+intervention was significantly lower than both driving+conversation (p<0.0001) and driving (p<0.0001).

To explore the influence of different types of intervention, we conducted a 3-way repeated measures ANOVA analysis on the trials with driving, conversation, and intervention, where Mode, Hold and Timing were the within subject variables, and Instance (1 or 2) was the between subject variable (for each repetition for each combination). Results showed a main effect of Mode (F(1,22)=8.3, p<0.009) - drivers missed less turns/minute when they received the longer message (M=0.09, S.D.=0.24) compared to the shorter message (M=0.18, S.D.=0.34), see Table 1. The more explicit intervention seemed to be more effective in directing the driver's attention to upcoming turns.

Effects of Interventions in Reducing Collisions

A collision was recorded when the driver hit another vehicle, a pedestrian, or lane markers in construction zones. An intervention message was delivered when there was a possibility of a collision ahead, but collisions could also occur in regular segments. An independent samples *t*-test for number of collisions /minute between critical (M=0.192, S.D.=0.15) and regular (M=0.038, S.D.=0.43) segments across all trials showed that drivers had more collisions during critical segments (t(420)=6.2, p<0.0001). This again validates the need to pay more attention while traversing a critical segment compared to a regular segment.

Looking only at the critical segments, a one-way ANOVA showed no significant differences in collisions per minute across driving (M=0.13, S.D.=0.34), driving+conversation (M=0.29, S.D.=0.59), and driving+conversation+ intervention (M=0.21, S.D.=0.46), but rate of collisions while conversing were slightly lower with interventions compared to no intervention. We explored whether there were any significant differences for the various intervention conditions. A three-way repeated measures ANOVA with Mode, Hold, and Timing as the within subject variables also did not show significant differences in collisions/minute. As seen in Table 1, the longer message caused less collisions/minute compared to the shorter message, though the differences did not reach significance.

Effects of Interventions in Forcing Roadside excursions

Roadside excursions were recorded when the vehicle deviated from its regular driving path for any reason, often due to lack of control. Unlike for turns and possibility of collisions where interventions provided prior alerts, roadside excursions were measured to understand potential side effects of an intervention, e.g. the prospect that the overhead of messaging would cause roadside excursions.

Driving, Conversation and Intervention		**Turning errors/minute**	**Collisions/ minute**
Factors	**Levels**	Driving Only: 0.54(0.75) Driving+Conv: 0.73(0.83)	Driving Only: 0.13(0.34) Driving+Conv: 0.29(0.59)
Mode	Shorter message	0.181(0.34)	0.263 (0.525)
	Longer message	0.088 (0.24)	0.16(0.366)
Hold	No hold	0.125(0.28)	0.156(0.355)
	Hold	0.149(0.32)	0.272(0.539)
Timing	Immediate	0.136 (0.31)	0.195(0.456)
	Breakpoint	0.138 (0.29)	0.236(0.463)

Table 1. Means (standard deviations in parenthesis) of rate of turning errors and collisions (per minute) across various levels of Mode, Hold, and Timing. Baselines are provided for comparison.

An independent samples *t*-test showed a higher incidence of roadside excursions per minute during critical (M=0.13, S.D.=0.37) compared to regular (M=0.07, S.D.=0.29) segments, $t(643)=2.33$, $p<0.03$, providing further evidence that managing driving safety during critical segments was more difficult than during regular segments. A one way ANOVA among driving, driving+conversation, and driving+ conversation+intervention showed no significant differences in roadside excursions/min, indicating that the intervention did not affect this measure negatively compared to only driving, or driving and conversing.

We explored whether one type of intervention had a more negative effect than others in the critical segments. A three-way repeated measures ANOVA with Mode, Hold, and Timing as within subjects variables showed an interaction effect between Mode and Hold ($F(1,22)=5.319$, $p<0.031$). Following up on the interaction effect between Mode and Hold, post hoc tests showed that for calls put on hold, longer messages caused more roadside excursions (M=0.27, S.D.=0.61) compared to shorter messages (M=0.08, S.D.=0.29). This suggests that the additional load of processing the longer message may cause drivers to swerve even after putting the conversation on hold.

Effects of Interventions on Red Light/Stop Sign Misses

As with roadside excursions, we measured the rate of red light and stop sign misses to assess if the intervention caused additional load inhibiting drivers' visual processing. An independent-samples *t*-test between critical (M=0.06, S.D.=0.23) and regular (M=0.12, S.D.=0.26) segments across all trials showed that drivers tend to miss red lights and stop signs less during critical segments ($t(675)=2.8$, $p<0.006$), which may be because drivers tend to drive slower during these segments.

Looking only at critical segments, a one-way ANOVA on Missed Red lights or Stop signs per minute did not show a significant difference across driving only, driving and conversation, and driving, conversation and intervention. A three-way repeated measures ANOVA also did not find differences in the effects of the different types of intervention. This may suggest that processing the intervention does not interfere with the perceptual task of recognizing and responding to red lights and stop signs.

Effects of Intervention on Conversation

To measure performance on the conversation, we examined the number of questions that the pair answered in a given amount of time. As with driving performance, we first compared answers per minute across regular and critical segments, then compared critical segments across conversation, conversation+driving, and conversation+ driving+ intervention. Finally, we studied effects of Mode, Hold, and Timing on the number of questions answered.

An independent samples *t*-test showed that users answered more questions per min during regular segments (M=7.53, S.D.=2.01) compared to critical segments (M=3.14, S.D.=3.57), $t(534)=19.7$, $p<0.0001$. A one-way ANOVA across only the critical segments showed that user-pairs answered significantly fewer questions per minute ($F(1,304)=58.8$, $p<0.00001$) during driving+conversation+ intervention (M=2.98, S.D.=3.3) compared to driving+ conversation (M=7.7, S.D.=3.29). This is to be expected, as for some of the trials with intervention, the call was put on hold, substantially affecting the number of questions that could be answered for that trial.

To understand the effect of the factors Mode, Hold, and Timing on the number of questions answered per minute, we ran a 3-way repeated measures ANOVA. Results showed a significant main effect of the Hold condition ($F(1,22)=431.6$ $p<0.0001$). Post Hoc tests showed that pairs answered more questions during the NoHold trials (M=5.9, S.D.=2.2) compared to the 0 during the Hold trials, which again is not unexpected.

Prior work has shown speech to slow down during dual-task situations in driving [14]. We explored whether the third task of intervention further slowed down answering questions, indicating additional load. We ran a one-way ANOVA on the rate of answering questions/minute comparing only the no hold-trials during the critical segments within driving+conversation+intervention, to the no-hold trials during driving +conversation (hold trials were excluded as no conversation took place for those). Results showed that the pairs answered significantly fewer ($F(1, 167)=13.06$, $p<0.0001$) questions during the driving+ conversation+ intervention (M=5.9, S.D.=2.11) compared to the driving+ conversation (M=7.6, S.D.=3.3) trials. This shows that the intervention does indeed slow down the conversation (while it did not necessarily affect driving performance), but with the added benefit of reducing driving errors, as shown in the previous section.

Subjective Feedback on Interventions

To get a sense of how users felt about the intervention experience, we asked them to rate their experiences on a variety of dimensions (see below) after each trial on a Likert scale of 1 to 5. Feedback was collected from both drivers and callers using role-specific questionnaires. However, some questions on the questionnaires were the same for both drivers and callers, allowing us to compare how the role affected perception. For analysis of the questions common to both roles, we added a fourth factor, Role, in addition to Mode, Hold and Timing.

Difficulty of trials

Both drivers and callers were asked to rate the difficulty of the trials on a Likert scale of 1 (very easy) to 5 (very difficult). A univariate ANOVA with Role (driver, caller) and Trial (driving only, conversation only, driving+ conversation and driving+conversation+intervention) as factors showed no differences in the ratings across Role; both driver ratings (M=2.06, S.D.=0.86) and caller ratings (M=2.04, S.D.=1.01) being on the easier side (3=neutral). A main effect of Trial ($F(3, 679)=25.74$, $p<0.0001$) was found. Post hoc Bonferroni tests showed that trials with driving, conversations, and interventions were rated to be significantly more difficult (M=2.21, S.D.=0.91), compared to driving only (M=1.46, S.D.=0.74), conversation only (M=1.39, S.D.=0.82) and driving+conversation (M=1.73, S.D.=0.84), $p<0.0001$ for all. This suggests that both drivers and callers perceived the intervention to add to the difficulty of the trials in terms of the shared goal (drive safely and answer questions), even though performance results suggested tradeoffs only in the conversations.

For only trials with driving, conversation, and intervention, we ran a repeated measures ANOVA with 4 within subjects factors (Mode, Hold, Timing and Role) on the difficulty ratings to understand effects of the various intervention conditions. Only a main effect of Hold ($F(1,17)=11.4$, $p<0.004$) was found. Trials where the conversation was put on hold were rated to be more difficult (M=2.29, S.D.=0.9) compared to trials where the conversation was not put on hold (M=2.02, S.D.=0.9). This suggests that difficulty ratings were being impacted by whether or not the conversation was being inhibited, which would impact the broader goal of overall performance on the trial.

Feedback on the intervention

There were three questions about the intervention that we asked both drivers and callers: whether they felt the intervention made driving safer, how disruptive the intervention was to the conversation and perceived 'rudeness' of the system (Figure 3). A Likert scale of 1 to 5 was used, 1 being strongly disagree, 5 being strongly agree.

On the question of whether the particular type of intervention for the trial made driving safer, we ran a four way repeated measures ANOVA with Mode, Hold, Timing, and Role as within subjects factors and Instance (1 or 2) as the between subjects factor. Results showed a main effect of Role ($F(1,13)=18.8$, $p<0.001$) and an interaction effect between Mode and Timing ($F(1,13)=10.156$, $p<0.007$). For the main effect of Role, drivers more strongly agreed (M=4.462, S.D.=0.84) that the intervention made driving safer, compared to the closer to neutral ratings of the callers (M=3.42, S.D.=0.97), see Figure 3. This difference may be explained by answers to a related question asked to callers only on whether they felt that they had enough information about the driver's state. Callers were again close to neutral on this point (M=3.52, S.D.=1.1), and a number of callers stated that since they did not have a view of the driver's environment (even though they could hear what was going on) it was difficult for them to fully evaluate safety.

On the question of whether the intervention disrupted conversation, a four-way repeated measures ANOVA showed a main effect of both Role ($F(1,14)=12,19$, $p<0.004$) and Hold ($F(1,14)=34.713$, $p<0.0001$), as well as an interaction effect between Role and Hold ($F(1,14)=13.87$, $p<0.002$), and between Mode and Timing ($F(1,14)=7.76$, $p<0.015$). Overall, callers more strongly agreed that the intervention disrupted the conversation (M=4.01), compared to the more neutral ratings of the drivers (M=2.98), see figure 3. Looking at the interaction

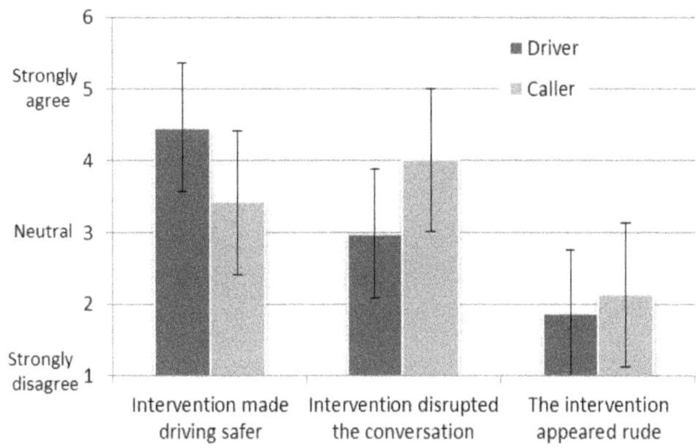

Figure 3: Comparison of driver and caller rating on driving safety, conversation disruption, and social attribution towards the intervention.

effect between Role and Hold, for trials where conversations were put on hold, callers had a higher rating of disruption (M=4.53, S.D.=0.62) compared to trials where conversations were not put on hold (M=3.48, S.D.=1.3, $p<0.0001$). The drivers' ratings of disruption of conversation did not vary significantly across the Hold condition. This again supports the observation that even in a cooperative environment with a broader common goal, individual roles of participants in a team can affect their judgments. For the interaction effect between Mode and Timing, the shorter message delivered immediately were considered to be more disruptive to the conversation (M=3.58, S.D.=1.23) compared to the longer messages delivered immediately (M=3.22, S.D.=1.28, $p<0.049$).

On the question of the perceived 'rudeness' of the intervention, the overall rating was low (M=1.988, S.D.=0.99) with drivers having a mean rating of 1.86 and callers having a mean rating of 2.11), see Figure 3. This suggests that the interventions were not deemed as unacceptable in terms of social norms. A repeated measures ANOVA showed no effect of Mode, Hold, Timing, or Role.

Drivers were also asked additional questions on specific effects of the intervention on the driving experience. On the question of whether they felt the intervention disrupted driving, they generally disagreed (M=1.9, S.D.=1.1) with no differences across Mode, Hold, or Timing. Drivers also agreed that the system provided the right amount of information (M=4.1, S.D.=0.9), but again were not biased towards any particular combination of the three factors. On a question of whether putting the conversation on hold helped, drivers leaned towards agreeing that it was useful (M=3.6, S.D.=1.2), but did not again show preference for any particular combination of factors.

Overall preferences

At the end of the study, both drivers and callers were asked about their overall opinion on the effectiveness of an intervention system that can help manage phone calls based on driving situations (Figure 4). Drivers were generally positive about the usefulness of such a system (17/18

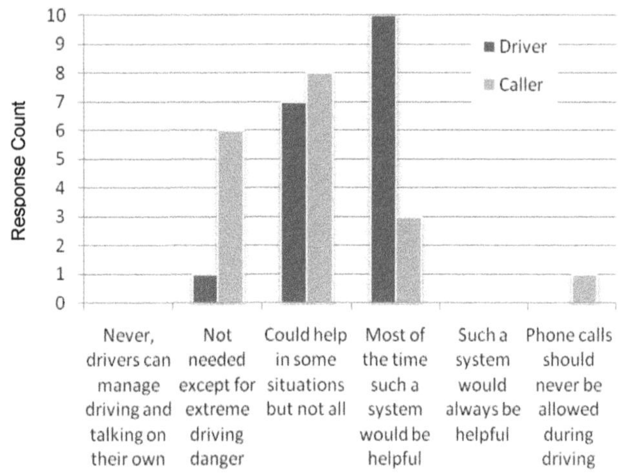

Figure 4: Histogram of preferences about intervention system for drivers and callers in the experiment. Majority of drivers were in favor of such a system, while majority of remote callers felt that such systems should be used occasionally at the best.

preferring such a system occasionally or most of the time). Interestingly, callers were less enthusiastic (14/18 preferring such a system occasionally, or only for extreme cases). This again suggests the need for callers to be more aware of effects of conversations on driving.

We also asked both drivers and callers to rank order their preferences for the various combinations of factors (Figure 5). Drivers mostly prefered the short message delivered at a breakpoint with the call put on hold, and remote callers mostly prefered the shorter message delivered at a breakpoint with the call not put on hold. Both drivers and callers least preferred the longer message that interrupted in the middle with the call on hold. No intervention was ranked 8 out of 9 for drivers, but was ranked 3 out of 9 for callers, indicating that drivers, through their more direct experience with the intervention during the study, perceived the benefits on driving more than their remote partners, who only experienced the effects on the conversation.

Drivers and callers also provided free form feedback on how they perceived the value of intervention. One driver commented: "*The prompts to pay attention were surprisingly useful. Wish I had them in my current auto system.*" Another driver commented: "*Announcement of turns was helpful.*" Of course, drivers did express their dislikes and preferences for the various forms of intervention. One driver had an initial comment of: "*Being put on hold doesn't help me, makes me wonder what happened...*" and after a few trials he remarked: "*After using it I seem to be getting used to the interruptions!*" A couple of drivers remarked that a visual indicator of when the call was on hold would have been helpful. Note that drivers and callers were informed right before the trial whether the call would be put on hold, but apart from silence from the caller's end after receiving the intervention message, there was no cue to the driver.

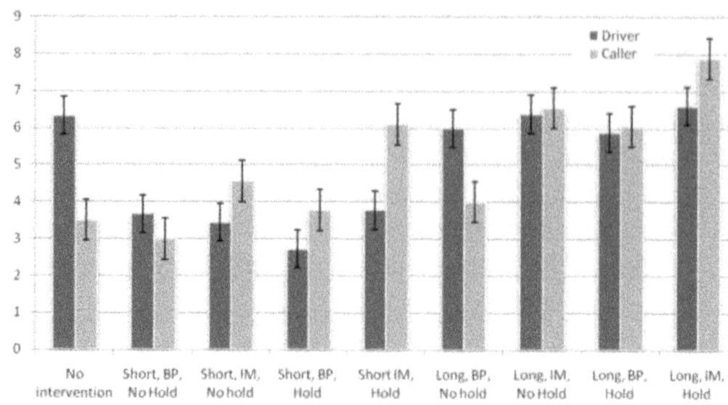

Figure 5. Average ranking for each experimental condition separated by drivers and callers. Lower scores indicate higher preferences (1= most preferred, 9= least preferred, shown on the *y-axis*). BP=breakpoint, IM=immediate.

The remote callers were less enthusiastic about the interventions. One caller commented: "*Not sure if I like my behavior dictated by a computer,*" while another remarked: "*hate being put on hold.*" One person found the hold being "*an annoyance,*" but also commented that "*but it gave me a few seconds to collect my thoughts.*" Another caller also voiced her preference towards the no-hold condition: "*Not putting on hold made the interventions ok to deal with as it is just a short break and the train of thought is not lost.*"

Callers generally prefered the shorter message as exemplified in the following feedback: "*I really like the shorter notifications – focus needed is plenty of info...*" and "*It was nice to have the detail about the driver was focusing – but shorter message is better.*" Overall, both drivers and callers seemed to see value in the interventions, but showed a preference towards being alerted and not necessarily to relinquish deeper control of the conversation to the system.

DISCUSSION

Our study on the effectiveness of various combinations of intervention factors revealed a positive effect of intervention on driving, resulting in lower incidence of turning errors and collisions as compared to trials without interventions. The mode of the intervention appeared to positively influence driving performance, with the more descriptive message being more effective in reducing driving errors. However, the intervention also affected performance on the conversation, and subsequently affected subjective preferences. Qualitatively, drivers showed strong preference towards interventions while callers, who did not directly benefit from interventions, were more neutral about the need for interventions while driving and conversing.

We also examined the effects of the additional cognitive load that interventions might place on a driver. We explored whether processing interventions for the critical events caused higher incidence of other driving errors such as roadside excursion and missing lights and signs. Results did not find interventions to affect these metrics compared to trials with only driving, or with driving and conversations, suggesting that the mediation did not significantly distract drivers. Pairing this with the benefits of improved performance on metrics for which interventions were provided, the positive ratings of drivers are understandable.

We found that interventions influenced conversations. For trials where calls were put on hold, the fluency of the conversation was understandably disrupted. Conversations slowed down during the critical events, even for cases where the call was not put on hold, compared to conversation during regular driving segments. This suggests that while facing a critical event, drivers were trading off performance on the conversation with driving safety, supporting findings in [14]. The shared intervention message provided callers with awareness of upcoming difficulty in driving, enabling them to assist with modulating conversations. In trials with no intervention, callers were unaware of the driving situation unless they were specifically told by the driver.

An overall preference was found towards short messages delivered at breakpoints during conversations, with drivers preferring the conversations to be also put on hold, even though longer messages were found be to be more effective. Callers, who generally found the call being put on hold annoying, could perhaps benefit from more information about the driving situation in addition to the sound bites, e.g. a visual abstraction of the driving scene [26].

Our study used a Wizard of Oz setup to perform an initial investigation of the effectiveness and acceptability of intervention during driving and conversing. To implement such a system in practice, an automated system could harness GPS, accelerometers, and proximity sensors along with information on the planned route, real-time traffic, accidents, detours, weather, etc., as well as statistics of events on upcoming segments to predict future criticality. The cognitive load of drivers could be estimated by considering the current driving situation (e.g. speed, braking, turning, and shifts in the overall complexity of driving) as well as physiological measures (e.g. heart rate [24]). The cognition required to perform the secondary task on top of driving (e.g. certain types of phone conversations may induce more cognitive engagement) might also be estimated. An alerting cost factor, representing a potential deficit of cognitive resources for driving, might be determined by considering the demands of the driving task and the demands of the secondary task. Such a cost factor could be applied to compute the overall expected cost of engaging in both tasks and the cost measure could be used to determine if, when, and how to best intervene.

An intervention system could be realized as an extension of in-vehicle systems equipped with the ability to interrupt and put ongoing calls on hold, or intercept incoming calls and direct them to a voice message system. While some of the technology exists today, further research is needed to determine the most effective form of such a system.

We note that such intervention systems are not a panacea for safe driving; people will likely continue to make driving mistakes regardless of whether they are talking on the phone or not. We expect that an intervention system would be able to help drivers better manage their attention while in a divided-attention scenario (e.g. taking on the role of a vigilant passenger), by directing their attention towards commonly backgrounded tasks of driving (e.g. details of the visual scene). The results on driving performance in our study appear to support this hypothesis, but further research is required to determine how interventions would work in the real world.

Many challenges remain with the design of such intervention systems. What are the most appropriate granularities of events that system should represent and direct the driver's attention to? What events are feasible to detect and which ones are not, and how should events be prioritized? More research is needed to understand how to determine critical upcoming events and tolerance for alerts about these events. Inappropriately low thresholds to alerting about events that would be recognized without notification can lead to situations where users ignore many of the interventions, including ones that may be more important. On the other hand, settings that are too conservative may lead to the suppression of alerts about potentially dangerous events. There are also risks associated with becoming dependent on an intervention system. Drivers might become less attentive towards road conditions expecting the system to alert them whenever a difficult situation is arising. Might such a growing dependence encourage multitasking while driving, with a new reliance on the cushion of being warned when attention needs to be directed towards the road? Future research is needed to address these questions.

Finally, despite having driving experience themselves, the callers in our study appeared overall to be agnostic about the usefulness of interventions, while the drivers in the study were more positive towards it. These differences are likely based in the roles that each of the participants had in the study which may have affected their perception. The results overall highlight the broader need to educate the population about the dangers of driving and multitasking, and awareness about the compromises that participating parties may have to make to ensure the safety of driving.

CONCLUSION AND FUTURE WORK

We conducted a study investigating the effectiveness and acceptability of informative alerting and communication mediation during simultaneous driving and phone conversation. Results showed that intervention with more explicit messages about upcoming critical conditions is effective in reducing turning errors and collisions, compared to situations with no intervention. No effects of additional load on the driver were found. However, the benefits on driving were traded off with a corresponding slowing down of the conversation. Overall, drivers showed preference towards the benefits of interventions, whereas callers tended to be more neutral. Our results provide insights on how different types of intervention during driving can help people drive more safely during conversations. Future work includes development of models of risk for combinations of driving situations and secondary tasks and the study of the engineering of context- and cognition-aware communication mediation systems.

ACKNOWLEGMENTS
We thank Ivan Tashev for his help with the driving simulator and also thank all the participants in our study.

REFERENCES

1. *Cell Phone and Texting Laws*. Dec. 2010, Retrieved from http://ghsa.org/html/stateinfo/laws/cellphone_laws.html
2. Alm, H. and Nilsson, L. The effects of a mobile telephone task on driver behavior in a car following situation. *Accident Analysis and Prevention*, *27* (5). 707-715.
3. Briem, V. and Hedman, L.R. Behavioral effects of mobile telephone use during simulated driving. *Ergonomics*, *38*. 2536-2562.
4. Brookhuis, K.A., De Vries, G. and De Waard, D. The effects of mobile telephoning on driving performance. *Accident Analysis and Prevention*, *23,* 309-316.
5. Brumby, D.P., Salvucci, D.D. and Howes, A. Focus on driving: How cognitive constraints shape the adaptation of strategy while dialing while driving. *Proc CHI*, 2009, 1629-1638.
6. Brumby, D.P., Salvucci, D.D., Mankowski, W. and Howes, A. A cognitive constraint model of the effects of portable music-player use on driver performance. *Proc HFES,* 2007, 1531-1535.
7. Cao, Y., Castronovo, S., Mahr, A. and Muller, C., On Timing and Modality Choice with Local Danger Warnings for Drivers. *Proc. AutomotiveUI*, 2009, 75-78.
8. Horrey, W.J. and Wickens, C.D. Examining the Impact of Cell Phone Conversations on Driving Using Meta-Analytic Techniques. *Human Factors*, *48* (1). 196-205.
9. Horvitz, E., Apacible, J. and Subramani, M. Balancing Awareness and Interruption: Investigation of Notification Deferral Policies. Ardissono, L., Brna, P. and Mitrovic, A. eds. *Proc. User Modeling*, 2005, 433-437.
10. Horvitz, E., Kadie, C.M., Paek, T. and Hovel, D. Models of Attention in Computing and Communications: From Principles to Applications. *CACM*, 2003, 52-59.
11. Horvitz, E., Koch, P., Kadie, C.M. and Jacobs, A. Coordinate: Probabilistic Forecasting of Presence and Availability. *Proc UAI*, 2002, 224-233.
12. Iqbal, S.T. and Bailey, B.P. Oasis: A Framework for Linking Notification Delivery to the Perceptual Structure of Goal-Directed Tasks. *ACM Transactions on Computer-Human Interaction*, 2010, *17* (4).
13. Iqbal, S.T. and Bailey, B.P., Understanding and Developing Models for Detecting and Differentiating Breakpoints during Interactive Tasks. *Proc. CHI*, 2007, 697-706.
14. Iqbal, S.T., Ju, Y.-C. and Horvitz, E. Cars, Calls, and Cognition: Investigating Driving and Divided Attention. *Proc. CHI*, 2010, 1281-1290.
15. Lee, J.D., Caven, B., Haake, S. and Brown, T. Speech-based Interaction with In-vehicle Computers: The Effect of Speech-based E-mail on Driver's attention to the Roadway. *Human Factors*, *43*. 631-640.
16. Levy, J. and Pashler, H. Task Prioritisation in Multitasking during Driving: Opportunity to Abort a Concurrent Task Does not Insulate Braking Responses from Dual Task Slowing. *Applied Cognitive Psychology*, *22*. 507-525.
17. Mahr, A., Pentcheva, M. and Muller, C., Towards System-Mediated Car Passenger Communication. *Proc. AutomotiveUI*, 2009, 79-80.
18. Manalavan, P., Samar, A., Schneider, M., Kiesler, S.B. and Siewiorek, D.P. In-car Cell Phone Use: Mitigating Risk by Signaling Remote Callers *CHI Extended Abstracts*, 2002, 790-791.
19. McFarlane, D.C. Comparison of four primary methods for coordinating the interruption of people in human-computer interaction. *Human Computer Interaction*, *17* (1). 63-139.
20. Meschtscherjakov, A., Wilfinger, D., Scherndl, T. and Tscheligi, M., Acceptance of Future Persuasive In-Car Interfaces Towards a more Economic Driving Behavior. *Proc AutomotiveUI*, 2009, 81-88.
21. Nunes, L.M. and Recarte, M.A. Cognitive Demands of hands-free-phone conversation while driving. *Transportation research Part F*, *5*. 133-144.
22. Redelmeier, D.A. and Tibshirani, R.J. Association between cellular-telephone calls and motor vehicle collisions. *New England Journal of Medicine*, *336* (7). 453-458.
23. Reed, N. and Robbins, R. The Effect of Text Messaging on Driver Behavior: A Simulator Study *Transport Research Lab Report*, 2008, PPR 367.
24. Riener, A., Ferscha, A. and Aly, M., Heart on the road: HRV analysis for monitoring a driver's affective state. *Proc. AutomotiveUI* 2009, 99-106.
25. Salvucci, D.D., Markley, D., Zuber, M. and Brumby, D.P. iPod distraction: effects of portable music-player use on driver performance *Proc. CHI* , 2007, 243-250.
26. Schneider, M. and Kiesler, S. Calling while driving: effects of providing remote traffic context. *Proc CHI*, 2005 561-569
27. Strayer, D.L. and Drews, F.A. Cell-Phone Induced Driver Distraction. *Current Directions in Psycological Science*, *16* (3). 128-131.
28. Strayer, D.L. and Johnston, W.A. Driven to distraction: Dual-task studies of simulated driving and conversing on a cellular phone. *Psychological Science*, *12*. 462-466.
29. Wickens, C.D. Processing Resources and Attention. in Parsuraman, R. and Davies, R. eds. *Varieties of Attention*, Academic Press, New York, 1984.

Fast or Safe? How Performance Objectives Determine Modality Output Choices While Interacting on the Move

Duncan P. Brumby, Samantha C.E. Davies, Christian P. Janssen, and Justin J. Grace
UCL Interaction Centre
University College London
London WC1E 6BT UK
Brumby@cs.ucl.ac.uk

ABSTRACT
In-car devices that use audio output have been shown to be less distracting than traditional graphical user interfaces, but can be cumbersome and slow to use. In this paper, we report an experiment that demonstrates how these performance characteristics impact whether people will elect to use an audio interface in a multitasking situation. While steering a simulated vehicle, participants had to locate a source of information in a short passage of text. The text was presented either on a visual interface, or using a text-to-speech audio interface. The relative importance of each task was varied. A no-choice/choice paradigm was used in which participants first gained experience with each of the two interfaces, before being given a choice on which interface to use on later trials. The characteristics of the interaction with the interfaces, as measured in the no-choice phase, and the relative importance of each task, had an impact on which output modality was chosen in the choice phase. Participants that prioritized the secondary task tended to select the (faster yet more distracting) visual interface over the audio interface, and as a result had poorer lane keeping performance. This work demonstrates how a user's task objective will influence modality choices with multimodal devices in multitask environments.

Author Keywords
Multitasking, visual interface, audio interface, driving, strategy selection, performance trade-offs.

ACM Classification Keywords
H.1.2 User/Machine Systems: human factors; H.5.2 User Interfaces: evaluation/methodology, interaction styles.

General Terms
Experimentation, Human Factors.

INTRODUCTION
In recent years there has been a steady flow of reports on people's propensity to use their mobile devices while driving – some even feel the need to keep their Twitter stream up-to-date from behind the wheel [5]. There is a large body of work showing that this kind of behavior is reckless and can increase the risk of a crash. For example, Horrey and Wickens [11] offer a meta-analysis of 23 different studies investigating mobile phone use while driving, each of which demonstrates negative effects on driving performance. Because mobile devices support so many of our daily activities, efforts to discourage drivers from using their devices have often failed to have an impact [6]. Hence, the HCI community might consider alternative design solutions to lessen some of these problems.

Audio interfaces offer a promising alternative to the traditional Graphical User Interface (GUI) for alleviating some of the deleterious problems associated with using a mobile device while driving. This is because audio output does not demand the user's visual attention and so limits perceptual interference between tasks [27,33]. Audio is already used extensively in many systems to signal events to users (e.g., that a file has finished downloading or that a new message has been received in an ongoing chat). Recently, the use of audio has been taken a step further in the development of *eyes-free* interfaces [21,34,35]. Studies have shown that using audio in this way is a safer alternative to a visual interface [19,20,22,29,34], though the potential for cognitive distraction remains [11,26]. Despite these benefits, task times using audio interfaces can be slower than with traditional GUIs [29,34].

There has been little discussion of whether such trade-offs between speed and safety across different output modalities on a multimodal device might present a problem. We question whether drivers might forfeit the safety benefit offered by an audio interface when they can access the same information more quickly by glancing at the device's screen. Despite the importance of this question to the HCI community, research has not considered whether performance objectives have a strong influence on modality choices with multimodal devices. Instead, previous work has focused on evaluating whether one output modality interferes more or less with driving performance than another [12,19,20,25,29,34], or in which environment particular output modalities work best [10].

In this paper, we investigate how performance objectives influence modality selection in a multitasking situation. In our experiment, participants were required to find the answer to a question in a short passage of text while controlling a simulated vehicle. This scenario resembles a situation in which someone is trying to read a text message while driving – a reckless activity, but alas one that is all too prevalent [6]. The text for the secondary task was presented either on a secondary display (visual interface) or was spoken by a text-to-speech program (audio interface). The driving task that we used was quite simple, in that, participants were only required to control the steering of the vehicle. Our steering task does therefore not allow us to investigate the full complexity of driver behavior [4,11], but lane keeping performance in a simulator can serve as a proxy for driver safety in the read-world [24].

We were primarily concerned with which output modality people will *choose* to interact with to complete a secondary task. To address this question we used a no-choice/choice paradigm [15,23,28,32]. This paradigm can be very useful for understanding factors that influence strategy selection. Alas its has been largely neglected in HCI research, though it was used in early studies to understand how users decide between different input techniques, namely, the mouse and the keyboard when on a desktop computer [23]. In the paradigm, participants first complete a series of trials using each of the available methods to complete the task at hand before being given the choice over which they would like to use. The benefits of this approach for investigating strategy selection are three-fold: (1) it gives an objective measure of the performance trade-offs at stake between different methods for achieving the same goal, (2) the user gains equal amounts of experience with each method (controlling for experience), and (3) it allows us to find out which option people choose and whether this choice varies under different conditions. This approach was useful here because it allowed us to move beyond the question that has occupied previous work, namely, whether in-car systems that use audio output are less distracting than interacting with a traditional GUI [12,19,20,25,29,34]. Instead, we focus on which output modality users will elect to use and whether this decision is sensitive to changes in the relative priority given to one task over another.

In the no-choice phase of the experiment, we expect to find that when the visual interface is used for the secondary task lane keeping performance will decline. This is because participants will have to shift their visual attention away from the road ahead to glance at the secondary display, and this will impact their ability to steer the vehicle [31]. In contrast, we expect the audio interface to be far less disruptive to steering performance because there is no competition for visual attention between the tasks [27,33].

In terms of time to complete the secondary task in the no-choice phase, we expect the audio interface to be slower because the audio output rate will be slower than a typical reading speed and participants will not be able to vary the rate at which the audio stream is outputted. With the visual interface, not only will participants be able to rapidly skim the content of the text to locate the target rapidly [7], but they will also be free to vary their strategy for interleaving attention between the two tasks [2,3,14,16-18]. In other words, participants can make longer or shorter glances to the secondary display before returning their attention to the road ahead. We do not investigate these fine-grained moment-to-moment interleaving patterns in detail here, as this has been studied extensively in previous work [2,3,14,16-18]. Instead, we use the no-choice phase to get a reliable measure of the performance trade-offs at stake between each option before giving participants a choice of output modality in the choice phase.

How might participants decide between these different modalities in the choice phase? It is well known that in single-task situations people tend to opt for the fastest method, even when it is only milliseconds faster [8]. Therefore we might expect participants to show a strong preference for the interface that allows them to complete the secondary task the fastest. Such a preference would mean that all participants might forfeit the safety benefits of using the audio output in order to complete the secondary task quickly. In contrast, the decision over which output modality to use might also be moderated by the users' *performance objective* (i.e., which of the two tasks is subjectively more important to them at that time).

To address the question of whether varying the relative value (or priority) of each task affects which modality is chosen, different instructions were given to participants. For half of the participants, the instructions emphasized that they should prioritize rapid completion of the secondary task, for the other half the instructions emphasized that they should prioritize safer steering performance. This manipulation reflects the idea that in many real world multitasking scenarios, a user might value one task more than another depending on what their goal is. For example, even a careful driver who usually avoids using their phone while driving might, on occasion, place a quick call if they are running late for a very important meeting. We therefore expect participants seeking to prioritize steering to forsake time and choose the audio interface. In contrast, participants seeking to prioritize the secondary task might forsake steering and choose the visual interface.

In summary, the aim of the study reported here is to investigate how people choose between different methods for completing a task in a dynamic multitask setting, and how these choices are affected by changes in the relative importance of one task relative to another. The value of this work is that it leads to a better understanding of how people interact with devices while multitasking, given their performance objectives and their experience with different output modalities. The expected trade-offs in modality choice have not been studied in depth until now. However, a better understanding is useful, particularly given the recent interest in the HCI community for multimodal interfaces that give feedback across multiple modalities at the same time [10,34,35] – essentially giving the user a choice over which modality to attend to. We consider how people might resolve such choices while driving a simulated vehicle.

METHOD

Participants

Twenty-four participants (10 female) took part in the study. Participants were unpaid volunteers, aged between 20- and 38-years (M = 27.0 years). All had a valid driver's license and at least two years of driving experience (M = 7.5 years). All the participants were highly proficient at reading and speaking in English (i.e., to the standard set by the University's admissions criteria), and most (20 out of 24) were native English speakers.

Materials

A dual-task setup was used in which the participant had to perform a secondary information look-up task while steering a simulated vehicle. Figure 1 shows a schematic representation of how the task equipment was arranged relative to the participant. The driving simulation environment was displayed on a 30-inch monitor and controlled by a Logitech G25 Racing Wheel. The secondary task used two output modalities (audio and visual). Audio output was projected using standard desktop speakers positioned behind the participant, while visual output was presented on a 7-inch secondary display positioned to the left of the main driving task display.

The driving task that was used required participants to navigate the center lane of a three-way highway environment. Participants were only required to steer the vehicle and maintain a central lane position, while the vehicle's speed was held at a constant 55 mph (88.5 km/h). We refer to this as the steering task. To reinforce safe lane keeping, safety cones were placed at either side of the driver's central lane. A lead vehicle was placed at a fixed distance in front of the participant's vehicle. Noise was added to the vehicle dynamics, causing the vehicle to gradually drift about in the lane. This meant that the participant had to actively control and monitor the vehicle's lateral position and heading to maintain a central lane position. This driving set-up is identical to the one used in other driver distraction studies [3,17,26].

The secondary task was designed to resemble a scenario in which a user is trying to locate a piece of information in a short passage of text, such as is common in e-mail and web browsing activities. Thirty different excerpts of text were sampled from various websites (e.g., www.wikipedia.org, www.bbc.co.uk) covering topics ranging from major historical events and figures, to popular culture. Each excerpt was edited so that it was approximately 150-180 words in length. For each text, two questions were set that could be easily answered based on the information presented within them. Care was taken to ensure that the location of the target information was balanced across texts. In particular, for one of the questions the target information appeared in the top half of the text and for the other question the target appeared in the bottom half of the text.

The text for the secondary task could be presented using either visual or audio output. For the visual output, text was presented on a 7-inch secondary display positioned to the left of the main driving task display in font Courier bold, size 18. This meant that approximately eight words (or 45 characters) were displayed per line. Words were not broken between lines. For the audio output, auditory information was generated using SmartRead text-to-speech software (http://www.smartysoft.com/index.php). Audio output was projected using standard desktop speakers positioned behind the participant. SmartRead was left at its default reading speed of approximately 167 words per minute (2.8 words per second). This meant that listening to a complete passage of text took approximately one minute.

The NASA-TLX questionnaire [9] was used to assess the subjective workload associated with using the audio and the visual interface for the secondary task. The NASA-TLX is a multi-dimensional questionnaire that derives an overall workload score for the task at hand based on the sum of responses to six subscales (mental demand, physical demand, temporal demand, performance, effort, frustration). The higher the NASA-TLX score, the more demanding the person believed the task to be.

Design

The experiment used a no-choice/choice design [15,23,28,32]. In the no-choice phase of the experiment, a 2x2 (modality x task priority) mixed factorial design was used. For the manipulation of modality, all participants had to complete a series of dual-task trials using the audio interface and the visual interface for the secondary task. Task priority was manipulated as a between-subjects factor, in that participants were instructed to either focus on completing the secondary search task as quickly as possible (the searching-focus condition) or to concentrate on keeping the car as close as possible to lane center (the steering-focus condition). There were three purposes for the no-choice phase of the experiment. First, it allowed us to get an objective measure of dual-task performance in each condition (i.e., for each interface x priority combination). Second, it allows us to find out which option people choose in a particular setting and how this might vary as a function of the instructed performance objective. Third, it gave all participants equal practice and experience at completing the secondary task with both of the available output modalities.

In the choice phase of the experiment, participants completed a second series of dual-task trials in which they were free to choose which of the two output modalities they wished to use. For this part of the experiment, a single between-subject factor design was used that manipulated task priority. Consistent with the no-choice phase, the same participants were again instructed to either prioritize completing the secondary task as quickly as possible or to prioritize keeping the car as close to the center of the middle lane as possible. The purpose of the choice phase of the experiment was to see whether changing the relative importance of each task had an impact on participants' preference for which output modality they used to access the information needed to complete the secondary task while steering.

For both phases of the experiment, the main dependent variables were the time taken to complete the secondary task and the impact that completing this task had on steering performance. Steering performance was indexed as the average distance that the vehicle drifted from lane center while the participant was working on the secondary task. The driving simulator logged the lateral distance of the vehicle at a rate of 200 Hz, and we report the root mean square error (RMSE) of these lateral deviation samples. Finally, we used the NASA-TLX questionnaire to get a measure of the subject workload associated with each condition in the no-choice phase of the experiment.

Procedure

Participants were informed that they would be required to find answers to questions in passages of text (as presented in audio or visual format) while steering a simulated vehicle. Participants were randomly assigned to one of the task priority conditions, though an effort was made to balance the distribution of gender and non-native English speakers across conditions. Participants in the steering-focus condition were told to prioritize the steering task and keep the vehicle as close to the lane center as possible while still completing the secondary task, whereas participants in the searching-focus condition were told to prioritize the secondary task and find the correct answer as quickly as possible while still maintaining lateral control over the vehicle. To emphasize these instructions, clear performance feedback on the relevant performance metric was given at the end of every dual-task trial. The whole experiment took about an hour to complete.

After receiving these instructions, participants were given an opportunity to practice each of the tasks separately. For the steering task, participants completed 10 practice trials in which they drove for a period of 30-seconds along a straight road. Participants were instructed to keep the vehicle as close to the center of the lane as possible. At the end of each trial, they received feedback on their steering performance (as RMSE lateral deviation). For the secondary task, participants completed two practice trials in which they had to find the answer to a question in a passage of text (as presented in audio or text format). Participants were instructed to inform the experimenter once they were confident that they had located the target information.

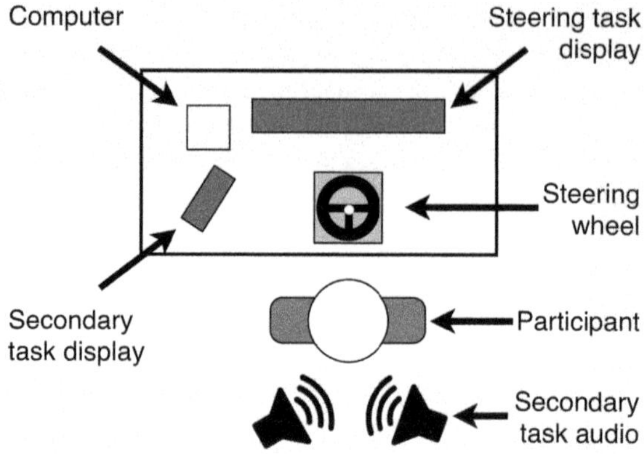

Figure 1. A schematic representation of how the displays for the steering and secondary task were arranged.

Participants were instructed to respond to the question as soon as they found the answer, either by reading it on the display, or by hearing it in the audio file. They indicated their intention to answer by saying, "got it" to the experimenter. At this time, the experimenter logged the event in the experimental software by pressing a key. After logging the event, the participant gave their answer and the experimenter coded this response as correct or incorrect. If an incorrect answer was given, then the trial was started over again until the correct answer was given. This was done to encourage participants not to give a fast (guessed) response for the secondary task, as repeating the trial took additional time. At the end of each trial, participants received feedback on task time.

Once familiar with the tasks, participants completed the no-choice phase of the experiment before completing the choice phase. For the no-choice phase, participants completed four dual-task trials using each of the two output modalities. The order in which each modality was experienced was randomized and counter-balanced across participants. For each dual-task trial, a pre-cue was shown on the driving display indicating which output modality was going to be used for the secondary task. The target question was then shown on the main driving task display, and participants were instructed to read the question out loud and inform the experimenter when they were ready to begin. Once ready, the driving environment was shown and when the vehicle had reached full-speed the participant was informed that they could start the secondary task. At this time, the audio output started playing or the passage of text was presented on the secondary display, depending on which modality was being used for the secondary task. A countdown on the main driving task indicated when the secondary task could be started. A trial ended when the participant told the experimenter the correct answer for the question. If an incorrect answer was given, then the trial was started over again until the correct answer was given. In addition, a trial was also repeated if no response was given within 100 seconds. When the correct answer was given, participants received feedback based on which condition they were in: participants in the steering-focus condition received feedback about the vehicle's RMSE lateral deviation, whereas participants in the searching-focus condition received feedback on the time taken to complete the secondary task. After completing all four trials with a given modality, participants completed the NASA-TLX questionnaire.

In the choice phase of the experiment, participants completed a block of nine dual-task trials. The structure of each trial was the same as that outlined above, except that participants could choose which output modality they wished to use when the question for the next trial was presented to them. Participants made their choice by saying either "audio" or "visual" to the experimenter, who then made the appropriate input command for the program controlling the experiment. If a trial had to be repeated, participants were again free to choose which modality they wished to use on each subsequent attempt.

Throughout the experiment steering performance was assessed. In between each block of dual-task trials participants completed two single-task steering-only trials, which were similar to the practice session outlined above. This allowed us to determine whether there were any systematic differences in steering ability between participants in each of the two experimental conditions, and to get a measure of base-line steering performance.

Finally, it should be noted that across the experiment each passage of text was only used for a single question. The question that was used with each passage was randomized for each participant with the constraint that target location was balanced across trials (i.e., the target appeared in the top-half of the text for half of the trials and the bottom-half for the other half of the trials). Moreover, participants were not given any information at the start of a trial that might help them guess the location of the target information in the passage of text.

RESULTS

We only consider data from trials in which the correct answer for the secondary task was given on the first attempt. Participants gave on average very few incorrect responses ($M = 1.42$ trials, $SD = 1.32$ trials, *range* 0-4), and in total, data from only 34 trials (8.33%) were excluded. Moreover, a correct response was always given on the second attempt at a question, meaning that no participant made more than one consecutive error on a given trial. Although errors are interesting, no solid conclusions can be drawn here given the low frequency of errors. We therefore excluded error trials from further statistical analysis.

In the following, we report separate analyses for the no-choice and choice phases of the experiment. For all statistical analyses, effects were judged significant if they reached a .05 significance level. First though, we briefly consider single-task steering performance to determine whether participants in either of the different task priority conditions were better at the steering task. For statistical analysis we use an independent samples *t*-test. As can be seen in Figure 2, there was no difference in participants' single-task baseline steering performance across the two conditions, $t < 1$; in both cases, RMSE lateral deviation was approximately 0.27 m from the lane center. This value is consistent with previous driving simulator studies [3,17,26].

No-Choice Trials

We first consider participants' performance when they were forced to use either the audio or the visual interface for the secondary task. We wanted to know if any interface was less distracting, and whether instructions on how to prioritize the tasks would lead to different dual-task performance trade-offs. We also use this no-choice phase to get a sense of participants' subjective assessment of using each output modality for the secondary task. For statistical analysis of these data, a 2x2 (modality x task priority) mixed factorial Analysis of Variance (ANOVA) was used.

Steering performance

Figure 2 shows the RMSE lateral deviation for each of the different conditions. For the no-choice data, it can be seen that steering performance was better (i.e., there was lower RMSE lateral deviation) when audio output was used for the secondary task than when visual output was used. It can also be seen that when audio was used steering performance was unaffected by task priority condition, and that steering performance was more or less equivalent to that observed in the single-task baseline condition. In contrast, when participants were forced to use the visual output and had to read the text on the secondary display, steering performance declined noticeably, in that the vehicle drifted further from the lane center. However, the extent to which the vehicle drifted was clearly moderated by which task the participant was choosing to prioritize: participants that had been instructed to prioritize the steering task maintained better lateral control of the vehicle (though still notably worse than when the audio interface was used).

Statistical analyses support these observations. There were main effects on steering performance of both modality type, $F(1, 22) = 73.28$, $p < .001$, $\eta_p^2 = .77$, and priority condition, $F(1, 22) = 7.06$, $p < .01$, $\eta_p^2 = .24$. Critically though the interaction was significant, $F(1, 22) = 12.06$, $p < .005$, $\eta_p^2 = .35$. Follow up tests of simple main effects found that there was no effect of task priority when participants used the audio interface, $F < 1$. There was however an effect of task priority when participants used the visual interface, $F(1, 22) = 9.27$, $p < .01$, $\eta_p^2 = .30$.

Task time performance

Figure 3 shows the mean time to complete the secondary task for each of the different conditions. For the no-choice data, it can be seen that trial times were slower, on average, when participants were forced to use the audio interface than when the visual interface was used for the secondary task. Interestingly, task times using the visual interface were clearly moderated by the participant's task priority:

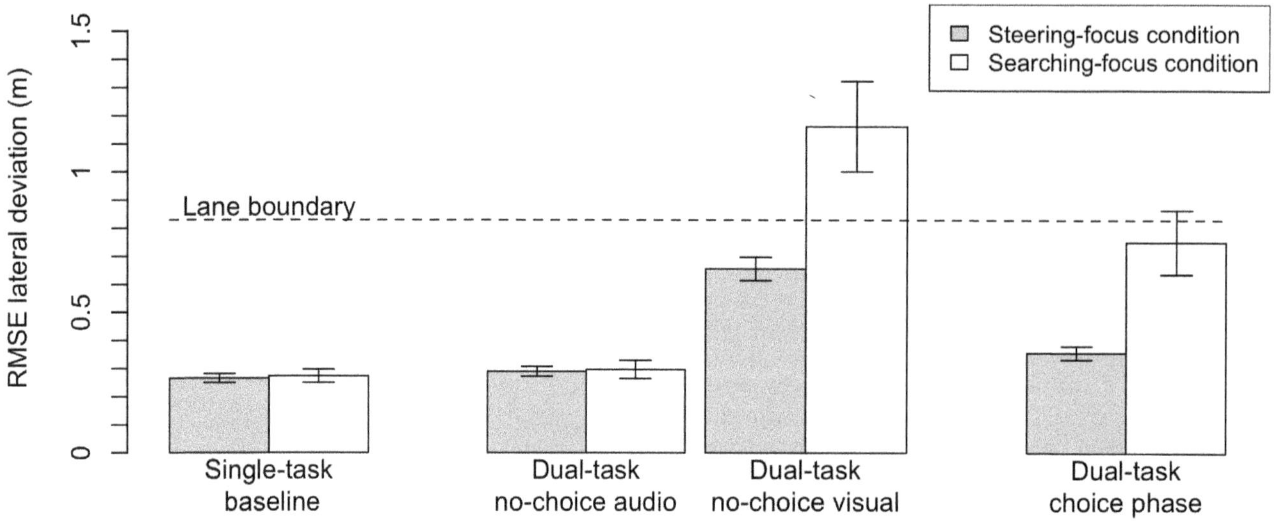

Figure 2. Steering performance for single-task baseline trials, dual-task no-choice trials with each output modality, and choice trials. Error bars depict standard errors.

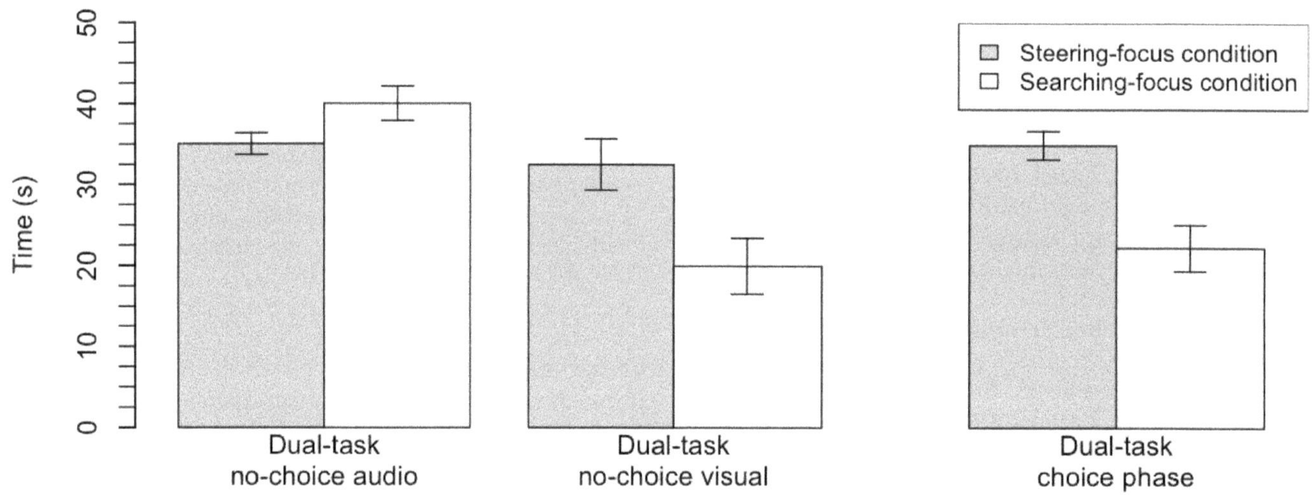

Figure 3. Task time for dual-task no-choice trials with each output modality, and choice trials. Error bars depict standard errors.

participants that had been instructed to prioritize the steering task were slower than those that had been instructed to prioritize the secondary task. There was no such influence of task priority when the audio interface was used – in fact, it is not really conceivable to think how there might have been given that the participant could not actively speed up or slow down the audio output stream.

Statistical analyses support these observations. Overall, there was a main effect of interface modality on task time, $F(1, 22) = 19.27$, $p < .001$, $\eta_p^2 = .47$. While there was no significant main effect of task priority, $F(1, 22) = 1.94$, $p = .18$, $\eta_p^2 = .08$, there was however a significant interaction between task priority and modality, $F(1, 22) = 11.51$, $p < .005$, $\eta_p^2 = .34$. Follow up tests of this interaction reflect what can patently be seen in the figure: there is a clear effect of priority on task time when the visual interface was used, $F(1, 22) = 7.20$, $p < .01$, $\eta_p^2 = .25$. But there is only a marginal effect of priority on task time when the audio interface was used, $F(1, 22) = 3.95$, $p = .06$, $\eta_p^2 = .15$. The astute reader will have noticed from the figure that this trend actually points in the opposite directions to what is expected: participants in the steering-focus condition were marginally faster than participants that had been instructed to complete the secondary task as quickly as possible. This would appear to be a fortuitous result, and in our estimation it is unlikely to replicate.

Subjective workload

The above measures provide an objective measure of participants' performance. But how was their subjective experience? To this end, NASA-TLX scores were analyzed to determine the subjective workload associated with both the audio and the visual interface for the secondary task. Results show that participants rated the audio interface as less demanding to use (M = 45.38, SD = 15.99) than the visual interface (M = 73.04, SD = 15.32), $F(1, 22) = 59.32$, $p < .001$, $\eta_p^2 = .73$. Moreover, this significant difference between conditions was reflected for each of the NASA-TLX subscales (i.e., mental demand, physical demand, temporal demand, performance, effort, frustration), p's < .001. There was no effect of task priority on workload ratings, nor was there a significant interaction, F's < 1.

Choice Trials

The above analysis demonstrates that when participants were forced to use the audio output for the secondary task, it took longer to complete a trial but steering performance was better. In contrast, when participants were forced to use the visual interface for the secondary task, they could complete the task faster but steering performance declined more because their eyes had to be taken off the road. However, the exact impact on steering performance of using the visual interfaces was moderated by the driver's priority. In addition, having to share visual attention between the steering and the search task was rated as being far more demanding than using the audio interface. Given these characteristics, which modality might participants prefer to use, and how might this choice be affected by differences in task priority instructions?

In the choice trials, participants were given a two-alternative forced-choice over which output modality they would like to use at the start of each trial. For all statistical analyses of the choice phase data, an independent samples t-test was used.

Figure 4 is a histogram showing the proportion of trials that each participant chose the audio interface for each priority condition. It can be seen in the figure that participants who were instructed to prioritize the steering task were more likely to select the audio interface (M = .88, SD = .16) than participants who were instructed to prioritize completing the secondary task quickly (M = .33, SD = .23), $t(22)$ = 6.77, $p < .001$, d = 2.77, 95% CI [.38, .71]. The figure also shows that 7 out of the 12 participants in the steering-focus condition chose the audio interface for every trial. Whereas, participants in the searching-focus condition did not show such a strong preference for one interface over another, choosing instead to flip between the audio and the visual interface on different trials. We next consider the impact of these choices on the main task performance metrics.

The two right-most columns of Figure 2 and 3 show respectively steering task performance (RMSE lateral deviation) and task time performance for the choice trials. In terms of steering performance, it can be seen that participants in the steering-focus condition maintained an RMSE lateral deviation equivalent to that observed in both the no-choice audio condition and at baseline single-task. In contrast, participants in the searching-focus condition deviate more from the lane center, and allowed the vehicle to drift out to the lane boundary. The inverse pattern can be found for task time data, in that participants in the steering-focus condition completed the task in the time associated with using the audio interface, whereas participants in the searching-focus condition were at the lower task times associated with using the visual interface in the no-choice searching-focus condition. These observations on dual-task performance are consistent with the choices made by participants in each priority condition. Statistical analysis support these observations, and show that participants in the steering-focus condition took significantly longer to complete the secondary task than participants in the searching-focus condition, $t(22)$ = 3.80, $p < .001$, d = 1.55, 95% CI [5.76, 19.62], but these participants had significantly better steering performance, $t(22)$ = 3.39, $p < .005$, d = 1.38, 95% CI [.15, .64].

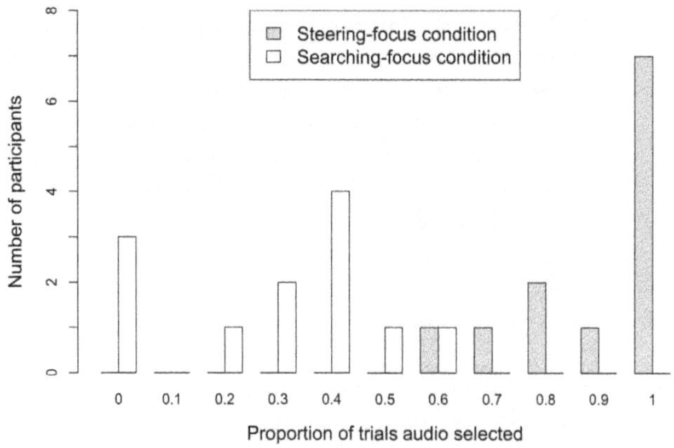

Figure 4. Histogram showing the proportion of trials that each participant selected the audio interface across choice trials

DISCUSSION

Audio output offers a promising interaction technique for alleviating some of the problems associated with using mobile devices while driving, such as visual distraction. However, the results of this study highlight that task completion time is a critical dimension for designing such audio interfaces. We found that participants that were encouraged to complete a secondary 'lookup' task quickly chose to forfeit the benefits of using audio output. Instead, they choose to glance over to a secondary display so that they could locate the target information quickly, resulting in a significant decline in lane keeping performance on the primary driving task. In contrast, participants that were encouraged to prioritize the driving task tended to select the slower audio output option so that they could maintain lateral control of the vehicle.

The results of this work have important implications for the design of multimodal interfaces that give feedback across multiple modalities at the same time [10,34,35], because such interfaces present the user with just the kind of choice over which modality to attend to as considered here. Our results show that the user's performance objective will have a strong influence on which modality is attended to on a multimodal device, and that audio and visual output can serve time and safety goals differently.

The use of a no-choice/choice paradigm [15,23,28,32] was essential for this work. The no-choice phase allowed participants to gain experience with each output modality and for us to gather an objective measure of the performance characteristics of each, before participants were given a choice about which method they preferred to use to meet a specific task objective. It was found that decisions about which modality to use were moderated by the users' *performance objective* (i.e., which of the two tasks was subjectively more important to them). Decisions were not made on the basis of simply selecting the fastest strategy for completing the task at hand [8].

These results contribute to a growing body of work on understanding how people adapt their behavior while multitasking to meet specific performance objectives [2,3,14,16-18]. The results of the current work are distinct from this previous line of research however, in that we focus here on how performance objectives influence modality *selection* rather than fine-grained task interleaving behavior. Our results show that people can make different overt choices between methods for completing a secondary task based upon the performance characteristics of each method and whether they meet the desired performance objective. In the following section, we consider a number of important limitations of the current study and some questions that future research in this area might examine.

Limitations and future research

One concern with generalizing the findings of this research to real-world contexts is that we were limited to using a low-fidelity driving simulator. Our driving task required participants only to control the steering of a vehicle as it travelled at a constant speed down a straight highway environment. This lane keeping performance measure can serve as a useful proxy for assessing drivers' attention, since steering control is an open-loop process that requires constant visual input [31]. However, this setup clearly does not allow us to investigate the full complexity of driver behavior. In particular, there is a concern that our lane keeping measure is not sensitive to the effects of cognitive distraction associated with performing a non-visual secondary task. Previous studies have found that such effects tend to have a stronger impact on a driver's ability to maintain a constant speed when following another vehicle, and their ability to react to unexpected events [1,11]. The effects of cognitive interference do show up on lane keeping performance metrics, but the effects can be small [26]. Consequently, there is a concern that our steering measure was maybe not sensitive enough to detect any negative effects of using the audio output for the secondary task. Our objective here however was not to show that an audio interface is not distracting for drivers, but instead to highlight the issue of how performance objectives will influence modality choices.

Future work might investigate people's modality choices in a more complex driving environment. It is reasonable to assume that people might have a stronger preference for using audio output in a more demanding environment, such as when there is heavy traffic or when driving at a high speed. In contrast, we might expect drivers to shift to using a visual interface when there is very little demand from the driving task, such as when waiting at a red light. The question would be whether such changes in modality preference would occur independent of the participant's objective (as manipulated here). There is some support for this view. A recent study by Iqbal et al. [16] showed that multitasking drivers give greater attention to the road when the driving environment is more challenging.

In contrast though, the results of a recent on-road driving study by Horrey and Lesch [13] showed that drivers show no preference for waiting until periods of decreased driving demand (i.e., when waiting at a red stop light) to engage in secondary in-car tasks. This latter finding would suggest that it is unlikely that drivers will spontaneously shift from one modality to another based on the changing demands of the road, or might they? A further possibility is that drivers might cope with the demands of performing a secondary in-car task in other ways, such as by reducing their speed [4,16]. Further research is required to address these questions.

One concern for generalizing from these results to how people might use multimodal devices in general is that we forced participants to make a choice between one of two output modalities. In contrast, we might have presented information via both output modalities simultaneously. Such a setup would allow the user to choose on the fly which modality to pay attention to, and to switch back and forth between different modalities while completing a task. The results of previous studies that have evaluated the use of multimodal interfaces while driving [22,34] are broadly consistent with those reported here: audio feedback is less distracting for the driver than visual feedback. Critically, it does not seem to matter whether multimodal audio+visual feedback is given or whether only audio feedback is given; the safety benefit is given by audio feedback.

Our results suggest that there might be considerable value in applications that disable visual output and present audio output in isolation. By having only a single output modality, the driver would not be tempted into glancing over to a device's display to complete a secondary task more quickly. This idea seems to have made its way into recent applications aimed for in-car use, such as DriveSafe.ly™ (http://www.drivesafe.ly/), which reads text (SMS) messages and emails aloud while not presenting the message on the phone's screen. Based upon the results of the current work, this would seem to be a promising approach as it removes the temptation to use an inappropriate visual modality. However, the potential for cognitive distraction from engaging in a secondary task while driving might remain [11,26]. Further work is required to unpack these issues more thoroughly.

Our results hinge on the assumption that the audio interface was slower for completing the secondary task than the visual interface. However, this does not have to be the case. There would be great value in pursuing design solutions that make audio interfaces faster to use so that users are not forced to make the kinds of trade-offs considered here. Interesting work has been done to evaluate various methods for compressing audio information so that it can be listened to more quickly while preserving critical information content [30]. We believe that such developments might hold promise for audio interfaces.

A second consideration is to allow the user more active control over the presentation of audio information. In our study, the audio output was read at the default reading speed of the software, which meant that listening to a complete passage of text took a fixed amount of time. The participant could not actively speed up or slow down the audio output stream, nor fast-forward or rewind it. This could be done differently in future studies. Indeed, examples of interactive audio interfaces abound, such as [21,34,35]. Zhao's earPod [34,35] for instance uses interruptible audio that plays the aural information associated with the currently highlighted menu option regardless of whether or not the previous audio file has completed. This allows the user to rapidly skim through menu options without having to exhaustively listen in full to each option.

There are then at least two ways in which the audio interface used here might be improved. First, audio content might be presented at a faster pace. Second, an interactive model might be developed to allow the user to skim though audio content to locate the relevant section more quickly. Both of these alternatives would conceivably work to allow the secondary task to be completed more quickly using the audio interface. We would expect this to have an impact on people's willingness to use the audio interface in the kind of multitask setup used here. This is because the results of the current study suggest that people consider the time taken to complete a task using each output option when deciding between them.

CONCLUSION

To summarize, a study was conducted to investigate whether people will choose to use a safer audio interface over a traditional GUI to complete a secondary task while driving in situations with different priorities. A no-choice/choice paradigm was used in which participants first completed a series of trials using each of the two output interface modalities before being given a choice on which to use. The benefit of using this paradigm are that we got both a reliable measure of the performance characteristics associated with each interface, and a measure of which interface participants preferred to use. Results from the no-choice phase showed that the audio interface did not interfere with driving performance but that it was slower to use than a traditional GUI. Given the choice of which interface modality to use and the performance characteristics associated with each, participants made different choices based on which task they were told to give greater emphasis to. Those participants that had been instructed to prioritize safer steering tended to select the audio interface, while those that had been encouraged to prioritize the secondary task chose the visual interface. These decisions had a large effect on dual-task performance metrics. The results of this work suggest that multimodal interfaces that make use of audio feedback offer a promising solution to alleviate some of the problems associated with using mobile devices in multitask environments. However, attention should be given to the time required to complete basic interactive tasks using audio feedback because if time is of the essence, people will likely forsake whatever safety benefits there are in order to achieve their goal quickly.

ACKNOWLEDGMENTS

The study was undertaken as part of the second author's MSc research project. All other authors were supported by EPSRC grant EP/G043507/1. We thank Andrew Howes for the idea to use no-choice/choice paradigms to investigate strategy use and selection. We thank Dario Salvucci for providing the initial code for the driving simulator. Finally, we thank the reviewers for their constructive comments.

REFERENCES

1. Brookhuis, K., De Vries, G., & De Waard, D. The effects of mobile telephoning on driving performance. *Accident Analysis & Prevention, 23,* (1991), 309-316.
2. Brumby, D.P., Salvucci, D.D., & Howes, A. Focus on driving: How cognitive constraints shape the adaptation of strategy when dialing while driving. In *Proc. CHI 2009*, ACM Press (2009), 1629-1638.
3. Brumby, D.P., Del Rosario, N., & Janssen, C.P. When to switch? Understanding how performance trade-offs shape dual-task strategy. In *Proc. ICCM 2010*, Drexel University (2010), 19-24.
4. Cnossen, F., Meijman, T., & Rothengatter, T. Adaptive strategy changes as a function of task demands: A study of car drivers. *Ergonomics, 47,* (2004), 218-236.
5. Crowd Science. Social media insights – twitter. http://www.crowdscience.com/blog/article/social_media_study_twitter_while_driving/, September 4th 2009.
6. Diels, C., Reed, N., and Weaver, L., *Drivers' attitudes to distraction and other motorists' behaviour: A focus group and observational study.* TRL Limited, Wokingham, UK, 2009.
7. Duggan, G.B. & Payne, S.J. Text skimming: The process and effectiveness of foraging through text under

time pressure. *Journal of Experimental Psychology: Applied, 15,* (2009), 228-242.

8. Gray, W.D. & Boehm-Davis, D.A. Milliseconds matter: An introduction to microstrategies and to their use in describing and predicting interactive behavior. *Journal of Experimental Psychology: Applied, 6,* (2000), 322-335.
9. Hart, S.G. & Staveland, L.E. Development of nasa-tlx (task load index): Results of empirical and theoretical research. *Human Mental Workload, 1,* (1988), 139–183.
10. Hoggan, E., Crossan, A., Brewster, S., & Kaaresoja, T. Audio or tactile feedback: Which modality when? In *Proc. CHI 2009*, ACM Press (2009), 2253-2256.
11. Horrey, W. & Wickens, C.D. Examining the impact of cell phone conversations on driving using meta-analytic techniques. *Human Factors, 48,* (2006), 196-205.
12. Horrey, W.J. & Wickens, C.D. Driving and side task performance: The effects of display clutter, separation, and modality. *Human Factors, 46,* (2004), 611-624.
13. Horrey, W.J. & Lesch, M.F. Driver-initiated distractions: Examining strategic adaptation for in-vehicle task initiation. *Accident Analysis and Prevention, 41,* (2009), 115-122.
14. Horrey, W.J., Wickens, C.D., & Consalus, K.P. Modeling drivers' visual attention allocation while interacting with in-vehicle technologies. *Journal of Experimental Psychology: Applied, 12,* (2006), 67-78.
15. Howes, A., Duggan, G.B., Kalidindi, K., Tseng, Y.-C., & Lewis, R.L. Bounded optimality in a cognitive utility learning paradigm. (under review).
16. Iqbal, S.T., Ju, Y.-C., & Horvitz, E. Cars, calls, and cognition: Investigating driving and divided attention. In *Proc. CHI 2010*, ACM Press. (2010), 1281-1290.
17. Janssen, C.P. & Brumby, D.P. Strategic adaptation to performance objectives in a dual-task setting. *Cognitive Science, 34,* (2010), 1548-1560.
18. Janssen, C.P., Brumby, D.P., Dowell, J., Chater, N., & Howes, A. Identifying optimum performance trade-offs using a cognitively bounded rational analysis model of discretionary task interleaving. *Topics in Cognitive Science, 3,* (2011), 123-139.
19. Lai, J., Cheng, K., Green, P., & Tsimhoni, O. On the road and on the web?: Comprehension of synthetic and human speech while driving. In *Proc. CHI 2001*, ACM Press (2001), 206-212.
20. Lee, J.D., Caven, B., Haake, S., & Brown, T.L. Speech-based interaction with in-vehicle computers: The effect of speech-based e-mail on drivers' attention to the roadway. *Human Factors, 43,* (2001), 631-640.
21. Li, K.A., Baudisch, P., & Hinckley, K. Blindsight: Eyes-free access to mobile phones. In *Proc. CHI 2008*, ACM Press (2008), 1389-1398.
22. Liu, Y. Comparative study of the effects of auditory, visual and multimodality displays on drivers' performance in advanced traveller information systems. *Ergonomics, 44,* (2001), 425-442.
23. MacLean, A., Barnard, P., & Wilson, M. Evaluating the human interface of a data entry system: User choice and performance measures yield different trade-off functions. In P. Johnson & S. Cook (Eds.), *People and Computers: Designing the Interface*. Cambridge University Press, 1985, 172-185.
24. Reed, M. & Green, P. Comparison of driving performance on-road and in a low-cost simulator using a concurrent telephone dialling task. *Ergonomics, 42,* (1999), 1015-1037.
25. Salvucci, D.D. Predicting the effects of in-car interface use on driver performance: An integrated model approach. *International Journal of Human Computer Studies, 55,* (2001), 85-107.
26. Salvucci, D.D. & Beltowska, J. Effects of memory rehearsal on driver performance: Experiment and theoretical account. *Human Factors, 50,* (2008), 834-44.
27. Salvucci, D.D. & Taatgen, N.A. Threaded cognition: An integrated theory of concurrent multitasking. *Psychological Review, 115,* (2008), 101-130.
28. Siegler, R.S. & Lemaire, P. Older and younger adults' strategy choices in multiplication: Testing predictions of ascm using the choice/no-choice method. *Journal of Experimental Psychology: General, 126,* (1997), 71-92.
29. Sodnik, J., Dicke, C., Tomazic, S., & Billinghurst, M. A user study of auditory versus visual interfaces for use while driving. *International Journal of Human-Computer Studies, 66,* (2008), 318-332.
30. Tucker, S. & Whittaker, S. Time is of the essence: An evaluation of temporal compression algorithms. In *Proc. CHI 2006*, ACM Press (2006), 329-338.
31. Wallis, G., Chatziastros, A., & Bülthoff, H. An unexpected role for visual feedback in vehicle steering control. *Current Biology, 12,* (2002), 295-299.
32. Walsh, M.M. & Anderson, J.R. The strategic nature of changing your mind. *Cognitive Psychology, 58,* (2009), 416-40.
33. Wickens, C.D. Multiple resources and performance prediction. *Theoretical Issues in Ergonomics Science, 3,* (2002), 159-177.
34. Zhao, S., *Earpod: Efficient hierarchical eyes-free menu selection*. Doctoral dissertation, Department of Computer Science, University of Toronto, 2009.
35. Zhao, S., Dragicevic, P., Chignell, M., Balakrishnan, R., & Baudisch, P. Earpod: Eyes-free menu selection using touch input and reactive audio feedback. In *Proc. CHI 2007*, ACM Press (2007), 1395-1404.

Gestural Interaction on the Steering Wheel – Reducing the Visual Demand

Tanja Döring[1], Dagmar Kern[1], Paul Marshall[2], Max Pfeiffer[1], Johannes Schöning[3], Volker Gruhn[1], Albrecht Schmidt[1,4]

[1] University of Duisburg-Essen, Paluno, Essen, Germany, {tanja.doering, dagmar.kern, max.pfeiffer, volker.gruhn}@uni-due.de
[2] University of Warwick, International Digital Laboratory, Coventry, UK, paul.marshall@warwick.ac.uk
[3] German Research Center for Artificial Intelligence, Saarbrücken, Germany, johannes.schoening@dfki.de
[4] University of Stuttgart, VIS, Stuttgart, Germany, albrecht.schmidt@acm.org

ABSTRACT
Cars offer an increasing number of infotainment systems as well as comfort functions that can be controlled by the driver. In our research, we investigate new interaction techniques that aim to make it easier to interact with these systems while driving. We suggest utilizing the steering wheel as an additional interaction surface. In this paper, we present two user studies conducted with a working prototype of a multi-touch steering wheel. In the first, we developed a user-defined steering wheel gesture set, and in the second, we applied the identified gestures and compared their application to conventional user interaction with infotainment systems in terms of driver distraction. The main outcome was that driver's visual demand is reduced significantly by using gestural interaction on the multi-touch steering wheel.

Author Keywords
Automotive user interfaces, multi-touch, gestural input, driver distraction, user-defined gestures, visual demand

ACM Classification Keywords
H.5.2 Information interfaces and presentation: User Interfaces - Input devices and strategies, H.5.1 Information interfaces and presentation: Multimedia Information Systems

General Terms
Design, Human Factors

INTRODUCTION
New media and communication technologies (like mobile phones, internet access, and MP3 players) provide increasing entertainment and communication opportunities while driving. Furthermore, functions like adaptive cruise control and lane-keeping assistance support drivers, reducing their mental workload, and increasing their capacity to share their attention between driving and consuming media content. Nevertheless, these tasks (also called tertiary tasks; see [3]) demand attention as they force the driver to interact with built-in systems or nomadic devices.

Automobile manufacturers sometimes provide buttons around a central display as well as multifunctional controllers or touch displays for controlling tertiary tasks. One trend for tertiary task input devices is to place them into spaces previously reserved for primary and secondary devices. The available space on the steering wheel for example is now often used for interacting with the entertainment system, navigation system or mobile phone [13]. The advantage of using space on the steering wheel is that the buttons or thumbwheels are very close to the driver's hand so there is no need to move the hand away from the steering wheel, improving safety. However, the arrangement of physical input devices is fixed and the space for mechanical buttons is limited. To further explore the potential of the steering wheel as a location for tertiary task input and output and the advantages that touch gestures might offer, we built a fully functional prototype of a multi-touch enabled steering wheel. Our research is motivated by the following:

1. Driver Distraction: Bringing tertiary tasks to the steering wheel has already proven to be a "best practice" in the design of many existing cars. Nevertheless, no scientific studies are yet publicly available that compare driver distraction regarding steering wheel and middle console input for infotainment systems.

2. Gestural Input: Gesture-based input on multi-touch surfaces allows the execution of many different commands in a limited space – from basic to complex – and for a variety of applications and tasks. At the same time, it raises many questions regarding the design, memorability and suitability of gestures for in-car usage (e.g., do thumb-, finger-, one hand, or two hand gestures work best?).

3. Graphical Input/Output: A multi-touch steering wheel can also contain a display, i.e. it can present flexible visualizations for input (e.g., input areas) and output (e.g., depending on the application). This leads to ques-

tions about how visual output on the steering wheel should appear, and how it might affect driving.

Thus, our overall goal is to find suitable input and output paradigms to interact with the steering wheel, taking driver safety and driver distraction [5, 19] into account.

Currently, the central surface of the steering wheel is not used as an input or output element as there is the airbag underneath in most designs. In the case of an accident the surface breaks to release the airbag. We expect that with emerging display technologies this is not longer a limitation, as displays will be constructed to break or will be made of segments that allow the airbag to open.

In this paper, we describe the design challenges and setup of a prototype multi-touch enabled steering wheel. We present two user studies. In study 1, we investigated which gestures users chose for a number of defined actions conducted on the steering wheel while driving. Study 2 builds on the results of study 1 and applies the identified gestures in a comparative study. Using eye tracking in a driving simulator, we measured the driver distraction when interacting with the steering wheel as well as with the middle console. The central finding is that interaction using a multi-touch steering wheel strongly reduces the visual demand to control a radio and to control a navigation system.

RELATED WORK

A number of researchers have investigated using the steering wheel for interaction, specifically for text input [4, 12, 21]. Kern et al. [12] investigated potential locations for text input via a touch display, finding "that handwritten text input using fingers on a touchscreen mounted on the steering wheel is well accepted by users and leads to 25% fewer corrections and remaining errors compared to text input in the central console". Sandnes et al. [21] kept buttons as an input device but provided text input via three finger chord sequences. González et al. [4] used a thumb-based input technique on a small touchpad mounted at a fixed position on the steering wheel to allow gestural interaction.

Bach et al. [1] presented an approach towards gestural interaction in the car, comparing haptic, touch, and gestural interaction to control a radio. For gestural input, a touch screen mounted on the vertical center stack was used. Their results indicate that gestural interaction is slower than touch or haptic interaction, but can reduce eye glances while interacting with the radio. Ecker et al. [2] combined direct touch gestures on a touch screen mounted on the center console with a pie menu idea for interacting with in-vehicle information systems. They observed an almost eyes-free interaction with the pie menu after a training phase. Harrison and Hudson [7] investigated a combination of a touch sensitive surface and physical buttons for nearly eyes-free interaction. They developed a visual display with deformable areas so that physical buttons can be produced flexibly but on fixed positions on the surface. Beside kiosks and ATM systems they investigated the use of a dashboard comprising such a flexible display. One could imagine using this on the steering wheel as well.

Multi-touch technologies allow direct gesture-based interactions with fingers on interactive surfaces [22]. While widely used on tabletops and interactive walls, the potential of this technology in the context of cars can only be found in ideas for concept cars (e.g., Chrysler's 200C concept[1]) and has not been investigated in more detail. As gestures can potentially support an intuitive form of interaction, an important research topic has been the design of free hand gestures on tabletop surfaces. Nevertheless, the design of a suitable set of gestures is a challenging task for system designers. Thus, Wobbrock et al. [23] conducted a study, where non-technical users had to develop their preferred gestures for certain tasks on a tabletop surface. Among their results was a user-defined set of gestures for 27 actions and the insight that users generally do not care about the number of fingers used for a gesture. As the identification of gesture sets for different contexts is a major current research question in HCI, a number of further research projects can be found, where user defined gesture sets have been developed (e.g. [14, 15, 17]. A discussion has also begun on the "intuitiveness" of so-called "natural" user interfaces [18], suggesting a critical look at the learnability and memorability of gestures.

In the following sections, we focus on the potential of gestural input on a steering wheel and on interacting with specific functions typical for in-car use.

DESIGN CHALLENGES

Derived from the three issues mentioned in the introduction, a number of design challenges have to be addressed on the use of a multi-touch steering wheel in cars. We focus on the following questions:

1. Driver Distraction: Can we reduce the cognitive load of interacting with infotainment systems with a multi-touch steering wheel? Obviously, the functioning of the steering wheel as well as the visibility of all instruments should not be affected.
2. Gestural Input: Can we find gestures such that the driver should not have to move her hands from the steering wheel or her eyes from the road? A closer look at thumb gestures appears to be promising.
3. Graphical Input/Output: By converting the steering wheel into a multi-touch surface, the whole space can be used for touch input and graphical output. This leads to questions of where to define interaction areas and what kind of visual feedback to display on the steering wheel.

We addressed these issues by building a multi-touch steering wheel prototype and integrating it into a driving simulation apparatus for two user studies. The prototype is de-

[1] http://wheels.blogs.nytimes.com/2009/04/09/chrysler-concept-imagines-a-car-without-buttons/ (last access: 2011-01-11).

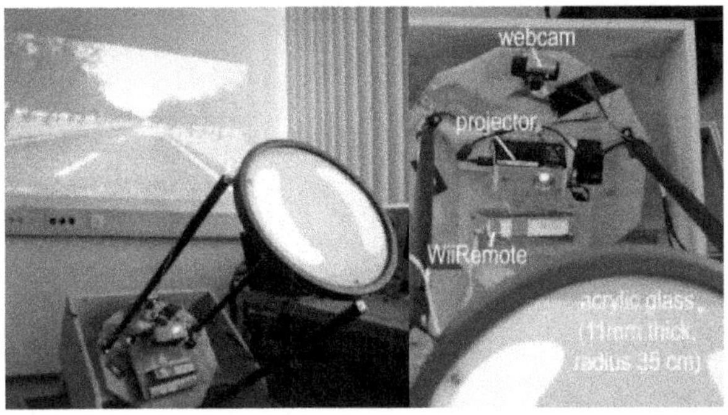

Figure 1. The multi-touch steering wheel hardware. General overview on the setting (left). Detailed screenshot of the foot well (right).

scribed in the following section. Thereafter, we describe study 1, which addressed questions regarding gestural input. Finally, study 2 built upon the results of study 1 and validated a set of identified user-defined gestures, comparing driver performance and driver distraction to middle console device interaction.

PROTOTYPE

To explore the design space we implemented a fully functional prototype (see figure 1; cf. [20]). An 11 mm thick round clear acrylic glass with a radius of 35 cm (standard steering wheel size) was fixed to a special mounting and used as the steering wheel "body". We applied the FTIR (frustrated total internal reflection) principle [6] to enable multi-touch input and attached infrared LEDs beneath the steering wheel cover as well as a silicone layer and tracing paper on top of the acrylic glass. The whole setup was mounted on a rotatable stand. A camera and a projector were attached on a board at the bottom of the mounting. For image processing we used the open source software CCV[2], which sent touch events in TUIO protocol format [11] to a Flash application that was responsible for the visual representation of interactive elements on the steering wheel.

In order to have a setting for identifying user-defined gestures and to investigate whether driver distraction could be reduced with multi-touch steering wheels, we installed a driving simulator setup in our lab (see figure 1). An HD projection of 3x2 meters was used to show driving scenarios. A WiiRemote was attached to the steering wheel and delivered steering information (i.e., the rotation angle of the wheel). BlueSoleil[3] and EIToolkit[4] were used for the communication between the WiiRemote and the driving simulations. EIToolkit is a component-based architecture that allows proxy-like objects to exchange messages over a general communication area, e.g., via UDP.

[2] CCV ("Community Core Vision") is an open source software solution for computer vision. It is available at: http://ccv.nuigroup.com/ (last access 2011-01-11).

[3] BlueSoleil: http://www.bluesoleil.com (last access 2011-01-11).

[4] EIToolkit: http://www.eitoolkit.de (last access 2011-01-11).

Menu	1. Music player	**Navigation System**	13. Zoom map in
	2. Navigation system		14. Zoom map out
	3. Help		15. Move map left
	4. Menu access		16. Move map right
List	5. List up		17. Move map up
	6. List down		18. Move map down
Music Player	7. Play		19. Rotate map
	8. Stop		20. New destination
	9. Next song		
	10. Previous song		
	11. Volume up		
	12. Volume down		

Table 1. The 20 commands performed on the multi-touch steering wheel while driving in the driving simulator.

STUDY 1: DEVELOPING A USER-DEFINED STEERING WHEEL GESTURE SET

In the first user study, we identified a user-defined gesture set for interacting with typical enter- and infotainment devices in cars.

Study Design

We proposed 20 commands that could be useful to perform directly on the steering wheel. We chose two exemplary applications, a music player and a navigation system, including commands for general menu access and list navigation. Table 1 gives an overview of the commands that participants were asked to perform on the steering wheel.

We provided a simple driving task and, after running several pilot studies, decided to restrict the interaction opportunities by equipping our multi-touch surface with two input fields close to the left and right edges of the steering wheel (see figure 1, left). Interactions on the screen were only recognized in these areas, so that the driver could leave both hands on the steering wheel, when choosing the thumbs for interaction. Apart from displaying the interaction areas, we did not provide visual feedback on the steering wheel during this study. Performed gestures were recorded by a screen record program capturing the finger detection images as well as by a webcam mounted above the setup. Thus, the video footage provided the finger movement as well as the gesture trails and was analyzed later to collect the user-defined gestures. We used the CARS driving simulation software[5] to provide a simple driving task without collecting driving performance measures. We presented the user a two lane endless highway, where participants had to change lane when an obstacle blocked their way.

Participants

12 participants (average age was 25.3 years) took part in our study. All participants had a driver's license, held for on average 7.1 years. Half of them had experience with touch technology. Five regularly used an iPhone and one had used a multi-touch table before.

[5] http://cars.pcuie.uni-due.de/ (last access: 2011-01-11).

Procedure

After being introduced to the driving setup, the participants carried out a test drive without any additional task to get used to the driving simulator. While driving thereafter, they were asked to create gestures for the 20 different commands as listed in table 1. All participants performed the commands in a randomly assigned order. The experimenter verbally introduced each task by asking a question, e.g., "What gesture would you perform to turn up the volume of the music player?". Participants could take as much time for each task as they wanted. Furthermore, they were free to choose which and how many fingers they would use for the gesture but at least one hand had to remain on the steering wheel during driving. They were instructed to think aloud. After accomplishing all 20 commands, participants filled out a questionnaire that contained questions concerning ratings of the gesture interaction on the steering wheel. Further open-text explanations for their statements were collected, e.g., advantages and disadvantages, as well as demographic data. Each experiment took between 20 and 30 minutes.

Results

Through video analysis we collected 240 gestures in total, 12 individual user-defined suggestions for each of the 20 commands. For each command, we selected the most frequently occurring gesture.

Overall, we observed that participants had little difficulty in inventing a gesture for each action. For commands like zooming where gestures had already been seen or used by the participants in other contexts and on other devices (e.g., mobile phones), we found similarities to existing gestures [23]. Nevertheless, driving has special constraints and the gestures had to be adapted. Gestures with thumbs were found to be especially well suited to the driving, where hands should ideally remain at the steering wheel.

In figure 2 we show 6 resulting map interactions with the navigation system, which were mainly conducted with two thumbs, one in each of the interaction areas. The two-thumb gestures provided basic operations for interaction with maps. In figure 2 a) and b) we show the zoom gestures, similar to zoom gestures on other multi-touch devices, as suggested by 9 of the 12 users. When asking the participants, it became clear that they had already formed a mental model for this type of interaction based on personal experience with multi-touch devices or having seen other people using them. The essential part of the zoom gestures is a convergent or divergent movement of two fingers or thumbs of the same or different hands. The gestures for moving the map left, right, or up and down were inspired by interactions that users would carry out if interacting with a physical map. The most popular gestures included touching and grasping a map with two fingers/thumbs and then moving both fingers/thumbs synchronously. This is shown for left and right in figure 2 c) and d) and for up and down in figure 2 e) and f). All 12 participants suggested very similar gestures for movements. Two further gestures to

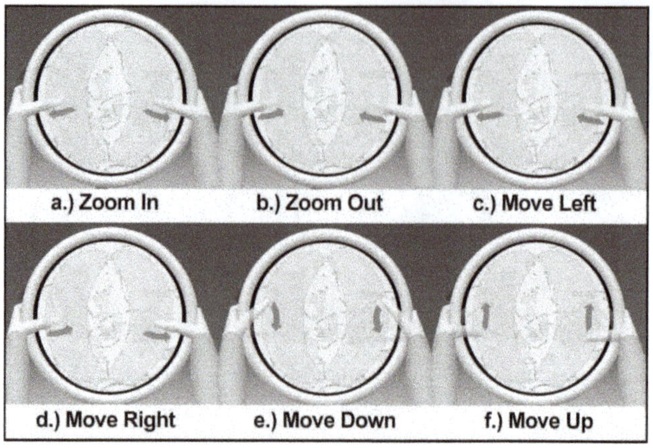

Figure 2. Gesture set for map interaction.

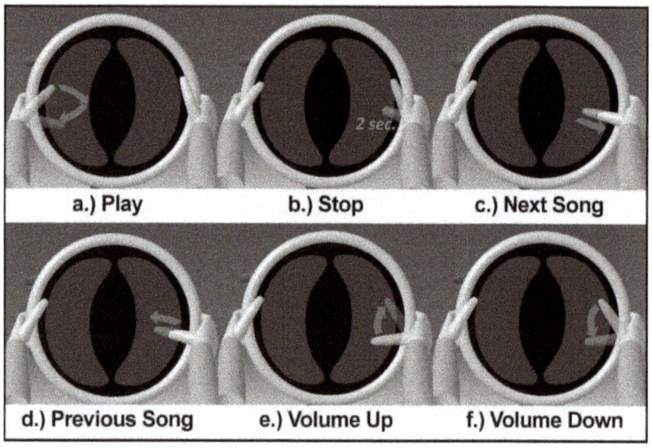

Figure 3. Gesture set for music player interaction.

control the navigation system were a "rotate map" command and the "new destination" command (see table 1). All 12 participants decided to execute the rotate command by putting either thumb and index finger of one hand onto the surface and rotating the hand 180 degrees or making a similar gesture trail using both thumbs. The agreement on the "new destination" command was the weakest: 3 of 12 participants chose to draw the first letter of the word "destination".

In contrast to the map interactions, interactions with the music player were all conducted with one finger or one thumb only (see figure 3). 4 participants traced the "play symbol" (triangle) used on HiFi systems. For gestures indicating the next and previous song a strong similarity in the gestures was observed. 9 of 12 made a gesture that represented moving the song to one of the sides as in figure 3 c) and d). Similarly, volume control was similar between participants. Increasing volume was associated with a moving up gesture and for reducing the volume the gesture was reversed as depicted in figure 3 e) and f). The least agreement was on a gesture for the stop action. 3 of the 12 users made a 2 second tap gesture on the screen, depicted in b).

For the general menu access, the agreement also was low: 3 participants decided to tap with two fingers/thumbs onto the steering wheel to trigger the menu. For the selection in the menu the agreement was higher: 6 people chose to draw a circle for "music player" and the first letter "N" for navigations system. 10 of 12 participants drew a question mark to enter the "help" command. On the list interaction, all participants agreed and performed an up/down movement with one thumb/finger as in the "volume up/down" command.

In order to analyze and structure gestures, Wobbrock et al. [23] have identified a number of taxonomic criteria. Among these, they suggest distinguishing between "symbolic", "physical", "metaphorical", and "abstract" gestures. If we analyze our user-defined gesture set for in-car interaction we find a number of symbolic gestures, e.g., for the menu gesture "music player" (a circle as symbol for a CD), for the music player gesture "play" (triangle symbol taken from HiFi systems), and for "help" (a question mark). For the menu command "navigation system" and the navigation system command "new destination" no real symbols were found by the participants and thus, the majority chose to draw the first letter of the command words as gestures. Abstract gestures can be found for the "menu access" command (a two finger tap) and for the music player "stop" command (a 2 second one finger tap). Most of the map interactions (rotate, move) are based on physical interactions (e.g., as if done with a paper map on a surface), whereas the zoom gestures have a metaphorical basis (imagining a stretchy material) (cf. [10]). Further –and fairly basic– metaphorical gestures were chosen for "list up/down" and music player interactions (next, previous, volume up/down) in the form of single finger or thumb strokes in the direction that participants mapped the interaction to (e.g., "upward" for louder, "to the right" for next song). These are well known mappings that are based on embodied conceptual metaphors (e.g., [9]).

Overall, the participants stated in the questionnaires that they preferred gestures, even compared to buttons on steering wheels. We found a strong desire to control a music player on touch-enabled steering wheels (11 of 12) whereas only 5 of 12 users stated that they would like to control a navigation system on the steering wheel. This might be due to participants' skepticism regarding having to look at the steering wheel to see the visual output.

STUDY 2: COMPARING GESTURES AND CONVENTIONAL CONTROLS IN CARS

For our second study, we selected the 6 navigation system gestures (zoom in, zoom out, move left, move right, move down and move up) presented in figure 2 and the 6 music player gestures (play, stop, next, previous, volume up and volume down) presented in figure 3 in order to validate them and to see, whether participants can remember and conduct them without errors. Furthermore, we were interested in the level of driving distraction caused by gestural interaction. In order to evaluate the gesture set we compared using gestures on a multi-touch steering wheel to a conventional car radio and navigation system in the middle console (see figure 4). While existing steering wheel buttons only offer certain input functionalities, middle console devices provide comparable input and output functions to those feasible on the multi-touch steering wheel (e.g., navigation systems are not normally controlled by steering wheel buttons). To simplify our setup, we compared the two UIs and left the steering wheel buttons out.

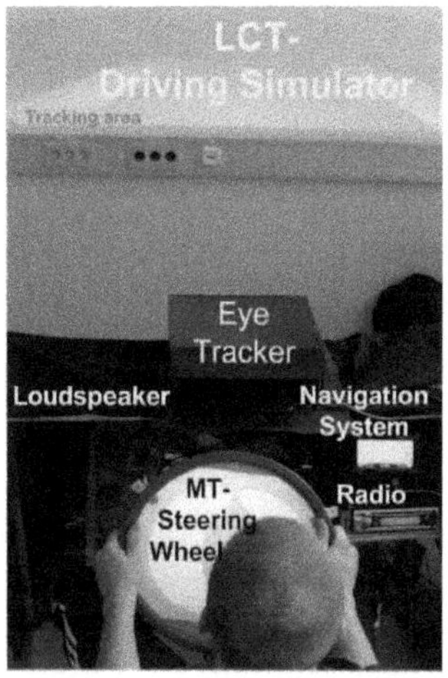

Figure 4. Experimental setup. The participant sits in front of the multi-touch steering wheel. A conventional navigation system and a radio are in the driver's reach on the right side. A 3x2 m projection shows the LCT driving simulation.

Setup

We developed a music player and a navigation application able to be controlled by gestures. The applications provided functions for each user generated gesture. For the navigation system, maps are shown directly on the screen of the multi-touch steering wheel. We performed the second user study using the same driving setup and added an eye tracker (Tobii X120) to analyze driver's gaze behavior. To get reliable and comparable driving performance data we used the Lane Change Task (LCT) [16] in this study. LCT calculates the mean deviation between a normative model and the actual path followed and is in the process of becoming an ISO standardized tool[6]. The main task of the LCT is steering the car along a 3-lane highway and changing lanes when overhead signs indicate this. Because LCT ISO draft prescribes a constant speed of 60 km/h we chose a setup without pedals and instead set the speed directly to 60 km/h. The experimental setup is shown in figure 4. As laboratory tests are the standard method for testing the impact of automotive UIs on driver distraction and offer a safe procedure during first tests, we chose a driving simulator setup for this user study (for a discussion on simulated driving versus real driving environments see [8]).

Study design

A within-subjects design was employed, with each subject performing the task in all conditions in counterbalanced order. We discriminated the following conditions: conventional middle console car radio (r), conventional middle console navigation system (n), touch gestures for the radio (rg), and touch gestures for navigation (ng). When interacting with the radio (r, rg) the users had to perform 6 different

[6] Lane Change Task: ISO Draft International Standard 26022.

actions (play, stop, next song, previous song, volume up, volume down). For interacting with the map (n, ng) we selected 6 different interaction tasks with the navigation system (zoom in, zoom out, move right, move left, move up, move down) while driving. The gestures for the multi-touch conditions (rg, ng) had to be executed as illustrated in figure 2 and figure 3, using thumbs or fingers, but always remaining one hand at the steering wheel. Only gestures performed on the interaction fields on the left and right side of the steering wheel (see figure 2 and 3) were recognized.

Each run lasted exactly 3 minutes and was dedicated to one of the four interaction conditions (r, rg, n, ng). Participants were asked to perform as many actions as they felt comfortable with during the run. Thus, in the analysis of driving behavior, rather than controlling for the frequency of actions during the experiment, which would limit the user's freedom during the driving task, we decided to make this a random variable that was controlled for after the fact by removing its effect on other dependent variables, if any, through analysis of covariance.

With the beginning of the run, the experimenter gave a verbal instruction, e.g., "Please move the map one step to the left side". After the participant had performed the action, the experimenter read the next instruction to him, in randomized order, and, if all 6 actions had been performed, starting over again. Thus, we could assess the number of actions performed (1) in each 3-minute-drive as one dependent variable. Further dependent variables included driving performance data (2) as well as data on the visual demand (3), i.e. number and duration of the user's glances at the steering wheel interface.

Participants

12 participants (5 female and 7 male) took part in the study. The average age of the participants was 26.7 years, 11 of the 12 had a driver's license and 5 had experience with touch user interfaces such as the iPhone.

Procedure

First, the participants received a brief introduction to the driving simulator setup and were asked about their radio and navigation usage while driving in a questionnaire. We showed the participants how to drive in the simulator with the LCT. The users could familiarize themselves with driving in order to explore how the virtual car reacted to their interaction with the steering wheel. As driving a virtual car with our prototype steering wheel differs a bit from steering a real car, users generally need some test-driving to get familiar with the steering.

Afterwards, the experimenter explained how to use the conventional radio and navigation system and demonstrated the different gestures for the radio and navigation application with his thumbs while leaving his hands at the steering wheel. Participants got 5 minutes time to try out all interactions and to commit them to memory. Before driving under each condition participants got the opportunity to try out all interactions again.

The first run after this introduction was recorded as the initial reference drive (RefS). The following 4 runs were performed while interacting with different media and modalities. After 4 runs interacting under the different conditions, one run was performed without interaction (middle reference run, RefM). In the second part, all 4 conditions were repeated (again randomized and counterbalanced). The final run was again a reference drive (RefE) without interacting with the system. A typical experiment would look like this: RefS, n, rg, r, ng, RefM, ng, rg, n, r, RefE. Each run, dedicated to one interface condition, lasted 3 minutes. At the end, participants received a second questionnaire and were asked to rate the conditions according to their preferences. Further open-text explanations for their statements were collected.

Results

As discussed in the study design section, we first compared the number of actions carried out with the different interfaces and then controlled for the frequency of actions during the experiment, where appropriate, in subsequent comparisons, through analysis of covariance.

Task Performance

In order to quantitatively assess the task performance in each condition, we recorded the number of successfully performed tasks during each run under each condition. The numbers of interface actions were compared with repeated measures ANOVAs for the radio task and for the navigation task. Mean numbers of interface actions are shown for each condition in figure 5.

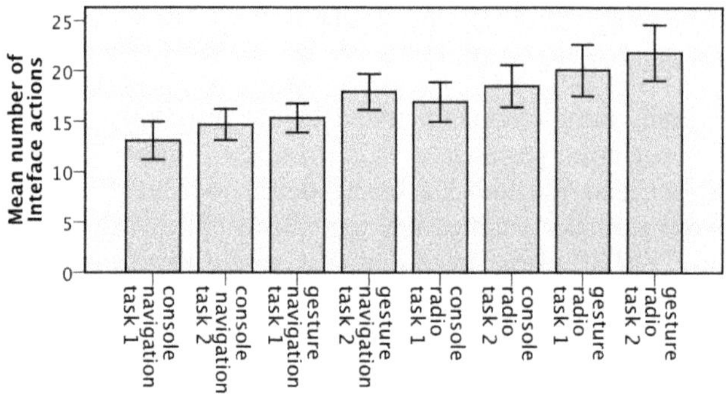

Figure 5. Mean number of actions carried out in each condition.

For the navigation task, there were main effects of both interface condition, $F(1,11)=24.80$, $p<0.01$, and time, $F(1,11)=64.25$, $p<0.01$, but no interaction, with more actions being carried out with the gestural interface and more actions tending to be carried out in the second trial than the first: on average participants carried out 17.2% more actions with the gestural interface in the first trial and 22.2% more in the second trial.

A similar pattern was found for the radio task, where there was also a main effect of interface condition, $F(1,11)=24.35$, $p<0.01$, and time, $F(1,11)=6.59$, $p<0.05$. Participants carried out 18.3% more actions with the gestural interface in the first trial and 18.0% more in the second trial.

As the frequency of interface actions varied between conditions, subsequent quantitative measures were compared controlling for this effect where appropriate as a covariate in an analysis of covariance.

Driving performance

For the navigation task, the covariate, frequency of actions, was significantly related to mean lane deviation, $F(1,43)=25.89$, $p<0.001$. However, controlling for the effect of frequency of actions, there was no effect of either interface condition, $F(1,43)=2.40$, $p>0.05$ or time, $F(1,43)=1.90$, $p>0.05$.

Similarly, frequency of actions was significantly related to mean lane deviation for the radio task, $F(1,43)=37.06$, $p<0.001$. Controlling for the effect of frequency of actions, there was a main effect of interface condition that approached significance, $F(1,43) = 3.80$, $p=0.058$, with participants tending to deviate less from the lane in the gestural conditions.

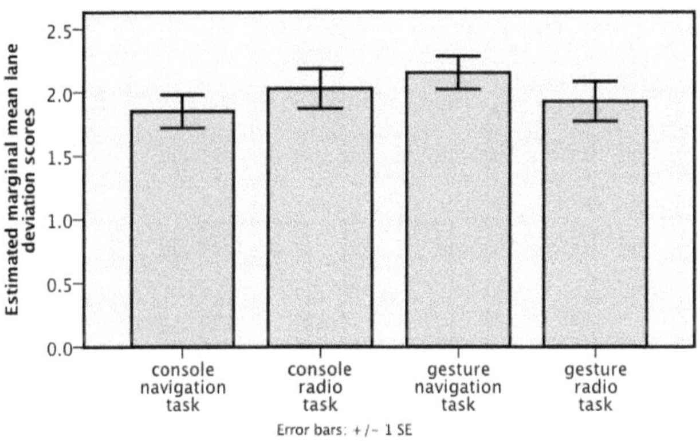

Figure 6. Estimated marginal mean lane deviation by condition. A lower deviation indicates a better driving performance.

If the driving performance was compared without controlling for the effect of frequency of actions, there was also no effect of interface condition for either the navigation task, $F(1,11) = 1.98$, $p>0.05$ or the radio task $F(1,11)=0.38$, $p>0.05$. Thus, participants were able to carry out more actions with the gestural interface without affecting driving performance. The estimated marginal mean lane deviation by condition is shown in figure 6.

Visual Demand

For the navigation task, the covariate, frequency of actions, was not significantly related to the number of glances at the interface for the navigation task, $F(1,43)=1.63$, $p>0.05$. There was a significant effect of interface condition, with participants looking at the interface less in the gestural conditions than the console conditions, $F(1,43)=17.65$, $p<0.001$. There was no main effect of time. Across the two trials, participants looked at the interface on average 58.1% less often with the gestural interface than with the console.

For the radio task, frequency of actions was related to the number of glances at the interface, $F(1,40)=4.33$, $p<0.05$. Controlling for this, there was a main effect of interface condition, $F(1,40)=85.36$, $p<0.001$, with participants looking at the interface less often when using the gestural interface. Looking at the estimated marginal means (controlling for the effect of frequency of actions), participants looked at the gestural interface 77.2% less often than they looked at the console. There was no effect of time. Figure 7 presents the estimated marginal means for the number of glances by condition.

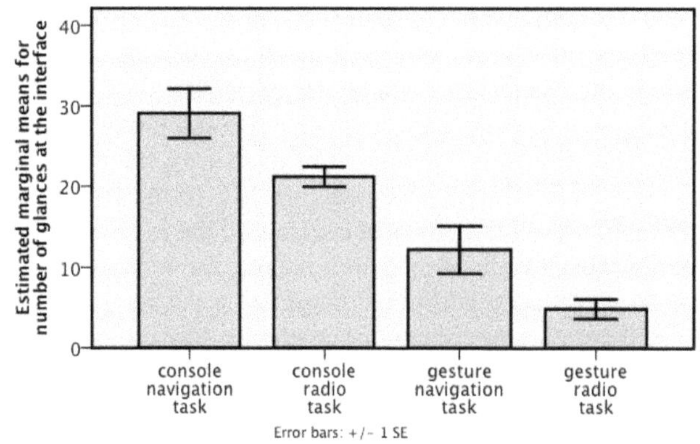

Figure 7. Estimated marginal mean number of glances at the interface by condition across both trials. Marginal means for the radio task control for the effect of frequency of actions.

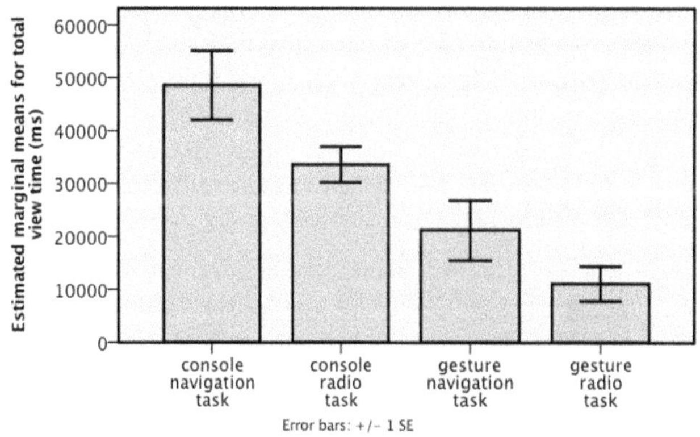

Figure 8. Estimated marginal mean time spent looking at the interface, by condition across both trials. Marginal means for the radio task control for the effect of frequency of actions.

For the second measure of visual demand, the total time spent looking at the interface, there was no relationship with the covariate, frequency of actions in the navigation task, $F(1,40)=0.25$, $p>0.05$. There was however a main effect of interface condition, $F(1,10)=15.55$, $p<0.01$, with participants spending on average 59.7% less time looking at the interface when using the gestural interface.

For the radio task, the covariate, frequency of actions, was significantly related to the total time participants spent looking at the interface, $F(1,40)=8.28$, $p<0.01$. Controlling for this, there was a main effect of interface condition, $F(1,40)=23.93$, $p<0.001$, with participants spending 67.1% less time (estimated marginal mean) looking at the interface when using the gestural interface. Figure 8 presents the estimated marginal mean time spent looking at the interface by conditions.

Operating a navigation system requires more visual attention than operating a radio. There is also a very clear and statistically significant difference for the same task using different interfaces. For both the navigation task and the radio task using the multi-touch surface in the steering wheel substantially reduced the required visual demand, operationalized as the number of glances and total time spent looking at the interface, compared to the conventional console interface.

Questionnaire Data - Subjective Ratings

In the questionnaire, we asked the active drivers (11 of 12) among the participants what types of devices they use while driving and in what way they use radio and navigation system. The radio was used by all of them very frequently and in most cases always when driving. All of the participants commonly used the physical controls of the radio located in the middle console of the car to operate the radio. Only 2 of the 11 were using additional controls on the steering wheel (e.g. for volume or changing stations). For the navigation system, 8 of the 11 participants reported that they used it at least once a week. All participants were used to operating navigation systems in the middle console (either built into the car or as an additional device).

Participants were asked to rate their expressed user experience with each system on a series of Likert scales relating to: how much they liked interacting with each of the systems (1=not at all to 5 very much) (see figure 9); how distracting they found each of the systems (1=not at all distracting to 5=very distracting)(see figure 10); and how easy they found each of the systems to use (1=difficult to 5=very easy) (see figure 11).

There was an effect of interface condition on participants' rated enjoyment ($\chi^2(3)=28.18$, $p<0.001$). Wilcoxon tests were used to follow up this finding. A Bonferroni correction was applied, so all effects are reported at a 0.0167 level of significance. The gestural radio interface was reported to be more enjoyable than the conventional radio interface (T=0, $p<0.01$). The gestural navigation interface was also reported as more enjoyable to use than the conventional radio interface (T=0, $p<0.01$). The gestural radio interface was also more enjoyable to use than the gestural navigation interface (T=0, $p<0.01$).

There was also an effect of interface condition on how distracting the participants found the task to be ($\chi^2(3) = 22.41$, $p<0.001$). Post-hoc Wilcoxon tests with a Bonferroni correction indicated that the conventional radio interface was more distracting than the gestural radio interface (T=7, $p<0.01$); that the conventional navigation interface was more distracting than the gestural navigation interface (T=0, $p<0.01$). Differences in ratings of how distracting the gestural radio and gestural navigation interfaces were approached significance (T=2.5, $p=0.047$, 2-tailed), with the navigation interface being rated as more distracting.

Finally, there was an effect of interface condition on how easy participants reported it was to use the interface, ($\chi^2(3)= 22.07$, $p<0.01$). The gestural radio interface was reported to be easier to use than the conventional radio interface (T=0, $p<0.01$); the gestural navigation interface was rated as easier to use than the console navigation interface (T=3, $p<0.01$); and the gestural radio interface was rated as easier to use than the gestural navigation interface (T=0, $p<0.01$).

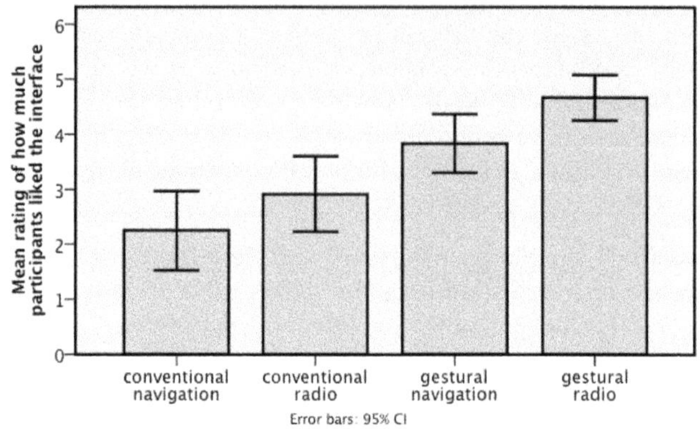

Figure 9. Mean rating of how much participants liked interacting with the different interfaces (1=not at all to 5=very much). Participants most liked gestural radio interaction.

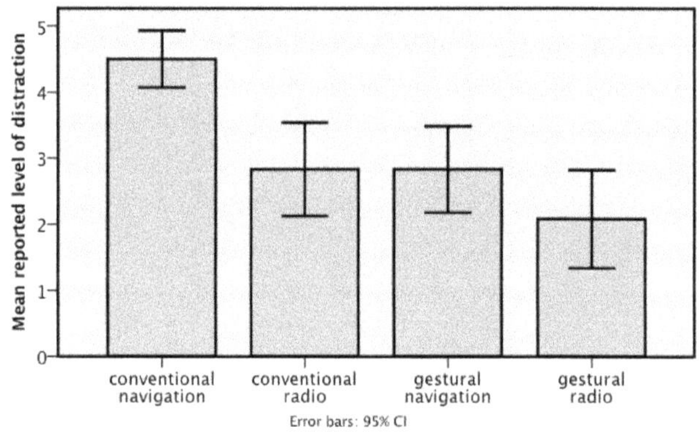

Figure 10. Mean ratings of distraction (1=not at all distracting, 5=very distracting).

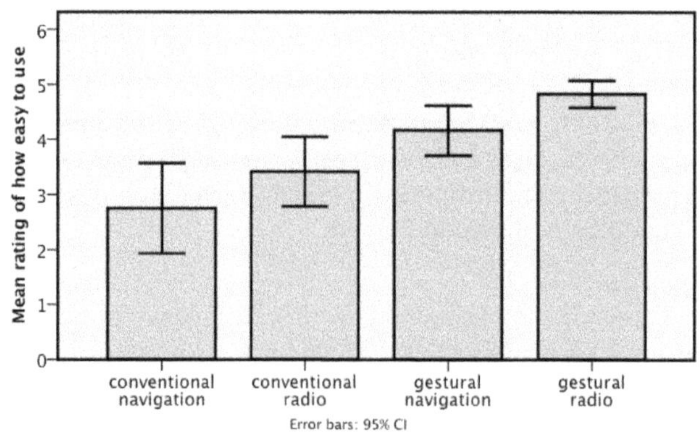

Figure 11. Mean rating of how easy to use (1=very difficult, 5=very easy).

DISCUSSION

Study setup and significance of the findings

In our experiment, we decided to compare interaction with the center console and the multi-touch steering wheel. We see both options as extreme positions: all controls and visualizations in the middle console versus all controls and visualization on the steering wheel. There are many cases in between, e.g., some controls and visualizations in the middle console and some on the steering wheel. Most cars currently on the market have the majority of controls and the visualization for infotainment systems in the middle console and a small set of additional physical controls on the steering wheel (e.g., volume, call button). In order to have an experiment with a small number of conditions and to make it easier reproducible we chose a clear separation and looked only at the two different options. As we found a number of significant results in our user study with 12 participants, especially with regard to required visual attention, we consider the chosen setup as a good initial data point to show that having flexible input and output unified on the steering wheel is potentially superior to interaction on the middle console. In future experiments, it could be useful to explore further variations on the study design (e.g., separation and distribution of controls and visualizations between locations) and integrate larger groups of participants.

Gestural interaction improves safety-relevant parameters

Our results indicate that gestural control on the steering wheel can serve as a viable option for future car user interfaces. The reduction in gaze time required to operate controls when using a multi-touch surface on the steering wheel is the major finding. Intuitively, one would expect that physical controls with haptic properties (e.g., the dial on a radio to change the volume) would help users to operate them without looking. However, our experiments showed that gestural input on the steering wheel is superior with regard to the visual demand compared to UIs in the middle console. One reason for this seems to be that users do not have to hit a specific spot to perform input. Users could keep their hands on the steering wheel all the time; potentially increasing safety. Overall, we have shown that two safety critical parameters, namely *demand on the driver's visual attention* and *positioning of the hands while driving*, can be improved by moving controls onto a multi-touch surface in the steering wheel.

Gestural interaction reduces the visual demand

Our experiments looked at two tasks with different visual demands. Controlling a radio has no inherent visual demand other than to find and use the controls, as the output is not visual. In contrast, manipulation of a map requires visual attention in order to complete a task. Our results show that tasks that have no inherent visual demand can potentially benefit significantly from using gestural input. The reduction of gaze time on the control by 67% and of number of glances at the interface by 77 % for the radio interface indicates that such tasks can benefit strongly from this type of interaction. For the navigation task, we see a reduction of gaze time of 58% and number of glances by 60% due to the fact that users have to look at the display to complete the task. However, during our experiments we observed that the time people look at the multi-touch steering wheel display is largely spent on the task and not for finding controls or interacting. Overall, our results indicate that the effect of moving controls onto a multi-touch steering wheel is strongest for applications that require little or no visual attention for the task itself.

Gestures have to fit the user's expectations and the usage environment

The user-defined gesture set identified in study 1 seemed well suited to many of the participants in study 2. It took little effort to learn the gestures and they commented positively on this. With many devices on the market, in particular smart phones and tablets, users have already learned what gestures they consider "natural". Several of our participants had no previous experience with gestural input on multi-touch surfaces personally, but their expectations and suggestions were driven by what they had seen other people doing or what they learned from advertising. Hence we expect, as gestures become very common in human-computer interaction, a basic set (e.g., zooming, moving, volume control) will become commonly agreed. And, as our study showed, users transfer those expectations from one device to another, e.g., from the phone to the steering wheel. Therefore, we think it is essential to support users by designing gestural interaction that conforms to their expectations, but also fits the interaction environment.

Flexibility for visualization and interaction is key

With using the entire surface of the steering wheel as an I/O surface, the flexibility to design interactive controls in the car increases. There are interesting options with regard to the positioning of content and controls: (1) they can stay horizontal, independent of the rotation of the steering wheel, (2) they can rotate with the steering and (3) they can stay next to the user's hand. Depending on the functionality provided, these options may be combined. E.g., a design for a phone book could include the contact details always horizontally in the middle (1) and the controls to make a call in reach of the driver's fingers (3). We have not investigated the usability of these combined visualizations yet, and we expect that further studies will explore the new design space of multi-touch steering wheels.

CONCLUSION

In this paper, we introduce the idea of a multi-touch steering wheel that allows gestural input as well as visual output. By integrating the interaction surface into the steering wheel, users can interact and still leave their hands in the preferred position for driving. In a first study with 12 participants we collected a gesture set for 20 typical interactions for controlling the infotainment system in a car. In a second experiment, we compared gestures on a multi-touch steering wheel with interaction via traditional physical controls positioned in the middle console.

The main finding is that interaction using a multi-touch steering wheel reduced the visual demand by a large degree. In the case of controlling typical functions of a radio, a reduction of 67-77% was observed, depending on the measure. In the case of a navigation task, where the task requires visual attention, a reduction of 58-60% was seen. Our observations during the user studies suggest that the multi-touch steering wheel is a step towards controls than can be used without visual attention and at the same time can offer visual feedback for fast recovery in the case of a problem. The driving performance measured with LCT showed no significant difference between the modalities. This means that participants conducted more actions with the gestural interface without affecting driving performance. In addition to the quantitative results participants provided very positive feedback on the gestural interface. They found the use of the multi-touch steering wheel instantly understandable and easy to use. In future research, we plan to integrate this technology into a car in order to explore the potential of a multi-touch steering wheel for different applications more comprehensively.

ACKNOWLEDGEMENTS

We would like to thank Roel Vertegaal, who provided us with valuable feedback on the statistical analysis of our data as well as the overall presentation. This work was funded by the DFG as part of the Project 'Embedded Interaction'.

REFERENCES

1. Bach, K. M., Jæger, M. G., Skov, M. B., Thomassen, N. G. You can touch, but you can't look: interacting with in-vehicle systems. Proc. of CHI '08, ACM, 1139-1148, 2008.
2. Ecker, R., Broy, V., Butz, A. and De Luca, A. pieTouch: A Direct Touch Gesture Interface for Interacting with In-Vehicle Information Systems, in Proc. of MobileHCI, ACM, 160-169, 2009.
3. Geiser, G. Man Machine Interaction in Vehicles. ATZ 87, 74-77, 1985.
4. González, I. E., Wobbrock, J. O., Chau, D. H., Faulring, A., and Myers, B. A. Eyes on the road, hands on the wheel: thumb-based interaction techniques for input on steering wheels. Proc. of GI '07, 95–102, 2007.
5. Green, P. Driver Distraction, Telematics Design, and Workload Managers: Safety Issues and Solutions. Convergence 2004, Detroit, MI, USA, 2004.
6. Han, J. Low-cost multi-touch sensing through frustrated total internal reflection, Proc. of UIST '05, ACM, 115-118, 2005.
7. Harrison, C. and Hudson, S. E. Providing dynamically changeable physical buttons on a visual display. In Proc. of CHI '09, ACM, 299-308, 2009.
8. Hoskins, A.H. and El-Gindy, M. Technical Report: Literature Survey on Driving Simulator Validation Studies, International Journal of Heavy Vehicle Systems, Vol. 13, No. 3, 241-252, 2006.
9. Hurtienne, J. and Israel, J. H. Image schemas and their metaphorical extensions: intuitive patterns for tangible interaction. In Proc. of TEI '07. ACM, 127-134, 2007.
10. Jacob, R. J., Girouard, A., Hirshfield, L. M., Horn, M. S., Shaer, O., Solovey, E. T., and Zigelbaum, J. 2008. Reality-based interaction: a framework for post-WIMP interfaces. In Proc. of CHI '08. ACM, 201-210, 2008.
11. Kaltenbrunner, M. reacTIVision and TUIO: A Tangible Tabletop Toolkit, Proc. of ITS '09, ACM, 9-16, 2009.
12. Kern, D., Schmidt, A., Arnsmann, J., Appelmann, T., Pararasasegaran, N., and Piepiera, B. Writing to your car: handwritten text input while driving. In Proc. of CHI '09 Extended Abstracts. ACM, 4705-4710, 2009.
13. Kern, D., Schmidt, A. Design space for driver-based automotive user interfaces. In Proc. of AutomotiveUI '09, ACM, 3-10, 2009.
14. Kray, C., Nesbitt, D., Dawson, J., and Rohs, M. User-defined gestures for connecting mobile phones, public displays, and tabletops. In Proc. of MobileHCI '10, ACM, 239-248, 2010.
15. Lee, S., Kim, S., Jin, B., Choi, E., Kim, B., Jia, X., Kim, D., and Lee, K. How users manipulate deformable displays as input devices. In Proc. of CHI '10, ACM, 1647-1656, 2010.
16. Mattes, S. The lane change task as a tool for driver distraction evaluation. In: Strasser, H., Rausch, H., and Bubb, H. (editors). Quality of Work and Products in Enterprises of the Future. Ergonomia, 2003.
17. Mauney, D., Howarth, J., Wirtanen, A., and Capra, M. Cultural similarities and differences in user-defined gestures for touchscreen user interfaces. In Proc. of CHI Extended Abstracts 2010. ACM, 4015-4020, 2010.
18. Norman, D. A. The way I see it: Natural user interfaces are not natural. *interactions* 17, 3, ACM, 6-10, 2010.
19. Pettitt, M. A., Burnett, G. E. and Stevens, A. Defining driver distraction. Proc. of 12th ITS World Congress, San Francisco, USA, ITS America, 2005.
20. Pfeiffer, M., Kern, D., Schöning J., Döring, T., Krüger, A., Schmidt, A. A multi-touch enabled steering wheel: exploring the design space. In Proc. of CHI Extended Abstracts 2010. ACM, 3355-3360, 2010.
21. Sandnes, F. E., Huang, Y.P., Huang, Y. M. An Eyes-Free In-car User Interface Interaction Style Based on Visual and Textual Mnemonics, Chording and Speech. In Proc. of MUE '08, 24-26, 2008.
22. Schöning, J., Hook, J., Motamedi, N., Olivier, P., Echtler, F., Brandl, P., Muller, L., Daiber, F., Hilliges, O., Löchtefeld, M., Roth, T., Schmidt, D., von Zadow, U. Building Interactive Multi-touch Surfaces. Journal of Graphics Tools, 2009.
23. Wobbrock, J. O., Morris, M. R., and Wilson, A. D. User-defined gestures for surface computing. In Proc. of CHI '09. ACM, 1083-1092, 2009.

Usability of Car Dashboard Displays for Elder Drivers

SeungJun Kim[1], Anind K. Dey[1], Joonhwan Lee[3], and Jodi Forlizzi[1,2]

[1]Human- Computer Interaction Institute and
[2]School of Design, Carnegie Mellon University
Pittsburgh PA 15213 USA
{sjunikim, anind, forlizzi}@cs.cmu.edu

[3]Neowiz Lab.
Seoul, Korea
joonhwan@neowiz.com

ABSTRACT
The elder population is rising worldwide; in the US, no longer being able to drive is a significant marker of loss of independence. One of the approaches to helping elders drive more safely is to investigate the use of automotive user interface technology, and specifically, to explore the instrument panel (IP) display design to help attract and manage attention and make information easier to interpret.

In this paper, we explore the premise that dashboard displays can be better designed to support elder drivers, their information needs, and their cognitive capabilities. We conducted a study to understand which display design features are critically linked to issues of divided attention and driving performance. We found that contrast of size and reduced clutter are instrumental in enhancing driving performance, particularly for the elder population. Surprisingly, our results showed that color elements have a negative effect on driving performance for elders, while color elements and fills slightly improve performance. We conclude with design implications generated from this work.

Author Keywords
Automotive UI, dashboard, dashboard display, senior drivers, eye tracking, divided attention, interface design

ACM Classification Keywords
H5.m. Information interfaces and presentation (e.g., HCI): Miscellaneous.

General Terms
Design.

INTRODUCTION
The elder population is rapidly rising worldwide. One of the significant losses of independence is when elders can no longer drive, especially as trips for shopping and social activities increase with age [4, 3, 10, 27]. At this point, elders relinquish all independence, and must rely on public transportation, formalized care, or a family member to leave one's primary home [22]. To fight against the inevitable loss of independence, elders often keep driving long after it is safe for them to do so. Impairments such as decay in vision, hearing, and general mobility issues which restrict range of motion and fine motor skills work to collectively reduce the performance of elderly drivers [32, 14, 25]. In particular, elders face a decline in the ability to perform secondary tasks while driving, which require attention switching between the primary task of driving and the secondary task of looking at in-vehicle information displays such as instrument panels or navigation displays [20, 12, 2, 17].

One approach is to investigate the use of automotive user interface technology to help elders drive safely for longer periods of time. Better sensing and display technologies can be placed in the car to augment the diligence that an individual needs while driving. This can help audiences like elder drivers with issues such as slowed reaction time and visual acuity. In addition, instrument panel (IP) display design can be explored to help attract and manage attention, make information easier to interpret, and facilitate the cognitive process of making sense of information and acting accordingly. In this paper, we explore the premise that dashboard displays can be better designed to support elder drivers, their information needs, and their cognitive capabilities. To do so, we conduct a study to understand which display design features are critically linked to issues of divided attention and driving performance.

We will explore two overarching questions: 1) What are the differences in the ways elders and non-elders manage attention when driving? 2) Can particular aspects of instrument panel (IP) display designs help elders better manage attention and perform better while driving? To answer these questions, 32 participants (18 elder drivers and 14 younger drivers) participated in a dual task experiment, evaluating a total of six displays while performing a simulated driving task. They were asked to locate and verbally read dashboard information while performing the driving task.

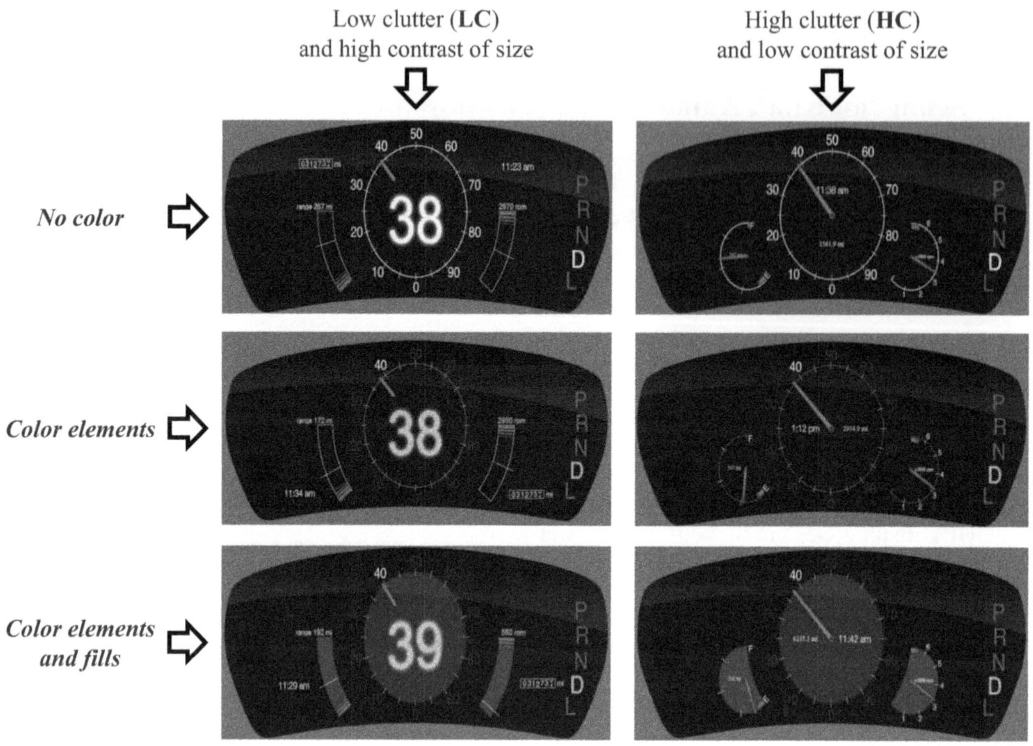

Figure 1: Six dashboard designs used for the study.

We developed two types of designs, high clutter designs and low clutter designs (Figure 1). We divided the dashboard into two areas, central and peripheral panels, and define *clutter* as the number of features per area. Within these two types of designs, we manipulated the contrast in size and color among dashboard elements to understand how useful, accessible, and legible each manipulation is (Figure 2).

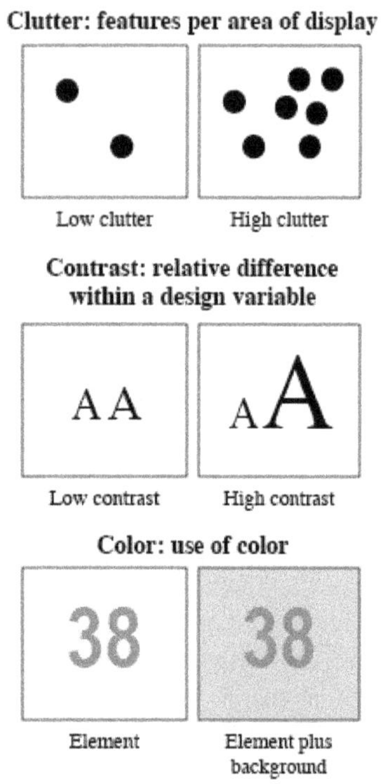

Figure 2. Design features used in the display designs.

The results of our study demonstrated that our designs caused variations in driving performance that were greater in elder than in younger drivers. There was a significant impact of clutter, affecting how both elder and younger drivers managed their attention. The speedometer designs in the central panel had the most distinct results in affecting driver performance and attention management. Elder drivers performed better and had shorter glance times using the speedometers in the low clutter designs. Therefore, we can conclude that dashboard displays can be better designed to support safer driving in the elderly population.

In what follows, we discuss related work on driving performance, icons, visual design features, and in-car information displays. Then we present the methods and findings from our study. We conclude with design implications that can be used to guide instrument panel display designs.

BACKGROUND WORK

Literature from three domains informed our research: research on in-vehicle information displays, cognitive psychology and attention demand, and icon design and research on visual design features that affect attention direction and information transfer.

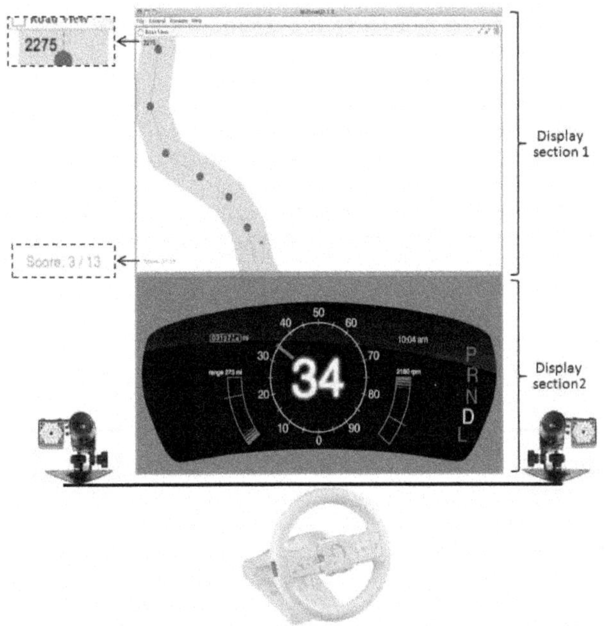

Figure 3: Dual task test-bed incorporated with a driving simulation game (primary display section 1 for driving task and secondary display section 2 for dashboard display), an eye tracker and a Wii-wheel joystick).

In-vehicle information displays

Attentive driving can be hindered when performing secondary interactive tasks, including eating or smoking, communicating with others, or using in-vehicle devices. In particular, in-vehicle information displays at times demand a driver's visual attention, causing significant issues of divided attention. To succeed in both safe driving and effective interaction, drivers have to manage their eye-off-road timings, patterns and frequency.

Human factors studies have shown that an average of 2.7 glances and a total of 4.1 seconds fixation time on a display are the maximum safely allowed when driving at 30km/h [33]. A driver takes approximately 0.78 seconds and 1.26 glances to read a speedometer [34]. Rockwell's two-second rule states that drivers should not take their eyes off the road for longer than a two-second interval [24]. That naturally limits the amount of interaction and information that can be consumed per distraction: for example, the amount of text-based information that can be safely read while driving is 6.2 Japanese or 11 Roman characters per second [15, 13]).

Fortunately, we find that visual attention demands can be positively impacted by the visual design of the instrument panel [20, 19, 17, 18]. For example, [19] used abstraction as a design strategy to minimize the complexity of route map visualizations in a navigation system, reducing fixation time and number of glances. Reduced attention demands led to positive effects on elders' driving-related task performance; by minimizing the number and length of transitions between a navigation display view and the primary driving view, the number of missed turns and pedestrians put in danger dropped by more than a factor of two [17]. Adding dynamic color to displays has eliminated the significant age-related decrease in reaction time seen when displays had no color [20]. As noted in [2], advanced automotive displays or UI technologies have the potential to improve safety and mobility if designed in accordance with the sensory/cognitive abilities of older drivers. We believe re-designing car dashboard displays can help increase elder drivers' visual search speed and decrease attention demands, and result in safer driving.

Visual search tasks and attention demand

Finding information on a visual display is a visual search task. The perceptual psychology literature has identified two types of visual search tasks: a top-down task, which is goal-driven and implements cognitive strategies; and bottom-up tasks, which are thought to work on raw sensory input, shifting attention to salient items in a visual field [7]. Typically, bottom-up processes are thought to act early on in the visual perception process, generally within 100 milliseconds.

Within bottom-up mechanisms, the concept of pop-out is important [28, 1]. Pop-out is the drawing of attention to an object, which occurs when an item in the visual field is somehow distinctive. This is done by using highly contrasting design variables, as shown in Figure 2. A range of design factors can cause pop-out effects, including color, brightness, and movement [5, 16, 29, 30]. Interestingly, the literature shows that size does not create a pop-out effect [1].

We can replicate the same visual search phenomena when searching for information in a dashboard display using the design features of clutter, contrast of size and color. When a driver searches for information, she will generally know what she is looking for. A top-down search will be invoked, and will be modified by particular design features that are the target of the user's search. For example, if the target of the driver's search has a pop-out effect, information will be discovered quickly. If other aspects of the display feature pop-out, they will hinder the driver's search for information.

Icon design and research on visual design features

Visual design is informed by research in many areas: cognitive science, human factors, and semiotics, among others. Research has explored identification and/or search speeds of text [9], color [8], high-symbolism icons [21], and combined text and high-symbolism pictures [6]. Visual search studies, on which many of the findings are based, are not representative of the dual-task paradigm that occurs during driving and that was used in our study.

Other research explores how individual design features holistically contribute to a design. Color as a design feature has been shown to result in faster search times compared to design features such as size, brightness, and geometric shape [8]. Another study showed that the discriminating effects of color lessen with learning [9]. Other research confirms that text can be processed faster than pictures [8], that concrete icons are more quickly interpreted than abstract ones [21], and that complex icons lead to slower search and identification times (whether the symbols are learned or unlearned by the viewer) [21].

From a rich body of empirical work, icon design guidelines have been created for in-vehicle usage [7] and public information [36]. Both sets of guidelines stress the importance of universal interpretability by using high-symbolism and simple drawings, because they assume viewers will have little or no training with the icons.

A body of dual-task research exists has examined interfaces for safety-critical situations, such as flying and driving. One dual-task study showed that finding items on a secondary display may not significantly hinder a primary task [26]. Other research has focused on icon-function relationships, exploring the relationship between visual design, complexity, and interpretation of particular designs. However, this work does not explore how a display might best convey information for a secondary task. This leaves open the exploration of designs and renditions that may use design features like contrast, color, and abstraction to quickly convey information.

From the literature, we can understand that the goal of minimizing complexity on a visual display is important. We also know that bottom-up search happens within 100ms of attending to a visual display. For this reason, we sought to design features that supported bottom-up processes, so that the driver's eye would be naturally directed to changes on the screen. Our designs explore clutter as a design strategy; increased clutter means there are more interface elements that can convey information, while decreased clutter means that there is less competition for user attention. Our designs also explore the impact of contrast in size and color as design variables. The details of particular design features relative to one another are important. To uncover them, we embarked on an iterative, user-centered design process to design the displays for our study.

PREDICTIONS

Because we view designs holistically, it is impossible to predict how individual design features such as color or size might directly affect performance on an experimental task. Therefore, we have developed the following predictions, based on our six designs:

a) Clutter type will impact a design's effect on driving performance more than design features.

b) Low clutter designs will require less fixation time and, therefore, less response time in answering a prompt for information. This difference will be greater for elder than younger drivers.

c) As predicted in the literature [1, 20], color will cause a greater attraction of attention than contrast in size for elder drivers. Designs using color will have faster interpretation time than designs using contrast in size. Designs using contrast in size plus color will demand the most attention and have the greatest effect on elders' driving performance.

DASHBOARD DESIGN

For the study, we designed six different car dashboard displays based on two design types, Low Clutter and High Clutter, and two design features: contrast in size and color (Figure 1).

To design the dashboard displays, we undertook an iterative, user-centered design process, which included interviews with elder and younger drivers, an expert interview with a driving rehab specialist, and a design and feature analysis of 36 existing dashboard designs on competitive car models. From this, we identified a set of design features for the focus of our study. A first round of designs was sketched by hand and evaluated by the driving specialist. From there, the set of features was narrowed to the final list and static designs were created using Adobe Illustrator. We then identified a set of interaction features for each dashboard (speed, gas gauge, engine light, *etc.*) and implemented these modified designs using Adobe Flash.

EXPERIMENTAL DESIGN

We conducted a dual-task experiment to test our predictions about our designs.

Test-bed setup

We presented a Java-based driving simulation game with two vertically separated areas of focus: a primary driving task display in the upper section and our dashboard displays in the lower section (See Figure 3). The overall screen size was 0.32×0.388 m with the resolution of 1024×1280 pixels. The screen resolution of the dashboard display section was 1024×512 pixels. The driving display featured blue coins arranged along a grey curve representing a road. Participants manipulated a red dot (representing their car) in this scene using a Bluetooth-based Wii steering wheel controller. As shown in Figure 3, a runtime timestamp and coin collection score can be seen on the top left and bottom left side of the task display screen, respectively. To assess where drivers were looking, their gaze was tracked using a Smart Eye Pro 5.5 contactless gaze tracker (http://www.smarteye.se).

The secondary display section showed dynamic images of the dashboard display. Our experiment featured six designs, using two clutter types, contrast in size, and variation in use of color (Figure 1). Each display consists of five dashboard components: speedometer, fuel gauge, clock, odometer, and tachometer. The HC dashboards combined speedometer, clock and odometer in a central panel, and fuel gauge and tachometer in a peripheral panel. The LC dashboard featured only the speedometer in the central panel.

Dual task

In the dual task experiment, participants were asked to complete a five-minute simulated driving game, and were verbally prompted to report information from the dashboard ten times during the game. The game incentive to collect coins was included to keep participants focused on the primary task of driving, rather than focusing on the dashboard. Drivers attempted to collect coins while maintaining the car's position in the center of the road. Five voice commands prompted for information twice in a counter-balanced order (*e.g.*, "speed", "fuel", "time", "odometer" and "tachometer"). Participants verbally reported the answers, referring to the dynamically updating dashboard display. For simplicity, we employed a top-view representation of a car in our driving task, rather than a driver-view representation.

Participants

We recruited 32 participants (age range/mean: 18-89/56.10, 10 males and 22 females) including 18 elder participants (65-89/74.24, 4 males and 14 females) and 14 younger participants (18-63/34.07, 6 males and 8 females). Elder participants were recruited through a lifelong learning institute at two local universities. We recruited younger participants through bulletin board ads placed around the university campus and in the local community. Participants provided demographic information and participated in an eye profiling and gaze calibration task, which took between 15 and 20 minutes.

All 18 elder participants reported having more than 30 years of driving experience. 78% did not report any impairment and three elders who reported visual or hearing impairments were excluded from the task performance/gaze analysis. None of the younger participants reported any impairment. Their driving experience varied from 0-2 years (14%), 3-4 years (14%), 5-10 years (29%), 11-20 years (7%), 21-30 years (7%) and more than 30 years (29%).

Measurement

Our automated measures for the primary task included *lane deviation* (LD), measuring the average distance from the center of the road, and *missed coins* (MC), measuring the total number of coins that drivers failed to collect during the experiment.

Our measures for the secondary task were collected using a video recording, with the timestamp on the driving display used to integrate the log of the automated measures and the recording. Auditory commands and participant answers were also time-coded. Our measures included *response time* (RT), time from when the voice command was announced to when the participant began to utter an answer, and *answer duration* (AD), time from the moment the participant begins responding until the time the answer is completed. These measures indicate how quickly participants searched the dashboard display and how long it took them to comprehend the visual designs and communicate the results. We also analyzed time-on-task by adding these two measures.

To create a measure of divided attention, we measured eye gaze movements and calculated eye-off-road times. We extracted the coordinates where a subject's gaze intersected

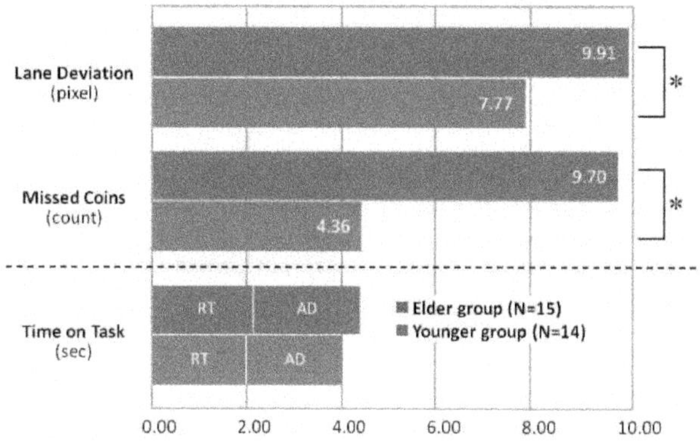

Figure 4: Primary and secondary task performance by age group.

with the screen. Using a high-pass noise filter combined with linear interpolation, we calculated *gaze dwell-on time*, indicating how long a subject's gaze remained on the dashboard display and on each of the dashboard components during our driving task, and *gaze drop-by frequency* that indicates how many times a subject's gaze was drawn to the dashboard display section and each of the dashboard components during our driving task.

For each test, we obtained a full dataset consisting of three output files: a driving log file, a gaze log file, and a video.

Questionnaires

Each participant filled out initial, interim and post-test questionnaires. An initial questionnaire surveyed participants about their driving patterns and general opinions about dashboard design properties. After each driving test, an interim questionnaire captured participants' subjective evaluations of the design. Participants rated each instrument panel in each dashboard display using a 6-point Likert scale. A post questionnaire captured comparative preferences for the dashboards.

RESULTS

We analyzed each design in four ways: by clutter type (high or low), by panel (central or peripheral), and by contrast of size and color. We examined post-hoc contrast results for more details.

Preliminary survey

The initial survey queried drivers about the relative importance of the instrument panels and what aspects of dashboard displays they felt could be improved. In terms of the dashboard display design, both elders and younger drivers rated the speedometer to be of primary importance to the driving task (89% and 79% respectively), followed by the fuel gauge (34% and 14% respectively). The tachometer was chosen as the least important instrument (78% and 57% respectively). Both groups selected the odometer and tachometer as the most difficult to find quickly. When asked what features of dashboard displays were most ripe for improvement, elder participants selected lighting brightness (67%) and display contrast (39%), followed by font size (33%).

Task performance

Primary task performance

The primary task was evaluated by two measures: missed coins (MC) and lane deviation (LD). We found significant performance measures for both, between the two age groups. On average, elder participants missed five more coins (2.22 times more, $F_{1,27}$=12.723, p<0.001) and had 1.28 times larger lane deviations ($F_{1,27}$=7.551, p<0.011), than younger participants (Figure 4).

In coin collecting performance, we found no significant impact either by clutter type or by color (including elements and background fills).

In lane deviation performance, elders showed 1.15 times larger lane deviations when using the color-added designs (bottom two rows of designs in Figure 1) than when using the no-color designs (top row in Figure 1) ($F_{1,139}$=5.317, p<0.023). Interestingly, however, when examining only the use of color elements and background fills together (*i.e.*, the 3rd row of designs in Figure 1), elders' lane deviation performance was NOT significantly different from when they used the no-color designs ($F_{1,135}$=0.488, p<0.486).

To summarize, younger participants performed better than elder participants on the primary driving task. Given the lane deviation results, one important implication is that dashboard display designs may draw attention away from driving safely, and that this effect is larger for elder drivers. To explore this issue further, we examined the participants' secondary task performance and gaze movement.

Secondary task performance

Secondary task performance was measured by time on task, time to answer (RT), and answer duration (AD). There were no significant differences between younger and elder participants in secondary task performance over all dashboards (Figure 4). However, we found design-specific differences in both age groups. Clutter type and contrast of size had an impact on RT and AD in some of the designs.

For example, when using LC dashboards, elders' time to respond to speedometer questions was 0.69s faster ($F_{1,135}$=17.276, p<.0001) and younger participants response time was 0.50s faster ($F_{1,135}$=8.319, p<0.005), than using HC dashboards. Faster average RTs were also found for the other dashboard components when using LC dashboards. Despite these results, participants had longer ADs when using LC dashboards, spending 0.26s more in reading information from the displays ($F_{1,135}$=6.304, p<0.013).

To understand this discrepancy, we conducted a post-hoc analysis by grouping the dashboard components into two panels: central and peripheral. Interestingly, we found that across all participants, both RT and AD in interacting with central panels were significantly shorter (0.91s and 0.70s per interaction) when using LC dashboards ($F_{1,135}$=59.423, p<.0001 and $F_{1,135}$=7.732, p<0.006, respectively). Further, these significantly shorter durations were seen in both younger and elder participants. The peripheral panel of the LC dashboards slowed the speed of responding to the prompt; here, participants' AD was 0.44s longer for the peripheral panel ($F_{1,135}$=15.627, p<.0001).

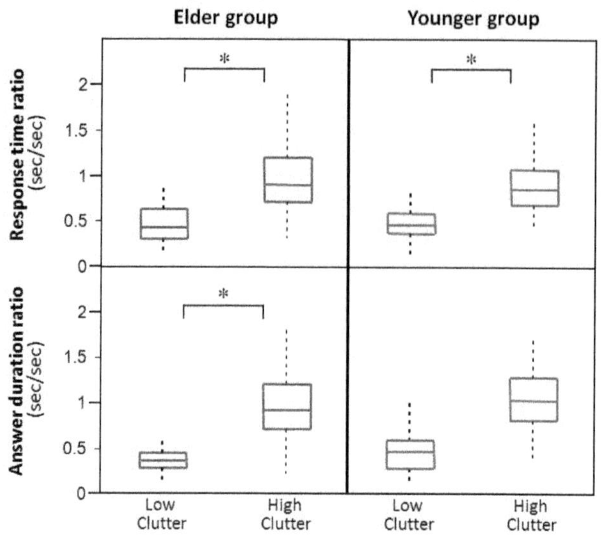

Figure 5: Ratios of response time and answer duration by panel zone (Average times taken for central panel / Average times taken for peripheral panel).

In other words, when using LC dashboards, RTs were generally faster across the panels overall and significantly faster for the central panel; ADs were shorter for the central panel, as expected, but they were significantly longer for the peripheral panel. Given these results, when glancing at the dashboard display, drivers may strategically manage their attention to ensure that they can continue to drive safely. This strategy may differ significantly depending on whether they are interacting with the central or peripheral panel. To explore this further, we examined the impact of the dashboard design factors.

In particular, when comparing high clutter and low clutter displays, we found that elder participants spent significantly different amounts of time attending to the central and peripheral panel zones. The average ratio of time spent on central vs. peripheral panels was closer to 0.5 for the LC dashboards, but closer to 1.0 for the HC dashboards (Figure 5, left). We interpret this to mean that elders changed their strategy for answering questions when using the LC and HC designs. This was not the case for younger participants, who exhibited no significant changes in AD by clutter type (Figure 5, bottom right) $F_{1,135}$=3.057, p<0.083).

To summarize, both elder and younger participants' secondary task performance was influenced by dashboard components and panels within the designs. LC dashboards with high contrast of size yielded a mostly faster response time for the secondary task, particularly in the central panel and particularly for elder drivers.

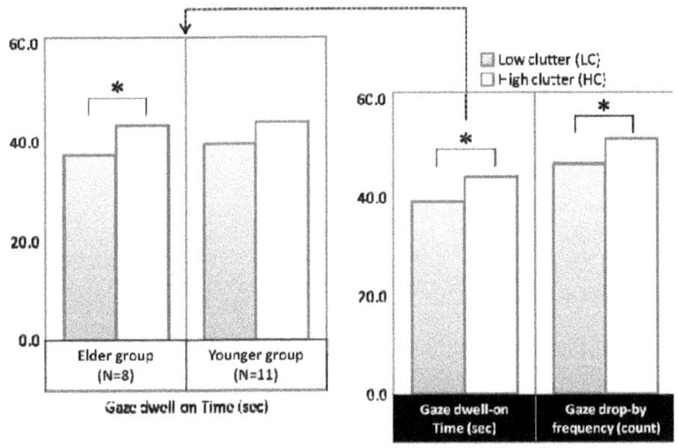

Figure 6: Analysis of gaze in the dashboard display zone, split by age group (left) and combined (right).

Gaze analysis

Our gaze analysis measures included gaze dwell-on time and gaze drop-by frequency; these measures represent how long and how often participants took their eyes off the road. Using gaze tracking data, we analyzed attention switching between the driving game and the dashboard display.

We found that clutter type, panel, and contrast in size all had a significant impact on both gaze dwell-on time and gaze drop-by frequency for the dashboard display. When using low clutter (LC) designs, participants gazed 4.92s less at the dashboard display and took their eyes off the road display 5.06 fewer times ($F_{1,77}$=6.985, $p<0.01$ and $F_{1,77}$=4.140, $p<0.045$, respectively); in particular, a *post hoc* analysis revealed that elder drivers' gaze-dwell on time was significantly affected by clutter type (5.96s less when using LC, $F_{1,77}$=4.434, $p<0.039$). (Figure 6).

When analyzing by panel, on average our participants spent 7.08s and 8.59 glances looking at dashboard components in the central panel and 4.47s and 6.302 glances for the peripheral components. LC dashboards required less gaze dwell-on time and lower gaze drop-by frequency than HC dashboards: 2.24s shorter ($F_{1,77}$=25.382, $p<.0001$) and 4.05 fewer glances ($F_{1,77}$=46.065, $p<.0001$) for the central component; 0.81s shorter ($F_{1,77}$=7.603, $p<0.007$) and 1.94 fewer glances ($F_{1,77}$=15.808, $p<0.0002$) for the peripheral component.

When analyzing by contrast of size, participants looked at the speedometer of the LC dashboards (*i.e.*, high size-contrast dashboards) for 10.42s less ($F_{1,77}$=224.775, $p<.0001$) and the clock for 1.68s less ($F_{1,77}$=41.892, $p<.0001$).

In conclusion, clutter type was more important than age factor in having an effect on gaze drop and gaze dwell time, although the degree of impact on gaze was greater in elder drivers. LC designs yielded a smaller gaze dwell-on time and lower gaze drop-by frequency (*i.e.*, a lower potential of eye-off-road issues) over all participants, for both the central and peripheral panels (Figure 7), but especially in the central panel.

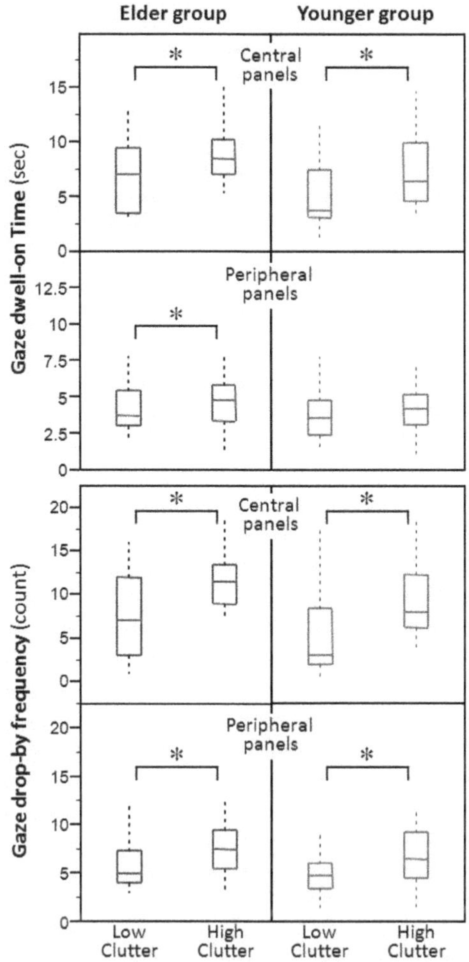

Figure 7: Analysis of gaze by panel (central or peripheral) and age group.

Design feature analysis

The color and contrast of size features resulted in distinct differences in task performance and gaze patterns between elder and younger drivers.

Contrast of size

Contrast of size did not cause a significant difference in primary task performance for younger participants. However, across all participants, secondary task performance and gaze movement varied depending on which contrast of size they saw in the design (Note: in this section we will summarize the results without replicating the numbers in clutter comparison).

Across all participants, both RT and AD in interacting with central panels were significantly shorter when using high size-contrast designs. Particularly for elder drivers, high size-contrast yielded a faster response time. We also found that contrast of size had a significant impact on both gaze dwell-on time and gaze drop-by frequency for the dashboard display. The lower potential for needing eyes-off-road, owing to large size contrast was clearly exhibited in the central panel.

In conclusion, our contrast of size design feature had an effect on both elder and younger drivers. In particular, elders' secondary task performance and eye-off-road time was more affected by contrast of size.

Color

Color as a design variable caused interesting effects on elder and younger drivers. Elder participants were 0.44s faster in response time (RT) for a dashboard component in the peripheral panel using the dashboards with background color fills ($F_{1,139}$=3.954, p<0.049). However, color did not have any significant impact on gaze movements for elder participants. Younger participants took on average about a second less to look at a peripheral component when using any of the colored dashboards (1.04s shorter $F_{1,81}$=5.508, p<0.021). Color did not cause any significant difference in either primary and secondary task performance for younger participants. This is in keeping with the findings in [20], which state that elders will have significantly better performance when using a dashboard display with color.

Contrast of size vs. Color

Most of our results show that the designs using high contrast of size provide the best results in secondary task performance and gaze durations. In addition, we also found some evidence that participants were affected by color fills in elements or background. One question we hoped to answer is which design feature, contrast of size or color, contributes to better performance.

We compared three combinations: 1) Large contrast of size + No color; 2) Large contrast of size + Color/Fill; and 3) Low contrast of size + Color/Fill. For the primary task, elder participants had better driving performance with the first combination than the second combination (1.20 times smaller lane deviation, $F_{1,139}$=4.261, p<0.041). Adding color to the high size-contrast dashboards reduced the legibility of the design for elders. In the secondary task, the third combination resulted in a slower RT than the other combinations, especially for the central panel (1.04s slower than the second combination and 1.22s slower than the first combination (*i.e.*, contrast dominant dashboards), $F_{1,139}$=27.115, p<.0001 and $F_{1,139}$=27.952, p<.0001, respectively).

The third combination also resulted in a longer gaze dwell-on time than the other dashboards, especially for the central panel (e.g., 2.65s longer gaze dwell-on time than the no color dashboards, $F_{1,81}$=16.097, p<.0001).

To summarize, size-contrast appears to be more dominant than color in improving performance.

Dashboard familiarity

In post-task questionnaires, all participants were asked about familiarity with the question "*Which dashboard most looks similar to your dashboard?*". We found no significant effect of participants' familiarity on task performance and gaze-related measures; however there was an effect of familiarity on overall rating, which was higher when dashboards were described as familiar. When analyzed with respect to age group, these results are almost the same.

DISCUSSION

In our study, we created six dashboard display designs using differing levels of clutter, contrast of size, and color elements and fills. Our experiment strove to understand the performance of these designs holistically, but in order to do so, we hoped to understand the relative strength of individual design features.

In general, both younger and elder drivers performed better using the LC, high contrast in size designs. Older drivers exhibited a greater variability in the measures of performance with different designs. In particular, the design of the speedometer panel in the LC designs — using high contrast of size and no color — resulted in the best performance measures for all participants.

Our first prediction, that clutter type would impact a design's effect on driving performance more than other design features, was partially supported. When using LC dashboards, drivers responded more quickly to the prompts for information generally faster across the panels overall and significantly faster for the central panel. Answer durations were also shorter for the central panel, as expected, but they were significantly longer for the peripheral panel.

Our second prediction, that low clutter designs will require less fixation time and, therefore, less response time in answering a prompt for information, and would be greater for elder than younger drivers, was supported. When driving with the LC dashboards, participants looked at the elements on the dashboard less (in particular, the speedometer), and answered questions more quickly.

Our third prediction was that color would cause a greater draw in attention than contrast of size, particularly for elder drivers. This prediction was made based on literature stating that color, not size, created an attraction of attention [1], and that color had been shown to assist in comprehension of driving displays in the elder population [20]. We believed that designs using color would have faster interpretation times than designs using contrast in size, and that designs using contrast in size plus color would communicate information quickly and have the greatest effect on elders' driving performance. This prediction, surprisingly, was not uniformly supported. The contrast dominant dashboards mostly performed better than the color dominant dashboards, especially in the central panel. It indicates that size-contrast was more dominant than color in improving performance. An interesting detail to note is that our color designs resulted in shorter than average glance durations. The literature cites 1.6 seconds threshold for in-vehicle glances (discussed by [35] as well as the recommended limits [22]), and our color displays averaged 0.84 seconds.

We also saw differences in the behavior of younger and elder drivers in interacting with the different designs. Elders had larger performance improvements with the LC designs, particularly with the speedometer design that featured high contrast of size. Elder drivers spent significantly different amounts of time attending to the central and peripheral panels depending on the types of clutter. We believe that this indicates that elders developed different strategies for responding to prompts for information using the two designs, so that they could maintain good driving performance over all designs. Color as a design element, however, did not uniformly improve elders' performance in driving. Designs with color elements-only especially caused larger lane deviations in elder drivers.

DESIGN IMPLICATIONS

Our design implications from this work are fairly straightforward, and generally follow the principles of good information design (*i.e.*, [31]). When designing dashboards to support elder drivers, the following considerations should be made:

Low clutter. Simple, low clutter designs should be used for the whole dashboard. Ample "white space" is needed, particularly between individual features of the dashboard.

Contrast of size. Reserve maximum contrast of size for the center panel, in particular the speedometer, since this feature is what elder drivers reference most often when driving.

Color. Use color for elements plus background fills, rather than for elements only. While the literature describes an increase in driving performance in elder drivers with the use of color, our findings do not uniformly support this work. Our research showed that contrast of size had more of an effect than color in increasing the performance of a design. For elders, designs with color and fill performed about the same as designs with no color. More research is needed to understand how color can help to make a dashboard display more legible in different lighting conditions.

Our future work will expand upon our renditions of high performing designs, placing them in the context of a real dashboard, rather than a lab, to test performance of legibility combined with human factors issues such as gaze distance, posture, and even driver fatigue.

CONCLUSION

No longer being able to drive is a significant marker of loss of independence. In this study, we sought to understand how the instrument panel (IP) display can be designed to help attract and manage attention in elder drivers, resulting in safer driving performance. Our dual-task study revealed which design features helped to increase driving performance and reduce eyes-off-road time. We found that contrast of size and reduced clutter are instrumental in enhancing driving performance for the elder population. Surprisingly, our results showed that color elements have a negative effect on driving performance for elders. By considering the outcomes of our work, combined with technical opportunities of future in-vehicle systems, we expect that better display systems can be designed and deployed that help elder drivers in the future.

ACKNOWLEDGMENTS

This work was generously funded by General Motors, the NSF and Quality of Life Engineering Research Center (EEEC-540865). We also thank Kimberley Nederlof for her assistance with data collection and all of our study participants.

REFERENCES

1. Baldassi, S., & Burr, D. C. "Pop-out" of targets modulated in luminance or colour: the eVect of intrinsic and extrinsic uncertainty. Vision Research, 44 (2004), 1227–1233.
2. Baldwin, C.L. Designing in-vehicle technologies for older drivers: Application of sensory-cognitive interaction theory. Theoretical Issues In Ergonomic Science, 3(4) (2002), 307-329.
3. Ball, K. and Owsley, C. Increasing mobility and reducing accidents of older drivers, in K. W. Schaie and M. Pietrucha (eds), Mobility and Transportation in the Elderly (New York: Springer) (2000), 213-250.
4. Ball, K., Owsley, C., Stalvey, B., Roenker, D.L., Sloane, M.E., & Graves, M. Driving avoidance and functional impairment in older drivers. Accident Analysis and Prevention, 30(3) (1998), 313-322.
5. Beck, J. Textural segmentation. In: Organization and Representation in Perception, Beck J, ed. Hillsdale, NJ: Erlbaum (1982), 285-317.
6. Booher, H.R. Relative comprehensibility of pictorial information and printed words in proceduralized instructions. Human Factors, 17 (1975), 266-277.
7. Campbell, J.L., Richman, J.B., Carney, C. and Lee, J.D. In-vehicle display icons and other information elements: Volume I: Guidelines, Federal Highway Administration, 2004.
8. Carney, C., Campbell, J.L. and Mitchell, E.A. In-vehicle display icons and other information elements: Literature review, Federal Highway Administration, 1998.
9. Christ, R.E. Research for evaluating visual display codes: An emphasis on colour coding. In Easterby, R. and Zwaga, H. eds. Information design: The design and evaluation of signs and printed materials, John Wiley & Sons (1984), 209-228.
10. Collia, D., Sharp, J. and Giesbrecht, L. The 2001 national household travel survey: A look into the travel patterns of older Americans. Journal of Safety Research 34 (2003), 461-470.

11. Connor, C.E., Egeth, H.E. and Yantis, S. Visual attention: Bottom-up vs. top-down. Current Biology, 14 (2004), 850-852.

12. Dingus, T.A., Hulse, M.C., Mollenhauer, M.A., Fleischman, R.N., Mcgehee, D.V. and Manakkal, N. Effects of age, system experience, and navigation technique on driving with and Advanced Traveler Information System, Human Factors, 39 (1997), 177-199

13. Green, P. Visual and Task Demands of Driver Information Systems. The University of Michigan Transportation Research Institute, Technical Report UMTRI-98-16. Ann Arbor, MI, 1998.

14. Hakamies-Blomqvist, L., Siren, A. and Davidse, R. Older drivers - a review. VTI rapport 497A, Swedish National Road and Transport Research Institute, 2004.

15. Ito, T. and Miki, Y. Japan's Safety Guideline on In-Vehicle Display Systems in Proceedings of the Fourth ITS World Congress. VERTIS, 1997.

16. Julesz, B. A brief outline of the textion theory of human vision. Trends in Neuroscience (1984), 41-45.

17. Kim, S. and Dey, A.K. Simulated augmented reality windshield display as a cognitive mapping aid for elder driver navigation. In *Proc. CHI 2009*, 133-142.

18. Kumar, M. and Kim, T. Dynamic speedometer: dashboard redesign to discourage drivers from speeding. *Ext. Abstracts CHI 2005*, 1573-1576.

19. Lee, J., Forlizzi, J., and Hudson, S.E. Studying the effectiveness of MOVE: a contextually optimized in-vehicle navigation system. In *Proc. CHI 2005*, 571-580.

20. Mayer, D. and Laux, L. Evaluating Vehicle Displays for Older Drivers. AAA Foundation for Traffic Safety, 1992.

21. McDougall, S., de Bruijn, O. and Curry, M. Exploring the effects of icon characteristics: Concreteness, complexity and distinctiveness. The J. of Experimental Psychology: Applied, 6(4) (2000), 291-306.

22. McGehee, D. V. New design guidelines aim to reduce driver distraction. Human Factors and Ergonomics Society Bulletin, Vol. 44, No. 10, (2001), 1-3.

23. Monash University Accident Research Centre. (2006). The Elderly and Mobility: A Review of the Literature. Sponsored by Swedish Road Administration (SRA), Report No. 255.

24. Rockwell, T.H. Spare Visual Capacity in Driving - Revisited: New Empirical Results of an Old Idea in Vision in Vehicles II. Amsterdam: Elsevier Science B.V. (North-Holland) (1988), 317-314.

25. Salthouse, T.A., Hancock, H.E., Meinz, E.J. and Hambrick, D.Z. Interrelations of age, visual acuity, and cognitive functioning. J Gerontol Psychol Sci; 51B (1996), 317-330

26. Somervell, J., McCrickard, D.S., North, C. and Shukla, M. An evaluation of information visualization in attention-limited environments. In *Proc. VISSYM 2002*.

27. Suen, S.L. & Sen, L. Mobility Options for Seniors. In Transportation in an Aging Society: A Decade of Experience. Transportation Research Board (2004), 97-113.

28. Treisman, A.M. and Sato, S. Conjunction search revisited. Journal of Experimental Psychology: Human Perception and Performance, 16 (1990), 451–478.

29. Treisman, A. Selection for perception for selection for action: A reply to Van der Heijden. Visual Cognition, 3 (1996), 353-357.

30. Treisman, A. Feature binding, attention and object perception. Philosophical Transactions of the Royal Society, Series B, 353 (1998), 1295-1306.

31. Tufte, E. Envisioning Information. Cheshire, CT: Graphics Press, 1990.

32. University of Michigan Transportation Research Institute. The assessment of older drivers capabilities: A review of the literature. Interim report for the GM/US DOT project entitled: Improvement of Older Driver Safety through Self-Evaluation, Report No. UMTRI-98-24, 1998.

33. VICS Promotion Council, VICS Promotion Council Safety Committee Report on Information Display. (Chapter 2 "Safety" Group). Tokyo, Japan: VICS Promotion Council, 1993.

34. Wierwille, W.W., Antin, J.F., Dingus, T.A., and Hulse, M.C. Visual Attentional Demand of an In-Car Navigation Display System in Vision in Vehicles II. Amsterdam: Elsevier Science B.V. (North-Holland) (1988), 307-316.

35. Wierwille, W.W. Visual and manual demands of in-car controls and displays. In B. Peacock and W.Karwowski (Eds.), Automotive Ergonomics. Taylor & Francis: Washington, D.C. (1993), 299-320.

36. Zwaga, H. and Easterby, R.S. Developing effective symbols for public information. In Easterby, R. & Zwaga, H. (eds.). Information design: The design and evaluation of signs and printed material, J. Wiley & Sons (1984), 277-297.

Synchronous Interaction Among Hundreds: An Evaluation of a Conference in an Avatar-based Virtual Environment

Thomas Erickson, N. Sadat Shami, Wendy A. Kellogg, David W. Levine
IBM T. J. Watson Research Center
P.O. Box 704, Yorktown Heights, NY 10598 USA
{snowfall,sadat,wkellogg,dwl}@us.ibm.com

ABSTRACT
This paper presents the first in-depth evaluation of a large multi-format virtual conference. The conference took place in an avatar-based 3D virtual world with spatialized audio, and had keynote, poster and social sessions. We studied it by drawing on logs, a survey and interviews with 30 participants. We develop a model – Coalescence, Focused Interaction, Remixing (CoFIRe) – of large synchronous interactions, and use it to discuss how the technology supported, or failed to support, the interactions that are the *raison d'etre* of conferences. We conclude by discussing the prospects for such large virtual gatherings.

Author Keywords
CSCW; collaboration, CVE; Second Life; spatialized audio; synchronous interaction; virtual environment; virtual world

ACM Classification Keywords
H5.3. Information Interfaces and Presentation: Group and Organization Interfaces: Synchronous Interaction.

General Terms
Design, Experimentation, Human Factors, Theory

INTRODUCTION
"*It was the first virtual meeting to cross the threshold to being useful!* [...] *But I'd still rather travel 30 hours.*"[FV]

While the exceptionally remote location of this informant was unusual, the ambivalence was not. In this study we describe a 500-person virtual conference, the activity that characterized it, and the experiences – positive and negative – that underlie its participants' ambivalence.

The conference in question came about in response to the worldwide economic downturn that began in 2008. Many organizations, including IBM, placed restrictions on travel. IBM restricted travel not related to client interactions, including the internal workshops, meetings and conferences that normally foster communication among employees. IBM challenged its employees to explore alternatives to face to face (FtF) gatherings. The conference that this paper examines was one of the responses to that challenge.

Large structured gatherings such as conferences and tradeshows are important for two reasons. First, they bring people together to share, discuss and develop knowledge. Second, they enable participants to interact with one another, offering the possibility of forming new relationships and strengthening existing ones. It is well established that fostering relationships among people from different contexts is an important means of enabling the spread of knowledge. As Granovetter says, "... social systems lacking in weak ties will be fragmented and incoherent. New ideas will spread slowly, scientific endeavors will be handicapped, and subgroups separated by race, ethnicity, geography, or other characteristics will have difficulty reaching a *modus vivendi.*" [10, p 202]. In sum, large structured gatherings play an important role in business, education and government by supporting the production and exchange of knowledge, *and* the creation and maintenance of the ties that underlie these processes.

The importance of such gatherings is underscored by their frequency and cost. For example, during 2008, there were over 7,400 international conferences with an average of 638 attendees (about 4.7 million trips) – this includes only annual conferences that rotate among at least 3 countries [13]. Looking only at the US, in 2008 businesses spent about $45 billion on travel to conferences and tradeshows [24]. Broadening the scope to include "business meetings," another source [23] estimates that more than $75 billion is spent annually in the US to attend over a million meetings and conventions. However one slices and dices it, the numbers are large. In addition to the direct costs, travel also has externalized environmental costs such as consumption of non-renewable fuels, and personal costs. So it makes sense to explore the utility of large virtual gatherings.

But how well do such large virtual gatherings actually work? How well do they support not just knowledge exchange but the 'social work' that underlies it? As we shall see, little is known. The aim of this paper is to describe one such gathering, assess how well it worked, and discuss the problems and prospects for such gatherings.

BACKGROUND
We know little about conferences, either online or FtF. Most studies come out of areas like tourism research or the

event management trade press (e.g., [23]). These focus on factors that affect decisions to attend conferences, but say little about how the work of the conference is carried on. An exception is Brecht, who provides a high level view of conference activity [2], but does not address the details of human interaction of interest to those in HCI. Finally, while HCI is exploring ways of augmenting FtF conferences (e.g., [18]), this line of work is informed by first-hand experience and by work on FtF dyadic and small group interaction (e.g., [8, 9, 15]), not by studies of conferences *per se*.

Likewise, virtual conferences have received little attention. Most work is either anecdotal (descriptions of attending conferences, e.g., [22]) – or prospective (proposing ways of augmenting virtual conferences, e.g., [4, 16, 21]). The closest to a rigorous evaluation is Jones' participant/observer account of two conferences held in ActiveWorlds [14]. He offers suggestions for organizing conferences, but notes that they are limited by the personal nature of the research and calls for work using a mix of methods. To the best of our knowledge, this paper is the first to address this call with a mixed method evaluation of a virtual conference.

Moving beyond conferences, there is a considerable amount of work that looks at dyadic and small group interactions in recreational and social virtual worlds (e.g., [3]). Many studies have noted the difficulties of customizing avatars, managing facial, gestural and postural expression, and maintaining mutual orientation (e.g. [11, 19]). Nevertheless, studies – especially recent work on World of Warcraft [1, 6, 20] – also show that virtual worlds can support rich interactions characterized by sophisticated collaboration, and the development of in-world norms, and communities.

How well this applies to large structured virtual gatherings is an open question. As we have noted, there is virtually no research on the interactional nature of conferences. There is also little work on the use of virtual worlds in business contexts (but see [7]). In this paper we address this gap, offering an in-depth study of a large virtual conference.

THE SETTING

IBM and its Academy of Technology

IBM is a global information technology firm with over 300,000 employees. Its businesses range from hardware to software to consulting. IBM places a premium on its ability to be a thought leader, to provide cutting edge technology and services to its clients, and to maintain and tap a vibrant worldwide network of technical leaders.

One manifestation of its emphasis on technical leadership is IBM's Academy of Technology. The Academy is an organization of IBM's technical leaders that has existed for over 20 years. Election to the Academy is viewed as quite prestigious, and new members gain access to a network of technical leaders and executives. Academy members participate in company-wide studies, workshops, and an annual conference, the Academy General Meeting (AGM), that brings members together with senior executives. It is this last activity that is the subject of this study.

The Technology Used for the Virtual Conference

Most of the AGM was held in a version of Second Life® [i] [17]. Second Life is an immersive 3D environment that represents users as avatars. Users control their avatars rather like puppets, using them to move about the virtual world, to communicate with other avatars via textual chat and speech, and to create, modify and interact with virtual objects such as clothing, devices, furniture, etc.

The version of Second Life used supported spatialized audio. Users wore headsets and as they spoke their in-world voices came from the correct direction, and varied in volume according to the distance between speaker and hearer. It also ran independently on servers inside IBM's firewall, making it suitable for confidential discussions, and displayed users' real names from the corporate directory.

Although the focus of this article is on the experience of attendees in Second Life, two other conference venues were deployed: a text-based discussion forum (open for the duration of the conference), and nine plenary talks held in physical locations around the world that were accessible in person, via streaming video, or via teleconference.

The AGM Virtual Conference Center

The setting for the AGM consisted of several spaces: conference halls for the Keynotes (Figure 1); areas for social events (Figure 2), and a posters area (Figure 3). These areas were designed to resemble their real world counterparts. Thus, the conference hall had a podium and

Figure1. A keynote

Figure 2. A social event

Figure 3. A poster session

seating interspersed with aisles, even though neither the podium nor the aisles were needed. Rather, these set the stage, signaling the type of activity and participants' roles. This literal approach was complemented with 'magical' features that supported the intended activity. Thus, upon taking a seat in the conference hall, the user's camera and audio settings were automatically adjusted so that the projected slides filled most of the screen, and ambient audio (except for the speaker) was suppressed. Similarly, the posters area included a "directory wall" that allowed users to browse poster abstracts and teleport to posters of interest. There are many other examples, but as this paper is not about the design of the environment we only provide details where needed to understand the interactions we discuss.

Events During and Prior to the Conference

The conference schedule (Figure 4) was single track for virtual events, with occasional overlaps for FtF plenaries. To accommodate the worldwide time zones, events were distributed throughout the 24-hour days.

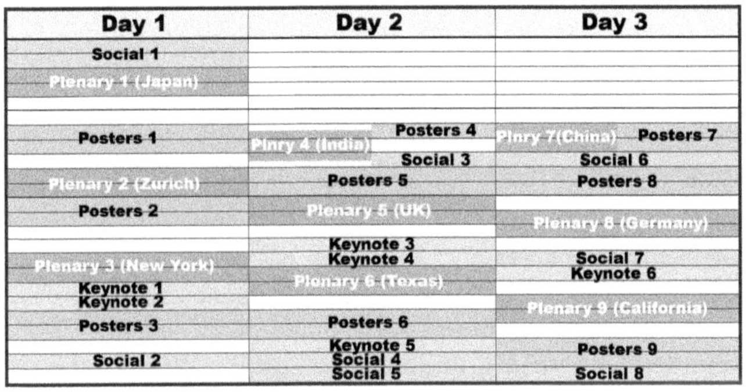

Figure 4. The Conference Schedule

Prior to the conference, 10 "on-boarding sessions" were held to acquaint users with the virtual world: how to move and navigate, customize their avatars, and interact with others (e.g., how to control their audio). While often such training is not widely used, the survey we will discuss later indicated that 73% of attendees reported spending 2 or more hours in preparation. In addition, an online forum for questions and problem reports was accessed by roughly half of those invited. Finally, invitees were sent email (cc'd to their managers) asking them to block out time on the calendaring system for the conference. All of this indicates that the AGM was positioned and received as a legitimate and important corporate event.

METHODS AND DATA

We used quantitative and qualitative methods to study the conference. Attendance was logged allowing determination of the identity and home countries of attendees. Immediately after the close of the conference, a link to an online survey was emailed to all those invited to the AGM.

We iteratively developed the survey by reviewing online discussions of prior virtual meetings held at IBM, and via a pilot study of a conference held in a similar environment by an unrelated group. The final survey consisted of about 40 questions, 25 related to this study (AGM administrators added their own questions), and took approximately 10 minutes to complete. It consisted of a mix of Likert scale and short answer questions. Questions used alternating valances when appropriate; positive forms are used in this paper. Likert responses are pooled into "agree" and "disagree" categories. The survey was distributed the day after the conference ended and was open for a week. It was distributed to the 1095 Academy members and guests (e.g., presenters) who were *invited* to the meeting, but did not necessarily attend it. It received 444 responses (40%), though not everyone responded to every question.

Qualitative data were also collected. Three authors attended the conference as observers, taking field notes and screenshots; one presented a poster. Authors were not involved in the design of the virtual world or the conference. The week after the conference we interviewed 30 informants using a semi-structured protocol. Interviews typically lasted 30 to 45 minutes. All interviews were recorded; most were conducted by two people, one guiding the interview and a second taking notes. Data were analyzed by repeatedly listening to recordings and working over transcripts to extract emergent themes. Names, quotes and images are altered to preserve confidentiality.

FINDINGS

What Happened? The Event Itself

As an event, the conference appears to have been successful. 502 people attended from around the world, most returning for 2 or 3 days (Figure 5). About 350 people attended each day for the first 2 days, with a drop on the third day, perhaps because it had only one Keynote rather than 2 or 3 as on the previous days.

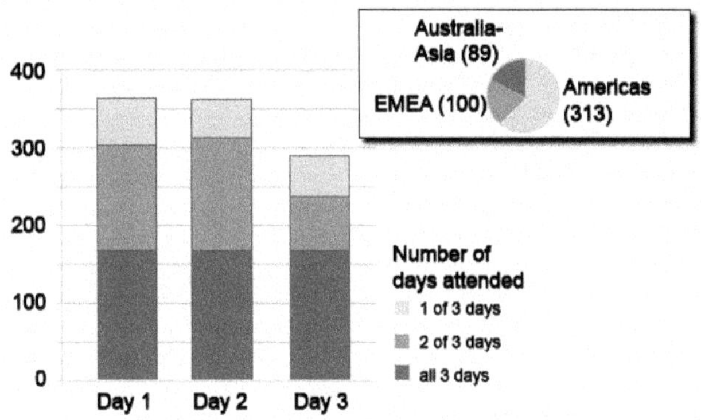

Figure 5. Attendance in Second Life by day and geography

All events we observed had significant attendance, and most participants appeared to use voice (spatialized audio) as their primary communication mode. Keynotes and Socials were well attended and often seemed crowded. Posters were not crowded. There were typically a few dozen people in an area that could accommodate hundreds (only a third of the posters were staffed per session). It was not uncommon to see a presenter standing alone, although there were also always posters with visitors.

How Well Did Things Go? Problems and Perceptions

The Second Life technology did not work flawlessly. Only 20% of the survey respondents reported that they experienced *no* problems. The rest experienced difficulties ranging from audio problems (52%) to server lag and machine crashes (35% and 31%), to difficulties logging on (27%). While a few participants experienced these problems to such a degree that they couldn't effectively participate in the conference, most experienced the problems intermittently or were able to work around them.

Two questions assessed respondents' feelings about the success of the conference as a whole (Table 1).

Questions\Responses	Agree	Disagree	N
Overall, the Virtual AGM was a good experience	66.2% (229)	33.8% (117)	346 of 444
The time invested in installing and using the technologies ... was worthwhile	73.1% (285)	26.9% (105)	390 of 444

Table 1. Success of the AGM in general

Three other questions asked whether particular technologies worked well for their portions of the conference. Of those who responded, 54% (172) agreed that Second Life worked well; larger majorities of 86% (186) and 81% (191) felt the text-based forum and the video broadcasts worked well. Finally, the survey asked about the interactions in which they engaged (Table 2). Majorities said they 'bumped into' acquaintances, had informal small group conversations, and spoke to strangers. 40% reported meeting at least one new person with whom they expected to maintain contact.

Question	Agree	Disagree	N
I unexpectedly encountered at least one acquaintance	59.4% (167)	40.6% (114)	281 of 444
I got into at least one informal conversation with a small group	64.7% (189)	35.3% (103)	292 of 444
I got into conversations with strangers	52.4% (155)	47.6% (141)	296 of 444
I met at least one new person that I expect to maintain connections with afterwards	40.0% (118)	60.0% (177)	295 of 444

Table 2. In-conference interactions

Experiencing the Conference

While it is interesting to see that a large scale virtual conference actually worked, so far this account leaves many questions unanswered. How did it work? What worked well? What was cumbersome? What did not work? To answer these questions we will look both at the fine-grained detail – how participants accomplished their interactions – and at the circumstances in which their participation was situated. We do this by drawing on interviews with 30 informants to assemble a richer picture of the AGM.

It is challenging to present qualitative data gleaned from interviews with many informants; the risk is that the reader will be overwhelmed by a multitude of details that form a fragmented picture of what transpired. To counter this, the qualitative data will be interleaved with a series of imagined accounts of users' experiences that present an accurate and coherent sense of what we observed. We emphasize that the details in the accounts are all real, drawn from the experiences of informants; what is fictional is the attribution of multiple details to a single user, and the narrative in which those details are embedded.

Experiencing the Conference: Avatars

Joost materialized in the Conference Center, surrounded by other avatars. To his surprise a few had quite outré appearances. But most hadn't spent much time on their appearance and looked eerily similar. He'd tried to make his avatar look like himself – but the settings seemed designed to make you look young and buffed, not 50, balding and a bit portly. So he'd settled for young and fit, with hair, and made sure that he looked business-like but distinctive. Now he was off to the conference, first walking and then flying. The system's performance was great, but that was thanks to his assistant who had upgraded his machine after problems during the on-boarding session.

Informants generally agreed that they couldn't recognize others by their avatars. This was not seen as a problem because avatars had their users' real names floating over them, something informants found *very* useful. They reported recognizing the names of people they'd been on conference calls with, and looking up names in IBM's online directory to find out more about them.

Informants' efforts to customize their avatars ranged from none to hours spent on the task. One said that "*after a while it was just a sea of people who amazingly looked like they all came from the same family.*"[IZ] Those who customized reported several motives. Some simply wanted to avoid appearing as the default avatar. Others, especially first timers, were interested in presenting an appearance that was appropriate: "*I just prefer to be in formal dress ... I think it's just making the person more approachable. Today if I go into an environment like this and someone has blue hair, I don't think someone will go up to them as easily as if they are just standing around in a suit.*"[OQ] Another said: "*I did go so far to get a business suit, etc. I tried to look like I would in a real business environment. And that was funny because a lot of people were in shorts and stuff; and that was kind of fun, but for me as a first-time attendee, it was important to look more professional.*"[DR]

A smaller number were interested in projecting a more individual identity. "*My avatar has blue hair and sparkly boots. ... I wouldn't say it's not professional – it looks different and unique. That's the kind of look I was going for.*"[QE] Yet at other times it can be important to portray one's membership in certain classes. The same informant said that as a female <ethnic> scientist involved in outreach activities, there were times – for example, speaking to groups in the <ethnic> community – that she would want to look <ethnic>. *"Sometimes you want to know how many women are here? How many <ethnics> are around here? That is hard to do in Second Life... and it's important to do if you are trying to encourage broader representation."* [QE]

Users reported trying to make their avatars look like themselves, with little success. One said, *"It seems like the avatars are aimed at somebody who is using virtual life as a game or escape, not for business. So they make everyone young or good-looking. And every feature that doesn't ... is hard to get."*[IV] Informants felt this was important because, *"You wanna see how the person looks in real life so in the future if you get a chance to go to that particular site, you know how the person looks like and it feels a little more real."*[BR] This holds true in reverse as well: *"Someone came by to my poster and I sort of recognized the name. The avatar looked very young and had sandy blonde hair and was very casual ... Later when I looked them up in <the directory>, it was like a General Manager, who was 40 years older than the avatar looked!"*[DR]

In summary, the role of the AGM in promoting connections among employees had effects on avatar customization. Many were interested in being "appropriate," either out of concern for making a good impression or being approachable. Most interesting was the desire of some for a stronger link between virtual and real appearance, reasons ranging from being identifiable in the real world to the expression of gender and ethnic identity.

Experiencing the Conference: Keynotes

Sue's first event was a keynote. Others had happened, but they were during the wee hours of the morning Toronto time, so she'd passed. Then, since she was in her office, she'd been dragged into an 'emergency' meeting with a client. Now, finally, she was in the conference hall. She pointed at a seat and issued the "Sit down" command: this sat her avatar in the chair and adjusted her settings so that the slides filled her view and the speaker's voice came through clearly. But the experience was not perfect: there was lag, with slides taking a while to fill in; worse was that sometimes an avatar would teleport onto the stage next to the speaker, and blunder around before figuring out where it was. Very distracting! Streaming video might be better! Still, there was a text window where people were chatting, and she could look around and read the name bubbles of who was there. Why, there was Tian whom she hadn't seen in ages! It was nice to feel like she was part of a group.

Many informants felt that the Keynotes were not worth the overhead, and that video streaming would have been better. They cited problems with lag, slide resolution, and sound (in line with the survey findings). Several noted (and we observed) that avatars would inadvertently teleport onto the stage during a presentation. And one informant remarked: *"You know how you see people on the stage doing dumb stuff? It's a little different when* ***your*** *name is on it!"*[UA]

A few liked having Keynotes in the virtual world. Some liked recognizing friends in the audience, or enjoyed the opportunity to converse in the chat channel. Most interestingly, some said they liked the feeling of being with others, in a way that video and web conferences didn't support: *"It's more participatory than a telephone conference call plus slides. I think some of it is you know you can if you want to look around, you can see other people in the virtual hall"*[IZC] Another remarked on a feeling of camaraderie: *"What was delightful was the number of people that showed up. ... It made it feel worthwhile that I stayed up until 1 in the morning."*[FV]

Experiencing the Conference: Social Events

It was evening in Bangalore, and Ramesh was logged in from home. His daughter had demanded a bedtime story, and he couldn't convince her that he was really "at" a conference – obviously, he was at home. But now she was asleep, and he was at the conference – lost! But he could cope: he'd IM'ed a colleague and she'd teleported him into the Social with her. This was his second Social. The first was conveniently at 8:30am his time, but few Europeans or North Americans had come at what were very late or early hours for them – the lazy bums. So to talk to the rest of the world ***he*** *was the one who would have to stay up late: That's life in a 'global' corporation – hah! At least* ***this*** *Social was going well. The host had everyone in a circle, introducing themselves one by one. It was rather organized for a Social, but it was working: he'd already made note of two people to contact later. In contrast, the other Social had been awkward. People had formed small groups, but it was hard to tell whether you were welcome to join. In real conferences people noticed as you approached, and smiled and made room. But in the virtual world people often didn't notice – peripheral vision wasn't as good. Instead, he'd approached a group unnoticed and ended up feeling like an eavesdropper when he'd overheard a private discussion.*

Our impression from observations and interviews is that not as many people attended the Socials as the other venues – as one person said, *"getting a virtual glass of wine isn't as attractive as a real glass of wine!"*[IV] But because those attending could cluster together (unlike the spatially distributed posters), the Socials felt busier. Some liked this: *"Part of the reason this was easy is that everyone was moving around with the same expectation* [of meeting people]*"*[ZI] And: *"It was just nice, like being in a café ... there were cups and you could take one, and there were people flying over. It just felt very comfortable, and like the poster session it was a good way to meet people."*[DR]

Most had more mixed reactions; several mentioned a highly structured Social that contrasted with the more informally organized Socials. *"The first Social worked better, I thought. Because it was an organized Social, if that makes any sense.* [The host] h*ad people introduce themselves and make comments – but it was a one-conversation Social. The other Social was more relaxed, but you couldn't really do one of those without running into other conversations that are going on.*"[IZ] Another said "*The first one was really good. Everyone was together. There was a common discussion... Everyone got introduced. I think that was fine. .... The second meeting was split up more quicker. I didn't get a sense of common things...* [small groups] *walked off in different areas to have private discussions.*"[ONK] Others echoed these sentiments, although one informant felt that the structured Social was "stupid" and "very artificial" and that while such organization would be "*fine for a group of ten people, it's not so great in a group of 25 people.*"[LT]

There are two underlying issues here. One has to do with group privacy. In general, voices carried much farther than people expected, and this led both to instances of inadvertent eavesdropping, and (once the 'loudness problem' was recognized) a concern that one's conversation would be overheard or would interrupt others. The conference setting did include "voice isolated areas," but most attendees weren't aware of them. Instead, some reported that they were reluctant to talk: "*There were times when I could have talked and didn't because I would have interrupted three other conversations that were going on quite a ways away from me.*"[IZ] Others compensated by moving their talks away from the main group: "*What I saw was people like* [C]. *He'd take someone and walk way up one of those ramps going to nowhere until* [he could have a private conversation]. *And that meant the Social wasn't working very well. You should be able to talk to this person and take a few steps and talk to that person, and not feel like you were broadcasting to a hundred people.*"[IZ]

The second issue had to do with the difficulty in knowing whether it was OK to join a group already engaged in conversation. "*In Second Life it becomes really strange to try to get into those discussion groups. It doesn't feel natural at all. It is hard to understand whether they've gone to the side because they don't want to disturb, or if they want to have a private discussion.*"[ONK] This is exacerbated because the cues used to assess if it's OK to join a group in real life are absent: "*I am missing all of this nonverbal communication forms: seeing someone, making sure they look back* [before I] *go and talk to this person.*" [ONK]

Although the Socials worked, they worked best when they were organized to support a single structured conversation. This avoids the privacy and joining-a-group difficulties, but some felt that these interactions were artificial or unnatural. Attempts to maintain group privacy by moving off succeeded, but tended to fragment the Social and undermine the spontaneous mixing that was one of its aims.

Experiencing the Conference: Poster Sessions

At first Tian had spent time in the poster directory area, where she'd browse the wall of poster abstracts and teleport to whatever interested her. But now she'd changed her approach, and she was strolling down the boulevard between the lines of posters. Sometimes she'd see a crowd and be drawn over out of curiosity; other times, she'd see a poster with only the presenter there, and go over because she felt sorry for the person. She'd presented a poster in another session, and knew how it felt. But she'd had some good chats at her poster and made some good contacts. She'd even talked to a VP! Unfortunately, she hadn't recognized him. His name had rung a bell, but she couldn't place it; later she looked him up in the corporate directory and immediately recognized him from his picture: his real life appearance – middle-aged, portly and balding – was not hinted at by his young, well-muscled avatar. Humph!

To our surprise, given that poster sessions never appeared crowded, our informants repeatedly told us that the posters were the most successful aspect of the virtual conference. "*I seriously almost felt like I was there – it was amazing. I've done a lot of posters in real life, and you almost got that same feeling because you could see people walking by. When I first got there, someone I knew flew down to say hello and it was just so cool bumping into them. And then when I gave my poster, I could see people walking by, and you got the same feeling: are they gonna stop to see it, are they going to come in? It was great because I met some people that I know in RL, and that was nice. I met some people that I've only met on the phone, and it felt like really meeting them, almost. And then some people who I never met before, but only knew their name. It was really great! It felt like I had really networked with them. So in the end, I was very pleased with how it worked and how I really felt, and on that first day when I had spent so many hours in it, I felt that I had been away – on a trip.*" [DR] Another said: "*I was very surprised that I actually found it useful. I did have interactions with people... Some of my friends came by, and I engaged in technical conversations while we were reading and exchanging information about certain posters. All in all it was a positive experience and it worked much better than I anticipated... I really didn't believe it was going to work, but I think it did!*" [BF]

While some teleported directly to posters of interest, many also reported more conventional forms of navigation: "*I went to* [DR]*'s poster session not because I looked at the schedule and decided to go; but because I was in the space and saw that the poster was by* [DR]. *So then I went over; and that stimulated the thought that I should share the benchmarking stuff with her. So that was all accidental. It mirrored a face to face type of meeting.*"[AB] A number of others reported being attracted to a poster because it had a crowd (i.e., social navigation [5]): "*And in one case I went in because there were several people there; so it kind of had the appeal of "oh, well, he's already talking to those people, even if it's something I'm not smart enough to ask questions about, I'll go and hear what he's saying to them.*"[AC] Or because they saw someone they knew at the poster: "*If I saw a person I knew who was looking at a poster, that was a natural magnet to see because I knew who this person was and what their interests were. Seeing who was attending which poster was helpful in guiding me in what I might be interested in as well.*"[BF]

The overhearing and other problems discussed in the case of the Socials tended not to occur in Posters. In part this was because the posters area was much larger and so participants were more spread out; and in part it was because the posters area was designed so poster booths were sonically isolated. That is, people walking through the posters area could see who was present, but could not hear conversations in the booths. Conversely, those in a booth could talk among themselves, but did not overhear or interrupt conversations in neighboring booths. This aspect of the design may be why Posters seemed better suited to spontaneous socializing than the Socials.

DISCUSSION

We've established that the virtual conference was fairly successful. Perhaps the most convincing metric is that of the 300-350 people who came each day, majorities returned for a second and sometimes even a third day (Figure 5). Furthermore, each event had active participation, and majorities of survey respondents agreed that the virtual AGM was "a good experience," and that Second Life "worked well." Given that 80% of the survey respondents experienced some sort of technical difficulty, we can take "worked well" as referring to supporting the aims of the conference, rather than delivering a flawless technical experience. Here majorities of survey respondents reported bumping into acquaintances, getting into small group conversations, and talking with strangers, just the sort of interactions one would hope that a conference would afford.

While it is interesting to establish that a virtual world *can* support a professionally-oriented synchronous gathering of hundreds of people, it is more interesting to understand *how* it does so, and what is effective and what is less so. Informants consistently reported that Posters were the most successful, providing a remarkably parallel enactment of FtF poster sessions and supporting the casual encounters and talk that are a core aspect of conferences. Those attending Socials reported enjoying them, although paradoxically the most-liked Social was highly structured. The more informal socials were marred by two factors: sound that carried too far, and the difficulty of knowing when it was OK to join a new group. Keynotes were least successful, with many believing that streaming video would have been more effective, although a minority enjoyed being in the audience and looking around, seeing who else was there, and engaging in textual side chat.

Interaction Among Hundreds: CoFIRe

While this paper's title refers to "Synchronous Interaction Among Hundreds," that should be qualified. While hundreds can interact simultaneously – think of an audience doing a standing ovation, or a large group doing a line dance – it is *not* the case that such large scale interaction is rich in interpersonal communications. Hundreds simply can't talk with one another simultaneously. Instead, the prospect that large gatherings offer is that one person will be brought into proximity with many others in a setting that allows some of the brief contacts to morph into interactions.

Remarkably, little work investigates the mechanics of such large scale interaction. To the best of our knowledge, only Goffman [8] looks at what he calls multi-focused gatherings (multiple small group interactions within larger unfocused gatherings), and his focus has been on the individual small groups, rather than on the interaction as a whole.

To frame our discussion we propose a model of large scale social interaction that begins with Goffman's observations, but takes a perspective that embraces the large scale interaction of multiple groups. Beginning with a large unfocused gathering, three things must happen to support productive large scale social interaction:

- **Coalescence**. First, interactants in a large gathering need to coalesce into small groups to enable coherent conversation. This includes both the formation of a group *ex nihilo*, and its growth as others join it.
- **Focused Interaction**. Second, a group needs to initiate and manage its focused interaction. In addition to the usual issues attending the conduct of talk [8, 9, 15], as Goffman has noted, small groups embedded in large gatherings face special challenges such as needing to "shield" their interactions from the gathering, while also managing the degree to which their interaction "drifts" from the settings' norms. [8, pp 151-190].
- **Remixing**. Third, as time goes on, groups must change their make up over time – a group dissolving *en mass*, or individuals joining and leaving it – to maximize the possible interactions. Only through this remixing can the promise of large scale interaction be realized.

Let's briefly reexamine the AGM in light of CoFIRe. While informants generally expressed satisfaction (if not unmarred by complaints) with both Posters and Socials, it is notable that the Socials did not work in the way they ought to. The Social that participants spoke most favorably of was the 'structured' social. It worked because the host transformed it into a round-the-table, "one-conversation" at a time event. In the less structured Socials, while participants formed small groups, the interaction broke down at that point. Because sound carried too far, the ability of the groups to manage their conversation was disrupted. While some groups moved away from the gathering to preserve group privacy, the increased inter-group distance inhibited remixing. Furthermore, as many reported, it was difficult to join an existing group. For people in an existing group, the restricted peripheral vision characteristic of virtual worlds meant it was difficult to notice someone on the periphery. Even if an outsider was noticed, it was cumbersome to produce the social cues – eye contact, nodding, smiling – that indicate welcome. And for the outsider, there was often a reluctance to approach closely enough to be noticed, for fear of intruding on a private conversation. In sum, problems with sound and difficulty with producing cues disrupted the social mechanisms that supported CoFIRe; the only social that 'worked,' was the one without CoFIRe.

Another example of inhibition of coalescence and remixing had to do with co-navigation. Two informants noted that at FtF gatherings, one thing that would happen is that they would encounter a more senior colleague, and end up walking around the conference together, with the senior colleague introducing the junior to new contacts. "*The one thing I miss most, being a new academy member, is that walking around with someone that I've known from before who is an old time academy member, and using that contact to get to know new people.*"[ONK] This didn't happen at the AGM because it is cumbersome for two people to walk around together: the subtle cues that enable people to co-navigate in real time are missing.

In contrast to the Socials, the Posters worked more like their real world counterparts. It is significant that Posters offer structural support for each stage of CoFIRe. A poster provides a concrete nucleus for a group to coalesce around. The poster also provides a focus for interaction, and a set of mutually understood roles – presenter and audience, and at the same time supports private group interaction by spatial separation and built-in sonic isolation for each poster booth. Finally, the posters area supports remixing by making it possible for newcomers to see (but not hear) nearby interactions, and to see who is in each group (taking advantage of participants' floating name bubbles). Remixing is also facilitated by the norm that poster presentations are public conversations. In sum, Posters largely avoided the problems that disrupted CoFIRe in the Socials, through the presence of structural features (sonic isolation; poster booths), and associated social norms.

Why Its Called "Second" Life

In the movie *Avatar*, the protagonist's mind is projected into an embodied avatar, enabling him to inhabit an alien world while his real body lies unconscious in a glass coffin. Unfortunately, those in Second Life have left behind real bodies that are neither unconscious nor sealed away.

As illustrated in the vignettes, that may mean that they are in their offices, at clients' sites, or at home. While a few were able to block their calendars and close their doors, the vast majority were visible and accessible. And sitting at their desks, typing on their computers and talking into headsets, they looked – to their colleagues and their families – just like they looked on every other day. Even if their managers agreed and their calendars were blocked, interruptions still happened. "*If I'm going out of town it's easy for me to say 'hey, I'm going out of town so I can't handle this client coming into my center and having a meeting.' It's expected if you're in town and in your office, that you don't prioritize an Academy meeting over a client.*"[QE] The same is true in the personal sphere: "*I only have a few times that I can rely on other people to, say, take my son to his piano lessons. If I were going away, I would bend over backward to get a neighbor to take him or cancel the lesson or something. But I didn't feel it was warranted here; I want to save those things.*" [DR]

These issues arise on a smaller scale too. Almost every informant admitted to multitasking while in the AGM. Some appreciated it as a benefit, and noted that they would do the same at FtF conferences. But most were ambivalent about multitasking: "*I think multitasking is necessary from time to time; it's not clear that you give your best to any of the activities that you do. ... The older I get the more I think multitasking is a bad practice; I think it trains you to have ADD; I think it's a societal issue, not the technology.*"[DR]

An interesting side effect of this was that people didn't hang out between sessions. As one said, "*When there was time between events I was here at work and so I'd get back to doing my normal day job.*"[QE] Thus, whereas in FtF conferences the best time for interaction is *between* events, in the virtual conference, that's precisely when many vanished (or at least abandoned their avatars). Similarly, the evenings – an important period for socializing during FtF conferences – did not function in the same way: "*Even in the evening... when you're here* [at the virtual conference] *I expect everyone goes home at night and puts their laptop away and that's the end of it. At* [a former, FtF AGM] *there's stuff all night, you're socializing with people and that's part of the whole meeting.*"[IV]

Indeed, several informants said that an advantage of FtF conferences was the spatial segregation from day to day life that it required. Besides the spatial segregation, which took you out of view of your colleagues, for those who had to travel long distances there was also a temporal segregation that lowered the likelihood of interruptions from work or family life: "*It is easier to block your time, it is easier to get wide acceptance that you are away on a conference when you go. Especially for us in Europe when we go to the U.S. So we're off the time zones. It is easier for us to be really isolated and work dedicated on the conference.*" [ONK].

CONCLUSION

The virtual AGM was reasonably successful. Hundreds of people came each day, and large majorities returned for one or two more days. Majorities were positive about the value of the conference and the virtual world technology, and majorities reported engaging in the sorts of social interactions a large gathering should afford.

In examining the conference venues, we found varying levels of success. The Posters, to our surprise, and to that of many of our informants, worked well, often feeling similar to 'real' poster sessions. Participants also said positive things about the Socials, but they worked best when they were least like a canonical, informal social. In the case of Socials, structure compensated for features of the virtual environment that disrupted the coalescence, focused interaction and remixing of small groups that characterizes large scale social interaction. Keynotes were least successful, although a few liked the feeling of being part of the audience, and the possibilities for peripheral and backchannel interaction it enabled.

However, while the explicitly designed AGM venues were generally successful, two entwined issues detracted from the overall atmosphere of the conference: the lack of interstitial periods, and the demands of "first life." First, unlike a FtF conference schedule, events in the AGM often immediately followed one another, for the obvious reason that time is not needed to support physical movement from one place to another, or for coffee breaks or snacks. Even when there was interstitial time, attendees would often 'step out' of the conference due to the second issue: the demands of 'first life'. Because of the demands of 'first life', and the fact that participants are not segregated from their family, friends and co-workers, virtual AGM attendees tended to vanish during gaps in the program to attend to business during the work day, and often preferred to spend non-work hours with family and friends. Overall, while the explicitly designed conference venues were successful in supporting many of the functions of a FtF conference, the lack of interstitial periods – which in FtF conferences afford communication and relationship building – was a clear shortcoming.

Having argued that the AGM was successful, we need to acknowledge some limitations on that claim. First, respondents tended to be those who actually participated in the conference. Although 54% of those invited did *not* attend, only 12% of the respondents were in that category. While this means that the survey provides a relatively high resolution picture of those who attended, it offers little insight on those who chose not to attend. Second, the population of IBM's Academy of Technology is not an ordinary one. Individuals are chosen, in part, for their technical acumen. The bottom line is that these results cannot be taken as an indication of how successful the technology would be for a general population. What the study *can* tell us is that under some conditions – for example, given a technically adept, motivated population – a large virtual conference can be successful.

One other issue deserves discussion here. Throughout the paper we have compared the virtual conference to its FtF counterparts. As many have argued (e.g., [12]), online interactions develop their own internal rationales and characteristics, and using their real world counterparts as a basis for a comparison may be a mistake. We agree, but in this particular instance we believe our approach is appropriate for two reasons. First, the virtual AGM that we studied was in fact a replacement for what had been a long tradition of FtF conferences. This was well known by our informants, and most made explicit and unsolicited comparisons between virtual and FtF conferences. Any account that reflects what our informants told us must necessarily take up the relationship between the virtual conference and its real counterpart. Moreover, the design of the conference setting mirrored many of the structural features of FtF conferences, even where unnecessary. Second, the majority of our informants were not "fluent" in Second Life, or in large virtual conferences. While online interactions do develop their own logics and structures, it takes time for this to happen, especially in events that involve so many participants. We believe, for this case, that it is premature to look for new interaction forms that have emerged to suit the characteristics of this new medium: virtual conferences are just beginning their evolution.

Prospects for Large Virtual Gatherings

While we characterize the virtual AGM as a success, it is important to recognize, as noted in our opening quote, that it was not an unqualified success. Not a single one of our informants felt that it was as good as being there. They viewed the AGM as a substitute for what had formerly been a FtF event.

While our informants recognized and generally accepted the reasons for this, they also were concerned about the longer range effects. "*I understand it's a huge expense bringing all these people together. But I wonder about the long-term ramifications of not having people meet face to face; I just wonder if that's going to pay off for us over the next ten years.*"[AB] A repeated theme was that while they met people at the virtual AGM, it was harder to really connect. "*I may have a name jotted down from someone I ran across in a poster session, but that's different from meeting and talking to them FtF.*"[QE]. And "*What I find is that if I can meet people once in RL, then I can get that to carry on for many years. Because I'll talk to them and network and sort of cement the relationship. So it's hard, because I feel like I didn't get the chance to do that and it'd be nice to have a FtF to meet a lot of these people just once. And then maybe year after year, it would work remotely. So maybe the solution is to find a way to do a FtF every 3 or 4 years.*"[DR] Others were less sanguine: "*At the end of the day the company's got to bite the bullet, you know? You can't build a culture virtually. You can't do it.*"[OV]

There is, obviously, no final answer here. Having begun this evaluation with skepticism about how effectively a virtual world could support a large conference, we find ourselves surprised. Clearly some aspects of the virtual world support the fluid interactions that are important to gatherings of this sort, whereas others fall short. It seems to us that some of the shortfalls – the difficulties with sound, the cumbersome nature of some interactions – can be ameliorated. Furthermore, careful design of event and environmental structures to facilitate CoFIRe may be able to compensate for disrupted or inhibited social mechanisms. For example, an artifact that produced a translucent cone of silence might address some of the problems of Socials, or a minimalist vehicle might enable dyads to effectively co-navigate and thus better support introductions.

On the other hand, some issues seem less tractable. Providing user interfaces that enable avatars to give (and give off) the social cues that underlie much of our interaction is a difficult problem. And so, at a more practical level, is the tension between first and second life, and the ensuing scarcity of opportunities for unstructured social interactions that create and reinforce social ties. Whether a virtual world can, on its own, sustain a vibrant culture over the long term is very much an open question.

NOTES

[i] Second Life is a trademark of Linden Research, Inc.

ACKNOWLEDGMENTS

Thanks to Chuck Goodwin, Christine Halverson, Pam Hinds, Bonnie Nardi and John Tang for literature help, and to our anonymous reviewers for useful comments. Thanks to the IBM CIO's office for funding portions of this work, and to the Academy for supporting our access to the AGM.

REFERENCES

1. Bardzell, S., Bardzell, J., Pace, T., and Reed, K. 2008. Blissfully productive: grouping and cooperation in world of warcraft instance runs. *Proc. CSCW 2008*, ACM Press (2008), 357-360.
2. Brecht, M. A. Study of Meeting and Conference Behavior. PhD Thesis, John Hopkins University, 1980.
3. Churchill, E. F., Snowdon, D. N. and Munro, A. J. (eds). *Collaborative Virtual Environments*, Springer, 2001.
4. De Lucia, A., Francese, R., Passero, I., and Tortora, G. SLMeeting: Supporting collaborative work in Second Life. *Proc. Advanced Visual interfaces*, ACM Press (2008), 301-304.
5. Dourish, P. and Chalmers, M. 1994. Running out of space: Models of information navigation. Short paper presented at *HCI'94* (Glasgow, UK).
6. Ducheneaut, N. and Moore, R. J. 2004. The social side of gaming: a study of interaction patterns in a massively multiplayer online game. *Proc. CSCW* 2004, ACM (2004), 360-369.
7. Ellis, J. B., Luther, K., Bessiere, K., and Kellogg, W. A. Games for virtual team building. *Proc. DIS* 2008, ACM Press (2008), 295-304.
8. Goffman E. *Behavior in Public Places: Notes on the Social Organization of Gatherings*. Doubleday Macmillan, New York, 1963.
9. Goodwin, C. *Conversational Organization: Interaction between Speakers and Hearers*. Academic Press, New York, 1981.
10. Granovetter, M. S. (1983) The strength of weak ties: a network theory revisited. *Sociological Theory 1* (1983), 201–233
11. Hindmarsh, J., Fraser, M., Heath, C., Benford, S. and Greenhalgh, C. Fragmented interaction: Establishing mutual orientation in virtual environments. *Proc. CSCW 1998*, ACM Press (1998), 217-226.
12. Hollan, J. and Stornetta, S. Beyond being there. In *Proc. CHI 1992*, ACM Press (1992), 119-125.
13. International Congress and Convention Association. Statistics Report: The International Association Meetings Market: Abstract for non-members. 2008.
14. Jones, M. L. 2000. Collaborative virtual conferences: Using exemplars to shape future research questions. *Proc. CVE 2000,* ACM Press (2000), 19-27.
15. Kendon, A. *Conducting Interaction: Patterns of Behavior in Focused Encounters*. Cambridge University Press, Cambridge, MA, 1990.
16. Lee, S. J., Fox, E. A., Marchionini, G., Velacso, J., Antunes, G., and Borbinha, J. Virtual DL poster sessions in second life. *Proc. 9th ACM/IEEE-CS Joint Conf. on Digital Libraries*, ACM Press (2009), 473-474.
17. Linden Labs, Inc. www.secondlife.com
18. McDonald, D.W., McCarthy, J.F., Soroczak, S., Nguyen, D.H., and Rashid, A.M. Proactive displays: Supporting awareness in fluid social environments. *ACM Trans. Comput.-Hum. Interact. 14*, 4 (2008), 1-31.
19. Moore, R.J., Ducheneaut, N. and Nickell, E. Doing virtually nothing: Awareness and accountability in massively multiplayer online worlds. *J Computer Supported Cooperative Work, 16*, 3 (2007) 265-305.
20. Nardi, B. and Harris, J. 2006. Strangers and friends: collaborative play in world of warcraft. *Proc. CSCW 2006*, ACM Press (2006), 149-158.
21. Shami, N.S., Cheng, L.-T., Rohall, S., Sempere, A. and Patterson, J. Avatars meet meetings: Design issues in integrating avatars in distributed corporate meetings. In *Proc. GROUP 2010*, ACM Press (2010), 35-44.
22. Teigland, R. Born virtuals and avapreneurship: A case study of achieving successful outcomes in Peace Train – a Second Life organization. *J. of Virtual Worlds Research, 2,* 4 (2010), 1-24.
23. Oppermann, M. and Chon, K. Convention participation decision-making process. *Annals of Tourism Research, 24,* 1 (1997), 178-191.
24. Oxford Economics USA. The return on investment of US business travel. September, 2009. Retrieved from http://www.ustravel.org/sites/default/files/09-10-09_Oxford%20Economics.pdf on January 13, 2011.

What did I miss? In-Meeting Review using Multimodal Accelerated Instant Replay (AIR) Conferencing

Sasa Junuzovic[1], Kori Inkpen[1], Rajesh Hegde[2], Zhengyou Zhang[2], John Tang[1], and Christopher Brooks[3]

Connect[1] and CCS[2] Groups
Microsoft Research, Redmond, WA
{sasajun, kori, rajeshh, zhang, johntang}@microsoft.com

Department of Computer Science[3]
University of Saskatchewan, Saskatoon, SK
cab938@mail.usask.ca

ABSTRACT

People sometimes miss small parts of meetings and need to quickly catch up without disrupting the rest of the meeting. We developed an Accelerated Instant Replay (AIR) Conferencing system for videoconferencing that enables users to catch up on missed content while the meeting is ongoing. AIR can replay parts of the conference using four different modalities: audio, video, conversation transcript, and shared workspace. We performed two studies to evaluate the system. The first study explored the benefit of AIR catch-up during a live meeting. The results showed that when the full videoconference was reviewed (i.e., all four modalities) at an accelerated rate, users were able to correctly recall a similar amount of information as when listening live. To better understand the benefit of full review, a follow-up study more closely examined the benefits of each of the individual modalities. The results show that users (a) preferred using audio along with any other modality to using audio alone, (b) were most confident and performed best when audio was reviewed with all other modalities, (c) compared to audio-only, had better recall of facts and explanations when reviewing audio together with the shared workspace and transcript modalities, respectively, and (d) performed similarly with audio-only and audio with video review.

Author Keywords

Telepresence, videoconferencing, CSCW, meetings, DVR, review, audio, video, shared workspace, transcript.

ACM Classification Keywords

H.5.1. Multimedia Information Systems; H.5.2. User Interfaces; H.5.3. Group and Organization Interfaces.

General Terms

Experimentation, human factors.

INTRODUCTION

Many people participate in meetings as part of their daily work. They often miss parts of meetings because of interruptions, distractions, or multitasking [7]. As a result, they may need to review the material they missed. The majority of the previous work in the area of meeting review has focused on *post-meeting review* [2,9,12]. Post-meeting review is beneficial when the missed segments are not critical for the rest of the discussion and can be reviewed after the meeting has finished. However, in other cases, the missed content provides necessary context for rest of the discussion, and participants would benefit from being able to review it during the meeting. In our work, we focus on enabling users to review during the meeting, which we refer to as *in-meeting review*. Since asking others about missed content can be disruptive, we investigated mechanisms that enable participants to privately catch up. Our initial focus is on providing in-meeting review for fully-distributed videoconference meetings. Additionally, our focus is on scenarios in which participants miss small portions (e.g., a minute or two) of the meeting.

A key requirement for in-meeting review is that it should enable users to review past content without missing new content being generated in the live discussion. One approach is to present only past information during review periods but present it in such a way that users can catch up to the live discussion. Recent work by Tucker et al. [14] demonstrated the benefits an audio-gisting technique which provides a compressed version of the missed audio. Their results showed that users understood the meeting better and were more confident in their understanding when they were able to review the missed content using audio-gisting.

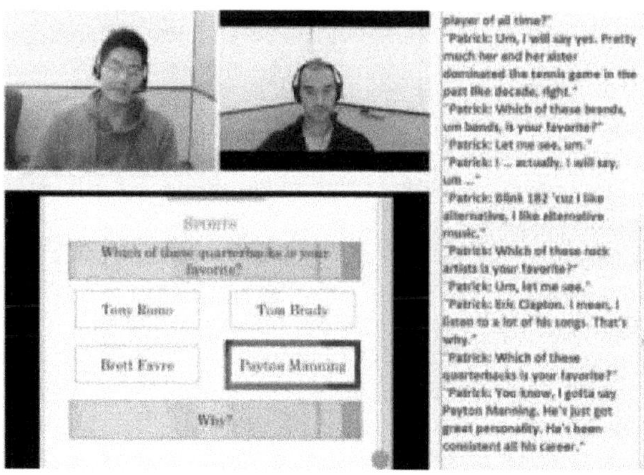

Figure 1. The AIR Conferencing window

Our work investigates the potential of accelerated *multimodal* review for in-meeting scenarios. We built a new system that enables users to review content in real-time during an ongoing meeting called Accelerated Instant Replay (AIR) Conferencing [5], shown in Figure 1. AIR incorporates DVR-like features, including pause, rewind, and accelerated review, to support several catch-up modalities including audio, video, shared workspace actions, and conversation transcript. We evaluated the benefit of AIR through two user studies. The first study explored the benefits of AIR catch-up during a live meeting. The results showed that when reviewing the full videoconference (i.e., all four modalities) at an accelerated rate, users were able to correctly recall a similar amount of information as when listening live. To better understand the benefit of full review, a follow up study more closely examined the benefits of each of the individual modalities. The results show that users (a) preferred using audio along with any other modality to using audio alone (b) were most confident and performed best when audio was reviewed with all other modalities, (c) compared to audio-only, had better recall of facts and explanations when reviewing audio together with the shared workspace and transcript modalities, respectively, and (d) performed similarly with audio-only and audio with video review.

Next, we present relevant work for in-meeting review. We then describe the AIR Conferencing system. Then, we describe the results of our initial study that evaluated the system in a three-way distributed meeting. Following this, we describe the results of our second, more in-depth study that more closely examined the benefits of each of the individual modalities. Finally, we conclude with discussions, the future potential of in-meeting catch-up systems, and the insights we gained from this work.

RELATED WORK

Providing users with the ability to review recorded meetings has been explored extensively in previous research. Prior work has investigated ways to facilitate automatic meeting capture [2,12], ways to automatically index meetings [6,13], and methods to replay multimedia content [9]. Compared to these approaches, our work focuses on fully distributed videoconferences and addresses techniques to review multimedia content.

Previous research has identified several key approaches for efficient multimedia playback including static summaries [4], linear compression [3], and video skims [1,8,10]. Static summary systems convert video segments into less rich modalities, such as a textual summary or a single image [4]. While they can be helpful for reviewing large amounts of content quickly, they reduce the fidelity of information by removing temporal aspects and serve as a lossy conclusion of what was presented. These issues can be solved by compressing content instead of changing its modality, which is the approach taken by linear compression systems. Linear compression systems compress multimedia content by dropping audio and video frames in a systematic fashion [3]. However, dropping frames may degrade the replay experience. While the resulting quality problems with video are difficult to solve, audio quality issues, such as pitch shift, can be corrected [10]. Experimental results suggest that a compression ratio of 2 is reasonable [11,15] for audio. The low computational overhead and the lossless features of this approach make it tractable as a method of catching up in a live videoconference. Linear compression, however, is not content driven. In many cases, certain sequences of audio and video are more important than others, and it would be useful to remove segments (e.g., dead air between speakers in an interview) or overlap segments (e.g. audio over a collage of video) to allocate more time to the important parts. Video skimming [1,8] is a technique that takes into account the context of content to create abbreviated content-driven summaries.

More recently Tucker et al. [14] introduced an in-meeting audio-catch-up mechanism that uses a skimming technique called gisting. Their tool summarizes an audio recording of a meeting using a three-stage post-production process: 1) an automated speech-to-text system generates a transcript; 2) a summarization scheme extracts the important information, the gist; and 3) an audio file containing only the gist is generated. Their system uses a compression ratio of 2.5.

Contrasting our catch-up approach to Tucker et al.'s gisting technique, we find that one of the key benefits of gisting is that it can often compress audio at higher rates than those provided by typical acceleration algorithms. However, the quality of the resulting gist depends on the accuracy of the mechanisms used to create the gist. Current state of the art speech-to-text systems typically require several hours of training for each user to gain reasonable levels of accuracy. Also, gisting can result in the loss of information because the gist summarizes most but not all content.

AIR CONFERENCING

The AIR (Accelerated Instant Replay) Conferencing system [5] is a multi-user desktop videoconferencing system with in-meeting review features. The videoconferencing portion of the system provides users with high quality audio and video of all participants, a shared workspace for data collaboration, and a real-time text transcript of the audio.

When observing the live content (i.e., when not using the in-meeting review feature), users interact with AIR through a window containing four panels shown in Figure 2 (left). The Video panel shows live video feeds for all remote users. The Shared Workspace panel provides a shared workspace that any user in the conference can interact with. The Transcript panel displays the conversation transcript generated by an automatic speech recognizer. Each user's text is preceded with the user's name and is shown in a different color than the text of other users. The Review panel contains review controls to mark catch-up sections and start in-meeting review.

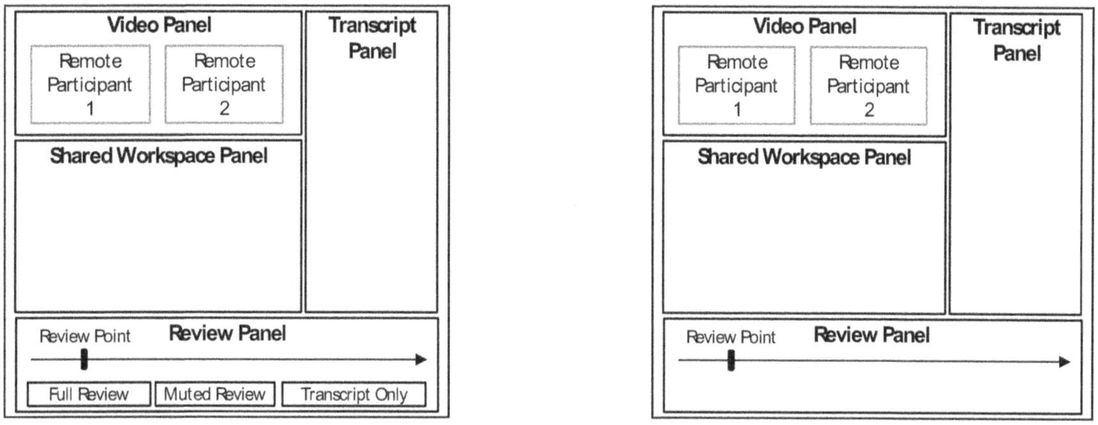

Figure 2. AIR Conferencing windows: (left) the live window and (right) review window

When using the in-meeting review feature, users interact with AIR using a separate window, shown in Figure 2 (right), that contains the same four panels as those in the live window with minimal differences. In particular, the Control panel displays a timeline allowing users to select a section of the conference to be reviewed. The other three panels display the reviewed content at an accelerated rate instead of the current meeting discussion.

Both the live and review windows are visible during catch-up sessions, enabling users to monitor the live meeting while simultaneously reviewing content from an earlier point in time. Users can choose whether to listen to the live meeting or past audio, but not both. By default, the playback is accelerated to a rate of 1.6 times normal to enable catching up to the live meeting. We solved the audio pitch and intelligibility issues that arise when audio is played back at an accelerated rate by using an audio speed-up technology that employs pitch correction and silence adjustment techniques to make sure the audio sounds meaningful even when played back at a faster rate [10].

USER STUDY #1

We performed a user study to get a preliminary evaluation of the AIR system. Our goals were two-fold. First, we wanted to measure general interest in a DVR-like approach for in-meeting review. Second, we wanted to evaluate the benefit of review mechanisms that go beyond just audio.

Participants and Procedure

We recruited eighteen participants (one female) between the ages of 24 and 45 (median 30), from a large software company. The participants all had a technical background, were comfortable with technology, and most (twelve) considered themselves to be early adopters of technology. Participants were recruited in groups of three. All members of a group knew each other well (for at least six months).

We first conducted 30 minute interviews with each participant to gather background data, measure interest in a system like AIR, and train the speech-to-text system used by our prototype. Next, the groups were brought into our research facility to take part in a distributed group meeting. The meeting took place in three adjacent usability lab rooms. Upon arrival the participants were given a brief introduction to the study and then asked to fill out a short background questionnaire. Participants were then given a ten-minute training session on the AIR Conferencing system, after which they began the main study task.

The main study task was designed to mimic a "status update" meeting, where each person is asked to give a short presentation on their project. These types of meetings are common in business environments. Instead of requiring our participants to prepare a presentation, we provided them with a presentation that prompted them for their preferences in a number of areas (e.g., technology, media, social) through multiple choice questions. Each participant was given twelve minutes to answer as many questions as possible (maximum seventy-six). For example, one question was "Which of these web browsers is your favorite?" The participant (a) read each question out loud, (b) picked one of the choices, and (c) gave a short explanation. The other group members were asked to remember answers and explanations. Each group member answered the same set of questions but in a different order than the other group members.

We wanted to simulate interruptions during real meetings. Thus, during each presentation, the participants experienced two interruptions where they left the experiment room and stayed out for 90 seconds before rejoining the meeting. This ensured that content from the live presentation was missed. After an interruption, the participants were instructed to review the portion of the meeting that they missed using one of three catch-up techniques.

At the end of the meeting, each participant completed two quizzes. Each quiz repeated the multiple choice questions answered during one of the presentations the participant observed. Each question also asked for the explanation given by the presenter. The question order in the quiz corresponded to that of the presentation.

Experimental Design

We explored three different review conditions in this study: *transcript-only*, *muted-review*, and *full-review*. In the transcript-only condition, users manually scrolled the speech-to-text window so that they could see a transcript of the conversation that they missed. No separate review window was launched and audio from the live meeting was still played. In the muted-review condition, a muted version of the video conference was reviewed in a separate window, including video, shared workspace (i.e., the presentation), and transcript. The live meeting was still visible in the live window, and its audio was still played. In the full-review condition, a full version of the video conference was reviewed in a separate window, including audio, video, shared workspace, and transcript. The live meeting was still visible in the live window, but its audio was muted.

In the muted and full-review conditions, content was reviewed at a rate of 1.6 times the normal speed. We chose this rate over 1.4 times, which was used previously [14], and 2.0 times the normal speed, which has been shown to be on the upper end of what users can understand [14,15]. Through our own pilot testing, we felt that this rate was a good compromise between speed and understandability.

As mentioned above, each participant gave one presentation for a total of three presentations per group. Each non-presenting participant was interrupted twice during a presentation. After an interruption, the participant used one of the catch-up conditions to catch up. All conditions and orders were counterbalanced to create eight orderings.

RESULTS OF USER STUDY #1

Background Interviews[1]

The background interview gathered information on users' previous experiences with missing parts of meetings, videoconferencing systems, DVR systems, and their interest in having a real-time review option during meetings. All of the participants reported sometimes missing parts of meetings, typically for less than five minutes. While they employ various strategies to review missed content, none of the strategies included viewing recordings of other participants or whiteboards. Thus, some content, such as facial expressions, gestures, and whiteboard data, are apparently never reviewed during meetings. Moreover, no participant brought up the idea of recording a meeting for in-meeting review, even though many of them use DVRs to pause, replay, and fast-forward TV content to handle scheduling conflicts, breaks, and interruptions.

When asked whether they felt it would be useful to review what they missed during a videoconference, ten participants indicated yes, seven indicated maybe, and only one indicated no. One participant explained, "*Often you miss critical conversations when you step out or are interrupted during a meeting and then you try to play catch-up during the rest of the meeting. Getting to know what was covered and who said it and the body language would put me back into the meeting very quickly.*"

While many of the participants felt that it would be beneficial to "*get context and avoid interrupting the meeting with questions that had already been covered,*" for a number of participants, the answer ultimately depended on the context of the meeting, how much they missed, and the type of catch-up mechanism. One participant explained, "*It would depend mostly upon the importance of the meeting, followed by the duration of how much I missed, and finally, on how discreetly I could review the video.*"

Some participants were concerned that the review might be disruptive to the rest of the meeting, "*If it can be done discreetly, then all the better.*" Also, there was concern that if they spent time catching up on missed information, they would end up missing more of the meeting, "*I wouldn't want to miss more information (while) reviewing missed parts.*" Another participant mentioned that "*Reviewing the video may force me to stay behind, but maybe if it looks like an unimportant or uninteresting (part of the) conversation is taking place and that gives me a window to catch up.*" One participant expressed desire for an accelerated review feature, "*If it was short and especially if I had a way of speeding up the content or seeing a transcript to help me multi-task and also not miss any (new) content.*"

These interviews suggest that users could benefit from a DVR-like in-meeting review system that allowed them to review missed content and catch up to the live discussion quickly.

Playback Options

We analyzed the participants' scores on the quizzes from the group session to assess the effectiveness of the catch-up techniques on participants' recall. The system crashed for one participant so we report on data from seventeen participants in this section. We calculated a baseline recall score for each participant based on the percentage of correct answers they had for the parts of the presentations they viewed live. We compared the participants' scores for the baseline, as well as the transcript-only, muted-review, and full-review techniques. We also examined these results for

Recall	Facts	Explanations
Baseline (Live)	78%[1]	43%[1]
Transcript Only	45%	16%
Muted Review	40%	13%
Full Review	80%[1]	49%[1]

Table 1. Percentage of correct quiz answers. [1]Recall was significantly higher in the baseline and full-review conditions compared to the transcript-only and muted-review conditions ($p<.05$). There were no significant differences between the full-review and baseline conditions, $p>.05$).

[1] Some of the results from the background interviews were presented in a poster at ACM Multimedia 2010 [5].

both the multiple choice answers (facts) as well as the short answers (explanations). The percentage correct for each category is shown in Table 1.

A 2-answer type {fact, explanation} x 4-experimental condition {baseline, transcript-only, muted-review, full-review} repeated measures ANOVA revealed significant main effects for answer type ($F_{1,16}$=74.8, $p<0.001$) and experimental condition ($F_{3,48}$=22.8, $p<0.001$), but no significant interaction effect ($F_{3,48}$=0.6, $p=0.63$).

Pair-wise post-hoc analyses of the experimental condition results (with Bonferroni corrections) revealed that participants' recall using the full-review condition was not significantly different than their baseline recall ($p=1.0$). However, recall in the transcript-only and muted-review conditions were significantly worse than both the full-review condition and the baseline recall ($p<0.01$).

Examining the results by answer type revealed that the participants performed significantly worse on the explanation answers than the fact answers, and this result was consistent across the experimental conditions ($p<.05$).

Final Questionnaire Data

After completing the main task and the quizzes, the participants were asked whether it would be useful to use a system like AIR to catch up on what they missing during a meeting. A 5-point scale (1 = strongly disagree and 5 = strongly agree) was used. Eleven participants strongly agreed that it would be useful to use a catch-up system like AIR, six somewhat agreed, and one somewhat disagreed.

Participants were also asked to report which of the three catch-up mechanisms they preferred. Significantly more participants choose the full-review condition (16) than the other two conditions ($\chi2$=25.33, $p<0.001$). These participants commented that:

- *"It was fast, easy to concentrate and auto catch-up"*
- *"Easier to playback and comprehend"*
- *"Ignore what was live as I had full fidelity"*
- *"Leads most smoothly into rejoining live"*
- *"The only one that let me digest information"*
- *"Seems like the only way to catch up in a focused way"*
- *"I feel like I can cheat in time with fast forward"*
- *"I can listen to audio while watching the live slide show and transcript"*

The other two participants chose the transcript-only condition because "*You can listen to current conversations and read transcripts*," and "*It is easier to multi-task*."

New Questions

Our initial study raised three new questions. First, the results indicated that when all four modalities are used for in-meeting review, users were able to correctly recall the same amount of information as when listening live. As described earlier, Tucker et al. [14] found that audio-only review is also a helpful catch-up mechanism. An important question is whether the additional modalities (video, shared workspace, and transcript) have additional benefits.

Second, despite the fact that we trained the speech-to-text system for each user, the quality of the conversation transcript was poor for many users. This effect likely had a significant impact on users' performance and preference. Four participants explicitly commented that they preferred the full-review condition because the "*transcript quality was low*" in the other conditions. We asked participants to re-rank the conditions assuming perfect transcription (Group 1 was not asked to answer this question, so n=15 for this result). Assuming perfect transcripts, there were no significant differences between the conditions ($\chi2$=2.80, $p=0.247$). The idea of a perfect transcript swayed some users away from the full-review to transcript-only and muted review: seven preferred transcript-only; six wanted full-review; and two desired muted-review. Therefore, it is important to reevaluate the benefit of transcript-only review when the speech-to-text system is perfect.

Third, the fact that users swayed away from full-review when the transcript is perfect indicated that they believe that they can use the transcript to catch up on past information while simultaneously listening to the live audio. To investigate further, we asked the participants to indicate whether it was difficult to attend to both the past and the present at the same time on a five point scale (strongly disagree to strongly agree). Fourteen people strongly agreed (six) or agreed (eight) that attending both the past and the present at the same time was difficult. Two participants found it neither easy nor difficult, and two found it somewhat easy. The debrief interviews revealed that while the participants had different preferences for whether or not they would like to hear live audio and read the past transcript or vice versa, one constant across all participants was that if the speech-to-text engine generated more accurate transcripts, it would have been easier to pay attention to both past and present at the same time. As it were, reading and understanding the transcript made it difficult to listen to audio concurrently.

Next, we describe a second user study of in-meeting review mechanisms that addressed the role of audio relative to other catch-up modalities and accuracy of the transcript. We leave the issue of divided attention for future work.

USER STUDY #2

Given the success of the AIR full-review configuration from the first study, we wanted to more closely examine the benefits of each of the individual modalities: audio, video, shared workspace, and conversation transcript.

Participants and Procedure

58 participants (25 female) between the ages of 18 and 60 (median of 39.5) were recruited for this study. Upon arrival, participants were introduced to the concept of accelerated

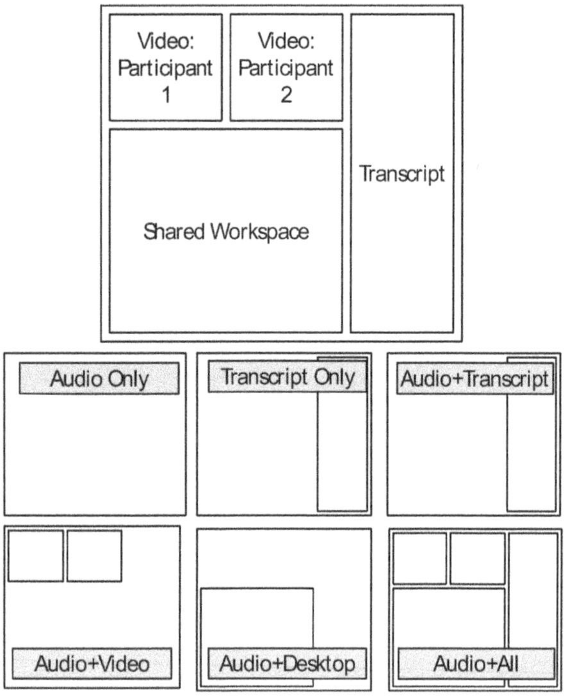

Figure 3. The mockup AIR system: (top) live window and (bottom) audio only, transcript only, audio+transcript, audio+video, audio+desktop, and audio+all review.

instant review and were told that they would be attending two, three-way distributed meetings using an in-house videoconferencing tool. They were also told that they would be interrupted and asked to catch-up on what they missed using two different catch-up mechanisms.

The simulated status meeting task from the first study was re-used in this study, modified slightly to have two presenters per meeting instead of one. To maintain consistency, two meetings were pre-recorded using two actors who answered questions from the shared presentation. The participants took on the role of the third person in the meeting (a passive attendee). For both meetings, the presentation, complete with audio, videos, and shared workspace, were recorded. The audio was also manually transcribed and synchronized with the audio and video to ensure a perfect transcript. The meetings were then played back using a system that matched the look and feel of AIR (see top image in Figure 3). Because of the divided attention challenges reported in the first study, this version of AIR showed either the review or the live window, but not both, and automatically switched between them.

Each meeting consisted of 40 questions, where the presenters alternated every five questions. Additionally, the presenters clicked on their answers in the shared workspace to provide visual confirmation of their choice. The first meeting was 7.5 minutes long and the second meeting was 8.25 minutes long. Each meeting had a 1 minute initial live portion, a 1.5 minute interruption, a 2.5 minute AIR catch-up portion, and a second live session 2.5 or 3.25 minutes long. The lengths were different because the actors took longer to answer questions in the second meeting.

After each meeting, the participants were asked to complete a quiz which contained all questions from the meeting but in a random order. The participants had to recall (a) the answer to the question, (b) the identity of the presenter who answered it, and (c) the explanation given for the answer. Following the quiz, the participants completed a questionnaire regarding their confidence in their answers and their experience during the live and review parts of the meeting. At the end of the session participants also completed a free-form questionnaire regarding their preferences for the catch-up mechanisms they used.

Experimental Design

Five different configurations of review modalities were examined in this study: 1) *audio only*; 2) *transcript only*; 3) *audio+transcript*; 4) *audio+video*; 5) *audio+workspace*; 6) *audio+all* (video, transcripts and shared workspace). These six conditions are shown in the six smaller images in Figure 3. We refer to conditions three through six as the *enhanced-audio review conditions*. The audio-only condition was used as a baseline for all 58 participants. The remaining five conditions were evaluated as a between subjects factor with each participant completing the task using one of these modalities (in addition to the audio-only condition). Each of the enhanced-audio conditions had twelve participants, while the transcript-only condition had ten. Condition and meeting order were counterbalanced across participants.

RESULTS OF USER STUDY #2

The main goal of this study was to explore whether video, shared workspace, and transcript added value over an audio-only catch-up. We first analyzed results for the four enhanced-audio conditions (audio+all, audio+workspace, audio+transcript, and audio+video) compared to audio-only and live (see Tables 2, 3, and 4), followed by a separate analysis of the transcript-only condition (see Table 5).

For the recall results, we analyzed participants' answers for the multiple choice questions (*facts*), the short answers (*explanations*), and identification of the person answering the question (*identifications*). We calculated recall scores for each participant based on the percentage of correct answers they had for the questions they viewed live, the catch-up questions in the audio-only condition, and the catch-up questions in the enhanced-audio or transcript-only conditions. For the preference and confidence ratings, we analyzed ratings from the post-meeting questionnaires which were based on a 7-point scale where 7 was extremely confident (see Table 4).

Enhanced Audio

Of the 48 participants who participated in the enhanced-audio review conditions, significantly more (40) preferred the enhanced-audio over the audio-only condition (χ^2=33.3, *p*<.001). This result was also supported by participants'

Recall	Fact	Explanation	Identification
Baseline (Live)	93%	77%	84%
Audio Only	74%	50%	61%
Enhanced Audio	83%[1]	62%[1]	72%[1]

Table 4. Percentage of correct answers for facts, explanations, and identifications. [1]Enhanced audio was sig. higher than audio only, but sig. lower than live, p<.05.

Recall	Fact	Explanation	Identification
Baseline (Live)	93%[1]	77%[1]	84%[1]
Audio Only	74%[2]	50%[2]	61%[2]
Audio+All	89%[1]	70%[1]	81%[1]
Audio+Workspace	90%[1]	65%[2]	72%[2]
Audio+Transcript	83%	67%[3]	66%
Audio+Video	70%[2]	48%[2]	68%[2]

Table 4. Percentage of correct answers for the enhanced-audio conditions. [1]Not statistically different from live but significantly better than audio only. [2]Not significantly different than audio only. [3]Recall of explanations significantly better than audio only, but significantly lower than live. Significance was measured as $p<.05$.

Confidence	Overall	Fact	Explanation	Ident.
Audio Only	2.7	3.8	3.4	3.7
Audio+All	[1]5.4	[1]5.1	[1]5.4	[1]5.9
Audio+Workspace	3.8	3.3	3.5	4.8
Audio+Transcript	4.9	3.6	4.5	4.6
Audio+Video	3.3	4.9	3.6	4.4

Table 4. Average responses to confidence level questions for being caught-up on all information during the catch-up phase (overall), and correctly answering multiple choice questions, explanations and identifications.

ratings of how much they liked each catch-up mechanism. They liked the enhanced-audio conditions significantly more (mean 4.9) than the audio-only condition (mean 3.1), ($F_{1,28}=26.49$, $p<.001$). Examining each of the enhanced-audio conditions separately, we found that all conditions were significantly preferred over the audio-only condition ($p<.05$) except for the audio+transcript condition ($p=.06$).

Recall results were analyzed using a mixed repeated measures ANOVA, with two within subject variables: *session* {live, audio, enhanced audio} and *question type* {fact, explanation, identification}; and two between subjects variables: *condition* {audio+all, audio+workspace, audio+transcript, audio+video} and *gender*. Bonferroni corrections were used for all post-hoc analyses. The results are shown in Table 2 and 3. A significant interaction effect was found for session and question type ($F_{4,152}=3.53$, $p=.009$), so we examined each question type separately. No significant effects were found for gender ($F_{1,38}=2.38$, $p=.13$).

Enhanced Audio: Significant main effects of session were found for all question types (facts: $F_{2,88}=48.42$, $p<.001$; explanations: $F_{2,84}=61.08$, $p<.001$; and identification: $F_{2,88}=48.52$, $p<.001$). Participants had significantly higher recall in the enhanced-audio session than the audio-only session but significantly lower recall when live ($p<.05$) as shown in Table 2.

Audio+All: For all question types, recall was significantly higher in the audio+all condition than the audio-only condition ($p<.05$), but not significantly different than live ($p>.05$) as shown in Table 3.

Audio+Workspace: For facts, recall was significantly higher in the audio+workspace condition than audio-only ($p<.05$) but not significantly different than live ($p>.05$). For explanations and identification, recall in the audio+workspace condition was significantly lower than live ($p<.05$) and not significantly different than the audio-only condition ($p>.05$).

Audio+Transcript: The results were mixed for the audio+transcript condition. For facts and identifications, the audio+transcript condition was not significantly different than either the live or the audio-only conditions ($p>.05$). For explanations however, the audio+transcript condition had significantly higher recall than the audio-only ($p<.05$), but significantly lower than the live condition ($p>.05$).

Audio+Video: For all question types, recall was significantly lower in the audio+video condition than the live condition ($p<.05$) but not significantly different than the audio-only condition ($p>.05$).

During the post-meeting questionnaire, we asked participants to rate their confidence in the accuracy of their answers overall and for facts, explanations, and identifications separately (see Table 4). Wilcoxon signed ranks tests revealed that for all confidence ratings, participants were significantly more confident in their answers in the audio+all condition than the audio-only condition ($p<.0125$). None of the other conditions had significantly different confidence ratings compared to audio-only.

Feedback from participants on the final questionnaire and during the debrief session provide insights on the benefits and weaknesses of the different enhanced-audio configurations. For example, some participants indicated that in the audio-only condition, the audio was disembodied and difficult to follow: "*The speeded up audio for me was difficult to understand sometimes*;" "*When it was audio only, I didn't have a place to look or focus at so I lost focus in the conversation. It was really difficult for me to focus on the audio.*" One participant stated that anything in addition to audio would help because there were no clues to understand audio when it went too fast, "*There was no other reference. A lot of things kind of blew by me ... I would have liked to have any other clue at that point.*" In the enhanced-audio conditions, audio could be correlated with other information and hence it was easier to understand and remember what was said.

For the audio+video review, participants indicated that the video review made it easier to remember which presenter answered each question, "*Being able to see who was talking during catch-up helped to associate a face, name, and voice with the answers given,*" and "*Video kept my attention and enabled me to focus on what and who said it.*" Others, however, found the video less useful, "*Video does not convey a whole lot,*" and "*The video on the catch-up, that added nothing to the ability to pick up (information).*"

For the audio+workspace and audio+transcript reviews, participants used the shared workspace and transcript as a reference to what they were hearing. One participant in the audio+transcript condition found that she had trouble following the accents of the actors, and she used the transcript to double-check what she heard, "*The written language was essential because the verbal was not enough for me.*" Others said that they were visual learners, "*I'm a visual learner, so I heard and remembered more.*"

Some participants who used the audio+all review mechanism noted that they mainly used the shared workspace to cross reference what they heard. However, when that cross-referencing was not sufficient for full understanding of the audio, they also cross-referenced the audio with the transcript. As one participant put it, "*I used the presentation to answer the questions, I used the audio to see who was talking, and every time I missed something, I had the transcript which kept a recording of everything and I could just look back at it.*" Others simply used the transcript to cross reference the audio and ignored the shared workspace, "*It's easy to listen and watch with the ability to check the transcript for the things you miss.*"

Overall, some participants simply said more is better, "*given the choice, the more information the better. It seemed very clear when you had all three of them (video, desktop, and workspace),*" while some others said that a minimalist approach works best "*I found that the more information that was there, the more confused I became. I think I did better during catch-up when I had audio-only.*"

Transcript-Only

Of the ten participants that took part in the transcript-only condition, only two preferred transcript-only. Feedback from the participants indicated that they found it more difficult to keep up with the text during review in the transcript-only condition as compared to the accelerated audio in the audio-only condition.

Table 5 shows the recall results for the transcript-only condition compared to audio-only. A significant interaction effect of condition and question type was found ($F_{2,18}$=9.67, p<.001). Examining each question type, recall was significantly higher for facts in the transcript-only condition compared to audio-only ($F_{1,9}$=5.16, p=.049) but no significant difference was found for explanations ($F_{1,9}$=0.16, p=.70). Identification recall for the transcript-only condition was significantly worse than the audio-only condition ($F_{1,9}$=6.02, p=.037). Finally, there were no significant differences in the participants' ratings of their confidence (p>.05).

Recall	Fact	Explanation	Identification
Audio Only	71%	50%	56%
Transcript Only	77%[1]	52%	43%[2]

Table 5. Percentage of correct answers. [12]Transcript only was significantly better than audio only for facts, but was significantly worse than audio only for identification, *p*<.05.

Feedback from the participants indicated that they found it more difficult to keep up with the text during review in the transcript-only condition than the accelerated-audio in the audio-only condition. As they put it, "*I had difficulty following the scrolling,*" "*I would much prefer to hear you talking faster. It was much easier to catch up than following the transcript,*" and "*Transcript alone was way too fast to really understand what was going on. I could kind of skim it and I got some information but I felt like I was just bouncing along.*" Others realized later that they were not actually reading all of the information in the transcript, "*I would read the words, but I would forgot to read the names.*" Several of them commented that it would have been better to allow manual scrolling through the transcript. While our mocked up version of AIR used in the study did not support this functionality, the real AIR system does.

Results Summary

The main results of this study demonstrate that enhanced-audio catch-up is superior to audio-only review. Both the subjective and objective results are consistent with this finding: overall, users preferred, felt more confident with, and performed better with enhanced-audio than with audio-only review. Closer examination of the individual modalities in the enhanced-audio conditions shows that compared to audio-only review, using all of the modalities to catch up showed the strongest benefit, with significantly higher user confidence and recall of facts, explanations, and identification. Additionally, using audio along with the shared workspace and transcript modalities for catching up significantly improved the recall of facts and explanations, respectively, compared to using audio-only. Finally, results from the transcript-only condition showed that this condition is slightly better than audio-only for fact recall, but was significantly worse for speaker identification. In terms of preference however, most participants did not like the transcript-only condition.

DISCUSSION

We have presented results that show the benefit of the AIR Conferencing system in a practical scenario – a status update meeting – when user absences are brief (a few minutes) and the number of users is small (three). In this section, we address our contributions with respect to their ecological validity and generalizability, and discuss other important issues concerning in-meeting review systems.

Data from the interviews in our first study indicate that a system like AIR would be useful in real meetings. Specifically, users reported that they arrive late for meetings or get interrupted, and they want to be able to catch up on information they missed. They also reported that these interruptions were relatively short (less than five minutes). In addition, most of the interviewed users had previous experience with both videoconferencing systems and DVR systems, and see benefits to both. Given that people frequently take advantage of DVR-like functionality (e.g., pause, replay, rewind) when they miss something, or do not understand something when watching television, it is plausible that this type of behavior could easily transition to videoconferencing. When asked about this possibility, most of the users in the study strongly felt that these features would be useful. Overall, these findings suggest that an accelerated review technique for in-meeting review could be useful for reviewing missed content.

Ecological Validity

In general, attaining ecological validity is a difficult task. The studies presented in this paper were designed to evaluate the usefulness of an in-meeting review system. Therefore, it was important to select a task that was both realistic and would allow for an objective evaluation. Given the conflicting nature of these requirements, we chose to focus on subparts of meetings that are common to many different types of meetings. Specifically, meetings typically have periods of presentation and recall. Our studies targeted these meeting subtasks. For instance, during presentations, facts are often presented, and when a participant wants to ask the presenter a question, the participant must recall some of these facts. During brainstorming sessions, factual data is often presented, such as the explanation of an idea or the reasons for pruning or choosing an idea. As brainstorming meetings are more interactive, people must recall not only facts and explanations, but also the participant who presented them.

Generalizability

The task we used in our studies focused on presentation and recall, which are common sub-tasks of real meetings; however, the structure of these in our task was simple and modular, consisting of alternating presentation and recall periods. While some real-world meetings are modular, many have a more complex structure. We did not evaluate how well in-meeting review systems support more complex meeting structures.

In addition to controlling the meeting structure, our study also controlled the interaction style. In particular, the non-presenting attendees were passive participants. They did not interrupt the presenter and were specifically told not to ask the presenter to catch them up when they returned from an interruption. In some real-world meetings, attendees are passive; however, in other kinds of meetings, all attendees have a stake in the outcome and are actively participating. In this case, an attendee may want to jump from replay to live if something interesting comes up in the live discussion. Similarly, a reviewing attendee may want to jump to the live meeting when asked a question. Handling these situations requires that users divide their attention between past and live content. In our first study, some participants did so by reading the transcript of one and listening to live audio of the other.

In general, participants could not act on divided attention cues because we controlled the replay to ensure consistency between participants and across conditions. Our participants always reviewed all content from the point in time at which they were interrupted and were not allowed to jump to the live discussion manually; instead, they had to wait for the replay mechanism to catch up to live. These replay restrictions allowed us to study replay effectiveness in absence of variables arising from control of the mechanisms; however, letting users choose when, what, and for how long to review would provide insights on how users multitask in meetings and help us better understand issues of divided attention.

Other Questions

The results of this work demonstrate the potential of in-meeting review; however, there are several questions that have not been answered by this work. One question is the social impact of review systems. For instance, in some cases, such as a fully-distributed videoconference, the review can be done privately. In such cases, in-meeting review may not have any social impact. However, in other cases, such as face-to-face meetings, the fact that an attendee is reviewing is going to be obvious to other attendees, which may have negative side effects. For instance, others may think that the reviewing attendee feels the current discussion is not important and is choosing not to participate live. In-meeting review systems may also impact meeting dynamics. For instance, what will happen if multiple attendees are reviewing at the same time? How is the conversation impacted? At what point does the meeting break down? What happens if all participants are reviewing? Before in-meeting review systems are introduced in real-world settings, the impact on social and meeting dynamics needs to be evaluated further.

Finally, we studied several modalities and their combinations as catch-up mechanisms. However, we did not study all possible combinations of modalities. Of particular interest is the combination that reviews everything but video. Since video is typically the most expensive modality in terms of computation and bandwidth resources, if lack of video does not significantly alter user preferences and performance, then future systems could review video only when resources are abundant. Also, some of the catch-up mechanisms we studied provided users with a computer generated speech-to-text transcript. Unfortunately, current state of the art speech-to-text systems require several hours of training on a per user basis to generate a fairly accurate (but not necessarily perfect) transcript, which may be a barrier for the adoption of speech-to-text systems. Until speech-to-text systems improve so that they are accurate with little or no training, the use of speech-to-text transcripts for catch-up purposes is going to be limited. Eventually, when they do improve, the use of audio+transcript with or without any additional modalities may become a viable catch-up mechanism.

CONCLUDING REMARKS AND FUTURE WORK

This work makes several significant contributions. We show that users prefer reviewing audio along with any additional modality to reviewing audio alone. We also show they are most confident and perform best when audio is reviewed simultaneously with video, shared workspace, and conversation transcript. Additionally, they had better recall of facts and explanations when reviewing audio along with the shared workspace and transcript, respectively, compared to reviewing audio only. However, when reviewing video along with audio, they performed similarly to when reviewing audio only. Also, the transcript-only review improved their recall of facts but degraded their recall of speaker identification compared to audio-only review. Finally, we designed a new in-meeting review system that goes beyond replaying just audio by incorporating audio, video, shared workspace actions, and a speech-to-text transcript into an accelerated review and demonstrated its usefulness in a live videoconference.

Our work also suggests several design considerations for future catch-up systems. Feedback from our research indicates that there is a cost/benefit tradeoff. The missed information needs to be important enough to warrant review and the system needs to be easy to use. If either of these two dimensions is off, users may not utilize the system. Additionally, users are concerned about disrupting the meeting or missing more of the meeting when trying to catch-up. Care must be taken when designing the user experience to ensure that the process is seamless and does not detract from or disrupt the flow of the meeting.

We have explored several catch-up mechanisms in our AIR system; however, we have barely scratched the surface of in-meeting support. We plan to explore the potential of catch-up mechanisms that use different combinations of the modalities we studied and other new modalities, such as spatial audio and shared workspaces that support pen and touch interaction. We also plan to study how well users can attend to both the past and the present through audio spatialization by leveraging the cocktail party effect. In addition, we intend to evaluate the social impact of in-meting review and study how it affects meeting dynamics.

REFERENCES

1. Christel, M. Evaluation and user studies with respect to video summarization and browsing. *Symposium on Eletronic Imaging 2006*, 17-19.
2. Cutler, R., Rui, Y., Gupta, A., Cadiz, JJ., Tashev, I., He, L. Colburn, A. Zhang, Z., Liu, Z. Silverberg, S. Distributed meetings: A meeting capture and broadcasting system. *ACM Multimedia 2002*, 503-512.
3. Dietz., P. H., and Yerazunis, W.S. Real-time audio buffering for telephone applications. *ACM UIST 2001*, 93-94.
4. He, L., Sanocki, E., Gupta, A., and Grudin, J. Auto-summarization of audio-video presentations. *ACM Multimedia 1999*, 489-498.
5. Inkpen, K., Hegde, R., Junuzovic, S., Brooks, C., Tang, J., and Zhang, Z. AIR Conferencing: Accelerated instant replay for in-meeting multimodal review. *ACM Multimedia 2010*. 663-666.
6. Kazman, R., Al-Halimi, R., Hunt, W., and Mantei, M. Four Paradigms for Indexing Video Conferences. *IEEE Multimedia 3,1 (1996)*, 63-73.
7. Meetings in America V: meeting of the minds. https://e-meetings.verizonbusiness.com/global/en/meetingsinamerica/uswhitepaper.php (2003).
8. Money, A. G., and Agius, H. Video summarization: A conceptual framework and survey of the state of the art. *Journal of Visual Communication and Image Recognition 19 (2008)*, 121-143.
9. Moran, T., Palen, L., Harrison, S., Chiu, P., Kimber, D., Minneman, S., van Melle, W., and Zellweger, P. I'll get that off the audio: A case study of salvaging multimedia meeting records. *ACM CHI 1997*, 202-209.
10. Omoigui, N., He, L., Gupta, A., Grudin, J., and Sanocki, E. Time-compression: Systems concerns, usage, and benefits. *ACM CHI 1999*, 136-143.
11. Orr, D.B. A perspective on the perception of time compressed speech. In P.M. Kjeldergaard, D.L. Horton, & J.J. Jenkins, (Eds.) Perception of Language, 108-119, Merrill, 1971.
12. Ranjan, A., Birnholtz, J. and Balakrishnan, R. Improving Meeting Capture by Applying Television Production Principles with Audio and Motion Detection. *ACM CHI 2008*, 227-236.
13. Tucker, S., and Whittaker, S. Accessing Multimodal Meeting Data: Systems, Problems, and Possibilities. Workshop on Multimodal Interaction and Related Machine Learning Algorithms, 2004.
14. Tucker, S., Bergman, O., Ramoorthy, A., and Whittaker, S. Catchup: A useful application of time-travel in meetings. *ACM CSCW 2010*.
15. Wildemuth, B., Marchionini, G., Yang, M., Geisler, G., Wilkens, T., Hughes, A., Gruss, R. How fast is too fast? Evaluating fast forward surrogates for digital video. *ACM/IEEE-CS Digital Libraries 2003*, 221-230.

MOGCLASS: Evaluation of a Collaborative System of Mobile Devices for Classroom Music Education of Young Children

Yinsheng Zhou, Graham Percival, Xinxi Wang, Ye Wang, Shengdong Zhao
School of Computing (SoC), National University of Singapore, Singapore 117417
{yzhou86, wangxinx, wangye, zhaosd}@comp.nus.edu.sg, graham@percival-music.ca

ABSTRACT
Composition, listening, and performance are essential activities in classroom music education, yet conventional music classes impose unnecessary limitations on students' ability to develop these skills. Based on in-depth fieldwork and a user-centered design approach, we created MOGCLASS, a multimodal collaborative music environment that enhances students' musical experience and improves teachers' management of the classroom.

We conducted a two-round system evaluation to improve the prototype and evaluate the system: Improvements were made based on the results from an iterative design evaluation, in which a trial system was implemented. The system then underwent a second round of evaluation through a three-week between-subject controlled experiment in a local primary school. Results showed that MOGCLASS is effective in motivating students to learn music, improving the way they collaborate with other students as well as helping teachers manage the classroom.

ACM Classification Keywords
H.5.5 Information Interfaces and Presentation: (e.g., HCI): Multimedia Information Systems: Sound and Music Computing; K.3.1 Computing Milieux: Computers and Education; J.5 Computer Applications: Arts and Humanities—*Music*

General Terms
Design, Experimentation, Human Factors.

Author Keywords
Mobile devices, music, education, musical instruments, children, user-centered design.

INTRODUCTION
Music education for young children integrates composition, listening, and performance. Performance and listening enrich students' repertoire of musicianship, allowing them to perform creatively and construct their ideas into new shapes and meanings. However, interaction among these musical activities is optimal only when the students have mastered the necessary technique to accomplish different tasks [20].

Conventional classroom music education constrains the development of students' musical skills [14]. Most instruments require years of practice to achieve competency, setting a technical demand which is too high for most students. The limited number of instruments available also restricts students' artistic expression. Furthermore, the chaos and noise produced by acoustic instruments during class-wide practice makes listening and self-analysis difficult. Teachers must spend a huge amount of time and effort keeping the class in order, which reduces the time for teaching technical instrumental skills or musical expression.

By carefully analyzing current practices in music education in classrooms, we designed MOGCLASS (Musical mObile Group for Classroom Learning And Study in Schools) [25], a collaborative system and multimodal music environment based on networked mobile devices. It supports students' music experience and assists teachers in managing the classroom. It enhances active listening, composition, and performance, which enables creative music making and engagement and makes lessons engaging, fun and effective.

Taking advantage of the sound synthesis technology and sensory capabilities in mobile devices, we were able to simulate playing a wide range of musical instruments through suitable body movements. Since the sounds were simulated, we could carefully control the level of complexity required to produce them. Extraneous movements were eliminated, allowing students to focus on musical understanding. It also allows the teacher to assist students through "scaffolding", a set of visual hints that guide students through the piece of music.

To support peer collaboration during practice sessions, we designed *virtual sound spaces*, allowing students within a group hear each other's sounds via headphones, but do not hear sounds produced by other groups. Consequently, students can collaborate better without disturbing others. Their devices can also be switched to *public performance mode*, which plays sound over loudspeakers so that everybody in the classroom can hear.

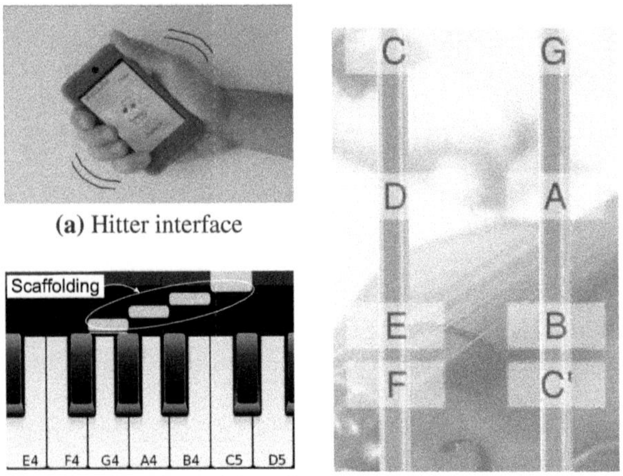

(a) Hitter interface

(b) Tapper interface with scaffolding

(c) Slider interface

Figure 1: Student interfaces in MOGCLASS

A device that acts as a remote control for all students' devices facilitates the teacher's management of the classroom. It can automate tasks for different instructive and disciplinary purposes such as changing the sounds and interfaces of students' devices, grouping students, activating or deactivating students' devices, and setting up group practices (through *virtual sound space*) or class rehearsal (using *public performance mode*).

Designing MOGCLASS required a significant understanding of the teachers' and students' characteristics (e.g., musical skills), requirements and the workflow of music classes. Two rounds of evaluation were conducted to refine and validate the design. The first round of evaluation consisted of an iterative design process with four separate music lessons given to three classes. The improved system was then evaluated in a between-subject controlled study of two groups of primary school students, one using MOGCLASS and the other using the recorder (a commonly-used music instrument), taking the same five-lesson course.

Our work makes the following contributions: 1) general design principles that will be useful for creating collaborative systems for improving classroom music education, 2) identification, through the iterative design evaluation, of specific challenges that these systems must meet, and 3) a tool for learning music that has a measurable impact on students.

USAGE SCENARIO

To illustrate the various functionalities of our system, we imagine MOGCLASS being used to teach a Grade 5 class (students aged 10-11 years).

At the beginning of the lesson, the teacher configures the students' devices to show a piano-like interface (Figure 1b) by pressing a few buttons on her device. To help the students learn a musical piece, she provides extra visual cues by enabling scaffolding. A set of bars drop down from the top of the screen of all devices. The location and size of each bar indicates a note and the duration it should be played. Students can press the buttons indicated by the bars allowing them to focus on the interface instead of splitting their attention between an instrument and a sheet of printed music.

After learning how to play the song on their devices, the students are allowed to do group improvisation. The teacher enables the headphones so that students within a group can hear each other's devices. She allows them choose any instrument, and turns off the visual cues. Students who choose percussion instruments produce sounds by shaking the device (Figure 1a). A few advanced students who choose to play the melody can make sounds such as an expressive glissando ("swooping in between" normal notes) using the interface in Figure 1c, which is easier to play than a real violin because of the "note regions" [1], yet is much more difficult than the other interfaces.

Five minutes later, the teacher enables the loudspeakers, and each group takes turns performing before the rest. However, while she is grading the first performance, some students in other groups are very excited and continue playing. The teacher identifies the misbehaving students through her device, and she mutes their devices so that they cannot disrupt the class.

RELATED WORK

Technology in music education has been growing rapidly over the last few decades. Programs such as GNU Solfege [2] and Practica-Musica [4] can be used for ear training and teaching music theory, while systems like i-Maestro [15] and the Digital Violin Tutor [23] provide interactive self-learning environments for studying how to play an instrument. Many schools teach composition using notation software [16], which allows students to hear their scores without the need for live musicians, while programs like Hyperscore [3] allow students to create music without any knowledge of music theory. However, most of these tools are geared towards non-performance activities (theory and composition), or were created for specific instruments (like violin). They are not suitable for classroom music education, which involves the use of a wide variety of instruments.

One solution is to create non-standard physical interfaces to act as controllers for synthesizers (e.g., Toy Symphony [10]). However, customized hardware limits the potential for widespread adaptation by schools. We adapted current mobile interfaces, especially since these devices are increasingly powerful and ubiquitous. One example of this approach is MoPhO [21], a new repertoire-based ensemble using mobile phones as primary musical instruments. Other projects have focused on accelerometers within commercial mobile phones [6, 7] or the Wii remote [22], using gesture recognition as input methods for musical instrument applications. Nevertheless, very few attempts to translate this approach so that it can be applied in large classrooms.

A few systems have been developed to support non-music classroom education. KidPad [8] developed a shared 2D

[1] The sound frequency within the note region is preset to help beginners to play in tune

drawing tool for storytelling. Livenotes[11] created a shared white board system using wireless communication and tablet PCs to support real-time communication within small groups of students during lectures. Mischief [13] is a platform that supports traditional classroom practices between a remote instructor and a group of students. Each student has a mouse but the class shares a single large display. Systems for special needs have also been developed. One example is vSked [9], an interactive and collaborative visual scheduling system that supports classroom activities for children with autism and eases teachers' workload.

DESIGN METHOD

We followed the *classroom-centered design* suggested by Loh [12]. This approach is aimed at "inquiry-oriented" education, which is a good fit for the current music curriculum in local primary schools [1]. It takes four factors into consideration: student collaboration, student-student and student-teacher communication, teachers as facilitators or guides, and the influence of the curriculum on the use of the tool.

We conducted several field trips and interviews in order to understand conventional music class practices. We visited three local primary schools, observing five classroom sessions in Grades 3-6 and interviewing four music teachers. Each class had 40 to 45 students, with a total of approximately 200 students. To support this project, we put together a multi-disciplinary team consisting of experts from HCI, sound technology, and music education. Paper prototypes were used to test designs within the team and with two music teachers.

To facilitate widespread deployment in public schools, the system has to be robust. It should, after a short period of training, be maintainable by music teachers who do not have a technical background. Setting up the system in the classroom and packing it away at the end of a class must be fast, and any problems during the class should be easy and quick for a teacher to solve.

Music Class Practices

We identified several essential music class practices that are common in classroom music education but are inadequately supported by existing learning tools.

A. Mastery of technical skills: Recorders are relatively easy to master at a basic level, but students still need to spend a significant amount of time to learn and develop the physical skills required to play them.[2] Students must learn those skills in conjunction with music theory, collaboration, and composition. Since none of the objectives of the music subject [1] is instrument technical skills, we could simplify the physical skills required to make music so that students would be able to spend more mental effort on the other three activities.

[2]These skills include hand position, fingering types, and breath control. Although the recorder is pre-tuned, it is very easy to change the pitch by over- or under-blowing. These often result in an unpleasant sound.

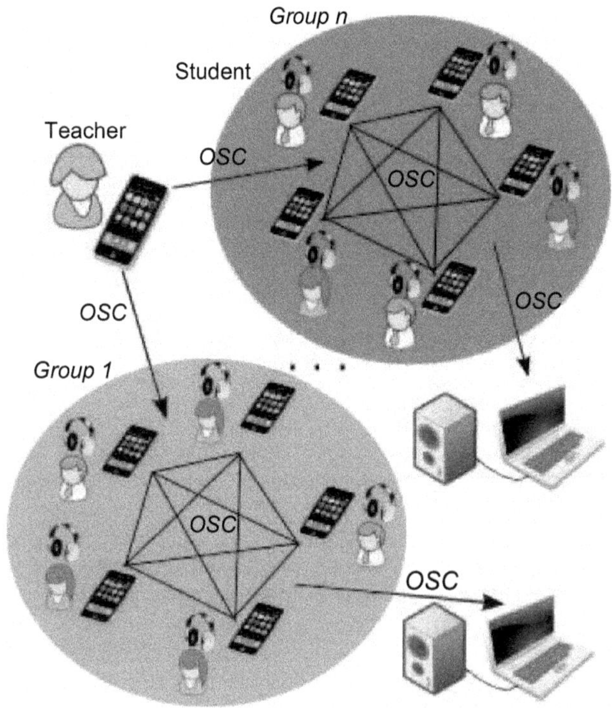

Figure 2: System diagram

B. Availability of instruments: For practical reasons, the use of musical instruments in the classroom is often restricted to simple percussion instruments (e.g., handbell) or affordable wind instruments (e.g., recorder or harmonica). Due to budget constraints and the lack of expertise in a wide range of instruments (be it Western classical or world music genres), music teachers introduce other instruments or genres through audio/visual samples such as YouTube videos [5], without giving students the ability to play and experiment with the instruments themselves.

C. Individual and group activities: There are frequent switches between individual practice, group activities, and class rehearsals. When students are allowed to practice on their own, cacophony ensues. This makes it difficult for each student to focus on the sound he is producing, reducing the effectiveness of solo practice. One teacher noted that this is the most terrible part of music class because it is too noisy, and hopes technology can be used to solve the problem.

D. Teacher's workload: Teachers handle many tasks, sometimes concurrently, such as giving musical instructions, organizing activities, guiding different students and groups, conducting performances, and maintaining classroom discipline. One particular challenge in music education for children is classroom management. Unlike in other school subjects where students sit at desks, music classes generally involve sitting on the floor in rows or in small groups. This freedom of movement, especially when combined with the opportunity to produce sounds with instruments, makes students excited and harder to manage. The teacher often spends a significant amount time giving warnings or punishments to noisy students.

Design Principles

Through our observations of the classes, we arrived at a set of core design objectives which became the basis for the final design of MOGCLASS.

A. Minimize instrument technical demands. Entry barriers such as the technical difficulty of music instruments should be reduced, allowing students to focus on musical creativity and improvisation. Lowering the technical demands of music increases the probability that children can organize and execute a course of action required to complete the designated performance, thereby enhancing their perceived competence and self-esteem in playing music.

B. Support a wide range of instruments and interactions. In order to adapt to a diverse musical repertoire and allow creative exploration, the system needs to support a wide range of functions and simulate sounds of a variety of musical instruments for children to actively explore and create with. The music curriculum allows time for such creative exploration; we should give students more sounds to discover.

C. Improve collaboration by separating performance and practice. To avoid disruptions in class, students should use headphones when practicing alone or in groups and speakers when performing. The wireless network allows students to be interconnected, supporting collaborative music making.

D. Facilitate teacher's task. Some activities can be automated: the teacher can carry out different classroom activities such as group performance, solo practice, and changing their instruments through her device. She can also get students' attention by sending a notification to their devices. The design should help the teacher accomplish tasks as she moves from group to group.

THE MOGCLASS SYSTEM

This section describes only the features of MOGCLASS after the iterative design evaluation. For a discussion of the interim features, see Iterative Design Evaluation. For technical details, see MOGCLASS [25]. The system diagram is in Figure 2.

Student and teacher interface

We implemented our system on the iPod Touch, a device with a multi-touch screen and an accelerometer. These two features are relatively new in commercial mobile devices, but we expect them to become widely used in the next few years.

Interfaces designed for young children should use intuitive metaphors as design elements [19], so we developed three users interfaces (hitter, tapper, and slider; Figure 1) based on the metaphors of drum, piano, and violin. Hitter uses the accelerometer. When the device detects a hand-shake, it produces a sound whose volume is proportional to the strength of the shake. Tapper and slider are controlled with the multi-touch display; tapper is played using discrete buttons, while the vertical position of a finger on the slider plays its note.

To help teachers monitor students' status and manage their

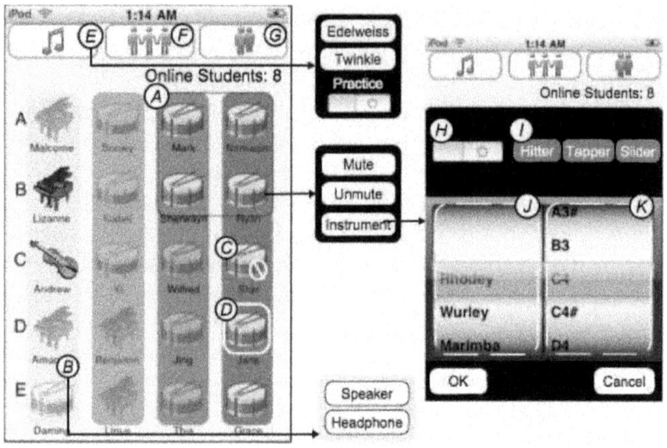

Figure 3: The workflow of the teacher's interface: the student icon represents hitter (drum), tapper (piano), slider (violin) that the student is using. Icons for students who are online are highlighted while the ones for those who are offline are semi-transparent. The students' names are displayed under each icon.

interfaces simultaneously, we designed an interface that integrates the teacher's functions in single display (Figure 3). Selecting individual students is done by dragging the finger to select students' icons (A) on the touchscreen, then clicking the "instrument" button in the pop-up menu. The teacher may allow students to choose any instrument (H), or specify their interface (I), sound (J), and starting note (K). The teacher may also disable or mute the student's device (C). A corresponding student icon flashes (D) when a device is being played, so the teacher always has class feedback.

Selecting an entire group (e.g., all Yellow ipods) is done by doing a long press in the group area (B). This lets the teacher choose between *public performance mode* (speakers) and *virtual sound spaces* (headphones). Scaffolding is enabled on all devices in the class (E), with the option of allowing students to practice by themselves, or having an ensemble practice. All devices can be selected with (F) for global administration. The teacher can also switch to display the other half class with (G).

Virtual Sound Space and Public Performances

In the *virtual sound space* (Figure 4), the students' devices are grouped according to how the teacher sets them. Each device sends all its user actions to other devices in the group, allowing the sounds to be synthesized in each device. In *public performance mode*, the group's loudspeakers will be enabled so that the group can perform their composition to all the students.

Scaffolding

The scaffolding is useful in guiding students through unfamiliar pieces of music. This gives students a chance to develop the necessary techniques to perform compositions in a consistent and developed manner [20]. The basic idea is similar to karaoke: students perform preset songs based on the visual hints. When the class is performing music together, all student devices are synchronized. The entire performance is started from the teacher's device.

Figure 4: Students working with MOGCLASS in a *virtual sound space* **under the teacher's direction.**

Table 1: Classroom session details. A: Bell pulling (hitter); B: Mechanical bells (hitter); C: Kangdi Qing Ge (Tapper); D: Frere Jaques (Tapper); E: Kangdi Qing Ge (Slider)

Grade	Time (min)	Lesson programs	Other activities
C-3A	50	A, B	Playing with animal sounds.
C-3A	50	C	Choosing new sounds to use. Practice with headphones.
C-6	90	A, B, C, D, E	Practice with headphones. Be free to use any interface and any sounds.
C-3B	50	A, C	No.

ITERATIVE DESIGN EVALUATION

We conducted four evaluations to test the usability of the initial prototype.

We tested our system on two groups of students in an actual classroom environment: Group 1 consisted of students aged 8 to 9 years (from two classes: C-3A, which has 44 students and C-3B, which has 42). This group was selected because they were at a key stage of music development where they can benefit from this type of technological enhancement. Group 2 consisted of students aged 11 to 12 years from one class C-6, which has 18 students). They represented the higher end of our target users, with better musical and analytical skills. These allowed us to collect more feedback for improving the system. All classes were roughly balanced in gender with 80% of them having some experience with mobile devices.

The first two sessions were carried out with class C-3A, the third session with C-6, and the final session with C-3B. A total of 104 students and 3 teachers participated in our evaluations.

To avoid excessively training the teachers on MOGCLASS's incomplete versions, the first three lessons were taught by one of the authors, who is also an experienced music teacher. The regular music teachers observed and gave comments after the lessons. The final evaluation was taught by a primary school teacher who was not previously exposed to MOGCLASS. This was done to test whether the system could be used effectively by a music teacher with no technical background.

Working closely with the teachers, we created lessons to evaluate the effectiveness of our system (see Table 1). These lessons aim to test with a variety of music from different cultures, instruments, and varying degree of difficulties. Lessons A, B, E represented a basic introduction to each music-making interface. Lesson C and D allowed students to play more challenging music which requires more coordination among different groups of students.

During each session, student feedback was collected via direct observation, video recordings, and questionnaires. We also conducted semi-structured interviews with the observing teachers.

Findings

Overall, the sessions were very successful in achieving our evaluation goals: testing the initial acceptance, learn-ability, and usability of MOGCLASS interface (both teacher and student interfaces), and to test the robustness of the system. Most of the feedback from students' and teachers' were positive. The response gathered from the students' questionnaire results were clearly favorable, with all classes reporting that MOGCLASS was fun and generally easy to use. All teachers, observing and participating, liked the system very much. Managing large groups of young students is typically a difficult task, but the mute function helped significantly. The teachers highly approved of this feature.

The prototype received a few complaints, which were caused by limitations intrinsic to mobile devices such as limited display and processing resources.

Feedback from Students

Students with a background in piano complained about the split-level notes in the original tapper interface [24] and the limited range (one octave). After discussions with music teachers, we adopted the piano for the metaphor of the tapper; and users can go up and down 3 octaves by sliding their fingers on the top of the screen. Some students were also unhappy with the hitter interface, as the synchronizing of the gesture and the sound produced is not accurate enough. We solved this problem by improving the algorithm using machine learning approach [25].

We observed that some students had difficulty reading sheet music – their eyes alternated between the musical notation and the screen of their device, with each change requiring half a second or more for them to "find their place." This motivated us to develop scaffolding.

Feedback from Teachers

In the teacher interface design of our initial prototype (Figure 5), the mute function (A) was not selective. It disabled all students' devices, so the teacher could not use it to silence the rest of the class when a group was performing. The teacher also did not have the option for selecting sounds and interfaces (B) for a specific group of student devices because the devices of the entire class were configured at once.

In the prototype, we only allowed each student to practice with headphones on their own. After the evaluation, teachers valued the headphone feature because it eliminated the chaos during music practice. Furthermore, teachers' suggestions inspired us to design the *virtual sound space* that students can do group practice without disrupting the rest of the class if their devices were shared with the group through headphones.

Some students were overly absorbed in the devices during the evaluations, repeatedly activating the instrument control even after the teachers disabled them. One suggestion we received was to provide the teacher device a function that identifies these students and freezes all the controls and displays on their devices.

The separate displays in the original interface of the teacher's device (Figure 5) should be streamlined. There are three main reasons we want to change the old teacher interface design: 1) the teacher has to switch among the three views to change the configurations of the students' devices; 2) class-wide control is provided but there is no control on individual device; and 3) the Connection Status display does not show whether a student's device is muted (in C of Figure 5, the cat and the whale represent the online and offline students, respectively. The red background means the student is pressing the buttons) and does not provide enough feedback on changes in the students' interfaces (hitter, tapper, or slider). Consequently, the separation of MOGCLASS functions into several separate displays increased teachers' cognitive load. We solved this problem by displaying all the functionalities in one screen.

CONTROLLED USER STUDY

The evaluations aimed to gather teachers' and students' initial reaction towards MOGCLASS, discover usability issues, and gather feedback for improvements. However, the lessons we conducted are insufficient for us to judge the system's educational value. It is also difficult to understand the advantages of teaching with MOGCLASS without comparing it with a traditional music class. Thus, we carried out a controlled user study to investigate further and answer the following research questions:

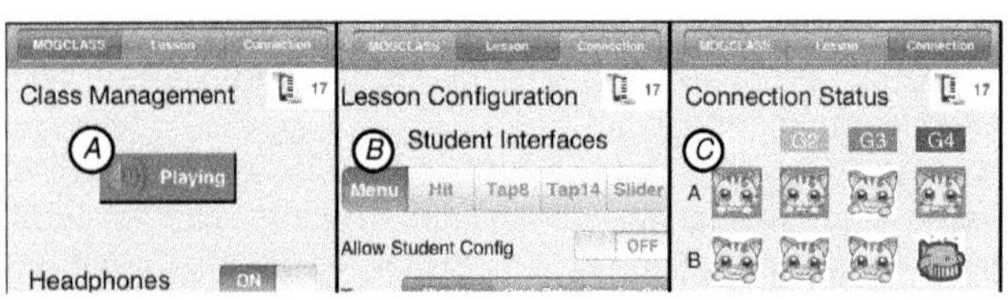

Figure 5: A partial view of the three seperate displays in the original teacher interface design

- Does MOGCLASS increase students' interest and motivation, and improve collaboration in music classes?
- Does MOGCLASS enhance the teacher's ability to organize and manage the class?
- Can MOGCLASS easily be integrated into the primary schools' current music curriculum?

Participants

Two classes (4A and 4B) consisting of 77 students in Primary 4 (Grade 4 in the US school system) and one music teacher participated in the study. The two classes were randomly chosen. Class 4A had 20 females and 19 males, while class 4B had 19 females and 19 males. Students in both classes were familiar with computers and mobile devices. Both classes were taught by the same music teacher. He was familiar with mobile devices, but did not have any previous experience with MOGCLASS.

Study Design and Procedure

The study adopts a between-subjects design. There is one independent variable (musical instrument) with two levels (MOGCLASS and recorder). Class 4A used MOGCLASS while Class 4B used recorders. All other variables – the teacher, the classroom where the lessons were conducted, the lesson plans, and the duration of the lessons – were controlled so that both groups worked in identical environments.

Prior to the study, we spent 30 minutes in the lab training the music teacher on the use of MOGCLASS. A survey and questionnaire were given at various stages of the lesson program.

Lesson Program

The music teacher created five-lesson program before the study. The lessons were conducted in 3 weeks. Each lesson lasted for 30 minutes. The details of the lessons are as follows:

1. Introduction of the musical instruments by playing the notes G, A, and B. At the end of the lesson, students are to answer questions Q2 - Q5 at the end of the lesson.
2. Learn how to play a simple song ("Mary had a little lamb") on the instruments. Students using MOGCLASS can use scaffolding.
3. Learn how to play a more advanced song ("Edelweiss") on the instruments. Students using MOGCLASS can use the scaffolding. Students are to answer questions Q1 - Q7 at the end of the lesson.
4. Repeat the same song ("Edelweiss") with proper timing. Students using MOGCLASS will no longer use scaffolding. Students are to work in small groups where some play the song while others add their own percussion compositions.

5. Evaluation: the teacher will assess and grade the performance of the groups in terms of creativity, style and technical proficiency. Students are to answer questions Q1 - Q7 at the end of the lesson.

Classroom Setup

Due to budget constraints, we only had 21 iPod Touches for use in the study (one for the teacher and 20 for the students). Students in 4A shared the devices in pairs. Students in 4B brought their own recorders. We brought in additional equipment for data collection: an HD camera positioned at the back of the room to record the whole class, 2 JVC camcorders to film two selected groups, and a pair of Cardio condenser microphones connected to a MacBook to pick up sound. The only difference in the classroom setup is the two laptops and four speakers we installed to support MOGCLASS in Class 4A's lesson.

Survey and Questionnaire

We used a survey and a questionnaire to evaluate the students' level of motivation and collaboration. The survey focused on general interest in music education. It was administrated before the first lesson and after the last lesson. The students ranked their interest in school's subjects (from 1 to 9, with higher numbers indicating more interest.)

The questionnaire (see Table 2) studied motivation in more detail, and was administered three times. The questions were based on Deci and Ryan's self-determination theory [18], which states three basic psychological factors contributing to self-intrinsic motivation:

- **Competence:** The feeling that one can reliably produce desired outcomes or avoid negative outcomes.
- **Autonomy:** The urge to engage in behavior on one's own initiative.
- **Relatedness:** The sense of being connected to a larger social experience, which is also a metric for student collaboration.

We created two questions on each factor, and included one question on "enjoyment". Each question was rated on a 7-point Likert scale, with higher numbers indicating stronger agreement with the given statement.

We also recorded and transcribed video from all classes to study and document the students' behaviors while using MOGCLASS. We conducted semi-structured interviews with the music teacher after each lesson, and had one group interview with four students from Class 4A regarding their attitudes towards using MOGCLASS.

Research Hypotheses

We established the following research hypotheses, with the null in each case indicating no difference in the mean scores for class 4A and class 4B.

H1: *Perceived enjoyment will be higher in Class 4A compared to Class 4B.*

Table 2: Questionnaire

#	Questions
Perceived Enjoyment	
Q1	I enjoyed the music lesson.
Perceived Competence	
Q2	I feel the instrument is easy to learn.
Q3	I can easily play music using the instrument.
Perceived Autonomy	
Q4	I would like to use the instrument frequently.
Q5	I would like to play more songs on this instrument.
Perceived Relatedness	
Q6	I enjoyed the music that our group performed in the class.
Q7	I am happy with my performance in our group.

H2: *Perceived competence will be higher in Class 4A compared to Class 4B.*

H3: *Perceived autonomy will be higher in Class 4A compared to Class 4B.*

H4: *Perceived relatedness will be higher in Class 4A compared to Class 4B.*

Results and Analysis

Students' Motivation, Interest, and Collaboration

In the survey, which presents a scale of 1 to 9 (1 being the least interesting, 9 being the most interesting), both classes perceived music as an interesting subject. Class 4A (MOGCLASS) with an initial rating of 7.31 and Class 4B (recorder) with an initial rating of 8.05. After the five lessons, Class 4A's rating increased significantly from 7.31 to 8.42 ($F(1,33) = 9.862$, $p = 0.004$) (see Table 3). For Class 4B, although the average rating also increased from 8.05 to 8.43, it was not significant ($F(1,28) = 1.451$, $p = 0.238$). The significant increase in the regard for music as an interesting subject demonstrates that MOGCLASS is effective in promoting students' interest. However, due to the higher initial rating of Class 4B, it is insufficient to conclude that MOGCLASS is more effective than recorders in increasing students' interest.

Since the students answered the questionnaire three times, we analyzed the results using the repeated-measures ANOVA test with the musical instrument as the between-subject factor (in Table 4 and Figure 6). Students using MOGCLASS had higher ratings on most of the questions except for Q1, where no significant difference was found. This indicates both classes enjoyed the five music lessons equally. However, since students using MOGCLASS initially had lower interest in the music (7.31 vs. 8.05), gaining comparable interest after the lessons seems to indicate greater improvement. For the other questions, MOGCLASS received signif-

Table 3: Survey Results: General Interest

Class	Before	After	F	p
4A	7.31	8.42	9.862	0.004
4B	8.05	8.43	1.451	0.238

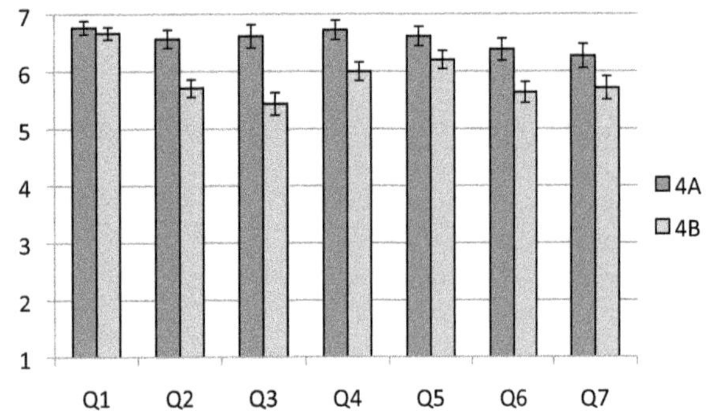

Figure 6: Graph of questionnaire results

icantly higher scores in Q2 and Q3, indicating that it was perceived as much easier to learn than the recorder. It also rated marginally higher in Q4 ($p < 0.1$), and significantly higher in Q5 ($p < 0.05$), indicating students had higher interest in using it and were likely to spend more time practicing it instead of recorders. The last two questions are related to the support of collaborative learning. MOGCLASS scored significantly higher than the recorder for Q6 ($p < 0.05$), and marginally higher for Q7 ($p < 0.1$), indicating it was more effective in facilitating and supporting group practices.

The questionnaire results support hypotheses **H2**, **H3**, and **H4**, proving MOGCLASS covered the components of self-intrinsic motivation. The survey shows that MOGCLASS increased Class 4A's interest in music education to the level of Class 4B. Thus, MOGCLASS has a significant effect on motivation.

Hypothesis **H1** is not supported by data, but since both classes reported such high values (up to a mean of 6.77 on a 7-point Likert scale!), it is not surprising that there is little difference. Future studies on MOGCLASS might attempt to reduce the overall "enjoyment" numbers by asking students to choose between one enjoyable activity and attending music class (i.e., extra music classes vs. lunch break).

In addition to between-subject effects between MOGCLASS and recorder, we also tested within-subject effects for each class across multiple lessons. We found no significant difference for within-subject effects ($p > 0.05$) , which means that both Class 4A and Class 4B maintained the same level of motivation throughout the five lesson period.

The field observation and interviews validated our questionnaire results. Teacher's assistance during song practice was much less in MOGCLASS lessons. Most students were able to practice playing "Edelweiss" on their own using the "scaffolding" feature without much involvement of teacher. As a result, some students fully mastered the playing of the music piece (Edelweiss) through classroom practice alone. On the other hand, the level of assistance in the recorder class was much higher. The teacher frequently approached students, but they still expressed the need for more assistance. As a result, none of the students learned to play Edelweiss during class even with more help from the teacher.

Table 4: Analysis of questionnaire results: one-way ANOVA test. (*$p < 0.1$; **$p < 0.05$)

#	C	Mean	Std. Error	$F(1,61)$	p
Q1	4A	6.767	0.114	0.404	0.527
	4B	6.667	0.109		
Q2	4A	6.567	0.161	14.9	< 0.001
	4B	5.707	0.154		
Q3	4A	6.611	0.205	17.236	< 0.001
	4B	5.434	0.196		
Q4	4A	6.611	0.169	3.085	0.084*
	4B	6.202	0.161		
Q5	4A	6.722	0.168	9.653	0.003**
	4B	6.000	0.160		
Q6	4A	6.383	0.192	7.926	0.007**
	4B	5.636	0.183		
Q7	4A	6.267	0.212	3.6	0.063*
	4B	5.712	0.202		

Many students strongly expressed the desire to have more MOGCLASS lessons in the future. They found MOGCLASS interesting and very easy to use, and liked that it made sounds of many musical instruments. They also "enjoyed the class", and felt "fortunate to be able to use an iPod Touch to learn music", and "look forward to my next music class". The students "highly recommend MOGCLASS to other schools".

On the other hand, feedback from the recorder class was mixed. Although most students agreed playing with recorder was "interesting and fun", "it is a little hard", and "noisy when practice in groups". The students felt that they want "more different instruments to learn". These confirmed that MOGCLASS is easier to use, and has higher perceived competence from students.

Video footage showed how students collaborated during group practice in a MOGCLASS lesson. It was a scene from any other music lesson, where each student was preoccupied with a certain idea, or wanted to do other things or cause mayhem. However, the music teacher reported that the major difference was the din of music practice, which can be overwhelming in a normal class, was gone. Except for occasional conversations among students, the noise level in Class 4A was inconsequential compared to the cacophony in Class 4B.

Classroom Management

Because MOGCLASS is a new system, it is expected that the teacher will take a while to learn and use its features. In the first lesson, the teacher did not use his device frequently. He still gave verbal orders to silence students instead of pressing the mute button on his device. As the study progressed, he became more familiar with the system and used the device more frequently. For example, before a group made a public performance, he would first put everybody else's devices on mute.

Managing the classroom using MOGCLASS also increased the teacher's competence in managing students' activities.

Since the status of students' devices are displayed in his device's interface, he could easily identify misbehaving students. This is especially helpful in a large class. The teacher liked the function that allows group practices using headphones because it was quieter. He also approved of the system's ability to simulate different musical instruments. It eliminated the need to buy new instruments since he can simply install new software applications.

Children are curious and active by nature. During the study, some students were overly absorbed in testing the instruments, continuing to play with them even when they were asked to place them on the floor. After one session with Class 4B, the teacher had to stop and explain to the class that he will not proceed with the lesson unless everyone listens. In Class 4A, the teacher simply disabled all the students' devices before giving verbal instructions. The group interview revealed that while one student found the classroom management functions of the teacher's device (particularly the mute function) restricted freedom, other students understand that they were necessary to keep order in the class.

Integration into the Music Curriculum

After using MOGCLASS for five lessons, the teacher is confident that it can be integrated into the current music curriculum at the primary level. MOGCLASS fulfills the objective specified in the General Music Programme for students to "sing and play melodic and rhythmic instruments individually and in groups." [1].

MOGCLASS's basic configuration, which was used in this study, has melodic elements (tapper and slider) and a percussion element (hitter). It allowed students to play almost all elements of classroom music making needs in terms of many common musical instrument sounds and the basic striking action of the percussion. It also provides an almost infinite expansion capability, requiring the devices only to be updated to receive new musical instrument sound and functionalities. As the teacher commented in the interview, MOGCLASS can be used for a variety of music lessons because of the options to play many musical instruments and its classroom management functionalities. He thinks it has a huge potential as a tool for music lessons that involve no instruments (e.g., singing) if a voice recording function can be added.

However, one of the most important objectives of classroom music education that traditional music technology fails to provide for is music making in groups [17]. This is also specified within the first objective of the 2008 General Music Programme Syllabus [1].

MOGCLASS is easy to deploy, requiring only five minutes for two students to set up and clean up the whole system in classroom. After a short training period, a typical music teacher was able to use the system smoothly. Once during the study, the students encountered some problems in the system (e.g., they could not log in) that the teacher was nevertheless able to solve without technical assistance. After the evaluation, the school purchased the system and continued to use it on a long-term basis. The potential challenge for schools with a tight budget is to find the means to obtain the necessary hardware and software. But with the ubiquity of mobile devices, the teacher foresees a day when everyone can bring their own mobile devices and use them to learn music.

By developing the music experience through three activities (listening, performance, and composition) MOGCLASS is effective in motivating students to study music and helping teachers manage the classroom. The survey and questionnaire results, field observation and interviews from the controlled study showed that MOGCLASS rated higher in questions regarding the three basic psychological factors described in the theory of self-intrinsic motivation in music education. The study also showed that MOGCLASS is effective in reducing teachers' workload in managing the classroom. There is a huge potential in deploying this system of networked mobile devices to enhance classroom music education.

LIMITATIONS

The physical actions of the Tapper and Slider interfaces bear little resemblance to the actions in playing an acoustic instrument. However, these interfaces still capture the essential interactivity of music performance: physical actions produce sounds, and sounds are analyzed to plan future actions. The development of this "action-sound-action" feedback loop is a crucial part of music education. Future work will compare MOGCLASS-trained and recorder-trained students' ability to learn a third musical instrument.

Unlike acoustic musical instruments, the playing time of an iPod Touch is constrained by its battery life. The iPod Touch can last 2.5 hours with the Wi-Fi in constant use. If a teacher wants to conduct a longer lesson or use the devices throughout several sessions, we would need to install a charging facility or prepare backup batteries or devices.

Although the interface of the teacher's device is easy to use, the limited size of the screen poses a challenge when many students are involved. The current interface was designed for up to 20 student devices; more students would result in a cluttered display. One possible solution is to use a tablet computer such as the iPad, which can display more student information and control functions on the screen.

Our study evaluated the progress of the students in the MOGCLASS class throughout the five-lesson program. In the future, we could work with the school to study the improvement on students' musical skills that can be attributed to the use of MOGCLASS over semesters.

CONCLUSION AND FUTURE WORK

Based on careful considerations of music education needs in schools we developed MOGCLASS. The interfaces of the teacher's and students' devices were designed to facilitate learning in a creative environment. It allows students to learn in a collaborative setting while exploring music in groups or as individuals. It can play sounds from a wide range of musical instruments and lowers the physical skills and time required to become proficient in playing music. MOGCLASS was developed to provide an active and motivating learning environment for children, while providing the teacher with an effective tool to manage classes.

Our iterative design evaluation and controlled user study have shown that MOGCLASS has achieved our goals. It was so enthusiastically received by our participants (students, teachers, and music education experts) that our proposed system and approach may prompt educators to rethinking current practices so that music education can be an active engaging experience.

This study will be helpful for designers and researchers who are interested in studying interactive classroom technologies. The success of this project makes us believe that MOGCLASS can be applied not only to music education but also to music therapy. We are currently working to adapt MOGCLASS as an assistive technology for children with physical disabilities (e.g., muscular dystrophy) to decrease their isolation, improve their social skills, and boost their self-confidence and self-esteem. We will continue to explore broader applications for MOGCLASS in our future work.

ACKNOWLEDGMENTS

We thank Ms. Chua Yu Gek from Henry Park Primary School, Mr. Weili Gan from Pasir Ris Primary School and their classes for assistance and participation in the user studies. Special thanks to Dr. Lum Chee Hoo for his kindly support and discussion, and Dillion Tan, Yang Zhao, Xiaoming Chen, Zhonghua Li for their support in system implementation. The work was supported by Singaporean Ministry of Education grant R-252-000-341-112.

REFERENCES

1. *2008 Syllabus, General Music Programme*. Ministry of Education, Singapore. [Online; accessed 24-Feb-2009].
2. Gnu solfege. `http://www.solfege.org/`.
3. Hyperscore. `http://www.hyperscore.com/`.
4. Practica musica. `http://www.ars-nova.com/aboutpm5/index.html`.
5. Youtube. `http://www.youtube.com`.
6. E.-S. Choi, W.-C. Bang, S.-J. Cho, J. Yang, D.-Y. Kim, and S.-R. Kim. Beatbox music phone: gesture-based interactive mobile phone using a tri-axis accelerometer. In *ICIT '05*.
7. A. Dekel and G. Dekel. Mogmi: Mobile gesture music instrument. In *5th International Mobile Music Workshop*, 2008.
8. A. Druin, J. Stewart, D. Proft, B. Bederson, and J. Hollan. Kidpad: a design collaboration between children, technologists, and educators. In *CHI '97*.
9. S. H. Hirano, M. T. Yeganyan, G. Marcu, D. H. Nguyen, L. A. Boyd, and G. R. Hayes. vsked: evaluation of a system to support classroom activities for children with autism. In *CHI '10*.
10. K. Jennings. Toy symphony: An international music technology project for children. *Music Education International*, (2):3–21, 2003.
11. M. Kam, J. Wang, A. Iles, E. Tse, J. Chiu, D. Glaser, O. Tarshish, and J. Canny. Livenotes: a system for cooperative and augmented note-taking in lectures. In *CHI '05*.
12. B. Loh, J. Radinsky, E. Russell, L. M. Gomez, B. J. Reiser, and D. C. Edelson. The progress portfolio: designing reflective tools for a classroom context. In *CHI '98*.
13. N. Moraveji, T. Kim, J. Ge, U. S. Pawar, K. Mulcahy, and K. Inkpen. Mischief: supporting remote teaching in developing regions. In *CHI '08*.
14. J. L. Mursell. The challenge to music education. *Music Educators Journal*, 36(5):20–22, 1950.
15. K. Ng and P. Nesi. i-maestro framework and interactive multimedia tools for technology-enhanced learning and teaching for music. In *AXMEDIS '08*.
16. M. D. Roblyer. *Integrating Educational Technology into Teaching*. Pearson Prentice Hall Publications, 2006.
17. A. Ruthmann. The composers' workshop: An approach to composing in the classroom–the way writing teachers approach composition can illuminate how we teach composing. *Music Educators Journal*, 93(4):38+, March 2007.
18. R. M. Ryan and E. L. Deci. *The Handbook of Self-Determination Research*. University of Rochester Press, 2007.
19. D. Stanton, V. Bayon, H. Neale, A. Ghali, S. Benford, S. Cobb, R. Ingram, C. O'Malley, J. Wilson, and T. Pridmore. Classroom collaboration in the design of tangible interfaces for storytelling. In *CHI '01*.
20. K. Swanwick and C. C. Franca. Composing, performing and audience-listening as indicators of musical understanding. *British Journal of Music Education*, 16(01):5–19, 1999.
21. G. Wang, G. Essl, and H. Penttinen. Do mobile phones dream of electric orchestras? In *ICMC '08*.
22. E. L. Wong, W. Y. F. Yuen, and C. S. T. Choy. Designing wii controller - a powerful musical instrument in an interactive music performance system. In *MoMM2008*.
23. J. Yin, Y. Wang, and D. Hsu. Digital Violin Tutor: an Integrated System for Beginning Violin Learners. In *ACM MM '05*.
24. Y. Zhou, Z. Li, D. Tan, G. Percival, and Y. Wang. Mogfun: musical mobile group for fun. In *ACM Multimedia '09*.
25. Y. Zhou, G. Percival, X. Wang, Y. Wang, and S. Zhao. Mogclass: a collaborative system of mobile devices forclassroom music education. In *ACM Multimedia '10*.

Buzzing to Play: Lessons Learned From an In the Wild Study of Real-time Vibrotactile Feedback

Janet van der Linden, Rose Johnson, Jon Bird, Yvonne Rogers, Erwin Schoonderwaldt
Department of Computing, The Open University,
Milton Keynes, MK7 6AA, UK
j.vanderlinden@open.ac.uk

ABSTRACT
Vibrotactile feedback offers much potential for facilitating and accelerating how people learn sensory-motor skills that typically take hundreds of hours to learn, such as learning to play a musical instrument, skiing or swimming. However, there is little evidence of this benefit materializing outside of research lab settings. We describe the findings of an in the wild study that explored how to integrate vibrotactile feedback into a real-world teaching setting. The focus of the study was on exploring how children of different ages, learning to play the violin, can use real-time vibrotactile feedback. Many of the findings were unexpected, showing how students and their teachers appropriated the technology in creative ways. We present some 'lessons learned' that are also applicable to other training settings, emphasizing the need to understand how vibrotactile feedback can switch between being foregrounded and backgrounded depending on the demands of the task, the teacher's role in making it work and when feedback is most relevant and useful. Finally, we discuss how vibrotactile feedback can provide a new language for talking about the skill being learned that may also play an instrumental role in enhancing learning.

Author Keywords
In the Wild Study, Children, Sensory-motor Learning, Vibrotactile Feedback, Violin Teaching, Motion Capture.

ACM Classification Keywords
H5. Information interfaces and presentation: User Interfaces: Evaluation/methodology; Haptic I/O.

General Terms
Design, Human Factors.

INTRODUCTION

Wearable technologies that are capable of providing real-time feedback on physical movement and posture offer new opportunities for improving people's health and well-being. The ability to measure a person's movements and analyze them from many angles is enabling automated personalized feedback in real-time that potentially can support people to train more effectively. Instead of performing exercises that are, say, videoed and having to wait until after the event to view and reflect upon them using a TV monitor, learners can now receive various kinds of 'body nudges' that can inform in real-time how well a particular part of the body is doing. A small buzz can be provided at what are considered key moments that 'pushes' or 'pulls' a limb, joint or other body part back towards a correct position. It can also be used to lightly 'touch' someone on their arm, leg wrist, etc., rewarding them for a correct limb or bodily movement. It is assumed that the immediacy of both kinds of feedback can be effective at consolidating and correcting body movements, leading to a more noticeable improvement in performance. Moreover, it offers an alternative teaching strategy as the actions of the learners and the feedback they receive are tightly coupled.

While some lab studies have been able to demonstrate how real-time feedback can result in enhanced practice, [21, 22], little is known as to how and whether they are borne out in the real world. The experience of a lesson is very different, often being subject to the vagaries of time, motivation, mood and other external factors. A key question, therefore, is how effective is this promising new technology when used in the wild?

Our research is concerned with how easy it is to integrate haptic technology into realistic teaching practices, and which aspects of teaching and learning they are particularly suited to. In particular, we are interested in how to enhance the practice of violin bowing by using real-time haptic feedback that is delivered to the upper limbs. Typically, learning to play the violin requires many years; a novice player takes around 700 practice hours to master basic bowing skills [13]. Our over-arching goal is to enable students and their teachers to use this new kind of feedback to reduce this practice time and, in so doing, encourage more children to persist with learning.

Our real-time feedback system, MusicJacket, uses a combination of motion capture and vibrotactile feedback in order to provide players with real-time feedback on some of the physical aspects of violin bowing. In this paper, we ask to what extent real users, in a realistic teaching setting, can use this system. Are students, often young children, able to attend to vibrotactile feedback while playing music? Do they find it helpful? What challenges do students face when learning the new motor skills required to play the violin? What techniques do teachers use to address the needs of individual students, and how can they use real-time vibrotactile feedback to support their teaching?

We describe an in the wild study using the MusicJacket with two teachers and ten pupils that lasted several months. We discuss the findings in terms of the problems that need to be overcome and the fine-tuning that needs to take place, in order to use such feedback effectively. We discuss the implications of these in the context of the cognitive load that is incurred through attending to vibrotactile feedback. Finally, we present some more general lessons learned for developing vibrotactile systems that can be used to train body movements.

BACKGROUND

Traditional teaching methods for violin playing include giving verbal instructions, physically guiding a pupil's arm through a bowing movement, or getting pupils to observe themselves in a mirror. Each of these methods has limitations. Students find it challenging to translate verbal instructions into complex motor actions; being guided by a teacher requires the students to be passive, rather than making active movements; and it is very difficult for a student to see whether they are bowing at the correct angle. In contrast, real-time vibrotactile feedback can enable players to physically engage in the learning process while still reading music and listening to the notes they are producing.

Haptic Feedback

A few studies have used motion capture technology to analyze violin bowing together with various kinds of augmented feedback to support the teaching of violin playing [15, 19]. For example, Ng *et al.* [15] tracked the precise movements of the bow and provided students with both visual and audio feedback to assist them. The visual feedback was in the form of graphs and an augmented mirror image of the player and their violin, and these gave players detailed information about bow speed, angle and other aspects of their bowing. However, interpreting such visual displays required significant attention by the players who were already busy with reading music notation and concentrating on finger positioning as well as listening to the sound they were producing. Audio feedback was also found to have its drawbacks, as users reported that the alerts that were used interfered with their music making.

Vibrotactile feedback mechanisms have been explored in a number of different contexts, including collision avoidance in virtual reality games [4], navigation systems for pedestrians [16] and rehabilitation exercises for stroke patients [2]. A commonly cited benefit of vibrotactile feedback is that it is useful when other modalities, such as hearing and vision, are under cognitive load [e.g., 7]. Researchers have started to explore whether vibrotactile feedback can be used in music educational contexts, where eyes and ears tend to be very busy. For example, Grosshauser and Hermann [6] gave vibrotactile feedback to violin students on aspects of their playing. The feedback was based on measurements of bowing movements from a variety of sensors attached to the bow and violin. Teaching with this type of feedback can involve the teacher providing 'silent hints' that are physical, rather than verbal. However, there is no systematic evaluation of how such hints are experienced by the pupil or for which type of activity they are most useful.

Haptic guidance, which is closely related to vibrotactile feedback, has also been used in a number of music educational approaches [5, 9, 10]. In the Haptic Drumkit [9] the players 'feel' the beat of a polyphonic rhythm in the form of vibrations on whichever limb is supposed to move and hit the drums. Rather than providing feedback on movements, this approach prompts when a movement should be made, giving the player the opportunity to passively experience the feel of the required rhythms.

Other systems have been designed to provide vibrotactile feedback in response to actual physical movement, with the aim of correcting the current posture or movement. An example is a jacket system developed by Lieberman and Breazeal [14]. To evaluate their system, they instructed participants to mimic the position of an expert's arm that was shown in a still image or to copy an arm movement that was shown in a short video. Eight actuators were placed on each participant's arm, four around the wrist and four around the elbow. The feedback took the form of a 'push' so that if, for example, the wrist was bent too far inward, then the actuator on the inside of the wrist would start to vibrate until the position was corrected, with a magnitude that was proportional to the error detected. Another example of an automated feedback system, is the Tactile Sleeve [4], which helped participants avoid collisions in virtual reality environments. The Tactile Sleeve was embedded with motion capture markers and 24 actuators (8 on the hand and 16 on the arm) that were arranged in bands of four. The part of the arm that was in collision with an obstacle was either marked as red in a display, for visual feedback, or was switched into vibration mode. The vibrotactile system was evaluated using a controlled experiment in a laboratory setting and its efficacy compared with visual feedback by measuring the accuracy and speed at which a set of specified movements could be performed with each of the feedback modalities. Participants were found to be faster when using vibrotactile feedback compared with visual feedback. However, findings from lab experiments do not always carry over to in the wild studies. Furthermore, sometimes quite different findings are demonstrated, questioning the validity of generalizing lab studies to different real world contexts [18].

Figure 1. A six year old participant wearing the MusicJacket

In the Wild Studies

A study by Spelmezan *et al.* [20] tested whether participants were able to identify feedback while they were snowboarding both in the lab and outdoors. They conducted two sessions in the lab, using simulators and Wii boards, and one session on the ski slopes. During each session participants received vibrotactile instructions to which they had to react. Even when the study was conducted outside the laboratory, it still had many characteristics of a controlled experiment. For example, the instructions were randomized and did not relate to moves the snowboarders needed to make on the piste. This randomization prevented such instructions being anticipated by experienced snowboarders, however, it also detracted from the realism of the scenario.

A different in the wild study was for a skiing application where skiers were equipped with cameras and accelerometers in order to record their performance to enhance their skiing experience [11]. The data from the sensors was stored and the skiers were able to playback and analyse their performance on mobile devices after each run. The purpose of this study was to identify the technical challenges involved in using this technology in the real world, and to see how users would appropriate the technology and the services it offered. They found to their surprise that the skiers did not look at their performance data during the day while they were out skiing, but only looked and discussed this with other skiers in the evening, after the day's skiing had finished. They argue that this in the wild approach can be a reliable means of identifying the real usage of a new technology, and in particular, can bring out when users initiate changes of usage that have not been anticipated.

Hoggan and Brewster [8] also stress the importance of in situ studies. They studied mobile devices with multimodal interfaces, and found that certain modalities work better in some environments. They also showed how people develop different habits under different workloads. They argue that different forms of usage cannot be uncovered in short duration laboratory experiments, but instead require a longitudinal approach. There is also evidence [12] that over time the novelty aspect of a new technology wears off and that after longer use people appreciate different aspects of a technology than they do on first encountering it.

RESEARCH AIMS

Findings from in the wild studies show different patterns of usage of new technologies compared with the results arising from lab studies. In so doing, they highlight how a variety of context factors, such as the physical environment, needs to be taken into account when deploying a new technology in situ. In the context of providing haptic feedback for learning a sensory-motor skill, factors that need to be considered are the role of the teacher, the age of the student, their motivation and prior experience. The aim of our study was to determine how such a system could be integrated into an existing music practice set-up. In contrast to most lab-based studies, including our own, the focus was on the effectiveness of vibrotactile feedback for a real use, namely, teaching the violin to children. The objective was to determine how a prototype feedback system would be appropriated by students and their teachers in a realistic setting, namely, where students have music lessons (classroom or home) when learning to play the violin.

THE MUSICJACKET SYSTEM

MusicJacket is a system we have built that uses inertial motion capture sensors to track a violinist's movements and posture during bowing and gives them real-time feedback using vibration motors placed on their arms and torso (Figure 1). It was used to improve the teaching of two basic violin-playing skills: correctly holding the violin and straight bowing. Novices initially find it difficult to hold the violin correctly and tend to let it drop down during playing. Straight bowing involves keeping the bow perpendicular to the strings during bowing and is a complex movement involving the coordination of the wrist, hand, elbow and shoulder.

An IGS-190-M mobile motion capture system was used to track the player's bowing action and violin position (developed by Animazoo [1]). The system operates in real-time, is easy to set up and use, and is portable. This motion capture system consists of inertial sensors containing 3-axis accelerometers, gyroscopes and a magnetometer. The sensors are attached to a Lycra suit and connected to a processing unit. The 3D orientation data from each sensor is computed and transmitted to a wireless receiver attached to a PC. Three dimensional position data are computed from the sensor data using a hierarchical skeleton model.

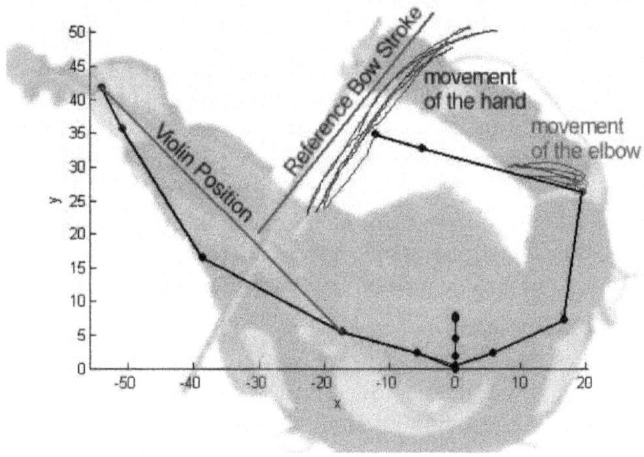

Figure 2: Bow stroke performed by a player, as seen from above, overlaid by reference bow stroke trajectories

The system can be configured to the body size of each user and features can be activated as appropriate. This versatility enables it to be used by participants from a range of ages and abilities. In order to deliver feedback appropriate for each player, we initially define a reference bow stroke or target path (Figure 2). This 'ideal' straight path is individual, depending on a number of factors, such as the build of the player, the way they hold the violin and the particular pedagogy of their teacher. The definition of the individual reference path is obtained by a calibration recording where the teacher guides the bowing movement of the student. By fitting a straight line to the measured bowing path we obtain a target path. Using appropriate tolerance margins, real-time feedback can be given on various aspects of the trajectory.

The feedback component of the system works by delivering a vibration, which feels like a gentle buzz, when the player's bowing moves too far from the target trajectory, whereas feeling no buzz means that they are on the correct path. If the player drops their violin position they also feel a buzz. The vibrotactile feedback is provided by 10mm shaftless DC vibration motors (310-101 Precision Microdrives) [17], similar to those found in mobile phones, which are attached to the motion capture suit. We use five actuators, placed on the arms and torso (Figure 3). On the bowing arm, motor 1 behind the elbow is designed to push the arm forward when it deviates too far from the reference path, and motor 2 on the wrist is designed to push the hand back. The up and downward movement of the violin is governed by motors 3, 4 and 5. Motor 5, behind the left elbow, makes the player aware that this arm needs to move upwards. Motors 3 and 4 are placed on the ribs and stimulate the lifting up of the whole body, including the violin. The precise location for the vibration motors has been gradually refined through user studies and expert advisors [21, 22].

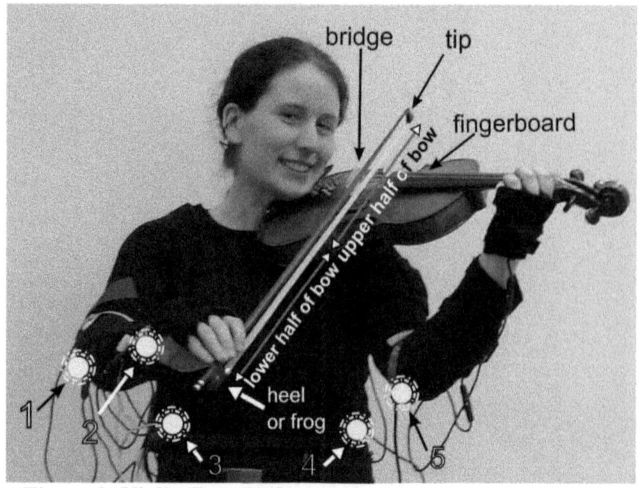

Figure 3: Violin Terminology and placement of motors for vibrotactile feedback

IN THE WILD STUDY

The in the wild study took place over two months with two teachers and ten children. The two teachers selected groups of pupils who they considered appropriate for the study. The teachers also helped to decide where the sessions should take place and how they should be set up so as to make the children to feel comfortable. The lesson materials and instructions were also discussed with the teachers.

The Teachers

Both teachers (teacher A and teacher B) had many years of experience of violin teaching. They were employed by the local Music Service to teach in schools, although they also had a number of private students, both children and adults.

The Pupils

There were two groups of pupils: group A taught by teacher A and group B taught by teacher B. Group A consisted of six girls who had started their violin lessons (with teacher A) only a few months prior to the start of the study. With the exception of one girl, aged nine, they were all just six years old. Their violin lessons took place during school hours in a spacious music room at their school. Teacher A had selected these children as they were absolute beginners and because she felt the children and their parents would be keen to participate. This group of pupils was normally taught as a group for a 20-minute session. A typical lesson when learning how to hold the violin involved singing and dancing, including an elephant song that was intended to help them put their violin on their shoulder and a story about a mouse on their arm to practice how to hold the bow. The aim of these fun exercises was to help pupils get to grips with the basics. The teacher considered an active movement to be very important. By the time our study commenced they had just moved on to learning the early stages of bowing.

Group B consisted of four pupils, also girls, aged between 10 and 13 years. They had all been playing for about three years. These pupils were used to having individual lessons with teacher B – one of them had private lessons outside school hours, but for the others the teaching was organized during school time. The teacher had selected these pupils as each of them had trouble with a particular aspect of bowing and she felt they could all benefit from focused bowing sessions.

The period of the study

We organised five sessions with each teacher over a period of two months, in which they gave individual lessons to each of their pupils using the MusicJacket system. This provided a total of approximately fifty lessons to work with the teachers and pupils. During this period the teachers also continued with their ordinary lessons and pupils practiced at home as usual. Each session took the form of a special bowing lesson, with two researchers present. The activities carried out in these lessons were varied and developed in close collaboration with the teachers. The sessions for group A took place during school time, in the classroom where they normally had their violin lessons (Figure 4), whilst for group B these were carried out in a home setting.

METHODOLOGY

We used a number of data collection methods to assess the suitability and effectiveness of the MusicJacket system for teaching the violin. We began by interviewing the two teachers and observing one of their normal lessons prior to the participants donning the MusicJacket. The MusicJacket sessions that then followed were videoed and field notes were made. During these sessions, observations were made together with informal conversations with the teachers and the pupils about the tasks they were doing and their perception and experience of using the MusicJacket in the context of their lessons. The MusicJacket system also logged each pupil's bowing movements and when they received vibrotactile feedback. Several months after these sessions, we conducted further interviews with the two teachers to reflect on the lessons and to discuss their impact on the children's bowing.

THE MUSICJACKET SESSIONS

There were three main parts to each MusicJacket session: preparation; physically exploring the technology; and playing exercises and pieces, during which different ways of providing feedback were investigated.

(i) Preparation

At the start of each session, the equipment was set up which took about 40 minutes. As each pupil arrived, they were dressed in the MusicJacket. This took about 10 minutes. This was followed by the actual lesson, which ranged from 10 minutes to half an hour. It took only 1 minute to remove the system at the end of a session.

(ii) Physically Exploring the Technology

The pupils were encouraged to physically explore the technology when wearing the MusicJacket to help them understand how it worked. During the first session, we introduced the concept of motion capture and encouraged the pupils to look at themselves using the Animazoo viewer software. This shows a stick figure moving in real-time

Figure 4: The set up during a typical session (the pupil is on right, the teacher in the middle and the researcher on the left)

with the wearer of the suit. Pupils were encouraged to move their arms, rotate their wrists, pretend to bow and make big arm movements. This exercise encouraged pupils to become more aware of their body movements. This was considered particularly useful for very young children who tend to have very little understanding of how their bodies work. In particular young children do not realize that arms can rotate around the elbow or that wrists can bend.

In subsequent weeks, vibrotactile feedback was introduced to the pupils by switching on each actuator in turn. Each pupil experienced how by moving their bowing arm in the right direction they could switch off the vibrotactile feedback and that this indicated that they were now in the correct position. This exercise was repeated for most of the weekly sessions.

(iii) Playing Exercises and Pieces

During the first two sessions, the research team introduced simple bowing exercises where the pupil was required to make long bowing movements on a single string without using fingering. However, these exercises were found to be not appropriate for either group of pupils: they were too difficult for group A and too easy for group B. In consultation with the teachers, we chose to change this approach. For the remaining sessions, the pupils were asked instead to play the exercises and pieces they were studying at that moment. This was thought to be a better strategy because it reinforced their current teaching.

By week 3, we also established that it was not appropriate to teach the technique of straight bowing to the pupils in group A, as their bowing technique was not sufficiently developed. However, the issue of 'holding up the violin' was very relevant for this group. This was the reverse of group B pupils, who had no issues with holding up their violin, but did need to improve their straight bowing.

Finally, a lesson plan was developed in which the early part contained an element of 'deliberately playing badly'. The pupil was encouraged to deliberately play in the wrong way in order to feel the feedback that resulted. This was done using one of their regular exercises – bowing a few strokes in the case of group A, and playing a scale in the case of group B. Later on in the lesson, they played one of their pieces, with the teacher giving verbal feedback on aspects of their playing (e.g., rhythm or intonation) while in the background the MusicJacket was providing real-time vibrotactile feedback on their posture or bowing.

FINDINGS

Both the teachers and the pupils in groups A and B were positive about using the MusicJacket when learning to play the violin. No pupils dropped out from the groups and all were excited at the prospect of having their next lesson using the MusicJacket. Vibrotactile feedback was found to be most successful in improving three aspects of pupils' playing: (i) holding up the violin; (ii) straight bowing, and (iii) using more bow. There was also evidence that as time progressed, both teachers and pupils gained in confidence in using the technology and began to change it for their own objectives. Below we describe in detail the three main improvements followed by the other findings.

(i) Holding up the violin

Holding up the violin was the most successful type of feedback for group A pupils. These pupils were still at a stage where they needed to practice bringing the violin up to their neck and positioning it in the correct place. It was not unusual to see the violin slip back out from underneath a child's chin whilst they were playing, so any teaching approach which encourages holding the violin up was particularly relevant to them at this stage of learning.

Pupils learnt to use the real-time vibrotactile feedback quickly, generally within the space of the first session. This showed both in the way their playing changed and also, for some, by their facial expressions. For one pupil, in particular, it was clear to see when the feedback was on, not only from her good arm movements, but also because she would wrinkle her brow slightly in a thoughtful expression or smile. Some of the other pupils showed when they felt the feedback by smiling or giggling, while others gave very few signals about what they were feeling but would tell us afterwards *"It buzzed about five times."*

Figure 5 shows a graph representing one pupil's playing that is representative for the whole of group A. The data were collected using the motion capture system. In the top part (panel A) of the figure her arm movement is shown without the feedback and in the bottom part (panel B) with the feedback switched on. Panel B shows that the violin is held higher, and in particular, held closer to the target line (at 0) set by the teacher during the calibration for this pupil. The recordings for these two graphs were made shortly after one another. In panel A, the pupil starts at -20cm, that is, the bow is slightly lowered, whereas for the second play through in panel B she starts at a better position, 0 cm.

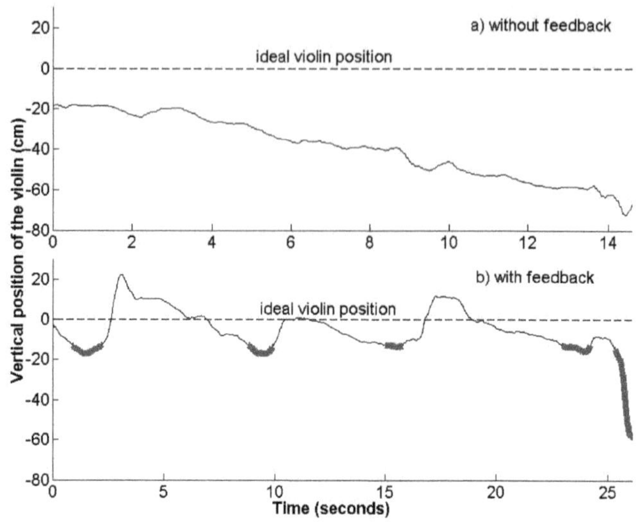

Figure 5: Panel A (no feedback) in top part and panel B (with feedback) in bottom part shows actual violin position relative to ideal position (thicker areas indicate when feedback is on)

This pupil, as well as some of the other pupils, would generally begin a piece holding the violin higher if the feedback was switched on, possibly anticipating what the feedback might tell her. Panel A also shows a general downward trend reflecting how the pupil gradually let the violin drop whilst playing. This was exhibited by many of the other pupils. Often they might deliberately do this at one point to get a better look at the strings and then never return the violin to its proper position. Panel B also shows a section of general downward gradient. However, whenever the feedback comes on there is a sharp upwards slope in the graph, showing that she pushed the violin up in response to the feedback. Overall she maintains a position close to the reference position when playing with feedback. The final trailing off is when she brings her violin down at the end of the piece.

It was also apparent that she took longer to play the piece when the feedback was switched on (25 seconds versus 14 seconds). This is because she played the piece twice in order to make up for an error she had made. We observed that she seemed to make more mistakes when the feedback was switched on, possibly because she was focused on reacting to it.

Analysis of the video and motion capture data showed that all six pupils in group A lowered their violin position at regular intervals in the absence of either vibrotactile feedback or prompting from their teacher. They responded to vibrotactile feedback by adjusting their violin position when playing familiar pieces. However, in situations where they experienced high cognitive load, such as when playing a new piece or when playing along to a CD, they did not respond to the vibrotactile feedback. In these cases they would tell us afterwards that they had not felt it.

Their teacher commented after the study that she thought this type of feedback had been *"useful"*. In one of the lessons she also mentioned how she *"thought the sound really improved when she suddenly held up the violin."* This comment was partly addressed to the researchers but also to her pupil whom she was praising for lifting her violin so well.

(ii) Straight bowing

The feedback on straight bowing was more successful with the group B pupils who were at the stage where they had many demands upon their attentional resources: reading or remembering complicated pieces of music; getting their fingers in the correct place; and bowing. These pupils knew how to bow correctly when this was their main focus but had difficulty doing it while focusing on these other areas. The youngest of the group had particular trouble doing this as she had progressed very quickly to playing more difficult pieces but her bowing had been left behind.

Taking this pupil as an example, the video data shows how the feedback made her glance down at the bow much more whilst she was playing. In her first lesson, without feedback, she only looked down at the bow once during the time she played two pieces. In the following lesson, when she had the vibrotactile feedback, she glanced down at the bow eleven times whilst playing two pieces. The lesson after that, again with the feedback, she looked at the bow fourteen times whilst playing three pieces. These glances are only momentary before she looks back up at the music, but they show that she is much more aware of what her bow is doing. Her teacher was pleased when she noticed this result of the feedback: *"it's quite good to have an eye on your bow and an eye on your music so you're swapping back from your music to your bow, music to your bow... You were doing that a bit more I've noticed today."*

The videos show that the result of this increased awareness was more controlled bowing and she was less likely to bow over the fingerboard, which she did in her initial lesson without feedback. This change was also observed by her teacher: *"you're not drifting as much on to the fingerboard as you have done. That's been a problem in the past."* Similar to many of the pupils in group A, her facial expression changed when she received the feedback. However, the particular change in expression suggests that she had a different kind of experience to the group A pupils. When she played, with or without feedback, she always had a look of concentration on her face. Without the feedback she would often smile with a more self-aware expression when she made a mistake or got to a certain part of a piece, such as the end of a phrase. When playing with feedback, her face moved more frequently but by smaller amounts, alternating between a slight smile and lips pursed together. When the feedback was switched on she seemed to become more tense, and her playing seemed to flow less. This suggests that she found the task more demanding when the feedback was switched on.

A lasting effect of the vibrotactile feedback was to provide the pupils and teachers with new shared terms to express aspects of the lesson that had previously been implicit. Teacher B used the experience of the MusicJacket system as a starting point for working on her pupils' bowing during the months following the study, both of them talking about their movements in terms of vibrotactile feedback. For example:

"We've talked about what we did – how she felt the feedback when she was going too far forward... and how she had to remember to counteract that by bringing her arm back, and she's got to try and do that herself and keep an eye on her bow... rather than just plowing through she's got to make conscious decisions about where she's bowing and how she's bowing."

(iii) Using more bow

One of the pupils in group B had a different problem with bowing, namely, she did not use enough bow. Figure 6a (top part) shows how she regularly used approximately only 10cm of bow (a typical bow is 75cm long). This was a concern for her teacher and she dedicated a large amount of the lesson time to encouraging her pupil to use more bow. The result of this is shown in Figure 6b where she had progressed by the end of the lesson to using 36cm on the longer notes.

When this pupil used the MusicJacket system to improve her straight bowing she did not receive much feedback. This is no surprise as it is easier to bow straight when using very little of the bow. Her teacher pushed her to use more bow by repeatedly reminding her whilst she was playing. However this additional focus upon bow length seemed to prevent her from noticing the feedback on straight bowing. After the session, the pupil reported she did not feel any vibrotactile feedback, even though the system recorded that it had triggered.

In a brainstorming session with the teacher and the pupil during the fourth lesson, we explored the possibility of adapting the MusicJacket system to suit the particular needs of this pupil. The following week we were able to present an adapted version which worked by providing vibrotactile feedback at each end of the bow length, if the student moved far enough along the bow. She was told to *aim* to feel the vibration as opposed to *avoiding* vibration in the usual set-up. Figure 6c is a result from that feedback session, in which she began to regularly use over 50cm of bow. The effect occurred almost as soon as she tried the feedback making it quicker than the lesson shown in Figure 6b. Clearly, this was a breakthrough moment, and both pupil and teacher were very pleased about the new approach. In an interview after the study her teacher noted *"it was very useful and I think that it worked really well"*.

Other findings

As the pupils became more familiar with the MusicJacket system they were more willing to explore its utility to help them learn and by the end of the study some of them had a very good understanding of how it worked. One of the pupils from group B displayed her knowledge when her

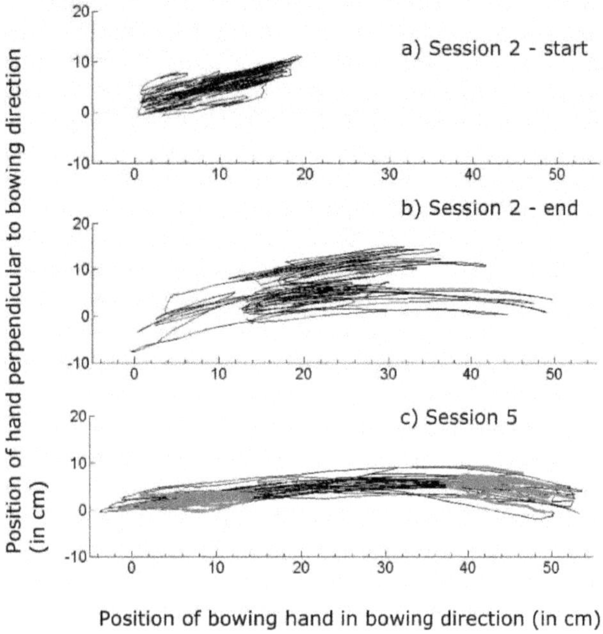

Figure 6: Change in bow length for one pupil over three sessions when provided vibrotactile feedback

ideal bow stroke was not very well calibrated. During her piece she struggled because her bow kept slipping back onto the bridge whilst she was playing and at one point she paused and made a very deliberate correction of her bow position. Afterwards we asked her whether it was the feedback which had made her stop and correct herself, to which she answered clearly: *"it [the feedback] wasn't telling me, it was just the noise of the violin [which told her]"*. She then made some suggestions about how she felt the system should have supported her. This demonstrates how she understood the limitations of the MusicJacket system and the way it inferred the bow stroke from the position of the hand. It took another two attempts to calibrate the system so that the system gave her feedback where she felt she needed it: stricter near the bridge than at the fingerboard.

Each time, she and her teacher were able to quickly evaluate the usefulness of the information it was giving her and decide whether a further calibration was needed. This questioning of the feedback shows a progression from her first feedback session where there was also a problem with the calibration. On that earlier occasion she told us *"it would always buzz when it got to there"*, and she did not phrase it confidently as a problem with the system. It was only when her teacher questioned the way she was playing, that we realized that there was a problem with the calibration, rather than her playing.

This example shows how pupil and teacher came to increasingly understand the feedback over the sessions, and consequently were able to articulate clearly what they needed the feedback to do. It also demonstrates how the teacher was important as a voice for questioning the system and backing up what the pupil expressed.

We also found the pupils enjoyed wearing the technology and were quite comfortable with the vibrations of the feedback. For example, one pupil described it as *"a bit bumpy, but I like it"*. Another pupil even found the vibrotactile feedback quite ticklish and managed to deliberately play her violin in such a way that the feedback stayed on the whole time. She was intentionally cheeky and playful, but through her action also showed a pretty good understanding of how the system worked. Teacher A also felt the bow hold of her pupils was improved when wearing the jacket simply because the sensor on the glove they wore was stiff, which helped keep their palm more open.

The study also revealed the importance of having teachers help in correcting behavior following the initial onset of vibrotactile feedback. When a vibration is set off, it indicates that a movement has left the desired path (or in the case of the violin hand, the instrument is being held in the wrong position), and there is only a minimal indication of how the student should correct their movement. This can be potentially ambiguous if not guided from the beginning. For example, on feeling a vibration on her elbow, one pupil from group A started to lift her elbow out to the side rather than lifting their whole arm to push the violin up. The teacher noticed and corrected her response by pushing her elbow down underneath the violin and then pushing the whole violin up from underneath. This was less an issue for the group B pupils, who had been playing the violin longer, who interpreted the feedback based upon their knowledge of how they ought to be playing, and with some experience of the vibrotactile feedback learned to flick their eyes briefly to their bow to make necessary corrections in the trajectory when they felt a vibration.

DISCUSSION

Our study has shown how vibrotactile feedback can improve violin playing in a real world context for a number of basic and advanced skills. Specifically, children as young as six can quickly learn how to interpret vibrotactile feedback and use it to improve a number of aspects of their violin playing: holding position; bowing straightness; and length of bow stroke. Older children can use it to help them increase their awareness of how they are playing and when they are making mistakes.

The in the wild study revealed that the effectiveness of the vibrotactile feedback was dependent on two factors. Firstly, it was important to have a teacher initially help the student understand how they should respond to the feedback as otherwise they could move their arm or torso inappropriately, as observed in one the pupils in our study. The feedback cannot tell the student the exact movement to make, only that their current path has strayed from the ideal. As noted by Spelmezan *et al.* [20], vibrations positioned on the body may be interpreted in a variety of ways. The teacher's role is important, therefore, in helping to show their pupils the response to the feedback that would be best for their playing.

Secondly, it is important to consider how other aspects of the playing and setting place demands on a pupil's attention. When there are high attentional demands from these factors, the pupil can pay less attention to the vibrotactile feedback, which means they can ignore or not notice it. For example, our study showed that if pupils are doing a difficult exercise, e.g., trying to play a new piece which requires all of their attention, then they often do not respond to the vibrotactile feedback, sometimes reporting that it had not been on or that they had not noticed it. Similarly, Bhargava *et al.* [3] reported that high cognitive load can reduce the ability to localize vibrotactile stimulation, that is, subjects' responses to vibrotactile feedback is diminished. A high demand on the pupil's attention can result in their responses to vibrotactile stimulation diminishing to the point where the buzzes no longer function as useful feedback to guide movement.

Hence, the effectiveness of vibrotactile feedback is variable, depending on the attentional demands on the player. This finding was uncovered through our in the wild study and was not evident in our previous lab studies. Our in the wild study also uncovered a number of ways the MusicJacket system could be used that we had not anticipated and that were only uncovered by taking the system into a realistic teaching scenario. This included the suitability of the feedback for different ability levels. In particular, we found that feedback on the hold of the violin was only useful for group A, and that group B only benefitted from the feedback for the straight bowing technique. The study also revealed new ways that vibrotactile feedback could be used in violin teaching that we had not considered when designing the MusicJacket system. For example, we discovered that the system could be modified with relative ease to teach long bowing, enabling the teacher to address the needs of a particular pupil. We were simply not aware that the calibration could be used as creatively as was done by the pupil who wanted to feel feedback at a particular point. Another discovery was that in contrast with other in-situ studies of haptic feedback, in which the device or technology under investigation can be handed over to participants with minimal training [e.g., 8, 11], ours required considerable time for the pupils to familiarize themselves with the technology and how to understand the buzzing experience relative to what they were normally used to in the lesson. This suggests the need to include training time with a haptic training system to explore its dimensions and understand what the feedback is meant to map onto.

LESSONS LEARNED

Based on the findings of our study we suggest there are three main areas that need to be considered when taking vibrotactile feedback out of the lab and into real world use. These are: task level; matching to the experience of the user; and how to involve the teachers in training.

Task level

Where learners are following elementary exercises they can attend to the vibrotactile feedback, resulting in them being able to respond to it appropriately and accurately report when it occurs. When learners are doing difficult exercises the vibrotactile feedback can recede into the background and remain unnoticed. The challenge is to find a task of intermediate difficulty where the vibrotactile feedback can play a useful role in guiding the students' playing but not make too many demands on their attention. The teacher can help by selecting appropriate tasks that are tailored to each student's ability.

Relevance of feedback

Vibrotactile feedback is most effective when it gives feedback on an aspect of motor learning that is relevant to a student's goals and level of learning. For example, older pupils found it effective for straight bowing and younger pupils for bow position. Vibrotactile feedback is most likely to be effective when it 'tells' the learners about a mistake they *regularly* make and which their teacher has informed them about.

Dialogue with teachers

Involving the teachers throughout the training process is critical to the effectiveness of using haptic feedback in a teaching context, especially in terms of selecting the appropriate exercises and exploring how the feedback works. This can help the students understand how a system works and also provides new terms that teacher and student can use to gauge their progress.

CONCLUSIONS

Our study has demonstrated the value and importance of in the wild studies when deploying haptic technology out into real world uses. We gained insights into the MusicJacket system that were not evident from our lab-based studies. These included the importance of working closely with teachers who have long experience of teaching and know their individual students very well. We also found that for real-time vibrotactile feedback to be effective at improving training it must be relevant to learning goals and should be used in conjunction with tasks which are the right level of difficulty. If these criteria are not met then the learner may feel overloaded and unable to attend to the feedback. Moreover, it is important to recognize that the addition of feedback can make a task more difficult. Finally, as the study progressed, we observed discussions between teachers and students about movements in terms of the vibrotactile feedback they would elicit. This was most noticeable with the more advanced pupils, where the teacher encouraged them to start evaluating their own performance and diagnosing their own problems. Asking 'whether the feedback came on' became a new line of questioning which was used to initiate a dialogue about movement. Hence, a novel benefit of using vibrotactile feedback for training body movements is that it can provide a common vocabulary for teachers and students to discuss body movements.

ACKNOWLEDGMENTS

We thank the children and teachers who participated in this study, and the reviewers for their thoughtful feedback. This research was supported by the eSense project, funded by the AHRC (AH/F011881/1) and The Open University.

REFERENCES

1. Animazoo IGS-190-M http://www.animazoo.com
2. Alamri, A., Eid, M., Iglesias, R., Shirmohammadi, S. and El Saddik, A. Haptic virtual rehabilitation exercises for poststroke diagnosis. *IEEE Trans. Instrumentation and Measurement*, 59, (2008), 1876-1884.
3. Bhargava, A., Scott, M., Traylor, R., Chung, R., Mrozek, K., Wolter, J. and Tan, H. Effect of cognitive load on tactor location identification in zero-g. *Proc 2005 World Haptics Conference (WHC05): First Joint Eurohaptics Conference and Symposium on Haptic Interfaces for Virtual Environment and Teleoperator Systems* (2005) 56-62.
4. Bloomfield, A. and Badler, N. Virtual training via vibrotactile arrays. *Presence,* 2008, vol. 17, 103-120.
5. Grindlay, G.C. The impact of haptic guidance on musical motor learning, *Masters Thesis*, Massachusetts Institute of Technology, 2006.
6. Grosshauser, T. and Hermann, T. Augmented Haptics–An Interactive Feedback System for Musicians. *Proc. Haptic and Audio Interaction Design*, (2009), 100-108.
7. Hale, K.S. and Stanney, K.M. Deriving haptic design guidelines from human physiological, psychophysical, and neurological foundations. *Computer Graphics and Applications*. 24(2), (2004) 33-39.
8. Hoggan, E. and Brewster, S.A. CrossTrainer: Testing the Use of Multimodal Interfaces in Situ. *Proc. CHI 2010*, ACM (2010), 333-342.
9. Holland, S., Bouwer, A.J., Dalgelish, M., and Hurtig, T.M. Feeling the beat where it counts: fostering multi-limb rhythm skills with the haptic drum kit. *Proc. TEI 2010*, ACM (2010), 21-28.
10. Huang, K., Starner, T., Do, E., Weiberg, G., Kohlsdorf, D., Ahlrichs, C. and Leibrandt, R. Mobile music touch: mobile tactile stimulation for passive learning, *Proc. CHI 2010*, ACM (2010), 791-800.
11. Jambon, F. and Meillon, B. User experience evaluation in the wild. In *Proc. CHI 2009, ACM (2009),* 4069-4074.
12. Karapanos, E., Zimmerman, J. Forlizzi, J. and Martens, J.B. User Experience Over Time: An Initial Framework. *Proc. CHI 2009, ACM (2009),* 719-738.
13. Konczak, J., vander Velden, H. and Jaeger, L. Learning to play the violin: Motor control by freezing, not freeing degrees of freedom. *Journal of Motor Behavior,* vol. 41, no. 3, (2009) *243-252.*
14. Lieberman, J. and Breazeal, C. TIKL: Development of a wearable vibrotactile feedback suit for improved human motor learning, In *IEEE Transactions on Robotics*, (2007), 919-926.
15. Ng, K.C., Weyde, T., Larkin, O., Neubarth, K., Koerselman, T. and Ong, B. 3D augmented mirror: a multimodal interface for string instrument learning and teaching with gesture support, *Proc. ICMI 2007*, ACM, (2007), 339-345.
16. Pielot, M. and Boll, S. Tactile Wayfinder: Comparison of Tactile Waypoint Navigation with Commercial pedestrian navigation Systems. *Proc Pervasive Computing, LNCS* (2010), 76-93.
17. Precision microdrive motors http://www.precisionmicrodrives.com
18. Rogers, Y., Connelly, K., Tedesco, L., Hazlewood, W., Kurtz, A., Hall, B., Hursey, J. and Toscos, T. Why it's worth the hassle: The value of in-situ studies when designing UbiComp. *UbiComp 2007 Proceedings, LNCS 4717,* Springer-Verlag, (2007) 336-353.
19. Schoonderwaldt, E. Mechanics and acoustics of violin bowing: Freedom, constraints and control in performance. *Ph.D. dissertation*, KTH—School Comput. Sci. Commun., Stockholm, Sweden, 2009.
20. Spelmezan, D., Jacobs, M., Hilgers, A. and Borchers, J. Tactile motion instructions for physical activities. In *Proc. CHI 2009*, ACM (2009), 2243-2252.
21. van der Linden, J. Schoonderwalt, E., Bird, J. and Johnson, R. MusicJacket: Combining Motion Capture and Vibrotactile Feedback to Teach Violin Bowing. In *IEEE Transactions on Instrumentation and Measurement*, 60 (1), 2011 (in press).
22. van der Linden, J., Schoonderwaldt, E. and Bird, J. Towards a real-time system for teaching novices good violin bowing technique. *Proc. IEEE HAVE*, (2009), 81-86.

PossessedHand: Techniques for Controlling Human Hands using Electrical Muscles Stimuli

Emi Tamaki
Graduate school of Interdisciplinary Information Studies,
The University of Tokyo.
hoimei@acm.org

Takashi Miyaki*
Interfaculty Initiative in Information Studies,
The University of Tokyo.
miyaki@acm.org

Jun Rekimoto
Interfaculty Initiative in Information Studies,
The University of Tokyo.
Sony Computer Science Laboratories, Inc.
rekimoto@acm.org

ABSTRACT
If a device can control human hands, the device can be useful for HCI and tangible application's output. To aid the controlling of finger movement, we present PossessedHand, a device with a forearm belt that can inform when and which fingers should be moved. PossessedHand controls the user's fingers by applying electrical stimulus to the muscles around the forearm. Each muscle is stimulated via 28 electrode pads. Muscles at different depths in the forearm can be selected for simulation by varying the stimulation level. PossessedHand can automatically calibrate the system for individuals. The automatic calibration system estimates relations between each electrode pad, stimulation level and muscle movement. Experiments show that PossessedHand can control the motion of 16 joints in the hand. Further, we also discuss an application based on this device to aid in playing a musical instrument.

Author Keywords
EMS, FES, Electric Stimulation, Hand Gesture, Musical Performance

ACM Classification Keywords
H.5 Information interfaces and presentation: [HCI]

General Terms
Design, Experimentation, Human Factors

INTRODUCTION
HCI and tangible devices use many actuators as outputs. On the other hand, human beings have many actuators such as their muscles in their body. In particular, human hands have the dexterous fingers which are used to output for communications, playing, touching and so on. However, human actuators have not been adapted to HCI and tangible devices. If a device can control human hands, the device would lead the next generation of HCI and tangle applications.

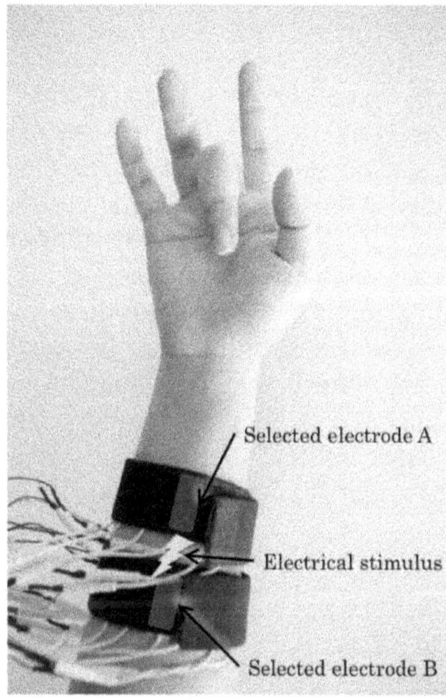

Figure 1. Our concept. PossessedHand controls user's finger.

In this paper, we introduce PossessedHand, a device with a forearm belt (Figure. 1) that can control several hand gestures and inform their timing; this device achieves this by providing electrical stimulus to the muscles in the forearm. However, a controlling the muscles requires special knowledge for the system setting because positions of the stimulation, the stimulation level and timing differ greatly in individuals. We also introduce an automatic calibration system of PossessedHand. On this calibration system, user can use PossessedHand without any special knowledge. Finally, we discuss applications of PossessedHand.

RELATED WORK
Many devices and systems that directly stimulate a user's fingers have been researched [14, 16]. However, users prefer to avoid wearing devices on area A, shown in Figure. 2, because this area is used to touch, hold, and pinch real objects. The skin on this area is important sensor for communication, touching, playing musical instruments or in other

*Karlsruhe Institute of Technology.(Author's current affiliation)

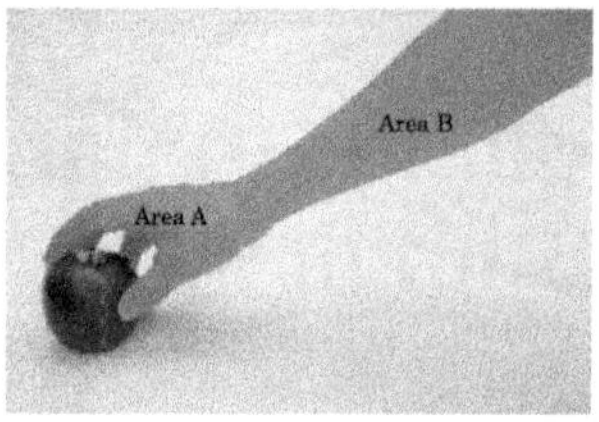

Figure 2. Area A: This area is involved in pinching, gripping, and holding motions. Area B: Electrical stimuli are provided to this area.

performing arts. Glove-type devices that dynamically and mechanically control a user's hand are available [29]. Such devices cover most of area A. Although a device that can be worn on the forearm has been developed, it is too large to be comfortably used for daily uses.

To solve these problems, we develop a small device, PossessedHand, that can control a user's hand without covering area A. PossessedHand can be used for controlling finger-joint movements; it operates by applying an electrical stimulus to the muscles in the forearm with noninvasive electrode pads. The muscles involved in finger motions are clustered in the forearm [23]. PossessedHand has electrode pads that are fastened to the forearm to stimulate these muscles. The tendons that are connected to the muscles move the finger joints. To date, there have been no research on controlling the position of the hand solely through electrical stimulation to the forearm. The electrical stimulation by PossessedHand is similar to *Electrical Muscle Stimulation*(EMS) [5, 6, 11] and *Functional Electrical Stimulation*(FES) [22, 9, 11, 17, 7, 26].

EMS has several applications. EMS is widely used in low-frequency therapeutic equipment and in devices used for ergotherapy [2, 33]. EMS allows in 15 min of continuous uses[2]. Akamatsu et al. used EMS in performing arts [19, 25]. EMS is similar to FES [8, 21, 31, 30, 32]. In FES, electrical currents are used to activate nerves innervating extremities that are affected by paralysis resulting from a stroke or other neurological disorders and spinal cord or head injuries. FES can be used to treat people with disabilities [34].

Watanabe et al. and Kruijff et al. presented a technique in which a user's wrist can be controlled with two degrees of freedom by stimulating four muscles [15, 30]. They observed that they could control wrist motion by electrically stimulating a muscle, which resulted in the motion of the tendon connected to the wrist. However, they did not consider the motion of finger-joints, which is important for controlling the position of the hand. Moreover, they used invasive electrodes embedded in the skin. Such electrodes are not suitable for playing musical instruments.

It is necessary to use noninvasive electrodes and to avoid fastening electrodes to the hands or fingers because the hands and fingers are used to hold or touch real objects. The haptic drum kit is developed by Simon et al [12]. This kit signals when a drum should be struck while playing drums by using vibrations. However, it is not effective for playing musical instruments other than drums such as piano and koto, because it cannot signal which finger should be moved.

We presented a designe of PossessedHand[28]. The paper shows that PossessedHand needs seven electrodes to control 1 finger joint angles of user's hand. Electrode pads, which is noninvasive electrodes, are set on user's forearm. However, a location setting of the pas took many time and required knowledges about muscle locations in forearm. We must make a personal belt for each user because the size of user's forearm differs widely in individuals. For widely uses, PossessedHand should have automatically calibration system.

PHASE OF DEVELOPMENT

There are four phases to control hand gestures as outputs of HCI and tangible applications. The applications are suggested on each phases. In this research, we identify three phases in which PossessedHand can be used.

Phase 1: Although the user cannot visually confirm the hand motion, he/she feels the motion owing to his/her somatic sense. (e.g., providing feedback for recognizing virtual objects)

Phase. 2: The user visually confirms the motion. The user's fingers are dependently controlled. (e.g., systems used in performing arts).

Phase 3: The user's fingers are independently controlled to perform grasping and opening motions (e.g., support systems for musical performances and sport activities, navigation systems, and sensory substitution systems for the visually impaired and the hearing impaired).

Phase 4: The user's hand is controlled to perform dexterous and powerful motions such as pinching by using the thumb and index finger (e.g., learning systems for finger languages and for making handicrafts)

OUR PLAN AND GOAL OF AN APPLICATION

Our goal of an application is to develop a support system for playing musical instruments with PossessedHand, that can teach the appropriate hand gestures and timing to a beginner playing a musical instrument. Beginners must devote considerable time to learning because it is difficult to simply observe a skillful performance and imitate the required hand gestures and their timing. This type of learning in which beginners compare their performance with a skillful performance leads to over fatigue. Skillful playing can be achieved if the appropriate hand gestures and timing can be taught to a beginner while he or she is playing a musical instrument.

First, we describe an experiment conducted to identify which and how finger-joints can be controlled by several stimulation levels. Second, we select the electric pads for daily uses. Third, we develop PossessedHand device and calibration systems about the location of the pads, the stimulation level, and stimulation timing. Forth, we verify that the each joint can be controlled, and users can correctly feel each joint movement induced by PossessedHand. In addition, we also discuss the results on the basis of the four phases discussed above. Finally, we will discuss a support system based on PossessedHand for playing musical instruments.

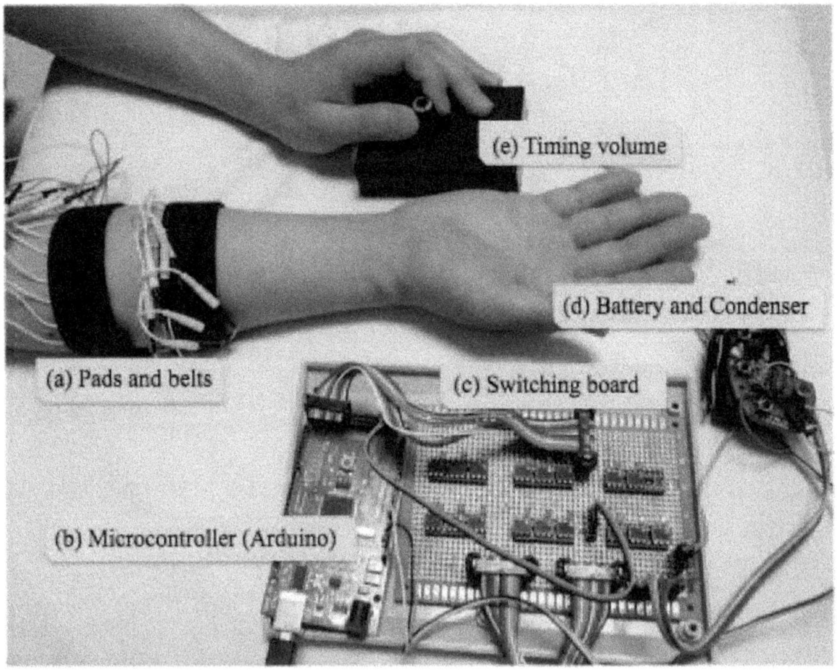

Figure 3. A prototype of PossessedHand.

SOLUTIONS

Muscles and stimulations for making hand postures

We use electrical pulses, 1 channels, and three levels of electrical stimulations to control the user's hand. The impulses generated by PossessedHand are transmitted to the muscles that are to be stimulated through electrode pads fastened to the skin. PossessedHand uses EMS to achieve its desired output energy and maintain a compact size [13, 27]. An electrical stimulus from PossessedHand is applied to the user's forearm because most of the muscles that control the fingers and the wrist are located the forearm. For this purpose, a forearm belt is used along with PossessedHand. The electrical stimuli are generated by an electronic pulse generator and transmitted via the electrode pads. The pads are arranged on the upper and lower parts of the user's forearm (Figure. 3-(a)). At least, five channels are needed to stimulate the muscles that are used to bend finger-joints, and two additional channels are needed to stimulate the muscles that are used to bend finger extensions and cause wrist flexions. PossessedHand stimulates seven muscles (the superficial flexor muscle, deep flexor muscle, long flexor muscle of the thumb, common digital extensor muscle, flexor carpi radialis muscle, long palmar muscle, and flexor carpi ulnaris muscle). These muscles are located in area B in Figure. 2. We can select a channel between a pad on the upper portion of the forearm and one on the lower portion of the forearm.

Stimulation levels and the pulse of electrical stimulation

PossessedHand selects the depth of the muscle by the stimulation levels. The flexor digitorum superficialis muscle is connected to the *proximal interphalangeal*(PIP) joint, the second joint in each finger. The flexor digitorum profundus muscle is connected to the *distal interphalangeal*(DIP) joint, the third joint in each finger. These muscles are located at the same position, however these muscle are at different depths in the user's forearm [3]. The existing electrical pads cannot be used to select muscles at different depths because the pads do not contact the muscles directly. Therefore, invasive needles are used when fine control of finger-joints is required. However, as previously described, controlling fingers by needles is difficult in daily life.

We tried to select the stimulated muscle by regulating voltages of stimulation. Moreover, we tried to stimulate both the flexor digitorum superficialis muscle and the flexor digitorum profundus muscle by applying higher voltages of stimulation. We conducted an experiment with various stimulation levels to see which muscle was selected. Figure. 5 shows the result of the experiment. The vertical axis indicates the joint angle. The horizontal axis shows voltages of the applied current generated by PossessedHand. In this experiment, subjects wore PossessedHand and were told to relax their muscles. We set the back of subjects' hand touched the flat of a desk. We measured joint angles starting from zero (when the finger is completely straight). Then, we raised the voltage by one volt and measured the joint angles.

The applied stimulation pulse frequency was set to Hz, and the pulse width was $.2\,ms$, and the pulse height (voltage) was in the range of 1 - 2 V (Figure. 4). The pulse reported is that which gives the user no pain, because it is similar to the human impulse to move muscles [5, 6, 11]. From this experiment, we found that the depth of the stimulated muscle could be selected by regulating voltages. The movement of each joint (PIP, DIP, and MP joints) was selected by different voltages. The PIP joint moved independently at 1 V. The PIP joint also moved at 1 V. Therefore,

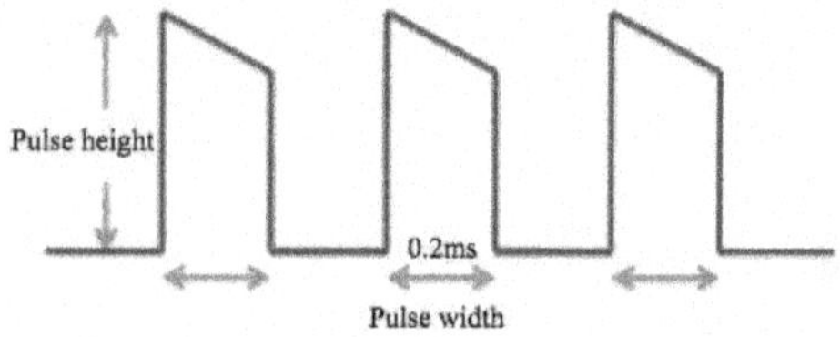

Figure 4. Pulse of electric stimulation by PossessedHand. The Pulse height is adjusted for the voltage. Pulse width is set 0.2ms to be similar to nervous signals in human muscles.

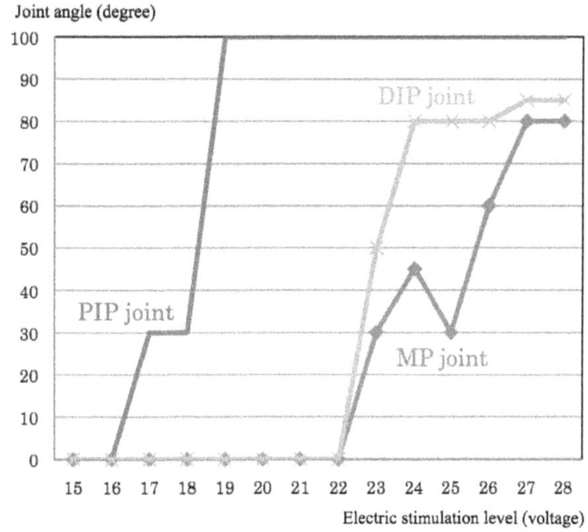

Figure 5. An example of the selected muscle depth and movement by the electric stimulation levels (voltage). Blue line with Diamond makers: MP joint movement. Red line: PIP joint movement. Green line with times makers: DIP joint movement.

we concluded that the voltage from 1 to 1 V stimulates the flexor digitorum superficialis muscle selectively. Voltages higher than 2 V also stimulated the flexor digitorum profundus muscle, resulting in the movement of the DIP joint and MP joint.

Operable joints

Our previous paper/,[28] reported that PossessedHand could control the motion of 16 joints in the hand. We conducted an experiment to confirm whether the finger-joints can be appropriately moved to achieve desired hand postures. We selected an anode from the seven electrodes placed on the upper arm and a ground electrode from the seven electrodes placed on the hand. We tested $-by-$ patterns of the electronic paths corresponding to each of three peak values of the pulse (1 V, 2 V, and 2 V); in other words, we performed 1 stimulations. We asked the subjects to eliminate strain in the hand. We confirmed that PossessedHand could control independent and 11 linked joints, 1 joints in total. We also found that a clasped hand could be opened by stimulating a common digital extensor muscle. Further, users could recognize the motion of their hands even when their eyes were closed. These results suggest that PossessedHand can control hand postures in phases 1, 2, and 3, as discussed above.

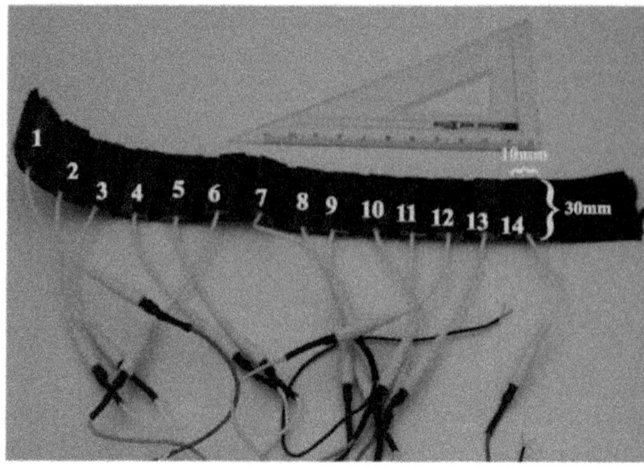

Figure 6. A belt and pads.

SYSTEM CONFIGURATION

Prototype of the device

We built a prototype of PossessedHand that consists of a battery, a condenser, a timing volume, a switching board (Photo-MOS Relays Series AQV221), a microcontroller, and 2 electrode pads on two belts(Figure. 3, Figure. 6). These devices are controlled by a graphical user interface (GUI) on a PC (Figure. 7). The microcontroller is connected to the PC via a USB cable. The dimensions of PossessedHand are 1 . $cm \times$. $cm \times$. cm, which are portable and suitable for daily uses and playing musical instruments. The pulse width is .2 ms, and the voltage is in the range of 1 - 2 V. For safety reasons, the electric are charged in the condenser that is limited.

Electric pads and pain

We used solid gel type electrodes (electrical pads) of sizes 1 $\times$ 1 mm or larger to prevent electric stimulations from causing pain. There are three types of noninvasive electrodes.

Dry type electric pads

These pads are made of metallic sheets. These pads are used to get galvanic skin response (GSR) values. The pads cause pain when the contact area is small.

Liquid gel type electric pads

Liquid gel type electric pads have a sponge base. The user must put some liquid gel on the base before placing the pad on the user's skin. The pads cause pain when the human skin becomes dry because the contact area becomes small with moisture conditions of the pads.

Solid gel type electric pads

Solid gel type electric pads include conductive gel on thin metallic sheets. User cause relatively little pain, because the pads attach to the skin surface with certainly, and the contact area does not decrease. *Self Stick Tyco gel Carbon Electrodes* [1] are adapted to PossessedHand.

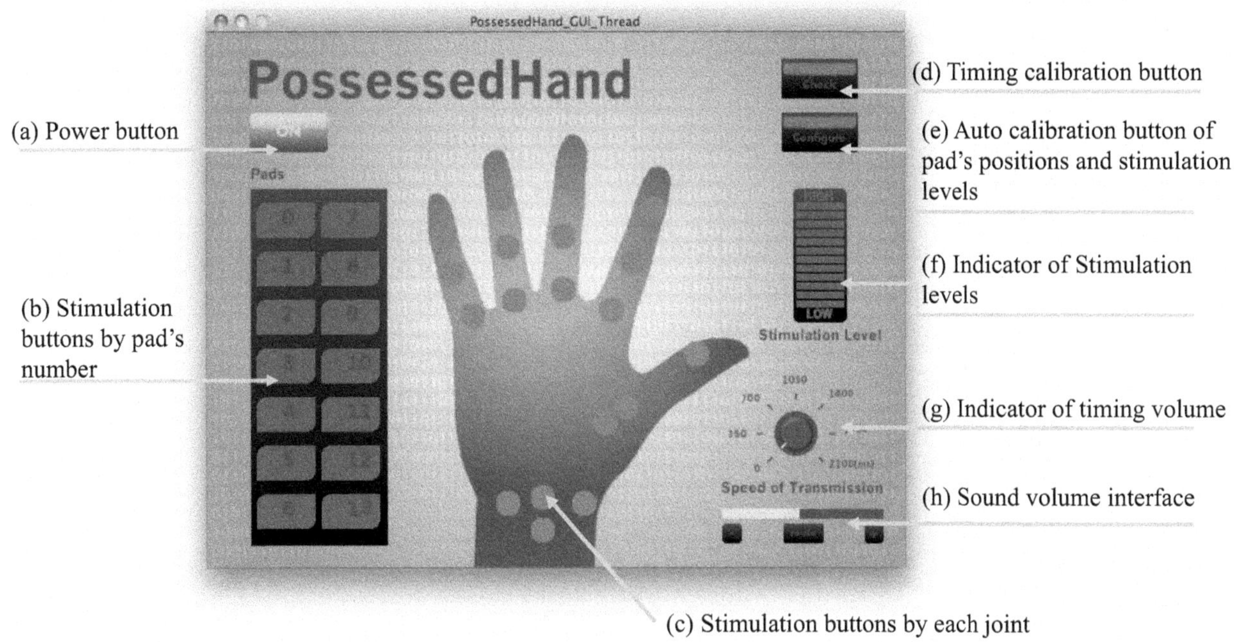

Figure 7. Screenshot of the PossessedHand GUI.

We also confirmed that users felt no pain from electrical stimulation (V, 1 mA, the pulse width = $.2\,ms$) with the 1 × 1 mm pads. In our experiments, we had ten subjects who wore an eye mask. We adopted solid gel type electric pads that were bigger than 1 × 1 mm in size. In this work, 1 × mm pads are used on the belts of PossessedHand. We cut the pads into pieces the same height size as the height of the belt.

Calibration system for individual variation

We suggest an automatic calibration system for PossessedHand that can calibrate the pads' positions and the electrical stimulation levels according to individual variations. It is difficult to fasten the seven pads and set the stimulation levels correctly on a user's forearm. To solve this problem, we include as many pads as possible on the belts. 1 pads can be set on a belt. PossessedHand has two belts, and 2 pads. The calibration system identifies the pads that are used to stimulate a user's muscles. The system also selects three optimal stimulation levels to move each joint from twelve stimulation levels. It works by software base. The calibration steps are given below:

STEP 1. Wear PossessedHand. Start the auto calibration system. (Figure. 7-(e) Auto-calibration button to calibrate pads' positions and stimulation levels)

STEP 2. The auto-calibration system gives 1 stimulation patterns that include 1 paths (via electric pads on the belts) and 12 stimulation levels.

STEP 3. Push the joint button on the GUI when the joints are moved. (Figure. 7-(c) Stimulation buttons for each joint)

STEP 4. The system checks the pads that can be used to move each joint.

STEP 5. The system also selects three optimal stimulation levels from twelve stimulation levels for use in moving each joint.

Calibration system for stimulation timing

It is also important that the timings for appropriate musical instruments are correctly set. We built a calibration system of stimulation timing on PossessedHand. A user can calibrate the stimulation timing by using a timing volume (Figure. 3-(e) Timing volume). There is always a lag between the sound timing and the stimulation timing because it takes some time to generate the electrical stimulations and for the stimulations to be felt. To synchronize the timing, we introduce a calibration system. The system gives sound and stimulation at the same time. A user can then adjust the timing using the timing volume (Figure. 3(e) Timing volume), (Figure. 7-(d) Timing calibration button, (g) Indicator of timing volume). For eight subjects, the average time lag was 0.34 s. The standard error was 0.16 s. In our experiments, all the subjects could adjust the timing.

EXPERIMENTS

Probability of each joint movement

We checked the probability of each joint movement by PossessedHand and the calibration systems. We had eight subjects. Table. 1 shows the results. We confirmed that PossessedHand could control independent and 11 linked joints, 1 joints in total, with the calibration systems. Figure. 10 shows over half of the probability of each joint movement from Table 1. Figure. 8 shows that PossessedHand was controlling each of the user's finger-joints. The results indicate

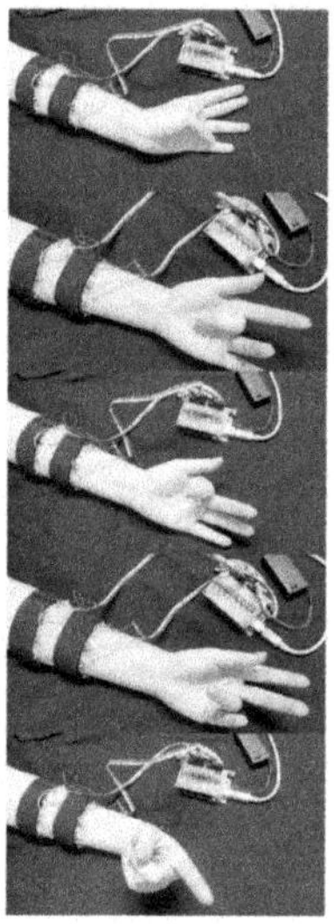

Figure 8. Examples of finger-joint movement by PossessedHand.

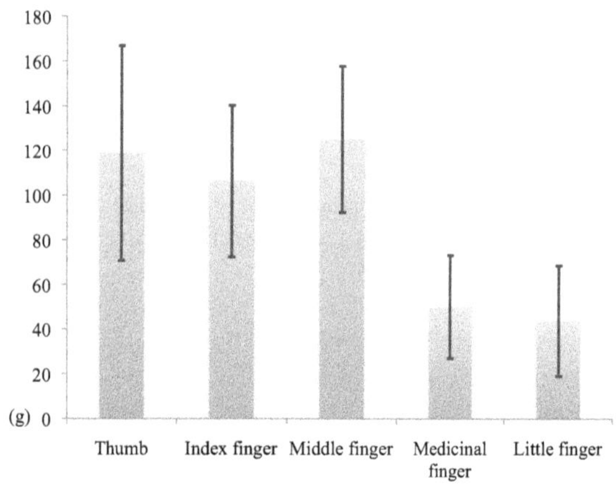

Figure 9. Measured forces for each finger.

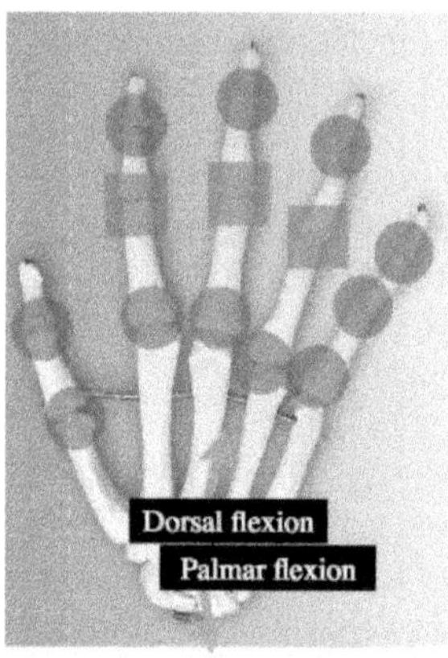

Figure 10. Operable joints. Squares indicate independently operable joints. Arrows and circles indicate ganed operable joints.

Table 1. Probability of each joint movement (%)

joint name	with other joints	independently
MP(Index finger)	100	0
MP(Middle finger)	100	0
MP(Medicinal finger)	100	0
MP(Littile finger)	100	0
PIP(IP) (Thumb)	100	0
PIP(Index finger)	100	100
PIP(Middle finger)	100	100
PIP(Medicinal finger)	100	100
PIP(Littile finger)	100	12.5
DIP(Thumb)	100	12.5
DIP(Index finger)	100	0
DIP(Middle finger)	87.5	0
DIP(Medicinal finger)	75	0
DIP(Littile finger)	87.5	0
Palmar flexion	100	0
Dorsal flexion	100	0
Radial flexion	37.5	0
Ulnar flexion	0	0

that PossessedHand and the calibration systems can realize Phases 1, 2, and 3.

Force per finger

We measured the force generated by PossessedHand on each finger with a spring balance. The eight subjects took part in this experiment, and did not move their fingers by themselves. The stimulation levels were set to the maximum possible values that did not cause pain to the subjects. The limit of voltage was $2V$. The locations of the pads were identified by our calibration system. PossessedHand moved MP, PIP and DIP joints in each finger at the same time. The fingers turned in. The force of each finger were measured by a spring scale, which mounted on a table and a finger. We set the back of subjects ’ hand touched the flat of a desk. We noted maximum values of the force in the three seconds.

In this experiment, all forces were too weak to grap real objects and to play musical instruments. Figure. 9 shows the results. The horizontal axis indicates fingers, while the vertical axis represents the forces (g). The error bars denote the standard error values. The number of trials per finger was three, and the total number of trials was 120. The average force was . g. The forces were not sufficient to grap and to play musical instruments however were enough to point out the fingers to be moved.

The Controlling the amount is next step of this research. That is feasible system, if the system calibrate the relation between the electric stimulation level and the amount of bend in a joint. It is reported that the muscle controlling method is similar to motor controlling method(proportional integral derivative controller, PID controller), on the electric stimulation experiment by using needle. It will be useful to tell correct hand postures, strength and weakness. In present system of PossessedHand can not reach the Phase. 4.

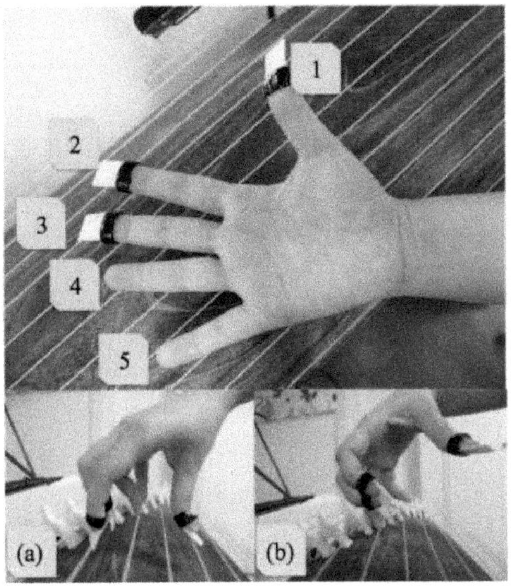

Figure 11. Playing styles of Koto. (a) one playing style using 1-3rd finger, (b) another playing style using 4 or 5th finger.

Somatesthesia

In this experiment, we confirmed that eight subjects could correctly feel each joint movement induced by PossessedHand. While wearing an eye mask, the subjects could correctly guess which joints were moved by PossessedHand. The stimulation levels and the locations of the pads were identified by our calibration system. For three seconds, PossessedHand moved MP, PIP and DIP joints in each finger. We conducted three trials for each fingers. The total number of the trials was 12 . The results show that PossessedHand can teach which finger must be moved to output information and to play musical instruments.

SUPPORT SYSTEM FOR MUSICAL INSTRUMENTS

PossessedHand can be used to help a beginner how to play musical instruments. In musical instruments, koto, subtle differences in tones are achieved by fine finger movements.

In this study, we developed an example application: a support system for playing koto. The koto is a traditional Japanese stringed instrument. Kotos are about 1 centimeters wide and made from paulownia wood. Koto has 1 strings that are strung over 1 movable bridges along the width of the instrument. Players can adjust the string pitches by moving these bridges before playing. A koto player uses all fingers to pluck the strings. The player puts three different picks on the thumb, index finger, and middle finger, respectively (Figure. 1). In playing koto, it is important when and which finger should be moved because each finger produces different sound and has a different playing style (Figure. 11).

It is difficult for performers to use visual or sound guides for the support of the Koto performance, because the performers should read a Koto score and listen to their own performances during their performances. On the score, string numbers, timings and finger numbers are written. The finger numbers guide which finger should be moved. However, performers' view points are almost set on the string numbers of the score for their performances. It is hard to read the string numbers, timings and finger numbers at the same time. Then, PossessedHand directly tells the finger number and timing to the performers.

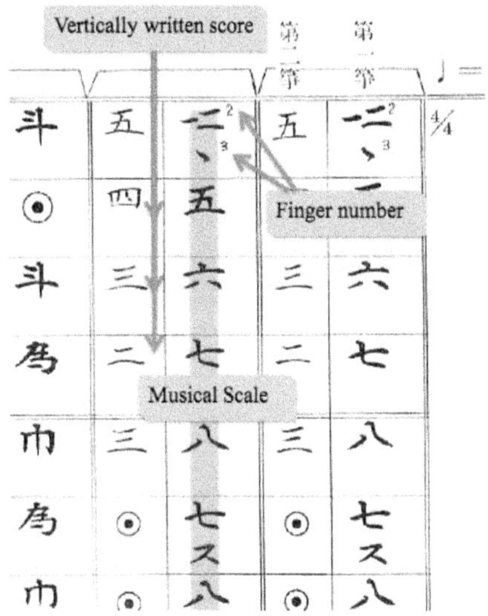

Figure 12. An example of koto score.

For a sample of perfect performances, we transcribe Japanese koto scores to PossessedHand scores. The Japanese koto scores included information on when and which fingers should be moved (Figure. 12). Two beginners (subjects) tried to play koto by wearing PossessedHand. In this experiment, we checked that beginners could get the rhythm and make fewer mistakes by wearing PossessedHand. We used a score, which was named "Usagi" [18]. The subject played 8-bar in quadruple time. For eight times, the subject alternated between normal playing and supported playing by wearing PossessedHand. The arm located by user-self. The result is shown in Table 2. It attests that PossessedHand supports beginners' playing. Furthermore, PossessedHand will help beginners move fingers appropriately when playing musical instruments.

DISCUSSION AND COMMENTS

In Table. 3, We list the comments of the subjects, who contributed to our experiments. Regarding the first comment, almost all subjects are not used to electric stimulation by PossessedHand. We must be careful to consider the feeling of terror. In our future work, PossessedHand's appearance will be improved to lessen the feeling of terror.

Table 2. The results of the experiment about the musical performance.

	supported	normal
mistakes about finger	3	4
timing errors	4	13

Table 3. Comments from the subjects.

subject's number	comment
1	Scary... just scary...
2	I felt like my forearm was pushed by someone.
3	I felt like when I got a cramp in my arm.
4	A kind of new sense!
5	I want to be controlled remotely.
6	It would be possible that I can do difficult task (such as driving helicopter) without training.
7	It will be useful when playing other instruments such as Piano or Sax other than koto.
8	I felt like my body was hacked.

As for the second comment, the current could stimulate not only muscles, however also sensory organs. In this case, pressure sensory organs in the surface of the skin were stimulated. This is unavoidable. However, selecting which ones to stimulate might be possible in the future by changing the stimulation frequency or controlling the stimulation depth.

As for the third comment, PossessedHand now applies current only to two points in one muscle. More elaborated application of current, such as adding current application points, would prevent cramp-like feeling.

As for the fourth and eighth comments, people believed their body was totally "under control", However PossessedHand raises questions about their control or "free will".

As for the sixth comment, PossessedHand now controls only the hand to enhance musical experiences. In the future, difficult tasks such as flying a helicopter might be possible. Applying current to the shoulder should be studied in the future. Moreover, combining PossessedHand with other technology such as context-recognition should be necessary.

As for the seventh comment, PossessedHand can be used to play any musical instruments. In this study, the koto was selected as the musical instrument in experiments because it was the only instrument with which the author was familiar.

We also feel that the use of PossessedHand can be extended to sports, learning finger languages, performing arts, and making handicrafts. To extend the use of PossessedHand, we have to consider reaction rates, accuracy, and muscle fatigue [4, 10, 24].

CONCLUSION

PossessedHand can inform the appropriate hand gestures and the timing of these gestures to a beginner playing a musical instrument. We used electric pulses, 14 channels, and three levels of electrical stimulations. The system stimulates the user's forearm muscles that are connected to each finger-joint. Auto-Calibration systems have been introduced to set pads' locations, levels of electrical stimulations and the timing. The calibration system gave 168 stimulation patterns that included 14 paths (via electric pads on the belts) and 12 stimulation levels. Than, the system selected the pad's locations and the levels of electrical stimulations from feedback of finger motions. To synchronize the timing, the system gave sounds and stimulations at the same time. The user can adjusted the timing by using a timing volume of PossessedHand.

PossessedHand can selectively apply simulations to muscles at different depths according to three levels of electrical stimulations, and it can control 5 independent and 11 linked joints, 16 joints in total, with our auto-calibration systems. In our experiments, subjects could correctly feel each joint movement induced by PossessedHand. We also measured the force generated by PossessedHand for each finger. The average force was $88.75\,g$. The forces were not sufficient to grap a real object and to play musical instruments were enough to indicate the fingers that needed to be moved.

We discussed a support system based on PossessedHand for playing koto, which is a traditional Japanese musical instrument. About the support system of the Koto performance, we are in the first stage. We must consider effective feedbacks, the controlling the amount of bend, motivations[20] and so on. In this paper, we confirmed that PossessedHand could tell a user which finger should be moved at which timing. When using PossessedHand, the subjects could maintain a correct rhythm and made fewer mistakes in finger selection.

ACKNOWLEDGEMENTS

The authors would like to thank our anonymous reviewers for their feedback and great suggestions. We thank a japanese Koto player, Mayuko Kobayashi for her advice. We also thank all subjects for their participation in the experiments, Lab-Cafe members and Ken Iwasaki for their help with the experiments, and Kenichi Kumatani for the discussion. This work was supported in part by the research fellowship for young scientists from the Japan Society for the Promotion of Science(JSPS).

REFERENCES

1. Self stick, tyco gel - carbon electrodes. Tyco.
2. Omron, omron battery-operated electronic nerve stimulator (ens), model e2 elite (hv-f127-e), 2009. http://www.omron-healthcare.com/export/sites/default/_global/EMC/EMCinfo-HV-F127-v01.pdf.
3. Adams, G., Harris, R., Woodard, D., and Dudley, G. Mapping of electrical muscle stimulation using mri. *Journal of applied physiology 2* (1993), 532— 537.
4. Boncompagni, S., Kern, H., Micaroni, M., Fano, G., Hofer, C., Forstner, C., Modlin, M., Mayr, M., Carraro, U., and Protasi, F. Functional electrical stimulation (fes) of long-term denervated and degenerated muscles (ddm) in humans: its effect on the rearrangement of the excitation-contraction coupling apparatus. *Journal of Muscle Research and Cell Motility. Abstracts: 32nd European Muscle Conference ' A link between fundamental research and therapeutic trials ' The Annual Meeting of the European Society for Muscle Research 24* (2003), 354.
5. E. C. Hummelsheim H, M.-L. M. The functional value of electrical muscle stimulation for the rehabilitation of the hand in stroke patients (1997). 3–10.
6. EB, M., and R, K. Functional walking in paralyzed patients by means of electrical stimulation. vol. 175 (1983), 30–36.
7. Faghri, P., Rodgers, M. M., Glaser, R., J. Bors, C. H., and Akuthota, P. The effects of functional electrical stimulation on shoulder subluxation, arm function recovery, and shoulder pain in hemiplegic stroke patients. *Archives of physical medicine and rehabilitation 75* (1994), 73–79.
8. Farbiz, F., Yu, Z. H., Manders, C., and Ahmad, W. An electrical muscle stimulation haptic feedback for mixed reality tennis game. In *ACM SIGGRAPH 2007 posters*, SIGGRAPH '07, ACM (New York, NY, USA, 2007).
9. Field-Fote, E. Combined use of body weight support, functional electric stimulation, and treadmill training to improve walking ability in individuals with chronic incomplete spinal cord injury. *In Archives of physical medicine and rehabilitation* (2001).
10. Griffin, L., Decker, M., Hwang, J., Wang, B., Kitchen, K., Ding, Z., and Ivy, J. Functional electrical stimulation cycling improves body composition, metabolic and neural factors in persons with spinal cord injury. *Journal of Electromyography and Kinesiology 19(4)* (2009), 614—622.
11. Hakansson, N., and Hull, M. Muscle stimulation waveform timing patterns for upper and lower leg muscle groups to increase muscular endurance in functional electrical stimulation pedaling using a forward dynamic model. vol. 56(9) (2009), 2263–70.
12. Holland, S., Bouwer, A. J., Dalgelish, M., and Hurtig, T. M. Feeling the beat where it counts: fostering multi-limb rhythm skills with the haptic drum kit. In *Proceedings of the fourth international conference on Tangible, embedded, and embodied interaction*, TEI '10, ACM (New York, NY, USA, 2010), 21–28.
13. Horst, H., Maier-Loth ML, and C, E. The functional value of electrical muscle stimulation for the rehabilitation of the hand in stroke patients. *Scandinavian journal of rehabilitation medicine 29(1)* (1997), 3.
14. Huang, K., Starner, T., Do, E., Weiberg, G., Kohlsdorf, D., Ahlrichs, C., and Leibrandt, R. Mobile music touch: mobile tactile stimulation for passive learning. In *Proceedings of the 28th international conference on Human factors in computing systems*, CHI '10, ACM (New York, NY, USA, 2010), 791–800.
15. Kruijff, E., Schmalstieg, D., and Beckhaus, S. Using neuromuscular electrical stimulation for pseudo-haptic feedback. In *Proceedings of the ACM symposium on Virtual reality software and technology*, VRST '06, ACM (New York, NY, USA, 2006), 316–319.
16. Kuroki, S., Kajimoto, H., Nii, H., Kawakami, N., and Tachi, S. Proposal for tactile sense presentation that combines electrical and mechanical stimulus. In *EuroHaptics Conference, 2007 and Symposium on Haptic Interfaces for Virtual Environment and Teleoperator Systems. World Haptics 2007. Second Joint* (2007), 121 –126.
17. Marsolais, E., and Kobetic, R. Functional electrical stimulation for walking in paraplegia. *In The Journal of Bone and Joint Surgery 69* (1987), 728–733.
18. N, M. Usagi, 1968.
19. Nagasawa, Y., Akamatsu, M., and Teruoka, M. Development of bio-feedback system and applications for musical performances. vol. 40 (2002), 27—32.
20. Percival, G., Wang, Y., and Tzanetakis, G. Effective use of multimedia for computer-assisted musical instrument tutoring. In *Proceedings of the international workshop on Educational multimedia and multimedia education*, Emme '07, ACM (New York, NY, USA, 2007), 67–76.
21. Poboroniuc, M., and Stefan, C. A method to test fes-based control strategies for neuroprostheses. In *Proceedings of the 9th WSEAS International Conference on International Conference on Automation and Information*, World Scientific and Engineering Academy and Society (WSEAS) (Stevens Point, Wisconsin, USA, 2008), 344–349.

22. Rushton, D. Functional electrical simulation and rehabilitationan hypothesis. *In Medical Engineering and Physics 25* (2003), 75–78.

23. Schuenke, M., Schulte, E., Schumacher, U., Lamperti, E. D., Ross, L. M., and Wesker, K. H. Atlas of anatomy: General anatomy and musculoskeletal system. Prometheus (2005).

24. Shioyama, T., Kondo, T., and ITo, K. Lower-limb joint torque and position controls by functional electrical stimulation(fes). *IEICE technical report. ME and bio cybernetics 104(757)* (2005), 25—28.

25. Stelarc. Ping body. http://stage.itp.nyu.edu/history/timeline/pingbody.html, 1996.

26. T. Thrasher, V. Z., McIlroy, W., and Popovic, M. Rehabilitation of reaching and grasping function in severe hemiplegic patients using functional electrical stimulation therapy. *Neurorehabilitation and neural repair 22, 6* (2008), 706.

27. Tachi, S., Tanie, K., and Abe, M. Effects of pulse height and pulse width on the magnitude sensation of electrocutaneous stimulus. *Japanese journal of medical electronics and biological engineering 15(5)* (1977), 315—320.

28. Tamaki, E., Miyaki, T., and Rekimoto, J. Possessedhand: a hand gesture manipulation system using electrical stimuli. In *Proceedings of the 1st Augmented Human International Conference*, AH '10, ACM (New York, NY, USA, 2010), 2:1–2:5.

29. Tsetserukou, D., Sato, K., Neviarouskaya, A., Kawakami, N., and Tachi., S. Flextorque: innovative haptic interface for realistic physical interaction in virtual reality. ACM (2009), 69.

30. Watanabe, T., Iibuchi, K., Kurosawa, K., and Hoshimiya, N. A method of multichannel pid control of two-degree-of-freedom wrist joint movements by functional electrical stimulation. *Systems and Computers in Japan 34(5)* (2003), 25–36.

31. Woo, S. H., J.Y.Jang, Jung, E. S., hyun Lee, J., Moon, Y. K., w Kim, T., Won, C. H., Choi, H. C., and Cho, J. H. Electrical stimuli capsule for control moving direction at the small intestine. ACTA Press (2006), 311—316.

32. Yagi, R., Sugimoto, Y., Nakatsuchi, Y., Yasunobu, H., Shimada, Y., Komatsu, S., Naito, A., Ichie, M., and Hoshimiya, N. Analysis of hand movement indubed by functional electrical stimulation in tetraplegic and hemiplegic patients. *The Japanese Journal of Rehabilitation Medicine 21(4)* (1984), 235—242.

33. Zatsiorsky, K. Science and practice of strength training - ems. *Human Kinetics* (2006), 132–133.

34. Zhang, D., Guan, T. H., Widjaja, F., and Ang, W. T. Functional electrical stimulation in rehabilitation engineering: a survey. In *Proceedings of the 1st international convention on Rehabilitation engineering; assistive technology: in conjunction with 1st Tan Tock Seng Hospital Neurorehabilitation Meeting*, i-CREATe '07, ACM (New York, NY, USA, 2007), 221–226.

Design Interventions for Open-Air Museums: Applying and Extending the Principles of "Assembly"

Marc McLoughlin
Interaction Design Centre, Dept. of CSIS
University of Limerick, Limerick, Ireland
marc.mcloughlin@ul.ie

Luigina Ciolfi
Interaction Design Centre, Dept. of CSIS
University of Limerick, Limerick, Ireland
luigina.ciolfi@ul.ie

ABSTRACT
This paper presents an empirical approach to designing and deploying technologies to support visitor activities in exhibition spaces. Specifically, we focus on the concept of "assembly" and how it was extended and applied to develop an interactive installation for an open-air museum. We argue that this approach to designing for a meaningful visitor experience is particularly suited to open-air visit scenarios; we describe how we have extended the approach and applied it, detailing the resulting multi-device installation that was deployed on site, and presenting some reflections on the usefulness of the assembly concept.

Author Keywords
Ubiquitous computing, design approaches, assemblies, museums.

ACM Classification Keywords
User interfaces, user-centred design, evaluation/methodology.

General Terms
Design, Theory.

INTRODUCTION
Open-air museums are popular visitor attractions whereby dwellings, man-made landscapes and other outdoor features are displayed in historically and/or thematically meaningful ways. They are interesting settings for technological augmentation, as they retain many of the qualities of museums based on room-sized exhibits (the role of the curator in arranging material, the use of themes for particular sections, etc.), which other outdoor heritage sites do not present. They also feature different challenges: their out-of-doors nature, the extended physical path and time frame of the visit, the importance of location and of movement between buildings and corners of the landscape. The HCI and Interaction Design communities have documented many examples of interactive technologies in museums and exhibitions (see for example [13][11][8][10] to mention but a few), however there is a need to extend current approaches to design interventions when considering sites that are spatially distributed and that are structured in ways different from the one-room/ one-exhibit approach. Applications for personal portable devices have been developed to support visitor trails in outdoor sites such as a city's historical centre, areas of natural beauty or other outdoor attractions [1][12][7]. Open-air museums, however, require an approach to design that takes into account not only their spatially distributed nature (whereby a mobile solution would appear the optimal one), but also their "narrative" quality, and their strong place identity, as they exhibit entire buildings in a reconstructed environment. Mobile applications alone are often detached from the lived physical context their content describes, and lack much of the character and material attractiveness of the site. Moreover, a case should be made for the value of shared visitor installations to facilitate social interaction and engagement among visitors during their exploration of a heritage site, a feature of exhibitions whose importance much research has highlighted [9]. A mobile component to an installation for these sites needs to be flanked with other opportunities for engagement, exchange and collaboration. There is a need to investigate how interaction unfolds and can be supported by multi-device systems in the context of large, distributed heritage sites.

A significant volume of work has isolated aspects of interaction with public systems, for example: how people interact with public installations [1], how social interaction shapes people's experiences [9], and how design can embody aspects of situated user experience [3][4]. Recent work [5][2][10][12][14] has concentrated on the role of portable artefacts, predominantly personal mobile devices, and how they can support engagement and interaction. However only a small amount of this work - specifically that of Fraser et al [6] - has looked at how to design systems that incorporate multiple heterogeneous points of interaction working together to support a coherent visit in a larger site. Fraser et al developed the concept of "*assembly*": an array of interactive technologies that are interrelated and that progressively provide elements of engagement for the visitor [6]. We will describe this notion and show its applicability in the case study of designing a multi-device installation for an open-air museum, also proposing ways of further extending the concept usefully for this particular domain.

DEFINING "ASSEMBLY"

Fraser et al suggest principles for designing an assembly of technologies that mediate specific parts of the museum experience: by understanding how to support the flow of the visit over numerous points of engagement, assemblies enable visitors to progressively make sense of the rich context they find themselves in. The exhibition space is seen as an arrangement of displays representing the points of engagement with the content at the core of the visit. To increase visitor engagement with each element on display, an overall meaningful activity should be introduced thus helping visitors to actively gather information as they progress. Central to the activity is an arrangement of interactive artefacts that support and facilitate interaction by offering points of engagement throughout the storyline and physical path of the visit. This approach does not focus only on designing arrays of ubiquitous technologies *per se*, but on providing guidance on how the whole experience could be flexibly formulated in order for participants to develop an understanding of what is happening. A duality exists with the term assembly. In one sense it relates to what people do to understand the situation they are in: they "assemble" sources of information to make sense of what they encounter. In another way, the term can be associated with an array of technologies that support this sense making. Fraser et al play on this duality to focus and guide design, and this is evident when examining the principles of the assembly approach [6].

1- Define a unifying overall activity that people can be engaged in.

2- Use an underlying information space that contains a variety of interrelated items that can be revealed as the activity progresses.

3- Use an assembly of interactive displays, with each display supporting a particular part of the overall activity and revealing a sub set of the common information space.

4- Use common interaction techniques to promote the coherence of the experience across the different displays.

5- Use a portable artefact that allows visitors to accumulate a record of their visit and/or support identification as they progress through the space.

APPLYING AND EXTENDING THE ASSEMBLY APPROACH

Activity Design Principles

Paramount to designing assemblies is the definition of an activity that is coherent and allows visitors to actively make sense of what they experience. Human activities are spatially situated, the complex array of interactions embedded in a place shapes how people carry out these activities [4]. Thus developing an understanding of how people experience place, its physical, social, cultural and emotional nature is critical to design, specifically when trying to support active participation. Conceptualizing how people experience situated knowledge is fundamental to the design of an activity that is integral to the environment and forms the basis of engagement. In the assembly approach, focus on situated experience, whereas this understanding is necessary to inform both the conceptual design process and the evaluation of concepts in terms of engagement potential and appropriateness to the setting, should be strengthened. In our case study, we extended the requirements for developing an overall activity by emphasizing the need for it to actively engage people *in situ*, and integrated a methodological approach focusing on place experience: a framework previously developed for studying place as an emergent experience at the intersection of personal, social, cultural and physical levels [3].

Technical Design Principles

The third assembly principle is about designing "interactive displays", meaning "exhibits", each supporting a part of the overall experience, and loci of interaction revealing a subset of the common information space. The physical design of these interactive standalone points should also be guided by an understanding of place [7]. The fourth principle is concerned with the ways people interact with the technology. This involves more than selecting different modes of interaction, but must examine how these individual modes complement people's situated activities and each other. The final requirement regards the role of a portable artefact: Fraser et al's view this as a coupler of the experience between the interactive displays and not as part of the technological assembly. However, the role of the portable artefact can also be extended, given the modalities of interaction that current mobile technologies afford.

Practical application

Design cases that have utilised the assembly approach [5][6] haven't explicitly outlined how the concept can be appropriated into other design practices. Due to its duality, it can be divided into concerns focused on developing novel ways for people to build a sense of what they are experiencing, and design of technological artefacts that create a supporting infrastructure. These two tasks and the requirements they represent are not mutually exclusive and the design process should include principles that guide the design of both the assembly as a "social accomplishment" and as the technical infrastructure that supports it. After having shown how the approach can be extended, we will now describe how we appropriated it in our case study.

CASE STUDY: DESIGN FOR BUNRATTY FOLK PARK

Bunratty Folk Park is an open-air museum, and one of Ireland's most popular tourist attractions. It attempts to recreate life from the late 19th century to the 1960s through a series of 32 dwellings arranged within a 26 acre site, including rural farmhouses, village shops and streets, all fitted and furnished as they would have appeared at their time. There are limited guidance and support resources for visitors, mainly consisting in a map of the site and in human animators who are present at some of the houses, taking roles such as the teacher, policeman and the "woman of the house". They engage in conversations with visitors regarding the setting and the activities they are performing, in order to convey a sense of authenticity and to personalise the visitor experience. A series of group sessions were carried out to develop concept and scenario design, starting with open brainstorming, and followed by more focused workshops as the design ideas were consolidated. Prior visitors to the Park were invited to participate. The sessions were organized around the discussion of themes from field data collected earlier in the project. The focus was to develop a basis for introducing the assembly principles by conceptualizing activities, information, technologies and modes of interaction in an open way. The assembly design concerns were introduced gradually to the participants so as to keep the sessions as open-ended as possible.

Developing the Assembly

Defining an overall activity in which people can engage and a common information space

In the design sessions several scenarios emerged, the initial assembly principles and relevant issues extracted from field data acted as a lens to analyse the scenarios: did a scenario provide a coherent overall activity? Did it articulate interaction around multiple entry points? Etc. The overall discussion was thus facilitated around the assembly principles. Of the ideas that were proposed, two were developed into the core of the overall unifying activity: the theme was that of memories of the past, and the exploration of the Park discovering not only details about the buildings' history or architecture, but about the lives of those who lived in them. This stemmed directly from one of the strongest findings from empirical work: how exploring the Park made visitors reminisce about their childhood and about memories of the past from parents and grandparents. Many of the conversations that visitors were having with the animators also related to personal stories and recollections.

The overall unifying activity involves visitors in a trail where they collect the memories of particular characters regarding past ways of life (e.g. butter making, turf cutting, etc) associated with certain areas of the Park. These memories are linked with different sites, and, as visitors progress, they can access them in two forms: digital content, and physical "tokens" which represent each point of call and also give clues on where to find more memories. Visitors also have the opportunity to leave their own memories or comments about the sites or activities in real time and to listen to memories or comments that other visitors have left.

Designing an assembly of interactive technologies and a set of common interaction techniques

Using the overall activity as a foundation, the technical design principles were then introduced and used to reflect on how an infrastructure could support it. Progressively a set of interactive technologies was defined that mediated the specific parts of the common information space. The final assembly consists of:

- A *central "portal"*: Here visitors could create a unique profile storing all the digital content they collected. They could also select the character they wished to hear memories from, and receive an initial clue about where to find the first memory of the trail. The portal was also where they collected the mobile device that they needed to gather the memories. When leaving the Park visitors would return to the portal, and view a map of their visit annotated with the memories they collected and recorded. Finally, the portal allowed them to share this content through email or social networking sites.

- A *mobile device*: a mobile phone was used to collect and record memories during the trail. At the different sites memories were represented by QR markers, visitors could scan them and receive an audio recording of the character's memory. They could also record and save their own using the handset's microphone.

- *Tangible tokens*: The physical tokens at each memory site where both a tangible representation of the memory and clues on how to proceed. They took the form of everyday objects of country life such as recipes, pieces of turf, small hanks of wool, etc. with embedded RFID tags. Visitors could take them home with them as mementos of their visit. The tokens could also be used at the interactive desk as keys to access memories other visitors left at the specific sites. They served to link the visitors' interaction at the particular sites with their interaction with another part of the assembly.

- An *interactive desk* was placed in the last site on the trail, the schoolhouse, where people could listen to memories that other visitors had left. Placed on the desk were books that related to each of the characters that visitors were collecting memories from. Also on the desk were a book holder and a basket: when one of the books was on the holder and a token was inside the basket the recordings left by other visitors were played back.

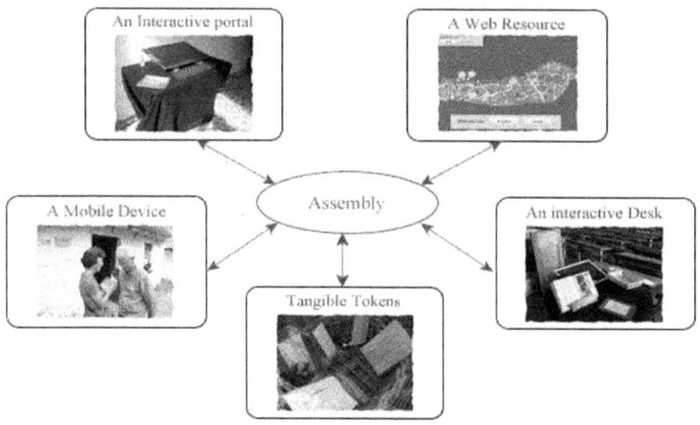

Figure 1: The underlying assembly of "Reminisce"

-A *Web Resource*, created to allow visitors to share their experience of the site after the visit, provided a map of their trail annotated with the memories they collected and recorded.

Each of these technologies served to support the overall activity and mediate the particular aspects of the information space. The design focus on the flow of interaction as visitors traversed the assembly was paramount. The principle of defining a set of common interaction techniques had a pivotal role in this, by making sure the forms of interaction were comprehensible and in keeping with how people experienced the site

REFLECTING ON 'REMINISCE' AS ASSEMBLY

The installation, titled "Reminisce" (Fig. 1), was deployed in the Folk Park over three full consecutive days. A detailed analysis of the participants' feedback goes beyond the scope of this note. We will present, however, some reflections regarding the experience of extending and using the assembly approach. The assembly concept complemented the UCD design frame by providing points of reflection throughout the design process and keeping focus on the 2 important themes of how people assemble knowledge during their activities and of how technology mediates this. For the design workshops, it was necessary to "translate" the principles into open questions, in terms understandable to participants, so that the discussion could develop on topic. This required some effort on our part to keep a focus on assembly as well as adapting the principles for the purpose of the workshops. The dual nature of assembly was another issue to be reckoned with: after examining the outcomes of the design sessions and having established an overall storyline, the technical design principles had to be brought in to progressively refine the elements of the assembly. Using the principles in this way ensured that that the two layers of the assembly (conceptual and infrastructural) would "fit". Having included into the approach an explicit regard for place and situated activities helped us keep thinking of the connection between the assembly and the setting: for example, in using tangible elements to help participants engage with the storyline, and ensuring that the interaction styles would be consistent with the nature of the site and across the components of the assembly (for example, having visitors scan memory codes with mobile phones in a way that is similar to picture taking on site). Having included the dimensions of place throughout helped keep the design work grounded, and we feel that without this the connection to the site would have been lost. On the basis of this experience, we feel that this approach is certainly a useful practical tool to guide design and development for open-air museum installations. As our setting was not too dissimilar from that described in Fraser et al.'s original paper but we nonetheless had to modify the approach to suit it, we cannot make universal claims as to its applicability. We do feel however that the extended assembly approach allows for technical and conceptual flexibility in a distributed environment, and for seamless integration with a complex exhibition structure. Therefore it can be highly useful for the design of public installations and other outdoor experiences - a type of interactive systems featuring increasingly in HCI research.

ACKNOWLEDGMENTS

This research is funded by Failte Ireland and by the University of Limerick Seed Funding. Thanks to Shannon Heritage and to all the participants in the project.

REFERENCES

1. Brignull, H. and Rogers, Y. 2003, 'Enticing People to Interact with Large Public Displays in Public Spaces', In Proc. INTERACT 2003, 17 - 24.
2. Brown, B., Chalmers, M., Bell, M., Hall, M., MacColl, I. and Rudman, P. 2005 'Sharing the Square: Collaborative Leisure in the City Streets', In Proc. ECSCW 2005, Paris, 427-447.
3. Ciolfi, L. 2004, 'Understanding space as places: extending interaction design paradigms', Cognition Technology and Work 6(1): 37-40.
4. Dourish, P. 2006, 'Re-space-ing place: "place" and "space" ten years on', In Proc. CSCW 2006, ACM, New York, 299 -308.
5. Ferris, K., Bannon, L., Ciolfi, L., Gallagher, P., Hall, T., and Lennon, M. 2004. 'Shaping experiences in the hunt museum: a design case study', In Proc. DIS '04, ACM, New York, 205-214
6. Fraser, M., Stanton, D., Hui Ng, K., Benford, S., O'Malley, C., Bowers, J., Taxén, G., Ferris, K., Hindmarsh, J. 2003, 'Assembling History: Achieving Coherent Experiences with Diverse Technologies', In Proc. ECSCW 2003, Helsinki, Finland, 179-198.
7. Giaccardi, E. and Palen, L. 2008, 'The Social Production of Heritage through Cross-media Interaction: Making Place for Place-making', International Journal of Heritage Studies, 14.3 (2008), 282-298
8. Grinter, R. E., Aoki, P.M., Hurst, A., Szymanski, M.H., Thornton, J.D. and Woodruff, A. 2002, 'Revisiting the Visit: Understanding How Technology Can Shape the Museum Visit', In Proc. CSCW 2002, New Orleans Nov. 2002, 146-155.
9. Hindmarsh, J., Heath, C., Vom Lehn, D., and Cleverly, J. 2005, 'Creating Assemblies in Public Environments: Social Interaction, Interactive Exhibits and CSCW', JCSCW, 14:1 (Feb. 2005), 1- 41.
10. Hsi, S. and Fait, H. 2005, 'RFID enhances visitors' museum experience at the Exploratorium', Communications of the ACM, 48:9 (Sep. 2005), 60-65.
11. Marti, P. 2001, 'Design for Art and Leisure', In Proc. ICHIM01, Philadelphia, 387 - 397.
12. O'Hara, K., Kindberg, T., Glancy, M., Baptista, L., Sukumaran, B., Kahana, G., and Rowbotham, J. 2007, 'Collecting and Sharing Location-based Content on Mobile Phones in a Zoo Visitor Experience', JCSCW 16:1-2 (Apr. 2007), 11-44.
13. Sparacino, F., Davenport, G., Pentland, A. 2000, 'Media in performance: Interactive spaces for dance, theater, circus, and museum exhibits', IBM Systems Journal, 39:3-4, 479-510.
14. Walker, K. 2007, 'Visitor-Constructed Personalized Learning Trails', In Proc. Museums and the Web 2007, Toronto. Consulted September 20 2010.

MoBoogie: Creative Expression Through Whole Body Musical Interaction

Megan Halpern[1], Jakob Tholander[2], Max Evjen[3], Stuart Davis[1] Andrew Ehlrich[1], Kyle Schustak[1], Eric P. S. Baumer[1], Geri Gay[1]

[1]Interaction Design Lab, Cornell University, 301 College Ave, Ithaca, NY, 14850, USA, {mkh46, std35, jae79, kos6, ericpsb, gkg1}@cornell.edu

[2] Mobile Life@Stockholm University Forum 100, 164 40, Kista, Sweden, jakobth@dsv.su.se

[3]Museum Studies, Johns Hopkins University, Washington, DC, 20036, USA, devjen1@jhu.edu

ABSTRACT
In this paper we describe MoBoogie, an application that allows users to manipulate and arrange music through movement. MoBoogie is designed to foster experiences in creative expression for children and potentially adults. The application responds to users' movements by changing variables in a continuous stream of music loops. Results from this study suggest that the creative expressions arose in the joint space of movement and music, and did not primarily have to be in one form or the other. This allowed users with limited experience in dance and music making to be creative in such forms of expression.

Author Keywords
Creative expression, whole-body interaction, music, mobile interaction.

ACM Classification Keywords
H5.m. Information interfaces and presentation (e.g., HCI): Miscellaneous.

General Terms
Design, Human Factors.

INTRODUCTION
There is a long-standing tradition of research and practice applying computational technologies in artistic contexts. In this note we explore the design of an interactive system to support creative expression through movement and music for users who are not trained or experienced in dance or music making. This led to a system called MoBoogie, an Android-based cell phone application designed for children to construct and manipulate music through dance and movement, allowing for an open-ended exploration of full body movement and creative dance and music experiences.

While designing MoBoogie, we strove to support a kind of proto-artistic expression. That is, we did not seek an interaction that results in a perfected or finished product, but rather a space conducive to having an experience in the act of expressing. Such opportunities have the potential to encourage a desire to engage in creative expression, and provide experiences that engage users in the skills used in such expressions.

This specific interest in combining new forms of creative expression with explorations of interaction that involve the body in novel ways aligns with 3rd wave HCI [1,9] and the increasing interest in aesthetic [13] and bodily [11] experiences in interaction design [e.g. 12]. Phenomenology and pragmatist philosophy have largely informed such work, typically represented by Heidegger [10] and Dewey [6].

RELATED WORK

Creative Expression
Throughout the design process we were inspired by Dewey's [6] notion of expression. When writing about artistic expression, Dewey defines acts of expression and objects of expression. Here, we are concerned with acts of expression, which, he says, are a function of both mind and body. An act of expression is not purely emotional or intellectual, but rather, it is purposeful and evokes emotion. Expression begins with what Dewey calls an impulsion: a "movement outward and forward of the whole organism to which special impulses are auxiliary" [6:60]. An impulsion is differentiated from an impulse because it is something we respond to as a whole, rather than in part. For Dewey, expression is ordered; it is a whole act that is carried through to completion. This suggests that to respond to an impulsion by expressing something requires some level of skill, and that skill is to be achieved through experience.

In the case of MoBoogie, we want to explore how technology can help inspire people to seek opportunities to engage in such a process. We aim to foster the ability to act in an expressive manner, even if the expression itself does not yield an object of expression. This kind of action may help young people and non-musicians or non-dancers begin to feel the intellectual and emotional rewards of creative expression; which, in turn, may lead them to seek future opportunities for creative experiences.

Systems for Whole-body Musical Interaction
Previous research has explored the design of gestural and whole-body [cf. 7] interfaces for musical expression. BodySpace [14] allows users to control a music player by placing a device on different body parts. Camurri et al.'s *The Bow is bent and drawn* [5] enabled a social active experience and dynamic molding of expressive content of a music piece. While not musical in the traditional sense, Williams et al.'s [15] evaluation of SignalPlay describes how participants' manipulation of augmented physical objects enabled them to construct, interpret, and manipulate connections between a physical space and a correlated soundscape. BodyBeats [16] used a number of different whole-body interaction prototypes designed to help children create music, exploring various approaches for gesture and full body movement to serve as an interface to music

Figures 1 and 2. Children and adults creatively exploring the phones response to movement

generation. Benveniste et al.'s [2] MINWii system used wiimotes and a virtual keyboard to create a form of music therapy for Alzheimer's patients. Bott et al. [4] developed a method for players of motion-based music games to switch instruments, and thus the sounds they are making, simply by moving the game controller in a different way (e.g., strumming a guitar, hitting a drum), and Blaine and Perkins [3] discussed a prototype of a collaborative drumming interaction in which both novices and experts could participate.

These last two systems closely resemble the creative expression we hoped to foster, and they speak to our decision to use Dewey's framework for acts of expression. McCarthy and Wright [12] draw extensively on Dewey in their discussion of experience, and this discussion parallels Dewey's ideas about expression in many ways. While there is a parallel between Dewey's artist/audience distinction and that of designer/user relationships in HCI, creating systems such as Blaine and Perkins' or MoBoogie require thinking about the experience of being an artist rather than viewing art.

DESIGN PROCESS

One important goal of this work was to explore tensions around the perceived locus of creative expression; would users consider the music generated by the device or their dancing and bodily movements as the primary form of expression? To explore the design qualities of the kind of creative expression we aimed to elicit, we conducted several small-scale user tests. In the first test we let users play with existing cell phone applications to explore issues of creative expression through movement and music with the sensing mechanisms of a state of the art mobile device. Some of these applications responded to users' movements, while others allowed them to explore novel methods of generating music with GUI-style interfaces. In the second and third tests we used an early version of MoBoogie. In these tests we observed users individually and asked them to complete a protocol that was later adapted and used for the evaluation (see below). They were led through a series of movements, for example, they were told to swing the phone like a baseball bat or conduct an orchestra. Then they were asked to play with the phone and explore how to move and make music with it. We asked them questions during and after the test.

From these tests a number of important design considerations emerged: a) Users systematically explored actions to which the systems responded in order to get a sense of the movements and the music that they could make with it. Central to that process was the character of the feedback e.g., precise vs. ambiguous changes in music, and the ways and extent to which the phone was responding to their movements. b) The modality used in the interaction influenced the character of the movements of the user. While visual interfaces with extensive information reduced the size and increased the precision of movements, interfaces with sound based feedback through the music fostered more open-ended, full body movements. c) Users initially expressed discomfort at the idea of dancing in front of researchers, or in public at all, but several of them still danced as they influenced the music through their dance. d) When the users started to get a sense for how to influence the application they moved freely and creatively in a variety of ways using their whole bodies. As they progressed, this engaged them in what we felt was the kind of increasingly engaging loop of creative movements for which we designed the application.

Though space limitations preclude us from elaborating on how we arrived at each specific element of the design, we found that these design considerations capture a number of tensions: between visual and audio feedback, between the desire to express one's self and apprehension over public performance, between precise responsiveness and allowance for open-ended movement. The next section describes the system design in which we attempted to balance these tensions.

MOBOOGIE: IMPLEMENTATION

A MoBoogie user is presented with a screen divided into colored thirds. The thirds represent, from top to bottom, a melody, bass, and drum track. Each of these three tracks corresponds to one of the three axes of the accelerometer. The music for each track is generated from sets of interchangeable, pre-recorded loops that change as the user moves. The simple display was designed to reduce the dominance of visual attention allowing users to focus on their movements and the music. When a user moves the phone, MoBoogie calculates the difference between subsequent accelerometer readings. If the difference along an axis surpasses a threshold and the current loop has played for a given interval, the track will randomly switch to a different loop in the same location. The interval and threshold values were selected based on user tests to provide a comfortable level of responsiveness, providing possibilities to gain a sense of control over how the music changed while still being open enough to allow free expression. Furthermore, the mapping of physical axes to music tracks encourages investigation of the workings of the application (i.e., a user can determine the impact of different motions) while maintaining a space for free expression. The user may touch and hold a track to mute it, or swipe a finger over one of tracks to lock it and prevent it from changing. These two features provide the opportunity for increased freedom of movement while at the same time allowing users increased control over the music.

FIELD TEST/EVALUATION

To gain a better understanding of how people might experience MoBoogie, we recruited ~100 children, ages 8 to 13 from local summer camps and eight of their adult camp counselors. While we developed the application primarily for children, we were also interested in how adults would respond to MoBoogie, so we gave opportunities for the counselors to participate as well. The findings below come primarily from analyzing the children's interactions. The children were divided into groups of between 6 and 10, and each group was paired with two researchers. The first gave a short explanation of how MoBoogie worked, while the second assisted in asking and answering questions while video-taping the session. The children were then given the opportunity to play, move, dance, and create music. At the beginning of their encounter with the app, the children were given a series of direct instructions such as "move as if you were conducting an orchestra" or "move as if you were boxing." The instructions served to show the children how to use the app while providing them an opportunity to move as a group, hopefully reducing any anxiety associated with dancing or moving creatively in public. After the direct instruction, children were asked first, to focus on their movements, then to focus on the music they were making, and then to play in whatever way they chose. Researchers intermittently asked questions of the children, such as: "How are the sounds related to your movements?" "What would you do if you took this home with you?" "Was there anything you didn't like about it?" "What else would you want to be able to do with it?" The authors conducted a group video analysis that focused on aspects of creative expression such as the character of the users' movement, the influence of the music, and how they related to the interface. Each author made notes on Post-Its about patterns or behaviors they saw, which were then iteratively and collaboratively grouped using affinity diagramming. The resulting thematic groups form the basis of the following findings.

Findings

As described above, one central tension was whether the locus of creative expression would be seen as the music or as the movement. The themes below help explicate users' perceptions and experiences of the relationship between the music and their movements.

Learning and Playing – Heidegger describes a distinction between present-at-hand to ready-to-hand [10] in the use of tools and artifacts. In previous studies, other [e.g. 15] researchers observed a general transition in the use of technology, where participants start acting *on* the object/interface, then gradually progress to acting *through* it. We saw something that appears to be related to these phenomena, but differs slightly. Users often started off with simple shaking or swinging, listening closely between each motion. After they were asked to try familiar actions (e.g., swing the phone like a tennis racket), they would complete the motion and then listen intently. As they became familiar with how the application reacted to their movement, they stopped listening between every motion and started actually dancing (see Figure 1) more fluidly, using the phone not as an interface for movement and music construction, but more as what appeared to us to be inspiration for creatively expressing themselves through dance and music.

Users spent a significant amount of time and effort trying to understand how the application reacted to their movements. This was true of the earlier user tests; however, in earlier tests, these manipulations were mostly conducted in a fairly mechanical fashion through simple, one-dimensional movements like horizontally swinging an arm from left to right. When using this version of MoBoogie, these explorations were done in a richer and more creative fashion through full-body moves. For instance, a group of camp counselors had the idea that the music stopped when they were completely off the ground, and they tested this theory using acrobatics (see Figure 2).

Creating and Owning – There were multiple examples of spontaneous, undirected movement. We observed users stopping listening to the music, dancing, stopping, listening, dancing, and, with each repetition, becoming more innovative in how they moved and interacted with the app. Rather than first trying out the devices in order to understand it, and then spending time playing with it [cf. 15], users in our study seemed to continuously reinvent new usages as they discovered different ways of experiencing and expressing themselves through the application.

Despite the examples of spontaneous, dance-like, movement, some users focused primarily on the music as the creative expression/product. When discussing their experiences with the researchers, subjects often referred to the music they "made" or "my" beat. These feelings of ownership resonate with our early design efforts as well as other studies such as Bott et al.'s [4] findings about users desiring a sense of control, even if they do not have total control over the music produced. Though they were effectively triggering events that randomly mixed pre-recorded samples, many participants felt that they were creating their own new music.

Socializing and Sharing – Though they were instructed to use MoBoogie individually, some users spontaneously formed groups and explored movement together. There were instances of social contagion, where one participant would start performing a particular dance move and then others would follow suit. Some groups formed conga lines, moving the phones in unison. Some users had participated in other camp programs in which they choreographed dances, so when they were playing with MoBoogie, they worked together and used pieces of their group dance. In some instances, counselors organized spontaneous "dance-offs", wherein groups would organize in a circle and take turns dancing for each other (see Figures 3 and 4).

We observed numerous examples of users sharing the music playing on their phones with others. In fact, the ability to record and share what they had made was among the most requested feature for future iterations. Users also watched other users, either to see what were acceptable ways to move, or to respond to other user's movements. Some users made specific comments about why the sharing was important to them. One user claimed that sharing the music with others was a way to share what he had "created." This creation was something to be proud of, even if there was not complete control over the music.

Participants readily participated in co-creating dance moves, but they were reluctant to co-create the music. For example, one participant would hold her phone up to a friend's ear, but when the friend reached for the phone, she would pull it back and prevent the friend from changing or manipulating her music. This reinforced the sense of individuality and creative ownership described by participants.

DISCUSSION

The findings described above indicate that the object of expression is not necessarily a dance, nor is it a piece of music. It may be described as something in between, or as neither. We aimed for a design supporting acts of

Figures 3 and 4. Dancing and performing for one another.

expression rather than objects, and our study shows that this kind of interaction often occurred. Here we return to the discussion of Dewey's definition of an act of expression. Users engaged in purposeful choices regarding both music and movement. These choices began with an impulsion, or a full body impulse. Often, they could not pinpoint the nature of their impulsion, but they did feel a sense of ownership over the music as well as the movement. They had the urge to share their expression with others. These observations indicate that MoBoogie has the potential to foster creative whole body musical expressions among users. The ambiguity surrounding the nature of that expression is potentially its greatest strength [8]. Users are not tied to an object of expression or a precise input scheme, but are free to experiment with the expression through open-ended whole body movements.

Our way of designing for bodily engagement was therefore not about trying to shape the interaction towards specific kinds of movements but rather about an overall process of letting dance and music interact to form a creative experience. This can be described as engaging users in a *positive loop* of dancing that occurs as the music changes along with their dance moves, and as their moves are guided by the music they are instantly creating. This reinforces a feeling of being in sync with the music.

CONCLUSION AND FUTURE WORK

MoBoogie was designed to provide opportunities for users to engage in creative expression; however, it does not encourage or demand that this expression result in the creation of a final or polished object of that expression. Our evaluation shows that the open-endedness in how users could use their bodies to interact with the system together with the use of pre-recorded musical elements created a joint space in which users could creatively engage in movement and music. MoBoogie users were compelled not only to use the application, but also to repeatedly explore how the application worked in conjunction with their movements. This continuous discovery and exploration may have added to a sense of ownership and the desire to share their music and movements with others. The inclination of users to share what they created indicates that the next logical step in the development of MoBoogie is to create an outlet for objects of expression. This could be done through a social networking service of some kind that would allow users to record their work to share with others. The tradeoff, in this case, might be twofold: first, while the creation of objects of expression may engender a more authentic act of expression in Dewey's terms, second, it may also shift the emphasis from expressing to creating an object of expression, losing some of the spontaneity of the act. Focusing on the object of expression would also likely force that object into existing categories (music or dance). The ambiguous nature of the expression seemed to be one of the things that made MoBoogie well-suited to the task of fostering creative experiences with dance and music.

ACKNOWLEDGMENTS

We would like to thank the Cornell Interaction Design Lab for help developing and implementing MoBoogie.

REFERENCES

1. Bødker, S. When second wave HCI meets third wave challenges. *NordiCHI*, (2006), 1-8.
2. Benveniste, S., Jouvelot, P., and Péquignot, R. The MINWii Project: Renarcissization of Patients Suffering from Alzheimer's Disease Through Video Game-Based Music Therapy. *ICEC*, (2010), 79–90.
3. Blaine, T. and Perkis, T. The Jam-O-Drum interactive music system: a study in interaction design. *DIS*, ACM (2000), 165–173.
4. Bott, J.N., Crowley, J.G., and LaViola, J.J. Exploring 3D gestural interfaces for music creation in video games. *FDG*, (2009), 18.
5. Camurri, A., Canepa, C., Coletta, P., Ferrari, N., Mazzarino, B., and Volpe, G. Social active listening and making of expressive music. *DIMEA*, (2008), 376.
6. Dewey, J. *Art as Experience*. Minton, Balch & company, New York, 1934.
7. England, D., Randles, M., Fergus, P., and Taleb-Bendiab, A. Towards an Advanced Framework for Whole Body Interaction. *Virtual and Mixed Reality 5622*, (2009), 32–40.
8. Gaver, W.W., Beaver, J., and Benford, S. Ambiguity as a resource for design. *SIGCHI*, ACM (2003), 233-240.
9. Harrison, S., Tatar, D., and Sengers, P. The Three Paradigms of HCI. *alt.chi*, (2007).
10. Heidegger, M. *Being and Time*. Harper, New York, 1962.
11. Larssen, A.T., Robertson, T., and Edwards, J. The feel dimension of technology interaction. *TEI*, (2007), 271.
12. McCarthy, J. and Wright, P. *Technology as Experience*. The MIT Press, 2007.
13. Petersen, M.G., Iversen, O.S., Krogh, P.G., and Ludvigsen, M. Aesthetic interaction. *DIS*, (2004), 269.
14. Strachan, S., Murray-Smith, R., and O'Modhrain, S. BodySpace. *ACM CHI Ext Abst*, (2007), 2001.
15. Williams, A., Kabisch, E., and Dourish, P. From Interaction to Participation: Configuring Space Through Embodied Interaction. *UbiComp*, (2005), 287.
16. Zigelbaum, J., Millner, A., Desai, B., and Ishii, H. BodyBeats. *ACM CHI Ext Abst*, (2006), 1595.

Life "Modes" in Social Media

Fatih Kursat Ozenc
Carnegie Mellon University
School of Design
5000 Forbes Avenue, Pittsburgh, PA 15213
kursat@cmu.edu

Shelly D. Farnham
Yahoo!
701 First Avenue
Sunnyvale, CA 94089
shellydfarnham@acm.org

ABSTRACT
Current social media products such as Facebook and Twitter have not sufficiently addressed how to help users organize people and content streams across different areas of their lives. We conducted a qualitative design research study to explore how we might best leverage natural models of social organization to improve experiences of social media. We found that participants organize their social worlds based on life 'modes', i.e., family, work and social. They strategically use communication technologies to manage intimacy levels within these modes, and levels of permeability through the boundaries between these modes. Mobile communication in particular enabled participants to aggregate and share content dynamically across life modes. While exploring problems with managing their social media streams, people showed a strong need for focused sharing – the ability to share content only with appropriate audiences within certain areas of life.

Author Keywords
Identity, faceted identity, social media, email, social networks, transitions, Facebook, privacy, roles, boundaries, modes.

ACM Classification Keywords
H5.2. User interfaces.

General Terms
Design

INTRODUCTION
People increasingly use social media to connect to others from different areas of their lives, especially through social networks that aggregate content from various online systems [10]. These networks however carry problematic assumptions in their implicit models of social organization: that one identity, and one social context, fits all. When examining offline world social dynamics, one may easily observe the richness of diverse roles people play across different social contexts [9], including friends, family, and coworkers. A misalignment between the sharing controls of social networks and users' roles and social contexts leads to awkward and inappropriate sharing [8, 25]. On the one hand, users may choose to over-share, with many of their connections receiving irrelevant or unimportant content [2]. On the other hand, users may choose to avoid sharing across their entire network [26], in which case they lose some of the advantages of network-based communication, i.e., connectedness and awareness. In this project, we explore how to leverage natural models of social organization from people's lives to improve their experiences of social media streams. We performed a design research project to examine how people might best a) organize their online content, b) transition between different areas of their lives online, and c) focus their sharing and consuming of online content within these areas. Our focus is holistic, rather than focusing on a particular communication channel or specific area of life, we consider the entire ecosystem of communication across areas of life. We present our theoretical framework and related prior work, and then report findings from our in-depth interviews, which included a life mapping activity and a needs validation session. We finally share our design recommendations to inform future work on socially intelligent social media design.

BACKGROUND

Faceted Identity
A person with a faceted identity performs different aspects of identity depending on social context [11]. For example, a person may project himself as a dad if he is surrounded by family members, or as a professor if he is amongst his students. Identity is thus formed and reinforced through these social role enactments [4, 16]. Past research has shown that the degree of identity faceting varies depending on the individual [11, 21]. In an online questionnaire study of 631 participants, Farnham and Churchill [11] found that a few life facets are fairly common and where people spend the majority of their time, particularly work, family or social life, while other facets are more idiosyncratic to individuals or groups. Contrary to more mainstream conceptions of the self -- that we should have a consistent, coherent personality -- identity and behavior meaningfully change depending on social situations that many seek to keep separate [11].

Segmentation and Transitions

Nippert-eng [21] developed a boundary model of work-home transitions, arguing that people vary in their levels of integration and segmentation across areas of life, and that other people, products, and activities help the person to manage transitions across boundaries. Clark similarly developed a work/family border theory [6] that spotlights the role of people, things, and schedules as border-keepers, which cue the person to change modes. Ashforth et al. [1] focused on the daily micro-transitions that happen across work, home and third places (e.g. church, grocery store, concert hall) and found that people often deploy rites of passage, or rituals, to facilitate transitions. See Figure 1. In our current work, we are particularly focused on exploring how to help people manage life facets and the micro-transitions between them online.

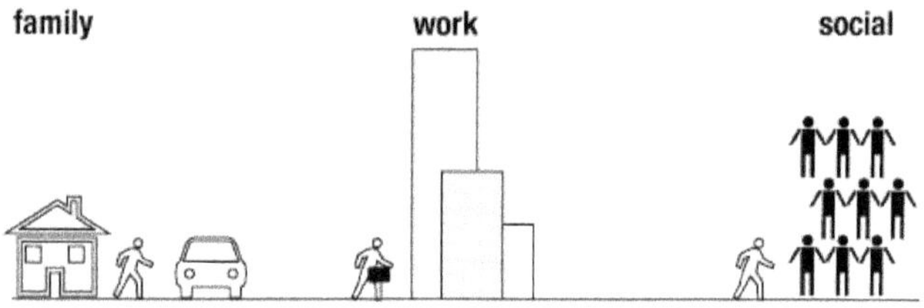

Figure 1. Daily transitions between different areas of life.

Sharing and Consuming Content Online

Relative to face-to-face encounters, users experience new challenges in online contexts as they cope with faceting identity and boundary management. In offline life contexts, people may segment their lives by location and time [20], and manage interruptions [1] and cross-boundary communication [6] accordingly. Online contexts, freed from the constraints of real-time communication and geographical co-location, posit a vulnerable openness across different areas of users' lives. On the one hand this openness increases boundary permeability and consequently the number of people with whom one may connect. On the other hand, it often results in the spill over of information that may be relevant in one context, but inappropriate in another [26, 11].

Many identity and sharing models have emerged to help users manage contextual sharing. Our own past research has found that users report the greatest level of control in email, where access is defined for each message [11]. People may further segment areas of their lives by creating different email accounts [14] or by using different social applications (such as Facebook and LinkedIn) to create bounded contexts [24]. It is particularly in the context of online social networks, where sharing is defined at the level of each connection, and then at the level of degree in the network, that users experience increasing difficulty in maintaining boundaries across areas of their lives [3, 11]. Networks do not easily enable specifying sharing by *type* of connection. As these networks further integrate with other social media systems, a message intended for just a few people may be transmitted to not only all of one's friends of friends on Facebook, but also across Twitter, YouTube, and any number of other social media sites. Social networks do not sufficiently consider the multifaceted nature of self and life modes in their design, which creates distress amongst users with incompatible life facets [11].

Thus, from a design research perspective, we seek to explore how we might help users leverage bounded, group-based sharing models in the context of online networks. To investigate possible representations of these models, we reviewed how both prominent technologies and past research projects helped users organize people, activities and groups, and what were the underlying organizing principles.

Representations of People, Activities and Groups

In prominent social technologies the most common representations of people are text-based, alphabetized lists, such as those found in contact management systems. The second most common representations of people are grids of photos such as found in Facebook. However these existing systems do not tend to organize people into groups or areas of life. A number of research projects have developed experimental visualizations with diverse organizing principles. See Table 1. The Personal Map [12] used a dynamic pie chart and eco-system metaphor, where people were organized into pie-wedged groups based on similarity in email communication history.

Type	Organizing Principle	Examples
List View	Alphabetically sorted lists	Yahoo-Mail, Gmail, Hotmail
Network Graph	Similarity, or connectedness, using nodes and edges	TouchGraph, Vizster
Pie Chart	Size of the group	Personal Map
Geo Map	Geographical location	Loccacino, Google Latitude
Tree Map	Recent activity and/or size of group, depicting importance	Netscan
Timeline	Time of day, or time in life	Rememble, Plurk

Table 1. Types of visual representations of people, groups, and activities and associated visual organizing principles.

Tree-maps partition groups into differently sized square areas, depicting topical or group hierarchies and importance [18, 28]. TouchGraph [27] and Vizster [15] used a network graph model, where people are organized by similarity to each other and segmented into color-coded groups using cluster analysis. Rememble [23] and Plurk [22] used timelines with activity tagging to represent activity within areas of one's life. Google Latitude [13] and Loccacino [29] used location-based mapping of people.

Based on our theoretical framework, prior work, and our review of existing technologies, we focused on four exploratory design themes for our study:

1) *Organize by facets.* How may we help users organize their online worlds based on common primary areas of life?
2) *Rituals for transitions.* How do people navigate between their different areas of lives and how might this translate to online situations?
3) *Focused sharing and consuming.* How might we help users share and consume content with the right people in the right context?
4) *Natural representations of facets.* How do users naturally mentally model areas of their lives, and what are natural and appealing visual representations of facets and groups?

DESIGN RESEARCH APPROACH

Design research generates knowledge through design artifacts, methods and processes, with the motivation of giving vision and depth to research and practice communities [30]. In this project, we chose a design research approach, framing the problem space through design artifacts to probe for future solutions, using a holistic process encompassing both understanding users and translating design themes into concrete solutions.

As a multidisciplinary field, human computer interaction research may draw from an arsenal of research approaches ranging from quantitative usage analysis to ethnographic interviews to prototyping systems. Design research augments these methodologies by taking an understanding of the needs and desires of people, considering the possibilities, constraints, and unanticipated effects of technology, and translating them into product concepts, ideas, and requirements.

Thus we use a design research approach to build on our prior, more quantitative work in this space [11], with the goal of a) deepening and validating our past findings that people vary in life segmentation, that there are fairly common life facets across users, and that users struggle to manage boundaries across these facets online, and b) exploring how to best translate our understanding into actual products that are meaningful and appealing to users by envisioning design concepts and seeking user feedback.

METHODOLOGY

We performed in-depth, two-hour interviews to explore how people naturally mentally model different areas of their lives, how they incorporate communication technologies to support them, and how we might improve their online experiences of managing their social media streams. Each session consisted of a life mapping activity, a need validation session, and a visual metaphors ranking activity.

Life Mapping Activity

Borrowing the concept of 'life mapping' from an earlier study [12], we had participants draw out pictures or diagrams of important areas of their lives on a large white board. See Figure 2 for specific instructions. Using their maps as a vehicle for conversation, we then instructed participants to describe how they used communication technologies to support different areas of their lives, how they maintained their life segmentation, and how they transitioned between areas of life.

> Imagine you wanted us to really know all about you and how you live your life, so you decided to **draw a picture -- like a map or a diagram**. What would this map look like?
>
> Use these **dry-erase markers** to draw out a picture, or a map, of your life using this whiteboard, and describe to us what you are drawing as you go along. Please draw a large map, using the **whole whiteboard**, since we'll be adding other notes later.
>
> Be sure to include the **different areas of your life** – who are the **different people** in your life, what are your **important roles or identities**, and what are your **important activities or hobbies**.

Figure 2. Instructions for life mapping activity.

Need Validation Session

Taking a design research approach, we created design concepts that enabled us inquire into 'what ought to be' products. We developed concept scenarios to manifest our design themes [5], and then used a speed dating method developed by Davidoff et al. [7] where we inquire into the needs, boundaries, and desires of people through their responses to a number of concept scenarios. The concept scenarios were in the form of storyboards consisting of four panels depicting the context, the problem, the interaction with the proposed design, and the desired outcome. To identify opportunity areas and possible future directions for social media products, we generated eleven concept scenarios on organizing contacts, focused sharing, focused consuming, and transitions.

These concept scenarios were developed based on a general underlying model where an organizing user interface enabled focused sharing and focused consuming of the users' social media streams. See Figure 3. We used the most common contexts of work, family and social life that emerged out of prior work [11]. These contexts may not only describe physical settings, but also conceptual places that include people, motivations, goals, and other situational factors. We asked participants to share what they liked and disliked about each concept scenario, and how they would suggest improving the proposed solution. Having gone through all the concept scenarios we then asked participants to rank them based on how much the problems and solutions resonated with their own situation.

Visual Representations

We incorporated diverse visual representations of people and groups into the study to help assess what are more natural ways to organize and visualize people. Based on our review of past research and current technologies we selected six visual representations and embedded them into the concept scenarios. Each representation probes a different way of organizing and visualizing people. All but one of the visual representations used the common facets of family, work and social with color-coding. We also created zoomed-in views for each visual representation, and had participants rank them before completing the study. See Figure 4.

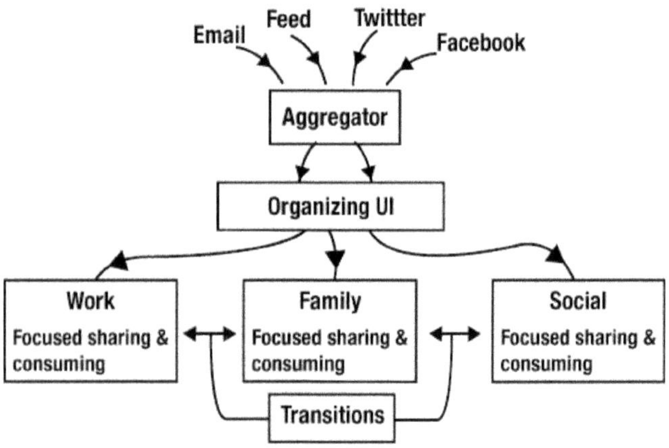

Figure 3. Underlying model for the concept scenarios.

STUDY RESULTS

Participants

16 participants were recruited through an online screening questionnaire that asked about age, gender, Internet usage, identity faceting, sociability and work status. Participants were included if they were anywhere from 21 to 55, had intermediate or higher levels of Internet usage, either worked full or part time or were students. Building on prior work [11], the goal of this qualitative study was to seek out participants who were likely to be involved in more than one life facet, and thus could provide meaningful feedback on concept scenarios that explore how to help people manage life facets online. Thus we further screened for individuals who scored intermediate or higher on personality measures of extroversion and identity faceting. For this screener we used the same identity faceting and extroversion questionnaires used in [11], for which about half of 631 participants had intermediate or higher levels of faceted identity. Extroversion questions included "I make new friends easily" and "I am skilled in handling social situations" [17], and life faceting questions included "I have many different sides of me, and the side I show depends on the social situation" and "I prefer to keep different parts of my life separate" [11]. The mean age of participants was 37, with 44% male, 56% female. Three were students, six worked part-time, and eight worked full time.

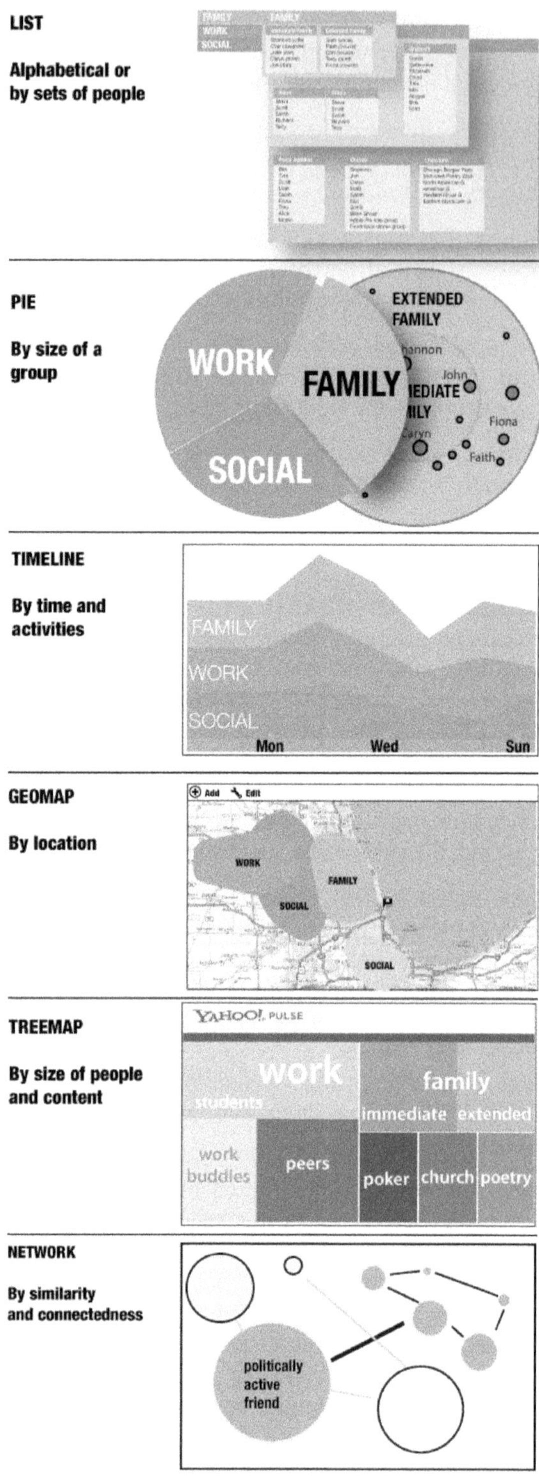

Figure 4. Visual representations of people.

Life Mapping Activity

Participants easily overcame any initial hesitation with drawing their life maps on a whiteboard. They were actively engaged in modeling their lives and happy to discuss their activities in detail. After completing our interviews, we performed a qualitative analysis by posting all the maps on the wall simultaneously and looking for emerging patterns.

As a part of our synthesis, we counted recurring categories and topics, reviewed our interview notes, and watched our recorded videos. We found that most of our participants drew one of two types of maps, namely, a social meme or timeline map, for modeling their lives. The remaining two visualizations are a list view, and a pi-chart.

Social Meme Maps

Social meme maps were the dominant type, drawn by 9 out of 16 participants. See Figure 5. We refer to this category of maps as *social meme maps* because while they resembled network graphs, consisting of nodes and edges, each node tended to represent social memes rather than individuals: areas of life, collections of people, activities, interests, and so forth. With this nuance, they are more like concept or mind maps, which were developed to facilitate learning and brainstorming [20]. Furthermore, the maps tended to be hierarchical; with lines indicating "is nested in" rather than "is connected to". 7 out of these 9 participants first drew 'me' in the middle, with lines from the self connecting important primary meme nodes to the self. Consistent with our prior quantitative work [11], family, work, and social (also labeled "friends" or "personal") were the most common primary nodes, representing categories of life. 15 out of 16 participants had family as a prominent category. The secondary nodes nested within the primary nodes were more idiosyncratic, such as specific sets of people (e.g. "soccer team"), important individuals (e.g. "mom"), hobbies (e.g. "sewing"), or events (e.g. "BBQ"). Interestingly, in a few cases, participants had "computer" or "Facebook" as primary or secondary nodes. Finally, another third level of nodes is best characterized as qualifier nodes, such as "San Francisco" as a qualifier node of "Friends".

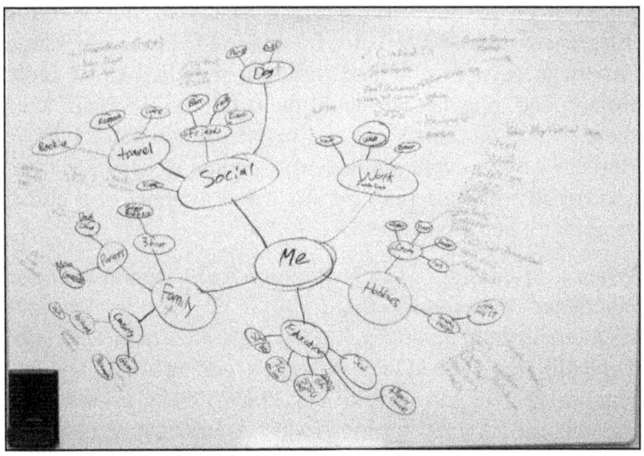

Figure 5. Type 1: Social meme map

Timeline Maps

A small yet significant number of participants (5 out of 16) drew timeline views of their lives. See Figure 6. Three of them depicted a view of their daily schedule and two depicted a long-term view of their lives. They tended to have both abstract and literal depictions of people and places. These timeline maps had a more collage flavor than did the social meme maps, with different types of images representing people, hobbies, and places dotted along the timelines. Another interesting note is that the daily timeline maps were both drawn by homemakers with children in school, whose timeline models of life indicated the demanding coordination activities required for maintaining their families' daily schedule.

Communication Practices

In the second round of the life-mapping interview, participants went through their maps with different colored markers and wrote down the communication technologies they used for each area or node, while describing out loud their communication practices. They reported that they used a wide array of communication technologies to support different areas of their lives, consisting of email, phone, texting, social networks, instant messaging, and video call (e.g. Skype). They accessed their communication media using laptops, desktops and mobile phones, from a diversity of places including work, home, and public places.

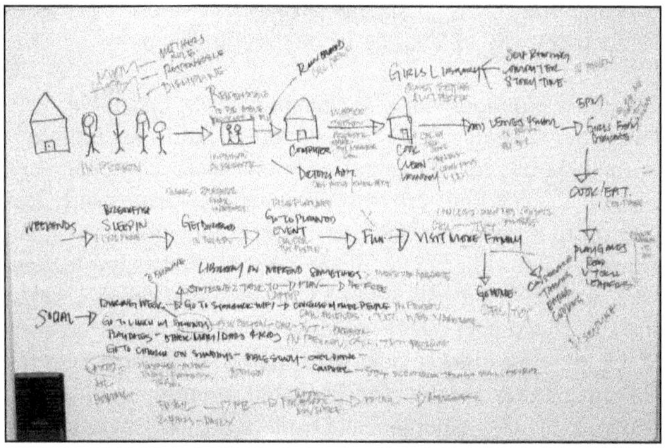

Figure 6. Type 2: Timeline map

By Closeness and Life Facets

They chose communication channels based on closeness, and based on different areas of their lives. The closer a person was to the self, the more they used a mix of all communication channels. For example, Alice[1] reported using a mix of texting, Facebook, and email to continually coordinate with her teenaged son, even when they were in the same house together. Communication with people who were less close to the self was restricted to fewer channels, such as Facebook for out of state friends. Mobile phones emerged as a dominant tool, both for aggregating across different communication channels and for hyper-coordination [19]. Texting was preferred as it is practical, more immediate, and less interruptive.

---

[1] Please note all participants' real names were changed to common names to preserve anonymity, matching participant gender.

When at work, our participants primarily used email and voice phone. Only a few participants also used instant messaging and texting. Most do not use Facebook while connecting to their coworkers. Communication practices within the family were more diverse, including phone calls, texting, email, and social networks. Their preferences depended on whether family members were part of their immediate or extended family, whether they were tech-savvy, and whether they were the same generation. As Mary stated:

> *"I try to be a good communicator...I try to keep everyone in the loop, you know I try to figure out where things come to crack, that is why I want to know a lot, except this daughter who doesn't check her emails. It is just trying to use whatever method works best for each person."*

While Facebook was preferred for connecting to extended family, younger people did not care to connect with their parents and immediate family in Facebook. In the social or friendship area of life, participants again reported using all kinds of channels. Texting and email stood out as coordination tools, whereas Facebook stood out as a lightweight way of keeping in touch with friends.

Boundary Management with Communication Channels

Participants strategically used communication technologies to manage boundaries across different social contexts. See Figure 7. When crossing boundaries they used less interruptive channels such as texting and email as small windows into other areas of their lives. For example, Joe, who is always on call as an IT professional, used a small Instant Messenger (IM) window as a boundary crosser. When playing video games at home he would open up his IM on another machine so he could keep an eye on and respond to any emergencies from work. If such an IM arrived, he would pause the game to read the message.

> *"If it is something that I think is important, I just stop playing the game... If it is something that can wait for 30 minutes or an hour I just message to that person, and then I say 'I'll take a look at it,' and go back to whatever I was doing."*

Similarly while at work, two participants reported they would only contact friends through Facebook (versus the phone) because they could "get away with it" in their cubicles. Participants indicated if they did not want to communicate across boundaries they simply cut off access to other contexts by turning off their devices and accounts.

Segmenting Areas of Life

We asked participants if they tried to keep different areas of their lives separate, and how comfortable they were blending different areas. Participants' responses illustrated that they varied along the segmented to integrated continuum, consistent with related research [1, 11, 21]. After our interviews we rated each person on a scale of 1 = extremely integrated life facets to 10 = extremely segmented life facets [1], and found an average of 4.7 with only one person on each extreme. Participants showed a lot diversity in how they desired to keep their lives segmented depending on the nuances of their individual situations, thus were rarely on either extreme.

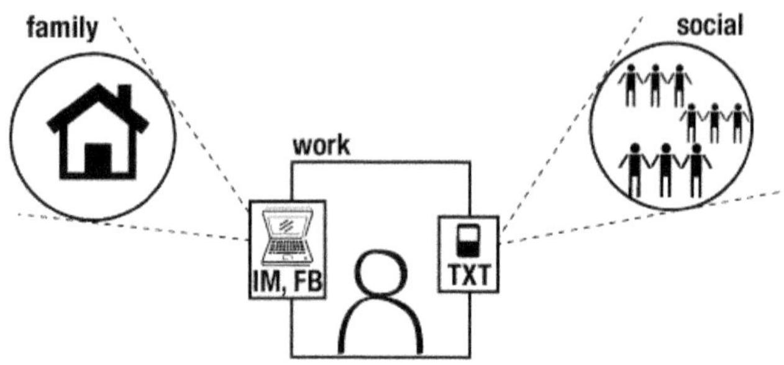

Figure 7. Crossing boundaries strategically using communication technologies.

Their level of segmentation depended on a number of factors including job type, personality, cultural differences across segments, and fear of being stigmatized. Joe and Todd both worked as managers in their companies, and they wanted to keep their social and work lives as separate as possible because of the differences between how they behaved in their job roles and how they behaved with friends. John is a musician and has a music group with his wife. For him, family, work, and social are all completely integrated facets, and he reported that it was an important part of his life style to be the same person all the time.

> *" Pretty much, there can be maybe some differences... but basically the same person. I try to be in the moment as much as I can, I don't try think of things as separations, I try to think things as inclusive...."*

For younger participants such as Deepak and Matt, cultural differences between their friends and first generation American parents -- where they felt impelled to be more formal and responsible with their family -- encouraged them to not mix their social lives with their family lives. Barbara was an event planner who wanted to keep her work and friends separate because she was a member of a nudist group with her friends.

When discussing segmentation and communication practices, we found that 100% of our participants segmented their email by having separate email accounts. Typically, they had at least one work, one personal, and one junk email account. Several also had a fourth professional account for personal business, such as sending resumes. In managing their online segmentation, participants used avoidance strategies, such as turning off and hiding devices, changing their status to invisible, or keeping separate phone numbers. In a few cases, participants indicated they would refuse any family or work "friend" requests in Facebook. Barbara created two Facebook profiles to keep her friends and coworkers separate.

Transitions

When describing transitions between areas of life, participants often used the language of changing 'modes' rather than that of changing their identities or facets. Which mode was active at any one time depended on participants' schedules, their geographical locations, who else was there, and the tasks of the moments.

Participants' transitions from one area of life to another were most often concurrent with external transitions such as moving through time or moving from one place to another. We found some participants had rituals that facilitated changing modes while transitioning. Susan for example used her shower as a ritual for mentally preparing for the day every morning.

> *"In the morning before I go to school, I take a shower, it is just like mandatory, in the shower, think over things -- what am I going to do at school, what am I going to wear. The kids are already gone to day care so that's out of the way. It is just transitioning from being mom to being a student about that time, during the shower."*

Participants often incorporated media into their routines and rituals when transitioning. From work to home, for example, Mary watched her favorite TV show.

> *"I come home, turn on Judge Judy and start making dinner."*

Joe played video games and Alice took off her shoes and listened to music to "wind down". From her personal mode to family mode, Sarah needed "winding up" with coffee and cheerful music before her niece visited her. Deepak and John used meditation and breathing exercises to transition from their work mode. Deepak, Matt, and Michael transitioned through behavioral enactments of their modes, changing their language and outfits when they were with their coworkers, family or friends.

Online transitions were subtler compared to offline world transitions, in part because online transitions were often concurrent with the offline world behaviors. Todd, for example physically left his work computer and its content, and went home to use his personal laptop. In other cases, participants made the work-home transition without any physical movement, by changing their tabs, switching accounts, closing folders, opening applications, or turning off access to certain devices.

Need Validation Session

In the need validation session we read aloud the scenarios for the participants and used them as a tool to facilitate conversation around their needs, wants, boundaries and desires. To compare participant ratings of scenarios we first averaged by scenario type (organization, transition, focused sharing, focused consuming) and then performed paired samples t-tests. We found that while users showed no preference for focused sharing over focused consuming scenarios, they preferred focused sharing over organizing ($t(14) = 4.82, p < .001$) and transitioning ($t(14) = 3.39, p < .004$) scenarios, and they preferred focused consuming over organizing ($t(15) = 3.39, p < .005$) and transitioning ($t(15) = 5.73, p < .001$) scenarios. There was no difference in preference between organizing and transitioning.

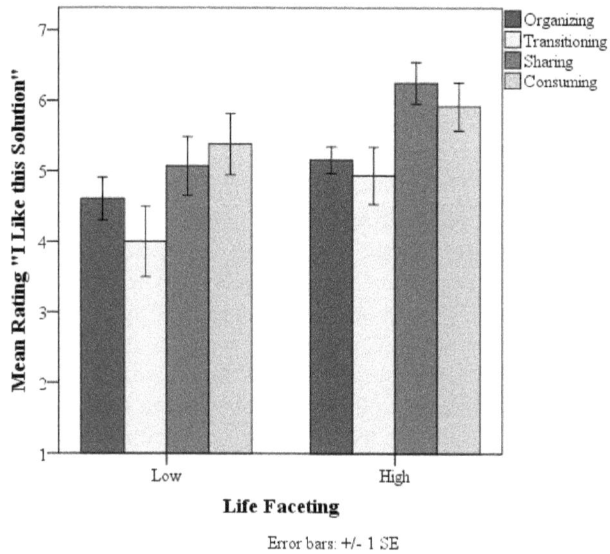

Figure 8. Ratings of "I like this solution" by concept type and degree of life faceting.

As expected, we also found that the people we categorized as having higher levels of life faceting (5 or higher on a scale of 1 to 10) were more likely to favor the focused sharing ($t(13) = 2.35$, $p < .04$) and organizing ($t(13) = 1.9$, $p < .09$) scenarios. See Figure 8. These results indicate that users do not feel a need to organize their social worlds online for the sake of organizing itself, but rather only if it enables focused sharing and consuming online.

In ranking the scenarios, they most preferred a focused sharing concept scenario. Participants expressed real concern about social "spam". Joanne liking the concept on filtering content is tired of getting irrelevant Facebook updates.

"..It is good for obnoxious people who you are not interact with a lot."

Similarly, they wanted to receive only what was important to them, and when sharing they wanted to be relevant to their social circles. Deepak for instance questioned relevancy of his Facebook friends while sharing.

> *"I have 800 hundred Facebook friends, 780 of them are even not real friends."*

In our discussion of the scenarios, participants further indicated they wanted dynamic and real-time maps crafted for sharing and consuming.

In organizing scenarios, we observed a strong tension between notions of manually and automatically organized content. With manual input, participants have a strong feeling of control, however they need to invest a lot of time and effort for the system to work. In scenarios with automatically organized content, they can let the system do the work, however, they lose the feeling of control and fear missing relevant people and content. Responding to one of these concept scenarios, Bob for instance stated:

"Not sure about automatically generated aspect, I would like to override it, I would like to be in control."

Similarly, Marta is skeptical about such system behavior.

"I know who to share info with, the computer doesn't need to know..."

In exploring which underlying organizing principles made the most sense, participants ranked views that prioritized and showed important people and content relative to the self more highly, favoring the tree map view the most of all. However they also favored the list view for its familiarity. They did not believe organizing facets by location mapped to their experiences, and a few found the pie chart was too clinical. They further indicated they favored concepts that showed holistic views of their people and groups.

EMERGING THEMES

Three important themes emerged from our findings: modes of the self, focused sharing, and mobile me.

"Modes" of the Self

We framed our project based on the theoretical frameworks of social identity, boundary work, and transitions. However, through the course of our interviews we came to the realization that there is a gap between the languages of these social science approaches and how people naturally talk about their lives. In the life-mapping interviews, when we directed our questions towards identity and segmentation, some participants had a hard time grasping the notion of identity faceting and role enactments. A couple of them responded strongly that they are the same person in every situation, even though they readily describe how they behave differently depending on the requirements of the social context. They felt that being a coherent, consistent self was a desirable character trait that improved the quality of their lives. In order to preserve this sense of a coherent self, participants would frame behavioral changes across areas of their lives as changes in life 'modes'. Changing modes had a more positive connotation than did changing identity facets, and when we adapted our own language from 'facets' to 'modes', participants more naturally described the differences across areas of their lives and how they maintained boundaries between them.

Focused Sharing vs. Privacy

Participants particularly favored the focused sharing and consuming concepts. These concepts highlight the fact that people have too many 'friends', and are overwhelmed by all the online content. Users of social media have a real need for improved relevancy in their social media streams. These results bring to light the problematic framing and practice of privacy settings.

Past work has noted *the privacy paradox* in social media [2] -- that people say they really care about their privacy, however they rarely change privacy settings and consequently tend to over share. On the one hand, these privacy settings may be badly designed, with inadequate or hard to use features. Our study results indicate an alternative explanation: that framing the relevancy and intimacy of sharing along one dimension – degree of privacy – is problematic and artificial. As suggested in [11], under the current circumstances, given the choice between over sharing or not sharing at all, participants will choose over sharing. We argue that *focused sharing* may be a more natural way of framing the problem by asking "which groups do you want to share with" rather than "do you want to share with friends or not". Focused sharing tools may bring a flexibility and feeling of control around balancing different life modes that is not found in the none-or-all approach of privacy settings.

Mobile Me as Social Aggregator

While developing the concept scenarios, our focus was on the social organization of shared content in online networks, rather than on communication devices. Our design concepts assumed that our organizing and sharing tools would live on a website designed for a desktop or laptop computer. Our conversations with participants during the interview, however, informed us that our more traditional view of the Internet as a desktop experience is out of date and the reality has shifted toward mobility. Participants naturally showed us their smart phones and how they used them, without any prompting from us. They used smart phones for aggregating content from their networks, email accounts, text messaging, and feeds. In other words, all significant communication channels are on the smart phone.

Not only was the mobile device actively used for light weight social updates and more heavy weight social coordination, it was a strategic tool for communication across their different areas of life. They particularly used texting as a boundary-crossing communication channel. When participants wanted absolute segmentation, they talked about turning off their phones to cut off access to the other modes. These results indicate that the future of social media is decreasingly desktop-based, and increasingly mobile and contextual.

DESIGN RECOMMENDATIONS

Reflecting on our study results and emerging themes, we have derived the following design recommendations for researchers and practitioners in the social media space.

Think Holistically

The life-mapping interview illustrated the richness of people's lives and how they choreograph different modes by using a wide array of communication technologies. The diversity of modes, devices, and software in use suggests a need for a holistic conception of the ecosystem of social organization and social technology. Future efforts should think broadly across different life modes, and across various communication practices.

Prioritize Focused Sharing Scenarios

Online networks have transformed the social experience of the Internet in their own unique yet challenging ways. Mapping offline world's social organization across life modes into the online world is one of those challenges. The excitement of connecting to people has led to a bewildering complexity and vulnerable openness across boundaries. Existing technologies attempt to address this complexity with network-based privacy settings. Future efforts should craft more natural ways for managing sharing, taking into consideration different sets of people across different areas of life. The notion of *focused sharing* in these efforts should be prioritized.

Organize Sharing by People and Life Modes

Primary Modes: Work, Family, Social

Our study has shown that people conceptualize a coherent yet dynamic self that changes modes depending on internal and external triggers. Internal triggers are more psychological and related to intention and mental preparation. External triggers are situational, and related to schedule, place, company, and the goal of the situation. Future efforts should frame organizing, sharing and transitioning in terms of these life modes. The most common modes of family, work, and social should be taken into account. While we found these modes are common to most people, their content and interactions were quite diverse and not necessarily reflective of stereotypical conceptions of family, friends, and work. Modes in this sense should be seen as frames for planning and action, taking shape according to the situation and depending on internal and external triggers, rather than universal sets of specific behaviors.

Relative to the Self: Importance

Consistent with past research [12], we found that the majority of life mapping drawings placed 'me' in the middle, indicating that people naturally model their social world in terms of relative importance to the self. Similarly, participants favored visual representations with indications of importance to self. Future efforts in social media design should emphasize this egocentric perspective, where importance or relative distance to the self is a prominent organizing principle, used to help users' focus on their most important people.

Prioritize Mobile as Aggregator and Facilitator

Our effort to understand the dynamics of the social Internet were elevated to another layer with the emergence of the *mobile me* theme. Mobility and smart phones give social media new meaning by blending physical and online worlds. Future efforts should leverage the mobile phone both as an aggregator and a facilitator of social interactions across boundaries. Aggregation increases awareness across channels, leading to improved facilitation and coordination.

Balance Agency

Our organizing scenarios brought to light the negative connotation of a technology knowing and acting too much on behalf of the person using the service. Future efforts seeking to craft 'smart' systems should carefully balance agency between the person and the technology. Users want technologies to take on cumbersome organizing tasks through automatic analyses, while at the same time desiring a final say or means to modify the outcome. Such smart technologies should leave a few unfinished details so that users may contribute to the system and retain a feeling of control.

Provide Tools for Transitioning between Life Modes

It was clear from our interviews that people were not very self-aware of the routines and rituals embedded in their transitions. When presented with concrete scenarios of transitions, however, people began elaborating on triggers that enabled them to switch modes, such as going to another room, playing music, or changing their clothes. External cues such as place and time are important triggers for switching modes, and routines and rituals are key activities that ease transitions between modes. Future efforts should consider mapping these external signals (such as a sense of place, who else is there, or a sense of time) and these routines and rituals (such as listening to music, or changing one's appearance) into the design of tools that facilitate transitions.

CONCLUSION

We conducted a design-driven qualitative research study to explore how people naturally think about and manage communications across their social worlds to inform future efforts in social media design. Our results indicate that people with higher levels of faceted identity have the problem of organizing, sharing and consuming online, especially while managing and transitioning between family, work, and social life modes. They strategically use communication technologies to manage intimacy levels within these modes, and levels of permeability across the boundaries between these modes. Feedback from our concept scenarios indicated two strong needs, the first for focused sharing and the second for focused consuming. Reactions to the concept scenarios and rankings of visual metaphors pointed to a need for organization tools that prioritize different areas of lives in simple, dynamic, yet holistic ways.

Although this study has all the limitations of qualitative research, it should be noted that we performed this design-focused investigation to build on our prior, more quantitative work [11] in order to provide a much richer picture of how participants manage communication across faceted areas of their lives – triangulating on a picture of our users using a multi-methodology approach. Given the focus of this particular study, our selection criterion was that participants scored intermediate or higher on a measure of faceted identity. Based on said prior quantitative work [11], we may expect that these findings would generalize to only approximately half of the population, those with self-reported higher levels of identity faceting.

Methodologically, we found the life mapping activity an effective vehicle for developing a fairly holistic view of the users' lives in a very short amount of time. For future efforts designing social media products, we recommend designers and researchers think about the user's communication ecology holistically, consider life 'modes' as one of the organizing principles, prioritize focused sharing and the mobile medium, and incorporate cues and signals when designing for transitions.

ACKNOWLEDGMENTS

We thank our participants.

REFERENCES

1. Ashforth, B., Kreiner, G. & Fugate, M. (2000). All in a day's work: Boundaries and micro-transitions. *Academy of Management Review* 25, 3, 472-491.
2. Barnes, S.B. (2006). A privacy paradox: Social networking in the United States, *First Monday* (2006),11, 9.
3. Boyd, D. (2004). Friendster and publicly articulated social networking. In *Proc. CHI 2004*, ACM Press
4. Brown, J. (1998). *The Self.* McGraw-Hill, Boston
5. Carroll, J. (2000). *Making use: Scenario-based design of Human- Computer Interaction.* MIT Press.
6. Clark, S. C. (2000). Work/family border theory: A new theory of work/family balance. *Human Relations,* 53, 747.
7. Davidoff, S., Lee, M. K., Dey, A. K., & Zimmerman, J. (2007). Rapidly exploring application design through speed dating.*UbiComp.*Springer-Verlag 429-446.
8. DiMicco et al. (2008). Motivations for social networking at work. In *Proc. of CSCW 2008*
9. DiMicco, J., & Millen, D. (2007). Identity Management: Multiple Presentations of Self in Facebook. *GROUP'07.*
10. Eldon, E. (2009). Facebook reaches 100 million monthly active users in the U.S. *Insidefacebook.com.*
11. Farnham, S., & Churchill, E. F. (2011). Faceted identity, faceted lives: Social and technical issues with being yourself online. In *Proc. CSCW 2011.*
12. Farnham et al. (2003). Personal Map: Automatically Modeling the User's Online Social Network. *Interact' 03* M. Rauterberg et al. (Eds.) IOS Press 567-574.
13. Google Latitude, www.google.com/latitude/intro.html
14. Gross, B. & Churchill, E. F. (2007). Addressing constraints: Multiple usernames, task spillage, and notions of identity. In *Proc. CHI 2007, Work-in-progress.* ACM Press.
15. Heer, J. & Boyd, D. (2005). Vizster: Visualizing Online Social Networks, *IEEE Symposium on Information Visualization, InfoVis.*
16. Heiss, J. (1992). Social roles. In Rosenberg, Morris, & Turner, Ralph (eds.). *Social Psychology: Sociological Perspectives.* Transaction Publishers.
17. John, O. P., & Srivastava, S. (1992). The Big Five trait taxonomy: History, measurement, and theoretical perspectives. In L. A. Pervin, & O. P. John (Eds.), *Handbook of personality: Theory and research* (pp. 102-138). New York: Guilford Press.
18. Johnson, B. & Shneiderman, B. (1999). Tree-Maps: a space-filling approach to the visualization of hierarchical information structures. In *Readings in information Visualization: Using Vision To Think*, Eds. Morgan Kaufmann Publishers, 152-159.
19. Ling, R. & Yttri, B. (2002). Hyper-coordination via mobile phones in Norway. In Katz, J. and Aakhus, M. (eds.) *Perpetual contact: Mobile communication, private talk, public performance.* Cambridge U. Press.
20. Novak, J. D. & Cañas, A. J. (2008). The Theory Underlying Concept Maps and How to Construct and Use Them, *Technical Report IHMC CmapTools*
21. Nippert-Eng, C. E. (1995). *Home and Work.* The University of Chicago Press, Chicago.
22. Plurk, http://www.plurk.com/aboutUs
23. Rememble, http://www.remember.com/
24. Schrammel, J., Koffel, C. & Tscheligi, M. (2009). How much do you tell? Information disclosure behavior in different types of online communities. *Communities and Technologies.*
25. Skeels, M. M. & Grudin, J. (2009). When social networks cross boundaries: A case study of workplace use of Facebook and LinkedIn. *GROUP'09.*
26. Strater, K., & Lipfort, H. (2008). Strategies and struggles with privacy in an online social networking community. *British Computer Society.*
27. Touchgraph, www.touchgraph.com/visplatform.html
28. Turner, T., Smith, M., Fisher, D. (2005). Picturing Usenet: Mapping computer-mediated collective action. *Journal of Computer-Mediated-Comm., 10*(4), 7.
29. Wagner et al.(2010).Hide and seek: location sharing practices with social media. *MobileHCI '10.* ACM Press, 55-58.
30. Zimmerman, J., Forlizzi, J., and Evenson, S. (2007). Research through design as a method for interaction design research in HCI. *In Proc. CHI 2007.* ACM Press 493-502.

Social Capital on Facebook: Differentiating Uses and Users

Moira Burke and Robert Kraut
Human-Computer Interaction Institute
Carnegie Mellon University
5000 Forbes Ave., Pittsburgh, PA 15213
{moira, robert.kraut} @cmu.edu

Cameron Marlow
Facebook
1601 S. California Ave.
Palo Alto, CA 94301
cameron@fb.com

ABSTRACT
Though social network site use is often treated as a monolithic activity, in which all time is equally "social" and its impact the same for all users, we examine how Facebook affects social capital depending upon: (1) types of site activities, contrasting one-on-one communication, broadcasts to wider audiences, and passive consumption of social news, and (2) individual differences among users, including social communication skill and self-esteem. Longitudinal surveys matched to server logs from 415 Facebook users reveal that receiving messages from friends is associated with increases in bridging social capital, but that other uses are not. However, using the site to passively consume news assists those with lower social fluency draw value from their connections. The results inform site designers seeking to increase social connectedness and the value of those connections.

Author Keywords
Social network sites, social capital, self-esteem, social skills, computer-mediated communication

ACM Classification Keywords
H.5.3 [Information Interfaces]: Group and Organization Interfaces - Collaborative computing, Web-based interaction, Computer-supported cooperative work

General Terms
Experimentation

INTRODUCTION
In its earliest days, when the Internet offered a small range of file transfer and communication services that were used by a relatively homogeneous population of early adopters, HCI researchers tended to treat both services and users monolithically. They implicitly assumed that all Internet use had similar effects on most users. For example, early studies of the Internet examined the association between overall time online, social capital, and loneliness [20,24]. However, as Internet services became richer and users more heterogeneous, researchers began to ask whether different types of Internet use, (e.g., communication with family and friends, meeting new people, and finding information) had different effects on those varying in demographics and social resources [5,27].

Social network sites (SNS) and research on their impact have reached a similar inflection point. Social network sites are designed to connect people with friends, family, and other strong ties, as well as to efficiently keep in touch with a larger set of acquaintances and new ties. Therefore, they have strong potential to influence users' social capital and the psychological well-being that often flows from social capital. While in their early days, sites like Facebook appealed to a homogeneous base of college students and supported only a small set of activities, today successful SNS are themselves rich platforms, allowing an enormous and diverse user base to join groups, play games, share photos, broadcast news, and exchange private messages. Therefore, just as researchers began to call for differentiated analyses of Internet use (e.g., [40]), researchers are recognizing that not all SNS use is equally "social" [8,12].

The goal of the present study is to examine how different uses of a large social network site influence different types of users' social capital. Combining longitudinal self-report surveys and Facebook server logs, we examine how direct communication with friends, broadcasting status updates to a wide audience, and reading of others' news predict changes in users' social capital. We examine how people varying in self-esteem and social communication skill engage in these activities and how their use differentially affects their social capital. By using behavioral logs of SNS usage, we overcome the self-report biases common in much of the existing literature. By using an eight-month longitudinal panel design, we go beyond the cross-sectional research common in this area and can make stronger causal claims about how SNS use changes social capital.

ONLINE COMMUNICATION AND SOCIAL CAPITAL
Social capital is "the actual or potential resources which are linked to a durable network of more or less institutionalized relationships of mutual acquaintance or recognition" [6]. It is the benefit derived from one's position in a social network, the number and character of the ties one maintains, and the resources those ties themselves possess [38]. Although sociologists and political scientists tend to use the term 'social capital,' psychologists refer to a related concept using the term 'social support.' Regardless of the discipline, a

large literature shows that people derive benefits from their interpersonal relationships and the groups they belong to, ranging from improved health, access to expertise, and financial resources [9].

Social capital is often described as two constructs: bonding and bridging [20,32]. Emotionally close relationships such as family members and good friends provide bonding social capital, which enables specific reciprocity, emotional support, and companionship [38]. On the other hand, a large number of diverse, weaker ties who travel in different circles generates bridging social capital. Bridging social capital provides access to novel information (e.g., job opportunities), because one's closest and strongest ties are likely to have redundant information [15]. Acquaintances expose us to diverse perspectives and external groups, but do not necessarily provide emotional support. Bridging and bonding are not mutually exclusive, but rather different dimensions of the resources in a social network.

Online communication in general and the use of social network sites in particular have the potential to change the costs of communication, the number and character of people with whom one keeps in touch, and the nature of the communication one has with them. As a result, many researchers have proposed that online communication and participation in social networking will influence one's social capital and the downstream psychological consequences. Wellman and colleagues crystallized the debate with a paper titled "Does the Internet increase, decrease, or supplement social capital?"[37]. Cross-sectional research shows that compared to light users, people who use the Internet heavily have better social integration. For example, heavier users participate more in organizations and are in more frequent contact with friends and relatives [37]. Bloggers and photo sharers are more likely to confide in someone of a different race or discuss important matters with someone from a different political party [16]. College students who use Facebook heavily report higher levels of social capital [11]. However, much like early studies of the Internet (e.g., [24]), these studies generally treat social media as a relatively monolithic activity.

More recent studies have examined different types of use, often differentiating social activities from others [23,40]. When researchers do differentiate uses they tend to find a positive link between social motives for use and positive psychological outcomes [5]. Adolescents use instant messenger with existing friends and so tend to disclose more, which improves the quality of their relationships [35]. On the other hand, uses for entertainment (e.g., games and online movies) and communication with strangers are negatively associated with social capital [5,37]. For example, adults with typical or high levels of offline social support who used the Internet to meet new people felt more depressed six months later [5].

DIFFERENTIATING SOCIAL NETWORK SITE ACTIVITIES

A few studies have begun to differentiate uses of SNS. College students motivated by "social information-seeking," using SNS to learn about people they have met offline, and "expressive information sharing," feel greater bridging social capital [12,31]. However, these studies generally differentiate social media use based on motivations, rather than actual behavior. This focus on motivation occurs in part because fine-grained behavioral data are not available, while survey measures of users' attitudes are easy to collect. In the current study, we focus on behavior—as recorded in server logs—and its impact on social capital, largely because motivations and actual behavior are rarely so cleanly connected. Undergraduates use Facebook out of "habit" and "time-passing" [31], which tells us how pervasive Facebook is in their lives, but does not clarify how users actually pass that time. They could be chatting with distant cousins or playing solitaire, and these different behaviors may have dramatically different outcomes.

Three kinds of social activities

We distinguish between three kinds of social behavior in social network sites. These behaviors are measurable through site logs on Facebook, but generalizable to other platforms. The first activity, **(1) directed communication with individual friends** consists of personal, one-on-one exchanges. Much like email and IM, Facebook supports targeted communication through messages, wall posts, and synchronous chat. Unlike previous platforms, it provides lightweight mechanisms such as the "like" button, inline comments, and photo tagging. In each of these actions, one friend singles out another friend, signaling that their relationship is meaningful enough to merit an action.

Directed communication has the potential to improve both bonding and bridging social capital for two conceptually distinct, although empirically interrelated reasons: the content of the communication and the strength of the relationship with the communication partner. By virtue of being directed at particular others, one-on-one messages are likely to be rich in content that strengthens relationships, such as self-disclosure, supportiveness and positivity [30]. Both the offering and the receiving of the intimate information increases relationship strength [10]. Providing a partner with personal information expresses trust, encourages reciprocal self-disclosure, and engages the partner in at least some of the details of one's daily life. Directed communication evokes norms of reciprocity, so may obligate partner to reply. The mere presence of the communication, which is relatively effortful compared to broadcast messages, also signals the importance of the relationship. Thus, because of its content, directed communication is likely useful for maintaining relationships with existing ties and encouraging the growth of new ones.

In addition to its content, directed communication may be especially important because it tends to be exchanged with those with whom one already has strong relationships. Although people typically maintain a moderate number of friends on social network sites (e.g., 150), they have reciprocal communication with a much smaller set (5-7) [26]. Ellison and colleagues [12] found that young adults only consider a small fraction of their Facebook friends "actual" friends (75 out of 300), and that only these "actual" friends correlate with social capital. Gilbert and Karahalios [13] demonstrated that features of directed communication—its recency, duration, intimacy, and amount—were strong predictors of Facebook tie strength. Because directed communication keeps one in touch with close ties, it should improve bonding social capital.

In contrast, the undirected messages that form the basis of **(2) passive consumption of social news**, when one reads others' updates, and **(3) broadcasting**, when one writes them for others' consumption, are not targeted at a particular other. Therefore, they are less likely to be rich in relationship-maintaining behaviors that characterize directed communication. These undirected messages are one of the novel features of SNS: an aggregate stream of news (known as the News Feed on Facebook). The News Feed contains general broadcasts, such as status updates, links, and photos, as well as public interactions between the user's friends and those friends' friends. In addition, profile pages and photo albums archive shared content generally viewable by any friend (modulo variations in privacy settings). By its very nature, this broadly targeted content is not tailored to a single recipient, and thus less likely to include the same degree of support and openness.

While the content of undirected messages may be less intimate than that of directed communication, they may still be valuable for relationship growth and maintenance. Profile information and status updates provide content for conversational grounding and reveal users' similarities. Hancock and colleagues found that college students who mined information from a stranger's Facebook profile were able to make that stranger like them more, by casually referencing shared interests [17].

News Feed content may be more similar to the small talk—informal superficial communication—that comprises roughly half of the content of face-to-face conversations [14]. While most scholars assume that communication involving support and openness are stronger drivers of tie strength than small talk, small talk can be valuable. Regular contact itself is at the heart of the relationships with friends [1]. The information exchanged by initiating and consuming broadcast messages allows one to keep in regular contact through a stream of small updates. Knapp and Vangelisti [22] argue that small talk "is critical to developing relationships," and "a proving ground for both new and established relationships."

Broadcast messages are much cheaper to produce and consume. Because the author doesn't know who has read it, it entails no obligation to reply, though it may elicit responses. Because of their relatively low cost, sending and consuming News Feed stories, profiles, and photos should allow a user to keep track of a much larger circle of friends and acquaintances—especially those she doesn't have the time to write to individually, or with whom some social barrier prevents her from directly engaging.

For these reasons, it is plausible that creating and consuming undirected messages, allowing users to keep in touch, will lead to increases in social capital. Compared to direct messages, undirected communication will have less intimate content and will be exchanged with a larger number of weaker ties. Therefore, its effects should be stronger on bridging social capital than bonding social capital.

In this paper, we do not focus on purely asocial Facebook activities, such as solitary game-playing, as we would not expect them to add to social capital. However, we do control for overall time spent on the site, and where games are social (e.g., by fostering game play with friends), we expect the results to hold.

INDIVIDUAL DIFFERENCES AND SOCIAL MEDIA USE

Though few studies of social network sites take them into account, individual differences influence whether and how people use the Internet and the effects it has on them. Less socially skilled individuals may gravitate toward computer-mediated communication because it reduces social boundaries, and thus they might have more to gain from technology than their more socially connected peers [3]. Personality components such as extroversion and neuroticism have been shown to affect one's choice of Internet activities and moderate the effect of those activities on affect, depression, and loneliness [5,23]. More introverted, less agreeable, and less conscientious college students spend more time online than their extroverted peers [25], which may be explained by extroverts spending their discretionary time in face-to-face social interactions, or introverts having fewer social obligations, freeing up additional time to spend online. Online channels allow greater control over self-presentation supporting the projection of an ideal self [36]. Caplan finds that some individuals with anxiety over self-presentation prefer interacting online because they feel "safer, more efficacious, more confident, and more comfortable" [9]. However, this preference for interacting online is linked to compulsive Internet use and negative consequences, such as missing work [9]. On the other hand, some introverts feel that they can better express themselves online and are thus more likely to form relationships that move offline [2, 28].

Of the numerous individual differences, we focus on two: social communication skill and self-esteem. Social communication skill gauges comfort with social "chitchat" and ability to recognize nonverbal signals (such as when a partner is getting bored). We focus on this trait because SNS offers many ways to connect socially (including the three forms presented here), any one of which may be better suited for those who are uncomfortable face-to-face [7].

Self-esteem has previously been demonstrated to moderate the relationship between overall SNS use and bridging social capital, and so we include it in the present study, to validate previous findings with a more diverse sample and investigate interaction effects with specific site activities. Ellison and colleagues [11] found that intensity of Facebook use (e.g., time spent on the site, number of friends, and agreement with attitudinal questions about the integration of Facebook in their daily lives) predicted higher levels of bridging social capital, even when controlling for self-esteem. Furthermore, they found that the effect was strongest for students with lower self-esteem. Therefore, we include self-esteem in the present study to validate those findings with an international, more diverse sample and investigate interaction effects with specific site activities.

Social communication skill and self-esteem are related but distinct concepts. In the present study, they correlate at 0.4, indicating a relationship, but 84% of the variance in either construct remains unexplained. Individuals with low self-esteem may be less comfortable communicating socially because they feel that they have few accomplishments to tout, or poor communication skills may reduce one's feeling of self-worth, indicating that it is quite possible that these constructs would affect an individual's choice of SNS activities differently, and so we examine both self-esteem and social communication skill separately.

IMPORTANCE OF LONGITUDINAL RESEARCH

In a cross-sectional study of approximately 1200 Facebook users, differentiating site activity revealed surprising differences in well-being outcomes. Communication one-on-one with friends was linked to positive outcomes, including higher levels of bonding social capital and lower loneliness but users who spent a lot of time passively consuming news reported lower bridging social capital and greater loneliness [8]. The cross-sectional analysis cannot determine causal direction: did the consumption cause the loneliness or the loneliness cause the consumption?

The problems making causal claims with observational data are well known. It is impossible to rule out the possibility that some third factor, such as self-esteem, accounts for the association between online activities and social capital. For example, Mikami et al. [29] show that adolescents' social disposition at age 13 predicted their SNS behavior nine years later. Those who were liked more by friends in adolescence had more friends online, communicated with them more and received more supportive messages from them. Rather than Internet use influencing their social capital, this research clearly shows that stable social dispositions can account for the association between Internet use and social capital.

Even the same dataset can lead to contradictory conclusions depending upon whether the researchers use cross-sectional or longitudinal data. For example, Shklovski and colleagues demonstrate that cross-sectional analyses show that people who use the Internet more have greater social capital [33]. They are more likely to dine out with friends or phone them. However, when using longitudinal data to examine changes in social capital, they showed that those who used the Internet for a wider variety of purposes decreased the amount that they visited friends in person.

To overcome these problems, the research reported here will use longitudinal panel data to determine the impact of SNS uses on changes in social capital over eight months.

METHOD

To analyze the relationship between SNS activity, individual differences, and social capital, we surveyed Facebook users in July 2009 and again in March 2010. The survey contained standard scales for social capital, social communication skill, and self-esteem. Survey responses were matched to server logs of the participants' activity on Facebook for the two months prior to the second wave.

Participants

Participants (N=1193) were recruited via an ad on Facebook targeted at English-speaking adults around the world, and 415 of the original 1193 completed the second wave. There were no differences between drop-outs and returnees in demographics, self-esteem, communication skill, social capital, number of friends, time spent on site, or amount of content produced or consumed ($p > .80$ for all comparisons). Therefore only users who responded at both time points are analyzed. Compared to a random sample of active Facebook users, survey takers were slightly older (M=33.7 vs. 33.0 years, $p < .05$), spent more time on the site[1] (M=1.7 hours per day vs. 0.5, $p < .001$), had more friends (M=185.6 vs. 170.0, $p < .001$), were more likely to be women (X^2=27.3, $p < .001$), and less likely to be from the U.S. (X^2=270.2, $p < .001$). Figure 1 presents demographics.

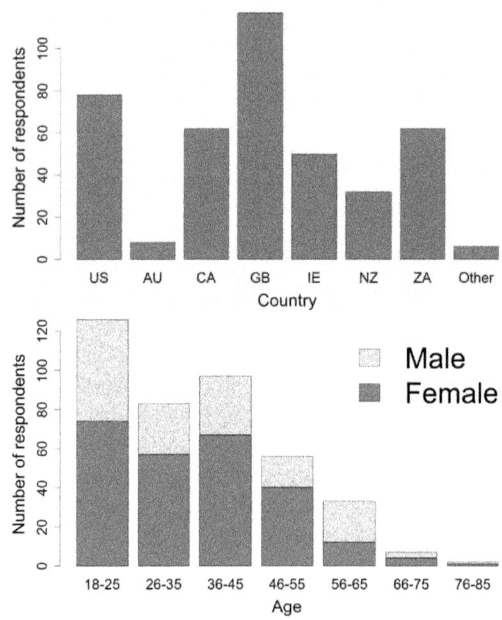

Figure 1. Participants by age, gender, and country.

[1] Log-transformed data were used for t-tests, but non-transformed means are reported for interpretability. Comparisons from July 2009.

	Median	Mean	SD
Age	34.0	35.2	13.9
Gender	63% female		
Friend count	171.0	241.2	288.4
Time on site (hours/day)	1.3	1.8	1.9
Directed communication scale (in) (α = 0.90)			
Distinct friends who initiated communication	41.0	53.1	47.3
Comments received	66.0	130.2	199.7
Messages received	30.0	70.8	147.8
Wall posts received	10.0	18.3	24.8
"Likes" received	29.0	61.5	116.7
Tags in photos	5.0	14.1	29.6
Directed communication scale (out) (α = 0.88)			
Distinct friends user communicated with	56.0	72.8	62.4
Comments written	127.0	232.2	344.8
Messages sent	34.0	92.3	226.2
Wall posts written	13.0	24.4	33.0
"Likes" given	34.0	93.6	231.3
Times tagged friends in photos	1.0	25.4	77.1
Passive consumption scale (α = 0.93)			
Times reloaded feed	773.0	1281.6	1577.2
Stories clicked in feed	179.0	341.1	498.3
Friends whose feed stories user clicked	65.0	101.2	109.9
Distinct photos viewed	4.0	11.5	20.5
Distinct profiles viewed	140.0	211.5	275.6
Broadcasting scale (α = 0.63)			
Status updates	24.0	41.3	58.6
Notes written	0.0	0.2	0.6
Photos shared	3.0	7.0	15.5
Application stories posted to own wall	17.0	126.0	352.5
Other items posted to own wall	2.0	10.6	28.0

Table 1. Participant demographics and activities over two-month period and aggregate scales.

	Directed comm. out	Consumption	Broadcast
Directed comm. in	0.88	0.60	0.65
Directed comm. out		0.67	0.71
Consumption			0.53

Table 2. Correlation between activity scales.

Survey content

Scales used in the survey include bonding and bridging social capital [39], social communication skill (a subscale of [4]), and self-esteem [32]. Major life came from [19]: pregnancy or new family member, move to a new city, personal injury or illness, fired or lost job, marriage or relationship reconciliation, divorce or relationship breakup, and death of close friend or family. Each was measured with single binary value indicating whether the event occurred between survey waves.

Bonding (5 items, scale alpha=0.75) includes "There are several people I trust to help solve my problems" and "There is someone I can turn to for advice about making very important decisions."

Bridging (10 items, alpha=0.86) includes "I come in contact with new people all the time," "I interact with people from different racial or ethnic backgrounds," and "Based on the people I interact with it is easy for me to hear about new job opportunities."

Social communication skill (10 items, alpha=0.63) includes "I enjoy social chitchat," "I know how to tell if someone listening to me is getting bored," and "I frequently find that I don't know how to keep a conversation going."

Self-esteem (7 items, alpha=0.87) includes "On the whole I am satisfied with myself," and "I feel that I have a number of good qualities."

Bridging, bonding and self-esteem were scored using the mean of 5-point agreement Likert scales. Communication skill was presented with the same scale for ease, but 1 point was given to "agree" or "strongly agree," 0.5 to "neither agree nor disagree," and 0 for "disagree" or "strongly disagree" (inverted for reverse-worded items). Scores were summed across the 10 items, so range from 0-10.

Site activity

Site activities for each survey participant for the 60 days before the second survey were counted. All variables were aggregated from server logs so that no individual's actions, friend networks, or identifiable information were used.

All activity variables follow heavy-tailed distributions, and so are log-transformed (base 2, after adding a start-value of 1) to control for skew and then standardized by centering at the mean and dividing by the standard deviation. Scales representing each kind of Facebook activity (directed communication, consumption, and broadcasting) were created by taking the means of the z-scores of the representative variables. Tables 1 and 2 present descriptive statistics for the raw variables, scale alphas, and correlations.

Controls

Participant age and gender were included as controls, as was time spent on the site (logged and standardized). Country did not improve the models, and so was dropped.

RESULTS

To determine how site use affects social capital change, we use a lagged dependent variable model of the form:

$$Y_t = \alpha Y_{t-1} + \beta_0 X_t + \varepsilon_t$$

For example:

$$Bridging_t = \alpha Bridging_{t-1} + \beta_0 TimeOnSite_t + \varepsilon_t$$

This form of autoregressive distributed lag model is common in econometrics and appropriate when the dependent variable is stationary (the mean and variance do not change over time, as is the case with our social capital measures) and model residuals are not highly autocorrelated. Lagged independent variables (previous site activity) are not included because they are highly collinear, and thus would produce biased estimates (see [21]).

Base model: Time on site and bridging social capital

Table 3 presents a series of models for bridging social capital. The base model includes the lagged dependent variable (bridging social capital reported eight months prior), demographic controls, and major life events in the intervening eight months. To determine which life events to include, we added each event separately to the base model and retained those that were at least marginally significant ($p < .10$): moving and losing a job. The base model shows that, controlling for demographics, major life changes, and previous level of bridging social capital, time spent on the site is a marginally significant predictor of increased bridging social capital ($p = .06$). This "monolithic" analysis of time on site suggests there is much room for improvement by differentiating site uses and users.

Model including Facebook activities

Next, holding time on site constant, we look at the impact of three kinds of SNS activities done during that time: directed communication with individual friends, consumption of social news, and broadcasting. Model 2 reveals that different activities on the site are not equally valuable. In particular, social capital increases with directed communication, but not with consumption or broadcasting.

Inbound and outbound directed communication are highly correlated ($r = 0.88$) and thus cannot be included in the same model. When included separately, inbound directed communication is a strong predictor of bridging social capital ($p < .01$), while outbound is not ($p = .20$). A combined measure is qualitatively similar to the inbound measure but slightly smaller ($\beta = .13$, $p = .02$). Since the research goal is to determine the impact of Facebook *on* the individual and identify levers available to site designers—such as nudging friends to contact another user—we include inbound directed communication in the model.

The intercept represents an average woman receiving the mean inbound directed communication (approximately 150 comments, "likes," wall posts, messages, and photo tags per month). She would have a bridging social capital score of 3.86 out of 5. For every doubling of that inbound communication, her bridging social capital would increase by .14 points. This is comparable to the social capital increase felt by people who moved to a new city between survey waves ($\beta = .14$), and about half the loss by those who became unemployed ($\beta = -0.32$).

Planned comparisons reveal that directed communication has a significantly larger impact on bridging social capital than broadcasting ($p = .04$), and marginally larger than consumption ($p = .10$). Broadcasting and consumption do not differ from each other ($p = .39$). Personalized, one-on-one communication with friends has a measurably greater impact on social capital than undirected communication.

A model testing reverse causation (not shown), in which current directed communication is the dependent variable, and lagged directed communication and lagged bridging social capital are independent variables, did not show an effect ($p = .23$ on lagged bridging). We do not find evidence that bridging social capital predicts future site activity.

Models 1 and 2 were repeated using bonding social capital as the outcome, and revealed no significant effects. Controlling for lagged bonding social capital, the three kinds of site use had no additional impact on bonding social capital. Potential explanations for this lack of findings are in the Discussion section.

	1. Base model			2. FB activity			3. Communication skill			4. Self-esteem		
	β		(SE)	β		(SE)	β		(SE)	β		(SE)
Intercept	3.86	***	(0.03)	3.86	***	(0.03)	3.85	***	(0.03)	3.86	***	(0.03)
Bridging social capital (lagged)	0.47	***	(0.04)	0.45	***	(0.04)	0.41	***	(0.04)	0.41	***	(0.04)
Age	0.00		(0.00)	0.00		(0.00)	0.00		(0.00)	0.00		(0.00)
Male	-0.17	***	(0.05)	-0.17	**	(0.05)	-0.14	**	(0.05)	-0.16	**	(0.05)
Major life changes												
Moved	0.14		(0.09)	0.14		(0.09)	0.12		(0.08)	0.13		(0.09)
Lost job	-0.34	**	(0.11)	-0.32	**	(0.11)	-0.25	*	(0.11)	-0.30	**	(0.11)
Time on Facebook	0.05	.	(0.03)	-0.05		(0.04)	-0.04		(0.04)	-0.04		(0.04)
Facebook activities												
Directed communication (in)				0.14	**	(0.05)	0.12	**	(0.05)	0.13	**	(0.05)
Passive consumption				0.05		(0.04)	0.04		(0.04)	0.04		(0.04)
Broadcasting				-0.02		(0.06)	0.01		(0.06)	0.00		(0.06)
Individual differences												
Communication skill							0.08	**	(0.03)			
‡Communication skill X Directed communication							-0.07	*	(0.03)			
‡Communication skill X Consumption							-0.07	*	(0.03)			
‡Communication skill X Broadcasting							0.00		(0.04)			
Self-esteem										0.06	*	(0.03)
‡Self-esteem X Directed communication										-0.07	**	(0.03)
‡Self-esteem X Consumption										-0.04	.	(0.02)
‡Self-esteem X Broadcasting										-0.01		(0.03)
	Adj. $R^2 = 0.30$			$R^2 = 0.32$			$R^2 = 0.34$			$R^2 = 0.34$		

*** $p < .001$ ** $p < .01$ * $p < .05$ · $p < .10$ N=415

Table 3. Models predicting bridging social capital, controlling for previous level of bridging social capital, major life changes, and time spent on Facebook. ‡Each interaction effect (e.g., between communication skill and directed communication in Model 3) was tested in a separate model due to multicollineary but each set of three is presented in a single column for space. Coefficients and standard errors for interaction effects with directed communication are shown and are qualitatively the same in other models.

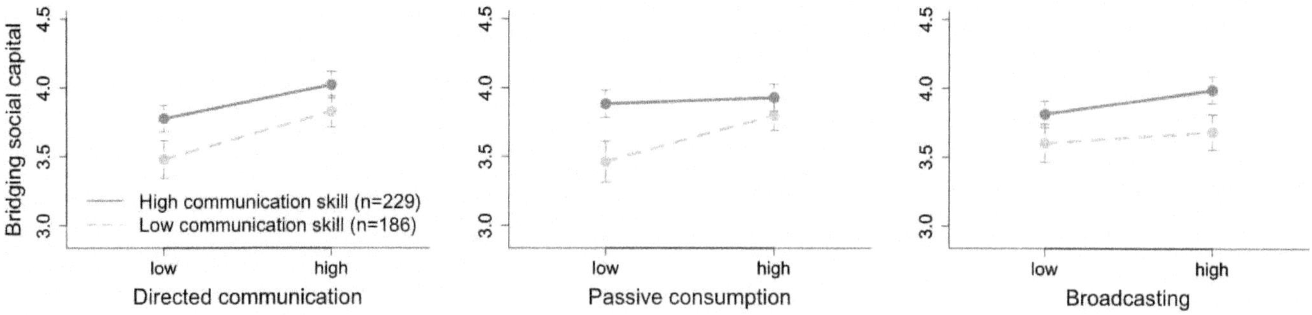

Figure 2. Interactions between social communication skill and site activity on bridging social capital (using median splits). There is a main effect for directed communication: users of all skill levels benefit from greater directed communication. There is an interaction effect for passive consumption; it benefits those with lower social communication skills, while has no effect on the bridging social capital of more socially skilled users. Broadcasting shows no effect for either group.

Models including self-esteem and communication skill

Next we examine individual differences. We first look to see if communication skill (M=8.1, SD=1.6) and self-esteem (M=3.9, SD=0.7) are related to differences in site use. Controlling for age and gender in an OLS regression (not shown), we see two differences in site use. Those with higher self-esteem and social communication skill have more friends: every standard deviation increase in self-esteem or communication skill is associated with 19 or 25 more friends, respectively ($p < .01$ for both). Additionally, those with lower communication skill initiate and receive less directed communication ($p < .05$). Every standard deviation decrease in communication skill is associated with approximately 150 fewer outbound and 90 fewer inbound directed communication actions. No other differences in site activity (including broadcasting, consumption, inbound directed communication, or time on site) are found based on self-esteem or social communication skill.

Now, we examine main and interaction effects based on social communication skill and self-esteem. Model 3 shows the effects for communication skill, and Model 4 shows them for self-esteem. There are main effects for each, such that those with higher communication skill or higher self-esteem have higher levels of bridging social capital.

For interaction effects with communication skill, we see negative coefficients for both directed communication and passive consumption. This indicates that the effects are greater for those with low social skill. Figure 2 shows this interaction effect more clearly using median splits. Participants are divided into "high" and "low" communication skill groups along the median. Those with exactly the median value (8.5) are included in the "high" group. The solid red lines represent those with higher skills, and the dashed blue lines represent those with lower skills. Each plot shows the relationship between one type of Facebook activity and bridging social capital. Each activity is also divided into "high" and "low" levels at the median. For directed communication, both lines have an upward slope, such that those who receive more directed communication feel higher levels of bridging social capital. But for consumption, there is a clearer difference in slopes, such that those with lower social communication skills who consume more social news experience higher social capital. Consumption has no effect on those with higher skills. For broadcasting, the lines are virtually horizontal, illustrating no significant effect for either group.

Results are qualitatively similar for self-esteem. Those with low self-esteem gain more through directed communication. The interaction effect with consumption is similar, though not statistically significant ($p = .11$).

DISCUSSION

Of the three types of social engagement provided by SNS, only directed, person-to-person exchanges were shown to be associated with increases in bridging social capital. Facebook users articulate a set of mutually agreed-upon relationships, but these ties do not directly equate to bridging social capital. For a tie to provide value, such as a job recommendation, an person must be aware that the tie has a resource (such as an "in" with the Human Resources department), and be able to ask the tie about it ("Hey, are you guys hiring?"). Through directed communication, friends keep a channel of interaction open, periodically maintaining the relationship. While undirected broadcasts and passive consumption may affect knowledge of friends' resources, they do not directly develop relationships or allow acquaintances to call on each other for help.

It is curious to note that while we see this relationship for inbound directed communication, we do not see it for outbound. This might be explained by the inherent asymmetric nature of new interactions: by sending a message, I am signaling to my friend that it is ok to get in touch with me in the future. Unless she reciprocates, this says nothing about the relationship from my perspective. In this manner, reaching out to a friend is tantamount to expanding his or her bridging social capital.

At first glance, the lack of connection between Facebook use and bonding social capital is surprising. Previous cross-sectional work has already demonstrated a connection exists [8,11], and so the power of the longitudinal analysis is the ability to tell that frequent Facebook users tend to be already rich in bonding social capital, and their use of the site does not directly increase the value of those relationships. Media multiplexity may help explain this finding: we tend to communicate with our closest friends over many channels, including face-to-face [18]. Therefore, the exchanges that maintain close relationships are less likely to appear in server logs. Facebook is one component in a diverse ecology of communication channels for strong relationships. Spouses and roommates know about each others' lives because they see each other every day, and so do not need Facebook to keep in touch as much as geographically distant friends do. Another explanation is that bonding social capital may be generated through one single good friend who can be relied upon in times of need, and so bonding is less sensitive to amount of communication. Facebook may not strengthen already-strong relationships, but it can increase the value of less strong and nascent relationships.

Similarly, the present results contrast with cross-sectional findings that passive consumption and bridging social capital are inversely correlated [8]. The previous analysis cannot determine whether passive consumption causes feelings of disconnectedness, or if that disconnectedness spurs consumption. With the benefit of time, we find that the latter explanation is more likely: those with lower initial bridging social capital may consume more, but the act of consumption does not make it worse. And, for those with lower social communication skills, consuming friends' status updates and photos makes it modestly better.

Another goal of this paper was to explore how individual differences in self-esteem and communication skill affect one's choice of activities and the benefits those activities bring them. Among the users we surveyed, we found very little difference in site use based on these individual qualities outside of users with higher self-esteem having more friends, and those with lower communication skill interacting one-on-one less. We see no difference in time on site, consumption, or broadcasting, suggesting the site, like many forms of computer-mediated communication, may help to "level the playing field" of self-expression and connection.

When we examine the interaction between communication skill and bridging social capital, we find that for users with lower communication skills, the effects of two kinds of Facebook uses are amplified. Receiving messages from friends, and consuming those friends' news increases their feelings of connectedness. There are a few possible explanations for why increased consumption may differentially help those with lower skills: those who are uncomfortable in social situations may have interacted less with their friends—especially weaker acquaintances—and as such will be less aware of the information and resources provided by those ties, or may be less comfortable asking them. These users may lack reasons to engage with their friends, and the added information provided by News Feed and profiles can catalyze conversations and provide context for discussion, online and offline.

We also find that some major life changes are associated with changes in bridging social capital. Moving has a positive relationship, most likely as a result of adding new relationships with diverse information in the new place of residence. Losing a job, on the other hand, is associated with a decrease, as the social context necessary to interact with former co-workers is lost. Other life changes, such as marriage, divorce, death, new family members, new jobs and illness do not have a relationship to bridging social capital, suggesting that these do not have as substantial an effect on one's wider social circle. When compared to events, where we would expect a major disruption in social capital, the effect of Facebook is clear: every doubling of directed communication is associated with the same gain as moving to a new city, and about half the change incurred by job loss.

Limitations and next steps

Though the sample of English-speaking adults from around the world is more diverse than a convenience sample of undergraduates, the sample is still a self-selected population willing to click on an ad and take multiple waves of surveys. The participants are also heavier site users and have more friends than average. In future waves, we plan to complement the current sample with another stratified by demographics and site use.

Like many large-scale observational social science studies, we cannot draw definitive causal conclusions, even with longitudinal data. By controlling for previous levels of social capital and observing the relationship between current site use and current social capital, we account for many exogenous factors, but other unmeasured variables may still affect both. We begin to address this by including major life changes, such as job loss, and demonstrating their correlation with changes in social capital. Furthermore, there are myriad individual differences that may affect Internet use and social benefits of that use, and social communication skill and self-esteem are just a first step in this large research space. Future studies will incorporate other potential variables, such as extroversion and social anxiety.

Social communication skill is a continuum, and everyone falls somewhere on the distribution. From an absolute perspective, most users surveyed were very highly skilled (with a median of 8.5 out of 10, and only 19 participants—4.6%—scoring below 5). Self-esteem is similarly top-heavy, with a median of 4 out of 5. Thus, we should be conservative in interpreting these results, as an especially unskilled population might have entirely different outcomes caused by varying degrees of use. However, among Facebook users, there is a range of social communication skill and self-esteem, and we don't see many behavioral differences in use across that range.

We employed an entirely content-free approach in order to maintain participant privacy. Though we found few quantitative differences in site use based on self-esteem and social communication skill, users of varying skill may express themselves in a qualitatively different way. Sociolinguistic features, such as hedge words, positive or negative emotion, or even informal web-speak (e.g., "lol") may differ and indicate ways in which communication content affects social capital.

Finally, the confound between communication channel and tie strength suggests the need for additional research to disentangle the two. Unlike traditional computer-mediated communication platforms, where channel and tie strength are more closely entwined (e.g., long phone calls are typically made to close friends and family, while online discussion forums revolve around exchanges with strangers who may share a common identity of interest, but have not met in person), social network sites foster many kinds of relationships over many kinds of channels. Users can passively consume the social news of weak or strong ties, send birthday wishes to best friends and work colleagues, and broadcast personal status updates to classmates and parents. To better understand how social capital is aggregated from dyadic relationships, we need to look at the interaction between communication channel and communication partner. In future waves, we intend to follow Gilbert and Karahalios's [13] method of asking users to report "closeness" for a set of Facebook friends, and identify features that correlate with tie strength. While many features will be related to communication channel (e.g., messages sent), others will be independent (e.g., number of friends in common in a geographic region, co-appearance in photos). We can use these features to add tie strength to our models of communication channel.

As social network sites grow, understanding the interaction between site features and individual differences in users will only become more important. This current study suggests a number of design implications for social media practitioners who may be interested in creating and optimizing social capital flows on their services. As both inbound communication and consumption are tied to bridging social capital in some respect, features which stimulate these behaviors may lead to systemic increases in social capital.

First, features which lower the barrier for initiating conversation will have positive effects on social capital. Many of the lightweight interactions, such as liking and poking have already increased the volume of interactions, and features to this end will result in the generation of more bridging social capital. Similarly, since new broadcast communications are the starting point for many conversations, SNS should consider creating incentives for users to produce stories that create opportunities for more inbound communication.

Second, by adapting the display of content, users can be prompted to interact with individuals who may benefit from direct communication. For example, Facebook's News Feed is an algorithmically controlled stream of information that displays the most relevant stories. This ranking could incorporate the potential value of a new communication. For instance, individuals who had recently lost their job could be ranked higher to increase the probability they will be the target of communications, relieving their feeling of lost bridging social capital. Services may also induce new communication by directly helping people maintain relationships. Suggestions to reconnect with old friends or reordering lists of people to highlight acquaintances over regular contacts would increase the likelihood that bridging social capital would result. This approach to catalyzing new communication comes with the cost of de-emphasizing friends with whom the user often communicates, possibly decreasing the overall interaction in the system. A system which took this ordering approach would need to account for this trade-off.

Finally, since much of the content on social media services has an ephemeral nature, disappearing from view a few weeks after it was shared, a final means of stimulating communication could be the resurfacing of prior content. For relationships that have been inactive for some time, services could choose to highlight prior interactions, such as a status update or photos with comments. These stories could spur nostalgic memories and create a context to re-engage.

CONCLUSION

The study presents compelling evidence for the need to differentiate *uses* and *users* in social media studies. Not all time is equally social, even on inherently social platforms, and individual mileage may vary. We find that, receiving messages—but not sending them—is linked to increases in bridging social capital. Furthermore, some effects depend on the person: passive consumption of friends' news has no effect on users with higher than average social skills, but does help those who are uncomfortable communicating in person, allowing them to benefit from the resources their relationships provide.

ACKNOWLEDGMENTS

We would like to thank Howard Seltman, Brian Junker, Adam Kramer, Tom Lento, Sara Kiesler, and Justine Cassell for feedback and assistance. This project was supported by NSF IIS-0729286 and an NSF Graduate Research Fellowship.

REFERENCES

1. Allan, G. (1979). *A Sociology of Friendship and Kinship*. London: George Allen & Unwin.
2. Amichai-Hamburger, Y., Wainapel, G., & Fox, S. (2002). "On the Internet No One Knows I'm an Introvert": Extroversion, Neuroticism, and Internet Interaction. *CyberPsychology & Behavior, 5*(2), 125-128.
3. Bargh, J., McKenna, K., & Fitzsimons, G. (2002). Can you see the real me? Activation and expression of the "true self" on the Internet. *J. Social Issues, 58*(1), 33-48.
4. Baron-Cohen, S., Wheelwright, S., Skinner, R., Martin, J., & Clubley, E. (2001). The Autism-Spectrum Quotient (AQ): Evidence from Asperger Syndrome/ High-Functioning Autism, Males and Females, Scientists and Mathematicians. *J. Autism and Developmental Disorders, 31*(1), 5-17.

5. Bessière, K., Kiesler, S., Kraut, R., & Boneva, B. (2008). Effects of Internet Use and Social Resources on Changes in Depression. *Information, Communication & Society, 11*(1), 47 - 70.
6. Bourdieu, P. (1985). The forms of capital. In JC Richardson (Ed.), *Handbook of Theory and Research for the Sociology of Education* (pp. 241-258). New York: Greenwood.
7. Burke, M., Kraut, R., Williams, D. (2010). Social use of computer-mediated communication by adults on the autism spectrum. In *Proc. CSCW 2010:* 425-434.
8. Burke, M., Marlow, C., & Lento, T. (2010). Social network activity and social well-being. In *Proc. CHI 2010*: 1902-1912.
9. Caplan, S. (2005). A social skill account of problematic Internet use. *J. Communication, 55*(4), 721. Coleman, J. S. (1988). Social Capital in the Creation of Human Capital. *The American Journal of Sociology, 94*, 95-120.
10. Collins, N., & Miller, L. (1994). Self-disclosure and liking: A meta-analytic review. *Psychological Bulletin, 116*(3), 457-475.
11. Ellison, N., Steinfield, C., & Lampe, C. (2007). The Benefits of Facebook" Friends:" Social Capital and College Students' Use of Online Social Network Sites. *JCMC, 12*(4), 143-1168.
12. Ellison, N., Steinfield, C. & Lampe, C. (In press). Connection Strategies: Social capital implications of Facebook-enabled communication practices. *New Media & Society.*
13. Gilbert, E., & Karahalios, K. (2009). Predicting tie strength with social media. *Proc. CHI 2009*, 211-220.
14. Goldsmith, D., & Baxter, L. (1996). Constituting relationships in talk: A taxonomy of speech events in social and personal relationship. *Human Communication Research*, 23(1), 87-114.
15. Granovetter, M. S. (1973). The strength of weak ties. *American journal of sociology, 78*(6), 1360.
16. Hampton, K. N., Sessions, L. F., & Her, E. J. (2009). Social Isolation and New Technology. *Pew Internet and American Life Project.*
17. Hancock, J., Toma, C., and Fenner, K. 2008. I know something you don't: the use of asymmetric personal information for interpersonal advantage. In *Proc. CSCW'08*. ACM, New York: 413-416.
18. Haythornthwaite, C., & Wellman, B. (1998). Work, friendship, and media use for information exchange in a networked organization. *J. the American Society for Information Science, 49*(12), 1101-1114.
19. Holmes T., and Rahe R. (1967). The Social Readjustment Rating Scale. *J Psychosomatic Research 11*(2): 213–8.
20. Katz, J., & Aspden, P. (1997). A nation of strangers? *Communications of the ACM*, 40(12), 81-86.
21. Keele, L., & Kelly, N. (2006). Dynamic Models for Dynamic Theories: The Ins and Outs of Lagged Dependent Variables. *Political Analysis, 14*(2), 186-205.
22. Knapp, M. L., & Vangeslisti, A. L. (2003). *Interpersonal communication and human relationships* (Vol. 5). Boston: Allyn and Bacon.
23. Kraut, R., Kiesler, S., Boneva, B., Cummings, J. N., Helgeson, V., & Crawford, A. M. (2002). Internet paradox revisited. *J. Social Issues, 58*(1), 49-74.
24. Kraut, R., Patterson, M., Lundmark, V., Kiesler, S., Mukhopadhyay, T., & Scherlis, W. (1998). Internet paradox: A social technology that reduces social involvement and psychological well-being? *American Psychologist, 53*(9), 1017-1031.
25. Landers, R., & Lounsbury, J. (2006). An investigation of Big Five and narrow personality traits in relation to Internet usage. *Computers in Human Behavior*, 22(2), 283-293.
26. Marlow, Cameron (2009). Maintained Relationships on Facebook. Retrieved from http://overstated.net/2009/03/09/maintained-relationships-on-facebook
27. McKenna, K., & Bargh, J. (1998). Coming out in the age of the Internet: Identity "demarginalization" through virtual group participation. *J. Personality & Social Psychology*, 75(3), 681-694.
28. McKenna, K., Green, A. S., & Gleason, M. (2002). Relationship formation on the Internet: What's the big attraction? *J. Social Issues*, 58(1), 9-31.
29. Mikami, A., Szwedo, D., Allen, J., Evans, M., & Hare, A. (2010). Adolescent Peer Relationships and Behavior Problems Predict Young Adultsí Communication on Social Networking Websites. *Developmental Psychology, 46*(1), 46.
30. Oswald, D. L., Clark, E. M., & Kelly, C. M. (2004). Friendship Maintenance: An Analysis of Individual and Dyad Behaviors. *J. Social and Clinical Psychology, 23*(3), 413-441.
31. Papacharissi, Z., & Mendelson, A. Toward a New (er) Sociability: Uses, Gratifications, and Social Capital on Facebook. Paper presented at the Internet Research conference, Copenhagen, Denmark, October 2008.
32. Rosenberg, M. (1989). Society and the adolescent self-image (Rev. ed.). *Middletown, CT: Wesleyan University.*
33. Shklovski, I., Kraut, R., & Rainie, L. (2004). The Internet and social participation: Contrasting cross-sectional and longitudinal Analyses. *JCMC, 10*(1).
34. Valenzuela, S., Park, N., & Kee, K. (2009). Is There Social Capital in a Social Network Site?: Facebook Use and College Students' Life Satisfaction, Trust, and Participation1. *JCMC, 14*(4), 875-901.
35. Valkenburg, P., & Peter, J. (2007). Internet communication and its relation to well-being: Identifying some underlying mechanisms. *Media Psychology, 9*(1), 43-58.
36. Walther, J. B. (1996). Computer-mediated communication: Impersonal, interpersonal, and hyperpersonal interaction. *Communication research, 23*(1), 3.
37. Wellman, B., Quan Haase, A., Witte, J., & Hampton, K. (2001). Does the Internet increase, decrease, or supplement social capital? Social networks, participation, and community commitment. *American Behavioral Scientist, 45*(3), 436-455.
38. Wellman, B., & Wortley, S. (1990). Different strokes from different folks: Community ties and social support. *American Journal of Sociology, 96*(3), 558-588.
39. Williams, D. (2006). On and off the 'net: Scales for social capital in an online era. *JCMC, 11*(2).
40. Zhao, S. (2006). Do Internet users have more social ties? A call for differentiated analyses of Internet use. *JCMC, 11*(3), 844.

Farmer's Tale: A Facebook Game to Promote Volunteerism

Don Sim Jianqiang[1], Xiaojuan Ma[2], Shengdong Zhao[1], Jing Ting Khoo[1], Swee Ling Bay[1], Zhenhui Jiang[2]

[1]Computer Science, [2]Information Systems, National University of Singapore

donsim85@gmail.com, {maxj, zhaosd, jingting, t0800128, jiang}@comp.nus.edu.sg

ABSTRACT
Volunteering is an important activity that brings great benefits to societies. However, encouraging volunteerism is difficult due to the altruistic nature of volunteer activities and the high resource demand in carrying them out. We have created a Facebook game called "*Farmer's Tale*" to attract and make it easier for people to volunteer. We evaluated people's acceptance to this novel idea and the results revealed great potential in such type of games.

Author Keywords
Volunteerism, Persuasive Games, Social Networking.

ACM Classification Keywords
J.4. Social and Behavioral Science.

General Terms
Design.

INTRODUCTION
Digital games are increasingly leveraged by researchers and practitioners as an effective tool/media to achieve goals in addition to passing time. One emerging genre of games is designed to "seek influence and change opinions and behaviors" (e.g. *persuasive games*) [4, 9]. Persuasive games have been explored in many areas (e.g. health promotion [8], reduction of energy consumption [1], etc.). However, one area with great importance for both individuals and the society has so far been under-investigated: using games to promote real world altruistic behaviors, e.g. volunteerism.

Volunteerism is "an unpaid activity undertaken of a person's own free will and involves the commitment of time and energy to actions of benefit to others and to society as a whole." [13] Top motivations to volunteer are altruism, personal growth (e.g. skills), gains in social relationship (e.g. friendship), and moral obligations [2, 12]. However, the actual practice depends on the availability and accessibility, the match to personal interests, and the potential social support and influence.

The most recent Individual Giving Surveys (2006 and 2008) [5, 6] showed a decrease in volunteer participation, from 48 million hours in 2006 to 45 million hours in 2008 in the local community. It is tough to remove constraints in volunteer work (e.g. competition in time), and thus, efforts to encourage volunteerism are mainly devoted to increasing accessibility and flexibility of altruistic activities.

For this purpose, *SG Cares* was established in 2009 to promote occasional volunteering by offering a variety of flexible activities throughout the year without minimum requirement for participation. Up to September 2010, *SG Cares* has successfully attracted 5000 volunteers [10]. However, given that the local city has multi-million residents, there is still a large need and potential to promote volunteering. This motivated us to work on a persuasive game that promotes volunteerism in the local community.

Nevertheless, encouragement of altruistic behaviors is much harder to achieve than the other goals in persuasive games. Volunteering consumes significant amount of time and physical efforts. In addition, the direct benefits of players' efforts are devoted to others, unlike the target behaviors (e.g. quit smoking [8]) in conventional persuasive games, which directly benefit the players. In other words, a game to promote physical volunteer activities has high *perceived cost* (time and physical efforts), but low *perceived benefit* other than the enjoyment of game playing, which imposes significant challenges to its design.

To make a persuasive game successful, its *perceived benefit* needs to out-weigh its *perceived cost* [3], and one way to increase the *perceived benefit* is to enhance the fun factor of playing the game. Currently, many persuasive games are not as engaging compared to other popular games, because most of them emphasize on the target behavior, which often significantly compromises the entertainment value.

In this paper, we took a different approach. Instead of designing a persuasive game for volunteerism from scratch and evolving the game play mechanics around the target behavior, we modeled our game "*Farmer's Tale*" (Figure 1) (apps.facebook.com/farmerstale) after an existing popular game on Facebook called *Farmville*. We inserted persuasive elements into the game by having a quest system which links virtual tasks to real world volunteer activities.

Figure 1. Screenshots of *Farmer's Tale*: game scene (left) and volunteer quest calendar (right).

Farmer's Tale was developed in collaboration with *SG Cares* [10]. It aims to increase awareness of volunteer activities, to encourage people to overcome the barrier of initial involvement, and to keep people engaged.

GAME USAGE SCENARIO

Tom is a young adult in his mid-twenties. He logs onto Facebook and his friend's newsfeed says, "Jane has been rewarded with an exclusive horse stable for completing a real world quest on *Farmer's Tale*! Click here to see how you can make a difference to someone else's life too!" Curious about how volunteering and farming can be combined together, Tom decides to try out *Farmer's Tale*.

In the game, he gets to be a farmer who can grow and harvest many kinds of localized crops. Tom finds out that there are virtual and real world quests by which he can receive reward to buy food and buildings for his farm. Tom clicks on the real world quests as it offers higher reward. He sees a calendar listing different volunteering opportunities. He comes across a beach cleaning activity that will be held this weekend and is nearby. The rewards for completing this activity are an exclusive "spa" and a "special diamond" to buy more rare farming tools. Tom clicks on "Beach clean up" to find out more details. He is pleasantly surprised to see that Jane's name is highlighted in the signup sheet. He feels more motivated to join the activity as he has a friend for company. He clicks on "Sign up for this activity" and spends a meaningful morning on the beach with friends.

One day after volunteering, he logs onto *Farmer's Tale* and sees that *SG Cares* has already sent him his reward. He happily claims his reward and posts it on his wall. *Farmer's Tale* has made volunteering a breeze for Tom. He cannot wait to tell his friends about this game, which combines the joy of farming with flexible volunteering opportunities. Being able to get exclusive rewards and join a community of like-minded people are attractive incentives too.

GAME DESIGN FOR VOLUNTEERISM

To ensure the popularity of our game and strike a fine balance of fun and persuasion so that the entertainment elements can function as a sufficient motivator without distracting people from the actual intention [14], we modeled our game after a successful Facebook game.

Selection of Platform and Successful Game Model

Given the social aspect of volunteering, we picked Facebook, a popular social website [11], as the platform to deploy our game. Through their friend network, Facebook users can quickly keep up and spread the news about game playing and any involvement of volunteer activities, and thus the influence can be magnified and propagated (a.k.a. snowball effect, Figure 2).

Two months into its first appearance on Facebook in June 2009, *Farmville* has consistently been the number one game application. At its peak, it has over 80 million active monthly users [11]. Farming, a commonly adopted game model, is advantageous because there is gender and age balance of its players which allows us to attract players from all backgrounds. Farming is also peaceful and blends well with volunteering. By adopting after *Farmville*, we inherited a number of key contributors to the popularity of successful games: simplistic tasks with high rewards, social enjoyment, invitation rebate, and personalization.

GAME MECHANISM

In *Farmer's Tale*, players will be able to grow crops, buy decorations (e.g. houses, animals etc), and take part in quests as those in *Farmville*. The game, however, also has some customized elements such as local delicacies and crops to make it more interesting for local players. Special items (such as spa buildings) are only awarded to players who complete volunteer tasks in real life.

Incorporation of Persuasive Element

In *Farmer's Tale*, Fogg's seven persuasion strategies [7] have been implemented in various elements (Figure 2). The volunteer recruitment mechanism was implemented as a new type of quest in addition to traditional tasks in farming games. The idea is to use virtual rewards that help advancement in the game to motivate players to perform volunteer work in real life. SG Cares will indicate the degree of difficulty and the urgency of sign up for each volunteer activity added into the game, and the appropriate level of reward will then be assigned to each task.

In order to determine the most appropriate virtual reward system that can effectively increase the perceived benefit without harming the flow of the game, six reward mechanisms with different underlying persuasive strategies were incorporated: 1) Heart points and food system to refill energy (player empowerment); 2) gold and diamond system to buy ordinary items for farming or decoration (player empowerment); 3) exclusive reward system such as special buildings not available on the general market (player empowerment); 4) clan contribution system - the received reward can be shared among friends (clan) (group empowerment); 5) simplistic game play and subtle system – no explicit reward but encouragement via verbal interaction with the volunteer coordinator (game interaction); and 6) volunteer status tracking system (points and achievement).

As with the volunteer status tracking system, *Farmer's Tale* displays information of existing players who have signed up for this quest and friends of the current player will be highlighted. This enhances group encouragement and peer influence. The tracking of the real-world quest activities is accomplished by updates in *SG Cares*' databases.

In general, deploying the game on Facebook helps to create a social environment for both existing volunteers and non-volunteers. The two groups of players can then interact socially both in the virtual and physical world. Once a non-volunteer registers in *SG Cares* and starts to participate in volunteer activity, he/she becomes a volunteer. The combination of game incentives, social influence, and the mixture of virtual and physical world reinforcement thus

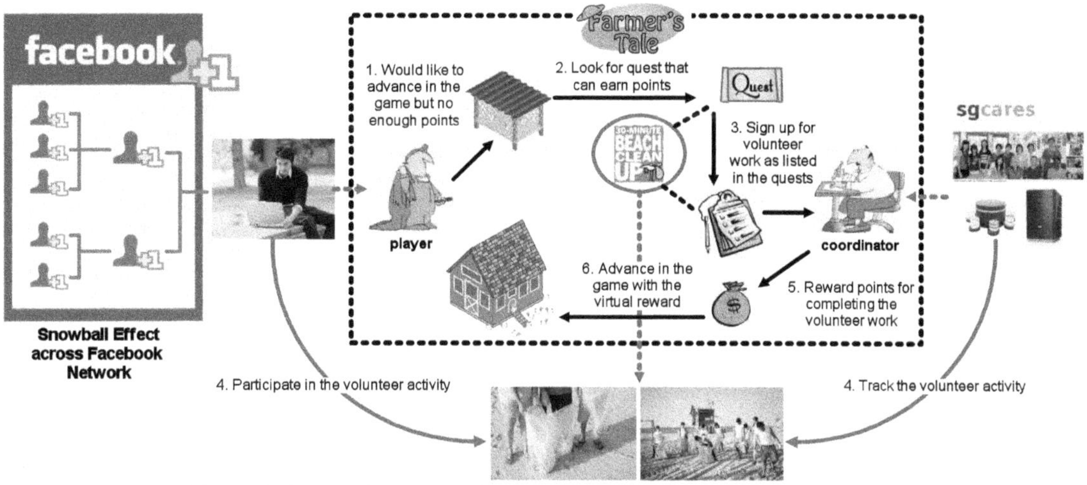

Figure 2. Interaction mechanism between virtual world and real world.

help to overcome the difficulty in promoting volunteerism. Different persuasive mechanisms are exemplified below.

EVALUATION OF ACCEPTANCE

We carried out an exploratory evaluation that involves a group of volunteers and non-volunteers for one week to determine the validity and acceptance of our approach, particularly on the six reward systems.

Experiment Design and Participants

The evaluation consisted of a pre-test survey on the players' gaming experience and volunteering status, daily surveys on the usability and acceptability of *Farmer's Tale* during the week-long game play, and a post-study survey gathering feedback. Twenty-eight players (10 males and 18 females, of age 15 to 50) participated in the study. We sent email invitations to the volunteer mailing list maintained by *SG Cares*. In three days, 48 volunteers signed up and 10 individuals were selected with the best gender, age and occupation mix. The 12 non-volunteers were recruited via email invitations to the undergraduate student mailing list in the local university. Volunteers and non-volunteers were playing together as a community in *Farmer's Tale*, and 20 of them had played Facebook games before. In addition, six volunteer leaders were recruited from *SG Cares* as Farming Quest Councilors to facilitate both groups of players.

Results and Analysis

Factors to Encourage Participation in Volunteerism

Overall, 25 (89.3%) players felt that the game has the potential to influence their willingness to volunteer.

We identified a few keys to encourage first-time volunteer participation based on responses from the non-volunteers: availability of volunteer activities that match personal interests (70%); accessibility of information on volunteering opportunities (70%); involvement of friends or family (70%); and being approached by volunteers (40%). None of the participants indicated complete unwillingness to start volunteering. These results clearly showed the possibility of attracting new volunteers through the game with the large variety of volunteer activities available, the ability to find out more about the activities, a platform to play the game with friends and family, and volunteer leaders placed into the game who will encourage and are willing to share their experiences as a volunteer and information about the different volunteer leaders.

Acceptance of the Novel Game Design

Our earlier surveys suggested that at the beginning, players were surprised that the volunteer elements in the game were not very conspicuous. However, players indicated in the later surveys that they had begun to explore the volunteer quests as the game progressed. Many players also mentioned that, they would use the chat box in the game to gather friends to join them if registering for a volunteer event. Some essential factors to acceptances were revealed:

1) **Fairness.** Players desired for a balance of the persuasive message and the fun factor. 2) **Social interaction.** Players were all in favor of the social features and felt that the community spirit they provide will be very powerful. Most players enjoyed competitions with friends, as it would make the game more fun. 3) **Personalization.** Players in general liked the localized food and crops in the game. They felt that they could identify with the game. 4) **Self-monitoring.** Players also liked the volunteer stats system and felt that it would give them a means to keep track of past volunteer work. 5) **Fun.** "*I have gotten to enjoy the game. I look forward to farming every day after a long day at work.*"

Although some players were concerned that it would make volunteer work incentivized, generally, players seemed positive about exchanging volunteer work with diamonds and to quote them, "*Effective usage of game and virtual activity to relate to real-life volunteerism*", "*It is interesting as it can encourage people to volunteer more in real life.*"

It is encouraging that players showed a high acceptance (Somewhat acceptable: 42.9%, Acceptable: 46.4%) to this novel approach of persuasive game design that focuses on game play and incorporates the persuasive elements. Players also presented clear preference for a farming game with optional but encouraged volunteerism over a game played with compulsory volunteerism (92.9%). This result showed that the majority of players were in fact in favor of our approach to the conventional persuasive game design.

Acceptance of Individual Persuasive Reward Systems

Acceptance of six reward systems from four persuasive strategies (Figure 3) was tested on a 5-point Likert scale. Overall, volunteers were generally positive towards all the reward systems. However, non-volunteers had many more concerns about how the heart points and food system might be biased towards people who carry out volunteer work and people who receive special items as a gift from their volunteer friends. Non-volunteers wanted an alternative way to get those exclusive rewards.

It was unexpected to find out that volunteers preferred to have the volunteer message subtle and inconspicuous with a simple game play design. On the contrary, some non-volunteers mentioned that they did not agree that reducing the game play complexity is a good idea as they felt that it would reduce the fun of the game. Non-volunteers enjoyed rewards that made them feel special and influential.

To sum up, the design of the persuasive reward systems must achieve a fine balance between encouraging practice of target behavior and maintaining the fairness of the game.

CONCLUSIONS, LIMITATIONS AND FUTURE WORK

Our evaluation of acceptance showed that the approach of using successful game models into which persuasion is built using Fogg's strategies is possible and promising.

Although the desired target behavior is participation in volunteer events, the study was unable to measure the actual practice demonstrated by the players due to the short experiment duration. We plan to carry out a controlled multi-month longitudinal study with invited users before fully launching the game on Facebook to the public. We believe that the work we have presented in this paper is valuable for future research on promoting volunteerism as a continuation of this project.

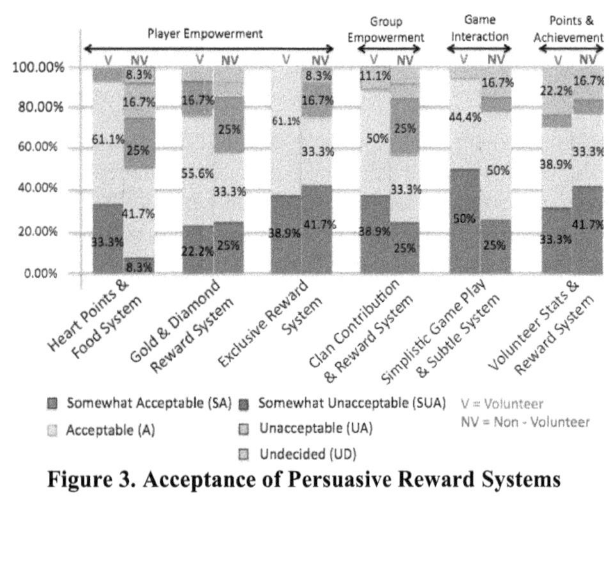

Figure 3. Acceptance of Persuasive Reward Systems

ACKNOWLEDGEMENT

We thank Kelvin, Hannah, Yit Chun, Yappy, Chris, Rachel, Jian Hao, Alwyn and Christopher for helping to develop the game. We thank Jocelyn, David, Tian from *SG Cares* for supporting the game. This research is supported by National University of Singapore Academic Research Fund R-252-000-375-133.

REFERENCES

1. Bang, M., Torstensson, C. and Katzeff, C. (2006) The PowerHouse: A Persuasive Computer Game Designed to Raise Awareness of Domestic Energy Consumpution. *Persuasive Technology*.3962: 123-132.
2. Cnaan, R. A. and Goldberg-Glen, R. S. (1991), Measuring motivation to volunteer in human services, *Journal of Applied Behavioural Sciences*, Vol. 27, No. 3, pp. 269-284
3. Cook, K. S., and R. M. Emerson. Power, equity and commitment in exchange networks. *American Sociological Review*, 43 (1978), 721–739.
4. Fogg, B. J. *Persuasive Technology: Using Computers to Change What We Think and Do*. Morgan Kaufmann Publishers, San Francisco, 2003.
5. Individual Giving Survey, 2006. http://www.nvpc.org.sg/Library/Documents/ResearchReports/IGS%202006.pdf
6. Individual Giving Survey, 2008. http://www.nvpc.org.sg/Library/Documents/ResearchReports/08IGS_SURVEY%20FINDINGS.pdf
7. Khaled, R., Biddle, R., Noble, J., Barr, P., and Fischer, R. Persuasive Interaction for Collectivist Cultures, In Proc. of *The Seventh Australasian User Interface Conference*, 50: 73-80. 2006.
8. Khaled R., Barr, P., Noble, J. and Fischer, R. (2007) Fine Tuning the Persuasion in Persuasive Games, In Proc. *Persuasive Technology*, 4744: 36-47.
9. Lavender, T. Games Just Wanna Have Fun Or Do They? Measuring the Effectiveness of Persuasive Games. *Loading*, 1(1). 2007.
10. *SG Cares*. http://www.sgcares.org/CheckAccess.aspx?url=/imagerepository/media/sgcaresanniversary_release_6sep2010.pdf. 2010.
11. Statistics on *Farmville*, http://www.appdata.com/apps/facebook/102452128776
12. Toppe, C.M., Kirsch, A.D., and Michel, J. (Independent Sector). *Volunteering and Giving in the United States: Findings from a National Survey*. 2001.
13. Volunteering in the European Union. EACEA. http://ec.europa.eu/citizenship/eyv2011/doc/Volunteering in the EU Final Report.pdf. September, 2010.
14. Wong, W. L., Shen, C., Nocera, L., Carriazo, E., Tang, F., Bugga, S., Narayanan, H., Wang, H. and Ritterfeld, U. (2007) Serious Video Game Effectiveness, In Proc. of *Advances in Computer Entertainment Technology*, 49-55

Identifying Social Capital in the Facebook Interface

Christian Yoder
School of Journalism and Mass Communication
University of North Carolina at Chapel Hill
Chapel Hill, NC
chrisnyoder@gmail.com

Fred Stutzman
School of Information and Library Science
University of North Carolina at Chapel Hill
Chapel Hill, NC
fred@fredstutzman.com

ABSTRACT
A number of studies have identified a robust relationship between the use of social network sites, particularly Facebook, and positive outcomes such as social capital. Social network site use is often measured as a function of use frequency, network size, and a range of subjective opinions about the value of the site. This research extends this understanding by exploring the relationship between the use of particular elements of the site and social capital. Our goal in this research is to identify where, in the interface, perceived social capital is most effectively produced and transmitted. We find that, as hypothesized, public, person-to-person communication is positively associated with perceived social capital. Through the use of a structural equation model, we are able to provide in-depth exploration of the relationship between the interface elements and the outcome, perceived social capital.

Author Keywords
Social network sites, social networking, Facebook, privacy, behavioral modeling, social capital

Classification Keywords
H5.3 Group and Organization Interfaces; Asynchronous interaction; Web-based interaction

General Terms
Measurement, theory, design

OUTCOMES OF SOCIAL NETWORK SITE USE
Previous research has identified a relationship between the use of social network sites (SNS) and positive outcomes such as perceived social capital [3, 7, 11, 12]. Acting as a mediator between dispersed groups, the SNS interface enables social awareness, facilitates interpersonal interaction, and allows for the maintenance of ties that may have otherwise gone dormant [7]. Through intensive participation in SNS, individuals may have greater access to informational, emotional, and tangible support. These benefits from the network can either be seen as bridging social capital or bonding social capital [4, 10].

Studies of Facebook use and social capital have generally identified a relationship between intensity of use and perceived social capital. First identified by Ellison et al. [7], intensity of use is generally measured by a construct composed of observed and latent variables. This measure has proven robust, with replications found in subsequent SNS studies [11,12]. Notably, intensity of Facebook use seems to be most positively associated with perceived bridging social capital, the form of social capital identified with the social, economic, and informational value of diverse, "weak-tie" relationships [10].

Recent work has coupled survey research with system-level observational data in exploring the relationship between Facebook use and social capital [3]. Employing regression analysis, the authors found that friend count was a robust predictor of both bridging and bonding social capital, while measures of directed communication and consumption had mixed results for social capital outcomes. In the following study, we wish to further elaborate the relationship between uses of Facebook and perceived social capital, particularly, the relationship between public and private communication practices within the site and perceived bridging social capital.

INTERACTION IN SOCIAL NETWORK SITES
Communication in SNS is generally executed through a range of interface-driven interactions. Facebook, for example, features chat interaction, a direct message feature, wall posts, and status updates as main interaction elements. Each of these interactions may differ on a number of axes, including the expected amount of content, anticipated response times of message recipients, and public-private visibility of content. This last characteristic is the basis for the taxonomy created for this study. Within these four primary interaction elements (chat, direct message, wall posts, status updates), content is either publicly visible to third parties or visible only to the creator and intended recipient of the content. We classify wall posts and status updates as third-party visible interactions because there is reasonable expectation that they will be observed by individuals other than the intended recipient(s) of the message. We classify chatting and direct messaging as one-to-one communication because the content of the message is only visible to the intended recipient(s).

We hypothesize that the level of disclosure provides insight into the mechanisms of social capital in a social network site. Private, one-to-one disclosures between individuals may serve to deepen interpersonal bonds in dyad [5,6]. However, in a heterogeneous media environment, it is likely that the bonding effects of one-to-one communication are spread over a range of devices, which may dampen the effects of a single form of media. Our first hypothesis (H1) is that increasing intensity of use of private-one-to-one communication tools in Facebook is associated with greater perceived bridging social capital.

A novel affordance of social network sites is the ability to create persistent public communication within a bound audience [2]. In Facebook, status updates and wall posts have a range of interesting properties. As public statements, they facilitate the construction of personal identity within the peer group [5, 8, 9]. These disclosures serve as identity cues, signaling individual attitudes towards individual ties and the group [6]. Creating wall posts both articulates a tie, and identifies features of the ties to the bounded group. Therefore, we hypothesize (H2) that the increasing intensity of use of third-party visible communication tools in Facebook is associated with greater perceived bridging social capital. Furthermore, we expect that third-party visible communication has a stronger relationship to bridging social capital than first-person communication.

SOCIAL CAPITAL IN THE INTERFACE

As Facebook use has been demonstrated to more strongly predict perceived bridging social capital [7, 11] than bonding social capital, this study focuses on the former relationship.

Methodology

Data for this study were collected through a web questionnaire, distributed to a random sample of 6,000 students at UNC-Chapel Hill. The questionnaire was created using Qualtrics software and contained 40 questions, including those used to gather demographic data. A total of 574 students responded to the questionnaire, resulting in a response rate of 9.6%. Incentives for participation were the chance to win one of three $20 gift cards, chosen via raffle.

Measures

The general analytic model is presented in Figure 1. We are interested in the relationship between intensity of interface element use and perceived bridging social capital.

Interface Element Intensity

Drawing on the Facebook Intensity Scale [7,11], we created *Interface Element Intensity* scales for Status Updates, Wall Posts, Chatting, and Direct Messaging. The instrument intensity scales were constructed from three items, designed to measure the amount of interface element use, dependence on the interface element for communication purposes, and the effectiveness of the interface element in communication. While the factors of the latent construct were standardized between instruments, the language of the questions was varied slightly for question quality. As questions were measured on different scales, responses were standardized prior to analysis. Individual reliability for the four scales was assessed with Cronbach's alpha; reliability ranged between .68 and .71, an acceptable level for a three-item scale.

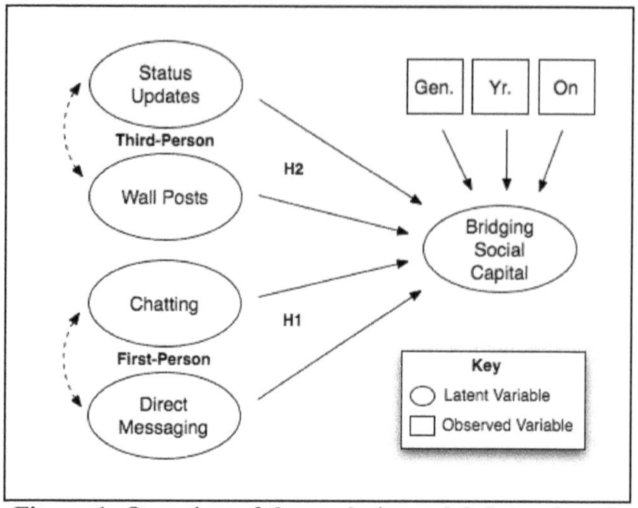

Figure 1: Overview of the analytic model. Intensity of status updating, wall posting, chatting and direct messaging are latent variables. Gender, school year and on-campus status are observed.

Bridging Social Capital

Perceived bridging social capital was measured with the bridging social capital scale [7], adapted for UNC-Chapel Hill. This scale measures, among other things, a student's attitudes toward the university, his or her connection to the larger community, and the diversity of connections he or she has established. Reliability for the bridging social capital scale was .91, measured with Cronbach's alpha.

Demographic Measures

Three demographic measures were included in the analysis. Gender is included because the campus population has an unbalanced gender ratio. School year is included, as individuals with more experience on campus may have accumulated more social capital. Residential status (on-campus status) is included because individuals living on campus may have more frequent access to university-related opportunities, thereby potentially increasing social capital.

RESULTS

Of the 574 total responses, the analytic data set was comprised of 557 responses. The average age of the respondent was 19.85, slightly older than the average student (expected: 19, p=0.000). Respondents were also more likely to be female (response: 78%, expected: 60%, p=0.000), and more likely to live on campus (response: 66%, expected: 47%, p=0.000). Respondents tended to be heavy internet users, with eighty percent of respondents using the internet for greater than 10 hours per week.

Measurement Model

In attempting to move from an omnibus measure of activity (the Facebook Intensity Scale) to sub-scales that explore activity within the interface, there are measurement challenges. Particular concern is focused on the reliability of the latent predictive elements (the Facebook interface measures) and potential covariance between the latent predictive elements.

Therefore, we employ structural equation modeling, a technique that provides estimation of latent construct validity through confirmatory factor analysis, as well as a reliable estimation of the predictive model accounting for measurement error. All latent variables (SU, W, C, DM) loaded on a single factor, with the primary factor responsible for greater than 60% of the variance in all cases. Descriptive results, as well as reliability estimates are presented in Table 1.

Regression Model

We then employed structural regression, with the outcome variable slightly modified from the bridging capital scale first described by Ellison et al. [7]. We entered the four latent predictive factors (status update, wall post, chat, and direct message) and the three observed covariates (gender, on campus status, and school year) into the regression model, allowing for covariance between the latent predictive factors (Table 2). Results of the regression analysis are presented in Table 3. Model identification is within acceptable criteria, with an RMSEA of 0.059.

ID	Question	μ	σ	α
SU1	About how many times do you update your FB status per week?	1.97	1.21	.707
SU2	I depend on the status update feature to communicate my thoughts	2.30	1.18	
SU3	The status update feature allows me to effectively express my ideas	2.94	1.21	
W1	About how many times per week do you create wall posts?	2.59	1.17	.684
W2	I depend on the wall posts feature to communicate ideas	3.35	1.09	
W3	I can effectively communicate with others using wall posts	3.98	.876	
C1	About how many times per week do you chat over Facebook?	3.42	1.66	.702
C2	I depend on the chat feature to connect with other users	2.56	1.33	
C3	I can effectively communicate with others using the chat feature	3.21	1.27	
DM 1	About how many times per week do you send direct messages over Facebook?	1.87	.916	.704
DM 2	I depend on the direct messaging feature to connect with others	3.43	1.15	
DM 3	I can effectively communicate with others using the direct message feature	4.11	.798	

SU1, W1, C1 and DM1 scored on following: 1: 1 or less, 2: 2-4 times, 3: 5-7 times, 4:8-10 times, 10: 10 or more times per week. Other questions on a 5 point Likert agreement scale where 1: Strongly agree and 5: Strongly disagree. Scales standardized in measurement model.

Table 1: Results and reliability estimates of the four latent factors.

In the analysis, we find that wall posting behavior is the only measured interface element that was a significant predictor of perceived bridging social capital (β=.405, p=.003). Of the three observed covariates, gender was the only variable that demonstrated significance. Because the latent factors were standardized to account for differences in the measurement scale, we can interpret the regression output to mean that a one standard deviation movement in an individual's wall posting intensity is associated with a .405 unit increase in an individual's bridging social capital.

Information Consumption and Social Capital

Of the four interface elements measured, wall post was the only significant predictor of perceived bridging social capital. We only find partial support for hypothesis one, and lack of support for hypothesis two. Our theoretical framework strongly couples the interpersonally communicative aspects of social network and bridging capital. That is, the process of social capital accumulation

	Status	Wall	Chat	DM
Wall Post	0.130*			
Chat	-0.067*	-0.066*		
Direct Msg.	0.050*	0.137*	-0.041*	
Gender (1=F)	-0.003	0.037*	0.015	0.028*
On Campus	0.052*	0.034*	-0.033*	0.012
School Year	-0.100*	-0.090*	0.116*	0.006

Table 2: Correlations within latent predictors and between observed variables. Starred correlations are significant at $p < .05$.

Hyp.	Predictor	Coefficient	P-Value
H1	Status Update	-0.098	0.418
H1	Wall Post	**0.405**	**0.003**
H2	Chat	0.094	0.259
H2	Direct Message	0.040	0.640
Cov	Gender	**-0.189**	**0.005**
Cov	On Campus	-0.033	0.646
Cov	School Year	-0.004	0.885

Model Parameters: RMSEA 0.059 (0.053-0.064), SRMR 0.043, Chi Square p=0.00. Standardized coefficients.

Table 3: Results of structural equation model predicting bridging capital. Wall posting is the significant predictor, and gender is a significant control variable.

through a SNS is associated with interpersonal communication. Of course, social network sites provide a range of awareness mechanisms that may affect an individual's social capital. For example, an individual that spends more time reading a News Feed may have a better sense of his or her local environment, contributing to increased social capital.

Recent research has identified a potentially negative association between consumptive social network behaviors and bridging social capital [3]. To test for consumption effects, we re-ran our full model, including a latent variable measuring News Feed consumption. The additional measure was not significant (β=.004, $p > 0.05$). Of course, the measurement and sample differ substantially from [3].

DISCUSSION

Wall posting is a form of semi-public interpersonal communication that remains fairly novel to SNS. According to [2], the semi-public communication that wall posts allow is one of the defining traits of an SNS. When comparing wall posts to chatting and direct messaging, we see that the one-to-one interaction exists across multiple tools. But why might wall posting emerge as a significant predictor, whereas status updates, another form of semi-public communication, do not?

One explanation might be in the focus of communication afforded by the interface. Wall posts are a primarily one-to-one, semi-public method of communication, whereas status updates are directed towards large, heterogeneous audiences. The nonspecific nature of the audience may be associated with a lack of connection between the poster and the audience, especially if the response to the status update is limited in terms of feedback. This explanation would suggest that more active and focused communication interfaces are predictive of perceived bridging social capital.

Wall posting is highly focused and inherently interactive. When an individual creates a wall post, they signal a relationship with an individual in the public's eye [5]. Furthermore, reciprocal wall posts act as a form of verification signal, providing observers direct evidence of a relationship [6]. The feeling of closeness associated with such a public display of connection may very well be linked to increased feelings of inclusion, awareness, and connectedness - all hallmarks of bridging social capital. Another peculiarity about wall posts is their relatively broad scope of communication. They are the only communication element on Facebook visible to friends' friends. This may be another explanation for the findings.

Conclusion and Limitations

A more thorough understanding of the mechanisms of social capital production and accumulation in SNS would assist site operators, designers, and policy builders [1]. In this work, we explored the relationship between interface elements and the production of perceived bridging social capital. Using structural equation modeling to account for inherent covariance between interface element use, we found that increasing intensity of wall posting is significantly associated with the accumulation of perceived bridging social capital. Wall posts represent an affordance unique to SNS, enabling a form of semi-public, directed, one-to-one (or more) communication. In future work, we wish to explore mechanisms similar to the wall post in other social network sites, to see if other semi-public, directed, one-to-one interface use is associated with the production of social capital. Similar findings in other sites may indicate perceived bridging social capital is associated with communication interfaces that are both publically visible and direct in their audience.

It is important to note that this research was conducted using only undergraduate college students from a single university. It may be concluded that the cultural norms among participants are relatively homogenous, and that results may differ significantly between groups with differing values concerning networks and social interaction. Other limitations include self-reported measures for use of communication elements that may not be as accurate as data from actual use. Without this hard data, we concluded that self-reported measures were the best alternative. Also, the low response rate could create a non-response bias.

ACKNOWLEDGMENTS

We would like to thank Jane Brown and Paul Jones for insight and supervision. This work was supported by the UNC Office for Undergraduate Research.

REFERENCES

1. Ala-Mutka, K. (2010). *The Impact of Social Computing on the EU Information Society and Economy*. JRC European Commission.

2. Boyd, D. and Ellison, N. B. Social Network Sites: Definition, History, and Scholarship. *JCMC 13*, 1 (2007).

3. Burke, M., Marlow, C., and Lento, T. Social Network Activity and Social Well-Being. *Proc. CHI 2010*, ACM Press (2010).

4. Coleman, J.S. Social capital in the creation of human capital. *Amer J Soc 94*, 1 (1988), 95.

5 Donath, J. and Boyd, D. Public displays of connection. *BT Technology Journal 22*, 4, (2004). 71-82.

6. Donath, J. Signals in Social Supernets. *JCMC 13*, 1 (2007).

7. Ellison, N. B., Steinfield, C., and Lampe, C. The Benefits of Facebook "Friends:" Social Capital and College Students' Use of Online Social Network Sites. *JCMC 12*, 4 (2007).

8. Kwon, O. and Wen, Y. An empirical study of the factors affecting social network service use. *Computers in Human Behavior 26*, 2 (2010). 254-263.

9. Preece, J. and Maloney-Krichmar, D. Online communities: focusing on sociability and usability. In Jacko, J. and Sears, A. (Eds.), *Handbook of human-computer interaction*. Lawrence Erlbaum Associates, Mahwah, NJ (2003) 596—620.

10. Putnam, R. *Bowling Alone : The Collapse and Revival of American Community*. Simon & Schuster, New York, NY. (2001).

11. Steinfield, C., Ellison, N. B., and Lampe, C. Social capital, self-esteem, and use of online social network sites: A longitudinal analysis. *Journal of Applied Developmental Psychology 29*. 6 (2008) 434-445.

12. Valenzuela, S., Park, N., and Kee, K. F.. Is There Social Capital in a Social Network Site?: Facebook Use and College Students' Life Satisfaction, Trust, and Participation. *JCMC 14*. 4 (2009) 875-901.

Competing Online Viewpoints and Models of Chronic Illness

[1]Jennifer Mankoff, [2]Kateryna Kuksenok, [3]Jennifer A. Rode, [1]Sara Kiesler, [4]Kelly Waldman
[1]Carnegie Mellon, Pittsburgh, PA 15213
[2]Univ. of Washington, Seattle, WA 98195
[3]Drexel University, Philadelphia, PA 19104
[4]Duke University, Durham, NC 27708

ABSTRACT
People with chronic health problems use online resources to understand and manage their condition, but many such resources can present competing and confusing viewpoints. We surveyed and interviewed with people experiencing prolonged symptoms after a Lyme disease diagnosis. We explore how competing viewpoints in online content affect participants' understanding of their disease. Our results illustrate how chronically ill people search for information and support, and work to help others over time. Participant identity and beliefs about their illness evolved, and this led many to take on new roles, creating content and advising others who were sick. What we learned about online content creation suggests a need for designs that support this journey and engage with complex issues surrounding online health resources.

Author Keywords
Health, Interviews, Search, Social Media, Community

ACM Classification Keywords
H.5.3. Information interfaces and presentation (HCI): Group and Organization Interfaces. General Terms: Human Factors

General Terms: Human Factors

INTRODUCTION
Although many people depend on their doctors to diagnose and treat acute conditions such as a sudden high fever or a broken ankle, patients tend to take a more active role in managing chronic conditions [10]. Chronic conditions are increasingly common [1], and people with chronic conditions face ongoing, often debilitating symptoms and uncertainty about the future. Most severe chronic conditions limit one or more activities of daily living (ADLs) [38]. Some conditions go into remission and then recur; others are a constant factor in a person's life. They may require lifestyle changes and complex medication regimens. Thus, "neither clinicians nor health systems... manage chronic disease, but rather patients themselves" ([10], p. 290). In the process, patients may leverage a diverse network of people and information as they develop an internal representation of their illness [15]. They may explore books, magazines, and a host of online resources for understanding and managing their condition and for finding others like themselves (*e.g.*, [2, 6, 31]).

Eight in ten Internet users have looked online for health information. Many say the Internet has had a significant impact on the way they care for themselves or for others [22]. For example, online support groups can influence how people understand their illness (*e.g.,* [4, 15]). Researchers have studied online health support for many chronic conditions including cancer [16, 18] hearing loss [14] chronic fatigue [4], mental health [30] and autism [7].

When people with chronic disease go online, they encounter resources that diverse individuals, groups, and organizations have created [3, 33]. The web can function as a support network, a source of information, a place to compare treatment options, and a mechanism for sharing information with caregivers, family, and friends [16, 21]. Despite the prevalence and promise of online health information technologies, problems exist. In particular, online information can be inaccurate, incomplete, controversial, misleading, and alarming for individuals with health questions [11, 16]. Online content can have a substantial impact on patient beliefs and actions [4, 15, 22]. Thus, it is important to understand how inconsistent or contradictory online information and discussion affects patients.

Our work answers this question by examining the holistic process by which engagement with online resources affects patients' *explanatory models* [29] of their illness over time, and how this in turn affects patients' online and offline actions, identity, and relationships. Even before the Internet became a major source of health information, Kleinman observed a gap between a patient's explanatory models of disease and doctors' more technical definition of it [29]. Patients evolve an explanatory model of their illness over time. This explanatory model is in part a social construct, and may be developed and refined in online settings (*e.g.*, [4, 15]). Yet the details of how understanding emerges from the use of online and offline information and discussion over time are not well understood.

We extend past work by examining how Internet resources that present competing information affect people with chronic illness. We present a study exploring how people with prolonged or recurring Lyme disease symptoms engage with conflicting information online. We describe participants' experiences of information online and how these experiences change their beliefs about Lyme disease. On the surface, patients went online to answer questions such as "what are my treatment options?" and their online activities included search, participation in online communities, and other things predicted by the literature. However, a deeper look shows that when standard medical information did not fit patients' experience, they moved to community-based resources, and adopted new theories and practices for managing their illness. As a result, patients' online needs shifted over time as their online activities led to changes in identity, beliefs about their condition, actions, and relationships with others. Along the way, participants took on new roles, such as interpreter of medical information and patient activist.

This work contributes to the body of HCI research concerned with information technology and health (*e.g.*, [3,7,18,35] and with sensemaking online (*e.g.*, [33]). Our work points to important questions that must be addressed by those creating online health resources. For instance, should search tools help people to find the latest scientific information or the prevailing medical consensus, or should they reveal the range of opinion and debate? We argue that any online technology that dictates a single explanatory model of a health condition may not meet the needs of patients going online. When there is no simple, single answer, online health resources must be understood and designed to address participative patient needs, even to the point of facilitating active debate and advocacy. However, technology that exposes conflicting explanatory models rather than attempting to unify them must engage with complex ethical issues, as its design may have an impact on both the debate and patient outcomes.

THE CASE OF LYME DISEASE

We studied the use of online resources for a condition called Lyme disease that is prevalent in North America and Europe. The basic facts about the disease are not in dispute. Lyme is an infectious disease caused by spirochetal bacteria in the genus *Borrelia,* carried by ticks. It can be diagnosed using a blood test, which detects the presence of antibodies to the spirochete. It can be treated with antibiotics. Lyme symptoms sometimes imitate those of other conditions such as flu or arthritis, and this can contribute to delayed diagnosis. Untreated patients may become sicker as time passes [13]. Delayed diagnosis can lead to complex psychiatric, neurological, or cognitive symptoms [8].

As we will describe, our participants confronted not just this basic explanation of Lyme disease, but at least two other explanatory models of their disease. These are described in depth in our results section, as they are grounded in our data. Given participants' uncertainty about their future and questions about how to manage their sometimes disabling symptoms, these models offered our participants different possibilities for treatment and new ways to understand their illness.

STUDY

Our study explores the holistic process by which online and offline experiences help to define a patient's explanatory model of Lyme disease over time, and how this model in turn affects patient behavior, identity, and use of online resources. Our focus was on the impact of multiple competing online viewpoints on this process. Online coherence is comparatively absent for those seeking information about Lyme disease diagnosis, treatment, treatment failure, prolonged symptoms, or prognosis.

Although our analysis focuses on data from our interviews and surveys, our interpretation of those data is also informed by the authors' experiences with chronic illness (including Lyme disease) and conversations with physicians, researchers, and patients aligned with multiple models of Lyme disease. Additionally, we attended support group meetings, visited doctors' offices aligned with multiple models, and immersed ourselves in reading online and offline content such as medical journal articles, books, forums, blogs, and web pages generated by a variety of stakeholders, about both primary explanatory models.

We began this work with a survey of Lyme patients to discover how they used health resources. We conducted interviews with a subsample of volunteer survey participants to gain more insight into their experiences.

Sample

Our goal was to include people both early and late in diagnosis, and from regions where Lyme is common as well as those where it is not. We advertised using emails to regional Lyme-related email lists (1 per USA state and a few international lists), in two popular support forums for Lyme disease, and by placing a poster in the office of a doctor who treats many individuals with Lyme disease. We obtained 150 survey participants; of those who said they were open to follow up, we recruited an interview subsample of 20 patients. For interviews, we oversampled men (n = 6) to obtain their perspective, but otherwise the interview sample was equivalent demographically and in the length and complexity of their illness to the survey participants.

The sample is not representative of all Lyme patients. People with difficult to treat or prolonged symptoms are probably more likely than others to seek support groups and subscribe to online lists. Our participants described more illness and more problems obtaining diagnoses and treatment than would be expected when Lyme is diagnosed and treated promptly. Thus, the results that we report reflect a sample of those with comparatively difficult experiences.

Procedure

We distributed a SurveyMonkey survey with a $50 raffle as an incentive to participate. The survey included rating scales and open-ended questions about the length of time participants had symptoms, the ease or difficulty of diagnosis, the number of doctors they had seen, and their use of online resources (social networks, general Internet resources, general health sites, Lyme-specific sites).

Our goal for the survey was to include resources that participants were likely to have used, so that survey answers would vary across participants. For this reason, we focused on popularity and the ease with which a resource could be found. In the case of health resources, we also wanted to include sites from a range of categories selected from the reviews by Sood [36], Eysenbach [16] and McManus [32]. We used Google page rank for the search "lyme disease" and popularity in the patient community (*i.e.*, mentioned in discussion posts and blogs) to ensure that we selected the most well known sites in each category. General health sites included Medline, PubMed, WebMD, Wikipedia, and CDC. Lyme-specific sites included CanLyme.com, ILADS.org, LymeDiseaseAssociation.org, LymeNet.org and LymeDisease.org.

We conducted the interviews by phone (in one case, Instant Messenger) in one to three sessions of 45 to 90 minutes. We paid participants $10/hour. Participants completed a pre-interview questionnaire to list the online and offline resources they depended on for support and information. We asked participants about their experience with their disease and their health practitioners, treatment goals, and satisfaction with treatment. They were asked to describe particularly helpful or unhelpful online resources mentioned in their questionnaire, and whether they were currently seeking different online resources. Much of the interview was open ended, to explore participants' disease experiences and use of online resources in depth.

We analyzed the interview data iteratively, generally following Strauss and Corbin's method [37]. The first step entailed the second author's open coding of the transcripts for concepts that were significant in the data such as usage of health information, experience of disease, relationships with people, online interactions, and so forth. The resulting list of over 100 original codes was then grouped into themes. As a group, the authors then integrated the themes into findings by contextualizing them within our problem space of chronic illness and online information and communication. These themes and interpretations shifted as we discussed them and also compared them with reports in the literature about other chronic conditions. We used descriptive labels to represent our interpretations of the experiences of the participants. All participants' names are fictionalized.

RESULTS

Of 150 survey participants, 140 described their online activities; 128 provided demographic information. Of the 128, 18% were male and 82% were female; 95% were white. The median age range was 41-50 (compared with a median of about 37 years for the US population as a whole). All but five resided in the USA; five were from Canada or the UK. Half had a university degree or above.

Seventy-one (55%) of the total sample of 150 participants were unable to work due to disability. Thus, this sample was distinctly ill. The median time since participants were first symptomatic was 6-10 years, but they had only been diagnosed for a median of 1-2 years, a lag of more than 5 years between onset and diagnosis. Eighty-one percent characterized their diagnosis as complicated rather than simple. Twenty percent had self-diagnosed. Another 103 had seen an average of 7.8 doctors prior to diagnosis.

To investigate how the experience of being ill affected online activity, we tested whether participants who had been sick longer differed in their use of online sites from those who had been sick for a shorter time, using mixed-models regression analyses. These analyses used participants as a random variable and included as control variables: gender, age, marital status, education level, and whether they used social media such as Facebook. We divided survey participants into two groups, those who had been symptomatic 5 years or less ($n = 51$) versus more than 5 years ($n = 98$). Overall Internet use did not differ but there was a significant difference in the frequency of use of different online resources. As shown in Figure 1, everyone visited Lyme-specific sites more often than general sites ($F[1, 123]=11.2, p < .01$). Additionally, those who had been sick longer were significantly more likely to use Lyme-specific sites (students t-test, $p < .05$). As we show below, the Lyme-specific sites offered a minority model of Lyme disease that contradicted the dominant model present in general health sites.

Explanatory Models of Lyme Disease: *Dominant*, *Minority*, and *Alternative*

We identified patients' explanatory models through an iterative process starting with bottom-up coding of interviews described earlier. Following practice for grounded theory data analysis [37], we compared our themes with (a) differing models of Lyme disease in the literature such as [39, 8] and (b) other literature on explanatory models. We then iterated on them as a group. Patient stories follow a temporal trajectory, so we divided the data into starting model and ending model to understand how patients' models changed over time.

From our interviews, it became evident that our participants had encountered conflicting accounts of the disease online, particularly two prevailing explanatory models of Lyme disease. We have named them the *Dominant* and *Minority*

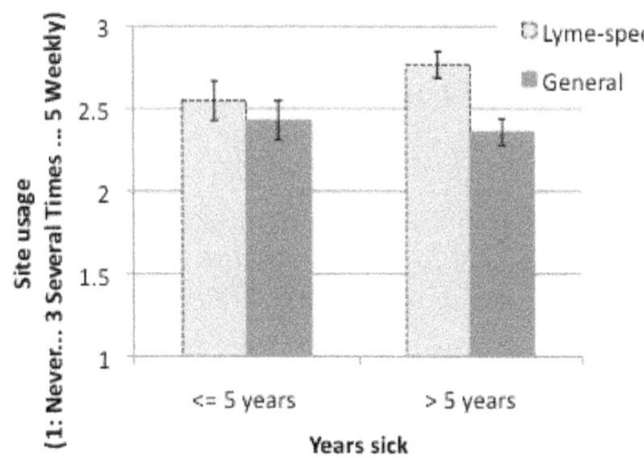

Figure 1: Use of general health vs. Lyme-specific websites. Darker bars show general health site usage, lighter bars (dashed outline) show Lyme-specific health site usage for people with recent onset of symptoms (5 or fewer years ago) versus those who have been symptomatic longer (more than 5 years). The general health sites were aligned with the dominant model; the Lyme-specific sites were aligned with the minority model. Regression analysis shows being sick longer is associated with more use of Lyme-specific, minority-model sites.

models. We categorized less prominent models (such as those based on non-Western medicine) as *Alternative.* We identified these models through our analysis of participants' narratives and terminology. For example, when participants spoke of "chronic Lyme disease" and talked about long-term antibiotics and "Lyme literate" doctors, we labeled this as aligned with the minority model. Both the dominant and minority models take a traditional Western medical view of the disease, but they are contradictory on several fronts, and this contradiction has led to disagreements about the diagnosis, treatment, and progression of prolonged Lyme symptoms (*e.g.*, [23, 12, 19, 8]). As a result, the models of patients and doctors were not always in alignment, and this misalignment was a force affecting participants' identities as patients. Below we describe the characteristic clusters of beliefs that we used to label which model participant statements reflected. All of the models we encountered represented beliefs not only of some patients, but also prevalent among some doctors, online websites, medical articles, and so on. Going forward, we will identify a specific set of beliefs found in our data using the shorthand "in the minority/dominant/alternative model."

Dominant: The dominant model is associated with the belief that Lyme disease is rare outside the USA northeast, most commonly presents with a bulls-eye rash and joint pain (although fatigue, headaches and neurological symptoms are possible [8]), can usually be diagnosed with a two-tiered blood test, and can be cured with approximately 10-28 days of antibiotic therapy, depending on how far the disease has progressed. If patients remain symptomatic, doctors are encouraged to test for other illnesses. Some patients are diagnosed with an untreatable auto-immune disorder, "post Lyme-disease syndrome" [8]. Chronic infection is not considered plausible after antibiotic therapy, although re-infection is possible. Once labeled as having post Lyme-disease syndrome, patients may still have symptoms, and treatment focuses on managing them. This view is dominant in the medical community, and the Infectious Disease Society of America (IDSA), a respected organization representing infectious disease (ID) doctors who treat a range of infectious diseases, including Lyme disease, is a proponent of this viewpoint.

Minority: The minority model is associated with the belief that Lyme disease is common, requires clinical diagnosis because blood tests are not reliable, presents with a rash in less than 50% of cases, and may include myriad other symptoms that may easily be mistaken for chronic fatigue, fibromyalgia, depression, ALS, and many other illnesses. Lyme disease, in this view, may be frequently complicated by co-infections also carried by ticks. Antibiotic therapy may need to extend over months and treatment should continue as long as it alleviates symptoms. If a patient is untreated or inadequately treated, and symptoms persist, the infection may have become chronic, labeled "chronic Lyme disease." In the words of a doctor introducing himself in his first blog post about treating chronic Lyme disease:

> *Physicians who treat this disease ... do so at their professional peril. Many Lyme advocates see this as a witch hunt against Lyme physicians. Physicians who treat chronic Lyme frequently refer to themselves as Lyme literate physician, or LLMDs. They point out that hundreds of publications in well respected medical journals back up their positions with regard to the disease. I am a physician who treats hundreds of patients with Lyme disease. AT this very time the medical board in my state is investigating my treatment of patients. I have opened this blog to vent my frustrations and to perhaps help some patients who may encounter my thoughts.*

Many LLMDs base their treatment approach on repeated clinical experience with patients who did not recover when treated under the dominant paradigm. The International Lyme and Associated Diseases Society (ILADS) represents LLMDs around the world.

As described in Weintraub's book [39], the two viewpoints do not have equal standing. Insurance companies have denied coverage of treatments advocated by the minority model to patients. Researchers aligned with the minority model have difficulty publishing their work. LLMDs treating within the minority model are vulnerable in front of medical boards because they do not follow the dominant standard. As a result, many LLMD patients try to protect the identities of their doctors, a behavior we did not see associated with the dominant model.

Alternative: In addition to dominant and minority models, we encountered a few social and informational sites advocating mixed or other models. The many varied alternative models we encountered were generally consistent with the minority model view that Lyme disease can be a persistent problem that is not easy to diagnose or treat, but advocated treatments outside of antibiotics or Western medicine.

To estimate the overall distribution and use of online resources, we collected a random sample of Lyme disease related websites from a popular social bookmarking tool, *delicious.com*. Delicious.com has an API for downloading data about bookmarks and their tags. We collected all links tagged with Lyme from all 181 delicious.com users who were bookmarking Lyme sites over a month in the spring of 2010. The users were chosen if they used the tag "Lyme" for at least one URL. We collected thousands of URLs this way and calculated popularity by grouping URLs with the same domain name and sorted by the number of users who bookmarked the URL. We coded the top 45 URLs (bookmarked by from 5 to 46 users) by author type (doctor, patient, or other) and model (dominant, mixed, or minority/alternative).

We found that 5 (11%) of these were dominant, 4 (9%) presented a mix of models, and 36 (80%) alternative or minority. Only one link was to the site of a doctor in the dominant model, and no patient-generated content was in the dominant model. To counter the clear bias toward minority sites in our *delicious.com* sample, we searched for "lyme disease treatment" on Google and selected the first 45 pages that reflected dominant or a mixture of models. When we combined these two lists, 43 (48%) were dominant, 11 (12%) were mixed, and 36 (40%) were minority or alternative. Patients had authored 28% of the minority or alternative content, and none of the dominant content. Only 6% of minority or alternative content had been authored by doctors, whereas 14% of the dominant content had been authored by doctors. Organizations or unknown authors were responsible for the remainder. No support groups or blogs were in the dominant category. One possible reason for the alignment of patient-generated content with the non-dominant models may lie in its definition of successful treatment: A patient with chronic symptoms who accepted the dominant model would not identify as having chronic Lyme disease.

Participants' Changing Explanatory Models

Encounters with content aligned with different models online influenced our interviewees' experience and identities. When they began to experience Lyme disease symptoms, ten were aligned with the dominant model, and ten with no clear model. All of the participants had become aligned with a non-dominant model (minority or alternative) by the time we spoke with them. Because so many of our participants shifted their beliefs over the course of their illness, our discussion focuses on the experiences leading to these changes.

Starting from the dominant model

Ten participants told us that at first they accepted facts associated with the dominant model of the disease and resisted contradictory viewpoints. These participants had been diagnosed in half the time (5 years on average) of other participants we spoke with. They cared about scientific evidence and current medical opinion. Jackie exemplifies this group. She is in her 40s, and is bedridden and on long-term disability. After Jackie was diagnosed, her symptoms did not disappear despite aggressive treatment in the dominant model (a few weeks of antibiotics).

> *... [my doctor] explained to me about this Post-Lyme Syndrome. And he said about 10% of people have it; that made sense to me, you know, that's what he said, he was my trusted physician.*

Jackie described being very skeptical of other views of Lyme disease initially, despite having a sister with Lyme in the minority model. She found online information complex.

> *... just too overwhelming, it's like, 'Oh my god, I can't look into all this, I can't do more than I'm doing.'*

Jackie's resistance to other viewpoints also derived from her wish to make decisions based on evidence and research rather than personal experience. She has a Master's degree, and spoke with great respect of support group members able to talk about current research.

> *I call them `braniacs,' ... they are scientists, they're PhD's.... And I know if I have a question ... I'm gonna get a lot of scientific information [from them], and get it answered.*

Jackie met an online acquaintance who persuaded her to think differently about her disease and treatment, but she continued to doubt opinions in the minority model. She responded with great skepticism when online support group members suggested that her son's difficulties might be caused by congenital Lyme.

> *Oh, for god's sakes ... [these people] think everything's Lyme disease. He has ADHD, you know, it's a biological thing.*

The failure of doctors to help her son eventually drove Jackie to take her son to an LLMD doctor (holding the minority model). Her son's treatment was successful, and she now speaks very positively about the minority model.

> *...it's just like such an unbelievable story, and such like-a miracle, that I wouldn't believe it if I wasn't living it.*

Once these participants aligned with a new model and began treatment, their skepticism faded, and improvements in health and wellbeing were attributed to the new viewpoint, and reinforced it.

Starting from rudimentary knowledge and no model

Unlike those participants who began in the dominant model, the other half of the interview participants understood only basic facts of the disease (carried by a tick, treated with antibiotics) or had no idea they had Lyme disease. Their initial encounter with the possibility of Lyme disease was not tied to the dominant model, and when they did discover it they did not find it persuasive. Instead as their symptoms progressed, they increasingly leaned toward the minority model or an alternative. With an average of 10 years until diagnosis (double that of the other group), many of these participants were treated without success for diseases other than Lyme. Unsure what was wrong, participants hoped for improvement. They began searching in earnest for an explanation when asked to accept blame or hopelessness. Twenty years later, Kate still remembers the doctor's statement that drove her to find answers:

> *'You will never be well again. You're 36 years old, you're gonna have to learn to live like this.' ... And I said, 'Absolutely not.'*

Because offline experiences caused them to initiate a search, when a person or website brought Lyme disease to the attention of these participants, they began to research it online. Thus, Kate and others like her were driven toward change initially not by what they found online, but by what they encountered offline.

The Influence of Online Resources

Participants used the Internet to find research related to their symptoms. Because of the uncertainty surrounding Lyme disease, participants did not find the same answers on every site. For participants who started in the dominant model, factual sites had more weight than the opinion of other patients. For example, Alex said:

Most of the online resources are littered with a lot of opinions and innuendo and lack of real facts. There's a lot of declarative stuff there without any reliability to it or validity.

In contrast, participants who started with no clear model seemed less likely to trust information that did not come from other patients [*cf.* 35]. An undergraduate student, Jane spent two years searching for a diagnosis. She had been diagnosed a few months before she was interviewed and had just begun treatment. When she began looking at factual pages, she found that:

It was obvious that Lyme wasn't very well understood, and I would get conflicting answers. Instead, I wanted to know what other people experienced, and I wasn't getting conflicting answers there.

These participants put trust in patient descriptions that had similarities to their own experiences. What Jenna found in support groups swayed her to pursue the possibility of Lyme disease:

...they had the symptoms and stuff like that listed [online] and with the symptoms I had, what they were listing they were pretty much, they were the same. Everything was the same.

Two participants described a mutual learning process with their doctors. These doctors learned about the minority model alongside their participants. Sarah had been in treatment for only three months after being sick for more than 6 years. She described a collaborative relationship with her doctor, in which she was encouraged to bring information to the doctor and ask questions.

...[my doctor] was so intrigued by my case, and the relief that doing this ... [has] made in my life, that she decided to go back to school and study this as her specialty.

While participants differed in their trust of the evidence in factual sites and in patient reports, they all shared a wish for answers, and they all viewed online information as a place to find them.

Interactions with online information

Information seeking, as described by our participants, was a social process. Participants posted new sources of information or followed up on each other. For example, Jenna noted,

...one person will write in something or another and they will have attachments with what they're writing about, and from that attachment it takes you on into another area of Lyme, and from there you gain even more knowledge about it. So it's not just a Lyme board that has people just talking about their symptoms all the time, no. They have so much information if you go on there.

In the end, participants settled into an iterative approach to online content that increased the trustworthiness of results. Seventeen participants described a research process that included triangulation across multiple sources, including support groups.

After they settled on an explanatory model, participants started to avoid information contradictory to it. Susan describes why:

... you know, we're going to disagree and I'm not going to change their minds by reading ... and they're not going to change my mind.

When they settled on a model, participants did not stop using online resources altogether. Instead they engaged in more discussion with like-minded patients. Gail, whose family and friends dismissed her pain and fatigue, told us:

...when I really feel desperate for something, you know, support, information, whatever it may be. At those times, all your life is websites.

Eleven participants, including Gail, described meeting new people online. Jackie explained the appeal of these relationships:

...there's such a disconnect with someone who's not sick.

As these examples suggest, online resources not only helped participants to adopt a new explanatory model of their disease, but to adopt a new group identity aligned with others having the same or similar illness.

The Explanatory Models of Other Stakeholders

As participants began to settle on their own interpretation of their disease, they found themselves increasingly out of alignment in their offline relationships. When doctors, friends, or family opposed the minority model, participants learned to associate the model with an anti-establishment and socially undesirable belief system. Rachel reported:

I had doctors that said you might want to look online and get in some support group [for a previously diagnosed disease] ... But then when I go to the same doctors, see them, or other specialists within the same clinic, I get truly yelled at for going online and trying to get support for the Lyme Disease.

Some participants also discovered that questions about their belief in the minority model led to questions about whether they were really sick. Despite the severity of their symptoms, their difficulties were not always visible to or accepted by others. Gail's husband and her best friend viewed her Lyme symptoms as insignificant. Overwhelmed with emotion, she retold stories of her illness being dismissed:

...[my husband] told me that I was crazy ...

...[my best friend] said, '... you know it really isn't as bad as that, because it's not like you have something that's really bad. You need to be grateful that all you have is Lyme disease and you don't have cancer.'

Jenna was made to feel as though she had hypochondria.

It was all in my head. I had ten noses on my face, I was making up stories.... And continual headaches all the time and you can't walk, you're paralyzed for no reason and nobody wants to take care of you. They think you're just putting on a show for them.

By contrast, Sarah's doctor helped to support her growing understanding of her disease, and Jane's family supported her in the minority model, financially and emotionally.

> *...they didn't think I was imagining things. I have a twin sister... [so] they can see that she isn't having any of the problems I'm having, so something IS wrong.*

Affirmation of this sort was a rare gift in the eyes of participants.

Changing others' models

Changing others' minds was an important part of participating in the Lyme community. Sarah, who told us how her physician had changed her specialty and practice, said,

> *I guess I feel pretty proud, that I could have that influence.*

This sense of accomplishment reflects her understanding that doctors aligned with the minority model are rare. Many patients travel for hours and across state lines to find a sympathetic or knowledgeable doctor [39].

Participants were also committed to helping other patients by encouraging them to accept beliefs associated with the minority model. John told us:

> *My ultimate goal, hopefully, is to try to help other people with this and tell them about ... the Marshall Protocol. It's the one thing that has worked for me the best.*

Kate describes her wish to publicize the problems she encountered:

> *I said... let me start blogging about the Lyme and see if I can get any attention to it... let people know my experiences and also my treatments and ... what's going on with me and pull their attention into everything I had to go through to get any treatment at all.*

Six participants started and contributed to blogs and other online resources to provide information to other patients, friends and family. However, only two participants reported that that the information they provided led to gains in respect and understanding among their friends and family.

An Active, Activist Online Community

Participants who contributed actively to online Lyme-related content did so in the context of a distributed online patient community in which, by the time of our study (2009), the minority model had become mainstream. In Lyme forums, which mix social interaction with the interpretation of online content, participants acted out community norms, such as protecting the names of doctors and supporting other patients. For example, a sense of community responsibility drove participants to provide ongoing social and emotional support.

> *...in [chat group] if someone's suicidal, we'll stay up all night with them.* (Jackie)

> *...if people are asking for help. If I have information I reach out.... So it's very comforting... and empowering to have real people out there that are trying to help that have been there.* (Rachel)

Here, Karen describes how forum members watch for hidden motives or shallow speculation about medical facts.

> *... as soon as somebody says, "I tried this new thing", they'll say, "I noticed that you never posted before. Are you trying to sell us something, or what's your connection to this?" So there's ... somebody who can kind of be policing that. And even regular posters, if they post about something that's a little outside the [minority model] mainstream... they will say, 'Do you have any studies to back that up? ... why is that true for you?'*

For some participants, attempts to shield the patient community went too far. In Alex's words,

> *There are webmasters who ... enforce a kind of public speak, something out of 1984... They don't like to say anything negative about the conventional [minority model] treatment ...*

Our participants' active participation in online Lyme sites also contributed to a vocal online advocacy movement. For example, participants had created or commissioned a social support site, a live group chat service, and a website that supports symptom tracking, visualization, and sharing with doctors.

Participants were also drawn into more traditional forms of activism. For example, there are state-by-state online mailing lists that provide information about local resources (*e.g.*, nearby doctors) and support local activism such as advocating for laws increasing education or protecting physicians who treat in the minority model from censure.

Altogether twelve of the twenty interview participants described numerous small and major acts that they did to protect or advance the interests of the minority model Lyme community with which they had become aligned.

DISCUSSION

Stigmatized groups have been studied by researchers of online health resources over the last two decades (*e.g.*, [4,30]). Outside the health domain, studies have shown how online groups can lead members to a new sense of security and self-esteem [31]. What distinguishes our study from others, we believe, is our discovery of the extent to which our participants used online resources to change their mental, behavioral, and social model of their disease.

These changes did not come overnight. One persuasive website did not make the difference. Our data shows that participants spent months to years struggling with conflicting viewpoints and engaging in discussion and information exchange with others. Many felt skeptical and experienced criticism, including that of doctors and family members, before and after they adopted a new model.

As participants began to align with the minority model, they were often confronted with a disconnect between their own beliefs and those of others they related to. Although some of this conflict focused on medical fact, much of it centered around personal trustworthiness, endurance, and even sanity. Thus, a participant's explanatory model was not only socially constructed, but also profoundly affected their interactions with others (doctors, friends, family, *etc.*).

For members of an out-group, structural conditions such as medical protocols, payment rules, and prescription rights reinforce the in-group majority, making it hard for patients to discover or act on non-dominant models. As Sewell argues [34], the cultural schemas enacted in a complex setting, such as healthcare, "empower and constrain social action and … tend to be reproduced by that social action." [34, p. 91]. Thus, there is a two-way connection between structures, as expressed in cultural schemas, and personal agency, that may evolve over time.

In the case of Lyme disease, the constraints of those cultural schemas led to negative feedback and frustration that drove participants away from the dominant model of Lyme disease. Over time, participants began to take on what Castells characterizes as a "defensive identity" that can lead to the formation of a community designed to resist, and ultimately change, the current cultural norm [9]. Thus the negative feedback participants received led them to identify with a new community of people, "Lymies," as they developed a new understanding of their disease. Defense (hiding doctors) and resistance (advocacy, activism) are defining parts of this community.

Participants worked to increase their new model's legitimacy by engaging in activist behaviors. Their passion for this cause is reflected in a level of emotional engagement that one might not normally associate with Internet health information, as Erica's words exemplify:

> *I would risk my life to get the truth out, and to get people who are suffering from this disease ... the right kind of treatment, just information.... I feel really strongly about that.*

Technological and Ethical Implications

Since this work does not provide evidence for what specific design solutions are likely to be successful, we instead focused on clarifying what need to be asked, and highlighting areas that would benefit from further effort.

Many policy makers and researchers have bemoaned the presence of inconsistent, wrong, or contradictory health information online (*e.g.,* [5, 17]), including contradictory information about Lyme disease [36]. However, there is another side to this concern. It is true that patients may get misleading information or become alarmed about symptoms that are in fact not serious, or they may focus too much attention on disease processes and symptoms, leading them to ruminate about their health [6]. Alarming websites could reinforce hypochondria or cause people unnecessary concern about their health status [25]. However, attempting to resolve this uncertainty by pointing people only to dominant or accepted models belies the changing nature of medical knowledge, in which accepted models of illness are frequently overturned. It also reflects a lack of understanding about the nature of online health behavior in situations where a person's needs are not being met.

***Expose multiple explanatory models, where they exist*:** In the many situations where knowledge of chronic disease is uncertain, people seek explanations from multiple types of online resources. We argue that, rather than causing harm, seeing the diversity of health resources online may lead to a more nuanced understanding of and involvement in the debates around a health condition. Because the scientific basis of disease, medical knowledge, treatments, and social and legal conditions for those with chronic conditions is continually changing, we argue that patients are better prepared to adjust their model of illness if they are exposed to diverse and proliferating viewpoints.

Technology could potentially help to make explicit the presence of multiple explanatory models. Researchers have begun to extract information about viewpoints in other domains (*e.g.,* [40]). Tools that extract and visualize different health models could help patients to familiarize themselves with, and filter, the complex and divergent information currently available online.

Help participants make informed decisions through credibility and triangulation: One possible way forward is technology that could also help individuals to identify more or less credible information by extracting and highlighting key features of credible sites such as those identified by Fogg [20]. Tools that help patients to keep track of, summarize, share, and rate information might also be valuable. Such a tool could be of value both to participants who are highly discerning and, as an educational tool, to those who are less knowledgeable about health information seeking.

Another option would be a search tool that facilitates a triangulation process by juxtaposing information from different kinds of resources (*e.g.,* patient-created content and doctor-created content). If the tool included support for teaching people about the value of triangulation, it could be especially valuable to those participants who engage in less sophisticated online information seeking behaviors. It could help participants more easily learn about information they have missed or show clearly what information is more marginalized. It could also help individuals to select for information consistent with their personal model of a condition once they have settled on one.

Acknowledge and engage with the ethics and value conflicts present in health care IT: There is no avoiding the ethical implications of working in this domain. Health resource designers who are cognizant of contradictory disease models need to decide how to position their practice. For instance, if a resource refers people to sites where an issue is debated or a side is taken, how are extremists to be handled? Should their comments be deleted? Should readers be warned but not protected? Who should judge who should or should not be given a voice in the debate? A design decision as simple as to give each viewpoint equivalent treatment thwarts the dominant model, gives legitimacy to the minority one, and has potentially serious legal consequences.

Although many sites focus on the debate we highlighted, there are also Lyme sites selling questionable cures. Many doctors might argue that any site not in the dominant model is selling questionable cures. What happens if a tool inadvertently highlights potentially harmful information that a patient might otherwise never have found?

Given that much American health care design work is sponsored by insurance companies, hospitals, and large health care repositories, the question of ethics in design becomes especially pertinent. Techniques such as value sensitive design [24], which explicitly address the perspectives and values of all stakeholders, could help with this process.

Limitations

A limitation of this study is its focus on a small group of people primarily located in the US. Also, we studied only a group with prolonged Lyme symptoms. Other patients (such as those cured and those who never went online), doctors, and family members and friends, to a large or small degree, inhabit the same medical, intellectual, and cultural context. We attempted to expand our view by extensive online research of Lyme resources, as described earlier, and by talking with doctors from all sides of the controversy, but these searches and discussions do not take the place of detailed examinations of experience. A study of patients and doctors' experiences in countries where Lyme disease seems to be spreading but where models have not yet been established would be valuable for understanding how models of disease enter a culture and interact with the emergence of online resources.

This study also does not address a larger social issue surrounding patient activism. Although patient activism can be seen as a case of democracy at work, and activism may encourage positive outcomes, it also can foster extremism and uncivil debate, especially in social media (*e.g.*, [28]). The clash of Lyme models has stimulated disrespectful commentary on each side. Here, a doctor aligned with the dominant model writes about proposed legislation that would require him to present both models to patients:

> *It's a free country, and if you want to ruin your health by allowing self-serving 'Lyme specialists' and the patient advocacy groups who fail to speak for the thousands of patients who have been harmed by them to present their laughable theories about [Lyme disease], go for it. But to compel me to allow anything other than objective evidence to shape my discussion with patients referred to me for a positive Lyme serology or an ECM rash is to practice the very shoddiest form of medicine.*

As this comment indicates, there is passion and commitment in the dominant model equal to anything we found in the minority model. Our work focuses primarily on the viewpoint of people currently aligned with the minority model, and does not cover the full range of debate online or its larger social implications.

CONCLUSIONS AND FUTURE WORK

Health researchers have learned a great deal about how people use online resources. As these sites have proliferated, health researchers have begun to turn their attention to the question of how individuals use online resources to manage their health (*e.g.*, [2, 11, 15, 16]). We contribute to this body of work and to the CHI community by exploring the ways in which online information and social interaction online contributes to an individual's shifting understanding of her chronic condition. Not unexpectedly, when patients are unable to resolve Lyme disease through conventional medical treatment, they search for high quality information online. However, we also found that offline and online interactions, along with continued health problems, drove online activities that ultimately resulted in a re-constructed identity that included roles such as educator and activist in addition to illness.

An important conclusion of this paper is that any online technology that dictates a single explanatory model of a health condition may not meet the needs of patients going online. While it is relatively easy to make the case for this with a disease that is as contentious as Lyme disease, there is evidence that the conflicting explanatory models described by Kleinman [29] are the rule with chronic illness, not the exception. For example, is asthma caused by disease or is it a side effect of socio-economic inequalities? Should it be managed by (possibly expensive) medication, a change in environment, or reduced activity? Causality, management, and cure may all be viewed differently by different stakeholders and in different cultural contexts. Online tools offer the possibility of helping patients understand these competing viewpoints. Yet helping designers to navigate the ethical, moral, legal, and practical consequences of this complexity remains a challenge for our community.

ACKNOWLEDGMENTS

Thanks to our participants for giving their time despite the difficulties involved. Thanks to Kristin Doughty for her tutorship on anthropological research and her pointers to relevant theory during our analysis. Thanks to the reviewers for their thoughtful comments. This work was funded by NSF IIS-0916459 and Google. IRB approval #HS10-658.

BIBLIOGRAPHY

1. Agency for Healthcare Research and Quality. (1998). *U.S. National Medical Expenditure Panel Survey*
2. Baker, L., Wagner, T. H., Singer, S., & Bundorf, M. K. (2003). Use of the Internet and e-mail for health care information: Results from a national survey. *JAMA,* **289**(18):2400-2406
3. Balka, E., Bjorn, P., Wagner, I. (2008). Steps toward a typology for health informatics. *CSCW '08,* 515-524
4. Barker, K. K. (2008). Electronic support groups, patient-consumers, and medicalization: The case of contested illness. *Journal of Health and Social Behavior* **49**(March):20-36

5. Benigeri, M., & Pluye, P. (2003). Shortcomings of health information on the Internet. *Health Promotion International, **18***(4):381-386

6. Bessière, K., Pressman, S., Kiesler, S., & Kraut, R. (2010). Effects of Internet use on health and depression: A longitudinal study. *Journal of Medical Internet Research*, **12**(1):e6

7. Burke, M., Kraut, R., & Williams, D. (2010). Social use of computer-mediated communication by adults on the autism spectrum. *CSCW'10*, 425-434

8. Cairns, V., & Godwin, J. (2005). Post-Lyme borreliosis syndrome: A meta-analysis of reported symptoms. *International Journal of Epidemiology, **34***(6):1340-1345

9. Castells, M. (1997). *The Power of Identity* (Information age: V. 2). Blackwell Publishers: MA, USA

10. Clark, N. M. (2003). Management of chronic disease by patients. *Annual Review of Public Health,* **24**, 289-313

11. Cline, R. J., & Haynes, K. M. (2001). Consumer health information seeking on the Internet: The state of the art. *Health Education Research,* **16**(6):671-692

12. Connecticut Attorney General's Office. (2008). Attorney General's investigation reveals flawed lyme disease guideline process, IDSA agrees to reassess guidelines, install independent arbiter. *Press Release*. www.ct.gov. Archived by WebCite® at http://webcitation.org/ 5jqlpUauz

13. Coyle, P. (2001). Lyme disease. *Current Neurology and Neuroscience Reports, **2***:479-487

14. Cummings, J., Sproull, L. S., & Kiesler, S. (2002). Beyond hearing: Where real-world and online support meet. *Group Dynamics: Theory, Research and Practice,* **6**(1):78-88

15. Davidson, K. P., Pennebaker, J. W. (1997). Chapter 16: Virtual Narratives: Illness representations in online support groups. In K. J. Petrie & J. A. Williams, *Perceptions of Health and Illness* (pp. 463-486). Hartwood Academic Publishers

16. Eysenbach, G. (2003). The impact of the internet on cancer outcomes. *CA: American Cancer Journal for Clinicians,* **54**:356-371

17. Eysenbach, G., Powell, J., Kuss, O., & Sa, E. R. (2002). Empirical studies assessing the quality of health information for consumers on the world wide web: A systematic review. *JAMA,* **287**(20):2691-2700

18. Farnham, S., Cheng, L., Stone, L., Zaner-Godsey, M., Hibbeln, C., Syrjala, K., *et al.* (2002). Hutchworld: Clinical study of computer-mediated social support for cancer patients and their caregivers. *CHI'02*, pp. 375-382

19. Feder, H. M., Johnson, B. J., O'Connell, S., Shapiro, E. D., Steere, A. C., Wormser, G. P., *et al.* (2007). A critical appraisal of "Chronic lyme disease". *NEJM,* **357**:1422-30

20. Fogg, B. J. (2002). *Persuasive Technology: Using Computers to Change What We Think and Do*. Morgan Kaufmann

21. Fox, S., & Purcell, K. (2010). Chronic disease and the Internet http://www.pewinternet.org/Reports/2010/ChronicDisease.aspx

22. Fox, S. (2009). The social life of health information. www.pewinternet.org/Reports/2009/8-The-Social-Life-of-Health-Information.aspx

23. France, D. (1999). Scientist at work: Allen C. Steere; Lyme expert developed big picture of tiny tick. www.NYTimes.com. Archived by WebCite® at http://www.webcitation.org/5jqHhP0DM

24. Friedman, B. & Borning, A. (2002). Value sensitive design as a pattern: Examples from informed consent in web browsers and from urban simulation. In *DIAC'02,* 109-113

25. Hardy, M. S., & Calhoun, L. G. (1997). Psychological distress and the "medical student syndrome" in abnormal psychology students. *Teaching of Psychology,* **24**(3):192-193

26. Harris Interactive, cited in the New York Times. (2007). Looking for answers. www.NYTimes.com. Archived by WebCite® at http://www.webcitation.org/5YtGjxB24

27. Hobson-West, P. (2003). Understanding Vaccination Resistance: Moving Beyond Risk. *Health, Risk, and Society*, **5**(3):273-283

28. Jacobs, D. Internet activism and the democratic emergency in the U.S. (2005). *ephemera*, **5**(1):68-77

29. Kleinman, A. (1989). *The illness narratives: Suffering, healing, and the human condition*. New York, NY: Basic Books

30. Kummervold, P. E., Gammon, D., Bergvik, S., Johnsen, J., Hasvold, T., & Rosenving, J. (2002). Social support in a wired world: Use of online mental health forums in Norway. *Nordic Journal of Psychiatry* , **56**:59-65

31. McKenna, K. & Bargh, J. A. (1998). Coming out in the age of the Internet: Identity "demarginalization" through virtual group participation. *Journal of Personality and Social Psych.* **75**(3):681-694

32. McManus, R. (2008). *Health 2.0 through the eyes of a diabetic - one year later.* ReadWriteWeb.com. Archived by WebCite® at http://www.webcitation.org/5jqlzPXLq

33. Paul, S. A. and Reddy, M. C. (2010). Understanding together: Sensemaking in collaborative information seeking. *CSCW'10*, pp. 321-330

34. Sewell, W. H. (1992). A Theory of Structure: Duality, Agency, and Transformation. *The American Journal of Sociology*, **98**(1):1-29

35. Sillence, E., Briggs, P., Fishwick, L., and Harris, P. 2004. Trust and mistrust of online health sites. *CHI '04*, pp. 663-670

36. Sood, S. K. (2002). Effective retrieval of Lyme disease information on the web. *Clinical Infectious Diseases,* **35**(4):451-464

37. Strauss, A. L., & Corbin, J. (1998). Basics of qualitative research: Techniques and procedures for developing grounded theory. Newbury Park, CA: Sage

38. Verbrugge, L. M., & Patrick, D. L. (1995). Seven chronic conditions: Their impact on U.S. adults' activity levels and use of medical services. *American Journal of Pub. Health* **85**(2):173-182

39. Weintraub, P. (2008). *Cure unknown: Inside the Lyme epidemic.* NY: St. Martin's Press.

40. Wilson, T., Hoffmann, P., Somasundaran, S., Kessler, J., Wiebe, J., Choi, Y., *et al.* (2005). OpinionFinder: A system for subjectivity analysis. *HLT/EMNLP'05,* Interactive Demonstrations.

Using Interface Cues in Online Health Community Boards to Change Impressions and Encourage User Contribution

Hyang-Sook Kim
Media Effects Research Laboratory
The Pennsylvania State University
University Park, PA 16802
hxk256@psu.edu

S. Shyam Sundar
Media Effects Research Laboratory
The Pennsylvania State University
University Park, PA 16802
sss12@psu.edu

ABSTRACT
Online health message boards have become popular, as users not only gain information from other users but also share their own experiences. However, as with most venues of user-generated content, there is need to constantly make quality evaluations as one sifts through enormous amounts of content. Can interface cues, conveying (1) pedigree of users posting content and (2) popularity of the posted content, help new users efficiently make credibility assessments? Furthermore, can the assignment of these same cues to their own posts serve to motivate content generation on their part? These questions were investigated in a 2-session between-subjects experiment (N = 99) with a prototype of a message-board that experimentally varied interface cues, and found that popularity indicators are more influential than pedigree indicators for both evaluation of existing content and contribution of new content. Findings also suggest theoretical mechanisms—involving such concepts as perceived authority, bandwagon effects, sense of agency and sense of community—by which cues affect user experience, providing rich implications for designing and deploying interface cues.

Author Keywords
Authority cues, Bandwagon cues, Heuristics, Sense of Agency, Sense of Community, User Contribution, Health Community Boards

ACM Classification Keywords
H5.m. Information interfaces and presentation (e.g., HCI): Miscellaneous.

General Terms
Design, Experimentation, Human Factors, Theory

INTRODUCTION
Kai recently signed up for membership on a health community website to obtain information about dietary supplements for weight training. Using his intuition, he clicked a post on the message board that was already viewed by many users. He also clicked a post that had many replies, although it was not read by as many users as the first post. While reading these posts, he found that some users had different membership statuses than his own, which was "registered user." Some posts came from "senior veterans." Other comments came from "junior members" who failed to receive much attention [18]. Kai tended to trust posts with greater number of views. Whenever he came across a post or reply that he thought was credible, he emailed it to a friend who was also looking for the same information about dietary supplements. After several weeks into his membership on the site, Kai thought about posting a review of a product that he used for his weight training. However, he was somewhat hesitant to do so because he was not sure how other users would react—whether they would read his post, find it helpful, post a reply, give feedback, and/or forward his post to others—given that he is only a "registered user."

As this scenario illustrates, online information sharing requires users to actively monitor existing content in the forum of interest before they contribute content themselves [6]. In emphasizing the critical role of users as active sources in online communities, studies conducted with recommendation systems [5, 8, 26, 28] and knowledge sharing [10] have found that certain features of the technology serve to stimulate user contributions to online communities. A set of visual cues (pertaining to membership status, # of views, # of replies, etc.) can not only be quite suggestive of the quality of the underlying information to other users, but also motivate subsequent actions, such as adding comments to an existing thread or initiating a new thread in a message board.

However, most studies on online information sharing have only investigated the effectiveness of such cues on one part of sharing activities—either user evaluations of content [8, 26, 28] or issues related to under contribution [5, 10], but not both. Given that online community users not only review information on message boards (and perhaps forward it to others) but also contribute information, it is important to examine how technological features, in the form of interface cues, stimulate both sides of the information-sharing process in the same online community.

With this in mind, the goal of the current study is to widen the scope of previous research in online information sharing by raising the following questions: How influential are interface cues in determining community users' evaluations of content? How likely are they to motivate user contribution to the community? Is there a certain combination of cues that promotes or discourages user activities in online community websites? We probed these questions in an online health community, arguably the most appropriate context for studying both reception and contribution of user-generated content.

THEORETICAL BACKGROUND

Fundamentally, cues on the interface attempting to convey the value of the underlying information are really cues about the quality of the source of the information [14]. In user-generated media, all receivers of content are also potentially sources of content, thus turning traditional models of communication on their head by blurring the distinction between senders and receivers of communication [25]. Given the absence of established journalistic standards or brand-names associated with good information quality (e.g., New York Times, BBC), users are having to constantly assess the source credibility of other users who contribute content online. Therefore, by conveying the pedigree of information, interface cues essentially serve as "credibility markers" [12] of otherwise unknown sources in online forums. For example, membership status in the scenario described above tells the reader something about the source of the post. Interface cues about aggregated actions (e.g., # of views) or opinions (# of people who found this helpful) are really channeling the collective will of other users of the forum, thereby making them, in a way, the source of communication. These cues serve as endorsements and confer status on posts in the same way that traditional media gatekeepers sway their audiences toward certain news events over others, by using cues such as headline size and air time.

In sum, there are two types of source cues on Internet forums—those that convey source expertise (e.g., the number of posts contributed by this user in the past, along with compatible membership badges) and those that convey the source's following (e.g., number of views, replies, star ratings of helpfulness). These two species of cues are akin to a newspaper touting in its masthead the year that it was established and its current circulation size, respectively.

Cues in Recommendation Systems

Several studies have examined the effects of interface cues pertaining to the value and quality of information through collaborative filtering systems in various communication settings. One study, using a mock-up of the Amazon.com site, found that two interface cues— star ratings and sales rank—had significant effects on participants' bandwagon perceptions. Statistical mediation analysis showed that the bandwagon perceptions explained why star ratings and sales ranks significantly affected purchase intentions [26]. A follow-up experiment showed that even the number of customer reviews served as a significant bandwagon cue signaling peer opinion [28].

Another study examined the effects of similar source cues—star ratings and sales volume—on users' decision making in an online bookstore [8]. The level of each source cue varied in the way that the star ratings were manipulated in three group comparisons (Group 1: five stars vs. one star, Group 2: four stars vs. two stars, Group 3: three stars vs. three stars), while similar manipulations were applied to sales volume (9000 vs. 3000 books, 6000 vs. 3000 books, 3000 vs. 3000 books for each group, respectively). The study found that Group 1 showed the greatest gap in participants' willingness to purchase a book for both star ratings and sales volume, followed by Groups 2 and 3 [8].

Indicators of peer review in e-commerce sites are a form of online information sharing, where others' opinions often influence users' evaluation of specific content. Even though the information is cumulated using collaborative filtering technologies rather than by users reacting to each other (as often happens in a group bulletin board), the essential outcome of these indicators is the same: they help individual users make rapid judgments about the utility of the content with just a cursory, rather than an effortful, examination of the actual information underlying the content. Dual-processing models in social psychology explain this type of quick information processing based on heuristic activation [7]. The MAIN Model argues that individuals tend to rely on interface cues, such as sales volume, number of clicks, and star ratings, that trigger superficial judgment rules that are accessible in their mind. When website users notice bandwagon cues in an e-commerce site, they are likely to activate a heuristic like "If others think that this product is good, then I should, too." [24]. Extant research in HCI suggests that bandwagon cues lead website users to readily form attitudes and make evaluations about information on the site [27]. Therefore, the current study proposed the following hypothesis:

H1. Cues signaling greater popularity and helpfulness of information provided by other users will produce more positive user attitudes toward the information (H1a) and the website (H1b), leading to more intentions to forward the information (H1c) as well as increased perceptions of the bandwagon effect (H1d) and credibility (H1e) in a health message board as compared to cues signaling lesser popularity and helpfulness.

Health message boards have become veritable hubs of user-generated content, not just because they offer vast potential for exchanging medical information and providing social support, but because "patient expertise" has increasingly become an accepted form of health communication [27]. This kind of peer-to-peer communication allows users to assess others' experiences in managing their own health, and will often need to ascertain the credibility of the person posting a given message. Source credibility can be particularly critical in health-related information [15].

However, little research has directly investigated the specific effects of interface cues in conveying source expertise in such collaborative systems. Instead, most of the previous studies have speculated about such effects in e-commerce settings [8 17, 26]. For example, Koh and Sundar [17] investigated the effects of source specialization on individuals' perceived trust as well as their purchase intentions in the context of e-commerce recommendations by simply labeling three different technology sources (i.e., web agent, website, and computer). They found that web agent specialization (i.e., Wine agent) yielded greater trust toward the agent and the site compared to a relatively generalist "E agent."

Clearly, interface cues impact individuals' perceptions of sources and the information that they provide, especially when they can readily signal source expertise. Dual-processing models also suggest that source credibility has a powerful cueing effect when presented along with expertise information [7]. Specifically, cues signaling expertise are called authority cues. These cues trigger a type of heuristic that allows individuals to readily "confer importance, believability, and pedigree to the content...and thereby positively impact its credibility" [24, p. 84].

Previous studies have examined the effects of authority cues on individuals' evaluations of information in recommendation systems. The power of other users as sources in collaborative filtering systems was demonstrated by Chen [8], who showed that other consumers' recommendations led to greater purchase intentions and trustworthiness than experts' recommendations, while the results were reversed for the perception of expertise in information provided by online bookstores. The mixed results with regard to these two credibility dimensions (trustworthiness vs. expertise) [12] indicate how important other users as sources are in collaborative filtering systems and how they gain authority in such settings. This concept can likely be applied to health message boards in the same manner; namely, other users may exhibit source expertise that is deployed by interface cues such as member labels.

In most online venues, both authority and bandwagon cues coexist. So, how do individuals evaluate information if both types of cues are presented in the interface together? In a study that examined this question [28], participants who viewed a review page of a camera with a credible authority cue (i.e., a CNET.com seal of approval) showed greater purchase intention only when they did not have an outlying negative review by a user. This, along with other results from the study, suggests that the combination of authority and bandwagon cues in recommendation systems are effective when the information values conveyed by both cues are positive rather than mixed. Thus, the findings from previous studies and the propositions from dual-process models lead us to the following hypotheses:

H2. Cues signaling higher expertise of other users as sources in a health message board will result in more positive user attitudes toward the information (H2a) and the website (H2b), leading to higher intention to forward the information (H2c) as well as increased perceptions of authority (H2d) and credibility (H2e), compared to cues signaling lower expertise.

H3. Users' psychological responses will be positive when the levels of both authority and bandwagon cues are higher than when they are inconsistent (i.e., higher authority cues + lower bandwagon cues or vice versa).

Although forty-one percent of Internet users report reading health information posted by other users in online news groups, websites, and blogs, only six percent actually generate health information [13]. Even though under-contribution is so common, research has neglected to explore ways in which technological cues could be leveraged to motivate users to move from lurking to producing original content. What would happen if the participant himself/herself is the source and is given low or high authority status on the board and receives low or high bandwagon cues for his/her posts? By asking this, our study expands the investigation of the effects of cues beyond user evaluation and into the domain of knowledge sharing.

Cues in Knowledge Sharing

Previous studies have probed users' motivations to contribute to online communities [30, 31] as well as the means by which to induce such motivations [5, 10]. Tedjamulia et al. listed eleven propositions in developing a model to explain the mechanisms behind information sharing in online communities [30]. They suggested different technological features conveying both authority and bandwagon cues, and argued that feedback (e.g., replies or comments on message boards) and visible reinforcements for source cues (e.g., membership seals, users' past activities/membership history or point rewards) are likely to constitute personal motivations for contributing content, such as self-efficacy, intrinsic motivation, need to achieve, and trust in the community. Ma and Agarwal also suggested that users' ranking/reputation and activity history, along with others' feedback, would positively impact user identity and therefore predict knowledge contribution [20]. Another study emphasized the relationship between users' motivations to enhance their reputation as well as tenure in an online community and their contribution to the site in terms of helpfulness and volume of their threads [31]. Although these studies hint at the importance of technological features on user motivations, they do not directly measure the effects of these features on user intentions to contribute.

Studies on under-contribution in online communities have tended to focus on increasing user motivation to solve this problem. Beenen et al. examined the effects of three different social-psychological considerations underlying users' intention to contribute to the website [5], and found that users' perceptions toward their unique membership and their specific goal-setting produced the most contributions.

Farzan et al. conducted a longitudinal study that deployed a reputational cue in an online employee community website that was likened to a Beehive [10]. The reputation cue was the image of a bee varying by point-based status classes (i.e., new bee, worker bee, busy bee, and super bee) among employees who used the site. The points were awarded to Beehive users based on their activities, such as uploading photos (5 points), updating their profiles by adding text (10 points), and commenting on others' profiles (15 points). Log data from six weeks revealed that the point-based reputation cue system led to greater contribution to the community site when employees could review overall point details than when they could not. In particular, when the Beehive users were not able to review how their own and other top bees' status was determined (i.e., control group), their contributions significantly dropped after the fifth week. Beenen et al. [5] and Farzan et al. [10] have both provided empirical support for the motivational benefits of signaling authorship value for information sharing online. Therefore, we propose that imbuing authority to the user is likely to encourage knowledge sharing online. Our fourth hypothesis reflects this prediction:

H4. A cue signaling higher expertise of the user himself/herself as a source in a health message board will produce more positive effects regarding the user's attitudes toward posting activities (H4a), intentions to post (H4b), sense of agency (H4c), and perceived empowerment (H4d) compared to a cue signaling lower expertise.

It must be noted that the studies reviewed above did not explicitly examine *why* people respond positively to authority cues or other forms of encouragement, such as email reinforcements of membership uniqueness. A study on (the empowerment potential of) blogging identified mediators that attempted to explain the "why" question [23]. The experimenters manipulated two cues on the blog interface—the number of site visits and number of comments—which served to enhance their sense of agency and sense of community en route to empowering them psychologically. In particular, the more site visits they ostensibly received, the more interest in blogging they showed. The number of comments, however, produced mixed effects that were interdependent with the type of blogs (personal vs. filtering) and the number of site visits. Given that blog-interface metrics such as number of site-visits and number of comments are analogous to authority and bandwagon cues, we can anticipate a similarly positive attitudinal effect in the context of a message board. Therefore, we propose the following hypotheses for study.

H5. Cues signaling the greater popularity and helpfulness of information contributed by the user him/herself as a source in a health message board will produce more positive effects regarding the participant's attitudes toward posting activities (H5a) and increased intentions to post (H5b), sense of community (H5c), and perceived empowerment (H5d), compared to those signaling lower levels of such values.

H6. Sense of agency and sense of community will explain the effects of authority and bandwagon cues, respectively, on persuasive outcomes via perceived empowerment with regard to online health information sharing.

METHODS

The current study employed two sessions, a week apart, of a 2 (authority cues high vs. low) x 2 (bandwagon cues high vs. low) fully-crossed factorial experiment to examine the effects of two source cues on both users' perceptions of a health community website and their intentions to contribute to the website, along with relevant psychological mediators. We developed a prototype of a health community website, modeled after Healthboards.com, as described in the Stimulus section below. Healthboards.com has recorded a large amount of user visits for a variety of health topics [3]. Two types of users contribute to Healthboards.com—"Posters" are users who ask a question about health issues, and "repliers" answer the question. These activities of both posters and repliers create a thread, which is a series of the conversations on the message board.

Ninety-nine undergraduates at a large US university participated in the study. The majority of the participants were females, comprising 80% of the sample. In fact, more females seek health information online than males [13].

Overview of Session 1

Stimulus. The experimental website, Health Q&A, was designed to have two layers of web pages, and participants were instructed to review one of the threads. The main page of the website included the topic of the bulletin board (i.e., fitness and nutrition – one of the most popular topics among college students) [4], the title and author information of the posts and four different bandwagon cues (see Figure 1). On this main page, participants clicked on the first thread that they were asked to read for the study. Only this target thread from the thread list in the main page was clickable, while the other threads were de-activated. When they clicked on the title of the thread on the main page, they were taken to the next layer, where they were able to read an original question posed by a user at the very top, followed by replies by other users.

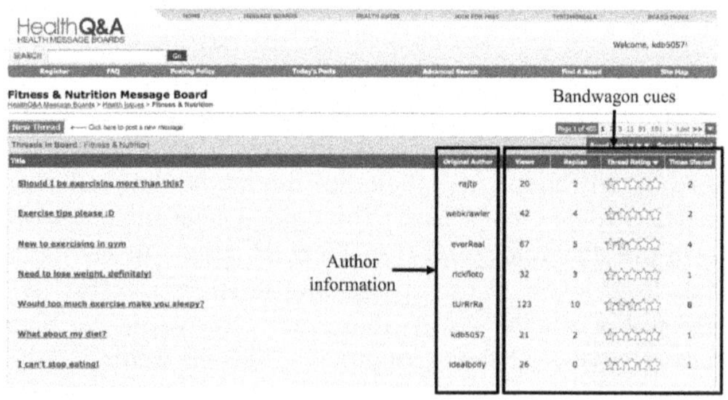

Figure 1. Screen capture of the main page of the experimental website

Independent Variables. Six different source cues constituted independent variables of Session 1. Two authority cues signaled repliers' level of source expertise in the online community. Each replier participating in the thread had a seal of membership status and a number-of-posts value. The high authority condition had 1) "online guru" as the membership seal with a corresponding image and 2) more than 100 posts (see Figure 2).

On the other hand, the low authority condition had 1) "member" as the membership seal and 2) fewer than 10 posts (see Figure 3). However, authority cues for the user who posted the question were identical across conditions—five posts and "member" as the membership seal.

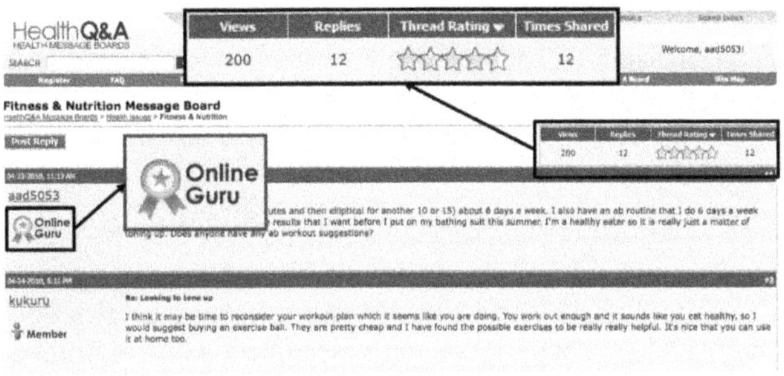

Figure 2. Screen capture of the stimulus website with interface cues for the thread page of the high authority x high bandwagon cues experimental condition

Another set of four metrics served as bandwagon cues: number of views (200 vs. 21), number of replies (12 vs. 2) that the thread had, number of times that the thread was shared (12 vs. 1), and a star rating of the thread's helpfulness (four-and-half stars vs. one star) (see Figures 2 and 3). These cues were indicators of other users' activities on the message board and thereby served to inform participants about other users' evaluations of the particular thread they read on this message board. The thread included identical content (i.e., the original question and core two replies) across all experimental conditions except for the agreement style of ten replies (e.g., I definitely agree with *Titchou*!) in high bandwagon conditions.

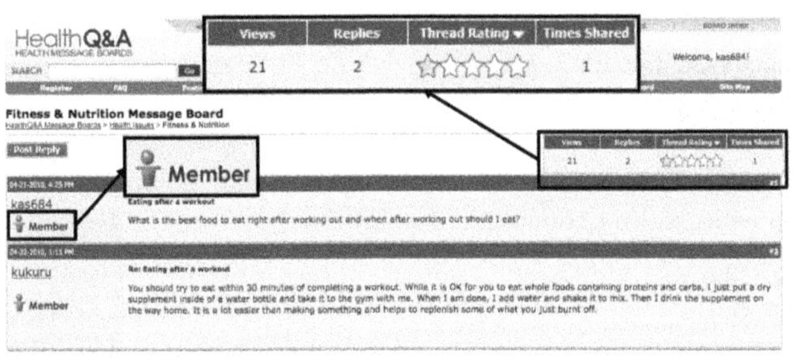

Figure 3. Screen capture of the stimulus website with interface cues for the thread page of the low authority x low bandwagon cues experimental condition

Seven-point scales were used for the measured variables throughout the study.

Manipulation Check Items. Participants were asked to rate their perception of the number of views that the thread had, on a scale anchored from "very few" to "a lot." The other three bandwagon cues (i.e., number of replies, number of times the post was shared, and the star ratings of the thread's helpfulness) and one authority cue manipulation (i.e., number of posts) were checked using similar questions. The manipulation of the other authority cue was assessed by a question in which participants indicated the membership seal—either online guru or member—and their perception of the seal on a scale anchored from very low to very high. The manipulation of the other authority cue was assessed by their perception of the seal on a scale anchored from very low to very high authority. These manipulation-check items were administered in both sessions.

Mediating Variables. Perceived authority measured participants' feelings toward the members who posted in the thread using a scale ("describes very poorly" to "describes very well") with 11 adjectives (e.g., reliable, informed, qualified; α = .93) [21]. In addition, perceived bandwagon was measured by seven items, each on a scale anchored from very unlikely to very likely. The items asked participants to report their opinions on the thread regarding its popularity and helpfulness [26] (e.g., How likely is it that other people would think this is a good thread?; α = .82). Participants also reported their perceptions of credibility for both the website and its content (i.e., the thread). They indicated their impressions of the thread (α = .92) and the web pages (α = .94) that they read on a scale using nine different adjectives (e.g., insightful, trustworthy, accurate) [22].

Dependent Variables. Six statements measured participants' evaluation of the content using a Likert scale [19] (e.g., The content of this website is accurate; α = .83). Attitudes toward the website were measured by asking participants to indicate the appropriateness of 13 adjectives for describing the webpages that they read (e.g., appealing, useful, positive; α = .94) [16]. Lastly, their intention to forward the thread was measured using a scale (extremely unlikely to very much likely) consisting of three items (e.g., I intend to email this thread to people that I know; α = .97) [2].

Procedure. Upon arrival at the study lab, participants were instructed to sit in front of an individual laptop computer designated for them, which was identified by his/her school email account at the top of the main page of the stimulus website. Once participants finished the pre-questionnaire, they browsed the stimulus website and were instructed to click the first thread from the thread list on the main page. After reading the thread, participants were instructed to post a question about the given topic in the health message board (i.e., about fitness and nutrition) in order for them to participate in Session 2. Once they posted a question, they returned to the main page of the stimulus website and clicked their own posting, which appeared at the bottom of the thread list, as a means of exiting to the main questionnaire online. When the participants finished answering the main questionnaire, they were informed about Session 2 before they left the lab.

Overview of Session 2

Stimulus. Researchers created html pages for each participant by changing the authority and bandwagon cues through the site's images and text. The images for Session 2 were identical to those used in Session 1. One html file for the main page of each participant's study webpages included information about bandwagon cue manipulations. In addition, a research assistant, who was blind to the manipulation, crafted replies to the question posted by the participant on the message board during Session 1.

Independent Variables. Four bandwagon cue manipulations were identical to Session 1. The images of the bandwagon cues appeared on both main and thread pages of the participants' own study webpages. Twelve replies were also created, including two core answers to the original participant's question and ten replies in agreement with the core replies for the high bandwagon condition. The core answers adequately addressed the participants' inquiries because the research assistant generated answers by giving participants tips for what they wanted to know about fitness and nutrition in their question. In the low bandwagon cues condition, only two core replies were presented on the participant's thread page. This method of crafting replies allowed us to minimize content effects.

The thread page of each participant included one of the membership seals, Online Guru or Member, with the same images used in Session 1 for the authority cue manipulation. The other authority manipulation—number of posts—was not used in Session 2 due to the nature of the experiment (it would be impossible for participants to have a history of posting in this particular message board).

Mediating Variables. A total of 22 items asked participants to rate the likelihood of the outcomes from their activities, i.e., posting a question or potentially replying to the thread. All items were placed on a scale, ("not at all" to "a lot") [23]. Based on an exploratory factor analysis, two indices of sense of agency and community were created. Three items for sense of agency referred to one's competence, assertiveness, and confidence (e.g., I have control over my own voice; α = .71), whereas 12 items for sense of community referred to one's expectations for interaction with other users in the network (e.g., It may well become very important to me to interact with others through this message board; α = .88). Perceived empowerment was measured by assessing psychological dimensions of autonomy, control and sense of influence regarding participants' posting activities (e.g., I feel more autonomous, I can motivate other people to become more involved in health issues; α = .86) [23].

Dependent Variables. Attitudes toward posting activities were measured by a scale ("describes very poorly" to "describes very well") consisting of six adjectives (e.g., good, beneficial, pleasant; α = .85) [2]. Intention to post was measured by a 3-item index that asked participants about the likelihood of them engaging in future posting activities in online communities, on a scale ranging from "extremely unlikely" to "very likely"; α = .90) [2].

Control Variables. The study administered a pre-questionnaire before the experiment in Session 1 in order to control potential influences from participants' prior experiences with e-community activities via Facebook, product review sites, and online health message boards. After Session 1, participants were asked to indicate the level of involvement with the health topic (i.e., fitness and nutrition) on a scale ("describes poorly" to "describes well") using 12 adjectives (e.g., important, of concern to me, relevant; α = .97) [33]. In Session 2, participants were asked to rate appropriateness of the membership badge that they received from the study website on a Likert-type scale using one item: "The membership status awarded to me is appropriate given my prior experience with these kinds of websites." All control variables were used as covariates in analysis.

Procedure. All of the procedures for Session 2 were online. Participants revisited the website on which they had posted a question about fitness and nutrition one week before. They received email instructions with the study link guiding them to their individual experiment webpages. The instructions emphasized the authority manipulation while describing the procedure for participants to follow. First, participants received information explaining how the website awarded a membership seal to them. The instructions said, "when you click on your own post, you will notice that you have been awarded a Membership Status. The membership has been assigned to you based on the information that you provided in Session 1 of the study regarding your day-to-day online activities." Furthermore, the instructions also informed them that the Online Guru status was considered a high membership status on the study website. Once participants clicked their own study link, they were able to read the exact same main page (i.e., HealthQ&A) that they visited during Session 1, but the page included their own question with their study identification (i.e., school email account) as the author information. Once participants clicked their own post, they accessed the thread page on which both the authority and bandwagon manipulations appeared. After browsing and reading the thread page, they clicked the questionnaire link on the bottom of the thread page and completed the questionnaire to conclude Session 2.

RESULTS

Session 1[1]

Manipulation Checks[2]. The membership status seal (online

---

[1] A series of 2 (authority cues high vs. low) x 2 (bandwagon cues high vs. low) factorial analyses of variance (ANOVA) was conducted to test the hypotheses proposed for Study 1.

[2] The following analyses used a total of ninety-three cases due to missing data.

guru vs. member) was clearly successful, χ^2 (1) = 20.17, $p <$ .0001, N = 93, with the vast majority of subjects correctly identifying the label (guru or member) assigned to their condition. However, the other item, asking participants to indicate their perceptions of the number of posts, failed to demonstrate the authority cue manipulation. Interestingly, this item ended up being an indicator of the bandwagon manipulation (t (91) = 2.93, p < .01). The bandwagon manipulation-check items (i.e., the number of views: t (91) = 3.11, p < .01; replies: t (91) = 5.08, p < .001; star ratings of thread's helpfulness: t (91) = 2.09, p < .05) were successful, except the number of forwards, t (91) = 1.69, *ns*.

Effects of Heuristic Cues on Persuasive Outcomes. Session 1 found near-significant interaction effects between the two different cue manipulations on attitudes toward both the content (F (3, 89) = 3.27, p = .07) and the website (F (3, 89) = 3.87, p = .05). A high level of bandwagon cues produced more positive attitudes toward the content (M = 4.74, SE = .20) and webpages (M = 4.25, SE = .19) than a low level of these cues (M = 4.52, SE = .20 for content; M = 4.00, SE = .19 for webpages), when there was a high level of authority cues in the condition as well. However, without high-status membership seals and a higher number of posts among contributors in the thread, the low level of bandwagon cues resulted in more positive attitudes toward the content (M = 4.86, SE = .21) and webpages (M = 4.24, SE = .20) than the high level of these cues (M = 4.33, SE = .21 for content; M = 3.72, SE = .20 for webpages) (see Figure 4).

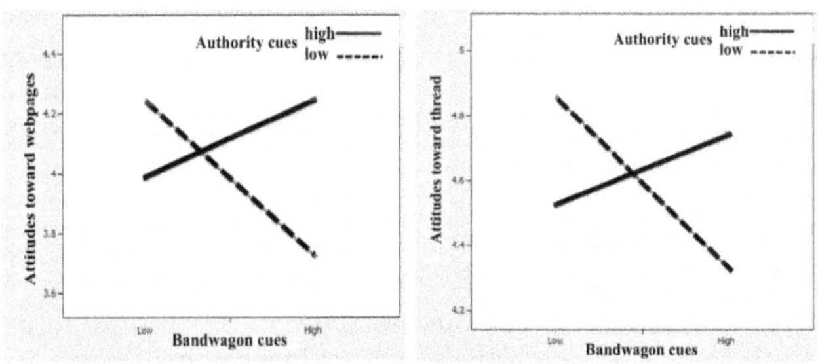

Figure 4. Interaction effects between authority and bandwagon cues on attitudes toward content (left) and webpages (right).

Therefore, H1a and H1b received partial support, in that the bandwagon effects were valid only in the presence of high authority cues. H3 was supported by the interaction effect.

Mediation Analysis. Session 1 showed that participants' perceptions of the number of posts and of the star ratings of the thread's helpfulness produced direct effects on perceived authority and perceived bandwagon respectively. Interestingly, perceived authority mediated the relationship between participants' perceptions of the number of posts and perceived bandwagon. The theoretical paths between the two perceived heuristics and the credibility of the content and the webpages were also significant, followed by significant direct effects between perceived credibility of the content and attitudes toward the thread as well as perceived credibility of the website and attitudes toward both the content and the website (see Figure 5). Regarding participants' behavioral intentions of sharing the thread, the credibility of website produced an indirect effect via attitudes toward the website. Therefore, the results from the mediation analysis suggest that a specific interface cue signaling a contributor's tenure in the site (i.e., the number of posts) [24] did predict users' attitudes toward the content and the website as well as their forwarding intentions, via perceived authority and credibility. The bandwagon effects from the star rating cue also predicted users' evaluations of the content, the website, and their forwarding intentions, consistent with findings from previous studies [8, 26, 28].

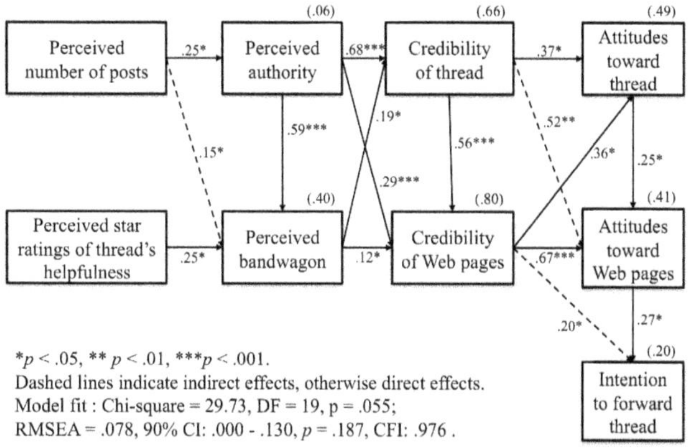

Figure 5. Standardized coefficients in the path model for Session 1. Numbers in parentheses indicate variance explained.

Session 2

Manipulation Checks[3]. Both source-cue manipulations were successful. For the authority cue manipulation, the participants' membership status showed significant differences between the low and high conditions as expected, χ^2 (1, 83) = 30.89, p < .0001 (i.e., What kind of membership seal did you receive from the website—Online Guru or Member?). All of the bandwagon-cue manipulations (the number of views: t (81) = 6.68, p < .001, the number of replies: t (81) = 9.63, p < .001, times of the post shared: t (81) = 5.36, p < .001 and the star rating of the thread's helpfulness: t (81) = 9.72, p < .001) showed significant differences between the low and high conditions for the manipulation-check items.

Effects of Cues on Persuasive Outcomes, Sense of Agency and Sense of Community. Session 2 found main effects of the bandwagon cues on participants' intentions to post (F (8, 74) = 6.74, p < .05) and sense of community (F (8, 74) = 4.29, p < .05). High bandwagon cues produced greater intentions to post (M = 4.30, SE = .52) and sense of community (M = 4.48, SE = .35) compared to low bandwagon cues (M = 3.41, SE = .46 for intention to post;

[3] From a total of ninety-five participants in Session 2, twelve cases were excluded due to missing data. Thus, data from only eighty-three participants were used for analysis.

$M = 4.00$, $SE = .31$ for sense of community). Thus, H5b and H5c were supported.

In addition, there was a near-significant interaction effect between source cues on sense of agency, $F(8, 74) = 3.47$, $p = .07$. While the high authority cue produced higher sense of agency in the low bandwagon condition, participants in the low authority condition actually showed a significant increase in their sense of agency when they had high bandwagon cues (see Figure 6).

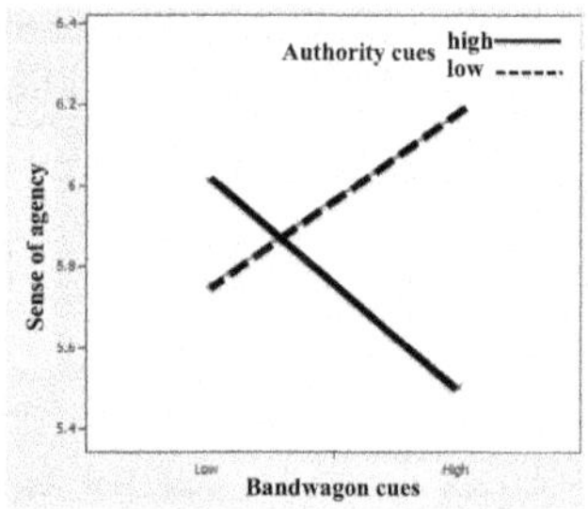

Figure 6. An interaction effect between authority and bandwagon cues on sense of agency.

Mediation Analysis. The final path model for Session 2 showed that one of the bandwagon cues—the number of times the posting was shared—to be a significant predictor of the sense of community, which in turn was associated with perceived empowerment and attitudes toward posting. It also had a direct effect on participants' intentions to post. Clearly, sense of community mediated the relationship between the perceived number of times the thread was shared and participants' intentions to post as well as their perceived empowerment, which also mediated the relationship between sense of community and attitudes toward posting (see Figure 7). Thus, H6 was partially supported.

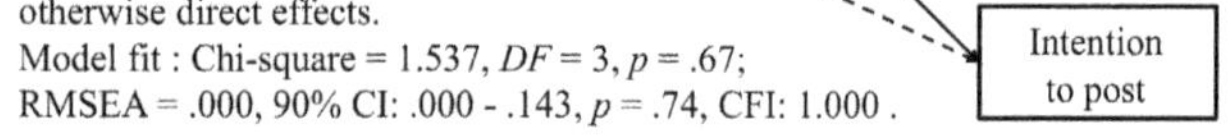

Figure 7. Standardized coefficients in the path model for Session 2. Numbers in parentheses indicate variance explained.

DISCUSSION

The current research examined the effectiveness of six different interface cues that readily inform users of health message boards about the quality of information on the site. Not only does this study test authority vs. bandwagon simultaneously, but it does so for both assessment of content and contribution of content in the same interface. Furthermore, most previous studies used live message boards that confounded content aspects with the presence of authority and bandwagon cues—our study is unique in that it is an experiment, not an observation, and minimized the effects of content by keeping it constant across conditions, thereby isolating the psychological effects of interface cues under study The findings from the two phases may be summarized as follows:

- Bandwagon cues appear to be more influential than authority cues in health message boards for both evaluating information and generating user contribution.
- Bandwagon cues boosted new members' sense of agency for posting activities in health message boards when authority cue was low rather than high.
- Inconsistent combinations of the level of authority and bandwagon cues reduced users' positive evaluations of the content and the webpages (see Figure 4).

The strong bandwagon effects noted in this study could be due to the nature of online health communities. Because it is natural in health message boards for users to interact with other lay people rather than health professionals, they might find the high membership status less meaningful in this kind of an online space. This result is consistent with recent research findings showing that bulletin boards exhibit greater influence on individuals' perceived credibility compared to other types of online sources such as websites and blogs [15]. It also lends empirical evidence to the notion of "information cascades" by showing that others' ratings tend to affect one's own decision-making [9]. In sum, the current study confirmed the notion of patient expertise [27] in the context of a health message bulletin boards, and the larger societal trend of showing faith in "the wisdom of crowds" [29].

A noteworthy contribution of the current study is that the interface elements and theoretical mechanisms for predicting content evaluation are quite different from those predicting content contribution, as evidenced by differences between the path models in Figure 5 and 7. When it comes to users' contribution of content to the board, support from other users (i.e., high bandwagon cues) served to boost participants' sense of agency and enhance future posting activities, especially when they were combined with low authority cue (see Figure 6). This result is particularly interesting because agency is typically associated with authority, not bandwagon [24]. Participants realized their controllability and assertiveness in the community through not only authority but also through bandwagon cues (in the absence of strong authority). Aside from agency, the initial study model for Session 2 (H6) anticipated that bandwagon cues would increase users' sense of community. The path model in Session 2 confirmed this relationship, thus indicating the importance of in-group bonds for encouraging users' contributions to online boards. This may explain the finding by Wu, et al. that peers' positive feedback helps users remain as contributors [32].

Next, our result shows that users are quite reactive to the process by which authority status is awarded to them. Random assignment of authority cues serves to lower the credibility of the label. This is also an interesting result because general wisdom in psychology would suggest that individuals gladly accept such flattery even when it is not warranted (i.e., Lake Wobegon effect) [1, p. 150]. One possible explanation for why the high authority cue did not enhance participants' intentions to contribute more on the site was due to limitations in the experimental setting. Although there was no significant difference among participants' perceptions of the appropriateness of the membership status awarded, the mean score of this item was not very high for both levels of the authority cue manipulation ($M_{\text{low authority}} = 4.35$, $M_{\text{high authority}} = 3.79$, on a 7-point scale). Therefore, the general lack of credibility surrounding the authority cue may have negatively impacted participants' desire to contribute. Previous studies that have found significant effects were conducted for more than two weeks [5, 10]. Thus, longer membership history in the community website appears to be necessary for authority cues to impact user contributions.

It is surprising that inconsistent combinations of authority and bandwagon cues devalue rather than compensate, which contradicts the general supposition in e-commerce studies that if bandwagon cues are equivocal, authority cues will become influential [28]. The negative impact of mixed signals between authority and bandwagon cues in Session 1 might be accounted for by participants' mental models of interpreting the relationship between the two types of interface cues. It would be logical for a user to expect that other users with high membership statuses would engage in a message discussion (i.e., thread) more actively than novice users, which, in turn, would lead to more replies/comments on the board. In fact, Fiore et al. [11] found that users are more willing to read a message from an author with high reputation ratings in Usenet newsgroups. They also found correlations between trust toward an author and rated helpfulness of the author's posts. In addition, authors who contributed more in threads showed more interaction with others in the group. There appears to be a psychological correlation between authority and bandwagon heuristics—something that designers of cue metrics ought to note because they tend to treat these as completely different from a UI design point of view.

CONCLUSION AND FUTURE WORK

The current research provides designers of community websites, particularly health message boards, with insight into utilizing interface cues that go beyond signaling information quality and value. Designers may need to deploy useful interface cues, such as the number of posts, views, replies, and the number of times the post was shared by other users, along with star ratings of threads' helpfulness. The specification of the psychological mechanisms by which interface cues lead to the two sides of sharing (evaluating and contributing content) is an important contribution of this study, because they offer ready implications for UI design, such as the following:

- If designers have to limit the number of interface cues, then they would not go wrong with the following two cues—the number of posts by a given contributor and star ratings for threads' helpfulness—which are shown by this study to optimally convey authority and bandwagon respectively, en route to positively affecting user attitudes toward the content and the site.
- When designers are developing metrics to award membership statuses to community users, they should be aware of the importance of making these metrics point in the same direction, given psychological expectation of a correlation between them.
- Cues conveying the number of times their posts are shared appear to be quite powerful in reinforcing community bonds, thereby enhancing users' contributions to message boards. To the extent site design can emphasize metrics reflecting the extent to which their posts were shared, users will feel energized and motivated to participate by contributing more.

Future studies may extend these findings by comparing the effectiveness of these interface cues to determine the most efficient way of displaying cues in the interface. Furthermore, the processes underlying cue effects revealed by the path models tested here as well as other types of cues (such as "sticky items" determined by the board moderator) can be used to design new and innovative interface cues for both promoting efficient consideration of content and stimulating user contributions to online forums.

ACKNOWLEDGMENTS

This research is supported by the U. S. National Science Foundation (NSF) via Standard Grant No. IIS-0916944 awarded to the second author, and by the Korea Science and Engineering Foundation under the WCU (World Class University) program funded through the Ministry of Education, Science and Technology, S. Korea (Grant No. R31-2008-000-10062-0, awarded to the Department of Interaction Science, Sungkyunkwan University, Seoul, where the second author is a visiting professor).

REFERENCES

1. Aronson, E., Wilson, T. D. and Akert, R. M. *Social psychology* (7th ed.). Upper Saddle River, NJ: Pearson Prentice Hall. 2010.
2. Ajzen, I. and Fishbein, M. *Understanding attitudes and predicting social behavior*. Englewood Cliffs, NJ: Prentice-Hall. 1980.
3. Alexa.com. http://www.alexa.com
4. Baxter, L., Egbert, N., and Ho, E. Everyday health communication experiences of college students. *Journal of American College Health, 56*, 4 (2008), 427-436.
5. Beenen, G., Ling., K., Wang, X., Chang, K., Frakowski, D., Resnick, P. and Kraut, R. E. Using social

psychology to motivate contributions to online communities. *In Proc. CSCW 2005,* ACM Press (2005), 212-221.

6. Bishop, J. Increasing participation in online communities: A framework for human–computer interaction. *Computers in Human Behavior, 23*, (2007), 1881–1893.

7. Chen, S. and Chaiken, S. The Heuristic-Systematic Model in its broader context. In S. Chaiken & Y. Trope (Eds.), *Dual-process theories in social psychology*, pp. 73-96. New York, NY: The Guilford Press. 1999.

8. Chen, Y. F. Herd behavior in purchasing books online. *Computers in Human Behavior, 24*, (2007), 1977-1992.

9. Duan, W., Gu, B. and Whinston, A. B. Informational cascades and software adoption on the Internet: An empirical investigation. *MIS Quaterly, 33*, 1 (2009), 23-48.

10. Farzan, R., DiMicco, J. M., Millen, D. R., Brownholtz, B., Geyer, W. and Dugan, C. Results from deploying a participation incentive mechanism within the enterprise. *In Proc. CHI 2008,* ACM Press (2008), 563-572.

11. Fiore, A. T., Tiernan, S. L. and Smith, M. A. Observed behavior and perceived value of authors in Usenet newsgroups: Bridging the gap. *In Proc. CHI 2002*, ACM Press (2002), 323-330.

12. Fogg, BJ. and Tseng, H. The elements of computer credibility. *In Proc. Human Factors in Computing Systems, CHI 1990*, ACM Press (1999), 80-87.

13. Fox, S. and Jones, S. The social life of health information. http://www.pewinternet.org/Reports/2009/8-The-Social-Life-of-Health-Information.aspx

14. Hilligoss, B. and Rieh, S. Y. Developing a unifying framework of credibility assessment: Construct, heuristics, and interaction in context. *Information Processing and Management, 44*, (2008), 1467-1484.

15. Hu, Y. and Sundar, S. S. Effects of online health sources on credibility and behavioral intentions. *Communication Research, 37*, (2010), 105-132.

16. Kalyanaraman, S. and Sundar, S. S. The psychological appeal of personalized online content in Web portals: Does customization affect attitudes and behavior? *Journal of Communication, 56*, (2006), 110-132.

17. Koh, Y J. and Sundar, S. S. Effects of specialization in computers, web sites, and web agents on e-commerce trust. *International Journal of Human-Computer Studies, 68,* 12 (2010), 899-912.

18. Lampe, C., Johnston, R. and Resnick, P. Follow the reader: Filtering comments on Slashdot. *In Proc. Human Factors in Computing Systems, CHI 2007,* ACM Press (2007), 1-10.

19. Lin, J. C-C. Online stickiness: Its antecedents and effect on purchasing intention. *Behavior & Information Technology, 26*, 6 (2007), 507-516.

20. Ma, M. and Agarwal, R. Through a class darkly: Information technology design, identity verification, and knowledge contribution in online communities. *Information System Research, 18,* 1 (2007), 42-67.

21. McCroskey, J. C. and Teven, J. J. Goodwill: A reexamination of the construct and its measurement. *Communication Monographs, 66*, (1999), 90-103.

22. Metzger, M. J. Making sense of credibility on the Web: Models for evaluating online information and recommendations for future research. *Journal of the American Society for Information Science and Technology, 58,* 13 (2007), 2078-2091.

23. Stavrositu, C. and Sundar, S. S. *Psychological empowerment derived from blogging: Is it agency or is it community? In Proc. the International Communication Association,* Montreal, Canada, 2008.

24. Sundar, S. S. The MAIN model: A heuristic approach to understanding technology effects on credibility. In M. J. Metzger & A. J. Flanagin (Eds.), *Digital media, youth, and credibility,* pp. 72-100. Cambridge, MA: The MIT Press 2008.

25. Sundar, S. S. and Nass, C. Conceptualizing sources in online news. *Journal of Communication, 51*, (2001), 52-72.

26. Sundar, S. S., Oeldorf-Hirsch, A. and Xu, Q. *The bandwagon effect of collaborative filtering technology. In Proc. CHI 2008,* ACM Press (2008), 3453-3458.

27. Sundar, S. S., Rice, R. E. and Kim, H. S. Trends in online health information: New conceptualizations for a new medium. *In Proc. the International Communication Association*, Singapore, 2010.

28. Sundar, S. S., Xu, Q. and Oeldorf-Hirsch, A. Authority vs. peer: How interface cues influence users. *In Proc. CHI 2009,* ACM Press (2009), 4231-4236.

29. Surowiecki, J. *The wisdom of crowds*. Random House, Inc. 2004.

30. Tedjamulia, S. J. J., Olsen, D. R., Dean, D. L. and Albrecht, C. C. Motivating content contributions to online communities: Toward a more comprehensive theory. *In Proc. the 38th Annual Hawaii International Conference on System Sciences,* (2005).

31. Wasko, M. M. and Faraj, S. Why should I share? Examining social capital and knowledge contribution in electronic networks of practice. *MIS Quarterly, 29*, 1 (2005), 35-57.

32. Wu, F., Wilkinson, D. M. and Huberman, B. A. Feedback loops of attention in peer production. *In Proc. Computational Science and Engeerning 2009*, 409-415.

33. Zaichkowsky, J. L. Measuring the involvement construct. *Journal of Consumer Research, 12*, (1985), 341-352.

ACES: Promoting Empathy Towards Aphasia Through Language Distortion Emulation Software

Joshua Hailpern[1], Marina Danilevsky[1], Andrew Harris[1], Karrie Karahalios[1], Gary Dell[2], Julie Hengst[3]
University of Illinois at Urbana Champaign
Urbana, IL USA 61801

[1]Department of Computer Science
(jhailpe2, kkarahal)@cs.uiuc.edu
(danilev1, harris78)@illinois.edu

[2]Department of Psychology
gdell@cyrus.psych.illinois.edu

[3]Department of Speech and Hearing Science
hengst@illinois.edu

ABSTRACT
Individuals with aphasia, an acquired communication disorder, constantly struggle against a world that does not understand them. This lack of empathy and understanding negatively impacts their quality of life. While aphasic individuals may appear to have lost cognitive functioning, their impairment relates to receptive and expressive language, not to thinking processes. We introduce a novel system and model, Aphasia Characteristics Emulation Software (ACES), enabling users (e.g., caregivers, speech therapists and family) to experience, firsthand, the communication-distorting effects of aphasia. By allowing neurologically typical individuals to "walk in another's shoes," we aim to increase patience, awareness and understanding. ACES was grounded in the communication science and psychological literature, and informed by an initial pilot study. Results from an evaluation of 64 participants indicate that ACES provides a rich experience that increases understanding and empathy for aphasia.

Author Keywords
Aphasia, Assistive Technology, Disabilities, Empathy, Emulation Software, Language, Speech

ACM Classification Keywords
H.5.0 General, K4.2 [Social Issues]: Assistive technologies for persons with disabilities

General Terms
Experimentation, Human Factors

INTRODUCTION
Receiving empathy and understanding are a constant need for those living with aphasia [17]. Aphasia is an acquired language disorder that impairs expressive and receptive language (both spoken and written)[18]. Over one million Americans are affected by aphasia [25]. There is considerable variability in the effects of aphasia, but all individuals with aphasia display difficulty producing words accurately and with ease. Specific disruptions in language include dropping key words, substituting incorrect words for the target word, mixing up sounds or letters within words, describing items that are difficult to name, having difficulty organizing coherent strings of words, and making multiple attempts to correct such production errors.

To an outsider it may appear that an aphasic individual has poor cognitive function. However, the problem resides in the individual's receptive and expressive language, not their ability to think. Aphasia most profoundly affects the ability to communicate with others, whose lack of understanding and empathy has the potential to "erode the social bonds that give life meaning" [17].

Our goal is to promote empathy and understanding of aphasia in unimpaired individuals. We made it possible for those without aphasia to metaphorically "walk in another's shoes" by interacting with a system which emulates the effects of aphasia through distortion of written text. This system has the potential to help family and friends of individuals with aphasia, and to serve as a training tool for physicians, nurses, and speech-language pathologists.

We introduce a novel system and model, called **A**phasia **C**haracteristics **E**mulation **S**oftware (ACES), that enables users to experience the speech-distorting effects of aphasia. This model adheres to the wealth of literature in language distortions resulting from aphasia. It was informed though a series of interviews and demonstrations (using an early prototype of ACES) with professionals and students from the field of aphasia and other language disorders.

The ACES system was designed to distort a user's Instant Messages (IMs) from the original message to one that appears like a message spoken by an individual with aphasia. Thus, the conversation that develops between the user and their IM partner has similar difficulties and hurdles to those experienced by an individual with aphasia. By experiencing these challenges firsthand, we hypothesize that users will have increased empathy, knowledge, and understanding of aphasia. Results from an evaluation of 64 participants indicate that ACES provides a rich experience that strongly increases understanding and empathy for aphasia.

The foremost contribution of our system is a demonstration of how existing literature about language distortions/errors due to cognitive impairment, age, or other language-based challenges can be extended to an interactive system that increases knowledge, empathy, and awareness. Our goal is not to perfectly emulate aphasia.

RELATED WORK

We describe aphasia, empathy and how our work builds upon, and extends, the literature related to aphasia.

Aphasia

Aphasia is a term used to describe an acquired language disorder that is caused by damage to the left or dominant hemisphere of the brain and impairs an individual's ability to produce and understand language in both written and spoken forms [1]. The severity and pattern of aphasic symptoms vary, depending in part on the specific locations of brain damage. Clinical researchers have developed classification systems that identify different patterns or sub-types of aphasia. For example, diagnostic batteries [12,27] based on the Boston classification system are designed to categorize an individual's aphasia symptoms as either a type of non-fluent aphasia (Broca's, Transcortical Motor, Global) or fluent aphasia (Wernicke, Transcortical Sensory, Conduction, Anomic). Of particular interest to the goals of the current study is that all individuals with aphasia will display at least some difficulty with writing, and although writing may be more or less impaired than spoken language, the linguistic deficits in writing will be generally consistent with those of the person's spoken language [2]. Recent research focusing on issues of treatment and functional recovery in aphasia[5] has drawn attention to the need for clinical interventions to attend not only to the areas of deficits in the patient with aphasia, but also to the person's communicative and social systems more broadly. This paper focuses on increasing empathy for those interacting with aphasics.

Empathy and Aphasia

Empathy is one of the fundamental underpinnings of interpersonal communication. It is an emotional response to the experiences of others, through which an empathetic person can understand and predict the feelings, emotions, and thoughts of others [10,29].

Non-technical approaches have been used to increase awareness and empathy in other situations by placing students in the "role" of an individual with an impairment. For example, students were tasked to spend a day in a wheelchair to develop an awareness of the challenges confronting a paraplegic [9]. In another course, students were given Augmentative and Alternative Communication (AAC) devices (such as text-to-speech systems which assist those with impairments or restrictions on the production or comprehension of spoken or written language) to emulate "non-vocal" communication while performing tasks such as going to a coffee shop [15].

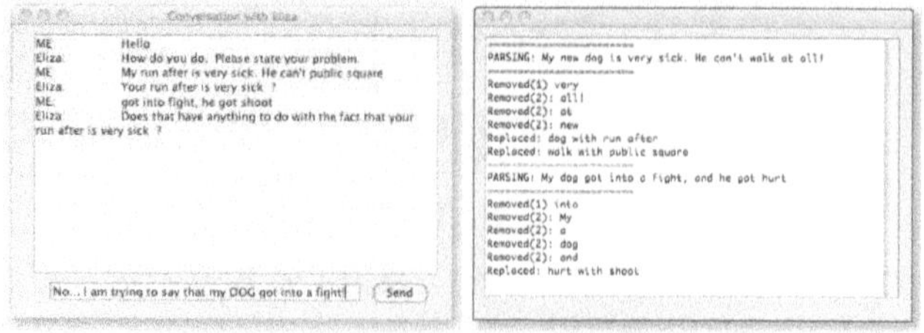

Figure 1. Prototype Chat Window (left) and Distortion Window (right)

Notice how the participant's text is hard to decipher after it has been distorted by the Aphasia Model. Removed (1) is a dropped Function word, Removed (2) is a random word drop and Replaced is when a word is substituted.

If individuals relating to those with aphasia lack empathy and understanding, it can greatly reduce quality of life for aphasic individuals [17]. Often, family members can deny or underestimate the severity and presence of aphasic errors [6]. Further, in speech therapy, empathy is necessary to motivate the aphasic client, with motivation being one of the three key aspects of effective treatment [28]. To date, research has shown that family member's ability to relate and empathize is based on how well they understand the distortions that their partners make [11].

Technology, Empathy and Aphasia

Technology has been used as a tool to enhance the functioning and communication of individuals with aphasia [7,20,30] and other speech and language disorders [16,24]. Specifically, work in the Human Computer Interaction (HCI) community has examined technological solutions to help with day planning [23], communication [3], and increased access to web-content [8] for aphasic individuals. Most of this HCI research has focused on providing support for the individual, their communication, and providing awareness of their activities to those around them. Unlike work that focuses on developing empathic agents [21], this work aims to increase empathy, knowledge, and understanding of aphasia for those who support aphasic individuals.

EARLY PROTOTYPE AND INITIAL INVESTIGATION

Although there is a wealth of technology that aids individuals with aphasia, to our knowledge there is none that aims to increase empathy among those associated with aphasic individuals. Following the existing work in other domains [9], we hypothesized that if individuals were to experience the effects of aphasia first hand, they might better understand the disorder and become more empathetic to its challenges.

To this end, we built a prototype chat client that randomly distorted messages sent by its user using an aphasia language model. We chose IM, because it eliminates any bias from voice inflection and focuses on communication and the language disorder itself.

To gain insight into aphasia, empathy, and the type of interaction design that may best support such a tool, we conducted an exploratory study (guided demonstrations and interviews) with ten individuals (students, professionals, and researchers) with experience in aphasia (speech and hearing science/psychology), averaging 10.3 years of experience in aphasia/language disorders, with mean age of 34.6 years.

The initial prototype (Figure 1) was built in Java and simulated an IM conversation between the user (whose text was distorted) and Eliza [31], a simple and unbiased text-based computerized conversational partner. The system provided a simplistic approximation of the effects of aphasia by randomly dropping the user's function words (16-33%), randomly dropping any words (20-40%), and randomly replacing non-function words with other random words from a dictionary file. While this prototype was a simplified representation of some effects of aphasia, it illustrated the concept and functionality of ACES in order to gather informed feedback. Users saw how their messages were distorted through an IM window, and through a log of distortions (Figure 1).

Each participant met with a researcher for one session of approximately 40 minutes duration. Sessions began with an explanation/demonstration of the prototype. Participants then used the prototype to have a conversation with Eliza. Following the IM conversation, researchers had a discussion with each participant, and concluded with a brief questionnaire using a 7-point Likert scale (7 agree, 1 disagree). There was no remuneration for participation.

Results And Lessons Learned

Overall, participants agreed that this tool could be used to teach empathy and understanding for aphasic individuals to: friends (mean=6.1), family (mean=6.2), clinicians (mean=5.9) and professionals (mean=6.1). In addition, participants provided explicit guidance on system improvements and general suggestions on the project. For example, one participant stated that:

> *This could be shown to people outside of the community of communication experts and their clients. It could teach empathy and acceptance to a group/ community as a whole. -P4*

Another participant stated that this software was critical for training clinicians:

> *I don't think treatment will be successful at all if the clinician is not understanding! They are the individuals who should be, and without that empathy, few gains will be achieved . -P5*

Another participant echoed P5 by stating that:

> *I believe that as a simulation of a disorder... this software could be used in classrooms as early as undergrad . -P3*

All participants stated the need for a customizable future system. Given the spectrum of aphasic disorders and the manifestation variety within each sub-disorder, such a tool needs to be robust enough to emulate different types of aphasia. Participants also felt that while the emulation would not need to be 'spot on,' it would need to emulate the key distortions of each condition reasonably well.

Participants suggested applications for an aphasia emulation system. One professional speech language pathologist suggested political applications, such as helping to raise awareness to increase both funding and accessibility. Another felt there to be a need for greater empathy by physicians and nurses in hospital and ER settings, who can seem dismissive of patient struggles. Most felt that an emulation system could be used by therapists with families that have a member with aphasia. All saw direct application of the software in the classroom. Some suggested that students use the software in class. Others suggested use at home, while attempting to communicate with friends for one evening. Participants mentioned that current practice in speech and hearing classrooms is to "role play" the effects of the aphasia (similar to acting). They reported that this approach is often awkward and inaccurate, indicating that an emulation system would be a large improvement over the status quo.

Perhaps the most tangible benefit of our study was the direct resources our participants provided. Students, faculty and professionals each mentioned key aspects of aphasia that should be emulated, if this system were to be useful.

ACES: APHASIA EMULATION SOFTWARE

ACES is a both an IM client and an instantiation of a model of linguistic distortions caused by aphasia. ACES distorts messages in a manner similar to those of an individual with aphasia. Our model determines the specific nature and rate of distortions, based upon feedback from study participants and the large body of related literature. In the following sections we describe the underlying model of aphasia distortions and the user interface components of ACES. While ACES was modeled on aphasia, our system could, in principle, be used to emulate other linguistic disorders.

Please note that the contribution of our work is to promote empathy and understanding in people through experiencing the linguistic challenges of aphasic individuals. It is not to perfectly emulate aphasia. Moreover, this project focuses on expressive language distortion, and does not address those with receptive language distortion.

Modeling The Effects of Aphasia

The effects of aphasia can vary widely based on the severity of the impairment, the type of aphasia, and even on the type of word that is subject to error. Therefore, we constructed a modeling system, **A**phasia **C**haracteristics **E**mulation **M**odel Editor (**ACE-ME**), providing controls that allows the user to configure the degree and type of distortions that will be applied to their messages (Figure 2).

ACE-ME sub-divides the distortions into 5 conceptual categories: Distortion of Content Words, Distortion of Inflections, Distortion of Function Words, Distortion of Fluency, and Other. Each category defines error types that affect similar types of words (e.g., only function words or only content words). By grouping similar errors together, we leverage existing literature that focuses on specific distortion types and provide an intuitive interface for users.

ACE-ME includes the breadth of distortions experienced by individuals with aphasia. Although not every aphasic linguistic error is included, our goal was not to create a linguistically exhaustive emulation tool, but one that was communicatively disruptive in a manner similar to those with aphasia. As knowledge of aphasia and natural language processing expand, so can the capabilities of our system.

Distortion of Content Words

Most forms of aphasia affect the production of content words (verbs, nouns, adjectives, and adverbs). However, the effect and frequency of each error type differs depending upon the disorder and severity. Schwartz [26] highlights five key ways that content word production can be distorted: Formal Errors, Nonword Errors, Semantic Errors, Unrelated Errors and Mixed Errors. ACE-ME implements the first four error types. We omit Mixed Errors due to their technical complexity and low incident rate.

- Formal errors occur when a user mistakenly says a content word that is phonetically similar, yet semantically different [26]. For example: intending to say 'population' but stating 'pollution.' Formal errors are common with most aphasic individuals. ACE-ME emulates formal errors by utilizing a spell check system, JaSpell [4]. We force JaSpell to return an alternative for a word users enter (even though spelled correctly). We then randomly select one of the possible alternatives as a replacement. By using a spell check system, the word replaced would be similar to the original word given that suggested "alternatives" are based on the spelling of the original word.
- Nonword errors occur when a generated word is not a valid English word [26]. The generated nonword can be phonetically similar to the source word. For example: the word 'castle' is changed to 'kaksel.' Nonword errors are common for many aphasic speakers, particularly those with conduction or Wernike's aphasia. ACE-ME emulates a nonword error by randomly replacing a random number of letters in the original word. Vowels are replaced by other vowels, and consonants are replaced by consonant digraphs (e.g., 'sh,' 'ch' etc) or other consonants (excluding x and z, which are uncommon in English). All generated words are then verified to not be 'real words.'
- Semantic errors occur when the target word is replaced by another word which is semantically similar [26]. For example: 'birthday' is replaced with 'anniversary,' or 'cake' with 'bread.' While anniversary is not a synonym for birthday, nor bread for cake, they are associated. This error occurs with all aphasic types. Because semantic errors are broader than synonyms, using a thesaurus would not capture the nuance of semantic errors. Therefore, ACE-ME identifies the root of the original word [19], searches the root in a ConceptNet database [14], and chooses a random word from possible semantic matches. ConceptNet is a NLP project that, among other things, attempts to group words together based on their semantic similarity. We extracted a relational database linking words to lists of semantically related terms.
- Unrelated errors are valid English words, that have no semantic or strong phonetic relationship to the original word [26]. These errors occur particularly in severe cases of aphasia. ACE-ME randomly selects another content word from a list and replaces the original word with the unrelated term.
- Mixed errors are similar to formal errors, except the target words are semantically similar [26]. For example: 'start' is distorted to 'stop,' or 'snail' to 'snake.' Mixed errors are are conceptually similar but programmatically very difficult. While we can readily generate semantically or phonetically similar words, we do not posses a large enough data set of either semantically or phonetically similar words to have a suitable intersection of the two. These errors are not very common, so not generating them should have little impact.

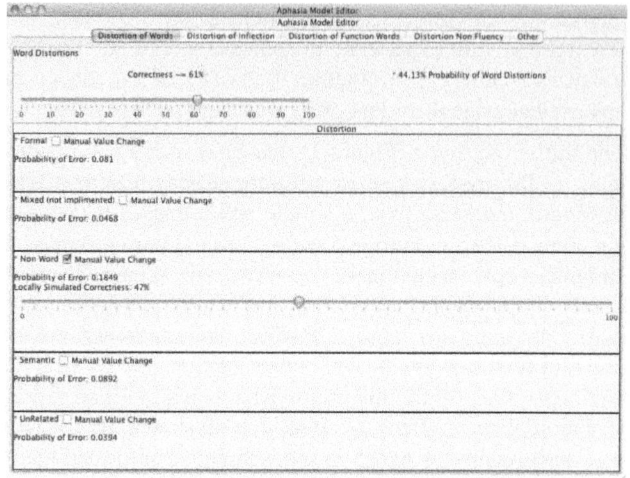

Figure 2. ACES Model Editor - Distortion of Word Tab
The overall correctness set to 61%, but the user has manually set the nonword errors to have a higher probability of occurring, increasing the overall probability of error to be 44.13%

To understand how severity of aphasia correlates with frequency of word errors, Schwartz [26] performed an analysis of errors made in picture naming tasks. Aphasic subjects were shown a picture and asked to identify it. Schwartz examined the errors and created regression models to predict how likely a given error was to occur based on a subject's overall level of impairment. Using the raw data published in Schwartz's paper, we re-generated the probability of each of the five error types based on subject impairment. We used these probabilistic models in ACE-ME to calculate estimated frequency of each error. The user can move a "correctness" slider to set the probability of each of the five content word errors based on Schwartz's work. ACE-ME also allows the user to manually set each specific content word distortion (Figure 2). ACE-ME displays the total probability of any content word error, calculated by summing the probabilities of all possible content word errors. If the user has not manually adjusted an error rate, the probability of content word error is one minus the correctness percentage.

Distortion of Inflections

Grammatical inflection is the modification of a word to express different grammatical categories such as tense, mood, voice, aspect, person, number, gender and case. English inflections are usually suffixes, such as the plural inflection on nouns ("apple" versus "apples").

ACE-ME distorts only verb inflection, the most common type of inflection error for aphasic individuals (especially for those with agrammatic speech). An example of such a distortion is changing "running" to its base form, "run." ACE-ME emulates verb inflection distortion by stemming verbs [19] and using the verb's infinitive form. Users can set the probability of Inflection Distortion with an interface slider labeled "Inflection Morphology of Verbs."

Distortion of Function Words

A common error made by aphasic individuals (especially those with agrammatic aphasia) is to omit function words. Function words are pronouns, articles, conjunctions, auxiliary verbs, interjections, particles, expletives, and prepositions. ACE-ME removes randomly selected function words. Users can set the probability of Function Word Distortion with an interface slider labeled "Dropping Function Words."

Distortion of Fluency

The fluency of sentence construction can also be affected by aphasia. ACE-ME targets three common types of distortions that can affect sentence fluency: Conduit d'approche, Omissions, and Semantic Description.

- *Conduit d'approche*: This commonly affects those with conduction aphasia. Conduit d'approche occurs when an individual adds/removes or distorts the production of a word, then iteratively repairs the errors until arriving at the intended production [13]. For example: a series of Conduit d'approche would be "brepple," "gresles," "glasles," and then completing the effort with "glasses." ACE-ME emulates Conduit d'approche errors by repeatedly applying a random number of nonword errors to the same word. The errors are then replayed in reverse order in the sent message, giving the appearance of correcting the specific word. Each attempt is put in a separate message followed by ellipses. The slight pause gives the impression that the sender is attempting to correct the word. Once the word is "correct," the remainder of the message is sent.
- *Omissions*: Most aphasic individuals omit or drop words from their sentences [18]. To emulate the effects of random omission, ACE-ME randomly drops words from a user's message.
- *Semantic Description:* Many aphasic individuals can describe the features of a target word when they cannot recall the specific word [18]. This is a semantic description error (unlike a semantic error which is a one-to-one substitution). For example, an individual trying to describe glasses may say, "seeing, head, face, eyes, round." ACE-ME utilizes the ConceptNet database [14], to search for a random number of semantically related terms and replaces the original word with a set of semantic descriptors (separated by ellipses).

Users can set the probability of all errors related to Fluency using ACE-ME interface sliders. As there is more than one type of Fluency error, ACE-ME also displays the total probability of a Fluency error occurring.

Other

There are two other effects common to aphasia that ACE-ME emulates. These are pauses and distortion awareness. Aphasic individuals often pause at atypical times. ACE-ME emulates these interruptions by randomly breaking up a message, sending each part as a separate IM.

People with certain types of aphasia (e.g., Wernicke's) can be unaware of the errors in their speech, while others (e.g., Broca's) are generally aware of their errors. To allow users to experience the frustration of not knowing why their conversation partner is confused (by not seeing the distorted message), as well as the frustration of not being able to send the intended message (e.g., seeing the distorted text), ACE-ME allows the user to toggle between displaying the original or the distorted message.

Users can set the probability of pauses by using the interface slider. Distortion awareness can be toggled by an interface check box in ACE-ME.

ACES Interface Components

Our system has three main components: an IM Window for engaging in instant message conversations; a Model Editor for configuring the distortions; and an Admin Window for login and switching between the IM and the Model Editor. Upon launch, users are presented with an Admin Window Users can input a user name, password, and subject ID (used for logging all conversations to protect privacy). Users can then launch the other two components.

The ACES Model Editor (Figure 2) consists of five tabs corresponding to the five categories of distortions. Users can switch between tabs and interact with all sliders and checkboxes. All changes made to the model editor affect the current IM conversation in real-time.

The IM Window (Figure 3) is a standard IM interface with a message history, text input field, send button, and buddy list. IM history is color coded for easy identification of message origin (red=user, blue=conversation partner).

Flexible Implementation

Our system leverages a plug-in architecture for distortions. Researchers, instructors, or therapists can create or customize a specific distortion type. The ACES system examines a directory where the distortion descriptions reside, including any new distortion from this directory.

ACES sends IMs over the AOL Instant Message network, though it can easily be extended to other protocols, because it leverages the JBuddy library [32] to facilitate connection with the AOL servers. JBuddy also supports ICQ, MSN, Yahoo, Google Talk, XMPP (Jabber), Lotus Sametime, Microsoft OCS 2007, and LCS 2005.

ACES was implemented using Java 1.6, allowing the software to execute on nearly any machine, though our system has only been tested on Apple's OSX. As a result, teachers, medical staff, and researchers need not invest in new hardware to run ACES.

ACES Logging

ACES is also conducive to post-conversation analysis and reflection because it logs all conversations in an HTML file of the perceived conversation (the user's sent messages), and in an XML file of the conversation (including the original message, the distorted message, and which distortion were applied). The HTML version is ideal for analyzing the conversation and reflecting upon difficulties in the user experience. The XML file allows researchers to analyze how users changed their behavior while trying to communicate with aphasic distortions.

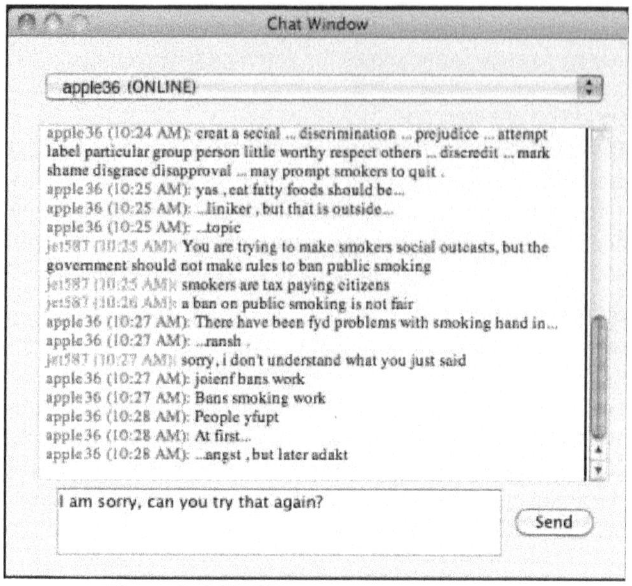

Figure 3. ACES Instant Message Window

The current (red) user's partner (blue) has their text distorted. Note: this is a log from an actual experiment conversation

USER STUDY

In order to observe the effects of using ACES on awareness and empathy, we conducted an in-depth user study. Sixty-four individuals (grouped in subject-pairs) engaged in IM conversations with each other. We wanted to see whether experiencing text distortions first-hand through IM conversations had an impact on a subject's level of empathy for individuals with aphasia. To test this, we utilized a between-subject 2x2 factorial design. The first factor in our factorial design compared a **Treatment Group** (where subjects experienced distortions first-hand) to a **Control Group** (where subjects did not experience aphasic distortions). The second factor in our factorial design compared subjects who had prior knowledge of aphasia, through formal education or personal exposure (**Informed Sub-population**) with subjects who did not (**Uninformed Sub-population**). Our *Independent Variable* was whether or not participants experienced distortions by ACES. All participants (both treatment and control groups and both informed and uninformed sub-populations) experienced the same experimental protocol, as they were given the same prompts. Therefore subjects were blind with respect to which group (treatment or control) they were assigned. Both subjects in any given subject-pair were from the same sub-population (Informed/Uninformed) and same group (Treatment/Control).

Experimental Protocol

Each study session consisted of four steps lasting a total of 45-60 minutes (Table 1). A session involved IMs between two participants (a subject-pair) who did not know each other. Subject-pairs remained physically separated. Each member of a pair was placed in separate identical rooms with a 23" iMac computer. All questionnaires were digital and administered using third-party software.

All participants completed both a demographic survey and a pre-study questionnaire to assess empathy using Mehrabian's measure[1] of emotional empathy [22]. Each participant also answered questions about their knowledge and background on aphasia. This allowed us to ensure equal background, pre-knowledge, and general empathy level across treatment and control groups. Pre-study demographic and background measures were not utilized to assess ACES effect on awareness and empathy.

Upon completion of the pre-study questionnaires, all participants were given an identical explanation of the study protocol. All participants (regardless of group or sub-population) were told that they would have two ten-minute IM conversations with each other.[2] During these conversations one member of the subject-pair would take on the **Aphasia Role**, while the other member of the subject-pair would take

	Description
Step #1	Demographic Questions
	Empathy Evaluation
	Pre-Study Questions on Aphasia
Step #2	Conversation with Partner, Prompt #1
Step #3	Conversation with Partner, Prompt #2
	Participant Roles are Switched
Step #4	Final Set of Questions

Table 1. Study Session Order

[1] Mehrabian's quantitative measure of empathy assigns an individual an empathy score based on responses to 33 questions. Scores range from -132 to +132. According to Mehrabian, a representative population should yield a mean score of 33 and S.D. of 24.

[2] Participants were logged into IM accounts created for this study, not requiring subjects to disclose their own user names or passwords.

on the **Typical Role**. After the first conversation, they would switch roles (ensuring that each participant would play both roles). All subjects (in both control and treatment groups) were told that the participant in the Aphasia role would have his/her text distorted by ACES, as though they had aphasia.

To guide their conversations, participants were instructed to have a "debate" or "discussion" around a specific topic. Further, each participant was assigned a position (**Pro** or **Con**), and was provided a suggested list of talking points to support their position (participants could also use their own talking points). Subjects were assigned one topic for the first conversation, and another topic for the second. The two debate topics were:

- *The age at which people gain the right to vote should be lowered to 16 years*
- *Smoking should be banned in all public places*

To conclude the study explanation, all participants were told *"Remember aphasia can be mild to severe, creating distortions that are obvious, to those which are not so easily noticed or apparent."* This statement was included in the instructions so participants in the "control" group would not be concerned if they did not notice any obvious distortions.

At the end of both IM conversations, participants were administered a single questionnaire to gauge their reaction to ACES and aphasia. Participants were then remunerated with a $10 gift certificate to Amazon.com.

Dependent Measure

A single post-study questionnaire was utilized to assess the effects of using ACES on awareness and empathy. Ten questions on the post-study questionnaire were scored on a 7-point Likert scale. Additionally short-response questions were included to obtain qualitative reactions to ACES.

Factorial Design, Counterbalancing, Treatment Effects

Our cohort of sixty-four individuals consisted of two sub-populations. Thirty-two subjects (one half of our subjects) had prior knowledge of aphasia either through formal education or personal exposure (Informed Sub-population), and the other thirty-two subjects did not (Uninformed Sub-population). Further, half of each sub-population was in the Control Group, and half was in the Treatment Group. Thus, we used a **2x2 Between-Subject Factorial Design** with 16 subjects (8 subject-pairs) in each of the following **Experimental Conditions**: Informed-Treatment, Informed-Control, Uninformed-Treatment and Uninformed-Control. By testing both a Informed and Uninformed population, we had the ability to test the potential applicability of ACES to both family members and clinicians/doctors in training.

Given the number of other factors inherently present in this type of experimental setup, there were at least three potential confounding effects (debate topic order, debate position and role order). To help control for these potential confounding effects, we used *counterbalancing*, a method commonly employed to help avoid confounding from order of task and

	% Male	Age (SD)	Empathy[1] (SD)
Overall	39.06	26.05 (7.30)	34.52 (25.82)
Overall - C	28.12	25.06 (7.27)	40.09 (22.60)
Overall - T	50.00	27.03 (7.30)	28.94 (27.92)
Informed	37.50	25.35 (6.83)	39.25 (25.38)
Informed - C	25.00	24.13 (6.54)	46.81 (21.28)
Informed - T	50.00	26.56 (7.11)	31.69 (27.51)
Uninformed	40.62	26.75 (7.78)	29.78 (25.76)
Uninformed - C	31.25	26.00 (8.04)	33.38 (22.50)
Uninformed - T	50.00	27.50 (7.69)	26.19 (28.95)

	Highest Level of Education Completed (%)		
	High School	*Bachelors*	*Graduate*
Overall	25.00	56.25	18.75
Overall - C	28.12	56.25	15.63
Overall - T	21.88	56.25	21.87
Informed	34.38	53.12	12.50
Informed - C	43.75	37.50	18.75
Informed - T	25.00	68.75	6.25
Uninformed	15.62	59.38	25.00
Uninformed - C	12.50	75.00	12.50
Uninformed - T	18.75	43.75	37.50

Table 2. Population Demographics & Empathy Scores
Empathy refers to Mehrabian's measure of emotional empathy[3]. Mean age and empathy scores are shown. C = Control T = Treatment

presentation. When counterbalancing, all permutations of the confounders are included in an attempt to minimize any bias due to these confounders that are not central to the experimental question. Thus, for each Experimental Condition (e.g., Informed/Uninformed and Treatment/Control), we needed 8 pairs of conversations to account for all permutations of Role (Aphasic/Typical), Topic (Voting/Smoking), and Debate Position (Pro/Con).

In addition, we attempted to control for "treatment effects." A treatment effect occurs when a participant has a reaction to a placebo simply because they are told they are going to receive a treatment. By effectively telling both Treatment and Control groups that they were going to be in the "treatment group," we attempted to control for the treatment effect. If we noticed a positive or negative response from participants in our control group, we would have confidence that it would be due to treatment effects, thus allowing us to better qualify the effects reported in the treatment group. Likewise, if no effects were observed in the control group, we would feel confident that the simple act of using IM in this experiment did not contribute to those results, and were due directly to ACES emulating the effects of aphasia.

Statistical Tests

To examine the effects of ACES we compared responses from the four Experimental Conditions to the post-study questionnaire in Step 4 (Table 1). A 2-way ANOVA (analysis of variance) was used to to test for differences between the four Experimental Conditions (Group by Sub-Population).

	Control Group		Treatment Group		2-Way ANOVA	
	Median	*Mean (SD)*	*Median*	*Mean (SD)*	*F Statistic*	*p -val*
1 In hindsight, this experience made me < > empathetic to individuals with aphasia.†	5 [4,5]	4.75 (0.80)	6 [6,6]	5.91 (0.77)	F(1,61)=34.84	0.0001
2 In hindsight, this experience made me < > empathetic to people who try to understand an individual with aphasia. †	4 [4,5]	4.62 (0.87)	6 [5,6]	5.59 (0.87)	F(1,61)=19.72	0.0001
3 This tool is useful for building empathy for family members‡	4 [4,5]	4.19 (1.47)	6.5* [5,7]	6.09 (1.06)	F(1,61)=34.96	0.0001
4 This tool is useful for building empathy for speech therapists‡	4 [4,5]	4.47 (1.59)	6 [5,7]	6.09 (1.03)	F(1,61)=23.28	0.0001
5 This tool is useful for building empathy for nurses and doctors‡	4.5* [4,5]	4.47 (1.54)	7 [5,7]	6.22 (0.91)	F(1,61)=30.13	0.0001
6 This tool is useful for building empathy for care givers‡	4 [4,5]	4.38 (1.50)	7 [6,7]	6.38 (0.91)	F(1,61)=41.12	0.0001
7 This tool is useful for education/training of individuals who treat/interact with individuals with aphasia‡	4 [4,6]	4.5 (1.65)	7 [6,7]	6.53 (0.80)	F(1,61)=39.02	0.0001
8 Which role helped you understand aphasia better?§	4 [3.5,4]	3.91 (1.42)	2 [1,3]	2.28 (1.55)	F(1,61)=18.79	0.0001
9 Which role increased your empathy for the the perspective of understanding an individual with aphasia? §	4 [4,4.5]*	4.5 (1.03)	1.5* [3.5,6]*	3.72 (2.40)	F(1,61)=1.02	0.317
10 Which role increased your empathy for the the perspective of an individual with aphasia? §	4 [3.5,4]*	3.69 (1.38)	2 [1,4.5]	2.72 (2.25)	F(1,61)=4.26	0.043

Table 3. Results

Median represents median value and interquartile range [IQ range] - 2-Way ANOVA Values represents Treatment vs. Control Factor

2-Way ANOVA Values for Informed Sub-population vs. Uninformed Sub-population (not shown) all p>0.05

* *Half values are due to even number of data points where the vale separating the higher half from the lower half lies between two different value, resulting in a median which is the average of the two values. For example a data set of [1,4,4,5,5,7] would have a median of 4.5 although 4.5 is not a possible value.*

† *Question Choices Were: 1=Much Less, 2=Less, 3=Slightly Less 4= No Change, 5= Slightly More, 6=More, 7=Much More*

‡ *Question Choices Were: 1= Disagree, 4=Neutral, 7 = Agree* § *Question Choices Were: 1= Aphasia, 4=Equal, 7=No Distortions/Normal*

An ANOVA test assumes that data are normally distributed and is robust to deviations in normality. Data is presented as median, inter-quartile range (the range of values that span the middle 50% of the data).

Subjects

Sixty-four participants completed the ACES experiment (Table 2). More than 75% of the Informed population had an educational background in psychology, speech and hearing science, or traditional sciences. Participants in the Uninformed population came from a wide variety of areas spanning engineering, science, and liberal arts.

The empathy scores of our subject population, as measured at the beginning of each session (Table 2), closely follow those of a standard population as presented in the original paper by Mehrabian[22]. With a balanced male/female population, Mehrabian expects a mean score of 33 (standard deviation of 24). Our study cohort had a mean empathy score of 34.5 (standard deviation of 25.8). This is nearly identical to Mehrabian. To ensure control and treatment groups were equivalent, we examined the empathy scores of the groups and the four initial self-response questions regarding participant knowledge of and sensitivity to the challenges of communication with aphasia. We examined any differences overall and within the Informed/Uninformed demographics. There were no statistically significant differences ($p = 0.08$, $z=1.75$) between the control and treatment groups in a priori disposition, knowledge of, or empathy towards individuals with aphasia (results not shown).

Results

Overall, participants in the group experiencing aphasic distortions by the ACES were strongly affected by their experience relative to the control group (Table 3, Questions 1 & 2). For example, participants indicated that the experience made them more empathetic to individuals with aphasia compared to the control group who felt only a slight change, with $p<0.0001$. Participants in the treatment group strongly agreed that ACES should be used in all applications explicitly listed, while the control group felt neutral as to the applicability of ACES (Table 3, Questions 3-7). Participants in the Treatment group strongly agreed that ACES could be used to increase empathy in caregivers, while participants that did not experience distortions felt neutral towards ACES use, with $p<0.0001$. Participants in the Treatment group felt that they gained understanding and empathy from having their text distorted, while the control group did not rank one role higher than another (Table 3, Questions 8 & 10).

When data was analyzed separately for the Informed and Uninformed groups, results were similar to those of the full cohort (results not shown). Finally, we compared the Informed treatment group with the Uninformed treatment group to see if a priori knowledge of aphasia influenced subject response. Both treatment groups found ACES beneficial in increasing knowledge and empathy.

Though not shown in Table 3, there was no significant difference in any of the post-study questions by Informed/ Uninformed Sub-Population. Furthermore, there were no interaction effects between the Treatment Group (Treatment/ Control) and Sub-Population (Informed/Uninformed) (data not shown - available from the authors upon request).

Figure 3 is a representative conversation between two subjects (taken from our study). The IM window is from jet587, whose partner, apple36, is having his text distorted.

Post Hoc Results

The one question with a non-significant value overall was question 9: "*Which role increased your empathy for the the perspective of understanding an individual with aphasia?*" Given the large inter-quartile range within the Treatment group, we hypothesized that the lack of significance was due to learning effects (having more exposure to the intervention makes you increasingly more empathetic). To test this hypothesis, we subdivided the Treatment Group by comparing the responses of subjects who were in the Aphasic Role first, to those in the Typical Role first. Because these are mutually exclusive subsets of the Treatment group we performed a between subject analysis comparing responses with a unpaired student T-test and found p=0.015 (-2.66=t). In particular, the mean response (2.69 $\pm$ 1.99) of participants whose first tole was Typical, indicated that the Aphasic role increased empathy more. In contrast, the mean response (4.75 $\pm$ 2.38) of participants whose first tole was Aphasic, indicated that the Typical role increased empathy more.

Thus, whichever role the participant experienced second was the role reported to have increased their empathy more. This post-hoc analysis suggests that it does not matter which role (Aphasic or Typical) participants take on first. Rather, we hypothesize that it is the opportunity to play both roles that may increase empathy. This would need to be validated in future experiments. We tested the other questions for learning effects and did not find any.

DISCUSSION

Participants who experienced the distortions of aphasia had a much stronger response than those in the control group. Those participants in the treatment group reported "strong" effects from the experiment, including increased empathy and envisioning a wide variety of potential uses of ACES. In contrast, participants who did not have their text distorted reported little or no change in their perception of or empathy towards aphasia. The median quantitative responses from the control group were almost unanimously at 4 (a neutral opinion/no change), with little deviation in inter-quartile ranges. The control group also saw no application for ACES to increase empathy or awareness of aphasia. This is in stark contrast to those with exposure to aphasic distortions.

There is always the possibility of a change in empathy resulting from being in an experimental condition (known as experimental demand). However, given the great difference in responses between the two groups (qualitatively and statistically), we are confident that ACES demonstrates a real impact on increasing awareness and empathy by experiencing distortions caused by aphasia. This is further supported in that both groups were given identical prompts, and the experiment was fully counterbalanced.

While quantitative feedback provides strong evidence of the effectiveness of ACES, qualitative feedback highlights how informative the ACES experience was for participants, and how supportive they are of the project. For example, one participant from the Informed Treatment group stated:

> *This was a wonderful way to gain empathy! I've learned about aphasia in classes, but this perspective was very helpful and will make a lasting impression.*

The qualitative feedback supported how prior experience with aphasia was not a prerequisite for gaining insight. One participant from the Uninformed Treatment group stated:

> *It was the most eye-opening from the point of view of having my text distorted. It was amazing how hard it can be sometimes to get a point across. From the aphasic side it is almost like experiencing it from both sides, because you see how difficult what you say can be for the 'normal' person.*

Participants also suggested that even short exposure could make a lasting impact, saying, *"it would only take a few minutes to gain perspective."*

In contrast, qualitative feedback from subjects in the control group supported our quantitative findings, indicating that this was not a meaningful experience. Given the stark difference in qualitative and quantitative responses between the control and treatment groups, we believe that ACES can provide a meaningful experience for all users who seek to better understand and empathize with aphasic individuals.

FUTURE WORK

Our experiment examined the impact of ACES on participants' empathy and understanding of aphasic individuals. However, our long term goal is to meaningfully improve real-world interactions, thereby improving quality of life and therapy for individuals with aphasia. We propose conducting a follow-up study to explore whether a subject's experience with ACES can positively impact their real-world interactions with individuals with aphasia. This study would directly involve individuals with aphasia in order to determine if they can perceive an increase in empathy present in users of ACES. We further wish to investigate the long-term impact of ACES, and how to integrate the software within a classroom of therapeutic setting

While ACES supports a robust set of distortions, there are always refinements and less common errors that can be implemented. Over time, we hope to increase the capabilities and functionality that ACES provides.

Though this project explicitly targets aphasia, our goal is to introduce language distortion emulation as a new approach to increasing empathy for those with other language impairments. We envision, for instance, a system similar to ACES that distorts text as though it comes from a young child. This can teach patience, understanding, and empathy to parents, teachers, and caregivers.

CONCLUSION

Empathy and understanding from family members, friends and clinicians can enhance the quality of life of aphasic individuals. Family members can deny or underestimate the severity and presence of aphasic errors. Without empathy, the quality of speech therapy can suffer, jeopardizing the speed and recovery of aphasic individuals. Our work has made several contributions to address these concerns stemming from a lack of empathy.

First, we leveraged speech-language and psychological theory to design and construct a model of aphasic distortions. Second, from an initial investigation we refined our model and designed a system to increase awareness and empathy with aphasic individuals. Third, we developed a novel system (ACES) that allows a neurologically typical individual to experience firsthand, the linguistic distortions of aphasia. Fourth, ACES was validated in an investigation with 64 participants (with and without background on aphasia). Results from this study strongly show that using ACES can increase empathy and awareness of aphasia.

Our model and system demonstrate how technology can play a central role in increasing empathy, awareness and understanding for individuals with a language disorder. Our approach can be used in many other domains where atypical language is present and can be emulated. It is through empathy that we learn to understand each other.

ACKNOWLEDGMENTS

We would like to thank our reviewers, participants, family and friends.

REFERENCES

1. Benson, D. F. Aphasia, Alexia and Agraphia: Clinical Neurology and Neurosurgery Monographs. Churchill Livingstone, New York, 1979.
2. Benson, D. F. The neurology of thinking. Oxford University Press, USA, 1994.
3. Boyd-Graber, J. L. et al. Participatory design with proxies: developing a desktop-PDA system to support people with aphasia. In In Proceedings of the CHI 06 (2006). ACM, Montreal, Canada.
4. Bruno Martins. JaSpell. http://jaspell.sourceforge.net/.
5. Chapey, R. Language intervention strategies in aphasia and related neurogenic communication disorders. Lippincott Williams & Wilkins, 2001.
6. Czvik, P. S. Assessment of family attitudes toward aphasic patients with severe auditory processing disorders. In Proceedings of Clinical Aphasiology (1977).
7. Daemen, E. et al. Designing a free style, indirect, and interactive storytelling application for people with aphasia. INTERACT 2007, 2010, 221-234.
8. Devlin, S. and Unthank, G. Helping aphasic people process online information. In Proc. of Assets '06 (2006). ACM, Portland, Oregon, USA New York, NY, USA.
9. Doerksen, S. Recreation for Persons with Disabilities (RPM 277). Pennsylvania State University Department of Recreation, Park and Tourism Management, Fall, 2009.
10. Dymond, R. F. A scale for the measurement of empathic ability. Journal of Consulting Psychology, 13(2), 1949, 127-133.
11. Furbacher, E. A. and Wertz, R. T. Simulation of Aphasia by Wives of Aphasic Patients. Clinical aphasiology, 1983, 227.
12. Goodglass, H., Goodglass, Kaplan. Boston Diagnostic Aphasia Examination: Stimulus Cards--Short Form. Lippincott Williams & Wilkins, 2001.
13. H. Goodglass and Kaplan, E. The Assessment of Aphasia and Other Neurological Disorders. Williams and Wilkins, Baltimore, MD, 1983.
14. Hugo Liu, Aingh, Push, and Eslick, Ian. ConceptNet. http://web.media.mit.edu/~hugo/conceptnet/.
15. Hengst, J. Augmentative and Alternative Communication (SHS 473). University of Illinois Department of Speech and Hearing Science, Spring, 2005.
16. Kitzing, P., Maier, A., and Åhlander, V. L. Automatic speech recognition (ASR) and its use as a tool for assessment or therapy of voice, speech, and language disorders. Logopedics Phonatrics Vocology, 34(2), 2009, 91-96.
17. Liechty, J. A. and Heinzekehr, J. B. Caring for Those Without Words: A Perspective on Aphasia. The Journal of Neuroscience Nursing, 39(5), 2007, 316.
18. Sarno, M. T. Acquired aphasia (Third Edition). Academic Press, San Diego, CA, 1998.
19. Martin Porter. Snowball: A language for stemming algorithms. 2010, http://snowball.tartarus.org/.
20. McCall, D. et al. Integrating technology and targeted treatment to improve narrative production in aphasia: A case study. Aphasiology, 23(4), 2009, 438-461.
21. McQuiggan, S. W. and Lester, J. C. Learning empathy: A data-driven framework for modeling empathetic companion agents. In Proceedings of Autonomous Agents and Multiagent Systems (2006). ACM, New York, NY.
22. Mehrabian, A. and Epstein, N. A measure of emotional empathy. Journal of personality, 40(4), 1972, 525-543.
23. Moffatt, K. et al. The participatory design of a sound and image enhanced daily planner for people with aphasia. In Proceedings of CHI 04 (2004). ACM, NY.
24. Mullennix, J. and Stern, S. Computer Synthesized Speech Technologies: Tools for Aiding Impairment. Medical Information Science Reference, Hershey, PA, 2010.
25. National Institute on Deafness and Other Communication Disorders. Aphasia. 2010, http://www.nidcd.nih.gov/health/voice/aphasia.htm.
26. Schwartz, M. F. et al. A case-series test of the interactive two-step model of lexical access: Evidence from picture naming. Journal of Memory and Language, 54(2), 2006, 228–264.
27. Shewan, C. M. and Kertesz, A. Reliability and validity characteristics of the Western Aphasia Battery (WAB). Journal of Speech and Hearing Disorders, 45(3), 1980, 308.
28. Shill, M. A. Motivational factors in aphasia therapy: Research suggestions. Journal of Communication Disorders, 12(6), 1979, 503–517.
29. Stotland, E. Exploratory investigations of empathy. Advances in experimental social psychology, 4, 1969, 271-314.
30. van de Sandt-Koenderman, M., Wiegers, J., and Hardy, P. A computerised communication aid for people with aphasia. Disability & Rehabilitation, 27(9), 2005, 529-533.
31. Weizenbaum, J. Contextual understanding by computers. Communications of the ACM, 10(8), 1967, 480.
32. Zion Software. JBuddy Messenger. http://www.zionsoftware.com/products/messenger/.

Cueing Swallowing in Parkinson's Disease

Roisin McNaney[1], Stephen Lindsay[1], Karim Ladha[1], Cassim Ladha[1], Guy Schofield[1], Thomas Plötz[1], Nils Hammerla[1], Daniel Jackson[1], Richard Walker[2], Nick Miller[2], Patrick Olivier[1]

[1] Culture Lab, School of Computing Science, Newcastle University, Newcastle Upon Tyne, UK
p.l.olivier@ncl.ac.uk

[2] Institute for Health and Society Newcastle University, Newcastle Upon Tyne, UK

ABSTRACT

We present the development of a socially acceptable cueing device for drooling in Parkinson's disease (PD). Sialorrhea, or drooling, is a significant problem associated with PD and has a strong negative emotional impact on those who experience it. Previous studies have shown the potential for managing drooling by using a cueing device. However, the devices used in these studies were deemed unacceptable by their users due to factors such as hearing impairment and social embarrassment. We conducted exploratory scoping work and high fidelity iterative prototyping with people with PD to get their input on the design of a cueing aid and this has given us an insight into challenges that confront users with PD and limit device usability and acceptability. The key finding from working with people with PD was the need for the device to be socially acceptable.

Author Keywords

Parkinson's disease, swallowing, drooling, participatory design.

ACM Classification Keywords

H5.m. Information interfaces and presentation: Miscellaneous.

General Terms

Design, Human Factors

INTRODUCTION

We are currently living within an ageing society. New advances in medical treatments, as well as a drive from the UK National Health Service (NHS) to implement initiatives around public health education, mean that life expectancy is increasing. Alongside this comes an increase in the prevalence of age-related diseases such as Parkinson's disease (PD), which currently affects approximately one in 500 of the UK population [11]. A significant symptom of PD is drooling, which has been found to be a problem for 70% of people with PD [3]. The existing literature suggests that drooling is associated with muscle rigidity and bradykinesia (slowness of movement) of the oral structures [9] coupled with a deterioration of the swallowing reflex rather than over-production of saliva. Drooling is not an incidental problem without consequences. The problem can impact an individual's quality of life socially, emotionally and physically. Drooling can cause social embarrassment for the person with PD and adds to the risk of aspiration (when food or liquid enters the lungs) which can result in choking or pneumonia [2]. Excessive loss of saliva can also cause related difficulties with eating and oral hygiene as saliva acts as a lubricant during chewing and swallowing and contains proteins with antibacterial effects [2]. Most current treatments for drooling in PD aim to decrease saliva production, predominantly with the use of pharmaceuticals or Botox injection into the salivary glands [6].

Previous studies have focused on testing the clinical effectiveness of using electronic cueing devices to manage drooling [7, 8]. These studies used a commercially available device in the form of a brooch which emits an auditory cue or prompt (beep) at regular intervals, to remind the wearer to swallow, thereby reducing drooling. Although such a device was found to be effective in the control of drooling problems, wearers reported several aspects that reduce their acceptability. For example, the auditory cue was a significant source of embarrassment for many wearers. In addition, hearing impaired people – who form a large percentage of the older population with PD – cannot use the device. The product used also incorporated a switch to turn the device on and off, yet many users needed assistance to operate this due to fine motor skill degeneration resulting from PD. Our work explored the design space for cueing devices and, to address the device's acceptability, explicitly incorporated the needs and desires of the PD population into the design process. This approach has been shown to be effective in previous work [1, 4]. The method also coincides with current pledges in NHS policy aimed at ensuring patients are involved in all aspects of their treatment, to promote their empowerment and motivation [5].

DESIGN PROCESS

The design process had two stages, scoping and high fidelity iterative design. The scoping stage was used to gather qualitative accounts from participants about everyday issues that affect accessibility such as hand tremors making small buttons difficult to operate. This stage allowed for more informed conceptualisation of the types of features the new device should have. High fidelity iterative design was then used to refine the device. Participants were recruited through the voluntary organization *Parkinson's UK* [11]. Twelve participants, eight with PD and four caregivers (age range 41-77 years old) took part in the scoping stage of the study. Three people with PD, who had taken part in the scoping stage, participated in the high fidelity iterative design (Table 1). Analysis of the discussions from the scoping stage revealed several recurrent themes. The consensus in the opinions expressed throughout all of the groups led to a set of design requirements being formulated.

Participant	Sex	Age	Years Since Diagnosis
One	Male	60	2
Two	Male	74	4
Three	Male	66	18

Table 1: High fidelity prototyping participant profiles.

SCOPING STAGE: PROCESS

This scoping stage discussion lasted approximately one hour. Participants were organized into three small groups of three to five people. Focus Groups were carried out in an exploratory manner using open ended questioning to allow free flowing discussion to develop and mature into topics of interest. Participants discussed PD and the impact its symptoms could or did have on their use of technology. They also discussed their feelings towards medical devices and previous negative and positive experiences with them. Within the same session participants brainstormed the types of features they would or would not want in a drooling management device. They discussed specific features, collectively deciding on the best options for them and the reasons behind their choices. At the end of the workshop the participants were shown two prototypes to act as prompts intended to stimulate or provoke discussion about concepts such as device size or appearance. Prior to prompt showing, these concepts were abstract for the participants

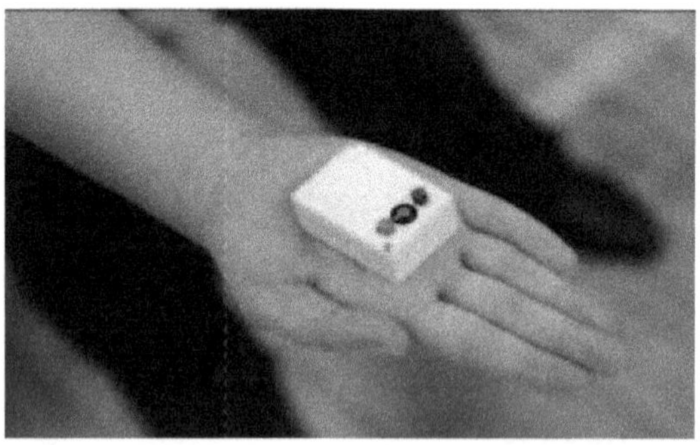

Figure 1. A prototype device shown as a prompt to elicit discussion about abstract concepts. Black and red buttons control vibration frequency on either side of an LED.

and many of them struggled to articulate their thoughts. One prototype was a rudimentary custom built device (see figure 1) and the other was an application that ran on a mobile phone. The scoping sessions were video recorded and the discussions transcribed. Subsequently, themes and sub-themes were extracted and used to develop a set of requirements for the first high fidelity prototype. Participants were contacted by telephone in the week following the data analysis to validate the requirements. This step was important as without it there was potential to obfuscate individuals concerns about the device.

SCOPING STAGE: RESULTS

Participants discussed the different modalities for **cueing** such as visual (a flashing light), auditory (a beeping noise) or vibration. The participants unanimously felt that the most acceptable modality for cueing was vibration because it reduced the attention drawn to the wearer if the device was worn in public. By contrast visual and auditory cues were considered potential sources of embarrassment in public.

In relation to **size**, participants' comments indicated that they would like to have a device that was small enough to be hidden to reduce embarrassment or social unease that might come about wearing it in public. However, they also commented that they would need a device that is large enough to be easily handled by a person with a tremor (a common symptom of PD) or other age-related conditions like arthritis in the hands.

Participants indicated that they would require help to change a **battery** due to their PD. They discussed the sense of dependency or disempowerment that this often caused when using other devices because they had to rely on someone else. As the design team considered it important to avoid this disempowerment and produce a device that someone with PD could use unassisted they built a large, easy to use plug in charger and a socket for it on the device.

In terms of **where to wear** the device most participants indicated a preference for a wrist worn device. They commented that it could then be designed to look like a commercial wristwatch, to avoid stigma that might be associated with a medical device. Discussion in one group produced the idea of using a hook and loop Velcro fastening. This eliminated many of the steps involved in putting the device on, thus making it more accessible for the user with PD further empowering them.

Participants said that pressing **buttons** on small devices like wristwatches could pose a significant problem for them. The groups felt that there needed to be some other way to operate a device. This theme was echoed throughout all of the Focus Groups and it was decided that a motion sensor feature would be employed to switch the device on and off. An accelerometer was used to recognize any form of motion and this served as a signal to put the device into 'on' mode and to switch off when the device was absolutely stationary (i.e. remaining on a stationary surface) for more than ten seconds.

Participants commented regularly on how much **stigma** they felt there was associated with the public's perceptions of PD. Because of their concern with this they believed it was vital to consider how the device's design related to potential stigma. The main issue that arose was that the participants were worried other people might see or hear the device when they were out in public which would lead to embarrassment. The feeling of stigma, from using medical devices, was highlighted during a discussion about wearing panic buttons (a medical device designed to alert emergency services if the wearer has a fall or medically dangerous incident). The participants involved in this discussion admitted not wearing these devices, even when alone at home, as it made them *"feel disabled"*. This showed the importance of designing a device that does not look like a disability aid, to prevent the feelings of being stigmatised becoming associated with the device. As one participant commented individuals with PD have:

"Enough to cope with, without also having to wear a device that advertises greater disability."

Stigma being associated with a device was felt to be a clear problem and, as part of this, so was the need for a device that could be worn somewhere discreet or disguised as an everyday piece of technology. Overall, these comments emphasize the importance of taking a design approach that more equally weights feelings evoked wearing a medical device with the devices actual functionality.

HIGH FIDELITY ITERATIVE DESIGN: PROCESS

This stage began two months after the scoping stage. Using the design specifications, a high fidelity prototype was made and given to three participants with PD so they could report their experiences of using the device over the course of a week. The participants were asked to use the device as they pleased. The design team was interested in the reasoning behind their choices e.g. when and where they chose to wear the device. The choices could then be analyzed to provide broader insights into their experiences using the technology. They each filled out a daily diary detailing the situations they had worn the device in and their feelings towards it. They were also interviewed at the end of the week. Recordings of the interviews were transcribed and, along with the diaries, thematically analyzed to identify aspects of the design that might impact the devices acceptability, usability or desirability. In response to this, alterations were made to the prototype and the process was repeated for the same participants. Interviews were transcribed and analyzed and further (more minor) improvements on the prototype were identified. A second device was then built in response to these perceived needs.

HIGH FIDELITY ITERATIVE DESIGN: RESULTS

The results and analysis in the scoping stage was used to construct a set of specifications that were then followed in the construction of a prototype. The prototypes that were produced vibrated once every minute independent of

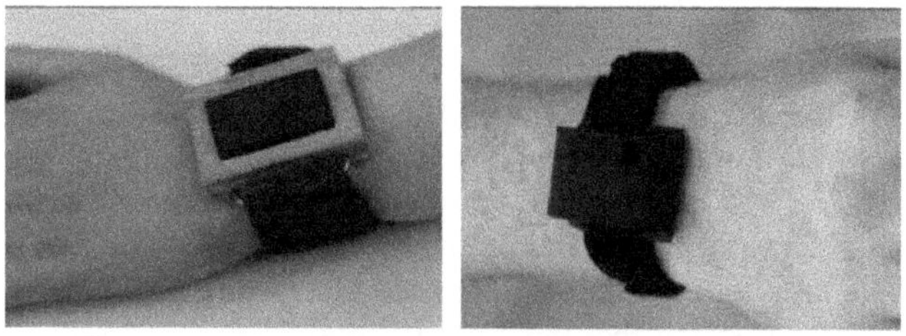

Figures 2: First (left) and second (right) versions of cueing device produced in the iterative design process.

swallowing actions to prompt the users to swallow any excess saliva. The time period was selected to correspond with the normal swallowing rate of adults. Once constructed, high fidelity prototypes (see figure 2) were given to three participants (see table 1 for their characteristics) for one week. Information regarding both their experiences with the device and their opinions about its design were then gathered through interviews.

This first in-situ study revealed several recurrent themes regarding specific device features that were expressed by all three participants. The consistency between their opinions made it simple to pinpoint the aspects of the device that needed to be improved. Only one negative aspect of the device itself was identified: that the vibration was too noisy and thus caused embarrassment in public contrary to the requirement for avoiding stigma discovered in the scoping work. All other faults discussed regarded the wrist worn band, within which the device was held. Participants felt that the band was too bulky causing it to catch on clothing, that it was too short making it difficult to put on and that it was aesthetically unpleasant (design shown in figure 2). Only one of the three participants said they would consider using the device in its current format and this same participant was the only one to wear it in public.

"I went shopping today and I was very pleased, I could talk to people much better than before."

He shared the opinions of the other participants about negative aspects of the device format. However, he experienced a reduction in his drooling problem and this was much more important to him. The main effect the reduction had for him was the improvement he experienced in his speech and he commented that other people also noticed a positive change.

"We were out with our friends and they were surprised at how much better my speech was."

His confidence increased dramatically whilst using the device. For him, the benefits it had given managing his drooling surpassed any problems he might have had with it. These comments show how much of a valuable contribution a device such as this could make to someone's life.

Changes to the prototype were made in response to participant critique and a second in-situ study was conducted with the same people. The same process was carried out using a second version of the high fidelity prototype (see figure 2). When discussing this new prototype all three participants said that they would use it again and all wore the device out of the home environment over the course of the week. The participants also all said they felt comfortable discussing the device with members of the public and that they preferred the second version of the device. When discussing the second device participants were also more likely to mention its effectiveness. One participant stated that the device *"controlled"* his drooling problem and that he felt *"more confident"* when using it. The only fault identified with this prototype version was that they still felt it was slightly too bulky.

REFLECTIONS

Whilst the research and design revealed interesting aspects that contributed to the acceptability of cueing aids for drooling in PD the study did not conduct quantitative work to evaluate the efficacy of the devices that were built. As such, we can only speculate on whether or not the perceived increase in efficacy actually correlated with a decrease in drooling. However, this study has contributed to our knowledge of how the emotional and physical aspects of living with PD can effect interactions with technology. Although there are commercial products for use in the management of drooling, there are aspects which make them unacceptable for users. The opinions of the participants in our study echoed those expressed by users of one such device [7, 8]. They wanted a product which was discreet and could be used independently, a product which would not draw attention to their drooling or incite curiosity from the general public.

During scoping we showed participants a mobile phone based cueing device. We considered this a cost-effective, simple solution to the issue. Our participants dismissed the idea as unrealistic. They listed multiple difficulties that might arise such as: the fact that a mobile cannot be used within hospitals, confusion that may occur when trying to distinguish between cueing vibrations and incoming SMS or calls, and the fact that female users often keep a mobile in their handbag and may not feel the cue. Although these comments seem obvious on reflection, they were not things that we had considered before. A noteworthy point was the increase in perceived effectiveness experienced by all participants with the second design. The functionality of the device had not changed which demonstrates the importance of having a desirable device that people want to interact with. There was also a shift in perception of the device, shown by the change in the way participants talked about it. Initially there was an overwhelming sense of being *"embarrassed"* because participants felt members of the public would associate it with a medical condition and in turn the stigma around PD. However, in final interviews all the participants were comfortable talking about the device. Participants did not make the same negative associations with the aesthetically pleasing device. Our findings agree with Norman's (2002) commentary on aesthetics. *"When we feel good, we overlook design faults. Use a pleasing design, one that looks good and feels- well- sexy, and the behavior seems to go along more smoothly, more easily and better. Attractive things work better"* [10, p.41].

ACKNOWLEDGEMENTS

This work has been funded by an Engineering and Physical Sciences Research Vacation Studentship and the Research Councils UK Digital Economy Research Hub SiDE: Social Inclusion through the Digital Economy (EP/G066019/1).

REFERENCES

1. Brown, R., Ditner, A., Findley, L. and Wessely, S.C. (2005). The Parkinson fatigue scale. *Parkinsonism & Related disorders, 11*, (1), 49-55.
2. Chou, K. L., Evatt, M., Hinson, V. and Kompoliti, K. (2007). Sialorrhea in Parkinson's disease: A review. *Movement Disorders, 22, (16)*, 2306-2313.
3. Edwards, L., Pfeifer, E., Quigley, E., Hofman, R. and Balluff, M. (1991). Gastrointestinal symptoms in Parkinson's disease. *Movement Disorders, 6*, 151-156.
4. Eisma, R., Dickinson, A., Goodman, J., Syme, A., Tiwari L. and Newell, A. (2004). Early user involvement in the development of information technology-related products for older people. *Universal Access in the Information Society, 3*, 131–140.
5. High Quality Care for all: NHS Next Stage Review final report. (2008). Retrieved October 5, 2009 from http://www.dh.gov.uk/en/publicationsandstatistics/publications/publicationspolicyandguidance/DH_085825.
6. Hyson, C.H., Johnson A.M., Jog, M.S. (2002). Sublingual atropine for sialorrhea secondary to Parkinsonism: A pilot study. *Movement Disorders, 17, (6)*, 1318-1320.
7. Marks, L., Turner, K., O'Sullivan, J., Deighton, B. and Lees, A. (2001). Drooling in Parkinson's disease: A novel speech and language therapy intervention. *International Journal of Language and Communication Disorders, 36*, 282-287.
8. Marron, A. (2004). Use of a metronome brooch reminder to improve drooling problems in patients with Parkinsonism. Retrieved 19/05/2009, from http://www.mepltd.co.uk/pdf/pd2004confreport.pdf
9. Nobrega, A.C., Rodrigues, B., Torres, A, Scarpel, R., Neves, C. and Melo, A. (2008). Is drooling secondary to a swallowing disorder in patients with Parkinson's disease? *Parkinsonism and Related Disorders, 14*, 243-245.
10. Norman, D. A., (2002). Emotion & design: Attractive things work better. *Interactions: new visions of human-computer interaction, 9 (4)*, 36-42.
11. Parkinson's Disease Society. Retrieved 25/03/2010, from http://www.parkinsons.org.uk/

Evaluating Swabbing: a Touchscreen Input Method for Elderly Users with Tremor

Chat Wacharamanotham, Jan Hurtmanns, Alexander Mertens, Martin Kronenbuerger, Christopher Schlick, Jan Borchers
RWTH Aachen University
52056 Aachen, Germany
{chat@cs, jan.hurtmanns@, a.mertens@iaw, c.schlick@iaw, borchers@cs}.rwth-aachen.de
mkronenbuerger@ukaachen.de

ABSTRACT
Elderly users suffering from hand tremor have difficulties interacting with touchscreens because of finger oscillation. It has been previously observed that sliding one's finger across the screen may help reduce this oscillation. In this work, we empirically confirm this advantage by (1) measuring finger oscillation during different actions and (2) comparing error rate and user satisfaction between traditional tapping and *swabbing* in which the user slides his finger towards a target on a screen edge to select it. We found that oscillation is generally reduced during sliding. Also, compared to tapping, swabbing resulted in improved error rates and user satisfaction. We believe that swabbing will make touchscreens more accessible to senior users with tremor.

Author Keywords
older adults, touchscreen, tremor, accuracy, evaluation, tapping, swabbing, input methods

ACM Classification Keywords
H.5.2 Information Interfaces and Presentation: User Interfaces—*Evaluation/methodology*

General Terms
Human factors, Experimentation

INTRODUCTION
Although tremor affects only 0.4% of the world population, when focusing on older adults, this number increases to 6.3% (age 60–65) and 21.7% (age $\geq$ 95) [8]. With the global increase of the senior population [11], tremor will be a significant concern in designing assistive technologies in the future.

Although touchscreens have several benefits—they provide direct hand-eye coordination, need minimal training, and require less space [10], users with tremor have difficulties using touchscreens. In particular, tremor-induced oscillations cause the finger to deviate from the target or to produce duplicate inputs. Although this can be alleviated by increasing target size and space between targets, this would require more screen space, which is often limited.

Our initial observations [9] indicated that sliding the finger across the screen during swabbing appeared to dampen deviation, but this observation has not been confirmed empirically. Neither has swabbing been compared to tapping, the basic touchscreen interaction technique.

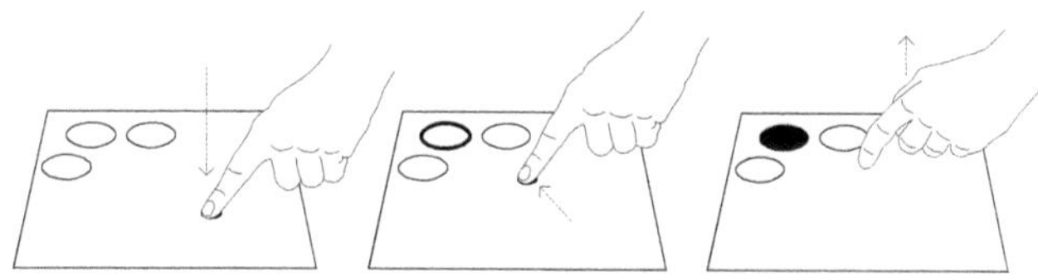

Figure 1. The three steps of swabbing: touch, slide towards the target, and lift.

After a review of related work, we report on a study of finger oscillation during swabbing and tapping in four actions of touchscreen interaction (hovering, tapping, sliding, and resting), and comparing error rate and user satisfaction between swabbing and tapping. We discuss our findings that (1) sliding reduces the oscillation of finger tips, and that (2) compared to tapping, swabbing resulted in improved error rates and user satisfaction.

RELATED RESEARCH
Swabbing Input on Touchscreens
Swabbing is a single-touch selection method proposed by Mertens et al. [9]. The user touches any area on the screen and slides his finger towards the target placed on an edge of the screen (see Figure 1). After the finger moved beyond a distance threshold, a linear regression is calculated from recent touch coordinates to determine the intended target, which is then highlighted. To select the target, the user either lifts his finger or slides it across the target and beyond the screen. To cancel the highlighting, the user slides the finger backward.

Swabbing can potentially reduce errors by reducing finger oscillation during sliding (visually observed in [9]) and by giving the user a chance to preview and correct an error in the highlighting step. The target placement eliminates the users' anxiety of overshooting and maximizes the opening angle from the initial touch point towards each target. Swabbing trades off input speed for accuracy because sliding always takes longer than tapping.

Other Input Techniques for Users with Tremor

Finger interactions differ from interactions using a stylus [1] or indirect pointing devices, e.g., a mouse [10]; these differences limit the adoption of existing input methods for touchscreens and for seniors. We review the limitations in adopting some methods and compare them to swabbing as follows.

With Goal Crossing [12], the user crosses the mouse cursor over the target to select it. The benefit, which is also maintained in swabbing, is that the user does not have to aim at a limited target area. Crossing targets on a touchscreen for a longer time, however, is demanding especially for elderly users because they cannot rest their hand on the surface—only the finger is supported. Since only trajectories are needed in swabbing, the sliding distance can be shorter than the distance to the target. Nevertheless, the swabbing technique also supports crossing.

With Barrier pointing [3], a physical screen edge and plane is used to catch the stylus or to guide stroke movements, which can increase selection accuracy. Nevertheless, when applied to finger interaction, the hand covers the targets during selection. Also, physical screen edges are disappearing on modern devices such as Apple's iPad.

With Touch [6], a target is selected if the stylus enters its bounds, and the stylus can be landed or lifted anywhere. Touch can increase input accuracy for older users but was not designed for users with tremor. The oscillation might cause neighbor targets to be touched. Increasing the space between targets is possible but often limited by screen space. With swabbing, the trajectory determines only one target at a time.

RESEARCH QUESTION

In order to evaluate the potential benefits of swabbing, we addressed the following research questions. (1) How does tremor oscillation change during different actions of touchscreen interaction for tapping and swabbing? (2) Will swabbing help users to select a target on a touchscreen more accurately than tapping? (3) Will users be satisfied with swabbing?

PARTICIPANTS

Users with *intention tremor*—tremor during target-directed movements— were recruited from a local hospital; none of them had used any touchscreen device before. Each participant drew a spiral (see Figure 2), to determine tremor strength: slight (< 0.5 cm), moderate (0.5–1 cm), marked (1–2 cm), and severe (> 2 cm)[1].

[1]As recommended by the Movement Disorder Society [2].

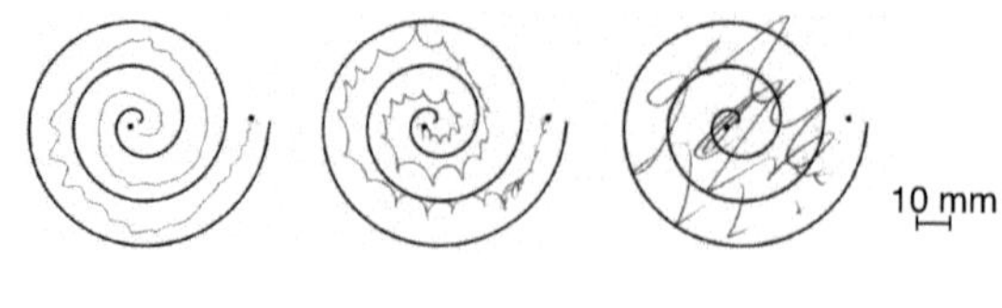

Figure 2. The spiral drawings from users with different tremor strengths (left to right: slight, marked, severe)

HARDWARE SETUP

As shown in Figure 3, we placed an HP TouchSmart tm2-1090eg[2] on a stand with the screen surface inclined 20° from the desk surface. The desk height was at the same level of the elbow when the user's arm was orthogonal to the ground. From the top view, the screen was placed in front of the user at a distance within the length of the forearm. Each participant used a fixed finger angle throughout the study.

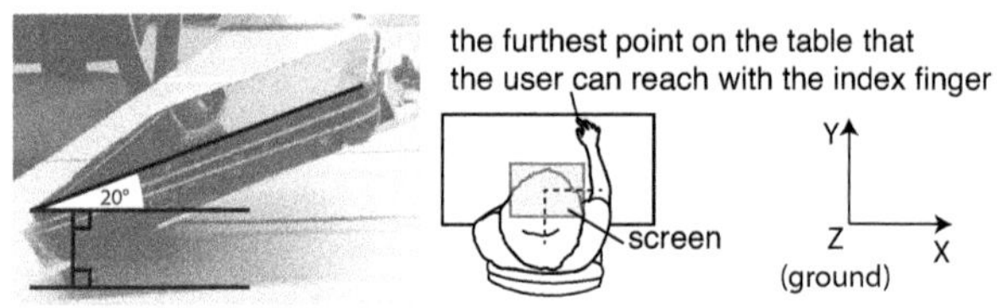

Figure 3. The hardware setup. Left: The screen surface is 20° inclined from the desk surface. Center: The top view of screen position. Right: Axes of the accelerometer.

EXPERIMENT 1: FINGER OSCILLATION

We hypothesized that the finger will exhibit less tremor while sliding on the screen. Therefore, we measured the acceleration of the fingertip in four actions: hovering over a spot, resting on a spot, repeatedly tapping on a spot, and sliding (to the left and right) in a designated area. We omitted visual feedback in order to prevent the bias to any feedback.

Procedure

Similar to [4], we used a velcro ring to attach a tri-axis accelerometer (GForce3D-3[3]) to the back of the extreme joint of the test finger; the entire tip of the finger was uncovered.

For each action, we recorded 10 seconds of acceleration data and discarded the first and the last second due to extreme variance, likely caused by the onset and the completion of the task. The data was transformed into the frequency domain by a Fast-Fourier Transform (See Figure 4 for an example.) The *peak magnitude* of each action was the highest magnitude within the tremor frequency (3–10 Hz) [4]. A *significant axis* has a peak magnitude of more than 0.1 G.

Result and Discussion

The results from all participants (age: 58–87, $M = 73$, $SD = 7.89$, $q1 = 70.50$, $q3 = 77.50$) are shown in Figure 5. In general, the peak magnitude in sliding was consistently lower than in the other actions. Although there were differences across users, the results suggest that sliding can lessen the oscillation magnitude in the significant axes.

[2]http://h10025.www1.hp.com/ewfrf/wc/product?product=4107117
[3]http://infusionsystems.com/catalog/product_info.php/products_id/157

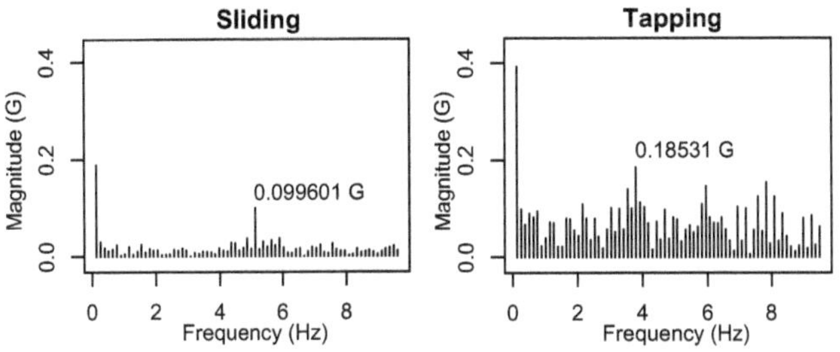

Figure 4. An example of a spectrum plot with the peak magnitude labeled. The peak magnitude in sliding is lower than in tapping.

Gender	Handedness	Tremor strength	Action with highest peak magnitude	Significant axes (ordered by intensity)	T: lower magnitude in tapping	S: lower magnitude in sliding
M	R	IIII	Rest	YZ	Z	Y
M	R	III	Rest	YZ	Y	Z
M	L	I	Hover	XYZ	Y	–
F	L	II	Hover	ZXY	–	XYZ
F	L	II	Hover	YXZ	–	XYZ
M	R	III	Hover	ZYX	XY	Z
M	L	III	Hover	–	–	XYZ
F	R	II	Hover	–	–	XYZ
M	L	IIII	Hover	YZX	–	XYZ
M	L	IIII	Hover	YZX	YZ	X

Tremor strength
I Slight
II Moderate
III Marked
IIII Severe

Axis direction
X: to the right
Y: to the front
Z: to the ground

Figure 5. Participant profile and finger oscillation results in sliding (S) versus tapping (T), with one participant per line. The peak magnitude was lower in sliding in severe axes in the majority of cases.

EXPERIMENT 2: ACCURACY AND USER SATISFACTION

Based on our results, we hypothesized that in a target selection task, swabbing will decrease the error rate and will increase the user's satisfaction compared to tapping.

Procedure

In each trial, participants performed either a tapping or swabbing action to select a designated target laid out as shown in Figure 6. In both methods, participants started each trial on a crosshair located on the same side as the hand. In swabbing, they had to start sliding from the center of the screen. The targets were in a square grid for tapping and were on the edges of the screen for swabbing. To prevent a learning effect, there was no hit/miss feedback. The targets were spread evenly across the screen because previous research has shown that finger selection accuracy can differ for different areas [5].

For this experiment, selection was initiated after the finger had moved beyond 50% of the average of the shortest distance from center point to target (a screen edge) and the longest distance (to a screen corner.) We omitted feedback (highlighting the target) to prevent users from developing a strategy for swabbing in the later trials.

We did a 2×3 within-group study ({tapping, swabbing} × {16, 25, 36} possible targets on the screen), with 15 trials per condition. The order of methods and number of targets was counterbalanced. Each participant had 10 trials for training with 9 targets on the screen before beginning with each method. We recorded the number of selection errors and timestamped touch movements (landing, sliding, and lifting). After the experiment, participants rated their satisfaction of each method with the Post-Study User Satisfaction Questionnaire (PSSUQ) [7] translated into German.

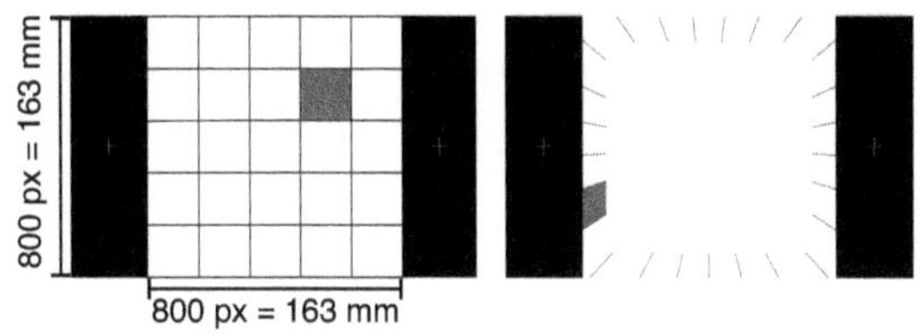

Figure 6. The screen layout for tapping (left) and swabbing (right).

Result and Discussion

Six users participated in this experiment (age: 70–87, M = 75, SD = 5.62, $q1$ = 71.50, $q3$ = 75.75); tremor strength: 1 slight, 1 moderate, 2 marked, 2 severe). As shown in Figure 7, the median error rate in swabbing was lower than in tapping. A two-way repeated measures ANOVA on error proportion with quasibinomial error distribution revealed no significant interaction effect among participants, number of targets, or methods. There were significant main effects of method, $F(1,35) = 5.258$, $p = .029$, and number of targets, $F(2,35) = 5.505$, $p < .001$, which supports H1.

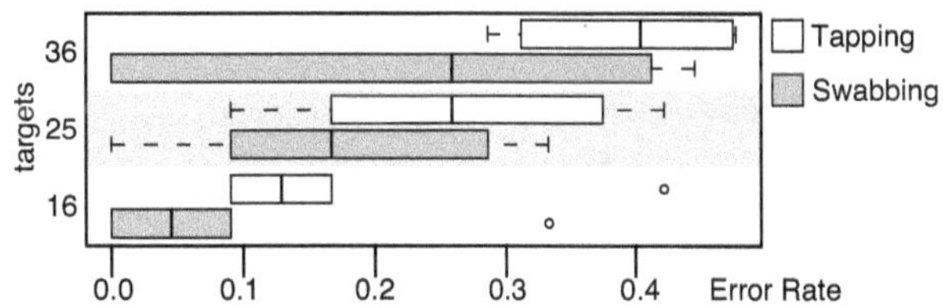

Figure 7. Summary of error rates. Swabbing has lower error rates in general, with a high variance in the 36 targets condition.

Although there was no significant interaction effect of method × number of targets on error rate, the positive impact of swabbing appeared to be strongest for the 16 targets layout. This is likely due to two reasons: (1) the high variance of error rates in 25 and 36 targets and (2) the lack of statistical power due to the small number of participants (power = 0.35 at effect size Cohen's $f = 4$).

Nevertheless, swabbing had a significant advantage for the 16 targets condition (grid target width = 41 mm). This could be especially useful for devices with numeric keypads such as a phone.

Although this study only compared tapping on a grid layout of targets to swabbing on a radial layout of targets, we conducted a preliminary study beforehand to test only nine targets and tapping on a swabbing layout. We found that most users could accurately tap in 9 targets (less than 20% error) because the target size was large (54 mm wide). We found no reduction of error rates in tapping on the swabbing layout.

As shown in Figure 8, swabbing was significantly slower than tapping for 25 and 36 targets, but the main effect of participants and the interaction between participants and method make it inconclusive. The time of tapping, which is a single-contact, and the time of swabbing, which is a continuous contact, cannot be directly compared because swabbing time depends on the contact area, pressure, finger humidity, angle, and direction of movement.

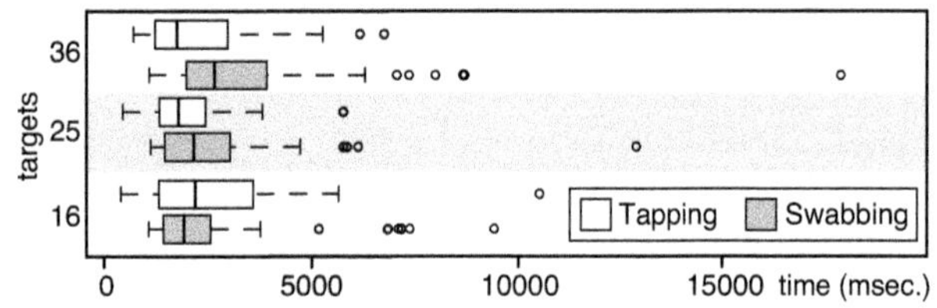

Figure 8. The summary of times to select each target. The time the user takes in swabbing is close to the time in tapping.

A summary of the PSSUQ results is shown in Figure 9. Friedman rank sum tests showed a significant effect of method on overall satisfaction, $\chi^2(1, N = 6) = 5$, $p = .025$, and on System Usage, $\chi^2(1, N = 6) = 6$, $p = .014$. There was no significant effect in Interface Quality, $\chi^2(1, N = 6) = 0.67$, $p = .414$. Although swabbing was inherently slower than tapping, participants were satisfied with this input method. The result indicates that users with tremor prefer more accurate input methods to faster ones. This supports H2.

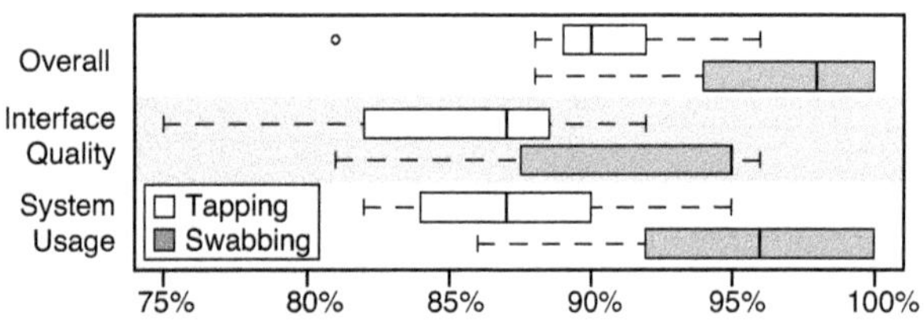

Figure 9. PSSUQ results. The overall rating and the rating for the System Usage was higher for swabbing.

CONCLUSION

We have compared swabbing to tapping as input methods for elderly users with tremor. In general, sliding can lessen finger tremor when interacting on a touchscreen. Overall, swabbing improved error rates and user satisfaction. Although this result is promising, future experiments with more participants are needed.

Based on our findings we derived at two design implications:

When to choose swabbing: Tapping is a viable choice for square targets that are at least 54 mm wide. When the target width is smaller than 41 mm, swabbing becomes a better alternative.

Speed-accuracy tradeoff: Elderly users with tremor may prefer a more accurate input method, even if it is slower.

ACKNOWLEDGEMENT

This work was partially funded by the German B-IT Foundation and the German Federal Ministry of Education and Research. We appreciate Leah Findlater for her shepherding.

REFERENCES

1. R. Balakrishnan and I. MacKenzie. Performance differences in the fingers, wrist, and forearm in computer input control. *Proc. CHI'97*, 303–310, 1997.
2. G. Deuschl, P. Bain, M. Brin, and A. H. S. Committee. Consensus statement of the movement disorder society on tremor. *MOVEMENT DISORD*, 13(S3):2–23, 1998.
3. J. Froehlich, J. Wobbrock, and S. Kane. Barrier pointing: Using physical edges to assist target acquisition on mobile device touch screens. *Proc. ASSETS'07*, 19–26, 2007.
4. B. Graham. Using an accelerometer sensor to measure human hand motion. *Master Thesis, MIT*, 2000.
5. T. Guerreiro, H. Nicolau, J. Jorge, and D. Goncalves. Assessing mobile touch interfaces for tetraplegics. *Proc. Mobile HCI'10*, 31–34, 2010.
6. J. Hourcade and T. Berkel. Simple pen interaction performance of young and older adults using handheld computers. *INTERACT COMPUT*, 20(1):166–183, 2008.
7. J. Lewis. Psychometric evaluation of the PSSUQ using data from five years of usability studies. *INT J HUM-COMPUT INT*, 14(3&4):463–488, 2002.
8. E. Louis and J. Ferreira. How common is the most common adult movement disorder? update on the worldwide prevalence of essential tremor. *MOVEMENT DISORD*, 25(5):534–541, 2010.
9. A. Mertens, N. Jochems, C. Schlick, D. Dünnebacke, and J. Dornberg. Design pattern TRABING: touchscreen-based input technique for people affected by intention tremor. *Proc. EICS'10*, 267–272, 2010.
10. W. Rogers, M. O'Brien, and A. McLaughlin. Selection and design of input devices for assistive technologies. *Proc. ICARCV'06*, 1–6, 2006.
11. K. Watkins, H. Fu, R. Fuentes, A. Ghosh, C. Giamberardini, C. Johansson, C. Kuonqui, A. Montes, D. Stewart, and C. Ugaz. Human development report 2005. *United Nations Development Programme*, 2005.
12. J. Wobbrock and K. Gajos. Goal crossing with mice and trackballs for people with motor impairments: Performance, submovements, and design directions. *TACCESS*, 1(1):4:1–4:37, 2008.

Direct Manipulation Through Surrogate Objects

Bum chul Kwon, Waqas Javed, Niklas Elmqvist, and Ji Soo Yi
Purdue University
West Lafayette, IN, USA
{kwonb, wjaved, elm, yij}@purdue.edu

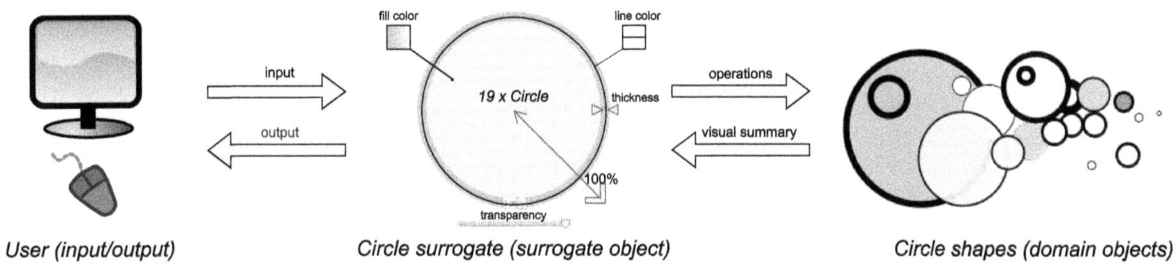

Figure 1. Conceptual diagram of Surrogate Interaction for a 2D vector editor. All interaction with the surrogate is forwarded to the shapes.

ABSTRACT
Direct manipulation has had major influence on interface design since it was proposed by Shneiderman in 1982. Although directness generally benefits users, direct manipulation also has weaknesses. In some cases, such as when a user needs to manipulate small, attribute-rich objects or multiple objects simultaneously, indirect manipulation may be more efficient at the cost of directness or intuitiveness of the interaction. Several techniques have been developed over the years to address these issues, but these are all isolated and limited efforts with no coherent underlying principle. We propose the notion of *Surrogate Interaction* that ties together a large subset of these techniques through the use of a surrogate object that allow users to interact with the surrogate instead of the domain object. We believe that formalizing this family of interaction techniques will provide an additional and powerful interface design alternative for interaction designers, as well as uncover opportunities for future research.

ACM Classification Keywords
H.5.2 Information Interfaces and Presentation: User Interfaces—*Interaction styles*; I.3.6 Computer Graphics: Methodology and Techniques—*Interaction techniques*

Author Keywords
Direct manipulation, instrumental interaction, design.

General Terms
Design, Theory

INTRODUCTION
For well over two decades, the direct manipulation paradigm [25, 26] has held sway in interface design, prompting designers to minimize indirection and to transform domain objects themselves into first-class interfaces. Despite being criticized for its deficiencies in managing abstract, group-based, or meta-level operations [12], challenged by agent-based and conversational approaches [17, 27], and extended with new measures for compatibility (similar to Norman's naturalness of mapping [18]) and integration of the input device, direct manipulation remains one of the basic tenets of user interface design to this day [28].

Although many novel approaches to resolve the weaknesses of the direct manipulation model have been proposed over the years, these tend to be isolated measures that do not seem to fit within a coherent framework. However, in this paper, we identify a subset of these techniques that share salient properties in how abstract, group-based, and meta-level operations are managed. We call this family of techniques *Surrogate Interaction* because they introduce *surrogate objects* that users can interact with instead of the real domain objects, and where changes are then propagated to the linked objects (Figure 1). While this increases indirection—albeit in a disciplined fashion—where direct manipulation stipulates decreasing it, this approach supports control over attribute-rich domain objects that would be difficult to access using direct manipulation, seamless and visible manipulation of multiple objects simultaneously, and access to abstract, intangible, meta-level properties and domain objects.

Consider a 2D vector editor such as Adobe Illustrator or the Open Source program Inkscape: graphical applications with multiple attribute-rich domain objects, i.e., geometric shapes. The standard solution is to provide multiple dialogs, control panels, and context menus to change graphical properties such as the line width, stippling, stroke color, fill, texture, transparency, and gradient of the shapes, only leaving a few attributes such as position, size, and rotation controlled by direct manipulation. Using the surrogate interaction approach, a 2D vector editor provides a single surrogate of the currently selected shape—or shapes—augmented with direct manipulation controls to change these graphical attributes. The surrogate looks like the selected shape and propagates all interaction to it, yet is larger, located in a well-defined place (a side panel or context menu), and can be annotated without interfering with the image being edited.

More specifically, by providing a surrogate of a domain object in a well-defined area of the screen, we can solve the access problem—the surrogate can be large and, by virtue of being a meta representation, is not required to convey information. It is thus easy to acquire and can be decorated with the necessary interface widgets. Furthermore, the surrogate also clearly shows that actions on it may affect multiple domain objects by indicating the selected objects, and its visual representation may unify the common attributes of the selection. Finally, surrogates can also be created for intangible properties, such as layout, ordering, or grid spacing.

In the following section, we give the background on direct manipulation and some of its weaknesses. We then derive the surrogate interaction framework from both new and existing academic and commercial applications that exhibit these commonalities. We go on to present a set of design examples for multidimensional visualization, vector drawing, and mobile devices for embodied interaction. We conclude with implications and constraints for user interface design.

BACKGROUND

Direct Manipulation

Introduced by Ben Shneiderman in 1982 [25, 26], the *direct manipulation* paradigm has held sway over user interface design for more than two decades. Before direct manipulation, the interaction between human and computer mostly relied on a conversation metaphor (e.g., a command-line interface), which is relatively indirect and abstract. As a backlash against this, direct manipulation promoted a more explicit way of interacting with computers. The paradigm is characterized by four main principles [26]:

1. Continuous representation of the object of interest;
2. Physical actions instead of complex syntax;
3. Rapid, incremental, and reversible operations whose impact on the object of interest is immediately visible; and
4. Layered or spiral approach to learning that permits usage with minimal knowledge.

These principles have helped make interaction more natural, intuitive, and predictable, thus causing applications to become easier and more efficient to learn and use.

However, direct manipulation did not win this reputation easily. Since its introduction, many researchers have criticized the paradigm [5, 7, 11, 12]. Among these, Frohlich [11, 12] provided a comprehensive review of the evolution and debate around direct manipulation. He argued that direct manipulation is not a panacea, and it actually has only limited utility because it is not abstract enough to fully express the user's intended interaction. More specifically, he listed seven tasks that are challenging to direction manipulation [12]—see Table 1. Based on these challenges, he predicted that the use of manipulation-based interaction would be limited and constrained. He further claimed that, as an alternative, conversation-based interaction (e.g., software agents) would complement manipulation-based interaction because it could provide users with more abstract and expressive interaction. The debate continued through the discussion between Shneiderman and Maes in 1997 [27].

In spite of (or thanks to) strong criticism, direct manipulation has evolved and appears to have stood the test of time. Numerous examples of academic research and commercial products explicitly and implicitly adopt the direct manipulation paradigm in their interaction design. The influences of direct manipulation are not limited to traditional WIMP (windows, icons, menus, pointer) interfaces, but are widely applied to other types of interfaces—often known as post-WIMP [35] or reality-based interaction [15]—such as information visualization (e.g., [37]), augmented/virtual reality (e.g., [22]) and direct touch interfaces (e.g., [23]).

Other researchers have expanded and refined the idea of direct manipulation, the most notable being the *instrumental interaction* model proposed by Michel Beaudouin-Lafon [3, 4]. The main idea of this model is to separate out the concept of an *instrument* as the mediator between users and domain objects in the interaction between human and computer. Instruments are first-class objects (e.g., a scroll bar and a paint brush) that can be used in many different contexts (e.g., a scrollbar that can operate on both a word processing document and a drawing canvas). Beaudouin-Lafon also introduced three properties to evaluate these instruments [3]:

1. *Degree of indirection:* a two-dimensional measure of the spatial and temporal distance introduced by instruments;
2. *Degree of integration:* the ratio between the degrees of freedom of the instrument and the input device; and
3. *Degree of compatibility:* a measure of similarity between actions on the instrument and the feedback on the object.

Given these properties, Beaudouin-Lafon argues that an instrument with low indirectness, high integration, and high compatibility will be a good instrument. These evaluation criteria could guide and generate the design for techniques and applications. Recently, Klokmose and Beaudouin-Lafon [16] further expanded the model by proposing the Views, Instruments, Governors and Objects (VIGO) architecture that allows many users to interact with multiple devices through diverse interfaces and on multiple surfaces.

We revisited the challenging tasks for direct manipulation that Frohlich listed [12]—see Table 1—and found that many of these challenges have been overcome through several variations of direct manipulation. When there are no proper visual representations of an object, visual representations are often created (or reified) to allow users to directly manipulate the object. For example, in order to allow a user to repeat

	Challenging Tasks	Solutions
1	Referring to previous actions	Interaction histories
2	Scheduling actions	Event scheduling
3	Identifying unseen objects	Shaking, jittering
4	Identifying groups of objects	Multi-object selection
5	Performing repetitive actions	Visual macros
6	Performing concurrent actions	Multitouch interaction
7	Specifying precise actions	Zooming

Table 1. Seven challenges for direct manipulation (adapted from [12]).

a certain action, visual macros (e.g., Apple Mac OS X Automator and Yahoo Pipes [38]) have been developed. When there already exists proper visual representations, other interaction techniques have been invented to overcome the identified issues (e.g., zooming to show the details of domain object). Furthermore, there still exists many examples of conversation-based interaction designs (e.g., the `cron` Unix command for scheduling repeated tasks) as well as compromises between conversation-based design and manipulation-based design (e.g., the Windows XP Scheduling Wizard). However, in general, direct manipulation seems to have tackled most of these challenges and has proliferated in interaction design for the last decades.

Challenges of Direct Manipulation

However, not all of these challenges have been effectively overcome for direct manipulation. Some of the limitations that Frohlich mentioned in 1993 still exist in current direct manipulation applications. In this work, we focus on the following issues (corresponding to challenges 7, 6, and 3):

- *Access:* Manipulating small, distant, or attribute-rich objects under limited space, high density, or high precision;
- *Multiple objects:* Manipulating multiple objects simultaneously as a group (including group attributes); and
- *Intangible properties:* Manipulating intangible object properties (abstract properties with no visual form).

The first of these challenges—**access**—is based on the fact that manipulating small objects can be cumbersome with direct manipulation. For example, when an object in a vector drawing application becomes too small, it may be difficult to select the object and to grab the handle instrument on the object in order to resize it. This problem is compounded if there are many objects in the same area of the screen, if the objects are located in a distant part of the screen, or even outside the screen in ubiquitous computing. Some of these issues can be partially solved by zooming the view for more detail and precision or other distortion techniques, but these approaches incur additional effort and cognitive load.

Another aspect of the same problem is manifested if the objects are rich in attributes. There may not be enough visual space to expose interface controls to manipulate all attributes, such as for a transistor object in an electric circuit CAD application. Alternatively, such controls detract from the visual appearance of the objects, such as information-carrying marks in a visualization, where adding such controls to the display would affect the visual representation.

The second problem we address is that interacting with **multiple objects** is often difficult using direct manipulation. When a user selects multiple domain objects with varying values (e.g., text with different font sizes), the aggregated properties of all selected objects typically cannot be properly presented, so the visual representation becomes ambiguous.

In addition, interacting with multiple objects using direct manipulation is often not nearly as intuitive as interacting with a single object. For example, suppose that a group of objects are selected, and the user resizes one of the objects in the group. How should the other objects in the group react to this user manipulation? One popular solution used in many applications, such as Microsoft PowerPoint, is that the single object that the user manipulates serves as a representative for the whole group, so the other objects in the group are also influenced by the same manipulation. This approach saves effort because it allows the user to resize all of the objects in the group by resizing a single representative. However, the approach could be criticized due to, again, its ambiguity. What if the selected objects have different shapes and sizes? Suppose that the user wants to increase the width of every object by 10 pixels—will resizing the representative object by 10 pixels cause the other objects to increase their widths by the same amount, or will their widths be increased proportionally? Much of the predictability of the direct manipulation interface has been lost in this situation.

Finally, the third problem we address deals with manipulating **intangible object properties**—abstract properties that have no natural visual form. For example, the spacing between multiple objects is not easily presented as a domain object, so it is difficult to allow direct manipulation of this attribute. Similar examples of intangible properties could be sorting order, layout, and object alignment. Many of these intangible properties arise from the multiple object challenge discussed earlier—these are attributes that do not exist other than for a group of objects, not for individual objects.

Currently, these intangible properties are manipulated in a relatively indirect manner. For example, Adobe Illustrator provides a toolbox for rearranging objects, allowing a user to choose between seven different layout types. Although the user might see the effects of layout changes immediately, there is significant spatial and cognitive distances between the domain objects and the instruments.

Data visualization gives rise to another type of intangible properties: summary statistics. These properties are especially challenging to turn into visible elements because they also do not belong to a single object but only become meaningful when multiple objects are related. Since these summary statistics might introduce visual clutter as well, it is often challenging to include them on the display.

The common denominator among the above problems is that they stem from the main strength of direct manipulation—the directness of the interaction (i.e., the low degree of indirection [3]). Attempting to resolve these issues would mean relaxing this central design principle. In the next sections, we will study how to do this in a disciplined fashion.

EVIDENCE OF SURROGATE INTERACTION

This paper proposes surrogate interaction as a unifying model for improving access, multiplicity, and intangibility in direct manipulation by introducing a small degree of indirectness between the user and the domain objects through surrogate objects. Below we review existing tools, both academic and commercial, for evidence of surrogate interaction.

3D Object Manipulation

Manipulating 3D objects is a difficult task, and different approaches have been designed to aid or solve it. Some of these draw on a surrogate interaction model to ease the interaction. Go-go interaction [22] deploys a surrogate hand to manipulate distant objects. World-In-Miniature [30] (WIM) are small-scale copies of the full 3D environment that the user is currently inhabiting. The miniature is linked to a physical plane the user is holding—yielding an out-of-body third-person view of the world—and rotating or moving the plane will affect the miniature world accordingly. Notably, the WIM itself is a first-class object, allowing the user to interact directly with objects visible in the miniature (but which may not be visible to the user in their first-person view of the world), thus causing the environment to be updated.

Even more relevant to surrogate interaction are the voodoo dolls proposed by Pierce et al. [21]: miniatures of actual first-class 3D objects in the world. Any interaction performed on the voodoo doll is immediately propagated to the real object it is linked to, and visual feedback is reflected on the doll to indicate state changes. However, the concept does not support manipulating more than one object at a time. The Monkey [9] (and commercial Monkey 2) device is essentially a physical Voodoo doll: a biped armature that can be used to control a virtual 3D character on screen.

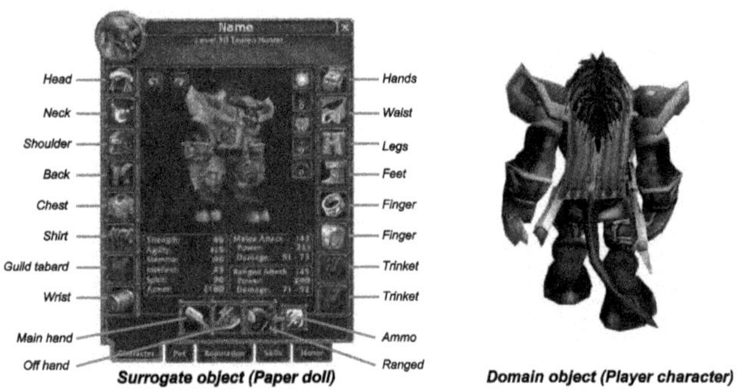

Figure 2. Paper doll interface in *World of Warcraft*. Changes in the doll (surrogate) will immediately affect the character (domain object).

Computer Games

Elements of surrogate interaction also exists in a number of computer games. For example, a common design mechanism, particularly for role-playing games (RPGs) where the player's character is wearing all manners of armor, weapons, and jewelry, is the *paper doll interface*. A paper doll is simply a miniature version of the player character where the user can access different equipment slots to dress the character in items from the inventory (just like a real paper doll). It is also often combined with information about the character's abilities, health, and bonuses (*World of Warcraft* in Figure 2).

The paper doll interface is clearly an example of surrogate interaction, where the doll is the surrogate for the player character (the domain object). Any changes to the equipment on the doll will be immediately reflected in the appearance of the character. More specifically, the mechanism solves the access problem—exposing all of these equipment slots on the 3D player character itself would cause visual clutter, and the paper doll is an elegant way to avoid this.

Interactive Legends

Legends have long been used as visual dictionaries in cartography, and this idea has also been extended to other applications—Edward Tufte [33] strongly advocate their use, and exemplify them, among other ways, through surrogate representations of people in photographs using silhouette legends [34]. With the advent of computerized maps, cartographers have begun to propose *active legends* that change color encodings as the user interacts with them [20].

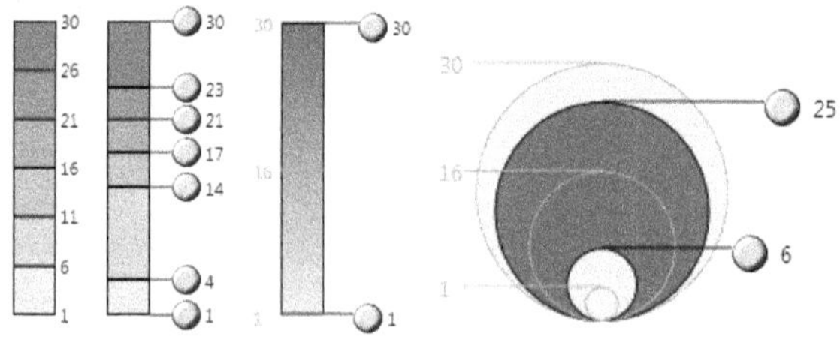

Figure 3. Interactive legends for filtering in visualization [24].

This trend has also carried across into visualization, prompting *interactive legends* as input devices that both save display space and are intrinsically integrated into the visual representation [32]. In particular, Riche et al. [24] evaluated the use of interactive legends for filtering and selection in multidimensional visualization (Figure 3), and found that they yield faster perception of data values. Similar to scented widgets [36], which incorporate visual displays into standard widgets, these interactive legends serve as surrogate objects representing visual elements in the visual representation, directly selected and filtered using the surrogate object.

Drawing Editors

Graphical editors are examples of interaction-heavy applications with attribute-rich domain objects (2D shapes). Perhaps for this reason, some editors already employ surrogate interaction concepts. Microsoft Office 2007 uses graphical depictions of what a selected shape will look like if different styles are applied. Inspectors in OmniGraffle [31] (Figure 4) are small windows containing visual surrogates that convey the state of the selection. Similarly, Apple's Keynote [2] incorporates inspectors for direct manipulation of shapes and slides, such as the Graphic Inspector (Figure 5).

In all of these examples, the surrogates are (to lesser or greater extent) visually reminiscient of the linked domain object, they summarize the state of the domain object, and they can be interacted with using direct manipulation, thus causing updates to propagate to the linked domain objects.

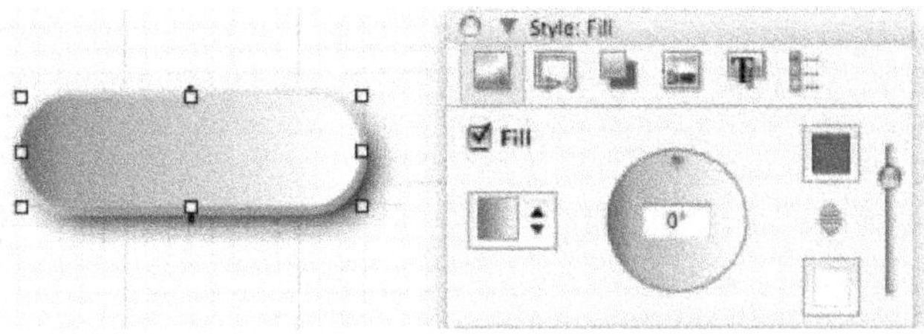

Figure 4. Style inspector in OmniGraffle Professional [31] for the Mac.

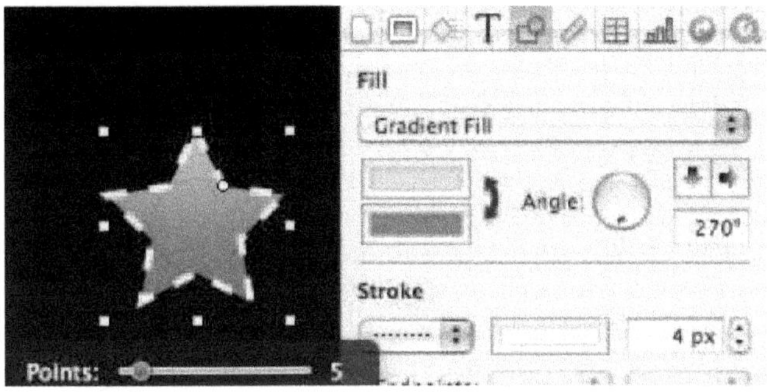

Figure 5. Graphic inspector in Apple Keynote [2].

SURROGATE INTERACTION

Instead of letting users control attributes of a domain object by interacting directly with its visual representation—as stipulated by both direct manipulation and instrumental interaction—surrogate interaction provides a *surrogate object* to interact with. The surrogate is an archetype of the domain objects, and any changes done to the surrogate will immediately affect the domain objects themselves.

More specifically, drawing on evidence in existing academic and commercial applications, we define *surrogate interaction* by means of the following characteristics:

1. Existence of surrogate objects that are visually reminiscent of the domain object/objects being manipulated;
2. Direct manipulation of object/meta attributes on the surrogate object that are propagated to the domain object; and
3. Visual summaries of the domain object state.

Consider a vector drawing editor where users can draw, move, and edit shapes by clicking and dragging with their pointer directly on the canvas using direct manipulation. Supporting surrogate interaction here would imply introducing a surrogate representation of a selected shape on the drawing canvas. This surrogate would allow users to change line style, width, and color as well as the fill color and style. Exposing control of these attributes in a direct manipulation fashion on the canvas itself is not practical due to space and layout constraints (not to mention being detrimental to the appearance of the image that the user is drawing), and would have had to be done using dialog boxes or context menus.

In the terms of the instrumental interaction model, introducing a surrogate object (or meta-object) such as this will increase the degree of spatial indirection in the interface. However, we are still obeying the design principles of direct manipulation by providing continuous visual representations of the domain objects with physical actions that are incremental, reversible, and provide immediate visual feedback. Surrogate interaction also solves the access, multiple object, and intangible property problems outlined earlier in this paper. In the following subsections, we shall see how.

Manipulating Single Objects

As we have seen, accessing domain objects using direct manipulation may be difficult if the visual space is limited or the number of attributes associated with the domain object is high. Furthermore, maintaining a high degree of compatibility between action and effect may be impossible in limited visual space. For surrogate interaction, we sidestep the access problem by allocating a part of the display outside of the main window to the visual representation of a large-scale surrogate of the domain object. Even though we now have introduced an additional level of spatial indirection, the surrogate is large and therefore easy to acquire and manipulate.

Having a surrogate representation for the domain object provides a number of additional benefits. Most importantly, by virtue of having more display space available in the surrogate than for the actual domain objects, we are able to integrate many more user interface components for controlling the attributes of the domain object in the visual representation of the surrogate. This way, surrogate interaction makes it possible to maintain a high degree of compatibility even for very rich domain object mappings.

The surrogate is a meta-object or archetype of its domain object. That means that it is not required to carry actual meaning (or it may carry aggregated meaning for several objects). Its visual representation can be stylized and decorated with annotations and explanations on how to interpret the data and how to interact with the surrogate and the domain objects.

Manipulating Multiple Objects

Surrogates can be linked to just a single domain object, or to several objects. Any changes to a surrogate will affect all of its linked domain objects. We have already seen that manipulating multiple objects using direct manipulation is complex due to the ambiguity and low predictability of operations performed on multiple operands. Surrogate interaction makes multiple object manipulation more visible and more predictable in two important ways:

- **Cardinality:** Each surrogate shows the number and type of the domain objects that will be affected by any operations performed on the surrogate.
- **Scope:** Surrogates communicate the scope of changes to an attribute by indicating the range of values for the underlying domain objects (see visual data aggregation below).

Furthermore, object manipulation can have several levels of *multiplicity*; the most common levels are the following:

- **Single object:** A single domain object, such as changes to a shape surrogate affecting a single shape on the canvas;
- **Set of objects:** A set of domain objects, such as formatting changes to a word surrogate affecting the selected region in a word processor; or

- **Class of objects:** All instances of a particular class of domain objects, such as changes to a bar chart surrogate affecting all bar charts in a scatterplot.

Depending on the type of the application, it may not make sense to support object manipulation for all levels. In the vector editor example, however, we would allow all three types of multiplicity levels depending on the selection: if a single object is selected, then changes will only affect that object, but if multiple objects are selected, then changes will affect them all. It would also make sense to be able to select the rectangle class, for instance, in order to be able to modify all rectangle objects on the canvas simultaneously.

Manipulating Intangible Properties

Unlike domain objects, surrogate objects do not necessarily have to portray actual visual entities. For direct manipulation, even abstract objects must have some visual form—or the designer must choose one—but the surrogate model relieves designers from this burden by allowing them to create only surrogates for such entities. Furthermore, this feature of the surrogate interaction model also promotes dividing different concerns of an application into separate surrogates.

For example, in the vector editor, we can create an entity representing the drawing canvas, where the user can change grid lines and snapping options through direct manipulation operations. Another example may be to expose the spacing between shapes as an actual tangible attribute in the shape surrogate—again, the user can directly change this spacing by manipulating the surrogate, something that would be difficult to achieve on the actual domain object.

Even properties that are difficult to manipulate using direct manipulation, such as choosing a color or selecting a stippling for a line, can be made more natural by situating the button to open the color selection dialog (or stippling drop-down box) on top of the the surrogate. While this does not improve the low directness of actually performing the task, it does increase the degree of compatibility of the interaction.

Visual Data Aggregation

Because the surrogate is an archetype of its linked domain objects (potentially several of them), it need not necessarily convey any specific information about the dataset. In our vector editor example, we may choose to show a stylized shape as a surrogate. On the other hand, this presents an opportunity in itself—the surrogate can be designed to serve as a visual representation of the aggregated data of its linked objects. In other words, for the vector editor example, we can use the surrogate shape to show data about the underlying shapes and their minimum and maximum line thickness, their different line and fill colors, and their relative sizes.

This concept can be extended to the domain object attributes controlled by user interface components in the surrogate. By using scented widgets similar to Willett et al. [36], we can communicate information about the number, range, and distribution of values for attributes controlled by a particular interface component. For example, a slider controlling line thickness in our vector drawing program may be combined with a histogram showing the totals of the linked shapes for each thickness value, exposing data about the drawing to the user. Of course, depending on the multiplicity level supported by the application, changing the value of such a widget would instantly change the underlying distribution of the linked objects (thereby instantly updating the histogram).

Cognitive Aspects

There is a fundamental cognitive difference between standard control panels and surrogate objects. Control panels are more or less haphazard collections of user interface controls (sliders, fields, buttons) and thus only have the most abstract relation to the domain object being manipulated. In contrast, a surrogate object—by virtue of the three characteristics above—embed the controls in interactions and visual representations that are *compatible* with the domain objects at a deep cognitive level. In other words, surrogate interaction allows us to strike a more precise and fine-grained balance between indirection and compatibility in the interface.

DESIGN EXAMPLES

In our experience, some general strategies are particularly useful when implementing actual surrogate interfaces:

- Surrogate objects can be seen as examples of both Prototype and Proxy design patterns [13]. They are prototypes because they act as archetypes of domain objects when instantiating new objects. They are proxies because all domain objects are manipulated through the surrogate.

- Domain objects can be seen as a simple registry of attributes (name-value pairs) controlled using surrogates. To support classes of domain objects, such as circles and squares in a drawing editor, objects can be arranged in a hierarchy that supports class narrowing of a set of objects.

In the examples below, we study surrogate objects applied to data visualization, vector drawing, and mobile interaction.

Scatterplot Visualization

Let us study how we can use surrogate interaction to augment a simple 2D scatterplot [6] visualization. A scatterplot is constructed by mapping two dimensions of the multidimensional dataset to visualize to the horizontal (X) and vertical (Y) axes. Entities in the dataset can now be drawn as points in the Cartesian space formed by the axes. Displaying additional dimensions can be done by varying the graphical properties of the points themselves, such as using their color, shape, and size to convey additional data. However, there is generally a limit to what these graphical properties can communicate. An alternative approach that may be more scalable is to turn the points themselves into miniature bar chart glyphs capable of displaying additional dimensions [1].

At this point, the scatterplot visualization is clearly a graphical application with rich domain objects: the axes and the bar charts. Controlling all of these attributes using direct manipulation on the visualization canvas is difficult due to the high data density and visual clutter. Instead, the practice in visualization applications is to provide menus and control panels where users can indirectly manipulate these settings.

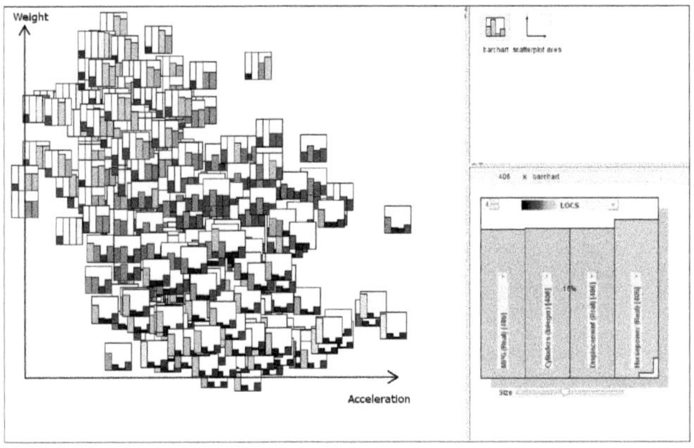

Figure 6. Scatterplot of the weight (Y) and acceleration (X) of around 400 cars. The bar charts show additional information about each car.

To improve this indirect mode of interaction, we have designed a scatterplot implementation that uses surrogate interaction to support access to all of the visualization attributes. Figure 6 shows a screenshot of the prototype. It exposes the two types of domain objects as surrogates in the palette:

- **Scatterplot axes:** The horizontal and vertical axes of the scatterplot, allowing the user to change which dimension to map to each axis as well as graphical attributes of the space (background color, tick marks, grid lines, etc).
- **Bar chart:** The bar charts that represent the points, allowing the user to control the number of bars (i.e., additional dimensions) to show for each data point, the color scale to use for the bars, and the size of the charts (Figure 7).

In this application, we need to maintain consistency across all bar charts, so we do not allow selecting individual glyphs. Instead, changing the surrogate will affect all bar charts.

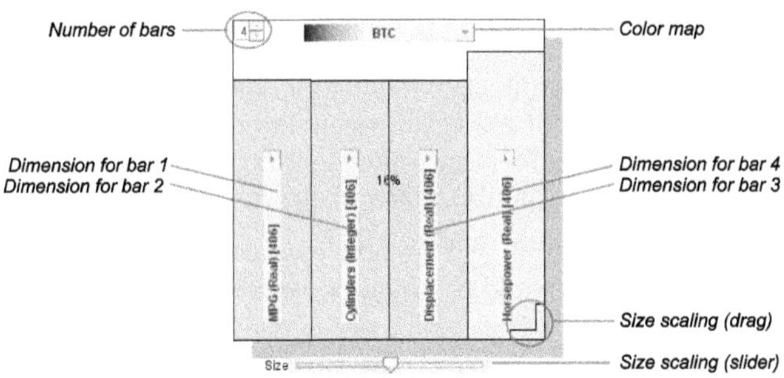

Figure 7. Bar chart surrogate for the scatterplot application.

Starplot Visualization

A starplot [29] is a multidimensional visualization where each item in a dataset becomes a circular glyph with its dimensions arranged around the radius of the glyph. A closed polygon connects values for each of the dimensions mapped to the radial axes. By creating a starplot for each data point in a dataset and laying them out on the visual space, the viewer can easily detect outliers and trends in the data.

Again, as is often the case in visualization, this is an example of an application consisting of heavyweight and attribute-rich domain objects. Instead of building menus or control panels to modify them, we apply surrogate interaction to create a visualization based on two surrogate objects (Figure 8):

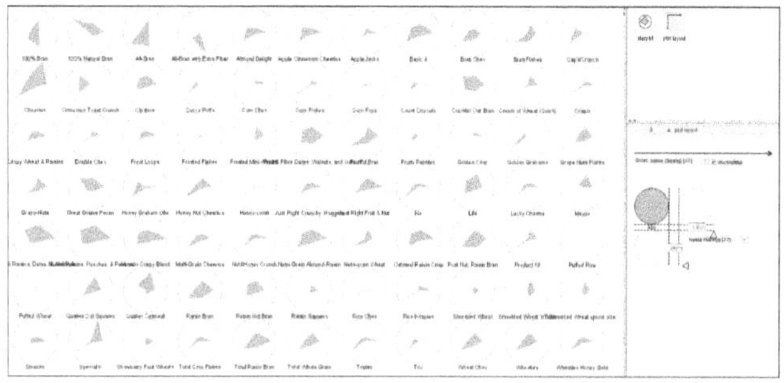

Figure 8. Starplots for 77 different cereals. Each plot shows calories, fiber, sodium, fat, and protein content for each cereal.

- **Starplot:** The starplot entities, enabling the user to change the number of dimensions to display and the mapping for each radial axis. Users can also use the surrogate to change color mapping and the glyph size.
- **Plot layout:** Layout is an intangible attribute that has no visual representation, but this surrogate enables users to change both horizontal and vertical glyph spacing as well as the sorting order for glyphs on the visualization canvas.

In particular, the layout surrogate (Figure 9) is useful because it provides a natural place for exposing intangible attributes. Glyph spacing could be seen as a glyph attribute (the amount of padding around each glyph), but the sorting order does not make sense anywhere else than in the layout surrogate (the standard solution is a menu or control panel).

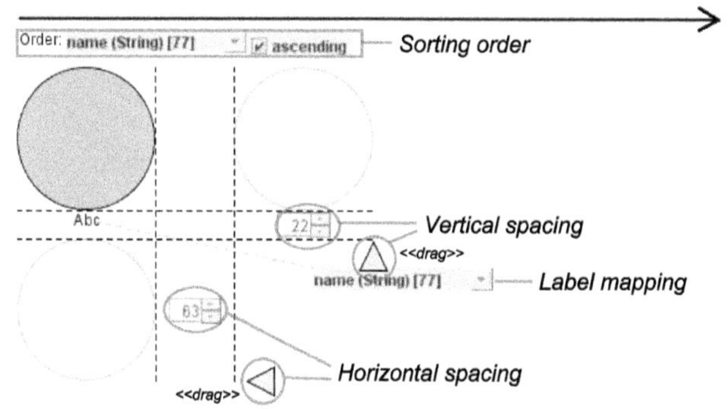

Figure 9. Plot surrogate object for the starplot application.

Vector Drawing Editor

Vector drawing editors have already been discussed extensively in this paper as an example of precisely the kind of application that is most suitable for surrogate interaction. Therefore, we have built such a vector editor based on surrogate interaction concepts. Figure 10 shows the basic structure the editor, closely mirroring that of the scatterplot and starplot applications. In this screenshot, the user has utilized the tools in the toolbar (top) to draw a set of shapes on the main canvas. The surrogate is showing that two shapes have been selected—note the visual aggregation in the surrogate representation for color and line thickness—and is exposing controls to change both shapes collectively.

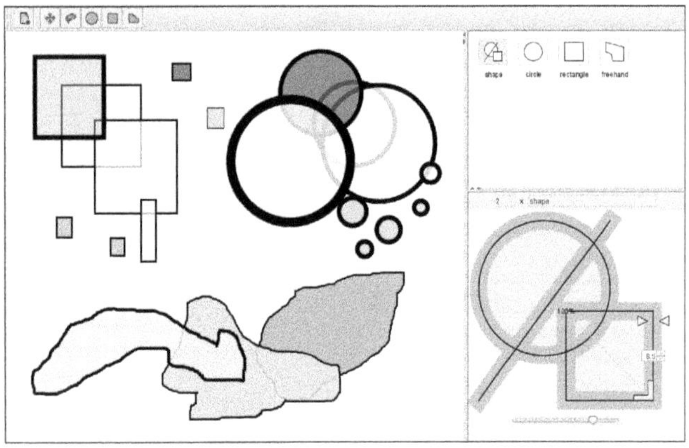

Figure 10. Vector drawing editor using surrogate interaction.

The surrogates that we support in the editor are organized in an inheritance hierarchy with the abstract **shape** class at the top—all concrete shapes inherit from this class. This makes for a structure that can be easily expanded for a realistic vector editor. When selecting shapes on the canvas using the lasso tool, the editor will automatically narrow the surrogate to the lowest common ancestor to the selected shapes in the shape hierarchy. This can clearly be seen in Figure 10—because the selected shapes are polymorphic, the surrogate has only been narrowed to the common shape base class.

The editor currently supports the following surrogate types:

- **Shape:** This surrogate exposes attributes that are common to shapes, such as line width, color, and transparency.
- **Circle:** Manipulation of the radius.
- **Rectangle:** Manipulation of height and width.
- **Freehand:** Editing individual vertices.

Figure 11 shows the surrogates in the vector editor. For some attributes, we expose both numeric and direct manipulation controls (signified by yellow shapes that the user can click and drag—e.g., Line thickness and Size scaling in the figure—whereas other attributes only have an indirect control. However, in this situation, the control is located in the context of its effect, thus minimizing indirection.

Interaction on Mobile Devices

Ubiquitous computing is on the rise, and concepts like *embodied interaction* [8] and *tangible computing* [14] are augmenting physical objects with computational abilities. However, the real world has the same limitations as the digital one: we still do not want to overload physical objects with too many controls, and we often lack metaphors for how to control many objects simultaneously. Surrogate interaction could be used to create surrogate interfaces of physical objects on mobile devices to control them (Figure 12).

IMPLICATIONS FOR DESIGN

There is no general panacea that resolves all issues of interaction design. Rather, interaction in an application should be

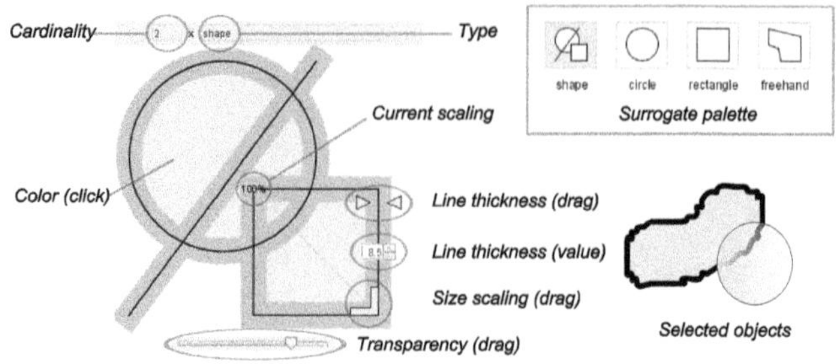

Figure 11. Basic components of the surrogate drawing editor. The surrogate palette (top right) is used to select different shape classes. The surrogate (left) is used to control the selected shapes (bottom right). Absolute and relative scaling can be toggled by clicking on the size indicator (percentage), giving a clear indication of scaling behavior.

Figure 12. Surrogate interface on a smartphone for interacting with home electronic devices using surrogates (mockup).

analyzed so that the appropriate interaction model (or models) can be chosen. While our design examples demonstrate that surrogate interaction can benefit many applications, we should note that the method is a complement to and not a replacement for direct manipulation and other methods. The most beneficial use of surrogate interaction is often in combination with direct manipulation, delegating complex, group-based, or intangible manipulation to a surrogate.

Some tasks are simply not suitable for surrogate interaction due to the information loss implicit in creating a surrogate object. Below we outline some of the tradeoffs that must be considered when applying surrogate interaction in a design:

- **Increased indirection.** Surrogate interaction clearly increases the spatial indirection in the interface.
- **Divided attention.** Surrogates are separate from the main display, forcing users to split their attention between them.
- **Ex situ.** Surrogates cannot convey positions because they are removed from their context, so absolute operations (e.g., move and resize) are best left to direct manipulation.
- **Visual representation.** Choosing a good visual representation, especially for abstract entities, can be challenging.

We discuss some aspects of these limitations and how to address them in the following subsections.

Surrogate Interaction in Context

There is already some evidence of surrogate interaction in the instrumental interaction model. Beaudouin-Lafon [3] discusses *meta-instruments* that operate on or organize other instruments; examples include toolboxes, menus, and instruments that modify other instruments. Surrogate interaction can be seen as an instance of *meta-objects*, a similar lifting of domain objects to a higher abstraction level.

In other words, a surrogate object is a reification of the abstract nature of domain objects. This abstraction enables surrogate interaction to more efficiently overcome the limitations of direct manipulation than other methods by better maintaining the cognitive link between meta-object and domain object. This way, despite introducing spatial indirection, surrogate interaction does not necessarily sacrifice the directness of the interaction; in fact, we believe that it may even *improve* directness in certain situations.

Activating Surrogates

Our design so far has positioned the surrogate object to the side of the main display, thus giving rise to the divided attention and ex situ problems listed above. However, it is possible to modify this design to remedy some of these issues by making the surrogate object activation dynamic:

- **Graphical context menu.** Similar to current textual context menus, typically activated by right-clicking on a certain object or area of the screen, we design our surrogate objects to appear as graphical context menus on selected domain objects. The obvious drawback is naturally that the surrogate object is invisible at all other times.
- **Trailing widget.** The surrogate object could be designed as a semi-transparent trailing widget [10] that follows the cursor, similar to the mini toolbar in Microsoft Office 2007. The surrogate would provide in-situ visual feedback without being disruptive, and a quick gesture would allow the user to acquire the surrogate for interaction.
- **In-situ replacement.** A third solution at the boundary between surrogate interaction and standard direct manipulation is to integrate the surrogate object with the domain object in-situ, allowing for the domain object itself to be replaced by the surrogate through an explicit interaction. Similar to semantic zooming [19], this design would temporarily assign more display space to the surrogate when it is active. Note that many direct manipulation interfaces already use a variant of this idea, for example displaying handles on graphical objects only when they are selected.

Visual Representations

A general difficulty with direct manipulation is choosing visual representations [26, 28], and this is compounded for surrogate interaction where the surrogates may represent multiple, abstract, or even intangible objects. For example, in our vector editor, we designed the visual representation of the abstract shape surrogate as a combination of a circle, a line, and a rectangle (Figure 10). This may be even more difficult for intangible attributes, such as spacing, sorting, or layout. In such instances, we found ourselves using indirect widgets such as combo boxes or spinners to control such attributes. However, by situating widgets in the context of their use—e.g., on the surrogates—we can still minimize the cognitive and spatial indirection. Moreover, surrogate interaction frees designers from having to create visual representations suitable for use in the actual display, a difficult task for abstract objects. Surrogates for abstract objects, on the other hand, can be heavily annotated to ease understanding and usage.

CONCLUSIONS AND FUTURE WORK

We have presented surrogate interaction, a framework that unifies a large set of existing commercial and academic techniques into a comprehensive interaction model. In the model, users interact with surrogates of an application's domain objects. Actions to a surrogate will affect the connected domain object. This avoids cluttering the display with the multitude of controls necessary to interact with attribute-rich objects. Furthermore, the surrogates can be used to interact with multiple objects simultaneously, and can even be created for intangible objects, such as layout or spacing, and for attributes that only exist in the context of a group, such as sorting order or alignment. We have also presented design examples that showcase the interaction model.

The design space defined by direct manipulation and instrumental interaction is clearly very large, and surrogate interaction is just one example of a part of this space that can be profitable for certain situations and for certain applications. We will continue to explore surrogate interaction and its applications in the future, but also the whole design space of this area. We also plan to investigate the concept of meta-instruments and their corresponding meta-objects.

REFERENCES

1. N. Andrienko and G. Andrienko. *Exploratory Analysis of Spatial and Temporal Data: A Systematic Approach.* Springer-Verlag, 2006.
2. Apple Inc. Keynote. `http://www.apple.com/iwork/keynote/`.
3. M. Beaudouin-Lafon. Instrumental interaction: an interaction model for designing post-WIMP user interfaces. In *Proceedings of the ACM CHI Conference on Human Factors in Computing Systems*, pages 446–453, 2000.
4. M. Beaudouin-Lafon. Designing interaction, not interfaces. In *Proceedings of the ACM Conference on Advanced Visual Interfaces*, pages 15–22, 2004.
5. B. Buxton. HCI and the inadequacies of direct manipulation systems. *SIGCHI Bulletins*, 25(1):21–22, 1993.
6. W. S. Cleveland and M. E. McGill, editors. *Dynamic Graphics for Statistics.* Wadsworth & Brooks/Cole, Pacific Grove, CA, USA, 1988.
7. P. R. Cohen, M. Dalrymple, D. B. Moran, F. C. N. Pereira, J. W. Sullivan, R. A. G. Jr, J. L. Schlossberg, and S. W. Tyler. Synergistic use of direct manipulation and natural language. In *Proceedings of the ACM CHI Conference on Human Factors in Computing Systems*, pages 227–233, 1989.

8. P. Dourish. *Where the Action Is: The Foundations of Embodied Interaction*. MIT Press, 2001.

9. C. Esposito, W. B. Paley, and J. Ong. Of mice and monkeys: A specialized input device for virtual body animation. In *Proceedings of the ACM Symposium on Interactive 3D Graphics*, pages 109–114, 1995.

10. C. Forlines, D. Vogel, and R. Balakrishnan. Hybrid-Pointing: fluid switching between absolute and relative pointing with a direct input device. In *Proceedings of the ACM Symposium on User Interface Software and Technology*, pages 211–220, 2006.

11. D. Frohlich. Direct manipulation and other lessons. In M. Helander, T. K. Landauer, and P. V. Prabhu, editors, *Handbook of Human-Computer Interaction*, pages 463–488. 1997.

12. D. M. Frohlich. The history and future of direct manipulation. *Behaviour & Information Technology*, 12(6):315–329, 1993.

13. E. Gamma, R. Helm, R. Johnson, and J. Vlissides. *Design Patterns: Elements of Reusable Object-Oriented Software*. Addison-Wesley, 1995.

14. H. Ishii and B. Ullmer. Tangible bits: Towards seamless interfaces between people, bits and atoms. In *Proceedings of the ACM CHI Conference on Human Factors in Computing Systems*, pages 234–241, 1997.

15. R. J. K. Jacob, A. Girouard, L. M. Hirshfield, M. S. Horn, O. Shaer, E. T. Solovey, and J. Zigelbaum. Reality-based interaction: a framework for post-WIMP interfaces. In *Proceedings of the ACM CHI Conference on Human Factors in Computing Systems*, pages 201–210, 2008.

16. C. N. Klokmose and M. Beaudouin-Lafon. VIGO: instrumental interaction in multi-surface environments. In *Proceedings of the ACM CHI Conference on Human Factors in Computing Systems*, pages 869–878, 2009.

17. P. Maes. Agents that reduce work and information overload. *Communications of the ACM*, 37(7):30–40, July 1994.

18. D. A. Norman. *The Design of Everyday Things*. The MIT Press, 1988.

19. K. Perlin and D. Fox. Pad: An alternative approach to the computer interface. In *Computer Graphics (Proceedings SIGGRAPH'93)*, pages 57–64, 1993.

20. M. P. Peterson. Active legends for interactive cartographic animation. *International Journal of Geographical Information Science*, 13(4):375–383, 1999.

21. J. S. Pierce, B. C. Stearns, and R. Randy Pausch. Voodoo dolls: Seamless interaction at multiple scales in virtual environments. In *Proceedings of the ACM Symposium on Interactive 3D Graphics*, pages 141–145, 1999.

22. I. Poupyrev, M. Billinghurst, S. Weghorst, and T. Ichikawa. The go-go interaction technique: Non-linear mapping for direct manipulation in VR. In *Proceedings of the ACM Symposium on User Interface Software and Technology*, pages 79–80, 1996.

23. J. Rekimoto. Pick-and-drop: A direct manipulation technique for multiple computer environments. In *Proceedings of the ACM Symposium on User Interface Software and Technology*, pages 31–39, 1997.

24. N. H. Riche, B. Lee, and C. Plaisant. Understanding interactive legends: a comparative study with standard widgets. *Computer Graphics Forum*, 29(3):1193–1202, 2010.

25. B. Shneiderman. The future of interactive systems and the emergence of direct manipulation. *Behaviour and Information Technology*, 1(3):237–256, 1982.

26. B. Shneiderman. Direct manipulation: A step beyond programming languages. *Computer*, 16(8):57–69, 1983.

27. B. Shneiderman and P. Maes. Direct manipulation vs. interface agents. *Interactions*, 4(6):42–61, 1997.

28. B. Shneiderman and C. Plaisant. *Designing the User Interface: Strategies for Effective Human-Computer Interaction*. Addison-Wesley, 5th edition, 2009.

29. J. H. Siegel, E. J. Farrell, R. M. Goldwyn, and H. P. Friedman. The surgical implication of physiologic patterns in myocardial infarction shock. *Surgery*, 72(1):126–141, 1972.

30. R. Stoakley, M. J. Conway, and R. Pausch. Virtual reality on a WIM: Interactive worlds in miniature. In *Proceedings of the ACM CHI Conference on Human Factors in Computing Systems*, pages 265–272, 1995.

31. The Omni Group. OmniGraffle Professional. `http://www.omnigroup.com/products/omnigraffle/`.

32. M. E. Tudoreanu and D. Hart. Interactive legends. In *Proceedings of the ACM Southeast Regional Conference*, pages 448–453, 2004.

33. E. Tufte. *The Visual Display of Quantitative Information*. Graphics Press, 1983.

34. E. Tufte. *Beautiful Evidence*. Graphics Press, 2006.

35. A. van Dam. Post-WIMP user interfaces. *Communications of the ACM*, 40(2):63–67, Feb. 1997.

36. W. Willett, J. Heer, and M. Agrawala. Scented widgets: Improving navigation cues with embedded visualizations. *IEEE Transactions on Visualization and Computer Graphics*, 13(6):1129–1136, Nov./Dec. 2007.

37. C. Williamson and B. Shneiderman. The Dynamic HomeFinder: Evaluating dynamic queries in a real-estate information exploration system. In *Proceedings of the ACM Conference on Research and Development in Information Retrieval*, pages 338–346, 1992.

38. Yahoo! Inc. Yahoo pipes. `http://pipes.yahoo.com`.

An Actuated Physical Puppet as an Input Device for Controlling a Digital Manikin

Wataru Yoshizaki[1,2], Yuta Sugiura[3,4], Albert C Chiou[4], Sunao Hashimoto[4], Masahiko Inami[3,4], Takeo Igarashi[4,5], Yoshiaki Akazawa[2], Katsuaki Kawachi[2], Satoshi Kagami[2], Masaaki Mochimaru[2]

[1]NAIST, Nara, Japan wataru-y@is.naist.jp

[2]DHRC AIST Tokyo, Japan {y-akazawa, k.kawachi, s.kagami, m-mochimaru}@aist.go.jp

[3]Keio Univ. Kanagawa, Japan inami@inami.info

[4]JST ERATO Tokyo, Japan hashimoto@designinterface.jp

[5]The Univ. of Tokyo Tokyo, Japan takeo@acm.org

ABSTRACT

We present an actuated handheld puppet system for controlling the posture of a virtual character. Physical puppet devices have been used in the past to intuitively control character posture. In our research, an actuator is added to each joint of such an input device to provide physical feedback to the user. This enhancement offers many benefits. First, the user can upload pre-defined postures to the device to save time. Second, the system is capable of dynamically adjusting joint stiffness to counteract gravity, while allowing control to be maintained with relatively little force. Third, the system supports natural human body behaviors, such as whole-body reaching and joint coupling. This paper describes the user interface and implementation of the proposed technique and reports the results of expert evaluation. We also conducted two user studies to evaluate the effectiveness of our method.

ACM Classification: I.3.6 [Computer Graphics]: Methodology and Techniques - Interaction Techniques; I.3.1 [Computer Graphics]: Hardware Architecture - Input devices.

General terms: Design, Human Factors

Keywords: input device, posture, force feedback, robot.

INTRODUCTION

A physical prop can be a powerful input device for controlling the posture of a rigged character [1, 15, 16, 23, 9, 10]. It offers many advantages compared with standard pointing devices such as the mouse. It provides a natural three-dimensional (3D) perspective, rather than just a two-dimensional (2D) screen, and both hands can be used to control 6 × 2 degrees of freedom (DOFs) without difficulty [13]. Moreover, the physical prop can provide direct tactile feedback, which is missing from abstract 3D input devices. Most importantly, the system can leverage a person's built in "hand intelligence" in operational tasks. However, existing prop-based input devices are mostly passive. The user sets the individual joint angles manually, but the system does not provide any active feedback. Also, these devices must usually be held by the user to maintain the desired posture against the force of gravity.

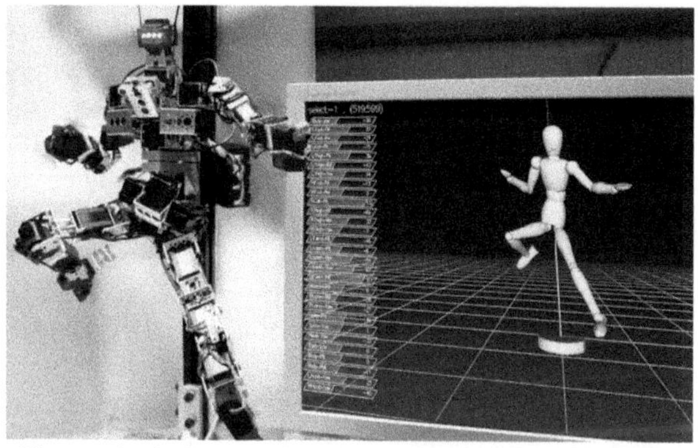

Figure 1: Active marionette system. The user controls the character by manipulating the device.

In this research, we add active control to a prop-based input device. A servomotor is attached to each DOF of a joint, and drives the joint. Actuation is useful in many ways. First, the user can upload pre-defined postures or the results of previous edits to the device to save time. Second, the system is capable of dynamically adjusting joint stiffness to counteract gravity, while allowing control to be maintained with relatively little force. Third, the system supports natural human body behaviors, such as whole-body reaching and joint coupling, by using measured human data.

Our primary target application is control of the digital or computer manikins used in product design [8,14]. A designer inserts a digital manikin in a virtual model of a product being designed in order to carry out ergonomics assessments of such factors as reachability and visibility. For example, an automotive designer places a virtual driver on the seat to ascertain that the driver can see and reach the console. Digital manikins have become a fundamental technology that is indispensable in industry. Various commercial products already exist (e.g., Jack from Siemens, RAMSIS from Human Solutions) and are widely used in the design of automobiles, airplanes, factory assembly lines, etc. However, a digital manikin has many degrees of freedom, and its control is notoriously difficult. Various techniques such as inverse kinematics have been proposed, but the problem has not yet been completely solved. We hope to address this issue by introducing a novel hardware solution and thus contribute to the manufacturing industry.

We first discuss related work and explain the basic user-interaction features of the device. We then describe the implementation of our prototype system, as well as the results of qualitative evaluations by experts and quantitative evaluations by test users. One evaluation compared our system with the standard mouse-based technique and a passive puppet device. Another compared the performance of our system with and without data-driven inverse kinematics. We conclude with a discussion of possible application scenarios for our system.

RELATED WORK

Several previous attempts have been made to use physical props as input devices for character posture control. Knep et al. [16] and Esposito et al. [9] developed systems for animating an articulated figure via a physical skeleton covered with sensors that monitor the orientations of the joints. Feng et al. [10] built a similar system with a vision sensor. Hinckley [13] introduced a prop-based, two-handed user interface for neurosurgical visualizations, allowing a surgeon to specify a cross-section for viewing by holding a plastic plate next to a miniature head. Weller et al. [23] introduced a hub-and-strut construction kit called Posey, in which the components report their physical configuration and relative orientation to a computer, which then constructs a corresponding virtual representation. Although these solutions have overcome a number of difficulties inherent in working with a 2D environment, the input devices are passive and thus can only pass information to the virtual environment without providing any feedback or active support to the user.

Force feedback is already popular in virtual reality applications such as surgical simulations [4] and remote manipulator control [22]. Some systems use force feedback for geometric editing [11] and painting [2], but their goal is to provide specific sensations to the user's finger or hand; the form factor of the device itself is not significant in these applications. In contrast, the shape of the input device is critical in character posing, and force feedback is used to assist in the control of a rigged character.

Although most of the research effort in robotics is focused on autonomous behavior, some systems do explicitly focus on interactivity. Sekiguchi et al. [20] developed the RobotPHONE system, in which two teddy bear robots are remotely connected through a network, and their postures are synchronized. Raffle et al. [18] created Topobo, a 3D constructive assembly system with kinetic memory, in which the actuator component recalls user operations and replays the motions. Shimizu et al. [21] introduced a teddy bear robot as a generic game controller. The main applications of these systems are entertainment and education. Our work builds on these attempts and uses a robot for the control of digital manikin with more DOFs in more goal-oriented tasks.

ACTUATED PUPPET INTERACTION

This section explains the features of our active puppet device from the user's point of view. Implementation details will be described in the next section. The basic idea is to add a servomotor to each joint of a puppet input device to support posture control by providing active feedback. In this work, we focus on the following three features: posture loading, gravity compensation, and active guidance using measured human data.

Posture loading

The posture design process rarely starts from scratch and often involves a small modification of an existing posture. The user might begin with a predefined canonical posture, such as sitting, standing, crouching, etc., and then adjust it to obtain a specific target posture. Alternatively, the user might start with the result of a previous editing task and further explore that result with additional modifications. Animation consists of a lengthy sequence of slightly different postures, and the design of a posture in a given frame usually begins with the posture in the previous frame.

Active joints can support this process by loading the existing posture into the puppet device. The user first selects the initial posture on the computer screen, loads the posture into the puppet device, and then modifies the posture by manipulating the puppet. This process is much simpler and faster than the use of a passive puppet, whose posture must be manually matched with the initial posture.

Intelligent Gravitational Compensation

Most existing passive puppet devices cannot independently maintain their postures against the force of gravity and must be held by the user. If each joint were stiff enough to counteract gravity on its own, the joints would be too hard to rotate manually.

Active joints address this problem by dynamically changing their stiffness. If the user is not controlling a joint, the system makes the joint stiff enough to hold its configuration against gravity. If the user is controlling the joint, the system makes the joint flexible enough to be freely rotated by the user.

Our current prototype puppet device successfully maintains its posture against the force of gravity, while allowing the rotation of a joint with a force as small as that typically applied by the little finger.

Active Guidance Using Measured Human Data

The human body has many hard and soft constraints, and it is important to design postures satisfying these constraints. Otherwise, the results will look very unrealistic. An active puppet can assist the user in complying with these constraints by providing active feedback based on measured human data.

One important point is that these constraints are not independent for each joint. If the constraints were simply a matter of an acceptable range of rotation angles for each joint, it would be straightforward to implement them with a passive puppet. However, some constraints involve multiple joints, and enforcement of these constraints is only possible with active feedback.

Our current prototype system supports natural reaching and joint coupling by using measured human data. Natural reaching takes the position of a hand as input and adjusts the joint angles to bring the hand to the desired position. The human body has redundant degrees of freedom for bringing an end effecter (e.g., a hand) to a position in space, and measured data resolve this ambiguity. Joint coupling is the interdependency between nearby joints, and our current prototype supports coupling between hip and knee joints. As the angle of the hip joint approaches 90 degrees, it becomes difficult to keep the knee joint straight.

IMPLEMENTATION

Our active puppet system consists of a handheld puppet device and a control program running on a host PC (Figure 2). All joints of the puppet device are actuated by servomotors made for hobby purposes by Futaba Co., with an RS485 serial interface to control and measure the parameters. The servomotors are connected to the host PC via cable. The host PC uses a simulation model of the puppet for physical simulations, and the postures of the puppet and the simulation model are synchronized at up to 15 Hz. A human interface program displays a 3D graphical model of the virtual puppet. This visualization model may have a different shape from the handheld puppet.

When the operator changes a joint angle of the handheld puppet, the system changes the corresponding joint angle of the simulation model, and this is reflected in the visualization model shown on the display via a mapping function. When the operator changes a joint angle of the visualization model, the change is passed to the simulation model, and the system changes the corresponding joint angle of the puppet device by controlling the appropriate servomotor.

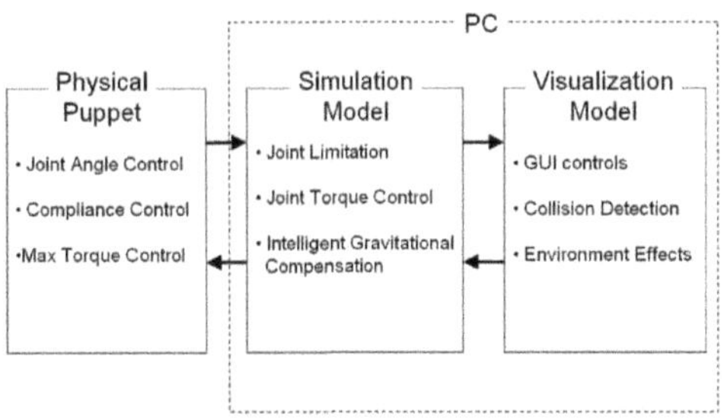

Figure 2: System configuration.

Handheld Puppet Hardware

The puppet is 40 cm in height and has 32 DOFs (joints). Figure 3 shows the overall configuration and joint specifications. The head and torso have 3 DOFs each to achieve human-like motion, such as standing on one leg. The shoulder has an extra degree of freedom to pull the arm to the front, allowing natural arm motion. The knee has a large joint angle to accommodate the "Seiza" posture (sitting down Japanese style, with the buttocks on top of the ankles).

Additionally, there is a hook for hanging the puppet by the waist joint to help generate free leg motion. With this, the user does not need to support the device manually. The hook has two DOFs to measure and control the roll and pitch of the entire body. (whole body part in Figure 3)

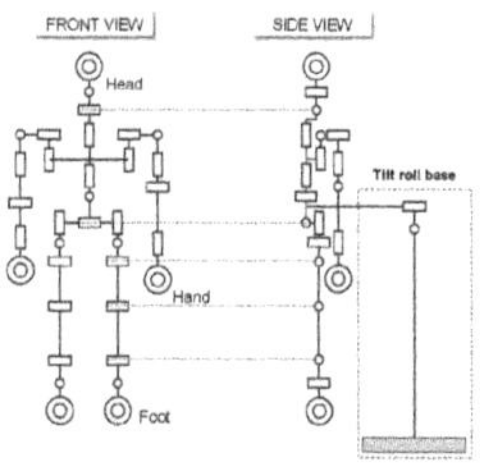

Body Part	Joint	Axis Direction	Servo
Arm	Shoulder	Roll, Yaw	RS302CD
		Pitch	RS301CR
	Elbow	Pitch	RS302CD
	Wrist	Yaw	
	Clavicle	Yaw	
Leg	Ankle	Pitch, Roll	RS301CR
	Knee	Pitch	
	Hip	Roll, Pitch, Yaw	
Torso	Waist	Roll, Pitch, Yaw	
Head	Neck	Roll, Pitch, Yaw	RS302CD
Whole body	Spine	Roll, Pitch	RS601CR

Figure 3: Hardware configuration.

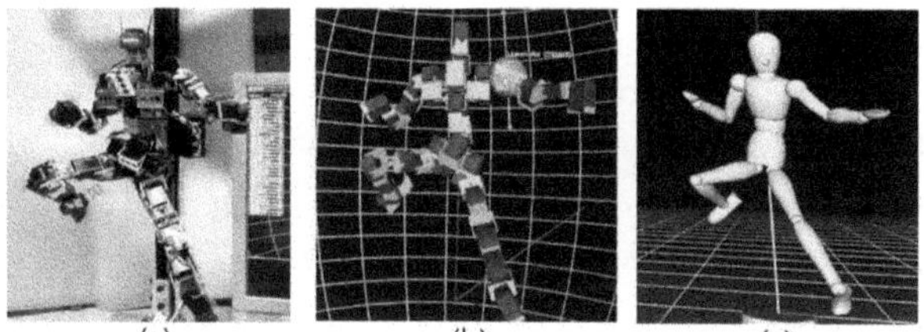

Figure 4: (a) puppet, (b) simulation model, (c) visualization model.

Communication between the Puppet and the Host PC

The servomotors (RS301CR, RS302CD, RS601CR, Futaba Co.) used for the puppet have RS485 serial communication to measure and control each joint. Table 1 shows their specifications. The parameters of these servomotors are target joint angle, servo gain, maximum torque, current joint angle, current torque, current temperature, and so on. The servo motors do not need any calibration. The servomotors are daisy chained and conduct two-way communications with the host PC using the RS-485 protocol. The host PC controls the target angle, servo gain, torque on/off, and maximum torque of each servomotor. The servo gain defines the relationship between the displacement angle and torque with which the system controls the stiffness of each joint. Each servomotor sends the current angle and temperature back to the host PC. The system then estimates the current torque from the current angle and servo gain setting (see Appendix for detail).

We use 115,200-bps serial communications in our current implementation, and the main control loop (which reads the data from the servomotors, computes the necessary torques, and sends the control commands to the servomotors) operates at approximately 10 fps. Hence, there is a delay of approximately 100 milliseconds before the user receives the force feedback from the system. This rate is significantly slower than standard haptic devices, but it is adequate because our goal is to assist the user's modeling operations, rather than to provide sensory illusions. Our current target is the design of static postures, and so this rate is acceptable. However, it might be necessary to support a faster loop for the design of animations by real-time performance.

Table 1 :Servomotor Specifications

	RS301	RS302	RS601
Torque	5	7.1	21
Baud rate [kbps]	9.6 ~ 460	9.6 ~ 460	9.6 ~ 1300
Weight [g]	21	27	91
Size [mm]	35.8 × 19.6 × 25.0	35.8 × 19.6 × 25.0	59 × 26 × 47.1
Speed [sec/60deg]	0.11	0.16	0.17
Angle Range [deg]	-150 ~ 150	-150 ~ 150	-120 ~ 120
Power [mA]	110	100	150

Simulation Model and Visualization Model

The simulation model maintains the configuration of the puppet device and its physical properties, such as the center of gravity and weight of each limb. The system matches the posture of the simulation model to that of the puppet device and uses the simulation model to predict the force that must be applied to each joint for gravitational compensation.

The visualization model represents the target character of the modeling task. The body configuration of the visualization model is freely adjustable. The mapping between the postures of the simulation model and the visualization model can be chosen arbitrarily, but in our current implementation we directly map raw joint angles. This can cause a mismatch between the postures of the device and the visualization model. For example, a posture that is possible for the visualization model may not be possible for the puppet device because of collisions, and vice versa.

However, the mismatch is usually not very large, and the user can obtain a reasonable posture with the puppet device. If the posture of the visualization model requires fine-tuning, the device can be controlled while looking at the visualization model on the screen, as with mouse-based control. Collisions can a problem, but they do not occur frequently because our targets are mostly reaching and manipulation, rather than folding arms or crossing legs.

Intelligent Gravitational Compensation

The system must make each joint stiff enough to resist the force of gravity when it is not being controlled by the user. This is accomplished by applying a torque to each servomotor. However, a joint that is too stiff is difficult for the user to rotate. The typical approach is to apply a constant stiffness to resist gravity, but we found this to be a hindrance to quick posture control. We therefore adaptively reduce the stiffness of a joint while the user is controlling it. The detailed procedure is as follows.

The system constantly adjusts the servo gain (stiffness) by computing the necessary torque at each joint to compensate for gravity, taking into account the physical properties of the device and the current posture. This keeps the joint angles constant as long as no user intervention occurs. When the user applies force to rotate a joint, the system observes a small rotation at the joint as a difference between the current (θ) and target angle (θ_d). Using this information, the system identifies the initiation of user control and reduces the stiffness by adjusting the servo gain. This allows the user to control the joint with a smaller amount of force. When control of the joint is relinquished, the user must hold the position for a short time. The system identifies this pause by detecting no change in the angle of rotation for a certain period, and then restores the original stiffness. Our method is based on a standard gravity compensation technique in the literature [5]. We tailored a popular method to work with our hardware configuration. Details are in the appendix.

Adaptive Range of Motion

There is a hardware limitation on each joint angle. A servomotor can usually rotate about 300 (deg), but this angle is sometimes too wide compared with the actual human range of motion, especially at the knees and elbows. Maximizing the torque when a joint angle reaches a human limitation assists users in generating realistic postures.

Joint Coupling

The joints of the human body are not independent, and they interfere with one another. For example, the knee joint and the hip joint are coupled. If the hip joint is rotated to 90°, it is difficult to hold the knee joint straight. We implement this joint coupling to facilitate the design of natural human postures. Because joint coupling is most prominent at the knee and hip joints, we do not include coupling of other joints in the current system. Figure 4 shows the acceptable region of hip and knee joint combinations. When the angles are outside this region, the system applies a torque to retract the limb to the nearest point inside the region. An expert in biomechanics defined the region manually based on his domain knowledge and the human posture database.

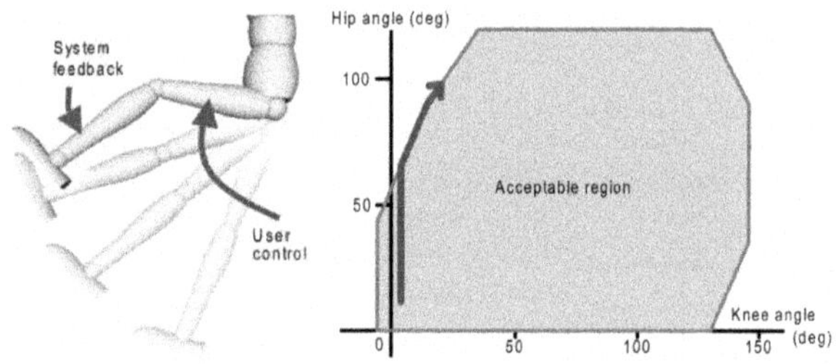

Figure 5: Joint coupling.

Natural Reaching by Data-driven Inverse-Kinematics

The active puppet system can generate natural whole body posture for a reaching action using measured human data. It calculates plausible whole body joint angles for the given hand position based on the posture database consisting of more than 1,500 different postures acquired from an optical motion capture system [24,19,12,17].

The data is obtained by measuring one subject person's pointing actions. He pointed given targets in both standing and sitting postures. The target points covered the surface of 100cm diameter cylinder around the subject's torso at 10cm grid. We captured 1536 sitting poses and 1584 standing poses.

When the user moves the puppet device, the system first computes the hand position from the current joint angles and simulation model configurations. The system then computes the desirable joint angles using the database and updates the posture of the puppet device as follows. We first compute a radial basis function (RBF) that interpolates the training data set. It takes hand position (in cylindrical polar coordinates around the body) as input and returns joint angles of the entire body as output. We then apply this RBF to the current hand position to obtain the desired whole-body pose. The hand position obtained by this interpolation does not exactly matches with the current hand position, so the system then applies standard inverse kinematics to match the hand position.

APPLICATION SCENARIOS

This section introduces several usage scenarios of the active puppet system in digital manikin applications, and reports on our informal experience with our prototype device.

Reachability assessment

One of popular applications of a digital manikin is to assess whether a specific position in a product is reachable from the user [6]. The designer places a digital manikin in the virtual scene and changes the posture of the manikin to examine if a target is reachable or not. For example, a designer places a digital manikin in front of a workbench and examines whether a tool on the bench is reachable, or places it on a car seat and determines whether control panels are reachable.

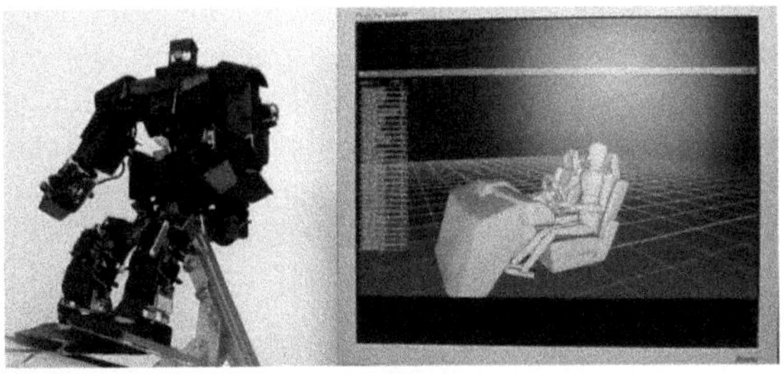

Figure 6: Reachability assessment.

We tested reachablity assessment for a car interior design scenario using our device. We prepared a 3D model of a car interior. It contains various devices that the user needs to touch and operate by hand while sitting on the seat, such as the steering wheel, driving handle, gearshift, and control panel for the air conditioner and audio system. The user places a digital manikin on the seat and reaches for these devices and tools by reaching the digital manikin's hand. If the hand touches a device, the device turns red to indicate that it is reachable. We tested this scenario with and without our active puppet device. It was much easier and more intuitive to operate using the device and we also found that the resulting postures are more natural compared to mouse control. Data-driven IK was particularly helpful because we can examine side effects of a reaching action caused by natural human body constraints such as the left arm moves as the user reaches with the right arm.

Load assessment

The other typical application of a digital manikin is to assess the load of each joint (or muscle, tendon, caput, socket, etc) under a given posture or task. If the load is too high, it causes damage to the user, so the product design needs to be changed. The active puppet system computes and displays the load of each joint in real time, so the user can easily evaluate and change the posture. The data-driven inverse kinematics further facilitates this process by automatically generating a natural posture for the given input.

We implemented an application in which the system computes the load applied to each joint from the current posture of the digital manikin. It shows joints with high load in red and those with low load in green as shown in Figure 7. We tested various postures on the application using the active puppet device and found that real-time feedback is very helpful to understand the relation between a posture and load distribution, as well as to find a posture with minimum load.

Figure 7: Load assessment

Visibility analysis

Visibility analysis examines whether specific targets are visible from the perspective of a person placed in the product. For example, the view from a car driver sitting in the driver's seat changes depending on the seat height and steering wheel position, and it is important to ensure that the driver clearly sees the outside environment. Visibility analysis is done by placing a digital manikin in a virtual environment and examining what is viewable from the digital manikin's eye position

We implemented an application in which a digital manikin sits on a driver seat and the system visualizes the visible area from the manikin's perspective. Visible area is shown as a pink cone as shown in Figure 8. Since the visible area depends on not only the head orientation but also overall posture of the character, it is beneficial to be able to control the entire body easily using the active puppet device. The active puppet device also makes it possible to control the posture while watching the manikin's view on the screen, which is very difficult for a mouse-based posture control.

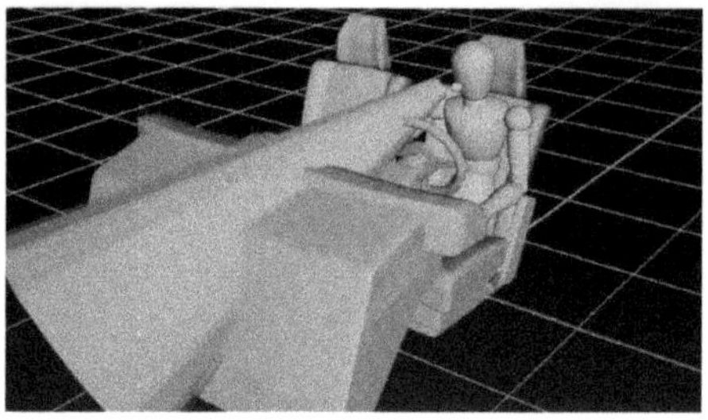

Figure 8: Visibility analysis

EVALUATION BY PROFESSIONAL USERS

We introduced our prototype system to professionals and asked them to evaluate it as potential users. We explained the concept, demonstrated the puppet system, and asked them to try it before soliciting feedback. We visited two companies. One was a game production company, and the other was a company that develops digital manikins.

Feedback from a Game Developer

We first visited the game production company and talked to a modeling expert. This individual is a member of the computer graphics department and works on geometry modeling and character posing. We introduced the device to him and then asked him to play with it for a while. The following is a summary of his feedback.

"The benefit of this device seems to be intuitive control. However, trained expert designers can fluently control character posture with a traditional user interface (manipulation of various widgets on the screen with a mouse), so the benefit of the puppet device is limited. I agree that it is nice to feel collisions with the environment as haptic feedback, but expert designers can easily design collision-avoiding postures with a traditional interface.

"A serious problem with the puppet device is that the joint structure is fixed. Game characters have various forms, and it is often necessary to handle a large variety of forms. Even human characters have a variety of configurations in a game. Furthermore, designers often assign special DOFs to control muscle bulging and flexible deformation of an arm, but these motions cannot be edited using the puppet.

"So I see limited value in this device for professional designers. However, I think the device might be useful for casual users to control character postures. For example, the puppet can be used as a controller for a character in a game. In this case, intuitive control without training is certainly attractive, and active feedback can be used to provide an engaging experience to the user. For example, the user can feel contact with the environment. It might be interesting to make the body difficult to control (stiffer) when the character is damaged in the game. "

Feedback from a Digital Manikin Developer

We then visited a company that develops various computer graphics softwares and devices. We talked to approximately 20 engineers who are working on the development of digital manikins and force feedback devices. We first introduced the device, and then asked them to play with it by themselves. The following is a summary of their comments.

"Digital manikins are used in the design of products such as furniture and car seats. The user can confirm that the size and form of the current design are ergonomically appropriate by placing the manikin in the product and checking for collisions without building a physical mock-up. A digital manikin usually provides a predefined set of body forms and postures that are transferable among different bodies. Some digital manikins have publicly available control APIs, so that control of existing commercial digital manikins is technically feasible with this puppet device.

"After playing with the device for a while, we feel that it is much easier to control character posture with the device than with a mouse. The users of digital manikins are mostly product designers and are not experts in character posing. Therefore, an intuitive control interface is very important. The ability of a device to maintain its own posture after release significantly contributes to productivity. Existing input devices such as Phantom and Polhemus cannot compensate for gravity and must be held by the user all the time. Active joints are also useful for representing various disabilities, such as paralysis on one side.

"We do see various limitations in the current implementation. First, there is a mismatch between the configuration of the puppet device and that of the digital manikin. This can cause unexpected collisions during control. The problem might be resolved to some extent by carefully tweaking the mapping, but this is not a perfect solution. It might be necessary to provide devices with different configurations or to make the puppet device physically reconfigurable. The number of joints might not be enough for some applications. We would probably need separate puppets for special purposes (for example, an arm-only device with many DOFs might be useful for detailed arm posturing). An active puppet seems to be useful for the design not only of static postures, but also of animations. It would be better to be able to use the device to represent a jumping motion by allowing vertical movement at the base."

COMPARISON WITH MOUSE AND PASSIVE PUPPET

We conducted two user studies. This section describes the first study, in which we compared our active puppet device with a mouse interface and a passive puppet device. The goal was to show that our active device with gravity compensation makes posture control easier and faster. Intelligent inverse kinematics had not been implemented at this point.

Participants

We invited 11 participants for the study. They were all male university students in computer science. Two of the participants had prior experience in character posing, whereas the other nine had no posing experience. They were all new to the puppet input device.

Methods

We compared the proposed active puppet system with a traditional mouse-based interface and a passive puppet device. We implemented a custom-designed mouse-based interface for controlling the character posture. The reason we decided not to use existing commercial programs was so that we could make all the test conditions as similar as possible. The sophisticated methods of commercial packages such as Maya and Poser have their own constraints and make it difficult to consistently use identical settings. In this study, the user controlled the joint angles either by using sliders or by dragging end effectors (such as hands and feet) with inverse kinematics. The user could also control the viewing direction by dragging the mouse. Figure 10 shows a screen shot of the mouse-based interface.

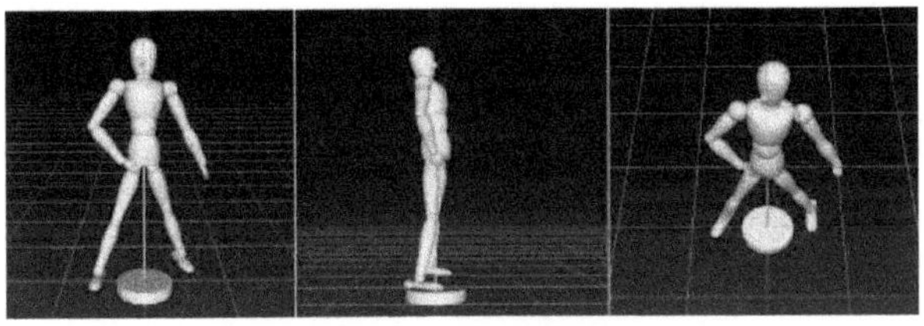

Figure 9: Example of a target posture shown to the participants.

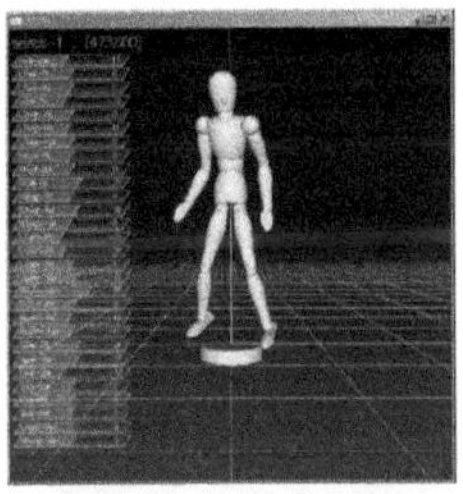

Figure 10: Screen shot of the mouse interface

The active puppet method used the system introduced in the previous section. We disabled uploading of pre-set postures because it provides too much advantage to the technique. Instead, we added a reset function so that the user could set the character posture back to a default position. We also disabled collision detection with the environment to minimize the factors influencing the results.

The passive puppet method used the same hardware as the active puppet method, but the puppet acted only as an input device. One way to implement this would be to turn off all the servomotors, but this would have been too difficult to control, as the user would have had to manually support all joints against the force of gravity. Therefore, we assigned a constant stiffness to each joint to compensate for gravity. This necessitated the use of more force to rotate a joint than with the active puppet used in this study.

Procedure

We used a within-subject procedure, in which each participant tested all three methods in a balanced order. Each participant designed three postures using each method, for a total of nine different postures in all. The same nine postures were assigned to all participants. The nine postures consisted of three groups of three postures: a group consisting of simple symmetric postures, a group consisting of asymmetric postures, and a group consisting of postures involving self-collision. The three control methods (passive, active, and mouse) were applied to these groups in a balanced way. Three screen shots of the character in the target posture, taken from different viewing angles, were printed on paper and presented to the participant, as shown in Figure 9. We imposed a cutoff time of three minutes to prevent excessively long operations. At the end of the session, we asked each participant to complete a questionnaire.

Results

Figure 11 and Figure12 show the task execution time and accuracy. We measured the accuracy as the sum of the squared errors of the joint angles. The error bar displays a 95% confidence interval. We analyzed the data via analysis of variance and found significant main effects for task execution time ($F_{2,20}$ = 33.72) and task execution accuracy ($F_{2,20}$=3.33). We then run a Tukey-Kramer post hoc pairwise comparison and the result is shown in Figure 11 and Figure12 as * marks (they show statistically significant differences ($p<0.05$)).

The active puppet was significantly faster than the mouse-based interface and the passive puppet ($p < 0.05$). Comments from the participants and our own observations showed that the automatic reduction of joint stiffness during control played an important role.

The active puppet was not significantly more accurate than the passive puppet ($p > 0.05$), but was significantly more accurate than the mouse-based interface ($p < 0.05$). This is somewhat counter intuitive (mouse seems to be more accurate), but the main reason is that many users failed to complete a task within the cut off time when using a mouse and this significantly increase the average errors.

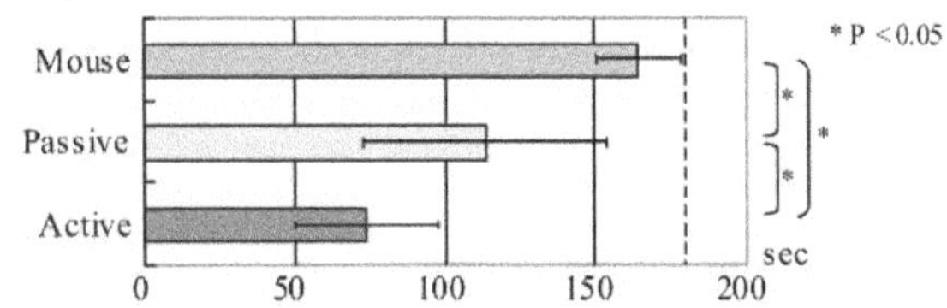

Figure 11: Task execution time.

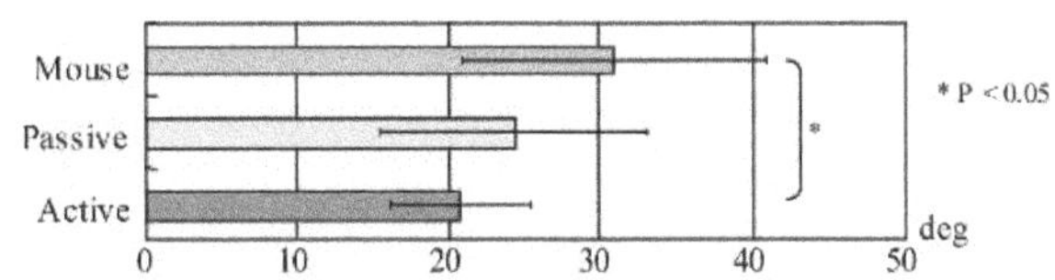

Figure12: Task execution accuracy.

Some participants complained that the end-effector positions of the virtual character were different from those of the puppet. This is because the physical structure (limb length and joint structure) of the virtual character is different from that of the physical puppet, which is a fundamental limitation of puppet devices. However, the users were still able to obtain most of the postures by controlling the individual joints while observing the posture of the virtual character on the screen. Although we did not explicitly explain this in the study, we feel that it will be necessary to include such an explanation in a tutorial for future first-time users.

Figure 13 shows the results of the questionnaire. We analyzed the data via analysis of variance and found a significant main effect on all questions ($F_{2,20}$=282.1, 301.9, 242.4, and 245). We run a non-parametric analysis (Steel-Dwass method) and the results are shown in Figure 13 as * marks (they show statistically significant differences ($p<0.05$)). Five of six participants chose the active puppet as the best method. One participant judged the active and passive puppets to be equal. This participant reported that the puppet device seemed too fragile, and he operated it very slowly, making it difficult to observe any differences between the active and passive methods.

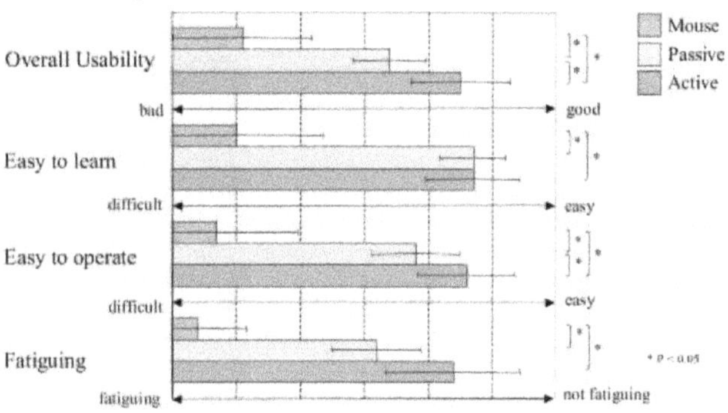

Figure 13: Questionnaire results.

The questionnaire results also showed that the active puppet caused the least amount of fatigue. We expected that the active puppet would cause less fatigue than the passive one, but it is significant that it also caused less fatigue than the mouse-based interface. Comments from the participants indicated that the active stiffness control and shorter operating time contributed to this result.

This result demonstrates the potential effectiveness of active feedback in this particular context, but it still cannot be concluded that our active puppet device is better than the best possible passive device. An ideal passive device would not have servomotors at each joint, and thus would be much lighter and easier to control. We did not test such a passive device because building special hardware solely for the purpose of this study would have been too costly. A perfectly fair comparison would be difficult to accomplish in any case if the form factors of the devices were significantly different.

EVALUATION OF DATA-DRIVEN INVERSE KINEMATICS

We ran a second user study to evaluate the effect of intelligent inverse kinematics (IK). In this evaluation, we asked the user to design reaching postures using our active puppet device with and without data-driven IK.

Participants

Ten participants joined the study. They were undergraduate or graduate students majoring in computer science. No participants except one had experience in virtual character posing using commercial software. Three users had joined the study described in the previous section.

Methods

The task was to pose a character using our active puppet device so that the hand reaches a target position in the environment. The participants designed given postures with and without data-driven IK and we compared task completion times and the quality of the resulting postures. We enabled gravity compensation in both conditions.

Procedure

We first described how to use the system for approximately 3 minutes to a participant and had him or her practice it for approximately 5 minutes. Figure 14 shows the virtual environment we used. The user points slots in the shelf highlighted in red by the right hand of the digital manikin. The digital manikin points at the top-left corner before starting a task. Starting from this configuration, the task was to point to the left-bottom, right-bottom, top-right, and top-left corner in that order. We measured the time need to complete this cycle (4 pointings). Each participant tested both conditions in a balanced order. They answered questionnaire at the end. They subjectively rated the quality of the postures they just designed in the questionnaire.

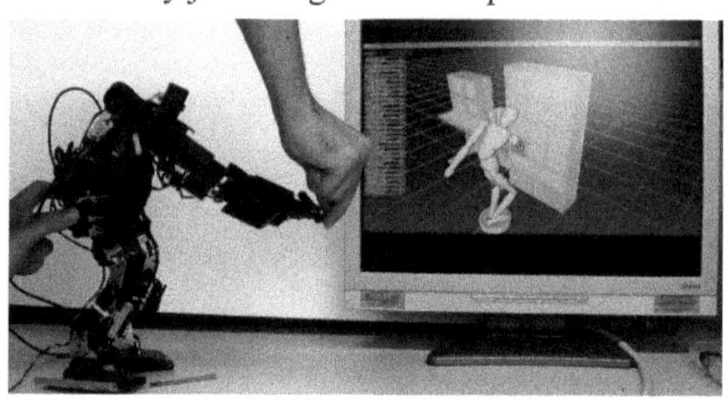

Figure 14: Environment used in the study.

Result

Figure 15 shows the task completion time. Error bars show the standard deviation. A paired t-test shows a significant difference between the two ($p < 0.05$). The graph shows that the participants completed the task approximately two times faster with data-driven IK. Figure 16 shows the results of the users' own subjective evaluation of the quality of the resulting postures (5 is the best). These results also shows that the posture designed with data-driven IK was significantly more satisfactory ($p<0.05$). We observed that the quality of the resulting postures showed large variations depending on the user's skill when designing without data-driven IK, while the quality was uniformly high when using data-driven IK.

Participants especially appreciated that data-driven IK automatically controls the lower body (waist and leg) joints when moving the hand. Control of the lower body was necessary when the user points to high or low targets. This was tedious when data-driven IK was not enabled, because the user needs to control the lower body manually.

Note that data-driven IK does not always produce an exact posture the user wants. The user may want to intentionally design a posture that is different from that in the database. We expect that the user will first posture the digital manikin approximately by using data-driven IK and then adjust the posture in detail by turning off data-driven IK.

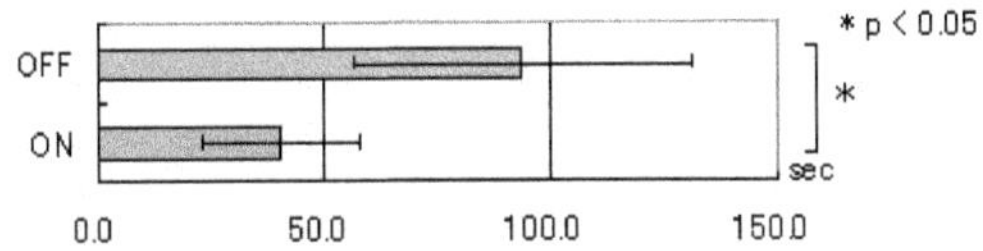

Figure 15: Task completion time

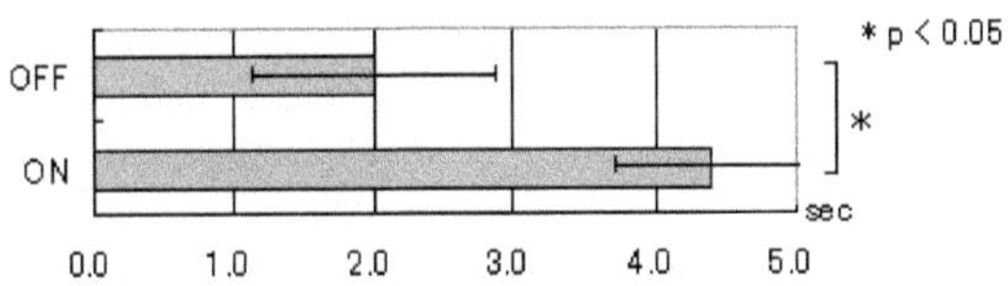

Figure 16: Subjective evaluation of the postures.

LIMITATIONS AND FUTURE WORK

One limitation of a physical puppet is that exactly matching the structure of the device to that of the target character is impossible. This results in a mismatch between the end-effector positions for the device and the virtual character. However, the user can still obtain most postures by controlling the individual joints while observing the posture of the virtual character. An exception to this would be when a collision occurs between the physical device and another object. In that case, it would be necessary to introduce some sort of clutching mechanism, or switch to a standard mouse interface to control the virtual character directly. In general we believe that the benefit of using active puppet outweigh these limitations especially in rapid prototyping phase.

Although we have focused on the design of static postures in this research, it should be possible to record dynamic motion with the device [7], and active feedback could be useful during such a procedure. For example, it might be possible for the user to swing one leg and let the system drive the other leg to design a walking motion [3]. Dynamic motion is more challenging because it requires faster actuation. However, the current hardware prototype can move reasonably fast, and we plan to explore this direction in the future.

Our current hardware implementation is an initial prototype and is built from off-the-shelf motors and frames, so the appearance is not very sophisticated. In the future, we plan to build a custom-made servo and frames to make a more human-like robot.

CONCLUSION

In this paper we proposed to add actuation to a physical puppet device and showed its feasibility with solid prototype implementation and a series of evaluations. The main technical novelty is in the data-driven inverse-kinematics applied to physical puppet. We showed that the active puppet method is faster than a mouse-based interface and the passive method with the same hardware in a study. We also showed that data-driven IK is useful for inexperienced users to obtain natural human postures. We demonstrated the device to developers of digital manikin and they saw value in rapid posture design made possible by the device.

REFERENCES

1. Arai, K. Cyber Bunraku. *ACM SIGGRAPH 97 Visual Proceedings,* (1997).
2. Baxter, B., Scheib, V., Lin, M. C., and Manocha, D. DAB: Interactive Haptic Painting with 3D Virtual Brushes. *Proc. SIGGRAPH '01*. (2001) ,461–468.
3. Chai, J., and Hodgins, J. Performance animation from low-dimensional control signals. *ACM Trans. Graph.* 24, 3 (July 2005), 686-696.
4. Cover, S. A., Ezquerra, N., O'Brien, J., Rowe, R., Gadacz, T., and Palm, E. Interactively Deformable Models for Surgery Simulation. *IEEE CG&A*, 13, 6. (1993), 68–75.
5. De Luca, A. and Panzieri, S. Learning gravity compensation in robots: Rigid arms, elastic joints, flexible links. *IJACSP*, 7, 5, (1993) 417-433.
6. Dempster, W. T. Space Requirements of the Seated Operator. *Technical Report WADC–TR–55–159*. Aerospace Medical Research Laboratory, Wright-Patterson Air Force Base, OH, (1955), 105–109.
7. Dontcheva, M., Yngve, G., Popović, Z. Layered Acting for Character Animation. *Proc. SIGGRAPH 2003*, (2003), 409–416.
8. Duffy, Vincent G. (eds.), *Handbook of Digital Human Modeling*, CRC Press, FL (2009)
9. Esposito, C., Paley, W. B., and Ong, J. Of mice and monkeys: a specialized input device for virtual body animation. *Proc. I3D '95*. (1995), 109-114.
10. Feng, T.C., Gunawardane, P., Davis, J., Jiang, B. Motion capture data retrieval using an artist's doll. *Proc. ICPR 2008*, (2008), 1-4.
11. Gaylean, T. A. and Hughes, J. F. Sculpting: An Interactive Volumetric Modeling Technique. *Proc. SIGGRAPH 1991*, (1991), 267–274.
12. Grochow, K., Martin, S. L., Hertzmann, A., and Popović, Z. Style-based Inverse Kinematics. *ACM Trans. Graph*. 23, 3 (Aug. 2004), 522–531.

13. Hinckley, K. Haptic Issues for Virtual Manipulation, Ph.D. Thesis, University of Virginia, (1997).

14. ISO 15536-2:2007(E) Ergonomics Comp. Manikins and Body Templates Part 2: Verification of Functions and Validation of Dimensions for Comp. Manikin Systems.

15. Johnson, M. P., Wilson, A., Blumberg, B., Kline, C., and Bobick, A. Sympathetic Interfaces: Using a Plush Toy to Direct Synthetic Characters. *Proc. CHI '99.*

16. Knep, B., Hayes, C., Sayre, R., and Williams, T. Dinosaur Input Device. *Proc. CHI 1995*, (1995), 304–309.

17. Mukai, T., Kuriyama, S. Geostatistical Motion Interpolation. *ACM Trans. Graph.* 24, 3 (2005), 1062-1070.

18. Raffle, H. S., Parkes, A. J., and Ishii, H. Topobo: A Constructive Assembly System with Kinetic Memory. *Proc. CHI '04*, (2004), 647–654.

19. Rose, C., Sloan, P., and Cohen, M. Artist-directed inverse-kinematics using radial basis function interpolation. *Computer Graphics Forum*, 20, (2001), 239–250.

20. Sekiguchi, D., Inami, M., and Tachi, S. RobotPHONE: RUI for Interpersonal Communication. *CHI '01 Extended Abstracts*, (2001), 277–278.

21. Shimizu, N., Koizumi, N., Sugimoto, M., Nii, H., Sekiguchi, D., and Inami, M. A Teddy-bear-based Robotic User Interface. *CIE* 4, 3 (July 2006), 8.

22. Tachi, S., Arai, H., and Maeda, T. Development of an Anthropomorphic Tele-existence Slave Robot. *Proc. ICAM '89*. JSME, (1989), 343–348.

23. Weller, M. P., Do, E. Y., and Gross, M. D. Posey: Instrumenting a Poseable Hub and Strut Construction Toy. *Proc. TEI '08*, (2008), 39–46.

24. Wiley D.J., Hahn J.K. Interpolation Synthesis of Articulated Figure Motion. *IEEE CG&A*, 17, 6, (1997), 39-45.

APPENDIX: GRAVITY COMPENSATION DETAILS

The servomotors have an RS485 serial interface, and the host PC controls them by reading the current angle θ and setting the servo gain K_{cw}, K_{ccw} and target angle θ_d (cw means clock-wise and ccw means counter-clock-wise). The output torque T is produced by the servomotor according to the current angle θ, target angle θ_d, and the given parameters via Eq. (1).Other parameters are T_p: punch, T_{max}: maximum torque, C_m: compliance margin. See figure below.

$$T^{t+1} = \begin{cases} \frac{T_{max} - T_p}{K_{cw}}(\theta^t - \theta_d^t - C_m) + T_p & (\theta_d^t - \theta^t > C_m) \\ 0 & (-C_m < \theta_d^t - \theta^t < C_m) \\ \frac{T_{max} - T_p}{K_{ccw}}(\theta^t - \theta_d^t + C_m) + T_p & (\theta_d^t - \theta^t < -C_m \end{cases} \quad (1)$$

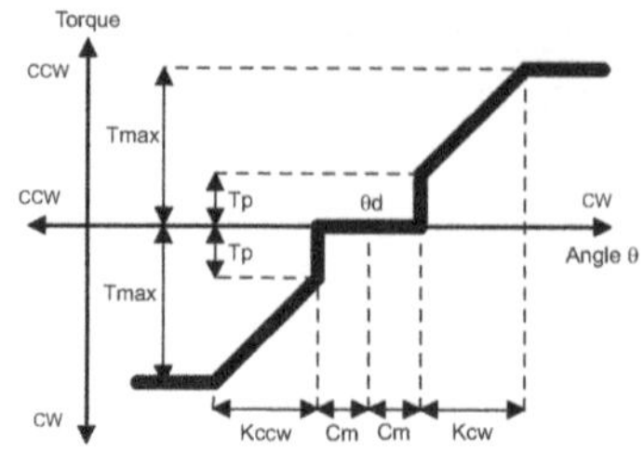

This will keep the difference in between the current angle θ and the target angle θ_d small unless a strong force is applied to the joint. If the difference exceeds a predefined threshold θ_{th}, the system assumes that the user intends to control the joint and updates the target angle θ_d as follows.

The torques T_{Tcw} and T_{Tccw} needed to overcome θ_{th} and thus start rotating the joint can be expressed as follows:

$$\theta_d^{t+1} = \begin{cases} \theta_d^t & (\theta_d^t - \theta^t > \theta_{th}) \text{ or } (\theta_d^t - \theta^t < -\theta_{th}) \\ \theta_d^{t+1} & (-\theta_{th} < \theta_d^t - \theta^t < \theta_{th}) \end{cases} \quad (2)$$

$$T_{Tcw}^t = \frac{T_{max} - T_p}{K_{cw}^t}(\theta_{th} - C_m) + T_p$$

$$T_{Tccw}^t = \frac{T_{max} - T_p}{K_{ccw}^t}(\theta_{th} - C_m) + T_p \quad (3)$$

T_{Tcw} and T_{Tccw} must be larger than gravitational forces T_{Gcw} and T_{Gccw} (one of which will be zero) applied to the joint in order to keep the current joint angle. The gravity forces are calculated via physical simulation. The force applied by the user's hand T_U is then obtained by subtracting T_G from T_T. We introduce a threshold T_{Uth} and start changing the θ_d when T_U exceeds T_{Uth}. So, we set T_{Tcw} and T_{Tccw} as follows

$$T_{Tcw}^t = T_{Gcw}^t + T_{Uth}$$

$$T_{Tccw}^t = T_{Gccw}^t + T_{Uth} \qquad (T_{Uth} \geq 0) \quad (4)$$

and then compute the gain as follows.

$$K_{cw}^{t+1} = \frac{T_{max} - T_p}{T_{Tcw}^t - T_p}(\theta_{th} - C_m)$$

$$K_{ccw}^{t+1} = \frac{T_{max} - T_p}{T_{Tccw}^t - T_p}(\theta_{th} - C_m) \quad (5)$$

This allows the system to compensate for gravity and yet be rotated via the small torque $T_U > T_{Uth}$ provided by the operator. As this gravity compensation technique is based on the difference between the current angle θ and the target angle θ_d, the cycle rate becomes critical if the user applies a quick rotation. Because our system is rather slow for haptic purposes, if the change in the target angle θ_F is greater than the threshold θ_{Fth}, the torque output is shut off to minimize the resistance.

In summary, the presudo code for the gravity compensation process is as followis

1. Read current angle θ
2. Calculate gravity force T_{Gcw} and T_{Gccw} by physical simulation
3. Calculate servo gain K_{cp} and K_{ccp}
4. Store current θ_d ($\theta_d' = \theta_d$)
5. If $\theta_d - \theta > \theta_{th}$ then $\theta_d = \theta$
6. If $\theta_d' - \theta_d > \theta_{Fth}$ then torque off else torque on
7. Go to 1

Roboshop: Multi-layered Sketching Interface for Robot Housework Assignment and Management

Kexi Liu[1&2], Daisuke Sakamoto[1], Masahiko Inami[1&3], Takeo Igarashi[1&4]

[1] JST ERATO IGARASHI Design Interface Project, 1-28-1-7F Koishikawa, Bunkyo, Tokyo 112-0002 Japan

[2] Department of Computer Science, Louisiana State University, 298 Coates Hall, Baton Rouge, LA 70803 USA

[3] Graduate School of Media Design, Keio University (KMD) 4-1-1 Hiyoshi, Kohoku, Yokohama, 223-8526 Japan

[4] Department of Computer Science, The University of Tokyo, 7-3-1 Hongo, Bunkyo, Tokyo, 113-0033 Japan

kliu9@tigers.lsu.edu, {sakamoto | inami}@designinterface.jp, takeo@acm.org

ABSTRACT

As various home robots come into homes, the need for efficient robot task management tools is arising. Current tools are designed for controlling individual robots independently, so they are not ideally suitable for assigning coordinated action among multiple robots. To address this problem, we developed a management tool for home robots with a graphical editing interface. The user assigns instructions by selecting a tool from a toolbox and sketching on a bird's-eye view of the environment. Layering supports the management of multiple tasks in the same room. Layered graphical representation gives a quick overview of and access to rich information tied to the physical environment. This paper describes the prototype system and reports on our evaluation of the system.

Author Keywords

Housework Management, Graphical User Interface, Sketching Interface, Home Robots, Human-Robot Interaction

ACM Classification Keywords

H5.2. Information interfaces and presentation (e.g., HCI): User Interfaces (D.2.2, H.1.2, I.3.6).

General Terms

Design

INTRODUCTION

Most people dream of having a personal assistant and living life like celebrities do. With a few words from the host, the personal assistant takes care of the host's household, screens his or her phone calls and E-mail, plans activities, and does other tasks to take care of the host. This dream has come partially true with the emergence of "electronic personal assistants", e.g., handheld devices. People are getting used to instructing these assistants to deal with their personal affairs, such as document and image editing, instant messaging, and web browsing, in information space.

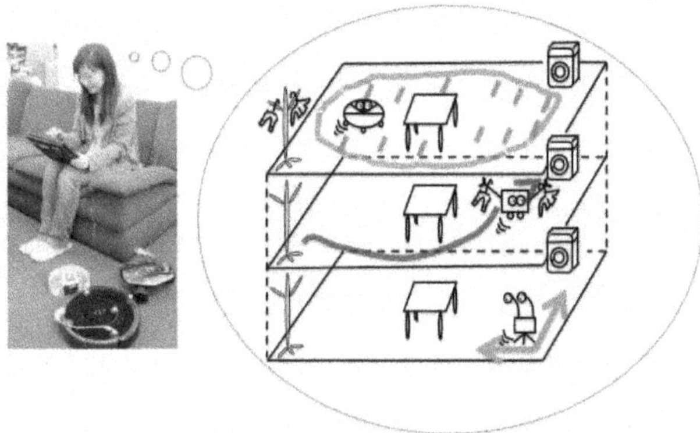

Figure 1: User sketching on the interface to assign tasks. She wants the vacuum robot to clean the living room at 8:00am, the grab&deliver robot to deliver clothes to the washer at 10:00am, and the video robot to record a video of the living room at 2:00pm.

However, help with activities in the physical world, e.g., house cleaning, object delivery, and dishwashing, by non-human assistants are still restricted and people tend to do those tasks themselves. One obvious reason is the shortage of advanced commercial home robots. Fortunately, significant efforts have been made by the electronics industry and we can now expect capable home robots to be on the market in the near future. However, if people use an independent robot control interface for each robot to assign tasks, then the users' separate manipulation efforts will still be unsatisfactory. A tool for managing coordinated action among multiple robots and appliances is needed.

Our goal is to provide an easy-to-use task management tool for multiple home robots so as to free people from the burden of setting up tasks. Users might like to have the whole house cleaned, with the windows opened to let in fresh air, and a vase of fresh flowers delivered to the living-room coffee table by a robot system. It might also be nice to have a robot system prepare for a dinner party, e.g., setting up the lighting, music, and gaming devices first and then getting cold beer and drinks out of refrigerator five minutes before the party starts. These scenarios require coordination among multiple robots: independent robot setting would introduce task organization problems.

To achieve such a goal, in this paper we propose a task management tool based on a graphical editing interface (Figure 1). Since the interface has a similar layout to Adobe® Photoshop®, we call it Roboshop. The user selects a tool from the toolbox and gives instructions to the robot system by sketching on a bird's-eye view of the environment. For example, the user might select the "vacuum" tool and specify the area to vacuum by coloring the area to be cleaned. We designed "Rainbow Sketch" to support multicolored freehand drawings with predesigned optional annotations. Rainbow Sketch aims to convey clear instructions to robots and also meaningful task details to users. The system also provides a layer mechanism to manage complex task composition as well as a grouping method to extract tasks of interest. Given that the system supports asynchronous heterogeneous robot controls, layers and grouping help users to review and manage the task sets efficiently. The overall advantage of using graphical representation is that it gives a quick overview of and access to information tied to the physical environment.

RELATED WORK

Intelligent Remote for Electronics

Along with the pervasiveness of home electronics, a universal remote control [33] is becoming a popular research topic, e.g., CRISTAL [26], Pronto [24] and inVoca [9]. A personal universal controller [21] is a slightly different interface since it supports self-programming. However, those studies did not focus on coordination among multiple robots. There are also many "smart home" projects, such as MIT's House_N [8], Smart house [18], "Ambient Intelligence" [3], "Living tomorrow" [16], and Roadie [15]. But those projects emphasize sensor technology or focus on the interface for controlling and debugging sets of appliances rather than on a tool for organizing multiple physical tasks to be executed by home robots.

Robot Control Medium in Home Environment

A realm of innovative robot instruction interfaces in the home environment, encompassing many interaction media, has been proposed since the emergence of home robots. Laser pointer-based user interfaces for giving robots instructions have been presented [1,10,14]. Matsumaru et al. [19,22] used a projected display and the interaction was based on a graphical user interface (GUI). Seifried et al. [26] developed a remote control system using touch-based actions on a multi-touch display in living areas. Zhao et al. [32] described a method that lets the user implicitly control a robot by issuing commands on real-world objects. While those systems allow users to invoke robot commands through various methods, they do not handle the reuse and editing of previous commands well: no direct strategy for managing command reuse through simple sketching, laser pointing, the use of remote controllers or paper cards. Roboshop's layers are intended to provide easy access to previously set commands and hence to enable them to be reused conveniently.

Sketch-based Interfaces

Various sketch-based interfaces have been intensively developed since tablets and PDAs have become our good friends. Chronis and Skubic [2] have developed a PDA interface through which the user sketches a route map as a means of directing a single robot along a designated path. Sakamoto et al. [25] present a synchronous control interface for commanding home robots by using stroke gestures on a computer display. Multi-modal robot interfaces that include the ability to sketch waypoints on top of a robot-sensed image have also been proposed [5, 23]. Lundberg et al. [17] have developed a similar PDA interface, which displays a map to designate a target location or a region to explore. Since these interfaces are designed for one-time robot control, the pen-stroke gestures are merely for dispatching simple commands to the robots, but not very suitable for describing and organizing multiple commands. Roboshop supports more structured sketching, called Rainbow Sketch, for the assignment and management of multiple tasks. In contrast to other sketch-based interfaces with plain trace-point drawing, Rainbow Sketch conveys rich information and task details with the predesigned supplementary annotations to users and dispatches concrete robot commands.

Robots for Household Tasks

Our work builds on various efforts to develop versatile robot platforms. The iRobot home robot series can perform a variety of house-cleaning tasks, such as vacuuming and mopping. HERB (home exploring robot butler) from a joint effort by Intel and CMU [28] is an autonomous mobile manipulator that performs useful manipulation tasks at home. Cody [12] from Georgia Tech Healthcare Robotics Lab is a humanoid mobile-manipulating robot. One distinctive feature of those two robots is that they can manipulate doors, cabinets, and other constrained objects using caging grasps (HERB) or equilibrium point controllers (Cody). Cooky [30] and Foldy [29] by Sugiura et al. can cook and fold clothes, respectively. The assistive robot EL-E [11] can fetch objects from flat surfaces. These robots, along with other education and entertainment home robots, will make robots into valuable members of many households. Our interface is thus designed to support a wide variety of home robots.

Multi-robot Control Interfaces

Several user interfaces that aim to control multiple robots have been implemented recently. Most of them instruct the robots directly. Kato et al. [13] developed a multi-touch interface to control multiple mobile robots simultaneously by manipulating a vector field in a bird's-eye view from a ceiling camera. This interface focused on driving multiple robots, rather instructing them to accomplish any tasks. Another existing system has been presented by Skubic et al. [27], who describe a system for communicating robot navigation tasks. The system works by having a user sketch a rough environment map and trajectory on a PDA. This interface is suitable when the environment is uncomplicated or the path-points need not be very precise. Glas et al. [6] introduced the teleoperation of multiple robots in the field of social robots, which lets a single operator simultaneously control up to four robots. These robots provide guidance in public places. Fong et al. [4] support multi-robot control and sketching waypoints on top of a map for remote robot driving. Both of these interfaces attempt to save limited resources, e.g., human attention, among multiple robots in order to make the synchronous control effective. Micire et al. tried to find the best gesture for controlling the team of robots in a multi-touch interface [20]. Our system lets users focus mostly on the tasks by supporting asynchronous workflow instructions to various robots in the home environment.

MOTIVATING SCENARIOS AND REQUIREMENTS

To clarify our goal, we first present some usage scenarios that motivated our research.

Scenarios

Scenario A: An old lady, Lily, lives alone. Her son intended to hire a housekeeper for her but she refused since she cannot fully trust an outsider. So instead he bought some home robots for his mother: an armed robot, which can pick up and deliver objects, and a vacuum-cleaning robot. Lily makes a simple sketch on her tablet screen to schedule the armed robot to get her pills for diabetes and hypertension twice a day at 9:00am and 3:00pm along with bottled water from the kitchen and bring them to the sofa so that she will never forget to take the pills even if she is preoccupied watching TV. After she has taken the day's pills, the robot should return the remaining pills and take the water back. Lily also sketches instructions for the vacuum robot to vacuum under the dining table at 1:30pm after lunch and at 7:00pm after dinner to remove crumbs on the floor. She also has it vacuum the whole house once a week.

This scenario shows that the interface needs to be easy to use, especially for elderly people. Users should be protected from the diversity and complexity of robot control panels. It is also preferable to be able to reuse the housework settings in the same environment.

Scenario B: A busy businessman, Bob, works from Monday through Friday until late. To keep his house in better condition, he bought three types of robots: a mobile camera robot, an armed robot, and a laundry robot. He usually does his grocery shopping weekly on Friday evening on his way home at around 7:00pm. Before he leaves work, he sketches on his tablet to instruct the mobile camera robot to photograph his kitchen, so he can check that the inventory of supplies is sufficient for the next week and also to take a photograph of the toilet so he can check the stock of toilet rolls and other daily needs. He sketches to instruct the armed robot and the laundry machine to collaborate in doing the laundry before he arrives home, so he can relax in peace and quiet without the noise of the washing machine.

This scenario shows that the system has to support asynchronous control. Besides, setting multiple tasks in a constrained location (Bob's apartment) requires spatial and temporal coordination. Assigning each task individually would create unintentional time overlaps or gaps. The interface needs a time scheduling mechanism to address possible task conflicts and inefficiencies.

Requirements

Below we summarize common operations that we hope will be executed by home robots.

Cleaning

Cleaning is a daily household chore and existing cleaning robots are very helpful, but have limitations. Cleaning dining areas after dinnertime as an everyday routine is trivial for a human but requires a considerable amount of setting up for robots, e.g., area specifications and time settings. When people encounter spots with stubborn dirt, they spend extra time cleaning them, but robots do not yet have such intelligence, so the users must explicitly specify an extended time. Moreover, if both vacuum and mop robots are present in the same room, coordinated action among them is necessary.

Delivery

Object delivery by robots saves a fair amount of labor. People might use a robot to tidy up the room after a party, e.g., gathering up gaming devices and storing them in a cupboard and throwing bottles into the recycle bin. The robot may also be capable of delivering clothes, newspaper/magazines, food and drinks from the fridge, and tools from the garage. These delivery tasks may require special instructions such as to move slowly when carrying fragile objects like wine glasses, avoid collisions with furniture, and collaborate with other robots to move a heavy object. Another benefit of robot delivery is the reliable automation of regular actions that a user might forget, as illustrated by the pill delivery in Lily's scenario.

Monitoring

Remote or automated monitoring of the home environment helps users check the house interior. A mobile webcam robot can not only monitor but also take photographs of specified spots. As indicated in scenario B, you can get an overview photograph of the kitchen worktop and the toilet in advance so you know what is needed at home, since it is irritating to discover after shopping that you bought something that you already have or missed some necessity, e.g., toilet paper. Although humans can adjust their angle of view to check objects at different heights, camera robots currently rely on preset camera angles.

SYSTEM DESIGN

The appearance of our system is similar to typical graphical editing systems, especially image editing tools such as Photoshop and GIMP. A *task* consists of *tool (housework)*, *place*, and *time*. Tools are in Housework Toolbox where users select a housework tool. The place is specified on the SketchPanel. Time will be selected on the Scheduler. Layer Palette manages the tasks, which is represented as a Layer.

Note that not all actions listed below are implemented in our current robot system. Some of the actions are included in our prototype user interface, but the robot system cannot execute the specified action. We include them for explanatory purposes only to clarify our vision for the future. We state clearly when we describe features that are not implemented in a working robot system. All other features are implemented and working.

Housework Toolbox & Property Panel

Housework Toolbox lists all available robot operations. Only one tool can be selected at a time: to select the tool, you click on the icon in the Toolbox. The Toolbox acts as a link between the icon and the actual robot. After selecting a tool, you draw a stroke on the sketch panel to command the robot to perform an action.

Our current software implementation supports five tools (Figure 2, left). The Mop and Vacuum tools instruct the robot system to mop and vacuum the specified area, respectively. The Grab&deliver tool tells the robot to collect a specified object and take it to a preset destination. The Push&deliver tool makes the robot move an object on the floor a short distance by pushing it. The Video&pics tool drives the robot to specified locations to take videos and still photographs.

Rainbow Sketch is designed to provide a quick overview of the given tasks. We use a set of rainbow-colored sketch pens to distinguish the chores, e.g., the yellow pen represents vacuuming. Since the inherent characteristics of housework differ, we use distinctive types of strokes for different operations. A freehand lasso circles the area to be mopped or vacuumed, drop and drag of the object icon for delivery, and a short arrow specifies the proper location and orientation for the camera robot.

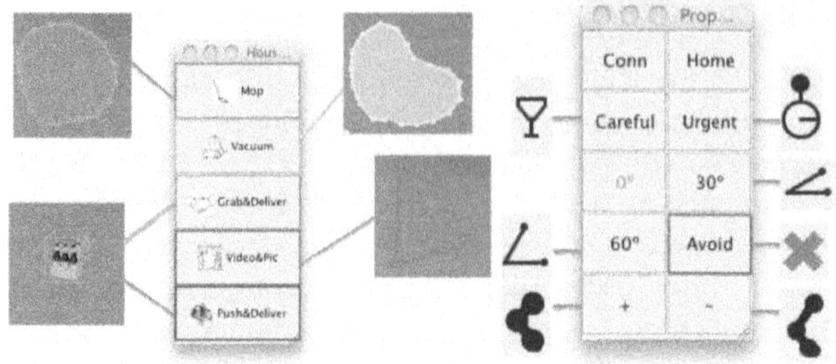

Figure 2: Housework Toolbox & Property Panel

Each stroke in Rainbow Sketch is associated with a set of properties. We provide a property panel for users to set these properties (Figure 2, right). Available properties differ according to the housework tool, and only buttons correspond to available properties appear in the panel. When the user clicks on a button, a corresponding annotation is attached to the stroke. Multiple annotations can be set for one stroke.

Our current Property Panel supports several types of annotations. "Careful" slows down the robot's moving pace to ensure careful delivery. This applies only to the Grab&Deliver and Push&Deliver tool. "Urgent" invokes immediate robot action. "0°/30°/60°" is designed for the Video&pics tool to specify the horizontal angle of the robot camera. "Weight Up(+)/Down(-)" raise or lower the weight assigned to an operation. It increases or decreases the size of the brush making the stroke. The meaning of the weight differs depending on the tool. For Push&Deliver jobs, more weight implies a larger number of pushing robots are required. In room-cleaning tasks, more weight means a longer cleaning time. "Avoid" makes the robot stay away of the specified area to protect fragile objects or private areas.

SketchPanel, ObjectCollection, and Scheduler

SketchPanel show the bird's-eye view of the room in which users assign location-specific instructions by sketching (Figure 3). We aim to support a set of housework in multiple rooms. One concern is that some furniture, e.g., cabinets contains other objects. The interface should have the capability to specify the objects inside. Therefore, furniture such as cabinets and wardrobes in the image should be designed to be clickable. When the users click on the furniture, the ObjectCollection window pops up to list the objects inside. Then users can select the target objects. This feature is not implemented in our current robot system. We envision that objects in these containers will all be tagged and tracked by means of some kind of tracking system.

Scheduler lets you set the time and date for an action. It has two parts: time-picker and date-picker. After you sketch the route map for the home robot, Scheduler calculates the time span for that task. You only need to assign a start time and date. Scheduler is intended to effectively avoid possible schedule conflicts, e.g., when the robot operations should obey some logical order. In our current implementation, vacuum tasks in a room are always executed before mop tasks. If you set a time for a mop task, Scheduler will display the time span of already set vacuum tasks for that room, so that you can set the mop task start time for after them. Scheduler also supports simple automatic multi-robot collaboration by getting all available suitable robots to engage in completing one task. If you set the task of vacuuming the whole house and more than one vacuum robot is available, the system commands all the available vacuum robots to work cooperatively.

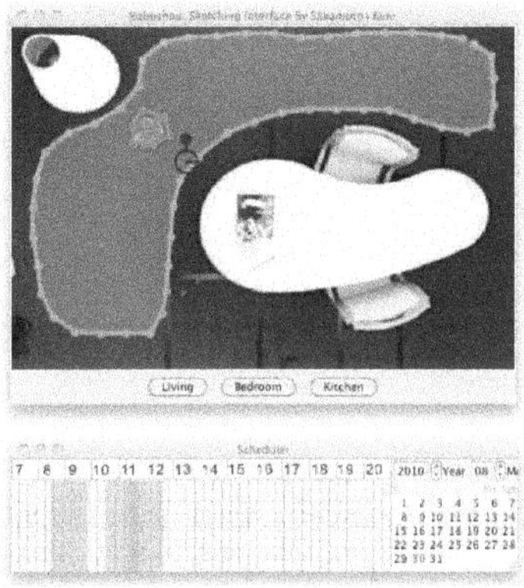

Figure 4:SketchPanel with mopping task. Scheduler shows the time span of preset vacuum tasks, so that the users set the mopping time later than that.

Layer Palette and Grouping Tool

Layer Palette is provided to manage multiple tasks (Figure 4). It has three columns: Layer Picker, Task Info, and Task Routine. The Layer Picker shows the task settings for that layer, Task Info displays the task element information (each task consists of the housework tool, the sketched room image, and the time), and Task Routine is used to set the task frequency. Only one type of task can be set in one layer, only one layer can be active at a time, and you can make changes to the task setting only for the active layer. Layers can be saved and retrieved for future use. The advantage of layers is that you can edit the task elements in one layer without disturbing the others. Layers of housework settings are presented as transparent sheets stacked on top of each other to perform a set of housework chores in the living space. You can use the Layer Palette to hide, display, duplicate, and delete layers.

The Room Grouping tool displays overlaid task contents in a particular room by collecting all the task settings scattered among separate layers. It provides you with a quick overview of the entire task set in one room.

SYSTEM IMPLEMENTATION

The system has several components: the Roboshop interface loaded on a handheld device, robots for actual household tasks, and a motion capture system to detect real-world objects. Motion Capture detects and recognizes the surroundings and objects. Roboshop then analyzes the

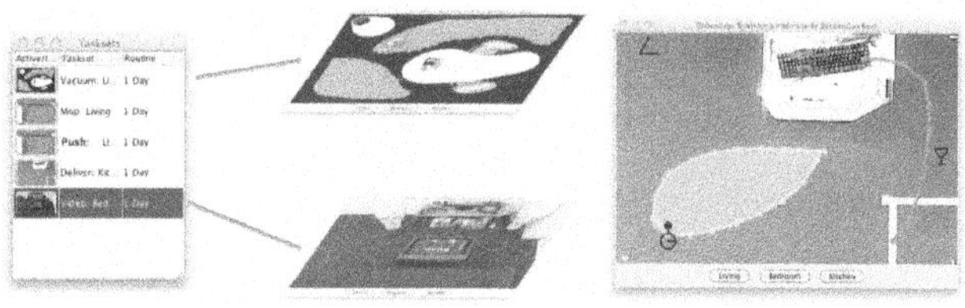

(a) (b)

Figure 3: (a) Layer Palette (b) Grouping tool collects all the tasks in one room.

user's sketch and executes the commands as specified by driving the robots in the real world.

System Overview

We run Roboshop on an Apple MacBook Pro and used the Wacom Bamboo Fun Tablet as our input device. In Roboshop, a bird's-eye view of the environment is shown to the user. This is not a live streaming video of the room, but a pre-shot still image. Webcams (Logitech, Qcam® Pro for Notebooks) are mounted on the ceiling of every room in the home to take pictures at appropriate intervals.

To detect objects and robots in the real world, we use MotionAnalysis, one of the major motion capture systems. It detects and tracks objects in the environment with eight cameras (Motion Analysis, Hawk Digital Camera) mounted on the ceiling very accurately with an error of 1 [mm] at 100 [fps]. All the objects that need to be detected by the system should be defined by the user, i.e., by attaching marker balls to them, and registered with the Motion Capture system in advance. Although the system initialization currently requires this procedure, we hope that future systems can avoid this need through the use of better technologies. Once the initial setup has been done, the Motion Capturing System detects the object in the environment. The system will send detected object with the name and markers' three-dimensional position to any applications via TCP/IP.

A Robot System manages home robots, which includes a server function to receive a command from the Roboshop application. The robot system first connects to the Motion Capturing System, and starts receiving the position of robots and objects. Then the robot system controls robots to perform housework in the environment.

Home Robots

iRobot Roomba and Create

iRobot Roomba and iRobot Create are commercially available products (Figure 5, left and right). Roomba can navigate through a living space containing obstacles while vacuuming the floor with a maximum speed of 500 mm/s. We attached a Bluetooth adaptor to each robot to provide connections to the computer running the main application, which controls Roomba and Create through Roomba Open Interface application programming interfaces (APIs). Users can control an iRobot's speed, direction, etc. In our current implementation, Roomba is used for cleaning and Create is used for object delivery.

Rovio

WowWee Rovio is a three-omni-wheeled mobile robot with a camera (Figure 5, center). Users can remotely control Rovio with the provided web-based interface or HTTP-based remote control APIs. Roivo uses these APIs to navigate and take photographs. This robot is used for monitoring.

Figure 5: iRobot Roomba (left), Rovio (center), and iRobot Create (right)

Robot System

The system supports three household tasks: vacuuming, object delivery, and house monitoring. The motion capture system provides accurate location information about the robots and objects, and the robot system uses this information to control the robots. An actual home environment has all kinds of furniture, such as chairs, tables, and bookshelves. These are not detected by the system automatically; you must specify them via the sketching interface. Then these objects will be detected by the system, and the robot will avoid interacting with them.

We use Roomba for vacuuming. In Roboshop, you circle the area to be vacuumed, set the vacuuming characteristics, e.g., the operation's weight (a higher weight means longer vacuuming time), and specify areas to avoid. The robot system then navigates Roomba to the specified vacuuming area to vacuum it. Roomba avoids the furniture and areas to avoid that you set. When Roomba has finished its task, it returns to its home base automatically.

Rovio is responsible for house monitoring (Figure 6, left). You specify Rovio's destination and the vertical and horizontal shooting angles, and Rovio moves to the specified position, sets the specified angle, and takes photographs and sends them to you. The photographs appear on the screen of your computer or PDA. Rovio then returns to its dock.

The object delivery task is more complicated since the iRobot Roomba we use to deliver objects does not have any pincers to hold objects. To support object push and delivery, the system includes a dipole-field object transportation mechanism [7]. This enables Create to push an object to the destination over a flat surface. We extend this idea to further support an object avoidance mechanism (Figure 6, right). The robot delivers (pushes) objects and avoids the furniture, which currently must be defined by the user, in the living space.

Figure 6: Monitoring by Rovio (left) and Object delivery by iRobot Roomba (right)

USER STUDY

We conducted a formal user study to collect feedback from participants for the purpose of improving future implementations. We did not perform a comparison study with other systems because our system focuses on household work management and arrangement, for which no other systems currently exist.

Environmental setup

We set up a simulated one-room home in our lab (Figure 7). The size was 4 [m] x 3 [m], which is a standard size for a Japanese living space. Cameras for the motion capturing system were mounted around the area. The room contained a couch. Along the wall opposite the couch was a bookshelf. On the other side was a table for the user.

Experimental Design

We recruited seven participants, aged 21–24 years old (average: 22.4 years, standard deviation (SD): 1.05 years), five male and two female, from the local university to participate in our study. Recruited participants had no prior associations or experience with our lab, group, or project. Students' majors included engineering, business, art and design. All participants were single: three live with their families and four live alone. Each participant was paid $20 per hour for taking part in the study.

The user study consisted of four parts: 1) pre-test questionnaire, 2) introduction of the system, 3) evaluation of the system, and 4) post-test questionnaire and interview.

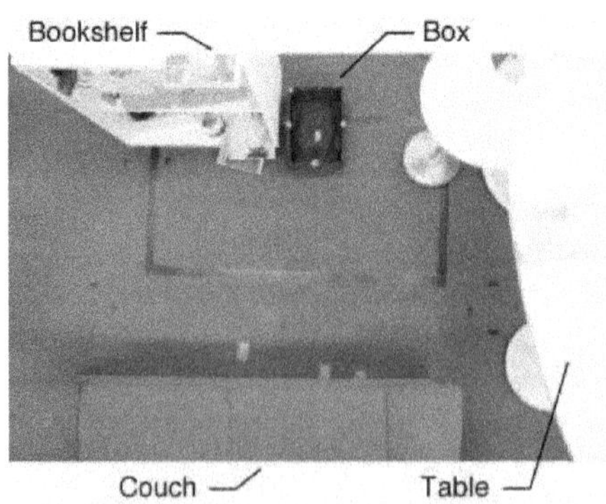

Figure 7: Environmental setup: bird's eye view.

For the user study, the interface supported three rooms: one for demonstrating the interface, one for user trial operations, and one for the actual evaluation, which was actually the working system with robots.

Before we started the user study, we asked participants to answer a demographic questionnaire. The aim was to understand their current life styles (e.g., living alone or with others), daily household chores, and so on. We started by showing our system demonstration and describing the motivation of our research. The participants just listened and watched how to use the interface and how it works. Next, the participants tried out the interface with an experimenter. Finally, the participants gave actual instructions to the robot system. They were shown the actual movements of the robot system that resulted from their instructions.

At the end of the study, all participants were asked to answer a post-experimental questionnaire. We also interviewed them and recorded their feedback.

Tasks

We asked participants to make three instructions to achieve three tasks:

1. Set a vacuuming area avoiding the couch in the environment and set the task start time for 10:00am.
2. Deliver to the vicinity of the couch a box containing glasses, requiring careful delivery, at 4:00pm.
3. Monitor the bookshelf at 2:00pm.

RESULTS AND ANALYSIS

All participants successfully made three instructions. Most of them created instructions in Roboshop without any help and said, "This is basically a very easy-to-use interface." The user study confirmed that the robots are able to successfully perform all the user-created instructions. The users watched and confirmed that the robot system actually worked with the Roboshop interface. However, we also got various suggestions for the future improvement: details of these and an analysis of the experiment are given below.

Usability

We asked six ease-of-use questions via questionnaire after the user study. The results are shown in Table 1, which shows the mean, SD, and percentage of positive responses (>4 on a 7-point Likert scale) to each question. Five users reported that the interface was easy-to-use (Q1: 5/7% of positive responses), they felt confident while using the interface (Q3), and thought most people would be able to use the interface (Q4). Furthermore, six users reported that they appreciated the interface for giving housework instructions (Q2: 6/7%). On the other hand, three users reported that they needed technical support and concentration to use it (Q5 and Q6: 3/7%).

Table 1: Results of Questionnaire

#	Question	Mean	SD	%
1	Was it easy to give the housework instructions?	5.29	1.90	5/7
2	Did you appreciate the system for household work?	5.29	1.57	6/7
3	Did you feel confident using the system?	5.43	2.29	5/7
4	Do you think most people would be able to use it?	4.86	2.48	5/7
5	Did you need technical support to use it?	4.29	0.57	3/7
6	Did you need concentration to use it?	4.00	3.67	3/7

Sketching / Drag & Drop instruction

Users reported through comments and feedback that the interface was visually understandable and easy-to-instruct the household works. "Rainbow Sketch was good to remind me of the current selected tool," because one color on the interface corresponds to one tool. The Drag & Drop instruction for the object delivery was easy and useful. Despite that users reported the sketching gestures were simple, they claimed that it was difficult to create dedicated instructions, saying, "I needed to concentrate to use." Some users were confused with sketching gesture for the monitoring operation; a user wrote an opposite angle to take a picture, and the other user tried to use arrow gesture to do that. Likewise, one user argued that the instruction of the vacuuming area does not need to use lasso gesture; it might be enough to specify several vertices around the area.

Property of the Instruction

From our analysis of post-questionnaire (7 pt Likert scale, 7 is best), even though all participants thought that having household performed by robots is very practical and helpful (*mean=6.57, SD=0.29*), they did not feel completely comfortable having robots execute some kinds of housework (*mean=4.29, SD=3.90*). They were concerned that fully automatic robots might break furniture, get stuck, or drop glasses and spill water while delivering them, and so forth. Some places in the house are private or need to be quiet, so robots are not welcome there.

At this point, they preferred to add a comment using property, to the instruction like "careful" to the task of delivering a fragile object or to increase the weight for the vacuuming task. Since Roboshop supports asynchronous control, which means the users may not be present to watch the robot when it performs the task, setting users' minds at ease is especially important. A few of users said, "The robot should detect the situation automatically," but the property will be necessary for Roboshop and future home robot interfaces.

Scheduler and Layer

The interface automatically estimates and displays the estimated time of the robot's housework. One user reported that the estimation function "was useful to understand the situation, and to plan multiple household work instructions" On the other hand, the current working prototype only supports rough time setting; it does not support specific time instruction, e.g., start vacuuming at 9:38am. The rough instruction "was easy-to-use," but some users "wanted to specify the exact time."

Regarding the layers, one user said "the thumbnail images in Layers enhance the speed of reviewing and retrieving the tasks," "[I think] the Save and Reuse will be useful for the future home." Rainbow Sketch represented the tool with its color, and it seems to help the user to grasp the instruction of the Layer. However, the interface only supports listing of Layers and one user was concerned "when the Layer number is increased, it will be difficult to search and select the Layer."

Room View for the Interface

Some users said that the interface should support multi-angle views and three-dimensional sketching. The bird's-eye view does not allow the user to specify the area under furniture, such as tables and chairs, or other tall furniture, such as lamps. Likewise, it does not allow the user to specify tasks that need to consider the "height", such as placing a book on the 3rd level of the bookshelf. The 3D image of the room and 3D sketching for the tasks will "have capability of supporting much more household works." Further, one user said, "hopefully the interface supports a live camera view of the room. It will be helpful to know the situation of the room."

DISCUSSION

Interface Design

Selecting sketching gesture to use in the interface is a significant challenge. Some users were confused with sketching gesture for the monitoring operation. One user argued that the instruction of the vacuuming area does not need to use sketching gesture. We consider that the design of the gesture for instruction of household work is still an open question. Especially, not many researches about the gesture control of the housework had been conducted in the around the area of robotics and HCI. Feedbacks from the users are very useful and valuable for improving the system.

The design of Layers should be improved as well. One Layer only has one task, and layers are only listed in the Layer palette. Even through the user can watch multiple tasks at the same time with the grouping tool, other functions will be necessary for the future implementation. A folder, which has multiple tasks, might be one solution.

Simplicity and Trust

To accomplish the housework tasks is the most important concern for the users, so the interface should provide them with quick access to the housework settings. Interface designers would keep the interaction styles simple and intuitive so that not much technique support would be needed for the users. An ambiguous or complicated interface would hesitate the users to touch it, particularly for elders and housewives. The results of our interviews reveal that if the delivery task setting takes too much time or thoughts, the users would rather do it by themselves.

At the same time, most of the users reported that if the instructions were merely simple drawing of the robot routes, then the tasks are so abstract that they feel difficult to trust the robots. "The property setting is much appreciated" to finalize some details of the tasks. All these concerns remind us at every stage of the designs that the interface needs a good balance between simplicity, intuitiveness and concreteness, accuracy.

Applicability

In this paper, we focused on the robot control with a common HCI technique, but it is not limited to robots. One user said, "I hope it will actuate the other things, like curtains, lights, air conditioners, etc." We consider that Roboshop will be able to support these home electronics and home automation systems by applying HCI technique. The CRISTAL system [26] was developed as a universal-remote for the home, but it did not support the asynchronous control, and the save and reuse function of the control. Roboshop can have the functions, which the CRISTAL system has, and manages them as Layers.

Also, one user reported that the system "will be used as a household work TODO management system." If a user noticed household works to do, s/he then just uses Roboshop to create instructions of the household work on the interface. After that, home robots will do the actual work no matter the user is in the home or not. At this point, the user does not need to care about the actual household works and home robots. They only manage and arrange the household work on the interface. We consider this as one of main future usage of the Roboshop at real home environment.

Autonomy

We designed the Roboshop user interface carefully to balance robot autonomy and user-control. If the system is mostly automatic, it is difficult for the users to customize control; if everything is manual, then interaction becomes too tedious. We use sketching and layers to allow the users to easily control the system with some autonomy while freeing them from low-level details. For example, the user specifies the region to vacuum, but does not specify detailed robot movement in the region. Low-level issues such as collision avoidance among robots are handled implicitly: it is taken care of by the system.

Multi-robot collaboration

A Heterogeneous group of robots is able to perform possibly different tasks simultaneously according to the layers; the Roboshop user interface (sketch + layers) can support various forms of robot collaborations as a framework. For a vacuum task that may require engaging multiple robots, the system can divide one vacuum area into multiple disjoint areas so that the robots clean those areas in parallel, applying specializations and avoiding collision etc. For an object delivery task, the system can divide it into several parts: picking an object out from a shelf, and delivering it to the user. The system performs this complex task by carefully utilizing single-function robots while avoiding space conflict and resource collisions.

Implications

Restricted by the current supply of the home robots, the system only supports limited robot actions. When the home robot interface is explored in near future, the design needs to be careful at several aspects.

- Since we use the specific stroke gesture to specify each task, as more housework types would be supported in near future, other styles of stroke gestures are needed. The fact that some users in our study misunderstood the gestures, which led to the misuse of them reveals that the unambiguity of the stroke gestures is one of the most important factors concerning the gesture design.
- Users expect to perform housework across the rooms. The capability of setting tasks across the rooms will provide the users with much more flexibility. For the current interface, we support tasks in multiple rooms, but one task must start and end at the same room. The further explorations of the home robot interface should take this into consideration.
- The system should ask the user to perform the instruction or not, because the system saves the user's instruction. A reminder function is "one of wanted function, because machines [which includes computers and robots] usually perform their work without asking."
- Users worry about the housework performed by the home robots. A housework recording and playing function will comfort the users. They will then be able to check the history of the housework by home robots.

LIMITATION AND FUTURE WORK

The current system is a proof-of-concept working prototype with limitations in terms of both users' and designers' prospects. The results of our study indicate that users would love to delegate as many types of housework to home robots as possible. However, the sketching mechanism itself sometimes delivers very limited instructions to the robots, e.g., laundry and folding the garment is impossible with the interface. Also, cooking instruction will be hard to design. These types of tasks are not very suitable for current Roboshop interface. We plan to improve our interface by integrating other GUI-based interaction technique and application to manage much more household works.

We confirmed that the property of the instruction helped end-users to specify the robot operations concretely, however, the current implemented property was limited. For example, our current implementation does not allow the users manually increase the number of robots for pushing and delivering heavy objects. Current working prototype did not support multi-robot collaboration work. With the development of the robot technology, we will improve our system for supporting much more properties of instructions.

For now, the motion capturing system is expensive equipment. Despite the high accuracy, it is unrealistic to install into the home. Recent years, with the development of the ubiquitous computing technology, RFID-based real-time location system had been developed [31]. Currently, these systems do not have enough speed and accuracy to control small home robots yet, however, they have possibility of being installed into the home because of the easiness and smallness. This will be a future work of the system.

CONCLUSION

We presented the Roboshop, a graphical user interface for managing and arranging the household work. Once the user sets up the instruction of housework, it will be performed by home robots whether the user is in the home or not. Roboshop supports various types of housework, composes detailed housework instructions, sets up the tasks in a coordinated time span and space, and lets users review and reuse tasks that are tied to the physical environment. A user study had conducted to evaluate the ease-of-use the interface and to collect users' feedbacks. The analysis of results showed that several important findings about users' attitudes and concerns towards future types of robot housework and instruction styles. We hope to enhance the capabilities of Roboshop as a physical assistant in room environments.

REFERENCES

1. Choi, Y., Anderson, C., Deyle, T., and Kemp, C. Human-Robot Interaction Studies for Autonomous Mobile Manipulation for the Motor Impaired. In *Experimental Design for Real-World Systems*, AAAI Spring Symposium '09, (2009).
2. Chronis, G., and Skubic, M. Robot navigation using qualitative landmark states from sketched route maps. In *Proc. ICRA'04*, IEEE (2004), 1530–1535.
3. de Ruyter, B. and Aarts, E. Ambient intelligence: visualizing the future. In *Proc. AVI '04*. ACM (2004), 203-208.
4. Fong, T., Thorpe, C., Baur, C. Multi-robot remote driving with collaborative control. *IEEE Transactions on Industrial Electronics 50*, 4 (2003), 699–704.

5. Fong, T., Thorpe, C., and Glass, B. PdaDriver: A Handheld System for Remote Driving. In *Proc. ICAR'03*, (2003).
6. Glas, D. F., Kanda, T., Ishiguro, H., and Hagita, N. Simultaneous teleoperation of multiple social robots. In *Proc. HRI '08*. ACM (2008), 311-318.
7. Igarashi, T. Kamiyama, Y. Inami, M. A dipole field for object delivery by pushing on a flat surface. In *Proc. ICRA '10*, IEEE (2010), 5114 – 5119.
8. Intille, S. S., Larson, K., Beaudin, J. S., Nawyn, J., Tapia, E. M., and Kaushik, P. A living laboratory for the design and evaluation of ubiquitous computing technologies. In *Ext. Abst. of CHI '05*. ACM (2005), 1941-1944.
9. inVoca, "inVoca Universal Remote" http://www.invoca.com.
10. Ishii K., Zhao S., Inami M., Igarashi T., and Imai M. Designing Laser Gesture Interface for Robot Control. In *Proc. INTERACT '09*, (2009), 479–492.
11. Jain, A. and Kemp, C. C. 2010. EL-E: an assistive mobile manipulator that autonomously fetches objects from flat surfaces. *Autonomous Robots 28*, 1 (2010), 45-64.
12. Jain, A., and Kemp, C. C. Pulling open doors and drawers: Coordinating an omni-directional base and a compliant arm with equilibrium point control. In *Proc. ICRA '10*, IEEE (2010), 1807 – 1814.
13. Kato, J., Sakamoto, D., Inami, M., and Igarashi, T. Multi-touch interface for controlling multiple mobile robots. In *Ext. Abst. of CHI '09*. ACM (2009), 3443-3448.
14. Kemp, C. C., Anderson, C. D., Nguyen, H., Trevor, A. J., and Xu, Z. A point-and-click interface for the real world: laser designation of objects for mobile manipulation. In *Proc. HRI '08*. ACM (2008), 241-248.
15. Lieberman, H. and Espinosa, J. A goal-oriented interface to consumer electronics using planning and commonsense reasoning. *Knowledge-Based Systems 20*, 6 (2007), 592-606.
16. "Living Tomorrow." http://www.livingtomorrow.com
17. Lundberg, C., Barck-Holst, C., Folkeson, J., Christensen, H.I. PDA interface for a field robot. In *Proc. IROS '03*, 3, IEEE (2003), 2882 – 2888.
18. Matsouoka, K. Smart house understanding human behaviors: Who did what, where, and when. In *Proc. WMSCI '04*, 3, (2004), 181- 185.
19. Matsumaru, T. Mobile Robot with Preliminary-announcement and Display Function of Forthcoming Motion using Projection Equipment. In *Proc. ROMAN '06*, IEEE (2006), 443–450.
20. Micire, M., Desai, M., Courtemanche, A., Tsui, K. M., and Yanco, H. A. Analysis of natural gestures for controlling robot teams on multi-touch tabletop surfaces. In *Proc. ITS '09*. ACM (2009), 41-48.
21. Nichols, J., Myers, B. A., Higgins, M., Hughes, J., Harris, T. K., Rosenfeld, R., and Pignol, M. Generating remote control interfaces for complex appliances. In *Proc. UIST '02*. ACM (2002), 161-170.
22. Park, J. and Kim, G. J. Robots with projectors: an alternative to anthropomorphic HRI. In *Proc. HRI '09*. ACM (2009), 221-222.
23. Perzanowski, D., Schultz, A.C., Adams, W., Marsh, E., and Bugajska, M. Building a Multimodal Human-Robot Interface, *Intelligent Systems 16*, 1 (2001), 16–20.
24. Philips, Pronto Intelligent Remote Control. Philips Consumer Electronics, (2001). http://www.pronto.philips.com/.
25. Sakamoto, D., Honda, K., Inami, M., and Igarashi, T. Sketch and run: a stroke-based interface for home robots. In *Proc. CHI '09*. ACM (2009), 197-200.
26. Seifried, T., Haller, M., Scott, S.D., Perteneder, F., Rendl, C., Sakamoto, D, and Inami, M. CRISTAL: a collaborative home media and device controller based on a multi-touch display. In *Proc. ITS '09*. ACM (2009), 33-40.
27. Skubic, M., Anderson D., Blisard S., Perzanowski D., and Schultz A. Using a hand-drawn sketch to control a team of robots. *Autonomous Robots 22*, 4 (2007), 399–410.
28. Srinivasa, S., Ferguson D., Helfrich, C., Berenson, D., Collet, A., Diankov, R., Gallagher, G., Hollinger, G., Kuffner, J., and Weghe M. HERB: a home exploring robotic butler. *Autonomous Robots 28*, 1 (2010), 5–20.
29. Sugiura, Y., Igarashi, T., Takahashi, H., Gowon, T. A., Fernando, C. L., Sugimoto, M., and Inami, M. Graphical instruction for a garment folding robot. In *ACM SIGGRAPH 2009 Emerging Technologies*. ACM (2009), 1.
30. Sugiura, Y., Sakamoto, D., Withana, A., Inami, M., and Igarashi, T. Cooking with robots: designing a household system working in open environments. In *Proc. CHI '10*. ACM (2010), 2427-2430.
31. Ubisense, http://www.ubisense.net/
32. Zhao, S., Nakamura, K., Ishii, K., and Igarashi, T. Magic cards: a paper tag interface for implicit robot control. In *Proc. CHI '09*. ACM (2009), 173-182.
33. Zimmermann, G., Vanderheiden, G., and Gilman, A. Prototype implementations for a universal remote console specification. In *Ext. Abst. of CHI '02*. ACM (2002), 510-511.

Examining the Impact of Collaborative Tagging on Sensemaking in Nutrition Management

Lena Mamykina[1], Andrew D. Miller[2], Yevgeniy Medynskiy[2], Catherine Grevet[2], Patricia R. Davidson[3], Michael A. Terry[4], Elizabeth D. Mynatt[2]

[1] Department of Biomedical Informatics, Columbia University, 622 West 168th St. VC5, New York, NY 10032

[2] GVU Center, Georgia Institute of Technology, 85 5th Street NW, Atlanta, GA 30332

[3] The Cardiovascular Care Group, Belleville, NJ, Saint Claires Hospital, Dover, NJ

[4] David R. Cheriton School of Computer Science, University of Waterloo, Waterloo, Canada

ABSTRACT
Collaborative tagging mechanisms are integral to social computing applications in a variety of domains. Their expected benefits include simplified retrieval of digital content, as well as enhanced ability of a community to makes sense of the shared content. We examine the impact of collaborative tagging in context of nutrition management. In a controlled experiment we asked individuals to assess the nutritional value of meals based on photographic images and observed the impact of different types of tags and tagging mechanisms on individuals nutritional sensemaking. The results of the study show that tags enhance individuals' ability to remember the viewed meals. However, we found that some types of tags can be detrimental to sensemaking, rather than supporting it. These findings stress the importance of tagging vocabularies and suggest a need for expert moderation of community sensemaking.

ACM Classification Keywords: H5.m. Information interfaces and presentation (e.g., HCI): Miscellaneous.
Author Keywords: Collaborative tagging, collective sensemaking, nutrition, wellness
General Terms: Experimentation

INTRODUCTION
In many areas of human enterprise, individuals rely on the collective wisdom of their peers rather than on expert advice alone. In the domain of health and wellness management, social applications such as TuDiabetes [1], Patients Like Me [2], and Eat.ly [3] help thousands of individuals share their experiences and receive advice and guidance from others. Compensating for the limited access to experts, these distributed communities help individuals fill gaps in their knowledge and understanding, and to contribute in kind.

One mechanism integral to these knowledge-sharing applications is *tagging*. Tagging allows individuals to assign free-form keywords to digitally stored content. For example, in the field of nutrition management, tags can be assigned to pictures of foods as part of a nutrition management program. The process of *collaborative tagging* allows individuals to share their tags with others, thus forming reusable, communal *tagging vocabularies*.

Tagging is generally thought to provide two types of benefits to users. At the most basic level, assigning meaningful keywords to digital data simplifies its retrieval. However, early advocates of collaborative tagging argued that tagging also promotes collaborative sensemaking and consensus building [21]. Sensemaking is a process through which individuals comprehend meaning of events and situations and decide on their course of action. When individuals tag items or events they assign them explicit labels and classify them into categories; both of these are essential steps of making sense of the world [23]. In collaborative tagging, explicit labeling allows individuals to compare their emergent understanding, and reach a consensus, thus enabling collective sensemaking.

In the context of health and wellness communities, these latter benefits would be highly desirable: They could enable development of a richer understanding of individuals' particular health concerns and help them create a shared vocabulary for health issues. Both of these effects could greatly enhance individual health management practices. In nutrition management, tags could highlight nutritional properties of meals, such as "good portion size," "poor proportions," or even "heart attack on a plate." Seeing these tags assigned to pictures of meals could help less experienced members adopt a shared operational vocabulary. Comparing tag assignments across pictures could also help individuals refine their own nutritional judgment, potentially leading to more informed choices in the future.

Despite these expectations, empirical studies of tagging in the context of text recognition and recall in educational settings have not demonstrated the expected benefits [4]. Thus, questions remain as to the potential benefits of tagging and whether tagging can facilitate comprehension, sensemaking, and consensus building.

In this paper we present results from an investigation of collaborative tagging mechanisms and their impact on nutritional judgment. Our primary research questions include the following:

1. How do individuals use social tagging mechanisms in context of nutrition management? What types of tags do they generate spontaneously?
2. Does assigning tags to meals affect individuals' sensemaking in the context of nutrition management? Are certain types of tags and tagging mechanisms more beneficial than others? Specifically, does tagging improve individuals' ability to remember meals and/or their ability to critically assess their nutritional value?
3. Does a socially (or otherwise) created tagging vocabulary have an impact on individuals' own tagging practices? How sustained is that impact?

To answer these questions, we conducted a controlled experiment. Participants were asked to view pictures of meals displayed on a computer screen and tag these meals using different tagging strategies, then answer a set of questions about the meals. Using a mixed-factors repeated measures design we assessed the general impact of tags, and differentiated between different tagging strategies, and types of tags.

Our experiment suggests that tagging helps individuals remember tagged content. However, we found that the *type* of tags suggested in a tagging vocabulary has a significant impact on individuals' ability to critically assess the nutritional value of these meals. In particular, *descriptive tags* that simply listed meals' ingredients (such as "meat", "potatoes") were actually detrimental to the individuals' ability to assess the meals. In contrast, *assessment tags* that focused participants' attention on nutritional properties of meals (such as "poor proportions" and "lacks vegetables") led to a slight improvement in their assessment abilities. Further, we found that individuals are more likely to spontaneously generate descriptive tags, rather than assessment tags. However, exposure to a tagging vocabulary containing assessment tags encouraged adoption of these more beneficial tagging strategies in individuals' own practice.

The results of this study have direct implications for the design of tagging mechanisms in general and for wellness and nutrition management sites in particular. For example, most of these sites allow individuals to collectively create tagging vocabularies without any supervision or moderation. Our study shows, however, that if these social vocabularies accrue only descriptive tags, they may inhibit sensemaking rather than promote it. To avoid this, such sites might consider interjecting expert-created assessment tags into the social vocabularies.

In the rest of this paper we discuss related work in the area of social tagging, enumerate our specific research questions, then present our experimental study, our findings, and their implications for the HCI community.

BACKGROUND AND RELATED WORK

Tagging and Collaborative Tagging

Collaborative tagging has become a popular mechanism for social web-based services. Examples of early communities that embraced tagging include Flikr, Del.icio.us, CiteULike, among many others. Tagging primarily allows individuals to assign free-form keywords to digital content, such as images or URLs.

One of the main advantages of collaborative tagging systems is to allow their users to converge on a shared meaning of the content that they tag. When multiple people use identical tags for items, aggregation of such tags leads to the emergence of a user-created categorization scheme, known as a "folksonomy"[22].

Tags present an alternative to the traditional method of an expert or group of experts developing a categorization scheme. Past research argues that expert-created taxonomies are not capable of responding to the changing understanding of the world, and result in loss of data when items in-between established categories [21]. In contrast, social tagging is seen as flexible and fluid, continuously responding to the changing understanding of the larger community. In addition, it allows for the emergence of multi-layer taxonomies, from more general categories to very low-level idiosyncratic ones, with no loss of data. However, there is some concern that folksonomies could reinforce misconceptions and stereotypes, and produce herding behavior [20].

Several researchers attempted to map out a theoretical model as well as design space for collaborative tagging systems. Marlow et al [15] present a three-tiered conceptual model, which includes such elements as resources, users, and tags. In the model, tags serve as connections between users and resources. The authors identify a number of design dimensions for social tagging mechanisms, including, for example, whether individuals are provided with tagging suggestions or whether they are asked to tag blindly, without access to tags by other people. The experimental conditions in our study were generally inspired by these variations in tagging mechanisms.

Encoding and Retrieval

While earlier writings on collaborative tagging examined their ability to foster collective sense-making, much of the recent literature focuses on these systems' capacity to simplify access to and retrieval of digital content. For example, Chi and Mytkovic [5] suggest that social tagging is "fundamentally a method for organizing objects for later use. It is a process of *encoding* objects with keywords so as to later *retrieve* those very same documents" (emphasis by authors). Within this perspective, researchers have focused on mathematically describing the dynamics of users' tagging behaviors, and on the evolution of tags and tagging vocabularies. In this research, the phrase "social bookmarking" often replaces "collaborative tagging," further stressing this work's focus on retrieval.

A common conclusion of this line of research (for example Golder and Huberman [7], and Halpin et al [8]) is the stabilization of tagging systems over time, essentially supporting the notion of consensus building. However, this research primarily focuses on the extrinsic value of the community-developed tagging vocabularies, namely their benefits for retrieval of content. What is not considered is how tags and the act of tagging affect their creators.

Sensemaking

Drawing inspiration from Karl Weick [23], we define sensemaking as a "process of transforming circumstances into a situation that is comprehended explicitly in words and that serves as a springboard to action". Weick includes bracketing (or classification) and labeling (or assigning explicit names) as two essential steps in the sensemaking process.

In nutrition sensemaking, individuals assess properties of a meal in the context of their existing knowledge, their nutritional goals, and their desires of the moment, and explicitly express their comprehension of the situation in words. This comprehension leads to their choice of action. On social networking sites dedicated to nutrition management (e.g., eat.ly), digital images of meals serve as a proxy of real meals. Users tag these meals, thus expressing their comprehension of the meal's value in words. In this scenario tagging becomes a mechanism for bracketing and labeling, and thus for sensemaking.

This view is consistent with other researchers' assessment of the potential of social tagging. For example, Golder and Huberman (2006) [7] assert, "Tagging is fundamentally about sensemaking. Sensemaking is a process in which information is categorized and labeled, and, critically, through which meaning emerges." They discuss the benefits of collaborative tagging in helping communities organize knowledge and coordinate action. Similarly, Pauen et al view tagging as sensemaking aid: "The act of assigning tags to categorize an object is an act of knowledge production as it makes apparent the mental models, or internal representations of knowledge, that one uses to associate with the object" [18].

Several researchers have explored the potential of social tagging to help communities of learners. For example, Yew et al [24] studied students taking an undergraduate Business Information Technology class. As part of class curriculum, the students were required to compose and tag blog posts discussing topics relevant to the class. The authors found a strong correlation between blogging frequency and higher overall grades. However they do not report on the impact of tags.

Oleksik et. al. [17] looked at how tagging supports information and activity management practices. They discuss four main tag usage scenarios: managing short-term/transient activities, revisiting resources and resuming activities, filtering resources and creating meta-organization of resources. Of these uses, the last one in particular could be seen as evidence for individuals use of tags to simplify retrieval, but also as sensemaking tools that helped them see patterns in their digital resources.

Hsieh et al examined the use of tags for synchronous collaboration in a workspace [9]. In their plugin to Lotus Sametime, users could assign tags to tasks. They found that tags could be used for temporal coordination.

Note Taking

While situated in a different context, research examining note-taking in educational settings is potentially relevant to tagging. Research in this space is extensive (see [10] for a review of the work in this area). Despite the different contexts, there are many parallels between the two activities. In both cases, individuals aim to externalize and capture in textual form their emerging understanding of particular concepts. Both are also relatively unstructured and emerge as part of individuals' evolving experience with the content. Finally, both are expected to aid in comprehension and later information retrieval.

Research in note-taking identifies a set of concepts that help structure an understanding of tagging as a cognitive activity. For example, it makes a distinction between note-taking *process* and its *product* (i.e., the actual notes), both of which are seen to have their benefits. In particular, there is evidence that the process of taking notes leads to a better understanding of the material, even if the notes are never reviewed [12]. Reviewing the notes at a later time also aids comprehension, indicating the value of the actual notes.

Prior research also distinguishes between different note-taking strategies and suggests differences in the benefits of these strategies. Specifically, studies show that *conceptual notes* are more likely to lead to deeper processing and comprehension than *factual notes*. However, students are more likely to spontaneously generate factual notes [11].

In the sections that follow, we adopt these frames of reference when considering the activity of tagging. In particular, we similarly distinguish between the tagging *process* itself (in which individuals are asked to assign tags to content) and the tagging *product* (how existing tagging vocabularies affect individuals' practices and comprehension). We also distinguish between *descriptive tags* and *assessment tags*, which are conceptually similar to the notions of factual notes and conceptual notes.

Lack of Strong Empirical Evidence

The body of work we discussed above establishes a strong theoretical foundation for collaborative tagging as facilitating sensemaking within a community. However, several recent studies that specifically examined the impact of tags on memory and sensemaking did not produce empirical evidence to support these claims. For example, Budiu *et al* [4] compared individuals' ability to remember part of written text with and without tags, also differentiating between two tagging mechanisms (typing tags, and selecting text as tags). They found that tags led to performance at best comparable with no tagging condition, but generated no improvement beyond it. Similarly, Nelson *et al* [16] investigated the impact of social tagging on making sense of novel information on the web. In their studies, tagging had a positive impact only when individuals used tags created by an expert, rather than tags of their own creation.

This seeming contradiction between a convincing theoretical foundation and the lack of strong empirical evidence calls for further investigations of collaborative tagging mechanisms. In our work we attempted to identify certain properties of collaborative tagging that may explain the lack of expected positive impact. Specifically, we hypothesized that there are substantial differences in the benefits afforded by different types of tags and tagging mechanisms: not all of them may be equally beneficial to comprehension and sensemaking. Our goal was to better understand what those properties are and what design solutions would help to maximize the positive impact.

RESEARCH QUESTIONS

Our focus on the effect of tagging in nutritional management applications led us to the following set of research questions:

1. How do individuals use social tagging mechanisms in context of nutrition management? What types of tags do they generate spontaneously?

Different applications impose different restrictions on the length and structure of tags. Some require single-word tags, others allow more complex compositions. Our first question was what style of tags individuals would choose in context of nutrition management, with no external restrictions. In addition, we were wondering what type of tags individuals would create spontaneously: descriptive or assessment. In agreement with note-taking literature, our expectation was that individuals would be more likely to spontaneously generate descriptive rather than assessment tags.

2. Does assigning tags to meals affect individuals' sensemaking in context of nutrition management?

As we mentioned earlier, sensemaking is a complex process involving a variety of components. In context of nutrition management it could involve an understanding of underlying physiological processes, different ways food affects them, and how to selectively manage diet to achieve one's nutritional goals. A fuller discussion of sensemaking in this context is beyond the scope of this paper. Here, we set to examine simpler components of sensemaking, including the following:

2.1 Does assigning tags to meals improve individuals' ability to remember these meals?

2.2 Does tagging lead to more accurate critical evaluation of food's nutritional value (as compared to the ground truth provided by a trained dietician)?

2.3 Is there a difference in the type and magnitude of impact for different tagging mechanisms (unassisted tagging and supported tagging), and different types of tags (descriptive and assessment)?

Our expectations were that collaborative tagging would positively affect both memory and evaluation. Furthermore, just as there is a difference between the effects of factual and conceptual note-taking practices, we expected that individuals who apply assessment tags would be able to better determine the nutritional value of a meal than those who merely used descriptive tags.

3. Does a socially-created tagging vocabulary have an impact on individuals' own tagging practices? For example, if individuals are presented with a vocabulary containing assessment tags, would they incorporate these into their own practices?

If in fact different types of tags have different effects on individual and collective sensemaking, the question becomes what mechanisms could be used to encourage the more beneficial practices. For example, if assessment tags have a more positive impact on memory and critical evaluation, how can designers and moderators of communities cultivate this approach to tagging? We expected that a pre-existing tagging vocabulary (e.g., one developed by the community) would influence individuals' tagging choices, leading to a convergence in practices.

METHOD

Design

To explore the research questions above, we designed a controlled laboratory experiment. The basic task of participants was to view digital images of meals with the goal of assessing nutritional value.

The study used a mixed-factorial design with repeated measures for within-group factors. The between-group factor corresponded to the type of tagging involved:

1. *Unassisted tagging*, in which individuals created free-form tags by typing them in the text box (Free, N=21),
2. *Supported tagging* with descriptive tags, in which individuals could select tags from a list as well as type them in a text-box; the list included descriptive tags ONLY (Descriptive, N=20),
3. *Supported tagging* with assessment tags, similar to the previous condition, with the list including assessment tags as well as descriptive tags (Assessment, N=17).

The within-group factor included the following conditions:

1. *Baseline*, in which individuals did not use any tagging,
2. *Intervention*, in which individuals were exposed to the 3 tagging mechanisms, depending on their between-group condition, and

3. *Retention,* in which all individuals were asked to use unsupported tagging to assess the residual effect of the tagging condition on individuals' own tagging approaches

The overall research questions and methods are summarized in Table 1 below:

Research questions	Methods
How do individuals use tagging in context of nutrition management	Classifying tags used by individuals in *Unassisted Tagging* condition during *Intervention* trial
Does assigning tags to meals improve individuals' ability to remember these meals?	Comparing performance on memory test between baseline (no tagging) and intervention trials for different between-subject conditions.
Does tagging lead to more accurate critical evaluation of food's nutritional value?	Comparing performance on assessment and choice tasks between baseline (no tagging) and intervention trials for different between-subject conditions
Is there a difference in the type and magnitude of impact for different tagging mechanisms and different types of tags?	Comparing performance on memory, assessment and choice tasks across different between-subject conditions.
Does a socially-created tagging vocabulary have an impact on individuals' own tagging practices?	Comparing individuals' choice of tags between intervention and retention trials for the two supported tagging conditions.

Table 1: Research questions and methods

Task

The task of participants was to assess overall nutritional value of meals based on their digital images. This type of task is becoming relatively common to the emerging health management applications. For example, several commercial services [3] and research platforms [13] allow individuals to take pictures of their meals, view them online, and share them with their peers or healthcare providers. The general premise of these applications is that viewing images of meals and their assessment by members of the community can increase individuals' nutritional literacy and help them maintain a healthy diet. In this study, we wanted to specifically investigate how these practices could be supported with social tagging mechanisms.

Procedures

Participants were seated in front of a desktop computer. Images of meals from a fictional individual were displayed on a screen one at a time. There was no restriction as to how long individuals could view the images. They were not allowed to use scrap paper or to take notes.

Participants were randomly assigned to one of the 3 conditions: Free Tagging, Descriptive Tagging, or Assessment Tagging. They were also randomly assigned to a particular starting case to avoid ordering effects. After a short, standardized introduction, the participants completed a paper-based demographic questionnaire and began the test. Each participant was asked to complete 3 trials that each included the following:

1. *Stimuli*: Individuals viewed images of meals on a computer screen (Figure 1). Each trial included 9 images that were arranged as 3 days of meals of a fictional person (breakfast, lunch, dinner, shown in that order). The participants were instructed to view the meals and think about how healthy the meals were.
2. *Evaluation*: Individuals were asked to answer a set of questions about the reviewed images; then they were presented with new images of meals (not seen before) and asked to either evaluate how healthy they were, or to choose the best meal in a set.

More specifically, the evaluation process included the following:

1. *Memory-recognition*: Participants viewed 9 images, 5 from the set they had seen before, 4 new ones, and were asked to judge whether they had seen that image before or not (see Figure 4).
2. *Evaluation-memory*: Participants were asked to assess the diet of the fictional individual, based on the 3 days of meals they viewed on a scale 1 to 5 (1–not at all healthy; 5-very healthy). They were also asked to explain their choice using free-form text
3. *Evaluation-new:* Participants viewed 3 new images of meals, one at a time (Figure 5). They were asked to decide how healthy these meals were using the same 1 to 5 scale, and to explain their decision using free-form text.
4. *Choice*: Participants viewed 2 sets of 3 new images (all 3 in a row) to decide which of these meals they would choose as the best option. They were asked to explain their choice using free-form text.

Figure 1: in a *stimuli* part of the test, individuals viewed images of meals and contemplated how healthy these meals were. In the baseline trial the individuals did not use any tagging mechanisms.

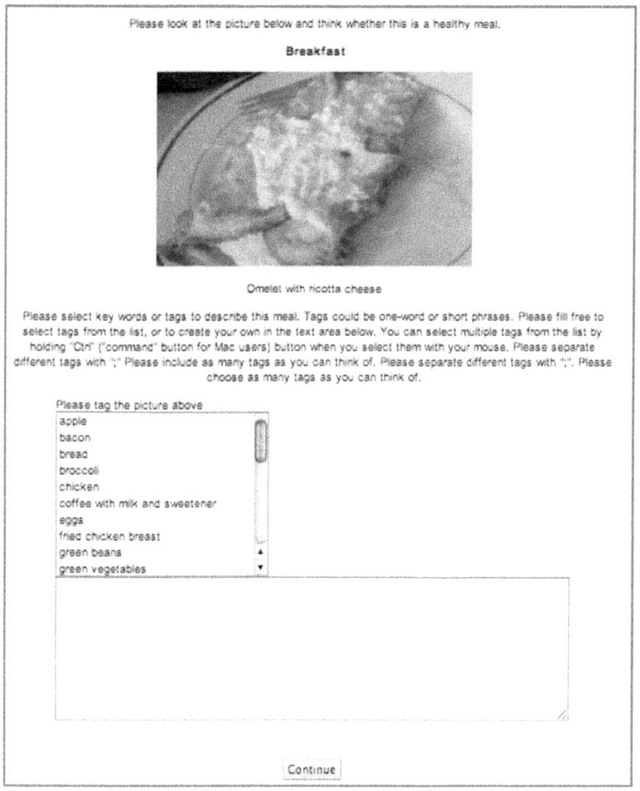

Figure 2: in the Intervention trial, individuals in both Descriptive and Assessment conditions could either enter their own tags or use tagging vocabulary that contained either descriptive tags (for Descriptive condition) or a combination of descriptive and assessment tags (for Assessment condition)

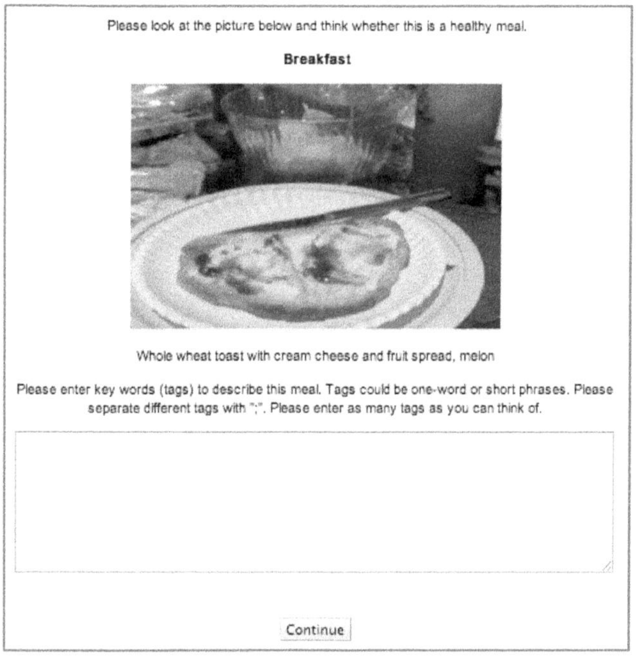

Figure 3: in the Retention trial, all participants used unsupported tags by typing them in the text box.

Figure 4: during the memory test, the individuals were asked to recognize whether the displayed meal was a part of the diet they viewed before.

Figure 5: after reviewing the images on meals, the individuals determined how healthy they were on a scale 1-5.

Materials

The images of meals used in the experiment were collected during previous deployment studies of a mobile application for wellness management [14]. This application allowed individuals to use cell phone cameras to capture pictures of their daily meals. As a result, all the images used for the experiment are authentic images of meals consumed by real individuals, rather than stock photography.

The images for the experiment were selected from the overall pool of collected images with the assistance of a diabetes educator/certified dietician. The dietician was instructed to select images that were either clearly healthy or clearly unhealthy to avoid potential ambiguity. The dietician was also asked to rate these images on a scale of 1-5, to provide an explanation of her judgment, and to assign both descriptive and assessment tags to the images.

The results of the expert assessment were used as the ground truth for individuals' assessment tasks. Furthermore, the tags developed by the dietician, consolidated across all images, were used as the tagging vocabulary for the assisted tagging conditions.

In the Descriptive condition, participants saw only descriptive tags. In the Assessment condition, participants saw both descriptive *and* assessment tags. The reason we chose to include both types of tags in the Assessment vocabulary is to increase ecological validity of the test. In a real world situation, replacing socially created vocabulary with the one created by an expert defeats its purpose. However, one could imagine using experts' help to populate the organically created social vocabulary with the more impactful tags.

Analysis

We used the following methods to analyze our data:

1. One-Way ANOVA comparing means of summed scores across repeated measures between Free, Descriptive, and Assessment conditions for each of the following: memory, assessment, and choice. This test showed us initial difference (or lack thereof) between our three groups to ensure that our randomization was successful and that there were no systematic differences between groups.

2. Repeated Measures General Linear Model test for Group*Trial to compare the differences in means between different groups (Free, Descriptive, Assessment) across different trials (Baseline, Intervention, Retention) for each of memory, assessment, and choice. This test allowed for assessment of the impact of each of the tagging mechanisms, and allowed us to compare the differences between them.

We also collected a substantial amount of qualitative data, including tags that individuals either selected or created and their explanations for their choices, written in free-form text. We incorporated these data in our analysis using the following method.

Tags were manually coded according to whether they were descriptive or assessment in nature. We used the following guidelines:

1. Tags that referred to meal ingredients (meat, potatoes), methods of cooking (fried), and style of cooling (Italian) were coded as Descriptive

2. Tags that referred to food groups (protein, carbohydrates), or any other nutritional attributes (comment on portion size, proportions of different food groups, etc.) were coded as Assessment

We then calculated the total number of tags of each type for each individual for the combinations of conditions and trials. In each of these groups, we determined whether individuals gave preference to descriptive tags or to assessment tags. We then used Chi-Square analysis to determine differences in proportions of tags between different between-group and within-group factors.

Explanations were reviewed and manually coded by a diabetes educator/dietician on their accuracy. The dietician read all the explanations, compared them with the actual images of meals, and rated them on a scale from 1-5, with a score of 1 indicating "absolutely wrong" and a score of 5 as "perfectly correct." We then aggregated the scores into 2 categories, correct and incorrect, and used Chi-Square analysis to evaluate the difference in distributions of answers across conditions and trials.

All the coding was done with researchers and dietician blinded to participants' assignment to conditions.

Participants

We recruited 58 participants among students enrolled in an Introduction to Psychology class, using the Experimetrix experiment scheduling software. The participants varied in age between 18 and 22 (Median=20), with an even split of Male/Female participants (28 Male, 30 Female). Not surprisingly, all of them were proficient with technology: over 95% reported using the Internet, SMS, email, and Facebook several times daily. However, only a few reported previous exposure to social tagging mechanisms (less than 8%). For those who used social tagging, Flickr, Del.icio.us, and Technorati were the services participants had experience with.

RESULTS

Tags and Tagging Vocabularies

In our data, we found a range of approaches to assigning tags to pictures of meals. Close to 70% of the tags were succinct, utilizing one-word or short phrase tags. However, the remaining 30% of tags included longer descriptions, at times including several sentences. Many of these longer tags were highly judgmental, and many humorous. Below are some examples of these longer tags:

- *Healthy meal, chips not needed but doesn't take away from anything*
- *Very healthy, juice as opposed to coffee would be better*

Considering the *types* of tags used (descriptive vs. assessment), the results supported our expectations that *without guidance, individuals are more likely to generate simpler descriptive tags*. In Intervention trials of Unassisted Tagging (Free) group, the ratio of Descriptive/Assessment tags was13/7, with a ratio of 12/8 for Retention trials.

At the same time, and consistent with our expectations, we found that *exposure to a tagging vocabulary affected individuals' own tagging strategies*: In the Descriptive Tagging condition, the majority of participants maintained the same preference for descriptive tags as the baseline group, with the ratio of Descriptive/Assessment tags of 16/4. In contrast, *those exposed to a vocabulary containing assessment tags adopted them in their own practice* (Descriptive/Assessment=3/14, difference from baseline: $\chi^2(1)=8.395$, $p<0.01$).

At the same time, this impact was not persistent: Many of those in the Assisted Tagging conditions switched back to using descriptive tags once the vocabulary was no longer visible. The ratio of tags in the Retention trial was Descriptive/Assessment=13/4, which was significantly different from Intervention trial: $\chi^2(1)=14.235$, $p<0.01$).

	Intervention	Retention
	Descriptive/Assessment	Descriptive/Assessment
Free	13/7	12/8
Descriptive	16/4	19/1
Assessment	3/14	13/4

Table 2: Proportions of Descriptive/Assessment tags for different conditions

Impact of tags

Baseline

To the impact of tags, we first needed to establish the baseline performance for the participants. A series of one-way ANOVA tests showed that the groups did not significantly vary in their ability to remember the images of meals; to accurately assess their nutritional values; or to select the best meal out of a set of 3. The participants' performance during the baseline trial did not differ significantly across the three groups.

Memory

As we expected, use of tagging mechanisms significantly and positively impacted individuals' ability to remember the meals as compared to no tagging baseline performance. As evident in Table 3, memory performance improved for all three groups (Free, Descriptive, and Assessment), creating a wsignificant effect of a within-group factor ($F=26.075$, $p<0.001$). There were no significant differences in how different types of tags impacted memory of the meals.

	Baseline	Intervention	Retention	Max
Free	8.42 (.81)	8.95 (.21)	8.76 (.53)	9
Descriptive	8.45 (.88)	8.9 (.30)	8.55 (.75)	9
Assessment	8.64 (0.49)	8.94 (.24)	8.54 (.60)	9

Table 3: Means and Standard Deviations for Recognition across Trials and Conditions

Assessment

The results of the assessment test were not as straightforward and contradicted some of our expectations. First of all, it showed a relatively low overall performance across conditions. In addition, instead of improving participants' ability to assess the meals, the introduction of tags led to a further drop in their performance, producing a significant negative impact of the within-group factor ($F=27.516$, $p<0.001$). *For the Free Tagging and Descriptive Tagging conditions, the introduction of tags significantly reduced individuals' ability to evaluate the meals.* However, the trend was different for the assisted tagging with assessment tags condition. These participants, while starting off at a slightly lower baseline, somewhat improved their scores on the assessment test for the Intervention trial, however this difference was not significant. Once the tagging vocabulary was removed this group's performance went down as well.

	Baseline	Intervention	Retention	Max
Free	2.04 (.74)	1.38 (.8)	1.33 (.65)	4
Descriptive	2.1 (.71)	1.5 (.76)	1.4 (.59)	4
Assessment	1.52 (1.06)	1.58 (.79)	1.11 (.69)	4

Table 4: Means for Assessment across Trials and Condition

Analysis of coded explanations produced similar results. The table below displays the proportions of correct/incorrect explanations for different conditions across trials.

	Baseline	Intervention	Retention
Free	94/32	87/39	99/27
Descriptive	102/18	94/26	107/13
Assessment	81/21	72/30	89/13

Table 5: Proportions of correct/incorrect explanations for answers for groups and trials

When comparing accuracy of explanations across groups and trials, we found that *using free-form tags during Intervention led to a decrease in the accuracy of explanations compared to baseline* ($\chi^2(1)=5.088$, $p<0.05$). However, *using free-form tags in Retention, after the exposure to Assisted tags, led to an increase in accuracy of explanations* ($\chi^2(1)=5.956$, $p<0.05$). No other trends were significant.

Choice

In regard to individuals' ability to select the best out of a set of 3 images, we found that the introduction of tagging mechanisms led to the drop in individuals' performance. The analysis showed a significant impact of both between-group factors ($F=1197.973$, $p<0.001$) and within-group factors ($F=28.02$, $p<0.001$). In the free-tagging Retention trial, however, all groups either returned to their baseline (Assessment Tagging condition) or exceeded it (Free Tagging and Descriptive Tagging conditions).

	Baseline	Intervention	Retention	Max
Free	1.47 (.81)	0.95 (.66)	1.61 (.49)	2
Descriptive	1.6 (.5)	1.00 (.64)	1.8 (.41)	2
Assessment	1.82 (.52)	0.94 (.65)	1.82 (.39)	2

Table 6: Means for Choice across Trials and Conditions

DISCUSSION

In our study, we set out to explore how social tagging mechanisms affect knowledge sharing communities in the area of health and wellness management. In particular, we wanted to investigate whether these mechanisms can help individuals improve their understanding of nutrition, as well as their ability to critically assess the nutritional value of the meals captured in photographs.

Richness of Tagging Approaches

The results of the study exposed a diversity of tagging approaches. Many individuals used concise single-word tags, whereas others wrote complete sentences that captured their sentiments in regards to the meals. Based on this observation, single-word tag restrictions, common to many collaborative tagging applications, might present a challenge to users in the context of nutrition management.

Mixed Impact of Collaborative Tagging

Limited impact of Tagging

First, our study shows that *all tagging mechanisms led to significant improvements in memory recall of meals as compared to the no tagging condition.* This is an encouraging finding, because it suggests that tagging online content helps individuals remember what they've seen. However, a prolonged exposure to the stimuli that likely occurred in tagging conditions presents an alternative explanation to this finding. Further research could help to distinguish between the two.

With respect to facilitating deeper processing, comprehension, and sensemaking, we found that tagging mechanisms can, in some circumstances, be detrimental. Specifically, we found that tagging can assist individuals only when the tagging scheme is consistent with the task individuals need to accomplish. Of the three experimental conditions—unassisted tagging, supported tagging with descriptive tags, and supported tagging with assessment tags—*only supported tagging with assessment tags did not lead to the decline in individuals' assessment abilities*. In contrast to other forms of tagging, this latter condition led to a non-significant improvement in their ability to critically evaluate nutritional value of meals. Drawing on previous work in classification and categorization, we propose that a mismatch between the tagging scheme and the task at hand produces *cognitive interference* [19], and presents barriers to sensemaking. In our case, when individuals composed or selected tags that highlighted meal composition (descriptive tags), they had a harder titime accurately assessing how healthy the meals were.

Conforming to Existing Vocabulary

While the study showed that assessment tags have the most potential in positively influencing sensemaking, we also discovered that this categorization scheme did not come naturally to study participants. *Without guidance, more individuals chose descriptive tags as opposed to assessment ones.* However, it appears to be possible to *influence individuals' choice of categorization scheme with examples in the tagging vocabulary.* In both supported tagging conditions (which exposed the participants to a particular tagging vocabulary), participants adopted the tagging style consistent with that vocabulary. Individuals with access to the vocabulary composed of descriptive tags adopted them for the duration of the study. Conversely, those with access to a vocabulary composed of both descriptive and assessment tags relied on assessment tags. This finding is consistent with the results reported by Fu et al [6], however, in our study the effect was short-lived and did not translate into a long-term impact; individuals who adopted assisted tags switched back to using descriptive ones when the vocabulary was no longer visible.

Design Implications

Collectively, these findings suggest that social tagging mechanisms have a complex cognitive basis, require further exploration, and should be used with caution. A vocabulary inconsistent with individuals' tasks or goals can lead to cognitive interference and be detrimental to their performance in these tasks. In the case of nutrition management, if the tagging vocabulary is disproportionately populated with tags that refer to meal ingredients, this vocabulary may interfere with individuals' ability to focus on the nutritional value of meals.

However, our study suggests ways to assist individuals in adopting more beneficial tagging practices. Specifically, they recommend the need to engage experts in monitoring and potentially adjusting tagging vocabularies that are generated by the community. This moderation can ensure that the vocabulary is consistent with the task and does not interfere with individuals' goals.

Limitations

The described study has a number of limitations. First of all, the choice of controlled experiment as our primary research methodology limits our ability to generalize our findings to real world situations. Tagging practices are spontaneous and highly context-sensitive. The tags individuals chose in the context of our experiment may be very different from what they would have chosen in a real-world environment. Our study design allowed us to explore several questions simultaneously; however it resulted in reduced number of trials for each type of assessment (only 9 for memory, 4 for assessment and 2 for choice). This also led to somewhat small effects; while we were able to detect some statistically significant differences, the effect sizes were small and are more suggesting than confirmatory. Finally, our findings might be specific to our study population (college students), thus limiting their applicability to other user groups. For example, our participants were more familiar with social tagging mechanisms than individuals of older age who are more common participants of health and wellness communities.

CONCLUSIONS

Well-designed tools can help individuals take advantage of their collective expertise. In the context of nutrition management, an ability to learn from others can increase individuals' nutritional literacy and help them adopt healthier eating habits. Collaborative tagging mechanisms have long been lauded for their potential to assist collective sensemaking. There is, however, a lack of empirical evidence to support these claims.

We conducted an experimental study to evaluate the impact of collaborative tagging on nutritional sensemaking, including memory and critical evaluation of meals. The results show that the composition of tagging vocabulary used by individuals has a significant impact on their ability to critically evaluate viewed digital content. This suggests a need for careful assessment and moderation of emerging tagging vocabularies.

ACKNOWLEDGEMENT

We are grateful to all our participants, to Dr. Wendy Rogers for her invaluable assistance with the design of the study and to Kliment Mamykin for assistance with the development of the experimental software.

REFERENCES

1. TuDiabetes. http://www.tudiabetes.org/.
2. PatientsLikeMe : Patients Helping Patients Live Better Every Day. http://www.patientslikeme.com/.
3. Eat.ly - Track, share, and discover great food. http://blog.eat.ly/.
4. Budiu, R., Pirolli, P., and Hong, L. Remembrance of things tagged: how tagging effort affects tag production and human memory. *Proceedings of the 27th international conference on Human factors in computing systems*, ACM (2009), 615-624.
5. Chi, E.H. and Mytkowicz, T. Understanding the efficiency of social tagging systems using information theory. *Proceedings of the ACM conference on Hypertext and hypermedia*, ACM (2008), 81-88.
6. Fu, W., Kannampallil, T., Kang, R., and He, J. Semantic imitation in social tagging. *ACM Trans. Comput.-Hum. Interact. 17*, 3 (2010), 1-37.
7. Golder, S.A. and Huberman, B.A. Usage patterns of collaborative tagging systems. *Journal of Information Science 32*, 2 (2006), 198 -208.
8. Halpin, H., Robu, V., and Shepherd, H. The complex dynamics of collaborative tagging. *Proceedings of the 16th international conference on World Wide Web*, ACM (2007), 211-220.
9. Hsieh, G., Lai, J., Hudson, S.E., and Kraut, R. Using tags to assist near-synchronous communication. *Proceeding of the SIGCHI conference on Human factors in computing systems*, ACM (2008), 223-226.
10. Kiewra, K.A. Notetaking and review: The research and its implications. *Instructional Science 16*, 3 (1987), 233-249.
11. Kiewra, K.A. A review of note-taking: The encoding-storage paradigm and beyond. *Educational Psychology Review 1*, 2 (1989), 147-172.
12. Kiewra, K.A. and Frank, B.M. Cognitive style: Effects of structure at acquisition and testing. *ED 23*, (1985), 261-072.
13. Mamykina, L., Mynatt, E., Davidson, P., and Greenblatt, D. MAHI: investigation of social scaffolding for reflective thinking in diabetes management. *Proceeding of the twenty-sixth annual SIGCHI conference on Human factors in computing systems*, ACM (2008), 477-486.
14. Mamykina, L., Mynatt, E., Davidson, P., and Greenblatt, D. MAHI: investigation of social scaffolding for reflective thinking in diabetes management. *Proceeding of the twenty-sixth annual SIGCHI conference on Human factors in computing systems*, ACM (2008), 477-486.
15. Marlow, C., Naaman, M., Boyd, D., and Davis, M. HT06, tagging paper, taxonomy, Flickr, academic article, to read. *Proceedings of the seventeenth conference on Hypertext and hypermedia*, ACM (2006), 31-40.
16. Nelson, L., Held, C., Pirolli, P., Hong, L., Schiano, D., and Chi, E.H. With a little help from my friends: examining the impact of social annotations in sensemaking tasks. *Proceedings of the 27th international conference on Human factors in computing systems*, ACM (2009), 1795-1798.
17. Oleksik, G., Wilson, M.L., Tashman, C., et al. Lightweight tagging expands information and activity management practices. *Proceedings of the 27th international conference on Human factors in computing systems*, ACM (2009), 279-288.
18. Pauen, S. Biobehavioral Development, Perception, and Action: Evidence for Knowledge–Based Category Discrimination in Infancy. *Child Development 73*, 4 (2002).
19. Sarason, I.G., Pierce, G.R., and Sarason, B.R. *Cognitive interference: theories, methods, and findings*. Psychology Press, 1996.
20. Sen, S., Lam, S.K., Rashid, A.M., et al. tagging, communities, vocabulary, evolution. *Proceedings of the 2006 20th anniversary conference on Computer supported cooperative work*, ACM (2006), 181-190.
21. Shirky, C. Shirky: Ontology is Overrated -- Categories, Links, and Tags. *Clay Shirky's Writings About the Intenet.* http://www.shirky.com/writings/ontology_overrated.html.
22. Vander Wal, T. Thomas Vander Wal: When Folksonomies Supplant Taxonomies « SpicyNodes Blog. *SpicyNodes Blog.* http://www.spicynodes.org/blog/2010/09/13/thomas-vander-wal-when-folksonomies-transplant-taxonomies/.
23. Weick, K.E., Sutcliffe, K.M., and Obstfeld, D. Organizing and the Process of Sensemaking. *ORGANIZATION SCIENCE 16*, 4 (2005), 409-421.
24. Yew, J., Gibson, F., and Teasley, S. Learning by tagging: group knowledge formation in a self-organizing learning community. *Proceedings of the 7th international conference on Learning sciences*, International Society of the Learning Sciences (2006), 1010-1011.

Using Tags to Encourage Reflection and Annotation on Data During Nomadic Inquiry

Alex Kuhn[1], Clara Cahill[2], Chris Quintana[2], Shannon Schmoll[3]

[1]Department of EECS
University of Michigan
2260 Hayward St.
Ann Arbor, MI 48109
kuhnalex@umich.edu

[2]School of Education
University of Michigan
610 East University
Ann Arbor, MI 48109
{claracah, quintana}@umich.edu

[3]Department of Astronomy
University of Michigan
500 Church Street
Ann Arbor, MI 48109
schmoll@umich.edu

ABSTRACT
Nomadic inquiry may benefit from tagging when used for educational purposes to support reflection and annotation during data collection. To that end we created Zydeco, a mobile system to scaffold learners through the science inquiry process in and out of the classroom, and tested it in a museum with 42 middle school students. Students report that tags encouraged reflection and annotation during data collection, suggesting that tagging can be used to support nomadic inquiry. From this work we present some emerging design recommendations for constructing similar systems.

Author Keywords
Mobile learning, learner-centered design, nomadic inquiry, scaffolding, tagging, mobile computing

ACM Classification Keywords
H.5.2 [Information Interfaces and Presentation]: User Interfaces – User-centered design

K.3.1 [Computers and Education]: Computer Uses in Education – Computer-assisted instruction

General Terms
Design

INTRODUCTION
Science inquiry, the process of posing questions and gathering and evaluating empirical evidence to find and explain the answers [6], is a central tenet of national reform efforts, and a key component of science education [1]. However, research has found that learners, particularly those new to the inquiry process, struggle with reflecting on what data to collect and how to annotate the data [7].

With the emergence of networked mobile technology, there is now interest in supporting mobile learning opportunities, or "nomadic inquiry"; inquiry that can occur among a variety of physical contexts, such as a museum or outdoor environment [6]. Challenges with collecting data for later synthesis emerge when students are away from the classroom and performing inquiry on-the-go:

- Organization – collecting and maintaining artifacts such as textual, pictorial, auditory, or numerical data from sensors, and then describing and storing this data for later usage and retrieval.
- Reflection and annotation – beyond merely describing the artifacts collected, the learner must reflect on the utility and purpose of the data and how it answers their inquiry, and use this reflection to take notes for later synthesis.

Previous work in mobile computing includes programs to help students collect data for later evaluation. BioKIDS enabled students to identify and track populations of organisms for later analysis [9], though data was only labeled with the identity of the organisms. Myartspace was a handheld program that enabled users to take photos and audio of data in a museum and access them later [10]. Students appreciated the chance to collect multimedia data during their museum visit, but the system did not organize data, so students had issues finding and using their data later. Ambient Wood used location-aware prompts, just-in-time information and multiple methods to collect data to guide inquiry in an outdoor environment [8]. However, this research relied on having an expert prompt the students at various stages to discuss and reflect on their task. While these studies supported data collection for later use, none of them were focused on encouraging students to reflect on and annotate their data during the nomadic inquiry process without having an expert (a teacher or similar) present.

Tagging functionality has the potential to provide this type of support. Tags are used to meet a variety of personal and social organizational and communicative functions [2]. For example, museums have used tagging as a way to empower visitors to interact socially around exhibits and to make sense of the content that they are exploring [4].

However, students need cognitive support to do meaningful tagging for personal and social annotation, reflection, and organization during science inquiry [2, 7]. One way to do this is to create potential tags in advance with the guidance of an expert [5]. These pre-created tags can be utilized as succinct notes describing the characteristics and purpose of the data, encouraging on-the-spot reflection about previously introduced concepts to help with data annotation- a task that research has shown learners do not perform well in science inquiry [7].

In this paper, we explore the use of tagging for educational purposes, in particular to support middle school students performing nomadic inquiry. To this end we created Zydeco, a mobile system to scaffold learners through the science inquiry process in and out of the classroom [3]. Current mobile devices provide the means to collect data and annotate it *in situ*. We wanted to discover whether kids were able to use tagging for nomadic inquiry, to determine the accuracy and usefulness of students' tags, to assess student perceptions on the tagging process, and understand whether tags can support students in reflecting and annotating on the data they collect.

SYSTEM OVERVIEW

Zydeco was iteratively designed over five rounds of pilot testing with middle school students at a local Natural History museum [3]. Zydeco is designed as part of a three-stage activity to scaffold the science inquiry process.

Stage One: The teacher leads a class discussion where students think about the driving question they are trying to answer and determine potential sub-questions that should be investigated. In our investigation, the driving question "Design an animal that could have survived near Michigan during the Cretaceous period" resulted in six sub-questions regarding topics such as defense traits, offensive traits, and other plants and animals (Figure 1). For each sub-question, the students, through a class discussion with the teacher, create a list of attributes that could potentially be used in describing the data they will collect to support their claims. For instance, tags created for defense traits include "claws" and "armor". This encourages the learner to reflect on what data they are going to collect in advance and helps prepare them to be more effective at collecting data later. During the mobile activity, the tags provide access to cognitive support and cues to remind them of their prior knowledge and experience, facilitating the annotation task.

Stage Two: The student uses a mobile device to collect data to answer each sub-question with the camera on the device. After a photo is taken, the user is prompted to enter in tags from the list they determined with expert help specific to the sub-question (Figure 1). The tags can be utilized as succinct notes describing the characteristics and purpose of the data they are collecting and the tagging process can serve as a point of reflection during the inquiry process.

Applied by tapping, Zydeco eliminates the need to type in a tag on a mobile device. Alternatively the user can enter in additional tags through the keyboard and record audio notes linked to the data.

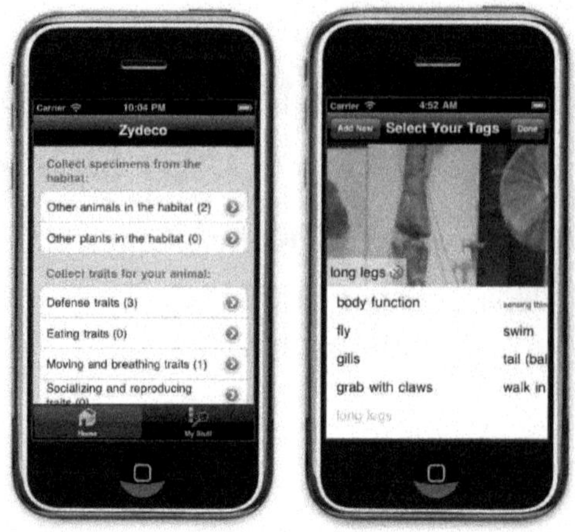

Figure 1. (Left) Sub-questions to collect data on. (Right) Tap to tag interface in Zydeco.

Stage Three: When the student has completed their data collection, the data and tags are uploaded to the Flickr website. In the classroom, students then revisit their data and sort through it using their tags to create an argument or explanation in response to the driving prompt or question.

EXPERIMENT

We tested Zydeco with 42 6th and 7th graders (aged 11-14) from a diverse suburban school district in which 50% of the students qualify for free or reduced-price lunch. The students attended two days of pre-visit activities after school to prepare them for the museum visit, and were introduced to the following inquiry problem: "Design an animal that could have survived near Michigan during the Cretaceous period." Teachers explained that students were going to visit the Natural History museum to collect data about the Cretaceous period and the strategies that animals used to survive the era. After activities introducing the students to life during the Cretaceous period, the teachers and students determined sub-questions and the types of data that they would need to answer them, devising tags to annotate the data. There were 57 different pre-determined tags entered into the Zydeco among the six sub-questions.

At the museum, students were issued iPhones loaded with Zydeco, pre- populated with the tags and sub-questions they had developed in class. Students were allowed 50 minutes to explore the museum, gather data, and annotate it with tags (max of four per photo), titles, and voice notes. This data was then uploaded to Flickr for later use.

After the museum visit, 23 of the students participated in an after-school activity to use the information gathered in the museum to develop explanations based on the information they collected. Students explored the data on Flickr while they developed these explanations.

At the culmination of the activity, 36 students were interviewed about their perceptions and experiences with Zydeco and about tagging in particular. Student responses to the tagging were evaluated for themes using open coding.

Tags applied to the data collected were also analyzed for utilization, accuracy and usefulness.

Analysis and Results

We analyzed three aspects of students' tagging: whether students tagged their data, the accuracy and usefulness of their tags, and their perceptions on tagging from the post activity interview.

Tag utilization

The 42 students participating in the activity took an average of 13 photos each during the visit. Of the 543 total photos taken, 457 (84.2%) of the images were tagged, with an average of two tags per photo. Preset tags created by the students in class prior to the field trip comprised 84% of the total tags used.

Every student took at least six photos, though there was no correlation between photos taken and tags applied per photo. It should be noted that two students avoided tagging any photo, and six additional students used few tags, averaging less than one tag per photo. In interviews, the two students who did not use any tags at all claimed that they had tagged their pictures, one explaining that he chose tags that, "would really go with that picture...so it could be sorted out" and the other explained that, "I would put for wings, fly, and for dinosaur's teeth, I would put tooth, and stuff like that..." These students wrote captions for their photographs that labeled the trait that the photograph was illustrating and overlapped with the terms used as tags. For these students, the captions may have served the purposes of organization, annotation, and reflection, making additional tags superfluous.

For the 34 students (81%) who regularly tagged their photographs, these results are promising as they show that students used tags to ascribe meaning to their photographs. Thus, we found that majority of the students will indeed use tagging to annotate their data.

Tag accuracy and usefulness

Each tag that students applied to their data during collection was analyzed for two attributes:

- Accuracy -- Was the tag true for the data collected? Here, "Fluffy" would not be an accurate tag for a tooth.
- Usefulness -- Would the tag be useful toward answering the Driving Question? A tag of "name means Edmonton lizard" accurately describes an Edmontosaurus, but is not useful toward the end goal of designing an animal that could have survived in the Cretaceous Period.

Two researchers independently rated the tags and achieved an inter-rater reliability of 90% agreement for accuracy and 89% for usefulness with 100% agreement after discussion.

When we evaluated students' tags for accuracy, we found that the mean accuracy of tags per student was 83% and the median was 85.5%. There was no correlation between the number of tags students collected and their accuracy. Only seven of the students had a tagging accuracy of less than 75%. This suggests that most students were mindful about assigning tags to the images they took.

The accurate tags were then evaluated for usefulness. Of the 783 accurate tags, only 38 (~5%) were not useful, suggesting that students were thoughtful during annotation.

Perceptions on tagging

Students were interviewed about their thoughts on the purpose and usage of tags. Several themes emerged from open coding of these interviews (Table 1). Interviews with the two students who did not tag any photos were excluded from analysis. Students appreciated tagging for a variety of reasons, mainly related to helping them learn about, organize, characterize, and store the data for later use. These responses suggest that the students found tagging helpful for meeting the two challenges of doing data collection for later synthesis in nomadic inquiry: data organization, and annotation and reflection.

Some other interesting data came out of the full interview. 31 of the 34 students reported enjoying and appreciating the tagging process, and found it useful. When students were asked what they liked about the system, they repeatedly mentioned that the tags were pre-entered and easy to apply.

However, four students found tagging somewhat confusing. One of them missed the pre-visit activities and felt that the tags didn't match the sub-questions, although he still felt that tagging was useful. Two of the students claimed that it was confusing because they were not able to find all of the information that they needed on the labels in the museum.

DISCUSSION & CONCLUDING REMARKS

Our data suggests that this system of tagging was relatively well-understood and well-received by students, as 81% (32) of the students were able to do tagging, the tags had high accuracy (mean of 83%) and usefulness (mean of 95%), and

	Percent of students who gave this response	Sample response
Labeling or identifying	74%	"I would add a tag that would describe it more, and then it would be easier to know what that animal does and do and eats and stuff..."
Recall	35%	"It was like footnotes, like you could forget it, and you could go back to the footnotes, and it could tell you everything about that kind of dinosaur."
Later use of data	35%	"Because if you just had the animal and the picture, it would make no sense what it would do, so you needed traits to describe that animal."
Categorizing	32%	"I was thinking about what category they fell under like if they ate plants or animals."
Learn more	18%	"[The purpose was] To help you learn more about the dinosaur that you took pictures of."
Unsure	9%	"I didn't use tags that much, because I didn't know how they would be useful really."

Table 1. Coded students' responses concerning their thoughts on the usage and purpose of tags.

student interview responses indicated that they understood the benefits and usefulness of tagging their photos.

In interviews, students identified three general benefits of using tags to support nomadic inquiry:

- Labeling and categorizing data in order to facilitate information retrieval and recall for later synthesis
- Prompting sensemaking and thoughtful data collection
- Expediting the note-taking process and avoiding typing difficulties (when using pre-set tags)

This suggests that using tags as a means of succinct note taking and having predefined attributes can encourage students to reflect upon and annotate their data during nomadic inquiry, something that is difficult for learners [7]. Reinforcing this idea is the fact that 84% percent of the tags applied to the photos were the preset ones, suggesting that students relied heavily on the cognitive support provided by creating the tags before the trip. It is unlikely, though possible, that these preset tags enabled students to randomly select an appropriate tag for their data as they had to choose what sub-question they were collecting the data under and had a potential of 57 different preset tags to choose from.

However, not all of the students utilized tagging or understood the purpose of tags. The issues these students had seemed to stem from not understanding the purpose of the tags and not being able to determine what to tag something based on the information in the museum. This may have occurred because students only spent 90 minutes engaged in pre-visit activities, the activities were unrelated to their daily class curriculum, and some students were absent during this preparation. In addition, a number of the labels at the museum exhibits used exclusively technical scientific terms with language geared towards university students, making it difficult for students to find the information they needed to choose or create their tags.

This was an early testing of the Zydeco system. Future work is needed to focus on what students are doing with the tagged data back in the classroom and determine the learning benefits that this system provides.

Some emerging design recommendations for others who want to utilize tagging for education are:

- Construct potential tags for questions in advance to provide a schema for the activity
- Provide a tap to tag or similar low-cost method to apply the tags *in situ*
- Categorize tags in a relevant way to reduce searching

ACKNOWLEDGMENTS

We would like to thank Linda Knox at the Digital Media Commons, which supported us with the GROCS Grant and the aid of Kira Berman and Amy Harris at the Exhibit Museum of Natural History. We would also like to thank the various teachers and students who gave their time and advice to the project. This material is based on work supported by the National Science Foundation under Grant No. DRL-1020027. Any opinions and findings expressed in this material are those of the authors and do not necessarily reflect those of the National Science Foundation.

REFERENCES

1. American Association for the Advancement of Science *Benchmarks for Science Literacy*. Oxford University Press, New York, 2009.
2. Ames, M. and Naaman, M. Why we tag: motivations for annotation in mobile and online media. In *Proc. Human Factors in Computing Systems (2007)*, 971-980.
3. Cahill, C., Kuhn, A., Schmoll, S., Pompe, A. and Quintana, C. Zydeco: using mobile and web technologies to support seamless inquiry between museum and school contexts. In *Proc. IDC (2010)*, 174-177.
4. Cosley, D., Baxter, J., Lee, S., Alson, B., Nomura, S., Adams, P., Sarabu, C. and Gay, G. A tag in the hand: supporting semantic, social, and spatial navigation in museums. In *Proc. Human Factors in Computing Systems (2009)*, 1953-1962.
5. Furnas, G., Fake, C., von Ahn, L., Schachter, J., Golder, S., Fox, K., Davis, M., Marlow, C. and Naaman, M. Why do tagging systems work? In *Proc. Human Factors in Computing Systems (2006)*, 36-39.
6. Hsi, S. A study of user experiences mediated by nomadic web content in a museum. *Computer Assisted Learning 19*, 3 (2003), 308-319.
7. Quintana, C., Reiser, B. J., Davis, E. A., Krajcik, J., Fretz, E., Duncan, R. G., Kyza, E., Edelson, D. and Soloway, E. A Scaffolding Design Framework for Software to Support Science Inquiry. *Journal of the Learning Sciences 13*, 3 (2004), 337 - 386.
8. Rogers, Y., Price, S., Randell, C., Fraser, D. S., Weal, M. and Fitzpatrick, G. Ubi-learning integrates indoor and outdoor experiences. *Communications of the ACM 48*, 1 (January 2005), 55-19.
9. Songer, N. B. BioKIDS: An animated conversation on the development of complex reasoning in science. In *The Cambridge Handbook of the Learning Sciences*, Cambridge University Press, 2006, 355-370.
10. Vavoula, G., Sharples, M., Rudman, P., Meek, J. and Lonsdale, P. Myartspace: Design and evaluation of support for learning with multimedia phones between classrooms and museums. *Computers & Education 53*, 2 (2009), 286-299.

User Perceptions of the Role and Value of Tags

Yong-Mi Kim
School of Information
University of Michigan
Ann Arbor, MI 48109-1285
kimym@umich.edu

Soo Young Rieh
School of Information
University of Michigan
Ann Arbor, MI 48109-1285
rieh@umich.edu

ABSTRACT
This study investigates user ideas about the role and value of tags in social media. An analysis of 45 interviews with heavy Web users reveals that user perceptions of tags differ from common assumptions held by researchers and designers of social tagging systems. Among beliefs held by participants were that tags were query suggestions or links to other pages, sites, or advertisements – although most identified tags as categories or keywords – and that tags were generated automatically by the computer system. Several participants believed that tags were intended for not only other users but also systems such as search engines. Our findings indicate that Web users, including those who are taggers themselves, experience a high level of uncertainty and confusion about the nature, purpose and value of tags.

Author Keywords
Social tagging, tags, user perceptions, value of tags.

ACM Classification Keywords
H5.m. Information interfaces and presentation (e.g., HCI): Miscellaneous.

General Terms
Human Factors

INTRODUCTION
Since its popularization through sites such as Delicious and Flickr, tags have now become part of the landscape of the Web. In recent years many more sites have emerged employing tags as a key feature. These include sites such as YouTube, LibraryThing, and Last.fm, as well as more specialized sites aimed at organizing and sharing academic research, such as Connotea and CiteULike. Tags are also visible on many blogs and newspaper sites.

Currently tags are a feature of the Web to which users are exposed with little or no guidance. For example, a user uploading photographs to Flickr sees an input field for tags, indicating that tags are expected and the user should already know what goes in that text box. In turn, Web pages display tags with no explanation of what they are. However, it is not clear whether Web users, in particular those who have no previous experience attaching tags to online materials, know or understand what tags are.

CHI 2011, May 7–12, 2011, Vancouver, BC, Canada.

When discussing tag use, it is helpful to distinguish tag *producers* and tag *consumers*, as frequently tag users are understood to be only tag producers, or taggers. In this paper we use the term *tag users* to refer to both tag consumers and tag producers. Tag producers have been extensively studied on a variety of systems such as Flickr [1,7], Delicious [12], enterprise tag applications [10], and research-motivated systems such as MovieLens [8,9] and MobiTag [2,11]. One of the few studies examining the value of tags to both taggers and non-taggers, [9] found that in general taggers had a more favorable view regarding the usefulness of tags than the overall mix of users. These studies have been valuable in contributing to our understanding of tag producers' perceptions regarding the role and value of tags.

Still, it is unclear whether user perceptions of tags match up with what researchers or designers of social tagging systems had in mind. We examine this issue through the following questions:

1. How do tag users conceptualize tags?
2. To what extent do tag users understand the value of tags?

This study addresses these questions through interviews with Web users, including both tag producers and consumers, without restrictions regarding the specific tagging system(s) they use.

METHODOLOGY
This paper is based on interview data taken from a larger study that examines people's use of tags during the search process. Semi-structured interviews were conducted with participants following their completion of four search tasks. These tasks involved the use of various search interfaces, which differed as to whether or not tags were present. No explanation or training regarding these interfaces was provided to participants, so as to replicate typical Web use conditions. In the interview after completion of the search tasks, participants were asked questions on their general experience, use, and perception of tags. Participants were first asked to list the Web sites they visit frequently, as well

as the frequency of their visits. They were then probed about their experience with and their perception of tags on these sites and any additional sites they could recall. At the conclusion of the interview, participants completed a background questionnaire with questions on their demographic information as well as their use of a number of popular tagging sites. Interviews were fully transcribed and analyzed to generate common themes.

Participants

Forty-five participants who reported having seen tags on the Web were included in this study. Participants were undergraduate students self-identified as native English speakers, recruited through on-campus flyers and Facebook advertisements. They were required to be heavy Web users, but were not required to be tag producers. The intent was to capture the experiences of tag users, without priming them beforehand on tags. These 45 participants (29 women and 16 men) ranged in age from 18 to 23 years old, with a mean age of 20 years. There were 25 different majors represented, from fields including engineering, social and natural sciences, business, and humanities.

In terms of tagging experience, 27 of the 45 participants had tagged on Facebook (15), YouTube (5), blogs (4), Flickr (3), Delicious (2), Twitter (1), and a university library-specific tagging application (1). Of these 27 participants, 13 had only Facebook tagging experience, 12 had non-Facebook tagging experience, and 2 had both. Because of the distinctive nature of tagging on Facebook, which was recognized by participants themselves, we reserve the term "taggers" for just those 14 participants who had experience tagging on systems other than Facebook. Twenty-seven participants were identified as tag consumers, of which 8 participants were pure tag consumers with no tagging experience. Tag consumption included clicking on a tag, as well as examining tags to get additional information or help with query terms. Ten participants could not recall specific instances of producing or consuming tags, but said they had seen and were aware of tags on the web. Our participant pool consisted of a mix of tag producers, tag consumers, and the tag-aware.

RESULTS

User Conceptualization of Tags

Three main questions about tags were asked: what are tags, where do they come from, and what is their purpose? The majority of participants supplied site-specific responses regarding tag creators and the purpose of tags, but when defining tags gave answers that applied to all sites.

What are tags according to users?

Participants were asked to describe tags in their own words. The following ideas of tags emerged from their responses:

- Categories: Tags are a way to group related material together (S30: "I think tags are ways to categorize your information, or information on the Web. Because, on your computer you can make folders and then put your documents into your folder, but on Websites you can't just make a folder and then put it into the folder. So, tags kind of work as folders would work on a regular computer.")
- Keywords: Tags describe key aspects of the document (S39: "crucial words that describe a page")
- Query suggestions: Tags are suggested queries (S41: "related terms that you might wish to check out as well")
- Links: Tags are links to other pages, sites, or advertisements (S29: "They're links that basically take you to articles or sites that have information that is like the name of the tag."; S01: "some of them might be ads.")

	Categories	Keywords	Queries	Links
Overall	15 (33%)	14 (31%)	7 (16%)	7 (16%)
Taggers	9 (64%)	3 (21%)	1 (7%)	0 (0%)

Table 1. Definition of tags.

The sites mentioned by participants as featuring tags provide some explanation as to why tags were considered to be query suggestions or links to other pages. Several participants mentioned seeing tags on Google, and what they described as tags turned out to be the list of related searches provided at the bottom of the search results. Some participants appeared to consider links in the text of Wikipedia or New York Times articles to be tags. As can be seen in Table 1, query suggestions and links were hardly mentioned by those with tagging experience.

Who or What Creates Tags?

Answers to the question of who or what creates tags were surprisingly diverse. In contrast to their more broadly applicable descriptions of tags, several participants identified different tag creators depending on the tagging system. For example, a participant who said that people uploading videos to YouTube tagged their own videos, also answered that Google generates tags.

Five types of tag sources were identified: content creator, site owner, system, general public, and people paid to tag (Table 2). Content creators or contributors were mentioned in connection with personal blogs and sites such as Flickr or YouTube. Site owners were mentioned for sites such as Engadget and Rotten Tomatoes that do not obviously rely on user-contributed content. Tags were also sometimes perceived as having been automatically generated in some way by "the system," and not by people. The general public, or people tagging content not their own, was mentioned by taggers with experience using Delicious. Several participants said they didn't know or were not sure, despite experience tagging on Facebook or using tags to find articles on a specific subject in blogs.

Three of the source types – site owners, system, and people paid to tag – are not typically considered taggers in social tagging research. Forty percent of the participants said they had never tagged anything themselves. Reasons provided included not being aware they could attach tags, and not knowing how to do so for a particular system. This may explain why some respondents did not mention other users like themselves when asked who attaches tags to online content.

What is the purpose of tags?

Participants were asked what they considered to be the purpose of tags. The purposes that emerged were findability (30 overall, 8 taggers), organization (12 overall, 8 taggers), leading people to content (4 overall, 0 taggers), and description (2 overall, 1 tagger). Several participants identified multiple purposes for tags.

Findability is about making tagged items easier to find with a search engine. Tags are thought of as links between the tagged item and the search engine (S17: "Search engines use tags as a way to reference searches. And people who create Websites use tags to identify to the search engines"). As a consequence, "people can search for it using those specific terms" (S12). In particular, several participants who had uploaded videos to YouTube and tagged these videos said the tags were for the system or search engine, so that their videos would turn up in searches. For these participants, the intended users of tags were search engines, not other people.

Organization is closely related to categorization, or grouping related items together. In this case the intended beneficiaries are people, both tag producers and tag consumers. This type of purpose was generally associated with tags in blogs (S46: "I tagged them because they were recipes … it was so I could click on something and make all of my recipes come up."). Tags are not for finding the tagged item itself, but for finding things in the same category as the tagged item.

Leading people to content is different from the other two types of purposes described above, in that the intent is not to help people find what they are looking for, but to manipulate or sometimes mislead people to certain sites by use of tags. These sites can be advertisements or simply misrepresented content. Tags are seen as a way to "string you along" (S5) or "lure people in" (S27), in effect describing tag spam [6].

	Overall	Taggers
Content creator	26 (58%)	11 (79%)
Site owner	11 (24%)	1 (7%)
System	7 (16%)	2 (14%)
General public	4 (9%)	3 (21%)
People paid to tag	2 (4%)	1 (7%)

Table 2. Perceived tag creators.

User understanding of tag value

Both tag producers and consumers in our study mentioned ignoring tags or not finding them useful. Tags were actively ignored (S14: "I usually just ignore the tags") or not noticed (S32: "I generally don't notice tags."). Some reasons given for ignoring tags were that tags led to content without regard to the user's needs (S36: "it's what they took a picture of and they want me to go look at it. So normally, I just ignore it."), or led to unwanted content (S23: "Tags, in terms of the context bring me to advertisements or lots of pop-ups come out, and I don't really wanna deal with that.") Tags were not considered necessary (S16: "I don't really need tags … I've never had any use for them."). Contributing to this was the perception that many of the tags were not relevant to the content being tagged (S13: "There are so many tags and it's not that relevant."; S46: "[tags on YouTube] tend to be really bizarre sometimes.").

Tags on blogs were regarded more positively. Participant S46, an avid blog reader, appreciated how tags "take me to large sections of awesome things." She also enjoyed how another blogger used tags for self-expression: "They make me smile because they're just PZ's [blog author's] way of viewing the things that he's responding to." Participants mentioned making use of tags that were topic-specific, as well as those that simply seemed interesting, to explore content in blogs.

Surprisingly, personal experience with tagging sometimes led to a negative perception of the value of tags. For example, for participant S42 exposure to tagging came through a class requiring the use of Delicious. This experience led to a distrust of tags:

S42: "I don't really have a trust for tags yet, because I feel anyone could tag it and it's just your opinion whether it's relevant to a topic or not"

This participant admitted to not expending much effort in tagging, and suspected that other people on the Web were doing likewise. That, in combination with the fact that anybody could tag, meant that tags could not be trusted.

Another participant was led to ignore tags due to "overtagging" by a person close to them:

S27: "I've always been kind of anti-tag and I feel that his [S27's boyfriend] overtagging makes me more so"

For S27, overtagging meant there were a large number of tags due to the inclusion of unnecessary or marginally related tags. She perceived her boyfriend's overtagging in his blog to be about self-presentation, showing how he was interested in diverse topics, and did not consider this to be an appropriate use of tags. She herself did not tag her own blog.

DISCUSSION

In general, our findings reveal that tags are as yet not well understood by Web users, and researchers and system designers should be cautious about assuming that Web users' understanding of tags is similar to their own. While categories and keywords are characterizations commonly found in studies of tagging [3,4,7], our study participants also saw query suggestions and links as tags. We also note that while tags are touted as being "user-generated," they were not uniformly perceived to be as such in our study. Our study participants also mentioned site owners, automatic generation, and people paid to tag in addition to the more typical content creators (e.g., Flickr) or the general public (e.g., Delicious). Participants' beliefs regarding who was doing the tagging varied depending on the site.

A surprising finding was that several participants reported that tags were produced for the consumption of search engines, rather than for other people. This included participants who had experience in uploading and tagging their videos on YouTube. One reason for this perception may be that on YouTube, tags are not visible to users by default. The system requests tags during the video upload, although tags are not visible otherwise, and this may engender the perception that tags are intended for the system, rather than other YouTube users.

Through studies of tag producers, HCI researchers have identified a variety of purposes for tagging, including organization [1,7], finding/search [1,7], self-expression [2,7], reflection or thinking about the tagged items [2], signaling of involvement and expertise [10,11], and adding context or annotation [1]. Our study findings indicate that non-taggers do not see such a rich variety of purposes for tags. The prevalence of YouTube use in our participants (44 out of 45 participants) likely influenced our findings. YouTube, being casual and entertainment-oriented, presents a different use environment than museums or enterprise tagging systems. In addition, YouTube tags have been found to have a number of significant differences from other tagging systems [5].

A limitation of this study is that our sample population of undergraduate students may not be representative of Web users. But, given their age range, participants are so-called "digital natives" for whom the Web has existed their entire lives. They have easy access to computers and Internet connections and are expected to use the Web regularly as part of their school and personal activities. The fact that a population very likely to have encountered tags on the Web had such varying conceptions of tags presents challenges to tagging system designers intending to appeal to wider and more diverse user bases.

The present study indicates the need for a large-scale survey investigating conceptualization and perception of the value of tags. Such a study can reveal perceptions of tagging related to additional social tagging systems not covered in our study. It is important to note that Web users still experience a great deal of uncertainty and confusion about the nature, purpose, and value of tags.

REFERENCES

1. Ames, M. and Naaman, M. Why we tag: motivations for annotation in mobile and online media. *Proc. CHI 2007*, ACM Press (2007), 971-980.
2. Cosley, D., Baxter, J., Lee, S., Alson, B., Nomura, S., Adams, P., Sarabu, C., and Gay, G. A tag in the hand: supporting semantic, social, and spatial navigation in museums. *Proc. CHI 2009*, ACM Press (2009), 1953-1962.
3. Golder, S.A., and Huberman, B. A. Usage Patterns of Collaborative Tagging Systems. *Journal of Information Science, 32*, 2 (2006), 198-208.
4. Hammond, T., Hannay, T., Lund, B., & Scott, J. Social Bookmarking Tools (I): A General Review. *D-Lib Magazine, 11*, 4 (2005).
5. Heckner, M., Neubauer, T., and Wolff, C. Tree, funny, to_read, google: what are tags supposed to achieve? a comparative analysis of user keywords for different digital resource types. *Proc. SSM '08*, ACM Press (2008), 3-10.
6. Heymann, P., Koutrika, G., and Garcia-Molina, H. Fighting Spam on Social Web Sites: A Survey of Approaches and Future Challenges. *IEEE Internet Computing, 11*, 6 (2007), 36-45.
7. Marlow, C., Naaman, M., Boyd, D., and Davis, M. HT06, tagging paper, taxonomy, Flickr, academic article, to read. *Proc. Hypertext 2006*, ACM Press (2006), 31-40.
8. Sen, S., Lam, S., K. (Tony), Rashid, A. M., Cosley, D., Frankowski, D., Osterhosuse, J. et al. tagging, communities, vocabulary, evolution (N. 4-8, Trans.). *Proc. CSCW 2006*, ACM Press (2006), 181-190.
9. Sen, S., Harper, F. M., LaPitz, A., & Riedl, J. The Quest for Quality Tags. *Proc. GROUP 2007*, ACM Press (2007), 361-370.
10. Thom-Santelli, J., Muller, M.J., and Millen, D.R. Social tagging roles: publishers, evangelists, leaders. *Proc. CHI 2008*, ACM Press (2008), 1041-1044.
11. Thom-Santelli, J., Cosley, D., and Gay, G. What do you know?: experts, novices and territoriality in collaborative systems, *Proc. CHI 2010*, ACM Press (2010), 1685-1694.
12. Wash, R. and Rader, E. Public bookmarks and private benefits: An analysis of incentives in social computing. In *Proc. ASIS&T '07*, 2007.

Towards a Feminist HCI Methodology: Social Science, Feminism, and HCI

Shaowen Bardzell
Indiana University
919 E 10th St.
Bloomington, IN, 47408
selu@indiana.edu

Jeffrey Bardzell
Indiana University
919 E 10th St.
Bloomington, IN, 47408
jbardzel@indiana.edu

ABSTRACT

With substantial efforts in ubiquitous computing, ICT4D, and sustainable interaction design, among others, HCI is increasingly engaging with matters of social change that go beyond the immediate qualities of interaction. In doing so, HCI takes on scientific and moral concerns. This paper explores the potential for feminist social science to contribute to and potentially benefit from HCI's rising interest in social change. It describes how feminist contributions to debates in the philosophy of science have helped clarify relationships among objectivity, values, data collection and interpretation, and social consequences. Feminists have proposed and implemented strategies to pursue scientific and moral agendas together and with equal rigor. In this paper, we assess the epistemologies, methodologies, and methods of feminist social science relative to prior and ongoing research efforts in HCI. We conclude by proposing an outline of a feminist HCI methodology.

Author Keywords

Feminism, design, theory, user research, feminist HCI, methodology, philosophy of science, post-positivism

ACM Classification Keywords

H5.m. Information interfaces and presentation (e.g., HCI): Miscellaneous.

General Terms

Design, Theory

INTRODUCTION

HCI's move out of the workplace and into everyday life has had a host of profound implications. Technologies, evaluation criteria, user research and scientific paradigms have all rushed to keep up with this change. In areas as diverse as affective computing, experience design, and domestic technologies, yesterday's preoccupations with productivity and efficiency seem quaint. Today, HCI is increasingly sensitive to its own influence on the broadest range of possible stakeholders, exemplified, for example, by sustainable interaction design.

In responding to these needs, HCI has turned to a wide range of cultural theories, from philosophical pragmatism to literary theory. A recent example of this trend is the notion of "feminist HCI," which [3] characterizes as the integration of feminist theory in HCI practice. Yet as promising as feminist HCI seems, beyond clearing a space for feminist HCI and introducing a set of qualities that characterize feminist interaction, [3] leaves open what exactly such an approach might look like in practice.

Feminism seems well positioned to support HCI's increasing awareness and accountability for its own social and cultural consequences, so developing feminist HCI is worthwhile. A particularly promising source is feminist social science, where researchers have practiced, theorized about, and debated scientific approaches committed to social progress. For example, feminist researchers Hanmer and Saunder [22] used community-based, at home interviews to study domestic violence in order to develop new forms of self-help and mutual aid among women. Naples [43] researched women on welfare and in college to reveal the problematic construction of welfare recipients as lacking work motivation. At its core, feminist social science research advocates for the integration of knowledge and responsible action, with a mandate for both individual and social change, reflecting a core value of feminism: critiquing and resisting the status quo [50]. However, feminist social science is not directed specifically at HCI, and any appropriation of this kind of research into HCI will take some work, though some work in HCI, including participatory design and other works that exhibit the values of feminist social science [10, 15, 36] are already working in this direction.

This paper explores the dynamic relations between values and different formulations of objectivity in the wake of post-positivist philosophy of science, stressing feminist contributions to these debates and arguing for their applicability to HCI today.

KNOWING TRUTH AND/OR DOING GOOD

At stake is the tension between traditional science (e.g., the logical positivism of Carnap and even much of contemporary post-positivism) and a science that sees itself as socially and politically engaged. Whereas traditional science champions the pursuit of truth and places values out of bounds, the latter argues that socio-cultural values are inevitably bound up in scientific practice and moreover that that's how it *ought* to be. To be responsive to this tension, science must negotiate between the Scylla and Charybdis of a nihilistic fetish for pure truth (the unwanted extreme of traditionalism) and an ideological battle where positions precede and determine facts (the unwanted extreme of politically oriented science). At the heart of this problem is the nature and implications of the intellectual value or ideal of *objectivity*.

Contemporary philosopher of science Harold Kincaid characterizes scientific objectivity as a "virtue" and a "symptom of good science," defining it as follows:

> [T]he ideal of an unbiased, disinterested pursuit of the truth is the hallmark of science. Science is objective when our beliefs reliably indicate the way the world is rather than the way we want it to be. [33]

Key to this definition of objectivity is the scientist's bracketing of the self, that is, excluding from scientific analysis one's values, goals, fears, and hopes—in short, one's perspective as a living individual. Accordingly, the scientist is able to assert "proposition *p*" and not "proposition *p*, in my opinion." In a recent philosophical essay on objectivity in science, ethics, and aesthetics, Richard Miller offers a two-pronged definition of an objective scientific truth claim, writing that it both (a) is perspective-independent and also (b) features data sufficient to compel agreement from qualified and rational others [42]. On this view, truth claims come from data, not from individuals, and the only question is whether the data is compelling enough to force assent to the claims they imply. Many of HCI's scientific claims are framed in this way: e.g., the performance increases of a new interface [e.g., 32], the features and organization of team-based collaboration [e.g., 45], and measurable aspects of the users' affective response to interaction [e.g., 48].

Yet one of the most valorized outcomes of scientific research in HCI is its implications for design. But design is an intervention, an intentional effort to create change. As design theorist Papanek defines it, design's job is "to transform man's environment and tools and, by extension, man himself," [47]. Papanek's definition here seems to foreground the very concerns—human values and intentions to bring about social change—that are backgrounded by scientific objectivity. Designs are consitituents of our artificial world, which we have made in the hopes of improving human quality of life and even protecting and developing our potential "futures" [19]. We can see this thread in HCI as well: these include ubiquitous computing [e.g., 51, 8], information communication technology for development (ICT4D) [e.g., 31], intimate interaction [46], sustainable interaction design [e.g., 6,14], HCI has shown a strong interest in recent years to participate in large-scale social change.

This tension between the disinterested pursuit of truth and the role of human social perspectives and values in science has been a major issue in the history and philosophy of science since the early 1950s, when Quine launched a series of eventually decisive attacks against logical positivism. Briefly, Quine argued that scientific theories are always underdetermined by any data and demonstrated that social and pragmatic concerns were inextricably tied up with science [58]. Building on Quine, other thinkers subsequently explored ways that values interact with science [e.g., 52, 41] and scientific practices emerge within social processes [e.g., 34]. Operating within this post-Quinean tradition, feminist science has demonstrated that gender has significantly influenced both scientific processes and products and feminists developed their own analyses of the roles of values in science as well as in the social nature of scientific practice.

As an applied scientific field, HCI inherits these tensions from the social and natural sciences as well. In recent years, work in HCI has increasingly raised concerns about the role of interaction designers' commitments to values and socio-political change, that is, the kinds of concerns that have, as we have argued, a complex relationship with good science. Lest such commitments lead interaction designers to imposing their own perspectives and values on others, designers have an ethical obligation to aspire toward a moral equivalent of scientific objectivity. *Moral objectivity*, as described by [42], involves both perspective-independent (moral) truth claims and truth-enhancing moral reasoning processes. Making perspective-independent truth claims about just or virtuous action must, for Miller, be based on "certain fundamental assumptions" (e.g., that "justice requires equal concern and respect for everyone willing to show equal concern and respect for all"), and these assumptions are comparable to the fundamental assumptions of science (e.g., that sense perception is basically reliable). By "certain processes [that are] truth-enhancing," Miller means that some processes of moral reasoning are more likely than others to lead to moral objectivity, such as maintaining standards for justice. The ideals or symptoms of good scientific versus good moral reasoning only partly overlap, however, so any scientist's integration of scientific and moral rationality is recognized as a non-trivial problem.

Inasmuch as HCI is to pursue a socially conscious agenda, it will need to develop its own strategies for achieving both scientific and moral objectivities, conflicts between the two notwithstanding. HCI has many resources on which to draw for this work: critical theory, philosophy, as well as design and design theory among them. We focus on the feminist philosophy of science, not only because it has grappled with these issues in ways that are recognized as "astonishingly complex and worthwhile" [30] even by non-feminist philosophers of science, but also because feminist philosophy of science, unlike much of critical theory, has been applied and developed in conjunction primarily with empirical science, bringing decades of case studies and examples with it.

FEMINISM AND SOCIAL SCIENCE

We explore feminist social science in detail below, but a brief overview should help orient readers new to this material. Perhaps most importantly, feminist social science research is not a monolithic unity, that is, a tight and coherent set of methodologies or a common set of domains [49]. It is often characterized as a family of loosely related approaches with some shared features [26,11,50,40,49]. Three philosophical commitments are common to feminist research. First is a categorical rejection of the notion that science is value-free. This rejection contradicts a key doctrine of logical positivism and remains controversial within post-positivism today [33]. We return to this concern below. The second commitment is to empirical accounts of human experience: "the experience of all human beings is valid and must not be excluded from our understandings," [50], a position compatible with HCI, which has been increasingly experience-oriented and broad-minded about what constitutes a stakeholder. Third is feminism's commitment to gender. It should be noted that this commitment is more than advancing the position of women; it is a commitment to ensure that gender remains, in Helen Longino's words, "a relevant axis of investigation," that gender is not "being disappeared" any more in science [cited in 44].

In addition to these three philosophical positions are methodological considerations, including a more transparent and reflexive relationship between researchers and research subjects, pluralist strategies to access and represent different ways of knowing, and a special emphasis on accounting for female voices. More recently, many feminist researchers have increasingly looked beyond women to other underprivileged groups as well, such as minorities, immigrants, children, homosexuals, and so forth. Finally, most feminist social science includes a reflexive dimension, which considers among other things whether and how it is itself "feminist."

Preliminary Notes Concerning Feminism and HCI

Before proceeding, it is also worth making the following points to preempt a number of common misconceptions.

There is no feminism but rather feminisms. As with any other field of its age and size, feminism has no shortage of internal factions, historical paradigms, and so forth. This paper focuses on the work of feminist philosophers of science and feminist methodologists (it is not concerned with, e.g., feminist literary critics or political activists). Feminist methodologists are a subgroup within feminism that began in feminism's second wave and gained momentum in its third.[1]

Feminism is not the investigation of gender. Or, restating as applies to our field, feminist HCI is not the same thing as gender and computing. Gender and computing is a domain of inquiry, but we have already shown that feminist social science is characterized more by a body of theories and methodologies—which, to be sure were historically achieved through interrogations of women's experiences—than it is by an overriding concern for offering traditional scientific representations of gendered states of affairs. As Star suggests, echoing feminist science's post-Quinean roots, "feminism does not have to have gender at its ground zero.... [i]t was about reclaiming a certain holistic way of looking at things" [60].

Feminist theory does not favor qualitative over quantitative approaches. Feminism is concerned with representing people on their own terms, as opposed to representing them from the unacknowledged (and even denied via the rhetoric of "objectivity") perspective of dominant social classes. Both quantitative and qualitative approaches can be used in distortive or unjust ways, and both can also be used with rigor and reflexivity to reveal salient aspects of gendered and/or social life [50, 55]. Indeed, some feminist social scientists have proposed a "critical quantitative methodology" to support quantitative research [56].

Feminism and HCI are not in conflict; HCI is not inherently "sexist" or "antifeminist"; and feminism does not operate in a privileged space over and above HCI. Indeed, we are committed to the position that placing feminism and HCI into a dialogue is mutually beneficial to both disciplines, as HCI and psychology, HCI and sociology, and HCI and design have all likewise enjoyed two-way relationships.

Epistemology, Methodology, and Methods

Thinking philosophically about science, one can identify different levels of theory and method and position them along a spectrum. Throughout this paper, we will refer to epistemology, methodology, and methods as constituting key levels of any approach to data gathering (in this, we are following [26, 55], and in HCI, [17, 7]). Feminist philosophers of science, along with many other post-positivist philosophers of science since Quine, have focused on this distinction as a way of demonstrating that data collection methods are tied to intellectual positions, that is, that methods are not simply tools found in the world that neutrally reveal data as it is. The focus found in many social science textbooks on the technicalities of particular methods often comes at the expense of reflection on the positions—philosophical, social, and political—embedded in our selection and use of such methods. Feminists' emphasis on this distinction helps expose the relationships between data collection and such positions, facilitating transparency and self-criticality in science.

At the most abstract and general end of the spectrum is an *epistemology*, which is a theory of knowledge, including to whom, by what means, and under what circumstances knowledge is produced. At the most concrete and particular end of this spectrum are individual data collection methods themselves. A *method* is "a technique for gathering and

---

[1] Second-wave feminism might be briefly characterized as emancipatory feminism, i.e., liberating women from informal forms of oppression (peaking in the 1960s and 70s); third-wave feminism includes postmodern, postcolonial, and/or multicultural feminism (peaking in the 1990s).

analyzing information," [55] such as observation, interview, survey, and so forth. Methods can be highly technical in nature, and social science textbooks are loaded with descriptions of them. In between and connecting these two extremes are methodologies. A *methodology* implements an epistemology by selecting and configuring methods in particular ways; methodology is "the terrain where philosophy and action meet, where the implications for what we believe for how we should proceed get worked out" [55]. Methodologies rely on implicit or explicit assumptions, often pointing back to an epistemology, and they can provide a coherent basis on which to decide on and explain the use of a given set of methods in a given research situation.

If, as Quine argued, theories are under-determined by data, then the *choice* of which theory to use becomes a vital concern to science. This 3-part distinction provides a normative model that clarifies the relationships among data, methods, holistic conceptual systems, and the socio-cultural value systems in which all of the above participate. The resulting clarity among these key aspects of scientific research provides a way of linking scientific and moral objectivities, hopefully supporting better reasoning in research design and better tools for evaluating the scientific and moral reasoning undergirding a given project.

Feminism's Critiques of Social Science

Feminist social science has in part developed an identity by defining itself in relation to traditional social science. That activity has involved both a philosophical critique of social science and it has also led to contributions to social science. We synthesize both the critique and the contributions in this paper, beginning with the critique.

Perhaps the most fundamental contribution of feminist philosophers of science has been their development of the critique (and its implications) of traditional science's aspirations to be value-free. Feminists offer two objections to the notion that science is value-free or neutral. First, feminists criticize scientists for performing the "God trick," that is, of speaking authoritatively and from nowhere [23, p4, the term "God trick" is from Haraway]. Harding notes that in performing the God trick, social scientists fail to disclose whose interests they are working in, typically in the name of powerful institutions, such as policy centers, schools, hospitals, unions, immigration services, law enforcement, etc. Yet these institutions, historically administered in the West by white men, have extraordinary control over the lives of all people: women, minorities, children, immigrants, and so forth. Yet most of these populations have no authorial voice in the scientific research about them and the resulting social policy used to manage them [23, 55]. The applicability of this critique to HCI is quite obvious: if interaction designers doing user research are not careful—e.g., they conflate "user experience" with "brand"—they similarly will contribute to an undemocratic and unjust state of affairs by framing their research to meet the needs of those powerful enough to pay for their services, rather than the needs of the users and stakeholders broadly conceived who will be affected by the system, as explored in e.g., [5].

A related issue is feminists' challenge to the idea of disembodied rationalism, as if scientists are purely rational beings, who are sexually indifferent, "a mind unlocated in space, time" [21]. Part of this critique is that disembodied rationalism overlooks two vital aspects of human life that are traditionally assigned to women: the care of our bodies and emotional labor. This oversight has implications for HCI: given the rise of embodiment as a theoretical orientation to interaction design [16], and the rise of affective computing as well as the role of emotion in user experience design [48, 35], failing to investigate women's perspectives in these areas, in service of an ungendered construction of "the user" [3], is problematic. Another critique of disembodied rationalism can be found in [23], which observes that underprivileged never asked for social research to be disembodied and purely rational; it is not hard to see, in fact, that any knowledge production divorced from everyday existence itself is more compatible for a group whose needs are already met, as opposed to underpriveleged groups, for whom such needs have not been met. As Harding puts it, "the questions an oppressed group wants answered are rarely requests for so-called pure truth. Instead, they are queries about how to change conditions."

The second objection to the neutrality claim is that it cuts science off from a productive source of good science: politically engaged research. In other words, whereas traditional science regards the political as an impediment to good science, feminists like Harding [23] argue that engaging in politics *directs* research and offers new avenues of insight:

> Hilary Rose argues that women's responsibility for their bodies and for emotional labor gives women a distinctive perspective on their own bodies and on the sciences. Patricia Hill Collins argues that Black women's distinctive activities in slavery, in the kinds of work Black women are assigned today, and in their ongoing struggles to support their families and communities gives them powerful critical perspectives on the limitations of mainstream sociology and the social institutions it services.

In these examples, turning to the experiences of the marginal is not only ethical, in the sense that it empowers a comparatively powerless population to participate in processes of social control, but it is also *good science*, because it introduces the potential for empirically derived insights harder to acquire by other means. Taken to an extreme, such an approach could lead to *essentialism*, i.e., the doctrine that women's experience is fundamentally different from men's, which implies that some insights are only available to women. Rejecting such essentialism is one of the central positions of third-wave feminism; however, it seems possible to promote the empirical study of marginal voices without committing to a strong essentialism.

Another critique feminists make against traditional science is that its framing of problem spaces is that it has often been neither politically neutral nor empirically justified. For example, [55] notes that social science research questions

> tend to be framed in terms of what is wrong with the person who is experiencing the problem, rather than in terms of what it is about the current social order that makes the problem likely. For example, a list of common research questions in the social sciences reads: What kind of people are likely to abuse drugs? ... Why is the working class so weak and disorganized? ... What is the influence of families and peers on discouraging African American children from succeeding in school? How can we teach people with developmental disabilities to have more self-determination?

Such framings seem to be a practical outcome of the voicelessness of the disenfranchised, because each of these framings reflects and perpetuates an outsider perspective on their lifeworlds.

The feminist alternative, turning to the disenfranchised as a source and guide of scientific inquiry, may lead to more benevolent framings. We can see this dynamic in a contemporary discourse surrounding women in Computer Science. This debate often frames the problem as one inhering in the women themselves: how can we raise girls' (deficient) confidence, (deficient) math competence, or (deficient) interest in technology so that they'll enroll in Computer Science? Underlying such conversations is what Harding calls an "add women" approach, in which traditional problems are addressed simply by adding data about women to the calculus, while leaving the traditional framing intact. So, "how can we raise undergraduate enrollments?" becomes "how can we raise undergraduate enrollments by adding more women?" The feminist alternative is to create knowledge about women *for women*, that is, answering questions to promote agendas that women care about (and one could apply this argument applies to any underprivileged group). Thus, if we want more women in computing, the feminist approach would suggest that rather than transforming women in primary and secondary education to better prepare them for undergraduate CS, we might also consider transforming undergraduate CS so that it more clearly relates to undergraduate women's own intellectual agendas.

[55] also cites other systematic framing problems in the social sciences. These include logical dichotomy, abstract individuation, and objectification. A *logical dichotomy* entails the analytic use of dichotomies, e.g., between work and leisure or paid and domestic labor, that seem natural to one class while failing to apply, or apply in the same ways, to underprivileged classes. An example of a logical dichotomy in HCI might be early/late adopter, which obviously has different significance for Silicon Valley professionals than it does for rural or urban youth in low social and economic status school districts. *Abstract individuation* refers to discussions of an individual "in isolation from and unconnected with its interpersonal, historical, or physical context," effectively reifying that person as a "type." In addition to examples of abstract individuation common in sociology—women of color, people with disabilities—HCI has added an important abstract individuation of its own: the user, which as [3] notes is a genderless, ahistorical individual who only exists in front of a software application. As we have seen earlier *objectification* denies the agency and subjecthood of people under study. In HCI, quite a bit of traditional usability evaluation is objectifying, because it is more concerned with task completion time and error rates than it is with the individual agency, lifeworlds, and personal goals of users. Again, in addition to the ethical concerns one can raise about these, feminists argue that they are not rational: "we social scientists do not derive [such framings] from empirical observation" [55]. Too often, we uncritically bring these framings to the data.

FEMINIST CONTRIBUTIONS TO SOCIAL SCIENCE

Feminist social scientists do not simply offer critiques from the sidelines; rather, they have distinctively contributed to both the philosophy and practice of science. In this section, we explore these contributions using the 3-part distinction introduced above: epistemology, methodology, and method.

Epistemology

Perhaps the most influential epistemological contribution of feminist social science has been standpoint theory. Feminist standpoint theory develops the idea that all knowledge is socially situated, as opposed to neutral and purely disinterested, into an epistemology. To move from the mere idea that knowledge is socially situated to an epistemology entails the fleshing out and structuring of that idea into theory, which is precisely what standpoint theory accomplishes.

It begins with a descriptive vocabulary for accounting for the situations from which scientific knowledge is produced, beginning with the researcher's unique place in and view on the world [1, 29]. In [24], Harding names the researcher's perspective a "standpoint" and continues on to identify four elements that compose it:

- **A physical location in nature**. Countering the "view from nowhere" and the "God trick," this element stresses that we are all in the physical world, and often differentially so. For example, from menstruation and lactation to their engagement with domestic labor, women inhabit a different world than men. Extending this logic, everyone, in one way or another, inhabits only certain parts/aspects of the natural and social worlds.
- **Interests in and about that location**. Because we occupy different spaces in the natural and social worlds, through natural difference and/or social segregation, we develop different interests and goals, which shape the work, including social science, that we undertake.
- **Discourses that shape sensemaking concerning the location**. To make possible understandings of locations, we use discourses, including "metaphors, models, and

narratives" [24, cited in 55] to structure our cognition and enable us to form intentions and express them to others. Such discourses are often created and maintained through powerful institutions, including universities, courts, the media, and governance.

- **A position in the social production of knowledge**. The pursuit, funding, and publication of scientific research, as well as its implications for one's reputation, tenure, etc., is also managed through institutions. People participate in these institutions differentially, from the quantity and quality of their publications, the nature of their professional networks, and so forth. Our position in the social production of knowledge shapes both what we are able to say and who hears us (and how).

Standpoint theory offers a model from which to understand articulate each scientist's "view from somewhere," providing greater transparency and accountability. Compatible approaches have been raised in HCI. For example, the "reflective HCI" series of workshops and papers [18, 53, 54] propose a more humanist, and less traditionally scientific, epistemology for HCI research and practice. Along similar lines, Star [57] warns that failing to engage seriously in the cultural context and using the facile rhetoric of user standardization should be replaced by a strong focus on "concrete situations," rather than abstract models for design.

Standpoint theory does more than flesh out what a standpoint is; it actually proposes a new strategy to achieve objectivity. Haraway [28, cited in 40] proposes "feminist versions of objectivity"; that is, limited knowledges that make explicit their positioning, their construction of power, and that seek to make visible the claims of the less powerful. Harding proposes such a strategy in [25]. There, she introduces what she calls a "strong objectivity," which engages the marginal in two independent ways. First, the experiences of marginal, rather than dominant, groups are the subject of research. As noted earlier, when privileged groups (such as academic, government, and corporate scientists) understand marginal experiences, a dialectic is staged that gives scientists a more heterogeneous view of the world. Second, Harding argues that the marginal should participate actively in setting the agenda for the scientific research, that is, answering the question, "what is this research *for*?" A second dialectic is thus staged between the moral interests (i.e., practical values and predispositions) of two groups. Foregrounding, rather than backgrounding, the moral perspectives of the participants makes this double dialectic possible, and it is this dialectic that prevents the unconscious encroachment of the assumptions and values of the privileged onto the whole project.

We note that the first of these strategies—the focus on the experiences of the marginal—is compatible with traditional scientific objectivity. The second of the strategies—the collaborative effort to decide what this research is for—is directed at moral objectivity. In other words, Harding's "strong objectivity" can be seen as an instantiation of a "scientific-moral objectivity," and as such is directly responsive to HCI's present dilemma to maintain scientific rigor while taking social issues more seriously. Such a double dialectic could serve as a template for empirical research in HCI, e.g., in ICT4D research.

Feminist Methodologies

"A *methodology* is a theory and analysis of how research does or should proceed.... For example, discussions of how functionalism (or Marxist political economy or phenomenology) should be or is applied in particular research areas are methodological analyses" [26, p3]. Methodologies are the glue that tie together our epistemologies and our methods: they help us choose which methods to use, and they become our tacit or explicit rationale for doing so. Feminist methodologies, therefore, should be seen not as a just-add-water procedure, but rather as loosely organized collection of compatible values, perspectives, and positions (many of which are not exclusively feminist). This collection in turn can inform reasoning about the selection and deployment of particular data collection methods as well as reasoning about what constitutes appropriate or desirable data sources.

We offer here a critical synthesis of issues common among the range of feminist methodologies. To lay out this synthesis, we describe these common issues using the four interrelated categories of intellectual positions, moral values, features and characteristics, and domains of inquiry. We note again that not all feminist methodologies avail themselves equally (or at all) of each of these issues and that moreover many of them are shared by other scientific and critical schools of thought.

Intellectual positions refer to normative research assumptions and goals common to many feminist social scientists. These intellectual positions have great range, and yet they also generally cohere with each other. Perhaps the most basic is that feminist methodologies are guided by feminist theory [50], that is, they are informed by "a normative framework that interrelates 'injustice,' a politics for 'women,' (however these categories are understood), ethical practices that eschew the 'unjust' exercise of power, and theory that conceptualizes gendered power within this normative framework" [49]. Research itself is implicated in power dynamics, and feminist methodologies generally seek to deal with that in some way: e.g., the injunction to be reflexive about the exercise of power [49], the importance of researchers being held morally, not merely intellectually, accountable for their practice [49], and the tendency of feminist researchers to cultivate relationships with their subjects [50].

Moral values are the positions feminists take that explicitly express their interestedness in the world. A commitment to a particular understanding of "justice," for example, is a moral value (known as a "non-epistemic value," because it is external to the "pure" pursuit of truth) that feminists argue should shape research. Such a value would be excluded from and stand in contrast to the sorts of values (known as "epistemic values") embraced by traditional science, such as a fit between data and theories, fruitfulness, predictability, reliability, etc. In a general sense, feminist methodologies are oriented toward the production "of knowledge that will be useful for the effective transformation of gendered injustice and subordination" [49]. This value is also formulated in terms of benefits for women, from establishing shelters for battered women to raising consciousness to women's issues [13, cited in 11]. Instrumental to commitments to social change are a number of other non-epistemic values: feminist methodologies seek to represent human diversity [50] and to shift social science knowledge production away from managing people to nurturing them [55]. Given the role of information systems in managing people today, this perspective is especially urgent.

Features and characteristics of feminist methodologies offer common ways to implement the positions and values just described into actual scientific practices. Feminist methodologies often embed a self-critique of their research [13, cited in 11; 50], one example being Harding's call for a stronger objectivity than that found in traditional social science [25]. Reinharz [50] notes that feminist methodologies tend to be multi-, inter-, and transdisciplinary, in part because feminism falls outside of traditional disciplines and because it leverages so many disciplines to pursue its goals. The use of multiple disciplines and the goal of being inclusive of marginal voices means that feminist methodologies often involve a multiplicity of methods [50]. These methods often include participatory methods, because these help implement the value of empowering research subjects to shape the research [13, cited in 11]. Implementing the goal of reflexivity often means that feminist methodologies include the researcher as a person [50]. Finally, Longino observes that because the critique and development of theory is a social process, heterogeneous scientific communities, with access to broader background assumptions, are likely to identify bad assumptions more quickly than homogeneous ones [37].

Domains of inquiry refer to common topic areas of research. Feminist methodologies are used in such a wide variety of domains that it is hard to identify any domains that are particularly interesting for feminist research. Obviously, gender and inequality in general remain hot topics, because exposing inequalities makes it easier to change them [13, cited in 11]. But inequalities such as these can be found throughout life and are hardly limited to any particular domain: they can be found in literature and film; in schools, hospitals, and prisons; in governments, media, and marketplaces to name a few. Another popular domain of inquiry is experience [13, cited in 11], but again, human experience is common to all areas of human life, so this too hardly pinpoints feminists to a particular domain.

This synthesis of common issues in feminist methodologies clearly does not add up to a tangible methodology, but it reveals some of the relationships among intellectual, moral, and scientific positions and practices, which can guide ways that feminist social scientists can make practical decisions about the fitness of theories and methods. The importance of methodology, as opposed to mere technical descriptions of valid methods, has come up recently in HCI, most notably in the discussion of ethnography and the use of cultural probes in the field [20, 17, 7]. This research has critiqued the application of methods in design situations in ways that lack corresponding methodologies. Growing differences in methodological dispositions is also quite evident in experience design, where some researchers (e.g., [39]) are proposing dialogic, critical frameworks to help designers interpret experience with technology, while other researchers seek to discover "valid useful user experience measurement" [35], an approach that is the genealogical descendent of the applied psychology approaches introduced into the field by [12]. Competence in UX design today surely entails more than skill with methods; practitioners also have to make practical decisions about methods that are based on their relationships to diverging UX methodologies and epistemologies.

Feminist Methods

As social scientists, feminists have often availed themselves of traditional quantitative and qualitative methods, including in-depth interviews, discourse analysis, observation, and so forth. At the same time, feminists have methodologically valorized a number of new or non-traditional methods. [50] offers a descriptive list of many of them. Over the decades, feminist-created social science methods include group diaries, dramatic role-play, (women's) genealogy and network-tracing, non-authoritative (participatory/conversational) research, studying unplanned personal experience, the talking-pictures technique (i.e., photos taken at intervals and included in an interview kit), and open-ended speech into a tape recorder and/or essay-type questionnaires.

A few aspects of this list are worth noting for HCI researchers and practitioners. First, though feminist methodologists may claim, as a matter of principle, that they are agnostic about quantitative versus qualitative methods, the actual methods they have put forward historically favor qualitative methods. This in no way invalidates their position of qualitative/quantitative agnosticism, but at the very least it suggests opportunities for feminists—including feminists in HCI—to innovate more in the area of quantitative methods.

Second, these methods are strong at collecting data about everyday experience, that is, subjectively felt life. Given feminism's emphasis on the importance of every type of human experience, this strength is not surprising. A cost of that emphasis is a move away from established scientific models and frameworks, which are treated with suspicion when it comes to facilitating the expression of authentic accounts of everyday experience, but which, to be fair, have other benefits. These feminist methods also seek to undercut the distance between the researcher and the research subject. At stake is an enhanced empathy between researcher and subject (for an HCI analogue, see [59]).

Third, many of these feminist methods are not unique to feminism; indeed, many of them already have analogues in HCI. For example, [9] introduce "pastiche scenarios," a method that bears striking resemblance to feminist dramatic role-play methods. [27] introduces a camera that subjects wear that takes pictures throughout the day, a method that is hard to distinguish from the feminist talking-pictures method. [4] uses open-ended prose essays as a method for collecting experiential reactions to viral videos. Again, feminist science has not so much invented new methods out of whole cloth, but rather situated methods within methodologies and epistemologies that enable them to work within the contexts of scientific and moral objectivities. Doing pastiche scenarios or reflective design does not make a project feminist. Thus, the opportunity for feminist scientists in HCI is to integrate these novel methods alongside traditional methods in a methodology and epistemology that is specifically feminist.

Finally, innovation in methods also has implications for the sources of data that are collected. As [50] has shown, feminists have also promoted historically marginal voices as data sources. For example, feminists have studied texts written by women and girls, who are not "important figures." Feminists have also developed a critical vocabulary that enables an analysis of artifacts to reveal the social construction of gender inscribed into them. They have also developed strategies to expose the sexism inscribed in medical textbooks, cookbooks, advertising, and scientific texts. It also clearly relates to emerging discourses surrounding interaction criticism (e.g., [2]).

TOWARDS A FEMINIST HCI METHODOLOGY

Throughout this paper, we have summarized feminist social science's dialogue with traditional social science and place that into a dialogue with recent methodological trends in HCI. By teasing out epistemological foundations, methodological positions, and the philosophical and scientific implications of research methods, we are in a position to propose a simple, and provisional, feminist HCI methodology. Every methodology points back to one or more epistemologies, which identify its participants (who is involved, and in what ways), its processes (i.e., its theory of how information is acquired, constructed, transformed, and articulated), and its normative criteria (i.e., how we know whether it is good). Feminist HCI methodology clearly leans on feminist epistemology, such as standpoint theory, feminist empiricism, or and feminist postmodernism [44]. A key strand of the feminist epistemologies we have seen is the emphasis on the experiences of marginalized peoples; as noted more than once, this is both an ethical imperative and also an epistemological one, as marginalized groups may be privileged in their ability to create certain kinds of accounts.

In addition to feminist HCI methodology's affiliation with feminist epistemologies, feminist HCI methodologies also need to participate in appropriate HCI epistemologies. Design epistemologies (e.g., [38]) share many compatibilities with feminist epistemology, so opportunities for harmonization presumably abound there. One of these is the feminist orientation to change individual and social reality to improve human life, a goal shared by designers. More challenging, but worth exploring, is integrating feminist epistemologies with the epistemologies behind much of the best quantitative work in HCI to provide the intellectual grounds for a feminist HCI quantitative methodology.

In the following, we outline some of the key methodological positions that we expect to compose a feminist HCI methodology:

- **A simultaneous commitment to scientific and moral objectivities.** Feminist methodologies are guided not only by the epistemic values of traditional science, but also by non-epistemic values, such as "ontological heterogeneity, complexity of relationships, diffusion of power, applicability to current human needs, and novelty" as well as foregrounding gender as an axis of research [44].
- **Connection to feminist theory**. Feminism is a diverse and heterogeneous body of theory, but in one way or another, feminist HCI methodologies should explicitly tie themselves to some part of that body of work. This connection to feminist thought, and not to the problem domain of gender and computing, is what makes an HCI methodology feminist.
- **A commitment to methodology**. A feminist methodology will not lose sight of the fact that methods must be chosen and used based on assumptions, commitments, and goals, and that these should cohere and be acknowledged as a methodology.
- **An empathic relationship with research participants focused on understanding their experiences**. Feminist social science maintains a strong commitment to people's experiences, and we expect that to come through. A similar HCI methodology can already be found in [59], though it is not offered vis-à-vis feminism.
- **Researcher/Practitioner Self-Disclosure**. Practice should involve a disclosure of the researcher's position in the world, her or his goals, as well as the researcher's position in her or his intellectual and, to an appropriate extent, political beliefs.
- **Co-construction of the core research activities and goals**. To the extent the following are appropriate, researchers and research subjects should collaboratively frame research questions (e.g., as opportunities to nurture, rather than control, populations), choose and implement methods, analyze data, and above all decide how the data and analysis will be used in the social world (e.g., its design and policy implications).
- **Diverse and/or mixed methods to support dialectic information gathering and knowledge production**. Feminist epistemologies stress the dialectic nature of social advances (a position shared also by Marxist epistemologies). Achieving this dialectic demands a genuine heterogeneity of data sources and interpretation, and this heterogeneity often can be achieved through transdisci-

plinary and multimethod approaches. A feminist HCI methodology sets such dialectics into play.

- **Reflexivity**. Research should be characterized by ongoing self-questioning about whether the research is delivering on its ambitions to be feminist, improve human quality of life, and undermine rather than reinforce oppressive social structures, etc.

CONCLUSIONS

Obviously, HCI professionals do research in many contexts and for many different reasons. As [57] reminds us, designing in response to concrete reality is not just a slogan, but a reminder to be epistemologically and methodologically flexible. Our proposed outline of a feminist HCI methodology is anything but a prescription for how to do feminist HCI. The concrete situations in which we find ourselves may make some of the above extremely or not at all important. Likewise, methodological issues not mentioned above may be paramount. Practitioners may have insights or experience with situations that we have not imagined.

HCI practice involves a negotiation of dialectics, between scientific and moral objectivities, between guiding theories and stubborn reality; between the interpretations and goals of HCI practitioners, those of users, and those of society. The goal of any methodology is ultimately pragmatic, not dogmatic: it is worthwhile only inasmuch as it helps to guide our everyday choices as we seek to contribute to knowledge about and design for better human life experiences and a social world in which to live and share them.

ACKNOWLEDGEMENTS

We are grateful for the feedback from Christine Satchell, Peter Wright, and our anonymous reviewers, along with the support of Elizabeth Churchill and Gilbert Cockton.

REFERENCES

1. Alcoff, L. and Potter, E. *Feminist Epistemologies*. Routledge, 1992.
2. Bardzell, J. Interaction criticism and aesthetics. *Proc. of CHI'09*, ACM Press (2009), 2357-2366.
3. Bardzell, S. Feminist HCI: Taking stock and outlining an agenda for design. *Proc. of CHI'10*, ACM Press (2010), 1301-1310.
4. Bardzell, S., Bardzell, J., Pace, T. Understanding affective interaction: Emotion, engagement, and Internet videos. *Proc. of 2009 IEEE International Conference on Affective Computing and Intelligent Interaction*. IEEE, 1-8.
5. Bjerknes, G., Ehn, P., and Kyng, M. *Computers and Democracy: A Scandavian Challenge*, Avebury, 1987.
6. Blevis, E. Sustainable interaction design: invention & disposal, renewal & reuse. *Proc. of CHI'07*, ACM Press (2007), 503-512.
7. Boehner, K., Vertesi, J., Sengers, P., Dourish, P. How HCI interprets the probes. In *Proc. of CHI'07*. NY: ACM Press. 1077-1086.
8. Bell, G, and Dourish, P. Yesterday's tomorrows: Notes on ubiquitous computing's dominant vision. *Personal and Ubiquitous Computing* (2006).
9. Blythe, M. Pastiche scenarios. *Interactions*. ACM Press (2004), 51-53.
10. Bødker, S. Creating conditions for participation: Conflicts and resources in system development. *Human Computer Interaction 11*, 3 (1996), 215-236.
11. Cancian, F. Feminist science: Methodologies that challenge inequality. *Gender & Society 6*, 1 (1992), 623-642.
12. Card, S., Moran, T., and Newell, A. *The Psychology of Human-Computer Interaction*. Lawrence Erlbaum Associates Publishers, 1983.
13. Cook, J. and Fonow, M. Knowledge and women's interests: Issues of epistemology and methodology in feminist sociological research. *Sociological Inquiry 56* (1986), 2-29.
14. DiSalvo, C., Brynjarsdóttir, B., and Sengers, P. Mapping the landscape of sustainable HCI. *Proc. of CHI 2010*, ACM Press (2010).
15. DiSalvo, C. Design and the construction of publics. *Design Issues 25*, 1 (2009), 48-63.
16. Dourish, P. *Where the Action is: The Foundations of Embodied Interaction*. MIT Press, 2006.
17. Dourish, P. Implications for design. *Proc. CHI'06*. NY: ACM Press, 541-550.
18. Dourish, P., Finlay, J., Sengers, P., & Wright, P. Reflective HCI: Towards a critical technical practice. In *CHI'04 Extended Abstracts*. ACM Press (2004), 1727-1728.
19. Fry, T. *New design philosophy: An Introduction to Defuturing*. University of New South Wales Press, 1999.
20. Gaver, W., Dunne, T., and Pacenti, E. Cultural probes. *Interactions*, (1996), 21-29.
21. Grosz, E. What is feminist theory? In Payne, C. and Grosz, E. (eds.). *Feminist Challenges: Social and Political Theory*. Northeaster UP, 1986, 190-204.
22. Hanmer, J., and Sanders, S. *Well-Founded Fear: A Community Study of Violence to Women*. Hutchinson, 1984.
23. Harding, S. *The Feminist Standpoint Theory Reader: Intellectual and Political Controversies*. Routledge, 2004.
24. Harding, S. *Is Science Multicultural?: Postcolonialisms, Feminisms, and Epistemologies*. Indiana University Press, 1998
25. Harding, S. Rethinking standpoint epistemology: What is "strong objectivity"? In Alcoff, L, and Potter, E. (eds.). *Feminist Epistemologies*. Routledge, 1992.

26. Harding, S. *Feminism and Methodology.* Indiana University Press, 1987.

27. Harper, R., Randall, D., Smythe, N., Evans, C., Heledd, L., and Moore, R. Thanks for the memory. In *Proc. of the 21st British HCI Group Annual Conference on HCI 2007.* British Computer Society, (2007), 39-42.

28. Haraway, D., J. *Simians, Cyborgs and Women: The Reinvention of Nature.* Free Association Books, London, 1991.

29. Hartsock, N. The feminist standpoint. In S. Harding and M. B. Hintikka (eds). *Discovering Reality.* D. Riedel Publishing Company, Holland, Boston, London, 1983, 283-310

30. Hollinger, R. Science and values. In Klemke, E.D., Hollinger, R., & Rudge, D.W., (eds.), *Introductory Readings in the Philosophy of Science.* 3rd ed. Prometheus Books, 1998.

31. Irani, L., Vertesi, J., Dourish, P., Philip, K., and Grinter, R. Postcolonial computing: A lens on design and development. *Proc. of CHI 2010*, ACM Press (2010), 1311-1320.

32. John, B. Information processing and skilled behavior. In Carroll, J. (ed.). *HCI Models, Theories, and Frameworks.* Morgan Kaufmann, 2003.

33. Kincaid, H. *Philosophical Foundations of the Social Sciences: Analyzing Controversies in Social Research.* Cambridge UP, 1996.

34. Kuhn, T. *The Structure of Scientific Revolutions.* University of Chicago Press, 1962.

35. Law. E. Preface: Meaningful measures: Valid useful user experience measurement. In *Proc. of the International Workshop on Meaningful Measures.* (2008), 3-4.

36. Light, A., Kleine, D and Vivent, M. Performing Charlotte: A tool to bridge cultures in participatory design. *International Journal of Sociotechnology and Knowledge Development, 2*, 1 (2010).

37. Longino, H. Can there be a feminist science? In Wyer, M., Barbercheck, M., Giesman, D., Öztürk, H., and Wayne, M. (eds.). *Women, Science, and Technology.* Routledge, New York, London, 2001, 216-222.

38. Löwgren, J. and Stolterman, E. *Thoughtful Interaction Design.* MIT Press, 2004.

39. McCarthy, J. and Wright, P. *Technology as Experience.* The MIT Press, 2004.

40. McDowell, L. Doing gender: Feminism, feminists, and research methods in human geography. *Transactions of the Institute of British Geographers 17*, 4 (1992), 399-416.

41. McMullen, E. Values in science. In Klemke, E.D., Hollinger, R., & Rudge, D.W., (eds.), *Introductory Readings in the Philosophy of Science.* 3rd ed. Prometheus Books, 1998.

42. Miller, R. (1998). Three versions of objectivity: aesthetic, moral, and scientific. In Levinson, J. (ed.), *Aesthetics and Ethics: Essays at the Intersection.* Cambridge: Cambridge University Press, 26-58.

43. Naples, N. *Feminism and Method: Ethnography, Discourse Analysis, and Activist Research.* Routledge, 2003.

44. Nelson, L.H. Feminist Philosophy of Science. In Machamer, P. & Silberstein, M. (eds.), *The Blackwell Guide to the Philosophy of Science.* Blackwell, 2002.

45. Olson, G., and Olson, J. Distance matters. *Human-Computer Interaction 15*, 1 (2000).

46. Pace, T., Bardzell, S., & Bardzell, J. (2010). The rogue in the lovely black dress: Intimacy in World of Warcraft. *Proc. of CHI'10*, ACM Press (2010), 233-242.

47. Papanek, V. *Design for the Real World: Human Ecology and Social Change.* Academy Chicago Publishers, 1985.

48. Picard, P. *Affective Computing.* The MIT Press, 2000.

49. Ramazanoğlu, C., and Holland, J. *Feminist Methodology: Challenges and Choices.* Sage, 2002.

50. Reinharz, S. *Feminist Methods in Social Research.* Oxford UP, 1992.

51. Rogers, Y. Moving on from Weiser's vision of calm computing: Engaging ubicomp experiences. Ubicomp 2006, LNCS 4206 (2006), 404-421.

52. Rudner, R. The scientist *qua* scientist makes value judgments. In Klemke, E.D., Hollinger, R., & Rudge, D.W., (eds.), *Introductory Readings in the Philosophy of Science.* 3rd ed. Prometheus Books, 1998.

53. Sengers P, Boehner K, David S, Kaye J. Reflective design. CC '05. ACM Press, New York (2005), 49-58.

54. Sengers, P., McCarthy, J. & Dourish, P. (2006). Reflective HCI: articulating an agenda for critical practice. Extended Abstracts, CHI '06, ACM Press, New York, NY, 1683-1686.

55. Sprague, J. *Feminist Methodologies for Critical Researchers: Bridging Differences.* AltaMira Press, 2005.

56. Sprague, J., and Zimmerman, M. Quality and quantity: Reconstructing feminist methodology. In *The American Sociologist, 20*, 1(1989), 71-86.

57. Star, S.L. Misplaced concretism and concrete situations: Feminism, method, and information technology. Gender-Nature-Culture feminist Research Network, working paper 11, (1994), Odense, Denmark.

58. Stroll, A. *Twentieth-Century Analytic Philosophy.* Columbia University Press, 2000.

59. Wright, P. and McCarthy, J. Empathy and experience in HCI. In *Proc. of CHI 2008*, ACM Press (2008).

60. Zachry, M. An interview with Susan Leigh Star. *Technical Communication Quarterly 17*, 4 (2008), 435-454.

Out There

Alex Taylor
Microsoft Research
7 J J Thomson Avenue, Cambridge, CB3 0FB, UK
ast@microsoft.com

ABSTRACT
"Out there" is increasingly becoming a topic of concern in HCI. Thanks to various clarion calls, researchers in the field are turning their attention to technology-mediated activities that are shaped less by Euro-American sensibilities and defined more by how they are culturally and geographically distinct. Fieldwork and ethnography researchers, for instance, are beginning to investigate ICT use at religious and spiritual sites, by the socially excluded and disenfranchised, and by people in developing regions. In this paper, I concentrate on the latter focus on development to reflect on HCI's disciplinary turn "out there". Specifically, I take the following three themes as common rhetorical devices in such work: (i) the network, (ii) difference and (iii) complexity. Through examples, I discuss how each of these themes has been mobilised. I then use materials from anthropology, science and technology studies, and to a lesser extent geography and postcolonial studies to complicate and in some cases question the interpretative frames that are being applied. Thus, my hope is that this paper is seen as a thought piece that deepens our thinking around HCI's efforts to look "out there" by paying critical attention to what is going on "in here".

Author Keywords: Anthropology, development, ethnography, fieldwork, ICT4D, networks, postcolonialism.

ACM Classification Keywords
H5.m. Information interfaces and presentation (e.g., HCI): Miscellaneous; K4.2 Computers and Society: Social Issues.

General Terms: Design, Human Factors.

INTRODUCTION
A consequence of HCI's third-wave [9], or third paradigm [23], has been the move to expand the field's empirical foci by looking, as it were, "out there". Alongside the efforts to take experience seriously and move on from limited notions of the user and performance/productivity, there have been a growing number of attempts to point the lens of HCI towards some very different kinds of practices and people. Not only are we turning our attention away from single users interacting with PCs and toward rich and nuanced forms of computer-mediated collaboration, we are also beginning to investigate unfamiliar communities, far flung places, and practices not ordinarily considered when thinking about information communication technology (ICT).

The general thrust of this movement has been motivated by the argument that HCI has neglected significant segments of society and sometimes overlooked sizeable yet marginalised members of the world's population. HCI, it is suggested, has been preoccupied with its own kind: largely white, middle-class men—and computer scientists, engineers and academics at that [6]. Thus we have paid little attention to the relationship women have with technology [7, 46] (and the role of feminism in HCI [4]); the role technology has and could have amongst society's disenfranchised [13, 14, 40, 47]; and that sizeable portion of the world's population making up what has been euphemistically called the Global South [8, 35, 38, 39, 41, 51, 56]. Moreover, the attention we've given to spirituality, religion [5, 53, 54, 55] and, surprisingly perhaps, even television viewing and sport has been decidedly wanting [6].

Without a doubt, the calls to address HCI's narrow foci are laudable. It is obvious that technology and, specifically, information technology has the potential to play and in many cases already plays a crucial role for many besides the Web surfing, Facebook using Twitterati. What I want to contemplate in this paper, however, are the motivations that underlie HCI's turn "out there" and what as a field it hopes to accomplish by pursuing such a move. I want to state emphatically, that my aim here is not to criticise the efforts to expand HCI, nor is it to judge, negatively, the attempts to redress some of its long-standing prejudices. I am hugely sympathetic to both projects. My intention is to better understand what seems to be a purposeful trend amongst my contemporaries and to ask how we might usefully frame and, in turn, direct it in constructive ways.

Before moving on, I want to also say that this is not intended as a design orientated paper in any conventional sense. I won't close with any design implications. Nor do I intend to produce what Dourish has suggested is ethnography's alternative: "models for thinking about... [social] settings and the work that goes on there" [17, p. 549]. What follows is targeted at deepening our thinking as HCI researchers and how it is we go about plying our trade. My hope, specifically, is to take seriously the attempts by many of us involved in fieldwork and ethnography in HCI to look beyond the field's established borders. If it is not too bold an aim, I want to begin the no doubt arduous journey of thinking deeply about what, exactly, we are doing in casting an eye "out there".

THE INSIDE OUT

In her book "The Network Inside Out" [36], Annelise Riles discusses a problem confronting the anthropology of still nebulous topics such as globalisation, transnationalism and networks. Riles, a legal anthropologist, examines the knowledge practices within and around international law and uses her empirical materials to demonstrate how anthropology might resist its long-established methods of separating and consequently (re-)constructing networks of relations 'characterised by systematic complexity'. She especially targets the anthropology of globalisation and what she sees as its counterpart, transnationalism. I cite her comments on transnationalism at length to offer a flavour of her position:

> "Consider for example, the methodological problems that anthropologists now understand as endemic to the ethnography of globalization. Despite the excitement surrounding this literature, in practice, studies of transnationalism have tended to yield familiar analytical paradigms writ large—notions such as "community" or "tradition" long outmoded in other anthropological domains. In my view, this traditionalism springs from a methodological source. What renders the field of transnationalism "new" is not so much the discovery of a new field site or the set of material conditions but rather the ethnographic encounter with knowledge practices already familiar to, and indeed in use by, the anthropologist at precisely the moment at which he or she seeks insight through fresh ethnographic observation. We might understand the impulse to exoticize through notions of community, identity, or tradition that characterizes this literature, then, as a methodological device, an effort to render the familiar strange so that it might be apprehended as ethnography." [36, p. 5]

Rather harshly, perhaps, Riles criticises the new anthropologies of transnationalism (using her points as illustrative of trends in research on globalisation) for exoticising communities, identities and traditions for its own ends. She contends the mechanism of exoticising—of 'making strange'—is pursued so that the work is seen as ethnographic. The analytical insights themselves, she intimates, bring nothing new to the underlying ideas and thinking in anthropology. Indeed, Riles argues that the predisposition to see the global, transnational or network "out there", or as she calls it "outside", obscures what might be going on, if you will, on the inside: "Anthropological analysis is reduced to restatement, to repetition, to generating reflexive modernity's 'doubles.' All one can do it seems, is to identify instances of globalisation..." [36, p. 5].

Through the anthropological studies of multi-national legal organisations, Riles is then making two important points: first she argues that in the rush to look "outside", anthropology has found itself restating the tropes of difference: that people are different, places are culturally distinct, and that any interconnections get very complicated because of these different ways of being. In effect, the anthropologists are extending their purview to look at the global and transnational, and lo and behold they discover the world is, well, multi-faceted and complex. This outcome Riles fairly points out is hardly surprising and merely succeeds "in the identification of new multisited 'places,' diasporic 'groups,' or technological phenomena for anthropological study" [36, p. 6].

Riles second point, arguably a more fundamental one, is that social science persists in seeing the network everywhere and describing just about any kind of collective or organisational practice in terms of the network. This she argues refigures what social science is accountable for. The analytical objectives are focused on animating, *ad nauseam*, the characteristics of the network, e.g., connectedness, mutuality, complexity, mutability, etc. etc., to such an extent that the social sciences have become accountable to nothing else.

These two points in Riles position are what I want to pick up on and use in setting out this paper. It is at the juncture of HCI turning its attention "out there" that I wonder whether we risk falling foul of the two-part trap that Riles describes. It's not that I think that HCI simulates this situation, exactly (or that Riles accurately represents social science); undoubtedly, there are some notable differences. Riles discussion, for instance, is limited to some of the peculiar and protracted methodological discussions in anthropology. Moreover, as a field, anthropology is for the most part concerned with new ways of making sense of and understanding cultural specificity, not the application of its results in engineering and design disciplines. Nevertheless, I can't help but wonder whether a number of us in HCI are caught up in an exercise of repeatedly looking further afield so that we can report back that things are different out there, that people's ways of knowing and practices are culturally situated, and, furthermore, that their activities are interconnected in complex ways. These are, of course, important points, but as a field that strives to produce new and hopefully provocative perspectives on human-computer interactions it seems we should be aiming to introduce something else besides these familiar ways of seeing.

Thus, what I'd like to do in the following is modestly follow Riles' example by turning, as she puts it, the network inside out. That is, I want to try to turn our interpretative frame inside out so that we might somehow catch sight of ourselves, looking out there. In attempting this contortion, three issues, in particular, will interest me:

1. how it is we are configuring the world out there;
2. the analytical resources we assemble to do so; and
3. our own roles in the processes of configuring "out there".

For the purposes of illustration, I approach these issues by focusing on recent research in HCI that has targeted development in emerging regions and has been referred to as ICT4D or, more recently, simply ICTD. As I see it, this research epitomises HCI's attempts to look beyond its traditional boundaries, tackling topics as wide-ranging as globalisation, transnationalism, colonialism, poverty, and the digital divide, as well as those topics more familiar to HCI. Inevitably, this focus on development and ICT narrows the applicability of some of the points I will make. Even so, my aim, as the paper's argument progresses, is also to draw out some points of general value.

IN HERE

Broadly, I hang the first part to this paper on what I see as three reoccurring themes in HCI's efforts to look out there: (i) *the network*; (ii) *difference;* and (iii) *complexity*. I use these ostensible themes not as a rigid taxonomic scheme but rather as a means to elucidate my points—to complicate and hopefully develop where it is I want to go with my argument and where it may be constructive for us to go as a research field.

My thinking in these terms has been informed by an eclectic collection of readings that grapple with pointing the empirical gaze out-there [2], and that query the ubiquity of the network as a conceptual apparatus [1, 15, 49]. The discussion specific to networks is informed by some relatively recent ideas in science and technology studies that engage, sometimes critically, with actor-network theory. In particular, I find inspiration in John Law's "After Method" [29] and look to a number of works that shift the framing of social (inter-)action to accommodate not just the agency of humans, but also that of things or non-humans [e.g., 3, 28, 45]. My critical discussion of networks also draws on anthropology, using the work from Riles, introduced above, and Marilyn Strathern's early but still apposite arguments about partiality and networks [43]. Borrowing from these readings, my hope is to show that HCI has tended to use the network as a taken for granted way of thinking about "out there" and, as a consequence, has potentially restricted its ideas of technology and its design.

The second thematic discussion, focused on the theme of difference, is informed by a longstanding debate in sociology and anthropology, one in which a critique is levelled at work that exoticises or "makes strange" foreign, "primitive" people [33, 52]. A principal point I wish to make here is that in mobilising the network as an analytical device, HCI risks rehearsing some of the weaknesses identified in the sociological and anthropological studies of far-off places and people. Specifically, by framing "out there" using the language and ideas of technologically mediated connections and relations (i.e., of networks), HCI runs the risk of promoting some troubling notions of difference. This difference-making sets ways of knowing originating through largely Euro-American sensibilities against those of other foreign, "less-developed" peoples. To consider an alternative view of difference, I find inspiration in the book "Science and African Logics" by historian and philosopher of science Helen Verran [50]. The proposal put forward is to see difference-making as on-going, contingent on the local and unfolding relations between people and things.

In the last of the three themes, I extend this argument to consider what Riles contends is another trope born of the network perspective, that is complexity (also see [48]). I argue that complexity is treated as a forgone conclusion in HCI research that views "out there" in terms of the network. Yet, crucially, this complexity is something seen and interpreted from "here" looking "out there", and thus something to be solved or ameliorated from the outside looking in. Referring again to Verran, I put forward the possibility of seeing complexity as something in the making, produced and re-produced "right there". This, I contend, shifts how and where we think of human-computer interactions and their design.

Next, then, I will discuss each of these three themes in greater detail. Following this, I will draw out what I think the broad implications to be for HCI.

The Network

As I see it, much of the published literature in HCI that seeks to look "out there" hinges on the notion of the network, sometimes implicitly and in some cases explicitly.[1] The use of the network in this context appears to be predicated on two basic ideas. One, we find an understanding and application of networks in relatively conventional terms; our attention is drawn to the groupings of people, communities and/or cultures that are related in some fashion. Both the nodes of the network and their many interconnections are viewed as empirical concerns that might be informative in systems design. Transnationalism and globalisation take this idea of the network as their starting point [36]. Technologically-mediated, social networks are an obvious derivative.

The second understanding of the network is an extension of the first. In this case, a principle concern is for people or things that move between the groupings—between nodes of the network—and how under some circumstances these people/things can transform, i.e., undergo some material change and/or change in how they are understood. This interest in movement or transformation adds both temporal and spatial dimensions to the network as an analytical device. These ideas are central to actor-network theory [29, 30], a programmatic view of the relations between humans and things that shaped contemporary science and technology studies and has had a significant impact on numerous fields in the social sciences.

A recent paper introducing contemporary thinking in post colonial studies to the HCI community makes explicit use of both these understandings of the network. Under the moniker "Postcolonial Computing" [25], the authors, Irani, Vertesi, Dourish, Philip and Grinter, articulate a clear and convincing argument for using postcolonial theories to advance a position on ICT in development contexts. In discussing how immigrant populations in the US enact their various cultural identities in dynamic ways, they write:

> "... the diaspora case illuminates the fluidity of cultural, regional, and transnational boundaries, as well as the variability of the what "home culture" can mean in daily life. People relate variably to a range of local and international networks, producing their cultural identities through a variety of signifying practices..." [25, pp. 1313-1314]

Irani et al. clearly describe the network as something that is made up of numerous elements (of various scales) and that is

---

[1] I'm aware that the word network and its associated nomenclature are not always used explicitly, but I believe it is reasonably uncontroversial to suggest that notions of separate-but-connected and, by implication, ideas of distributed networks of people and technology are commonplace in both the empirical and design oriented works focused on culturally and geographically distinct places and practices (see, for example, [7, 19, 38, 55]).

dynamic, fluid and multi-faceted, thus invoking the first of the two understandings of the network I've described. Later, they also make specific reference to the possibilities of transformation that I identified in the second. Through an example of a Brazilian company's efforts to build computers compatible with the Macintosh operating system, they describe how legal, economic, corporate and local interests can come together, shaping not only the use and appropriation of computing, but also how technology figures in ideas of innovation. As the authors explain more generally:

> "... the insights of postcolonial studies and STS [Science and Technology Studies] speak at once to the highly local and contingent practices that we see at work in different specific sites of technology design and use, while at the same time recognizing the ways that those localisms are conditioned and embedded within global and historical flows of material, people, capital, knowledge, and technology." [25, pp. 1316-1317]

Here, then, we see the reference to movement and transformation through the network. In a clever inversion, the paper's authors develop their argument by situating HCI's practices in these very same flows and transformations. Using the terms *articulation* and *translation*—and in doing so echoing two key concepts in actor-network theory—they situate design practice *vis-à-vis* the production of culturally specific representational forms (articulation) and the movement of things and meanings between cultures (translation). Design, amongst other things, thus threads its way through the network, existing as something that is at once locally contingent and global, mobile yet immutable [27].

In referring to this example, I want to address the seeming neatness of the network as a framing device. Although I think this paper does a particularly nice job of shifting ideas in, around and between their materials and their own empirical/design practices, I want to suggest the network persists here (and elsewhere in HCI) as a taken for granted analytical device. It provides a seductive theoretical perspective that neatly joins things up when looking from "here" "out there" and, coincidentally, offers a convenient parallel to the technological metaphor of networks. Thus, in looking out there, I would contend we are seldom inclined to see or challenge the ontological status of the network. Again, Riles' words are pointed, but germane:

> "It appeals to our collective fantasy about linking up with our subjects and finding in the "data" exactly what we set out to find. The idea of the Network, as the term is used here... as a form that supersedes analysis and reality, might also be imagined to borrow from the reflexive turn in the social sciences—from the notion that there is no longer such a thing as dependent and independent variables, that causes and effects are all mutually constituted in an endless feedback loop." [36, p. 174]

As I've suggested, Riles' answer to this quandary is to turn things inside out, to look back in on ourselves and our own systems and methods of practice and accounting. Such exercises in looking inward are inexhaustible, boundless. There are though, some tentative steps we might take to complicate and get us thinking more critically about the network "out there", from "in here".

The anthropologist Marilyn Strathern offers us a starting point or more aptly, perhaps, an ending place in her article "Cutting the Network":

> "However, the power of such analytical networks is also their problem: theoretically, they are without limit. If diverse elements make up a description, they seem as extensible or involuted as the analysis is extensible or involuted. Analysis appears able to take into account, and thus create, any number of forms. And one can always discover networks within networks; this is the fractal logic that renders any length a multiple of other lengths, or a link in a chain of further links. Yet analysis, like interpretation, must have a point, it must be enacted as a stopping place." [42, p. 523].

Some point? A stopping place? Might this be a point of departure? Can we ask where is it the networks are "cut", where they stop, where the stabilising flows of articulation and translation come to a halt? And, most importantly for Strathern, in what ways the networks cut everywhere else, besides, "back here"? In this way, Strathern turns our attention to the analyst's view, reminding us that it is but one of many possible renderings of lengths, links and chains—of networks. Such a position, I would contend, are the means by which we disrupt the loops, the fractal logics.

Riles usefully provides an example of going about such a venture in her field studies of the private world of self-regulated, global swap markets [37]. She illustrates how these markets and specifically the related practices of unregulated, private law operate in what she calls the *anti-network*. Even though it is global and at some level falls under the aegis of state-sanctioned law, Riles demonstrates that aspects of private law are locally produced and maintained through routine form-filling and mundane document workflows (something those from CSCW will be intimately familiar [e.g., 11, 20, 24]). These locally managed legal technicalities "make it possible for global actors to deal with one another without trust, without shared norms, without a thick web of personal relations..." [37, pp. 623-624]. Furthermore, the networks come apart because the sheer sophistication and complexity of the financial and legal instruments mean that expertise is organisationally and physically divided. Lawyers, for example, know they don't understand the relationships between all the agents and, indeed, are mandated by regulators to be physically separated from their trading counterparts. The neat systems of articulation and translation, Riles contests, thus sit uneasily with the locally achieved, mundane routines that are observed in practice.

To return to the paper from Irani and her colleagues, it would thus be fair to ask not only of the strands of transnationalism and the flows along them, but also about where it is they stop and how this stopping is enacted? Similarly, we might ask not how technologies move and undergo translations, but how it is they and their concomitant design practices stay just where they are? Mindful of simplistic binaries, we might turn to the words from the geographer Harrison and his invitation to consider relationalities counter-point, the *non-relational* [22], as well as those breaks, gaps, and moments of pause: the *caesuras* [21]. As he laments "[a]nd yet I wonder in all of this where the concern is—and care—for distance, withdrawal, and disappearance" [22, p. 593].

Difference

These points, I realise, are not especially perspicacious. Even though I'd argue there's been little evidence of it, it doesn't take a big leap of imagination to ask what else there might be besides the network. In turning, next, to consider difference, I thus want to delve a little deeper, moving I hope closer to Riles' inward-outward looking move.

As it happens, in proposing their "Postcolonial Computing", Irani et al. [25] set out a nuanced position on difference. Making reference to postcolonial theory, they complicate the lines between us, "in here", and those "out there". Much of the literature in HCI, however, adopts a more problematic perspective. I want to use work from the anthropologist Genevieve Bell—who will be familiar to many in HCI—as illustrative of what I see as troubling.

In a paper published in the UbiComp 2006 conference proceedings [5], Bell uses a series of empirical observations to highlight the ways that modern ICTs are routinely combined with culturally-bound, spiritual practices. In one example, she describes the Chinese government's encouragement of online ancestor worship through virtual memorial halls and cemeteries. Users of these services are able to choose from a selection of virtual tombstones, and to "burn e-incense, and leave e-flowers" [5, p. 152]. Explicitly invoking the network, Bell also describes how these portals are also facilitating worship from afar and connecting the dispersed Chinese diaspora through the online memorialising of the deceased.

Now I understand that Bell's mission is somewhat unique, driven as she is to convince here multinational organisation to see beyond its national borders, and to disrupt, as she recounts it, their once troubling nomenclature for anywhere "out there", i.e., RoW (Rest of World) [6]. Indeed, I feel she deserves a considerable amount of credit for transforming her organisation's international outlook and, indeed, their *modus operandi*. Yet, what unnerves me about work such as this is that it repeatedly relies on the same strategy to report "out there". One sees the juxtaposition of digital technology, such as mobile phones and the world wide web, against a set of culturally specific practices or rituals. I take this to be a means of accentuating locally contingent practices and the often surprising appropriation of technologies originally intended for neoliberal, Euro-American sensibilities. However, an unfortunate side effect is that it promotes an exoticising or making-strange of the "other". It sets "out there" in relational terms to "in here".

To explain why I see this as a problem, I want to reflect on fieldwork I did about three years ago in the Dharavi Slum in the outskirts of Mumbai. In total, I spent a month dividing my time between two homes, both made up of three generations of extended family members. One of the many things that struck me in Dharavi was the relationship instituted with water. In most of the slums of Mumbai, water is rationed for between 4 to 6 hours a day, meaning that the majority of dwellers need to go to shared taps at prescribed times of day to use and collect water for washing, cleaning, cooking and drinking. For example, in one of the households I spent time with, the water was available at their "local tap" between 4-8A.M. The household's "daughter in-law" recounted to me that it was her job to get up and do the necessary chores that relied on the flow of water within these hours, as well as collect water in containers for other water-dependent activities during the day. She also told me she never went to the water source before 6A.M. because it took two hours of the water flowing before she considered it clean enough.

Another aspect of water flow I found hard to ignore was the unremitting presence of sewage. In the areas of Dharavi I spent time in, most of the narrow roughly carved out streets, surfaced with loose soil and gravel, were lined with 1 to 2 metre-wide open or barely covered sewers. Houses had their own off-shoots or arteries to this larger sewage system so that they could discard their waste from within the bounds of their property.

On seeing (and indeed writing about) the labour intensive, arduous and in some cases demoralising water-related activities in the households in Dharavi, and the ever-present smell of effluent, my impulse is to ponder on how different things are over there. How is it that people can live in such squalor? How do they tolerate the heat, the dampness, the dirt, the smell? And how do some appear so bright and happy despite it all? Intellectually, I also find myself resorting to the longstanding comparative tradition in anthropology, using my materials to reflect on our own Euro-American routines and rituals. As a matter of fact, on returning to my ordered and sanitised home and workplace in the UK, my initial questions centred on what if any parallels I could draw with life back here. What were the scarcity of resources that my home-life revolved around? What flows were ever-present and socially organising in my life? The flow of time, perhaps?

Taking such a standpoint of looking from here out there, it is virtually impossible not to see difference and to draw out comparisons. The trouble is, such a perspective really tells us very little about what is going on "out there", or in the way I would prefer to phase it "right there". As Verran writes:

> "Either way, a distinct "us" and "them" are locked forever together, and apart, through the specter of originality/mimicry. This is just what we would expect of a difference "outside worlds"—not real or doable. The only way to tell such a difference is to pull "their" world into "ours." [50, p. 31]

Thus, it seems to me that a genuine interest in the cultural specificities of places like Dharavi cannot come from an articulation of how different "there" is from "here". To do so simply achieves pulling worlds such as Dharavi into "ours". I would contend, if difference is to matter at all, our concern should be for how it is enacted there, right there. How in Strathern's [42] terms is the network cut "right there"?

We catch a glimpse of this alternate view of cutting the network through a memorable question that I was asked in Dharavi. One household member I interviewed wanted to know what other jobs I had. Involved in numerous entrepreneurial activities himself, my informant assumed I, similarly, had more than one job. Also, the way he made sense of me hanging around and asking inane questions was to view me as an NGO employee (having witnessed other NGO staff behaving in a similar fashion). This, he extolled, was obviously a woman's job, so it would make sense I must be making a more honest living through other means. This line of inquiry by a father-figure in a house in Dharavi deserves some considerably unpacking that I, unfortunately, do not have the luxury of doing here. What I want to suggest, however, is that it is just this form of making different (or making same) that offers a way out of us casting "out there" in relational terms to "in here". It re-specifies difference so that it is treated as a local member's category rather than belonging to someone peering "out there" from "back here". At the same time, it also allows us to see another rendering of the network, but again it is not mine, the analysts, that reveals itself but one that is constituted through the lines of sameness and difference cast from "right there".

Complexity

I hope, then, that some progress is being made in turning the inside out, laying bare our own analytical apparatus in enacting "out there". By considering complexity, as the last of my three themes, my aim is to take things one stage further, this time situating ourselves within the interpretative frame(s).

An indication of HCI and, more generally, computing's interest in developing regions is evidenced by the proliferation of related position pieces in computing journals [10, 18, 32], workshops [34], and conference panels [12, 26] all seeking to address the challenges faced. By and large, the depictions painted in these talks and published materials is of a world out there that is complex. The manifold relations between different people, technologies, agents and infrastructures are projected as the constituents of complexity and consequently viewed, in their networked assembly, as challenging.

But this, I want to argue, is only one side of the story of complexity and a side that arguably rehearses, as Riles suggests, modernity's doubles or to use Verran's phrase "the modern figuring of the world" [50, p. 35]. Again, we see the assembling of networks, relationality, difference and so on figuring the world out there as something other, something complex and yet, at the same time, something we can bring (our) order to. My hope in what follows is to show that another side of the complexity story is exposed when we turn the network inside out; we find that our own webs of ordering and knowing begin to unravel, revealing complexity underway—in the making—and thus things unordered and insoluble.

To pursue this thought, I will use an example from Verran's book *Science and African Logic* [50]. In her text, Verran builds and exemplifies her ideas using three case studies with the Yoruba-speaking people living in Southwestern Nigeria. The second of these revolves around a set of experiments she conducted in the late 1980s that contrasted the ways Yoruba-speaking children and English-speaking Australian children apply generalised rules to recognise the persistence of matter. To construct the experimental conditions, various substances (e.g., water, Coke and peanuts) and "measurement" containers (e.g., cups, bottles, bowls, and bean balances) were used, and the children were asked whether the quantity of substances changed as they were moved between the containers. The experiments are reminiscent of Piaget's famous studies of children's mental development.

Verran's aim was to contest a universalist perspective (that Yoruba speakers learn how to generalise when they are older with impoverished skills) with a relativist account (that English and Yoruba-speakers fundamentally differ in the ways they make generalisations). She accomplished this by demonstrating that between the ages of 6 to 11, English-speaking children develop a notion of persistence of matter using the abstract concepts "thingness" and volume. In contrast, Yoruba-speaking children begin applying a concept Verrran calls "unicity" from the age of 5/6 and use it confidently by 12. Unicity refers to the treatment of substances as units, e.g., one unit, half a unit, two units, etc. of peanuts. In short, the experiments showed that both sets of children were able to apply general rules about the persistence of matter, but did so using quite different features of the physical world.

This, then, typifies the kind of problematic difference-making I discussed earlier. Even the relativist position situates the Yoruba within the structures of modern scientific ways of knowing so that "out there" is still cast from "in here"—albeit in this case seen via an interpretative frame that is, analytically, one-step removed, and predicated on separateness but equity (something Verran herself calls the "trivialising of difference" [50, p. 154]).

Fortunately, Verran offers a thorough critique of her original results. In her *a posteriori* account, she places her own systems of ordering in view:

> "I messed around with the children, words, water, Coke, peanuts, bottles, bowls, bean balances, tape recorders, translators, transcriptions, index cards, tabulations of numbers, and so on, ordering them all into an almost smooth operation. Nothing would have happened without my energy, my organising, my bringing and carrying, my telling others to do this and to do that, my arranging by putting this here and that there, saying this and that with a zealous and obsessive bossiness." [50, p. 146].

For our purposes, this recognition of her own work achieves two important results. First, it acknowledges that ways of knowing are never outside of the work of ordering. In the original experiment, the work of ordering the conditions: of placing subjects in front of tables; objects into other objects; recording machines in close proximity; interviewers posing questions; researchers bossing obsessively; etc. were necessary by-products in eliciting the strategies children use to generalise, but crucially they not worthy of mention in reporting the results. Thus, embedded in the practical work of doing science are its epistemic underpinnings, yet these are carefully kept separate [also see 52]. As Verran succinctly puts it: "[t]he endless messy mediating ordering work must not pollute the delicate separating" [50, p. 152].

Her *a posteriori* commentary consequently serves to shift her and her orderings/knowings into the frame of analysis. The ordering of the conditions become self-evidently bound up with a system of knowing—first and foremost of science as a foundational epistemology. Also, they show from the outset that taken as given were the divisions between knowing, knower and matter: the ontological supposition that knowing is separate from body/thing. This outside-inside move may on the face of it seem trivial, but what it draws attention to is our own participation in the ongoing figurations of knowing and being. It reveals that despite our best efforts, we always are and always have been "inside", busying ourselves in ordering and dividing the many "in heres" from "out theres" [see 3].

The second implication of Verran's insertion of herself into the frame teases this out a little further. The point she makes is that the continual figuring—the bringing about of some way of ordering—is not achieved through the separation of the experimenter from the subject; the subjects from the objects; the English-speakers from the Yoruba-speakers; "in here" from "out there". Quite the opposite. She writes of it as "the collective going-on that was my experiment..." [50, p. 159]; the ordering of the world is, as a consequence, situated right there, "going-on" set amongst all the people and things involved in the experiment, and an emergent feature of their specific and contingent arrangement.

To offer another view on this, let us return for a moment to my visit to Dharavi and my conversation with my entrepreneurial informant. My reply to his question was that, yes, hanging around and asking questions was, indeed, the only job I had. This was the source of both immediate consternation and laughter for my informant as well as his family. I suspect similar reactions would have probably been provoked if I had been foolhardy enough to convey my unease and discomfort with the dirt and smells of the slum, and with the proximity of the dwellings to the flows of effluent. I can imagine the family thinking how simple life must be back there with one job, and how pedantic my divisions seem between clean and dirt (the sacred and the profane [see 16]). Life here in Dharavi, they might contemplate, is so much more complicated, so much more complex.

This is, of course, mere speculation. The issue I want to illustrate, however, is that, as in Verran's case study, if we pay careful attention to the situations we are in, it is possible to catch sight of the ways that we all collectively busy ourselves enacting an "out there", drawing lines, separating and rejoining. Everywhere, we see the ongoing and unremarkable assemble of machinery, amassed to as neatly as possible see the world in terms of networks, differences and complexities, amongst many other things. It is through our actual routine orderings, as Verran explains, "a vast amount of irrelevant complexity is excluded, and momentarily, ongoing collective life becomes extremely simple" [50, p. 159]. It is these moments of collective going-on, of mutually enacted orderings, that Verran teaches us we must place ourselves into (inside of), and that we must treat with concern and care.

GOING-ON

These latter points, especially, are complicated to convey as well as hold in view. To close, let me try, however, to summarise the points I have developed above. I'll then draw out why I think they are of importance to HCI and how they get us to a position from which we might go on.

As I set out above, my main intention in this paper has been to think about the turning of HCI's gaze "out there". Specifically, I've sought to consider the ways we might deepen and complicate this turn through three main themes. First, I've argued we must be mindful of using disciplinary tropes such as networks. That is not to say the network is the only trope we are guilty of deferring to. Nor is it to deny the network as an important topic of concern and/or framing device. Rather, I've wanted to remind the reader that we bring certain ways of ordering to the world when we cast ourselves "in here", looking "out there".

I've also suggested we be careful about claims of difference and that we aim to better understand what we may be doing by making-strange some of the practices we observe "out there". I understand that reasserting the lines between us, "in here", and them, "out there", does a particular kind of work in HCI, namely it offers a reminder to a largely Euro-American audience that people in different places do things differently. My point, though, is that this is still a making-different in terms of our own foundational ideas of organising and knowing the world; in seeing difference "out there", from here, "... it stabilizes necessary separations by superficial reconciliation." [50, p. 145].

Lastly, I've considered the ways we draw lines between the many different humans and things "out there" and, by doing so, enact complexity. What I've hopefully demonstrated is that this complexity (amongst other things) is something that is emergent. The collective assemblies of people and things in any space/time continually organise the world to both enact phenomenon like complexity and then do work to order it. Thus, looking "out there" from "in here", we are not outside of those processes. Complexity, in short, is a work-in-progress, and we are embedded in that work.

To give these points a greater purchase in HCI, I tentatively outline what I've chosen to call three orienting frames. I say tentatively because I'm conscious they will not prescribe a concrete approach or method to the issues I've discussed. Nor do they circumscribe a tidy or workable model of social settings. The aim here is to present them in the manner of going-on, of leaving room for more, much more, to come.

Right there

The first of my orienting frames takes up the idea of collective orderings. Again, by collective orderings I refer to the in-just-that-moment assemblage of people and things that enact just-that-way-of-seeing/understanding the world. My proposal is that we work to turn the network inside out, so that it is not just our ways of ordering we rehearse, but we attend to the orderings as they are achieved "right there" on the ground. Crucially, and to persist in looking from the inside out, I also mean to situate our own practices and rituals inside of that momentary, collective assemblage. The unit of analysis should thus also include the apparatus we bring to bear in ordering "out there". This isn't merely a call for reflexivity, in all its various guises [see 31]. It is to recognise that we are "in there" when we shift ourselves "out there", that we are unavoidably part and parcel of the practices and rituals of ordering.

The first of the orienting frames is thus an invitation to turn the network inside out; in turning our attention out there, I encourage us to also place what it is we do "back here" within the unit of analysis.

Collective configurations of technology

The second of the orienting frames finds inspiration in a paper Suchman [44] has written discussing the relationship between industrial research and innovation in the United States and technology uptake in developing countries. Early in the paper, she raises a number of pertinent questions:

> "So one question that could animate our projects is: What are the opportunities to interrupt these asymmetric flows and redirect them? What alternative configurations of technologies and practices might then be possible? And perhaps a prior question: In what ways are these flows already, in fact, more multidirectional than the mainstream discourse of globalizing information systems would suggest?" [44, p. 139]

One reading of Suchman's call could be to see it as a (re)articulation of transnationalism, serving to complicate the lines of globalising flows. In terms of the issues that I've been tackling, however, I take her thoughts to point to a recognition of and the possibilities for a collective "configuration of technologies". I don't consider this to be another proposal for participatory design or, for that matter, a recognition of the Global South's artful re-appropriations of technologies originally designed in wealthy, industrialised countries. What I want to suggest is that by attending with concern and care to the mutual practices and rituals of ordering—in which "in heres" and "out theres" are continually folding into themselves—we might start to imagine technological configurations that could be incorporated into the collective going-on. This configuration of technologies would *not* be equivalent to the assemblage of "words, water, Coke, peanuts, bottles, bowls, bean balances, tape recorders, translators, transcriptions, index cards, tabulations of numbers, and so on," that enforce an order on others. They would, instead, aim to provide practical and ordinary tools for collective ordering right here, right now.

The second of the orienting frames is thus a call to imagine human-computer systems that enrich the locally organising practices of emergent assemblies, rather than reasserting the lines between in here and out there. The question I intentionally leave unanswered is how we might situate design and HCI in those collectively enacted logics and dialogues emerging "right here, right now".

Instabilities

Unanswered questions lead me to the third of my orienting frames. In HCI, leaving things unanswered and still messy is often equated with messy thinking and research. However, something I see as crucial in peering "out there" is to recognise that our orderings are always collectively going-on—there are no neat, stable orders for us to report back. The networks of difference and complexity are not immutable "out theres" to be tidied up or solved; they are just the scrappy, messy and unfinished enactments of ordering that are going on. Thus, in the same way Harrison writes of the pauses, disjunctures and resistance to producing solutions in Wittgenstein's later writings, we might also learn to be more comfortable with our own pauses and moments of going on:

> "Wittgenstein will not tell us what to do, his work will not add-up, will not provide (yet) another theory. However an engagement with his work can give a different understanding of what to expect by and from an explanation and thereby intimate a different, perhaps suppler, more hospitable, way of going-on..." [21, p. 489]

The third of the orienting frames thus suggests a position from which we may apply a suppler idea of what we are hoping to achieve by looking "out there". Our accounts and explanations might allow for the unsettling of what we know, why we know it, and how we apply it; we might find ways to leave complexity just as it is.

CONCLUSION

I'm conscious in closing that I could reasonably be accused of conflating themes such as transnationalism, globalisation, postcolonialism, and networks, and choosing from what are, on the face of it, a motley collection of arguments to make my points. I also think there are reasonable grounds for accusing me of armchair theorising, intellectually posturing in ways that detract from what are without doubt some very real and practical issues "out there". "How", it might be fairly asked, "is this helping?" In conclusion, I thus want to open up my thoughts to a wider discussion in the hope of explaining why these possibly confusing and seemingly esoteric matters are of importance as HCI shifts its gaze further afield.

Something I've tried to convey in the points above is the trouble fields like anthropology and sociology run into when they set out to describe and account for the world using their own existing theories and concepts. In short, I've suggested this can lead to confusion over the substance and purpose of the work: whether it succeeds in describing what, exactly, is going on in a setting or whether it is, instead, engaging in some protracted disciplinary dialogue. Often the latter is confusingly presented as the former.

In its efforts to investigate "out there", I've argued that HCI runs the risk of repeating this same confusion. I've borrowed on old and new arguments alike to suggest that the reference to networks and the related themes of difference and complexity in HCI speak to the conceptual apparatus mobilised in certain areas of sociology, anthropology, etc., and is thus in danger of losing sight of or worse still misrepresenting the phenomena it seeks to report on and design for.

My wish here, however, is not to doggedly dismiss *a priori* theory or to question the value of importing concepts from other disciplines. Such a perspective is an old one in HCI that continues to have both its entrenched proponents and detractors. What I want to suggest is that the implications of the presented argument extend beyond the specific theoretical apparatus of networks and for that matter the particular issues of HCI and development/ICTD. The wider relevance, as I see it, is to disciplinary perspectives and the way that HCI as a discipline positions itself *vis-à-vis* "out there"—i.e., how it frames people who think, work, and play differently, and who have different rights and privileges. In these broad terms, I want to highlight what I see as two general lessons.

First, my hope is the above discussion points towards how we might pursue an integrity to our research as we turn to look "out there". Hopefully, it invites us to repeatedly ask what we are accomplishing by setting up some place or people as "out there" and to question the methods and concepts we use to do so. Rather than succumbing to the urgency to identify and investigate new sites and ever-different "out theres", and rehearsing familiar conceptual arguments because they have some disciplinary caché, we see how we might examine a world from "inside", from "right here". This, I want to suggest, is the broader consequence of turning the network inside out; it is an invitation to shift ourselves into the frame of analysis—where, as I have tried to argue, we have always been—and to apply care and concern for what, exactly, is going on around us.

Second, and relatedly, the above shows how we might begin to see ourselves within the processes of going on. Rather than "back here" reporting "out there", it gives form to an HCI that situates itself inside of the on-going interactions between humans and humans, humans and machines, machines and machines, etc. This is not a rehearsal of participatory design where the user is the designer, thereby democratising the design process. The call is a broader and more fundamental one that recognises the mutual, unfolding enactments of ordering, classifying, producing and ultimately designing technology. This collapses the us-them, human-machine, inside-outside binaries and allows us to see technology and its design not as a recapitulation of disciplinary tropes or tidy conceptual categories, but as a means of participating in unfolding ways of knowing, being and doing. The lesson here then is to recognise our inextricable participation in these enactments, to see that we to are part and parcel of just those human-computer interactions we are studying and designing for.

How then is this helping? As Gary Marsden—deservedly honoured by SIGCHI for his contribution to research in development—once put to me, "I just want to make people's lives better". I couldn't agree more with Gary's sentiment. And yet, I find myself struggling with what this better might be. How will we know it when we see it, and how will we know who's better it is? If we might momentarily look beyond this paper's conceptual meanderings, my hope is that at the very least it offers a basis for asking more questions, challenging our own practices and, in turning our attention "out there", keeping an eye on what we are doing "right here".

ACKNOWLEDGMENTS

I am indebted to many kind friends and colleagues for reading drafts of this paper. Listing their names hardly does justice, but I hope it is some recompense for their time and thoughts. Many thanks to Barry Brown, Richard Harper, Lara Houston, Lucian Leahu, Kenton O'Hara, Nimmi Rangaswamy, Daniela Rosner, Laurel Swan and Janet Vertesi.

REFERENCES

1. Anderson, W. From subjugated knowledge to conjugated subjects: science and globalisation, or postcolonial studies of science? *Postcolonial Studies*, 12, 4 (2009), 389-400.
2. Anderson, W. and Adams, V. Pramoedya's Chickens: Postcolonial Studies of Technoscience. In E. Hackett, O. Amsterdamska, M. Lynch and J. Wajcman (Eds.), *The Handbook of Science and Technology Studies*. MIT Press, London, 2007, 181-204.
3. Barad, K. *Meeting the Universe Halfway: Quantum Physics and the Entanglement of Matter and Meaning*. Duke University, London, 2007.
4. Bardzell, S. Feminist HCI: taking stock and outlining an agenda for design. In *Proc. CHI '10* (Atlanta, GA, 2010). ACM, NY, NY, 1301-1310.
5. Bell, G. No More SMS from Jesus: Ubicomp, Religion and Techno-spiritual Practices. In *Proc. Ubicomp '06 (Berlin, 2006)*. Springer-Verlag, Heidelberg, Germany, 141-158.
6. Bell, G. Messy Futures: culture, technology and research. *Keynote address, CHI '10* (Atlanta, GA, 2010). ACM, NY, NY.
7. Bell, G. and Dourish, P. Yesterday's tomorrows: notes on ubiquitous computing's dominant vision. *Personal Ubiquitous Computing*, 11, 2 (2007), 133-143.
8. Bidwell, N. J., Reitmaier, T., Marsden, G. and Hansen, S. Designing with mobile digital storytelling in rural Africa. In *Proc. CHI '10* (Atlanta, GA, 2010). ACM, NY, NY, 1593-1602.
9. Bødker, S. When second wave HCI meets third wave challenges. In *Proc. NordiCHI '06* (Oslo, Norway, 06). ACM, NY, NY, 1-8.
10. Brewer, E., Demmer, M., Ho, M., Honicky, R. J., Pal, J., Plauche, M. and Surana, S. The Challenges of Technology Research for Developing Regions. *IEEE Pervasive Computing*, 5, 2 (2006), 15-23.
11. Button, G. and Sharrock, W. The production of order and the order of production: possibilities for distributed organisations, work and technology in the print industry. In *Proc. ECSCW '97* (Lancaster, UK, 1997). Kluwer Academic, Dordrecht, NL, 1-16.
12. Churchill, E., Dray, S., Elliott, A., Larvie, P. and Siegel, D. Addressing challenges in doing international field research. In *Proc. CHI EA '10* (Atlanta, GA, 2010). ACM, NY, NY, 3127-3130.
13. Dantec, C. A. L. and Edwards, W. K. Designs on dignity: perceptions of technology among the homeless. In *Proc. CHI '08* (Florence, Italy, 2008). ACM, NY, NY, 627-636.
14. Dantec, C. A. L. and Edwards, W. K. The view from the trenches: organization, power, and technology at two nonprofit home-

less outreach centers. In *Proc. CSCW '08* (San Diego, CA, 2008). ACM, NY, NY, 589-598.

15. de Laet, M. and Mol, A. The Zimbabwe Bush Pump: Mechanics of a Fluid Technology. *Social Studies of Science*, 30, 2 (2000), 225-263.
16. Douglas, M. *Purity and Danger*. Routledge, London, 2002.
17. Dourish, P. Implications for design. In *Proc. CHI '06* (Montréal, Canada, 2006). ACM, NY, NY, 541-550.
18. Dray, S. M., Siegel, D. A. and Kotzé, P. Indra's Net: HCI in the developing world. *Interactions*, 10, 2 (2003), 28-37.
19. Gitau, S., Marsden, G. and Donner, J. After access: challenges facing mobile-only internet users in the developing world. In *Proc. CHI '10* (Atlanta, GA, 2010). ACM, NY, NY, 2603-2606.
20. Harper, R., Procter, R., Randall, D. and Rouncefield, M. 'Safety in numbers': calculation and document re-use in knowledge work. In *Proc. GROUP '01* (Boulder, CO, 2001). ACM, NY, NY, 242-251.
21. Harrison, P. The Caesura: remarks on Wittgenstein's interruption of theory, or, why practices elude explanation. *Geoforum*, 33, 4 (2002), 487-503.
22. Harrison, P. " How shall I say it...?" Relating the nonrelational. *Environment and Planning A*, 39, 3 (2007), 590-608.
23. Harrison, S., Tatar, D. and Sengers, P. The three paradigms of HCI. In *Proc. alt.chi, CHI '07* (San Jose, CA, 07). ACM, NY, NY.
24. Heath, C. and Luff, P. Documents and professional practice: "bad" organisational reasons for "good" clinical records. In *Proc. CSCW '96* (Boston, MA, 1996). ACM, NY, NY, 354-363.
25. Irani, L., Vertesi, J., Dourish, P., Philip, K. and Grinter, R. E. Postcolonial computing: a lens on design and development. In *Proc. CHI '10* (Atlanta, GA, 2010). ACM, NY, NY, 1311-1320.
26. Kam, M., Dray, S., Toyama, K., Marsden, G., Parikh, T. and Cutrell, E. Computing technology in international development: who, what, where, when, why and how? In *Proc. CHI EA '10* (Atlanta, GA, 2010). ACM, NY, NY, 3135-3138.
27. Latour, B. Visualization and cognition: Drawing things together. In M. Lynch and S. Woolgar (Eds.), *Representation in scientific activity*. MIT Press, Cambridge, MA, 1990, 19-68.
28. Latour, B. *Pandora's Hope: Essays on the Realities of Science Studies*. Harvard University Press, Cambridge, MA, 1999.
29. Law, J. *After Method: Mess in Social Science Research*. Routledge, London, 2004.
30. Law, J. and Hassard, J. *Actor Network Theory and After*. Blackwell Publishing, London, 1999.
31. Lynch, M. Against reflexivity as an academic virtue and source of privileged knowledge. *Theory, Culture & Society*, 17, 3 (2000), 26.
32. Marsden, G. UNDER DEVELOPMENT: The six habits of highly effective "humanitarian" projects. *Interactions*, 16, 5 (2009), 36-39.
33. Miner, H. (1956). Body Ritual among the Nacirema. *American Anthropologist, 58*(3), 503-507.
34. Oyugi, C., Nocera, J. A., Dunckley, L. and Dray, S. The challenges for participatory design in the developing world. In *Proc. PDC '08* (Bloomington, IN, 2008). Indiana University, 295-296.
35. Parmar, V., Groeneveld, G., Jalote-Parmar, A. and Keyson, D. Tangible user interface for increasing social interaction among rural women. In *Proc. TEI '09* (Cambridge, UK, 2009). ACM, NY, NY, 139-145.
36. Riles, A. *The Network Inside Out*. The University of Michigan Press, Ann Arbor, MI, 2001.
37. Riles, A. The anti-network: Private global governance, legal knowledge, and the legitimacy of the state. *American Journal of Comparative Law*, 56(2008), 605-630.
38. Sambasivan, N., Cutrell, E., Toyama, K. and Nardi, B. Intermediated technology use in developing communities. In *Proc. CHI '10* (Atlanta, GA, 2010). ACM, NY, NY, 2583-2592.
39. Sambasivan, N., Rangaswamy, N., Cutrell, E. and Nardi, B. Ubicomp4D: infrastructure and interaction for international development--the case of urban indian slums. In *Proc. Ubicomp '09* (Orlando, FL, 2009). ACM, NY, NY, 155-164.
40. Sawhney, N. Voices beyond walls: the role of digital storytelling for empowering marginalized youth in refugee camps. In *Proc. Conference on Interaction Design and Children* (Como, Italy, 2009). ACM, NY, NY, 302-305.
41. Smyth, T. N., Kumar, S., Medhi, I. and Toyama, K. Where there's a will there's a way: mobile media sharing in urban india. In *Proc. CHI '10* (Atlanta, GA, 2010). ACM, NY, NY, 753-762.
42. Strathern, M. Cutting the network. *Journal of the Royal Anthropological Institute*, 2, 3 (1996), 517-535.
43. Strathern, M. *Partial Connections*. Rowman & Littlefield Publishers, Oxford, 2004.
44. Suchman, L. Practice-based design of information systems: Notes from the hyperdeveloped world. *The Information Society*, 18, 2 (2002), 139-144.
45. Suchman, L. A. *Human-Machine Reconfigurations: Plans and Situated Actions*. Cambridge University Press, Cambridge, 2007.
46. Taylor, A. S. and Swan, L. Artful systems in the home. In *Proc. CHI '05* (Portland, OR, 2005). ACM, NY, NY, 641-650.
47. Taylor, N. and Cheverst, K. Social interaction around a rural community photo display. *Int. J. Hum.-Comput. Stud.*, 67, 12 (2009), 1037-1047.
48. Thrift, N. The place of complexity. *Theory, Culture & Society*, 16, 3 (1999), 31-69.
49. Tsing, A. The global Situation. *Cultural Anthropology*, 15, 3 (2000), 327-360.
50. Verran, H. *Science and African Logic*. University of Chicago Press, London, 2001.
51. Williams, A., Anderson, K. and Dourish, P. Anchored mobilities: mobile technology and transnational migration. In *Proc. DIS '08* (Cape Town, South Africa, 2008). ACM, NY, NY, 323-332.
52. Winch, P. Understanding a Primitive Society. *American Philosophical Quarterly*, 1, 4 (1964), 307-324.
53. Woodruff, A., Augustin, S. and Foucault, B. Sabbath day home automation: "it's like mixing technology and religion". In *Proc. CHI '07* (San Jose, CA, 2007). ACM, NY, NY, 527-536.
54. Wyche, S. P., Hayes, G. R., Harvel, L. D. and Grinter, R. E. Technology in spiritual formation: an exploratory study of computer mediated religious communications. In *Proc. CSCW '06* (Banff, Canada, 2006). ACM, NY, NY, 199-208.
55. Wyche, S. P., Magnus, C. M. and Grinter, R. E. Broadening Ubicomp's vision: an exploratory study of charismatic pentecostals and technology use in Brazil. In *Proc. Ubicomp '09* (Orlando, FL, 2009). ACM, NY, NY, 145-154.
56. Wyche, S. P., Smyth, T. N., Chetty, M., Aoki, P. M. and Grinter, R. E. Deliberate interactions: characterizing technology use in Nairobi, Kenya. In *Proc. CHI '10* (Atlanta, GA, 2010). ACM, NY, NY, 2593-2602.

How HCI Talks about Sexuality: Discursive Strategies, Blind Spots, and Opportunities for Future Research

Gopinaath Kannabiran, Jeffrey Bardzell, Shaowen Bardzell
School of Informatics and Computing, Indiana University
919, E 10 Street, Bloomington, IN 47408
gopikann@indiana.edu, jbardzel@indiana.edu, selu@indiana.edu

ABSTRACT
The topic of sexuality has been increasingly researched inside the field of HCI. At the same time, and for many reasons, research gaps remain. In this paper, we present a critical analysis of 70 works on this topic spanning the past two decades to understand how we as an academic field talk about sexuality. We use Foucauldian discourse analysis to identify and analyze the various rules of knowledge production on this topic inside our field. By doing so, we expose not only existing gaps in current research literature, but we also gain an understanding of why some of them exist. We suggest some opportunities to make the field more amenable to this kind of research and point out future research directions on sexuality inside the field of HCI.

Author Keywords
Sexuality, HCI, erotic, intimacy, gender, epistemology, discourse, Foucault, critical HCI, SHCI

ACM Classification Keywords
H5.m. Information interfaces and presentation (e.g., HCI): Miscellaneous.

General Terms
Design, Theory

INTRODUCTION
Works on various facets of sexuality, including gender, sensuality, intimacy, agency, embodiment, etc., have been published in the field of HCI for the past two decades. For example, in 2004, [17] explicitly calls for research and conversation about sexuality, pornography specifically, in HCI. [17] cites the then-unpublished manuscript of [11], published the following year, which labels pornography as the "elephant in the room" that everyone in the HCI community knows that it exists but does not talk about. Also in 2004, [36] and [38] were published both exploring intimacy mediated through interactive technology. While it is difficult to trace the history of works in this area, due to the trans/interdisciplinary nature of the field and the topic in hand, it is our observation that there have been spurts of research interest spanning over the past two decades on sexuality. These works focus on different aspects of sexuality in the context of a range of areas such as aesthetics [7,8,13], affective computing [30,33,50], product design [54,62], CSCW [59], human factors [23,26], ubiquitous computing [12,49], CSCL [3,60], robotics [25], domestic technology [11,36,41,42], wearable computing [29,33,49,50,61], tactile/tangible interfaces [23,26,30,48,49, 55,60,61], and participatory design [33,38,49,60], to name a few.

Clearly, the emergence of this discourse in human sexuality in HCI is well underway and is gaining momentum. At the same time, it does not seem to us to have achieved a critical cogency; that is, it feels fractured, filled with gaps and missed opportunities, as well as contributions that seem to have more potential for HCI generally than is recognized. To address these issues, we use discourse analysis to critically examine this body of research, both to clarify and synthesize what has been done, but more deeply to explore the tacit rules that seem to govern what can be said about sexuality inside HCI, who can say it, and to what ends. Our hope in doing so is to facilitate both future contributions in sexuality and HCI by, for example, helping young researchers find their voices, and also to facilitate the integration of sexuality research in HCI more broadly into the rest of the HCI research community.

RELATED WORKS
Many researchers have stressed the importance of discussing sexuality in HCI, beyond those already mentioned. For example, [6] expounds how paying attention "to intersections of technology and symbolically and emotionally dense cultural experiences", such as sex, can be illuminating, while [13] argues that erotic life is a "useful provocation" in maturing the field of HCI. Proposing the Sexual Interactions workshop at CHI2006, [21] draws to attention how research on sexuality can help bring new perspectives to existing works, legitimize alternate directions of inquiry and underscore the potential to inspire novel interfaces. Genevieve Bell, in the opening keynote of CHI2010, also advocated for research on sex and HCI.

Yet gaps in the research remain. [4] calls attention to the fact that HCI literature is mostly silent about cybersex. [13] shows how the erotic aspects of life are marginalized in

HCI research. [29] points out the insufficient attention that has been given to designs that facilitate sexual practices. The present work is an attempt to understand why such gaps exist as well as how the field might seek to legitimate a broader and better discourse on sex and HCI.

We approach this issue by charting out how we as a field deal with the topic of sexuality. In this regard, our work aligns itself along with other works that attempt to identify themes of knowledge production on the topic of sexuality. For example, [12] points out three broad manifestations of works that deal with intimacy in the technological literature from a ubiquitous computing standpoint: intimacy as cognitive and emotional closeness with technology, intimacy as physical closeness with technology, and intimacy through technology. A more generic overview about the majority of research conducted on intimacy and technology is summarized in [46] as an emphasis on "enhancing, replacing or creating more intimate experiences via either new or repurposed technologies." [13] presents two different viewpoints about how design of domestic technology might contribute to erotic life. The first focuses on designing interactive technologies that directly support erotic experiences, and the second looks at how the design of everyday domestic technology influences conditions for erotic life.

Instead of focusing on what is being done in a particular context or work, we focus on how we as a field deal and make sense of sexuality. This critical attitude stems from works on critical HCI such as [5,14,24,34]. In particular, this paper follows in the footsteps of [19] and [24], the latter of which claims, "careful, critical analysis of differing perspectives on research in the field and their relationship to deeper underlying intellectual commitments and trends can benefit HCI by providing reflective scaffolding for future research." The present work does not offer models of sexuality that could be leveraged directly in interaction design practice; rather, we hope to support future endeavors by providing a critical synthesis of existing works and pointing out potential areas for further exploration.

METHODOLOGY

The overall methodology of this work is discourse analysis, and in particular the strand of discourse analysis that owes its epistemological and ethical orientations to the work of sociologist and philosopher Michel Foucault. In his work, Foucault offered "archaeologies" and "genealogies" of social science domains (e.g., sciences of crime, pedagogy, psychiatry) and key concepts (e.g., fearless public speech, personal identity), seeking to understand them as discursive traditions, that is, as corpuses of texts, which are created and read within a context of rules and institutional practices. By discovering these rules and practices, Foucault hoped to expose them to the possibility of change.

More recently, scholars [45, 47] have abstracted Foucault's critical strategies into a research methodology, discourse analysis. (Note that there is also a quantitative empirical methodology, sometimes called "content analysis," e.g., [43], that also sometimes goes by the name of "discourse analysis"; the present work uses discourse analysis in its critical/Foucauldian sense, which we explain below.) It's worth noting also that Foucault himself wrote three books offering a genealogy of sexual discourses in the West, so he is in more senses than one an inspiration for the present work. He summarizes his own approach to the study of sexual discourses in the social sciences as follows:

> The central issue... is not to determine whether one says yes or no to sex, whether one formulates prohibitions or permissions, whether one asserts its importance or denies its effects, or whether one refines the words one uses to designate it; but to account for the fact that it is spoken about, to discover who does the speaking, the positions and viewpoints from which they speak... What is at issue, briefly, is the over-all 'discursive fact,' the way in which sex is 'put into discourse.' [27]

With the present work, we take a similar approach, seeking less to comment on the substance of scientific work in HCI and sexuality and instead seek to understand how such work enters the discourse of HCI. With that methodological background, we now summarize how we constructed our corpus and analyzed it as a discourse.

Constructing the Corpus

Over the last 15 months, we have surveyed archival papers, workshop proceedings, journal entries, magazine articles, posters, project websites, and book chapters that deal with aspects of sexuality. For this work, we use an inclusive definition of sexuality: by *sexuality*, we accept [53]'s definition as "the way in which we experience and express ourselves as sexual beings," a definition that deliberately includes broader dimensions of human sexuality, such as gender and intimacy.

A total of 70 items made it to our corpus based on our evaluation strategies. The selection followed a two-stage process. Initially, we searched for author keywords in ACM digital library on the words "sex", "sexuality," "erotic," "intimacy," "porn," and "gender." After this, we reference crawled the initial corpus, a strategy that also led us to works outside of the ACM library as well. These works were then evaluated for inclusion in the corpus study. We used two criteria to evaluate inclusion in our corpus. First, the work had to be already published or available in a public domain and affiliate itself to HCI or its cognate fields. Second, the work had to deal with at least one aspect of sexuality, as defined above.

Sexuality can be raised explicitly, implicitly, and through its conspicuous absence. For work on online pornography, for example, the sexual content is explicit. A more subtle way to report on sex-related research is to discuss it under the umbrella term of "intimacy." For example, [6] justifies its choice of the word "intimacy" over "sexuality" to "emphasize the broadest and most inclusive notions of human sexuality," though its authors were also responding to strong editorial pressure to do so. [9] labels "sharing physical encounters ranging from proximity to sexuality" as "physical intimacy," which is itself offered as one of five characteristics of intimacy. The most subtle way to report on sexuality is to do so through silence: for example, research about gender tends to remain silent about the sexual aspects of gender, even when they are relevant.

Regardless of whether papers discussed sexuality explicitly or implicitly, we sought to include representatives of them all. This raises the additional point of how we dealt with different positions with regard to sexuality. For example, [11,17] underscore that pornography is an important area of research that HCI can benefit from. Contradicting them, [56] argues that studying pornography will actually harm HCI rather than benefit it, especially if porn research prevents researchers from taking on other, richer areas of sexual life. [32] pushes forward the agenda to rethink our conceptualization of what online pornography is. Regardless of the varied stances these works take towards their object of inquiry and their mode of inquiry, all four works qualify themselves to be in our corpus since they deal with aspects of sexuality.

Finally, it is important to stress that exhaustiveness is neither possible nor desirable for the purposes of our work. Our goal is to collect works that are collectively sufficient to study as making up a discourse, including its key speakers, aims and contributions, and assumptions. We are aiming for a collection that is thematically and rhetorically representative of the whole, not literally comprehensive or even statistically representative of the whole.

Critical discourse analysis

As noted above, Foucauldian discourse analysis seeks to expose rules and mechanisms involved in the production, circulation, and validation of texts in a discourse. Discourse theory has since emerged as a field in itself, and providing a succinct account of it is beyond the scope of this work (note that [47] provides an excellent introduction to Foucauldian discourse). However, we introduce a few key concepts that are important to the present work.

Discourse

Foucault does not provide one single conception or theory of what discourse is but defines it in a number of ways throughout his works. He uses the word *discourse* to refer to "the general domain of all statements, sometimes as an individualizable group of statements, and sometimes as a regulated practice that accounts for a number of statements" [28]. In this work, we use the notion of discourse as a set of regulated practices "that systematically form the objects of which they speak" [28]. In other words, our operating theory of discourse is as follows:

- *Discourse* is understood as a corpus of statements that is both regulated and systematic.
- The production of such statements is governed by a set of rules that is internal to the discourse itself. This set of rules includes within itself the rules of combination with other discourses (for example, how does sexuality interact with tangible computing) and rules that help to establish the differences from other categories of discourse (for example, scientific versus literary).
- These rules delimit what can count as a legitimate statement inside a specific discourse.
- These rules create discursive spaces within which new statements can be made. Thus, like a grammar, they simultaneously delimit what can be said but also make possible new statements, in this case by providing the conceptual frameworks, models, analogies and theories, these rules with which research operates.

A discourse analysis, then, aims not at providing a summary of what is said per se, but rather an attempt to expose the discursive rules, demonstrate their operations and consequences, and subject them to the possibility of intentional change. Stated more concretely, the rules help us understand what can/cannot be said about sexuality in HCI, and we hope that by making them visible, we, as a community, can change the rules and make room for new kinds of research contributions, hitherto lacking a grammar allowing their formulation.

MAPPING THE TERRITORY

In this section, we present a quick survey of the works in our corpus and analyze them based on their content and intent. Using both these lenses, we identify and discuss some emergent themes. These emergent themes do not cover all the works in the corpus since some of them cannot be categorized based on the criteria chosen for differentiation, and also because the works cited under each of these emergent themes are not necessarily mutually exclusive.

Relationship between sexuality and technology

To analyze the works based on their content, we look at how these works approach the relationship between sexuality and technology. Using this relationship as the variable for differentiation, we identified three major emergent clusters that are presented below: technology as a facilitator of sexuality, sexuality as an explanatory variable, and sexuality as a critical lens.

Technology as a facilitator of sexuality

Works under this theme view technology as a tool that facilitates to fulfill a need, solve a problem, overcome hurdles and/or enhance existing situations in the subject's sexual life. These works have their allegiances rooted in engineering and design in that technology is positioned as a solution to an existing human problem. A vast majority of works in our corpus falls under this theme and is spread over multiple areas of research. For example, [9,12,15,25,29,31,35,36,38,41,42,48,60,61] all involve situations where technological solutions are designed for mediating intimacy between two or more people. Another variation of this approach would be works that deal with exploring aspects of intimacy in tangible and tactile interfaces [23,26,30,48,49,55,60,61]. Common to all of these is that technology is a solution to a pre-existing, well defined problem, and the research can explore the solution space without engaging with, or being held to account for, that problem space.

Sexuality as an explanatory variable

Works in this cluster view aspects of sexuality as explanatory variables for analysis of subjects' behavior or as a rationale for design choices. These works commonly have their epistemic roots in cognitive and behavioral sciences. For example, [2] presents some insights about the way subjects interact with, make sense of, and build relationships with virtual conversational agents based on the gender of the agent. Abusive sexual comments towards virtual conversational agents are explored in [3] and [20]. Specifically, [20] tries to examine the role of gender impressions behind such abusive behavior. While the above works view sexuality as an explanatory variable for subject's behavior, works also use characteristics of sexuality as a rationale for design choices. For instance, [10] uses "formative works" to understand the existence of gender-relevant design features based on which they design and implement new features on their research prototype. [16] points out the often overlooked or ignored aspects of sexuality, namely sexual orientation and gender identity, and the effects of ignoring these can have on establishing trust in avatar-based technologies.

Sexuality as a critical lens

In this third cluster, works tend to use human sexuality as a lens to critically interrogate and/or generate fresh perspectives on under-explored areas of research. This approach draws from various cultural and critical theories. In these works, sexuality is neither the goal nor the explanation but rather is the mode of analysis through which investigation occurs. These works, though few in number, are increasing along with the advent of critical and cultural HCI. [11], for instance, brings to surface how the notion of private space is constructed in different cultural contexts by analyzing the activity of browsing pornography in the domestic space. "Passages," an interactive installation that is designed to facilitate intimacy between people separated geographically, has helped view distance as a "creative object," which is otherwise considered in a negative way [15]. By analyzing online intimacy practices, [6] explores users as subjects that express themselves through aestheticized online performances. Going a step further, [7,8] analyze the virtual BDSM community of SecondLife and its practices and propose a new domain of aesthetic inquiry, interaction aesthetics, that can be observed and analyzed in online sexual practices such as this community. In [38], the authors critically reflect on conceptual sketches for mediated intimacy in order to open the discussion on the subject of "customized technology," raising important questions about "generalizability" while designing solutions. [41] explores the realm of rich interpretation in intimate communication between couples in long distance relationship by reducing the bandwidth of communication. While deception is usually considered a poor design decision, [46] critically reflects on the use of thumbnail gallery posts in ad-driven websites providing links to purportedly free pornography to explore alternative design spaces on the topic of online trust. Using three experimental prototypes that were designed to facilitate minimal, implicit, and expressive communication, [58cl] explores the concept of awareness and the characteristics of communication that contrasts with most CSCW work. Common to each of these approaches is the critical use of sexuality as a lens to gain access to and theorize about dense subjective experiences.

Each of these proposed relationships between technology and sexuality can be seen as instantiating a paradigm of HCI sexuality research. In each of these paradigms, scientific problems, disciplinary and methodological traditions, and scientific claims form coherent and already accepted clusters within HCI; moreover, in a point that we return to later, sexuality is carefully scoped to a single level of the project (i.e., design objective, explanatory variable, or critical lens, respectively).

Intended contribution of the work

Whereas the first criterion of differentiation—how sex and technology are claimed to relate to one another—effectively situated sexuality and HCI research into paradigms, our second criterion considers the authors intellectual goals, i.e., what they hoped to affect or change with their research. In our analysis we considered aims in terms of their scope, from the most general to the most specific goals. We accordingly distinguished among three levels: agenda setting (most general), domain exploration, and problem exploration.

Agenda setting

Works under this theme try to propose an agenda or point at directions for future work in this area of research. For example, [12] attempts to develop an agenda for intimate computing, [13] outlines theoretical and empirical perspectives to establish erotic life as a new frontier in HCI, and [29] suggests an agenda for designing technologies that facilitates sexual interactivity in the context of strong-tie, intimate relationships. Amongst the works that suggest future directions, [44] stresses the need to address the joint effects of race, class and gender in contexts beyond the workplace while [57] advocates that current works in sexual HCI must strive to humanize the technology.

Domain exploration

These works aim to explore a particular research domain or specific issues within a domain. Common domains of inquiry included mediating intimacy using interactive technology between two people in a romantic relationship [26,30,31,35,38,41,48,61], members of the family [25,31], individuals of a society to support city communities [9], and random strangers to facilitate "anonymous expressions of desire and sexuality" [15]. Another major motif of exploration is online sexuality. These works range from exploring sexual interactions between virtual agents [4,20,59] to expression and exploration of the sexual self through online interactions such as gender swapping in virtual reality environments [22] and intimate experiences in MMORPGs [52]. Exploring the role of design in gendered division of domestic space and labor is another area of reflective research found in works such as [11,18].

One interesting observation we found while analyzing these exploratory works is the marked absence of works that deal with aspects of sexual orientation or gender beyond traditional norms, that is, heterosexuality experienced by men and women. With a few exceptions, such as [16] and [51], homosexuality and transsexuality remain largely neglected topics.

Problem exploration

Works that contribute this theme deal with a specific problem by attempting to design an optimal solution or understand the factors involved. For instance, [10] aims to understand gender related differences while designing end user problem-solving software such as spreadsheets and CAD. [50] presents a design solution for peripheral safety and feedback system for practitioners of BDSM. The most specific of the intended contributions, research in this category is arguably the closest to directly changing conditions in everyday life.

It is possible, even from the categorizations we have made so far, to begin to make inferences about how sex is discursively regulated in HCI research. We have seen that it tends to be talked about in tightly scoped ways, constraining it to one well-demarcated portion of a broader (and otherwise "acceptable") project (e.g., sex as a variable, a constituent of a user research methodology, or a marginal subdomain of the field requiring valorization and agenda-setting). It is also presented fairly orthodox ways, both in terms of general cultural norms (i.e., emphasis on traditional gender and sexual categories) and HCI research norms (i.e., sexual needs as a problem amenable to a technological solution). Such discursive rules have a real impact on what kind of work can be published and presented in the field, a concern we turn to next.

THE DISCOURSE OF SEXUALITY

In this section, we analyze the corpus to provide an understanding of how sexuality enters the discourse of HCI and the problems that are associated with it. By *entering the discourse of HCI*, we refer to the manifold ways that a given work is able to legitimate itself, including establishing its subject-matter authority and situating itself vis-à-vis the rest of the field, and claim to make a novel scientific contribution. The primary aim of such critical project is neither to evaluate the existing works nor to make predictions about future works but rather to observe the mechanisms through which such works come into existence.

The intent behind focusing on these aspects is to critically question the assumptions, common-sense notions, and values that are inscribed in them to understand their implications. For example, works that deal with mediated intimacy almost always frame their user group as couples in a relationship or members of a family. An example of this would be Mutsugoto, a novel design that its creators describe as "an intimate communication device … meant to be used by romantic couples in long distance relationships…. Mutsugoto is meant to be installed in the bedrooms of two distant partners." [35]. The device could just as easily be used by anonymous long-distance partners (i.e., the partners don't have to be in a relationship) or by polyamorous lovers (i.e., the device is not strictly limited to only two users). Our aim in raising this example here is neither to criticize this particular work nor to provide our own normative standard. Rather, by questioning such seemingly commonsensical assumptions, we hope to raise critical questions about its implications for the stakeholders involved in it.

Sexuality and the sayable: A research opportunity

One common theme observed in all the works in our corpus is that sexuality can be discussed inside HCI only with respect to the way technoscience thinks about technology. In other words, not only does sexuality have to be linked to technology—a rather obvious requirement for HCI and sexuality—but sexual discourse must be framed and articulated in terms of technical discourse. Underlying this point is Foucault's notion of an episteme. An *episteme* "may be understood as the ground of thought on which at a particular time some statements – and not others – will count as knowledge" [45]. This "ground of thought" includes within itself philosophical commitments, academic lineage, methodologies, etc. making it possible only for certain kind of works to be considered as knowledge within a given discipline. (Foucault's reasoning here is similar to fellow sociologist of science Thomas Kuhn's notion of a scientific paradigm.)

Since HCI ultimately concerns itself with the interaction between technology and human subjects, sexuality can be discussed inside our field only with respect to technology. For example, let us consider the case of browsing pornography online. A work that addresses enhancing user experience while browsing pornography online [1], or a work that advocates paying attention to porn browsing practices to understand the concept of enjoyability [11], can be legitimated in HCI because the field seeks case studies understanding user experience. A Lacanian psychoanalysis arguing that the experienced pleasure of an interaction comes from a subject's subconscious yearnings for sexual domination, an intellectual strategy that would be at home in film studies, would be hard to sell in today's HCI. At stake is the extent to which HCI's existing episteme and corresponding discursive traditions are better suited to some sexuality and HCI projects than they are to others, which ones, and above all whether we can do anything to improve the situation.

The second implication is that sexuality-related works done in HCI need not (and should not) be mere attempts to import, after the fact, research on sexuality going on in other fields, be they applied health sciences, gender studies, or psychology. Rather than playing catch-up, HCI is a legitimate (and relatively new) domain of human sexuality in its own right and is worthy of study as such.

One unfortunate state of affairs—both for science and for public health—is that at present no academic discipline rigorously deals with the combination of technology and sexuality. Fields tend to prefer one or the other. HCI, which is historically quite strong on both technology and psychology (the latter obviously being a major contributor for sexual health sciences), and is now increasingly taking on human experience with various imports from traditional design and the humanities (which have investigated the role of sexuality, gender, and pleasure, etc., in film and literature), is arguably positioned as well as any discipline to develop this expertise. HCI research might thus contribute in important ways to scientific understandings of sexuality, which could in turn be leveraged to improve quality of human life, which may or may not involve technological solutions.

Complicating progress toward this agenda is that HCI research is typically validated by a double-blind peer review process, which demands that works stand on their own merit (i.e., not on the reputations of the scientists behind them) *in such a way that they are perceivable and appreciable by an audience of peers*. This merit is rhetorically established among a social community (i.e., HCI peer reviewers) through a combination of problem framings, demonstration of conceptual mastery, adequate quantity and relevance of literature referenced, and so forth. Because HCI has only tenuous relationships with disciplines that commonly research human sexuality—sexual health sciences and gender studies in particular—sexuality and HCI research is more likely to be successful by demonstrating technological scholarship, as opposed to sexuality scholarship, in other words, by circumscribing sexual discourse within a more recognizably rigorous technoscience discourse.

Two modalities through which sexuality enters HCI

We found that sexuality is commonly circumscribed in technoscience discourse using one of two common modalities. *Modality* here refers to how a work situates itself in a particular domain, establishes legitimacy, contributes to the field's knowledge and carries within the potential for furthering itself through future works. The two modalities are as follows:

- Presenting sexuality as a methodological apparatus
- Presenting sexuality as the object of inquiry

The first form of modality views sexuality as a mode of knowing, a methodological apparatus. Works employing this form of modality attribute themselves primarily to an HCI-related domain that is not sexuality, and sexuality becomes a strategy to gain insight about that domain. For example, [11] situates itself primarily as a work in the domain of domestic technology. One of the key contributions of this work was to introduce the technique of *defamiliarization* to help gain a critical distance while designing domestic technology. Gendered division of labor and consumption of pornography are two major facets of sexuality that the work uses to draw novel insights on how the concept of space and privacy is constructed inside a home.

We argue that the sexuality-based lenses in this paper do much more than add a bit of spice and point to a couple of interesting insights. Rather, aspects of sexuality are shown to reveal profound aspects of the lived experience of domestic space, in particular with regard to domestic privacy. An implication of this argument is that sexuality is an important dimension of the study of domestic life, along with concepts like privacy. This in turn suggests that sexuality should become a common dimension of domestic technology research. Yet [11] does not make this claim explicit, and there is little evidence that the paper, whose impressive citation history attests to its overall influence, has made sexuality a commonplace consideration in domestic technology research.

The concern we have for works in this modality is that the sexual angle is perceived as a one-off that has no further trajectory in HCI beyond the paper. And because these works are about the other domain (e.g., in [11]'s case, domestic technology), they are not usually viewed as contributing to the discourse of sexuality, either. The consequence is that sexuality, which is frequently an integral aspect in that particular domain, is not recognized as such in a lasting way, and the potential insights related to sexuality's role in that domain, are not subsequently developed.

Works that employ the second modality treat sexuality as the object of inquiry and situate themselves primarily as works in the domain of sexuality. This view stems from the assumption that the discourse of sexuality is separable from other discourses inside HCI and that other domains do not have anything to benefit from these works. Yet sexuality pervades many if not all aspects of human life, and understanding human life is ostensibly the very core of HCI, so the discursive marginalization of sexuality work in HCI seems hard to defend.

An active discourse can be enriched by new entrants, which have the potential to disrupt existing rule structures and thereby create new discursive spaces. Thus, the marginalization of sexual discourses in HCI not only limits the field's scientific understanding of human experience today, but it also might foreclose the possibility of subsequent works building on them. A positive example is [38] presents a preliminary study on intimate objects, technological devices for maintaining intimacy at a distance between couples. A year later [40], "inspired" by [38] and [42], proposes VIO (virtual intimacy objects), which use minimal communication to mediate intimacy and discusses user logbook data and journal entries to draw insights about minimal communication. Based on the VIO logbook entries, [41] raises important questions about evaluation strategies for context-based, interpretation rich, minimal and affective communications. In other words, research originally centered on sexuality subsequently yielded implications for more "mainstream" affective computing research where sexuality was much more tangential.

An implication of our analysis of research within these two modalities is that as a field, we are constraining the constructive influence a more scientific understanding of sexuality could potentially provide. For works that use sexuality-related concerns methodologically to build understandings of other domains, we should allow those relations to persist and develop; that is, subsequent researchers operating in the same domain might consider using sexuality-related lenses themselves to do their research, extending, refuting, or validating the prior work. For works that are about sexuality, they should both reach out to related domains and articulate those relations, and as a community we need to recognize the linkages when they are made and, again, build on, validate, or refute them. In both cases, sexuality is scoped too tightly to realize its potential in HCI—but why?

Barriers to entry

By identifying and discussing some of the documented barriers works in this domain face, we hope to identify some of the issues that hinder research in this area. The problems identified here are closely linked to each other, and is not an exhaustive list of all the problems these works face.

Taboo

The topic of sexuality has generally been mythicized as a taboo due to various reasons in varying degrees. While there is nothing intrinsic to the topic that makes it difficult to talk about, "once a subject is tabooed, that status begins to feel self-evident" [47]. Sexuality in HCI is a taboo topic, and attempts to address it have elicited reactions anywhere between politely ignoring it to outright moral high-handed judgment. For instance, [17] describes how "placing pornography in an academic context can still cause…a "moral panic"" while [1] expresses genuine concern about furthering their work of designing better interfaces for browsing pornography online since they are concerned about what their University ethics committee, colleagues, and partners would say about it. The authors of [6] were forced, as a condition of publication, to reframe their *interactions* magazine article to be about "intimacy" rather than "sexuality," and an anonymous editor unilaterally redlined dozens of examples, including projects sponsored by a nationally regarded center for public health, before the article was published in radically altered form. The organizers of the Sexual Interactions workshop at CHI 2006 [21] share a review comment about their workshop proposal where one of the reviewers wrote: "I'd feel a whole lot better if some of them had…signed statements from their psychotherapists attesting to their motives in promoting the workshop" [39]. While it is surprising in a scientific community to see such reactions to legitimate research, the growing interest in the topic over the recent years shows an increase in general acceptance and scholarly attitude towards sexuality in HCI.

Lack of definition

Human sexuality is a complex and intricate phenomenon that defies a single all-encompassing definition. Its lack of definition poses a pragmatic challenge to researchers working on this domain since "there is no generally accepted language for describing and discussing intimacy, especially in relation to designing technologies for its support" [42]. The lack of a single universal definition can also be viewed as a healthy stimulant that enriches the domain, allowing for multiple rich interpretations that enable researchers to focus on various facets of sexuality without reducing the complexity of it. This burdens researchers to operationalize "sexuality" in their research, an act that could be intimidating for someone new to the domain.

Intractability

Sexuality crosses the physical, emotional, psychological, social, cultural, political, legal, philosophical, moral, ethical, spiritual and religious dimensions of both everyday life and academic disciplines. This irreducible complexity makes it difficult to work with as researchers, even as the so-called third wave or third paradigm of HCI is likewise grappling with such issues [34]. As [39] points out, one of the reasons why sexuality is difficult to deal with is "not that it is naughty, but rather that it is so complex that it challenges and tests the limits of the tenuously rigorous design methods that we hold so dear." The seemingly insurmountable complexity of the topic makes it harder to approach and at the same time making it a rich ground for research. While it "presents the researcher with a number of unique and interesting challenges" [42], "the resoundingly personal nature of sex pushes user-centered design to new heights" [39].

MOVING FORWARD

In this section we build upon the findings that we have made so far to provide a few stimulants for future directions of research in this area. We have argued that there already exists a discourse of sexuality in the field of HCI. More importantly, we believe that we have been able to show that we are increasingly taking on the complex human experience sexuality, albeit with limits and lacunae. We hope that the present work, standing on the shoulders of this corpus, has helped legitimate this body research and identified opportunities for improving it. We conclude by offering a number of specific prescriptions.

Broaden the scope of "sexuality" in HCI. As we have argued, the extent to which we have, as a field, circumscribed sexuality (e.g., as a methodology, an independent variable, or a specialized domain) to a small part of a broader technological research project has probably limited its impact. We also know that sexuality is a fundamental aspect of human life, and it needs to come out of the margins of HCI research, especially in related areas, such as domestic computing, experience design, embodied interaction, feminist HCI, aesthetic interaction, and so forth.

Explicitly recognize sexuality-oriented HCI as a significant domain of HCI. One way to do so is to name it. [17] proposes "Human Computer (Sexual) Interactions." However, the phrase "Human Computer (Sexual) Interactions" is not representative of all the existing works in the field since "sexual interactions" connotes that the interaction itself is inherently sexual. Such a definition narrows "sexuality" to one, admittedly significant, aspect of it. We propose instead "Sexuality and HCI," to be abbreviated as SHCI and pronounced "shy." This definition leaves in place a broad—and endlessly contestable—framing of the domain.

Establish HCI as the expert domain of sexuality and technology in academic and corporate research. This means treating technology and sexuality with equal rigor, an outcome that could be facilitated both by strongly and urgently improving HCI's linkages to disciplines strong on sexuality, such as sexual health sciences and gender studies, and also by broadening the scope of sexuality in HCI to the foreground in domains where it makes sense to do so. It also means generating analytic understandings of sexual health-related designs. Works on sexual technology such as pornography, sex toys and health equipment are very few in number. Works such as [54], which discusses the design of the vaginal speculum, are much needed and can have immediate and positive effects on human life. The impact of these works extends well beyond the individual and affects larger social concerns such as safe sex practices, as in the case of [62], which presents the design of a condom applicator that increases the effectiveness of condom usage.

Set aside sexual prejudices (e.g., refusal to acknowledge the significance of homosexuality, transsexuality, and pornography). The rejection of prejudices is, of course, just good science, but some prejudices are harder than others to set aside, especially if they have been naturalized in systems of cultural norms and taboos. A closer connection to sexual health sciences and gender studies should also contribute toward this goal. A focus on the socio-cultural aspects of sexuality with respect to technology can help us question the assumptions and expose the politics involved in the design of the technology. For example, [44] talks about how race, gender and class politics affect women in technology, while [16] brings to light the heteronormativity embedded in virtual worlds. [27] critically examines the politics involved in framing gender within the binary norms.

Maintain an ongoing critical reflection about what we are researching sexuality in HCI for. A topic as wide-ranging and complex as sexuality can be of interest for any number of projects. [29] asks what *should* be our stance as researchers in the field towards "the 'unsentimental' facets of intimacy"? This question implies that we as a field are still not comfortable talking about sexuality outside the purview of a romantic relationship. [32] points out that "research related to sexual content online is framed by the need to draw clear regulatory lines to control such communication," the keyword being "control." Such observations help us to critically reflect whether the research we do is based on good reasoning or commonsense prejudices.

That technology and sexuality share a common past is just a matter of history. The role of pornography in the emergence of the World Wide Web and e-commerce is well known. HCI is a scientific discipline that designs technologies to support, enhance, and improve human life. To relegate sexuality to the margins is to shirk that responsibility; doing so has consequences for the progress of the field, for innovation and commerce, and for public health and wellness.

ACKNOWLEDGEMENTS
We would also like to thank the reviewers for their constructive criticism; the work has improved considerably as a result. We are grateful for the support and guidance of Erik Stolterman. Finally, we would like to thank all the authors in our corpus for making this work possible.

REFERENCES
1. Agarawala, A., Tang, A., and Greenberg, S. Browsing Pornography: An Interface Design Perspective. *CHI 2006 Sexual Interactions Workshop Paper*, (2006), 1-4.
2. Angeli, A.D. and Brahnam, S. Sex Stereotypes and Conversational Agents. *AVI 2006 Gender and Interaction: Real and Virtual Women in a Male World Workshop paper*, (2006), 1-4.
3. Angeli, A.D. and Brahnam, S. I hate you! Disinhibition with virtual partners. *Interacting with Computers 20, 3 (2008)*, 302-310.
4. Angeli, A.D. Seduced by computers! Sexual conversations with artificial partners. *CHI 2006 Sexual Interactions Workshop Paper*, (2006).
5. Bardzell, J. Interaction Criticism and Aesthetics. *Proc. of CHI 2009*, ACM Press (2009), 2357-2366.
6. Bardzell, J. and Bardzell, S. Intimate Interactions: Online Representation and Software of the Self. *interactions 15, 5* (2008), 11-15.
7. Bardzell, S. and Bardzell, J. Sex-Interface-Aesthetics: The Docile Avatars and Embodied Pixels of Second Life BDSM. *CHI 2006 Sexual Interactions Workshop Paper*, (2006).
8. Bardzell, S. and Bardzell, J. Docile Avatars: Aesthetics, Experience, and Sexual Interaction in Second Life. *Proc. of British HCI 2007*, British Computer Society (2007), 3-12.

9. Battarbee, K., Baerten, N., Hinfelaar, M., et al. Pools and Satellites - Intimacy in the City. *Proc. of DIS 2002*, ACM Press (2002), 237 - 245.
10. Beckwith, L., Burnett, M., Wiedenbeck, S., and Grigoreanu, V. Gender HCI: Results To Date Regarding Issues in Problem-Solving Software. *AVI 2006 Gender and Interaction: Real and Virtual Women in a Male World Workshop paper*, (2006), 1-4.
11. Bell, G., Blythe, M., and Sengers, P. Making by Making Strange: Defamiliarization and the Design of Domestic Technologies. *TOCHI 12, 2*, ACM Press (2005), 149-173.
12. Bell, G., Brooke, T., Churchill, E., and Paulos, E. Intimate (Ubiquitous) Computing. *UbiComp 2003 Intimate Ubiquitous Computing Workshop Proposal*, (2003).
13. Bertelsen, O.W. and Petersen, M.G. Erotic Life as a New Frontier in HCI. *Proc. of British HCI 2008*, British Computer Society (2007), 7-10.
14. Bertelsen, O.W. and Pold, S. Criticism as an Approach to Interface Aesthetics. *Proc. of NordiCHI 2004*, ACM Press (2004), 23-32.
15. Bitton, J. Distance and Sexuality: where HCI meets convenience and affinity. *CHI 2006 Sexual Interactions Workshop Paper*, (2006).
16. Blodgett, B.M., Xu, H., and Trauth, E.M. Lesbian, Gay, Bisexual and Transgender (LGBT) Issues in Virtual Worlds. *ACM SIGMIS Database 38, 4*, ACM Press (2007), 97-99.
17. Blythe, M. and Jones, M. Human computer (sexual) interactions. *interactions 11, 5* (2004), 75 - 76.
18. Blythe, M. and Monk, A. Notes towards an ethnography of domestic technology. *Proc. of DIS 2002*, ACM Press (2002), 277.
19. Boehner, K., Vertesi, J., Sengers, P., and Dourish, P. How HCI interprets the probes. *Proc. of CHI 2007*, ACM Press (2007), 1077 - 1086.
20. Branham, S. Gendered Bods and Bot Abuse. *CHI 2006 Misuse and Abuse of Interactive Technologies Workshop Paper*, (2006).
21. Brewer, J., Kaye, J., Williams, A., and Wyche, S. Sexual Interactions: Why we should talk about sex in HCI. *Ext. Abstracts CHI 2006*, ACM Press (2006), 1695-1698.
22. Bruckman, A.S. Gender Swapping on the Internet. *Proc. of INET 1993*, (1993).
23. Chang, A., Resner, B., Koerner, B., Wang, X., and Ishii, H. LumiTouch: an emotional communication device. *Ext. Abstracts CHI 2001*, ACM (2001), 313 - 314.
24. DiSalvo, C., Sengers, P., and Brynjarsdóttir, H. Mapping the landscape of sustainable HCI. *Proc. of CHI 2010*, ACM Press (2010), 1975-1984.
25. Disalvo, C., Gemperle, F., Forlizzi, J., and Montgomery, E. The Hug: An Exploration of Robotic Form For Intimate Communication. *Proc. of Ro-Man 2003*, (2003).
26. Dodge, C. The bed: a medium for intimate communication. *Ext. Abstracts CHI 1997*, ACM Press (1997), 371 - 372.
27. Foucault, M. *The History of Sexuality: An Introduction Volume 1.* Vintage Books, (1990).
28. Foucault, M. *The Archaeology of Knowledge & the Discourse of Language.* Pantheon (1972).
29. Gibbs, M., Howard, S., Kjeldskov, J., Vetere, F., and Satchell, C. 'Was it good for you darling?' – Intimacy, Sex and Critical Technical Practice. *CHI 2006 Sexual Interactions Workshop Paper*, (2006), 1-4.
30. Gibbs, M., Vetere, F., Bunyan, M., and Howard, S. SynchroMate: a phatic technology for mediating intimacy. *Proc. of DUX 2005*, AIGA: American Institute of Graphic Arts (2005), 2-6.
31. Goodman, E. and Misilim, M. The Sensing Beds. *UbiComp 2003 Intimate Ubiquitous Computing Workshop Paper*, (2003).
32. Halavais, A.C. Small Pornographies. *ACM SIGGROUP Bulletin 25, 2*, ACM Press (2005), 19-22.
33. Hansen, L.K. and Kozel, S. Embodied imagination: a hybrid method of designing for intimacy. *Digital Creativity 18, 4* (2007), 207-220.
34. Harrison, S., Tatar, D., and Sengers, P. The Three Paradigms of HCI. *Proc. of alt.chi 2007*, (2007), 1-18.
35. Hayashi, T., Agamanolis, S., Karau, M. *Mutsugoto - http://vimeo.com/2007048* Retrieved on: January 12, 2011.
36. Howard, S., Vetere, F., Gibbs, M., et al. Mediating Intimacy: digital kisses and cut and paste hugs. *Proc. of British HCI 2004*, (2004).
37. Kannabiran, G., Petersen, M. Politics at the Interface: A Foucauldian power analysis. *Proc. of NordiCHI 2010*, ACM Press (2010).
38. Kaye, J. and Goulding, L. Intimate Objects. *Proc. of DIS 2004*, ACM Press (2004), 341 - 344.
39. Kaye, J., Brewer, J., and Williams, A. Sex - Let's Talk About It. *Ambidextrous, Issue 10*, 2008, 8.
40. Kaye, J.J., Levitt, M.K., Nevins, J., Golden, J., and Schmidt, V. Communicating Intimacy One Bit at a Time. *Ext. Abstracts CHI 2005*, ACM Press (2005), 1529-1532.
41. Kaye, J.J. I Just Clicked To Say I Love You: Rich Evaluations of Minimal Communication. Ext. Abstracts CHI 2006, ACM Press (2006), 363-368.

42. Kjeldskov, J., Gibbs, M., Vetere, F., Howard, S., Pedell, S., and Mecoles, K. Using cultural probes to explore mediated intimacy. *Australian Journal of Information Systems 12, 1*, Australian Computer Society (2005), 102-115.

43. Krippendorff, K. *Content Analysis: An Introduction to Its Methodology*. Sage Publications (2003).

44. Kvasny, L. Triple Jeopardy: Race, Gender and Class Politics of Women in Technology. *Proc. of SIGMIS 2003*, ACM Press (2003), 112-116.

45. Macdonnell, D. *Theories of Discourse*. Blackwell (1986).

46. Medynskiy, Y.E. Lies in the Interface: Free " Smut " As License for Deception. *CHI 2006 Sexual Interactions Workshop Paper*, (2006).

47. Mills, S. Michel Foucault. Routledge (2003).

48. Motamedi, N. Keep in Touch: A Tactile-Vision Intimate Interface. *Proc. of TEI 2007*, ACM Press (2007), 21-22.

49. Mueller, F.'., Vetere, F., Gibbs, M., Kjeldskov, J., Pedell, S., and Howard, S. Hug over a distance. *Ext. Abstracts CHI 2005*, ACM Press (2005), 1673 - 1676.

50. Noessel, C. Master John: Peripheral safety and feedback system for practitioners of BDSM. *CHI 2006 Sexual Interactions Workshop Paper*, (2006).

51. O'Riordan, K. From Usenet To Gaydar: A Comment On Queer Online Community. *ACM SIGGROUP Bulletin 25, 2*, ACM Press (1994), 28-32.

52. Pace, T., Bardzell, S., and Bardzell, J. The Rogue in the Lovely Black Dress: Intimacy in World of Warcraft. *Proc. of CHI 2010*, ACM Press (2010), 233-242.

53. Rathus, A. S., Nevid, J. S., Fichner-Rathus, L. *Human Sexuality: In a World of Diversity*. Allyn & Bacon, 2007.

54. Rossman, J.S. Built to Spec? *Ambidextrous, Issue 10*, 2008, 47-49.

55. Schiphorst, T., Nack, F., Kauwatjoe, M., et al. PillowTalk: Can We Afford Intimacy? *Proc. of TEI 2007*, ACM Press (2007), 23-30.

56. Silverburg, C. Problematizing Porn: Ideas on Sexuality, Intimacy and the Place of Pornography in HCI Research. *CHI 2006 Sexual Interactions Workshop Paper*, (2006).

57. Stein, A. Sexual Human Computer Interfaces in 2006 and our Future Responsibility in its Development. *CHI 2006 Sexual Interactions Workshop Paper*, 2006.

58. Strong, R. and Gaver, B. Feather, Scent, and Shaker: Supporting Simple Intimacy. *Proc. of CSCW 1996*, (1996), 29 - 30.

59. Veletsianos, G., Scharber, C., and Doering, A. When sex, drugs, and violence enter the classroom: Conversations between adolescents and a female pedagogical agent. *Interacting with Computers 20, 3*, Elsevier Science Inc. (2008), 292-301.

60. Vetere, F., Gibbs, M., Kjeldskov, J., et al. Mediating Intimacy: Designing Technologies to Support Strong-Tie Relationships. *Proc. of SIGCHI 2005*, ACM Press (2005), 471 - 480.

61. Werner, J., Wettach, R., and Hornecker, E. United-Pulse: Feeling Your Partner's Pulse. *Proc. of MobileHCI 2008*, ACM Press (2008), 535-538.

62. Williams, A. Getting it On Gets Faster… and that's a good thing. *Ambidextrous, Issue 10*, 2008, 17-18.

In the Shadow of Misperception: Assistive Technology Use and Social Interactions

Kristen Shinohara and Jacob O. Wobbrock
The Information School
DUB Group
University of Washington
Seattle, WA 98195
{kshino, wobbrock}@uw.edu

ABSTRACT

Few research studies focus on how the use of assistive technologies is affected by social interaction among people. We present an interview study of 20 individuals to determine how assistive technology use is affected by social and professional contexts and interactions. We found that specific assistive devices sometimes marked their users as having disabilities; that functional access took priority over feeling self-conscious when using assistive technologies; and that two misperceptions pervaded assistive technology use: (1) that assistive devices could functionally eliminate a disability, and (2) that people with disabilities would be helpless without their devices. Our findings provide further evidence that accessibility should be built into mainstream technologies. When this is not feasible, assistive devices should incorporate cutting edge technologies and strive to be designed for social acceptability, a new design approach we propose here.

Author Keywords: Accessibility, product design, interface design, stigma, social interactions, assistive devices.

ACM Classification Keywords: K.4.2 [Computers and society]: Social issues—*assistive technologies for persons with disabilities.*

General Terms: Design, Human Factors.

INTRODUCTION

People with disabilities use assistive technologies for various tasks in their everyday lives. Assistive technologies are defined by the Technical Assistance to the States Act as "any item, piece of equipment, or product system, whether acquired commercially off the shelf, modified, or customized, that is used to increase, maintain or improve functional capabilities of individuals with disabilities" [6]. This definition describes any technology appropriated for the specific purpose of aiding people with disabilities, created with the express purpose of enabling access to environment, technology, information, and services. But assistive technologies are abandoned at high rates [20,22], and surprisingly, this is often due to personal meaning associated with such devices [18]. If assistive technologies are built to be functional and usable, but people are abandoning them, how effective are they in helping people with disabilities accomplish daily tasks? Research involving assistive technologies generally focuses on functionality and usability [10], yet technology use does not happen in a social vacuum. Rather, personal preferences in social contexts may dictate whether and how a device is used [24]. This implies an effect on technology use arising from social contexts. We present this study investigating the effects of assistive technology use in social and professional contexts from the perspective of people with disabilities, a perspective often lacking in assistive technology research.

We conducted an interview study to find how 20 people with disabilities feel about using assistive technologies in social and professional contexts. We found that while assistive technology empowers and enables people to work, socialize, and orchestrate their lives, it still lives in the shadow of social misperceptions. These misperceptions may perpetuate social barriers to accessibility. Assistive technologies are used in social situations and not in isolated laboratories; therefore, design of such technologies must be assessed for impacts on social and professional interactions.

BACKGROUND

In previous work [24], it was found that unwanted attention brought on by an assistive device made the individual feel self-conscious in some social contexts. Indeed, assistive technologies often bridge functionally *and* socially-situated experiences. To understand how social contexts may affect assistive technology use, we turn to literature on the disabilities rights movement, the meaning of objects, and the psychology of stigma.

Disability Rights: An Enabling Environment

As researchers who do not have disabilities, we believe it is important to endeavor to understand social and cultural issues of disability rights, and how these affect assistive technology adoption and use. In *Nothing About Us Without Us,* Charlton describes the social issues which drove the disabilities rights movement [5]. Fueled by the Civil Rights Movements of the 1960s in the United States, people with disabilities rallied for equal rights and equal access. The movement rejected the idea of disability as a medical condition, and instead adopted a socially constructed view, emphasizing that disability lies not in the person, but in the environment; access or in-access are situational and societal constructs. Rather than creating technologies and environments excluding people of varying abilities, this socially constructed view says the environment should be built to *enable* access. We take this one step further: *technology* should also be built not to disable, but to enable.

Personal Objects and Meaning

To understand how the built environment affects social interactions, we turn to literature on objects and meaning. People associate personal meaning with objects they use in everyday life [7] and may view their objects as defining part of their identity in some way. We negotiate how we present ourselves to others, cultivating our own desired identity [14]. Thus, we associate identifying characteristics with things others use and ways they present themselves. Through these social expectations, people determine and interpret social norms in order to navigate relationships with others. In this way, we make judgments based on first impressions and unconscious expectations [9], determining socially acceptable ways of interacting with others.

Disability and Social Stigma

If a person's self-presentation does not meet expected social norms, that person may be found to deviate from others and social interaction is disrupted. It is then that people may be marked for their difference from social norms. Goffman defines this as *stigma*: when an "attribute that is deeply discrediting" is associated with an individual [15]. He emphasizes that crediting or discrediting individuals occurs when negotiating social relationships. Thus, stigma is a socially constructed phenomenon; social norms influence the way social interactions are negotiated. Many social norms are based in societal underpinnings, which are out of scope to enumerate for this paper. However, we do focus on how people identify themselves and others through objects (assistive technologies) they use, and how objects affect perceived differences among people. If assistive devices mark users as "other," this may create social barriers to access even while such devices should help overcome them.

Elliot *et al.* [11] explain that people with disabilities lose legitimacy (are discredited) and incur stigma when it is determined, through social interaction, that they may not meet the implicit expectations of others. Elements of discrediting attributes include: visibility, pervasiveness in everyday life, centrality of a "problematic" attribute, and an inability to remove stigma. When these characteristics come together, they bring attention to the bearer, interrupting social discourse. Fine and Asch [12] argue that disability is a socially constructed phenomena. The environment and attitudes of others create "barriers of discrimination" and inaccessibility, and not necessarily physical impairment. In this way, it is a social responsibility to provide for accessibility in the creation of environments and artifacts.

RELATED WORK

Most research regarding assistive technologies focus on improving functionality or user interaction [10]. Some focus on how assistive technologies are used from the perspective of those who use them [16,23]. Few examine the effect of social situations, or the perceptions of those who use them. Here, we discuss some studies that do, and how this study differs.

Meaning of Assistive Technologies

Pape *et al.* [18] surveyed previous rehabilitation and assistive technology literature, examining where *meaning* and *significance* were reported as factors affecting assistive technology abandonment or use. They found that people with disabilities were more likely to abandon an assistive device if they did not accept their disability, if the device socially excluded them (made them feel different from peers), or if the device significantly clashed with cultural values. Pape *et al.* concluded that many social factors pervade choices in using assistive technologies, not just usability and functionality.

Assistive Technology and Stigma

Parette and Scherer [19] evaluated previous rehabilitation studies where individuals felt stigmatized by assistive devices. Elements contributing to stigmatization included aesthetics, gender and age, social acceptability and deference of rehabilitation professionals. While their paper is a thorough description of how assistive technologies may stigmatize individuals, it retains a rehabilitation perspective and does not describe its own empirical study, as we do here. Jacobson [17] explores modifications individuals incorporate as a way to manage stigma. Through individual cases illustrating how devices are personalized, she focuses on customization, supporting our work here on image and identity. Bispo and Branco [2,3] propose to eliminate stigmatizing effects of devices through design. Their work does not cite an empirical study, but their idea of "replacing the prejudices and the assumptions related to disability with an image of normality" by creating "new symbolic imagery" via design supports work we have done here.

Assistive technology is used in and around social interactions, and is subject to social expectations, but how? How much does perception shape meaning of assistive technologies in socially situated contexts? In what ways might assistive technologies mark users, perpetuating misperceptions about people with disabilities? These are some of the questions our empirical investigation addresses.

STUDY METHOD

Twenty participants were interviewed in sessions ranging from 60 to 90 minutes. Interviews were held in our university facility or at participants' place of work or home. Participants were recruited through various local assistive technology center email lists and were compensated for their time. Eleven participants were blind; 3 lost their sight later in life. Three participants had low vision, 1 due to macular degeneration. Four participants were deaf or hard of hearing, 1 lost hearing later in life. One participant was deaf-blind, 1 had cerebral palsy. Table 1 lists participants and technologies discussed or shared.

	Disability	Age	Sex	Employment	Technology (previously used devices)
1	Totally blind, born with vision in one eye	57	M	Retired fisherman, Sports Supervisor	JAWS, BrailleNote, HTC Touch Pro cell phone with MobileSpeak & MobileGeo, white cane, netbook, (Victor Reader), (Perkins Brailler), BookSense, guide dog
2	Leber's Congenital Amaurosis (blind)	28	M	Assistive Technology Specialist	accessible cell phone, BrailleNote, KNFBReader, Victor Reader Stream
3	Congenitally blind, losing hearing	58	M	Retired	JAWS, hearing aids, Perkins Brailler, (slate and stylus), (BrailleLite), Braille Display, (Duxbury), (books on record), (Optacon), white cane, cell phone - not accessible, talking watch
4	Lost sight 5 years prior, totally blind	30	F	Student	JAWS, talking watch, Nokia cell phone with MobileSpeak, white cane, Victor Reader
5	Born with low vision	44	F	Mental Health Counselor	ZoomText, Victor Reader, monocular, (books on CD), (books on cassette), (books on record), glasses for low vision, (CCTV), (large print typewriter)
6	Lost sight due to Retinitis Pigmentosa	71	F	Retired Librarian	VoiceNote, JAWS, Screen magnification, Screen contrast, CCTV, books on tape, Victor Reader Stream, Verizon LG cell phone - not voice accessible
7	Congenitally blind	58	F	Unemployed	JAWS, Braille, Victor Reader Stream, Slate and Stylus, (books on reel-to-reel books), (books on tape), Braille Display, (Braille N Speak), (portable typewriter)
8	Congenitally blind	58	F	Transition and Independent Living Specialist	(books on reel-to-reel tape), (books on tape), (books on record), BrailleNote, white cane, Nokia 6682 cell phone with Talks accessibility program, (Optacon), scanner with Kurzweil software, Duxbury
9	Low vision	49	F	Assistive Technology Instructor	white cane, speech program on computer, Nokia N86 with voice accessibility, BrailleNote, talking scale, (tape player for note taking), (Perkins Brailler), (Slate and Stylus), (regular typewriter), (books on reel-to-reel tape), (CCTV)
10	Congenitally blind, losing hearing	56	F	Unemployed	Perkins Brailler, hearing aids, Screen Reader, (optacon), Slate and Stylus, (portable typewriter)
11	Congenitally blind	61	F	Retired Social Worker	PacMate, iPhone, KNFBReader, scanner, Braille Display, talking microwave
12	Low vision, Macular Degeneration	72	F	Retired Professor	iPhone, iPad, magnifying glasses, glasses, monocular, JAWS
13	Deaf-blind, Usher's Syndrome	39	M	between jobs	Deaf-Blind Communicator, white cane, TTY, ZoomText
14	Deaf	38	F	Director, Human Services	iPod, videophones, phone captioning, pager with IP relay, TTY, Video Relay Service, (FM System), netbook, cell phone, flashing doorbell, flashing and vibrating bed alarm
15	Hard of hearing	59	M	Salesman	hearing aids, iPhone, headphones for home use, captioning, (ASL)
16	Hard of hearing, low vision (Usher's Syndrome)	52	M	Retired	hearing aids, white cane, Computer Aided Real Time captioning, guide dog, cell phone
17	Hard of hearing	56	F	Freelance Editor	cell phone with bluetooth, TTY, hearing aids,
18	Cerebral palsy	69	F	Advocate	Pathfinder Communication device
19	Congenitally blind	59	M	Singer	Victor Reader Stream, talking watch, BrailleLite, (Perkin's Brailler)
20	Lost sight due to Retinitis Pigmentosa	48	F	Unemployed/ Retired	CCTV, ZoomText, JAWS

Table 1. Participants and assistive technologies.

Participants were asked about assistive technologies used, how technologies were used, and what they thought of their technologies. Wherever possible, they were encouraged to show their technologies. If participants had a disability since birth or childhood, they were asked to compare past and current devices. They were asked what it was like to use assistive devices around others in social or work contexts. They were also asked if they thought there were misperceptions surrounding their technologies, and if they ever felt self-empowered or self-conscious when using their assistive devices.

Analysis

All interviews were recorded and transcribed verbatim. Using a grounded theory approach [13,25], transcripts were coded using open and axial coding; similar categories and concepts were combined, then compared with concepts in subsequent interviews. Early interviews were initially open coded for specific concepts to pursue in later interviews. From the developed categories, dimensions and properties were drawn out as well as connections to other categories.

RESULTS

We found that people with disabilities balance complex relationships with their environment and with others while using their assistive technologies. When using their devices, participants negotiated feeling self-conscious with the desire to be independent and the need to be productive, especially at work. Participants used a wide variety of proprietary and mainstream technologies, as shown in Table 1, over a range of social and personal activities, including: for education, traveling, entertainment, engaging with friends, at work, and safety. Devices discussed included electronic note takers, hearing aids, the Victor Reader Stream (digital book player), monoculars, magnifying glasses, and video relay services. Some participants also used mainstream devices, such as the Apple iPhone and iPad, netbooks, cell phones, laptops, and desktop computers. A range of devices and systems bridged proprietary and mainstream technologies, including Bluetooth-compatible hearing aids, and JAWS (Job Access With Speech) software. Even proprietary devices such as the Victor Reader Stream integrated with SD (Secure Digital memory) cards, and several blind participants used scanners with OCR (Optical Character Recognition) technology to access print books.

Figure 1. The Pathfinder Communication Device used by P18.

Assistive Technology in a Social World

We found assistive devices played both central and peripheral roles in social interactions. For instance, the Pathfinder (Figure 1) and the Deaf-Blind Communicator were used as primary communication tools for P18 and P13, respectively. In comparison, the Victor Reader Stream and software like ZoomText and JAWS were peripheral in most social interactions. Technologies in central social roles were more conspicuous than others. While peripheral technologies were not usually central to interactions, many influenced how social interactions played out, particularly at work. If peripheral technologies were more visible and "weird" or "strange" looking, they tended to attract attention from others. Smaller devices and those that looked like mainstream counterparts attracted the least attention.

Participants were aware their devices attracted attention by the kinds of questions and comments they received. In some cases, participants were sensitive to the reactions of others around them, for instance, taking note when another person seemed uncomfortable, sent furtive looks, or by their tone of voice. Despite this, participants did not significantly alter device use, although they reported feeling self-conscious about attention in a few situations: (1) if they had an "invisible disability," one that may not be apparent without explicit disclosure; (2) when using traditional and socially recognizable devices, such as a white cane or hearing aids; and (3) when design attracted attention to differences from mainstream counterparts, for example, voice accessible phones that spoke aloud commands everyone could hear.

Just Like Everyone Else

Participants valued technology enabling equal access because it allowed them to do things *just like everyone else.* Two caveats to this perspective were that participants felt they should retain disability-specific training (for example, blindness skills, or American Sign Language), and that not all technologies leveled the playing field of access. P18 explained that her device allowed others to "see I can communicate like any person," resulting in improved social interactions. P7 felt empowered because she had access just like everyone else:

... it's just neat that I can do things,... that other people can do. Like, I can have books to read that I want to read... when I first got my scanner I was really excited about it because then I could ... buy books that weren't available, and I could read those books,...I would say your technology is your lifeline...it opens up worlds of opportunity.

Still, participants reported assistive technologies lagged behind current technical standards, meaning they did not truly have access like everyone else. P2 discusses the appeal of mainstream technologies and how people feel about assistive technology always being a step behind:

You know, if someone's using an iPhone, and I'm using an iPhone, that's normal, right? It's the same thing... like universal design, you build the accessibility directly into the products, then you're not using some clunky, blindness specific product. A term that gets thrown around sometimes is blind ghetto products. ... cell phones have, like, all these neat features and stuff, but, ...the BrailleNote's just catching up. When you know, it doesn't even have like, 802.11n, which is the new networking standard. You know, but it costs six grand. I mean, come on.

An important point must be made: participants recognized that no assistive technology would fully replace sight, hearing, or any kind of functioning. Rather, they most valued *having access* to the information and services *everyone else had.* Finally, as seen in these comments, many participants expressed the importance of *being seen* with assistive or mainstream devices in order to demonstrate how they were capable of doing just as much as anyone else.

Design and Aesthetics

As mentioned previously, participants were aware of how their technologies differed from the mainstream status quo in quality of access and function. They were also aware how their technologies looked different than mainstream technologies. Device design and aesthetics were divided into appealing and unappealing characteristics, based on look and feel. It was noted that manufacturers of proprietary technology do not appear to make an effort to make their devices aesthetically appealing. P2 described his experience upon discovering the color of his BrailleNote[1] earbuds:

The original BrailleNote used to ship- I don't remember what color they were- but they were the ugliest earbuds you

[1] http://www.humanware.com

could possibly- like, bright orange or something. It came with these hideous earbuds. And, I had one of my friends- sighted friends- is like, 'man, you- those things are awful, dude. You should never[2] use those.' And I had no idea. But, of course, they just thought, since it was a bunch of blind people they're shipping this stuff to, it didn't matter.

P10 explained she cared about the design of things she used because it could be a reflection on her:

I like things attractive. Whatever adaptive equipment, I want it to look nice. You know, you got everybody with their iPods and their iPads and their Blackberries, you know, and they're whipped out, they're small... and they're nice looking. Cause –Apple would not be selling their "i" stuff if it wasn't good looking. And, as a blind person, yeah, maybe I don't see it, but other people see it, and I want it to be, you know, just as glamorous as the next guy.

If a device looked similar to mainstream devices, or if few alternatives existed (for instance, electronic note takers are the only devices providing portable refreshable Braille), participants did not report feeling self-conscious. But, if devices looked unlike anything else (monoculars), or were altered versions of mainstream counterparts (extra thick glasses, large print typewriters), participants were more likely to report feeling self-conscious (Figure 2). This last category was compounded by the fact that many who used such devices also had "invisible disabilities" and could pass as having no disability (if they were not using assistive devices). Illustrating this point, P8, a transition specialist for young blind and low vision students, observed:

So anything that might be cosmetic, is a real big--... like the monoculars, or big thick glasses, or a hand held magnifier, you know. Some of those things are more of a cosmetic kind of thing. They're real visual... And even the large print books, because if you're carrying those around, they're probably, legal size paper, if not bigger. You know, so they really are huge compared to what other kids carry around. And so they don't like to carry those around.

Two of the three participants with low-vision reported they could pass as non-disabled *if they were not using their devices*. Speaking to this, P5 explained how she negotiated self-consciousness and utility:

...a device is no use to you if you won't use it. So, I think there's some holes between shame and utilitarianism... Like, this is gonna be efficient for me, and I'm gonna do it. You know, and on the other end of it is, I'll just figure out any way to do this where I won't be noticed. And I've been on both ends of that and everywhere in between.

Internal battles between self-consciousness and utility were most prominent among the low-vision participants. Other participants also overcame feelings of self-consciousness through adopting utilitarian viewpoints, but to a lesser extent. Like P5, participants recognized their devices as tools enabling them to do things such as write papers for school or contact work clients. Finally, while acknowledging different-looking devices attracted attention, some participants reported not feeling self-conscious.

Figure 2. From left: Victor Reader Stream, monocular, glasses.

Avoidance

Many participants reported they avoided using certain technologies as much as possible at one time or another. P8 describes what she perceived cane-use to mean and how she did not want "that" to be her:

...when I was a teenager I wasn't gonna use a white cane because I was blind and I didn't want – The only example I had of a blind person using a cane, it sounded like they were shuffling their feet, and they had their head down, and they were... you know? ...so I wasn't gonna use the cane.

Similarly, P9 explained why she refused to use a cane at first: "because I felt it really caused me to stand out." She wanted to avoid being marked as the blind person P8 envisioned. Many of the blind and low-vision participants echoed this sentiment. But where P8 and P9 eventually did start using their canes, it was something P12, who had macular degeneration, still had not adopted:

The kind of thing that I have a problem with, and I do not use, is a white cane. I mean, that is – that is a hurdle that, boy, that's gonna be awhile before I get over that one.... Because, it just immediately, kind of marks you out as different, as having vision problems. Most people who meet me, until I tell them, have no idea. And, I guess I kind of prefer that.

Although not as prevalent, some participants with hearing loss also experienced a reluctance to wearing hearing aids so often associated with the elderly. P15 describes why:

...it's just the acceptance of it, which is much harder, compared to, say like, glasses, which you know,... it's universal, it's socially accepted... Again, the frame of reference being that the people you knew who wore hearing aids was your grandfather. And, so there's that part of it.

[2] All emphasis in original.

...I think it's some sort of social stigma. And I still experience that now.

While P15 felt glasses were more socially acceptable than hearing aids, P10, herself congenitally blind, had a hard time accepting hearing loss and hearing aids:

The hardest thing for me was to accept – was having to use a hearing aid. And, it took me a really long time. I was really kind of surprised at myself, 'cause I am pretty matter of fact. But it was just coming to terms with the fact that I wasn't hearing as well as I used to... I was afraid it would look awful.

Although the white cane is not an electronic assistive technology, it is an assistive device, and connotations our participants associated with it tell us much about the social meaning they attributed to this device. They were aware of the social stigma of these devices, and it did not matter if the participants were totally blind, had low vision, were born deaf or became deaf later in life. This tells us some assistive devices do, in fact, have strong social meaning associated with them. It is hard to guess how such perceptions came to be a part of these devices, but we can see our participants did not want to be associated with these perceptions. As we saw in P8's comment about using the white cane, they felt such perceptions did not represent who they were at all.

Safety

In contrast to avoidance, some participants purposefully chose to call attention to their disability, usually for safety reasons, through the use of their devices. P9 describes how she began to use her cane:

...once I kind of... got over my inhibitions, and all the concerns that I felt about what people would think of me in high school, I found that it was so much easier. I mean, a cane gives information to the world. It says to people, 'this person is blind'...You know, 'give her another couple seconds before you blast on your horn when she's crossing the street,' you know? Um, 'just go easy.' ... So, to me, the cane was one of the most empowering things, but it was also... one of the most difficult things for me to sort of admit that I needed.

Not all assistive technology used for safety reasons were appropriated to identify the person with a disability. For instance, P14 used a pager with an IP address service in case of an emergency where she might need to call for help. P1 avoided any technology with wearable straps, wary that such devices might invite attackers to "yank" them off his neck. P20 explains why safety was an important concern:

I would say it's a more perceived feeling of being threatened, or being less safe. And a lot of that is because there's a realization, first of all, we don't know our surroundings. Other than from what we can hear. And we can't run. And, maybe you can fight, but... you don't know who you're fighting and what they may have in their hand. And if you fight, you gotta get up close, and then – even then, what happens if you win? You still – what are you gonna do, grab your cane, and click clack, click clack, click clack down the street? So... you start thinking of all the implications, like, okay, hmm, I just need to be more aware of – that I keep myself out of situations that may be unsafe.

These descriptions give credence to the safety concerns of people with disabilities, while also highlighting important concepts of device design, use, and safety. It is important for people with disabilities to be able to identify and communicate something about their disability, depending on the context, but only *if they so choose*. Recall that P9 used her cane to identify her as visually-impaired so people would know she may not see them. At the same time, P1 did not want people to recognize his blindness-specific technologies; thus, he did not wear them visibly for others to see, and he was wary of designs implicating a device be worn. Finally, expensive proprietary technologies are hard to replace and require extra security.

Help

Themes of help arose out of many of the social interactions participants described. Not all kinds of help involved assistive technology directly, but we include them because they were strongly tied to perspectives on identity, which in turn, was tied to assistive technology use. Participants negotiated when they asked for help, especially if they had an assistive device at hand. P4 was careful when asking for help so as not to burden friends or family, and also because she did not want them to think less of her. Here, P4 associates asking for help with her own abilities, and consequently, how she wants others to identify her. She is concerned with what is portrayed about her if she asks for help too much:

I don't want people to – just view me as a disabled person. I want them to view me as Karen,[3] so, it's like when I ask them questions, it's like, okay, I'm this disabled person asking questions. It's not Karen asking questions. And it's just sort of like – sometimes if I ask questions a lot, then it's like my – it's like I'm losing my... personality.

Participants reported that strangers offered unwanted help, grabbing, pushing or pulling blind participants, assuming they knew where the participant was headed. People over-articulated or spoke loudly, trying to compensate for deaf participants' hearing loss. P5 received emails in large font by people who knew she had low vision and assumed she had no accommodations (in fact, she used ZoomText[4]). This "discombobulated" her (her word), requiring her to adjust software settings. In unwanted help, the helper identified the participant as having a disability, was unaware of the participant's abilities or accommodations, made assumptions, and took it upon themselves to "help."

---

[3] Names changed to maintain confidentiality of participants.

[4] http://www.aisquared.com/zoomtext

Issues of help were significant because they occurred often and because participants felt that if others saw them getting help, they would consider them less able. Issues of help have implications for assistive technology design. As we have seen, participants did not want to be identified as helpless, they wanted others to see how assistive devices made them independent and capable. Thus, it was important for participants to be able to use devices confidently, and it was just as important for others to see this as well.

Ignorance and Misperceptions

When participants were offered unwanted help, it was often because others did not know what the participants could do. Many social interactions involved participants answering questions about their disability or devices; some questions overstepped social and privacy boundaries, such as, "how did you lose your sight?" or, "What's that?" interrupting participants about an assistive device they were using. Most participants welcomed the chance to educate others about having a disability, although some felt such questions were too personal and an invasion of privacy.

People asked questions because they were unfamiliar with assistive technology. One problem with this general unfamiliarity was that people then made incorrect assumptions. P6 described how the reactions of others made her feel self-conscious about what they were actually thinking about her using a VoiceNote[5]:

When you're in a group of sighted – especially sighted people, you know, and you bring out something like this. They'll say, 'Oh, what's that? What's that? Oh, isn't that wonderful?' And they'll get sort of patronizing. They'll say, 'oh, isn't that wonderful? You can have that?'

P6 discusses how this patronizing perspective from others leads to misperceptions about what her device can do:

I have a friend and we were talking about being disabled. She said, 'well, you have your VoiceNote.' It's like people think you can be normal... because you have some technology...you're still not visually normal. But... I don't know, she had the misperception that, well, I could just live a normal life because I had a VoiceNote... Well, I can live better. But I don't... see, I'm comparing it to a visual life. And, I thought, I still don't live a visual life, even though I have assistive technology. But, I know the difference between sighted life and not sighted life.

While others think her device is "wonderful" and will make her "normal," P6 instead views her device as just another tool that improves her life. P6's encounters were not unique among our participants. They felt empowered and grateful to have assistive technologies, but as P10 explains, most participants considered their devices just another tool:

I don't think it represents me as a person. It's a device. The same way as a sighted person using a blackberry or whatever – it doesn't represent them. It's just a tool that they have, it's a toy they play with all the time... that makes life a little bit more convenient... and that's the way I look at whatever adaptive technology I use. It's the same thing as my sighted neighbor using their computer toys.

Our participants rejected supercilious comments about their devices because they patronized what participants felt was their ability to do just as anyone else. Thus, the perspective that assistive devices were "wonderful" and could make people with disabilities "normal" was a charitable view on assistive technology use, and was not accurate or realistic. The two most commonly reported misperceptions by others about assistive technologies were that (1) assistive technologies functionally eliminated a person's disability (made them "normal"), and (2) that without an assistive technology, a person was helpless and could do nothing. The first misperception was rooted in ignorance about what assistive technologies do; the second was an assumption that the presence of an assistive technology meant a continual need for assistance.

Employment

Participants viewed assistive technologies as a means to an end in employment situations. As important as having access and the ability to work was the *perception* on the part of others that participants had the ability to get a job done. For example, P4's employer, a small firm, was unaware of the technologies that would allow P4 access at work. Although she received a large monitor and JAWS software, her employer knew little about what might help her access print material with her sight nearly gone. In the end, she was demoted and given fewer responsibilities. P20 purchased his own assistive technology for work, and negotiated office interactions in new ways as a result:

...you have to put your earphones on, so you don't annoy everybody around... and I didn't necessarily like ...being cut off from people. I like to sit in a room and hear what's going on... you know, get a sense of what's going on in... my team around me. And so that was my way of keeping track without being, you know, nosy. And so when I... was working with JAWS and had the earphones in, then I kind of felt a little cut off, and so that... took some getting used to.

Similarly, P14, who was deaf, found small workarounds so her vibrating pager would not attract unwanted attention at the office: "I finally got a mouse pad just to put the pager on so it *wouldn't* vibrate all over the table and make a loud noise and have people look at me." As an example of how choices affected work, P1 was hired for one job only when he described how he could get the job done:

In the individual interview, they asked me one question, 'How you gonna do the paperwork and stuff we have?' I says, 'I got a Dell laptop that has screen reading software and if you can send it to me I can do it.' The head of human resources says, 'Well, you got the job, congratulations.' I says, 'What about the rest of the interview?' He says, 'You

[5] http://www.humanware.com

don't need it. You impressed us at the group interview, so we only had one question for you.'

At one point, he opted to use the BrailleNote, but eventually abandoned it for his Dell. The BrailleNote's proprietary software was incompatible with his employer's software.

The most serious concerns were about losing jobs, not based on abilities, but on *perceptions* of disabilities by others. For these reasons, if they could, participants chose not to disclose their disabilities. P6 explains why she did not tell her employer she was losing her sight, and that technologies could alleviate the perceptions she feared:

I must admit, I kept it from them so they didn't know. ...because I didn't want to lose my job. Because I know- this was back in the 80s, and I saw how the workplace was. The people with disabilities were often... let go for various reasons. So... I think if you look more mainstream, you look more able, then you're more likely ... to be employed.

The reported barriers to employment seemed to have little to do with participants' actual abilities. Incompatibility issues and negotiating new office norms added to the effort required to gain access at work. However, more serious misperceptions about ability and the unfamiliarity with assistive technologies significantly affected employment.

DISCUSSION

People with disabilities feel empowered when using their devices, but they are also aware of misperceptions others have about assistive technologies. These misperceptions may be inherent to social stereotypes about disabilities, but how are they influenced by assistive technologies? Some participants did not want to use white canes and hearing aids because the social stigma associated with these identified them as less capable. While they did not associate the same stereotypes with current electronic assistive devices, they acknowledged aesthetic and design issues distinguished their devices from mainstream devices with similar functionality. How does this affect access? We discuss here why we think electronic assistive technologies run the risk of perpetuating social barriers, and what we believe this means for assistive technology design.

Implications of Misperceptions

We found two common misperceptions of assistive technologies: (1) that assistive technologies functionally eliminate a disability, and (2) the presence of assistive technologies mean that people with disabilities are helpless without assistive technologies. Although our participants were not concerned that electronic assistive technologies marked them in the way white canes and hearing aids might, we believe these misperceptions are problematic because they incorrectly draw assumptions about the abilities of the people who use them.

Misperceptions about Ability

Several participants were concerned about appearing unable to use their technologies; they did not want to contribute to misperceptions that they were not capable. For example, some assistive technologies had steep learning curves or required special training. Although participants patiently learned to use their technologies, as we saw in issues with help, they were concerned that making mistakes would make them appear less capable. Appearing incompetent might perpetuate the misperception that people with disabilities were unable to do things for themselves.

Misperceptions about Mainstream Technologies

Misperceptions also support stereotypes that people with disabilities cannot use mainstream technologies due to disability. We recall P2 mentioned, "if someone's using an iPhone, and I'm using an iPhone, that's normal, right? It's the same thing." This implies a special, proprietary cell phone indicates the *person* using it is not normal. In turn, it implies that person's disability precludes them from using mainstream phones like everyone else. But, if a person cannot use a device because the device is inaccessible, and not necessarily because of the person's disability, this becomes an unfair and inaccurate misperception. P10 explains why device appeal is important for social perception:

I'm a person. Not... you know? That's why I like to see things a little more attractive, compact... where people might not notice them as much. So that they treat it ... like anybody else's toys.

Misperceptions imply an ambiguous social construct. As we have seen, electronic assistive technologies are relatively unknown to many people. Despite the fact that our participants felt enabled by the technologies they used, ambiguous social constructs gave way to supercilious and patronizing misunderstandings on the part of others of what assistive technologies do. We contrast this misperception with evidence that two of our blind and low-vision participants used the iPhone, an example of mainstream technologies usable by people with disabilities because of its accessibility features. Given this, misperceptions about assistive technologies may run the risk of marking people with disabilities by implying an inability to use comparable, mainstream technologies.

A Case for Mainstream Accessibility

The misperceptions reported in this study appear to do little to assuage common stereotypes, and may perpetuate them instead. We believe this means social misperceptions hinder true access. Ideally, there would be no misperceptions of disability, and stereotypes of people with disabilities would be that they are technically savvy and employable. Yet, this is not so. And while we may not be able change social misperceptions of disability, perhaps we can design technologies to alleviate such misperceptions by making mainstream technologies more accessible, or proprietary technologies more socially acceptable. *Design for social acceptance* could be a new design approach that goes beyond functionality and usability to prioritize the social contexts in which assistive technologies are used, thereby avoiding the creation of designs that mark or stigmatize.

Functional differences between assistive technologies and their mainstream counterparts influenced misperceptions. For example, when participants described assistive devices using mainstream terminology, such as "iPod-like" or "iPod-esque," it illuminated differences. Why is a device iPod-like, but not an iPod? Whether functional or perceived, inequalities perpetuated the notion that assistive technologies are built only for people with disabilities because they cannot use mainstream devices. In addition, both functional and perceived differences do nothing to indicate what abilities people with disabilities *have*.

Figure 3. P1's BookSense digital MP3 player.

We do not believe this means all devices and services must be mainstream technologies. The Victor Reader Stream was a popular device among participants, partly because of the free downloadable book service offered by the National Library Service (NLS) [1]. Still, P1 preferred to use the smaller BookSense[6] (Figure 3), as he describes here: "Half the size of the Victor Stream ...But this is like, cool. See I like this 'cause I can put this in a coat pocket... on a bus if I'm going a long way somewhere." The BookSense is a proprietary device and P1 still used the NLS for free books to load on his device. While both the BookSense and the Victor Reader have phone keypads, in almost all other ways, the BookSense is aesthetically more appealing. P1's preference for the BookSense demonstrates that the proprietary nature of a device does not mean it should not have a better design. Therefore, the social acceptability of assistive device design should not be overlooked.

Limitations

Due to random recruitment, this study lacks representation from people other than those with sensory disabilities. We took pains to combat this by paying careful attention to the concepts that arose through each interview using the grounded theory approach. However, we recognize the importance of appropriate sampling. Therefore, future work will include more interviews or surveys to compare concepts for people with other disabilities. We also did not examine perspectives of non-disabled people who witness the use of assistive devices. What do they think of these devices, and how are their perceptions shaped? We consider this an equally important perspective, but this study's goals were to focus on what people with disabilities thought about social interactions around their devices. Another interview study of a non-disabled population to find out their perceptions would address this limitation.

FUTURE WORK

We believe more socially acceptable design might draw less unnecessary attention and change misperceptions about assistive devices. If "strange looking" devices mark a person as being dis-abled, perhaps socially acceptable, "cool" devices would indicate a person is capable of as much as everyone else. As Pullin emphasizes, addressing creative tensions between function and "fashion" in assistive technology may support "positive images of disability" [21]. Therefore, we plan to develop *design for social acceptance* (DSA), an approach considering not only functionality and usability, but perception, misperception, stigma, affect, and aesthetics to maximize a device's social acceptability. A three-part DSA methodology will help determine how to incorporate social inclusiveness through design, prototyping, and *in situ* study. First, analyzing differences between mainstream and proprietary devices with similar functioning will be done through mock-up prototypes embodying design differences of varying degrees, as done in prior work [8]. Evaluations by people with and without disabilities will empirically determine aspects of design contributing to different perceptions. Next, iterative prototyping with people with disabilities will evaluate systems on both traditional HCI metrics, such as time and usability [4], and on social-acceptability metrics, like appeal, familiarity, and identity-assessment. This part may involve modifying existing design practices, such as paper prototyping with blind participants. Lastly, prototypes will be tested *in situ,* over an extended period of time and in social spaces where reactions can be gauged. Longitudinal evaluation will determine how prototypes fare in socially situated situations.

CONCLUSION

In this study, we found that misperceptions rooted in differences between assistive and mainstream technologies led to socially constructed ambiguities around a person's ability. To that end, we found two common misperceptions of assistive technologies. First, that assistive technologies eliminate a person's disability, making them functionally equivalent to a person with no disability. And second, that people with disabilities can do nothing without their devices. We believe these indicate assistive technologies do not bridge social misperceptions of disability, and therefore may not meet their potential for enabling access. Design of

[6] http://www.gwmicro.com/Booksense/

assistive technology, whether proprietary or mainstream, should address not only function, usability, and cost, but also aesthetics and social acceptance. Furthermore, if people with disabilities use the same technology as everyone else, perceptions of what they can and cannot do may be re-aligned. After all, the technology now exists to provide them with this access, we should consider what this means for reducing stigma and changing perceptions. We introduced *design for social acceptance* as one possibility for combating this tendency. We end with a quote from P5, encapsulating social implications uncovered in this study:

*Well, it's difficult being a disabled person in this society, and people are…not kind. But you get this sense of- there's something wrong with me, people don't like me, I'm unappealing, I look pathetic, I look un-sexy, you know, whatever it is. And, people are staring at me, and they are. I'm not making this up. I'm not paranoid. I mean, they are! And, it's because they wonder what that is (points to device). They haven't seen that before. They want to know what's up with the person using it…I don't want to look helpless, I don't want to look pathetic, or something… so it took me a long time to…now I think I can just do it without really worrying about it at all, but what I had to do at first—this was many years of work—but what I had to do at first was cultivate this sort of 'f*** you' attitude, you know?*

ACKNOWLEDGMENTS

Thanks to Michael Lee, Shaun K. Kane, Parmit K. Chilana, Eun Kyoung Choe, and Batya Friedman. This work was supported in part by Intel and by National Science Foundation grant IIS-0952786.

REFERENCES

1. National Library Service for the Blind and Physically Handicapped. http://www.loc.gov/nls/. September 2010.
2. Bispo, R. and Branco, R. (2008). Designing out stigma: the role of objects in the construction of disabled people's identity. *Dare to Desire: 6th Int'l Design & Emotion Conf.* Hong Kong.
3. Bispo, R. and Branco, V. (2009). Designing out stigma: the potential of contradictory symbolic imagery. *Proc. Include 2009*. London.
4. Card, S. K., Moran, T. P. and Newell, A. (1983). *The Psychology of Human-Computer Interaction*. Lawrence Erlbaum Associates, Hillsdale, NJ.
5. Charlton, J. I. (1998). *Nothing about us without us: disability oppression and empowerment*. Univ. of California Press, Berkeley, CA.
6. Cook, A. M. and Hussey, S. M. (2002). *Assistive Technologies: Principles and Practice*. Second Ed. Mosby, Inc., St. Louis, MO.
7. Csikszentmihalyi, M. and Rochberg-Halton, E. (1981). *The meaning of things*. Cambridge Univ. Press, NY.
8. Denning, T., Borning, A., Friedman, B., Gill, B. T., Kohno, T. and Maisel, W. H. (2010). Patients, pacemakers, and implantable defibrillators: human values and security for wireless implantable medical devices. *Proc. CHI '10*. Atlanta, GA, ACM, 917-926.
9. Dijksterhuis, A. and Nordgren, L. F. (2006). A theory of unconscious thought. *Persp. on Psych. Sci.* 1 (2), 95-109.
10. Edwards, A. D. N. (1995). *Extra-Ordinary Human-Computer Interaction: Interfaces for Users with Disabilities*. Univ. of Cambridge Press, Cambridge.
11. Elliott, G. C., Ziegler, H. L., Altman, B. M. and Scott, D. R. (1982). Understanding stigma. *Deviant Behavior.* 3 (3), 275-300.
12. Fine, M. and Asch, A. (1988). Disability Beyond Stigma: Social Interaction, Discrimination, and Activism. *Journal of Social Issues.* 44 (1), 3-21.
13. Glaser, B. G. and Strauss, A. L. (1967). *The Discovery of Grounded Theory.* Aldine Publishing Co, Chicago, IL.
14. Goffman, E. (1959). *The presentation of self in everyday life*. Doubleday, Garden City, NY.
15. Goffman, E. (1963). *Stigma; notes on the management of spoiled identity*. Prentice-Hall, Englewood Cliffs, NJ.
16. Gray, D. B., Quatrano, L. A. and Lieberman, M. L. (1998). *Designing and using assistive technology: the human perspective*. P.H. Brookes Pub. Co., Baltimore.
17. Jacobson, S. (2010). Overcoming Stigma Associated with Assistive Devices. *7th Int'l Conf. on Design and Emotion*. Chicago, IL.,
18. Pape, T. L.-B., Kim, J. and Weiner, B. (2002). The shaping of individual meanings assigned to assistive technology: a review of personal factors. *Disability and Rehabilitation.* 24 (1/2/3), 5-20.
19. Parette, P. and Scherer, M. (2004). Assistive Technology Use and Stigma. *Education and Training in Developmental Disabilities.* 39 (3), 217-226.
20. Phillips, B. and Zhao, H. (1993). Predictors of assistive technology abandonment. *Assistive technology: the official journal of RESNA.* 5 (1), 36-45.
21. Pullin, G. (2009). *Design meets disability*. MIT Press, Cambridge, MA.
22. Riemer-Reiss, M. L. and Wacker, R. R. (2000). Factors Associated with Assistive Technology Discontinuance Among Individuals with Disabilities. *Journal of Rehabilitation.* 66 (3), 44-50.
23. Scherer, M. J. (1993). *Living in the state of stuck: how technologies affect the lives of people with disabilities*. Brookline Books, Cambridge, MA.
24. Shinohara, K. and Tenenberg, J. (2009). A blind person's interactions with technology. *Comm. ACM.* 52 (8), 58-66.
25. Strauss, A. L. and Corbin, J. M. (1998). *Basics of qualitative research.* Sage Publications, Thousand Oaks, CA.

Identifying Emotional States using Keystroke Dynamics

Clayton Epp, Michael Lippold, and Regan L. Mandryk
Department of Computer Science, University of Saskatchewan
176 Thorvaldson Bldg., 110 Science Place, Saskatoon, SK, S7N5C9, Canada
clayton.epp@usask.ca, mike.lippold@usask.ca, regan@cs.usask.ca

ABSTRACT
The ability to recognize emotions is an important part of building intelligent computers. Emotionally-aware systems would have a rich context from which to make appropriate decisions about how to interact with the user or adapt their system response. There are two main problems with current system approaches for identifying emotions that limit their applicability: they can be invasive and can require costly equipment. Our solution is to determine user emotion by analyzing the rhythm of their typing patterns on a standard keyboard. We conducted a field study where we collected participants' keystrokes and their emotional states via self-reports. From this data, we extracted keystroke features, and created classifiers for 15 emotional states. Our top results include 2-level classifiers for confidence, hesitance, nervousness, relaxation, sadness, and tiredness with accuracies ranging from 77 to 88%. In addition, we show promise for anger and excitement, with accuracies of 84%.

Author Keywords
Affective computing, keystroke dynamics, emotion sensing

ACM Classification Keywords
H5.2.h [User Interfaces]: Input devices and strategies.

General Terms
Human Factors.

INTRODUCTION
Despite progress in graphics capabilities and processing power, interactive applications still have considerable usability problems. One main reason for these problems is that applications do not understand or adapt to users' context, such as their location, expertise, or emotional state. As a result, applications often act inappropriately: they provide inappropriate feedback, interrupt the user at the wrong time, and increase frustration. To solve these problems, we must make advances in two key areas: first, a set of mechanisms for gathering and modeling user context; and second, a set of techniques for adapting user interfaces and system behavior based on contextual information.

User context includes information such as the user's location, situation, or expertise, but one often ignored type of context that could radically change our computer interactions is the user's emotional state. If a user of a safety-critical application was frustrated or distracted, it could dangerously affect their performance. If a user of an online tutoring system was frustrated or distracted, the system could adapt its presentation of learning materials to better suit that student's learning style. For users of ordinary computer applications, frustration or distraction may not be dangerous, but can lead to increased errors. Systems that detect and respond to a user's emotional state could improve user performance as well as satisfaction. In addition, emotionally intelligent systems could also aid in computer-mediated communication by incorporating the user's emotional state into messages and by allowing users to naturally express emotional content to others.

Many approaches for detecting user emotions have been investigated, including voice intonation analysis, facial expression analysis, physiological sensors attached to the skin, and thermal imaging of the face. Although these explorations have seen varying rates of success, they still exhibit one or both of two main problems preventing wide-scale use: they can be intrusive to the user, and can require specialized equipment that is expensive and not found in typical home or office environments.

Our solution is to detect users' emotional states through their typing rhythms on the common computer keyboard. Called keystroke dynamics, this is an approach from user authentication research that shows promise for emotion detection in human-computer interaction (HCI). Identifying emotional state through keystroke dynamics addresses the problems of previous methods by using standard equipment that it is also non-intrusive to the user.

To investigate the efficacy of keystroke dynamics for determining emotional state, we conducted a field study that gathered keystrokes as users performed their daily computer tasks. Using an experience-sampling approach, users labeled the data with their level of agreement with 15 emotional states and provided additional keystrokes by typing fixed pieces of text. Our approach allowed users' emotions to emerge naturally with minimal influence from our study, or through emotion elicitation techniques.

From the raw keystroke data, we extracted a number of features derived mainly from key duration (dwell time) and key latency (flight time). We then created decision-tree classifiers for 15 emotional states, using the derived feature set. We successfully modeled six emotional states, including confidence, hesitance, nervousness, relaxation, sadness, and tiredness, with accuracies ranging from 77.4% to 87.8%. We also identify two emotional states (anger and excitement) that show potential for future work in this area.

RELATED WORK

Modeling affective state using typing rhythms draws from two fields: affective computing and keystroke dynamics.

Affective Computing

Affective computing refers to "computing that relates to, arises from, or deliberately influences emotions" [27]. We are interested in identifying a user's emotional state, so we must first consider how emotions are described, and what other approaches have been used to classify emotion. The terms affect and emotion are often used interchangeably; we will use *emotional state* to refer to the internal dynamics (cognitive and physiological) that are present during an emotional episode, and *emotional experience* as what an individual perceives of their emotional state [27].

Describing Emotions

Two main approaches have been used to describe emotions: categorical and dimensional. The categorical approach applies specific labels to different emotional states through language (e.g. sadness, fear, joy) [12]. The dimensional approach [28] uses two orthogonal axes called arousal and valence. *Arousal* is related to the energy of the feeling and is typically described in terms of low (e.g. sleepiness) to high (e.g. excitement) arousal. *Valence* describes the pleasure (positive) or displeasure (negative) of a feeling. Labels for different emotional states can be represented in this two-dimensional space. For example, anger would be a high-arousal, low-valence state.

Sensing Emotional State

Both the categorical and dimensional models of emotion have been used in prior approaches of identifying emotional state. Some approaches use features easily discernable by other humans, such as facial expressions, gestures, vocal intonation, and language [27]. For example, face-tracking software is used to analyze facial expressions gathered from webcam images to infer users' affective states [9,26]. This approach has been extended to use thermal imaging to identify changes in blood flow patterns of the face that are synonymous with different facial expressions [22].

Other approaches use features that are less discernable to other humans, but can be measured by specialized equipment. For example, significant research has been conducted on measuring physiological changes that occur in the body during emotional episodes using sensors such as galvanic skin response, electromyography of the face, and heart activity (see [14] for an overview). In HCI, researchers have used physiological sensors to measure the affective state of a user interacting with technology. Results have been produced by studying users playing video games [24], navigating web pages [32], using video conferencing software [33], and using mobile technology [7].

The above approaches have two main problems that prevent their widespread use: the sensing technology is obtrusive, and requires expensive specialized equipment. For example, EKG is measured using electrodes attached directly to the user's skin. In some cases, the area where the electrodes are placed needs to be shaved to prevent interference [30]. Although research is underway to integrate these sensors into interaction devices, they are currently intrusive and their mere presence may alter the user's emotional state. In [22], a thermal camera is used is measure blood flow to a user's face. Although unobtrusive, the equipment is specialized and not found in typical home or office settings. To eliminate the need for intrusive and costly equipment, we propose to determine affective state via typing rhythms.

Keystroke Dynamics

Keystroke dynamics is the study of the unique timing patterns in an individual's typing, and typically includes extracting keystroke timing features such as the duration of a key press and the time elapsed between key presses.

Much of the previous research in keystroke dynamics has been in authentication systems, with the premise that, just as with handwritten signatures, the way that an individual types can be unique enough to identify them [21]. The use of keystroke dynamics for user authentication has been an active area of research, producing many studies [3,10,21,25], patents [2], and systems [1], whereby users are authenticated by providing the correct user name, password, and typing rhythm (see [13] for an overview). Anecdotal evidence suggests that strong emotional states can interfere with authentication [25]; however, little is mentioned of this and it is unclear whether the timing variance associated with these emotional states is similar between individuals.

Most of the authentication systems [3,21,25] use fixed-text models – that is, they use the same static piece of text (entered during authentication) that the model was trained on. There have been fewer approaches [10,16,25] that use models based on free text (text that is not prescribed to the user), as they do not perform as well as fixed-text models [25]. The length of the required training text varies between different studies; some require a few words [3] or full pages of text [15], which can create better performing models [4].

Although fixed-text models generally perform better than free-text models, the potential applications of free-text models are desirable. Recent work has explored free-text models for use in continuous verification, where users are continually monitored to identify masqueraders at any time (not just during authentication), and have shown potential given enough samples of sufficient length [16]. Free-text models have even been able to identify individuals typing in different languages [17] as long as the two languages have enough similar valid digraphs. Most free-text studies require users to enter any 'valid' text as sample text [16]; however, in [10] keystroke activity was monitored as a background process during normal computer use. This method had three benefits: the user was less disturbed by the collection method, the data was obtained unobtrusively, and it reduced the cognitive load on the user by avoiding situations where they must think of something to type.

Classification algorithms for the analysis of keystroke dynamics for user authentication include neural networks [5], distance measures [21,25], decision trees [29], and other statistical methods [3,10,25]. Due to the differences in data collection approaches and classification methods, a comparison of performance across studies is difficult [3].

Keystroke Dynamics & Affective Computing

There has been very little previous work applying keystroke dynamics to affective computing.

Zimmerman et al. [35] describe a method to correlate user interactions (keyboard and mouse) with affective state. Affective states were induced using films. Physiological sensors were used in conjunction with the Self-Assessment Manikin (SAM) [23], a method of subjectively expressing affective state. The authors found significant differences between the neutral state and other emotional states, but were unable to distinguish between the induced states.

Recent work by Vizer et al. [31] used keystroke timing features of free text in conjunction with linguistic features to identify cognitive and physical stress. They achieved correct classifications of 62.5% for physical stress and 75% for cognitive stress (for 2 classes), which they state is comparable to other affective computing solutions. They also state that their solutions should be tested with varying typing abilities and keyboards, with varying physical and cognitive abilities, and in real-world stressful situations.

METHODOLOGY

The two primary components of this work are the data collection process and the data processing required to create classifications of emotional state. The data collection process consisted of gathering and labeling users' keystroke data. The data processing consisted of extracting relevant keystroke features to build classifiers.

Experience Sampling of Emotional Keystroke Data

We wanted to gather keystroke data *in situ* – as participants performed their daily computer activities – but also needed to label each data point with the emotional state of the user. To accomplish both of these goals, we used an experience-sampling methodology (ESM), whereby we periodically collect user keystroke data and user responses to emotional state questionnaires. In ESM [19], participants are asked to record their experiences periodically in real-time during their daily activities. The purpose is to gather temporal data 'in the moment' rather than retrospectively, which avoids problems of incorrect reconstruction or forgetfulness of the user. The drawback is that researchers cannot control or balance the different states tested.

We chose an experience-sampling methodology for two reasons. First, we were interested in emotional data gathered in the real-world, rather than induced in a laboratory setting through emotion-elicitation methods [8]. Our results are intended for use in real-world systems, and gathering the data for modeling from naturally occurring emotions increases our ecological validity. Second, as this is a new affect sensing technique, we wanted to explore a wide range of emotional states, and emotional induction, in the laboratory, is limited to one or two emotional states.

In experience-sampling studies, users are typically outfitted with a signaling device that alerts them to complete a self-report on their current state and/or situation [19]. We developed custom software for our signaling device and data collection that participants installed on their personal computers for use while they performed their daily tasks.

Data Collection Software

The data collection software was written in C# and used a low-level windows hook to scan each keystroke as it was entered by the user. This program ran in the background, gathering keystrokes regardless of the application that was currently in focus. The only visible sign that the application was running was an icon in the desktop system tray.

Based on the user's level of computer activity, the program prompted the user throughout their day. At each prompt, the user was presented with their keystroke text from the previous 10 minutes to review, then with an emotional state questionnaire, and then with some fixed text to type. The user could opt out of data collection at any time during the prompt if they were too busy or did not want to share their keystroke data (e.g., contained sensitive information like a password). Initial keystroke data was called *free text* as it was not constrained or influenced by our study.

The emotional state questionnaire contained 15 5-point Likert scale questions regarding a user's current emotional state: *I am frustrated, I am focused, I am angry, I am happy, I feel overwhelmed, I feel confident, I feel hesitant, I feel stressed, I feel relaxed, I feel excited, I am distracted, I feel bored, I feel sad, I feel nervous, I feel tired.* For each statement, the user would: *strongly disagree, disagree, neither agree nor disagree, agree,* or *strongly agree.*

The user was then asked to enter a randomly selected piece of text from *Alice's Adventures in Wonderland* [6]; this was how we collected the *fixed text* from users. To prevent copying and pasting, the user was unable to select the fixed text. The user then had a chance to review what s/he just entered before submitting the data remotely to our data collection server. The data collection server allowed us to preserve participant anonymity and supported remote users.

Field Study

The field study was conducted from July to October, 2009 with users participating for an average of four weeks. Participants installed the software on the computer that they used the most. There were no restrictions on their activities during the study; they had the freedom to work unimpeded.

Demographics

Upon installation of the software, the participant was presented with a one-time demographic questionnaire. We originally had 26 users take part in the study; however, not all participants completed enough study questionnaires to be included in the analysis – some completed as few as 2 over the duration of the experiment. Unlike a laboratory experiment, the field study did not allow us to control the amount of participation. To determine an informed threshold for inclusion in the study, we considered how many responses were needed to ensure that users were familiar with the study questionnaires and were calibrating their responses appropriately. Participants who completed more than one questionnaire per day on average for at least half of the study duration were likely familiar enough with the questionnaires and the process to be considered to have finished the study. Thus, we removed users with fewer than 50 responses, leaving 12 participants. This process occurred prior to the analyses and all remaining results are based on this reduced dataset. We had 10 male and 2 female users aged 24-34 (mean=28.5, s.d.=2.7), who were university students (9), admin personnel (2), and technicians (1).

Overall, participants were proficient with word processing, email, and instant messaging applications, with usages of 3-7 hours a week (3), 1-2 hours a day (2), and more than 2 hours a day (7). Ten participants indicated they spent at least half of their time on the computer that was collecting data. Work computers accounted for 8 of the installations with the remaining 4 installations on home computers. Most participants used desktop computers (10); few used laptops (2). One of these installations was on a virtual machine. We only included English-speaking participants because we focused on English character sequences in the features.

Feature Extraction

Once the data was gathered, we needed to transform the raw keystroke data files into a feature set that could be used as input to models. We extracted three different categories of information from the data: keystroke/content features, emotional state classes, and additional data points.

Keystroke Features

The raw keystroke data consisted of key press and release events, unique codes for each key, and a timestamp of when the key event occurred. Extensive processing grouped these keys into graphs of 2 or 3 symbols. Our keystroke features were mainly derived from the timing of single keystrokes as well as digraphs (two-letter combinations) and trigraphs (three-letter combinations). Initially, we extracted all key-specific features (e.g., duration of 'ie' digraph); however, this caused a number of problems. The number of features grew to over 100,000, making training unrealistic and our data set very sparse (e.g. one user may use the digraph 'aa' often and others may not, leading to missing data points).

To narrow the scope, we used only aggregate features for this analysis and removed all key/graph specific features. For each feature, we extracted the mean and standard deviation because during a sample period, the user could enter the same sequence of keys more than once (e.g., entering 'th' twice during the 10-minute sampling period). Keystroke features used in our models are shown in Table 1 and the categories of features are described further.

Code	Description
2G_1D2D	The duration between 1st and 2nd down keys of the digraphs.
2G_1Dur	The duration of the 1st key of the digraphs.
2G_1KeyLat	Duration between 1st key up and next key down of the digraphs.
2G_2Dur	The duration of the 2nd key of the digraphs.
2G_Dur	The duration of the digraphs from 1st key down to last key up.
2G_NumEvents	The number of key events that were part of the graph.
3G_1D2D	The duration between 1st and 2nd down keys of the trigraphs.
3G_1Dur	The duration of the 1st key of the trigraphs.
3G_1KeyLat	Duration between 1st key up and next key down of trigraphs.
3G_2D2D	The duration between 2nd and 3rd down keys of the trigraphs.
3G_2Dur	The duration of the 2nd key of the trigraphs.
3G_2KeyLat	Duration between 2nd key up and next key down of trigraphs.
3G_3Dur	The duration of the third key of the trigraphs.
3G_Dur	The duration of the trigraphs from 1st key down to last key up.
3G_NumEvents	The number of key events that were part of the graph.

Table 1. Coded keystroke features with descriptions.

Keystroke Duration Features (dwell): Keystroke duration features have been used extensively in previous keystroke dynamics work [3,4,5,17,25]. For our analysis, duration features were included for both single key features as well as graph features (i.e., digraphs and trigraphs).

For single keys, the duration was the time elapsed between 'key press' to 'key release'. Each key of the digraphs were extracted separately (e.g. 2G_1Dur was the duration of the 1st key of all digraphs). Key duration features included 2G_1Dur, 2G_2Dur, 3G_1Dur, and 3G_2Dur in Table 1.0. For graph duration features (2G_Dur and 3G_Dur), duration was measured as the time elapsed from the first 'key press' event to the last key's 'key release' event. For example, for the digraph 'the' the 3G_Dur would be the time from the 't' press event to the 'e' release event.

Keystroke Latency Features (flight): Keystroke latency features have been used in previous keystroke dynamics studies in authentication [3,5,25]. Keystroke latency is the time elapsed from one key release event to the next key press event or the 'time between keys'. Unlike the duration features, latency always involves two keys so there are no single key latency features. Our keystroke latency features (2G_1KeyLat, 3G_1KeyLat, 3G_2KeyLat) were separated for each pair of keys found in the graph.

Other Keystroke Features: We included features that combined some aspects of the duration and latency features. This included the "key down to down" features (2G_1D2D,

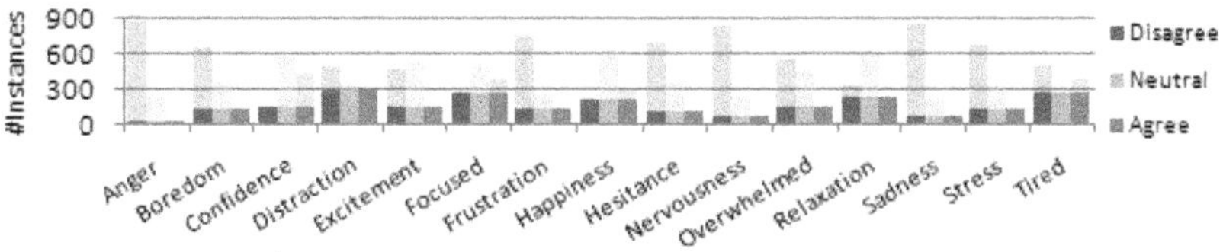

Figure 1. Distribution of responses (classes) before under-sampling (faded) and after.

3G_1D2D, 3G_2D2D), which contain the elapsed time from the first key down to the next key down event.

We calculated the number of events that were found in each digraph and trigraph (2G_NumEvents, 3G_NumEvents). Although most digraphs contain 4 events (first key press, first key release, second key press, second key release) and trigraphs contain 6, there are scenarios where the user could type more. For example, a user could press keys in quick succession and release them out of order (e.g. 1st key press, 2nd key press, 1st key release, 3rd key press, 2nd key release). This would result in 5 key events in a digraph. This may be indicative of a user's emotional state, and has not been used previously in keystroke dynamics, to our knowledge.

Keystroke Feature Overlap: Some of the keystroke features that we described overlap slightly; however, in the classification section, we describe how we reduced this set using supervised attribute selection.

Content Features

We included a few features based on the content extracted (text) from the free keystrokes, including separate features for the number of characters, numbers, punctuation marks, uppercase characters, and the number and percentage of 'special characters' (numbers, uppercase characters, punctuation marks). These features were used in only the free text models as we provided the fixed text to the user.

The number of mistakes (backspace + delete key) was calculated for both fixed and free text models. There are many different ways to correct mistakes (e.g., selection with the mouse and replacement with keystrokes). It was not possible to catch all of the possible correction scenarios as keystrokes were collected from different applications that we did not control. However, this feature does give a general idea of the number of mistakes being made.

Emotional State Classes

All of our features needed to be labeled with the user's emotional state for classification. We used discrete emotion categories to collect emotional state responses from users because these categories are close to the language commonly used to describe their emotional state.

As mentioned, we collected Likert Scale responses for 15 emotional states (e.g. "I feel stressed"). The available options that were presented for each statement (strongly disagree, disagree, neither agree nor disagree, agree, strongly agree) became the target classes during classification. Many users avoided the 'extreme' categories of the 5-point scale, resulting in highly under-represented classes (class skew). We grouped the 'strongly agree' and 'strongly disagree' categories with the 'agree' and 'disagree' categories respectfully, resulting in 3 classes for each emotional state: agree, neutral, and disagree.

Additional Data Points

We extracted a number of additional data points to assist in our analysis, including the active process name for each collected keystroke, which would allow us to analyze our data set differentially depending on application.

Additional Data Processing

Our keystroke feature extraction did not take into account large pauses in typing, when a user might have switched to another mode of input (e.g. mouse) or have taken a break from the computer. To remove these pauses, we calculated outliers for all of the features that involved multiple keys (e.g. digraph latency). Outliers were removed by calculating the mean and standard deviation for all keystroke timing features for each participant and then removing the samples that were 12 standard deviations greater than the mean for that participant. A large number of standard deviations were used to only remove trials where very long pauses were present. We then recalculated all of the features with the filtered instance set. This resulted in the removal of 0.07% of the samples collected. This method of outlier removal was similar to the approach taken in [21]. All values were normalized for each user to facilitate the aggregate analysis.

CLASSIFICATION

Due to the large variations in the number of responses per user, we did not create user-specific models, but aggregated the data across participants for 1129 valid instances. Models were created using the C4.5 supervised machine learning algorithm as it is implemented in Weka [34].

Although there are many classification algorithms, we used decision trees as a simple low-cost solution to investigate this new approach to identifying emotion. Decision trees can be reduced into a set of rules and allow generalization (e.g. pruning). The chosen decision tree algorithm also handles missing values, which we have in our data set.

Supervised Attribute Selection

Although we identified 31 fixed text features and 37 free text features, we needed to first identify which of these features were important to keep and which had little predictive value. We used the correlation-based feature subset attribute selection method described by Hall in [18] and implemented in Weka [34] to select salient features in our set for each emotional state model separately.

Model Variations

We trained a number of model variations using different text types (i.e., free and fixed text), numbers of target classes, and adjustments to compensate for class skew.

In addition to the 3 class-level (agree, neutral, disagree) variations explained in the Feature Extraction section, we included variations that had 2 class-levels (agree, disagree), removing instances in the neutral category to determine if keystrokes could differentiate between two opposing states.

Responses were not distributed evenly across all levels of each emotional state (see Figure 1). For example, the responses to the phrase, "I am angry" were skewed to the strongly disagree and disagree categories. This is expected as users generally would not be very angry as often as not at all angry. Class skew such as this can lead to unreliable classification rates. To eliminate class skew, we used a method called under-sampling [11], which randomly removes instances from the majority classes to equal the class with the fewest instances, creating a uniform distribution (see Figure 1). We included models built using under-sampling and the original distribution. For each emotional state model that used under-sampling, we repeated the classification process 10 times and report the mean classification accuracy and variance.

Evaluation

We used 10-fold cross-validation from the stratified training results to evaluate our models, which is standard practice when the data set's size is limited [34].

To more easily describe our top results, we defined a hierarchy of evaluation categories: Bronze, Silver, Gold, and Platinum (see Table 2). Each category is based on the classification rates and the top three also incorporate false positive rate. To be considered for one of our categories, the sample-to-feature ratio had to be greater than 10. During the creation of the different model variations, instances were sometimes removed (e.g., instances of the majority classes were removed in under-sampling). In classifier design, it is generally accepted that there must be 10 times more instances (training samples) per class than the number of features [20]. Another criterion for inclusion was that the Kappa statistic had to be greater than 0.4. The Kappa statistic indicates how much the classification rate was a true reflection of the model or how much could be attributed to chance alone; Kappa values range from 0 (chance agreement) to 1 (perfect agreement) [34].

Type	Description
Bronze	Overall classification rate > 75%.
Silver	TP rates > 75%, FP rates < 25% for each class.
Gold	TP rates > 80%, FP rates < 20% for each class.
Platinum	TP rates > 85%, FP rates < 15% for each class.

Table 2. Evaluation categories used to describe the results.

RESULTS

We gathered both fixed text and free text data and created separate models for each of these data types. We are presenting the results of only the fixed text models as there were no free text models that made our top evaluation categories. For performance of the free text models, see [13]; in the discussion of this paper, we discuss potential improvement to the free text models. After removal of participants with fewer than 50 responses, the number of samples collected per participant ranged from 51 to 219 (mean=94.1, s.d.= 52.7).

Top Emotional State Models

Figure 2 shows the classification rates for our top-performing emotional state models. These top-performing models are all two-class models (agree and disagree), and perform appreciably better than chance (50%).

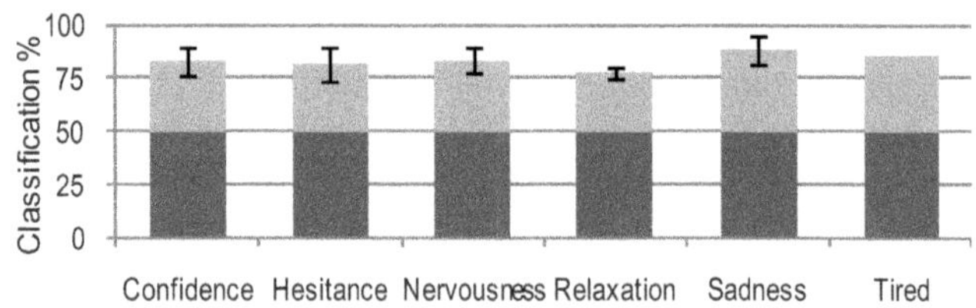

Figure 2. Classification rates for our top-performing models. Light bars show how our models improve upon random classification (chance). Error bars represent the variance in the classification rates after 10 random samplings.

We were very conservative in categorizing models as top-performing, to limit models to those with high classification rates, but also with little or no class skew, low false positive rates, high samples-to-features ratios, and high kappa values. We considered models that achieved our top 3 evaluation categories as our top emotional state models. Table 3 shows the results using 10-fold cross-validation. The Bronze category is not included because it was susceptible to class skew as it only looked at overall classification rates and not classification rates for individual class levels. Models in the Bronze category are presented in the next section as they show potential for future study.

Our top results were all based on 2 class levels (agree and disagree) and most of them used under-sampling. This means that these models were built using a reduced data set (reduced initially by removing the neutral category and further during under-sampling). Despite this reduction, we are still achieving satisfactory samples to features ratios (N:M) as seen in Table 3. N:M ranges from 11 to 49 with the most samples being used by the 'tired' model that used the original distribution of data (i.e., no under-sampling).

For 7 of the 8 top results in Table 3, under-sampling was used, and the correctly classified rate (CC) and Kappa statistic show averages from the 10 random-samplings models that were used during under-sampling. The variance columns in Table 3 (CC Var, Kap Var) indicate the variance from these 10 random samplings models. The 'tired' and 'relaxation' models have the lowest variance in both the classification rate and the Kappa statistic, and also have the highest sample-to-feature ratio, which may suggest that the variance can be lowered for the other emotional

State	CC	CC Var	Kap	Kap Var	M	N	N:M	Silv	Gold	Plat
Confidence	83.0	6.74	0.66	0.0027	8	286	18	X	X	
Hesitance	81.9	7.69	0.64	0.0031	9	204	11	X	X	
Nervousness	83.3	5.60	0.67	0.0022	5	152	15	X	X	
Relaxation	77.4	2.33	0.55	0.0009	8	442	28	X		
Sadness	87.8	6.52	0.76	0.0026	4	156	20	X	X	X
Tired	84.1	0.47	0.68	0.0002	9	758	42	X	X	
Tired*	85.1	0.00	0.70	0.0000	9	861	48	X	X	

Table 4. Top 3 evaluation category results. CC = correctly classified rate, Var = variance, Kap = Kappa statistic, M = #features used, N = #samples used, * = no under-sampling

state models given additional samples. Lower variance in the classification rates would suggest that the model results are truer indications of the predictive power of keystroke dynamics for emotional state detection.

When considering all of the factors (under-sampling, variance, sample-size) for the models in Table 3, the 'tired' model performs the best. The original distribution of responses for the 'tired' query was more balanced than the other emotional states (see Figure 1). This resulted in two 'tired' models reaching our top results, one using under-sampling and the other using the original distribution. These two models are quite similar, with similar numbers of instances, classification rates, and Kappa statistics.

Emotional State Models with Potential

As mentioned in the previous section, we considered emotional state models that made it to our Bronze category as emotional states with potential for future study, rather than as top-performing classifiers. This is because these models exhibited uneven distributions (class skew), which can lead to artificially-inflated classification rates. Each of the Bronze models in Table 4 are from unbalanced data.

Each emotional state from our top results in Table 3 also appeared in the Bronze category with an unbalanced version (no under-sampling), except for the tired state, which had an unbalanced version in Table 3. In addition, there were new representations from the 'excitement' and 'anger' emotional states. As Table 4 shows, classification rates were high; however, these models are also highly skewed. For example, the 2-state excitement model has an overall classification rate of 84.3%; however, when looking at the individual true/false positives for agree and disagree, we see that the 'disagree' class has a 92.7% classification rate whereas the 'agree' class has only 56.9%. Also, the 'disagree' class has 87.5% of the total number of samples. The same pattern exists for the anger emotional state.

It makes sense why such class skew exists in both of the anger and excitement states. These states have very high activation; it would be unusual for someone to be in a heightened state of anger or excitement for extended periods of time over the course of a normal workday. Because of the class skew for these two states, there were not enough instances remaining after under-sampling for these models to achieve our top-performing categories (see Figure 2). However, the high classification rates show that

State	CL	CC	Kap	D TP	D FP	N TP	N FP	A TP	A FP
Anger	3	83.9	0.53	92.0	38.4	64.6	9.2	0.0	0.0
Confidence	2	86.2	0.63	69.9	8.3	n/a	n/a	91.7	30.1
Excitement	2	84.3	0.53	92.7	43.3	n/a	n/a	56.7	7.3
Hesitance	2	92.3	0.67	94.9	25.5	n/a	n/a	74.5	5.1
Hesitance	3	76.3	0.55	86.9	26.9	63.3	10.4	48.0	6.5
Nervousness	2	93.0	0.52	96.9	48.7	n/a	n/a	51.3	3.1
Nervousness	3	81.6	0.51	95.2	40.7	46.5	5.4	38.2	3.4
Relaxation	2	78.9	0.56	82.4	26.2	n/a	n/a	73.8	17.6
Sadness	2	93.8	0.55	97.9	50.0	n/a	n/a	50.0	2.1
Sadness	3	82.9	0.55	93.8	33.3	56.0	6.2	35.9	3.9

Table 3. Emotional state models in the Bronze category. CL = class-level, CC = correctly classified rate, Var = variance, Kap = Kappa statistic, D = disagree, N = neutral, A = agree, TP = true-positive, FP = false-positive.

anger and excitement should not be ruled out as candidates for keystroke-based emotion modeling simply because of class skew in our particular data set. Future studies on these emotional states should consider using a laboratory-based emotion-elicitation method [8] rather than a field study.

Selected Features

Among the top emotional state models, the number of features were reduced from 31 (fixed text) to an average of 7.4 (s.d.=2.1). Using the correlation-based feature subset attribute selection method [18] allowed us to increase the sample-to-feature ratio with minimal loss to the classification rate. Table 5 lists the features that were used for each of the top classifiers (see Table 1 for a description of each feature). These features contain a fairly even number of both key latency and duration features with the 2G_1KeyLat_Mean and 2G_2Dur_Mean used in most of the models. Features that were not used in any of the models include the means of 3G_2Dur, 2G_Dur, and 3G_2KeyLat as well as the standard deviations of 2G_1D2D, 2G_1KeyLat, 2G_Dur, 3G_1D2D, 3G_1Dur, 3G_1KeyLat, 3G_2D2D, 3G_3Dur, 3G_Dur as well as our content features (NumMistakes).

Feature	C	H	N	R	S	T
2G_1D2D_Mean	X			X		X
2G_1Dur_Mean			X		X	X
2G_1Dur_Std						X
2G_1KeyLat_Mean	X	X	X	X	X	
2G_2Dur_Mean	X	X	X	X	X	X
2G_2Dur_Std		X		X		
2G_NumEvents_Mean	X			X		X
2G_NumEvents_Std	X	X			X	
3G_1D2D_Mean	X	X		X		X
3G_1Dur_Mean	X					
3G_1KeyLat_Mean		X	X			
3G_2D2D_Mean	X					X
3G_2Dur_Std		X				
3G_2KeyLat_Std				X		
3G_3Dur_Mean		X				
3G_Dur_Mean						X
3G_NumEvents_Mean			X			
3G_NumEvents_Std		X		X		X

Table 5. Features selected for each top emotional state model. C=Confidence, H=Hesitance, N=Nervousness, R=Relaxation, S=Sadness, T=Tired.

DISCUSSION

Our results show that keystroke dynamics can accurately classify at least two levels of seven emotional states (confidence, hesitance, nervousness, relaxation, sadness, and tired). In addition, we identified two other emotional states (anger, excitement) that have potential for keystroke-based classification. In this section, we discuss the benefits and drawbacks of using experience-sampling, the use of fixed text versus free text in keystroke-based modeling, aggregate versus individual analyses, the limitations of our data set, and opportunities for extensions to our work.

Experience-Sampling for Emotion Modeling

One of the goals of our research was to fill the gap in the related literature on the real-world applicability of affective computing solutions. Our choice to use keystroke dynamics was partly guided by this goal to create classifiers that are unobtrusive and inexpensive enough to be deployed in users' homes or workplaces. Experience-sampling allowed us to focus on the eventual application of our keystroke-based approach. Users' emotional states emerged naturally as compared to emotion-elicitation experiments [8].

Experience-sampling also provided us with the opportunity to perform exploratory research in this new field. Before our study, there was no guidance on which emotional states might be identifiable using keystrokes; experience-sampling allowed us to take a broad approach to the problem and narrow down which emotional states we should target with future work. This broad approach would be unfeasible using emotion elicitation because participants would have to be induced into each emotional state (neutral states as well) in individual experiments. In addition, mood induction does not necessarily work on all participants. Collecting data using experience-sampling and remote data submission allowed us to collect labeled emotional state data with minimal administration overhead.

However, experience-sampling introduced some drawbacks with implications for our analyses. Due to the uncontrolled nature of this methodology, we could not balance the distribution of classes for each emotional state, which led to class skew in the data. These uneven distributions limited our interpretation of the results for unbalanced models, and limited the number of instances available for our balanced models that used under-sampling.

Despite this disadvantage, we feel that experience-sampling provides a data-collection methodology that can be beneficial when studying a wide range of naturally-emerging emotions in new areas of research.

Free Text Models

Our free text models did not perform well enough to achieve our top evaluation categories and were not included in the results section. We believe that this was due to setting the user activity threshold too low. A low activity threshold caused the questionnaire to be presented to the user with fewer free text keystrokes than needed for analysis. Although the mean number of collected keystrokes were similar between the free (169) and fixed text (166), the standard deviation for the free text was quite high (302.8). A high standard deviation implies that some samples had very few free text keystrokes whereas the fixed text remained relatively consistent. Future studies should ensure that enough free text data is collected.

Aggregated versus Individual Participant Analyses

We created emotional state models for the entire data set across all participants to maximize the number of samples, especially in the under-sampled versions of the models. Creating models at the level of individual participants was not viable due to the number of collected samples with which to work. The mean number of samples per participant was 94.1, and this number would have been reduced when adjusting for class skew using under-sampling and in 2 class-level models. Having so few instances would have caused our sample to feature ratio to be too small and our results to be less accurate and reliable.

However, we do not know whether there are large individual differences in how keystroke dynamics change with emotional state. With enough samples per participant, personalized models could improve our classification rates. The success of keystroke dynamics for user authentication is based on the fact that each person's typing rhythm is unique enough to identify them. This suggests that individuals might have unique keystroke-level reactions to different emotional states. For example, when stressed, some individuals may type faster and other may pause in their typing more frequently. Accounting for these personal differences may allow us to build better performing models.

Limitations of our Data Set

We took care to ensure that we did not artificially inflate our classification rates by ignoring the two main limitations of our data set: its limited size and its uneven distribution.

Half of the participants in our study submitted fewer than 50 samples over the course of 4 weeks. For ethical reasons, we allowed participants to opt out of submitting data for each sample, but we tried to encourage participation through the use of data-based incentives (for each week that users submitted at least 15 samples, they were entered into a draw for a cash prize). After including only the active participants (more than 50 total samples), we had 1129 samples over all participants. This total was further reduced in the 2 class-level models though the elimination of the neutral category and in the under-sampled models by balancing the samples per class. In future work, we would prefer larger data sets with enough samples to perform individual-level models. Collecting user data for a longer time period and providing better incentives for active participation would increase our data set size.

The second problem with our data set was unequal distributions of responses across some of the emotional states. This is understandable as our feelings over the course of the day are not evenly distributed. To address this problem of class skew, we used under-sampling, which reduced our data set size. In our field study software, we prompted the user at random times to fill out the experience-sampling questionnaire. We also allowed them to select the questionnaire explicitly if they wanted to submit their data. Coaching participants to use this explicit submit feature when they were experiencing low-frequency emotions like anger could help improve the distribution of responses. With the preliminary models provided by our work, we could deploy an adaptive version of the software that conducts modeling in the background and prompts the experience-sampling questionnaire when it detects that the user might be in a low-frequency emotional state.

Opportunities for Future Work

Our work is the first to classify a broad range of emotional states using typing rhythms. We have demonstrated the efficacy of this technique, which opens up opportunities for future research to refine, improve, and utilize this approach.

Because of our limited data set, we used all of the available samples in our models. Filtering the samples based on the application context could improve classification rates. For example, the keystroke dynamics gathered using word processing software are likely different than when writing code in an integrated development environment. Samples could be filtered based on the application that was active during each keystroke entered, which would allow for application-specific models. Although we did not filter samples based on the active application, our software did collect this information in anticipation of future analysis. In addition, we would like to investigate how models personalized to individual users change classification rates, as described in the section on aggregated analysis.

When selecting our features, we used only generalized features, such as the flight time between two keys in a digraph. We could also investigate specific features, such as the flight time between two keys in a specific digraph (e.g., 'th'), or a number of specific digraphs (e.g., the 20 most common digraphs in the English language). We calculated these features from our raw data [13], but due to our data set size, we focused on the general features.

Rather than use individual features in a model directly, feature aggregation through an approach like Principle Component Analysis (PCA) could be used. We investigated using PCA to select and aggregate features, but found that this process did not improve overall classification rates [13]. In addition, the resulting decision trees were difficult to interpret due to the feature aggregation. We could also use aggregation of the target classes to improve our results. Informal analysis of the 15 emotional states found many correlations. Combining the co-varying states could improve classification rates and the potential application.

Adding other interaction-based features could improve classification. Adding linguistic features as model attributes (similar to [31]) is an approach that could be applied to the free-text models (fixed text and the resulting linguistic features is, by definition, prescribed). Adding low-level features based on mouse kinematics might also improve classification. In addition, using a multi-modal approach could provide better generalization of the models to different computer-based tasks that require varying amounts of typing or aiming. Our software collected linguistic data and mouse kinematics, in anticipation of future analysis. We could also combine our approach with established methods (e.g., physiological models) for a more complete and robust model of user experience.

We used our own custom questionnaire to take a broad approach to collecting a variety of user states. Using a validated emotional state scale [8] would provide additional validity to the keystroke dynamics approach. Also, distinguishing between different emotions rather than levels of a single emotion would be beneficial.

Finally, although we used decision trees as our classification algorithm, there are other machine learning algorithms (e.g. support vector machines) that might provide better-performing classifiers.

CONCLUSION

The ability to recognize emotions is an important part of building intelligent computers. Systems that could extract the emotional aspects of a situation would have a rich context from which to make appropriate decisions about how to interact with the user or adapt their system response. There are two main problems with current approaches for identifying emotions that limit their applicability: they can be invasive and may require expensive equipment. We presented a solution that determines user emotion by analyzing the rhythm of users' typing patterns on a standard keyboard. To gather emotionally-labeled data, we conducted a field study where participants' keystrokes were collected and their emotional states were recorded via self report using an experience-sampling methodology. From this data, we extracted keystroke features, and reduced our feature set using correlation-based feature subset attribute selection. We created classifiers for 15 emotional states.

Our top results include 2-level classifiers for confidence, hesitance, nervousness, relaxation, sadness, and tiredness with accuracies ranging from 77.4 to 87.8%. In addition, our results show promise for anger and excitement, with accuracies of 84%. This work presents the first use of naturally-gathered typing rhythms to identify the emotional state of a computer user, and the first method of sensing a variety of emotional states unobtrusively and inexpensively. This work is important as it moves us closer to creating emotionally-aware computers that can be widely deployed.

ACKNOWLEDGEMENTS

Thanks to NSERC for funding and the University of Saskatchewan HCI lab for feedback.

REFERENCES

1. Admit One Security. *AdmitOneSecurity*. http://www.admitonesecurity.com.
2. Bender, S. and Postley, H. Key sequence rhythm recognition system and method. .
3. Bergadano, F., Gunetti, D., and Picardi, C. Identity verification through dynamic keystroke analysis. *Intell. Data Anal. 7*, 5 (2003), 469-496.
4. Bergadano, F., Gunetti, D., and Picardi, C. User authentication through keystroke dynamics. *ACM Trans. Inf. Syst. Secur. 5*, 4 (2002), 367-397.
5. Brown, M. and Rogers, S.J. User identification via keystroke characteristics of typed names using neural networks. *Int. J. Man-Mach. Stud. 39*, 6 (1993), 999-1014.
6. Carroll, L. *Alice's Adventures in Wonderland*. The Gutenberg Project, 2008.
7. Chen, D. and Vertegaal, R. Using mental load for managing interruptions in physiologically attentive user interfaces. *CHI '04 ext. abst. on Human fac. in comp. systems*, ACM (2004), 1513-1516.
8. Coan, J. and Allen, J. *Handbook of Emotion Elicitation and Assessment*. Oxford University Press, New York, USA, 2007.
9. De Silva, L. and Suen Chun, H. Real-time facial feature extraction and emotion recognition. *Infor., Comm., and Sig. Proc. 2003 and the 4th Pac. Rim Conf. on Multimedia*, (2003).
10. Dowland, P. and Furnell, S. A Long-term trial of keystroke profiling using digraph, trigraph, and keyword latencies. In *IFIP Intern. Fed. for Infor. Processing*. Springer Boston, 2004, 275-289.
11. Drummond, C. and Holte, R. C4.5, class imbalance, and cost sensitivity: why under-sampling beats over-sampling. (2003).
12. Ekman, P. *Basic Emotions*. John Wiley & Sons, Ltd, 2005.
13. Epp, C. Identifying emotional states through keystroke dynamics. 2010. http://library2.usask.ca/theses/available/etd-08312010-131027/.
14. Fairclough, S. Fundamentals of physiological computing. *Inter. with Comp. 21*, 1-2 (2009), 133-145.
15. Gaines, R., Lisowski, W., Press, S., and Shapiro, N. Authentication by keystroke timing: some preliminary results. 1980.
16. Gunetti, D. and Picardi, C. Keystroke analysis of free text. *ACM Trans. Inf. Syst. Secur. 8*, 3 (2005), 312-347.
17. Gunetti, D., Picardi, C., and Ruffo, G. Keystroke analysis of different languages: a case study. In *Lecture Notes in Computer Science*. Springer Berline / Heidelberg, 2005, 133-144.
18. Hall, M. Correlation-based feature subset selection for machine learning. 1999.
19. Hektner, J., Schmidt, J., and Csikszentmihalyi, M. *Experience Sampling Method: Measuring the Quality of Everyday Life*. Sage Publications, Thousand Oaks, 2007.
20. Jain, A., Duin, R., and Mao, J. Statistical pattern recognition: a review. *IEEE Transactions on Pattern Analysis and Machine Intelligence 22*, 1 (2000), 4-37.
21. Joyce, R. and Gupta, G. Identity authentication based on keystroke latencies. *Commun. ACM 33*, 2 (1990), 168-176.
22. Khan, M.M., Ingleby, M., and Ward, R.D. Automated facial expression classification and affect interpretation using infrared measurement of facial skin temperature variations. *ACM Trans. Auton. Adapt. Syst. 1*, 1 (2006), 91-113.
23. Lang, P. Behavioral treatment and bio-behavioral assessment: computer applications. *Technology in mental health care delivery systems*, (1980), 119-137.
24. Mandryk, R.L. and Atkins, M.S. A fuzzy physiological approach for continuously modeling emotion during interaction with play technologies. *Int. J. Hum.-Comput. Stud. 65*, 4 (2007), 329-347.
25. Monrose, F. and Rubin, A.D. Keystroke dynamics as a biometric for authentication. *Future Gener. Comput. Syst. 16*, 4 (2000), 351-359.
26. Partala, T., Surakka, V., and Vanhala, T. Real-time estimation of emotional experiences from facial expressions. *Interact. Comput. 18*, 2 (2006), 208-226.
27. Picard, R.W. *Affective Computing*. MIT Press, Cambridge, 2007.
28. Russell, J. Core affect and the psychological construction of emotion. *Psychological Review 110*, 1 (2003), 145-172.
29. Sheng, Y., Phoha, V., and Rovnyak, S. A parallel decision tree-based method for user authentication based on keystroke patterns. *IEEE Transactions on Systems, Man, and Cybernetics 35*, 4 (2005), 826-833.
30. Stern, R.M., Ray, W.J., and Quigley, K.S. *Psychophysiological recording*. Oxford University Press, New York, 2001.
31. Vizer, L.M., Zhou, L., and Sears, A. Automated stress detection using keystroke and linguistic features: An exploratory study. *Int. J. Hum.-Comput. Stud. 67*, 10 (2009), 870-886.
32. Ward, R.D. and Marsden, P.H. Physiological responses to different web page designs. *Int. J. Hum.-Comput. Stud. 59*, 1-2 (2003), 199-212.
33. Wilson, G. and Sasse, M. Do users always know what's good for them? Utilizing physiological responses to assess media quality. (2000), 327-339.
34. Witten, I. and Frank, E. *Data Mining: Practical machine learning tools and techniques*. Morgan Kaufmann, San Francisco, 2005.
35. Zimmermann, P., Guttormsen, S., Danuser, B., and Gomez, P. Affective computing - a rationale for measuring mood with mouse and keyboard. *Inter. J. of Occ. Saf. and Ergo. 9*, 4 (2003), 539-551.

PAM: A Photographic Affect Meter for Frequent, In Situ Measurement of Affect

J.P. Pollak, Phil Adams, Geri Gay
Information Science
Cornell University
301 College Ave, Ithaca, NY 14850
{jpp9, pja22, gkg1}@cornell.edu

ABSTRACT

The assessment of emotion, or affect, is critical for anyone trying to understand human behavior. But there is a problem: affect as a state is frequently changing and difficult to recall and express, yet in research, we typically only assess it via a single questionnaire at the end of a study. This work presents PAM, the Photographic Affect Meter, a novel tool for measuring affect in which users select from a wide variety of photos the one which best suits their current mood. Our findings indicate that PAM—which takes seconds to complete and is designed to run on modern mobile phones and mobile computing devices—demonstrates strong construct validity across two studies and is very well suited for frequent sampling in context. This work provides a tool to researchers in need of frequent assessment of affect and guidance to others interested in developing similar measurement tools.

Author Keywords

Affect, mobile computing, health.

ACM Classification Keywords

H5.m. Information interfaces and presentation, miscellaneous.

General Terms

Design, Experimentation, Measurement.

INTRODUCTION

Emotion is an omnipresent aspect of human existence that influences nearly every facet of our behavior [23,35,41]. As such, scientists often require at least a basic understanding of the emotional state of research subjects. The measurement and study of emotion, or affect, is commonplace in the behavioral sciences [3,21,31,37,38] and is particularly prevalent in health-related research, where it has become clear that numerous relationships exist between emotion and health [35]. As evidence of this, the paper detailing PANAS [45], among the most widely used measure of affect, has been cited over 7,000 times [17].

There exists, however, a problem with most measures of affect: they are lengthy questionnaire-based methods that are generally only administered at the beginning and end of studies. Yet, we know that affective state varies significantly over time [12,16] and that recall of affect is limited and often distorted [42,20]. Because of this disconnect between reality and measurement, the effectiveness of many research studies is threatened [26]. Based on the above literature, what is needed to solve this problem is a tool that (1) reliably measures affect, (2) is unobtrusive and pleasant enough to administer at least daily, and (3) can be administered in situ.

Here we present a novel system called the Photographic Affect Meter, or PAM, designed to address each of these three points. PAM has been developed for researchers seeking a brief, objective measure of affect that can be administered on mobile phones, and the work extends that in single-item affect assessment by Russell [37] and Lang [3,21] as well as research in Ecological Momentary Assessment [12,22,42]. In the system, users are shown a grid containing photos of varying subject matter, each in some way depicting an emotional state. In the first of two studies, individuals self-reported their current emotional state using PAM as well as standard measures of affect, and the scores were compared to demonstrate the effectiveness of PAM as a measure of affect. In the second study, PAM was deployed to measure affect in a field experiment to demonstrate effectiveness in actual use. From these two studies, we concluded that we can in fact reliably use a subject's choice of photo from PAM as a measure of affect and that PAM is very well suited for use on mobile phones for collecting affective data in situ.

The implications of these findings are important for several reasons. First and foremost, we offer an instrument with which researchers can reliably and frequently measure affect via mobile phones and over the web. PAM is a testament to the ability of these technologies to deliver media, interact with users at key moments in context, and collect incredibly useful information. Second, this work represents further validation of a number of premises important to emotion research, notably the link between imagery and emotion [21,6], the utility of single-item affect instruments [4], and the importance of frequent sampling of affect in context [32,42,12]. System designers and Human-Computer Interaction researchers can turn to PAM and the methodology behind this work to inform future development of quick, reliable means of assessing various aspects of the state of their users in context.

BACKGROUND AND RELATED WORK

The Argument for Frequent Assessment of Affect

The assessment of subjects at the beginning and end of a study by self-report is a standard practice with a long history in experimental and clinical investigations. This makes sense logistically for a number of reasons including convenience, practicality, managing participant burden, and of course, lack of suitable methods for more frequent sampling. There are, however, two serious drawbacks to employing this approach when dealing with affect. First, numerous studies have found reports of specific past events to be distorted [42], generally based on the most intensely experienced emotions and the state at the time of reporting [20]. Such distortion of memory clearly threatens the effectiveness of research [26].

The second manner in which baseline-closeout studies struggle measuring affect relates to the duality of emotional experience. When affect is measured, what is captured is either the more stable, general affective condition of a subject (trait affect, or dispositional affect) or a short-term bout of emotion being experienced in that given moment (state affect, or possibly mood) [16]. Hence, when affect is measured at the end of a study, what is generally captured is trait affect, possibly influenced by current state affect, or perhaps just state affect at the time of closeout. Either way, the moment-by-moment, day-by-day emotional experience of the subject cannot be captured by this single assessment.

There does exist a theoretical framework dealing with the importance of collecting various in-the-moment assessments during research. Ecological Momentary Assessment, or EMA, is a class of data collection methods that attempt to alleviate the problem of recall bias and big picture emphasis by instead assessing subjects in context at opportune moments [32,42], usually with some sort of mobile computing device [1]. For example, Experience Sampling [1,12,15,22] is a notable subset of EMA methodology in which users are prompted by messages on their phone to complete some sort of assessment. Reis and Gabel [36] highlight the importance and benefits of sampling a subject's experience day-to-day in terms of salience, recency, and memorability of events, each of which are likely to impact recall and reporting of affect. Because of this, EMA has a significant advantage over standard data collection methods in that it permits more sensitive, detailed, and wide-ranging measurements of mood and behavior [32]. Epstein and colleagues [14], for example have demonstrated success with this approach measuring and modeling affective states at the time of cravings and relapses in substance abusers.

One prerequisite for the use of EMA and similar frequent measurement constructs is that brief, reliable, unobtrusive instruments must exist to measure the variables in question at precise times throughout the day or in the context of specific behaviors. It is not clear that such an instrument exists to measure affect. That is not, by any means, to say that this work represents the first brief measure of affect; there have been a number of previous attempts to create less time-consuming measures. Of course, there are numerous challenges in creating a brief measure of affect, not the least of which is the highly complex and oft-debated nature of affect itself. Much of that will be avoided here, but a short discussion on the subject should suffice to convey the difficulty of the task as well as frame this work from a theoretical perspective.

Measuring Affect

The most common manner of conceptualizing affect for objective measurement is to consider it as existing in two dimensions: valence (unpleasurable to pleasurable or negative to positive) and arousal (low activation to high activation), perhaps best described by Russell's Circumplex Model of Affect [38]. Granted, the first dimensional model of affect [46] and many subsequent models have involved a third dimension (dominance, tension, control, etc.), but most current emotion scholars work within the more manageable two-dimensional framework [39]. Various discrete and independent emotions can be mapped in two-dimensional affect space, as can an individual's current affective state, which may involve one or many of those discrete emotions. In order to meaningfully measure and report affect, an instrument must capture to some extent an individual's state in regards to both of these dimensions. Mehrabian and Russell created a Semantic Differential Scale in attempt to capture the full dimensionality of emotion and included a third dimension, dominance [28]. While thorough, this scale is somewhat unwieldy both in practice and analysis [37].

Watson, et al, presented a different approach with their Positive And Negative Affect Schedule, or PANAS, essentially combining dimensions of arousal and valence into two measures, one for positive affect (PA) and one for negative affect (NA) [45]. PANAS consists of 20 items—single emotion or feeling words that represent positively and negatively valenced feelings as well as arousal/activation. For the PA scale, higher arousal and more pleasurable selections result in higher scores; low arousal and less pleasure result in a low score. The NA scale functions the same with respects to arousal but features negatively valenced items. More recently, PANAS has been suggested to be more reflective of positive activation than of pleasure, as items such as happiness are not directly assessed [10,44], which could lead to misleading interpretation if PA is assumed to be pleasure-driven.

Examination of PANAS scores in subjects experiencing extreme state anger has highlighted this issue, as the high level of activation from anger leads to confusingly high PANAS Positive scores [18]. Still, the validity and reliability of the measure is difficult to question; the relative simplicity combined with repeatability across thousands of studies has given PANAS a place among the more widely used measures in all of science.

Brief Measures of Affect

Researchers have sought to streamline the process of measuring affect for some time. Ironically, even Watson et al originally referred to the 20-item PANAS as "brief measures of positive and negative affect" [45]. PANAS may be brief in comparison to prior work, but certainly not to the point that it would be suitable for use in the context of Ecological Momentary Assessment or frequent measurement. In fairness, PANAS was not developed to be used as a frequent, in situ measure, but there have been several efforts to develop more suitable single-item measures of affect meeting with varying degrees of success.

The first work that is relevant to this research is Russell's Affect Grid [37]. In short, the Affective Grid is a pen and paper based instrument in which subjects are presented a 10x10 empty grid representing two-dimensional affect space with valence in the x-axis and arousal in the y-axis. Subjects check the cell of the grid that represents how they currently feel, and that location can be mapped to a score that correlates strongly with the Semantic Differential Scale and PANAS Positive. The most significant issue with the Affect Grid is the difficulty that it presents subjects; the instructions are lengthy in order to explain the less-than-clear concepts described above and even then, subjects must be able to cognitively process their current emotional state and quantify it on a box in a grid.

A second important single-item measure of affect is Bradley and Lang's Self Assessment Manikin, or SAM [3]. SAM presents users three sets of five drawings of a simple character, each set representing the range of states in the pleasure, arousal, and dominance dimensions. Subjects identify the character in each set that represents their current state in that particular dimension. SAM scores correlate highly with scores from Semantic Differential, particularly in the Valence and Arousal dimensions but were not reported as validated against PANAS. SAM attempts to simplify the cognitively difficult task of locating ones affective state in two-dimensional space by instead leveraging the human response to imagery, a subject in which Lang is expert [21].

To a certain extent, the two measures described above could be considered as the conceptual predecessors to most of the more recent work in this area. Perhaps the best example of how modern mobile devices can be combined with these classic theoretically grounded measures of affect is the work of Morris, et al [31], who assess affect on mobile phones with a colored two-dimensional Mood Map. The system is essentially an abstract version of the original Affect Grid that has been designed to run on the MyExperience experience sampling application [15]. The simplistic but seemingly effective Mood Map is perfectly suited for such applications, however it has not been validated against reliable measures of affect, and given the level of abstraction of the grid space and arbitrary color use, it may prove difficult to validate. Other examples of mobile phone-based assessments include Isomursu's Feedback [19], although this is more focused at emotional response to a mobile app for use in usability testing and Meschtscherjakov's emoticon-based work, which is promising, but also not yet validated [29].

If we revisit the three criteria from above, namely that the system must (1) reliably measure affect, (2) be unobtrusive and pleasant enough to administer at least daily, and (3) be able to be administered in situ, we find that no single instrument fully satisfies all three criteria. Russell's and Lang's work certainly satisfy the reliability criterion. The Affect Grid could easily be implemented on a mobile phone, but due to the above-discussed issues would remain a cumbersome instrument. Lang's SAM is quicker and more pleasant, but requires three distinct decisions to be made regarding one's emotional state. The Mood Map and other similar works are ideally suited for frequent, in context measurement but have in general not been validated as reliable measures of affect. Designing a mobile phone-based tool for frequently assessing a user's emotions in context sounds decidedly like a problem for the HCI research community, yet there has been little work done along these lines. Taking aim at the problem with what research in HCI has taught us about mobile technology, context, usability, design, and affective computing seems likely to yield significant contributions.

Figure 1. An instance of PAM on an Android mobile device.

PAM: THE PHOTOGRAPHIC AFFECT METER

From a user's perspective, PAM, like its predecessors, is laid out in a grid (Figure 1). The subject is presented with 16 photographs that represent a diversity of emotions (description to follow) arranged into a 4x4 grid, and is prompted to select a photo that best describes how they feel right now. Below the grid, a button to choose more photos reloads the grid with a different set of PAM images should the user not be able to comfortably express their state with one of the photos currently displayed. Upon selection of a representative photo, the other images are removed, allowing the subject to review his/her selection before touching the report mood button.

Design Decisions and Prototyping

Research in affective computing suggests that computers are inherently bad at detecting users' emotional states and that designers should steer clear of falling into this trap [2]. In this context, our approach was to (1) use a representation of emotion that offered opportunity for interpretation and personal meaning and (2) allow users (rather than the designers or the system) to determine the meaning of each representation of emotion. Therefore, we decided to incorporate the ambiguity of emotion into the design of the system [40] but then use rigorous quantitative validation to produce an objective measure a la PANAS [45].

Along these lines, the first important consideration was choosing a medium for representing emotion. Text-based instruments are obtrusive in the amount of time they take to complete, and even simplified measures like Russell's Affect Grid can be unwieldy. Others, such as SAM and Mood Map, instead make use of graphical representations, taking a successful step towards an abbreviated scale. Along these lines, color has been a popular medium for representing emotion in the HCI community [30,43]. A body of research connects color with emotion [27,33] but suggests that interpretation of color would prove to be too equivocal to be useful for assessment purposes [13].

Photographs offer a richer and more engaging representation of affect. The link between photographs and emotion is well researched, with evidence suggesting that photos themselves can be emotionally charged and can have universal emotional legibility [21], but also can have very private meaning based on prior or shared experiences [6]. We hoped this tension between emotional legibility and private meaning would offer users a range of interpretive flexibility from images with more specific emotional content (such as an expressive human face) to something more ambiguous (a drop of water rippling in a glass).

In selecting a photo set to use for PAM, we first considered using Lang's International Affective Picture System (IAPS), an archive of photos that make up a validated instrument for evoking a variety of emotional responses [21]. However, in order for these photos to consistently evoke such responses, the subject matter they depict falls at extreme ends of the spectrum (including violence, sexuality, etc.), and our pilot testers indicated that most images in IAPS would not be photos they would choose for themselves. Further, the IAPS photos have been chosen to provoke emotional response, whereas the goal of PAM is assessment.

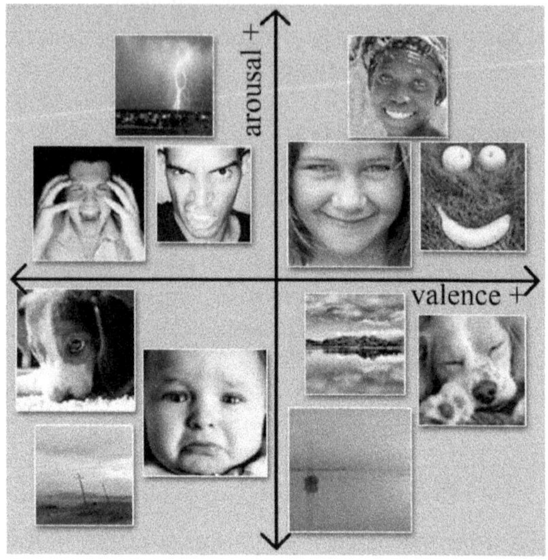

Figure 2. Example PAM images in Russell's affective space.

Instead, we turned to the online photo-sharing service Flickr. Using the Flickr API, we downloaded roughly 9,000 Creative Commons-licensed images that had been tagged by the community of Flickr users with one of Russell's 28 words of affect [38] in hopes of finding photos that PAM users would find representative of a variety of emotions. After removing images with inappropriate content, 7,714 photos remained. To prototype the concept and illuminate the subset of these images with which people would be most likely to identify, testers (N=70) were encouraged to use an early version of PAM to select photos to represent their current emotional state repeatedly over a period of one to two weeks. From these data, we identified the most frequently user-selected photos. It should be noted that the communal tagging of a photo with an emotion word on Flickr has the potential to be somewhat arbitrary, loaded, or unrelated to the image. As such, we used the photos' tag words in the initial sorting and handling of the images only—our assumptions moving forward about the relationship of a given image to affect are always based on empirical evidence rather than the emotion-word tags.

We decided to arrange the photos in a grid, from low arousal and negative valence in the bottom left corner, to high arousal and positive valence in the top right, imitating Russell's Affect Grid. Brief testing on a variety of smart phones such as Android, iPhone, and Blackberry indicated that a 4x4 grid was an appropriate balance of photo size given limited screen size. To deal with the openness for interpretation of photos described above, multiple images would be assigned to each grid cell, and those images would rotate randomly each time PAM loads. Under this solution, hopefully with use of the 'more photos' button and repeated use, users will select an appropriate photo the majority of the time.

Finally, we chose our list of most frequently selected photos and arranged them in the grid based on the dimensions of valence and arousal and Russell's itemization of emotion words [38]. Starting with a list of 100 or so photos, the prototype system was piloted with 70 more testers who also completed PANAS after selecting a PAM image, and these results determined the final photoset (3 images per grid cell) as well as the location each would appear in the grid.

Scoring System

PAM produces four separate "scores" upon completion. The first, just referred to as PAM, is a 1-16 score that maps to PANAS PA. In keeping with the conceptualization of PANAS PA as ranging from low pleasure and low arousal to high pleasure and high arousal at the high end, the PAM Score is derived by starting a counter at the negative valence, low arousal corner of the grid and working increasingly in arousal then valence toward the positive valence, high arousal corner of the grid (Figure 3).

High Arousal

6	8	14	16
5	7	13	15
2	4	10	12
1	3	9	11

Negative Valence (left) — Positive Valence (right)

Low Arousal

Figure 3. PAM scoring in the grid layout.

The other three PAM values are also derivatives of position within the grid (Figure 3). The PAM Quadrant is the valence and arousal quadrant of the grid from which the subjects' selection was made, and is represented by a score of 1 (Negative/ Low), 2 (Negative/ High), 3 (Positive/ Low), or 4 (Positive/ High). PAM Valence is a score of -2 to 2 (excluding 0) that represents the absolute position in the grid in absolute terms on the x-axis, and is a measure of the extent of displeasure to pleasure the subject is feeling. PAM Arousal is also a -2 to 2 (excluding 0) score, instead derived from the position on the y-axis. PAM Arousal represents the subject's state of arousal or activation ranging from low to high.

METHODS

The goal of this research is to establish the validity of the PAM as a usable tool to frequently measure affect. To that end, we conducted two studies using PAM: the first was designed to validate the instrument against PANAS, the most widely used measure of affect; the second was designed to test the use of PAM in the context of an actual behavioral experiment. The question did arise as to which existing measure PAM scores should be compared to. The Affect Grid would have been a good choice from the perspective of fit with PAM. The Semantic Differential Scale and SAM would have made good choices from the perspective of in-depth evaluation of PAM in multi-dimensional affective space. However, PANAS was selected, partly because it is somewhat of a summary measure of these others, and partly because of its wide use in health [9,14], the area of interest of this research team.

Study 1: Validation of PAM with PANAS

Subjects were 315 individuals (45% male; Asian 21.3%, Black or African American 7.8%, Hispanic or Latino 8.5%, White 54.6%, Other 7.8%) recruited through a combination of university departmental and student list serves, snowball sampling, flyers, and postings on a variety of websites. Subjects who participated were given the option of providing an email address to be entered into a drawing to win an iPod.

Subjects logged into the study website and completed the PAM assessment with the prompt "Select the image that best captures how you feel right now." Next, subjects were taken to a web-based version of PANAS, with the time scale of the PANAS prompt also changed to be "Indicate to what extent you feel this way *right now*, that is, at the present moment." Finally, subjects were asked to provide basic demographic information. This provided a data set with which to examine the relationship between each subject's PAM and PANAS results, both theoretically representing measures of *state* affect.

Study 2: Use of PAM in a Field Experiment

Subjects were 34 individuals (14 male) recruited via university departmental and student list serves and flyers for participation in a mobile phone-based research study examining healthy decision making processes. Subjects were compensated for participation in the main study, but not for the ancillary study. The primary research study consisted of subjects using an application called VERA, in which users are asked to take photographs documenting health-related decisions (take the stairs or ride the elevator, eat a piece of cake or pass it up, etc.) that they make throughout the course of the day. In the system, users take a photo of their health behavior, toggle whether the behavior was something they did or avoided (took the stairs, avoided the piece of cake), rate the decision on a scale of -3 (most unhealthy) to +3 (most healthy), and optionally add a short text comment. The photos and notes are then posted to a social system in which other users in a group can view and comment on one another's photos.

To examine how PAM might work in an experimental context, the instrument was integrated into the VERA system as the last step in the posting process. Immediately after each user-behavior photo was taken and rated, users were prompted to select the PAM photo that best represented their mood at the time of the activity. As part of pre-study training, users were instructed to choose the photo that best represented how they felt at the time of the behavior, not necessarily how they felt about their health-related decision. Following the study, subjects completed PANAS, prompted to indicate how they felt *in the last two weeks* over the duration of the study. Note that in study one, PAM and PANAS were both intended to represent state affect. However, in study two, while PAM represents *state* affect, PANAS—with a prompted duration of two weeks—represents *trait* affect [35].

The goal of this study was two-fold: first, to ensure that subjects would not mind regularly completing PAM and that it wouldn't grow burdensome, and second, to further validate PAM as a measure of affect. While the former is straightforward, the latter is somewhat more involved. Based on the premise that there is a well-documented link between affect and health—chiefly that higher positive affect is associated with healthier behaviors across the board [9,35]—the expectation is to find a correlation between PAM and healthiness. This is complicated, however, by the fact that the VERA system is aimed at in-the-moment decisions on health behaviors, and as such is more a question of *state* than *trait* affect [35]. The true expectation, then, is for healthier behaviors to be associated with higher PAM scores but not necessarily with higher PANAS PA scores.

RESULTS

The results of these two studies represent strong evidence of construct validity for PAM as well as suggest that the instrument is effective in field experiments.

Study 1: Validation of PAM with PANAS

The primary point of comparison of this study is subjects' PAM scores and PANAS scores, both representing state affect. In this sample (N=315), mean scores for each measure were PAM, M=9.72, SD=4.06; PANAS PA, M=25.75, SD=7.64; and PANAS NA, M=15.65, SD=6.20. Figure 4 depicts a scatterplot of PANAS PA vs. PAM.

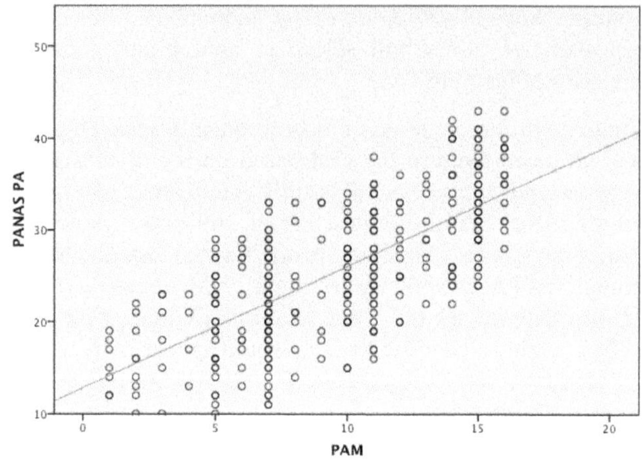

Figure 4. Scatterplot of PANAS PA vs PAM

PAM strongly correlates with PANAS Positive (.71, Table 1). PAM scores are in fact a good indicator of positive affect. Note that there is a weak negative correlation (-.37) between PAM and PANAS Negative, which is consistent both with theoretical expectations [45] and with the correlation between PANAS Positive and PANAS Negative (-.30). While it is difficult to compare correlations between studies, it is worth noting that Russell's Affect Grid produced a correlation of only .62 with PANAS PA.

Given the dimensionality of PAM, it is also important to examine the component data (arousal and valence) as well as just the compiled PAM score. Remember that PANAS Positive is in reality a combination of valence and arousal, with lower arousal and obviously negative valence indicative of lower scores and higher arousal and positive valence indicating higher scores. The graphs in Figure 5 clearly demonstrate the same pattern, providing strong evidence of the validity of the PAM valence and arousal components. It is interesting to note that PANAS Positive scores are slightly higher at Arousal=1 than Arousal=2 (although not significantly so), as this suggests that the scores are somewhat valence (pleasure) dominated.

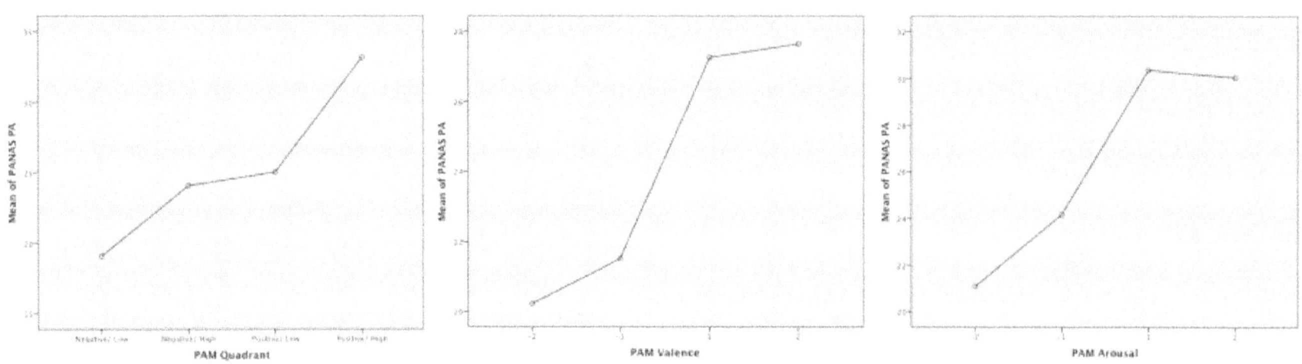

Figure 5. Plot of mean PANAS scores by PAM Quadrant, Valence, and Arousal. ANOVA for each significant at $p < 0.001$. Difference in means (t-test) are all significant at $p < 0.001$ except for Negative/ High vs. Positive/ Low, Valence = -2 vs Valence = -1. Valence = 2 vs. Valence = 1, Arousal = 2 vs. Arousal = 1.

	PANAS Positive	PANAS Negative
PAM	.71	-.37
PANAS Positive		-.30

Table 1. Correlations between PAM scores and PANAS scores, N=315 ($p < 0.001$ for all values).

Study 2: Use of PAM in a Field Experiment

In the second study, 34 subjects posted and recorded affect with PAM 1,169 times. The focal point of analysis for the second study is comparison of the healthiness of decisions and the corresponding PAM state affect results as well as to PANAS PA trait affect assessed at post-test. To frame this analysis, it should be pointed out that a significant literature links emotions and health-related behaviors, as extensively reviewed by Pressman and Cohen [35].

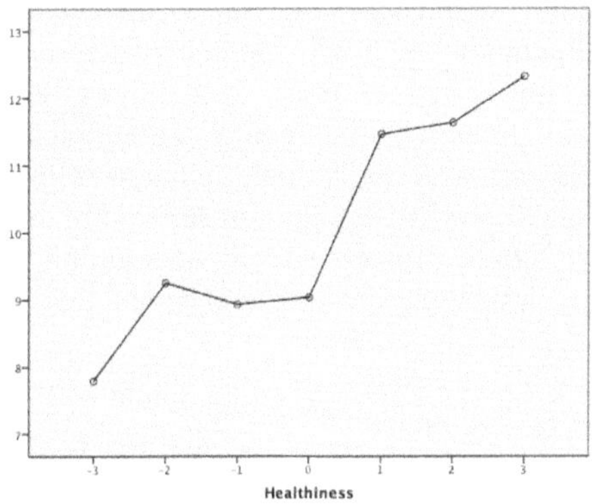

Figure 6. Mean PAM Score vs. Healthiness, ANOVA significant at $p < 0.001$.

Given that subjects recorded a wide variety of health-related behaviors and those behaviors cannot always be associated with one's current emotional state, there is substantial variability in these data. Yet, the expected moderate, significant positive correlation of 0.52 ($p < 0.01$) between PAM and healthiness of behavior is found. Figure 6 shows the mean PAM scores generally increasing with healthiness, the expected result [9,35]. A comparison of the mean PAM scores of healthy choices (M=11.68, SD=4.19, N=711) vs. unhealthy choices (M=8.95, SD=4.61, N=437) finds healthy choices to be associated with significantly higher PAM Scores, $t(1146)=10.30$, $p < 0.001$. This is of course what we would expect from a theoretical perspective [9,35] and provides evidence that PAM is an effective measure of affect in a field experiment such as this.

Further analysis of PAM scores in the dimensions of valence and arousal with healthiness make this relationship quite clear. An analysis of the valence and arousal components of PAM produces similar results. The graphs in Figure 7 clearly depict the desired, theoretically grounded trend of increasing likelihood of healthy behavior with increases in positive affect. Comparing the mean Healthiness of decisions identified by positively valenced PAM scores (M=.79, SD=1.53, N=861) to those of negatively valenced PAM scores (M=-.33, SD=1.68, N=308) shows that positively valenced PAM scores are associated with significantly healthier decisions, $t(1167)=10.74$, $p < 0.001$. The same can be said for Arousal, with PAM high Arousal Healthiness scores (M=.79, SD=1.63, N=638) significantly greater, $t(1167)=6.744$, $p < 0.001$, than the PAM low Arousal scores (M=.15, SD=1.61, N=531).

Up to this point, the assessments of affect discussed have been measures of *state affect.* In study two, however, PANAS PA was employed as a measure of *trait affect*, creating an interesting comparison point. Remember that state affect has been shown to be more influential over acute health issues and spur of the moment, seemingly less consequential decisions [35], whereas trait affect is more associated with long term health issues and influence over more serious issues [9,35]. Here then, the expected outcome is a link between healthiness and state affect, measured by PAM (which has been clearly demonstrated above), but not necessarily between health and trait affect, measured by PANAS PA. This is in fact what the data from this study show, finding no significant correlation

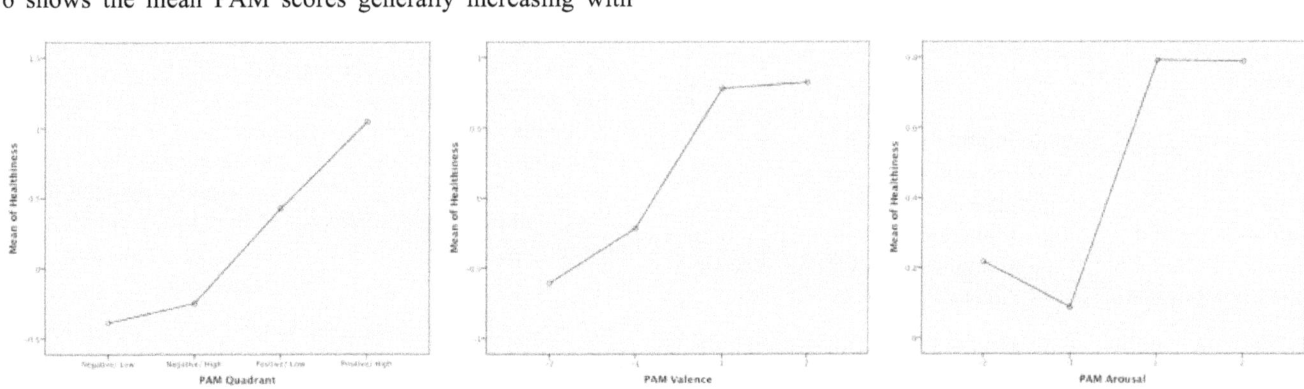

Figure 7. Plot of healthiness by PAM Quadrant, Valence, and Arousal. ANOVA all significant at $p < 0.001$. Difference in means (t-test) are all significant at $p < 0.001$ except for Negative/ High vs. Positive/ Low, Valence = -2 vs Valence = -1. Valence = 2 vs. Valence = 1, Arousal = 2 vs. Arousal = 1, Arousal -2 vs. Arousal -1.

between the mean healthiness of an individual's behaviors and their PANAS PA score. Further, while one would expect a complete record of affective states to, on average, be consistent with trait affect [12,35], the same would not be said for a sampling of state affect as we have here, because of the extreme variability [12,16]. Indeed, there is no significant correlation between the mean of PAM scores recorded at the time of healthy decisions for an individual and their PANAS PA score recorded at post-test.

Lastly, subjects were asked about their use of PAM in post-test surveys and interviews. Of the 34 subjects who participated, only one had a problem of any kind with PAM—he didn't like the subject matter of the imagery. Not one of the subjects found the use of PAM obtrusive, annoying, or burdensome, in spite of the fact that the 34 subjects used PAM 1,169 times over the two-week period of the study for an average of 2.5 times per day each.

DISCUSSION

Validity and Effectiveness of PAM

These results clearly demonstrate that PAM can be utilized as a brief, reliable measure of affect. Establishing the validity of any measure can be an arduous task involving the exhaustive assessment of various forms of validity [5,8] and thorough contextual analysis of both measure and theory for fit and boundary conditions [24]. Chronbach describes the process as iterative and nearly unending [11]. At this stage, our approach has been to establish construct validity for PAM—that is, that PAM is in fact measuring affect and doing so in a way that is meaningful and fits within expectations—and to examine the use of PAM in the context of its most likely usage scenario and see if it holds.

Campbell and Fiske [5] classically identify convergent validity (the extent to which the measure converges with other similar or theoretically correlated measures) and discriminant validity (the extent to which the measure does not converge with theoretically unrelated measures) as the two requisite components to establish construct validity in a new measure. This argument is very simple: in study one, PAM scores strongly correlate with PANAS Positive state affect scores, and analysis of the valence and arousal components of PAM leads to expected results when compared to PANAS. This is strong evidence of convergent validity considering that PANAS is the measure we have selected as most representative of our desired construct of affect. Discriminant validity is somewhat more complicated, but we find evidence of this in study two in the fact that the limited sampling of state affect PAM scores do not correlate with a trait affect measured by PANAS.

Equally as important as establishing construct validity, the findings above demonstrate the viability and effectiveness of PAM for use as a tool for Ecological Momentary Assessment [22] in field studies. The fact that PAM was used with such frequency over a two-week period with little or no complaint is a testament to both the design and the theoretical construct of a photo-based grid representation of affect. To wit, users of PAM need not be given instructions other than a brief prompt, in contrast to Russell's Affect Grid [37], for example, which requires lengthy instruction. Design and implementation undoubtedly play a role in the effectiveness of PAM; a touch screen interface with one step that is built into existing apps is far from obtrusive. Further, the grid layout of photos, whose underlying structure is not spelled out explicitly to users, may still become familiar over time, increasing the ease of response. Another possibility is that the emotional representation of images allows for a very rapid response. Lang suggests that images elicit a visceral response [21]; perhaps users are forming almost precognitive decisions about their current emotional state in response to the imagery. All the above is certainly subject matter for future experimentation.

It should be noted that work on PAM has yet to investigate how cultural differences may shape the interpretation of emotional photos, or even whether this model of affect would be appropriate to apply cross-culturally. While the sample used in both studies was relatively racially diverse, the participants were individuals living, working, or going to school in the United States. Those looking to incorporate PAM into future projects should be mindful of this fact until more work along these lines is conducted.

Who Should Use PAM?

PAM is not intended as a substitute for PANAS or other more substantial measures of affect. While there is evidence that shorter scales are not always necessarily worse than more complete ones [4], PAM is really designed for circumstances that necessitate a more efficient or portable instrument, particularly when assessment would be best carried out on a mobile device or computer. A prudent approach would be to combine frequent measurement with PAM to capture variability around daily events or key happenings with a more substantial assessment of affect at the beginning and/ or end of the study.

The field experiment described above using the VERA application is a perfect example of the value of PAM. As the findings demonstrate, simply assessing subjects' affect with PANAS after the study period (the classic approach) would not have shed light on a link between emotion and health behavior in that study. Yet the PAM scores recorded at the time of each health decision demonstrated a clear relationship with health behavior. Hence, by employing PAM in situ as well as PANAS at post-test, a relationship emerged highlighting the importance of state over trait affect for day-to-day health-related decisions.

Two general cases comprised of classic examples of Ecological Momentary Assessment make up the most likely usage scenarios for PAM. First, PAM could be used in cases where researchers need to know about subjects' affective states during certain events or decision making processes, such as linking affect to dietary choices [25], exercise behavior [7], lapses in substance abuse [14], or around traumatic events [34]. Second, PAM would be a logical tool to incorporate into any experience sampling or other similar scenarios, such as examining the variability of affect over time [1,12], around use of an app or system [19], or around scheduled happenings like key political addresses or the FIFA World Cup. The majority of examples that fall into these two categories emphasize the importance of measuring affect in situ. As such, they beg for the use of mobile devices, particularly a user's primary mobile phone that would be with them at all times and on hand whenever the key moment of assessment might take place.

Researchers and developers of mobile and web applications should be particularly interested in PAM. Android, iPhone, and web-based PAM widgets already exist and will be made available to researchers at http://cornellhci.org/pam. If these widgets are incorporated into existing applications as an additional single-click step of login, posting, or other common workflow processes, developers can immediately begin collecting affective data about their users. PAM offers substantial value to researchers developing behavioral interventions that want to collect affect data for their analysis as highlighted by the VERA example above. Developers building experience sampling, diary, reflective, or other creative apps in which affect might play a role might also find value in a simple measure of affect. Even developers simply looking to better understand their users might find some value in the ability to quickly and easily measure their users' affective state, perhaps in response to various stimuli either in the app or their surroundings.

CONCLUSION

This research has demonstrated that PAM, the Photographic Affect Meter, is a viable solution for measuring state affect frequently and in situ. In a first study, PAM was found to correlate strongly with PANAS PA, among the most widely accepted measures of affect, establishing it as a valid measure of affect. In a second study, PAM was deployed as part of a mobile phone-based health behavior field experiment and was not only found to be unobtrusive and efficient, but to produce a measure of state affect that was completely consistent with theoretical expectations.

Given this evidence, researchers in the behavioral, medical, and computer sciences should consider the use of PAM in future studies where frequent measurement of affect would be of value. Those developing mobile device applications in particular should take note because of the ease with which they could incorporate the measurement of affect into their new or existing applications. While PAM may not represent the first validated brief measure of affect or the first measure to work on mobile phones, it may well prove to be the most effective combination of the two—a combination that will open the door to original uses of affect in a broad range of research disciplines.

ACKNOWLEDGMENTS

We would like to thank our colleagues who helped in the development of PAM, both technically and conceptually, particularly Drs. John Leonard, Mary Charlson, and Andy Dannenberg of Weill Cornell Medical College.

REFERENCES

1. Barrett, L.F. & Barrett, D.J. An introduction to computerized experience sampling in psychology. *Social Science Computer Review, 19,2* (2001), 175-185.
2. Boehner, K, DePaula, R, Dourish, P, Sengers, P. How emotion is made and measured. *Intl J Human-Computer Studies, 65,4* (2007), 275-291.
3. Bradley, M.M. & Lang, P.J. Measuring emotion: the self-assessment manikin and the semantic differential. *J Behavioral Therapy and Experimental Psychiatry*, 25,1 (1994), 49-59.
4. Burisch, M. You don't always get what you pay for: Measuring depression with short and simple versus long and sophisticated scales. *J Research in Personality 18,1* (1984), 81-98.
5. Campbell, D.T. & Fiske, D.W. Convergent and discriminant validity by the multitrait-multimethod matrix. *Psychological Bulletin, 56,2* (1959), 81-105.
6. Chalfen, R. *Snapshot Versions of Life*. Bowling Green, 1987.
7. Charlson, M.E., Boutin-Foster, C., Mancuso, C.A., Peterson, J.C., Ogedegbe, G., Briggs, W.M., Robbins, L., Isen, A.M., Allegrante, J.P. Randomized controlled trials of positive affect and self-affirmation to facilitate healthy behaviors in patients with cardiopulmonary diseases: rationale, trial design, and methods. *Contemporary clinical trials, 28,6* (2007), 748-62.
8. Cook, T.D. & Campbell, D.T. Quasi-experimentation design & analysis for field settings. Houghton Mifflen, Boston, 1979.
9. Cohen, S. & Pressman, S.D. Positive affect and health. *Current Directions in Psych Sci, 15,3* (2006), 122-125.
10. Crawford, J.R. & Henry, J.D. Positive and Negative Affect Schedule (PANAS): Construct validity, measurement properties and normative data in a large non-clinical sample. *British Journal of Clinical Psychology, 44* (2004), 245-265.
11. Cronbach, L.J. Five perspectives on validity argument. In Wainer, H. & Braun, H.I. (Eds.) *Test validity*. Lawrene Erlbaum Assoc., New Jersey, 1988.
12. Csikszentmihalyi, K. & Hunter, M. Happiness in everyday life: The uses of experience sampling. *J Happiness Studies, 4* (2003), 185-199.
13. D'Andrade, R. & Egan, M. The Colors of Emotion. *American Ethnologist, 1,1* (1974), 49-63.

14. Epstein, D.H., Willner-Reid, J., Vahabzadeh, M., Mezghanni, M., Lin, J.L., Preston, K.L. Real-time electronic diary reports of cue exposure and mood in the hours before cocaine and heroin craving and use. *Arch Gen Psychiatry, 66,1* (2009), 88-94.

15. Froehlich, J., Chen, M.Y., Consolvo, S. MyExperience: a system for in situ tracing and capturing of user feedback on mobile phones. *Proc Mobysis 2007,* (2007).

16. George, J.M. Trait and State Affect. In K.R. Murphy (Ed) *Individual Differences and Behavior in Organizations*, (1996), 145-171.

17. Google Scholar, www.google.com/scholar, 9/23/10.

18. Harmon-Jones, E., Harmon-Jones, C., Abramson, L., Peterson, C.K. PANAS Positive Activation Is Associated With Anger. *Emotion, 9,2* (2009), 183-196.

19. Isomursu, M., Tähti, M., Väinämö, S., Kuutti, K. Experimental evaluation of five methods for collecting emotions in field settings with mobile applications. *Int'l J. of Human-Computer Studies, 65* (2007), 404-418.

20. Kahneman, D., Objective Happiness. Kahneman, D., Diener, E. and Schwarz, N. (Eds.) *Well-Being: The Foundations of Hedonic Psychology*, (1999), 3-25.

21. Lang, P. The Emotion Probe: Studies of Motivation and Attention. *American Psychologist, 50,5* (1995), 372-85.

22. Larson, R. & Csikszentmihalyi, M. The Experience Sampling Method. *New Directions for Methodology of Social and Behavioral Science, 15* (1983), 41-56.

23. Lazarus, R. & Lazarus, B. *Passion and Reason: Making Sense of Our Emotions*. Oxford U. Press, 1994.

24. McGuire, W.J. A contextualist theory of knowledge: Its implications for innovation and reform in psychological research. In Berkowitz, L. (Ed) *Advances in experimental social psychology, Vol 16*. (1983), 1-43.

25. Macht, M., How emotions effect eating: a five-way model. *Appetite, 50,1* (2008), 1-11.

26. Mancuso, C.A. & Charlson, M.E. Does Recollection Error Threaten the Validity of Cross-Sectional Studies of Effectiveness? *Med Care, 33,4* (1995), AS77-AS88.

27. Mayer, J., DiPaulo, M., Salovey, P. Perceiving Affective Content in Ambiguous Visual Stimuli: A Component of Emotional Intelligence. *J. Personality Assessment, 54,3* (1990) 772-781.

28. Mehrabian, A. & Russell, J.A. *An approach to environmental psychology*. MIT Press, Boston, 1974.

29. Meschtscherjakov, A., Weiss, A., Scherndl, T. Utilizing Emoticons on mobile devices within ESM studies to measure emotions in the field. *MobileHCI 2009* (2009)

30. MoodJam Research Group. MoodJam. www.moodjam.org (Verified, 9/23/2010).

31. Morris, M.E., Kathawala, Q., Leen, T.K., Gorenstein, E.E., Guilak, F., Labhard, M., Deleeuw, W. Mobile therapy: case study evaluations of a cell phone application for emotional self-awareness. *Journal of Medical Internet Research, 12,2* (2010), e10.

32. Moskowitz, D.S. & Young, S.N. Ecological momentary assessment: what it is and why it is a method of the future in clinical psychopharmacology. *J Psychiatry Neurosci, 31,1* (2006), 13-20.

33. Naz, K & Helen, H. Color-Emotion Associations: Past Experience and Personal Preference. *Proc. AIC 2004*, (2004).

34. Pennebaker, J., Zech, E., Rimé, B. Disclosing and Sharing Emotion: Psychological, Social, and Health Consequences. *Handbook of Bereavement Research: Consequences*. APA, Washington, DC, 2001.

35. Pressman, S.D. & Cohen, S. Does Positive Affect Influence Health? *Psych Bulletin, 131,6* (2005), 925-71.

36. Reis, H.T., Gable, S.L. Event-sampling and other methods for studying everyday experience. Reis, H.T., and Judd, C.M. (Eds) *Handbook of Research Methods in Social and Personality Psychology,* (2000).

37. Russell, J.A., Weiss, A., Mendelsohn, G.A. Affect Grid: A Single-Item Scale of Pleasure and Arousal. *J Personality and Social Psych, 57,3* (1989), 493-502.

38. Russell, J. A Circumplex Model of Affect. *J. Personality and Social Psych, 39,4* (1980) 1161-1178.

39. Scherer, K.R. What are emotions? And how can they be measured? *Social Science Info*, 44,4 (2005), 695-729.

40. Sengers, P., Boehner, K., Mateas, M., Gay, G. The Disenchantment of Affect. *Personal and Ubiquitous Computing, 12(5)*, (2008).

41. Slovic, P., Finuane, M.L., Peters, E. The affect heuristic. *Eur J of Operational Research, 177* (2007), 1333-1352.

42. Stone, A.A. & Shiffman, S. Capturing momentary, self-report data: A proposal for reporting guidelines. *Annals of Behavioral Medicine, 24,3* (2002), 236-43.

43. Sundström, P., Ståhl, A., Höök, K. In Situ Informants Exploring an Emotional Mobile Messaging System in Their Everyday Practice. *Intl. J. Human-Computer Studies* (2007).

44. Watson, D., Wiese, D., Vaidya, J., Tellegen, A. The Two General Activation Systems of Affect: Structural Findings, Evolutionary Considerations, and Psychobiological Evidence. *J of personality and social psychology, 76,5* (1999), 820-38.

45. Watson, D., Clark, L.A., Tellegen, A. Development and Validation of Brief Measures of Positive and Negative Affect: The PANAS Scales. *J Personality and Social Psychology, 54,6* (1988), 1063-1070.

46. Wundt, W., Fundamentals of physiological psychology, 1905

Affective Computational Priming and Creativity

Sheena Lewis[1], Mira Dontcheva[2], Elizabeth Gerber[1,3]
Technology and Social Behavior[1], Segal Institute of Design[3]
Northwestern University
Evanston, IL 60208 USA
sheena@u.northwestern.edu, egerber@northwestern.edu
Advanced Technology Labs[2]
Adobe Systems
San Francisco, CA 94103 USA
mirad@adobe.com

ABSTRACT
While studies have shown that affect influences creativity, few investigate how affect influences creative performance with creativity support tools. Drawing from methods commonly used in psychology research, we present affective computational priming, a new method for manipulating affect using digitally embedded stimuli. We present two studies that explore computational techniques for inducing positive, neutral, and negative affect and examine their impact on idea generation with creativity support tools. Our results suggest that positive affective computational priming positively influences the quality of ideas generated. We discuss opportunities for future HCI research and offer practical applications of affective computational priming.

Author Keywords
creativity support tools, design, computational primes

ACM Classification Keywords
H5.m. Information interfaces and presentation (e.g., HCI): Miscellaneous.

General Terms
Design

INTRODUCTION
Creative professionals, such as engineers, scientists, and designers, increasingly rely on technology to complete creative tasks at work. They use web browsers to conduct research and search for inspiration. They document projects on wikis in order to collaborate with others. They depend on graphic design software and word processors to design and create. In response, human-computer interaction (HCI) researchers have started building creativity support tools, or software to enhance creative performance [38].

To inform the design of creativity support tools, HCI researchers have turned to psychological research on the cognitive aspects of individual and group creativity. For example, Hewett suggests that creativity support tools should allow users to formulate, re-formulate, and solve problems as their domain or state of the problem changes [21]. While this perspective has spawned new software and interfaces that enhance the cognitive variation necessary for creativity [38], few HCI researchers have yet to take an affective perspective on creativity, despite extensive psychological research in the domain [e.g. 14, 24].

Figure 1. Our studies show that a picture of a hammer (left) induces neutral affect, while a picture of a laughing baby (right) induces positive affect. Positive affect positively influences the quality of ideas generated in a creativity task.

Affect, the experience of emotion [43], has been shown to be a source of the cognitive variation necessary for creativity [4, 15, 23]. In the laboratory, experimenters induced positive affect by showing participants funny videos or giving them candy bars and asked them to perform established creativity tasks, such as generating alternative uses for a brick [19]. These studies show that positive affect leads to increased creative performance. But does positive affect lead to increased creative performance with real-world creativity support tools? How might we induce positive affect in a more contextualized and unobtrusive way?

In this paper we present two studies that demonstrate that affect has a positive influence on creativity support tool use. We introduce *affective computational priming*, a new method for manipulating affect using digitally embedded stimuli that influence a later response. In our studies, the embedded stimuli are images (see Figure 1), and we study their influence on creative idea generation tasks. In a first study with 240 participants generating unusual uses for common objects [19], we find that affective computational priming influences creative performance and that embedded images can be used as affective computational primes.

Images are already part of creativity support tools in the form of sample materials, tutorials, and startup screens, and therefore, they offer an opportunity for studying the link between affect and creativity in a contextualized unobtrusive way. In a second study with 31 participants and an existing creativity support tool, a sketching application, we find that positive affective computational priming positively influences the quality of created sketches. This study is the first to empirically demonstrate how computationally induced affect influences creative performance in the context of a creativity support tool.

This research contributes to design and HCI by introducing psychological research on affect to creativity support tool research, demonstrating the effectiveness of affective computational priming, and providing design implications for creativity support tools.

BACKGROUND

Creativity is defined as the generation of novel and useful ideas [2]. According to Simonton's [39] evolutionary theory of creativity, the probability of generating novel ideas increases with the number and breadth of cognitive elements available for association and considered relevant to the problem. For example, when developing an interface for CAD software, the likelihood of generating a novel interface increases if the designer combines a broad number of insights gathered from architects, engineers, construction managers, builders, etc. rather than a few insights generated from a single user. The more insights used to inform the new design, the greater likelihood that a novel idea will emerge [39]. Because creativity depends on novelty, which is a function of cognitive variation, increasing variation is likely to increase creativity. Psychologists find that affect supports cognitive variation leading to creativity [4, 15, 23]. For example, Isen and colleagues found that when subjects were primed for positive affect, they exhibited a more original and diverse range of word associations as compared to control subjects [25].

While HCI researchers have designed creativity support tools to increase cognitive variation in order to improve creative performance, few have considered the use of affective stimuli in creativity support tools.

Affect and Creativity

Affect is the experience of emotion that can occur without extensive perceptual and cognitive encoding and is often the first reaction to a given stimuli [43]. Affect constitutes the primary motivational system for human beings, modifying, controlling, and directing cognitive processes and task performance [27]. Affect may have two forms: trait (stable) or state (temporary); the latter may be induced by external stimuli [27].

Isen [23] proposes that positive affect influences cognitive activity in three ways. First, positive affect increases the number of cognitive elements available for processing, thereby increasing the number of elements available for association. Second, positive affect supports defocused attention, therefore broadening attention and leading to an increase in the numbers of cognitive elements treated as relevant to the problem. Third, positive affect increases cognitive flexibility, thereby increasing the probability of association between diverse cognitive elements [23, 24].

Similarly, Fredrickson [15] proposes a broaden-and-build model of positive emotion, which proposes that positive emotions (such as joy, contentment, interest, and love) broaden a person's scope of attention and cognition, increasing the number of available cognitive elements and breadth of those elements relevant to the problem. According to Simonton's evolutionary theory [39], breadth of relevant cognitive elements should increase creative performance.

In laboratory studies, Isen and colleagues have established an extensive repertoire (see [23] for a review) of ways to experimentally induce state (temporary) positive affect. In Isen's studies, participants are most often given gifts and treats, shown a clip of a comedy film, or played an excerpt from affect-laden music. For example, in two separate experiments with college students, participants were shown a clip of the movie Gag Reel or given a small bag of candy to induce affect [24]. In both cases, positive affect improved performance on creative ingenuity tasks, such as Mednick's Remote Associates Task[1] [32] and Duncker's Candle Task[2] [12]. This study suggests the possibility of HCI researchers designing creativity support tools to induce positive affect as a way of supporting idea production.

Positive affect has also been shown to influence performance by influencing the cognitive processes underlying motivation [9]. Scholars posit that positive affect influences expectancy (belief that effort will result in good performance), which in turn influences goal commitment, goal setting, persistence, and performance [13]. In a study of 97 undergraduate students, researchers induced positive affect by giving the students a bag of candy and then asked them to solve 10 anagrams. The study found that participants induced with positive affect performed better, were more persistent, tried harder, and reported higher levels of motivation than those in the neutral condition who did not receive a bag of candy.

Based on this literature, we formulated the following hypotheses:

Hypothesis 1

People who are computationally primed for positive affect will generate a greater number of ideas and ideas that are rated as more creative than those primed for negative or neutral affect.

[1] In Mendick's Remote Associates Task, participants are given three words and asked to give a fourth word that relates to the original three words.

[2] In Duncker's Candle Task, participants are given a candle, a book of matches, and a box of thumbtacks and asked to fix a lighted candle to a corkboard such that the candle wax won't drip on the table.

Hypothesis 2

People who are computationally primed for positive affect will generate a greater number of ideas and ideas that are rated as more creative than those who are not computationally primed.

Next, we discuss our study design and then describe our experiments in detail.

STUDY DESIGN

To study the influence of affect on creative performance with creativity support tools, we chose to use images as affective computational primes, because images are commonly used in startup screens, sample materials, and learning resources in modern software applications. We first created a dataset of affect-laden images and evaluated their influence on a common creativity task used in psychology, Guilford's Alternative Uses Task [19], to confirm that affective computational primes influence creativity. In Guilford's Alternative Uses Task, participants are asked to generate as many unusual uses as possible for a common object (e.g., brick).

In a second experiment, we embedded the same affect-laden images in a creativity support tool, the digital sketching application Adobe Ideas, and studied the impact of positive, neutral, and negative computational primes on idea generation in another common creativity task, the Torrance Test of Creativity Circles [42]. In this task participants are asked to sketch as many real objects as possible incorporating a circle.

We chose Guilford's Alternative Uses Task [19] and the Torrance Test of Creativity Circles [42], because they have been extensively developed and validated as a measure of ability to generate ideas in hundreds of studies on creativity over the past 30 years [31].

Amazon Mechanical Turk

To create a dataset of affect-laden images and to carry out our first experiment, we made use of Amazon Mechanical Turk. Mechanical Turk is an micro-task market where people, referred to as Turkers, use the web to complete one or more small tasks in exchange for micro-payments that typically range from $0.01 to $0.10 per task. Mechanical Turk has been shown to be an effective platform for crowd-sourcing users studies [29]. Hence, we use Mechanical Turk in our studies, because it provides low recruitment costs and immediate access to hundreds of participants. While limitations of Mechanical Turk do not allow us to verify accurate demographic information of the participants, previous studies [22, 36, 40] have reported that the demographics of Mechanical Turkers are similar to typical Internet users, i.e., the majority are between 18-40 years old and slightly more educated than the general US population. The ratio of male to female is 45% to 55%.

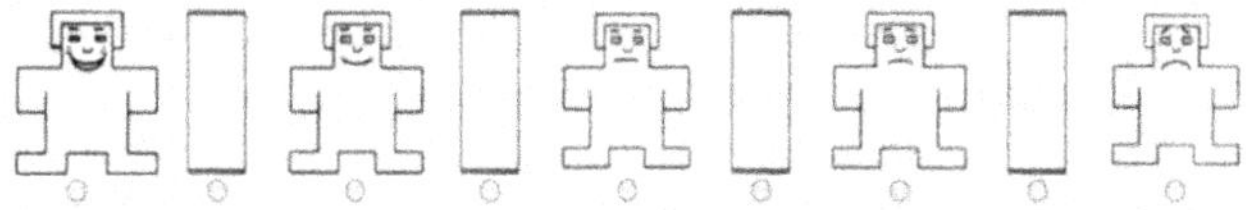

Figure 2. Self-Assessment Manikin [30] used to rate emotion

Affect	Image Description	IAPS Rating Mean (Std. Dev.)	MTurk Rating Mean (Std. Dev.)
Positive	Laughing baby	8.20 (1.31)	8.65 (0.67)
	Puppy	8.34 (1.12)	8.25 (1.16)
	Dessert	7.53 (1.73)	8.15 (1.31)
	Beach	8.22 (1.08)	8.00 (1.62)
	Bunny	7.89 (1.26)	7.90 (1.33)
	Bride	7.64 (1.46)	7.85 (1.46)
	Couple	7.80 (1.55)	7.70 (1.38)
	Mountain lake	7.27 (1.59)	7.45 (1.50)
	Sunflower	7.16 (1.56)	7.45 (1.23)
	Salsa	7.25 (1.83)	7.20 (1.47)
	Mountain top	7.61 (1.46)	6.90 (1.55)
	Athlete	7.09 (1.36)	6.45 (1.57)
Neutral	Cutlery	5.27 (1.09)	6.85 (1.46)
	Shoes	4.82 (1.20)	6.80 (1.70)
	Umbrella	4.72 (1.00)	6.65 (1.57)
	Clothes rack	4.82 (0.99)	6.10 (1.52)
	Stool	4.63 (1.17)	6.00 (1.38)
	File cabinet	4.45 (1.36)	5.90 (1.97)
	Hammer	4.95 (0.87)	5.70 (1.34)
	Factory worker	4.87 (1.06)	5.55 (1.70)
	Secretary	4.72 (1.36)	5.50 (1.43)
	Trashcan	4.43 (1.16)	5.45 (1.73)
Negative	Oil spill	3.89 (1.58)	3.60 (2.16)
	Natural disaster	3.49 (1.87)	3.30 (2.15)
	Medical	3.28 (1.64)	2.80 (1.79)
	Homeless	2.87 (1.28)	2.58 (1.26)
	Dead body	2.78 (1.71)	2.50 (1.79)
	Explosion	1.62 (1.20)	2.45 (1.43)
	Stitches	2.06 (1.23)	2.25 (1.48)
	Deformed	2.26 (1.57)	2.15 (1.53)
	Burn victim	1.79 (1.30)	2.05 (2.19)
	Dead pet	1.97 (1.16)	1.52 (1.10)
	Dead bodies	1.53 (1.25)	1.50 (1.31)

Table 1. We created an image database for our experiments using Mechanical Turk. The Mechanical Turk ratings were consistent with the IAPS database ratings.

Stimuli

To select images that induce positive, neutral, and negative affect, we referenced the International Affective Picture System (IAPS) manual. IAPS is a database of images for experimental investigations of affect [30]. We created our own database of affect-inducing images, because IAPS administrators stipulate that images from the IAPS database cannot be posted on the Internet or shared with anyone outside of the study participants. To create our own dataset, we selected images from iStockphoto.com based on the image descriptions (e.g., "laughing baby") in the IAPS manual and gathered ratings for each image using the 9-point Self-Assessment Manikin (SAM) Scale [30]. Figure 2 shows SAM, which uses graphical figures to depict human emotions ranging from smiling (i.e. happy) to frowning (i.e. unhappy). The blocks between each figure allow participants to indicate if their emotion falls between two figures. After viewing the instructions on how to use SAM, participants were shown an image for five seconds and then asked to *"Select the figure that most closely corresponds to how you felt viewing the previous image"* using SAM. Our rating method is similar to the method used to generate the IAPS affect image ratings.

The main difference between our rating approach and the approach employed by Lang et al. [30] is that we collected ratings using Mechanical Turk, while they collected ratings in a laboratory setting. We collected data for 33 images (12 positive, 10 neutral, 11 negative), and each image received an average of 20 ratings. To validate that the ratings were genuine, we asked participants to complete a validation test. After users rated an image, they were asked to describe the image they were rating and the reasons for their rating. Participants who failed the validation test were excluded from our analysis. Table 1 compares our image ratings to the IAPS database.

EXPERIMENT 1: ALTERNATIVE USES TASK

While our broader goal is to understand the influence of affect on the use of creativity support tools, in our first experiment, we wanted to determine whether affective computational primes have a similar impact as previously studied primes. Thus, for our first experiment, we followed previous experiments and studied an established creativity task, Guilford's Alternative Uses Task. We asked participants to generate unusual uses for two common objects, a brick and a quarter. The brick is frequently used as the object in the unusual uses task, but because we were concerned that participants may use one of the numerous websites that list unusual uses for a brick, we chose to also use a quarter as the object, which to our knowledge has not been used in such experiments.

Participants

We recruited 240 participants from Mechanical Turk that reside in the United States and had successfully completed at least 80% of prior Amazon Mechanical Turk tasks. Participants were either paid $0.05 for completing the brick task or $0.50 for the quarter task. Consistent with previous findings [20], we found that offering people more money did not influence the quality of the data but did influence the rate at which Turkers responded, thereby allowing us to collect data more quickly for the quarter task.

Measures

Researchers have long debated how to best assess creativity in a way that consistently captures the complex dimensions of creativity [35]. The most commonly adopted approach [1, 5, 17] and the one we employ is to ask domain experts to subjectively make scale-rated assessments of creativity. Typically, domain experts rate originality, feasibility, elaboration, and flexibility and count the number of ideas generated [3].

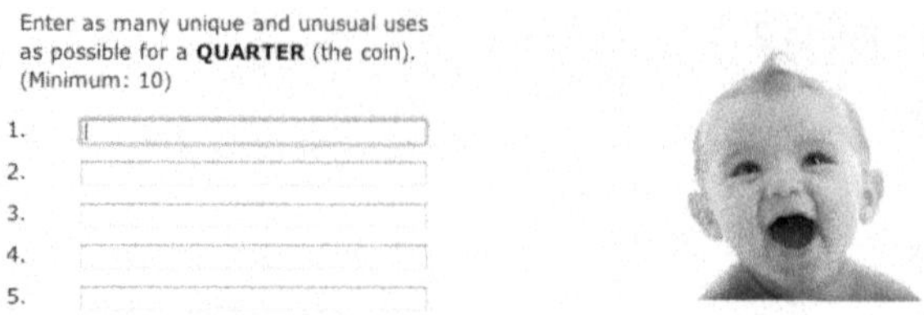

Figure 3. Screenshot of the unusual uses task on Mechanical Turk for the positive condition.

Procedure

Each Turker was assigned to one of four conditions: positive affect, neutral affect, negative affect, and no affect (our baseline). The instructions on completing the task (adopted from [19]) were as follows:

In this task, your goal is to think of as many unique and unusual uses for a common object. For example, using a paper clip as an earring is an unusual and unique use. However, using a paper clip to bind papers is not unique or unusual. Try to think of as many unique and unusual uses as possible. DO NOT use any external sources (e.g., websites, people) to complete this task.

To the right of the instructions was a 350 x 233 pixel image. This image served as the affective computational prime and varied under the different conditions. For the baseline, we did not include an image. We did not provide information about why the image was present. Using our database of affective images, we selected the image with the highest rating (a laughing baby) and the lowest rating (dead bodies after the 2010 earthquake in Haiti) for the positive and negative conditions, respectively. For the neutral condition, we selected the image with a rating closest to the median rating of 5 and with the lowest standard deviation (a hammer).

To proceed, Turkers clicked a next button. They were then presented with a web form (see Figure 3), which asked them to enter as many unique and unusual uses for an object (either a brick or a quarter) as possible. They were required to enter a minimum of 10 responses but had the option of entering up to 20 responses. The affective computational prime remained visible throughout the task.

Each Turker either completed the task for a brick or a quarter, not both. For the brick task, we collected responses from 20 Turkers for each condition (positive, negative, neutral, and baseline). For the quarter task, we collected responses from 40 Turkers for each condition.

Analysis

Out of the 240 total Turkers recruited on Mechanical Turk, we excluded responses from 14 Turkers, because they did not follow directions. The remaining 226 Turkers (75 in the brick task; 151 in the quarter task) produced 2,463 responses (836 for the brick task and 1627 for the quarter task). Though previous studies [20] suggest task completion times provided by Mechanical Turk are unreliable, we note that the average completion time was six minutes.

Creativity

We collected expert ratings for all responses. For the brick task, we collected ratings from two expert raters. Both were members of the research team and each has over 10 years experience as design professionals.

For the quarter task, we collected ratings from three expert raters, who we recruited through an e-mail distribution list of a graduate design program on the west coast in the United States. Two were current design graduate students, who have worked as design professionals for at least 4 years, and the other was an alumni, who had 8 years of experience as a design professional.

All expert raters were blind to the conditions. Inter-rater reliability for the raters of the brick and quarter tasks were Cohen's Kappa = 0.77, 0.68 ($p<0.01$, 0.05) respectively.

We asked the expert raters to rate each response on a scale of 1-5 according to *originality*, *feasibility*, *elaboration*, and *flexibility* [19]. *Originality* refers to how unique the response is as compared to others. *Feasibility* refers to whether the described use is possible. *Elaboration* refers to the amount of detail in a response. *Flexibility* refers to the variety of categories for all of the responses given by a particular participant. For example, the raters rated using a brick as "a doorstop" with 1 for originality because most participants also generated this use for a brick, 5 for feasibility because the use of a brick as a doorstop is feasible, 1 for elaboration because there is minimal detail included in the description of the use, and 5 for flexibility because the participant suggested no other related ideas within their own set of responses. In contrast, the raters rated using a brick "to mark a spot where a treasure is buried" with 4 for originality, 5 for feasibility, 4 for elaboration, and 5 for flexibility because there were no other ideas within the participant's response that were related to using a brick as a marker.

In order to calibrate their ratings, the raters first rated a small subset of the responses and discussed their ratings until they agreed on a strategy for rating. After they reached agreement, the expert raters continued rating their portion of the responses. The brick expert raters each rated approximately 450 responses. The quarter expert raters each rated approximately 600 responses.

Results

Our data suggests that although the effect is not very large, positive affect-laden images positively influence idea generation in both the brick and quarter tasks, validating the influence of affective computational primes on creative performance. We used Welch's t-test to measure significance for all reported findings and report mean ratings (μ) and their standard deviations (σ).

Quality of Ideas

As predicted in Hypothesis 1 and 2, positive affect positively influenced the quality of ideas. For both the brick and quarter tasks, we find that Turkers who were computationally primed to feel positive affect generate ideas rated as more original than those primed for neutral affect. The responses from Turkers primed with positive-laden stimuli were rated as significantly more original (brick: μ=2.76 σ=1.31, quarter: μ=2.76 σ=0.96) than the responses from participants primed to feel no affect in the neutral condition (brick: μ=2.58 σ=1.22, $p<0.04$, quarter: μ=2.56 σ=0.94, $p<0.008$). Surprisingly, the responses from Turkers primed with negative-laden stimuli were also rated as significantly more original (brick: μ=2.85 σ=1.30, quarter: μ=2.71 σ=0.87) than those primed to feel neutral affect (brick: μ=2.58 σ=1.22, $p<0.05$, quarter: μ=2.56 σ=0.94, $p<0.02$).

In the brick task, we find that Turkers who are computationally primed with positive affect generate ideas rated as significantly more original (μ=2.76 σ=1.30) than those who are not computationally primed (μ=2.54 σ=1.32, $p<0.02$). Additionally, Turkers who were computationally primed for negative affect in the brick task also generate ideas that were rated as significantly more original (μ=2.85 σ=1.30) than those who are not computationally primed (μ=2.54 σ=1.32 $p<0.03$).

In the quarter task, we did not find significant differences between the positive and baseline conditions. Additional data is needed to understand this difference between the brick and quarter tasks.

In both tasks, we did not find significant differences in the feasibility, elaboration, and flexibility ratings.

Quantity of Ideas

We did not find significant differences in the number of ideas generated between the positive, neutral, negative, and baseline conditions (Hypothesis 1 and 2).

EXPERIMENT 2: CREATIVITY SUPPORT TOOLS

The goal of the second experiment was to examine how computationally primed affect influences creativity with an existing creativity support tool. Since creativity support tools on the desktop can be complex, for our experimental platform, we selected a simple sketching application (Adobe Ideas) on a tablet (iPad). We felt the tablet was a particularly useful platform to explore, as creative professionals are increasingly using tablets to generate and capture ideas.

Participants

We recruited 31 participants (12 women) through email distribution lists at a small college and medium-size software company located on the west coast of the United States. Data from four participants was removed (2 did not follow instructions, 2 were familiar with the task prior to the study). The remaining 27 participants (9 women) ranged in age (24-56 years old) and occupation (engineers, designers, managers, IT specialists, and marketing professionals). Two participants owned or had extensive experience using a tablet PC. Four participants had used Adobe Ideas prior to the study. Participants were given $20 gift cards for their participation.

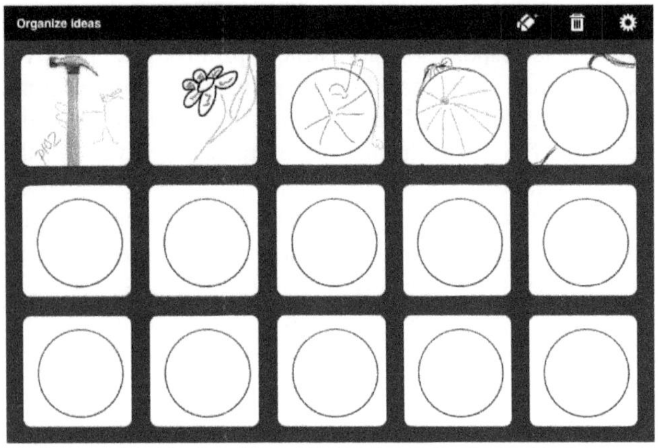

Figure 4. This screenshot shows a portion of the screen for a completed circles task in the neutral condition. The participants were given 20 circles as part of the task.

Stimuli

To induce positive, neutral, and negative affect, we used the same images as in Experiment 1.

Measures

Creativity. Expert raters assessed originality, elaboration, and flexibility and counted the number of sketches generated by each participant.

Procedure

The participants were randomly assigned to one of the four conditions: positive affect, neutral affect, negative affect, and no affect (baseline). Each study session included two to four participants.

First, the participants completed a web survey on the iPad that included measures for creative efficacy [41] and confidence levels using a tablet (adapted from [10]) as well as basic demographic information. The study moderator then led the participants through a brief tutorial on how to use the sketching software including information about how to draw, erase, scale, undo, and change the color/size of the pen. After participants confirmed that they felt comfortable using the tool, their mood was accessed using the SAM mood rating. Participants in the positive, neutral, and negative conditions were told about an additional feature of the software, which allows images to be used as a background for a drawing. They were instructed on how to insert an image in their drawing from the photo library. Each participant's library depended on the condition to which they were assigned. The participants in the positive condition had a library that included only positive affect-inducing images, while participants in the negative condition saw only negative affect-inducing images in their photo library.

Participants were told to select the photo of the laughing baby in the positive condition, the photo of the hammer in the neutral condition, and the photo of the dead bodies in Haiti in the negative condition. Participants in the baseline condition were not told how to embed images in the background of a drawing. After drawing on the embedded image for approximately one minute, the participants were told it was time to start the study. We replicated one of the Torrance Creative Thinking Tests [42], the circles task. The participants were given the following written and verbal instructions.

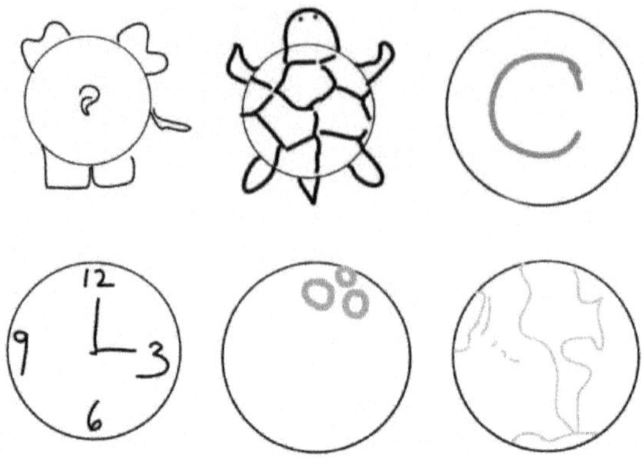

Figure 5. Sketches of an elephant, a turtle, and a copyright sign (top) received high originality ratings, while sketches of a clock, bowling ball, and globe received low originality ratings (bottom).

"For the next 5 minutes, draw as many sketches as you can using the circles provided. Avoid drawing abstract sketches. Be sure to use the circles as a part of the picture (not just a border around a picture).

1. *Draw as many sketches as possible.*
2. *Make the sketches as unusual or different as you can.*
3. *Quality (or "prettiness") doesn't matter.*

The participants were given 20 circles as part of the task (see Figure 4) and after five minutes they were asked to stop. In contrast to Experiment 1, the participants only saw the affect-laden images during the tutorial and not during the sketching task. After completing the task, participants were again asked to complete the SAM affect survey. They were asked if they had ideas about the reason for the study. Only two indicated that they had previous knowledge of the task (data from these participants was removed).

Analysis

We collected 226 sketches with 72 from the positive condition, 56 from the neutral, 46 from the negative, and 52 from those who were not primed.

One expert rater who was blind to the conditions rated the originality, elaboration, and flexibility of all the sketches. A second rater rated 10% of the sketches, and since the inter-rater reliability between the two raters was high (Cohen's Kappa=0.83 $p<0.001$), we used ratings from the first rater. Both raters were members of the research team. Figure 5 shows sketches with high and low originality ratings.

Condition	Total Participants	0-2 *Creative* Sketches	3-5 *Creative* Sketches	6-8 *Creative* Sketches
Baseline	7	4	3	0
Negative	6	2	4	0
Neutral	7	2	4	1
Positive	7	0	3	4

Table 2. The distribution of participants with respect to the number of *creative* sketches they generated.

Results

Our results indicate that positive affect positively influences the quality (originality and elaboration) of ideas generated. The results did not show any correlation to the age, gender, or occupation of the participants; nor was previous experience using tablets or Adobe Ideas related to the results.

Quality of ideas - Originality

As predicted in Hypothesis 1, people primed to feel positive affect generated sketches rated as significantly more original ($\mu=2.65$ $\sigma=1.2$) than those primed to feel negative affect ($\mu=2.15$ $\sigma=1.13$, $p<0.02$).

As predicted in Hypothesis 2, people primed to feel positive affect created sketches rated as significantly more original ($\mu=2.65$ $\sigma=1.2$) than those who were not primed ($\mu=2.03$ $\sigma=1.12$, $p<0.001$).

We also found that those in the neutral condition generated sketches rated as significantly more original ($\mu=2.66$ $\sigma=1.18$) than those in the negative ($\mu=2.15$ $\sigma=1.13$) and baseline ($\mu=2.03$ $\sigma=1.12$) conditions (p-value<0.02, 0.001, respectively).

In a deeper analysis, we examined the distribution of originality ratings for the drawings of each participant. Specifically, we calculated the number of sketches that were rated 3 or above (on a 5-point scale with 5 being extremely original) for each participant. For the rest of this discussion, we refer to sketches with an originality rating of 3 or above as *creative*. Table 2 shows the distribution of *creative* sketches per person across the four conditions.

Those primed to feel positive affect generated the most *creative* sketches. All participants in the positive condition generated at least 3 *creative* sketches. In fact, four out of seven of the participants in the positive condition created between 6 and 8 *creative* sketches. In contrast, in the baseline condition four out of seven participants created between 0 and 2 *creative* sketches. Although we did not see big differences between the number of participants who had *creative* sketches in the neutral and negative conditions, we suspect that a larger sample will illustrate that negative affect leads to fewer participants with *creative* sketches than neutral affect.

Figure 6. Example of a sketch with a low elaboration rating (left) and a sketch with a high elaboration rating (right).

Quality of Ideas - Elaboration

In addition to differences in originality, we observed differences in the amount of elaboration per condition (see Figure 6). Consistent with past research, we find that positive affect expands the number of cognitive elements associated with a task, supporting elaboration. Those primed for positive affect were more likely to elaborate ($\mu=2.67$ $\sigma=0.96$) than those primed for negative affect ($\mu=2.04$ $\sigma=0.69$) and those who were not primed ($\mu=2.13$ $\sigma=0.95$, p-value<0.001, 0.001, respectively). As shown in Figure 6, elaboration includes drawing additional elements, such as bananas and apples, in addition to the primary response, the orange.

Those in the neutral condition ($\mu=2.49$ $\sigma=1.00$) also elaborated on their sketches significantly more than those in the negative ($\mu=2.04$ $\sigma=0.69$) and baseline ($\mu=2.13$ $\sigma=0.95$) condition (p-value < 0.01, 0.04, respectively).

Quantity of Ideas

People primed to feel positive affect created more sketches ($\mu=10.29$ $\sigma=4.27$) than those primed to feel negative ($\mu=7.66$ $\sigma=3.27$) and neutral ($\mu=8.00$ $\sigma=4.12$) affect as well as those who were not primed ($\mu=7.43$ $\sigma=2.76$). Although the differences are not significant ($p<0.21$ for negative, $p<0.25$ for neutral, $p<0.15$ for baseline), there are trends that suggest that people in the positive condition may generate a larger quantity of sketches. While this result is consistent with research that finds that positive affect influences persistence and performance [8, 9], more data is needed to verify these trends.

DISCUSSION

Consistent with past research on affect and creativity [23] we found that positive affect positively influences the quality of ideas generated when using a creativity support tool. Psychology researchers reason that positive affect leads to improved creative performance by increasing the number of cognitive elements available for processing and association as well as by broadening attention to those elements treated as relevant to the problem [23] and supporting goal-setting, expectancy, and persistence during a task [13]. Somewhat surprisingly, in Experiment 2 we also found that neutral affect also has a positive influence on the quality of ideas generated, while negative affect is indistinguishable from the baseline condition. This implies that the effect is not due to the presence of images but is tied to the content of the image. Although the mean creativity ratings for the neutral and positive are similar, the distribution of creative sketches across participants for the two conditions is quite different; hence, we suspect that the positive-laden prime may have a stronger effect. We plan to study this further in future work.

Also, in Experiment 1 we unexpectedly found that negative affect also positively influences creative performance. While most experimental studies of affect find a positive relationship between experimentally induced positive affect and creative performance, a few studies find that both positive and negative affect support creativity. Kaufmann and Vosburg [28] suggest that positive affect supports a satisficing solution strategy and negative affect supports an optimizing solution strategy, both of which are useful for creative problem solving. We suspect that the nature of the platform may influence the effect of negative primes. People may be less sensitive to negative primes on the web, because they commonly see such images through news and entertainment channels, while negatively-laden images are uncommon in design applications.

Our experiments employed two different types of computational primes: passive and active. In Experiment 1, the computational primes were embedded as background images and user interactions with the primes were passive, as we did not force any direct user interaction with the images. On the other hand, in Experiment 2, the computational primes were part of instructional tutorials, and the participants were asked to draw on top of the images, thereby actively engaging with the primes. The active computational priming technique offers a higher guarantee that the user sees the affect-laden image; but users may not actively engage in such an instructional tutorial before every use. We suspect that active affective computational primes may have a stronger impact on creativity; however, more research is necessary to confirm this hypothesis.

Collectively, our findings demonstrate that affective computational primes, or interaction embedded stimuli, influence technology use. To our knowledge, this is the first investigation to demonstrate this effect. While web-based companies are increasingly using A-B testing to make small manipulations that improve their websites, it is not always understood how and why such design changes influence behavior. We provide a theoretical explanation and empirical demonstration of how affect could serve as a mechanism for influencing human-computer interaction.

Design Implications for Creativity Support Tools

Since our data shows that computationally primed positive affect positively influences the quality of ideas generated during creativity tasks, designers of creativity support tools should consider the affective influences of all materials associated with tools including startup screens, background images, sample material, and learning content. To test for the affective nature of materials, designers can make use of crowd-sourcing platforms such as Mechanical Turk.

Furthermore, given reported practices regarding multi-tasking [11], it is quite possible that users are engaged with multiple applications at once and may be influenced by them. For example, reading the news or answering email while engaging in a creative task may have an unanticipated influence on a user's creativity. Therefore, designers of creativity support tools should consider ways to reengage users after task switching during a creative task.

Since a link between affect, goal-setting, expectancy, and persistence has been established by others [9, 13] and demonstrated in our experiments, affect-laden primes may offer a technique for re-engaging users when productivity declines. Alternatively, affect may also be useful as a consideration for adaptive user interface models that not only predict user needs in order to optimize productivity, but also offer affect-appropriate suggestions. Including affect in computational models is part of research in affective computing, which aims to understand how computers can be more emotionally intelligent to reduce people's negative emotions [34].

LIMITATIONS

As other scholars have acknowledged [35], there are concerns with using expert raters to assess creativity, as their ratings can be subjective and ultimately taint the results. While we are satisfied with inter-rater reliability and reliance on extensive and established means for rating creativity, we intend to consider crowd-sourcing creativity ratings to acquire aggregate creativity ratings rather than relying on the opinions of a few raters.

Although Amazon Mechanical Turk has many benefits to researchers, because it is a low cost, low time commitment, and short turnaround platform, it may not be the best platform for creativity studies. There are two factors that had an impact on our experiments. First, because the platform is web-based, Turkers have access to other resources and can readily turn to the Web to search for answers. Guilford's Unusual Uses Task (Experiment 1) is commonly done with a brick, and there are a number of websites with solutions. This makes it difficult to evaluate whether a participant generated all of the responses or copied some or all of them from external sources. Second, creativity is linked to domain expertise, which increases over time [1], but Turkers are not incentivized to spend a long time completing a task, but rather to complete many small tasks quickly in order to make more money. It remains to be seen whether crowd-sourcing platforms are environments appropriate for creative tasks.

FUTURE RESEARCH

Our study suggests a number of areas for future research. First, we plan to explore different techniques for integrating affective computational primes into existing creativity support tools. Affective images, for example, could be placed on the start-up screen or help menu of a creativity support tool. Other stimuli that could be manipulated to induce affect include colors, textures, and sound. For example, a computational prime for a search tool might involve affect-laden search icons. Additionally, many software programs currently include videos in tutorials that instruct users on new features. Videos may turn out to be stronger primes because they stimulate both the visual and auditory senses.

Affect has been shown to influence user behavior in other domains beyond creativity. Affect has been empirically related to the evaluation of others [6], risk-taking [26], negotiation skills [7], and helping behavior [16]. Affective computational priming may be useful in human resource software, project management and decision-making software, and browser and search interfaces.

In addition to affect, computational primes can be used to induce a variety of mental states that influence behavior. While this study focuses on priming affect, we can imagine computationally priming for things such as power [18], individualism, and collectivism, which have all been shown to influence subsequent behavior.

Another area for future research is examining the length of time in which computational primes influence behavior. Previous findings suggest that experimentally induced affect may last up to 30 minutes [33]. Therefore, we might consider how to effectively schedule the use of computational primes in technology. Future research may not only explore the limits of the duration of computational priming in technology use but also consider ways to computationally prime users the entire time a tool is used.

CONCLUSION

Affect influences how people feel, think, and act. For this reason, as HCI researchers and designers, it is imperative that we understand the role of affect on the use of technology, which people use to complete their daily work. Although this study focused on the role of affect and creativity tool use in response to a grand challenge posed to the HCI community [37], we see this as a small window into a wealth of opportunities for the human-computer interaction community to understand users and design technology through the lens of affect and behavior. Thirty years ago, by considering the cognitive functioning of users, HCI researchers expanded the understanding of technology from functionality to usability. Now, by integrating an understanding of affective functioning into HCI, we have the opportunity to further advance HCI for increased acceptance, use, and performance. We suggest that understanding how to design technologies such that they mesh with affective functioning is the next critical step for the HCI community. Ultimately, as HCI designers, we will design systems that respond to human affective, cognitive, and behavioral processes.

ACKNOWLEDGEMENTS

We thank our study participants and expert raters for their time. We especially thank Wendy Ju for helping with participant recruitment. We would also like to thank our reviewers, Joel Brandt, Jeremy Barksdale, and Kyla McMullen for their insightful comments on previous versions of this paper. We appreciate the input received from Adobe's Creative Technologies Lab, Scott Klemmer, and Don Norman on this work. The first author is supported by the National Science Foundation Graduate Research Fellowship.

REFERENCES

1. Amabile, T. *Creativity in Context*. Westview Press, Boulder, CO, 1996.
2. Amabile, T. The social psychology of creativity: A componential conceptualization. *Journal of Personality and Social Psychology*, *45*, 357-376 (1983).
3. Amabile, T. Social psychology of creativity: A consensual assessment technique. *Journal of Personality and Social Psychology*, *43*, 5 (1982), 997-1013.
4. Amabile, T., Barsade, S., Mueller, J. and Staw, B. Affect and Creativity at Work. *Administrative Science Quarterly*, *50* (2005), 367-403.
5. Bao, P., Gerber, E., Gergle, D. and Hoffman, D. Momentum: getting and staying on topic during a brainstorm. In *Proc. CHI 2010*, ACM (2010), 1233-1236.
6. Cardy, R.L. and Dobbins, G.H. Affect and appraisal accuracy: Liking as an integratl dimension in evaluating performance. *Journal of Applied Psychology*, *71* (1986), 672-678.
7. Carnevale, P. and Isen, A. The influence of positive affect and visual access on the discovery of integrative solutions in bilateral negoation. *Organizational Behavior and Human Decision Processes*, *37* (1986), 1-13.
8. Carver, C. and Scheier, M. Origins and functions of positive and negative affect: a control-process view. *Psychological Review*, *97* (1990), 19-35.
9. Clore, G. Why emotions are felt. in Ekman, P. and Davidson, R. eds. *The nature of emotion: fundamental questions*, Oxford University Press, New York, 1994, 103-111.
10. Compeau, D. and Higgins, C.A. Computer Self-Efficacy: Development of a Measure and Initial Test. *MIS Quarterly*, *19*, 2 (1995), 189-211.
11. Czerwinski, M., Horvitz, E. and Wilhite, S. A diary study of task switching and interruptions. In *Proc. CHI 2004*, ACM (2004), 175-182.
12. Duncker, K. On problem solving. *Psychological Monographs*, *58*, 5 (1945), Whole No. 270.
13. Erez, A. and Isen, A.M. The influence of positive affect on the components of expectancy motivation. *Journal of Applied Psychology*, *87*, 6 (2002), 1055-1067.

14. Estrada, C., Isen, A. and Young, M. Positive affect improves creative problem solving and influences reported source of practice satisfaciton in physicians. *Motivation and Emotion*, *18*, 4 (1994), 285-299.

15. Frederickson, B. What good are postive emotions? *Review of General Psychology*, *2* (1998), 300-319.

16. George, J. and Brief, A. Feeling good-doing good: A conceptual analysis of the mood at work - organizational spontaneity. *Psychological Bulletin*, *112* (1992), 310-329.

17. George, J. and Zhou, J. Understanding when bad mood fosters creativity and good ones don't: The role of context and clarity of feelings. *Journal of Applied Psychology*, *87* (2002), 687-697.

18. Gerber, E. and Lewis, S. Priming Approach Behavior in Mobile Devices. Northwestern University, (2010), Technical Report No.: NWU-DSGN-11-02.

19. Guilford, J.P. *The Nature of Human Intelligence*. McGraw-Hill, New York, 1967.

20. Heer, J. and Bostock, M. Crowdsourcing graphical perception: using mechanical turk to assess visualization design. In *Proc. CHI 2010*, ACM (2010), 203-212.

21. Hewett, T., Czerwinski, M., Terry, M., Nunamaker, J., Candy, L., Kules, B. and Sylvan, E. Creativity Support Tool Evaluation Methods and Metrics. In *Creativity Support Tools: A workshop sponsored by the National Science Foundation* (2005), 10-24.

22. Ipeirotis, P.G., Provost, F. and Wang, J. Quality management on Amazon Mechanical Turk. In *Proc. ACM SIGKDD Workshop on Human Computation*, ACM (2010), 64-67.

23. Isen, A. Positive Affect. in Dalgleish, T. and Power, M. eds. *The Handbook of Cognition and Emotion*, Wiley, New York, 1999, 521-539.

24. Isen, A., Daubman, K. and Nowicki, G.P. Positive affect facilitates creative problem solving. *Journal of Personality and Social Psychology*, *52* (1987), 1122-1131.

25. Isen, A., Johnson, M., Mertz, E. and Robinson, G. The influence of positive affect on the unusualness of word associations. *Journal of Personality and Social Psychology*, *48* (1985), 1413-1426.

26. Isen, A., Nygren, T. and Ashby, G. The influence of positive affect on subjective utility of gains and losses: It's not worth the risk. *Journal of Personality and Social Psychology*, *55*, 710-717 (1988).

27. Izard, C.E. *Human Emotions*. Plenum Press, New York, 1977.

28. Kauffman, G. and Vosburg, S. The Effects of Mood on Early and Late Idea Production. *Creativity Research Journal*, *14*, 3 (2002), 317-330.

29. Kittur, A., Chi, E.H. and Suh, B. Crowdsourcing user studies with Mechanical Turk. In *Proc. CHI 2008*, ACM (2008), 453-456.

30. Lang, P., Bradley, M., Cuthbert, B. International Affective Picture System: Affective ratings of pictures and instruction manual, NIMH Center for the Study of Emotion & Attention, University of Florida, 2008.

31. Lee, K., C. K. and Cassidy, T. Principles of design leadership for industrial design teams in Taiwan. *Design Studies*, *10*, 16 (2007), 1-26.

32. Mednick, M.T., Mednick, S.A. and Mednick, E.V. Incubation of creative performance and specific associative priming. *Journal of Abnormal and Social Psychology*, *69*, 84-88 (1964).

33. Morris, W. *Mood: The frame of mind*. Springer-Verlag, New York, 1989.

34. Picard, R. *Affective computing*. The MIT Press, 2000.

35. Puccio, G. and Murdock, M. *Creativity Assessment: Readings and Resources*. Creative Education Foundation, Buffalo, NY, 1999.

36. Ross, J., Irani, L., Silberman, M.S., Zaldivar, A. and Tomlinson, B. Who are the crowdworkers?: shifting demographics in mechanical turk. In *Proc. Ext. Abstracts CHI 2010*, ACM (2010), 2863-2872.

37. Shneiderman, B. (ed.), *Creativity Support Tools: A Grand Challenge for HCI Researchers*, London, 2009.

38. Shneiderman, B., Fischer, G., Czerwinski, M., Resnick, M., Myers, B., Candy, L., Edmonds, E., Eisenberg, M., Giaccardi, E., Hewett, T., Jennings, P., Kules, B., Nakakoji, K., Nunamaker, J., Pausch, R., Selker, T., Sylvan, E. and Terry, M. Creativity Support Tools: Report From a U.S. National Science Foundation Sponsored Workshop. *International Journal of Human-Computer Interaction*, *20*, 2 (2006), 61-77.

39. Simonton, D.K. *Origins of Genius: Darwinian Perspective on Creativity*. Oxford University Press, New York, 1999.

40. Slepian, M., Weisbuch, M., Rutchick, A., Newman, L. and Ambady, N. Shedding light on insight: Priming bright Ideas. *Journal of Experimental Social Psychology*, *46* (2010), 696-700.

41. Tierney, P. and Farmer, S. Creative self-efficacy: potential antecedents: Potential antecedents and relationship to creative performance. *Academy of Management Journal*, *45* (2002), 1137-1148.

42. Torrance, E.P. *Torrance Tests of Creative Thinking*. Scholastic Testing Services, 1974.

43. Zajonc, R.B. Feeling and thinking: Preferences need no inferences. *American Psychologist*, *35*, 2 (1980), 151-175.

Upset Now?: Emotion Contagion in Distributed Groups

Jamie Guillory, Jason Spiegel, Molly Drislane, Benjamin Weiss,
Walter Donner, & Jeffrey T. Hancock
Cornell University
306 Kennedy Hall, Ithaca, New York, USA contact author: jeg258@cornell.edu

ABSTRACT
The importance of emotion to group outcomes in FtF highlights the need to understand emotion contagion in distributed groups. The present study examines the transfer of negative emotion in online groups. Negative emotion was induced in one of three group members completing a task in CMC. The data suggest that emotion contagion took place at the group level, with partners experiencing more negative emotion, more disagreement, higher verbosity, and use of more complex language in induced groups compared to control groups. Induced groups also performed better on the group task, raising questions about the effects of negative emotion contagion in online groups.

Author Keywords
Computer-mediated communication, affect, group, emotion.

ACM Classification Keywords
J4 Social and behavioral sciences: Psychology
Experimentation

General Terms: Experimentation

INTRODUCTION
Distributed groups are an integral part of interaction in modern society. Groups interacting via text-based media can experience misunderstandings and destructive behaviors stemming from differences in location and a lack of cues available face-to-face (FtF) [1]. Current systems have limitations in conveying interpersonal emotions (i.e.,emotions arising via interaction between people), despite their importance in affecting group outcomes [2][3].

One emotional phenomenon that has recently been of interest in text-based communication is emotion contagion, a process by which group members influence the emotions or behavior of other members via conscious or unconscious transfer of emotions, behaviors and attitudes. Shared emotion can lead to increased levels of cooperation, performance and lower levels of conflict in groups, which makes understanding how emotions operate in text-based contexts especially important [3].

Previous research shows that when one member of a FtF group experiences a particular emotion it can lead the other members of the group to experience the same emotion [3].Emotion contagion is much less understood in text-based CMC. One study demonstrates contagion of sadness between dyads in CMC [4], showing that contagion is possible in text-based communication, and that non-verbal cues available FtF are not essential for contagion to occur.

Many questions about contagion in textual interaction remain. First, does contagion scale up from dyadic to group levels? Research suggests that as the number of communicators in an interaction increases, individual group members' contributions diminish [5]. The diffusion of attention required for group conversation combined with fewer contributions may inhibit emotion contagion. The escalation of negative emotions in text-based online groups is well-known (e.g., flame wars), especially to moderators who facilitate online groups (e.g., newsgroups, blog comments, email lists). However, the dynamics of how emotions spread in group communication online are surprisingly poorly understood, especially from a contagion perspective.

A second issue is the very limited nature of the emotions studied in text-based CMC (i.e., mildly positive [6] or negative emotions [4]). Mild emotions are not of much interest to the moderator trying to manage an online group, for example. Instead, highly arousing emotions, such as anger or fear, have the most potential for disrupting or motivating online group communication. How do these high-energy emotions, which are more visible and potentially elicit greater amounts of attention, propagate emotion contagion in online groups?

To address these questions, we build on previous work on contagion in text-based CMC [4] by examining the spread of negative emotions, especially those that are characterized as being high arousal and negative (e.g., anger, tension, fear, etc.), within groups performing a problem-solving task in text-based CMC. Consistent with emotion contagion, our first hypothesis is:

H1: When one person in a group experiences negative emotion the rest of the group will report feeling more negative emotion compared to control group members.

Another dimension of interest to this study is the cues related to emotional expression and detection online. Earlier work suggests that nonverbal cues are essential for sharing emotion given that ostentatious displays of emotion are discouraged and expression via more subtle, physical cues is preferred [7]. Despite this assumption, some argue that relationships developed exclusively online can reach the same level of closeness as FtF over time [8].

Emotion appears to be detectable linguistically in text-based communication via word choice, word count, punctuation, and timing [6]. Experience of sadness in text-based CMC is related to the use of fewer words, more disagreement, and slower response times compared to happiness [4][6]. These cues were sufficient for detection of emotion by partners, who recognized sadness in a partner induced with sadness after a short interaction [4]. Studies in negotiation settings also show that people who experience more conflict and negative emotion use more discrepancy words, which are indicative of disagreement [9][10]. We expect that more intense emotions should be detectable linguistically as well in a group interaction. Based on findings from previous studies, we predict the following:

H2: Groups sharing negative emotion will use more negative affect words and disagree more often compared to control group members

Though previous research showed that inducing sadness led to the use of fewer words and less punctuation in text-based CMC [4], we believe that higher arousal negative emotion will lead to the use of more words and punctuation, which is associated with talkativeness and verbal fluency [11]. Because the experience of negative emotion in groups is often associated with group conflict, groups experiencing negative emotion and conflict should spend more time negotiating the group task, engaging in more group discussion, thus:

H3: Groups sharing negative emotion will use more words and more punctuation than control group members.

A final question relates to group performance. Previous work suggests that negative emotion leads to group conflict, while positive emotion elicits cooperation and higher performance [3]. This work focused primarily on valence, failing to assess the nature of specific emotions' intensity. Research on stress and performance demonstrates that people perform better at moderate stress levels, suggesting that an emotion's energy level may also impact performance [12], thus we propose the following question:

RQ1: How will groups sharing negative emotion differ in performance compared to control group members?

METHODS

Participants

The participants (*N*= 84, 47 females) were students who received class credit or $10 for their participation and ranged in age from 18 to 26 years. Participants signed up in groups of three friends. Sixteen groups (10 same-sex) were randomly assigned to the *negative emotion* group and twelve groups (7 same-sex) were randomly assigned to the *neutral* group.

Procedure

Phase I: After being assigned to one of the two group types, participants were led to separate rooms and told that they would be participating in two unrelated studies, the first being a "perceptions of film" study. Participants then watched a 7-minute video clip. In the *negative emotion* groups, one participant (the *experiencer*) was randomly assigned to view a clip from the film *My Bodyguard* depicting instances of bullying and injustice that reliably induces anger and other negative emotions [13]. The other two *partners* watched a clip from *Before Sunset,* a neutral film chosen to have no effect on affect [4]. In the *neutral* condition, all three participants watched the *Before Sunset* clip.

After watching clips, participants in all conditions and roles filled out a questionnaire measuring emotion with the full Positive And Negative Affect Schedule (PANAS) [14], which asked about feelings on a 7-point Likert scale for twenty affect words (e.g., hostile, guilty, inspired, etc.). A negative affect factor was created using all negative PANAS items (Cronbach's □= .91) and an intense, negative affect factor using a subset of higher arousal, negative PANAS items (Cronbach's □= .92) were created.

Phase II: All participants were then informed that they would begin the next study on multi-tasking in CMC, which would involve text-based chatting, listening to music and solving word scrambles. Their main task was to chat with group members via AOL IM to generate a list of "3 Tips for Surviving Freshman Year." To motivate discussion of personal experiences, each tip was to be accompanied by an example of the tip's personal relevance. The manipulation was presented as a study on how multiple stimuli affect group productivity. As a performance incentive, participants were told that the group with the best tips would be awarded $20 gift certificates.

In the *negative emotion* groups the *experiencer* simultaneously listened to loud, abrasive heavy metal music and completed word scrambles that solved to words with an anger-related prime (e.g., limaec > malice) to maintain the affect induction. *Partners* and all *neutral* group participants listened to light jazz music and completed word scrambles that solved to neutral primes (e.g., ldbna > bland).

Following the task, participants in all conditions and roles filled out a second questionnaire measuring their emotional state on a 7-point likert scale using all affect words from Russell's Circumplex Affect Scale [15]. This affect scale was used in place of PANAS to prevent participants from discovering that the two phases of the experiment were part of the same study. Participants were also questioned about perceptions of group members' performance and emotions. Participants were then debriefed and given cookies to ensure that participants in the *negative emotion* groups did not feel negative emotion after the clip and activity.

Linguistic Analyses

The language of group chats was analyzed using the Linguistic Inquiry and Word Count (LIWC) data analysis program [11]. LIWC counts the frequency of a variety of linguistic and psychologically meaningful dimensions. In the present study negative emotion words, discrepancy words, word count, and punctuation were evaluated.

RESULTS AND DISCUSSION

Manipulation Check

The induction of negative emotion with the *My Bodyguard* clip was successful, with no gender effects. *Experiencers* who watched this clip reported having significantly more negative emotion on the PANAS ($M = 2.21$, $SE = .12$) than participants who watched the neutral clip ($M = 1.20$, $SE = .06$), $F(1, 71.64) = 55.32$, $p < .001$. Analysis with the higher arousal, negative emotion factor also revealed that *experiencers* demonstrated more negative emotions ($M = 2.43$, $SE = .14$) than participants who watched the neutral clip ($M = 1.22$, $SE = .07$), $F(1, 71.73) = 66.01$, $p < .001$.

Emotion contagion

A series of linear mixed models nesting participants within their group were used to test the hypotheses and research question. H1 predicted that the induced emotion of the *experiencer* would be shared via emotion contagion with the rest of the group. If this was the case, *partners* who interacted with *experiencers* in the *negative emotion* groups should report more negative emotion than participants in *neutral* groups. Descriptive data are in Table 1. Comparing only *partners* to the *neutral* groups revealed that *partners* reported being significantly more tense than *neutral* group members, $F(1, 21) = 6.96$, $p < .05$. The same negative emotion, tension, was transferred within groups sharing negative emotion, supporting H1. No other significant differences between *partners* and *neutral* groups were observed.

Analyses were also conducted to explore differences in emotions felt between roles and across conditions to see how the emotional induction affected *experiencers, partners* and *neutral* participants differently. *Partners* felt more glad and content than *experiencers,* which may reflect relief from the mental exhaustion of interacting with *experiencers*. *Experiencers* and *partners* also felt more alarmed than *neutral* participants, reflecting the increased arousal elicited by interaction with a participant induced with negative emotion (see Table 1).

	Negative Emotion		Control
Emotion	**Experiencer**	**Partner**	**All Members**
Tense	1.81^{a} (.26)	1.64^{a} (.17)	1.18^{b} (.06)
Glad	2.31^{a} (.30)	3.25^{b} (.21)	2.81^{ab} (.18)
Content	2.75^{a} (.23)	3.54^{b} (.19)	3.39^{ab} (.16)
Alarmed	1.63^{a} (.30)	1.25^{ab} (.13)	1.05^{b} (.04)

Table 1. Post-activity emotion means (standard errors) by role and condition. Comparisons between experiencer, partner and neutral means, specified by lowercase superscripts, are horizontal only. Cell means that do not share a letter differ at p < .05 using Tukey's HSD.

Linguistic Differences

The remaining hypotheses explored whether there would be linguistic differences between *negative emotion* and *neutral* groups. Group transcripts for five groups were lost due to technical difficulties; linguistic analyses include data from the remaining groups. Linguistic analyses are reported at the group level as no linguistic differences were seen within the *negative emotion* condition (see Table 2 for means).

H2 predicted that participants in the *negative emotion* condition would use more negative affect words and disagree more than *neutral* participants. While there were not differences in use of negative emotion words between groups ($F(2, 59) = 1.03$, $p = .36$), differences in the number of discrepancy words used (e.g., should've, wouldn't, need) emerged with *negative emotion* groups using more discrepancy words than *neutral* groups, $F(2, 59) = 6.39$, $p < .01$. Thus H2 was partially supported.

H3, which explored whether *negative emotion* groups used more words and punctuation than *neutral* groups, was partially supported. *Partners* and *experiencers* used more words than *neutral* groups, $F(2, 59) = 3.79$, $p < .05$, but punctuation use did not differ, $F(2, 59) = .64$, $p = .53$. These findings advance our understanding of linguistic expression of emotion by demonstrating that emotional arousal impacts verbosity. While we did not manipulate emotional arousal in the study, former contagion studies using negative emotions considered low in arousal exhibited the opposite pattern, suggesting that the intensity of specific emotions impacts word count.

	Condition		
Category	**Angry**	**Neutral**	***p***
Word Count	229.75 (15.75)	171.03 (13.98)	.03
CogMech	17.68 (.52)	14.10 (.67)	.00
Discrepancy	1.98 (.18)	1.13 (.16)	.00

Table 2. Profiles of emotion across angry and neutral groups.

In addition to our hypothesized findings, we found that participants in *negative emotion* groups used more cognitive mechanism words (e.g., suppose, thought, reasonable, recall) (see Table 2). These words are indicative of more complex language and are used more frequently in complex sections of texts (e.g., discussion sections of research articles) [11]. Negative moods (compared to positive moods) guide cognitive processing by narrowing people's attention and encouraging more analytical thinking [16], suggesting higher levels of task focus in the *negative emotion* groups.

Group Performance

RQ1 explored whether *negative emotion* groups performed better on the task than *neutral* groups. Participants' task sheets were rated by two independent coders for practicality and overall quality (Krippendorf's □= .77; .86). *Negative emotion* groups were rated higher in their tips' practicality ($M = 4.33$; $SE = .18$) and marginally higher in their tips' overall quality ($M = 3.98$; $SE = .19$) than *neutral* groups ($M = 3.78$; $SE = .21$; $M = 3.50$; $SE = .22$; $F(1, 26) = 4.10$, $p = .05$; $F(1, 26) = 2.71$, $p = .11$). The findings parallel research suggesting that performance is optimal at moderate stress levels, while too much or too little stress negatively impacts performance [10]. While more research is required, the data suggest emotional intensity as well as valence, influence performance [3].

Perception of Group Members

Did participants perceive differences in emotionality of their partners? No significant differences within or between groups in perceived emotion of group members, ratings of closeness to group members, or task performance of group members were observed, suggesting that participants were unaware of differences with respect to emotions or behaviors. No gender differences emerged.

The fact that emotional differences were felt individually, but not detected in fellow group members, indicates that the emotion contagion observed here takes place at a level below awareness. Further, the nature of the emotion contagion was not simply one to one. While *experiencers* reported feeling more frustration and annoyance, their partners did not. Instead, *experiencers* and *partners* felt more tension than *neutral* participants. The expression of frustration and annoyance may be socially inappropriate [7] and *experiencers* appeared to try to hold back these emotions. Indeed, negative emotion words were not used more frequently by *experiencers* than *neutral* participants, suggesting 1) restraint on the part of *experiencers,* and 2) that emotion contagion does not simply spread via emotion-related words.

CONCLUSION

Though researchers in affective computing have made strides in designing systems that convey emotion in text-based settings, these systems have limitations in sharing interpersonal emotions [2]. The present study demonstrates that despite these limitations interpersonal emotions can be shared in distributed groups via linguistic cues.

The present work also highlights the importance of the intensity of specific emotions in understanding the way that emotions impact text-based communication and suggests that the process of emotion contagion in this setting is more complex than previously thought. The finding that *negative emotion* groups exhibited higher performance than *neutral* groups is of particular interest, given that previous studies in FtF contexts exhibited similar effects with positive emotion [3]. Arousal associated with a shared emotion's intensity may provide a plausible explanation for performance differences, but future work must tease apart effects of an emotion's intensity and valence on performance as both factors were held constant in this study.

In terms of practical significance, findings from this study are particularly important for anyone who must manage or facilitate online, chat-based groups that deal with intense emotional topics, such as moderators of support groups, managers of blogs, and even listserv administrators. Indeed, users and designers of text-based communication spaces should consider the power of emotions in textual communication given the dominant assumption that emotion cannot be expressed without nonverbal cues. Lastly, these findings are useful for distributed group members who should be cognizant of the potential influence of fellow group members' emotions, even when those emotions are not directly perceptible.

ACKNOWLEDGEMENTS

This research was supported by NSF Grant 0904822 awarded to Hancock. The authors are also grateful to students in Comm 4500 – Language and Technology class.

REFERENCES

1. Bazarova, N. N. and Walther, J. B. (2009). Attribution of blame in distributed groups. In P. Lutgen-Sandvik & B. Davenport-Sypher eds., *The Destructive Side of Organizational Communication: Processes, Consequences, and Constructive Ways of Organizing*. Routledge/LEA, Mahwah, NJ, USA, 252-266.
2. Parkinson, B. (1995). *Ideas and realities of emotion*. Routledge, London, UK.
3. Barsade, S.G. (2002). The ripple effect: Emotion contagion and its influence on group behavior. *Admin Sci Quart, 47* (4), 644 – 675.
4. Hancock, J.T., Gee, K., Ciaccio, K., and Lin, J. M. I'm sad you're sad: Emotion contagion in CMC. In *Proc. CSCW 2008*. ACM Press, 295-298.
5. Valacich, J.S., Wheeler, B.C., Mennecke, B.E. and Wachter, R. (1995). The effects of numerical and logical group size on computer-mediated idea generation. *Org Behavior and Human Decision Processes, 62* (3), 318- 329.
6. Hancock, J.T., Landrigan, C., and Silver, C. Expressing emotion in text-based communication. In *Proc. CHI 2007.* ACM Press, 929 - 932.
7. Mehrabian, A. (1972). *Nonverbal communication*. Aldine-Atherton, Chicago, 1972.
8. Walther, J.B. (1996). Interpersonal effects in computer-mediated interaction: A relational perspective. *Comm. Research, 19* (1), 52-90.
9. Brett, J.M., Olekalns, M., Friedman, R., Goates, N., Anderson, C., and Lisco, C.C. (2007). Sticks and stones: Language, face, and online dispute resolution. *Acad of Mgmt J., 50*(1), 85-99.
10. Taylor, P.J., and Thomas, S. (2008). Linguistic style matching and negotiation outcome. *Negotiation and Conflict Mgmt Research, 1*(3), 263-281.
11. Tausczik, Y.R., and Pennebaker, J.W. (in press). The psychological meaning of words: LIWC and computerized text analysis methods. *J. Lang and Soc Psych*, 1-52.
12. Anderson, C.R. (1976). Coping behaviors as intervening mechanisms in the inverted-U stress-performance relationship. *J. Applied Psych., 61* (1), 30-34.
13. Lobbestael, J., Arntz, A. and Wiers, R.W. (2008). How to push someone's buttons: A comparison of four anger induction methods. *Cognition and Emotion, 22* (2), 354-373.
14. Watson, D., Clark, L.A. and Tellegen, A. (1988). Development and validation of brief measures of positive and negative affect: The PANAS scales. *JPSP, 54* (6), 1063-1070.
15. Russell, J.A. (1980). A circumplex model of affect. *JPSP, 39,* (6), 1161-1178.
16. Schwarz, N. (1990). Feelings as information: Informational and motivational functions of affective states. In E.T. Higgins & R. Sorrentino eds., *Handbook of Motivation and Cognition: Foundations of Social Behavior*. Guilford, New York, 527-561.

Emotion Regulation for Frustrating Driving Contexts

Helen Harris
Stanford University, Dept. of Communication
450 Serra Mall, Building 120
Stanford, CA. 94305-2050
helenh@stanford.edu

Clifford Nass
Stanford University, Dept. of Communication
450 Serra Mall, Building 120
Stanford, CA. 94305-2050
nass@stanford.edu

ABSTRACT
Driving is a challenging task because of the physical, attentional, and emotional demands. When drivers become frustrated by events their negative emotional state can escalate dangerously. This study examines behavioral and attitudinal effects of cognitively reframing frustrating events. Participants (N = 36) were asked to navigate a challenging driving course that included frustrating events such as long lights and being cut-off. Drivers were randomly assigned to three conditions. After encountering a frustrating event, drivers in a *reappraisal-down* condition heard voice prompts that reappraised the event in an effort to deflate negative reactions. Drivers in the second group, *reappraisal-up,* heard voice prompts that brought attention to the negative actions of vehicles and pedestrians. Drivers in a *silent* condition drove without hearing any voice prompts. Participants in the *reappraisal-down* condition had better driving behavior and reported less negative emotions than participants in the other conditions.

Author Keywords
In-car interfaces, emotion regulation, voice interfaces.

ACM Classification Keywords
H5.2. Information interfaces and presentation: User interfaces.

INTRODUCTION
Often frustration is referred to as a gateway emotion that leads to anger, and ultimately to aggressive road rage [2]. As the number of vehicles on the roadways increase, drivers encounter more frustration-inducing scenarios. As a result, road rage is now an escalating problem and is the primary cause of many accidents and driving fatalities. Given the implications of driving under the influence of negative emotional states, it is important to be able to minimize driver frustrations when possible. While some previous work has addressed the question of how to address drivers if their emotional state is known [9], near-term solutions should use available knowledge of the road to anticipate driver frustrations.

Emotion Regulation
The field of psychology provides a significant body of work to aid in addressing negative emotions and promoting healthier states. The process model of emotion regulation [3, 5] posits that emotions may be regulated at one of five points during the time course of emotion: selection of the situation; modification of the situation; deployment of attention; change of cognitions; and modulation of the response. If we aim to improve frustration during everyday circumstances, not all of these stages are feasible points for an intervention.

Considering the selection of the situation, drivers can choose low-traffic routes or travel during off-peak hours, but these choices may not be available given schedules and might not entirely prevent the driver from encountering frustrating situations. Modifying the situation is also difficult. Driving occurs in a complex environment of pedestrians, cyclists, cars, and traffic signals, so there a little opportunity to the driver to personally minimize frustrating events. Attentional deployment could increase driver distraction, and modulation of responses by means of suppression would likely increase the experience of negative emotions.

Because of the timing and distraction issues posed by the other points of emotion regulation, we see the most obvious opportunity for an intervention to be changing cognitions immediately after frustrating events. Although driving is a complex task and there are issues of fatigue [1] and workload [12] with the cognitive effort required to reframe the situation, it might remain possible to change cognitions, and this is what the current study addresses. Cognitive reappraisal is one method of changing cognitions and in other contexts it has been more effective than other interventions [e.g., 4]; it requires that the potentially emotion-inducing event is reframed immediately after its occurrence in order to diminish or prevent a negative response before a full emotional response can occur.

Implementing an Effective Voice Interface
Considerable research has been done under the "computers are social actors" paradigm [10] to show that people respond to computers, technology, and media, as if they

were other people [7, 8, 10]. In a variety of domains we find that interfaces can affect liking, attitudes, task performance, and behavior. Whether the interaction is with a desktop computer, through a web interface, or with an in-car voice interface, properly designed media has the power to affect users at emotional, cognitive, and physiological levels. It is for this reason that we believe that an effective yet unobtrusive strategy for emotion regulation is to design a voice interface that encourages cognitive reappraisal.

Technology for Context-aware Responses

To test the effects of cognitive reappraisal on drivers, a challenging course and the ability to respond to frustrating events was required. With the driving simulator software STISIM *Drive* [11] we created events and placed obstacles in a driving course that would cause frustration. Pre-recorded cognitive reappraisal voice prompts would be played precisely after an incident occurred, but before the event was fully cognitively processed. Simulating a context-aware car interface in this way is straightforward, and even though all of the necessary technologies are not widespread now, it is foreseeable that future vehicles will be more intelligent via on-board sensors and networked information.

Cognitive Reappraisal Implementation

In contrast to some previous studies of emotion regulation, and to make the implementation more realistic for the driving context, drivers were not given any cognitive reappraisal training or instructions before beginning the driving task. There were two implementations of cognitive reappraisal: *reappraisal-down* and *reappraisal-up*. The *reappraisal-down* prompts were designed to decrease driver frustration by reframing the frustrating events the occurred in the course so that the driver did not believe the actions of others were as offensive potentially interpreted initially. By contrast, the *reappraisal-up* prompts were designed to increase negative driver emotion by suggesting the actions of others were intentional or careless. A *silent* condition was added to compare the effects of the voice conditions to standard driving conditions.

The *reappraisal-up* condition was included so that we could distinguish the effects of a voice in the car from the effects of the voice interface's content. It is possible that the calmness of the voice (the same for both conditions) could cause emotional contagion, and result in a more positive state of the driver, regardless of the content. Without the *reappraisal-up* condition, we would not have enough evidence to prove the effect of the voice interface content. Thus, we arrive at our research question: will employing a supportive social agent with cognitive reappraisal commentary have the same or any effects as cognitive reappraisal training and approaches found in less-cognitively demanding settings?

- H1: Drivers who experience the *reappraisal-down* prompts will be less negatively affected by the frustrating driving scenario than drivers with *reappraisal-up* prompts or no voice at all, and consequently have better driving performance.
- H2: Drivers with the *reappraisal-up* reinforcement will be adversely affected and exhibit poorer performance than drivers in the silent condition.
- H3: Drivers in the *reappraisal-down* condition will be in a more positive emotional state and have more favorable attitudes towards the driving partner than drivers in the *reappraisal-up* condition.

STUDY DESIGN

Participants

Thirty-six participants were included in this study, with eighteen males and eighteen females balanced between conditions. Participants were university students ages 18 to 24 years old and had between two and ten years of driving experience (M = 5.1, SD = 1.84). Participants were randomly assigned to one of three conditions: *reappraisal-down* (n = 12), *reappraisal-up* (n = 12), and *silent* (n = 12).

Procedure

After arriving at the lab participants drove a five minute practice course while being supervised by an experimenter. The role of the experimenter was to make sure the participant was comfortable in the driving seat and understood the essential operations of the driving simulator (brakes, accelerator, shifting views, etc.). Before beginning the drive participants were reminded to obey all traffic rules and to drive as safely as possible. Drivers who were in the voice conditions were also told that as they would hear a driving partner comment on the driving scenario

The 38,500-foot course was filled with challenging elements such as heavy traffic, merging cars, long stoplights, curvy roads, slippery surfaces, and low-visibility. The course elements were programmed based on distance in the course, not elapsed time, so all participants experienced the same course elements at the same positions in the course. All participants completed the course without technical problems or experiencing simulator sickness.

Participants in the voice conditions heard ten statements, each following one of the frustrating events (Table 1).

Event	Reappraise-Up	Reappraise-Down
traffic	The behavior of overly aggressive and inconsiderate drivers leads to traffic congestion.	Heavy traffic results from limited routes, not the behavior of other drivers.
cut-off	The driver must have chosen to change lanes despite the danger of running into your car.	The driver must not have seen you; otherwise, he would not have chosen to change lanes.

Table 1. Example Prompts

Participants in the *silent* condition drove without prompts.

After the drive, participants completed a questionnaire that included items about their emotional state, their attitudes about the car, and the driving experience.

Measures

Bad Driving

The software used to create the driving simulation, STISIM *Drive,* collects behavioral data during each drive. The following measures were automatically recorded during the test drives: *off-road accidents, collisions, speeding tickets, traffic light tickets, stop signs missed, centerline crossings,* and *road edge excursions.* These items were combined to create a *bad driving* measure ($M = 0$, $SD = 1$).

Run Length

Run length (in seconds) was the time it took participants to complete the course ($M = 1094.3$, $SD = 300.9$).

Car Evaluation

Participants rated the following descriptions and statements in response to "How well do the following statements describe how you feel about the car?": *trustworthy, friendly, annoying, boring, intelligent, frustrating, I would buy, fun to use, well-designed, I would want to have, high in quality, helpful, likeable, I would use again, reliable,* and *I would recommend it to a friend or family member.* The items were rated on a 10-point Likert scale with anchors "Describes very poorly" and "Describes very well." Negative items were reverse coded; a higher score represented a more positive evaluation ($M = 0$, $SD = 1$).

Negative Emotion

Participants were asked to respond to "How well do the following words describe your present feelings or emotions?" on the following items: *angry, disgusted, aggressive, distaste, distressed, ashamed, fearful, hostile, mad, repulsion, sad, scared, shocked, afraid, dislike, upset, and frightened.* The items were rated on a 10-point Likert scale with the same anchors as above. A higher score represented more negative feelings ($M = 0$, $SD = 1$).

RESULTS

A one-way analysis of variance was used to compare the between-group differences, with Fisher's least significant difference (LSD) test used for the post-hoc comparisons. Error bars represent 95% confidence intervals.

Bad Driving

The ANOVA revealed a significant difference in the *bad driving* behavior between groups ($F(2, 33) = 3.75$, $p = .034$). The post-hoc tests revealed significant differences for two out of the three comparisons. For both *silent* versus *reappraise-down* ($p = .022$), and *reappraise-down* versus *reappraise-up* ($p = .026$), participants in the *reappraise-down* condition had lower bad-driving scores than their counterparts in the other conditions (see Figure 1).

Run Length

There was also a significant difference between groups for the time it took to complete the course ($F(2, 33) = 4.03$, $p = .027$). Participants in the *reappraise-down* condition took a longer time to complete the course than those in the *reappraise-up* ($p = .013$) or *silent* ($p = .033$) conditions (Figure 2). Although slower driving can sometimes signal indecision or confusion in the case of older drivers [6], with this younger population we interpret slower driving as indicating more careful, cautious behavior, and therefore a positive effect.

Car Evaluation

There was a significant difference between groups ($F(2,33) = 3.71$, $p = .035$), with post-hoc tests showing a difference between the *silent* and *up* groups ($p = .01$), and a marginal difference between the *reappraise-up* and *reappraise-down* groups ($p = .10$). In all comparisons, the *up* participants rated the car lower than the *silent* or *down* drivers (see Figure 3).

Negative Emotion

There was a marginal significant difference ($F(2, 33) = 2.65$, $p = .086$) for negative emotion; this likely resulted from a dampening effect associated with the similarity of the *silent* and *reappraisal-up* groups (see Figure 4).

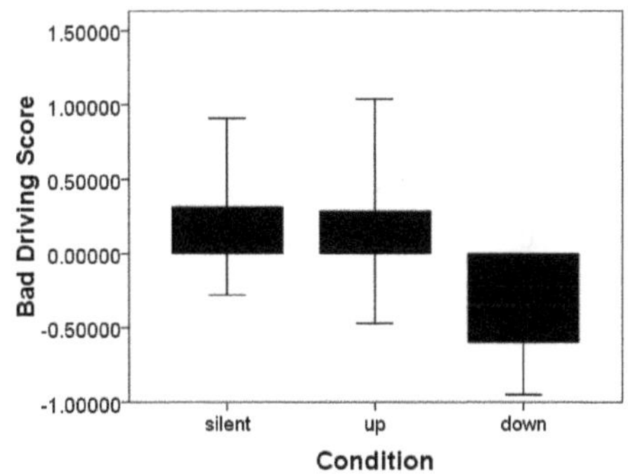

Figure 1. Bad Driving Score.

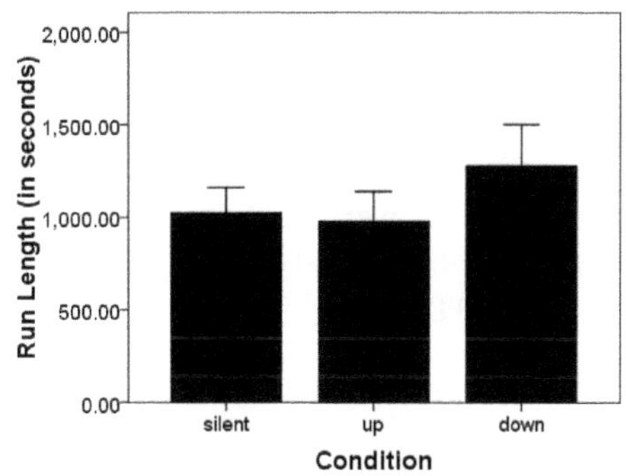

Figure 2. Run Length.

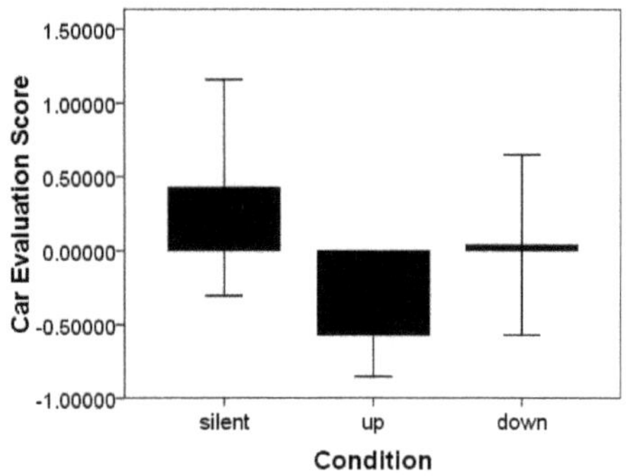

Figure 3. Car Evaluation Score.

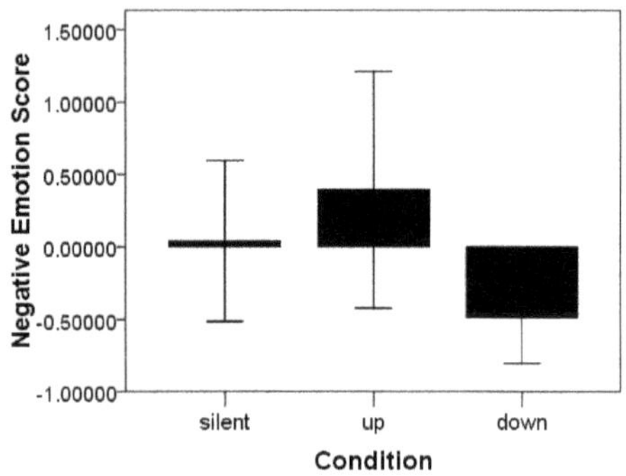

Figure 4: Negative Emotion Score.

DISCUSSION

The results from the study largely support the original hypotheses and point towards a hopeful solution for preventing driver frustration with a conversational in-car interface. We confirmed that carefully implementing a voice interface by situating reframing comments throughout a driving course yields dramatic effects on behavior, self-reported emotions, and attitudes. As hypothesized, the *reappraisal-down* participants had better driving performance and a better outcome emotional state than drivers in the *reappraisal-up* condition. More importantly, the system speaking in the *down* reframing condition did not have adverse effects in terms of performance or interface perceptions. On the contrary, the *down* participants drove better than those in the *silent* condition, and the two groups did not differ in terms of negative emotion or car evaluation. We did not find attitudinal differences between the *down* and the *silent* condition, but given that the prompts were subtle and not overly personal or emotional, the lack of significant differences is not necessarily surprising.

Limitations and Future Work

The study was an initial attempt to apply psychological theory and an emotion regulation strategy to the driving context. Although the results demonstrated the benefits of cognitive reappraisal, there was no real-time record of participants' frustration, attention, or cognitive load. The frustrating events were selected based on researcher experience and artifacts available through the software; additional studies should examine the effects of emotion regulation strategies on specific causes of driving frustration such as continuous (traffic) versus momentary (being cut-off) triggers. While this study provides promising evidence that drivers can be positively influenced without prior training or disruptive alerts, in order for these findings to be implementable reappraisal should be examined within the context of other car applications and in more realistic settings. As infotainment applications grow in the car, reappraisal prompts like the ones used in this paper could be weaved into the everyday interactions with a social or informational interface.

REFERENCES

1. Baumeister, R.F. and Heatherton, T.F. Self Regulation Failure: An Overview. *Psychological Inquiry 7, 1* (1996), 1-15.
2. Galovski, T.E. and Blanchard, E.B. Road Rage: A domain for psychological intervention? *Aggression and Violent Behavior 9,2* (2004), 105-127.
3. Gross, J. Antecedent- and Response-Focused Emotion Regulation: Divergent Consequences for Experience, Expression, and Physiology. *Journal of Personality and Social Psychology 74, 1* (1998), 224-237.
4. Gross, J. The Emerging Field of Emotion Regulation: An Integrative Review. *Review of General Psychology 2,3* (1998), 271-299.
5. Gross, J.J. and Thompson, R.A. Emotion regulation: Conceptual foundations. In J.J. Gross's *Handbook of Emotion Regulation*, The Guilford Press, (2007), 3-24.
6. Jonsson, I.-M., Zajicek, M., Harris, H. and Nass, C. Thank you, I did not see that: in-car speech based information systems for older adults. *Ext. Abstracts CHI 2005*, ACM Press, (2005), 1953-1956.
7. Nass, C. and Moon, Y. Machines and mindlessness: Social responses to computers. *Journal of Social Issues 56, 1* (2000), 81-103.
8. Nass, C. and Brave, S.B. *Wired for speech: How voice activates and advances the human-computer relationship.* MIT Press, Cambridge, MA, 2005.
9. Nass, C., Jonsson, I.M., Harris, H., Reaves, B., Endo, J., Brave, S. and Takayama, L. Improving Automotive Safety by Pairing Driver Emotion and Car Voice Emotion. In *Proc. CHI*, ACM Press (2005), 1973-1976.
10. Reeves, B. and Nass, C. *The Media Equation: How people treat computers, television, and new media like real people and places.* Cambridge University Press, New York, 1996.
11. Systems Technology Inc. http://www.stisimdrive.com/, 2010.
12. Wegner, D.M. Ironic processes of mental control. *Psychological Review 101, 1* (1994), 34-52.

Introverted Elves & Conscientious Gnomes: The Expression of Personality in World of Warcraft

Nick Yee[1], Nicolas Ducheneaut[1], Les Nelson[1], Peter Likarish[2]

[1]Palo Alto Research Center
3333 Coyote Hill Road, Palo Alto, CA
[nyee, nicolas, lnelson]@parc.com

[2]University of Iowa
Iowa City, IA
peter-likarish@uiowa.edu

ABSTRACT

Personality inference can be used for dynamic personalization of content or system customization. In this study, we examined whether and how personality is expressed in Virtual Worlds (VWs). Survey data from 1,040 *World of Warcraft* players containing demographic and personality variables was paired with their VW behavioral metrics over a four-month period. Many behavioral cues in VWs were found to be related to personality. For example, Extraverts prefer group activities over solo activities. We also found that these behavioral indicators can be used to infer a player's personality.

Author Keywords

Virtual worlds, online games, personality, Big 5, inference.

ACM Classification Keywords

H5.m. Information interfaces and presentation (e.g., HCI): Miscellaneous.

General Terms

Human Factors

INTRODUCTION

Games can be character revealing. One of the author's fathers once noted that he enjoys playing golf with his business partners because it lets him see which of them cheats on the golf course. The underlying implication, of course, is that how someone behaves on a golf course says something about how they may behave during a business transaction. And online gamers who have developed romantic relationships in virtual worlds [34] often say something similar:

"The game WAS the reason we fell in love. Going through all the adventures and quests together really built our relationship. We found out how the other person is when they are mad, tired, sad, happy, excited, annoyed, etc." [City of Villains, Female, Age 25]

The unique affordances of virtual worlds offer an unparalleled platform for examining the intersections between personality and behaviors in virtual environments. On the other hand, unlike personality expression in physical settings, online games allow, or even encourage, users to behave in a manner inconsistent with their everyday identities. Thus, in this study, we ask:

- Is it true that a person's personality can be inferred from how they behave in a virtual world?
- And if so, what specific virtual cues are highly indicative of a person's introversion or conscientiousness (for example)?

Being able to infer a user's personality from online cues has direct relevance to HCI research, given the field's long-standing interest in interface personalization and system customization [e.g., 16, 24]. Indeed, knowing more about a user's personality could help design systems more responsive to users' needs in areas as diverse as e-commerce, social software, and recommender systems, to name a few.

In this paper, we use data from the widely popular massively multiplayer online game (MMOG), *World of Warcraft* (WoW), to answer the two questions above. We then use our results to discuss how personality data could be used in the design of future online systems, being mindful of some important limitations and potential pitfalls also suggested by our research.

The Expression of Personality

Studies in personality psychology have repeatedly shown that judgments of personality at zero acquaintance (i.e., by strangers) are moderately accurate. More importantly, the specific cues used to infer different personality traits are consensually shared. In other words, personality is readily expressed in specific cues in everyday life. This has been shown to be true for brief face-to-face encounters [9, 15]. For example, in an earlier study involving video-taped face-to-face conversations [9], Extraverted individuals spoke louder, with more enthusiasm and energy, and were more expressive with gestures.

Other studies have researched personality inference by examining an individual's bedroom or office [12], or their music collection [23]. For example, in the study of personal spaces, Conscientious individuals had well-lit, neat, and well-organized bedrooms. And individuals who scored high on Openness to Experience had more varied books and magazines.

This line of research has also extended to computer-mediated communication (CMC). In particular, studies have shown that moderately accurate personality impressions can be formed based on an individual's personal website [18, 28], Facebook profile [3], email content [10], blog content [32], and even an individual's email address—the thinnest slice of CMC possible [2]. For example, in terms of linguistic output on blogs, Agreeable individuals were more likely to use the first person singular, words related to family, and words related to positive emotions (e.g., happy, joy). Conscientious individuals were more likely to use words related to achievement.

These studies illustrate that we leave behind personality traces in both the physical and digital spaces that we inhabit. Given that the average online gamer spends over 20 hours a week in a virtual world [31, 33], it is not difficult to imagine that some amount of personality traces could be gleaned from logs of their virtual interactions as well.

Limits to Personality Expression?

On the other hand, there are also reasons to believe that personality may not be readily expressed in virtual worlds. First of all, previous studies have largely focused on personality expression in everyday settings or linguistic output online. It is unclear how or whether personality is expressed via non-human bodies doing non-human things in a fantasy world (e.g., gnomish priests resurrecting the dead with magical light rays).

Related to this point, some scholars, like Turkle, have suggested that VWs allow us to constantly reinvent ourselves [27]. If the strongest interpretation of this notion were true, it would imply that there might be a clean break between personality and how a person behaves in a VW. In other words, people could express or reinvent themselves idiosyncratically in VWs, such that shared cues of personality would not exist. And finally, there is also evidence that users do alter their behaviors in online games. For example, studies have shown that role-players tend to be more imaginative and thus willing to experiment with their online personas [5, 26]. And studies of online dating [13] and online gaming [4] have shown that users in both settings tend to idealize their online personas to some degree. In particular, some studies have revealed that tendencies to idealize self-representation online are moderated by poor self-esteem [4, 7]. Thus, identity experimentation and individual variations in that experimentation may suppress stable personality expression cues in virtual worlds.

The Collection of Personality Data

Previous studies of personality expression have tended to rely on linguistic output or behavioral traces. These traces are often artifacts of behaviors over time. For example, a person who is low on Conscientiousness may often forget to water their plant. A withered plant in a bedroom is an example of a behavioral trace. Of course, as some researchers have suggested [20], we should also study actual behaviors as they occur. These researchers argue that observations of individuals in their natural settings and "humdrum lives" (pg. 862) may yield a better understanding of the link between personality and behavior.

The problem is that the recording of behaviors in natural settings and the subsequent coding are daunting tasks using traditional tools. Shadowing and video recording individuals is a laborious method that significantly constrains sample size. Recent technology has begun to offset the daunting nature of behavioral data collection, however. For example, in a study of how personality is related to everyday linguistic output [20], researchers used an electronically activated recorder which was programmed to record a participant's acoustic space for 30 seconds every 12 minutes. A dictionary-based software tool was then used to generate quantitative linguistic metrics of these recordings.

Behavioral Data Collection in Virtual Worlds

Virtual Worlds (VWs) offer unique affordances for studying the link between personality and behavior. For the purposes of this paper, we define VWs as graphical environments that enable geographically-distant individuals to interact via avatars (i.e., digital representations of users). It is also important to note that VWs are no longer academic prototypes or niche cultures, but have become mainstream interaction platforms. For example, *WoW* has over 11 million active monthly subscribers [30], and the *Facebook* game *FarmVille* has over 80 million active monthly users.

VWs offer three unique features in terms of collection of natural behavioral data. First, unlike the physical world where it would be unfeasible to follow everyone around with video cameras, VWs come inherently instrumented. The computer systems running the VWs already track the movement and behavior of every avatar to make interactions possible (e.g., orienting avatars so that they can look at each other). Second, these high-precision sensors operate at all times. Thus, it is possible to generate not only snapshot data, but longitudinal behavior profiles for every user in a particular VW (e.g., see [8]). And finally, all these observations can be performed unobtrusively, thereby significantly reducing the observer effect [29]—participants cannot react to the camera if the camera is invisible.

Indeed, a recent study has illustrated that there are connections between personality and virtual behaviors in the VW *Second Life* [35]. In that study, 76 students were asked to participate in *Second Life* for six weeks while "wearing" a scripted virtual tracking device that captured some of their behaviors and linguistic output. The findings revealed some interesting correlations. For example, high Conscientiousness was positively correlated with geographical movement.

There were several weaknesses in that study, however. First and foremost, it is difficult to capture natural behavior by assigning users to participate in a VW not of their own choosing. Being able to observe actual users would likely yield more reliable data. Second, only data from one VW was collected. Given that much of SL resembles suburban America [1], it would be helpful to gather data from additional VWs (and in particular fantasy-based online games) to see if the results generalize. Third, participants in that study were only asked to spend six hours each week in *Second Life*. On the other hand, we know that players of other VWs spend on average 20 hours a week (without being asked to) in games like WoW [33]. In other words, the participant sample may not be representative of VW users in either demographics or usage patterns. And finally, many of the correlations found in that study did not align with trait definitions of the personality variables used—e.g., virtual behaviors that correlated with Agreeableness were not related in obvious ways to Agreeableness. Thus, a replication in a different VW with existing users may help clarify whether the results are an artifact of the nature of *Second Life* or how people behave in VWs in general.

Research Questions

We focus on two research questions in this paper. While previous studies have examined personality expression in everyday settings, we were interested in examining whether and how personality is expressed in online games. To clarify and expand upon previous findings of personality correlates in VWs, we focus on the online game *World of Warcraft* in this paper with a sample of active players. Our first research question is thus:

RQ1. What are the behavioral correlates of personality in an online game?

If indeed personality is expressed in consistent cues in VWs, a pertinent question is whether these cues can be used specifically for personality inference. Thus, our second research question is:

RQ2. How well can we infer someone's personality from only observing their virtual behaviors?

METHOD

Given our focus on the online game WoW, we will begin by first briefly describing the game context to lay the foundation for understanding the variables we use as behavioral indicators.

World of Warcraft

WoW is currently one of the more popular online games available commercially [30]. Unlike *Second Life* (SL) where users create most of the in-world content (including buildings, clothing, hair styles, and avatar bodies), content in WoW is almost entirely created and designed by the company running the game. And unlike the open sandbox nature of SL, WoW uses a typical "leveling up" formula seen in computer role-playing games. Specifically, players start at level 1 and kill monsters to become higher level and acquire better weapons and armor in order to kill bigger monsters. Along the way, the game encourages players in different ways to collaborate with other players. Users can also create characters with different skill sets that complement each other. For example, heavily-armored *tank* classes shield the group from enemy attacks while lightly-armored damage dealing *DPS* (damage per second) classes deal damage to enemies and *healing* classes restore health lost in combat. In short, WoW is a collaborative virtual environment [22].

WoW draws from an established lore from the Warcraft franchise. Briefly, players must choose to belong to one of two primary factions—the Alliance or the Horde. Each faction has five distinct races, e.g., Night Elves or Trolls. A variety of rules dictate where and when players may attack and kill each other. Thus, a distinction is made between PvP (player-vs-player) activities and PvE (player-vs-environment) activities. PvP activites can range from one-to-one duels to large 40 vs. 40 battlegrounds (BGs). And in general, it is a player's choice as to how much PvP activity they want to engage in.

Players in WoW communicate via typed chat and might also use VoIP tools to communicate via speech. The game also provides a modest set of emotes (e.g., /hug). Players are also able to specialize in crafting professions and convert collected raw ingredients into finished goods, such as in tailoring or cooking.

There is also a system of Achievements that keeps track of a wide variety of combat and non-combat based objectives. There are Achievements for zones explored, for dungeons completed, for number of hugs given, and for cooking proficiency. These Achievement scores provide a good sense of how a player chooses to spend their time in WoW.

Thus, overall, WoW offers a wide and varied set of rich behavioral cues to draw from. From class choice to amount of PvP activity, from number of emotes used to amount of world exploration, the game context offers a range of measurable behaviors. This is also a point of differentiation from SL. Due to the open nature of SL, most higher-level conceptual behaviors are not defined in the environment and it is up to individual users to define their creations. Thus, there is no overarching set of metrics beyond fairly low level behaviors, whereas in WoW, the game keeps track of many behaviors and activities using a standardized lexicon.

The World of Warcraft Armory

Indeed, the standardized lexicon and data format inherently lends itself to automated data collection. Blizzard, the developer of WoW, is unique in that they have provided public access to much of their internally-collected data at a website known as the Armory. In short, by searching for a character's name, anyone can view details about their past activities, including how many hugs they have given, the quality of their equipment, the class they prefer to play, etc. More importantly, these metrics have been tracked since the character was first created. With a few clicks, we can gather a character profile that has cumulative data over many months of game play. It bears emphasizing the tremendous social science research opportunities that are made possible by this publicly-available database of longitudinal behavioral metrics. It is from the Armory that we gathered the behavioral metrics for this study.

Participants

1,040 WoW players were included in the study. We recruited participants from forums dedicated to WoW, publicity on popular gaming sites (e.g., WoW.com), word-of-mouth on social media like Twitter, and mailing lists from previous studies of online gamers. We note that due to human subjects regulations, minors were excluded from participating in the study. Nevertheless, we were still able to gather data from a very wide age range (18-65). The average age of our sample was 27.03 (SD = 8.21). 26% of participants were women.

Procedure

Participants began by completing a web-based survey that gathered their demographic and personality information. Participants were also asked to list up to 6 WoW characters they were actively playing. Once these characters were in our database, an automated data collection system was activated. The system launches a web scraper that gathers character profiles (large XML files) from the WoW Armory. The Armory updates itself once per day (in the early morning) if a character has been active the previous day. Thus, our script follows this schedule with a daily interval and collects any updated profiles. For the results, we analyzed data from a contiguous 4-month period in the spring and summer of 2010.

Personality Measures

In personality psychology, the Big-5 model is the gold standard. The model measures five traits: Extraversion, Agreeableness, Conscientiousness, Emotional Stability, and Openness to Experience.

For comparability, we also used an inventory that measured these 5 factors. A 20-item scale measuring the Big-Five Factor structure was drawn from the International Personality Item Pool [11]. Participants rated themselves on the inventory items using a scale that ranged from 1 (Very Inaccurate) to 5 (Very Accurate).

Behavioral Measures in WoW

There are two main complexities we encountered when dealing with the Armory data. First, Armory profiles consist of hundreds of variables, oftentimes in a hierarchy. For example, there is a system of Achievements in WoW that tracks progress in a variety of defined goals, such as Exploration Achievements and Dungeon Achievements. Under Exploration Achievements, there is a category for each continent. Under each continent, there is a listing for each zone. To avoid being inundated by low-level variables or including overlapping variables, we adopted an analytic strategy of looking at or generating high level variables where possible. This in turn produces more stable variables that map to psychologically meaningful concepts. For example, a notion of geographical exploration would seem to be better tracked by the overall count of zones explored rather than looking at any one particular zone.

A second complexity is that most players have multiple active characters at the same time and it is not at first clear how to combine metrics across characters to derive participant-level aggregates. For example, a level 80 character can do much more damage than a level 60 character (and the function is non-linear). Thus, there is no way to easily combine damage done across characters. While these metrics needed to be normalized, there wasn't one single variable they could all be normalized against.

We therefore adopted the following normalization and variable generation strategies:

1) Static character attributes were normalized against total number of characters. E.g., ratio of male characters = male characters / total characters.

2) Variable character attributes were normalized against overall time played. E.g., for combat roles, we calculated how often each character was a tank/healer/DPS, and then calculated a participant-level ratio for each of those roles. A 0.24 tank ratio meant that across all of a participant's characters, they spent 0.24 of their total playing time as a tank.

3) Metrics that could be normalized against another variable were normalized accordingly. E.g., the score of Exploration Achievements could be divided by the score of All Achievements to generate an Exploration ratio. This thus filtered out the raw difference between someone with many and someone with few achievements, and focused instead on how they focus their game-play.

4) For metrics that could not be normalized and were highly dependent on character level, we extracted the maximum. E.g., it is very different having one character that has 80 vanity pets compared with having 4 characters with 20 vanity pets each. In these cases, we found the maximum number of vanity pets across a participant's characters.

5) For metrics that could not be normalized and were not dependent on character level, we calculated the sum. E.g., any level character can emote /hug as often as they'd like. In these cases, we summed up the count of hugs across all of their characters.

It is important to mention that we are not claiming to have extracted all possible variables for analysis in this paper, but rather, that we have extracted a meaningful and manageable subset of higher-level variables that covers a wide range of behaviors in WoW. A description of each derived variable, along with its mean and standard deviation are presented in Table 1 below. Note that we excluded outliers that were more than 2 standard deviations away from the mean when deriving these metrics. For brevity we will only describe high-level trends in the text, but for ease of reference, we will include the table row index in round brackets after each mentioned correlate.

#	Variable	Description	M (SD)	E	A	C	ES	O
1	Ratio of Alliance Characters	= Alliance Chars / Total Chars	0.53 (0.47)	0.00	0.05	**0.07**	0.04	0.02
2	Ratio of Opposite Gender Characters	= Opposite Gender Chars / Total Chars	0.27 (0.36)	**-0.07**	**-0.14**	-0.03	**0.07**	0.00
3	Total Character Count	Count of all active characters reported by participant	2.79 (1.51)	**-0.12**	0.03	**0.07**	0.02	**0.10**
4	Number of Days Played Since Start of Study	Count of unique active days since start of study	65.47 (34.89)	-0.04	0.00	0.01	-0.03	-0.01
5	Total Realm Count	Count of realms participant has active characters on	1.11 (0.31)	-0.05	0.06	0.01	-0.03	**0.09**
6	Max of Guild Changes	Highest number of guild change events	.78 (1.05)	**0.07**	-0.01	0.00	-0.05	0.03
7	Sum of Kills	Includes both kills against computer monsters and other players	162353.84 (108633.20)	-0.03	-0.03	0.00	-0.00	**-0.07**
8	Sum of Kills in BGs	Number of kills in battlegrounds	2705.70 (3589.28)	-0.01	**-0.06**	0.00	0.04	0.00
9	Sum of PvP Kills	Number of all PvP-related kills	10437.22 (12026.80)	-0.04	**-0.08**	0.05	**0.09**	-0.05
10	Sum of Deaths	Total number of deaths from any cause	1849.12 (1440.63)	0.05	**-0.07**	0.00	**0.05**	-0.04
11	Sum of Deaths in Raid Dungeons	Number of deaths in dungeons	1018.84 (899.94)	**0.06**	**-0.07**	0.01	0.02	**-0.08**
12	Sum of Deaths from Falling	Number of deaths from falling from high places	32.64 (69.10)	0.02	-0.05	**-0.07**	-0.02	0.00
13	Sum of Hugs	Number of /hug emote	38.57 (69.10)	-0.02	**0.11**	**0.10**	-0.03	**0.09**
14	Sum of LOLs	Number of /lol emote	63.73 (147.57)	0.01	0.01	-0.03	-0.02	0.05
15	Sum of Cheers	Number of /cheer emote	47.05 (90.40)	**-0.09**	**0.13**	**0.07**	0.04	**0.13**
16	Sum of Waves	Number of /wave emote	79.77 (140.21)	-0.06	**0.10**	**0.09**	**0.08**	**0.14**
17	Max Number of Mounts	Mounts increase travel speed and are both functional and collectible	32.08 (29.62)	-0.05	0.03	0.05	-0.02	0.01
18	Max Number of Vanity Pets	Vanity pets are small non-functional and largely decorative companions	39.45 (31.80)	**-0.07**	**0.07**	**0.08**	-0.05	**0.07**
19	Ratio of Need Rolls	= Need Rolls / Total Rolls	0.17 (0.11)	**0.10**	**-0.14**	**-0.08**	-0.06	**-0.09**
20	Max Equipment Score	Sum of all equipment item levels	3867.90 (813.20)	0.02	**-0.10**	-0.04	0.01	-0.06
21	Sum of Count of Respecs	Number of times player has changed skill specializations	27.02 (28.06)	0.03	**-0.09**	-0.02	0.03	-0.05
22	Max of Achievement Score	Total Achievement score	413.06 (195.44)	-0.01	-0.04	0.02	0.00	-0.03
23	Ratio of Quest Achievements	= Quest Achs / Total Achs (based on Sums)	.07 (.02)	**-0.10**	**0.07**	0.02	0.01	-0.01
								Table Continued

#	Variable	Description	M (SD)	E	A	C	ES	O
24	Ratio of Exploration Achievements	= Exploration Achs / Total Achs (based on Sums)	.10 (.05)	-0.04	**0.09**	0.06	0.02	**0.13**
25	Ratio of PvP Achievements	= PvP Achs / Total Achs (based on Sums)	.10 (.05)	0.00	**-0.12**	-0.03	**0.07**	-0.01
26	Ratio of Dungeon Achievements	= Dungeons Achs / Total Achs (based on Sums)	.36 (.12)	**0.12**	**-0.17**	**-0.12**	0.01	**-0.17**
27	Ratio of Profession Achievements	= Profession Achs / Total Achs (based on Sums)	.10 (.06)	-0.04	**0.13**	**0.07**	-0.02	**0.12**
28	Ratio of Reputation Achievements	= Reputation Achs / Total Achs (based on Sums)	.03 (.01)	-0.03	-0.02	-0.03	-0.01	**-0.12**
29	Ratio of World Event Achievements	= World Achs / Total Achs (based on Sums)	.13 (.07)	**-0.08**	**0.16**	**0.10**	-0.04	**0.11**
30	Max of Cooking Achievements	Highest cooking score	6.33 (4.85)	**-0.07**	**0.07**	**0.07**	-0.01	0.05
31	Max of Fishing Achievements	Highest fishing score	7.26 (6.02)	**-0.06**	**0.07**	**0.07**	0.01	0.05
32	Sum of End Game 10-man Raids Done	Total 10-man end-game raids completed	16.78 (17.83)	0.06	**-0.11**	-0.05	0.00	**-0.13**
33	Sum of End Game 25-man Raids Done	Total 25-man end-game raids completed	18.13 (22.99)	**0.08**	**-0.09**	-0.05	0.00	**-0.12**
34	Ratio of Healing Done	= Healing Done / Damage Done (based on Sums)	.32 (.46)	0.00	0.00	-0.03	-0.02	0.01
35	Sum of Arenas Played	Number of Arenas entered	55.57 (155.31)	-0.01	**-0.09**	0.01	0.06	0.01
36	Sum of BGs Played	Number of BGs entered	98.36 (147.11)	**-0.07**	**-0.07**	0.02	0.05	0.04
37	Sum of Duels Played	Number of Duels entered	52.80 (94.73)	**0.11**	**-0.07**	-0.04	-0.05	-0.03
38	Ratio of Arena Wins	= Arena Wins / Arenas Entered	.33 (.18)	**-0.10**	**-0.12**	0.03	**0.08**	-0.01
39	Ratio of BG Wins	= BG Wins / BGs Entered	.48 (.18)	-0.02	**-0.06**	-0.01	-0.01	0.01
40	Ratio of Duel Wins	= Duel Wins / Duels Entered	.46 (.21)	**-0.06**	0.02	**0.07**	0.04	-0.01
41	Sum of Flight Paths Taken	Flight paths are used to fly from one fixed location to another	1424.42 (1117.06)	**-0.08**	**0.07**	0.05	-0.02	-0.01
42	Sum of Hearths	Hearthstones allow a character to teleport to a pre-determined location	454.08 (310.49)	0.00	0.02	-0.01	-0.03	-0.03
43	Ratio of Melee DPS Role	Ratio of time spent in hand-to-hand DPS role (e.g., fury warriors, rogues)	.30 (.30)	**-0.08**	-0.01	0.03	0.02	0.05
44	Ratio of Ranged DPS Role	Ratio of time spent in ranged DPs role (e.g, hunters, mages)	.38 (.32)	0.06	0.05	0.01	**-0.08**	0.04
45	Ratio of Healing Role	Ratio of time spent in healing role (e.g., holy priests, restoration druids)	.20 (.24)	0.04	-0.05	-0.05	-0.01	-0.05
46	Ratio of Tank Role	Ratio of time spent in tanking role (e.g., protection warrior, protection paladin)	.13 (.20)	-0.01	-0.01	-0.01	**0.11**	-0.07

Table 1. Means, standard deviations, and correlation coefficients of VW behavioral measures. Correlation coefficients in bold are $p < .05$.

RESULTS

To analyze how personality is expressed in VWs, we examined the correlations between the virtual behaviors and the personality factors. Given the increased risk of experiment-wise error in large correlation tables with 46 variables against the five personality factors, we used an analytic method developed by Sherman and Funder [25] to address this specific issue. The method employs a Monte Carlo simulation of repeatedly randomized data within each participant. Thus, the method preserves the statistical properties of the data gathered. The method creates 1,000 instances of these randomized data sets and tabulates the number of observed significant correlations (at alpha of .05). The probability of the actual number of significant correlations is then calculated based on where it lies on the distribution of these 1,000 randomizations. In other words, this technique answers whether we found a significantly higher number of significant correlations in our data set than would be expected by chance alone. In our case, using an alpha of .05, we had 83 observed significant correlations where only 11.50 would be expected by chance based on the simulations. According to this Monte Carlo method, the probability of this number of observed correlations is $p < .001$. This provides assurance that the observed correlations, as a whole, are non-random.

We will now describe each of the Big 5 personality factors and the virtual behaviors they were correlated with. We will not discuss every significant correlation, but instead try to find clusters of correlations that trace out the bigger picture.

Extraversion

According to the trait definition, individuals who score high on Extraversion tend to be outgoing, gregarious, and energetic, while those who score low on Extraversion tend to be reserved, shy, and quiet.

In terms of behavioral indicators in VWs, individuals who score high on Extraversion tend to prefer group activities. They have a higher ratio of Dungeon Achievements (26), which requires collaboration with other players. They have also completed a higher number of end-game 25-man raid dungeons (33). Their higher number of guild changes also implies social promiscuity (6).

On the other hand, players who score low on Extraversion prefer solo activities, such as questing (23), cooking (30), and fishing (33). They also are more likely to have more vanity pets (18), which are silent pet-like companions.

We also see that players who score low on Extraversion have a preference and higher win ratios for some PvP activities (36, 37, 38, & 40), but it is less obvious what the connection is. The same is true for the higher ratio of opposite gender characters (2) among those who score low on Extraversion.

Agreeableness

According to the trait definition, individuals who score high on Agreeableness tend to be friendly, caring, and cooperative, while those who score low on Agreeableness tend to be suspicious, antagonistic, and competitive.

In terms of behavioral indicators in VWs, individuals who score high on Agreeableness give out more positive emotes (13. 15, 16), i.e., hugs, cheers, and waves, and prefer non-combat activities such as exploration (24), crafting (13), world events (29), cooking (30), and fishing (31).

On the other hand, players who score low on Agreeableness prefer the more competitive and antagonistic aspects of game-play. They enjoy killing other players (8 & 9). They also have more deaths (10), focus more on getting better equipment (20), and have engaged in more PvP activities (25), including BGs (35), Arenas (36), and duels (37). Their competitive edge also translates to a higher winning ratio in Arenas (38) and BGs (39).

The negative correlation with ratio of need rolls (19) is also telling. Valuable equipment drops from monsters are given to players according to dice rolls. Players select to roll based on "Need" or "Greed", of which the former is given higher priority. We found that players who are low on Agreeableness often insist on being given higher priority over others by rolling "Need". While this is tolerated in some cases, abusing Need rolls is often seen as anti-social (there is even a specific epithet used by the community to describe these players: ninja looters).

Conscientiousness

According to the trait definition, individuals who score high on Conscientiousness are organized, self-disciplined, and dutiful, while those who score low on Conscientiousness are careless, spontaneous, and easy-going.

In terms of behavioral indicators in VWs, individuals who score high on Conscientiousness seem to enjoy disciplined collections in non-combat settings. This is reflected in having a large number of vanity pets (18) which must be collected one at a time, and having high cooking (30) and fishing scores (31) which reflect self-discipline in collecting unique recipes and visiting unique fishing locations (as well as patiently staying put for significant amounts of time in these locations, since fishing in the game is surprisingly close to its real-world equivalent: catches can be few and far between). The same is true for world event achievements (29) which often require disciplined collections of items and visiting a set of locations around the world.

On the other hand, individuals who score low on Conscientiousness seem to be more careless and are more likely to die from falling from high places (12).

Emotional Stability

According to the trait definition, individuals who score high on Emotional Stability are calm, secure, and confident, while those who score low on Emotional Stability are nervous, sensitive, and vulnerable.

While there were significant correlations between behavioral metrics and this personality trait, these correlations were more difficult to interpret as a whole. Individuals who score low on Emotional Stability prefer PvP related activities, including having a higher PvP achievement score (25) and higher wins in the Arena (38). Individuals who score higher on Emotional Stability are more likely to have characters of the opposite gender (2).

It is worth noting that previous studies have also had difficulty identifying meaningful behavioral correlates for

Emotional Stability [12, 17], so our findings here may reflect an overall weaker behavioral expression of this trait.

Openness to Experience

According to the trait definition, individuals who score high on Openness to Experience are abstract thinkers, imaginative, and intellectually curious, while those who score low on Openness to Experience are down-to-earth, conventional, and traditional.

In terms of behavioral indicators in VWs, we see a cluster of correlates that reflect exploration and curiosity. For example, individuals who score higher on Openness have more characters (3). They also have characters on more realms (5), i.e., game servers or parallel worlds that each character resides on. And they spend more of their play-time exploring the world (reflected by the higher exploration achievement ratio, 24). They also spend more time participating in non-combat activities, such as crafting professions (27) and world events (29).

On the other hand, individuals who score low on Openness prefer the more traditional, combat-oriented aspects of game-play, spending more time in dungeons and raids (26, 32, & 33).

Personality Inference from Behavioral Metrics

To examine how well personality can be inferred from virtual behavioral metrics alone, we conducted a series of multiple regressions on each of the personality factors using the respective ten highest behavioral correlates. We note that this method is imperfect and creates a "double-dipping" concern, but provides a rough sense of how well personality can be inferred. The results are shown in Table 2.

All of the multiple regressions were significant at $p < .05$; four were significant at $p < .001$. This suggests that virtual behavioral metrics can be used to provide statistically significant models of a player's personality. According to Cohen [6], an R of .30 is a medium effect size, while an R of .10 is a small effect size. Thus, many of our regression models had around medium effect sizes.

Variable	R	R^2	Adj. R^2	STE	F	p
Extrav.	0.30	0.09	0.07	0.93	4.73	< .001
Agreeable.	0.30	0.09	0.07	0.67	4.67	< .001
Conscient.	0.20	0.04	0.03	0.79	4.86	< .001
Emo. Sta.	0.21	0.04	0.02	0.79	2.13	0.03
Openness	0.26	0.07	0.06	0.75	4.93	< .001

Table 2. Multiple regressions on each of the personality factors.

DISCUSSION

The availability of fine-grained virtual behavioral metrics in the WoW Armory allowed us to gather longitudinal profiles of actual VW users. While studies in the past have examined links between personality and linguistic output online (in emails or blogs), our study is the first to examine the links between personality and virtual behavior in an online game. Our findings reveal that our personalities are expressed in VWs via consistent cues, and that most of these cues reflect trait definitions of standard personality factors. For example, players who score high on Extraversion prefer group-oriented activities. And players who score high on Agreeableness use more positive emotes and prefer non-combat activities. More importantly, our multiple regressions reveal that behavioral cues in VWs can be used to infer an individual's personality. These findings suggest that while some degree of identity experimentation is occurring in virtual worlds, basic personality is still being readily expressed.

While an earlier study of personality expression in VWs [35] had trouble finding trait-aligned behavioral correlates in *Second Life*, we were able to find much more coherent behavioral clusters that were consistent with personality trait definitions in our study. Findings in the earlier study may have been impacted by participants with no prior experience with the VW. Also, it bears pointing out that the WoW Armory allowed us to gather a set of more conceptually meaningful variables. Due to constraints in the scripting language and sandbox nature of *Second Life*, there is no standardized set of high-level behavioral variables that are shared. Thus the earlier study relied on lower-level variables such as distance walked or ratio of time sitting down, which may be less powerful in capturing personality expression, as opposed to behaviors such as hugging someone.

Knowing the specific behavioral correlates for personality expression in virtual worlds is also important for several reasons. First, it helps researchers triage the large number of behavioral variables gathered in future studies, and helps prioritize where to start looking. Second, it helps psychologists understand whether certain personality traits are more easily predicted via behavioral indicators. And finally, comparing the findings across these studies will help us understand whether these behavioral correlates are consistent or idiosyncratic among different virtual worlds.

Implications for CHI

Personalized interfaces and system customization have long been of interest to the HCI community [16, 24]. It is reasonable to assume that information needs vary based on a user's personality – for instance, extroverts using an online shopping website might be more interested in other customers' reviews, while introverts might prefer seeing mostly technical data about the product instead. Our paper points at the possibility of inferring users' personalities based on their activity traces (which need not come from online games) and customizing their experience based on the results.

Another possibility directly applicable to online games but also other forms of social software would be to use inferred personality information to assist in the formation of groups, perhaps by recommending compatible partners based on the task to be accomplished. For instance, groups requiring a diversity of opinions might benefit from the inclusion of a wide range of personality types [14]. In other contexts, a more homogeneous mix could be beneficial. And it is worth pointing out that we are not suggesting an automated system that would kick some players out of groups because they are low on Agreeableness. After all, the competitive nature of these players can be an asset in PvP settings, and an assertive nature can also be an asset for raid leaders. In a related fashion, personality data could also be used in recommender systems: recommendations from other users with similar personality profiles could be given more or less weight, depending on the user's desire for more homogeneity or diversity in the options they are presented with [19].

Limitations and Future Research Directions

There were several limitations to our study. First, we only collected data from one VW. It is unclear whether the behavioral cues we identified generalize to other similar online games. Moreover, it is difficult to say how our indicators translate to VWs that do not employ the dragon-slaying role-playing paradigm. Nevertheless, our findings hint at potential metrics to collect and analyze in future studies. For example, emotes (for Agreeableness) or geographical movement (for Openness) have analogous metrics across many types of VWs.

A related limitation to generalizability is that WoW users are highly-engaged users who spend on average 20 weeks producing behaviorally-rich metrics. This usage profile is likely atypical of normal website or mobile app usage. Whether the more typical casual engagement with websites and mobile apps would allow personality inference is certainly an avenue for future research.

Third, while the correlation coefficients appear to be quite low (ranging from .06-.17), a similar large-scale study (i.e., >500 participants) of linguistic output among bloggers yielded similar effect sizes [32]. Given the larger variances in demographics (with an age range of 16-85 in our sample) and unavoidable noise among natural setting samples, these smaller effect sizes are probably not surprising in hindsight.

And finally, we relied on the set of variables that Blizzard shares publicly via the Armory. It is possible that other unshared variables, such as logged chat, may be even more predictive of personality. Given the existing work on linguistic predictors of personality [21, 32], it would be interesting to be able to directly compare the predictive power of linguistic and behavioral cues.

Overall, it is important to continue exploring how personality is expressed across a range of VWs (using a variety of metrics) to understand how generalizable these findings are.

Ending Thoughts

VWs provide a novel research platform with unique affordances and challenges. The automated longitudinal data collection across a wide range of behaviors is impossible to mirror using traditional data collection techniques, and similar techniques could also be used to study other social phenomena, such as the emergence of group norms or leadership.

On the other hand, VWs come with unique challenges as well. Above all, the ability to create tracking systems that essentially shadow a user wherever they go in a VW raises privacy concerns. In our study, the consent process spelled out the data collection scripts to participants, but given that VWs like WoW are a kind of pseudonymous public space, data collection studies (without a survey component like ours) largely fall into the exempt category for human subjects Institutional Review Board (IRB) review. The gray area arises due to the fact that the public space of WoW is unlike any physical public space we know--with microphones and video cameras that could follow every user unobtrusively.

This becomes even more complicated when the game developer makes public what would otherwise be private data. Such is the case with the WoW Armory. After all, before the WoW Armory, players could make the case that they had a reasonable expectation of privacy in WoW (with regard to IRB review). This expectation is no longer reasonable with the release of the Armory. In short, VWs create new research platforms, but at the same time, force us to address our role as researchers in the face of such powerful data collection tools.

It is easy to imagine that VWs allow us to become whatever we want to be, but our findings show that our personalities remain even when we don virtual bodies. These findings of personality expression in VWs suggest that our first lives still play an important role even when we are in *Second Life*. And our personalities are readily expressed even when we are Elves and Gnomes.

ACKNOWLEDGMENTS

This research is sponsored by the Air Force Research Laboratory.

REFERENCES

1. Au, W. Linden Suburban Home Owners More Likely To Treat Their Place As Extension of the Real Life Self, Academic Suggests. *New World Notes*. http://nwn.blogs.com/nwn/2010/04/linden-homes-study.html
2. Back, M., Schukle, S. and Egloff, B. How extraverted is honey.bunny77@hotmail.de? Inferring personality from e-mail addresses. *Journal of Research in Personality, 42* (2008), 1116-1122.
3. Back, M., Stopfer, J., Vazire, S., Gaddis, S., Schmukle, S., Egloff, B. and Gosling, S. Facebook profiles reflect

actual personality not self-idealization. *Psychological Science*, *21* (2010), 372-374.

4. Bessiere, K., Seay, A. and Kiesler, S. The Ideal Elf: Identity Exploration in World of Warcraft. *CyberPsychology and Behavior*, *10* (2007), 530-535.
5. Carroll, J. and Carolin, P. Relationship between game playing and personality. *Psychological Reports*, *64* (1989), 705-706.
6. Cohen, J. *Statistical Power Analysis*. Lawrence Erlbaum Associates, 1988.
7. Ducheneaut, N., Wen, M., Yee, N. and Wadley, G. Body and mind: a study of avatar personalization in three virtual worlds. *Proceedings of CHI*, *1* (2009), 1151-1160.
8. Ducheneaut, N., Yee, N., Nickell, E. and Moore, R. The life and death of online gaming communities: a look at guilds in World of Warcraft. *CHI 2007 Proceedings* (2007), 839-848.
9. Funder, D. and Sneed, C. Behavioral Manifestations of Personality: An Ecological Approach to Judgmental Accuracy. *Journal of Personality and Social Psychology*, *64* (1993), 479-490.
10. Gill, A., Oberlander, J. and Austin, E. Rating E-mail Personality at Zero Acquaintance. *Personality and Individual Differences*, *40* (2006), 497-507.
11. Goldberg, L. A broad-bandwidth, public domain, personality inventory measuring the lower-level facets of several five-factor models. in Mervielde, I., Deary, I., De Fruyt, F. and Ostendorf, F. eds. *Personality Psychology in Europe*, Tilburg University Press, Tilburg, The Netherlands, 1999, 7-28.
12. Gosling, S., Ko, S., Mannarelli, T. and Morris, M. A Room with a cue: Judgments of personality based on offices and bedrooms. *Journal of Personality and Social Psychology*, *82* (2002), 379-398.
13. Hancock, J., Toma, C. and Ellison, N. The truth about lying in online dating profiles. *Proceedings of CHI 2007*, *1* (2007), 449-452.
14. Harper, F., Frankowski, D., Drenner, S., Ren, Y.Q., Kiesler, S., Terveen, L., Kraut, R. and Riedl, J. Talk Amongst Yourselves: Inviting Users to Participate in Online Conversations. *IUI 2007* (2007), 62-71.
15. Kenny, D., Horner, C., Kashy, D. and Chu, L. Consensus at zero acquaintance: Replication, behavioral cues, and stability. *Journal of Personality and Social Psychology*, *62* (1992), 88-97.
16. Mackay, W. Triggers and Barriers to Customizing Software. *Proceedings of SIGCHI 1991*, *1* (1991), 153-160.
17. Mairesse, F. and Walker, M. Automatic Recognition of Personality in Conversation. *Proceedings of the Human Language Technology Conference*, *1* (2006), 85-88.
18. Marcus, B., Machilek, F. and Schutz, A. Personality in Cyberspace: Personal Web Sites as Media for Personality Expressions and Impressiosn. *Journal of Personality and Social Psychology*, *90* (2006), 1014-1031.
19. McNee, S., Riedl, J. and Konstan, J. Making Recommendations Better: An Analytic Model for Human-Recommender Interaction. *CHI 2006* (2006), 1103-1108.
20. Mehl, M., Gosling, S. and Pennebaker, J. Personality in Its Natural Habitat: Manifestations and Implicit Folk Theories of Personality in Daily Life. *Journal of Personality and Social Psychology*, *90* (2006), 862-877.
21. Mehl, M. and Pennebaker, J. The Sounds of Social Life: A Psychometric Analysis of Students' Daily Social Environment and Natural Conversations. *Journal of Personality and Social Psychology*, *84* (2003), 857-870.
22. Nardi, B. and Harris, J. Strangers and Friends: Collaborative Play in World of Warcraft. *CSCW 2006* (2006), 149-158.
23. Rentfrow, P. and Gosling, S. Message in a Ballad: The Role of Music Preferences in Interpersonal Perception. *Psychological Science*, *17* (2006), 236-242.
24. Riecken, D. Personalized Views of Personalization. *Communications of the ACM*, *43* (2000), 26-28.
25. Sherman, R. and Funder, D. Evaluating correlations in studies of personality and behavior: Beyond the number of significant findings to be expected by chance. *Journal of Research in Personality*, *43* (2009), 1053-1063.
26. Simon, A. Emotional stability pertaining to the game of Dungeons and Dragons. *Psychology in the Schools*, *24* (1987), 329-332.
27. Turkle, S. *Life on the Screen: Identity in the Age of the Internet*. New York: Simon and Schuster., 1995.
28. Vazire, S. and Gosling, S. e-Perceptions: Personality Impressions Based on Personal Websites. *Journal of Personality and Social Psychology*, *87* (2004), 123-132.
29. Webb, E., Campbell, D., Schwartz, R. and Sechrest, L. *Unobtrusive measures: non-reactive research in the social sciences*. Rand McNalley, Chicago, 1966.
30. White, P. MMOGData: Charts. *2009* (2008).
31. Williams, D., Yee, N. and Caplan, S. Who plays, how much, and why? Debunking the stereotypical gamer profile. *Journal of Computer-Mediated Communication*, *13* (2008), 993-1018.
32. Yarkoni, T. Personality in 100,000 Words: A large scale analysis of personality and word use among bloggers. *Journal of Research in Personality* (in press).
33. Yee, N. The demographics, motivations, and derived experiences of users of massively multi-user online graphical environments. *Presence: Teleoperators and Virtual Environments*, *15* (2006), 309-329.
34. Yee, N. The "Impossible" Romance. *The Daedalus Project*. http://www.nickyee.com/daedalus/archives/001534.php
35. Yee, N., Harris, H., Jabon, M. and Bailenson, J. The Expression of Personality in Virtual Worlds. *Social Psychological & Personality Science* (in press).

Starcraft from the Stands: Understanding the Game Spectator

Gifford Cheung
Information School
University of Washington
giffordc@u.washington.edu

Jeff Huang
Information School
University of Washington
chi@jeffhuang.com

ABSTRACT

Video games are primarily designed for the players. However, video game spectating is also a popular activity, boosted by the rise of online video sites and major gaming tournaments. In this paper, we focus on the spectator, who is emerging as an important stakeholder in video games. Our study focuses on Starcraft, a popular real-time strategy game with millions of spectators and high level tournament play. We have collected over a hundred stories of the Starcraft spectator from online sources, aiming for as diverse a group as possible. We make three contributions using this data: i) we find nine personas in the data that tell us who the spectators are and why they spectate; ii) we strive to understand how different stakeholders, like commentators, players, crowds, and game designers, affect the spectator experience; and iii) we infer from the spectators' expressions what makes the game entertaining to watch, forming a theory of distinct types of information asymmetry that create suspense for the spectator. One design implication derived from these findings is that, rather than presenting as much information to the spectator as possible, it is more important for the stakeholders to be able to decide *how* and *when* they uncover that information.

Author Keywords

Spectators, Video Games, Starcraft.

ACM Classification Keywords

H.5.m. Information interfaces and presentation (e.g., HCI): Miscellaneous.

General Terms

Human Factors.

INTRODUCTION

Video games are primarily designed for the players. However, the players are not the only people engaged with the game. In this paper, we turn our attention to the spectators, those who watch but do not directly interact with the game.

Spectating has been common in physical sports as well as contests of mental wits: spectators gathering in the park to watch chess champion Garry Kasparov or audiences watching game shows on television. The presence of a large spectating audience can generate more attention to the game, drive sales of the game, increase advertising revenue, and even improve the experience for the players themselves. Additionally, spectators have been found to meet social needs for the community [6]. We want to know more about the context of their spectating so that game designers can better design video games as spectator activities. To achieve this, we ask three fundamental research questions about spectators.

RQ1 Who are the spectators and why do they spectate?

RQ2 How do different stakeholders affect the spectator experience?

RQ3 What makes spectating a game *enjoyable*?

We have selected Starcraft, a popular real-time strategy computer game, to study in depth. Originally released in the United States by Blizzard Entertainment, Starcraft became popular in Internet cafes throughout South Korea in 1998 [10]. The cafes fostered competition and spectatorship. As the phenomenon grew, competition became tournaments and leagues; spectators became fans and community. Dedicated television channels broadcast Starcraft matches in South Korea. This has fostered a complex supporting infrastructure of professional leagues, teams, and superstars. Furthermore, more than a decade after its release, Blizzard Entertainment has released a sequel (Starcraft 2) with intentions of furthering it as an electronic spectator sport [18]. We chose to focus on the Starcraft series because it is the most successful case of video game spectating, with large audiences and wide appeal. In Korea, Starcraft closely resembles spectator sports in its presentation and audience, a game played by many and watched by many.

First we define spectating and introduce Starcraft, the target of our empirical study. Next we describe the method and data gathered in the study. Then we analyze the data from the study and present theories addressing our research questions. We develop a framework of the spectator ecosystem, and explore information asymmetry as a source of spectator entertainment. The theories lead to implications for design and a better understanding of game spectators.

How do we define spectating?

Spectators are people who follow the in-game experience, but are not direct participants in the game. This definition includes many contexts: the mother who watches Dad and the boys launch 'threes' in NBA 2K10 but refuses to play; a crowd in a conference ballroom cheering on Street Fighter 4 tournament contenders; or the kid looking over his brother's shoulder, advising him on how best to catch a rare Pokémon. Those scenarios, and more, are worth consideration from game designers.

RELATED WORK

Game Studies and Play Theory

Cultural anthropologist Johan Huizinga's study of the *play* element in culture [11] is a widely cited definition of play. In his work, we find ideas for defining the spectator. Huizinga's major conceptualization of players is that they hold a hedged existence '*outside* ordinary life'; this concept is referred to as the "magic circle" by Salen and Zimmerman [17]. Our challenge is to determine the proper position of the spectator with respect to the magic circle: *inside or outside*? The answer may be both.

On one hand, a spectator can be just as immersed in the reality of the game as players who have a direct hand in the final outcome of the game. Throughout Huizinga's book we find many descriptions of spectators as participants. The audience plays along with the emotional theatrics of a savage ritual (pp. 23–24). Onlookers share the tension of play, from games of chance to challenges of great difficulty (pp. 47–49). It should be noted that in-game tension is over stakes that, Huizinga reminds us, do not necessarily have any outside meaning; they are "unimportant and a matter of indifference" (pp. 49). These spectators have adopted the values of the game-world, a position squarely *inside* the magic circle. Also related to spectatorship, Huizinga defends the playful spirit of the whole Roman civilization despite the fact that ancient gladiatorial games were played only by a fraction of that society, its slaves. Huizinga describes this as a "shift" of the competitive impulse "from the protagonist to the spectator", but not as a disappearance of play. Rather, he points out that the spectator adopts a "vicarious attitude" and the gladiators represent and fight on behalf of the spectators (pp. 74–75). This blurred line between spectator and player is also pointed out by Sutton-Smith [21]. He describes fantasy play that is 'rooted in the mind' as a kind of vicarious play, a parallel to 'active' play. In this respect, the act of spectating is an active form of playing-along. These examples from the games literature give us three themes: commitment to the in-game values, investment in the tension of play, and the vicarious relationship between players and spectators.

However, can spectators exist *outside* of the magic circle? From Huizinga's description of play, we find barriers between "ordinary life" and the play world. One is the barrier of understanding; the values of the play world do not make sense in the ordinary. The other is a barrier of adoption; the values of the play world are not adopted by the outsiders. This is evident by Huizinga's descriptions of the outsider perspective. A game is "ridiculous" (pp. 198), effectively nonexistent (pp. 21), "unimportant" and unprofitable (pp. 49). Do spectators exhibit these views of the game they watch? Consider the person who registers the events of a game but does not understand the shared fiction of its players: a family member who happens upon a game in progress can see that there are pieces on a board, watch the pieces move, but due to a lack of understanding or interest may remain outside of the "magic circle". Also consider the meta-gamer: a person who is playing a different game over the same in-game events. For example, griefers actively dismiss the values of the game their victims are playing. In Second Life, an online game world, the leader of a group of griefers expresses his motivation to annoy the Second Lifers "who take their 'metaverse' seriously" [8]. This outsider understands the values, but refuses to adopt them. Overall, we are guided by two themes of outsiders: misunderstanding and non-adoption. In summary, game literature challenges us to watch for both participatory and non-participatory aspects of spectating.

Game Design and HCI

Drucker et al. [5] recognize that the growing popularity of video and board games includes a widening audience of spectators. They contribute design ideas for making online games more engaging and entertaining for non-players watching the game. Drucker et al. reason that key pieces of this are cinematography, commentating, awareness of the size of the audience, rich spectator interaction (e.g. kibitzing[1]), and support for promoting star players and fan-based activities. Design solutions explore the technical possibilities of animation, rendering, editing, replays, automatic cameras, commentator agents, and architectural solutions.

Game design has a close relationship with spectating. Ducheneaut et al. [6], in their analysis of the social dynamics of massively multiplayer online games, call for designers to consider the importance of designing for spectators. Su [20] describes a rich community of competitive Street Fighter IV players. He notes that one of the most commonly requested features is a spectator system to allow participants to view live matches.

Reeves et al. [16] broadens the attention to spectators in any human-computer interaction. They present a taxonomy of the spectator's view based on the visibility of manipulations and effects, which can be affected by performers and interface design. We build on this theory in our conceptualization of information asymmetry. Dalsgaard [3] carries Reeves et al.'s conversation further by thinking about the user as a simultaneous operator, performer, and spectator.

---

[1] According to Merriam-Webster, a kibitzer is a Yiddish term for "one who looks on and often offers unwanted advice or comment <a *kibitzer* at a card game>".

Dalsgaard et al. draw on the arcade game, Dance Dance Revolution, as an example: *we may denote the proficient player's experience as one of immersion...: well-timed responses to the game, socioculturally recognizable gestures and utterances such as raising ones arms in celebration, nods and comments to friends, pleasure in displaying expertise in front of strangers in a public place, adrenaline rushing in the knowledge of the imminent risk of failing.* (pp. 23)

Overall, these articles exhibit technical creativity and rich design sense. Our empirical contribution can fill speculative gaps and contribute to this discussion by providing more data about the nature and diversity of spectating.

Sports Spectating

Some sports have similarities to video games in that they have competitive players as well as spectators. Numerous studies have identified who the spectators in sporting events are, why they spectate, and how sports commentary affects the spectator experience.

Trail et al. conducted a study of why spectators watched sporting events [23]. The Motivation Scale for Sport Consumption revealed factors of aesthetics, achievement (feeling good when the team did well), drama, escape (as an escape from life), knowledge (learning about the game), physical skills, social, and family. We found that spectators watched Starcraft for many of the same reasons. Melnick elaborates further on the social motivation behind American sports spectating [13]. He notes that sports spectating is one of the last few social outlets in urban environments. The publicness and playfulness of being a sports spectator can alleviate loneliness. An empirical study of race rally attendees [7] teaches that live spectators can be disoriented in a 'viewer's paradox': present for a close, live, rich experience, but obstructed from grasping the whole sporting event. Also, they find an active attitude in spectators as they seek out information and follow the sporting event closely.

Commentators have been a common presence in many spectator sports such as hockey, golf, and professional wrestling. Some studies have examined how they affect the spectator experience. Sports commentary has commonly been divided into two personas: color commentators and play-by-play analysts. Color commentators provide background information on the players and teams as well as light humor, while play-by-play analysts describe what is happening in the game. These two types of commentators often annotate a match together, the color commentator filling in when action is not occurring on the field [2]. Bryant et al. [1] found that subjects watching a tennis match found the experience more enjoyable, exciting, involving, and interesting when the commentary depicted the players as enemies, rather than friends or neutral parties. The projected animosity between the players because of the commentators created suspense throughout the game. Cominsky et al. [2] showed that even commentators that simply report what was occurring on the screen make watching the game more entertaining and enjoyable for subjects.

STARCRAFT: A CASE STUDY

What is Starcraft?

The Starcraft games are a popular "real-time strategy" (RTS) series. RTS games can be described as war games where each player commands an army and production buildings from a bird's eye (top-down) perspective. We focus on the two major games in the Starcraft franchise: Starcraft 1 (1998) and Starcraft 2 (2010). While each game has a single player campaign as well as a multi-player mode, our study is about the multi-player mode which is more popular and commonly spectated.

In Starcraft, each player competes on a map containing key locations where resources can be mined and spent on buildings and military units. The player's vision of the board or map is limited to his or her own units and buildings, a concept called "fog of war"; this prevents them from seeing their opponent unless they perform reconnaissance. Worker units collect resources and build specialized buildings that can create marines, fighters, tanks, air units, and more. These units have a more elaborate version of a "rock-paper-scissors" dynamic. Some units are also better suited to certain strategies such as an armored "Blitzkrieg" through the enemy base, wave after wave of cheap disposable units, or sneak attacks behind enemy lines. The first player to destroy all of the opponent's buildings is the winner.

Spectator Technologies in Starcraft

In addition to watching a player's computer screen over the shoulder, there are a number of software tools available for spectating and commentating Starcraft games. Each Starcraft game can be digitally captured and then shared and replayed by the players, allowing others watch the game after it has taken place. Alternatively, the games can be arranged with an in-game observer. This client is granted the ability to see everything, but does not participate in the game. Thus, a game can be observed and broadcast in real-time. Either of these viewings can be recorded using standard video capture software, and optionally, commentary can be overlaid over the video. From here, videos are often uploaded to video sharing sites like YouTube. The original Starcraft game had a number of community-developed tools that allowed the observer to monitor each player's resources and APM (actions per minute, a metric often used to judge a player's skill). Starcraft 2 built many of these metrics into the game's spectator interface.

Why study Starcraft?

Starcraft is popular and established as an e-sport. Online videos of pro-gaming Starcraft matches are uploaded regularly to the internet and watched by fans worldwide. In South Korea, StarCraft has an active professional competition circuit. The two major game channels in South Korea, Ongamenet and MBCGame, each run a Starleague (Ongamenet Starleague, MBCgame Starleague), viewed by millions on television. Starting in about 2002, pro-gamers started organizing into teams, sponsored by large South Korean companies like Samsung, SK Telecom and KTF.

StarCraft is also the most popular computer game competition at the annual World Cyber Games, one of the world's largest game competitions in terms of prize money, global coverage and participants. In other parts of the world, Starcraft is still quite popular and watching the games is rapidly gaining traction, such as online video websites or tournaments (Figure 1). One American commentator, HDStarcraft, noted that it took one year to reach 100,000 subscribers on his Youtube channel but this has tripled to over 300,000 subscribers within the last few months. Due to the game's popularity, there were many Starcraft online communities from which we could collect data.

Figure 1: Spectators watching a Starcraft 2 match at a tournament in Raleigh, United States on August 28, 2010. Permission granted for this image by Major League Gaming.

Method

This study was conducted from a Naturalistic perspective [12] and guided by Grounded Theory [19]. We collected material from public, online sources such as videos, blog articles, forum posts, and comments, using maximum variation sampling [15]. When we approached theoretical saturation in some areas, we actively sought greater variety in types of people or contexts. This allowed us to explore the many different types of Starcraft spectators and take a broader picture of the spectating.

For analysis, we endeavored to draw theory from the data rather than to impose personal assumptions or biases on the analysis. Data-centricity required familiarity with the area as well as caution against personal biases or imposed interpretations of the data. Familiarity with the area was important in our situation because, i) games defy understanding when the analysts have never played them or a similar game and, ii) the level of jargon in the competitive communities (phrases such as “2Fac”, “gg”, “Micro/Macro”, “APM”) can be nonsense to outsiders. Both authors drew on independent personal experiences as Starcraft players in single- and multi-player contexts and Starcraft spectators in online and live Starcraft tournaments.

We sought to protect against personal bias in how we approached the data. Grounded Theory cautions its researchers from imposing a prior theory over the existing data; instead, as the name suggests, codes, categories, and theories are meant to arise from the ‘ground up’. This does not require analysts to attempt bring a ‘blank slate’ towards analysis by avoiding related literature, but to accord to that literature its proper place during analysis. We follow Strauss and Corbin [19] by regarding related work and personal spectating experiences as knowledge meant to aid our sensitivity. “Sensitivity” (pp. 46–48) is the analyst’s ability to seek association and meaning in the data.

For keeping the analysts unbiased, Grounded Theory relies on the open/axial/selective method of coding. Open coding is the process of discovering instances and initial categories; axial coding, the discovery of broader, aggregate categories; and selective coding, the completion of the larger categories through theoretical reasoning and the effort of explaining every instance in the data. The thick interrelationship of data instances ensures that the data itself is the primary driver for interpretation rather than prior theory or biases. In addition, we used a paired approach to analysis. The coding phases were conducted by both authors of this paper. Rather than splitting up the analysis, both authors were present during all phases of analysis. During the initial coding period where instances were labeled with basic descriptive categories, each author would validate the other’s choices, deterring the use of pet theories or forced interpretations. If disagreements arose, the authors would return to the original sources for resolution.

Procedurally, the analysis took the following form. After data collection, the two authors together wrote annotations for each data instance. Example annotations were "follows tournaments and favorite players", "watches and listens to commentary to improve their game", and "never played but enjoys watching with friends". These annotations acted as concise summaries of spectating instances.

The two authors together reviewed the data in the backdrop of the annotations to cluster them through the lens of the research questions. The first step was to look at who the spectators were and why they were spectating (RQ1). The authors clustered the data (usually anecdotes) into personas to identify commonalities between different types of spectators (Figure 2). Next, the authors clustered the annotations themselves to form spectating themes. We regard these steps as the open coding step: producing basic instances grouped into 9 personas and into themes of spectating.

The goal of the axial coding step which followed was to find larger patterns within the initial groupings. The authors used the research questions (RQ2 and RQ3) as lenses to identify two major themes: insights on the spectator environment and stakeholders, and what made spectating entertaining. As these major themes took shape, the selective coding steps took place. This involved reflection over the forming themes and categories to generate new questions for returning to the data. The resulting three conceptualizations are spectating personas, the ecology of spectatorship, and spectator enjoyment.

Sample Characteristics

We collected a total of 127 comments and videos from the web, from users sharing their story of spectating Starcraft. These spectator stories came from a diverse set of sources: commentary on popular Starcraft matches, opinion pieces from veteran players, initial reactions from a first-time Starcraft spectator, etc.. Common sources were social news sites like Reddit, Metafilter, and Slashdot; Blizzard Forums, Starcraft player sites, and commentary community forums (especially the Introduce Yourself sections) provided perspectives from active spectators and commentators. We organized these data in a large spreadsheet. There were 5 articles, 10 article comments, 8 blog posts, 36 comments, 39 forum posts, 19 videos, and 9 video comments.

Figure 2: Spectator stories printed from online sources being annotated and clustered on a table.

PERSONAS

We identified nine personas from the data to understand each spectator as a person. These personas are not mutually exclusive; a person may be a mix of multiple personas.

The Bystander – *"i remember watching AoE at the austrian WCG finals (never played it tho) it looked so boring, and when one of the 2 players left, i didnt even know why :D"* The Bystander is the least engaged of the spectators. He or she is exemplified by an outsider's perspective. We distinguish between two different groups of Bystanders.

The first is the bystander who has little to no understanding of the mechanics of the game. This is the *uninformed bystander*. He or she lacks knowledge for explaining the meaning of the in-game actions. For example, a person may visit her boyfriend and see that he is playing Starcraft; or, as in the quote above, a conference attendee may come across a tournament for a game he has never played. In addition to the serendipitous encounter with the game, the uninformed bystander finds much of the game incomprehensible.

The second is the bystander who is not originally invested in the game—ignorant of the players, what the techniques are, what the plays are, or who the winner will be. This is the *uninvested bystander*. In their introductory posts, many Starcraft forum members talked about how they "stumbled" onto a Youtube video and eventually became engaged in the professional-gaming scene. A common element in their story is that they played Starcraft many years ago, but had stopped playing the game long before this recent rediscovery. We interpret the proper description of them at the moment of stumbling as "uninvested". Their outsider status is not "uninformed" because they have a basic understanding of Starcraft; but, they are outsiders because there is no investment in the game.

The Curious – *"Once I ... learn all of this for myself, it will become far less fascinating, but right now it's all new and exciting." "Before i thought SC was slow, ugly, and ponderous like a drunkin elephant, but as i watched pro gamers go at it, i realized that SC was fast, harsh, and hardcore. I started watching more and more commentary's[sic], learning more about SC then i had ever thought possible."* The Curious spectator focuses his or her attention on knowledge-gaps about the game. As long as there is something that is incomprehensible and that can be discovered by spectating, the experience remains engrossing. In the data, spectators report fascination with understanding the basics of the game, depth of the game (comparing it to Chess), the nature of the game ("fast, harsh, and hardcore"), idiosyncrasies of the game engine, new strategies, and different players. The Curious has the following criteria: engagement only as long as there is more to learn.

The Inspired – *"Starcraft 2 played by experts is absolutely great to watch. I could definitely get behind some of the players out there. It actually makes me want to fire the game up and try the same shit." "Watching all the talent and hearing all of these in-depth analyses of advanced strategy has inspired me to go buy the game myself and start playing playerVsplayer online for the first time."* After spectating, the Inspired is eager to play the game himself/herself. Sometimes it is to try the same strategies that they witnessed; sometimes the enthusiasm is more broadly directed at the game itself. The experience of watching is, for the Inspired, a catalyst for putting themselves in front of a computer and playing for themselves. The purpose is to evoke the same thrill that they experienced as a spectator.

The Pupil – *"At the same time I learned the benefits of watching replays of matches where I'd gotten panned, because I'd always come away with some trick or idea (hard not to when SC2 lets you watch how your opponent moved his camera and cursor)"* Much like the Curious, the Pupil wants to understand the game and the techniques of the players. However, what distinguishes the Pupil is the emphasis on translating knowledge to practice. The Pupil's question is not merely "How did he do that?" it is also, "How does this information change how I play?" This emphasis reframes what medium of watching is favored by the Pupil. As a result, compared to others, the Pupil is more interested in spectating content with high amounts of detailed information: videos that show the screen of the player ("first-person video on demand" or FPVOD) and replays.

The Unsatisfied – *"I started playing the single player game with my son and he is constantly bugging me to play so it is likely I will only get to watch him play and see the story"* The Unsatisfied sees the act of spectating as a weaker substitute for the activity he or she would rather do. Overall, the spectating experience is inadequate because, for example, the Unsatisfied would rather be playing the game. What is particular about this category for Starcraft (and we believe for gaming in general) is the close connection between watching a game and playing it. For example, as a spectator grows more inspired by watching a game, the desire to play begins to compete with the desire to watch the game.

The Entertained – *"On the other hand, I have never really played SC but I enjoy watching it greatly. My girlfriend has never played games at all and she loves watching SC. Not WC3. Why would that be?"* On the opposite end of the spectrum of Playing vs. Watching are those who find satisfaction in watching, which many prefer over playing. For these, watching affords the experience of playing without the stress. The Entertained watches for entertainment, much like a person watches a television show or movie. Watching solely for entertainment was a very common story from our dataset. From fandom to the spectacle and more, the reasons for enjoying the game were so diverse that we will elaborate further in the section titled 'Entertaining the Spectator'.

The Assistant – *"When Starcraft came out my brother always played it (since we had only 1 computer) and I would always sit next to him and helping him like telling him he is under attack in that section, your research is complete (I know the computer gives you this messages but you can't handle everything at once), it was like I was playing the in-game assistant."* Spectators often have the opportunity to impact the game in-progress. Two examples of this are to act as an advisor to the player and to help the player focus on the game. The advisor acts as a second pair of eyes, giving the player reminders about what to do and alerts about key events that may have gone unnoticed. The other example is generally external to the game where the assistance is meant to make it easier for the player to focus on the game. Feeding snacks to the gamer is an example of this: *"[My ex] gets stressed out playing herself, but she found watching just as fun. She would goad me into playing long into the night, getting me sandwiches and beers."*

The Commentator – *"I really appreciate the insight [commentators] give on players, about their past accomplishments and how they've been doing recently, coming into a match. It's much more enjoyable when you know the players and the stakes."* The Commentator or "shoutcaster" is both spectator and a performer. He shapes the viewing experience of other spectators by providing a running commentary of the game. Amateur commentators on Youtube are sometimes dependent on the 'camera' operator, known as the 'observer' (hereafter, "observer-cameraman"), who controls the game UI to show the audience what is happening, while the commentator provides the voiceover. For example, an American caster named Moletrap casting a pre-recorded professional Korean match could not control when the video revealed game information relevant to his commentary. Unable to order the observer-cameraman to focus on a unit to show its upgrade level, he (helplessly) mutters, "click on a muta, click on a muta." In other cases, the observer-cameraman and the commentator are the same person, juggling both responsibilities.

A commentator is capable of conveying excitement and emotion that draws the crowd in to similar emotional reactions to the game. *"[Korean commentators] go crazy. Hell, I loved watching [videos on demand] from the time when Heman and Madfrog were in Korea, back in the glory days. The REACTIONS are what make watching these things fun."* Conversations drawn from the data were filled with meta-commentary about casting styles and favorite commentators. This parallels the previously described studies in sports commentary that make the game more enjoyable to the spectators [6]. Paired commentary is not uncommon, with spectators noting that one commentator is more technical while the other does more lightweight banter, like in many sportscasts [2]. Technically, commentators are valued for their ability to expose the depth of the game. Our analysis suggests that, as information gatekeepers, the commentator (along with the observer-cameraman) is the person who has the most influence on the audience. Our 'Information Asymmetry' section covers this later.

The Crowd – *"I know if something insane happens, there's going to be an insane reaction. From the crowd, from the commentators, from the players and coaches even! The fact that there's a scene makes a huge difference."* There is a strong communal aspect to spectating and a pleasure in watching a game as a group that matches behavior for traditional sporting events. We uncovered insights on group watching that we elaborate on in the following section.

THE SPECTATOR ECOSYSTEM

Spectating involves a communal aspect where fans derive a common social experience [1,2,3,6]. Here we present some key themes that we observed.

The Spectator Ecosystem— We use the term *ecosystem* to convey a sense of the inter-related aspect of game spectatorship. What is relevant about this characterization are the interrelated ties—ties that also include the players. Information dependencies arise as Pupils look towards the Commentators. Emotional experiences are shared. Social norms are established: players promise not to disappoint their fans and spectators judge players according to an understanding of sportsmanship and "bad-mannered" play.

Circles of watching— Although the game sits in the center-stage, it does not mean that the only performers are the players. The work of the broadcasters (observer-cameramen and Commentators) is another level of performance. Beyond that, the Crowd engages in little performances, trying to out-commentate the official commentators with their own analysis and prediction, or stirring up the emotions of their peers, and other reactionary performances. Dalsgaard et al. [3] describe a similar pattern for a performance at a public arcade: *This assembly of game, player, and immediate spec-*

tators can be said to exist as one situation of interaction, circumscribed by another one, namely that of spectators in the games arcade observing the friends playing. To spectators outside of the group of friends, the group of people taking turns playing make up a performative spectacle in its own right. The attention of the player and the bystanding friends are somewhat more unfocused when it comes to this second layer of performance. However, the group of alternating players is in no way oblivious to the fact that they may be the center of attention for passers-by.

Co-laboring in Spectatorship— Spectators work together to produce an enjoyable spectating experience. Most obviously, the commentators and observer-cameramen labor to shape the experience for their consumers. Venues provide food and refreshments for tournament spectators. Members of the crowd find narratives to latch onto. Informal information sharing is at work throughout. Even individuals preparing themselves to enjoy the game will actively avoid spoiling the game's outcome beforehand.

ENTERTAINING THE SPECTATOR

We now explore the anticipated question, what makes spectating a game enjoyable? Why are people entertained by an activity they have no control over? What is it about Starcraft that gives it multiple dedicated television channels in South Korea? The community crowns players as dominant stars. Fans avidly track careers as they rise, peak, and slump. How can a single game serve as a vessel for excitement, despair, and triumph?

As we combed through the stories and revelations in our data, we focused on the entertaining points that spectators mentioned when referring to Starcraft. As expected, spectators appreciated aspects of the game such as the spectacle of battles and graphics, user interface features and a game designed to enable spectators perceive the action, tactics and units in competitive play, and the emotions evoked during competition. Spectators commented on the excitement of watching a professional player's plans unfold. They noted that the graphics allowed them to understand who had the advantage, what the units were doing, and detect tense moments in the game. These were things Starcraft did especially well. However, we also began to find something that was intrinsic to Starcraft but less common in other games that was a source of entertainment. We now introduce a concept that we call *information asymmetry*, sensitized by Reeves et al.'s manipulations and effects [16] described by an article (from the data) by a documentary producer who is also a Starcraft spectator [22] and supported by diverse comments from the data.

Information Asymmetry

The spectator and players each have different slices of game information. Starcraft information includes strategic plans in the players' minds, the unit locations on the map, or the outcome of a sneak attack. Information asymmetry is the imbalance of information between the player and spectator, where due to the game design, one party is privy to some information and the other is not. We have collected evidence that information asymmetry is a fundamental source of entertainment in video games, with examples from Starcraft and other media. We list the different forms of information asymmetry and explain how they drive enjoyment in watching the game. Table 1 summarizes several examples that we elaborate on next.

One form of information asymmetry is information that is known to the player(s) but not the spectator. For example, each player knows their game plan and capabilities. They may have a well-practiced strategy or battle tactic that delights the spectator when it is executed flawlessly. Reeves et al. [16] give players credit for enhancing the spectators' experience through deliberately hiding or showing manipulations or effects. Spectators observing the manipulations can marvel at the skill of the player, while hidden manipulations creates a gap in information between the player and spectator. The spectator cannot see what the player is doing that affects the game later. In American football, elaborate plays are developed by the coaches before the players jog on to the field, and the spectator watches them unfold. Thus the spectator enjoys the show of skill, but "*You can only marvel at a brilliant move... after it happens*" [22].

The spectator does not know what will happen and this builds tension. The spectator wonders, "will they go for a field goal or touchdown?" or "will they make a running or passing play?" They are pleasantly surprised and cheer when a play is well executed. Starcraft has many of these scenarios; one is the building build order and army compo-

Table 1: Examples of information asymmetry in Starcraft. In the first two cases, information is unknown to both the spectator and player. In the next four cases, information is known only to either the spectator or the player.

Information		Example
Spectator	Player	
Unknown	Unknown	Outcome of a close battle (often dependent on "micro", careful skilled control of each unit by the player)
Unknown	Unknown	Unpredictable attacks: Reaver Scarabs may fizzle or decimate an army, Banelings roll over grouped marines but only if they can get close enough, Hunter Seeker Missiles track and home in on enemies
Known	Unknown	The positions and compositions of opposing players' units; enemy armies may unintentionally collide
Known	Unknown	Traps laid by one player for another, causing catastrophic damage at inopportune times
Unknown	Known	Planned build order during the opening, especially "cheese" (unorthodox trick opening play)
Unknown	Known	Attack strategy, e.g. a multi-pronged invasion, distracting the front while dropping in behind defenses

sition, which skilled players practice before the match. These often creative permutations determine the style of play for much of the game. The excitement of watching the players play out their strategies is a learning experience for some spectators such as the Pupil and the Curious, and an enjoyable surprise to others. This is especially true in games involving "cheese", where a player performs a risky unorthodox play at the start of the game to catch their opponent off-guard. For example, a player might construct buildings inside the enemy base without their knowing. If left undiscovered by the opponent, the player can overwhelm his opponent with an unexpected attack behind enemy lines. At first, the spectator may be confused by the player's actions, but then delights in seeing such a rare scenario once they understand the strategy.

A second form of information asymmetry occurs in nearly all games, when information is unknown to both the player and the spectator. The unknown information may be due to chance or skill and is a source of excitement for the players and spectators. In poker games, the players and spectators stand up in anticipation of the crucial upcoming card which decides who will win the pot of money in the center of the table. This causes a build-up of excitement that spectators enjoy. In Starcraft 2, one player may control a group of Banelings, rolling bombs that decimate enemy marines but only if they can get up close, surviving enemy fire en route. Micro-managed furiously by opposing players, the banelings and marines perform a dance, appearing as though they are about to engage but then pulling back at the last moment, each trying to gain a positional advantage. In Starcraft games, this form of missing information sometimes follows from the previous type. The player will begin with an information advantage over the spectator, but eventually the spectator catches up as the player executes their actions. At some point, the player and spectator have the same known and unknown information, and the excitement steers towards revealing the unknown.

The third form of information asymmetry is when the spectator has information about the game that the player(s) do not. In games like Street Fighter, Counterstrike, chess, or sports like tennis and soccer, spectators do not have any information advantage over the player. However, in Texas Hold'em poker, which gained popularity through televised tournaments, spectators could see the two cards held by each player (hole cards), but the players could only see their own cards. Spectators would know when a player was bluffing, eliciting empathetic emotions from the spectator as the uninformed player agonized over tough decisions. Starcraft and many other RTS games have a similar concept called "fog of war", where a player can only see the area near their units. Neither player can see the other player's buildings or armies, but, in broadcasted games or replays, the spectator can see both. The spectator has greater knowledge of both players' army and economy. This develops into dramatic scenarios: watching a transport vessel slowly scoot behind defensive lines for a tank drop which may devastate a player's economy, a player warping their main fighting force into an undetected minefield, or an invisible Dark Templar lying in wait for their opponent's vulnerable workers to come by. The Storyteller adds, *"Or, later in the game, the hold lurker strategy, the goliaths hanging around the spot that the dropships are passing by, the DT chillin' out at the expo, waiting to strike..."* [22]. These situations cause the spectator to wonder, "Will the player find out before it's too late?"

Commentators can also take advantage of information asymmetry. Suspense is sometimes orchestrated by the observer-cameraman, *"Korean obs are much better at making the spectating of SC2 more exciting. That was a great choice to NOT show TLO's tanks at the back door, and finally show it right as the roaches get in range. ... I've seen a lot of this stuff in Korean matches where someone is setting up an ambush or building lots of a surprise unit, and the obs focuses on other [parts of the map] and shows the stuff at the last moment."*

This effected emotion matches one author's experience at a Starcraft 2 tournament, where he witnessed the crowd going wild when the observer-cameraman 'discovered' a hidden group of tanks in the corner of the map. There was excited cheering, laughter, and clapping from the audience.

Leading to Suspense

All information asymmetry is reduced and eliminated as the game progresses. But as the information is revealed, the spectator is entertained in the process. The revelation of this information, slowly teased out, creates suspense for spectators and players. In an article of "why Starcraft attracts crowds so often" listing 14 examples of exciting spectacles [4], the majority were cases of information asymmetry leading to suspense. The examples were: crazy unexpected strategies (player has information advantage), air chases, mine drags, storm blankets, reavers, and the clash (outcomes are highly variable and thus unknown), lurker hold position trick, arbiter recall on mines, and nukes (the spectator has an information advantage over the victim player). For example, as flying transportation vessels float over enemy frontlines, spectators watch in anticipation, wondering if they will be shot down by the opponent's turrets or if they will make it to the mining workers, devastating the opponent's economy. Starcraft's strength in attracting spectators lies in its many situations of long teasing information asymmetries of all three types. These drawn out unknowns build suspense for the spectators and their release is a source of entertainment.

Suspense is also a product of other events in the game. Comebacks, where players are nearly beaten but return to parity after spectacular play provides suspense. Epic games, long matches which go back and forth a lot, are another source of suspense, where the spectator feels that so much has already been invested into the game that when one player loses, it will be all for naught. Situations that result in suspense in Starcraft are frequent, increasing the overall spectator enjoyment of the game.

DISCUSSION

Spectatorship and the Magic Circle

We return to a question raised in our literature review: where the Spectator fits in the Magic Circle. From the readings, our criteria for inclusion are understanding and adoption. From our analysis, we find that this is the fence on which the Bystander sits. The examples of information and investment and the personas match thematically with the exception of the "griefer" persona which paints a picture of an outside player whose actions interfere with the game experience of the game players. This exception can be explained by architectural differences: a Starcraft match cannot be as easily interrupted in the same manner as a World of Warcraft raid. This leaves room for inquiry about the relationship between game design and spectator-as-griefer. That aside; we can safely state that spectators are typically informed and invested, and that the spectator's relationship to the Magic Circle can be mapped inside or outside according to these two variables.

Furthermore, we have seen that Starcraft is a game where information is always in demand and that information and investment exist at *different levels.* The Pupil persona and the investment levels seen in Information Asymmetry confirm this. When there is more to understand about the game, there is greater involvement in the play. The picture of the Magic Circle for spectators changes thus: there are *many* circles. They are circumscribed according to varying levels of knowledge and investment.

Something more can be said about the nature of such depth. Our analysis suggests that both informational and investment depth come to an inevitable end (at least for Starcraft). Knowledge about a game comes to a plateau. Emotional investments in the outcome of a game are closed when the outcome is decided. This anticipated finish for spectating can be seen in traditional baseball when crowds begin to empty a stadium in the 7th or 8th inning.

Finally, we believe that our data helps untangle the "vicarious attitude" of spectatorship. In our data, we noted two distinct attitudes towards playing vs. watching. For some, playing is the preferred activity. For others, such as the Unsatisfied and Inspired, spectating fuels a desire to play. Our interpretation is that vicariousness in spectatorship should be divided into two: the satisfying and the unsatisfying. This sentiment extends the conversation on spectatorship in ways that may lead researchers to ask why, in the aftermath of a worldwide Starcraft tournament, the servers are flooded with like-minded gamers; and why some people can identify deeply with the game, follow favorite players, attend matches, and yet never play themselves.

The idea of *circles of watching* in the spectator ecology inspires reference to Goffman's dramaturgical lens [9]. Certainly, within the "Crowd" we can say that a group identity is being acted out. There is concern, for example, over how gamers are seen by society: violent and time-wasting instead of people healthily engaged in community events. Delving into the 'backstage' of one of these communities, we found a debate over the use of offensive words like 'rape' in the gamer community[2]; one issue was how such language impacted outsider perception. Another example is the concerted effort by the performers, the gamers (and, in part, the commentators) in representing themselves as athletes engaged in a match of wits and skill. Many online posters constantly compared Starcraft to other sports—chess in particular—appealing to the case that Starcraft holds equal ground in balance, depth and respectability. These portrayals impact playing style. Further investigations could examine how players balance their goal of winning the game alongside their self-portrayal as athletes, as gamers, or as celebrities.

Implications for Design

Among the possibilities of design (taking an ecological approach to spectating communities, applying personas to design, engaging the Entertained, etc...) the primacy of information leads us to share the following insight.

One naïve perspective may be that games should be designed to give as much information to the spectator as possible. In some cases, this makes sense: spectators will better understand the status of the game from seeing the banked resources each player has or the unit counts on the field, or in fighting games, statistics about the attacks or players' match history. Games need to reveal enough information for the spectator to know what is going on, who is winning, etc. Otherwise, they are hard to watch and understand. Esbjörnsson et al. [7] recognize that race rally attendees can miss out on the whole picture of a race when they watch one corner of a race from the sidelines. However, we found that spectators enjoy situations that start with information asymmetry—that the suspense is in the revelation.

Consider game "spoilers". Taken in light of Information Asymmetry, we can define a spoiler as information that prematurely collapses the desired game suspense for a spectator. Even information about the length of the game shown on the video playback can spoil the game for the spectator. One spectator describes a make-shift solution (and his frustrations) as he actively hides such spoilers from himself: *"if I watch [videos] on youtube i use paper+ducktape to cover the scores at the top of the screen and the "time-tracker" or how you wanna call it at the bottom, so I don't know the scores and the length of the match... BUT: I have to switch to fullscreen - so I have to close my eyes so that I can barely see anything and quickly switch to fullscreen without seeing the score or the length of the [video]."*

Stakeholders in the spectator ecosystem take opportunities to intentionally create information asymmetry. The example of a commentator purposely ignoring attack preparation only to show them at an opportune time demonstrates this. In fact, players might benefit from the ability to hide certain

[2] http://www.teamliquid.net/forum/viewmessage.php?topic_id=143803

information from the spectator, such as a crucial tank factory in Starcraft. Several professional Starcraft players already attempt to play in a style that is more fun to watch. HDStarcraft during a Google Tech Talk suggested, "*the spectators love watching interesting and creative play; and for those of you guys that don't know, if play terran, you can go for nukes, nuclear missiles, which are very hard to use, but they're always a crowd pleaser. and tlo, the little one, uses nukes so effectively and that's one of the reasons why he's become so successful.*" Information hiding would be a natural next step. Perhaps the proper question for designers to ask is not "how do we give *more* information to spectators?", but rather, as spectators participate in and *co-construct* their own experience as a body of viewers, "*where* should we place control over the game information?"

CONCLUSIONS

In this paper we have defined the video game spectator: a person whose intentions range from watching the game casually to being a fan at competitive gaming tournaments. We collected over a hundred stories of the Starcraft spectator from online sources, aiming for as diverse a group as possible. Using a grounded theory approach, we then analyzed the data, annotated instances, and clustered them in different facets. These facets corresponded to the lens of our research questions, asking i) who are the spectators and why do they spectate, ii) how different stakeholders affect the spectator's experience, and iii) what a spectator finds entertaining. We drew upon the data to construct different spectator personas evident in the stories. From this, we built theoretical frameworks of the spectator ecosystem and information asymmetry. These led to design implications for improving the game watching experience for spectators.

Spectating games is a growing activity. Starcraft popularity, previously confined to Korea, has been spreading to the rest of the world thanks to the rise of video sharing sites and the release of Starcraft 2. An era when game designers and even players attend to the spectator does not seem too distant. Our paper presents a better understanding of the spectator that may support these stakeholders. These are the lessons we have learned from spectating the spectator.

REFERENCES

1. Bryant, J., Brown, D., Comisky, P.W., and Zillmann, D. 1982. Sports and Spectators: Commentary and Appreciation. *Journal of Communication*, 32(1), 109–119.
2. Cominsky, P., Bryant, J., and Zillmann, D. 1977. Commentary as a substitute for action. *Journal of Communication*, 27(3), 150–153.
3. Dalsgaard, P. and Hansen, L.K. 2008. Performing perception—staging aesthetics of interaction. *ACM Transactions of Computer-Human Interaction*, 15(3), 1–33.
4. Ddengster. 2010. Spectator moments in Starcraft. Team Liquid Forums. Retrieved September 14, 2010 from http://www.teamliquid.net/forum/viewmessage.php?topic_id=145848
5. Drucker, S., He, L., Cohen, M., Wong, C., and Gupta, A. 2002. Spectator games: A new entertainment modality of networked multiplayer games. Technical report, Microsoft Research.
6. Ducheneaut, N., Yee, N., Nickell, E., and Moore, R. J. 2006. "Alone together?": exploring the social dynamics of massively multiplayer online games. In *Proceedings of CHI '06*, 407–416.
7. Esbjörnsson, M., Brown, B., Juhlin, O., Normark, D., Östergren, M., and Laurier, E. 2006. Watching the cars go round and round: designing for active spectating. In *Proceedings of CHI '06*, 1221–1224.
8. Giles, J. 2007. Virtual entrepreneurs and 'griefers' spoil the fantasy of online worlds. *New Scientist*, September 2007, 28–29.
9. Goffman, E. 1959. *The Presentation of Self in Everday Life.* Anchor Books, Doubleday.
10. Huhh, J. 2008. Culture and Business of PC Bangs in Korea. *Games and Culture*, 3(1), 26–37.
11. Huizinga, J. 1938. *Homo Ludens*. Beacon Press.
12. Lincoln, Y. S. and Guba, E. G. 1985. *Naturalistic Inquiry*. Sage, Newbury Park, CA.
13. Melnick, M. 1993. Searching for Sociability in the Stands: A Theory of Sports Spectating. *Journal of Sports Management*, 7(1), 44–60.
14. Nardi, B. 2010. *My Life as a Night Elf Priest: An Anthropological Account of World of Warcraft.* University of Michigan Press.
15. Patton, M.Q. 2001. *Qualitative Research and Evaluation Methods*, 234–235.
16. Reeves, S., Benford, S., O'Malley, C., and Fraser, M. 2005. Designing the spectator experience. In *Proceedings of CHI '05*, 741–750.
17. Salen, K and Zimmerman, E. 2003. *Rules of Play: Game Design Fundamentals.* The MIT Press.
18. Shea, C. 2008. Blizzard Entertainment's Frank Pearse: AU Interview. Australia, August 3, 2008. Retrieved September 23, 2010 from http://pc.ign.com/articles/896/896078p1.html
19. Strauss, A. and Corbin, J. 1990. *Basics of Qualitative Research.* Sage, Newbury Park, CA.
20. Su, N. 2010. Street Fighter IV: Braggadocio Off and On-Line. In *Proceedings of CSCW '10*, 361–370.
21. Sutton-Smith, B. 2001. *The Ambiguity of Play*. Harvard University Press.
22. The Storyteller. 2009. Tension in SC. Team Liquid Forums. Retrieved July 25, 2010 from http://www.teamliquid.net/forum/viewmessage.php?topic_id=87117
23. Trail, G.T., Fink, J.S., and Anderson, D.F. 2003. Sport spectator consumption behavior. *Sport Marketing Quarterly*, 12(1), 8–17.

Do Men Heal More When in Drag? Conflicting Identity Cues Between User and Avatar

Nick Yee[1], Nicolas Ducheneaut[1], Mike Yao[2], Les Nelson[1]

[1]Palo Alto Research Center
3333 Coyote Hill Road, Palo Alto, CA
[nyee, nicolas, lnelson]@parc.com

[2]Department of Media and Communication
City University of Hong Kong
mike.yao@cityu.edu.hk

ABSTRACT
Studies in the Proteus Effect have shown that users conform to stereotypes associated with their avatar's appearance. In this study, we used longitudinal behavioral data from 1,040 users in a virtual world to examine the behavioral outcome of conflicting gender cues between user and avatar. We found that virtual gender had a significant effect on in-game behaviors for both healing and player-vs-player activity.

Author Keywords
Avatar, identity, stereotypes, Proteus Effect, gender.

ACM Classification Keywords
H5.m. Information interfaces and presentation (e.g., HCI): Miscellaneous.

General Terms
Human Factors

INTRODUCTION
Digital environments allow us to create and customize our avatars (i.e., digital representations of ourselves) at the click of a button. Whether choosing to be an orc or an elf in a fantasy online game like *World of Warcraft*, or the exact shade of eye color in the user-created world of *Second Life*, virtual worlds (VWs) allow us to dramatically alter our self-representation. Understanding how people create avatars [2] and how social interaction is influenced by avatar appearance [10] are core research interests in the HCI community.

While it is easy to think of avatar creation as a one-way, user-directed process, studies have shown a more provocative two-way process between user and avatar. Specifically, the Proteus Effect [9] describes the observed phenomenon where users conform to expected behaviors and attitudes associated with their avatar's appearance. For example, users given taller avatars negotiate more aggressively in a bargaining task than users given shorter avatars. But what happens when an avatar's identity is in direct conflict with the user's identity? Given that avatar creation is typically a user-driven choice in VWs, it is difficult to know whether findings from randomly assigned avatars in laboratory studies generalize to natural settings.

In this paper, we describe a study that uses longitudinal data from actual users in a VW to examine the Proteus Effect when user and avatar identity cues are in conflict.

Outcomes of Conflicting Identity Cues
A conflict between physical and virtual identity cues may lead to a variety of plausible outcomes:

1) According to deindividuation theory, identity cues hold more sway when individuals are in VWs [4]. Thus, physical identity cues are deemphasized, and users conform to virtual cues, regardless of physical cues.
2) On the other hand, when virtual identity cues are made salient (especially when they are in direct conflict with the physical identity of a user), it allows for conscious monitoring and filtering of stereotypes [1]. Thus, users may not be influenced by the virtual cues at all. This seems particularly plausible in natural settings where users choose their own avatars.
3) But in more extreme cases, conscious monitoring may lead to overcompensation. This is similar to the ironic nature of mental control [5], such as asking someone to not think of a pink elephant. In much the same way, asking someone to not be aggressive may cause them to overcompensate and become overly docile.

A recent study [3] using longitudinal data from *EverQuest II* (EQ2) examined this conflict between players who do and do not gender-bend (i.e., play a character of the opposite gender). The activities they analyzed were combat, quest completion, player vs. player, and chatting. Among men, they found no differences between players who do and do not gender-bend. Among women, they found a mixture of overcompensation and deindividuation effects. In short, these findings lend some support to all three outcomes listed above.

We seek to expand upon these prior findings in two ways. First, we want to identify actual game-related gender stereotypes held by gamers. In the above-mentioned study, stereotypes from the physical world were assumed to transfer into a fantasy game context. As the authors in that paper noted, this translation resulted in broad measures of combat and questing that may not have been sensitive enough to detect gendered differences. Secondly, additional data from another online gaming context may help us more clearly see the outcome of conflicting identity cues. To address these two points, we gathered and analyzed stereotype and longitudinal behavioral data from the online game *World of Warcraft* (WoW).

METHOD

In order to identify stereotypically gendered behaviors to further analyze, we first conducted a web-based survey to explore which in-game behaviors were most strongly stereotyped in terms of gender. Below, we briefly describe the context of WoW. Then, we report the findings of the pretest survey of stereotypes and the analyses of in-game behaviors.

World of Warcraft

WoW is currently one of the more popular online games available commercially, with roughly 11 million active subscribers world-wide [6]. WoW uses a typical "leveling up" formula seen in computer role-playing games. The game encourages players in different ways to collaborate with other players. For example, users can create characters with different skill sets that complement each other (i.e., classes). Heavily-armored *tank* classes shield the group from enemy attacks while lightly-armored damage dealing *DPS* (damage per second) classes deal damage to enemies and *healing* classes restore health lost in combat. Player vs. Player (PvP) combat is allowed, but a set of rules defines where and whether players can attack and kill each other. And finally, it is important to note that in WoW, male and female avatars have the same abilities and skills. Thus avatar gender is entirely cosmetic and does not lead to any functional difference in terms of game-play.

Pretest of Player Stereotypes

Given that the Proteus Effect operates on shared social stereotypes, it is important to first understand what gender stereotypes WoW players have. 252 participants were recruited from message boards and websites catering to WoW players. Participants were asked to rate a set of six activities in WoW along a 5-point rating scale of whether they believed men or women had a preference for that activity: -2 (women strongly prefer), 0 (no difference), and 2 (men strongly prefer). We show the means and standard deviations for each activity in Table 1.

A paired t-test revealed that the stereotype valence for Healing was significantly different from that of Crafting ($t[251] = -8.20$, $p < .001$), and thus would be significantly different from all other activities as well. Thus, for a stereotypically female activity, we selected Healing to further analyze. And for a stereotypically male activity, we selected PvP. We did not select Tanking for the male activity to analyze because it is much more difficult to create a metric for Tanking from the current database of player activities (the WoW Armory, described in more detail below).

Activity	Mean	SD
Tank	1.08	0.76
PvP	0.98	0.76
Melee DPS	0.88	0.73
Ranged DPS	-0.23	0.65
Crafting	-0.25	0.6
Healing	-0.7	0.68

Table 1. Means and standard deviations for gender stereotypes in WoW, ordered from strongest male preferred activity to strongest female preferred activity.

Participants

1,084 WoW players were included in the next phase of the study. We recruited participants from forums dedicated to WoW, publicity on popular gaming sites (e.g., WoW.com), word-of-mouth on social media like Twitter, and mailing lists from previous studies of WoW players. We note that due to human subjects regulations, minors were excluded from participating in the study. Nevertheless, we were still able to gather data from a very wide age range (18-65). The average age of our sample was 27.03 (SD = 8.21). 26% of participants were women. These demographic variables are mostly consistent with previous studies of online gamers [8].

Procedure

Participants began by completing a web-based survey that gathered their demographic information. Participants were also asked to list up to 6 WoW characters they were actively playing. Once these characters were in our database, an automated data collection system was activated. The system then launched a daily web scraper to gather these characters' profiles (large XML files) from the WoW Armory over a 5 month period.

The WoW Armory is a public database maintained by Blizzard, the developer of WoW, which contains hundreds of longitudinal game-play metrics of every character, including total career kills, deaths, equipment currently worn, and even the number of hugs (i.e., emotes) given to other players. The Armory is updated daily.

Measures

To create a metric for healing, we calculated the ratio of total healing done against total damage done for each participant's primary character (i.e., the character that had the most days played during the 5 month period, $M = 53.66$, $SD = 39.71$). Calculating a ratio of healing against damage circumvents the potential problem of comparing hardcore players from casual players. In other words, it is important to remove the noise of players who have a high amount of cumulative healing due to playing many more hours of WoW than the average. Thus, the ratio focuses more directly on the concept of preference—how does the player allocate between healing and dealing damage on a particular character? We also note that healing as reported on the Armory includes some noise from passive healing abilities that are beyond a player's control, but that these weak passive heals are easily overshadowed by direct healing spells in dungeon and raiding contexts. Similar to this healing metric, to create a metric for PvP, we calculated the ratio of PvP-related kills against total kills.

RESULTS

We first report some descriptive statistics for base rates of gender-bending, and then present the results for the research question.

Gender-Bending Base Rates

In our sample of 1,084 participants, we had 281 women and 801 men. On average, they had 2.79 (SD = 1.51) characters. Among men, 53.3% had a character of the opposite gender. On average for men, 33.4% of their characters were of the opposite gender. Among women, 18.5% had at least one character of the opposite gender. On average for women, 9.1% of their characters were of the opposite gender. The same trends were true for the primary character. 7.5% of women's primary characters were male. 29.3% of men's primary characters were female. This disparity between men and women is consistent with past data [7]. Also consistent with this past data, gender-bending is positively correlated with age among men ($r = .10, p < .01$), but not women ($r = .08, p = .16$).

Healing Metric

We conducted an ANOVA using Player Gender and Character Gender as the factors and the Healing Ratio (of each participant's primary character) as the dependent variable. We removed any outliers that were more than 2 SDs away from the mean.

The main effect of Player Gender was not significant ($F[1, 1024] = .20, p = .67$). In terms of Healing Ratio in the game, men ($M = .33, SE = .02$) and women ($M = .30, SE = .06$) were quite similar.

The main effect of Character Gender was significant ($F[1, 1024] = 5.13, p = .02$). Female characters ($M = .39, SE = .03$) had a significantly higher Healing Ratio than male characters ($M = .23, SE = .06$). Post-hoc comparisons revealed that this was true for both men and women (p's < .05). See Figure 1. The interaction effect was not significant ($F[1, 1024] = .67, p = .41$).

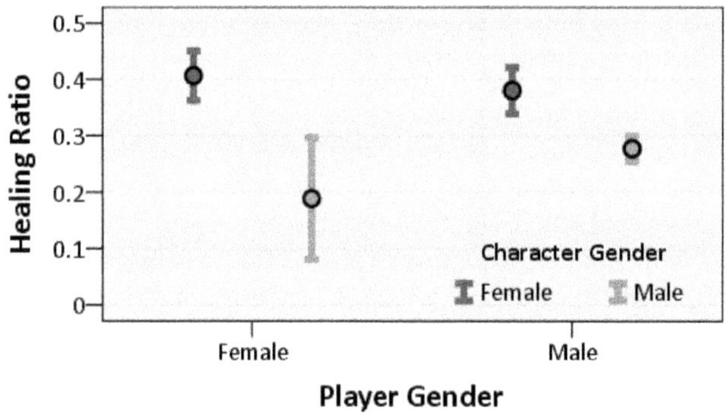

Figure 1. Plot of player gender and character gender interaction with standard error bars. Note that larger F-M variance in this and next graph are due to much smaller sample size of women who gender-bend.

PvP Metric

We conducted a similar ANOVA with the PvP metric. The main effect of Player Gender was approaching significance ($F[1, 1096] = 3.29, p = .07$). Men had a higher PvP Ratio ($M = .06, SE = .002$) than women ($M = .04, SE = .007$).

The main effect of Character Gender was significant ($F[1, 1096] = 3.99, p = .04$). Male characters had a higher PvP Ratio ($M = .06, SE = .007$) than female characters ($M = .04, SE = .003$). The interaction effect was not significant ($F[1, 1096] = .00, p = .81$). See Figure 2.

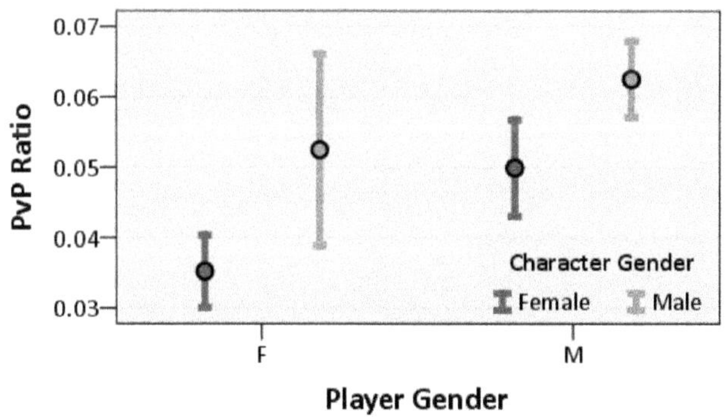

Figure 2. Plot of player gender and character gender interaction with standard error bars.

DISCUSSION

Our findings show that when identity cues conflict among actual VW users, users conform to their virtual identity. In terms of both healing and PvP activity, character gender had a significant effect on in-game behavior. This in turn suggests that deindividuation in virtual environments allows virtual cues to take precedence over physical cues.

On the other hand, even though there were some similarities, discrepancies with the earlier study of EQ2 data [3] complicate the picture. Similar to that study, we observed the Proteus Effect for PvP activity, but we found the effect for both men and women. And overall, we found more consistent support for the Proteus Effect in the current data set, where both metrics showed a significant main effect for character gender.

We propose several reasons for these discrepancies. First, we conducted a survey to target gender-stereotyped in-game behaviors and likely identified more sensitive measures. Indeed, the PvP measure was largely comparable in both studies. Moreover, our survey results show that "combat" may be too broad as a metric, but finer-grained distinctions between Melee and Ranged DPS might show gendered differences. Secondly, different cultural norms and personality profiles among players in WoW and EQ2 may contribute to observed differences as well. For example, the EQ2 study found that 17.4% of men gender-bended, whereas in the WoW sample, 53.3% of men gender-bended. It is likely that another demographic or game-related variable is lurking as a moderating variable. In short, we can't take for granted that findings from one virtual world generalize to other virtual worlds, and we need to continue exploring identity cue conflicts in other virtual environments.

Social Construction of Gender

The data on healing presents a particularly provocative illustration of the social construction of gender. While WoW players share a strong stereotype of women preferring to heal, our findings show that this stereotype isn't true. We did not find a significant difference in terms of player gender. What we did find was that players enact this stereotype when gender-bending. Thus, the stereotype becomes true in the VW—female characters heal more than male characters. These findings illustrate how gender differences can be socially constructed, and how gender is being produced in VWs.

Implications for CHI

The Proteus Effect has implications for avatar-mediated systems in general, whether 2D or 3D. For example, these studies in the Proteus Effect suggest that providing more athletic and fit avatars in the context of a health game may lead to better outcomes than providing an avatar that resembles the user. Our findings suggest that any cue conflicts between user and avatar are likely to be resolved in favor of the avatar.

Limitations

There are significant trade-offs between lab experiments and natural observations. Given that character creation, and especially gender-bending, is a user choice, it makes sense to try to study this behavior in a natural setting instead of forcing users to adopt particular avatars. On the other hand, we lose experimental control in doing so.

This introduces several limitations to our study. First, it is possible that other players have a significant role in shaping a female avatar's behavior, via social pressure (i.e., behavior confirmation). It is also difficult to tease out whether an underlying personality variable is driving both gender-bending and healing preference. Nevertheless, our study illustrates the outcome of conflicting identity cues between user and avatar in an actual VW. While we cannot pin the causality precisely on the Proteus Effect, the findings are consistent with the theoretical prediction.

These limitations also point directly at possible future studies where avatar gender is incongruent between user and other players—i.e., a man playing a female character is perceived as a male character by other players. Such a setup would allow us to pit the Proteus Effect against behavioral confirmation directly.

Conclusion

Creating an avatar is a fascinating two-way process. Our findings in the current study suggest that we conform to the roles that are expected of our avatars, independent of who we are in the physical world. While one might assume that the infinite fluidity in VWs helps free us of our physical identities and norms, the opposite appears to be more accurate in this case. And in the particular case of healing, we in fact found that a gender stereotype that isn't true in the physical world becomes true in the virtual world.

ACKNOWLEDGMENTS

This research is sponsored by the Air Force Research Laboratory

REFERENCES

1. Devine, P. Stereotypes and prejudice: Their automatic and controlled components. *Journal of Personality and Social Psychology, 56* (1989), 5-18.
2. Ducheneaut, N., Wen, M., Yee, N. and Wadley, G. Body and mind: a study of avatar personalization in three virtual worlds. *Proceedings of CHI 2009* (2009).
3. Huh, S. and Williams, D. Dude looks like a lady: Gender swapping in an online game. in Bainbridge, W. ed. *Online Worlds: Convergence of the real and the virtual*, Springer, New York, 2009.
4. Johnson, R. and Downing, L. Deindividuation and valence of cues: Effects on prosocial and antisocial behavior. *Journal of Personality and Social Psychology, 37* (1979), 1532-1538.
5. Wegner, D. Ironic processes of mental control. *Psychological Review, 101* (1994), 34-52.
6. White, P. MMOGData: Charts. *2009* (2008).
7. Yee, N. The Demographics of Gender-Bending. *The Daedalus Project.* http://www.nickyee.com/daedalus/archives/000551.php
8. Yee, N. The demographics, motivations, and derived experiences of users of massively multi-user online graphical environments. *Presence: Teleoperators and Virtual Environments, 15* (2006), 309-329.
9. Yee, N. and Bailenson, J. The Proteus Effect: The effect of transformed self-representation on behavior. *Human Communication Research, 33* (2007), 271-290.
10. Yee, N., Bailenson, J.N. and Rickertsen, K. A Meta-Analysis of the Impact of the Inclusion and Realism of Human-Like Faces on User Experiences in Interfaces. *CHI 2007 Proceedings* (2007), 1-10.

Is the Media Equation a Flash in the Pan? The Durability and Longevity of Social Responses to Computers

Laura M. Pfeifer, Timothy Bickmore
College of Computer and Information Science
Northeastern University
360 Huntington Avenue, Boston, MA 02115
{laurap, bickmore}@ccs.neu.edu

ABSTRACT
Research on social responses to computers often assesses only first-impression reactions during a single experimental session, providing limited knowledge about the lasting effect of the results. In this work, we assess the lasting strength of social desirability bias effects on an interface designed to track exercise, manipulated to have high or low personalization (text vs. anthropomorphic conversational character). After 40 days of daily interactions by 25 participants, we found that self-reported exercise was more accurate when reported to the character vs. text. We also find that, for both conditions, participants' decision to initiate a session is greater when they have done more exercise. Moreover, we show that this effect significantly increases over time for participants in the character condition, and decreases for participants in the text condition. This study demonstrates that Media Equation effects can grow stronger or weaker over time, depending upon the presentation of the interface.

Author Keywords
Media Equation, self-report, longitudinal assessments

ACM Classification Keywords
H5.2. Information interfaces and presentation (e.g., HCI): User Interfaces—Evaluation/methodology, Graphical user interfaces, Interaction styles.

General Terms
Experimentation, Human Factors

INTRODUCTION

Since the introduction of the Media Equation hypothesis and the Computers as Social Actors paradigm, there have been several experiments showing that people respond socially to computers, in ways that are similar to how people respond socially to humans [12]. For example, people have been shown to assign gender and personality traits to computers and interact in ways that are biased by those social assignments [9,12].

CHI 2011, May 7–12, 2011, Vancouver, BC, Canada.

With years of research behind us, there is scientific support for the Media Equation hypothesis. However, research studies on the social responses to computers have typically only assessed a person's first-reaction response, and have not evaluated the potential for changes over time. A reasonable hypothesis is that when people interact with a social interface repeatedly, over long periods of time, their reactions to the interface might change. They may realize that the interface is not as capable or competent as a human is at being a social actor, or they may become conscious of their misattribution and as a result, their social responses to the computer may diminish with time. In this work, we explore the durability and longevity of social responses to computer interfaces, in a longitudinal context.

Social Desirability Bias

During social interactions, it is well-established that humans continually edit themselves to create a desirable presentation to their peers [5]. In survey or interview responses, a well-known form of self-editing is referred to as social desirability bias. This bias in self-reported data typically involves the over-reporting of socially desirable behaviors (voting, exercise, etc) and under- or non-reporting of socially undesirable behaviors (illicit drug use, etc) [4]. For example, self-reported information from online dating profiles is frequently inaccurate, with members describing themselves in a more socially positive light, e.g. men reporting themselves as taller and women reporting themselves as thinner [6].

When eliciting self-reports of potentially sensitive information, a well-known mechanism to reduce the effects of social desirability bias is to make the data collection medium as anonymous as possible. For example, computerized interviews have been shown to collect higher quality data than face-to-face interviews [2,10].

Nonetheless, even computerized interviews can elicit socially desirable responses. A classic study by Nass, et al., shows that people give significantly more polite responses when completing an evaluation about a computer, if the evaluation takes place on the same computer they recently interacted with, versus a different computer in the same room [8].

However, simple personalization manipulations of computer interfaces do not always elicit strong social cues. In an experiment examining the personalization of questionnaires and the corresponding effects of social desirability bias on self-reported data, Couper, et. al.. failed to demonstrate socially biased reports on sensitive topics when elicited via a web survey that included a photo of the researcher, compared to the same survey without this personalization [13].

Cassell & Miller propose using embodied conversational agents – animated characters that simulate face-to-face interaction - as a medium for boosting perceptions of personalization, manipulating social bias effects, and for systematically studying self-report behaviors, since they encompass features of both a computer and a human [3]. They have the ability to build rapport, trust and accountability with the interviewee, as well as provide a sense of anonymity. Initial research has shown that people do give socially desirable responses to these high-personalization computer interfaces, at least during an initial session with the character [7].

In this paper, we extend previous work by exploring how social desirability bias effects, as witnessed in human-computer interactions, hold up over time. We describe a randomized longitudinal experiment, in which participants completed an assessment about their exercise behavior (walking), each day, for six weeks. The assessment was either conducted through dialogue with an anthropomorphic conversational character or via displayed text (Figure 1). We compare these self-report data to data collected via a wearable sensor (pedometer) worn by participants throughout the course of the study.

EXPERIMENTAL METHODS

The experiment was conducted in our Virtual Laboratory, a framework for running longitudinal experiments with a standing group of study participants [1]. For the current implementation, participants interacted with a computer character designed to emulate an exercise counselor and promote walking behavior. The daily conversation with the virtual exercise counselor took place on participants' home computers and lasted approximately 10 minutes. It included a discussion about the participant's walking behavior, and problem-solved any barriers to exercise. After the conversation with the virtual counselor was over, participants were given the opportunity to complete a single-item assessment, self-reporting the number of minutes they walked on the previous day. We chose this self-report measure as the target of this study because of its ability to be independently verified through the use of a wearable sensor: a pedometer.

Participants were randomized into one of two conditions, either completing the assessment via a continued conversation with their virtual counselor (CHARACTER, high personalization) or via displayed text (TEXT, low personalization). All participants received the exercise counseling session with the character, and at the end of the interaction participants were asked - either spoken by the virtual counselor (CHARACTER) or via displayed text (TEXT) - "Do you have time for one more question?" If the participant responded *yes*, the participant was asked "How many minutes of walking did you do yesterday?" and the system displayed a keypad for the participant to enter their answer (Figure 1). This completed the participant's daily interaction with the system.

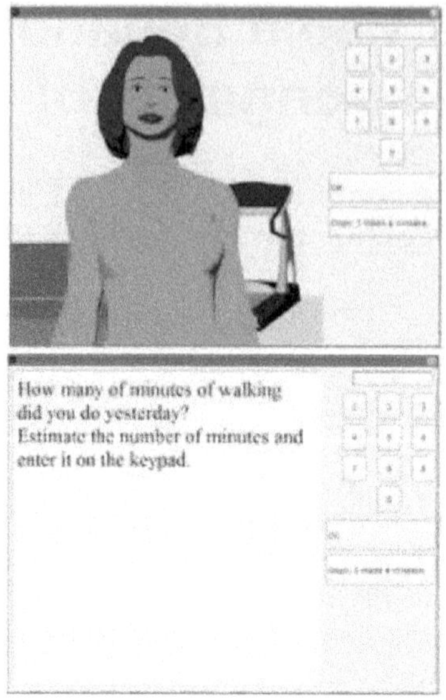

Figure 1. CHARACTER and TEXT condition.

We independently measured walking behavior through the use of an Omron HJ-720ITC pedometer worn by each participant throughout the course of the experiment, with steps uploaded to the computer via USB cable. The pedometers displayed daily step counts but did not display any information regarding time spent walking.

Our hypotheses are that: (H1) the more physical activity the participants performed, the more likely they will be to report it to the system - and that this effect will be greater when reporting to the virtual human versus the displayed text; but that (H2) the effect will dissipate over time, as participants receive increased exposure to the computer system; and finally, (H3) data gathered via the character interface will be more accurate (verified by data from the pedometer) than data gathered via the text interface.

Participants

A total of 25 participants (23 female, ages 55-68) took part in the study. All participants were compensated $1 per day that they interacted with the system. Thirteen participants were randomized into the CHARACTER condition and 12 were randomized into the TEXT condition. The experiment lasted for six weeks.

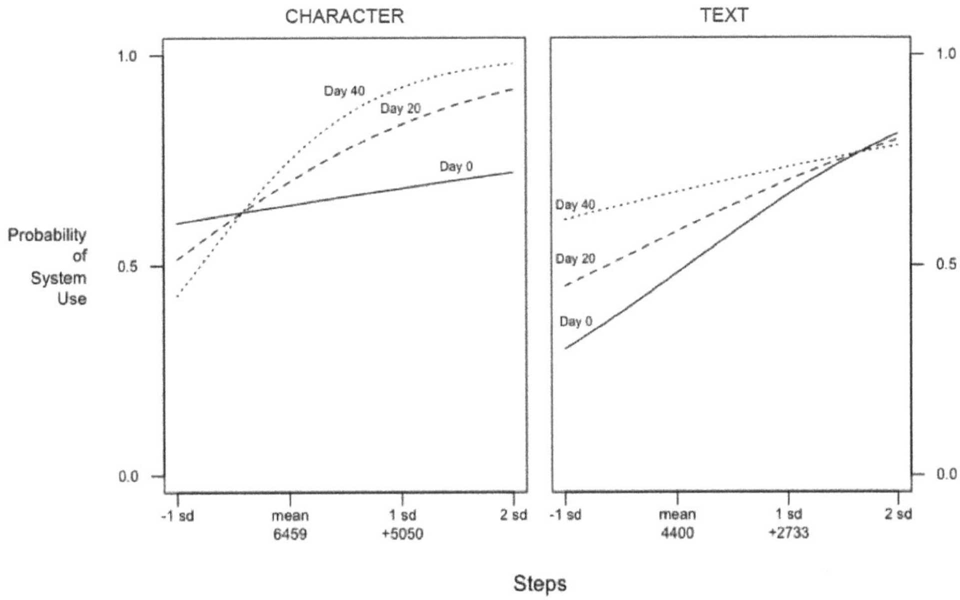

Figure 2. Effects of steps walked (pedometer-measured) on system use over time. Steps are mean-centered, by condition.

RESULTS

System usage and the self-reported walking behavior were analyzed as binary outcomes, by fitting a logistic mixed-effect regression model to the data. Logistic mixed-effect regression is a generalization of logistic regression, suitable for analyzing repeated binary measurements. All analyses were performed using R 2.9.1 with the lme4 package [11].

To examine H1 and H2, we first analyzed the likelihood of participants logging in and having a daily session with the system. Our model included fixed effects of study day, condition, and the pedometer step count from the previous day, along with corresponding interaction effects (Table1). Results show a significant three-way interaction between the previous day's step count, study condition, and study day on system use. This interaction is visualized in Figure 2. Throughout the entirety of the study (days 0, 20 and 40 in Figure 2) we see that for both conditions, the more steps a participant walked, the more likely they were to use the system, providing partial support for H1. Initially, the effect is stronger in the TEXT condition than the CHARACTER condition.

Furthermore, we see significant differences between conditions on the lasting effect of this finding. By longitudinally examining the effect of the previous day's step count on daily system use, we find that in concordance with H2, this effect *decreased* over time for participants in the TEXT condition, but in contrast, it *increased* over time for participants in the CHARACTER condition. By the end of the study, the amount of walking done by a participant in the TEXT condition had little effect on their likelihood to use the system. In contrast, the amount of walking done by participants in the CHARACTER condition greatly determined the likelihood that they would interact with the system.

We also examined the likelihood of participants to self-report their minutes of walking once they initiated an interaction with the system. Our model included fixed effects of study day, condition, and the previous day's pedometer step count. Results show that participants in the TEXT condition were more likely to self-report their number of minutes walked, regardless of the number of steps they actually walked and regardless of the study day, compared to participants in the CHARACTER condition, $B = 1.817$, $p < 0.01$. We hypothesize this may be due to the TEXT interface being more efficient to use.

Table 1. Logistic Mixed-Effect Regression Estimate of Effects of Condition, Previous Day's Step Count, and Study Day on System Use. Condition 0 = CHARACTER, 1 = TEXT.

Random Effects	Std. Dev.		
Intercept	0.8457		
Fixed Effects	**Estimate**	**Std. Error**	***p***
Intercept	0.5858	0.3306	0.0764
Condition	-0.6632	0.4699	0.1581
Previous Day's Steps	0.1788	0.3055	0.5583
Study Day	0.0125	0.0103	0.2243
Cond*Steps	0.5917	0.4062	0.1453
Cond*Day	0.0074	0.0139	0.5940
Steps*Day	0.0300	0.0139	0.0306
Cond*Steps*Day	-0.0422	0.0172	**0.0140**

Finally, we examined the accuracy of the collected data. There was a significant positive correlation between pedometer step counts and self-reported minutes of walking, for both conditions, with a stronger correlation present for the CHARACTER condition, $r = 0.75$, $p < 0.001$; [95% CI, 0.69-0.81], vs. the TEXT condition: $r = 0.50$, $p < 0.001$; [95% CI, 0.40-0.59], providing support for H3.

CONCLUSION

Prior research indicates that people respond socially to computers, in similar ways to how they respond socially to other humans. In this work, we examine the durability of these effects in a longitudinal context. We show that social responses to computers change over time, and moreover, that this change varies depending upon the personalization of the interface. In a system designed for tracking exercise, we find that participants' actual walking behavior influences their daily decision to use the system. The more steps a participant walks, the more likely she is to use the system and conversely, the less she walks, the less likely she is to use the system. Furthermore, we find that with repeated interactions over time, this effect grows *smaller* for participants using a text-based interface and grows *larger* for participants using a character-based interface.

This study also examines the quantity and quality of data reported to the system. We find that participants are more likely to provide data to the text-based system, but that data provided to the character-based system were more accurate. It is possible that the character interface elicited higher-quality data due to increased feelings of trust and rapport, or because the time associated with reporting to the character - conversing with the character takes longer than reading text - caused participants to reflect more deeply about their answer, prior to reporting it to the system. Further research is needed to examine the exact reasons behind this finding.

One limitation of this study is that the experimental population is heavily biased towards women and older adults. Despite these limitations, this study provides support for the hypothesis that social desirability bias effects witnessed in human-computer interactions are not static, but can increase or decrease over time, and that these changes are influenced by the presentation of the computer interface.

ACKNOWLEDGMENTS

We thank Jenna Zaffini her assistance with this experiment and Daniel Schulman for his statistical insights. This work was supported by NSF CAREER IIS-0545932.

REFERENCES

1. Bickmore, T., Schulman, D., and Yin, L.: Maintaining Engagement in Long-term Interventions with Relational Agents. International Journal of Applied Artificial Intelligence 24, 6 (2010) 648-666.
2. Booth-Kewley, S., Larson, G. E., and Miyoshi, D. K.: Social desirability effects on computerized and paper-and-pencil questionnaires. Computers in Human Behavior 23, 1 (2007) 463-477.
3. Cassell, J. and Miller, P.: Is it Self-Administration if the Computer Gives you Encouraging Looks? In F. G. Conrad and M. F. Schober, Eds.: Envisioning the Survey Interview of the Future, John Wiley & Sons, (2007) 161-178.
4. Crowne, D. and Marlowe, D., *The approval motive; studies in evaluative dependence,* Wiley, (1964).
5. Goffman, E., *The presentation of self in everyday life,* Harmondsworth, (1978).
6. Hancock, J. T., Toma, C., and Ellison, N.: The truth about lying in online dating profiles. Proceedings of the SIGCHI conference on Human factors in computing systems (2007) 452.
7. Hoffmann, L., Krämer, N., Lam-chi, A., Kopp, S., Ruttkay, Z., Kipp, M., Nijholt, A., and Vilhjálmsson, H.: Media Equation Revisited: Do Users Show Polite Reactions towards an Embodied Agent? In Intelligent Virtual Agents, Volume 5773, Springer Berlin / Heidelberg, (2009) 159-165.
8. Nass, C., Moon, Y., and Carney, P.: Are People Polite to Computers? Responses to Computer-Based Interviewing Systems. Journal of Applied Social Psychology 29, 5 (1999) 1093-1109.
9. Nass, C., Steuer, J., and Tauber, E.: Computers are social actors. CHI '94: Proceedings of the SIGCHI conference on Human factors in computing systems (1994) 72-78.
10. Newman, J., Des, Turner, C., Gribble, J., Cooley, P., and Paone, D.: The Differential Effects of Face-to-Face and Computer Interview Modes. Am J Public Health 92, 2 (2002) 294-297.
11. R. Development Core Team, *R: A Language and Environment for Statistical Computing,* (2009).
12. Reeves, B. and Nass, C., *The media equation: how people treat computers, television, and new media like real people and places,* CSLI Publications, (1996).
13. Tourangeau, R., Couper, M., and Steiger, D.: Humanizing self-administered surveys: experiments on social presence in web and IVR surveys. Computers in Human Behavior 19, 1 (2003) 1-24.

What Drives Customization? Control Or Identity?

Sampada Marathe
Media Effects Research Laboratory
The Pennsylvania State University
University Park, PA 16802
ssm161@psu.edu

S. Shyam Sundar
Media Effects Research Laboratory
The Pennsylvania State University
University Park, PA 16802
sss12@psu.edu

ABSTRACT
Customization – an attribute that lets users take control and make changes to the presentation and functionality of the interface – is becoming a hallmark of today's interactive media devices. What do users experience when they change interface aspects like fonts and colors, skins on mobile phones, speed dial numbers, privacy settings on social networks and different command menus in software? Do they feel in control? Do they see the customized interface as a reflection of who they are? More importantly, is the feeling of being in control a major driver of usage, or does sense of identity – a personal connection with the interface – prove more vital? This paper discusses the psychology of customization, reports an empirical user study designed to explore the relationship between customization, sense of control, and sense of identity, and outlines implications for design of customizable interfaces based on the findings.

Author Keywords
Customization, sense of control, sense of identity, user experience

ACM Classification Keywords
H5.m. Information interfaces and presentation (e.g., HCI): Miscellaneous theory and methods.

General Terms
Experimentation, theory.

INTRODUCTION
Customization is a means to an end and is not typically designed to be an end in itself. It is assumed to be a secondary activity because users customize interfaces and devices in order to better facilitate a task at hand. Managing privacy settings on a social networking website, getting an avatar ready in a video game and organizing contacts in a cell phone are all preparatory activities for the actual task of communicating and networking, playing the video game and making phone calls respectively.

Customizable products offer users a chance to play an active role in influencing their technology and media consumption. Instead of having to passively consume content, customization allows users to enhance their experience with a product by adapting it to their own needs and desires. User interaction with an interface evolves over time and varies across place as a result of many different factors. As users spend more time interacting with a device, they "learn" the interface, their needs evolve (dynamics), their expertise with using the interface improves and they also adapt the interface to be used in many different situations (situatedness) [11]. For example, a cell phone is used to make calls at various times in personal, work and social contexts. Similarly, the activities of calling vs. texting vs. browsing vary in all the above situations.

In theory, these customization actions are supposed to be ancillary to a primary activity. However, evidence suggests that they are becoming a primary activity themselves, as more and more users spend considerable amount of time customizing their interfaces with a great deal of interest and involvement. Many among us expect to be able to customize our avatars and tools in video game play, ringtones on our cell phones, backgrounds and wallpapers on our computers, and don't think twice about the fact that our iPods and TiVos allow us to essentially create our own media channels. In fact, changing appearances, rearranging components, inserting or removing user interface widgets and adapting interfaces to personal needs have become an inherent part of technology use for many users [5]. However, we have very little generalizable knowledge about user experience of customization.

Although there are countless customization features on most interfaces, they are generally solitary and dispersed throughout the interface without much attention to the core user experience that they help create. Interactive and customizable products tend to be seen as mere tools for fulfilling users' instrumental goals. Instead of simply deploying the coolest new customization features and heading into the trap of trying to find users after building the interface customization features, we should be asking – what does customization fundamentally entail? What are users experiencing when they change interface features? This will help us build a coherent and comprehensive theory about customization tools and practices, with implications for user-centered design.

PSYCHOLOGY OF CUSTOMIZATION
As the popularity of the so-called 'participatory web' [22] increases, users are increasingly becoming active producers of content rather than passive consumers [29]. This user

activity has been fueled by access to numerous products and interfaces that allow users to create content as well as customize the "functionality, interface, information content or distinctiveness of a system" [4].

The hallmark of customization is letting users themselves modify some aspect of an interface to a certain degree so as to increase its personal relevance. For instance, most portal websites allow users to change the font or color on the website while others like MyYahoo! allow users to add/delete content and change the layout of webpages. iGoogle™ allows users to add/delete different widgets and choose different personal themes according to one's own taste. Google News even lets its users create different news categories based on their own preferences. For example, a user can create an entire section dedicated to news about mangoes or the movie Harry Potter or even the social media phenomenon Twitter, if they so choose. While mobile phones allow users to choose their own background wallpaper or ringtones., iPods allow their users to create their own idiosyncratic playlists. Most video games allow users to choose their own avatars, difficulty levels, opponents, and some even let them create entirely new environments and scenarios within the original game (modding). Figure 1 shows an iPhone with a user customized cover. Customizing a mobile phone by putting such covers or skins, diamond encrusted cases, or different charms is quite common in many cultures. While different types of customization features can be classified as appearance-based or functionality-based changes [24], we consider all user changes to content as *resulting* from one or both of these type of customization activities.

Figure 1. An example of a customized iPhone

Psychologically, customization can imbue a strong sense of personal agency [35] by letting users specify their preferences and modify the product or an interface to make it more relevant to them, thereby ensuring the utility of the resultant content. By placing the user at the center of the interaction, a customizable interface places the locus of control within the user. Indeed, a review of the extant literature reveals that users generally report engaging in customization and exert control for one or more of the following reasons: 1) to make a system's goals fit their own (e.g. [12]) 2) to make the system more efficient (e.g. [20]; [28]) 3) to manage complexity 4) to dictate outcome and 5) to manage information overload.

For example, various games allow players to remap certain functions in UI controls. Dyck et al., [12] found that remapping the right and left keys to create a 'crouch down' function, allows players to influence the progress of the game and finally the game outcome. Similarly, studies have also found that the most common type of customization options used in word processors by their participants were to add/move toolbars, change menus and write short macros to fit the software to their needs [28]. Providing such options makes it easy for users to personally decide which operations they would perform repeatedly and then automate those operations.

User Control

User control over the performance of the technology appears to be a critical aspect of the psychology of customization. A survey of 513 respondents [23] showed a significant correlation between one's need for control and the amount of customization they engage in during their technology usage. It appears that those who exhibit high need for control are psychologically attracted to interfaces that gratify this need.

Customizable interfaces afford control to the user in four ways – by being modifiable, by offering predictability, by letting users initiate the action, and by offering many options (i.e., choice) in their interaction with the interface. By their very nature of promoting active user participation, customizable systems let users explore, manipulate and rearrange our technological surroundings [17]. Sundar [35] equates the manipulability of such interfaces with one's sense of agency (see also [18]) – a feeling of being the source of an interaction or being a relevant actor in a given situation. Such a feeling of agency, he posits, gives a sense of immediate control to the user. Hence, the sheer *modifiability* of an interface can contribute to one's sense of control [37].

An example of such modifiability can be found on Jordan's Furniture website. Their 'room planner' tool lets users create virtual rooms (dining room, bedroom, living room, office), determine room dimensions, and arrange furniture in order to help them visualize and plan their purchases. Figure 2 shows a completely modifiable living room where the users can change the position, dimensions, colors and even the orientation of the furniture, as well as the room itself.

Sense of control could emerge from either customization of interface elements or formal features. From a psychological point of view, the ability to alter the tools offered by the interface (e.g., room planner on the Jordan's website) is no different from the ability to alter an element on the interface itself (e.g., layout of widgets).

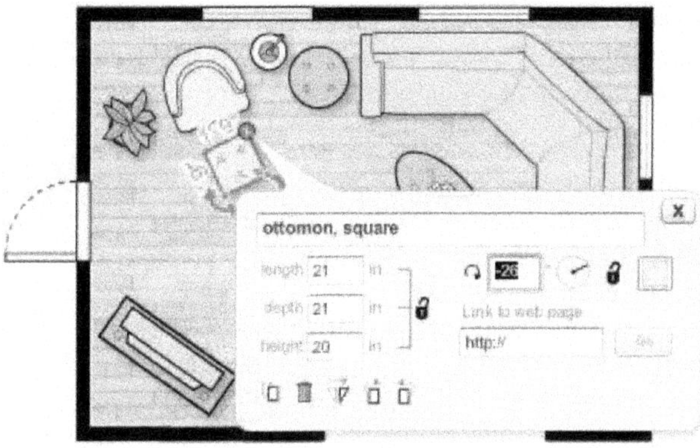

Figure 2. An example of a customizable room planner on Jordan's Furniture website

Investigations of user interactions with various adaptable interfaces have also shown that when users are allowed to add or remove functions, or more them around, the systems become more efficient for the specific tasks at hand [26]. Beyond that, however, letting users make such changes can help reduce the clutter and complexity that arises out of the growing functionality. When users are able to put away those functions that they do not foresee being used, it empties up their visual space for more useful functionality [8].

Customization also affords *predictability* to user interaction with the interface. For example, by creating a customized playlist, a user can reliably expect to hear the specific songs one after another that he/she put into the list. Similarly, by creating a new category for Entertainment news about actress Angelina Jolie, and placing the category on the top right hand corner of the Google News page, a user can reliably predict that s/he will be able to read about the actress on the top right corner of their webpage every day. Klug and Schell [18] equate this sense of predictability with controllability. Direct-manipulation interfaces bring such predictability to the interface by affording greater user control [32]. Essentially, this predictability, and thereby controllability, arises from being able to make decisions that affect the path to an outcome or sometimes even the outcome itself. Indeed, most game players thrive on this kind of controllability in interfaces that allow them to maximize the efficiency of game play. Such adaptable interfaces [8], by way of user manipulation, afford greater predictability in terms of what comes up on the interface and hence place users in control of the interface.

Customizable interfaces also encourage users to initiate action, instead of driving the interaction on their behalf. These systems are designed to wait for the user to specifically make changes and ask for system help when needed in the tasks that they perform. Research related to technology-assisted learning environments has shown that the opportunity to *initiate actions* in such environments provides a strong sense of control to the learner [19].

Finally, customizable interfaces let users choose between different options rather than make their choices for them. Barkhuus and Dey [3] found that users felt a significant loss of control when the system personalized information for them (fully context aware), but felt in control when they were allowed to customize the application themselves. This feeling of control came from being able to choose between different services offered on mobile phones rather than the device making the choices for them (e.g., ringing profiles, location tracking). Different types of systems can offer different types of choice options. In video game play, users are able to choose between many difficulty levels based on their proficiency, thus ensuring optimum levels of challenge. This choice determines how the game will be played and ultimately contributes to game outcome. Similarly, in many games, users are able to determine the tools and weapons that they can use, which affects their 'skills' and 'powers' during play.

On a portal website, this same choice can manifest itself in the form of selecting which news source to display on the webpage or on some cell phones where users are able to customize and (re)define the tools that are summoned for specific keystrokes. Such customization activities let users influence how their systems should behave. Such activities have been shown to positively affect one's sense of control over their environment [6], [13].

However, it would be erroneous to assume that all users who are faced with customizable interfaces deal with them in a similar way, or even experience a uniform feeling of control. An empirical study conducted to test how power users and non-power users respond to customization [36] demonstrated that the non-power users of technology showed negative attitudes toward the interface when asked to customize the interface, whereas they showed significantly positive attitudes when presented with ready-made tailored (personalized) content. Power users, on the other hand, showed significantly positive attitudes toward the interface when allowed to customize and negative attitudes when presented with automatic ready-made tailored content, thereby demonstrating an affinity toward controlling their experiences with technology. However, a follow-up study done by these researchers found that this finding held true, only under conditions of low privacy, i.e. when users felt a loss of control over their private browsing data [36]. Furthermore, the study also found that under low privacy, sense of control increased with power usage for those who were allowed to customize their own interface. In other words, power users felt much more in control of the interface than non-power users when they were allowed to make changes to the interface themselves.

Beyond Control

While actively changing interface elements places the element of control in a user's hand, it also serves to enhance their connection with the device. New media technologies offer extensive opportunities for users to express their *identity* by way of actively engaging in media selection and use [29]. From wearing a specific brand of clothes to buying a specific car, we surround ourselves with possessions that we think tell others about the kind of a person we are. We are known to go to extensive lengths of self-presentation to ensure that our possessions reflect how we want to be seen by others [14, 16, 41]. The connection between pleasure-inducing hedonic attributes of various products and self-identity have been established in the literature in HCI and user experience. Researchers have found that instead of simply helping us achieve our instrumental goals, products also help us establish an emotional connection and communicate our identity [14, 15, 27].

Simply by choosing to use one device versus another, individuals try to impress their personality on others around them. For example, owning and displaying an Apple product is a great example of how users have been known to present an image of themselves they want others to see, establish their group identity, and at the same time distinguish themselves from the general masses. Individuals initiate specific behavioral choices and decisions by actively engaging in actions that convey their identity ([33], [34]) and thus try to be agentic in their interactions. Being able to customize an interface according to one's choice can thus be linked to one's sense of identity, a personal connection with the device.

Examples of interfaces allowing users to customize the look and feel to convey personality are plentiful. E-commerce sites have capitalized on this tendency by offering customers numerous options and opportunities to customize the products they purchase. The shoe giant Nike, for instance, allows its customers to make changes to the look of their basic shoe design. Figure 3 shows an example of a customized shoe on Nike.com.

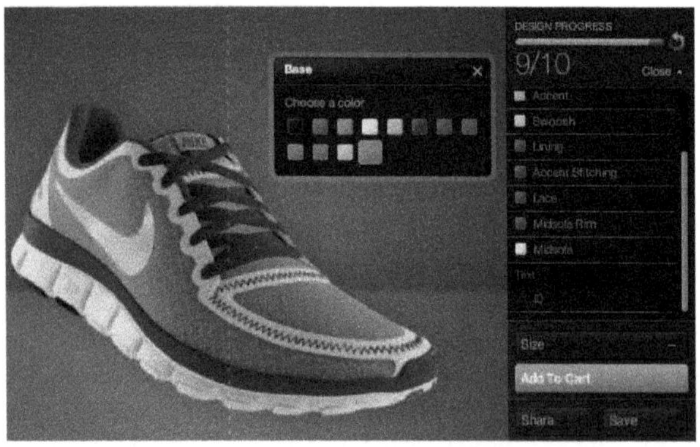

Figure 3. A customized shoe on Nike.com

Consumers can customize the base, overlay, lining, stitching, midsole and many other attributes to their liking before buying shoes on the website. They are able to express their choice and personality by determining the look of the shoes. The Vermont Teddy Bear company allows their customers to customize their chosen toy's appearance by selecting different colors of fur and eyes for the bears. By allowing users to specify preferences, these sites provide numerous opportunities for expressing one's identity.

Even outside the content of what we peruse and purchase, self-presentation in digital/online environments has become a means to build/convey one's identity, with easy access to design elements, background, color, font, layout, text, video, music, graphics, profile photo, photo albums and blogs. Schau and Gilly [31] collected data from personal web spaces and interviews with 35 respondents who managed their own websites, and overwhelmingly found support for the notion of designing and building websites and using text, audio, images, icons, hyperlinks, and animations in order to construct and convey a digital self. Such 'appearance customization' is immensely popular among mobile phone users throughout the world. An international study conducted in eleven cities around the world [10] has shown that users customize their mobile phones with covers, straps and/or stickers to promote themselves and convey their style and identity.

A similar study was conducted by Tractinsky and Zmiri [38] with 60 undergraduates, where they were asked to evaluate and choose from 12 different skins for Microsoft's Media Player, and then perform a set of tasks with each of the skins they chose. These researchers defined skins as "alternative interfaces to commonly used applications that allow users to change the appearances of their applications while preserving their functionality" (p. 2). They found that 80% of their participants had chosen to deviate from the default skin to one of the remaining 11 skins and hence concluded that users show an unmistakable need to customize their applications. This finding provides interesting insight into the variety in user preferences. Not only did a majority of their participants engage in customization, their preferences spanned all the available options in skins. Thus, customization allows each user a choice among many options to modify the interface and make it unique and distinct.

The agency model of customization [35] posits that by letting a user function as a source of action, customization imbues a greater sense of agency in the user, consequently contributing to and helping project one's sense of identity. Marathe [23] found a strong correlation between one's need for uniqueness and the amount of customization.

While the concept of users actively customizing interfaces and managing their digital identities is not new, no empirical research has been reported that tests and contrasts the notion of control and identity as connected with customization. Exactly what underlies our tendency to customize? Is it simply control or a sense of identity or both? An answer to this question can help us design customization tools that better address the psychological needs and expectations of users. Therefore, we conducted an experimental study to specifically explore the relationship between customization, sense of control (SOC), and sense of identity (SOI).

We proposed the following research questions:

RQ1: What is the relationship between customization, sense of identity (SOI) and sense of control (SOC)?

RQ2: Do power users and non-power users differ in their experience of sense of identity (SOI) and sense of control (SOC) after engaging in customization?

RQ3: Is sense of identity (SOI) a more significant factor in influencing the user experience surrounding customization, or is sense of control (SOC)?

Figure 4 shows the theoretical model of the study.

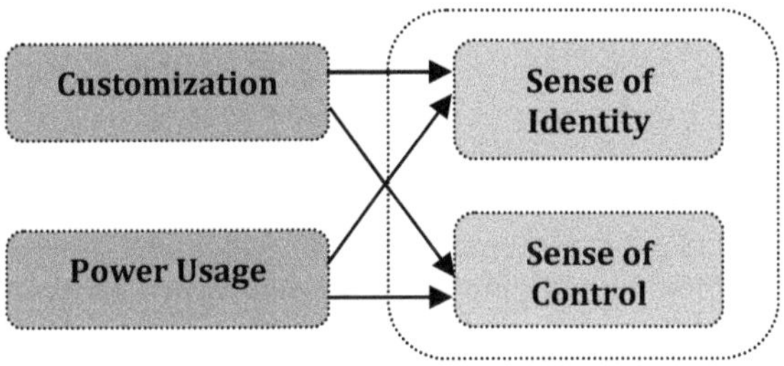

Figure 4. Theoretical model

STUDY DETAILS

We conducted a between-participants experimental user study in which participants were either asked to customize an interface and browse, or asked to simply browse, followed by an online questionnaire that evaluated their sense of identity and sense of control with the interface.

Participants

133 participants (mean age 19.61 years, 52% female) were recruited from a university campus in the US, and participated in this study for extra credit. They were randomly assigned to either the 'customization' (N=76) or 'no customization' (N=57) condition.

Stimulus

The Netvibes portal (www.netvibes.com) allows users to manage information consumption by letting them choose widgets from diverse sources such as email, weather, entertainment, news, and shopping on a single webpage. The 'Add content' button on the left top of the page, as shown in figure 5, lets users add widgets as they want on different topics.

Users are able to add different widgets to their personal page, create different tabs for different types of content, (e.g. general, work, fun etc) and manage their digital life through one interface. All the widgets are customizable by the users and can also be dragged and moved around and arranged as the user pleases. The portal website also lets the user give a page title, change color of widgets, change theme and background, and perform many other widget-specific changes.

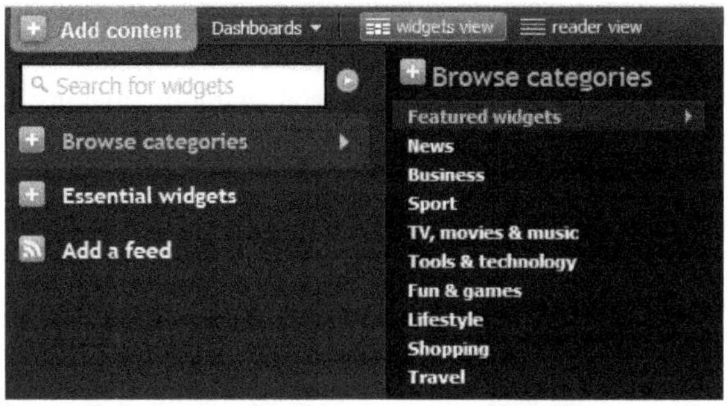

Figure 5. A customization menu on Netvibes.com that lets users add content and manage the portal

Figure 6 shows an example of the customization options in the Flickr widget.

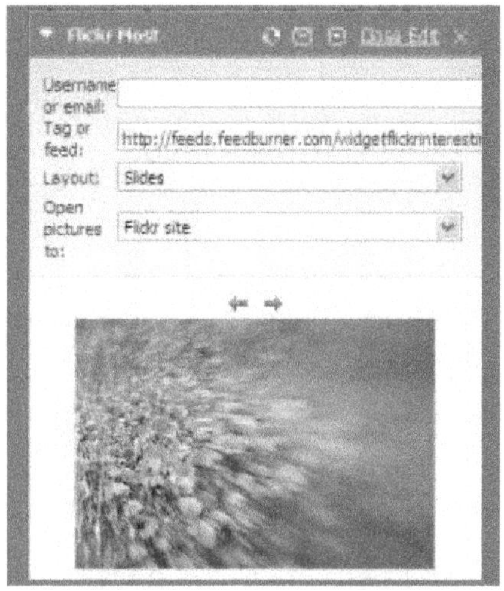

Figure 6. An example of a customization options on a Flickr widget on Netvibes.com

Procedure

Participants came to the research lab, and were asked to read and sign an informed consent form before their participation. They were given preliminary information about the study and the procedure, and were asked to answer a brief online questionnaire designed to assess their level of general technological prowess. This power -usage scale [23] asked them about their extent of technology use in daily life, their attitudes and efficacy with using devices, as well as their expertise with technological devices.

All participants were given an identical Netvibes portal page, with the same widgets arranged in a specific order on the page. Each participant in the customization condition was then introduced to the customization options that were available on the portal and asked to customize it according to their taste. For example, participants were shown how to add new widgets, change settings for the widgets and customize page elements like background and theme. All participants in the customization condition were then given about 10 minutes to customize the stimulus portal website as they wanted and then asked to browse the website (and its resulting customized content) for about 10 minutes.

Those in the 'no customization' condition were simply told that Netvibes allows users to manage their digital lives and then asked to browse the portal without making any changes. They were not introduced to any specific customization features on the portal. At the end of their session, all participants in both conditions were asked to answer a questionnaire that assessed their sense of control (SOC) and sense of identity (SOI) with the interface.

At the end of each study session, once the participants left the lab, their customized Netvibes portal pages were retrieved and saved. Figure 7 shows a Netvibes portal page with multiple widgets and tabs, customized by one of the study participants. All the changes made by the participants in the customization condition were counted and measured based off of the original portal template used for the study.

Figure 7. Netvibes.com portal (www.netvibes.com)

Measured Variables

Power usage

Power usage was one of the measured independent variables. The scale was adapted from Marathe et al. [23] and consisted of 20 items about participants' liking of technology, extent of their technology use, dependence on different technologies and attitude toward using different technologies, among other things. All items were measured on a 7-point Likert-type scale, each anchored between 'Strongly Disagree' and 'Strongly Agree'. 3 of the items were reverse coded for consistency. An exploratory factor analysis revealed 4 factors based on Eigen values, together explaining 59.02% of the variance. However, contrary to the original work, a principal-components analysis with Varimax rotation revealed multiple cross loadings and no meaningful theoretical distinctions among factors. Hence, all items were combined to form a single index of power usage (Cronbach's $\alpha = .89$).

Sense of Identity

Measures for sense of identity were adapted from Tractinsky and Zmiri [38] and Ball and Tasaki [2]. All questions were measured on a 7-point Likert-type scale anchored between 'Not at all' and 'Very much'. The questions pertained to participants' belief about the interface reflecting personal identity, reflecting personality, interface being a true representation of self, a feeling of ownership toward the interface, and interface feeling personal. An exploratory factor analysis with these seven items yielded a single factor. They were combined to form the sense of identity index (Cronbach's $\alpha = .96$).

Sense of control

Measures for sense of control were adapted from Ariely [1], Venkatesh [39] and Witmer and Singer [40], and consisted of 15 items about participants' beliefs about being able to transform the interface, interface being rigid and inflexible, being able to adapt interface to personal taste, being able to initiate actions to modify interface, feeling in charge of the interface, free to decide how to browse, free to make different choices, able to influence widgets, able to influence how portal looked, able to influence how portal worked and environment being responsive to the interaction. All questions were measured on a 7-point Likert-type scale anchored between 'Not at all' and 'Very much'. One of the items was reverse-coded for consistency. An exploratory principal-components factor analysis with Varimax rotation revealed 2 factors based on the examination of Eigen values. Together, they explained 65.08% of the variance. A close examination of the items in both factors did not reveal a meaningful theoretical distinction. Hence, all 15 items were combined to form the sense of control index (Cronbach's $\alpha = .93$).

Manipulation Check

In order to preserve some form of validity to the customization activity, the instructions did not specify what changes participants in the customization condition should make, rather simply introduced them to the changes they could make. Also, since the stimulus interface was not restrictive in any way, in theory, participants in the 'no customization' condition were free to ignore instructions and use any customization features they discovered. It was thus extremely necessary to conduct a manipulation check. To that effect, each participant's Netvibes page was retrieved as soon as they left, saved and used to count the number of customization changes they had made. Two separate t-tests revealed that the manipulation was successful and that there was no significant relationship between power usage and amount of customization.

STUDY RESULTS

Several omnibus General Linear Model (GLM) analyses were conducted with customization and power usage as independent variables, and sense of identity (SOI) and sense of control (SOC) as dependent variables. These data analyses revealed some interesting insights.

RQ1: Customization, sense of identity, sense of control: Participants who engaged in customization reported a higher sense of control (SOC) with the interface ($M = 5.98$, $SE = .11$) than those who did not ($M = 4.94$, $SE = .13$), $F(1, 129) = 34.46$, $p < .0001$. Customization also significantly predicted sense of identity (SOI), F (1, 129) = 48.82, $p<$ .0001, such that those who engaged in customization reported a higher sense of identity with the interface (M = 4.95, SE = .15) than those who did not (M = 3.26, SE = .18).

RQ2: Power usage: We found a significant positive relationship between power usage and sense of control, (β = .22, $p<$ .001), such that those on the higher end of the power usage scale reported more sense of control with the interface than those on the lower end of the scale, F (1, 129) = 7.28, $p<$ .01, adjusted R^2 = .23. A significant positive relationship between power usage and sense of identity (SOI) (β = .22, $p<$ .001) was also seen, such that those on the higher end of the power usage scale reported more sense of identity with the interface than those on the lower end of the scale, F (1, 129) = 5.38, $p<$ .05, adjusted R^2 = .28.

RQ3: Is SOI more important or SOC? Several omnibus analyses of covariance (ANCOVAs) were conducted to investigate the relative importance of SOI and SOC.

Sense of Control as covariate

As noted above, customization significantly affected one's sense of identity with the interface. The magnitude of the effect went down when sense of control was introduced as a covariate in the analysis, from F = 48.82 to F (1, 128) = 12.45, $p<$ .001, thus indicating that sense of control functions as a partial mediator, and is only *one* of the reasons why those who customize feel higher sense of identity with the interface.

Previous analysis had also found that power usage was significantly related to sense of identity (SOI). However, once SOC was introduced into the analysis as a covariate, this significant relationship between power usage and sense of identity (SOI) disappeared, thereby suggesting that sense of control fully mediates the effect of power usage on sense of identity. It appears that those on the higher end of the power usage scale (power users) tend to derive their identity from the control afforded by customization.

Sense of Identity as covariate

As reported earlier, those who engaged in customization showed significantly higher sense of control with the interface, than those who did not customize the interface. Interestingly, when sense of identity was introduced as a covariate in this analysis, the effect of customization on sense of control ceased to be significant. This implies that customization changes that do not engender a sense of identity do not provide a sense of control to the user.

Similarly, a previously significant relationship between power usage and sense of control ceased to be significant once sense of identity was added as a covariate. Moreover, the same analysis also revealed an interaction between power usage and customization that approached significance, F (1, 128) = 3.53, p = .06. Specifically, engaging in customization, compared to simple browsing on the interface, gave more sense of control to power users. However, whether or not they engaged in customization did not change the sense of control for users on the lower end of the power usage scale. Figure 8 shows the graphical representation of this interaction between power usage and customization on sense of control. The red line on the top represents participants who were in the 'customization' condition, and the blue dashed line on the bottom represents participants who were in the 'no customization' condition.

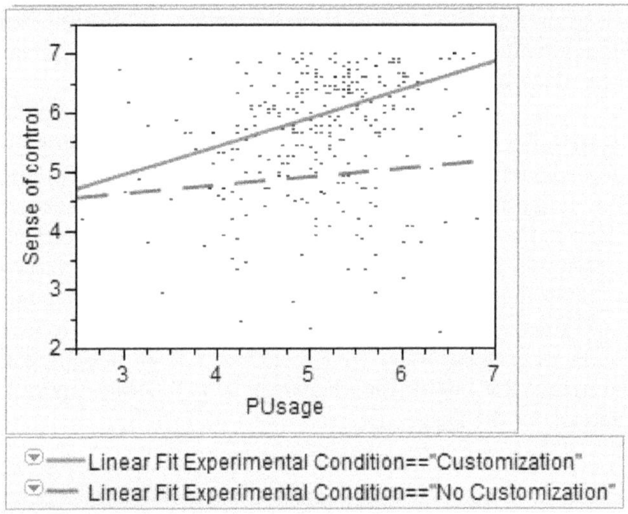

Figure 8. Interaction between power usage and customization on sense of control

INTERPRETATION OF RESULTS

First and foremost, this user study revealed that customization indeed has deep psychological value, when users take time to engage in it and make changes according to their preferences. As suggested by the agency model of customization [35], the ability of the user to serve as source or gatekeeper of content is critical for realizing the benefits of self-agency.

Data show that customization is associated with two psychologically meaningful gratifications – namely, sense of identity (SOI), and sense of control (SOC). We found that customization shows two distinct patterns of effects on sense of identity and sense of control. While the effect of customization on sense of control was fully mediated by sense of identity, its effect on sense of identity was only partially mediated by sense of control. This means that sense of identity is the main reason why those who engage in customization feel a sense of control. However, feeling a sense of control is only one of the reasons why those who engage in customization feel a heightened sense of identity. While sense of control emerges as an important factor, its value is underscored by the presence of sense of identity – a sense of conveying one's self-representation through use of technological tools. Psychologically this means that having control is all about being able to express one's identity, but feeling a sense of identity has implications beyond feeling sense of control. Therefore, user experience with customization tools is fundamentally tied to the perceived sense of connection and self-representation one experiences while expressing identity. These results suggest that interface features can serve as potential tools for self-realization even among the uninitiated. By allowing users of all skill levels to self-tailor their information universe, customization features can be quite influential in helping shape one's self-representation, both for oneself and others.

The interaction effect we found between power usage and customization on sense of control, after controlling for sense of identity, approached significance. Clearly, the act of making changes to the interface that goes beyond serving an identity-enhancing purpose brings with it the ability to exert control over the interface, but this ability is appreciated by power users more than regular users. Do these findings imply that non-power users are somehow inhibited in their use of customization features that keeps them from experiencing control? Theoretically, this finding implies that the sense of agency one experiences while customizing has somewhat different meanings for power users and regular users, such that control is an integral part of agency for the former whereas identity is a key aspect of agency for the latter.

Since this study was conducted in a university town, we relied on a convenience sample of undergraduate students as study participants. However, we believe that the applicability of our findings does not suffer for two reasons. First, various surveys conducted by the Pew Internet and American Life Project show that teens (ages 12-17) and young adults (ages 18-29) lead in the usage of internet, cell phone, gaming, as well as social networking websites, compared to other age groups, thus making them a dominant demographic in technology usage [21]. Second, we believe that the applicability of the results is enhanced by the inclusion of the power usage variable. Some scholars have proposed that the digital divide today is not based simply on age or access (information haves and have-nots), but rather in our "readiness, willingness, and ability to productively use technological interfaces." Bucy and Newhagen [7] call it 'psychological access.' We account for such variance in technological usage by including power usage in our analyses, thereby strengthening the validity of our findings.

IMPLICATIONS FOR HCI

It is clear from the results of this study that customization is tied to two psychological constructs – sense of identity (SOI) and sense of control (SOC) – and shows significant effect on both constructs, compared to simple browsing of content. Regardless of the nature of customization outcomes, offering some features that are manipulable by users will undoubtedly create a richer agentic experience for them than offering no customization at all.

However, this implication comes with a caveat. Our study also shows that power users experience a high sense of control and a high sense of identity when they engage in customization. Interestingly however, engaging in customization does not enhance non-power users' sense of control with the interface, in the absence of identity enhancement. Designers thus need to be conscious of the identity-enhancing potential of customization options, given its ability to affect users' sense of control. Clearly, non-power users cannot be considered 'blank slates' [9]. Indeed, it is entirely possible that many novice users, although on the lower end of the power usage scale, are actually experts in the content domain and hence may have evolved functional needs from an interface. For example, an already skilled musician learning to use a digital musical instrument might want to be able to customize many different settings (e.g., pitch) on the instrument. But, our data clearly show that customizing that interface will not enhance their sense of control, if they do not feel a connection with the interface itself. Hence if the goal of the device is to empower users by letting them customize aspects of the interface, then designers need to make sure that identity enhancement is an important design goal. Otherwise, customization will only truly help the initiated – those users who are already at the higher end of the power usage scale.

Beyond these implications however, the true contribution of this study lies in the insight it provides on the intertwined relationship between the two psychological gratifications – sense of identity (SOI) and sense of control (SOC). We found that customization changes that do not engender a sense of control within a user can still enhance their sense of identity. An example of such customization change can be found on the weight tracker tool on the medhelp.org health portal.

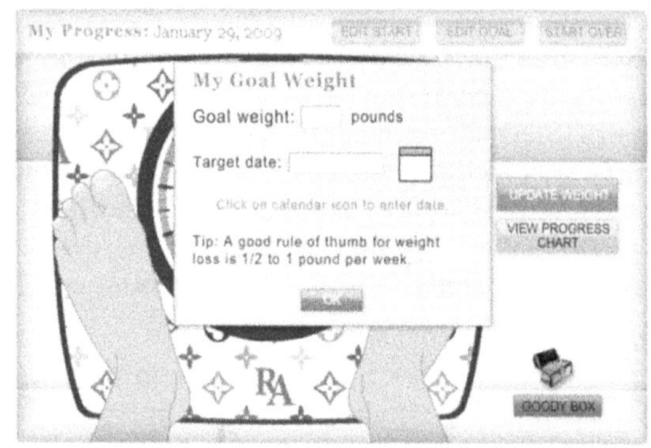

Figure 9. Weight tracker tool on www.medhelp.org

This portal allows its users to change color or pattern on the weighing scale in the weight widget. Figure 9 shows this weighing scale. Clearly, changing the pattern on the weighing scale will surely be considered a very low-end manifestation of customization. It does not provide any sort of control over how the weighing scale functions or how the weight tracker tool works. Our data show that although apparently insignificant, even such customization changes can invoke a strong psychological connection with the interface. From an interface design perspective, providing surface customization options that deal with aspects of interface and presentation should be more easily deployable than other task-based customization options that affect the functioning of the system, and thus provide an easier fix to the challenge of creating a psychological connection with the users. Whether it is changing the color of a webpage or dressing up an avatar in a video game, users are able to express their desires and preferences through various seemingly trivial cosmetic changes. Sense of identity can thus be compellingly linked to making cosmetic (presentation-based) changes [24] and warrants further investigation.

In designing interface features, UI designers need to consider what gratification each customization feature will imbue in the user and strategically include it based on the larger design goals of the system. Thinking about interfaces as identity-enhancing or control-enhancing tools provides us with a chance to actually design user experiences with systems, rather than solitary and dispersed customization features. Thinking about an entire product experience lets designers define and create harmonious user experiences and frees them from having to design any single customization feature in one part of the system. Design of user experiences also brings to the fore a simple but elegant fact – by fulfilling higher-order needs like enhancing identity or control, designers can create an interface that is an end in itself rather than a means. This approach will undoubtedly also guide designers away from the trap of deploying the coolest new features and then trying to find uses and users for the tools. When the primary focus of a design is based on generating value for users, it ensures attention to user goals and the psychological aspects of customization.

Although quite insightful, these data have some limitations. We designed the user study to investigate the causal relationship between customization and its effects, leading to an experimental manipulation of customization that would provide strong internal validity to the findings. The study was not designed to answer the question –do users customize, or how do they customize? It was designed to answer the question – what happens when users customize? We believe that in designing the study so, we have achieved that goal. However, experimentally manipulating customization takes away from the external validity of the study. This can be addressed with field-based studies in the future that are more naturalistic, and therefore better positioned to offer specific practical suggestions for development and deployment of customization tools.

ACKNOWLEDGMENTS
This research is supported in part by the Korea Science and Engineering Foundation under the WCU (World Class University) program funded through the Ministry of Education, Science and Technology, S. Korea (Grant No. R31-2008-000-10062-0, awarded to the Department of Interaction Science, Sungkyunkwan University, Seoul, where the second author is a visiting professor).

REFERENCES
1. Ariely, D., & Levav, J. Sequential choice in group settings: Taking the road less traveled and less enjoyed. *Journal of Consumer Research 27,* 3(2000), 279-290.
2. Ball, A. D., & Tasaki, L. H. The Role and Measurement of Attachment in Consumer Behavior. *Journal of Consumer Psychology 1,* 2(1992), 155-172.
3. Barkhuus, L., & Dey, A. *Is Context-Aware Computing Taking Control away from the User? Three Levels of Interactivity Examined.* In *Proc. UbiComp2003*, ACM Press (2003).
4. Blom, J. *Personalization – A taxonomy. Ext. Abstracts CHI 2000*, ACM Press (2000), 313-314.
5. Bolin, M., Webber, M., Rha, P., Wilson, T., & Miller, R. C. *Automation and Customization of Rendered Web Pages.* In *Proc. UIST 2005*, ACM Press (2005), 163-172.
6. Botti, S., McGill, A. L., & Iyengar, S. S. Preference for control and its effect on evaluation of consumption experience. *Advances in Consumer Research, 2003.*
7. Bucy, E. P., & Newhagen, J. E. *Media access: Social and psychological dimensions of new technology.* Mahwah, NJ: Lawrence Elrbaum Associates, 2004.
8. Bunt, A., Conati, C., & McGrenere, J. *What role can adaptive support play in an adaptable system?* In *Proc. IUI 2004*, ACM Press (2004), 117-124.
9. Carroll, J., & Rosson, M. B. *Paradox of the Active User.* In J. Carroll (Ed.), Interfacing Thought: Cognitive Aspects of Human-Computer Interaction (pp. 80-111). Cambridge, MA: MIT Press, 1987.
10. Cui, Y., Chipchase, J., & Ichikawa, F.*A Cross Culture Study on Phone Carrying and Physical Personalization.* In N. Aykin (Ed.), Usability and Internationalization: HCI and Culture (Vol. 4559, pp. 483-492): Springer Berlin / Heidelberg, 2007.
11. Dix, A. Designing for appropriation. In Proc. BCS HCI Group Conference, 2007.
12. Dyck, J., Pinelle, D., Brown, B., & Gutwin, C. *Learning from games: HCI design innovations in entertainment software.* In Proc. Graphics Interface, 2003.
13. Grodal, T. *Video games and the pleasures of control.* In D. Zillmann & P. Vorderer (Eds.), Media entertainment: The psychology of its appeal (pp. 197-213). Mahwah, NJ: Lawrence Erlbaum Associates, 2000.
14. Hassenzahl, M. The thing and I: *Understanding the relationship between user and product.* In M.A. Blythe, A. F. Monk, K. Overbeeke & P. C. Wright (Eds.), Funology: From usability to enjoyment (pp 31-42). Kluwer Academic Publishers. Netherlands, 2003.
15. Karapanos, E., Zimmerman, J., Forlizzi, J., & Martens, J-B. User experience over time: An initial framework. In Proc. CHI 2009. 729-738.

16. Kleine, S. S., Kleine III, R. E., & Allen, C. T. How is a possession "me" or "not me"? Characterizing types and an antecedent of material possession attachment. *Journal of Consumer Research 22,* 3 (1995), 327-343.

17. Klimmt, C., & Hartmann, T. *Effectance, self-efficacy, and the motivation to play video games.* In P. Vorderer& J. Bryant (Eds.), Playing video games: Motives, responses, and consequences (pp. 133-145). Mahwah, NJ: Lawrence Erlbaum Associates, 2006.

18. Klug, G. C., & Schell, J. *Why people play games: An industry perspective.* In P. Vorderer & J. Bryant (Eds.), Playing video games: Motives, responses, and consequences (pp. 91-100). Mahwah, NJ: Lawrence Erlbaum Associates, 2006.

19. Lepper, M. R., & Chabay, R. W. Intrinsic motivation and instruction: Conflicting views on the role of motivational processes in computer-based education. *Educational Psychologist 20,* 4 (1985), 217-230.

20. Mackay, W. *Triggers and barriers to customizing software.* In *Proc. CHI 1991.*

21. Madden, M. *Four or more: The new demographic*: Pew Internet Project, 2010.

22. Madden, M., & Fox, S. *Riding the waves of "Web 2.0": More than a buzzword, but still not easily defined*: Pew Internet Project, 2006

23. Marathe, S. S. If you build it, they will come - Or will they? Need for uniqueness and need for control as psychological predictors of customization. In Proc. of the Annual Conference of the International Communication Association, ICA (2007).

24. Marathe, S. S. Investigating the psychology of task-based and presentation-based UI customization. *Ext. Abstracts, CHI 2009*, 3129-3132.

25. Marathe, S. S., Sundar, S. S., Bijvank, M. N., van Vugt, H., &Veldhuis, J. Who are these power users anyway? Building a psychological profile. In Proc. of the Annual Conference of the International Communication Association, ICA (2007).

26. McGrenere, J., Baecker, R. M., & Booth, K. S. An Evaluation of a Multiple Interface Design Solution for Bloated Software. In Proc. CHI 2002.

27. Mugge, R., Schoormans, J. & Schifferstein, H. Emotional bonding with personalised products. *Journal of Engineering Design 20,* 5 (2009), 467-476.

28. Page, S. R., Johnsgard, T. J., Albert, U., & Allen, C. D. (1996). *User customization of a word processor.* In Proc. CHI 1996, ACM Press (1996).

29. Papacharissi, Z. The presentation of self in virtual life: Characteristics of personal home pages. *Journalism and Mass Communication Quarterly 79,* 3 (2002), 643-660.

30. Rubin, A. M. Audience activity and media use. *Communication Monographs 60,* 1 (1993), 98-105.

31. Schau, H. J., & Gilly, M. C. We are what we post? Self-presentation in personal web space. *Journal of Consumer Research 30,* 3 (2003), 385-404.

32. Shneiderman, B., & Maes, P. Direct manipulation vs. interface agents. *Interactions 4,* 6 (1997), 42-61.

33. Sparks, P., & Shepherd, R. Self-identity and the theory of planned behavior: Assessing the role of identification with "green consumerism". *Social Psychology Quarterly 55*, 1992, 388-399.

34. Stets, J. E., & Burke, P. J. *A sociological approach to self and identity.* In M. R. Leary & J. P. Tangney (Eds.), Handbook of self and identity (pp. 128-152). New York, NY: The Guilford Press, 2003.

35. Sundar, S. S. Self as source: Agency and customization in interactive media. In E. Konijn, S. Utz, M. Tanis & S. Barnes (Eds.), *Mediated interpersonal communication,* 2008.

36. Sundar, S. S., & Marathe, S. S. Personalization vs. customization: The importance of agency, privacy and power usage. *Human Communication Research 36,* 2010, 298-322.

37. Sundar, S. S., Marathe, S. S., & Kang, H. *Beyond tailoring: Customization in health websites.* In Proc. of the 95th Annual Convention of the National Communication Association, NCA (2009).

38. Tractinsky, N., & Zmiri, D. *Exploring attributes of skins as potential antecedents of emotion in HCI.* In P. Fishwick (Ed.), Aesthetic Computing (pp. 405-422): MIT Press, 2006.

39. Venkatesh, V. Determinants of perceived ease of use: Integrating control, intrinsic motivation, and emotion into the technology acceptance model. *Information Systems Research 11,* 4 (2000), 342-365.

40. Witmer, B. G., & Singer, M. J. Measuring Presence in Virtual Environments: A Presence Questionnaire. *Presence 7,* 3 (1998), 225-240.

41. Zimmerman, J. Designing for the self: Making products that help people become the person they desire to be. In Proc. CHI 2009, 395-404.

Your Noise is My Command: Sensing Gestures Using the Body as an Antenna

Gabe Cohn[1,2], Dan Morris[1], Shwetak N. Patel[1,2,3], Desney S. Tan[1]

[1]Microsoft Research
Redmond, WA (USA)
{dan, desney}@microsoft.com

[2]Electrical Eng., [3]Computer Science & Eng.
UbiComp Lab, DUB Group, Univ. of Washington
Seattle, WA (USA)
{gabecohn, shwetak}@uw.edu

ABSTRACT

Touch sensing and computer vision have made human-computer interaction possible in environments where keyboards, mice, or other handheld implements are not available or desirable. However, the high cost of instrumenting environments limits the ubiquity of these technologies, particularly in home scenarios where cost constraints dominate installation decisions. Fortunately, home environments frequently offer a signal that is unique to locations and objects within the home: electromagnetic noise. In this work, we use the body as a receiving antenna and leverage this noise for gestural interaction. We demonstrate that it is possible to robustly recognize touched locations on an uninstrumented home wall using no specialized sensors. We conduct a series of experiments to explore the capabilities that this new sensing modality may offer. Specifically, we show robust classification of gestures such as the position of discrete touches around light switches, the particular light switch being touched, which appliances are touched, differentiation between hands, as well as continuous proximity of hand to the switch, among others. We close by discussing opportunities, limitations, and future work.

Author Keywords

Input, touch interaction, surface interaction, electrical noise

ACM Classification Keywords

H.5.2 Information interfaces and presentation: User Interfaces - Input devices and strategies.

General Terms

Design, Experimentation, Measurement

INTRODUCTION

As computers become more mobile and more ubiquitous, people increasingly expect always-available computing, either with devices that they carry on their bodies, or using devices embedded in the environment. We see an increasing need for interaction modalities that go beyond the keyboard and mouse, and furthermore, that do not require mediated interaction with specialized devices such as styluses.

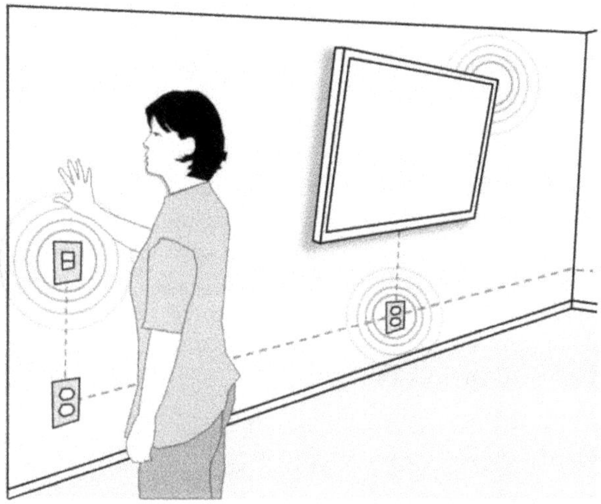

Figure 1: The human body behaves as an antenna in the presence of noise radiated by power lines and appliances. Our approach analyzes this noise, turning the whole home into an interaction surface.

Researchers have addressed this need through a variety of input channels. Speech recognition enables hands-free interaction for a variety of desktop and mobile applications. Similarly, computer vision enables machines to recognize faces, track movement, recognize gestures, and reconstruct 3D scenes. Various techniques, most notably capacitive sensing, have been used to instrument surfaces such a tables, walls, and mobile devices in order to provide touch sensing. In addition, specialized depth cameras that allow users to interact with their computers using whole-body gestures are becoming commercially available to consumers (e.g., Microsoft Kinect).

Speech input comes at a relatively low cost of instrumentation, but is limited in input bandwidth and may not be appropriate in many scenarios. Vision- and touch-based technologies offer an array of subtle, natural interaction techniques, but are limited in the potential scale of deployment due to their associated installation burden and cost. Consequently, we will likely not see homes or workplaces that allow truly ubiquitous input in the foreseeable future using these modalities.

Other researchers, realizing these limitations, have explored sensors that exploit characteristics of the human body itself to turn it into an inherently portable interaction device. Harrison et al. utilize bio-acoustic sensors to determine the location of taps on the body, and thereby turn it into a touchscreen [12]. Saponas et al. use electrical recordings of forearm muscles to sense muscle activity and infer finger gestures [16]. However, these on-body input systems are to date limited to a small number of discrete inputs, and do not offer the large-scale interaction that is provided by touch-sensitive surfaces.

In this paper, we present a novel interaction modality that utilizes the human body as an antenna to receive electromagnetic (EM) noise that already exists in our environments (Figure 1). While this noise is bothersome to nearly every other EM sensing application, we treat it as the core of our signal. By observing the properties of the noise picked up by the body, we can infer gestures on and around existing surfaces and objects, specifically the walls and appliances in the home. We targeted our initial proof-of-concept work to the home both because there is growing demand for computing in the home, but also because power lines in the home have been shown to be a relatively good transmitting antenna that creates a particularly noisy (i.e., signal-rich) environment for us.

Specifically, the contributions of this paper are:

1) A novel technique that uses the human body to sense EM noise already present in the environment to infer gestures such as touch and hover around various uninstrumented objects.

2) A core experiment conducted by 10 people in 10 homes validating the operation and robustness of the technique. Results from this experiment show that we can accurately classify the location in the home where the interaction occurred and the contact positions around light switches.

3) A set of smaller experiments to explore additional capabilities and limitations of our approach. Results from these experiments suggest that we can infer proximity to walls, multi-hand gestures, touched appliances, and continuous position along a touched wall.

BACKGROUND AND RELATED WORK

The Human Body as an Antenna

A basic receiving antenna can be thought of as an apparatus that converts electromagnetic waves into electrical current. An antenna consists of a set of conductors that can be arranged in a variety different ways, where the size, geometry, and material dictate its effectiveness at receiving a particular frequency. One of the simplest antennas is just a loop of wire (commonly used for AM and FM radio), whose length determines its effective frequency response. In addition, any wire or conductor carrying current or a wire exposed to an electromagnetic field may exhibit unintentional antenna characteristics. For instance, it is not uncommon to hear AM or CB radio through a set of speakers that is not plugged into a radio. Home electrical wiring also makes an effective antenna [4, 13, 15, 20], a phenomenon which we leverage in this work.

It turns out that the human body is also a very effective antenna over a broad frequency range. The human body is an electrical conductor, and thus when exposed to electromagnetic fields, it behaves as an antenna with a frequency resonance determined by various factors including height, posture, etc. Research suggests that since the human body is a lossy conductor (dielectric) with a complex geometry, it does not have a single effective resonance frequency, but rather a broadly distributed response [7], capturing frequencies from 40 Hz all the way to 400 MHz [8].

Sometimes referred to as the "body antenna effect," this phenomenon poses significant problems for systems employing body area networks (i.e., using the body as a conductor to send data from one part of the body to another) and for systems analyzing electrical phenomena within the body (e.g., muscle activity). Consequently, researchers have gone through great lengths to mitigate the problems of ambient electromagnetic noise being coupled to the body [2]. In contrast, our focus in the present work is to *leverage* the ambient electromagnetic noise picked up by the human body as a signal for classifying human interaction with the environment.

Related research has focused on using the human body as a conductor for body area networks [6, 10, 22]. For example, in the HCI community, Fukumoto and Tonomura demonstrated the FingeRing [6], a finger-worn sensor that communicates to a wrist mounted receiver by using the body as an "electric wire." Although their approach did not use the body as an antenna, they noted that touching a surface greatly reduced communication reliability because of the body being grounded and acting as a human antenna. Other work has explored using the human body as a transmission/reception antenna for inter-body communication [1, 3, 10].

Also in the HCI community, near-field electric field sensing has been a popular approach for touch and motion gestures, where the human body has been used as a disturbance and a radiator of an electric field [18, 21]. The DiamondTouch [5] employs the human body as both a signal conductor and an antenna by passing electromagnetic waves from a conductive pad into the body; these waves are in turn picked up by antennas embedded in a tabletop interaction surface. In the present work, we are interested in picking up noise signals using the body *without* instrumenting the environment. We use the particular properties of the measured noise to infer the gestures performed by the human user. We are not aware of other work that has explicitly looked at using ambient electromagnetic noise picked up by the human body for user interaction.

Home Power Infrastructure

There are many sources of electromagnetic noise in the

environment, but the home power line infrastructure is a major source. A home typically consists of electrical wiring that supplies power to outlets, appliances, and lighting via wall switches. The electrical wiring branches from a central circuit breaker, but the ground and neutral wires in the home are all tied together. Thus, signals occurring on the power line in one part of the house can be measured in other parts as well. In addition, the walls of the home are dielectrics and will radiate electromagnetic fields even if there are no power lines in the wall.

Also, as mentioned earlier, the electrical wiring in the home can act as both a reception and transmission antenna. Past work has used this phenomenon for indoor location tracking, where a tracking signal is radiated off the power line [13, 20]. Similarly, [4] used the power line as a large antenna for receiving data wirelessly from ultra-low-power sensor nodes. All of these approaches use a known signal that is either injected through or received by the power lines. Other work has looked at passively monitoring the power line using a high-frequency sampling of the voltage at a single electrical outlet to infer the activation of appliances and electrical devices in the home based on the appearance of electrical noise from those devices [9, 14].

Although similar in spirit, our work monitors only the electromagnetic noise radiated off of the power lines and received by the human body to determine where in the home the person is and what type of gesture they are performing.

Electrical Noise

The AC signal itself is one of the largest sources of electromagnetic noise in the home: this signal typically oscillates at 60 Hz[1]. However, appliances and electronic devices attached to the power line also contribute some noise. There are roughly three general classes of electrical noise sources that may be found in a home: resistive loads, inductive loads such as motors, and loads with solid state switching (also known as switched-mode power supplies).

Purely resistive loads, such as incandescent lamps or electric stoves, do not create detectable amounts of electrical noise while in operation, although just like a resistor, they can be expected to produce trace amounts of thermal noise at an undetectable level. A motor, such as in a fan or a blender, is modeled as both a resistive and inductive load. The continuous breaking and connecting by the motor brushes creates a voltage noise synchronous to the AC power at 60 Hz (and at 120 Hz). Solid state switching devices, such as those found in computer power supplies, compact fluorescent light (CFL) bulbs, modern TVs, TRIAC dimmer switches and microwave ovens, emit noise that varies among devices and whose frequency is determined by an internal oscillator [14].

The drive towards smaller and more efficient consumer electronics has made use of switched-mode power supplies (SMPS) increasingly prevalent. In a modern SMPS this modulation happens at a very high rate (10 kHz – 1 MHz). A side effect of an SMPS's operation is that the modulation of the inductor's magnetic field produces large amounts of unintentional electromagnetic interference (EMI) centered at or around the modulation frequency. Due to the physical contact between the power line and the power supply, this EMI gets coupled onto the power line, which then propagates the noise throughout the entire electrical infrastructure of a home. This is known as conducted EMI, which in turn is radiated by the power line as radiated EMI. The appliance or device itself can also exhibit radiated EMI. Because such EMI may cause problems in the operation of certain electronic devices, the US Federal Communications Commission (FCC) sets rules for any device that connects to the power line and limits the amount of EMI it can conduct and radiate. However, despite these limits, significant and detectable EMI is still coupled back over the power line.

There are also several significant sources of electrical noise on the power line which originate outside the home. Radio broadcasts, including commercial AM and FM radio, are picked up by the power line, which acts as a receiving antenna over a wide range of frequencies. In addition, noise from elsewhere in the neighborhood is often coupled through the earth ground connection as well. Pilot tests showed that even when we turned off the main power coming into a home, there was still significant baseline noise present in the home, and radiated from the power line.

Combining Power Line Noise and "Body as an Antenna"

Past work in power line noise analysis and using the human body as an antenna has largely explored disparate applications. Recognizing the potential of using electrical noise as a signal and the human body as a receiving antenna, our work seeks to enable new user interaction capabilities in the home that require no additional instrumentation to the environment, and only a simple analog-to-digital converter on the body itself. Based on the prior work, we hypothesized that the complex shape of the power line infrastructure provides enough spatial differentiability in the signal space to allow us to uniquely identify locations and contact points relative to electrical devices and wiring. In other words, by looking at a various characteristics of the frequencies (presence, amplitude, shape, etc.) observed on body, it is possible to detect gestures.

CORE EXPERIMENT: VALIDATING THE TECHNIQUE

Participants and Homes

We conducted the experiment in 10 homes selected to represent a variety of constructions, in the Pacific Northwest region of the United States. These homes were single-family and townhouses built between 1948 and 2006 (μ=1981). They ranged in size between 120 and 290 square meters (μ=215), and had between 1 and 3 floors, some of them basements. The owner of each of these homes participated in our experiment. These 10 participants (5 female) were between 28 and 61 years old (μ=38), weighed be-

[1] This work was conducted in North America and thus refers to 60 Hz AC power; other parts of the world use 50 Hz.

tween 52 and 82 kg (μ=64), and were between 150 and 188 cm tall (μ=169 cm).

Apparatus

Electromagnetic signals radiating from the power lines and walls and picked up by the human body antenna can be measured as voltages. Since the body is relatively conductive, we can measure these voltages by placing a conductive pad, connected by a wire to an analog-to-digital converter, nearly anywhere on the body. In this experiment, we chose to measure voltages on the back of the neck because it is a stable point on the body that does not move significantly while a person is gesturing with their hands. The neck was also a convenient place because it is near our data collection equipment, which was housed in a backpack worn by the participant (Figure 2). We will validate in additional experiments that wearing the contact pad on a different part of the body still permits robust classification of hand gestures.

We made electrical contact to the skin using a standard grounding strap, typically worn around the wrist when working with sensitive electronics. We ran a small wire from the contact pad to a National Instruments USB-6216 data acquisition unit, which sampled the voltages at 400 kS/s. We biased the voltage on the contact point to a local ground signal on the data acquisition unit through a 10 MΩ resistor in order to remove most of the DC offset of the single-ended voltage. The data acquisition unit's local ground is internally isolated from the laptop's ground so that the measurements are referenced only to the small local ground on the data acquisition unit. The signal was digitized at 16-bit resolution and streamed to disk on an attached laptop for subsequent processing.

Experimental Procedure

We selected 5 light switches and 1 spot above an electrical outlet on a blank wall for testing in each of the 10 homes. In order to test whether or not we could differentiate between locations in close proximity, we ensured that two of the chosen light switches were located in the same room. The

Figure 2: Experimental setup. A laptop and a USB data acquisition device are worn in a backpack. A wire connects the data acquisition device to a conductive pad in contact with the back of the participant's neck.

other locations were distributed around the home with at least one location on each floor.

To minimize the number of variables that changed during the experimental session, we turned off appliances to which we had reasonable access and that periodically change their state, including most computers, as well as heating and air conditioning units. We left all light switches used in the experiment on, and we did not change the state of any lights or appliances once the experiment started.

Participants stood at arm's length away from the wall and performed 6 specific gestures around each interaction point (i.e., light switch or wall). The first was a "rest" gesture in which participants placed both hands at their sides. The other five involved contacting the wall with the right palm, placed flat against the wall for 6 seconds at different positions around the switch. These positions included directly on the light switch plate and at points approximately 20 cm above, below, right of, and left of the light switch. In the case of the blank wall, the same positions were used, but in reference to an arbitrary point at about the height of a light switch above the outlet marked on the wall. Each participant performed these six gestures at all six locations (5 switches, 1 wall) around their home. Figure 2 shows a participant in contact with the wall in the "above light switch" position.

To help participants and to ensure consistency, we marked each of the contact points with tape. When obstacles prevented the touch from occurring at 20 cm in any direction from the center position, we placed the tape as close as possible to the target position and noted this. We also taped over the ground screws on each light switch to ensure that the participant would not be shorted to ground while touching the switch. This was done to ensure that each contact with the switch was conducted under the same known conditions. Subsequent experiments confirmed that the ground screw provides a unique signal unto itself that is easy to robustly discriminate from the other positions in our experiment.

Software running on the data collection laptop issued verbal commands in order to guide participants through the experiment. In addition, all experiments involved a second person as an observer to check for mistakes and inconsistencies. The observer stood at least 1 m away from the participant to ensure that his presence did not significantly alter the received signals. At each location, the software issued commands about which position around the switch the participant should touch, followed by a 2-second beep, allowing the participant time to move to that position. Data was then collected for 6 seconds before the next command was issued. We randomized the order of the gestures at each light switch to eliminate any potential temporal bias and to ensure that the participant remained cognitively engaged. Participants moved from location to location in a predetermined order, and repeated the entire procedure 4 times (144 total gestures performed).

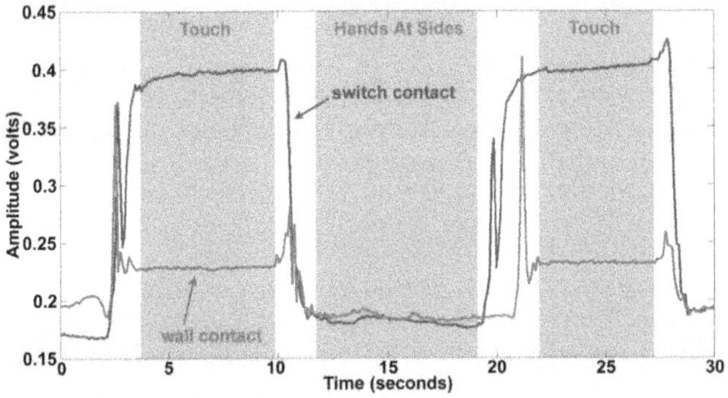

Figure 3: Signal captured from a participant during two touches on a wall (red) and a light switch (blue). Green highlights (left and right) indicate periods of contact, the orange highlight (center) indicates the "rest" period of non-contact. Differences between these signals, and between the contact and no-contact "rest" states, form the basis of our approach.

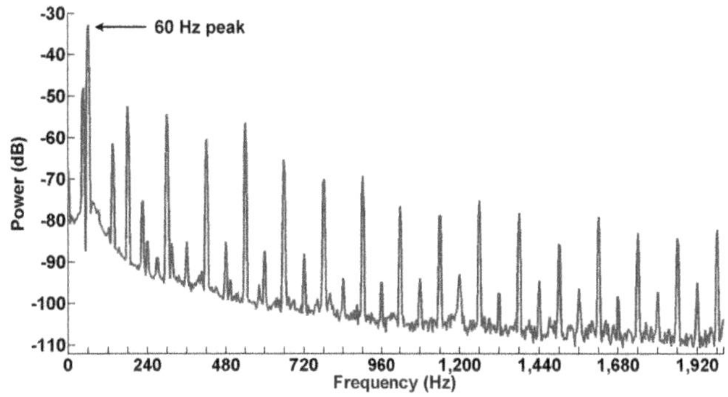

Figure 4: A frequency-domain representation of a signal captured during contact between a participant and a light switch. The 60 Hz peak and its harmonics are clearly visible throughout the low-frequency spectrum.

Analysis

Our primary goal is to inform the development of interactive systems that use the sampled signal to recognize gestures. Hence we treated our analysis as a machine learning classification problem. Specifically, we used the Sequential Minimal Optimization (SMO) implementation of the support vector machine (SVM) found in the Weka machine learning toolkit [11]. An SVM uses labeled data to construct a set of hyperplanes that separate labels in a high-dimensional feature space, which can then be used for classification. Fully exploring possible machine learning techniques is outside the scope of this paper; our results can be treated as a baseline that may be further optimized.

In order to prepare data for the SVM, we first segmented the 6-second gestures, removing a half-second from the front and end of this period to account for potential reaction time and anticipatory effects. We then divided the raw voltage signal into consecutive 82-millisecond windows. This window size allows for very low latency in gesture detection; however the results of the classification can be improved by smoothing over longer windows. In our analyses, each of these windows was treated as being independent data points. We then generated the following 1002 features for each window, which we used to train our SVM.

Time-Domain Features (2)

The most basic feature was the mean of the voltage (DC value). We also calculated the root-mean-square, or RMS value. The RMS value represents the AC amplitude of the voltage, which changes significantly between different gestures, as shown in Figure 3.

Low-Frequency Features (582)

Since the power lines are used to carry low-frequency AC power (at 60 Hz), it is not surprising that most of the energy radiated off of the power line and received by the human body antenna is in the low-frequency range. Figure 4 shows that the power spectrum is dominated by 60 Hz and its harmonics. As a result, these frequencies are important for machine learning. We used all of the raw frequency bins between DC and 2 kHz (12 Hz resolution) produced from a 32768-point FFT as features. Since the SVM is a linear classifier, we included both the linear and log (dB) versions of these features (332 features total). In addition, the harmonics of 60 Hz seem to become negligible at frequencies higher than about 25 kHz, and hence we create a second set of low frequency features containing FFT bins between DC and 25 kHz at 200 Hz resolution, again using both the linear and log (dB) versions (250 features total).

High-Frequency Peak Features (18)

Through an initial exploration of the signals received on the human body antenna, it became obvious that several high-frequency peaks were indicative of certain types of gestures. As a result, we also include the maximum value of several of these high-frequency peaks as features. The peaks that we included are 20k, 30k, 50k, 60k, 80k, 90k, 110k, 140k, and 150 kHz, again using both the linear and log (dB) versions (18 features total).

Full Frequency Range Features (400)

In order to encode the general shape of the frequency spectrum, we use features containing frequency samples between DC and 200 kHz with a 1 kHz resolution, again using both the linear and log (dB) versions (400 features total).

Results

To calculate how accurately we could classify various conditions, we conducted multiple four-fold cross-validations. Each fold was made up of data points from a single "round" through all locations in the home. This ensured that training and testing data points were separated within a fold, and that training data and testing data were separated by several minutes in time (to avoid over-fitting to transient variations in the environment). These numbers are representative of what we would expect to see in an interactive system. We report average accuracies and standard deviations.

Wall Touch

Looking only at the time-domain signals (Figure 3), it is easy to see the difference between the time when the participant is touching the wall (green) and the time when they are not (orange). Therefore, not surprisingly, the classification results for this kind of analysis were quite high.

Two-class classification of wall-touch vs. no-wall-touch

performed at 98.5%, σ=4.1 (chance=50%) when averaged across the participants in all 10 homes. Since the strength of the signal received on the body is related to the proximity to the radiating source, in this case the power lines, we expected that our wall touch classification would perform better on light switches than on the blank walls above outlets. However, our results show that the classification worked just as well on the blank walls, indicating that gestures do not need to be confined to the area around light switches. In fact, touches on most walls are detectable because of the wiring elsewhere in the wall.

Location in Home

The 6-location classification of interaction location in the home performed at 99.1%, σ=1.3 (chance=16.7%) when using data from all gestures around each light switch in each home. This is a very impressive result, made even more impressive by noting that by experimental design, two of the walls in each classification were located in the *same* room. This suggests the possibility to classify which wall a user is interacting with, rather than just which room.

Perhaps even more interestingly, the same level of accuracy can be obtained without even touching the wall. Using only the data from when the participant was standing at rest at arm's length from the wall (hands at sides), the 6-location classification performed at 99.5% σ=1.2 (chance=16.7%). This is a promising result, because it hints at the possibility of determining the location of people throughout the home, even when they are not interacting directly with the walls. This could enable location-aware systems that use in-air gestures in addition to on-wall gestures.

Touch Position on Wall

The 5-position classification of gesture position around the light switches performed at 87.4%, σ=10.9% (chance=20%). The touch position on the blank walls can be classified at 74.3%, σ=16.1% (chance=20%). This is an interesting result, as it suggests that it may be possible to classify arbitrary touch positions on blank walls, not just touches that are near light switches. We explore this further in the exploratory experiments described in the next section.

Location in Home and Touch Position on Wall

By combining the classification of *both* the location in home *and* the touch position on the wall, we have a 30-class problem, which performed at 79.8%, σ=7.0 (chance=3.3%). While this number may not seem high, recall that these are unoptimized classifications on individual time-windows and that these numbers should increase for entire touches, even simply using naïve voting schemes across multiple windows. With no additional instrumentation to the home, these results are quite promising in terms of the ability to both classify touch locations in the home as well as the absolute position on the wall.

Summary

Based on the classification results presented in this section, we can determine the location of the user in the home, with near 100% accuracy, and can determine whether the user is touching a wall or not with 98% accuracy. With 87% accuracy, we are able to determine the position around a light switch on a wall. We can even simultaneously identify the location in the home and the position on the wall of a given touch with 80% accuracy.

EXPLORING ADDITIONAL CAPABILITIES

Our core experiments, described above, confirmed our hypothesis that electromagnetic noise in the home is unique to specific locations, allowing discrimination of locations within the home and touched wall positions. In order to guide future work and understand the boundaries of this approach, we conducted a series of additional experiments to determine other capabilities that our approach might offer. We also wanted to confirm that decisions we made for consistency in experimental design (e.g., choosing the neck as the body contact location) are not restrictions that are fundamental to our approach.

We used the data acquisition system and methodology presented in the previous sections, but the following experiments were performed by two participants (instead of ten), each in one (different) home. This reduced participant pool allowed us to explore a variety of techniques, while still ensuring that results were not unique to a single person or home. Unless otherwise indicated, classification results are based on the same SVM described above, classifying 82-millisecond windows within our 5-second gestures, with 4-fold cross-validation across 4 "rounds" through all gestures in an experiment.

Each subsection introduces an experimental question that we aimed to answer in this additional exploration, along with results that provide preliminary answers to those questions.

Experiments and Results

Body Contact Location

In our core experiment, we placed the contact pad on the participant's neck, which allowed us to eliminate movement of the pad for the sake of experimental consistency. However, for real-world scenarios, connecting a computing device to a user's skin would much more likely sit near a location on which we already wear computing devices (e.g., the wrist). We thus repeated our core 5-position classification experiment around a single light switch in each of 2 homes, with the contact pad placed on the participant's forearm, instead of the neck. The 5-position classification of position around the switch performed at 98% and 97% (chance=20%) for our two participants.

This indicates that our approach performs well with the contact pad placed on the arm (where it might be connected to a watch), which is more practical for consumer scenarios.

Appliance Classification

Home appliances are known to emit a significant amount of electromagnetic noise. In addition, they have large sections of metal which are well grounded to the home's power line

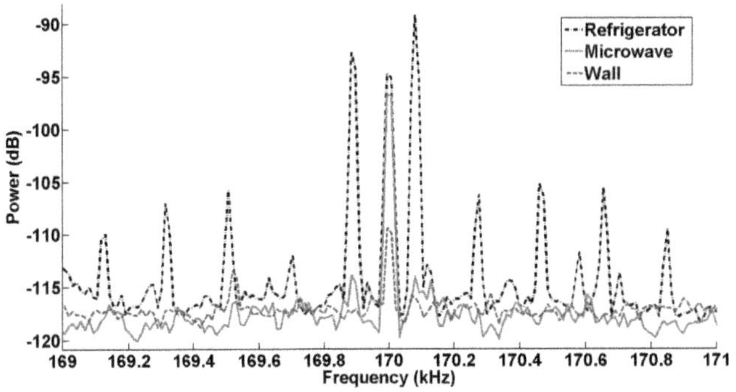

Figure 5: Frequency-domain differences of measured signal between a refrigerator, microwave, and a wall touch. Peaks show characteristic changes in amplitude that allow our classifiers to discriminate among touched objects. Here we show just one set of peaks from the high-frequency spectrum; similar characteristic peaks occur throughout the spectrum.

infrastructure. We hypothesized that this would allow us to robustly classify contact between a user and a home appliance, suggesting a variety of interaction techniques based on touching uninstrumented appliances. In order to address this hypothesis, participants touched each of six appliances in the same kitchen: refrigerator, freezer, stove, microwave, dishwasher, and faucet. All appliances were plugged in, but not actively running, during the experiment.

Consistent with our hypothesis, the measured electromagnetic noise while touching these appliances was quite dramatic, even compared to the noise observed during wall touches, and showed strong differences in our feature space among appliances (Figure 5). Consequently, classification among these six appliances was 100% for both participants (chance=16.7%).

This indicates that direct contact with appliances provides a robust signal for classification, suggesting the potential to turn uninstrumented appliances into real-world "buttons".

Number of Hands

In the experiments presented in the previous section, participants used only their right hand. We hypothesized that asymmetries in body conductivity, subtle asymmetries in contact pad placement, and differences in contact area would allow us to robustly discriminate left-, right-, and two-handed contact with a wall or light switch. As a preliminary investigation of this hypothesis, participants made left-, right-, or two-handed contact with a single light switch, and we attempt to classify among these contact types.

Consistent with our hypothesis, dramatic differences in our acquired signal were visible among these states, resulting in classification accuracies of 96% and 99% for our two participants (chance=33.3%).

This indicates that our approach allows robust discrimination among left-, right-, and two-handed contact.

Proximity to Wall

Based on initial observations that the amplitude of the signal received on the human body antenna changes continuously as participants' hands approached the wall prior to a touch, we hypothesized that the captured signal would provide a robust indication of the distance between a person's hand and the wall when no touch is occurring.

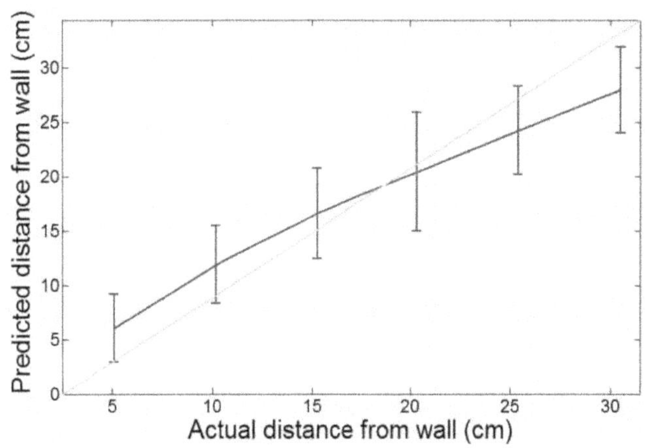

Figure 6: Regressing captured data onto a participant's distance from the wall (hand movement only). Error bars represent standard deviations. Light gray line indicates correct prediction values.

To investigate this hypothesis, participants rested their right hands above a measuring device for several seconds at 5, 10, 15, 20, 25, and 30 cm away from a light switch (along a line perpendicular to the wall). The participant's body did not move throughout this experiment, only the hand.

We used the same features as in our core experiment, and the same cross-validation procedure, but within each fold, rather than training a support vector machine classifier (which discriminates among discrete states), we trained a regression of our features onto the user's distance to the wall, using Weka's implementation of the SMO regression algorithm [17], which uses a support vector machine to map features into a high-dimensional space (as in an SVM classifier) and performs a linear regression in that space. Figure 6 shows the results across all regressions. The overall RMS error was 4.1 cm.

This indicates that our approach provides an indication of a user's distance from a wall containing electrical wires, with a resolution on the order of several centimeters.

Continuous Position Along Wall

The success of the "blank wall" results in the core experiment described earlier suggested that noise radiated from the power lines would vary continuously and predictably *along* a wall, offering the possibility of *continuous* touch localization. To assess this hypothesis, we again used a regression approach. In this case, participants rested their right-hand index finger against a wall at distances from 10 cm to 60 cm away from a light switch, *along* the wall, in one horizontal direction, at 10 cm increments (i.e., 10, 20, 30, 40, 50, and 60 cm). Figure 7 shows the results across all regressions. The overall RMS error was 8.1 cm.

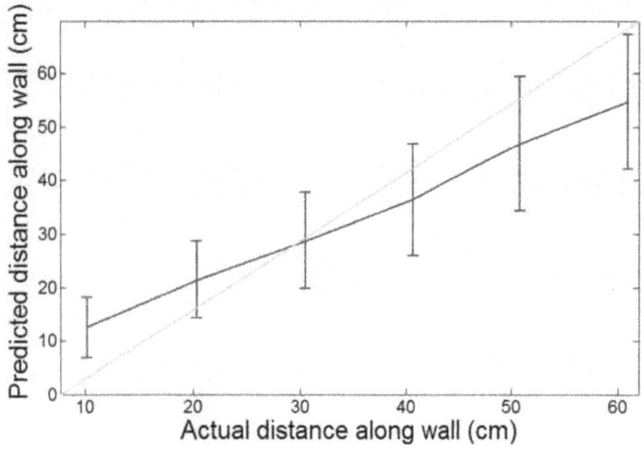

Figure 7: Regressing captured data onto a participant's touch position along a wall; distances indicate cm away from a light switch. Error bars represent standard deviations. Light gray line indicates correct prediction values.

This indicates that our approach provides an indication of a user's position along a noise-radiating wall, with a resolution on the order of several centimeters.

Interaction Switch Off

Our core experiments focused solely on light switches that were on (i.e., passing current). The noise environment at a light switch, however, is a function of the complete wiring pattern in the wall and the house, suggesting that passing current through the light switch at the center of interaction may not be necessary. We thus repeated our 5-position classification experiment around a single light switch in each of two homes, with the contact switch *off*. Classification performed at 99% and 97% (chance=20%) for our two participants.

This indicates that our approach performs well even for determining position relative to a light switch that is off.

Number of Fingers

Our ability to discriminate among one- and two-handed contact suggested that changes in contact area would be reflected in our signal, and that it might be possible to discriminate finer changes in contact area, such as the difference between single-finger and multi-finger contact.

To assess this hypothesis, our two participants conducted 5-second touches on a light switch using 1, 2, 3, 4, and 5 fingers on a single hand. Classification performed at 53% and 59% (chance=20%).

This is significantly lower than classification performance for the other capabilities explored in this section, but indicates that there is a relationship between contact area and our signal features. Additional work may be required to robustly discriminate fine changes in contact area.

DISCUSSION AND FUTURE WORK

Through our core experiment, we found that by measuring the electromagnetic noise received by the human body antenna, we can classify a person's location in the home with nearly 100% accuracy, and the position that a person is touching around a light switch with 87% accuracy on average. Through our additional explorations, we have demonstrated the ability to differentiate right and left hands, and determine which appliance is being touched. In addition, we have shown the ability to estimate the distance between a wall and a hand in the air, as well as the position of a hand along a wall.

These are promising results, which we believe can be integrated into an interactive real-time system for gesture sensing in uninstrumented homes. However, note that all of the classification accuracies reported in this work are on 82-millisecond windows. In an interactive system, it would be more natural to classify at the level of individual touches, which will likely *improve* classification performance, since smoothing can be performed over multiple windows.

Classification Features

We analyzed the classifiers built for our experiments to determine which features were most informative, by ranking the feature weights generated for each classifier. Over several hundred classifiers, the raw FFT amplitude spanning 60 Hz was the feature most frequently in the top ten highest-weighted features. Other features frequently ranked highly in our classifiers included the RMS amplitude and the FFT amplitude at 48 Hz (most likely a distortion of the 60 Hz signal). Perhaps more surprisingly, though, is the fact that several of our "high frequency peak" features in the kilohertz range were assigned large weights by most classifiers, motivating further exploration of these informative signals (Figure 5).

In addition to further exploring the "high frequency peaks", we would like to conduct an in-depth analysis of the feature space for this type of gesture sensing. We are currently using a naïve feature set, and are confident that our results can be improved – and several of our current limitations can be addressed – by using more appropriate features. For example, we have found examples of high-frequency peaks whose center frequency shifts as a function of the gesture. Exploration of these features remains future work.

Limitations and Future Improvements

Although our approach holds some promise, there are a number of limitations that we observed which will require further examination. The first is the generalizability of the observed noise signals. Since the electrical noise is a side effect of the power line infrastructure, there are no simple predictive models to infer what the signal will look like at different locations. Thus, the fingerprinting (classification) approach used here appears to be the most viable solution for now. This would require a user to calibrate and train the relevant gestures and locations for their home.

However, there are some simple techniques that could be used to help inform the user if a particular location would perform well. For example, the relative noise spread at a given location compared to the observed baseline noise in the house, and the observed signal strength, could be used to indicate a good location. Since it is possible to model certain electronic devices in the home, such as the noise emitted from a switching power supply, this could allow us to actively reject or select certain features to improve the performance at a particular location.

Alternatively and perhaps more interestingly, if we allow ourselves to marginally instrument the environment, previous work shows that we may be able to infer activities such as which light switch has been flipped (and hence touched) [15]. Using this system, we might be able to passively train the system as the user goes about their daily activities, turning lights on and off.

With the electrical wiring being embedded in the walls, it may be difficult to determine good locations for interaction. Appliances, TVs, light switches, and outlets can all be used as a general guide and anchor points. For blank walls, since it is hard to see the actual electrical wiring, we could imagine using a "stud finder" approach with our system, in which the user runs their hand on the surface and audible feedback is played to indicate that the area under the hand contains enough signal for interaction.

Large inductive loads or very noisy dimmer switches may pose problems since they generate broadband noise that can potentially mask or overwhelm a previously observed noise signal. Some of these may only cause localized problems, while others may propagate throughout the entire home. Similarly, other loads operating in the home may temporally change the signature of a particular location. A potential solution may be to have the wearable device synchronized to a single device plugged into an outlet that is continuously monitoring the power line noise and computing difference vectors for classification. This may only work for a certain number of noisy devices, since the response of the power line is not necessarily linear and superposition may not hold. Another approach may be to have a plug-in device that generates a known broadband signal and injects it into the power line, similar to [13].

In all of our experiments, the electrical state of the home (i.e., which appliances and lights were turned on) remained constant throughout the testing session. We performed an informal exploration of the effects associated with changing the electrical state of the home. We found that the classification works well when the home is in the same state as it was during training; however, causing large changes in state (i.e., turning on the air conditioning, or all lights in the home) causes the classification accuracy to drop. Smaller changes to the electrical state of the home appear to reduce the classification accuracy to a lesser extent. We plan to develop a feature set that is more robust to these kinds of changes. Additionally, the user could train the system using a few significantly different electrical states (e.g., all lights off, all lights on, and air conditioning on). Using existing systems [9, 14, 15] is possible to passively determine when each of the electrical appliances in the home change states, and therefore our classifier can change its model based on the electrical state of the home.

During our core experiment, we taped over the ground screws of all light switches to ensure consistency between these touches. We hypothesized that touching the ground screw would short the human body antenna to ground, and would therefore significantly affect the received signal. We performed an informal experiment to test this theory. Based on our results, it appears that the received signal is significantly different when the body is grounded through the screws on the light switch. Not surprisingly, the signal looks similar to those seen when touching grounded appliances. Since the signal is significantly different when touching the ground screws, these can be considered an additional type of gestural input on each switch.

Our initial results suggest the contact pad may be located anywhere on the body. We would like to further explore non-intrusive form factors for connecting a computing device to the body, such as a wrist watch. Another possibility is to explore how well a short range air-coupled connection to the body may work. In this case, we could imagine having sensors integrated into a mobile device, which could either reside on belt clip or in a pocket. It would need to be able to sense the electromagnetic noise received by the human body without any physical contact to the body.

As we described earlier, the shape of an antenna dictates the received frequency response. We intend to explore free-space gestures conducted near the electrical power lines. Changes in posture and hand gestures could result in discernable frequency shifts, which may indicate a gesture.

We attempted to characterize the side-effects of our particular hardware, and minimize all effects of noise and interference; however, it is possible that the data collection hardware (i.e., the data acquisition unit and laptop) may have been injecting noise in the environment (though almost certainly not in a gesture-specific manner). We plan to more carefully characterize the side-effects of our equipment, and if it turns out that noise generated by the current hardware is beneficial to the operation or robustness of the system, future designs can intentionally generate these signals.

Applications

The ability to turn almost any wall surface or electrical device in the home into an interactive input system enables a breadth of applications. In the light switch scenario, we can imagine mapping a collection of gestures to digital lighting in a room without having to add additional physical switches to the space. Since we are able to identify the location of the gesture, the interaction can be mapped to specific parts of the home. This enables having arbitrary widgets being placed in the environment. Another application is a simple gesture that can be used to control the home's thermostat from anywhere in the house. For instance, tapping on the wall above and below any light switch could be mapped to increasing and decreasing the thermostat temperature. Similarly, these gestures could be mapped to controlling the music playing through the intercom or whole-home audio system.

In addition, the wearable computing unit has the side benefit of identifying the user performing the gesture. Thus, each person in a home could have their own device and can create custom gestures and map them to their own applications. The ability to scale the entire home into an input system also enables a breadth of new gaming and general computing applications that could easily be deployed in any home. Exploring and building these applications remains future work.

CONCLUSION

We have demonstrated the feasibility of a new interaction modality that utilizes the human body as a receiving antenna for ambient electromagnetic noise already in existence in our environments. While this noise poses problems for many sensing applications, we have used this phenomenon as our signal, thereby reducing the need to instrument the environment. By examining the noise picked up by the body, we have shown that we can infer the absolute touch position around a light switch or blank wall near electrical wiring within the home with nearly 87% accuracy. The location of which wall in the home a person is touching has nearly 100% classification accuracy. We also demonstrated the potential for hovering and continuously tracking a hand on a wall to enable a richer set of interaction techniques. Interacting with electrical devices and appliances also produces discernable changes in the received signal which could provide additional opportunities for further exploration. Although our initial experiments were conducted with rather bulky test equipment, this sensing modality only requires a wearable contact pad and an analog-to-digital converter, suggesting incorporation into an easy-to-deploy form factor such as a watch or mobile phone.

REFERENCES

1. Chen, W.T. and Chuang, H.R. Numerical Computation of the EM Coupling between a Circular Loop Antenna and a Full-Scale Human-Body Model. *IEEE Trans Microwave theory and Techniques,* 46.10 (1998).
2. Cho, N., Yan, L., Bae, J., Yoo, H.J. 60 kb/s-10 Mb/s Adaptive Frequency Hopping Transceiver for Interference-Resilient Body Channel Communication. *IEEE Jour Solid-State Circuits*, 44.3 (2009).
3. Chuang, H.R. and Chen, W.T. Computer Simulation of the Human-Body Effects on a Circular-Loop-Wire Antenna for Radio-Pager Communications at 152, 280, and 400 MHz. *IEEE Trans Vehicular Tech*, 36.3 (1997).
4. Cohn, G., Stuntebeck, E., Pandey, J., Otis, B., Abowd, G.D., Patel, S.N. SNUPI: Sensor Nodes Utilizing Powerline Infrastructure. *Proc ACM Ubicomp 2010.*
5. Dietz, P. and Leigh, D. DiamondTouch: A Multi-User Touch Technology. *Proc ACM UIST 2001.*
6. Fukumoto, M. and Tonomura, Y. Body Coupled FingeRing: Wireless Wearable Keyboard. *Proc ACM CHI 1997.*
7. Gabriel, S., Lau, R.W., Gabriel, C. The dielectric properties of biological tissues: II. Measurements in the frequency range 10 Hz to 20 GHz. *Phys Med Biol*, 41 (1996).
8. Gabriel, S., Lau, R.W., Gabriel, C. The dielectric properties of biological tissues: I. Literature Survey. *Phys Med Biol* 41 (1996).
9. Gupta, S., Reynolds, M.S., Patel, S.N. ElectriSense: Single-Point Sensing Using EMI for Electrical Event Detection and Classification in the Home. *Proc ACM Ubicomp 2010.*
10. Hall, P.S. and Hoa, Y. Antennas and Propagation for Body Centric Communications. *Proc Euro Conf on Antennas and Propagation 2006.*
11. Hall, M., Frank, E., Holmes, G., Pfahringer, B., Reutemann, P., Witten, I.H. The WEKA Data Mining Software: An Update. *SIGKDD Explorations*, 11.1 (2009).
12. Harrison, C., Tan, D. Morris, D. Skinput: Appropriating the Body as an Input Surface. *Proc ACM CHI 2010.*
13. Patel, S.N., Truong, K.N., Abowd, G.D. PowerLine Positioning: A Practical Sub-Room-Level Indoor Location System for Domestic Use. *Proc ACM Ubicomp 2006.*
14. Patel, S.N., Robertson, T., Kientz, J.A., Reynolds, M.S., Abowd, G.D. At the Flick of a Switch: Detecting and Classifying Unique Electrical Events on the Residential Power Line. *Proc ACM Ubicomp 2007.*
15. Patel, S.N., Stuntebeck, E.P., Robertson, T. PL-Tags: Detecting Batteryless Tags through the Power lines in a Building. *Proc Pervasive 2009.*
16. Saponas, S., Tan, D., Morris, D., Balakrishnan, R., Turner, J., Landay, J. Enabling Always-Available Input with Muscle-Computer Interfaces. *Proc ACM UIST 2009.*
17. Shevade, S.K., Keerthi, S.S., Bhattacharyya, C., Murthy, K.R.K. Improvements to the SMO Algorithm for SVM Regression. *IEEE Trans Neural Networks*, 11.5 (2000).
18. Smith, J.R. Field Mice: Extracting hand geometry from electric field measurements. *IBM Systems Journal*, 35.3 (1996).
19. Smola, A.J. and Schoelkopf, B. A tutorial on support vector regression. *Statistics and Computing*, 14.3 (2004).
20. Stuntebeck, E.P., Patel, S.N., Robertson, T., Reynolds, M.S., Abowd, G.D. Wideband power line positioning for indoor localization. *Proc ACM Ubicomp 2008.*
21. Zimmerman, T., Smith, J., Paradiso, J., Allport, D., Gershenfeld, N. Applying Electric Field Sensing to Human-Computer Interfaces. *Proc ACM CHI 1995.*
22. Zimmerman, T.G., Personal Area Networks: Nearfield intrabody communication. *IBM Systems Journal*, 35.3 (1996).

Sensor Synaesthesia: Touch in Motion, and Motion in Touch

Ken Hinckley[1], Hyunyoung Song[1,2]
[1]Microsoft Research
One Microsoft Way, Redmond, WA 98052
kenh@microsoft.com
[2]University of Maryland
Computer Science: College Park, MD 20742
hsong@cs.umd.edu

ABSTRACT
We explore techniques for hand-held devices that leverage the multimodal combination of touch and motion. Hybrid touch + motion gestures exhibit interaction properties that combine the strengths of multi-touch with those of motion-sensing. This affords *touch-enhanced motion* gestures, such as one-handed zooming by holding one's thumb on the screen while tilting a device. We also consider the reverse perspective, that of *motion-enhanced touch*, which uses motion sensors to probe what happens underneath the surface of touch. Touching the screen induces secondary accelerations and angular velocities in the sensors. For example, our prototype uses motion sensors to distinguish gently swiping a finger on the screen from "drags with a hard onset" to enable more expressive touch interactions.

Author Keywords
Sensors, touch, gestures, multimodal input, mobile devices

ACM Classification Keywords
H.5.2 Information Interfaces and Presentation: Input

General Terms
Human Factors

INTRODUCTION
Touch-screen input is ubiquitous in mobile interaction. But mobile devices also include motion sensors such as accelerometers and gyroscopes to support contextual sensing [19,31], digital photography [23], and games. The widespread availability of mobile devices with both touch and motion-sensing presents an opportunity to explore novel interaction techniques that leverage synergistic roles for *touch and motion* as complementary modalities.

Synaethesia is a secondary sensation, such as color, experienced by some people in response to an actual perception, such as listening to music. In the context of touch input, there is a corresponding *sensor synaesthesia* of accelerations, angular velocities, and torques that mobile devices can perceive coincident to the contacts detected by a touch-screen. These secondary sensor responses may offer hints about touch that enhance the expressiveness of touch-screen interaction. We build on a few prior examples (e.g. [12,17,29]) to show how touch+motion represents a promising design space of synaesthetic gestures that has not been recognized or systematically explored before.

CHI 2011, May 7–12, 2011, Vancouver, BC, Canada.

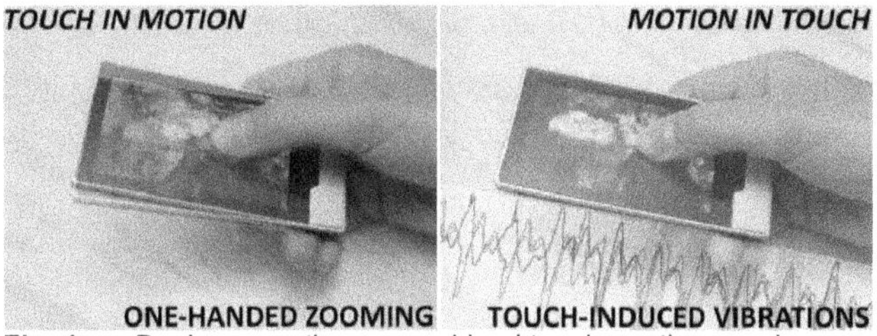

Fig. 1. Dual perspective on combined touch+motion sensing.

Touch-enhanced motion techniques put "touch in motion" to produce new gestures (*Fig. 1, left*). These gestures can include information from the touch, such as the number of contacts and their positions, as parameters to a motion gesture. For example, the user can tilt the device (motion) to zoom into a specific screen location (touch).

Motion-enhanced touch techniques (*Fig. 1, right*) put the "motion in touch" to enable more expressive touch interactions, such as soft vs. hard taps, or gentle swipes vs. drags with a hard onset. These techniques use the incidental vibratory motion induced by finger contact to add nuances to the expression of touch, or to infer context of use (e.g., how the user held the device when he touched the screen).

Collectively these perspectives represent a "hidden dimension of touch" that we seek to explore in the design space of motion sensing techniques that we propose, the novel techniques that we implement, and in the informal user study evaluating these new techniques that follows.

Synaesthetic Touch + Motion Techniques
To explore the design space of touch + motion, we implemented several techniques on a handheld device.

Touch-Enhanced Motion Techniques
***1) Tilt-to-zoom*:** The user can zoom in or out relative to a specific point on the screen by holding the tip of the thumb at that point and tilting the device. The user's touch input cues the system to "listen" for motion gestures. This delimits *Tilt-to-zoom* from other incidental movements of the device. This also affords direct control over the center of expansion via the *(x,y)* coordinate indicated by the user's thumb. This offers one-handed continuous zooming, unlike pinch-to-zoom, which requires one hand to hold the device, and the other hand to articulate the pinch gesture.

***2) Pivot-to-lock*:** The user can touch the screen while pivoting the device to a new viewing orientation. This locks the screen at its current landscape/portrait format, for usage scenarios such as browsing the web while lying in bed.

3) Hold-and-shake: The user can touch an icon and shake the device to apply a command, such as *Undo,* to that icon. This integrates selection with the motion gesture itself [17].

4) Tip-to-select: The user can frame a portion of the screen with two thumbs and then tilt the device to select the indicated region. This shows how multi-touch combines with motion to fluidly support additional desirable interactions, without interfering with pinch-to-zoom.

Motion-Enhanced Touch Techniques

The four techniques above illustrate new synaesthetic touch-motion gestures. The following techniques employ motion sensors to lend secondary nuances to touch.

5) Soft-vs-Hard-Tap: Softly tapping an item activates it, but tapping an item harder "drills into it" to allow direct navigation to a secondary target. For example, a soft tap on the calendar tile of our device's home screen navigates to the *day view* showing all appointments for the day, but a hard tap navigates directly to the current appointment.

6) Swipe-vs-Hard-Drag: Gently swiping the screen scrolls or pans the display as usual, but a drag with a hard onset (that is, striking an item and dragging it) allows the user to directly drag and rearrange items in the view, without having to activate an "edit" mode (e.g. via tap-and-hold).

7) Context of Touch: We also explore how accelerometer and gyroscope signals may help infer the context of touches.

Design Attributes of Touch + Motion

Synaesthetic touch+motion gestures exhibit a number of desirable design properties that collectively offer designers a new implement in the toolbox of mobile interaction. To explore the design space of touch+motion gestures, we carefully considered the design properties of this class of gestures. We then deliberately chose the techniques enumerated above to populate this space of touch+motion gestures with examples that illustrate each property. Here, we briefly discuss these properties, and indicate the corresponding techniques that illustrate each of them.

State transitions for motion gestures. We use *FingerDown* and *FingerUp* events to delimit motion gestures from other movements of a device. This affords chunking and phrasing [4] of touch+motion gestures in a kinesthetic mode that is salient to the user [35]. When motion sensing is used to enhance touch, the onset (or release) of touch indicates when to pull the corresponding motion data out of the sensor stream. Example: All seven techniques listed above.

Mixed-mode Parameters. A touch-screen indicates an (x,y) position in addition to the *FingerDown* and *FingerUp* events. Meanwhile, tilt can apply a continuous control to the indicated location. Example technique: *Tilt-to-zoom.*

A comfortable and imprecise target to delimit motion. Systems must distinguish motion gestures from other incidental handling of a device. A button can serve this role but diverts attention [19] and requires constant muscular strain while moving the device. Some of our touch-motion gestures let the user gently rest a finger anywhere on the screen while moving the device. Such motions demand less attention, do not impose a particular hand-grip, and may be more comfortable to articulate. Example: *Pivot-to-lock.*

Contextual commands. Some motion gestures can use the touch point to indicate specific objects on the screen. This enables motion gestures that apply to a specific icon [17], photo, or region of the screen. Example: *Hold-and-shake* a specific icon to *Delete* an icon, or *Undo* that deletion.

Multi-touch motion gestures. Unlike a physical button, touch allows for multiple points of contact, which can be combined with motion to afford additional interaction states. Example: *Tip-to-select* a region of the screen, as indicated by the bounding rectangle of two thumbs.

Fluidly interleave touch and motion. Some techniques may interleave motion gestures with complementary direct-touch movements. For example, a user can hold his thumb still and tilt-to-zoom, but then slide his thumb to transition directly to panning. Examples: *tilt-to-zoom*; *tip-to-select* interleaves two-thumb zooming with rectangular selection.

Expressive Touches. By leveraging the motion sensors in more of a background-sensing role [19], different nuances of touch can be sensed. This also allows simply resting a finger on an object to be treated differently than a distinct tap on an object, for example. Examples: *Soft-vs-Hard-Tap*, *Swipe-vs-Hard-Drag*, and *Context of Touch* techniques.

RELATED WORK

Combining motion gestures with touch is a simple idea that has been little explored. Hassan's "Chucking" technique [17] uses a simultaneous touch+motion gesture to toss a file from a mobile device to a wall display. The user holds a finger on the file's icon, while indicating where to place the file via a motion gesture. Rahman [29] also uses touch + motion to measure wrist deflection angles. We contribute novel examples of touch+motion gestures, and we reveal the larger design space of touch+motion by articulating its properties and charting a taxonomy of related techniques.

On digital cameras, sampling device motion at the moment that the user depresses the shutter button can yield enhanced image deblurring [23]. Skinput [16] uses vibratory signals to infer the location of taps on one's forearm. These techniques hint at the strategy of *looking for the motion in touch* that we adopt in some of our techniques.

Several efforts have considered accelerometers as a proxy for pressure input. For example, accelerometer-inferred pressure is not satisfactory for the musical expression of piano-forte on touchscreen-based mobile devices [12], but can support a few discrete states for "expressive typing" on the keys of an accelerometer-enhanced laptop [22].

Motion has also been used as a cue for grip-sensing mobile devices. For example, an accelerometer can trigger implicit grip sensing when a mobile device is held still [24]. Graspables [36] use accelerometers to sense the orientation of objects and to trigger grip sensing at the right moment.

Several efforts consider touch in combination with other modalities. Herot [18] describes a touch screen that senses shear and torque forces. PACER [26] interleaves touch gestures with camera-based motion gestures. Spilling [28] and TouchProjector [2] use direct input on the screen of a device, in combination with movement of the device itself, to augment physically situated interactions. Touch + motion also echoes other examples of synergistic modalities, such as speech + gesture [10] and pen + touch [20].

Motion Sensing and Delimiters

Many works have explored motion-sensing gestures, as well as background sensing of motion as a contextual cue. As this implies, motions may be explicitly triggered by the user, but motions also occur incidental to handling and transporting a mobile device. While several tradeoffs have been explored (e.g. [1,14,19,21]), a fundamental problem for motion sensing is to either map gestures to motions unlikely to occur by accident, or to explicitly delimit motion gestures from other handling of the device. Indeed, delimiters and state transitions [5] are fundamental building blocks of interactive techniques.

Some motion gestures are distinctive enough to serve as delimiters. TimeTilt employs tapping the back of a device, or jerking it forward and back, to signal state changes [30]. Particular patterns of hard contact forces (such as whacking a device [21]) can provide motion gestures that are fairly robust to false positive recognition errors. However, to avoid false positives, these approaches limit the space of motion gestures. Articulating the delimiters also may slow down some of the resulting interactions.

Many systems instead employ mechanical button presses to delimit motion gestures and manipulations (e.g. [9,37]). This opens up a larger space of permissible motions, but requires that the user find and hold a pushbutton on the device. This may force the user to adopt a particular hand grip, or reduce the range of hand and wrist motions [29] that are comfortable to articulate. Some systems have used *indirect* touch [14,19,24], but few systems have considered direct touch [17,29] to delimit motion gestures.

For manipulative motion gestures, tilt dynamics are often based on rate mappings to compensate for the limited range of motion that is possible when tilting a device [1,14,19]. The exact transfer function and appropriate feedback for such mappings can be tricky to optimize [8,11]. Other systems use larger-scale absolute movements to support a metaphor of direct spatial navigation [2,9,13,28].

Additional Considerations for Mobile Interaction

One-handed input is widely recognized as a desirable property for mobile interaction (e.g. [17,29]). Yet the ubiquitous pinch-to-zoom gesture requires both hands on mobile devices: one hand holds the device while the other hand pinches. As such, an effective one-handed method for continuous zooming could prove valuable to mobile users.

Attention is a precious resource in mobile interaction [19,21,31]; indeed, limiting the visual demands of interfaces has motivated many motion-sensing techniques. Many of our proposed touch+motion gestures implicitly require some degree of visual attention, since they involve interaction with the touch-screen. Yet our techniques complement existing motion-sensing techniques, and they populate a middle ground of gestures that offload some aspects of what would otherwise be purely touch-based visual interactions onto the motion channel.

DESIGN SPACE OF MOTION SENSING TECHNIQUES

We can now map out the design space of motion sensing techniques. The following tableau (Fig. 2), informed by previous taxonomies [3,6], delineates the design space by the *property sensed* versus the *activation mechanism*.

	INDIRECT		DIRECT		
	Mech. Buttons	**Indirect Touch & Pressure**	**Direct Touch**	**None (pure motion)**	
Acceleration (linear accelerometer)	Virtual Shelves [9]		***Pivot-to-lock***	Auto screen rotation [19]	Absolute (Θ)
	Tilt for text [37]	Tilt scrolling [14,19]	***Tilt-to-zoom*** Measuring wrist angles [29]	Rock'n'Scroll [1]	Relative (ΔΘ)
	Expressive Typing [22]		***Hard-tap*** ***Hard-drag*** Piano forte [12]	Whack gestures [21]	Hard contact force
			Hold+shake ***Tip-to-select*** Chucking [17]	TimeTilt [30]	Motion gesture
		Graspables [36] Grip sensing [24]			Stability (no motion)
Angular Velocity	Deblur image on shutter press (accel. + gyro) [23]		***Thumb vs. finger usage***	***Tapping corners*** Dual-screen Reader [7]	
Vibratory		Scratch input [15]	Skinput [16]	Bone conduction microphones	
Shear, Torque		Gummi bendable computer [34]	Vector touch-screen [18]		
Position-based motion sensing	Chameleon [13] (Hold button + sensed motion of device)		TouchProjector [2], Spilling [28], (Direct input on screen + sensed motion of device)	PhoneTouch [32] (motion signal on phone, at same time as phone contact with surface)	

Fig. 2. Design space of motion sensing techniques, organized by the *property sensed* (rows) versus *activation mechanism* (columns).

The property sensed is the primary axis of organization. We classify it as *acceleration* (sensed by linear accelerometer), *angular velocity* (gyroscope), *vibratory* signals, *shear & torque* forces, or *position-based* motion sensing. Within the acceleration category, the rightmost column characterizes the techniques based on how they use the accelerometer.

The columns of the table classify techniques by the *activation mechanism* employed to trigger an interactive response to sensed motions. *Indirect* activation mechanisms include mechanical buttons as well as touch, pressure, or grip sensors integrated with the device. *Direct* activation mechanisms include direct-touch contact with the display, as well as "none" (that is, no activation mechanism), for techniques that employ always-active motion sensing.

We populate each cell of the resulting matrix with references to representative systems and techniques. The new techniques described in this paper are shown in **bold**.

The taxonomy of Fig. 2 situates our techniques within a constellation of related motion-sensing techniques, but does not emphasize mixed-mode mappings for touch + motion gestures. Thus, we enumerate our techniques in a second table (*Fig. 3*) that shows combinations we have explored.

TECHNIQUE	State Transitions	Touch Parameter	Motion Parameter
Tilt-to-zoom	2 (Hold)	**(x,y) point** for focus of expansion	Change in forward-back tilt angle ($\Delta\Theta_x$)
Pivot-to-lock	2 (Hold)	**Entire screen** (touch anywhere)	Absolute rotation (Θ_z)
Rotate object (variant of Pivot-to-lock)	2 (Hold)	**(x,y) point** for center of rotation	Change in rotation ($\Delta\Theta_z$)
Hold-and-shake	2 (Hold)	**Select object** or icon	Gesture: three spikes in (Θ_{xy})
Tip-to-select	2 (Two-finger Hold)	**Rectangle** (two touch points)	Gesture: one quick jerk in (Θ_{xy})
Hard-tap	**0→2→0** (Hard contact on rapid FingerDown-FingerUp event sequence)	**Select object** or icon	Hard contact force: Spike in (Θ_z)
Hard-drag	**0→2** (Hard contact on FingerDown event, with no FingerUp)	**Select object** + **drag path**.	Hard contact force: Spike in (Θ_z)
Tap-and-hold (e.g. for context menus)	**0→2** (No sensed motion and no dragging after FingerDown)	**Select object** or icon	Stability (no motion)

Fig. 3. Mixed-modality mappings explored by our techniques.

The *state transitions* show how we incorporate the motion signal into the interactive technique, in terms of Buxton's 3-state model [5], where state 0 is *out-of-range* (no finger contact) and state 2 is dragging (finger on screen).

The *touch parameter* is the aspect of the touch signal that the technique leverages, which can be any of the following:

- **Entire screen**: a touch anywhere on the screen.
- **(x,y) point**: the centroid of the touch point.
- **Drag path**: the path followed by the finger.
- **Select object**: the user touches a specific icon, object, or region of the screen to select it.
- **Rectangle** (two touch points): a bounding box.
- **Contact / Shape**: the geometry of the touch(es).

Our techniques currently do not include any examples of *Contact / Shape* parameters for touch+motion gestures, as our prototyping devices do not report this information. Nonetheless these parameters suggest paths for future work.

The *motion parameter* specifies the contribution of the motion signal to the mixed-mode parameters of a gesture. These use the same nomenclature as the attributes from the rightmost column of Fig. 2; we also note which axes of the accelerometer each technique employs.

IMPLEMENTATION

We implemented our techniques as 3rd party applications for Windows Phone 7 (WP7). We also implemented some techniques on a Zune HD. Both devices have capacitive multi-touch screens and an integrated three-axis linear accelerometer. WP7 supports sampling the accelerometer at 30Hz, whereas the Zune HD supports 60Hz. We used both platforms because of limited availability of WP7 devices, and to user-test *Tilt-to-zoom* at the 60Hz sampling rate.

We have implemented a WP7 photo browser which includes all of our techniques except Tilt-to-zoom; this remains a separate application. However, we believe that a well-considered implementation could support all of our gestures simultaneously (using approaches suggested by [1,19,30], for example). Here we focus on optimizing the individual techniques to assess their value to users.

Motivation for Application Scenarios & Techniques

Several of our techniques are motivated by pain-points that we have observed in current mobile user interfaces. These include the inability to articulate continuous one-handed zooming, the difficulty of browsing the web while lying in bed due to undesired automatic screen rotation, and the tedium of performing a succession of taps to drill down to commonly used options or views. We also intentionally chose examples that populate our design space of touch+motion gestures, so that each technique illustrates specific design properties. Most of the techniques were implemented in a WP7 photo browser; we chose this as a demonstration application because all of the touch+motion gestures of interest have useful semantics in the context of browsing, organizing, cropping, and viewing individual photos or collections of photos [8].

TOUCH-ENHANCED MOTION TECHNIQUES

Tilt-to-Zoom

As noted earlier, pinch-to-zoom is difficult to perform, one-handed. As such, touch-screen devices often use double-tap for one-handed zooming, but double-tap only supports discrete zooming. Furthermore, in the context of zooming within a web browser, the first of the two taps is prone to accidentally activating links. This forces the user to hunt for "empty" space, or text that is not hyperlinked, to successfully zoom via double-tap. Thus, a reliable and effective way to zoom with one hand is desirable for mobile devices. Because one-handed continuous zooming would open up many mobile usage scenarios, such as a user referring to a map while encumbered with shopping bags or holding a child's hand, such a technique complements pinch-to-zoom even if it is not necessarily faster.

The user zooms into a point on the screen by holding his thumb at the desired location, and tilting the device. Tilt-to-zoom thus affords directly zooming into locations such as the corners of a web page. Pinch-to-zoom cannot directly express this because there is not room to expand two fingers at the edges of the screen. Yet our technique is compatible with pinch-to-zoom; a device can support both techniques. This lets the user employ the approach that best suits his current usage context.

Implementation Issues & Considerations

We implemented Tilt-to-zoom in a simple map navigation application. Touching down a finger on the screen starts an ambiguous "pan-or-zoom" mode. We say the mode is ambiguous because at the moment of the *FingerDown* event, the system does not yet know if the user will pan or zoom the display. Sliding the thumb beyond a minimum distance threshold triggers the standard panning behavior. If the user instead tilts the device while the finger remains still, this triggers tilt-to-zoom. Lifting the finger from the screen exits the mode. The user can also hold the thumb still at the end of a panning motion, and then tilt, to transition directly to zooming. Our technique therefore fluidly interleaves both panning and zooming.

Tilting the top edge of the screen *away from yourself* is mapped to zoom-out, while tilting the top edge of the screen *closer to yourself* is mapped to zoom-in. In early pilot testing, we found that slightly more than half of users preferred this mapping, but some users with a different mental model preferred the opposite mapping. The zooming speed is a rate-based function of the *change* in forward-back tilt angle [14,19]. The zooming speed is therefore determined *relative to the angle at which the user starts touching the device*: that is, whenever the user touches the screen, this resets the "resting" orientation (where the speed of zooming is zero) to the current forward-back tilt angle. We chose a transfer function with a rate of expansion that seemed "about right" in early pilot tests, balancing rapid zooming against the desire for fine control of the zoom.

Fig. 1. Tilt-to-Zoom: No zooming occurs while the device is held normally (left). Touching the screen enters the zooming mode (middle). Zooming is then mapped to the change in tilt angle (right).

To avoid accidentally triggering tilt-to-zoom with small motions, the user must pass through a dead-band of $\pm 5°$ around the starting orientation before zooming starts. Zooming uses tilt along the device's forward-back axis, which corresponds to ulnar/radial deviation of the wrist [29] for a typical single-handed grip (Fig. 1). However, it is possible to tilt the device without significant deviation of the wrist by adopting a precision grip on the device, and using the fingertips to subtly tilt it forward and back like a miniature seesaw. The rate-based transfer function enables zooming a long distance with a small change in the tilt.

Visual Affordance for Motion Gestures

There has been little exploration of visual languages for motion gestures [25] that show the desired direction or degree of tilting required by an interaction. To convey that tilt-to-zoom requires forward-back tilting, we provide a *perspective box* near the borders of the map that appears axis-aligned at the start of a tilt motion, but becomes perspective-distorted as the user tilts further from the starting angle. The vanishing point appears to be either somewhere above the screen, when zooming in, or somewhere below the screen, when zooming out. This conveys the current zoom direction as well as the tilt axis that responds to zooming. Our pilot testing suggested that the perspective box enforces the metaphor, while providing feedback of the correct direction to tilt the device.

Pivot-to-Lock

Automatic screen rotation [19] is commonplace on mobile devices, but in some usage contexts the technique can lead to undesired changes in the screen orientation. Attempting to read a web page while lying down on a couch, or in bed, are common examples that many of us have experienced. To address this, the Apple iPad and iPhone include a global screen lock (a hardware button for the iPad, and a software setting for the iPhone) to disable automatic screen rotation, but this makes it tedious to change orientation. The *MobileRSS* iPhone app (tinyurl.com/yb37rac) pops up an icon when the user reorients the screen. Users can touch this icon to toggle between the *lock* and *automatic* screen rotation option. This icon appears for two seconds every single time the user reorients the device. This may distract the user, and it interferes with reading the underlying text.

Implementation Issues & Considerations

The interaction metaphor of *Pivot-to-Lock* is that the user can "pin down" the screen to keep it at its current viewing orientation. That is, holding a finger on the screen while pivoting the device to a new viewing orientation locks the screen at its current landscape or portrait format.

Fig. 2. Pivoting the device while holding the screen locks the current viewing orientation. A small padlock icon provides feedback.

For this technique, the location of the touch point does not matter. Thus it is an example of a touch-motion gesture that uses the imprecision of a touch anywhere on the entire screen as a way to delimit motion-sensing gestures from other incidental movements of the device. Although this is the only example of such a gesture that we implemented, it is clear that motion-sensing gestures for other "global commands" that act on the entire screen (or on the currently active application) could be added, so long as the required motions do not conflict with one another.

We implement standard automatic rotation to any of the four canonical screen orientations, but we check to see if the user is holding a finger on the display before we respond. Like the *Tilt-to-zoom* technique, on a *FingerDown* event *Pivot-to-lock* starts in an ambiguous mode. If the user touches down and slides his finger, this again triggers panning. If the device rotates substantially with little movement of the finger, we turn off the panning interpretation. When the device has rotated far enough to represent a new viewing orientation, we trigger *Pivot-to-lock* instead of automatically rotating the screen.

Visual feedback in the form of a padlock icon (🔒) appears to indicate that the screen has entered the lock state. The screen remains locked after the user lifts his finger. The obvious design question is how the user can later deactivate the lock. To prevent the screen lock from becoming a heavyweight mode, we opted to leave the lock on as long as the user remains at the current viewing orientation. As soon as the user rotates the device to a new orientation (without pinning down the screen), this turns off the lock and restores the automatic screen rotation functionality. This solution ensures that the user cannot become "trapped" in a mode that they do not know how to escape.

Tip-to-Select

Selecting or clipping content from the current screen view can be problematic for touch-only interfaces, if only because many of the obvious input events and state transitions available to the interaction designer must be assigned to other, higher-priority tasks. For example, to select a region of text on the Apple iPad, the user must tap and then manipulate small blue selection handles to indicate the desired passage. Indicating a rectangular selection by framing it with two fingers is an oft-demonstrated technique in the literature, but in typical mobile device interfaces, two-finger manipulation is already consumed by the pinch-to-zoom gesture.

Fig. 3. Holding the screen with two thumbs (top) and then tipping the device away (middle) selects the indicated region (bottom).

Implementation Issues & Considerations

Our photo browser supports two-fingered zooming on individual photographs. However, with the *Tip-to-Select* technique, if the user holds both fingers stationary and quickly tips the device away and back, this triggers a state transition to the *selection mode*. The user can then use the two fingers to directly manipulate the opposite corners of a marquee selection (*Fig. 3*). When the user lifts his fingers, this crops the selected region from the photo.

Note that *Tip-to-Select* fluidly interleaves two-fingered zooming with the selection mode. The user can start by zooming to the desired portion of a photograph, for example, and then keep the fingers in contact with the display while tipping the device to trigger selection.

Tip-to-Select responds to a change in orientation from the start of the motion signal. The user must quickly depart from the current orientation by at least ±15°to trigger the transition to selection mode. The user can tip by this amount in any direction. The user then returns to the original orientation within a short time-out. Hence, *Tip-to-Select* represents a gesture that is recognized as a whole, rather than continuously interpreted as a direct manipulation. The motion component of *Tip-to-Select* is related to the jerk gesture employed by TimeTilt [30].

Hold-and-Shake

Context menus (e.g. for photos, icons) can be difficult to access on a mobile device. Bringing up the menu via tap-and-hold is a standard solution. The user must search through the menu for the desired option, and then tap on it via hand-eye coordination. Hence context menus are slow to activate, and demand significant visual attention.

On iPhone and Android devices, shaking applies to the entire application (e.g. undo, shuffle playlist). However, a problem with shaking as a pure-motion gesture is that it is prone to unintended activation. As a result, a system must be careful what it accepts as "shaking," which makes it more difficult to articulate the gesture when it is intended.

Fig. 4. Holding a photo (left) while shaking the device (middle) deletes the photo (right). Shaking again undoes the deletion.

Implementation Issues & Considerations

We instead explore *Hold-and-Shake* as a contextual touch+motion gesture. This gesture simultaneously demonstrates two interaction properties of interest. First, it illustrates how holding touch indicates a mode switch from the "neutral" mode, where incidental motions can be ignored, to a "gesture" mode where the system looks for motion gestures. Second, *Hold-and-Shake* illustrates how this transition to gesture mode can be integrated with object selection, by selecting the underlying object or icon that falls underneath the (x,y) coordinate of the touch. Clearly the concept of *touching an object to integrate mode switching with object selection* [20] could be applied to other contextual motion gestures, such as holding a photo and moving the device in various directions [17,30].

The user can hold a photo and shake the device to delete the indicated photo. Instead of asking the user to confirm whether the photo should be deleted, our prototype just replaces the photo with a red square that says *Deleted*. The user can later undo the operation by holding on the former location of the photo and again shaking the device to *Undo* the action. This leads to a nice symmetry between the original action and the gesture needed to reverse its effects.

Like our other gestures, *Hold-and-Shake* starts in an ambiguous mode. For example, touching down but then sliding the finger on the screen scrolls the list of photos, and deactivates motion-sensing mode. If the user instead touches down while the finger does not slide, we then recognize the shaking gesture by a heuristic that looks for three successive peaks in the motion signal (within a 2s time interval). Once motion starts, but before the shaking gesture has completed, we relax the distance threshold (for the transition from holding to scrolling) because the touch contact point may move while the user shakes the device.

Note that the standard tap-and-hold interaction can still be supported in the presence of *Hold-and-Shake*. The system just recasts tap-and-hold as a touch that occurs while the device is not sensing significant motion.

MOTION-ENHANCED TOUCH TECHNIQUES

The techniques detailed in the sections above focus on touch-enhanced motion gestures. We now turn our attention to the complementary perspective of techniques that sense motion consequent to touching a device's screen. We implement *Soft-vs-Hard-Tap* and *Swipe-vs-Hard-Drag* to demonstrate this approach. We conclude this section with some further possibilities for augmenting touch with gyroscope + accelerometer motion sensing.

Soft-vs-Hard-Tap

Touch interfaces for small-screen devices often tradeoff breadth for depth: fewer options are presented on any one screen, so that more taps are required to navigate to a particular option. To address this, we implement *Hard-vs-Soft-Tap* in a mock-up of the WP7 home screen "tiles" and a Calendar application with *daily agenda* and *current appointment* views. This exhibits the depth-first nature typical of navigational structures on mobile phones. The home screen offers a context where making the interactions less tedious (and more fun) seems particularly appropriate.

By introducing a distinction between soft-taps and hard-taps, and the design rule that *two soft taps equals one hard tap,* our technique allows users to selectively jump ahead: softly tapping an item activates it, but tapping an item more forcefully "drills into" it to allow direct navigation to a secondary target. For example, in our prototype, a soft-tap on the calendar tile in the device's home screen navigates to the *day view* with all appointments for the day, but a hard tap navigates directly to the current appointment.

This technique also enlivens interaction with the home screen, while providing feedback for hard vs. soft taps, by animating the tile that the user taps in proportion to the force exerted. Lightly tapping an icon subtly expands the tile to show that it has been activated, but striking it more forcefully causes it to animate with more of a "splat."

We distinguish hard vs. soft taps by looking at the difference between the accelerometer peaks in the first 200ms of the touch. If the separation is larger than 0.3g, it is a hard tap. This heuristic could be improved by considering the force of the touch in relation to ongoing background movements, such as walking [21].

Swipe-vs-Hard-Drag

Many views on mobile devices can be scrolled or panned, but at the same time, the user may want to rearrange the items in the view by standard drag-and-drop actions. Examples of such views include home screen icons, photos in an album, or web bookmarks. The problem is that making a swipe motion to scroll conflicts with drag-and-drop, so the system typically must introduce a special "edit" mode to support rearranging items.

Our technique offers a new way to finesse this problem by using motion sensing to distinguish gentle swipes from hard drags. In our prototype, gentle swipes scroll through a list of photos. Hard drags "grab" the photo that the user lands on, to drag it to a new position. The user thus has direct access to both scrolling and dragging. This technique is similar to *Soft-vs-Hard-Tap*, except that the finger remains in contact with the display and specifies the dragging path.

Further Possibilities: Accelerometers, Gyros, & Touch

We have fewer example techniques for *motion-enhanced touch*, but we believe this perspective is equally important. Our devices only include integrated accelerometers, which limits their sensitivity to some types of motions [23].

Users employ various hand grips on mobiles, such as interacting with a thumb, versus the index finger of the opposite hand. If we can sense such nuances, they may form valuable contextual cues that can be used to fine-tune the handling of the touch input signal itself. For example, the software might adjust interaction thresholds to make scrolling a web page with a thumb more forgiving. Or, a soft-keyboard might be able to optimize its input model if it knows whether a given tap is a thumb, or an index finger.

To explore such possibilities, we attached an external gyroscope to a Zune HD and produced sensor traces. As shown below (*Fig. 5*), performing vertical swipes on the screen with a *Thumb,* versus a *Finger,* results in distinct motion-sensor signals. We found the gyro signal (top trace) more sensitive to these types of subtle motions than the accelerometer. Furthermore the gyro senses motion in the reference frame of the device, as opposed to the world coordinate system of the accelerometer, thus making it easier to recognize the device-centric motions of interest.

This suggests that such contextual inferences could be made with appropriate recognition techniques, and a sufficient corpus of training data. We implemented a simple user-specific recognizer as a proof of concept, but more work must be done to generalize and validate this. For example, the gyroscope and accelerometer have complementary properties that can be combined to help enhance recognition (e.g. by unifying the sensors into a 6DOF inertial reference frame via the *direct cosine matrix* [27] or other algorithms).

We also tried recognizing finger taps on the inert rear casing of the device. Our video illustrates the recognizer responding to the user's finger tapping the case at the top-left corner, and the top-right corner. Tapping each corner produces a distinct motion which we recognize as a different type of tap (e.g. for forward/back gestures in a web browser). Thus, the gyro and accelerometer signals can be used to localize "touch" interactions to some degree, without any true touch sensing being used at all [15,16].

Our recognizer uses a typical training-data approach. We manually register several templates for the desired motion. Template matching is performed on a candidate temporal data sequence. If the sum of Euclidean distances between the input values and the template is within an error threshold, the recognizer reports a match.

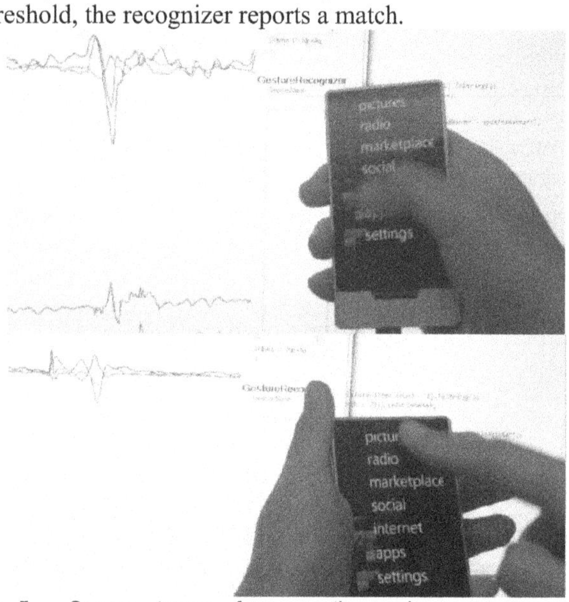

Fig. 5. Sensor traces from a three-axis gyroscope and accelerometer for one-handed scrolling with the thumb (top) versus two-handed scrolling with the index finger (bottom). See also video.

While we believe these are intriguing possibilities, they nonetheless remain to be adequately explored and validated by future work. For example, the motion signals coincident with touch interactions also might form valuable sources of contextual data for probabilistic interaction frameworks, such as that proposed by Schwarz et al. [33].

INFORMAL EVALUATION & REACTIONS FROM USERS

In addition to our early pilot studies which helped to iteratively refine the initial implementation of our techniques, we conducted an informal evaluation to garner feedback on our techniques from test users. The goal of the evaluation was to assess each technique's value proposition, as well as its strengths and weaknesses, with test users. We also sought ideas for possible enhancements by observing users' experiences, as well as their comments.

Participants

We recruited 10 Microsoft volunteers (3 female, 7 male, ages 22-55, none affiliated with our team). Each received $10 for participation. Nine participants were touch screen phone users (5 iPhone, 3 Windows Mobile, 1 Android), and one participant was a generic flip style mobile phone user.

Procedure

The experimenter demonstrated each of the six primary touch+motion gestures discussed above. Participants then tried each feature, and spent about 10 minutes using each one. For the Tilt-to-Zoom gesture, users tried both the WP7 prototype (which offered the *perspective box* feedback) and the Zune HD prototype (which offered 60Hz sampling rate for more responsive tilt control, but no perspective box).

After trying each technique, users filled out 7-point Likert scale questions, and we asked users what the best and worst thing was about each technique. After trying all six techniques, users rank-ordered them for overall preference.

Results

Overall, the Likert questions revealed positive to strongly positive responses to memory load, learning curve, and ease of control. Many users commented that the features were simple, fluent, seamless, or intuitive. The general area that indicated the most concern by users was ease of discovery, which tended towards neutral to mildly positive responses on the Likert scale questions. Although our current focus is not on self-revelation mechanisms for motion gestures [25], this does suggest we should improve discoverability. In general, this is a little explored topic in motion sensing.

Learning Touch+Motion Gestures

The physical metaphors that many of our techniques exploit appeared to help users learn the techniques, while also making the interaction memorable. For example, one user commented that *Pivot-to-lock* "mimics a natural technique to prevent things from moving." Another user described *Hold-and-shake* as a "salt and pepper" metaphor. *Hard-tap* and *Hard-drag* correspond to real-world experiences with striking objects: as one user stated, "the splat animation is a natural mapping between gesture and the resulting action."

Although all users found the gestures easy to learn, we observed that in the early going, in general there are four steps that most users progress through:

(1) Learn the device reacts to motion. One user stated "I'm not accustomed to shaking the phone," while another's initial reaction was "tilting may not be natural." However, most users had seen or used motion-sensing before.

(2) Holding the screen starts listening to motion. Because of the limited screen real estate, users had a tendency not to touch the screen unless there was a clear purpose. (One user stated: "I don't keep my finger on the screen if there isn't a target," while another said that "at first, holding a finger against the screen was unintuitive"). However, most users had no problem holding the screen while moving.

(3) Users must generate motion in synchrony with touching the screen. With Tilt-to-zoom, some users made anticipatory tilting motions before their finger actually touched down on the screen, which made the technique seem less responsive.

(4) The user must learn how tilt is mapped to the interface control. This was easy for direct angular mappings (e.g. *Pivot-to-Lock, Tip-to-Select*) but took some getting used to for the rate-based *Tilt-to-Zoom*. Our rate-based zooming function appeared to be a bit over-sensitive, leading to overshoot, and hence should be further refined [11]. A couple of users suggested the alternative of imparting discrete zooming steps by making "whip" tilting motions. Nonetheless, despite these limitations, *Tilt-to-zoom* (and *Pivot-to-lock*) resonated very strongly with most test-users.

Semantics Matter

It is important to map touch+motion gestures to suitable interaction semantics. There were several users who did not like *Hard-tap*, but reacted positively to *Hard-drag*, which is based on a very similar motion. These users commented that if they make a mistake with *Hard-tap*, they first have to realize this, and then figure out how to go back. On the other hand, if the user intends to do *Hard-drag* but scrolls a bit by mistake instead, the cost of this error is essentially zero, and the user can just try hard-dragging the item again.

We observed a similar issue with *Pivot-to-lock*. All users liked being able to lock the screen orientation, but several users wanted the lock to be persistent (for example, one who really liked *Pivot-to-lock* also stated that "auto unlock is a horrible feature"). Several users wanted the device to remain at a fixed screen orientation if they showed the screen to someone else, or passed the device to that person.

Lightweight Interactions

Users appreciated that they could use movements of the device for *Pivot-to-lock* and *Tilt-to-zoom*, or intensity of the movement for *Hard-tap* and *Hard-drag*, to address common problems that they experience in mobile device interaction. Compared to tedious sequences of time-outs or touch gestures, users liked how they could combine wrist, finger, and device motion to articulate lightweight interactions with less "friction" in the user interface. For example, users commented that the techniques were "intuitive and easy to transition to different modes," "easy and magical," or that "the icons are alive!"

Physical Effort and Ergonomics

On the other hand, for motion based interaction to be useful, the interactions must carefully consider appropriate grips as well as the wrist's range-of-motion [29]. For example, although we designed *Pivot-to-lock* with the idea that users would "pinch" the device between their fingers, and spin the device (somewhat like a propeller), many users performed *Pivot-to-lock* by adopting a rigid grip on the device while using ulnar/radial deviation of the wrist to turn the device on its side. This is somewhat uncomfortable as the wrist has limited mobility along this axis. However, in a more naturalistic usage context, where the user actually lies down in a bed while rigidly gripping the device, no wrist motion would be required. Nonetheless, this leads us to consider teaching users the appropriate grip on the device as part of the self-revelation strategy for our gestures.

Likewise, the simplistic recognition heuristics that we currently use for some of our gestures, such as *Hard-tap* and *Hard-drag* ("Hard tapping is too hard on my fingers"), or *Hold-and-shake* ("I had to shake vigorously"), currently requires the user to make more forceful or effortful motions than perhaps is necessary.

Overall Preference for the Techniques

Users' preference rankings for the techniques reflected the everyday problems that they experience using their mobile phones. The need to support effective one-handed zooming, as well as to avoid undesired automatic screen rotation, strongly resonated with many of the users. Five of the ten users explicitly mentioned "one-handed" interaction as the best thing about *Tilt-to-zoom*. Another user loved the fact that the center of expansion is controllable, unlike pinching. Users of the iPhone in particular felt that having a simple gesture to lock the screen orientation was valuable. Several users particularly appreciated shortcuts for common interactions ("avoiding unnecessary taps is always nice"). *Hold-and-shake* was the only technique that nobody chose as their favorite technique (or runner up), largely because shaking took too much effort, and took too much time. However, because our study only includes 10 subjects, keep in mind that the difference between the rankings is not significant (Kruskal-Wallis test, $\chi^2_{(5)}=16.74$, $p>0.05$).

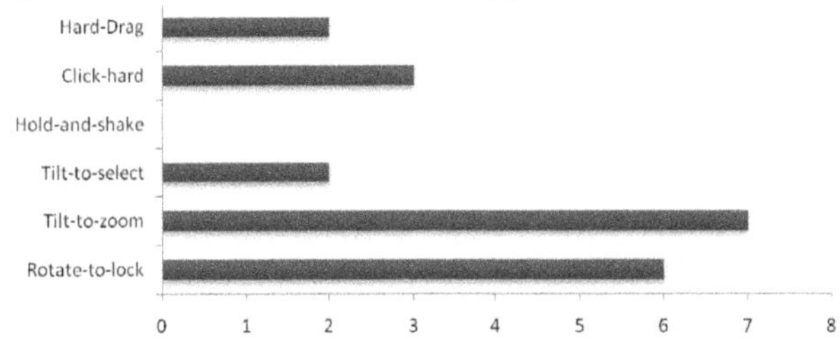

Fig. 6. Number of participants who chose each technique as their favorite technique, or as the runner-up, in their rank orderings.

CONCLUSION AND FUTURE WORK

Our interactions are designed to take unique advantage of the properties of handheld mobile devices, while the user is interacting with the device at hand. However, because of this, it is unclear how touch+motion techniques would translate to other form-factors, such as slate devices, or to other usage contexts, such as employing a device while it rests flat on a desk. For example, the motions for *Tilt-to-zoom*, *Pivot-to-lock*, and *Tip-to-select* cannot be applied when the device is resting flat on a surface such as a desk.

In our current prototype, we deliberately picked interactions that work well with an accelerometer. However, integrating accelerometers with gyros, proximity sensors, or vibratory and shear/torque sensors could greatly enrich the vocabulary of motion at our disposal. For example, combining accelerometers and gyros into an inertial reference frame enables each sensor to make up for shortcomings of the other, which could help to improve our existing techniques, or open up possibilities for others.

We have shown how the multimodal combination of *touch-enhanced motion* enables new types of motion gestures such as holding the device and tilting it to zoom; pivoting the device to a new orientation to lock the screen rotation; framing a portion of the screen with two thumbs and then tilt the device to select the indicated region; or holding an icon on the screen and shaking the device to apply a command to that specific icon.

We have also explored *motion-enhanced touch* techniques that tease out further nuances of touch when the user strikes the screen. Sensors such as accelerometers and gyros can pick up the subtle ripples in the motion stream that spread out from the point of impact. We have implemented hard-tapping and hard-dragging as examples of this perspective, while also presenting sensor traces that suggest further contextual sensing techniques may be possible.

Collectively, all of these techniques help to reveal the hidden dimension of touch. Direct interaction is about much more than just the touch modality itself. This work provides one example of how touch interactions can be extended and enriched by considering the interplay of touch with other modalities, including touch + motion sensing.

ACKNOWLEDGEMENTS

We thank Andy Wilson, Hrvoje Benko, Daniel Wigdor, and Michel Pahud as well as our test users and the reviewers.

REFERENCES

1. Bartlett, J.F., Rock 'n' Scroll Is Here to Stay. IEEE Computer Graphics and Applications, 2000(May/June 2000): p. 40-45.
2. Boring, S., Baur, D., Butz, A., Gustafson, S., Baudisch, P. Touch Projector: Mobile Interaction Through Video. *CHI'10*.
3. Buxton, W., Lexical and Pragmatic Considerations of Input Structure. Computer Graphics, 1983. **17**(1): p. 31-37.
4. Buxton, W. Chunking and Phrasing and the Design of Human-Computer Dialogues. *IFIP Information Processing `86*. Amsterdam: North Holland Publishers.
5. Buxton, W. Three-state model of graphical input. *Human-computer interaction - INTERACT'90*. Amsterdam: Elsevier Science Publishers B. V. (North-Holland).
6. Card, S., Mackinlay, J., Robertson, G. The Design Space of Input Devices. *CHI'90*.
7. Chen, N., et al. Navigation Techniques for Dual-Display E-Book Readers. *CHI'08*.
8. Cho, Murray-Smith, & Kim. Multi-Context Photo Browsing on Mobile Devices Based on Tilt Dynamics. *Mobile HCI'07*.
9. Chun Yat Li, F., Dearman, D., Truong, K. Virtual Shelves: Interactions with Orientation-Aware Devices. *UIST'09*.
10. Cohen, P.R., Dalrymple, M., Moran, D.B., Pereira, F.C., Sullivan, J.W. Synergistic use of direct manipulation and natural language. *CHI'89*.
11. Eslambolchilar, P., Murray-Smith, R. Tilt-Based Automatic Zooming and Scaling in Mobile Devices. *Mobile HCI'04*.
12. Essl, G., Rohs, M., Kratz, S. Use the Force (or something) - Pressure and Pressure-Like Input for Mobile Music Performance. *NIME 2010 Conf. on New Interfaces for Musical Expression*.
13. Fitzmaurice, G., Buxton, W. The Chameleon: spatially aware palmtop computers. *CHI'94*.
14. Harrison, B.L., Fishkin, K.P., Gujar, A., Mochon, C., Want, R. Squeeze me, hold me, tilt me! An exploration of manipulative user interfaces. *CHI'98*.
15. Harrison, C., Hudson, S. Scratch Input: Creating Large, Inexpensive, Unpowered and Mobile Finger Input Surfaces. *UIST'08*.
16. Harrison, C., Tan, C., Morris, D. Skinput: Appropriating the Body as an Input Surface. *CHI'10*.
17. Hassan, N., Rahman, M., Irani, P., Graham, P. Chucking: A One-Handed Document Sharing Technique. *INTERACT'09*.
18. Herot, C., Weinzapfel, G., One-Point Touch Input of Vector Information from Computer Displays. Computer Graphics, 1978. **12**(3): p. 210-216.
19. Hinckley, K., Pierce, J., Sinclair, M., Horvitz, E. Sensing techniques for mobile interaction. *UIST 2000*.
20. Hinckley, K., et al. Manual Deskterity: An Exploration of Simultaneous Pen + Touch Direct Input. *CHI 2010 Ext. Abstracts*.
21. Hudson, S., Harrison, C., Harrison, B., LaMarca, A. Whack Gestures: Inexact and Inattentive Interaction with Mobile Devices. *TEI 2010 Conf. Tangible & Embedded Interaction*.
22. Iwasaki, K., Miyaki, T., Rekimoto, J. Expressive Typing: A New Way to Sense Typing Pressure and Its Applications. *CHI'09*.
23. Joshi, N., Kang, S.B., Zitnik, C.L., Szeliski, R. Image Deblurring using Inertial Measurement Sensors. *Proc. SIGGRAPH 2010*.
24. Kim, K.-E., et al. Hand Grip Pattern Recognition for Mobile User Interfaces. *Proceedings of AAAI/IAAI-2006: Innovative Applications of Artificial Intelligence*. 2006.
25. Kratz, S., Ballagas, R. Unravelling Seams: Improving Mobile Gesture Recognition with Visual Feedback Techniques. *CHI'09*.
26. Liao, C., Liu, Q., Liew, B., Wilcox, L. PACER: Fine-Grained Interactive Paper via Camera-Touch Hybrid Gestures on a Cell Phone. *CHI'10*.
27. Mahoney, R., Nonlinear Complementary Filters on the Special Orthogonal Group. IEEE Trans. on Automatic Control, 2008. **53**(5): p. 1203-18.
28. Olsen, D.R., Clement, J., Pace, A. Spilling: Expanding Hand-held Interaction to Touch Table Displays. *IEEE TableTop '07*.
29. Rahman, M., Gustafson, S., Irani, P., Subramanian, S. Tilt Techniques: Investigating the Dexterity of Wrist-Based Input. *CHI'09*.
30. Roudaut, A., Baglioni, M., Lecolinet, E. TimeTilt: Using Sensor-Based Gestures to Travel through Multiple Applications on a Mobile Device. *Interact '09*.
31. Schmidt, A., et al. Advanced interaction in context. *Handheld and Ubiquitous Computing (HUC'99)*.
32. Schmidt, D., Chehimi, F., Rukzio, E., Gellersen, H. PhoneTouch: A Technique for Direct Phone Interaction on Surfaces. *UIST'10*.
33. Schwarz, J., Hudson, S., Mankoff, J., Wilson, A.D. A framework for robust and flexible handling of inputs with uncertainty. *UIST'10*.
34. Schwesig, C., Poupyrev, I., Mori, E. Gummi: A Bendable Computer. *CHI'04*.
35. Sellen, A., Kurtenbach, G., Buxton, W., The prevention of mode errors through sensory feedback. Human Computer Interaction, 1992. **7**(2): p. 141-164.
36. Taylor, B., Bove Jr., V. Graspables: Grasp-Recognition as a User Interface. *CHI'09*.
37. Wigdor, D., Balakrishnan, R. TiltText: Using tilt for text input to mobile phones. *UIST'03*.

Data Miming: Inferring Spatial Object Descriptions from Human Gesture

Christian Holz[1,2] and Andrew D. Wilson[2]

[1]Hasso Plattner Institute
Potsdam, Germany
christian.holz@hpi.uni-potsdam.de

[2]Microsoft Research
Redmond, WA 98052 USA
awilson@microsoft.com

ABSTRACT

Speakers often use hand gestures when talking about or describing physical objects. Such gesture is particularly useful when the speaker is conveying distinctions of shape that are difficult to describe verbally. We present *data miming*—an approach to making sense of gestures as they are used to describe concrete physical objects. We first observe participants as they use gestures to describe real-world objects to another person. From these observations, we derive the data miming approach, which is based on a voxel representation of the space traced by the speaker's hands over the duration of the gesture. In a final proof-of-concept study, we demonstrate a prototype implementation of matching the input voxel representation to select among a database of known physical objects.

Author Keywords

Gestures, shape descriptions, 3D modeling, depth camera, object retrieval.

ACM Classification Keywords

H5.2 [Information interfaces and presentation]: User Interfaces. Input devices & strategies.

General Terms

Design, Experimentation, Human Factors.

INTRODUCTION

In conversation we sometimes resort to using hand gestures to assist in describing a shape, particularly when it would be cumbersome to describe with words alone. For example, the roofline of a new car might be conveyed by a swoop of the outstretched hand, or a particular chair style might be indicated to a shopkeeper by a series of gestures that describe the arrangement of surfaces unique to that chair. In such cases, the speaker often appears to trace the precise 3D shape of the described object. Meanwhile, the listener appears to effortlessly integrate the speaker's gestures over time to recreate the 3D shape. This exchange strikes us as a remarkably efficient and useful means of communicating the mental imagery of the speaker.

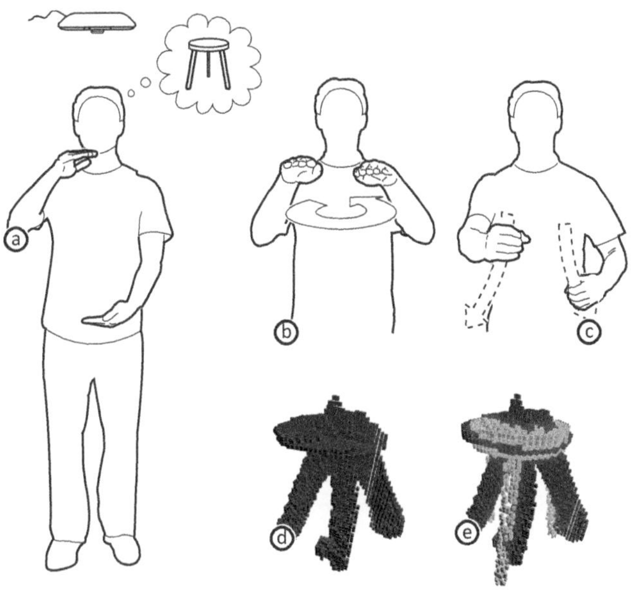

Figure 1: Data miming walkthrough. The user performs gestures in 3-space, as they might during conversations with another person, to query the database for a specific object that they have in mind (here a 3-legged stool). Users thereby visualize their mental image of the object not only by indicating the dimensions of the object (a), but more importantly the specific attributes, such as (b) the seat and (c) the legs of the chair. Our prototype system tracks the user's gestures with an overhead camera (a) and derives an internal representation of the user's intended image (d). (e) The query to the database returns the most closely matching object (green).

In this paper, we consider the use of gestures to describe physical objects. We present *data miming* as an approach to enable users to spatially describe existing 3D objects to a computer just as they would to another person.

We make two contributions in this paper. First is an *observation* of how people use gestures in a *natural way* to describe physical objects (i.e., without telling them how to use a certain gesture to specify a certain part of an object). From these observations, we derive the *data miming* approach to making sense of gestures as they are used to describe physical objects (i.e., which object was described). Our second contribution is a prototype system, which allows for walk-up use with a single overhead depth camera to sense the user's gestures. Our system follows a query-by-demonstration approach and retrieves the model in a database that most closely matches the user's descriptions.

We envision a number of practical applications for data miming. For example, shoppers in a furniture warehouse could approach a kiosk to perform gestures describing an object that they are looking for. The system would look up the closest matches in a database and present the results alongside the locations to the user. In an immersive video game (e.g., Kinect [31]), a player could summon objects by describing them spatially. The game might tailor the object to the precise dimensions indicated by the player's gestures.

DATA MIMING

In such scenarios, data miming *observes* and *makes sense* of human gesture, exploits the human sense of spatial references, and uses the richness of hand shape and motion when describing objects to *infer* the described objects (Figure 1). Similar to using gestures when talking to a human observer, data miming observes passively, thereby providing no feedback during the gesture (a-c). The user, therefore, works solely from a mental image of the described object and their gestures are used to *implicitly* create a virtual representation of the mental image (d).

The virtual representation can be used to *classify* the described object (e.g., "stool"), but also to extract the object's *specifics* in order to distinguish it from other instances in that class. For example, a user may describe *a* chair (where no further detail is required), but may also describe a *particular and existing* chair that has three legs, slanted from the center, and two feet tall (Figure 1). Without those specific details, the reference to that particular chair would be unclear.

Method

We approach this topic as follows. In an initial user study, we observe participants describing real-world objects to another person using gestures. We instruct participants to describe objects just as they would in a conversation. The purpose of this study is to determine *how* participants describe the various objects, i.e., what gestures they use, and on which parts of objects they concentrate. We analyze the patterns that recur when participants specify object dimensions and boundaries, define object faces and the shape of single parts. In addition, we observe how participants distinguish between deliberately describing meaningful parts of an object and transitioning between such parts.

From our observations, we derive the *data miming* approach, which describes how to create a virtual representation of the user's mental image from the performed gestures. We implement a prototype system that observes the user with a single depth-sensing camera and then matches the virtual representation against objects in a database.

We then run a proof-of-concept study on our prototype system to determine if the features extracted from users' actions suffice to classify and match a described object. We find that our system correctly identifies described objects in 60% of all cases from a set of 10 potential matches.

RELATED WORK

Data miming is related to sculpting, hand tracking through computer vision, three-dimensional shape querying, spatial memory, gesture input, and linguistic models of gesture.

Sculpting

Similar to our *data miming* approach, many sculpting systems make use of the expressiveness of human gesture. While some systems allow the user to shape and transform 3D objects using their hands (e.g., Gesture-based 3D modeling [19], *SketchMaker* [22], *Twister* [17], *Surface Drawing* [24]), others equip the user's hands with tools (e.g., *Volume sculpting* [28], heat gun and sandpaper in *Sculpting* [8]). Other systems derive 3D models from the user's sketches in the air using a stylus (e.g., *3-Draw* [23], *Spatial Sketch* [29], *HoloSketch* [5]). Users typically create and refine the 3D model iteratively based on the visual feedback provided by the sculpting application, which allows them to create high-quality 3D models. For example, different hand postures result in different brush widths in *Surface Drawing* [24] and users create high-quality virtual models with a physical brush in *CavePainting* [14].

While sculpting applications enable users to *create* new high-quality models, our *data miming* approach focuses on enabling users to specify *existing* objects. Sculpting applications are inherently *interactive*, which causes a feedback loop on the user's end; to create the intended model, a user verifies if their actions had the intended outcomes (i.e., all input needs to be rendered). The user thus directly works on the visual representation of the model. *Data miming*, in contrast, passively *observes* how the user *acts* and does not provide any feedback; the user thus works solely from their conceptual model of the object.

Spatial Memory

As it provides no feedback, *data miming* assumes that users maintain a frame of reference when performing gestures. Hinckley et al. found that the user's body becomes the spatial reference [12] in this situation; users do not rely on visual feedback when using both hands together [11]. Humans further have the ability to know where both hands are relative in space [12, 23] and can maintain a spatial anchor outside their body over a brief amount of time [3]. Baddeley and Hitch attributed this short-term visual memory for maintaining spatial relationships to the visuospatial sketchpad, a part of the working memory [1]. Gustafson et al. exploit this, such that users set a reference frame for interaction using their left hand, and draw or pick locations with their right hand without visual feedback [10].

Natural Gesture

Linguists have studied how speakers use gesture in conversation. MacNeill [18] places a series of gesture types (originally described by Kendon [15]) along a continuum according to the degree to which gesture *complements* speech. Kendon's *gesticulation* category includes those gestures that complement speech the most. MacNeill further categorizes gesticulation to include the ubiquitous *beat* gestures, which are used for emphasis, *deictic* gestures for indicating objects (pointing), *metaphoric* gestures to convey abstract meaning, and *iconic* gestures. Iconic gestures depict a concrete object or event, bear a close formal relationship to the content of the speech, and are used when trying to describe the shape or form of an object. Moving along Kendon's continuum, *emblems* include signs that carry meaning only by convention, such as the "OK" sign. *Pantomime* gestures are similar to iconic gestures in that they depict objects or actions, but do not require speech (and are distinct from gestures used in theatrical miming). Finally, sign languages stand in place of spoken languages and therefore complement speech the least.

Data miming performs matching against stored 3D models of objects. Because these models are not based on convention but rather the actual shape of real physical objects, we argue that data miming gestures are iconic or pantomime gestures, not emblems. While in the case of specifying the class by speech (e.g., "chair"), gesture and speech are clearly complementary; the dependence of one on the other does not have the complexity typical of natural iconic gestures. The gestures modeled in the present work are therefore probably best called 'pantomime' gestures.

Gesture-based systems

Many gesture-based input systems allow users to control applications. While such gestures ideally resemble corresponding real-world gestures (e.g., pushing a set of floating objects aside in *g-speak* [20], pointing in the *Perceptive Workbench* [26]), other operations do not afford a "natural" gesture and need to be defined (e.g., an input vocabulary for controlling presentations in *Charade* [2]). *Gesture Pendant* recognizes the user's hand pose and movement for the continuous control of devices [25].

Hand pose and position recognition

Many of the previously mentioned systems use gloves and motion capture devices to determine the stylus' or hand's location and pose in space. While this approach of tracking input is reliable, it requires the user to wear a device.

Alternatively, hand poses and gestures have been sensed with body-attached cameras (e.g., [10], [25]), side-view image and cast shadows (*Perceptive Workbench* [26]), and stereo images (e.g., [16]). Pavlovic et al.'s survey provides further information on modeling hands and interpretation of hand gestures [21].

Related work has often used props to distinguish between meaningful parts of gesture input from random hand motions, such as pressing a button (e.g., [14],[17],[29], aligning the thumb [24]) or pointing at a specific region to perform gestures (e.g., pointing at the screen in *Charade* [2]).

Query-by-3D model

While our prototype does not focus on the speed of matching 3D models, related work has addressed efficient 3D queries to object databases through efficient matching algorithms [7]. *Modeling-by-example* allows partial matching of 3D objects based on single parts [6]. (Tangelder and Veltkamp present a thorough review [27].)

EXPERIMENT: HOW DO USERS DESCRIBE OBJECTS?

When humans describe objects by gesture, they have a number of means to express geometry. The purpose of this user study was to find recurring patterns in those gestural descriptions. We also examined how participants distinguished between the aforementioned meaningful and random parts of gestures.

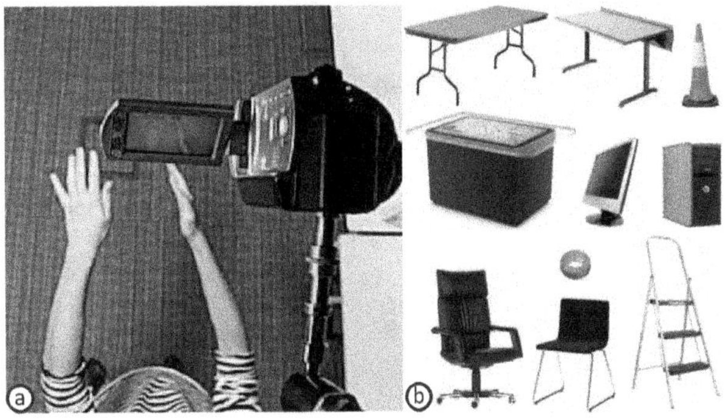

Figure 2: (a) Study setup. Participants described objects using gestures to the experimenter, recorded by an overhead camera for later analysis. (b) Participants described 10 objects.

Task and Procedure

Figure 2a shows a participant during the study, describing one of the ten objects (b). All objects were located behind the participant. For each object, the participant took a close look at the object, then turned away from the object, and described the object through gestures to the experimenter. Participants were only instructed to describe objects using gestures—not postures (e.g., assuming the posture in an office chair to augment their descriptions), but received no instructions as to which gestures to use. Participants did not use speech during the study, received no feedback, and could not see what the camera recorded. Participants finished a description of an object by lowering their arms.

As shown in Figure 2b, the objects included primitive shapes (e.g., PC = box shape, cone, tape), objects of medium complexity (table), as well as more elaborate objects (office chair, ladder). Our intention was to find the degree to which participants' descriptions agree, and the features they include when describing more complex objects.

All participants were recorded with an overhead video camera for later investigation. Overall, participants described all objects in less than six minutes. Afterwards, they filled out a questionnaire on prior experience with 3D modeling applications to determine if the tools in such applications inspired and influenced their performances.

Apparatus and Participants

The overhead video camera was mounted to the ceiling 8ft from the ground. This setup allowed the camera to capture a top-down volume of 5ft (W) × 3ft (H) × 5ft (D). We recruited 12 participants (4 female) from our institution. All participants were between 21 and 46 years old (*M*=29.5, *SD*=6.2).

Results and Observations

All participants not only maintained relative proportions of an object's parts, but also maintained relative scale across objects. For example, participants used a large fraction of their arm's length to describe the two tables, while describing the chairs smaller as appropriate. It was interesting to see participants' notion of space in each of the three dimensions (Figure 3); particularly for larger objects, participants seemed to scale objects non-uniformly to adapt sizes relative to the area covered by arm's length in each direction. This implied that, by nature of the human body, objects could always be wider than tall, and taller than deep.

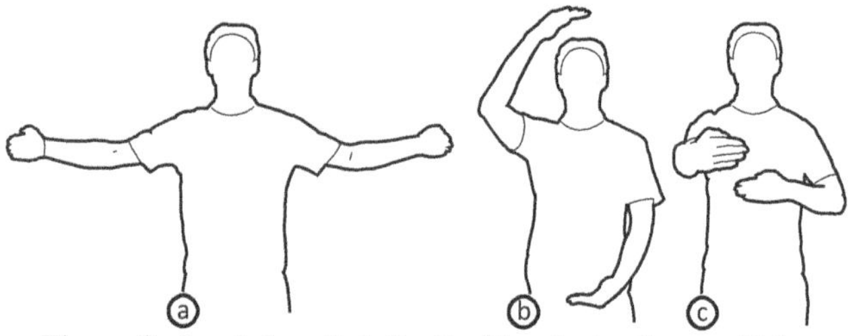

Figure 3: Arm's length is the limiting factor for specifying dimensions. When necessary, participants seemed to describe objects in non-uniform scale according to the available span for each dimension. Objects can thereby be (a) wider than (b) tall, and taller than (c) deep.

Participants mostly used a top-down approach to describe objects; after larger, more apparent surfaces they described the smaller parts. It was apparent that all participants distinguished between surfaces (e.g., flat faces of PC, monitor, Microsoft Surface, table, but also curved surfaces, such as frame of the ladder, seat and backrest of the chairs) and smaller components, such as struts and connections. We thus analyze them separately.

Surfaces and Faces of the Object

Symmetry was most apparent during participants' descriptions; all twelve used both hands in a parallel pose, facing one another to define symmetric elements of an object (e.g., PC, monitor, Microsoft Surface). Those symmetric parts did not necessarily represent the dimensions of the entire object, but would specify certain parts. Participants also used simultaneous and symmetric hand movement to describe smaller parts such as legs of chair, or frame of the ladder.

Dimensions: When the shape of objects resembled that of a box, all participants defined the dimensions of parts of objects (e.g., PC, Microsoft Surface, and monitor). Seven participants simultaneously moved both hands in a flat pose back and forth along the bounding dimensions of the object repeatedly. Three others held both hands flat in place to define those boundaries. Two participants drew wireframes of objects in box shape.

Large surfaces: All but two participants used their hands to "trace" surfaces, i.e. they moved their flat hands along surfaces, as if wiping them with their hands (e.g., tables, top of Microsoft Surface, seats of the chairs). Six of them even wiped the area within boundaries to "fill" it (Figure 4a).

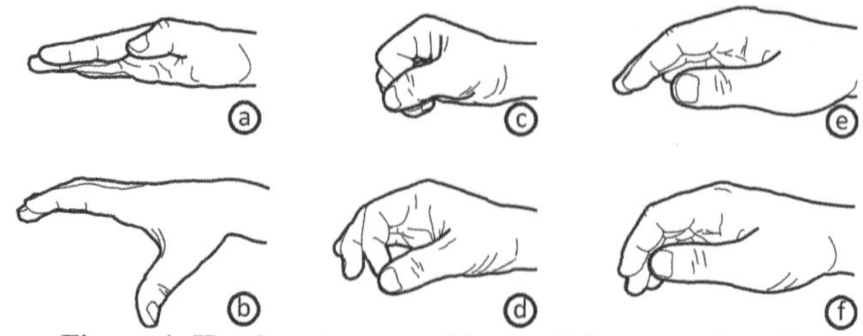

Figure 4: Hand postures used by participants to describe (a) flat and (b) curved surfaces, (c&d) struts and legs. (e&f) Hands were relaxed when not tracing a surface.

Medium surfaces: Four participants specified the outline of surfaces with their flat hands and, again, wiped the enclosed area to "fill" it (e.g., monitor, backrest of the office chair). The other eight participants abstracted those medium surfaces to a mere stroke of their flat hand, which they performed repeatedly. This was most noticeable for the two chairs. Four participants sometimes described a surface only by waving their hand repeatedly, roughly in the place of a surface (e.g., monitor, seats).

Small surfaces: All participants used their hand to "trace" smaller components of objects (e.g., steps of the ladder, outside frame of the ladder).

Curved/non-planar surfaces: All 12 participants adapted the shape of their hand to match the curved surface and "wiped" up and down the surface repeatedly. To describe the cone, for example, all participants formed a closed circle using both thumbs and index fingers and then moved their hands down, thereby driving them apart. Their fingers thereby maintained the original shape (Figure 4b).

Smaller Components

Symmetry: As with object faces, participants moved both hands symmetrically and simultaneously if the object afforded it.

Bars, struts, and legs: 6 participants used a fist and moved it along the bar to represent a straight bar (e.g., legs of the table, tripod, chair, pole of the office chair, Figure 4c). The other 6 pinched their thumb and index fingers and moved them along the bar (Figure 4d).

Interestingly, only 4 participants tried to match the actual size of a bar with their hand and only when describing objects with connected bars of varying diameters (e.g., tripod, table). The shape of their hand symbolized grabbing around bars, and they opened their hand accordingly if the bar was too big to fit inside (e.g., leg of the table).

For bigger struts, 6 participants brought their hands to a close distance, held them parallel or connected fingers and palms of both hands to enclose the space between the hands, and moved both hands to trace the shape of a component (e.g., pole and legs of the chairs, monitor stand).

Level of detail: 3 participants abstracted the complex shape of the office chair's foot base to a single disc. All other participants ignored the base and indicated the stand only.

Questionnaire: While nine of the 12 participants reported prior usage of 3D modeling applications (e.g., AutoCAD, Sketchup and the like), only two participants stated that those tools influenced their descriptions. They reported trying to perform extrusion/push and pull operations by moving their hands, and other times they performed sweeping and revolving.

Discussion and Analysis of Patterns

All participants began describing an object spatially in a top-down fashion immediately after looking at it. While participants received no instructions as to the detail of their description, all participants followed a similar approach. They abstracted the form of the object, often specified large components and faces first, and finally described some of the characteristic, but smaller components. For instance, while all participants indicated the armrests, the pole and foot of the office chair, few described the support of the armrests or the bars connecting the backrest to the seat. Similarly, participants described the ladder by indicating all three steps and then highlighting the outer frame.

Participants often described those parts first that most clearly represented the function of the object (e.g., backrest, seat of the chairs, top of MS Surface, steps of the ladder). They then described the parts that hold the object together.

Participants made use of symmetric appearances whenever possible; they used both hands with mirrored gestures to describe the shape. Likewise, participants used both hands to specify dimensions, either by defining constraining planes or "drawing" the bounding box. The actual dimensions of medium- and small-sized surfaces seemed to be unimportant to participants, as only a few times did a participant constrain the dimensions of such objects.

The majority of participants adapted the shape of their hand to that of the described object or component, stretching (to describe a planar surface, Figure 4a) or curling and bringing together fingers (for a round surface, Figure 4b) as necessary. In contrast, when participants moved their hands to the next part of an object, they would relax their hands and allow them to assume their natural posture (Figure 4e&f).

For smaller components of an object, such as bars and stands, participants had similar conceptual models for their description. They either formed a fist or pinched their thumb and index finger to indicate both round and square bars, along whose shape they then moved the hand. The majority of participants thereby ignored the actual diameter of those bars, using hand motion to indicate the shape of such bars (Figure 4c&d).

Expressiveness of the user's hand: hand postures

While participants mostly varied hand yaw and roll, they typically varied hand pitch only when indicate parallel parts by a vertical pose (Figure 3c). We assume this to be due to the limited range of angles for hand pitch. When the hand is vertical, however, moving the elbow can extend this range. In contrast, hand roll and yaw cover a larger range; elbow movement also supports the range of hand yaw.

We observed that participants focused on using their hands to describe shapes, and not their arms. This coincides with participants' statements.

Delimiters: meaningful vs. random parts of gestures

In addition to stretching the hand to indicate activity as mentioned above, all participants generally deliberately described parts of the object more slowly, while moving their hands faster when transitioning to another object part. For smaller surfaces, participants dwelled in one position for a brief amount of time. For lager surfaces, participants repeatedly described the surface and often more carefully than when moving their hands to another part.

Whenever two components were closely collocated, participants did not dwell between components, but rather treated them as a compound part and changed hand orientation while they were moving their hands (e.g., connected backrest and seat of a chair). Participants often repeatedly indicated this compound component through gestures.

THE DATA MIMING APPROACH

The previous observations allow us to design *data miming* as an approach to translate the observed gestures, as they occur, into implications for a virtual representation that seeks to reproduce the user's mental image. In particular, we argue that we need not rely on predefined gestures that manifest themselves as a particular part of an object upon recognition.

Basic Approach

The analysis of participants' gestures in the previous study showed that they often traced an object's surfaces and structural elements, thereby essentially recreating the object based on their spatial memory. That they often repeatedly traced those identifying parts suggests that the virtual representation of the user's description should also build up over time. Those parts that the user has spent more time describing should be weighted more strongly than parts they have covered only briefly.

Since participants mostly described surfaces of different sizes by waving their hand in the respective area, the user's hand should create a trace in the virtual representation. Since the actual path of the gesture is less important, the position and orientation of the user's hands are essential to translate motions correctly. In conjunction with the time-aware sensing of gestures, such traces become more meaningful to the virtual representation as the user repeatedly or more slowly covers a certain part of the object. The analysis of gestures thereby entirely focuses on the user's hands and neglects position and posture of the user's arms and body.

Meaningful vs. Random Motions

Ideally, our approach recognizes and translates only the meaningful parts of a user's gesture, while ignoring motions that only serve to transition the hands to the next part of the object.

Our first study showed that participants briefly relax their muscles while moving the hands to another part of the object, whereas they typically align or stretch their fingers, or flex their muscles to signal a meaningful hand pose. While it would be desirable to capture this distinction, changes in finger postures and curvature are fairly subtle (Figure 5).

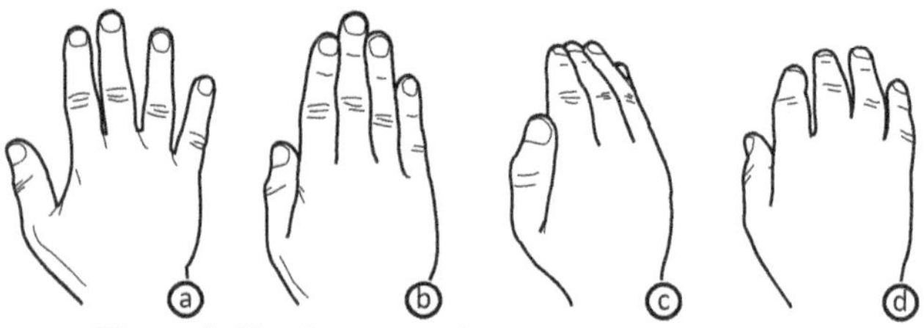

Figure 5: Hand poses and corresponding meanings. (a) Stretched hand, used to indicate a shape (e.g., flat surface), (b) stretched hand, fingers together, which also shows intention to indicate a shape, (c) curved hand shape and fingers together, suggesting that this motion is meaningful, and (d) relaxed pose when transitioning (cf. Figure 4e&f).

Considering the difficulty of sensing muscle relaxation with a camera, *data miming* forgoes the interpretation of finger curvature to derive the meaning of the current gesture. Instead, the user's hands constantly leave a footprint in the virtual representation whose position and orientation corresponds to those of the user's hands in the real world. That is, the orientation and posture of the hand at all times determines the volume of the component added to the virtual representation (i.e., a flat, tilted hand makes a flat, slanted small-sized impact on the virtual representation).

By simply replicating the volumes of the user's hands and representing them in the virtual space, our approach allows for sensing flat and curved hand postures (e.g., flat surfaces, surface of a sphere) and also accounts for smaller elements when users form a fist or pinch their fingers (e.g., legs of a chair). It also allows us to consider both hands separately.

Modeling the Scene

Data miming creates a virtual representation of the user's description in a discretized 3D volume consisting of $l \times m \times n$ voxels. This *voxel space* represents the "memory" of the system. Each voxel is either active or inactive. A scene begins with only inactive voxels and over the course of observing the user's gestures, voxels are activated as appropriate. Voxels also have a certain weight, which is increased as the user repeatedly activates the voxel. This allows us to capture how users trace the parts of the object: slower and more careful tracing indicates a more meaningful part and thus increased weight, while a faster (random) motion indicates a less meaningful part of the description (as in [13]). The set of voxels below a certain weight are thus ignored, leaving only meaningful parts of the gestures.

The 3D-scene approach we use is world-anchored, such that its location and orientation does not adapt to the user's position or orientation. While the center of the scene is always in front of the user (i.e., world anchored), users are able to maintain this spatial anchor [3], as object descriptions take only a few seconds in our case.

Retrieving matching objects from the database

To retrieve the identity of the user-described object, our approach relies on a database of candidate objects in voxel representation. Data miming selects the most closely matching object from the database as follows. For each candidate object, the user-created model is aligned with the database model for comparison and measurement of similarity. As byproduct we obtain the scale and rotation difference from the user's creation.

Account for the user's under-specification

As objects are mostly assembled from characteristic components, humans describe such characteristic parts separately. People also seem to make implicit assumptions about their audience; they do not describe less significant parts, parts that seem implicitly necessary (e.g., connecting parts between surfaces, such as backrest and seat in a chair) or features that do not serve to uniquely identify the object.

We reflect this *fragmentary* modeling on the user's part in the matching process by allowing the user to omit any part of the object, trusting that the user will specify enough detail given some familiarity with the class of objects under consideration and the variability of shape within that class. In the study of discourse, Grice's maxims of co-operation describe the tendency for speakers to lead the listener to a correct understanding. In particular, Grice's Maxim of Quantity holds that the speaker will make their contribution as informative as required, and no more [9].

IMPLEMENTATION OF THE DATA MIMING SYSTEM

We implemented a prototype system based on the *data miming* approach described in the previous section. This prototype works on an end-user system and requires only a single depth-sensing camera that is mounted above the user.

Hardware and Processing

Our prototype system uses a Microsoft Kinect camera which provides depth images at 30Hz and a resolution of 640×480 (Figure 6a). The camera has a diagonal field-of-view of 70°. The prototype processes each camera frame in less than 15ms, thus providing real-time processing of the user's gestures and translation into *voxel* representation.

Our prototype system first transforms every pixel in the input image into world coordinates and then crops coordinates (i.e., pixels) outside a volume of 3ftW × 2ftH × 2.5ftD (Figure 6b). This removes the floor, walls, and potential other objects from the depth image (e.g., the chair and table in Figure 6a). The prototype then identifies the user's arms in the image, distinguishing between contiguous regions with only gradually changing depth values to account for overlapping arms, and extracts the user's hands from those regions (c). The prototype system thereby assumes that the user's arms enter from outside and reach into the volume (as in [26]). Our prototype then finds the most-distant point of the hand, measuring distance as the length of a path *within* the shape of the arm (i.e., not Euclidean distance), to account for bent elbows and wrists. To extract the user's hands, we assume a constant hand length (depending on the distance to the camera), which has proven to work well in our tests. Our prototype also provides an optional calibration for the user's particular hand size.

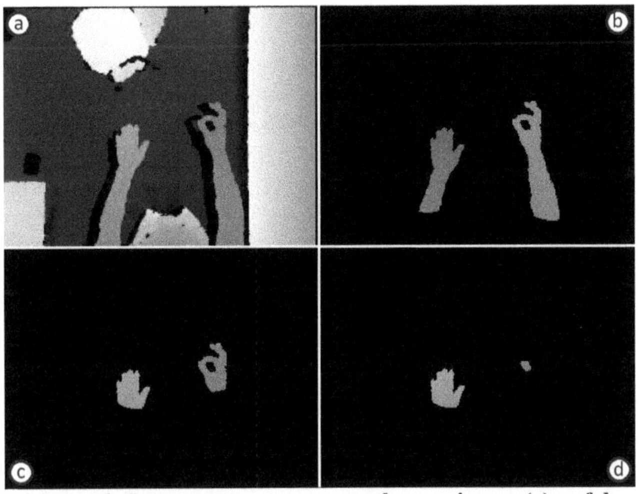

Figure 6: Our prototype processes the raw image (a) as follows: (b) crop to world coordinates (background removal), (c) extract hands, and (d) check for enclosed regions. Detected regions and hands add to the *voxel space* (cf. Figure 1d).

Our prototype calculates the orientation and volume of both hands by tracking the visible area of the hand over time; the system calculates the roll and pitch angle of each hand from the changes in depth values across the visible area. If the visible area is too small, such as for vertical hand roll (only thumb and index finger are visible top-down), our prototype estimates based on prior observations how much of the hand must be occluded, and determines the hand orientation accordingly. Calculating the yaw angle of the hand is straightforward considering the camera is mounted above the user's head. From the observations over time, our system reconstructs the posture of each hand in 3-space, as well as its precise extent in the z-axis (i.e., the axis of line-of-sight of the camera).

Having calculated the orientation of the hands, our prototype then directly translates the position and orientation of the hand into locations of voxels in the *voxel space*. As mentioned before, this comprises activating all voxels in an area that has the same depth, location, and orientation as the user's hand. To account for fast hand motions, the system additionally considers the direction of hand movement and activates voxels between the two positions of the same hand in consecutive camera frames.

Our prototype system detects users' intentions to create finer elements by pinching their fingers and thumb together or moving both hands together. As shown in Figure 6d, as soon as our prototype detects such an enclosed region, it processes this region as opposed to the hand (as in [30]). It samples the depth values for this region from the surrounding area (i.e., the hand). Voxels become active if they share a location with this enclosed region; the prototype dismisses the actual shape of the hand if it encloses a region. This allows users to indicate thinner elements, such as table legs or tripod struts. The same applies if the user connects both thumbs and index fingers, thereby enclosing a bigger area.

Modeling the time-aware scene (*voxel space*)

Our prototype implements the *voxel space* as a three-dimensional array of positive numbers, effectively a 3D histogram. Each voxel has a constant width, height, and depth (10mm in our implementation). We placed the center of the *voxel space* directly in front of the user, roughly at torso level (Figure 6a).

Activating a voxel in the system increases its count in the histogram. This implies that voxels through which the user passes repeatedly or more slowly (i.e., meaningful parts of the object description) will have a higher count than voxels the user passes through when moving the arms to the next, meaningful location. Simple thresholding across all voxels in the space leaves the meaningful and relevant parts.

Matching

We implemented two different techniques to match objects represented in *voxel spaces*. While an interactive system would benefit from real-time matching, our proof-of-concept implementation is not focused on execution speed.

Iterative alignment uses the iterative closest point (ICP) algorithm to register two models [32]. The prototype runs ICP after pre-aligning both models (by translating and rotating to match the principal components). This preparation additionally adapts the scale of both models uniformly.

Brute force tests four levels of quarter-rotation around the z-axis (vertical) and any combination of translations within 16cm×16cm×16cm. We neglected rotations around x and y (horizontal), as users often maintain an object's orientation around those axes, while they tend to "turn" objects towards them when describing (i.e., they rotate about the z axis). The number of z rotations for this algorithm ideally corresponds to the number of vertical faces in the object, often four. This algorithm also pre-aligns both models and adapts their scale uniformly.

While ICP is computationally expensive and takes around 8s to compare two models in our prototype, brute force takes less than 1s, because it operates in the discrete *voxel space* (looking up voxels is fast). However, ICP is more flexible in that it rotates the objects around all three axes to find the best match.

PROOF-OF-CONCEPT EXPERIMENT

The purpose of this study was to verify the relevance of our observations during the first user study and determine if our prototype implementation is capable of recognizing users' descriptions. In addition, we were also curious to see how our prototype system performs during walk-up use.

Task

As in the first study, participants' task was to describe a 3D object through gestures to the experimenter (Figure 7). Each trial started with a projection of the object onto the wall *behind* the experimenter, such that only the participant could see it. After the participant had studied the object, the projection was turned off and the participant described the object based on their mental representation. The experimenter then tried to guess the object and noted it down.

Figure 7: A participant describes an object to the experimenter (here portrayed by an actor). The object had been previously shown to the participant in the projection area, which the experimenter could not see.

In order to encourage participants to provide a sufficiently detailed description of each object, the experimenter never saw the object projected on the wall. This required the participant to perform careful and understandable gestures.

As in the first study, participants were instructed to describe objects using gestures and not complement their gestures with speech. They received no feedback from the system or the experimenter, as this might have impacted how they perform descriptions.

Procedure

Participants described objects from four different categories (Figure 8), each of which contained ten objects. The choice of categories allowed us to separately examine the suitability of our prototype system for simplistic 3D objects, as well as more complex, real-world objects.

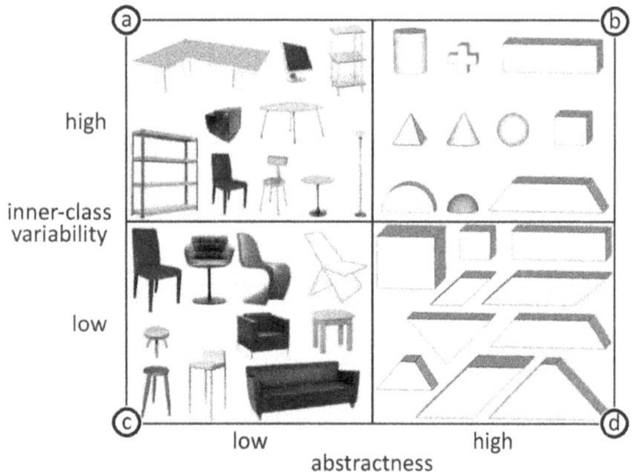

Figure 8: The objects used in the study were split into 2x2 categories: (a) office furniture, (b) primitive solids, (c) chairs, and (d) parallelepipeds.

Before the study, the experimenter presented all categories and objects to the participant, such that the participant could become familiar with the set of objects and learn about the level of detail necessary in the description to uniquely determine the object. (Some objects were in more than one category; depending on the other objects in each category, however, different levels of detail might be necessary to provide an unambiguous description.) The experimenter announced the category at the beginning of each trial and held up a printed sheet illustrating all contained objects to remind the participant.

The study consisted of two sessions: *walk-up* and *instructed*. Participants always began with the walk-up session, in which they described two objects from each category without any instructions. After completing the first session, the experimenter explained to the participant that the system derives faces and legs/struts from the participant's gestures and that single postures did not add to object recognition. The experimenter additionally encouraged the participant to describe each object's elements carefully in the second session. Overall, participants described three objects from each category during the second session.

Participants were instructed to stand on an X on the ground and face the experimenter when gesturing. While this did not preclude participants from gesturing outside the capture volume or occluding their hands, it ensured that the camera would capture most of the gestures.

To avoid priming participants, we made no reference to "miming" during instructions. The absence of feedback for participants during the study ensured that we could test the gestures participants would use when describing objects to a person as opposed to a camera. The use of an experimenter thus precluded participants from falling into an unnaturally detailed and slow demonstration mode.

Categories as well as object selection from the categories were counterbalanced across participants. Overall, each participant completed all 20 trials (4 conditions × (2 objects in the first and 3 objects in the second session)) in less than 20 minutes. Participants filled out a questionnaire on experience with 3D modeling tools after the study.

Apparatus and Participants

Our system captured all interaction with a Microsoft Kinect camera. During the study, the system recorded a video of participants' gestures at 640×480 pixels resolution with depth information at 30Hz. We processed and evaluated all study videos post-hoc with our prototype. The system was running Windows 7 Ultimate, powered by an Intel Core2Duo 2.13 GHz processor and 6GB of RAM. We used an off-the-shelf projector to present objects to participants.

We recruited 15 participants (5 female) from our institution. Participants were between 26 and 47 years old (M=33.6, SD=7.6) and received a small gratuity for their time.

Results

Outliers and limitations

We experienced two types of outliers during the study. The first relates to occlusion and the limits of the capture volume; while we experienced only five such cases in the walk-up session, because participants leaned into the capture volume with their head, we removed ten more trials from the instructed session (of 300 overall). In some of these cases, participants held one hand up, though inactive, and thereby obstructed the camera view onto their other hand, which was gesturing. In other cases, they moved their hands outside the capture volume, or leaned back also gesturing outside. (We removed no more than two trials from one participant, and never more than one per category.)

The second type of outlier relates to variations in human behavior. In some cases, participants performed gestures too fast to be captured by the camera, finishing a trial in less than two seconds. Two participants, for example, held their fingers and arms together to indicate the cross (Figure 8b). While data miming does not account for recognizing shapes from a single posture, we chose not to remove these "outliers" for the analysis of this study.

We take a two-fold approach in measuring the recognition rate of our prototype. We check if the most-closely matching model from the database is the model the participant had to describe ("*top-match*"), as well as if the described object is among the three most-closely matching models ("*closest-three*"). All numbers compare against chance = 10% for the first approach and 34% for the second.

As shown in Figure 9a, our prototype system retrieved the participant's described object in 60% of all trials (i.e., both sessions and all categories). In 87% of all cases, our prototype retrieved the intended object amongst the three most-closely matching models. We now break out these numbers into the different factors.

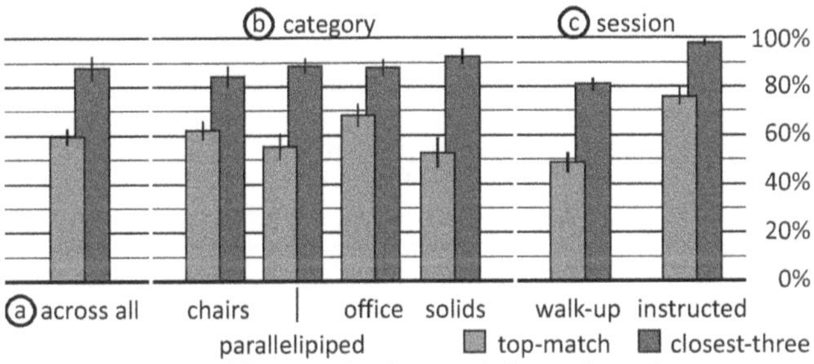

Figure 9: Matching results for participants' performances, showing success rates for *top-match* (green; the matching returned the described object) and *closest-three* (blue; the described object is among the three most-closely matched objects). (a) Accuracy across all trials, (b) broken down to the four categories, and (c) the two sessions. Error bars encode standard error of the mean.

Categories

A two-way ANOVA on recognition rate with participant as the random variable did not find an effect of category on *top-match* performance (p=0.18) or *closest-three* matches (p=0.3). The numbers, however, exhibit interesting patterns (Figure 9b). While the matched object for descriptions of primitive solids was only correct in about half of all cases, this number increased substantially for the *closest-three* approach (92%). The accuracy of matching parallelepipeds exhibits a similar pattern.

Session

A paired-samples t-test comparing accuracy of matches between the walk-up session and the instructed session of our study found a significant increase of correct matches in the instructed part for both *top-match* (t_{14}=4.276, p<0.002) and *closest-three* (t_{14}=6.035, p<0.001). As shown in Figure 9c, our prototype correctly matched participants' descriptions in ¾ of all cases during the instructed part (98% for *closest-three*).

A two-way ANOVA on category and session did not find a significant interaction between the two for *top-match* (p=0.126) nor *closest-three* (p=0.7).

Questionnaire

While four participants stated to have prior experience with 3D modeling tools, none reported to have thought about operations in such tools during the study.

Discussion

The results of the study support our *data miming* approach, which performed particularly well after participants had been given a few instructions (increasing success in 50% more of the cases to obtain the described object as the top match) or when returning several most-closely matching objects. Surprisingly, however, the recognition rate of the primitive solids and parallelepipeds was lower than that of the other two categories when considering the most closely matching object. The considerable difference to *closest-three*, however, suggests that this low performance is due to the similarity of objects in those two categories in general.

Our study also supports findings in the related work. Working solely on their mental image and receiving no feedback, participants' gestures resulted in 3D representations that could mostly be recognized ([1, 10], no-feedback condition in [29]). Participants used fluid and directed gestures to describe object parts, such that straight lines (e.g., shelf, struts) and faces (e.g., seats) looked proper and not jagged [29].

Our results also confirm that participants were able to maintain a spatial reference while performing gestures using both hands [3, 11, 12]. While some object parts were displayed (see video figure), most have only slight offsets (e.g. legs in Figure 1). Participants maintained relative scale and references when gesturing due to their visuospatial memory [1], which also reflects prior insights [10, 11, 12, 23].

We suspect that our study differs from the real world in that users might be more familiar with the object they are describing. On the other hand, our study design matches the case where the user only roughly knows what they want and "sketches" the desired object. A system for such a task would benefit from the *closest-three* approach; a user specifies an object through gestures, upon which the system returns the three most-closely matching objects. The user then picks one, starts over, or continues to gesture more detail, because it has become apparent that they underspecified the object.

Alternatively, the *closest-three* results might be consumed by a larger system that models the context of the interaction, such as the spoken dialogue (e.g., [4]). This extra information might easily disambiguate the user's input and narrow the class of objects under consideration (and, conversely, gesture might disambiguate other aspects of the interaction, such as speech). For example, the user could say "chair" and then specify a particular chair by gesturing to indicate a uniquely identifying feature (or set of features) of the chair's shape. Interactive systems can thus use data miming for input as users describe objects focusing on their mental image.

CONCLUSIONS AND FUTURE WORK

We have presented *data miming* as an approach to inferring spatial objects from the user's gestures when describing physical objects. Our approach results from observations in a user study, in which participants described real-world objects to another person using gestures. We implemented a proof-of-concept prototype system, which passively observes the user's gestures with a depth camera and models the trace of the user's hands with a discrete and time-aware voxel representation. Data miming proved useful in a final study and recognized participants' iconic or pantomime gestures while describing physical objects. That our implementation performs as well as it does suggests that people do carry 3D mental images of objects, and that they readily replicate this 3D imagery in gesture with surprising fidelity.

Although promising, our results show that next versions of data miming need to incorporate multiple cameras to mitigate occlusion, and also recognize compound hand postures. While easy to detect for humans, future prototypes need to recognize distorted and out-of-shape objects. While the findings reported in this paper are limited to the tested objects, we believe they extend to others that consist of struts and faces.

Of course, linguists have observed many gesture strategies that do not follow a 3D model. For example, a participant might have indicated the red 'S'-shaped chair (Figure 8c) with a "wavy" motion of the hand. While the form of this gesture might not match the actual 3D shape of the chair's back, it instead conveys an abstract quality of the shape. A more feature-based or machine-learning approach driven by training examples might capture some non-literal aspects of gesture behavior. Extending data miming to handle such metaphoric gestures is an interesting avenue of future work.

ACKNOWLEDGMENTS

We thank Hrvoje Benko, Ken Hinckley, and Johnny Lee for valuable feedback and discussions, as well as all participants of our studies for their time.

REFERENCES

1. Baddeley, A.D., and Hitch, G. 1974. Working memory. In G.H. Bower (Ed.), *The Psychology of Learning and Motivation: Advances in Research and Theory 8*, 47-89.
2. Baudel, T. and Beaudouin-Lafon, M. Charade: remote control of objects using free-hand gestures. *CACM* 36, 7(1993), 28-35.
3. Billinghurst M., Bowskill J., Dyer N., and Morphett, J. Spatial information displays on a wearable Computer. *IEEE CG&A* 18, (1998), 24-30.
4. Bohus, D., Horvitz, E. 2009. Dialog in the Open World: Platform and Applications. *Proc. ICMI '09*, 31-38.
5. Deering, M. F. HoloSketch: a virtual reality sketching/animation tool. *ACM Trans. Comput.-Hum. Interact.* 2, 3(1995), 220-238.
6. Funkhouser, T., Kazhdan, M., Shilane, P., Min, P., Kiefer, W., Tal, A., Rusinkiewicz, S., and Dobkin, D. Modeling by example. *ACM Trans. Graph.* 23, 3(2004), 652-663.
7. Funkhouser, T., Min, P., Kazhdan, M., Chen, J., Halderman, A., Dobkin, D., and Jacobs, D. A search engine for 3D models. *ACM Trans. Graph.* 22, 1(2003), 83-105.
8. Galyean, T.A., Hughes, J.F. Sculpting: an interactive volumetric modeling technique. *SIGGRAPH Comput. Graph.* 25, 4(2004), 267-274.
9. Grice, P. Studies in the Way of Words. Harvard University Press: Cambridge. 1989.
10. Gustafson, S., Bierwirth, D., and Baudisch, P. Imaginary Interfaces: Spatial Interaction with Empty Hands and Without Visual Feedback. *Proc. UIST'10.*
11. Hinckley, K., Pausch, R., and Proffitt, D. Attention and visual feedback: the bimanual frame of reference. *Proc. I3D '97*, 121-ff.
12. Hinckley, K., Pausch, R., Goble, J. C., and Kassell, N. F. A survey of design issues in spatial input. *Proc. UIST '94*, 213-222.
13. Holz, C. and Feiner, S. Relaxed Selection Techniques for Querying Time-Series Graphs. *Proc. UIST '09*, 213-222.
14. Keefe, D. F., Feliz, D. A., Moscovich, T., Laidlaw, D. H., and LaViola, J. J. CavePainting: a fully immersive 3D artistic medium and interactive experience. *Proc. I3D '01*, 85-93.
15. Kendon, A. How gesture can become like words. In F. Payatos (ed.), *Cross-Cultural Perspectives in Nonverbal Communication,* 131-141. Toronto: Hogrefe.
16. Lee, J. and Kunii, T. L. Model-Based Analysis of Hand Posture. *IEEE Comput. Graph. Appl.* 15, 5(1995), 77-86.
17. Llamas, I., Kim, B., Gargus, J., Rossignac, J., and Shaw, C. D. Twister: a space-warp operator for the two-handed editing of 3D shapes. *ACM Trans. Graph* 22, 3(2003), 663-668.
18. McNeill, D. Hand and Mind: What Gesture Reveal about Thought. Chicago: University of Chicago Press. 1992.
19. Nishino, H., Utsumiya, K., and Korida, K. 3D object modeling using spatial and pictographic gestures. *Proc. VRST '98*, 51-58.
20. oblong g-speak. http://www.oblong.com
21. Pavlovic, V.I., Sharma, R., Huang, T.S. Visual interpretation of hand gestures for human-computer interaction: a review. *IEEE Trans. Pattern Analysis and Machine Intelligence* 19, 7(1997), 677-695.
22. Pratini, E. New Approaches to 3D Gestural Modeling – the 3D SketchMaker Project. *Proc. eCAADe '01*, 466-471.
23. Sachs, E., Roberts, A., and Stoops, D. 3-Draw: A Tool for Designing 3D Shapes. *IEEE Comput. Graph* 11, 6(1991), 18-26.
24. Schkolne, S., Pruett, M., and Schröder, P. Surface drawing: creating organic 3D shapes with the hand and tangible tools. *Proc. CHI '01*, 261-268.
25. Starner, T., Auxier, J., Ashbrook, D., and Gandy, M. The Gesture Pendant: A Self-illuminating, Wearable, Infrared Computer Vision System for Home Automation Control and Medical Monitoring. *Proc. ISWC '00*, 87-94.
26. Starner, T., Leibe, B., Minnen, D., Westeyn, T.L., Hurst, A., Weeks, J. The perceptive workbench: Computer-vision-based gesture tracking, object tracking, and 3D reconstruction for augmented desks. *Machine Vision and Appl.* 14, 1(2003), 59-71.
27. Tangelder, J. W. and Veltkamp, R. C. A survey of content based 3D shape retrieval methods. *Multimedia Tools Appl.* 39, 3(2008), 441-471.
28. Wang, S. W. and Kaufman, A. E. Volume sculpting. *Proc. I3D '95*, 151-156.
29. Willis, K. D., Lin, J., Mitani, J., and Igarashi, T. Spatial sketch: bridging between movement & fabrication. *Proc. TEI '10*, 5-12.
30. Wilson, A.D. Robust computer vision-based detection of pinching for one and two-handed gesture input. *Proc. UIST '06*, 255-258.
31. Xbox Kinect. http://www.xbox.com/kinect.
32. Zhang, Z. Iterative point matching for registration of free-form curves and surfaces. *Int. J. Comput. Vision* 13, 2(1994), 119-152.

Understanding Naturalness and Intuitiveness in Gesture Production: Insights for Touchless Gestural Interfaces

Sukeshini A. Grandhi, Gina Joue, Irene Mittelberg
Natural Media and Engineering, HumTec, RWTH Aachen University, Germany
{grandhi, joue, mittelberg}@humtec.rwth-aachen.de

ABSTRACT
This paper explores how interaction with systems using touchless gestures can be made intuitive and natural. Analysis of 912 video clips of gesture production from a user study of 16 subjects communicating transitive actions (manipulation of objects with or without external tools) indicated that 1) dynamic pantomimic gestures where imagined tool/object is explicitly held are performed more intuitively and easily than gestures where a body part is used to represent the tool/object or compared to static hand poses and 2) gesturing while communicating the transitive action as how the user habitually performs the action (pantomimic action) is perceived to be easier and more natural than gesturing while communicating it as an instruction. These findings provide guidelines for the characteristics of gestures and user mental models one must consciously be concerned with when designing and implementing gesture vocabularies of touchless interaction.

Author Keywords
Gestures, intuitiveness, naturalness, user centric interaction design, cognitive semiotic principles, metonymy

ACM Classification Keywords
H.5.2 Information Interfaces and Presentation: User Interfaces

General Terms
Design, Human Factors, Experimentation.

INTRODUCTION
Touchless gestural interfaces have many potential applications such as in sterile/clean room environments, collocated shared technology and robotics [13,14]. However, unlike touch gestures, touchless gestures remain largely a notion developed in science fiction (as depicted in the popular sci-fi movie *Minority Report*) and have only been implemented to a limited degree in a few proof-of-concept research applications (e.g. [1,2]) and video games (e.g. Sony Eye Toy, Microsoft Kinect). This limited implementation of touchless gestures is due to challenges in 1) achieving accurate and meaningful gesture recognition [1,2] and 2) identifying natural, intuitive and meaningful gesture vocabularies appropriate for the tasks in question [10]. While computer vision researchers have long been working on gesture recognition, the challenge of generating natural and intuitive touchless gesture vocabulary while keeping user experience in mind, has received relatively very little research attention. The gesture vocabulary used has often been an ad-hoc choice made by the designer to trigger certain pre-assigned actions (e.g. the gesture of clapping one's hands to turn on the computer). Mostly chosen for their ease of implementation to facilitate distinctive recognition and segmentation, such gestures have arbitrary mappings that require users to learn a set of gestures and the associated commands they trigger. This often puts a strain on user memory and defeats the purpose of using gestures as a way to facilitate intuitive and natural interaction [5,10]. The aim of the work presented in this paper is to take a small step towards understanding what makes touchless gesture production natural and intuitive to provide design guidelines for such interfaces. We adopt a vernacular definition of "natural" as being marked by spontaneity and "intuitive" as coming naturally without excessive deliberation. While several classifications of gestures and their functions exist [5,11,12,16], we adopt a semiotic or communicative approach to gestures [12] for HCI, which corresponds to Caldoz's classification of *semiotic* hand movements [4], or movements that communicate information from shared common ground. Since 90% of semiotic gestures are accompanied by speech [11], we look at gestures in association with speech.

RESEARCH QUESTIONS
In particular, this paper focuses on the communication of transitive actions, or actions involving the manipulation of objects with or without external tools. For example, how do we communicate to the system using gestures that a screen be erased? Specifically we view gesture forms in terms of its relationship to what is being communicated or represented. This was motivated by neuropsychology, psychiatry and developmental psychology literature which all suggest that for transitive gestures (e.g. brushing teeth with a toothbrush), it is more normal for the hand itself to hold an imagined object (e.g. holding an imaginary toothbrush) rather than representing a body part as the object itself (e.g. finger representing the toothbrush itself). Using the hand to represent the object itself is termed as "body-part-as-object" in neuropsychology, and is an example of "object substitution" in developmental

psychology. In neurological examinations, this type of action is considered an error associated with movement planning disorders [7]. The ability to perform hand actions where the hand holds an imagined object, referred to as pantomimed action with an imagined object in neuropsychology, is considered the proper developmental trend in children [3]. Based on semiotic theory, "body-part-as-object" gestures are referred to as exhibiting "internal metonymy", and "holding-imagined-object" gestures are referred to as "external metonymy" [12]. Therefore, we hypothesize that body-part-as-object gestures, i.e. reflecting internal metonymy, are generally not as intuitive as hand actions holding-imagined-objects, i.e. reflecting external metonymy. In order to develop design principles for effective communication of transitive actions to a system using gestures, we considered the following two broad research questions:

1. What aspects of a gesture (such as motion, hand shape and form) are natural and intuitive when communicating a transitive action? In particular, are gestures using hand actions holding-imagined-objects more intuitive and natural than using body-part-as-object?
2. Is it easier to gesture a transitive action when the user communicates as how s/he habitually performs the action or when the user communicates it as an instruction? That is, should one gesture as "this is how I do it" or "this is how you should do it"?

USER STUDY

Procedure

In order to address the above research questions we adopted a user-centric approach [13,15,16]. Participants were told that the study explored people's intuitive preferences and natural tendencies in verbal and non-verbal expressions. Sixteen (8 female) native or near-native American English speakers of different U.S. regions were recruited from a university visitor pool. All except one (over 60 years old) were between 20-30 years old, and 68.8% were strongly right-handed based on the Edinburgh Handedness Survey.

Participants were presented pairs of pictures showing a "before" and "after" scenario. These scenarios (Table 1) reflected simple computer tasks (e.g. cut, erase), but were camouflaged as everyday non-computer scenarios to minimize the influence of conceptual models of performing these tasks on pre-existing input devices. Our definitions of intuitive and natural translate into the assumption that spontaneous and more frequently produced gestures in common tasks can indicate what is more "natural and intuitive," and how well people can maintain a so-called unintuitive gesture, can shed further light on naturalness.

As soon as the picture pair disappeared, participants were asked to speak aloud while performing a gesture to "explain and show" the experimenter (seated in front of them in a position where the pictures could not be seen), what needed to be done to achieve what was in the after-picture from the before-picture. Each picture pair was shown for 3 seconds on a 24″ monitor at a resolution of 1024 x 768 (stimulus visual angle of 7.15°). A total of 19 pairs of before-after pictures were used. The scenarios were divided into three categories: Transitive actions usually done 1) with an external tool (e.g. slicing an apple with a knife), 2) without an external tool (e.g. laying plates on a table) and 3) with or without an external tool (e.g. wiping a surface with bare hands or a cloth). Participants performed the "explain and show" scenario for the above tasks under three conditions to distinguish between the styles of communication (Instructional vs. Habitual) and to understand naturalness and intuitiveness of performing gestures with internal metonymy (body-part-as-tool).

1. Instructional: Participants instructed the experimenter on what needed to be done and began their instructions with the sentence frame, "You need to..."
2. Habitual: Participants explained how they normally would perform what needed to be done, beginning their explanations with the sentence frame, "This is how I..."
3. Instructional using body-part-as-tool: Participants repeated the Instructional condition, but they additionally were required to use their hands to represent any tool they might need to use (internal metonymy).

pile coins CT: arrange	erase board CT: erase/clear	break banana CT: cut/slice	fill glass CT: fill
sort coins CT: arrange	clear crumbs CT: erase/clear	cut paper CT: cut	beat eggs CT: mix/blend
arrange plates CT: arrange	clear leaves CT: erase/clear	slice apple CT: cut/slice	fix nail CT: place/fix
arrange folders CT: arrange	clear coins CT: erase/clear	crack open eggs CT: open	hang poster CT: place/fix
	clear toys CT: erase/clear	close book CT: close	write a sign CT: write/sketch

Table 1 The 19 scenarios and corresponding computing task (CT)

The order of the three conditions as well as the 19 scenarios within each condition was randomized for each participant to minimize order effects. At the end of the study, participants were interviewed on their perspectives on the naturalness and intuitiveness of the communicating styles and tool/object representation in their gestures (internal or external metonymy). All sessions were recorded using two high-speed video cameras from two visual perspectives.

FINDINGS

Data from 912 video clips (16 participants x 19 scenarios x 3 conditions) were blindly annotated by a coder. Parts of the annotations were verified for consistency by the authors, and a second annotator blindly coded 25% of the data. The inter-rater reliability for the annotators was good (Cohen's $\kappa = 0.64$, $p<0.001$). Annotations consisted of 1) right- or left-hand use; 2) number of hands used; 3) use of body-part as tool/object vs. pantomimed action of imagined tool/object use; 4) dynamic (moving gesture) vs. static gesture poses; 5) distinctions between gestures involving a tool (device used to perform the dominant action, e.g. knife used for cutting) or object (entity upon which the dominant action is performed, e.g. the apple that is cut); and 6) distinctions between gestures that set up the context vs. execute the dominant action of the transitive action.

Gestures exhibited motion than static poses

Gestures representing the dominant action were seldom shown as static hand forms or poses (e.g. palm held sideways with extended fingers to represent cutting), but were almost always (95.7%) dynamic motions demonstrating the "use of tool".

Pantomimed actions of holding-imagined-tool were more intuitive and easier than body-part-as-tool

In conditions 1 and 2 where participants were not told how to represent tools in their gestures, participants gestured holding an imaginary tool significantly more often than representing a part of their hand as a tool ($\chi^2(4) = 54.5$, $p < 0.001$). Figure 1 and Video Clip 1 (video file uploaded with the paper) show a subject holding an imaginary knife in the right hand to cut an imaginary apple held in the left. Figure 2 and Video Clip 2 show the right palm to represent a knife. In gestures where no external tool was used and the dominant action was pantomimed, the object, by default, was manipulated (Video Clip 3). In condition 3 where participants were explicitly asked to use body-part-as-tool to represent any tool used in the action, they failed to do so 77.5% of the time when an external tool was necessary. Only 3.7% of these participants "corrected" themselves to the instructions of the condition without prompting (Video Clip 4). The intuitiveness and ease of pantomiming with an imaginary tool in hand is further corroborated by participants' comments such as the following that were typical: *"most difficult was using my hand as a tool. That really didn't come naturally", "It felt weird to use my finger as the tool because I don't do that. It's just more usual to use the tool…it's kind of awkward."*

Gestures represented objects explicitly rather implicitly

In all the three conditions, bimanual gestures were performed three times more often than one-handed gestures. Objects on which an action was performed, be it with an external tool or the hand itself, were depicted explicitly 45% of the time, as opposed to implicitly assuming its presence in one of three forms (illustrated in Figures 1-3 by the left hand for an apple being cut): pantomimed action of holding-imagined-object (52.5% in all conditions, Fig 1), using a hand to situate the space in which an object is placed (34.0% in all conditions, Fig 3) and part of hand as object when not explicitly asked to do so (18.1% in conditions 1 and 2, Fig 2).

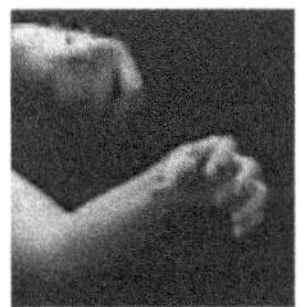
Figure 1

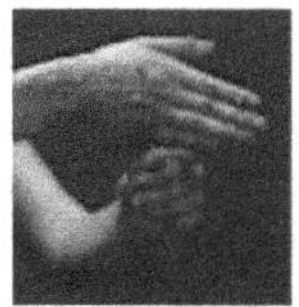
Figure 2

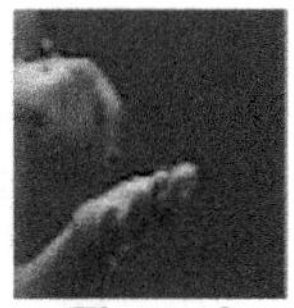
Figure 3

Communicating as "actor" easier than as commander"

Almost all participants reported that gesturing how they habitually perform an action was easier and more intuitive than gesturing an instruction. Comments such as the following were typical from the participants: *"it was easier to visualize and pantomime what I would normally do than relay that information to you…", "I found showing how I do it easier because it was more natural because I know how to do it and instructing you I don't know if you will understand my hand gestures".* Video Clip 5 exemplifies the struggle and awkwardness in terms of body orientation of a participant gesturing while instructing.

DISCUSSION AND IMPLICATIONS

Our findings suggest that communicating with a system through gestures may be easier when designers adopt an embodied approach [6]. Namely, user experience can be enhanced when the gesture vocabulary is developed based on the understanding that actions are embodied, i.e. situated in real-life social and physical scenarios. In particular, our findings provide the following key guiding principles for the design of touchless gestures involving transitive actions.

Firstly our findings have implications for how designers should communicate the presence and use of touchless gestural interactions in a system, be it in the form of text, symbols or illustrations and demonstrations [15]. Gestures triggering manipulation of objects should be dynamic iconic representations of the motion required for the manipulation, rather than static iconic hand poses. For example, a gesture to trigger "delete" should be a "wiping" hand movement rather than a static hand sign. Instructions for use of such gestures may also be helpful as illustrations of the pantomimed action. For example, rather than showing an image of a knife to indicate the gesture to use, an illustration of hand holding a knife performing the cutting act could be shown.

Secondly, gestures to trigger tasks that suggest the use of a tool should not impose body-part-as-tool compositions because such gestures do not seem to come naturally and intuitively. Instead designers should consider selecting gestures that pantomime the actual action with imagined tool in hand. For example, a gesture to slice could be a pantomiming motion of cutting with an imaginary knife in hand rather than the gesture, open palm moving vertically up and down. However, it must be noted that when the hand shape can represent the tool or object, or draw attention to an important aspect of the tool/object being communicated, in an unambiguous way due to anatomy [13], using body-part-as-tool may make more sense. This may be why certain body-part-as-object gestures have become emblematic, e.g. index and middle fingers showing scissors for cutting.

Thirdly, gestures in space to trigger manipulation of objects should be two-handed, as the non-dominant hand often appears to provide a reference frame while the dominant hand performs the transitive gesture. This is consistent with principles of Guiard's kinematic chain model of asymmetric bimanual actions [8] and other research, which suggests that two hands together provide a better sense of virtual space than one hand for task execution [9].

Finally, since gestures performed in habitual conditions were reported to be easier and more intuitive, adopting an egocentric rather than an allocentric (viewer's) frame of reference to gesture may ease the awkwardness of interacting with a system for the user, which is often a major concern in human robotic communication [14]. That is, instilling the mental model of an actor egocentrically pantomiming the action, i.e. with a communicative perspective of "I would like to do Task X", reduces the propensity of users to re-orient their reference frames to position gestures in space when communicating the perspective of "You do Task X for me".

LIMITATIONS AND FUTURE WORK

In this study we concentrated on hand forms, motion and communication style. However, many other characteristics such as the intensity of hold and other gesture kinematics may also afford insights on what comes naturally and intuitively. Consequently, promising directions for future work include using motion capture data to identify other characteristics of gestures which may help define intuitive and natural interaction, such as distance, speed, trajectory, image schemas and gestural space.

Although learned behavior can become common and even "natural", we wanted to avoid the preconceived assumptions of how one is familiar with interacting with existing system interfaces and disguised our tasks as everyday tasks. Of course, this also gives rise to limitations as to how translatable these tasks are to specific computer applications. We acknowledge that a good gesture vocabulary is typically task/context-specific, and it is a challenge to develop generic principles that can be applied across different contexts [13]. However, this challenge can be met if researchers collectively bring together their findings from diverse tasks/contexts. Thus, work presented here makes a small yet significant contribution towards the understanding of the core design principles to create intuitive and natural user experience for touchless gestural interfaces.

ACKNOWLEDGMENTS

This work has been funded by the Excellence Initiative of the German Research Foundation.

REFERENCES

1. Baudel, T. and Beaudouin-Lafon, M. Charade: Remote Control of Objects Using Free-Hand Gestures. *Communications of the ACM 36*, 7 (1993), 28-35.
2. Bolt, R. "Put-that-there": Voice and gesture at the graphics interface, Proceedings of the 7th annual conference on Computer graphics and interactive techniques, ACM, New York, NY (1980), 262-270.
3. Boyatzis, C.J. and Watson, M.W. Preschool children's symbolic representation of objects through gestures. *Child Development 64* (1993), 729-735.
4. Cadoz, C. (1994). Les realites virtuelles. Dominos, Flammarion.
5. Cassell, J. A Framework For Gesture Generation and Interpretation. In R. Cipolla and A. Pentland (eds.), *Computer Vision in Human-Machine Interaction*. Cambridge University Press, New York (1998), 191-215.
6. Dourish, P. *Where the Action Is: The Foundations of Embodied Interaction*. MIT Press, Cambridge, 2001.
7. Goodglass, H., and Kaplan, E. Disturbance of gesture and pantomine in aphasia. *Brain 86* (1963), 703-720.
8. Guiard, Y., "Asymmetric Division of Labor in Human Skilled Bimanual Action: The Kinematic Chain as a Model," The Journal of Motor Behavior, 19 (4), 1987, pp. 486-517.
9. Hinckley, K., Pausch, R., and Proffitt, D. Attention and visual feedback: the bimanual frame of reference. *Proc. Symposium on Interactive 3D Graphics*, ACM Press (1997), 121-126.
10. Lee, J.C. In search of a natural gesture. *XRDS: Crossroads, The ACM Magazine for Students 16*, 4 (2010), 9-12.
11. McNeill, D. *Hand and mind: What gestures reveal about thought*. University of Chicago Press, Chicago, 1992.
12. Mittelberg, I. and Waugh, L.R. Metonymy first, metaphor second: A cognitive-semiotic approach to multimodal figures of speech in co-speech gesture. In C. Forceville and E. Urios-Aparisi (eds.), *Multimodal Metaphor*. Mouton de Gruyter, Berlin (2009), 329-358.
13. Nielsen, M., Moeslund, T., Storring, M. and Granum, E. A procedure for developing intuitive and ergonomic gesture interfaces for HCI. In A. Camurri and G. Volpe (eds.). *Gesture-Based Communication in Human-Computer Interaction: 5th International Gesture Workshop, GW 2003*, LNCS 2915, Springer, Berlin (2004), 409-420.
14. Powers, A. What Robotics Can Learn from HCI. *ACM Interactions Magazine 15*, 2 (2008), 67-69.
15. Saffer, D. *Designing Gestural Interfaces*. O'Reilly Media, 2008.
16. Wobbrock, J.O., Morris, M.R. and Wilson, A.D. User-defined gestures for surface computing. *Proc. of the 27th Int. Conf. on Human Factors in Computing Systems,* ACM, New York, NY (2009), 1083-1092.

The Impact on Musculoskeletal System during Multitouch Tablet Interactions

Cecil Lozano[1], Devin Jindrich[2], and Kanav Kahol[1]
Arizona State University
[1]501 E. Tyler Mall, Tempe, AZ 85287, USA
[2]427 E. Tyler Mall, LSE 216, Tempe, AZ 85287-45041, USA
{Cecil.Lozano, Devin.Jindrich, Kanav.Kahol}@asu.edu

ABSTRACT
HCI researchers and technologists have heralded multitouch interaction as the technology to drive computing systems into the future. However, as we move towards a world where interaction is based on human body movements that are not well documented or studied, we face a serious and a grave risk of creating technology and systems that may lead to musculoskeletal disorders (MSD's). Designers need to be empowered with objective data on the impact of multitouch interactions on the musculoskeletal system to make informed choices in interaction design. In this paper we present an experiment that documents kinematic (movement) and kinetic measures (EMG) when interacting with a multitouch tablet. Results show that multitouch interaction can induce significant stress that may lead to MSDs and care must be taken when designing multitouch interaction.

Author Keywords
Ergonomic Multitouch tablet interfaces.

ACM Classification Keywords
H.5.2 User Interfaces (D.2.2, H.1.2, I.3.6) Ergonomics.

General Terms
Experimentation, human factors, measurement, performance, design.

INTRODUCTION
The advent of numerous commercial devices and software such as iPhone® (www.apple.com/iphone), Microsoft Surface® (www.microsoft.com/surface/index.html), Windows 7® (www.microsoft.com/windows/windows-7/), HP's new touch screen PC and CNN's Multitouch collaboration Wall has heralded a new era of multitouch interaction. Multitouch interaction enables a natural, veridical interface to digital media [2]. It allows for users to experience content through multimodal interaction enabling a high degree of interactivity and impressiveness, which in turn makes the technology suitable to become the default human computer interaction standard of the near future. However, as we move towards a world where interaction is based on human body movements that are not well documented or studied, we face a serious and a grave risk of creating technology and systems that may lead to musculoskeletal disorders.

Often interfaces such as keyboards, mouse and touch screens are designed without considering the effect of interaction on musculoskeletal system [1]. The increase in workplace computer usage since 1980 has been accompanied by a corresponding increase in incidence rates of chronic musculoskeletal disorders reported in the United States [1]. Conservative estimates of the annual cost to the U.S. economy for all musculoskeletal disorders range from $45 to $54 billion [5].

Poor design strategies can cause biomechanical and physical stress to the musculoskeletal system and are associated with work-related musculoskeletal disorders (MSDs) [1]. Additionally, even when users are allowed to define their gestures for interactions with touch based systems, the lack of knowledge about the impact of gestures may cause users to choose unsafe gestures. Thus, there is the need of generating ergonomic standards of interaction in which a diversity of current and novel gestures can be assessed and can therefore aid designers (and users) in making appropriate choices in terms of ergonomic impact of gestures on the user's musculoskeletal system (MSS).

This paper presents an initial attempt to define scientific principles to build such standards. To that goal it is required a methodology of analysis where gestures are carefully controlled to evaluate their independent and isolated impact to the MSS. With such information a designer can indeed choose which gestures should have higher frequency and which should be used sparingly. This information would be critical in developing data driven guidelines for interactions.

Furthermore, we believe that an important initial element of these investigations needs to focus on generation of gestures, as this is the technology's novelty and there is no knowledge of their effect on the MSS. Thus in this work we investigated the effect of a set of free stroke gestures that represent one and two finger type of interactions on device conditions relevant to mobile devices and to building design guidelines (see below). Tapping/typing motions also require investigation but were not included as they involve different confounding variables that will be tested independently.

Through this initial experiment, we have developed objective measures of musculoskeletal stress introduced by gestures on tablet system. The short-term aim of this research is to provide designers with objective measures of the impact of gestures and configurations of tablet on musculoskeletal system. This would empower multitouch interaction designers to make informed choices of interaction design. The long-term aim of this research is to develop a software toolkit that would enable designers to input a target gesture and ascertain its impact on the musculoskeletal system, which would allow for safe and effective designs.

METHODS

Experimental design

The goals of this experiment were to measure physiological impact of using gestures for multitouch technology, specifically the iPad, and to provide a glance of some parameters to consider for designing guidelines. We tested 3 different conditions: gesture type, device position and context.

We chose 8 gestures using only index and thumb fingers of participant's dominant (right) hand: rotating to the right and left, zooming in, zooming out, panning with the index to the right, left, up and down. These gestures represent "free" form strokes that involve dragging using single and multiple fingers and are being used in most devices for common HCI actions. We incorporated also an important usability factor of mobile devices by having gestures being executed in 2 device positions: exocentric or fixed on a table in a 15° angle in front of the participant and egocentric while the participant held the device with their non-dominant (left) hand. And finally, we included a factor of context geared for design guidelines. Gestures were performed in 2 contextual scenarios: non-contextual when device was off and contextual as participants interacted with mapping software Google Earth (as this application allowed for the use of all the tested gestures). This factor is particularly important to estimate the difference in the effect of novel gestures at the non-contextual design phase and the applied phase in realistic scenarios.

To assess the effects of these factors, we measured muscle activation and finger joint angles. Muscle activation was measured using bipolar surface electromyography (EMG; Bortec AMT-8). We recorded from the dominant forearm extensor digitorum communis (wrist and finger extension) and the anterior deltoid (forward shoulder flexion). We also included the non-dominant biceps (forearm flexion) and anterior deltoid. Placement of electrodes achieved through palpation and signal response to isometric test contractions [3]. For the ground reference we used the non-dominant ulnar styloid process. Amplification for each muscle was adjusted to maximize the information captured. Finger movement (kinematic) information was obtained for the dominant hand with a CyberGlove® 22 sensor system that captures angular excursions of the finger joints. We focused our analysis on the index finger as it has the maximum use in the multitouch interactions.

Participants

Eight right-handed healthy participants (6 males and 2 females, ages 20 to 27) volunteered for one experimental session that lasted 3-4 hours. Handedness was selected to represent the majority of the population and to minimize confounding factors that need to be address separately. Participants reported to be frequent users of multitouch technology (more than 40 hours), which eliminated familiarization time. Note that level of experience with the iPad was not assessed since the interaction studied was not task oriented. Subjects also reported to be free of any musculoskeletal disorder of the upper extremities. Procedures were approved by the Institutional Review Board at our University and were in accordance with the declaration of Helsinki.

Experimental protocol

Participants comfortably sat in front of a table with the device in front of them. They performed each of the 8 gestures for each of the device position and contextual conditions a total of 3 times (total of 8x2x2x3 = 96 trials). In each recorded trial, participants first waited 5 s with their arms resting on the device's side, which was used as starting point and allowed recording of baseline signal of minimal muscle activation. They then were cued to repeat the gesture in turn for 20 s until they were cued to stop. A fixed time allowed for collecting enough data for analysis and for statistical comparison between gestures. Participants were asked to perform the gestures in the middle of the device using only the fingers required (index and thumb for rotating and zooming and index for panning), while the arm wasn't supported. In the conditions when the device was held, participants were requested to lift the device with their non-dominant arm to the previously chosen comfortable position and hold it throughout the time of performing the gesture without resting the arm. We asked participants to look at the center of the device while doing the gestures even when it was off.

We ran 3 sets (replications) of 8 gestures for each combination of device position and contextual condition. The order of the gestures was randomized within set and the order of the device position and contextual conditions among participants were presented in a complete counterbalance for immediate sequential effects order. We included 20 s rests between trials to allow recovery of gesture in turn, 1 m rest between sets of trials and at least 5 m between changes of position-contextual device condition change to minimize mental/physical fatigue.

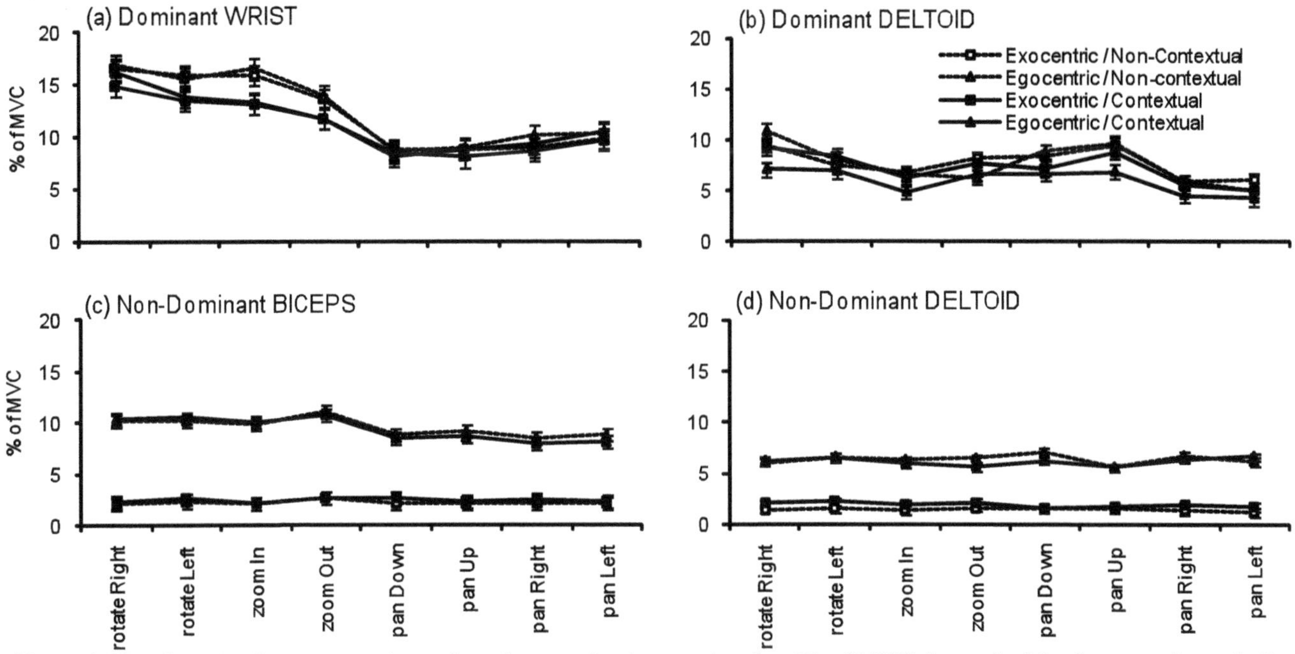

Figure 1. Muscle activation as percentage of maximum voluntary contraction (% of MVC) for each of the four muscles and all the conditions with error bars representing least significant differences. Axis labels of (a & b) same as (c & d).

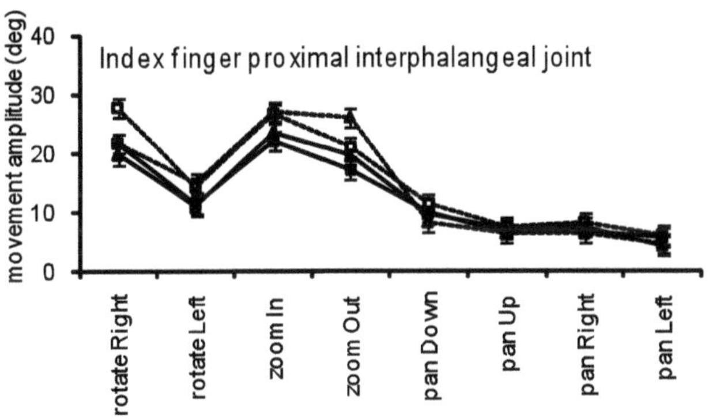

Figure 2. Average rotation amplitude of the index finger interphalangeal joint during gestures.

We obtained two maximum voluntary contractions (MVCs) for each muscle at the beginning and at the end of the experimental session. These measures were used for both normalizing the EMG data and measuring possible fatigue of the individual muscles after producing all the tested gestures.

Data analysis

We evaluated muscle activation as the percentage of MVC, since each muscle had different EMG amplification. We first calculated the root mean square of the EMG signal for the 10 to 20 s of the 25 s trial to assure we didn't include the transitions within the trial (e.g., beginning and end of doing the correspondent gesture). We then normalized it with the maximum EMG obtained from the MVCs. The maximum EMG values from both MVCs were extracted after smoothing the signal with a 1 s moving average window.

The kinematic data from the three joints of the index finger yielded angular changes in gestures presented in degrees. We obtained statistical comparisons using the average of the 3 replications of each condition for each participant (i.e., 8 values per condition). We used the ANOVA output of Design Expert for a general factorial design of the 3 factors with 8, 2 and 2 levels corresponding to gestures, device position and contextual conditions. This analysis allowed the removal of any variation attributed to blocks of data (each participant data assigned to one block). Significance was set at 5% (i.e., $\alpha = 0.05$ or p-value < 0.05).

RESULTS

Gestures

Gesture type had a statistical effect on the dominant arm doing the gesture.

The average dominant wrist extensor muscle activity was generally greater for the gestures where both fingers (thumb and index) were involved than when only the index finger was used for the gesture (factor's p-value < 0.0001; see Figure 1a). In average rotating to the right produced the highest (16.1% of MVC) and panning down the lowest muscle activation (8.5% of MVC). It should be noted that the average muscle activation is higher to reported maximum activation of computer mouse use [4].

For the dominant deltoid, rotating to the right and panning up produced the highest muscle activation (9.2 and 8.7 % of MVC, respectively), while panning sideways produced the least activation (5.1% and 5.4% of MVC; factor's p-value < 0.0001; see Figure 1b).

Kinematic data analysis showed similar trends to the EMG. The difference between gestures was statistically significant (Figure 2). Rotation and Zooming gesture produced high levels of rotation up to 40 degrees.

Device position

Device position had statistical effect on the non-dominant arm muscle activations. Activation was higher when the device was held (egocentric) than when it was fixed on the table (exocentric; factor's p-value < 0.0001; see Figure 1c and 1d). Additionally, when holding the device, the activity of the biceps with respect to the maximum voluntary contraction was greater for the biceps (9.5% of MVC) than the deltoid (6.3% of MVC). Device position had no significant impact on the kinematic activations.

Task context

The task context had an effect on muscle activation of the dominant arm only. The average non-contextual gestures (device off) produced higher wrist muscle activation (12.5% of MVC) than contextual gestures (interacting with Google Earth; 11.2% of MVC; factor's p-value < 0.05). This difference was more noticeable for the two finger gestures, especially for zooming in (see Figure 1a). Similar to the wrist, the non-contextual gestures produced higher deltoid muscular activation (7.7% of MVC) than contextual gestures (6.6% of MVC; Figure 1b). From a kinematic perspective, task context had a significant impact with contextual interaction providing higher joint rotation amplitudes.

Maximum voluntary contractions

The biceps was the muscle that had the largest tendency for lower MVCs at the end of the experiment. This shows that holding the device may produce unsafe fatigue.

DISCUSSION

It was expected that gestures require the activation of local (e.g., wrist muscles) and non-local (e.g., deltoid) muscles. Our experiments show that indeed multitouch interaction has impact on the entire hand shoulder system and in some cases the impact can be at risk levels (higher than the lowest recommended). This is an important experimental result, which seems to suggest that caution must be observed when considering interaction design. Multitouch interaction can indeed be very engaging and users may have the tendency to develop MSDs without conscious knowledge of the developing conditions.

As expected we also found that holding the device (egocentric) would have greater muscle activation of the non-dominant arm (both biceps and deltoid). The activation of the biceps was around 10% of the MVC, which is about 50% of the average activation found for a similar posture in an experiment for dumbbell biceps curl exercises [6]. Although these and higher levels of muscle activation are used for training, a sustained muscle activation of even 5% of MVC may cause musculoskeletal disorders [7].

Non-contextual gestures produced slightly higher activation of the arm involved, especially for two-finger gestures. This outcome indicates that context might have a different effect depending on the type of gestures. Greater activation could partially be driven by factors such as force and motion amplitude. Our experimental results showed that at least the motion amplitude partially explains the activation patterns.

CONCLUSIONS

The presented data provides important insights for designers to consider ergonomic factors when designing multitouch interaction. It suggests that gestures that involve two fingers (e.g., rotation), can introduce high levels of muscle activations. Furthermore, certain conditions such as egocentric device positioning (such as the condition in using tablets as book readers and hand documentation units) can introduce additional stress. Thus it is important that HCI designers develop applications and devices that encourage safe practices while limiting unsafe practices. Note that the results of this study represent only a portion of the vast repertoire of factors that may affect interaction with multitouch technology. In future work, we aim to asses additional factors to develop guidelines and provide a toolkit for designers to aid in selection process for gestures. For example assess gestures in contexts such as "opening a web page and finding a recipe" etcetera.

REFERENCES

1. (BLS), B.o.L.S., Reports on survey of occupational injuries and illnesses in 1977-2001. (2002).
2. Buxton, B. Multitouch Systems that I have known and loved. www.billbuxton.com/multitouchOverview.html, (2008).
3. Cram, J. and E. Criswell, Introduction to surface electromyography. Second ed. (2010): *David Cella*. 412.
4. Laursen, B., B.R. Jensen, and A. Ratkevicius, Performance and muscle activity during computer mouse tasks in young and elderly adults. *European Journal of Applied Physiology*. 84(4), (2001), 329-336.
5. NSR/IOM, N.R.C.a.I.o.M.C., Musculoskeletal disorders and the workplace: low back and upper extremities. (2001), Washington, D.C.: *National Academy Press*.
6. Oliveira, L.F., et al., Effect of the shoulder position on the biceps brachii EMG in different dumbbell curls. *Journal of Sports Science and Medicine*. 8(1), (2009), 24-29.
7. Sommerich, C.M., W.S. Marras, and M. Parnianpour, A method for developing biomechanical profiles of hand-intensive tasks. *Clinical Biomechanics*. 13(4-5), (1998), 261-271.

TorusDesktop: Pointing via the Backdoor is Sometimes Shorter

Stéphane Huot[1,2] huot@lri.fr

Olivier Chapuis[1,2] chapuis@lri.fr

Pierre Dragicevic[2] dragice@lri.fr

[1]LRI - Univ. Paris-Sud & CNRS
F-91405 Orsay, France

[2]INRIA
F-91405 Orsay, France

ABSTRACT
When pointing to a target on a computer desktop, we may think we are taking the shortest possible path. But new shortcuts become possible if we allow the mouse cursor to jump from one edge of the screen to the opposite one, i.e., if we turn the desktop into a torus. We discuss the design of TORUSDESKTOP, a pointing technique that allows to wrap the cursor around screen edges to open this pointing backdoor. A dead zone and an off-screen cursor feedback make the technique more usable and more compatible with everyday desktop usage. We report on three controlled experiments conducted to refine the design of the technique and evaluate its performance. The results suggest clear benefits of using the backdoor when target distance is more than 80% the screen size in our experimental conditions.

Author Keywords
Pointing Technique, Cursor Wrapping, Torus.

ACM Classification Keywords
H.5.2 Information Interfaces and Presentation: User interfaces—*Graphical user interfaces.*

General Terms
Human Factors, Experimentation.

INTRODUCTION
When flying from New-York to San Francisco, one usually does not fly around the globe across the Atlantic and the Pacific Oceans. Yet we often do it on our computers: we routinely move our mouse pointer from one side of the screen to the opposite side – e.g., to select a tool or invoke a menu command – ignoring potential trajectory shortcuts. Such shortcuts would only require a small modification to the mouse behavior: when the pointer goes past a screen edge it re-appears on the opposite side, as in the Asteroids or Pac-Man video-games (see Figure 1).

We introduce TORUSDESKTOP, a pointing technique which opens these shortcuts on our computer desktops. Although many pointing facilitation techniques have been already proposed, most of them are *target-aware* [26, 3], i.e., they require knowledge of all the potential targets the user may acquire. These techniques can be extremely efficient but they are sensitive to distractors and are difficult to integrate to existing systems. Only a few *target-agnostic* pointing facilitation techniques have been introduced and the results have been mixed. TORUSDESKTOP is target-agnostic, making it easy to integrate to existing systems and compatible with most existing pointing facilitation techniques.

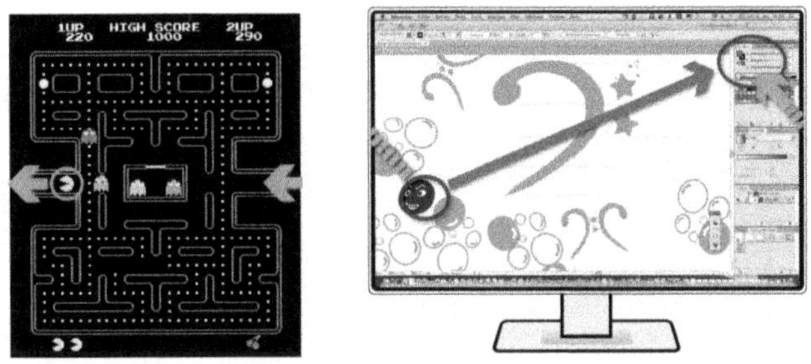

Figure 1. The Pac-Man video-game and a case scenario where pointing through screen edges could be beneficial.

TORUSDESKTOP teleports the mouse cursor to the opposite side of the screen when it goes past one of the screen's edges. This technique is sometimes referred to as *cursor wrapping*. One consequence of this wrapping behavior is that the shortest path between two points is not necessarily the on-screen segment that connects them. Although this may evoke a sphere topology, wrapping the cursor around screen edges actually turns the computer desktop into a torus.

The idea of wrapping the mouse cursor around screen or window edges is not new. In addition to video games from the early 80's, a few system tweaks and mouse drivers support this technique. But current implementations are all under-designed as the cursor immediately jumps when it reaches a screen edge. This can yield several problems: first, it is easy to trigger the wrapping inadvertently. Second, it might be difficult to find the new location of the cursor. Third, the technique prevents the user from using the border to acquire targets that are located on screen edges. TORUSDESKTOP addresses these issues by introducing a wrapping dead zone and visual feedback to anticipate cursor jumps.

As cursor wrapping has never been studied experimentally, it is not clear whether it should be supported natively by operating systems and better publicized among end users, or simply abandoned. Our initial Fitt's Law simulations (considering all possible pointing tasks on a 2560x1600 display with 40-pixel targets) suggest that cursor wrapping should outperform direct pointing in more than 40% of all possible pointing tasks. But it is unlikely that the question can be adequately answered by a naive Fitts' Law simulation: choosing to use cursor wrapping or not might have an impact on efficiency, and large cursor jumps might be distracting to users and could result in a drop in performance.

Thus we conducted three controlled experiments to refine our design and evaluate its performance. The results of the two first experiments identify the best off-screen feedback, and suggest that a dead zone of $5 - 10\%$ the size of the screen should be provided to enable edge pointing. Our final experiment confirms that our naive Fitts' Law simulation is overly optimistic as it does not account for factors such as the distraction produced by cursor teleportation or the cost of having to chose whether or not to use the backdoor. Nevertheless, our experiment reveals that TORUSDESKTOP is still faster than direct pointing for targets whose distance is greater than 80% the width of a 2560-pixel wide display. This suggests that enabling cursor wrapping is worthwhile, especially in situations where commonly-accessed widgets are located close to the edges of the screen (Figure 1) or when going back-and-forth between two very distant targets.

RELATED WORK

A fundamental tool in the area of target acquisition is Fitts' law [20]. This law models the movement time to acquire a target of size W at distance D as a linear function of an index of difficulty ID usually defined as $\log_2\left(\frac{D}{W}+1\right)$. According to this law, techniques that try to facilitate pointing increase W, reduce D or do both [3]. They are either target-aware or target-agnostic.

Target-Aware Techniques

Most techniques that increase W are target-aware. They either expand the targets themselves [21] – sometimes in the motor space only [27, 9] – or expand the cursor's activation area [15, 12]. Target-aware techniques for reducing D try to predict the target(s) the user wants to acquire. They then bring the cursor closer to the target [2, 16] or bring potential targets closer to the cursor [4]. Another way to reduce D is to use a grid of cursors and a target-aware algorithm that tries to select the appropriate cursor [19].

However, target-aware techniques fail when there are a large number of potential targets, and they are difficult to implement at a system-wide level because they require access to target information that is solely available at a system-level.

Target-Agnostic Techniques

Effective target-agnostic pointing facilitation techniques are relatively rare. Speed-adaptive C-D gain has been modeled as a technique that increases W in motor space, but experiments did not confirm the improvements predicted by the model [11]. Angle Mouse adapts C-D gain to trajectory curvature, but it has been shown to only benefit motor-impaired users [26]. Finally, visual and motor-space uniform magnification (i.e., W and D increased in the same proportion) have been shown to improve pointing performance, but only for very small targets [24].

Other techniques employ more than one input device at a time. For example, D can be reduced in a target-agnostic manner using eye tracking. MAGIC [28] uses eye tracking to define an area where the pointer is automatically warped. The Rake cursor uses a grid of cursors and eye tracking for cursor selection [10, 25]. These techniques benefit from the increase in input bandwidth provided by gaze tracking, but they cannot be implemented on standard computer hardware.

Adaptive [18] and adaptable [13] methods have also been considered: DirtyDesktops [18] creates magnetic fields around frequently-selected locations on the screen and UIMarks [13] lets users specify on-screen locations whose acquisition will be facilitated. However, adaptative techniques improve pointing only for frequently-selected targets and adaptable techniques require user intervention.

Edge and Displayless Pointing

HCI practitioners early noticed that targets on screen edges are easier to acquire because screen edges stop the cursor, effectively increasing W in the motor space. Edge pointing has been studied experimentally in [14, 1].

Edge pointing becomes problematic in multi-display environments: by default, desktop environments treat multiple displays as a single space, disabling edge pointing between them. Mouse Ether [5] takes into account the space between the displays as well as display size and resolution to compute a motor space – the *ether* – that lies between the displays. This re-enables edge pointing, since stopping the mouse in the ether warps the pointer to the closest display edge.

Mouse Ether is conceptually similar to our dead zones: they both add off-screen pointing space that (among other things) enable edge pointing. One problem with Mouse Ether is the absence of visual feedback when the cursor is in the ether. Several techniques have been proposed to visualize the location of off-screen objects: Halo [7] surrounds off-screen objects with rings large enough to reach the edge of the display, and Wedge [17] uses a triangle pointing towards the off-screen object. A recent study suggested that augmenting Mouse Ether with Halo helps, while also suggesting that Mouse Ether itself (with or without feedback) hurts performance when displays are sufficiently far apart [23].

Cursor Warping vs. Cursor Wrapping

Cursor warping refers to the sudden teleportation of the mouse cursor to a possibly distant place. It has been used to reduce pointing distance in some target-aware pointing techniques [2, 16] as well as in target-agnostic ones [28]. Manually-triggered cursor warping has also been used for rapidly switching between displays in multi-monitor environments [8]. However, it is also believed that sudden cursor jumps can be confusing to users and can slow them down [6].

Cursor wrapping should not be confused with cursor warping: wrapping the mouse cursor around screen edges involves a specific type of cursor warping, going from one edge of the screen to the opposite one. Several applications exist that support cursor wrapping. More than 15 years ago, the FVWM X Window Manager could be configured to en-

Figure 2. Wrapping dead zone (right) and expansion of targets located on the screen edge (left).

able it. Today, system-level tools provide the same feature[1]. But as discussed previously, none of these applications provide a dead zone or off-screen feedback. Moreover, to our knowledge, such techniques have never been evaluated.

THE TORUSDESKTOP TECHNIQUE

The TORUSDESKTOP extends direct cursor wrapping techniques with two additional features in order to make it usable and compatible with everyday desktop usage:

- a *wrapping dead zone* that adds a displayless pointing space around screen edges in order to help users anticipate cursor jumps and to re-enable edge pointing;
- a *wrapping feedback* that provides visual feedback on the cursor's location inside the dead zone to further increase user's control over cursor wrapping.

Wrapping Dead Zone

The *wrapping dead zone* is a displayless frame added around the screen edges. When the cursor reaches a screen edge, the user needs to cross this space before the cursor gets teleported to the opposite edge (Figure 2). This design presents three advantages:

Prevention of accidental triggering. In situations where users do not want to cross the screen, the wrapping dead zone prevents them from wrapping the cursor accidentally. Accidental wrapping can be distracting – especially repetitive wrapping when following a screen edge – and can slow users down since they have to bring the cursor back once they realize it has jumped. They may even lose the cursor altogether if they do not realize it has moved to the opposite side. The dead zone addresses this issue by making it more difficult to trigger the wrapping and allowing to cancel it.

Support for anticipation. In cases users want to cross the screen, the wrapping dead zone helps them anticipate the cursor jump and gives them time to switch their visual attention to the region where the cursor will re-appear. Additionally, it provides users with more flexibility, as they can adapt their mouse movement while crossing the dead zone to control where and when the cursor will re-appear.

Compatibility with edge pointing. As discussed previously, targets located on screen edges are faster to acquire, a feature that is now commonly used in window management systems and desktops (e.g., Mac OS' menu bars and MS Windows' task bar). While a naive implementation of the wrapping technique defeats edge pointing, using a large enough dead zone re-enables this feature as clicks within the dead zone are dispatched to the screen edge where the cursor comes from (Figure 2 left).

However, using a dead zone raises two issues. First, it increases the distance users have to cover during cursor wrapping so it may reduce the number of cases where the technique is useful. Second, it is not clear which dead zone sizes are small enough not to impede cursor wrapping, while being large enough to allow comfortable edge pointing. These questions will be later addressed in our experiment sections.

Wrapping Feedback

When crossing a dead zone, a standard mouse cursor would stop on the screen's edge and the user would have to blindly move a virtual cursor within the dead zone. It has been suggested that visual feedback about the position of an off-screen cursor helps pointing in displayless space [23], so we chose to augment the dead zone with visual feedback. Since there are many possible designs, we identified the three following requirements for TORUSDESKTOP visual feedback:

Position along the edge. The feedback needs to show where the cursor is located along the screen edge: for example if the exiting edge is vertical, users need to keep track of the cursor's y-coordinate to be able to predict where it will re-appear on the opposite edge.

Position within the dead zone. The feedback also needs to show the cursor's position in the orthogonal direction, i.e., how deep the cursor is in the dead zone. This is necessary for users to be able to predict when the cursor will be teleported and better anticipate its arrival. This also allows users to see how far they can go before the cursor jumps to prevent accidental triggering, especially during edge pointing.

Feedback mirroring. The two pieces of information above should be shown both near the edge where the cursor exits the screen and near the opposite edge. Thus, users can use the feedback whether they are focusing on the exiting side – i.e., when moving close to the edge or when doing edge pointing – or on the reentering side – i.e., when using cursor wrapping to point to a distant target.

We experimented with three feedback methods: *Halos*, *Arrow* and *Ghost*. Figure 3 explains these three techniques in detail: DZ is the dead zone size, d is the cursor's distance to the dead zone entrance and the constant k is Halo's intrusion distance. Gray arrows depict how cursor movements map to movements of visual feedback.

Halos. *Halo* [7] is a technique for providing on-screen feedback for off-screen objects, e.g., showing the location of points of interest in a map on a handheld device. It shows an arc of circle next to the screen edge; the circle is centered on the off-screen object in order to convey its direction and distance. In our case the off-screen object is the cursor itself, so when it enters the dead zone, we display a Halo both on the exit and on the entrance sides of the screen (Figure 3a). As in the original technique, the arcs stick out from the displayless space with a fixed intrusion distance k.

[1]E.g., www.networkactiv.com/SoundyMouse.html, www.digicowsoftware.com/detail?_app=Wraparound

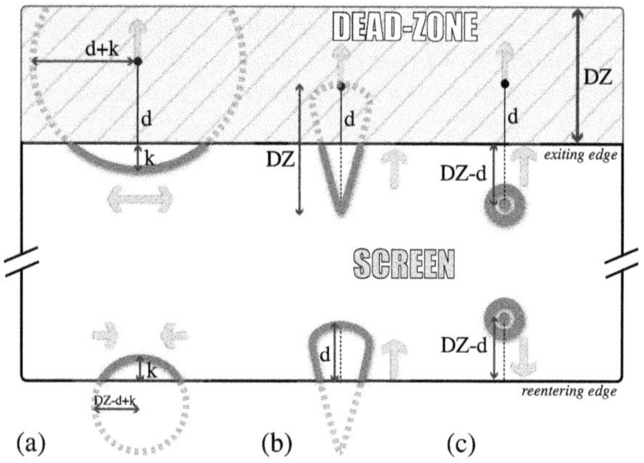

Figure 3. Halos, Arrow and Ghost TORUSDESKTOP feedback techniques for a top-to-bottom cursor wrapping.

Arrow. The Arrow feedback is inspired from a variant of Halo called *Wedge* [17]. Arrow's triangular shape is similar to Wedge's but unlike Wedge, its intrusion distance is not fixed and its shape does not change. Instead, it is a solid triangle of constant size, always perpendicular to the screen edge, that sticks out on both sides (Figure 3b). On the exit side, its flat end is attached to the cursor and its tail sticks out. On the entrance side, its tail is attached to the cursor and its flat end sticks out. The angle formed by the flat end conveys the cursor's distance in a way similar to Wedge.

Ghost. Finally, we propose a simpler visual feedback called *Ghost*, specifically designed for wrapping dead zones. Next to the dead zone's exit (bottom of Figure 3c), a circular shape is displayed whose distance to the edge is the same as the cursor's. In other terms, the edge acts like a mirror and the circular shape is like the cursor's reflection on that mirror. The same circular shape is displayed at the same distance near the dead zone's entrance.

Even if these wrapping feedback techniques fulfill the requirements we identified, it is not clear how much they help, if they help at all. We investigate this question in our study.

Corners

In a torus topology, the four screen corners are equivalent. So when the cursor reaches a corner, it is not clear where it should exit. Besides, the behavior of the cursor in the vicinity of a corner can be disturbing. For example, a cursor going to the top-right corner will re-appear either on the top-left or on the bottom-right. These two locations are nevertheless close to each other on the torus, so if the user approaches a corner with a 45-degree angle, the cursor will eventually appear on the opposite corner no matter which path it takes. However, the cursor will rapidly jump twice on the screen, which can be visually disturbing. To address these issues, we added four *corner zones* of 20 pixels each. When the cursor reaches one of these zones, it simply re-appears on the diagonally opposite corner after the dead zone crossing.

PRELIMINARY EXPERIMENTS

We conducted two preliminary experiments in order to refine the design of the technique before comparing it with direct pointing. The first experiment compares the feedback techniques and provides a first sense of the impact of the dead zone on movement time. The second one investigates the compatibility of TORUSDESKTOP with edge pointing.

Apparatus & Participants

The two experiments were conducted on a workstation running Mac OS X and with a 2560×1600 30" LCD monitor [2]. Such large displays are becoming more and more common and are likely to become a standard once their price drops. The TORUSDESKTOP software was implemented in Java. The mouse was a standard optical mouse with 500 dpi resolution and default system acceleration.

Eight unpaid volunteers, all male and right-handed, participated in the experiments. Participants were experienced mouse users with ages ranging from 24 to 31 (median 26.5). Each participant took about 60 minutes to complete each experiment after which they were given a short questionnaire.

Experiment 1: Feedback & Dead Zone

This experiment addresses the following questions:

- *Q1: Which wrapping feedback (including no feedback) is the best, with and without a dead zone?*
- *Q2: Does dead zone size affect movement time?*

Task & Design. A trial was a TORUSDESKTOP pointing task requiring subjects to cross either the left or the right edge of the screen. Subjects had to click on a *start target* at a distance DB1 to its closest edge and then acquire a *goal target* at a distance DB2 to the opposite edge by crossing the closest edge. Both start and goal targets were circles of 40 pixels. Targets were lying on the screen's horizontal centerline or placed above and below the centerline at a distance of 300 pixels, depending on the factor ALIGN (see Figure 4a). Task direction was either left to right (DIR = LR) or right to left (DIR = RL).

The experiment was a within-subject design with the main factors: (i) Feedback: FB = *None*, *Halos*, *Arrow*, *Ghost*; and (ii) Dead zone size: DZ $= 0, 125, 250, 500$.

Auxiliary factors were: (i) Distance of the start target to its closest edge, DB1 (Distance to Border 1) $= 50, 150$; (ii) Distance of the goal target to the opposite edge, DB2 (Distance to Border 2) $= 50, 150, 300$; (iii) ALIGN and DIR.

Concerning the values we chose for dead zone size, 0 is the baseline condition implemented in former cursor wrapping techniques. 125 and 250 seem to be realistic values for edge pointing [1]. We added 500 for completeness although we expect it to be too large to be used in practice. Note that for DZ = 0, the feedback condition is irrelevant and we only need to test the condition for feedback = *None*.

We grouped trials into blocks according to DZ × FB. We used 2 orders of presentation for DZ, increasing and decreasing, and counterbalanced the presentation order of FB. Before each DZ × FB condition, participants did one block of 24 practice trials then 2 blocks of measured trials. We hence collected 8 (PARTICIPANT) × 48 × (4(DZ)×1(FB=*None*) + 3(DZ=125,250,500)×3(FB)) = 4992 trials for analysis.

[2] Yielding 100.63 ppi and a pixel size of 0.025 cm.

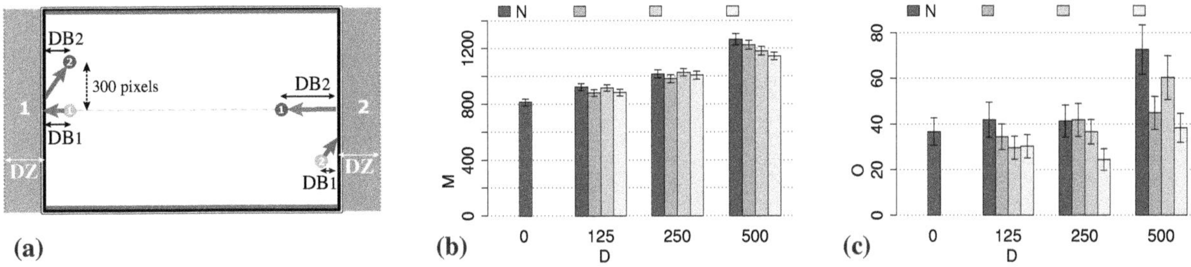

Figure 4. (a) Examples of target placement in experiment 1. Start targets are green, goal targets are red. Case 1: ALIGN **= yes,** DIR **= RL,** DZ **on the left. Case 2:** ALIGN **= no,** DIR **= LR,** DZ **on the right. (b)** MT **per deadzone and feedback. (c)** *OverShoot* **per deadzone and feedback.**

We collected three measures: (i) *MT*, the time from the click on the start target to a successful click on the goal target; (ii) *Error*, whether or not there was a click outside the target; and (iii) *OverShoot*, the distance in pixels of the furthest point reached by the pointer to the goal target.

Quantitative Results. We removed 0.75% outliers (trials with a *MT* that is 3 standard deviations apart from the mean *MT* within the condition) and duplicated the data for DZ = 0 for each FB in order to perform a full factorial analysis: FB × DZ × Random(PARTICIPANT) with *MT*, *Error* and *OverShoot*.

An analysis of variance reveals an effect of DZ on *MT* ($F_{3,21} = 80.0, p < 0.0001$). A Tukey post-hoc test shows a significant difference in means between all DZ, with *MT* increasing with DZ (Figure 4b). We observed no significant effect of FB on *MT*. However, we found a significant interaction FB × DZ ($F_{9,63} = 2.62, p = 0.0123$), which can be observed in Figure 4b: the difference between mean *MT*s for each FB value is the largest for DZ = 500. Indeed a post-hoc test shows no significant difference between the FBs for DZ $\leq$ 250, whereas for DZ = 500, *Ghost* is significantly faster than *Halos* and *None*, and *Arrow* is significantly faster than *None*.

We found an average error rate of 7.9%. An analysis of variance using a nominal logistic test for the model *Error* $\sim$ FB × DZ reveals no significant effect, error rates being very close for each FB × DZ (min 5.0%, max 9.9%).

For *OverShoot*, we found a significant effect of both FB ($F_{3,21} = 6.32, p = 0.0032$) and DZ ($F_{3,21} = 8.01, p = 0.0010$) (see Figure 4c). Post-hoc Tukey tests show that *Ghost* exhibits significantly less *OverShoot* than other feedback and that *OverShoot* is significantly larger for DZ = 500. However, there is a significant interaction FB × DZ ($F_{9,63} = 3.82, p = 0.0007$), which can be observed in Figure 4c: *OverShoot* is significantly lower for *Ghost* than for all other FB when DZ = 250. For DZ = 125, the only significant difference is between *Ghost* and *None*. For DZ = 500 we observe more *OverShoot* for *None* than for other feedback and less for *Ghost* than for *Arrow*.

Qualitative Results. In the post-experiment questionnaire, participants were asked to rank the feedback techniques globally and for each dead zone size. Among the eight participants, five globally ranked *Ghost* first, and each of the three other techniques was ranked first by one participant (*Ghost* was ranked second, third and last in these cases). Rankings by DZ are consistent with global ranking. Only three participants ranked *None* higher for DZ = 125.

Summary. Back to our first question *Q1*, *Ghost* seems to be the best choice for TORUSDESKTOP for all dead zone sizes: even if it does not exhibit a significantly better performance – except for the limit case DZ = 500 – it yields the smallest *OverShoot* and was preferred by participants. Concerning *Q2*, it is confirmed that *MT* increases with DZ.

Experiment 2: Edge Pointing

The questions this second experiment addresses are:

- *Q1: Does a dead zone help users performing edge-pointing tasks? If yes, is there an optimal dead zone size?*
- *Q2: Does wrapping feedback help or impede users during edge pointing?*

Stimuli & Design. A trial consisted in an edge pointing task where the subject had to click on a circular *start target* and then acquire a *goal target* on a screen edge. The goal target was located to the left or right end of the screen, and was vertically centered (Figure 5a). It had a width of 40 pixels and two possible heights H $= 40, 125$ – a size comparable to buttons on typical task bars and menu bars. Start targets were located on a 3 × 3 grid designed to cover several angles of approach. Their location was defined by DB $= 200, 1200, 2200$, their distance to the edge where the goal target was, and DH $= 0, 600, -600$, their distance to the horizontal centerline of the screen.

The experiment was a within-subject design with the same main factors as the first experiment: (i) Feedback: FB = *None*, *Ghost*; and (ii) Dead zone: DZ $= 0, 125, 250, 500,$ inf. Given the findings of the first experiment, we only tested the *None* and *Ghost* feedback techniques in this experiment. We used the same dead zone sizes as in the first experiment and added an 'infinite' size (i.e., no cursor wrapping) as a baseline condition to test standard edge pointing.

Trials were grouped into blocks by DZ × FB. For each DZ × FB condition, participants started with one practice block of 2 × 2(H) × 3(DB) × 3(DH) = 36 trials, then proceeded with two measured blocks. Thus, for each participant, we collected 2 × 36 × (2(DZ=0,inf) + 2(FB) × 3(DZ=125,250,500)) = 576 trials for analysis.

In addition to *MT* and *Error* (defined as in previous experiment), we measured the dead zone distance effectively used *UseDistDZ* – i.e., the maximum horizontal travel distance inside the dead zone – and the number of times the cursor went past the dead zone *DZOverShoot*.

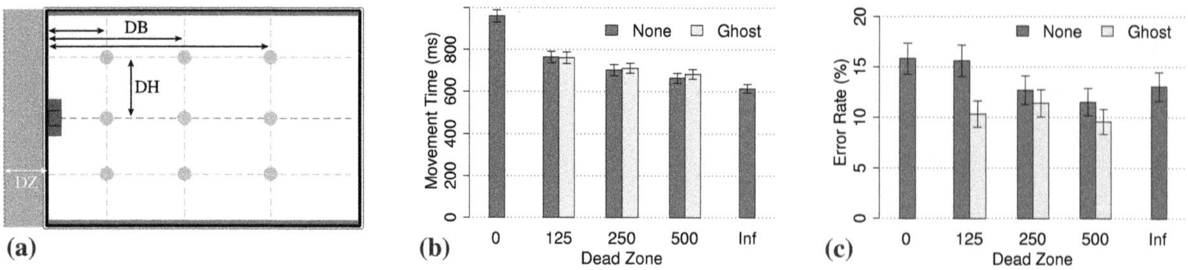

Figure 5. (a) Target placement in experiment 2. (b) MT per deadzone and feedback. (c) Error rate per deadzone and feedback.

Quantitative Results. We removed 0.97% outliers and duplicated the data for DZ = 0 and DZ = inf with the *Ghost* feedback to be able to perform a full factorial analysis FB × DZ × Random(PARTICIPANT).

An analysis of variance reveals an effect of DZ on *MT* ($F_{4,28} = 38.6, p < 0.0001$). As expected *MT* decreases as DZ increases (Figure 5b). A post-hoc Tukey test shows that (i) DZ = 0 is significantly slower than DZ $\geq$ 125; (ii) DZ = 125 is significantly slower than DZ $\geq$ 500; (iii) DZ = 250 is significantly slower than DZ = inf; and that (iv) difference is not significant for other DZ pairs. Indeed, we observe that the biggest improvement is from DZ = 0 to DZ = 125 (a 20% speed up).

As Figure 5b suggests, an analysis of variance reveals no effect of FB ($F_{1,7} = 0.42, p = 0.5463$) and no interaction FB × DZ ($F_{4,28} = 0.55, p = 0.6989$) on *MT*. Practical equivalence tests with a threshold of 20 ms (less than 3% of the grand mean) give positive results ($p \leq 0.02$), confirming there is no difference in MT between *None* and *Ghost*.

Regarding error, a nominal logistic ANOVA for the model FB × DZ ~ *Error* (on the data set where 125 $\leq$ DZ $\leq$ 500) shows a significant effect of FB ($\chi^2 = 6.12, p = 0.0134$) but no effect of DZ ($\chi^2 = 2.79, p = 0.2477$) and no interaction FB × DZ ($\chi^2 = 1.99, p = 0.3697$). Figure 5c shows that *Ghost* is less error-prone than *None*.

For *DZOverShoot*, the percentage of trials with accidental cursor wrapping is significantly higher without a dead zone (24.37% for DZ = 0 and less than 7% for DZ > 0). We noticed small differences between *Ghost* and *None* – *Ghost* always yielding less overshoots – but these are not significant.

Regarding *UseDistDZ*, i.e., the distance covered in the dead zone, we observed that the 90% quantile is close to half the dead zone size for all DZ < inf. It is close to 600 pixels for DZ = inf, a result consistent with previous studies [1].

Qualitative Results. After the experiment, participants were asked to tell (i) whether the *Ghost* feedback helped them select the target and (ii) whether they found the feedback distracting. Six participants out of eight agreed or strongly agreed that the feedback helped (one was neutral and one disagreed). However, half the participants agreed or strongly agreed that the feedback was also distracting.

Summary. Back to our first question *Q1*, this study confirms that when cursor wrapping is enabled, users are more efficient at selecting targets on the screen edges if a dead zone is provided. Not only a dead zone expands these targets ($W = 40 + DZ$), but it also prevents accidental cursor wrapping that can be time-costly to recover from. The high cost of accidental wrapping is confirmed by participants' conservative use of dead zones when doing edge pointing. As Figure 5b does not exhibit an asymptote for DZ < inf, the study does not suggest an optimal dead zone size. It however reveals that a small deadzone (125 pixels) is enough to reduce movement time by 20%.

Regarding *Q2*, we observe that the *Ghost* feedback does not impair performance but does not improve it either. However, it significantly reduces errors, suggesting that feedback makes users more accurate. Since in real systems pointing errors can have a high cost in terms of time and user frustration, this further confirms that *Ghost* feedback should be provided. Some users might however find the feedback distracting, as suggested by answers to our questionnaire.

COMPARING DIRECT POINTING & TORUSDESKTOP

In the two previous experiments, we validated and refined the design of TORUSDESKTOP by confirming the benefits of a wrapping dead zone and by identifying the best wrapping feedback technique. The goal of this third experiment is to evaluate TORUSDESKTOP by comparing it with conventional pointing (i.e., is it worth opening the backdoor?).

To this end, we presented subjects with various pointing tasks and had them either use direct pointing only (condition *Direct*) or use the backdoor only (condition *Wrapping*). The goal was to assess if TORUSDESKTOP can help, and when. But since in real settings deciding whether or not to use cursor wrapping may take time and/or yield suboptimal choices, we added a more realistic condition where it was up to the subject to go through the backdoor or not (condition *Torus*).

Figure 6b qualitatively illustrates our initial expectations. Using *Direct*, the further apart the start and the goal targets are, the higher the movement time. *Wrapping* is likely to show the opposite trend since the further apart the targets are, the closer they are on a torus topology (but note that Fitts' law cannot account for possible distracting effects of cursor wrapping). We hypothesized that performance under the *Torus* condition would roughly follow the minimum of *Direct* and *Wrapping*, plus a possible penalty due to choice.

Apparatus & Participants

The apparatus was the same as in the previous experiments. We recruited a total of 18 participants (5 female), all right-handed and experienced mouse users, with ages ranging from 23 to 35 (median 27.8). 14 of them participated in at least one of the previous experiments or pilot studies.

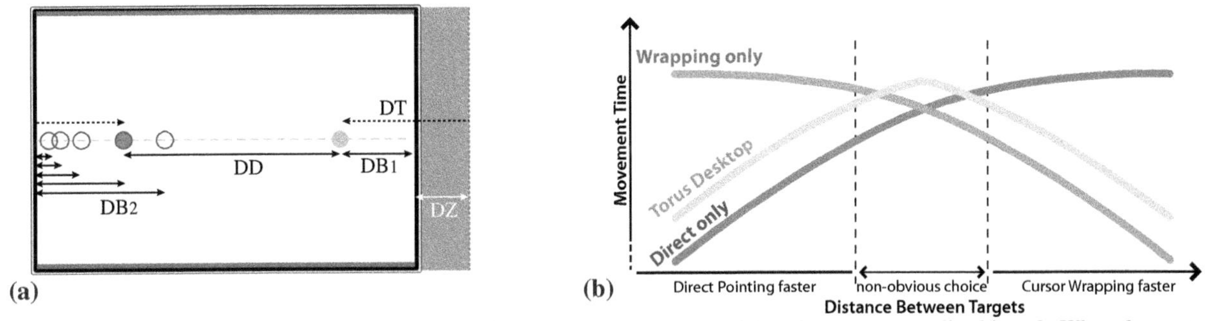

Figure 6. (a) Targets placement in experiment 3. The start target is green and potential goal targets are outlined in red. When the start target is acquired, the actual goal target appears with a solid color and other targets disappear. (b) Expected performance model. TORUSDESKTOP should behave as the most efficient technique according to the distance, though a penalty may be considered because of the choice between the techniques.

Stimuli & Design

Given the results of previous experiments, we used the *Ghost* feedback and a dead zone of 125 pixels for *Wrapping* and *Torus*. Recall this dead zone size yields a reasonable trade-off that meets the demands of both edge pointing and Torus pointing (i.e., neither of them is strongly penalized). As before, subjects had to click on a start target and acquire a goal target as fast as possible. Both targets were located on the horizontal centerline of the screen and were 40-pixel large[3].

At the beginning of a trial, all potential goal targets were shown. When the subject acquired the start target, the actual goal target appeared with a solid color and non-targets disappeared (see Figure 6a). This design was motivated by the inclusion of the *Torus* condition. In real settings, users might or might not know exactly where to click when they initiate a pointing movement. Our design is a trade-off between these two situations, since it reminds users of the possible target locations, but does not give them complete information about the task to prevent them from carefully deciding whether or not use the backdoor before the timing starts.

In addition to the pointing conditions TECH, the experiment included the factor DB1, the distance from the start target to the closest screen edge; and DB2, the distance from the goal target to the opposite edge. These two factors fully define the pointing tasks, whose direct pointing distance is DD = $2560 - (\text{DB1}+\text{DB2})$, where 2560 is the screen width; and whose torus pointing distance is DT = $\text{DB1}+\text{DB2}+125$, where 125 is the size of the dead zone (Figure 6a). Both DB1 and DB2 values were $\{50, 125, 250, 500, 750\}$. We chose these values according to an extensive pilot study suggesting that among all possible pointing tasks defined by these DB1×DB2 pairs, 7 clearly favor *Wrapping*, 7 clearly favor *Direct* and the remaining 11 yield comparable performances.

The presentation order of the techniques was counterbalanced. Prior to the experiment, the *Direct* and *Wrapping* techniques were introduced to the participants with two short practice sessions. Then, the experiment was divided in two parts. First, participants performed 4 series of 25 trials per technique. A series of trials included all the possible combinations of DB1 and DB2 and was fully randomized. This part was exclusively a training session. Then, participants performed 1 series of practice trials followed by 5 series of measured trials per technique. Thus, for each participant, we collected a total of 3 (TECH) × 5 (repetition) × 5 (DB1) × 5 (DB2) = 375 trials for analysis.

We collected movement time (*MT*) and errors (*Error*) defined as in previous experiments. The experiment lasted about 45 minutes after which participants were given a short questionnaire and were interviewed about the strategies they developed in the *Torus* condition.

Quantitative Results

We removed 0.76% outliers defined as in previous experiments and performed a full factorial analysis with the model TECH×DD×Random(PARTICIPANT) and the finer model TECH×DB1×DB2×Random(PARTICIPANT). We found no learning effect and no significant difference in performance between the 14 subjects who were involved in preliminary experiments and the 4 new subjects.

Average Performance. The ANOVA reveals no effect of TECH on *MT* ($F_{2,34} = 0.245, p = 0.7836$ for the DD model and $F_{2,34} = 0.612, p = 0.5481$ for the DB1×DB2 model). Mean *MT* are close for *Direct* (1091 ms), *Wrapping* (1094 ms) and *Torus* (1108 ms). These similarities confirm that we chose well-balanced pairs of DB1×DB2 for *Wrapping* and *Direct*, but also suggest that the improvement promised by *Torus* may have been outweighted by the cost of choice. This will be discussed later.

We found a significant effect of TECH on *ErrorRate* ($F_{2,34} = 7.74, p = 0.0017$ for the DD model and $F_{2,34} = 7.40, p = 0.0021$ for the DB1×DB2 model). A post-hoc Tukey test shows that *Wrapping* and *Torus* are significantly less error-prone than *Direct*, with an error rate of about 6.6% for *Wrapping* and *Torus* versus 9.2% for *Direct*. A possible explanation is that participants were more careful with *Wrapping* and *Torus*, as they were less familiar with these techniques than with *Direct*.

Effect of Direct Distance. The ANOVA reveals a significant effect of DD ($F_{13,221} = 14.0, p < 0.0001$) and a significant interaction TECH×DD on *MT* ($F_{26,442} = 12.5, p < 0.0001$). We found no significant effect or interaction on *ErrorRate*.

Figure 7 shows *MT* as a function of DD for the three techniques. In accordance with our first intuitions, *Direct* gets slower as DD increases and *Wrapping* gets faster, although the

[3]Pilots studies did not show any effect of target size when comparing TORUSDESKTOP and direct pointing.

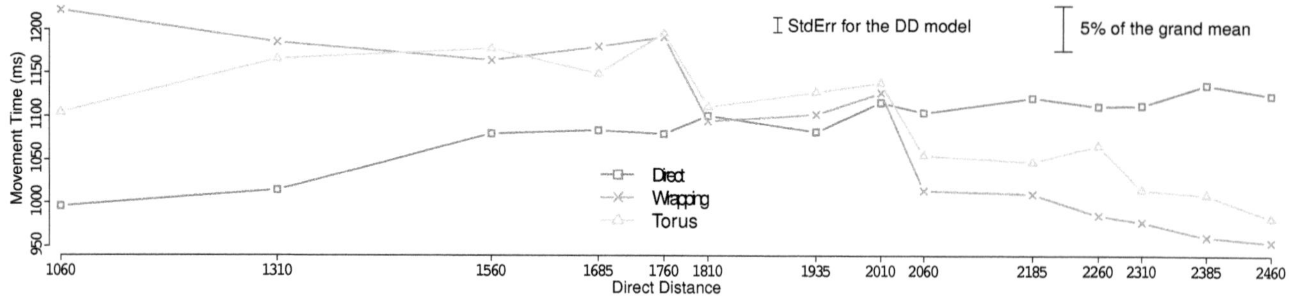

Figure 7. *Direct* **vs.** *Wrapping* **vs.** *Torus* **as a function of DD. Since the y-axis has its origin at 950, scale bars of error and grand mean are shown.**

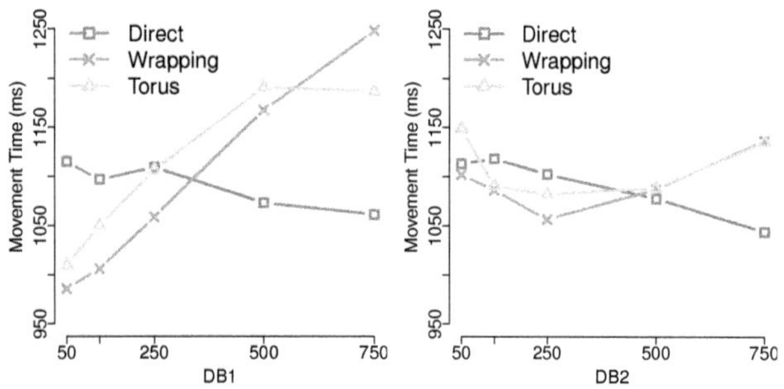

Figure 8. *MT* **as a function of DB1 (left) and DB2 (right) per TECH.**

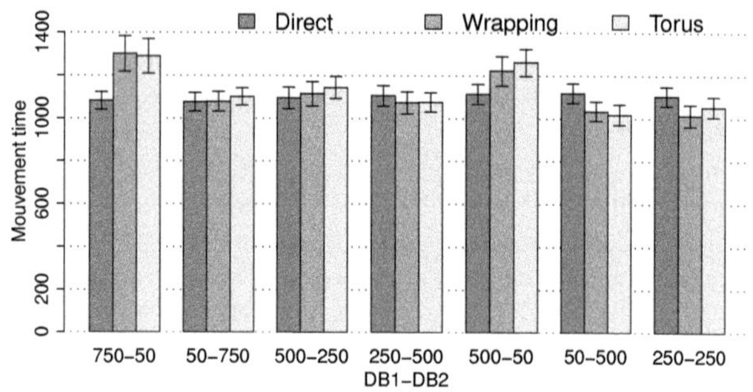

Figure 9. *MT* **as a fct. of certain critical DB1-DB2 couples per TECH.**

curve exhibits some irregularities (which will be explained when analyzing DB1 and DB2). The two techniques are comparable where the two curves cross, i.e., between DD=1810 and 2010 pixels. This corresponds to a Torus travel distance of only DT=675 to 875 pixels, suggesting that *Wrapping* is slower than what Fitts' law would have predicted. Taking trials where DD$\sim$DT, we estimate this penalty to about $200\,ms$ [4]. This penalty is likely due to the difficulty in reacquiring the mouse cursor, but far from invalidating the whole approach, it merely increases the target distance above which *Wrapping* starts to be beneficial. Indeed, post-hoc tests show clear benefits for *Wrapping* above DD=2010 pixels, i.e., 80% the screen size in our experimental setup.

Figure 7 shows that the behavior of *Torus* is similar to *Wrapping* for DD>2010 pixels, where it exhibits a choice penalty of about $50\,ms$ but still clearly outperforms *Direct*. For DD=1810 to 2010 the 3 conditions exhibit similar performance. The left part of the curve is however less consistent with our initial expectations: for DD<1810, the performance with *Torus* is close to *Wrapping* instead of being close to *Direct* as in Figure 6b. One explanation is that participants failed to choose direct pointing when it was more efficient (our later experimental data confirms this). However, *Torus* also gets closer to *Direct* as DD decreases, which suggests that subjects might still favor *Direct* when it is clearly beneficial.

Effects of DB1 *and* DB2. We found significant effects of both DB1 ($F_{4,68} = 68.9$, $p < 0.0001$) and DB2 ($F_{4,68} = 3.68$, $p < 0.0090$) on *MT*. We also found significant interactions DB1×DB2 ($F_{16,272} = 6.29$, $p < 0.0001$), DB1×TECH ($F_{8,136} = 28.5$, $p < 0.0001$) and DB2×TECH ($F_{8,136} = 6.67$, $p < 0.0001$). We found no significant effect or interaction on *ErrorRate*.

[4]This value is consistent with a Fitts' law analysis we conducted on an extensive pilot study comparing *Wrapping* with *Direct*.

The interaction DB1×TECH can be observed in Figure 8 left. As DB1 increases, *MT* decreases for *Direct* (because DD decreases) and increases for *Wrapping* (because DT increases). For *Torus*, *MT* behaves like *Wrapping* up to DB1=750, suggesting *Direct* was preferred when the start target was very far from the edge. Ideally, *MT* should have followed *Direct*'s trend starting from DB1=500, but both the cost of the choice and the overuse of the backdoor seem to have prevented this.

Surprisingly, the interaction DB2×TECH is quite different (see Figure 8 right). For the same reasons as above, *MT* decreases with DB2 for *Direct*. But for *Wrapping*, *MT* follows a catenary curve with a minimum at DB2=250. Since *Wrapping* should normally increase with DB2, this suggests an issue with goal targets being very close to the edge. This issue also impacts the *Torus* condition, which exhibits the same minimum at DB2=250.

The asymmetric effects of DB1 and DB2 are further detailed in Figure 9, which shows *MT* by TECH for each DB1-DB2 pair that yields a DD value of 1760, 1810, 2010 or 2060. These values correspond to the irregularities we previously observed in Figure 7. Figure 9 confirms that *Wrapping* does poorly when DB2 is small. For example, *Wrapping* does much worse with the pair 750-50 than the pair 50-750, despite these pairs yielding the same DD=1760. This is the cause for the peak in Figure 7. This peak is followed by a sharp decline at DD=1810 which involves the more balanced pairs 500-250 and 250-500. *Torus* exhibits the same irregularities.

This asymmetry can be explained in the light of the optimized dual sub-movement model [22] and by considering *when* in the pointing movement cursor warping occurs. Using *Wrapping*, the mouse cursor first travels the distance DB1 + DZ, then warps and re-appears on the opposite side, after which it travels a distance DB2 before reaching the target. If DB2 is small compared to DB1 + DZ, the warping occurs at

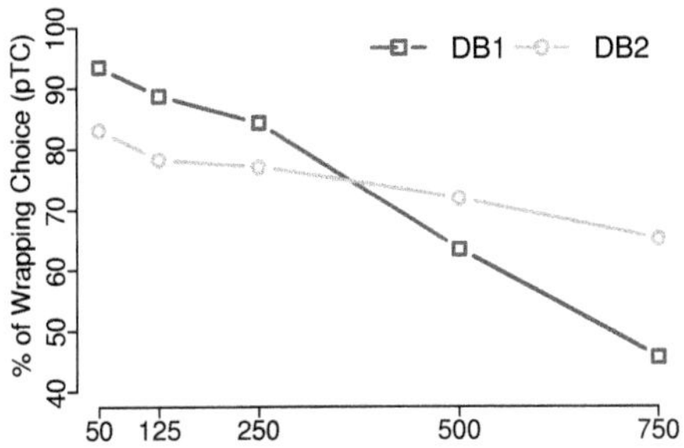

Figure 10. Percentage of *Wrapping* choice for DB1 and DB2.

the end of the movement – i.e., the corrective phase where visual feedback is the most crucial. Cursor warping requires attention shift, which likely disrupts the corrective process and slows users down. Conversely, if DB2 is large compared to DB1 + DZ, the warping happens during the initial ballistic phase of the movement where visual feedback is not used, thus its impact on performance is less severe.

Note that we could have ran a post-hoc analysis, but doing so with such a large number of data points is subject to methodological issues (high risks of type I or type II errors) and a correct analysis would have required a fair amount of space to justify and report. Since the significant interactions we found and the Figures 7, 8 and 9 are already quite informative we chose not to perform theses analyses.

Choice Strategies

So far, our results show that using the backdoor was beneficial when more than 80% of the screen had to be traveled. However, we observed mixed results when subjects had to make a choice, especially when direct pointing was the best choice. Therefore, we further analyze the choices made in the *Torus* condition. We consider the measure *pTC*, i.e., the % of the time where subjects chose wrapping, the model DD×Random(PARTICIPANT) and the finer model DB1×DB2×Random(PARTICIPANT) for this condition.

Unsurprisingly, DD has an effect on *pTC* ($F_{13,221} = 25.2$, $p < 0.0001$) and *pTC* increases with DD: the larger the distance to travel, the more often the backdoor was used.

DB1 and DB2 also have an effect on *pTC* ($F_{4,68} = 28.0$, $p < 0.0001$ and $F_{4,68} = 9.61$, $p < 0.0001$ respectively), with no DB1×DB2 interaction. As can be seen in Figure 10, the closer to the edges the targets were, the more often cursor wrapping was used. The dissimilar slopes further suggest that subjects gave more weight to the distance of the start target when they had to make a choice. This might be due to the fact that this information was available before DB2.

During the post-experiment interviews, participants reported using different strategies that can be summarized as:

- START: only wrap when the start target is close to the edge.
- GOAL: only wrap when the goal target is close to the edge.
- WRAP: always wrap the mouse cursor.
- DIRECT: always use direct pointing.
- NOCLUTCH: take the path that minimizes mouse clutching.
- RANDOM: choose more or less randomly.

10 participants reported relying mostly on START and 3 reported using it as a secondary strategy. 5 participants reported using WRAP as their primary strategy and 1 mentioned it as a secondary strategy. All the other strategies have been mentioned as a main strategy only once. GOAL was mentioned as a secondary strategy 3 times. Reported strategies were consistent with mean *pTC* per participant and with our analyses of the effects of DB1 and DB2 on *pTC*, except for two participants who reported using START and DIRECT but actually chose wrapping 93% and 76% of the time.

Overall, participants overused the backdoor: the global mean of *pTC* is 75% (std dev. 15%, median 74%). Even in the worst case scenario (DB1=DB2=750, DD=1060 and DT=1625), wrapping was used about 30% of the time. This trend could be partly due to a "good user" effect. It is also likely that participants were not accurate enough at estimating when cursor wrapping would beat direct pointing. It could be that with more training, users would develop a habit of the technique and start making close-to-optimal choices. But since we used an extensive training session and did not find a learning effect – even for subjects who were not involved in preliminary experiments – TORUSDESKTOP could probably benefit from visual clues that help users make optimal choices and develop more rational strategies.

Another question concerns the cognitive load associated with the choice. Although we did not measure cognitive load formally, we gave a post-experiment questionnaire where we asked subjects if they found it difficult to choose between direct pointing and wrapping. Out of 18, 4 strongly disagreed and 9 disagreed, suggesting cognitive load is moderate.

CONCLUSION AND FUTURE DIRECTIONS

Despite being an old idea, cursor wrapping is a simple and target-agnostic way of reducing target distance in pointing tasks. We discussed how such a technique should be designed and proposed the TORUSDESKTOP technique: it includes a dead zone that prevents accidental cursor warping and facilitates edge pointing, and a visual feedback that helps keeping track of the cursor inside the dead zone.

We tested several variations over this design and found that our *Ghost* off-screen feedback reduces overshoots during both edge pointing and cursor wrapping and is well-received by end-users, and that a 125-pixel dead zone (5% the screen size[5]) yields good performance for edge pointing while not sacrificing cursor wrapping performance. Recall the optimal dead zone size is infinite for edge pointing and is zero for cursor wrapping. However, a 125-pixel dead zone size is a reasonable trade-off where neither task is strongly penalized.

We also compared TORUSDESKTOP with direct pointing and uncovered the following potential sources of difficulties with the cursor wrapping approach:

- Cursor teleportation adds a time penalty of ~200ms,
- Targets very close to the edges are harder to acquire,
- Chosing whether or not to use the backdoor has some cost.

[5]All figures are given according to our experimental setup that involves a 30" 2560x1600 display.

In our study, the cost of choice took the form of a small time penality (~50ms) when cursor wrapping was the most beneficial, and of suboptimal choices (overuse of the backdoor) when direct pointing was the best option.

However, rather than invalidating the whole approach, these difficulties merely increase the travel distance above which TORUSDESKTOP starts being beneficial. Indeed, our study shows that cursor wrapping outperforms direct pointing above a travel distance of 2010 pixels (80% the screen size), and these benefits are preserved when users have to choose between direct pointing and cursor wrapping. These benefits can translate to much higher gains when one needs to regularly acquire targets close to an edge (e.g., toolbar buttons), or when going back-and-forth between two very distant targets (e.g., toolbars placed at opposite sides of the screen). However, despite extensive training, our study participants were not very accurate at estimating which technique will be the most efficient under a given condition. We are investigating how to augment TORUSDESKTOP with visual clues and feedforward techniques to help users make optimal choices and develop better strategies in the long run.

Further design is also required to support TORUSDESKTOP in multi-display environments. Several strategies can be considered such as disabling cursor wrapping on adjacent screen edges, restricting wrapping to the active screen or supporting on-demand wrapping/screen jump.

Finally, a field study of TORUSDESKTOP is clearly needed to validate the approach and ensure that cursor wrapping can be adopted and effectively used by end users in their everyday desktop usage. As a first step towards this goal, we implemented an application that enables TORUSDESKTOP at the system-level on Mac OS X and that is freely available at `http://insitu.lri.fr/TorusDesktop`.

REFERENCES

1. C. Appert, O. Chapuis, and M. Beaudouin-Lafon. Evaluation of pointing performance on screen edges. In *AVI '08*, 119–126. ACM, 2008.
2. T. Asano, E. Sharlin, Y. Kitamura, K. Takashima, and F. Kishino. Predictive interaction using the delphian desktop. In *UIST '05*, 133–141. ACM, 2005.
3. R. Balakrishnan. "Beating" Fitts' law: virtual enhancements for pointing facilitation. *IJHCS*, 61(6):857–874, 2004.
4. P. Baudisch, E. Cutrell, M. Czerwinski, D. Robbins, P. Tandler, B. Bederson, and A. Zierlinger. Drag-and-pop and drag-and-pick: techniques for accessing remote screen content on touch- and pen-operated systems. In *Interact '03*, 57–64. IOS, 2003.
5. P. Baudisch, E. Cutrell, K. Hinckley, and R. Gruen. Mouse ether: accelerating the acquisition of targets across multi-monitor displays. In *CHI '04 EA*, 1379–1382. ACM, 2004.
6. P. Baudisch, E. Cutrell, and G. Robertson. High-density cursor: a visualization technique that helps users keep track of fast-moving mouse cursors. In *Interact '03*, 236–243. IOS, 2003.
7. P. Baudisch and R. Rosenholtz. Halo: a technique for visualizing off-screen objects. In *CHI '03*, 481–488. ACM, 2003.
8. H. Benko and S. Feiner. Pointer warping in heterogeneous multi-monitor environments. In *GI '07*, 111–117. ACM, 2007.
9. R. Blanch, Y. Guiard, and M. Beaudouin-Lafon. Semantic pointing: improving target acquisition with control-display ratio adaptation. In *CHI '04*, 519–526. ACM, 2004.
10. R. Blanch and M. Ortega. Rake cursor: improving pointing performance with concurrent input channels. In *CHI '09*, 1415–1418. ACM, 2009.
11. G. Casiez, D. Vogel, R. Balakrishnan, and A. Cockburn. The impact of control-display gain on user performance in pointing tasks. *HCI*, 23(3):215–250, 2008.
12. O. Chapuis, J.-B. Labrune, and E. Pietriga. Dynaspot: speed-dependent area cursor. In *CHI '09*, 1391–1400. ACM, 2009.
13. O. Chapuis and N. Roussel. UIMarks: Quick graphical interaction with specific targets. In *UIST '10*, 173–182. ACM, 2010.
14. J. Farris, K. Jones, and B. Anders. Factors affecting the usefulness of impenetrable interface element borders. *Human factors*, 44(4):578, 2002.
15. T. Grossman and R. Balakrishnan. The bubble cursor: enhancing target acquisition by dynamic resizing of the cursor's activation area. In *CHI '05*, 281–290. ACM, 2005.
16. Y. Guiard, R. Blanch, and M. Beaudouin-Lafon. Object pointing: a complement to bitmap pointing in guis. In *GI '04*, 9–16. CHCC Society, 2004.
17. S. Gustafson, P. Baudisch, C. Gutwin, and P. Irani. Wedge: clutter-free visualization of off-screen locations. In *CHI '08*, 787–796. ACM, 2008.
18. A. Hurst, J. Mankoff, A. Dey, and S. Hudson. Dirty desktops: using a patina of magnetic mouse dust to make common interactor targets easier to select. In *UIST '07*, 183–186. ACM, 2007.
19. M. Kobayashi and T. Igarashi. Ninja cursors: using multiple cursors to assist target acquisition on large screens. In *CHI '08*, 949–958. ACM, 2008.
20. S. MacKenzie. Fitts' law as a research and design tool in human-computer interaction. *HCI*, 7:91–139, 1992.
21. M. McGuffin and R. Balakrishnan. Fitts' law and expanding targets: experimental studies and designs for user interfaces. *ACM ToCHI*, 12(4):388–422, 2005.
22. D. Meyer, J. Smith, S. Kornblum, R. Abrams, and C. Wright. Optimality in human motor performance: Ideal control of rapid aimed movements. *Psych. Review*, 95(3):340–370, 1988.
23. M. Nacenta, R. Mandryk, and C. Gutwin. Targeting across displayless space. In *CHI '08*, 777–786. ACM, 2008.
24. G. Ramos, A. Cockburn, R. Balakrishnan, and M. Beaudouin-Lafon. Pointing lenses: Facilitating stylus input through visual- and motor-space magnification. In *CHI '07*, 757–766, 2007.
25. K.-J. Räihä and O. Spakov. Disambiguating Ninja cursors with eye gaze. In *CHI '09*, 1411–1414. ACM, 2009.
26. J. Wobbrock, J. Fogarty, S.-Y. Liu, S. Kimuro, and S. Harada. The angle mouse: target-agnostic dynamic gain adjustment based on angular deviation. In *CHI '09*, 1401–1410. ACM, 2009.
27. A. Worden, N. Walker, K. Bharat, and S. Hudson. Making computers easier for older adults to use: area cursors and sticky icons. In *CHI '97*, 266–271. ACM, 1997.
28. S. Zhai, C. Morimoto, and S. Ihde. Manual and gaze input cascaded (MAGIC) pointing. In *CHI '99*, 246–253. ACM, 1999.

Comet and Target Ghost: Techniques for Selecting Moving Targets

Khalad Hasan[1], Tovi Grossman[2], Pourang Irani[3]

[1]Department of Computer Science
University of Manitoba,
Winnipeg, Manitoba, Canada
khalad@cs.umanitoba.ca

[2]Autodesk Research
210 King St. East,
Toronto, Ontario, Canada
tovi.grossman@autodesk.com

[3]Department of Computer Science
University of Manitoba,
Winnipeg, Manitoba, Canada
irani@cs.umanitoba.ca

ABSTRACT
Numerous applications such as simulations, air traffic control systems, and video surveillance systems are inherently composed of spatial objects that move in a scene. In many instances, users can benefit from tools that allow them to select these targets in real-time, without having to pause the dynamic display. However, selecting moving objects is considerably more difficult and error prone than selecting stationary targets. In this paper, we evaluate the effectiveness of several techniques that assist in selecting moving targets. We present Comet, a technique that enhances targets based on their speed and direction. We also introduce Target Ghost, which allows users to select a static proxy of the target, while leaving the motion uninterrupted. We found a speed benefit for the Comet in a 1D selection task in comparison to other cursor and target enhancements. For 2D selection, Comet outperformed Bubble cursor but only when Target Ghost was not available. We conclude with guidelines for design.

ACM Classification: H5.2 [Information interfaces and presentation]: User Interfaces. - Graphical user interfaces.

General terms: Design, Human Factors.

Keywords: Moving targets selection, Comet, Target Ghost.

INTRODUCTION
Animations consisting of moving targets are ubiquitous and are found in applications such as video surveillance systems, molecular simulations and air traffic control displays. Pointing is a fundamental task in direct manipulation interfaces and users can benefit from being able to directly select one or more moving targets. For example, an air traffic controller may select an airplane to view its flight plan. Similarly, video tracking software can allow users to select objects in real-time, to retrieve statistics on a basketball player, in mid-play.

Selecting a moving target is challenging. The user must continually track the target and simultaneously plan to move the cursor over it. If the user stops moving the cursor, clicking on the mouse button for selection could cause the target to slip away from the pointer. Currently, we possess limited knowledge on which interaction techniques can best support this task.

One option is to allow users to pause the motion for selection. However, this may cause viewers to miss important information [5] in certain real-time applications such as air traffic control systems or video games.

Figure 1 – Moving objects can be enhanced with a Comet to enlarge their activation area. We show its value in the case of a video feed (vehicle paths were annotated manually). When a car is selected more information (top left corner) is available.

In this paper we evaluate the performance of various existing and new techniques that can assist in selecting moving targets. We present *Comet* and *Target Ghost*. Comet enhances a target based on its movement trajectory and speed to facilitate selection. With Comet the target's activation size is increased with an appended tail, analogous to comets that are seen in the sky. Faster targets have longer tails than slower targets, thus leveling the field for selecting targets with various movement speeds (Figure 1).

We implement a variation of pausing by designing Target Ghost, a proxy-based technique [2, 4]. Target Ghost creates static proxies of all the objects in the scene based on their position at time of invocation, but does not disrupt the overall movement of objects. Users can then select the motionless targets. Ghosting can be used in conjunction with new or existing techniques, such as the Area cursor [16] and Bubble cursor [11].

We conducted a 1D moving target acquisition experiment, and found that user performance was significantly improved with Comet over the Bubble cursor and variants of Target Ghost, including the Basic and Bubble Ghosts. In a 2D experiment, we also manipulated the predictability of the object's movement path, to create conditions where objects' movements were highly predictable (i.e. straight line) or less predictable (i.e. random movement). Our results reveal that Comet still outperforms the Bubble cursor, but only without using it with Target Ghost.

Our contributions in this work are: 1) an evaluation of competing interfaces for selecting moving objects; 2) designs of Comet and Target Ghost that work in 2D; 3) techniques for selecting targets with high and low predictability movement paths; 4) a set of guidelines for assisting interface designers in supporting moving target selection.

LITERATURE REVIEW

Our work is inspired by work done on the selection of motion-less and motion-based targets.

Selection of motionless targets

Pointing tasks with motionless targets can be generally captured by Fitts' law [10, 17]. The movement time T needed to point to a target of width W and at distance (or amplitude) A can be expressed as:

$$T = a + b \log_2 (A/W + 1) \qquad (1)$$

where a and b are empirically determined constants [17]. The logarithmic term log (A/W + 1) is referred to as the Index of Difficulty (ID) (measured in "bits") of the task. Researchers have also extended Fitts' law to model two- and three dimensional targets [17] and also to targets of varying shapes [12]. Based on the above equation, performance benefits can be obtained by increasing the width of the target, decreasing its amplitude, or by doing both. Since virtual pointing tasks are less constrained than pointing in the physical world, researchers have shown that altering the properties of the virtual object or of the cursor can lead to significant performance benefits [1].

The Area cursor [16] converts a point cursor by giving it a larger width and thereby increases its effective activation area. The Area cursor has been shown to follow the properties of Fitts' law where the width of the target is instead replaced by the width of the cursor [16] in equation (1).

Grossman and Balakrishnan [11] built upon the concept of the area cursor with the introduction of the Bubble cursor. Their technique dynamically resizes the cursor's activation area based on the number and proximity of targets, and ensures that only one is selected from any given cursor position. The Bubble cursor is known to be effective under a variety of contexts [11]. However, there has not been any systematic evaluation of the bubble or area cursors for selecting moving targets.

One concern in using cursor enhancements for selecting moving targets is their lack of precision in a dense and dynamically changing field of targets. This would require the cursor to constantly adapt to disambiguate selection. An alternative to enhancing the cursor is to change the target properties. Such enhancements are generally based on alterations to the target itself [18, 19], to the target's position [2, 4], or even on the workspace [3].

An example of such target enhancements is to expand its size (as with buttons on some operating systems). McGuffin and Balakrishnan [18] found a clear advantage to expanding targets, even when the expansion started after 90% of the total movement to the target. However, when targets are densely populated, target expansion creates problems with targets overlapping one another [18]. To mitigate this problem, alterations can be made to the workspace. Baudisch et al. [3] presented Starburst, a space-partitioning algorithm that identifies the available areas of screen space and places each target into a different tessellated region on the screen. The user can simply click on the associated region of the workspace to select the target. For this method to work with dynamically refreshed targets, the partitioning would have to constantly occur, thus changing the visual and motor properties of the workspace as targets move around. Our design of Comet is inspired by target expansion techniques as it enlarges the target's activation area.

Instead of modifying properties of the target one can reduce the distance to the target. In drag-and-pop [2] and the vacuum filter [4], the user can invoke a replica of the target that is placed in proximity to the cursor, thus shrinking A in equation (1). The user then needs to only move the cursor minimally to select the target. These techniques have shown benefits for selecting targets at large distances. In the case of moving targets, shrinking the target distance as it moves away is an appealing solution, and one we used as a basis for our Target Ghost techniques.

Selection of moving targets

Researchers in the fields of cognitive psychology have explored users' performance in selecting moving targets. Jagacinski et al [15] demonstrated that selection of moving target is highly correlated to the velocity of the object and offered an analytical model for movement time estimation:

$$T = a + bA + c(V+1)(1/W-1)$$

where A is the initial amplitude, V is the target velocity, W its width, and a, b, c, are empirically determined constants.

Despite the growing abundance of data displayed in a dynamic manner, only a few studies in HCI have explored the selection of moving targets. Faure et al [9] investigated the acquisition of pop-up and animated targets, as found on some operating systems such as the Mac OS X. They examined the effects of different transition and animation delays on pop-up targets and found no significant difference with selecting static targets.

Ilich's [14] recent investigation into the selection of moving targets was done on interactive video browsing. Ilich showed that when pausing the entire scene with a Click-to-Pause technique, the selection of moving targets comes close to that of static targets. Click-to-Pause involves first depressing the mouse button to pause all onscreen moving objects; once the cursor moves over the item of interest, releasing the button selects it. In a user evaluation, Ilich found that Click-to-Pause results in lower selection times than the unassisted pointer for small and/or fast targets [14]. Target Ghost was partly inspired by this approach, but instead of pausing the scene we created static in-place proxies to aid selection. This has the added benefit of working in environments where pausing is not possible or when the users do not wish to not miss any information [5].

DESIGN CONSIDERATIONS

A number of factors can influence the design and performance of techniques for selecting moving targets. We outline those that have guided the design of the Comet and Target Ghost. These include: target speed, movement direction, movement type and feedback type.

Target speed

Studies on moving targets [13, 15, 21] show that the objects' speed is a strong determinant of targeting performance. In Jagacinski's model [15], the index of difficulty is directly proportional to target velocity (faster targets are more difficult to select than slower ones). It is possible that new enhancements would only help in acquiring faster targets instead of slower ones. Our techniques dampen the impact of fast movements by either increasing the target's activation area or by creating static proxies of the targets.

Movement direction

In a study by Tresilian and Lonegram [21] participants were required to select a moving target by intercepting it, by hitting a ball with a baseball bat. This task was found to be considerably different than prior work on moving targets [13, 15] where participants were instead pursuing the targets. Tresilian's model also differed considerably than Jagacinski's and was attributed to the different motor control processes between both task types. These results suggest that the direction of motion, i.e. away, toward or orthogonal to the cursor can result in different targeting strategies and motor control movements. This factor played an important role in the design of 2D Comet's design.

Movement type

Movement type is a multidimensional attribute consisting of the level of predictability of a target's trajectory vector, the shape of the path (straight, curved, random), and the rate of changes in these. For example in the video feedback of a hockey game, players can move in highly unpredictable paths, changing directions at random moments. There are numerous types of movement paths, either in nature or simulated (i.e. in video games) and the design of techniques for acquiring moving targets needs to consider this factor.

Feedback type

Target feedback type can also affect the selec-tion of moving targets. Mould and Gutwin [20] investigated target feedback on multiple moving objects in a gaming environment. They compared selection performance for conditions of no target feedback, feedback on the target only and feedback on all items. Feedback on the target or on all items significantly improved task completion. Since feedback on all targets can result in too many distracters, target-only feedback was proposed as being practical.

TECHNIQUES

We describe our designs of Comet and Target Ghost.

The Comet

The *Comet* is based on the concept of target expansion used in static environments [18]. The technique has a physical resemblance to the astronomical comet that displays a trailing blaze of dust and ice as it moves along the sky, and is similar to the past position trails displayed in some air traffic control systems. The design of comet tail was motivated by motor control theory which proposes that target acquisition consists of an initial ballistic movement, followed by corrective sub-movements [10]. With a tail length proportional to the target speed, we could improve the chance that after the user's initial ballistic movement towards the original target position, the cursor would be in the general region of the comet, even if the target had moved away.

Figure 2 illustrates how the Comet behaves. As shown, each target has a tail whose size is based on the speed and width of a target. A slower target will have a shorter tail than a target that is moving faster. This means that if the user aims at the original target position, the cursor will land on the tail if it misses it. Similarly the thickness of the tail is dictated by the width of the target. For example, a target moving at a speed of 500 pixels/sec and of size 50 pixels had a Comet tail of 337 pixels (where Tail length = Speed/c + Width/2, where c is a constant scale factor in our case, 1.6 which was tuned after initial pilot testing). When the cursor enters the trigger area, the tail becomes a solid object, denoting that it is selectable (Figure 2.b). Furthermore, if the tail overlaps with another target, it is rendered below the target so it does not occlude the target (Figure 2.c).

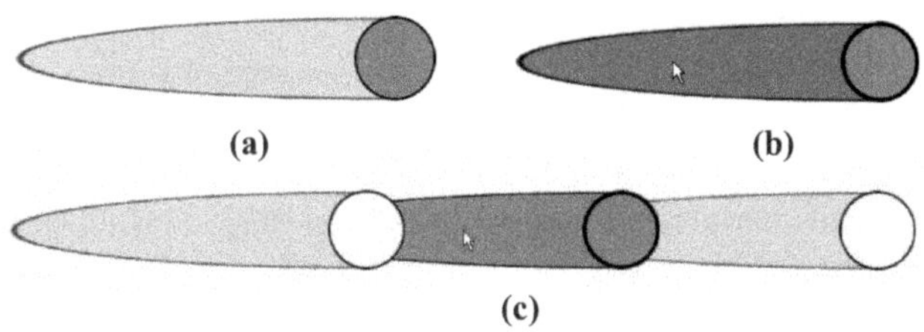

Figure 2. (a) Target and its comet tail; (b) the tail gets highlighted as the cursor moves over it; (c) tails can be overlapped by adjacent targets.

Target Ghost

Target Ghost is inspired by proxy-based techniques [2, 4] that bring the target closer to the user's cursor. The exception here is that the proxies do not come closer to the cursor, since this would cause clutter and thus require additional layout algorithms. Instead, as the targets are ghosted, they leave behind a proxy in the position at the moment when the user invoked the *Ghost* (Figure 3). The ghosted targets are rendered in a dimmer shade making them less visible, but moving along their paths. Showing continued motion is critical in environments where users cannot stop the scene or wish to not lose continuity between frames [5].

Ghosting is invoked by pressing the Shift key with the non-dominant hand. To select a target users simply move their cursor over the target's proxy and select it with a mouse click. If the user does not select the target and instead releases her finger off the Shift key, the targets get un-ghosted and continue moving along their trajectory. Since Target Ghost is not a cursor based enhancement, any cursor technique can be applied in conjunction with Target Ghost, to create a Bubble Ghost or Comet Ghost, for example. Note that the user can only select the proxy of the ghosted target and not the target itself.

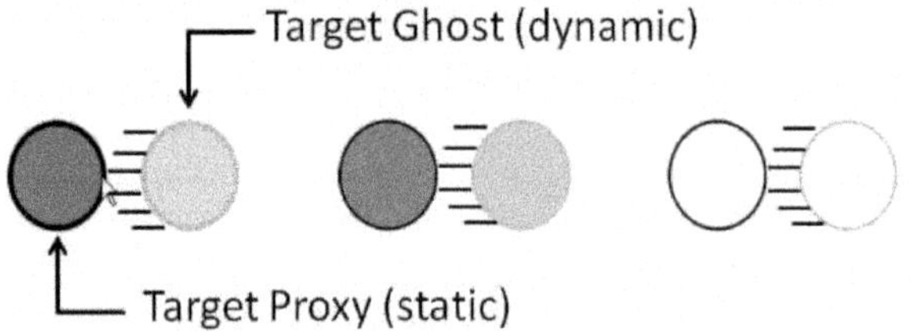

Figure 3. (Arrows and annotations are only for illustration) Target Ghost technique with the basic cursor. When Ghosted, the original target is faded (as a ghost) but keeps moving along its trajectory. A much sharper proxy of the object remains at the target's position when the Shift key was depressed and becomes enabled for selection. Note that the user can only click on the proxy to select the target.

EXPERIMENT 1 – 1D TARGET SELECTION

Goal

In our first experiment we compared the performance of different cursor techniques in a 1D selection task. Each cursor technique was also accompanied with its Ghost equivalent. In this experiment the targets were always moving along the horizontal axis and cursor movement was restricted along the same axis. Based on the properties of our techniques, we hypothesized the following:

H1: the dynamically enlarged activation area or Comet will result in greater reduction in selection time compared to the Basic cursor and Area cursor;

H2: the constantly changing size of the Bubble cursor may be visually distracting to the user and would thus negatively affect targeting performance;

H3: both the Comet and the Bubble cursor techniques will result in fewer click errors than the Basic and Area cursors as the former two techniques result in selecting targets with a larger activation area;

H4: since Ghosting results in selecting static targets, these will show faster selection times and fewer errors than their un-ghosted counterparts.

Methods

Apparatus

The experiment ran on a Windows XP PC equipped with a 22 inch LCD monitor with a resolution of 1680 * 1050 pixels (1 pixel = 0.28 mm in real world units) and a Microsoft mouse that used the default Windows XP settings. The experimental system is a standard Windows gaming application, developed using the Microsoft XNA framework.

Subjects

Twelve participants (9 male and 3 female) who ranged in age from 21-35, participated in this experiment. All of them were right-handed. They were all frequent mouse users and occasional computer gamers. Participants were paid a small sum of money for volunteering.

Task

The experimental system required that the user select a moving goal target in a 1D environment by moving their cursor from the Start position to the target. All targets and distracters were solid circles. The target was drawn in red and placed between two white distracters. The distracter targets were placed on opposite sides and were equidistant from the target center, controlling effective width for the bubble cursor and comet techniques. The task was successful when the user selected the goal target, which was highlighted in green when selected. An error was recorded if the user missed the target. Users could keep attempting to select the object until it disappeared off the screen.

Design

A within-subject design was used to compare the performance of each technique. The independent variables we selected were *Technique*, *Target Speed*, *Target Width* or *Width*, and *Distracter Distance*.

The eight *Techniques* were:

- *Basic cursor:* this is the basic Windows pointer and served as a baseline;
- *Area cursor:* this was implemented as a circular cursor with a width of 100 pixels, which was the same as the maximum target width;
- *Bubble cursor:* this was implemented as originally designed [11];
- *Comet*: this technique was implemented as described above. Target speed and target width were the determining factors for assigning a size to the Comet's tail;
- *Ghosts*: each of the above techniques also included a version of its ghost, resulting in Basic Ghost, Bubble Ghost, Area Ghost and Comet Ghost. The user would trigger the Ghost by pressing the Shift key using their non-dominant hand.

We chose *Speeds* of: 500 pxs/sec, 650 pxs/sec and 800 pxs/sec, which are values that could occur in video streams, video games, and simulations of natural phenomenon. Targets were set to *Widths*: 50 pixels, 75 pixels and 100 pixels. *Distracter distances* were set at 250 pixels, 300 pixels and 350 pixels. We settled on levels of these factors through iterative pilot testing, to provide a reasonable spectrum of difficulty levels. Participants were shown the various techniques and the experimenter demonstrated the task. They were given at least 2-3 practice trials and more if needed. When ready, subjects performed four test trials with each condition, yielding 8×3×3×3×4=864 trials per subject, or 10,368 trials in total. All of them completed the experiment in one session, lasting approximately 45 minutes. The trials were grouped by technique, and the techniques order of presentation was randomized among participants.

Experimental Setup

The goal target always began at a constant distance (300 pixels) from the start button and had a pre-determined movement direction. The target to be selected was colored red, and the distracters were rendered in white. When participants correctly selected the target, it turned green. The target was always moving away from the pointer at the start of the trial. If the target crossed the application window, it was marked as a failed trial. At the start of each technique, the program displayed an instruction on the screen.

Measures

In this experiment, we collected the trial completion time, pointer movement distance and error rates for our data analysis. *Trial completion time* was the time from when the user clicked the start button to when they successfully selected the target. *Errors* were logged if users clicked the mouse button but failed to select the target. Upon completion, participants ranked (Likert scale: 1-5) the techniques according to their preference.

Results

We used the univariate ANOVA test and Tamhane post-hoc pair-wise tests (unequal variances) for all our analyses.

Task Completion Time

Outliers defined by 3 s.d. away from the mean for selection technique were removed, resulting in less than 2% of all trials being excluded from the analysis. Results showed a main effect of *Technique*, *Target Speed*, *Target Width*, and *Distracter Distance* (all $p<0.001$) on trial completion time with $F_{1,7}=656.2$, $F_{1,2}=15.3$, $F_{1,2}=76.4$, and $F_{1,2}=7.1$, respectively. There were significant interaction effects (all $p<0.005$) for *Technique×Target Speed* ($F_{1,14}=3.7$), *Technique×Target Width* ($F_{1,14}=20.9$), and *Technique×Distracter Distance* ($F_{1,14}=2.4$). Other interaction effects were not significant.

Post-hoc pair-wise comparisons of *Techniques* yielded significant differences across all pairs of techniques ($p<0.01$), with the exception of the Area cursor vs. Bubble Ghost ($p=1.0$). Participants were fastest with the Comet (381ms), then the Bubble cursor (415ms), followed by the Comet Ghost (435ms), the Area cursor and Bubble Ghost (470ms), then the Basic Ghost (689ms) and finally the Basic cursor (785ms) (Figure 4).

Post-hoc pair-wise comparisons of *Target Speed* yielded significant differences in trial completion times between 500 and 800 pxs/sec ($p=0.003$) and between 650 and 800 pxs/sec ($p=0.001$). Post-hoc pair-wise comparison of *Target Width* yielded significant differences (all $p<0.01$) in trial completion times for all pairs of widths. Post-hoc pair-wise comparison of *Distracter Distance* yielded significant differences only between the largest two distances, 250 and 350 pixels ($p=0.004$) in trial completion times.

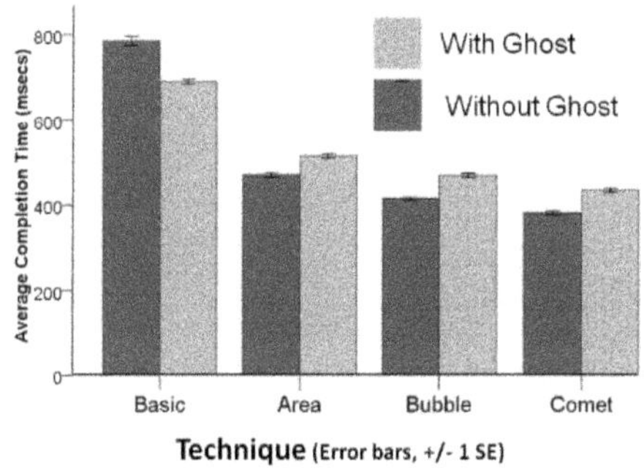

Figure 4. Task completion times across techniques with and without the Ghost.

Number of Errors

Results showed a main effect of *Technique*, *Target Speed*, *Target Width*, and *Distracter Distance* (all $p<0.002$) on trial completion time with $F_{1,7}=349.1$, $F_{1,2}=6.3$, $F_{1,2}=28.2$, and $F_{1,2}=9.6$ respectively. There were significant interaction effects (all $p<0.05$) for *Technique×Target Speed* ($F_{1,14}=2.4$), *Technique×Target Width* ($F_{1,14}=19.1$), and *Technique×Distracter Distance* ($F_{1,14}=1.9$). Other interaction effects were not significant.

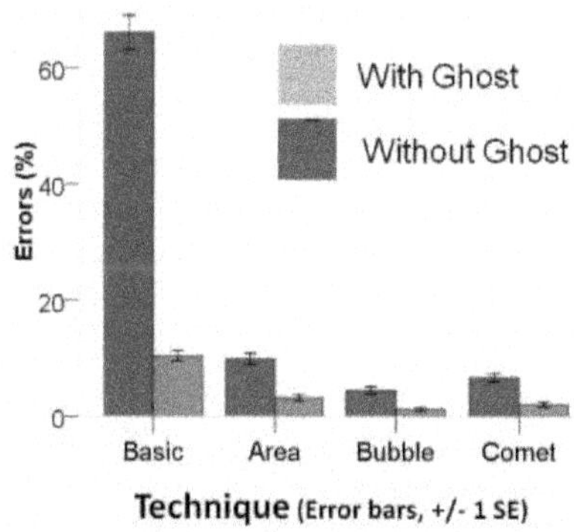

Figure 5. Error rates across techniques with and without the Ghost.

Post-hoc pair-wise comparisons of *Techniques* yielded significant differences between the Basic cursor and all other techniques ($p<0.01$). The Ghosted techniques were also all significantly less error prone than the non-ghosted techniques ($p<0.05$), except for the Bubble cursor which was on par with the Area Ghost ($p=0.983$). With the exception of the Basic Ghost (10% error rate), the other ghosted techniques exhibited error rates less than 3% (Area Ghost=3%, Comet Ghost=2%, Bubble Ghost=1%). In the non-ghosted techniques, the Basic cursor had the highest error rate (66%), followed by the Area cursor (10%), the Comet (7%) and the Bubble (4%) (Figure 5). It is not surprising that users have to click less in the ghosted version of the techniques, as the proxies of the moving targets are stationary. However, interestingly the Basic Ghost (i.e. unassisted by other enhancements) performs either at the same level or worse than the basic cursor enhancement techniques.

Post-hoc pair-wise comparisons of *Target Speed* yielded no significant differences in the number of errors between pairs of speeds. Post-hoc pair-wise comparison of *Target Width* yielded significant differences in the number of errors between 50 and 100 pixel target sizes ($p<0.001$). Similarly, a post-hoc pair-wise comparison of *Distracter Distance* only yielded significant differences between distances of 250 and 350 pixels ($p<0.001$) in number of errors.

Subjective feedback

In an exit survey, participants ranked (the Likert scale consisted of equally spaced scalar values from 1 – least preferred - to 5 – most preferred), the Bubble and Comet Ghost, 3.66 and 4.16 respectively. This order is reflected in the error rates. These were then followed by the Bubble, Comet and Area cursor techniques. A similar pattern prevailed concerning the level of control for each technique.

Discussion

Technique

The results of our study show that participants were fastest with an enhancement to the target, such as with the Comet over cursor based enhancements (supporting H1). The Comet tail increases the effective width of the target thus facilitating the selection. Based on our exit survey, participants did not seem affected by the rapidly changing cursor size with the Bubble, thus rejecting H2.

The Basic cursor performed the slowest and was also the most error prone. Interestingly, the interaction effect of technique and speed is most apparent with the basic cursor as users were faster at higher speeds than at lower ones. This effect has been previously reported in the literature [14] but primarily when users have intercepted the target (i.e. waiting ahead on the target's path so that the target falls under the cursor). Indeed, in observing users select targets with this cursor type, we found that once an error occurred (i.e. they missed the target), they would convert their motion into one involving interception instead of pursuit. This occurred less with the other cursor types.

The only Ghost technique that showed any improvement in time performance in comparison to its counterpart was the Basic Ghost. All other Ghost techniques were slower, thus rejecting H4. This was in part due to pressing the Shift key to create the proxies of the moving objects, causing an overhead of around 200 ms. However, we found that the Ghost techniques exhibited the lowest error rates. It is also interesting to observe the wide range in error rates from the Basic technique compared to all the other cursor types, supporting our hypothesis that selecting moving targets (at the levels tested) requires significant assistance. Our results also support H3, suggesting that the increase in activation area resulting from the Comet and Bubble would minimize errors in comparison to the Basic and Area cursors.

Distance to target

We looked at the cursor-to-target distance when selection occurred. If this distance was large, it means that users did not move their cursor too far to select. This gives us insight as to whether users were taking advantage of the enhanced activation areas of the Comet and Bubble cursors. Interestingly, we see that the distance-to-target is not only a function of the distracter distance, but also of the speed of the targets. As we see in Figure 6.a, this distance is highly affected by the target speed. In contrast, we see a lesser effect of distracter distance on distance-to-target (Figure 6.b). Interestingly, the largest variance with respect to distracter distance was with the Comet technique and not the Bubble cursor as we would have expected. This happens because when the Bubble cursor is highlighting the correct target, users needed to readjust their motor movement before they complete the selection as fast moving distracters could cancel out the Bubble cursor's selection. For this reason, enhancements to the target may have a slighter advantage over techniques with cursor enhancements for this task.

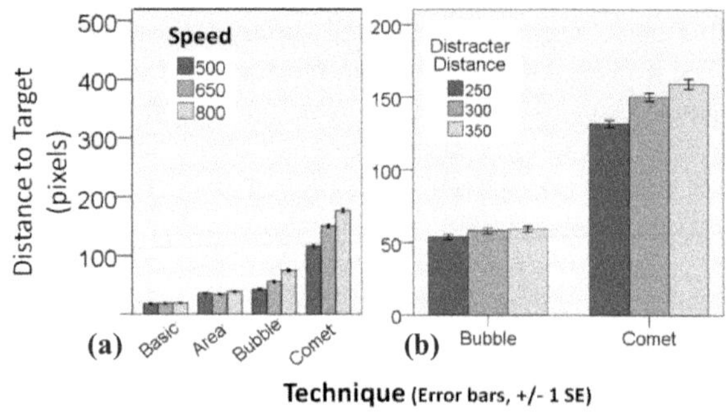

Figure 6. Distance-to-target (a) across techniques without the Ghost; (b) by technique and distracter distance.

Target Speed

As expected, faster targets are harder and more error prone to select. Static proxies of the targets, as with Ghosting reduce the error rates slightly. However this is not significantly different than leaving the targets in full movement, suggesting that bringing targets to a full halt may not necessarily resolve erroneous selection. Other alternatives, discussed later are needed to reduce such errors.

Overshooting the target

We found that with the Area and Bubble cursors participants would select a target when the pointer was in front of it. We found that this occurred more often with the Area cursor (11% of all trials with this cursor) than the Bubble cursor (7%). These trends are also very similar for the Area and Bubble Ghost techniques. Surprisingly, this occurred more frequently at the lower target speeds.

COMET AND TARGET GHOST FOR 2D SELECTION

In the 1D experiment subjects were able to quickly access targets using the activation area introduced by the comet tail. However, pilot tests for the 2D setup revealed that the 1D Comet design was weak on two aspects. The first consisted of the shape of the tail. In the 1D Comet, tail thickness degrades gradually providing an elliptical activation area for the cursor to land on. However, results from the first study show that participants largely selected targets when the cursor was at the tip of the tail. This part of the tail needed a significantly larger activation area and we therefore increased the thickness of the tail at its tip by a factor of target width×1.5 (Figure 7).

In this design the shape of the tail follows the changes in the object's movement direction (Figure 7.b). As a result, users do not need to make drastic changes to the cursor's path when the target is moving along less predictable trajectories. Clicking the mouse button when the cursor is over the comet tail or on the target selects the object. If two comet tails overlap the closest target gets selected.

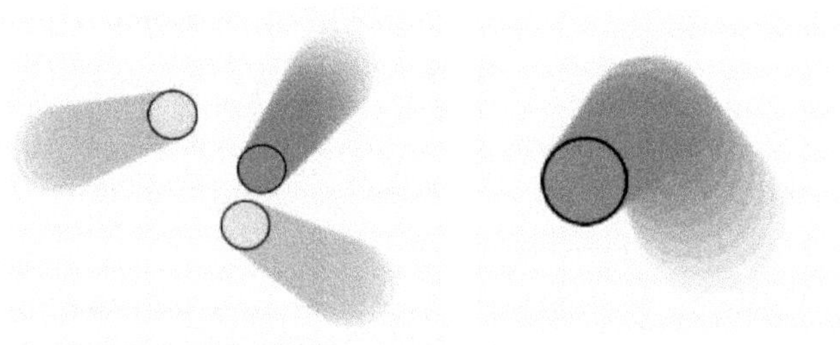

(a) (b)

Figure 7. (a) The tail's thickness grows towards its end. (b) Tails bend and turn based on the target's movement path. This helps users in not having to alter their initial ballistic movement that was aimed at the target before it moved.

The tail gradually increases in transparency until it completely blends with the background. We rendered the tail using a series of slightly wider circles positioned along the target's movement path. The part of the tail closest to the target is solid and then gradually becomes more transparent toward its end. The purpose of this gradual transformation was to reduce the amount of clutter that would appear on the screen particularly in more densely populated scenes.

Target Ghost did not vary significantly from the 1D setup (Figure 8.a). In Comet Ghost, a proxy of both the target and the tail were created. To reduce clutter, the Ghosted object was drawn in a transparent blue shade. The target proxies are red and those of the distracters are grey.

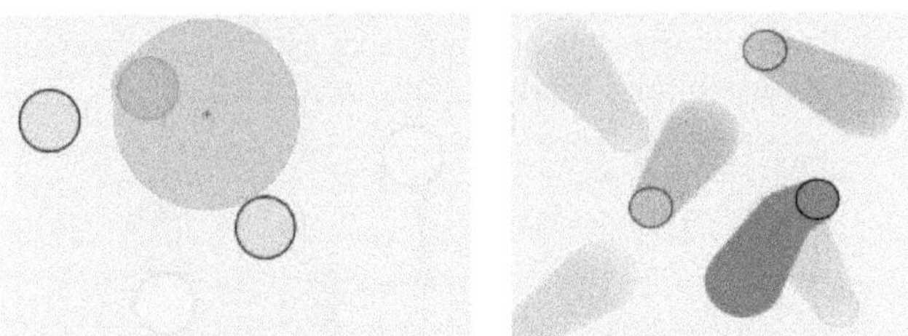

(a) (b)

Figure 8. (a) Bubble Ghost, and (b) Comet Ghost. With Comet Ghost targets were transparent to reduce clutter.

EXPERIMENT 2 – 2D TARGET SELECTION

Goal

Results of experiment 1 showed the potential of the Comet as a selection technique for 1D moving targets, due to its increased activation area. However, it could be possible that the Comet may not be suitable for more complex target acquisition tasks that one commonly encounters in real 2D GUI interfaces. Using the Bubble cursor, a user can select the target with the closest distance to the pointer. However, in Comet, the selection area is only enlarged along the movement vector. Therefore if the cursor movement is orthogonal to the tail or the Comet, then selection could be impaired as the activation region may be less beneficial [18]. To investigate the performance of the various cursor types and their ghosted versions, we conducted a second experiment with targets moving in 2D. Since the movement vector has shown to effect acquisition times [21], we also examined the effect of a less predictable target paths on selection performance. We excluded the Area cursor from this experiment as it did not show significant benefits in the 1D task. We hypothesized that:

H5: the ghosted techniques will outperform the others in selection times and errors as users will select a static target;

H6: the enlarged activation area brought by the Comet will mainly show benefits in the absence of ghosting.

Methods

Apparatus

The apparatus used was the same as in experiment 1.

Subjects

12 right-handed participants (8 male) whose age ranged from 21 to 30, volunteered for this experiment. All of them were right-handed. They are frequent mouse users and occasionally play computer games.

Task

We used 20 distracters along with the target. Users were asked to select the goal target, which was moving based on its movement predictability and speed. Targets were also allowed to bounce off the edges of the application window.

Design

We used a within-subject design to compare the performance of the techniques in the 2D environment. Here, the independent variables were *Technique*, *Path Predictability*, *Target Speed*, and *Density*.

The *Techniques* selected were, the Basic cursor, Bubble cursor, Comet, and their ghosted equivalent.

Path predictabilities were defined as:

- High - the target moved in a straight line.
- Medium - the target changed direction between 15° and 45 °, at intervals of 400-600 msecs.
- Low - the target changed direction between 45° and 315 °, at intervals of 200-400 msecs.

Target speed was set to 400 pixels/sec, 550 pixels/sec and 700 pixels/sec.

The width of the targets and distracters was fixed at 75 pixels. The design was balanced based on cursor type (6 types), with 3 blocks of trials for each technique. Within each block we used 3 path predictabilities × 3 target speeds × 2 distracter distances × 3 repetitions for each condition, yielding 972 trials per subject or 11,664 trials in total. All the participants completed the experiment in one session, lasting approximately 50 minutes. Before starting the trials, subjects were given practice trials with each technique. The techniques order of presentation was counterbalanced among participants using a Latin Square design.

Experimental Setup

At the start of each trial, the target and the distracters were initialized with a random movement vector. When targets hit the edge of the application window, we redirected the path at an angle of reflection equal to that of the incidence. After each successful selection, a new target and a set of distracter targets were displayed, with the goal target appearing at a fixed distance (400 pixels) from the start button but at different *x-y* positions. To test the effect of movement type, we used three different path predictabilities (see above). In the case of high path predictability, the targets started with a random vector, and only the direction vector changed when it bounced off the edges. Targets with medium path predictability also started with a random initial vector, but the vector changed after a longer random time interval and with a smaller random angle. Low path predictability had the same initial conditions, but the vector changed at a high variance and at a higher angular degree. The target to be selected was colored red, and the distracters were rendered as light gray with the same width as the goal target. When selected correctly the target turned green.

Measures

In this experiment, we also collected the trial completion time and error rates. We asked participants to fill out a post-experiment survey to rank the techniques according to preference and perceived level of control.

Results

We used the univariate ANOVA test and Tamhane post-hoc pair-wise tests (unequal variances) for all our analyses.

Task Completion Time

Outliers defined by 3 s.d. away from the mean for selection technique were removed, resulting in less than 5% of all trials being excluded from the analysis. Results showed a main effect of *Technique*, *Target Speed*, and *Path Predictability* (all p<0.001) on trial completion time with $F_{1,5}$=1660.09, $F_{1,2}$=146.03, $F_{1,2}$=108.35, and $F_{1,1}$=6.04 respectively. There were significant interaction effects (all p<0.005) for *Technique×Target Speed* ($F_{1,10}$=30.74), *Technique×Path Predictability* ($F_{1,10}$=59.74). Other interaction effects were not significant.

Post-hoc pair-wise comparisons of *Techniques* yielded significant differences across all pairs of techniques (p<0.01), with the exception of the Bubble cursor vs. Basic Ghost (p=1.0). Participants completed the target selection task in less time using all the ghosted techniques than their non-ghosted version. Participants were fastest with the Bubble Ghost (609ms), then the Comet Ghost (709ms), followed by the Comet (753ms), the Bubble cursor (794ms), then the Basic Ghost (810ms) and finally the Basic cursor (1,841ms) (Figure 9.a).

Post-hoc pair-wise comparisons of Target Speed yielded significant differences in trial completion times between all pairs of speeds. Post-hoc pair-wise comparisons of *Path predictability* yielded significant differences in trial completion times between *High* and *Low* and no significant difference between other pairs. Figure 9.b shows the effect of path predictability on performance.

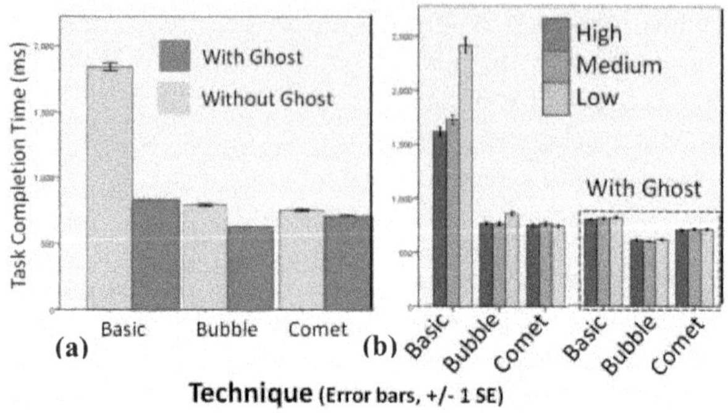

Figure 9. Task completion times (a) across techniques with and without the Ghost; (b) by path predictability.

Number of Errors

Results showed a main effect of *Technique, Path Predictability,* and *Target Speed* (all p<0.001) on errors with $F_{1,5}$=1030.2, $F_{1,2}$=10.36, $F_{1,2}$=109.05, and $F_{1,1}$=14.5 respectively. There were significant interaction effects (all p<0.05) for *Technique×Target Speed* ($F_{1,10}$=15.08), and *Technique×Path Predictability* ($F_{1,10}$=6.49). Other interaction effects were not significant.

Post-hoc pair-wise comparisons of *Techniques* yielded significant differences between the Basic cursor and all other techniques (p<0.01). The Ghosted techniques were also all significantly less error prone than the non-ghosted techniques (p<0.01). The ghosted techniques exhibited error rates less than 10% (Comet Ghost=5%, Bubble Ghost=2% and Basic Ghost = 9%). In the non-ghosted techniques, the Basic cursor had the highest error rate (74%), followed by the Bubble cursor (38%) and then Comet (33%) (Figure 10). This sharp difference between the ghosted techniques and their counterpart is not surprising particularly since low path predictabilities result in many mis-clicks.

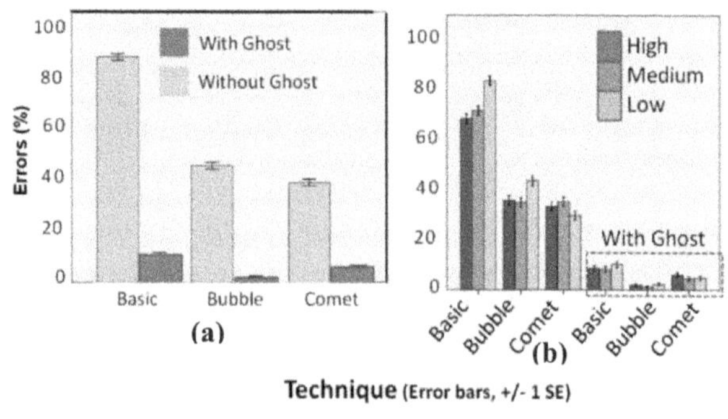

Figure 10. Error rates (a) across techniques with and without Ghost; (b) by technique and path predictability.

Post-hoc pair-wise comparisons of *Target Speed* yielded significant differences (p<0.001) in the number of errors between pairs of speeds. Post-hoc pair-wise comparison of

Path Predictability yielded no significant differences in number of errors between pairs of path predictabilities.

Subjective feedback

On a Likert scale from 1 (lowest preference) to 5 (highly preferred), the Bubble and Comet Ghosts were the most preferred techniques (4.16 for both) followed by the Comet and then the Bubble. Understandably, Basic cursor was the least preferred among all techniques.

DISCUSSION

We first discuss our results from experiment 2.

Discussion of results from Experiment 2

Our results show that additional cursor enhancements such as target expansion or static proxies are necessary for selecting moving targets. With different path movement types, ghosted techniques had faster selections and fewer errors than without ghosting (supporting H5). However, without the ghosting, we see that the Comet's activation area is again beneficial to users, as they are faster and less error prone than the Bubble cursor (partial support for H6). Our results strongly support the use of cursor or target enhancements even with static proxies. This is not surprising in terms of performance times, but in terms of errors we see that significantly fewer errors occur with the Bubble Ghost and Comet Ghost than the Basic Ghost. This result can be partly explained by users over/undershooting targets whose proxies stop abruptly. One solution might be to bring the static proxies into a gradual halt.

We were surprised to see that in the second experiment, even with ghosting, i.e. creating static proxies, we were not able to completely remove all errors. Users still needed some form of enhancement, such as the Comet or Bubble cursor to complement proxy selection. In the case of the enhanced cursor types, a large part of the errors resulted from clicking the wrong target, suggesting that finer improvements are needed to make selection practical. One solution might be to list all objects 'under' the cursor such that the user can then select one from the list. Our technique would then work as a pre-filter to provide the user with a list of potential items. Another possibility might be to disambiguate selection by correlating the movement direction with the cursor's movement path. Movements that are deemed parallel may indicate a strong likelihood of a user wanting to select these targets.

Applications

Many applications can benefit from the results obtained here. We implemented our techniques in a video browsing environment, to emulate what a user of a video tracking system may have. Direct manipulation interfaces in such an environment have shown to significantly improve user interactions [7,8]. To do this, we captured video footage of cars on a highway. We then manually annotated the motion paths by extracting them from all the frames. This allowed us to separate moving objects from the background, to which we then applied our techniques (Figure 1, and video). Other applications that can benefit from these techniques include molecular or weather simulations and educational tools that are based on animated displays. Typically, animations such as these are only viewable and accept very little input from the user. However, direct manipulation can aid in better understanding the information being displayed. For example, as video tracking becomes more commonplace one can foresee target selection available for multiple media types, including televised games. In these scenarios, it might be particularly difficult to pause the entire scene. With the use of our techniques, users can select players or other items of interest to briefly inspect relevant statistics. Finally, video games include a large number of moving objects. Typically, designers select the right level of difficulty to provide a sufficient balance. This avoids losing game players who either get bored because it is easy, or who give up because of the difficulty level. Our results can assist designers in selecting the appropriate balance by introducing techniques at the right level of user expertise.

Pausing vs. Ghosting

Ghosting is inspired by proxy-based techniques [2, 4] but also borrows properties of pausing an animated scene. While pausing is also possible, there are cases where Target Ghosts would be more useful. For example, in air-traffic control, pausing the display would not be a viable option since releasing the pause would create a disjointed view between frames. In contrast, the continuity that is available with Ghosting would still allow the user to inspect the ghosted targets whose movements are not interrupted. Future work is required to find applications where either type of interaction is the most appropriate.

Guidelines for Designers

From our results we propose the following guidelines:

- designers should take the cost of an error into account when selecting a design;
- for target movements in 1D, Comet should be the technique of choice;
- in 2D, selection of moving targets is best achieved with static proxies, such as Target Ghost;
- cursor enhancements such as the Comet or Bubble cursor should be employed, even when using static proxies of moving objects.

Limitations

Comet and Target Ghost also present some limitations. For example, in scenes with a large number of objects, Comet can add clutter. This makes it more difficult to select those targets that may lie beneath the clutter. One solution might be to create more intelligent techniques that only add comet tails to those objects that are needed or that fall in line with the cursor's movement. Similarly, the duplicates of objects with Target Ghost also create clutter that can be difficult to manage in a scene. One approach to resolve the clutter might be to create proxies of only a few targets that are in the vicinity of the cursor. Furthermore, performance of the comet may degrade when two tails overlap. It would be interesting to investigate this further using advanced heuristic methods for overlapping tails. Finally, if targets all have similar appearance, it should be investigated how well users can keep track of their goal target after activating the Target Ghost technique.

Another concern worth mentioning is the small number of participants used for higher number of conditions in the experiments. While the parameters used in our studies are consistent with similar HCI studies, we feel that a larger number of participants could further ascertain our claims.

CONCLUSION AND FUTUREWORK

In this work we present techniques that aid in selecting moving targets. We demonstrate through two experiments the need for assisting the basic cursor in selecting such types of targets. Comet enhances objects by adding a selectable tail. This increases the activation area for selection. Target Ghost creates proxies of the moving object. These proxies are static and created at the moment of invocation. In a 1D selection task, Comet outperformed existing techniques such as the Area and Bubble cursors. Comet also outperformed Ghosted versions of all techniques. In a 2D selection task, Comet outperformed the Bubble, but only in conditions without the ghost. Our results show that even if the user were to create static versions of the moving objects, an enhancement such as the Comet or Bubble is critical to assist in selecting these.

In future work we will test the performance of our techniques in real applications. This could lead to new improvements to the Comet and Target Ghost, such as reducing the amount of clutter and minimizing the overhead of creating static proxies. We will also test these techniques with different input devices, for example, by simulating a TV remote control. Finally, we are also interested in studying whether the selection of targets moving in 3D has different features than the ones we describe here.

REFERENCES

1. Balakrishnan, R. (2004). Beating Fitts' law: virtual enhancements for pointing facilitation. Int. J. Hum.-Comput. Stud. 61, 6, 857-874.
2. Baudisch, P., Cutrell, E., Robbins, D., Czerwinski, M., Tandler, P. Bederson, B., and Zierlinger, A. Drag-and-Pop and Drag-and-Pick (2003). Techniques for Accessing Remote Screen Content on Touch- and Pen-operated Systems. *Proc. of Interact'03*, pp. 57-64.
3. Baudisch, P., Zotov, A., Cutrell, E., and Hinckley, K. (2008). Starburst: a target expansion algorithm for non-uniform target distributions. *Proc. of AVI '08*, 129-137.
4. Bezerianos, A., Balakrishnan, R. (2005). The Vacuum: Facilitating the manipulation of distant objects. *Proc. of CHI'05*, 361-370.
5. Bezerianos, A., Dragicevic, P., and Balakrishnan, R. 2006. Mnemonic rendering: an image-based approach for exposing hidden changes in dynamic displays. *Proc. of UIST '06*, 159-168.
6. Chapuis, O., Labrune, J., and Pietriga, E. (2009). DynaSpot: speed-dependent area cursor. *Proc. of CHI '09*, 1391-1400.
7. Cheng, K., Luo, S., Chen, B., and Chu, H. (2009). SmartPlayer: user-centric video fast-forwarding. *Proc. of CHI '09*, 789-798.
8. Dragicevic, P., Ramos, G., Bibliowitcz, J., Nowrouzezahrai, D., Balakrishnan, R., and Singh, K. (2008). Video browsing by direct manipulation. *Proc. of CHI '08*, 237-246.
9. Faure, G., Chapuis, O., and Beaudouin-Lafon, M. (2009). Acquisition of Animated and Pop-Up Targets. *Proc. of INTERACT '09*, 372-385.
10. Fitts, P. M. (1954). The information capacity of the human motor system in controlling the amplitude of movement. *Journal of Experimental Psychology*, 47, 381-39.
11. Grossman, T. and Balakrishnan, R. (2005). The bubble cursor: enhancing target acquisition by dynamic resizing of the cursor's activation area. *Proc. of CHI '05*, 281-290.
12. Grossman, T., Kong, N., Balakrishnan, R. (2007): Modeling pointing at targets of arbitrary shapes. *Proc. of CHI'07*, 463-472.
13. Hoffmann, E. R., (1991) Capture of Moving Targets: a Modification of Fitts' Law. *Ergonomics*, 34, 211–220.
14. Ilich, M.V. (2010) Moving Target Selection in Interactive Video, *M.Sc. Thesis, University of British Columbia*, pp. 110.
15. Jagacinski, R. J., Repperger, D. W., Ward, S. L., and Moran, M. S. (1980). A test of Fitts' law with moving targets. *Human Factors*, 22(2):225-233.
16. Kabbash, P. and Buxton, W. (1995). The "Prince" technique: Fitts' law and selection using area cursors. *Proc. of CHI'95*, p. 273-279.
17. MacKenzie, I. S. and Buxton, W. (1992). Extending Fitts' law to two-dimensional tasks. *Proc. of CHI '92*, 219-226.
18. McGuffin, M. and Balakrishnan, R. (2002). Acquisition of expanding targets. *Proc. of CHI '02*, 57-64.
19. McGuffin, M. J. and Balakrishnan, R. (2005). Fitts' law and expanding targets: Experimental studies and designs for user interfaces. *TOCHI*, 12, 4, 388-422.
20. Mould, D. and Gutwin, C. (2004). The effects of feedback on targeting with multiple moving targets. *Proc. of Graphics interface 2004*, 25-32.
21. Tresilian, J. R. & Lonergan, A. (2002) Intercepting moving objects: effect of temporal precision and movement amplitude. *Experimental Brain Research*, 142, 193-207.

Acquiring and Pointing: An Empirical Study of Pen-Tilt-Based Interaction

Yizhong Xin[1,2], Xiaojun Bi[3], Xiangshi Ren[1]

[1]School of Information
Kochi University of Technology, Japan
ren.xiangshi@kochi-tech.ac.jp

[2]School of Information
Shenyang University of Technology, China
xyz@sut.edu.cn

[3]Department of Computer Science, University of Toronto, Canada
xiaojun@dgp.toronto.edu

ABSTRACT
Research literature has shown that pen tilt is a promising input modality in pen-based interaction. However, the human capability to control pen tilt has not been fully evaluated. This paper systematically investigates the human ability to perform discrete target selection tasks by varying the pen stylus' tilt angle through two controlled experiments: tilt acquiring (Experiment 1) and tilt pointing (Experiment 2). Results revealed a decreasing power relationship between angular width and selection time in Experiment 1. The results of Experiment 2 confirmed that pen tilt pointing can be modeled by Fitts' law. Based on our quantitative analysis, we discuss the human ability to control pen tilt and the implications of pen tilt use. We also propose a taxonomy of pen tilt based interaction techniques and showcase a series of possible pen tilt technique designs.

Author Keywords
Pen-based interfaces, pen tilt input, pen tilt techniques.

ACM Classification Keywords
H5.2 User Interfaces: Input devices and strategies.

General Terms
Design, Experimentation, Human Factors.

INTRODUCTION
The pen is favored over other input devices such as keyboards and mice in mobile computing environments due to its portability, outdoor accessibility, short-time learning curve, and ease of manipulation. Consequently, research into pen-based interaction has intensified in recent years (e.g., [12, 27, 16]).

Typically, only x-y pen tip movement is used for interaction, but this unnecessarily limits the communication bandwidth between pen and computer, and restrains users from taking advantage of the great expressiveness of a pen. Fortunately, tablets these days can accurately detect pen pressure, and pen tilt and rolling angles. A trend in pen computing is towards fully utilizing these extra degrees of freedom. Rigorous studies have been conducted to investigate users' ability to control pen pressure [24] and rolling [2].

Among the various characteristics of a pen, tilt has unique properties compared to pen pressure and rolling: the tilt anlge of a pen is tightly related to the workplane-orientation [3], and the pen barrel can visually indicate the tilt angle of a pen anytime during pen use, which could be beneficial for eye-free interaction. Thus, pen tilt is a promising input modality [21, 32].

In spite of its potential, the human ability to control pen tilt has been overlooked and it has become a timely issue. Comprehensive evaluation will help guide developers/ researchers to design effective tilt-based interfaces.

We, therefore, systematically invesitigate the human ability to control pen tilt through two controlled experiments: (1) tilt acquiring and (2) tilt pointing. According to the aforementioned previous works, current pen-tilt-based interaction techniques can be classified into two types: (1) *Tilt acquiring*: users adjust the pen to a designate tilt angle either before or after placing the pen tip on the surface (e.g., using pen tilt to control the cursor [36] or to choose a pen mode once the pen tip contacts the tablet), and (2) *Tilt pointing*: users tilt the pen from one angle to another only after the pen tip is in contract with the surface (e.g., "tilt menu" [33], controlling a virtual human figure [21], 3D navigation [4, 31]). Based on the study results, we discuss the implications for designing pen-tilt-based user interfaces.

RELATED WORK
The tilt of an interactive device has been widely explored as an additional input channel. Research literature has presented plenty of compelling interaction techniques based on the physical manipulation of a small screen device such as a PDA. Earlier work by Fitzmaurice et al. [9] investigated the use of positions and tilting actions based on the Chameleon system. They explored the potential of the tilting action as a natural way to issue commands, e.g., to scroll up or down. Rekimoto [25] presented an interaction technique that uses variations in the tilt of a small screen device as input commands to build several interaction techniques for

navigating menus, maps, and 3-D scenes. During operation, only one hand was required to both hold and control the device, which was especially useful for field workers. TiltType [22] and TiltText [34] are text entry techniques for mobile devices. The tilt direction and angle of a mobile device were used to aid character selection from a range of given candidates. Rekimoto and Sciammarella [26] proposed the ToolStone that can sense physical manipulations of the device itself such as rotating, flipping or tilting to expand the functionalities of a single input device.

Harrison et al. [11], Fishkin et al. [6], Hinckley et al. [13], Small and Ishii [30], and Bartlett [1] used tilt sensors to scroll through and select information on a hand-held device. Eissele et al. [5] used tilt operations to achieve successive scroll and link-step actions. Wigdor and Balakrishnan [34] proposed a new technique, TiltText, for entering text into a mobile phone: the phone could be tilted in one of four directions to choose which character on a particular key to enter. Similar work has been done by Partridge et al. [22] and Sazawal et al. [28]. Tilt and orientation have also been used to allow spatially aware display. Fitzmaurice et al. [8] studied how artists took advantage of their ability to reorient their work surface while sketching and writing. They also introduced and explored many issues relating to Rotating User Interfaces (RUIs) including applications and toolkits for pen-based computing systems that take into account work-plane orientation, angle of rotation relative to the user around the axis perpendicular to the user's work surface. Rahman et al. [23] analyzed the design space of wrist-based interactions and the level of wrist control. By investigating the factors that could influence tilt control, they concluded that users could comfortably control at least 16 levels on the pronation/supination axis. Leitner et al. [19] compared the performance of a multi-touch surface with a pen based tilting surface and presented the different usages of tilt change.

In addition to the studies and techniques exploring the tilt of interactive devices in which sensors were mounted on the screens (or devices), there was a sizable amount of research focused on pen tilt. Blaskó et al. [3] presented two complementary methods to achieve more fine-grained awareness of user-to-device orientation for a hand-held writing surface, one using computer vision techniques, the other based on stylus-pose. Kuroki and Kawai [17] observed that people hold three physical tools (a syringe, a pen, and a cutter) differently and proposed that the use of tilt information for pen interfaces should be based on this observation. Oshita [21] designed a virtual human figure movement manipulation system that used not only pen pressure but also pen tilt to control a virtual human figure. Tian and colleagues [32, 33] showed that using pen tilt information could improve the stimulus-response compatibility and their "Tilt Cursor" utilized pen tilt to extend selection capability. Futhermore, Zhou and Ren [36] showed that tilt input performed relatively better than pressure input for cursor control. Bridson [4] used both translation and tilt of a pen to control viewpoint in a 3D scene, treating the pen as a handle attached to a selected point on the surface.

Despite the sizable amount of research integrating pen tilt into normal pen interfaces, no literature quantitatively investigated the human ability to control pen tilt in acquiring and/or pointing tasks. This paper is aimed at shedding some light in this area.

EXPERIMENT 1: TILT ACQUIRING

This experiment was to investigate how well a user can acquire a target using an absolute pen tilt angle. The user can adjust the pen tilt either before or after landing the pen tip on the surface.

Participants

Twelve participants (2 females, 10 males), ranging in age from 20 to 33, participated in the experiment. To minimize experimental bias caused by handedness, we ensured that all participants were right-handed according to self-report.

Apparatus

A Wacom Cintiq 21UX interactive LCD graphics display tablet and a wireless stylus with an isometric tip were used in the experiment. The Cintiq 21UX can detect the tilt angle of the stylus in the range from 30° to 90°. 90° tilt angle means that the stylus is perpendicular to the tablet surface. The experimental program was designed in the Java Environment and ran on a 2.13 GHz Intel Core2 CPU PC with Windows XP Professional SP2. The resolution of the display was set to 1280 by 1024 pixels at 96 dpi (0.27 mm per pixel).

Task and Procedure

Figure 1 is the schematic diagram of the experimental tool. As shown in Figure 1, we extended the pen tilt range from [30°, 90°] to [30°, 150°] using pen azimuth angles. The tilt angle is within the range [30°, 90°] if the azimuth angle is between 0°, 179°, while it is within [91°, 150°] if the azimuth angle is between [180°, 359°]. As a result, the tilt angle range in our experiment is from 30° to 150° (120° wide).

The pen tilt angle was mapped uniformly to a circumferential angle with a radius of 300 pixels on the screen. (e.g., 80° pen tilt is mapped to an 80° circumferential angle). Pen tilt was utilized to guide the rotation movement of a pink cursor around a fixed point, either clockwise or anticlockwise. A set of equal and consecutive sectors which presented the targets' angular width were drawn by dashed lines around a fixed point on the screen. Subjects were seated in front of the display tablet which was placed in the horizontal plane. The display edge was parallel to the subject's torso. In our pilot studies, we found that the preferred display-table angle varied for different users. Thus, we decided to place the tablet horizontally to eliminate potential effects caused by different display-table angles. The horizontal angle is also a common tablet usage, e.g., where users flatten a tablet laptop and place it on their laps or on a desk.

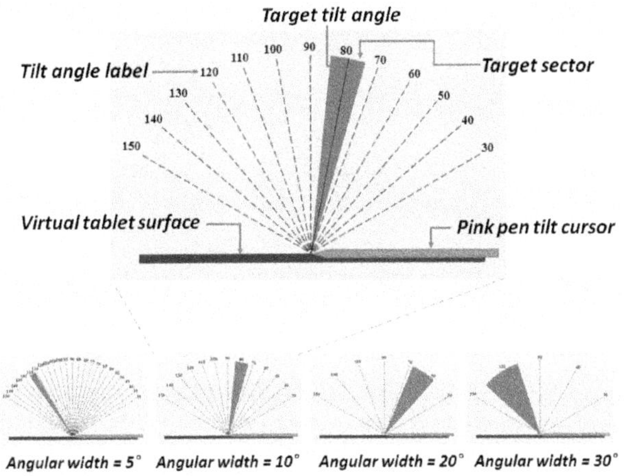

Figure 1. Schematic diagram of the tilt acquiring experiment.

During each trial, one of the target sectors was highlighted in red. The pink cursor indicating the pen tilt angle was displayed once the pen was in contact with the tablet surface. Subjects were instructed to land the pen on the tablet surface with the appropriate amount of pen tilt to guide the pink cursor to the desired target. The tilt cursor indicated the pen tilt angle at any time the pen was in contact with the tablet surface. For example, if a user landed the pen with the tilt angle of 80°, the tilt cursor jumped to 80°. When the pink cursor entered the target sectors, the target sector color changed to green. The subject confirmed the selection by pressing the space bar with the non-dominant hand on the keyboard. Subjects were told to strive for both accuracy and speed. If an incorrect selection was made, a failure "ding"' sound cue was given to the subject.

A within-subject full factorial design with repeated measures was used. The independent variables were *angular width* (5°, 10°, 20°, and 30°) and *target tilt angle* (35°, 57°, 79°, 101°, 123°, 145°). The target tilt angle refers to the angle between the middle line of the target sector and the 0 degree line (Figure 1). A Latin Square was used to counterbalance the order of the appearance of the targets. To explore the learning effects, 5 blocks of trials were completed by each subject. Each block consisted of 24 target acquiring tasks repeated once. Presentation of trials within a block was randomized. In total, the experiment consisted of:

12 subjects ×
4 angular widths ×
6 target tilt angles ×
5 blocks ×
2 times
=2880 target selection trials

Results

Selection Time

Selection time is the elasped time from the moment the pen tip comes into contact with the tablet's surface until the moment the subject confirmed the selection by pressing the space bar. Results showed that the narrower the angular width, the more time subjects needed to select the target. A further regression analysis of *angular width* × *target tilt angle* on selection time showed strong fits to the power relationship of $MT = a*W^b$ with a correlation of $R^2 > 0.98$ where MT is selection time, W is angular width, and a, b are empirical constants. Figure 2 illustrates the results.

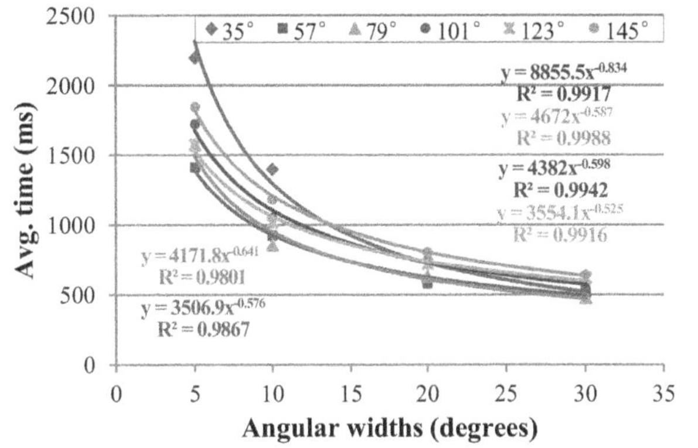

Figure 2. Average selection time per angular width × target tilt angle.

Repeated measures analysis of variance showed a significant main effect on selection time for *target tilt angle* ($F_{5, 55} = 6.27$, $p < .001$) and *angular width* ($F_{3, 33} = 61.30$, $p < .001$). Moreover, there was a significant interaction effect on selection time for *target tilt angle* × *angular width* ($F_{15, 165} = 4.05$, $p < .001$). On average, participants selected the targets in the shortest selection time when the *target tilt angle* was 57°. The second shortest selection time was achieved when the *target tilt angle* was 79°. The *target tilt angle* of 145° produced the longest time. This result is consistent with the finding from our pilot studies in which participants were asked to naturally and comfortably place the pen tip on the tablet surface. Pilot studies revealed that the comfortable and natural range for pen tilt was 58.8° with an *SD* of 8.6°.

In Experiment 1, we also observed that participants encountered trouble selecting targets with *target tilt angle* 35° because the pen was obstructed by the hand when the pen tail was oriented towards the participant's arm. Even when the angular width of a target increased to 10°, the selection time was still very long, indicating the strong influence imposed by hand obstruction. *Post hoc* pair-wise comparisons showed significant differences between all angular width pairs ($p < .005$) and target tilt angle pairs (35°, 57°), (35°, 79°), (57°, 145°), (79°, 101°), and (79°, 145°), (all $p < .01$). The significant *target tilt angle* × *angular width* interaction for time indicates that the adverse impact of hand occlusion was obviously reduced when angular width increased.

Selection Error

Selection error rate was defined as the percentage of trials in which subjects made erroneous selections. Subjects committed the fewest errors (3.33%) when angular width was 30°, and the most errors (32.38%) when angular width was 5°. For *target tilt angle*, subjects committed the fewest errors when the target tilt angle was 145°, and the most errors when the target tilt angle was 101°. Repeated measures analysis of variance showed a significant main effect on error rate for *target tilt angle* ($F_{5, 55} = 7.46$, $p < .001$) and *angular width* ($F_{3, 33} = 341.42$, $p < .001$). Moreover, there was a significant main effect on error rate for *target tilt angle* × *angular width* ($F_{15, 165} = 2.28$, $p < .01$). Figure 3 illustrates the results.

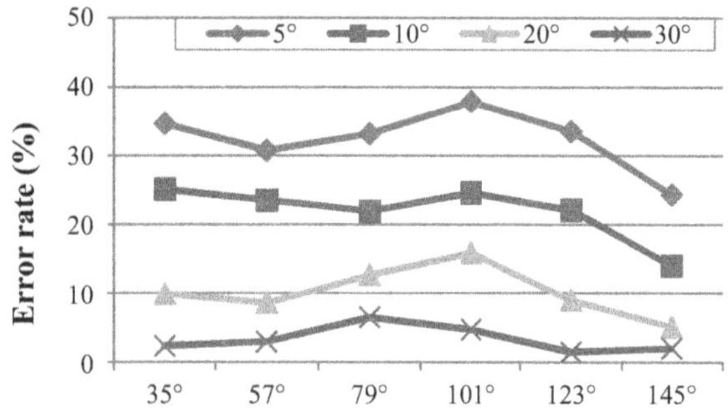

Figure 3. Error rate per angular width × target tilt angle.

Post hoc pairwise comparisons showed significant differences between all angular width pairs ($p < .001$) and target tilt angle pairs (35°, 145°), (57°, 145°), (79°, 145°), (101°, 123°), and (101°, 145°), ($p < .005$). The significant interaction effect of *target tilt angle* × *angular width* on time indicates that with the increase of angular width, subjects tended to commit a similar number of errors for different target tilt angles.

Number of Crossings

When rotating the pink tilt cursor to select a target, subjects sometimes crossed the target more than once. Number of crossings, NC, is defined as the number of times the pink tilt cursor enters or leaves a target for a particular trial, minus 1. Repeated measures analysis of variance showed a significant main effect on NC for *target tilt angle* ($F_{5, 55} = 10.25$, $p < .001$) and *angular width* ($F_{3, 33} = 61.52$, $p < .001$). Moreover, there was an interaction effect on NC for *target tilt angle* × *angular width* ($F_{15, 165} = 3.96$, $p < .001$).

As illustrated in Figure 4, a narrower angular width leads to a higher number of NC. In particular, subjects managed to select the target without extra crossings when angular width was 30°.

Analyzing NC by *target tilt angle*, subjects crossed the target with the least NC when target tilt angle was 145°; the largest NC occurred when the target tilt angle was 101°. These results indicate that NC increases as the pen becomes perpendicular to the tablet surface. *Post hoc* pairwise comparisons show significant differences between all angular width pairs ($p < .001$) and target tilt angle pairs (35°, 79°), (35°, 101°), (57°, 101°), (79°, 145°), (101°, 123°), and (101°, 145°) (all $p < .005$).

Learning effect

We collected 5 blocks of data to investigate the learning effect. Results showed that the selection time dropped as the block number increased.

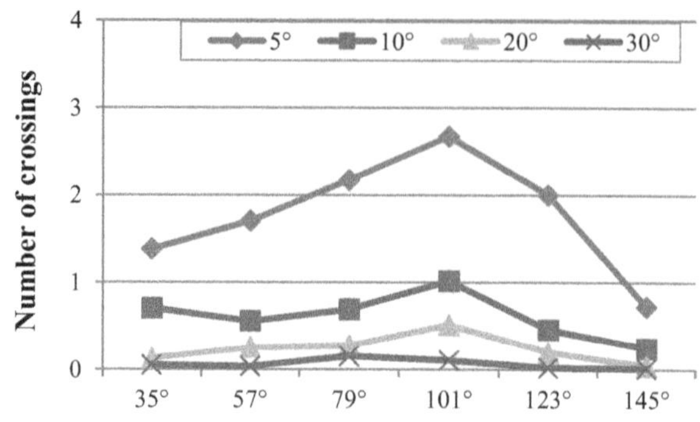

Figure 4. Number of crossings per angular width × target tilt angle.

Repeated measures analysis of variance showed a significant main effect for *block* on selection time ($F_{4, 44} = 10.55$, $p < .001$) and on NC ($F_{4, 44} = 4.31$, $p < .01$). Pairwise mean comparisons showed significant differences between block 1 and each of the other blocks (all $p < .05$). However, no significant differences were found between blocks 2, 3, 4 and 5 in pairs, indicating that participants reached a steady performance after the first block. No significant main effect was found for *block* on Error rate. Figure 5 illustrates the results.

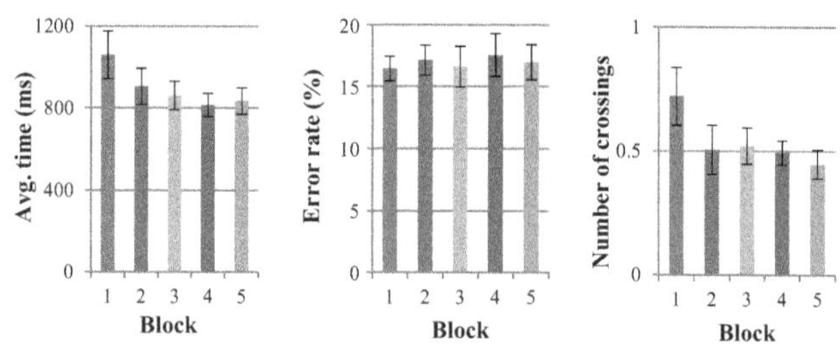

Figure 5. Learning effects of selection time, error rate, and NC × block.

Subjective Evaluation

At the end of the experiment, a questionnaire was administrated to gather subjective opinions. Participants were asked to rate *angular width* and *target tilt angle* on 7-point Likert Scales regarding *difficulty*, *stress*, and *fatigue*.

The final *preference* ratings were based on the average value of the answers given by the subjects (1 = lowest preference, and 7 = highest preference). Repeated measures analysis of variance showed a significant main effect on *angular width* ($F_{3, 33} = 61.40$, $p < .001$). The preference and the standard deviation values of *angular widths* 5°, 10°, 20°, and 30° were (2.72, 1.58), (4.97, 0.97), (6.44, 0.41) and (6.89, 0.30) respectively. 5° was rated the lowest and 30° the highest. A significant main effect on *target tilt angle* was found ($F_{5, 55} = 13.39$, $p < .001$). The preference and the standard deviation values of target tilt angles 35°, 57°, 79°, 101°, 123°, and 145° were (3.31, 2.03), (5.50, 1.18), (6.03, 0.94), (5.36, 1.58), (4.39, 1.15), and (2.44, 1.09) respectively. 145° was rated the lowest and 79° the highest.

Discussion

One main objective of this study was to investigate the comfort zones for pen tilt. Our results indicate that users performed experimental tasks efficiently during the tilt range [30°, 150°] with angular width >=30°, and tilt range [30°, 80°] & [100°, 150°] with angular width >=20°. We highly recommend these ranges as "comfortable zones" for pen tilt. Within these ranges, the selection times are all less than 1 second with error rate<=10% and NC<=1. Once the angular width drops to 10°, the error rate drastically increases to above 20%. Utilizing the tilt angle within these "comfortable zones" will lead to shorter performance time and lower error rate.

We observed that participants adjusted the pen tilt angles using the following two approaches: 1) by roughly tilt the pen in the air, and finely adjust the tilt angle after landing the pen on the tablet; 2) by not adjusting the tilt angle until the pen tip is in contact with the tablet. Since our purpose is to investigate how users naturally tilt the pen, participants could freely choose either of these two approaches during the experiment. Interestingly, most of the pen tilt adjustments fell within the approach #1, especially for tilt angles within [90°, 180°]. This is probably because approach #1 allowed participants to see both the pen tip and visual objects most of the time. The pen tip is occluded when the tilt angel falls within [90°, 180°] in approach #2.

EXPERIMENT 2: TILT POINTING

This experiment investigated the human ability to control pen tilt when the pen tip is in contact with the tablet. Also, we planned to test whether tilt-based pointing tasks can be modeled by Fitts' law [7].

Participants and Apparatus

The same 12 individuals who participated in Experiment 1 took part in Experiment 2. The same apparatus with the same experimental setup was used as in Experiment 1.

Task and Procedure

Figure 6 is the schematic diagram of the tilt pointing experimental tool. Pen tilt was utilized to control the rotation movement of a pink cursor around a fixed point, either clockwise or anticlockwise. As in Experiment 1, the pen tilt angle was mapped to the circumferential angle of the pink cursor in a one-to-one manner (e.g., 80° pen tilt is mapped to an 80° rotation). A set of equal and consecutive sectors presenting targets with various angular widths were drawn using dashed lines around the fixed point on the screen. During each trial, two of the target sectors were highlighted in red and yellow respectively. Subjects had to land the pen tip in the input area and apply the appropriate amount of pen tilt to rotate the pink cursor into the first desired target, the red one. When the pink cursor entered the first target, the target sector color changed to green. The subject confirmed the selection by pressing the space bar with the non-dominant hand on the keyboard. After the first selection, the color of the first target sector changed to gray and the color of the second target sector changed to red. The subject had to tilt the pen to select the second target. The subject could not select the second target without correctly selecting the first target. Subjects were told to strive for both accuracy and speed. An error was defined as selecting the second target wrongly. If an incorrect selection was made, a failure "ding" sound cue was given to the subject.

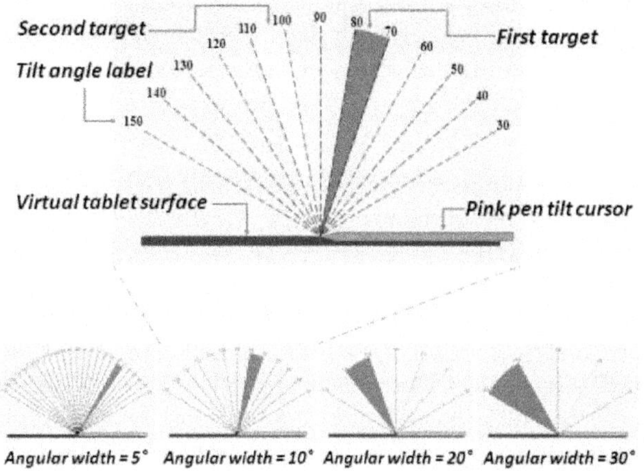

Figure 6. Schematic diagram of the tilt pointing experimental tool.

A within-subject full factorial design with repeated measures was used. The independent variables were angular widths, *ID* (index of difficulty), and tilt directions (left-to-right, and right-to-left). To ensure that the targets were symmetrical along the vertical line of the tablet and the ID values were relatively decentralized, we designated the following values of angular widths and angular distances (see Table 1). The *ID* values were calculated according to $ID = log_2$ *(Angular distance/Angular width+1)*.

Angular Width	5°			10°			20°			30°		
Angular Distance	25°	65°	115°	30°	70°	110°	20°	60°	100°	30°	60°	90°
ID	2.58	3.81	4.58	2	3	3.58	1	2	2.58	1	1.58	2

Table 1. Angular widths vs. angular distances in Experiment 2.

A Latin Square was used to counterbalance the order of the appearance of angular widths and angular distances. To explore the learning effects, 5 blocks of trials were completed by every subject. Each block consisted of 24 target acquiring tasks repeated once. Presentation of trials within a block was randomized. Before the formal experiment, subjects were allowed to perform a warm-up practice session until they could understand the task and perform it correctly. In total, the experiment consisted of:

12 subjects ×
4 angular widths ×
3 angular distances ×
2 tilting directions ×
5 blocks ×
2 times
=2880 target selection trials

Results

Selection Time

Selection time is elapsed time from the moment when the subject confirmed the first target selection correctly until the time when the subject executed the second target selection by pressing the space bar on the keyboard. Similar to the results of the first experiment, the narrower the angular width, the more time subjects needed to select the target. The subjects generally tilted the pen from the left to the right side (right pointing, towards the dominant hand) faster than from the right to the left side (left pointing, towards the non-dominant hand).

Repeated measures analysis of variance showed a significant main effect on selection time for *angular width* ($F_{3,\ 33}$ = 176.86, $p < .001$), *tilting direction* ($F_{1,11}$ = 5.45, $p < .05$) and *ID* ($F_{7,\ 77}$ = 47.52, $p < .001$). However, there was no significant effect on selection time for *angular width × direction* ($F_{3,33}$ = 2.69, p = 0.062) and *ID × direction* ($F_{7,77}$ = 0.682, p = 0.687). *Post hoc* pairwise comparisons showed significant differences between all angular width pairs (p < .001).

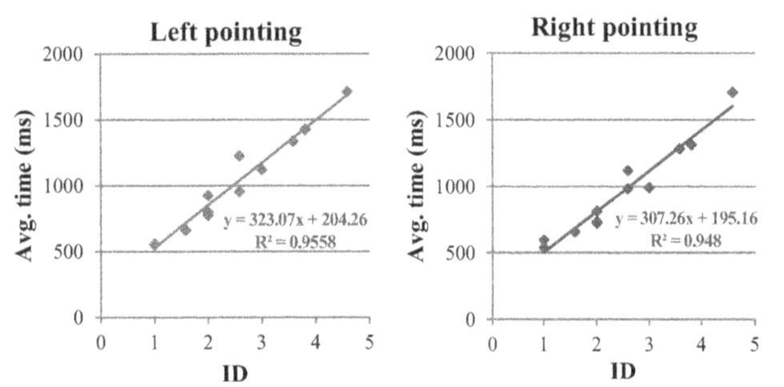

Figure 7. Selection time of left and right pointing for each ID.

As shown in Figure 7, linear regression of the experimental data *MT* by *ID* showed high correlations with Fitts' law. In both left and right pointing, R-Squares were greater than 0.94. We also performed linear regression of *MT* by *ID* separately with each angular width. R-Squares were all greater than 0.90. These results show that pen tilt-controlled target pointing tasks obey Fitts' law. For right-handed subjects, left pointing was a closer fit to Fitts' law than right pointing.

Selection Error

The error rate was defined as the percentage of trials in which the subjects made erroneous selections of the second target. Results indicate that narrower angular widths lead to higher error rates. ANOVA showed a significant main effect on error rate for *angular width* ($F_{3,33}$ = 5.86, $p < .005$) and *ID* ($F_{7,77}$ = 3.11, $p < .01$). However, there were no significant effects on error for *tilting direction*, angular width × *direction* and *ID × direction*.

Number of Crossings

The NC was calculated in the second target selections. Repeated measures analysis of variance showed a significant main effect on NC for *angular width* ($F_{3,33}$ = 82.62, $p < .001$) and *ID* ($F_{7,77}$ = 16.81, $p < .001$). However, there were no significant effects on NC for *tilting direction*, angular width × *direction* and *ID × direction*.

Learning effect

The experimental results showed a sight learning effect for tilt pointing. Selection time decreased as the number of blocks increased. Repeated measures analysis of variance showed a significant main effect on selection time for *block* ($F_{4,44}$ = 7.08, $p < .001$). Pairwise mean comparisons showed significant differences between block 1 and each of the other blocks (all $p < .05$). However, no significant differences were found between blocks 2, 3, 4 and 5 in pairs, indicating that participants reached a steady performance after performing block 1. This result showed that the leaning effect was minor and participants could quickly learn tilt pointing operations. Moreover, there was a significant interaction effect on selection time for *tilt direction × block* ($F_{4,44}$ = 3.17, $p < .05$). Subjects achieved a better learning effect in tilting to the left than in tilting to the right. In block 5, subjects used almost the same time to accomplish the target selections.

For error rate, repeated measures analysis of variance showed no significant effect on error rate for *block*. Moreover, there was no significant interaction effect on error rate for *tilt direction × block*.

For NC, repeated measures analysis of variance showed no significant effect on NC for *block* ($F_{4,44}$ = 0.087, p = 0.986). Moreover, there was no significant interaction effect on NC for *tilt direction × block*. Figure 8 illustrates the results.

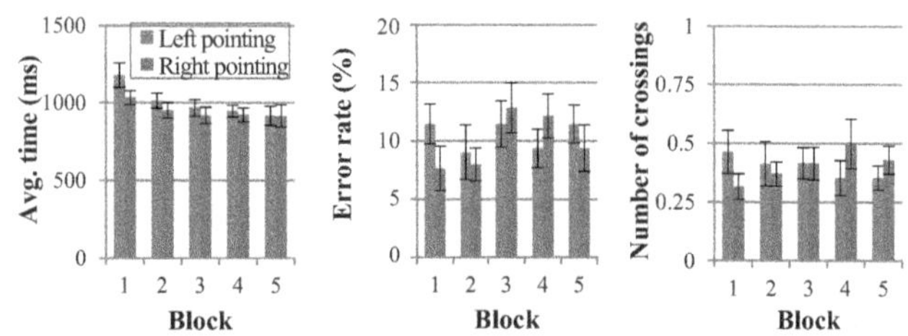

Figure 8. Learning effects of selection time, error rate, and NC for block × tilting direction.

Subjective Evaluation

At the end of the experiment, a questionnaire was administrated to gather subjective opinions. Participants were asked to rate *tilting direction*, *angular distance* and *angular width* on 7-point Likert Scales regarding *difficulty*, *stress*, and *fatigue*.

The final *preference* ratings were based on the average value of the answers given by the subjects (1 = lowest preference, and 7 = highest preference). Repeated measures analysis of variance showed a significant main effect on *angular width* ($F_{3,33}$ = 55.99, $p < .001$). The preference and the standard deviation values of *angular widths* 5°, 10°, 20°, and 30° were (2.61, 1.48), (4.92, 1.08), (6.49, 0.38) and (6.75, 0.29) respectively. The *angular distances* were classified as "far", "middle", and "near". A significant main effect on *angular distances* was found ($F_{2,22} = 12.86, p < .001$). The preference and the standard deviation values of *angular distances* "far", "middle", and "near" were (3.79, 1.18), (4.20, 1.63), and (5.67, 0.86) respectively. However, no significant main effect was found on *tilting direction*.

Discussion

Experimental results indicate that users can control pen tilt well when angular widths are equal or above 20°. Regarding selection time, subjects selected the target within 0.8 second for tilt angular widths of 20° and 30°, but very close or above 1 second when tilt angular width is 10° or 5°. The selection times in the 5th block for tilt angular widths 5°, 10°, 20°, and 30° were 1.34s, 0.99s, 0.77s, and 0.59s, respectively. For error rate, subjects committed less than 10% errors for angular widths 10°, 20°, and 30° in the 5th block. The average NCs were less than 1 except for angular width 5°. In the 5th block, the NCs for all target tilts were less than 1. Right pointing (towards the dominant hand) leads to better performance than Left pointing (towards the non-dominant hand) in terms of selection time, error rate, and NC.

Though the tilt-based pointing task in Experiment 2 was different from the traditional pointing tasks, interestingly, experimental results indicate that the tilt pointing task can also be modeled by Fitts' law in both left pointing and right pointing. Thus, the related applications and theories of Fitts' law could be widened to include tilt pointing tasks.

GENERAL DISCUSSION

Implications for Design

Experiments 1 and 2 investigate the user's ability to control tilt acquiring and pointing tasks respectively. The experimental results lead to the following important implications for pen tilt based interface design:

- The results reveal the comfort zones (tilt range [30°, 150°] with angular width >=30°, and tilt range [30°, 80°] & [100°, 150°] with angular width >=20°) for pen tilt in both *target-acquiring* and *target-pointing* situations. Since users can achieve high performance in these zones, we recommend their use for common pen tilt interaction. For example, if pen tilt angle is used to trigger mode switches, these angles should be distributed within the range [30°, 150°], and the angular width of each mode should be at least 20° wide. If pen tilt is used to control a virtual human figure [21] or for 3D navigation [4], using tilt angels within the "comfortable zones" could lead to better performance.
- The results give guidance to the continuous pen tilt space discretization. Study results show that users performed *tilt pointing* tasks with good performance when the angular width was equal or above 20°. Therefore, to obtain high performance, the angular width of a discrete unit should be equal to or above 20°.
- Selection time for acquisition by tilting can be modeled as a power relation while selection time for tilt pointing can be modeled by Fitts' law. These results can help designers improve design, e.g., to adjust the number of items in a pen-tilt-based pie menu.

We note that a direct input device was used in our experiments. The results might vary slightly in different situations such as with the use of indirect devices and in mobile postures. Furthermore, though absolute mapping was used in the experiment, (e.g., if the user lands the pen with the tilt angle of 80 degrees, the tilt cursor jumps to 80 degrees), we believe that the human ability to control pen tilt will not be changed even when using a relative mapping function. However, using different mapping functions like [29, 35] in pressure studies should be investigated in future work.

Method for conforming selection

How to conform the target selection in both tilt acquiring and pointing tasks is a key issue. At the design stage of the study, we conducted a series of experiments to decide the target selection technique. The five candidates considered were 1) Barrel-Button-Click: pressing the stylus' barrel button; 2) Dwell: keeping the tilt cursor within the target for 1 second; 3) Quick-Release: quickly lifting the pen from the tablet's surface; 4) Stroke: quickly drawing a circle; and 5) Key-Pressing: pressing a key on the keyboard using the non-dominant hand.

The results indicated that the Key-Pressing method was the most appropriate for investigating pen tilt control for the following reasons: 1) Barrel-Button-Click [20] and Stroke [15] often caused inadvertent pen-tip movement and easily led to pen tilt changes. Besides, subjects often rotated the stylus, thus the button may not always be in a position that facilitates pressing; 2) Dwell requires subjects to maintain pen tilt for a given time, which may lead to user fatigue and pen tilt change. Ramos et al.'s study [24] also showed that the time cost for Dwell was high; 3) Quick-release method requires the user to lift pen tip up after the selection. This method is a poor fit for the "tilt pointing" task because the user had to select the first and the second targets in succession, in which case he/she had to keep the pen tip in contact with the surface. 4) Previous work indicated that better performance in selection time and error rate could be achieved with bi-manual rather than with uni-manual interaction [8, 10, 14, 28].

We also asked the subjects to evaluate the five selection techniques according to fatigue, difficulty, nervousness, and preference on a 7-point Likert scale. Key-Pressing was ranked best, followed by Quick-Release, Barrel-Button-Click, Dwell, and Stroke. Because our purpose was to investigate the human ability to control pen tilt, it was necessary to minimize the factors that affected the results. Thus in this study, we regarded the space bar selection method as optimal. We note that pressing a button may not always be available in real applications which only involve one-handed operation, thus other selections method should be considered.

An alternative is to confirm the selection by pressing the pen tip. However, since a tablet can not reliably detect the pen pressure at a large pen tilt angle and exerting force on the pen tip could affect the tilt angle which might compromise the experiments, we did not use this method in our experiments.

Effects of Handedness

To avoid bias caused by handedness, we deliberately choose right-handed participants in our experiments. Since the structures of left and right hands are symmetrical, we expect that findings in our studies also apply to left-handed users by symmetrically adjusting the coordinate system. In our experiment, tilt angle range [30°, 90°] is mapped to azimuth angle range [0°, 179°]. For left-handed users, most of the conclusions still hold if the tilt angle range [30°, 90°] is mapped to the azimuth angle range [180°, 359°]. Investigating how handedness affects the human ability to control pen tilt is one of our future research directions, but it is not within the scope of the current paper.

PEN TILT INTERACTION TECHNIQUES

As an additional input modality, pen tilt can be used in both discrete selections, e.g., choosing an item from a list or a pie menu, and consecutive variant manipulations, e.g. varying brush size in a painting system. Moreover, in a concrete pen based interface, pen tilt changes can be mapped either to displace a cursor in the interface, or to change the angle/orientation of a target, or to adjust the granularity of a manipulation of a parameter. Taking into account the factors mentioned above, we developed a taxonomy of pen tilt utilization which describes the characteristics of the pen tilt techniques we proposed (see Table 2).

	Manner of Pen tilt manipulation	
	Discrete	Consecutive
Target	Fan menu 3D manipulation Sub-objects creation	Granularity widget 3D manipulation
Cursor	Magic Pen Mode switching	Projection cursor

Table 2. A taxonomy for the design of pen tilt techniques.

Based on our experimental results, a series of interactive techniques are proposed to demonstrate the potential of pen tilt to enhance pen-based interactions (see Figure 9).

Fan menu

A pie menu is divided into different sectors and each sector is mapped to a certain range of pen tilt angle (Figure 9a). By changing pen tilt angle with the pen tip in contact with the tablet, users can switch between different menu items. Moreover, the pen tilt could also be used in a marking menu [18] to extend the number of available items. According to the results of our experiment, it is better to set the sector in a tilt menu no smaller than 20° to achieve more comfortable manipulation.

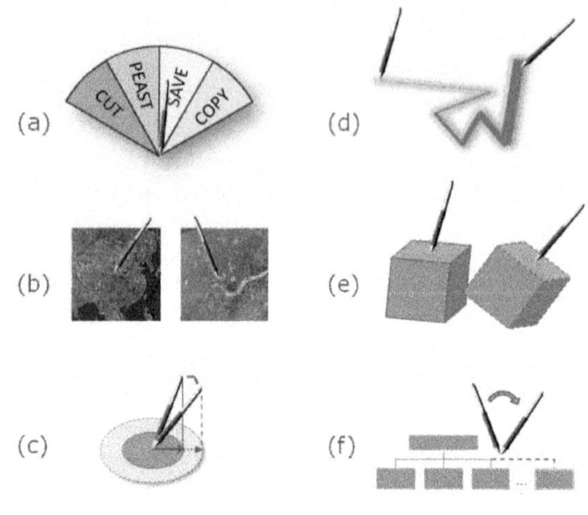

Figure 9. The conceptual designs of pen tilt techniques: (a) Fan menu; (b) Granularity widget; c) Projection cursor; (d) Magic Pen with implicit mode switching; (e) 3D manipulation; (f) Sub-objects creation.

Granularity widget

Pen tilt can be used to manipulate a parameter with varied precision. A slider is an object in a GUI with which the user sets a value by moving an indicator. The slider can be augmented with pen tilt (Figure 9b) so that the sliding action is produced by varying the pen tip x-y coordinate position, and the granularity of the sliding is adjusted by controlling pen tilt. As indicated in the experimental results, pen tip displacement could be found when the pen is tilted. In order to achieve accurate manipulation, a special procedure to reduce the influence of displacement is recommended. This mechanism can be used to adjust the granularity of a control such as the number of steps in scrolling, or the speed of the fast forward function in a video replay. For example, in map navigation, the reader can easily navigate the map to either coarse or fine scale by adjusting the pen tilt.

Projection cursor

As the pen tilt angle changes, its projected shadow varies accordingly. We proposed a projected cursor whose size changes according to the pen's tilt angle (Figure 9c). The cursor size shrinks as the pen is tilted towards the line perpendicular to the tablet surface, while the size of a cursor expands when it is tilted towards the tablet surface. This cursor is useful for selecting multiple targets, or for specifying an area. Also, the cursor size provides user visual feedback about the pen tilt angle.

Magic Pen with implicit mode switching

Mode switching is always challenging in pen interface design. Pen tilt has the potential to smooth the mode switching process. For example, in our Magic Pen design (Figure 9d), a digital pen has two painting modes ("hard" pen and "soft" pen). In drawing tasks, a large pen tilt angle results in a "hard" pen mode in which stroke width is consistent. A small pen tilt angle invokes "soft" pen in which stroke width varied according to pen pressure. Our experimental results show that a target angle near 90° is difficult to acquire. Since hard pen mode is seldom used in pen design, we suggest mapping this area (e.g., [80°, 100°]) to "hard pen" mode.

3D manipulation

Through the manipulation of a 3D object with pen tilt, more intuitive interaction may be achieved (Figure 9e). For example, a 3D object could be rotated according to variations in pen tilt. If the azimuth angle of a pen is also used to control the azimuth angle of the rotated target, the user can manipulate multiple degrees-of-freedom simultaneously.

Sub-objects creation

Since users can tilt a pen without moving the pen tip position drastically, using pen tilt can ease the sub-objects creation process in the drawing of an organizational chart or a flowchart. For example, we can slide the pen tip downward to create subordinates or left & right to create colleagues. During a pen sliding process, we can also tilt the pen to determine the number of sub-objects (Figure 9f). Because our experimental results indicate that an angle of more than 20° in width is identifiable, the pen tilt space [30°, 150°] can be divided into six regions at most thus reflecting the maximum number of sub-objects in one instance of pen tilting. If more sub-objects are needed, we can use a multiple-tilting method: after the first tilt is finished, the pen can be slid upwards over a threshold distance and the pen can be tilted again to continue sub-object creation.

CONCLUSIONS

This paper presented two controlled experiments, pen tilt target acquiring and pointing, that empirically investigated the human ability to use pen tilt to perform discrete target selection tasks. Results revealed a decreasing power relationship between angular width and selection time. This paper also verified the applicability of Fitts' law in the pen tilt pointing experiment. Results also indicate that 20 degrees of angular width presented the optimal performance regarding selection time, error, number of crossings, and number of tilt divisions. The human ability to control pen tilt and the implications of pen tilt utilization are discussed. In addition, a taxonomy of pen tilt based techniques along with a series of possible pen tilt scenarios is given. This paper presents a general understanding of pen tilt utilization, which may be useful in pen-based user interface design.

ACKNOWLEDGEMENTS

This study has been partially supported by Grant-in-Aid for Scientific Research (No.20500118), Microsoft Research Asia Mobile Computing in Education Theme and Exploratory Software Project of IPA (information technology promotion agency in Japan). The authors are grateful for the work and support of all the members of the Ren Lab in Kochi University of Technology. The authors thank Jibin Yin and Tomoaki Tsuchida for their contributions to earlier work on this project.

REFERENCES

1. Bartlett, J.F. (2000). Rock n' scroll is here to stay. *IEEE Computer. Graphics and Applications.* 20(3), 40-50.
2. Bi, X., Moscovich, T., Ramos, G., Balakrishnan, R. and Hinckley, K. (2008). An exploration of pen rolling for pen-based interaction, *Proc. UIST,* 191-200.
3. Blaskó, G., Beaver, W., Kamvar, M. and Feiner, S. (2004). Workplane-orientation sensing techniques for tablet PCs, *Proc. UIST,* 24-27.
4. Bridson, R. (2009) SpikeNav: using stylus tilt in three-dimensional navigation, *ACM UIST* Poster Session
5. Eissele, M., Stegmaier, S., Weiskopf, D. and Ertl, T. (2004). Orientation as an additional user interface in mixed-reality environments. *Workshop GI-Fachgruppe AR/VR,* 79-90.
6. Fishkin, K.P., Moran, T.P. and Harrison, B.L. (1998). Embodied user interfaces: towards invisible user interfaces. *Proc. EHCI,* 1-18.
7. Fitts, P. M. (1954). The information capacity of the human motor system in controlling the amplitude of movement. *Journal of Experimental Psychology.* 47, 381-391.
8. Fitzmaurice, G.W., Balakrishnan, R., Kurtenbach, G. and Buxton, B. (1999). An exploration into supporting artwork orientation in the user interface. *Proc. CHI,* 167-174.
9. Fitzmaurice, G.W., Zhai, S. and Chignell, M.H. (1993). Virtual reality for palmtop computers. *ACM Transactions on Information Systems,* 11(3), 197-218.
10. Guiard, Y. and Ferrand, T. (1987). Asymmetric division of labor in human skilled bimanual action: the kinematic chain as a model. *Journal of Motor Behavior,* 19(4), 486-517.
11. Harrison, B.L., Fishkin, K.P., Gujar, A., Mochon, C. and Want, R. (1998). Squeeze me, hold me, tilt me! an exploration of manipulative user interfaces. *Proc. CHI,* 17-24.
12. Hinckley, K., Baudisch, P., Ramos, G. and Guimbretiere, F. (2005). Design and analysis of delimiters for selection-action pen gesture phrases in scriboli. *Proc. CHI,* 451-460.
13. Hinckley, K., Pierce, J., Sinclair, M. and Horvitz, E. (2000). Sensing techniques for mobile interaction. *Proc. UIST,* 91-100.
14. Kabbash, P., Buxton, W. and Sellen, A.G. (1994). Two-handed input in a compound task. *Proc. CHI,* 417-423.
15. Krishnan, S.N. and Moriya, S. (1996). One stroke operations: a new pen-based user interface that can

integrate or separate operand specification, menu opening and selection, and action execution, in one or more strokes. *Information Processing Society of Japan,* 37(12), 2419-2437.

16. Kristensson, P.-O. and Zhai, S. (2004). SHARK2: a large vocabulary shorthand writing system for pen-based computers. *Proc. UIST,* 43-52.

17. Kuroki, T. and Kawai, S. (1999). An interface technology for pen devices using tilt information. *Proc. Interactive Systems and Software VII,* 1-6.

18. Kurtenbach, G. and Buxton, W. (1993). The limits of expert performance using hierarchical marking menus. *Proc. CHI,* 35-42.

19. Leitner, J., Powell, J., Brandl, P., Seifried, T., Haller, M., Dorray, B. and To, P. (2009). Flux: a tilting multi-touch and pen based surface. *Proc. CHI EA,* 3211-3216.

20. Lin, J., Newman, M.W., Hong, J.I. and Landay, J.A. (2000). DENIM: finding a tighter fit between tools and practice for Web site design. *Proc. CHI,* 510-517.

21. Oshita M. (2004). Pen-to-mime: a pen-based interface for interactive control of a human figure. *EUROGRAPHICS workshop on sketch-based interfaces and modeling,* 43-52.

22. Partridge, K., Chatterjee, S., Sazawal, V., Borriello, G. and Want, R. (2002). TiltType: accelerometer-supported ext entry for very small devices. *Proc. UIST,* 201-204.

23. Rahman, M., Gustafson, S., Irani, P. and Subramanian, S. (2009). Tilt techniques: investigating the dexterity of wrist-based input. *Proc. CHI,* 1943-1952.

24. Ramos, G., Boulos, M. and Balakrishnan, R. (2004). Pressure Widgets. *Proc. CHI,* 487-494.

25. Rekimoto, J. (1996). Tilting operations for small screen interfaces. *Proc. UIST,* 167-168.

26. Rekimoto, J. and Sciammarella, E. (2000). ToolStone: effective use of the physical manipulation vocabularies of input devices. *Proc. UIST,* 109-117.

27. Ren, X. and Moriya, S. (2000). Improving selection performance on pen-based systems: a study of pen-input interaction for selection tasks. *ToCHI,* 7(3), 384-416.

28. Sazawal, V., Want, R. and Borriello, G. (2002). The unigesture approach. one-handed text entry for small devices. *Proc. MobileHCI,* 256-270.

29. Shi, K., Irani, P., Gustafson, S. and Subramanian, S. (2008). PressureFish: a method to improve control of discrete pressure-based input. *Proc. CHI,* 1295-1298.

30. Small, D. and Ishii, H. (1997). Design of spatially aware graspable displays. *Proc. CHI,* 367-368.

31. Szalavári, Z. and Gervautz, M. (1997). The Personal Interaction Panel - a Two-Handed Interface for Augmented Reality. *Computer Graphics Forum,* 16(3), 335-346.

32. Tian, F., Ao, X., Wang, H., Setlur, V. and Dai, G. (2007). The tilt cursor: enhancing stimulus-response compatibility by providing 3D orientation cue of pen. *Proc. CHI,* 303-306.

33. Tian, F., Xu, L., Wang, H., Zhang, X., Liu, Y., Setlur, V. and Dai, G. (2008). Tilt menu: using the 3D orientation information of pen devices to extend the selection capability of pen-based user interfaces. *Proc. CHI,* 1371-1380.

34. Wigdor, D. and Balakrishnan, R. (2003). TiltText: using tilt for text input to mobile phones. *Proc. UIST,* 81-90.

35. Xin, Y. and Ren, X. (2010). An investigation of adaptive pen pressure discretization method based on personal pen pressure use profile, *IEICE Transactions on Information and Systems,* E93-D(5), 1205-1213.

36. Zhou, X. and Ren, X. (2009). A comparison of pressure and tilt input techniques for cursor control, *IEICE Transactions on Information and Systems,* E92-D(9), 1683-1691.

On the Costs of Multiple Trajectory Pointing Methods

Philip Quinn,[1] Andy Cockburn,[1] Kari-Jouko Räihä,[2] Jérôme Delamarche[3]
[1]Dept. of Computer Science, University of Canterbury, New Zealand;
philip.quinn@canterbury.ac.nz, andy@cosc.canterbury.ac.nz
[2]School of Information Sciences, University of Tampere, Finland; kari-jouko.raiha@cs.uta.fi
[3]Polytech' Paris-Sud, Orsay, France; jerome.delamarche@gmail.com

ABSTRACT
Several enhanced pointing techniques aim to reduce the Fitts' law targeting distance by providing multiple target trajectories in the hope that a shorter path is available. However, these techniques introduce a search or decision component to pointing – users must examine the alternatives available and decide upon the trajectory to use. We analyse these difficulties, present a methodology for examining them as well as other behaviour issues, and report empirical results of performance with pointer wrapping and Ninja cursors. Results show that offering multiple trajectories incurs a significant search or decision cost, and that users are therefore poor at capitalising on the theoretical benefits of reduced target distance.

Author Keywords
Pointing, Fitts' law, Ninja cursors, wrapping cursors, multiple trajectories, search/decision.

ACM Classification Keywords
H5.2. Information interfaces and presentation: User Interfaces – Evaluation/methodology.

General Terms
Human Factors, Theory, Verification

INTRODUCTION
Several approaches to improving pointing performance with a mouse focus on reducing the index of difficulty (*ID*) of the pointing task, as described by Fitts' law [8]. That is, by manipulating the representations of the cursor or the target, they reduce the target distance or increase target width.

One approach for reducing target distance is to provide multiple pointing trajectories. Kobayashi and Igarashi describe *Ninja cursors* [7], in which multiple cursors are controlled in unison with a single mouse, allowing a different trajectory for each cursor. Another multiple trajectory approach is to allow the cursor to 'wrap around' the screen edge: for example, exiting the East side enters the West.

However, such approaches introduce a search or decision element to the task of pointing. When there is only one trajectory, the choice of how to move the cursor is obvious; but when multiple alternatives are introduced, users must first select a trajectory and then execute the movement. There is a risk that the search/decision cost could reduce (or eliminate) the benefits of providing these shortcut paths. Figure 1 illustrates efficient (black) and inefficient (red) trajectories for pointer wrapping and Ninja cursors when moving from the right to left targets.

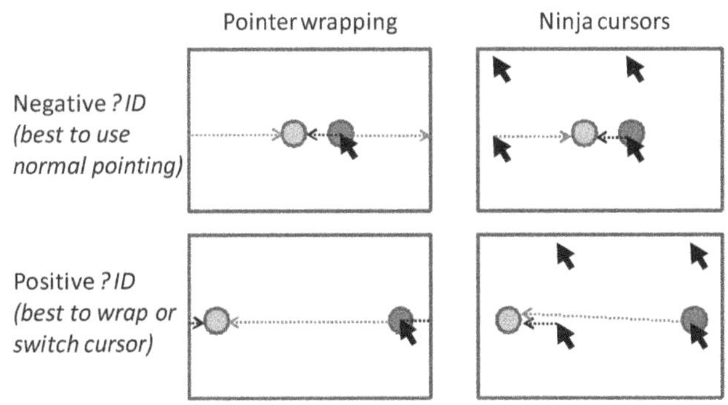

Figure 1. Multiple trajectories for pointer wrapping (left) and Ninja cursors (right). Top row shows a cost to using the alternative trajectory; bottom row shows a benefit.

We developed a methodology for examining the decision component of pointing techniques by comparing them to a user's expected direct pointing performance as described by Fitts' law. We were also interested in examining the selected trajectories chosen when presented with these techniques – do users make the right decisions?

The following section briefly reviews research on pointing models and multiple trajectory techniques. We then present a method for examining performance with these techniques. Finally, we report experimental results for *pointer wrapping*, where the cursor can wrap around screen borders, and *Ninja cursors* in configurations of four and nine cursors.

BACKGROUND
Fitts' law [8] is a well-established model of target acquisition, predicting movement time $MT = a + b \times ID$, where $ID = \log_2(D/W + 1)$, and D and W are target distance and width. Since the seminal work of Card *et al.* [2], decision times in interaction have also been examined in HCI, with recent examples including Hinckley *et al.*'s [6] analysis of 'Springboard' mode control mechanisms, and Cockburn and Gutwin's [3] investigation of hierarchical navigation.

Pointing Techniques

Ninja cursors [7] display multiple cursors that are moved in unison with the mouse. While only one cursor can be 'active' at any time, users can use any cursor to acquire a target. To prevent targeting ambiguity a queuing algorithm determines which cursor is 'active'. For each cursor on the screen, an independent *ID* and *MT* can be calculated; with a good distribution of cursors, the minimum *ID* can be significantly less than that of single-cursor pointing.

Kobayashi and Igarashi [4] evaluated Ninja cursors in several cursor configurations and distracter densities, using tasks that intentionally removed the search/decision component of pointing. Ninja cursors significantly outperformed traditional pointing, except in conditions with high target density. Researchers have subsequently used eye gaze to eliminate the inefficiency of the queuing algorithm [1, 9]. Blanch and Ortega [1] separately analysed reaction time and movement time, observing high reaction times for their *Rake Cursor* technique, which they attributed to the need to decide between alternative cursors.

Another technique, *pointer wrapping*, uses a single cursor with the traditional appearance. However, the cursor does not stop when it reaches the edge of the screen; instead, it 'wraps' around to the opposite edge of the display. For example, when the cursor tries to move beyond the bottom of the display, it re-appears at the corresponding horizontal position at the top of the display (and similarly for the left and right edges). Pointer wrapping introduces multiple trajectories through the possible wrapping actions: users can either move directly, or wrap around edges of the screen.

Related techniques eliminate all non-target space: the *Bubble Cursor* [4] enlarges the cursor activation area to always enclose a target, and *Object Pointing* [5] analyses motion kinematics to jump between targets. These techniques may incur search/decision costs, even though they do not create multiple trajectories.

EVALUATING DECISION COSTS

Ninja cursors and pointer wrapping both introduce a search or decision component to pointing interactions by giving users a choice between multiple valid trajectories. Our goals are to examine the size and impact of this component on performance and to examine how well users select paths.

Neither of these techniques alters the representation of the cursor or target; once a trajectory/cursor has been chosen, the task is a direct pointing task and can be modelled by Fitts' law. With this observation, if the Fitts component is known, then whatever additional time remains in the pointing task can be attributed to search/decision factors. Therefore, by calibrating the Fitts *a* and *b* parameters for a user, their expected pointing times can be calculated and compared to actual pointing times with other techniques.

In order to examine trajectory choice, the benefits of each possible trajectory must be controlled. Pointing experiments typically control the *ID* of the target selection; however, this is insufficient when there are multiple possible *ID*s available, as single *ID* does not control the cost or benefit of choosing a different trajectory over the direct pointing path.

When multiple pointing trajectories are present, the user needs to determine: (1) if they need to switch cursors; and (2) which path to switch to. For Ninja cursors, this is a decision between cursors against the one that has their present focus (assumed to be the one used to select the previous target). For pointer wrapping, the decision is between direct pointing or wrapping around the screen (for brevity, we will refer to both of these activities as 'switching').

The switching decision requires a comparison between all possible *ID*s, but ultimately the decision is between the best possible *ID* for not switching and the *ID* for switching: that is, $\Delta ID = ID_{ns} - ID_s$. Controlling ΔID allows isolation of the switching cost/benefit. It also allows examination of how switching behaviour varies with theoretical benefit.

ID_{ns} is the direct pointing *ID*, when not switching cursors or wrapping around the screen. ID_s is the minimum *ID* achievable when switching cursors – the *ID* from the closest cursor (exclusive of the one currently used), or when wrapping around an edge of the screen. A negative ΔID indicates a theoretical cost to switching, while a positive ΔID indicates a benefit, as illustrated in Figure 1.

EXPERIMENT

We conducted an experiment to investigate pointing and decision time behaviour in three interfaces: pointer wrapping, Ninja cursors with four cursors ('Ninja-4'; in a 2×2 arrangement), and Ninja cursors with nine cursors ('Ninja-9'; in a 3×3 arrangement). Additionally, each participant completed a Fitts' law calibration phase.

Our implementation of Ninja cursors matched that described by Kobayashi and Igarashi [7]. Cursors were spaced evenly across the screen, matching the aspect-ratio of the display. As there were no distracter targets, no queuing algorithm was necessary and there were no limitations on which cursor could be used to make selections. Cursors wrapped to the opposing edge when they reached the edge of the display, but targets were controlled so that on-screen cursors were initially closer to the target than wrapped ones.

Apparatus and Participants The experiment ran on an Intel Core 2 Duo machine running Fedora 12 and was presented on a 22□ LCD monitor at a resolution of 1680×1050. Input was collected through a Microsoft Wheel Mouse Optical.

Fifteen volunteers (three female) participated in the experiment. All were post-graduate computer science students and each received a $10 gift certificate.

Task and Stimuli All participants completed four experimental stages: a Fitts calibration (direct pointing) first, and then pointer wrapping, Ninja-4, and Ninja-9 in a counterbalanced order.

Two target acquisition tasks were used: *random* selections and *bi-directional tapping*. In *random* tasks, targets were selected randomly from the collection of possible targets (see below); each target was a red circle, 40 pixels in diameter and was the only element visible on the screen (aside from the cursor(s)). In *bi-directional tapping* tasks, pairs of targets were chosen and presented to participants; the target to select was presented as a solid red circle, while the paired target was shown as a hollow black outline. The order of *random* and *bi-directional tapping* within each stage was counter-balanced between participants.

In *random* stages, participants selected 46 targets (the first target was discarded, as its position relative to the cursor was not controlled). In *bi-directional tapping* stages, fifteen pairs of targets were presented serially, and participants selected each target in the pair four times (the first target of the pair was selected five times, but the initial selection was discarded). *Random* and *bi-directional tapping* tasks were used to provide insights into how users make trajectory decisions in different types of activities. *Random* tasks involve a unique decision for every target, but *bi-directional tapping* involves repeated reciprocal trajectories, so the costs of an initial decision can be dissipated across improved performance in many trials.

In the Fitts calibration stage, participants selected or tapped between targets with *ID*s of {1, 2, 3, 4, 5} bits, within a tolerance of 0.0001 bits. Each *ID* value was used for nine trials. The remaining stages used a similar process, except targets were generated for ΔIDs {-0.5, 0, 0.5, 1, 1.5} with wrapping and {-1, 0, 1, 2, 3} for Ninja cursors. The ΔID ranges differ between wrapping and Ninja cursors due to target distance being bounded by cursor separation in Ninja cursors. Consequently, results cannot be directly compared between the wrapping and Ninja cursors conditions.

Additionally, the distance of the target was controlled to ensure that targets at high ΔIDs for the Ninja-9 condition were distributed over the full range of possible targets.

Procedure and Design The dependent measure was selection time: from the instant the target was displayed to successful acquisition. It was analyzed for each interface using a 2×5 within-subjects ANOVA for the factors *task* (*random* selection and *bi-directional tapping*) and ΔID.

Each trial continued until successful target selection. After each selection, the cursor was snapped to the centre of the target to ensure an accurate *ID* in the following trial.

In summary, the experiment consisted of:

4 interfaces × 5 *ID*s or ΔIDs ×
(3 tap pairs × 8 trials per pair + 9 random targets/trials)
= 660 target selection trials per participant

Prior to each stage, participants were instructed on the interface and completed fifteen sample *random* selection trials. Participants were instructed to perform the tasks as quickly and accurately as possible; they could take breaks between each task, and completed a questionnaire after each stage. The experiment lasted approximately 20 minutes.

RESULTS

For each participant, the Fitts calibration data stage was used to determine their *a* and *b* parameters. These values were used to calculate the participant's expected pointing times with the three multi-trajectory interfaces (wrapping, Ninja-4, Ninja-9), each analysed separately below.

Pointer Wrapping

An analysis of variance revealed significant main effects on the selection time for the factors *task* ($F_{1,14} = 75.9, p < .001$) and ΔID ($F_{4,56} = 18.4, p < .001$).

Figure 2(a) shows results for pointer wrapping in the *random* (left) and *bi-directional tapping* tasks (middle). Each plot shows actual mean times as well as Fitts' predictions for direct (ID_{ns}) and wrapping (ID_s). They show that actual performance was substantially slower than Fitts' law predictions for both the optimal trajectory *and* for the suboptimal trajectory (when the user takes the wrong path). The rightmost plot shows the difference between actual and predicted optimal performance. Even with *bi-directional tapping*, where users could recover the initial decision cost through multiple trials, actual performance was substantially worse than the optimum Fitts' predictions. It is interesting that actual performance was best when the theoretical costs of switching were highest (negative ΔID) and worst when ΔID was slightly positive (representing a marginal benefit for switching). This suggests that hard decisions, where the trajectories are evenly balanced, take longer to make (nearly 700 ms, as shown in Figure 2(c)), making performance much worse than if the multiple trajectory option was absent.

Enabling multiple trajectories reduced participants' performance beyond that attainable with normal pointing – the decision costs of between 380 and 677 ms (for *random* targets) overwhelmed any potential benefit in all conditions.

Ninja cursors

Analysis of variance also revealed significant main effects on the selection time for the Ninja-4 interface for the factors *task* ($F_{1,14} = 250.7$, $p < .001$) and ΔID ($F_{4,56} = 39.1$, $p < .001$); and similarly for Ninja-9, *task* ($F_{1,14} = 144.5$, $p < .001$) and ΔID ($F_{4,56} = 28.7$, $p < .001$). Figures 2(b,c) show results for Ninja-4 and Ninja-9 respectively.

With *random* Ninja-4 targets (Figure 2(b), left), participants' actual performance matched that of normal pointing ('expected direct') at $\Delta ID = 2$, and outperformed it at $\Delta ID = 3$, showing that for very distant targets Ninja cursors can offer a performance benefit. However, the plot also shows that Ninja cursors' multiple trajectories reduced performance beyond that expected for normal pointing with ΔID in the range □1 to +1. The plots for Ninja-9 (Figure 2(c)) show similar performance trends: for *random* trials it reduced performance beyond normal pointing in all but the most favourable conditions. The search/decision costs for *random* targets ranged from 148 to 310 ms with Ninja-4, and from 102 to 436 ms with Ninja-9. Overall, Ninja cursors reduced performance with *random* targets.

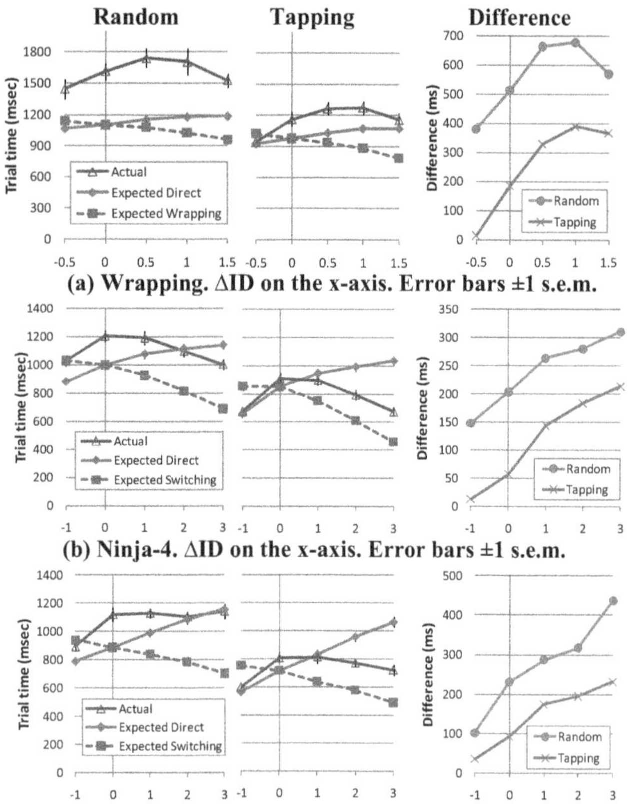

(a) Wrapping. ΔID on the x-axis. Error bars ±1 s.e.m.

(b) Ninja-4. ΔID on the x-axis. Error bars ±1 s.e.m.

(c) Ninja-9. ΔID on the x-axis. Error bars ±1 s.e.m.

Figure 2. Results for the three interface conditions with random and tapping tasks (left and middle columns). Lines show actual and Fitts' predicted times. The right column shows the difference between actual and Fitts' predicted optimal times.

Performance was better in *bidirectional tapping*, with both Ninja-4 and 9 showing performance benefits when $\Delta ID > 1$.

DISCUSSION

In almost all conditions, actual performance was substantially slower than the optimal Fitts' law predictions. Performance with multiple trajectory methods was also worse than normal pointing Fitts' law models (without multiple trajectories) in all but the most favourable conditions.

The search/decision times associated with pointer wrapping overwhelmed any potential advantage of shortened trajectory – even when the theoretical advantages or penalties (allowing it to be easily ignored) of wrapping were large.

Participant comments identified major differences in the nature of the search/decision costs between pointer wrapping and Ninja cursors. With wrapping, participants referred to *'getting confused'*, *'hard to decide'*, and *'easier to ignore'*, indicating that it demanded a cognitive decision about the trajectory, as supported by the high time difference between theoretical and actual times (nearly 700 ms, Figure 2a, right). With Ninja cursors, however, participants referred to *'seeing the nearest cursor straight after beginning'*, indicating a visual search pop-out effect. The rightmost plots in Figures 2(b,c) also show comparatively small differences between theoretical and actual performance with Ninja cursors (up to 300 ms with Ninja-4 and up to 450 ms with Ninja-9).

Very few experimental conditions showed benefits for multiple trajectory techniques with *random* targets (only Ninja-4 in the $\Delta ID = 3.0$ level). This shows a major challenge for multiple trajectory techniques because the random condition best resembles real world pointing (users seldom repeatedly tap between targets as tested with *bi-directional tapping*). In all other conditions, the decision cost of these interfaces was too high for their theoretical advantages to be realized. It might be tempting to think that users could be given the option to 'turn on' Ninja cursors for distant targets, but these results suggest that each additional decision costs time, and adding further decision points is likely to further harm performance unless targets are very distant.

CONCLUSIONS AND FUTURE WORK

We presented an examination of the search/decision cost in pointing interfaces that provide multiple possible target trajectories. We carried out a controlled experiment where pointing with two such interfaces – pointer wrapping and Ninja cursors – were tested and compared with Fitts' law predictions for optimal trajectories and for traditional pointing with a single cursor. Results showed that actual performance was far from optimal, and that traditional pointing outperforms multiple trajectories in many conditions – the search/decision costs overwhelm the benefits.

Further work includes evaluating multiple trajectories with very large screens and multi-monitor environments, further analysis of the independent effects of target distance and width, and analysis of other enhanced pointing techniques such as Bubble Cursor [4] and Object Pointing [5].

REFERENCES

1. Blanch, R. and Ortega, M. Rake cursor: improving pointing performance with concurrent input channels. in *Proc. CHI'09*, ACM, (2009), 1415-1418.
2. Card, S.K., Moran, T.P. and Newell, A. *The Psychology of HCI.* Lawrence Erlbaum Associates, 1983.
3. Cockburn, A. and Gutwin, C. A predictive model of human performance with scrolling and hierarchical lists. *HCI J. 24*, 3 (2009), 273-314.
4. Grossman, T. and Balakrishnan, R. The bubble cursor. in *Proc. CHI'05*, ACM, (2005), 281-290.
5. Guiard, Y., Blanch, R. and Beaudouin-Lafon, M. Object pointing: a complement to bitmap pointing in GUIs. in *Proc. Graphics Interface'04*, (2004), 9-16.
6. Hinckley, K., Guimbretiere, F., Baudisch, P., Sarin, R., Agrawala, M. and Cutrell, E. The Springboard: multiple modes in one spring-loaded control. in *Proc. CHI'06*, ACM, (2006), 181-190.
7. Kobayashi, M. and Igarashi, T. Ninja cursors: using multiple cursors to assist target acquisition on large screens. in *Proc. CHI'08*, ACM, (2008), 949-958.
8. MacKenzie, I.S. Fitts' law as a research and design tool in human-computer interaction. *HCI J. 7* (1992), 91-139.
9. Räihä, K. and Špakov, O. Disambiguating Ninja cursors with eye gaze. in *Proc. CHI'09*, (2009), 1411-1414.

Cursor Relocation Techniques to Help Older Adults Find 'Lost' Cursors

Nic Hollinworth
School of Systems Engineering
University of Reading, Whiteknights
Reading, RG6 6AY, UK
n.d.p.hollinworth@reading.ac.uk

Faustina Hwang
School of Systems Engineering
University of Reading, Whiteknights
Reading, RG6 6AY, UK
f.hwang@reading.ac.uk

ABSTRACT
Older adult computer users often lose track of the mouse cursor and so resort to methods such as mouse shaking or searching the screen to find the cursor again. Hence, this paper describes how a standard optical mouse was modified to include a touch sensor, activated by releasing and touching the mouse, which automatically centers the mouse cursor to the screen, potentially making it easier to find a 'lost' cursor. Six older adult computer users and six younger computer users were asked to compare the touch sensitive mouse with cursor centering with two alternative techniques for locating the mouse cursor: manually shaking the mouse and using the Windows sonar facility. The time taken to click on a target following a distractor task was recorded, and results show that centering the mouse was the fastest to use, with a 35% improvement over shaking the mouse. Five out of six older participants ranked the touch sensitive mouse with cursor centering as the easiest to use.

Author Keywords
Computer mouse, touch sensor, mouse cursor, fieldmouse

ACM Classification Keywords
H5.2. [Information interfaces and presentation (e.g., HCI)]: Input devices and strategies, interaction styles

General Terms
Human factors

INTRODUCTION
Losing the mouse cursor is not uncommon amongst older adult computer users [8, 10, 17], who may experience age-related declines in vision that make it more difficult to locate a stationary cursor or track a moving cursor. Some of the difficulties may be explained by declines in visual sensitivity [9], and declines in selective and divided attention [12, 15] which can directly affect visual search ability. A reduction in the width of the visual field is common too [16], and means that peripheral stimuli need to be either nearer to the center of the screen, or stronger in order to be detected [18]. There is also a reduced ability to detect flicker (potentially causing difficulties in locating a flashing cursor), changes in contrast, reduction in color sensitivity and greater difficulties shutting out distracting visual stimuli, meaning that screens need to be kept simple and free from distractions [5].

Declines in visual search ability [e.g. 12, 5] make it more difficult to locate a target (such as the mouse cursor) against a distracting background or track a moving target [13] and this becomes more difficult as the contrast between target and background is reduced, or the competing non-target stimuli increases. Thus, users often resort to methods such as shaking the mouse from side to side in order to try and make the cursor more noticeable, or searching the entire screen. In addition, older adults are slower at processing visual stimuli, so that for accurate identification they need to see objects for longer [16].

RELATED WORK
Very few studies have considered the problem that older adult computer users have with losing the mouse cursor, although various solutions to make the mouse more visible have been developed for computer users in general, such as PinPoint 3 (for the Mac) [11] and the Windows Mouse sonar, both of which display some form of additional graphic feature to help make the mouse cursor more noticeable. There is also support in most operating systems for increasing the cursor size, though it is not known whether this offers any real advantage.

Ball and North [2] interviewed experienced and inexperienced computer users and found that losing the mouse pointer on screen was a common and frustrating experience. They cite three techniques used by the interviewees for finding the mouse cursor when it becomes lost (in order of most often to least often used):

- quickly moving the mouse back and forth in a small area to use human visual motion detection
- scanning the entire display until finding the cursor
- moving the mouse cursor to an extreme edge (e.g. moving it to the bottom right corner of the screen)

Benko et al [4] used cursor centering as one of the strategies for (re)placing a mouse cursor following a shift from one screen to another when using a multiple monitor configuration. In their implementation, a Windows sonar animation is used in conjunction with centering to help in finding the mouse cursor when it is moved to a different screen. The centering is automatic, in that it is repositioned whenever the user moves between screens, rather than controlled by the user.

Robertson [14] addressed the problem of losing the mouse cursor by introducing an Auto-Locator cursor which is similar to the Windows mouse sonar, but is invoked whenever the cursor moves a long distance across the display at a rapid speed. Ashdown [1] used a flashing star to help users locate the mouse cursor when switching between monitors in a multiple monitor configuration and Baudisch [3] developed a technique for making the mouse cursor more visible when moving it, by using a trail of mouse cursors. Apart from the technique used by Benko, a feature common to all these techniques is that they all rely on a visual search of the screen to find the mouse cursor.

TOUCH ENABLED MOUSE

Given the difficulties reported with finding a lost cursor, a novel technique was developed to make finding the mouse cursor easier, but does *not* rely upon visual search of the screen, the memorization of any sequences of key presses or mouse clicks, and it is not automated, giving users control over when the technique operates. The technique uses a Quantum QT113 touch sensor, placed in the body of a standard optical mouse, which automatically centers the mouse pointer whenever the mouse is fully-released and then touched again [6]. In general use, the touch sensor does not interfere with normal mouse operation.

Pilot Study

Prior to the current study, a pilot study was conducted [7] to get user feedback on different cursor relocation techniques activated by the touch sensitive mouse (nicknamed 'FieldMouse'). Three techniques were trialed by two older adult volunteers (aged 52 and 76), and one younger volunteer (age 26), each of whom had more than 3 years experience of using a computer on a regular basis.

The three techniques were as follows:

- placing the mouse cursor at the screen center
- displaying a flashing red ring around the mouse cursor
- visually wiggling the mouse cursor from side to side

The flashing mouse was found to be unhelpful in practice and one participant remarked that they often saw the mouse cursor *before* they noticed the flashing ring, and that the flashing ring was just distracting. The wiggling mouse cursor was found to be time-consuming to use, and the wiggling motion unhelpful when searching for the mouse cursor. The technique of centering the mouse was the most popular, and all three of the volunteers remarked that it was quicker to use as the mouse cursor was always placed at the screen center, and so no searching of the screen was required. This latter technique was therefore chosen for inclusion in the current study, for comparisons with more standard techniques.

EXPERIMENT

A study was conducted to compare three techniques that could help in finding the mouse cursor after attention has been diverted to a non-mouse task:

1. *Touch centering*: centering the mouse cursor in the screen using the FieldMouse
2. *Mouse shaking*: manually shaking a standard mouse from side to side
3. *Windows mouse sonar*: aims to make the cursor more visible by displaying animated concentric circles around the cursor when the control key is pressed

It was hypothesized that it will be faster to click on a target after using *Touch centering*, than *Mouse shaking* or using the *Windows mouse sonar*, because with touch centering the screen needs the least amount of visual searching to locate the cursor. Also, participants will find mouse centering easier to use than the other techniques, as there are no additional tasks to remember and no key presses involved.

Participants

6 older adult volunteers (3 male and 3 female, aged between 52 and 81, mean age = 66.2 years) and 6 younger adult volunteers (4 male and 2 female, aged between 18 and 28, mean age = 23.3 years) participated in the study. All were experienced computer users, having used a computer at least every other day for a minimum of one year. None of the participants had previously used touch centering, nor used windows sonar, but they had all used mouse shaking.

Method

Participants were initially interviewed to gather information on their prior computing experience and any health-related conditions that could affect their participation in the study. Each participant was then asked to perform 3 blocks of 16 trials for each of the 3 techniques, where the order of presentation of techniques was balanced across participants. A short practice session of 10 trials was provided to familiarize the participant with each of the three techniques.

Comparison of the techniques was made by displaying two words, randomly selected from a list of 100, near the center of the screen. Participants were then asked to type the words into a text field and press the return key, the idea being that they were forced to release the mouse and divert their attention to another task. If a mistake was made, the text field was highlighted in red and the error had to be corrected before continuing. After the words had been entered correctly and the return key pressed, a circular target of 46 pixels in diameter was displayed (see Figure 1). Each target was randomly selected from a set of 16 targets arranged in a circular configuration of diameter 700px, and used once only for the 16 trials. Participants were asked to click on the target as quickly and as accurately as possible, and once selected, the next two-words were displayed. Words were of mixed case so that both hands would be needed to type the correct characters. The speed of typing and any errors made whilst typing the phrases were not factors in the study, and did not affect the outcomes.

Figure 1: The current target is displayed as a red circle. The upper rectangle is used to display the two word phrase, and the lower rectangle is used to type in the words of the phrase.

A distracter background was used to make the task of locating the cursor more realistic, so that the contrast between the background and the mouse cursor was similar to that when using a typical windows application such as MS Word. Paragraphs of random selections from Finnegans Wake were used, with a font size equal to that of the text displayed in the rectangular field containing the words.

The program recorded the time taken (in milliseconds) between pressing the return key after the two words were entered and successfully clicking on the target. This could then be used as a measure of how quickly the mouse pointer was located after the distracter task of typing in the two words. Data was also captured on the mouse cursor location, so that analysis could be made of the movements.

RESULTS

A repeated measures ANOVA showed a significant main effect ($F_{2,20} = 8.7$, $p = 0.002$) of technique on the time taken between pressing the return key after entering the two word phrase, and successfully clicking on the target. For both groups of participants, *Touch centering* was quickest and *Windows sonar* was the slowest. A summary of the mean times is given in table 1 below.

	Touch centering	Mouse shaking	Windows mouse sonar
Older adults	2.57s	3.95s	4.87s
Younger	1.45s	1.65s	1.99s

Table 1: mean selection times, given in seconds

Post-hoc comparisons using paired t-tests (with Bonferroni corrections) revealed that older participants performed significantly better when using *Touch centering*, than when using *Windows sonar* ($t(5) = 2.89$, $p = 0.034$), and younger participants performed significantly better using *Touch centering* than with *Mouse shaking* ($t(5) = 2.85$, $p = 0.036$) or with Windows mouse sonar ($t(5) = 2.76$, $p = 0.040$). Although not significant, the results suggest there may also be a difference between *Touch centering* and *Mouse shaking* for older participants ($t(5) = 1.86$, $p = 0.122$).

There was a significant main effect of age group on the selection time ($F_{1,10} = 7.12$, $p = 0.024$) where the older group took more than twice as long to select the target for the mouse shaking and sonar conditions as the younger group. This can be seen in Figure 2. The interaction between technique and group approached significance ($F_{2,20} = 3.4$, $p = 0.053$)

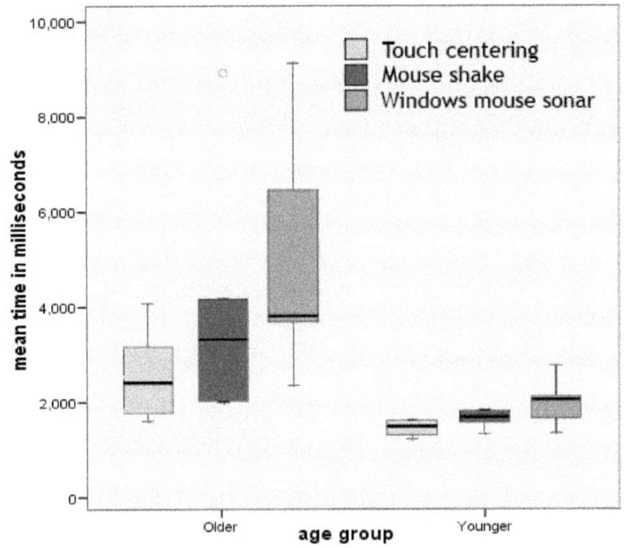

Figure 2: Mean time taken (in milliseconds) between pressing return key and successfully clicking on a target.

During a brief interview following the experiment, each participant was asked to rank the technique in the order which they thought was the easiest to use, with a rank of 1 being the easiest and rank 3 the hardest. Table 2 shows the techniques which were given a rank of 1 by each group, and Table 3 shows the techniques that were given a rank of 3.

	Mouse shake	Sonar	Centering
Older	0	1	5
Younger	4	0	2

Table 2: The number of participants who thought a particular technique was the easiest to use.

	Mouse shake	Sonar	Centering
Older	3	3	0
Younger	1	3	2

Table 3: Number of participants who thought a particular technique to be the most difficult to use.

DISCUSSION

For both groups of users, *Touch centering* was the quickest method of finding the mouse cursor (supporting the first hypothesis) and *Windows mouse sonar* was the slowest. The older adult users performed over two seconds faster using *Touch centering* than when using *Windows sonar*, and more than one second faster than with *Mouse shaking*. In the former case, the additional time needed for a key press may account for this larger difference. To illustrate the differences, Figure 3 shows the cursor traces for two of the techniques *Touch centering* and *Mouse shake*. It is clear that when using the Touch mouse, the path to the target is more direct, and so faster.

Five of the older adult participants stated that they thought *Touch centering* was the easiest to use and did not find the technique intrusive. Comments suggest that this is because it does not require additional tasks, such as key presses, to operate it. However, it does require that the user looks at the screen center - one older adult participant forgot that the cursor was placed in the center when the mouse was released and touched again.

Despite the effectiveness of mouse centering and the improvement in speed, only two of the younger group rated it as the easiest technique, with the remaining four opting for the mouse shake. One explanation is that the younger group are already more accustomed to mouse shaking. For both groups the slowest technique was the *Mouse sonar*, probably because this requires pressing the CTRL key in addition to searching the screen for the animated effect.

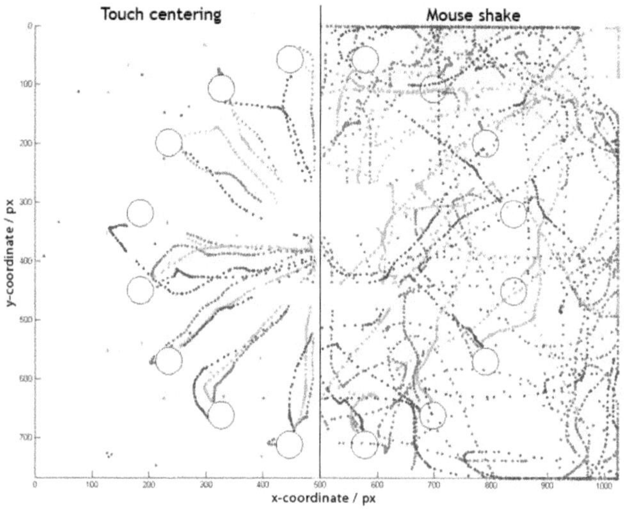

Figure 3: The left side of the image shows cursor traces for Touch centering; the right side shows traces for Mouse shake

CONCLUSIONS

Touch centering is quicker than either *Mouse shaking* or the *Windows mouse sonar*, requires no additional tasks, is controllable by the user and does not necessitate the user to perform visual searches of the screen to locate the mouse cursor. Therefore it is better suited to older adult users who need a transparent method of finding a lost mouse cursor without the need for visual search, nor having to memorize new tasks that can distract from their immediate goal.

ACKNOWLEDGMENTS

Thanks to the staff and volunteers at Age UK Reading, Age UK Banbury, and the University of Reading. This work is funded by School of Systems Engineering.

REFERENCES

1. Ashdown, M., Oka, K., Sato, Y. (2005) Combining head tracking and mouse input for a GUI on multiple monitors, In *Ext. Abstracts CHI 05*, 1180–91.
2. Ball, R. and North, C. (2005) Effects of tiled high-resolution display on basic visualization and navigation tasks, In *Ext. Abstracts CHI 05*, 1196-99.
3. Baudisch, P., Cutrell, E. and Robertson, G. (2003) High-Density Cursor: A Visualization Technique that Helps Users Keep Track of Fast-Moving Mouse Cursors. In *Proc. Interact 2003,* IOS Press, 236-43.
4. Benko, H and Feiner, S. (2005) Multi-Monitor Mouse, In *Ext. Abstracts CHI 05,* 1208-11.
5. Czaja, S. and Lee, C.C. (2008) Information Technology and Older Adults, The Human Computer Interaction Handbook, CRC Press, 777-792.
6. Hinckley, K. and Sinclair, M. (1999) Touch-sensing input devices, *SIGCHI conference on Human Factors in Computer Systems*, Pittsburgh, Pennsylvania, 223-230.
7. Hollinworth, N. (2010) Helping Older Adults Locate 'Lost' Cursors using FieldMouse, *ASSETS 2010,* 315-316.
8. Kosnik, W., Winslow, L., Kline, D., Rasinski, K. and Sekuler, R. (1988) Visual Changes in Daily Life Throughout Adulthood, *Journal of Gerontology*, 43(3), 63-70.
9. Owsley, C., Ball, K. and Keeton, D.M. (1994) Relationship Between Visual Sensitivity and Target Localisation in Older Adults, *Vision Res.* 35(4), 579-87.
10. Paradise, J., Trewin, S. and Keates, S. (2005) Using Pointing Devices: Difficulties Encountered and Strategies Employed, *3rd International Conference on Universal Access and Human-Computer Interaction.*
11. PinPoint 3, http://www.2point5fish.com/
12. Plude, D.J. and Hoyer, W.J. (1986) Age and the Selectivity of Visual Information Processing, *Journal of Psychology and Aging*, 1(1), 4-10.
13. Riviere, C. N. and N. V. Thakor (1996) Effects of age and disability on tracking tasks with a computer mouse: Accuracy and linearity, *Journal of Rehabilitation Research and Development*, 33(1), 6-15.
14. Robertson, G., Czerwinski, M., Baudisch, P., Meyers, B., Robbins, D., Smith, G. and Tan, D. (2005) Large Display User Experience, *IEEE Computer Graphics and Applications*, 44-45.
15. Rogers, W. (2000) Attention and Aging, In Park, D. and Schwarz, N. (eds) *Cognitive Aging, A Primer*, Psychology Press, Sussex.
16. Stuart-Hamilton, I. (2006) *The Psychology of Ageing: An Introduction*, J Kingsley Publishers, London.
17. Vigouroux, N., Rumeau, P., Vella, F. and Vellas, B. (2009) Studying Point-Select-Drag Interaction Techniques for Older People with Cognitive Impairment, *Proc. of the 5th International Conference on Universal Access in HCI*, 422-428.
18. Wood, E., Willoughby, T., Rushing, A., Bechtel, L. and Gilbert, J. (2005) Use of Computer Input Devices by Older Adults, *Journal of Applied Gerontology*, 24(5), 419-438.

CHI 2011 Author Index

CHI 2011 Author Index

Volume 1 Pages: 1–866

Volume 2 Pages: 867–1864

Volume 3 Pages: 1865–2816

Volume 4 Pages: 2817–3478

CHI 2011 Author Index

CHI 2011 Author Index

CHI 2011 Author Index

CHI 2011 Author Index

CHI 2011 Author Index

CHI 2011 Author Index

CHI 2011 Author Index

CHI 2011 Author Index

CHI 2011 Author Index

CHI 2011 Author Index

CHI 2011 Author Index

CHI 2011 Author Index

CHI 2011 Author Index

CHI 2011 Author Index

CHI 2011 Author Index

www.ingramcontent.com/pod-product-compliance
Ingram Content Group UK Ltd.
Pitfield, Milton Keynes, MK11 3LW, UK
UKHW051454290926
15471UKWH00008B/1202

9 781450 313520